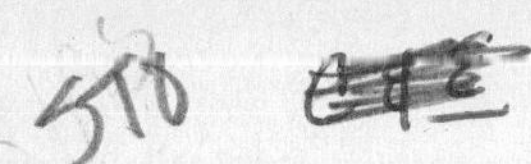

PETERSON'S

COLLEGES WITH PROGRAMS FOR STUDENTS WITH LEARNING DISABILITIES OR ATTENTION DEFICIT DISORDERS

FIFTH EDITION

Peterson's
Princeton, New Jersey

About Peterson's

Peterson's is the country's largest educational information/communications company, providing the academic, consumer, and professional communities with books, software, and on-line services in support of lifelong education access and career choice. Well-known references include Peterson's annual guides to private schools, summer programs, colleges and universities, graduate and professional programs, financial aid, international study, adult learning, and career guidance. Peterson's Web site at petersons.com is the only comprehensive—and most heavily traveled—education resource on the Internet. The site carries all of Peterson's fully searchable major databases and includes financial aid sources, test-prep help, job postings, direct inquiry and application features, and specially created Virtual Campuses for every accredited academic institution and summer program in the U.S. and Canada that offers in-depth narratives, announcements, and multimedia features.

Visit Peterson's Education Center on the Internet (World Wide Web) at http://www.petersons.com

ISBN 1-56079-853-X

Printed in the United States of America

10 9 8 7 6 5 4 3 2 1

CONTENTS

▶ FOREWORD ◀

The American Council on Education has sponsored the HEATH Resource Center since 1980, first as a model/demonstration program and, since 1984, as the National Clearinghouse on Postsecondary Education for Individuals with Disabilities, which is funded by the U.S. Department of Education. HEATH collects and disseminates information about education after high school for students with any disability. Opportunities for students with disabilities have grown exponentially in the time since the beginning of the HEATH Resource Center. When I began as Director there were about thirty-five colleges and universities in our Campus Resource File that indicated that they served students with learning disabilities. Many campus disability support staff, however, were contacting us to find out how they could serve the growing number of students with learning disabilities who were indeed enrolling. Now, nearly twenty years later, our small staff responds to more than 30,000 inquiries annually. These inquiries come to us by telephone, mail, fax, and the Internet. Those asking about resources and other information include students and their parents, grandparents, and significant others, as well as professionals who teach and advise them. We also hear from college administrators, vocational rehabilitation officials, journalists, librarians, and federal, state, and local education officials.

More than half the questions to the HEATH staff concern students with learning disabilities. In the last several years we have had numerous questions about students with attention deficit disorders. The questions are similar: *Where can I study? What accommodations can I expect, and what do I do to receive them? How can I get assistance to pay for the education?* and recently, *I want to go to law school (or other professional or graduate school),* followed by the same questions as above.

The HEATH Resource Center publishes a number of resource papers on many topics, and we have several papers that assist readers to learn how to respond to these questions. We do not list any colleges but rather teach how to structure the search for a postsecondary institution. We do, however, consistently recommend *Peterson's Colleges with Programs for Students with Learning Disabilities* as a comprehensive listing of colleges to explore. The publication of this fifth edition of *Peterson's Colleges with Programs for Students with Learning Disabilities or Attention Deficit disorders,* which now contains information about services to students with attention deficit disorders and contains more than 1,000 colleges and universities that serve students with learning disabilities is tangible testimony to the changes that have occurred over the last two decades.

For more than seventeen years as Director of the HEATH Resource Center, I have both witnessed and proactively encouraged these changes. When HEATH began, our task was to provide technical assistance to colleges and universities about how to make their campuses and programs accessible to students with disabilities. Few in higher education at that time had heard of learning disabilities. There was little information about how to provide support services to such students or where researchers could turn to observe successful college programs. The first HEATH paper on the topic of students with learning disabilities in postsecondary education in 1981 listed and described nine programs. It was from this core of programs that many colleges and universities based their initial provision of services for students with learning disabilities. Since that time, HEATH's mission has expanded to assist postsecondary educational entities of all varieties to be accessible and to provide information to students with disabilities, their families, and those who work with them to achieve the goal of pursuing education after high school.

Over this period of time, there has been a significant increase in the number and percentage of college students with disabilities. In 1978, the first year disability-related data on college students were reported in *American Freshman: National Norms,* 2.6 percent of full-time, first-time freshmen indicated that they had a disability. In the most recent data, *College Freshmen with Disabilities: A Triennial Statistical Profile,* published by HEATH/American Council on Education in 1995, 9.2 percent of college freshmen reported a disability. Of these, one third of them (more than 45,000) report having a learning disability, which is the fastest growing disability category.

While data have not yet been collected about college students with attention deficit disorders, professionals writing in the *Journal of Postsecondary Education and Disability* estimate that between 1 and 3 percent of college students have attention deficit disorders. They also report that many support services emerging on campuses for this population are an extension or adaptation of programs originally developed for students with learning disabilities. The literature, once unavailable, on the topic of accommodations and preferred policies for college students with attention deficit disorders is now growing. Publication of this fifth edition of Peterson's guide recognizes the phenomenon of increasing numbers of students with attention deficit disorders who are seeking college enrollment.

A combination of factors has led to the increase in the number of college learning disability services and programs as well as a dramatic increase in the number of students seeking such programs. In the mid-1970s two significant pieces of legislation became law: the Education of the Handicapped Act (now called the Individuals with Disabilities Education Act—IDEA) and the Rehabilitation Act of 1973, followed by the 1977 regulations implementing Section 504 of that act. Together they reflected Americans' concern about including people with disabilities in regular education (and other federally funded activities) and led to the changes necessary in those programs so that these people, including those with learning disabilities, could participate.

These concerns were further validated with the enactment of the Americans with Disabilities Act (ADA) of 1990. ADA has also had the effect of raising the awareness of educational institutions about their responsibilities to people with disabilities, and that has renewed access activity on many campuses. In addition, at both the secondary and postsecondary levels, educators have increased efforts to teach students with disabilities—including those with learning disabilities—self-advocacy skills, which have heightened their self-determination. Such skills have emboldened students to come forward and request disability-specific accommodations, which may account for the increasing number of students who self-identify. On the other hand, self-advocacy groups, together with ADA, have also resulted in increased litigation about academic accommodations and documentation of disabilities, especially for people with learning disabilities and attention deficit disorders. The resolution of such litigation will continue to shape the nature of *required* modifications and may change the types of special services for which a college or university can charge a fee over and above tuition.

Another factor that must not be overlooked is the significant role that federal funding of demonstration projects in postsecondary education has played in spreading the word about what both campus administrators and students with learning disabilities need to know to succeed. Much of the expanded variety of postsecondary programs for students with learning disabilities can be attributed to the federal initiatives to create model programs to demonstrate support services and related activities in community colleges, four-year colleges, and universities, as well as programs to facilitate the transition from high school to college for students with learning disabilities. During the 1980s, approximately seventy-five demonstration postsecondary programs for students with learning disabilities were federally supported for two- and three-year periods. Many of these were later incorporated into the regular college programming and are included in this guide.

As students have become better prepared, as their aspirations are raised by supportive parents and teachers, and as colleges and universities come to understand the strengths and potential that such students add to campus life, the number of programs for students with learning disabilities has multiplied.

In the past, those of us concerned with information about postsecondary education and disability have hesitated to recommend or endorse directories, guides, or listings of accessible places, for usually such lists imply that only schools on the list serve people with disabilities. I have come to believe, however, that the past several editions of *Peterson's Colleges with Programs for Students with Learning Disabilities* has consistently offered such a wealth of information about so many institutions that we regularly recommend this guide to most inquirers as an excellent reference tool and starting place for those in the process of investigating college choices. In addition to the descriptions of the schools, Peterson's guide provides a great deal of information to enhance one's search. The editors, Stephen Strichart and Charles Mangrum, have prepared useful, *on-target* background material, essays, and specific steps to take to assist readers to select their personal best schools. There is, of course, no substitute for actually visiting a campus firsthand and talking with the disability support services directors as well as other students with disabilities. *Peterson's Colleges with Programs for Students with Learning Disabilities or Attention Deficit Disorders* is an excellent resource to use as one begins the investigation.

Rhona C. Hartman, Director
HEATH Resource Center
National Clearinghouse on Postsecondary Education for Individuals with Disabilities
American Council on Education
Washington, D.C.

▶ PREFACE ◀

During the 1970s, when we both began our work with students with learning disabilities (LD), there were few colleges providing programs or even services for such students. Those that existed were difficult to find; the few published guides and lists that identified such schools were not very accurate. We had to rely primarily on word of mouth from other professors and parents of students who had LD. As our work continued into the early 1980s, we became increasingly aware of the number of colleges and universities adding programs and services for students with LD. But still there was no single, reliable source listing such schools.

In our efforts to update our own lists, we visited and made phone calls to the schools we had heard were making accommodations for students with LD. We asked them about their programs and services, about the numbers of students with LD enrolled or taking classes with them. And we read everything we could find about expanding college opportunities for students with LD.

We published what we had learned in our first book, *College and the Learning Disabled Student* (Grune and Stratton, 1984, 1988). The information in that book was used by many colleges establishing new programs and expanding existing ones for students with LD.

We then began working with the editors at Peterson's on the ambitious task of collecting data on all the colleges and universities in the United States that were responding to the special needs of students with LD. The result was the first edition of this book, published in 1985. Expanded, updated editions published in 1988, 1992, and 1994 included two-year colleges as well as four-year colleges and universities, information about colleges and universities in Canada, and Academic Options—a computer search software that, among other features, enabled users to quickly identify the colleges or universities in this guide that best meet the specific needs and preferences of individual LD students.

Now, we are pleased to see the publication of this, the fifth edition of *Peterson's Colleges with Programs for Students with Learning Disabilities or Attention Deficit Disorders*. As reflected in the expanded title, the fifth edition now includes information on services available to the increasing number of students with attention deficit disorders (ADD) attending college. Section 504 of the Rehabilitation Act of 1973 and the Americans with Disabilities Act (ADA) of 1990 require that all colleges and universities receiving federal funds take action to meet the needs of students with disabilities. Many colleges and universities comply with these laws but lack the resources and/or philosophical commitment to go beyond only compliance. The colleges and universities included in this guide go far beyond compliance with these laws. They reach out to students with LD and ADD with an array of resources and a strong commitment to do everything necessary to ensure that these students succeed. The Academic Options CD-ROM accompanying the guide will make it more convenient than ever for users of the guide to obtain the important information they need to identify those colleges or universities that best meet the needs of an LD or ADD student.

A Word of Caution

As confident as we are with the care and effort that has gone into preparing this new edition, we still want to offer these words of caution: No guide can provide all the information that one needs to make a well-informed college choice. The decision about where to go to college—where to spend one's time, effort, and money—is a very important one, and this book can only be the beginning of that selection process. Studying school catalogs and visiting campuses (or, at the least, speaking by phone to the LD contact people listed at the end of each profile in this guide) will ensure that you have the most accurate and up-to-date college information on which to base your decision.

Charles T. Mangrum II and Stephen S. Strichart

▸ INTRODUCTION ◂

Since the publication of the first edition of this guide in 1985, more and more students diagnosed with learning disabilities (LD) and attention deficit disorders (ADD) are going to college, succeeding there, and graduating. They are going to all types of colleges and universities, participating in the mainstream of college life, including advancement to graduate and professional programs. With appropriate knowledge about college programs for students with LD, the right preparation, and proper guidance, such students can choose a suitable college, major in any area of study, and graduate successfully.

To prepare this guide, we mailed questionnaires to all accredited two-year and four-year colleges and universities in the United States, U.S. territories, and Canada that grant associate or bachelor's degrees (more than 3,250) to identify those with programs or services for students with LD or ADD. The detailed questionnaires were completed by the responsible professionals at the colleges. These professionals were asked to describe special provisions for students with LD or ADD at their institutions. The results are shared in this guide.

HOW TO USE THIS GUIDE

Types of Assistance Available

Here you will find basic information about how colleges and universities throughout the country are responding to the specific needs of students with LD or ADD through their comprehensive programs or special services. This section contains definitions of the criteria we use to qualify for inclusion the 1,053 programs we have selected to be profiled in this book and explanations of the major components of a higher education learning disabilities program.

Selecting a College

This section provides you with step-by-step guidelines for narrowing your college selections, finding out more about these schools, applying to your top choices, and preparing for a campus visit.

Making the Most of Your College Visit offers advice about when to visit a school and who to speak with while you're there. It includes one list of questions to ask the admission officer or LD Program Director and another to ask of students with LD on campus. The Personal Summary Chart helps you to organize and compare features of different colleges that you are considering.

The two sample letters here may be helpful to you when writing for more information about a school and then requesting an appointment for a campus visit.

The Personal Summary Chart is organized to serve as a useful worksheet for you to fill out as you consider the college profiles. It will provide a structured format to compare the relative ways that different schools may meet your needs.

Information Resources

This is a listing of organizations that can be contacted to provide more information related to higher education for individuals with LD or ADD.

Quick-Reference Chart

Organized geographically, this chart provides essential information elements about every college profiled in the guide. You can use it as a quick way to narrow your search. It also functions as a geographic index to the colleges.

College Profile Listings

Here is detailed information about learning disabilities programs and services at specific colleges. The profiles are organized into two primary divisions: four-year colleges, followed by two-year colleges. These two primary divisions are further subdivided into Colleges with Comprehensive Programs—programs specially designed for students with LD or ADD, and Colleges with Special Services—programs that may not be complete but do provide a considerable number of special services to students with LD. Advice is provided in the Selecting a College chapter on page 6 about how to decide which category of programs or services you may desire. The four sections of individual college profiles are presented in this order: Four-Year Colleges with Comprehensive Programs; Four-Year Colleges with Special Services; Two-Year Colleges with Comprehensive Programs; Two-Year Colleges with Special Services.

In both categories, the information of special interest to the student with LD appears first, followed by general information about the school.

Academic Options CD-ROM—

The CD-ROM that accompanies this guide is an optional tool that enables the user to identify colleges quickly. The program can be used to begin your search process, but the guide should be used when evaluating schools and selecting a final list of schools that will best meet your needs. In addition to this enhanced selection capability, the CD-ROM contains models of letters of inquiry that you can customize to serve as your own. Peterson's Universal Application, accepted now by more than 650 colleges, and AT&T WorldNet Service are useful added features on the CD-ROM.

► TYPES OF ASSISTANCE AVAILABLE ◄

Colleges provide many kinds of assistance to help students with LD or ADD succeed. The descriptions in the College Profile Listings section of this guide identify the assistance provided by each college. In this section of the guide, the kinds of assistance provided to students with LD are explained in detail. Most colleges that offer assistance to students with LD also offer the assistance to students with ADD.

WHAT ARE THE DIFFERENCES BETWEEN COLLEGES WITH COMPREHENSIVE PROGRAMS AND THOSE WITH SPECIAL SERVICES?

This guide distinguishes between colleges that offer comprehensive programs designed specifically for students with LD and colleges that make a number of special services available but do not offer comprehensive programs.

The typical components of a comprehensive program are diagnostic testing, tutoring, remediation, advisement, special courses, counseling, and a range of auxiliary aids and services. The keys to such a program are that its components are provided in a manner specifically designed to meet the needs of students with LD and that it is staffed with personnel with appropriate training and experience.

Colleges without comprehensive programs may offer many of the same services as those offered by comprehensive programs, but there are several important differences. First, these colleges generally do not offer quite as wide a range of services as do programs. Second, the services are not uniquely designed for students with LD but are usually part of the general services available to the entire student population. Third, colleges offering services do not typically have staff who have significant training or experience working specifically with college students with LD. Nevertheless, these services can often be very helpful and may be all the assistance some students with LD need to succeed in college.

Generally, students whose learning disabilities were diagnosed early and who spent much of their school career in special programs or classes might need a comprehensive program, while students who were successful in regular high school classes with some outside assistance might find special services sufficient. Students and their families should examine colleges' offerings and then compare them to the student's needs to find the best fit.

Diagnostic Testing

Diagnostic testing is needed to assess cognitive abilities, academic skills, language abilities, perceptual-motor skills, social development, emotional development, and work and study habits. Information from diagnostic tests is used to prescribe services for the student. Frequently, this information is used to develop an individual educational program (IEP), which specifies the assistance that will be provided to a student with LD. The format for the IEP varies from college to college, but the basic information included is fairly consistent. Typically, an IEP will include information about the following:

- Academic and learning strengths and deficits
- Effective learning strategies to be used by the student
- Effective teaching strategies to be used with the student
- Areas in need of remediation
- Courses in which the student requires tutoring
- Problems for which the student requires counseling
- Special courses that will help the student develop the skills necessary to succeed in college
- Auxiliary aids and services that will help the student compensate for the learning disability

Tutoring

Tutoring is designed to help students understand and master the content of their courses. The major objective is to help students pass their courses. Because they see immediate results, students frequently report that tutoring is the most helpful form of assistance. It is most often provided in English, mathematics, physical sciences, and social sciences. It is usually given individually or in small groups by professional tutors who are experts in their subject areas. Sometimes students without learning disabilities who excel in a subject are used as peer tutors.

Remediation

College students with LD need remediation to improve their basic skills in reading, writing, language, and mathematics. They also need assistance in developing compensatory strategies that will minimize the impact of their learning disabilities upon their achievement in college courses. A student's need for remediation depends upon three factors: the severity of the academic and learning deficits, the level of proficiency in the academic skills needed for success in the student's program of studies, and the student's desire to achieve. Remediation is typically provided in individual or small-group sessions. Those providing remediation should be skilled teachers who are knowledgeable about learning disabilities.

Advisement

College students with LD need careful and ongoing academic advisement for these reasons:

- They frequently enroll in courses that are too difficult for them
- They tend to enroll in the wrong courses
- They often misperceive the progress they are making in courses
- They rarely seek out services they need to overcome academic and social difficulties
- They frequently are overwhelmed by the registration process
- They tend to accept poor advice from well-intentioned peers

It is important for advisers to ensure that such students do not end up with overly difficult course loads, courses out of sequence, or a poorly planned schedule. It is essential that advisers be familiar with the assistance available to students with LD and the characteristics and needs of these students.

Special Courses

Frequently, special courses are offered for students with LD. These courses provide such students with the prerequisite skills and social and emotional awareness necessary to succeed in college. They may be credit or noncredit courses and may or may not count in a student's overall grade point average. Examples of special courses are:

- Developmental reading
- English composition
- Fundamentals of communication
- Language remediation
- Study skills
- Notetaking techniques
- Writing research papers
- Speed writing
- Typing
- Word processing
- Memory improvement
- Personal psychology
- College survival
- Social relationships

Counseling

To meet social needs, counseling is often necessary. It offers students with LD a sounding board for their feelings and provides an opportunity for them to develop self-understanding and more effective peer relationships. Counseling available may include group counseling, individual counseling, and career counseling. The major goals are to help college students with LD reduce anxiety, increase self-confidence and socialization, learn life skills, understand their disability, and achieve a sense of normalcy. At many colleges, students with LD have begun their own support groups.

Auxiliary Aids and Services

Colleges provide a number of auxiliary aids and services to help students with LD succeed.

Tape Recorders and Taped Textbooks

Students with LD often have difficulty taking notes from class lectures. The tape recorder becomes a valuable auxiliary aid for them. They are able to tape-record a lecture at the same time they take notes. Later, they can replay the tapes to check their notes for completeness and accuracy. Variable speech-control tape recorders allow students to play back taped material at slower or faster rates than the rate at which the material was originally recorded. The use of a tape recorder reduces the heavy demands upon their auditory memory, language processing, and writing skills. Because of the value of tape recorders, professors are encouraged to allow students with LD to use them in their classes.

Taped textbooks are used by students with LD who have difficulty reading college-level materials. College personnel help such students obtain taped textbooks from Recording for the Blind & Dyslexic. The role of staff members is primarily a facilitative one. They familiarize students with the services of Recording for the Blind & Dyslexic and help them complete the necessary application forms. They also help students determine the textbooks needed for future courses to enable the students to submit applications for taped textbooks in sufficient time to receive books prior to the beginning of a new term.

Technological Aids

The expansion of computer technology has produced many benefits for students with LD. Calculators can be used by students who are not strong in computational skills. Word processors can be used by students who have poorly developed handwriting skills that interfere with their ability to produce written assignments; they are also useful for writing term papers because students are able to store what they write and make revisions as necessary. Spell checking and proofing programs may be used by students to identify and correct errors in the mechanics of writing. Computer programs are now available to help students organize and construct their papers.

Students whose oral language abilities exceed their written language abilities benefit from speech recognition programs that allow them to operate a computer by speaking to it. These students also benefit from speech synthesis programs that read back text displayed on the computer screen. Optical character recognition (OCR) technology, such as the Kurzweil scanning system, allows students to convert print in books into spoken words. Personal data managers assist students in managing their time effectively.

Notetakers

Typically, notetakers are students without LD who are in the same classes as the students who do have LD. They have been identified as good notetakers who are reliable, are competent in the subject, and have legible handwriting. A duplicate set of notes is given to the student with LD. Usually the notetaker does not know the identity of the student receiving the notes.

Alternative Examination Arrangements

Alternative arrangements are provided for students who have difficulty taking examinations in the usual manner. Often, students with LD have difficulty completing a test within a specified time limit, accurately reading test questions, and writing answers. Arrangements are made with professors to allow students to take course examinations with one of a number of alternatives:

- Extended time limits
- Questions dictated onto an audio tape
- Questions read by a proctor
- Responses dictated to a proctor
- Responses dictated onto audio tapes
- Responses typed rather than handwritten
- Questions presented in a different format, e.g., multiple choice in place of essay
- Take-home examinations or projects in place of written examinations

Advocacy

College staff members often serve as advocates for students with LD. They work with professors to ensure that students are given every legitimate opportunity to succeed in their courses. The goal is to have students become their own advocates. Ideally, the activities and roles performed by staff members are phased out as students develop increasing independence. Some of the advocacy activities performed include:

- Requesting lists of required textbooks for taping
- Obtaining permission for students with LD to tape-record lectures
- Obtaining permission to use a non–class member as a notetaker
- Requesting opportunities for students to take tests in alternative ways
- Arranging for incomplete grades when students need more time to complete a course
- Arranging for withdrawal from a course without a grade penalty when extra time is not the answer
- Helping professors understand the needs of students with LD

▸ SELECTING A COLLEGE ◂

Users of this guide can conduct a manual or a computer-assisted search for colleges that will best meet the needs of students with learning disabilities (LD) or attention deficit disorders (ADD), which include the disability called attention deficit hyperactivity disorder (ADHD). The manual search requires only the use of the guide. The computer-assisted search requires the use of the enclosed Academic Options CD-ROM and the guide.

All of the colleges described in the guide and CD-ROM provide services or programs for students with learning disabilities. Most also provide these services and programs for students with ADD. In some cases colleges provide additional services to students with ADD. This can be determined by examining the profile of the colleges identified in your basic search. In the two sections of program descriptions of colleges that offer comprehensive programs, the second check-off box in the left column is labeled *ADD services* and will contain a check if students with ADD are provided services. In the sections that contain colleges that offer special services but not comprehensive programs, the last sentence in the first paragraph that starts the profile will say: "Students diagnosed with ADD/ADHD *are* eligible for the same services available to students with LD," or "Students diagnosed with ADD/ADHD *are not* eligible for the same services available to students with LD." All college profiles contain this sentence in this same location. The entries in the profile section of this guide identify those colleges that extend their services for students with LD to students with ADD, as well as those that offer additional services to students with ADD.

After you have chosen either to conduct a manual search or a computer-assisted search, please follow the steps outlined below.

Manual Search Using the Guide

1. Decide how much assistance you need to succeed in college:
   a. Should you attend a college that offers **Special Services** to its students with LD? Colleges with special services provide one or more of the following: tutoring, alternative test arrangements, notetakers, taped textbooks, basic skills remediation, diagnostic testing, priority registration, and advocates.
   b. Or, should you attend a college that offers a **Comprehensive Program** especially designed for its students with LD? Colleges offering comprehensive programs provide the services listed in (a.) above as part of a comprehensive program uniquely designed for students. Most often, special admission procedures must be followed by students with LD who wish to gain admission to colleges with these programs.
2. Decide whether you want to attend a:
   Two-year college, or Four-year college.
3. Decide in which U.S. states or Canadian provinces you wish to attend college.
4. Use the **Quick-Reference Chart of Colleges** (pages 12–39) to identify the colleges that meet the criteria you selected in steps 1–3.
5. For each college identified in step 4, enter the name of the college on the **Personal Summary Chart** on page 9.
6. For each of these colleges, read the complete entry in the **College Profile Listings** section of the guide to obtain the information needed to complete the checklist.
7. From the completed checklist, select those colleges that seem most appropriate. Colleges with the most "yes" responses are most likely to meet your specific needs.
8. Write to each college selected in step 7 to request additional information and application forms.
9. Complete and submit application forms to up to six colleges.
10. Visit the colleges to which you have been accepted. Use the sample letter on page 8 to arrange these visits.
11. When visiting campuses, be sure to take copies of the "General Questions" and "Questions to Ask of Students with LD or ADD" (found on page 7) with you.
12. Make your final decision and enroll.

Computer-Assisted Search Using the Academic Options CD-ROM and the Guide

1. Place the Academic Options disk in your computer. An introductory screen will appear.
2. Follow the directions on each succeeding screen to produce a printed list of the colleges that are most appropriate for you.

Following these procedures will help you make a final decision about which college to attend. The program will also helps you print appropriate letters to send to each college's Admissions Office and prepare an Application Checklist to help you through the process.

MAKING THE MOST OF YOUR COLLEGE VISIT

Reading the profiles in this guide and studying the school catalogs you receive will give you general descriptions about facilities, programs, services, and the like. It won't, however, give you the real feel for a school the way a campus visit will. Walking around campus, visiting the facilities, and getting impressions of the students and faculty will give you a much better sense of what it would be like to go to school there. It will also give you an excellent opportunity to get more detailed and up-to-date information about the things that interest you most at the college.

When to Visit, Who and What to See

If at all possible, see the school or schools in which you're most interested before you apply. This may not be possible when your top choices are far away. Then you may have to visit them after you've been accepted or rely on school brochures and phone calls to get as much information as you can. Plan a visit while classes are in session. Call ahead of time to make an appointment with the admission office and to request a tour of the school. Also ask if the office can arrange for you to meet with some students, including some with LD or ADD. Allow yourself time to walk around campus on your own and, if possible, to drive around the area to see nearby towns and surrounding neighborhoods.

Ask Questions

Write a list of questions about the college to take with you on your campus visit. Use the following questions as a guide for writing your own:

1. Is the campus attractive?
2. Are the residence halls appealing?
3. Do I have a choice of meal plans?
4. Is there a good library?
5. What is the surrounding community like?
6. Can I keep a car on campus?
7. Is travel between college and home easy?
8. Are there good recreational facilities?
9. Is there a comprehensive student health center?
10. Overall, is this a place where I would like to spend my college days? Would I feel comfortable here?

Also, write a list of questions to ask of students with LD or ADD on campus. Use the following questions as a guide for writing your own:

1. Do the staff members understand your needs?
2. Do the staff members provide you with the help, materials, and equipment that you need to succeed in college?
3. Is there a staff member you can go to when things are really going poorly?
4. Do your professors understand your needs and try to help you?
5. Do you feel comfortable here?

Student's street address
City, State Zip
Date

Name of College Contact
Name of College or University
Address
City, State Zip

Dear (Dr., Mr., or Ms.) (last name of contact):

I am a student with a learning disability (attention deficit disorder) and am completing my (junior or senior) year at (name of high school). I expect to graduate in (date) and then go on to college.

Please send me information about the assistance you offer to students with learning disabilities. Also send admission forms, a catalog, and any other specific information that you believe will be helpful to me.

Thank you for your assistance.

Sincerely,

Name of student

Sample Letter Requesting Information

Sample Letter Requesting a Campus Visit

Student's street address
City, State Zip
Date

Name of College Contact
Name of College or University
Address
City, State Zip

Dear (Dr., Mr., or Ms.) (last name of contact):

I am a student with a learning disability (attention deficit disorder) who has been acceptd to your college (university). To help me make a final decision about attending, I wish to visit your campus. During this visit I hope to talk to you regarding the assistance available to students with learning disabilities (attention deficit disorder). I also hope to see the campus and meet some of the students with learning disabilities (attention deficit disorder) who attend your college (university). If possible, would you please arrange a visit for me on any of the following dates: (list two or three available dates)?

I look forward to hearing from you and visiting your campus.

Sincerely,

Name of student

▶ THE PERSONAL SUMMARY CHART ◀

Directions: Write the names of the colleges that you identified in step 4 at the top of each column. For each question of interest to you, write Yes or No based on the information provided in the college profile.

1. Are services provided for graduate students?
2. Is there a special fee for services?
3. Is there an official written policy regarding:
   –Substitutions and waivers of admissions requirements?
   –Substitutions and waivers of graduation requirements?
   –Substitutions and waivers of degree requirements?
   –Grade forgiveness?
4. Is there a special summer program for new students?
5. Is there a special orientation for new students?
6. Is diagnostic testing available?
7. Is subject-area tutoring available?
8. Is basic skills remediation available?
9. Can students take fewer than 12 credits and maintain full-time status?
10. Are special courses available?
11. Are the following auxiliary aids available?
    –Taped textbooks
    –Tape recorders
    –Calculators
    –Typewriters
    –Word processors with spell check
    –Personal computers
    –Optical character readers
    –Talking computers
12. Are the following auxiliary services available?
    –Alternative test arrangements
    –Notetakers
    –Priority registration
    –Advocates
13. Are the following counseling services available?
    –Individual
    –Small-group/discussion groups
    –Career
    –Self-advocacy
14. Is there a student organization?
15. Is there financial aid available of the type desired?

► INFORMATION RESOURCES ◄

Association on Higher Education and Disability (AHEAD)
P.O. Box 21192
Columbus, OH 43221-0192
614-488-4972
Fax: 614-488-1174
http://www.ahead.org/

Attention Deficit Disorder Association (ADDA)
P.O. Box 972
West Newbury, MA 01985
800-487-2282 (toll-free)
http://www.add.org/

Attention Deficit Information Network, Inc. (AD-IN)
475 Hillside Avenue
Needham, MA 02194
617-455-0585 or 444-5466

Children and Adults with Attention Deficit Disorders (CHADD)
499 Northwest 70th Avenue
Suite 101
Plantation, FL 33317
305-587-3700
800-233-4050 (toll-free)
Fax: 305-587-4599
http://www.chadd.org/

Council for Exceptional Children (CEC)
Division for Learning Disabilities (DLD)
1920 Association Drive
Reston, VA 22091-1589
703-620-3660
800-328-0272 (toll-free)
Fax: 703-264-9494
http://www.cec.sped.org/

Council for Learning Disabilities (CLD)
P.O. Box 40303
Overland Park, KS 66204
913-492-8755
Fax: 913-492-2546
http://www1.winthrop.edu/cld/

HEATH Resource Center
National Clearinghouse on Postsecondary Education for Individuals with Disabilities
American Council on Education
One Dupont Circle, NW, Suite 800
Washington, DC 20036-1193
202-939-9322
800-544-3284 (toll-free)
Fax: 202-833-4760
http://ace-info-server.nche.edu/Programs/HEATH/

International Dyslexia Association
The Chester Building,
8600 LaSalle Road
Suite 382
Baltimore, MD 21286-2044
410-296-0232
800-222-3123 (toll-free)
Fax: 410-321-5069
http://www.interdys.org/

Learning Disabilities Association of America, Inc. (LDA)
4156 Library Road
Pittsburgh, PA 15234-1349
412-341-1515
Fax: 412-344-0224
http://www.ldanatl.org/

Learning Disabilities Association of Canada (LDAC)
323 Chapel Street,
Ottawa, Ontario K1N 7Z2
613-238-5721
http://edu-ss10.educ.queensu.ca/lda/

Learning Disabilities Center
331 Milledge Hall
University of Georgia
Athens, GA 30602-5875
706 542-4589
Fax: 706 542-4532
http://www.coe.uga.edu/ldcenter/

Learning Disabilities Network
72 Sharp Street
Suite A-2
Hingham, MA 02043
617-340-5605
Fax: 617-340-5603

National Adult Literacy and Learning Disabilities Center (National ALLD Center)
Academy for Educational Development
1875 Connecticut Avenue, NW
Washington, DC 20009-1202
202-884-8185
800-953-2553 (toll-free)
Fax: 202-884-8422
http://www.nifl.gov/nalldtop.htm/

National Center for Law and Learning Disabilities (NCLLD)
P.O. Box 368
Cabin John, MD 20818
301-469-8308
Fax: 301-469-9466

National Center for Learning Disabilities (NCLD)
381 Park Avenue
Suite 1420
New York, NY 10016
212-545-7510
Fax: 212-545-9665
http://www.ncld.org/

National Information Center for Children and Youth with Disabilities (NICHCY)
P.O. Box 1492
Washington, DC 20013
202-884-8200;
800-695-0285 (toll-free)
Fax: 202-884-8441
http://www.nichcy.org/

Information about nonstandard testing arrangements for the ACT and SAT may be obtained from:

ACT Test Administration
P.O. Box 4028
Iowa City, IA 52243
319-337-1332
Fax: 319-339-3020

SAT Services for Students with Disabilities
College Board
P.O. Box 6226
Princeton NJ 08541-6226
609-771-7137
Fax: 609-771-7681

Information about obtaining recorded textbooks may be obtained from:

Recording for the Blind & Dyslexic
20 Roszel Road
Princeton, NJ 08540
609-452-0606
Fax: 609-520-7990
http://www.rfbd.org/

► QUICK-REFERENCE CHART ◄

	Comp. Program	Special Services	Two-Year	Four-Year	No Special Fee Charged	Page
ALABAMA						
Auburn University at Montgomery		✓		✓	✓	130
Bishop State Community College		✓	✓		✓	461
George C. Wallace State Community College, Dothan		✓	✓		✓	511
James H. Faulkner State Community College		✓	✓		✓	528
John C. Calhoun State Community College		✓	✓		✓	531
John M. Patterson State Technical College		✓	✓		✓	531
Northeast Alabama Community College		✓	✓		✓	574
Southeastern Bible College		✓		✓	✓	280
Troy State University, Troy		✓		✓	✓	303
Troy State University Dothan		✓		✓	✓	304
The University of Alabama, Tuscaloosa		✓		✓		307
The University of Alabama in Huntsville		✓		✓	✓	308
University of Montevallo		✓		✓	✓	327
University of South Alabama		✓		✓		338
ALASKA						
Sheldon Jackson College		✓		✓	✓	278
University of Alaska Fairbanks		✓		✓	✓	308
ARIZONA						
Arizona State University	✓			✓	✓	44
Arizona State University West		✓		✓	✓	128
DeVry Institute of Technology		✓		✓	✓	168
Eastern Arizona College		✓	✓			498
Northern Arizona University		✓		✓	✓	237
Northland Pioneer College		✓	✓		✓	579
Pima Community College		✓	✓		✓	591
South Mountain Community College		✓	✓		✓	620
University of Arizona	✓			✓		95
Yavapai College		✓	✓		✓	653
ARKANSAS						
Arkansas State University		✓		✓	✓	129
East Arkansas Community College		✓	✓		✓	497

	Comp. Program	Special Services	Two-Year	Four-Year	No Special Fee Charged	Page
Garland County Community College		✓	✓		✓	509
Harding University		✓		✓	✓	193
Southern Arkansas University–Magnolia		✓		✓	✓	283
University of Arkansas, Fayetteville		✓		✓	✓	309
University of the Ozarks	✓			✓		110
CALIFORNIA						
Allan Hancock College		✓	✓		✓	452
American River College	✓		✓		✓	378
Antelope Valley College		✓	✓		✓	453
Bakersfield College		✓	✓		✓	458
Biola University		✓		✓		134
Brooks Institute of Photography		✓		✓	✓	138
Butte College	✓		✓		✓	382
Cabrillo College	✓		✓			382
California Polytechnic State University, San Luis Obispo		✓		✓	✓	141
California State Polytechnic University, Pomona		✓		✓	✓	141
California State University, Bakersfield		✓		✓	✓	142
California State University, Chico		✓		✓	✓	143
California State University, Fresno		✓		✓	✓	143
California State University, Fullerton		✓		✓	✓	144
California State University, Long Beach	✓			✓	✓	50
California State University, Northridge	✓			✓	✓	51
California State University, Sacramento		✓		✓	✓	144
California State University, San Bernardino	✓			✓	✓	51
California State University, San Marcos		✓		✓	✓	145
California State University, Stanislaus		✓		✓	✓	146
Cañada College	✓		✓		✓	383
Cerritos College	✓		✓		✓	386
Cerro Coso Community College	✓		✓		✓	387
Chaffey College	✓		✓		✓	388
Chapman University		✓		✓		150
Citrus College	✓		✓		✓	389
City College of San Francisco		✓	✓		✓	477
College of Alameda	✓		✓		✓	391
College of Marin	✓		✓		✓	391
College of San Mateo	✓		✓		✓	392
College of the Canyons		✓	✓			482
College of the Desert		✓	✓		✓	483
College of the Redwoods	✓		✓		✓	392
College of the Sequoias		✓	✓		✓	484
Contra Costa College	✓		✓		✓	395
Crafton Hills College	✓		✓		✓	397
Cuesta College	✓		✓		✓	397

	Comp. Program	Special Services	Two-Year	Four-Year	No Special Fee Charged	Page
Cuyamaca College		✓	✓		✓	490
Cypress College		✓	✓		✓	490
De Anza College	✓		✓		✓	399
Diablo Valley College	✓		✓		✓	400
East Los Angeles College		✓	✓		✓	499
Evergreen Valley College		✓	✓		✓	502
Feather River Community College District	✓		✓		✓	401
Foothill College	✓		✓		✓	402
Fresno City College		✓	✓		✓	506
Fullerton College		✓	✓		✓	507
Gavilan College	✓		✓			402
Glendale Community College	✓		✓			403
Grossmont College	✓		✓		✓	404
Hartnell College		✓	✓			514
Humboldt State University		✓		✓	✓	195
Imperial Valley College		✓	✓		✓	522
Irvine Valley College		✓	✓		✓	524
Kings River Community College	✓		✓		✓	407
Laney College	✓		✓		✓	408
Long Beach City College	✓		✓		✓	409
Los Angeles Harbor College		✓	✓		✓	545
Los Angeles Pierce College	✓		✓			410
Los Angeles Southwest College		✓	✓		✓	545
Los Angeles Valley College		✓	✓		✓	546
Los Medanos College	✓		✓		✓	411
Marymount College, Palos Verdes, California		✓	✓			549
Mendocino College	✓		✓		✓	411
Merced College		✓	✓		✓	553
MiraCosta College		✓	✓		✓	559
Modesto Junior College	✓		✓		✓	415
Monterey Peninsula College	✓		✓		✓	415
Moorpark College	✓		✓		✓	417
Mt. San Antonio College	✓		✓		✓	418
Mt. San Jacinto College	✓		✓		✓	419
Napa Valley College	✓		✓			420
Orange Coast College	✓		✓		✓	426
Oxnard College		✓	✓			585
Pacific Union College		✓		✓		247
Palomar College		✓	✓		✓	586
Pasadena City College		✓	✓		✓	587
Porterville College	✓		✓		✓	429
Rancho Santiago College	✓		✓		✓	430
Rio Hondo College	✓		✓		✓	430
Riverside Community College		✓	✓		✓	597
Sacramento City College	✓		✓			431

	Comp. Program	Special Services	Two-Year	Four-Year	No Special Fee Charged	Page
Saddleback College		✓	✓		✓	599
San Bernardino Valley College		✓	✓		✓	606
San Diego City College		✓	✓		✓	607
San Diego Mesa College		✓	✓			607
San Diego Miramar College		✓	✓			608
San Diego State University		✓		✓	✓	273
San Francisco State University		✓		✓	✓	274
Santa Barbara City College		✓	✓		✓	609
Santa Clara University		✓		✓		275
Santa Monica College	✓		✓		✓	433
Santa Rosa Junior College		✓	✓			611
Shasta Bible College		✓		✓	✓	277
Shasta College		✓	✓		✓	614
Sierra College	✓		✓		✓	434
Skyline College	✓		✓		✓	434
Solano Community College	✓		✓		✓	435
Sonoma State University		✓		✓	✓	280
Stanford University		✓		✓	✓	288
Taft College	✓		✓		✓	437
University of California, Berkeley		✓		✓	✓	310
University of California, Irvine	✓			✓	✓	96
University of California, Los Angeles		✓		✓	✓	311
University of California, Riverside		✓		✓	✓	312
University of California, San Diego		✓		✓	✓	312
University of California, Santa Barbara		✓		✓	✓	313
University of Redlands		✓		✓	✓	335
University of Southern California		✓		✓	✓	341
University of the Pacific		✓		✓		345
Vista Community College		✓	✓			645
West Los Angeles College	✓		✓		✓	444
West Valley College	✓		✓		✓	444
COLORADO						
Arapahoe Community College		✓	✓			454
Colorado Mountain College, Alpine Campus		✓	✓			484
Colorado Northwestern Community College		✓	✓		✓	485
Colorado School of Mines		✓		✓	✓	160
Colorado State University		✓		✓	✓	161
Community College of Aurora		✓	✓		✓	487
Community College of Denver	✓		✓			395
Front Range Community College		✓	✓			507
Lamar Community College		✓	✓		✓	539
Morgan Community College		✓	✓		✓	563
Northeastern Junior College		✓	✓		✓	575
Pikes Peak Community College	✓		✓		✓	428

	Comp. Program	Special Services	Two-Year	Four-Year	No Special Fee Charged	Page
Pueblo Community College		✓	✓		✓	594
Regis University	✓			✓		85
Trinidad State Junior College		✓	✓		✓	633
University of Colorado at Boulder	✓			✓		96
University of Colorado at Colorado Springs	✓			✓	✓	97
University of Denver	✓			✓		99
CONNECTICUT						
Briarwood College		✓	✓		✓	464
Central Connecticut State University		✓		✓	✓	149
Eastern Connecticut State University		✓		✓	✓	172
Housatonic Community-Technical College	✓		✓		✓	405
Manchester Community-Technical College		✓	✓		✓	548
Mitchell College	✓		✓			414
Naugatuck Valley Community–Technical College		✓	✓		✓	567
Norwalk Community-Technical College	✓		✓		✓	424
Southern Connecticut State University		✓		✓	✓	283
University of Connecticut, Storrs	✓			✓	✓	98
University of Hartford	✓			✓	✓	100
University of New Haven		✓		✓	✓	328
DELAWARE						
Delaware State University		✓		✓	✓	167
DISTRICT OF COLUMBIA						
Georgetown University		✓		✓		186
The George Washington University		✓		✓	✓	186
FLORIDA						
Barry University	✓			✓		46
Brevard Community College		✓	✓		✓	464
Central Florida Community College		✓	✓		✓	472
Chipola Junior College		✓	✓		✓	476
Florida Agricultural and Mechanical University	✓			✓		64
Florida Atlantic University		✓		✓	✓	180
Florida Baptist Theological College		✓		✓		181
Florida International University		✓		✓	✓	181
Florida State University		✓		✓		182
Hillsborough Community College		✓	✓		✓	517
Johnson & Wales University		✓		✓	✓	203
Lake City Community College		✓	✓		✓	537
Lake-Sumter Community College		✓	✓		✓	538
Lynn University	✓			✓		73
Manatee Community College		✓	✓		✓	547

	Comp. Program	Special Services	Two-Year	Four-Year	No Special Fee Charged	Page
Miami-Dade Community College		✓	✓		✓	554
Okaloosa-Walton Community College		✓	✓		✓	583
Pensacola Junior College		✓	✓		✓	590
Ringling School of Art and Design		✓		✓	✓	257
St. Johns River Community College		✓	✓		✓	602
St. Petersburg Junior College		✓	✓		✓	604
Santa Fe Community College		✓	✓		✓	610
Seminole Community College		✓	✓		✓	613
Southeastern College of the Assemblies of God		✓		✓	✓	281
Tallahassee Community College		✓	✓		✓	629
University of Florida		✓		✓		315
University of Miami		✓		✓	✓	325
GEORGIA						
Albany State University		✓		✓	✓	123
Andrew College		✓	✓			452
Armstrong Atlantic State University		✓		✓	✓	129
Atlanta Metropolitan College		✓	✓		✓	456
Augusta State University		✓		✓	✓	131
Bainbridge College		✓	✓		✓	457
Brenau University	✓			✓		49
Clayton College & State University		✓		✓	✓	152
Columbus State University		✓		✓	✓	162
Darton College		✓	✓		✓	492
DeKalb College		✓	✓		✓	494
Emory University		✓		✓	✓	177
Floyd College		✓	✓			504
Georgia Southern University		✓		✓		187
Georgia State University		✓		✓		188
Middle Georgia College		✓	✓		✓	555
Morehouse College		✓		✓	✓	227
Reinhardt College	✓			✓		86
Savannah State University		✓		✓	✓	275
Southern Polytechnic State University		✓		✓	✓	285
State University of West Georgia		✓		✓	✓	296
Truett-McConnell College		✓	✓		✓	634
University of Georgia	✓			✓		100
Valdosta State University		✓		✓	✓	356
Waycross College		✓	✓		✓	647
HAWAII						
University of Hawaii at Hilo		✓		✓	✓	316
University of Hawaii–Hawaii Community College		✓	✓		✓	636
University of Hawaii–Leeward Community College	✓		✓		✓	438

	Comp. Program	Special Services	Two-Year	Four-Year	No Special Fee Charged	Page
IDAHO						
College of Southern Idaho		✓	✓		✓	482
University of Idaho		✓		✓		318
ILLINOIS						
Barat College	✓			✓		46
Belleville Area College		✓	✓		✓	460
Black Hawk College, Moline		✓	✓		✓	462
Carl Sandburg College		✓	✓		✓	469
City Colleges of Chicago, Harry S Truman College		✓	✓			478
City Colleges of Chicago, Malcolm X College	✓		✓		✓	390
College of Lake County		✓	✓		✓	481
Columbia College		✓		✓	✓	161
Danville Area Community College		✓	✓		✓	491
DePaul University	✓			✓		58
Eastern Illinois University		✓		✓	✓	173
Elgin Community College		✓	✓		✓	501
Illinois Central College		✓	✓		✓	519
Illinois Eastern Community Colleges, Frontier Community College		✓	✓		✓	519
Illinois Eastern Community Colleges, Lincoln Trail College		✓	✓		✓	520
Illinois Eastern Community Colleges, Olney Central College		✓	✓		✓	520
Illinois Eastern Community Colleges, Wabash Valley College		✓	✓		✓	521
Illinois Institute of Technology		✓		✓	✓	196
Illinois State University		✓		✓	✓	196
Illinois Valley Community College		✓	✓		✓	521
John A. Logan College		✓	✓		✓	530
John Wood Community College		✓	✓		✓	532
Kankakee Community College		✓	✓		✓	533
Kishwaukee College		✓	✓		✓	536
Lincoln Land Community College		✓	✓		✓	543
MacMurray College		✓		✓	✓	214
McHenry County College		✓	✓		✓	552
Moraine Valley Community College		✓	✓			562
The National College of Chiropractic		✓		✓	✓	231
National-Louis University		✓		✓	✓	232
North Central College		✓		✓	✓	236
Northern Illinois University		✓		✓		238
Oakton Community College		✓	✓			582
Olivet Nazarene University		✓		✓	✓	245
Parkland College	✓		✓		✓	426

	Comp. Program	Special Services	Two-Year	Four-Year	No Special Fee Charged	Page
Prairie State College		✓	✓		✓	593
Roosevelt University	✓			✓		88
Saint Xavier University		✓		✓		272
Sauk Valley Community College		✓	✓		✓	611
School of the Art Institute of Chicago		✓		✓	✓	276
Shawnee Community College		✓	✓		✓	614
Southeastern Illinois College		✓	✓		✓	618
Southern Illinois University at Carbondale	✓			✓		91
Southern Illinois University at Edwardsville		✓		✓	✓	284
Spoon River College		✓	✓		✓	623
University of Illinois at Chicago		✓		✓		319
University of Illinois at Urbana–Champaign		✓		✓		319
Waubonsee Community College	✓		✓			442
Western Illinois University		✓		✓	✓	366
William Rainey Harper College	✓		✓			445
INDIANA						
Anderson University	✓			✓	✓	43
Indiana State University		✓		✓	✓	197
Indiana University Bloomington		✓		✓	✓	197
Indiana University Northwest		✓		✓	✓	198
Indiana University Southeast		✓		✓	✓	199
Indiana Wesleyan University		✓		✓	✓	200
Ivy Tech State College–Central Indiana		✓	✓		✓	525
Ivy Tech State College–Kokomo		✓	✓		✓	525
Ivy Tech State College–Northcentral		✓	✓		✓	526
Ivy Tech State College–Northeast		✓	✓		✓	526
Ivy Tech State College–Southeast		✓	✓		✓	526
Ivy Tech State College–Southwest		✓	✓		✓	527
Ivy Tech State College–Whitewater		✓	✓		✓	527
Manchester College		✓		✓	✓	214
Oakland City University		✓		✓	✓	240
Purdue University, West Lafayette		✓		✓	✓	252
Purdue University North Central		✓		✓	✓	252
Taylor University		✓		✓	✓	298
University of Evansville		✓		✓	✓	314
University of Indianapolis	✓			✓		101
University of Southern Indiana		✓		✓	✓	341
Vincennes University	✓		✓			440
IOWA						
Clinton Community College		✓	✓		✓	479
Coe College		✓		✓	✓	154
Des Moines Area Community College		✓	✓		✓	495

	Comp. Program	Special Services	Two-Year	Four-Year	No Special Fee Charged	Page
Ellsworth Community College	✓		✓			400
Graceland College		✓		✓		188
Grinnell College		✓		✓	✓	190
Hawkeye Community College		✓	✓		✓	514
Indian Hills Community College		✓	✓		✓	522
Iowa Central Community College		✓	✓			523
Iowa State University of Science and Technology		✓		✓		200
Iowa Wesleyan College		✓		✓	✓	201
Iowa Western Community College		✓	✓		✓	523
Loras College	✓			✓		72
Marshalltown Community College		✓	✓		✓	549
Morningside College		✓		✓	✓	229
Muscatine Community College	✓	✓	✓		✓	420
Northeast Iowa Community College, Calmar Campus		✓	✓		✓	576
Northeast Iowa Community College, Peosta Campus		✓	✓		✓	576
North Iowa Area Community College		✓	✓		✓	577
Northwest Iowa Community College		✓	✓		✓	580
St. Ambrose University		✓		✓	✓	268
Southeastern Community College, North Campus, West Burlington		✓	✓		✓	618
Southwestern Community College		✓	✓			621
The University of Iowa		✓		✓		320
Waldorf College	✓		✓			441
Western Iowa Tech Community College		✓	✓		✓	649
KANSAS						
Barton County Community College		✓	✓		✓	459
Bethany College		✓		✓	✓	133
Bethel College		✓		✓	✓	133
Butler County Community College		✓	✓		✓	467
Cloud County Community College		✓	✓		✓	479
Colby Community College		✓	✓		✓	480
Donnelly College		✓	✓		✓	496
Fort Scott Community College		✓	✓		✓	505
Garden City Community College		✓	✓		✓	508
Labette Community College		✓	✓		✓	536
MidAmerica Nazarene University		✓		✓	✓	222
Neosho County Community College		✓	✓		✓	567
University of Kansas		✓		✓		320
Wichita State University		✓		✓	✓	372
KENTUCKY						
Clear Creek Baptist Bible College		✓		✓	✓	153
Eastern Kentucky University	✓			✓		60

	Comp. Program	Special Services	Two-Year	Four-Year	No Special Fee Charged	Page
Morehead State University		✓		✓	✓	227
Murray State University		✓		✓	✓	230
Northern Kentucky University		✓		✓	✓	239
Thomas More College		✓		✓	✓	302
University of Kentucky, Hazard Community College		✓	✓		✓	636
University of Kentucky, Lexington Community College		✓	✓		✓	637
University of Kentucky, Somerset Community College		✓	✓		✓	637
Western Kentucky University		✓		✓		366
LOUISIANA						
Louisiana College	✓			✓		73
Louisiana State University and Agricultural and Mechanical College		✓		✓	✓	210
Loyola University New Orleans		✓		✓	✓	212
Our Lady of the Lake College		✓	✓		✓	584
University of Southwestern Louisiana		✓		✓	✓	342
MAINE						
Kennebec Valley Technical College		✓	✓		✓	534
Southern Maine Technical College		✓	✓		✓	619
Unity College	✓			✓	✓	93
University of Maine, Orono		✓		✓	✓	321
University of Maine at Farmington		✓		✓	✓	322
University of Maine at Fort Kent		✓		✓	✓	322
University of Maine at Machias		✓		✓	✓	323
University of New England	✓			✓		105
MARYLAND						
Baltimore City Community College		✓	✓		✓	458
Carroll Community College		✓	✓		✓	469
Charles County Community College		✓	✓		✓	475
Dundalk Community College		✓	✓		✓	497
Frederick Community College		✓	✓		✓	506
Frostburg State University		✓		✓	✓	184
Hagerstown Junior College		✓	✓		✓	512
Harford Community College		✓	✓		✓	513
Howard Community College	✓		✓		✓	406
Loyola College		✓		✓		212
Montgomery College–Rockville Campus	✓		✓		✓	416
Morgan State University		✓		✓		228
University of Baltimore		✓		✓	✓	309
University of Maryland, Baltimore County		✓		✓	✓	323
University of Maryland, College Park		✓		✓	✓	324

	Comp. Program	Special Services	Two-Year	Four-Year	No Special Fee Charged	Page
Washington College		✓		✓	✓	360
Western Maryland College	✓			✓		116
Wor-Wic Community College		✓	✓		✓	652
MASSACHUSETTS						
American International College	✓			✓		42
Anna Maria College		✓		✓	✓	126
Aquinas College at Newton		✓	✓		✓	454
Bentley College		✓		✓	✓	133
Berkshire Community College		✓	✓		✓	461
Boston University	✓			✓		47
Bradford College	✓			✓		48
Brandeis University		✓		✓	✓	136
Bristol Community College		✓	✓		✓	465
Cape Cod Community College	✓		✓		✓	384
Clark University		✓		✓	✓	152
Curry College	✓			✓		56
Dean College		✓	✓			493
Fitchburg State College	✓			✓	✓	63
Hampshire College		✓		✓	✓	192
Lesley College	✓			✓		69
Massasoit Community College		✓	✓		✓	550
Middlesex Community College	✓		✓		✓	412
Mount Holyoke College		✓		✓	✓	229
Mount Ida College	✓		✓			418
Mount Wachusett Community College		✓	✓		✓	565
North Adams State College	✓			✓	✓	83
North Shore Community College		✓	✓		✓	579
Smith College		✓		✓	✓	279
Springfield College		✓		✓	✓	288
Springfield Technical Community College		✓	✓		✓	624
Stonehill College		✓		✓	✓	296
Tufts University		✓		✓	✓	304
University of Massachusetts Amherst	✓			✓		102
Wellesley College		✓		✓	✓	364
Wheelock College		✓		✓	✓	371
MICHIGAN						
Adrian College		✓		✓	✓	122
Alma College		✓		✓	✓	124
Aquinas College		✓		✓	✓	127
Baker College of Jackson		✓	✓		✓	457
Calvin College		✓		✓	✓	146
Charles Stewart Mott Community College		✓	✓		✓	475

	Comp. Program	Special Services	Two-Year	Four-Year	No Special Fee Charged	Page
Glen Oaks Community College		✓	✓		✓	511
Grand Valley State University		✓		✓	✓	189
Jackson Community College		✓	✓		✓	528
Kellogg Community College		✓	✓		✓	533
Kendall College of Art and Design		✓		✓	✓	205
Kirtland Community College		✓	✓		✓	535
Lansing Community College		✓	✓		✓	540
Michigan Technological University		✓		✓	✓	222
Mid Michigan Community College		✓	✓		✓	556
Montcalm Community College		✓	✓		✓	561
Muskegon Community College		✓	✓		✓	565
North Central Michigan College		✓	✓		✓	572
Oakland Community College	✓		✓		✓	424
Oakland University		✓		✓		241
Olivet College		✓		✓	✓	244
Saginaw Valley State University		✓		✓	✓	268
St. Clair County Community College		✓	✓		✓	600
Schoolcraft College		✓	✓		✓	612
Suomi College	✓		✓		✓	436
University of Michigan–Dearborn		✓		✓		325
Washtenaw Community College		✓	✓		✓	647
Wayne State University		✓		✓		362
MINNESOTA						
Alexandria Technical College		✓	✓		✓	451
Anoka-Ramsey Community College	✓		✓		✓	378
Augsburg College	✓			✓	✓	45
Bemidji State University		✓		✓	✓	132
Central Lakes College		✓	✓		✓	473
Century Community and Technical College		✓	✓		✓	474
College of St. Catherine		✓		✓		156
College of St. Catherine–Minneapolis		✓		✓	✓	157
College of St. Scholastica		✓		✓	✓	158
Gustavus Adolphus College		✓		✓	✓	191
Hamline University		✓		✓	✓	192
Hibbing Community College		✓	✓		✓	515
Itasca Community College		✓	✓		✓	524
Macalester College		✓		✓	✓	213
Mankato State University		✓		✓	✓	215
Mesabi Range Community and Technical College		✓	✓		✓	554
Minneapolis Community and Technical College		✓	✓		✓	557
Minnesota West Community and Technical College–Granite Falls Campus		✓	✓		✓	557
Minnesota West Community and Technical College–Worthington Campus		✓	✓		✓	558

	Comp. Program	Special Services	Two-Year	Four-Year	No Special Fee Charged	Page
Moorhead State University		✓		✓	✓	226
Normandale Community College		✓	✓		✓	571
Northland Community and Technical College		✓	✓		✓	578
Northwest Technical College		✓	✓		✓	581
Rainy River Community College		✓	✓		✓	594
Ridgewater College		✓	✓		✓	596
Riverland Community College		✓	✓		✓	597
Rochester Community and Technical College		✓	✓		✓	598
St. Cloud State University		✓		✓	✓	270
St. Cloud Technical College		✓	✓		✓	601
Saint John's University		✓		✓	✓	271
St. Paul Technical College		✓	✓		✓	604
South Central Technical College		✓	✓		✓	616
Southwest State University		✓		✓	✓	287
University of Minnesota, Duluth		✓		✓	✓	326
University of St. Thomas		✓		✓	✓	337
Vermilion Community College		✓	✓		✓	643
MISSISSIPPI						
Meridian Community College		✓	✓		✓	553
Mississippi Delta Community College		✓	✓		✓	559
Mississippi State University		✓		✓	✓	224
William Carey College		✓		✓	✓	373
MISSOURI						
Evangel College		✓		✓	✓	177
Jefferson College		✓	✓		✓	529
Kansas City Art Institute		✓		✓	✓	205
Longview Community College	✓		✓			409
Maple Woods Community College		✓	✓		✓	548
Missouri Southern State College		✓		✓	✓	225
Moberly Area Community College		✓	✓		✓	560
North Central Missouri College		✓	✓		✓	573
Saint Charles County Community College		✓	✓		✓	600
St. Louis Community College at Florissant Valley		✓	✓		✓	602
St. Louis Community College at Forest Park		✓	✓		✓	603
St. Louis Community College at Meramec		✓	✓		✓	603
Southeast Missouri State University		✓		✓		282
Washington University		✓		✓	✓	361
Westminster College	✓			✓		117
MONTANA						
Dawson Community College		✓	✓		✓	493
Flathead Valley Community College		✓	✓		✓	504

	Comp. Program	Special Services	Two-Year	Four-Year	No Special Fee Charged	Page
Montana State University–Billings		✓		✓	✓	225
Montana State University College of Technology–Great Falls		✓	✓		✓	561
Montana State University–Northern		✓		✓	✓	226
Rocky Mountain College		✓		✓	✓	259
Salish Kootenai College		✓	✓		✓	605
The University of Montana–Missoula		✓		✓	✓	326
Western Montana College of The University of Montana		✓		✓	✓	367
NEBRASKA						
Central Community College–Hastings Campus		✓	✓		✓	471
Central Community College–Platte Campus		✓	✓		✓	472
Concordia College		✓		✓	✓	163
Creighton University		✓		✓	✓	164
Doane College		✓		✓	✓	170
Northeast Community College		✓	✓		✓	575
Peru State College		✓		✓	✓	249
Southeast Community College, Beatrice Campus		✓	✓			617
Southeast Community College, Milford Campus		✓	✓		✓	617
Union College	✓			✓		92
Wayne State College		✓		✓	✓	362
NEVADA						
Truckee Meadows Community College	✓		✓			438
University of Nevada, Reno	✓			✓		104
Western Nevada Community College		✓	✓		✓	649
NEW HAMPSHIRE						
Colby-Sawyer College		✓		✓	✓	154
New England College		✓		✓	✓	233
New Hampshire Community Technical College, Manchester/Stratham		✓	✓		✓	568
New Hampshire Technical Institute		✓	✓		✓	569
Rivier College		✓		✓	✓	258
NEW JERSEY						
Atlantic Community College		✓	✓			456
Bergen Community College		✓	✓		✓	460
Brookdale Community College	✓		✓			381
Camden County College		✓	✓		✓	468
Centenary College	✓			✓		53
The College of New Jersey		✓		✓	✓	155
County College of Morris	✓		✓		✓	396
Cumberland County College	✓		✓		✓	398

	Comp. Program	Special Services	Two-Year	Four-Year	No Special Fee Charged	Page
Fairleigh Dickinson University, Teaneck–Hackensack	✓			✓	✓	62
Gloucester County College		✓	✓		✓	511
Hudson County Community College		✓	✓		✓	518
Kean College of New Jersey	✓			✓	✓	68
Middlesex County College	✓		✓		✓	413
New Jersey Institute of Technology		✓		✓	✓	233
Ocean County College	✓		✓		✓	425
Ramapo College of New Jersey		✓		✓	✓	253
Raritan Valley Community College		✓	✓		✓	595
The Richard Stockton College of New Jersey		✓		✓	✓	256
Rider University		✓		✓	✓	256
Rutgers, The State University of New Jersey, Camden College of Arts and Sciences		✓		✓		260
Rutgers, The State University of New Jersey, College of Engineering		✓		✓		261
Rutgers, The State University of New Jersey, College of Pharmacy		✓		✓		261
Rutgers, The State University of New Jersey, Cook College		✓		✓		262
Rutgers, The State University of New Jersey, Douglass College		✓		✓		263
Rutgers, The State University of New Jersey, Livingston College		✓		✓		263
Rutgers, The State University of New Jersey, Mason Gross School of the Arts		✓		✓		264
Rutgers, The State University of New Jersey, Newark College of Arts and Sciences		✓		✓	✓	265
Rutgers, The State University of New Jersey, Rutgers College		✓		✓		265
Rutgers, The State University of New Jersey, University College–Camden		✓		✓		266
Rutgers, The State University of New Jersey, University College–Newark		✓		✓	✓	267
Rutgers, The State University of New Jersey, University College–New Brunswick		✓		✓		267
Sussex County Community College	✓		✓		✓	436
Warren County Community College		✓	✓		✓	646
NEW MEXICO						
Albuquerque Technical Vocational Institute		✓	✓		✓	451
Clovis Community College		✓	✓		✓	480
College of Santa Fe		✓		✓	✓	158
Doña Ana Branch Community College		✓	✓		✓	496
Eastern New Mexico University–Roswell		✓	✓			498
New Mexico Junior College		✓	✓		✓	569
New Mexico State University		✓		✓	✓	234
Northern New Mexico Community College	✓		✓		✓	422
San Juan College		✓	✓		✓	609

	Comp. Program	Special Services	Two-Year	Four-Year	No Special Fee Charged	Page
Santa Fe Community College		✓	✓		✓	610
University of New Mexico–Valencia Campus		✓	✓		✓	637
NEW YORK						
Adelphi University	✓			✓		42
Adirondack Community College		✓	✓		✓	450
Broome Community College		✓	✓		✓	466
Bryant and Stratton Business Institute, Rochester		✓	✓		✓	466
Bryant and Stratton Business Institute, Syracuse		✓	✓		✓	467
Canisius College		✓		✓	✓	147
Cazenovia College		✓		✓	✓	149
Clinton Community College		✓	✓		✓	479
College of New Rochelle		✓		✓	✓	156
College of Staten Island of the City University of New York		✓		✓	✓	159
Columbia College		✓		✓	✓	162
Columbia-Greene Community College		✓	✓		✓	486
Concordia College	✓			✓		55
Cornell University		✓		✓	✓	164
Corning Community College		✓	✓		✓	489
Dowling College	✓			✓		58
D'Youville College		✓		✓	✓	170
Fashion Institute of Technology		✓		✓	✓	179
Finger Lakes Community College		✓	✓		✓	503
Fiorello H. LaGuardia Community College of the City University of New York		✓	✓		✓	503
Fordham University		✓		✓		183
Genesee Community College		✓	✓		✓	510
Hamilton College		✓		✓	✓	191
Hobart and William Smith Colleges		✓		✓	✓	193
Hofstra University	✓			✓		66
Houghton College		✓		✓	✓	194
Hudson Valley Community College		✓	✓		✓	518
Hunter College of the City University of New York		✓		✓	✓	195
Iona College, New Rochelle	✓			✓		67
Jamestown Community College		✓	✓		✓	529
Jefferson Community College		✓	✓		✓	530
John Jay College of Criminal Justice, the City University of New York		✓		✓	✓	202
Long Island University, C.W. Post Campus	✓			✓		71
Manhattan College	✓			✓	✓	74
Manhattanville College	✓			✓		75
Marist College	✓			✓		76
Marymount College		✓		✓	✓	217
Marymount Manhattan College	✓			✓		78

	Comp. Program	Special Services	Two-Year	Four-Year	No Special Fee Charged	Page
Mater Dei College		✓	✓		✓	550
Medaille College		✓		✓	✓	220
Mercy College	✓			✓		78
Mohawk Valley Community College		✓	✓		✓	560
Molloy College	✓			✓		80
Nassau Community College		✓	✓		✓	566
Nazareth College of Rochester		✓		✓	✓	232
New York University	✓			✓	✓	82
Niagara County Community College		✓	✓		✓	570
Niagara University		✓		✓	✓	234
Paul Smith's College of Arts and Sciences		✓	✓		✓	588
Queens College of the City University of New York		✓		✓	✓	253
Rensselaer Polytechnic Institute		✓		✓	✓	255
Roberts Wesleyan College		✓		✓	✓	258
Rochester Institute of Technology	✓			✓		87
Rockland Community College		✓	✓		✓	598
St. Bonaventure University		✓		✓	✓	269
St. Lawrence University		✓		✓	✓	271
St. Thomas Aquinas College	✓			✓		89
Schenectady County Community College		✓	✓		✓	612
State University of New York at Binghamton		✓		✓	✓	289
State University of New York at Buffalo		✓		✓	✓	289
State University of New York at Farmingdale		✓	✓		✓	625
State University of New York at New Paltz		✓		✓	✓	290
State University of New York at Oswego		✓		✓	✓	291
State University of New York at Stony Brook		✓		✓	✓	291
State University of New York College at Brockport		✓		✓	✓	292
State University of New York College at Old Westbury		✓		✓	✓	293
State University of New York College at Oneonta		✓		✓	✓	293
State University of New York College at Plattsburgh		✓		✓		294
State University of New York College at Potsdam		✓		✓	✓	295
State University of New York College of Agriculture and Technology at Cobleskill		✓	✓		✓	625
State University of New York College of Environmental Science and Forestry		✓		✓	✓	295
State University of New York College of Technology at Alfred		✓	✓		✓	626
State University of New York College of Technology at Canton		✓	✓		✓	627
Suffolk County Community College–Ammerman Campus		✓	✓		✓	627
Suffolk County Community College–Eastern Campus		✓	✓		✓	628
Sullivan County Community College		✓	✓		✓	628

	Comp. Program	Special Services	Two-Year	Four-Year	No Special Fee Charged	Page
Syracuse University		✓		✓	✓	297
Trocaire College		✓	✓		✓	633
University at Albany, State University of New York		✓		✓		306
University of Rochester		✓		✓	✓	336
Utica College of Syracuse University		✓		✓		355
Utica School of Commerce		✓	✓		✓	642
Villa Maria College of Buffalo		✓	✓		✓	644
Westchester Community College		✓	✓		✓	648
NORTH CAROLINA						
Alamance Community College		✓	✓		✓	451
Appalachian State University		✓		✓	✓	127
Asheville-Buncombe Technical Community College		✓	✓		✓	455
Blue Ridge Community College	✓		✓		✓	380
Brevard College		✓	✓		✓	463
Caldwell Community College and Technical Institute		✓	✓		✓	468
Carteret Community College		✓	✓		✓	470
Catawba Valley Community College	✓		✓		✓	384
Central Piedmont Community College	✓		✓		✓	386
Davidson College		✓		✓		166
Davidson County Community College		✓	✓		✓	492
East Carolina University		✓		✓		171
Elon College		✓		✓	✓	176
Gardner-Webb University		✓		✓	✓	185
Haywood Community College		✓	✓		✓	515
Johnson C. Smith University		✓		✓	✓	204
Mayland Community College		✓	✓		✓	551
McDowell Technical Community College		✓	✓		✓	551
North Carolina Agricultural and Technical State University		✓		✓	✓	235
North Carolina State University		✓		✓	✓	235
Piedmont Bible College		✓		✓	✓	250
Randolph Community College		✓	✓		✓	595
Sandhills Community College		✓	✓		✓	606
Southwestern Community College		✓	✓		✓	622
The University of North Carolina at Chapel Hill	✓			✓	✓	106
University of North Carolina at Charlotte		✓		✓	✓	328
University of North Carolina at Greensboro		✓		✓	✓	329
University of North Carolina at Pembroke		✓		✓	✓	330
University of North Carolina at Wilmington		✓		✓	✓	330
Vance-Granville Community College		✓	✓		✓	642
Wake Technical Community College	✓		✓		✓	441
Western Carolina University		✓		✓	✓	365

	Comp. Program	Special Services	Two-Year	Four-Year	No Special Fee Charged	Page
Wilkes Community College		✓	✓		✓	651
Wilson Technical Community College		✓	✓		✓	651
Wingate University		✓		✓	✓	374
NORTH DAKOTA						
Bismarck State College		✓	✓		✓	462
Dickinson State University		✓		✓	✓	169
Mayville State University		✓		✓	✓	218
Minot State University–Bottineau		✓	✓		✓	558
North Dakota State College of Science		✓	✓		✓	574
North Dakota State University		✓		✓	✓	237
University of North Dakota		✓		✓	✓	331
University of North Dakota–Lake Region		✓	✓		✓	638
Valley City State University		✓		✓	✓	356
OHIO						
Antioch College		✓		✓	✓	126
Art Academy of Cincinnati		✓		✓	✓	130
Central Ohio Technical College	✓		✓		✓	385
College of Mount St. Joseph	✓			✓		54
Cuyahoga Community College, Eastern Campus		✓	✓		✓	489
Denison University		✓		✓	✓	168
Franklin University		✓		✓	✓	183
Hocking College		✓	✓		✓	517
Kent State University		✓		✓	✓	206
Kent State University, Stark Campus		✓	✓		✓	534
Lakeland Community College		✓	✓		✓	537
Lima Technical College		✓	✓		✓	542
Lorain County Community College		✓	✓		✓	544
Lourdes College		✓		✓	✓	211
Miami University		✓		✓	✓	221
Miami University–Middletown Campus		✓	✓		✓	555
Muskingum Area Technical College		✓	✓		✓	565
Muskingum College	✓			✓		81
Northwestern College		✓	✓		✓	580
Northwest State Community College		✓	✓		✓	581
Oberlin College	✓			✓	✓	84
Ohio State University Agricultural Technical Institute		✓	✓			582
The Ohio State University at Lima		✓		✓		242
The Ohio State University at Marion		✓		✓		242
Ohio State University–Mansfield Campus		✓		✓		242
Ohio State University–Newark Campus		✓		✓	✓	243
Owens Community College, Toledo		✓	✓		✓	585
Shawnee State University		✓		✓	✓	277

	Comp. Program	Special Services	Two-Year	Four-Year	No Special Fee Charged	Page
Sinclair Community College		✓	✓		✓	615
Terra State Community College		✓	✓		✓	629
The University of Akron		✓		✓	✓	306
The University of Akron–Wayne College		✓	✓		✓	635
University of Cincinnati		✓		✓	✓	313
The University of Findlay		✓		✓	✓	314
University of Toledo	✓			✓	✓	111
Urbana University		✓		✓	✓	354
Ursuline College	✓			✓		115
Washington State Community College		✓	✓		✓	646
Wright State University	✓			✓	✓	119
Wright State University, Lake Campus		✓	✓		✓	652
Xavier University		✓		✓	✓	375
OKLAHOMA						
Northern Oklahoma College		✓	✓		✓	576
Oklahoma State University		✓		✓	✓	243
Oklahoma State University, Oklahoma City		✓	✓		✓	583
Oral Roberts University		✓		✓	✓	245
Phillips University		✓		✓	✓	249
St. Gregory's College		✓	✓			601
Seminole State College		✓	✓		✓	614
Southeastern Oklahoma State University		✓		✓	✓	281
Tulsa Community College		✓	✓		✓	634
University of Oklahoma		✓		✓	✓	332
OREGON						
Blue Mountain Community College	✓		✓		✓	380
Chemeketa Community College		✓	✓		✓	476
Clackamas Community College		✓	✓		✓	478
Eastern Oregon University		✓		✓	✓	173
Lane Community College		✓	✓		✓	540
Linfield College		✓		✓	✓	209
Linn-Benton Community College		✓	✓		✓	543
Mt. Hood Community College		✓	✓		✓	564
Oregon Institute of Technology		✓		✓	✓	246
Oregon State University		✓		✓	✓	246
Portland Community College		✓	✓		✓	592
Reed College		✓		✓	✓	255
Rogue Community College		✓	✓		✓	599
Treasure Valley Community College		✓	✓		✓	632
Umpqua Community College		✓	✓		✓	635
Western Baptist College		✓		✓	✓	365
Western Oregon University		✓		✓	✓	367

	Comp. Program	Special Services	Two-Year	Four-Year	No Special Fee Charged	Page
PENNSYLVANIA						
Albright College		✓		✓	✓	124
Bryn Mawr College		✓		✓		139
Bucknell University		✓		✓	✓	140
Bucks County Community College		✓	✓		✓	467
California University of Pennsylvania	✓			✓		52
Clarion University of Pennsylvania		✓		✓	✓	151
College Misericordia	✓			✓	✓	54
Community College of Allegheny County	✓		✓		✓	394
Community College of Beaver County		✓	✓		✓	487
Community College of Philadelphia		✓	✓		✓	488
Delaware County Community College	✓		✓		✓	399
Delaware Valley College		✓		✓	✓	167
Drexel University	✓			✓	✓	59
Eastern College		✓		✓	✓	172
East Stroudsburg University of Pennsylvania		✓		✓	✓	174
Edinboro University of Pennsylvania	✓			✓		62
Gannon University	✓			✓		65
Harcum College	✓		✓			404
Harrisburg Area Community College		✓	✓		✓	513
Indiana University of Pennsylvania		✓		✓	✓	199
Johnson Technical Institute		✓	✓		✓	532
King's College	✓			✓		68
Kutztown University of Pennsylvania		✓		✓	✓	207
Lehigh Carbon Community College		✓	✓		✓	541
Luzerne County Community College		✓	✓		✓	546
Mansfield University of Pennsylvania		✓		✓	✓	216
Marywood University		✓		✓	✓	218
Mercyhurst College	✓			✓		79
Messiah College		✓		✓	✓	220
Northampton County Area Community College		✓	✓		✓	572
Peirce College		✓	✓		✓	588
Pennsylvania College of Technology		✓	✓		✓	589
Pennsylvania State University Altoona College		✓		✓	✓	247
Pennsylvania State University Delaware County Campus of the Commonwealth College	✓		✓		✓	428
Pennsylvania State University Harrisburg Campus of the Capital College		✓		✓	✓	248
Pennsylvania State University Mont Alto Campus of the Commonwealth College		✓	✓		✓	589
Pennsylvania State University University Park Campus		✓		✓		248
Pennsylvania State University Wilkes-Barre Campus of the Commonwealth College		✓	✓		✓	590
Pittsburgh Technical Institute		✓	✓		✓	592

	Comp. Program	Special Services	Two-Year	Four-Year	No Special Fee Charged	Page
Reading Area Community College		✓	✓		✓	596
Rosemont College		✓		✓	✓	260
Temple University, Philadelphia		✓		✓	✓	299
University of Pennsylvania		✓		✓		333
University of Pittsburgh	✓			✓	✓	106
University of Pittsburgh at Greensburg		✓		✓	✓	333
University of the Arts	✓			✓	✓	109
Washington and Jefferson College		✓		✓	✓	360
West Chester University of Pennsylvania		✓		✓	✓	364
Westminster College		✓		✓	✓	369
Widener University		✓		✓	✓	372
PUERTO RICO						
Polytechnic University of Puerto Rico		✓		✓	✓	251
University of Puerto Rico, Humacao University College		✓		✓	✓	334
University of Puerto Rico, Río Piedras		✓		✓	✓	334
RHODE ISLAND						
Brown University		✓		✓	✓	139
Community College of Rhode Island		✓	✓		✓	488
Johnson & Wales University		✓		✓	✓	203
New England Institute of Technology		✓	✓		✓	568
Providence College		✓		✓	✓	251
Salve Regina University		✓		✓	✓	273
University of Rhode Island		✓		✓	✓	335
SOUTH CAROLINA						
Aiken Technical College		✓	✓		✓	450
The Citadel, The Military College of South Carolina		✓		✓		150
Clemson University		✓		✓		153
Limestone College	✓			✓		70
Spartanburg Technical College		✓	✓		✓	622
Trident Technical College		✓	✓		✓	632
University of South Carolina, Columbia		✓		✓	✓	338
University of South Carolina–Aiken		✓		✓	✓	339
University of South Carolina–Spartanburg		✓		✓	✓	339
York Technical College	✓		✓		✓	446
SOUTH DAKOTA						
Augustana College		✓		✓	✓	131
Black Hills State University		✓		✓	✓	135
Dakota Wesleyan University		✓		✓	✓	165
National American University		✓		✓	✓	231

	Comp. Program	Special Services	Two-Year	Four-Year	No Special Fee Charged	Page
Northern State University		✓		✓	✓	239
University of Sioux Falls		✓		✓	✓	337
University of South Dakota		✓		✓	✓	340
TENNESSEE						
David Lipscomb University		✓		✓		166
Lee University		✓		✓	✓	208
Middle Tennessee State University		✓		✓	✓	223
Motlow State Community College		✓	✓		✓	563
Nashville State Technical Institute		✓	✓		✓	566
Pellissippi State Technical Community College	✓		✓		✓	427
Shelby State Community College		✓	✓		✓	615
Southern Adventist University		✓		✓	✓	282
State Technical Institute at Memphis		✓	✓		✓	624
Tennessee State University		✓		✓	✓	299
Tennessee Technological University		✓		✓	✓	300
Union University		✓		✓	✓	305
The University of Memphis	✓			✓	✓	103
University of Tennessee at Chattanooga	✓			✓		107
The University of Tennessee at Martin	✓			✓		108
University of Tennessee, Knoxville		✓		✓		342
TEXAS						
Abilene Christian University		✓		✓		122
Angelina College		✓	✓		✓	453
The Art Institute of Houston		✓	✓		✓	455
Bee County College		✓	✓		✓	459
Blinn College	✓		✓		✓	379
Brookhaven College		✓	✓		✓	465
Cedar Valley College		✓	✓		✓	471
Central Texas College		✓	✓		✓	474
Cisco Junior College		✓	✓		✓	477
College of the Mainland		✓	✓		✓	483
Collin County Community College	✓		✓		✓	393
Del Mar College		✓	✓		✓	494
Eastfield College		✓	✓		✓	499
El Centro College		✓	✓		✓	500
El Paso Community College		✓	✓		✓	501
Galveston College		✓	✓		✓	508
Hill College of the Hill Junior College District		✓	✓		✓	516
Kilgore College		✓	✓		✓	535
Lamar University–Port Arthur		✓	✓		✓	539
Lee College		✓	✓		✓	541
Lon Morris College		✓	✓		✓	543

	Comp. Program	Special Services	Two-Year	Four-Year	No Special Fee Charged	Page
McLennan Community College		✓	✓		✓	552
Midland College		✓	✓		✓	556
Midwestern State University		✓		✓	✓	223
Mountain View College		✓	✓		✓	564
North Harris College		✓	✓		✓	577
North Lake College		✓	✓		✓	578
Paris Junior College		✓	✓		✓	586
St. Philip's College		✓	✓		✓	605
San Antonio College	✓		✓		✓	432
San Jacinto College–Central Campus		✓	✓		✓	608
San Jacinto College–North Campus		✓	✓		✓	609
Schreiner College	✓			✓		90
Southern Methodist University		✓		✓		285
South Texas Community College		✓	✓		✓	621
Southwest Texas State University	✓			✓	✓	92
Tarleton State University		✓		✓	✓	298
Texas A&M University, College Station		✓		✓	✓	301
Texas A&M University–Kingsville		✓		✓		301
Texas State Technical College–Harlingen		✓	✓		✓	630
Texas State Technical College–Waco/Marshall Campus		✓	✓		✓	630
Texas Wesleyan University		✓		✓	✓	302
Tomball College		✓	✓		✓	631
University of Houston		✓		✓	✓	317
University of Houston–Downtown		✓		✓	✓	318
University of North Texas		✓		✓		331
The University of Texas at Arlington		✓		✓	✓	343
The University of Texas at Austin		✓		✓	✓	344
The University of Texas at El Paso		✓		✓	✓	344
The University of Texas at San Antonio		✓		✓		345
UTAH						
Brigham Young University		✓		✓	✓	137
College of Eastern Utah		✓	✓		✓	481
Dixie College		✓	✓		✓	495
Salt Lake Community College	✓		✓		✓	432
Southern Utah University		✓		✓	✓	286
University of Utah		✓		✓	✓	346
Utah State University		✓		✓		354
Utah Valley State College	✓		✓		✓	439
Weber State University		✓		✓	✓	363
VERMONT						
Burlington College		✓		✓	✓	140
College of St. Joseph		✓		✓	✓	157

	Comp. Program	Special Services	Two-Year	Four-Year	No Special Fee Charged	Page
Green Mountain College		✓		✓	✓	190
Johnson State College		✓		✓	✓	204
Landmark College	✓		✓		✓	407
Norwich University		✓		✓	✓	240
Southern Vermont College		✓		✓	✓	287
University of Vermont	✓			✓		112
Vermont Technical College		✓	✓		✓	643
VIRGINIA						
Bluefield College		✓		✓	✓	135
College of William and Mary		✓		✓	✓	159
Community Hospital of Roanoke Valley–College of Health Sciences		✓		✓	✓	163
Dabney S. Lancaster Community College		✓	✓		✓	491
Eastern Mennonite University	✓			✓	✓	61
Emory & Henry College		✓		✓		176
Ferrum College		✓		✓	✓	180
George Mason University		✓		✓	✓	185
James Madison University		✓		✓	✓	202
Liberty University		✓		✓	✓	209
Longwood College		✓		✓	✓	210
Lord Fairfax Community College		✓	✓		✓	544
Mary Washington College		✓		✓	✓	217
New River Community College	✓		✓		✓	421
Patrick Henry Community College		✓	✓		✓	587
Piedmont Virginia Community College		✓	✓		✓	591
Thomas Nelson Community College		✓	✓		✓	631
University of Virginia		✓		✓	✓	347
Virginia Commonwealth University		✓		✓	✓	357
Virginia Highlands Community College		✓	✓		✓	644
Virginia Intermont College		✓		✓	✓	357
Virginia Polytechnic Institute and State University		✓		✓	✓	358
Virginia Western Community College		✓	✓		✓	645
WASHINGTON						
Centralia College		✓	✓		✓	473
Columbia Basin College		✓	✓		✓	486
Eastern Washington University		✓		✓	✓	174
Edmonds Community College		✓	✓		✓	500
Everett Community College		✓	✓		✓	502
The Evergreen State College		✓		✓	✓	178
Green River Community College		✓	✓		✓	512
Highline Community College		✓	✓		✓	516
Lutheran Bible Institute of Seattle		✓		✓	✓	213
Olympic College		✓	✓		✓	584

	Comp. Program	Special Services	Two-Year	Four-Year	No Special Fee Charged	Page
Saint Martin's College		✓		✓	✓	272
Seattle Central Community College		✓	✓		✓	613
Seattle Pacific University		✓		✓	✓	276
Skagit Valley College		✓	✓		✓	616
South Seattle Community College		✓	✓		✓	620
Spokane Falls Community College		✓	✓			623
Walla Walla College		✓		✓	✓	359
Washington State University		✓		✓	✓	361
Wenatchee Valley College		✓	✓		✓	648
Western Washington University		✓		✓	✓	368
Whitman College		✓		✓	✓	371
WEST VIRGINIA						
Bluefield State College		✓		✓	✓	136
Davis & Elkins College	✓			✓		57
Fairmont State College		✓		✓	✓	179
Marshall University	✓			✓		77
Potomac State College of West Virginia University		✓	✓		✓	593
Southern West Virginia Community and Technical College		✓	✓		✓	619
West Liberty State College		✓		✓	✓	369
West Virginia State College		✓		✓	✓	370
West Virginia University		✓		✓		370
West Virginia Wesleyan College	✓			✓		118
WISCONSIN						
Alverno College		✓		✓	✓	125
Blackhawk Technical College		✓	✓		✓	463
Cardinal Stritch University		✓		✓	✓	148
Chippewa Valley Technical College	✓		✓		✓	388
Edgewood College		✓		✓	✓	175
Fox Valley Technical College		✓	✓		✓	505
Gateway Technical College		✓	✓		✓	509
Lakeshore Technical College		✓	✓		✓	538
Lawrence University		✓		✓	✓	208
Madison Area Technical College		✓	✓		✓	547
Marquette University		✓		✓		216
Milwaukee Area Technical College	✓		✓		✓	413
Moraine Park Technical College		✓	✓		✓	562
Nicolet Area Technical College		✓	✓		✓	571
Northcentral Technical College		✓	✓		✓	573
Northeast Wisconsin Technical College	✓		✓		✓	421
Ripon College		✓		✓	✓	257
Southwest Wisconsin Technical College		✓	✓		✓	622

	Comp. Program	Special Services	Two-Year	Four-Year	No Special Fee Charged	Page
University of Wisconsin Center–Baraboo/Sauk County		✓	✓		✓	638
University of Wisconsin Center–Fox Valley		✓	✓		✓	639
University of Wisconsin Center–Marathon County		✓	✓			639
University of Wisconsin Center–Marinette County		✓	✓		✓	640
University of Wisconsin Center–Marshfield/Wood County		✓	✓		✓	640
University of Wisconsin Center–Rock County		✓	✓		✓	641
University of Wisconsin Center–Sheboygan County		✓	✓		✓	641
University of Wisconsin–Eau Claire		✓		✓	✓	349
University of Wisconsin–Green Bay		✓		✓	✓	350
University of Wisconsin–La Crosse		✓		✓	✓	350
University of Wisconsin–Madison		✓		✓		351
University of Wisconsin–Milwaukee		✓		✓		351
University of Wisconsin–Oshkosh	✓			✓	✓	113
University of Wisconsin–Stout		✓		✓		352
University of Wisconsin–Superior		✓		✓	✓	352
University of Wisconsin–Whitewater	✓			✓		114
Viterbo College		✓		✓	✓	359
Waukesha County Technical College	✓		✓			443
Western Wisconsin Technical College		✓	✓		✓	649
Wisconsin Indianhead Technical College, Ashland Campus	✓		✓		✓	446
Wisconsin Indianhead Technical College, Superior Campus		✓	✓		✓	652
WYOMING						
Casper College		✓	✓		✓	470
Eastern Wyoming College		✓	✓		✓	499
Laramie County Community College		✓	✓		✓	541
Northwest College	✓		✓		✓	423
University of Wyoming		✓		✓	✓	353
Western Wyoming Community College		✓	✓		✓	650
CANADA						
ALBERTA						
Alberta College of Art and Design		✓		✓	✓	123
University of Alberta	✓			✓		94
BRITISH COLUMBIA						
Simon Fraser University		✓		✓	✓	279
University of British Columbia		✓		✓	✓	310

	Comp. Program	Special Services	Two-Year	Four-Year	No Special Fee Charged	Page
MANITOBA						
The University of Winnipeg		✓		✓	✓	348
NEW BRUNSWICK						
Mount Allison University	✓			✓	✓	81
NOVA SCOTIA						
St. Francis Xavier University		✓		✓	✓	270
Saint Mary's University	✓			✓	✓	88
ONTARIO						
Brock University		✓		✓	✓	138
Carleton University		✓		✓	✓	148
Laurentian University		✓		✓	✓	207
McMaster University		✓		✓		219
Queen's University at Kingston	✓			✓	✓	85
Redeemer College		✓		✓	✓	254
Trent University		✓		✓	✓	303
University of Guelph		✓		✓	✓	316
University of Waterloo		✓		✓	✓	347
The University of Western Ontario		✓		✓	✓	348
University of Windsor	✓			✓	✓	113
Wilfrid Laurier University		✓		✓		373
York University	✓			✓		120
QUEBEC						
McGill University		✓		✓	✓	219

▸ FOUR-YEAR COLLEGES ◂

WITH COMPREHENSIVE PROGRAMS

ADELPHI UNIVERSITY

Garden City, New York

Students with LD	100	Subject-Area Tutoring	
ADD services	✓	Special Courses	✓
Staff	12 full-time	Taped Textbooks	✓
Special Fee	✓	Alternative Test Arrang.	✓
Diagnostic Testing	✓	Notetakers	✓
Basic Skills Remediation	✓	LD Student Organization	

LEARNING DISABILITIES PROGRAM INFORMATION

The Program for College Students with Learning Disabilities began offering services in 1979. Currently the program serves 100 undergraduates with LD. Services are also available to graduate students. Students diagnosed with ADD/ADHD are eligible for the same services available to students with LD.
Staff: 12 full-time staff members, including director. Services provided by tutors, counselors, test proctors, LD specialists.
Special Fees: $3800 per year.
Applications and admissions: *Required:* high school transcript, extended time SAT I, personal interview, autobiographical statement, letters of recommendation, psychoeducational report completed within 3 years, diagnosis by LD specialist, WAIS-R. Students may begin taking classes in summer only (freshmen); transfer students may begin taking classes in any term. *Application deadline:* continuous.

PROGRAM AND SERVICE COMPONENTS

Special preparation or orientation: Summer program (required for some) held prior to entering college. Orientation (required for some) held during summer prior to enrollment (5 weeks).
Diagnostic testing: Reading, math, handwriting, written language, study skills, learning strategies.
Academic advising: Provided by LD staff members during freshman year; academic advisers in consultation with LD staff members provide program planning for sophomore, junior and senior students. Students with LD may take up to 17 credits each term; most take 12 to 16 credits; 12 credits required to maintain full-time status and be eligible for financial aid.
Counseling services: Individual counseling, small-group counseling, career counseling, self-advocacy training, family counseling.
Basic skills remediation: Offered one-on-one by LD teachers. Available in written language, learning strategies, study skills, time management, social skills, word processing.
Special courses: College survival skills, communication skills, composition. All offered for credit; all enter into overall grade point average.
Auxiliary aids: Taped textbooks, word-processors with spell-check, personal computers.
Auxiliary services: Alternative test arrangements, notetakers, priority registration, advocacy, readers, scribes.

GENERAL COLLEGE INFORMATION

Independent, coed. Awards bachelor's, master's, doctoral degrees. Founded 1896. *Setting:* 75-acre suburban campus with easy access to New York City. *Endowment:* $37.9 million. *Research spending 1995–96:* $249,606. *Total enrollment:* 5,969. *Faculty:* 549 (199 full-time, 71% with terminal degrees, 350 part-time); student–undergrad faculty ratio is 12:1.
Enrollment Profile: 2,787 students from 34 states and territories, 38 other countries. 66% women, 34% men, 32% part-time, 91% state residents, 20% live on campus, 13% transferred in, 5% international, 41% 25 or older, 0% Native American, 7% Hispanic, 16% black, 5% Asian or Pacific Islander. *Retention:* 73% of 1995 full-time freshmen returned. *Areas of study chosen:* 18% health professions and related sciences, 13% liberal arts/general studies, 10% business management and administrative services, 10% education, 5% biological and life sciences, 4% psychology, 3% mathematics, 2% communications and journalism, 2% performing arts, 1% foreign language and literature, 1% philosophy, 1% physical sciences, 1% social sciences. *Most popular recent majors:* business administration/commerce/management, nursing, psychology.
First-Year Class: 337 total; 1,947 applied, 71% were accepted, 24% of whom enrolled. 18% from top 10% of their high school class, 47% from top quarter, 77% from top half.
Graduation Requirements: 120 credits; computer course for business, accounting, management, banking and money management, earth science, secondary education, math majors; internship (some majors); senior project.
Computers on Campus: 450 computers available on campus for general student use. Computer purchase/lease plans available. A campus-wide network can be accessed from student residence rooms. Students can contact faculty members and/or advisers through e-mail. Computers for student use in computer center, learning resource center, library, gymnasium, Nursing Learning Center provide access to the Internet/World Wide Web, on-campus e-mail addresses. Staffed computer lab on campus. *Academic computing expenditure 1995–96:* $154,465.

EXPENSES AND FINANCIAL AID

Expenses for 1996–97: *Application fee:* $35. Comprehensive fee of $20,520 includes full-time tuition ($13,830), mandatory fees ($170), and college room and board ($6520). College room only: $3620. Part-time tuition: $420 per credit. Part-time mandatory fees: $184 per year.
Undergraduate Financial Aid: 71% of all full-time undergraduates enrolled in fall 1996 applied for aid; of these,100% were judged to have need according to Federal Methodology, of whom 98% were aided. On average, 100% of need was met. *Financial aid deadline (priority):* 2/15. *Financial aid forms:* FAFSA required; state form acceptable. Institutional form, CSS Business Supplement required for some.
LD Program Contact: Ms. Susan Spencer, Assistant Dean for Learning Resources, Adelphi University, Box 701, Eddy Hall, Garden City, NY 11530, 516-877-4710. Fax: 516-877-4711. Email: spencer@adlibv.adelphi.edu.

AMERICAN INTERNATIONAL COLLEGE

Springfield, Massachusetts

Students with LD	96	Subject-Area Tutoring	✓
ADD services	✓	Special Courses	
Staff	10 full-, 4 part-time	Taped Textbooks	✓
Special Fee	Varies	Alternative Test Arrang.	✓
Diagnostic Testing		Notetakers	
Basic Skills Remediation	✓	LD Student Organization	

LEARNING DISABILITIES PROGRAM INFORMATION

The Supportive Learning Services Program began offering services in 1977. Currently the program serves 96 undergraduates with LD. Services are also available to graduate students. Students diagnosed with ADD/ADHD are eligible for the same services available to students with LD.
Staff: 10 full-time, 4 part-time staff members, including coordinator, assistant coordinator. Services provided by remediation specialists, tutors, diagnostic specialists.
Special Fees: Range from $1000 to $3300 per year.
Applications and admissions: *Required:* high school transcript, grade point average, class rank, courses completed, untimed SAT I, personal interview, letters of recommendation, psychoeducational report completed within 2 years; *recom-*

mended: high school extracurricular activities, IEP (Individualized Education Program), extended time SAT I, autobiographical statement, evaluations from high school counselors. Students may begin taking classes in fall, spring, or summer. *Application deadline:* continuous.

Special policies: The college has written policies regarding grade forgiveness.

PROGRAM AND SERVICE COMPONENTS

Special preparation or orientation: Required orientation held during registration.

Academic advising: Provided by LD staff members, academic advisers. Students with LD may take up to 16 credits each term; most take 12 to 15 credits; 12 credits required to maintain full-time status and be eligible for financial aid.

Counseling services: Individual counseling, career counseling.

Basic skills remediation: Offered one-on-one by LD teachers. Available in reading, math, spelling, handwriting, written language, learning strategies, study skills, time management, computer skills.

Subject-area tutoring: Offered one-on-one by professional teachers. Available in all subjects.

Auxiliary aids: Taped textbooks, tape recorders, word-processors with spell-check, personal computers.

Auxiliary services: Alternative test arrangements, advocacy.

GENERAL COLLEGE INFORMATION

Independent, comprehensive, coed. Awards associate, bachelor's, master's, doctoral degrees. Founded 1885. *Setting:* 58-acre urban campus. *Endowment:* $9.3 million. *Educational spending 1995–96:* $3724 per undergrad. *Total enrollment:* 1,986. *Undergraduate faculty:* 93 (72 full-time, 70% with terminal degrees, 21 part-time); student–undergrad faculty ratio is 16:1.

Enrollment Profile: 1,420 students from 26 states and territories, 24 other countries. 52% women, 48% men, 17% part-time, 59% state residents, 58% live on campus, 39% transferred in, 7% international, 9% 25 or older, 5% Hispanic, 13% black, 2% Asian or Pacific Islander. *Retention:* 68% of 1995 full-time freshmen returned. *Graduation:* 58% graduate in 4 years, 60% in 5 years, 61% in 6 years. *Areas of study chosen:* 23% health professions and related sciences, 16% education, 12% business management and administrative services, 12% social sciences, 10% biological and life sciences, 4% premed, 3% physical sciences, 2% English language/literature/letters, 2% prelaw, 1% communications and journalism, 1% computer and information sciences, 1% foreign language and literature, 1% mathematics, 1% philosophy. *Most popular recent majors:* criminal justice, accounting, nursing.

First-Year Class: 261 total; 1,117 applied, 77% were accepted, 30% of whom enrolled. 6% from top 10% of their high school class, 21% from top quarter, 75% from top half. 8 class presidents, 2 valedictorians.

Graduation Requirements: 120 credits for bachelor's; 2 semesters of lab science; computer course for business, math, physical therapy, occupational therapy, criminal justice majors; internship (some majors); senior project (some majors).

Computers on Campus: 50 computers available on campus for general student use. Computer purchase/lease plans available. Students can contact faculty members and/or advisers through e-mail. Computers for student use in computer center, computer labs, learning resource center, library. Staffed computer lab on campus provides training in use of computers, software. *Academic computing expenditure 1995–96:* $78,850.

EXPENSES AND FINANCIAL AID

Expenses for 1997–98: Comprehensive fee of $16,936 includes full-time tuition ($10,718), mandatory fees ($526), and college room and board ($5692). Part-time tuition: $325 per credit. Part-time mandatory fees: $20 per semester.

Undergraduate Financial Aid: 97% of all full-time undergraduates enrolled in fall 1996 applied for aid; of these, 80% were judged to have need according to Federal Methodology, of whom 100% were aided. On average, 80% of need was met. *Financial aid deadline (priority):* 4/15. *Financial aid forms:* FAFSA, institutional form required.

LD Program Contact: Ms. Mary Saltus, Coordinator, Supportive Learning Services Program, American International College, 1000 State Street, Springfield, MA 01109-3189, 413-747-6426. Fax: 413-737-2803.

ANDERSON UNIVERSITY

Anderson, Indiana

Students with LD	55	Subject-Area Tutoring	✓
ADD services	✓	Special Courses	✓
Staff	1 full-, 1 part-time	Taped Textbooks	✓
Special Fee	None	Alternative Test Arrang.	✓
Diagnostic Testing		Notetakers	
Basic Skills Remediation	✓	LD Student Organization	

LEARNING DISABILITIES PROGRAM INFORMATION

The Kissinger Learning Center began offering services in 1987. Currently the program serves 55 undergraduates with LD. Services are also available to graduate students. Students diagnosed with ADD/ADHD are eligible for the same services available to students with LD.

Staff: 1 full-time, 1 part-time staff members, including director, coordinator. Services provided by remediation specialist, tutors, diagnostic specialist.

Special Fees: No special fees are charged for services to students with LD.

Applications and admissions: *Required:* high school transcript, grade point average, class rank, courses completed, untimed SAT I or ACT, personal interview, autobiographical statement, letters of recommendation, psychoeducational report completed within 2 years. Students may begin taking classes in fall only. *Application deadline:* continuous.

PROGRAM AND SERVICE COMPONENTS

Special preparation or orientation: Required orientation held during registration.

Academic advising: Provided by LD staff members, academic advisers. Students with LD may take up to 13 semester hours the first semester; afterwards as many as individual can handle each term; most take 12 to 15 semester hours; 12 semester hours required to maintain full-time status and be eligible for financial aid.

Counseling services: Individual counseling, small-group counseling, career counseling.

Basic skills remediation: Offered one-on-one and in small groups by LD teachers, teacher trainees. Available in reading, math, written language, learning strategies, study skills, social skills.

Subject-area tutoring: Offered one-on-one and in small groups by professional teachers, peer tutors. Available in all subjects.

Special courses: College survival skills, study skills. All offered for credit; none enter into overall grade point average.

Auxiliary aids: Taped textbooks, word-processors with spell-check, optical character readers.

Auxiliary services: Alternative test arrangements.

GENERAL COLLEGE INFORMATION

Independent, comprehensive, coed, affiliated with Church of God. Awards associate, bachelor's, master's, doctoral, first professional degrees. Founded 1917. *Setting:* 100-acre suburban

Anderson University (continued)

campus with easy access to Indianapolis. *Endowment:* $3.3 million. *Educational spending 1995–96:* $4744 per undergrad. *Total enrollment:* 2,136. *Faculty:* 197 (134 full-time, 66% with terminal degrees, 63 part-time); student–undergrad faculty ratio is 14:1.

Enrollment Profile: 1,949 students from 40 states and territories, 14 other countries. 58% women, 42% men, 12% part-time, 62% state residents, 8% transferred in, 1% international, 17% 25 or older, 1% Native American, 1% Hispanic, 5% black, 1% Asian or Pacific Islander. *Retention:* 69% of 1995 full-time freshmen returned. *Graduation:* 31% graduate in 4 years, 47% in 5 years, 50% in 6 years. *Areas of study chosen:* 26% education, 14% business management and administrative services, 12% social sciences, 8% health professions and related sciences, 8% theology/religion, 5% biological and life sciences, 5% communications and journalism, 4% fine arts, 4% performing arts, 4% psychology, 3% vocational and home economics, 2% computer and information sciences, 2% premed, 1% English language/literature/letters, 1% physical sciences, 1% prelaw. *Most popular recent majors:* elementary education, social work, nursing.

First-Year Class: 421 total; 1,214 applied, 77% were accepted, 45% of whom enrolled. 32% from top 10% of their high school class, 59% from top quarter, 92% from top half. 12 valedictorians.

Graduation Requirements: 62 semester hours for associate, 124 semester hours for bachelor's; 4 semester hours each of math and science; 6 semester hours of a foreign language; computer course for business administration, accounting, economics, psychology, political science majors; internship (some majors); senior project (some majors).

Computers on Campus: 130 computers available on campus for general student use. Computer purchase/lease plans available. Computers for student use in computer center, computer labs, classrooms, library, instructional materials center provide access to microcomputer software. Staffed computer lab on campus. *Academic computing expenditure 1995–96:* $214,147.

EXPENSES AND FINANCIAL AID

Expenses for 1997–98: *Application fee:* $20. Comprehensive fee of $16,850 includes full-time tuition ($12,500), mandatory fees ($200), and college room and board ($4150). College room only: $2310. Part-time tuition: $521 per semester hour. Part-time mandatory fees per semester (6 to 11 semester hours): $100.

Undergraduate Financial Aid: 85% of all full-time undergraduates enrolled in fall 1996 applied for aid; of these, 90% were judged to have need according to Federal Methodology, of whom 98% were aided. On average, 100% of need was met. *Financial aid deadline (priority):* 3/1. *Financial aid forms:* FAFSA required.

LD Program Contact: Ms. Rinda S. Vogelgesang, Director, Special Educational Services, Kissinger Learning Center, Anderson University, 1100 East Fifth Street, Anderson, IN 46012-3495, 765-641-4226. Fax: 317-641-3851.

ARIZONA STATE UNIVERSITY

Tempe, Arizona

Students with LD	473	Subject-Area Tutoring	✓
ADD services	✓	Special Courses	
Staff	3 full-time	Taped Textbooks	✓
Special Fee	None	Alternative Test Arrang.	✓
Diagnostic Testing		Notetakers	✓
Basic Skills Remediation		LD Student Organization	

LEARNING DISABILITIES PROGRAM INFORMATION

The Disability Resources for Students began offering services in 1982. Currently the program serves 473 undergraduates with LD. Services are also available to graduate students. Students diagnosed with ADD/ADHD are eligible for the same services available to students with LD.

Staff: 3 full-time staff members, including coordinators, Senior Coordinator. Services provided by tutors, academic aides, testers, computer lab assistants, library aides, readers/braillers.

Special Fees: No special fees are charged for services to students with LD.

Applications and admissions: *Required:* high school transcript, courses completed, untimed SAT I or ACT, transfer transcript; *recommended:* letters of recommendation. Students may begin taking classes any term. *Application deadline:* continuous.

PROGRAM AND SERVICE COMPONENTS

Special preparation or orientation: Required orientation held before classes begin.

Academic advising: Provided by LD staff members, academic advisers. Most students with LD take 12 credits each term; 12 credits required to maintain full-time status; source of aid determines number of credits required to be eligible for financial aid.

Counseling services: Individual counseling, small-group counseling, career counseling.

Subject-area tutoring: Offered one-on-one and in small groups by peer tutors. Available in some subjects.

Auxiliary aids: Taped textbooks, tape recorders, calculators, typewriters, word-processors with spell-check, personal computers, talking computers, optical character readers, FM systems.

Auxiliary services: Alternative test arrangements, notetakers, priority registration, advocacy, readers/braillers.

GENERAL COLLEGE INFORMATION

State-supported, coed. Awards bachelor's, master's, doctoral, first professional degrees. Founded 1885. *Setting:* 814-acre suburban campus with easy access to Phoenix. *Endowment:* $77.1 million. *Research spending 1995–96:* $53 million. *Total enrollment:* 38,664. *Faculty:* 1,913 (1,705 full-time, 84% with terminal degrees, 208 part-time); student–undergrad faculty ratio is 17:1.

Enrollment Profile: 30,680 students from 54 states and territories, 87 other countries. 51% women, 49% men, 21% part-time, 72% state residents, 17% live on campus, 58% transferred in, 4% international, 26% 25 or older, 2% Native American, 10% Hispanic, 3% black, 4% Asian or Pacific Islander. *Retention:* 71% of 1995 full-time freshmen returned. *Graduation:* 17% graduate in 4 years, 39% in 5 years, 46% in 6 years. *Areas of study chosen:* 18% business management and administrative services, 10% engineering and applied sciences, 8% education, 7% communications and journalism, 6% social sciences, 5% psychology, 4% biological and life sciences, 3% architecture, 3% fine arts, 3% health professions and related sciences, 3% performing arts, 2% English language/literature/letters, 1% agriculture, 1% area and ethnic studies, 1% computer and information sciences, 1% foreign language and literature, 1% liberal arts/general studies, 1% mathematics, 1% natural resource sciences, 1% philosophy, 1% physical sciences, 1% prelaw, 1% premed, 1% theology/religion, 1% vocational and home economics. *Most popular recent majors:* business administration/commerce/management, psychology, elementary education.

First-Year Class: 4,245 total; 14,383 applied, 78% were accepted, 38% of whom enrolled. 24% from top 10% of their high school class, 49% from top quarter, 82% from top half. 35 National Merit Scholars.

Graduation Requirements: 120 credits; 6 credits of math; 8 credits of lab science; computer course for engineering, business, architecture, design, public programs majors; senior project for honors program students.

Computers on Campus: 808 computers available on campus for general student use. Computer purchase/lease plans available. A campus-wide network can be accessed from student residence rooms and from off-campus. Students can contact faculty members and/or advisers through e-mail. Computers for student use in computer center, computer labs, learning resource center, classrooms, library, dorms provide access to the Internet/World Wide Web. Staffed computer lab on campus (open 24 hours a day) provides training in use of computers, software.

EXPENSES AND FINANCIAL AID

Expenses for 1997–98: State resident tuition: $1988 full-time. Nonresident tuition: $8640 full-time, $360 per credit part-time. Part-time mandatory fees per semester range from $18 to $36. Part-time tuition for state residents: $105 per credit for 1 to 6 credits, $994 per semester for 7 or more credits. Full-time mandatory fees: $71. College room and board: $3260 (minimum). College room only: $2100 (minimum).

Undergraduate Financial Aid: Of all full-time undergraduates enrolled in fall 1996, 100% of those judged to have need according to Federal Methodology were aided. On average, 88% of need was met. *Financial aid deadline (priority):* 3/1. *Financial aid forms:* FAFSA required.

LD Program Contact: Gale Johnson, Pre-entry Program Coordinator, Learning Disabilities, Arizona State University, Matthews Center, Tempe, AZ 85287, 602-965-1234. Fax: 602-965-2120. Email: lcghj@asuvm.inre.asu.edu.

AUGSBURG COLLEGE

Minneapolis, Minnesota

Students with LD	117	Subject-Area Tutoring	✓
ADD services	✓	Special Courses	✓
Staff	6 full-time	Taped Textbooks	✓
Special Fee	None	Alternative Test Arrang.	✓
Diagnostic Testing		Notetakers	✓
Basic Skills Remediation	✓	LD Student Organization	✓

LEARNING DISABILITIES PROGRAM INFORMATION

The Center for Learning and Adaptive Student Services (CLASS) began offering services in 1984. Currently the program serves 117 undergraduates with LD. Services are also available to graduate students. Students diagnosed with ADD/ADHD are eligible for the same services available to students with LD.

Staff: 6 full-time staff members, including coordinator, accommodations specialist, disabilities specialists. Services provided by tutors, proctors, textbook tapers, computer classroom attendants, notetakers.

Special Fees: No special fees are charged for services to students with LD.

Applications and admissions: *Required:* high school transcript, grade point average, class rank, courses completed, extended time ACT, personal interview, autobiographical statement, psychoeducational report completed within 3 years; *recommended:* high school extracurricular activities, untimed ACT, letters of recommendation, history of supportive services. Students may begin taking classes any term. *Application deadline:* continuous.

Special policies: The college has written policies regarding substitutions and waivers of admissions and graduation requirements.

PROGRAM AND SERVICE COMPONENTS

Special preparation or orientation: Required orientation held before registration, during registration, after classes begin.

Academic advising: Provided by LD staff members, academic advisers. Students with LD may take up to 4 courses each term; most take 3 to 4 courses; 3 courses required to maintain full-time status; 8 courses per year required to be eligible for financial aid.

Counseling services: Individual counseling, small-group counseling, career counseling.

Basic skills remediation: Offered one-on-one and in small groups by LD teachers, Director of Learning Center. Available in reading, math, spelling, written language, learning strategies, study skills, time management, social skills, computer skills.

Subject-area tutoring: Offered one-on-one and in small groups by professional teachers, peer tutors. Available in all subjects.

Special courses: College survival skills, learning strategies, word processing, math, study skills, career planning, conversational Spanish. Most offered for credit; some enter into overall grade point average.

Auxiliary aids: Taped textbooks, tape recorders, calculators, typewriters, word-processors with spell-check, personal computers, talking computers, optical character readers, Franklin Speller, Dragon Dictate, reading machines.

Auxiliary services: Alternative test arrangements, notetakers, advocacy, computer lab assistance.

Campus support group: A special student organization is available to students with LD.

GENERAL COLLEGE INFORMATION

Independent Lutheran, comprehensive, coed. Awards bachelor's, master's degrees. Founded 1869. *Setting:* 23-acre urban campus. *Endowment:* $14.4 million. *Research spending 1995–96:* $583,210. *Educational spending 1995–96:* $5199 per undergrad. *Total enrollment:* 2,862. *Faculty:* 325 (127 full-time, 83% with terminal degrees, 198 part-time); student–undergrad faculty ratio is 15:1.

Enrollment Profile: 2,559 students from 28 states and territories, 35 other countries. 54% women, 46% men, 8% part-time, 83% state residents, 37% transferred in, 5% international, 20% 25 or older, 2% Native American, 2% Hispanic, 4% black, 5% Asian or Pacific Islander. *Retention:* 74% of 1995 full-time freshmen returned. *Graduation:* 29% graduate in 4 years, 43% in 5 years, 46% in 6 years. *Areas of study chosen:* 15% business management and administrative services, 13% education, 6% fine arts, 6% social sciences, 5% psychology, 4% biological and life sciences, 3% communications and journalism, 3% computer and information sciences, 3% English language/literature/letters, 3% natural resource sciences, 2% foreign language and literature, 2% mathematics, 2% performing arts, 2% premed, 1% engineering and applied sciences, 1% interdisciplinary studies, 1% prelaw, 1% theology/religion. *Most popular recent majors:* business administration/commerce/management, education, communication.

First-Year Class: 291 total; 710 applied, 82% were accepted, 50% of whom enrolled. 21% from top 10% of their high school class, 44% from top quarter, 73% from top half.

Graduation Requirements: 33 courses; 2 math/science courses; 2 courses in a foreign language; computer course for honors program students, math, business majors; internship; senior project for honors program students and some majors.

Computers on Campus: 160 computers available on campus for general student use. Computer purchase/lease plans available. A campus-wide network can be accessed from student residence rooms and from off-campus. Students can contact faculty members and/or advisers through e-mail. Computers for student use in computer center, learning resource center, library, dorms, departmental study centers provide access to the Internet/World Wide Web, on- and off-campus e-mail addresses. Staffed computer lab on campus provides training in use of computers, software. *Academic computing expenditure 1995–96:* $351,516.

Augsburg College (continued)

EXPENSES AND FINANCIAL AID

Expenses for 1997–98: *Application fee:* $20. Comprehensive fee of $18,982 includes full-time tuition ($13,850), mandatory fees ($146), and college room and board ($4986). Part-time tuition: $1497 per course.

Undergraduate Financial Aid: 87% of all full-time undergraduates enrolled in fall 1996 applied for aid; of these, 88% were judged to have need according to Federal Methodology, of whom 99% were aided. On average, 82% of need was met. *Financial aid deadline (priority):* 4/15. *Financial aid forms:* FAFSA, institutional form required; CSS Financial Aid PROFILE, state form acceptable.

LD Program Contact: Ms. Diane Glorvigen or Ms. Lisa King, LD Specialists, Augsburg College, 2211 Riverside Avenue, Minneapolis, MN 55454-1351, 612-330-1053. Fax: 612-330-1137.

BARAT COLLEGE

Lake Forest, Illinois

Students with LD	46	Subject-Area Tutoring	✓
ADD services		Special Courses	
Staff	2 full-, 4 part-time	Taped Textbooks	✓
Special Fee	Varies	Alternative Test Arrang.	✓
Diagnostic Testing	✓	Notetakers	✓
Basic Skills Remediation	✓	LD Student Organization	

LEARNING DISABILITIES PROGRAM INFORMATION

The Learning Opportunities Program began offering services in 1980. Currently the program serves 46 undergraduates with LD. Services are also available to graduate students.

Staff: 2 full-time, 4 part-time staff members, including director, assistant director. Services provided by remediation specialists, tutors, counselors, diagnostic specialists.

Special Fees: Range from $1350 to $3600 per year according to number of meeting hours per week with LD specialist. $750 for diagnostic testing.

Applications and admissions: *Required:* high school transcript, grade point average, class rank, courses completed, untimed or extended time ACT, extended time SAT I, autobiographical statement, letters of recommendation, psychoeducational report completed within 4 years, WAIS-R (within last 4 years); *recommended:* high school extracurricular activities. Students may begin taking classes in fall or spring. *Application deadline:* continuous.

PROGRAM AND SERVICE COMPONENTS

Diagnostic testing: Intelligence, reading, math, spelling, handwriting, spoken language, written language, motor abilities, perceptual skills, study skills, social skills, hearing, learning strategies, vision.

Academic advising: Provided by LD staff members. Students with LD may take up to 16 credit hours each term; most take 12 credit hours; 12 credit hours required to maintain full-time status; 6 credit hours (part-time), 12 credit hours (full-time) required to be eligible for financial aid.

Counseling services: Individual counseling, small-group counseling, career counseling, self-advocacy training.

Basic skills remediation: Offered one-on-one, in small groups, and in class-size groups by LD teachers, regular teachers. Available in reading, math, spelling, written language, learning strategies, study skills, time management, social skills.

Subject-area tutoring: Offered one-on-one and in small groups by professional teachers, peer tutors. Available in most subjects.

Auxiliary aids: Taped textbooks, tape recorders, calculators, typewriters, word-processors with spell-check, personal computers, optical character readers.

Auxiliary services: Alternative test arrangements, notetakers, advocacy.

GENERAL COLLEGE INFORMATION

Independent Roman Catholic, 4-year, coed. Awards bachelor's degrees. Founded 1858. *Setting:* 30-acre suburban campus with easy access to Chicago and Milwaukee. *Educational spending 1995–96:* $3290 per undergrad. *Total enrollment:* 757. *Faculty:* 120 (42 full-time, 83% with terminal degrees, 78 part-time).

Enrollment Profile: 757 students from 23 states and territories, 16 other countries. 67% women, 33% men, 49% part-time, 43% state residents, 27% live on campus, 40% transferred in, 7% international, 39% 25 or older, 0% Native American, 5% Hispanic, 13% black, 4% Asian or Pacific Islander. *Areas of study chosen:* 15% social sciences, 13% performing arts, 8% education, 6% communications and journalism, 5% fine arts. *Most popular recent majors:* business administration/commerce/management, psychology, education.

First-Year Class: 128 total; 281 applied, 77% were accepted, 60% of whom enrolled. 14% from top 10% of their high school class, 33% from top quarter, 61% from top half.

Graduation Requirements: 120 credit hours; algebra proficiency; 1 math course; computer course for management, business, math majors; senior project.

Computers on Campus: 72 computers available on campus for general student use. Computers for student use in computer center, computer labs, library, dorms provide access to the Internet/World Wide Web, on- and off-campus e-mail addresses. Staffed computer lab on campus. *Academic computing expenditure 1995–96:* $44,000.

EXPENSES AND FINANCIAL AID

Expenses for 1997–98: *Application fee:* $20. Comprehensive fee of $17,536 includes full-time tuition ($12,570) and college room and board ($4966). Part-time tuition: $419 per credit hour.

Undergraduate Financial Aid: On average, 97% of need was met. *Financial aid deadline (priority):* 4/15. *Financial aid forms:* FAFSA, institutional form required; CSS Financial Aid PROFILE acceptable. State form, state income tax form required for some.

Financial aid specifically for students with LD: work-study: college work study.

LD Program Contact: Dr. Pamela Adelman, Director, Learning Opportunities Program, Barat College, 700 Westleigh, Lake Forest, IL 60045-3297, 847-604-6321. Fax: 847-604-6260. Email: padelma@barat.edu.

BARRY UNIVERSITY

Miami Shores, Florida

Students with LD	35	Subject-Area Tutoring	✓
ADD services	✓	Special Courses	✓
Staff	3 full-, 15 part-time	Taped Textbooks	✓
Special Fee	✓	Alternative Test Arrang.	✓
Diagnostic Testing	✓	Notetakers	✓
Basic Skills Remediation	✓	LD Student Organization	

LEARNING DISABILITIES PROGRAM INFORMATION

The Barry University Center for Advanced Learning began offering services in 1994. Currently the program serves 35 undergraduates with LD. Services are also available to graduate students. Students diagnosed with ADD/ADHD are eligible for the same services available to students with LD.

Staff: 3 full-time, 15 part-time staff members, including director, associate director. Services provided by remediation specialists, tutors, counselors, diagnostic specialists, speech pathologist, psychologist.
Special Fees: $3500 per year.
Applications and admissions: *Required:* high school transcript, grade point average, class rank, courses completed, extracurricular activities, IEP (Individualized Education Program), untimed SAT I or ACT, personal interview, autobiographical statement, letters of recommendation, psychoeducational report completed within 3 years; *recommended:* extended time SAT I or ACT. Students may begin taking classes in fall or spring. *Application deadline:* continuous.
Special policies: The college has written policies regarding grade forgiveness; substitutions and waivers of admissions, graduation, and degree requirements.

PROGRAM AND SERVICE COMPONENTS

Special preparation or orientation: Optional summer program offered prior to entering college. Orientation offered before registration and during registration.
Diagnostic testing: Intelligence, reading, math, spelling, spoken language, written language, perceptual skills, study skills, personality, social skills, learning strategies, vocational interest.
Academic advising: Provided by LD staff members. Students with LD may take up to 15 credits each term; most take 12 to 13 credits; 12 credits required to maintain full-time status; 6 credits required to be eligible for financial aid.
Counseling services: Individual counseling, small-group counseling, career counseling, self-advocacy training.
Basic skills remediation: Offered one-on-one and in small groups by LD teachers, regular teachers; computer-aided instruction also offered. Available in reading, math, spelling, spoken language, written language, learning strategies, perceptual skills, study skills, time management, social skills, computer skills, higher-order thinking skills.
Subject-area tutoring: Offered one-on-one and in small groups by professional teachers. Available in all subjects.
Special courses: College survival skills, reading, vocabulary development, communication skills, composition, learning strategies, word processing, time management, math, personal psychology, study skills, career planning, stress management, English as a Second Language (ESL), Transition in Language and Culture Program, summer transition program. Some offered for credit; some enter into overall grade point average.
Auxiliary aids: Taped textbooks, word-processors with spell-check, talking computers, optical character readers, computers with editing, spell check and voice synthesizers.
Auxiliary services: Alternative test arrangements, notetakers, priority registration, advocacy, writing center, mathematics lab.

GENERAL COLLEGE INFORMATION

Independent Roman Catholic, comprehensive, coed. Awards bachelor's, master's, doctoral degrees. Founded 1940. *Setting:* 90-acre suburban campus with easy access to Miami. *Endowment:* $11 million. *Educational spending 1995–96:* $5830 per undergrad. *Total enrollment:* 7,016. *Faculty:* 550 (238 full-time, 80% with terminal degrees, 312 part-time); student–undergrad faculty ratio is 14:1.
Enrollment Profile: 4,773 students from 38 states and territories, 58 other countries. 67% women, 33% men, 42% part-time, 27% live on campus, 65% transferred in, 3% international, 67% 25 or older, 0% Native American, 27% Hispanic, 17% black, 2% Asian or Pacific Islander. *Retention:* 75% of 1995 full-time freshmen returned. *Areas of study chosen:* 46% liberal arts/general studies, 18% health professions and related sciences, 12% business management and administrative services, 6% biological and life sciences, 3% education, 2% premed, 2% social sciences, 1% communications and journalism, 1% computer and information sciences, 1% English language/literature/letters, 1% fine arts, 1% foreign language and literature, 1% interdisciplinary studies, 1% mathematics, 1% performing arts, 1% predentistry, 1% prelaw, 1% psychology.
First-Year Class: 270 total; 910 applied, 77% were accepted, 39% of whom enrolled. 29% from top 10% of their high school class, 56% from top quarter, 80% from top half.
Graduation Requirements: 120 credits; 9 credits of math/science; computer course for business-related majors; internship (some majors); senior project for honors program students and some majors.
Computers on Campus: 500 computers available on campus for general student use. Computer purchase/lease plans available. A computer is recommended for some students. A campus-wide network can be accessed from off-campus. Students can contact faculty members and/or advisers through e-mail. Computers for student use in computer center, computer labs, learning resource center, classrooms, library provide access to the Internet/World Wide Web, on- and off-campus e-mail addresses. Staffed computer lab on campus provides training in use of computers, software. *Academic computing expenditure 1995–96:* $948,930.

EXPENSES AND FINANCIAL AID

Expenses for 1997–98: *Application fee:* $30. Comprehensive fee of $19,460 includes full-time tuition ($13,290), mandatory fees ($260), and college room and board ($5910). Part-time tuition: $385 per credit. Part-time mandatory fees: $10 per credit.
Undergraduate Financial Aid: 76% of all full-time undergraduates enrolled in fall 1996 applied for aid; of these, 70% were judged to have need according to Federal Methodology, of whom 98% were aided. On average, 100% of need was met. *Financial aid deadline (priority):* 2/15. *Financial aid forms:* FAFSA, state form, institutional form required.
LD Program Contact: Mr. Bruce L. Smitley, Assistant Director, Barry University, 11300 Northeast 2nd Avenue, Miami Shores, FL 33161, 305-899-3461. Fax: 305-899-3778. Email: smitley@bu4090.barry.edu.

BOSTON UNIVERSITY

Boston, Massachusetts

Students with LD	200	Subject-Area Tutoring	✓
ADD services	✓	Special Courses	
Staff	2 full-, 11 part-time	Taped Textbooks	✓
Special Fee	✓	Alternative Test Arrang.	✓
Diagnostic Testing		Notetakers	✓
Basic Skills Remediation	✓	LD Student Organization	

LEARNING DISABILITIES PROGRAM INFORMATION

The Disability Services began offering services in 1988. Currently the program serves 200 undergraduates with LD. Services are also available to graduate students. Students diagnosed with ADD/ADHD are eligible for the same services available to students with LD.
Staff: 2 full-time, 11 part-time staff members, including director, coordinator. Services provided by tutors, learning specialists.
Special Fees: $2600 per year; scholarships are available to cover the fee.
Applications and admissions: *Required:* high school transcript, letters of recommendation, essay; *recommended:* high school grade point average. Students may begin taking classes in fall or summer. *Application deadline:* 1/15 (fall term), 11/15 (spring term).

Boston University (continued)

Special policies: The college has written policies regarding grade forgiveness; substitutions and waivers of admissions, graduation, and degree requirements.

PROGRAM AND SERVICE COMPONENTS

Special preparation or orientation: Optional summer program offered prior to entering college. Optional orientation offered during summer prior to enrollment.

Academic advising: Provided by LD staff members, academic advisers. Students with LD may take up to 18 credits each term; most take 12 credits; 12 credits required to maintain full-time status and be eligible for financial aid.

Counseling services: Individual counseling.

Basic skills remediation: Offered one-on-one by regular teachers. Available in math, foreign language.

Subject-area tutoring: Offered one-on-one and in small groups by professional teachers. Available in most subjects.

Auxiliary aids: Taped textbooks, tape recorders, word-processors with spell-check, personal computers, optical character readers, audible computers.

Auxiliary services: Alternative test arrangements, notetakers, priority registration, readers.

GENERAL COLLEGE INFORMATION

Independent, coed. Awards bachelor's, master's, doctoral, first professional degrees. Founded 1839. *Setting:* 123-acre urban campus. *Endowment:* $443.7 million. *Research spending 1995–96:* $71.3 million. *Educational spending 1995–96:* $11,527 per undergrad. *Total enrollment:* 29,664. *Faculty:* 2,834 (1,933 full-time, 80% with terminal degrees, 901 part-time); student–undergrad faculty ratio is 13:1.

Enrollment Profile: 15,414 students from 54 states and territories, 87 other countries. 57% women, 43% men, 3% part-time, 25% state residents, 8% transferred in, 10% international, 3% 25 or older, 1% Native American, 6% Hispanic, 4% black, 14% Asian or Pacific Islander. *Retention:* 84% of 1995 full-time freshmen returned. *Graduation:* 56% graduate in 4 years, 67% in 5 years, 69% in 6 years. *Areas of study chosen:* 11% social sciences, 10% business management and administrative services, 10% communications and journalism, 10% liberal arts/general studies, 8% engineering and applied sciences, 7% biological and life sciences, 6% health professions and related sciences, 6% psychology, 3% education, 3% English language/literature/letters, 3% fine arts, 3% physical sciences, 2% computer and information sciences, 2% performing arts, 1% foreign language and literature, 1% interdisciplinary studies, 1% mathematics, 1% philosophy, 1% theology/religion. *Most popular recent majors:* business administration/commerce/management, social science, communication.

First-Year Class: 3,969 total; 25,991 applied, 53% were accepted, 29% of whom enrolled. 55% from top 10% of their high school class, 88% from top quarter, 99% from top half. 36 National Merit Scholars, 103 valedictorians.

Graduation Requirements: 128 credits; computer course for communication, engineering, math, management, science majors; internship (some majors); senior project (some majors).

Computers on Campus: 500 computers available on campus for general student use. Computer purchase/lease plans available. A campus-wide network can be accessed from student residence rooms and from off-campus. Students can contact faculty members and/or advisers through e-mail. Computers for student use in computer center, computer labs, research center, learning resource center, classrooms, library, student center, dorms, departmental labs provide access to the Internet/World Wide Web, on- and off-campus e-mail addresses, research and educational networks. Staffed computer lab on campus (open 24 hours a day) provides training in use of computers, software. *Academic computing expenditure 1995–96:* $7.9 million.

EXPENSES AND FINANCIAL AID

Expenses for 1997–98: *Application fee:* $50. Comprehensive fee of $29,848 includes full-time tuition ($21,970), mandatory fees ($308), and college room and board ($7570). College room only: $4640. Part-time tuition: $687 per credit. Part-time mandatory fees: $40 per semester.

Undergraduate Financial Aid: 63% of all full-time undergraduates enrolled in fall 1996 applied for aid; of these, 92% were judged to have need according to Federal Methodology, of whom 96% were aided. On average, 89% of need was met. *Financial aid deadline (priority):* 2/15. *Financial aid forms:* FAFSA, CSS Financial Aid PROFILE required. State form, financial aid transcript (for mid-year transfers) required for some.

Financial aid specifically for students with LD: Scholarship: tutoring assistance scholarship; loans.

LD Program Contact: Dr. Lorraine Wolf, Clinical Director, Learning Disabilities Support Services, Boston University, 19 Deerfield Street, Boston, MA 02215, 617-353-3658. Fax: 617-353-5891.

BRADFORD COLLEGE

Bradford, Massachusetts

Students with LD	45	Subject-Area Tutoring	✓
ADD services		Special Courses	
Staff	3 full-, 4 part-time	Taped Textbooks	
Special Fee	Varies	Alternative Test Arrang.	
Diagnostic Testing		Notetakers	
Basic Skills Remediation	✓	LD Student Organization	✓

LEARNING DISABILITIES PROGRAM INFORMATION

The College Learning Program (CLP) began offering services in 1979. Currently the program serves 45 undergraduates with LD.

Staff: 3 full-time, 4 part-time staff members, including assistant director, Director of Academic Support. Services provided by tutors, counselor, LD specialists.

Special Fees: Range from $1600 to $4000 per year.

Applications and admissions: *Required:* high school transcript, personal interview, letters of recommendation, psychoeducational report completed within 3 years, reading test, WAIS-R, achievement battery; *recommended:* high school grade point average, courses completed, extracurricular activities, extended time SAT I, record of accommodations used in high school. Students may begin taking classes in fall or spring. *Application deadline:* continuous.

PROGRAM AND SERVICE COMPONENTS

Special preparation or orientation: Required orientation held before registration.

Academic advising: Provided by LD staff members, academic advisers. Students with LD may take up to 15 credits each term; most take 12 to 15 credits; 12 credits required to maintain full-time status and be eligible for financial aid.

Counseling services: Self-advocacy training.

Basic skills remediation: Offered in small groups and in class-size groups by LD teachers. Available in learning strategies, study skills, time management.

Subject-area tutoring: Offered one-on-one and in small groups by professional teachers. Available in most subjects.

Campus support group: A special student organization is available to students with LD.

GENERAL COLLEGE INFORMATION

Independent, 4-year, coed. Awards bachelor's degrees. Founded 1803. *Setting:* 75-acre small-town campus with easy access to Boston. *Endowment:* $20.4 million. *Educational spending 1995–96:* $7402 per undergrad. *Total enrollment:* 568. *Faculty:* 77 (35 full-time, 85% with terminal degrees, 42 part-time); student–undergrad faculty ratio is 12:1.

Enrollment Profile: 568 students from 25 states and territories, 34 other countries. 63% women, 37% men, 6% part-time, 52% state residents, 75% live on campus, 24% transferred in, 16% international, 14% 25 or older, 1% Native American, 5% Hispanic, 6% black, 2% Asian or Pacific Islander. *Retention:* 65% of 1995 full-time freshmen returned. *Graduation:* 31% graduate in 4 years, 35% in 5 years, 36% in 6 years. *Areas of study chosen:* 10% social sciences, 5% business management and administrative services, 4% fine arts, 4% performing arts, 3% English language/literature/letters, 2% biological and life sciences, 2% communications and journalism, 1% philosophy. *Most popular recent majors:* psychology, art/fine arts, marketing/retailing/merchandising.

First-Year Class: 195 total; 1,020 applied, 78% were accepted, 24% of whom enrolled. 5% from top 10% of their high school class, 30% from top quarter, 75% from top half.

Graduation Requirements: 121 credits; 1 course each in math and science; computer course for management, natural science, math majors; internship (some majors); senior project.

Computers on Campus: 60 computers available on campus for general student use. A campus-wide network can be accessed from student residence rooms and from off-campus. Students can contact faculty members and/or advisers through e-mail. Computers for student use in computer center, computer labs, learning resource center, library, dorms provide access to the Internet/World Wide Web, on- and off-campus e-mail addresses. Staffed computer lab on campus provides training in use of computers, software. *Academic computing expenditure 1995–96:* $184,565.

EXPENSES AND FINANCIAL AID

Expenses for 1997–98: Comprehensive fee of $23,035 includes full-time tuition ($15,850), mandatory fees ($465), and college room and board ($6720). College room only: $3770. Part-time tuition: $525 per credit.

Undergraduate Financial Aid: Of all full-time undergraduates enrolled in fall 1996, 71% of those who applied for aid were judged to have need according to Federal Methodology, of whom 100% were aided. On average, 95% of need was met. *Financial aid deadline (priority):* 2/15. *Financial aid forms:* FAFSA, institutional form, nontaxable income verification required. State form required for some.

LD Program Contact: Ms. Patricia Davison, Associate Director of Admissions/CLP Admissions Coordinator, Bradford College, South Main Street, Bradford, MA 01835, 508-372-7161 Ext. 271. Fax: 508-372-5240. Email: pdavison@bnet.bradford.edu.

BRENAU UNIVERSITY

Gainesville, Georgia

Students with LD	40	Subject-Area Tutoring	✓
ADD services	✓	Special Courses	✓
Staff	2 full-, 1 part-time	Taped Textbooks	✓
Special Fee	Varies	Alternative Test Arrang.	✓
Diagnostic Testing		Notetakers	
Basic Skills Remediation	✓	LD Student Organization	✓

LEARNING DISABILITIES PROGRAM INFORMATION

The Learning Center began offering services in 1984. Currently the program serves 40 undergraduates with LD. Services are also available to graduate students. Students diagnosed with ADD/ADHD are eligible for the same services available to students with LD.

Staff: 2 full-time, 1 part-time staff members, including director, associate director, remedial skills specialist. Services provided by remediation specialists, tutors, counselors.

Special Fees: Range from $1800 to $7200 per year.

Applications and admissions: *Required:* high school transcript, grade point average, courses completed, personal interview, letters of recommendation, psychoeducational report completed within 2 years; *recommended:* high school extracurricular activities, untimed or extended time SAT I or ACT, autobiographical statement. Students may begin taking classes any term. *Application deadline:* continuous.

PROGRAM AND SERVICE COMPONENTS

Special preparation or orientation: Summer program (required for some) held prior to entering college. Required orientation held before registration.

Academic advising: Provided by LD staff members. Students with LD may take up to 15 semester hours each term; most take 12 to 15 semester hours; 12 semester hours required to maintain full-time status and be eligible for financial aid.

Counseling services: Individual counseling, career counseling.

Basic skills remediation: Offered one-on-one by academic specialist. Available in reading, math, spoken language, written language, learning strategies, study skills, social skills, computer skills.

Subject-area tutoring: Offered one-on-one by professional teachers. Available in all subjects.

Special courses: College survival skills, reading, composition, learning strategies, word processing, time management, math, study skills, career planning, stress management. Some offered for credit; some enter into overall grade point average.

Auxiliary aids: Taped textbooks, tape recorders, calculators, typewriters, word-processors with spell-check, personal computers, optical character readers, Franklin Speller.

Auxiliary services: Alternative test arrangements, priority registration, advocacy.

Campus support group: A special student organization is available to students with LD.

GENERAL COLLEGE INFORMATION

Independent, comprehensive, primarily women. Awards bachelor's, master's degrees. Founded 1878. *Setting:* 50-acre small-town campus with easy access to Atlanta. *Endowment:* $17.1 million. *Educational spending 1995–96:* $1970 per undergrad. *Total enrollment:* 2,225. *Faculty:* 230 (68 full-time, 88% with terminal degrees, 162 part-time); student–undergrad faculty ratio is 13:1.

Enrollment Profile: 1,423 students from 22 states and territories, 9 other countries. 97% women, 3% men, 10% part-time, 83% state residents, 44% transferred in, 4% international, 22% 25 or older, 1% Native American, 2% Hispanic, 7% black, 1% Asian or Pacific Islander. *Retention:* 62% of 1995 full-time freshmen returned. *Areas of study chosen:* 29% business management and administrative services, 25% education, 18% health professions and related sciences, 6% fine arts, 6% social sciences, 5% liberal arts/general studies, 4% performing arts, 3% communications and journalism, 2% biological and life sciences, 2% psychology, 1% English language/literature/letters, 1% mathematics, 1% prelaw. *Most popular recent majors:* education, business administration/commerce/management, nursing.

Brenau University (continued)

First-Year Class: 262 total; 434 applied, 74% were accepted, 81% of whom enrolled. 26% from top 10% of their high school class, 45% from top quarter, 63% from top half.

Graduation Requirements: 120 semester hours; 3 semester hours of math; 6 semester hours of science; foreign language requirement varies according to degree program; computer course for students without computer competency; internship (some majors); senior project for honors program students and some majors.

Computers on Campus: 112 computers available on campus for general student use. Computer purchase/lease plans available. A campus-wide network can be accessed from student residence rooms and from off-campus. Students can contact faculty members and/or advisers through e-mail. Computers for student use in computer labs, library, dorms provide access to the Internet/World Wide Web, on- and off-campus e-mail addresses. Staffed computer lab on campus provides training in use of computers, software. *Academic computing expenditure 1995–96:* $132,000.

EXPENSES AND FINANCIAL AID

Expenses for 1997–98: *Application fee:* $30. Comprehensive fee of $17,070 includes full-time tuition ($10,740) and college room and board ($6330). Part-time tuition: $358 per semester hour. Part-time tuition for evening and weekend classes: $235 per semester hour.

Undergraduate Financial Aid: 65% of all full-time undergraduates enrolled in fall 1996 applied for aid; of these, 87% were judged to have need according to Federal Methodology, of whom 100% were aided. On average, 88% of need was met. *Financial aid deadline (priority):* 5/1. *Financial aid forms:* FAFSA required. State form, institutional form required for some.

LD Program Contact: Dr. Vince Yamilkoski, Director, Learning Disability Program, Brenau University, One Centennial Circle, Gainesville, GA 30501-3697, 404-534-6133.

CALIFORNIA STATE UNIVERSITY, LONG BEACH

Long Beach, California

Students with LD	300	Subject-Area Tutoring	✓
ADD services	✓	Special Courses	✓
Staff	1 full-, 18 part-time	Taped Textbooks	✓
Special Fee	None	Alternative Test Arrang.	✓
Diagnostic Testing	✓	Notetakers	✓
Basic Skills Remediation		LD Student Organization	

LEARNING DISABILITIES PROGRAM INFORMATION

The Stephen Benson Program for Students with Learning Disabilities began offering services in 1980. Currently the program serves 300 undergraduates with LD. Services are also available to graduate students. Students diagnosed with ADD/ADHD are eligible for the same services available to students with LD.

Staff: 1 full-time, 18 part-time staff members, including coordinator, academic adviser, lead counselor, assessment specialist, secretary. Services provided by counselors.

Special Fees: No special fees are charged for services to students with LD.

Applications and admissions: *Required:* high school transcript, grade point average, courses completed, untimed SAT I, autobiographical statement, letters of recommendation, psychoeducational report completed within 3 years; *recommended:* high school class rank, extracurricular activities, IEP (Individualized Education Program), extended time SAT I, personal interview. Students may begin taking classes in fall or spring. *Application deadline:* 4/1 (fall term), 10/1 (spring term).

PROGRAM AND SERVICE COMPONENTS

Special preparation or orientation: Optional orientation offered before registration.

Diagnostic testing: Intelligence, reading, math, spelling, spoken language, written language, perceptual skills.

Academic advising: Provided by LD staff members, academic advisers. Most students with LD take 12 units each term; 12 units (9 with special permission) required to maintain full-time status; 12 units required to be eligible for financial aid.

Counseling services: Individual counseling, small-group counseling, career counseling, self-advocacy training.

Subject-area tutoring: Offered one-on-one, in small groups, and in class-size groups by peer tutors. Available in most subjects.

Special courses: Composition, learning strategies, word processing, Internet use, personal psychology, study skills, career planning. Some offered for credit; most enter into overall grade point average.

Auxiliary aids: Taped textbooks, tape recorders, word-processors with spell-check, optical character readers.

Auxiliary services: Alternative test arrangements, notetakers, priority registration, advocacy.

GENERAL COLLEGE INFORMATION

State-supported, comprehensive, coed. Part of California State University System. Awards bachelor's, master's degrees. Founded 1949. *Setting:* 320-acre suburban campus with easy access to Los Angeles. *Total enrollment:* 27,431. *Faculty:* 1,423 (863 full-time, 90% with terminal degrees, 560 part-time); student–undergrad faculty ratio is 20:1.

Enrollment Profile: 22,052 students from 45 states and territories, 106 other countries. 55% women, 45% men, 28% part-time, 97% state residents, 7% live on campus, 55% transferred in, 30% 25 or older, 1% Native American, 20% Hispanic, 8% black, 25% Asian or Pacific Islander. *Retention:* 78% of 1995 full-time freshmen returned. *Areas of study chosen:* 16% business management and administrative services, 11% health professions and related sciences, 8% engineering and applied sciences, 8% fine arts, 8% vocational and home economics, 6% biological and life sciences, 6% liberal arts/general studies, 6% psychology, 6% social sciences, 3% communications and journalism, 3% computer and information sciences, 3% English language/literature/letters, 3% performing arts, 1% area and ethnic studies, 1% foreign language and literature, 1% interdisciplinary studies, 1% mathematics, 1% philosophy, 1% physical sciences, 1% theology/religion.

First-Year Class: 2,477 total; 8,551 applied, 83% were accepted, 35% of whom enrolled. 96% from top half of their high school class.

Graduation Requirements: 124 units; 3 units of math; 6 units of science; computer course for business, engineering, math majors; internship (some majors); senior project for honors program students and some majors.

Computers on Campus: 2,500 computers available on campus for general student use. Computer purchase/lease plans available. A computer is recommended for some students. A campus-wide network can be accessed from off-campus. Students can contact faculty members and/or advisers through e-mail. Computers for student use in computer center, computer labs, library, departmental labs provide access to the Internet/World Wide Web, on- and off-campus e-mail addresses. Staffed computer lab on campus provides training in use of computers, software.

EXPENSES AND FINANCIAL AID

Expenses for 1997–98: State resident tuition: $0 full-time. Nonresident tuition: $7626 full-time, $246 per unit part-time. Part-time mandatory fees: $590 per semester. Full-time mandatory fees: $1864. College room and board: $5049.
Undergraduate Financial Aid: Of all full-time undergraduates enrolled in fall 1996, 75% of those who applied for aid were judged to have need according to Federal Methodology, of whom 94% were aided. On average, 60% of need was met. *Financial aid deadline (priority):* 3/2. *Financial aid forms:* FAFSA required.
LD Program Contact: Ms. Kathryn Holmes, Coordinator, California State University, Long Beach, 1250 Bellflower Boulevard, ED-172, Long Beach, CA 90840-2201, 562-985-4430. Fax: 562-985-2413.

CALIFORNIA STATE UNIVERSITY, NORTHRIDGE

Northridge, California

Students with LD	396	Subject-Area Tutoring	✓
ADD services	✓	Special Courses	
Staff	1 full-, 3 part-time	Taped Textbooks	✓
Special Fee	None	Alternative Test Arrang.	✓
Diagnostic Testing	✓	Notetakers	✓
Basic Skills Remediation		LD Student Organization	

LEARNING DISABILITIES PROGRAM INFORMATION

The Learning Disability Program began offering services in 1985. Currently the program serves 396 undergraduates with LD. Services are also available to graduate students. Students diagnosed with ADD/ADHD are eligible for the same services available to students with LD.
Staff: 1 full-time, 3 part-time staff members, including LD specialists. Services provided by tutors, counselors, diagnostic specialists.
Special Fees: No special fees are charged for services to students with LD.
Applications and admissions: *Recommended:* personal interview, letters of recommendation, psychoeducational report completed within 3 years. Students may begin taking classes any term. *Application deadline:* continuous.
Special policies: The college has written policies regarding grade forgiveness; substitutions and waivers of admissions, graduation, and degree requirements.

PROGRAM AND SERVICE COMPONENTS

Special preparation or orientation: Optional orientation offered before registration.
Diagnostic testing: Intelligence, reading, math, spelling, handwriting, spoken language, written language, motor abilities, cognitive skills.
Academic advising: Provided by LD staff members, academic advisers. Students with LD may take up to 19 units each term; most take 12 units; 12 units required to maintain full-time status and be eligible for financial aid.
Counseling services: Individual counseling, career counseling.
Subject-area tutoring: Offered one-on-one by peer tutors, graduate students. Available in most subjects.
Auxiliary aids: Taped textbooks, tape recorders, calculators, typewriters, word-processors with spell-check, personal computers, talking computers, optical character readers.
Auxiliary services: Alternative test arrangements, notetakers, priority registration, advocacy, individual assistance with test taking strategies, mnemonics, time management, and study skills.

GENERAL COLLEGE INFORMATION

State-supported, comprehensive, coed. Part of California State University System. Awards bachelor's, master's degrees. Founded 1958. *Setting:* 353-acre urban campus with easy access to Los Angeles. *Total enrollment:* 25,020. *Undergraduate faculty:* 1,453 (832 full-time, 621 part-time).
Enrollment Profile: 20,024 students from 47 states and territories, 101 other countries. 55% women, 45% men, 31% part-time, 98% state residents, 11% transferred in, 1% international, 31% 25 or older, 1% Native American, 21% Hispanic, 8% black, 13% Asian or Pacific Islander. *Most popular recent majors:* business administration/commerce/management, psychology, liberal arts/general studies.
First-Year Class: 2,138 total. Of the students who applied, 79% were accepted, 29% of whom enrolled.
Graduation Requirements: 124 units; 1 math course; 3 science courses including at least 1 lab science course; computer course for business, health administration, engineering, physics majors.
Computers on Campus: 1,700 computers available on campus for general student use. Computers for student use in computer center, library, student labs, departmental labs provide access to the Internet/World Wide Web. Staffed computer lab on campus provides training in use of computers, software.

EXPENSES AND FINANCIAL AID

Expenses for 1997–98: *Application fee:* $55. State resident tuition: $0 full-time. Nonresident tuition: $7626 full-time, $246 per unit part-time. Part-time mandatory fees: $657 per semester. Full-time mandatory fees: $1980. College room only: $4190.
Undergraduate Financial Aid: Of all full-time undergraduates enrolled in fall 1996, 78% of those who applied for aid were judged to have need according to Federal Methodology, of whom 100% were aided. On average, 74% of need was met. *Financial aid deadline (priority):* 3/2. *Financial aid forms:* FAFSA, state form required. Institutional form required for some.
LD Program Contact: Dr. Lee Axelrod or Dr. Jennifer Zvi, Learning Disabilities Specialists, California State University, Northridge, 18111 Nordhoff Street, Northridge, CA 91330-8264, 818-677-2684. Email: lee.axelrod@csun.edu.

CALIFORNIA STATE UNIVERSITY, SAN BERNARDINO

San Bernardino, California

Students with LD	140	Subject-Area Tutoring	
ADD services	✓	Special Courses	✓
Staff		Taped Textbooks	✓
Special Fee	None	Alternative Test Arrang.	✓
Diagnostic Testing	✓	Notetakers	✓
Basic Skills Remediation		LD Student Organization	✓

LEARNING DISABILITIES PROGRAM INFORMATION

The Services to Students with Disabilities began offering services in 1988. Currently the program serves 140 undergraduates with LD. Services are also available to graduate students. Students diagnosed with ADD/ADHD are eligible for the same services available to students with LD.
Staff: Includes director, coordinator. Services provided by student assistants.
Special Fees: No special fees are charged for services to students with LD.
Applications and admissions: *Required:* high school transcript, WAIS-R, WRAT; contact Lydia Ortega in Admissions concerning Special Admission Option. Students may begin taking classes in fall, winter, or spring. *Application deadline:* continuous.

Special policies: The college has written policies regarding substitutions and waivers of degree requirements.

PROGRAM AND SERVICE COMPONENTS

Special preparation or orientation: Optional orientation offered before registration.
Diagnostic testing: Intelligence, reading, math, perceptual skills, learning strategies.
Academic advising: Provided by LD staff members, academic advisers. Students with LD may take up to 19 quarter units each term; most take 8 to 15 quarter units; 12 quarter units required to maintain full-time status and be eligible for financial aid.
Counseling services: Individual counseling, small-group counseling, career counseling.
Special courses: College survival skills, learning strategies, time management, study skills, career planning, University Study Skills. All offered for credit; all enter into overall grade point average.
Auxiliary aids: Taped textbooks, tape recorders, calculators, typewriters, word-processors with spell-check, personal computers, talking computers, optical character readers.
Auxiliary services: Alternative test arrangements, notetakers, priority registration, advocacy, proofreading, paper writing assistance, library research and lab assistance.
Campus support group: A special student organization is available to students with LD.

GENERAL COLLEGE INFORMATION

State-supported, comprehensive, coed. Part of California State University System. Awards bachelor's, master's degrees. Founded 1965. *Setting:* 430-acre suburban campus with easy access to Los Angeles. *Total enrollment:* 12,153. *Faculty:* 571 (421 full-time, 93% with terminal degrees, 150 part-time); student–undergrad faculty ratio is 19:1.
Enrollment Profile: 9,094 students from 31 states and territories, 84 other countries. 59% women, 41% men, 34% part-time, 96% state residents, 3% live on campus, 13% transferred in, 3% international, 38% 25 or older, 1% Native American, 20% Hispanic, 9% black, 8% Asian or Pacific Islander. *Most popular recent majors:* business administration/commerce/management, humanities, social science.
First-Year Class: 942 total; 2,875 applied, 70% were accepted, 47% of whom enrolled.
Graduation Requirements: 186 units; 4 units of math; 5 units of science; computer course for administration, communication, health science, physics, math majors.
Computers on Campus: 1,300 computers available on campus for general student use. A campus-wide network can be accessed from student residence rooms and from off-campus. Students can contact faculty members and/or advisers through e-mail. Computers for student use in computer center, learning resource center, classrooms, library, dorms, student rooms provide access to the Internet/World Wide Web, on-campus e-mail addresses. Staffed computer lab on campus (open 24 hours a day).

EXPENSES AND FINANCIAL AID

Expenses for 1997–98: *Application fee:* $55. State resident tuition: $0 full-time. Nonresident tuition: $7544 full-time, $164 per unit part-time. Part-time mandatory fees per quarter range from $410 to $632. Full-time mandatory fees: $1896. College room and board: $4174.
Undergraduate Financial Aid: *Financial aid deadline (priority):* 3/1. *Financial aid forms:* FAFSA, state form required; CSS Financial Aid PROFILE acceptable.
LD Program Contact: Ms. Elizabeth Watson, Learning Disabilities Specialist, California State University, San Bernardino, 5500 University Parkway, San Bernardino, CA 92407-2397, 909-880-5243. Fax: 909-880-7090. Email: ewatson@wiley.csusb.edu.

CALIFORNIA UNIVERSITY OF PENNSYLVANIA

California, Pennsylvania

Students with LD	90	Subject-Area Tutoring	✓
ADD services		Special Courses	✓
Staff	1 full-, 14 part-time	Taped Textbooks	✓
Special Fee	Varies	Alternative Test Arrang.	✓
Diagnostic Testing		Notetakers	✓
Basic Skills Remediation	✓	LD Student Organization	

LEARNING DISABILITIES PROGRAM INFORMATION

The Center for Academic Research and Enhancement (CARE)/Specialized Support Service Program (SSSP) began offering services in 1988. Currently the program serves 90 undergraduates with LD. Services are also available to graduate students.
Staff: 1 full-time, 14 part-time staff members, including director, Administrator. Services provided by remediation specialists, tutors, staff monitors, university personnel.
Special Fees: Range from $1410 to $2075 per year.
Applications and admissions: *Required:* high school transcript, separate application, LD documentation (submitted to the CARE project); *recommended:* high school grade point average, class rank, courses completed, extracurricular activities, untimed or extended time SAT I, personal interview, autobiographical statement, letters of recommendation. Students may begin taking classes in fall, spring, or summer. *Application deadline:* continuous.

PROGRAM AND SERVICE COMPONENTS

Special preparation or orientation: Required orientation held before registration, during registration, after classes begin.
Academic advising: Provided by LD staff members, academic advisers. Most students with LD take 12 to 15 credits each term; 12 credits required to maintain full-time status.
Counseling services: Individual counseling, small-group counseling, career counseling, self-advocacy training.
Basic skills remediation: Offered in small groups by LD teachers, peer tutors. Available in learning strategies, study skills, time management, workshops predominately focused on study and course management skills.
Subject-area tutoring: Offered one-on-one and in small groups by professional teachers, peer tutors. Available in all subjects.
Special courses: College survival skills, time management, study skills, individualized course work. None offered for credit; none enter into overall grade point average.
Auxiliary aids: Taped textbooks, tape recorders, calculators, typewriters, word-processors with spell-check, optical character readers.
Auxiliary services: Alternative test arrangements, notetakers, advocacy, test readers; accommodations are individually arranged based upon needs of students.

GENERAL COLLEGE INFORMATION

State-supported, comprehensive, coed. Part of Pennsylvania State System of Higher Education. Awards associate, bachelor's, master's degrees. Founded 1852. *Setting:* 148-acre small-town campus with easy access to Pittsburgh. *Endowment:* $293,783. *Research spending 1995–96:* $65,649. *Total enrollment:* 5,636. *Faculty:* 355 (315 full-time, 64% with terminal degrees, 40 part-time); student–undergrad faculty ratio is 18:1.
Enrollment Profile: 4,779 students from 35 states and territories, 22 other countries. 51% women, 49% men, 13% part-time, 94% state residents, 32% transferred in, 1% international, 21% 25

or older, 1% Native American, 1% Hispanic, 5% black, 1% Asian or Pacific Islander. *Retention:* 80% of 1995 full-time freshmen returned. *Areas of study chosen:* 29% education, 8% engineering and applied sciences, 7% communications and journalism, 5% social sciences, 3% interdisciplinary studies, 3% natural resource sciences, 2% premed, 1% performing arts, 1% prevet. *Most popular recent majors:* education, business administration/commerce/management, accounting.

First-Year Class: 834 total; 2,271 applied, 83% were accepted, 44% of whom enrolled. 7% from top 10% of their high school class, 23% from top quarter, 55% from top half.

Graduation Requirements: 64 credits for associate, 128 credits for bachelor's; 9 credits of math/science; computer course (varies by major); internship (some majors); senior project for honors program students and some majors.

Computers on Campus: 708 computers available on campus for general student use. Computer purchase/lease plans available. Computers for student use in computer center, computer labs, learning resource center, classrooms, library, student center provide access to the Internet/World Wide Web, on- and off-campus e-mail addresses. Staffed computer lab on campus provides training in use of computers, software.

EXPENSES AND FINANCIAL AID

Expenses for 1996–97: *Application fee:* $25. State resident tuition: $3368 full-time, $140 per credit part-time. Nonresident tuition: $8566 full-time, $357 per credit part-time. Part-time mandatory fees: $39.50 per credit. Full-time mandatory fees: $936. College room and board: $3992.

Undergraduate Financial Aid: Of all full-time undergraduates enrolled in fall 1996, 88% of those who applied for aid were judged to have need according to Federal Methodology, of whom 95% were aided. On average, 79% of need was met. *Financial aid deadline (priority):* 4/1. *Financial aid forms:* FAFSA required.

LD Program Contact: Ms. Cheryl Bilitski, Director, College CARE Program, California University of Pennsylvania, 250 University Avenue, Box 66, California, PA 15419-1394, 412-938-5781.

CENTENARY COLLEGE

Hackettstown, New Jersey

Students with LD	25	Subject-Area Tutoring	✓
ADD services	✓	Special Courses	
Staff	1 full-, 1 part-time	Taped Textbooks	✓
Special Fee	✓	Alternative Test Arrang.	✓
Diagnostic Testing		Notetakers	✓
Basic Skills Remediation	✓	LD Student Organization	

LEARNING DISABILITIES PROGRAM INFORMATION

The Learning Differences Program began offering services in 1990. Currently the program serves 25 undergraduates with LD. Services are also available to graduate students. Students diagnosed with ADD/ADHD are eligible for the same services available to students with LD.

Staff: 1 full-time, 1 part-time staff members, including director. Services provided by tutor.

Special Fees: $1850 per year.

Applications and admissions: *Required:* high school transcript, grade point average, class rank, untimed SAT I, personal interview, autobiographical statement, psychoeducational report completed within 3 years; *recommended:* extended time SAT I, letters of recommendation. Students may begin taking classes in fall or spring. *Application deadline:* continuous.

Special policies: The college has written policies regarding grade forgiveness.

PROGRAM AND SERVICE COMPONENTS

Special preparation or orientation: Summer program (required for some) held prior to entering college. Required orientation held before registration.

Academic advising: Provided by LD staff members, academic advisers. Students with LD may take up to 12 credits each term; most take 12 to 15 credits; 12 credits required to maintain full-time status and be eligible for financial aid.

Counseling services: Individual counseling, career counseling.

Basic skills remediation: Offered one-on-one and in small groups by regular teachers, tutors. Available in reading, math, written language.

Subject-area tutoring: Offered one-on-one and in small groups by professional teachers, peer tutors, professional tutor in math and English. Available in all subjects.

Auxiliary aids: Taped textbooks, word-processors with spell-check.

Auxiliary services: Alternative test arrangements, notetakers, advocacy.

GENERAL COLLEGE INFORMATION

Independent, comprehensive, coed, affiliated with United Methodist Church. Awards associate, bachelor's, master's degrees. Founded 1867. *Setting:* 42-acre suburban campus with easy access to New York City. *Endowment:* $1.7 million. *Total enrollment:* 968. *Faculty:* 106 (42 full-time, 62% with terminal degrees, 64 part-time); student–undergrad faculty ratio is 13:1.

Enrollment Profile: 931 students from 13 states and territories, 8 other countries. 78% women, 22% men, 48% part-time, 85% state residents, 49% transferred in, 6% international, 53% 25 or older, 1% Native American, 2% Hispanic, 5% black, 1% Asian or Pacific Islander. *Areas of study chosen:* 28% business management and administrative services, 12% education, 11% psychology, 7% English language/literature/letters, 5% interdisciplinary studies, 4% computer and information sciences, 4% social sciences, 2% communications and journalism, 2% mathematics. *Most popular recent majors:* business administration/commerce/management, education, equestrian studies.

First-Year Class: 88 total; 292 applied, 84% were accepted, 36% of whom enrolled. 2% from top 10% of their high school class, 19% from top quarter, 46% from top half.

Graduation Requirements: 64 credits for associate, 128 credits for bachelor's; 6 credits of math; 4 credits of science including at least 1 lab science course; computer course for business, math, fashion, American culture majors; senior project (some majors).

Computers on Campus: 30 computers available on campus for general student use. A computer is strongly recommended for all students. Computers for student use in computer center, computer labs, learning resource center provide access to the Internet/World Wide Web. Staffed computer lab on campus provides training in use of computers, software. *Academic computing expenditure 1995–96:* $93,085.

EXPENSES AND FINANCIAL AID

Expenses for 1997–98: *Application fee:* $25. Comprehensive fee of $19,060 includes full-time tuition ($12,900), mandatory fees ($220), and college room and board ($5940). Part-time tuition: $240 per credit. Part-time mandatory fees: $10 per semester.

Undergraduate Financial Aid: 77% of all full-time undergraduates enrolled in fall 1996 applied for aid; of these, 91% were judged to have need according to Federal Methodology, of

Centenary College (continued)

whom 100% were aided. On average, 87% of need was met. *Financial aid deadline (priority):* 5/1. *Financial aid forms:* FAFSA, institutional form required. Nontaxable income verification required for some.

LD Program Contact: Mr. Dennis Kelly, Dean of Admissions, Centenary College, 400 Jefferson Street, Hackettstown, NJ 07840-2100, 908-852-1400 Ext. 2170. Fax: 908-852-3454.

COLLEGE MISERICORDIA

Dallas, Pennsylvania

Students with LD	57	Subject-Area Tutoring	✓
ADD services		Special Courses	
Staff	5 full-time	Taped Textbooks	✓
Special Fee	None	Alternative Test Arrang.	✓
Diagnostic Testing		Notetakers	✓
Basic Skills Remediation	✓	LD Student Organization	

LEARNING DISABILITIES PROGRAM INFORMATION

The Alternative Learners Project began offering services in 1979. Currently the program serves 57 undergraduates with LD. Students diagnosed with ADD/ADHD are not eligible for the same services available to students with LD.

Staff: 5 full-time staff members, including director, coordinators. Services provided by program coordinators, career counselor.

Special Fees: No special fees are charged for services to students with LD.

Applications and admissions: *Required:* high school transcript, grade point average, class rank, courses completed, extracurricular activities, untimed SAT I, personal interview, autobiographical statement, letters of recommendation, psychoeducational report, WAIS-R. Students may begin taking classes in fall or summer. *Application deadline:* continuous.

Special policies: The college has written policies regarding grade forgiveness; substitutions and waivers of admissions, graduation, and degree requirements.

PROGRAM AND SERVICE COMPONENTS

Special preparation or orientation: Required summer program offered prior to entering college. Required orientation held during 3-week summer program prior to enrollment.

Academic advising: Provided by LD staff members, academic advisers. Students with LD may take up to 12 credits each term; most take 12 credits; 12 credits required to maintain full-time status and be eligible for financial aid.

Counseling services: Individual counseling, career counseling.

Basic skills remediation: Offered in small groups by regular teachers. Available in learning strategies, study skills.

Subject-area tutoring: Offered one-on-one, in small groups, and in class-size groups by peer tutors with LD training. Available in all subjects.

Auxiliary aids: Taped textbooks, tape recorders, calculators, typewriters, word-processors with spell-check, personal computers, optical character readers, talking calculators, Wilsonline Workstation.

Auxiliary services: Alternative test arrangements, notetakers, priority registration, advocacy, editing services.

GENERAL COLLEGE INFORMATION

Independent Roman Catholic, comprehensive, coed. Awards bachelor's, master's degrees. Founded 1924. *Setting:* 100-acre small-town campus. *Endowment:* $4.6 million. *Educational spending 1995–96:* $3681 per undergrad. *Total enrollment:* 1,736. *Faculty:* 158 (93 full-time, 52% with terminal degrees, 65 part-time); student–undergrad faculty ratio is 13:1.

Enrollment Profile: 1,590 students from 17 states and territories, 1 other country. 73% women, 27% men, 24% part-time, 80% state residents, 8% transferred in, 1% international, 23% 25 or older, 0% Native American, 1% Hispanic, 1% black, 1% Asian or Pacific Islander. *Retention:* 83% of 1995 full-time freshmen returned. *Graduation:* 52% graduate in 5 years, 55% in 6 years. *Areas of study chosen:* 55% health professions and related sciences, 11% social sciences, 9% business management and administrative services, 9% education, 3% biological and life sciences, 3% liberal arts/general studies, 3% psychology, 2% English language/literature/letters, 2% prelaw, 1% computer and information sciences, 1% mathematics, 1% premed. *Most popular recent majors:* physical therapy, occupational therapy, elementary education.

First-Year Class: 248 total; 1,276 applied, 61% were accepted, 32% of whom enrolled. 26% from top 10% of their high school class, 54% from top quarter, 70% from top half. 3 valedictorians.

Graduation Requirements: 120 credits; 6 credits each of math and science; computer course for biology, pre-medicine, math, business, chemistry majors; internship (some majors); senior project for honors program students.

Computers on Campus: 50 computers available on campus for general student use. Computer purchase/lease plans available. A campus-wide network can be accessed. Students can contact faculty members and/or advisers through e-mail. Computers for student use in computer center, computer labs, learning resource center, library provide access to the Internet/World Wide Web, on- and off-campus e-mail addresses. Staffed computer lab on campus provides training in use of computers, software. *Academic computing expenditure 1995–96:* $129,915.

EXPENSES AND FINANCIAL AID

Expenses for 1997–98: Comprehensive fee of $19,760 includes full-time tuition ($13,120), mandatory fees ($710), and college room and board ($5930). College room only: $3400. Part-time tuition: $330 per credit.

Undergraduate Financial Aid: 96% of all full-time undergraduates enrolled in fall 1996 applied for aid; of these, 97% were judged to have need according to Federal Methodology, of whom 100% were aided. On average, 68% of need was met. *Financial aid deadline (priority):* 3/1. *Financial aid forms:* FAFSA, institutional form required; CSS Financial Aid PROFILE acceptable. State form required for some.

LD Program Contact: Dr. Joseph Rogan, Director, Alternative Learners Project, College Misericordia, 301 Lake Street, Dallas, PA 18612-1098, 717-674-6347. Fax: 717-675-2441. Email: jrogan@misery.edu.

COLLEGE OF MOUNT ST. JOSEPH

Cincinnati, Ohio

Students with LD	57	Subject-Area Tutoring	✓
ADD services	✓	Special Courses	✓
Staff	3 full-, 8 part-time	Taped Textbooks	✓
Special Fee	Varies	Alternative Test Arrang.	✓
Diagnostic Testing	✓	Notetakers	✓
Basic Skills Remediation	✓	LD Student Organization	✓

LEARNING DISABILITIES PROGRAM INFORMATION

The Project EXCEL began offering services in 1982. Currently the program serves 57 undergraduates with LD. Services are also available to graduate students. Students diagnosed with ADD/ADHD are eligible for the same services available to students with LD.

Staff: 3 full-time, 8 part-time staff members, including director, assistant director, administrative secretary. Services provided by remediation specialists, tutors, diagnostic specialists, LD specialists.
Special Fees: Range from $1500 to $3000 per year. $900 for diagnostic testing.
Applications and admissions: *Required:* high school transcript, grade point average, courses completed, personal interview, letters of recommendation, psychoeducational report completed within 3 years, specific Project EXCEL application forms; *recommended:* high school class rank, extracurricular activities, untimed or extended time SAT I or ACT, autobiographical statement. Students may begin taking classes any term. *Application deadline:* continuous.

PROGRAM AND SERVICE COMPONENTS

Special preparation or orientation: Required orientation held before general freshman orientation.
Diagnostic testing: Intelligence, reading, math, spelling, spoken language, written language, perceptual skills, personality.
Academic advising: Provided by LD staff members. Most students with LD take 12 to 15 semester hours each term; 12 semester hours required to maintain full-time status and be eligible for financial aid.
Counseling services: Career counseling.
Basic skills remediation: Offered one-on-one, in small groups, and in class-size groups by LD teachers, regular teachers; computer-aided instruction also offered. Available in reading, math, written language, study skills, time management.
Subject-area tutoring: Offered one-on-one and in small groups by professional teachers, peer tutors. Available in all subjects.
Special courses: Study skills, "Study For Success" (college survival skills, time management, reading in content areas, notetaking skills, test taking skills, career planning). All offered for credit; all enter into overall grade point average.
Auxiliary aids: Taped textbooks, tape recorders, calculators, typewriters, word-processors with spell-check, personal computers, voice recognition software.
Auxiliary services: Alternative test arrangements, notetakers, advocacy.
Campus support group: A special student organization is available to students with LD.

GENERAL COLLEGE INFORMATION

Independent Roman Catholic, comprehensive, coed. Awards associate, bachelor's, master's degrees. Founded 1920. *Setting:* 75-acre suburban campus. *Endowment:* $10.4 million. *Research spending 1995–96:* $15,000. *Educational spending 1995–96:* $4122 per undergrad. *Total enrollment:* 2,205. *Faculty:* 210 (102 full-time, 46% with terminal degrees, 108 part-time); student–undergrad faculty ratio is 15:1.
Enrollment Profile: 2,083 students from 14 states and territories, 18 other countries. 74% women, 26% men, 45% part-time, 85% state residents, 13% live on campus, 15% transferred in, 3% international, 34% 25 or older, 1% Native American, 1% Hispanic, 7% black, 1% Asian or Pacific Islander. *Retention:* 83% of 1995 full-time freshmen returned. *Graduation:* 59% graduate in 4 years, 62% in 5 years, 63% in 6 years. *Areas of study chosen:* 24% business management and administrative services, 19% education, 16% health professions and related sciences, 14% social sciences, 6% liberal arts/general studies, 5% fine arts, 3% biological and life sciences, 3% communications and journalism, 3% computer and information sciences, 2% English language/literature/letters, 2% mathematics, 2% natural resource sciences, 1% performing arts, 1% psychology, 1% theology/religion. *Most popular recent majors:* business administration/commerce/management, nursing, liberal arts/general studies.
First-Year Class: 227 total; 745 applied, 80% were accepted, 38% of whom enrolled. 19% from top 10% of their high school class, 53% from top quarter, 86% from top half. 4 class presidents, 2 valedictorians.
Graduation Requirements: 64 semester hours for associate, 128 semester hours for bachelor's; 7 semester hours of math/science; computer course for business, physical therapy majors; internship (some majors); senior project (some majors).
Computers on Campus: 181 computers available on campus for general student use. A computer is recommended for all students. A campus-wide network can be accessed from student residence rooms and from off-campus. Students can contact faculty members and/or advisers through e-mail. Computers for student use in computer labs, classrooms, library, dorms provide access to the Internet/World Wide Web. Staffed computer lab on campus provides training in use of computers, software. *Academic computing expenditure 1995–96:* $609,000.

EXPENSES AND FINANCIAL AID

Expenses for 1997–98: *Application fee:* $25. Comprehensive fee of $17,000 includes full-time tuition ($11,900), mandatory fees ($50), and college room and board ($5050). College room only: $2600. Part-time tuition: $305 per semester hour.
Undergraduate Financial Aid: Of all full-time undergraduates enrolled in fall 1996, 89% of those who applied for aid were judged to have need according to Federal Methodology, of whom 100% were aided. On average, 90% of need was met. *Financial aid deadline (priority):* 3/1. *Financial aid forms:* FAFSA required.
LD Program Contact: Ms. Jane Pohlman, Director, Project EXCEL, College of Mount St. Joseph, 5701 Delhi Road, Cincinnati, OH 45233-1670, 513-244-4623. Fax: 513-244-4222. Email: jane_pohlman@mail.msj.edu.

CONCORDIA COLLEGE

Bronxville, New York

Students with LD	22	Subject-Area Tutoring	✓
ADD services	✓	Special Courses	
Staff	1 full-, 2 part-time	Taped Textbooks	
Special Fee	✓	Alternative Test Arrang.	✓
Diagnostic Testing	✓	Notetakers	✓
Basic Skills Remediation	✓	LD Student Organization	

LEARNING DISABILITIES PROGRAM INFORMATION

The Concordia Connection Program began offering services in 1993. Currently the program serves 22 undergraduates with LD. Students diagnosed with ADD/ADHD are eligible for the same services available to students with LD.
Staff: 1 full-time, 2 part-time staff members, including director, associate director. Services provided by remediation specialists, tutors, counselors, diagnostic specialists.
Special Fees: $3000 per year.
Applications and admissions: *Required:* high school transcript, grade point average, class rank, courses completed, IEP (Individualized Education Program), personal interview, autobiographical statement, letters of recommendation, psychoeducational report completed within 2 years; *recommended:* high school extracurricular activities, untimed or extended time SAT I, extended time ACT. Students may begin taking classes in fall or spring. *Application deadline:* continuous.

PROGRAM AND SERVICE COMPONENTS

Special preparation or orientation: Required orientation held before registration.

Concordia College (continued)

Diagnostic testing: Intelligence, reading, math, spelling, handwriting, spoken language, written language, motor abilities, perceptual skills, study skills, personality, social skills, learning strategies.

Academic advising: Provided by LD staff members. Students with LD may take up to 18 credit hours each term; most take 15 credit hours; 12 credit hours required to maintain full-time status and be eligible for financial aid.

Counseling services: Individual counseling, small-group counseling, career counseling, self-advocacy training.

Basic skills remediation: Offered one-on-one and in small groups by regular teachers, school psychologist; computer-aided instruction also offered. Available in reading, math, spelling, written language, learning strategies, study skills, time management.

Subject-area tutoring: Offered one-on-one and in small groups by professional teachers, peer tutors. Available in most subjects.

Auxiliary aids: Tape recorders, calculators, typewriters, word-processors with spell-check, personal computers, microfiche reader.

Auxiliary services: Alternative test arrangements, notetakers, priority registration, advocacy.

GENERAL COLLEGE INFORMATION

Independent Lutheran, 4-year, coed. Part of Concordia University System. Awards associate, bachelor's degrees. Founded 1881. *Setting:* 33-acre suburban campus with easy access to New York City. *Total enrollment:* 556. *Faculty:* 46 (34 full-time, 79% with terminal degrees, 12 part-time); student–undergrad faculty ratio is 13:1.

Enrollment Profile: 556 students from 15 states and territories, 32 other countries. 55% women, 45% men, 15% part-time, 82% state residents, 29% transferred in, 18% international, 18% 25 or older, 0% Native American, 8% Hispanic, 17% black, 6% Asian or Pacific Islander. *Retention:* 70% of 1995 full-time freshmen returned. *Most popular recent majors:* education, business administration/commerce/management.

First-Year Class: 104 total; 408 applied, 85% were accepted, 30% of whom enrolled. 11% from top 10% of their high school class, 41% from top quarter, 70% from top half.

Graduation Requirements: 62 credit hours for associate, 122 credit hours for bachelor's; 3 credit hours of algebra; computer course; internship (some majors).

Computers on Campus: 30 computers available on campus for general student use. Computers for student use in computer center, library provide access to the Internet/World Wide Web, on- and off-campus e-mail addresses. Staffed computer lab on campus provides training in use of computers, software.

EXPENSES AND FINANCIAL AID

Expenses for 1997–98: Comprehensive fee of $17,540 includes full-time tuition ($11,990) and college room and board ($5550). Part-time tuition: $348 per credit hour.

Undergraduate Financial Aid: 75% of all full-time undergraduates enrolled in fall 1996 applied for aid; of these, 82% were judged to have need according to Federal Methodology, of whom 100% were aided. On average, 78% of need was met. *Financial aid deadline (priority):* 4/1. *Financial aid forms:* FAFSA required; state form acceptable.

LD Program Contact: Mr. George Groth, Psy.D, Director, Concordia College, 171 White Plains Road, Bronxville, NY 10708, 914-337-9300 Ext. 2361.

CURRY COLLEGE

Milton, Massachusetts

Students with LD	385	Subject-Area Tutoring	✓
ADD services	✓	Special Courses	
Staff	14 full-, 10 part-time	Taped Textbooks	✓
Special Fee	✓	Alternative Test Arrang.	✓
Diagnostic Testing		Notetakers	
Basic Skills Remediation	✓	LD Student Organization	

LEARNING DISABILITIES PROGRAM INFORMATION

The Program for Advancement of Learning (PAL) began offering services in 1970. Currently the program serves 385 undergraduates with LD. Services are also available to graduate students. Students diagnosed with ADD/ADHD are eligible for the same services available to students with LD.

Staff: 14 full-time, 10 part-time staff members, including director, coordinator. Services provided by tutors, counselors, diagnostic specialists, professional mentors.

Special Fees: $3576 for full-time students; $1926 for part-time students.

Applications and admissions: *Required:* high school transcript, grade point average, courses completed, autobiographical statement, letters of recommendation, psychoeducational report completed within 18 months, WAIS-R; *recommended:* high school class rank, extracurricular activities, IEP (Individualized Education Program), untimed or extended time SAT I, personal interview. Students may begin taking classes in fall or spring. *Application deadline:* continuous.

Special policies: The college has written policies regarding substitutions and waivers of admissions requirements.

PROGRAM AND SERVICE COMPONENTS

Special preparation or orientation: Optional summer program offered prior to entering college. Required orientation held during registration and during summer prior to enrollment.

Academic advising: Provided by LD staff members, academic advisers. Students with LD may take up to 18 credit hours each term; most take 12 to 15 credit hours; 12 credit hours required to maintain full-time status and be eligible for financial aid.

Counseling services: Individual counseling, career counseling.

Basic skills remediation: Offered one-on-one and in small groups by professional mentors. Available in reading, math, spelling, spoken language, written language, learning strategies, motor abilities, study skills, time management, social skills.

Subject-area tutoring: Offered one-on-one and in small groups by professional teachers, peer tutors. Available in most subjects.

Auxiliary aids: Taped textbooks, tape recorders, word-processors with spell-check.

Auxiliary services: Alternative test arrangements.

GENERAL COLLEGE INFORMATION

Independent, comprehensive, coed. Awards bachelor's, master's degrees. Founded 1879. *Setting:* 120-acre suburban campus with easy access to Boston. *Total enrollment:* 1,909. *Faculty:* 170 (75 full-time, 55% with terminal degrees, 95 part-time).

Enrollment Profile: 1,867 students from 32 states and territories, 23 other countries. 48% women, 52% men, 40% part-time, 62% state residents, 33% transferred in, 4% international, 13% 25 or older, 0% Native American, 1% Hispanic, 4% black, 1% Asian or Pacific Islander. *Retention:* 70% of 1995 full-time freshmen returned. *Areas of study chosen:* 20% health professions and related sciences, 18% communications and journalism, 10% business management and administrative services, 7% psychology, 4% social sciences, 2% English language/literature/letters, 2% fine arts, 1% biological and life sciences, 1% education, 1%

interdisciplinary studies, 1% liberal arts/general studies, 1% library and information studies, 1% philosophy, 1% physical sciences. *Most popular recent majors:* business administration/commerce/ management, communication, nursing.

First-Year Class: 294 total; 1,063 applied, 86% were accepted, 32% of whom enrolled. 6% from top 10% of their high school class, 22% from top quarter, 49% from top half.

Graduation Requirements: 120 credit hours; 1 science course; computer course for communication, business management, education majors; internship (some majors); senior project for honors program students and some majors.

Computers on Campus: 50 computers available on campus for general student use. Computer purchase/lease plans available. A campus-wide network can be accessed from student residence rooms and from off-campus. Students can contact faculty members and/or advisers through e-mail. Computers for student use in computer center, computer labs, learning resource center, library, learning center, nursing buildings provide access to the Internet/World Wide Web. Staffed computer lab on campus provides training in use of computers, software.

EXPENSES AND FINANCIAL AID

Expenses for 1997–98: *Application fee:* $40. Comprehensive fee of $21,515 includes full-time tuition ($15,250), mandatory fees ($450), and college room and board ($5815 minimum). College room only: $3215 (minimum). Part-time tuition: $508.33 per credit hour.

Undergraduate Financial Aid: 69% of all full-time undergraduates enrolled in fall 1996 applied for aid; of these, 94% were judged to have need according to Federal Methodology, of whom 100% were aided. On average, 72% of need was met. *Financial aid deadline (priority):* 3/15. *Financial aid forms:* FAFSA, institutional form required.

LD Program Contact: Ms. Joan Manchester, Assistant to Director, Learning Center, Curry College, 1071 Blue Hill Avenue, Milton, MA 02186-9984, 617-333-0500 Ext. 2250. Fax: 617-333-6860. Email: jmanches@curry.edu.

DAVIS & ELKINS COLLEGE

Elkins, West Virginia

Students with LD	65	Subject-Area Tutoring	✓
ADD services		Special Courses	
Staff	3 full-, 1 part-time	Taped Textbooks	✓
Special Fee	Varies	Alternative Test Arrang.	✓
Diagnostic Testing	✓	Notetakers	✓
Basic Skills Remediation	✓	LD Student Organization	

LEARNING DISABILITIES PROGRAM INFORMATION

The Learning Disabilities Special Services began offering services in 1987. Currently the program serves 65 undergraduates with LD. Students diagnosed with ADD/ADHD are not eligible for the same services available to students with LD.

Staff: 3 full-time, 1 part-time staff members, including director. Services provided by remediation specialists, tutors, counselors, diagnostic specialists.

Special Fees: Range from $1150 to $2250 per year.

Applications and admissions: *Required:* high school transcript, grade point average, courses completed, IEP (Individualized Education Program), untimed or extended time ACT, untimed SAT I, letters of recommendation, psychoeducational report; *recommended:* high school class rank, extracurricular activities, extended time SAT I, personal interview, autobiographical statement. Students may begin taking classes in summer only. *Application deadline:* continuous.

Special policies: The college has written policies regarding grade forgiveness.

PROGRAM AND SERVICE COMPONENTS

Special preparation or orientation: Required orientation held the week before classes begin.

Diagnostic testing: Study skills, personality, social skills, learning strategies.

Academic advising: Provided by LD staff members. Students with LD may take up to 12 credit hours each term; most take 12 to 14 credit hours; 12 credit hours required to maintain full-time status.

Counseling services: Individual counseling, small-group counseling, career counseling.

Basic skills remediation: Offered one-on-one by LD teachers. Available in reading, math, spelling, handwriting, spoken language, written language, learning strategies, study skills, time management, social skills, speech.

Subject-area tutoring: Offered one-on-one and in small groups by professional teachers, peer tutors. Available in all subjects.

Auxiliary aids: Taped textbooks, tape recorders, calculators, typewriters, word-processors with spell-check, personal computers.

Auxiliary services: Alternative test arrangements, notetakers, advocacy.

GENERAL COLLEGE INFORMATION

Independent Presbyterian, 4-year, coed. Awards associate, bachelor's degrees. Founded 1904. *Setting:* 170-acre small-town campus. *Endowment:* $9.4 million. *Educational spending 1995–96:* $4133 per undergrad. *Total enrollment:* 732. *Faculty:* 80 (49 full-time, 72% with terminal degrees, 31 part-time); student–undergrad faculty ratio is 13:1.

Enrollment Profile: 732 students from 24 states and territories, 9 other countries. 60% women, 40% men, 13% part-time, 60% state residents, 42% live on campus, 2% international, 21% 25 or older, 0% Native American, 0% Hispanic, 3% black, 3% Asian or Pacific Islander. *Retention:* 63% of 1995 full-time freshmen returned. *Graduation:* 20% graduate in 4 years, 29% in 5 years, 30% in 6 years. *Areas of study chosen:* 22% business management and administrative services, 10% education, 10% health professions and related sciences, 7% psychology, 6% biological and life sciences, 4% performing arts, 4% social sciences, 3% computer and information sciences, 1% communications and journalism, 1% English language/literature/letters, 1% fine arts, 1% mathematics. *Most popular recent majors:* business administration/commerce/management, education, psychology.

First-Year Class: 154 total; 430 applied, 91% were accepted, 39% of whom enrolled. 12% from top 10% of their high school class, 31% from top quarter, 63% from top half. 2 valedictorians.

Graduation Requirements: 62 credit hours for associate, 124 credit hours for bachelor's; 3 credit hours of math; 7 credit hours of natural science; computer course; internship (some majors); senior project for honors program students and some majors.

Computers on Campus: 99 computers available on campus for general student use. Computers for student use in computer center, computer labs, learning resource center, library, academic resources, science centers provide access to the Internet/ World Wide Web. Staffed computer lab on campus provides training in use of computers, software.

EXPENSES AND FINANCIAL AID

Expenses for 1997–98: *Application fee:* $25. Comprehensive fee of $15,460 includes full-time tuition ($10,580 minimum), mandatory fees ($200), and college room and board ($4680). College room only: $2000. Part-time mandatory fees: $50 per semester. Full-time tuition ranges up to $11,000 according to class level. Part-time tuition: $350 per credit hour for 1 to 6 credit hours, $420 per credit hour for 7 or more credit hours.

Davis & Elkins College (continued)

Undergraduate Financial Aid: 85% of all full-time undergraduates enrolled in fall 1996 applied for aid; of these, 92% were judged to have need according to Federal Methodology, of whom 100% were aided. On average, 95% of need was met. *Financial aid deadline (priority):* 5/1. *Financial aid forms:* FAFSA, CSS Financial Aid PROFILE required.

LD Program Contact: Dr. Margaret N. Turner, Director, Special Services for College Learning Disabled Students, Davis & Elkins College, 104 Albert Hall, Elkins, WV 26241-3996, 304-637-1384.

DEPAUL UNIVERSITY

Chicago, Illinois

Students with LD	70	Subject-Area Tutoring	
ADD services	✓	Special Courses	
Staff	1 full-, 6 part-time	Taped Textbooks	
Special Fee	Varies	Alternative Test Arrang.	✓
Diagnostic Testing	✓	Notetakers	
Basic Skills Remediation	✓	LD Student Organization	

LEARNING DISABILITIES PROGRAM INFORMATION

The Productive Learning Strategies (PLuS) began offering services in 1984. Currently the program serves 70 undergraduates with LD. Services are also available to graduate students. Students diagnosed with ADD/ADHD are eligible for the same services available to students with LD.

Staff: 1 full-time, 6 part-time staff members, including director. Services provided by remediation specialists, diagnostic specialists, adviser, LD specialists.

Special Fees: Range from $750 to $1350 per year. $250 to $500 for diagnostic testing.

Applications and admissions: *Required:* high school transcript, grade point average, class rank, courses completed, untimed or extended time SAT I or ACT, personal interview, letters of recommendation, psychoeducational report completed within 3 years, history of supportive services including evaluations from high school counselors; *recommended:* high school extracurricular activities. Students may begin taking classes any term. *Application deadline:* continuous.

PROGRAM AND SERVICE COMPONENTS

Diagnostic testing: Intelligence, reading, math, spelling, handwriting, spoken language, written language, motor abilities, perceptual skills, study skills.

Academic advising: Provided by LD staff members, academic advisers. Students with LD may take up to 20 quarter hours each term; most take 8 to 12 quarter hours; 12 quarter hours required to maintain full-time status; 6 quarter hours required to be eligible for financial aid.

Counseling services: Individual counseling, self-advocacy training.

Basic skills remediation: Offered one-on-one by LD specialists. Available in reading, math, spelling, spoken language, written language, learning strategies, perceptual skills, study skills, time management, social skills, computer skills.

Auxiliary aids: Word-processors with spell-check, personal computers.

Auxiliary services: Alternative test arrangements, priority registration, advocacy.

GENERAL COLLEGE INFORMATION

Independent Roman Catholic, coed. Awards bachelor's, master's, doctoral, first professional degrees. Founded 1898. *Setting:* 36-acre urban campus. *Endowment:* $76.5 million. *Research spending 1995–96:* $1.8 million. *Total enrollment:* 17,294. *Faculty:* 1,344 (527 full-time, 88% with terminal degrees, 817 part-time); student–undergrad faculty ratio is 16:1.

Enrollment Profile: 10,438 students from 50 states and territories, 44 other countries. 59% women, 41% men, 38% part-time, 75% state residents, 25% live on campus, 37% transferred in, 1% international, 45% 25 or older, 1% Native American, 11% Hispanic, 13% black, 7% Asian or Pacific Islander. *Areas of study chosen:* 34% liberal arts/general studies, 27% business management and administrative services, 6% education, 6% performing arts, 4% communications and journalism, 4% computer and information sciences, 4% psychology, 4% social sciences, 1% area and ethnic studies, 1% engineering and applied sciences, 1% fine arts, 1% interdisciplinary studies, 1% mathematics, 1% natural resource sciences, 1% philosophy, 1% predentistry, 1% prelaw, 1% premed, 1% prevet. *Most popular recent majors:* accounting, finance/banking, communication.

First-Year Class: 1,157 total; 4,966 applied, 78% were accepted, 30% of whom enrolled. 27% from top 10% of their high school class, 57% from top quarter, 87% from top half. 40 National Merit Scholars, 20 valedictorians.

Graduation Requirements: 188 quarter hours; 3 math/science courses; computer course for math, geography, science, business-related majors; internship (some majors); senior project for honors program students and some majors.

Computers on Campus: 850 computers available on campus for general student use. Computer purchase/lease plans available. A campus-wide network can be accessed from student residence rooms and from off-campus. Students can contact faculty members and/or advisers through e-mail. Computers for student use in computer center, computer labs, classrooms, library, student center, dorms, various locations provide access to the Internet/World Wide Web, on-campus e-mail addresses. Staffed computer lab on campus provides training in use of computers, software.

EXPENSES AND FINANCIAL AID

Expenses for 1997–98: *Application fee:* $25. Comprehensive fee of $21,296 includes full-time tuition ($13,458 minimum), mandatory fees ($30), and college room and board ($7808). College room only: $3639. Part-time tuition: $275 per quarter hour (minimum). Part-time mandatory fees: $10 per quarter. Tuition for music program: $14,898 full-time, $311 per quarter hour part-time. Tuition for theater program: $15,849 full-time, $394 per quarter hour part-time.

Undergraduate Financial Aid: 88% of all full-time undergraduates enrolled in fall 1996 applied for aid; of these, 94% were judged to have need according to Federal Methodology, of whom 95% were aided. On average, 65% of need was met. *Financial aid deadline (priority):* 4/1. *Financial aid forms:* FAFSA required; CSS Financial Aid PROFILE, state form acceptable. Institutional form required for some.

LD Program Contact: Mr. Brian Lynch, Associate Director, Admissions, DePaul University, 2320 North Kenmore, #103, Chicago, IL 60614, 773-325-7000 Ext. 2985.

DOWLING COLLEGE

Oakdale, New York

Students with LD	25	Subject-Area Tutoring	
ADD services	✓	Special Courses	
Staff	2 full-, 25 part-time	Taped Textbooks	
Special Fee	✓	Alternative Test Arrang.	✓
Diagnostic Testing	✓	Notetakers	✓
Basic Skills Remediation	✓	LD Student Organization	

LEARNING DISABILITIES PROGRAM INFORMATION

The Program for College Students with Learning Disabilities began offering services in 1987. Currently the program serves 25 undergraduates with LD. Services are also available to graduate students. Students diagnosed with ADD/ADHD are eligible for the same services available to students with LD.

Staff: 2 full-time, 25 part-time staff members, including director, associate director. Services provided by tutors, graduate students (with extensive training).

Special Fees: $3000 per year.

Applications and admissions: *Required:* high school transcript, IEP (Individualized Education Program), extended time SAT I, personal interview, letters of recommendation, psychoeducational report completed within 3 years. Students may begin taking classes in fall or spring. *Application deadline:* continuous.

Special policies: The college has written policies regarding substitutions and waivers of graduation requirements.

PROGRAM AND SERVICE COMPONENTS

Special preparation or orientation: Required orientation held after classes begin.

Diagnostic testing: Reading, spelling, written language.

Academic advising: Provided by LD staff members, academic advisers. Students with LD may take up to 12 credit hours each term; most take 12 credit hours; 12 credit hours required to maintain full-time status and be eligible for financial aid.

Counseling services: Individual counseling, career counseling, self-advocacy training.

Basic skills remediation: Offered one-on-one by graduate assistants/tutors. Available in learning strategies, study skills, time management.

Auxiliary aids: Word-processors with spell-check.

Auxiliary services: Alternative test arrangements, notetakers, priority registration, advocacy.

GENERAL COLLEGE INFORMATION

Independent, comprehensive, coed. Awards bachelor's, master's degrees. Founded 1955. *Setting:* 156-acre suburban campus with easy access to New York City. *Total enrollment:* 6,046. *Faculty:* 424 (107 full-time, 96% with terminal degrees, 317 part-time); student–undergrad faculty ratio is 9:1.

Enrollment Profile: 3,812 students from 17 states and territories, 40 other countries. 55% women, 45% men, 76% part-time, 95% state residents, 11% live on campus, 53% transferred in, 2% international, 34% 25 or older, 0% Native American, 5% Hispanic, 6% black, 2% Asian or Pacific Islander. *Retention:* 82% of 1995 full-time freshmen returned. *Graduation:* 22% graduate in 4 years, 31% in 5 years, 33% in 6 years. *Areas of study chosen:* 30% business management and administrative services, 19% education, 16% interdisciplinary studies, 8% liberal arts/general studies, 6% computer and information sciences, 6% psychology, 4% engineering and applied sciences, 3% English language/literature/letters, 3% social sciences, 2% biological and life sciences, 1% fine arts, 1% mathematics, 1% performing arts. *Most popular recent majors:* business administration/commerce/management, liberal arts/general studies, education.

First-Year Class: 320 total; 1,038 applied, 93% were accepted, 33% of whom enrolled.

Graduation Requirements: 122 credit hours; computer course for aeronautics, business-related, natural science, math majors.

Computers on Campus: 118 computers available on campus for general student use. Computer purchase/lease plans available. A campus-wide network can be accessed. Students can contact faculty members and/or advisers through e-mail. Computers for student use in computer center, computer labs, research center, learning resource center, student center provide access to the Internet/World Wide Web, on- and off-campus e-mail addresses. Staffed computer lab on campus provides training in use of computers, software.

EXPENSES AND FINANCIAL AID

Expenses for 1997–98: *Application fee:* $25. Tuition: $11,940 full-time. Part-time mandatory fees per semester range from $113 to $230. Part-time tuition (1 to 9 credit hours): $398 per credit hour. Full-time mandatory fees: $690. College room only: $3600 (minimum). Tuition guaranteed not to increase for student's term of enrollment.

Undergraduate Financial Aid: On average, 85% of need was met. *Financial aid deadline (priority):* 6/1. *Financial aid forms:* FAFSA, state form, institutional form required; CSS Financial Aid PROFILE acceptable.

Financial aid specifically for students with LD: Scholarship: Lotte Kaliski Foundation for Gifted Children Scholarship.

LD Program Contact: Dr. Dorothy A. Stracher, Director, Dowling College, Idle Hour Boulevard, Oakdale, NY 11769, 516-244-3306. Fax: 516-589-6644.

DREXEL UNIVERSITY

Philadelphia, Pennsylvania

Students with LD	75	Subject-Area Tutoring	
ADD services	✓	Special Courses	✓
Staff		Taped Textbooks	✓
Special Fee	None	Alternative Test Arrang.	✓
Diagnostic Testing		Notetakers	✓
Basic Skills Remediation		LD Student Organization	

LEARNING DISABILITIES PROGRAM INFORMATION

The Office of Disability Services currently serves 75 undergraduates with LD. Services are also available to graduate students. Students diagnosed with ADD/ADHD are eligible for the same services available to students with LD.

Staff: Includes co-directors, tutorial manager. Services provided by counselors, learning specialist, disability specialist.

Special Fees: No special fees are charged for services to students with LD.

Applications and admissions: *Required:* high school transcript, untimed SAT I or ACT, essay, possible attendance at four-week program focusing on basic skills remediation (for students not meeting minimum requirements); *recommended:* extended time SAT I or ACT. Students may begin taking classes in fall only. *Application deadline:* 3/1.

PROGRAM AND SERVICE COMPONENTS

Special preparation or orientation: Summer program (required for some) held prior to entering college. Required orientation held prior to orientation.

Academic advising: Provided by LD staff members, academic advisers. Students with LD may take up to 20 credit hours each term; most take 15 credit hours; 12 credit hours required to maintain full-time status and be eligible for financial aid.

Counseling services: Individual counseling, small-group counseling, career counseling.

Special courses: College survival skills, math, study skills (all held during a free 4-week summer session for entering freshmen who are academically at risk). None offered for credit.

Auxiliary aids: Taped textbooks, tape recorders, calculators, personal computers, Visualtek machine, close view computer work station, reading machine.

Auxiliary services: Alternative test arrangements, notetakers, advocacy, readers, proofreaders, interpreters.

Drexel University (continued)

GENERAL COLLEGE INFORMATION

Independent, coed. Awards bachelor's, master's, doctoral degrees. Founded 1891. *Setting:* 38-acre urban campus. *Endowment:* \$103.6 million. *Research spending 1995–96:* \$10.7 million. *Total enrollment:* 9,590. *Faculty:* 732 (360 full-time, 96% with terminal degrees, 372 part-time); student–undergrad faculty ratio is 12:1.

Enrollment Profile: 6,805 students from 43 states and territories, 87 other countries. 33% women, 67% men, 25% part-time, 67% state residents, 5% transferred in, 8% international, 23% 25 or older, 1% Native American, 2% Hispanic, 10% black, 10% Asian or Pacific Islander. *Retention:* 80% of 1995 full-time freshmen returned. *Areas of study chosen:* 39% engineering and applied sciences, 7% fine arts, 7% physical sciences, 5% architecture, 3% library and information studies, 2% biological and life sciences, 2% social sciences, 1% area and ethnic studies, 1% communications and journalism, 1% education. *Most popular recent majors:* electrical engineering, accounting, finance/banking.

First-Year Class: 1,305 total; 5,050 applied, 74% were accepted, 35% of whom enrolled. 25% from top 10% of their high school class, 63% from top quarter, 88% from top half.

Graduation Requirements: 180 credit hours; 2 math courses; computer course; senior project (some majors).

Computers on Campus: 6,500 computers available on campus for general student use. Computer purchase/lease plans available. A computer is required for all students. A campus-wide network can be accessed from student residence rooms and from off-campus. Students can contact faculty members and/or advisers through e-mail. Computers for student use in computer center, computer labs, learning resource center, classrooms, library, dorms, student rooms, departmental labs provide access to the Internet/World Wide Web, on- and off-campus e-mail addresses. Staffed computer lab on campus provides training in use of computers, software. *Academic computing expenditure 1995–96:* \$2.4 million.

EXPENSES AND FINANCIAL AID

Expenses for 1997–98: *Application fee:* \$35. Comprehensive fee of \$23,350 includes full-time tuition (\$15,294 minimum), mandatory fees (\$820), and college room and board (\$7236). College room only: \$4296 (minimum). Part-time tuition: \$360 per credit hour. Part-time mandatory fees: \$63 per quarter. Full-time tuition ranges up to \$17,784 according to program and class level. Part-time tuition for evening classes: \$192 per credit hour.

Undergraduate Financial Aid: *Financial aid deadline (priority):* 5/1. *Financial aid forms:* FAFSA, state form, institutional form required.

LD Program Contact: Mr. Bill Welsh and Ms. Marilyn Longo, Coordinators, Disability Services, Drexel University, 32nd and Chestnut Streets, Philadelphia, PA 19104-2875, 215-895-2960. Fax: 215-895-6810.

EASTERN KENTUCKY UNIVERSITY

Richmond, Kentucky

Students with LD	45	Subject-Area Tutoring	✓
ADD services	✓	Special Courses	✓
Staff	1 full-, 27 part-time	Taped Textbooks	✓
Special Fee	None	Alternative Test Arrang.	✓
Diagnostic Testing	✓	Notetakers	✓
Basic Skills Remediation	✓	LD Student Organization	✓

LEARNING DISABILITIES PROGRAM INFORMATION

The Project SUCCESS/The Office of Services for Students with Disabilities began offering services in 1992. Currently the program serves 45 undergraduates with LD. Services are also available to graduate students. Students diagnosed with ADD/ADHD are eligible for the same services available to students with LD, as well as support group, distraction-free testing environment.

Staff: 1 full-time, 27 part-time staff members, including director, coordinators, peer tutors, notetakers. Services provided by remediation specialists, tutors, counselors, diagnostic specialists.

Special Fees: \$15 to \$60 for diagnostic testing.

Applications and admissions: *Required:* high school transcript, grade point average, untimed or extended time ACT, psychoeducational report completed within 3 years; *recommended:* high school class rank, courses completed, extracurricular activities, IEP (Individualized Education Program), untimed or extended time SAT I, personal interview, autobiographical statement, letters of recommendation. Students may begin taking classes any term. *Application deadline:* continuous.

Special policies: The college has written policies regarding grade forgiveness; substitutions and waivers of admissions, graduation, and degree requirements.

PROGRAM AND SERVICE COMPONENTS

Special preparation or orientation: Optional summer program offered prior to entering college. Orientation (required for some) held during registration.

Diagnostic testing: Intelligence, reading, math, spelling, handwriting, spoken language, written language, perceptual skills, study skills, personality, social skills, speech, hearing, learning strategies.

Academic advising: Provided by academic advisers. Students with LD may take up to 18 semester hours each term; most take 12 semester hours; 12 semester hours required to maintain full-time status and be eligible for financial aid.

Counseling services: Individual counseling, career counseling, self-advocacy training.

Basic skills remediation: Offered in small groups and in class-size groups by regular teachers. Available in reading, math, written language, learning strategies, study skills, time management, social skills, speech.

Subject-area tutoring: Offered one-on-one by peer tutors. Available in most subjects.

Special courses: College survival skills, reading, vocabulary development, communication skills, learning strategies, word processing, Internet use, time management, math, study skills, career planning. None offered for credit; none enter into overall grade point average.

Auxiliary aids: Taped textbooks, tape recorders, calculators, word-processors with spell-check, personal computers, optical character readers, spell checkers (hand-held).

Auxiliary services: Alternative test arrangements, notetakers, advocacy.

Campus support group: A special student organization is available to students with LD.

GENERAL COLLEGE INFORMATION

State-supported, comprehensive, coed. Part of Kentucky Council on Higher Education. Awards associate, bachelor's, master's degrees. Founded 1906. *Setting:* 350-acre small-town campus. *Research spending 1995–96:* \$369,900. *Educational spending 1995–96:* \$2461 per undergrad. *Total enrollment:* 16,060. *Undergraduate faculty:* 855 (529 full-time, 326 part-time); student–undergrad faculty ratio is 23:1.

Enrollment Profile: 14,154 students from 49 states and territories, 37 other countries. 57% women, 43% men, 21% part-time, 90% state residents, 1% international, 29% 25 or older, 1% Native American, 5% Hispanic, 5% black, 1% Asian or Pacific Islander. *Most popular recent major:* nursing.
First-Year Class: 2,351 total; 5,114 applied, 95% were accepted, 48% of whom enrolled.
Graduation Requirements: 64 semester hours for associate, 128 semester hours for bachelor's; 9 semester hours of science; computer course for business, science, math, education majors.
Computers on Campus: 500 computers available on campus for general student use. Computer purchase/lease plans available. Computers for student use in computer center, computer labs, classrooms, library, dorms, academic buildings. Staffed computer lab on campus provides training in use of computers, software. *Academic computing expenditure 1995–96:* $687,431.

EXPENSES AND FINANCIAL AID

Expenses for 1997–98: State resident tuition: $2060 full-time, $86 per semester hour part-time. Nonresident tuition: $5660 full-time, $236 per semester hour part-time. College room and board: $3160. College room only: $1370 (minimum).
Undergraduate Financial Aid: *Financial aid deadline (priority):* 4/1. *Financial aid forms:* FAFSA, institutional form required.
Financial aid specifically for students with LD: Scholarships.
LD Program Contact: Ms. Teresa Belluscio, Project SUCCESS Director/Disabilities Coordinator, Eastern Kentucky University, 1 Turley House, Richmond, KY 40475-3136, 606-622-1500. Fax: 606-622-1020. Email: disbellu@acs.eku.edu.

EASTERN MENNONITE UNIVERSITY

Harrisonburg, Virginia

Students with LD	53	Subject-Area Tutoring	✓
ADD services	✓	Special Courses	✓
Staff	1 full-, 8 part-time	Taped Textbooks	✓
Special Fee	None	Alternative Test Arrang.	✓
Diagnostic Testing	✓	Notetakers	✓
Basic Skills Remediation	✓	LD Student Organization	

LEARNING DISABILITIES PROGRAM INFORMATION

The Learning Center, Academic Support Services began offering services in 1993. Currently the program serves 53 undergraduates with LD. Services are also available to graduate students. Students diagnosed with ADD/ADHD are eligible for the same services available to students with LD.
Staff: 1 full-time, 8 part-time staff members, including director. Services provided by tutors.
Special Fees: No special fees are charged for services to students with LD.
Applications and admissions: *Required:* high school transcript, extracurricular activities, extended time SAT I or ACT, autobiographical statement, letters of recommendation, psychoeducational report completed within 3 years; *recommended:* high school grade point average, class rank, courses completed, IEP (Individualized Education Program), personal interview. Students may begin taking classes in fall or spring. *Application deadline:* continuous.
Special policies: The college has written policies regarding grade forgiveness.

PROGRAM AND SERVICE COMPONENTS

Special preparation or orientation: Orientation (required for some) held before registration.
Diagnostic testing: Intelligence, reading, math, spelling, handwriting, spoken language, written language, motor abilities, perceptual skills, personality, psychoneurology, learning strategies.
Academic advising: Provided by LD staff members, academic advisers. Students with LD may take up to 16 semester hours each term; most take 12 semester hours; 11 semester hours (fewer with special permission) required to maintain full-time status and be eligible for financial aid.
Counseling services: Individual counseling, small-group counseling, career counseling, self-advocacy training, mentoring.
Basic skills remediation: Offered one-on-one and in class-size groups by regular teachers, peer tutors; computer-aided instruction also offered. Available in reading, math, spoken language, written language, learning strategies, study skills, time management, computer skills.
Subject-area tutoring: Offered one-on-one and in small groups by professional teachers, peer tutors. Available in some subjects.
Special courses: Reading, composition, math. All offered for credit; all enter into overall grade point average.
Auxiliary aids: Taped textbooks, tape recorders, calculators, typewriters, word-processors with spell-check, personal computers, talking computers, optical character readers.
Auxiliary services: Alternative test arrangements, notetakers, priority registration, advocacy, proofreading.

GENERAL COLLEGE INFORMATION

Independent Mennonite, comprehensive, coed. Awards associate, bachelor's, master's, first professional degrees. Founded 1917. *Setting:* 92-acre small-town campus. *Endowment:* $10.4 million. *Research spending 1995–96:* $2490. *Educational spending 1995–96:* $5208 per undergrad. *Total enrollment:* 1,150. *Faculty:* 122 (89 full-time, 66% with terminal degrees, 33 part-time); student–undergrad faculty ratio is 13:1.
Enrollment Profile: 989 students from 37 states and territories, 14 other countries. 61% women, 39% men, 10% part-time, 40% state residents, 60% live on campus, 6% transferred in, 4% international, 19% 25 or older, 0% Native American, 2% Hispanic, 4% black, 2% Asian or Pacific Islander. *Retention:* 75% of 1995 full-time freshmen returned. *Graduation:* 44% graduate in 4 years, 59% in 5 years, 60% in 6 years. *Areas of study chosen:* 25% education, 17% biological and life sciences, 13% health professions and related sciences, 10% business management and administrative services, 10% social sciences, 6% psychology, 4% English language/literature/letters, 3% computer and information sciences, 3% liberal arts/general studies, 3% theology/religion, 2% mathematics, 1% agriculture, 1% fine arts, 1% foreign language and literature, 1% performing arts. *Most popular recent majors:* education, biology/biological sciences, nursing.
First-Year Class: 231 total; 525 applied, 92% were accepted, 48% of whom enrolled. 18% from top 10% of their high school class, 46% from top quarter, 73% from top half. 3 National Merit Scholars, 12 valedictorians.
Graduation Requirements: 64 semester hours for associate, 128 semester hours for bachelor's; 3 math/science courses including at least 1 lab science course; computer course for business, math, chemistry, education, biology majors; internship (some majors); senior project for honors program students and some majors.
Computers on Campus: 75 computers available on campus for general student use. Computer purchase/lease plans available. A computer is recommended for all students. A campus-wide network can be accessed from student residence rooms and from off-campus. Students can contact faculty members and/or advisers through e-mail. Computers for student use in computer labs, learning resource center, library, science center provide access to the Internet/World Wide Web, on- and off-campus e-mail addresses. Staffed computer lab on campus provides training in use of computers, software. *Academic computing expenditure 1995–96:* $170,000.

Eastern Mennonite University (continued)

EXPENSES AND FINANCIAL AID

Estimated Expenses for 1997–98: *Application fee:* $25. Comprehensive fee of $16,620 includes full-time tuition ($12,000), mandatory fees ($120), and college room and board ($4500). College room only: $2250. Part-time tuition: $500 per semester hour.

Undergraduate Financial Aid: 95% of all full-time undergraduates enrolled in fall 1996 applied for aid; of these, 76% were judged to have need according to Federal Methodology, of whom 100% were aided. On average, 94% of need was met. *Financial aid deadline (priority):* 3/15. *Financial aid forms:* FAFSA, institutional form required; CSS Financial Aid PROFILE acceptable. State form required for some.

LD Program Contact: Ms. Joyce Coryell Hedrick, Director, Disability Support Services, Eastern Mennonite University, 1200 Park Road, Harrisonburg, VA 22801, 540-434-4233. Fax: 540-432-4977. Email: hedrickj@emu.edu.

EDINBORO UNIVERSITY OF PENNSYLVANIA

Edinboro, Pennsylvania

Students with LD	202	Subject-Area Tutoring	
ADD services	✓	Special Courses	
Staff		Taped Textbooks	✓
Special Fee	Varies	Alternative Test Arrang.	✓
Diagnostic Testing	✓	Notetakers	
Basic Skills Remediation	✓	LD Student Organization	✓

LEARNING DISABILITIES PROGRAM INFORMATION

The Office for Students with Disabilities began offering services in 1985. Currently the program serves 202 undergraduates with LD. Services are also available to graduate students. Students diagnosed with ADD/ADHD are eligible for the same services available to students with LD.

Staff: Includes co-directors, coordinator, occupational therapist, coordinator of physical activity, computer analyst, registered nurse, secretary. Services provided by student peer mentors.

Special Fees: Range from $356 to $1320 per year.

Applications and admissions: *Required:* high school transcript, grade point average, class rank, courses completed, untimed SAT I or ACT, psychoeducational report completed within 5 years; *recommended:* high school extracurricular activities, extended time SAT I or ACT, personal interview, autobiographical statement, letters of recommendation. Students may begin taking classes any term. *Application deadline:* continuous.

Special policies: The college has written policies regarding grade forgiveness; substitutions and waivers of degree requirements.

PROGRAM AND SERVICE COMPONENTS

Diagnostic testing: Intelligence, reading, math, spelling, handwriting, written language, learning styles.

Academic advising: Provided by LD staff members, academic advisers. Students with LD may take up to 18 credits each term; most take 12 credits; 9 credits (with waiver) required to maintain full-time status; 12 credits required to be eligible for financial aid.

Basic skills remediation: Offered one-on-one and in small groups by regular teachers. Available in written language, learning strategies, study skills, time management.

Auxiliary aids: Taped textbooks, word-processors with spell-check, personal computers, optical character readers.

Auxiliary services: Alternative test arrangements, priority registration, advocacy, readers.

Campus support group: A special student organization is available to students with LD.

GENERAL COLLEGE INFORMATION

State-supported, comprehensive, coed. Part of Pennsylvania State System of Higher Education. Awards associate, bachelor's, master's degrees. Founded 1857. *Setting:* 585-acre small-town campus. *Endowment:* $1.5 million. *Research spending 1995–96:* $97,703. *Total enrollment:* 7,178. *Faculty:* 313 (287 full-time, 62% with terminal degrees, 26 part-time); student–undergrad faculty ratio is 17:1.

Enrollment Profile: 6,509 students from 25 states and territories, 29 other countries. 57% women, 43% men, 16% part-time, 93% state residents, 30% live on campus, 6% transferred in, 1% international, 20% 25 or older, 1% Native American, 1% Hispanic, 5% black, 1% Asian or Pacific Islander. *Retention:* 70% of 1995 full-time freshmen returned. *Areas of study chosen:* 24% education, 12% liberal arts/general studies, 12% social sciences, 9% fine arts, 8% business management and administrative services, 7% communications and journalism, 6% health professions and related sciences, 6% psychology, 3% biological and life sciences, 3% English language/literature/letters, 2% computer and information sciences, 2% natural resource sciences, 2% physical sciences, 1% engineering and applied sciences, 1% foreign language and literature, 1% interdisciplinary studies, 1% mathematics. *Most popular recent majors:* elementary education, criminal justice, psychology.

First-Year Class: 1,296 total; 3,693 applied, 78% were accepted, 45% of whom enrolled.

Graduation Requirements: 60 credits for associate, 128 credits for bachelor's; 12 credits of math/science; computer course for math majors; internship (some majors); senior project for honors program students and some majors.

Computers on Campus: 218 computers available on campus for general student use. Computers for student use in computer center, computer labs, classrooms, library, student center, dorms provide access to the Internet/World Wide Web. Staffed computer lab on campus provides training in use of software. *Academic computing expenditure 1995–96:* $1 million.

EXPENSES AND FINANCIAL AID

Expenses for 1997–98: *Application fee:* $25. State resident tuition: $3468 full-time, $144 per credit part-time. Nonresident tuition: $8824 full-time, $368 per credit part-time. Part-time mandatory fees: $30.20 per credit. Full-time mandatory fees: $725. College room and board: $3616. College room only: $1936.

Undergraduate Financial Aid: Of all full-time undergraduates enrolled in fall 1996, 94% of those who applied for aid were judged to have need according to Federal Methodology, of whom 100% were aided. On average, 95% of need was met. *Financial aid deadline (priority):* 5/1. *Financial aid forms:* FAFSA required.

LD Program Contact: Ms. Kathleen K. Strosser, Assistant to the Director, Office for Students with Disabilities, Edinboro University of Pennsylvania, Edinboro, PA 16444, 814-732-2462. Fax: 814-732-2866. Email: strosser@edinboro.edu.

FAIRLEIGH DICKINSON UNIVERSITY, TEANECK–HACKENSACK

Teaneck, New Jersey

Students with LD	112	Subject-Area Tutoring	✓
ADD services		Special Courses	✓
Staff	6 full-, 6 part-time	Taped Textbooks	✓
Special Fee	None	Alternative Test Arrang.	✓

Diagnostic Testing	✓	Notetakers	
Basic Skills Remediation	✓	LD Student Organization	

LEARNING DISABILITIES PROGRAM INFORMATION

The Regional Center for College Students with Learning Disabilities began offering services in 1988. Currently the program serves 112 undergraduates with LD. Students diagnosed with ADD/ADHD are not eligible for the same services available to students with LD.

Staff: 6 full-time, 6 part-time staff members, including director, assistant directors. Services provided by counselors, diagnostic specialists, LD specialists.

Special Fees: No special fees are charged for services to students with LD.

Applications and admissions: *Required:* high school transcript, courses completed, letters of recommendation, psychoeducational report completed within 2 years; *recommended:* high school grade point average, class rank. Students may begin taking classes in fall or spring. *Application deadline:* continuous.

PROGRAM AND SERVICE COMPONENTS

Special preparation or orientation: Required orientation held after classes begin and during summer prior to enrollment and throughout freshman year.

Diagnostic testing: Intelligence, reading, math, spelling, handwriting, spoken language, written language, motor abilities, perceptual skills, study skills, learning strategies.

Academic advising: Provided by LD staff members, academic advisers. Students with LD may take up to 15 credits each term; most take 12 credits; 12 credits required to maintain full-time status and be eligible for financial aid.

Counseling services: Individual counseling, small-group counseling, career counseling.

Basic skills remediation: Offered in small groups by LD teachers; computer-aided instruction also offered. Available in reading, math, spelling, learning strategies, study skills, time management, social skills, computer skills, word processing.

Subject-area tutoring: Offered one-on-one and in small groups by professional teachers. Available in most subjects.

Special courses: College survival skills, learning strategies, time management, study skills, career planning. All offered for credit; all enter into overall grade point average.

Auxiliary aids: Taped textbooks, tape recorders, calculators, typewriters, word-processors with spell-check, personal computers, talking computers, optical character readers, spelling calculators, audiovisual aids, study guides, text scanner.

Auxiliary services: Alternative test arrangements, priority registration, advocacy, lecture taping, note lending.

GENERAL COLLEGE INFORMATION

Independent, comprehensive, coed. Awards associate, bachelor's, master's, doctoral degrees. Founded 1942. *Setting:* 125-acre suburban campus with easy access to New York City. *Endowment:* $16 million. *Research spending 1995–96:* $903,000. *Educational spending 1995–96:* $5980 per undergrad. *Total enrollment:* 6,934. *Faculty:* 767 (263 full-time, 81% with terminal degrees, 504 part-time).

Enrollment Profile: 3,934 students from 25 states and territories, 43 other countries. 55% women, 45% men, 32% part-time, 81% state residents, 37% live on campus, 11% transferred in, 7% international, 34% 25 or older, 1% Native American, 7% Hispanic, 12% black, 4% Asian or Pacific Islander. *Retention:* 76% of 1995 full-time freshmen returned. *Graduation:* 23% graduate in 4 years, 35% in 5 years, 42% in 6 years. *Areas of study chosen:* 32% business management and administrative services, 15% liberal arts/general studies, 10% psychology, 9% health professions and related sciences, 8% social sciences, 7% biological and life sciences, 4% English language/literature/letters, 3% communications and journalism, 3% computer and information sciences, 3% engineering and applied sciences, 3% fine arts, 2% physical sciences, 1% mathematics. *Most popular recent majors:* business administration/commerce/management, psychology, nursing.

First-Year Class: 708 total; 3,197 applied, 65% were accepted, 34% of whom enrolled. 14% from top 10% of their high school class, 34% from top quarter, 66% from top half.

Graduation Requirements: 72 credits for associate, 128 credits for bachelor's; 6 credits of math; 3 credits of science; computer course for business, math, engineering, engineering technology, biochemistry, environmental science, sociology, chemistry, nursing majors; internship (some majors); senior project for honors program students and some majors.

Computers on Campus: 300 computers available on campus for general student use. Computer purchase/lease plans available. A computer is recommended for all students. A campus-wide network can be accessed from student residence rooms and from off-campus. Students can contact faculty members and/or advisers through e-mail. Computers for student use in computer center, computer labs, learning resource center, library, dorms, student rooms, academic buildings provide access to the Internet/World Wide Web, on- and off-campus e-mail addresses. Staffed computer lab on campus provides training in use of computers, software. *Academic computing expenditure 1995–96:* $1.3 million.

EXPENSES AND FINANCIAL AID

Expenses for 1997–98: *Application fee:* $35. Comprehensive fee of $20,752 includes full-time tuition ($13,996), mandatory fees ($716 minimum), and college room and board ($6040). College room only: $3562. Part-time tuition: $431 per credit. Part-time mandatory fees: $91 per course.

Undergraduate Financial Aid: 80% of all full-time undergraduates enrolled in fall 1996 applied for aid; of these, 90% were judged to have need according to Federal Methodology, of whom 94% were aided. On average, 76% of need was met. *Financial aid deadline (priority):* 3/15. *Financial aid forms:* FAFSA required.

LD Program Contact: Ms. Lisa Chambers-Smith, Campus Director, Florham-Madison, Fairleigh Dickinson University, Teaneck–Hackensack, 285 Madison Avenue, M102E, Madison, NJ 07940, 732-443-8734. Fax: 732-443-8089. Above services are also available to students attending the following Fairleigh Dickinson University colleges: Fairleigh Dickinson University, Florham-Madison Campus; Fairleigh Dickinson University, Edward Williams College.

FITCHBURG STATE COLLEGE

Fitchburg, Massachusetts

Students with LD	109	Subject-Area Tutoring	✓
ADD services	✓	Special Courses	✓
Staff	1 full-, 3 part-time	Taped Textbooks	✓
Special Fee	None	Alternative Test Arrang.	✓
Diagnostic Testing		Notetakers	✓
Basic Skills Remediation	✓	LD Student Organization	

LEARNING DISABILITIES PROGRAM INFORMATION

The Disability Services began offering services in 1993. Currently the program serves 109 undergraduates with LD. Services are also available to graduate students. Students diagnosed with ADD/ADHD are eligible for the same services available to students with LD.

Fitchburg State College (continued)

Staff: 1 full-time, 3 part-time staff members, including coordinator, student assistant, learning specialist, secretary. Services provided by remediation specialists, tutors, trained peer tutoring, adaptive computer lab monitors.

Special Fees: No special fees are charged for services to students with LD.

Applications and admissions: *Required:* high school transcript; *recommended:* high school grade point average, class rank, courses completed, extracurricular activities, untimed or extended time SAT I or ACT, personal interview, autobiographical statement, letters of recommendation, psychoeducational report completed within 3 years. Students may begin taking classes any term. *Application deadline:* continuous.

Special policies: The college has written policies regarding substitutions and waivers of degree requirements.

PROGRAM AND SERVICE COMPONENTS

Special preparation or orientation: Optional orientation offered before the start of each semester.

Academic advising: Provided by LD staff members. Students with LD may take up to 18 semester hours each term; most take 12 semester hours; 12 semester hours required to maintain full-time status and be eligible for financial aid.

Counseling services: Individual counseling, small-group counseling, career counseling, self-advocacy training.

Basic skills remediation: Offered one-on-one and in small groups by regular teachers. Available in reading, math, spelling, written language, learning strategies, study skills, time management.

Subject-area tutoring: Offered one-on-one, in small groups, and in class-size groups by peer tutors. Available in all subjects.

Special courses: Study skills. None offered for credit.

Auxiliary aids: Taped textbooks, tape recorders, calculators, typewriters, word-processors with spell-check, personal computers, optical character readers.

Auxiliary services: Alternative test arrangements, notetakers.

GENERAL COLLEGE INFORMATION

State-supported, comprehensive, coed. Part of Massachusetts Public Higher Education System. Awards bachelor's, master's degrees. Founded 1894. *Setting:* 45-acre small-town campus with easy access to Boston. *Endowment:* $3.4 million. *Total enrollment:* 3,701. *Faculty:* 415 (207 full-time, 74% with terminal degrees, 208 part-time); student–undergrad faculty ratio is 12:1.

Enrollment Profile: 3,153 students from 19 states and territories, 18 other countries. 59% women, 41% men, 19% part-time, 96% state residents, 40% live on campus, 27% transferred in, 1% international, 18% 25 or older, 1% Native American, 3% Hispanic, 5% black, 2% Asian or Pacific Islander. *Retention:* 64% of 1995 full-time freshmen returned. *Graduation:* 32% graduate in 4 years, 46% in 5 years, 49% in 6 years. *Areas of study chosen:* 16% education, 15% health professions and related sciences, 14% communications and journalism, 13% business management and administrative services, 8% liberal arts/general studies, 8% psychology, 6% biological and life sciences, 5% engineering and applied sciences, 5% social sciences, 4% English language/literature/letters, 4% interdisciplinary studies, 2% computer and information sciences, 1% mathematics, 1% physical sciences. *Most popular recent majors:* business administration/commerce/management, communication, nursing.

First-Year Class: 466 total; 2,651 applied, 59% were accepted, 30% of whom enrolled. 4% from top 10% of their high school class, 19% from top quarter, 66% from top half.

Graduation Requirements: 120 semester hours; 4 math/science courses; computer course; internship (some majors); senior project for honors program students and some majors.

Computers on Campus: 500 computers available on campus for general student use. Computer purchase/lease plans available. A computer is recommended for some students. A campus-wide network can be accessed from off-campus. Students can contact faculty members and/or advisers through e-mail. Computers for student use in computer labs, classrooms, library, dorms provide access to the Internet/World Wide Web, on-campus e-mail addresses. Staffed computer lab on campus (open 24 hours a day).

EXPENSES AND FINANCIAL AID

Expenses for 1997–98: *Application fee:* $10. State resident tuition: $1270 full-time, $52.92 per semester hour part-time. Nonresident tuition: $5950 full-time, $247.92 per semester hour part-time. Part-time mandatory fees: $86.50 per semester hour. Full-time mandatory fees: $2076. College room and board: $4410. College room only: $2590.

Undergraduate Financial Aid: Of all full-time undergraduates enrolled in fall 1996, 88% of those who applied for aid were judged to have need according to Federal Methodology, of whom 100% were aided. On average, 89% of need was met. *Financial aid deadline (priority):* 3/1. *Financial aid forms:* FAFSA, institutional form required.

LD Program Contact: Ms. Debra Roberts, Coordinator of Disability Services, Fitchburg State College, 160 Pearl Street, Fitchburg, MA 01420, 508-665-3427. Fax: 508-665-3693. Email: droberts@fsc.edu.

FLORIDA AGRICULTURAL AND MECHANICAL UNIVERSITY

Tallahassee, Florida

Students with LD	150	Subject-Area Tutoring	✓
ADD services	✓	Special Courses	✓
Staff	5 full-, 5 part-time	Taped Textbooks	✓
Special Fee	✓	Alternative Test Arrang.	✓
Diagnostic Testing	✓	Notetakers	✓
Basic Skills Remediation	✓	LD Student Organization	✓

LEARNING DISABILITIES PROGRAM INFORMATION

The Learning Development and Evaluation Center began offering services in 1985. Currently the program serves 150 undergraduates with LD. Services are also available to graduate students. Students diagnosed with ADD/ADHD are eligible for the same services available to students with LD.

Staff: 5 full-time, 5 part-time staff members, including director, assistant director, coordinator, tutoring supervisor. Services provided by remediation specialist, tutors, counselor, diagnostic specialist, technology specialist.

Special Fees: $900 for summer transition program (one-time charge).

Applications and admissions: *Required:* high school transcript, courses completed, untimed SAT I or ACT, personal interview, letters of recommendation, psychoeducational report completed within 3 years, documentation of disability, completion of College Study Skills Institute during a recent summer at FAMU; *recommended:* high school extracurricular activities, extended time SAT I or ACT. Students may begin taking classes any term. *Application deadline:* 5/30 (fall term), 11/10 (spring term).

Special policies: The college has written policies regarding grade forgiveness; substitutions and waivers of admissions, graduation, and degree requirements.

PROGRAM AND SERVICE COMPONENTS

Special preparation or orientation: Required summer program offered prior to entering college. Required orientation held before registration. Students may complete up to 3 summer transition programs.

Diagnostic testing: Intelligence, reading, math, spelling, handwriting, spoken language, written language, perceptual skills, study skills, personality, social skills, psychoneurology, learning strategies.

Academic advising: Provided by LD staff members, academic advisers. Students with LD may take up to 12 semester hours each term; most take 12 semester hours; 12 semester hours (9 with prior approval) required to maintain full-time status and be eligible for financial aid.

Counseling services: Individual counseling, small-group counseling, career counseling.

Basic skills remediation: Offered in small groups and in class-size groups by LD teachers, regular teachers, graduate students. Available in reading, math, spelling, handwriting, spoken language, written language, learning strategies, study skills, time management, social skills, computer skills.

Subject-area tutoring: Offered one-on-one and in small groups by professional teachers, peer tutors, clubs (e.g. Economics Club volunteers). Available in most subjects.

Special courses: College survival skills, reading, vocabulary development, composition, learning strategies, word processing, time management, study skills, stress management, computer skills. Most offered for credit; most enter into overall grade point average.

Auxiliary aids: Taped textbooks, tape recorders, calculators, typewriters, word-processors with spell-check, personal computers, optical character readers.

Auxiliary services: Alternative test arrangements, notetakers, advocacy.

Campus support group: A special student organization is available to students with LD.

GENERAL COLLEGE INFORMATION

State-supported, coed. Part of State University System of Florida. Awards associate, bachelor's, master's, doctoral, first professional degrees. Founded 1887. *Setting:* 419-acre urban campus. *Research spending 1995–96:* $19 million. *Total enrollment:* 10,448. *Faculty:* 727 (723 full-time, 53% with terminal degrees, 4 part-time); student–undergrad faculty ratio is 16:1.

Enrollment Profile: 9,251 students from 41 states and territories, 44 other countries. 59% women, 41% men, 18% part-time, 75% state residents, 11% transferred in, 1% international, 18% 25 or older, 0% Native American, 1% Hispanic, 89% black, 1% Asian or Pacific Islander. *Retention:* 80% of 1995 full-time freshmen returned. *Areas of study chosen:* 13% liberal arts/general studies, 12% social sciences, 9% business management and administrative services, 9% health professions and related sciences, 8% engineering and applied sciences, 7% education, 5% biological and life sciences, 4% computer and information sciences, 3% architecture, 3% communications and journalism, 2% agriculture, 2% English language/literature/letters, 2% premed, 2% psychology, 1% area and ethnic studies, 1% fine arts, 1% mathematics, 1% physical sciences. *Most popular recent majors:* education, business administration/commerce/management.

First-Year Class: 1,494 total; 4,851 applied, 60% were accepted, 51% of whom enrolled. 1 National Merit Scholar.

Graduation Requirements: 60 semester hours for associate, 120 semester hours for bachelor's; 6 semester hours of math; 8 semester hours of science; computer course for business, engineering, graphic arts, journalism, math, technology majors; internship (some majors); senior project (some majors).

Computers on Campus: 100 computers available on campus for general student use. Computer purchase/lease plans available. A campus-wide network can be accessed from student residence rooms and from off-campus. Students can contact faculty members and/or advisers through e-mail. Computers for student use in computer center, departmental labs provide access to the Internet/World Wide Web, on- and off-campus e-mail addresses. Staffed computer lab on campus provides training in use of computers, software. *Academic computing expenditure 1995–96:* $311,702.

EXPENSES AND FINANCIAL AID

Expenses for 1997–98: *Application fee:* $20. State resident tuition: $1981 full-time, $66.03 per semester hour part-time. Nonresident tuition: $7898 full-time, $263.25 per semester hour part-time. Part-time mandatory fees per semester (6 to 11 semester hours): $62.10. Full-time mandatory fees: $124. College room and board: $3198. College room only: $1954.

Undergraduate Financial Aid: *Financial aid deadline (priority):* 4/1. *Financial aid forms:* FAFSA, institutional form required.

Financial aid specifically for students with LD: Scholarship: Theodore and Vivian P. Johnson Award.

LD Program Contact: Dr. William Hudson, Instructional Specialist, Learning Development and Evaluation Center, Florida Agricultural and Mechanical University, Tallahassee, FL 32307, 904-599-3180. Fax: 904-561-2513.

GANNON UNIVERSITY

Erie, Pennsylvania

Students with LD	60	Subject-Area Tutoring	✓
ADD services	✓	Special Courses	✓
Staff	3 full-, 3 part-time	Taped Textbooks	✓
Special Fee	✓	Alternative Test Arrang.	✓
Diagnostic Testing		Notetakers	
Basic Skills Remediation	✓	LD Student Organization	

LEARNING DISABILITIES PROGRAM INFORMATION

The Program for Students with Learning Disabilities began offering services in 1986. Currently the program serves 60 undergraduates with LD. Students diagnosed with ADD/ADHD are eligible for the same services available to students with LD.

Staff: 3 full-time, 3 part-time staff members, including director, assistant director. Services provided by tutors.

Special Fees: $600 per year.

Applications and admissions: *Required:* high school transcript, grade point average, class rank, courses completed, untimed SAT I or ACT, personal interview, autobiographical statement, letters of recommendation, psychoeducational report completed within 2 years (any year that identifies the student as learning disabled is acceptable); *recommended:* high school extracurricular activities, extended time SAT I or ACT. Students may begin taking classes in fall only. *Application deadline:* continuous.

PROGRAM AND SERVICE COMPONENTS

Special preparation or orientation: Required orientation held specific times during general orientation.

Academic advising: Provided by LD staff members, academic advisers. Students with LD may take up to 18 credits (may take overload if GPA is 3.0 or better) each term; most take 15 credits; 12 credits required to maintain full-time status; 24 credits per year required to be eligible for financial aid.

Counseling services: Individual counseling, career counseling, self-advocacy training.

Gannon University (continued)

Basic skills remediation: Offered one-on-one and in class-size groups by program instructors. Available in reading, math, written language, learning strategies, study skills, time management, social skills.
Subject-area tutoring: Offered one-on-one and in small groups by professional teachers. Available in all subjects.
Special courses: Advocacy seminar (includes study skills). All offered for credit; all enter into overall grade point average.
Auxiliary aids: Taped textbooks, tape recorders, calculators, word-processors with spell-check, personal computers, optical character readers, copy machine (for fee), Franklin Speller, dictionaries, encyclopedias (some in Spanish).
Auxiliary services: Alternative test arrangements, advocacy, peer mentors.

GENERAL COLLEGE INFORMATION

Independent Roman Catholic, comprehensive, coed. Awards associate, bachelor's, master's degrees. Founded 1925. *Setting:* 13-acre urban campus with easy access to Cleveland. *Endowment:* $16.4 million. *Research spending 1995–96:* $932,000. *Educational spending 1995–96:* $5300 per undergrad. *Total enrollment:* 3,327. *Faculty:* 290 (169 full-time, 55% with terminal degrees, 121 part-time); student–undergrad faculty ratio is 13:1.
Enrollment Profile: 2,826 students from 28 states and territories, 15 other countries. 57% women, 43% men, 16% part-time, 82% state residents, 3% transferred in, 2% international, 23% 25 or older, 1% Hispanic, 3% black, 2% Asian or Pacific Islander. *Retention:* 78% of 1995 full-time freshmen returned. *Graduation:* 45% graduate in 4 years, 62% in 5 years, 64% in 6 years. *Areas of study chosen:* 25% health professions and related sciences, 12% business management and administrative services, 9% biological and life sciences, 8% social sciences, 7% engineering and applied sciences, 6% education, 5% psychology, 4% communications and journalism, 4% physical sciences, 3% prelaw, 3% premed, 2% computer and information sciences, 1% English language/literature/letters, 1% liberal arts/general studies, 1% theology/religion, 1% vocational and home economics. *Most popular recent majors:* biology/biological sciences, criminal justice, elementary education.
First-Year Class: 491 total; 2,274 applied, 76% were accepted, 28% of whom enrolled. 27% from top 10% of their high school class, 65% from top quarter, 98% from top half.
Graduation Requirements: 64 credits for associate, 128 credits for bachelor's; math/science requirements vary according to program; computer course for business, math, engineering majors; internship (some majors); senior project (some majors).
Computers on Campus: 375 computers available on campus for general student use. A computer is recommended for some students. A campus-wide network can be accessed from student residence rooms and from off-campus. Students can contact faculty members and/or advisers through e-mail. Computers for student use in computer center, computer labs, learning resource center, library, dorms, departmental labs provide access to the Internet/World Wide Web, on- and off-campus e-mail addresses. Staffed computer lab on campus provides training in use of computers, software. *Academic computing expenditure 1995–96:* $528,000.

EXPENSES AND FINANCIAL AID

Expenses for 1996–97: *Application fee:* $25. Comprehensive fee of $16,404 includes full-time tuition ($11,410 minimum), mandatory fees ($284), and college room and board ($4710). College room only: $2540. Part-time mandatory fees: $8 per credit. Full-time tuition ranges up to $12,100 according to program. Part-time tuition per credit ranges from $365 to $385 according to program.
Undergraduate Financial Aid: 89% of all full-time undergraduates enrolled in fall 1996 applied for aid; of these, 88% were judged to have need according to Federal Methodology, of whom 100% were aided. On average, 80% of need was met. *Financial aid deadline:* Applications processed continuously. *Financial aid forms:* FAFSA required. Institutional form required for some.
LD Program Contact: Ms. Jennifer Pelkowski, Associate Director of Freshman Admissions, Gannon University, University Square, Erie, PA 16541-0001, 814-871-7409. Fax: 814-871-5803. Email: pelkowski@cluster.gannon.edu.

HOFSTRA UNIVERSITY

Hempstead, New York

Students with LD	150	Subject-Area Tutoring	✓
ADD services		Special Courses	✓
Staff	3 full-, 2 part-time	Taped Textbooks	✓
Special Fee	✓	Alternative Test Arrang.	✓
Diagnostic Testing	✓	Notetakers	✓
Basic Skills Remediation	✓	LD Student Organization	

LEARNING DISABILITIES PROGRAM INFORMATION

The Program for Academic Learning Skills (PALS) began offering services in 1979. Currently the program serves 150 undergraduates with LD. Services are also available to graduate students.
Staff: 3 full-time, 2 part-time staff members, including director, assistant director. Services provided by remediation specialists, tutors, counselors, diagnostic specialists.
Special Fees: $4400 for freshman year only.
Applications and admissions: *Required:* high school transcript, personal interview, WAIS-R; *recommended:* untimed SAT I, autobiographical statement, psychoeducational report. Students may begin taking classes in fall or spring. *Application deadline:* continuous.
Special policies: The college has written policies regarding substitutions and waivers of admissions and degree requirements.

PROGRAM AND SERVICE COMPONENTS

Diagnostic testing: Intelligence, reading, spelling, handwriting, written language, study skills.
Academic advising: Provided by LD staff members. Students with LD may take up to 18 semester hours each term; most take 16 semester hours; 12 semester hours required to maintain full-time status and be eligible for financial aid.
Counseling services: Individual counseling, small-group counseling, career counseling.
Basic skills remediation: Offered one-on-one and in small groups by LD teachers. Available in spelling, spoken language, written language, learning strategies, study skills, time management, social skills.
Subject-area tutoring: Offered one-on-one by professional teachers, peer tutors. Available in all subjects.
Special courses: Learning strategies, personal psychology. All offered for credit; all enter into overall grade point average.
Auxiliary aids: Taped textbooks, tape recorders, calculators, typewriters, word-processors with spell-check, optical character readers, voice-activated computers.
Auxiliary services: Alternative test arrangements, notetakers, advocacy.

GENERAL COLLEGE INFORMATION

Independent, coed. Awards bachelor's, master's, doctoral, first professional degrees. Founded 1935. *Setting:* 238-acre suburban campus with easy access to New York City. *Endowment:* $59.8

million. *Research spending 1995–96:* $938,446. *Total enrollment:* 12,279. *Faculty:* 978 (449 full-time, 90% with terminal degrees, 529 part-time); student–undergrad faculty ratio is 15:1.
Enrollment Profile: 7,149 students from 45 states and territories, 67 other countries. 53% women, 47% men, 16% part-time, 83% state residents, 50% live on campus, 34% transferred in, 4% international, 11% 25 or older, 1% Native American, 5% Hispanic, 5% black, 5% Asian or Pacific Islander. *Retention:* 80% of 1995 full-time freshmen returned. *Areas of study chosen:* 38% business management and administrative services, 9% psychology, 8% communications and journalism, 8% social sciences, 7% liberal arts/general studies, 6% education, 4% biological and life sciences, 4% English language/literature/letters, 3% engineering and applied sciences, 3% performing arts, 2% computer and information sciences, 1% area and ethnic studies, 1% fine arts, 1% foreign language and literature, 1% interdisciplinary studies, 1% mathematics, 1% natural resource sciences, 1% philosophy, 1% physical sciences. *Most popular recent majors:* psychology, accounting, marketing/retailing/merchandising.
First-Year Class: 1,746 total; 7,689 applied, 88% were accepted, 29% of whom enrolled. 23% from top 10% of their high school class, 57% from top quarter, 93% from top half. 40 valedictorians.
Graduation Requirements: 124 semester hours; 9 semester hours of math/science; computer course for business, engineering majors; senior project for honors program students and some majors.
Computers on Campus: 350 computers available on campus for general student use. Computer purchase/lease plans available. Computers for student use in computer center, computer labs, learning resource center, classrooms, library, student center, dorms, word processing area provide access to the Internet/World Wide Web. Staffed computer lab on campus provides training in use of computers, software. *Academic computing expenditure 1995–96:* $635,005.

EXPENSES AND FINANCIAL AID

Expenses for 1997–98: *Application fee:* $25. Comprehensive fee of $19,910 includes full-time tuition ($12,790), mandatory fees ($754), and college room and board ($6366 minimum). College room only: $3976 (minimum). Part-time tuition: $420 per semester hour. Part-time mandatory fees per semester range from $111 to $182.
Undergraduate Financial Aid: Of all full-time undergraduates enrolled in fall 1996, 81% of those who applied for aid were judged to have need according to Federal Methodology, of whom 100% were aided. On average, 57% of need was met. *Financial aid deadline (priority):* 3/1. *Financial aid forms:* FAFSA, CSS Financial Aid PROFILE required. Institutional form required for some.
LD Program Contact: Dr. Ignacio Götz, Director, Program for Academic Learning Skills, Hofstra University, 202 Roosevelt Hall, Hempstead, NY 11550-1090, 516-463-5840. Fax: 516-463-4832. Email: nucizg@vaxb.hofstra.edu.

IONA COLLEGE

New Rochelle, New York

Students with LD	62	Subject-Area Tutoring	
ADD services	✓	Special Courses	
Staff	2 full-, 8 part-time	Taped Textbooks	
Special Fee	✓	Alternative Test Arrang.	✓
Diagnostic Testing		Notetakers	
Basic Skills Remediation	✓	LD Student Organization	

LEARNING DISABILITIES PROGRAM INFORMATION

The College Assistance Program (CAP) began offering services in 1981. Currently the program serves 62 undergraduates with LD. Students diagnosed with ADD/ADHD are eligible for the same services available to students with LD.
Staff: 2 full-time, 8 part-time staff members, including director, assistant director. Services provided by remediation specialists, tutors, counselors.
Special Fees: $2000 per year.
Applications and admissions: *Required:* high school transcript, grade point average, class rank, courses completed, extracurricular activities, IEP (Individualized Education Program), untimed or extended time SAT I, personal interview, letters of recommendation, psychoeducational report completed within 2 years, WAIS-R. Students may begin taking classes in fall only. *Application deadline:* continuous.

PROGRAM AND SERVICE COMPONENTS

Special preparation or orientation: Required summer program offered prior to entering college. Required orientation held before registration.
Academic advising: Provided by LD staff members, academic advisers. Students with LD may take up to 15 credits (12 credits freshman year) each term; most take 12 credits; 12 credits required to maintain full-time status and be eligible for financial aid.
Counseling services: Individual counseling, small-group counseling, career counseling, self-advocacy training.
Basic skills remediation: Offered one-on-one by LD teachers. Available in reading, math, spelling, written language, learning strategies, study skills, time management, social skills.
Auxiliary aids: Tape recorders, calculators, word-processors with spell-check, personal computers.
Auxiliary services: Alternative test arrangements, priority registration.

GENERAL COLLEGE INFORMATION

Independent, comprehensive, coed. Awards associate, bachelor's, master's degrees. Founded 1940. *Setting:* 35-acre suburban campus with easy access to New York City. *Endowment:* $10.4 million. *Educational spending 1995–96:* $5126 per undergrad. *Total enrollment:* 5,588. *Faculty:* 400 (175 full-time, 76% with terminal degrees, 225 part-time); student–undergrad faculty ratio is 17:1.
Enrollment Profile: 4,079 students from 21 states and territories, 45 other countries. 57% women, 43% men, 27% part-time, 91% state residents, 18% live on campus, 3% transferred in, 33% 25 or older, 0% Native American, 13% Hispanic, 19% black, 2% Asian or Pacific Islander. *Retention:* 67% of 1995 full-time freshmen returned. *Areas of study chosen:* 33% business management and administrative services, 17% liberal arts/general studies, 13% social sciences, 9% communications and journalism, 7% psychology, 5% computer and information sciences, 4% education, 4% English language/literature/letters, 4% health professions and related sciences, 3% biological and life sciences, 1% foreign language and literature. *Most popular recent majors:* communication, education, accounting.
First-Year Class: 646 total; 3,031 applied, 72% were accepted, 29% of whom enrolled. 10% from top 10% of their high school class, 26% from top quarter, 54% from top half.
Graduation Requirements: 60 credits for associate, 120 credits for bachelor's; 3 credits each of math and science; computer course.
Computers on Campus: 500 computers available on campus for general student use. Computers for student use in computer center, computer labs, learning resource center, classrooms, dorms

Iona College (continued)

provide access to the Internet/World Wide Web. Staffed computer lab on campus provides training in use of computers, software. *Academic computing expenditure 1995–96:* $1.9 million.

EXPENSES AND FINANCIAL AID

Expenses for 1997–98: *Application fee:* $25. Comprehensive fee of $21,160 includes full-time tuition ($13,100), mandatory fees ($320), and college room and board ($7740). Part-time tuition: $440 per credit. Part-time mandatory fees: $160 per term.

Undergraduate Financial Aid: Of all full-time undergraduates enrolled in fall 1996, 90% of those who applied for aid were judged to have need according to Federal Methodology, of whom 90% were aided. On average, 72% of need was met. *Financial aid deadline (priority):* 4/15. *Financial aid forms:* FAFSA, institutional form required. State form required for some.

LD Program Contact: Ms. Madeline Packerman, Director, Iona College, 715 North Avenue, New Rochelle, NY 10801, 914-633-2582. Fax: 914-633-2025.

KEAN COLLEGE OF NEW JERSEY

Union, New Jersey

Students with LD	25	Subject-Area Tutoring	✓
ADD services		Special Courses	✓
Staff	3 part-time	Taped Textbooks	
Special Fee	None	Alternative Test Arrang.	✓
Diagnostic Testing	✓	Notetakers	
Basic Skills Remediation	✓	LD Student Organization	

LEARNING DISABILITIES PROGRAM INFORMATION

The Project Excel began offering services in 1991. Currently the program serves 25 undergraduates with LD. Services are also available to graduate students. Students diagnosed with ADD/ADHD are not eligible for the same services available to students with LD.

Staff: 3 part-time staff members, including director, mentors. Services provided by remediation specialist, diagnostic specialist.

Special Fees: No special fees are charged for services to students with LD.

Applications and admissions: *Required:* high school transcript, grade point average, class rank, courses completed, IEP (Individualized Education Program), untimed SAT I, Child Study Team evaluation; *recommended:* high school extracurricular activities, extended time SAT I, autobiographical statement, letters of recommendation. Students may begin taking classes any term. *Application deadline:* 6/15 (fall term), 11/1 (spring term).

PROGRAM AND SERVICE COMPONENTS

Special preparation or orientation: Optional orientation offered upon admission.

Diagnostic testing: Intelligence, reading, math, spelling, handwriting, spoken language, written language, motor abilities, perceptual skills, study skills, personality, social skills, psychoneurology, speech, hearing, learning strategies.

Academic advising: Provided by LD staff members, academic advisers. Most students with LD take fewer than 15 semester hours each term; 12 semester hours required to maintain full-time status and be eligible for financial aid.

Counseling services: Individual counseling, small-group counseling, career counseling.

Basic skills remediation: Offered one-on-one by regular teachers, teacher trainees, graduate students. Available in reading, math, handwriting.

Subject-area tutoring: Offered one-on-one and in small groups by professional teachers, learning disability teacher consultants. Available in all subjects.

Special courses: Learning strategies. All offered for credit; all enter into overall grade point average.

Auxiliary aids: Tape recorders, typewriters, word-processors with spell-check, personal computers.

Auxiliary services: Alternative test arrangements, advocacy.

GENERAL COLLEGE INFORMATION

State-supported, comprehensive, coed. Part of New Jersey State College System. Awards bachelor's, master's degrees. Founded 1855. *Setting:* 151-acre urban campus with easy access to New York City. *Research spending 1995–96:* $132,000. *Total enrollment:* 10,404. *Undergraduate faculty:* 916 (343 full-time, 78% with terminal degrees, 573 part-time); student–undergrad faculty ratio is 19:1.

Enrollment Profile: 9,134 students: 63% women, 37% men, 35% part-time, 98% state residents, 43% transferred in, 2% international, 37% 25 or older, 0% Native American, 18% Hispanic, 17% black, 6% Asian or Pacific Islander. *Retention:* 80% of 1995 full-time freshmen returned. *Graduation:* 8% graduate in 4 years, 22% in 5 years, 32% in 6 years. *Areas of study chosen:* 21% education, 5% fine arts, 5% social sciences, 3% communications and journalism, 3% engineering and applied sciences, 1% performing arts. *Most popular recent majors:* accounting, business administration/commerce/management.

First-Year Class: 1,064 total. 11% from top 10% of their high school class, 62% from top half.

Graduation Requirements: 124 semester hours; 7 semester hours of math/science; computer course for management science, industrial technology, accounting majors; internship (some majors); senior project (some majors).

Computers on Campus: 528 computers available on campus for general student use. A computer is recommended for some students. A campus-wide network can be accessed from off-campus. Students can contact faculty members and/or advisers through e-mail. Computers for student use in computer center, computer labs, learning resource center, classrooms, library, academic buildings provide access to the Internet/World Wide Web, on- and off-campus e-mail addresses.

EXPENSES AND FINANCIAL AID

Expenses for 1997–98: *Application fee:* $15. State resident tuition: $2928 full-time, $98 per semester hour part-time. Nonresident tuition: $4400 full-time, $147 per semester hour part-time. Part-time mandatory fees: $22.10 per semester hour. Full-time mandatory fees: $741. College room and board: $5120.

Undergraduate Financial Aid: 64% of all full-time undergraduates enrolled in fall 1996 applied for aid; of these, 83% were judged to have need according to Federal Methodology, of whom 87% were aided. On average, 68% of need was met. *Financial aid deadline (priority):* 5/1. *Financial aid forms:* FAFSA, CSS Financial Aid PROFILE, institutional form required. Federal work study application, parent PLUS loan data sheet required for some.

LD Program Contact: Dr. Marie Segal, Director, Project Excel, Kean College of New Jersey, Morris Avenue, Union, NJ 07083, 908-527-2380. Fax: 908-527-2738.

KING'S COLLEGE

Wilkes-Barre, Pennsylvania

Students with LD	24	Subject-Area Tutoring	✓
ADD services	✓	Special Courses	✓
Staff	2 full-, 1 part-time	Taped Textbooks	✓

Special Fee	✓	Alternative Test Arrang.	✓
Diagnostic Testing		Notetakers	✓
Basic Skills Remediation	✓	LD Student Organization	

LEARNING DISABILITIES PROGRAM INFORMATION

The Freshman Academic Year Program began offering services in 1995. Currently the program serves 24 undergraduates with LD. Students diagnosed with ADD/ADHD are eligible for the same services available to students with LD.

Staff: 2 full-time, 1 part-time staff members, including director, coordinator. Services provided by remediation specialists, tutors, tutorial coordinator, writing center coordinator.

Special Fees: $1800 per year.

Applications and admissions: *Required:* high school transcript, grade point average, courses completed, untimed or extended time SAT I, personal interview, letters of recommendation, psychoeducational report completed within 3 years; *recommended:* high school class rank, extracurricular activities, autobiographical statement. Students may begin taking classes in fall or summer. *Application deadline:* 4/1.

PROGRAM AND SERVICE COMPONENTS

Special preparation or orientation: Summer program (required for some) held prior to entering college. Required orientation held before registration.

Academic advising: Provided by LD staff members, academic advisers. Students with LD may take up to 15 credits each term; most take 12 to 15 credits; 12 credits required to maintain full-time status and be eligible for financial aid.

Counseling services: Individual counseling, career counseling.

Basic skills remediation: Offered one-on-one and in small groups by LD teachers. Available in reading, spelling, written language, learning strategies, study skills, time management, speech.

Subject-area tutoring: Offered one-on-one, in small groups, and in class-size groups by professional teachers, peer tutors, learning specialist. Available in most subjects.

Special courses: College survival skills, reading, vocabulary development, communication skills, composition, learning strategies, word processing, time management, study skills, career planning. Some offered for credit; some enter into overall grade point average.

Auxiliary aids: Taped textbooks, tape recorders, word-processors with spell-check.

Auxiliary services: Alternative test arrangements, notetakers, priority registration, advocacy.

GENERAL COLLEGE INFORMATION

Independent Roman Catholic, comprehensive, coed. Awards associate, bachelor's, master's degrees. Founded 1946. *Setting:* 48-acre suburban campus. *Endowment:* $24.6 million. *Research spending 1995–96:* $275,998. *Educational spending 1995–96:* $3927 per undergrad. *Total enrollment:* 2,279. *Faculty:* 176 (98 full-time, 84% with terminal degrees, 78 part-time); student–undergrad faculty ratio is 17:1.

Enrollment Profile: 2,151 students from 23 states and territories, 14 other countries. 51% women, 49% men, 19% part-time, 77% state residents, 36% live on campus, 6% transferred in, 2% international, 22% 25 or older, 0% Native American, 1% Hispanic, 2% black, 1% Asian or Pacific Islander. *Retention:* 83% of 1995 full-time freshmen returned. *Graduation:* 74% graduate in 4 years, 79% in 5 years. *Areas of study chosen:* 25% business management and administrative services, 14% social sciences, 10% health professions and related sciences, 9% biological and life sciences, 6% education, 6% psychology, 5% communications and journalism, 4% computer and information sciences, 4% English language/literature/letters, 1% foreign language and literature, 1% mathematics, 1% performing arts, 1% philosophy, 1% physical sciences, 1% theology/religion. *Most popular recent majors:* accounting, communication, business administration/commerce/management.

First-Year Class: 439 total; 1,611 applied, 74% were accepted, 37% of whom enrolled. 19% from top 10% of their high school class, 47% from top quarter, 80% from top half.

Graduation Requirements: 60 credit hours for associate, 120 credit hours for bachelor's; 3 math/science courses; computer course for all business, some science majors; senior project for honors program students and some majors.

Computers on Campus: 160 computers available on campus for general student use. Computer purchase/lease plans available. A campus-wide network can be accessed. Students can contact faculty members and/or advisers through e-mail. Computers for student use in computer center, computer labs, library, dorms provide access to the Internet/World Wide Web, on- and off-campus e-mail addresses. Staffed computer lab on campus provides training in use of computers, software. *Academic computing expenditure 1995–96:* $400,530.

EXPENSES AND FINANCIAL AID

Expenses for 1997–98: *Application fee:* $30. Comprehensive fee of $20,120 includes full-time tuition ($13,390), mandatory fees ($610), and college room and board ($6120). College room only: $2860. Part-time tuition: $331 per credit hour.

Undergraduate Financial Aid: 91% of all full-time undergraduates enrolled in fall 1996 applied for aid; of these, 91% were judged to have need according to Federal Methodology, of whom 96% were aided. On average, 85% of need was met. *Financial aid deadline:* Applications processed continuously. *Financial aid forms:* FAFSA, institutional form required; CSS Financial Aid PROFILE, state form acceptable.

LD Program Contact: Ms. Jacintha Burke, Director, Academic Skills Center, King's College, 133 North River Street, Wilkes-Barre, PA 18711-0801, 717-826-5800. Fax: 717-825-9049. Email: jaburke@rs.02.kings.edu.

LESLEY COLLEGE

Cambridge, Massachusetts

Students with LD	65	Subject-Area Tutoring	✓
ADD services	✓	Special Courses	✓
Staff	9 full-, 18 part-time	Taped Textbooks	✓
Special Fee	✓	Alternative Test Arrang.	✓
Diagnostic Testing		Notetakers	
Basic Skills Remediation	✓	LD Student Organization	✓

LEARNING DISABILITIES PROGRAM INFORMATION

The Threshold Program began offering services in 1982. Currently the program serves 65 undergraduates with LD. Students diagnosed with ADD/ADHD are eligible for the same services available to students with LD.

Staff: 9 full-time, 18 part-time staff members, including director, assistant directors. Services provided by remediation specialists, counselors, instructors.

Special Fees: $26,000 per year includes tuition, room, board and insurance.

Applications and admissions: *Required:* high school transcript, courses completed, personal interview, letters of recommendation, psychoeducational report completed within 1 year, TAT or Rorschach. Students may begin taking classes in fall only. *Application deadline:* 3/1.

Special policies: The college has written policies regarding substitutions and waivers of admissions requirements.

Lesley College (continued)

PROGRAM AND SERVICE COMPONENTS

Special preparation or orientation: Required orientation held after classes begin and at beginning of school year.
Academic advising: Provided by LD staff members, academic advisers.
Counseling services: Individual counseling, small-group counseling, career counseling, self-advocacy training, social skills training.
Basic skills remediation: Offered one-on-one, in small groups, and in class-size groups by LD teachers; computer-aided instruction also offered. Available in reading, math, spelling, handwriting, spoken language, written language, learning strategies, perceptual skills, study skills, time management, social skills, computer skills.
Subject-area tutoring: Offered one-on-one, in small groups, and in class-size groups by professional teachers, private tutors. Available in all subjects.
Special courses: College survival skills, reading, vocabulary development, communication skills, composition, learning strategies, word processing, Internet use, time management, math, typing, personal psychology, study skills, career planning, stress management, health and nutrition, social relationships, vocational, social and independent living skills. All offered for credit; none enter into overall grade point average.
Auxiliary aids: Taped textbooks, tape recorders, calculators, typewriters, word-processors with spell-check, personal computers, optical character readers.
Auxiliary services: Alternative test arrangements, advocacy.
Campus support group: A special student organization is available to students with LD.

GENERAL COLLEGE INFORMATION

Independent, comprehensive, women only. Awards associate, bachelor's, master's, doctoral degrees. Founded 1909. *Setting:* 5-acre urban campus with easy access to Boston. *Endowment:* $14 million. *Research spending 1995–96:* $491,154. *Total enrollment:* 6,166. *Faculty:* 920 (140 full-time, 70% with terminal degrees, 780 part-time); student–undergrad faculty ratio is 14:1.
Enrollment Profile: 490 students from 28 states and territories, 8 other countries. 100% women, 0% men, 6% part-time, 65% state residents, 12% transferred in, 6% international, 4% Hispanic, 6% black, 3% Asian or Pacific Islander. *Retention:* 80% of 1995 full-time freshmen returned. *Areas of study chosen:* 60% education, 30% health professions and related sciences, 10% business management and administrative services. *Most popular recent majors:* education, human services, business administration/commerce/management.
First-Year Class: 103 total; 305 applied, 75% were accepted, 45% of whom enrolled. 6% from top 10% of their high school class, 36% from top quarter, 72% from top half.
Graduation Requirements: 64 credits for associate, 128 credits for bachelor's; 14 credits of math/science; computer course; internship; senior project.
Computers on Campus: 125 computers available on campus for general student use. Computer purchase/lease plans available. A campus-wide network can be accessed from student residence rooms and from off-campus. Students can contact faculty members and/or advisers through e-mail. Computers for student use in computer center, computer labs, learning resource center, classrooms, dorms provide access to the Internet/World Wide Web, on-campus e-mail addresses. Staffed computer lab on campus provides training in use of computers, software. *Academic computing expenditure 1995–96:* $1.2 million.

EXPENSES AND FINANCIAL AID

Expenses for 1997–98: *Application fee:* $35. Comprehensive fee of $21,306 includes full-time tuition ($14,300), mandatory fees ($306), and college room and board ($6700). College room only: $4050. Part-time tuition: $421 per credit. Part-time mandatory fees: $75 per year.
Undergraduate Financial Aid: Of all full-time undergraduates enrolled in fall 1996, 89% of those who applied for aid were judged to have need according to Federal Methodology, of whom 100% were aided. On average, 84% of need was met. *Financial aid deadline (priority):* 2/1. *Financial aid forms:* FAFSA, state form, institutional form, financial aid transcript (for transfers) required.
Financial aid specifically for students with LD: Scholarship: Threshold Endowment.
LD Program Contact: Mr. Jim Wilbur, Admissions Coordinator, Lesley College, 29 Everett Street, Cambridge, MA 02138-2790, 617-349-8181. Fax: 617-349-8189. Email: jwilbur@mail.lesley.edu.

LIMESTONE COLLEGE

Gaffney, South Carolina

Students with LD	22	Subject-Area Tutoring	✓
ADD services	✓	Special Courses	✓
Staff	1 part-time	Taped Textbooks	✓
Special Fee	Varies	Alternative Test Arrang.	✓
Diagnostic Testing	✓	Notetakers	✓
Basic Skills Remediation	✓	LD Student Organization	

LEARNING DISABILITIES PROGRAM INFORMATION

The Program for Alternative Learning Styles (PALS) began offering services in 1991. Currently the program serves 22 undergraduates with LD. Students diagnosed with ADD/ADHD are eligible for the same services available to students with LD.
Staff: 1 part-time staff member (director). Services provided by remediation specialist, tutors, counselors.
Special Fees: Range from $1500 to $3000 per year.
Applications and admissions: *Required:* high school transcript, grade point average, class rank, courses completed, untimed SAT I or ACT, personal interview, psychoeducational report completed within 3 years; *recommended:* high school extracurricular activities, extended time SAT I or ACT. Students may begin taking classes in fall only. *Application deadline:* continuous.

PROGRAM AND SERVICE COMPONENTS

Special preparation or orientation: Required orientation held before registration.
Diagnostic testing: Math, written language.
Academic advising: Provided by LD staff members. Students with LD may take up to 17 semester hours each term; most take 12 semester hours; 12 semester hours required to maintain full-time status and be eligible for financial aid.
Counseling services: Individual counseling.
Basic skills remediation: Offered one-on-one and in small groups by regular teachers; computer-aided instruction also offered. Available in reading, math, written language, learning strategies, study skills, time management.
Subject-area tutoring: Offered one-on-one and in small groups by peer tutors. Available in all subjects.
Special courses: College survival skills, reading, learning strategies, word processing, time management, study skills, career planning, stress management. All offered for credit; some enter into overall grade point average.

Auxiliary aids: Taped textbooks, tape recorders, calculators, word-processors with spell-check.
Auxiliary services: Alternative test arrangements, notetakers, priority registration, advocacy.

GENERAL COLLEGE INFORMATION

Independent, 4-year, coed. Awards associate, bachelor's degrees. Founded 1845. *Setting:* 115-acre small-town campus with easy access to Charlotte. *Total enrollment:* 366. *Faculty:* 84 (35 full-time, 60% with terminal degrees, 49 part-time); student–undergrad faculty ratio is 11:1.

Enrollment Profile: 366 students from 25 states and territories, 5 other countries. 48% women, 52% men, 5% part-time, 66% state residents, 65% live on campus, 24% transferred in, 2% international, 0% 25 or older, 0% Native American, 0% Hispanic, 18% black, 1% Asian or Pacific Islander. *Retention:* 90% of 1995 full-time freshmen returned. *Areas of study chosen:* 28% education, 18% business management and administrative services, 12% fine arts, 7% biological and life sciences, 7% social sciences, 6% psychology, 5% English language/literature/letters, 5% liberal arts/general studies, 4% prelaw, 3% computer and information sciences, 3% mathematics, 2% physical sciences. *Most popular recent majors:* business administration/commerce/management, education, music.

First-Year Class: 96 total; 351 applied, 76% were accepted, 36% of whom enrolled. 15% from top 10% of their high school class, 35% from top quarter, 70% from top half. 4 class presidents, 2 valedictorians.

Graduation Requirements: 120 semester hours for bachelor's; 1 math course; 2 lab science courses; computer course; internship (some majors); senior project for honors program students.

Computers on Campus: 55 computers available on campus for general student use. A campus-wide network can be accessed. Students can contact faculty members and/or advisers through e-mail. Computers for student use in computer center, computer labs, library provide access to the Internet/World Wide Web, on- and off-campus e-mail addresses. Staffed computer lab on campus provides training in use of computers, software.

EXPENSES AND FINANCIAL AID

Expenses for 1997–98: *Application fee:* $25. Comprehensive fee of $12,500 includes full-time tuition ($8600) and college room and board ($3900). Part-time tuition: $360 per semester hour.

Undergraduate Financial Aid: 98% of all full-time undergraduates enrolled in fall 1996 applied for aid; of these, 83% were judged to have need according to Federal Methodology, of whom 100% were aided. On average, 98% of need was met. *Financial aid deadline (priority):* 5/1. *Financial aid forms:* FAFSA, institutional form required. CSS Financial Aid PROFILE, state form required for some.

LD Program Contact: Ms. Sherry Horton, Director of Admissions, Limestone College, 1115 College Drive, Gaffney, SC 29340-3798, 864-489-7151 Ext. 300. Fax: 864-487-8706.

LONG ISLAND UNIVERSITY, C.W. POST CAMPUS

Brookville, New York

Students with LD	125	Subject-Area Tutoring	✓
ADD services	✓	Special Courses	
Staff	2 full-, 19 part-time	Taped Textbooks	✓
Special Fee	✓	Alternative Test Arrang.	✓
Diagnostic Testing	✓	Notetakers	✓
Basic Skills Remediation	✓	LD Student Organization	

LEARNING DISABILITIES PROGRAM INFORMATION

The Academic Resource Center began offering services in 1985. Currently the program serves 125 undergraduates with LD. Students diagnosed with ADD/ADHD are eligible for the same services available to students with LD.

Staff: 2 full-time, 19 part-time staff members, including director, associate director, graduate assistants. Services provided by remediation specialists, tutors, graduate assistants.

Special Fees: $3000 per year.

Applications and admissions: *Required:* high school transcript, grade point average, class rank, courses completed, extracurricular activities, untimed or extended time SAT I, extended time ACT, personal interview, letters of recommendation, psychoeducational report completed within 1 year; *recommended:* high school IEP (Individualized Education Program). Students may begin taking classes in fall only. *Application deadline:* 4/1.

Special policies: The college has written policies regarding substitutions and waivers of admissions and graduation requirements.

PROGRAM AND SERVICE COMPONENTS

Special preparation or orientation: Required orientation held before classes begin in September.

Diagnostic testing: Intelligence, reading, math, spelling, handwriting, spoken language, written language, perceptual skills, study skills, speech, hearing, learning strategies.

Academic advising: Provided by LD staff members, academic advisers. Students with LD may take up to 12 credits each term; most take 12 credits; 12 credits required to maintain full-time status and be eligible for financial aid.

Counseling services: Individual counseling, career counseling.

Basic skills remediation: Offered in class-size groups by regular teachers. Available in reading, written language, learning strategies, time management, speech.

Subject-area tutoring: Offered one-on-one and in small groups by professional teachers, peer tutors, graduate assistants. Available in all subjects.

Auxiliary aids: Taped textbooks, tape recorders, calculators, word-processors with spell-check, personal computers.

Auxiliary services: Alternative test arrangements, notetakers, advocacy, readers (for textbooks).

GENERAL COLLEGE INFORMATION

Independent, comprehensive, coed. Part of Long Island University. Awards associate, bachelor's, master's, doctoral degrees. Founded 1954. *Setting:* 305-acre small-town campus with easy access to New York City. *Endowment:* $15.1 million. *Research spending 1995–96:* $2.5 million. *Total enrollment:* 9,172. *Faculty:* 956 (302 full-time, 90% with terminal degrees, 654 part-time); student–undergrad faculty ratio is 10:1.

Enrollment Profile: 4,670 students from 26 states and territories, 40 other countries. 64% women, 36% men, 22% part-time, 89% state residents, 31% live on campus, 47% transferred in, 1% international, 24% 25 or older, 2% Native American, 7% Hispanic, 8% black, 4% Asian or Pacific Islander. *Retention:* 72% of 1995 full-time freshmen returned. *Areas of study chosen:* 21% education, 20% business management and administrative services, 13% health professions and related sciences, 7% fine arts, 7% performing arts, 7% social sciences, 6% psychology, 5% biological and life sciences, 5% communications and journalism, 3% liberal arts/general studies, 2% computer and information sciences, 1% interdisciplinary studies, 1% mathematics, 1% physical sciences. *Most popular recent majors:* liberal arts/general studies, business administration/commerce/management, education.

First-Year Class: 729 total; 3,415 applied, 76% were accepted, 28% of whom enrolled. 10% from top 10% of their high school class, 42% from top quarter, 78% from top half.

Long Island University, C.W. Post Campus (continued)

Graduation Requirements: 64 credits for associate, 129 credits for bachelor's; 8 credits of lab science; 6 credits of a foreign language or the equivalent; computer course; internship (some majors); senior project for honors program students and some majors.

Computers on Campus: 357 computers available on campus for general student use. Computer purchase/lease plans available. A computer is recommended for all students. A campus-wide network can be accessed from student residence rooms and from off-campus. Students can contact faculty members and/or advisers through e-mail. Computers for student use in computer center, computer labs, learning resource center, classrooms, library, dorms, school of visual and performing arts, writing center provide access to the Internet/World Wide Web. Staffed computer lab on campus provides training in use of computers, software. *Academic computing expenditure 1995–96:* $931,000.

EXPENSES AND FINANCIAL AID

Expenses for 1996–97: *Application fee:* $30. Comprehensive fee of $19,640 includes full-time tuition ($13,120), mandatory fees ($570), and college room and board ($5950). College room only: $3650. Part-time tuition: $408 per credit. Part-time mandatory fees: $160 per semester.

Undergraduate Financial Aid: 85% of all full-time undergraduates enrolled in fall 1996 applied for aid; of these, 94% were judged to have need according to Federal Methodology, of whom 100% were aided. On average, 75% of need was met. *Financial aid deadline:* Applications processed continuously. *Financial aid forms:* FAFSA, state form required. CSS Financial Aid PROFILE required for some.

LD Program Contact: Ms. Carol Rundlett, Director, Long Island University, C.W. Post Campus, Northern Boulevard, Brookville, NY 11548-1300, 516-299-2937.

LORAS COLLEGE

Dubuque, Iowa

Students with LD	65	Subject-Area Tutoring	✓
ADD services	✓	Special Courses	✓
Staff	2 full-time	Taped Textbooks	✓
Special Fee	Varies	Alternative Test Arrang.	✓
Diagnostic Testing	✓	Notetakers	✓
Basic Skills Remediation		LD Student Organization	

LEARNING DISABILITIES PROGRAM INFORMATION

The Learning Disabilities Program began offering services in 1986. Currently the program serves 65 undergraduates with LD. Services are also available to graduate students. Students diagnosed with ADD/ADHD are eligible for the same services available to students with LD.

Staff: 2 full-time staff members, including director, associate director. Services provided by tutors, notetakers, study group leaders.

Special Fees: $2490 for first-year students; $2015 thereafter; $1430 for support services only.

Applications and admissions: *Required:* high school transcript, grade point average, class rank, extended time SAT I or untimed ACT, personal interview, psychoeducational report completed within 2 years; *recommended:* high school extracurricular activities, letters of recommendation. Students may begin taking classes in fall only. *Application deadline:* 10/1.

PROGRAM AND SERVICE COMPONENTS

Special preparation or orientation: Required orientation held by special arrangement during summer prior to enrollment and during general orientation.

Diagnostic testing: Reading, math, spelling, handwriting, spoken language, written language, study skills, personality.

Academic advising: Provided by LD staff members, academic advisers. Most students with LD take 12 to 15 credits each term; 12 credits required to maintain full-time status and be eligible for financial aid.

Counseling services: Individual counseling, career counseling, LD support staff.

Subject-area tutoring: Offered one-on-one and in small groups by professional teachers, peer tutors. Available in all subjects.

Special courses: College survival skills, reading, vocabulary development, communication skills, composition, learning strategies, time management, study skills, career planning, stress management. All offered for credit; all enter into overall grade point average.

Auxiliary aids: Taped textbooks, tape recorders, word-processors with spell-check, personal computers, optical character readers, Reading Edge.

Auxiliary services: Alternative test arrangements, notetakers, priority registration.

GENERAL COLLEGE INFORMATION

Independent Roman Catholic, comprehensive, coed. Awards associate, bachelor's, master's degrees. Founded 1839. *Setting:* 60-acre suburban campus. *Endowment:* $24.5 million. *Research spending 1995–96:* $118,090. *Educational spending 1995–96:* $4130 per undergrad. *Total enrollment:* 1,815. *Faculty:* 136 (111 full-time, 79% with terminal degrees, 25 part-time); student–undergrad faculty ratio is 13:1.

Enrollment Profile: 1,736 students from 24 states and territories, 15 other countries. 52% women, 48% men, 14% part-time, 55% state residents, 65% live on campus, 16% transferred in, 2% international, 2% 25 or older, 0% Native American, 0% Hispanic, 3% black. *Areas of study chosen:* 24% business management and administrative services, 12% communications and journalism, 12% education, 12% English language/literature/letters, 12% psychology, 9% social sciences, 6% biological and life sciences, 2% computer and information sciences, 2% foreign language and literature, 2% mathematics, 2% physical sciences, 1% engineering and applied sciences, 1% fine arts, 1% interdisciplinary studies, 1% philosophy, 1% theology/religion. *Most popular recent majors:* business administration/commerce/management, social science, education.

First-Year Class: 355 total; 1,041 applied, 82% were accepted, 42% of whom enrolled. 15% from top 10% of their high school class, 35% from top quarter, 62% from top half. 14 valedictorians.

Graduation Requirements: 60 credits for associate, 120 credits for bachelor's; 12 credits of math/science; computer course for business, accounting, finance, marketing, sociology, psychology majors; senior project for honors program students and some majors.

Computers on Campus: 100 computers available on campus for general student use. Computer purchase/lease plans available. A campus-wide network can be accessed from student residence rooms and from off-campus. Students can contact faculty members and/or advisers through e-mail. Computers for student use in computer labs, classrooms, library provide access to the Internet/World Wide Web, on- and off-campus e-mail addresses. Staffed computer lab on campus provides training in use of computers, software. *Academic computing expenditure 1995–96:* $349,708.

EXPENSES AND FINANCIAL AID

Expenses for 1996–97: *Application fee:* $25. Comprehensive fee of $17,205 includes full-time tuition ($12,660) and college room and board ($4545). Part-time tuition: $320 per credit.

Undergraduate Financial Aid: Of all full-time undergraduates enrolled in fall 1996, 100% of those judged to have need according to Federal Methodology were aided. On average, 94% of need was met. *Financial aid deadline (priority):* 4/15. *Financial aid forms:* FAFSA required; CSS Financial Aid PROFILE acceptable.

LD Program Contact: Ms. Theresa Waldron, LD Liaison-Admissions Office, Loras College, 1450 Alta Vista Street, Dubuque, IA 52004-0178, 319-588-7739. Fax: 319-588-7964. Email: twaldron@loras.edu.

LOUISIANA COLLEGE

Pineville, Louisiana

Students with LD	35	Subject-Area Tutoring	✓
ADD services	✓	Special Courses	
Staff	2 full-, 2 part-time	Taped Textbooks	✓
Special Fee	Varies	Alternative Test Arrang.	✓
Diagnostic Testing		Notetakers	✓
Basic Skills Remediation	✓	LD Student Organization	

LEARNING DISABILITIES PROGRAM INFORMATION

The Program to Assist Student Success (PASS) began offering services in 1991. Currently the program serves 35 undergraduates with LD. Students diagnosed with ADD/ADHD are eligible for the same services available to students with LD, as well as specialized types of tutoring, monitoring and testing arrangements.

Staff: 2 full-time, 2 part-time staff members, including director. Services provided by tutors, counselor.

Special Fees: Range from $250 to $850 per year.

Applications and admissions: *Required:* high school transcript, grade point average, class rank, courses completed, personal interview, autobiographical statement, letters of recommendation, psychoeducational report completed within 3 years; *recommended:* untimed or extended time SAT I or ACT. Students may begin taking classes in fall, spring, or summer. *Application deadline:* continuous.

Special policies: The college has written policies regarding substitutions and waivers of admissions, graduation, and degree requirements.

PROGRAM AND SERVICE COMPONENTS

Special preparation or orientation: Required orientation held before registration.

Academic advising: Provided by LD staff members, academic advisers. Students with LD may take up to 15 credit hours each term; most take 12 credit hours; 12 credit hours required to maintain full-time status and be eligible for financial aid.

Counseling services: Individual counseling, small-group counseling, career counseling.

Basic skills remediation: Offered one-on-one and in small groups by LD teachers. Available in reading, math, spelling, written language, learning strategies, study skills, time management, computer skills.

Subject-area tutoring: Offered one-on-one and in small groups by professional teachers, peer tutors. Available in all subjects.

Auxiliary aids: Taped textbooks, tape recorders, word-processors with spell-check, personal computers, optical character readers.

Auxiliary services: Alternative test arrangements, notetakers, advocacy, typing of required papers and projects.

GENERAL COLLEGE INFORMATION

Independent Southern Baptist, 4-year, coed. Awards associate, bachelor's degrees. Founded 1906. *Setting:* 81-acre small-town campus. *Endowment:* $22.1 million. *Educational spending 1995–96:* $4122 per undergrad. *Total enrollment:* 959. *Faculty:* 96 (61 full-time, 62% with terminal degrees, 35 part-time); student–undergrad faculty ratio is 15:1.

Enrollment Profile: 959 students from 18 states and territories, 3 other countries. 60% women, 40% men, 13% part-time, 95% state residents, 42% live on campus, 7% transferred in, 1% international, 22% 25 or older, 1% Native American, 1% Hispanic, 7% black, 1% Asian or Pacific Islander. *Retention:* 65% of 1995 full-time freshmen returned. *Areas of study chosen:* 17% education, 14% biological and life sciences, 13% health professions and related sciences, 10% business management and administrative services, 8% social sciences, 5% theology/religion, 4% communications and journalism, 4% psychology, 1% computer and information sciences, 1% English language/literature/letters, 1% foreign language and literature, 1% interdisciplinary studies, 1% liberal arts/general studies, 1% mathematics, 1% performing arts. *Most popular recent majors:* business administration/commerce/management, nursing, education.

First-Year Class: 206 total; 525 applied, 78% were accepted, 50% of whom enrolled. 34% from top 10% of their high school class, 62% from top quarter, 86% from top half.

Graduation Requirements: 62 credit hours for associate, 127 credit hours for bachelor's; 3 credit hours of math; 4 credit hours of science; 3 credit hours of a foreign language for bachelor's degree; computer course for business majors; internship (some majors); senior project (some majors).

Computers on Campus: 142 computers available on campus for general student use. A computer is recommended for some students. A campus-wide network can be accessed from off-campus. Students can contact faculty members and/or advisers through e-mail. Computers for student use in computer center, classrooms, library, dorms provide access to the Internet/World Wide Web, on- and off-campus e-mail addresses. Staffed computer lab on campus provides training in use of computers, software. *Academic computing expenditure 1995–96:* $47,000.

EXPENSES AND FINANCIAL AID

Expenses for 1997–98: *Application fee:* $25. Comprehensive fee of $9799 includes full-time tuition ($6272), mandatory fees ($491), and college room and board ($3036). Part-time tuition: $196 per credit hour. Part-time mandatory fees per semester range from $39.50 to $235.25.

Undergraduate Financial Aid: On average, 55% of need was met. *Financial aid deadline (priority):* 5/1. *Financial aid forms:* FAFSA, state form, institutional form required; CSS Financial Aid PROFILE acceptable.

LD Program Contact: Ms. Vickie Y. Kelly, Director, Louisiana College, Box 545, Pineville, LA 71359-0545, 318-487-7629. Fax: 318-487-7191.

LYNN UNIVERSITY

Boca Raton, Florida

Students with LD	150	Subject-Area Tutoring	✓
ADD services	✓	Special Courses	✓
Staff	6 full-, 4 part-time	Taped Textbooks	✓
Special Fee	Varies	Alternative Test Arrang.	✓
Diagnostic Testing		Notetakers	✓
Basic Skills Remediation	✓	LD Student Organization	

Lynn University (continued)

LEARNING DISABILITIES PROGRAM INFORMATION

The Advancement Program began offering services in 1991. Currently the program serves 150 undergraduates with LD. Services are also available to graduate students. Students diagnosed with ADD/ADHD are eligible for the same services available to students with LD.

Staff: 6 full-time, 4 part-time staff members, including director, associate director, assistant directors, coordinators. Services provided by remediation specialists, tutors, counselors.

Special Fees: Range from $3800 to $7700 per year according to level of services required.

Applications and admissions: *Required:* high school transcript, courses completed, untimed or extended time SAT I, letters of recommendation, psychoeducational report completed within 4 years; *recommended:* extended time ACT, personal interview, autobiographical statement. Students may begin taking classes in fall only. *Application deadline:* continuous.

PROGRAM AND SERVICE COMPONENTS

Special preparation or orientation: Summer program (required for some) held prior to entering college.

Academic advising: Provided by LD staff members, academic advisers. Students with LD may take up to 18 credit hours each term; most take 14 to 16 credit hours; 9 credit hours required to maintain full-time status; 12 credit hours required to be eligible for financial aid.

Counseling services: Individual counseling, career counseling.

Basic skills remediation: Offered in class-size groups by regular teachers. Available in grammar.

Subject-area tutoring: Offered one-on-one and in small groups by professional teachers, community volunteers. Available in all subjects.

Special courses: Language and learning, research and writing. All offered for credit; all enter into overall grade point average.

Auxiliary aids: Taped textbooks, typewriters, word-processors with spell-check.

Auxiliary services: Alternative test arrangements, notetakers, priority registration, advocacy.

GENERAL COLLEGE INFORMATION

Independent, comprehensive, coed. Awards associate, bachelor's, master's degrees. Founded 1962. *Setting:* 123-acre suburban campus with easy access to Fort Lauderdale. *Total enrollment:* 1,652. *Faculty:* 168 (63 full-time, 70% with terminal degrees, 105 part-time); student–undergrad faculty ratio is 19:1.

Enrollment Profile: 1,508 students from 37 states and territories, 58 other countries. 45% women, 55% men, 24% part-time, 30% state residents, 50% live on campus, 34% transferred in, 18% international, 24% 25 or older, 1% Native American, 5% Hispanic, 4% black, 1% Asian or Pacific Islander. *Retention:* 85% of 1995 full-time freshmen returned. *Areas of study chosen:* 63% business management and administrative services, 10% education, 7% communications and journalism, 7% social sciences, 5% health professions and related sciences, 5% liberal arts/general studies, 3% fine arts, 1% premed. *Most popular recent majors:* hotel and restaurant management, international business, business administration/commerce/management.

First-Year Class: 264 total; 1,388 applied, 80% were accepted, 24% of whom enrolled. 80% from top half of their high school class.

Graduation Requirements: 62 credit hours for associate, 124 credit hours for bachelor's; 6 credit hours of math; 8 credit hours of science; computer course; internship (some majors); senior project for honors program students and some majors.

Computers on Campus: 125 computers available on campus for general student use. A computer is recommended for all students. Computers for student use in computer center, computer labs, learning resource center, classrooms, library provide access to the Internet/World Wide Web, off-campus e-mail addresses. Staffed computer lab on campus.

EXPENSES AND FINANCIAL AID

Expenses for 1997–98: *Application fee:* $25. Comprehensive fee of $22,950 includes full-time tuition ($16,300), mandatory fees ($400), and college room and board ($6250). Tuition for evening program: $175 per credit hour.

Undergraduate Financial Aid: 77% of all full-time undergraduates enrolled in fall 1996 applied for aid; of these, 43% were judged to have need according to Federal Methodology, of whom 100% were aided. On average, 100% of need was met. *Financial aid deadline (priority):* 5/1. *Financial aid forms:* FAFSA required; CSS Financial Aid PROFILE, state form acceptable.

LD Program Contact: Mr. James P. Sullivan, Director of Admission, Lynn University, 3601 North Military Trail, Boca Raton, FL 33431-5598, 561-994-0770. Fax: 561-241-3552. Email: admission@lynn.edu.

MANHATTAN COLLEGE

Riverdale, New York

Students with LD	60	Subject-Area Tutoring	
ADD services	✓	Special Courses	
Staff	2 full-, 1 part-time	Taped Textbooks	✓
Special Fee	None	Alternative Test Arrang.	✓
Diagnostic Testing		Notetakers	✓
Basic Skills Remediation	✓	LD Student Organization	

LEARNING DISABILITIES PROGRAM INFORMATION

The Learning Disabilities Program began offering services in 1991. Currently the program serves 60 undergraduates with LD. Services are also available to graduate students. Students diagnosed with ADD/ADHD are eligible for the same services available to students with LD.

Staff: 2 full-time, 1 part-time staff members, including director, coordinator. Services provided by remediation specialists, counselors.

Special Fees: No special fees are charged for services to students with LD.

Applications and admissions: *Required:* high school transcript, grade point average, class rank, courses completed, untimed SAT I, letters of recommendation; *recommended:* high school extracurricular activities, extended time SAT I, personal interview. Students may begin taking classes any term. *Application deadline:* continuous.

Special policies: The college has written policies regarding grade forgiveness; substitutions and waivers of admissions, graduation, and degree requirements.

PROGRAM AND SERVICE COMPONENTS

Academic advising: Provided by academic advisers. Students with LD may take up to 18 credit hours each term; most take 12 to 15 credit hours; 12 credit hours required to maintain full-time status and be eligible for financial aid.

Basic skills remediation: Offered one-on-one by remediation specialists. Available in learning strategies, study skills, time management, social skills.

Auxiliary aids: Taped textbooks, tape recorders, calculators, typewriters, word-processors with spell-check, personal computers, talking computers, optical character readers.

Auxiliary services: Alternative test arrangements, notetakers, priority registration, advocacy.

GENERAL COLLEGE INFORMATION

Independent, comprehensive, coed, affiliated with Roman Catholic Church. Awards bachelor's, master's degrees. Founded 1853. *Setting:* 50-acre urban campus with easy access to New York City. *Endowment:* $15 million. *Research spending 1995–96:* $1.1 million. *Educational spending 1995–96:* $6003 per undergrad. *Total enrollment:* 3,076. *Undergraduate faculty:* 244 (164 full-time, 92% with terminal degrees, 80 part-time); student–undergrad faculty ratio is 14:1.

Enrollment Profile: 2,601 students from 27 states and territories, 49 other countries. 45% women, 55% men, 9% part-time, 85% state residents, 44% live on campus, 21% transferred in, 1% international, 8% 25 or older, 0% Native American, 15% Hispanic, 7% black, 7% Asian or Pacific Islander. *Retention:* 85% of 1995 full-time freshmen returned. *Graduation:* 56% graduate in 4 years, 69% in 5 years, 71% in 6 years. *Areas of study chosen:* 22% business management and administrative services, 20% engineering and applied sciences, 10% education, 6% biological and life sciences, 5% computer and information sciences, 5% psychology, 5% social sciences, 4% health professions and related sciences, 3% communications and journalism, 3% English language/literature/letters, 2% mathematics, 1% fine arts, 1% foreign language and literature, 1% interdisciplinary studies, 1% liberal arts/general studies, 1% philosophy, 1% physical sciences, 1% theology/religion. *Most popular recent majors:* marketing/retailing/merchandising, civil engineering, finance/banking.

First-Year Class: 564 total; 2,986 applied, 77% were accepted, 25% of whom enrolled.

Graduation Requirements: 128 credit hours; 3 credit hours each of math and science; computer course; senior project (some majors).

Computers on Campus: 375 computers available on campus for general student use. Computer purchase/lease plans available. A campus-wide network can be accessed from student residence rooms and from off-campus. Students can contact faculty members and/or advisers through e-mail. Computers for student use in computer center, computer labs, research center, library, dorms, engineering center provide access to the Internet/World Wide Web, on- and off-campus e-mail addresses. Staffed computer lab on campus provides training in use of computers. *Academic computing expenditure 1995–96:* $893,641.

EXPENSES AND FINANCIAL AID

Expenses for 1997–98: *Application fee:* $25. Comprehensive fee of $21,805 includes full-time tuition ($14,400 minimum), mandatory fees ($155), and college room and board ($7250 minimum). College room only: $5050 (minimum). Part-time tuition: $400 per credit hour. Full-time tuition ranges up to $16,000 according to program. One-time mandatory fee: $200.

Undergraduate Financial Aid: Of all full-time undergraduates enrolled in fall 1996, 74% of those who applied for aid were judged to have need according to Federal Methodology, of whom 100% were aided. On average, 79% of need was met. *Financial aid deadline (priority):* 2/15. *Financial aid forms:* FAFSA, state form, institutional form required.

LD Program Contact: Dr. Ross Pollack, Director, Specialized Resource Center, Manhattan College, Manhattan College Parkway, Riverdale, NY 10471, 718-862-7101. Fax: 718-862-7821. Email: rpollack@manhattan.edu.

MANHATTANVILLE COLLEGE

Purchase, New York

Students with LD	32	Subject-Area Tutoring	✓
ADD services		Special Courses	✓
Staff	4 full-, 7 part-time	Taped Textbooks	
Special Fee	✓	Alternative Test Arrang.	✓
Diagnostic Testing	✓	Notetakers	
Basic Skills Remediation	✓	LD Student Organization	

LEARNING DISABILITIES PROGRAM INFORMATION

The Higher Education Learning Program began offering services in 1983. Currently the program serves 32 undergraduates with LD. Students diagnosed with ADD/ADHD are not eligible for the same services available to students with LD.

Staff: 4 full-time, 7 part-time staff members, including director. Services provided by remediation specialists, tutors, assistant professor.

Special Fees: $3000 per year.

Applications and admissions: *Required:* high school transcript, grade point average, class rank, courses completed, extracurricular activities, extended time SAT I, autobiographical statement, letters of recommendation, psychoeducational report completed within 1 year; *recommended:* high school IEP (Individualized Education Program), personal interview. Students may begin taking classes any term. *Application deadline:* continuous.

PROGRAM AND SERVICE COMPONENTS

Special preparation or orientation: Orientation (required for some) held before registration.

Diagnostic testing: Reading, math, written language, study skills, learning strategies.

Academic advising: Provided by LD staff members, academic advisers. Most students with LD take 12 to 15 credits each term; 12 credits required to maintain full-time status; 12 credits (full-time) required to be eligible for financial aid.

Counseling services: Individual counseling, career counseling.

Basic skills remediation: Offered one-on-one by LD teachers. Available in reading, written language, learning strategies, study skills, time management.

Subject-area tutoring: Offered one-on-one and in small groups by peer tutors. Available in most subjects.

Special courses: Composition, learning strategies, study skills. All offered for credit; all enter into overall grade point average.

Auxiliary aids: Tape recorders, word-processors with spell-check.

Auxiliary services: Alternative test arrangements.

GENERAL COLLEGE INFORMATION

Independent, comprehensive, coed. Awards bachelor's, master's degrees. Founded 1841. *Setting:* 100-acre suburban campus with easy access to New York City. *Total enrollment:* 1,500. *Undergraduate faculty:* 207 (76 full-time, 90% with terminal degrees, 131 part-time).

Enrollment Profile: 835 students from 44 states and territories, 25 other countries. 67% women, 33% men, 20% part-time, 67% state residents, 25% transferred in, 15% international, 4% 25 or older, 1% Native American, 15% Hispanic, 7% black, 7% Asian or Pacific Islander. *Retention:* 81% of 1995 full-time freshmen returned. *Graduation:* 52% graduate in 4 years, 58% in 5 years, 60% in 6 years. *Areas of study chosen:* 26% social sciences, 13% psychology, 12% business management and administrative services, 10% English language/literature/letters, 10% fine arts, 9% biological and life sciences, 7% performing arts, 3% computer and information sciences, 3% interdisciplinary studies, 3% math-

Manhattanville College (continued)

ematics, 2% foreign language and literature, 1% philosophy, 1% physical sciences. *Most popular recent majors:* economics, business administration/commerce/management, political science/government.

First-Year Class: 274 total; 988 applied, 75% were accepted, 37% of whom enrolled. 30% from top 10% of their high school class, 45% from top quarter, 90% from top half. 3 valedictorians.

Graduation Requirements: 120 credits; 8 credits of math/science; computer course for math, management majors; senior project.

Computers on Campus: 60 computers available on campus for general student use. Computers for student use in computer center, learning resource center, library provide access to the Internet/World Wide Web. Staffed computer lab on campus provides training in use of computers.

EXPENSES AND FINANCIAL AID

Expenses for 1997–98: *Application fee:* $35. Comprehensive fee of $25,300 includes full-time tuition ($16,760), mandatory fees ($540), and college room and board ($8000). Part-time tuition: $395 per credit. Part-time mandatory fees: $30 per semester.

Undergraduate Financial Aid: Of all full-time undergraduates enrolled in fall 1996, 94% of those who applied for aid were judged to have need according to Federal Methodology, of whom 100% were aided. On average, 95% of need was met. *Financial aid deadline (priority):* 3/1. *Financial aid forms:* FAFSA, CSS Financial Aid PROFILE, state form required.

LD Program Contact: Dr. Rebecca Rich, Professor of Education/Director, Higher Education Learning Program, Manhattanville College, 2900 Purchase Street, Purchase, NY 10577, 914-323-5143. Fax: 914-323-5493.

MARIST COLLEGE

Poughkeepsie, New York

Students with LD	70	Subject-Area Tutoring	✓
ADD services		Special Courses	
Staff	2 full-, 3 part-time	Taped Textbooks	✓
Special Fee	✓	Alternative Test Arrang.	✓
Diagnostic Testing		Notetakers	✓
Basic Skills Remediation	✓	LD Student Organization	

LEARNING DISABILITIES PROGRAM INFORMATION

The Learning Disabilities Support Program began offering services in 1982. Currently the program serves 70 undergraduates with LD.

Staff: 2 full-time, 3 part-time staff members, including director, LD specialists. Services provided by tutors, LD specialists.

Special Fees: $2400 per year.

Applications and admissions: *Required:* high school transcript, untimed SAT I, personal interview, autobiographical statement, letters of recommendation, psychoeducational report completed within 3 years. Students may begin taking classes in fall or spring. *Application deadline:* 3/1.

PROGRAM AND SERVICE COMPONENTS

Special preparation or orientation: Required orientation held one day prior to the arrival of all freshmen.

Academic advising: Provided by LD staff members, academic advisers. Students with LD may take up to 15 credits each term; most take 12 credits; 12 credits required to maintain full-time status and be eligible for financial aid.

Counseling services: Individual counseling, career counseling.

Basic skills remediation: Offered one-on-one by LD teachers. Available in written language, learning strategies, study skills, time management, social skills.

Subject-area tutoring: Offered one-on-one by peer tutors, math lab staff, writing center staff. Available in most subjects.

Auxiliary aids: Taped textbooks, tape recorders, calculators, word-processors with spell-check, personal computers, optical character readers, Kurzweil Reading Edge.

Auxiliary services: Alternative test arrangements, notetakers, advocacy, scribes, readers.

GENERAL COLLEGE INFORMATION

Independent, comprehensive, coed. Awards bachelor's, master's degrees. Founded 1929. *Setting:* 120-acre small-town campus with easy access to Albany and New York City. *Endowment:* $7 million. *Research spending 1995–96:* $72,255. *Educational spending 1995–96:* $4491 per undergrad. *Total enrollment:* 4,372. *Undergraduate faculty:* 415 (81% of full-time faculty have terminal degrees); student–undergrad faculty ratio is 15:1.

Enrollment Profile: 3,842 students from 27 states and territories, 11 other countries. 56% women, 44% men, 14% part-time, 68% state residents, 11% transferred in, 1% international, 15% 25 or older, 0% Native American, 5% Hispanic, 5% black, 2% Asian or Pacific Islander. *Retention:* 91% of 1995 full-time freshmen returned. *Graduation:* 64% graduate in 4 years, 65% in 5 years. *Areas of study chosen:* 24% communications and journalism, 17% psychology, 16% business management and administrative services, 11% social sciences, 7% liberal arts/general studies, 5% computer and information sciences, 4% biological and life sciences, 4% English language/literature/letters, 3% education, 3% physical sciences, 2% prelaw, 1% health professions and related sciences, 1% interdisciplinary studies, 1% mathematics, 1% premed. *Most popular recent majors:* communication, business administration/commerce/management, psychology.

First-Year Class: 876 total; 4,710 applied, 65% were accepted, 29% of whom enrolled. 16% from top 10% of their high school class, 37% from top quarter, 83% from top half. 1 National Merit Scholar, 15 class presidents, 11 valedictorians.

Graduation Requirements: 120 credits; 6 credits each of math and science; computer course; internship (some majors); senior project (some majors).

Computers on Campus: 401 computers available on campus for general student use. Computer purchase/lease plans available. A campus-wide network can be accessed from student residence rooms and from off-campus. Students can contact faculty members and/or advisers through e-mail. Computers for student use in computer center, computer labs, learning resource center, classrooms, library, student center, dorms, academic buildings provide access to the Internet/World Wide Web, on- and off-campus e-mail addresses. Staffed computer lab on campus (open 24 hours a day) provides training in use of computers, software. *Academic computing expenditure 1995–96:* $1.6 million.

EXPENSES AND FINANCIAL AID

Expenses for 1997–98: *Application fee:* $35. Comprehensive fee of $19,870 includes full-time tuition ($12,734), mandatory fees ($364), and college room and board ($6772). College room only: $4202 (minimum). Part-time tuition: $352 per credit. Part-time mandatory fees: $20 per semester. One-time mandatory fee: $25.

Undergraduate Financial Aid: Of all full-time undergraduates enrolled in fall 1996, 86% of those who applied for aid were judged to have need according to Federal Methodology, of whom 100% were aided. On average, 65% of need was met. *Financial aid deadline (priority):* 3/1. *Financial aid forms:* FAFSA required. State form required for some.

LD Program Contact: Ms. Linda Cooper, Director, Special Services, Marist College, 290 North Road, Poughkeepsie, NY 12601-1387, 914-575-3274. Fax: 914-575-3011.

MARSHALL UNIVERSITY

Huntington, West Virginia

Students with LD	200	Subject-Area Tutoring	✓
ADD services	✓	Special Courses	✓
Staff	8 full-, 60 part-time	Taped Textbooks	✓
Special Fee	Varies	Alternative Test Arrang.	✓
Diagnostic Testing	✓	Notetakers	✓
Basic Skills Remediation	✓	LD Student Organization	✓

LEARNING DISABILITIES PROGRAM INFORMATION

The Higher Education for Learning Problems (HELP) began offering services in 1981. Currently the program serves 200 undergraduates with LD. Services are also available to graduate students. Students diagnosed with ADD/ADHD are eligible for the same services available to students with LD.

Staff: 8 full-time, 60 part-time staff members, including director, assistant director, coordinators, LD specialists. Services provided by remediation specialists, tutors, counselor, diagnostic specialists.

Special Fees: Range from $200 to $2000 per year. $600 for diagnostic testing.

Applications and admissions: *Required:* high school transcript, grade point average, courses completed, extended time SAT I or ACT, personal interview, autobiographical statement, letters of recommendation, psychoeducational report completed within 1 year, college records for transfers. Students may begin taking classes any term. *Application deadline:* continuous.

Special policies: The college has written policies regarding substitutions and waivers of admissions and graduation requirements.

PROGRAM AND SERVICE COMPONENTS

Special preparation or orientation: Required orientation held during summer prior to first term of enrollment.

Diagnostic testing: Intelligence, reading, math, spelling, perceptual skills, study skills, personality, social skills.

Academic advising: Provided by LD staff members, academic advisers. Students with LD may take up to 15 semester hours each term; most take 12 semester hours; 12 semester hours required to maintain full-time status and be eligible for financial aid.

Counseling services: Individual counseling, small-group counseling, career counseling.

Basic skills remediation: Offered one-on-one and in small groups by LD teachers; computer-aided instruction also offered. Available in reading, math, spelling, handwriting, written language, learning strategies, perceptual skills, study skills, time management, social skills.

Subject-area tutoring: Offered one-on-one by professional teachers, trained graduate assistants. Available in all subjects.

Special courses: College survival skills, reading, vocabulary development, learning strategies, word processing, time management, math, study skills, career planning, stress management, social relationships. Some offered for credit; most enter into overall grade point average.

Auxiliary aids: Taped textbooks, tape recorders, word-processors with spell-check, optical character readers.

Auxiliary services: Alternative test arrangements, notetakers, priority registration, advocacy, readers.

Campus support group: A special student organization is available to students with LD.

GENERAL COLLEGE INFORMATION

State-supported, comprehensive, coed. Part of University System of West Virginia. Awards associate, bachelor's, master's, doctoral, first professional degrees. Founded 1837. *Setting:* 70-acre urban campus. *Endowment:* $25.8 million. *Research spending 1995–96:* $4.9 million. *Educational spending 1995–96:* $3900 per undergrad. *Total enrollment:* 11,066. *Faculty:* 719 (504 full-time, 80% with terminal degrees, 215 part-time); student–undergrad faculty ratio is 20:1.

Enrollment Profile: 8,778 students from 41 states and territories, 34 other countries. 52% women, 48% men, 24% part-time, 85% state residents, 7% transferred in, 1% international, 27% 25 or older, 1% Native American, 1% Hispanic, 4% black, 1% Asian or Pacific Islander. *Retention:* 70% of 1995 full-time freshmen returned. *Graduation:* 12% graduate in 4 years, 28% in 5 years, 37% in 6 years. *Areas of study chosen:* 15% education, 14% business management and administrative services, 7% biological and life sciences, 7% health professions and related sciences, 4% premed, 4% psychology, 3% communications and journalism, 3% engineering and applied sciences, 3% liberal arts/general studies, 3% social sciences, 2% English language/literature/letters, 2% fine arts, 2% physical sciences, 2% prelaw, 1% computer and information sciences, 1% foreign language and literature, 1% interdisciplinary studies, 1% mathematics, 1% natural resource sciences, 1% vocational and home economics. *Most popular recent majors:* elementary education, criminal justice, psychology.

First-Year Class: 1,642 total; 3,480 applied, 90% were accepted, 52% of whom enrolled.

Graduation Requirements: 64 semester hours for associate, 128 semester hours for bachelor's; 3 semester hours of math; 8 semester hours of science; computer course; internship (some majors); senior project.

Computers on Campus: 550 computers available on campus for general student use. Computer purchase/lease plans available. A campus-wide network can be accessed from student residence rooms. Students can contact faculty members and/or advisers through e-mail. Computers for student use in computer center, computer labs, research center, learning resource center, classrooms, library, dorms provide access to the Internet/World Wide Web, on- and off-campus e-mail addresses. Staffed computer lab on campus. *Academic computing expenditure 1995–96:* $716,568.

EXPENSES AND FINANCIAL AID

Expenses for 1997–98: *Application fee:* $10. State resident tuition: $2184 full-time, $91.25 per semester hour part-time. Nonresident tuition: $6066 full-time, $253 per semester hour part-time. Tuition for Kentucky residents of Boyd, Carter, Greenup, and Lawrence counties and Ohio residents of Lawrence county: $4076 full-time, $170 per semester hour part-time. College room and board: $4420. College room only: $2266.

Undergraduate Financial Aid: Of all full-time undergraduates enrolled in fall 1996, 82% of those who applied for aid were judged to have need according to Federal Methodology, of whom 97% were aided. On average, 83% of need was met. *Financial aid deadline (priority):* 2/1. *Financial aid forms:* FAFSA required.

LD Program Contact: Dr. Barbara Guyer, Director, HELP Program, Marshall University, Myers Hall, 520 18th Street, Huntington, WV 25755-2020, 304-696-6256. Fax: 304-696-3231. Email: guyerb@marshall.edu.

MARYMOUNT MANHATTAN COLLEGE

New York, New York

Students with LD	16	Subject-Area Tutoring	✓
ADD services		Special Courses	
Staff	4 part-time	Taped Textbooks	
Special Fee	✓	Alternative Test Arrang.	✓
Diagnostic Testing		Notetakers	✓
Basic Skills Remediation	✓	LD Student Organization	

LEARNING DISABILITIES PROGRAM INFORMATION

The Learning Disabled College Students Program began offering services in 1990. Currently the program serves 16 undergraduates with LD.

Staff: 4 part-time staff members, including director. Services provided by remediation specialists.

Special Fees: $3000 per year.

Applications and admissions: *Required:* high school transcript, grade point average, class rank, courses completed, extended time SAT I, personal interview, letters of recommendation, psychoeducational report completed within 2 years, WAIS-R; *recommended:* extended time ACT. Students may begin taking classes in fall or spring. *Application deadline:* 7/1 (fall term), 11/15 (spring term).

PROGRAM AND SERVICE COMPONENTS

Special preparation or orientation: Optional summer program offered prior to entering college. Required orientation held during registration and after classes begin.

Academic advising: Provided by LD staff members, academic advisers. Students with LD may take up to 15 credits each term; most take 12 credits; 12 credits required to maintain full-time status and be eligible for financial aid.

Counseling services: Individual counseling, small-group counseling.

Basic skills remediation: Offered one-on-one by LD teachers. Available in reading, math, spelling, written language, learning strategies, study skills, time management, speech, computer skills.

Subject-area tutoring: Offered one-on-one by professional teachers. Available in most subjects.

Auxiliary aids: Tape recorders, calculators, word-processors with spell-check.

Auxiliary services: Alternative test arrangements, notetakers, priority registration, advocacy.

GENERAL COLLEGE INFORMATION

Independent, 4-year, coed. Awards bachelor's degrees. Founded 1936. *Setting:* 1-acre urban campus. *Endowment:* $4.2 million. *Educational spending 1995–96:* $2783 per undergrad. *Total enrollment:* 2,015. *Faculty:* 156 (62 full-time, 75% with terminal degrees, 94 part-time); student–undergrad faculty ratio is 17:1.

Enrollment Profile: 2,015 students from 42 states and territories, 60 other countries. 82% women, 18% men, 42% part-time, 74% state residents, 15% live on campus, 34% transferred in, 2% international, 45% 25 or older, 1% Native American, 16% Hispanic, 20% black, 7% Asian or Pacific Islander. *Retention:* 79% of 1995 full-time freshmen returned. *Graduation:* 60% graduate in 4 years, 64% in 5 years, 67% in 6 years. *Areas of study chosen:* 26% liberal arts/general studies, 22% performing arts, 15% business management and administrative services, 10% communications and journalism, 10% psychology, 5% social sciences, 4% biological and life sciences, 4% English language/literature/letters, 4% fine arts. *Most popular recent majors:* business administration/commerce/management, theater arts/drama, psychology.

First-Year Class: 288 total; 1,103 applied, 79% were accepted, 33% of whom enrolled. 17% from top 10% of their high school class, 34% from top quarter, 78% from top half.

Graduation Requirements: 120 credits; 2 math courses; 1 science course; computer course for business, accounting majors.

Computers on Campus: 60 computers available on campus for general student use. A computer is recommended for some students. Computers for student use in library, academic offices provide access to the Internet/World Wide Web. Staffed computer lab on campus provides training in use of computers, software. *Academic computing expenditure 1995–96:* $66,800.

EXPENSES AND FINANCIAL AID

Expenses for 1996–97: *Application fee:* $30. Comprehensive fee of $17,500 includes full-time tuition ($11,650), mandatory fees ($250), and college room and board ($5600). Part-time tuition: $330 per credit. Part-time mandatory fees: $85 per semester.

Undergraduate Financial Aid: 72% of all full-time undergraduates enrolled in fall 1996 applied for aid; of these, 90% were judged to have need according to Federal Methodology, of whom 100% were aided. On average, 80% of need was met. *Financial aid deadline (priority):* 2/15. *Financial aid forms:* FAFSA required. State form required for some.

LD Program Contact: Dr. Ann Jablon, Director, Marymount Manhattan College, 221 East 71st Street, New York, NY 10021-4597, 212-517-0501. Fax: 212-517-0413.

MERCY COLLEGE

Dobbs Ferry, New York

Students with LD	45	Subject-Area Tutoring	✓
ADD services	✓	Special Courses	✓
Staff	3 full-, 7 part-time	Taped Textbooks	✓
Special Fee	✓	Alternative Test Arrang.	✓
Diagnostic Testing		Notetakers	✓
Basic Skills Remediation	✓	LD Student Organization	

LEARNING DISABILITIES PROGRAM INFORMATION

The Program for College Students with Learning Disabilities began offering services in 1985. Currently the program serves 45 undergraduates with LD. Students diagnosed with ADD/ADHD are eligible for the same services available to students with LD.

Staff: 3 full-time, 7 part-time staff members, including director, assistant director. Services provided by remediation specialists, tutors, counselors, diagnostic specialists, LD teachers, consulting psychologist.

Special Fees: $2500 per year.

Applications and admissions: *Required:* high school transcript, courses completed, IEP (Individualized Education Program), personal interview, letters of recommendation, psychoeducational report completed within 1 year; *recommended:* high school extracurricular activities, autobiographical statement. Students may begin taking classes in fall or spring. *Application deadline:* 7/1 (fall term), 12/1 (spring term).

Special policies: The college has written policies regarding grade forgiveness; substitutions and waivers of graduation and degree requirements.

PROGRAM AND SERVICE COMPONENTS

Special preparation or orientation: Required orientation held before registration.

Academic advising: Provided by LD staff members, academic advisers. Students with LD may take up to 15 credits each term; most take 12 credits; 12 credits required to maintain full-time status; source of aid determines number of credits required to be eligible for financial aid.

Counseling services: Individual counseling, small-group counseling, career counseling.
Basic skills remediation: Offered one-on-one and in small groups by LD teachers, regular teachers. Available in reading, math, spelling, spoken language, written language, learning strategies, study skills, time management, social skills, speech.
Subject-area tutoring: Offered one-on-one and in small groups by professional teachers. Available in all subjects.
Special courses: College survival skills, reading, vocabulary development, composition, math, study skills. Most offered for credit; most enter into overall grade point average.
Auxiliary aids: Taped textbooks, tape recorders, calculators, typewriters, word-processors with spell-check.
Auxiliary services: Alternative test arrangements, notetakers, advocacy, scribes, readers.

GENERAL COLLEGE INFORMATION

Independent, comprehensive, coed. Awards associate, bachelor's, master's degrees. Founded 1951. *Setting:* 20-acre small-town campus with easy access to New York City. *Total enrollment:* 7,364. *Faculty:* 665 (165 full-time, 500 part-time); student–undergrad faculty ratio is 14:1.
Enrollment Profile: 6,759 students from 6 states and territories, 49 other countries. 70% women, 30% men, 30% part-time, 91% state residents, 54% transferred in, 8% international, 58% 25 or older, 1% Native American, 19% Hispanic, 22% black, 6% Asian or Pacific Islander. *Most popular recent majors:* business administration/commerce/management, computer science, behavioral sciences.
First-Year Class: 1,242 total; 2,408 applied, 90% were accepted, 65% of whom enrolled. 1% from top 10% of their high school class, 5% from top quarter, 45% from top half.
Graduation Requirements: 60 credits for associate, 120 credits for bachelor's; 12 credits of math/science including at least 1 algebra course; 1 semester of a foreign language; computer course for business administration, accounting, math, nursing, psychology, sociology, behavioral sciences, social work majors.
Computers on Campus: 138 computers available on campus for general student use. Computer purchase/lease plans available. A computer is recommended for all students. A campus-wide network can be accessed from off-campus. Students can contact faculty members and/or advisers through e-mail. Computers for student use in computer center, computer labs, library, Honors Center provide access to the Internet/World Wide Web, on- and off-campus e-mail addresses. Staffed computer lab on campus provides training in use of computers, software.

EXPENSES AND FINANCIAL AID

Expenses for 1996–97: *Application fee:* $35. Comprehensive fee of $13,800 includes full-time tuition ($7200) and college room and board ($6600 minimum). Part-time tuition: $285 per credit.
Undergraduate Financial Aid: *Financial aid deadline (priority):* 2/15. *Financial aid forms:* CSS Financial Aid PROFILE, institutional form required.
LD Program Contact: Ms. Terry Rich DeMartino, Director, Program for College Students with Learning Disabilities, Mercy College, 555 Broadway, Dobbs Ferry, NY 10522, 914-674-7218. Fax: 914-674-7410.

MERCYHURST COLLEGE

Erie, Pennsylvania

Students with LD	45	Subject-Area Tutoring	✓
ADD services	✓	Special Courses	✓
Staff	1 full-, 4 part-time	Taped Textbooks	
Special Fee	Varies	Alternative Test Arrang.	✓
Diagnostic Testing		Notetakers	✓
Basic Skills Remediation	✓	LD Student Organization	✓

LEARNING DISABILITIES PROGRAM INFORMATION

The Program for Students with Learning Differences began offering services in 1986. Currently the program serves 45 undergraduates with LD. Students diagnosed with ADD/ADHD are eligible for the same services available to students with LD.
Staff: 1 full-time, 4 part-time staff members, including director, assistant director, graduate assistant. Services provided by remediation specialists, tutors, counselors, faculty advisers.
Special Fees: Range from $0 to $1000 per year.
Applications and admissions: *Required:* high school transcript, grade point average, class rank, courses completed, extracurricular activities, untimed SAT I or ACT, personal interview, letters of recommendation, psychoeducational report completed within 2 years; *recommended:* high school IEP (Individualized Education Program), extended time SAT I or ACT, autobiographical statement, writing sample. Students may begin taking classes in summer only. *Application deadline:* continuous.

PROGRAM AND SERVICE COMPONENTS

Special preparation or orientation: Required summer program offered prior to entering college. Required orientation held during summer prior to enrollment.
Academic advising: Provided by LD staff members, academic advisers. Students with LD may take up to 12 credits each term; most take 9 credits; 9 credits required to maintain full-time status; 8 credits required to be eligible for financial aid.
Basic skills remediation: Offered one-on-one, in small groups, and in class-size groups by LD teachers, regular teachers, teacher trainees, peer tutors. Available in reading, math, written language, learning strategies, study skills, time management.
Subject-area tutoring: Offered one-on-one by peer tutors, graduate students. Available in all subjects.
Special courses: Reading, vocabulary development, composition, word processing, math. Some offered for credit; most enter into overall grade point average.
Auxiliary aids: Word-processors with spell-check, optical character readers.
Auxiliary services: Alternative test arrangements, notetakers, priority registration, advocacy, student assistants.
Campus support group: A special student organization is available to students with LD.

GENERAL COLLEGE INFORMATION

Independent Roman Catholic, comprehensive, coed. Awards associate, bachelor's, master's degrees. Founded 1926. *Setting:* 88-acre suburban campus with easy access to Buffalo. *Endowment:* $5.3 million. *Educational spending 1995–96:* $6610 per undergrad. *Total enrollment:* 2,712. *Undergraduate faculty:* 164 (106 full-time, 55% with terminal degrees, 58 part-time); student–undergrad faculty ratio is 20:1.
Enrollment Profile: 2,635 students from 38 states and territories, 16 other countries. 53% women, 47% men, 20% part-time, 64% state residents, 16% transferred in, 3% international, 17% 25 or older, 1% Native American, 2% Hispanic, 6% black, 2% Asian or Pacific Islander. *Retention:* 80% of 1995 full-time freshmen returned. *Graduation:* 55% graduate in 4 years, 56% in 5 years, 57% in 6 years. *Areas of study chosen:* 15% business management and administrative services, 15% liberal arts/general studies, 11% social sciences, 11% vocational and home economics, 9% education, 7% health professions and related sciences, 5% performing arts, 3% fine arts, 3% physical sciences, 3% premed, 3% psychology, 2% communications and journalism, 2% English language/literature/letters, 2% prelaw, 2% prevet, 1% biological

Mercyhurst College (continued)

and life sciences, 1% computer and information sciences, 1% engineering and applied sciences, 1% foreign language and literature, 1% mathematics, 1% predentistry, 1% theology/religion. *Most popular recent majors:* business administration/commerce/management, archaeology, music.

First-Year Class: 456 total; 1,733 applied, 76% were accepted, 34% of whom enrolled. 16% from top 10% of their high school class, 42% from top quarter, 86% from top half. 12 class presidents, 9 valedictorians.

Graduation Requirements: 60 credits for associate, 128 credits for bachelor's; 1 course each in math and lab science; computer course for math, accounting, business majors; internship (some majors); senior project for honors program students and some majors.

Computers on Campus: 190 computers available on campus for general student use. Computers for student use in computer center, computer labs, learning resource center, library, dorms, academic buildings provide access to the Internet/World Wide Web. Staffed computer lab on campus (open 24 hours a day) provides training in use of computers, software. *Academic computing expenditure 1995–96:* $259,615.

EXPENSES AND FINANCIAL AID

Expenses for 1997–98: *Application fee:* $25. Comprehensive fee of $17,640 includes full-time tuition ($12,192), mandatory fees ($750), and college room and board ($4698). Part-time tuition: $381 per credit. Part-time mandatory fees: $212 per term.

Undergraduate Financial Aid: On average, 85% of need was met. *Financial aid deadline (priority):* 5/1. *Financial aid forms:* FAFSA, institutional form required; CSS Financial Aid PROFILE acceptable. State form required for some.

LD Program Contact: Mr. Matthew Whelan, Director of Admissions, Mercyhurst College, 501 East 38th Street, Erie, PA 16546, 814-824-2202. Fax: 814-824-2071.

PROGRAM AND SERVICE COMPONENTS

Special preparation or orientation: Required summer program offered prior to entering college. Required orientation held after classes begin.

Diagnostic testing: Reading, math, English.

Academic advising: Provided by academic advisers. Most students with LD take 12 to 16 credits each term; 12 credits required to maintain full-time status and be eligible for financial aid.

Counseling services: Individual counseling, small-group counseling, career counseling, self-advocacy training.

Basic skills remediation: Offered one-on-one, in small groups, and in class-size groups by LD teachers, regular teachers, qualified students. Available in reading, math, written language, learning strategies, study skills, time management, social skills, word processing.

Subject-area tutoring: Offered one-on-one and in small groups by professional teachers, peer tutors. Available in all subjects.

Special courses: College survival skills, reading, composition, learning strategies, word processing, time management, personal psychology, study skills, career planning. Some offered for credit; none enter into overall grade point average.

Auxiliary aids: Taped textbooks, tape recorders, calculators, typewriters, word-processors with spell-check.

Auxiliary services: Alternative test arrangements, notetakers, advocacy.

MOLLOY COLLEGE

Rockville Centre, New York

Students with LD	23	Subject-Area Tutoring	✓
ADD services	✓	Special Courses	✓
Staff		Taped Textbooks	✓
Special Fee	✓	Alternative Test Arrang.	✓
Diagnostic Testing	✓	Notetakers	✓
Basic Skills Remediation	✓	LD Student Organization	

LEARNING DISABILITIES PROGRAM INFORMATION

The Success Through Expanded Education Program (STEEP) began offering services in 1991. Currently the program serves 23 undergraduates with LD. Services are also available to graduate students. Students diagnosed with ADD/ADHD are eligible for the same services available to students with LD.

Staff: Includes director, co-director, Liaison for Students with Handicapping Conditions. Services provided by tutors, staff members.

Special Fees: $600 per year.

Applications and admissions: *Recommended:* high school IEP (Individualized Education Program), untimed or extended time ACT, untimed SAT I, autobiographical statement, letters of recommendation, psychoeducational report completed within 3 years. Students may begin taking classes any term. *Application deadline:* continuous.

Special policies: The college has written policies regarding grade forgiveness; substitutions and waivers of admissions, graduation, and degree requirements.

GENERAL COLLEGE INFORMATION

Independent, comprehensive, coed. Awards associate, bachelor's, master's degrees. Founded 1955. *Setting:* 25-acre suburban campus with easy access to New York City. *Total enrollment:* 2,346. *Undergraduate faculty:* 278 (136 full-time, 26% with terminal degrees, 142 part-time); student–undergrad faculty ratio is 12:1.

Enrollment Profile: 2,148 students: 83% women, 17% men, 18% part-time, 97% state residents, 58% transferred in, 3% international, 29% 25 or older, 1% Native American, 5% Hispanic, 13% black, 2% Asian or Pacific Islander. *Retention:* 90% of 1995 full-time freshmen returned. *Most popular recent majors:* nursing, social work, psychology.

First-Year Class: 152 total; 457 applied, 77% were accepted, 43% of whom enrolled. 2% from top 10% of their high school class, 24% from top quarter, 78% from top half.

Graduation Requirements: 64 credits for associate, 128 credits for bachelor's; 9 credits of math/science including at least 3 credits each of math and science; 6 credits of a foreign language; internship (some majors).

Computers on Campus: 120 computers available on campus for general student use. Computers for student use in computer center, computer labs provide access to the Internet/World Wide Web. Staffed computer lab on campus provides training in use of computers, software.

EXPENSES AND FINANCIAL AID

Expenses for 1997–98: *Application fee:* $25. Tuition: $10,000 full-time, $335 per credit part-time. Part-time mandatory fees per term range from $55 to $100. Full-time mandatory fees: $304.

Undergraduate Financial Aid: 90% of all full-time undergraduates enrolled in fall 1996 applied for aid; of these, 87% were judged to have need according to Federal Methodology, of whom 100% were aided. On average, 75% of need was met. *Financial aid deadline (priority):* 3/1. *Financial aid forms:* FAFSA, CSS Financial Aid PROFILE, institutional form required. State form required for some.

LD Program Contact: Sr. Therese Forker, Director of Success Through Expanded Education Program (STEEP), Molloy College, 1000 Hempstead Avenue, Rockville Centre, NY 11571-5002, 516-678-5000 Ext. 381. Fax: 516-678-7295.

MOUNT ALLISON UNIVERSITY

Sackville, New Brunswick, Canada

Students with LD	40	Subject-Area Tutoring	✓
ADD services		Special Courses	✓
Staff	2 full-, 1 part-time	Taped Textbooks	✓
Special Fee	None	Alternative Test Arrang.	✓
Diagnostic Testing	✓	Notetakers	
Basic Skills Remediation		LD Student Organization	

LEARNING DISABILITIES PROGRAM INFORMATION

The Meighen Centre for Learning Assistance and Research began offering services in 1987. Currently the program serves 40 undergraduates with LD. Students diagnosed with ADD/ADHD are not eligible for the same services available to students with LD.

Staff: 2 full-time, 1 part-time staff members, including director, coordinator. Services provided by tutors, learning skills assistant.

Special Fees: No special fees are charged for services to students with LD.

Applications and admissions: *Required:* high school transcript, courses completed, letters of recommendation, psychoeducational report completed within 1 year, completed supplemental form, unedited and edited writing samples; *recommended:* high school extracurricular activities, IEP (Individualized Education Program), personal interview. Students may begin taking classes in fall only. *Application deadline:* 1/5.

PROGRAM AND SERVICE COMPONENTS

Special preparation or orientation: Required orientation held during registration and after classes begin.

Diagnostic testing: Intelligence, reading, math, spelling, handwriting, spoken language, written language, motor abilities, study skills, psychoneurology, learning strategies.

Academic advising: Provided by LD staff members, academic advisers. Students with LD may take up to 4 full courses (first year), 5 full courses (subsequent years) each term; most take 4 half courses; 3 half courses required to maintain full-time status and be eligible for financial aid.

Counseling services: Individual counseling.

Subject-area tutoring: Offered one-on-one by peer tutors. Available in most subjects.

Special courses: Reading, composition, learning strategies, time management, listening and notetaking, critical thinking, test taking strategies. None offered for credit; none enter into overall grade point average.

Auxiliary aids: Taped textbooks, tape recorders, word-processors with spell-check.

Auxiliary services: Alternative test arrangements, advocacy.

GENERAL COLLEGE INFORMATION

Province-supported, comprehensive, coed. Awards bachelor's, master's degrees. Founded 1839. *Setting:* 50-acre small-town campus. *Total enrollment:* 2,498. *Undergraduate faculty:* 184 (124 full-time, 60 part-time); student–undergrad faculty ratio is 12:1.

Enrollment Profile: 2,493 students from 12 provinces and territories, 35 other countries. 58% women, 42% men, 7% part-time, 97% province residents, 60% live on campus, 15% transferred in, 3% international, 6% 25 or older, 1% Native American, 0% Hispanic, 1% black, 1% Asian or Pacific Islander. *Most popular recent majors:* English, psychology, sociology.

First-Year Class: 650 total; 2,000 applied, 75% were accepted, 43% of whom enrolled. 25% from top 10% of their high school class, 50% from top quarter, 95% from top half.

Graduation Requirements: 120 credits; computer course for accounting, management, math, engineering majors; internship (some majors); senior project for honors program students and some majors.

Computers on Campus: 100 computers available on campus for general student use. A campus-wide network can be accessed from student residence rooms and from off-campus. Students can contact faculty members and/or advisers through e-mail. Computers for student use in computer center, computer labs, research center, learning resource center, library, dorms, departmental labs provide access to the Internet/World Wide Web. Staffed computer lab on campus provides training in use of computers, software.

EXPENSES AND FINANCIAL AID

Expenses for 1997–98: *Application fee:* $40. Canadian resident tuition: $3850 full-time, $770 per course part-time. Nonresident tuition: $7475 full-time, $1495 per course part-time. (All figures are in Canadian dollars.). Full-time mandatory fees: $167. College room and board: $5410 (minimum). College room only: $2850 (minimum).

Undergraduate Financial Aid: *Financial aid deadline (priority):* 3/15. *Financial aid forms:* FAFSA, institutional form required.

LD Program Contact: Ms. Jane Drover, Coordinator/Learning Specialist, Mount Allison University, Sackville, NB EOA 3CO, Canada, 506-364-2527. Fax: 506-364-2219.

MUSKINGUM COLLEGE

New Concord, Ohio

Students with LD	124	Subject-Area Tutoring	✓
ADD services	✓	Special Courses	
Staff	16 full-, 3 part-time	Taped Textbooks	✓
Special Fee	✓	Alternative Test Arrang.	✓
Diagnostic Testing		Notetakers	✓
Basic Skills Remediation		LD Student Organization	✓

LEARNING DISABILITIES PROGRAM INFORMATION

The PLUS Program began offering services in 1983. Currently the program serves 124 undergraduates with LD. Services are also available to graduate students. Students diagnosed with ADD/ADHD are eligible for the same services available to students with LD.

Staff: 16 full-time, 3 part-time staff members, including director, coordinators. Services provided by tutors.

Special Fees: $3750 per year with $1875 designated for maintenance program.

Applications and admissions: *Required:* high school transcript, grade point average, courses completed, untimed SAT I or ACT, personal interview, autobiographical statement, letters of recommendation, psychoeducational report completed within 3 years; *recommended:* high school class rank, extracurricular activities, IEP (Individualized Education Program), extended time SAT I or ACT. Students may begin taking classes in fall or spring. *Application deadline:* continuous.

Special policies: The college has written policies regarding grade forgiveness.

PROGRAM AND SERVICE COMPONENTS

Special preparation or orientation: Optional summer program offered prior to entering college. Required orientation held before registration.

Academic advising: Provided by LD staff members, academic advisers. Students with LD may take up to 18 credit hours each term; most take 14 to 15 credit hours; individual need determines the number of credit hours required to maintain full-time status and be eligible for financial aid.

Muskingum College (continued)

Counseling services: Individual counseling.
Subject-area tutoring: Offered one-on-one and in small groups by professional teachers. Available in all subjects.
Auxiliary aids: Taped textbooks, tape recorders, typewriters, word-processors with spell-check, personal computers.
Auxiliary services: Alternative test arrangements, notetakers, advocacy.
Campus support group: A special student organization is available to students with LD.

GENERAL COLLEGE INFORMATION

Independent, comprehensive, coed, affiliated with Presbyterian Church (U.S.A.). Awards bachelor's, master's degrees. Founded 1837. *Setting:* 215-acre small-town campus with easy access to Columbus. *Endowment:* $27 million. *Total enrollment:* 1,411. *Faculty:* 105 (81 full-time, 92% with terminal degrees, 24 part-time); student–undergrad faculty ratio is 15:1.
Enrollment Profile: 1,302 students from 27 states and territories, 11 other countries. 49% women, 51% men, 6% part-time, 85% state residents, 10% transferred in, 1% international, 4% 25 or older, 1% Native American, 1% Hispanic, 3% black, 2% Asian or Pacific Islander. *Retention:* 79% of 1995 full-time freshmen returned. *Graduation:* 51% graduate in 4 years, 62% in 5 years, 63% in 6 years. *Areas of study chosen:* 17% business management and administrative services, 15% education, 11% social sciences, 9% psychology, 8% prelaw, 6% communications and journalism, 5% premed, 4% English language/literature/letters, 4% health professions and related sciences, 3% mathematics, 2% biological and life sciences, 2% computer and information sciences, 2% interdisciplinary studies, 1% engineering and applied sciences, 1% fine arts, 1% physical sciences, 1% prevet. *Most popular recent majors:* business administration/commerce/management, elementary education, secondary education.
First-Year Class: 394 total; 1,348 applied, 82% were accepted, 35% of whom enrolled. 21% from top 10% of their high school class, 51% from top quarter, 80% from top half. 18 valedictorians.
Graduation Requirements: 124 credits; 2 lab science courses; 1 math course; computer course for business, math, psychology majors; senior project (some majors).
Computers on Campus: 50 computers available on campus for general student use. Computer purchase/lease plans available. A computer is recommended for all students. A campus-wide network can be accessed from student residence rooms and from off-campus. Students can contact faculty members and/or advisers through e-mail. Computers for student use in computer center, computer labs, learning resource center, classrooms, library, dorms provide access to the Internet/World Wide Web, on- and off-campus e-mail addresses. Staffed computer lab on campus provides training in use of computers, software.

EXPENSES AND FINANCIAL AID

Expenses for 1997–98: *Application fee:* $20. Comprehensive fee of $15,285 includes full-time tuition ($10,450 minimum), mandatory fees ($335), and college room and board ($4500). College room only: $2130. Full-time tuition ranges up to $15,100 according to class level. One-time mandatory fee: $100. Part-time tuition per credit ranges from $109 to $290 according to course load.
Undergraduate Financial Aid: 86% of all full-time undergraduates enrolled in fall 1996 applied for aid; of these, 95% were judged to have need according to Federal Methodology, of whom 100% were aided. On average, 91% of need was met. *Financial aid deadline (priority):* 3/15. *Financial aid forms:* FAFSA, institutional form required; CSS Financial Aid PROFILE acceptable. State form required for some.
Financial aid specifically for students with LD: Scholarship: PLUS Program Endowment Fund; work-study.

LD Program Contact: Ms. Jen Navicky, Director, Center for Advancement of Learning, Muskingum College, 223 Montgomery Hall, New Concord, OH 43762, 614-826-8284. Fax: 614-826-8404. Email: navicky@muskingum.edu.

NEW YORK UNIVERSITY

New York, New York

Students with LD	230	Subject-Area Tutoring	
ADD services	✓	Special Courses	
Staff	2 full-, 5 part-time	Taped Textbooks	✓
Special Fee	None	Alternative Test Arrang.	✓
Diagnostic Testing		Notetakers	✓
Basic Skills Remediation		LD Student Organization	✓

LEARNING DISABILITIES PROGRAM INFORMATION

The Access to Learning began offering services in 1984. Currently the program serves 230 undergraduates with LD. Services are also available to graduate students. Students diagnosed with ADD/ADHD are eligible for the same services available to students with LD.
Staff: 2 full-time, 5 part-time staff members, including director, assistant director. Services provided by LD specialists.
Special Fees: No special fees are charged for services to students with LD.
Applications and admissions: *Required:* high school transcript, grade point average, courses completed, extended time SAT I, letters of recommendation, psychoeducational report completed within 3 years; *recommended:* high school class rank, extracurricular activities, IEP (Individualized Education Program), untimed SAT I. Students may begin taking classes any term. *Application deadline:* 1/15 (fall term), 12/1 (spring term).
Special policies: The college has written policies regarding substitutions and waivers of graduation and degree requirements.

PROGRAM AND SERVICE COMPONENTS

Special preparation or orientation: Optional orientation offered during general orientation.
Academic advising: Provided by LD staff members, academic advisers. Most students with LD take 12 to 16 credits each term; 12 credits required to maintain full-time status and be eligible for financial aid.
Counseling services: Individual counseling, small-group counseling, career counseling, self-advocacy training.
Auxiliary aids: Taped textbooks, tape recorders, typewriters, word-processors with spell-check, optical character readers, voice-synthesized computer.
Auxiliary services: Alternative test arrangements, notetakers, advocacy, readers, library assistance.
Campus support group: A special student organization is available to students with LD.

GENERAL COLLEGE INFORMATION

Independent, coed. Awards associate, bachelor's, master's, doctoral, first professional degrees. Founded 1831. *Setting:* 28-acre urban campus. *Endowment:* $793.1 million. *Research spending 1995–96:* $182.2 million. *Total enrollment:* 36,056. *Faculty:* 4,722 (2,274 full-time, 99% with terminal degrees, 2,448 part-time); student–undergrad faculty ratio is 12:1.
Enrollment Profile: 17,063 students from 52 states and territories, 120 other countries. 59% women, 41% men, 16% part-time, 59% state residents, 8% transferred in, 6% international, 0% Native American, 8% Hispanic, 10% black, 19% Asian or Pacific Islander. *Retention:* 88% of 1995 full-time freshmen returned. *Areas of study chosen:* 22% business management and administrative services, 9% health professions and related sciences, 8%

liberal arts/general studies, 7% performing arts, 6% biological and life sciences, 6% interdisciplinary studies, 5% English language/literature/letters, 5% psychology, 5% social sciences, 4% communications and journalism, 4% fine arts, 4% premed, 3% education, 3% prelaw, 2% computer and information sciences, 1% area and ethnic studies, 1% engineering and applied sciences, 1% foreign language and literature, 1% mathematics, 1% philosophy, 1% physical sciences, 1% predentistry. *Most popular recent majors:* business administration/commerce/management, theater arts/drama, social science.

First-Year Class: 3,090 total; 18,986 applied, 44% were accepted, 37% of whom enrolled. 56% from top 10% of their high school class, 90% from top quarter, 99% from top half. 72 National Merit Scholars, 4 Westinghouse recipients.

Graduation Requirements: 60 credits for associate, 128 credits for bachelor's; computer course for business, math, science majors; internship (some majors); senior project (some majors).

Computers on Campus: 859 computers available on campus for general student use. Computer purchase/lease plans available. A computer is strongly recommended for all students. A campus-wide network can be accessed from student residence rooms and from off-campus. Students can contact faculty members and/or advisers through e-mail. Computers for student use in computer center, computer labs, classrooms, library, student center, dorms provide access to the Internet/World Wide Web, on- and off-campus e-mail addresses. Staffed computer lab on campus (open 24 hours a day) provides training in use of computers, software.

EXPENSES AND FINANCIAL AID

Expenses for 1997–98: *Application fee:* $45. Comprehensive fee of $29,900 includes full-time tuition ($21,730 minimum) and college room and board ($8170). Part-time tuition: $605 per credit. Full-time tuition for students enrolled in the Tisch School of the Arts: $22,840.

Undergraduate Financial Aid: 70% of all full-time undergraduates enrolled in fall 1996 applied for aid; of these, 91% were judged to have need according to Federal Methodology, of whom 98% were aided. On average, 67% of need was met. *Financial aid deadline (priority):* 2/15. *Financial aid forms:* FAFSA required. State form required for some.

LD Program Contact: Ms. Georgeann du Chossois, Coordinator, Access to Learning, New York University, Room 701, 566 LaGuardia Place, New York, NY 10012-1019, 212-998-4980. Fax: 212-995-4114. Email: duchosss@is2.nyu.edu.

NORTH ADAMS STATE COLLEGE

North Adams, Massachusetts

Students with LD	35	Subject-Area Tutoring	✓
ADD services	✓	Special Courses	✓
Staff	5 full-, 1 part-time	Taped Textbooks	✓
Special Fee	None	Alternative Test Arrang.	✓
Diagnostic Testing	✓	Notetakers	✓
Basic Skills Remediation	✓	LD Student Organization	

LEARNING DISABILITIES PROGRAM INFORMATION

The Center for Academic Advancement began offering services in 1982. Currently the program serves 35 undergraduates with LD. Services are also available to graduate students. Students diagnosed with ADD/ADHD are eligible for the same services available to students with LD.

Staff: 5 full-time, 1 part-time staff members, including director, assistant director, coordinators. Services provided by remediation specialist, tutors, counselors, diagnostic specialist.

Special Fees: No special fees are charged for services to students with LD.

Applications and admissions: *Required:* high school transcript, IEP (Individualized Education Program), psychoeducational report completed within 3 years, recent assessment of skills, recent WAIS (may be substituted for SAT/ACT scores); *recommended:* extended time SAT I or ACT, personal interview. Students may begin taking classes in summer only. *Application deadline:* 6/1 (fall term), 1/1 (spring term).

Special policies: The college has written policies regarding substitutions and waivers of admissions, graduation, and degree requirements.

PROGRAM AND SERVICE COMPONENTS

Special preparation or orientation: Optional orientation offered before registration.

Diagnostic testing: Intelligence, reading, math, spelling, written language, study skills, psychoneurology, learning strategies.

Academic advising: Provided by LD staff members, academic advisers. Students with LD may take up to 15 credits each term; most take 10 to 15 credits; 12 credits required to maintain full-time status; 6 credits required to be eligible for financial aid.

Counseling services: Individual counseling, small-group counseling, career counseling.

Basic skills remediation: Offered in class-size groups by regular teachers. Available in reading, math, written language, learning strategies.

Subject-area tutoring: Offered in small groups by peer tutors. Available in some subjects.

Special courses: Composition, learning strategies, math. All offered for credit; all enter into overall grade point average.

Auxiliary aids: Taped textbooks, tape recorders, word-processors with spell-check, personal computers.

Auxiliary services: Alternative test arrangements, notetakers, priority registration, advocacy.

GENERAL COLLEGE INFORMATION

State-supported, comprehensive, coed. Part of Massachusetts Public Higher Education System. Awards bachelor's, master's degrees. Founded 1894. *Setting:* 80-acre small-town campus. *Endowment:* $808,405. *Educational spending 1995–96:* $4804 per undergrad. *Total enrollment:* 1,745. *Undergraduate faculty:* 136 (98 full-time, 75% with terminal degrees, 38 part-time); student–undergrad faculty ratio is 15:1.

Enrollment Profile: 1,617 students from 20 states and territories. 58% women, 42% men, 14% part-time, 80% state residents, 13% transferred in, 1% international, 24% 25 or older, 1% Native American, 1% Hispanic, 3% black, 1% Asian or Pacific Islander. *Retention:* 66% of 1995 full-time freshmen returned. *Areas of study chosen:* 18% business management and administrative services, 16% social sciences, 12% education, 11% psychology, 7% English language/literature/letters, 6% communications and journalism, 5% biological and life sciences, 3% computer and information sciences, 3% interdisciplinary studies, 1% health professions and related sciences, 1% mathematics, 1% philosophy, 1% physical sciences. *Most popular recent majors:* English, sociology, psychology.

First-Year Class: 333 total; 1,433 applied, 68% were accepted, 34% of whom enrolled. 1% from top 10% of their high school class, 20% from top quarter, 61% from top half.

Graduation Requirements: 120 credits; 12 credits of math/science; computer course for business administration, math majors; internship (some majors); senior project (some majors).

Computers on Campus: 200 computers available on campus for general student use. Computer purchase/lease plans available. A campus-wide network can be accessed from student residence rooms and from off-campus. Students can contact faculty members and/or advisers through e-mail. Computers for student

North Adams State College (continued)

use in computer center, computer labs, classrooms, library provide access to the Internet/World Wide Web, on- and off-campus e-mail addresses. Staffed computer lab on campus provides training in use of computers, software.

EXPENSES AND FINANCIAL AID

Expenses for 1997–98: *Application fee:* $10. State resident tuition: $1270 full-time, $52.92 per credit part-time. Nonresident tuition: $5850 full-time, $243.75 per credit part-time. Part-time mandatory fees: $71.67 per credit. Tuition for nonresidents who are eligible for the New England Regional Student Program: $1905 full-time, $79.38 per credit part-time. Full-time mandatory fees: $2167. College room and board: $4901 (minimum). College room only: $2660 (minimum).

Undergraduate Financial Aid: 84% of all full-time undergraduates enrolled in fall 1996 applied for aid; of these, 86% were judged to have need according to Federal Methodology, of whom 100% were aided. On average, 78% of need was met. *Financial aid deadline (priority):* 4/1. *Financial aid forms:* FAFSA, institutional form required.

LD Program Contact: Ms. Claire Smith, Coordinator of Disabled Students, North Adams State College, Church Street, North Adams, MA 01247, 413-662-5318. Fax: 413-663-3300.

OBERLIN COLLEGE

Oberlin, Ohio

Students with LD	125	Subject-Area Tutoring	✓
ADD services	✓	Special Courses	✓
Staff	4 full-, 2 part-time	Taped Textbooks	✓
Special Fee	None	Alternative Test Arrang.	✓
Diagnostic Testing	✓	Notetakers	✓
Basic Skills Remediation	✓	LD Student Organization	✓

LEARNING DISABILITIES PROGRAM INFORMATION

The Learning Assistance Program began offering services in 1983. Currently the program serves 125 undergraduates with LD. Students diagnosed with ADD/ADHD are eligible for the same services available to students with LD, as well as additional counseling and therapy.

Staff: 4 full-time, 2 part-time staff members, including coordinator. Services provided by remediation specialists, tutors, counselors, diagnostic specialist.

Special Fees: No special fees are charged for services to students with LD.

Applications and admissions: *Required:* high school transcript, extracurricular activities, extended time SAT I; *recommended:* high school grade point average, class rank, courses completed, untimed SAT I or extended time ACT, letters of recommendation, psychoeducational report completed within 3 years. Students may begin taking classes in fall only. *Application deadline:* continuous.

Special policies: The college has written policies regarding grade forgiveness.

PROGRAM AND SERVICE COMPONENTS

Special preparation or orientation: Orientation (required for some) held before registration and during registration.

Diagnostic testing: Intelligence, reading, math, spelling, handwriting, written language, motor abilities, perceptual skills, study skills, social skills, learning strategies.

Academic advising: Provided by LD staff members, academic advisers. Students with LD may take up to 16 credit hours each term; most take 12 credit hours; 12 credit hours required to maintain full-time status; 12 credit hours (unless waived) required to be eligible for financial aid.

Counseling services: Individual counseling.

Basic skills remediation: Offered in small groups by LD teachers. Available in reading, math, spelling, written language, learning strategies, perceptual skills, study skills, time management.

Subject-area tutoring: Offered one-on-one and in small groups by professional teachers, peer tutors. Available in most subjects.

Special courses: College survival skills, reading, learning strategies, time management, study skills. Most offered for credit; all enter into overall grade point average.

Auxiliary aids: Taped textbooks, tape recorders, calculators, typewriters, word-processors with spell-check, Arkenstone Reader.

Auxiliary services: Alternative test arrangements, notetakers, advocacy.

Campus support group: A special student organization is available to students with LD.

GENERAL COLLEGE INFORMATION

Independent, 4-year, coed. Awards bachelor's degrees. Founded 1833. *Setting:* 440-acre small-town campus with easy access to Cleveland. *Endowment:* $326.3 million. *Research spending 1995–96:* $529,857. *Educational spending 1995–96:* $9274 per undergrad. *Total enrollment:* 2,861. *Faculty:* 251 (179 full-time, 92% with terminal degrees, 72 part-time); student–undergrad faculty ratio is 12:1.

Enrollment Profile: 2,861 students from 52 states and territories, 53 other countries. 58% women, 42% men, 2% part-time, 9% state residents, 75% live on campus, 2% transferred in, 5% international, 1% 25 or older, 1% Native American, 4% Hispanic, 7% black, 9% Asian or Pacific Islander. *Retention:* 90% of 1995 full-time freshmen returned. *Graduation:* 80% graduate in 6 years. *Areas of study chosen:* 22% social sciences, 18% English language/literature/letters, 17% interdisciplinary studies, 11% biological and life sciences, 6% fine arts, 5% psychology, 4% performing arts, 3% foreign language and literature, 3% theology/religion, 2% area and ethnic studies, 2% computer and information sciences, 2% mathematics, 2% philosophy, 2% physical sciences. *Most popular recent majors:* English, history, biology/biological sciences.

First-Year Class: 671 total; 3,863 applied, 65% were accepted, 27% of whom enrolled. 46% from top 10% of their high school class, 80% from top quarter, 99% from top half. 34 National Merit Scholars, 19 valedictorians.

Graduation Requirements: 112 credit hours; 1 quantitative proficiency certification course or completion of advanced placement calculus exam; internship (some majors); senior project for honors program students.

Computers on Campus: 240 computers available on campus for general student use. Computer purchase/lease plans available. A computer is recommended for all students. A campus-wide network can be accessed from student residence rooms and from off-campus. Students can contact faculty members and/or advisers through e-mail. Computers for student use in computer center, computer labs, classrooms, library, student center, dorms provide access to the Internet/World Wide Web, on- and off-campus e-mail addresses. Staffed computer lab on campus provides training in use of computers, software. *Academic computing expenditure 1995–96:* $1.8 million.

EXPENSES AND FINANCIAL AID

Expenses for 1997–98: *Application fee:* $45. Comprehensive fee of $28,796 includes full-time tuition ($22,282), mandatory fees ($156), and college room and board ($6358). College room only: $3166. Part-time tuition: $930 per credit hour. Part-time mandatory fees: $78 per term.

Undergraduate Financial Aid: 69% of all full-time undergraduates enrolled in fall 1996 applied for aid; of these, 84% were judged to have need according to Federal Methodology, of

whom 100% were aided. On average, 100% of need was met. *Financial aid deadline:* Applications processed continuously. *Financial aid forms:* FAFSA, CSS Financial Aid PROFILE, institutional form required. State form required for some.
LD Program Contact: Dr. Dean Kelly, Coordinator, Disabled Students, Oberlin College, Room 6, Peters Hall, Oberlin, OH 44074-1090, 216-775-8467. Fax: 216-775-6724. Email: pkelly@oberlin.edu.

QUEEN'S UNIVERSITY AT KINGSTON

Kingston, Ontario, Canada

Students with LD	145	Subject-Area Tutoring	✓
ADD services	✓	Special Courses	
Staff	1 full-, 1 part-time	Taped Textbooks	✓
Special Fee	None	Alternative Test Arrang.	✓
Diagnostic Testing	✓	Notetakers	✓
Basic Skills Remediation		LD Student Organization	

LEARNING DISABILITIES PROGRAM INFORMATION

The Student Counselling Service began offering services in 1989. Currently the program serves 145 undergraduates with LD. Services are also available to graduate students. Students diagnosed with ADD/ADHD are eligible for the same services available to students with LD.
Staff: 1 full-time, 1 part-time staff members, including coordinator. Services provided by tutors, counselors, diagnostic specialists.
Special Fees: No special fees are charged for services to students with LD.
Applications and admissions: *Required:* high school transcript; *recommended:* psychoeducational report. Students may begin taking classes in fall only.

PROGRAM AND SERVICE COMPONENTS

Diagnostic testing: Intelligence, reading, math, spelling, handwriting, written language, perceptual skills, personality, learning strategies.
Academic advising: Provided by academic advisers. Most students with LD take 3 to 4 courses each term; 3 courses required to maintain full-time status and be eligible for financial aid.
Counseling services: Individual counseling, small-group counseling, career counseling, self-advocacy training.
Subject-area tutoring: Offered one-on-one by peer tutors. Available in most subjects.
Auxiliary aids: Taped textbooks, tape recorders, word-processors with spell-check, personal computers, talking computers, optical character readers.
Auxiliary services: Alternative test arrangements, notetakers, priority registration, advocacy, scribes, notetakers.

GENERAL COLLEGE INFORMATION

Province-supported, coed. Awards bachelor's, master's, doctoral degrees. Founded 1841. *Setting:* 160-acre urban campus. *Endowment:* $113.5 million. *Research spending 1995–96:* $45.5 million. *Educational spending 1995–96:* $5221 per undergrad. *Total enrollment:* 16,662. *Faculty:* 1,164 (965 full-time, 199 part-time); student–undergrad faculty ratio is 15:1.
Enrollment Profile: 14,162 students from 12 provinces and territories, 80 other countries.
First-Year Class: 2,550 total; 17,085 applied, 47% were accepted, 32% of whom enrolled.
Graduation Requirements: 15 courses; computer course for math, geological science with physics, biochemistry, mathematical physics, statistics, applied science, commerce majors.
Computers on Campus: 500 computers available on campus for general student use. Computer purchase/lease plans available. A computer is recommended for some students. A campus-wide network can be accessed from student residence rooms and from off-campus. Students can contact faculty members and/or advisers through e-mail. Computers for student use in computer labs, various locations provide access to the Internet/World Wide Web, on- and off-campus e-mail addresses. Staffed computer lab on campus (open 24 hours a day) provides training in use of computers, software. *Academic computing expenditure 1995–96:* $3.3 million.

EXPENSES AND FINANCIAL AID

Expenses for 1997–98: *Application fee:* $75. Canadian resident tuition: $3228 (minimum) full-time, $645.60 per course part-time. Nonresident tuition: $9717 (minimum) full-time. Nonresident part-time tuition per course ranges from $1943 to $3168. Part-time mandatory fees: $20 per course (minimum). Full-time tuition ranges up to $3505 for Canadian residents, $15,842 for nonresidents, according to program. (All figures are in Canadian dollars.). Full-time mandatory fees: $502. College room and board: $5586. College room only: $3080.
Undergraduate Financial Aid: 34% of all full-time undergraduates enrolled in fall 1996 applied for aid; of these, 94% were judged to have need according to Federal Methodology, of whom 100% were aided. *Financial aid deadline:* Applications processed continuously. *Financial aid forms:* FAFSA, state form, institutional form required; CSS Financial Aid PROFILE acceptable.
LD Program Contact: Mr. Mike Condra, Director, Queen's University at Kingston, St. Lawrence Building, Kingston, ON K7L 3N6, Canada, 613-545-6000. Fax: 613-545-6740. Email: condram@post.queensu.ca.

REGIS UNIVERSITY

Denver, Colorado

Students with LD	50	Subject-Area Tutoring	✓
ADD services	✓	Special Courses	✓
Staff	2 full-, 2 part-time	Taped Textbooks	✓
Special Fee	✓	Alternative Test Arrang.	✓
Diagnostic Testing		Notetakers	✓
Basic Skills Remediation	✓	LD Student Organization	

LEARNING DISABILITIES PROGRAM INFORMATION

The Commitment Program began offering services in 1976. Currently the program serves 50 undergraduates with LD. Students diagnosed with ADD/ADHD are eligible for the same services available to students with LD.
Staff: 2 full-time, 2 part-time staff members, including director, assistant director, tutoring coordinator. Services provided by tutors, instructors.
Special Fees: $1300 per year.
Applications and admissions: *Required:* high school transcript, grade point average, courses completed, extracurricular activities, untimed or extended time SAT I, autobiographical statement, letters of recommendation; *recommended:* untimed or extended time ACT, psychoeducational report completed within 3 years. Students may begin taking classes in fall or spring. *Application deadline:* continuous.
Special policies: The college has written policies regarding substitutions and waivers of degree requirements.

PROGRAM AND SERVICE COMPONENTS

Special preparation or orientation: Required orientation held before registration.

Regis University (continued)

Academic advising: Provided by LD staff members, academic advisers. Students with LD may take up to 16 semester hours each term; most take 12 to 13 semester hours; 12 semester hours required to maintain full-time status and be eligible for financial aid.

Counseling services: Individual counseling, career counseling.

Basic skills remediation: Offered in small groups by Learning Center instructors. Available in reading, math, written language, learning strategies, study skills.

Subject-area tutoring: Offered one-on-one and in small groups by peer tutors. Available in all subjects.

Special courses: Reading, vocabulary development, composition, learning strategies, math, study skills. All offered for credit; all enter into overall grade point average.

Auxiliary aids: Taped textbooks, tape recorders, calculators, typewriters, word-processors with spell-check.

Auxiliary services: Alternative test arrangements, notetakers, priority registration, advocacy.

GENERAL COLLEGE INFORMATION

Independent Roman Catholic (Jesuit), comprehensive, coed. Awards bachelor's, master's degrees. Founded 1877. *Setting:* 90-acre suburban campus. *Endowment:* $16.3 million. *Total enrollment:* 7,039. *Undergraduate faculty:* 109 (69 full-time, 93% with terminal degrees, 40 part-time); student–undergrad faculty ratio is 16:1.

Enrollment Profile: 1,160 students: 56% women, 44% men, 5% part-time, 62% state residents, 9% transferred in, 4% international, 11% 25 or older, 1% Native American, 9% Hispanic, 2% black, 3% Asian or Pacific Islander. *Retention:* 79% of 1995 full-time freshmen returned. *Graduation:* 33% graduate in 4 years, 40% in 5 years, 46% in 6 years. *Most popular recent majors:* nursing, business administration/commerce/management, communication.

First-Year Class: 224 total; 919 applied, 89% were accepted, 27% of whom enrolled. 12 class presidents, 12 valedictorians.

Graduation Requirements: 128 semester hours; 1 course each in math and lab science; proven competence in a foreign language at the intermediate level; computer course for business administration, accounting, economics majors; senior project.

Computers on Campus: 300 computers available on campus for general student use. Computer purchase/lease plans available. A computer is recommended for some students. A campus-wide network can be accessed from student residence rooms and from off-campus. Students can contact faculty members and/or advisers through e-mail. Computers for student use in computer center, computer labs, research center, learning resource center, classrooms, library, student center, dorms, student rooms provide access to the Internet/World Wide Web, on-campus e-mail addresses. Staffed computer lab on campus (open 24 hours a day) provides training in use of computers, software. *Academic computing expenditure 1995–96:* $265,833.

EXPENSES AND FINANCIAL AID

Expenses for 1997–98: *Application fee:* $40. Comprehensive fee of $20,870 includes full-time tuition ($14,900), mandatory fees ($70), and college room and board ($5900). College room only: $3200. Part-time tuition: $465 per semester hour. Part-time mandatory fees: $50 per semester.

Undergraduate Financial Aid: 74% of all full-time undergraduates enrolled in fall 1996 applied for aid; of these, 85% were judged to have need according to Federal Methodology, of whom 98% were aided. On average, 79% of need was met. *Financial aid deadline (priority):* 3/5. *Financial aid forms:* FAFSA required. State form, institutional form required for some.

LD Program Contact: Mr. H. Greg Miller, Admissions Officer, Regis University, 3333 Regis Boulevard, Denver, CO 80221-1099, 303-458-4900.

REINHARDT COLLEGE

Waleska, Georgia

Students with LD	55	Subject-Area Tutoring	✓
ADD services	✓	Special Courses	
Staff	4 full-time	Taped Textbooks	✓
Special Fee	Varies	Alternative Test Arrang.	✓
Diagnostic Testing		Notetakers	✓
Basic Skills Remediation		LD Student Organization	

LEARNING DISABILITIES PROGRAM INFORMATION

The Academic Support Office began offering services in 1982. Currently the program serves 55 undergraduates with LD. Students diagnosed with ADD/ADHD are eligible for the same services available to students with LD.

Staff: 4 full-time staff members, including director. Services provided by counselors.

Special Fees: Range from $1350 to $4050 per year.

Applications and admissions: *Required:* high school transcript, grade point average, class rank, courses completed, IEP (Individualized Education Program), untimed SAT I, personal interview, letters of recommendation, psychoeducational report completed within 3 years, on-site essay, application supplement; *recommended:* high school extracurricular activities, extended time SAT I or ACT. Students may begin taking classes in fall, winter, or spring. *Application deadline:* continuous.

PROGRAM AND SERVICE COMPONENTS

Special preparation or orientation: Required orientation held after classes begin.

Academic advising: Provided by LD staff members. Students with LD may take up to 17 quarter hours each term; most take 12 to 17 quarter hours; 12 quarter hours required to maintain full-time status and be eligible for financial aid.

Counseling services: Individual counseling.

Subject-area tutoring: Offered one-on-one and in small groups by professional teachers. Available in most subjects.

Auxiliary aids: Taped textbooks, word-processors with spell-check, personal computers, optical character readers.

Auxiliary services: Alternative test arrangements, notetakers, priority registration, advocacy.

GENERAL COLLEGE INFORMATION

Independent, 4-year, coed, affiliated with United Methodist Church. Awards associate, bachelor's degrees. Founded 1883. *Setting:* 600-acre rural campus with easy access to Atlanta. *Endowment:* $32.3 million. *Educational spending 1995–96:* $2597 per undergrad. *Total enrollment:* 959. *Faculty:* 48 (32 full-time, 38% with terminal degrees, 16 part-time); student–undergrad faculty ratio is 18:1.

Enrollment Profile: 959 students from 10 states and territories, 16 other countries. 60% women, 40% men, 16% part-time, 95% state residents, 6% transferred in, 3% international, 20% 25 or older, 1% Native American, 1% Hispanic, 3% black, 1% Asian or Pacific Islander. *Retention:* 60% of 1995 full-time freshmen returned. *Areas of study chosen:* 26% liberal arts/general studies, 24% business management and administrative services, 12% education, 7% biological and life sciences, 4% fine arts, 3% health professions and related sciences, 1% mathematics, 1% prelaw. *Most popular recent majors:* liberal arts/general studies, business administration/commerce/management, science.

First-Year Class: 271 total; 476 applied, 83% were accepted, 68% of whom enrolled. 9% from top 10% of their high school class, 30% from top quarter, 63% from top half. 5 class presidents.
Graduation Requirements: 97 quarter hours for associate, 197 quarter hours for bachelor's; 10 quarter hours each of math and science; computer course for business majors; internship (some majors).
Computers on Campus: 90 computers available on campus for general student use. A campus-wide network can be accessed. Students can contact faculty members and/or advisers through e-mail. Computers for student use in computer center, computer labs, classrooms, library provide access to the Internet/World Wide Web. Staffed computer lab on campus provides training in use of computers, software. *Academic computing expenditure 1995–96:* $149,133.

EXPENSES AND FINANCIAL AID

Expenses for 1997–98: *Application fee:* $15. Comprehensive fee of $11,235 includes full-time tuition ($6762) and college room and board ($4473). Part-time tuition: $138 per quarter hour.
Undergraduate Financial Aid: 95% of all full-time undergraduates enrolled in fall 1996 applied for aid. On average, 100% of need was met. *Financial aid deadline (priority):* 5/1. *Financial aid forms:* state form, institutional form required; CSS Financial Aid PROFILE acceptable. FAFSA required for some.
LD Program Contact: Ms. Sylvia Robertson, Director, Academic Support Office, Reinhardt College, 7300 Reinhardt College Parkway, Waleska, GA 30183, 770-720-5567. Fax: 770-720-5602. Email: srr@mail.reinhardt.edu.

ROCHESTER INSTITUTE OF TECHNOLOGY

Rochester, New York

Students with LD	360	Subject-Area Tutoring	✓
ADD services	✓	Special Courses	✓
Staff	1 full-time	Taped Textbooks	✓
Special Fee	Varies	Alternative Test Arrang.	✓
Diagnostic Testing	✓	Notetakers	✓
Basic Skills Remediation	✓	LD Student Organization	✓

LEARNING DISABILITIES PROGRAM INFORMATION

The Learning Development Center's Alternative Learning Department (ALD) began offering services in 1983. Currently the program serves 360 undergraduates with LD. Services are also available to graduate students. Students diagnosed with ADD/ADHD are eligible for the same services available to students with LD.
Staff: 1 full-time staff member (Chair). Services provided by remediation specialists, tutors, counselor, diagnostic specialists, LD specialist, math instructor, academic coordinator.
Special Fees: Range from $280 to $840 per year. $250 for diagnostic testing.
Applications and admissions: *Required:* psychoeducational report. Students may begin taking classes any term. *Application deadline:* continuous.
Special policies: The college has written policies regarding grade forgiveness; substitutions and waivers of admissions, graduation, and degree requirements.

PROGRAM AND SERVICE COMPONENTS

Special preparation or orientation: Optional summer program offered prior to entering college.
Diagnostic testing: Intelligence, reading, math, spelling, handwriting, written language, perceptual skills, study skills, personality, learning strategies.
Academic advising: Provided by LD staff members, academic advisers. Most students with LD take 12 quarter credits each term; 12 quarter credits required to maintain full-time status and be eligible for financial aid.
Counseling services: Individual counseling, small-group counseling, career counseling, self-advocacy training, workshops.
Basic skills remediation: Offered one-on-one, in small groups, and in class-size groups by LD teachers, regular teachers, developmental specialist. Available in reading, math, spelling, spoken language, written language, learning strategies, motor abilities, study skills, time management, speech, problem solving.
Subject-area tutoring: Offered one-on-one and in small groups by peer tutors. Available in all subjects.
Special courses: College survival skills, reading, vocabulary development, communication skills, composition, learning strategies, time management, math, personal psychology, study skills, career planning, transition workshop. None offered for credit.
Auxiliary aids: Taped textbooks, tape recorders, calculators, typewriters, word-processors with spell-check, optical character readers, spelling calculator.
Auxiliary services: Alternative test arrangements, notetakers, advocacy.
Campus support group: A special student organization is available to students with LD.

GENERAL COLLEGE INFORMATION

Independent, comprehensive, coed. Awards associate, bachelor's, master's, doctoral degrees. Founded 1829. *Setting:* 1,300-acre suburban campus with easy access to Buffalo. *Endowment:* $292.1 million. *Research spending 1995–96:* $10 million. *Total enrollment:* 12,933. *Faculty:* 1,076 (676 full-time, 75% with terminal degrees, 400 part-time); student–undergrad faculty ratio is 13:1.
Enrollment Profile: 10,755 students from 50 states and territories, 70 other countries. 34% women, 66% men, 25% part-time, 60% state residents, 60% live on campus, 33% transferred in, 5% international, 29% 25 or older, 1% Native American, 3% Hispanic, 5% black, 5% Asian or Pacific Islander. *Retention:* 86% of 1995 full-time freshmen returned. *Graduation:* 61% graduate in 6 years. *Areas of study chosen:* 30% engineering and applied sciences, 20% fine arts, 13% business management and administrative services, 13% interdisciplinary studies, 6% computer and information sciences, 5% biological and life sciences, 3% premed, 3% social sciences, 2% physical sciences, 2% prelaw, 1% communications and journalism, 1% health professions and related sciences, 1% mathematics. *Most popular recent majors:* engineering (general), engineering technology, art/fine arts.
First-Year Class: 1,774 total; 5,924 applied, 76% were accepted, 39% of whom enrolled. 27% from top 10% of their high school class, 61% from top quarter, 87% from top half. 8 National Merit Scholars, 20 valedictorians.
Graduation Requirements: 90 credit hours for associate, 180 credit hours for bachelor's; computer course for most majors; internship (some majors); senior project (some majors).
Computers on Campus: 800 computers available on campus for general student use. Computer purchase/lease plans available. A computer is recommended for some students. A campus-wide network can be accessed from student residence rooms and from off-campus. Students can contact faculty members and/or advisers through e-mail. Computers for student use in computer center, computer labs, classrooms, library, dorms provide access to the Internet/World Wide Web, on- and off-campus e-mail

Rochester Institute of Technology (continued)

addresses, course registration and student account information. Staffed computer lab on campus provides training in use of computers, software. *Academic computing expenditure 1995–96:* $1.8 million.

EXPENSES AND FINANCIAL AID

Expenses for 1997–98: *Application fee:* $40. Comprehensive fee of $22,776 includes full-time tuition ($16,083), mandatory fees ($276), and college room and board ($6417). College room only: $3486. Part-time tuition: $384 per credit hour. Part-time mandatory fees: $19 per quarter.
Undergraduate Financial Aid: 71% of all full-time undergraduates enrolled in fall 1996 applied for aid; of these, 95% were judged to have need according to Federal Methodology, of whom 100% were aided. *Financial aid deadline (priority):* 3/15. *Financial aid forms:* FAFSA required. State form, institutional form required for some.
Financial aid specifically for students with LD: Scholarship: Bennett Scholarship.
LD Program Contact: Ms. Jacqueline Lynch Czamanske, Chair for LDC-ALD, Rochester Institute of Technology, One Lomb Memorial Drive, Rochester, NY 14623-5604, 716-475-2215.

ROOSEVELT UNIVERSITY

Chicago, Illinois

Students with LD	23	Subject-Area Tutoring	✓
ADD services	✓	Special Courses	
Staff	1 full-, 2 part-time	Taped Textbooks	✓
Special Fee	✓	Alternative Test Arrang.	✓
Diagnostic Testing		Notetakers	✓
Basic Skills Remediation	✓	LD Student Organization	

LEARNING DISABILITIES PROGRAM INFORMATION

The Learning and Support Services Program (LSSP) began offering services in 1980. Currently the program serves 23 undergraduates with LD. Services are also available to graduate students. Students diagnosed with ADD/ADHD are eligible for the same services available to students with LD.
Staff: 1 full-time, 2 part-time staff members, including director, assistant director. Services provided by remediation specialists.
Special Fees: $2000 per year.
Applications and admissions: *Required:* high school transcript, grade point average, courses completed, IEP (Individualized Education Program), extended time SAT I, psychoeducational report completed within 3 years, documentation of learning disability; *recommended:* untimed SAT I or ACT. Students may begin taking classes any term. *Application deadline:* continuous.
Special policies: The college has written policies regarding substitutions and waivers of admissions requirements.

PROGRAM AND SERVICE COMPONENTS

Special preparation or orientation: Required orientation held before registration and during registration.
Academic advising: Provided by LD staff members, academic advisers. Students with LD may take up to 15 semester hours each term; most take 9 semester hours; 12 semester hours required to maintain full-time status; 6 semester hours required to be eligible for financial aid.
Counseling services: Individual counseling, small-group counseling, career counseling.
Basic skills remediation: Offered one-on-one by LD teachers. Available in reading, math, spelling, handwriting, spoken language, written language, learning strategies, perceptual skills, study skills, time management, social skills.
Subject-area tutoring: Offered one-on-one by professional teachers. Available in all subjects.
Auxiliary aids: Taped textbooks, tape recorders, typewriters, word-processors with spell-check, personal computers.
Auxiliary services: Alternative test arrangements, notetakers, advocacy.

GENERAL COLLEGE INFORMATION

Independent, comprehensive, coed. Awards bachelor's, master's, doctoral degrees. Founded 1945. *Setting:* urban campus. *Total enrollment:* 6,663. *Faculty:* 530 (165 full-time, 80% with terminal degrees, 365 part-time); student–undergrad faculty ratio is 13:1.
Enrollment Profile: 4,279 students from 20 states and territories, 65 other countries. 62% women, 38% men, 65% part-time, 95% state residents, 5% live on campus, 18% transferred in, 74% 25 or older, 1% Native American, 9% Hispanic, 27% black, 4% Asian or Pacific Islander. *Retention:* 45% of 1995 full-time freshmen returned. *Areas of study chosen:* 30% business management and administrative services, 27% social sciences, 11% computer and information sciences, 8% education, 7% performing arts, 5% communications and journalism, 5% liberal arts/general studies, 2% biological and life sciences, 2% English language/literature/letters, 1% health professions and related sciences, 1% mathematics, 1% physical sciences. *Most popular recent majors:* accounting, social science, psychology.
First-Year Class: 235 total; 750 applied, 92% were accepted, 34% of whom enrolled. 15% from top 10% of their high school class, 35% from top quarter, 65% from top half.
Graduation Requirements: 120 semester hours; computer course for business, public administration majors; internship (some majors); senior project (some majors).
Computers on Campus: 180 computers available on campus for general student use. Computer purchase/lease plans available. A computer is recommended for all students. A campus-wide network can be accessed from off-campus. Students can contact faculty members and/or advisers through e-mail. Computers for student use in computer center, computer labs, learning resource center, library provide access to the Internet/World Wide Web, on- and off-campus e-mail addresses. Staffed computer lab on campus provides training in use of computers, software.

EXPENSES AND FINANCIAL AID

Expenses for 1997–98: *Application fee:* $25. Comprehensive fee of $16,530 includes full-time tuition ($10,830), mandatory fees ($200), and college room and board ($5500). Part-time tuition: $361 per semester hour. Part-time mandatory fees: $100 per semester.
Undergraduate Financial Aid: *Financial aid deadline (priority):* 5/1. *Financial aid forms:* FAFSA required; CSS Financial Aid PROFILE acceptable.
LD Program Contact: Ms. Nancy Litke, Director, Learning and Support Services Program, Roosevelt University, 430 South Michigan Avenue, Chicago, IL 60605-1394, 312-341-3810.

SAINT MARY'S UNIVERSITY

Halifax, Nova Scotia, Canada

Students with LD	60	Subject-Area Tutoring	✓
ADD services	✓	Special Courses	
Staff	1 full-, 2 part-time	Taped Textbooks	✓
Special Fee	None	Alternative Test Arrang.	✓
Diagnostic Testing		Notetakers	✓
Basic Skills Remediation	✓	LD Student Organization	

LEARNING DISABILITIES PROGRAM INFORMATION

The Learning Disabilities Support Program with the Atlantic Centre began offering services in 1990. Currently the program serves 60 undergraduates with LD. Services are also available to graduate students. Students diagnosed with ADD/ADHD are eligible for the same services available to students with LD.

Staff: 1 full-time, 2 part-time staff members, including director, coordinator. Services provided by counselors.

Special Fees: No special fees are charged for services to students with LD.

Applications and admissions: *Required:* high school transcript, courses completed, personal interview, letters of recommendation, psychoeducational report. Students may begin taking classes any term. *Application deadline:* continuous.

PROGRAM AND SERVICE COMPONENTS

Special preparation or orientation: Required orientation held before registration.

Academic advising: Provided by LD staff members. Students with LD may take up to 5 courses each term; most take 3 to 4 courses; 3 courses required to maintain full-time status.

Counseling services: Individual counseling, career counseling, self-advocacy training.

Basic skills remediation: Offered one-on-one by LD counsellor. Available in reading, learning strategies, study skills, time management, computer skills.

Subject-area tutoring: Offered one-on-one and in small groups by professional teachers, peer tutors. Available in most subjects.

Auxiliary aids: Taped textbooks, tape recorders, calculators, typewriters, word-processors with spell-check, personal computers, talking computers, optical character readers.

Auxiliary services: Alternative test arrangements, notetakers, priority registration, advocacy.

GENERAL COLLEGE INFORMATION

Province-supported, comprehensive, coed. Awards bachelor's, master's degrees. Founded 1802. *Setting:* 30-acre urban campus. *Total enrollment:* 7,019. *Faculty:* 492 (205 full-time, 90% with terminal degrees, 287 part-time); student–undergrad faculty ratio is 13:1.

Enrollment Profile: 6,616 students from 12 provinces and territories, 48 other countries. 50% women, 50% men, 29% part-time, 86% province residents, 6% transferred in, 4% international, 31% 25 or older. *Areas of study chosen:* 29% business management and administrative services, 23% liberal arts/general studies, 5% social sciences, 4% psychology, 3% biological and life sciences, 3% engineering and applied sciences, 3% English language/literature/letters, 2% computer and information sciences, 2% physical sciences, 1% education, 1% foreign language and literature, 1% mathematics.

First-Year Class: 1,678 total.

Graduation Requirements: 15 courses; computer course for math, business administration majors; internship (some majors); senior project for honors program students and some majors.

Computers on Campus: 500 computers available on campus for general student use. A campus-wide network can be accessed from student residence rooms and from off-campus. Students can contact faculty members and/or advisers through e-mail. Computers for student use in computer center, computer labs provide access to the Internet/World Wide Web, on- and off-campus e-mail addresses. Staffed computer lab on campus provides training in use of computers, software.

EXPENSES AND FINANCIAL AID

Expenses for 1997–98: *Application fee:* $30. Canadian resident tuition: $3635 full-time, $727 per course part-time. Nonresident tuition: $6785 full-time, $1357 per course part-time. Part-time mandatory fees: $19 per semester. (All figures are in Canadian dollars.). Full-time mandatory fees: $108. College room and board: $3920 (minimum).

Undergraduate Financial Aid: On average, 80% of need was met. *Financial aid deadline (priority):* 5/25. *Financial aid forms:* institutional form required; FAFSA, CSS Financial Aid PROFILE acceptable. State form required for some.

LD Program Contact: Mr. Keith Bain, Coordinator, Saint Mary's University, c/o Atlantic Centre, Halifax, NS B3H 3C3, Canada, 902-496-8741. Fax: 902-496-8122. Email: keith.bain@stmarys.ca.

ST. THOMAS AQUINAS COLLEGE

Sparkill, New York

Students with LD	85	Subject-Area Tutoring	
ADD services	✓	Special Courses	✓
Staff	5 full-, 7 part-time	Taped Textbooks	✓
Special Fee	✓	Alternative Test Arrang.	✓
Diagnostic Testing	✓	Notetakers	✓
Basic Skills Remediation		LD Student Organization	✓

LEARNING DISABILITIES PROGRAM INFORMATION

The Saint Thomas Aquinas College (STAC) Exchange began offering services in 1981. Currently the program serves 85 undergraduates with LD. Services are also available to graduate students. Students diagnosed with ADD/ADHD are eligible for the same services available to students with LD, as well as self-confidence seminars, drug therapy discussions.

Staff: 5 full-time, 7 part-time staff members, including director. Services provided by diagnostic specialists, mentor-counselor.

Special Fees: $3000 per year.

Applications and admissions: *Required:* high school transcript, courses completed, extracurricular activities, personal interview, autobiographical statement, letters of recommendation, psychoeducational report completed within 1 year; *recommended:* high school grade point average, IEP (Individualized Education Program), extended time SAT I or ACT. Students may begin taking classes in summer only. *Application deadline:* continuous.

Special policies: The college has written policies regarding grade forgiveness.

PROGRAM AND SERVICE COMPONENTS

Special preparation or orientation: Required summer program offered prior to entering college. Required orientation held during summer prior to enrollment (1-week program).

Diagnostic testing: Intelligence, spoken language, personality, social skills, learning strategies, career interests.

Academic advising: Provided by LD staff members, academic advisers. Students with LD may take up to 16 credits each term; most take 15 credits; 12 credits required to maintain full-time status and be eligible for financial aid.

Counseling services: Individual counseling, small-group counseling, career counseling, self-advocacy training, self-assessment inventories/strategies for enhancing self-image.

Special courses: College survival skills, communication skills, composition, learning strategies, word processing, Internet use, time management, typing, personal psychology, study skills, career planning, stress management; seminars are also available in college survival skills, perceptual skills, spoken language, written language, work skills, social skills, listening skills and non-verbal communication skills. None offered for credit.

Auxiliary aids: Taped textbooks, tape recorders, calculators, typewriters, word-processors with spell-check, personal computers, talking computers, spellers/thesaurus.
Auxiliary services: Alternative test arrangements, notetakers, priority registration, advocacy, scribes.
Campus support group: A special student organization is available to students with LD.

GENERAL COLLEGE INFORMATION

Independent, comprehensive, coed. Awards bachelor's, master's degrees. Founded 1952. *Setting:* 46-acre suburban campus with easy access to New York City. *Total enrollment:* 2,100. *Undergraduate faculty:* 115 (70 full-time, 75% with terminal degrees, 45 part-time); student–undergrad faculty ratio is 17:1.
Enrollment Profile: 1,500 students from 14 states and territories, 7 other countries. 60% women, 40% men, 30% part-time, 68% state residents, 34% live on campus, 40% transferred in, 2% international, 19% 25 or older, 1% Native American, 12% Hispanic, 6% black, 4% Asian or Pacific Islander. *Retention:* 74% of 1995 full-time freshmen returned. *Most popular recent majors:* education, business administration/commerce/management, psychology.
First-Year Class: 262 total; 1,100 applied, 71% were accepted, 34% of whom enrolled. 15% from top 10% of their high school class, 30% from top quarter, 90% from top half. 2 National Merit Scholars, 8 class presidents, 1 valedictorian.
Graduation Requirements: 120 credits; 1 semester each of math and science; 1 year of a foreign language; computer course; internship (some majors); senior project (some majors).
Computers on Campus: 170 computers available on campus for general student use. A computer is recommended for all students. A campus-wide network can be accessed from student residence rooms and from off-campus. Students can contact faculty members and/or advisers through e-mail. Computers for student use in computer labs, library, student rooms, academic counseling center provide access to the Internet/World Wide Web, on- and off-campus e-mail addresses. Staffed computer lab on campus provides training in use of computers, software.

EXPENSES AND FINANCIAL AID

Estimated Expenses for 1997–98: *Application fee:* $25. Comprehensive fee of $16,900 includes full-time tuition ($10,200), mandatory fees ($200), and college room and board ($6500). College room only: $3600. Part-time tuition: $350 per credit. Part-time mandatory fees: $50 per term.
Undergraduate Financial Aid: *Financial aid deadline (priority):* 2/15. *Financial aid forms:* FAFSA, institutional form required.
Financial aid specifically for students with LD: Scholarship: Mooney Scholarship.
LD Program Contact: Dr. Marijanet Doonan, Director of The STAC Exchange, St. Thomas Aquinas College, Route 340, Sparkill, NY 10976, 914-398-4230. Fax: 914-359-9537.

SCHREINER COLLEGE

Kerrville, Texas

Students with LD	95	Subject-Area Tutoring	✓
ADD services	✓	Special Courses	
Staff	4 full-, 25 part-time	Taped Textbooks	✓
Special Fee	Varies	Alternative Test Arrang.	✓
Diagnostic Testing		Notetakers	✓
Basic Skills Remediation		LD Student Organization	

LEARNING DISABILITIES PROGRAM INFORMATION

The Learning Support Services began offering services in 1978. Currently the program serves 95 undergraduates with LD. Students diagnosed with ADD/ADHD are eligible for the same services available to students with LD.
Staff: 4 full-time, 25 part-time staff members, including director, coordinator, administrative assistants. Services provided by tutors, counselor.
Special Fees: Range from $2850 to $3750 per year.
Applications and admissions: *Required:* high school transcript, grade point average, class rank, personal interview, psychoeducational report completed within 1 year, statement of disability, WAIS-R, individually administered achievement tests; *recommended:* extended time SAT I or ACT. Students may begin taking classes in fall only. *Application deadline:* 4/1.
Special policies: The college has written policies regarding substitutions and waivers of admissions, graduation, and degree requirements.

PROGRAM AND SERVICE COMPONENTS

Special preparation or orientation: Required orientation held before registration.
Academic advising: Provided by LD staff members, academic advisers. Students with LD may take up to 15 credit hours each term; most take 12 credit hours; 12 credit hours required to maintain full-time status and be eligible for financial aid.
Counseling services: Individual counseling, career counseling.
Subject-area tutoring: Offered one-on-one and in small groups by professional teachers, peer tutors, tutors with Bachelor's degrees. Available in all subjects.
Auxiliary aids: Taped textbooks, word-processors with spell-check.
Auxiliary services: Alternative test arrangements, notetakers, advocacy.

GENERAL COLLEGE INFORMATION

Independent Presbyterian, 4-year, coed. Awards associate, bachelor's degrees. Founded 1923. *Setting:* 175-acre small-town campus with easy access to San Antonio. *Endowment:* $7 million. *Educational spending 1995–96:* $3361 per undergrad. *Total enrollment:* 675. *Faculty:* 56 (40 full-time, 71% with terminal degrees, 16 part-time); student–undergrad faculty ratio is 13:1.
Enrollment Profile: 675 students from 12 states and territories, 10 other countries. 56% women, 44% men, 17% part-time, 86% state residents, 11% transferred in, 8% international, 26% 25 or older, 0% Native American, 15% Hispanic, 3% black, 1% Asian or Pacific Islander. *Retention:* 69% of 1995 full-time freshmen returned. *Areas of study chosen:* 35% business management and administrative services, 15% education, 10% biological and life sciences, 10% health professions and related sciences, 7% English language/literature/letters, 7% psychology, 3% engineering and applied sciences, 3% premed, 2% fine arts, 2% mathematics, 2% philosophy, 2% prelaw, 1% liberal arts/general studies, 1% theology/religion. *Most popular recent majors:* business administration/commerce/management, mathematics, psychology.
First-Year Class: 202 total; 641 applied, 80% were accepted, 39% of whom enrolled. 20% from top 10% of their high school class, 45% from top quarter, 80% from top half.
Graduation Requirements: 64 credit hours for associate, 128 credit hours for bachelor's; math/science requirements vary according to program; 9 credit hours of a foreign language; computer course; internship (some majors); senior project.
Computers on Campus: 32 computers available on campus for general student use. Computers for student use in computer labs, learning resource center, classrooms. Staffed computer lab on campus provides training in use of computers, software.

EXPENSES AND FINANCIAL AID

Expenses for 1996–97: *Application fee:* $20. Comprehensive fee of $16,791 includes full-time tuition ($10,095), mandatory fees ($40), and college room and board ($6656). College room only: $3040. Part-time tuition: $310 per credit hour.

Undergraduate Financial Aid: *Financial aid deadline (priority):* 4/15. *Financial aid forms:* FAFSA required for some.

Financial aid specifically for students with LD: Scholarships.

LD Program Contact: Mr. Charles Tait, Senior Associate Director of Admissions, Schreiner College, 2100 Memorial Boulevard, Kerrville, TX 78028, 210-896-5411. Fax: 210-896-3232.

SOUTHERN ILLINOIS UNIVERSITY AT CARBONDALE

Carbondale, Illinois

Students with LD	175	Subject-Area Tutoring	✓
ADD services	✓	Special Courses	✓
Staff	5 full-, 15 part-time	Taped Textbooks	✓
Special Fee	Varies	Alternative Test Arrang.	✓
Diagnostic Testing	✓	Notetakers	✓
Basic Skills Remediation	✓	LD Student Organization	

LEARNING DISABILITIES PROGRAM INFORMATION

The Achieve Program began offering services in 1978. Currently the program serves 175 undergraduates with LD. Services are also available to graduate students. Students diagnosed with ADD/ADHD are eligible for the same services available to students with LD.

Staff: 5 full-time, 15 part-time staff members, including coordinator, assistant coordinators. Services provided by remediation specialists, tutors, counselors, diagnostic specialists, graduate students.

Special Fees: Range from $925 to $1850 per year. $1000 for diagnostic testing.

Applications and admissions: *Required:* high school transcript, grade point average, class rank, untimed or extended time ACT, extended time SAT I, program application. Students may begin taking classes in fall or spring. *Application deadline:* continuous.

Special policies: The college has written policies regarding substitutions and waivers of graduation requirements.

PROGRAM AND SERVICE COMPONENTS

Special preparation or orientation: Required orientation held one week before classes begin.

Diagnostic testing: Intelligence, reading, math, spelling, handwriting, spoken language, written language, motor abilities, perceptual skills, psychoneurology, speech, hearing, learning strategies.

Academic advising: Provided by academic advisers. Most students with LD take 15 to 16 semester hours each term; 12 semester hours required to maintain full-time status and be eligible for financial aid.

Counseling services: Individual counseling, small-group counseling, career counseling.

Basic skills remediation: Offered one-on-one by LD staff. Available in reading, math, spelling, written language, learning strategies, study skills, time management.

Subject-area tutoring: Offered one-on-one by peer tutors. Available in all subjects.

Special courses: Composition. None offered for credit.

Auxiliary aids: Taped textbooks, tape recorders, calculators, word-processors with spell-check.

Auxiliary services: Alternative test arrangements, notetakers, priority registration, advocacy.

GENERAL COLLEGE INFORMATION

State-supported, coed. Part of Southern Illinois University. Awards associate, bachelor's, master's, doctoral, first professional degrees. Founded 1869. *Setting:* 1,128-acre small-town campus. *Endowment:* $25.5 million. *Research spending 1995–96:* $31.7 million. *Educational spending 1995–96:* $5761 per undergrad. *Total enrollment:* 21,863. *Faculty:* 1,612 (89% of full-time faculty have terminal degrees); student–undergrad faculty ratio is 13:1.

Enrollment Profile: 17,725 students from 51 states and territories, 74 other countries. 42% women, 58% men, 12% part-time, 83% state residents, 26% live on campus, 53% transferred in, 5% international, 31% 25 or older, 1% Native American, 2% Hispanic, 13% black, 2% Asian or Pacific Islander. *Retention:* 66% of 1995 full-time freshmen returned. *Graduation:* 33% graduate in 4 years, 38% in 5 years. *Areas of study chosen:* 13% education, 8% business management and administrative services, 8% engineering and applied sciences, 7% social sciences, 5% biological and life sciences, 5% health professions and related sciences, 5% vocational and home economics, 4% agriculture, 4% fine arts, 3% communications and journalism, 3% liberal arts/general studies, 3% psychology, 2% computer and information sciences, 2% English language/literature/letters, 1% architecture, 1% foreign language and literature, 1% interdisciplinary studies, 1% natural resource sciences, 1% physical sciences, 1% prelaw. *Most popular recent majors:* vocational education, industrial engineering technology, aviation administration.

First-Year Class: 2,366 total; 9,925 applied, 72% were accepted, 33% of whom enrolled. 11% from top 10% of their high school class, 32% from top quarter, 66% from top half.

Graduation Requirements: 60 semester hours for associate, 120 semester hours for bachelor's; 1 math course; 2 lab science courses for bachelor's degree; computer course for most majors; internship (some majors); senior project for honors program students and some majors.

Computers on Campus: 450 computers available on campus for general student use. Computer purchase/lease plans available. A campus-wide network can be accessed from student residence rooms and from off-campus. Students can contact faculty members and/or advisers through e-mail. Computers for student use in computer center, computer labs, research center, learning resource center, classrooms, library, dorms, departmental labs. Staffed computer lab on campus provides training in use of computers, software.

EXPENSES AND FINANCIAL AID

Expenses for 1997–98: State resident tuition: $2700 full-time, $90 per semester hour part-time. Nonresident tuition: $8100 full-time, $270 per semester hour part-time. Part-time mandatory fees per semester range from $29.49 to $256.89. Full-time mandatory fees: $560. College room and board: $3472.

Undergraduate Financial Aid: Of all full-time undergraduates enrolled in fall 1996, 100% of those judged to have need according to Federal Methodology were aided. On average, 100% of need was met. *Financial aid deadline (priority):* 4/1. *Financial aid forms:* FAFSA required; state form acceptable.

Financial aid specifically for students with LD: Scholarship: Achieve Program Fee Waivers.

LD Program Contact: Dr. Tim Kaufman, Skills Specialist, Southern Illinois University at Carbondale, Clinical Center, Carbondale, IL 62901-6806, 618-453-2369. Fax: 618-453-3711.

SOUTHWEST TEXAS STATE UNIVERSITY

San Marcos, Texas

Students with LD	130	Subject-Area Tutoring	✓
ADD services	✓	Special Courses	✓
Staff	6 full-time	Taped Textbooks	✓
Special Fee	None	Alternative Test Arrang.	✓
Diagnostic Testing		Notetakers	✓
Basic Skills Remediation	✓	LD Student Organization	

LEARNING DISABILITIES PROGRAM INFORMATION

The Office of Disability Services began offering services in 1980. Currently the program serves 130 undergraduates with LD. Services are also available to graduate students. Students diagnosed with ADD/ADHD are eligible for the same services available to students with LD, as well as quiet testing room.

Staff: 6 full-time staff members, including director. Services provided by counselor, diagnostic specialist, graduate student.

Special Fees: No special fees are charged for services to students with LD.

Applications and admissions: *Required:* high school transcript, class rank, untimed SAT I or ACT; *recommended:* high school grade point average, letters of recommendation. Students may begin taking classes in fall, spring, or summer. *Application deadline:* 7/1 (fall term), 12/1 (spring term).

Special policies: The college has written policies regarding substitutions and waivers of admissions, graduation, and degree requirements.

PROGRAM AND SERVICE COMPONENTS

Academic advising: Provided by LD staff members, academic advisers. Students with LD may take up to 18 semester hours each term; most take 12 to 15 semester hours; 12 semester hours required to maintain full-time status and be eligible for financial aid.

Counseling services: Individual counseling, small-group counseling, career counseling.

Basic skills remediation: Offered one-on-one, in small groups, and in class-size groups by regular teachers, peer teachers. Available in reading, math, spelling, written language, learning strategies, study skills.

Subject-area tutoring: Offered one-on-one and in small groups by peer tutors. Available in most subjects.

Special courses: College survival skills, learning strategies, personal psychology, study skills. None offered for credit; none enter into overall grade point average.

Auxiliary aids: Taped textbooks, tape recorders, calculators, typewriters, word-processors with spell-check, personal computers, optical character readers, scanner.

Auxiliary services: Alternative test arrangements, notetakers, priority registration, advocacy, special seating, permission to tape lectures.

GENERAL COLLEGE INFORMATION

State-supported, comprehensive, coed. Part of Texas State University System. Awards bachelor's, master's, doctoral degrees. Founded 1899. *Setting:* 423-acre small-town campus with easy access to San Antonio and Austin. *Endowment:* $19.5 million. *Research spending 1995–96:* $4.6 million. *Total enrollment:* 20,776. *Faculty:* 931 (686 full-time, 75% with terminal degrees, 245 part-time); student–undergrad faculty ratio is 26:1.

Enrollment Profile: 17,677 students from 45 states and territories, 49 other countries. 54% women, 46% men, 22% part-time, 97% state residents, 26% live on campus, 48% transferred in, 1% international, 24% 25 or older, 1% Native American, 18% Hispanic, 5% black, 2% Asian or Pacific Islander. *Retention:* 64% of 1995 full-time freshmen returned. *Graduation:* 7% graduate in 4 years, 23% in 5 years, 29% in 6 years. *Areas of study chosen:* 15% business management and administrative services, 12% education, 11% health professions and related sciences, 9% engineering and applied sciences, 8% social sciences, 7% biological and life sciences, 5% communications and journalism, 5% computer and information sciences, 5% psychology, 4% performing arts, 3% fine arts, 3% natural resource sciences, 3% vocational and home economics, 2% agriculture, 2% English language/literature/letters, 1% area and ethnic studies, 1% foreign language and literature, 1% mathematics, 1% philosophy, 1% physical sciences. *Most popular recent majors:* elementary education, accounting, business administration/commerce/management.

First-Year Class: 2,472 total; 7,375 applied, 68% were accepted, 49% of whom enrolled. 15% from top 10% of their high school class, 50% from top quarter, 94% from top half.

Graduation Requirements: 128 semester hours; 3 semester hours of math; 7 semester hours of science; 2 years of a foreign language in high school or 6 semester hours in college; computer course for criminal justice, applied sociology, family and consumer science, education, recreational administration, sound recording technology, math, medical technology, applied sociology majors; internship (some majors); senior project for honors program students and some majors.

Computers on Campus: 582 computers available on campus for general student use. A campus-wide network can be accessed from off-campus. Students can contact faculty members and/or advisers through e-mail. Computers for student use in computer center, computer labs, library, dorms, academic buildings provide access to the Internet/World Wide Web, on- and off-campus e-mail addresses. Staffed computer lab on campus provides training in use of computers, software.

EXPENSES AND FINANCIAL AID

Expenses for 1997–98: *Application fee:* $25. State resident tuition: $1088 full-time. Nonresident tuition: $7936 full-time, $248 per semester hour part-time. State resident part-time tuition per semester ranges from $120 to $374. Part-time mandatory fees per semester range from $165 to $665. Full-time mandatory fees: $1610. College room and board: $3901.

Undergraduate Financial Aid: Of all full-time undergraduates enrolled in fall 1996, 77% of those who applied for aid were judged to have need according to Federal Methodology, of whom 91% were aided. On average, 95% of need was met. *Financial aid deadline (priority):* 4/1. *Financial aid forms:* FAFSA required.

LD Program Contact: Ms. Susan Maher, Student Development Specialist, Southwest Texas State University, 601 University Drive, San Marcos, TX 78666, 512-245-3451. Fax: 512-245-3452. Email: sm17@swt.edu.

UNION COLLEGE

Lincoln, Nebraska

Students with LD	50	Subject-Area Tutoring	✓
ADD services	✓	Special Courses	✓
Staff	1 full-, 4 part-time	Taped Textbooks	✓
Special Fee	✓	Alternative Test Arrang.	✓
Diagnostic Testing	✓	Notetakers	✓
Basic Skills Remediation	✓	LD Student Organization	✓

LEARNING DISABILITIES PROGRAM INFORMATION

The Teaching Learning Center began offering services in 1984. Currently the program serves 50 undergraduates with LD. Students diagnosed with ADD/ADHD are eligible for the same services available to students with LD.

Staff: 1 full-time, 4 part-time staff members, including director. Services provided by remediation specialists, tutors, diagnostic specialists.
Special Fees: $425 per year. $200 for diagnostic testing.
Applications and admissions: *Required:* high school transcript, untimed ACT, personal interview, letters of recommendation, psychoeducational report completed within 3 years, previous LD evaluations; *recommended:* extended time ACT. Students may begin taking classes in fall or spring. *Application deadline:* continuous.

PROGRAM AND SERVICE COMPONENTS

Special preparation or orientation: Required orientation held after classes begin.
Diagnostic testing: Intelligence, reading, math, spelling, written language.
Academic advising: Provided by LD staff members, academic advisers. Students with LD may take up to as many semester hours as approved by adviser each term; most take 12 to 15 semester hours; 12 semester hours required to maintain full-time status and be eligible for financial aid.
Basic skills remediation: Offered one-on-one and in small groups by LD teachers, regular teachers. Available in reading, math, spelling, written language, learning strategies, study skills, time management.
Subject-area tutoring: Offered one-on-one and in small groups by professional teachers, peer tutors. Available in most subjects.
Special courses: Reading, vocabulary development, composition. Some offered for credit; some enter into overall grade point average.
Auxiliary aids: Taped textbooks, tape recorders, word-processors with spell-check, optical character readers, Dragon Dictate, assistive technology lab.
Auxiliary services: Alternative test arrangements, notetakers, advocacy, scribes.
Campus support group: A special student organization is available to students with LD.

GENERAL COLLEGE INFORMATION

Independent Seventh-day Adventist, 4-year, coed. Awards associate, bachelor's degrees. Founded 1891. *Setting:* 26-acre suburban campus with easy access to Omaha. *Total enrollment:* 553. *Faculty:* 77 (45 full-time, 98% with terminal degrees, 32 part-time); student–undergrad faculty ratio is 10:1.
Enrollment Profile: 553 students from 36 states and territories, 19 other countries. 55% women, 45% men, 23% part-time, 21% state residents, 7% transferred in, 9% international, 1% Native American, 5% Hispanic, 2% black, 2% Asian or Pacific Islander. *Retention:* 78% of 1995 full-time freshmen returned. *Areas of study chosen:* 13% health professions and related sciences, 11% business management and administrative services, 11% education, 6% premed, 6% theology/religion, 5% biological and life sciences, 4% computer and information sciences, 3% communications and journalism, 3% psychology, 3% social sciences, 2% English language/literature/letters, 2% fine arts, 2% physical sciences, 1% mathematics. *Most popular recent majors:* nursing, business administration/commerce/management, education.
First-Year Class: 142 total; 320 applied, 90% were accepted, 49% of whom enrolled. 4 class presidents, 12 valedictorians.
Graduation Requirements: 62 semester hours for associate, 124 semester hours for bachelor's; 3 semester hours of math; 4 semester hours of lab science; computer course; internship; senior project.
Computers on Campus: 520 computers available on campus for general student use. A campus-wide network can be accessed from student residence rooms and from off-campus. Students can contact faculty members and/or advisers through e-mail. Computers for student use in computer center, computer labs, learning resource center, library, student center, dorms, student rooms provide access to the Internet/World Wide Web, on- and off-campus e-mail addresses. Staffed computer lab on campus provides training in use of computers, software.

EXPENSES AND FINANCIAL AID

Expenses for 1997–98: *Application fee:* $10. Comprehensive fee of $13,166 includes full-time tuition ($9926) and college room and board ($3240). College room only: $1940. Part-time tuition: $414 per semester hour.
Undergraduate Financial Aid: 59% of all full-time undergraduates enrolled in fall 1996 applied for aid; of these, 94% were judged to have need according to Federal Methodology, of whom 97% were aided. On average, 55% of need was met. *Financial aid deadline (priority):* 6/15. *Financial aid forms:* FAFSA required; CSS Financial Aid PROFILE acceptable.
LD Program Contact: Ms. Jennifer Forbes, Director, Teaching Learning Center, Union College, 3800 South 48th, Lincoln, NE 68506, 402-486-2506. Fax: 402-486-2895. Email: jeforbes@ucollege.edu.

UNITY COLLEGE

Unity, Maine

Students with LD	27	Subject-Area Tutoring	✓
ADD services	✓	Special Courses	✓
Staff	7 full-, 1 part-time	Taped Textbooks	✓
Special Fee	None	Alternative Test Arrang.	✓
Diagnostic Testing		Notetakers	✓
Basic Skills Remediation	✓	LD Student Organization	

LEARNING DISABILITIES PROGRAM INFORMATION

The Learning Resource Center began offering services in 1977. Currently the program serves 27 undergraduates with LD. Students diagnosed with ADD/ADHD are eligible for the same services available to students with LD.
Staff: 7 full-time, 1 part-time staff members, including director, LD specialist, psychologist, writing specialist, secretary, counselor, math specialists. Services provided by remediation specialist, tutors, counselor, peer tutors, faculty tutors.
Special Fees: No special fees are charged for services to students with LD.
Applications and admissions: *Required:* high school transcript, courses completed, letters of recommendation, psychoeducational report completed within 2 years; *recommended:* untimed or extended time SAT I or ACT, personal interview. Students may begin taking classes in summer only. *Application deadline:* continuous.

PROGRAM AND SERVICE COMPONENTS

Special preparation or orientation: Summer program (required for some) held prior to entering college. Orientation (required for some) held before registration.
Academic advising: Provided by LD staff members, academic advisers. Students with LD may take up to 16 semester hours each term; most take 12 to 13 semester hours; 12 semester hours required to maintain full-time status and be eligible for financial aid.
Counseling services: Individual counseling, small-group counseling, career counseling.
Basic skills remediation: Offered one-on-one and in class-size groups by LD teachers, regular teachers. Available in reading, math, spelling, written language, learning strategies.
Subject-area tutoring: Offered one-on-one and in small groups by professional teachers, peer tutors. Available in most subjects.

Unity College (continued)

Special courses: College survival skills, reading, composition, learning strategies, math, study skills. Most offered for credit; most enter into overall grade point average.
Auxiliary aids: Taped textbooks, tape recorders, calculators, typewriters, word-processors with spell-check.
Auxiliary services: Alternative test arrangements, notetakers, advocacy.

GENERAL COLLEGE INFORMATION

Independent, 4-year, coed. Awards associate, bachelor's degrees. Founded 1965. *Setting:* 205-acre rural campus. *Endowment:* $1 million. *Educational spending 1995–96:* $3500 per undergrad. *Total enrollment:* 512. *Faculty:* 57 (35 full-time, 50% with terminal degrees, 22 part-time); student–undergrad faculty ratio is 14:1.
Enrollment Profile: 512 students from 24 states and territories, 2 other countries. 40% women, 60% men, 1% part-time, 33% state residents, 22% transferred in, 2% international, 3% 25 or older, 0% Native American, 0% Hispanic, 0% black, 0% Asian or Pacific Islander. *Retention:* 51% of 1995 full-time freshmen returned. *Graduation:* 24% graduate in 4 years, 30% in 5 years, 33% in 6 years. *Areas of study chosen:* 96% natural resource sciences, 2% interdisciplinary studies, 1% liberal arts/general studies, 1% prelaw.
First-Year Class: 188 total; 522 applied, 89% were accepted, 41% of whom enrolled.
Graduation Requirements: 60 semester hours for associate, 120 semester hours for bachelor's; 3 semester hours of math; 9 semester hours of science; computer course; internship (some majors).
Computers on Campus: 42 computers available on campus for general student use. Computers for student use in computer center, computer labs, learning resource center, library, dorms provide access to the Internet/World Wide Web, on- and off-campus e-mail addresses. Staffed computer lab on campus provides training in use of computers, software. *Academic computing expenditure 1995–96:* $100,000.

EXPENSES AND FINANCIAL AID

Expenses for 1997–98: *Application fee:* $25. Comprehensive fee of $16,150 includes full-time tuition ($10,750), mandatory fees ($200), and college room and board ($5200). Part-time tuition: $360 per semester hour. One-time mandatory fee: $150.
Undergraduate Financial Aid: 89% of all full-time undergraduates enrolled in fall 1996 applied for aid; of these, 90% were judged to have need according to Federal Methodology, of whom 95% were aided. On average, 74% of need was met. *Financial aid deadline (priority):* 4/15. *Financial aid forms:* FAFSA, state form, institutional form required.
LD Program Contact: Ms. Ann Dailey, Learning Disability Specialist, Unity College, HC 78, Box 1, Unity, ME 04988, 207-948-3131. Fax: 207-948-5626.

UNIVERSITY OF ALBERTA

Edmonton, Alberta, Canada

Students with LD	35	Subject-Area Tutoring	
ADD services	✓	Special Courses	✓
Staff	2 full-time	Taped Textbooks	
Special Fee	✓	Alternative Test Arrang.	✓
Diagnostic Testing	✓	Notetakers	
Basic Skills Remediation	✓	LD Student Organization	✓

LEARNING DISABILITIES PROGRAM INFORMATION

The Program for Students with Learning Disabilities (PSLD) began offering services in 1986. Currently the program serves 35 undergraduates with LD. Services are also available to graduate students. Students diagnosed with ADD/ADHD are eligible for the same services available to students with LD.
Staff: 2 full-time staff members, including director, coordinator. Services provided by remediation specialists, counselor, diagnostic specialist.
Special Fees: $2000 per year. $250 for diagnostic testing.
Applications and admissions: *Required:* high school courses completed, personal interview, psychoeducational report completed within 2 years; *recommended:* extended time ACT, letters of recommendation. Students may begin taking classes any term. *Application deadline:* continuous.

PROGRAM AND SERVICE COMPONENTS

Special preparation or orientation: Required orientation held during registration.
Diagnostic testing: Intelligence, reading, spelling, written language, motor abilities, perceptual skills.
Academic advising: Provided by LD staff members, academic advisers. Most students with LD take 9 to 12 credits each term; 9 credits required to maintain full-time status.
Counseling services: Individual counseling.
Basic skills remediation: Offered one-on-one and in small groups by LD teachers; computer-aided instruction also offered. Available in reading, spelling, written language, learning strategies, study skills, time management, computer skills.
Special courses: College survival skills, reading, vocabulary development, communication skills, composition, learning strategies, word processing, Internet use, time management, typing, personal psychology, study skills, career planning, stress management. None offered for credit; none enter into overall grade point average.
Auxiliary aids: Tape recorders, typewriters, word-processors with spell-check, personal computers, talking computers, optical character readers.
Auxiliary services: Alternative test arrangements, advocacy.
Campus support group: A special student organization is available to students with LD.

GENERAL COLLEGE INFORMATION

Province-supported, coed. Awards bachelor's, master's, doctoral degrees. Founded 1906. *Setting:* 154-acre urban campus. *Total enrollment:* 29,924. *Undergraduate faculty:* 2,129 (1,579 full-time, 550 part-time); student–undergrad faculty ratio is 12:1.
Enrollment Profile: 25,652 students: 54% women, 46% men, 12% part-time, 81% province residents, 14% transferred in, 6% international, 35% 25 or older.
First-Year Class: 6,655 total; 18,518 applied, 44% were accepted, 81% of whom enrolled.
Graduation Requirements: 120 credits; computer course for business, engineering, education majors; internship (some majors); senior project for honors program students and some majors.
Computers on Campus: 721 computers available on campus for general student use. Computer purchase/lease plans available. A campus-wide network can be accessed from student residence rooms and from off-campus. Students can contact faculty members and/or advisers through e-mail. Computers for student use in computer center, computer labs, research center, learning resource center, classrooms, library, student center, dorms, student rooms, various locations provide access to the Internet/World Wide Web.

EXPENSES AND FINANCIAL AID

Expenses for 1997–98: *Application fee:* $60. Canadian resident tuition: $3056 full-time, $611.28 per course part-time. Nonresident tuition: $6113 full-time, $1223 per course part-time. Part-time mandatory fees: $103.96 per term. (All figures are in Canadian dollars.). Full-time mandatory fees: $390. College room and board: $3400.

Undergraduate Financial Aid: *Financial aid deadline:* 7/15. *Financial aid forms:* state form, institutional form required for some.

LD Program Contact: Ms. Teddi Allan, Instructor, Program for Students with Learning Disabilities, University of Alberta, 2-800 Students' Union Building, Edmonton, AB T6G 2J7, Canada, 403-492-3381. Fax: 403-492-6701. Email: teddi.allan@ualberta.ca.

UNIVERSITY OF ARIZONA

Tucson, Arizona

Students with LD	500	Subject-Area Tutoring	✓
ADD services	✓	Special Courses	✓
Staff	18 full-, 1 part-time	Taped Textbooks	✓
Special Fee	Varies	Alternative Test Arrang.	✓
Diagnostic Testing		Notetakers	✓
Basic Skills Remediation		LD Student Organization	

LEARNING DISABILITIES PROGRAM INFORMATION

The Strategic Alternatives Learning Techniques Center for Learning Disabilities began offering services in 1980. Currently the program serves 500 undergraduates with LD. Students diagnosed with ADD/ADHD are eligible for the same services available to students with LD.

Staff: 18 full-time, 1 part-time staff members, including director, associate director, Admissions Coordinator, tutoring coordinator, computer lab specialist. Services provided by tutors, counselors, education specialists, writing specialist.

Special Fees: Range from $1100 to $3300 per year.

Applications and admissions: *Required:* high school transcript, courses completed, extended time SAT I or ACT, autobiographical statement, letters of recommendation, psychoeducational report completed within 3 years; *recommended:* high school grade point average, class rank, extracurricular activities, personal interview. Students may begin taking classes in fall, spring, or summer. *Application deadline:* continuous.

Special policies: The college has written policies regarding grade forgiveness; substitutions and waivers of degree requirements.

PROGRAM AND SERVICE COMPONENTS

Special preparation or orientation: Optional orientation offered before registration.

Academic advising: Provided by LD staff members, academic advisers. Most students with LD take 12 to 15 semester hours each term; 12 semester hours required to maintain full-time status; source of aid determines number of semester hours required to be eligible for financial aid.

Counseling services: Individual counseling, career counseling, self-advocacy training.

Subject-area tutoring: Offered one-on-one and in small groups by peer tutors. Available in most subjects.

Special courses: College survival skills, learning strategies, time management, personal psychology, study skills. All offered for credit; all enter into overall grade point average.

Auxiliary aids: Taped textbooks, tape recorders, word-processors with spell-check, personal computers, optical character readers.

Auxiliary services: Alternative test arrangements, notetakers, priority registration, advocacy.

GENERAL COLLEGE INFORMATION

State-supported, coed. Awards bachelor's, master's, doctoral, first professional degrees. Founded 1885. *Setting:* 347-acre urban campus. *Endowment:* $82 million. *Research spending 1995–96:* $207.9 million. *Educational spending 1995–96:* $5683 per undergrad. *Total enrollment:* 33,504. *Faculty:* 1,592 (1,359 full-time, 97% with terminal degrees, 233 part-time).

Enrollment Profile: 25,293 students from 53 states and territories, 79 other countries. 51% women, 49% men, 19% part-time, 72% state residents, 8% transferred in, 3% international, 19% 25 or older, 2% Native American, 15% Hispanic, 3% black, 6% Asian or Pacific Islander. *Retention:* 75% of 1995 full-time freshmen returned. *Graduation:* 18% graduate in 4 years, 44% in 5 years, 51% in 6 years. *Areas of study chosen:* 19% liberal arts/general studies, 14% social sciences, 12% business management and administrative services, 9% engineering and applied sciences, 8% agriculture, 8% biological and life sciences, 8% fine arts, 4% education, 4% English language/literature/letters, 3% communications and journalism, 2% architecture, 2% computer and information sciences, 2% health professions and related sciences, 2% interdisciplinary studies, 2% physical sciences, 1% mathematics. *Most popular recent majors:* psychology, political science/government, elementary education.

First-Year Class: 4,168 total; 14,394 applied, 84% were accepted, 34% of whom enrolled. 32% from top 10% of their high school class, 58% from top quarter, 87% from top half. 65 National Merit Scholars.

Graduation Requirements: 125 semester hours; 1 semester of math; 2 semesters of science; computer course for business administration, public administration, engineering, mining, science majors; internship (some majors); senior project (some majors).

Computers on Campus: 1,750 computers available on campus for general student use. Computer purchase/lease plans available. A computer is recommended for all students. A campus-wide network can be accessed from student residence rooms and from off-campus. Students can contact faculty members and/or advisers through e-mail. Computers for student use in computer center, computer labs, research center, learning resource center, classrooms, library, dorms, student rooms provide access to the Internet/World Wide Web, on- and off-campus e-mail addresses. Staffed computer lab on campus provides training in use of computers, software. *Academic computing expenditure 1995–96:* $2.8 million.

EXPENSES AND FINANCIAL AID

Expenses for 1997–98: State resident tuition: $1988 full-time. Nonresident tuition: $8640 full-time, $360 per semester hour part-time. Part-time mandatory fees per semester range from $6 to $36. Part-time tuition for state residents: $105 per semester hour for 1 to 6 semester hours, $994 per semesterfor 7 or more semester hours. Full-time mandatory fees: $72. College room and board: $3525 (minimum). College room only: $1595 (minimum).

Undergraduate Financial Aid: Of all full-time undergraduates enrolled in fall 1996, 75% of those who applied for aid were judged to have need according to Federal Methodology, of whom 98% were aided. On average, 81% of need was met. *Financial aid deadline (priority):* 3/1. *Financial aid forms:* FAFSA, CSS Financial Aid PROFILE, institutional form acceptable.

LD Program Contact: Ms. Shirley Ramsey, Admissions Coordinator, University of Arizona, Old Main, Room 117, Tucson, AZ 85721, 520-621-8493. Fax: 520-621-9448.

UNIVERSITY OF CALIFORNIA, IRVINE

Irvine, California

Students with LD	100	Subject-Area Tutoring	✓
ADD services	✓	Special Courses	
Staff	3 full-, 1 part-time	Taped Textbooks	✓
Special Fee	None	Alternative Test Arrang.	✓
Diagnostic Testing		Notetakers	✓
Basic Skills Remediation		LD Student Organization	✓

LEARNING DISABILITIES PROGRAM INFORMATION

The Office for Disability Services began offering services in 1979. Currently the program serves 100 undergraduates with LD. Services are also available to graduate students. Students diagnosed with ADD/ADHD are eligible for the same services available to students with LD.

Staff: 3 full-time, 1 part-time staff members, including director, coordinators. Services provided by tutors, counselor, tutor coordinator.

Special Fees: No special fees are charged for services to students with LD.

Applications and admissions: *Required:* high school transcript, grade point average, courses completed, untimed SAT I, completed application form; *recommended:* extended time SAT I, psychoeducational report completed within 3 years. Students may begin taking classes any term. *Application deadline:* 11/30.

Special policies: The college has written policies regarding substitutions and waivers of degree requirements.

PROGRAM AND SERVICE COMPONENTS

Special preparation or orientation: Optional orientation offered before registration, during registration, after classes begin.

Academic advising: Provided by LD staff members, academic advisers. Students with LD may take up to 20 quarter units each term; most take 12 to 16 quarter units; 12 quarter units required to maintain full-time status and be eligible for financial aid.

Counseling services: Individual counseling, small-group counseling, career counseling.

Subject-area tutoring: Offered one-on-one and in small groups by peer tutors. Available in all subjects.

Auxiliary aids: Taped textbooks, tape recorders, calculators, typewriters, word-processors with spell-check, personal computers, talking computers, optical character readers, Easy Listener, computer speech output, special computer software programs.

Auxiliary services: Alternative test arrangements, notetakers, priority registration, advocacy, priority housing, reading services, proofreaders.

Campus support group: A special student organization is available to students with LD.

GENERAL COLLEGE INFORMATION

State-supported, coed. Part of University of California System. Awards bachelor's, master's, doctoral degrees. Founded 1965. *Setting:* 1,489-acre suburban campus with easy access to Los Angeles. *Total enrollment:* 17,281. *Faculty:* 997 (99% of full-time faculty have terminal degrees); student–undergrad faculty ratio is 19:1.

Enrollment Profile: 13,833 students from 37 states and territories, 41 other countries. 53% women, 47% men, 6% part-time, 97% state residents, 32% live on campus, 29% transferred in, 2% international, 8% 25 or older, 1% Native American, 13% Hispanic, 3% black, 50% Asian or Pacific Islander. *Areas of study chosen:* 25% business management and administrative services, 19% social sciences, 7% engineering and applied sciences, 7% physical sciences, 4% computer and information sciences, 4% fine arts. *Most popular recent majors:* biology/biological sciences, economics, English.

First-Year Class: 2,910 total; 15,819 applied, 73% were accepted, 25% of whom enrolled. 85% from top 10% of their high school class, 100% from top quarter.

Graduation Requirements: 180 quarter units; 3 science courses; computer course for social science, engineering, math majors; internship (some majors); senior project for honors program students.

Computers on Campus: 500 computers available on campus for general student use. Computer purchase/lease plans available. A campus-wide network can be accessed from student residence rooms and from off-campus. Students can contact faculty members and/or advisers through e-mail. Computers for student use in computer center, computer labs, library, student center provide access to the Internet/World Wide Web. Staffed computer lab on campus (open 24 hours a day).

EXPENSES AND FINANCIAL AID

Estimated Expenses for 1997–98: *Application fee:* $40. State resident tuition: $0 full-time. Nonresident tuition: $8394 full-time, $1399 per quarter part-time. Part-time mandatory fees: $2507 per year. Full-time mandatory fees: $4050. College room and board: $5565 (minimum).

Undergraduate Financial Aid: Of all full-time undergraduates enrolled in fall 1996, 86% of those who applied for aid were judged to have need according to Federal Methodology, of whom 94% were aided. On average, 100% of need was met. *Financial aid deadline (priority):* 3/2. *Financial aid forms:* FAFSA, state form required; CSS Financial Aid PROFILE acceptable.

LD Program Contact: Ms. Diane Crary, LD Coordinator, University of California, Irvine, Irvine, CA 92697-5250, 714-824-7494. Email: dcrary@uci.edu.

UNIVERSITY OF COLORADO AT BOULDER

Boulder, Colorado

Students with LD	250	Subject-Area Tutoring	
ADD services	✓	Special Courses	
Staff	1 full-, 3 part-time	Taped Textbooks	
Special Fee	None	Alternative Test Arrang.	✓
Diagnostic Testing	✓	Notetakers	✓
Basic Skills Remediation		LD Student Organization	

LEARNING DISABILITIES PROGRAM INFORMATION

The Learning Disabilities Program began offering services in 1979. Currently the program serves 250 undergraduates with LD. Services are also available to graduate students. Students diagnosed with ADD/ADHD are eligible for the same services available to students with LD.

Staff: 1 full-time, 3 part-time staff members, including coordinator. Services provided by remediation specialists, diagnostic specialists.

Special Fees: $250 for diagnostic testing.

Applications and admissions: *Required:* high school transcript, grade point average, class rank, courses completed, psychoeducational report completed within 3 years, documentation of disability; *recommended:* high school extracurricular activities, untimed or extended time SAT I or ACT, personal interview, autobiographical statement, letters of recommendation. Students may begin taking classes any term. *Application deadline:* 2/15 (fall term), 11/15 (spring term).

PROGRAM AND SERVICE COMPONENTS

Diagnostic testing: Intelligence, reading, math, spelling, handwriting, written language, perceptual skills.
Academic advising: Provided by LD staff members, academic advisers. Students with LD may take up to as many credit hours as an individual can handle each term; most take 12 to 15 credit hours; 12 credit hours required to maintain full-time status and be eligible for financial aid.
Auxiliary aids: Tape recorders, typewriters, word-processors with spell-check, talking computers, optical character readers.
Auxiliary services: Alternative test arrangements, notetakers, priority registration, advocacy, readers.

GENERAL COLLEGE INFORMATION

State-supported, coed. Part of University of Colorado System. Awards bachelor's, master's, doctoral, first professional degrees. Founded 1876. *Setting:* 600-acre suburban campus with easy access to Denver. *Research spending 1995–96:* $114.4 million. *Educational spending 1995–96:* $5574 per undergrad. *Total enrollment:* 24,622. *Faculty:* 1,500 (1,215 full-time, 95% with terminal degrees, 285 part-time); student–undergrad faculty ratio is 14:1.
Enrollment Profile: 19,845 students from 52 states and territories, 91 other countries. 47% women, 53% men, 7% part-time, 68% state residents, 7% transferred in, 4% international, 11% 25 or older, 1% Native American, 5% Hispanic, 2% black, 6% Asian or Pacific Islander. *Retention:* 81% of 1995 full-time freshmen returned. *Graduation:* 36% graduate in 4 years, 61% in 5 years, 66% in 6 years. *Areas of study chosen:* 18% liberal arts/general studies, 12% business management and administrative services, 10% engineering and applied sciences, 10% social sciences, 9% biological and life sciences, 6% communications and journalism, 6% health professions and related sciences, 6% psychology, 4% fine arts, 3% architecture, 3% English language/literature/letters, 2% computer and information sciences, 2% foreign language and literature, 2% natural resource sciences, 2% physical sciences, 1% area and ethnic studies, 1% education, 1% mathematics, 1% performing arts, 1% philosophy. *Most popular recent majors:* psychology, English, environmental biology.
First-Year Class: 3,952 total; 14,850 applied, 80% were accepted, 33% of whom enrolled. 23% from top 10% of their high school class, 59% from top quarter, 92% from top half.
Graduation Requirements: 120 credit hours; math/science requirements vary according to program; foreign language requirement varies according to division; computer course for business, engineering majors; internship (some majors); senior project for honors program students.
Computers on Campus: 1,500 computers available on campus for general student use. Computer purchase/lease plans available. A computer is recommended for all students. A campus-wide network can be accessed from student residence rooms and from off-campus. Students can contact faculty members and/or advisers through e-mail. Computers for student use in computer center, computer labs, research center, learning resource center, classrooms, library, student center, dorms, academic buildings provide access to the Internet/World Wide Web, on- and off-campus e-mail addresses, standard and academic software. Staffed computer lab on campus (open 24 hours a day) provides training in use of computers, software. *Academic computing expenditure 1995–96:* $6.9 million.

EXPENSES AND FINANCIAL AID

Expenses for 1996–97: *Application fee:* $40. Part-time mandatory fees per semester range from $91 to $259.12. Full-time tuition ranges from $2322 to $2726 for state residents, $13,914 to $14,508 for nonresidents, according to program. Part-time tuition per credit hour ranges from $138 to $165 for state residents, $741 to $806 for nonresidents, according to program. Full-time mandatory fees: $518. College room and board: $4370.
Undergraduate Financial Aid: Of all full-time undergraduates enrolled in fall 1996, 63% of those who applied for aid were judged to have need according to Federal Methodology, of whom 100% were aided. On average, 80% of need was met. *Financial aid deadline (priority):* 4/1. *Financial aid forms:* FAFSA required.
Financial aid specifically for students with LD: Scholarship: Vinnick Scholarship; work-study.
LD Program Contact: Ms. Terri Bodhaine, Learning Disabilities Coordinator, University of Colorado at Boulder, Campus Box 107, Boulder, CO 80309-0107, 303-492-8671. Fax: 303-492-5601.

UNIVERSITY OF COLORADO AT COLORADO SPRINGS

Colorado Springs, Colorado

Students with LD	62	Subject-Area Tutoring	✓
ADD services	✓	Special Courses	✓
Staff	1 full-time	Taped Textbooks	✓
Special Fee	None	Alternative Test Arrang.	✓
Diagnostic Testing	✓	Notetakers	✓
Basic Skills Remediation		LD Student Organization	

LEARNING DISABILITIES PROGRAM INFORMATION

The Supplemental Services began offering services in 1991. Currently the program serves 62 undergraduates with LD. Services are also available to graduate students. Students diagnosed with ADD/ADHD are eligible for the same services available to students with LD, as well as self-directed behavioral management, coaching.
Staff: 1 full-time staff member (coordinator). Services provided by remediation specialists, tutors.
Special Fees: No special fees are charged for services to students with LD.
Applications and admissions: *Required:* high school transcript, grade point average, class rank, courses completed, psychoeducational report completed within 3 years, untimed SAT I or ACT or extended time ACT; *recommended:* high school extracurricular activities, personal interview, autobiographical statement, letters of recommendation. Students may begin taking classes any term. *Application deadline:* continuous.

PROGRAM AND SERVICE COMPONENTS

Special preparation or orientation: Orientation offered before registration and during registration.
Diagnostic testing: Reading, math, spelling, written language, study skills, learning strategies.
Academic advising: Provided by LD staff members, academic advisers. Students with LD may take up to 18 credit hours (more with special permission) each term; most take 9 to 15 credit hours; 12 credit hours required to maintain full-time status and be eligible for financial aid.
Subject-area tutoring: Offered one-on-one by professional teachers, peer tutors. Available in all subjects.
Special courses: Reading, learning strategies, time management, study skills, stress management. None offered for credit.
Auxiliary aids: Taped textbooks, tape recorders, calculators, word-processors with spell-check.
Auxiliary services: Alternative test arrangements, notetakers, advocacy, library assistance.

University of Colorado at Colorado Springs (continued)

GENERAL COLLEGE INFORMATION

State-supported, comprehensive, coed. Part of University of Colorado System. Awards bachelor's, master's, doctoral degrees. Founded 1965. *Setting:* 400-acre suburban campus with easy access to Denver. *Endowment:* $338,861. *Research spending 1995–96:* $1.2 million. *Total enrollment:* 5,840. *Faculty:* 390 (210 full-time, 92% with terminal degrees, 180 part-time); student–undergrad faculty ratio is 13:1.

Enrollment Profile: 4,157 students from 48 states and territories, 26 other countries. 57% women, 43% men, 36% part-time, 88% state residents, 5% live on campus, 13% transferred in, 1% international, 42% 25 or older, 1% Native American, 9% Hispanic, 4% black, 4% Asian or Pacific Islander. *Retention:* 62% of 1995 full-time freshmen returned. *Areas of study chosen:* 15% business management and administrative services, 13% psychology, 13% social sciences, 10% biological and life sciences, 10% communications and journalism, 10% engineering and applied sciences, 7% computer and information sciences, 5% English language/literature/letters, 3% fine arts, 3% natural resource sciences, 3% physical sciences, 3% premed, 1% education, 1% foreign language and literature, 1% interdisciplinary studies, 1% mathematics, 1% philosophy. *Most popular recent majors:* business administration/commerce/management, psychology, communication.

First-Year Class: 441 total; 1,121 applied, 76% were accepted, 52% of whom enrolled. 15% from top 10% of their high school class, 39% from top quarter, 77% from top half.

Graduation Requirements: 124 credit hours; 3 credit hours of math; 12 credit hours of natural science; computer course for business, engineering, education majors; senior project (some majors).

Computers on Campus: 100 computers available on campus for general student use. A campus-wide network can be accessed from student residence rooms and from off-campus. Students can contact faculty members and/or advisers through e-mail. Computers for student use in computer center, library, student labs provide access to the Internet/World Wide Web. Staffed computer lab on campus provides training in use of computers, software. *Academic computing expenditure 1995–96:* $481,836.

EXPENSES AND FINANCIAL AID

Expenses for 1996–97: *Application fee:* $40. Part-time mandatory fees per semester range from $68 to $143. Full-time tuition ranges from $2122 to $2316 for state residents, $8422 to $8904 for nonresidents, according to class level and program. Part-time tuition per credit hour ranges from $90 to $99 for state residents, $340 to $358 for nonresidents, according to class level and program. Full-time mandatory fees: $371. College room and board: $4700 (minimum).

Undergraduate Financial Aid: *Financial aid deadline (priority):* 4/1. *Financial aid forms:* FAFSA required.

LD Program Contact: Ms. JoAnne Hill, Coordinator, Supplemental Services, University of Colorado at Colorado Springs, Main Hall 132, PO Box 7150, Colorado Springs, CO 80933-7150, 719-262-3065. Email: jhill@mail.uccs.edu.

UNIVERSITY OF CONNECTICUT

Storrs, Connecticut

Students with LD	150	Subject-Area Tutoring	
ADD services		Special Courses	✓
Staff	1 full-, 6 part-time	Taped Textbooks	✓
Special Fee	None	Alternative Test Arrang.	✓
Diagnostic Testing		Notetakers	
Basic Skills Remediation		LD Student Organization	✓

LEARNING DISABILITIES PROGRAM INFORMATION

The University Program for College Students with Learning Disabilities (UPLD) began offering services in 1984. Currently the program serves 150 undergraduates with LD. Services are also available to graduate students.

Staff: 1 full-time, 6 part-time staff members, including director, assistant director. Services provided by tutors, learning specialists.

Special Fees: No special fees are charged for services to students with LD.

Applications and admissions: *Required:* high school transcript, courses completed, untimed SAT I; *recommended:* high school grade point average, class rank, extended time SAT I, psychoeducational report completed within 3 years, WAIS-R, Achievement Tests. Students may begin taking classes in fall or spring. *Application deadline:* 4/1 (fall term), 10/15 (spring term).

Special policies: The college has written policies regarding substitutions and waivers of admissions and graduation requirements.

PROGRAM AND SERVICE COMPONENTS

Academic advising: Provided by academic advisers. Students with LD may take up to 18 credits each term; most take 12 credits; individual arrangement determines the number of credits required to maintain full-time status; source of aid determines number of credits required to be eligible for financial aid.

Special courses: College survival skills, reading, composition, learning strategies, time management, study skills. None offered for credit.

Auxiliary aids: Taped textbooks, tape recorders, calculators, word-processors with spell-check, personal computers, talking computers, optical character readers.

Auxiliary services: Alternative test arrangements.

Campus support group: A special student organization is available to students with LD.

GENERAL COLLEGE INFORMATION

State-supported, coed. Awards associate, bachelor's, master's, doctoral, first professional degrees. Founded 1881. *Setting:* 4,000-acre rural campus. *Endowment:* $5.5 million. *Research spending 1995–96:* $57.2 million. *Educational spending 1995–96:* $11,139 per undergrad. *Total enrollment:* 15,541. *Faculty:* 1,148 (1,106 full-time, 93% with terminal degrees, 42 part-time); student–undergrad faculty ratio is 14:1.

Enrollment Profile: 11,336 students: 50% women, 50% men, 9% part-time, 84% state residents, 65% live on campus, 17% transferred in, 1% international, 9% 25 or older, 1% Native American, 4% Hispanic, 4% black, 6% Asian or Pacific Islander. *Retention:* 86% of 1995 full-time freshmen returned. *Graduation:* 33% graduate in 4 years, 62% in 5 years, 67% in 6 years. *Areas of study chosen:* 13% business management and administrative services, 12% health professions and related sciences, 9% social sciences, 8% education, 7% engineering and applied sciences, 6% biological and life sciences, 5% psychology, 4% agriculture, 4% communications and journalism, 4% fine arts, 3% English language/literature/letters, 3% liberal arts/general studies, 3% vocational and home economics, 1% computer and information sciences, 1% foreign language and literature, 1% interdisciplinary studies, 1% mathematics, 1% performing arts, 1% physical sciences. *Most popular recent majors:* psychology, English, political science/government.

First-Year Class: 2,165 total; 10,183 applied, 67% were accepted, 32% of whom enrolled. 23% from top 10% of their high school class, 59% from top quarter, 95% from top half. 11 National Merit Scholars.

Graduation Requirements: 120 credits for bachelor's; 2 courses each in math and science; 3 years of a foreign language in high school or 2 years in high school and 1 year in college; computer course.

Computers on Campus: 1,800 computers available on campus for general student use. Computer purchase/lease plans available. A campus-wide network can be accessed from student residence rooms and from off-campus. Students can contact faculty members and/or advisers through e-mail. Computers for student use in computer center, library, student center, dorms, departmental labs provide access to the Internet/World Wide Web, on- and off-campus e-mail addresses. Staffed computer lab on campus provides training in use of computers, software. *Academic computing expenditure 1995–96:* $10.3 million.

EXPENSES AND FINANCIAL AID

Estimated Expenses for 1997–98: *Application fee:* $40. State resident tuition: $4158 full-time. Nonresident tuition: $12,676 full-time. Full-time mandatory fees: $938. College room and board: $5461.

Undergraduate Financial Aid: Of all full-time undergraduates enrolled in fall 1996, 78% of those who applied for aid were judged to have need according to Federal Methodology, of whom 96% were aided. On average, 77% of need was met. *Financial aid deadline (priority):* 3/1. *Financial aid forms:* FAFSA, institutional form required.

LD Program Contact: Dr. Joan McGuire, Director, University Program for College Students with Learning Disabilities, University of Connecticut, U-64, School of Education, 249 Glenbrook Road, Storrs, CT 06269-2064, 860-486-0178. Fax: 860-486-5037. Email: mcguire@uconnvm.uconn.edu.

UNIVERSITY OF DENVER

Denver, Colorado

Students with LD	134	Subject-Area Tutoring	✓
ADD services	✓	Special Courses	
Staff	4 full-, 3 part-time	Taped Textbooks	✓
Special Fee	✓	Alternative Test Arrang.	✓
Diagnostic Testing	✓	Notetakers	
Basic Skills Remediation	✓	LD Student Organization	✓

LEARNING DISABILITIES PROGRAM INFORMATION

The Learning Effectiveness Program began offering services in 1982. Currently the program serves 134 undergraduates with LD. Services are also available to graduate students. Students diagnosed with ADD/ADHD are eligible for the same services available to students with LD.

Staff: 4 full-time, 3 part-time staff members, including director, clinical director. Services provided by tutors, counselors.

Special Fees: $2442 per year. $150 to $600 for diagnostic testing.

Applications and admissions: *Required:* current WAIS-R or Woodcock-Johnson Revised, Achievement Tests. Students may begin taking classes in fall, winter, or spring. *Application deadline:* continuous.

Special policies: The college has written policies regarding substitutions and waivers of admissions, graduation, and degree requirements.

PROGRAM AND SERVICE COMPONENTS

Special preparation or orientation: Required orientation held before registration.

Diagnostic testing: Intelligence, reading, math, spelling, handwriting, written language, perceptual skills, personality.

Academic advising: Provided by LD staff members, academic advisers. Students with LD may take up to as many quarter hours as an individual can handle each term; most take 12 to 15 quarter hours; 12 quarter hours required to maintain full-time status and be eligible for financial aid.

Counseling services: Individual counseling, small-group counseling, career counseling.

Basic skills remediation: Offered one-on-one by Center of Academic Resources staff. Available in learning strategies, study skills, time management.

Subject-area tutoring: Offered one-on-one and in small groups by professional teachers, peer tutors, LEP professional staff. Available in most subjects.

Auxiliary aids: Taped textbooks, word-processors with spell-check, personal computers, optical character readers.

Auxiliary services: Alternative test arrangements, priority registration, advocacy.

Campus support group: A special student organization is available to students with LD.

GENERAL COLLEGE INFORMATION

Independent, coed. Awards bachelor's, master's, doctoral, first professional degrees. Founded 1864. *Setting:* 125-acre suburban campus. *Endowment:* $81.2 million. *Research spending 1995–96:* $11.4 million. *Educational spending 1995–96:* $7387 per undergrad. *Total enrollment:* 8,714. *Faculty:* 420 (402 full-time, 90% with terminal degrees, 18 part-time); student–undergrad faculty ratio is 13:1.

Enrollment Profile: 2,949 students from 52 states and territories, 56 other countries. 52% women, 48% men, 4% part-time, 41% state residents, 41% live on campus, 5% transferred in, 11% international, 9% 25 or older, 1% Native American, 6% Hispanic, 3% black, 6% Asian or Pacific Islander. *Retention:* 86% of 1995 full-time freshmen returned. *Graduation:* 46% graduate in 4 years, 59% in 5 years, 60% in 6 years. *Areas of study chosen:* 31% business management and administrative services, 11% social sciences, 9% biological and life sciences, 8% communications and journalism, 6% psychology, 5% performing arts, 4% engineering and applied sciences, 4% interdisciplinary studies, 3% English language/literature/letters, 3% fine arts, 3% physical sciences, 2% computer and information sciences, 2% foreign language and literature, 1% mathematics, 1% philosophy. *Most popular recent majors:* biology/biological sciences, communication, marketing/retailing/merchandising.

First-Year Class: 716 total; 2,996 applied, 94% were accepted, 25% of whom enrolled. 28% from top 10% of their high school class, 57% from top quarter, 83% from top half.

Graduation Requirements: 183 quarter hours; 8 quarter hours of math; 12 quarter hours of science; computer course; internship (some majors); senior project for honors program students and some majors.

Computers on Campus: 600 computers available on campus for general student use. Computer purchase/lease plans available. A computer is recommended for all students. A campus-wide network can be accessed from student residence rooms and from off-campus. Students can contact faculty members and/or advisers through e-mail. Computers for student use in computer center, computer labs, research center, learning resource center, classrooms, library, student center, dorms provide access to the Internet/World Wide Web. Staffed computer lab on campus provides training in use of computers, software. *Academic computing expenditure 1995–96:* $1.1 million.

EXPENSES AND FINANCIAL AID

Expenses for 1997–98: *Application fee:* $40. Comprehensive fee of $23,424 includes full-time tuition ($17,532), mandatory fees ($354), and college room and board ($5538). Part-time tuition: $487 per quarter hour.

Undergraduate Financial Aid: Of all full-time undergraduates enrolled in fall 1996, 74% of those who applied for aid were judged to have need according to Federal Methodology, of whom 100% were aided. On average, 85% of need was met. *Financial aid deadline (priority):* 2/19. *Financial aid forms:* FAFSA required. State form required for some.

University of Denver (continued)

LD Program Contact: Ms. Gail E. Nickels, Assistant to Director, Learning Effectiveness Program, University of Denver, 2050 East Evans Avenue, Denver, CO 80208-2372, 303-871-4155. Fax: 303-871-3939. Email: gnickels@du.edu.

UNIVERSITY OF GEORGIA

Athens, Georgia

Students with LD	201	Subject-Area Tutoring	
ADD services		Special Courses	
Staff	7 full-, 13 part-time	Taped Textbooks	✓
Special Fee	None	Alternative Test Arrang.	✓
Diagnostic Testing	✓	Notetakers	✓
Basic Skills Remediation		LD Student Organization	✓

LEARNING DISABILITIES PROGRAM INFORMATION

The Learning Disabilities Center began offering services in 1982. Currently the program serves 201 undergraduates with LD. Services are also available to graduate students.

Staff: 7 full-time, 13 part-time staff members, including director, associate director, coordinators, psychologist. Services provided by remediation specialists, tutors, counselor, diagnostic specialist, graduate assistants, licensed psychologist.

Special Fees: $300 for diagnostic testing.

Applications and admissions: *Required:* high school transcript, grade point average, courses completed, untimed SAT I or ACT, psychoeducational report completed within 3 years; *recommended:* high school class rank, extended time SAT I. Students may begin taking classes any term. *Application deadline:* 3/1.

Special policies: The college has written policies regarding substitutions and waivers of admissions and degree requirements.

PROGRAM AND SERVICE COMPONENTS

Special preparation or orientation: Optional orientation offered individually by special arrangement.

Diagnostic testing: Intelligence, reading, math, spelling, handwriting, spoken language, written language, motor abilities, perceptual skills, study skills, personality, social skills, psychoneurology, speech, hearing.

Academic advising: Provided by LD staff members, academic advisers. Students with LD may take up to 18 quarter hours each term; most take 10 to 15 quarter hours; 12 quarter hours required to maintain full-time status and be eligible for financial aid.

Counseling services: Individual counseling, small-group counseling, career counseling, self-advocacy training.

Auxiliary aids: Taped textbooks, tape recorders, calculators, typewriters, word-processors with spell-check, personal computers, talking computers.

Auxiliary services: Alternative test arrangements, notetakers, priority registration, advocacy, readers, lab assistants.

Campus support group: A special student organization is available to students with LD.

GENERAL COLLEGE INFORMATION

State-supported, coed. Part of University System of Georgia. Awards associate, bachelor's, master's, doctoral, first professional degrees. Founded 1785. *Setting:* 1,601-acre suburban campus with easy access to Atlanta. *Research spending 1995–96:* $172.6 million. *Total enrollment:* 29,404. *Faculty:* 3,173 (2,871 full-time, 94% with terminal degrees, 302 part-time).

Enrollment Profile: 22,946 students from 52 states and territories, 99 other countries. 54% women, 46% men, 11% part-time, 84% state residents, 26% live on campus, 24% transferred in, 2% international, 5% 25 or older, 1% Native American, 1% Hispanic, 7% black, 3% Asian or Pacific Islander. *Retention:* 87% of 1995 full-time freshmen returned. *Graduation:* 35% graduate in 4 years, 61% in 5 years, 66% in 6 years. *Areas of study chosen:* 19% business management and administrative services, 15% education, 9% social sciences, 7% communications and journalism, 7% English language/literature/letters, 6% biological and life sciences, 5% psychology, 5% vocational and home economics, 4% agriculture, 4% health professions and related sciences, 3% fine arts, 2% natural resource sciences, 1% architecture, 1% area and ethnic studies, 1% computer and information sciences, 1% engineering and applied sciences, 1% foreign language and literature, 1% interdisciplinary studies, 1% liberal arts/general studies, 1% mathematics, 1% philosophy, 1% physical sciences, 1% predentistry, 1% prelaw, 1% premed, 1% prevet. *Most popular recent majors:* English, accounting, political science/government.

First-Year Class: 3,480 total; 12,930 applied, 56% were accepted, 48% of whom enrolled. 1 National Merit Scholar.

Graduation Requirements: 95 quarter hours for associate, 195 quarter hours for bachelor's; 20 quarter hours of math/science; computer course for business majors; internship (some majors); senior project (some majors).

Computers on Campus: 800 computers available on campus for general student use. A computer is recommended for all students. A campus-wide network can be accessed from student residence rooms and from off-campus. Students can contact faculty members and/or advisers through e-mail. Computers for student use in computer center, computer labs, research center, library, student center, dorms, various locations provide access to the Internet/World Wide Web. Staffed computer lab on campus (open 24 hours a day) provides training in use of computers, software.

EXPENSES AND FINANCIAL AID

Expenses for 1996–97: *Application fee:* $25. State resident tuition: $2115 full-time, $59 per quarter hour part-time. Nonresident tuition: $7296 full-time, $203 per quarter hour part-time. Full-time mandatory fees: $579. College room and board: $4045. College room only: $2115.

Undergraduate Financial Aid: 71% of all full-time undergraduates enrolled in fall 1996 applied for aid; of these, 56% were judged to have need according to Federal Methodology, of whom 97% were aided. *Financial aid deadline (priority):* 3/1. *Financial aid forms:* FAFSA required.

LD Program Contact: Ms. Sebrena Mason, Support Staff, Learning Disabilities Center, University of Georgia, 331 Milledge Hall, Athens, GA 30602-7155, 706-542-4589. Fax: 706-542-4532.

UNIVERSITY OF HARTFORD

West Hartford, Connecticut

Students with LD	318	Subject-Area Tutoring	✓
ADD services	✓	Special Courses	
Staff	1 full-, 5 part-time	Taped Textbooks	
Special Fee	None	Alternative Test Arrang.	✓
Diagnostic Testing		Notetakers	
Basic Skills Remediation	✓	LD Student Organization	✓

LEARNING DISABILITIES PROGRAM INFORMATION

The Learning Plus began offering services in 1986. Currently the program serves 318 undergraduates with LD. Services are also available to graduate students. Students diagnosed with ADD/ADHD are eligible for the same services available to students with LD, as well as support group.

Staff: 1 full-time, 5 part-time staff members, including director. Services provided by remediation specialists.

Special Fees: No special fees are charged for services to students with LD.
Applications and admissions: *Required:* high school transcript, grade point average, courses completed, psychoeducational report completed within 3 years; *recommended:* untimed or extended time SAT I or ACT, personal interview, autobiographical statement, letters of recommendation. Students may begin taking classes in summer only. *Application deadline:* continuous.
Special policies: The college has written policies regarding substitutions and waivers of admissions and degree requirements.

PROGRAM AND SERVICE COMPONENTS

Special preparation or orientation: Optional orientation offered before classes begin.
Academic advising: Provided by LD staff members, academic advisers. Students with LD may take up to 16 credits each term; most take 13 to 16 credits; 12 credits (fewer with special permission) required to maintain full-time status; 12 credits required to be eligible for financial aid.
Counseling services: Individual counseling, small-group counseling, career counseling, self-advocacy training.
Basic skills remediation: Offered one-on-one by LD teachers, regular teachers. Available in reading, math, spelling, written language, learning strategies, study skills, time management.
Subject-area tutoring: Offered one-on-one by professional teachers. Available in some subjects.
Auxiliary aids: Tape recorders, word-processors with spell-check, personal computers.
Auxiliary services: Alternative test arrangements, advocacy.
Campus support group: A special student organization is available to students with LD.

GENERAL COLLEGE INFORMATION

Independent, comprehensive, coed. Awards associate, bachelor's, master's, doctoral degrees. Founded 1877. *Setting:* suburban campus with easy access to Hartford. *Total enrollment:* 7,068. *Faculty:* 904 (315 full-time, 79% with terminal degrees, 589 part-time); student–undergrad faculty ratio is 11:1.
Enrollment Profile: 5,354 students from 40 states and territories, 55 other countries. 52% women, 48% men, 23% part-time, 44% state residents, 22% transferred in, 5% international, 18% 25 or older, 0% Native American, 3% Hispanic, 6% black, 2% Asian or Pacific Islander. *Retention:* 73% of 1995 full-time freshmen returned. *Areas of study chosen:* 23% liberal arts/general studies, 13% engineering and applied sciences, 12% health professions and related sciences, 10% business management and administrative services, 8% education, 8% fine arts, 7% performing arts, 6% communications and journalism, 6% social sciences, 3% psychology, 2% biological and life sciences, 1% computer and information sciences, 1% English language/literature/letters.
First-Year Class: 1,276 total; 5,065 applied, 82% were accepted, 31% of whom enrolled. 11% from top 10% of their high school class, 35% from top quarter, 69% from top half.
Graduation Requirements: 60 credits for associate, 120 credits for bachelor's; computer course for business, engineering, math, physics, technology, teacher education, human service majors.
Computers on Campus: 380 computers available on campus for general student use. A campus-wide network can be accessed from student residence rooms and from off-campus. Students can contact faculty members and/or advisers through e-mail. Computers for student use in computer center, computer labs, learning resource center, classrooms, library, dorms, academic buildings provide access to the Internet/World Wide Web, on- and off-campus e-mail addresses. Staffed computer lab on campus provides training in use of computers, software.

EXPENSES AND FINANCIAL AID

Expenses for 1997–98: Comprehensive fee of $24,210 includes full-time tuition ($16,380), mandatory fees ($940), and college room and board ($6890). College room only: $4250. Part-time tuition: $260 per credit. Part-time mandatory fees per semester range from $60 to $150.
Undergraduate Financial Aid: 62% of all full-time undergraduates enrolled in fall 1996 applied for aid; of these, 92% were judged to have need according to Federal Methodology, of whom 98% were aided. On average, 70% of need was met. *Financial aid deadline (priority):* 2/1. *Financial aid forms:* FAFSA, institutional form required.
LD Program Contact: Ms. Sharon Truex, Director, University of Hartford, 200 Bloomfield Avenue, West Hartford, CT 06117-1599, 860-768-4522. Fax: 860-768-4940.

UNIVERSITY OF INDIANAPOLIS

Indianapolis, Indiana

Students with LD	61	Subject-Area Tutoring	✓
ADD services	✓	Special Courses	✓
Staff	3 full-, 6 part-time	Taped Textbooks	✓
Special Fee	✓	Alternative Test Arrang.	✓
Diagnostic Testing	✓	Notetakers	✓
Basic Skills Remediation	✓	LD Student Organization	

LEARNING DISABILITIES PROGRAM INFORMATION

The Baccalaureate for University of Indianapolis Learning Disabled (B.U.I.L.D.) began offering services in 1990. Currently the program serves 61 undergraduates with LD. Services are also available to graduate students. Students diagnosed with ADD/ADHD are eligible for the same services available to students with LD.
Staff: 3 full-time, 6 part-time staff members, including co-directors, coordinator. Services provided by tutors, counselors.
Special Fees: $3700 per year.
Applications and admissions: *Required:* high school transcript, class rank, courses completed, untimed SAT I or extended time ACT, personal interview, letters of recommendation, psychoeducational report completed within 3 years; *recommended:* high school grade point average, extracurricular activities, extended time SAT I, autobiographical statement. Students may begin taking classes any term. *Application deadline:* continuous.

PROGRAM AND SERVICE COMPONENTS

Special preparation or orientation: Required orientation held before registration.
Diagnostic testing: Intelligence, reading, math, spelling, handwriting, spoken language, written language, motor abilities, study skills, learning strategies.
Academic advising: Provided by LD staff members, academic advisers. Students with LD may take up to 12 credit hours (more if GPA warrants) each term; most take 12 credit hours; 9 credit hours required to maintain full-time status; 12 credit hours required to be eligible for financial aid.
Counseling services: Individual counseling, small-group counseling, career counseling.
Basic skills remediation: Offered in small groups and in class-size groups by LD teachers. Available in learning strategies, motor abilities, study skills, time management, social skills.
Subject-area tutoring: Offered one-on-one and in small groups by professional teachers, peer tutors. Available in all subjects.
Special courses: College survival skills, math, study skills, English, modern languages. Some offered for credit; some enter into overall grade point average.

University of Indianapolis (continued)

Auxiliary aids: Taped textbooks, tape recorders, calculators, typewriters, word-processors with spell-check, personal computers, optical character readers.

Auxiliary services: Alternative test arrangements, notetakers, priority registration, advocacy.

GENERAL COLLEGE INFORMATION

Independent, comprehensive, coed, affiliated with United Methodist Church. Awards associate, bachelor's, master's, doctoral degrees. Founded 1902. *Setting:* 60-acre suburban campus. *Endowment:* $35.8 million. *Educational spending 1995–96:* $4925 per undergrad. *Total enrollment:* 3,861. *Faculty:* 337 (134 full-time, 60% with terminal degrees, 203 part-time); student–undergrad faculty ratio is 13:1.

Enrollment Profile: 2,906 students from 26 states and territories, 57 other countries. 67% women, 33% men, 47% part-time, 83% state residents, 19% transferred in, 4% international, 1% Native American, 1% Hispanic, 7% black, 1% Asian or Pacific Islander. *Retention:* 69% of 1995 full-time freshmen returned. *Graduation:* 40% graduate in 4 years, 52% in 5 years, 53% in 6 years. *Areas of study chosen:* 31% health professions and related sciences, 17% business management and administrative services, 13% education, 7% biological and life sciences, 7% social sciences, 5% psychology, 3% communications and journalism, 2% fine arts, 2% prelaw, 2% premed, 1% computer and information sciences, 1% engineering and applied sciences, 1% English language/literature/letters, 1% foreign language and literature, 1% mathematics, 1% philosophy, 1% predentistry, 1% prevet, 1% theology/religion. *Most popular recent majors:* nursing, physical therapy, elementary education.

First-Year Class: 449 total; 1,649 applied, 89% were accepted, 31% of whom enrolled. 26% from top 10% of their high school class, 49% from top quarter, 77% from top half. 19 valedictorians.

Graduation Requirements: 62 credit hours for associate, 124 credit hours for bachelor's; 2 math/science courses; competence in a foreign language; computer course; senior project for honors program students.

Computers on Campus: 200 computers available on campus for general student use. Computer purchase/lease plans available. A campus-wide network can be accessed from student residence rooms and from off-campus. Students can contact faculty members and/or advisers through e-mail. Computers for student use in computer center, computer labs, classrooms, library, dorms provide access to the Internet/World Wide Web, on- and off-campus e-mail addresses. Staffed computer lab on campus provides training in use of computers, software. *Academic computing expenditure 1995–96:* $395,515.

EXPENSES AND FINANCIAL AID

Expenses for 1997–98: *Application fee:* $20. Comprehensive fee of $17,540 includes full-time tuition ($12,990) and college room and board ($4550). Part-time tuition: $542 per credit hour. Part-time tuition for evening program: $164 per credit hour.

Undergraduate Financial Aid: 80% of all full-time undergraduates enrolled in fall 1996 applied for aid; of these, 91% were judged to have need according to Federal Methodology, of whom 99% were aided. On average, 89% of need was met. *Financial aid deadline (priority):* 3/1. *Financial aid forms:* FAFSA, institutional form required; CSS Financial Aid PROFILE acceptable.

LD Program Contact: Dr. Patricia A. Cook and Dr. Nancy E. O'Dell, Company Directors, University of Indianapolis, 1400 East Hanna Avenue, Indianapolis, IN 46227, 317-788-3285. Fax: 317-788-3300.

UNIVERSITY OF MASSACHUSETTS AMHERST

Amherst, Massachusetts

Students with LD	530	Subject-Area Tutoring	✓
ADD services	✓	Special Courses	✓
Staff		Taped Textbooks	✓
Special Fee	None	Alternative Test Arrang.	✓
Diagnostic Testing	✓	Notetakers	✓
Basic Skills Remediation	✓	LD Student Organization	✓

LEARNING DISABILITIES PROGRAM INFORMATION

The Learning Disabilities Support Services (LDSS) began offering services in 1984. Currently the program serves 530 undergraduates with LD. Services are also available to graduate students. Students diagnosed with ADD/ADHD are eligible for the same services available to students with LD.

Staff: Includes director, coordinator, Office Manager, graduate assistants. Services provided by remediation specialists, tutors, counselors, diagnostic specialists, graduate assistants.

Special Fees: $450 for diagnostic testing.

Applications and admissions: *Required:* high school transcript, grade point average, class rank, courses completed, IEP (Individualized Education Program), autobiographical statement, letters of recommendation, psychoeducational report completed within 3 to 5 years; *recommended:* high school extracurricular activities, untimed or extended time SAT I. Students may begin taking classes in fall or spring. *Application deadline:* 2/1 (fall term), 10/15 (spring term).

Special policies: The college has written policies regarding grade forgiveness; substitutions and waivers of admissions and degree requirements.

PROGRAM AND SERVICE COMPONENTS

Special preparation or orientation: Optional orientation offered during registration.

Diagnostic testing: Intelligence, reading, math, spelling, handwriting, spoken language, written language, motor abilities, perceptual skills, study skills, personality, social skills, psychoneurology, speech, hearing.

Academic advising: Provided by LD staff members, academic advisers. Students with LD may take up to 15 credits each term; most take 12 credits; 12 credits required to maintain full-time status and be eligible for financial aid.

Counseling services: Individual counseling, small-group counseling, career counseling.

Basic skills remediation: Offered one-on-one, in small groups, and in class-size groups by LD teachers, teacher trainees. Available in reading, math, learning strategies.

Subject-area tutoring: Offered one-on-one and in small groups by graduate students. Available in most subjects.

Special courses: Study skills, career planning. None offered for credit.

Auxiliary aids: Taped textbooks, tape recorders, calculators, typewriters, word-processors with spell-check.

Auxiliary services: Alternative test arrangements, notetakers, advocacy, course modification plans, individual written plans.

Campus support group: A special student organization is available to students with LD.

GENERAL COLLEGE INFORMATION

State-supported, coed. Part of University of Massachusetts. Awards associate, bachelor's, master's, doctoral degrees. Founded 1863. *Setting:* 1,463-acre small-town campus. *Endowment:* $18.9 million. *Research spending 1995–96:* $60.5 million. *Educational spend-*

ing 1995–96: $6658 per undergrad. *Total enrollment:* 23,108. *Faculty:* 1,310 (1,164 full-time, 96% with terminal degrees, 146 part-time); student–undergrad faculty ratio is 18:1.

Enrollment Profile: 18,209 students from 51 states and territories, 71 other countries. 48% women, 52% men, 5% part-time, 73% state residents, 57% live on campus, 22% transferred in, 2% international, 8% 25 or older, 1% Native American, 4% Hispanic, 5% black, 6% Asian or Pacific Islander. *Retention:* 78% of 1995 full-time freshmen returned. *Graduation:* 41% graduate in 4 years, 57% in 5 years, 60% in 6 years. *Areas of study chosen:* 17% business management and administrative services, 14% social sciences, 7% communications and journalism, 7% psychology, 6% health professions and related sciences, 6% natural resource sciences, 5% agriculture, 5% engineering and applied sciences, 5% fine arts, 4% biological and life sciences, 3% English language/literature/letters, 2% foreign language and literature, 2% interdisciplinary studies, 2% liberal arts/general studies, 2% prelaw, 1% architecture, 1% area and ethnic studies, 1% computer and information sciences, 1% education, 1% mathematics, 1% physical sciences, 1% vocational and home economics. *Most popular recent majors:* psychology, communication, hotel and restaurant management.

First-Year Class: 3,985 total; 17,705 applied, 74% were accepted, 30% of whom enrolled. 12% from top 10% of their high school class, 38% from top quarter, 78% from top half.

Graduation Requirements: 60 credits for associate, 120 credits for bachelor's; 3 science courses; 1 course each in basic math and analytical reasoning; computer course for business, engineering, math, science majors; senior project for honors program students and some majors.

Computers on Campus: 1,000 computers available on campus for general student use. Computer purchase/lease plans available. A campus-wide network can be accessed from student residence rooms and from off-campus. Students can contact faculty members and/or advisers through e-mail. Computers for student use in computer center, computer labs, research center, learning resource center, classrooms, library, dorms, academic buildings provide access to the Internet/World Wide Web, on- and off-campus e-mail addresses. Staffed computer lab on campus provides training in use of computers, software.

EXPENSES AND FINANCIAL AID

Expenses for 1997–98: *Application fee:* $25. State resident tuition: $2004 full-time, $83.50 per credit part-time. Nonresident tuition: $9017 full-time, $373 per credit part-time. One time mandatory fee: $143. Tuition for nonresidents who are eligible for the New England Regional Student Program: $3006 full-time, $125.25 per credit part-time. Part-time mandatory fees per semester range from $474.25 to $1189 for state residents, $485 to $1210 for nonresidents, according to course load. Full-time mandatory fees: $3325. College room and board: $4274 (minimum). College room only: $2488 (minimum).

Undergraduate Financial Aid: 79% of all full-time undergraduates enrolled in fall 1996 applied for aid; of these, 91% were judged to have need according to Federal Methodology, of whom 88% were aided. On average, 81% of need was met. *Financial aid deadline:* Applications processed continuously. *Financial aid forms:* FAFSA required.

LD Program Contact: Mrs. Amanda Zygmont, Office Manager, University of Massachusetts Amherst, 123 Berkshire House, Amherst, MA 01003-0640, 413-545-4602. Fax: 413-545-2699.

THE UNIVERSITY OF MEMPHIS

Memphis, Tennessee

Students with LD	358	Subject-Area Tutoring	✓
ADD services	✓	Special Courses	✓
Staff	6 full-, 6 part-time	Taped Textbooks	✓
Special Fee	None	Alternative Test Arrang.	✓
Diagnostic Testing		Notetakers	✓
Basic Skills Remediation	✓	LD Student Organization	

LEARNING DISABILITIES PROGRAM INFORMATION

The Student Disability Services began offering services in 1980. Currently the program serves 358 undergraduates with LD. Services are also available to graduate students. Students diagnosed with ADD/ADHD are eligible for the same services available to students with LD.

Staff: 6 full-time, 6 part-time staff members, including director, coordinator. Services provided by tutors, adaptive lab coordinator, learning specialist, graduate assistant.

Special Fees: No special fees are charged for services to students with LD.

Applications and admissions: *Required:* high school transcript, grade point average, courses completed, untimed or extended time ACT; *recommended:* high school extracurricular activities, personal interview, autobiographical statement, letters of recommendation, psychoeducational report completed within 1 year. Students may begin taking classes in fall, spring, or summer. *Application deadline:* 8/1 (fall term), 12/1 (spring term).

PROGRAM AND SERVICE COMPONENTS

Special preparation or orientation: Optional orientation offered during registration.

Academic advising: Provided by LD staff members, academic advisers. Students with LD may take up to 20 semester hours each term; most take 9 to 12 semester hours; 12 semester hours required to maintain full-time status; source of aid determines number of semester hours required to be eligible for financial aid.

Counseling services: Individual counseling, small-group counseling, career counseling.

Basic skills remediation: Offered in class-size groups by regular teachers. Available in reading, math, written language, study skills, time management.

Subject-area tutoring: Offered one-on-one and in small groups by professional teachers, peer tutors, graduate students. Available in most subjects.

Special courses: College survival skills, communication skills, learning strategies, word processing, time management, study skills, Academics 1100 (an Introduction to the University). Some offered for credit; some enter into overall grade point average.

Auxiliary aids: Taped textbooks, tape recorders, calculators, typewriters, word-processors with spell-check, personal computers, talking computers, optical character readers.

Auxiliary services: Alternative test arrangements, notetakers, priority registration, advocacy.

GENERAL COLLEGE INFORMATION

State-supported, coed. Part of State University and Community College System of Tennessee. Awards bachelor's, master's, doctoral, first professional degrees. Founded 1912. *Setting:* 1,100-acre urban campus. *Endowment:* $88.3 million. *Research spending 1995–96:* $15.7 million. *Educational spending 1995–96:* $2206 per undergrad. *Total enrollment:* 19,271. *Faculty:* 1,217 (775 full-time, 80% with terminal degrees, 442 part-time); student–undergrad faculty ratio is 20:1.

Enrollment Profile: 14,298 students from 45 states and territories, 32 other countries. 57% women, 43% men, 28% part-time, 87% state residents, 15% live on campus, 11% transferred in, 4% international, 19% 25 or older, 1% Hispanic, 27% black, 3% Asian or Pacific Islander. *Retention:* 69% of 1995 full-time freshmen returned. *Graduation:* 5% graduate in 4 years, 21% in 5 years, 31% in 6 years. *Areas of study chosen:* 11% business management and administrative services, 6% social sciences, 4% health professions and related sciences, 3% communications and journalism, 3% fine arts, 3% interdisciplinary studies, 3% psychology, 2% biological and life sciences, 2% English language/literature/letters, 2% performing arts, 1% computer and information sciences, 1% education, 1% foreign language and literature, 1% mathematics, 1% philosophy, 1% physical sciences, 1% vocational and home economics. *Most popular recent majors:* finance/banking, accounting, business administration/commerce/management.

First-Year Class: 1,642 total; 4,353 applied, 70% were accepted, 54% of whom enrolled.

Graduation Requirements: 132 semester hours; 6 semester hours of science; computer course; internship (some majors); senior project (some majors).

Computers on Campus: 2,100 computers available on campus for general student use. Computer purchase/lease plans available. A campus-wide network can be accessed from off-campus. Students can contact faculty members and/or advisers through e-mail. Computers for student use in computer center, computer labs, research center, learning resource center, classrooms, library, student center, dorms, departmental labs provide access to the Internet/World Wide Web, on- and off-campus e-mail addresses. Staffed computer lab on campus (open 24 hours a day) provides training in use of computers, software. *Academic computing expenditure 1995–96:* $1 million.

EXPENSES AND FINANCIAL AID

Expenses for 1996–97: *Application fee:* $5. State resident tuition: $2112 full-time, $92 per semester hour part-time. Nonresident tuition: $6448 full-time, $282 per semester hour part-time. Part-time mandatory fees per semester range from $4 to $34. Full-time mandatory fees: $68. College room only: $1680.

Undergraduate Financial Aid: 69% of all full-time undergraduates enrolled in fall 1996 applied for aid; of these, 85% were judged to have need according to Federal Methodology, of whom 90% were aided. On average, 60% of need was met. *Financial aid deadline:* Applications processed continuously. *Financial aid forms:* FAFSA, institutional form required.

LD Program Contact: Ms. Susan TePaske, Learning Disabilities Coordinator, The University of Memphis, 215 Scates Hall, Memphis, TN 38152, 901-678-2880. Fax: 901-678-3070. Email: stepaske@cc.memphis.edu.

UNIVERSITY OF NEVADA, RENO

Reno, Nevada

Students with LD	90	Subject-Area Tutoring	✓
ADD services	✓	Special Courses	
Staff	1 full-time	Taped Textbooks	✓
Special Fee	None	Alternative Test Arrang.	✓
Diagnostic Testing	✓	Notetakers	✓
Basic Skills Remediation		LD Student Organization	

LEARNING DISABILITIES PROGRAM INFORMATION

The Disability Resource Services began offering services in 1980. Currently the program serves 90 undergraduates with LD. Services are also available to graduate students. Students diagnosed with ADD/ADHD are eligible for the same services available to students with LD.

Staff: 1 full-time staff member (coordinator). Services provided by tutors, counselors.

Special Fees. A fee is charged for diagnostic testing.

Applications and admissions: *Required:* high school transcript, grade point average, class rank, courses completed, extracurricular activities, untimed SAT I or ACT; *recommended:* extended time SAT I or ACT, personal interview, autobiographical statement, letters of recommendation. Students may begin taking classes in summer only. *Application deadline:* 7/1.

Special policies: The college has written policies regarding grade forgiveness; substitutions and waivers of admissions, graduation, and degree requirements.

PROGRAM AND SERVICE COMPONENTS

Special preparation or orientation: Optional orientation offered before registration.

Diagnostic testing: Intelligence.

Academic advising: Provided by LD staff members. Students with LD may take up to 18 credits each term; most take 15 credits; 12 credits required to maintain full-time status and be eligible for financial aid.

Counseling services: Individual counseling, career counseling.

Subject-area tutoring: Offered one-on-one and in small groups by peer tutors. Available in most subjects.

Auxiliary aids: Taped textbooks, tape recorders, calculators, typewriters, word-processors with spell-check, personal computers, optical character readers, voice-activated computers, screen magnifiers.

Auxiliary services: Alternative test arrangements, notetakers, advocacy.

GENERAL COLLEGE INFORMATION

State-supported, coed. Part of University and Community College System of Nevada. Awards bachelor's, master's, doctoral, first professional degrees. Founded 1874. *Setting:* 200-acre urban campus. *Endowment:* $60.6 million. *Research spending 1995–96:* $33.8 million. *Total enrollment:* 11,652. *Faculty:* 649 (586 full-time, 74% with terminal degrees, 63 part-time).

Enrollment Profile: 8,558 students from 52 states and territories, 65 other countries. 52% women, 48% men, 27% part-time, 80% state residents, 12% live on campus, 9% transferred in, 4% international, 26% 25 or older, 1% Native American, 5% Hispanic, 2% black, 6% Asian or Pacific Islander. *Retention:* 74% of 1995 full-time freshmen returned. *Areas of study chosen:* 15% education, 14% health professions and related sciences, 14% social sciences, 12% engineering and applied sciences, 6% biological and life sciences, 6% business management and administrative services, 6% communications and journalism, 5% psychology, 3% English language/literature/letters, 3% natural resource sciences, 2% computer and information sciences, 2% fine arts, 2% liberal arts/general studies, 2% performing arts, 2% physical sciences, 2% vocational and home economics, 1% agriculture, 1% foreign language and literature, 1% mathematics, 1% prevet. *Most popular recent majors:* education, psychology, criminal justice.

First-Year Class: 1,224 total; 2,527 applied, 86% were accepted, 56% of whom enrolled.

Graduation Requirements: 128 credits; 1 algebra course; computer course for business, engineering science, journalism majors; internship (some majors); senior project (some majors).

Computers on Campus: 130 computers available on campus for general student use. Computer purchase/lease plans available. A campus-wide network can be accessed from student residence rooms and from off-campus. Students can contact faculty members and/or advisers through e-mail. Computers for student use in computer center, computer labs, library, student center, dorms, academic buildings provide access to the Internet/World Wide Web. Staffed computer lab on campus provides training in use of computers, software. *Academic computing expenditure 1995–96:* $276,483.

EXPENSES AND FINANCIAL AID

Expenses for 1997–98: *Application fee:* $20. State resident tuition: $2128 full-time, $66.50 per credit part-time. Nonresident tuition: $7563 full-time. Nonresident part-time tuition per semester ranges from $130.50 to $3449. Part-time mandatory fees per smester (6 to 11 credits): $57. Full-time mandatory fees: $114. College room and board: $4795. College room only: $2800.
Undergraduate Financial Aid: 84% of all full-time undergraduates enrolled in fall 1996 applied for aid; of these, 95% were judged to have need according to Federal Methodology, of whom 88% were aided. On average, 73% of need was met. *Financial aid deadline (priority):* 3/1. *Financial aid forms:* FAFSA required.
LD Program Contact: Ms. Mary Zabel, Coordinator, Disability Resource Services, University of Nevada, Reno, Thompson 107, Reno, NV 89557-0072, 702-784-6000. Fax: 702-784-1353.

UNIVERSITY OF NEW ENGLAND

Biddeford, Maine

Students with LD	28	Subject-Area Tutoring	✓
ADD services		Special Courses	✓
Staff		Taped Textbooks	✓
Special Fee	Varies	Alternative Test Arrang.	✓
Diagnostic Testing	✓	Notetakers	
Basic Skills Remediation	✓	LD Student Organization	

LEARNING DISABILITIES PROGRAM INFORMATION

The Individual Learning Program began offering services in 1983. Currently the program serves 28 undergraduates with LD. Services are also available to graduate students.
Staff: Includes director, learning specialist, writing support tutor. Services provided by remediation specialists, tutors, diagnostic specialist.
Special Fees: Range from $1500 to $3600 per year depending on level of services.
Applications and admissions: *Required:* high school transcript, grade point average, courses completed, personal interview, autobiographical statement, letters of recommendation, psychoeducational report completed within 1 year, WAIS-R, individualized achievement battery; *recommended:* high school class rank, extracurricular activities, untimed or extended time SAT I or ACT. Students may begin taking classes in fall or spring. *Application deadline:* 2/15 (fall term), 10/30 (spring term).
Special policies: The college has written policies regarding substitutions and waivers of graduation and degree requirements.

PROGRAM AND SERVICE COMPONENTS

Special preparation or orientation: Required orientation held after classes begin.
Diagnostic testing: Intelligence, reading, math, spelling, handwriting, spoken language, written language, motor abilities, perceptual skills, study skills, social skills, learning strategies.
Academic advising: Provided by LD staff members, academic advisers. Students with LD may take up to 18 credits each term; most take 12 to 18 credits; 12 credits required to maintain full-time status and be eligible for financial aid.
Counseling services: Individual counseling, small-group counseling, career counseling, self-advocacy training.
Basic skills remediation: Offered one-on-one and in small groups by LD teachers. Available in reading, math, spelling, written language, learning strategies, study skills, time management.
Subject-area tutoring: Offered one-on-one and in small groups by professional teachers, peer tutors. Available in all subjects.
Special courses: College survival skills, reading, composition, learning strategies, word processing, time management, typing, study skills, career planning, stress management. Some offered for credit; none enter into overall grade point average.
Auxiliary aids: Taped textbooks, tape recorders, word-processors with spell-check, personal computers.
Auxiliary services: Alternative test arrangements, advocacy, peer notesharing.

GENERAL COLLEGE INFORMATION

Independent, comprehensive, coed. Awards associate, bachelor's, master's, first professional degrees. Founded 1953. *Setting:* 410-acre small-town campus. *Endowment:* $3.6 million. *Research spending 1995–96:* $15,479. *Educational spending 1995–96:* $6300 per undergrad. *Total enrollment:* 1,892. *Faculty:* 181 (107 full-time, 70% with terminal degrees, 74 part-time); student–undergrad faculty ratio is 19:1.
Enrollment Profile: 1,000 students from 32 states and territories, 3 other countries. 70% women, 30% men, 6% part-time, 53% state residents, 35% live on campus, 12% transferred in, 1% international, 15% 25 or older, 1% Asian or Pacific Islander. *Areas of study chosen:* 57% health professions and related sciences, 11% biological and life sciences, 11% premed, 8% business management and administrative services, 5% liberal arts/general studies, 4% education, 4% social sciences. *Most popular recent majors:* occupational therapy, physical therapy, nursing.
First-Year Class: 273 total; 1,456 applied, 66% were accepted, 28% of whom enrolled. 18% from top 10% of their high school class, 48% from top quarter, 82% from top half.
Graduation Requirements: 70 credits for associate, 129 credits for bachelor's; 3 credits of math; 7 credits of science including at least 4 credits of lab science; computer course for business, physical therapy, occupational therapy, nursing majors; internship (some majors); senior project.
Computers on Campus: 52 computers available on campus for general student use. Computer purchase/lease plans available. A computer is recommended for all students. A campus-wide network can be accessed from off-campus. Students can contact faculty members and/or advisers through e-mail. Computers for student use in computer center, library provide access to the Internet/World Wide Web, on- and off-campus e-mail addresses. Staffed computer lab on campus. *Academic computing expenditure 1995–96:* $250,000.

EXPENSES AND FINANCIAL AID

Expenses for 1997–98: *Application fee:* $40. Comprehensive fee of $19,680 includes full-time tuition ($13,575), mandatory fees ($510), and college room and board ($5595). Part-time tuition: $455 per credit. Part-time mandatory fees per year (7 to 11 credits): $510.
Undergraduate Financial Aid: Of all full-time undergraduates enrolled in fall 1996, 91% of those who applied for aid were judged to have need according to Federal Methodology, of whom 100% were aided. On average, 65% of need was met. *Financial aid deadline (priority):* 5/1. *Financial aid forms:* FAFSA, state form, institutional form required; CSS Financial Aid PROFILE acceptable.
LD Program Contact: Director, Individual Learning Program, University of New England, Hills Beach Road, Biddeford, ME 04005-9526, 207-283-0171 Ext. 2443. Fax: 207-282-6379.

THE UNIVERSITY OF NORTH CAROLINA AT CHAPEL HILL

Chapel Hill, North Carolina

Students with LD	120	Subject-Area Tutoring	✓
ADD services	✓	Special Courses	✓
Staff	5 full-, 4 part-time	Taped Textbooks	✓
Special Fee	None	Alternative Test Arrang.	✓
Diagnostic Testing	✓	Notetakers	✓
Basic Skills Remediation	✓	LD Student Organization	✓

LEARNING DISABILITIES PROGRAM INFORMATION

The Learning Disability Services began offering services in 1980. Currently the program serves 120 undergraduates with LD. Services are also available to graduate students. Students diagnosed with ADD/ADHD are eligible for the same services available to students with LD.

Staff: 5 full-time, 4 part-time staff members, including director, assistant director, LD specialists, graduate students, test coordinator, secretary, student worker. Services provided by tutors, counselors, diagnostic specialist, LD specialists.

Special Fees: No special fees are charged for services to students with LD.

Applications and admissions: *Required:* high school transcript, courses completed, untimed SAT I or ACT, psychoeducational report completed within 3 years, documentation of disability. Students may begin taking classes in fall or summer. *Application deadline:* 1/15.

Special policies: The college has written policies regarding substitutions and waivers of graduation requirements.

PROGRAM AND SERVICE COMPONENTS

Special preparation or orientation: Optional summer program offered prior to entering college. Optional orientation offered during registration.

Diagnostic testing: Intelligence, reading, math, written language, perceptual skills, personality, social skills, learning strategies, various other areas as appropriate.

Academic advising: Provided by LD staff members, academic advisers. Students with LD may take up to 17 credit hours each term; most take 12 credit hours; 12 credit hours required to maintain full-time status and be eligible for financial aid.

Counseling services: Individual counseling, small-group counseling.

Basic skills remediation: Offered one-on-one and in small groups by LD specialist. Available in reading, spoken language, written language.

Subject-area tutoring: Offered one-on-one and in small groups by peer tutors, graduate students. Available in some subjects.

Special courses: Metacognitive development. All offered for credit; none enter into overall grade point average.

Auxiliary aids: Taped textbooks, tape recorders, calculators, typewriters, word-processors with spell-check, voice-activated computer.

Auxiliary services: Alternative test arrangements, notetakers, priority registration, advocacy.

Campus support group: A special student organization is available to students with LD.

GENERAL COLLEGE INFORMATION

State-supported, coed. Part of University of North Carolina System. Awards bachelor's, master's, doctoral, first professional degrees. Founded 1789. *Setting:* 789-acre suburban campus with easy access to Raleigh-Durham. *Endowment:* $390.2 million. *Research spending 1995–96:* $156 million. *Total enrollment:* 24,141. *Faculty:* 2,640 (2,417 full-time, 93% with terminal degrees, 223 part-time).

Enrollment Profile: 15,363 students from 53 states and territories, 55 other countries. 60% women, 40% men, 6% part-time, 82% state residents, 41% live on campus, 8% transferred in, 1% international, 6% 25 or older, 1% Native American, 1% Hispanic, 10% black, 5% Asian or Pacific Islander. *Retention:* 95% of 1995 full-time freshmen returned. *Graduation:* 63% graduate in 4 years, 80% in 5 years, 83% in 6 years. *Areas of study chosen:* 22% social sciences, 13% biological and life sciences, 13% health professions and related sciences, 9% psychology, 6% business management and administrative services, 6% communications and journalism, 5% English language/literature/letters, 5% liberal arts/general studies, 4% area and ethnic studies, 4% education, 4% physical sciences, 1% computer and information sciences, 1% engineering and applied sciences, 1% fine arts, 1% foreign language and literature, 1% interdisciplinary studies, 1% mathematics, 1% performing arts, 1% philosophy, 1% theology/religion. *Most popular recent majors:* biology/biological sciences, business administration/commerce/management, psychology.

First-Year Class: 3,278 total; 15,249 applied, 38% were accepted, 56% of whom enrolled. 69% from top 10% of their high school class, 92% from top quarter, 99% from top half. 254 National Merit Scholars, 220 class presidents, 226 valedictorians.

Graduation Requirements: 120 credit hours; 2 math courses; 3 semesters of a foreign language or the equivalent; computer course (varies by major).

Computers on Campus: 460 computers available on campus for general student use. Computer purchase/lease plans available. Computers for student use in computer center, computer labs, learning resource center, classrooms, library, student center, dorms provide access to the Internet/World Wide Web. Staffed computer lab on campus provides training in use of computers, software. *Academic computing expenditure 1995–96:* $10 million.

EXPENSES AND FINANCIAL AID

Estimated Expenses for 1997–98: State resident tuition: $1386 full-time. Nonresident tuition: $9918 full-time. Part-time tuition per semester ranges from $482.66 to $888.66 for state residents, $1550 to $4088 for nonresidents. Full-time mandatory fees: $779. College room and board: $4520. College room only: $2320.

Undergraduate Financial Aid: Of all full-time undergraduates enrolled in fall 1996, 67% of those who applied for aid were judged to have need according to Federal Methodology, of whom 97% were aided. On average, 95% of need was met. *Financial aid deadline (priority):* 3/1. *Financial aid forms:* FAFSA, CSS Financial Aid PROFILE required.

LD Program Contact: Ms. Jane Byran, Director of Learning Disability Services, The University of North Carolina at Chapel Hill, 315 Wilson Library, CB #3447, Chapel Hill, NC 27599, 919-962-7227.

UNIVERSITY OF PITTSBURGH

Pittsburgh, Pennsylvania

Students with LD	611	Subject-Area Tutoring	✓
ADD services	✓	Special Courses	✓
Staff	5 full-time	Taped Textbooks	✓
Special Fee	None	Alternative Test Arrang.	✓
Diagnostic Testing		Notetakers	✓
Basic Skills Remediation	✓	LD Student Organization	

LEARNING DISABILITIES PROGRAM INFORMATION

The Office of Disability Resources and Services began offering services in 1980. Currently the program serves 611 undergraduates with LD. Services are also available to graduate students. Students diagnosed with ADD/ADHD are eligible for the same services available to students with LD.

Staff: 5 full-time staff members, including coordinators, student services specialist. Services provided by learning strategy assistant, adaptive technology specialist, LD specialist, realtime reporter.

Special Fees: No special fees are charged for services to students with LD.

Applications and admissions: *Required:* high school transcript, courses completed, untimed SAT I or ACT, psychoeducational report completed within 3 years; *recommended:* high school grade point average, class rank, extracurricular activities, IEP (Individualized Education Program), extended time SAT I or ACT, personal interview, autobiographical statement, letters of recommendation. Students may begin taking classes any term. *Application deadline:* continuous.

Special policies: The college has written policies regarding substitutions and waivers of degree requirements.

PROGRAM AND SERVICE COMPONENTS

Special preparation or orientation: Summer program (required for some) held prior to entering college. Orientation (required for some) held before registration.

Academic advising: Provided by LD staff members. Students with LD may take up to 18 credits each term; most take 12 credits; 12 credits required to maintain full-time status and be eligible for financial aid.

Counseling services: Individual counseling, small-group counseling, career counseling, self-advocacy training.

Basic skills remediation: Offered one-on-one by LD teachers, teacher trainees; computer-aided instruction also offered. Available in reading, math, written language, learning strategies, perceptual skills, study skills, time management, social skills, computer skills.

Subject-area tutoring: Offered one-on-one and in small groups by professional teachers, peer tutors. Available in some subjects.

Special courses: College survival skills, time management, career planning, stress management, social relationships, self-advocacy. None offered for credit.

Auxiliary aids: Taped textbooks, tape recorders, calculators, word-processors with spell-check, personal computers, talking computers, optical character readers, assistive listening devices.

Auxiliary services: Alternative test arrangements, notetakers.

GENERAL COLLEGE INFORMATION

State-related, coed. Part of University of Pittsburgh System. Awards bachelor's, master's, doctoral, first professional degrees. Founded 1787. *Setting:* 132-acre urban campus. *Endowment:* $518.4 million. *Research spending 1995–96:* $158 million. *Total enrollment:* 25,479. *Faculty:* 3,465 (2,882 full-time, 91% with terminal degrees, 583 part-time); student–undergrad faculty ratio is 14:1.

Enrollment Profile: 16,049 students from 50 states and territories, 61 other countries. 53% women, 47% men, 20% part-time, 87% state residents, 39% live on campus, 1% international, 21% 25 or older, 1% Native American, 1% Hispanic, 9% black, 4% Asian or Pacific Islander. *Retention:* 85% of 1995 full-time freshmen returned. *Areas of study chosen:* 44% interdisciplinary studies, 8% engineering and applied sciences, 8% health professions and related sciences, 7% social sciences, 6% English language/literature/letters, 5% business management and administrative services, 4% psychology, 3% biological and life sciences, 3% computer and information sciences, 2% performing arts, 1% area and ethnic studies, 1% communications and journalism, 1% education, 1% foreign language and literature, 1% liberal arts/general studies, 1% mathematics, 1% philosophy, 1% physical sciences, 1% vocational and home economics. *Most popular recent majors:* business administration/commerce/management, psychology, speech/rhetoric/public address/debate.

First-Year Class: 2,202 total; 9,455 applied, 67% were accepted, 35% of whom enrolled. 26% from top 10% of their high school class, 58% from top quarter, 93% from top half.

Graduation Requirements: 120 credits; algebra proficiency; 3 natural science courses; proven proficiency in a foreign language; computer course for math, business, engineering, information science, health information management majors; senior project for honors program students and some majors.

Computers on Campus: 620 computers available on campus for general student use. Computer purchase/lease plans available. A computer is recommended for some students. A campus-wide network can be accessed from off-campus. Students can contact faculty members and/or advisers through e-mail. Computers for student use in computer center, computer labs, library, dorms provide access to the Internet/World Wide Web, on- and off-campus e-mail addresses. Staffed computer lab on campus provides training in use of computers, software. *Academic computing expenditure 1995–96:* $5.5 million.

EXPENSES AND FINANCIAL AID

Expenses for 1997–98: *Application fee:* $35. Part-time tuition per credit ranges from $197 to $248 for state residents, $425 to $527 for nonresidents. Part-time mandatory fees: $58 per semester. Full-time tuition ranges from $5658 to $7280 for state residents, $12,422 to $15,874 for nonresidents, according to school and program. Part-time tuition per credit ranges from $197 to $248 for state residents, $425 to $527 for nonresidents, according to school and program. Full-time mandatory fees: $506. College room and board: $5414. College room only: $3164.

Undergraduate Financial Aid: 75% of all full-time undergraduates enrolled in fall 1996 applied for aid; of these, 85% were judged to have need according to Federal Methodology, of whom 100% were aided. On average, 85% of need was met. *Financial aid deadline (priority):* 3/1. *Financial aid forms:* FAFSA, institutional form required. State form required for some.

LD Program Contact: Ms. Marcie Roberts, Coordinator, Disability Resources and Services, University of Pittsburgh, 216 William Pitt Union, Pittsburgh, PA 15260, 412-648-7890. Fax: 412-624-3346. Email: mcrobtst@pitt.edu.

UNIVERSITY OF TENNESSEE AT CHATTANOOGA

Chattanooga, Tennessee

Students with LD	160	Subject-Area Tutoring	✓
ADD services	✓	Special Courses	✓
Staff	4 full-, 1 part-time	Taped Textbooks	✓
Special Fee	✓	Alternative Test Arrang.	✓
Diagnostic Testing	✓	Notetakers	✓
Basic Skills Remediation	✓	LD Student Organization	

LEARNING DISABILITIES PROGRAM INFORMATION

The College Access Program began offering services in 1984. Currently the program serves 160 undergraduates with LD. Students diagnosed with ADD/ADHD are eligible for the same services available to students with LD, as well as screenings/assessments, computer lab.

Staff: 4 full-time, 1 part-time staff members, including director, coordinator, assessment counselor. Services provided by remediation specialists, tutors, counselor, diagnostic specialist.

Special Fees: $1000 per year. $400 for diagnostic testing.

Applications and admissions: *Required:* high school transcript, grade point average, courses completed, untimed SAT I or ACT, personal interview, autobiographical statement, letters of recommendation, psychoeducational report completed within 3 years, brief handwritten essay; *recommended:* extended time SAT I or ACT. Students may begin taking classes any term. *Application deadline:* 4/1 (fall term), 11/1 (spring term).

Special policies: The college has written policies regarding grade forgiveness.

PROGRAM AND SERVICE COMPONENTS

Special preparation or orientation: Required summer program offered prior to entering college. Required orientation held prior to fall enrollment and the week before classes begin.

Diagnostic testing: Intelligence, reading, math, spelling, handwriting, spoken language, written language, perceptual skills, study skills, personality, social skills, learning strategies.

Academic advising: Provided by LD staff members, academic advisers. Students with LD may take up to 20 semester hours each term; most take 12 to 15 semester hours; 12 semester hours required to maintain full-time status; 12 to 15 semester hours required to be eligible for financial aid.

Counseling services: Individual counseling, small-group counseling, career counseling, self-advocacy training.

Basic skills remediation: Offered one-on-one, in small groups, and in class-size groups by LD teachers, regular teachers, College Access Program staff; computer-aided instruction also offered. Available in reading, math, spelling, handwriting, spoken language, written language, learning strategies, study skills, time management, social skills, computer skills.

Subject-area tutoring: Offered one-on-one, in small groups, and in class-size groups by professional teachers, peer tutors, graduate assistants. Available in all subjects.

Special courses: College survival skills, reading, vocabulary development, communication skills, composition, learning strategies, word processing, time management, math, personal psychology, study skills, career planning, stress management, social relationships. Some offered for credit; some enter into overall grade point average.

Auxiliary aids: Taped textbooks, tape recorders, calculators, typewriters, word-processors with spell-check, personal computers, optical character readers.

Auxiliary services: Alternative test arrangements, notetakers, priority registration, advocacy.

GENERAL COLLEGE INFORMATION

State-supported, comprehensive, coed. Part of University of Tennessee System. Awards bachelor's, master's degrees. Founded 1886. *Setting:* 101-acre urban campus with easy access to Atlanta. *Research spending 1995–96:* $2.8 million. *Total enrollment:* 8,296. *Faculty:* 547 (325 full-time, 80% with terminal degrees, 222 part-time); student–undergrad faculty ratio is 17:1.

Enrollment Profile: 7,021 students from 46 states and territories, 49 other countries. 56% women, 44% men, 23% part-time, 89% state residents, 17% live on campus, 9% transferred in, 2% international, 27% 25 or older, 1% Native American, 1% Hispanic, 13% black, 3% Asian or Pacific Islander. *Retention:* 69% of 1995 full-time freshmen returned. *Areas of study chosen:* 17% business management and administrative services, 13% education, 11% health professions and related sciences, 7% engineering and applied sciences, 6% biological and life sciences, 6% psychology, 4% communications and journalism, 4% social sciences, 4% vocational and home economics, 3% agriculture, 3% computer and information sciences, 3% English language/literature/letters, 3% physical sciences, 2% fine arts, 2% performing arts, 1% mathematics, 1% philosophy, 1% theology/religion. *Most popular recent majors:* business administration/commerce/management, secondary education, nursing.

First-Year Class: 1,027 total; 2,372 applied, 53% were accepted, 81% of whom enrolled.

Graduation Requirements: 128 semester hours; 3 semester hours of math; 4 semester hours of science; computer course for business administration, engineering, math, science and math education majors; internship (some majors); senior project for honors program students and some majors.

Computers on Campus: 300 computers available on campus for general student use. A campus-wide network can be accessed from off-campus. Students can contact faculty members and/or advisers through e-mail. Computers for student use in computer center, computer labs, classrooms, library, dorms provide access to the Internet/World Wide Web. Staffed computer lab on campus.

EXPENSES AND FINANCIAL AID

Expenses for 1997–98: *Application fee:* $25. State resident tuition: $2200 full-time, $100 per semester hour part-time. Nonresident tuition: $6796 full-time, $260 per semester hour part-time. College room only: $1650 (minimum).

Undergraduate Financial Aid: 91% of all full-time undergraduates enrolled in fall 1996 applied for aid; of these, 96% were judged to have need according to Federal Methodology, of whom 88% were aided. On average, 78% of need was met. *Financial aid deadline (priority):* 3/1. *Financial aid forms:* FAFSA required; CSS Financial Aid PROFILE acceptable. State form required for some.

LD Program Contact: Mrs. Carolyn Bush, Principal Secretary, University of Tennessee at Chattanooga, 615 McCallie Avenue, Chattanooga, TN 37403, 423-755-4006. Fax: 423-785-2288. Email: carolyn-bush@utc.edu.

THE UNIVERSITY OF TENNESSEE AT MARTIN

Martin, Tennessee

Students with LD	65	Subject-Area Tutoring	✓
ADD services	✓	Special Courses	✓
Staff	1 full-, 5 part-time	Taped Textbooks	✓
Special Fee	✓	Alternative Test Arrang.	✓
Diagnostic Testing	✓	Notetakers	✓
Basic Skills Remediation	✓	LD Student Organization	

LEARNING DISABILITIES PROGRAM INFORMATION

The Program Access for College Enhancement (PACE) began offering services in 1992. Currently the program serves 65 undergraduates with LD. Services are also available to graduate students. Students diagnosed with ADD/ADHD are eligible for the same services available to students with LD.

Staff: 1 full-time, 5 part-time staff members, including director, coordinator. Services provided by remediation specialists, tutors, diagnostic specialist, notetakers, tapers, readers, graduate assistants.

Special Fees: $1000 per year.

Applications and admissions: *Required:* high school transcript, grade point average, courses completed, untimed or extended time ACT, autobiographical statement, letters of recommendation, psychoeducational report completed within 2 years; *recommended:* high school extracurricular activities, previous testing records. Students may begin taking classes in fall, spring, or summer. *Application deadline:* continuous.

Special policies: The college has written policies regarding substitutions and waivers of admissions, graduation, and degree requirements.

PROGRAM AND SERVICE COMPONENTS

Special preparation or orientation: Required summer program offered prior to entering college. Orientation (required for some) held before registration.

Diagnostic testing: Reading, math, spelling, handwriting, spoken language, written language, perceptual skills, study skills, personality, social skills, learning strategies.

Academic advising: Provided by LD staff members, academic advisers. Most students with LD take 12 to 15 semester hours each term; 12 semester hours required to maintain full-time status; source of aid determines number of semester hours required to be eligible for financial aid.

Counseling services: Individual counseling, small-group counseling, career counseling, discussion groups.

Basic skills remediation: Offered one-on-one and in small groups by LD teachers, PACE staff; computer-aided instruction also offered. Available in reading, math, spelling, handwriting, written language, learning strategies, study skills, time management, social skills.

Subject-area tutoring: Offered one-on-one and in small groups by professional teachers, peer tutors, graduate assistants. Available in all subjects.

Special courses: College survival skills, reading, composition, learning strategies, Internet use, time management, math, study skills, career planning, social relationships. Most offered for credit; most enter into overall grade point average.

Auxiliary aids: Taped textbooks, tape recorders, calculators, typewriters, word-processors with spell-check, personal computers, talking computers, optical character readers, Franklin Speller.

Auxiliary services: Alternative test arrangements, notetakers, advocacy.

GENERAL COLLEGE INFORMATION

State-supported, comprehensive, coed. Part of University of Tennessee System. Awards bachelor's, master's degrees. Founded 1927. *Setting:* 250-acre small-town campus. *Endowment:* $7.5 million. *Research spending 1995–96:* $680,192. *Educational spending 1995–96:* $3713 per undergrad. *Total enrollment:* 5,491. *Faculty:* 376 (280 full-time, 75% with terminal degrees, 96 part-time); student–undergrad faculty ratio is 14:1.

Enrollment Profile: 5,113 students from 36 states and territories, 32 other countries. 57% women, 43% men, 13% part-time, 90% state residents, 60% live on campus, 8% transferred in, 4% international, 24% 25 or older, 1% Native American, 1% Hispanic, 14% black, 1% Asian or Pacific Islander. *Retention:* 62% of 1995 full-time freshmen returned. *Areas of study chosen:* 15% business management and administrative services, 14% agriculture, 14% health professions and related sciences, 12% education, 9% social sciences, 4% engineering and applied sciences, 4% psychology, 3% biological and life sciences, 3% communications and journalism, 3% liberal arts/general studies, 3% natural resource sciences, 2% computer and information sciences, 2% premed, 2% vocational and home economics, 1% English language/literature/letters, 1% fine arts, 1% foreign language and literature, 1% mathematics, 1% performing arts, 1% philosophy, 1% physical sciences, 1% predentistry, 1% prevet. *Most popular recent majors:* marketing/retailing/merchandising, health education, accounting.

First-Year Class: 979 total; 1,129 applied, 97% were accepted, 90% of whom enrolled. 19 valedictorians.

Graduation Requirements: 129 semester hours; 3 semester hours of math; internship (some majors); senior project for honors program students and some majors.

Computers on Campus: 350 computers available on campus for general student use. Computer purchase/lease plans available. A computer is recommended for all students. A campus-wide network can be accessed from student residence rooms and from off-campus. Students can contact faculty members and/or advisers through e-mail. Computers for student use in computer center, computer labs, learning resource center, classrooms, library, student center, dorms, student rooms provide access to the Internet/World Wide Web. Staffed computer lab on campus provides training in use of computers, software. *Academic computing expenditure 1995–96:* $374,903.

EXPENSES AND FINANCIAL AID

Expenses for 1997–98: *Application fee:* $25. State resident tuition: $2240 full-time, $95 per semester hour part-time. Nonresident tuition: $6706 full-time, $286 per semester hour part-time. College room and board: $3104. College room only: $1600.

Undergraduate Financial Aid: Of all full-time undergraduates enrolled in fall 1996, 94% of those who applied for aid were judged to have need according to Federal Methodology, of whom 95% were aided. On average, 75% of need was met. *Financial aid deadline (priority):* 3/1. *Financial aid forms:* FAFSA or CSS Financial Aid PROFILE required. State form required for some.

LD Program Contact: Dr. Barbara Gregory, Director, Program Access for College Enhancement (PACE), The University of Tennessee at Martin, 240 Gooch Hall, Martin, TN 38238, 901-587-7195. Fax: 901-587-7956. Email: bgregory@utm.edu.

UNIVERSITY OF THE ARTS

Philadelphia, Pennsylvania

Students with LD	20 to 25	Subject-Area Tutoring	✓
ADD services	✓	Special Courses	
Staff	1 part-time	Taped Textbooks	✓
Special Fee	None	Alternative Test Arrang.	✓
Diagnostic Testing		Notetakers	✓
Basic Skills Remediation	✓	LD Student Organization	

LEARNING DISABILITIES PROGRAM INFORMATION

The Learning Specialist's Office began offering services in 1980. Currently the program serves 20 to 25 undergraduates with LD. Students diagnosed with ADD/ADHD are eligible for the same services available to students with LD.

Staff: 1 part-time staff member (coordinator). Services provided by remediation specialists, tutors, counselors.

Special Fees: No special fees are charged for services to students with LD.

Applications and admissions: *Required:* high school transcript, grade point average, class rank, courses completed, autobiographical statement, letters of recommendation, psychoeducational report completed within 3 years; *recommended:* high school extracurricular activities, IEP (Individualized Education Program), untimed or extended time SAT I or ACT, personal interview. Students may begin taking classes in fall or spring. *Application deadline:* continuous.

PROGRAM AND SERVICE COMPONENTS

Academic advising: Provided by LD staff members, academic advisers. Students with LD may take up to 18 credits each term; most take 12 to 18 credits; 12 credits required to maintain full-time status; 6 credits required to be eligible for financial aid.

Counseling services: Individual counseling, career counseling.

Basic skills remediation: Offered one-on-one by regular teachers, learning specialist. Available in reading, written language, learning strategies, study skills, time management, computer skills.

University of the Arts (continued)

Subject-area tutoring: Offered one-on-one by professional teachers, peer tutors. Available in all subjects.
Auxiliary aids: Taped textbooks, tape recorders, typewriters, word-processors with spell-check.
Auxiliary services: Alternative test arrangements, notetakers, priority registration, advocacy, taped lectures, time extensions for assignments; other arrangements as needed.

GENERAL COLLEGE INFORMATION

Independent, comprehensive, coed. Awards bachelor's, master's degrees. Founded 1870. *Setting:* urban campus. *Endowment:* $9.9 million. *Educational spending 1995–96:* $7400 per undergrad. *Total enrollment:* 1,399. *Faculty:* 256 (88 full-time, 63% with terminal degrees, 168 part-time); student–undergrad faculty ratio is 9:1.
Enrollment Profile: 1,268 students from 37 states and territories, 20 other countries. 50% women, 50% men, 4% part-time, 47% state residents, 10% transferred in, 3% international, 11% 25 or older, 1% Native American, 4% Hispanic, 10% black, 4% Asian or Pacific Islander. *Retention:* 76% of 1995 full-time freshmen returned. *Areas of study chosen:* 62% fine arts, 38% performing arts. *Most popular recent majors:* dance, illustration, art/fine arts.
First-Year Class: 330 total; 958 applied, 81% were accepted, 43% of whom enrolled. 8% from top 10% of their high school class, 24% from top quarter, 70% from top half.
Graduation Requirements: 123 credits; computer course for industrial design, graphic design, animation majors; internship (some majors); senior project (some majors).
Computers on Campus: 135 computers available on campus for general student use. A computer is required for some students. Students can contact faculty members and/or advisers through e-mail. Computers for student use in computer center, computer labs, learning resource center, classrooms, library, departmental electronic media labs provide access to the Internet/World Wide Web. Staffed computer lab on campus provides training in use of computers, software. *Academic computing expenditure 1995–96:* $278,533.

EXPENSES AND FINANCIAL AID

Expenses for 1997–98: *Application fee:* $30. Tuition: $14,570 full-time, $630 per credit part-time. Full-time mandatory fees: $500. College room only: $4100.
Undergraduate Financial Aid: On average, 65% of need was met. *Financial aid deadline (priority):* 2/15. *Financial aid forms:* FAFSA required.
LD Program Contact: Ms. Marilyn Longo, Learning Specialist, University of the Arts, 1500 Pine Street, Philadelphia, PA 19102, 215-875-2254. Fax: 215-875-5003.

UNIVERSITY OF THE OZARKS

Clarksville, Arkansas

Students with LD	61	Subject-Area Tutoring	✓
ADD services	✓	Special Courses	✓
Staff	16 full-, 1 part-time	Taped Textbooks	✓
Special Fee	✓	Alternative Test Arrang.	✓
Diagnostic Testing	✓	Notetakers	✓
Basic Skills Remediation	✓	LD Student Organization	

LEARNING DISABILITIES PROGRAM INFORMATION

The Jones Learning Center began offering services in 1971. Currently the program serves 61 undergraduates with LD. Students diagnosed with ADD/ADHD are eligible for the same services available to students with LD, as well as more structured assistance with time management skills.
Staff: 16 full-time, 1 part-time staff members, including director, assistant director. Services provided by remediation specialists, tutors, diagnostic specialist, auxiliary service coordinator, program coordinator, LD assistants, peer tutors.
Special Fees: $9800 per year. $600 for diagnostic testing.
Applications and admissions: *Required:* high school transcript, grade point average, personal interview, psychoeducational report completed within 1 year, 2-day session of on-campus psychoeducational testing; *recommended:* high school class rank, courses completed, extracurricular activities, untimed or extended time SAT I or ACT, letters of recommendation. Students may begin taking classes in fall or spring. *Application deadline:* continuous.
Special policies: The college has written policies regarding substitutions and waivers of admissions and graduation requirements.

PROGRAM AND SERVICE COMPONENTS

Special preparation or orientation: Optional orientation offered before registration.
Diagnostic testing: Intelligence, reading, math, spelling, handwriting, spoken language, written language, motor abilities, perceptual skills, personality, hearing, learning strategies.
Academic advising: Provided by LD staff members, academic advisers. Students with LD may take up to 21 credits each term; most take 12 credits; 9 credits required to maintain full-time status and be eligible for financial aid.
Counseling services: Career counseling, self-advocacy training.
Basic skills remediation: Offered one-on-one and in small groups by LD teachers. Available in reading, math, spelling, written language, learning strategies, study skills, time management.
Subject-area tutoring: Offered one-on-one and in small groups by peer tutors, program coordinators, remediation specialists, LD assistants. Available in all subjects.
Special courses: Reading, vocabulary development, composition, time management, study skills, career planning, understanding learning disabilities. Some offered for credit; some enter into overall grade point average.
Auxiliary aids: Taped textbooks, tape recorders, calculators, word-processors with spell-check, personal computers, talking computers, optical character readers, Dragon Dictate.
Auxiliary services: Alternative test arrangements, notetakers, advocacy, typing services.

GENERAL COLLEGE INFORMATION

Independent Presbyterian, 4-year, coed. Awards associate, bachelor's degrees. Founded 1834. *Setting:* 56-acre small-town campus with easy access to Little Rock. *Endowment:* $28 million. *Total enrollment:* 575. *Faculty:* 56 (41 full-time, 85% with terminal degrees, 15 part-time); student–undergrad faculty ratio is 15:1.
Enrollment Profile: 575 students from 26 states and territories, 9 other countries. 54% women, 46% men, 10% part-time, 65% state residents, 10% transferred in, 13% international, 1% Native American, 1% Hispanic, 6% black, 1% Asian or Pacific Islander. *Retention:* 64% of 1995 full-time freshmen returned. *Areas of study chosen:* 27% business management and administrative services, 12% education, 11% social sciences, 7% communications and journalism, 6% biological and life sciences, 5% fine arts, 4% performing arts, 3% health professions and related sciences, 3% mathematics, 2% engineering and applied sci-

ences, 2% natural resource sciences, 2% psychology, 1% premed. *Most popular recent majors:* business administration/commerce/ management, elementary education, secondary education.
First-Year Class: 125 total; 298 applied, 96% were accepted, 44% of whom enrolled. 18% from top 10% of their high school class, 61% from top quarter, 98% from top half. 2 National Merit Scholars, 12 valedictorians.
Graduation Requirements: 60 semester hours for associate, 128 semester hours for bachelor's; 6 semester hours of math/ science including at least 3 semester hours of math; computer course; senior project (some majors).
Computers on Campus: 125 computers available on campus for general student use. A campus-wide network can be accessed from student residence rooms and from off-campus. Students can contact faculty members and/or advisers through e-mail. Computers for student use in computer labs, classrooms, library, student rooms, departmental labs provide access to the Internet/ World Wide Web, on-campus e-mail addresses. Staffed computer lab on campus provides training in use of computers, software.

EXPENSES AND FINANCIAL AID

Expenses for 1997–98: *Application fee:* $10. Comprehensive fee of $10,990 includes full-time tuition ($7250), mandatory fees ($140), and college room and board ($3600). Part-time tuition: $305 per semester hour. Part-time mandatory fees per semester (9 to 11 semester hours): $70.
Undergraduate Financial Aid: 70% of all full-time undergraduates enrolled in fall 1996 applied for aid; of these, 94% were judged to have need according to Federal Methodology, of whom 100% were aided. On average, 57% of need was met. *Financial aid deadline (priority):* 2/15. *Financial aid forms:* FAFSA required; CSS Financial Aid PROFILE acceptable.
Financial aid specifically for students with LD: Scholarship: Jones Learning Center Scholarships.
LD Program Contact: Mrs. Emma Lee Morrow, Secretary, Jones Learning Center, University of the Ozarks, 415 North College Avenue, Clarksville, AR 72830-2880, 501-979-1403. Fax: 501-979-1429. Email: jlc@dobson.ozarks.edu.

Special policies: The college has written policies regarding grade forgiveness; substitutions and waivers of admissions, graduation, and degree requirements.

PROGRAM AND SERVICE COMPONENTS

Special preparation or orientation: Optional summer program offered prior to entering college. Optional orientation offered before registration and during registration, before classes begin.
Academic advising: Provided by LD staff members, academic advisers. Students with LD may take up to 16 semester hours each term; most take 12 semester hours; 12 semester hours required to maintain full-time status; 6 semester hours required to be eligible for financial aid.
Counseling services: Individual counseling, career counseling.
Basic skills remediation: Offered one-on-one and in small groups by regular teachers. Available in reading, math, learning strategies, study skills, time management, social skills.
Subject-area tutoring: Offered one-on-one by professional teachers, peer tutors, graduate students. Available in all subjects.
Special courses: Learning strategies, time management, study skills, career planning. All offered for credit; all enter into overall grade point average.
Auxiliary aids: Taped textbooks, tape recorders, calculators, word-processors with spell-check, personal computers, optical character readers.
Auxiliary services: Alternative test arrangements, notetakers, priority registration, advocacy, interpreters, tutors, proctors.
Campus support group: A special student organization is available to students with LD.

UNIVERSITY OF TOLEDO
Toledo, Ohio

Students with LD	638	Subject-Area Tutoring	✓
ADD services	✓	Special Courses	✓
Staff	5 full-, 10 part-time	Taped Textbooks	✓
Special Fee	None	Alternative Test Arrang.	✓
Diagnostic Testing		Notetakers	✓
Basic Skills Remediation	✓	LD Student Organization	✓

LEARNING DISABILITIES PROGRAM INFORMATION

The Center for the Physically and Mentally Challenged began offering services in 1982. Currently the program serves 638 undergraduates with LD. Services are also available to graduate students. Students diagnosed with ADD/ADHD are eligible for the same services available to students with LD.
Staff: 5 full-time, 10 part-time staff members, including director, assistant directors, coordinators. Services provided by tutors.
Special Fees: No special fees are charged for services to students with LD.
Applications and admissions: *Required:* high school transcript, extended time SAT I or ACT, psychoeducational report completed within 5 years. Students may begin taking classes any term. *Application deadline:* continuous.

GENERAL COLLEGE INFORMATION

State-supported, coed. Awards associate, bachelor's, master's, doctoral, first professional degrees. Founded 1872. *Setting:* 407-acre suburban campus with easy access to Detroit. *Endowment:* $25.1 million. *Research spending 1995–96:* $6.3 million. *Educational spending 1995–96:* $4990 per undergrad. *Total enrollment:* 21,692. *Faculty:* 1,355 (643 full-time, 87% with terminal degrees, 712 part-time); student–undergrad faculty ratio is 18:1.
Enrollment Profile: 18,187 students from 44 states and territories, 81 other countries. 53% women, 47% men, 21% part-time, 88% state residents, 13% live on campus, 6% transferred in, 4% international, 31% 25 or older, 1% Native American, 2% Hispanic, 13% black, 2% Asian or Pacific Islander. *Retention:* 73% of 1995 full-time freshmen returned. *Graduation:* 11% graduate in 4 years, 30% in 5 years, 37% in 6 years. *Areas of study chosen:* 17% education, 15% business management and administrative services, 14% vocational and home economics, 10% engineering and applied sciences, 7% interdisciplinary studies, 7% liberal arts/general studies, 4% social sciences, 3% communications and journalism, 3% psychology, 2% biological and life sciences, 2% physical sciences, 1% English language/literature/letters, 1% fine arts, 1% mathematics, 1% performing arts. *Most popular recent majors:* communication, marketing/retailing/merchandising.
First-Year Class: 2,442 total; 5,827 applied, 97% were accepted, 43% of whom enrolled. 38 National Merit Scholars.
Graduation Requirements: 124 semester hours for bachelor's; 19 quarter hours of math/science; computer course for engineering, business administration majors; internship (some majors); senior project for honors program students and some majors.
Computers on Campus: 2,750 computers available on campus for general student use. Computer purchase/lease plans available. A campus-wide network can be accessed from student residence rooms and from off-campus. Students can contact faculty members and/or advisers through e-mail. Computers for student use in computer center, computer labs, research center, learning resource center, classrooms, library, student center, dorms pro-

University of Toledo (continued)

vide access to the Internet/World Wide Web, on- and off-campus e-mail addresses. Staffed computer lab on campus (open 24 hours a day) provides training in use of computers, software. *Academic computing expenditure 1995–96:* $1.3 million.

EXPENSES AND FINANCIAL AID

Expenses for 1997–98: *Application fee:* $30. State resident tuition: $3171 full-time, $132.12 per semester hour part-time. Nonresident tuition: $8763 full-time, $365.12 per semester hour part-time. Part-time mandatory fees: $32.55 per semester hour. Full-time mandatory fees: $781. College room and board: $4194.
Undergraduate Financial Aid: 58% of all full-time undergraduates enrolled in fall 1996 applied for aid; of these, 99% were judged to have need according to Federal Methodology, of whom 94% were aided. On average, 78% of need was met. *Financial aid deadline (priority):* 3/1. *Financial aid forms:* FAFSA, institutional form required; CSS Financial Aid PROFILE acceptable.
Financial aid specifically for students with LD: Scholarship: Ketlholtz Scholarship.
LD Program Contact: Ms. Pamela J. Errich, Interim Director, Office of Accessibility, University of Toledo, 2801 West Bancroft Street, Toledo, OH 43606-3398, 419-530-4981. Fax: 419-530-6137.

UNIVERSITY OF VERMONT
Burlington, Vermont

Students with LD	484	Subject-Area Tutoring	✓
ADD services	✓	Special Courses	
Staff	5 full-, 3 part-time	Taped Textbooks	✓
Special Fee	None	Alternative Test Arrang.	✓
Diagnostic Testing	✓	Notetakers	✓
Basic Skills Remediation	✓	LD Student Organization	

LEARNING DISABILITIES PROGRAM INFORMATION

The Office of Specialized Student Services began offering services in 1981. Currently the program serves 484 undergraduates with LD. Services are also available to graduate students. Students diagnosed with ADD/ADHD are eligible for the same services available to students with LD.
Staff: 5 full-time, 3 part-time staff members, including director, assistant director. Services provided by remediation specialist, tutors, diagnostic specialist.
Special Fees: $50 to $300 for diagnostic testing.
Applications and admissions: *Required:* high school transcript, grade point average, courses completed, extracurricular activities; *recommended:* high school class rank, IEP (Individualized Education Program), untimed or extended time SAT I or ACT, personal interview, autobiographical statement, letters of recommendation, psychoeducational report completed within 3 years. Students may begin taking classes in fall only. *Application deadline:* 2/1.
Special policies: The college has written policies regarding substitutions and waivers of admissions, graduation, and degree requirements.

PROGRAM AND SERVICE COMPONENTS

Special preparation or orientation: Optional orientation offered before registration.
Diagnostic testing: Intelligence, reading, math, spelling, spoken language, written language, motor abilities, perceptual skills, study skills, psychoneurology, speech, hearing, learning strategies.
Academic advising: Provided by LD staff members, academic advisers. Students with LD may take up to 18 credits each term; most take 12 to 15 credits; 12 credits (fewer with permission) required to maintain full-time status.
Counseling services: Individual counseling, small-group counseling, career counseling.
Basic skills remediation: Offered one-on-one by LD specialists, Learning Cooperative staff. Available in reading, math, written language, learning strategies, study skills, time management, speech.
Subject-area tutoring: Offered one-on-one and in small groups by professional teachers, peer tutors. Available in most subjects.
Auxiliary aids: Taped textbooks, tape recorders, word-processors with spell-check.
Auxiliary services: Alternative test arrangements, notetakers, priority registration, advocacy, scribes.

GENERAL COLLEGE INFORMATION

State-supported, coed. Awards associate, bachelor's, master's, doctoral, first professional degrees. Founded 1791. *Setting:* 425-acre small-town campus. *Endowment:* $137.3 million. *Total enrollment:* 8,929. *Faculty:* 1,030 (888 full-time, 86% with terminal degrees, 142 part-time); student–undergrad faculty ratio is 13:1.
Enrollment Profile: 7,375 students from 48 states and territories, 28 other countries. 54% women, 46% men, 6% part-time, 41% state residents, 47% live on campus, 4% transferred in, 1% international, 6% 25 or older, 1% Native American, 1% Hispanic, 1% black, 2% Asian or Pacific Islander. *Retention:* 81% of 1995 full-time freshmen returned. *Graduation:* 51% graduate in 4 years, 68% in 5 years, 72% in 6 years. *Areas of study chosen:* 11% social sciences, 10% liberal arts/general studies, 10% natural resource sciences, 9% biological and life sciences, 9% business management and administrative services, 9% health professions and related sciences, 8% education, 6% psychology, 5% agriculture, 5% engineering and applied sciences, 5% English language/literature/letters, 3% fine arts, 2% vocational and home economics, 1% area and ethnic studies, 1% computer and information sciences, 1% foreign language and literature, 1% mathematics, 1% performing arts, 1% philosophy, 1% physical sciences, 1% theology/religion. *Most popular recent majors:* business administration/commerce/management, political science/government, psychology.
First-Year Class: 1,799 total; 8,578 applied, 75% were accepted, 28% of whom enrolled. 16% from top 10% of their high school class, 54% from top quarter, 90% from top half.
Graduation Requirements: 60 credits for associate, 122 credits for bachelor's; computer course for mathematical science, business administration, engineering, wildlife biology majors; internship (some majors).
Computers on Campus: 500 computers available on campus for general student use. Computer purchase/lease plans available. A computer is strongly recommended for all students. A campus-wide network can be accessed from student residence rooms. Computers for student use in computer center, computer labs, library, student center, dorms, engineering and business administration buildings provide access to the Internet/World Wide Web, on- and off-campus e-mail addresses. Staffed computer lab on campus provides training in use of computers, software.

EXPENSES AND FINANCIAL AID

Expenses for 1997–98: State resident tuition: $7032 full-time, $293 per credit part-time. Nonresident tuition: $17,580 full-time, $732.50 per credit part-time. Full-time mandatory fees: $498. College room and board: $5272. College room only: $3432 (minimum).

Undergraduate Financial Aid: Of all full-time undergraduates enrolled in fall 1996, 97% of those who applied for aid were judged to have need according to Federal Methodology, of whom 100% were aided. On average, 90% of need was met. *Financial aid deadline (priority):* 2/7. *Financial aid forms:* FAFSA required. State form, institutional form required for some.
LD Program Contact: Ms. Susan Krasnow, Learning Disabilities Specialist, Specialized Student Services, University of Vermont, A170 Living Learning Center, Burlington, VT 05405-0160, 802-656-7753.

UNIVERSITY OF WINDSOR

Windsor, Ontario, Canada

Students with LD	111	Subject-Area Tutoring	✓
ADD services	✓	Special Courses	✓
Staff	3 full-time	Taped Textbooks	✓
Special Fee	None	Alternative Test Arrang.	✓
Diagnostic Testing	✓	Notetakers	✓
Basic Skills Remediation		LD Student Organization	✓

LEARNING DISABILITIES PROGRAM INFORMATION

The Special Needs Department/Student Affairs began offering services in 1988. Currently the program serves 111 undergraduates with LD. Services are also available to graduate students. Students diagnosed with ADD/ADHD are eligible for the same services available to students with LD, as well as counselling for specific social problems.
Staff: 3 full-time staff members, including coordinator, technology adviser, secretary/exam coordinator. Services provided by counselor, diagnostic specialist, special needs adviser.
Special Fees: No special fees are charged for services to students with LD.
Applications and admissions: *Required:* high school transcript, grade point average, courses completed, psychoeducational report completed within 3 years; *recommended:* high school IEP (Individualized Education Program). Students may begin taking classes in fall or spring. *Application deadline:* 5/1 (fall term), 12/1 (spring term).
Special policies: The college has written policies regarding grade forgiveness; substitutions and waivers of admissions, graduation, and degree requirements.

PROGRAM AND SERVICE COMPONENTS

Special preparation or orientation: Optional orientation offered during registration and after classes begin.
Diagnostic testing: Intelligence, reading, math, spelling, handwriting, spoken language, written language, motor abilities, perceptual skills, study skills, personality, psychoneurology, learning strategies.
Academic advising: Provided by LD staff members. Students with LD may take up to 5 courses (6 with special permission) each term; most take 4 courses; 4 courses required to maintain full-time status; source of aid determines number of courses required to be eligible for financial aid.
Counseling services: Individual counseling, small-group counseling, career counseling, self-advocacy training, relaxation training, peer support group.
Subject-area tutoring: Offered one-on-one and in small groups by peer tutors, graduate assistants. Available in most subjects.
Special courses: College survival skills, reading, vocabulary development, communication skills, composition, learning strategies, word processing, time management, math, study skills, career planning. None offered for credit; none enter into overall grade point average.
Auxiliary aids: Taped textbooks, tape recorders, calculators, typewriters, personal computers, optical character readers.
Auxiliary services: Alternative test arrangements, notetakers, advocacy, priority registration (if student attends summer orientation).
Campus support group: A special student organization is available to students with LD.

GENERAL COLLEGE INFORMATION

Province-supported, coed. Awards bachelor's, master's, doctoral, first professional degrees. Founded 1857. *Setting:* 125-acre urban campus with easy access to Detroit. *Total enrollment:* 13,720. *Faculty:* 800 (500 full-time, 90% with terminal degrees, 300 part-time); student–undergrad faculty ratio is 17:1.
Enrollment Profile: 12,797 students from 10 provinces and territories, 38 other countries. 54% women, 46% men, 25% part-time, 79% province residents, 16% live on campus, 6% transferred in, 4% international. *Areas of study chosen:* 38% social sciences, 17% business management and administrative services, 5% education, 5% engineering and applied sciences. *Most popular recent majors:* social science, business administration/commerce/management, engineering and applied sciences.
First-Year Class: 3,200 total; 10,000 applied, 52% were accepted, 62% of whom enrolled.
Graduation Requirements: 30 courses; computer course for business administration, engineering, math majors; internship (some majors); senior project (some majors).
Computers on Campus: 62 computers available on campus for general student use. Computer purchase/lease plans available. A campus-wide network can be accessed from off-campus. Students can contact faculty members and/or advisers through e-mail. Computers for student use in computer center, computer labs, classrooms, faculty of business building, school of computer science, faculty of human kinetics building provide access to the Internet/World Wide Web, on- and off-campus e-mail addresses. Staffed computer lab on campus provides training in use of computers, software.

EXPENSES AND FINANCIAL AID

Expenses for 1997–98: *Application fee:* $75. Canadian resident tuition: $318 per course part-time. Nonresident part-time tuition per course ranges from $880 to $1155. Part-time mandatory fees per semester range from $42.57 to $52.57. Full-time tuition: $3181 to $3454 for Canadian residents, $8800 to $11,815 for nonresidents, according to program. (All figures are in Canadian dollars.). Full-time mandatory fees range from $382 to $429. College room and board: $6136.
Undergraduate Financial Aid: *Financial aid deadline (priority):* 7/1. *Financial aid forms:* state form required. Institutional form required for some.
LD Program Contact: Ms. Margaret Crawford, Special Needs Coordinator, University of Windsor, Room 117, Dillon Hall, Windsor, ON N9B 3P4, Canada, 519-253-4232 Ext. 3298. Fax: 519-973-7046. Email: crawfm@uwindsor.ca.

UNIVERSITY OF WISCONSIN–OSHKOSH

Oshkosh, Wisconsin

Students with LD	180	Subject-Area Tutoring	✓
ADD services	✓	Special Courses	✓
Staff	2 full-, 1 part-time	Taped Textbooks	
Special Fee	None	Alternative Test Arrang.	
Diagnostic Testing	✓	Notetakers	
Basic Skills Remediation	✓	LD Student Organization	✓

University of Wisconsin–Oshkosh (continued)

LEARNING DISABILITIES PROGRAM INFORMATION

The Project Success began offering services in 1979. Currently the program serves 180 undergraduates with LD. Services are also available to graduate students. Students diagnosed with ADD/ADHD are eligible for the same services available to students with LD, as well as specific training in the use of explicit sequencing concepts and in the identification of Requisite Antecedent Behavior for tasks common to human beings.
Staff: 2 full-time, 1 part-time staff members, including director, associate director, program manager. Services provided by remediation specialists, tutors, diagnostic specialist.
Special Fees: No special fees are charged for services to students with LD.
Applications and admissions: *Required:* high school transcript, untimed SAT I or ACT, personal interview, personal assessment including on-campus testing; *recommended:* extended time SAT I or ACT. Students may begin taking classes in summer only. *Application deadline:* continuous.
Special policies: The college has written policies regarding substitutions and waivers of admissions and degree requirements.

PROGRAM AND SERVICE COMPONENTS

Special preparation or orientation: Required summer program offered prior to entering college. Required orientation held during summer prior to enrollment.
Diagnostic testing: Reading, math, spelling, handwriting, spoken language, written language, motor abilities, social skills.
Academic advising: Provided by academic advisers. Students with LD may take up to 15 credits each term; most take 12 credits; 12 credits required to maintain full-time status and be eligible for financial aid.
Counseling services: Individual counseling, career counseling.
Basic skills remediation: Offered one-on-one, in small groups, and in class-size groups by LD teachers, teacher trainees. Available in reading, math, spelling, handwriting, written language, learning strategies, social skills.
Subject-area tutoring: Offered one-on-one, in small groups, and in class-size groups by professional teachers, professional tutors. Available in all subjects.
Special courses: Reading, vocabulary development, communication skills, composition, math, study skills. Most offered for credit; all enter into overall grade point average.
Campus support group: A special student organization is available to students with LD.

GENERAL COLLEGE INFORMATION

State-supported, comprehensive, coed. Part of University of Wisconsin System. Awards associate, bachelor's, master's degrees. Founded 1871. *Setting:* 192-acre suburban campus. *Research spending 1995–96:* $1.6 million. *Total enrollment:* 10,382. *Faculty:* 529 (401 full-time, 79% with terminal degrees, 128 part-time); student–undergrad faculty ratio is 19:1.
Enrollment Profile: 8,751 students from 30 states and territories, 34 other countries. 57% women, 43% men, 15% part-time, 96% state residents, 35% live on campus, 9% transferred in, 1% international, 20% 25 or older, 1% Native American, 1% Hispanic, 1% black, 2% Asian or Pacific Islander. *Retention:* 71% of 1995 full-time freshmen returned. *Graduation:* 9% graduate in 4 years, 36% in 5 years, 47% in 6 years. *Areas of study chosen:* 20% education, 16% social sciences, 10% business management and administrative services, 8% health professions and related sciences, 7% communications and journalism, 3% biological and life sciences, 3% fine arts, 3% psychology, 2% computer and information sciences, 1% English language/literature/letters, 1% foreign language and literature, 1% mathematics, 1% philosophy, 1% physical sciences, 1% theology/religion. *Most popular recent majors:* nursing, marketing/retailing/merchandising, elementary education.
First-Year Class: 1,563 total; 3,727 applied, 49% were accepted, 85% of whom enrolled. 11% from top 10% of their high school class, 34% from top quarter, 85% from top half. 1 National Merit Scholar.
Graduation Requirements: 60 credits for associate, 120 credits for bachelor's; 3 credits of math; 8 credits of natural science; computer course for business-related, some science majors; internship (some majors).
Computers on Campus: 350 computers available on campus for general student use. Computer purchase/lease plans available. A computer is recommended for some students. A campus-wide network can be accessed from student residence rooms and from off-campus. Students can contact faculty members and/or advisers through e-mail. Computers for student use in computer center, computer labs, library, dorms provide access to the Internet/World Wide Web, on- and off-campus e-mail addresses. Staffed computer lab on campus (open 24 hours a day) provides training in use of computers, software. *Academic computing expenditure 1995–96:* $1.2 million.

EXPENSES AND FINANCIAL AID

Expenses for 1996–97: *Application fee:* $28. State resident tuition: $2417 full-time, $101 per credit part-time. Nonresident tuition: $7881 full-time, $328 per credit part-time. Tuition for Minnesota residents: $2747 full-time, $115.28 per credit part-time. Full-time mandatory fees: $2. College room and board: $2511. College room only: $1551.
Undergraduate Financial Aid: Of all full-time undergraduates enrolled in fall 1996, 48% of those who applied for aid were judged to have need according to Federal Methodology, of whom 100% were aided. On average, 95% of need was met. *Financial aid deadline (priority):* 3/15. *Financial aid forms:* FAFSA required.
LD Program Contact: Dr. Robert T. Nash, Director, Project Success, University of Wisconsin–Oshkosh, Room #27, Nurse Education Building, Oshkosh, WI 54901, 414-424-1033. Fax: 414-424-0858.

UNIVERSITY OF WISCONSIN–WHITEWATER

Whitewater, Wisconsin

Students with LD	200	Subject-Area Tutoring	✓
ADD services	✓	Special Courses	✓
Staff	1 full-, 2 part-time	Taped Textbooks	✓
Special Fee	Varies	Alternative Test Arrang.	✓
Diagnostic Testing	✓	Notetakers	✓
Basic Skills Remediation	✓	LD Student Organization	✓

LEARNING DISABILITIES PROGRAM INFORMATION

The Project ASSIST began offering services in 1977. Currently the program serves 200 undergraduates with LD. Services are also available to graduate students. Students diagnosed with ADD/ADHD are eligible for the same services available to students with LD.
Staff: 1 full-time, 2 part-time staff members, including director, assistant director. Services provided by tutors.
Special Fees: Range from $295 to $900 per year. $200 to $350 for diagnostic testing.

Applications and admissions: *Required:* high school transcript, grade point average, courses completed, extended time ACT, letters of recommendation, psychoeducational report completed within 2 years; *recommended:* high school class rank, extracurricular activities, IEP (Individualized Education Program), personal interview. Students may begin taking classes in fall or summer. *Application deadline:* continuous.
Special policies: The college has written policies regarding grade forgiveness.

PROGRAM AND SERVICE COMPONENTS

Special preparation or orientation: Summer program (required for some) held prior to entering college. Orientation (required for some) held during summer prior to enrollment (4-week program).
Diagnostic testing: Intelligence, reading, math, spelling, spoken language, written language, perceptual skills, social skills, speech, hearing.
Academic advising: Provided by LD staff members, academic advisers. Students with LD may take up to 13 credits (freshman year) each term; most take 12 to 13 credits; 12 credits required to maintain full-time status; source of aid determines number of credits required to be eligible for financial aid.
Counseling services: Individual counseling, small-group counseling, career counseling.
Basic skills remediation: Offered one-on-one, in small groups, and in class-size groups by teacher trainees, peer tutors, Project Director, Assistant Director. Available in reading, math, spelling, handwriting, written language, learning strategies, study skills, time management, social skills, speech, computer skills.
Subject-area tutoring: Offered one-on-one and in small groups by peer tutors, teacher trainees, Program Director, Assistant Director. Available in all subjects.
Special courses: College survival skills, study skills, career planning. Most offered for credit; all enter into overall grade point average.
Auxiliary aids: Taped textbooks, tape recorders, calculators, typewriters, word-processors with spell-check, personal computers.
Auxiliary services: Alternative test arrangements, notetakers, advocacy.
Campus support group: A special student organization is available to students with LD.

GENERAL COLLEGE INFORMATION

State-supported, comprehensive, coed. Part of University of Wisconsin System. Awards associate, bachelor's, master's degrees. Founded 1868. *Setting:* 385-acre small-town campus with easy access to Milwaukee. *Endowment:* $2.4 million. *Research spending 1995–96:* $415,042. *Educational spending 1995–96:* $3496 per undergrad. *Total enrollment:* 10,398. *Undergraduate faculty:* 471 (347 full-time, 69% with terminal degrees, 124 part-time); student–undergrad faculty ratio is 21:1.
Enrollment Profile: 9,337 students from 24 states and territories, 35 other countries. 55% women, 45% men, 15% part-time, 94% state residents, 40% live on campus, 7% transferred in, 2% international, 10% 25 or older, 1% Native American, 2% Hispanic, 3% black, 1% Asian or Pacific Islander. *Retention:* 74% of 1995 full-time freshmen returned. *Areas of study chosen:* 32% business management and administrative services, 22% education, 12% social sciences, 11% communications and journalism, 6% psychology, 3% performing arts, 2% biological and life sciences, 2% computer and information sciences, 2% English language/literature/letters, 2% fine arts, 2% foreign language and literature, 1% interdisciplinary studies, 1% mathematics, 1% physical sciences, 1% prelaw. *Most popular recent majors:* business administration/commerce/management, accounting, marketing/retailing/merchandising.
First-Year Class: 1,841 total; 4,152 applied, 83% were accepted, 54% of whom enrolled. 11% from top 10% of their high school class, 35% from top quarter, 82% from top half.
Graduation Requirements: 60 credits for associate, 120 credits for bachelor's; 3 credits of algebra or completion of proficiency test; 5 credits of lab science; computer course for secondary math education, business-related majors; internship (some majors); senior project (some majors).
Computers on Campus: 700 computers available on campus for general student use. Computer purchase/lease plans available. A campus-wide network can be accessed from student residence rooms. Students can contact faculty members and/or advisers through e-mail. Computers for student use in computer center, computer labs, learning resource center, classrooms, library, dorms, academic buildings provide access to the Internet/World Wide Web. Staffed computer lab on campus provides training in use of computers, software.

EXPENSES AND FINANCIAL AID

Expenses for 1996–97: *Application fee:* $28. State resident tuition: $2586 full-time, $107.78 per credit part-time. Nonresident tuition: $8050 full-time, $335.54 per credit part-time. Tuition for Minnesota residents: $2906 full-time, $121.50 per credit part-time. College room and board: $2702. College room only: $1556.
Undergraduate Financial Aid: *Financial aid deadline (priority):* 4/15. *Financial aid forms:* FAFSA required; CSS Financial Aid PROFILE acceptable.
LD Program Contact: Ms. Deborah Hall, Director, University of Wisconsin–Whitewater, Roseman 2019, Whitewater, WI 53190, 414-472-5239. Fax: 414-472-5716.

URSULINE COLLEGE

Pepper Pike, Ohio

Students with LD	5	Subject-Area Tutoring	
ADD services		Special Courses	
Staff	1 full-, 1 part-time	Taped Textbooks	✓
Special Fee	✓	Alternative Test Arrang.	✓
Diagnostic Testing		Notetakers	✓
Basic Skills Remediation	✓	LD Student Organization	

LEARNING DISABILITIES PROGRAM INFORMATION

The Program for Students with Learning Disabilities (PSLD) began offering services in 1995. Currently the program serves 5 undergraduates with LD. Services are also available to graduate students.
Staff: 1 full-time, 1 part-time staff members, including Learning Disability Specialist. Services provided by remediation specialists, writing specialist.
Special Fees: $1000 per year.
Applications and admissions: *Required:* high school transcript, IEP (Individualized Education Program), personal interview, psychoeducational report completed within 3 years (or since age twenty), extended time SAT I or ACT (for students under 23 years old). Students may begin taking classes in fall or spring. *Application deadline:* 3/1 (fall term), 11/1 (spring term).
Special policies: The college has written policies regarding substitutions and waivers of graduation and degree requirements.

PROGRAM AND SERVICE COMPONENTS

Special preparation or orientation: Required orientation held before the start of each semester.
Academic advising: Provided by LD staff members. Most students with LD take 12 semester hours each term; 9 semester hours required to maintain full-time status; 6 semester hours required to be eligible for financial aid.

Ursuline College (continued)

Basic skills remediation: Offered one-on-one by LD teachers, writing skills specialist. Available in written language, learning strategies, study skills, time management.

Auxiliary aids: Taped textbooks, tape recorders, word-processors with spell-check, personal computers, talking computers, optical character readers, personal spell checkers, electronic dictionaries, talking calculators.

Auxiliary services: Alternative test arrangements, notetakers, priority registration, weekly support group.

GENERAL COLLEGE INFORMATION

Independent Roman Catholic, comprehensive, primarily women. Awards bachelor's, master's degrees. Founded 1871. *Setting:* 112-acre suburban campus with easy access to Cleveland. *Endowment:* $9.7 million. *Total enrollment:* 1,312. *Faculty:* 133 (73 full-time, 45% with terminal degrees, 60 part-time); student–undergrad faculty ratio is 14:1.

Enrollment Profile: 1,153 students from 11 states and territories, 1 other country. 95% women, 5% men, 44% part-time, 98% state residents, 8% live on campus, 13% transferred in, 1% international, 58% 25 or older, 1% Native American, 1% Hispanic, 18% black, 1% Asian or Pacific Islander. *Retention:* 48% of 1995 full-time freshmen returned. *Areas of study chosen:* 45% health professions and related sciences, 11% business management and administrative services, 9% fine arts, 7% education, 7% psychology, 7% social sciences, 3% biological and life sciences, 3% English language/literature/letters, 1% communications and journalism, 1% interdisciplinary studies, 1% mathematics, 1% philosophy, 1% prelaw, 1% premed, 1% theology/religion, 1% vocational and home economics. *Most popular recent majors:* nursing, psychology, business administration/commerce/management.

First-Year Class: 80 total; 261 applied, 84% were accepted, 36% of whom enrolled. 15% from top 10% of their high school class, 37% from top quarter, 69% from top half.

Graduation Requirements: 128 semester hours; 6 semester hours of science; computer course for business administration, health services management majors.

Computers on Campus: 45 computers available on campus for general student use. Computers for student use in computer center, learning resource center provide access to the Internet/World Wide Web. Staffed computer lab on campus provides training in use of computers, software. *Academic computing expenditure 1995–96:* $383,208.

EXPENSES AND FINANCIAL AID

Expenses for 1997–98: *Application fee:* $25. Comprehensive fee of $16,588 includes full-time tuition ($11,424), mandatory fees ($704), and college room and board ($4460 minimum). Part-time tuition: $357 per semester hour. Part-time mandatory fees: $22 per semester hour.

Undergraduate Financial Aid: 91% of all full-time undergraduates enrolled in fall 1996 applied for aid; of these, 96% were judged to have need according to Federal Methodology, of whom 100% were aided. On average, 89% of need was met. *Financial aid deadline (priority):* 3/1. *Financial aid forms:* FAFSA, institutional form required.

LD Program Contact: Ms. Beverly Brodsky, Learning Disability Specialist, Ursuline College, 2550 Lander Road, Pepper Pike, OH 44124-4398, 216-449-2046. Fax: 216-646-8318. Email: bbrodsky@main.ursuline.edu.

WESTERN MARYLAND COLLEGE

Westminster, Maryland

Students with LD	125	Subject-Area Tutoring	✓
ADD services	✓	Special Courses	✓
Staff	2 full-, 6 part-time	Taped Textbooks	✓
Special Fee	Varies	Alternative Test Arrang.	✓
Diagnostic Testing	✓	Notetakers	✓
Basic Skills Remediation	✓	LD Student Organization	

LEARNING DISABILITIES PROGRAM INFORMATION

The Academic Skills Center began offering services in 1984. Currently the program serves 125 undergraduates with LD. Services are also available to graduate students. Students diagnosed with ADD/ADHD are eligible for the same services available to students with LD.

Staff: 2 full-time, 6 part-time staff members, including director, assistant director. Services provided by tutors.

Special Fees: Range from $0 to $1200 per year according to program level. $1200 for diagnostic testing.

Applications and admissions: *Required:* high school transcript, grade point average, class rank, courses completed, untimed SAT I, autobiographical statement, letters of recommendation, psychoeducational report completed within 2 years; *recommended:* high school extracurricular activities, untimed or extended time ACT, extended time SAT I. Students may begin taking classes in fall or spring. *Application deadline:* 3/15.

Special policies: The college has written policies regarding substitutions and waivers of graduation and degree requirements.

PROGRAM AND SERVICE COMPONENTS

Special preparation or orientation: Required orientation held during registration.

Diagnostic testing: Intelligence, reading, math, spelling, handwriting, spoken language, written language, motor abilities, perceptual skills, study skills, personality, social skills, learning strategies, various academic areas (curriculum-based assessment).

Academic advising: Provided by LD staff members, academic advisers. Students with LD may take up to 20 semester hours each term; most take 12 to 15 semester hours; 12 semester hours required to maintain full-time status and be eligible for financial aid.

Counseling services: Individual counseling, small-group counseling, career counseling.

Basic skills remediation: Offered one-on-one, in small groups, and in class-size groups by LD teachers. Available in learning strategies, study skills, time management, social skills.

Subject-area tutoring: Offered one-on-one and in small groups by peer tutors, graduate students. Available in all subjects.

Special courses: College survival skills. None offered for credit; none enter into overall grade point average.

Auxiliary aids: Taped textbooks, tape recorders, word-processors with spell-check.

Auxiliary services: Alternative test arrangements, notetakers, priority registration, advocacy.

GENERAL COLLEGE INFORMATION

Independent, comprehensive, coed. Awards bachelor's, master's degrees. Founded 1867. *Setting:* 160-acre small-town campus with easy access to Baltimore and Washington, DC. *Endowment:* $28.3 million. *Research spending 1995–96:* $275,627. *Educational spending 1995–96:* $6305 per undergrad. *Total enrollment:* 2,592. *Faculty:* 204 (82 full-time, 96% with terminal degrees, 122 part-time); student–undergrad faculty ratio is 13:1.

Enrollment Profile: 1,382 students from 29 states and territories, 19 other countries. 54% women, 46% men, 5% part-time, 66% state residents, 6% transferred in, 3% international, 8% 25 or older, 1% Native American, 1% Hispanic, 5% black, 1% Asian or Pacific Islander. *Retention:* 83% of 1995 full-time freshmen returned. *Graduation:* 51% graduate in 4 years, 60% in 5 years, 61% in 6 years. *Areas of study chosen:* 17% social sciences, 10% biological and life sciences, 7% business management and administrative services, 7% communications and journalism, 7% physical sciences, 6% English language/literature/letters, 6% psychology, 4% fine arts, 3% mathematics, 1% foreign language and literature, 1% performing arts, 1% philosophy, 1% theology/religion. *Most popular recent majors:* sociology, physical education, biology/biological sciences.
First-Year Class: 385 total; 1,500 applied, 83% were accepted, 31% of whom enrolled. 36% from top 10% of their high school class, 55% from top quarter, 84% from top half. 1 National Merit Scholar, 21 valedictorians.
Graduation Requirements: 128 semester hours; 8 semester hours of math/science including at least 4 semester hours of lab science and math proficiency; 8 semester hours of a foreign language; computer course for math, physics majors; senior project.
Computers on Campus: 170 computers available on campus for general student use. Computer purchase/lease plans available. A campus-wide network can be accessed from student residence rooms and from off-campus. Students can contact faculty members and/or advisers through e-mail. Computers for student use in computer labs, classrooms, library provide access to the Internet/World Wide Web, on- and off-campus e-mail addresses. Staffed computer lab on campus provides training in use of computers, software. *Academic computing expenditure 1995–96:* $904,128.

EXPENSES AND FINANCIAL AID

Expenses for 1997–98: *Application fee:* $30. Comprehensive fee of $22,200 includes full-time tuition ($16,850) and college room and board ($5350). College room only: $2540 (minimum). Part-time tuition: $528 per semester hour. One-time mandatory fee: $300.
Undergraduate Financial Aid: 73% of all full-time undergraduates enrolled in fall 1996 applied for aid; of these, 89% were judged to have need according to Federal Methodology, of whom 100% were aided. On average, 97% of need was met. *Financial aid deadline (priority):* 3/1. *Financial aid forms:* FAFSA, institutional form required.
LD Program Contact: Ms. Denise Marjarum, Director, Academic Skills Center, Western Maryland College, 2 College Hill, Westminster, MD 21157-4390, 410-857-2504.

WESTMINSTER COLLEGE

Fulton, Missouri

Students with LD	36	Subject-Area Tutoring	✓
ADD services	✓	Special Courses	✓
Staff	2 full-time	Taped Textbooks	✓
Special Fee	Varies	Alternative Test Arrang.	✓
Diagnostic Testing		Notetakers	✓
Basic Skills Remediation	✓	LD Student Organization	

LEARNING DISABILITIES PROGRAM INFORMATION

The Learning Disabilities Program began offering services in 1975. Currently the program serves 36 undergraduates with LD. Students diagnosed with ADD/ADHD are eligible for the same services available to students with LD.
Staff: 2 full-time staff members, including director, assistant director. Services provided by tutors, counselors, diagnostic specialist, LD specialist.
Special Fees: Range from $1500 to $3000 per year according to program level.
Applications and admissions: *Required:* high school transcript, grade point average, courses completed, untimed ACT, personal interview, letters of recommendation, psychoeducational report completed within 3 years; *recommended:* high school class rank, extracurricular activities, untimed SAT I. Students may begin taking classes in fall only. *Application deadline:* continuous.

PROGRAM AND SERVICE COMPONENTS

Special preparation or orientation: Required orientation held before registration.
Academic advising: Provided by LD staff members. Students with LD may take up to 16 credit hours each term; most take 12 to 15 credit hours; 10 credit hours required to maintain full-time status; 12 credit hours required to be eligible for financial aid.
Counseling services: Individual counseling, career counseling.
Basic skills remediation: Offered one-on-one and in class-size groups by LD teachers. Available in reading, spelling, spoken language, written language, learning strategies, study skills, time management, computer skills.
Subject-area tutoring: Offered one-on-one and in small groups by professional teachers, peer tutors, LD specialists. Available in all subjects.
Special courses: College survival skills, reading, vocabulary development, composition, learning strategies, word processing, time management, study skills. All offered for credit; all enter into overall grade point average.
Auxiliary aids: Taped textbooks, tape recorders, word-processors with spell-check, personal computers, talking computers, optical character readers, computer dictation programs (speech-to-text technology).
Auxiliary services: Alternative test arrangements, notetakers, advocacy.

GENERAL COLLEGE INFORMATION

Independent, 4-year, coed, affiliated with Presbyterian Church. Awards bachelor's degrees. Founded 1851. *Setting:* 65-acre small-town campus. *Endowment:* $28.7 million. *Total enrollment:* 653. *Faculty:* 64 (47 full-time, 75% with terminal degrees, 17 part-time); student–undergrad faculty ratio is 12:1.
Enrollment Profile: 653 students from 24 states and territories, 12 other countries. 45% women, 55% men, 2% part-time, 60% state residents, 7% transferred in, 7% international, 1% 25 or older, 2% Native American, 2% Hispanic, 2% black, 3% Asian or Pacific Islander. *Retention:* 76% of 1995 full-time freshmen returned. *Graduation:* 55% graduate in 4 years, 57% in 5 years, 60% in 6 years. *Areas of study chosen:* 20% business management and administrative services, 15% social sciences, 8% biological and life sciences, 8% psychology, 5% education, 2% interdisciplinary studies, 2% mathematics. *Most popular recent majors:* business administration/commerce/management, political science/government, English.
First-Year Class: 216 total; 636 applied, 89% were accepted, 38% of whom enrolled. 30% from top 10% of their high school class, 54% from top quarter, 78% from top half.
Graduation Requirements: 122 credit hours; 2 math courses; 2 natural science courses including at least 1 lab science course; computer course for business, accounting, math, sociology majors; senior project for honors program students and some majors.
Computers on Campus: 280 computers available on campus for general student use. Computer purchase/lease plans available. A computer is recommended for all students. A campus-wide

network can be accessed from student residence rooms. Students can contact faculty members and/or advisers through e-mail. Computers for student use in computer center, computer labs, learning resource center, classrooms, library, academic buildings provide access to the Internet/World Wide Web, on- and off-campus e-mail addresses. Staffed computer lab on campus provides training in use of computers, software. *Academic computing expenditure 1995–96:* $121,617.

EXPENSES AND FINANCIAL AID

Expenses for 1996–97: *Application fee:* $25. Comprehensive fee of $16,270 includes full-time tuition ($11,700), mandatory fees ($240), and college room and board ($4330). Part-time tuition: $490 per credit hour.

Undergraduate Financial Aid: Of all full-time undergraduates enrolled in fall 1996, 92% of those who applied for aid were judged to have need according to Federal Methodology, of whom 100% were aided. On average, 94% of need was met. *Financial aid deadline (priority):* 3/22. *Financial aid forms:* FAFSA required; CSS Financial Aid PROFILE acceptable.

LD Program Contact: Mr. Henry F. Ottinger, Director, Learning Disabilities Program, Westminster College, Westminster Hall, Fulton, MO 65251-1299, 573-592-1304. Fax: 573-642-1217. Email: ottingh@micro.wcmo.edu.

WEST VIRGINIA WESLEYAN COLLEGE

Buckhannon, West Virginia

Students with LD	246	Subject-Area Tutoring	✓
ADD services	✓	Special Courses	✓
Staff	12 full-, 9 part-time	Taped Textbooks	✓
Special Fee	Varies	Alternative Test Arrang.	✓
Diagnostic Testing	✓	Notetakers	✓
Basic Skills Remediation	✓	LD Student Organization	

LEARNING DISABILITIES PROGRAM INFORMATION

The Special Support Services Program began offering services in 1982. Currently the program serves 246 undergraduates with LD. Services are also available to graduate students. Students diagnosed with ADD/ADHD are eligible for the same services available to students with LD.

Staff: 12 full-time, 9 part-time staff members, including director, coordinators, supervisor of learning center lab, staff assistants. Services provided by remediation specialists, tutors, counselors, LD specialists, reading specialists, writing specialists, math specialist.

Special Fees: $3700 for the first year; $2000 for the second year; $1000 for the third year; $500 for the fourth year.

Applications and admissions: *Required:* high school transcript, grade point average, autobiographical statement, letters of recommendation, psychoeducational report completed within 3 years, WAIS-R, WISC-R, Woodcock-Johnson Achievement Battery; *recommended:* extended time SAT I, personal interview. Students may begin taking classes in fall only. *Application deadline:* 3/1.

Special policies: The college has written policies regarding grade forgiveness.

PROGRAM AND SERVICE COMPONENTS

Special preparation or orientation: Required orientation held before registration.

Diagnostic testing: Reading, written language, study skills, learning strategies, learning styles.

Academic advising: Provided by LD staff members, academic advisers. Students with LD may take up to 16 credit hours each term; most take 12 to 15 credit hours; 12 credit hours required to maintain full-time status and be eligible for financial aid.

Counseling services: Individual counseling, small-group counseling, career counseling, self-advocacy training.

Basic skills remediation: Offered one-on-one and in small groups by LD teachers, regular teachers. Available in reading, math, spelling, written language, learning strategies, study skills, time management, social skills.

Subject-area tutoring: Offered one-on-one and in small groups by professional teachers, peer tutors. Available in all subjects.

Special courses: College survival skills, reading, composition, learning strategies, word processing, time management, math, typing, study skills, auditory processing, memory skills. All offered for credit; all enter into overall grade point average.

Auxiliary aids: Taped textbooks, tape recorders, calculators, word-processors with spell-check, personal computers, talking computers, Franklin Speller.

Auxiliary services: Alternative test arrangements, notetakers, priority registration, advocacy.

GENERAL COLLEGE INFORMATION

Independent, comprehensive, coed, affiliated with United Methodist Church. Awards bachelor's, master's degrees. Founded 1890. *Setting:* 80-acre small-town campus. *Endowment:* $25 million. *Total enrollment:* 1,592. *Faculty:* 144 (75 full-time, 71% with terminal degrees, 69 part-time); student–undergrad faculty ratio is 15:1.

Enrollment Profile: 1,531 students from 33 states and territories, 27 other countries. 54% women, 46% men, 7% part-time, 45% state residents, 87% live on campus, 7% transferred in, 4% international, 11% 25 or older, 1% Native American, 1% Hispanic, 5% black, 1% Asian or Pacific Islander. *Retention:* 78% of 1995 full-time freshmen returned. *Graduation:* 39% graduate in 4 years, 49% in 5 years, 52% in 6 years. *Areas of study chosen:* 18% social sciences, 11% business management and administrative services, 11% education, 8% biological and life sciences, 4% English language/literature/letters, 3% engineering and applied sciences, 3% performing arts, 2% communications and journalism. *Most popular recent majors:* business administration/commerce/management, biology/biological sciences, education.

First-Year Class: 377 total; 1,366 applied, 85% were accepted, 32% of whom enrolled. 24% from top 10% of their high school class, 50% from top quarter, 81% from top half. 2 National Merit Scholars, 17 valedictorians.

Graduation Requirements: 128 credit hours; 2 courses each in math and science; computer course for education, business, economics, nutrition/dietetics, physics, adult fitness majors; internship (some majors); senior project for honors program students and some majors.

Computers on Campus: 150 computers available on campus for general student use. Computer purchase/lease plans available. A computer is strongly recommended for all students. A campus-wide network can be accessed from student residence rooms and from off-campus. Students can contact faculty members and/or advisers through e-mail. Computers for student use in computer center, computer labs, learning resource center, library, departmental labs provide access to the Internet/World Wide Web. Staffed computer lab on campus provides training in use of computers, software. *Academic computing expenditure 1995–96:* $150,000.

EXPENSES AND FINANCIAL AID

Expenses for 1996–97: *Application fee:* $25. Comprehensive fee of $19,150 includes full-time tuition ($14,975), mandatory fees ($200), and college room and board ($3975). College room only: $1800. Part-time tuition: $625 per credit hour.

Undergraduate Financial Aid: 95% of all full-time undergraduates enrolled in fall 1996 applied for aid. *Financial aid deadline (priority):* 2/15. *Financial aid forms:* FAFSA required. Institutional form required for some.

Financial aid specifically for students with LD: Scholarships: Barosh Scholarship, Hall Liles Scholarship, Allen Manfuso Scholarship.

LD Program Contact: Ms. Phyllis Coston, Director of Learning Center, West Virginia Wesleyan College, 59 College Avenue, Buckhannon, WV 26201, 304-473-8380. Fax: 304-472-2571.

WRIGHT STATE UNIVERSITY

Dayton, Ohio

Students with LD	378	Subject-Area Tutoring	✓
ADD services	✓	Special Courses	✓
Staff	8 full-, 1 part-time	Taped Textbooks	✓
Special Fee	None	Alternative Test Arrang.	✓
Diagnostic Testing	✓	Notetakers	
Basic Skills Remediation	✓	LD Student Organization	✓

LEARNING DISABILITIES PROGRAM INFORMATION

The Office of Disability Services began offering services in 1975. Currently the program serves 378 undergraduates with LD. Services are also available to graduate students. Students diagnosed with ADD/ADHD are eligible for the same services available to students with LD.

Staff: 8 full-time, 1 part-time staff members, including director, associate director, assistant director, adapted technology specialist, academic support services specialist, test proctoring coordinator. Services provided by tutors, counselors, test proctors, readers, advocates.

Special Fees: No special fees are charged for services to students with LD.

Applications and admissions: *Required:* high school transcript, grade point average, class rank, courses completed, untimed SAT I or ACT, personal interview, psychoeducational report completed within 3 years; *recommended:* extended time SAT I or ACT, autobiographical statement, letters of recommendation. Students may begin taking classes any term. *Application deadline:* continuous.

Special policies: The college has written policies regarding grade forgiveness; substitutions and waivers of admissions, graduation, and degree requirements.

PROGRAM AND SERVICE COMPONENTS

Special preparation or orientation: Optional orientation offered before classes begin.

Diagnostic testing: Intelligence, reading, math, spelling, written language, perceptual skills, learning strategies.

Academic advising: Provided by academic advisers. Most students with LD take 12 to 14 credit hours each term; 12 credit hours required to maintain full-time status and be eligible for financial aid.

Counseling services: Individual counseling, small-group counseling, career counseling, self-advocacy training.

Basic skills remediation: Offered in class-size groups by regular teachers. Available in reading, math, spelling, written language, learning strategies, study skills, time management.

Subject-area tutoring: Offered one-on-one by peer tutors. Available in all subjects.

Special courses: College survival skills, reading, vocabulary development, communication skills, composition, learning strategies, time management, math, study skills, career planning. Most offered for credit; none enter into overall grade point average.

Auxiliary aids: Taped textbooks, tape recorders, word-processors with spell-check, personal computers, talking computers, optical character readers.

Auxiliary services: Alternative test arrangements, advocacy, readers.

Campus support group: A special student organization is available to students with LD.

GENERAL COLLEGE INFORMATION

State-supported, coed. Awards associate, bachelor's, master's, doctoral, first professional degrees. Founded 1964. *Setting:* 557-acre suburban campus with easy access to Cincinnati and Columbus. *Endowment:* $3.6 million. *Research spending 1995–96:* $12.5 million. *Total enrollment:* 15,697. *Undergraduate faculty:* 950 (700 full-time, 80% with terminal degrees, 250 part-time); student–undergrad faculty ratio is 20:1.

Enrollment Profile: 11,843 students from 47 states and territories, 59 other countries. 55% women, 45% men, 27% part-time, 97% state residents, 8% transferred in, 1% international, 31% 25 or older, 1% Native American, 1% Hispanic, 7% black, 2% Asian or Pacific Islander. *Retention:* 67% of 1995 full-time freshmen returned. *Areas of study chosen:* 24% liberal arts/general studies, 20% business management and administrative services, 13% education, 9% engineering and applied sciences, 7% health professions and related sciences, 5% biological and life sciences, 5% psychology, 5% social sciences, 4% fine arts, 3% communications and journalism, 2% computer and information sciences, 2% English language/literature/letters, 1% physical sciences. *Most popular recent majors:* accounting, nursing, psychology.

First-Year Class: 2,046 total; 4,092 applied, 90% were accepted, 56% of whom enrolled. 19% from top 10% of their high school class, 40% from top quarter, 65% from top half.

Graduation Requirements: 96 credit hours for associate, 187 credit hours for bachelor's; 3 credit hours of math; 12 credit hours of lab science; computer course for engineering, business, geological sciences, math, physics, psychology majors.

Computers on Campus: 450 computers available on campus for general student use. A campus-wide network can be accessed from student residence rooms and from off-campus. Students can contact faculty members and/or advisers through e-mail. Computers for student use in computer center, computer labs, classrooms, library, student center, dorms provide access to the Internet/World Wide Web, on- and off-campus e-mail addresses. Staffed computer lab on campus provides training in use of computers, software.

EXPENSES AND FINANCIAL AID

Expenses for 1997–98: *Application fee:* $30. State resident tuition: $3708 full-time. Nonresident tuition: $7416 full-time. Part-time tuition (1 to 10 credit hours): $115 per credit hour for state residents, $230 per credit hour for nonresidents. College room and board: $3900 (minimum).

Undergraduate Financial Aid: *Financial aid deadline (priority):* 3/1. *Financial aid forms:* FAFSA, institutional form required. State form required for some.

LD Program Contact: Mr. Stephen H. Simon, Director, Office of Disability Services, Wright State University, Colonel Glenn Highway, Dayton, OH 45435, 937-775-5680. Fax: 937-775-5795.

YORK UNIVERSITY

North York, Ontario, Canada

Students with LD	300	Subject-Area Tutoring	
ADD services	✓	Special Courses	✓
Staff		Taped Textbooks	✓
Special Fee	Varies	Alternative Test Arrang.	✓
Diagnostic Testing	✓	Notetakers	
Basic Skills Remediation	✓	LD Student Organization	✓

LEARNING DISABILITIES PROGRAM INFORMATION

The Learning Disabilities Programme (LDP) began offering services in 1985. Currently the program serves 300 undergraduates with LD. Services are also available to graduate students. Students diagnosed with ADD/ADHD are eligible for the same services available to students with LD, as well as coaching (life skills).

Staff: Includes assistant directors, coordinator, secretary, exam coordinators. Services provided by remediation specialist, counselors, diagnostic specialist.

Special Fees: $800 for diagnostic testing.

Applications and admissions: *Required:* high school transcript, grade point average, courses completed, IEP (Individualized Education Program), letters of recommendation, psychoeducational report completed within 5 years; *recommended:* high school extracurricular activities, personal interview, autobiographical statement. Students may begin taking classes any term. *Application deadline:* 4/1.

PROGRAM AND SERVICE COMPONENTS

Special preparation or orientation: Optional orientation offered during registration.

Diagnostic testing: Intelligence, reading, math, spelling, handwriting, spoken language, written language, motor abilities, perceptual skills, study skills, personality, learning strategies.

Academic advising: Provided by LD staff members, academic advisers. Students with LD may take up to 30 credits each term; most take 21 to 24 credits; 18 credits required to maintain full-time status; 12 credits required to be eligible for financial aid.

Counseling services: Individual counseling, small-group counseling, career counseling, self-advocacy training.

Basic skills remediation: Offered one-on-one by LD teachers, tutors. Available in reading, math, written language, learning strategies, study skills, time management, social skills.

Special courses: Learning and language seminar. All offered for credit; all enter into overall grade point average.

Auxiliary aids: Taped textbooks, tape recorders, word-processors with spell-check, personal computers, optical character readers.

Auxiliary services: Alternative test arrangements, priority registration, advocacy.

Campus support group: A special student organization is available to students with LD.

GENERAL COLLEGE INFORMATION

Province-supported, coed. Awards bachelor's, master's, doctoral, first professional degrees. Founded 1959. *Setting:* 650-acre urban campus with easy access to Toronto. *Total enrollment:* 37,900. *Faculty:* 2,228 (1,123 full-time, 100% with terminal degrees, 1,105 part-time); student–undergrad faculty ratio is 16:1.

Enrollment Profile: 33,999 students: 59% women, 41% men, 28% part-time, 97% province residents, 6% live on campus, 2% international, 34% 25 or older. *Areas of study chosen:* 19% business management and administrative services, 13% social sciences, 10% prelaw, 10% premed, 8% interdisciplinary studies, 7% English language/literature/letters, 7% fine arts, 6% psychology, 4% physical sciences, 3% biological and life sciences, 3% computer and information sciences, 3% education, 2% engineering and applied sciences, 2% liberal arts/general studies, 1% communications and journalism, 1% foreign language and literature, 1% health professions and related sciences, 1% mathematics, 1% natural resource sciences, 1% philosophy. *Most popular recent majors:* business administration/commerce/management, psychology, social science.

First-Year Class: 6,117 total; 20,523 applied, 66% were accepted, 45% of whom enrolled.

Graduation Requirements: 15 courses; computer course for administration majors; internship (some majors); senior project (some majors).

Computers on Campus: 1,200 computers available on campus for general student use. A computer is recommended for all students. A campus-wide network can be accessed from student residence rooms and from off-campus. Students can contact faculty members and/or advisers through e-mail. Computers for student use in computer center, computer labs, library, dorms provide access to the Internet/World Wide Web, on- and off-campus e-mail addresses. Staffed computer lab on campus (open 24 hours a day) provides training in use of computers, software.

EXPENSES AND FINANCIAL AID

Expenses for 1997–98: *Application fee:* $85. Canadian resident tuition: $3748 full-time, $749.64 per course part-time. Nonresident tuition: $10,746 full-time, $2149 per course part-time. Full-time mandatory fees for nonresidents: $546. (All figures are in Canadian dollars.). College room and board: $4595 (minimum). College room only: $3897.

Undergraduate Financial Aid: *Financial aid deadline:* Applications processed continuously. *Financial aid forms:* state form, institutional form required.

LD Program Contact: Dr. Marc Wilchesky, Coordinator, LDP, York University, 4700 Keele Street, 145 BSB, North York, ON M3J 1P3, Canada, 416-736-5297. Fax: 416-736-5633. Email: marc@yorku.ca.

▸ FOUR-YEAR COLLEGES ◂

WITH SPECIAL SERVICES

ABILENE CHRISTIAN UNIVERSITY

Abilene, Texas

LEARNING DISABILITIES SERVICES INFORMATION

Alpha Academic Services (Student Support Services) began offering services in 1987. Currently the program serves 134 undergraduates with LD. Students diagnosed with ADD/ADHD are eligible for the same services available to students with LD, as well as coaching.
Staff: 3 full-time, 26 part-time staff members, including director, coordinators. Services provided by tutors.
Special Fees: $10 to $200 for diagnostic testing.
Applications and admissions: *Required:* high school transcript, grade point average, class rank, courses completed, personal interview, autobiographical statement, letters of recommendation, psychoeducational report completed within 5 years (preferred); *recommended:* high school extracurricular activities, IEP (Individualized Education Program), extended time SAT I or ACT. Students may begin taking classes in fall or summer. *Application deadline:* continuous.
Special policies: The college has written policies regarding grade forgiveness.

PROGRAM AND SERVICE COMPONENTS

Diagnostic testing: Intelligence, reading, math, spelling, handwriting, spoken language, written language, motor abilities, perceptual skills, study skills, personality, social skills, psychoneurology, speech, hearing, learning strategies.
Academic advising: Provided by unit staff members, academic advisers. Students with LD may take up to 15 semester hours each term; most take 12 to 13 semester hours; 12 semester hours required to maintain full-time status and be eligible for financial aid.
Counseling services: Individual counseling, small-group counseling, career counseling, self-advocacy training.
Subject-area tutoring: Offered one-on-one and in small groups by professional teachers, peer tutors. Available in most subjects.
Auxiliary aids: Taped textbooks, tape recorders, calculators, typewriters, word-processors with spell-check, personal computers, optical character readers.
Auxiliary services: Alternative test arrangements, notetakers.

GENERAL COLLEGE INFORMATION

Independent, comprehensive, coed, affiliated with Church of Christ. Awards associate, bachelor's, master's, doctoral, first professional degrees. Founded 1906. *Setting:* 208-acre suburban campus. *Endowment:* $67 million. *Research spending 1995–96:* $378,990. *Educational spending 1995–96:* $3708 per undergrad. *Total enrollment:* 4,397. *Faculty:* 278 (186 full-time, 77% with terminal degrees, 92 part-time); student–undergrad faculty ratio is 19:1.
Enrollment Profile: 3,754 students from 47 states and territories, 53 other countries. 53% women, 47% men, 12% part-time, 64% state residents, 47% live on campus, 8% transferred in, 5% international, 12% 25 or older, 1% Native American, 5% Hispanic, 5% black, 3% Asian or Pacific Islander. *Retention:* 70% of 1995 full-time freshmen returned. *Graduation:* 26% graduate in 4 years, 44% in 5 years, 50% in 6 years. *Areas of study chosen:* 18% business management and administrative services, 13% education, 7% biological and life sciences, 7% communications and journalism, 6% theology/religion, 4% health professions and related sciences, 4% psychology, 4% social sciences, 3% performing arts, 3% vocational and home economics, 2% agriculture, 2% English language/literature/letters, 2% fine arts, 2% physical sciences, 1% computer and information sciences, 1% engineering and applied sciences, 1% foreign language and literature, 1% mathematics. *Most popular recent majors:* elementary education, biology/biological sciences, nursing.
First-Year Class: 896 total; 1,826 applied, 52% were accepted, 94% of whom enrolled. 23% from top 10% of their high school class, 49% from top quarter, 78% from top half. 8 National Merit Scholars, 44 valedictorians.
Graduation Requirements: 64 semester hours for associate, 128 semester hours for bachelor's; 3 semester hours of math; 6 semester hours of science; computer course for business, education, accounting, science, English, industrial technology, math, journalism, management, sociology, social work majors; internship (some majors); senior project for honors program students and some majors.
Computers on Campus: 500 computers available on campus for general student use. Computer purchase/lease plans available. A computer is recommended for some students. A campus-wide network can be accessed from student residence rooms and from off-campus. Students can contact faculty members and/or advisers through e-mail. Computers for student use in computer center, computer labs, learning resource center, classrooms, library, dorms, learning labs provide access to the Internet/World Wide Web, on- and off-campus e-mail addresses. Staffed computer lab on campus (open 24 hours a day) provides training in use of computers, software. *Academic computing expenditure 1995–96:* $1 million.

EXPENSES AND FINANCIAL AID

Expenses for 1997–98: *Application fee:* $25. Comprehensive fee of $13,640 includes full-time tuition ($9312), mandatory fees ($440), and college room and board ($3888). College room only: $1830. Part-time tuition: $291 per semester hour. Part-time mandatory fees: $15 per semester hour.
Undergraduate Financial Aid: Of all full-time undergraduates enrolled in fall 1996, 82% of those who applied for aid were judged to have need according to Federal Methodology, of whom 89% were aided. On average, 70% of need was met. *Financial aid deadline (priority):* 3/1. *Financial aid forms:* FAFSA, institutional form required; CSS Financial Aid PROFILE, state form acceptable.
LD Services Contact: Ms. Gloria Bradshaw, Director, Abilene Christian University, 222 W. Brown Library, Box 29204, Abilene, TX 79699-9204, 915-674-2750. Fax: 915-674-6847. Email: bradshawg@nicanor.acu.edu.

ADRIAN COLLEGE

Adrian, Michigan

LEARNING DISABILITIES SERVICES INFORMATION

EXCEL Program began offering services in 1980. Currently the program serves 51 undergraduates with LD. Students diagnosed with ADD/ADHD are eligible for the same services available to students with LD.
Staff: 4 full-time, 1 part-time staff members, including director, tutoring coordinator. Services provided by remediation specialists, tutors, counselors, reading specialist, learning specialist.
Special Fees: No special fees are charged for services to students with LD.
Applications and admissions: *Required:* high school transcript, grade point average, class rank, courses completed, psychoeducational report completed within 3 years of matriculation date; *recommended:* high school extracurricular activities, untimed or extended time SAT I or ACT, personal interview, autobiographical statement, letters of recommendation. Students may begin taking classes in fall or spring. *Application deadline:* 8/15.

PROGRAM AND SERVICE COMPONENTS

Diagnostic testing: Reading, math, spelling, handwriting, spoken language, written language, study skills, personality, learning strategies.
Academic advising: Provided by unit staff members, academic advisers. Students with LD may take up to 17 credit hours (12 to 13 recommended academic load) each term; most take 12 to 14 credit hours; 12 credit hours required to maintain full-time status; 12 credit hours (full-time) required to be eligible for financial aid.
Counseling services: Individual counseling, small-group counseling, career counseling, self-advocacy training.
Basic skills remediation: Offered one-on-one and in class-size groups by regular teachers, learning specialist, reading specialist, Director. Available in reading, math, written language, learning strategies, study skills, time management, speech.
Subject-area tutoring: Offered one-on-one and in small groups by peer tutors. Available in most subjects.
Special courses: College survival skills, reading, vocabulary development, composition, learning strategies, word processing, time management, math, study skills, career planning. Some offered for credit; all enter into overall grade point average.
Auxiliary aids: Taped textbooks, tape recorders, calculators, word-processors with spell-check, personal computers, talking computers, optical character readers.
Auxiliary services: Alternative test arrangements, notetakers, advocacy.

GENERAL COLLEGE INFORMATION

Independent, 4-year, coed, affiliated with United Methodist Church. Awards associate, bachelor's degrees. Founded 1859. *Setting:* 100-acre small-town campus with easy access to Detroit and Toledo. *Endowment:* $21.2 million. *Educational spending 1995–96:* $5022 per undergrad. *Total enrollment:* 1,049. *Faculty:* 92 (62 full-time, 79% with terminal degrees, 30 part-time); student–undergrad faculty ratio is 16:1.

Enrollment Profile: 1,049 students from 22 states and territories, 11 other countries. 49% women, 51% men, 8% part-time, 79% state residents, 75% live on campus, 3% transferred in, 1% international, 61% 25 or older, 3% Native American, 1% Hispanic, 7% black, 1% Asian or Pacific Islander. *Retention:* 74% of 1995 full-time freshmen returned. *Graduation:* 35% graduate in 4 years, 50% in 5 years, 52% in 6 years. *Areas of study chosen:* 14% business management and administrative services, 14% social sciences, 11% education, 6% biological and life sciences, 6% English language/literature/letters, 6% fine arts, 5% psychology, 4% communications and journalism, 4% natural resource sciences, 3% physical sciences, 2% computer and information sciences, 2% foreign language and literature, 2% mathematics, 2% prelaw, 2% premed, 1% performing arts, 1% theology/religion. *Most popular recent majors:* business administration/commerce/management, biology/biological sciences.
First-Year Class: 298 total; 1,228 applied, 89% were accepted, 27% of whom enrolled. 20% from top 10% of their high school class, 40% from top quarter, 80% from top half.
Graduation Requirements: 62 credit hours for associate, 124 credit hours for bachelor's; 8 credit hours of math/science; computer course for math, chemistry, education, physics, business majors; internship (some majors); senior project for honors program students and some majors.
Computers on Campus: 57 computers available on campus for general student use. Computer purchase/lease plans available. A campuswide network can be accessed from student residence rooms and from off-campus. Students can contact faculty members and/or advisers through e-mail. Computers for student use in computer labs, research center, classrooms, library, dorms, academic buildings provide access to the Internet/World Wide Web, on- and off-campus e-mail addresses. Staffed computer lab on campus provides training in use of computers, software. *Academic computing expenditure 1995–96:* $119,000.

EXPENSES AND FINANCIAL AID

Expenses for 1997–98: *Application fee:* $20. Comprehensive fee of $16,710 includes full-time tuition ($12,730), mandatory fees ($100), and college room and board ($3880 minimum). College room only: $1880 (minimum). Part-time tuition: $300 per credit hour. Part-time mandatory fees: $25 per semester.
Undergraduate Financial Aid: 90% of all full-time undergraduates enrolled in fall 1996 applied for aid; of these, 89% were judged to have need according to Federal Methodology, of whom 100% were aided. On average, 92% of need was met. *Financial aid deadline (priority):* 3/15. *Financial aid forms:* FAFSA required. Institutional form required for some.
LD Services Contact: Ms. Jane McCloskey, Director, EXCEL Program, Adrian College, Jones Hall, Adrian, MI 49221, 517-265-5161 Ext. 4413. Fax: 517-264-3331.

ALBANY STATE UNIVERSITY

Albany, Georgia

LEARNING DISABILITIES SERVICES INFORMATION

Disability Student Services began offering services in 1993. Currently the program serves 26 undergraduates with LD. Services are also available to graduate students. Students diagnosed with ADD/ADHD are eligible for the same services available to students with LD.
Staff: Includes associate director.
Special Fees: No special fees are charged for services to students with LD.
Applications and admissions: *Required:* high school transcript, grade point average, class rank, courses completed, personal interview, psychoeducational report completed within 3 years; *recommended:* high school extracurricular activities, IEP (Individualized Education Program), extended time SAT I or ACT. Students may begin taking classes any term. *Application deadline:* 9/1 (fall term), 3/1 (spring term).
Special policies: The college has written policies regarding substitutions and waivers of admissions, graduation, and degree requirements.

PROGRAM AND SERVICE COMPONENTS

Academic advising: Provided by academic advisers. Students with LD may take up to 15 quarter hours each term; most take 12 to 15 quarter hours; 12 quarter hours required to maintain full-time status; 6 quarter hours required to be eligible for financial aid.
Counseling services: Individual counseling, career counseling.
Basic skills remediation: Offered in class-size groups by regular teachers. Available in reading, math, written language, study skills.
Subject-area tutoring: Offered one-on-one by peer tutors. Available in most subjects.
Auxiliary aids: Taped textbooks, tape recorders, typewriters, word-processors with spell-check.
Auxiliary services: Alternative test arrangements, notetakers, priority registration, advocacy.

GENERAL COLLEGE INFORMATION

State-supported, comprehensive, coed. Part of University System of Georgia. Awards associate, bachelor's, master's degrees. Founded 1903. *Setting:* 131-acre urban campus. *Total enrollment:* 3,150. *Undergraduate faculty:* 173 (156 full-time, 17 part-time); student–undergrad faculty ratio is 20:1.
Enrollment Profile: 2,801 students: 64% women, 36% men, 20% part-time, 93% state residents, 4% transferred in, 15% 25 or older, 1% Native American, 1% Hispanic, 89% black, 1% Asian or Pacific Islander. *Areas of study chosen:* 14% health professions and related sciences, 12% fine arts, 10% computer and information sciences, 8% business management and administrative services, 8% education, 8% interdisciplinary studies.
First-Year Class: 515 total; 1,617 applied, 70% were accepted, 46% of whom enrolled.
Graduation Requirements: 95 quarter hours for associate, 186 quarter hours for bachelor's; 10 quarter hours each of math and science; computer course for business, math, office administration majors; internship (some majors); senior project (some majors).
Computers on Campus: 500 computers available on campus for general student use. A campus-wide network can be accessed. Students can contact faculty members and/or advisers through e-mail. Computers for student use in computer labs, library, departmental labs provide access to the Internet/World Wide Web, on- and off-campus e-mail addresses. Staffed computer lab on campus provides training in use of computers, software.

EXPENSES AND FINANCIAL AID

Expenses for 1996–97: *Application fee:* $10. State resident tuition: $1440 (minimum) full-time. Nonresident tuition: $4320 (minimum) full-time. Part-time tuition per quarter hour ranges from $40 to $44 for state residents, $120 to $151.75 for nonresidents. Full-time tuition ranges up to $1584 for state residents, $5463 for nonresidents. Part-time mandatory fees per quarter (6 to 11 quarter hours): $140. Full-time mandatory fees: $420. College room and board: $3180. College room only: $1515.
Undergraduate Financial Aid: Of all full-time undergraduates enrolled in fall 1996, 84% of those who applied for aid were judged to have need according to Federal Methodology, of whom 94% were aided. On average, 85% of need was met. *Financial aid deadline (priority):* 4/15. *Financial aid forms:* FAFSA required; CSS Financial Aid PROFILE acceptable. State form, institutional form required for some.
LD Services Contact: Ms. Deborah J. Moore, Acting Associate Director of Counseling, Testing and Career Development, Albany State University, 504 College Drive, Albany, GA 31705, 912-430-4667. Fax: 912-430-3826.

ALBERTA COLLEGE OF ART AND DESIGN

Calgary, Alberta, Canada

LEARNING DISABILITIES SERVICES INFORMATION

Student Services began offering services in 1985. Currently the program serves 20 undergraduates with LD. Students diagnosed with ADD/ADHD are eligible for the same services available to students with LD.
Staff: 1 full-time staff member (Counsellor). Services provided by counselors.
Special Fees: No special fees are charged for services to students with LD.
Applications and admissions: *Required:* high school transcript, autobiographical statement; *recommended:* high school grade point average, courses completed, IEP (Individualized Education Program), personal interview, psychoeducational report. Students may begin taking classes in fall, winter, or spring.

PROGRAM AND SERVICE COMPONENTS

Special preparation or orientation: Optional orientation offered after classes begin.

Alberta College of Art and Design (continued)

Academic advising: Provided by academic advisers. Most students with LD take 10 to 15 credits each term; 9 credits required to maintain full-time status and be eligible for financial aid.
Counseling services: Individual counseling, career counseling.
Subject-area tutoring: Offered by peer tutors, Counsellor. Available in most subjects.
Special courses: College survival skills, reading, communication skills, learning strategies, time management, career planning, stress management. None offered for credit.
Auxiliary aids: Tape recorders, word-processors with spell-check, personal computers.
Auxiliary services: Alternative test arrangements, notetakers.

GENERAL COLLEGE INFORMATION

Province-supported, 4-year, specialized, coed. Awards bachelor's degrees. Founded 1926. *Setting:* 1-acre urban campus. *Endowment:* $1.3 million. *Educational spending 1995–96:* $5150 per undergrad. *Total enrollment:* 730. *Faculty:* 87 (35 full-time, 46% with terminal degrees, 52 part-time).
Enrollment Profile: 730 students from 9 provinces and territories, 14 other countries. 55% women, 45% men, 8% part-time, 74% province residents, 19% transferred in, 3% international, 26% 25 or older. *Retention:* 90% of 1995 full-time freshmen returned. *Areas of study chosen:* 100% fine arts. *Most popular recent majors:* painting/drawing, graphic arts, illustration.
First-Year Class: 220 total; 425 applied, 52% were accepted, 100% of whom enrolled.
Graduation Requirements: 132 credits; computer course for visual communications, photographic arts majors; senior project.
Computers on Campus: 35 computers available on campus for general student use. Computer purchase/lease plans available. Computers for student use in computer labs provide access to the Internet/World Wide Web. Staffed computer lab on campus provides training in use of computers, software. *Academic computing expenditure 1995–96:* $1.5 million.

EXPENSES AND FINANCIAL AID

Expenses for 1997–98: *Application fee:* $25. Canadian resident tuition: $1997 (minimum) full-time, $101 per credit part-time. Nonresident tuition: $8847 (minimum) full-time. Full-time tuition and fees range up to $2022 for Canadian residents, $8872 for nonresidents, according to class level. Part-time tuition and fees for nonresidents range from $202 to $482 per credit, according to class level. (All figures are in Canadian dollars.).
Undergraduate Financial Aid: *Financial aid deadline (priority):* 5/1. *Financial aid forms:* institutional form, Canada Student Loan form required for some.
LD Services Contact: Mr. Paul Roberge, Counsellor, Alberta College of Art and Design, 1407 14th Avenue, NW, Calgary, AB T2R 0Z7, Canada, 403-284-7666. Fax: 403-284-7636. Email: paul.roberge@acad.ab.ca.

ALBRIGHT COLLEGE

Reading, Pennsylvania

LEARNING DISABILITIES SERVICES INFORMATION

Counseling Center began offering services in 1984. Currently the program serves 15 undergraduates with LD. Students diagnosed with ADD/ADHD are eligible for the same services available to students with LD.
Staff: 1 part-time staff member (coordinator). Services provided by tutors, Associate Academic Dean, Coordinator.
Special Fees: No special fees are charged for services to students with LD.
Applications and admissions: *Required:* high school transcript, grade point average, untimed SAT I or ACT, autobiographical statement, letters of recommendation, psychoeducational report completed within 3 years; *recommended:* high school IEP (Individualized Education Program), extended time SAT I or ACT, personal interview. Students may begin taking classes in fall, spring, or summer. *Application deadline:* continuous.
Special policies: The college has written policies regarding grade forgiveness; substitutions and waivers of admissions, graduation, and degree requirements.

PROGRAM AND SERVICE COMPONENTS

Special preparation or orientation: Optional orientation offered during first week of classes.
Academic advising: Provided by academic advisers, registrar, associate dean. Students with LD may take up to 4 course units each term; most take 3 to 4 course units; 3 course units required to maintain full-time status and be eligible for financial aid.
Counseling services: Individual counseling, small-group counseling, career counseling, family counseling.
Subject-area tutoring: Offered one-on-one and in small groups by peer tutors. Available in all subjects.
Auxiliary aids: Taped textbooks, word-processors with spell-check, personal computers.
Auxiliary services: Alternative test arrangements, notetakers, priority registration, advocacy.

GENERAL COLLEGE INFORMATION

Independent, 4-year, coed, affiliated with United Methodist Church. Awards bachelor's degrees. Founded 1856. *Setting:* 110-acre suburban campus with easy access to Philadelphia. *Endowment:* $19.8 million. *Total enrollment:* 1,193. *Faculty:* 109 (63 full-time, 92% with terminal degrees, 46 part-time); student–undergrad faculty ratio is 12:1.
Enrollment Profile: 1,193 students from 13 states and territories, 5 other countries. 53% women, 47% men, 8% part-time, 66% state residents, 80% live on campus, 3% transferred in, 3% international, 2% 25 or older, 1% Native American, 3% Hispanic, 5% black, 3% Asian or Pacific Islander. *Retention:* 82% of 1995 full-time freshmen returned. *Graduation:* 61% graduate in 4 years, 66% in 5 years, 67% in 6 years. *Areas of study chosen:* 20% liberal arts/general studies, 17% biological and life sciences, 12% interdisciplinary studies, 12% psychology, 11% social sciences, 10% business management and administrative services, 4% education, 4% English language/literature/letters, 2% computer and information sciences, 2% physical sciences, 1% fine arts, 1% foreign language and literature, 1% mathematics, 1% philosophy, 1% theology/religion, 1% vocational and home economics. *Most popular recent majors:* business administration/commerce/management, biology/biological sciences, psychology.
First-Year Class: 354 total; 1,197 applied, 85% were accepted, 35% of whom enrolled. 23% from top 10% of their high school class, 46% from top quarter, 70% from top half. 8 valedictorians.
Graduation Requirements: 32 courses; 2 science courses including at least 1 lab science course; 3 courses in a foreign language or proven competence; computer course for business, education, math, accounting majors; internship (some majors); senior project for honors program students and some majors.
Computers on Campus: 225 computers available on campus for general student use. Computer purchase/lease plans available. A computer is recommended for all students. A campus-wide network can be accessed from student residence rooms and from off-campus. Students can contact faculty members and/or advisers through e-mail. Computers for student use in computer center, computer labs, classrooms, library, student center, dorms provide access to the Internet/World Wide Web. Staffed computer lab on campus provides training in use of computers, software. *Academic computing expenditure 1995–96:* $90,196.

EXPENSES AND FINANCIAL AID

Expenses for 1997–98: *Application fee:* $25. Comprehensive fee of $23,760 includes full-time tuition ($17,710), mandatory fees ($600), and college room and board ($5450). College room only: $3050. Part-time tuition: $2060 per course. Part-time tuition for evening classes: $705 per course.
Undergraduate Financial Aid: 86% of all full-time undergraduates enrolled in fall 1996 applied for aid; of these, 84% were judged to have need according to Federal Methodology, of whom 100% were aided. On average, 90% of need was met. *Financial aid deadline (priority):* 3/1. *Financial aid forms:* FAFSA, institutional form required; CSS Financial Aid PROFILE acceptable. State form required for some.
LD Services Contact: Coordinator, LD Services, Albright College, PO Box 15234, Reading, PA 19612, 610-921-7630. Fax: 610-921-7235.

ALMA COLLEGE

Alma, Michigan

LEARNING DISABILITIES SERVICES INFORMATION

Center for Student Development began offering services in 1990. Currently the program serves 15 undergraduates with LD. Students diagnosed with ADD/ADHD are eligible for the same services available to students with LD.

Staff: 1 full-time, 1 part-time staff members, including director, associate director. Services provided by tutors, counselors, graduate intern.
Special Fees: No special fees are charged for services to students with LD.
Applications and admissions: *Required:* high school transcript, grade point average, courses completed, extracurricular activities, psychoeducational report completed within 5 years; *recommended:* extended time SAT I or ACT, personal interview, autobiographical statement, letters of recommendation. Students may begin taking classes in fall or winter. *Application deadline:* continuous.

PROGRAM AND SERVICE COMPONENTS

Academic advising: Provided by unit staff members, academic advisers. Students with LD may take up to 15 credits each term; most take 13 to 15 credits; 13 credits required to maintain full-time status and be eligible for financial aid.
Counseling services: Individual counseling, small-group counseling, career counseling, self-advocacy training.
Basic skills remediation: Offered in class-size groups by regular teachers, professional staff. Available in math, written language, learning strategies, study skills, time management, social skills.
Subject-area tutoring: Offered one-on-one by peer tutors. Available in most subjects.
Special courses: Reading, communication skills, learning strategies, word processing, time management, study skills, career planning. None offered for credit.
Auxiliary aids: Typewriters, word-processors with spell-check.
Auxiliary services: Alternative test arrangements, notetakers, advocacy.
Campus support group: A special student organization is available to students with LD.

GENERAL COLLEGE INFORMATION

Independent Presbyterian, 4-year, coed. Awards bachelor's degrees. Founded 1886. *Setting:* 100-acre small-town campus. *Endowment:* $69.6 million. *Research spending 1995–96:* $83,552. *Educational spending 1995–96:* $4872 per undergrad. *Total enrollment:* 1,363. *Faculty:* 147 (85 full-time, 86% with terminal degrees, 62 part-time); student–undergrad faculty ratio is 14:1.
Enrollment Profile: 1,363 students from 18 states and territories, 6 other countries. 55% women, 45% men, 4% part-time, 96% state residents, 84% live on campus, 2% transferred in, 1% international, 2% 25 or older, 1% Native American, 1% Hispanic, 1% black, 1% Asian or Pacific Islander. *Retention:* 86% of 1995 full-time freshmen returned. *Graduation:* 58% graduate in 4 years, 68% in 5 years, 69% in 6 years. *Areas of study chosen:* 16% biological and life sciences, 15% business management and administrative services, 11% education, 10% health professions and related sciences, 8% English language/literature/letters, 8% social sciences, 7% psychology, 6% physical sciences, 4% communications and journalism, 4% mathematics, 3% fine arts, 2% computer and information sciences, 2% foreign language and literature, 2% performing arts, 1% philosophy, 1% theology/religion. *Most popular recent majors:* business administration/commerce/management, physical fitness/exercise science, biology/biological sciences.
First-Year Class: 377 total; 1,194 applied, 90% were accepted, 35% of whom enrolled. 40% from top 10% of their high school class, 74% from top quarter, 95% from top half. 10 National Merit Scholars, 16 class presidents, 19 valedictorians.
Graduation Requirements: 136 credits; basic math proficiency; 12 credits of science; computer course for physics, chemistry, math majors; internship (some majors); senior project for honors program students and some majors.
Computers on Campus: 627 computers available on campus for general student use. Computer purchase/lease plans available. A campus-wide network can be accessed from student residence rooms and from off-campus. Students can contact faculty members and/or advisers through e-mail. Computers for student use in computer center, computer labs, research center, classrooms, library, dorms, academic offices provide access to the Internet/World Wide Web, on- and off-campus e-mail addresses. Staffed computer lab on campus provides training in use of computers, software. *Academic computing expenditure 1995–96:* $861,718.

EXPENSES AND FINANCIAL AID

Estimated Expenses for 1997–98: *Application fee:* $20. Comprehensive fee of $18,728 includes full-time tuition ($13,690), mandatory fees ($133), and college room and board ($4905). Part-time tuition: $527 per credit. Part-time mandatory fees: $66.50 per term.
Undergraduate Financial Aid: Of all full-time undergraduates enrolled in fall 1996, 90% of those who applied for aid were judged to have need according to Federal Methodology, of whom 100% were aided. On average, 84% of need was met. *Financial aid deadline (priority):* 2/15. *Financial aid forms:* FAFSA required; CSS Financial Aid PROFILE acceptable.
LD Services Contact: Kalindi Trietley, Dean of Student Development, Alma College, 614 West Superior, Alma, MI 48801, 517-463-7225. Fax: 517-463-7277. Email: trietley@alma.edu.

ALVERNO COLLEGE

Milwaukee, Wisconsin

LEARNING DISABILITIES SERVICES INFORMATION

Instructional Services began offering services in 1986. Currently the program serves 60 undergraduates with LD. Services are also available to graduate students. Students diagnosed with ADD/ADHD are eligible for the same services available to students with LD.
Staff: 8 full-time, 2 part-time staff members, including director, assistant director, coordinator. Services provided by teachers.
Special Fees: No special fees are charged for services to students with LD.
Applications and admissions: *Required:* high school transcript, grade point average, class rank, untimed ACT, psychological report (if accommodations are requested); *recommended:* extended time ACT, autobiographical statement. Students may begin taking classes in fall or spring. *Application deadline:* continuous.

PROGRAM AND SERVICE COMPONENTS

Special preparation or orientation: Optional orientation offered through individual interviews before classes begin or during first two weeks of classes.
Academic advising: Provided by academic advisers. Most students with LD take 8 to 12 units each term; 12 units required to maintain full-time status; 6 units required to be eligible for financial aid.
Counseling services: Individual counseling, self-advocacy training, academic support group.
Basic skills remediation: Offered one-on-one and in small groups by regular teachers. Available in reading, math, written language, learning strategies, study skills, time management.
Subject-area tutoring: Offered one-on-one and in small groups by professional teachers, peer tutors. Available in all subjects.
Special courses: Reading, composition, learning strategies, math, study skills, critical thinking, integrated reading/writing. Some offered for credit.
Auxiliary aids: Taped textbooks, tape recorders, calculators, typewriters, word-processors with spell-check, personal computers, electronic dictionaries.
Auxiliary services: Alternative test arrangements, notetakers, advocacy.

GENERAL COLLEGE INFORMATION

Independent Roman Catholic, comprehensive, women only. Awards associate, bachelor's, master's degrees (also offers weekend program with significant enrollment not reflected in profile). Founded 1887. *Setting:* 46-acre suburban campus. *Endowment:* $11.6 million. *Research spending 1995–96:* $453,211. *Educational spending 1995–96:* $4087 per undergrad. *Total enrollment:* 2,191. *Undergraduate faculty:* 197 (115 full-time, 87% with terminal degrees, 82 part-time); student–undergrad faculty ratio is 13:1.
Enrollment Profile: 2,161 students from 13 states and territories, 2 other countries. 100% women, 42% part-time, 96% state residents, 7% live on campus, 10% transferred in, 1% international, 67% 25 or older, 1% Native American, 7% Hispanic, 18% black, 2% Asian or Pacific Islander. *Retention:* 87% of 1995 full-time freshmen returned. *Graduation:* 45% graduate in 4 years, 50% in 5 years, 55% in 6 years. *Areas of study chosen:* 31% business management and administrative services, 20% health professions and related sciences, 16% communications and journalism, 12% education, 6% psychology, 4% biological and life sciences, 4% English language/literature/letters, 3% fine arts, 2% social sciences, 1% mathematics, 1% physical sciences. *Most popular recent majors:* nursing, business administration/commerce/management, communication.
First-Year Class: 235 total; 691 applied, 65% were accepted, 52% of whom enrolled. 7% from top 10% of their high school class, 29% from top quarter, 62% from top half. 1 National Merit Scholar, 1 valedictorian.
Graduation Requirements: 32 units for associate, 40 units for bachelor's; math proficiency; 2 semesters of science; computer course; internship; senior project.

Alverno College (continued)

Computers on Campus: 196 computers available on campus for general student use. Computer purchase/lease plans available. Computers for student use in computer center, computer labs, library, dorms provide access to the Internet/World Wide Web. Staffed computer lab on campus provides training in use of computers, software. *Academic computing expenditure 1995–96:* $293,550.

EXPENSES AND FINANCIAL AID

Expenses for 1997–98: *Application fee:* $10. Comprehensive fee of $13,762 includes full-time tuition ($9672 minimum), mandatory fees ($50), and college room and board ($4040). Part-time tuition: $403 per unit (minimum). Part-time mandatory fees: $25 per semester. Tuition for engineering and nursing programs: $10,392 full-time, $433 per unit part-time.
Undergraduate Financial Aid: 83% of all full-time undergraduates enrolled in fall 1996 applied for aid; of these, 87% were judged to have need according to Federal Methodology, of whom 100% were aided. On average, 75% of need was met. *Financial aid deadline (priority):* 4/1. *Financial aid forms:* FAFSA, institutional form required; CSS Financial Aid PROFILE acceptable.
LD Services Contact: Ms. Colleen Barnett, Coordinator for Disability Services, Alverno College, PO Box 343922, Milwaukee, WI 53234-3922, 414-382-6026. Fax: 414-382-6354.

ANNA MARIA COLLEGE

Paxton, Massachusetts

LEARNING DISABILITIES SERVICES INFORMATION

Learning Center began offering services in 1982. Currently the program serves 15 undergraduates with LD. Services are also available to graduate students. Students diagnosed with ADD/ADHD are eligible for the same services available to students with LD.
Staff: 1 full-time staff member (director). Services provided by tutors, counselor.
Special Fees: No special fees are charged for services to students with LD.
Applications and admissions: *Required:* high school transcript, grade point average, class rank, courses completed, untimed SAT I, letters of recommendation, psychoeducational report completed within 3 years; *recommended:* high school extracurricular activities, extended time SAT I, personal interview, autobiographical statement. Students may begin taking classes in fall or winter. *Application deadline:* continuous.

PROGRAM AND SERVICE COMPONENTS

Academic advising: Provided by unit staff members, academic advisers. Students with LD may take up to 12 credit hours each term; most take 9 to 12 credit hours; 10 credit hours required to maintain full-time status; 12 credit hours required to be eligible for financial aid.
Counseling services: Individual counseling, career counseling.
Basic skills remediation: Offered one-on-one, in small groups, and in class-size groups by regular teachers. Available in reading, math, written language, learning strategies, study skills.
Subject-area tutoring: Offered one-on-one and in small groups by professional teachers, peer tutors. Available in most subjects.
Auxiliary aids: Taped textbooks, tape recorders, word-processors with spell-check, personal computers.
Auxiliary services: Alternative test arrangements, notetakers.

GENERAL COLLEGE INFORMATION

Independent Roman Catholic, comprehensive, coed. Awards associate, bachelor's, master's degrees. Founded 1946. *Setting:* 180-acre rural campus with easy access to Boston. *Endowment:* $1.7 million. *Educational spending 1995–96:* $6293 per undergrad. *Total enrollment:* 1,927. *Faculty:* 85 (34 full-time, 33% with terminal degrees, 51 part-time); student–undergrad faculty ratio is 15:1.
Enrollment Profile: 866 students from 12 states and territories, 5 other countries. 60% women, 40% men, 51% part-time, 90% state residents, 20% transferred in, 4% international, 10% 25 or older, 1% Native American, 2% Hispanic, 2% black, 2% Asian or Pacific Islander. *Retention:* 79% of 1995 full-time freshmen returned. *Graduation:* 45% graduate in 4 years, 51% in 5 years. *Areas of study chosen:* 45% social sciences, 13% business management and administrative services, 10% health professions and related sciences, 6% education, 6% performing arts, 5% liberal arts/general studies, 5% psychology, 3% fine arts, 2% biological and life sciences, 1% English language/literature/letters, 1% foreign language and literature, 1% predentistry, 1% prelaw, 1% premed. *Most popular recent majors:* criminal justice, business administration/commerce/management, elementary education.
First-Year Class: 112 total; 426 applied, 88% were accepted, 30% of whom enrolled. 3% from top 10% of their high school class, 27% from top quarter, 60% from top half. 1 valedictorian.
Graduation Requirements: 60 credit hours for associate, 120 credit hours for bachelor's; 3 math/science courses including at least 1 course each in math and lab science; 1 course in intermediate level foreign language or culture; computer course for business, elementary education majors; internship (some majors); senior project (some majors).
Computers on Campus: 40 computers available on campus for general student use. A campus-wide network can be accessed from student residence rooms. Students can contact faculty members and/or advisers through e-mail. Computers for student use in computer center, learning resource center, library, dorms, ESL lab provide access to the Internet/World Wide Web. Staffed computer lab on campus (open 24 hours a day) provides training in use of computers, software. *Academic computing expenditure 1995–96:* $99,789.

EXPENSES AND FINANCIAL AID

Expenses for 1997–98: *Application fee:* $30. Comprehensive fee of $17,676 includes full-time tuition ($11,600), mandatory fees ($640), and college room and board ($5436). Part-time tuition: $177 per credit hour. Part-time mandatory fees: $3 per credit hour.
Undergraduate Financial Aid: 83% of all full-time undergraduates enrolled in fall 1996 applied for aid; of these, 99% were judged to have need according to Federal Methodology, of whom 100% were aided. On average, 91% of need was met. *Financial aid deadline (priority):* 3/1. *Financial aid forms:* FAFSA, CSS Financial Aid PROFILE, state form required.
LD Services Contact: Ms. Olivia Tarleton, Director, Learning Center, Anna Maria College, Sunset Lane, Paxton, MA 01612, 508-849-3356.

ANTIOCH COLLEGE

Yellow Springs, Ohio

LEARNING DISABILITIES SERVICES INFORMATION

Learning Center began offering services in 1993. Students diagnosed with ADD/ADHD are eligible for the same services available to students with LD.
Staff: 7 part-time staff members, including coordinator. Services provided by tutors.
Special Fees: No special fees are charged for services to students with LD.
Applications and admissions: *Required:* high school transcript, letters of recommendation, 2 essays; *recommended:* high school extracurricular activities, untimed or extended time SAT I or ACT, personal interview, autobiographical statement, psychoeducational report completed within 3 years. Students may begin taking classes in fall, spring, or summer. *Application deadline:* 2/1 (fall term), 11/1 (spring term).

PROGRAM AND SERVICE COMPONENTS

Academic advising: Provided by unit staff members, academic advisers. Students with LD may take up to 18 semester hours each term; most take 12 to 16 semester hours; 12 semester hours required to maintain full-time status and be eligible for financial aid.
Counseling services: Individual counseling, self-advocacy training.
Basic skills remediation: Offered one-on-one by peer tutors; computer-aided instruction also offered. Available in math, spelling, written language, learning strategies, study skills, time management.
Subject-area tutoring: Offered one-on-one and in small groups by peer tutors. Available in most subjects.
Special courses: College survival skills, composition, learning strategies, word processing, time management, math, typing, study skills. Some offered for credit; none enter into overall grade point average.
Auxiliary aids: Personal computers, academic software.
Auxiliary services: Alternative test arrangements, advocacy.
Campus support group: A special student organization is available to students with LD.

GENERAL COLLEGE INFORMATION

Independent, 4-year, coed. Part of Antioch University. Awards bachelor's degrees. Founded 1852. *Setting:* 100-acre small-town campus with

easy access to Dayton. *Research spending 1995–96:* $186,855. *Total enrollment:* 640. *Faculty:* 84 (51 full-time, 69% with terminal degrees, 33 part-time); student–undergrad faculty ratio is 9:1.
Enrollment Profile: 640 students from 45 states and territories, 4 other countries. 60% women, 40% men, 19% state residents, 95% live on campus, 25% transferred in, 2% international, 4% 25 or older, 1% Native American, 4% Hispanic, 6% black, 3% Asian or Pacific Islander. *Retention:* 67% of 1995 full-time freshmen returned. *Areas of study chosen:* 5% interdisciplinary studies, 4% psychology, 2% communications and journalism, 2% English language/literature/letters, 2% performing arts, 1% biological and life sciences, 1% business management and administrative services, 1% computer and information sciences, 1% education, 1% fine arts, 1% foreign language and literature, 1% mathematics, 1% natural resource sciences, 1% philosophy, 1% social sciences.
First-Year Class: 143 total. Of the students who applied, 74% were accepted, 33% of whom enrolled. 16% from top 10% of their high school class, 44% from top quarter, 78% from top half.
Graduation Requirements: 107 credits and 60 cooperative education credits; 4 math/science courses; proven competence in a foreign language; senior project.
Computers on Campus: 37 computers available on campus for general student use. Computer purchase/lease plans available. A campus-wide network can be accessed from off-campus. Students can contact faculty members and/or advisers through e-mail. Computers for student use in computer labs, learning resource center, library, student center, dorms provide access to the Internet/World Wide Web, on- and off-campus e-mail addresses. Staffed computer lab on campus provides training in use of computers, software. *Academic computing expenditure 1995–96:* $6411.

EXPENSES AND FINANCIAL AID

Expenses for 1997–98: *Application fee:* $35. Comprehensive fee of $22,485 includes full-time tuition ($16,812), mandatory fees ($1675), and college room and board ($3998). College room only: $1906.
Undergraduate Financial Aid: *Financial aid deadline (priority):* 3/1. *Financial aid forms:* FAFSA, institutional form, W-2 forms, federal income tax form, Divorced/Separated Parents' Statement (first year only) required; CSS Financial Aid PROFILE acceptable. State form required for some.
LD Services Contact: Prof. Cheryl Keen, Director, Antioch College, 795 Livermore Street, Yellow Springs, OH 45387, 937-767-7331. Fax: 937-767-6470. Email: ckeen@antioch_college.edu.

APPALACHIAN STATE UNIVERSITY

Boone, North Carolina

LEARNING DISABILITIES SERVICES INFORMATION

Learning Disability Program began offering services in 1979. Currently the program serves 270 undergraduates with LD. Services are also available to graduate students. Students diagnosed with ADD/ADHD are eligible for the same services available to students with LD.
Staff: 1 full-time, 1 part-time staff members, including coordinator. Services provided by tutors, counselors, graduate assistants.
Special Fees: No special fees are charged for services to students with LD.
Applications and admissions: *Required:* high school transcript, grade point average, class rank, courses completed, untimed SAT I or ACT; *recommended:* high school extracurricular activities, extended time SAT I or ACT, autobiographical statement, letters of recommendation. Students may begin taking classes in fall, spring, or summer. *Application deadline:* continuous.
Special policies: The college has written policies regarding grade forgiveness; substitutions and waivers of graduation and degree requirements.

PROGRAM AND SERVICE COMPONENTS

Academic advising: Provided by unit staff members, LD coordinator. Students with LD may take up to 17 semester hours each term; most take 12 to 16 semester hours; 12 semester hours required to maintain full-time status and be eligible for financial aid.
Counseling services: Individual counseling, small-group counseling, career counseling.
Basic skills remediation: Offered one-on-one and in class-size groups by regular teachers, teacher trainees. Available in reading, math, spoken language, written language, study skills, time management.
Subject-area tutoring: Offered one-on-one by peer tutors, graduate students. Available in all subjects.
Special courses: College survival skills, reading, communication skills, composition, learning strategies, word processing, Internet use, study skills, career planning. Some offered for credit; some enter into overall grade point average.
Auxiliary aids: Tape recorders, word-processors with spell-check, optical character readers.
Auxiliary services: Alternative test arrangements, notetakers, priority registration.

GENERAL COLLEGE INFORMATION

State-supported, comprehensive, coed. Part of University of North Carolina System. Awards bachelor's, master's, doctoral degrees. Founded 1899. *Setting:* 255-acre small-town campus. *Total enrollment:* 11,909. *Faculty:* 763 (580 full-time, 95% with terminal degrees, 183 part-time); student–undergrad faculty ratio is 15:1.
Enrollment Profile: 10,878 students from 41 states and territories, 32 other countries. 51% women, 49% men, 7% part-time, 89% state residents, 8% transferred in, 10% 25 or older, 0% Native American, 1% Hispanic, 3% black, 1% Asian or Pacific Islander. *Retention:* 87% of 1995 full-time freshmen returned. *Graduation:* 33% graduate in 4 years, 59% in 5 years. *Areas of study chosen:* 18% education, 17% business management and administrative services, 7% social sciences, 6% communications and journalism, 5% biological and life sciences, 5% psychology, 4% English language/literature/letters, 3% computer and information sciences, 3% health professions and related sciences, 3% physical sciences, 2% fine arts, 2% mathematics, 2% performing arts, 2% vocational and home economics, 1% foreign language and literature, 1% interdisciplinary studies. *Most popular recent majors:* business administration/commerce/management, communication, elementary education.
First-Year Class: 2,032 total; 8,664 applied, 61% were accepted, 38% of whom enrolled. 20% from top 10% of their high school class, 63% from top quarter, 95% from top half.
Graduation Requirements: 122 semester hours; 4 semester hours of algebra; computer course for business, geography, planning majors; internship (some majors); senior project for honors program students and some majors.
Computers on Campus: 500 computers available on campus for general student use. A campus-wide network can be accessed from student residence rooms. Computers for student use in computer center, computer labs, research center, learning resource center, classrooms, library, student center, dorms provide access to the Internet/World Wide Web. Staffed computer lab on campus provides training in use of computers, software.

EXPENSES AND FINANCIAL AID

Expenses for 1997–98: *Application fee:* $25. State resident tuition: $874 full-time. Nonresident tuition: $8028 full-time. Part-time tuition per semester ranges from $109 to $328 for state residents, $1004 to $3011 for nonresidents. Part-time mandatory fees per semester range from $132 to $470. Full-time mandatory fees: $940. College room and board: $3008. College room only: $1740.
Undergraduate Financial Aid: 44% of all full-time undergraduates enrolled in fall 1996 applied for aid; of these, 74% were judged to have need according to Federal Methodology, of whom 95% were aided. On average, 100% of need was met. *Financial aid deadline (priority):* 3/15. *Financial aid forms:* CSS Financial Aid PROFILE required; institutional form acceptable. FAFSA required for some.
LD Services Contact: Ms. Arlene J. Lundquist, Coordinator, Learning Disability Program, Appalachian State University, Boone, NC 28608, 704-262-2291.

AQUINAS COLLEGE

Grand Rapids, Michigan

LEARNING DISABILITIES SERVICES INFORMATION

Academic Achievement Center began offering services in 1986. Currently the program serves 41 undergraduates with LD. Services are also available to graduate students. Students diagnosed with ADD/ADHD are eligible for the same services available to students with LD.
Staff: Includes director, coordinator. Services provided by remediation specialists, tutors, counselor, peer tutors.
Special Fees: No special fees are charged for services to students with LD.
Applications and admissions: *Required:* high school transcript, grade point average, courses completed, untimed SAT I or ACT; *recommended:* high school class rank, extracurricular activities, extended time

Aquinas College (continued)

SAT I or ACT, personal interview, autobiographical statement, letters of recommendation, psychoeducational report completed within 3 years. Students may begin taking classes in fall or winter. *Application deadline:* continuous.

PROGRAM AND SERVICE COMPONENTS

Special preparation or orientation: Optional orientation offered during registration.
Academic advising: Provided by academic advisers. Students with LD may take up to 15 credits each term; most take 12 to 15 credits; 12 credits required to maintain full-time status and be eligible for financial aid.
Counseling services: Individual counseling, small-group counseling, career counseling, self-advocacy training.
Basic skills remediation: Offered one-on-one and in small groups by LD teachers, regular teachers, teacher trainees. Available in reading, math, spelling, written language, learning strategies, study skills, time management, social skills.
Subject-area tutoring: Offered one-on-one and in small groups by professional teachers, peer tutors. Available in most subjects.
Auxiliary aids: Taped textbooks, tape recorders, calculators, typewriters, word-processors with spell-check, talking computers, optical character readers, Franklin Speller.
Auxiliary services: Alternative test arrangements, notetakers, priority registration, advocacy.
Campus support group: A special student organization is available to students with LD.

GENERAL COLLEGE INFORMATION

Independent Roman Catholic, comprehensive, coed. Awards associate, bachelor's, master's degrees. Founded 1886. *Setting:* 107-acre suburban campus with easy access to Detroit and Chicago. *Endowment:* $4.7 million. *Educational spending 1995–96:* $2524 per undergrad. *Total enrollment:* 2,385. *Undergraduate faculty:* 173 (75 full-time, 66% with terminal degrees, 98 part-time); student–undergrad faculty ratio is 16:1.
Enrollment Profile: 1,825 students from 19 states and territories, 12 other countries. 66% women, 34% men, 34% part-time, 95% state residents, 42% transferred in, 1% international, 36% 25 or older, 1% Native American, 3% Hispanic, 6% black, 1% Asian or Pacific Islander. *Retention:* 75% of 1995 full-time freshmen returned. *Graduation:* 29% graduate in 4 years, 34% in 5 years, 45% in 6 years. *Areas of study chosen:* 28% business management and administrative services, 14% social sciences, 12% education, 7% communications and journalism, 7% liberal arts/general studies, 7% psychology, 6% English language/literature/letters, 4% fine arts, 4% health professions and related sciences, 3% computer and information sciences, 2% biological and life sciences, 2% foreign language and literature, 2% mathematics, 2% philosophy, 1% physical sciences. *Most popular recent majors:* business administration/commerce/management, English, psychology.
First-Year Class: 283 total; 769 applied, 92% were accepted, 40% of whom enrolled. 18% from top 10% of their high school class, 43% from top quarter, 71% from top half. 2 class presidents, 3 valedictorians.
Graduation Requirements: 64 credits for associate, 124 credits for bachelor's; 9 credits of science; 12 credits of a foreign language; computer course for business administration, economics, accounting, psychology, math, political science majors.
Computers on Campus: 130 computers available on campus for general student use. Computer purchase/lease plans available. A computer is recommended for all students. A campus-wide network can be accessed. Students can contact faculty members and/or advisers through e-mail. Computers for student use in computer center, computer labs, classrooms, library, dorms provide access to the Internet/World Wide Web, on- and off-campus e-mail addresses. Staffed computer lab on campus provides training in use of computers, software. *Academic computing expenditure 1995–96:* $312,812.

EXPENSES AND FINANCIAL AID

Expenses for 1997–98: *Application fee:* $25. Comprehensive fee of $17,274 includes full-time tuition ($12,910), mandatory fees ($40 minimum), and college room and board ($4324). Full-time mandatory fees range from $40 to $60. Part-time mandatory fees: $5 per course. Part-time tuition: $265 per credit for 1 to 6 credits, $403 per credit for 7 or more credits.
Undergraduate Financial Aid: 88% of all full-time undergraduates enrolled in fall 1996 applied for aid; of these, 91% were judged to have need according to Federal Methodology, of whom 99% were aided. On average, 91% of need was met. *Financial aid deadline (priority):* 3/31. *Financial aid forms:* FAFSA required.
Financial aid specifically for students with LD: Scholarship: Burkowitz Scholarship.
LD Services Contact: Ms. Karen Broekstra, Disability Coordinator, Aquinas College, AB-320, Grand Rapids, MI 49506-1799, 616-459-8281 Ext. 3741. Fax: 616-732-4487.

ARIZONA STATE UNIVERSITY WEST

Phoenix, Arizona

LEARNING DISABILITIES SERVICES INFORMATION

Disability Resource Center began offering services in 1991. Currently the program serves 60 undergraduates with LD. Services are also available to graduate students. Students diagnosed with ADD/ADHD are eligible for the same services available to students with LD.
Staff: 3 full-time, 1 part-time staff members, including coordinators. Services provided by program assistant, administrative assistant.
Special Fees: No special fees are charged for services to students with LD.
Applications and admissions: *Required:* adequate transfer GPA and college transcript. Students may begin taking classes any term. *Application deadline:* continuous.
Special policies: The college has written policies regarding grade forgiveness; substitutions and waivers of admissions, graduation, and degree requirements.

PROGRAM AND SERVICE COMPONENTS

Special preparation or orientation: Optional orientation offered before registration.
Academic advising: Provided by unit staff members, academic advisers. Most students with LD take 9 to 12 credit hours each term; 12 credit hours required to maintain full-time status; 6 credit hours required to be eligible for financial aid.
Auxiliary aids: Taped textbooks, tape recorders, calculators, word-processors with spell-check, talking computers, optical character readers, assistive listening devices, word prediction software, voice recognition computer, spell checker.
Auxiliary services: Alternative test arrangements, notetakers, priority registration, advocacy.
Campus support group: A special student organization is available to students with LD.

GENERAL COLLEGE INFORMATION

State-supported, upper-level, coed. Part of Arizona State University. Awards bachelor's, master's degrees. Founded 1984. *Setting:* 300-acre urban campus. *Research spending 1995–96:* $260,000. *Educational spending 1995–96:* $6953 per undergrad. *Total enrollment:* 3,898. *Faculty:* 301 (224 full-time, 94% with terminal degrees, 77 part-time); student–undergrad faculty ratio is 12:1.
Enrollment Profile: 3,391 students from 12 states and territories, 22 other countries. 65% women, 35% men, 55% part-time, 99% state residents, 100% transferred in, 69% 25 or older, 1% Native American, 11% Hispanic, 3% black, 3% Asian or Pacific Islander. *Areas of study chosen:* 33% education, 27% business management and administrative services, 21% social sciences, 7% communications and journalism, 5% psychology, 2% English language/literature/letters, 1% area and ethnic studies, 1% biological and life sciences, 1% fine arts, 1% interdisciplinary studies. *Most popular recent majors:* elementary education, business administration/commerce/management, communication.
First-Year Class: 908 total; 1,237 applied, 91% were accepted, 81% of whom enrolled.
Graduation Requirements: 126 credit hours; 6 credit hours of math; 8 credit hours of natural science; computer course for education, business majors; internship (some majors); senior project for honors program students and some majors.
Computers on Campus: 319 computers available on campus for general student use. Computer purchase/lease plans available. A campus-wide network can be accessed from off-campus. Students can contact faculty members and/or advisers through e-mail. Computers for student use in computer center, computer labs, learning resource center, classrooms, library, student center, statistics lab provide access to the Internet/World Wide Web, on- and off-campus e-mail addresses. Staffed computer lab on campus provides training in use of computers, software. *Academic computing expenditure 1995–96:* $1.8 million.

EXPENSES AND FINANCIAL AID

Expenses for 1996–97: State resident tuition: $1940 full-time. Nonresident tuition: $8308 full-time, $346 per credit hour part-time. Part-time tuition and fees for state residents (1 to 6 credit hours): $102 to $612. Full-time mandatory fees: $68.
Undergraduate Financial Aid: Of all full-time undergraduates enrolled in fall 1996, 91% of those who applied for aid were judged to have need according to Federal Methodology, of whom 97% were aided. *Financial aid deadline (priority):* 3/1. *Financial aid forms:* FAFSA required. Institutional form required for some.
LD Services Contact: Ms. Denise Labrecque, Program Coordinator, Senior Outreach and Education, Arizona State University West, 4701 West Thunderbird Road, Phoenix, AZ 85069, 602-543-8145. Fax: 602-543-8233. Email: dlabrecque@asu.edu.

ARKANSAS STATE UNIVERSITY

State University, Arkansas

LEARNING DISABILITIES SERVICES INFORMATION

Disability Services currently serves undergraduate and graduate students with LD. Students diagnosed with ADD/ADHD are eligible for the same services available to students with LD.
Staff: Includes director, language development instructor, secretary, graduate assistants. Services provided by remediation specialist, counselor.
Special Fees: No special fees are charged for services to students with LD.
Applications and admissions: *Required:* high school transcript, grade point average; *recommended:* untimed or extended time ACT, psychoeducational report completed within 3 years. Students may begin taking classes any term. *Application deadline:* 8/13 (fall term), 1/2 (spring term).

PROGRAM AND SERVICE COMPONENTS

Special preparation or orientation: Orientation (required for some) held during summer prior to enrollment.
Diagnostic testing: Intelligence, reading, spelling, spoken language, written language, study skills, speech, hearing.
Academic advising: Provided by unit staff members, academic advisers. Students with LD may take up to 18 credit hours each term; most take 15 credit hours; 12 credit hours required to maintain full-time status and be eligible for financial aid.
Counseling services: Individual counseling, career counseling.
Special courses: Reading, composition, math, study skills. Some offered for credit; some enter into overall grade point average.
Auxiliary aids: Taped textbooks, tape recorders, calculators, typewriters, word-processors with spell-check, talking computers, optical character readers, Reading Edge, brailler, enlarger, scanner.
Auxiliary services: Alternative test arrangements, notetakers, priority registration, readers.
Campus support group: A special student organization is available to students with LD.

GENERAL COLLEGE INFORMATION

State-supported, comprehensive, coed. Awards associate, bachelor's, master's, doctoral degrees. Founded 1909. *Setting:* 800-acre small-town campus with easy access to Memphis. *Endowment:* $6.8 million. *Research spending 1995–96:* $1.6 million. *Educational spending 1995–96:* $3380 per undergrad. *Total enrollment:* 9,828. *Faculty:* 481 (405 full-time, 84% with terminal degrees, 76 part-time); student–undergrad faculty ratio is 23:1.
Enrollment Profile: 8,762 students from 44 states and territories, 54 other countries. 57% women, 43% men, 18% part-time, 86% state residents, 19% live on campus, 9% transferred in, 3% international, 24% 25 or older, 0% Native American, 1% Hispanic, 10% black, 1% Asian or Pacific Islander. *Retention:* 67% of 1995 full-time freshmen returned. *Graduation:* 11% graduate in 4 years, 25% in 5 years, 33% in 6 years. *Areas of study chosen:* 20% liberal arts/general studies, 16% business management and administrative services, 13% education, 13% health professions and related sciences, 8% social sciences, 5% agriculture, 5% biological and life sciences, 4% communications and journalism, 4% engineering and applied sciences, 4% fine arts, 3% psychology, 2% English language/literature/letters, 1% computer and information sciences, 1% mathematics, 1% physical sciences. *Most popular recent majors:* elementary education, accounting, business administration/commerce/management.
First-Year Class: 1,653 total; 2,093 applied, 87% were accepted, 91% of whom enrolled.
Graduation Requirements: 62 credit hours for associate, 124 credit hours for bachelor's; 3 credit hours of math; 8 credit hours of science; computer course for business, engineering, economics, printing, secondary education, math, physics majors; internship (some majors); senior project for honors program students and some majors.
Computers on Campus: 421 computers available on campus for general student use. Computer purchase/lease plans available. A computer is recommended for some students. A campus-wide network can be accessed from student residence rooms and from off-campus. Students can contact faculty members and/or advisers through e-mail. Computers for student use in computer center, computer labs, classrooms, dorms, departmental labs provide access to the Internet/World Wide Web, on- and off-campus e-mail addresses. Staffed computer lab on campus provides training in use of computers, software. *Academic computing expenditure 1995–96:* $1.8 million.

EXPENSES AND FINANCIAL AID

Expenses for 1997–98: *Application fee:* $15. State resident tuition: $2000 full-time, $84 per credit hour part-time. Nonresident tuition: $5090 full-time, $213 per credit hour part-time. Part-time mandatory fees per semester range from $15 to $125. Full-time mandatory fees: $290. College room and board: $2620 (minimum).
Undergraduate Financial Aid: 70% of all full-time undergraduates enrolled in fall 1996 applied for aid; of these, 92% were judged to have need according to Federal Methodology, of whom 86% were aided. On average, 76% of need was met. *Financial aid deadline (priority):* 4/1. *Financial aid forms:* FAFSA required; state form, institutional form acceptable.
LD Services Contact: Dr. Jenifer Rice-Mason, Director of Disability Services/Assistant Dean of Students, Arkansas State University, PO Box 360, State University, AR 72467, 501-972-3964. Fax: 501-972-3843. Email: jrmason@chickasaw.astate.edu.

ARMSTRONG ATLANTIC STATE UNIVERSITY

Savannah, Georgia

LEARNING DISABILITIES SERVICES INFORMATION

Office of Disability Services began offering services in 1992. Currently the program serves 20 undergraduates with LD. Services are also available to graduate students. Students diagnosed with ADD/ADHD are eligible for the same services available to students with LD.
Staff: 1 full-time staff member (director).
Special Fees: No special fees are charged for services to students with LD.
Applications and admissions: *Required:* high school transcript, grade point average, courses completed; *recommended:* untimed or extended time SAT I or ACT. Students may begin taking classes any term. *Application deadline:* continuous.
Special policies: The college has written policies regarding substitutions and waivers of degree requirements.

PROGRAM AND SERVICE COMPONENTS

Special preparation or orientation: Optional orientation offered individually by arrangement.
Academic advising: Provided by academic advisers. Students with LD may take up to 20 quarter hours each term; most take 10 to 15 quarter hours; 12 quarter hours required to maintain full-time status; 6 quarter hours (part-time), 12 quarter hours (full-time) required to be eligible for financial aid.
Counseling services: Individual counseling.
Auxiliary aids: Taped textbooks, tape recorders, calculators, word-processors with spell-check.
Auxiliary services: Alternative test arrangements, notetakers.

GENERAL COLLEGE INFORMATION

State-supported, comprehensive, coed. Part of University System of Georgia. Awards associate, bachelor's, master's degrees. Founded 1935. *Setting:* 250-acre suburban campus. *Educational spending 1995–96:* $2387 per undergrad. *Total enrollment:* 5,617. *Faculty:* 349 (238 full-time, 65% with terminal degrees, 111 part-time); student–undergrad faculty ratio is 14:1.

Armstrong Atlantic State University (continued)

Enrollment Profile: 5,042 students from 48 states and territories, 49 other countries. 70% women, 30% men, 36% part-time, 93% state residents, 3% live on campus, 34% transferred in, 2% international, 57% 25 or older, 1% Native American, 2% Hispanic, 21% black, 2% Asian or Pacific Islander. *Retention:* 61% of 1995 full-time freshmen returned. *Graduation:* 17% graduate in 5 years. *Areas of study chosen:* 13% education, 10% health professions and related sciences, 3% psychology, 3% social sciences, 2% biological and life sciences, 2% computer and information sciences, 2% engineering and applied sciences, 2% English language/literature/letters, 2% fine arts, 2% liberal arts/general studies, 2% physical sciences, 1% performing arts, 1% premed. *Most popular recent majors:* education, nursing, criminal justice.
First-Year Class: 654 total; 1,119 applied, 78% were accepted, 75% of whom enrolled.
Graduation Requirements: 93 quarter hours for associate, 191 quarter hours for bachelor's; 4 math/science courses including at least 1 math course and 2 lab science courses; computer course for political science, English, chemistry, elementary education majors; internship (some majors); senior project (some majors).
Computers on Campus: 90 computers available on campus for general student use. Computer purchase/lease plans available. A computer is recommended for some students. A campus-wide network can be accessed from off-campus. Students can contact faculty members and/or advisers through e-mail. Computers for student use in computer center, computer labs, learning resource center, library, departmental labs provide access to the Internet/World Wide Web, on- and off-campus e-mail addresses. Staffed computer lab on campus provides training in use of computers, software.

EXPENSES AND FINANCIAL AID

Estimated Expenses for 1997–98: *Application fee:* $15. State resident tuition: $1836 full-time. Nonresident tuition: $5715 full-time. Part-time tuition per quarter ranges from $128 to $568 for state residents, $236 to $1756 for nonresidents. College room and board: $3921.
Undergraduate Financial Aid: On average, 80% of need was met. *Financial aid deadline (priority):* 4/15. *Financial aid forms:* FAFSA, institutional form required; state form acceptable.
LD Services Contact: Jan S. Jones, Director, Disability Services, Armstrong Atlantic State University, 11935 Abercorn Street, Savannah, GA 31419, 912-927-5271. Fax: 912-921-5497. Email: jan_jones@mailgate.armstrong.edu.

ART ACADEMY OF CINCINNATI

Cincinnati, Ohio

LEARNING DISABILITIES SERVICES INFORMATION

Office of Dean of Students began offering services in 1985. Currently the program serves 5 to 10 undergraduates with LD. Services are also available to graduate students. Students diagnosed with ADD/ADHD are eligible for the same services available to students with LD.
Staff: 1 part-time staff member (director).
Special Fees: No special fees are charged for services to students with LD.
Applications and admissions: *Required:* high school transcript, grade point average, courses completed, untimed SAT I or ACT, personal interview, letters of recommendation. Students may begin taking classes in fall only. *Application deadline:* continuous.

PROGRAM AND SERVICE COMPONENTS

Academic advising: Provided by academic advisers. Students with LD may take up to 18 credit hours each term; most take 12 credit hours; 12 credit hours required to maintain full-time status and be eligible for financial aid.
Counseling services: Individual counseling.
Basic skills remediation: Offered one-on-one, in small groups, and in class-size groups by regular teachers. Available in reading, written language, learning strategies, study skills, time management, computer skills.
Special courses: College survival skills, composition, learning strategies, time management, study skills. None offered for credit; none enter into overall grade point average.
Auxiliary aids: Taped textbooks, tape recorders, typewriters, word-processors with spell-check, electronic/speaking dictionaries.
Auxiliary services: Alternative test arrangements, notetakers, advocacy.

GENERAL COLLEGE INFORMATION

Independent, comprehensive, specialized, coed. Awards associate, bachelor's, master's degrees. Founded 1887. *Setting:* 184-acre urban campus. *Endowment:* $6 million. *Total enrollment:* 168. *Faculty:* 51 (19 full-time, 99% with terminal degrees, 32 part-time).
Enrollment Profile: 158 students from 10 states and territories, 4 other countries. 48% women, 8% men, 15% part-time, 65% state residents, 30% transferred in, 1% international, 30% 25 or older, 5% black, 2% Asian or Pacific Islander. *Retention:* 84% of 1995 full-time freshmen returned. *Areas of study chosen:* 100% fine arts.
First-Year Class: 42 total; 118 applied, 76% were accepted, 47% of whom enrolled.
Graduation Requirements: 65 credit hours for associate, 129 credit hours for bachelor's; 6 credit hours of math/natural science; computer course for communication design majors; internship (some majors); senior project.
Computers on Campus: 25 computers available on campus for general student use. Computers for student use in computer center, learning resource center, classrooms. Staffed computer lab on campus.

EXPENSES AND FINANCIAL AID

Expenses for 1997–98: *Application fee:* $25. Tuition: $10,800 full-time, $385 per credit hour part-time. Full-time mandatory fees: $125.
Undergraduate Financial Aid: Of all full-time undergraduates enrolled in fall 1996, 92% of those who applied for aid were judged to have need according to Federal Methodology, of whom 100% were aided. *Financial aid deadline:* continuous. *Financial aid forms:* FAFSA required. State form required for some.
LD Services Contact: Ms. Marcia Schoeni, Director of Services for Learning Disabled Students, Art Academy of Cincinnati, 1125 St. Gregory Street, Cincinnati, OH 45202, 513-562-8766. Fax: 513-562-8778.

AUBURN UNIVERSITY AT MONTGOMERY

Montgomery, Alabama

LEARNING DISABILITIES SERVICES INFORMATION

Center for Special Services began offering services in 1986. Currently the program serves 150 undergraduates with LD. Services are also available to graduate students. Students diagnosed with ADD/ADHD are eligible for the same services available to students with LD.
Staff: 4 full-time, 3 part-time staff members, including director, assistant director, coordinator. Services provided by tutors, peer counselors, proctors.
Special Fees: No special fees are charged for services to students with LD.
Applications and admissions: *Required:* high school transcript, grade point average; *recommended:* extended time SAT I or ACT, psychoeducational report completed within 3 years. Students may begin taking classes any term. *Application deadline:* continuous.
Special policies: The college has written policies regarding substitutions and waivers of admissions and degree requirements.

PROGRAM AND SERVICE COMPONENTS

Special preparation or orientation: Optional orientation offered before registration.
Academic advising: Provided by unit staff members, academic advisers. Students with LD may take up to 20 quarter hours each term; most take 12 quarter hours; 12 quarter hours required to maintain full-time status and be eligible for financial aid.
Counseling services: Individual counseling, small-group counseling, career counseling, self-advocacy training.
Subject-area tutoring: Offered one-on-one by professional teachers, peer tutors. Available in all subjects.
Special courses: Composition, math, study skills. All offered for credit; none enter into overall grade point average.
Auxiliary aids: Taped textbooks, tape recorders, calculators, typewriters, word-processors with spell-check, personal computers, optical character readers, voice-synthesized computers.
Auxiliary services: Alternative test arrangements, notetakers, priority registration, advocacy, readers, writers, taped lectures, interpreters.

GENERAL COLLEGE INFORMATION

State-supported, comprehensive, coed. Part of Auburn University. Awards bachelor's, master's degrees. Founded 1967. *Setting:* 500-acre suburban campus. *Endowment:* $9.4 million. *Research spending 1995–96:* $273,422. *Total enrollment:* 5,645. *Faculty:* 364 (195 full-time, 22% with terminal degrees, 169 part-time).

Enrollment Profile: 4,771 students from 25 states and territories, 15 other countries. 61% women, 39% men, 33% part-time, 99% state residents, 1% international, 30% 25 or older, 1% Native American, 1% Hispanic, 29% black, 2% Asian or Pacific Islander. *Areas of study chosen:* 21% business management and administrative services, 17% education, 9% health professions and related sciences, 7% liberal arts/general studies, 6% biological and life sciences, 6% engineering and applied sciences, 5% physical sciences, 4% computer and information sciences, 4% fine arts, 4% mathematics, 4% psychology, 3% communications and journalism, 2% social sciences, 1% English language/literature/letters, 1% foreign language and literature. *Most popular recent majors:* elementary education, nursing, secondary education.

First-Year Class: 844 total; 1,006 applied, 92% were accepted, 91% of whom enrolled. 38% from top quarter of their high school class.

Graduation Requirements: 200 quarter hours; 15 quarter hours of math; 10 quarter hours of science; computer course; internship (some majors); senior project (some majors).

Computers on Campus: 120 computers available on campus for general student use. Computer purchase/lease plans available. A computer is strongly recommended for all students. A campus-wide network can be accessed. Students can contact faculty members and/or advisers through e-mail. Computers for student use in computer center, computer labs, learning resource center, classrooms, library provide access to the Internet/World Wide Web, on- and off-campus e-mail addresses. Staffed computer lab on campus (open 24 hours a day) provides training in use of computers, software. *Academic computing expenditure 1995–96:* $331,140.

EXPENSES AND FINANCIAL AID

Expenses for 1997–98: *Application fee:* $25. State resident tuition: $2289 full-time, $58 per quarter hour part-time. Nonresident tuition: $6867 full-time, $174 per quarter hour part-time. Part-time mandatory fees: $30 per quarter. College room only: $1830.

Undergraduate Financial Aid: On average, 75% of need was met. *Financial aid deadline (priority):* 3/15. *Financial aid forms:* FAFSA, institutional form required.

LD Services Contact: Ms. Lynne Stokley, Student Services Coordinator, Auburn University at Montgomery, 9th Floor, Library Tower, Montgomery, AL 36124-4023, 334-244-3468. Fax: 334-244-3837.

AUGUSTANA COLLEGE

Sioux Falls, South Dakota

LEARNING DISABILITIES SERVICES INFORMATION

Student Services began offering services in 1990. Currently the program serves 15 undergraduates with LD. Services are also available to graduate students. Students diagnosed with ADD/ADHD are eligible for the same services available to students with LD.

Staff: 1 part-time staff member (coordinator). Services provided by tutors, notetakers.

Special Fees: No special fees are charged for services to students with LD.

Applications and admissions: *Required:* high school transcript, grade point average, class rank, courses completed, extracurricular activities, untimed or extended time ACT, letters of recommendation, psychoeducational report completed within 3 years; *recommended:* high school IEP (Individualized Education Program), personal interview. Students may begin taking classes any term. *Application deadline:* continuous.

PROGRAM AND SERVICE COMPONENTS

Academic advising: Provided by academic advisers. Students with LD may take up to 18 credits each term; most take 14 to 15 credits; 10 credits required to maintain full-time status and be eligible for financial aid.

Counseling services: Individual counseling.

Subject-area tutoring: Offered one-on-one by peer tutors. Available in all subjects.

Auxiliary aids: Tape recorders, talking computers, optical character readers.

Auxiliary services: Alternative test arrangements, notetakers.

Campus support group: A special student organization is available to students with LD.

GENERAL COLLEGE INFORMATION

Independent, comprehensive, coed, affiliated with Evangelical Lutheran Church in America. Awards associate, bachelor's, master's degrees. Founded 1860. *Setting:* 100-acre urban campus. *Endowment:* $22.8 million. *Research spending 1995–96:* $637,868. *Educational spending 1995–96:* $5364 per undergrad. *Total enrollment:* 1,750. *Faculty:* 159 (121 full-time, 76% with terminal degrees, 38 part-time); student–undergrad faculty ratio is 12:1.

Enrollment Profile: 1,589 students from 32 states and territories, 8 other countries. 65% women, 35% men, 8% part-time, 45% state residents, 60% live on campus, 6% transferred in, 3% international, 5% 25 or older, 1% Native American, 1% Hispanic, 1% black, 1% Asian or Pacific Islander. *Retention:* 79% of 1995 full-time freshmen returned. *Graduation:* 43% graduate in 4 years, 54% in 5 years, 57% in 6 years. *Areas of study chosen:* 16% education, 13% biological and life sciences, 13% business management and administrative services, 13% health professions and related sciences, 10% social sciences, 7% liberal arts/general studies, 4% communications and journalism, 4% psychology, 3% English language/literature/letters, 3% performing arts, 3% physical sciences, 2% computer and information sciences, 2% fine arts, 2% mathematics, 1% engineering and applied sciences, 1% foreign language and literature, 1% natural resource sciences, 1% philosophy, 1% theology/religion. *Most popular recent majors:* biology/biological sciences, education, business administration/commerce/management.

First-Year Class: 386 total; 1,088 applied, 92% were accepted, 39% of whom enrolled. 25% from top 10% of their high school class, 58% from top quarter, 86% from top half. 2 National Merit Scholars, 26 valedictorians.

Graduation Requirements: 66 credits for associate, 130 credits for bachelor's; 3 credits of math; 7 credits of science including at least 1 lab science course; 6 credits of a foreign language or proven proficiency; computer course; internship (some majors); senior project.

Computers on Campus: 115 computers available on campus for general student use. A campus-wide network can be accessed from off-campus. Students can contact faculty members and/or advisers through e-mail. Computers for student use in computer center, computer labs, classrooms, library, student center, dorms, student rooms, departmental labs provide access to the Internet/World Wide Web, on- and off-campus e-mail addresses. Staffed computer lab on campus (open 24 hours a day) provides training in use of computers, software. *Academic computing expenditure 1995–96:* $598,137.

EXPENSES AND FINANCIAL AID

Expenses for 1997–98: *Application fee:* $25. Comprehensive fee of $17,015 includes full-time tuition ($12,968), mandatory fees ($144), and college room and board ($3903 minimum). College room only: $1904 (minimum). Part-time tuition (1 to 9 credits) ranges from $200 to $3510 per semester. Tuition guaranteed not to increase for student's term of enrollment.

Undergraduate Financial Aid: Of all full-time undergraduates enrolled in fall 1996, 80% of those who applied for aid were judged to have need according to Federal Methodology, of whom 97% were aided. On average, 96% of need was met. *Financial aid deadline (priority):* 3/1. *Financial aid forms:* FAFSA required. State form, institutional form required for some.

LD Services Contact: Ms. Katie Poole, Student Services Assistant, Augustana College, 29th and Summit, Box 729, Sioux Falls, SD 57197, 605-336-4496. Fax: 605-336-4901. Email: poole@inst.augie.edu.

AUGUSTA STATE UNIVERSITY

Augusta, Georgia

LEARNING DISABILITIES SERVICES INFORMATION

Office of Disability Services (ODS) currently serves 54 undergraduates with LD. Services are also available to graduate students. Students diagnosed with ADD/ADHD are eligible for the same services available to students with LD.

Staff: 1 full-time, 1 part-time staff members, including coordinator. Services provided by student assistant.

Special Fees: No special fees are charged for services to students with LD.

Applications and admissions: *Required:* high school transcript, courses completed, psychoeducational report; *recommended:* high school grade point average, class rank, extracurricular activities, extended time SAT I. *Application deadline:* continuous.

Special policies: The college has written policies regarding substitutions and waivers of degree requirements.

Augusta State University (continued)

PROGRAM AND SERVICE COMPONENTS

Academic advising: Provided by academic advisers.
Counseling services: Individual counseling, career counseling, self-advocacy training.
Auxiliary aids: Taped textbooks, tape recorders, typewriters, word-processors with spell-check.
Auxiliary services: Alternative test arrangements, notetakers, advocacy.

GENERAL COLLEGE INFORMATION

State-supported, comprehensive, coed. Part of University System of Georgia. Awards associate, bachelor's, master's degrees. Founded 1925. *Setting:* 72-acre urban campus. *Endowment:* $172,202. *Research spending 1995–96:* $50,816. *Total enrollment:* 5,561. *Faculty:* 275 (191 full-time, 62% with terminal degrees, 84 part-time).
Enrollment Profile: 4,733 students: 64% women, 36% men, 34% part-time, 88% state residents, 8% transferred in, 1% international, 31% 25 or older, 1% Native American, 2% Hispanic, 19% black, 4% Asian or Pacific Islander. *Retention:* 56% of 1995 full-time freshmen returned. *Graduation:* 4% graduate in 4 years, 13% in 5 years, 19% in 6 years. *Areas of study chosen:* 17% biological and life sciences, 12% business management and administrative services, 11% education, 9% social sciences, 7% health professions and related sciences, 6% psychology, 4% communications and journalism, 4% computer and information sciences, 3% English language/literature/letters, 2% physical sciences, 1% foreign language and literature, 1% interdisciplinary studies, 1% mathematics, 1% performing arts. *Most popular recent majors:* nursing, early childhood education, biology/biological sciences.
First-Year Class: 843 total; 1,411 applied, 79% were accepted, 75% of whom enrolled.
Graduation Requirements: 90 quarter hours for associate, 180 quarter hours for bachelor's; 10 quarter hours each of math and science; computer course for business administration majors; internship (some majors).
Computers on Campus: 147 computers available on campus for general student use. A campus-wide network can be accessed from off-campus. Students can contact faculty members and/or advisers through e-mail. Computers for student use in computer center, computer labs, library, reading, tutorial labs provide access to the Internet/World Wide Web, on- and off-campus e-mail addresses. Staffed computer lab on campus (open 24 hours a day) provides training in use of computers, software. *Academic computing expenditure 1995–96:* $830,261.

EXPENSES AND FINANCIAL AID

Expenses for 1996–97: *Application fee:* $10. State resident tuition: $1584 full-time, $44 per quarter hour part-time. Nonresident tuition: $5463 full-time, $152 per quarter hour part-time. Part-time mandatory fees: $72 per quarter. Full-time mandatory fees: $216.
Undergraduate Financial Aid: Of all full-time undergraduates enrolled in fall 1996, 93% of those judged to have need according to Federal Methodology were aided. On average, 62% of need was met. *Financial aid deadline (priority):* 4/15. *Financial aid forms:* FAFSA required. State form required for some.
LD Services Contact: Ms. Rosemary Meredith, Disability Services Coordinator, Augusta State University, 2500 Walton Way, Augusta, GA 30904, 706-737-1471. Fax: 706-667-4350. Email: rmeredit@aug.edu.

BEMIDJI STATE UNIVERSITY

Bemidji, Minnesota

LEARNING DISABILITIES SERVICES INFORMATION

Office for Students with Disabilities began offering services in 1972. Currently the program serves 55 undergraduates with LD. Services are also available to graduate students. Students diagnosed with ADD/ADHD are eligible for the same services available to students with LD.
Staff: 1 full-time staff member (Disabilities Specialist).
Special Fees: No special fees are charged for services to students with LD.
Applications and admissions: *Required:* high school transcript, untimed ACT; *recommended:* high school courses completed, letter of self-identification for proper referral. Students may begin taking classes any term. *Application deadline:* continuous.

PROGRAM AND SERVICE COMPONENTS

Special preparation or orientation: Required orientation held as part of a one credit class (schedule undetermined).
Academic advising: Provided by unit staff members, academic advisers. Students with LD may take up to 17 quarter hours each term; most take 12 quarter hours; 12 quarter hours required to maintain full-time status; 12 quarter hours and appropriate GPA (full assistance), 3 to 9 quarter hours and appropriate GPA (partial assistance) required to be eligible for financial aid.
Counseling services: Individual counseling, career counseling, self-advocacy training.
Basic skills remediation: Offered one-on-one, in small groups, and in class-size groups by LD teachers, regular teachers, student lab instructors. Available in reading, math, spelling, written language, learning strategies, study skills, time management.
Subject-area tutoring: Offered one-on-one and in small groups by peer tutors. Available in most subjects.
Auxiliary aids: Taped textbooks, typewriters, personal computers, Arkenstone Scanner with Vocal Eyes, taped journal articles.
Auxiliary services: Alternative test arrangements, notetakers, priority registration, advocacy, handouts and taped lectures as needed.

GENERAL COLLEGE INFORMATION

State-supported, comprehensive, coed. Part of Minnesota State Colleges and Universities System. Awards associate, bachelor's, master's degrees. Founded 1919. *Setting:* 83-acre small-town campus. *Research spending 1995–96:* $150,758. *Educational spending 1995–96:* $3167 per undergrad. *Total enrollment:* 4,019. *Undergraduate faculty:* 201 (190 full-time, 70% with terminal degrees, 11 part-time); student–undergrad faculty ratio is 20:1.
Enrollment Profile: 3,905 students from 45 states and territories, 31 other countries. 53% women, 47% men, 14% part-time, 88% state residents, 43% transferred in, 6% international, 23% 25 or older, 4% Native American, 1% Hispanic, 1% black, 1% Asian or Pacific Islander. *Retention:* 72% of 1995 full-time freshmen returned. *Graduation:* 13% graduate in 4 years, 32% in 5 years, 37% in 6 years. *Areas of study chosen:* 13% business management and administrative services, 13% education, 11% social sciences, 7% biological and life sciences, 7% fine arts, 6% engineering and applied sciences, 6% psychology, 5% health professions and related sciences, 5% physical sciences, 4% communications and journalism, 4% computer and information sciences, 3% English language/literature/letters, 3% natural resource sciences, 3% prelaw, 2% interdisciplinary studies, 2% mathematics, 2% performing arts, 1% area and ethnic studies, 1% foreign language and literature, 1% liberal arts/general studies, 1% philosophy. *Most popular recent majors:* elementary education, business administration/commerce/management, industrial engineering technology.
First-Year Class: 576 total; 1,183 applied, 68% were accepted, 72% of whom enrolled. 14% from top 10% of their high school class, 39% from top quarter, 73% from top half.
Graduation Requirements: 96 quarter hours for associate, 192 quarter hours for bachelor's; 12 quarter hours of science; computer course for business, math, science, psychology, geography majors; internship (some majors); senior project for honors program students and some majors.
Computers on Campus: 200 computers available on campus for general student use. A campus-wide network can be accessed from student residence rooms and from off-campus. Students can contact faculty members and/or advisers through e-mail. Computers for student use in computer center, classrooms, library, dorms provide access to the Internet/World Wide Web, on- and off-campus e-mail addresses. Staffed computer lab on campus provides training in use of computers, software. *Academic computing expenditure 1995–96:* $469,227.

EXPENSES AND FINANCIAL AID

Expenses for 1996–97: *Application fee:* $20. State resident tuition: $2520 full-time, $52.50 per quarter hour part-time. Nonresident tuition: $5631 full-time, $117.30 per quarter hour part-time. Part-time mandatory fees per quarter range from $17 to $135. Tuition for nonresidents who are eligible for the Midwest Student Exchange Program: $3780 full-time, $78.75 per quarter hour part-time. Full-time mandatory fees: $405. College room and board: $3300.
Undergraduate Financial Aid: Of all full-time undergraduates enrolled in fall 1996, 74% of those who applied for aid were judged to have need according to Federal Methodology, of whom 82% were aided. *Financial aid deadline (priority):* 5/15. *Financial aid forms:* FAFSA, institutional form required. Financial aid transcript (for transfers) required for some.
LD Services Contact: Ms. Kathi Hagen, Disabilities Specialist, Bemidji State University, 14 Sanford Hall, Bemidji, MN 56601-2699, 218-755-3883. Fax: 218-755-4115. Email: fishlady@vax1.bemidji.msus.edu.

BENTLEY COLLEGE

Waltham, Massachusetts

LEARNING DISABILITIES SERVICES INFORMATION

Office of Counseling and Student Development began offering services in 1978. Currently the program serves 20 undergraduates with LD. Services are also available to graduate students. Students diagnosed with ADD/ADHD are eligible for the same services available to students with LD.

Staff: 4 full-time, 2 part-time staff members, including director, associate director. Services provided by counselors, psychology interns.

Special Fees: No special fees are charged for services to students with LD.

Applications and admissions: *Required:* high school transcript, courses completed, untimed or extended time SAT I, untimed ACT, letters of recommendation; *recommended:* WAIS-R, writing samples, educational history. Students may begin taking classes any term. *Application deadline:* 2/15 (fall term), 12/1 (spring term).

PROGRAM AND SERVICE COMPONENTS

Academic advising: Provided by unit staff members, academic advisers. Most students with LD take 9 to 15 credits each term; 12 credits required to maintain full-time status and be eligible for financial aid.

Counseling services: Individual counseling, small-group counseling, career counseling.

Auxiliary aids: Taped textbooks, tape recorders, word-processors with spell-check, optical character readers.

Auxiliary services: Alternative test arrangements, notetakers, priority registration.

GENERAL COLLEGE INFORMATION

Independent, comprehensive, coed. Awards bachelor's, master's degrees. Founded 1917. *Setting:* 110-acre suburban campus with easy access to Boston. *Endowment:* $95.4 million. *Research spending 1995–96:* $807,831. *Total enrollment:* 6,169. *Faculty:* 360 (194 full-time, 82% with terminal degrees, 166 part-time); student–undergrad faculty ratio is 18:1.

Enrollment Profile: 4,162 students from 37 states and territories, 65 other countries. 45% women, 55% men, 34% part-time, 64% state residents, 4% transferred in, 10% international, 25% 25 or older, 0% Native American, 3% Hispanic, 3% black, 6% Asian or Pacific Islander. *Retention:* 91% of 1995 full-time freshmen returned. *Graduation:* 62% graduate in 4 years, 68% in 5 years, 71% in 6 years. *Areas of study chosen:* 89% business management and administrative services, 5% computer and information sciences, 4% interdisciplinary studies, 2% communications and journalism. *Most popular recent majors:* accounting, marketing/retailing/merchandising, finance/banking.

First-Year Class: 754 total; 3,836 applied, 66% were accepted, 30% of whom enrolled. 19% from top 10% of their high school class, 51% from top quarter, 85% from top half.

Graduation Requirements: 40 courses; 2 courses each in math and science; computer course.

Computers on Campus: 3,200 computers available on campus for general student use. Computer purchase/lease plans available. A computer is required for all students. A campus-wide network can be accessed from student residence rooms and from off-campus. Students can contact faculty members and/or advisers through e-mail. Computers for student use in computer center, library, student center, various locations provide access to the Internet/World Wide Web, on- and off-campus e-mail addresses. Staffed computer lab on campus provides training in use of computers, software. *Academic computing expenditure 1995–96:* $1.5 million.

EXPENSES AND FINANCIAL AID

Expenses for 1997–98: *Application fee:* $35. Comprehensive fee of $23,305 includes full-time tuition ($16,400), mandatory fees ($95), and college room and board ($6810 minimum). College room only: $3560 (minimum). Part-time tuition: $1640 per course. Part-time mandatory fees: $10 per semester. Part-time tuition for evening classes: $832 per course.

Undergraduate Financial Aid: Of all full-time undergraduates enrolled in fall 1996, 92% of those who applied for aid were judged to have need according to Federal Methodology, of whom 97% were aided. On average, 77% of need was met. *Financial aid deadline:* 2/1. *Financial aid forms:* FAFSA, CSS Financial Aid PROFILE required.

LD Services Contact: Dr. Brenda K. Hawks, Associate Director, Office of Counseling and Student Development, Bentley College, 175 Forest Street, Waltham, MA 02154-4705, 617-891-2274.

BETHANY COLLEGE

Lindsborg, Kansas

LEARNING DISABILITIES SERVICES INFORMATION

Academic Support Center began offering services in 1990. Currently the program serves 6 undergraduates with LD. Students diagnosed with ADD/ADHD are eligible for the same services available to students with LD.

Staff: 1 full-time staff member (director). Services provided by remediation specialist, tutors, counselor, diagnostic specialist.

Special Fees: No special fees are charged for services to students with LD.

Applications and admissions: *Required:* high school transcript, grade point average, class rank, untimed or extended time ACT. Students may begin taking classes in fall only. *Application deadline:* continuous.

Special policies: The college has written policies regarding grade forgiveness.

PROGRAM AND SERVICE COMPONENTS

Diagnostic testing: Intelligence, reading, math, spoken language, written language, perceptual skills, study skills, learning strategies.

Academic advising: Provided by unit staff members, academic advisers. Students with LD may take up to 17 semester hours each term; most take 12 to 13 semester hours; 12 semester hours required to maintain full-time status and be eligible for financial aid.

Counseling services: Individual counseling, career counseling.

Basic skills remediation: Offered in class-size groups by LD teachers. Available in math, written language, study skills, time management.

Subject-area tutoring: Offered one-on-one, in small groups, and in class-size groups by professional teachers, peer tutors. Available in most subjects.

Special courses: College survival skills, reading, composition, learning strategies, word processing, time management, math, study skills, career planning. Some offered for credit; some enter into overall grade point average.

Auxiliary aids: Taped textbooks, tape recorders, calculators, word-processors with spell-check, personal computers.

Auxiliary services: Alternative test arrangements, notetakers, advocacy.

GENERAL COLLEGE INFORMATION

Independent Lutheran, 4-year, coed. Awards bachelor's degrees. Founded 1881. *Setting:* 80-acre small-town campus.

EXPENSES AND FINANCIAL AID

Expenses for 1996–97: *Application fee:* $10. Comprehensive fee of $12,670 includes full-time tuition ($9875), mandatory fees ($105), and college room and board ($2690 minimum). College room only: $1495 (minimum). Part-time tuition per semester hour ranges from $158 to $315.

Undergraduate Financial Aid: 85% of all full-time undergraduates enrolled in fall 1996 applied for aid; of these, 94% were judged to have need according to Federal Methodology, of whom 100% were aided. On average, 72% of need was met. *Financial aid deadline (priority):* 3/15. *Financial aid forms:* institutional form required; FAFSA, CSS Financial Aid PROFILE acceptable. State form required for some.

LD Services Contact: Ms. Martha Robertson, Director of Academic Support, Bethany College, 421 North First Street, Lindsborg, KS 67450, 913-227-3380 Ext. 8200. Fax: 913-227-2860. Email: robertsom@bethanylb.edu.

BETHEL COLLEGE

North Newton, Kansas

LEARNING DISABILITIES SERVICES INFORMATION

Center for Academic Development currently serves 65 undergraduates with LD. Students diagnosed with ADD/ADHD are eligible for the same services available to students with LD, as well as special testing areas, assistance with organizational skills.

Bethel College (continued)

Staff: 14 part-time staff members, including director. Services provided by tutors.

Special Fees: No special fees are charged for services to students with LD.

Applications and admissions: *Required:* high school transcript, letters of recommendation; *recommended:* high school IEP (Individualized Education Program), untimed or extended time SAT I or ACT, personal interview. Students may begin taking classes in fall only. *Application deadline:* continuous.

Special policies: The college has written policies regarding grade forgiveness; substitutions and waivers of admissions, graduation, and degree requirements.

PROGRAM AND SERVICE COMPONENTS

Diagnostic testing: Reading, math, spelling, learning strategies.

Academic advising: Provided by academic advisers. Students with LD may take up to 16 credit hours each term; most take 13 credit hours; 12 credit hours required to maintain full-time status and be eligible for financial aid.

Counseling services: Individual counseling.

Basic skills remediation: Offered one-on-one and in small groups by regular teachers. Available in reading, math, spelling, spoken language, written language, learning strategies, study skills, time management.

Subject-area tutoring: Offered one-on-one and in small groups by peer tutors. Available in most subjects.

Auxiliary aids: Taped textbooks, tape recorders, calculators, word-processors with spell-check, optical character readers.

Auxiliary services: Alternative test arrangements, notetakers.

GENERAL COLLEGE INFORMATION

Independent, 4-year, coed, affiliated with General Conference Mennonite Church. Awards bachelor's degrees. Founded 1887. *Setting:* 60-acre small-town campus with easy access to Wichita. *Endowment:* $11.7 million. *Educational spending 1995–96:* $4189 per undergrad. *Total enrollment:* 618. *Faculty:* 78 (50 full-time, 66% with terminal degrees, 28 part-time); student–undergrad faculty ratio is 12:1.

Enrollment Profile: 618 students from 34 states and territories, 17 other countries. 60% women, 40% men, 14% part-time, 68% state residents, 33% transferred in, 5% international, 20% 25 or older, 1% Native American, 5% Hispanic, 3% black, 1% Asian or Pacific Islander. *Retention:* 80% of 1995 full-time freshmen returned. *Graduation:* 39% graduate in 4 years, 46% in 5 years, 47% in 6 years. *Areas of study chosen:* 33% health professions and related sciences, 12% business management and administrative services, 9% social sciences, 8% education, 5% English language/literature/letters, 5% performing arts, 4% biological and life sciences, 4% communications and journalism, 4% fine arts, 4% mathematics, 3% foreign language and literature, 3% psychology, 2% engineering and applied sciences, 2% physical sciences, 2% theology/religion. *Most popular recent majors:* nursing, education, business administration/commerce/management.

First-Year Class: 101 total; 419 applied, 89% were accepted, 27% of whom enrolled. 20% from top 10% of their high school class, 36% from top quarter, 67% from top half. 8 valedictorians.

Graduation Requirements: 124 credit hours; math proficiency; 6 credit hours of science; computer course; senior project (some majors).

Computers on Campus: 38 computers available on campus for general student use. Computers for student use in computer center, computer labs, classrooms, library provide access to the Internet/World Wide Web, on-campus e-mail addresses. Staffed computer lab on campus provides training in use of computers, software. *Academic computing expenditure 1995–96:* $20,937.

EXPENSES AND FINANCIAL AID

Expenses for 1997–98: Comprehensive fee of $14,490 includes full-time tuition ($10,290) and college room and board ($4200 minimum). Part-time tuition: $270 per credit hour for 1 to 5 credit hours, $360 per credit hour for 6 or more credit hours.

Undergraduate Financial Aid: 87% of all full-time undergraduates enrolled in fall 1996 applied for aid; of these, 99% were judged to have need according to Federal Methodology, of whom 98% were aided. On average, 87% of need was met. *Financial aid deadline (priority):* 3/1. *Financial aid forms:* FAFSA required.

LD Services Contact: Ms. Sandee Zerger, Director, Center for Academic Development, Bethel College, Box B, 300 East 27th, North Newton, KS 67117, 316-283-0656. Fax: 316-284-5286.

BIOLA UNIVERSITY

La Mirada, California

LEARNING DISABILITIES SERVICES INFORMATION

Learning Assistance Services (LAS), Office of Student Affairs began offering services in 1971. Currently the program serves 7 undergraduates with LD. Services are also available to graduate students. Students diagnosed with ADD/ADHD are eligible for the same services available to students with LD.

Staff: 2 full-time, 1 part-time staff members, including director, coordinators. Services provided by tutor, peer tutors.

Special Fees: A fee is charged for diagnostic testing.

Applications and admissions: *Required:* psychoeducational report completed within 3 years, certification of learning disability, documentation of diagnosis. Students may begin taking classes in fall or spring. *Application deadline:* 6/1.

Special policies: The college has written policies regarding substitutions and waivers of graduation and degree requirements.

PROGRAM AND SERVICE COMPONENTS

Diagnostic testing: Intelligence, reading, math, spelling, handwriting, written language, motor abilities, perceptual skills, personality.

Academic advising: Provided by academic advisers. Students with LD may take up to 12 units each term; most take 12 units; 12 units required to maintain full-time status.

Counseling services: Individual counseling, career counseling.

Basic skills remediation: Offered in class-size groups by regular teachers. Available in reading, math, spelling, spoken language, written language, learning strategies, study skills.

Subject-area tutoring: Offered one-on-one and in small groups by peer tutors. Available in some subjects.

Special courses: College survival skills, composition, learning strategies, personal psychology, study skills, career planning. Some offered for credit; some enter into overall grade point average.

Auxiliary aids: Taped textbooks, tape recorders, calculators, word-processors with spell-check, optical character readers.

Auxiliary services: Alternative test arrangements, notetakers, priority registration, advocacy.

GENERAL COLLEGE INFORMATION

Independent interdenominational, coed. Awards bachelor's, master's, doctoral degrees. Founded 1908. *Setting:* 95-acre suburban campus with easy access to Los Angeles. *Endowment:* $8.2 million. *Total enrollment:* 3,039. *Faculty:* 240 (136 full-time, 65% with terminal degrees, 104 part-time); student–undergrad faculty ratio is 19:1.

Enrollment Profile: 1,926 students from 27 states and territories, 19 other countries. 62% women, 38% men, 5% part-time, 75% state residents, 65% live on campus, 49% transferred in, 4% international, 1% Native American, 9% Hispanic, 2% black, 12% Asian or Pacific Islander. *Areas of study chosen:* 10% communications and journalism, 10% psychology, 9% business management and administrative services, 8% health professions and related sciences, 5% education, 5% theology/religion, 4% liberal arts/general studies, 3% biological and life sciences, 3% English language/literature/letters, 3% social sciences, 2% computer and information sciences, 2% mathematics, 1% physical sciences, 1% premed. *Most popular recent majors:* business administration/commerce/management, communication, psychology.

First-Year Class: 407 total; 1,616 applied, 55% were accepted, 46% of whom enrolled.

Graduation Requirements: 130 units; 3 units each of math and science; 3 semesters of a foreign language or the equivalent for bachelor of arts degree, 1 semester of a foreign language or the equivalent for bachelor of science degree; computer course for math, education majors; internship (some majors); senior project (some majors).

Computers on Campus: 55 computers available on campus for general student use. Computer purchase/lease plans available. A campus-wide network can be accessed from student residence rooms and from off-campus. Students can contact faculty members and/or advisers through e-mail. Computers for student use in computer center, computer labs provide access to the Internet/World Wide Web, on- and off-campus e-mail addresses. Staffed computer lab on campus provides training in use of computers, software. *Academic computing expenditure 1995–96:* $155,203.

EXPENSES AND FINANCIAL AID

Expenses for 1997–98: *Application fee:* $35. Comprehensive fee of $18,754 includes full-time tuition ($14,286) and college room and board ($4468 minimum). College room only: $2546. Part-time tuition: $595 per unit.
Undergraduate Financial Aid: Of all full-time undergraduates enrolled in fall 1996, 91% of those who applied for aid were judged to have need according to Federal Methodology, of whom 100% were aided. On average, 82% of need was met. *Financial aid deadline (priority):* 3/2. *Financial aid forms:* FAFSA, institutional form required. State form required for some.
LD Services Contact: Dr. Michael Trigg, Dean for Student Affairs, Biola University, 13800 Biola Avenue, La Mirada, CA 90639-0001, 562-903-4874. Fax: 562-906-4567.

BLACK HILLS STATE UNIVERSITY

Spearfish, South Dakota

LEARNING DISABILITIES SERVICES INFORMATION

Student Support Services Program began offering services in 1973. Currently the program serves 40 undergraduates with LD. Students diagnosed with ADD/ADHD are eligible for the same services available to students with LD.
Staff: 4 full-time, 25 part-time staff members, including director, coordinators, faculty member. Services provided by remediation specialists, tutors, counselors.
Special Fees: No special fees are charged for services to students with LD.
Applications and admissions: *Required:* high school transcript, grade point average, class rank, courses completed, untimed SAT I or ACT, GED (in lieu of high school diploma). Students may begin taking classes any term. *Application deadline:* continuous.
Special policies: The college has written policies regarding grade forgiveness; substitutions and waivers of degree requirements.

PROGRAM AND SERVICE COMPONENTS

Academic advising: Provided by unit staff members, academic advisers. Students with LD may take up to 24 credits each term; most take 10 to 12 credits; 12 credits required to maintain full-time status; 1 credit required to be eligible for financial aid.
Counseling services: Individual counseling, small-group counseling, career counseling.
Basic skills remediation: Offered one-on-one and in class-size groups by regular teachers, peer teachers. Available in reading, math, spelling, written language, learning strategies, study skills, time management, social skills.
Subject-area tutoring: Offered one-on-one, in small groups, and in class-size groups by professional teachers, peer tutors. Available in all subjects.
Special courses: College survival skills, composition, math, study skills. Most offered for credit; most enter into overall grade point average.
Auxiliary aids: Taped textbooks, tape recorders, calculators, typewriters, word-processors with spell-check, personal computers, talking computers, optical character readers.
Auxiliary services: Alternative test arrangements, notetakers, advocacy.

GENERAL COLLEGE INFORMATION

State-supported, comprehensive, coed. Awards associate, bachelor's, master's degrees. Founded 1883. *Setting:* 123-acre small-town campus. *Endowment:* $4 million. *Research spending 1995–96:* $29,474. *Educational spending 1995–96:* $2357 per undergrad. *Total enrollment:* 2,866. *Faculty:* 105 (all full-time, 72% with terminal degrees); student–undergrad faculty ratio is 21:1.
Enrollment Profile: 2,769 students from 37 states and territories, 13 other countries. 58% women, 42% men, 18% part-time, 71% state residents, 24% live on campus, 13% transferred in, 1% international, 30% 25 or older, 4% Native American, 1% Hispanic, 1% black, 1% Asian or Pacific Islander. *Retention:* 44% of 1995 full-time freshmen returned. *Areas of study chosen:* 21% education, 19% business management and administrative services, 9% social sciences, 5% communications and journalism, 4% psychology, 3% philosophy, 3% physical sciences, 2% English language/literature/letters, 2% fine arts, 2% mathematics, 1% foreign language and literature, 1% natural resource sciences, 1% performing arts, 1% prelaw, 1% premed. *Most popular recent majors:* education, business administration/commerce/management.
First-Year Class: 451 total; 796 applied, 99% were accepted, 57% of whom enrolled. 7% from top 10% of their high school class, 22% from top quarter, 52% from top half.
Graduation Requirements: 64 credits for associate, 128 credits for bachelor's; 6 credits each of math and lab science; computer course for business, travel industry management, elementary education, majors; internship (some majors); senior project (some majors).
Computers on Campus: 200 computers available on campus for general student use. Computer purchase/lease plans available. A campuswide network can be accessed from student residence rooms and from off-campus. Students can contact faculty members and/or advisers through e-mail. Computers for student use in computer center, library, dorms, departmental labs provide access to the Internet/World Wide Web. *Academic computing expenditure 1995–96:* $386,535.

EXPENSES AND FINANCIAL AID

Expenses for 1997–98: *Application fee:* $15. State resident tuition: $1728 full-time, $54 per credit part-time. Nonresident tuition: $5496 full-time, $171.75 per credit part-time. Part-time mandatory fees: $35.93 per credit. Minnesota residents pay state resident tuition rates. Tuition for nonresidents who are eligible for the Western Undergraduate Exchange: $2592 full-time, $81 per credit part-time. Full-time mandatory fees: $1150. College room and board: $2958. College room only: $1382.
Undergraduate Financial Aid: Of all full-time undergraduates enrolled in fall 1996, 85% of those who applied for aid were judged to have need according to Federal Methodology, of whom 95% were aided. On average, 80% of need was met. *Financial aid deadline (priority):* 3/1. *Financial aid forms:* FAFSA required. State form required for some.
LD Services Contact: Ms. Ann M. Anderson, Disability Services Coordinator, Black Hills State University, 1200 University USB 9510, Spearfish, SD 57799-9510, 605-642-6622. Fax: 605-642-6214.

BLUEFIELD COLLEGE

Bluefield, Virginia

LEARNING DISABILITIES SERVICES INFORMATION

Learning Center began offering services in 1987. Currently the program serves 13 undergraduates with LD. Students diagnosed with ADD/ADHD are eligible for the same services available to students with LD.
Staff: 1 full-time, 3 part-time staff members, including director. Services provided by tutors, diagnostic specialist.
Special Fees: No special fees are charged for services to students with LD.
Applications and admissions: *Required:* high school transcript, grade point average, class rank, courses completed, untimed or extended time ACT, untimed SAT I, autobiographical statement, letters of recommendation, psychoeducational report; *recommended:* high school extracurricular activities, extended time SAT I. Students may begin taking classes any term. *Application deadline:* continuous.
Special policies: The college has written policies regarding grade forgiveness.

PROGRAM AND SERVICE COMPONENTS

Special preparation or orientation: Orientation (required for some) held before registration.
Diagnostic testing: Various areas as appropriate.
Academic advising: Provided by academic advisers. Students with LD may take up to 17 semester hours each term; most take 12 to 15 semester hours; 12 semester hours required to maintain full-time status and be eligible for financial aid.
Counseling services: Individual counseling, career counseling, spiritual counseling.
Basic skills remediation: Offered one-on-one and in small groups by regular teachers, tutors; computer-aided instruction also offered. Available in reading, math, spelling, spoken language, written language, learning strategies, study skills, time management, social skills, speech.
Subject-area tutoring: Offered one-on-one and in small groups by professional teachers, peer tutors. Available in most subjects.
Special courses: Freshman seminar. All offered for credit; all enter into overall grade point average.
Auxiliary aids: Taped textbooks, tape recorders, word-processors with spell-check.
Auxiliary services: Alternative test arrangements, notetakers, advocacy.

Bluefield College (continued)

GENERAL COLLEGE INFORMATION

Independent Southern Baptist, 4-year, coed. Awards associate, bachelor's degrees. Founded 1922. *Setting:* 85-acre small-town campus. *Endowment:* $1.8 million. *Total enrollment:* 758. *Faculty:* 53 (37 full-time, 60% with terminal degrees, 16 part-time); student–undergrad faculty ratio is 16:1.

Enrollment Profile: 758 students from 23 states and territories, 9 other countries. 52% women, 48% men, 10% part-time, 53% state residents, 31% transferred in, 1% international, 28% 25 or older, 1% Native American, 1% Hispanic, 5% black, 1% Asian or Pacific Islander. *Retention:* 61% of 1995 full-time freshmen returned. *Graduation:* 38% graduate in 4 years, 42% in 5 years, 44% in 6 years. *Areas of study chosen:* 24% business management and administrative services, 12% education, 8% interdisciplinary studies, 7% psychology, 7% social sciences, 6% biological and life sciences, 3% communications and journalism, 3% mathematics, 1% computer and information sciences, 1% English language/literature/letters, 1% fine arts, 1% prelaw, 1% premed. *Most popular recent majors:* business administration/commerce/management, education, psychology.

First-Year Class: 144 total; 367 applied, 93% were accepted, 42% of whom enrolled. 10% from top 10% of their high school class, 30% from top quarter, 60% from top half.

Graduation Requirements: 32 semester hours for associate, 126 semester hours for bachelor's; 1 math course, 2 lab science courses for associate degree; 2 math courses, 3 lab science courses for bachelor's degree; computer course; internship (some majors); senior project for honors program students and some majors.

Computers on Campus: 75 computers available on campus for general student use. Computers for student use in computer labs, learning resource center, library, writing center provide access to the Internet/World Wide Web. Staffed computer lab on campus provides training in use of computers. *Academic computing expenditure 1995–96:* $87,100.

EXPENSES AND FINANCIAL AID

Expenses for 1997–98: *Application fee:* $15. Comprehensive fee of $13,710 includes full-time tuition ($8770), mandatory fees ($330), and college room and board ($4610). College room only: $1750. Part-time tuition per semester hour ranges from $165 to $340. Part-time mandatory fees per semester (5 to 11 semester hours): $85.

Undergraduate Financial Aid: Of all full-time undergraduates enrolled in fall 1996, 99% of those judged to have need according to Federal Methodology were aided. On average, 65% of need was met. *Financial aid deadline (priority):* 3/10. *Financial aid forms:* FAFSA, state form, institutional form required; CSS Financial Aid PROFILE acceptable.

LD Services Contact: Ms. Lenora Buckland, Interim Director, Bluefield College, 3000 College Drive, Bluefield, VA 24605, 540-326-4286. Fax: 540-326-4288.

BLUEFIELD STATE COLLEGE

Bluefield, West Virginia

LEARNING DISABILITIES SERVICES INFORMATION

Student Support Services began offering services in 1990. Currently the program serves 4 undergraduates with LD. Students diagnosed with ADD/ADHD are eligible for the same services available to students with LD.

Staff: 5 full-time, 1 part-time staff members, including director. Services provided by remediation specialist, tutors, counselor.

Special Fees: No special fees are charged for services to students with LD.

Applications and admissions: *Required:* high school transcript, grade point average, class rank, courses completed, IEP (Individualized Education Program), extended time ACT, psychoeducational report completed within 2 years; *recommended:* high school extracurricular activities. Students may begin taking classes in summer only. *Application deadline:* continuous.

Special policies: The college has written policies regarding grade forgiveness.

PROGRAM AND SERVICE COMPONENTS

Academic advising: Provided by unit staff members, academic advisers. Students with LD may take up to 16 semester hours each term; most take 9 semester hours; 12 semester hours required to maintain full-time status and be eligible for financial aid.

Counseling services: Individual counseling, small-group counseling, career counseling.

Basic skills remediation: Offered one-on-one and in small groups by regular teachers; computer-aided instruction also offered. Available in reading, math, written language, learning strategies, study skills, time management.

Special courses: College survival skills, reading, time management, math, study skills, career planning, stress management. Some offered for credit; some enter into overall grade point average.

Auxiliary aids: Taped textbooks, tape recorders, calculators, typewriters, word-processors with spell-check, personal computers.

Auxiliary services: Alternative test arrangements, notetakers, advocacy.

GENERAL COLLEGE INFORMATION

State-supported, 4-year, coed. Part of State College System of West Virginia. Awards associate, bachelor's degrees. Founded 1895. *Setting:* 45-acre small-town campus. *Endowment:* $4.5 million. *Total enrollment:* 2,609. *Faculty:* 162 (82 full-time, 45% with terminal degrees, 80 part-time); student–undergrad faculty ratio is 18:1.

Enrollment Profile: 2,609 students from 8 states and territories, 9 other countries. 57% women, 43% men, 38% part-time, 92% state residents, 7% transferred in, 2% international, 35% 25 or older, 1% Native American, 1% Hispanic, 8% black, 1% Asian or Pacific Islander. *Areas of study chosen:* 30% business management and administrative services, 26% liberal arts/general studies, 13% health professions and related sciences, 12% engineering and applied sciences, 5% education, 4% computer and information sciences, 3% social sciences, 2% premed, 1% architecture, 1% mathematics, 1% prevet. *Most popular recent majors:* business administration/commerce/management, nursing, education.

First-Year Class: 533 total; 1,287 applied, 65% were accepted, 63% of whom enrolled. 10% from top 10% of their high school class, 25% from top quarter, 65% from top half. 8 class presidents, 8 valedictorians.

Graduation Requirements: 64 semester hours for associate, 128 semester hours for bachelor's; 3 semester hours of math; 8 semester hours of science; computer course; senior project (some majors).

Computers on Campus: 425 computers available on campus for general student use. A campus-wide network can be accessed from off-campus. Students can contact faculty members and/or advisers through e-mail. Computers for student use in computer center, computer labs, classrooms, library provide access to the Internet/World Wide Web, on- and off-campus e-mail addresses. Staffed computer lab on campus provides training in use of computers, software.

EXPENSES AND FINANCIAL AID

Expenses for 1997–98: State resident tuition: $2044 full-time. Nonresident tuition: $4968 full-time. Part-time tuition per semester ranges from $85 to $935 for state residents, $207 to $2277 for nonresidents.

Undergraduate Financial Aid: On average, 36% of need was met. *Financial aid deadline (priority):* 3/1. *Financial aid forms:* FAFSA, CSS Financial Aid PROFILE, institutional form required.

LD Services Contact: Ms. Kathy M. Epperly, Director, Student Support Services, Bluefield State College, 219 Rock Street, Bluefield, WV 24701-2198, 304-327-4098. Fax: 304-327-4098. Email: kepperly@bscvax.wvnet.edu.

BRANDEIS UNIVERSITY

Waltham, Massachusetts

LEARNING DISABILITIES SERVICES INFORMATION

Office of Academic Affairs began offering services in 1985. Currently the program serves 64 to 75 undergraduates with LD. Services are also available to graduate students.

Staff: 2 part-time staff members, including co-directors.

Special Fees: No special fees are charged for services to students with LD.

Applications and admissions: *Recommended:* psychoeducational report completed within 3 years. Students may begin taking classes in fall, spring, or summer. *Application deadline:* 2/1.

Special policies: The college has written policies regarding grade forgiveness; substitutions and waivers of admissions, graduation, and degree requirements.

PROGRAM AND SERVICE COMPONENTS

Special preparation or orientation: Required orientation held during registration.

Academic advising: Provided by unit staff members, academic advisers. Students with LD may take up to 20 credits each term; most take 12 to 16 credits; 12 credits required to maintain full-time status and be eligible for financial aid.
Counseling services: Individual counseling, small-group counseling, career counseling.
Basic skills remediation: Offered in small groups. Available in study skills, time management.
Subject-area tutoring: Offered one-on-one and in small groups by peer tutors. Available in most subjects.
Auxiliary aids: Taped textbooks, tape recorders, calculators, typewriters, word-processors with spell-check, personal computers.
Auxiliary services: Alternative test arrangements, notetakers.

GENERAL COLLEGE INFORMATION

Independent, coed. Awards bachelor's, master's, doctoral degrees. Founded 1948. *Setting:* 250-acre suburban campus with easy access to Boston. *Endowment:* $235 million. *Research spending 1995–96:* $28.9 million. *Educational spending 1995–96:* $10,563 per undergrad. *Total enrollment:* 4,219. *Faculty:* 485 (351 full-time, 96% with terminal degrees, 134 part-time); student–undergrad faculty ratio is 10:1.
Enrollment Profile: 3,020 students from 45 states and territories, 56 other countries. 55% women, 45% men, 2% part-time, 28% state residents, 85% live on campus, 1% transferred in, 5% international, 2% 25 or older, 1% Native American, 3% Hispanic, 3% black, 9% Asian or Pacific Islander. *Retention:* 91% of 1995 full-time freshmen returned. *Areas of study chosen:* 38% social sciences, 14% area and ethnic studies, 13% psychology, 10% biological and life sciences, 10% English language/literature/letters, 3% fine arts, 3% foreign language and literature, 3% philosophy, 2% computer and information sciences, 2% physical sciences, 1% interdisciplinary studies, 1% mathematics, 1% performing arts. *Most popular recent majors:* political science/government, English, psychology.
First-Year Class: 770 total; 5,513 applied, 53% were accepted, 26% of whom enrolled. 57% from top 10% of their high school class, 80% from top quarter, 99% from top half. 8 National Merit Scholars.
Graduation Requirements: 32 courses; 1 course each in quantitative reasoning and science; proven competence in a foreign language; senior project (some majors).
Computers on Campus: 100 computers available on campus for general student use. Computer purchase/lease plans available. A campus-wide network can be accessed from student residence rooms and from off-campus. Students can contact faculty members and/or advisers through e-mail. Computers for student use in computer center, computer labs, research center, learning resource center, classrooms, library, student center, dorms, science library provide access to the Internet/World Wide Web, on- and off-campus e-mail addresses, educational software. Staffed computer lab on campus provides training in use of computers, software. *Academic computing expenditure 1995–96:* $1.4 million.

EXPENSES AND FINANCIAL AID

Expenses for 1997–98: *Application fee:* $50. Comprehensive fee of $29,821 includes full-time tuition ($22,360), mandatory fees ($491), and college room and board ($6970). College room only: $3890. Part-time tuition: $2795 per course.
Undergraduate Financial Aid: Of all full-time undergraduates enrolled in fall 1996, 100% of those judged to have need according to Federal Methodology were aided. *Financial aid deadline (priority):* 2/15. *Financial aid forms:* FAFSA, CSS Financial Aid PROFILE, institutional form required. State form required for some.
LD Services Contact: Ms. Betty Lloyd, Associate Director of Admissions, Brandeis University, 415 South Street, Waltham, MA 02254-9110, 617-736-3500.

BRIGHAM YOUNG UNIVERSITY

Provo, Utah

LEARNING DISABILITIES SERVICES INFORMATION

Services for Students with Disabilities began offering services in 1983. Currently the program serves 200 undergraduates with LD. Services are also available to graduate students. Students diagnosed with ADD/ADHD are eligible for the same services available to students with LD, as well as medical consultation.
Staff: 4 full-time, 3 part-time staff members, including director, coordinators. Services provided by counselors, diagnostic specialists, notetakers, readers, technology volunteers.
Special Fees: No special fees are charged for services to students with LD.
Applications and admissions: *Required:* high school transcript, grade point average, class rank, untimed ACT; *recommended:* extended time ACT. Students may begin taking classes any term. *Application deadline:* 2/15 (fall term), 10/1 (spring term).

PROGRAM AND SERVICE COMPONENTS

Special preparation or orientation: Optional orientation offered before classes begin.
Diagnostic testing: Intelligence, reading, math, spelling, written language, perceptual skills, study skills, personality, psychoneurology, learning strategies.
Academic advising: Provided by unit staff members, academic advisers. Students with LD may take up to 18 credits each term; most take 10 to 12 credits; 8.5 credits required to maintain full-time status; 12 credits required to be eligible for financial aid.
Counseling services: Individual counseling, career counseling, self-advocacy training.
Subject-area tutoring: Offered one-on-one and in small groups by peer tutors. Available in most subjects.
Auxiliary aids: Taped textbooks, tape recorders, calculators, word-processors with spell-check, talking computers, optical character readers.
Auxiliary services: Alternative test arrangements, notetakers, priority registration, readers.
Campus support group: A special student organization is available to students with LD.

GENERAL COLLEGE INFORMATION

Independent, coed, affiliated with Church of Jesus Christ of Latter-day Saints. Awards bachelor's, master's, doctoral, first professional degrees. Founded 1875. *Setting:* 638-acre suburban campus. *Total enrollment:* 30,563. *Faculty:* 1,691 (1,370 full-time, 78% with terminal degrees, 321 part-time); student–undergrad faculty ratio is 29:1.
Enrollment Profile: 27,706 students from 52 states and territories, 97 other countries. 48% women, 52% men, 4% part-time, 33% state residents, 19% live on campus, 35% transferred in, 4% international, 17% 25 or older, 1% Native American, 3% Hispanic, 1% black, 3% Asian or Pacific Islander. *Retention:* 87% of 1995 full-time freshmen returned. *Graduation:* 12% graduate in 4 years, 25% in 5 years, 42% in 6 years. *Areas of study chosen:* 13% social sciences, 10% business management and administrative services, 10% engineering and applied sciences, 10% interdisciplinary studies, 9% biological and life sciences, 7% education, 7% health professions and related sciences, 6% English language/literature/letters, 6% fine arts, 4% communications and journalism, 3% area and ethnic studies, 3% foreign language and literature, 3% psychology, 2% computer and information sciences, 2% mathematics, 2% physical sciences, 1% agriculture, 1% performing arts, 1% philosophy. *Most popular recent majors:* business administration/commerce/management, elementary education, zoology.
First-Year Class: 4,277 total; 6,817 applied, 77% were accepted, 82% of whom enrolled. 53% from top 10% of their high school class, 86% from top quarter, 98% from top half. 169 National Merit Scholars.
Graduation Requirements: 128 credits; 1 math course beyond college algebra (in lieu of foreign language requirement); 9 credits of science; 1 course in advanced literature, reading, or history taught in a foreign language (in lieu of math requirement); computer course for engineering, business majors; internship (some majors); senior project for honors program students and some majors.
Computers on Campus: 1,800 computers available on campus for general student use. A computer is recommended for some students. A campus-wide network can be accessed from student residence rooms and from off-campus. Students can contact faculty members and/or advisers through e-mail. Computers for student use in computer center, computer labs, research center, learning resource center, classrooms, library, student center, dorms provide access to the Internet/World Wide Web. Staffed computer lab on campus.

EXPENSES AND FINANCIAL AID

Expenses for 1997–98: *Application fee:* $25. Comprehensive fee of $6435 includes full-time tuition ($2630 minimum) and college room and board ($3805). Part-time tuition: $135 per credit (minimum). Tuition for non-church members: $3950 full-time, $200 per credit part-time.
Undergraduate Financial Aid: 74% of all full-time undergraduates enrolled in fall 1996 applied for aid; of these, 53% were judged to have need according to Federal Methodology, of whom 88% were aided. On average, 52% of need was met. *Financial aid deadline (priority):* 3/1. *Financial aid forms:* FAFSA, institutional form required.

Brigham Young University (continued)

LD Services Contact: Dr. Paul B. Byrd, Director, Services for Students with Disabilities, Brigham Young University, 155 Spencer W. Kimball Tower, Provo, UT 84602-5541, 801-378-2767. Email: byrd@st/gate.byc.edu.

BROCK UNIVERSITY

St. Catharines, Ontario, Canada

LEARNING DISABILITIES SERVICES INFORMATION

Student Development Centre/Special Needs Services began offering services in 1990. Currently the program serves 90 undergraduates with LD. Services are also available to graduate students. Students diagnosed with ADD/ADHD are eligible for the same services available to students with LD.

Staff: 1 full-time, 3 part-time staff members, including director. Services provided by remediation specialists, special needs assistant.

Special Fees: No special fees are charged for services to students with LD.

Applications and admissions: *Required:* high school transcript, courses completed, psychoeducational report completed within 5 years, letter from school outlining previous accommodations; *recommended:* high school IEP (Individualized Education Program), SAT I. Students may begin taking classes any term. *Application deadline:* 6/1.

Special policies: The college has written policies regarding substitutions and waivers of admissions requirements.

PROGRAM AND SERVICE COMPONENTS

Special preparation or orientation: Optional orientation offered during registration.

Academic advising: Provided by academic advisers. Students with LD may take up to 5 credits each term; most take 3 to 5 credits; 3 credits required to maintain full-time status; 1 credit required to be eligible for financial aid.

Counseling services: Individual counseling, career counseling, self-advocacy training.

Basic skills remediation: Offered one-on-one and in small groups by LD specialist, learning skills instructors. Available in reading, spelling, written language, learning strategies, perceptual skills, study skills, time management, memory strategies.

Special courses: Communication skills, learning strategies, time management, study skills, stress management, essay writing. None offered for credit; none enter into overall grade point average.

Auxiliary aids: Taped textbooks, tape recorders, calculators, word-processors with spell-check, talking computers, optical character readers.

Auxiliary services: Alternative test arrangements, notetakers, assistance with registration.

GENERAL COLLEGE INFORMATION

Province-supported, comprehensive, coed. Awards bachelor's, master's degrees. Founded 1964. *Setting:* 540-acre urban campus with easy access to Toronto. *Total enrollment:* 11,299. *Faculty:* 338 (325 full-time, 80% with terminal degrees, 13 part-time); student–undergrad faculty ratio is 43:1.

Enrollment Profile: 10,655 students from 10 provinces and territories, 18 other countries. 59% women, 41% men, 30% part-time, 96% province residents, 19% live on campus, 10% transferred in, 3% international, 40% 25 or older. *Areas of study chosen:* 27% social sciences, 22% liberal arts/general studies, 17% business management and administrative services, 15% health professions and related sciences, 15% physical sciences, 4% education. *Most popular recent majors:* liberal arts/general studies, psychology, education.

First-Year Class: 2,043 total; 8,539 applied, 73% were accepted, 33% of whom enrolled.

Graduation Requirements: 15 courses; computer course for accounting, business administration, business economics, environmental science, geography, geological sciences, health studies, physics, sociology, urban and environmental studies majors; senior project for honors program students and some majors.

Computers on Campus: 275 computers available on campus for general student use. A campus-wide network can be accessed from student residence rooms and from off-campus. Students can contact faculty members and/or advisers through e-mail. Computers for student use in computer center, computer labs, library provide access to the Internet/World Wide Web. Staffed computer lab on campus provides training in use of computers, software.

EXPENSES AND FINANCIAL AID

Expenses for 1997–98: Canadian resident tuition: $3427 full-time, $685.40 per course part-time. Nonresident tuition: $9425 full-time, $1885 per course part-time. Mandatory fee for nonresidents: $570.43 per year. (All figures are in Canadian dollars.). College room and board: $4743 (minimum). College room only: $2410 (minimum).

Undergraduate Financial Aid: *Financial aid deadline:* Applications processed continuously. *Financial aid forms:* state form required.

Financial aid specifically for students with LD: Scholarship: Special Needs Bursary.

LD Services Contact: Ms. Maureen Kemeny, Learning Disabilities Specialist, Brock University, 500 Glenridge Avenue, St. Catharines, ON L2S 3A1, Canada, 905-688-5550 Ext. 3240. Fax: 905-685-1188.

BROOKS INSTITUTE OF PHOTOGRAPHY

Santa Barbara, California

LEARNING DISABILITIES SERVICES INFORMATION

The Learning Disabilities special services program currently serves 1 undergraduate with LD. Services are also available to graduate students. Students diagnosed with ADD/ADHD are eligible for the same services available to students with LD.

Special Fees: No special fees are charged for services to students with LD.

Applications and admissions: *Required:* high school transcript, grade point average, autobiographical statement, psychoeducational report; *recommended:* personal interview, letters of recommendation. Students may begin taking classes any term. *Application deadline:* continuous.

PROGRAM AND SERVICE COMPONENTS

Academic advising: Provided by academic advisers. Students with LD may take up to 18 semester hours each term; most take 15 to 18 semester hours; 12 semester hours required to maintain full-time status.

Auxiliary aids: Typewriters, word-processors with spell-check.

Auxiliary services: Alternative test arrangements.

GENERAL COLLEGE INFORMATION

Proprietary, comprehensive, specialized, coed. Awards bachelor's, master's degrees. Founded 1945. *Setting:* 25-acre suburban campus. *Total enrollment:* 351. *Faculty:* 39 (19 full-time, 100% with terminal degrees, 20 part-time); student–undergrad faculty ratio is 14:1.

Enrollment Profile: 324 students from 27 states and territories, 22 other countries. 40% women, 60% men, 5% part-time, 35% state residents, 100% transferred in, 36% international, 50% 25 or older. *Retention:* 63% of 1995 full-time freshmen returned. *Areas of study chosen:* 100% fine arts.

First-Year Class: 115 total; 294 applied, 39% were accepted, 100% of whom enrolled.

Graduation Requirements: 153 credits; 1 course each in math and science; computer course; senior project (some majors).

Computers on Campus: 15 computers available on campus for general student use. Students can contact faculty members and/or advisers through e-mail. Computers for student use in computer center provide access to the Internet/World Wide Web, on- and off-campus e-mail addresses. Staffed computer lab on campus provides training in use of computers, software.

EXPENSES AND FINANCIAL AID

Estimated Expenses for 1997–98: *Application fee:* $35. Tuition: $14,700 full-time. Full-time mandatory fees: $210.

Undergraduate Financial Aid: *Financial aid deadline (priority):* 7/1. *Financial aid forms:* FAFSA, institutional form required.

LD Services Contact: Ms. Inge B. Kautzmann, Director of Admissions, Brooks Institute of Photography, 801 Alston Road, Santa Barbara, CA 93108, 805-966-3888 Ext. 217. Fax: 805-565-1386. Email: admissions@brooks.edu.

BROWN UNIVERSITY

Providence, Rhode Island

LEARNING DISABILITIES SERVICES INFORMATION

Dean of the College Office began offering services in 1984. Currently the program serves 180 undergraduates with LD. Services are also available to graduate students. Students diagnosed with ADD/ADHD are eligible for the same services available to students with LD.
Staff: 1 full-time, 1 part-time staff members, including director.
Special Fees: No special fees are charged for services to students with LD.
Applications and admissions: *Required:* high school transcript, grade point average, class rank, courses completed, extracurricular activities, untimed SAT I, autobiographical statement, letters of recommendation; *recommended:* extended time SAT I. Students may begin taking classes in fall only. *Application deadline:* 1/1.
Special policies: The college has written policies regarding substitutions and waivers of admissions, graduation, and degree requirements.

PROGRAM AND SERVICE COMPONENTS

Special preparation or orientation: Optional orientation offered during registration.
Academic advising: Provided by unit staff members, academic advisers. Students with LD may take up to 20 credits each term; most take 16 credits; 12 credits required to maintain full-time status; type of aid determines number of credits required to be eligible for financial aid.
Counseling services: Individual counseling, career counseling, self-advocacy training.
Basic skills remediation: Offered one-on-one by LD teachers. Available in reading, math, spelling, handwriting, spoken language, written language, learning strategies, motor abilities, perceptual skills, study skills, time management, social skills, speech.
Subject-area tutoring: Offered one-on-one by peer tutors. Available in some subjects.
Auxiliary services: Alternative test arrangements, notetakers, advocacy.
Campus support group: A special student organization is available to students with LD.

GENERAL COLLEGE INFORMATION

Independent, coed. Awards bachelor's, master's, doctoral, first professional degrees. Founded 1764. *Setting:* 140-acre urban campus with easy access to Boston. *Total enrollment:* 7,626. *Faculty:* 682 (540 full-time, 98% with terminal degrees, 142 part-time); student–undergrad faculty ratio is 8:1.
Enrollment Profile: 5,963 students from 52 states and territories, 66 other countries. 53% women, 47% men, 6% part-time, 3% state residents, 85% live on campus, 2% transferred in, 9% international, 1% 25 or older, 1% Native American, 5% Hispanic, 6% black, 15% Asian or Pacific Islander. *Retention:* 96% of 1995 full-time freshmen returned. *Graduation:* 76% graduate in 4 years, 89% in 5 years, 91% in 6 years. *Areas of study chosen:* 47% social sciences, 18% biological and life sciences, 12% physical sciences, 7% fine arts, 6% English language/literature/letters, 3% foreign language and literature, 2% philosophy, 2% theology/religion, 1% performing arts. *Most popular recent majors:* biology/biological sciences, history, psychology.
First-Year Class: 1,511 total; 15,012 applied, 19% were accepted, 53% of whom enrolled. 88% from top 10% of their high school class, 97% from top quarter, 99% from top half.
Graduation Requirements: 30 courses; computer course for applied math majors; senior project for honors program students and some majors.
Computers on Campus: 400 computers available on campus for general student use. Computer purchase/lease plans available. A campuswide network can be accessed from student residence rooms and from off-campus. Students can contact faculty members and/or advisers through e-mail. Computers for student use in computer center, computer labs, learning resource center, library, student center, dorms provide access to the Internet/World Wide Web, on- and off-campus e-mail addresses. Staffed computer lab on campus provides training in use of computers, software.

EXPENSES AND FINANCIAL AID

Expenses for 1997–98: *Application fee:* $55. Comprehensive fee of $29,900 includes full-time tuition ($22,592), mandatory fees ($532), and college room and board ($6776). College room only: $4154. Part-time tuition: $2824 per course.
Undergraduate Financial Aid: Of all full-time undergraduates enrolled in fall 1996, 89% of those who applied for aid were judged to have need according to Federal Methodology, of whom 100% were aided. On average, 100% of need was met. *Financial aid deadline:* 1/22. *Financial aid forms:* FAFSA, CSS Financial Aid PROFILE, institutional form required. State form, Divorced/Separated Parents' Statement, Business/Farm Supplement required for some.
LD Services Contact: Mr. Robert A. Shaw, Associate Dean of the College, Brown University, Providence, RI 02912.

BRYN MAWR COLLEGE

Bryn Mawr, Pennsylvania

LEARNING DISABILITIES SERVICES INFORMATION

Undergraduate Deans Office currently serves 18 undergraduates with LD. Students diagnosed with ADD/ADHD are eligible for the same services available to students with LD.
Staff: 1 part-time staff member (coordinator). Services provided by remediation specialists, tutors, diagnostic specialists.
Special Fees: $200 to $800 for diagnostic testing.
Applications and admissions: *Required:* high school transcript, letters of recommendation, essay; *recommended:* personal interview. *Application deadline:* continuous.
Special policies: The college has written policies regarding substitutions and waivers of graduation and degree requirements.

PROGRAM AND SERVICE COMPONENTS

Diagnostic testing: Intelligence, reading, math, spelling, handwriting, spoken language, written language, motor abilities, perceptual skills, study skills, personality, social skills, psychoneurology, speech, hearing, learning strategies.
Academic advising: Provided by academic advisers. Students with LD may take up to 4 units each term; most take 4 units; 3 units required to maintain full-time status; 3 to 4 units required to be eligible for financial aid.
Counseling services: Individual counseling, small-group counseling, career counseling.
Basic skills remediation: Offered one-on-one and in small groups by regular teachers. Available in reading, learning strategies, study skills, time management, social skills.
Subject-area tutoring: Offered one-on-one and in small groups by peer tutors. Available in all subjects.
Auxiliary aids: Taped textbooks, tape recorders, word-processors with spell-check, personal computers, optical character readers.
Auxiliary services: Alternative test arrangements, notetakers, priority registration, advocacy.

GENERAL COLLEGE INFORMATION

Independent, women only. Awards bachelor's, master's, doctoral degrees. Founded 1885. *Setting:* 135-acre suburban campus with easy access to Philadelphia. *Endowment:* $245 million. *Research spending 1995–96:* $2.2 million. *Educational spending 1995–96:* $12,600 per undergrad. *Total enrollment:* 1,886. *Faculty:* 232 (148 full-time, 99% with terminal degrees, 84 part-time); student–undergrad faculty ratio is 9:1.
Enrollment Profile: 1,205 students from 49 states and territories, 43 other countries. 100% women, 3% part-time, 14% state residents, 97% live on campus, 5% transferred in, 11% international, 3% 25 or older, 1% Native American, 3% Hispanic, 4% black, 18% Asian or Pacific Islander. *Retention:* 94% of 1995 full-time freshmen returned. *Graduation:* 88% graduate in 4 years, 92% in 5 years, 94% in 6 years. *Areas of study chosen:* 28% social sciences, 16% interdisciplinary studies, 14% foreign language and literature, 14% physical sciences, 12% English language/literature/letters, 10% biological and life sciences, 8% psychology, 7% mathematics, 5% area and ethnic studies, 2% philosophy, 1% fine arts, 1% performing arts, 1% theology/religion. *Most popular recent majors:* history, political science/government, English.
First-Year Class: 360 total; 1,619 applied, 58% were accepted, 38% of whom enrolled. 60% from top 10% of their high school class, 90% from top quarter, 100% from top half.
Graduation Requirements: 32 courses; basic math proficiency; 2 lab science courses; 2 courses in a foreign language or proven competence.
Computers on Campus: 150 computers available on campus for general student use. Computer purchase/lease plans available. A campuswide network can be accessed from student residence rooms and from off-campus. Students can contact faculty members and/or advisers through e-mail. Computers for student use in computer center, computer labs,

Bryn Mawr College (continued)

research center, classrooms, library, dorms provide access to the Internet/World Wide Web, on- and off-campus e-mail addresses. Staffed computer lab on campus provides training in use of computers, software. *Academic computing expenditure 1995–96:* $753,695.

EXPENSES AND FINANCIAL AID

Expenses for 1997–98: *Application fee:* $40. Comprehensive fee of $28,930 includes full-time tuition ($21,020), mandatory fees ($410), and college room and board ($7500).

Undergraduate Financial Aid: Of all full-time undergraduates enrolled in fall 1996, 84% of those who applied for aid were judged to have need according to Federal Methodology, of whom 100% were aided. On average, 100% of need was met. *Financial aid deadline:* 1/15. *Financial aid forms:* FAFSA, CSS Financial Aid PROFILE, institutional form required. State form required for some.

LD Services Contact: Ms. Lois Méndez Catlin, Assistant Dean, Bryn Mawr College, 101 North Merion Avenue, Bryn Mawr, PA 19010, 610-526-5375. Fax: 610-526-7450. Email: lmendez@brynmawr.edu.

BUCKNELL UNIVERSITY

Lewisburg, Pennsylvania

LEARNING DISABILITIES SERVICES INFORMATION

Office of the Dean of Students began offering services in 1992. Currently the program serves 32 undergraduates with LD. Services are also available to graduate students. Students diagnosed with ADD/ADHD are eligible for the same services available to students with LD.

Staff: 5 part-time staff members, including coordinators. Services provided by tutors.

Special Fees: No special fees are charged for services to students with LD.

Applications and admissions: *Required:* high school transcript, grade point average, class rank, courses completed, extracurricular activities, untimed ACT, letters of recommendation; *recommended:* untimed or extended time SAT I, extended time ACT, personal interview, psychoeducational report. Students may begin taking classes in fall only. *Application deadline:* 1/1.

PROGRAM AND SERVICE COMPONENTS

Academic advising: Provided by academic advisers. Students with LD may take up to 4 courses each term; most take 4 courses; 3 courses required to maintain full-time status and be eligible for financial aid.

Counseling services: Individual counseling, small-group counseling, career counseling.

Auxiliary aids: Tape recorders, word-processors with spell-check, optical character readers.

Auxiliary services: Alternative test arrangements, notetakers.

GENERAL COLLEGE INFORMATION

Independent, comprehensive, coed. Awards bachelor's, master's degrees. Founded 1846. *Setting:* 300-acre small-town campus. *Endowment:* $204.5 million. *Research spending 1995–96:* $942,000. *Educational spending 1995–96:* $8195 per undergrad. *Total enrollment:* 3,573. *Faculty:* 280 (261 full-time, 98% with terminal degrees, 19 part-time); student–undergrad faculty ratio is 13:1.

Enrollment Profile: 3,347 students from 43 states and territories, 31 other countries. 50% women, 50% men, 1% part-time, 33% state residents, 84% live on campus, 1% transferred in, 2% international, 1% 25 or older, 0% Native American, 2% Hispanic, 2% black, 4% Asian or Pacific Islander. *Retention:* 93% of 1995 full-time freshmen returned. *Graduation:* 86% graduate in 4 years, 89% in 5 years. *Areas of study chosen:* 18% engineering and applied sciences, 11% biological and life sciences, 9% social sciences, 8% business management and administrative services, 5% education, 3% English language/literature/letters, 3% physical sciences, 2% interdisciplinary studies, 2% mathematics, 2% psychology, 1% computer and information sciences, 1% fine arts, 1% foreign language and literature, 1% natural resource sciences, 1% performing arts, 1% philosophy, 1% theology/religion. *Most popular recent majors:* biology/biological sciences, economics, English.

First-Year Class: 894 total; 7,364 applied, 49% were accepted, 25% of whom enrolled. 53% from top 10% of their high school class, 85% from top quarter, 99% from top half. 2 National Merit Scholars, 31 class presidents, 28 valedictorians.

Graduation Requirements: 32 courses; computer course for all majors except humanities; senior project for honors program students and some majors.

Computers on Campus: 350 computers available on campus for general student use. A computer is recommended for all students. A campus-wide network can be accessed from student residence rooms and from off-campus. Students can contact faculty members and/or advisers through e-mail. Computers for student use in computer center, computer labs, classrooms, library, dorms provide access to the Internet/World Wide Web, on- and off-campus e-mail addresses. Staffed computer lab on campus provides training in use of computers, software. *Academic computing expenditure 1995–96:* $3 million.

EXPENSES AND FINANCIAL AID

Expenses for 1997–98: *Application fee:* $45. Comprehensive fee of $26,410 includes full-time tuition ($21,080), mandatory fees ($130), and college room and board ($5200). College room only: $2785. Part-time tuition: $2410 per course.

Undergraduate Financial Aid: Of all full-time undergraduates enrolled in fall 1996, 85% of those who applied for aid were judged to have need according to Federal Methodology, of whom 100% were aided. On average, 99% of need was met. *Financial aid deadline (priority):* 1/1. *Financial aid forms:* FAFSA, CSS Financial Aid PROFILE, state form required.

LD Services Contact: Ms. Maureen Murphy, Associate Dean, Arts and Sciences, Bucknell University, 113 Marts Hall, Lewisburg, PA 17837, 717-524-1031. Fax: 717-524-3760.

BURLINGTON COLLEGE

Burlington, Vermont

LEARNING DISABILITIES SERVICES INFORMATION

Educational Resources Center began offering services in 1985. Currently the program serves 11 undergraduates with LD. Students diagnosed with ADD/ADHD are eligible for the same services available to students with LD.

Staff: 1 full-time, 5 part-time staff members, including director, coordinator. Services provided by tutors, counselor, peer helpers, faculty tutors, social worker.

Special Fees: No special fees are charged for services to students with LD.

Applications and admissions: *Required:* high school transcript, personal interview; *recommended:* psychoeducational report, writing samples. Students may begin taking classes any term. *Application deadline:* continuous.

Special policies: The college has written policies regarding substitutions and waivers of admissions, graduation, and degree requirements.

PROGRAM AND SERVICE COMPONENTS

Special preparation or orientation: Optional orientation offered after classes begin.

Diagnostic testing: Reading, math, spelling, written language, learning strategies.

Academic advising: Provided by unit staff members, academic advisers. Students with LD may take up to 18 credits each term; most take 6 to 12 credits; 12 credits required to maintain full-time status; 6 credits required to be eligible for financial aid.

Counseling services: Individual counseling, career counseling, self-advocacy training.

Basic skills remediation: Offered one-on-one and in small groups by Student Support Services staff. Available in reading, math, spelling, handwriting, spoken language, written language, learning strategies, study skills, time management, social skills.

Subject-area tutoring: Offered one-on-one by professional teachers, peer tutors. Available in most subjects.

Auxiliary aids: Tape recorders, calculators, word-processors with spell-check, personal computers.

Auxiliary services: Alternative test arrangements, advocacy.

GENERAL COLLEGE INFORMATION

Independent, 4-year, coed. Awards associate, bachelor's degrees. Founded 1972. *Setting:* 1-acre urban campus. *Endowment:* $20,025. *Educational spending 1995–96:* $1593 per undergrad. *Total enrollment:* 198. *Faculty:* 57 (all part-time); student–undergrad faculty ratio is 4:1.

Enrollment Profile: 198 students from 20 states and territories, 5 other countries. 60% women, 40% men, 48% part-time, 95% state residents,

40% transferred in, 1% international, 75% 25 or older, 3% Native American, 3% Hispanic, 5% black, 1% Asian or Pacific Islander. *Areas of study chosen:* 38% social sciences, 15% interdisciplinary studies, 11% fine arts. *Most popular recent majors:* psychology, humanities, human services.
First-Year Class: 15 total; 28 applied, 100% were accepted, 54% of whom enrolled.
Graduation Requirements: 60 credits for associate, 120 credits for bachelor's; 9 credits of natural science; 3 credits of math; internship; senior project.
Computers on Campus: 21 computers available on campus for general student use. Computers for student use in computer center, library provide access to the Internet/World Wide Web. Staffed computer lab on campus provides training in use of computers, software. *Academic computing expenditure 1995–96:* $35,000.

EXPENSES AND FINANCIAL AID

Expenses for 1997–98: *Application fee:* $30. Tuition: $8190 full-time, $273 per credit part-time. Part-time mandatory fees: $115 per semester. Full-time mandatory fees for seniors: $530. Part-time mandatory fees for nonmatriculated students: $30 per semester. Tuition for External Degree Program: $6800 full-time, $2000 per semester part-time. Full-time mandatory fees: $230 (minimum).
Undergraduate Financial Aid: 100% of all full-time undergraduates enrolled in fall 1996 applied for aid; of these, 92% were judged to have need according to Federal Methodology, of whom 100% were aided. On average, 75% of need was met. *Financial aid deadline:* continuous. *Financial aid forms:* FAFSA, institutional form required; CSS Financial Aid PROFILE acceptable. State form required for some.
LD Services Contact: Mr. Don Huffman, Director of Student Support Services, Burlington College, 95 North Avenue, Burlington, VT 05401-2998, 802-862-9616 Ext. 46. Fax: 802-658-0071. Email: huffmand@burlcol.edu.

CALIFORNIA POLYTECHNIC STATE UNIVERSITY, SAN LUIS OBISPO

San Luis Obispo, California

LEARNING DISABILITIES SERVICES INFORMATION

Disability Resource Center began offering services in 1980. Currently the program serves 400 undergraduates with LD. Services are also available to graduate students. Students diagnosed with ADD/ADHD are eligible for the same services available to students with LD.
Staff: 2 full-time, 1 part-time staff members, including director. Services provided by diagnostic specialists, LD specialist, disability management specialist.
Special Fees: No special fees are charged for services to students with LD.
Applications and admissions: *Required:* high school transcript. Students may begin taking classes any term with special admission in fall quarter only. *Application deadline:* 11/30.
Special policies: The college has written policies regarding grade forgiveness; substitutions and waivers of admissions and graduation requirements.

PROGRAM AND SERVICE COMPONENTS

Special preparation or orientation: Optional orientation offered before registration and during summer prior to enrollment.
Diagnostic testing: Intelligence, reading, math, spelling, handwriting, spoken language, written language, perceptual skills, study skills, speech.
Academic advising: Provided by unit staff members, academic advisers. Most students with LD take 12 to 14 quarter units each term; 12 quarter units required to maintain full-time status; 6 quarter units required to be eligible for financial aid.
Counseling services: Individual counseling, career counseling, self-advocacy training.
Subject-area tutoring: Offered one-on-one and in small groups by peer tutors, graduate students. Available in most subjects.
Special courses: College survival skills, math, study skills. All offered for credit; none enter into overall grade point average.
Auxiliary aids: Taped textbooks, tape recorders, calculators, typewriters, word-processors with spell-check, personal computers, optical character readers, spell checkers.
Auxiliary services: Alternative test arrangements, notetakers, priority registration, advocacy, writing/computer skills assistance.
Campus support group: A special student organization is available to students with LD.

GENERAL COLLEGE INFORMATION

State-supported, comprehensive, coed. Part of California State University System. Awards bachelor's, master's degrees. Founded 1901. *Setting:* 6,000-acre small-town campus. *Endowment:* $2.7 million. *Research spending 1995–96:* $4.8 million. *Total enrollment:* 17,000. *Faculty:* 888 (611 full-time, 67% with terminal degrees, 277 part-time); student–undergrad faculty ratio is 19:1.
Enrollment Profile: 15,947 students from 50 states and territories, 44 other countries. 43% women, 57% men, 8% part-time, 96% state residents, 16% live on campus, 36% transferred in, 1% international, 13% 25 or older, 2% Native American, 14% Hispanic, 2% black, 13% Asian or Pacific Islander. *Retention:* 87% of 1995 full-time freshmen returned. *Graduation:* 4% graduate in 4 years, 30% in 5 years. *Areas of study chosen:* 24% engineering and applied sciences, 17% agriculture, 13% business management and administrative services, 7% architecture, 7% social sciences, 6% biological and life sciences, 3% computer and information sciences, 3% liberal arts/general studies, 3% psychology, 2% communications and journalism, 2% English language/literature/letters, 2% natural resource sciences, 1% fine arts, 1% mathematics, 1% philosophy, 1% physical sciences. *Most popular recent majors:* business administration/commerce/management, agricultural business, mechanical engineering.
First-Year Class: 2,827 total; 11,675 applied, 58% were accepted, 42% of whom enrolled. 40% from top 10% of their high school class, 68% from top quarter, 91% from top half.
Graduation Requirements: 186 units; 1 algebra course or completion of proficiency test; computer course; internship (some majors); senior project.
Computers on Campus: 1,600 computers available on campus for general student use. Computer purchase/lease plans available. A campus-wide network can be accessed from student residence rooms and from off-campus. Students can contact faculty members and/or advisers through e-mail. Computers for student use in computer center, computer labs, learning resource center, classrooms, library, student center, departmental labs provide access to the Internet/World Wide Web, on- and off-campus e-mail addresses. Staffed computer lab on campus (open 24 hours a day) provides training in use of computers, software. *Academic computing expenditure 1995–96:* $4.6 million.

EXPENSES AND FINANCIAL AID

Expenses for 1997–98: *Application fee:* $55. State resident tuition: $0 full-time. Nonresident tuition: $7544 full-time, $164 per unit part-time. Part-time mandatory fees: $526 per quarter. Full-time mandatory fees: $2244. College room and board: $5164.
Undergraduate Financial Aid: 58% of all full-time undergraduates enrolled in fall 1996 applied for aid; of these, 78% were judged to have need according to Federal Methodology, of whom 97% were aided. *Financial aid deadline (priority):* 3/2. *Financial aid forms:* FAFSA required; CSS Financial Aid PROFILE acceptable. State form required for some.
LD Services Contact: Ms. Ann Fryer, Learning Specialist, California Polytechnic State University, San Luis Obispo, San Luis Obispo, CA 93407, 805-756-1395. Fax: 805-756-5451.

CALIFORNIA STATE POLYTECHNIC UNIVERSITY, POMONA

Pomona, California

LEARNING DISABILITIES SERVICES INFORMATION

Disabled Student Services currently serves 1,400 undergraduates with LD. Services are also available to graduate students. Students diagnosed with ADD/ADHD are eligible for the same services available to students with LD.
Staff: 9 full-time, 2 part-time staff members, including director, associate director, coordinators. Services provided by diagnostic specialist.
Special Fees: No special fees are charged for services to students with LD.
Applications and admissions: *Required:* high school transcript, grade point average, courses completed, psychoeducational report completed within 3 years. Students may begin taking classes any term. *Application deadline:* continuous.

California State Polytechnic University, Pomona (continued)

PROGRAM AND SERVICE COMPONENTS

Special preparation or orientation: Required orientation held throughout the year.

Diagnostic testing: Intelligence, reading, math, spelling, spoken language, written language, perceptual skills.

Academic advising: Provided by academic advisers. Most students with LD take 12 units each term; 12 units required to maintain full-time status and be eligible for financial aid.

Subject-area tutoring: Offered one-on-one by peer tutors. Available in most subjects.

Auxiliary aids: Taped textbooks, calculators, word-processors with spell-check, optical character readers.

Auxiliary services: Alternative test arrangements, notetakers, priority registration, advocacy.

GENERAL COLLEGE INFORMATION

State-supported, comprehensive, coed. Part of California State University System. Awards bachelor's, master's degrees. Founded 1938. *Setting:* 1,400-acre urban campus with easy access to Los Angeles. *Endowment:* $2.7 million. *Research spending 1995–96:* $6.4 million. *Total enrollment:* 16,803. *Faculty:* 994 (627 full-time, 76% with terminal degrees, 367 part-time); student–undergrad faculty ratio is 19:1.

Enrollment Profile: 15,038 students from 32 states and territories, 62 other countries. 42% women, 58% men, 24% part-time, 90% state residents, 10% live on campus, 11% transferred in, 3% international, 24% 25 or older, 1% Native American, 21% Hispanic, 4% black, 29% Asian or Pacific Islander. *Retention:* 80% of 1995 full-time freshmen returned. *Graduation:* 7% graduate in 4 years, 26% in 5 years, 41% in 6 years. *Areas of study chosen:* 23% business management and administrative services, 22% engineering and applied sciences, 10% computer and information sciences, 7% biological and life sciences, 6% social sciences, 5% agriculture, 5% architecture, 5% interdisciplinary studies, 3% psychology, 2% communications and journalism, 2% education, 2% fine arts, 1% English language/literature/letters, 1% mathematics, 1% performing arts, 1% physical sciences, 1% vocational and home economics. *Most popular recent majors:* computer information systems, electronics engineering, marketing/retailing/merchandising.

First-Year Class: 1,922 total; 6,678 applied, 60% were accepted, 48% of whom enrolled. 3 National Merit Scholars.

Graduation Requirements: 186 units; 16 units of math/science including at least 1 lab science course; computer course for business, economics, engineering, some science, architecture majors; internship (some majors); senior project (some majors).

Computers on Campus: 1,858 computers available on campus for general student use. Computer purchase/lease plans available. A computer is recommended for all students. A campus-wide network can be accessed from student residence rooms and from off-campus. Students can contact faculty members and/or advisers through e-mail. Computers for student use in computer labs, learning resource center, library, student center, student rooms provide access to the Internet/World Wide Web, on- and off-campus e-mail addresses. Staffed computer lab on campus (open 24 hours a day) provides training in use of computers, software. *Academic computing expenditure 1995–96:* $3.3 million.

EXPENSES AND FINANCIAL AID

Expenses for 1997–98: State resident tuition: $0 full-time. Nonresident tuition: $7544 full-time, $164 per unit part-time. Part-time mandatory fees: $419 per quarter. Full-time mandatory fees: $1923. College room and board: $5300.

Undergraduate Financial Aid: Of all full-time undergraduates enrolled in fall 1996, 90% of those who applied for aid were judged to have need according to Federal Methodology, of whom 94% were aided. On average, 74% of need was met. *Financial aid deadline (priority):* 3/2. *Financial aid forms:* FAFSA required. State form required for some.

LD Services Contact: Mr. Fred D. Henderson Jr., Director, California State Polytechnic University, Pomona, 3801 West Temple Avenue, Pomona, CA 91768, 909-869-3333. Fax: 909-869-3271. Email: fdhenderson@csupomona.edu.

CALIFORNIA STATE UNIVERSITY, BAKERSFIELD

Bakersfield, California

LEARNING DISABILITIES SERVICES INFORMATION

Services for Students with Disabilities began offering services in 1989. Currently the program serves 200 undergraduates with LD. Services are also available to graduate students. Students diagnosed with ADD/ADHD are eligible for the same services available to students with LD.

Staff: 2 full-time, 2 part-time staff members, including director, coordinator, LD specialist. Services provided by tutors, counselors, diagnostic specialists.

Special Fees: No special fees are charged for services to students with LD.

Applications and admissions: *Required:* high school transcript, courses completed, untimed SAT I or ACT, college transcript. Students may begin taking classes any term. *Application deadline:* continuous.

Special policies: The college has written policies regarding grade forgiveness; substitutions and waivers of admissions requirements.

PROGRAM AND SERVICE COMPONENTS

Diagnostic testing: Intelligence, reading, math, spelling, written language, motor abilities, perceptual skills, personality.

Academic advising: Provided by unit staff members, academic advisers. Students with LD may take up to 19 quarter units each term; most take 12 to 15 quarter units; 12 quarter units required to maintain full-time status and be eligible for financial aid.

Counseling services: Individual counseling, career counseling, self-advocacy training, support group.

Basic skills remediation: Offered in small groups and in class-size groups by regular teachers. Available in reading, math, spelling, written language, learning strategies, time management.

Subject-area tutoring: Offered one-on-one and in small groups by peer tutors. Available in most subjects.

Special courses: College survival skills, word processing, career planning. All offered for credit; none enter into overall grade point average.

Auxiliary aids: Taped textbooks, tape recorders, calculators, word-processors with spell-check, optical character readers, adaptive software programs.

Auxiliary services: Alternative test arrangements, notetakers, priority registration, readers, self-advocacy assistance.

GENERAL COLLEGE INFORMATION

State-supported, comprehensive, coed. Part of California State University System. Awards bachelor's, master's degrees. Founded 1970. *Setting:* 575-acre urban campus. *Educational spending 1995–96:* $5200 per undergrad. *Total enrollment:* 5,435. *Faculty:* 315 (242 full-time, 73 part-time); student–undergrad faculty ratio is 19:1.

Enrollment Profile: 4,189 students from 16 states and territories, 48 other countries. 62% women, 38% men, 24% part-time, 97% state residents, 4% live on campus, 86% transferred in, 2% international, 37% 25 or older, 2% Native American, 29% Hispanic, 7% black, 8% Asian or Pacific Islander. *Areas of study chosen:* 16% business management and administrative services, 15% liberal arts/general studies, 9% health professions and related sciences, 7% psychology, 5% education, 4% biological and life sciences, 4% English language/literature/letters, 3% communications and journalism, 3% computer and information sciences, 3% social sciences, 2% mathematics, 1% fine arts, 1% foreign language and literature, 1% philosophy. *Most popular recent majors:* education, business administration/commerce/management.

First-Year Class: 432 total; 1,202 applied, 68% were accepted, 53% of whom enrolled.

Graduation Requirements: 186 quarter units; 5 quarter units of math; 10 quarter units of science; computer course for business administration, biology, chemistry, geology, math, health science, economics, medical technology, physics majors; senior project (some majors).

Computers on Campus: 600 computers available on campus for general student use. Computer purchase/lease plans available. A computer is recommended for all students. A campus-wide network can be accessed from student residence rooms and from off-campus. Students can contact faculty members and/or advisers through e-mail. Computers for student use in computer center, computer labs, learning resource center, classrooms, library, academic building provide access to the Internet/

World Wide Web, on- and off-campus e-mail addresses. Staffed computer lab on campus provides training in use of computers, software. *Academic computing expenditure 1995–96:* $2 million.

EXPENSES AND FINANCIAL AID

Expenses for 1997–98: *Application fee:* $55. State resident tuition: $0 full-time. Nonresident tuition: $7544 full-time, $164 per unit part-time. Part-time mandatory fees: $433 per quarter. Full-time mandatory fees: $1965. College room and board: $4185.
Undergraduate Financial Aid: Of all full-time undergraduates enrolled in fall 1996, 91% of those who applied for aid were judged to have need according to Federal Methodology, of whom 94% were aided. On average, 76% of need was met. *Financial aid deadline (priority):* 3/2. *Financial aid forms:* FAFSA required.
LD Services Contact: Jan Freshwater, Learning Disabilities Specialist, California State University, Bakersfield, 9001 Stockdale Highway, Bakersfield, CA 93311-1099, 805-664-3360. Fax: 805-664-2171. Email: jfreshwater@csubak.edu.

CALIFORNIA STATE UNIVERSITY, CHICO

Chico, California

LEARNING DISABILITIES SERVICES INFORMATION

Disabled Student Services began offering services in 1979. Currently the program serves 350 undergraduates with LD. Services are also available to graduate students. Students diagnosed with ADD/ADHD are eligible for the same services available to students with LD.
Staff: 5 full-time, 1 part-time staff members, including director. Services provided by counselor, LD specialists, support specialists.
Special Fees: No special fees are charged for services to students with LD.
Applications and admissions: *Required:* high school transcript, grade point average, courses completed, untimed SAT I, letters of recommendation, psychoeducational report, petition letter; *recommended:* extended time SAT I or ACT. Students may begin taking classes any term. *Application deadline:* continuous.
Special policies: The college has written policies regarding grade forgiveness; substitutions and waivers of admissions, graduation, and degree requirements.

PROGRAM AND SERVICE COMPONENTS

Special preparation or orientation: Optional orientation offered before classes begin.
Diagnostic testing: Intelligence, reading, math, spelling, spoken language, written language, motor abilities, perceptual skills, study skills, psychoneurology, learning strategies.
Academic advising: Provided by unit staff members, academic advisers. Students with LD may take up to 17 units each term; most take 12 to 15 units; 12 units required to maintain full-time status; source of aid determines number of units required to be eligible for financial aid.
Counseling services: Individual counseling, small-group counseling, career counseling, support group.
Subject-area tutoring: Offered one-on-one and in small groups by peer tutors. Available in some subjects.
Auxiliary aids: Taped textbooks, tape recorders, calculators, word-processors with spell-check, personal computers, optical character readers.
Auxiliary services: Alternative test arrangements, notetakers, priority registration, advocacy, readers, computer lab.
Campus support group: A special student organization is available to students with LD.

GENERAL COLLEGE INFORMATION

State-supported, comprehensive, coed. Part of California State University System. Awards bachelor's, master's degrees. Founded 1887. *Setting:* 119-acre small-town campus. *Endowment:* $9.7 million. *Research spending 1995–96:* $2.8 million. *Educational spending 1995–96:* $4938 per undergrad. *Total enrollment:* 13,919. *Faculty:* 816 (589 full-time, 70% with terminal degrees, 227 part-time); student–undergrad faculty ratio is 19:1.
Enrollment Profile: 12,298 students from 30 states and territories, 50 other countries. 51% women, 49% men, 11% part-time, 98% state residents, 12% live on campus, 14% transferred in, 27% 25 or older, 2% Native American, 10% Hispanic, 3% black, 5% Asian or Pacific Islander. *Retention:* 77% of 1995 full-time freshmen returned. *Graduation:* 12% graduate in 4 years, 40% in 5 years, 49% in 6 years. *Areas of study chosen:* 15% social sciences, 14% business management and administrative services, 12% liberal arts/general studies, 10% interdisciplinary studies, 7% communications and journalism, 7% engineering and applied sciences, 6% education, 5% psychology, 4% English language/literature/letters, 4% fine arts, 4% health professions and related sciences, 3% agriculture, 3% biological and life sciences, 3% computer and information sciences, 1% foreign language and literature, 1% mathematics, 1% physical sciences, 1% vocational and home economics. *Most popular recent majors:* business administration/commerce/management, liberal arts/general studies, psychology.
First-Year Class: 1,561 total; 5,343 applied, 83% were accepted, 35% of whom enrolled.
Graduation Requirements: 124 units; 3 units of math; 6 units of science; computer course for business, industrial technology, communication studies, physical science, civil engineering, mechanical engineering, electrical/electronic engineering, social science, sociology majors; internship (some majors); senior project for honors program students and some majors.
Computers on Campus: 660 computers available on campus for general student use. A campus-wide network can be accessed from student residence rooms and from off-campus. Students can contact faculty members and/or advisers through e-mail. Computers for student use in computer center, computer labs, library, student center, dorms, interdepartmental student workstations provide access to the Internet/World Wide Web, on- and off-campus e-mail addresses. Staffed computer lab on campus provides training in use of computers, software. *Academic computing expenditure 1995–96:* $3.9 million.

EXPENSES AND FINANCIAL AID

Expenses for 1997–98: *Application fee:* $55. State resident tuition: $0 full-time. Nonresident tuition: $7626 full-time, $246 per unit part-time. Part-time mandatory fees: $702.50 per semester. Full-time mandatory fees: $2075. College room and board: $5179.
Undergraduate Financial Aid: *Financial aid deadline (priority):* 3/1. *Financial aid forms:* FAFSA required.
LD Services Contact: Mr. Ed Daniels, Associate Director, Retention Services, California State University, Chico, 400 West First Street, Chico, CA 95929-0726, 916-898-5959. Fax: 916-898-4411.

CALIFORNIA STATE UNIVERSITY, FRESNO

Fresno, California

LEARNING DISABILITIES SERVICES INFORMATION

Disabled Student Services began offering services in 1980. Currently the program serves 180 undergraduates with LD. Services are also available to graduate students. Students diagnosed with ADD/ADHD are eligible for the same services available to students with LD.
Staff: 3 full-time staff members, including coordinator. Services provided by counselor.
Special Fees: No special fees are charged for services to students with LD.
Applications and admissions: *Required:* verification of disability. Students may begin taking classes any term.
Special policies: The college has written policies regarding grade forgiveness.

PROGRAM AND SERVICE COMPONENTS

Academic advising: Provided by unit staff members. Most students with LD take 12 units each term; 12 units required to maintain full-time status and be eligible for financial aid.
Counseling services: Individual counseling, small-group counseling, career counseling.
Auxiliary aids: Taped textbooks, tape recorders, calculators, typewriters, word-processors with spell-check, talking computers, optical character readers.
Auxiliary services: Alternative test arrangements, notetakers, priority registration, advocacy.
Campus support group: A special student organization is available to students with LD.

GENERAL COLLEGE INFORMATION

State-supported, comprehensive, coed. Part of California State University System. Awards bachelor's, master's, doctoral degrees. Founded 1911. *Setting:* 1,410-acre urban campus. *Endowment:* $31.1 million.

California State University, Fresno (continued)

Research spending 1995–96: $296,528. *Educational spending 1995–96:* $8132 per undergrad. *Total enrollment:* 17,213. *Faculty:* 950 (654 full-time, 296 part-time); student–undergrad faculty ratio is 18:1.
Enrollment Profile: 14,100 students from 40 states and territories, 78 other countries. 54% women, 46% men, 8% part-time, 91% state residents, 7% live on campus, 14% transferred in, 3% international, 29% 25 or older, 1% Native American, 28% Hispanic, 6% black, 11% Asian or Pacific Islander. *Retention:* 81% of 1995 full-time freshmen returned. *Areas of study chosen:* 17% business management and administrative services, 14% health professions and related sciences, 12% education, 10% social sciences, 7% engineering and applied sciences, 5% agriculture, 5% biological and life sciences, 5% psychology, 3% communications and journalism, 2% computer and information sciences, 2% English language/literature/letters, 2% fine arts, 1% foreign language and literature, 1% mathematics, 1% performing arts, 1% vocational and home economics. *Most popular recent majors:* business administration/commerce/management, early childhood education, criminology.
First-Year Class: 1,546 total; 4,758 applied, 71% were accepted, 46% of whom enrolled.
Graduation Requirements: 124 units; computer course for business, engineering majors.
Computers on Campus: 605 computers available on campus for general student use. Computer purchase/lease plans available. A computer is recommended for all students. A campus-wide network can be accessed from off-campus. Students can contact faculty members and/or advisers through e-mail. Computers for student use in computer center, computer labs, learning resource center, library, dorms, academic buildings provide access to the Internet/World Wide Web, on- and off-campus e-mail addresses. Staffed computer lab on campus. *Academic computing expenditure 1995–96:* $3.8 million.

EXPENSES AND FINANCIAL AID

Expenses for 1997–98: State resident tuition: $0 full-time. Nonresident tuition: $7626 full-time, $246 per unit part-time. Part-time mandatory fees: $570 per semester. Full-time mandatory fees: $1806. College room and board: $4709.
Undergraduate Financial Aid: 80% of all full-time undergraduates enrolled in fall 1996 applied for aid; of these, 89% were judged to have need according to Federal Methodology, of whom 96% were aided. On average, 88% of need was met. *Financial aid deadline (priority):* 3/1. *Financial aid forms:* financial aid transcript (for transfers) required. FAFSA, CSS Financial Aid PROFILE, state form, institutional form required for some.
LD Services Contact: Mr. Robert Lundal, Coordinator, Disabled Student Services, California State University, Fresno, 5200 North Barton, MS #125, Fresno, CA 93740, 209-278-2811. Fax: 209-278-4214.

CALIFORNIA STATE UNIVERSITY, FULLERTON

Fullerton, California

LEARNING DISABILITIES SERVICES INFORMATION

Disability Resource Services began offering services in 1985. Currently the program serves 225 undergraduates with LD. Services are also available to graduate students. Students diagnosed with ADD/ADHD are eligible for the same services available to students with LD.
Staff: 2 full-time staff members, including coordinator. Services provided by counselors, diagnostic specialists.
Special Fees: No special fees are charged for services to students with LD.
Applications and admissions: *Required:* high school transcript, grade point average, courses completed, extended time SAT I or ACT, autobiographical statement, letters of recommendation, psychoeducational report completed within 3 years, documentation of disability. Students may begin taking classes in fall, spring, or summer. *Application deadline:* continuous.
Special policies: The college has written policies regarding grade forgiveness.

PROGRAM AND SERVICE COMPONENTS

Special preparation or orientation: Optional orientation offered after classes begin.
Diagnostic testing: Intelligence, reading, math, spelling, handwriting, written language, perceptual skills, study skills, personality, psychoneurology, learning strategies.
Academic advising: Provided by unit staff members, academic advisers. Most students with LD take 6 to 12 semester units each term; 12 semester units required to maintain full-time status and be eligible for financial aid.
Counseling services: Individual counseling, small-group counseling, self-advocacy training.
Auxiliary aids: Taped textbooks, tape recorders, calculators, typewriters, word-processors with spell-check, personal computers, optical character readers, electronic dictionary/thesaurus.
Auxiliary services: Alternative test arrangements, notetakers, priority registration, advocacy, readers, scribes.

GENERAL COLLEGE INFORMATION

State-supported, comprehensive, coed. Part of California State University System. Awards bachelor's, master's degrees. Founded 1957. *Setting:* 225-acre suburban campus with easy access to Los Angeles. *Research spending 1995–96:* $8.2 million. *Educational spending 1995–96:* $3093 per undergrad. *Total enrollment:* 24,040. *Faculty:* 1,228 (540 full-time, 88% with terminal degrees, 688 part-time); student–undergrad faculty ratio is 22:1.
Enrollment Profile: 20,090 students from 38 states and territories, 78 other countries. 56% women, 44% men, 33% part-time, 80% state residents, 2% live on campus, 12% transferred in, 4% international, 30% 25 or older, 1% Native American, 18% Hispanic, 3% black, 18% Asian or Pacific Islander. *Areas of study chosen:* 30% business management and administrative services, 9% communications and journalism, 9% social sciences, 6% psychology, 5% biological and life sciences, 5% vocational and home economics, 4% engineering and applied sciences, 4% fine arts, 4% health professions and related sciences, 4% liberal arts/general studies, 3% computer and information sciences, 3% English language/literature/letters, 2% performing arts, 2% physical sciences, 1% area and ethnic studies, 1% foreign language and literature, 1% mathematics. *Most popular recent majors:* communication, finance/banking, child psychology/child development.
First-Year Class: 2,205 total; 8,453 applied, 84% were accepted, 31% of whom enrolled.
Graduation Requirements: 124 semester units; 12 semester units of math/science including at least 3 semester units each of math, biology, and physical science; computer course for business administration, engineering majors; internship (some majors); senior project (some majors).
Computers on Campus: 1,000 computers available on campus for general student use. A campus-wide network can be accessed from student residence rooms and from off-campus. Students can contact faculty members and/or advisers through e-mail. Computers for student use in computer center, computer labs, learning resource center provide access to the Internet/World Wide Web, on- and off-campus e-mail addresses. Staffed computer lab on campus provides training in use of computers, software. *Academic computing expenditure 1995–96:* $2.6 million.

EXPENSES AND FINANCIAL AID

Expenses for 1997–98: *Application fee:* $55. State resident tuition: $0 full-time. Nonresident tuition: $7626 full-time, $246 per unit part-time. Part-time mandatory fees: $640.50 per semester. Full-time mandatory fees: $1947. College room only: $3662.
Undergraduate Financial Aid: 53% of all full-time undergraduates enrolled in fall 1996 applied for aid; of these, 83% were judged to have need according to Federal Methodology, of whom 91% were aided. On average, 64% of need was met. *Financial aid deadline (priority):* 3/1. *Financial aid forms:* FAFSA, state form required.
LD Services Contact: Ms. Debra J. Fletcher, Learning Disabilities Specialist, California State University, Fullerton, Box 34080, Fullerton, CA 92834-9480, 714-278-3117. Fax: 714-278-2408. Email: dfletcher@fullerton.edu.

CALIFORNIA STATE UNIVERSITY, SACRAMENTO

Sacramento, California

LEARNING DISABILITIES SERVICES INFORMATION

Learning Disabilities Program began offering services in 1980. Currently the program serves 450 undergraduates with LD. Services are also

available to graduate students. Students diagnosed with ADD/ADHD are eligible for the same services available to students with LD.

Staff: Includes director, associate director, coordinator/LD specialist. Services provided by tutors, counselors, diagnostic specialist, computer skills instructor/lab supervisor.

Special Fees: No special fees are charged for services to students with LD.

Applications and admissions: *Required:* high school transcript, grade point average, untimed SAT I or ACT, personal interview, letters of recommendation, psychoeducational report completed within 3 years; *recommended:* extended time SAT I or ACT. Students may begin taking classes any term. *Application deadline:* continuous.

Special policies: The college has written policies regarding grade forgiveness.

PROGRAM AND SERVICE COMPONENTS

Special preparation or orientation: Required orientation held after classes begin.

Diagnostic testing: Intelligence, reading, math, spelling, handwriting, written language, perceptual skills, speech, hearing.

Academic advising: Provided by unit staff members, academic advisers. Students with LD may take up to 21 units each term; most take 15 units; 12 units required to maintain full-time status and be eligible for financial aid.

Counseling services: Individual counseling, small-group counseling, career counseling, self-advocacy training.

Basic skills remediation: Offered one-on-one and in small groups by LD teachers, teacher trainees, peer teachers. Available in reading, math, spelling, handwriting, spoken language, written language, learning strategies, perceptual skills, study skills.

Subject-area tutoring: Offered one-on-one by professional teachers, peer tutors. Available in all subjects.

Special courses: Learning strategies, word processing, math, study skills. Most offered for credit.

Auxiliary aids: Taped textbooks, tape recorders, calculators, word-processors with spell-check, personal computers, optical character readers.

Auxiliary services: Alternative test arrangements, notetakers, priority registration, advocacy, readers.

Campus support group: A special student organization is available to students with LD.

GENERAL COLLEGE INFORMATION

State-supported, comprehensive, coed. Part of California State University System. Awards bachelor's, master's degrees. Founded 1947. *Setting:* 288-acre urban campus. *Research spending 1995–96:* $9.9 million. *Educational spending 1995–96:* $4161 per undergrad. *Total enrollment:* 23,420. *Faculty:* 1,214 (640 full-time, 78% with terminal degrees, 574 part-time).

Enrollment Profile: 18,713 students from 40 states and territories, 101 other countries. 54% women, 46% men, 27% part-time, 97% state residents, 5% live on campus, 71% transferred in, 2% international, 35% 25 or older, 1% Native American, 12% Hispanic, 6% black, 15% Asian or Pacific Islander. *Retention:* 75% of 1995 full-time freshmen returned. *Areas of study chosen:* 17% business management and administrative services, 9% engineering and applied sciences, 7% social sciences, 6% education, 6% liberal arts/general studies, 6% psychology, 5% biological and life sciences, 5% communications and journalism, 5% health professions and related sciences, 3% English language/literature/letters, 2% computer and information sciences, 2% fine arts, 2% vocational and home economics, 1% foreign language and literature, 1% interdisciplinary studies, 1% mathematics, 1% natural resource sciences, 1% performing arts, 1% physical sciences. *Most popular recent majors:* business administration/commerce/management, liberal arts/general studies, engineering (general).

First-Year Class: 1,523 total; 5,182 applied, 53% were accepted, 55% of whom enrolled.

Graduation Requirements: 124 units; 3 units of math; 6 units of science; intermediate level competence in a foreign language; computer course for business administration, engineering majors; internship (some majors); senior project (some majors).

Computers on Campus: 700 computers available on campus for general student use. A campus-wide network can be accessed from student residence rooms. Students can contact faculty members and/or advisers through e-mail. Computers for student use in computer center, computer labs, learning resource center, classrooms, library, student center, dorms, student labs provide access to the Internet/World Wide Web, on-campus e-mail addresses. Staffed computer lab on campus provides training in use of computers, software. *Academic computing expenditure 1995–96:* $3.8 million.

EXPENSES AND FINANCIAL AID

Expenses for 1997–98: *Application fee:* $55. State resident tuition: $0 full-time. Nonresident tuition: $7626 full-time, $246 per unit part-time. Part-time mandatory fees: $658 per semester. Full-time mandatory fees: $1982. College room and board: $4962 (minimum).

Undergraduate Financial Aid: 62% of all full-time undergraduates enrolled in fall 1996 applied for aid; of these, 90% were judged to have need according to Federal Methodology, of whom 95% were aided. *Financial aid deadline (priority):* 3/2. *Financial aid forms:* FAFSA, state form, institutional form required.

Financial aid specifically for students with LD: Scholarship: CAPED Scholarship; work-study.

LD Services Contact: Ms. Kathleen A. Cronin, Learning Disability Specialist, California State University, Sacramento, 6000 J Street, Sacramento, CA 95819-6048, 916-278-6955. Email: cronink@csus.edu.

CALIFORNIA STATE UNIVERSITY, SAN MARCOS

San Marcos, California

LEARNING DISABILITIES SERVICES INFORMATION

Disabled Student Services began offering services in 1990. Currently the program serves 40 undergraduates with LD. Services are also available to graduate students. Students diagnosed with ADD/ADHD are eligible for the same services available to students with LD.

Staff: 1 full-time staff member (coordinator). Services provided by tutors, counselors, diagnostic specialists.

Special Fees: No special fees are charged for services to students with LD.

Applications and admissions: *Required:* psychoeducational report completed within 3 years. Students may begin taking classes in fall, spring, or summer. *Application deadline:* continuous.

Special policies: The college has written policies regarding grade forgiveness; substitutions and waivers of graduation and degree requirements.

PROGRAM AND SERVICE COMPONENTS

Special preparation or orientation: Optional orientation offered during registration.

Diagnostic testing: Cognition, academic skills (Woodcock-Johnson-Revised), intellectual functioning (WAIS-R).

Academic advising: Provided by unit staff members, academic advisers. Students with LD may take up to 19 units each term; most take 9 to 12 units; 12 units required to maintain full-time status.

Counseling services: Individual counseling, small-group counseling, self-advocacy training.

Subject-area tutoring: Offered one-on-one and in small groups by peer tutors. Available in most subjects.

Auxiliary aids: Taped textbooks, tape recorders, calculators, word-processors with spell-check, personal computers, talking computers, optical character readers, spell checkers.

Auxiliary services: Alternative test arrangements, notetakers, priority registration, advocacy.

GENERAL COLLEGE INFORMATION

State-supported, comprehensive, coed. Part of California State University System. Awards bachelor's, master's degrees. Founded 1990. *Setting:* 302-acre suburban campus with easy access to San Diego. *Endowment:* $679,012. *Research spending 1995–96:* $870,705. *Total enrollment:* 3,841. *Undergraduate faculty:* 264 (122 full-time, 95% with terminal degrees, 142 part-time).

Enrollment Profile: 3,511 students: 63% women, 37% men, 51% part-time, 99% state residents, 89% transferred in, 52% 25 or older, 2% Native American, 16% Hispanic, 4% black, 8% Asian or Pacific Islander. *Areas of study chosen:* 26% business management and administrative services, 22% liberal arts/general studies, 14% psychology, 14% social sciences, 7% English language/literature/letters, 6% biological and life sciences, 2% foreign language and literature, 2% mathematics, 1% computer and information sciences, 1% performing arts, 1% physical sciences.

First-Year Class: 339 total; 1,130 applied, 79% were accepted, 38% of whom enrolled.

California State University, San Marcos (continued)

Graduation Requirements: 124 units; 12 units of math/natural science; 3 semesters of a foreign language; computer course; internship (some majors); senior project for honors program students and some majors.

Computers on Campus: 220 computers available on campus for general student use. Computer purchase/lease plans available. A campus-wide network can be accessed from student residence rooms and from off-campus. Students can contact faculty members and/or advisers through e-mail. Computers for student use in computer center, computer labs, library provide access to the Internet/World Wide Web, on- and off-campus e-mail addresses. Staffed computer lab on campus provides training in use of computers, software. *Academic computing expenditure 1995–96:* $986,869.

EXPENSES AND FINANCIAL AID

Expenses for 1997–98: *Application fee:* $55. State resident tuition: $0 full-time. Nonresident tuition: $7626 full-time, $246 per unit part-time. Part-time mandatory fees: $517 per semester. Full-time mandatory fees: $1720. College room only: $3114.

Undergraduate Financial Aid: On average, 36% of need was met. *Financial aid deadline (priority):* 3/2. *Financial aid forms:* FAFSA required. State form required for some.

LD Services Contact: Mr. John Segoria, Coordinator of Student Support Services, California State University, San Marcos, San Marcos, CA 92096-0001, 760-750-4905. Fax: 760-750-4030.

CALIFORNIA STATE UNIVERSITY, STANISLAUS

Turlock, California

LEARNING DISABILITIES SERVICES INFORMATION

Disabled Student Services began offering services in 1979. Currently the program serves 130 undergraduates with LD. Services are also available to graduate students. Students diagnosed with ADD/ADHD are eligible for the same services available to students with LD.

Staff: 3 full-time, 5 part-time staff members, including director, coordinator. Services provided by remediation specialists, counselors, diagnostic specialists, student assistants.

Special Fees: No special fees are charged for services to students with LD.

Applications and admissions: *Required:* high school transcript; *recommended:* untimed or extended time SAT I or ACT. Students may begin taking classes any term. *Application deadline:* continuous.

Special policies: The college has written policies regarding grade forgiveness; substitutions and waivers of admissions, graduation, and degree requirements.

PROGRAM AND SERVICE COMPONENTS

Diagnostic testing: Intelligence, reading, math, spelling, handwriting, spoken language, written language, perceptual skills, study skills, learning strategies.

Academic advising: Provided by academic advisers. Most students with LD take 10 to 14 units each term; 10 units (2 during winter term) required to maintain full-time status and be eligible for financial aid.

Counseling services: Individual counseling, career counseling, self-advocacy training.

Basic skills remediation: Offered one-on-one and in small groups by LD specialist, disabled student services coordinator, counselors. Available in reading, math, spelling, handwriting, written language, learning strategies, study skills, time management, social skills.

Special courses: Communication skills, time management, personal psychology, study skills, career planning, stress management, social relationships. None offered for credit; none enter into overall grade point average.

Auxiliary aids: Taped textbooks, tape recorders, calculators, word-processors with spell-check, personal computers, optical character readers.

Auxiliary services: Alternative test arrangements, notetakers, priority registration, advocacy, readers.

Campus support group: A special student organization is available to students with LD.

GENERAL COLLEGE INFORMATION

State-supported, comprehensive, coed. Part of California State University System. Awards bachelor's, master's degrees. Founded 1957. *Setting:* 220-acre small-town campus. *Research spending 1995–96:* $825,558. *Total enrollment:* 6,100. *Faculty:* 345 (249 full-time, 90% with terminal degrees, 96 part-time); student–undergrad faculty ratio is 18:1.

Enrollment Profile: 4,817 students from 31 states and territories, 59 other countries. 79% women, 21% men, 24% part-time, 99% state residents, 20% transferred in, 39% 25 or older, 2% Native American, 22% Hispanic, 4% black, 10% Asian or Pacific Islander. *Retention:* 79% of 1995 full-time freshmen returned. *Graduation:* 16% graduate in 4 years, 33% in 5 years, 40% in 6 years. *Areas of study chosen:* 19% liberal arts/general studies, 17% business management and administrative services, 7% psychology, 6% biological and life sciences, 5% interdisciplinary studies, 4% computer and information sciences, 4% English language/literature/letters, 3% communications and journalism, 3% education, 2% health professions and related sciences, 2% mathematics, 2% physical sciences, 1% area and ethnic studies, 1% foreign language and literature, 1% philosophy. *Most popular recent majors:* liberal arts/general studies, business administration/commerce/management, psychology.

First-Year Class: 433 total; 887 applied, 95% were accepted, 51% of whom enrolled.

Graduation Requirements: 124 units; 3 units of math; 6 units of science; computer course for business, math, science majors.

Computers on Campus: 150 computers available on campus for general student use. Computer purchase/lease plans available. A computer is required for some students. A campus-wide network can be accessed from student residence rooms and from off-campus. Students can contact faculty members and/or advisers through e-mail. Computers for student use in computer center, computer labs, research center, learning resource center, library, student center, dorms provide access to the Internet/World Wide Web, on-campus e-mail addresses. Staffed computer lab on campus provides training in use of computers, software.

EXPENSES AND FINANCIAL AID

Expenses for 1997–98: *Application fee:* $55. State resident tuition: $0 full-time. Nonresident tuition: $7626 full-time, $246 per unit part-time. Part-time mandatory fees: $536.50 per term. Full-time mandatory fees: $1915. College room and board: $5461.

Undergraduate Financial Aid: 86% of all full-time undergraduates enrolled in fall 1996 applied for aid; of these, 76% were judged to have need according to Federal Methodology, of whom 77% were aided. On average, 72% of need was met. *Financial aid deadline (priority):* 3/1. *Financial aid forms:* FAFSA, state form required; CSS Financial Aid PROFILE acceptable.

LD Services Contact: Dr. Anne Reith, Learning Disabilities Specialist, California State University, Stanislaus, 801 West Monte Vista Avenue, Turlock, CA 95382, 209-667-3159. Fax: 209-667-3585. Email: reith_anne@macmail.csustan.edu.

CALVIN COLLEGE

Grand Rapids, Michigan

LEARNING DISABILITIES SERVICES INFORMATION

Services to Students with Disabilities/Office of Student Academic Services currently serves 41 undergraduates with LD. Services are also available to graduate students. Students diagnosed with ADD/ADHD are eligible for the same services available to students with LD.

Staff: 2 full-time staff members, including director, coordinator. Services provided by diagnostic specialists.

Special Fees: No special fees are charged for services to students with LD.

Applications and admissions: *Required:* high school transcript, grade point average, courses completed, untimed SAT I or ACT, letters of recommendation, psychoeducational report completed within 3 years; *recommended:* high school class rank, extracurricular activities, extended time SAT I or ACT, personal interview, autobiographical statement. Students may begin taking classes in fall only. *Application deadline:* continuous.

Special policies: The college has written policies regarding substitutions and waivers of admissions and graduation requirements.

PROGRAM AND SERVICE COMPONENTS

Diagnostic testing: Intelligence, reading, math, spelling, written language, perceptual skills, study skills, learning strategies.

Academic advising: Provided by unit staff members, academic advisers. Students with LD may take up to 17 semester hours each term; most take 14 to 15 semester hours; 12 semester hours required to maintain full-time status and be eligible for financial aid.

Counseling services: Individual counseling, small-group counseling, career counseling.

Subject-area tutoring: Offered one-on-one and in small groups by peer tutors. Available in most subjects.

Special courses: Composition, math, study skills. None offered for credit; none enter into overall grade point average.

Auxiliary aids: Taped textbooks, tape recorders, word-processors with spell-check, personal computers.

Auxiliary services: Alternative test arrangements, notetakers, priority registration.

GENERAL COLLEGE INFORMATION

Independent, comprehensive, coed, affiliated with Christian Reformed Church. Awards bachelor's, master's degrees. Founded 1876. *Setting:* 370-acre suburban campus. *Endowment:* $34.4 million. *Research spending 1995–96:* $943,630. *Educational spending 1995–96:* $5215 per undergrad. *Total enrollment:* 4,051. *Faculty:* 324 (263 full-time, 81% with terminal degrees, 61 part-time); student–undergrad faculty ratio is 16:1.

Enrollment Profile: 3,993 students from 49 states and territories, 26 other countries. 56% women, 44% men, 8% part-time, 55% state residents, 57% live on campus, 10% transferred in, 8% international, 6% 25 or older, 0% Native American, 1% Hispanic, 1% black, 2% Asian or Pacific Islander. *Retention:* 83% of 1995 full-time freshmen returned. *Graduation:* 43% graduate in 4 years, 61% in 5 years, 64% in 6 years. *Areas of study chosen:* 14% business management and administrative services, 14% social sciences, 11% health professions and related sciences, 10% education, 8% biological and life sciences, 8% English language/literature/letters, 6% fine arts, 6% psychology, 5% engineering and applied sciences, 4% communications and journalism, 3% foreign language and literature, 3% physical sciences, 2% computer and information sciences, 2% interdisciplinary studies, 2% mathematics, 1% philosophy, 1% theology/religion. *Most popular recent majors:* education, business administration/commerce/management, engineering (general).

First-Year Class: 962 total; 1,852 applied, 97% were accepted, 54% of whom enrolled. 30% from top 10% of their high school class, 56% from top quarter, 85% from top half. 20 National Merit Scholars, 38 valedictorians.

Graduation Requirements: 124 semester hours; 1 math course; 2 science courses; 2 years of a foreign language or proven competence; computer course for business, math, sociology, psychology, engineering majors; internship (some majors); senior project (some majors).

Computers on Campus: 500 computers available on campus for general student use. Computer purchase/lease plans available. A computer is recommended for all students. A campus-wide network can be accessed from off-campus. Students can contact faculty members and/or advisers through e-mail. Computers for student use in computer center, computer labs, research center, classrooms, library, student center, dorms provide access to the Internet/World Wide Web, on- and off-campus e-mail addresses. Staffed computer lab on campus (open 24 hours a day) provides training in use of computers, software. *Academic computing expenditure 1995–96:* $2.4 million.

EXPENSES AND FINANCIAL AID

Expenses for 1996–97: *Application fee:* $35. Comprehensive fee of $15,840 includes full-time tuition ($11,655), mandatory fees ($25), and college room and board ($4160). Part-time tuition: $440 per semester hour.

Undergraduate Financial Aid: Of all full-time undergraduates enrolled in fall 1996, 98% of those who applied for aid were judged to have need according to Federal Methodology, of whom 100% were aided. On average, 77% of need was met. *Financial aid deadline (priority):* 2/15. *Financial aid forms:* FAFSA, institutional form required; CSS Financial Aid PROFILE acceptable.

Financial aid specifically for students with LD: Scholarship: Berkowitz Scholarship.

LD Services Contact: Ms. Margaret Vriend, Coordinator of Services to Students with Disabilities, Calvin College, 3201 Burton Street, SE, Grand Rapids, MI 49546, 616-957-6077. Fax: 616-957-8551. Email: vriend@calvin.edu.

CANISIUS COLLEGE

Buffalo, New York

LEARNING DISABILITIES SERVICES INFORMATION

Disability Support Services (DSS) began offering services in 1976. Currently the program serves 25 undergraduates with LD. Services are also available to graduate students. Students diagnosed with ADD/ADHD are eligible for the same services available to students with LD.

Staff: 2 full-time, 6 part-time staff members, including director, coordinator, basic skills instructors. Services provided by counselors, peer tutors, interpreters.

Special Fees: No special fees are charged for services to students with LD.

Applications and admissions: *Required:* high school transcript, grade point average, courses completed, untimed SAT I or ACT; *recommended:* high school class rank, extracurricular activities, extended time SAT I or ACT, personal interview, autobiographical statement, letters of recommendation. Students may begin taking classes in fall only. *Application deadline:* continuous.

PROGRAM AND SERVICE COMPONENTS

Diagnostic testing: Reading, math.

Academic advising: Provided by academic advisers. Students with LD may take up to 18 credit hours each term; most take 14 credit hours; 12 credit hours required to maintain full-time status; 12 credit hours (for New York State aid) required to be eligible for financial aid.

Counseling services: Individual counseling, career counseling.

Basic skills remediation: Offered in class-size groups by regular teachers. Available in reading, math, written language.

Subject-area tutoring: Offered one-on-one by peer tutors. Available in most subjects.

Special courses: College survival skills, reading, composition, math, study skills. Some offered for credit.

Auxiliary aids: Taped textbooks, Arkenstone Reader.

Auxiliary services: Alternative test arrangements, notetakers, advocacy.

Campus support group: A special student organization is available to students with LD.

GENERAL COLLEGE INFORMATION

Independent Roman Catholic (Jesuit), comprehensive, coed. Awards associate, bachelor's, master's degrees. Founded 1870. *Setting:* 26-acre urban campus. *Endowment:* $41.4 million. *Educational spending 1995–96:* $4410 per undergrad. *Total enrollment:* 4,746. *Faculty:* 383 (195 full-time, 88% with terminal degrees, 188 part-time); student–undergrad faculty ratio is 18:1.

Enrollment Profile: 3,275 students from 27 states and territories, 26 other countries. 47% women, 53% men, 13% part-time, 94% state residents, 30% live on campus, 18% transferred in, 2% international, 11% 25 or older, 1% Native American, 3% Hispanic, 6% black, 2% Asian or Pacific Islander. *Retention:* 80% of 1995 full-time freshmen returned. *Graduation:* 37% graduate in 4 years, 54% in 5 years, 57% in 6 years. *Areas of study chosen:* 22% business management and administrative services, 20% social sciences, 17% education, 10% English language/literature/letters, 9% biological and life sciences, 5% communications and journalism, 4% computer and information sciences, 4% premed, 2% physical sciences, 1% engineering and applied sciences, 1% foreign language and literature, 1% health professions and related sciences, 1% mathematics, 1% philosophy. *Most popular recent majors:* psychology, business administration/commerce/management, physical education.

First-Year Class: 692 total; 2,424 applied, 84% were accepted, 34% of whom enrolled. 19% from top 10% of their high school class, 38% from top quarter, 63% from top half. 2 National Merit Scholars, 8 valedictorians.

Graduation Requirements: 60 credit hours for associate, 120 credit hours for bachelor's; 6 credit hours of science; 6 credit hours of a foreign language; computer course for business, biology, secondary education, medical technology, physics majors; senior project for honors program students.

Computers on Campus: 140 computers available on campus for general student use. Computer purchase/lease plans available. A computer is recommended for all students. A campus-wide network can be accessed from student residence rooms and from off-campus. Students can contact faculty members and/or advisers through e-mail. Computers for student use in computer center, computer labs, classrooms, library, dorms provide access to the Internet/World Wide Web, on- and off-

Canisius College (continued)

campus e-mail addresses. Staffed computer lab on campus provides training in use of computers, software. *Academic computing expenditure 1995–96:* $531,222.

EXPENSES AND FINANCIAL AID

Expenses for 1996–97: *Application fee:* $25. Comprehensive fee of $18,751 includes full-time tuition ($12,600), mandatory fees ($326), and college room and board ($5825). Part-time tuition: $355 per credit hour. Part-time mandatory fees: $9 per credit hour.
Undergraduate Financial Aid: Of all full-time undergraduates enrolled in fall 1996, 94% of those who applied for aid were judged to have need according to Federal Methodology, of whom 100% were aided. *Financial aid deadline (priority):* 1/31. *Financial aid forms:* FAFSA, state form, institutional form required.
LD Services Contact: Dr. Dan Ryan, Director, Canisius College, 2001 Main Street, Buffalo, NY 14208-1098, 716-888-3748. Fax: 716-888-3190. Email: ryan@canisius.edu.

CARDINAL STRITCH UNIVERSITY

Milwaukee, Wisconsin

LEARNING DISABILITIES SERVICES INFORMATION

Academic Support Center, Conditional Acceptance Program began offering services in 1990. Currently the program serves 5 undergraduates with LD. Services are also available to graduate students.
Staff: Includes director, learning specialist. Services provided by remediation specialists, tutors, counselors, diagnostic specialists.
Special Fees: No special fees are charged for services to students with LD.
Applications and admissions: *Required:* high school transcript, grade point average, class rank, untimed ACT, letters of recommendation; *recommended:* psychoeducational report. Students may begin taking classes any term. *Application deadline:* continuous.

PROGRAM AND SERVICE COMPONENTS

Special preparation or orientation: Required orientation held individually by special arrangement.
Diagnostic testing: Intelligence, reading, math, written language, study skills, learning strategies.
Academic advising: Provided by academic advisers. Students with LD may take up to 15 credits each term; most take 12 credits; 12 credits required to maintain full-time status and be eligible for financial aid.
Counseling services: Individual counseling, career counseling.
Basic skills remediation: Offered one-on-one and in class-size groups by teachers with developmental education expertise. Available in reading, math, written language, learning strategies, study skills, time management.
Special courses: Reading, composition, math, study skills. All offered for credit; none enter into overall grade point average.
Auxiliary services: Alternative test arrangements, advocacy.

GENERAL COLLEGE INFORMATION

Independent Roman Catholic, comprehensive, coed. Awards associate, bachelor's, master's degrees. Founded 1937. *Setting:* 40-acre suburban campus. *Total enrollment:* 5,526. *Faculty:* 572 (74 full-time, 65% with terminal degrees, 498 part-time); student–undergrad faculty ratio is 17:1.
Enrollment Profile: 3,161 students from 18 states and territories, 14 other countries. 73% women, 27% men, 15% part-time, 80% state residents, 25% live on campus, 31% transferred in, 1% international, 73% 25 or older, 1% Native American, 3% Hispanic, 11% black, 2% Asian or Pacific Islander. *Retention:* 82% of 1995 full-time freshmen returned. *Graduation:* 24% graduate in 4 years, 47% in 5 years. *Areas of study chosen:* 25% health professions and related sciences, 20% education, 8% business management and administrative services, 5% social sciences, 4% fine arts, 3% biological and life sciences, 3% communications and journalism, 3% theology/religion, 2% computer and information sciences, 1% foreign language and literature, 1% mathematics. *Most popular recent majors:* business administration/commerce/management, education, nursing.
First-Year Class: 169 total; 378 applied, 78% were accepted, 57% of whom enrolled. 10% from top 10% of their high school class, 32% from top quarter, 55% from top half. 10 class presidents, 4 valedictorians.
Graduation Requirements: 64 credits for associate, 128 credits for bachelor's; 2 math/science courses; senior project.
Computers on Campus: 58 computers available on campus for general student use. Computer purchase/lease plans available. Computers for student use in computer labs provide access to the Internet/World Wide Web, on- and off-campus e-mail addresses. Staffed computer lab on campus provides training in use of computers, software.

EXPENSES AND FINANCIAL AID

Expenses for 1996–97: *Application fee:* $20. Comprehensive fee of $12,890 includes full-time tuition ($8960), mandatory fees ($50), and college room and board ($3880 minimum). College room only: $1240. Part-time tuition: $280 per credit (minimum). Part-time mandatory fees: $37 per year. Part-time tuition for nursing program: $310 per credit.
Undergraduate Financial Aid: *Financial aid deadline (priority):* 8/1. *Financial aid forms:* institutional form required; FAFSA, CSS Financial Aid PROFILE acceptable.
LD Services Contact: Ms. Marcia L. Laskey, Director, Academic Support Center, Cardinal Stritch University, 6801 North Yates Road, Milwaukee, WI 53211, 414-352-5400 Ext. 389. Fax: 414-351-7516.

CARLETON UNIVERSITY

Ottawa, Ontario, Canada

LEARNING DISABILITIES SERVICES INFORMATION

Paul Menton Centre for Persons with Disabilities began offering services in 1987. Currently the program serves 264 undergraduates with LD. Services are also available to graduate students. Students diagnosed with ADD/ADHD are eligible for the same services available to students with LD.
Staff: 2 full-time, 4 part-time staff members, including coordinators, learning specialist, administrator. Services provided by tutors, counselors, diagnostic specialists, counseling interns.
Special Fees: No special fees are charged for services to students with LD.
Applications and admissions: *Required:* high school transcript, grade point average, courses completed, IEP (Individualized Education Program), letters of recommendation, psychoeducational report completed within 3 years. Students may begin taking classes any term. *Application deadline:* 6/1.

PROGRAM AND SERVICE COMPONENTS

Special preparation or orientation: Optional orientation offered after classes begin.
Academic advising: Provided by unit staff members, academic advisers. Students with LD may take up to 5 courses each term; most take 3 to 4 courses; 3.5 courses required to maintain full-time status.
Counseling services: Individual counseling, self-advocacy training, peer support group.
Basic skills remediation: Offered one-on-one and in small groups by specially trained peer instructors. Available in written language, learning strategies, study skills, time management.
Subject-area tutoring: Offered one-on-one by peer tutors. Available in some subjects.
Auxiliary aids: Taped textbooks, tape recorders, word-processors with spell-check, personal computers, talking computers, optical character readers, Dragon Dictate.
Auxiliary services: Alternative test arrangements, notetakers, priority registration, advocacy, limited free photocopy services.

GENERAL COLLEGE INFORMATION

Province-supported, coed. Awards bachelor's, master's, doctoral degrees. Founded 1942. *Setting:* 152-acre urban campus. *Total enrollment:* 18,194. *Faculty:* 686 (667 full-time, 19 part-time); student–undergrad faculty ratio is 18:1.
Enrollment Profile: 15,840 students from 12 provinces and territories, 100 other countries. 47% women, 53% men, 29% part-time, 80% province residents, 9% live on campus, 10% transferred in, 7% international, 20% 25 or older.
First-Year Class: 3,500 total; 15,173 applied, 65% were accepted, 36% of whom enrolled.
Graduation Requirements: 15 full-year courses; computer course for commerce, engineering, statistics, operations research majors; internship (some majors); senior project for honors program students and some majors.
Computers on Campus: 350 computers available on campus for general student use. A computer is recommended for some students. A campus-wide network can be accessed from off-campus. Students can

contact faculty members and/or advisers through e-mail. Computers for student use in computer center, computer labs, classrooms, library provide access to the Internet/World Wide Web, on- and off-campus e-mail addresses. Staffed computer lab on campus provides training in use of computers, software.

EXPENSES AND FINANCIAL AID

Expenses for 1997–98: *Application fee:* $50. Canadian resident tuition: $3528 (minimum) full-time. Nonresident tuition: $9158 (minimum) full-time. Full-time tuition and fees range up to $4033 for Canadian residents, $10,233 for nonresidents, according to program. Part-time tuition and fees per course range from $696.70 to $709.70 for Canadian residents, $2022.20 to $2035.70 for nonresidents, according to program. (All figures are in Canadian dollars.). College room and board: $4965.
Undergraduate Financial Aid: *Financial aid deadline:* continuous. *Financial aid forms:* government loan forms required.
LD Services Contact: Dr. Nancy McIntyre, Learning Specialist, Carleton University, Paul Menton Centre, 500 Univ. Centre, 1125 Colonel By Drive, Ottawa, ON K1S 5B6, Canada, 613-520-6608. Fax: 613-520-3995. Email: nancy_mcintyre@carleton.ca.

CAZENOVIA COLLEGE

Cazenovia, New York

LEARNING DISABILITIES SERVICES INFORMATION

Learning Resources Center began offering services in 1980. Currently the program serves 65 undergraduates with LD. Students diagnosed with ADD/ADHD are eligible for the same services available to students with LD.
Staff: 1 full-time, 2 part-time staff members, including director, associate director, clerk. Services provided by remediation specialists, tutors, counselors.
Special Fees: No special fees are charged for services to students with LD.
Applications and admissions: *Required:* high school transcript, grade point average, psychoeducational report completed within 3 years; *recommended:* high school IEP (Individualized Education Program), personal interview. Students may begin taking classes in fall, winter, or summer. *Application deadline:* continuous.

PROGRAM AND SERVICE COMPONENTS

Special preparation or orientation: Orientation offered.
Diagnostic testing: Reading, math, written language, study skills.
Academic advising: Provided by academic advisers. Students with LD may take up to 15 credits each term; most take 12 credits; 12 credits required to maintain full-time status.
Counseling services: Individual counseling, career counseling.
Basic skills remediation: Offered one-on-one and in small groups by regular teachers. Available in reading, math, written language, learning strategies, study skills, time management.
Subject-area tutoring: Offered one-on-one and in small groups by professional teachers, peer tutors, professional tutors. Available in most subjects.
Auxiliary aids: Taped textbooks, tape recorders, calculators, typewriters, word-processors with spell-check.
Auxiliary services: Alternative test arrangements, notetakers.

GENERAL COLLEGE INFORMATION

Independent, 4-year, coed. Awards associate, bachelor's degrees. Founded 1824. *Setting:* 40-acre small-town campus with easy access to Syracuse. *Endowment:* $38.6 million. *Educational spending 1995–96:* $5320 per undergrad. *Total enrollment:* 727. *Faculty:* 136 (46 full-time, 63% with terminal degrees, 90 part-time); student–undergrad faculty ratio is 14:1.
Enrollment Profile: 727 students from 16 states and territories, 1 other country. 65% women, 35% men, 10% part-time, 90% state residents, 86% live on campus, 19% transferred in, 1% international, 6% 25 or older, 1% Native American, 4% Hispanic, 12% black, 1% Asian or Pacific Islander. *Retention:* 59% of 1995 full-time freshmen returned. *Areas of study chosen:* 36% fine arts, 20% business management and administrative services, 20% liberal arts/general studies, 9% health professions and related sciences, 7% education. *Most popular recent majors:* liberal arts/general studies, interior design.
First-Year Class: 177 total; 816 applied, 86% were accepted, 25% of whom enrolled. 6% from top 10% of their high school class, 28% from top quarter, 57% from top half.
Graduation Requirements: 60 credits for associate, 120 credits for bachelor's; internship (some majors); senior project (some majors).
Computers on Campus: 70 computers available on campus for general student use. A campus-wide network can be accessed from student residence rooms. Students can contact faculty members and/or advisers through e-mail. Computers for student use in computer center, learning resource center, library, learning center provide access to the Internet/World Wide Web, on- and off-campus e-mail addresses. Staffed computer lab on campus provides training in use of computers, software. *Academic computing expenditure 1995–96:* $84,605.

EXPENSES AND FINANCIAL AID

Estimated Expenses for 1997–98: *Application fee:* $25. Comprehensive fee of $17,116 includes full-time tuition ($11,232), mandatory fees ($416), and college room and board ($5468). College room only: $2734. Part-time tuition: $282 per credit.
Undergraduate Financial Aid: Of all full-time undergraduates enrolled in fall 1996, 100% of those judged to have need according to Federal Methodology were aided. On average, 34% of need was met. *Financial aid deadline (priority):* 3/15. *Financial aid forms:* FAFSA required; CSS Financial Aid PROFILE acceptable. State form required for some.
LD Services Contact: Ms. Cynthia-Anne Tietje, Director of Special Services, Cazenovia College, Cazenovia, NY 13035-1084, 315-655-9446 Ext. 308. Fax: 315-655-2190.

CENTRAL CONNECTICUT STATE UNIVERSITY

New Britain, Connecticut

LEARNING DISABILITIES SERVICES INFORMATION

Special Student Services began offering services in 1977. Currently the program serves 300 undergraduates with LD. Services are also available to graduate students. Students diagnosed with ADD/ADHD are eligible for the same services available to students with LD.
Staff: 1 full-time, 1 part-time staff members, including director, university assistant. Services provided by remediation specialists, tutors, counselors, diagnostic specialists.
Special Fees: No special fees are charged for services to students with LD.
Applications and admissions: *Required:* high school transcript, grade point average, courses completed, IEP (Individualized Education Program), psychoeducational report completed within 2 years; *recommended:* high school class rank, extracurricular activities, untimed or extended time SAT I, personal interview, autobiographical statement, letters of recommendation.
Special policies: The college has written policies regarding grade forgiveness.

PROGRAM AND SERVICE COMPONENTS

Special preparation or orientation: Optional orientation offered before registration.
Academic advising: Provided by unit staff members. Students with LD may take up to 17 credit hours each term; most take 12 credit hours; 12 credit hours (fewer with special permission) required to maintain full-time status; 12 credit hours required to be eligible for financial aid.
Counseling services: Individual counseling, small-group counseling, career counseling, self-advocacy training.
Special courses: College survival skills, learning strategies, math, remedial English. None offered for credit.
Auxiliary aids: Taped textbooks, tape recorders, calculators, typewriters, word-processors with spell-check, personal computers, talking computers.
Auxiliary services: Alternative test arrangements, notetakers, priority registration, advocacy.

GENERAL COLLEGE INFORMATION

State-supported, comprehensive, coed. Part of Connecticut State University System. Awards bachelor's, master's degrees. Founded 1849. *Setting:* 176-acre suburban campus. *Research spending 1995–96:* $329,570. *Educational spending 1995–96:* $3231 per undergrad. *Total enrollment:* 9,520. *Faculty:* 729 (367 full-time, 73% with terminal degrees, 362 part-time); student–undergrad faculty ratio is 17:1.
Enrollment Profile: 7,798 students from 32 states and territories, 32 other countries. 55% women, 45% men, 27% part-time, 95% state residents, 30% live on campus, 55% transferred in, 1% international, 31% 25

Central Connecticut State University (continued)

or older, 1% Native American, 5% Hispanic, 7% black, 2% Asian or Pacific Islander. *Retention:* 67% of 1995 full-time freshmen returned. *Graduation:* 15% graduate in 4 years, 40% in 5 years, 48% in 6 years. *Areas of study chosen:* 20% business management and administrative services, 9% psychology, 8% education, 7% engineering and applied sciences, 7% liberal arts/general studies, 7% social sciences, 4% English language/literature/letters, 3% computer and information sciences, 3% health professions and related sciences, 3% mathematics, 2% biological and life sciences, 2% communications and journalism, 2% fine arts, 1% foreign language and literature, 1% performing arts, 1% physical sciences. *Most popular recent majors:* elementary education, accounting, psychology.
First-Year Class: 1,093 total; 4,068 applied, 67% were accepted, 40% of whom enrolled. 3% from top 10% of their high school class, 13% from top quarter, 42% from top half.
Graduation Requirements: 122 credit hours; 6 credit hours each of math and science; 2 courses in a foreign language; computer course for business, math majors.
Computers on Campus: 230 computers available on campus for general student use. Computer purchase/lease plans available. Computers for student use in computer center, computer labs, research center, library, student center provide access to the Internet/World Wide Web. Staffed computer lab on campus provides training in use of computers, software. *Academic computing expenditure 1995–96:* $476,000.

EXPENSES AND FINANCIAL AID

Expenses for 1997–98: State resident tuition: $2062 full-time, $155 per credit hour part-time. Nonresident tuition: $6674 full-time, $155 per credit hour part-time. Part-time mandatory fees: $42 per semester. Full-time tuition for nonresidents who are eligible for the New England Regional Student Program: $3093. Full-time mandatory fees: $1552 for state residents and nonresidents who are eligible for the New England Regional Student Program, $2418 for other nonresidents. College room and board: $4850 (minimum). College room only: $2800 (minimum).
Undergraduate Financial Aid: Of all full-time undergraduates enrolled in fall 1996, 74% of those who applied for aid were judged to have need according to Federal Methodology, of whom 100% were aided. On average, 80% of need was met. *Financial aid deadline (priority):* 4/22. *Financial aid forms:* FAFSA required.
LD Services Contact: Dr. George R. Tenney, Director of Special Student Services, Central Connecticut State University, Willard Hall, Room 100, New Britain, CT 06050, 860-832-1957. Fax: 860-832-1650. Email: tenney@ccsua.ctstateu.edu.

CHAPMAN UNIVERSITY

Orange, California

LEARNING DISABILITIES SERVICES INFORMATION

Academic Resources Center began offering services in 1980. Currently the program serves 40 undergraduates with LD. Services are also available to graduate students. Students diagnosed with ADD/ADHD are eligible for the same services available to students with LD.
Staff: 3 full-time staff members, including director, assistant director, coordinator. Services provided by remediation specialist, tutors, diagnostic specialists.
Special Fees: $350 for diagnostic testing.
Applications and admissions: *Required:* high school transcript, grade point average, courses completed, extended time SAT I, letters of recommendation. Students may begin taking classes in fall only. *Application deadline:* continuous.

PROGRAM AND SERVICE COMPONENTS

Diagnostic testing: Intelligence, reading, math, written language, perceptual skills, study skills, learning strategies.
Academic advising: Provided by academic advisers. Students with LD may take up to 12 credits each term; most take 12 credits; 12 credits required to maintain full-time status.
Counseling services: Individual counseling.
Basic skills remediation: Offered in class-size groups by regular teachers. Available in reading, math, written language.
Subject-area tutoring: Offered one-on-one and in small groups by peer tutors. Available in some subjects.
Auxiliary services: Alternative test arrangements, notetakers, priority registration, advocacy.

GENERAL COLLEGE INFORMATION

Independent, comprehensive, coed, affiliated with Christian Church (Disciples of Christ). Awards bachelor's, master's, first professional degrees. Founded 1861. *Setting:* 40-acre suburban campus with easy access to Los Angeles. *Endowment:* $47.9 million. *Educational spending 1995–96:* $5768 per undergrad. *Total enrollment:* 3,673. *Faculty:* 352 (188 full-time, 80% with terminal degrees, 164 part-time); student–undergrad faculty ratio is 11:1.
Enrollment Profile: 2,299 students from 38 states and territories, 38 other countries. 56% women, 44% men, 8% part-time, 90% state residents, 40% live on campus, 50% transferred in, 4% international, 20% 25 or older, 1% Native American, 14% Hispanic, 6% black, 8% Asian or Pacific Islander. *Retention:* 82% of 1995 full-time freshmen returned. *Graduation:* 25% graduate in 4 years, 41% in 5 years, 44% in 6 years. *Areas of study chosen:* 19% performing arts, 15% business management and administrative services, 10% health professions and related sciences, 10% social sciences, 8% communications and journalism, 7% psychology, 5% English language/literature/letters, 5% liberal arts/general studies, 2% fine arts, 2% premed, 1% biological and life sciences, 1% computer and information sciences, 1% foreign language and literature, 1% interdisciplinary studies, 1% natural resource sciences, 1% philosophy, 1% physical sciences, 1% vocational and home economics. *Most popular recent majors:* communication, business administration/commerce/management, liberal arts/general studies.
First-Year Class: 392 total; 1,266 applied, 76% were accepted, 41% of whom enrolled. 24% from top 10% of their high school class, 59% from top quarter, 84% from top half. 2 class presidents, 5 valedictorians.
Graduation Requirements: 124 credits; 12 credits of math/science; 2 years of a foreign language in high school or 1 year in college; computer course for business, applied math majors; internship (some majors); senior project for honors program students and some majors.
Computers on Campus: 170 computers available on campus for general student use. A computer is recommended for some students. A campus-wide network can be accessed from off-campus. Students can contact faculty members and/or advisers through e-mail. Computers for student use in computer labs, library, dorms provide access to the Internet/World Wide Web, on- and off-campus e-mail addresses. Staffed computer lab on campus provides training in use of computers, software.

EXPENSES AND FINANCIAL AID

Expenses for 1997–98: *Application fee:* $30. Comprehensive fee of $25,556 includes full-time tuition ($18,510), mandatory fees ($240), and college room and board ($6806 minimum). Part-time tuition: $575 per credit. Part-time mandatory fees: $120 per term.
Undergraduate Financial Aid: 92% of all full-time undergraduates enrolled in fall 1996 applied for aid; of these, 89% were judged to have need according to Federal Methodology, of whom 95% were aided. On average, 96% of need was met. *Financial aid deadline (priority):* 3/1. *Financial aid forms:* FAFSA required. State form required for some.
LD Services Contact: Dr. Lynn Mayer, Director, Academic Resources Center, Chapman University, 333 North Glassell Street, Orange, CA 92866, 714-997-6828. Fax: 714-744-7699. Email: lmayer@chapman.edu.

THE CITADEL, THE MILITARY COLLEGE OF SOUTH CAROLINA

Charleston, South Carolina

LEARNING DISABILITIES SERVICES INFORMATION

Special Services Department began offering services in 1979. Currently the program serves 150 undergraduates with LD. Services are also available to graduate students. Students diagnosed with ADD/ADHD are eligible for the same services available to students with LD.
Staff: 1 full-time, 3 part-time staff members, including director. Services provided by tutors, graduate assistants.
Special Fees: $150 for diagnostic testing.
Applications and admissions: *Required:* high school transcript, untimed SAT I or ACT, history of LD accommodations or current diagnostic report; *recommended:* high school IEP (Individualized Education Program), extended time SAT I or ACT, letters of recommendation. Students may begin taking classes in fall or summer. *Application deadline:* 7/1.
Special policies: The college has written policies regarding substitutions and waivers of admissions, graduation, and degree requirements.

PROGRAM AND SERVICE COMPONENTS

Special preparation or orientation: Optional summer program offered prior to entering college. Required orientation held before classes begin.

Diagnostic testing: Intelligence, reading, math, spelling, handwriting, written language, perceptual skills, personality, psychoneurology, learning strategies.

Academic advising: Provided by unit staff members, academic advisers. Students with LD may take up to 21 semester hours each term; most take 12 to 15 semester hours; 12 semester hours required to maintain full-time status and be eligible for financial aid.

Counseling services: Individual counseling, career counseling.

Basic skills remediation: Offered one-on-one by graduate assistants; computer-aided instruction also offered. Available in learning strategies, study skills, time management.

Subject-area tutoring: Offered one-on-one and in small groups by professional teachers, peer tutors. Available in some subjects.

Special courses: Composition, learning strategies, time management, study skills, stress management. None offered for credit; none enter into overall grade point average.

Auxiliary aids: Taped textbooks, word-processors with spell-check, personal computers, videos.

Auxiliary services: Alternative test arrangements, notetakers, priority registration, advocacy.

GENERAL COLLEGE INFORMATION

State-supported, comprehensive, coed. Awards bachelor's, master's degrees. Founded 1842. *Setting:* 130-acre urban campus. *Endowment:* $22 million. *Research spending 1995–96:* $196,619. *Educational spending 1995–96:* $4560 per undergrad. *Total enrollment:* 4,319. *Faculty:* 190 (151 full-time, 90% with terminal degrees, 39 part-time); student–undergrad faculty ratio is 13:1.

Enrollment Profile: 1,967 students from 46 states and territories, 18 other countries. 1% women, 99% men, 4% part-time, 50% state residents, 15% transferred in, 2% international, 6% 25 or older, 0% Native American, 2% Hispanic, 7% black, 2% Asian or Pacific Islander. *Retention:* 80% of 1995 full-time freshmen returned. *Graduation:* 67% graduate in 4 years, 75% in 5 years, 77% in 6 years. *Areas of study chosen:* 32% business management and administrative services, 21% social sciences, 15% engineering and applied sciences, 10% education, 7% biological and life sciences, 4% computer and information sciences, 4% psychology, 3% English language/literature/letters, 2% physical sciences, 1% foreign language and literature, 1% mathematics. *Most popular recent majors:* business administration/commerce/management, political science/government, civil engineering.

First-Year Class: 475 total; 1,330 applied, 86% were accepted, 42% of whom enrolled. 13% from top 10% of their high school class, 37% from top quarter, 73% from top half.

Graduation Requirements: 118 semester hours; 6 semester hours of math; computer course for electrical engineering, civil engineering, math, business administration majors; internship (some majors); senior project (some majors).

Computers on Campus: 350 computers available on campus for general student use. Computer purchase/lease plans available. A computer is strongly recommended for all students. A campus-wide network can be accessed from student residence rooms and from off-campus. Students can contact faculty members and/or advisers through e-mail. Computers for student use in computer center, library, dorms, writing lab. Staffed computer lab on campus provides training in use of computers, software. *Academic computing expenditure 1995–96:* $577,901.

EXPENSES AND FINANCIAL AID

Expenses for 1997–98: *Application fee:* $25. State resident tuition: $3499 full-time. Nonresident tuition: $8149 full-time. Deposit required to defray the cost of uniforms and supplies: $3900 for freshmen, $1200 for upperclassmen. Full-time mandatory fees: $830. College room and board: $3950.

Undergraduate Financial Aid: 49% of all full-time undergraduates enrolled in fall 1996 applied for aid; of these, 78% were judged to have need according to Federal Methodology, of whom 97% were aided. On average, 86% of need was met. *Financial aid deadline:* Applications processed continuously. *Financial aid forms:* FAFSA required.

LD Services Contact: Dr. Barbara A. Zaremba, Director of Academic Support, The Citadel, The Military College of South Carolina, MSC 33, Charleston, SC 29409, 803-953-1820. Fax: 803-953-7084. Email: zarembab@citadel.edu.

CLARION UNIVERSITY OF PENNSYLVANIA

Clarion, Pennsylvania

LEARNING DISABILITIES SERVICES INFORMATION

Student Support Services began offering services in 1982. Currently the program serves 40 undergraduates with LD. Services are also available to graduate students. Students diagnosed with ADD/ADHD are eligible for the same services available to students with LD.

Staff: 3 full-time staff members, including director. Services provided by counselor, learning skills specialist.

Special Fees: No special fees are charged for services to students with LD.

Applications and admissions: *Required:* high school transcript, grade point average, class rank, courses completed, extracurricular activities, untimed SAT I, autobiographical statement, letters of recommendation, psychoeducational report completed within 3 years; *recommended:* extended time SAT I, personal interview. Students may begin taking classes in summer only. *Application deadline:* continuous.

PROGRAM AND SERVICE COMPONENTS

Special preparation or orientation: Required orientation held during registration.

Academic advising: Provided by unit staff members. Students with LD may take up to 18 credit hours each term; most take 12 to 15 credit hours; 12 credit hours required to maintain full-time status and be eligible for financial aid.

Counseling services: Individual counseling, career counseling, self-advocacy training.

Basic skills remediation: Offered one-on-one by graduate students, peer tutors; computer-aided instruction also offered. Available in math, written language, learning strategies, time management.

Subject-area tutoring: Offered one-on-one and in small groups by peer tutors. Available in some subjects.

Special courses: College survival skills, learning strategies. All offered for credit; all enter into overall grade point average.

Auxiliary aids: Taped textbooks, tape recorders, typewriters, word-processors with spell-check.

Auxiliary services: Alternative test arrangements, notetakers, priority registration, advocacy.

Campus support group: A special student organization is available to students with LD.

GENERAL COLLEGE INFORMATION

State-supported, comprehensive, coed. Part of Pennsylvania State System of Higher Education. Awards associate, bachelor's, master's degrees. Founded 1867. *Setting:* 100-acre rural campus. *Research spending 1995–96:* $155,504. *Educational spending 1995–96:* $4916 per undergrad. *Total enrollment:* 5,886. *Faculty:* 366 (340 full-time, 68% with terminal degrees, 26 part-time); student–undergrad faculty ratio is 18:1.

Enrollment Profile: 5,410 students from 28 states and territories, 21 other countries. 61% women, 39% men, 10% part-time, 97% state residents, 37% live on campus, 6% transferred in, 1% international, 19% 25 or older, 0% Native American, 0% Hispanic, 4% black, 0% Asian or Pacific Islander. *Retention:* 71% of 1995 full-time freshmen returned. *Graduation:* 27% graduate in 4 years, 52% in 5 years, 57% in 6 years. *Areas of study chosen:* 28% education, 18% business management and administrative services, 8% health professions and related sciences, 7% communications and journalism, 4% biological and life sciences, 4% psychology, 3% computer and information sciences, 3% physical sciences, 2% liberal arts/general studies, 1% English language/literature/letters, 1% fine arts, 1% mathematics. *Most popular recent majors:* elementary education, secondary education, communication.

First-Year Class: 1,313 total; 3,088 applied, 89% were accepted, 48% of whom enrolled.

Graduation Requirements: 62 credits for associate, 128 credits for bachelor's; 9 credits of math/science including at least 3 credits each in math and science; computer course.

Computers on Campus: 354 computers available on campus for general student use. A campus-wide network can be accessed from student residence rooms and from off-campus. Students can contact faculty members and/or advisers through e-mail. Computers for student use in computer center, computer labs, library, student center, dorms, aca-

Clarion University of Pennsylvania (continued)

demic buildings provide access to the Internet/World Wide Web, on- and off-campus e-mail addresses. Staffed computer lab on campus provides training in use of computers, software.

EXPENSES AND FINANCIAL AID

Expenses for 1996–97: *Application fee:* $25. State resident tuition: $3368 full-time, $140 per credit part-time. Nonresident tuition: $8566 full-time, $357 per credit part-time. Part-time mandatory fees per semester range from $49.95 to $359.01. Full-time mandatory fees range from $870 to $900. College room and board: $3140 (minimum). College room only: $1860 (minimum).

Undergraduate Financial Aid: 85% of all full-time undergraduates enrolled in fall 1996 applied for aid; of these, 89% were judged to have need according to Federal Methodology, of whom 94% were aided. On average, 79% of need was met. *Financial aid deadline:* Applications processed continuously. *Financial aid forms:* FAFSA, state form required; institutional form acceptable.

LD Services Contact: Mr. Gregory K. Clary, Director, Clarion University of Pennsylvania, 216 Davis Hall, Clarion, PA 16214, 814-226-2347. Fax: 814-226-2368.

CLARK UNIVERSITY

Worcester, Massachusetts

LEARNING DISABILITIES SERVICES INFORMATION

Special Needs Program began offering services in 1983. Currently the program serves 145 undergraduates with LD. Students diagnosed with ADD/ADHD are eligible for the same services available to students with LD.

Staff: 1 full-time staff member (director). Services provided by counselor/diagnostic specialist.

Special Fees: No special fees are charged for services to students with LD.

Applications and admissions: *Required:* high school transcript, untimed SAT I or ACT, letters of recommendation, psychoeducational report completed within 3 years; *recommended:* extended time SAT I or ACT, personal interview, autobiographical statement. Students may begin taking classes in fall only. *Application deadline:* 2/15.

Special policies: The college has written policies regarding grade forgiveness; substitutions and waivers of graduation requirements.

PROGRAM AND SERVICE COMPONENTS

Special preparation or orientation: Optional orientation offered before registration.

Academic advising: Provided by unit staff members. Students with LD may take up to 16 credit hours each term; most take 16 credit hours; 12 credit hours required to maintain full-time status and be eligible for financial aid.

Counseling services: Individual counseling, small-group counseling, career counseling, peer advising.

Auxiliary services: Alternative test arrangements, notetakers, priority registration, advocacy, readers.

GENERAL COLLEGE INFORMATION

Independent, coed. Awards bachelor's, master's, doctoral degrees. Founded 1887. *Setting:* 50-acre urban campus with easy access to Boston. *Endowment:* $87.5 million. *Total enrollment:* 2,732. *Faculty:* 172 (all full-time, 99% with terminal degrees); student–undergrad faculty ratio is 11:1.

Enrollment Profile: 1,869 students from 38 states and territories, 70 other countries. 58% women, 42% men, 2% part-time, 37% state residents, 70% live on campus, 11% transferred in, 16% international, 2% Hispanic, 4% black, 5% Asian or Pacific Islander. *Retention:* 83% of 1995 full-time freshmen returned. *Graduation:* 63% graduate in 4 years, 71% in 5 years, 72% in 6 years. *Areas of study chosen:* 44% liberal arts/general studies, 16% social sciences, 9% psychology, 5% biological and life sciences, 4% business management and administrative services, 3% English language/literature/letters, 3% premed, 2% communications and journalism, 2% fine arts, 2% foreign language and literature, 2% natural resource sciences, 2% performing arts, 1% computer and information sciences, 1% interdisciplinary studies, 1% mathematics, 1% philosophy, 1% physical sciences, 1% predentistry, 1% prelaw, 1% prevet. *Most popular recent majors:* psychology, political science/government, business administration/commerce/management.

First-Year Class: 534 total; 2,949 applied, 79% were accepted, 23% of whom enrolled. 27% from top 10% of their high school class, 61% from top quarter, 89% from top half.

Graduation Requirements: 32 courses; 1 math/science course; computer course (varies by major); internship (some majors); senior project for honors program students and some majors.

Computers on Campus: 100 computers available on campus for general student use. Computer purchase/lease plans available. A computer is recommended for some students. A campus-wide network can be accessed from student residence rooms and from off-campus. Students can contact faculty members and/or advisers through e-mail. Computers for student use in computer center, computer labs, classrooms, library, academic buildings, departmental labs provide access to the Internet/World Wide Web, on- and off-campus e-mail addresses. Staffed computer lab on campus provides training in use of computers, software.

EXPENSES AND FINANCIAL AID

Expenses for 1997–98: *Application fee:* $40. Comprehensive fee of $25,190 includes full-time tuition ($20,500), mandatory fees ($440), and college room and board ($4250). College room only: $2250. Part-time tuition: $2563 per course.

Undergraduate Financial Aid: Of all full-time undergraduates enrolled in fall 1996, 94% of those who applied for aid were judged to have need according to Federal Methodology, of whom 100% were aided. On average, 94% of need was met. *Financial aid deadline (priority):* 2/1. *Financial aid forms:* FAFSA, financial aid transcript (for transfers) required. CSS Financial Aid PROFILE, institutional form required for some.

LD Services Contact: Mr. Alan C. Bieri, Director, Special Needs, Clark University, 950 Main Street, Worcester, MA 01610-1477, 508-793-7468. Fax: 508-793-7500.

CLAYTON COLLEGE & STATE UNIVERSITY

Morrow, Georgia

LEARNING DISABILITIES SERVICES INFORMATION

Counseling and Career Planning Center began offering services in 1982. Currently the program serves 70 undergraduates with LD. Students diagnosed with ADD/ADHD are eligible for the same services available to students with LD.

Staff: 1 full-time staff member (coordinator).

Special Fees: No special fees are charged for services to students with LD.

Applications and admissions: *Required:* high school transcript, untimed SAT I, psychoeducational report completed within 3 years; *recommended:* extended time SAT I, personal interview. Students may begin taking classes any term. *Application deadline:* 9/6 (fall term), 3/6 (spring term).

Special policies: The college has written policies regarding substitutions and waivers of degree requirements.

PROGRAM AND SERVICE COMPONENTS

Special preparation or orientation: Optional orientation offered before registration.

Diagnostic testing: Intelligence, reading, math, spelling, spoken language, written language, personality, learning strategies, cognitive abilities.

Academic advising: Provided by academic advisers. Students with LD may take up to 15 quarter hours each term; most take 10 to 12 quarter hours; 12 quarter hours required to maintain full-time status; 6 quarter hours required to be eligible for financial aid.

Counseling services: Individual counseling, career counseling, self-advocacy training.

Basic skills remediation: Offered in class-size groups by developmental studies instructors. Available in reading, math, handwriting, spoken language, written language, speech.

Auxiliary aids: Taped textbooks, tape recorders, calculators, typewriters, word-processors with spell-check, magnifiers, talking calculator, DecTalk speech synthesizer.

Auxiliary services: Alternative test arrangements, notetakers, advocacy.

GENERAL COLLEGE INFORMATION

State-supported, 4-year, coed. Part of University System of Georgia. Awards associate, bachelor's degrees. Founded 1969. *Setting:* 163-acre suburban campus with easy access to Atlanta. *Endowment:* $582,000.

Total enrollment: 4,687. *Faculty:* 250 (128 full-time, 55% with terminal degrees, 122 part-time); student–undergrad faculty ratio is 22:1.
Enrollment Profile: 4,687 students from 23 states and territories, 80 other countries. 65% women, 35% men, 59% part-time, 97% state residents, 40% transferred in, 1% international, 37% 25 or older, 0% Native American, 2% Hispanic, 26% black, 2% Asian or Pacific Islander. *Retention:* 50% of 1995 full-time freshmen returned. *Graduation:* 10% graduate in 4 years, 15% in 5 years, 20% in 6 years. *Most popular recent majors:* business administration/commerce/management, nursing, dental services.
First-Year Class: 847 total.
Graduation Requirements: 90 quarter hours for associate, 180 quarter hours for bachelor's; 1 math course; computer course for business majors; internship (some majors); senior project (some majors).
Computers on Campus: 110 computers available on campus for general student use. A campus-wide network can be accessed from off-campus. Students can contact faculty members and/or advisers through e-mail. Computers for student use in computer labs, learning resource center, library, technology building provide access to the Internet/World Wide Web, on- and off-campus e-mail addresses. Staffed computer lab on campus provides training in use of computers, software. *Academic computing expenditure 1995–96:* $262,845.

EXPENSES AND FINANCIAL AID

Expenses for 1996–97: *Application fee:* $20. State resident tuition: $1584 full-time, $44 per quarter hour part-time. Nonresident tuition: $5463 full-time, $152 per quarter hour part-time. Part-time mandatory fees: $86 per quarter. Full-time mandatory fees: $258.
Undergraduate Financial Aid: 75% of all full-time undergraduates enrolled in fall 1996 applied for aid; of these, 80% were judged to have need according to Federal Methodology, of whom 99% were aided. *Financial aid deadline (priority):* 6/1. *Financial aid forms:* FAFSA, institutional form required.
LD Services Contact: Mr. R. Wayne Stewart, Disability Services Coordinator, Clayton College & State University, PO Box 285, Morrow, GA 30260, 770-961-3515. Fax: 770-960-2166. Email: stewart@dd.clayton.edu.

CLEAR CREEK BAPTIST BIBLE COLLEGE

Pineville, Kentucky

LEARNING DISABILITIES SERVICES INFORMATION

Dean of Students Office began offering services in 1952. Currently the program serves 8 undergraduates with LD. Students diagnosed with ADD/ADHD are not eligible for the same services available to students with LD.
Staff: 1 part-time staff member (director).
Special Fees: No special fees are charged for services to students with LD.
Applications and admissions: Open admissions. Students may begin taking classes in fall only. *Application deadline:* 7/15.

PROGRAM AND SERVICE COMPONENTS

Diagnostic testing: Reading, spoken language, written language, study skills.
Academic advising: Provided by academic advisers. Students with LD may take up to 16 semester hours each term; most take 12 to 16 semester hours; 12 semester hours required to maintain full-time status; 6 semester hours required to be eligible for financial aid.
Counseling services: Individual counseling.
Basic skills remediation: Offered one-on-one by regular teachers. Available in reading, spoken language, written language, learning strategies.
Subject-area tutoring: Offered one-on-one by professional teachers. Available in some subjects.

GENERAL COLLEGE INFORMATION

Independent Southern Baptist, 4-year, specialized, primarily men. Awards associate, bachelor's degrees. Founded 1926. *Setting:* 700-acre rural campus. *Total enrollment:* 150. *Faculty:* 17 (7 full-time, 50% with terminal degrees, 10 part-time); student–undergrad faculty ratio is 12:1.
Enrollment Profile: 150 students from 39 states and territories, 1 other country. 10% women, 90% men, 5% part-time, 70% state residents, 2% transferred in, 1% international, 90% 25 or older, 0% Native American, 0% Hispanic, 1% black, 0% Asian or Pacific Islander. *Retention:* 75% of 1995 full-time freshmen returned.
First-Year Class: 48 total; 60 applied, 100% were accepted, 80% of whom enrolled. 0% from top 10% of their high school class, 4% from top quarter, 16% from top half.
Graduation Requirements: 66 semester hours for associate, 130 semester hours for bachelor's; 1 course each in math and science; internship.
Computers on Campus: 4 computers available on campus for general student use. A computer is strongly recommended for all students. Computers for student use in computer labs provide access to the Internet/World Wide Web, on- and off-campus e-mail addresses. Staffed computer lab on campus provides training in use of computers, software.

EXPENSES AND FINANCIAL AID

Expenses for 1996–97: *Application fee:* $40. Comprehensive fee of $4850 includes full-time tuition ($2170 minimum), mandatory fees ($200), and college room and board ($2480 minimum). College room only: $1060. Part-time tuition: $105 per semester hour (minimum). Part-time mandatory fees: $50 per semester. Tuition for non-church members: $2610 full-time, $130 per semester hour part-time.
Undergraduate Financial Aid: 84% of all full-time undergraduates enrolled in fall 1996 applied for aid; of these, 91% were judged to have need according to Federal Methodology, of whom 100% were aided. On average, 41% of need was met. *Financial aid deadline (priority):* 7/31. *Financial aid forms:* FAFSA, institutional form, federal income tax form required; CSS Financial Aid PROFILE acceptable.
LD Services Contact: Mr. Charles Rice, Assistant Academic Dean, Clear Creek Baptist Bible College, 300 Clear Creek Road, Pineville, KY 40977-9754, 606-337-3196. Fax: 606-337-2372.

CLEMSON UNIVERSITY

Clemson, South Carolina

LEARNING DISABILITIES SERVICES INFORMATION

Orientation, Leadership, and Disability Services began offering services in 1988. Currently the program serves 250 undergraduates with LD. Services are also available to graduate students. Students diagnosed with ADD/ADHD are eligible for the same services available to students with LD, as well as medication evaluation (in Health Services), FM systems, ADDvantage (ADD support group).
Staff: 1 full-time, 5 part-time staff members, including director, coordinator.
Special Fees: $300 to $500 for diagnostic testing.
Applications and admissions: *Required:* high school transcript, grade point average, class rank, courses completed, extended time SAT I, personal interview, psychoeducational report completed within 3 years. Students may begin taking classes any term. *Application deadline:* continuous.
Special policies: The college has written policies regarding substitutions and waivers of graduation and degree requirements.

PROGRAM AND SERVICE COMPONENTS

Diagnostic testing: Intelligence, reading, math, spelling, handwriting, spoken language, written language, motor abilities, perceptual skills, study skills, personality, social skills, psychoneurology, speech, hearing, learning strategies, foreign language.
Academic advising: Provided by unit staff members, academic advisers. Students with LD may take up to 21 credits each term; most take 12 to 18 credits; 12 credits (6 to 9 with special permission) required to maintain full-time status; 12 credits required to be eligible for financial aid.
Counseling services: Individual counseling, small-group counseling, career counseling, self-advocacy training.
Auxiliary aids: Taped textbooks, tape recorders, calculators, typewriters, word-processors with spell-check, talking computers, optical character readers.
Auxiliary services: Alternative test arrangements, notetakers, priority registration, advocacy.
Campus support group: A special student organization is available to students with LD.

GENERAL COLLEGE INFORMATION

State-supported, coed. Awards bachelor's, master's, doctoral degrees. Founded 1889. *Setting:* 1,400-acre small-town campus. *Endowment:* $140.9 million. *Research spending 1995–96:* $64.3 million. *Educational spending 1995–96:* $5730 per undergrad. *Total enrollment:* 16,537. *Faculty:* 1,301 (1,122 full-time, 75% with terminal degrees, 179 part-time); student–undergrad faculty ratio is 16:1.

Clemson University (continued)

Enrollment Profile: 12,717 students from 50 states and territories, 52 other countries. 45% women, 55% men, 7% part-time, 72% state residents, 52% live on campus, 7% transferred in, 1% international, 3% 25 or older, 1% Native American, 1% Hispanic, 8% black, 1% Asian or Pacific Islander. *Retention:* 85% of 1995 full-time freshmen returned. *Graduation:* 38% graduate in 4 years, 64% in 5 years, 70% in 6 years. *Areas of study chosen:* 15% business management and administrative services, 14% engineering and applied sciences, 10% education, 6% agriculture, 6% health professions and related sciences, 5% biological and life sciences, 4% architecture, 4% social sciences, 3% computer and information sciences, 3% English language/literature/letters, 3% psychology, 2% fine arts, 2% natural resource sciences, 2% physical sciences, 1% communications and journalism, 1% foreign language and literature, 1% mathematics, 1% philosophy, 1% premed. *Most popular recent majors:* nursing, business administration/commerce/management, accounting.
First-Year Class: 2,546 total; 7,956 applied, 78% were accepted, 41% of whom enrolled. 30% from top 10% of their high school class, 62% from top quarter, 92% from top half. 28 National Merit Scholars, 80 valedictorians.
Graduation Requirements: 128 hours; 6 hours of math; 11 hours of science; computer course for engineering, management, nursing, some natural science, agriculture, architecture, economics majors; internship (some majors); senior project for honors program students.
Computers on Campus: 1,000 computers available on campus for general student use. A campus-wide network can be accessed from student residence rooms and from off-campus. Students can contact faculty members and/or advisers through e-mail. Computers for student use in computer center, library, academic buildings provide access to the Internet/World Wide Web. Staffed computer lab on campus (open 24 hours a day) provides training in use of computers, software. *Academic computing expenditure 1995–96:* $1.8 million.

EXPENSES AND FINANCIAL AID

Expenses for 1997–98: *Application fee:* $35. State resident tuition: $3062 full-time, $126 per hour part-time. Nonresident tuition: $8486 full-time, $356 per hour part-time. Part-time mandatory fees: $6 per hour. Full-time mandatory fees: $330. College room and board: $3094. College room only: $1560 (minimum).
Undergraduate Financial Aid: Of all full-time undergraduates enrolled in fall 1996, 68% of those who applied for aid were judged to have need according to Federal Methodology, of whom 90% were aided. On average, 73% of need was met. *Financial aid deadline (priority):* 4/1. *Financial aid forms:* FAFSA required.
LD Services Contact: Ms. Bonnie S. Martin, Coordinator, Clemson University, 707 University Union, Clemson, SC 29634-4002, 864-656-0515. Fax: 864-656-0514. Email: bmartin@clemson.edu.

COE COLLEGE

Cedar Rapids, Iowa

LEARNING DISABILITIES SERVICES INFORMATION

Educational Support Program currently serves 10 undergraduates with LD. Students diagnosed with ADD/ADHD are eligible for the same services available to students with LD.
Staff: 3 full-time, 1 part-time staff members, including director, tutoring coordinator. Services provided by remediation specialist, tutors, counselor, math specialist.
Special Fees: No special fees are charged for services to students with LD.
Applications and admissions: *Required:* high school transcript, grade point average, untimed SAT I or ACT, essay; *recommended:* high school class rank, courses completed, extracurricular activities, extended time SAT I, personal interview, psychoeducational report. Students may begin taking classes in fall, spring, or summer. *Application deadline:* continuous.

PROGRAM AND SERVICE COMPONENTS

Academic advising: Provided by academic advisers. Students with LD may take up to 4 courses each term; most take 3 to 4 courses; 3 courses required to maintain full-time status and be eligible for financial aid.
Counseling services: Individual counseling, career counseling, self-advocacy training.
Basic skills remediation: Offered one-on-one by counselor, peer teachers, reading specialist. Available in reading, math, written language, learning strategies, study skills, time management.
Subject-area tutoring: Offered one-on-one and in small groups by peer tutors. Available in most subjects.
Special courses: College survival skills, composition, study skills. All offered for credit; all enter into overall grade point average.
Auxiliary aids: Taped textbooks, tape recorders, word-processors with spell-check.
Auxiliary services: Alternative test arrangements, notetakers, priority registration, advocacy.

GENERAL COLLEGE INFORMATION

Independent, comprehensive, coed, affiliated with Presbyterian Church. Awards bachelor's, master's degrees. Founded 1851. *Setting:* 55-acre urban campus. *Endowment:* $45 million. *Research spending 1995–96:* $125,000. *Total enrollment:* 1,247. *Faculty:* 143 (85 full-time, 87% with terminal degrees, 58 part-time); student–undergrad faculty ratio is 12:1.
Enrollment Profile: 1,202 students from 34 states and territories, 18 other countries. 54% women, 46% men, 16% part-time, 62% state residents, 71% live on campus, 6% transferred in, 4% international, 7% 25 or older, 0% Native American, 1% Hispanic, 2% black, 2% Asian or Pacific Islander. *Retention:* 80% of 1995 full-time freshmen returned. *Areas of study chosen:* 35% business management and administrative services, 19% social sciences, 6% education, 5% biological and life sciences, 2% fine arts, 2% interdisciplinary studies, 2% premed, 1% engineering and applied sciences. *Most popular recent majors:* business administration/commerce/management, psychology, biology/biological sciences.
First-Year Class: 248 total; 855 applied, 90% were accepted, 32% of whom enrolled. 24% from top 10% of their high school class, 47% from top quarter, 81% from top half. 12 valedictorians.
Graduation Requirements: 36 courses; 2 natural science courses including at least 1 lab science course; computer course for physics majors; senior project for honors program students.
Computers on Campus: 126 computers available on campus for general student use. Computer purchase/lease plans available. A computer is recommended for all students. A campus-wide network can be accessed from student residence rooms and from off-campus. Students can contact faculty members and/or advisers through e-mail. Computers for student use in computer center, computer labs, library provide access to the Internet/World Wide Web, on- and off-campus e-mail addresses. Staffed computer lab on campus provides training in use of computers, software. *Academic computing expenditure 1995–96:* $162,062.

EXPENSES AND FINANCIAL AID

Expenses for 1997–98: *Application fee:* $25. Comprehensive fee of $20,890 includes full-time tuition ($16,170), mandatory fees ($150), and college room and board ($4570). College room only: $2030. Part-time tuition: $820 per course.
Undergraduate Financial Aid: 97% of all full-time undergraduates enrolled in fall 1996 applied for aid; of these, 96% were judged to have need according to Federal Methodology, of whom 100% were aided. On average, 100% of need was met. *Financial aid deadline (priority):* 3/1. *Financial aid forms:* FAFSA required; CSS Financial Aid PROFILE acceptable. State form, institutional form required for some.
LD Services Contact: Ms. Lois Kabela-Coates, Director of Educational Support Program, Coe College, 1220 1st Avenue, NE, Cedar Rapids, IA 52402, 319-399-8546. Fax: 319-399-8869.

COLBY-SAWYER COLLEGE

New London, New Hampshire

LEARNING DISABILITIES SERVICES INFORMATION

Academic Development Center began offering services in 1989. Currently the program serves 51 undergraduates with LD. Students diagnosed with ADD/ADHD are eligible for the same services available to students with LD, as well as single rooms (upon request).
Staff: 1 full-time, 2 part-time staff members, including director, learning specialists. Services provided by tutors.
Special Fees: No special fees are charged for services to students with LD.
Applications and admissions: *Required:* high school transcript, grade point average, extended time SAT I, personal interview, autobiographical statement, letters of recommendation, psychoeducational report completed within 3 years. Students may begin taking classes in fall or spring. *Application deadline:* continuous.
Special policies: The college has written policies regarding substitutions and waivers of admissions, graduation, and degree requirements.

PROGRAM AND SERVICE COMPONENTS

Special preparation or orientation: Optional orientation offered after registration during the first week of classes.
Academic advising: Provided by academic advisers. Students with LD may take up to 15 credit hours (depending on the complexity of the courses) each term; most take 12 to 15 credit hours; 12 credit hours required to maintain full-time status; 12 credit hours (for institutional aid), 6 credit hours (for federal aid) required to be eligible for financial aid.
Basic skills remediation: Offered one-on-one by LD teachers, learning specialists. Available in reading, written language, learning strategies, study skills, time management.
Auxiliary aids: Taped textbooks, tape recorders, calculators, word-processors with spell-check, personal computers.
Auxiliary services: Alternative test arrangements, notetakers, priority registration, advocacy.

GENERAL COLLEGE INFORMATION

Independent, 4-year, coed. Awards associate, bachelor's degrees. Founded 1837. *Setting:* 196-acre small-town campus. *Endowment:* $4 million. *Research spending 1995–96:* $29,679. *Educational spending 1995–96:* $3113 per undergrad. *Total enrollment:* 755. *Faculty:* 90 (40 full-time, 78% with terminal degrees, 50 part-time); student–undergrad faculty ratio is 12:1.
Enrollment Profile: 755 students from 25 states and territories, 7 other countries. 65% women, 35% men, 4% part-time, 34% state residents, 82% live on campus, 15% transferred in, 3% international, 5% 25 or older, 1% Native American, 1% Hispanic, 1% black, 1% Asian or Pacific Islander. *Retention:* 84% of 1995 full-time freshmen returned. *Graduation:* 48% graduate in 4 years, 51% in 5 years, 52% in 6 years. *Areas of study chosen:* 35% health professions and related sciences, 16% education, 9% business management and administrative services, 8% fine arts, 7% psychology, 5% communications and journalism, 4% biological and life sciences, 3% vocational and home economics, 2% English language/literature/letters, 1% interdisciplinary studies, 1% liberal arts/general studies. *Most popular recent majors:* sports medicine, child psychology/child development, business administration/commerce/management.
First-Year Class: 227 total; 1,121 applied, 81% were accepted, 25% of whom enrolled.
Graduation Requirements: 60 credit hours for associate, 120 credit hours for bachelor's; 1 math course; 2 science courses; computer course; internship (some majors); senior project (some majors).
Computers on Campus: 70 computers available on campus for general student use. Computer purchase/lease plans available. A computer is recommended for all students. Students can contact faculty members and/or advisers through e-mail. Computers for student use in computer labs, library provide access to the Internet/World Wide Web, on-campus e-mail addresses. Staffed computer lab on campus provides training in use of computers, software.

EXPENSES AND FINANCIAL AID

Expenses for 1997–98: *Application fee:* $40. Comprehensive fee of $22,550 includes full-time tuition ($16,310) and college room and board ($6240). College room only: $3430. Part-time tuition: $545 per credit hour.
Undergraduate Financial Aid: 87% of all full-time undergraduates enrolled in fall 1996 applied for aid; of these, 89% were judged to have need according to Federal Methodology, of whom 91% were aided. On average, 77% of need was met. *Financial aid deadline (priority):* 3/1. *Financial aid forms:* FAFSA, institutional form required.
LD Services Contact: Dr. Tom Mooney, Learning Specialist, Colby-Sawyer College, Main Street, New London, NH 03257, 603-526-3713. Fax: 603-526-3452. Email: tmooney@colby-sawyer.edu.

THE COLLEGE OF NEW JERSEY

Trenton, New Jersey

LEARNING DISABILITIES SERVICES INFORMATION

Office for Students with Differing Abilities began offering services in 1988. Currently the program serves 35 undergraduates with LD. Services are also available to graduate students. Students diagnosed with ADD/ADHD are eligible for the same services available to students with LD.
Staff: 1 full-time staff member (coordinator). Services provided by tutors, counselors.
Special Fees: No special fees are charged for services to students with LD.
Applications and admissions: *Required:* high school transcript, grade point average, class rank, courses completed, extracurricular activities, untimed SAT I; *recommended:* extended time SAT I, letters of recommendation, psychoeducational report completed within 2 years. Students may begin taking classes in summer only. *Application deadline:* 3/1.

PROGRAM AND SERVICE COMPONENTS

Academic advising: Provided by academic advisers. Students with LD may take up to 18 semester hours each term; most take 12 to 15 hours; 12 semester hours (9 with permission) required to maintain full-time status; 12 semester hours required to be eligible for financial aid.
Counseling services: Individual counseling, small-group counseling, career counseling, self-advocacy training.
Basic skills remediation: Offered in class-size groups by regular teachers. Available in reading, math, spelling, written language.
Subject-area tutoring: Offered one-on-one by professional teachers, peer tutors, graduate students. Available in most subjects.
Auxiliary aids: Taped textbooks, tape recorders, calculators, typewriters, word-processors with spell-check, personal computers.
Auxiliary services: Alternative test arrangements, notetakers, priority registration, advocacy.
Campus support group: A special student organization is available to students with LD.

GENERAL COLLEGE INFORMATION

State-supported, comprehensive, coed. Awards bachelor's, master's degrees. Founded 1855. *Setting:* 255-acre suburban campus with easy access to Philadelphia. *Endowment:* $3 million. *Research spending 1995–96:* $1.6 million. *Educational spending 1995–96:* $5749 per undergrad. *Total enrollment:* 6,704. *Faculty:* 612 (319 full-time, 85% with terminal degrees, 293 part-time); student–undergrad faculty ratio is 14:1.
Enrollment Profile: 5,744 students from 23 states and territories, 20 other countries. 61% women, 39% men, 11% part-time, 95% state residents, 59% live on campus, 4% transferred in, 1% international, 13% 25 or older, 1% Native American, 5% Hispanic, 6% black, 6% Asian or Pacific Islander. *Retention:* 93% of 1995 full-time freshmen returned. *Graduation:* 17% graduate in 4 years, 54% in 5 years, 74% in 6 years. *Areas of study chosen:* 18% education, 15% business management and administrative services, 12% social sciences, 9% liberal arts/general studies, 7% biological and life sciences, 7% English language/literature/letters, 6% psychology, 5% fine arts, 4% engineering and applied sciences, 4% health professions and related sciences, 3% communications and journalism, 3% mathematics, 2% computer and information sciences, 2% performing arts, 2% physical sciences, 1% foreign language and literature. *Most popular recent majors:* elementary education, biology/biological sciences, English.
First-Year Class: 1,014 total; 6,329 applied, 45% were accepted, 36% of whom enrolled. 54% from top 10% of their high school class, 89% from top quarter, 98% from top half. 50 valedictorians.
Graduation Requirements: 128 semester hours; 6 semester hours of math; 8 semester hours of science; computer course for art, business, education, engineering, law and justice, science, math majors; senior project for honors program students and some majors.
Computers on Campus: 500 computers available on campus for general student use. A computer is recommended for all students. A campus-wide network can be accessed from student residence rooms and from off-campus. Students can contact faculty members and/or advisers through e-mail. Computers for student use in computer center, computer labs, classrooms, library, student center, dorms, academic buildings provide access to the Internet/World Wide Web, on- and off-campus e-mail addresses. Staffed computer lab on campus provides training in use of computers, software. *Academic computing expenditure 1995–96:* $3 million.

EXPENSES AND FINANCIAL AID

Expenses for 1997–98: *Application fee:* $50. State resident tuition: $3791 full-time, $129 per semester hour part-time. Nonresident tuition: $6620 full-time, $226 per semester hour part-time. Part-time mandatory fees: $36.45 per semester hour. Full-time mandatory fees: $1134. College room and board: $5996.
Undergraduate Financial Aid: *Financial aid deadline (priority):* 4/1. *Financial aid forms:* FAFSA, institutional form required; CSS Financial Aid PROFILE acceptable.
LD Services Contact: Ms. Ann DeGennaro, Coordinator, The College of New Jersey, Suite 159, Community Commons, Trenton, NJ 08650-4700, 609-771-2571. Fax: 609-771-3379. Email: degennar@tcnj.edu.

COLLEGE OF NEW ROCHELLE

New Rochelle, New York

LEARNING DISABILITIES SERVICES INFORMATION

Learning Support Services currently serves 20 undergraduates with LD. Services are also available to graduate students. Students diagnosed with ADD/ADHD are eligible for the same services available to students with LD.

Staff: 2 full-time, 20 part-time staff members, including director, assistant director. Services provided by tutors.

Special Fees: No special fees are charged for services to students with LD.

Applications and admissions: *Required:* high school transcript, untimed SAT I or ACT, essay, recommendations and personal interview (for some programs); *recommended:* extended time SAT I or ACT. Students may begin taking classes any term. *Application deadline:* continuous.

PROGRAM AND SERVICE COMPONENTS

Academic advising: Provided by unit staff members, academic advisers. Students with LD required to take 12 credits to maintain full-time status and be eligible for financial aid.

Counseling services: Individual counseling, career counseling.

Basic skills remediation: Offered one-on-one, in small groups, and in class-size groups by regular teachers, teacher trainees. Available in reading, math, spoken language, written language, learning strategies, study skills, time management, social skills.

Subject-area tutoring: Offered one-on-one, in small groups, and in class-size groups by professional teachers, peer tutors. Available in most subjects.

Special courses: College survival skills, reading, composition, learning strategies, word processing, time management, math, study skills, career planning. Some offered for credit; some enter into overall grade point average.

Auxiliary aids: Taped textbooks, tape recorders, calculators, word-processors with spell-check.

Auxiliary services: Alternative test arrangements, notetakers.

GENERAL COLLEGE INFORMATION

Independent, comprehensive, primarily women. Awards bachelor's, master's degrees. Founded 1904. *Setting:* 20-acre suburban campus with easy access to New York City. *Endowment:* $8.8 million. *Total enrollment:* 2,698. *Faculty:* 219 (71 full-time, 80% with terminal degrees, 148 part-time).

Enrollment Profile: 1,116 students from 13 states and territories, 4 other countries. 97% women, 3% men, 36% part-time, 90% state residents, 58% live on campus, 14% transferred in, 1% international, 13% 25 or older, 1% Native American, 18% Hispanic, 32% black, 6% Asian or Pacific Islander. *Retention:* 70% of 1995 full-time freshmen returned. *Graduation:* 9% graduate in 4 years, 26% in 5 years, 30% in 6 years. *Areas of study chosen:* 65% health professions and related sciences, 7% psychology, 6% communications and journalism, 5% social sciences, 4% fine arts, 3% biological and life sciences, 3% business management and administrative services, 2% English language/literature/letters, 1% education, 1% foreign language and literature, 1% interdisciplinary studies, 1% mathematics, 1% physical sciences. *Most popular recent majors:* psychology, communication, art/fine arts.

First-Year Class: 167 total; 742 applied, 65% were accepted, 35% of whom enrolled. 23% from top 10% of their high school class, 48% from top quarter, 85% from top half.

Graduation Requirements: 120 credits; 6 credits of math/science; computer course for business, education, math, physics, psychology, social work majors; senior project for honors program students and some majors.

Computers on Campus: 72 computers available on campus for general student use. Computer purchase/lease plans available. Computers for student use in computer center, classrooms. *Academic computing expenditure 1995–96:* $207,544.

EXPENSES AND FINANCIAL AID

Expenses for 1997–98: *Application fee:* $20. Comprehensive fee of $16,800 includes full-time tuition ($11,000), mandatory fees ($100), and college room and board ($5700). Part-time tuition: $370 per credit. Part-time mandatory fees: $50 per year.

Undergraduate Financial Aid: On average, 100% of need was met. *Financial aid deadline (priority):* 9/1. *Financial aid forms:* FAFSA, state form, institutional form, federal income tax form required; state income tax form required for some; CSS Financial Aid PROFILE acceptable.

Financial aid specifically for students with LD: Scholarships.

LD Services Contact: Ms. Joan Bristol, Vice President for Student Services, College of New Rochelle, 29 Castle Place, New Rochelle, NY 10805-2308, 914-654-5364.

COLLEGE OF ST. CATHERINE

St. Paul, Minnesota

LEARNING DISABILITIES SERVICES INFORMATION

Services for Students with Disabilities, O'Neill Center for Academic Development began offering services in 1986. Currently the program serves 45 undergraduates with LD. Services are also available to graduate students. Students diagnosed with ADD/ADHD are eligible for the same services available to students with LD.

Staff: 2 part-time staff members, including assistant director, coordinator.

Special Fees: $300 for diagnostic testing.

Applications and admissions: *Required:* high school transcript, grade point average, untimed SAT I; *recommended:* letters of recommendation. Students may begin taking classes any term. *Application deadline:* continuous.

PROGRAM AND SERVICE COMPONENTS

Special preparation or orientation: Orientation offered before classes begin in the Fall.

Diagnostic testing: Intelligence, reading, math, spelling, written language, perceptual skills.

Academic advising: Provided by academic advisers. Most students with LD take 12 to 16 credits each term; 12 credits required to maintain full-time status; source of aid determines number of credits required to be eligible for financial aid.

Basic skills remediation: Offered one-on-one by Disabilities staff. Available in study skills, time management.

Auxiliary aids: Taped textbooks, tape recorders, word-processors with spell-check, optical character readers.

Auxiliary services: Alternative test arrangements, notetakers, priority registration.

GENERAL COLLEGE INFORMATION

Independent Roman Catholic, comprehensive, women only. Awards bachelor's, master's degrees. Founded 1905. *Setting:* 110-acre urban campus. *Endowment:* $28.6 million. *Research spending 1995–96:* $121,305. *Educational spending 1995–96:* $4168 per undergrad. *Total enrollment:* 2,695. *Undergraduate faculty:* 161 (120 full-time, 83% with terminal degrees, 41 part-time); student–undergrad faculty ratio is 14:1.

Enrollment Profile: 2,248 students from 18 states and territories, 9 other countries. 100% women, 24% part-time, 85% state residents, 58% transferred in, 2% international, 43% 25 or older, 1% Native American, 2% Hispanic, 2% black, 4% Asian or Pacific Islander. *Retention:* 79% of 1995 full-time freshmen returned. *Graduation:* 32% graduate in 4 years, 45% in 5 years, 56% in 6 years. *Areas of study chosen:* 37% health professions and related sciences, 12% education, 10% business management and administrative services, 5% communications and journalism, 5% English language/literature/letters, 5% social sciences, 4% biological and life sciences, 4% psychology, 3% vocational and home economics, 2% computer and information sciences, 2% fine arts, 2% library and information studies, 1% foreign language and literature, 1% interdisciplinary studies, 1% liberal arts/general studies, 1% mathematics, 1% philosophy, 1% theology/religion. *Most popular recent majors:* business administration/commerce/management, nursing, occupational therapy.

First-Year Class: 216 total; 612 applied, 90% were accepted, 39% of whom enrolled. 21% from top 10% of their high school class, 80% from top half. 3 valedictorians.

Graduation Requirements: 32 courses; 2 math/science courses; 4 semesters of a foreign language or the equivalent; computer course; senior project for honors program students and some majors.

Computers on Campus: 350 computers available on campus for general student use. Computer purchase/lease plans available. A campus-wide network can be accessed from student residence rooms and from off-campus. Students can contact faculty members and/or advisers through e-mail. Computers for student use in computer center, learning resource center, classrooms, library, student center, dorms provide access to the Internet/World Wide Web. Staffed computer lab on campus provides training in use of computers, software. *Academic computing expenditure 1995–96:* $485,000.

EXPENSES AND FINANCIAL AID

Expenses for 1996–97: *Application fee:* $20. Comprehensive fee of $18,284 includes full-time tuition ($13,472), mandatory fees ($230), and college room and board ($4582). College room only: $2590. Part-time tuition: $421 per credit. Part-time mandatory fees: $115 per term.
Undergraduate Financial Aid: 86% of all full-time undergraduates enrolled in fall 1996 applied for aid; of these, 88% were judged to have need according to Federal Methodology, of whom 100% were aided. On average, 100% of need was met. *Financial aid deadline (priority):* 4/1. *Financial aid forms:* FAFSA, institutional form required.
LD Services Contact: Ms. Elaine McDonough, Assistant Director, O'Neill Center, College of St. Catherine, Mail #4152, 2004 Randolph Avenue, St. Paul, MN 55105, 612-690-6563. Fax: 612-690-6718. Email: emmcdonough@stkate.edu.

COLLEGE OF ST. CATHERINE–MINNEAPOLIS

Minneapolis, Minnesota

LEARNING DISABILITIES SERVICES INFORMATION

Learning Center began offering services in 1989. Currently the program serves 30 undergraduates with LD. Services are also available to graduate students. Students diagnosed with ADD/ADHD are eligible for the same services available to students with LD.
Staff: 3 full-time, 1 part-time staff members, including director, coordinator, Disabilities/Learning Specialist, Study Skills/Writing Specialist and Tutor Coordinator, Testing and Alternate Format Specialist. Services provided by tutors.
Special Fees: No special fees are charged for services to students with LD.
Applications and admissions: *Required:* high school transcript, letters of recommendation, essay; *recommended:* psychoeducational report completed within 5 to 7 years. Students may begin taking classes any term. *Application deadline:* continuous.

PROGRAM AND SERVICE COMPONENTS

Special preparation or orientation: Optional summer program offered prior to entering college. Optional orientation offered individually by special arrangement.
Academic advising: Provided by unit staff members, academic advisers. Most students with LD take 8 to 12 semester credits each term; 6 semester credits required to maintain full-time status and be eligible for financial aid.
Counseling services: Individual counseling, small-group counseling, self-advocacy training.
Basic skills remediation: Offered one-on-one and in small groups by LD teachers, teacher trainees, study skills specialist, peer tutors; computer-aided instruction also offered. Available in reading, math, spelling, written language, learning strategies, study skills, time management.
Subject-area tutoring: Offered one-on-one and in small groups by professional teachers, peer tutors. Available in all subjects.
Auxiliary aids: Taped textbooks, tape recorders, word-processors with spell-check, assistive listening device for Auditory Processing Disorder and Attention Deficit Disorder.
Auxiliary services: Alternative test arrangements, notetakers, priority registration, advocacy.
Campus support group: A special student organization is available to students with LD.

GENERAL COLLEGE INFORMATION

Independent Roman Catholic, 2-year, coed. Administratively affiliated with College of St. Catherine. Awards associate, master's degrees. Founded 1964. *Setting:* 1-acre urban campus. *Total enrollment:* 1,237. *Undergraduate faculty:* 116 (51 full-time, 85% with terminal degrees, 65 part-time).
Enrollment Profile: 1,115 students from 16 states and territories. 88% women, 12% men, 78% part-time, 94% state residents, 7% live on campus, 84% transferred in, 0% international, 64% 25 or older, 1% Native American, 2% Hispanic, 7% black, 2% Asian or Pacific Islander. *Retention:* 74% of 1995 full-time freshmen returned. *Areas of study chosen:* 96% health professions and related sciences, 3% liberal arts/general studies, 1% education. *Most popular recent majors:* nursing, physical therapy.
First-Year Class: 528 total; 876 applied, 86% were accepted, 70% of whom enrolled.
Graduation Requirements: 60 semester credits; math/science requirements vary according to program; computer course; internship (some majors).
Computers on Campus: 40 computers available on campus for general student use. Computer purchase/lease plans available. A campus-wide network can be accessed from student residence rooms and from off-campus. Students can contact faculty members and/or advisers through e-mail. Computers for student use in computer center, computer labs, learning resource center, library, dorms provide access to the Internet/World Wide Web, on- and off-campus e-mail addresses. Staffed computer lab on campus provides training in use of computers, software. *Academic computing expenditure 1995–96:* $57,000.

EXPENSES AND FINANCIAL AID

Expenses for 1997–98: *Application fee:* $20. Tuition: $10,200 full-time, $340 per credit part-time. College room only: $1600.
Undergraduate Financial Aid: *Financial aid deadline (priority):* 6/1. *Financial aid forms:* FAFSA, institutional form required; CSS Financial Aid PROFILE acceptable.
LD Services Contact: Ms. Kathleen Whaley, Disabilities/Learning Specialist, College of St. Catherine–Minneapolis, 601 25th Avenue South, Minneapolis, MN 55454, 612-690-7848. Fax: 612-690-7849.

COLLEGE OF ST. JOSEPH

Rutland, Vermont

LEARNING DISABILITIES SERVICES INFORMATION

Project Success began offering services in 1990. Currently the program serves 25 undergraduates with LD. Students diagnosed with ADD/ADHD are eligible for the same services available to students with LD.
Staff: 4 full-time, 3 part-time staff members, including director. Services provided by remediation specialists, tutors, counselors, Evening Learning Center Coordinator.
Special Fees: No special fees are charged for services to students with LD.
Applications and admissions: *Required:* high school transcript, grade point average, class rank, IEP (Individualized Education Program), letters of recommendation, SAT I (untimed) or extended time ACT; *recommended:* personal interview, psychoeducational report. Students may begin taking classes in fall, spring, or summer. *Application deadline:* continuous.

PROGRAM AND SERVICE COMPONENTS

Special preparation or orientation: Orientation (required for some) held before registration.
Diagnostic testing: Intelligence, reading, written language, study skills, personality, social skills, learning strategies.
Academic advising: Provided by academic advisers. Students with LD may take up to 17 credits each term; most take 12 to 15 credits; 12 credits required to maintain full-time status; 6 credits (half-time) required to be eligible for financial aid.

GENERAL COLLEGE INFORMATION

Independent Roman Catholic, comprehensive, coed. Awards associate, bachelor's, master's degrees. Founded 1954. *Setting:* 99-acre small-town campus. *Endowment:* $300,000. *Total enrollment:* 478. *Undergraduate faculty:* 61 (13 full-time, 65% with terminal degrees, 48 part-time); student–undergrad faculty ratio is 11:1.
Enrollment Profile: 353 students from 12 states and territories, 3 other countries. 66% women, 34% men, 39% part-time, 66% state residents, 8% transferred in, 2% international, 40% 25 or older, 1% Native American, 1% Hispanic, 2% black, 1% Asian or Pacific Islander. *Retention:* 85% of 1995 full-time freshmen returned. *Graduation:* 42% graduate in 4 years, 49% in 5 years, 51% in 6 years. *Areas of study chosen:* 30% education, 21% business management and administrative services, 21% psychology, 7% computer and information sciences, 7% social sciences, 5% English language/literature/letters, 3% communications and journalism, 3% prelaw, 2% liberal arts/general studies, 1% interdisciplinary studies.
First-Year Class: 70 total; 149 applied, 93% were accepted, 51% of whom enrolled. 2% from top 10% of their high school class, 10% from top quarter, 40% from top half. 3 class presidents, 1 valedictorian.
Graduation Requirements: 60 credits for associate, 127 credits for bachelor's; 6 credits each of math and science; computer course; internship (some majors); senior project (some majors).

Computers on Campus: 35 computers available on campus for general student use. Computers for student use in computer center, learning resource center, library. Staffed computer lab on campus provides training in use of computers, software.

EXPENSES AND FINANCIAL AID

Estimated Expenses for 1997–98: *Application fee:* $25. Comprehensive fee of $15,900 includes full-time tuition ($10,000), mandatory fees ($100), and college room and board ($5800). Part-time tuition: $170 per credit.
Undergraduate Financial Aid: On average, 87% of need was met. *Financial aid deadline (priority):* 3/1. *Financial aid forms:* FAFSA required; CSS Financial Aid PROFILE acceptable.
LD Services Contact: Mr. William Lucci Jr., Director of Student Support Services, College of St. Joseph, 71 Clement Road, Rutland, VT 05701-3899, 802-773-5900 Ext. 260. Fax: 802-773-5900 Ext. 258.

COLLEGE OF ST. SCHOLASTICA

Duluth, Minnesota

LEARNING DISABILITIES SERVICES INFORMATION

Academic Support Services began offering services in 1985. Currently the program serves 15 undergraduates with LD. Students diagnosed with ADD/ADHD are eligible for the same services available to students with LD.
Staff: 1 part-time staff member (director). Services provided by tutors.
Special Fees: No special fees are charged for services to students with LD.
Applications and admissions: *Required:* high school transcript, class rank, untimed ACT; *recommended:* autobiographical statement, letters of recommendation. Students may begin taking classes in fall, winter, or spring. *Application deadline:* continuous.
Special policies: The college has written policies regarding substitutions and waivers of admissions, graduation, and degree requirements.

PROGRAM AND SERVICE COMPONENTS

Diagnostic testing: Intelligence, reading, math, written language, study skills, personality, learning strategies.
Academic advising: Provided by academic advisers. Students with LD may take up to 18 credits each term; most take 16 credits; 12 credits required to maintain full-time status; 15 credits (full-time) required to be eligible for financial aid.
Counseling services: Individual counseling, small-group counseling, career counseling, self-advocacy training.
Subject-area tutoring: Offered one-on-one and in small groups by peer tutors. Available in most subjects.
Auxiliary aids: Taped textbooks, tape recorders, word-processors with spell-check, Arkenstone Reader.
Auxiliary services: Alternative test arrangements, notetakers, priority registration, advocacy.

GENERAL COLLEGE INFORMATION

Independent, comprehensive, coed, affiliated with Roman Catholic Church. Awards bachelor's, master's degrees. Founded 1912. *Setting:* 160-acre suburban campus. *Endowment:* $12 million. *Educational spending 1995–96:* $5597 per undergrad. *Total enrollment:* 2,101. *Faculty:* 160 (122 full-time, 72% with terminal degrees, 38 part-time); student–undergrad faculty ratio is 13:1.
Enrollment Profile: 1,474 students from 19 states and territories, 6 other countries. 74% women, 26% men, 9% part-time, 88% state residents, 44% live on campus, 10% transferred in, 1% international, 19% 25 or older, 2% Native American, 1% Hispanic, 1% black, 1% Asian or Pacific Islander. *Retention:* 77% of 1995 full-time freshmen returned. *Graduation:* 49% graduate in 4 years. *Areas of study chosen:* 56% health professions and related sciences, 11% business management and administrative services, 7% education, 6% biological and life sciences, 4% psychology, 3% communications and journalism, 3% English language/literature/letters, 2% computer and information sciences, 2% social sciences, 2% vocational and home economics, 1% interdisciplinary studies, 1% liberal arts/general studies, 1% mathematics, 1% theology/religion. *Most popular recent majors:* nursing, business administration/commerce/management, health services administration.
First-Year Class: 292 total; 777 applied, 92% were accepted, 41% of whom enrolled. 30% from top 10% of their high school class, 64% from top quarter, 94% from top half.
Graduation Requirements: 192 credits; 4 credits of math; 8 credits of science; 3 years of a foreign language in high school or 8 credits in college; computer course for management, health services administration majors; internship (some majors); senior project (some majors).
Computers on Campus: 100 computers available on campus for general student use. A campus-wide network can be accessed from off-campus. Students can contact faculty members and/or advisers through e-mail. Computers for student use in computer labs, classrooms, library, dorms provide access to the Internet/World Wide Web. Staffed computer lab on campus provides training in use of computers, software. *Academic computing expenditure 1995–96:* $843,190.

EXPENSES AND FINANCIAL AID

Expenses for 1997–98: *Application fee:* $25. Comprehensive fee of $17,952 includes full-time tuition ($13,905), mandatory fees ($90), and college room and board ($3957). Part-time tuition: $290 per credit. Part-time mandatory fees per quarter (9 to 11 credits): $30.
Undergraduate Financial Aid: 86% of all full-time undergraduates enrolled in fall 1996 applied for aid; of these, 97% were judged to have need according to Federal Methodology, of whom 100% were aided. On average, 87% of need was met. *Financial aid deadline (priority):* 3/15. *Financial aid forms:* state form required; CSS Financial Aid PROFILE acceptable. FAFSA, institutional form required for some.
LD Services Contact: Mr. Jay Newcomb, Director, Academic Support Services, College of St. Scholastica, 1200 Kenwood Avenue, Duluth, MN 55811, 218-723-6552.

COLLEGE OF SANTA FE

Santa Fe, New Mexico

LEARNING DISABILITIES SERVICES INFORMATION

Center for Academic Excellence began offering services in 1988. Currently the program serves 22 undergraduates with LD. Services are also available to graduate students. Students diagnosed with ADD/ADHD are eligible for the same services available to students with LD.
Staff: 4 full-time, 3 part-time staff members, including director, secretary. Services provided by remediation specialists, Academic Support Coordinator, peer tutors.
Special Fees: No special fees are charged for services to students with LD.
Applications and admissions: *Required:* high school transcript, grade point average, courses completed, autobiographical statement, letters of recommendation; *recommended:* high school class rank, extracurricular activities, IEP (Individualized Education Program), untimed or extended time SAT I or ACT, personal interview, psychoeducational report completed within 3 years, campus visit. Students may begin taking classes in fall, spring, or summer. *Application deadline:* continuous.

PROGRAM AND SERVICE COMPONENTS

Academic advising: Provided by unit staff members, academic advisers. Students with LD may take up to 18 semester hours (more with Dean's approval) each term; most take 12 to 18 semester hours; 12 semester hours required to maintain full-time status; 6 semester hours required to be eligible for financial aid.
Counseling services: Individual counseling, small-group counseling, career counseling.
Basic skills remediation: Offered one-on-one and in small groups by professional staff; computer-aided instruction also offered. Available in reading, math, spelling, written language, learning strategies, study skills, time management, computer skills.
Subject-area tutoring: Offered one-on-one, in small groups, and in class-size groups by peer tutors, professional staff. Available in most subjects.
Auxiliary aids: Taped textbooks, tape recorders, calculators, talking computers, optical character readers.
Auxiliary services: Alternative test arrangements, notetakers, priority registration, advocacy.

GENERAL COLLEGE INFORMATION

Independent, comprehensive, coed. Awards associate, bachelor's, master's degrees. Founded 1947. *Setting:* 98-acre suburban campus with easy access to Albuquerque. *Endowment:* $5.8 million. *Educational*

spending 1995–96: $2547 per undergrad. *Total enrollment:* 1,469. *Undergraduate faculty:* 178 (60 full-time, 75% with terminal degrees, 118 part-time); student–undergrad faculty ratio is 14:1.
Enrollment Profile: 1,290 students from 42 states and territories, 5 other countries. 64% women, 36% men, 35% part-time, 70% state residents, 30% live on campus, 50% transferred in, 2% international, 17% 25 or older, 3% Native American, 27% Hispanic, 3% black, 1% Asian or Pacific Islander. *Retention:* 77% of 1995 full-time freshmen returned. *Graduation:* 53% graduate in 4 years, 60% in 5 years, 62% in 6 years. *Areas of study chosen:* 21% business management and administrative services, 15% education, 14% performing arts, 13% fine arts, 8% communications and journalism, 5% psychology, 4% biological and life sciences, 4% natural resource sciences, 3% prelaw, 3% social sciences, 2% English language/literature/letters, 2% liberal arts/general studies, 2% premed, 2% prevet, 1% computer and information sciences, 1% theology/religion. *Most popular recent majors:* film and video production, education, business administration/commerce/management.
First-Year Class: 165 total; 532 applied, 80% were accepted, 39% of whom enrolled. 17% from top 10% of their high school class, 42% from top quarter, 75% from top half. 2 valedictorians.
Graduation Requirements: 64 semester hours for associate, 128 semester hours for bachelor's; 8 semester hours of math and science; computer course for business administration, accounting, education majors; internship (some majors); senior project (some majors).
Computers on Campus: 25 computers available on campus for general student use. A computer is recommended for some students. Students can contact faculty members and/or advisers through e-mail. Computers for student use in computer center, computer labs, learning resource center, library provide access to the Internet/World Wide Web, on- and off-campus e-mail addresses. Staffed computer lab on campus provides training in use of computers, software. *Academic computing expenditure 1995–96:* $266,461.

EXPENSES AND FINANCIAL AID

Expenses for 1997–98: *Application fee:* $25. Comprehensive fee of $17,964 includes full-time tuition ($13,000), mandatory fees ($240), and college room and board ($4724). College room only: $2308. Part-time tuition: $433 per semester hour.
Undergraduate Financial Aid: 85% of all full-time undergraduates enrolled in fall 1996 applied for aid; of these, 86% were judged to have need according to Federal Methodology, of whom 100% were aided. On average, 78% of need was met. *Financial aid deadline (priority):* 3/1. *Financial aid forms:* FAFSA, institutional form, federal verification worksheet and tax returns required; CSS Financial Aid PROFILE acceptable.
LD Services Contact: Dr. Madelyn P. Pressley, Director, Center for Academic Excellence, College of Santa Fe, 1600 St. Michael's Drive, Santa Fe, NM 87505-7615, 505-473-6112. Fax: 505-473-6124. Email: pressley@fogelson.csf.edu.

COLLEGE OF STATEN ISLAND OF THE CITY UNIVERSITY OF NEW YORK

Staten Island, New York

LEARNING DISABILITIES SERVICES INFORMATION

Special Student Services began offering services in 1980. Currently the program serves 87 undergraduates with LD. Services are also available to graduate students. Students diagnosed with ADD/ADHD are eligible for the same services available to students with LD.
Staff: 2 full-time, 1 part-time staff members, including director, assistant director. Services provided by tutors.
Special Fees: No special fees are charged for services to students with LD.
Applications and admissions: *Required:* documentation of learning disability (test results, evaluation results, resource room referral). Students may begin taking classes any term. *Application deadline:* 3/15.

PROGRAM AND SERVICE COMPONENTS

Special preparation or orientation: Optional orientation offered before registration and after classes begin.
Academic advising: Provided by unit staff members. Most students with LD take 8 to 12 credits each term; 12 credits required to maintain full-time status; 6 credits (for part-time), 12 credits (for full-time) required to be eligible for financial aid.
Counseling services: Individual counseling, small-group counseling.
Basic skills remediation: Offered one-on-one by peer teachers, local retired teachers; computer-aided instruction also offered. Available in reading, math, spelling, learning strategies, study skills, time management, social skills.
Subject-area tutoring: Offered one-on-one and in small groups by peer tutors. Available in most subjects.
Auxiliary aids: Taped textbooks, tape recorders, calculators, typewriters, word-processors with spell-check, personal computers, talking computers, optical character readers.
Auxiliary services: Alternative test arrangements, notetakers, priority registration, advocacy.

GENERAL COLLEGE INFORMATION

State and locally supported, comprehensive, coed. Part of City University of New York System. Awards associate, bachelor's, master's degrees. Founded 1955. *Setting:* 204-acre urban campus. *Research spending 1995–96:* $45,000. *Educational spending 1995–96:* $4244 per undergrad. *Total enrollment:* 12,208. *Faculty:* 765 (257 full-time, 80% with terminal degrees, 508 part-time); student–undergrad faculty ratio is 23:1.
Enrollment Profile: 10,709 students from 6 states and territories, 93 other countries. 60% women, 40% men, 46% part-time, 95% state residents, 5% transferred in, 4% international, 47% 25 or older, 1% Native American, 8% Hispanic, 9% black, 7% Asian or Pacific Islander. *Retention:* 68% of 1995 full-time freshmen returned. *Most popular recent majors:* business administration/commerce/management, psychology.
First-Year Class: 1,816 total; 3,527 applied, 100% were accepted, 51% of whom enrolled.
Graduation Requirements: 60 semester hours for associate, 120 semester hours for bachelor's; 1 math course; 11 semester hours of science; computer course for science, engineering majors.
Computers on Campus: 750 computers available on campus for general student use. A campus-wide network can be accessed from off-campus. Students can contact faculty members and/or advisers through e-mail. Computers for student use in computer center, computer labs, learning resource center, library provide access to the Internet/World Wide Web, on-campus e-mail addresses. Staffed computer lab on campus (open 24 hours a day) provides training in use of computers, software. *Academic computing expenditure 1995–96:* $445,781.

EXPENSES AND FINANCIAL AID

Expenses for 1996–97: State resident tuition: $3200 full-time, $135 per semester hour part-time. Nonresident tuition: $6800 full-time, $285 per semester hour part-time. Part-time mandatory fees: $32 per semester. Full-time mandatory fees: $116.
Undergraduate Financial Aid: *Financial aid deadline (priority):* 5/29. *Financial aid forms:* FAFSA required.
LD Services Contact: Dr. Audrey Glynn, Director, Special Student Services, College of Staten Island of the City University of New York, 2800 Victory Boulevard, Staten Island, NY 10314-6600, 718-982-2510. Fax: 718-982-2117. Email: glynn@postbox.csi.cuny.edu.

COLLEGE OF WILLIAM AND MARY

Williamsburg, Virginia

LEARNING DISABILITIES SERVICES INFORMATION

Disabled Student Services began offering services in 1983. Currently the program serves 100 undergraduates with LD. Services are also available to graduate students. Students diagnosed with ADD/ADHD are eligible for the same services available to students with LD.
Staff: 1 full-time staff member (director). Services provided by tutors, counselors, diagnostic specialists, study skills specialist, student assistants.
Special Fees: No special fees are charged for services to students with LD.
Applications and admissions: *Required:* high school transcript, grade point average, class rank, courses completed, extracurricular activities, untimed SAT I, autobiographical statement, letters of recommendation; *recommended:* untimed or extended time ACT, extended time SAT I, psychoeducational report completed within 3 years. Students may begin taking classes in fall or spring. *Application deadline:* 1/15.
Special policies: The college has written policies regarding substitutions and waivers of graduation and degree requirements.

PROGRAM AND SERVICE COMPONENTS

Diagnostic testing: Intelligence, reading, math, spelling, written language, motor abilities, perceptual skills, study skills, personality, learning strategies.

College of William and Mary (continued)

Academic advising: Provided by unit staff members, academic advisers. Students with LD may take up to 18 credit hours each term; most take 15 credit hours; 12 credit hours required to maintain full-time status; 6 credit hours required to be eligible for financial aid.

Counseling services: Individual counseling, small-group counseling, career counseling, self-advocacy training.

Basic skills remediation: Offered one-on-one and in small groups by study skills specialist. Available in learning strategies, study skills, time management.

Subject-area tutoring: Offered one-on-one by peer tutors. Available in all subjects.

Auxiliary aids: Taped textbooks, tape recorders, calculators, typewriters, word-processors with spell-check, personal computers, talking computers, optical character readers, adapted computer software and hardware.

Auxiliary services: Alternative test arrangements, notetakers, priority registration, advocacy.

GENERAL COLLEGE INFORMATION

State-supported, coed. Awards bachelor's, master's, doctoral, first professional degrees. Founded 1693. *Setting:* 1,200-acre small-town campus with easy access to Richmond. *Endowment:* $124.8 million. *Research spending 1995–96:* $10.2 million. *Total enrollment:* 7,722. *Faculty:* 696 (575 full-time, 92% with terminal degrees, 121 part-time); student–undergrad faculty ratio is 10:1.

Enrollment Profile: 5,618 students from 50 states and territories, 47 other countries. 59% women, 41% men, 3% part-time, 66% state residents, 77% live on campus, 3% transferred in, 2% international, 3% 25 or older, 1% Native American, 2% Hispanic, 7% black, 7% Asian or Pacific Islander. *Retention:* 96% of 1995 full-time freshmen returned. *Graduation:* 78% graduate in 4 years, 88% in 5 years, 89% in 6 years. *Areas of study chosen:* 19% liberal arts/general studies, 12% biological and life sciences, 10% English language/literature/letters, 9% psychology, 8% social sciences, 7% physical sciences, 5% area and ethnic studies, 3% computer and information sciences, 2% fine arts, 2% foreign language and literature, 2% interdisciplinary studies, 2% mathematics, 2% performing arts, 2% philosophy, 1% theology/religion. *Most popular recent majors:* business administration/commerce/management, biology/biological sciences, English.

First-Year Class: 1,333 total; 6,733 applied, 48% were accepted, 41% of whom enrolled. 74% from top 10% of their high school class, 95% from top quarter, 99% from top half. 25 National Merit Scholars, 23 class presidents, 75 valedictorians.

Graduation Requirements: 120 credit hours; 3 math/science courses including at least 1 lab science course; 4 years of a foreign language in high school or 4 semesters in college; computer course for business, math majors; senior project for honors program students and some majors.

Computers on Campus: 300 computers available on campus for general student use. Computer purchase/lease plans available. A computer is recommended for all students. A campus-wide network can be accessed from student residence rooms and from off-campus. Students can contact faculty members and/or advisers through e-mail. Computers for student use in computer labs, library, dorms, academic buildings provide access to the Internet/World Wide Web, on- and off-campus e-mail addresses. Staffed computer lab on campus (open 24 hours a day) provides training in use of computers, software. *Academic computing expenditure 1995–96:* $1.1 million.

EXPENSES AND FINANCIAL AID

Expenses for 1997–98: *Application fee:* $40. State resident tuition: $2890 full-time, $153 per credit hour part-time. Nonresident tuition: $13,262 full-time, $480 per credit hour part-time. Full-time mandatory fees: $2142. College room and board: $4586. College room only: $2606.

Undergraduate Financial Aid: 47% of all full-time undergraduates enrolled in fall 1996 applied for aid; of these, 65% were judged to have need according to Federal Methodology, of whom 100% were aided. On average, 85% of need was met. *Financial aid deadline (priority):* 2/15. *Financial aid forms:* FAFSA required.

LD Services Contact: Lisa Bickley, Assistant Dean of Students, College of William and Mary, Room 109, Campus Center, Williamsburg, VA 23187-8795, 757-221-2510. Fax: 757-221-2538.

COLORADO SCHOOL OF MINES

Golden, Colorado

LEARNING DISABILITIES SERVICES INFORMATION

Student Support Services began offering services in 1994. Currently the program serves 12 undergraduates with LD. Students diagnosed with ADD/ADHD are eligible for the same services available to students with LD.

Staff: 3 full-time staff members, including director, coordinator. Services provided by tutors, counselors, interpreters/signers.

Special Fees: No special fees are charged for services to students with LD.

Applications and admissions: *Required:* high school transcript, grade point average, class rank, courses completed, untimed SAT I or ACT; *recommended:* extended time SAT I or ACT, letters of recommendation, psychoeducational report.

Special policies: The college has written policies regarding substitutions and waivers of graduation and degree requirements.

PROGRAM AND SERVICE COMPONENTS

Academic advising: Provided by academic advisers. Students with LD may take up to 21 semester hours each term; most take 12 to 15 semester hours; 12 semester hours required to maintain full-time status and be eligible for financial aid.

Counseling services: Individual counseling, small-group counseling, career counseling.

Subject-area tutoring: Offered one-on-one, in small groups, and in class-size groups by peer tutors. Available in most subjects.

Special courses: College survival skills, reading, learning strategies, time management, math, study skills, career planning, stress management. None offered for credit.

Auxiliary aids: Taped textbooks, tape recorders, word-processors with spell-check, personal computers.

Auxiliary services: Alternative test arrangements, notetakers, priority registration.

GENERAL COLLEGE INFORMATION

State-supported, coed. Awards bachelor's, master's, doctoral degrees. Founded 1874. *Setting:* 307-acre small-town campus with easy access to Denver. *Endowment:* $49.1 million. *Research spending 1995–96:* $20.1 million. *Educational spending 1995–96:* $11,670 per undergrad. *Total enrollment:* 3,203. *Faculty:* 290 (200 full-time, 95% with terminal degrees, 90 part-time); student–undergrad faculty ratio is 14:1.

Enrollment Profile: 2,353 students from 51 states and territories, 96 other countries. 24% women, 76% men, 3% part-time, 69% state residents, 35% live on campus, 20% transferred in, 5% international, 2% 25 or older, 1% Native American, 7% Hispanic, 1% black, 5% Asian or Pacific Islander. *Retention:* 85% of 1995 full-time freshmen returned. *Areas of study chosen:* 87% engineering and applied sciences, 6% mathematics, 6% physical sciences, 1% business management and administrative services. *Most popular recent majors:* engineering (general), chemical engineering, computer science.

First-Year Class: 557 total; 1,712 applied, 87% were accepted, 37% of whom enrolled. 52% from top 10% of their high school class, 84% from top quarter, 100% from top half.

Graduation Requirements: 137 semester hours; 2 years of calculus; 1.5 years of chemistry; computer course; senior project.

Computers on Campus: 250 computers available on campus for general student use. A campus-wide network can be accessed from student residence rooms and from off-campus. Students can contact faculty members and/or advisers through e-mail. Computers for student use in computer center, computer labs, research center, library, student center, dorms, academic buildings provide access to the Internet/World Wide Web, on- and off-campus e-mail addresses. Staffed computer lab on campus provides training in use of computers, software. *Academic computing expenditure 1995–96:* $1.3 million.

EXPENSES AND FINANCIAL AID

Estimated Expenses for 1997–98: *Application fee:* $25. State resident tuition: $4494 full-time, $150 per semester hour part-time. Nonresident tuition: $13,980 full-time, $466 per semester hour part-time. Full-time mandatory fees: $575. College room and board: $4730.

Undergraduate Financial Aid: 77% of all full-time undergraduates enrolled in fall 1996 applied for aid; of these, 94% were judged to have need according to Federal Methodology, of whom 100% were aided. On

average, 100% of need was met. *Financial aid deadline (priority):* 3/1. *Financial aid forms:* FAFSA, institutional form required.
LD Services Contact: Mr. Harold Cheuvront, Vice President of Student Life/Dean of Students, Colorado School of Mines, 1500 Illinois Street, Golden, CO 80401, 303-273-3357. Email: hcheuvro@mines.edu.

COLORADO STATE UNIVERSITY

Fort Collins, Colorado

LEARNING DISABILITIES SERVICES INFORMATION

Resources for Disabled Students began offering services in 1980. Currently the program serves 600 undergraduates with LD. Services are also available to graduate students. Students diagnosed with ADD/ADHD are eligible for the same services available to students with LD.
Staff: 3 full-time, 7 part-time staff members, including director, assistant director, coordinator. Services provided by counselors, paraprofessional staff.
Special Fees: No special fees are charged for services to students with LD.
Applications and admissions: *Required:* high school transcript, grade point average, untimed SAT I or ACT, documentation of disability; *recommended:* extended time SAT I or ACT, personal interview, autobiographical statement, letters of recommendation. Students may begin taking classes in fall, spring, or summer. *Application deadline:* 7/1.

PROGRAM AND SERVICE COMPONENTS

Diagnostic testing: Intelligence, reading, math, spelling, written language, perceptual skills, study skills, personality, social skills, psychoneurology, speech, hearing.
Academic advising: Provided by unit staff members, academic advisers. Students with LD may take up to 16 credits each term; most take 9 to 15 credits; 12 credits required to maintain full-time status and be eligible for financial aid.
Counseling services: Individual counseling, small-group counseling, career counseling.
Subject-area tutoring: Offered one-on-one, in small groups, and in class-size groups by peer tutors. Available in most subjects.
Auxiliary aids: Taped textbooks, tape recorders, calculators, typewriters, word-processors with spell-check, optical character readers.
Auxiliary services: Alternative test arrangements, notetakers, priority registration, advocacy.
Campus support group: A special student organization is available to students with LD.

GENERAL COLLEGE INFORMATION

State-supported, coed. Part of Colorado State University System. Awards bachelor's, master's, doctoral, first professional degrees. Founded 1870. *Setting:* 666-acre urban campus with easy access to Denver. *Endowment:* $41.7 million. *Research spending 1995–96:* $87.9 million. *Educational spending 1995–96:* $5740 per undergrad. *Total enrollment:* 21,970. *Faculty:* 1,004 (all full-time, 88% with terminal degrees); student–undergrad faculty ratio is 22:1.
Enrollment Profile: 18,451 students from 55 states and territories, 52 other countries. 51% women, 49% men, 12% part-time, 78% state residents, 25% live on campus, 9% transferred in, 1% international, 16% 25 or older, 1% Native American, 5% Hispanic, 2% black, 3% Asian or Pacific Islander. *Retention:* 83% of 1995 full-time freshmen returned. *Graduation:* 22% graduate in 4 years, 48% in 5 years, 54% in 6 years. *Areas of study chosen:* 9% biological and life sciences, 9% engineering and applied sciences, 8% business management and administrative services, 8% natural resource sciences, 8% social sciences, 7% agriculture, 7% health professions and related sciences, 4% psychology, 4% vocational and home economics, 3% communications and journalism, 3% computer and information sciences, 3% fine arts, 3% liberal arts/general studies, 2% English language/literature/letters, 2% physical sciences, 2% prevet, 1% architecture, 1% education, 1% foreign language and literature, 1% mathematics, 1% performing arts, 1% philosophy, 1% predentistry, 1% prelaw. *Most popular recent majors:* business administration/commerce/management, liberal arts/general studies, physical fitness/exercise science.
First-Year Class: 2,733 total; 9,628 applied, 77% were accepted, 37% of whom enrolled. 24% from top 10% of their high school class, 61% from top quarter, 93% from top half.
Graduation Requirements: 128 credits; 3 credits of math; 7 credits of science; computer course (varies by major); internship (some majors); senior project for honors program students and some majors.
Computers on Campus: 3,500 computers available on campus for general student use. Computer purchase/lease plans available. A computer is strongly recommended for all students. A campus-wide network can be accessed from student residence rooms and from off-campus. Students can contact faculty members and/or advisers through e-mail. Computers for student use in computer center, computer labs, research center, learning resource center, classrooms, library, student center, dorms, student rooms provide access to the Internet/World Wide Web, on- and off-campus e-mail addresses. Staffed computer lab on campus provides training in use of computers, software. *Academic computing expenditure 1995–96:* $3.5 million.

EXPENSES AND FINANCIAL AID

Expenses for 1996–97: *Application fee:* $30. State resident tuition: $2224 full-time, $93 per credit part-time. Nonresident tuition: $9160 full-time, $382 per credit part-time. Part-time mandatory fees per semester range from $27.15 to $135.75. Full-time mandatory fees: $631. College room and board: $4152 (minimum).
Undergraduate Financial Aid: Of all full-time undergraduates enrolled in fall 1996, 58% of those who applied for aid were judged to have need according to Federal Methodology, of whom 100% were aided. *Financial aid deadline (priority):* 3/1. *Financial aid forms:* FAFSA required; CSS Financial Aid PROFILE acceptable.
LD Services Contact: Ms. Kathleen Ivy, Counselor, Colorado State University, Fort Collins, CO 80523-8002, 970-491-6385. Fax: 970-491-3457.

COLUMBIA COLLEGE

Chicago, Illinois

LEARNING DISABILITIES SERVICES INFORMATION

Office of Academic Advising began offering services in 1990. Currently the program serves 50 undergraduates with LD. Services are also available to graduate students. Students diagnosed with ADD/ADHD are eligible for the same services available to students with LD.
Staff: 3 full-time, 3 part-time staff members, including director, Assistant Dean. Services provided by tutors, counselor.
Special Fees: No special fees are charged for services to students with LD.
Applications and admissions: *Required:* high school transcript, courses completed, psychoeducational report completed within 3 years, any other supportive documentation of the student's disability; *recommended:* high school grade point average, class rank. Students may begin taking classes in fall, spring, or summer. *Application deadline:* continuous.
Special policies: The college has written policies regarding substitutions and waivers of graduation and degree requirements.

PROGRAM AND SERVICE COMPONENTS

Special preparation or orientation: Optional orientation offered before registration.
Academic advising: Provided by academic advisers. Students with LD may take up to 16 credit hours each term; most take 12 credit hours; 12 credit hours required to maintain full-time status; 6 credit hours (part-time), 12 credit hours (full-time) required to be eligible for financial aid.
Counseling services: Individual counseling.
Subject-area tutoring: Offered one-on-one by professional teachers, peer tutors. Available in most subjects.
Special courses: College survival skills, reading, composition, learning strategies, time management, math, study skills. Some offered for credit; some enter into overall grade point average.
Auxiliary aids: Taped textbooks, word-processors with spell-check.
Auxiliary services: Alternative test arrangements, notetakers, priority registration, advocacy.

GENERAL COLLEGE INFORMATION

Independent, comprehensive, coed. Awards bachelor's, master's degrees. Founded 1890. *Setting:* urban campus. *Endowment:* $590,066. *Research spending 1995–96:* $1.5 million. *Educational spending 1995–96:* $4011 per undergrad. *Total enrollment:* 8,066. *Faculty:* 1,148 (192 full-time, 40% with terminal degrees, 956 part-time); student–undergrad faculty ratio is 7:1.
Enrollment Profile: 7,510 students from 40 states and territories, 51 other countries. 48% women, 52% men, 26% part-time, 84% state residents, 5% live on campus, 17% transferred in, 1% international, 28% 25 or older, 1% Native American, 11% Hispanic, 20% black, 7% Asian or

Pacific Islander. *Areas of study chosen:* 38% communications and journalism, 22% fine arts, 11% business management and administrative services, 9% performing arts, 6% English language/literature/letters. *Most popular recent majors:* film and video production, art/fine arts, radio and television studies.
First-Year Class: 1,136 total; 2,014 applied, 90% were accepted, 63% of whom enrolled. 18% from top quarter of their high school class, 42% from top half.
Graduation Requirements: 124 semester hours; 9 semester hours of math/science; computer course.
Computers on Campus: 230 computers available on campus for general student use. A campus-wide network can be accessed. Computers for student use in computer center, computer labs, library, dorms provide access to the Internet/World Wide Web. Staffed computer lab on campus. *Academic computing expenditure 1995–96:* $1.2 million.

EXPENSES AND FINANCIAL AID

Expenses for 1997–98: Tuition: $8498 full-time, $291 per semester hour part-time. Part-time mandatory fees: $40 per semester. Full-time mandatory fees: $100. College room only: $4523.
Undergraduate Financial Aid: 61% of all full-time undergraduates enrolled in fall 1996 applied for aid. *Financial aid deadline:* continuous. *Financial aid forms:* FAFSA required; CSS Financial Aid PROFILE acceptable.
LD Services Contact: Ms. Gigi Posejpal, Assistant Dean/International Student Affairs, Columbia College, 600 South Michigan Avenue, Suite 301, Chicago, IL 60605, 312-663-1600.

COLUMBIA COLLEGE

New York, New York

LEARNING DISABILITIES SERVICES INFORMATION

Office of Disability Services began offering services in 1990. Currently the program serves 80 undergraduates with LD. Services are also available to graduate students. Students diagnosed with ADD/ADHD are eligible for the same services available to students with LD.
Staff: 2 full-time staff members, including director, coordinator.
Special Fees: No special fees are charged for services to students with LD.
Applications and admissions: *Required:* high school transcript, grade point average, class rank, courses completed, extracurricular activities, extended time SAT I, autobiographical statement, letters of recommendation. Students may begin taking classes in fall only. *Application deadline:* 1/1.

PROGRAM AND SERVICE COMPONENTS

Special preparation or orientation: Orientation optional.
Academic advising: Provided by unit staff members, academic advisers. Most students with LD take 12 to 15 credits each term; 12 credits required to maintain full-time status and be eligible for financial aid.
Counseling services: Individual counseling.
Auxiliary aids: Taped textbooks, tape recorders, word-processors with spell-check, talking computers.
Auxiliary services: Alternative test arrangements, notetakers, advocacy.

GENERAL COLLEGE INFORMATION

Independent, 4-year, coed. Part of Columbia University. Awards bachelor's degrees. Founded 1754. *Setting:* 35-acre urban campus. *System endowment:* $2.2 billion. *Total university enrollment:* 19,000. *Faculty:* 581 full-time, 99% with terminal degrees; student–undergrad faculty ratio is 7:1.
Enrollment Profile: 3,726 students from 48 states and territories, 45 other countries. 49% women, 51% men, 0% part-time, 19% state residents, 5% transferred in, 5% international, 0% 25 or older, 1% Native American, 8% Hispanic, 9% black, 19% Asian or Pacific Islander. *Retention:* 96% of 1995 full-time freshmen returned. *Graduation:* 80% graduate in 4 years, 90% in 6 years. *Most popular recent majors:* English, history, political science/government.
First-Year Class: 975 total; 10,247 applied, 21% were accepted, 45% of whom enrolled. 84% from top 10% of their high school class, 94% from top half.
Graduation Requirements: 124 credits; 3 semesters of science (2 fields); competence in a foreign language; computer course for economics majors; senior project for honors program students.
Computers on Campus: 400 computers available on campus for general student use. Computer purchase/lease plans available. A campus-wide network can be accessed from student residence rooms. Computers for student use in computer center, library, dorms. Staffed computer lab on campus provides training in use of computers, software.

EXPENSES AND FINANCIAL AID

Expenses for 1997–98: *Application fee:* $45. Comprehensive fee of $29,872 includes full-time tuition ($22,072), mandatory fees ($578), and college room and board ($7222 minimum). College room only: $4222 (minimum).
Undergraduate Financial Aid: 55% of all full-time undergraduates enrolled in fall 1996 applied for aid; of these, 89% were judged to have need according to Federal Methodology, of whom 100% were aided. On average, 100% of need was met. *Financial aid deadline:* 2/10. *Financial aid forms:* FAFSA, CSS Financial Aid PROFILE, institutional form required. State form required for some.
LD Services Contact: Ms. Lynne Bejoian, Director of Disability Services, Columbia College, 305 Low Library, New York, NY 10027, 212-854-6794. Fax: 212-854-3448. Above LD services are available to students attending the following Columbia University colleges: Columbia University, School of Engineering and Applied Sciences; Columbia University, School of General Studies; Columbia University, School of Nursing.

COLUMBUS STATE UNIVERSITY

Columbus, Georgia

LEARNING DISABILITIES SERVICES INFORMATION

Special Needs Office began offering services in 1972. Currently the program serves 95 undergraduates with LD. Services are also available to graduate students. Students diagnosed with ADD/ADHD are eligible for the same services available to students with LD, as well as peer counseling, referrals.
Staff: 2 full-time, 1 part-time staff members, including director. Services provided by tutors, sign language interpreter, graduate assistants, student assistant, notetakers, readers, transcribers.
Special Fees: No special fees are charged for services to students with LD.
Applications and admissions: *Required:* high school transcript, grade point average, courses completed, untimed SAT I, psychoeducational report completed within 5 years; *recommended:* high school class rank. Students may begin taking classes any term. *Application deadline:* continuous.
Special policies: The college has written policies regarding grade forgiveness; substitutions and waivers of admissions, graduation, and degree requirements.

PROGRAM AND SERVICE COMPONENTS

Special preparation or orientation: Optional orientation offered during registration.
Diagnostic testing: Intelligence, reading, math, spelling, written language, study skills.
Academic advising: Provided by academic advisers. Students with LD may take up to 19 quarter hours each term; most take 10 to 15 quarter hours; 12 quarter hours required to maintain full-time status; 5 quarter hours required to be eligible for financial aid.
Counseling services: Individual counseling, small-group counseling, career counseling.
Basic skills remediation: Offered in class-size groups by regular teachers. Available in reading, math, written language.
Subject-area tutoring: Offered one-on-one and in small groups by professional teachers, peer tutors. Available in all subjects.
Special courses: College survival skills. All offered for credit; all enter into overall grade point average.
Auxiliary aids: Taped textbooks, tape recorders, personal computers, optical character readers.
Auxiliary services: Alternative test arrangements, notetakers, advocacy.
Campus support group: A special student organization is available to students with LD.

GENERAL COLLEGE INFORMATION

State-supported, comprehensive, coed. Part of University System of Georgia. Awards associate, bachelor's, master's degrees. Founded 1958. *Setting:* 132-acre suburban campus with easy access to Atlanta. *Total enrollment:* 5,536. *Faculty:* 221 (64% of full-time faculty have terminal degrees); student–undergrad faculty ratio is 24:1.

Enrollment Profile: 4,766 students from 35 states and territories, 18 other countries. 61% women, 39% men, 38% part-time, 81% state residents, 5% live on campus, 8% transferred in, 1% international, 36% 25 or older, 3% Hispanic, 23% black, 3% Asian or Pacific Islander. *Retention:* 61% of 1995 full-time freshmen returned. *Graduation:* 20% graduate in 5 years. *Areas of study chosen:* 25% education, 18% health professions and related sciences, 15% business management and administrative services, 14% social sciences, 6% computer and information sciences, 3% biological and life sciences, 3% engineering and applied sciences, 3% performing arts, 2% communications and journalism, 1% English language/literature/letters. *Most popular recent majors:* liberal arts/general studies, criminal justice, elementary education.

First-Year Class: 707 total; 1,274 applied, 73% were accepted, 76% of whom enrolled.

Graduation Requirements: 95 quarter hours for associate, 190 quarter hours for bachelor's; 2 courses each in math and lab science for bachelor's degree; computer course for business, math majors; internship (some majors).

Computers on Campus: 300 computers available on campus for general student use. A campus-wide network can be accessed from student residence rooms. Computers for student use in computer center, computer labs, classrooms, library, school of business provide access to the Internet/World Wide Web. Staffed computer lab on campus provides training in use of computers, software.

EXPENSES AND FINANCIAL AID

Expenses for 1996–97: *Application fee:* $20. State resident tuition: $1845 full-time, $82 per quarter hour part-time. Nonresident tuition: $5724 full-time, $190 per quarter hour part-time. Full-time mandatory fees: $261. College room and board: $3825.

Undergraduate Financial Aid: 81% of all full-time undergraduates enrolled in fall 1996 applied for aid; of these, 68% were judged to have need according to Federal Methodology, of whom 100% were aided. On average, 60% of need was met. *Financial aid deadline (priority):* 7/1. *Financial aid forms:* institutional form required; CSS Financial Aid PROFILE acceptable. FAFSA required for some.

LD Services Contact: Mr. Roderick Jungbaner, Special Needs Coordinator, Columbus State University, 4225 University Avenue, Columbus, GA 31907-5645, 706-568-2330. Fax: 706-569-3096.

COMMUNITY HOSPITAL OF ROANOKE VALLEY–COLLEGE OF HEALTH SCIENCES

Roanoke, Virginia

LEARNING DISABILITIES SERVICES INFORMATION

TRIAGE began offering services in 1993. Currently the program serves 6 undergraduates with LD. Students diagnosed with ADD/ADHD are eligible for the same services available to students with LD, as well as instruction in study skills and time management.

Staff: 1 full-time staff member (coordinator). Services provided by tutors.

Special Fees: No special fees are charged for services to students with LD.

Applications and admissions: *Required:* high school transcript, grade point average, class rank, courses completed, psychoeducational report completed within 1 year; *recommended:* high school extracurricular activities, untimed or extended time SAT I or ACT. *Application deadline:* continuous.

PROGRAM AND SERVICE COMPONENTS

Academic advising: Provided by academic advisers. Most students with LD take 9 credit hours each term; 12 credit hours required to maintain full-time status and be eligible for financial aid.

Counseling services: Individual counseling, self-advocacy training.

Subject-area tutoring: Offered one-on-one by peer tutors. Available in most subjects.

Auxiliary aids: Taped textbooks, tape recorders, personal computers, optical character readers.

Auxiliary services: Alternative test arrangements, notetakers, advocacy.

GENERAL COLLEGE INFORMATION

Independent, 4-year, specialized, coed. Awards associate, bachelor's degrees. Founded 1982. *Setting:* urban campus. *Total enrollment:* 561. *Faculty:* 49 (34 full-time, 86% with terminal degrees, 15 part-time); student–undergrad faculty ratio is 11:1.

Enrollment Profile: 561 students from 7 states and territories. 76% women, 24% men, 54% part-time, 99% state residents, 15% live on campus, 75% transferred in, 66% 25 or older, 6% black, 2% Asian or Pacific Islander. *Areas of study chosen:* 100% health professions and related sciences. *Most popular recent majors:* nursing, physical therapy, occupational therapy.

First-Year Class: 6 total; 132 applied, 42% were accepted, 11% of whom enrolled.

Graduation Requirements: 66 credit hours for associate, 121 credit hours for bachelor's; 2 anatomy and physiology courses; computer course; internship (some majors).

Computers on Campus: 18 computers available on campus for general student use. A computer is required for some students. A campus-wide network can be accessed from off-campus. Students can contact faculty members and/or advisers through e-mail. Computers for student use in computer labs, learning resource center. Staffed computer lab on campus provides training in use of computers, software.

EXPENSES AND FINANCIAL AID

Expenses for 1996–97: *Application fee:* $25. Tuition: $4500 (minimum) full-time. Part-time tuition per credit hour ranges from $150 to $160. Full-time tuition ranges up to $4800 according to course level. Tuition for summer session ranges from $2250 to $2400 according to course level. College room only for summer session: $475. College room only: $1300.

Undergraduate Financial Aid: *Financial aid deadline (priority):* 4/1. *Financial aid forms:* FAFSA, institutional form required; state form acceptable.

LD Services Contact: Ms. Dianne Caldwell, Coordinator of Counseling, Community Hospital of Roanoke Valley–College of Health Sciences, 920 South Jefferson Street, Roanoke, VA 24016, 540-985-8501.

CONCORDIA COLLEGE

Seward, Nebraska

LEARNING DISABILITIES SERVICES INFORMATION

Academic Support Services began offering services in 1982. Currently the program serves 10 undergraduates with LD. Students diagnosed with ADD/ADHD are eligible for the same services available to students with LD.

Staff: 2 part-time staff members, including director, coordinator. Services provided by tutors, counselors.

Special Fees: No special fees are charged for services to students with LD.

Applications and admissions: *Required:* high school transcript, untimed ACT; *recommended:* psychoeducational report completed within 3 years. Students may begin taking classes in fall, winter, or summer. *Application deadline:* continuous.

PROGRAM AND SERVICE COMPONENTS

Academic advising: Provided by unit staff members, academic advisers. Students with LD may take up to 16 credit hours each term; most take 12 to 14 credit hours; 12 credit hours required to maintain full-time status; 12 credit hours (9 with special permission) required to be eligible for financial aid.

Counseling services: Individual counseling, career counseling.

Basic skills remediation: Offered one-on-one and in small groups by regular teachers; computer-aided instruction also offered. Available in reading, math, written language, learning strategies, study skills, time management.

Subject-area tutoring: Offered one-on-one and in small groups by peer tutors. Available in most subjects.

Auxiliary aids: Taped textbooks, tape recorders, word-processors with spell-check.

Auxiliary services: Alternative test arrangements, notetakers.

GENERAL COLLEGE INFORMATION

Independent, comprehensive, coed, affiliated with Lutheran Church–Missouri Synod. Awards bachelor's, master's degrees. Founded 1894. *Setting:* 120-acre small-town campus with easy access to Omaha. *Endow-*

ment: $7.3 million. *Educational spending 1995–96:* $3590 per undergrad. *Total enrollment:* 951. *Faculty:* 135 (80 full-time, 65% with terminal degrees, 55 part-time); student–undergrad faculty ratio is 9:1.
Enrollment Profile: 913 students from 37 states and territories, 10 other countries. 55% women, 45% men, 9% part-time, 35% state residents, 7% transferred in, 3% international, 8% 25 or older, 1% Native American, 1% Hispanic, 1% black, 1% Asian or Pacific Islander. *Retention:* 81% of 1995 full-time freshmen returned. *Graduation:* 30% graduate in 4 years, 35% in 5 years. *Areas of study chosen:* 55% education, 10% fine arts, 6% business management and administrative services, 6% health professions and related sciences, 5% theology/religion, 4% liberal arts/general studies, 4% social sciences, 2% communications and journalism, 2% premed, 1% English language/literature/letters, 1% performing arts, 1% predentistry, 1% prelaw. *Most popular recent majors:* education, business administration/commerce/management, commercial art.
First-Year Class: 248 total. Of the students who applied, 84% were accepted, 47% of whom enrolled. 2 National Merit Scholars.
Graduation Requirements: 128 credit hours; 3 credit hours of math; 9 credit hours of science; computer course; internship (some majors); senior project (some majors).
Computers on Campus: 75 computers available on campus for general student use. A computer is strongly recommended for all students. A campus-wide network can be accessed from student residence rooms and from off-campus. Students can contact faculty members and/or advisers through e-mail. Computers for student use in computer center, computer labs, library, dorms, art departmental lab, business school provide access to the Internet/World Wide Web, on- and off-campus e-mail addresses. Staffed computer lab on campus (open 24 hours a day) provides training in use of computers, software. *Academic computing expenditure 1995–96:* $238,689.

EXPENSES AND FINANCIAL AID

Expenses for 1997–98: *Application fee:* $15. Comprehensive fee of $14,290 includes full-time tuition ($10,650) and college room and board ($3640). Part-time tuition per credit hour ranges from $176 to $328 according to course load.
Undergraduate Financial Aid: Of all full-time undergraduates enrolled in fall 1996, 100% of those judged to have need according to Federal Methodology were aided. On average, 81% of need was met. *Financial aid deadline (priority):* 8/15. *Financial aid forms:* FAFSA, institutional form required; CSS Financial Aid PROFILE acceptable.
LD Services Contact: Ms. Grace-Ann Dolak, Director of Academic Support Services, Concordia College, 800 North Columbia, Seward, NE 68434-1599, 402-643-2750. Email: gdolak@seward.ccsn.edu.

CORNELL UNIVERSITY

Ithaca, New York

LEARNING DISABILITIES SERVICES INFORMATION

Disability Services (Office of Equal Opportunity) began offering services in 1986. Currently the program serves 188 undergraduates with LD. Services are also available to graduate students. Students diagnosed with ADD/ADHD are eligible for the same services available to students with LD.
Staff: 1 full-time staff member (coordinator). Services provided by tutors, counselors.
Special Fees: No special fees are charged for services to students with LD.
Applications and admissions: *Required:* high school transcript, grade point average, class rank, courses completed, untimed SAT I or ACT, letters of recommendation. Students may begin taking classes any term. *Application deadline:* 1/1.
Special policies: The college has written policies regarding substitutions and waivers of degree requirements.

PROGRAM AND SERVICE COMPONENTS

Academic advising: Provided by academic advisers. Most students with LD take 12 to 16 credit hours each term; 12 credit hours required to maintain full-time status; 9 credit hours (with verification from coordinator) required to be eligible for financial aid.
Counseling services: Individual counseling.
Subject-area tutoring: Offered one-on-one by peer tutors, teaching assistants, Learning Skills Center staff. Available in all subjects.
Special courses. College survival skills, reading, study skills, career planning. Some offered for credit; some enter into overall grade point average.
Auxiliary aids: Taped textbooks, tape recorders, word-processors with spell-check, talking computers, optical character readers, specialized software, Arkenstone Reader.
Auxiliary services: Alternative test arrangements, notetakers, priority registration, advocacy, readers.
Campus support group: A special student organization is available to students with LD.

GENERAL COLLEGE INFORMATION

Independent, coed. Awards bachelor's, master's, doctoral, first professional degrees. Founded 1865. *Setting:* 745-acre small-town campus with easy access to Syracuse. *Endowment:* $1.5 billion. *Research spending 1995–96:* $171.9 million. *Total enrollment:* 18,849. *Faculty:* 1,541 (1,485 full-time, 96% with terminal degrees, 56 part-time); student–undergrad faculty ratio is 9:1.
Enrollment Profile: 13,512 students from 55 states and territories, 78 other countries. 47% women, 53% men, 0% part-time, 43% state residents, 47% live on campus, 3% transferred in, 6% international, 3% 25 or older, 1% Native American, 6% Hispanic, 4% black, 17% Asian or Pacific Islander. *Retention:* 96% of 1995 full-time freshmen returned. *Graduation:* 79% graduate in 4 years, 87% in 5 years, 89% in 6 years. *Areas of study chosen:* 18% business management and administrative services, 15% social sciences, 13% agriculture, 12% biological and life sciences, 12% engineering and applied sciences, 5% architecture, 3% communications and journalism, 3% interdisciplinary studies, 3% liberal arts/general studies, 2% computer and information sciences, 2% English language/literature/letters, 2% natural resource sciences, 2% physical sciences, 2% psychology, 1% area and ethnic studies, 1% education, 1% fine arts, 1% foreign language and literature, 1% mathematics, 1% performing arts. *Most popular recent majors:* biology/biological sciences, economics, hotel and restaurant management.
First-Year Class: 3,212 total; 21,004 applied, 33% were accepted, 47% of whom enrolled. 81% from top 10% of their high school class, 94% from top quarter, 99% from top half. 312 National Merit Scholars, 2 Westinghouse recipients.
Graduation Requirements: 120 credit hours; computer course for engineering majors; internship (some majors); senior project for honors program students and some majors.
Computers on Campus: Computer purchase/lease plans available. A campus-wide network can be accessed from student residence rooms and from off-campus. Students can contact faculty members and/or advisers through e-mail. Computers for student use in computer center, computer labs, research center, library, student center, dorms, student rooms, various locations provide access to the Internet/World Wide Web. Staffed computer lab on campus provides training in use of computers, software.

EXPENSES AND FINANCIAL AID

Expenses for 1997–98: *Application fee:* $65. Comprehensive fee of $29,092 includes full-time tuition ($21,840), mandatory fees ($74), and college room and board ($7178). College room only: $4238. Tuition for state-supported programs: $9300 full-time, part-time for state residents; $17,950 full-time, part-time for nonresidents.
Undergraduate Financial Aid: Of all full-time undergraduates enrolled in fall 1996, 80% of those who applied for aid were judged to have need according to Federal Methodology, of whom 100% were aided. On average, 100% of need was met. *Financial aid deadline (priority):* 2/15. *Financial aid forms:* FAFSA, CSS Financial Aid PROFILE, state form, institutional form required.
LD Services Contact: Ms. Joan B. Fisher, Assistant Director, Disability Services/Office of Equal Opportunity, Cornell University, 234 Day Hall, Ithaca, NY 14853-2801, 607-255-3976. Fax: 607-255-7481. Email: jbf1@cornell.edu.

CREIGHTON UNIVERSITY

Omaha, Nebraska

LEARNING DISABILITIES SERVICES INFORMATION

Student Support Services Program began offering services in 1990. Currently the program serves 70 undergraduates with LD. Services are also available to graduate students. Students diagnosed with ADD/ADHD are eligible for the same services available to students with LD.

Staff: Includes coordinator, assistant coordinator. Services provided by remediation specialists, tutors, counselor.
Special Fees: No special fees are charged for services to students with LD.
Applications and admissions: *Required:* high school transcript, grade point average, class rank, psychoeducational report completed within 3 years (only if accommodations are requested); *recommended:* untimed SAT I or ACT, personal interview, autobiographical statement, letters of recommendation. Students may begin taking classes in fall, spring, or summer. *Application deadline:* continuous.

PROGRAM AND SERVICE COMPONENTS

Diagnostic testing: Intelligence, reading, math, motor abilities, study skills, personality, learning strategies, Woodcock-Johnson, WAIS-R.
Academic advising: Provided by academic advisers. Students with LD may take up to 18 credits each term; most take 12 to 15 credits; 12 credits required to maintain full-time status; 12 credits for full-time required to be eligible for financial aid.
Counseling services: Individual counseling, career counseling.
Basic skills remediation: Offered one-on-one by Bachelor's and Master's level staff. Available in reading, math, spelling, written language, learning strategies, study skills, time management, natural sciences.
Subject-area tutoring: Offered one-on-one and in small groups by peer tutors, Bachelor's and Master's level staff. Available in most subjects.
Special courses: College survival skills, word processing, study skills. All offered for credit; all enter into overall grade point average.
Auxiliary aids: Taped textbooks, tape recorders, word-processors with spell-check, optical character readers.
Auxiliary services: Alternative test arrangements, notetakers, priority registration, advocacy.

GENERAL COLLEGE INFORMATION

Independent Roman Catholic (Jesuit), coed. Awards associate, bachelor's, master's, doctoral, first professional degrees. Founded 1878. *Setting:* 85-acre urban campus. *Endowment:* $92.9 million. *Research spending 1995–96:* $9.4 million. *Educational spending 1995–96:* $10,044 per undergrad. *Total enrollment:* 6,158. *Faculty:* 1,361 (695 full-time, 92% with terminal degrees, 666 part-time); student–undergrad faculty ratio is 14:1.
Enrollment Profile: 3,679 students from 45 states and territories, 50 other countries. 59% women, 41% men, 15% part-time, 46% state residents, 44% live on campus, 12% transferred in, 3% international, 5% 25 or older, 1% Native American, 3% Hispanic, 3% black, 8% Asian or Pacific Islander. *Retention:* 85% of 1995 full-time freshmen returned. *Graduation:* 51% graduate in 4 years, 65% in 5 years, 67% in 6 years. *Areas of study chosen:* 21% health professions and related sciences, 17% business management and administrative services, 11% biological and life sciences, 10% psychology, 9% physical sciences, 8% social sciences, 4% communications and journalism, 4% English language/literature/letters, 3% education, 3% mathematics, 2% fine arts, 2% foreign language and literature, 2% natural resource sciences, 1% computer and information sciences, 1% performing arts, 1% philosophy, 1% theology/religion. *Most popular recent majors:* nursing, psychology, finance/banking.
First-Year Class: 881 total; 3,369 applied, 92% were accepted, 28% of whom enrolled. 37% from top 10% of their high school class, 60% from top quarter, 91% from top half.
Graduation Requirements: 64 credits for associate, 128 credits for bachelor's; 1 course each in natural science and math; computer course for business majors; senior project for honors program students and some majors.
Computers on Campus: 520 computers available on campus for general student use. Computer purchase/lease plans available. A computer is recommended for some students. A campus-wide network can be accessed from student residence rooms and from off-campus. Students can contact faculty members and/or advisers through e-mail. Computers for student use in computer center, computer labs, learning resource center, classrooms, library, dorms provide access to the Internet/World Wide Web, on- and off-campus e-mail addresses. Staffed computer lab on campus provides training in use of computers, software. *Academic computing expenditure 1995–96:* $288,000.

EXPENSES AND FINANCIAL AID

Expenses for 1997–98: *Application fee:* $30. Comprehensive fee of $17,696 includes full-time tuition ($12,246), mandatory fees ($510), and college room and board ($4940). College room only: $2740. Part-time tuition: $382 per credit. Part-time mandatory fees: $26 per semester.
Undergraduate Financial Aid: Of all full-time undergraduates enrolled in fall 1996, 86% of those who applied for aid were judged to have need according to Federal Methodology, of whom 100% were aided. *Financial aid deadline (priority):* 4/1. *Financial aid forms:* FAFSA, institutional form required; CSS Financial Aid PROFILE acceptable.
LD Services Contact: Mr. Wade Pearson, Coordinator of Services for Students with Disabilities, Creighton University, Markoe Hall, 2500 California, Omaha, NE 68178, 402-280-2749. Fax: 402-280-5579.

DAKOTA WESLEYAN UNIVERSITY

Mitchell, South Dakota

LEARNING DISABILITIES SERVICES INFORMATION

Student Support Services began offering services in 1980. Currently the program serves 4 undergraduates with LD. Students diagnosed with ADD/ADHD are eligible for the same services available to students with LD.
Staff: 4 full-time staff members, including director, coordinator. Services provided by tutors, counselors.
Special Fees: No special fees are charged for services to students with LD.
Applications and admissions: *Required:* high school transcript, grade point average, class rank, courses completed, IEP (Individualized Education Program), psychoeducational report completed within 3 years; *recommended:* letters of recommendation. Students may begin taking classes any term. *Application deadline:* continuous.

PROGRAM AND SERVICE COMPONENTS

Diagnostic testing: Intelligence, reading, math, written language, perceptual skills, study skills, personality, social skills, psychoneurology, speech, hearing, learning strategies.
Academic advising: Provided by unit staff members, academic advisers. Most students with LD take 14 to 15 semester hours each term; 12 semester hours required to maintain full-time status; minimum of 6 semester hours (part-time), 12 semester hours (full-time) required to be eligible for financial aid.
Counseling services: Individual counseling, career counseling.
Basic skills remediation: Offered one-on-one and in small groups by regular teachers, teacher trainees; computer-aided instruction also offered. Available in math, spelling, written language, learning strategies, study skills, time management, social skills.
Subject-area tutoring: Offered one-on-one and in small groups by professional teachers, peer tutors. Available in all subjects.
Auxiliary aids: Taped textbooks, tape recorders, calculators, typewriters, word-processors with spell-check, personal computers.
Auxiliary services: Alternative test arrangements, notetakers, advocacy.

GENERAL COLLEGE INFORMATION

Independent United Methodist, comprehensive, coed. Awards associate, bachelor's, master's degrees (master's degree in education only). Founded 1885. *Setting:* 40-acre small-town campus. *Endowment:* $388,622. *Total enrollment:* 710. *Undergraduate faculty:* 66 (36 full-time, 26% with terminal degrees, 30 part-time); student–undergrad faculty ratio is 15:1.
Enrollment Profile: 710 students from 11 states and territories, 4 other countries. 62% women, 38% men, 22% part-time, 84% state residents, 35% live on campus, 10% transferred in, 1% international, 16% 25 or older, 4% Native American, 1% Hispanic, 3% black, 1% Asian or Pacific Islander. *Retention:* 80% of 1995 full-time freshmen returned. *Areas of study chosen:* 26% social sciences, 13% business management and administrative services, 12% education, 7% biological and life sciences, 5% psychology, 3% communications and journalism, 3% English language/literature/letters, 3% fine arts, 1% mathematics. *Most popular recent majors:* nursing, business administration/commerce/management, education.
First-Year Class: 148 total; 405 applied, 75% were accepted, 49% of whom enrolled.
Graduation Requirements: 62 semester hours for associate, 125 semester hours for bachelor's; 1 math course; 2 natural science courses; computer course for business majors; internship (some majors); senior project (some majors).
Computers on Campus: 65 computers available on campus for general student use. A campus-wide network can be accessed. Students can contact faculty members and/or advisers through e-mail. Computers for student use in computer center, computer labs, classrooms, library, dorms, departmental labs provide access to the Internet/World Wide Web, on- and off-campus e-mail addresses. Staffed computer lab on campus provides training in use of computers, software.

Dakota Wesleyan University (continued)

EXPENSES AND FINANCIAL AID

Estimated Expenses for 1997–98: *Application fee:* $15. Comprehensive fee of $12,065 includes full-time tuition ($8825) and college room and board ($3240). Part-time tuition: $180 per semester hour (minimum).
Undergraduate Financial Aid: 100% of all full-time undergraduates enrolled in fall 1996 applied for aid; of these, 73% were judged to have need according to Federal Methodology, of whom 100% were aided. On average, 82% of need was met. *Financial aid deadline (priority):* 4/1. *Financial aid forms:* institutional form, Education Assistance Corporation's Application for Student Aid required; FAFSA, CSS Financial Aid PROFILE acceptable. State form required for some.
LD Services Contact: Mr. Paul Szabo, Academic Specialist, Dakota Wesleyan University, 1200 West University Avenue, Mitchell, SD 57301-4398, 605-995-2682. Fax: 605-995-2900. Email: pszabo@cc.dwu.edu.

DAVID LIPSCOMB UNIVERSITY

Nashville, Tennessee

LEARNING DISABILITIES SERVICES INFORMATION

Academic Counseling Center began offering services in 1991. Currently the program serves 42 undergraduates with LD. Services are also available to graduate students. Students diagnosed with ADD/ADHD are eligible for the same services available to students with LD, as well as self/academic management coaching.
Staff: 2 part-time staff members, including coordinator. Services provided by diagnostic specialist.
Special Fees: $100 for diagnostic testing.
Applications and admissions: *Required:* high school transcript, grade point average, class rank, courses completed, untimed or extended time SAT I or ACT, letters of recommendation, psychoeducational report completed within 3 years; *recommended:* high school extracurricular activities, IEP (Individualized Education Program), personal interview. Students may begin taking classes in fall only. *Application deadline:* continuous.
Special policies: The college has written policies regarding substitutions and waivers of graduation and degree requirements.

PROGRAM AND SERVICE COMPONENTS

Diagnostic testing: Intelligence, reading, math, spelling, written language, perceptual skills, personality, social skills.
Academic advising: Provided by unit staff members, academic advisers. Most students with LD take 12 semester hours each term; 12 semester hours required to maintain full-time status; 12 semester hours (14 for institutional aid) required to be eligible for financial aid.
Counseling services: Individual counseling, career counseling.
Auxiliary aids: Personal computers, optical character readers.
Auxiliary services: Alternative test arrangements, notetakers, advocacy.

GENERAL COLLEGE INFORMATION

Independent, comprehensive, coed, affiliated with Church of Christ. Awards bachelor's, master's degrees. Founded 1891. *Setting:* 65-acre urban campus. *Endowment:* $38.1 million. *Research spending 1995–96:* $8244. *Total enrollment:* 2,543. *Undergraduate faculty:* 183 (99 full-time, 79% with terminal degrees, 84 part-time); student–undergrad faculty ratio is 18:1.
Enrollment Profile: 2,457 students from 44 states and territories, 41 other countries. 56% women, 44% men, 15% part-time, 65% state residents, 50% live on campus, 5% transferred in, 3% international, 15% 25 or older, 1% Hispanic, 4% black, 2% Asian or Pacific Islander. *Retention:* 75% of 1995 full-time freshmen returned. *Graduation:* 23% graduate in 4 years, 39% in 5 years. *Areas of study chosen:* 16% business management and administrative services, 11% education, 7% biological and life sciences, 5% premed, 5% psychology, 5% social sciences, 4% health professions and related sciences, 3% communications and journalism, 3% engineering and applied sciences, 3% physical sciences, 2% computer and information sciences, 2% English language/literature/letters, 2% fine arts, 2% prelaw, 2% theology/religion, 2% vocational and home economics, 1% foreign language and literature, 1% liberal arts/general studies, 1% mathematics, 1% predentistry. *Most popular recent majors:* business administration/commerce/management, education, history.
First-Year Class: 544 total; 1,318 applied, 89% were accepted, 46% of whom enrolled. 34% from top 10% of their high school class, 57% from top quarter, 82% from top half. 5 National Merit Scholars.
Graduation Requirements: 132 semester hours; 3 semester hours of math; 6 semester hours of lab science; computer course for business, public administration, fashion merchandising, dietetics, physics, engineering science, applied chemistry, food systems management, health, math, clinical psychology majors; internship (some majors); senior project for honors program students and some majors.
Computers on Campus: 232 computers available on campus for general student use. Computer purchase/lease plans available. A computer is recommended for all students. A campus-wide network can be accessed from student residence rooms and from off-campus. Students can contact faculty members and/or advisers through e-mail. Computers for student use in computer center, computer labs, learning resource center, classrooms, library, dorms provide access to the Internet/World Wide Web, on- and off-campus e-mail addresses. Staffed computer lab on campus provides training in use of computers, software. *Academic computing expenditure 1995–96:* $603,102.

EXPENSES AND FINANCIAL AID

Expenses for 1997–98: *Application fee:* $35. Comprehensive fee of $13,283 includes full-time tuition ($9273), mandatory fees ($40), and college room and board ($3970). College room only: $1980. Part-time tuition: $281 per semester hour. Part-time mandatory fees: $12 per semester.
Undergraduate Financial Aid: 78% of all full-time undergraduates enrolled in fall 1996 applied for aid; of these, 67% were judged to have need according to Federal Methodology, of whom 90% were aided. On average, 95% of need was met. *Financial aid deadline (priority):* 2/28. *Financial aid forms:* FAFSA required; CSS Financial Aid PROFILE acceptable. State form required for some.
LD Services Contact: Ms. Kathryn Fowler, Coordinator of Academic Counseling, David Lipscomb University, 3901 Granny White Pike, Nashville, TN 37204-3951, 615-269-1781. Fax: 615-269-1815. Email: fowlerkf@dlu.edu.

DAVIDSON COLLEGE

Davidson, North Carolina

LEARNING DISABILITIES SERVICES INFORMATION

Special Services, Dean of Students Office began offering services in 1990. Currently the program serves 42 undergraduates with LD. Students diagnosed with ADD/ADHD are eligible for the same services available to students with LD.
Staff: 2 part-time staff members, including coordinators. Services provided by tutors, counselor, diagnostic specialist.
Special Fees: $300 to $450 for diagnostic testing.
Applications and admissions: *Required:* high school transcript, grade point average, courses completed, extracurricular activities, untimed SAT I or ACT, letters of recommendation, psychoeducational report; *recommended:* high school class rank, extended time SAT I or ACT, personal interview, autobiographical statement. Students may begin taking classes in fall only. *Application deadline:* 1/15 (fall term), 11/15 (spring term).
Special policies: The college has written policies regarding substitutions and waivers of admissions, graduation, and degree requirements.

PROGRAM AND SERVICE COMPONENTS

Diagnostic testing: Intelligence, reading, math, spelling, spoken language, written language, motor abilities, perceptual skills, study skills, personality, learning strategies.
Academic advising: Provided by unit staff members, academic advisers. Students with LD may take up to 5 courses each term; most take 3 to 4 courses; 3 courses (with special permission) required to maintain full-time status and be eligible for financial aid.
Counseling services: Individual counseling, career counseling, self-advocacy training.
Subject-area tutoring: Offered one-on-one by peer tutors. Available in all subjects.
Auxiliary aids: Taped textbooks, tape recorders, calculators, typewriters, word-processors with spell-check, personal computers.
Auxiliary services: Alternative test arrangements, notetakers, advocacy, readers.

GENERAL COLLEGE INFORMATION

Independent Presbyterian, 4-year, coed. Awards bachelor's degrees. Founded 1837. *Setting:* 464-acre small-town campus with easy access to Charlotte. *Endowment:* $172.8 million. *Research spending 1995–96:*

$190,290. *Educational spending 1995–96:* $11,106 per undergrad. *Total enrollment:* 1,613. *Faculty:* 151 (139 full-time, 96% with terminal degrees, 12 part-time); student–undergrad faculty ratio is 12:1.
Enrollment Profile: 1,613 students from 46 states and territories, 39 other countries. 49% women, 51% men, 0% part-time, 20% state residents, 92% live on campus, 1% transferred in, 2% international, 1% 25 or older, 1% Native American, 2% Hispanic, 4% black, 3% Asian or Pacific Islander. *Retention:* 94% of 1995 full-time freshmen returned. *Graduation:* 84% graduate in 4 years, 88% in 5 years. *Areas of study chosen:* 34% social sciences, 15% English language/literature/letters, 14% biological and life sciences, 9% psychology, 7% foreign language and literature, 5% interdisciplinary studies, 5% mathematics, 4% physical sciences, 3% fine arts, 2% philosophy, 1% performing arts, 1% theology/religion. *Most popular recent majors:* history, English, biology/biological sciences.
First-Year Class: 442 total; 2,829 applied, 37% were accepted, 42% of whom enrolled. 76% from top 10% of their high school class, 96% from top quarter, 100% from top half. 21 National Merit Scholars, 2 Westinghouse recipients, 57 valedictorians.
Graduation Requirements: 32 courses; 3 math/science courses including at least 1 course each in math and lab science; 3 courses in a foreign language or the equivalent; computer course for math majors; senior project (some majors).
Computers on Campus: 130 computers available on campus for general student use. Computer purchase/lease plans available. Computers for student use in computer center, computer labs, research center, classrooms, library, academic buildings provide access to the Internet/World Wide Web, on- and off-campus e-mail addresses. Staffed computer lab on campus provides training in use of computers, software. *Academic computing expenditure 1995–96:* $946,474.

EXPENSES AND FINANCIAL AID

Expenses for 1997–98: *Application fee:* $45. Comprehensive fee of $26,513 includes full-time tuition ($19,883), mandatory fees ($712), and college room and board ($5918). College room only: $3129.
Undergraduate Financial Aid: 43% of all full-time undergraduates enrolled in fall 1996 applied for aid; of these, 88% were judged to have need according to Federal Methodology, of whom 99% were aided. On average, 95% of need was met. *Financial aid deadline:* 2/15. *Financial aid forms:* FAFSA, CSS Financial Aid PROFILE required. State form required for some.
LD Services Contact: Ms. Leslie M. Marsicano, Associate Dean of Students, Davidson College, PO Box 1719, Davidson, NC 28036-1719, 704-892-2225. Fax: 704-892-2005.

DELAWARE STATE UNIVERSITY

Dover, Delaware

LEARNING DISABILITIES SERVICES INFORMATION

Office of Disabilities Services began offering services in 1994. Currently the program serves 24 undergraduates with LD. Services are also available to graduate students. Students diagnosed with ADD/ADHD are eligible for the same services available to students with LD.
Staff: Includes coordinator, student worker. Services provided by tutors, readers, notetakers.
Special Fees: No special fees are charged for services to students with LD.
Applications and admissions: *Required:* high school transcript, grade point average, courses completed, psychoeducational report completed within 3 years; *recommended:* high school class rank, extracurricular activities, IEP (Individualized Education Program), untimed or extended time SAT I or ACT, personal interview, autobiographical statement, letters of recommendation. Students may begin taking classes in fall only. *Application deadline:* continuous.

PROGRAM AND SERVICE COMPONENTS

Special preparation or orientation: Optional summer program offered prior to entering college.
Diagnostic testing: Reading, math, spelling, handwriting, written language, study skills, learning strategies.
Academic advising: Provided by unit staff members, academic advisers. Students with LD may take up to 15 credit hours each term; most take 12 credit hours; 12 credit hours required to maintain full-time status and be eligible for financial aid.
Counseling services: Individual counseling, small-group counseling, career counseling, self-advocacy training.
Basic skills remediation: Offered one-on-one and in class-size groups by LD teachers, regular teachers; computer-aided instruction also offered. Available in reading, math, written language, learning strategies, study skills, time management, social skills.
Subject-area tutoring: Offered one-on-one by peer tutors. Available in all subjects.
Auxiliary aids: Taped textbooks, tape recorders, calculators, word-processors with spell-check, talking computers, optical character readers.
Auxiliary services: Alternative test arrangements, notetakers, advocacy.

GENERAL COLLEGE INFORMATION

State-supported, comprehensive, coed. Part of Delaware Higher Education Commission. Awards bachelor's, master's degrees. Founded 1891. *Setting:* 400-acre small-town campus. *Research spending 1995–96:* $2.3 million. *Educational spending 1995–96:* $3918 per undergrad. *Total enrollment:* 3,328. *Undergraduate faculty:* 176 (60% of full-time faculty have terminal degrees); student–undergrad faculty ratio is 14:1.
Enrollment Profile: 3,030 students from 45 states and territories, 17 other countries. 58% women, 42% men, 20% part-time, 59% state residents, 6% transferred in, 4% international, 25% 25 or older, 0% Native American, 1% Hispanic, 72% black, 1% Asian or Pacific Islander. *Retention:* 53% of 1995 full-time freshmen returned. *Areas of study chosen:* 19% business management and administrative services, 13% computer and information sciences, 11% health professions and related sciences, 6% biological and life sciences, 5% communications and journalism, 5% psychology, 4% agriculture, 2% English language/literature/letters, 2% mathematics, 2% prelaw, 2% social sciences, 2% vocational and home economics. *Most popular recent majors:* business administration/commerce/management, education, social work.
First-Year Class: 604 total; 1,786 applied, 69% were accepted, 49% of whom enrolled.
Graduation Requirements: 121 credit hours; 6 credit hours each of math and science; computer course for math, social work, sociology, administrative office management majors; internship (some majors); senior project (some majors).
Computers on Campus: 346 computers available on campus for general student use. A campus-wide network can be accessed. Computers for student use in computer center, computer labs, library, departmental labs provide access to the Internet/World Wide Web, on- and off-campus e-mail addresses. Staffed computer lab on campus provides training in use of computers, software.

EXPENSES AND FINANCIAL AID

Expenses for 1997–98: *Application fee:* $10. State resident tuition: $2810 full-time, $110 per credit hour part-time. Nonresident tuition: $6470 full-time, $263 per credit hour part-time. Part-time mandatory fees: $40 per semester. Full-time mandatory fees: $160. College room and board: $4862.
Undergraduate Financial Aid: 77% of all full-time undergraduates enrolled in fall 1996 applied for aid; of these, 90% were judged to have need according to Federal Methodology, of whom 97% were aided. On average, 77% of need was met. *Financial aid deadline (priority):* 3/1. *Financial aid forms:* FAFSA required.
LD Services Contact: Ms. Laura H. Kurtz, Coordinator, Delaware State University, 1200 North DuPont Highway, Dover, DE 19901, 302-739-5310. Fax: 302-739-7499.

DELAWARE VALLEY COLLEGE

Doylestown, Pennsylvania

LEARNING DISABILITIES SERVICES INFORMATION

Learning Support Services began offering services in 1980. Currently the program serves 74 undergraduates with LD. Students diagnosed with ADD/ADHD are eligible for the same services available to students with LD.
Staff: 1 full-time staff member (Learning Support Specialist). Services provided by tutors, counselors.
Special Fees: No special fees are charged for services to students with LD.
Applications and admissions: *Required:* high school transcript, letters of recommendation. Students may begin taking classes in fall only. *Application deadline:* continuous.
Special policies: The college has written policies regarding substitutions and waivers of graduation and degree requirements.

PROGRAM AND SERVICE COMPONENTS

Academic advising: Provided by academic advisers. Students with LD may take up to 18 credits each term; most take 12 to 14 credits; 12 credits required to maintain full-time status and be eligible for financial aid.

Counseling services: Individual counseling, self-advocacy training.

Auxiliary aids: Taped textbooks, tape recorders, calculators, typewriters, word-processors with spell-check, personal computers.

Auxiliary services: Alternative test arrangements, notetakers, priority registration.

GENERAL COLLEGE INFORMATION

Independent, 4-year, coed. Awards associate, bachelor's degrees. Founded 1896. *Setting:* 600-acre suburban campus with easy access to Philadelphia. *Endowment:* $8.8 million. *Research spending 1995–96:* $388,499. *Total enrollment:* 1,380. *Faculty:* 129 (81 full-time, 69% with terminal degrees, 48 part-time); student–undergrad faculty ratio is 18:1.

Enrollment Profile: 1,380 students from 28 states and territories, 7 other countries. 50% women, 50% men, 30% part-time, 74% state residents, 70% live on campus, 23% transferred in, 1% international, 29% 25 or older, 0% Native American, 1% Hispanic, 2% black, 1% Asian or Pacific Islander. *Retention:* 72% of 1995 full-time freshmen returned. *Areas of study chosen:* 48% agriculture, 17% business management and administrative services, 7% biological and life sciences, 6% computer and information sciences, 6% natural resource sciences, 6% prevet, 4% education, 4% social sciences, 1% English language/literature/letters, 1% mathematics. *Most popular recent majors:* business administration/commerce/management, ornamental horticulture, animal sciences.

First-Year Class: 395 total; 1,370 applied, 73% were accepted, 40% of whom enrolled. 8% from top 10% of their high school class, 17% from top quarter, 61% from top half.

Graduation Requirements: 65 credits for associate, 126 credits for bachelor's; 1 year each of math and science; computer course.

Computers on Campus: 150 computers available on campus for general student use. A campus-wide network can be accessed. Students can contact faculty members and/or advisers through e-mail. Computers for student use in computer center, computer labs, learning resource center, classrooms, library, dorms provide access to the Internet/World Wide Web. Staffed computer lab on campus provides training in use of computers, software. *Academic computing expenditure 1995–96:* $125,609.

EXPENSES AND FINANCIAL AID

Expenses for 1997–98: *Application fee:* $35. Comprehensive fee of $20,584 includes full-time tuition ($14,929) and college room and board ($5655). College room only: $2485. Part-time tuition: $345 per credit. Part-time tuition for evening classes: $240 per credit.

Undergraduate Financial Aid: On average, 86% of need was met. *Financial aid deadline (priority):* 5/1. *Financial aid forms:* FAFSA, institutional form required; CSS Financial Aid PROFILE acceptable. State form required for some.

LD Services Contact: Ms. Karen Kay, Director of Counseling and Learning Services, Delaware Valley College, 700 East Butler Avenue, Doylestown, PA 18901-2697, 215-489-2309. Fax: 215-230-2964.

DENISON UNIVERSITY

Granville, Ohio

LEARNING DISABILITIES SERVICES INFORMATION

Office of Academic Support currently serves 100 undergraduates with LD. Students diagnosed with ADD/ADHD are eligible for the same services available to students with LD, as well as distraction-free testing area.

Staff: Includes director, assistant directors. Services provided by tutors, counselors.

Special Fees: No special fees are charged for services to students with LD.

Applications and admissions: *Required:* high school transcript, grade point average, class rank, courses completed, extracurricular activities, untimed SAT I or ACT, letters of recommendation, psychoeducational report completed within 3 years; *recommended:* extended time SAT I or ACT, personal interview. Students may begin taking classes in fall only. *Application deadline:* 2/1.

Special policies: The college has written policies regarding substitutions and waivers of graduation and degree requirements.

PROGRAM AND SERVICE COMPONENTS

Special preparation or orientation: Optional orientation offered before general orientation for all students prior to the first day of classes.

Academic advising: Provided by academic advisers. Students with LD may take up to 18 credit hours each term; most take 16 credit hours; 12 credit hours required to maintain full-time status and be eligible for financial aid.

Counseling services: Individual counseling, career counseling.

Subject-area tutoring: Offered one-on-one by peer tutors. Available in most subjects.

Auxiliary aids: Taped textbooks, word-processors with spell-check, personal computers, talking computers, Reading Edge.

Auxiliary services: Alternative test arrangements, notetakers, priority registration, readers, taped lectures.

GENERAL COLLEGE INFORMATION

Independent, 4-year, coed. Awards bachelor's degrees. Founded 1831. *Setting:* 1,200-acre small-town campus with easy access to Columbus. *Endowment:* $201.1 million. *Research spending 1995–96:* $270,739. *Educational spending 1995–96:* $8178 per undergrad. *Total enrollment:* 2,017. *Faculty:* 163 (150 full-time, 97% with terminal degrees, 13 part-time); student–undergrad faculty ratio is 12:1.

Enrollment Profile: 2,017 students from 45 states and territories, 33 other countries. 52% women, 48% men, 1% part-time, 39% state residents, 93% live on campus, 1% transferred in, 4% international, 1% 25 or older, 0% Native American, 2% Hispanic, 4% black, 3% Asian or Pacific Islander. *Retention:* 81% of 1995 full-time freshmen returned. *Graduation:* 75% graduate in 4 years, 78% in 5 years. *Areas of study chosen:* 28% social sciences, 10% biological and life sciences, 10% English language/literature/letters, 8% communications and journalism, 8% psychology, 6% fine arts, 5% physical sciences, 4% education, 4% foreign language and literature, 2% computer and information sciences, 2% mathematics, 2% natural resource sciences, 2% performing arts, 2% theology/religion, 1% area and ethnic studies, 1% philosophy. *Most popular recent majors:* English, psychology, economics.

First-Year Class: 644 total; 2,569 applied, 82% were accepted, 30% of whom enrolled. 35% from top 10% of their high school class, 65% from top quarter, 86% from top half. 13 National Merit Scholars, 54 valedictorians.

Graduation Requirements: 127 credit hours; 3 science courses; 3 semesters of a foreign language or proven proficiency; computer course for math majors; senior project for honors program students and some majors.

Computers on Campus: 160 computers available on campus for general student use. Computer purchase/lease plans available. A computer is recommended for some students. A campus-wide network can be accessed from student residence rooms and from off-campus. Students can contact faculty members and/or advisers through e-mail. Computers for student use in computer center, computer labs, learning resource center, library, dorms, departmental labs provide access to the Internet/World Wide Web, on- and off-campus e-mail addresses. *Academic computing expenditure 1995–96:* $1 million.

EXPENSES AND FINANCIAL AID

Expenses for 1997–98: *Application fee:* $35. Comprehensive fee of $25,620 includes full-time tuition ($19,310), mandatory fees ($940), and college room and board ($5370). College room only: $2960. Part-time tuition: $600 per credit hour.

Undergraduate Financial Aid: 53% of all full-time undergraduates enrolled in fall 1996 applied for aid; of these, 89% were judged to have need according to Federal Methodology, of whom 96% were aided. On average, 74% of need was met. *Financial aid deadline (priority):* 3/1. *Financial aid forms:* FAFSA, institutional form required.

LD Services Contact: Ms. Lenora Barnes-Wright, Associate Dean/Director of Academic Support, Denison University, 104 Doane, Granville, OH 43023, 614-587-6224. Fax: 614-587-6319. Email: barnes@denison.edu.

DEVRY INSTITUTE OF TECHNOLOGY

Phoenix, Arizona

LEARNING DISABILITIES SERVICES INFORMATION

Student Services Department began offering services in 1969. Currently the program serves 35 undergraduates with LD. Students diagnosed with ADD/ADHD are eligible for the same services available to students with LD.

Staff: 2 full-time staff members, including director, co-director. Services provided by counselors.
Special Fees: No special fees are charged for services to students with LD.
Applications and admissions: *Required:* high school transcript, grade point average, courses completed, personal interview; *recommended:* high school class rank, untimed or extended time ACT, untimed SAT I. Students may begin taking classes in fall, spring, or summer. *Application deadline:* continuous.

PROGRAM AND SERVICE COMPONENTS

Academic advising: Provided by unit staff members, academic advisers. Most students with LD take 8 to 12 credit hours each term; 12 credit hours required to maintain full-time status; 6 credit hours required to be eligible for financial aid.
Counseling services: Individual counseling, career counseling.
Special courses: Reading, composition, math. All offered for credit; all enter into overall grade point average.
Auxiliary aids: Tape recorders, calculators, typewriters, word-processors with spell-check, personal computers.
Auxiliary services: Alternative test arrangements, priority registration, advocates; accommodations are individually arranged based upon the needs of the student.

GENERAL COLLEGE INFORMATION

Proprietary, 4-year, coed. Part of DeVry Inc./Keller Graduate School of Management. Awards associate, bachelor's degrees. Founded 1967. *Setting:* 18-acre urban campus. *Total enrollment:* 2,862. *Faculty:* 85 (64 full-time, 21 part-time); student–undergrad faculty ratio is 34:1.
Enrollment Profile: 2,862 students from 44 states and territories, 22 other countries. 21% women, 79% men, 20% part-time, 57% state residents, 1% transferred in, 1% international, 42% 25 or older, 4% Native American, 11% Hispanic, 5% black, 6% Asian or Pacific Islander. *Retention:* 47% of 1995 full-time freshmen returned. *Areas of study chosen:* 54% engineering and applied sciences, 32% computer and information sciences, 14% business management and administrative services. *Most popular recent majors:* electronics engineering technology, computer information systems, electrical and electronics technologies.
First-Year Class: 773 total; 1,511 applied, 73% were accepted, 70% of whom enrolled.
Graduation Requirements: 88 credit hours for associate, 132 credit hours for bachelor's; math/science requirements vary according to program; computer course; senior project.
Computers on Campus: 361 computers available on campus for general student use. A computer is recommended for all students. A campus-wide network can be accessed. Students can contact faculty members and/or advisers through e-mail. Computers for student use in computer labs, academic support center. Staffed computer lab on campus provides training in use of computers, software.

EXPENSES AND FINANCIAL AID

Expenses for 1997–98: *Application fee:* $25. Tuition: $6968 full-time, $235 per credit hour part-time.
Undergraduate Financial Aid: On average, 82% of need was met. *Financial aid deadline (priority):* 10/28. *Financial aid forms:* FAFSA required.
LD Services Contact: Ms. Molly Abt, Dean of Student Services, DeVry Institute of Technology, 2149 West Dunlap Avenue, Phoenix, AZ 85021, 602-870-9222. Fax: 602-870-1209. Email: mabt@primenet.com.

DICKINSON STATE UNIVERSITY

Dickinson, North Dakota

LEARNING DISABILITIES SERVICES INFORMATION

Office of Student Support Services currently serves 10 undergraduates with LD. Students diagnosed with ADD/ADHD are eligible for the same services available to students with LD.
Staff: 2 full-time staff members, including director. Services provided by remediation specialist.
Special Fees: No special fees are charged for services to students with LD.
Applications and admissions: *Required:* high school transcript; *recommended:* high school grade point average, courses completed, IEP (Individualized Education Program). Students may begin taking classes in fall, spring, or summer. *Application deadline:* continuous.
Special policies: The college has written policies regarding grade forgiveness; substitutions and waivers of admissions, graduation, and degree requirements.

PROGRAM AND SERVICE COMPONENTS

Academic advising: Provided by unit staff members, academic advisers. Students with LD may take up to 22 credit hours each term; most take 12 to 15 credit hours; 12 credit hours required to maintain full-time status; 3 credit hours (grants), 6 credit hours (loans) required to be eligible for financial aid.
Counseling services: Individual counseling, small-group counseling, career counseling, self-advocacy training.
Basic skills remediation: Offered one-on-one by Director, learning specialist; computer-aided instruction also offered. Available in reading, math, spelling, handwriting, spoken language, written language, learning strategies, study skills, time management, social skills, speech, computer skills.
Subject-area tutoring: Offered one-on-one and in small groups by peer tutors. Available in all subjects.
Special courses: College survival skills, reading, vocabulary development, communication skills, composition, learning strategies, word processing, time management, math, typing, study skills, career planning, stress management, social relationships. Some offered for credit; some enter into overall grade point average.
Auxiliary aids: Taped textbooks.
Auxiliary services: Alternative test arrangements, notetakers, priority registration.
Campus support group: A special student organization is available to students with LD.

GENERAL COLLEGE INFORMATION

State-supported, 4-year, coed. Part of North Dakota University System. Awards associate, bachelor's degrees. Founded 1918. *Setting:* 100-acre small-town campus. *Endowment:* $2.3 million. *Educational spending 1995–96:* $2866 per undergrad. *Total enrollment:* 1,701. *Faculty:* 103 (72 full-time, 56% with terminal degrees, 31 part-time); student–undergrad faculty ratio is 16:1.
Enrollment Profile: 1,701 students from 21 states and territories, 7 other countries. 58% women, 42% men, 15% part-time, 75% state residents, 27% live on campus, 9% transferred in, 2% international, 25% 25 or older, 2% Native American, 1% Hispanic, 1% black, 1% Asian or Pacific Islander. *Areas of study chosen:* 26% education, 25% business management and administrative services, 12% liberal arts/general studies, 11% health professions and related sciences, 4% agriculture, 4% computer and information sciences, 3% biological and life sciences, 3% prelaw, 3% premed, 1% communications and journalism, 1% English language/literature/letters, 1% fine arts, 1% foreign language and literature, 1% mathematics, 1% natural resource sciences, 1% performing arts, 1% predentistry, 1% social sciences. *Most popular recent majors:* business administration/commerce/management, education, nursing.
First-Year Class: 429 total; 625 applied, 100% were accepted, 69% of whom enrolled. 11% from top 10% of their high school class, 22% from top quarter, 52% from top half.
Graduation Requirements: 64 semester hours for associate, 128 semester hours for bachelor's; 1 semester each of math and lab science; computer course; internship (some majors); senior project (some majors).
Computers on Campus: 125 computers available on campus for general student use. A campus-wide network can be accessed from student residence rooms and from off-campus. Students can contact faculty members and/or advisers through e-mail. Computers for student use in computer center, computer labs, learning resource center, classrooms, library, dorms provide access to the Internet/World Wide Web, on- and off-campus e-mail addresses. Staffed computer lab on campus provides training in use of computers, software. *Academic computing expenditure 1995–96:* $124,718.

EXPENSES AND FINANCIAL AID

Expenses for 1996–97: *Application fee:* $25. State resident tuition: $1680 full-time, $70 per semester hour part-time. Nonresident tuition: $4486 full-time, $186.92 per semester hour part-time. Part-time mandatory fees: $12.08 per semester hour. Tuition for Manitoba, Montana, Saskatchewan and South Dakota residents: $2100 full-time, $94.83 per semester hour part-time. Tuition for nonresidents who are eligible for the Western Undergraduate Exchange: $2520 full-time, $112.33 per semester hour part-time. Full-time mandatory fees: $290. College room and board: $2328.
Undergraduate Financial Aid: Of all full-time undergraduates enrolled in fall 1996, 100% of those judged to have need according to Federal

Dickinson State University (continued)

Methodology were aided. *Financial aid deadline (priority):* 4/15. *Financial aid forms:* FAFSA, institutional form required. State form required for some.

LD Services Contact: Mr. Philip D. Covington, Director of Student Support Services, Dickinson State University, 291 Campus Drive, Dickinson, ND 58601, 701-227-2029. Fax: 701-227-2006. Email: pcovington@dsu1.dsu.nodak.edu.

DOANE COLLEGE

Crete, Nebraska

LEARNING DISABILITIES SERVICES INFORMATION

Student Support Services began offering services in 1980. Currently the program serves 9 undergraduates with LD. Students diagnosed with ADD/ADHD are eligible for the same services available to students with LD.

Staff: 1 full-time, 3 part-time staff members, including director, associate director, math specialist, writing specialist. Services provided by tutors, writing, math and reading/study skills specialists.

Special Fees: No special fees are charged for services to students with LD.

Applications and admissions: *Required:* high school transcript, grade point average, class rank, courses completed, extracurricular activities, letters of recommendation, predicted GPA; if less than 2.0 student must submit writing sample and complete Nelson-Denny Reading Test; *recommended:* extended time SAT I or ACT, personal interview, autobiographical statement. Students may begin taking classes any term. *Application deadline:* continuous.

Special policies: The college has written policies regarding substitutions and waivers of admissions, graduation, and degree requirements.

PROGRAM AND SERVICE COMPONENTS

Diagnostic testing: Reading, math, written language.

Academic advising: Provided by unit staff members, academic advisers. Students with LD may take up to 17 credit hours (more with special permission) each term; most take 12 to 17 credit hours; 12 credit hours required to maintain full-time status; 6 credit hours (federal aid) required to be eligible for financial aid.

Counseling services: Individual counseling, career counseling, academic counseling.

Basic skills remediation: Offered one-on-one by math specialist. Available in math.

Subject-area tutoring: Offered one-on-one and in small groups by professional teachers, peer tutors. Available in most subjects.

Special courses: Reading, composition, learning strategies, time management, math, study skills. Most offered for credit; all enter into overall grade point average.

Auxiliary aids: Taped textbooks, tape recorders, calculators, typewriters, word-processors with spell-check, personal computers, optical character readers.

Auxiliary services: Alternative test arrangements, notetakers, priority registration, advocacy.

GENERAL COLLEGE INFORMATION

Independent, comprehensive, coed, affiliated with United Church of Christ. Awards bachelor's, master's degrees (Nontraditional undergraduate programs and graduate programs offered at Lincoln campus. Undergraduate information given is for Crete campus only). Founded 1872. *Setting:* 300-acre small-town campus with easy access to Omaha. *Endowment:* $40.2 million. *Educational spending 1995–96:* $4511 per undergrad. *Total enrollment:* 1,795. *Undergraduate faculty:* 112 (58 full-time, 76% with terminal degrees, 54 part-time); student–undergrad faculty ratio is 13:1.

Enrollment Profile: 902 students from 24 states and territories, 4 other countries. 52% women, 48% men, 3% part-time, 80% state residents, 77% live on campus, 3% transferred in, 3% international, 3% 25 or older, 0% Native American, 1% Hispanic, 2% black, 0% Asian or Pacific Islander. *Retention:* 80% of 1995 full-time freshmen returned. *Graduation:* 45% graduate in 4 years, 54% in 5 years. *Areas of study chosen:* 24% education, 16% business management and administrative services, 11% biological and life sciences, 10% social sciences, 6% performing arts, 6% psychology, 5% communications and journalism, 5% mathematics, 4% computer and information sciences, 4% English language/literature/letters, 3% interdisciplinary studies, 2% physical sciences, 1% foreign language and literature, 1% philosophy. *Most popular recent majors:* education, business administration/commerce/management, sociology.

First-Year Class: 274 total; 933 applied, 90% were accepted, 33% of whom enrolled. 20% from top 10% of their high school class, 46% from top quarter, 80% from top half. 19 valedictorians.

Graduation Requirements: 132 credit hours; 1 math course; 2 natural science courses; computer course; internship (some majors); senior project for honors program students and some majors.

Computers on Campus: 90 computers available on campus for general student use. Computer purchase/lease plans available. A computer is recommended for some students. A campus-wide network can be accessed from student residence rooms and from off-campus. Students can contact faculty members and/or advisers through e-mail. Computers for student use in computer center, computer labs, learning resource center, classrooms, library, dorms provide access to the Internet/World Wide Web, on- and off-campus e-mail addresses. Staffed computer lab on campus provides training in use of computers, software. *Academic computing expenditure 1995–96:* $353,589.

EXPENSES AND FINANCIAL AID

Expenses for 1997–98: *Application fee:* $15. Comprehensive fee of $14,920 includes full-time tuition ($11,180), mandatory fees ($270), and college room and board ($3470). Part-time tuition: $373 per credit hour. Part-time mandatory fees per term range from $35 to $135.

Undergraduate Financial Aid: 87% of all full-time undergraduates enrolled in fall 1996 applied for aid; of these, 91% were judged to have need according to Federal Methodology, of whom 100% were aided. On average, 82% of need was met. *Financial aid deadline (priority):* 3/15. *Financial aid forms:* institutional form required; CSS Financial Aid PROFILE acceptable. FAFSA required for some.

LD Services Contact: Ms. Sherri Hanigan, Director, Doane College, 1014 Boswell Avenue, Crete, NE 68333, 402-826-8554. Fax: 402-826-8278. Email: shanigan@doane.edu.

D'YOUVILLE COLLEGE

Buffalo, New York

LEARNING DISABILITIES SERVICES INFORMATION

Learning Center began offering services in 1987. Currently the program serves 16 undergraduates with LD. Services are also available to graduate students. Students diagnosed with ADD/ADHD are eligible for the same services available to students with LD.

Staff: 10 full-time, 2 part-time staff members, including director, assistant director, coordinator. Services provided by remediation specialists, tutors, counselors.

Special Fees: No special fees are charged for services to students with LD.

Applications and admissions: *Required:* high school grade point average, courses completed, extended time SAT I or ACT; *recommended:* personal interview, letters of recommendation. Students may begin taking classes in fall only. *Application deadline:* continuous.

PROGRAM AND SERVICE COMPONENTS

Special preparation or orientation: Optional summer program offered prior to entering college.

Academic advising: Provided by unit staff members, academic advisers. Students with LD may take up to 19 credit hours each term; most take 12 to 15 credit hours; 12 credit hours (fewer with special permission) required to maintain full-time status; 6 credit hours (part-time), 12 credit hours (full-time; fewer with special permission) required to be eligible for financial aid.

Counseling services: Individual counseling, career counseling, self-advocacy training.

Basic skills remediation: Offered one-on-one, in small groups, and in class-size groups by LD teachers, regular teachers; computer-aided instruction also offered. Available in reading, math, spelling, handwriting, spoken language, written language, learning strategies, study skills, time management, social skills, computer skills, critical thinking.

Subject-area tutoring: Offered one-on-one and in small groups by professional teachers, peer tutors. Available in most subjects.

Auxiliary aids: Taped textbooks, computer lab.

Auxiliary services: Alternative test arrangements, notetakers, priority registration, advocacy.

GENERAL COLLEGE INFORMATION

Independent, comprehensive, coed. Awards bachelor's, master's degrees. Founded 1908. *Setting:* 7-acre urban campus. *Endowment:* $8 million. *Educational spending 1995–96:* $3540 per undergrad. *Total enrollment:* 1,915. *Faculty:* 164 (91 full-time, 60% with terminal degrees, 73 part-time); student–undergrad faculty ratio is 15:1.

Enrollment Profile: 1,445 students from 19 states and territories, 9 other countries. 73% women, 27% men, 27% part-time, 68% state residents, 20% live on campus, 50% transferred in, 18% international, 37% 25 or older, 1% Native American, 3% Hispanic, 9% black, 2% Asian or Pacific Islander. *Retention:* 75% of 1995 full-time freshmen returned. *Graduation:* 50% graduate in 4 years, 55% in 5 years, 62% in 6 years. *Areas of study chosen:* 63% health professions and related sciences, 17% education, 5% business management and administrative services, 4% liberal arts/general studies, 3% biological and life sciences, 1% premed. *Most popular recent majors:* physical therapy, occupational therapy, nursing.

First-Year Class: 238 total; 1,036 applied, 53% were accepted, 44% of whom enrolled. 21% from top 10% of their high school class, 55% from top quarter, 89% from top half. 4 valedictorians.

Graduation Requirements: 120 credit hours; 1 math course; 2 science courses; computer course; internship (some majors).

Computers on Campus: 58 computers available on campus for general student use. Computer purchase/lease plans available. A computer is recommended for all students. A campus-wide network can be accessed from off-campus. Students can contact faculty members and/or advisers through e-mail. Computers for student use in computer center, computer labs, library, dorms provide access to the Internet/World Wide Web, on- and off-campus e-mail addresses. Staffed computer lab on campus provides training in use of computers, software. *Academic computing expenditure 1995–96:* $500,000.

EXPENSES AND FINANCIAL AID

Expenses for 1997–98: *Application fee:* $20. Comprehensive fee of $14,740 includes full-time tuition ($9840), mandatory fees ($200), and college room and board ($4700). Part-time mandatory fees: $100 per semester. Part-time tuition: $270 per credit hour for 1 to 8 credit hours, $295 per credit hour for 9 or more credit hours.

Undergraduate Financial Aid: Of all full-time undergraduates enrolled in fall 1996, 99% of those who applied for aid were judged to have need according to Federal Methodology, of whom 99% were aided. On average, 85% of need was met. *Financial aid deadline (priority):* 4/15. *Financial aid forms:* FAFSA required. State form, financial aid transcript (for transfers) required for some.

LD Services Contact: Ms. Carolyn L. Boone, Coordinator of Disability Services, D'Youville College, 320 Porter Avenue, Buffalo, NY 14201-1084, 716-881-7728. Fax: 716-881-7790.

EAST CAROLINA UNIVERSITY

Greenville, North Carolina

LEARNING DISABILITIES SERVICES INFORMATION

Handicapped Student Services began offering services in 1980. Currently the program serves 178 undergraduates with LD. Services are also available to graduate students. Students diagnosed with ADD/ADHD are eligible for the same services available to students with LD.

Staff: 2 full-time, 3 part-time staff members, including director, associate director, coordinator, reading specialist. Services provided by tutors, counselor, diagnostic specialists.

Special Fees: $150 for diagnostic testing.

Applications and admissions: *Required:* high school transcript, grade point average, class rank, courses completed, extended time SAT I, psychoeducational report; *recommended:* high school IEP (Individualized Education Program), untimed or extended time ACT, untimed SAT I. Students may begin taking classes any term. *Application deadline:* continuous.

Special policies: The college has written policies regarding grade forgiveness; substitutions and waivers of admissions, graduation, and degree requirements.

PROGRAM AND SERVICE COMPONENTS

Diagnostic testing: Intelligence, reading, math, spelling, written language, perceptual skills, study skills, speech, hearing.

Academic advising: Provided by unit staff members, academic advisers. Students with LD may take up to 18 semester hours each term; most take 13 semester hours; 12 semester hours required to maintain full-time status and be eligible for financial aid.

Counseling services: Individual counseling, small-group counseling, career counseling.

Basic skills remediation: Offered in small groups and in class-size groups by regular teachers, teacher trainees. Available in reading, math, spelling, written language, learning strategies, perceptual skills, study skills, time management, social skills, speech.

Subject-area tutoring: Offered one-on-one and in small groups by peer tutors, graduate assistants. Available in all subjects.

Special courses: Reading, vocabulary development, composition, math, study skills, career planning. Some offered for credit; some enter into overall grade point average.

Auxiliary aids: Taped textbooks, word-processors with spell-check, talking computers, optical character readers.

Auxiliary services: Alternative test arrangements, notetakers, priority registration.

GENERAL COLLEGE INFORMATION

State-supported, coed. Part of University of North Carolina System. Awards bachelor's, master's, doctoral, first professional degrees. Founded 1907. *Setting:* 465-acre urban campus. *Endowment:* $24.9 million. *Research spending 1995–96:* $5.8 million. *Educational spending 1995–96:* $7708 per undergrad. *Total enrollment:* 16,805. *Faculty:* 1,181 (1,134 full-time, 81% with terminal degrees, 47 part-time); student–undergrad faculty ratio is 19:1.

Enrollment Profile: 14,313 students from 49 states and territories, 28 other countries. 58% women, 42% men, 12% part-time, 86% state residents, 32% live on campus, 37% transferred in, 1% international, 16% 25 or older, 1% Native American, 1% Hispanic, 11% black, 1% Asian or Pacific Islander. *Retention:* 77% of 1995 full-time freshmen returned. *Graduation:* 17% graduate in 4 years, 41% in 5 years, 49% in 6 years. *Areas of study chosen:* 16% education, 15% health professions and related sciences, 12% fine arts, 11% vocational and home economics, 10% social sciences, 9% business management and administrative services, 6% biological and life sciences, 6% engineering and applied sciences, 4% communications and journalism, 3% English language/literature/letters, 3% psychology, 2% physical sciences, 1% computer and information sciences, 1% foreign language and literature, 1% mathematics, 1% performing arts, 1% philosophy. *Most popular recent majors:* business administration/commerce/management, nursing, elementary education.

First-Year Class: 2,807 total; 8,898 applied, 77% were accepted, 41% of whom enrolled. 15% from top 10% of their high school class, 44% from top quarter, 83% from top half.

Graduation Requirements: 120 semester hours; 3 semester hours of math; 8 semester hours of science; computer course for math, business, health sciences, applied physics, political science, technical education, economics majors; internship (some majors); senior project (some majors).

Computers on Campus: 2,000 computers available on campus for general student use. Computer purchase/lease plans available. A computer is strongly recommended for all students. A campus-wide network can be accessed from student residence rooms and from off-campus. Students can contact faculty members and/or advisers through e-mail. Computers for student use in computer center, computer labs, research center, learning resource center, classrooms, library, dorms provide access to the Internet/World Wide Web, on- and off-campus e-mail addresses. Staffed computer lab on campus provides training in use of computers, software. *Academic computing expenditure 1995–96:* $3.1 million.

EXPENSES AND FINANCIAL AID

Expenses for 1996–97: *Application fee:* $35. State resident tuition: $874 full-time. Nonresident tuition: $8028 full-time. Part-time tuition per semester ranges from $109 to $328 for state residents, $1004 to $3011 for nonresidents. Part-time mandatory fees per semester range from $110 to $330. Full-time mandatory fees: $878. College room and board: $3480. College room only: $1660.

Undergraduate Financial Aid: Of all full-time undergraduates enrolled in fall 1996, 85% of those who applied for aid were judged to have need according to Federal Methodology, of whom 90% were aided. On average, 90% of need was met. *Financial aid deadline (priority):* 4/15. *Financial aid forms:* FAFSA required; CSS Financial Aid PROFILE, state form acceptable.

LD Services Contact: Mr. C. C. Rowe, Director, Department for Disability Support Services, East Carolina University, A-117 Brewster Building, Greenville, NC 27858-4353, 919-328-6799. Fax: 919-328-4883. Email: hsrowe@ecuvm.cis.edu.

EASTERN COLLEGE

St. Davids, Pennsylvania

LEARNING DISABILITIES SERVICES INFORMATION

Cushing Center for Counseling and Academic Support began offering services in 1996. Currently the program serves 17 undergraduates with LD. Services are also available to graduate students. Students diagnosed with ADD/ADHD are eligible for the same services available to students with LD, as well as screening, medical evaluation, medication dispensing and monitoring, support group.

Staff: 3 full-time, 15 part-time staff members, including director, coordinator. Services provided by remediation specialist, tutors, diagnostic specialist.

Special Fees: No special fees are charged for services to students with LD.

Applications and admissions: *Required:* high school transcript, grade point average, class rank, courses completed, letters of recommendation; *recommended:* high school extracurricular activities, IEP (Individualized Education Program), untimed or extended time SAT I, personal interview, psychoeducational report. Students may begin taking classes in summer only. *Application deadline:* continuous.

PROGRAM AND SERVICE COMPONENTS

Special preparation or orientation: Summer program (required for some) held prior to entering college.

Diagnostic testing: Intelligence, reading, math, spelling, handwriting, written language, personality.

Academic advising: Provided by unit staff members, academic advisers. Most students with LD take 12 to 15 credits each term; 12 credits required to maintain full-time status and be eligible for financial aid.

Special courses: College survival skills, reading, vocabulary development, composition, word processing, time management, study skills, stress management. Some offered for credit; some enter into overall grade point average.

Auxiliary aids: Taped textbooks, tape recorders, word-processors with spell-check, personal computers.

Auxiliary services: Alternative test arrangements, notetakers, advocacy.

GENERAL COLLEGE INFORMATION

Independent American Baptist, comprehensive, coed. Awards associate, bachelor's, master's degrees. Founded 1932. *Setting:* 107-acre small-town campus with easy access to Philadelphia. *Endowment:* $5 million. *Total enrollment:* 2,348. *Faculty:* 207 (59 full-time, 80% with terminal degrees, 148 part-time); student–undergrad faculty ratio is 15:1.

Enrollment Profile: 1,594 students from 36 states and territories, 21 other countries. 67% women, 33% men, 20% part-time, 66% state residents, 39% live on campus, 58% transferred in, 3% international, 41% 25 or older, 1% Native American, 2% Hispanic, 12% black, 1% Asian or Pacific Islander. *Retention:* 76% of 1995 full-time freshmen returned. *Graduation:* 28% graduate in 4 years, 35% in 5 years, 38% in 6 years. *Areas of study chosen:* 30% business management and administrative services, 30% liberal arts/general studies, 11% health professions and related sciences, 8% social sciences, 7% education, 4% theology/religion, 2% communications and journalism, 2% performing arts, 2% psychology, 1% agriculture, 1% biological and life sciences, 1% English language/literature/letters, 1% foreign language and literature, 1% mathematics, 1% physical sciences. *Most popular recent majors:* business administration/commerce/management, elementary education, nursing.

First-Year Class: 250 total; 635 applied, 88% were accepted, 45% of whom enrolled. 17% from top 10% of their high school class, 47% from top quarter, 75% from top half.

Graduation Requirements: 60 credits for associate, 127 credits for bachelor's; computer course for business administration, chemistry, health, math majors; internship (some majors); senior project for honors program students and some majors.

Computers on Campus: 57 computers available on campus for general student use. A campus-wide network can be accessed from student residence rooms and from off-campus. Computers for student use in computer labs, library, dorms, student rooms provide access to the Internet/World Wide Web, on- and off-campus e-mail addresses. Staffed computer lab on campus provides training in use of computers, software. *Academic computing expenditure 1995–96:* $172,550.

EXPENSES AND FINANCIAL AID

Expenses for 1997–98: *Application fee:* $25. Comprehensive fee of $18,140 includes full-time tuition ($12,700) and college room and board ($5440). College room only: $2660. Part-time tuition: $305 per credit.

Undergraduate Financial Aid: 92% of all full-time undergraduates enrolled in fall 1996 applied for aid; of these, 93% were judged to have need according to Federal Methodology, of whom 100% were aided. On average, 90% of need was met. *Financial aid deadline:* continuous. *Financial aid forms:* FAFSA, institutional form, financial aid transcript (for transfers) required.

LD Services Contact: Dr. Bruce A. Naylor, Director, Cushing Center for Counseling and Academic Support, Eastern College, 1300 Eagle Road, St. Davids, PA 19087-3696, 610-341-5838. Fax: 610-341-1705.

EASTERN CONNECTICUT STATE UNIVERSITY

Willimantic, Connecticut

LEARNING DISABILITIES SERVICES INFORMATION

Special Services for Students with Disabilities, Office of Student Affairs began offering services in 1978. Currently the program serves 76 undergraduates with LD. Services are also available to graduate students. Students diagnosed with ADD/ADHD are eligible for the same services available to students with LD.

Staff: 1 part-time staff member (coordinator). Services provided by tutors, counselor.

Special Fees: No special fees are charged for services to students with LD.

Applications and admissions: *Required:* high school transcript, grade point average, class rank, courses completed, untimed or extended time SAT I, letters of recommendation; *recommended:* high school extracurricular activities, IEP (Individualized Education Program), personal interview, psychoeducational report completed within 3 years (in most cases). Students may begin taking classes any term. *Application deadline:* continuous.

Special policies: The college has written policies regarding substitutions and waivers of admissions, graduation, and degree requirements.

PROGRAM AND SERVICE COMPONENTS

Academic advising: Provided by academic advisers. Students with LD may take up to 17 credit hours each term; most take 12 to 15 credit hours; 12 credit hours required to maintain full-time status and be eligible for financial aid.

Counseling services: Individual counseling, small-group counseling, career counseling.

Auxiliary aids: Taped textbooks, tape recorders, personal computers, talking computers.

Auxiliary services: Alternative test arrangements, notetakers, priority registration, advocacy, readers.

GENERAL COLLEGE INFORMATION

State-supported, comprehensive, coed. Part of Connecticut State University System. Awards associate, bachelor's, master's degrees. Founded 1889. *Setting:* 174-acre small-town campus. *Total enrollment:* 4,590. *Undergraduate faculty:* 199 (134 full-time, 78% with terminal degrees, 65 part-time); student–undergrad faculty ratio is 17:1.

Enrollment Profile: 4,312 students from 33 states and territories, 39 other countries. 53% women, 47% men, 33% part-time, 90% state residents, 35% transferred in, 3% international, 35% 25 or older, 1% Native American, 6% Hispanic, 10% black, 1% Asian or Pacific Islander. *Areas of study chosen:* 30% business management and administrative services, 13% education, 9% communications and journalism, 8% social sciences, 7% psychology, 5% biological and life sciences, 5% computer and information sciences, 4% fine arts, 4% liberal arts/general studies, 4% natural resource sciences, 3% English language/literature/letters, 3% mathematics, 2% foreign language and literature, 1% predentistry, 1% prelaw, 1% premed. *Most popular recent majors:* business administration/commerce/management, education, psychology.

First-Year Class: 695 total; 2,127 applied, 80% were accepted, 41% of whom enrolled. 6% from top 10% of their high school class, 42% from top quarter, 73% from top half.

Graduation Requirements: 60 credit hours for associate, 120 credit hours for bachelor's; 2 courses each in math and natural science; 2 semesters in foreign language or proven proficiency; computer course; senior project for honors program students.

Computers on Campus: 200 computers available on campus for general student use. Computer purchase/lease plans available. Computers for student use in computer center, computer labs, learning resource center, classrooms, library, student center, academic buildings, advisement and media centers provide access to the Internet/World Wide Web. Staffed computer lab on campus provides training in use of computers, software.

EXPENSES AND FINANCIAL AID

Expenses for 1997–98: State resident tuition: $2062 full-time, $149 per credit hour part-time. Nonresident tuition: $6674 full-time, $149 per credit hour part-time. Part-time mandatory fees: $17.50 per credit hour. Full-time tuition for nonresidents who are eligible for the New England Regional Student Program: $3094. Full-time mandatory fees: $1532 for state residents and nonresidents who are eligible for the New England Regional Student Program, $2398 for other nonresidents. College room and board: $5048. College room only: $3500.
Undergraduate Financial Aid: Of all full-time undergraduates enrolled in fall 1996, 64% of those who applied for aid were judged to have need according to Federal Methodology, of whom 70% were aided. On average, 90% of need was met. *Financial aid deadline (priority):* 3/15. *Financial aid forms:* FAFSA, institutional form required.
LD Services Contact: Dr. Deb Cohen, Counselor/Coordinator, Disabled Student Services, Eastern Connecticut State University, Counseling Services, 185 Birch Street, Willimantic, CT 06226-2295, 860-465-4527. Fax: 860-465-4560. Email: cohendeb@ecsuc.ctstateu.edu.

EASTERN ILLINOIS UNIVERSITY

Charleston, Illinois

LEARNING DISABILITIES SERVICES INFORMATION

Office of Disability Services began offering services in 1985. Currently the program serves 78 undergraduates with LD. Services are also available to graduate students. Students diagnosed with ADD/ADHD are eligible for the same services available to students with LD.
Staff: 2 full-time, 1 part-time staff members, including coordinator. Services provided by adaptive technology specialist.
Special Fees: No special fees are charged for services to students with LD.
Applications and admissions: *Required:* high school transcript, class rank, untimed ACT, psychoeducational report completed within 3 years; *recommended:* high school IEP (Individualized Education Program). Students may begin taking classes any term. *Application deadline:* continuous.

PROGRAM AND SERVICE COMPONENTS

Academic advising: Provided by academic advisers. Most students with LD take 12 to 15 semester hours each term; 12 semester hours (unless documentation specifies otherwise) required to maintain full-time status; 9 semester hours (with supportive documentation) required to be eligible for financial aid.
Basic skills remediation: Offered in class-size groups by regular teachers, speech/language pathologists, Disability Services staff. Available in reading, math, written language, time management, speech.
Auxiliary aids: Taped textbooks, tape recorders, calculators, word-processors with spell-check, personal computers, talking computers, optical character readers, talking dictionary.
Auxiliary services: Alternative test arrangements, notetakers, priority registration, advocacy, taped lectures, alternate assignments, lighter course load, course substitution.

GENERAL COLLEGE INFORMATION

State-supported, comprehensive, coed. Awards bachelor's, master's degrees. Founded 1895. *Setting:* 320-acre small-town campus. *Endowment:* $13.8 million. *Research spending 1995–96:* $333,920. *Educational spending 1995–96:* $4429 per undergrad. *Total enrollment:* 11,711. *Faculty:* 659 (596 full-time, 73% with terminal degrees, 63 part-time); student–undergrad faculty ratio is 15:1.
Enrollment Profile: 10,106 students from 35 states and territories, 15 other countries. 57% women, 43% men, 9% part-time, 97% state residents, 51% live on campus, 24% transferred in, 1% international, 10% 25 or older, 2% Hispanic, 5% black, 1% Asian or Pacific Islander. *Retention:* 79% of 1995 full-time freshmen returned. *Graduation:* 65% graduate in 6 years. *Areas of study chosen:* 25% education, 15% business management and administrative services, 7% English language/literature/letters, 7% social sciences, 6% biological and life sciences, 5% psychology, 4% vocational and home economics, 3% liberal arts/general studies, 2% engineering and applied sciences, 2% fine arts, 2% health professions and related sciences, 2% interdisciplinary studies, 2% mathematics, 2% performing arts, 1% communications and journalism, 1% foreign language and literature, 1% physical sciences. *Most popular recent majors:* elementary education, liberal arts/general studies, psychology.
First-Year Class: 1,739 total; 5,872 applied, 76% were accepted, 39% of whom enrolled. 9% from top 10% of their high school class, 38% from top quarter, 85% from top half.
Graduation Requirements: 120 semester hours; 1 semester of math; 1 year of a foreign language; computer course for business, math majors; internship (some majors); senior project (some majors).
Computers on Campus: 785 computers available on campus for general student use. A campus-wide network can be accessed from off-campus. Students can contact faculty members and/or advisers through e-mail. Computers for student use in computer center, computer labs, library, dorms provide access to the Internet/World Wide Web. Staffed computer lab on campus provides training in use of computers, software. *Academic computing expenditure 1995–96:* $1.4 million.

EXPENSES AND FINANCIAL AID

Estimated Expenses for 1997–98: *Application fee:* $25. State resident tuition: $2124 full-time, $88.50 per semester hour part-time. Nonresident tuition: $6372 full-time, $265.50 per semester hour part-time. Part-time mandatory fees: $32.30 per semester hour. Full-time mandatory fees: $792. College room and board: $3362.
Undergraduate Financial Aid: Of all full-time undergraduates enrolled in fall 1996, 81% of those who applied for aid were judged to have need according to Federal Methodology, of whom 75% were aided. *Financial aid deadline (priority):* 4/15. *Financial aid forms:* FAFSA required.
LD Services Contact: Ms. Martha P. Jacques, C.R.C., Director, Eastern Illinois University, Office of Disability Services, Charleston, IL 61920-3099, 217-581-6583.

EASTERN OREGON UNIVERSITY

La Grande, Oregon

LEARNING DISABILITIES SERVICES INFORMATION

Student Support Services currently serves 36 undergraduates with LD. Students diagnosed with ADD/ADHD are eligible for the same services available to students with LD.
Staff: 3 part-time staff members, including director. Services provided by tutors, counselors.
Special Fees: No special fees are charged for services to students with LD.
Applications and admissions: *Required:* high school transcript, grade point average, courses completed, untimed SAT I, psychoeducational report; *recommended:* high school extracurricular activities, extended time SAT I, autobiographical statement, letters of recommendation. *Application deadline:* continuous.

PROGRAM AND SERVICE COMPONENTS

Special preparation or orientation: Optional orientation offered before registration, during registration, after classes begin.
Academic advising: Provided by unit staff members, academic advisers. 12 credit hours are required each term to be eligible for financial aid.
Counseling services: Individual counseling, small-group counseling, career counseling, self-advocacy training.
Basic skills remediation: Offered one-on-one, in small groups, and in class-size groups. Available in reading, math, spelling, handwriting, spoken language, written language, learning strategies, study skills, social skills, speech.
Subject-area tutoring: Offered one-on-one and in small groups by professional teachers, peer tutors. Available in most subjects.
Special courses: College survival skills, reading, vocabulary development, communication skills, composition, learning strategies, word processing, time management, math, personal psychology, study skills, career planning. Some offered for credit; some enter into overall grade point average.
Auxiliary aids: Tape recorders, calculators, typewriters, word-processors with spell-check.
Auxiliary services: Alternative test arrangements, notetakers.

GENERAL COLLEGE INFORMATION

State-supported, comprehensive, coed. Part of Oregon State System of Higher Education. Awards associate, bachelor's, master's degrees.

Eastern Oregon University (continued)

Founded 1929. *Setting:* 121-acre rural campus. *Endowment:* $646,448. *Research spending 1995–96:* $171,127. *Educational spending 1995–96:* $3786 per undergrad. *Total enrollment:* 1,876. *Undergraduate faculty:* 103 (83 full-time, 84% with terminal degrees, 20 part-time); student–undergrad faculty ratio is 14:1.
Enrollment Profile: 1,849 students from 32 states and territories, 23 other countries. 52% women, 48% men, 11% part-time, 71% state residents, 25% live on campus, 14% transferred in, 3% international, 24% 25 or older, 2% Native American, 4% Hispanic, 1% black, 3% Asian or Pacific Islander. *Retention:* 55% of 1995 full-time freshmen returned. *Areas of study chosen:* 23% education, 15% liberal arts/general studies, 13% business management and administrative services, 6% agriculture, 6% biological and life sciences, 6% social sciences, 4% health professions and related sciences, 4% psychology, 3% English language/literature/letters, 3% performing arts, 2% fine arts, 2% physical sciences, 1% engineering and applied sciences, 1% mathematics, 1% predentistry, 1% prelaw, 1% premed, 1% prevet. *Most popular recent majors:* education, business economics, biology/biological sciences.
First-Year Class: 378 total; 878 applied, 61% were accepted, 70% of whom enrolled. 1 National Merit Scholar, 25 class presidents, 43 valedictorians.
Graduation Requirements: 93 credit hours for associate, 186 credit hours for bachelor's; computer course for business, agribusiness, chemistry, physics, engineering majors; internship (some majors); senior project (some majors).
Computers on Campus: 75 computers available on campus for general student use. Computer purchase/lease plans available. A campuswide network can be accessed from off-campus. Students can contact faculty members and/or advisers through e-mail. Computers for student use in computer center, computer labs, learning resource center, library, dorms provide access to the Internet/World Wide Web. Staffed computer lab on campus provides training in use of computers, software. *Academic computing expenditure 1995–96:* $390,635.

EXPENSES AND FINANCIAL AID

Expenses for 1996–97: *Application fee:* $50. Comprehensive fee of $6977 includes full-time tuition ($2316), mandatory fees ($695), and college room and board ($3966). One-time mandatory fee: $50. Part-time tuition per quarter ranges from $132 to $972 according to course load.
Undergraduate Financial Aid: Of all full-time undergraduates enrolled in fall 1996, 95% of those judged to have need according to Federal Methodology were aided. On average, 95% of need was met. *Financial aid deadline (priority):* 1/31. *Financial aid forms:* state form, Institutional Scholarship Applications required; FAFSA acceptable.
LD Services Contact: Dr. Thacher Carter, Director, Counseling Center, Eastern Oregon University, 1410 L Avenue, La Grande, OR 97850, 541-962-3744. Fax: 541-962-3335.

EASTERN WASHINGTON UNIVERSITY

Cheney, Washington

LEARNING DISABILITIES SERVICES INFORMATION

Disability Support Services began offering services in 1991. Currently the program serves 65 undergraduates with LD. Services are also available to graduate students. Students diagnosed with ADD/ADHD are eligible for the same services available to students with LD.
Staff: 1 full-time staff member (coordinator). Services provided by tutors, counselors, learning skills specialists.
Special Fees: No special fees are charged for services to students with LD.
Applications and admissions: *Required:* high school transcript, grade point average, courses completed, untimed SAT I or ACT, personal interview, psychoeducational report completed within 5 years (for receipt of services), Washington Pre-College Test; *recommended:* extended time SAT I or ACT. Students may begin taking classes any term. *Application deadline:* 2/15 (fall term), 2/1 (spring term).

PROGRAM AND SERVICE COMPONENTS

Academic advising: Provided by unit staff members, academic advisers. Students with LD may take up to 18 quarter hours each term; most take 5 to 12 quarter hours; 10 quarter hours required to maintain full-time status; 12 quarter hours required to be eligible for financial aid.
Counseling services: Individual counseling, small-group counseling, career counseling.
Basic skills remediation: Offered one-on-one and in small groups by regular teachers, teaching assistants. Available in reading, math, written language, learning strategies, study skills, time management.
Subject-area tutoring: Offered one-on-one by peer tutors, learning skills specialists. Available in most subjects.
Special courses: Reading, communication skills, composition, learning strategies, word processing, time management, math, typing, personal psychology, study skills, career planning. Most offered for credit; most enter into overall grade point average.
Auxiliary aids: Taped textbooks, tape recorders, word-processors with spell-check, talking computers, optical character readers.
Auxiliary services: Alternative test arrangements, notetakers, priority registration, advocacy, referrals to writing lab, math lab and learning skills center.

GENERAL COLLEGE INFORMATION

State-supported, comprehensive, coed. Part of Washington Higher Education Coordinating Board. Awards bachelor's, master's degrees. Founded 1882. *Setting:* 335-acre small-town campus. *Endowment:* $1.9 million. *Research spending 1995–96:* $1 million. *Total enrollment:* 7,589. *Faculty:* 538 (381 full-time, 62% with terminal degrees, 157 part-time); student–undergrad faculty ratio is 16:1.
Enrollment Profile: 6,326 students from 44 states and territories, 35 other countries. 58% women, 42% men, 7% part-time, 91% state residents, 14% live on campus, 21% transferred in, 8% international, 39% 25 or older, 2% Native American, 4% Hispanic, 2% black, 3% Asian or Pacific Islander. *Retention:* 74% of 1995 full-time freshmen returned. *Areas of study chosen:* 11% education, 11% social sciences, 6% biological and life sciences, 6% business management and administrative services, 4% English language/literature/letters, 3% health professions and related sciences, 2% communications and journalism, 2% fine arts, 2% foreign language and literature, 2% liberal arts/general studies, 2% psychology, 1% computer and information sciences, 1% engineering and applied sciences, 1% interdisciplinary studies, 1% mathematics, 1% physical sciences. *Most popular recent majors:* business administration/commerce/management, reading education, liberal arts/general studies.
First-Year Class: 707 total; 1,978 applied, 90% were accepted, 39% of whom enrolled.
Graduation Requirements: 180 quarter hours; intermediate algebra competence; 1 geometry course; 2 natural science courses; computer course for math, business majors; internship (some majors); senior project for honors program students and some majors.
Computers on Campus: 300 computers available on campus for general student use. Computer purchase/lease plans available. A campuswide network can be accessed from off-campus. Students can contact faculty members and/or advisers through e-mail. Computers for student use in computer center, computer labs, library, student center provide access to the Internet/World Wide Web, on- and off-campus e-mail addresses. Staffed computer lab on campus provides training in use of computers, software. *Academic computing expenditure 1995–96:* $1.3 million.

EXPENSES AND FINANCIAL AID

Expenses for 1997–98: *Application fee:* $35. State resident tuition: $2526 full-time, $84.20 per quarter hour part-time. Nonresident tuition: $8961 full-time, $298.70 per quarter hour part-time. College room and board: $4294. College room only: $2188.
Undergraduate Financial Aid: Of all full-time undergraduates enrolled in fall 1996, 91% of those judged to have need according to Federal Methodology were aided. On average, 90% of need was met. *Financial aid deadline (priority):* 2/15. *Financial aid forms:* FAFSA required.
Financial aid specifically for students with LD: Scholarship: Disabled Student Scholarship.
LD Services Contact: Ms. Karen Raver, Director, Disability Support Services/ADA Compliance Officer, Eastern Washington University, Mail Stop 60, Cheney, WA 99004-2496, 509-359-2293. Fax: 509-359-4673. Email: kraver@ewu.edu.

EAST STROUDSBURG UNIVERSITY OF PENNSYLVANIA

East Stroudsburg, Pennsylvania

LEARNING DISABILITIES SERVICES INFORMATION

Office of Disability Services began offering services in 1990. Currently the program serves 170 undergraduates with LD. Services are also

available to graduate students. Students diagnosed with ADD/ADHD are eligible for the same services available to students with LD.

Staff: 2 full-time staff members, including coordinator. Services provided by counselor.

Special Fees: No special fees are charged for services to students with LD.

Applications and admissions: *Required:* high school transcript, grade point average, class rank, courses completed, extended time SAT I, psychoeducational report completed since age 15 or older; *recommended:* high school extracurricular activities, IEP (Individualized Education Program). Students may begin taking classes in fall or summer. *Application deadline:* 3/1.

PROGRAM AND SERVICE COMPONENTS

Academic advising: Provided by unit staff members, academic advisers. Students with LD may take up to 18 credits each term; most take 12 to 15 credits; 12 credits required to maintain full-time status and be eligible for financial aid.

Counseling services: Individual counseling, small-group counseling, career counseling, self-advocacy training.

Auxiliary aids: Taped textbooks, tape recorders, calculators, typewriters, word-processors with spell-check, personal computers, optical character readers.

Auxiliary services: Alternative test arrangements, notetakers, priority registration, advocacy.

Campus support group: A special student organization is available to students with LD.

GENERAL COLLEGE INFORMATION

State-supported, comprehensive, coed. Part of Pennsylvania State System of Higher Education. Awards associate, bachelor's, master's degrees. Founded 1893. *Setting:* 183-acre small-town campus. *Endowment:* $3.8 million. *Research spending 1995–96:* $478,513. *Educational spending 1995–96:* $5193 per undergrad. *Total enrollment:* 5,552. *Faculty:* 277 (260 full-time, 74% with terminal degrees, 17 part-time); student–undergrad faculty ratio is 19:1.

Enrollment Profile: 4,647 students from 23 states and territories, 25 other countries. 57% women, 43% men, 13% part-time, 84% state residents, 45% live on campus, 27% transferred in, 1% international, 18% 25 or older, 0% Native American, 3% Hispanic, 2% black, 1% Asian or Pacific Islander. *Retention:* 71% of 1995 full-time freshmen returned. *Graduation:* 20% graduate in 4 years, 44% in 5 years, 47% in 6 years. *Areas of study chosen:* 30% education, 15% health professions and related sciences, 11% liberal arts/general studies, 10% business management and administrative services, 8% biological and life sciences, 7% social sciences, 5% psychology, 3% communications and journalism, 2% computer and information sciences, 2% English language/literature/letters, 2% physical sciences, 1% fine arts, 1% foreign language and literature, 1% mathematics, 1% premed. *Most popular recent majors:* elementary education, physical education, business administration/commerce/management.

First-Year Class: 902 total; 3,936 applied, 67% were accepted, 34% of whom enrolled. 4% from top 10% of their high school class, 22% from top quarter, 69% from top half.

Graduation Requirements: 60 credits for associate, 128 credits for bachelor's; 15 credits of math/science; computer course for chemistry, economics, hospitality management, math, recreation/leisure services, management majors; internship (some majors); senior project for honors program students.

Computers on Campus: 250 computers available on campus for general student use. Computer purchase/lease plans available. A computer is recommended for all students. A campus-wide network can be accessed from off-campus. Students can contact faculty members and/or advisers through e-mail. Computers for student use in computer center, computer labs, learning resource center, classrooms, library, student center provide access to the Internet/World Wide Web, on- and off-campus e-mail addresses. Staffed computer lab on campus provides training in use of computers, software. *Academic computing expenditure 1995–96:* $1.8 million.

EXPENSES AND FINANCIAL AID

Expenses for 1997–98: *Application fee:* $25. State resident tuition: $3468 full-time, $144 per credit part-time. Nonresident tuition: $8824 full-time, $368 per credit part-time. Part-time mandatory fees: $35.60 per credit. Full-time mandatory fees: $854. College room and board: $3670. College room only: $2282.

Undergraduate Financial Aid: 75% of all full-time undergraduates enrolled in fall 1996 applied for aid; of these, 81% were judged to have need according to Federal Methodology, of whom 93% were aided. *Financial aid deadline:* 3/1. *Financial aid forms:* FAFSA required. Institutional form required for some.

Financial aid specifically for students with LD: Scholarship: Kravitz Scholarship.

LD Services Contact: Dr. Edith F. Miller, Disability Services Coordinator, East Stroudsburg University of Pennsylvania, 200 Prospect Street, East Stroudsburg, PA 18301-2999, 717-422-3825. Fax: 717-422-3819. Email: emiller@po-box.esu.edu.

EDGEWOOD COLLEGE

Madison, Wisconsin

LEARNING DISABILITIES SERVICES INFORMATION

Assistance to Students with Learning Differences (ASLD) began offering services in 1989. Currently the program serves 19 undergraduates with LD. Services are also available to graduate students. Students diagnosed with ADD/ADHD are eligible for the same services available to students with LD.

Staff: 1 full-time staff member (director). Services provided by remediation specialists, tutors, reading instructors, math instructors.

Special Fees: No special fees are charged for services to students with LD.

Applications and admissions: *Required:* high school transcript, grade point average, class rank, courses completed, untimed ACT, personal interview, autobiographical statement, letters of recommendation, psychoeducational report completed within 18 months; *recommended:* extended time ACT. Students may begin taking classes in fall or spring. *Application deadline:* continuous.

Special policies: The college has written policies regarding substitutions and waivers of graduation requirements.

PROGRAM AND SERVICE COMPONENTS

Special preparation or orientation: Required orientation held the week prior to the beginning of classes.

Academic advising: Provided by unit staff members, academic advisers. Students with LD may take up to 18 credits (more with dean's permission) each term; most take 12 to 14 credits; 12 credits required to maintain full-time status and be eligible for financial aid.

Auxiliary aids: Taped textbooks, word-processors with spell-check.

Auxiliary services: Alternative test arrangements, notetakers.

GENERAL COLLEGE INFORMATION

Independent Roman Catholic, comprehensive, coed. Awards associate, bachelor's, master's degrees. Founded 1927. *Setting:* 55-acre urban campus. *Endowment:* $3 million. *Total enrollment:* 2,032. *Faculty:* 152 (69 full-time, 77% with terminal degrees, 83 part-time); student–undergrad faculty ratio is 15:1.

Enrollment Profile: 1,500 students from 19 states and territories, 24 other countries. 73% women, 27% men, 35% part-time, 87% state residents, 24% live on campus, 10% transferred in, 6% international, 42% 25 or older, 1% Native American, 1% Hispanic, 1% black, 2% Asian or Pacific Islander. *Retention:* 66% of 1995 full-time freshmen returned. *Graduation:* 18% graduate in 4 years, 35% in 5 years, 41% in 6 years. *Areas of study chosen:* 22% business management and administrative services, 18% education, 14% health professions and related sciences, 8% psychology, 6% social sciences, 5% biological and life sciences, 5% computer and information sciences, 5% English language/literature/letters, 1% foreign language and literature, 1% mathematics, 1% performing arts, 1% physical sciences, 1% theology/religion. *Most popular recent majors:* nursing, business administration/commerce/management, education.

First-Year Class: 218 total; 555 applied, 80% were accepted, 49% of whom enrolled. 12% from top 10% of their high school class, 29% from top quarter, 74% from top half. 5 class presidents, 4 valedictorians.

Graduation Requirements: 60 credits for associate, 120 credits for bachelor's; 1 semester of math; 2 semesters of physical science; 1 year of a foreign language or the equivalent; computer course; internship (some majors); senior project.

Computers on Campus: 57 computers available on campus for general student use. Computer purchase/lease plans available. A campus-wide network can be accessed from student residence rooms and from off-campus. Students can contact faculty members and/or advisers through e-mail. Computers for student use in computer center, computer labs, learning resource center, library provide access to the Internet/World

Edgewood College (continued)

Wide Web. Staffed computer lab on campus provides training in use of computers, software. *Academic computing expenditure 1995–96:* $195,788.

EXPENSES AND FINANCIAL AID

Expenses for 1997–98: *Application fee:* $25. Comprehensive fee of $14,660 includes full-time tuition ($10,100), mandatory fees ($180), and college room and board ($4380). College room only: $2070. Part-time tuition: $299 per credit. Part-time mandatory fees: $50 per term.
Undergraduate Financial Aid: 88% of all full-time undergraduates enrolled in fall 1996 applied for aid; of these, 76% were judged to have need according to Federal Methodology, of whom 97% were aided. On average, 80% of need was met. *Financial aid deadline (priority):* 4/1. *Financial aid forms:* FAFSA, institutional form required; CSS Financial Aid PROFILE acceptable.
LD Services Contact: Ms. Kathie Moran, Learning Resource Center Director, Edgewood College, 855 Woodrow Street, Madison, WI 53711, 608-257-4861 Ext. 2247. Fax: 608-257-1455. Email: moran@edgewood.edu.

ELON COLLEGE

Elon College, North Carolina

LEARNING DISABILITIES SERVICES INFORMATION

Academic Advising began offering services in 1991. Currently the program serves 90 undergraduates with LD. Services are also available to graduate students. Students diagnosed with ADD/ADHD are eligible for the same services available to students with LD.
Staff: 1 part-time staff member (coordinator). Services provided by advisers, teachers, learning specialist.
Special Fees: No special fees are charged for services to students with LD.
Applications and admissions: *Required:* high school transcript, grade point average, class rank, courses completed; *recommended:* high school extracurricular activities, untimed or extended time SAT I, autobiographical statement, letters of recommendation. Students may begin taking classes any term. *Application deadline:* 7/1 (fall term), 1/1 (spring term).
Special policies: The college has written policies regarding substitutions and waivers of graduation requirements.

PROGRAM AND SERVICE COMPONENTS

Special preparation or orientation: Optional orientation offered individually as requested.
Diagnostic testing: Foreign language.
Academic advising: Provided by unit staff members, academic advisers. Students with LD may take up to 18 semester hours each term; most take 12 to 16 semester hours; 8 semester hours required to maintain full-time status and be eligible for financial aid.
Auxiliary aids: Taped textbooks, tape recorders, calculators, typewriters, word-processors with spell-check, personal computers.
Auxiliary services: Alternative test arrangements, notetakers, priority registration, advocacy, student mentor; other services as requested and supported by documentation.

GENERAL COLLEGE INFORMATION

Independent, comprehensive, coed, affiliated with United Church of Christ. Awards bachelor's, master's degrees. Founded 1889. *Setting:* 330-acre suburban campus with easy access to Raleigh. *Endowment:* $28.1 million. *Educational spending 1995–96:* $3456 per undergrad. *Total enrollment:* 3,588. *Faculty:* 235 (154 full-time, 84% with terminal degrees, 81 part-time); student–undergrad faculty ratio is 17:1.
Enrollment Profile: 3,427 students from 40 states and territories, 23 other countries. 57% women, 43% men, 5% part-time, 30% state residents, 55% live on campus, 10% transferred in, 1% international, 1% 25 or older, 0% Native American, 1% Hispanic, 6% black, 1% Asian or Pacific Islander. *Retention:* 80% of 1995 full-time freshmen returned. *Graduation:* 43% graduate in 4 years, 57% in 5 years, 58% in 6 years. *Areas of study chosen:* 14% social sciences, 12% business management and administrative services, 11% communications and journalism, 11% education, 7% health professions and related sciences, 5% psychology, 4% biological and life sciences, 4% foreign language and literature, 3% English language/literature/letters, 2% computer and information sciences, 2% fine arts, 2% performing arts, 2% physical sciences, 1% engineering and applied sciences, 1% mathematics, 1% philosophy, 1% theology/religion. *Most popular recent majors:* business administration/commerce/management, communication, education.
First-Year Class: 948 total; 4,504 applied, 70% were accepted, 30% of whom enrolled. 18% from top 10% of their high school class, 43% from top quarter, 81% from top half. 6 valedictorians.
Graduation Requirements: 132 semester hours; 3 math/science courses including at least 1 lab science course; computer course for business, accounting, economics, elementary education, math; internship (some majors); senior project for honors program students and some majors.
Computers on Campus: 200 computers available on campus for general student use. A computer is recommended for all students. A campus-wide network can be accessed from student residence rooms and from off-campus. Students can contact faculty members and/or advisers through e-mail. Computers for student use in computer center, computer labs, learning resource center, classrooms, library, student center, dorms, curriculum lab provide access to the Internet/World Wide Web, on- and off-campus e-mail addresses. Staffed computer lab on campus provides training in use of computers, software. *Academic computing expenditure 1995–96:* $387,500.

EXPENSES AND FINANCIAL AID

Expenses for 1997–98: *Application fee:* $25. Comprehensive fee of $15,782 includes full-time tuition ($11,322), mandatory fees ($220), and college room and board ($4240). College room only: $1900. Part-time tuition: $230 per semester hour for 1 to 8 semester hours, $355 per semester hour for 9 or more semester hours. Part-time mandatory fees per semester (9 to 11 semester hours): $110.
Undergraduate Financial Aid: 53% of all full-time undergraduates enrolled in fall 1996 applied for aid; of these, 79% were judged to have need according to Federal Methodology, of whom 98% were aided. On average, 65% of need was met. *Financial aid deadline (priority):* 4/1. *Financial aid forms:* FAFSA, CSS Financial Aid PROFILE, institutional form required.
LD Services Contact: Ms. Priscilla Haworth, Associate Director of Academic Advising and Coordinator of Services for Students with Special Needs, Elon College, 2284 CB, Elon College, NC 27244, 910-584-2212. Fax: 910-538-2735. Email: haworthp@numen.elon.edu.

EMORY & HENRY COLLEGE

Emory, Virginia

LEARNING DISABILITIES SERVICES INFORMATION

Academic Support Center began offering services in 1990. Currently the program serves 40 undergraduates with LD. Students diagnosed with ADD/ADHD are eligible for the same services available to students with LD.
Staff: Includes director, associate director, administrative assistant. Services provided by tutors, supplemental instructors.
Special Fees: A fee is charged for diagnostic testing.
Applications and admissions: *Required:* high school transcript, grade point average, class rank, courses completed, untimed SAT I, autobiographical statement, psychoeducational report completed within 4 years; *recommended:* high school extracurricular activities, extended time SAT I, personal interview, letters of recommendation. Students may begin taking classes in fall or summer. *Application deadline:* continuous.
Special policies: The college has written policies regarding grade forgiveness; substitutions and waivers of admissions and degree requirements.

PROGRAM AND SERVICE COMPONENTS

Special preparation or orientation: Orientation (required for some) held for 4 weeks in the summer.
Diagnostic testing: Intelligence, reading, math, written language, perceptual skills, study skills.
Academic advising: Provided by unit staff members, academic advisers. Students with LD may take up to 15 semester hours each term; most take 12 semester hours; 12 semester hours required to maintain full-time status.
Counseling services: Individual counseling, career counseling.
Basic skills remediation: Offered one-on-one and in small groups by regular teachers. Available in math, written language.
Subject-area tutoring: Offered one-on-one and in small groups by peer tutors. Available in some subjects.
Special courses: Study skills, career planning. Some offered for credit; some enter into overall grade point average.
Auxiliary aids: Taped textbooks, word-processors with spell-check.

Auxiliary services: Alternative test arrangements, advocacy.

GENERAL COLLEGE INFORMATION

Independent United Methodist, 4-year, coed. Awards bachelor's degrees. Founded 1836. *Setting:* 150-acre rural campus. *Research spending 1995–96:* $135,474. *Total enrollment:* 917. *Faculty:* 82 (59 full-time, 82% with terminal degrees, 23 part-time); student–undergrad faculty ratio is 14:1.

Enrollment Profile: 917 students from 14 states and territories, 6 other countries. 49% women, 51% men, 3% part-time, 82% state residents, 71% live on campus, 22% transferred in, 1% international, 5% 25 or older, 0% Native American, 0% Hispanic, 5% black, 1% Asian or Pacific Islander. *Retention:* 79% of 1995 full-time freshmen returned. *Graduation:* 51% graduate in 4 years, 62% in 5 years, 64% in 6 years. *Areas of study chosen:* 16% business management and administrative services, 14% social sciences, 12% English language/literature/letters, 12% interdisciplinary studies, 11% psychology, 10% biological and life sciences, 7% education, 5% communications and journalism, 4% mathematics, 3% computer and information sciences, 2% foreign language and literature, 2% physical sciences, 1% engineering and applied sciences, 1% fine arts, 1% health professions and related sciences. *Most popular recent majors:* business administration/commerce/management, English, education.

First-Year Class: 257 total; 838 applied, 86% were accepted, 36% of whom enrolled. 29% from top 10% of their high school class, 56% from top quarter, 87% from top half. 5 class presidents, 6 valedictorians.

Graduation Requirements: 116 semester hours; 1 natural science course; computer course for biology, accounting, economics, management, engineering, math, physics, psychology, some education majors; internship (some majors); senior project (some majors).

Computers on Campus: 85 computers available on campus for general student use. Computer purchase/lease plans available. A computer is recommended for some students. Students can contact faculty members and/or advisers through e-mail. Computers for student use in computer labs, library, writing center provide access to the Internet/World Wide Web, on- and off-campus e-mail addresses. Staffed computer lab on campus provides training in use of computers, software.

EXPENSES AND FINANCIAL AID

Expenses for 1997–98: *Application fee:* $25. Comprehensive fee of $16,372 includes full-time tuition ($11,572) and college room and board ($4800). Part-time tuition: $454 per semester hour. Part-time mandatory fees: $28 per semester.

Undergraduate Financial Aid: Of all full-time undergraduates enrolled in fall 1996, 90% of those who applied for aid were judged to have need according to Federal Methodology, of whom 99% were aided. On average, 92% of need was met. *Financial aid deadline (priority):* 4/1. *Financial aid forms:* FAFSA, institutional form required; CSS Financial Aid PROFILE acceptable. State form required for some.

LD Services Contact: Ms. Karen Kilgore, Associate Director, Emory & Henry College, PO Box 947, Emory, VA 24327-0947, 540-944-6873. Fax: 540-944-6934. Email: kkilgore@ehc.edu.

EMORY UNIVERSITY

Atlanta, Georgia

LEARNING DISABILITIES SERVICES INFORMATION

Disability Services and Compliance began offering services in 1979. Currently the program serves 41 undergraduates with LD. Services are also available to graduate students. Students diagnosed with ADD/ADHD are eligible for the same services available to students with LD.

Staff: 4 full-time, 2 part-time staff members, including director, coordinators, program administrator.

Special Fees: No special fees are charged for services to students with LD.

Applications and admissions: *Required:* high school transcript, untimed SAT I or ACT, letters of recommendation, psychoeducational report completed within 3 years, essay; *recommended:* extended time SAT I or ACT. Students may begin taking classes in fall, spring, or summer. *Application deadline:* 1/15 (fall term), 11/1 (spring term).

PROGRAM AND SERVICE COMPONENTS

Special preparation or orientation: Optional orientation offered before registration and after classes begin.

Academic advising: Provided by academic advisers. Students with LD may take up to 21 semester hours each term; most take 17 semester hours; 12 semester hours required to maintain full-time status and be eligible for financial aid.

Counseling services: Individual counseling, small-group counseling, career counseling.

Subject-area tutoring: Offered one-on-one, in small groups, and in class-size groups by peer tutors, teaching assistants. Available in most subjects.

Auxiliary aids: Taped textbooks, tape recorders, word-processors with spell-check, personal computers, talking computers.

Auxiliary services: Alternative test arrangements, notetakers, priority registration, advocacy.

Campus support group: A special student organization is available to students with LD.

GENERAL COLLEGE INFORMATION

Independent Methodist, coed. Awards bachelor's, master's, doctoral, first professional degrees. Founded 1836. *Setting:* 631-acre suburban campus. *Endowment:* $3.2 billion. *Total enrollment:* 11,270. *Faculty:* 2,486 (2,061 full-time, 98% with terminal degrees, 425 part-time); student–undergrad faculty ratio is 10:1.

Enrollment Profile: 5,400 students from 49 states and territories, 44 other countries. 53% women, 47% men, 2% part-time, 19% state residents, 63% live on campus, 2% transferred in, 2% international, 0% 25 or older, 0% Native American, 4% Hispanic, 10% black, 12% Asian or Pacific Islander. *Retention:* 92% of 1995 full-time freshmen returned. *Graduation:* 88% graduate in 4 years, 90% in 5 years, 92% in 6 years. *Areas of study chosen:* 36% social sciences, 16% biological and life sciences, 14% interdisciplinary studies, 13% psychology, 11% business management and administrative services, 7% English language/literature/letters, 3% performing arts, 1% education. *Most popular recent majors:* psychology, biology/biological sciences, political science/government.

First-Year Class: 1,160 total; 10,040 applied, 44% were accepted, 26% of whom enrolled. 81% from top 10% of their high school class, 98% from top quarter, 100% from top half. 32 National Merit Scholars.

Graduation Requirements: 132 semester hours; 3 math/science courses including at least 1 lab science course; computer course for math, business majors; senior project for honors program students and some majors.

Computers on Campus: 500 computers available on campus for general student use. Computer purchase/lease plans available. A campus-wide network can be accessed from student residence rooms and from off-campus. Students can contact faculty members and/or advisers through e-mail. Computers for student use in computer center, computer labs, learning resource center, classrooms, library, student center, dorms, law school, theological school buildings provide access to the Internet/World Wide Web. Staffed computer lab on campus (open 24 hours a day) provides training in use of computers, software.

EXPENSES AND FINANCIAL AID

Expenses for 1997–98: *Application fee:* $40. Comprehensive fee of $27,142 includes full-time tuition ($20,870), mandatory fees ($250), and college room and board ($6022). College room only: $4222.

Undergraduate Financial Aid: 51% of all full-time undergraduates enrolled in fall 1996 applied for aid; of these, 86% were judged to have need according to Federal Methodology, of whom 97% were aided. On average, 86% of need was met. *Financial aid deadline (priority):* 2/15. *Financial aid forms:* FAFSA, CSS Financial Aid PROFILE required. State form required for some.

LD Services Contact: Ms. Tricia Jacob, Coordinator of Disability Services for Students, Emory University, 110 Administration Building, Atlanta, GA 30322, 404-727-6016. Fax: 404-727-1126. Email: tjaco04@emory.edu.

EVANGEL COLLEGE

Springfield, Missouri

LEARNING DISABILITIES SERVICES INFORMATION

Center for Effective Learning began offering services in 1969. Currently the program serves 4 undergraduates with LD. Students diagnosed with ADD/ADHD are eligible for the same services available to students with LD.

Staff: 2 full-time staff members, including coordinator. Services provided by remediation specialist, tutors, diagnostic specialists.

Special Fees: No special fees are charged for services to students with LD.

Applications and admissions: *Required:* high school transcript, grade point average, class rank, untimed or extended time ACT, extended time

SAT I, autobiographical statement, letters of recommendation. Students may begin taking classes in fall or spring. *Application deadline:* continuous.

PROGRAM AND SERVICE COMPONENTS

Diagnostic testing: Intelligence, reading, math, written language, study skills, learning strategies.
Academic advising: Provided by unit staff members. Students with LD may take up to 13 credit hours each term; most take 13 credit hours; 12 credit hours required to maintain full-time status and be eligible for financial aid.
Counseling services: Individual counseling, small-group counseling, career counseling.
Basic skills remediation: Offered in class-size groups by regular teachers, tutors. Available in reading, math, spelling, written language, learning strategies, study skills, time management.
Subject-area tutoring: Offered one-on-one by peer tutors. Available in some subjects.
Special courses: Reading, vocabulary development, composition, math, study skills. All offered for credit; all enter into overall grade point average.
Auxiliary aids: Taped textbooks, tape recorders, word-processors with spell-check.
Auxiliary services: Alternative test arrangements, advocacy, readers.

GENERAL COLLEGE INFORMATION

Independent, 4-year, coed, affiliated with Assemblies of God. Awards associate, bachelor's degrees. Founded 1955. *Setting:* 80-acre urban campus. *Total enrollment:* 1,574. *Faculty:* 122 (84 full-time, 50% with terminal degrees, 38 part-time); student–undergrad faculty ratio is 18:1.
Enrollment Profile: 1,574 students from 48 states and territories, 13 other countries. 58% women, 42% men, 8% part-time, 40% state residents, 8% transferred in, 2% international, 2% 25 or older, 1% Native American, 1% Hispanic, 5% black. *Retention:* 76% of 1995 full-time freshmen returned. *Graduation:* 51% graduate in 4 years. *Areas of study chosen:* 17% education, 16% computer and information sciences, 14% business management and administrative services, 9% fine arts, 8% communications and journalism, 8% social sciences, 8% theology/religion, 7% psychology, 6% biological and life sciences, 3% performing arts. *Most popular recent majors:* business administration/commerce/management, education, communication.
First-Year Class: 405 total; 722 applied, 91% were accepted, 62% of whom enrolled. 19% from top 10% of their high school class, 45% from top quarter, 77% from top half. 15 valedictorians.
Graduation Requirements: 60 credit hours for associate, 124 credit hours for bachelor's; 7 credit hours of science; computer course; senior project (some majors).
Computers on Campus: 64 computers available on campus for general student use. A computer is recommended for all students. Computers for student use in computer center, computer labs, learning resource center, library. Staffed computer lab on campus provides training in use of computers, software.

EXPENSES AND FINANCIAL AID

Expenses for 1997–98: *Application fee:* $25. Comprehensive fee of $11,505 includes full-time tuition ($7700), mandatory fees ($365), and college room and board ($3440). Part-time tuition: $300 per credit hour. Part-time mandatory fees per semester range from $40 to $50.
Undergraduate Financial Aid: 81% of all full-time undergraduates enrolled in fall 1996 applied for aid; of these, 86% were judged to have need according to Federal Methodology, of whom 99% were aided. On average, 68% of need was met. *Financial aid deadline (priority):* 4/1. *Financial aid forms:* FAFSA required.
LD Services Contact: Dr. Eleanor G. Syler, Coordinator, Evangel College, 1111 North Glenstone, Springfield, MO 65802-2191, 417-865-2811 Ext. 7232. Fax: 417-865-1574.

THE EVERGREEN STATE COLLEGE

Olympia, Washington

LEARNING DISABILITIES SERVICES INFORMATION

Access Services for Students with Disabilities currently serves 300 undergraduates with LD. Services are also available to graduate students. Students diagnosed with ADD/ADHD are eligible for the same services available to students with LD.

Staff. 1 full-time, 4 part-time staff members, including director, coordinator, student assistants. Services provided by tutors, counselors, notetakers, readers.

Special Fees: No special fees are charged for services to students with LD.

Applications and admissions: *Required:* high school transcript, documentation of disability. Students may begin taking classes any term. *Application deadline:* continuous.

Special policies: The college has written policies regarding grade forgiveness; substitutions and waivers of admissions, graduation, and degree requirements.

PROGRAM AND SERVICE COMPONENTS

Academic advising: Provided by unit staff members, academic advisers. Students with LD may take up to 16 credit hours each term; most take 12 to 16 credit hours; 12 credit hours required to maintain full-time status and be eligible for financial aid.

Counseling services: Individual counseling, career counseling.

Subject-area tutoring: Offered one-on-one by peer tutors. Available in all subjects.

Auxiliary aids: Taped textbooks, tape recorders, calculators, typewriters, word-processors with spell-check.

Auxiliary services: Alternative test arrangements, notetakers, priority registration, advocacy, tutors, readers.

Campus support group: A special student organization is available to students with LD.

GENERAL COLLEGE INFORMATION

State-supported, comprehensive, coed. Awards bachelor's, master's degrees. Founded 1967. *Setting:* 1,000-acre small-town campus with easy access to Seattle. *Research spending 1995–96:* $1.2 million. *Educational spending 1995–96:* $3530 per undergrad. *Total enrollment:* 3,714. *Faculty:* 183 (151 full-time, 75% with terminal degrees, 32 part-time); student–undergrad faculty ratio is 24:1.

Enrollment Profile: 3,498 students from 44 states and territories, 16 other countries. 57% women, 43% men, 13% part-time, 76% state residents, 28% live on campus, 22% transferred in, 1% international, 38% 25 or older, 4% Native American, 4% Hispanic, 4% black, 4% Asian or Pacific Islander. *Retention:* 70% of 1995 full-time freshmen returned. *Areas of study chosen:* 100% interdisciplinary studies. *Most popular recent majors:* human services, environmental studies, public affairs and policy studies.

First-Year Class: 494 total; 1,831 applied, 88% were accepted, 31% of whom enrolled.

Graduation Requirements: 80 quarter hours.

Computers on Campus: 150 computers available on campus for general student use. Computer purchase/lease plans available. A computer is recommended for all students. A campus-wide network can be accessed from student residence rooms and from off-campus. Students can contact faculty members and/or advisers through e-mail. Computers for student use in computer center, computer labs, classrooms, library, science labs provide access to the Internet/World Wide Web. Staffed computer lab on campus provides training in use of computers, software. *Academic computing expenditure 1995–96:* $404,182.

EXPENSES AND FINANCIAL AID

Expenses for 1996–97: *Application fee:* $35. State resident tuition: $2439 full-time, $81.30 per quarter hour part-time. Nonresident tuition: $8625 full-time, $287.50 per quarter hour part-time. Full-time mandatory fees: $105. College room and board: $4470. College room only: $1958 (minimum).

Undergraduate Financial Aid: Of all full-time undergraduates enrolled in fall 1996, 90% of those who applied for aid were judged to have need according to Federal Methodology, of whom 98% were aided. On average, 76% of need was met. *Financial aid deadline (priority):* 2/15. *Financial aid forms:* FAFSA required. Institutional form required for some.

LD Services Contact: Ms. Erin Rowland, Administrative Coordinator, The Evergreen State College, 2700 Evergreen Parkway NW, Library 1407D, Olympia, WA 98505, 360-866-6000 Ext. 6348. Fax: 360-866-6823.

FAIRMONT STATE COLLEGE

Fairmont, West Virginia

LEARNING DISABILITIES SERVICES INFORMATION

Learning Skills Center began offering services in 1973. Currently the program serves 35 undergraduates with LD. Students diagnosed with ADD/ADHD are eligible for the same services available to students with LD.

Staff: 10 full-time staff members, including coordinator. Services provided by remediation specialists, tutors, lab assistant.

Special Fees: No special fees are charged for services to students with LD.

Applications and admissions: *Required:* high school transcript, grade point average, class rank, courses completed, extracurricular activities, untimed or extended time SAT I or ACT, psychoeducational report completed within 3 years. Students may begin taking classes in fall only. *Application deadline:* 6/15.

Special policies: The college has written policies regarding grade forgiveness.

PROGRAM AND SERVICE COMPONENTS

Special preparation or orientation: Optional orientation offered after classes begin.

Diagnostic testing: Reading, math, spelling, written language.

Academic advising: Provided by academic advisers. Students with LD may take up to 18 credits each term; most take 12 to 15 credits; 12 credits required to maintain full-time status; 6 credits required to be eligible for financial aid.

Counseling services: Individual counseling, small-group counseling, career counseling.

Basic skills remediation: Offered in small groups and in class-size groups by regular teachers. Available in reading, math, spelling, written language, learning strategies, study skills.

Subject-area tutoring: Offered one-on-one by peer tutors, lab assistant. Available in most subjects.

Special courses: College survival skills, reading, vocabulary development, composition, math, study skills. None offered for credit.

Auxiliary aids: Taped textbooks, tape recorders, typewriters, word-processors with spell-check, personal computers, optical character readers.

Auxiliary services: Alternative test arrangements, notetakers, priority registration.

Campus support group: A special student organization is available to students with LD.

GENERAL COLLEGE INFORMATION

State-supported, 4-year, coed. Part of State College System of West Virginia. Awards associate, bachelor's degrees. Founded 1865. *Setting:* 80-acre small-town campus. *Endowment:* $4.6 million. *Research spending 1995–96:* $104,817. *Total enrollment:* 6,555. *Faculty:* 437 (191 full-time, 38% with terminal degrees, 246 part-time); student–undergrad faculty ratio is 23:1.

Enrollment Profile: 6,555 students from 26 states and territories, 6 other countries. 55% women, 45% men, 33% part-time, 95% state residents, 7% live on campus, 5% transferred in, 1% international, 29% 25 or older, 1% Native American, 1% Hispanic, 3% black, 1% Asian or Pacific Islander. *Retention:* 76% of 1995 full-time freshmen returned. *Graduation:* 34% graduate in 4 years, 66% in 5 years, 100% in 6 years. *Areas of study chosen:* 11% education, 9% business management and administrative services, 7% engineering and applied sciences, 5% health professions and related sciences, 5% psychology, 5% social sciences, 2% architecture, 2% computer and information sciences, 2% vocational and home economics, 1% biological and life sciences, 1% communications and journalism, 1% English language/literature/letters, 1% foreign language and literature, 1% interdisciplinary studies, 1% liberal arts/general studies, 1% mathematics, 1% performing arts, 1% physical sciences, 1% predentistry, 1% premed. *Most popular recent majors:* criminal justice, accounting, education.

First-Year Class: 1,214 total; 2,148 applied, 99% were accepted, 57% of whom enrolled. 2 National Merit Scholars, 10 valedictorians.

Graduation Requirements: 64 credits for associate, 128 credits for bachelor's; 3 credits of math; 8 credits of science; computer course for sociology majors; internship (some majors); senior project (some majors).

Computers on Campus: 1,250 computers available on campus for general student use. A computer is recommended for some students. A campus-wide network can be accessed from off-campus. Students can contact faculty members and/or advisers through e-mail. Computers for student use in computer center, computer labs, library provide access to the Internet/World Wide Web, on-campus e-mail addresses. Staffed computer lab on campus provides training in use of computers, software. *Academic computing expenditure 1995–96:* $103,772.

EXPENSES AND FINANCIAL AID

Expenses for 1997–98: State resident tuition: $2040 full-time, $85 per credit part-time. Nonresident tuition: $4840 full-time, $202 per credit part-time. College room and board: $3358 (minimum). College room only: $1630 (minimum).

Undergraduate Financial Aid: Of all full-time undergraduates enrolled in fall 1996, 57% of those who applied for aid were judged to have need according to Federal Methodology, of whom 61% were aided. On average, 90% of need was met. *Financial aid deadline (priority):* 2/14. *Financial aid forms:* FAFSA required. State form required for some.

LD Services Contact: Ms. Martha French, Coordinator, Learning Skills Center, Fairmont State College, 200 Jaynes Hall, Fairmont, WV 26554, 304-367-4299. Fax: 304-366-4870. Email: msf@fscuax.wvnet.edu.

FASHION INSTITUTE OF TECHNOLOGY

New York, New York

LEARNING DISABILITIES SERVICES INFORMATION

Learning Disabilities Program, Educational Skills Department began offering services in 1985. Currently the program serves 103 undergraduates with LD. Students diagnosed with ADD/ADHD are eligible for the same services available to students with LD.

Staff: Includes director, coordinator. Services provided by tutors, counselor.

Special Fees: No special fees are charged for services to students with LD.

Applications and admissions: *Required:* high school transcript, essay. Students may begin taking classes any term (services available in fall and spring). *Application deadline:* 1/15 (fall term), 10/15 (spring term).

PROGRAM AND SERVICE COMPONENTS

Academic advising: Provided by unit staff members, academic advisers. Most students with LD take 12 to 15 credits each term; 12 credits required to maintain full-time status and be eligible for financial aid.

Counseling services: Individual counseling, small-group counseling, career counseling.

Basic skills remediation: Offered one-on-one, in small groups, and in class-size groups by regular teachers, tutors. Available in reading, math, spelling, handwriting, spoken language, written language, learning strategies, study skills, time management.

Subject-area tutoring: Offered one-on-one and in small groups by college graduates experienced in working with LD students. Available in all subjects.

Special courses: Reading, vocabulary development, composition, learning strategies, word processing, time management, study skills. Most offered for credit; most enter into overall grade point average.

Auxiliary aids: Taped textbooks, typewriters, word-processors with spell-check, optical character readers.

Auxiliary services: Alternative test arrangements, notetakers, advocacy.

GENERAL COLLEGE INFORMATION

State and locally supported, comprehensive, coed. Part of State University of New York System. Awards associate, bachelor's, master's degrees. Founded 1944. *Setting:* 5-acre urban campus. *Educational spending 1995–96:* $7750 per undergrad. *Total enrollment:* 8,489. *Undergraduate faculty:* 844 (169 full-time, 675 part-time); student–undergrad faculty ratio is 14:1.

Enrollment Profile: 8,430 students from 51 states and territories, 65 other countries. 79% women, 21% men, 55% part-time, 79% state residents, 9% transferred in, 6% international, 50% 25 or older, 0% Native American, 14% Hispanic, 12% black, 24% Asian or Pacific Islander. *Retention:* 78% of 1995 full-time freshmen returned. *Graduation:* 63% graduate in 4 years. *Areas of study chosen:* 35% vocational and home economics, 7% business management and administrative services, 6% communications and journalism, 2% fine arts. *Most popular recent majors:* fashion merchandising, fashion design and technology, advertising.

First-Year Class: 1,973 total; 5,362 applied, 50% were accepted, 73% of whom enrolled. 8% from top 10% of their high school class, 25% from top quarter, 70% from top half.

Fashion Institute of Technology (continued)

Graduation Requirements: 70 credits for associate, 133 credits for bachelor's; 6 credits of math/science; computer course; internship (some majors); senior project (some majors).

Computers on Campus: 450 computers available on campus for general student use. Computer purchase/lease plans available. Computers for student use in computer labs, learning resource center, classrooms. Staffed computer lab on campus (open 24 hours a day) provides training in use of computers, software. *Academic computing expenditure 1995–96:* $835,897.

EXPENSES AND FINANCIAL AID

Expenses for 1996–97: *Application fee:* $25. Part-time mandatory fees: $5 per term. Full-time tuition for associate degree program: $2400 for state residents, $5750 for nonresidents. Full-time tuition for bachelor's degree program: $2885 for state residents, $6600 for nonresidents. Part-time tuition per credit for associate degree program: $78 for state residents, $200 for nonresidents. Part-time tuition per credit for bachelor's degree program: $88 for state residents, $220 for nonresidents. Full-time mandatory fees: $210. College room and board: $5340. College room only: $3007.

Undergraduate Financial Aid: Of all full-time undergraduates enrolled in fall 1996, 83% of those who applied for aid were judged to have need according to Federal Methodology, of whom 83% were aided. On average, 69% of need was met. *Financial aid deadline (priority):* 3/15. *Financial aid forms:* FAFSA required. State form, federal income tax form required for some.

LD Services Contact: Ms. Gail Ballard, Program Coordinator, Fashion Institute of Technology, Seventh Avenue at 27th Street, New York, NY 10001, 212-217-7522. Fax: 212-217-7965.

FERRUM COLLEGE

Ferrum, Virginia

LEARNING DISABILITIES SERVICES INFORMATION

Academic Resources Center (ARC) began offering services in 1972. Currently the program serves 102 undergraduates with LD. Students diagnosed with ADD/ADHD are eligible for the same services available to students with LD.

Staff: 2 full-time, 2 part-time staff members, including director, coordinator, accommodations coordinator. Services provided by tutors, counselors, academic advisers.

Special Fees: No special fees are charged for services to students with LD.

Applications and admissions: *Required:* high school transcript, grade point average, class rank, untimed SAT I or ACT; *recommended:* high school IEP (Individualized Education Program), personal interview, letters of recommendation, psychoeducational report completed within 3 years, writing sample. Students may begin taking classes in fall only. *Application deadline:* continuous.

PROGRAM AND SERVICE COMPONENTS

Special preparation or orientation: Optional summer program offered prior to entering college. Optional orientation offered before registration and after classes begin.

Academic advising: Provided by unit staff members, academic advisers. Students with LD may take up to 19 credit hours each term; most take 13 to 15 credit hours; 12 credit hours required to maintain full-time status and be eligible for financial aid.

Counseling services: Individual counseling, small-group counseling, career counseling, self-advocacy training.

Subject-area tutoring: Offered one-on-one and in small groups by professional teachers, peer tutors. Available in most subjects.

Auxiliary aids: Taped textbooks, tape recorders, word-processors with spell-check, personal computers, optical character readers.

Auxiliary services: Alternative test arrangements, notetakers, advocacy, special academic advisers.

GENERAL COLLEGE INFORMATION

Independent United Methodist, 4-year, coed. Awards bachelor's degrees. Founded 1913. *Setting:* 720-acre rural campus. *Endowment:* $27.9 million. *Educational spending 1995–96:* $3703 per undergrad. *Total enrollment:* 1,075. *Faculty:* 97 (71 full-time, 66% with terminal degrees, 26 part-time); student–undergrad faculty ratio is 14:1.

Enrollment Profile: 1,075 students from 23 states and territories, 12 other countries. 44% women, 56% men, 6% part-time, 82% state residents, 75% live on campus, 17% transferred in, 1% international, 10% 25 or older, 1% Native American, 1% Hispanic, 13% black, 1% Asian or Pacific Islander. *Retention:* 61% of 1995 full-time freshmen returned. *Graduation:* 18% graduate in 4 years, 27% in 5 years, 29% in 6 years. *Areas of study chosen:* 20% social sciences, 16% business management and administrative services, 10% natural resource sciences, 8% education, 4% liberal arts/general studies, 4% psychology, 3% agriculture, 3% computer and information sciences, 3% health professions and related sciences, 2% biological and life sciences, 2% fine arts, 1% foreign language and literature, 1% mathematics, 1% performing arts, 1% theology/religion. *Most popular recent majors:* business administration/commerce/management, psychology, history.

First-Year Class: 307 total; 1,180 applied, 74% were accepted, 35% of whom enrolled. 7% from top 10% of their high school class, 22% from top quarter, 44% from top half.

Graduation Requirements: 127 credit hours; 6 credit hours of math; 8 credit hours of science; computer course for business, math, accounting, recreation and leisure majors; internship (some majors); senior project (some majors).

Computers on Campus: 100 computers available on campus for general student use. A campus-wide network can be accessed from off-campus. Students can contact faculty members and/or advisers through e-mail. Computers for student use in computer labs, library, dorms, academic buildings provide access to the Internet/World Wide Web, on- and off-campus e-mail addresses. Staffed computer lab on campus provides training in use of computers, software. *Academic computing expenditure 1995–96:* $110,861.

EXPENSES AND FINANCIAL AID

Expenses for 1997–98: *Application fee:* $25. Comprehensive fee of $15,600 includes full-time tuition ($10,750) and college room and board ($4850). Part-time tuition: $245 per credit hour for 1 to 6 credit hours, $335 per credit hour for 7 or more credit hours.

Undergraduate Financial Aid: 88% of all full-time undergraduates enrolled in fall 1996 applied for aid; of these, 87% were judged to have need according to Federal Methodology, of whom 100% were aided. On average, 88% of need was met. *Financial aid deadline (priority):* 4/1. *Financial aid forms:* FAFSA, state form required; CSS Financial Aid PROFILE acceptable.

LD Services Contact: Ms. Nancy Beach, Coordinator of LD Services and Academic Accommodations, Ferrum College, PO Box 1000, Ferrum, VA 24088, 540-365-4262. Fax: 540-365-4203. Email: nbeach@ferrum.edu.

FLORIDA ATLANTIC UNIVERSITY

Boca Raton, Florida

LEARNING DISABILITIES SERVICES INFORMATION

Office for Students with Disabilities currently serves 230 undergraduates with LD. Services are also available to graduate students. Students diagnosed with ADD/ADHD are eligible for the same services available to students with LD.

Staff: 3 full-time staff members, including director, coordinators.

Special Fees: No special fees are charged for services to students with LD.

Applications and admissions: *Required:* high school transcript, psychoeducational report completed within 3 years; *recommended:* high school extracurricular activities, untimed or extended time SAT I or ACT, autobiographical statement, letters of recommendation. Students may begin taking classes any term. *Application deadline:* continuous.

Special policies: The college has written policies regarding grade forgiveness; substitutions and waivers of admissions, graduation, and degree requirements.

PROGRAM AND SERVICE COMPONENTS

Academic advising: Provided by unit staff members, academic advisers. Most students with LD take 9 to 12 semester hours each term; 12 semester hours required to maintain full-time status and be eligible for financial aid.

Counseling services: Individual counseling, career counseling.

Subject-area tutoring: Offered one-on-one by peer tutors. Available in most subjects.

Auxiliary aids: Taped textbooks, tape recorders, calculators, typewriters, word-processors with spell-check, personal computers, talking computers, optical character readers, Reading Edge, Dragon Dictate, large screen computers.

Auxiliary services: Alternative test arrangements, notetakers, advocacy.
Campus support group: A special student organization is available to students with LD.

GENERAL COLLEGE INFORMATION

State-supported, coed. Part of State University System of Florida. Awards associate, bachelor's, master's, doctoral degrees. Founded 1961. *Setting:* 850-acre suburban campus with easy access to Miami. *Research spending 1995–96:* $12.9 million. *Total enrollment:* 18,362. *Faculty:* 688 (677 full-time, 93% with terminal degrees, 11 part-time); student–undergrad faculty ratio is 18:1.
Enrollment Profile: 15,995 students from 51 states and territories, 130 other countries. 59% women, 41% men, 55% part-time, 92% state residents, 7% live on campus, 14% transferred in, 4% international, 55% 25 or older, 1% Native American, 10% Hispanic, 11% black, 4% Asian or Pacific Islander. *Areas of study chosen:* 21% business management and administrative services, 15% education, 8% biological and life sciences, 7% social sciences, 6% engineering and applied sciences, 6% health professions and related sciences, 6% liberal arts/general studies, 6% psychology, 5% computer and information sciences, 3% communications and journalism, 3% fine arts, 3% performing arts, 2% English language/literature/letters, 2% physical sciences, 1% foreign language and literature, 1% mathematics, 1% philosophy. *Most popular recent majors:* elementary education, biology/biological sciences, accounting.
First-Year Class: 1,010 total; 3,478 applied, 74% were accepted, 39% of whom enrolled.
Graduation Requirements: 60 semester hours for associate, 120 semester hours for bachelor's; 2 college algebra courses or higher level math; computer course for business, engineering majors; internship (some majors); senior project for honors program students and some majors.
Computers on Campus: 377 computers available on campus for general student use. A computer is recommended for some students. A campus-wide network can be accessed from student residence rooms and from off-campus. Students can contact faculty members and/or advisers through e-mail. Computers for student use in computer center, computer labs, library, academic buildings provide access to the Internet/World Wide Web, on- and off-campus e-mail addresses. Staffed computer lab on campus provides training in use of computers. *Academic computing expenditure 1995–96:* $1.5 million.

EXPENSES AND FINANCIAL AID

Expenses for 1997–98: *Application fee:* $20. State resident tuition: $2023 full-time, $67.42 per semester hour part-time. Nonresident tuition: $7939 full-time, $264.64 per semester hour part-time. College room and board: $4680. College room only: $2360.
Undergraduate Financial Aid: Of all full-time undergraduates enrolled in fall 1996, 52% of those who applied for aid were judged to have need according to Federal Methodology, of whom 97% were aided. On average, 49% of need was met. *Financial aid deadline (priority):* 4/1. *Financial aid forms:* FAFSA, financial aid transcript (for transfers) required; CSS Financial Aid PROFILE acceptable.
LD Services Contact: Ms. Beverly Warde, Director, Florida Atlantic University, PO Box 3091, Boca Raton, FL 33431, 561-367-3880.

FLORIDA BAPTIST THEOLOGICAL COLLEGE

Graceville, Florida

LEARNING DISABILITIES SERVICES INFORMATION

Cook Learning Center began offering services in 1986. Currently the program serves 13 undergraduates with LD. Students diagnosed with ADD/ADHD are eligible for the same services available to students with LD.
Staff: 1 full-time, 2 part-time staff members, including director. Services provided by tutors, lab assistant/aide.
Special Fees: $30 per year.
Applications and admissions: *Required:* high school transcript, grade point average, courses completed, untimed SAT I or ACT, autobiographical statement, letters of recommendation, psychoeducational report completed within 5 years; *recommended:* extended time SAT I or ACT. Students may begin taking classes in fall, spring, or summer. *Application deadline:* continuous.
Special policies: The college has written policies regarding grade forgiveness; substitutions and waivers of admissions, graduation, and degree requirements.

PROGRAM AND SERVICE COMPONENTS

Special preparation or orientation: Orientation (required for some) held between general orientation and registration.
Diagnostic testing: Reading, math, spelling, written language, study skills, learning strategies.
Academic advising: Provided by academic advisers. Students with LD may take up to 12 semester hours each term; most take 12 semester hours; 12 semester hours required to maintain full-time status; type of program determines the number of semester hours required to be eligible for financial aid.
Counseling services: Individual counseling, career counseling, LD counseling.
Basic skills remediation: Offered one-on-one and in small groups by learning center director; computer-aided instruction also offered. Available in reading, math, spelling, written language, learning strategies, study skills, speech.
Subject-area tutoring: Offered one-on-one and in small groups by professional teachers, peer tutors, Learning Center Director. Available in some subjects.
Special courses: Reading, vocabulary development, composition, learning strategies, word processing, math, typing. Some offered for credit; some enter into overall grade point average.
Auxiliary aids: Taped textbooks, tape recorders, calculators, typewriters, personal computers, Tachistoscope/Scotopic Sensitivity materials.
Auxiliary services: Alternative test arrangements, notetakers, scribes, readers.

GENERAL COLLEGE INFORMATION

Independent Southern Baptist, 4-year, coed. Awards associate, bachelor's degrees. Founded 1943. *Setting:* 150-acre small-town campus. *Total enrollment:* 529. *Faculty:* 24 (13 full-time, 85% with terminal degrees, 11 part-time).
Enrollment Profile: 529 students from 25 states and territories, 4 other countries. 26% women, 74% men, 17% part-time, 62% state residents, 36% live on campus, 63% transferred in, 1% international, 88% 25 or older, 0% Native American, 3% Hispanic, 3% black, 1% Asian or Pacific Islander. *Retention:* 55% of 1995 full-time freshmen returned. *Areas of study chosen:* 60% theology/religion, 21% education, 12% performing arts. *Most popular recent majors:* theology, religious education, sacred music.
First-Year Class: 55 total; 191 applied, 37% of whom enrolled.
Graduation Requirements: 66 semester hours for associate, 130 semester hours for bachelor's; 4 semester hours of math; 3 semester hours of science.
Computers on Campus: 14 computers available on campus for general student use. A campus-wide network can be accessed. Computers for student use in computer center provide access to the Internet/World Wide Web. Staffed computer lab on campus provides training in use of computers, software.

EXPENSES AND FINANCIAL AID

Expenses for 1997–98: *Application fee:* $20. Tuition: $2850 full-time, $90 per semester hour part-time. Part-time mandatory fees: $42 per term. Full-time mandatory fees: $84. College room only: $1500.
Undergraduate Financial Aid: Of all full-time undergraduates enrolled in fall 1996, 100% of those judged to have need according to Federal Methodology were aided. On average, 54% of need was met. *Financial aid deadline (priority):* 4/1. *Financial aid forms:* FAFSA, institutional form required; CSS Financial Aid PROFILE acceptable.
LD Services Contact: Dr. Paul Robinson, Director, Cook Learning Center, Florida Baptist Theological College, PO Box 1306, Graceville, FL 32440, 904-263-3261 Ext. 467. Fax: 904-263-7506.

FLORIDA INTERNATIONAL UNIVERSITY

Miami, Florida

LEARNING DISABILITIES SERVICES INFORMATION

Disabled Student Services began offering services in 1976. Currently the program serves 163 undergraduates with LD. Services are also available to graduate students. Students diagnosed with ADD/ADHD are eligible for the same services available to students with LD.
Staff: 5 full-time, 1 part-time staff members, including director, associate director, coordinators, senior secretary. Services provided by readers, proctors, scribes, clerks.

Florida International University (continued)

Special Fees: No special fees are charged for services to students with LD.

Applications and admissions: *Required:* high school transcript, grade point average, untimed SAT I or ACT, psychoeducational report completed within 2 years; *recommended:* high school courses completed, extracurricular activities, extended time SAT I or ACT, personal interview, autobiographical statement, letters of recommendation. Students may begin taking classes any term. *Application deadline:* continuous.

Special policies: The college has written policies regarding grade forgiveness; substitutions and waivers of admissions, graduation, and degree requirements.

PROGRAM AND SERVICE COMPONENTS

Special preparation or orientation: Optional orientation offered after classes begin.

Academic advising: Provided by academic advisers. Most students with LD take 9 to 12 credit hours each term; 12 credit hours required to maintain full-time status; source of aid determines number of credit hours required to be eligible for financial aid.

Counseling services: Individual counseling, career counseling.

Auxiliary aids: Taped textbooks, tape recorders, calculators, word-processors with spell-check, personal computers, talking computers, optical character readers.

Auxiliary services: Alternative test arrangements, notetakers, priority registration, advocacy, taped lectures.

Campus support group: A special student organization is available to students with LD.

GENERAL COLLEGE INFORMATION

State-supported, coed. Part of State University System of Florida. Awards bachelor's, master's, doctoral degrees. Founded 1965. *Setting:* 573-acre urban campus. *Endowment:* $12.9 million. *Research spending 1995–96:* $33 million. *Total enrollment:* 24,413. *Faculty:* 821 full-time, 96% with terminal degrees, 397 part-time; student–undergrad faculty ratio is 15:1.

Enrollment Profile: 20,314 students from 52 states and territories, 114 other countries. 57% women, 43% men, 46% part-time, 91% state residents, 8% live on campus, 67% transferred in, 6% international, 33% 25 or older, 0% Native American, 54% Hispanic, 14% black, 4% Asian or Pacific Islander. *Retention:* 89% of 1995 full-time freshmen returned. *Graduation:* 41% graduate in 4 years, 50% in 5 years, 53% in 6 years. *Areas of study chosen:* 32% business management and administrative services, 14% education, 8% engineering and applied sciences, 8% health professions and related sciences, 8% psychology, 8% social sciences, 4% communications and journalism, 4% computer and information sciences, 3% biological and life sciences, 3% English language/literature/letters, 2% physical sciences, 1% architecture, 1% fine arts, 1% foreign language and literature, 1% mathematics, 1% performing arts, 1% philosophy. *Most popular recent majors:* psychology, biology/biological sciences, accounting.

First-Year Class: 1,157 total; 3,846 applied, 64% were accepted, 47% of whom enrolled. 42% from top 10% of their high school class, 89% from top quarter, 99% from top half. 2 National Merit Scholars, 9 valedictorians.

Graduation Requirements: 120 credit hours; 6 credit hours of math; 8 credit hours of science; 8 credit hours of a foreign language; computer course for business, math, engineering majors; internship (some majors); senior project (some majors).

Computers on Campus: 600 computers available on campus for general student use. Computer purchase/lease plans available. A campus-wide network can be accessed from student residence rooms and from off-campus. Students can contact faculty members and/or advisers through e-mail. Computers for student use in computer center, computer labs, research center, learning resource center, classrooms, library, student center provide access to the Internet/World Wide Web. Staffed computer lab on campus provides training in use of computers, software. *Academic computing expenditure 1995–96:* $2 million.

EXPENSES AND FINANCIAL AID

Expenses for 1996–97: *Application fee:* $20. State resident tuition: $1783 full-time, $59.43 per credit hour part-time. Nonresident tuition: $7028 full-time, $234.27 per credit hour part-time. Part-time mandatory fees: $46 per semester. Full-time mandatory fees: $92. College room only: $2400 (minimum).

Undergraduate Financial Aid: Of all full-time undergraduates enrolled in fall 1996, 91% of those who applied for aid were judged to have need according to Federal Methodology, of whom 94% were aided. On average, 54% of need was met. *Financial aid deadline (priority):* 3/15. *Financial aid forms:* FAFSA required.

Financial aid specifically for students with LD: Scholarship: Theodore R. and Vivian Johnson Scholarship.

LD Services Contact: Ms. Diane Russell, Coordinator, Florida International University, University Park, GC 190, Miami, FL 33199, 305-348-3532. Fax: 305-348-3850.

FLORIDA STATE UNIVERSITY

Tallahassee, Florida

LEARNING DISABILITIES SERVICES INFORMATION

Disabled Student Services began offering services in 1980. Currently the program serves 600 undergraduates with LD. Services are also available to graduate students. Students diagnosed with ADD/ADHD are eligible for the same services available to students with LD.

Staff: 3 full-time, 3 part-time staff members, including director, assistant director, Assistant to the Director. Services provided by remediation specialists, tutors, counselors, notetakers, readers, graduate assistants.

Special Fees: A fee is charged for diagnostic testing.

Applications and admissions: *Required:* high school transcript, grade point average, courses completed, untimed SAT I or ACT; *recommended:* extended time SAT I or ACT. Students may begin taking classes in fall or summer. *Application deadline:* 3/1.

Special policies: The college has written policies regarding grade forgiveness; substitutions and waivers of admissions, graduation, and degree requirements.

PROGRAM AND SERVICE COMPONENTS

Special preparation or orientation: Optional orientation offered before classes begin.

Diagnostic testing: Intelligence, reading, math, spelling, handwriting, spoken language, written language, motor abilities, perceptual skills, personality, psychoneurology, speech, hearing, medical evaluation.

Academic advising: Provided by unit staff members, academic advisers. Students with LD may take up to 18 semester hours each term; most take 12 semester hours; 12 semester hours required to maintain full-time status and be eligible for financial aid.

Counseling services: Individual counseling, small-group counseling, career counseling.

Basic skills remediation: Offered one-on-one and in small groups by counselors, LD specialists. Available in learning strategies, study skills, time management, social skills.

Subject-area tutoring: Offered one-on-one by peer tutors, graduate students. Available in all subjects.

Special courses: Math. All offered for credit; all enter into overall grade point average.

Auxiliary aids: Taped textbooks, tape recorders, word-processors with spell-check, personal computers, talking computers, optical character readers.

Auxiliary services: Alternative test arrangements, notetakers, advocacy.

Campus support group: A special student organization is available to students with LD.

GENERAL COLLEGE INFORMATION

State-supported, coed. Part of State University System of Florida. Awards associate, bachelor's, master's, doctoral, first professional degrees. Founded 1857. *Setting:* 451-acre suburban campus. *Endowment:* $84.7 million. *Research spending 1995–96:* $66.4 million. *Educational spending 1995–96:* $6275 per undergrad. *Total enrollment:* 30,264. *Faculty:* 1,470 (1,434 full-time, 87% with terminal degrees, 36 part-time).

Enrollment Profile: 22,408 students from 51 states and territories, 109 other countries. 55% women, 45% men, 11% part-time, 89% state residents, 22% live on campus, 10% transferred in, 1% international, 13% 25 or older, 1% Native American, 9% Hispanic, 10% black, 3% Asian or Pacific Islander. *Graduation:* 31% graduate in 4 years, 59% in 5 years, 64% in 6 years. *Areas of study chosen:* 20% business management and administrative services, 9% social sciences, 8% education, 7% biological and life sciences, 5% communications and journalism, 5% psychology, 5% vocational and home economics, 4% engineering and applied sciences, 4% English language/literature/letters, 4% fine arts, 4% health professions and related sciences, 2% computer and information sciences, 2% physical sciences, 1% foreign language and literature, 1% mathematics, 1% performing arts. *Most popular recent majors:* biology/biological sciences, criminology, psychology.

First-Year Class: 3,228 total; 14,216 applied, 75% were accepted, 30% of whom enrolled. 47% from top 10% of their high school class, 72% from top quarter, 95% from top half. 73 National Merit Scholars.

Graduation Requirements: 60 semester hours for associate, 120 semester hours for bachelor's; 1 math course; 2 science courses including at least 1 lab science course; computer course for business, chemistry, engineering, math, math education, meteorology, science education, statistics majors; internship (some majors); senior project for honors program students and some majors.
Computers on Campus: 780 computers available on campus for general student use. Computer purchase/lease plans available. A campus-wide network can be accessed from student residence rooms and from off-campus. Students can contact faculty members and/or advisers through e-mail. Computers for student use in computer center, computer labs, classrooms, library, student center, dorms provide access to the Internet/World Wide Web, on- and off-campus e-mail addresses. Staffed computer lab on campus provides training in use of computers, software. *Academic computing expenditure 1995–96:* $2.4 million.

EXPENSES AND FINANCIAL AID

Expenses for 1997–98: *Application fee:* $20. State resident tuition: $1988 full-time, $66.26 per semester hour part-time. Nonresident tuition: $7904 full-time, $263.48 per semester hour part-time. College room and board: $4570. College room only: $2540.
Undergraduate Financial Aid: 64% of all full-time undergraduates enrolled in fall 1996 applied for aid; of these, 88% were judged to have need according to Federal Methodology, of whom 85% were aided. On average, 100% of need was met. *Financial aid deadline (priority):* 3/1. *Financial aid forms:* FAFSA, institutional form required.
LD Services Contact: Dr. Robin Leach, Director, Student Disability Resource Center, Florida State University, 08 Kellum Hall, Tallahassee, FL 32306-4066, 904-644-9566. Email: rleach@admin.fsu.edu.

FORDHAM UNIVERSITY

New York, New York

LEARNING DISABILITIES SERVICES INFORMATION

Student Affairs/Student Services began offering services in 1982. Currently the program serves 50 undergraduates with LD. Services are also available to graduate students. Students diagnosed with ADD/ADHD are eligible for the same services available to students with LD.
Staff: 3 full-time, 12 part-time staff members, including director, associate director, coordinator. Services provided by remediation specialists, tutors, counselors, diagnostic specialists.
Special Fees: $500 to $700 for diagnostic testing.
Applications and admissions: *Required:* high school transcript, grade point average, class rank, courses completed, extracurricular activities, IEP (Individualized Education Program), untimed or extended time SAT I or ACT, personal interview, autobiographical statement, letters of recommendation, psychoeducational report. Students may begin taking classes in fall only. *Application deadline:* 2/1.
Special policies: The college has written policies regarding substitutions and waivers of degree requirements.

PROGRAM AND SERVICE COMPONENTS

Special preparation or orientation: Required summer program offered prior to entering college. Required orientation held before registration.
Diagnostic testing: Intelligence, reading, math, spelling, written language, motor abilities, perceptual skills, study skills, personality, social skills, psychoneurology, learning strategies.
Academic advising: Provided by unit staff members, academic advisers. Students with LD may take up to 16 credits each term; most take 12 to 16 credits; 12 credits required to maintain full-time status and be eligible for financial aid.
Counseling services: Individual counseling, small-group counseling, career counseling, self-advocacy training.
Basic skills remediation: Offered in small groups by LD teachers, regular teachers, counseling center tutor. Available in reading, math, written language, learning strategies, study skills, time management, social skills, computer skills.
Subject-area tutoring: Offered one-on-one and in small groups by professional teachers, peer tutors. Available in all subjects.
Special courses: College survival skills, communication skills, learning strategies, Internet use, time management, math, study skills, career planning, stress management, health and nutrition, social relationships. None offered for credit; none enter into overall grade point average.
Auxiliary aids: Taped textbooks, tape recorders, calculators, typewriters, word-processors with spell-check, personal computers, talking computers, optical character readers.
Auxiliary services: Alternative test arrangements, notetakers, priority registration, advocacy.

GENERAL COLLEGE INFORMATION

Independent Roman Catholic (Jesuit), coed. Awards bachelor's, master's, doctoral, first professional degrees (branch locations: an 85-acre campus at Rose Hill and an 8-acre campus at Lincoln Center). Founded 1841. *Setting:* 85-acre urban campus. *Endowment:* $136.3 million. *Research spending 1995–96:* $3.7 million. *Educational spending 1995–96:* $5512 per undergrad. *Total enrollment:* 13,723. *Faculty:* 1,139 (525 full-time, 97% with terminal degrees, 614 part-time); student–undergrad faculty ratio is 17:1.
Enrollment Profile: 5,822 students from 49 states and territories, 50 other countries. 59% women, 41% men, 23% part-time, 60% state residents, 7% transferred in, 5% international, 0% Native American, 15% Hispanic, 6% black, 5% Asian or Pacific Islander. *Retention:* 93% of 1995 full-time freshmen returned. *Graduation:* 78% graduate in 5 years. *Areas of study chosen:* 25% business management and administrative services, 22% social sciences, 20% liberal arts/general studies, 6% communications and journalism, 6% psychology, 5% English language/literature/letters, 4% biological and life sciences, 4% mathematics, 2% computer and information sciences, 2% foreign language and literature, 2% physical sciences, 1% fine arts, 1% performing arts. *Most popular recent majors:* business administration/commerce/management, communication, English.
First-Year Class: 1,211 total; 5,357 applied, 70% were accepted, 32% of whom enrolled. 26% from top 10% of their high school class, 58% from top quarter, 88% from top half.
Graduation Requirements: 124 credits; 3 math/science courses; computer course for business, math majors; senior project for honors program students and some majors.
Computers on Campus: 400 computers available on campus for general student use. Computer purchase/lease plans available. A campus-wide network can be accessed from student residence rooms and from off-campus. Students can contact faculty members and/or advisers through e-mail. Computers for student use in computer center, computer labs, research center, classrooms, library provide access to the Internet/World Wide Web, on- and off-campus e-mail addresses. Staffed computer lab on campus provides training in use of computers, software. *Academic computing expenditure 1995–96:* $2 million.

EXPENSES AND FINANCIAL AID

Expenses for 1996–97: *Application fee:* $50. Comprehensive fee of $23,125 includes full-time tuition ($15,800), mandatory fees ($200), and college room and board ($7125 minimum). Part-time tuition per credit ranges from $375 to $410 for nontraditional students.
Undergraduate Financial Aid: 76% of all full-time undergraduates enrolled in fall 1996 applied for aid; of these, 93% were judged to have need according to Federal Methodology, of whom 99% were aided. On average, 79% of need was met. *Financial aid deadline (priority):* 2/1. *Financial aid forms:* FAFSA, institutional form required. CSS Financial Aid PROFILE, state form required for some.
Financial aid specifically for students with LD: Scholarships; loans; work-study.
LD Services Contact: Ms. Christine Mone, Associate Director of Student Support Services, Fordham University, B1 Hughes Hall, New York, NY 10458, 718-817-4822.

FRANKLIN UNIVERSITY

Columbus, Ohio

LEARNING DISABILITIES SERVICES INFORMATION

Disability Services began offering services in 1982. Currently the program serves 37 undergraduates with LD. Services are also available to graduate students. Students diagnosed with ADD/ADHD are eligible for the same services available to students with LD.
Staff: Includes coordinator, assistant. Services provided by tutors, counselors, developmental teachers.
Special Fees: No special fees are charged for services to students with LD.
Applications and admissions: *Required:* high school transcript, personal interview, psychoeducational report completed within 3 years; *recommended:* high school IEP (Individualized Education Program). Students may begin taking classes in fall, winter, or summer. *Application deadline:* continuous.

Franklin University (continued)

Special policies: The college has written policies regarding grade forgiveness; substitutions and waivers of graduation requirements.

PROGRAM AND SERVICE COMPONENTS

Academic advising: Provided by unit staff members. Students with LD may take up to 18 credit hours each term; most take 12 credit hours; 12 credit hours required to maintain full-time status and be eligible for financial aid.

Counseling services: Individual counseling, career counseling, professional and personal development workshops.

Subject-area tutoring: Offered one-on-one and in small groups by professional teachers, peer tutors. Available in most subjects.

Special courses: College survival skills, reading, vocabulary development, composition, learning strategies, math, study skills, career planning. Some offered for credit; none enter into overall grade point average.

Auxiliary aids: Taped textbooks, tape recorders, calculators, word-processors with spell-check.

Auxiliary services: Alternative test arrangements, notetakers, advocacy.

GENERAL COLLEGE INFORMATION

Independent, comprehensive, coed. Awards associate, bachelor's, master's degrees. Founded 1902. *Setting:* 14-acre urban campus. *Educational spending 1995–96:* $1650 per undergrad. *Total enrollment:* 4,049. *Faculty:* 230 (48 full-time, 58% with terminal degrees, 182 part-time); student–undergrad faculty ratio is 18:1.

Enrollment Profile: 3,669 students: 59% women, 41% men, 72% part-time, 68% transferred in, 6% international, 74% 25 or older, 1% Native American, 1% Hispanic, 13% black, 2% Asian or Pacific Islander. *Areas of study chosen:* 72% business management and administrative services, 8% health professions and related sciences, 7% computer and information sciences, 7% engineering and applied sciences, 3% communications and journalism, 3% social sciences. *Most popular recent majors:* business administration/commerce/management, accounting, marketing/retailing/merchandising.

First-Year Class: 108 total; 250 applied, 100% were accepted, 43% of whom enrolled.

Graduation Requirements: 64 credit hours for associate, 124 credit hours for bachelor's; 1 course each in math and science; computer course; senior project.

Computers on Campus: 150 computers available on campus for general student use. A computer is recommended for some students. A campus-wide network can be accessed. Students can contact faculty members and/or advisers through e-mail. Computers for student use in computer center, computer labs, learning resource center provide access to the Internet/World Wide Web. Staffed computer lab on campus provides training in use of computers, software. *Academic computing expenditure 1995–96:* $1.9 million.

EXPENSES AND FINANCIAL AID

Expenses for 1996–97: Tuition: $4991 full-time, $161 per credit hour part-time. Part-time mandatory fees: $25 per trimester. Full-time mandatory fees: $75.

Undergraduate Financial Aid: 59% of all full-time undergraduates enrolled in fall 1996 applied for aid; of these, 78% were judged to have need according to Federal Methodology, of whom 100% were aided. *Financial aid deadline (priority):* 5/30. *Financial aid forms:* FAFSA, institutional form required. State form required for some.

LD Services Contact: Mr. Rick McIntosh, Student Services Associate, Disability Services, Franklin University, 201 South Grant Avenue, Columbus, OH 43215-5399, 614-341-6415.

FROSTBURG STATE UNIVERSITY

Frostburg, Maryland

LEARNING DISABILITIES SERVICES INFORMATION

Disabled Student Services began offering services in 1983. Currently the program serves 240 undergraduates with LD. Students diagnosed with ADD/ADHD are eligible for the same services available to students with LD.

Staff: 5 full-time, 1 part-time staff members, including director, assistant director, counselors, academic advisers, study skills/math specialist. Services provided by remediation specialists, tutors, counselors, diagnostic specialists.

Special Fees: No special fees are charged for services to students with LD.

Applications and admissions: *Required:* high school transcript, grade point average, courses completed, SAT I; *recommended:* personal interview, letters of recommendation. Students may begin taking classes in fall or summer. *Application deadline:* continuous.

Special policies: The college has written policies regarding substitutions and waivers of admissions, graduation, and degree requirements.

PROGRAM AND SERVICE COMPONENTS

Special preparation or orientation: Orientation (required for some) held before registration or later by individual arrangement.

Diagnostic testing: Intelligence, reading, math, spelling, handwriting, spoken language, written language, motor abilities, perceptual skills, study skills, personality, hearing, learning strategies.

Academic advising: Provided by unit staff members, academic advisers. Students with LD may take up to 18 credit hours each term; most take 12 to 13 credit hours; 12 credit hours required to maintain full-time status.

Counseling services: Individual counseling, small-group counseling, career counseling.

Basic skills remediation: Offered one-on-one, in small groups, and in class-size groups by regular teachers, basic skills instructors. Available in reading, math, written language, learning strategies, study skills, time management, social skills.

Subject-area tutoring: Offered one-on-one, in small groups, and in class-size groups by professional teachers, peer tutors, study skills/math specialist. Available in most subjects.

Special courses: College survival skills, reading, communication skills, composition, learning strategies, word processing, time management, math, personal psychology, study skills, career planning. Most offered for credit; all enter into overall grade point average.

Auxiliary aids: Taped textbooks, tape recorders, word-processors with spell-check, spell checkers.

Auxiliary services: Alternative test arrangements, notetakers, priority registration, advocacy.

Campus support group: A special student organization is available to students with LD.

GENERAL COLLEGE INFORMATION

State-supported, comprehensive, coed. Part of University of Maryland System. Awards bachelor's, master's degrees. Founded 1898. *Setting:* 260-acre small-town campus. *Research spending 1995–96:* $1.9 million. *Educational spending 1995–96:* $4133 per undergrad. *Total enrollment:* 5,418. *Undergraduate faculty:* 314 (232 full-time, 77% with terminal degrees, 82 part-time); student–undergrad faculty ratio is 17:1.

Enrollment Profile: 4,543 students from 32 states and territories, 16 other countries. 50% women, 50% men, 9% part-time, 87% state residents, 45% live on campus, 9% transferred in, 1% international, 13% 25 or older, 1% Native American, 1% Hispanic, 8% black, 1% Asian or Pacific Islander. *Retention:* 76% of 1995 full-time freshmen returned. *Graduation:* 26% graduate in 4 years, 57% in 5 years. *Areas of study chosen:* 17% education, 17% social sciences, 15% business management and administrative services, 5% psychology, 4% biological and life sciences, 4% communications and journalism, 4% computer and information sciences, 3% physical sciences, 2% agriculture, 2% English language/literature/letters, 2% fine arts, 2% natural resource sciences, 1% foreign language and literature, 1% interdisciplinary studies, 1% liberal arts/general studies, 1% mathematics, 1% performing arts, 1% philosophy. *Most popular recent majors:* business administration/commerce/management, education, criminal justice.

First-Year Class: 992 total; 2,785 applied, 85% were accepted, 42% of whom enrolled. 90% from top half of their high school class.

Graduation Requirements: 120 credit hours; 1 math course; 2 lab science courses; computer course for most majors; internship (some majors); senior project (some majors).

Computers on Campus: 237 computers available on campus for general student use. Computer purchase/lease plans available. A computer is required for some students. A campus-wide network can be accessed from off-campus. Students can contact faculty members and/or advisers through e-mail. Computers for student use in computer center, computer labs, learning resource center, library, dorms, academic buildings provide access to the Internet/World Wide Web, on- and off-campus e-mail addresses. Staffed computer lab on campus provides training in use of computers, software. *Academic computing expenditure 1995–96:* $429,150.

EXPENSES AND FINANCIAL AID

Expenses for 1997–98: *Application fee:* $30. State resident tuition: $3544 full-time, $128 per credit hour part-time. Nonresident tuition: $7530 full-time, $214 per credit hour part-time. College room and board: $4786. College room only: $2489.
Undergraduate Financial Aid: 59% of all full-time undergraduates enrolled in fall 1996 applied for aid; of these, 72% were judged to have need according to Federal Methodology, of whom 96% were aided. On average, 83% of need was met. *Financial aid deadline (priority):* 4/1. *Financial aid forms:* FAFSA, institutional form required; CSS Financial Aid PROFILE acceptable. State form required for some.
LD Services Contact: Ms. Suzanne Carroll Hull, Director, Department of Support Services, Frostburg State University, 113 Pullen Hall, Frostburg, MD 21532-1099, 301-687-4481. Fax: 301-687-4671.

GARDNER-WEBB UNIVERSITY

Boiling Springs, North Carolina

LEARNING DISABILITIES SERVICES INFORMATION

Noel Programs for the Disabled began offering services in 1988. Currently the program serves 20 undergraduates with LD. Services are also available to graduate students. Students diagnosed with ADD/ADHD are eligible for the same services available to students with LD.
Staff: 4 full-time, 1 part-time staff members, including director. Services provided by remediation specialists, counselors.
Special Fees: No special fees are charged for services to students with LD.
Applications and admissions: *Required:* high school transcript, grade point average, class rank, courses completed, extracurricular activities; *recommended:* untimed or extended time SAT I or ACT, psychoeducational report completed within 3 years. Students may begin taking classes in fall only. *Application deadline:* continuous.
Special policies: The college has written policies regarding grade forgiveness.

PROGRAM AND SERVICE COMPONENTS

Special preparation or orientation: Required orientation held individually by arrangement.
Academic advising: Provided by unit staff members, academic advisers. Students with LD may take up to 18 semester hours each term; most take 12 to 16 semester hours; 12 semester hours required to maintain full-time status and be eligible for financial aid.
Counseling services: Individual counseling.
Basic skills remediation: Offered in class-size groups by regular teachers. Available in reading, math, written language.
Subject-area tutoring: Offered one-on-one and in small groups by peer tutors. Available in all subjects.
Auxiliary aids: Taped textbooks, tape recorders, word-processors with spell-check, personal computers, optical character readers.
Auxiliary services: Alternative test arrangements, notetakers, priority registration, advocacy, readers.

GENERAL COLLEGE INFORMATION

Independent Baptist, comprehensive, coed. Awards associate, bachelor's, master's degrees. Founded 1905. *Setting:* 200-acre small-town campus with easy access to Charlotte. *Total enrollment:* 2,739. *Faculty:* 174 (90 full-time, 84 part-time); student–undergrad faculty ratio is 16:1.
Enrollment Profile: 2,436 students from 23 states and territories, 35 other countries. 60% women, 40% men, 16% part-time, 52% state residents, 38% transferred in, 1% international, 36% 25 or older, 0% Native American, 0% Hispanic, 12% black, 1% Asian or Pacific Islander. *Retention:* 67% of 1995 full-time freshmen returned. *Most popular recent majors:* business administration/commerce/management, education, biology/biological sciences.
First-Year Class: 319 total; 1,445 applied, 88% were accepted, 25% of whom enrolled. 22% from top 10% of their high school class, 42% from top quarter, 75% from top half.
Graduation Requirements: 64 semester hours for associate, 128 semester hours for bachelor's; 3 semester hours of math; 8 semester hours of science; computer course for business, management information systems majors; internship (some majors); senior project (some majors).
Computers on Campus: 55 computers available on campus for general student use. Computer purchase/lease plans available. A computer is recommended for all students. A campus-wide network can be accessed from student residence rooms and from off-campus. Students can contact faculty members and/or advisers through e-mail. Computers for student use in library, math, business departmental labs provide access to the Internet/World Wide Web, on- and off-campus e-mail addresses. Staffed computer lab on campus provides training in use of computers, software.

EXPENSES AND FINANCIAL AID

Expenses for 1997–98: *Application fee:* $20. Comprehensive fee of $14,250 includes full-time tuition ($9620) and college room and board ($4630). College room only: $2190. Part-time tuition (1 to 9 semester hours): $210 per semester hour.
Undergraduate Financial Aid: Of all full-time undergraduates enrolled in fall 1996, 100% of those judged to have need according to Federal Methodology were aided. On average, 84% of need was met. *Financial aid deadline (priority):* 4/1. *Financial aid forms:* FAFSA acceptable. CSS Financial Aid PROFILE, state form required for some.
LD Services Contact: Ms. Sharon D. Jennings, Director, Noel Programs for the Disabled, Gardner-Webb University, Box 7274, Boiling Springs, NC 28017, 704-434-2371. Fax: 704-434-2371.

GEORGE MASON UNIVERSITY

Fairfax, Virginia

LEARNING DISABILITIES SERVICES INFORMATION

Disability Support Services began offering services in 1980. Currently the program serves 400 undergraduates with LD. Services are also available to graduate students. Students diagnosed with ADD/ADHD are eligible for the same services available to students with LD.
Staff: Includes assistant director, coordinator, assistant coordinator.
Special Fees: No special fees are charged for services to students with LD.
Applications and admissions: *Required:* high school transcript, grade point average, class rank, courses completed, college transcript; *recommended:* high school extracurricular activities, extended time SAT I, psychoeducational report. Students may begin taking classes in summer only. *Application deadline:* 2/1 (fall term), 12/1 (spring term).
Special policies: The college has written policies regarding substitutions and waivers of graduation requirements.

PROGRAM AND SERVICE COMPONENTS

Special preparation or orientation: Optional orientation offered individually by special arrangement.
Academic advising: Provided by unit staff members, academic advisers. Students with LD may take up to 18 credit hours each term; most take 12 to 13 credit hours; 12 credit hours required to maintain full-time status.
Counseling services: Individual counseling, small-group counseling, career counseling.
Auxiliary aids: Taped textbooks, word-processors with spell-check, Arkenstone Reader.
Auxiliary services: Alternative test arrangements, notetakers, priority registration, advocacy, TDD/(703)993-2474.

GENERAL COLLEGE INFORMATION

State-supported, coed. Awards bachelor's, master's, doctoral, first professional degrees. Founded 1957. *Setting:* 677-acre suburban campus with easy access to Washington, DC. *Endowment:* $17.9 million. *Research spending 1995–96:* $32.5 million. *Educational spending 1995–96:* $4413 per undergrad. *Total enrollment:* 24,368. *Faculty:* 1,350 (800 full-time, 95% with terminal degrees, 550 part-time); student–undergrad faculty ratio is 17:1.
Enrollment Profile: 13,832 students from 45 states and territories, 101 other countries. 56% women, 44% men, 29% part-time, 91% state residents, 12% live on campus, 15% transferred in, 3% international, 29% 25 or older, 1% Native American, 5% Hispanic, 8% black, 15% Asian or Pacific Islander. *Retention:* 75% of 1995 full-time freshmen returned. *Graduation:* 25% graduate in 4 years, 43% in 5 years, 48% in 6 years. *Areas of study chosen:* 18% business management and administrative services, 13% social sciences, 10% health professions and related sciences, 8% psychology, 6% biological and life sciences, 6% communications and journalism, 6% English language/literature/letters, 5% computer and information sciences, 4% engineering and applied sciences, 4% liberal arts/general studies, 2% interdisciplinary studies, 2% physical sciences, 1% fine arts, 1% foreign language and literature, 1% mathematics, 1% performing arts, 1% philosophy. *Most popular recent majors:* business administration/commerce/management, psychology, English.

George Mason University (continued)

First-Year Class: 1,953 total; 5,449 applied, 69% were accepted, 52% of whom enrolled. 12% from top 10% of their high school class, 30% from top quarter, 75% from top half. 16 National Merit Scholars, 3 Westinghouse recipients, 42 class presidents, 35 valedictorians.
Graduation Requirements: 120 credit hours; 8 credit hours of lab science; 3 credit hours of math; computer course for economics, math, psychology, public administration, business majors; internship (some majors); senior project (some majors).
Computers on Campus: 900 computers available on campus for general student use. Computer purchase/lease plans available. A computer is recommended for all students. A campus-wide network can be accessed from student residence rooms and from off-campus. Students can contact faculty members and/or advisers through e-mail. Computers for student use in computer center, computer labs, learning resource center, library, student center, dorms, departmental labs provide access to the Internet/World Wide Web, on- and off-campus e-mail addresses. Staffed computer lab on campus (open 24 hours a day) provides training in use of computers, software. *Academic computing expenditure 1995–96:* $6.7 million.

EXPENSES AND FINANCIAL AID

Expenses for 1997–98: *Application fee:* $30. State resident tuition: $4296 full-time, $179 per credit hour part-time. Nonresident tuition: $12,240 full-time, $510 per credit hour part-time. College room and board: $5120. College room only: $3300.
Undergraduate Financial Aid: 75% of all full-time undergraduates enrolled in fall 1996 applied for aid; of these, 84% were judged to have need according to Federal Methodology, of whom 86% were aided. On average, 68% of need was met. *Financial aid deadline (priority):* 3/1. *Financial aid forms:* FAFSA required.
LD Services Contact: Mr. Paul Bousel, Assistant Director, Academic Advising Center/Disability Support Services, George Mason University, Mail Stop 2E6, Fairfax, VA 22030-4444, 703-993-2474. Fax: 703-993-2478.

GEORGETOWN UNIVERSITY

Washington, District of Columbia

LEARNING DISABILITIES SERVICES INFORMATION

Learning Services began offering services in 1981. Currently the program serves 116 undergraduates with LD. Services are also available to graduate students. Students diagnosed with ADD/ADHD are eligible for the same services available to students with LD, as well as medication monitoring by Counseling and Psychiatric Center physicians.
Staff: 1 full-time staff member (director).
Special Fees: A fee is charged for diagnostic testing.
Applications and admissions: *Required:* high school transcript, grade point average, class rank, courses completed, extracurricular activities, letters of recommendation; *recommended:* psychoeducational report completed within 3 years. Students may begin taking classes in summer only.
Special policies: The college has written policies regarding substitutions and waivers of admissions, graduation, and degree requirements.

PROGRAM AND SERVICE COMPONENTS

Special preparation or orientation: Optional orientation offered individually after classes begin.
Diagnostic testing: Intelligence, reading, math, spelling, handwriting, written language, motor abilities, perceptual skills, study skills, learning strategies.
Academic advising: Provided by academic advisers. Students with LD may take up to 15 credit hours each term; most take 12 credit hours; 9 credit hours required to maintain full-time status; 12 credit hours required to be eligible for financial aid.
Counseling services: Individual counseling.
Basic skills remediation: Offered one-on-one and in small groups by Director of Learning Services. Available in reading, spelling, handwriting, spoken language, written language, learning strategies, study skills, time management.
Auxiliary aids: Taped textbooks, tape recorders, word-processors with spell-check.
Auxiliary services: Alternative test arrangements, notetakers, priority registration.

GENERAL COLLEGE INFORMATION

Independent Roman Catholic (Jesuit), coed. Awards bachelor's, master's, doctoral, first professional degrees. Founded 1789. *Setting:* 110-acre urban campus. *Endowment:* $448 million. *Research spending 1995–96:* $97.6 million. *Total enrollment:* 12,629. *Faculty:* 2,085 (1,576 full-time, 90% with terminal degrees, 509 part-time).
Enrollment Profile: 6,338 students from 52 states and territories, 128 other countries. 52% women, 48% men, 5% part-time, 3% district residents, 75% live on campus, 15% transferred in, 10% international, 4% 25 or older, 1% Native American, 6% Hispanic, 6% black, 8% Asian or Pacific Islander. *Retention:* 95% of 1995 full-time freshmen returned. *Graduation:* 83% graduate in 4 years, 89% in 5 years. *Areas of study chosen:* 33% social sciences, 20% business management and administrative services, 11% foreign language and literature, 6% health professions and related sciences, 4% biological and life sciences, 4% English language/literature/letters, 3% psychology, 2% physical sciences, 1% area and ethnic studies, 1% computer and information sciences, 1% fine arts, 1% interdisciplinary studies, 1% mathematics, 1% philosophy, 1% theology/religion. *Most popular recent majors:* international relations, political science/government, English.
First-Year Class: 1,415 total; 13,010 applied, 23% were accepted, 47% of whom enrolled. 79% from top 10% of their high school class, 95% from top quarter, 99% from top half. 204 class presidents, 110 valedictorians.
Graduation Requirements: 120 credit hours; computer course for business administration, math, nursing majors; senior project for honors program students and some majors.
Computers on Campus: 300 computers available on campus for general student use. Computer purchase/lease plans available. A computer is recommended for all students. A campus-wide network can be accessed from student residence rooms and from off-campus. Students can contact faculty members and/or advisers through e-mail. Computers for student use in computer center, computer labs, library, dorms provide access to the Internet/World Wide Web, on- and off-campus e-mail addresses. Staffed computer lab on campus provides training in use of computers, software.

EXPENSES AND FINANCIAL AID

Expenses for 1997–98: *Application fee:* $50. Comprehensive fee of $27,069 includes full-time tuition ($21,216), mandatory fees ($189), and college room and board ($5664 minimum). College room only: $4560 (minimum). Part-time tuition: $884 per credit hour. Part-time mandatory fees: $189 per year.
Undergraduate Financial Aid: Of all full-time undergraduates enrolled in fall 1996, 85% of those who applied for aid were judged to have need according to Federal Methodology, of whom 100% were aided. On average, 100% of need was met. *Financial aid deadline:* continuous. *Financial aid forms:* CSS Financial Aid PROFILE required. District form required for some.
LD Services Contact: Dr. Norma Jo Eitington, Director of Learning Services, Georgetown University, One Darnall Hall, Washington, DC 20057, 202-687-6985. Fax: 202-687-6069.

THE GEORGE WASHINGTON UNIVERSITY

Washington, District of Columbia

LEARNING DISABILITIES SERVICES INFORMATION

Disability Support Services began offering services in 1978. Currently the program serves 156 undergraduates with LD. Services are also available to graduate students. Students diagnosed with ADD/ADHD are eligible for the same services available to students with LD, as well as one-on-one support for time management.
Staff: 2 full-time staff members, including director, LD specialist. Services provided by readers, proctors, aides, graduate assistants.
Special Fees: No special fees are charged for services to students with LD.
Applications and admissions: *Required:* high school transcript, grade point average, class rank, courses completed, untimed SAT I or ACT, letters of recommendation, essay; *recommended:* high school extracurricular activities, extended time SAT I or ACT, personal interview, psychoeducational report completed within 3 years, achievement tests (untimed or standard). Students may begin taking classes any term. *Application deadline:* 2/1 (fall term), 11/1 (spring term).

Special policies: The college has written policies regarding grade forgiveness.

PROGRAM AND SERVICE COMPONENTS

Special preparation or orientation: Optional orientation offered before registration.

Academic advising: Provided by unit staff members, academic advisers. Students with LD may take up to 17 semester hours each term; most take 12 to 15 semester hours; 12 semester hours required to maintain full-time status and be eligible for financial aid.

Counseling services: Individual counseling, small-group counseling, career counseling.

Subject-area tutoring: Offered one-on-one by professional teachers, peer tutors. Available in all subjects.

Auxiliary aids: Taped textbooks, tape recorders, word-processors with spell-check, personal computers, optical character readers, voice-synthesized computer.

Auxiliary services: Alternative test arrangements, notetakers, advocacy, laboratory assistance.

Campus support group: A special student organization is available to students with LD.

GENERAL COLLEGE INFORMATION

Independent, coed. Awards associate, bachelor's, master's, doctoral, first professional degrees. Founded 1821. *Setting:* 36-acre urban campus. *Endowment:* $497.1 million. *Total enrollment:* 18,986. *Faculty:* 2,214 (1,428 full-time, 92% with terminal degrees, 786 part-time); student–undergrad faculty ratio is 14:1.

Enrollment Profile: 6,581 students from 54 states and territories, 94 other countries. 55% women, 45% men, 7% part-time, 9% district residents, 49% live on campus, 13% transferred in, 9% international, 7% 25 or older, 1% Native American, 4% Hispanic, 7% black, 12% Asian or Pacific Islander. *Retention:* 88% of 1995 full-time freshmen returned. *Graduation:* 54% graduate in 4 years, 61% in 5 years, 63% in 6 years. *Areas of study chosen:* 33% liberal arts/general studies, 23% social sciences, 14% business management and administrative services, 6% engineering and applied sciences, 6% health professions and related sciences, 3% biological and life sciences, 3% English language/literature/letters, 3% psychology, 2% communications and journalism, 2% computer and information sciences, 1% area and ethnic studies, 1% interdisciplinary studies, 1% performing arts, 1% philosophy, 1% physical sciences. *Most popular recent majors:* international studies, biology/biological sciences, psychology.

First-Year Class: 1,657 total; 10,356 applied, 58% were accepted, 28% of whom enrolled. 41% from top 10% of their high school class, 78% from top quarter, 98% from top half. 42 National Merit Scholars.

Graduation Requirements: 60 semester hours for associate, 120 semester hours for bachelor's; 9 semester hours of lab science; 6 semester hours of math or statistics; computer course for business, engineering, some liberal arts majors; senior project for honors program students and some majors.

Computers on Campus: 550 computers available on campus for general student use. Computer purchase/lease plans available. A computer is recommended for all students. A campus-wide network can be accessed from student residence rooms and from off-campus. Students can contact faculty members and/or advisers through e-mail. Computers for student use in computer center, computer labs, classrooms, library, student center, dorms provide access to the Internet/World Wide Web, on- and off-campus e-mail addresses. Staffed computer lab on campus (open 24 hours a day) provides training in use of computers, software.

EXPENSES AND FINANCIAL AID

Expenses for 1997–98: *Application fee:* $50. Comprehensive fee of $27,250 includes full-time tuition ($19,650), mandatory fees ($990), and college room and board ($6610 minimum). College room only: $4590 (minimum). Part-time tuition: $655 per semester hour. Part-time mandatory fees: $33 per semester hour.

Undergraduate Financial Aid: 56% of all full-time undergraduates enrolled in fall 1996 applied for aid; of these, 84% were judged to have need according to Federal Methodology, of whom 95% were aided. On average, 90% of need was met. *Financial aid deadline (priority):* 1/31. *Financial aid forms:* FAFSA, CSS Financial Aid PROFILE required. Institutional form required for some.

LD Services Contact: Ms. Stefanie Coale, Learning Specialist, The George Washington University, Marvin Center, Suite 436, 800 21st Street, NW, Washington, DC 20052, 202-994-8250. Fax: 202-994-7610. Email: stef@gwis2.circ.gwu.edu.

GEORGIA SOUTHERN UNIVERSITY

Statesboro, Georgia

LEARNING DISABILITIES SERVICES INFORMATION

Student Disability Resource Center began offering services in 1989. Currently the program serves 235 undergraduates with LD. Services are also available to graduate students. Students diagnosed with ADD/ADHD are eligible for the same services available to students with LD.

Staff: 4 full-time, 2 part-time staff members, including director, associate director. Services provided by tutors.

Special Fees: $300 for diagnostic testing.

Applications and admissions: *Required:* high school transcript, grade point average, class rank, courses completed, untimed SAT I, psychoeducational report completed within 3 years; *recommended:* high school extracurricular activities, letters of recommendation. Students may begin taking classes any term. *Application deadline:* continuous.

PROGRAM AND SERVICE COMPONENTS

Diagnostic testing: Intelligence, reading, math, spelling, handwriting, spoken language, written language, motor abilities, perceptual skills, personality, speech, hearing.

Academic advising: Provided by unit staff members, academic advisers. Students with LD may take up to 18 quarter hours each term; most take 12 quarter hours; 12 quarter hours required to maintain full-time status and be eligible for financial aid.

Counseling services: Individual counseling, career counseling.

Basic skills remediation: Offered in class-size groups by regular teachers. Available in reading, math, written language, learning strategies.

Subject-area tutoring: Offered one-on-one by graduate assistants. Available in some subjects.

Special courses: Learning strategies, time management, study skills, career planning, stress management, health and nutrition. None offered for credit; none enter into overall grade point average.

Auxiliary aids: Taped textbooks, tape recorders, calculators, typewriters, word-processors with spell-check, personal computers, talking computers.

Auxiliary services: Alternative test arrangements, notetakers, priority registration, advocacy.

GENERAL COLLEGE INFORMATION

State-supported, comprehensive, coed. Part of University System of Georgia. Awards associate, bachelor's, master's, doctoral degrees. Founded 1906. *Setting:* 601-acre small-town campus with easy access to Savannah. *Total enrollment:* 14,312. *Undergraduate faculty:* 650 (594 full-time, 60% with terminal degrees, 56 part-time); student–undergrad faculty ratio is 25:1.

Enrollment Profile: 12,650 students from 50 states and territories, 67 other countries. 54% women, 46% men, 8% part-time, 88% state residents, 24% live on campus, 5% transferred in, 1% international, 11% 25 or older, 1% Native American, 2% Hispanic, 26% black, 1% Asian or Pacific Islander. *Most popular recent majors:* early childhood education, marketing/retailing/merchandising, finance/banking.

First-Year Class: 4,020 total; 8,629 applied, 70% were accepted, 66% of whom enrolled.

Graduation Requirements: 95 quarter hours for associate, 190 quarter hours for bachelor's; 4 math/science courses including at least 2 lab science courses; computer course for business, math majors; internship (some majors); senior project (some majors).

Computers on Campus: 275 computers available on campus for general student use. Computer purchase/lease plans available. A campus-wide network can be accessed from student residence rooms and from off-campus. Students can contact faculty members and/or advisers through e-mail. Computers for student use in computer center, computer labs, learning resource center, library, dorms provide access to the Internet/World Wide Web, on- and off-campus e-mail addresses. Staffed computer lab on campus (open 24 hours a day) provides training in use of computers, software.

EXPENSES AND FINANCIAL AID

Expenses for 1996–97: *Application fee:* $10. State resident tuition: $1584 full-time, $44 per quarter hour part-time. Nonresident tuition: $5463 full-time, $152 per quarter hour part-time. Part-time mandatory fees per quarter (6 to 11 quarter hours): $157. Full-time mandatory fees: $471. College room and board: $3675.

Undergraduate Financial Aid: Of all full-time undergraduates enrolled in fall 1996, 96% of those who applied for aid were judged to have need

according to Federal Methodology, of whom 100% were aided. On average, 58% of need was met. *Financial aid deadline (priority):* 5/1. *Financial aid forms:* FAFSA required; CSS Financial Aid PROFILE acceptable.
LD Services Contact: Mr. Wayne Akins, Director, Student Disability Resource Center, Georgia Southern University, PO Box 8037, Statesboro, GA 30460, 912-871-1566. Fax: 912-871-1419.

GEORGIA STATE UNIVERSITY

Atlanta, Georgia

LEARNING DISABILITIES SERVICES INFORMATION

Office of Disability Services began offering services in 1974. Currently the program serves 133 undergraduates with LD. Services are also available to graduate students. Students diagnosed with ADD/ADHD are eligible for the same services available to students with LD.
Staff: 7 full-time staff members, including director, student development specialist. Services provided by remediation specialist, tutors, counselor, diagnostic specialist, peer helpers, student aides, graduate lab assistant.
Special Fees: $300 for diagnostic testing.
Applications and admissions: *Required:* high school transcript, grade point average, class rank, courses completed, untimed or extended time SAT I; *recommended:* high school IEP (Individualized Education Program), autobiographical statement, psychoeducational report completed within 3 years. Students may begin taking classes any term. *Application deadline:* 7/15 (fall term), 2/15 (spring term).
Special policies: The college has written policies regarding substitutions and waivers of admissions, graduation, and degree requirements.

PROGRAM AND SERVICE COMPONENTS

Special preparation or orientation: Optional orientation offered during registration and after classes begin, individually during registration and after classes begin.
Diagnostic testing: Intelligence, reading, math, spelling, handwriting, spoken language, written language, motor abilities, perceptual skills, study skills, personality, social skills, psychoneurology, speech, hearing, learning strategies.
Academic advising: Provided by unit staff members, academic advisers. Students with LD may take up to 15 quarter hours each term; most take 10 to 15 quarter hours; 10 quarter hours required to maintain full-time status; source of aid determines number of quarter hours required to be eligible for financial aid.
Counseling services: Individual counseling, small-group counseling, career counseling, self-advocacy training.
Basic skills remediation: Offered one-on-one, in small groups, and in class-size groups by regular teachers, tutors; computer-aided instruction also offered. Available in reading, math, spelling, spoken language, written language, learning strategies, study skills, time management, social skills.
Subject-area tutoring: Offered one-on-one by peer tutors. Available in some subjects.
Special courses: College survival skills, reading, vocabulary development, communication skills, composition, learning strategies, word processing, time management, math, typing, personal psychology, study skills, career planning. None offered for credit; none enter into overall grade point average.
Auxiliary aids: Taped textbooks, tape recorders, calculators, typewriters, word-processors with spell-check, optical character readers, Arkenstone Reader, closed-captioned television with print magnification.
Auxiliary services: Alternative test arrangements, notetakers, advocacy, readers, TDD/(404)651-2206.

GENERAL COLLEGE INFORMATION

State-supported, coed. Part of University System of Georgia. Awards associate, bachelor's, master's, doctoral, first professional degrees. Founded 1913. *Setting:* 24-acre urban campus. *Endowment:* $22.3 million. *Research spending 1995–96:* $29.7 million. *Total enrollment:* 23,410. *Faculty:* 1,437 (840 full-time, 87% with terminal degrees, 597 part-time); student–undergrad faculty ratio is 14:1.
Enrollment Profile: 16,320 students from 50 states and territories, 107 other countries. 60% women, 40% men, 46% part-time, 90% state residents, 8% live on campus, 46% transferred in, 3% international, 58% 25 or older, 1% Native American, 2% Hispanic, 17% black, 6% Asian or Pacific Islander. *Areas of study chosen:* 9% business management and administrative services, 8% education, 7% computer and information sciences, 6% health professions and related sciences, 5% biological and life sciences, 5% communications and journalism, 5% psychology, 3% English language/literature/letters, 3% fine arts, 1% foreign language and literature, 1% mathematics, 1% philosophy, 1% physical sciences, 1% social sciences. *Most popular recent majors:* business administration/commerce/management, mathematics, accounting.
First-Year Class: 1,705 total; 4,626 applied, 70% were accepted, 52% of whom enrolled.
Graduation Requirements: 90 quarter hours for associate, 180 quarter hours for bachelor's; 20 quarter hours of math/science; computer course for business administration majors; internship (some majors).
Computers on Campus: 425 computers available on campus for general student use. A computer is recommended for all students. A campus-wide network can be accessed from student residence rooms and from off-campus. Computers for student use in computer center, library provide access to the Internet/World Wide Web. Staffed computer lab on campus (open 24 hours a day) provides training in use of computers, software. *Academic computing expenditure 1995–96:* $4.5 million.

EXPENSES AND FINANCIAL AID

Expenses for 1996–97: *Application fee:* $25. State resident tuition: $2124 full-time, $47.20 per quarter hour part-time. Nonresident tuition: $8379 full-time, $186.20 per quarter hour part-time. Part-time mandatory fees: $87 per quarter. Full-time mandatory fees: $261. College room only: $3790.
Undergraduate Financial Aid: Of all full-time undergraduates enrolled in fall 1996, 100% of those judged to have need according to Federal Methodology were aided. *Financial aid deadline (priority):* 4/15. *Financial aid forms:* FAFSA required. State form required for some.
LD Services Contact: Dr. Carole L. Pearson, Director, Office of Disability Services, Georgia State University, University Plaza, Atlanta, GA 30303-3083, 404-651-2206. Fax: 404-651-1404.

GRACELAND COLLEGE

Lamoni, Iowa

LEARNING DISABILITIES SERVICES INFORMATION

Chance began offering services in 1987. Currently the program serves 34 undergraduates with LD. Students diagnosed with ADD/ADHD are eligible for the same services available to students with LD.
Staff: 3 full-time, 2 part-time staff members, including coordinator. Services provided by remediation specialists, diagnostic specialists.
Special Fees: $2100 per year. $80 for diagnostic testing.
Applications and admissions: *Required:* personal interview, psychoeducational report, on-campus testing; *recommended:* high school transcript, grade point average, class rank, courses completed. Students may begin taking classes any term. *Application deadline:* continuous.

PROGRAM AND SERVICE COMPONENTS

Special preparation or orientation: Summer program (required for some) held prior to entering college.
Diagnostic testing: Intelligence, reading, spelling, spoken language, perceptual skills.
Academic advising: Provided by unit staff members. Students with LD may take up to 18 semester hours each term; most take 12 semester hours; 12 semester hours required to maintain full-time status and be eligible for financial aid.
Counseling services: Individual counseling, small-group counseling, career counseling.
Basic skills remediation: Offered one-on-one by trained clinicians. Available in reading, math, spelling, written language, learning strategies, perceptual skills, study skills.
Subject-area tutoring: Offered one-on-one by professional teachers, peer tutors. Available in most subjects.
Special courses: College survival skills, reading, vocabulary development, communication skills, composition, learning strategies, time management, math, study skills, career planning. All offered for credit; all enter into overall grade point average.
Auxiliary aids: Tape recorders, calculators, typewriters, word-processors with spell-check.
Auxiliary services: Alternative test arrangements, notetakers, priority registration, advocacy.

GENERAL COLLEGE INFORMATION

Independent Reorganized Latter Day Saints, comprehensive, coed. Awards bachelor's, master's degrees. Founded 1895. *Setting:* 169-acre small-town campus. *Endowment:* $17.2 million. *Educational spending 1995–96:* $5788 per undergrad. *Total enrollment:* 1,260. *Undergraduate faculty:* 95 (85 full-time, 61% with terminal degrees, 10 part-time); student–undergrad faculty ratio is 15:1.

Enrollment Profile: 1,260 students from 42 states and territories, 31 other countries. 54% women, 46% men, 9% part-time, 32% state residents, 10% transferred in, 11% international, 17% 25 or older, 1% Native American, 3% Hispanic, 4% black, 3% Asian or Pacific Islander. *Retention:* 71% of 1995 full-time freshmen returned. *Graduation:* 27% graduate in 4 years, 43% in 5 years, 46% in 6 years. *Areas of study chosen:* 18% business management and administrative services, 15% education, 12% health professions and related sciences, 11% social sciences, 8% biological and life sciences, 7% fine arts, 6% English language/literature/letters, 4% psychology, 3% computer and information sciences, 3% engineering and applied sciences, 2% foreign language and literature, 2% mathematics, 2% performing arts, 1% liberal arts/general studies, 1% theology/religion. *Most popular recent majors:* nursing, business administration/commerce/management, education.

First-Year Class: 297 total; 974 applied, 63% were accepted, 48% of whom enrolled. 15% from top 10% of their high school class, 40% from top quarter, 74% from top half.

Graduation Requirements: 128 semester hours; 6 semester hours of math or 3 semester hours each of math and science; computer course for math, business administration, accounting, clinical lab science, commercial design majors; internship (some majors); senior project for honors program students and some majors.

Computers on Campus: 97 computers available on campus for general student use. Computer purchase/lease plans available. A computer is strongly recommended for all students. A campus-wide network can be accessed from student residence rooms and from off-campus. Students can contact faculty members and/or advisers through e-mail. Computers for student use in computer center, computer labs, learning resource center, library provide access to the Internet/World Wide Web, on- and off-campus e-mail addresses. Staffed computer lab on campus provides training in use of computers, software. *Academic computing expenditure 1995–96:* $179,056.

EXPENSES AND FINANCIAL AID

Expenses for 1997–98: *Application fee:* $25. Comprehensive fee of $14,480 includes full-time tuition ($10,750), mandatory fees ($110), and college room and board ($3620). College room only: $1420. Part-time mandatory fees: $55 per term. Part-time tuition (1 to 9 semester hours): $336 per semester hour.

Undergraduate Financial Aid: 89% of all full-time undergraduates enrolled in fall 1996 applied for aid; of these, 91% were judged to have need according to Federal Methodology, of whom 99% were aided. On average, 91% of need was met. *Financial aid deadline (priority):* 4/15. *Financial aid forms:* FAFSA required for some.

LD Services Contact: Ms. Susan Knotts, Chance Program Coordinator, Graceland College, 700 College Avenue, Lamoni, IA 50140, 515-784-5226. Fax: 515-784-5449. Email: knotts@graceland.edu.

GRAND VALLEY STATE UNIVERSITY

Allendale, Michigan

LEARNING DISABILITIES SERVICES INFORMATION

Office of Academic Support (OAS) began offering services in 1993. Currently the program serves 230 undergraduates with LD. Services are also available to graduate students. Students diagnosed with ADD/ADHD are eligible for the same services available to students with LD.

Staff: 5 full-time staff members, including coordinators, counselors, secretary, student workers. Services provided by counselors.

Special Fees: No special fees are charged for services to students with LD.

Applications and admissions: *Required:* extended time ACT, documentation of disability. Students may begin taking classes any term. *Application deadline:* continuous.

Special policies: The college has written policies regarding substitutions and waivers of admissions, graduation, and degree requirements.

PROGRAM AND SERVICE COMPONENTS

Special preparation or orientation: Optional orientation offered after classes begin as special section of Freshman Seminar.

Academic advising: Provided by academic advisers. Students with LD may take up to 16 semester hours (14 recommended) each term; most take 12 to 14 semester hours; 12 semester hours required to maintain full-time status; 6 semester hours required to be eligible for financial aid.

Counseling services: Individual counseling.

Basic skills remediation: Offered one-on-one and in small groups by peer tutors. Available in math, written language, study skills, time management.

Subject-area tutoring: Offered one-on-one and in small groups by peer tutors. Available in most subjects.

Special courses: College survival skills, learning strategies, time management, study skills, career planning. All offered for credit; none enter into overall grade point average.

Auxiliary aids: Taped textbooks, word-processors with spell-check, optical character readers, Phonic Ear.

Auxiliary services: Alternative test arrangements, notetakers, priority registration, advocacy.

Campus support group: A special student organization is available to students with LD.

GENERAL COLLEGE INFORMATION

State-supported, comprehensive, coed. Awards bachelor's, master's degrees. Founded 1960. *Setting:* 900-acre small-town campus with easy access to Grand Rapids. *Endowment:* $26.1 million. *Research spending 1995–96:* $1.9 million. *Educational spending 1995–96:* $3589 per undergrad. *Total enrollment:* 14,662. *Faculty:* 769 (470 full-time, 84% with terminal degrees, 299 part-time); student–undergrad faculty ratio is 22:1.

Enrollment Profile: 11,734 students from 35 states and territories, 24 other countries. 59% women, 41% men, 22% part-time, 97% state residents, 16% live on campus, 45% transferred in, 1% international, 21% 25 or older, 1% Native American, 2% Hispanic, 5% black, 2% Asian or Pacific Islander. *Retention:* 75% of 1995 full-time freshmen returned. *Areas of study chosen:* 17% business management and administrative services, 17% social sciences, 15% health professions and related sciences, 9% psychology, 7% communications and journalism, 6% biological and life sciences, 5% English language/literature/letters, 4% engineering and applied sciences, 3% computer and information sciences, 3% fine arts, 3% physical sciences, 2% mathematics, 1% foreign language and literature, 1% liberal arts/general studies, 1% natural resource sciences. *Most popular recent majors:* health science, business administration/commerce/management, psychology.

First-Year Class: 2,114 total; 6,022 applied, 85% were accepted, 41% of whom enrolled. 16% from top 10% of their high school class, 47% from top quarter, 86% from top half.

Graduation Requirements: 120 semester hours; 1 algebra course; 2 math/science courses including at least 1 lab science course; computer course for business, engineering, education, majors; internship (some majors); senior project for honors program students and some majors.

Computers on Campus: 2,200 computers available on campus for general student use. Computer purchase/lease plans available. A computer is strongly recommended for all students. A campus-wide network can be accessed from student residence rooms and from off-campus. Students can contact faculty members and/or advisers through e-mail. Computers for student use in computer center, computer labs, research center, learning resource center, classrooms, library, student center, dorms, student rooms, tutorial labs provide access to the Internet/World Wide Web, on- and off-campus e-mail addresses. Staffed computer lab on campus provides training in use of computers, software. *Academic computing expenditure 1995–96:* $1.7 million.

EXPENSES AND FINANCIAL AID

Expenses for 1996–97: *Application fee:* $20. State resident tuition: $2866 full-time, $128 per semester hour part-time. Nonresident tuition: $6650 full-time, $287 per semester hour part-time. Part-time mandatory fees per semester range from $48 to $128. Full-time mandatory fees: $360. College room and board: $4380.

Undergraduate Financial Aid: 77% of all full-time undergraduates enrolled in fall 1996 applied for aid; of these, 78% were judged to have need according to Federal Methodology, of whom 100% were aided. On average, 98% of need was met. *Financial aid deadline (priority):* 2/1. *Financial aid forms:* FAFSA required.

Financial aid specifically for students with LD: Scholarships.

LD Services Contact: Mr. John Pedraza, Coordinator, Grand Valley State University, 1 Campus Drive, Allendale, MI 49401-9403, 616-895-2490. Fax: 616-895-3440. Email: pedrazaj@gvsu.edu.

GREEN MOUNTAIN COLLEGE

Poultney, Vermont

LEARNING DISABILITIES SERVICES INFORMATION

Learning Center began offering services in 1995. Currently the program serves 25 undergraduates with LD. Students diagnosed with ADD/ADHD are eligible for the same services available to students with LD.
Staff: 2 full-time, 2 part-time staff members, including director, associate director, writing instructor, math instructor. Services provided by remediation specialists, tutors.
Special Fees: No special fees are charged for services to students with LD.
Applications and admissions: *Required:* high school transcript, grade point average, class rank, courses completed, extracurricular activities, extended time SAT I, personal interview, autobiographical statement, letters of recommendation; *recommended:* high school IEP (Individualized Education Program), untimed SAT I or extended time ACT, psychoeducational report completed within 3 years. Students may begin taking classes in fall or spring. *Application deadline:* continuous.
Special policies: The college has written policies regarding substitutions and waivers of graduation and degree requirements.

PROGRAM AND SERVICE COMPONENTS

Academic advising: Provided by unit staff members, academic advisers. Students with LD may take up to 18 credits each term; most take 12 to 15 credits; 12 credits required to maintain full-time status and be eligible for financial aid.
Counseling services: Individual counseling, small-group counseling, career counseling, self-advocacy training.
Basic skills remediation: Offered one-on-one, in small groups, and in class-size groups by LD teachers. Available in reading, math, written language, learning strategies, study skills, time management.
Subject-area tutoring: Offered one-on-one and in small groups by professional teachers, peer tutors. Available in most subjects.
Auxiliary aids: Taped textbooks, tape recorders, word-processors with spell-check, personal computers.
Auxiliary services: Alternative test arrangements, notetakers, priority registration, advocacy, scribes.

GENERAL COLLEGE INFORMATION

Independent, 4-year, coed, affiliated with United Methodist Church. Awards bachelor's degrees. Founded 1834. *Setting:* 155-acre small-town campus. *Total enrollment:* 585. *Faculty:* 59 (35 full-time, 86% with terminal degrees, 24 part-time); student–undergrad faculty ratio is 14:1.
Enrollment Profile: 585 students from 30 states and territories, 10 other countries. 51% women, 49% men, 7% part-time, 89% live on campus, 8% international, 4% 25 or older, 1% Native American, 1% Hispanic, 2% black, 1% Asian or Pacific Islander. *Most popular recent majors:* behavioral sciences, business administration/commerce/management.
First-Year Class: 215 total; 1,006 applied, 85% were accepted, 25% of whom enrolled. 8% from top 10% of their high school class, 22% from top quarter, 53% from top half.
Graduation Requirements: 120 credits; 3 math/science courses; computer course for business, behavioral sciences majors; internship (some majors); senior project for honors program students and some majors.
Computers on Campus: 268 computers available on campus for general student use. Computer purchase/lease plans available. A computer is recommended for some students. Students can contact faculty members and/or advisers through e-mail. Computers for student use in computer center, computer labs, learning resource center, classrooms, library provide access to the Internet/World Wide Web, on- and off-campus e-mail addresses. Staffed computer lab on campus provides training in use of computers, software.

EXPENSES AND FINANCIAL AID

Expenses for 1997–98: *Application fee:* $20. Comprehensive fee of $18,460 includes full-time tuition ($14,940), mandatory fees ($200), and college room and board ($3320).
Undergraduate Financial Aid: Of all full-time undergraduates enrolled in fall 1996, 92% of those who applied for aid were judged to have need according to Federal Methodology, of whom 100% were aided. *Financial aid deadline (priority):* 2/15. *Financial aid forms:* FAFSA required. State form, institutional form required for some.

LD Services Contact: Ms. Kristin Wiedmann, Director, Green Mountain College, One College Circle, Poultney, VT 05764, 802-287-8287. Fax: 802-287-8099.

GRINNELL COLLEGE

Grinnell, Iowa

LEARNING DISABILITIES SERVICES INFORMATION

Academic Advising Office currently serves 25 undergraduates with LD. Students diagnosed with ADD/ADHD are eligible for the same services available to students with LD.
Staff: 2 part-time staff members, including director, academic advising counselor. Services provided by tutors, counselors, professional writing lab, reading lab and math/science lab staff.
Special Fees: No special fees are charged for services to students with LD.
Applications and admissions: *Required:* high school transcript, grade point average, class rank, courses completed, extracurricular activities, untimed SAT I or ACT, letters of recommendation, psychoeducational report completed within 3 years; *recommended:* extended time SAT I or ACT. Students may begin taking classes in fall only. *Application deadline:* 2/1.

PROGRAM AND SERVICE COMPONENTS

Diagnostic testing: Reading, spelling, personality, vocational interest (Strong Interest Inventory).
Academic advising: Provided by unit staff members, academic advisers. Students with LD may take up to 18 credits each term; most take 16 credits; 12 credits required to maintain full-time status and be eligible for financial aid.
Counseling services: Individual counseling, small-group counseling, career counseling.
Subject-area tutoring: Offered one-on-one, in small groups, and in class-size groups by professional teachers, peer tutors. Available in all subjects.
Special courses: Reading, vocabulary development, composition, math. All offered for credit; none enter into overall grade point average.
Auxiliary aids: Tape recorders, word-processors with spell-check.
Auxiliary services: Alternative test arrangements, notetakers, priority registration, reduced course load, readers.

GENERAL COLLEGE INFORMATION

Independent, 4-year, coed. Awards bachelor's degrees. Founded 1846. *Setting:* 95-acre small-town campus. *Endowment:* $571.5 million. *Research spending 1995–96:* $291,173. *Educational spending 1995–96:* $10,656 per undergrad. *Total enrollment:* 1,314. *Faculty:* 155 (141 full-time, 99% with terminal degrees, 14 part-time); student–undergrad faculty ratio is 10:1.
Enrollment Profile: 1,314 students from 51 states and territories, 42 other countries. 55% women, 45% men, 0% part-time, 14% state residents, 85% live on campus, 3% transferred in, 9% international, 1% 25 or older, 0% Native American, 4% Hispanic, 4% black, 4% Asian or Pacific Islander. *Retention:* 96% of 1995 full-time freshmen returned. *Graduation:* 72% graduate in 4 years, 81% in 5 years, 83% in 6 years. *Areas of study chosen:* 34% social sciences, 11% biological and life sciences, 9% physical sciences, 8% English language/literature/letters, 8% foreign language and literature, 7% psychology, 4% mathematics, 4% performing arts, 3% area and ethnic studies, 3% fine arts, 2% computer and information sciences, 2% theology/religion, 1% interdisciplinary studies, 1% philosophy. *Most popular recent majors:* biology/biological sciences, English, history.
First-Year Class: 355 total; 1,820 applied, 73% were accepted, 27% of whom enrolled. 63% from top 10% of their high school class, 89% from top quarter, 98% from top half. 33 National Merit Scholars, 7 class presidents, 31 valedictorians.
Graduation Requirements: 24 credits.
Computers on Campus: 281 computers available on campus for general student use. Computer purchase/lease plans available. A campus-wide network can be accessed from off-campus. Students can contact faculty members and/or advisers through e-mail. Computers for student use in computer center, computer labs, classrooms, library, dorms, science building, Carnegie Hall provide access to the Internet/World Wide Web, on- and off-campus e-mail addresses. Staffed computer lab on campus provides training in use of computers, software. *Academic computing expenditure 1995–96:* $1.4 million.

EXPENSES AND FINANCIAL AID

Expenses for 1997–98: *Application fee:* $25. Comprehensive fee of $22,720 includes full-time tuition ($17,142), mandatory fees ($426), and college room and board ($5152). College room only: $2342.
Undergraduate Financial Aid: Of all full-time undergraduates enrolled in fall 1996, 78% of those who applied for aid were judged to have need according to Federal Methodology, of whom 99% were aided. On average, 100% of need was met. *Financial aid deadline (priority):* 2/1. *Financial aid forms:* FAFSA, institutional form required; CSS Financial Aid PROFILE acceptable.
LD Services Contact: Ms. Jo Calhoun, Associate Dean/Director of Academic Advising, Grinnell College, PO Box 805, Grinnell, IA 50112-0805, 515-269-3702. Fax: 515-269-3710. Email: calhoun@admin.grin.edu.

GUSTAVUS ADOLPHUS COLLEGE

St. Peter, Minnesota

LEARNING DISABILITIES SERVICES INFORMATION

Advising Center currently serves 7 undergraduates with LD. Students diagnosed with ADD/ADHD are eligible for the same services available to students with LD, as well as coaching, goal setting and time management meetings.
Staff: 1 full-time staff member.
Special Fees: No special fees are charged for services to students with LD.
Applications and admissions: *Required:* high school transcript, IEP (Individualized Education Program), letters of recommendation, psychoeducational report completed in 11th or 12th grade; *recommended:* high school grade point average, class rank, extracurricular activities, untimed or extended time SAT I or ACT, personal interview. Students may begin taking classes in fall, winter, or spring. *Application deadline:* 4/1.

PROGRAM AND SERVICE COMPONENTS

Academic advising: Provided by unit staff members, academic advisers. Most students with LD take 4 courses each term; 3 courses required to maintain full-time status; 3 courses (fewer than 3 courses prorated) required to be eligible for financial aid.
Counseling services: Individual counseling, career counseling, self-advocacy training.
Subject-area tutoring: Offered one-on-one by peer tutors. Available in most subjects.
Auxiliary aids: Taped textbooks.
Auxiliary services: Alternative test arrangements, notetakers, priority registration, advocacy.

GENERAL COLLEGE INFORMATION

Independent, 4-year, coed, affiliated with Evangelical Lutheran Church in America. Awards bachelor's degrees. Founded 1862. *Setting:* 309-acre small-town campus with easy access to Minneapolis–St. Paul. *Endowment:* $47 million. *Research spending 1995–96:* $99,755. *Educational spending 1995–96:* $6181 per undergrad. *Total enrollment:* 2,376. *Faculty:* 225 (164 full-time, 87% with terminal degrees, 61 part-time); student–undergrad faculty ratio is 13:1.
Enrollment Profile: 2,376 students from 45 states and territories, 23 other countries. 55% women, 45% men, 2% part-time, 69% state residents, 90% live on campus, 5% transferred in, 2% international, 0% 25 or older, 0% Native American, 1% Hispanic, 2% black, 3% Asian or Pacific Islander. *Retention:* 89% of 1995 full-time freshmen returned. *Graduation:* 74% graduate in 4 years, 77% in 5 years. *Areas of study chosen:* 21% social sciences, 11% psychology, 9% biological and life sciences, 9% business management and administrative services, 8% education, 8% physical sciences, 7% fine arts, 7% health professions and related sciences, 5% communications and journalism, 4% foreign language and literature, 3% English language/literature/letters, 2% computer and information sciences, 2% interdisciplinary studies, 2% theology/religion, 1% mathematics, 1% philosophy. *Most popular recent majors:* psychology, biology/biological sciences, political science/government.
First-Year Class: 627 total; 1,883 applied, 81% were accepted, 41% of whom enrolled. 37% from top 10% of their high school class, 72% from top quarter, 97% from top half. 15 National Merit Scholars, 49 valedictorians.
Graduation Requirements: 35 courses; 1 course each in math and lab science; senior project for honors program students and some majors.
Computers on Campus: 200 computers available on campus for general student use. Computer purchase/lease plans available. A computer is recommended for all students. A campus-wide network can be accessed from student residence rooms and from off-campus. Students can contact faculty members and/or advisers through e-mail. Computers for student use in computer center, computer labs, classrooms, library, dorms provide access to the Internet/World Wide Web, on- and off-campus e-mail addresses. Staffed computer lab on campus provides training in use of computers, software. *Academic computing expenditure 1995–96:* $661,106.

EXPENSES AND FINANCIAL AID

Expenses for 1997–98: *Application fee:* $25. Comprehensive fee of $20,150 includes full-time tuition ($15,940), mandatory fees ($200), and college room and board ($4010). College room only: $1900. Part-time tuition: $1700 per course. Part-time mandatory fees: $100 per year.
Undergraduate Financial Aid: Of all full-time undergraduates enrolled in fall 1996, 91% of those who applied for aid were judged to have need according to Federal Methodology, of whom 98% were aided. *Financial aid deadline (priority):* 4/15. *Financial aid forms:* FAFSA, institutional form required; CSS Financial Aid PROFILE acceptable.
LD Services Contact: Ms. Jody Donnelly, Academic Counselor, Gustavus Adolphus College, 800 West College Avenue, St. Peter, MN 56082, 507-933-7027. Email: jdonnell@gac.edu.

HAMILTON COLLEGE

Clinton, New York

LEARNING DISABILITIES SERVICES INFORMATION

Writing Center, Peer Tutoring Center currently serves 30 undergraduates with LD. Students diagnosed with ADD/ADHD are eligible for the same services available to students with LD.
Staff: 7 full-time, 1 part-time staff members, including director, coordinator. Services provided by tutors, counselors.
Special Fees: No special fees are charged for services to students with LD.
Applications and admissions: *Required:* high school transcript, grade point average, class rank, courses completed, extracurricular activities, untimed or extended time SAT I, autobiographical statement, letters of recommendation; *recommended:* high school IEP (Individualized Education Program), untimed or extended time ACT. Students may begin taking classes in fall or spring. *Application deadline:* 1/15.

PROGRAM AND SERVICE COMPONENTS

Academic advising: Provided by academic advisers. Students with LD may take up to 4 courses each term; most take 4 courses; 3 courses required to maintain full-time status; 3 to 4 courses required to be eligible for financial aid.
Auxiliary aids: Word-processors with spell-check, personal computers.

GENERAL COLLEGE INFORMATION

Independent, 4-year, coed. Awards bachelor's degrees. Founded 1812. *Setting:* 1,200-acre rural campus. *Endowment:* $222.7 million. *Research spending 1995–96:* $581,000. *Educational spending 1995–96:* $10,706 per undergrad. *Total enrollment:* 1,715. *Faculty:* 201 (173 full-time, 98% with terminal degrees, 28 part-time); student–undergrad faculty ratio is 10:1.
Enrollment Profile: 1,715 students from 42 states and territories, 38 other countries. 47% women, 53% men, 2% part-time, 39% state residents, 96% live on campus, 1% transferred in, 4% international, 1% 25 or older, 1% Native American, 3% Hispanic, 2% black, 3% Asian or Pacific Islander. *Retention:* 91% of 1995 full-time freshmen returned. *Graduation:* 88% graduate in 4 years, 92% in 5 years. *Areas of study chosen:* 39% social sciences, 14% English language/literature/letters, 9% biological and life sciences, 8% psychology, 5% fine arts, 5% foreign language and literature, 5% mathematics, 4% physical sciences, 3% area and ethnic studies, 3% philosophy, 2% computer and information sciences, 1% interdisciplinary studies, 1% performing arts, 1% theology/religion. *Most popular recent majors:* economics, English, political science/government.
First-Year Class: 499 total; 4,045 applied, 44% were accepted, 28% of whom enrolled. 46% from top 10% of their high school class, 81% from top quarter, 98% from top half. 11 National Merit Scholars, 18 valedictorians.
Graduation Requirements: 32 courses; 2 math/science courses; senior project.
Computers on Campus: 200 computers available on campus for general student use. Computer purchase/lease plans available. A computer

Hamilton College (continued)

is strongly recommended for all students. A campus-wide network can be accessed from student residence rooms and from off-campus. Students can contact faculty members and/or advisers through e-mail. Computers for student use in computer center, classrooms, library, student center, reading/writing center provide access to the Internet/World Wide Web, on- and off-campus e-mail addresses. Staffed computer lab on campus provides training in use of computers, software. *Academic computing expenditure 1995–96:* $378,431.

EXPENSES AND FINANCIAL AID

Expenses for 1997–98: *Application fee:* $50. Comprehensive fee of $28,350 includes full-time tuition ($22,700) and college room and board ($5650). College room only: $2850.
Undergraduate Financial Aid: 59% of all full-time undergraduates enrolled in fall 1996 applied for aid; of these, 89% were judged to have need according to Federal Methodology, of whom 100% were aided. On average, 100% of need was met. *Financial aid deadline:* 2/1. *Financial aid forms:* FAFSA, CSS Financial Aid PROFILE, institutional form required.
LD Services Contact: Ms. Louise Peckingham, Assistant to the President, Hamilton College, 198 College Hill Road, Clinton, NY 13323, 315-859-4106.

HAMLINE UNIVERSITY

St. Paul, Minnesota

LEARNING DISABILITIES SERVICES INFORMATION

Study Resource Center currently serves 28 undergraduates with LD. Services are also available to graduate students. Students diagnosed with ADD/ADHD are eligible for the same services available to students with LD.
Staff: 2 full-time staff members, including director, assistant director. Services provided by tutors.
Special Fees: No special fees are charged for services to students with LD.
Applications and admissions: *Required:* high school transcript, grade point average, class rank, courses completed, personal interview, autobiographical statement, psychoeducational report completed within 3 years; *recommended:* high school extracurricular activities, IEP (Individualized Education Program), untimed or extended time SAT I, extended time ACT, letters of recommendation. Students may begin taking classes any term. *Application deadline:* continuous.

PROGRAM AND SERVICE COMPONENTS

Academic advising: Provided by unit staff members, academic advisers. Students with LD may take up to 20 semester hours each term; most take 12 to 16 semester hours; 12 semester hours required to maintain full-time status; 8 semester hours required to be eligible for financial aid.
Counseling services: Individual counseling, small-group counseling, career counseling.
Auxiliary aids: Taped textbooks, tape recorders, word-processors with spell-check.
Auxiliary services: Alternative test arrangements, notetakers, priority registration, advocacy.

GENERAL COLLEGE INFORMATION

Independent, comprehensive, coed, affiliated with United Methodist Church. Awards bachelor's, master's, doctoral, first professional degrees. Founded 1854. *Setting:* 50-acre urban campus. *Endowment:* $36.6 million. *Research spending 1995–96:* $220,156. *Educational spending 1995–96:* $5141 per undergrad. *Total enrollment:* 3,335. *Faculty:* 296 (154 full-time, 98% with terminal degrees, 142 part-time); student–undergrad faculty ratio is 13:1.
Enrollment Profile: 1,655 students from 41 states and territories, 36 other countries. 58% women, 42% men, 9% part-time, 72% state residents, 50% live on campus, 7% transferred in, 2% international, 7% 25 or older, 1% Native American, 1% Hispanic, 3% black, 5% Asian or Pacific Islander. *Retention:* 77% of 1995 full-time freshmen returned. *Graduation:* 59% graduate in 4 years, 63% in 5 years, 64% in 6 years. *Areas of study chosen:* 34% social sciences, 14% psychology, 9% English language/literature/letters, 8% business management and administrative services, 7% biological and life sciences, 6% physical sciences, 6% prelaw, 5% communications and journalism, 5% natural resource sciences, 4% fine arts, 3% foreign language and literature, 3% interdisciplinary studies, 3% liberal arts/general studies, 2% mathematics, 2% performing arts, 2% philosophy, 1% computer and information sciences, 1% theology/religion. *Most popular recent majors:* psychology, political science/government, English.
First-Year Class: 371 total; 1,133 applied, 84% were accepted, 39% of whom enrolled. 33% from top 10% of their high school class, 69% from top quarter, 94% from top half. 5 National Merit Scholars.
Graduation Requirements: 32 courses; 2 lab science courses; computer course; internship (some majors); senior project for honors program students and some majors.
Computers on Campus: 196 computers available on campus for general student use. Computer purchase/lease plans available. A campus-wide network can be accessed from student residence rooms and from off-campus. Students can contact faculty members and/or advisers through e-mail. Computers for student use in computer center, computer labs, research center, learning resource center, classrooms, library, student center, dorms, student rooms, science building provide access to the Internet/World Wide Web, on- and off-campus e-mail addresses. Staffed computer lab on campus provides training in use of computers, software. *Academic computing expenditure 1995–96:* $625,509.

EXPENSES AND FINANCIAL AID

Expenses for 1997–98: *Application fee:* $25. Comprehensive fee of $19,653 includes full-time tuition ($14,678), mandatory fees ($176), and college room and board ($4799). College room only: $2580. Part-time tuition: $1835 per course.
Undergraduate Financial Aid: 95% of all full-time undergraduates enrolled in fall 1996 applied for aid; of these, 80% were judged to have need according to Federal Methodology, of whom 100% were aided. *Financial aid deadline (priority):* 4/15. *Financial aid forms:* FAFSA required; CSS Financial Aid PROFILE acceptable. State form, institutional form required for some.
Financial aid specifically for students with LD: Scholarship: Walter Benjamin Scholarship/Grant.
LD Services Contact: Ms. Patricia Chase, Assistant Dean, Hamline University, 1536 Hewitt, C-1909, St. Paul, MN 55104, 612-641-2417. Fax: 612-641-2055. Email: pchase@seq.hamline.edu.

HAMPSHIRE COLLEGE

Amherst, Massachusetts

LEARNING DISABILITIES SERVICES INFORMATION

Advising Office began offering services in 1988. Currently the program serves 26 undergraduates with LD. Students diagnosed with ADD/ADHD are eligible for the same services available to students with LD, as well as counseling with a different emphasis.
Staff: 1 part-time staff member (coordinator). Services provided by remediation specialists, tutors, counselors, diagnostic specialists.
Special Fees: No special fees are charged for services to students with LD.
Applications and admissions: *Required:* high school transcript, courses completed, extracurricular activities, autobiographical statement, letters of recommendation, analytic writing sample or graded academic paper; *recommended:* high school grade point average, personal interview, psychoeducational report. Students may begin taking classes in fall or spring. *Application deadline:* 2/1 (fall term), 11/15 (spring term).

PROGRAM AND SERVICE COMPONENTS

Academic advising: Provided by unit staff members, academic advisers.
Counseling services: Individual counseling.
Subject-area tutoring: Offered one-on-one and in small groups by professional teachers, peer tutors. Available in some subjects.
Auxiliary aids: Taped textbooks, tape recorders, word-processors with spell-check, personal computers, optical character readers.
Auxiliary services: Alternative test arrangements, notetakers, priority registration, readers.

GENERAL COLLEGE INFORMATION

Independent, 4-year, coed. Awards bachelor's degrees. Founded 1965. *Setting:* 800-acre rural campus. *Endowment:* $14.2 million. *Research spending 1995–96:* $650,000. *Educational spending 1995–96:* $6055 per undergrad. *Total enrollment:* 1,068. *Faculty:* 94 (84 full-time, 85% with terminal degrees, 10 part-time); student–undergrad faculty ratio is 11:1.
Enrollment Profile: 1,068 students from 47 states and territories, 27 other countries. 56% women, 44% men, 0% part-time, 18% state residents, 95% live on campus, 13% transferred in, 4% international, 4% 25

or older, 1% Native American, 3% Hispanic, 5% black, 3% Asian or Pacific Islander. *Retention:* 89% of 1995 full-time freshmen returned. *Areas of study chosen:* 20% fine arts, 13% social sciences, 11% English language/literature/letters, 11% interdisciplinary studies, 11% performing arts, 7% biological and life sciences, 4% computer and information sciences, 4% psychology, 4% theology/religion, 3% education, 3% philosophy, 2% area and ethnic studies, 2% communications and journalism, 2% physical sciences, 1% mathematics, 1% prelaw, 1% premed. *Most popular recent majors:* art/fine arts, biology/biological sciences, film studies.

First-Year Class: 291 total; 1,691 applied, 70% were accepted, 25% of whom enrolled. 30% from top 10% of their high school class, 84% from top quarter, 88% from top half. 9 valedictorians.

Graduation Requirements: Natural science project or 2 approved courses; senior project.

Computers on Campus: 125 computers available on campus for general student use. Computer purchase/lease plans available. A campuswide network can be accessed from student residence rooms and from off-campus. Students can contact faculty members and/or advisers through e-mail. Computers for student use in computer center, computer labs, research center, library, student rooms provide access to the Internet/World Wide Web, on- and off-campus e-mail addresses. Staffed computer lab on campus provides training in use of computers, software. *Academic computing expenditure 1995–96:* $185,000.

EXPENSES AND FINANCIAL AID

Expenses for 1997–98: *Application fee:* $45. Comprehensive fee of $30,045 includes full-time tuition ($23,480), mandatory fees ($300), and college room and board ($6265). College room only: $3955.

Undergraduate Financial Aid: 78% of all full-time undergraduates enrolled in fall 1996 applied for aid; of these, 83% were judged to have need according to Federal Methodology, of whom 100% were aided. On average, 100% of need was met. *Financial aid deadline (priority):* 2/1. *Financial aid forms:* FAFSA, CSS Financial Aid PROFILE, institutional form required.

LD Services Contact: Ms. Karyl Lynch, Assistant Dean of Advising, Hampshire College, 893 West Street, Amherst, MA 01002, 413-582-5498.

HARDING UNIVERSITY

Searcy, Arkansas

LEARNING DISABILITIES SERVICES INFORMATION

Student Support Services began offering services in 1986. Currently the program serves 76 undergraduates with LD. Students diagnosed with ADD/ADHD are eligible for the same services available to students with LD.

Staff: 5 full-time staff members, including director, Administrative Assistant. Services provided by remediation specialists, tutors, counselors, diagnostic specialist, math, reading, English and study skills instructors.

Special Fees: No special fees are charged for services to students with LD.

Applications and admissions: *Required:* high school transcript, untimed SAT I or ACT, letters of recommendation; *recommended:* high school courses completed, extended time SAT I or ACT, psychoeducational report completed within 3 years. Students may begin taking classes in fall, spring, or summer. *Application deadline:* continuous.

PROGRAM AND SERVICE COMPONENTS

Special preparation or orientation: Required orientation held after classes begin.

Diagnostic testing: Intelligence, reading, math, spelling, handwriting, spoken language, written language, motor abilities, perceptual skills, study skills, personality, social skills, speech, hearing, learning strategies, auditory discrimination, intersensory integration.

Academic advising: Provided by unit staff members, academic advisers. Most students with LD take 12 to 15 semester hours each term; 9 semester hours required to maintain full-time status and be eligible for financial aid.

Counseling services: Individual counseling, small-group counseling, career counseling.

Basic skills remediation: Offered one-on-one and in small groups by regular teachers, counselors. Available in reading, math, written language, learning strategies, study skills, time management, social skills, speech.

Subject-area tutoring: Offered one-on-one and in small groups by peer tutors. Available in all subjects.

Auxiliary aids: Taped textbooks, tape recorders, word-processors with spell-check, personal computers, optical character readers, Optelec print enlarger.

Auxiliary services: Alternative test arrangements, notetakers, priority registration, advocacy.

GENERAL COLLEGE INFORMATION

Independent, comprehensive, coed, affiliated with Church of Christ. Awards associate, bachelor's, master's degrees. Founded 1924. *Setting:* 200-acre small-town campus with easy access to Little Rock. *Endowment:* $48 million. *Research spending 1995–96:* $36,429. *Educational spending 1995–96:* $4730 per undergrad. *Total enrollment:* 4,081. *Faculty:* 246 (212 full-time, 70% with terminal degrees, 34 part-time); student–undergrad faculty ratio is 16:1.

Enrollment Profile: 3,540 students from 50 states and territories, 36 other countries. 55% women, 45% men, 5% part-time, 31% state residents, 70% live on campus, 7% transferred in, 5% international, 8% 25 or older, 1% Native American, 1% Hispanic, 3% black, 1% Asian or Pacific Islander. *Retention:* 73% of 1995 full-time freshmen returned. *Graduation:* 39% graduate in 4 years, 53% in 5 years, 58% in 6 years. *Areas of study chosen:* 18% business management and administrative services, 12% education, 11% health professions and related sciences, 8% social sciences, 7% biological and life sciences, 5% communications and journalism, 5% fine arts, 5% psychology, 5% theology/religion, 4% premed, 3% computer and information sciences, 3% vocational and home economics, 2% English language/literature/letters, 2% liberal arts/general studies, 2% physical sciences, 2% predentistry, 1% engineering and applied sciences, 1% foreign language and literature, 1% interdisciplinary studies, 1% mathematics, 1% natural resource sciences, 1% performing arts. *Most popular recent majors:* business administration/commerce/management, elementary education, communication.

First-Year Class: 848 total; 1,713 applied, 64% were accepted, 77% of whom enrolled. 35% from top 10% of their high school class, 60% from top quarter, 87% from top half. 17 National Merit Scholars, 40 valedictorians.

Graduation Requirements: 64 semester hours for associate, 128 semester hours for bachelor's; 1 course each in math and science; computer course for business, science, design, math, health sciences majors; internship (some majors); senior project for honors program students and some majors.

Computers on Campus: 140 computers available on campus for general student use. Computer purchase/lease plans available. Computers for student use in computer center, computer labs, learning resource center, classrooms, library provide access to the Internet/World Wide Web, on- and off-campus e-mail addresses. Staffed computer lab on campus provides training in use of computers, software. *Academic computing expenditure 1995–96:* $368,000.

EXPENSES AND FINANCIAL AID

Expenses for 1997–98: *Application fee:* $25. Comprehensive fee of $11,698 includes full-time tuition ($6528), mandatory fees ($1184), and college room and board ($3986). College room only: $1874. Part-time tuition: $204 per semester hour. Part-time mandatory fees: $37 per semester hour.

Undergraduate Financial Aid: 93% of all full-time undergraduates enrolled in fall 1996 applied for aid; of these, 66% were judged to have need according to Federal Methodology, of whom 99% were aided. On average, 88% of need was met. *Financial aid deadline (priority):* 3/1. *Financial aid forms:* FAFSA, institutional form required; CSS Financial Aid PROFILE acceptable. State form required for some.

LD Services Contact: Dr. Linda R. Thompson, Director, Student Support Services, Harding University, PO Box 2235, 900 East Center, Searcy, AR 72149-0001, 501-279-4416. Fax: 501-279-4217. Email: lthompson@harding.edu.

HOBART AND WILLIAM SMITH COLLEGES

Geneva, New York

LEARNING DISABILITIES SERVICES INFORMATION

Center for Academic Support Services began offering services in 1991. Currently the program serves 82 undergraduates with LD. Students diagnosed with ADD/ADHD are eligible for the same services available to students with LD.

Hobart and William Smith Colleges (continued)

Staff: 2 full-time, 1 part-time staff members, including director, administrative assistant. Services provided by learning specialist.

Special Fees: No special fees are charged for services to students with LD.

Applications and admissions: *Required:* high school transcript, courses completed, autobiographical statement, letters of recommendation; *recommended:* high school grade point average, class rank, extracurricular activities. Students may begin taking classes in fall, winter, or spring. *Application deadline:* 2/1.

PROGRAM AND SERVICE COMPONENTS

Academic advising: Provided by unit staff members, academic advisers. Students with LD may take up to 3 courses each term; most take 3 courses; 2 courses required to maintain full-time status and be eligible for financial aid.

Basic skills remediation: Offered one-on-one by LD specialist. Available in reading, written language, learning strategies, study skills, time management.

Auxiliary aids: Word-processors with spell-check, readers.

Auxiliary services: Alternative test arrangements, notetakers, advocacy.

Campus support group: A special student organization is available to students with LD.

GENERAL COLLEGE INFORMATION

Independent, 4-year, coed. Awards bachelor's degrees. Founded 1822. *Setting:* 200-acre small-town campus with easy access to Rochester and Syracuse. *Endowment:* $63.5 million. *Research spending 1995–96:* $427,847. *Educational spending 1995–96:* $7984 per undergrad. *Total enrollment:* 1,794. *Faculty:* 159 (128 full-time, 97% with terminal degrees, 31 part-time); student–undergrad faculty ratio is 13:1.

Enrollment Profile: 1,794 students from 41 states and territories, 28 other countries. 52% women, 48% men, 1% part-time, 49% state residents, 81% live on campus, 6% transferred in, 3% international, 0% 25 or older, 1% Native American, 4% Hispanic, 5% black, 2% Asian or Pacific Islander. *Retention:* 85% of 1995 full-time freshmen returned. *Graduation:* 67% graduate in 4 years, 72% in 5 years, 73% in 6 years. *Areas of study chosen:* 29% social sciences, 17% English language/literature/letters, 17% interdisciplinary studies, 13% psychology, 8% biological and life sciences, 5% fine arts, 4% foreign language and literature, 3% physical sciences, 1% computer and information sciences, 1% mathematics, 1% philosophy, 1% theology/religion. *Most popular recent majors:* English, economics, interdisciplinary studies.

First-Year Class: 532 total; 2,805 applied, 78% were accepted, 24% of whom enrolled. 25% from top 10% of their high school class, 60% from top quarter, 87% from top half. 17 National Merit Scholars, 15 class presidents, 7 valedictorians.

Graduation Requirements: 36 courses; computer course for math majors; senior project for honors program students.

Computers on Campus: 146 computers available on campus for general student use. Computer purchase/lease plans available. A campus-wide network can be accessed from student residence rooms and from off-campus. Students can contact faculty members and/or advisers through e-mail. Computers for student use in computer center, computer labs, research center, learning resource center, classrooms, library, honors room provide access to the Internet/World Wide Web, on- and off-campus e-mail addresses. Staffed computer lab on campus provides training in use of computers, software. *Academic computing expenditure 1995–96:* $386,420.

EXPENSES AND FINANCIAL AID

Expenses for 1997–98: *Application fee:* $45. Comprehensive fee of $28,944 includes full-time tuition ($21,927), mandatory fees ($453), and college room and board ($6564). College room only: $3333. Part-time tuition: $2437 per course.

Undergraduate Financial Aid: 69% of all full-time undergraduates enrolled in fall 1996 applied for aid; of these, 95% were judged to have need according to Federal Methodology, of whom 100% were aided. On average, 82% of need was met. *Financial aid deadline (priority):* 2/15. *Financial aid forms:* FAFSA, CSS Financial Aid PROFILE required. State form required for some.

LD Services Contact: Ms. Joyce Yamaguchi Dillon, Director, Hobart and William Smith Colleges, Harris House, Geneva, NY 14456, 315-781-3351. Fax: 315-781-3862. Email: jdillon@hws.edu.

HOUGHTON COLLEGE

Houghton, New York

LEARNING DISABILITIES SERVICES INFORMATION

Student Academic Services began offering services in 1985. Currently the program serves 22 undergraduates with LD. Students diagnosed with ADD/ADHD are eligible for the same services available to students with LD.

Staff: 2 part-time staff members, including director, coordinator. Services provided by tutors.

Special Fees: No special fees are charged for services to students with LD.

Applications and admissions: *Required:* high school transcript, grade point average, class rank, extracurricular activities, untimed SAT I or ACT, autobiographical statement, psychoeducational report completed within 3 years, verification of learning disability by clinical psychologist; *recommended:* extended time SAT I or ACT, personal interview. Students may begin taking classes in fall only. *Application deadline:* 3/1.

Special policies: The college has written policies regarding substitutions and waivers of admissions, graduation, and degree requirements.

PROGRAM AND SERVICE COMPONENTS

Academic advising: Provided by unit staff members, academic advisers. Students with LD may take up to 16 credit hours each term; most take 12 to 15 credit hours; 12 credit hours required to maintain full-time status and be eligible for financial aid.

Counseling services: Individual counseling.

Basic skills remediation: Offered in class-size groups by regular teachers. Available in study skills.

Subject-area tutoring: Offered in small groups by peer tutors. Available in some subjects.

Auxiliary aids: Taped textbooks, tape recorders.

Auxiliary services: Alternative test arrangements, advocacy.

GENERAL COLLEGE INFORMATION

Independent Wesleyan, 4-year, coed. Awards associate, bachelor's degrees. Founded 1883. *Setting:* 1,300-acre rural campus with easy access to Buffalo and Rochester. *Endowment:* $10 million. *Research spending 1995–96:* $4681. *Educational spending 1995–96:* $4092 per undergrad. *Total enrollment:* 1,249. *Faculty:* 133 (100 full-time, 80% with terminal degrees, 33 part-time); student–undergrad faculty ratio is 15:1.

Enrollment Profile: 1,249 students from 40 states and territories, 22 other countries. 64% women, 36% men, 3% part-time, 60% state residents, 74% live on campus, 15% transferred in, 6% international, 7% 25 or older, 1% Native American, 1% Hispanic, 2% black, 1% Asian or Pacific Islander. *Retention:* 88% of 1995 full-time freshmen returned. *Graduation:* 63% graduate in 4 years, 64% in 5 years, 65% in 6 years. *Areas of study chosen:* 24% education, 12% biological and life sciences, 12% psychology, 11% fine arts, 7% business management and administrative services, 5% premed, 4% communications and journalism, 4% English language/literature/letters, 4% social sciences, 4% theology/religion, 3% performing arts, 2% foreign language and literature, 2% mathematics, 2% prelaw, 1% interdisciplinary studies, 1% physical sciences, 1% predentistry, 1% prevet. *Most popular recent majors:* elementary education, biology/biological sciences, psychology.

First-Year Class: 282 total; 1,031 applied, 77% were accepted, 35% of whom enrolled. 39% from top 10% of their high school class, 67% from top quarter, 91% from top half. 25 National Merit Scholars, 30 valedictorians.

Graduation Requirements: 62 credit hours for associate, 125 credit hours for bachelor's; 1 math course; 2 science courses; 2 years of a foreign language or the equivalent; computer course for business administration majors; internship (some majors); senior project for honors program students and some majors.

Computers on Campus: 130 computers available on campus for general student use. Computer purchase/lease plans available. A computer is required for all students. A campus-wide network can be accessed from student residence rooms and from off-campus. Students can contact faculty members and/or advisers through e-mail. Computers for student use in computer center, computer labs, library, dorms, divisional offices. Staffed computer lab on campus (open 24 hours a day) provides training in use of computers, software. *Academic computing expenditure 1995–96:* $633,565.

EXPENSES AND FINANCIAL AID

Expenses for 1997–98: *Application fee:* $25. Comprehensive fee of $16,962 includes full-time tuition ($12,344), mandatory fees ($380), and college room and board ($4238). College room only: $2118. Part-time tuition per credit hour ranges from $279 to $398.
Undergraduate Financial Aid: 89% of all full-time undergraduates enrolled in fall 1996 applied for aid; of these, 90% were judged to have need according to Federal Methodology, of whom 100% were aided. On average, 83% of need was met. *Financial aid deadline (priority):* 3/15. *Financial aid forms:* FAFSA, institutional form required; CSS Financial Aid PROFILE acceptable. State form required for some.
LD Services Contact: Dr. Susan M. Hice, Director of Academic Support Center, Houghton College, One Willard Avenue, Houghton, NY 14744, 716-567-9622 Ext. 202. Fax: 716-567-9570.

HUMBOLDT STATE UNIVERSITY

Arcata, California

LEARNING DISABILITIES SERVICES INFORMATION

Disabled Student Services began offering services in 1976. Currently the program serves 300 undergraduates with LD. Services are also available to graduate students. Students diagnosed with ADD/ADHD are eligible for the same services available to students with LD.
Staff: 3 full-time, 2 part-time staff members, including director, LD psychologist. Services provided by diagnostic specialist.
Special Fees: No special fees are charged for services to students with LD.
Applications and admissions: *Required:* high school transcript, grade point average, courses completed, untimed SAT I or ACT, autobiographical statement, letters of recommendation, psychoeducational report completed within 3 years; *recommended:* personal interview. Students may begin taking classes in fall or spring. *Application deadline:* 11/30 (fall term), 8/31 (spring term).
Special policies: The college has written policies regarding substitutions and waivers of graduation requirements.

PROGRAM AND SERVICE COMPONENTS

Special preparation or orientation: Required orientation held before registration, during registration, after classes begin.
Diagnostic testing: Intelligence, reading, math, spelling, spoken language, written language, motor abilities, perceptual skills, psychoneurology, speech, hearing.
Academic advising: Provided by unit staff members, academic advisers. Students with LD may take up to as many semester units as an individual can handle each term; most take 12 to 14 semester units; 12 semester units required to maintain full-time status and be eligible for financial aid.
Counseling services: Individual counseling.
Subject-area tutoring: Offered one-on-one by peer tutors. Available in all subjects.
Auxiliary aids: Taped textbooks, tape recorders, word-processors with spell-check, personal computers, talking computers.
Auxiliary services: Alternative test arrangements, notetakers, priority registration, advocacy.

GENERAL COLLEGE INFORMATION

State-supported, comprehensive, coed. Part of California State University System. Awards bachelor's, master's degrees. Founded 1913. *Setting:* 161-acre rural campus. *Endowment:* $9.1 million. *Research spending 1995–96:* $6.7 million. *Educational spending 1995–96:* $4732 per undergrad. *Total enrollment:* 7,686. *Faculty:* 637 (340 full-time, 71% with terminal degrees, 297 part-time); student–undergrad faculty ratio is 17:1.
Enrollment Profile: 6,862 students from 45 states and territories, 23 other countries. 51% women, 49% men, 9% part-time, 98% state residents, 20% live on campus, 43% transferred in, 1% international, 32% 25 or older, 3% Native American, 8% Hispanic, 2% black, 4% Asian or Pacific Islander. *Retention:* 80% of 1995 full-time freshmen returned. *Areas of study chosen:* 16% natural resource sciences, 13% biological and life sciences, 10% education, 8% social sciences, 5% business management and administrative services, 5% engineering and applied sciences, 5% psychology, 4% English language/literature/letters, 4% fine arts, 3% health professions and related sciences, 3% performing arts, 2% communications and journalism, 2% physical sciences, 1% computer and information sciences, 1% foreign language and literature, 1% interdisciplinary studies, 1% mathematics, 1% philosophy. *Most popular recent majors:* biology/biological sciences, elementary education, business administration/commerce/management.
First-Year Class: 842 total; 3,866 applied, 76% were accepted, 29% of whom enrolled. 75% from top quarter of their high school class.
Graduation Requirements: 124 semester units; 3 semester units each of math, biology, and physical science; computer course for all business, economics, some social science, science, natural resources majors; internship (some majors); senior project (some majors).
Computers on Campus: 370 computers available on campus for general student use. Students can contact faculty members and/or advisers through e-mail. Computers for student use in computer labs, library provide access to the Internet/World Wide Web, on- and off-campus e-mail addresses. Staffed computer lab on campus. *Academic computing expenditure 1995–96:* $1.5 million.

EXPENSES AND FINANCIAL AID

Expenses for 1997–98: *Application fee:* $55. State resident tuition: $0 full-time. Nonresident tuition: $7626 full-time, $246 per unit part-time. Part-time mandatory fees: $630 per semester. Full-time mandatory fees: $1926. College room and board: $5194. College room only: $3040.
Undergraduate Financial Aid: Of all full-time undergraduates enrolled in fall 1996, 87% of those who applied for aid were judged to have need according to Federal Methodology, of whom 95% were aided. On average, 70% of need was met. *Financial aid deadline (priority):* 3/2. *Financial aid forms:* FAFSA required; CSS Financial Aid PROFILE acceptable. State form required for some.
Financial aid specifically for students with LD: Scholarship: Hart-Pollack Scholarship.
LD Services Contact: Ms. Theresa A. Jordan, Director, Disabled Student Services, Humboldt State University, Arcata, CA 95521-8299, 707-826-4678. Fax: 707-826-5397. Email: jordant@laurel.humboldt.edu.

HUNTER COLLEGE OF THE CITY UNIVERSITY OF NEW YORK

New York, New York

LEARNING DISABILITIES SERVICES INFORMATION

Services for Students with Disabilities currently serves undergraduate students with LD. Students diagnosed with ADD/ADHD are eligible for the same services available to students with LD.
Staff: 4 full-time, 3 part-time staff members, including director, assistant director, coordinator. Services provided by tutors, counselors, readers, writers.
Special Fees: No special fees are charged for services to students with LD.
Applications and admissions: *Required:* high school transcript, evaluation of learning disability. *Application deadline:* 1/15.
Special policies: The college has written policies regarding grade forgiveness.

PROGRAM AND SERVICE COMPONENTS

Subject-area tutoring: Offered one-on-one and in small groups by peer tutors. Available in most subjects.

GENERAL COLLEGE INFORMATION

State and locally supported, comprehensive, coed. Part of City University of New York System. Awards bachelor's, master's degrees. Founded 1870. *Setting:* urban campus. *Total enrollment:* 18,250. *Faculty:* 1,095 (644 full-time, 85% with terminal degrees, 451 part-time); student–undergrad faculty ratio is 18:1.
Enrollment Profile: 13,980 students from 25 states and territories. 73% women, 27% men, 36% part-time, 93% state residents, 5% international, 60% 25 or older, 1% Native American, 25% Hispanic, 22% black, 16% Asian or Pacific Islander. *Retention:* 76% of 1995 full-time freshmen returned. *Areas of study chosen:* 18% psychology, 10% health professions and related sciences, 9% English language/literature/letters, 5% performing arts, 4% biological and life sciences, 3% communications and journalism, 3% education, 3% foreign language and literature, 3% physical sciences, 1% mathematics, 1% philosophy, 1% theology/religion. *Most popular recent majors:* psychology, sociology, English.
First-Year Class: 1,186 total; 6,640 applied, 41% were accepted, 44% of whom enrolled.

Hunter College of the City University of New York (continued)

Graduation Requirements: 125 credits; 10 credits of math/science; computer course (varies by major); internship (some majors); senior project for honors program students and some majors.
Computers on Campus: 300 computers available on campus for general student use. Computers for student use in computer center, computer labs, learning resource center, library provide access to the Internet/World Wide Web. Staffed computer lab on campus.

EXPENSES AND FINANCIAL AID

Expenses for 1996–97: *Application fee:* $35. State resident tuition: $3200 full-time, $135 per credit part-time. Nonresident tuition: $6800 full-time, $285 per credit part-time. Part-time mandatory fees: $61.60 per semester. (College housing is available through Brookdale Health Sciences Campus only.). Full-time mandatory fees: $118.
Undergraduate Financial Aid: *Financial aid deadline (priority):* 5/1. *Financial aid forms:* FAFSA, state form, institutional form required.
LD Services Contact: Ms. Sandra LaPorta, Office for Students with Disabilities, Hunter College of the City University of New York, 695 Park Avenue, New York, NY 10021-5085, 212-772-4857.

ILLINOIS INSTITUTE OF TECHNOLOGY

Chicago, Illinois

LEARNING DISABILITIES SERVICES INFORMATION

Center for Disability Resources and Educational Development currently serves 2 undergraduates with LD. Services are also available to graduate students. Students diagnosed with ADD/ADHD are eligible for the same services available to students with LD.
Staff: 3 part-time staff members, including director, coordinators. Services provided by tutors.
Special Fees: No special fees are charged for services to students with LD.
Applications and admissions: *Required:* high school transcript, grade point average, class rank, courses completed, extracurricular activities, untimed SAT I or ACT, autobiographical statement, letters of recommendation; *recommended:* extended time SAT I or ACT, personal interview. Students may begin taking classes in fall only. *Application deadline:* 3/1.

PROGRAM AND SERVICE COMPONENTS

Diagnostic testing: Intelligence, reading, math, spelling, personality.
Academic advising: Provided by academic advisers. Students with LD may take up to 18 semester hours (more with special permission) each term; 12 semester hours required to maintain full-time status and be eligible for financial aid.
Counseling services: Individual counseling, small-group counseling, career counseling, self-advocacy training.
Subject-area tutoring: Offered one-on-one and in small groups by peer tutors. Available in all subjects.
Auxiliary aids: Taped textbooks, tape recorders, word-processors with spell-check.
Auxiliary services: Alternative test arrangements, notetakers, advocacy.

GENERAL COLLEGE INFORMATION

Independent, coed. Awards bachelor's, master's, doctoral, first professional degrees. Founded 1890. *Setting:* 120-acre urban campus. *Endowment:* $111.6 million. *Research spending 1995–96:* $11.3 million. *Total enrollment:* 6,287. *Undergraduate faculty:* 535 (295 full-time, 90% with terminal degrees, 240 part-time); student–undergrad faculty ratio is 12:1.
Enrollment Profile: 1,959 students from 51 states and territories, 56 other countries. 23% women, 77% men, 27% part-time, 63% state residents, 44% live on campus, 11% transferred in, 13% international, 29% 25 or older, 0% Native American, 8% Hispanic, 11% black, 13% Asian or Pacific Islander. *Retention:* 80% of 1995 full-time freshmen returned. *Graduation:* 45% graduate in 6 years. *Areas of study chosen:* 62% engineering and applied sciences, 13% architecture, 10% computer and information sciences, 1% biological and life sciences, 1% mathematics, 1% physical sciences, 1% psychology, 1% social sciences. *Most popular recent majors:* electrical engineering, mechanical engineering, architecture.
First-Year Class: 245 total; 2,340 applied, 67% were accepted, 16% of whom enrolled. 51% from top 10% of their high school class, 83% from top quarter, 98% from top half. 1 Westinghouse recipient.
Graduation Requirements: 126 semester hours; 5 semester hours of math; 11 semester hours of natural science or engineering; computer course; senior project.
Computers on Campus: 250 computers available on campus for general student use. A computer is strongly recommended for all students. A campus-wide network can be accessed from student residence rooms and from off-campus. Students can contact faculty members and/or advisers through e-mail. Computers for student use in computer center, computer labs, learning resource center, classrooms, library, dorms, academic buildings provide access to the Internet/World Wide Web, on- and off-campus e-mail addresses. Staffed computer lab on campus provides training in use of computers, software. *Academic computing expenditure 1995–96:* $970,715.

EXPENSES AND FINANCIAL AID

Estimated Expenses for 1997–98: *Application fee:* $30. Comprehensive fee of $21,080 includes full-time tuition ($16,400), mandatory fees ($60), and college room and board ($4620 minimum). Part-time tuition: $515 per semester hour. Part-time mandatory fees: $1.50 per semester hour.
Undergraduate Financial Aid: 76% of all full-time undergraduates enrolled in fall 1996 applied for aid; of these, 88% were judged to have need according to Federal Methodology, of whom 99% were aided. On average, 91% of need was met. *Financial aid deadline (priority):* 3/15. *Financial aid forms:* FAFSA required; CSS Financial Aid PROFILE, state form acceptable.
LD Services Contact: Mr. Charles Merbitz, Director, Illinois Institute of Technology, IIT Center, Chicago, IL 60616, 312-567-8862. Fax: 312-567-8948.

ILLINOIS STATE UNIVERSITY

Normal, Illinois

LEARNING DISABILITIES SERVICES INFORMATION

Disability Concerns Office began offering services in 1978. Currently the program serves 100 undergraduates with LD. Services are also available to graduate students. Students diagnosed with ADD/ADHD are eligible for the same services available to students with LD.
Staff: Includes director, assistant director, coordinators. Services provided by remediation specialists, tutors, counselors.
Special Fees: No special fees are charged for services to students with LD.
Applications and admissions: *Required:* high school transcript, grade point average, class rank, courses completed, untimed ACT, psychoeducational report completed since age 17 or older; *recommended:* untimed SAT I, personal interview. Students may begin taking classes any term. *Application deadline:* 6/30.

PROGRAM AND SERVICE COMPONENTS

Diagnostic testing: Spoken language, speech, hearing.
Academic advising: Provided by unit staff members, academic advisers. Students with LD may take up to 17 credits each term; most take 12 credits; 12 credits required to maintain full-time status; minimum of 6 credits (aid is proportional to credits taken) required to be eligible for financial aid.
Counseling services: Individual counseling, small-group counseling, career counseling, self-advocacy training.
Subject-area tutoring: Offered one-on-one and in small groups by professional teachers, peer tutors, Learning Assistance lab technician. Available in most subjects.
Special courses: Communication skills, learning strategies, time management, study skills, career planning. None offered for credit.
Auxiliary aids: Taped textbooks, tape recorders, word-processors with spell-check, personal computers, Arkenstone Reader.
Auxiliary services: Alternative test arrangements, notetakers, advocacy, scribes, proofreading, typing services.
Campus support group: A special student organization is available to students with LD.

GENERAL COLLEGE INFORMATION

State-supported, coed. Awards bachelor's, master's, doctoral degrees. Founded 1857. *Setting:* 850-acre urban campus. *Endowment:* $11.3 million. *Research spending 1995–96:* $12.3 million. *Educational spending 1995–96:* $3370 per undergrad. *Total enrollment:* 19,409. *Faculty:* 944 (774 full-time, 85% with terminal degrees, 170 part-time); student–undergrad faculty ratio is 21:1.
Enrollment Profile: 16,763 students from 32 states and territories, 40 other countries. 56% women, 44% men, 10% part-time, 98% state residents, 42% live on campus, 40% transferred in, 1% international, 12% 25

or older, 0% Native American, 2% Hispanic, 9% black, 2% Asian or Pacific Islander. *Retention:* 73% of 1995 full-time freshmen returned. *Graduation:* 28% graduate in 4 years, 50% in 5 years, 54% in 6 years. *Areas of study chosen:* 18% education, 16% business management and administrative services, 11% social sciences, 6% fine arts, 5% communications and journalism, 4% computer and information sciences, 4% health professions and related sciences, 3% biological and life sciences, 3% engineering and applied sciences, 3% English language/literature/letters, 3% psychology, 2% agriculture, 2% physical sciences, 2% vocational and home economics, 1% foreign language and literature, 1% mathematics. *Most popular recent majors:* elementary education, accounting, special education.
First-Year Class: 2,896 total; 10,134 applied, 78% were accepted, 36% of whom enrolled. 11% from top 10% of their high school class, 33% from top quarter, 77% from top half. 3 National Merit Scholars.
Graduation Requirements: 120 credits; computer course for business, math, industrial technology, home economics majors; internship (some majors); senior project (some majors).
Computers on Campus: 6,423 computers available on campus for general student use. A campus-wide network can be accessed from student residence rooms and from off-campus. Students can contact faculty members and/or advisers through e-mail. Computers for student use in computer center, computer labs, library, dorms, academic buildings provide access to the Internet/World Wide Web, on- and off-campus e-mail addresses. Staffed computer lab on campus (open 24 hours a day) provides training in use of computers, software.

EXPENSES AND FINANCIAL AID

Expenses for 1997–98: State resident tuition: $2952 full-time, $98.40 per credit part-time. Nonresident tuition: $8856 full-time, $295.20 per credit part-time. Part-time mandatory fees: $35.05 per credit. Full-time mandatory fees: $1052. College room and board: $3996. College room only: $2118.
Undergraduate Financial Aid: 64% of all full-time undergraduates enrolled in fall 1996 applied for aid; of these, 79% were judged to have need according to Federal Methodology, of whom 96% were aided. On average, 93% of need was met. *Financial aid deadline (priority):* 3/1. *Financial aid forms:* FAFSA required.
LD Services Contact: Ms. Ann M. Caldwell, Coordinator of Learning Disabilities, Illinois State University, Campus Box 1290, Normal, IL 61790-1290, 309-438-5853. Fax: 309-438-7713.

INDIANA STATE UNIVERSITY

Terre Haute, Indiana

LEARNING DISABILITIES SERVICES INFORMATION

Student Support Services began offering services in 1982. Currently the program serves 75 undergraduates with LD. Students diagnosed with ADD/ADHD are eligible for the same services available to students with LD.
Staff: 4 full-time staff members, including director, coordinators, English instructor, academic coordinator. Services provided by tutors, counselors.
Special Fees: No special fees are charged for services to students with LD.
Applications and admissions: *Required:* high school transcript, grade point average, class rank, courses completed, untimed SAT I or ACT, documentation of learning disability and academic need verification; *recommended:* high school extracurricular activities, IEP (Individualized Education Program), extended time SAT I or ACT, personal interview, autobiographical statement, letters of recommendation, psychoeducational report completed within 4 years. Students may begin taking classes in fall only. *Application deadline:* 8/1 (fall term), 12/1 (spring term).

PROGRAM AND SERVICE COMPONENTS

Special preparation or orientation: Required orientation held during registration.
Diagnostic testing: Intelligence, reading, math, spelling, written language.
Academic advising: Provided by unit staff members, academic advisers. Students with LD may take up to 17 credit hours each term; most take 12 credit hours; 12 credit hours required to maintain full-time status; 3 credit hours (for Pell Grant) required to be eligible for financial aid.
Counseling services: Individual counseling, small-group counseling, career counseling.
Basic skills remediation: Offered one-on-one by tutors. Available in reading, written language, learning strategies, study skills, time management, computer skills.
Subject-area tutoring: Offered one-on-one, in small groups, and in class-size groups by peer tutors. Available in most subjects.
Special courses: Composition, math, study skills, career planning. All offered for credit; all enter into overall grade point average.
Auxiliary aids: Tape recorders, typewriters, word-processors with spell-check, personal computers, optical character readers, Recordings for the Blind.
Auxiliary services: Alternative test arrangements, advocacy, vocational rehabilitation.

GENERAL COLLEGE INFORMATION

State-supported, coed. Awards associate, bachelor's, master's, doctoral degrees. Founded 1865. *Setting:* 91-acre suburban campus with easy access to Indianapolis. *Endowment:* $974,950. *Research spending 1995–96:* $5.5 million. *Educational spending 1995–96:* $4819 per undergrad. *Total enrollment:* 10,934. *Faculty:* 706 (563 full-time, 78% with terminal degrees, 143 part-time); student–undergrad faculty ratio is 15:1.
Enrollment Profile: 9,490 students from 51 states and territories, 38 other countries. 51% women, 49% men, 18% part-time, 90% state residents, 34% live on campus, 6% transferred in, 4% international, 16% 25 or older, 1% Native American, 1% Hispanic, 8% black, 1% Asian or Pacific Islander. *Retention:* 64% of 1995 full-time freshmen returned. *Graduation:* 18% graduate in 4 years, 33% in 5 years, 38% in 6 years. *Areas of study chosen:* 17% business management and administrative services, 17% health professions and related sciences, 16% education, 15% engineering and applied sciences, 11% social sciences, 4% performing arts, 3% communications and journalism, 3% psychology, 2% computer and information sciences, 2% English language/literature/letters, 2% liberal arts/general studies, 2% vocational and home economics, 1% architecture, 1% biological and life sciences, 1% mathematics, 1% natural resource sciences, 1% physical sciences, 1% prelaw. *Most popular recent majors:* elementary education, criminology, nursing.
First-Year Class: 1,921 total; 4,550 applied, 88% were accepted, 48% of whom enrolled. 10% from top 10% of their high school class, 31% from top quarter, 66% from top half.
Graduation Requirements: 62 credit hours for associate, 124 credit hours for bachelor's; 11 credit hours of math/science; computer course for math, business, technology majors; internship (some majors); senior project (some majors).
Computers on Campus: 371 computers available on campus for general student use. Computer purchase/lease plans available. A computer is recommended for some students. A campus-wide network can be accessed from student residence rooms and from off-campus. Students can contact faculty members and/or advisers through e-mail. Computers for student use in computer center, computer labs, learning resource center, classrooms, library, student center, dorms provide access to the Internet/World Wide Web, on- and off-campus e-mail addresses. Staffed computer lab on campus (open 24 hours a day) provides training in use of computers, software. *Academic computing expenditure 1995–96:* $2 million.

EXPENSES AND FINANCIAL AID

Expenses for 1997–98: *Application fee:* $20. State resident tuition: $3196 full-time, $114.50 per credit hour part-time. Nonresident tuition: $7916 full-time, $277.50 per credit hour part-time. College room and board: $4143.
Undergraduate Financial Aid: 72% of all full-time undergraduates enrolled in fall 1996 applied for aid; of these, 87% were judged to have need according to Federal Methodology, of whom 98% were aided. On average, 49% of need was met. *Financial aid deadline (priority):* 3/1. *Financial aid forms:* CSS Financial Aid PROFILE, institutional form required. FAFSA required for some.
LD Services Contact: Ms. Rita Worrall, Director of Student Support Services, Indiana State University, 204A Gillum Hall, Terre Haute, IN 47809-1401, 812-237-2300. Fax: 812-237-8353. Email: sacworra@ruby.indstate.edu.

INDIANA UNIVERSITY BLOOMINGTON

Bloomington, Indiana

LEARNING DISABILITIES SERVICES INFORMATION

Office of Disabled Student Services and Veterans' Affairs began offering services in 1982. Currently the program serves 220 undergraduates with LD. Services are also available to graduate students. Students diagnosed with ADD/ADHD are eligible for the same services available to students with LD.

Indiana University Bloomington (continued)

Staff: Includes director, LD specialist. Services provided by tutors, counselors, proctors, readers, notetakers.
Special Fees: No special fees are charged for services to students with LD.
Applications and admissions: *Required:* high school transcript, grade point average, courses completed, untimed SAT I or ACT, psychoeducational report completed within 3 years; *recommended:* high school class rank. Students may begin taking classes any term. *Application deadline:* continuous.
Special policies: The college has written policies regarding substitutions and waivers of degree requirements.

PROGRAM AND SERVICE COMPONENTS

Special preparation or orientation: Optional orientation offered individually by appointment.
Diagnostic testing: Intelligence, reading, math, spelling, handwriting, written language, perceptual skills, speech, hearing, learning strategies.
Academic advising: Provided by unit staff members, academic advisers. Students with LD may take up to 21 credit hours each term; most take 12 credit hours; 12 credit hours required to maintain full-time status; 6 to 11 credit hours (part-time), 12 credit hours (full-time) required to be eligible for financial aid.
Counseling services: Individual counseling, small-group counseling, career counseling.
Subject-area tutoring: Offered one-on-one by peer tutors, upperclassmen and graduate students. Available in most subjects.
Special courses: College survival skills, reading, word processing, time management, study skills, career planning, stress management. Some offered for credit.
Auxiliary aids: Taped textbooks, tape recorders, calculators, typewriters, personal computers, talking computers, optical character readers.
Auxiliary services: Alternative test arrangements, notetakers, advocacy.

GENERAL COLLEGE INFORMATION

State-supported, coed. Part of Indiana University System. Awards associate, bachelor's, master's, doctoral, first professional degrees. Founded 1820. *Setting:* 1,800-acre small-town campus with easy access to Indianapolis. *Endowment:* $103.6 million. *Research spending 1995–96:* $48.7 million. *Total enrollment:* 34,700. *Undergraduate faculty:* 1,635 (1,430 full-time, 205 part-time); student–undergrad faculty ratio is 17:1.
Enrollment Profile: 25,451 students from 53 states and territories, 135 other countries. 54% women, 46% men, 6% part-time, 73% state residents, 3% transferred in, 2% international, 6% 25 or older, 0% Native American, 2% Hispanic, 4% black, 3% Asian or Pacific Islander. *Retention:* 80% of 1995 full-time freshmen returned. *Graduation:* 47% graduate in 4 years, 67% in 5 years, 71% in 6 years. *Most popular recent majors:* liberal arts/general studies, business administration/commerce/management, education.
First-Year Class: 5,837 total; 16,725 applied, 83% were accepted, 42% of whom enrolled. 24% from top 10% of their high school class, 52% from top quarter, 97% from top half. 117 valedictorians.
Graduation Requirements: 60 credit hours for associate, 122 credit hours for bachelor's; 1 semester of math; computer course for business, education majors; senior project (some majors).
Computers on Campus: 2,000 computers available on campus for general student use. Computer purchase/lease plans available. A campus-wide network can be accessed from student residence rooms and from off-campus. Students can contact faculty members and/or advisers through e-mail. Computers for student use in computer center, computer labs, learning resource center, classrooms, library, student center, dorms, academic buildings provide access to the Internet/World Wide Web, on- and off-campus e-mail addresses, various software packages. Staffed computer lab on campus (open 24 hours a day) provides training in use of computers, software. *Academic computing expenditure 1995–96:* $20.3 million.

EXPENSES AND FINANCIAL AID

Expenses for 1997–98: *Application fee:* $35. State resident tuition: $3486 full-time, $108.80 per credit hour part-time. Nonresident tuition: $11,410 full-time, $356.55 per credit hour part-time. Part-time mandatory fees per semester range from $50.50 to $221.55. Full-time mandatory fees: $443. College room and board: $4900.
Undergraduate Financial Aid: Of all full-time undergraduates enrolled in fall 1996, 78% of those who applied for aid were judged to have need according to Federal Methodology, of whom 94% were aided. On average, 66% of need was met. *Financial aid deadline (priority):* 3/1. *Financial aid forms:* FAFSA, institutional form required; CSS Financial Aid PROFILE acceptable.

LD Services Contact: Ms. Lynn Flinders, Learning Disability Specialist, Indiana University Bloomington, Franklin Hall 331, Bloomington, IN 47405-2801, 812-855-3508. Fax: 812-855-5381. Email: lflinder@indiana.edu.

INDIANA UNIVERSITY NORTHWEST

Gary, Indiana

LEARNING DISABILITIES SERVICES INFORMATION

Special Counseling began offering services in 1981. Currently the program serves 45 undergraduates with LD. Services are also available to graduate students. Students diagnosed with ADD/ADHD are eligible for the same services available to students with LD.
Staff: 2 full-time, 6 part-time staff members, including director, coordinator. Services provided by remediation specialists, tutors, counselors.
Special Fees: No special fees are charged for services to students with LD.
Applications and admissions: *Recommended:* personal interview, autobiographical statement, letters of recommendation, psychoeducational report completed within 3 years. Students may begin taking classes any term. *Application deadline:* continuous.

PROGRAM AND SERVICE COMPONENTS

Special preparation or orientation: Optional orientation offered before registration.
Diagnostic testing: Reading, math, written language.
Academic advising: Provided by unit staff members. Students with LD may take up to 12 credits each term; most take 9 to 12 credits; 12 credits required to maintain full-time status; 6 credits required to be eligible for financial aid.
Counseling services: Individual counseling, career counseling, self-advocacy training.
Basic skills remediation: Offered one-on-one, in small groups, and in class-size groups by regular teachers, teacher trainees, graduate students. Available in reading, math, spelling, spoken language, written language, learning strategies, perceptual skills, study skills, time management, social skills.
Subject-area tutoring: Offered one-on-one and in small groups by professional teachers, peer tutors. Available in most subjects.
Special courses: College survival skills, reading, vocabulary development, math, study skills, career planning. Some offered for credit.
Auxiliary aids: Taped textbooks, tape recorders, calculators, typewriters, word-processors with spell-check, personal computers.
Auxiliary services: Alternative test arrangements, notetakers, advocacy.
Campus support group: A special student organization is available to students with LD.

GENERAL COLLEGE INFORMATION

State-supported, comprehensive, coed. Part of Indiana University System. Awards associate, bachelor's, master's degrees. Founded 1959. *Setting:* 27-acre urban campus with easy access to Chicago. *Endowment:* $82,502. *Research spending 1995–96:* $121,733. *Total enrollment:* 5,149. *Faculty:* 350 (173 full-time, 85% with terminal degrees, 177 part-time); student–undergrad faculty ratio is 14:1.
Enrollment Profile: 4,620 students: 67% women, 33% men, 52% part-time, 99% state residents, 24% transferred in, 49% 25 or older, 0% Native American, 9% Hispanic, 24% black, 1% Asian or Pacific Islander. *Retention:* 63% of 1995 full-time freshmen returned. *Areas of study chosen:* 27% health professions and related sciences, 17% business management and administrative services, 12% education, 6% liberal arts/general studies, 3% psychology, 2% biological and life sciences, 2% physical sciences, 2% social sciences, 1% communications and journalism, 1% computer and information sciences, 1% English language/literature/letters, 1% fine arts, 1% foreign language and literature, 1% mathematics, 1% performing arts. *Most popular recent majors:* business administration/commerce/management, accounting, nursing.
First-Year Class: 723 total; 1,771 applied, 53% were accepted, 77% of whom enrolled. 7% from top 10% of their high school class, 20% from top quarter, 46% from top half.
Graduation Requirements: 60 credits for associate, 120 credits for bachelor's; 1 course each in math and science; computer course for business, medical records technology, public affairs, environmental affairs majors; senior project for honors program students and some majors.
Computers on Campus: 170 computers available on campus for general student use. Computer purchase/lease plans available. A campus-

wide network can be accessed from off-campus. Students can contact faculty members and/or advisers through e-mail. Computers for student use in computer center, academic offices, clusters provide access to the Internet/World Wide Web, on- and off-campus e-mail addresses. Staffed computer lab on campus provides training in use of computers, software. *Academic computing expenditure 1995–96:* $1.1 million.

EXPENSES AND FINANCIAL AID

Expenses for 1997–98: State resident tuition: $2715 full-time, $90.50 per credit part-time. Nonresident tuition: $7044 full-time, $234.80 per credit part-time. Part-time mandatory fees: $6 per credit. Full-time mandatory fees: $180.
Undergraduate Financial Aid: Of all full-time undergraduates enrolled in fall 1996, 85% of those who applied for aid were judged to have need according to Federal Methodology, of whom 98% were aided. On average, 61% of need was met. *Financial aid deadline (priority):* 3/1. *Financial aid forms:* FAFSA, institutional form required; CSS Financial Aid PROFILE acceptable.
LD Services Contact: Mr. Ronald Thorton, Coordinator for Students, Indiana University Northwest, 3400 Broadway, Gary, IN 46408-1197, 219-980-6798. Fax: 219-980-6624.

INDIANA UNIVERSITY OF PENNSYLVANIA

Indiana, Pennsylvania

LEARNING DISABILITIES SERVICES INFORMATION

Advising and Testing Center began offering services in 1984. Currently the program serves 150 undergraduates with LD. Services are also available to graduate students. Students diagnosed with ADD/ADHD are eligible for the same services available to students with LD.
Staff: 3 full-time staff members, including director, assistant director, adviser. Services provided by graduate assistant.
Special Fees: No special fees are charged for services to students with LD.
Applications and admissions: *Required:* high school transcript, grade point average, class rank, courses completed, untimed SAT I or ACT, letters of recommendation; *recommended:* extended time SAT I or ACT, psychoeducational report completed within 3 years. Students may begin taking classes any term. *Application deadline:* continuous.

PROGRAM AND SERVICE COMPONENTS

Academic advising: Provided by unit staff members, academic advisers. Students with LD may take up to 17 semester hours each term; most take 13 to 15 semester hours; 12 semester hours required to maintain full-time status.
Counseling services: Individual counseling, career counseling, self-advocacy training.
Auxiliary aids: Taped textbooks, tape recorders, calculators, word-processors with spell-check, optical character readers.
Auxiliary services: Alternative test arrangements, notetakers, priority registration, advocacy.

GENERAL COLLEGE INFORMATION

State-supported, coed. Part of Pennsylvania State System of Higher Education. Awards associate, bachelor's, master's, doctoral degrees. Founded 1875. *Setting:* 341-acre small-town campus with easy access to Pittsburgh. *Endowment:* $16.2 million. *Research spending 1995–96:* $978,340. *Total enrollment:* 13,680. *Faculty:* 823 (742 full-time, 83% with terminal degrees, 81 part-time); student–undergrad faculty ratio is 19:1.
Enrollment Profile: 12,144 students from 45 states and territories, 70 other countries. 54% women, 46% men, 7% part-time, 96% state residents, 34% live on campus, 5% transferred in, 1% international, 13% 25 or older, 1% Native American, 1% Hispanic, 5% black, 1% Asian or Pacific Islander. *Retention:* 77% of 1995 full-time freshmen returned. *Graduation:* 30% graduate in 4 years, 52% in 5 years, 62% in 6 years. *Areas of study chosen:* 4% biological and life sciences, 4% fine arts, 3% computer and information sciences, 2% prelaw, 1% liberal arts/general studies, 1% military science, 1% predentistry, 1% premed. *Most popular recent majors:* criminology, elementary education, accounting.
First-Year Class: 1,928 total; 7,515 applied, 63% were accepted, 41% of whom enrolled. 22% from top 10% of their high school class, 51% from top quarter, 85% from top half.
Graduation Requirements: 60 semester hours for associate, 124 semester hours for bachelor's; 3 semester hours of math; 8 semester hours of science; computer course for business, science, math, communication media majors.
Computers on Campus: Computer purchase/lease plans available. A campus-wide network can be accessed from student residence rooms. Computers for student use in computer center, computer labs, classrooms, library, dorms provide access to the Internet/World Wide Web, on- and off-campus e-mail addresses. Staffed computer lab on campus provides training in use of computers, software. *Academic computing expenditure 1995–96:* $1.1 million.

EXPENSES AND FINANCIAL AID

Expenses for 1997–98: State resident tuition: $3468 full-time, $144 per semester hour part-time. Nonresident tuition: $8824 full-time, $368 per semester hour part-time. Part-time mandatory fees: $171 per semester. Full-time mandatory fees: $736. College room and board: $2696 (minimum). College room only: $1952 (minimum).
Undergraduate Financial Aid: 91% of all full-time undergraduates enrolled in fall 1996 applied for aid; of these, 70% were judged to have need according to Federal Methodology, of whom 86% were aided. On average, 75% of need was met. *Financial aid deadline:* Applications processed continuously. *Financial aid forms:* FAFSA required.
LD Services Contact: Ms. Catherine Dugan, Director, Advising and Testing Center, Indiana University of Pennsylvania, 106 Pratt Hall, Indiana, PA 15705, 412-357-4067. Fax: 412-357-4079.

INDIANA UNIVERSITY SOUTHEAST

New Albany, Indiana

LEARNING DISABILITIES SERVICES INFORMATION

Office of Services for Students with Disabilities began offering services in 1976. Currently the program serves 100 undergraduates with LD. Services are also available to graduate students. Students diagnosed with ADD/ADHD are eligible for the same services available to students with LD.
Staff: 3 full-time staff members, including director, coordinators. Services provided by remediation specialist, tutors.
Special Fees: No special fees are charged for services to students with LD.
Applications and admissions: *Required:* psychoeducational report completed within 3 years; *recommended:* high school transcript, untimed or extended time SAT I or ACT, personal interview. Students may begin taking classes any term. *Application deadline:* continuous.
Special policies: The college has written policies regarding grade forgiveness; substitutions and waivers of admissions, graduation, and degree requirements.

PROGRAM AND SERVICE COMPONENTS

Academic advising: Provided by unit staff members, academic advisers. Students with LD may take up to 15 credit hours each term; most take 6 to 12 credit hours; 12 credit hours required to maintain full-time status and be eligible for financial aid.
Counseling services: Individual counseling, small-group counseling, career counseling.
Basic skills remediation: Offered one-on-one, in small groups, and in class-size groups by regular teachers, peer tutors. Available in reading, math, written language, learning strategies, study skills, time management.
Subject-area tutoring: Offered one-on-one and in small groups by professional teachers, peer tutors. Available in all subjects.
Special courses: College survival skills, reading, vocabulary development, composition, learning strategies, word processing, time management, math, personal psychology, study skills, career planning. All offered for credit; most enter into overall grade point average.
Auxiliary aids: Taped textbooks, tape recorders, word-processors with spell-check, optical character readers.
Auxiliary services: Alternative test arrangements, notetakers, advocacy, readers.
Campus support group: A special student organization is available to students with LD.

GENERAL COLLEGE INFORMATION

State-supported, comprehensive, coed. Part of Indiana University System. Awards associate, bachelor's, master's degrees. Founded 1941. *Setting:*

Indiana University Southeast (continued)

177-acre suburban campus with easy access to Louisville. *Total enrollment:* 5,396. *Faculty:* 376 (136 full-time, 85% with terminal degrees, 240 part-time); student–undergrad faculty ratio is 19:1.

Enrollment Profile: 4,854 students: 62% women, 38% men, 51% part-time, 98% state residents, 2% transferred in, 1% international, 40% 25 or older, 1% Native American, 1% Hispanic, 2% black, 1% Asian or Pacific Islander. *Retention:* 83% of 1995 full-time freshmen returned. *Most popular recent majors:* business administration/commerce/management, education.

First-Year Class: 1,073 applied, 99% were accepted, 75% of whom enrolled.

Graduation Requirements: 63 credit hours for associate, 120 credit hours for bachelor's; 3 credit hours of math; computer course.

Computers on Campus: 200 computers available on campus for general student use. Computer purchase/lease plans available. A campus-wide network can be accessed from off-campus. Students can contact faculty members and/or advisers through e-mail. Computers for student use in computer center, computer labs, learning resource center, classrooms, library provide access to the Internet/World Wide Web, on- and off-campus e-mail addresses.

EXPENSES AND FINANCIAL AID

Expenses for 1997–98: *Application fee:* $25. State resident tuition: $2715 full-time, $90.50 per credit hour part-time. Nonresident tuition: $7044 full-time, $234.80 per credit hour part-time. Part-time mandatory fees: $6 per credit hour. Full-time mandatory fees: $180.

Undergraduate Financial Aid: Of all full-time undergraduates enrolled in fall 1996, 86% of those who applied for aid were judged to have need according to Federal Methodology, of whom 93% were aided. On average, 49% of need was met. *Financial aid deadline (priority):* 3/1. *Financial aid forms:* FAFSA, institutional form required; CSS Financial Aid PROFILE acceptable.

LD Services Contact: Ms. Jodi Taylor, Coordinator, Indiana University Southeast, LB-006, New Albany, IN 47150-6405, 812-941-2243. Fax: 812-941-2556. Email: jetaylor@iusmail.ius.indiana.edu.

INDIANA WESLEYAN UNIVERSITY

Marion, Indiana

LEARNING DISABILITIES SERVICES INFORMATION

Student Support Services began offering services in 1981. Currently the program serves 20 undergraduates with LD. Students diagnosed with ADD/ADHD are eligible for the same services available to students with LD, as well as readers.

Staff: 3 full-time staff members, including director, assistant director, counselor. Services provided by remediation specialists, tutors, counselors.

Special Fees: No special fees are charged for services to students with LD.

Applications and admissions: *Required:* high school transcript, untimed SAT I or ACT, personal interview, letters of recommendation, psychoeducational report. Students may begin taking classes in fall or spring. *Application deadline:* continuous.

PROGRAM AND SERVICE COMPONENTS

Diagnostic testing: Reading, math, study skills, personality, learning strategies.

Academic advising: Provided by unit staff members, academic advisers. Students with LD may take up to 12 semester hours each term; most take 12 semester hours; 11 semester hours required to maintain full-time status; 12 semester hours required to be eligible for financial aid.

Counseling services: Individual counseling, career counseling.

Basic skills remediation: Offered one-on-one and in small groups by LD teachers. Available in reading, handwriting.

Subject-area tutoring: Offered one-on-one by peer tutors. Available in all subjects.

Special courses: Reading, vocabulary development. None offered for credit.

Auxiliary aids: Tape recorders, word-processors with spell-check, personal computers, talking computers, optical character readers.

Auxiliary services: Alternative test arrangements, notetakers, advocacy.

GENERAL COLLEGE INFORMATION

Independent Wesleyan, comprehensive, coed. Awards associate, bachelor's, master's degrees. Founded 1920. *Setting:* 132-acre small-town campus with easy access to Indianapolis. *Endowment:* $7 million. *Research spending 1995–96:* $2000. *Total enrollment:* 5,069. *Faculty:* 133 (83 full-time, 51% with terminal degrees, 50 part-time); student–undergrad faculty ratio is 17:1.

Enrollment Profile: 3,899 students from 47 states and territories, 16 other countries. 61% women, 39% men, 14% part-time, 61% state residents, 2% international, 20% 25 or older, 0% Native American, 2% Hispanic, 2% black, 1% Asian or Pacific Islander. *Retention:* 69% of 1995 full-time freshmen returned. *Areas of study chosen:* 17% health professions and related sciences, 14% education, 12% social sciences, 12% theology/religion, 6% fine arts, 6% psychology, 5% business management and administrative services, 4% biological and life sciences, 3% communications and journalism, 2% premed, 1% computer and information sciences, 1% English language/literature/letters, 1% performing arts. *Most popular recent majors:* nursing, psychology, ministries.

First-Year Class: 396 total; 1,099 applied, 72% were accepted, 50% of whom enrolled.

Graduation Requirements: 62 semester hours for associate, 124 semester hours for bachelor's; 7 semester hours of math/science including at least 4 semester hours of lab science; computer course for education, business-related majors; internship (some majors); senior project (some majors).

Computers on Campus: 70 computers available on campus for general student use. Computers for student use in computer center, computer labs, learning resource center, library, student center, dorms provide access to the Internet/World Wide Web. Staffed computer lab on campus provides training in use of computers, software. *Academic computing expenditure 1995–96:* $733,000.

EXPENSES AND FINANCIAL AID

Expenses for 1997–98: *Application fee:* $15. Comprehensive fee of $14,880 includes full-time tuition ($10,722) and college room and board ($4158). College room only: $1752. Part-time tuition per term ranges from $229 to $4235.

Undergraduate Financial Aid: 90% of all full-time undergraduates enrolled in fall 1996 applied for aid; of these, 95% were judged to have need according to Federal Methodology, of whom 100% were aided. *Financial aid deadline (priority):* 3/1. *Financial aid forms:* FAFSA, institutional form required.

LD Services Contact: Dr. Neil McFarlane, Director, The Center for Student Support Services, Indiana Wesleyan University, 4201 South Washington Street, Marion, IN 46953, 765-677-2257. Fax: 765-677-2140. Email: nmcfarla@indwes.edu.

IOWA STATE UNIVERSITY OF SCIENCE AND TECHNOLOGY

Ames, Iowa

LEARNING DISABILITIES SERVICES INFORMATION

Disability Resources, Dean of Students Office began offering services in 1989. Currently the program serves 200 undergraduates with LD. Services are also available to graduate students. Students diagnosed with ADD/ADHD are eligible for the same services available to students with LD, as well as support group.

Staff: 1 full-time, 2 part-time staff members, including coordinator. Services provided by LD specialist, graduate assistant.

Special Fees: $35 for diagnostic testing.

Applications and admissions: *Required:* high school transcript, grade point average, class rank, courses completed; *recommended:* extended time SAT I or ACT. Students may begin taking classes in fall, spring, or summer. *Application deadline:* continuous.

PROGRAM AND SERVICE COMPONENTS

Diagnostic testing: Intelligence, reading, math, spelling, motor abilities, perceptual skills, study skills, personality, psychoneurology, speech, hearing.

Academic advising: Provided by unit staff members, academic advisers. Most students with LD take 12 semester hours each term; 12 semester hours required to maintain full-time status and be eligible for financial aid.

Counseling services: Individual counseling, small-group counseling, career counseling, self-advocacy training.

Basic skills remediation: Offered one-on-one by LD teachers. Available in learning strategies, study skills, time management, social skills.

Subject-area tutoring: Offered one-on-one and in small groups by professional teachers, peer tutors, departmental tutors. Available in most subjects.

Auxiliary aids: Taped textbooks, tape recorders, calculators, word-processors with spell-check, personal computers, optical character readers, Arkenstone Reader.

Auxiliary services: Alternative test arrangements, notetakers, priority registration, advocacy, readers, test proctors, scribes, TDD/(515)294-1021.

Campus support group: A special student organization is available to students with LD.

GENERAL COLLEGE INFORMATION

State-supported, coed. Awards bachelor's, master's, doctoral, first professional degrees. Founded 1858. *Setting:* 1,736-acre suburban campus. *Endowment:* $161 million. *Research spending 1995–96:* $120 million. *Educational spending 1995–96:* $6461 per undergrad. *Total enrollment:* 24,899. *Faculty:* 1,568 (1,385 full-time, 90% with terminal degrees, 183 part-time); student–undergrad faculty ratio is 13:1.

Enrollment Profile: 20,503 students from 52 states and territories, 85 other countries. 43% women, 57% men, 9% part-time, 77% state residents, 34% live on campus, 29% transferred in, 6% international, 13% 25 or older, 0% Native American, 2% Hispanic, 3% black, 2% Asian or Pacific Islander. *Retention:* 82% of 1995 full-time freshmen returned. *Graduation:* 19% graduate in 4 years, 51% in 5 years, 60% in 6 years. *Areas of study chosen:* 20% engineering and applied sciences, 15% business management and administrative services, 10% education, 9% agriculture, 6% biological and life sciences, 6% liberal arts/general studies, 5% architecture, 4% fine arts, 4% social sciences, 3% communications and journalism, 3% computer and information sciences, 3% English language/literature/letters, 3% psychology, 3% vocational and home economics, 2% health professions and related sciences, 1% mathematics, 1% physical sciences, 1% premed, 1% prevet. *Most popular recent majors:* finance/banking, mechanical engineering, elementary education.

First-Year Class: 3,610 total; 8,990 applied, 90% were accepted, 44% of whom enrolled. 26% from top 10% of their high school class, 57% from top quarter, 91% from top half. 154 National Merit Scholars, 176 valedictorians.

Graduation Requirements: 120.5 semester hours; math/science requirements vary according to program; computer course for engineering, business, agriculture, most science majors; internship (some majors); senior project for honors program students and some majors.

Computers on Campus: 2,200 computers available on campus for general student use. Computer purchase/lease plans available. A computer is recommended for some students. A campus-wide network can be accessed from student residence rooms and from off-campus. Students can contact faculty members and/or advisers through e-mail. Computers for student use in computer center, computer labs, learning resource center, classrooms, library, student center, dorms provide access to the Internet/World Wide Web, on- and off-campus e-mail addresses. Staffed computer lab on campus (open 24 hours a day) provides training in use of computers, software. *Academic computing expenditure 1995–96:* $6 million.

EXPENSES AND FINANCIAL AID

Expenses for 1997–98: *Application fee:* $20. State resident tuition: $2566 full-time. Nonresident tuition: $8608 full-time. Part-time tuition per semester ranges from $214 to $1177 for state residents, $214 to $3949 for nonresidents. Part-time mandatory fees per semester range from $57 to $97. Full-time mandatory fees: $200 (minimum). College room and board: $3647. College room only: $1879.

Undergraduate Financial Aid: 70% of all full-time undergraduates enrolled in fall 1996 applied for aid; of these, 82% were judged to have need according to Federal Methodology, of whom 100% were aided. On average, 100% of need was met. *Financial aid deadline (priority):* 3/1. *Financial aid forms:* FAFSA required.

LD Services Contact: Ms. Gwen Woodward, Learning Disabilities Specialist, Iowa State University of Science and Technology, 210 Student Services Building, Ames, IA 50011-2222, 515-294-1020. Fax: 515-294-5670.

IOWA WESLEYAN COLLEGE

Mount Pleasant, Iowa

LEARNING DISABILITIES SERVICES INFORMATION

Learning Center began offering services in 1980. Currently the program serves 5 undergraduates with LD. Students diagnosed with ADD/ADHD are eligible for the same services available to students with LD.

Staff: Includes director, assistant director. Services provided by tutors, counselors.

Special Fees: No special fees are charged for services to students with LD.

Applications and admissions: *Required:* high school transcript, grade point average, class rank, courses completed, untimed ACT; *recommended:* psychoeducational report. Students may begin taking classes in fall, winter, or spring. *Application deadline:* continuous.

PROGRAM AND SERVICE COMPONENTS

Academic advising: Provided by unit staff members, academic advisers. Students with LD may take up to 15 credit hours each term; most take 12 credit hours; 10 credit hours required to maintain full-time status; 12 credit hours required to be eligible for financial aid.

Counseling services: Career counseling.

Basic skills remediation: Offered one-on-one and in small groups by regular teachers; computer-aided instruction also offered. Available in reading, spelling, spoken language, written language, learning strategies, study skills, time management, speech.

Subject-area tutoring: Offered one-on-one and in small groups by professional teachers, peer tutors. Available in some subjects.

Special courses: College survival skills, reading, vocabulary development, communication skills, composition, learning strategies, time management, study skills. All offered for credit.

Auxiliary aids: Word-processors with spell-check.

Auxiliary services: Alternative test arrangements, notetakers.

GENERAL COLLEGE INFORMATION

Independent United Methodist, 4-year, coed. Awards bachelor's degrees. Founded 1842. *Setting:* 60-acre small-town campus. *Endowment:* $5.1 million. *Educational spending 1995–96:* $2972 per undergrad. *Total enrollment:* 794. *Faculty:* 56 (37 full-time, 41% with terminal degrees, 19 part-time); student–undergrad faculty ratio is 12:1.

Enrollment Profile: 794 students from 22 states and territories, 11 other countries. 62% women, 38% men, 44% part-time, 79% state residents, 62% transferred in, 3% international, 51% 25 or older, 0% Native American, 2% Hispanic, 8% black, 2% Asian or Pacific Islander. *Retention:* 48% of 1995 full-time freshmen returned. *Graduation:* 30% graduate in 4 years, 44% in 5 years, 46% in 6 years. *Areas of study chosen:* 23% business management and administrative services, 16% health professions and related sciences, 13% education, 7% social sciences, 6% psychology, 5% biological and life sciences, 3% fine arts, 2% communications and journalism, 2% computer and information sciences, 2% English language/literature/letters, 1% interdisciplinary studies, 1% mathematics, 1% physical sciences, 1% premed. *Most popular recent majors:* business administration/commerce/management, elementary education, nursing.

First-Year Class: 103 total; 336 applied, 83% were accepted, 37% of whom enrolled. 2% from top 10% of their high school class, 16% from top quarter, 57% from top half.

Graduation Requirements: 124 credit hours; 1 problem-solving course; computer course; internship; senior project (some majors).

Computers on Campus: 43 computers available on campus for general student use. Students can contact faculty members and/or advisers through e-mail. Computers for student use in library, academic buildings. Staffed computer lab on campus provides training in use of computers, software. *Academic computing expenditure 1995–96:* $35,000.

EXPENSES AND FINANCIAL AID

Expenses for 1997–98: *Application fee:* $15. Comprehensive fee of $15,540 includes full-time tuition ($11,640) and college room and board ($3900). Part-time tuition: $270 per credit hour. Part-time tuition for evening students: $180 per credit hour.

Undergraduate Financial Aid: 98% of all full-time undergraduates enrolled in fall 1996 applied for aid; of these, 97% were judged to have need according to Federal Methodology, of whom 100% were aided. On average, 85% of need was met. *Financial aid deadline (priority):* 4/1. *Financial aid forms:* FAFSA required.

Iowa Wesleyan College (continued)

LD Services Contact: Ms. Linda C. Widmer, Director, Learning Center, Iowa Wesleyan College, 601 North Main Street, Mount Pleasant, IA 52641-1398, 319-385-6332.

JAMES MADISON UNIVERSITY

Harrisonburg, Virginia

LEARNING DISABILITIES SERVICES INFORMATION

Office of Disability Services began offering services in 1981. Currently the program serves 122 undergraduates with LD. Services are also available to graduate students. Students diagnosed with ADD/ADHD are eligible for the same services available to students with LD.

Staff: 1 full-time staff member (coordinator). Services provided by student employees, volunteers, graduate assistants.

Special Fees: No special fees are charged for services to students with LD.

Applications and admissions: *Required:* high school transcript, grade point average, class rank, courses completed, untimed SAT I, autobiographical statement; *recommended:* high school extracurricular activities, extended time SAT I. Students may begin taking classes any term. *Application deadline:* 1/15 (fall term), 11/1 (spring term).

Special policies: The college has written policies regarding grade forgiveness; substitutions and waivers of graduation and degree requirements.

PROGRAM AND SERVICE COMPONENTS

Academic advising: Provided by unit staff members, academic advisers. Most students with LD take 12 credit hours each term; 12 credit hours required to maintain full-time status and be eligible for financial aid.

Counseling services: Individual counseling, small-group counseling, career counseling, self-advocacy training.

Subject-area tutoring: Offered one-on-one by peer tutors. Available in some subjects.

Special courses: Learning strategies, self-determination skills. None offered for credit.

Auxiliary aids: Taped textbooks, tape recorders, typewriters, word-processors with spell-check, optical character readers, Arkenstone Reader.

Auxiliary services: Alternative test arrangements, notetakers, priority registration, advocacy, mentor program, specialized academic advising, academic support services, reading and writing support labs, math lab.

GENERAL COLLEGE INFORMATION

State-supported, comprehensive, coed. Awards bachelor's, master's, doctoral degrees. Founded 1908. *Setting:* 472-acre small-town campus. *Endowment:* $10.5 million. *Research spending 1995–96:* $778,450. *Educational spending 1995–96:* $3695 per undergrad. *Total enrollment:* 12,963. *Faculty:* 758 (559 full-time, 80% with terminal degrees, 199 part-time); student–undergrad faculty ratio is 19:1.

Enrollment Profile: 11,643 students from 48 states and territories, 49 other countries. 55% women, 45% men, 4% part-time, 68% state residents, 49% live on campus, 5% transferred in, 1% international, 4% 25 or older, 1% Native American, 2% Hispanic, 5% black, 4% Asian or Pacific Islander. *Retention:* 90% of 1995 full-time freshmen returned. *Graduation:* 58% graduate in 4 years, 80% in 5 years, 81% in 6 years. *Areas of study chosen:* 20% business management and administrative services, 18% social sciences, 11% psychology, 9% health professions and related sciences, 8% communications and journalism, 7% English language/literature/letters, 6% fine arts, 5% biological and life sciences, 5% computer and information sciences, 3% physical sciences, 2% education, 1% foreign language and literature, 1% liberal arts/general studies, 1% mathematics, 1% vocational and home economics. *Most popular recent majors:* psychology, biology/biological sciences, English.

First-Year Class: 3,258 total; 13,322 applied, 63% were accepted, 39% of whom enrolled. 5 National Merit Scholars.

Graduation Requirements: 120 credit hours; 3 credit hours of math; 6 credit hours of natural science; computer course; internship (some majors); senior project for honors program students and some majors.

Computers on Campus: 500 computers available on campus for general student use. Computer purchase/lease plans available. A campus-wide network can be accessed from student residence rooms and from off-campus. Students can contact faculty members and/or advisers through e-mail. Computers for student use in computer center, computer labs, classrooms, library, dorms, academic buildings provide access to the Internet/World Wide Web, on- and off-campus e-mail addresses. Staffed computer lab on campus (open 24 hours a day) provides training in use of computers, software.

EXPENSES AND FINANCIAL AID

Expenses for 1997–98: *Application fee:* $25. State resident tuition: $4148 full-time. Nonresident tuition: $8816 full-time. Part-time tuition per semester ranges from $271 to $1721 for state residents, $739 to $3446 for nonresidents. College room and board: $4846. College room only: $2612.

Undergraduate Financial Aid: On average, 70% of need was met. *Financial aid deadline (priority):* 2/15. *Financial aid forms:* FAFSA required; CSS Financial Aid PROFILE acceptable. Financial aid transcript (for transfers) required for some.

LD Services Contact: Mr. Lou Hedrick, Coordinator, Office of Disability Services, James Madison University, Harrisonburg, VA 22807, 540-568-6705. Fax: 540-568-3780. Email: hedriclj@jmu.edu.

JOHN JAY COLLEGE OF CRIMINAL JUSTICE, THE CITY UNIVERSITY OF NEW YORK

New York, New York

LEARNING DISABILITIES SERVICES INFORMATION

Office of Services for Students with Learning Disabilities currently serves undergraduate and graduate students with LD. Students diagnosed with ADD/ADHD are eligible for the same services available to students with LD.

Staff: 3 full-time, 9 part-time staff members, including director, coordinator. Services provided by tutors, counselor, diagnostic specialist.

Special Fees: No special fees are charged for services to students with LD.

Applications and admissions: *Recommended:* high school IEP (Individualized Education Program). Students may begin taking classes in fall, spring, or summer. *Application deadline:* continuous.

PROGRAM AND SERVICE COMPONENTS

Special preparation or orientation: Optional orientation offered before registration.

Diagnostic testing: Intelligence, reading, math, foreign language.

Academic advising: Most students with LD take 9 to 15 credit hours each term; 12 credit hours required to maintain full-time status.

Counseling services: Individual counseling, small-group counseling, career counseling.

Subject-area tutoring: Offered one-on-one, in small groups, and in class-size groups by professional teachers, peer tutors. Available in some subjects.

Special courses: Composition.

Auxiliary aids: Optical character readers.

Auxiliary services: Alternative test arrangements, notetakers, priority registration, support groups.

GENERAL COLLEGE INFORMATION

State and locally supported, comprehensive, coed. Part of City University of New York System. Awards associate, bachelor's, master's degrees. Founded 1964. *Setting:* urban campus. *Total enrollment:* 10,724. *Undergraduate faculty:* 689 (205 full-time, 85% with terminal degrees, 484 part-time); student–undergrad faculty ratio is 18:1.

Enrollment Profile: 9,790 students from 10 states and territories, 12 other countries. 53% women, 47% men, 29% part-time, 97% state residents, 35% transferred in, 1% international, 35% 25 or older, 1% Native American, 34% Hispanic, 29% black, 3% Asian or Pacific Islander. *Retention:* 72% of 1995 full-time freshmen returned. *Most popular recent majors:* criminal justice, public administration, forensic sciences.

First-Year Class: 1,812 total. Of the students accepted, 54% enrolled. 20% from top quarter of their high school class, 66% from top half.

Graduation Requirements: 60 credits for associate, 120 credits for bachelor's; 6 credits of math; 8 credits of science or the equivalent; 1 year of a foreign language or the equivalent; computer course for legal studies, public administration majors.

Computers on Campus: 250 computers available on campus for general student use. A campus-wide network can be accessed from off-campus. Students can contact faculty members and/or advisers through e-mail. Computers for student use in computer center, computer labs, library provide access to the Internet/World Wide Web. Staffed computer lab on campus provides training in use of computers, software.

EXPENSES AND FINANCIAL AID

Expenses for 1996–97: *Application fee:* $40. Part-time mandatory fees: $44.85 per semester. Full-time tuition ranges from $2950 to $3200 for state residents, $6550 to $6800 for nonresidents, according to class level. Part-time tuition per credit ranges from $125 to $135 for state residents, $275 to $285 for nonresidents, according to class level. Full-time mandatory fees: $109.

Undergraduate Financial Aid: On average, 85% of need was met. *Financial aid deadline (priority):* 6/30. *Financial aid forms:* FAFSA required.

LD Services Contact: Farris Forsythe, Director of Services for Students, John Jay College of Criminal Justice, the City University of New York, 449 West 59th Street, New York, NY 10019, 212-237-8122. Fax: 212-237-8742.

JOHNSON & WALES UNIVERSITY

North Miami, Florida

LEARNING DISABILITIES SERVICES INFORMATION

Department of Student Success currently serves 60 undergraduates with LD. Students diagnosed with ADD/ADHD are eligible for the same services available to students with LD.

Staff: 1 full-time staff member (director). Services provided by tutors, counselor.

Special Fees: No special fees are charged for services to students with LD.

Applications and admissions: *Required:* high school transcript; *recommended:* high school class rank, extracurricular activities, IEP (Individualized Education Program), untimed or extended time SAT I or ACT, psychoeducational report completed within 3 years. Students may begin taking classes in fall only. *Application deadline:* continuous.

PROGRAM AND SERVICE COMPONENTS

Academic advising: Provided by unit staff members. Students with LD may take up to 18 quarter credit hours each term; most take 15 quarter credit hours; 12 quarter credit hours required to maintain full-time status; 6 quarter credit hours required to be eligible for financial aid.

Counseling services: Individual counseling, career counseling.

Basic skills remediation: Available in math, spelling, written language, computer skills.

Subject-area tutoring: Offered one-on-one and in small groups by professional teachers, peer tutors. Available in all subjects.

Auxiliary services: Alternative test arrangements, notetakers, priority registration, advocacy.

GENERAL COLLEGE INFORMATION

Independent, 4-year, coed. Administratively affiliated with Johnson & Wales University (RI). Awards associate, bachelor's degrees. Founded 1992. *Setting:* 8-acre suburban campus with easy access to Miami. *System endowment:* $57.2 million. *Educational spending 1995–96:* $6056 per undergrad. *Total enrollment:* 875. *Faculty:* 31 (21 full-time, 10 part-time); student–undergrad faculty ratio is 22:1.

Enrollment Profile: 875 students from 36 states and territories, 5 other countries. 34% women, 66% men, 4% part-time, 69% state residents, 37% live on campus, 40% transferred in, 4% international, 36% 25 or older, 1% Native American, 23% Hispanic, 17% black, 2% Asian or Pacific Islander. *Retention:* 63% of 1995 full-time freshmen returned. *Areas of study chosen:* 88% vocational and home economics. *Most popular recent major:* culinary arts.

First-Year Class: 386 total; 1,237 applied, 76% were accepted, 41% of whom enrolled.

Graduation Requirements: 99 quarter credit hours for associate, 193.5 quarter credit hours for bachelor's; internship (some majors).

Computers on Campus: 26 computers available on campus for general student use. A campus-wide network can be accessed from off-campus. Computers for student use in computer labs, learning resource center, library provide access to the Internet/World Wide Web. Staffed computer lab on campus provides training in use of computers, software.

EXPENSES AND FINANCIAL AID

Expenses for 1997–98: Tuition: $11,526 (minimum) full-time, $96 per credit hour part-time. Full-time tuition ranges up to $14,376 according to program. Full-time mandatory fees: $426. College room only: $3180.

Undergraduate Financial Aid: 78% of all full-time undergraduates enrolled in fall 1996 applied for aid; of these, 91% were judged to have need according to Federal Methodology, of whom 98% were aided. On average, 67% of need was met. *Financial aid deadline (priority):* 5/1. *Financial aid forms:* FAFSA required.

LD Services Contact: Ms. Susan Rosbottom, Director, Student Success, Johnson & Wales University, 1701 Northeast 127th Street, North Miami, FL 33181, 305-892-7046. Fax: 305-892-7019.

JOHNSON & WALES UNIVERSITY

Providence, Rhode Island

LEARNING DISABILITIES SERVICES INFORMATION

Special Needs began offering services in 1984. Currently the program serves 550 undergraduates with LD. Services are also available to graduate students. Students diagnosed with ADD/ADHD are eligible for the same services available to students with LD.

Staff: 4 full-time, 2 part-time staff members, including director. Services provided by tutors, counselors.

Special Fees: No special fees are charged for services to students with LD.

Applications and admissions: *Required:* high school transcript, grade point average, courses completed; *recommended:* high school class rank, extracurricular activities. Students may begin taking classes any term. *Application deadline:* continuous.

PROGRAM AND SERVICE COMPONENTS

Special preparation or orientation: Optional orientation offered before registration.

Academic advising: Provided by academic advisers. Students with LD may take up to 18 credit hours each term; most take 13.5 credit hours.

Counseling services: Individual counseling, career counseling, self-advocacy training.

Basic skills remediation: Offered one-on-one, in small groups, and in class-size groups by Special Needs Coordinator, tutors. Available in reading, math, spelling, written language, learning strategies, perceptual skills, study skills, time management, social skills, speech, computer skills.

Subject-area tutoring: Offered one-on-one and in small groups by professional teachers, peer tutors, Learning Center staff. Available in all subjects.

Auxiliary aids: Taped textbooks, typewriters, word-processors with spell-check.

Auxiliary services: Alternative test arrangements, notetakers, priority registration, advocacy.

Campus support group: A special student organization is available to students with LD.

GENERAL COLLEGE INFORMATION

Independent, comprehensive, coed. Awards associate, bachelor's, master's, doctoral degrees (branch locations: Charleston, SC; Vail, CO; North Miami, FL; Norfolk, VA; Worcester, MA; Gothenberg, Sweden). Founded 1914. *Setting:* 47-acre urban campus with easy access to Boston. *System endowment:* $57.2 million. *Educational spending 1995–96:* $3257 per undergrad. *Total enrollment:* 7,851. *Faculty:* 319 (229 full-time, 21% with terminal degrees, 90 part-time); student–undergrad faculty ratio is 30:1.

Enrollment Profile: 7,266 students from 50 states and territories, 77 other countries. 47% women, 53% men, 15% part-time, 16% state residents, 41% live on campus, 20% transferred in, 9% international, 11% 25 or older, 0% Native American, 5% Hispanic, 10% black, 2% Asian or Pacific Islander. *Retention:* 64% of 1995 full-time freshmen returned. *Graduation:* 72% graduate in 4 years, 80% in 5 years, 82% in 6 years. *Areas of study chosen:* 34% vocational and home economics, 25% business management and administrative services, 4% communications and journalism, 3% computer and information sciences, 2% engineering and applied sciences, 1% health professions and related sciences. *Most popular recent majors:* culinary arts, hotel and restaurant management, hospitality services.

First-Year Class: 2,310 total; 15,267 applied, 86% were accepted, 18% of whom enrolled.

Graduation Requirements: 90 credit hours for associate, 180 credit hours for bachelor's; 2 math/science courses; computer course for all majors except culinary arts, pastry arts; internship (some majors); senior project (some majors).

Johnson & Wales University (continued)

Computers on Campus: 340 computers available on campus for general student use. A campus-wide network can be accessed from off-campus. Students can contact faculty members and/or advisers through e-mail. Computers for student use in computer center, computer labs, learning resource center, classrooms, library provide access to the Internet/World Wide Web, on- and off-campus e-mail addresses. Staffed computer lab on campus provides training in use of computers, software.

EXPENSES AND FINANCIAL AID

Expenses for 1997–98: Comprehensive fee of $17,289 includes full-time tuition ($11,526 minimum), mandatory fees ($426), and college room and board ($5337 minimum). Part-time tuition: $96 per credit hour. Full-time tuition ranges up to $14,376 according to program.

Undergraduate Financial Aid: 74% of all full-time undergraduates enrolled in fall 1996 applied for aid; of these, 91% were judged to have need according to Federal Methodology, of whom 98% were aided. On average, 65% of need was met. *Financial aid deadline (priority):* 5/1. *Financial aid forms:* FAFSA required.

LD Services Contact: Ms. Meryl Berstein, Director of Learning Centers and Academic Support, Johnson & Wales University, 8 Abbott Park Place, Providence, RI 02903, 401-598-4689. Fax: 401-598-4657. Email: mert@loa.com.

JOHNSON C. SMITH UNIVERSITY

Charlotte, North Carolina

LEARNING DISABILITIES SERVICES INFORMATION

Student Support Services began offering services in 1990. Currently the program serves 5 undergraduates with LD. Students diagnosed with ADD/ADHD are not eligible for the same services available to students with LD.

Staff: 3 part-time staff members, including director, coordinator. Services provided by tutor.

Special Fees: No special fees are charged for services to students with LD.

Applications and admissions: *Required:* high school transcript, grade point average, class rank, courses completed, extracurricular activities; *recommended:* high school IEP (Individualized Education Program), untimed or extended time SAT I or ACT, personal interview, autobiographical statement, letters of recommendation, psychoeducational report. Students may begin taking classes in fall only. *Application deadline:* continuous.

PROGRAM AND SERVICE COMPONENTS

Diagnostic testing: Various areas as appropriate.

Academic advising: Provided by academic advisers. Students with LD may take up to 15 semester hours each term; most take 12 semester hours; 12 semester hours (9 with special permission) required to maintain full-time status and be eligible for financial aid.

Subject-area tutoring: Offered one-on-one by professional teachers, peer tutors. Available in all subjects.

Auxiliary aids: Taped textbooks, tape recorders, calculators, typewriters, word-processors with spell-check.

Auxiliary services: Alternative test arrangements, notetakers, priority registration, advocacy.

GENERAL COLLEGE INFORMATION

Independent, 4-year, coed. Awards bachelor's degrees. Founded 1867. *Setting:* 105-acre urban campus. *Endowment:* $14.9 million. *Educational spending 1995–96:* $3055 per undergrad. *Total enrollment:* 1,427. *Faculty:* 88 (81 full-time, 74% with terminal degrees, 7 part-time); student–undergrad faculty ratio is 17:1.

Enrollment Profile: 1,427 students from 30 states and territories, 2 other countries. 58% women, 42% men, 6% part-time, 19% state residents, 77% live on campus, 4% transferred in, 6% 25 or older, 100% black. *Retention:* 67% of 1995 full-time freshmen returned. *Areas of study chosen:* 19% social sciences, 17% business management and administrative services, 10% communications and journalism, 10% education, 10% psychology, 7% biological and life sciences, 7% English language/literature/letters, 5% computer and information sciences, 5% fine arts, 2% engineering and applied sciences, 2% health professions and related sciences, 2% mathematics, 2% physical sciences, 2% prelaw. *Most popular recent majors:* business administration/commerce/management, communication, computer science.

First-Year Class: 394 total; 2,132 applied, 61% were accepted, 30% of whom enrolled. 7% from top 10% of their high school class, 25% from top quarter, 48% from top half.

Graduation Requirements: 122 semester hours; 6 semester hours of math; 8 semester hours of science; 6 semester hours of a foreign language; computer course; internship (some majors); senior project.

Computers on Campus: 250 computers available on campus for general student use. Computer purchase/lease plans available. A computer is recommended for some students. A campus-wide network can be accessed from student residence rooms and from off-campus. Students can contact faculty members and/or advisers through e-mail. Computers for student use in computer labs, learning resource center, library, dorms. Staffed computer lab on campus provides training in use of computers, software. *Academic computing expenditure 1995–96:* $36,488.

EXPENSES AND FINANCIAL AID

Expenses for 1997–98: *Application fee:* $20. Comprehensive fee of $11,797 includes full-time tuition ($7702), mandatory fees ($767), and college room and board ($3328). Part-time tuition: $187 per semester hour. Part-time mandatory fees: $383.50 per semester.

Undergraduate Financial Aid: On average, 100% of need was met. *Financial aid deadline (priority):* 5/1. *Financial aid forms:* FAFSA required.

LD Services Contact: Mr. James Cuthbertson, Disability Services Coordinator, Johnson C. Smith University, 100 Beatties Ford Road, Charlotte, NC 28216, 704-378-1282. Fax: 704-378-1181.

JOHNSON STATE COLLEGE

Johnson, Vermont

LEARNING DISABILITIES SERVICES INFORMATION

Student Support Services began offering services in 1975. Currently the program serves 50 undergraduates with LD. Services are also available to graduate students. Students diagnosed with ADD/ADHD are eligible for the same services available to students with LD.

Staff: 4 full-time, 2 part-time staff members, including director, coordinators. Services provided by tutors, counselor, diagnostic specialist.

Special Fees: No special fees are charged for services to students with LD.

Applications and admissions: *Required:* high school transcript, grade point average, courses completed, untimed SAT I or ACT, letters of recommendation, psychoeducational report completed within 3 years, essay; *recommended:* high school class rank, extracurricular activities, extended time SAT I or ACT, personal interview, autobiographical statement. Students may begin taking classes in summer only. *Application deadline:* continuous.

Special policies: The college has written policies regarding grade forgiveness; substitutions and waivers of admissions, graduation, and degree requirements.

PROGRAM AND SERVICE COMPONENTS

Diagnostic testing: Reading, math, spelling, handwriting, spoken language, written language, motor abilities, perceptual skills, learning strategies, attention skills.

Academic advising: Provided by unit staff members, academic advisers. Students with LD may take up to 18 credits each term; most take 12 to 15 credits; 12 credits required to maintain full-time status and be eligible for financial aid.

Counseling services: Individual counseling, small-group counseling, career counseling, self-advocacy training.

Subject-area tutoring: Offered one-on-one, in small groups, and in class-size groups by peer tutors. Available in all subjects.

Special courses: College survival skills, reading, composition. Some offered for credit; all enter into overall grade point average.

Auxiliary aids: Taped textbooks, tape recorders, typewriters, word-processors with spell-check, personal computers, Franklin Spellers.

Auxiliary services: Alternative test arrangements, notetakers, advocacy, readers, scribes.

Campus support group: A special student organization is available to students with LD.

GENERAL COLLEGE INFORMATION

State-supported, comprehensive, coed. Part of Vermont State Colleges System. Awards associate, bachelor's, master's degrees. Founded 1828. *Setting:* 350-acre rural campus with easy access to Montreal. *Endowment:* $414,000. *Educational spending 1995–96:* $3150 per undergrad.

Total enrollment: 1,591. *Faculty:* 114 (66 full-time, 80% with terminal degrees, 48 part-time); student–undergrad faculty ratio is 18:1.
Enrollment Profile: 1,313 students from 24 states and territories, 6 other countries. 54% women, 46% men, 20% part-time, 72% state residents, 27% transferred in, 2% international, 30% 25 or older, 2% Native American, 1% Hispanic, 1% black, 1% Asian or Pacific Islander. *Retention:* 51% of 1995 full-time freshmen returned. *Graduation:* 24% graduate in 4 years, 40% in 5 years, 42% in 6 years. *Areas of study chosen:* 20% interdisciplinary studies, 12% business management and administrative services, 11% education, 11% liberal arts/general studies, 8% natural resource sciences, 7% health professions and related sciences, 6% psychology, 5% English language/literature/letters, 5% fine arts, 5% performing arts, 5% social sciences, 4% biological and life sciences, 1% mathematics. *Most popular recent majors:* biology/biological sciences, education, business administration/commerce/management.
First-Year Class: 273 total; 761 applied, 88% were accepted, 41% of whom enrolled. 2% from top 10% of their high school class, 15% from top quarter, 46% from top half.
Graduation Requirements: 60 credits for associate, 120 credits for bachelor's; 2 math courses; 1 lab science course; computer course for business majors; internship (some majors); senior project (some majors).
Computers on Campus: 131 computers available on campus for general student use. A computer is recommended for all students. A campus-wide network can be accessed from student residence rooms and from off-campus. Students can contact faculty members and/or advisers through e-mail. Computers for student use in computer center, computer labs, learning resource center, classrooms, library, student center, dorms provide access to the Internet/World Wide Web, on- and off-campus e-mail addresses. Staffed computer lab on campus provides training in use of computers, software. *Academic computing expenditure 1995–96:* $147,640.

EXPENSES AND FINANCIAL AID

Expenses for 1997–98: *Application fee:* $30. State resident tuition: $3780 full-time, $158 per credit part-time. Nonresident tuition: $8760 full-time, $365 per credit part-time. Part-time mandatory fees per semester range from $110.10 to $325.60. Tuition for nonresidents who are eligible for the New England Regional Student Program: $5688 full-time, $237 per credit part-time. Full-time mandatory fees: $736. College room and board: $5086. College room only: $2928.
Undergraduate Financial Aid: 93% of all full-time undergraduates enrolled in fall 1996 applied for aid; of these, 95% were judged to have need according to Federal Methodology, of whom 100% were aided. On average, 73% of need was met. *Financial aid deadline (priority):* 3/1. *Financial aid forms:* FAFSA required; state form acceptable.
LD Services Contact: Ms. Sara Henry, Learning Specialist, Johnson State College, RR2, Box 75, Johnson, VT 05656, 802-635-1259. Fax: 802-635-1248. Email: henrys@badger.jsc.vsc.edu.

KANSAS CITY ART INSTITUTE

Kansas City, Missouri

LEARNING DISABILITIES SERVICES INFORMATION

Academic Resource Center currently serves 25 undergraduates with LD. Students diagnosed with ADD/ADHD are eligible for the same services available to students with LD.
Staff: 1 full-time, 1 part-time staff members, including director, learning specialist.
Special Fees: No special fees are charged for services to students with LD.
Applications and admissions: *Required:* high school transcript, grade point average, class rank, courses completed, untimed SAT I or ACT, letters of recommendation; *recommended:* high school extracurricular activities, extended time SAT I or ACT, personal interview, autobiographical statement, psychoeducational report completed within 3 years. Students may begin taking classes in fall or spring. *Application deadline:* continuous.

PROGRAM AND SERVICE COMPONENTS

Special preparation or orientation: Optional orientation offered individually by special arrangement.
Diagnostic testing: Intelligence, reading, spoken language, written language, personality, learning strategies, general intellectual ability (WAIS-R).
Academic advising: Provided by unit staff members, academic advisers. Students with LD may take up to 18 credit hours each term; most take 12 to 15 credit hours; 12 credit hours required to maintain full-time status and be eligible for financial aid.
Counseling services: Individual counseling, career counseling.
Basic skills remediation: Offered one-on-one and in small groups by LD teachers, regular teachers, professional tutors. Available in reading, spelling, written language, learning strategies, study skills, time management, social skills.
Subject-area tutoring: Offered one-on-one and in small groups by Liberal Arts instructors, professional tutors. Available in most subjects.
Auxiliary aids: Taped textbooks, tape recorders, typewriters, word-processors with spell-check.
Auxiliary services: Alternative test arrangements, advocacy.

GENERAL COLLEGE INFORMATION

Independent, 4-year, specialized, coed. Awards bachelor's degrees. Founded 1885. *Setting:* 12-acre urban campus. *Endowment:* $11.1 million. *Educational spending 1995–96:* $4852 per undergrad. *Total enrollment:* 598. *Faculty:* 75 (47 full-time, 98% with terminal degrees, 28 part-time); student–undergrad faculty ratio is 12:1.
Enrollment Profile: 598 students from 42 states and territories, 11 other countries. 44% women, 56% men, 3% part-time, 24% state residents, 25% live on campus, 17% transferred in, 2% international, 96% 25 or older, 1% Native American, 5% Hispanic, 2% black, 3% Asian or Pacific Islander. *Retention:* 87% of 1995 full-time freshmen returned. *Graduation:* 33% graduate in 4 years, 43% in 5 years, 46% in 6 years. *Areas of study chosen:* 100% fine arts.
First-Year Class: 146 total; 397 applied, 70% were accepted, 52% of whom enrolled.
Graduation Requirements: 129 credit hours; internship (some majors); senior project.
Computers on Campus: 50 computers available on campus for general student use. Computers for student use in computer center, learning resource center, classrooms, library, CAD, computer graphics, photo, visual departmental labs provide access to the Internet/World Wide Web. Staffed computer lab on campus provides training in use of computers, software. *Academic computing expenditure 1995–96:* $72,000.

EXPENSES AND FINANCIAL AID

Expenses for 1997–98: *Application fee:* $25. Comprehensive fee of $21,015 includes full-time tuition ($16,320) and college room and board ($4695).
Undergraduate Financial Aid: 95% of all full-time undergraduates enrolled in fall 1996 applied for aid; of these, 84% were judged to have need according to Federal Methodology, of whom 100% were aided. *Financial aid deadline (priority):* 2/15. *Financial aid forms:* FAFSA required.
LD Services Contact: Ms. Mary Majors, Director, Academic Resource Center, Kansas City Art Institute, 4415 Warwick Boulevard, Kansas City, MO 64111-1820, 816-561-4852 Ext. 264. Fax: 816-561-6404.

KENDALL COLLEGE OF ART AND DESIGN

Grand Rapids, Michigan

LEARNING DISABILITIES SERVICES INFORMATION

Counseling Office, Student Affairs began offering services in 1989. Currently the program serves 7 undergraduates with LD. Students diagnosed with ADD/ADHD are eligible for the same services available to students with LD.
Staff: 1 full-time staff member (coordinator). Services provided by tutors, counselor.
Special Fees: No special fees are charged for services to students with LD.
Applications and admissions: *Required:* high school transcript, untimed SAT I or ACT, personal interview, autobiographical statement; *recommended:* high school grade point average, letters of recommendation, psychoeducational report completed within 2 years. Students may begin taking classes any term. *Application deadline:* continuous.

PROGRAM AND SERVICE COMPONENTS

Special preparation or orientation: Optional orientation offered individually by special arrangement.

Kendall College of Art and Design (continued)

Academic advising: Provided by academic advisers. Students with LD may take up to 12 credits each term; most take 12 credits; 12 credits required to maintain full-time status; 6 credits required to be eligible for financial aid.
Counseling services: Individual counseling.
Basic skills remediation: Offered one-on-one by counselor, tutor. Available in learning strategies, study skills, time management, social skills.
Subject-area tutoring: Offered one-on-one and in small groups by peer tutors. Available in all subjects.
Special courses: College survival skills, learning strategies, time management, study skills, career planning. None offered for credit.
Auxiliary aids: Typewriters, word-processors with spell-check, personal computers.
Auxiliary services: Alternative test arrangements, notetakers, advocacy.

GENERAL COLLEGE INFORMATION

Independent, 4-year, specialized, coed. Awards bachelor's degrees. Founded 1928. *Setting:* urban campus. *Endowment:* $1.5 million. *Educational spending 1995–96:* $3704 per undergrad. *Total enrollment:* 527. *Faculty:* 59 (26 full-time, 54% with terminal degrees, 33 part-time); student–undergrad faculty ratio is 11:1.
Enrollment Profile: 527 students from 15 states and territories, 10 other countries. 52% women, 48% men, 33% part-time, 91% state residents, 45% transferred in, 3% international, 36% 25 or older, 1% Native American, 2% Hispanic, 4% black, 2% Asian or Pacific Islander. *Retention:* 59% of 1995 full-time freshmen returned. *Graduation:* 30% graduate in 4 years, 36% in 5 years. *Areas of study chosen:* 100% fine arts. *Most popular recent majors:* communication, illustration, interior design.
First-Year Class: 88 total; 217 applied, 72% were accepted, 56% of whom enrolled. 3% from top 10% of their high school class, 16% from top quarter, 54% from top half.
Graduation Requirements: 120 credits; 3 credits of math/science; computer course for illustration, interior design, visual communication, furniture design, industrial design majors.
Computers on Campus: 100 computers available on campus for general student use. Computer purchase/lease plans available. A computer is recommended for some students. Computers for student use in computer center, classrooms, library provide access to the Internet/World Wide Web. Staffed computer lab on campus provides training in use of computers, software. *Academic computing expenditure 1995–96:* $78,248.

EXPENSES AND FINANCIAL AID

Estimated Expenses for 1997–98: *Application fee:* $35. Tuition: $10,500 full-time, $350 per credit part-time. Part-time mandatory fees: $25 per semester. Full-time mandatory fees: $50.
Undergraduate Financial Aid: 89% of all full-time undergraduates enrolled in fall 1996 applied for aid; of these, 80% were judged to have need according to Federal Methodology, of whom 100% were aided. On average, 74% of need was met. *Financial aid deadline (priority):* 2/21. *Financial aid forms:* FAFSA required; CSS Financial Aid PROFILE acceptable. State form required for some.
LD Services Contact: Ms. Kathy Jordan, Counselor, Kendall College of Art and Design, 111 Division Avenue North, Grand Rapids, MI 49503, 616-451-2787 Ext. 136.

KENT STATE UNIVERSITY

Kent, Ohio

LEARNING DISABILITIES SERVICES INFORMATION

Student Disability Services currently serves 230 undergraduates with LD. Services are also available to graduate students. Students diagnosed with ADD/ADHD are eligible for the same services available to students with LD, as well as seminars with psychologists regarding living skills and medication management.
Staff: 2 full-time, 2 part-time staff members, including coordinators, part-time graduate students. Services provided by remediation specialists, tutors, counselors, developmental specialists.
Special Fees: No special fees are charged for services to students with LD.
Applications and admissions: *Required:* high school IEP (Individualized Education Program), personal interview, psychoeducational report completed in 10th, 11th or 12th grade (multifactor evaluation); *recommended:* high school transcript, grade point average, class rank, courses completed, extended time SAT I or ACT. Students may begin taking classes in summer only. *Application deadline:* continuous.
Special policies: The college has written policies regarding grade forgiveness.

PROGRAM AND SERVICE COMPONENTS

Academic advising: Provided by unit staff members, academic advisers. Students with LD may take up to 18 semester hours each term; most take 12 to 14 semester hours; 12 semester hours (fewer with special permission) required to maintain full-time status; 12 semester hours required to be eligible for financial aid.
Counseling services: Individual counseling, small-group counseling, career counseling, self-advocacy training, peer support groups.
Basic skills remediation: Offered one-on-one, in small groups, and in class-size groups by regular teachers, tutors. Available in reading, math, written language, learning strategies, study skills, time management, speech.
Subject-area tutoring: Offered one-on-one and in small groups by professional teachers, peer tutors, graduate students. Available in some subjects.
Special courses: Reading, composition, learning strategies, time management, math, study skills, career planning, peer group counseling session. Some offered for credit; some enter into overall grade point average.
Auxiliary aids: Taped textbooks, calculators, word-processors with spell-check, talking computers, optical character readers.
Auxiliary services: Alternative test arrangements, notetakers, priority registration, advocacy, peer mentors.

GENERAL COLLEGE INFORMATION

State-supported, coed. Part of Kent State University System. Awards bachelor's, master's, doctoral degrees. Founded 1910. *Setting:* 1,200-acre small-town campus with easy access to Cleveland. *Endowment:* $15.6 million. *Total enrollment:* 20,600. *Faculty:* 1,351 (798 full-time, 77% with terminal degrees, 553 part-time); student–undergrad faculty ratio is 17:1.
Enrollment Profile: 15,958 students from 41 states and territories, 64 other countries. 57% women, 43% men, 17% part-time, 92% state residents, 40% live on campus, 22% transferred in, 1% international, 18% 25 or older, 1% Native American, 1% Hispanic, 6% black, 1% Asian or Pacific Islander. *Retention:* 72% of 1995 full-time freshmen returned. *Areas of study chosen:* 13% business management and administrative services, 11% education, 10% computer and information sciences, 7% social sciences, 6% health professions and related sciences, 5% communications and journalism, 5% fine arts, 5% liberal arts/general studies, 5% psychology, 5% vocational and home economics, 4% biological and life sciences, 2% architecture, 2% English language/literature/letters, 2% mathematics, 2% physical sciences, 2% predentistry, 2% premed, 1% engineering and applied sciences, 1% foreign language and literature, 1% performing arts, 1% prelaw, 1% prevet.
First-Year Class: 2,811 total; 8,287 applied, 88% were accepted, 38% of whom enrolled. 10% from top 10% of their high school class, 29% from top quarter, 62% from top half.
Graduation Requirements: 129 semester hours; math proficiency; 6 semester hours of science; computer course for business, math, fashion design, fashion merchandising, aerospace majors; internship (some majors); senior project for honors program students and some majors.
Computers on Campus: 800 computers available on campus for general student use. Computer purchase/lease plans available. A computer is recommended for some students. A campus-wide network can be accessed from off-campus. Students can contact faculty members and/or advisers through e-mail. Computers for student use in computer center, computer labs, research center, learning resource center, classrooms, library, student center, dorms, departmental labs provide access to the Internet/World Wide Web, on- and off-campus e-mail addresses. Staffed computer lab on campus provides training in use of computers, software. *Academic computing expenditure 1995–96:* $4.7 million.

EXPENSES AND FINANCIAL AID

Expenses for 1997–98: State resident tuition: $4460 full-time. Nonresident tuition: $8920 full-time. Part-time tuition (1 to 10 semester hours): $202.75 per semester hour for state residents, $405.50 per semester hour for nonresidents. College room and board: $4152. College room only: $2448.
Undergraduate Financial Aid: 84% of all full-time undergraduates enrolled in fall 1996 applied for aid. *Financial aid deadline (priority):* 2/15. *Financial aid forms:* FAFSA, state form required. Summer aid application required for some.

LD Services Contact: Ms. Anne L. Jannarone, Disability Specialist, Kent State University, 181 Michael Schwartz Center, Kent, OH 44242, 330-672-3391. Fax: 330-672-2073. Email: ajannaro@kent.edu.

KUTZTOWN UNIVERSITY OF PENNSYLVANIA

Kutztown, Pennsylvania

LEARNING DISABILITIES SERVICES INFORMATION

Office of Human Diversity began offering services in 1984. Currently the program serves 174 undergraduates with LD. Services are also available to graduate students. Students diagnosed with ADD/ADHD are eligible for the same services available to students with LD, as well as separate testing location.
Staff: 4 full-time, 1 part-time staff members, including director, reading specialists. Services provided by remediation specialists, tutors, counselors.
Special Fees: No special fees are charged for services to students with LD.
Applications and admissions: *Required:* high school transcript, grade point average, class rank, courses completed, untimed SAT I; *recommended:* extended time SAT I, personal interview, letters of recommendation. Students may begin taking classes in fall or summer. *Application deadline:* continuous.
Special policies: The college has written policies regarding substitutions and waivers of degree requirements.

PROGRAM AND SERVICE COMPONENTS

Academic advising: Provided by academic advisers. Students with LD may take up to 18 credits each term; most take 12 credits; 12 credits required to maintain full-time status and be eligible for financial aid.
Counseling services: Individual counseling.
Basic skills remediation: Offered one-on-one by regular teachers. Available in reading, math, written language, learning strategies, study skills, time management, speech.
Subject-area tutoring: Offered one-on-one and in small groups by peer tutors, graduate assistants. Available in most subjects.
Special courses: Reading, composition, math, study skills. None offered for credit.
Auxiliary aids: Taped textbooks, tape recorders, word-processors with spell-check, optical character readers.
Auxiliary services: Alternative test arrangements, notetakers, priority registration, advocacy.

GENERAL COLLEGE INFORMATION

State-supported, comprehensive, coed. Part of Pennsylvania State System of Higher Education. Awards bachelor's, master's degrees. Founded 1866. *Setting:* 325-acre small-town campus with easy access to Philadelphia. *Endowment:* $3.1 million. *Research spending 1995–96:* $34,671. *Educational spending 1995–96:* $4737 per undergrad. *Total enrollment:* 7,843. *Faculty:* 430 (346 full-time, 59% with terminal degrees, 84 part-time); student–undergrad faculty ratio is 19:1.
Enrollment Profile: 6,925 students from 19 states and territories, 27 other countries. 58% women, 42% men, 12% part-time, 91% state residents, 35% live on campus, 8% transferred in, 1% international, 12% 25 or older, 1% Native American, 2% Hispanic, 3% black, 1% Asian or Pacific Islander. *Retention:* 76% of 1995 full-time freshmen returned. *Graduation:* 23% graduate in 4 years, 46% in 5 years, 49% in 6 years. *Areas of study chosen:* 28% education, 14% business management and administrative services, 9% fine arts, 8% social sciences, 6% biological and life sciences, 6% psychology, 3% English language/literature/letters, 3% health professions and related sciences, 3% physical sciences, 2% computer and information sciences, 2% performing arts, 1% library and information studies. *Most popular recent majors:* marketing/retailing/merchandising, early childhood education.
First-Year Class: 1,411 total; 4,798 applied, 73% were accepted, 40% of whom enrolled. 6% from top 10% of their high school class, 25% from top quarter, 77% from top half.
Graduation Requirements: 128 credits; computer course for math, science majors; internship (some majors); senior project for honors program students and some majors.
Computers on Campus: 350 computers available on campus for general student use. Computer purchase/lease plans available. A campuswide network can be accessed from off-campus. Students can contact faculty members and/or advisers through e-mail. Computers for student use in computer center, computer labs, classrooms, library, student center, academic buildings provide access to the Internet/World Wide Web, on- and off-campus e-mail addresses. Staffed computer lab on campus. *Academic computing expenditure 1995–96:* $1.5 million.

EXPENSES AND FINANCIAL AID

Expenses for 1996–97: *Application fee:* $25. State resident tuition: $3368 full-time, $140 per credit part-time. Nonresident tuition: $8566 full-time, $357 per credit part-time. Part-time mandatory fees: $49 per semester. Full-time mandatory fees: $730. College room and board: $3258. College room only: $2240.
Undergraduate Financial Aid: Of all full-time undergraduates enrolled in fall 1996, 80% of those who applied for aid were judged to have need according to Federal Methodology, of whom 80% were aided. On average, 75% of need was met. *Financial aid deadline (priority):* 3/15. *Financial aid forms:* FAFSA required.
LD Services Contact: Ms. Barbara N. Peters, Coordinator, Program for Diversity, Kutztown University of Pennsylvania, Kutztown, PA 19530, 610-683-4108. Fax: 610-683-4010.

LAURENTIAN UNIVERSITY

Sudbury, Ontario, Canada

LEARNING DISABILITIES SERVICES INFORMATION

Special Needs currently serves 75 undergraduates with LD. Services are also available to graduate students. Students diagnosed with ADD/ADHD are eligible for the same services available to students with LD.
Staff: 2 full-time staff members, including coordinator. Services provided by tutors, counselors.
Special Fees: No special fees are charged for services to students with LD.
Applications and admissions: *Required:* high school transcript, courses completed; *recommended:* high school extracurricular activities, autobiographical statement, letters of recommendation. Students may begin taking classes in fall or spring. *Application deadline:* continuous.
Special policies: The college has written policies regarding substitutions and waivers of degree requirements.

PROGRAM AND SERVICE COMPONENTS

Special preparation or orientation: Optional orientation offered before registration and during registration.
Diagnostic testing: Intelligence, reading, math, spelling, handwriting, spoken language, written language, motor abilities, perceptual skills, personality, psychoneurology.
Academic advising: Provided by academic advisers. Students with LD may take up to 5 courses each term; most take 4 courses; 3.5 courses required to maintain full-time status; 1 course required to be eligible for financial aid.
Counseling services: Individual counseling, career counseling.
Subject-area tutoring: Offered one-on-one by peer tutors. Available in all subjects.
Auxiliary aids: Taped textbooks, tape recorders, calculators, typewriters, word-processors with spell-check, personal computers, optical character readers.
Auxiliary services: Alternative test arrangements, notetakers, advocacy.

GENERAL COLLEGE INFORMATION

Province-supported, comprehensive, coed. Awards bachelor's, master's degrees. Founded 1960. *Setting:* 700-acre suburban campus. *Endowment:* $2.6 million. *Research spending 1995–96:* $5 million. *Educational spending 1995–96:* $6587 per undergrad. *Total enrollment:* 6,587. *Faculty:* 436 (312 full-time, 100% with terminal degrees, 124 part-time); student–undergrad faculty ratio is 16:1.
Enrollment Profile: 6,257 students from 12 provinces and territories, 26 other countries. 55% women, 45% men, 32% part-time, 97% province residents, 1% international. *Areas of study chosen:* 32% social sciences, 16% liberal arts/general studies, 15% health professions and related sciences, 13% physical sciences, 9% business management and administrative services, 3% computer and information sciences, 3% education, 3% engineering and applied sciences, 2% philosophy, 1% foreign language and literature, 1% mathematics.
First-Year Class: 1,628 total; 6,014 applied, 70% were accepted, 39% of whom enrolled.
Graduation Requirements: 90 credits; computer course for commerce, science, engineering majors; senior project (some majors).
Computers on Campus: 125 computers available on campus for general student use. Computers for student use in computer labs, class-

Laurentian University (continued)

rooms, library provide access to the Internet/World Wide Web. Staffed computer lab on campus provides training in use of computers, software. *Academic computing expenditure 1995–96:* $981,360.

EXPENSES AND FINANCIAL AID

Expenses for 1997–98: *Application fee:* $50. Canadian resident tuition: $3230 full-time, $646 per course part-time. Nonresident tuition: $7000 full-time, $1400 per term part-time. Part-time mandatory fees: $12 per course. Full-time mandatory fees for nonresidents: $885. (All figures are in Canadian dollars.). Full-time mandatory fees: $315 (minimum). College room and board: $3940. College room only: $2290.
Undergraduate Financial Aid: *Financial aid deadline:* Applications processed continuously. *Financial aid forms:* institutional form required.
Financial aid specifically for students with LD: Scholarships: companies' scholarships, government scholarships, private scholarships.
LD Services Contact: Mr. Earl Black, Coordinator, Special Needs, Laurentian University, Ramsey Lake Road, Sudbury, ON P3E 2C6, Canada, 705-675-1151 Ext. 3324. Fax: 705-675-4547.

LAWRENCE UNIVERSITY

Appleton, Wisconsin

LEARNING DISABILITIES SERVICES INFORMATION

Student Academic Services Office began offering services in 1991. Currently the program serves 60 undergraduates with LD. Students diagnosed with ADD/ADHD are eligible for the same services available to students with LD.
Staff: Includes faculty advisers, Director of Academic Support. Services provided by tutors, counselors, psychologists.
Special Fees: No special fees are charged for services to students with LD.
Applications and admissions: *Recommended:* psychoeducational report completed within 3 to 4 years, diagnostic report. Students may begin taking classes in fall only. *Application deadline:* continuous.
Special policies: The college has written policies regarding substitutions and waivers of graduation requirements.

PROGRAM AND SERVICE COMPONENTS

Academic advising: Provided by unit staff members, academic advisers. Students with LD may take up to 3 courses each term; most take 2 to 3 courses; 2.5 courses required to maintain full-time status; source of aid determines number of courses required to be eligible for financial aid.
Counseling services: Individual counseling, career counseling, peer support group.
Subject-area tutoring: Offered one-on-one by peer tutors. Available in all subjects.
Auxiliary services: Alternative test arrangements, notetakers, text taping, readers, tutors.
Campus support group: A special student organization is available to students with LD.

GENERAL COLLEGE INFORMATION

Independent, 4-year, coed. Awards bachelor's degrees. Founded 1847. *Setting:* 84-acre small-town campus. *Endowment:* $100.4 million. *Research spending 1995–96:* $1.2 million. *Educational spending 1995–96:* $8129 per undergrad. *Total enrollment:* 1,218. *Faculty:* 158 (114 full-time, 95% with terminal degrees, 44 part-time); student–undergrad faculty ratio is 11:1.
Enrollment Profile: 1,218 students from 42 states and territories, 38 other countries. 53% women, 47% men, 7% part-time, 46% state residents, 98% live on campus, 3% transferred in, 8% international, 4% 25 or older, 1% Native American, 2% Hispanic, 1% black, 4% Asian or Pacific Islander. *Retention:* 86% of 1995 full-time freshmen returned. *Graduation:* 61% graduate in 4 years, 65% in 5 years, 67% in 6 years. *Areas of study chosen:* 26% social sciences, 15% biological and life sciences, 14% performing arts, 12% psychology, 10% English language/literature/letters, 10% foreign language and literature, 10% physical sciences, 9% fine arts, 8% education, 4% philosophy, 3% interdisciplinary studies, 3% mathematics, 3% theology/religion, 1% computer and information sciences. *Most popular recent majors:* biology/biological sciences, English, psychology.
First-Year Class: 317 total; 1,587 applied, 61% were accepted, 33% of whom enrolled. 47% from top 10% of their high school class, 73% from top quarter, 95% from top half. 16 National Merit Scholars, 35 valedictorians.
Graduation Requirements: 36 courses; 1 course each in math and lab science; 1 course in intermediate level foreign language; computer course for math, physics majors; senior project for honors program students and some majors.
Computers on Campus: 140 computers available on campus for general student use. Computer purchase/lease plans available. A computer is recommended for all students. A campus-wide network can be accessed from student residence rooms. Students can contact faculty members and/or advisers through e-mail. Computers for student use in computer center, computer labs, learning resource center, library, dorms, academic buildings provide access to the Internet/World Wide Web. Staffed computer lab on campus provides training in use of computers, software. *Academic computing expenditure 1995–96:* $549,152.

EXPENSES AND FINANCIAL AID

Expenses for 1997–98: *Application fee:* $30. Comprehensive fee of $23,961 includes full-time tuition ($19,494), mandatory fees ($126), and college room and board ($4341).
Undergraduate Financial Aid: Of all full-time undergraduates enrolled in fall 1996, 92% of those who applied for aid were judged to have need according to Federal Methodology, of whom 100% were aided. On average, 100% of need was met. *Financial aid deadline (priority):* 3/15. *Financial aid forms:* FAFSA, institutional form required; CSS Financial Aid PROFILE acceptable.
LD Services Contact: Mr. Geoff Gajewski, Director, Academic Support, Lawrence University, Box 599, Appleton, WI 54912-0599, 414-832-6767. Fax: 414-832-6884.

LEE UNIVERSITY

Cleveland, Tennessee

LEARNING DISABILITIES SERVICES INFORMATION

Academic Support Services began offering services in 1980. Currently the program serves 85 undergraduates with LD. Services are also available to graduate students. Students diagnosed with ADD/ADHD are eligible for the same services available to students with LD.
Staff: 2 full-time, 3 part-time staff members, including director, coordinator, tutorial coordinator. Services provided by tutors, counselors.
Special Fees: No special fees are charged for services to students with LD.
Applications and admissions: *Recommended:* high school transcript, IEP (Individualized Education Program), untimed or extended time ACT, untimed SAT I, psychoeducational report completed in 11th grade. Students may begin taking classes in fall, winter, or spring. *Application deadline:* continuous.

PROGRAM AND SERVICE COMPONENTS

Diagnostic testing: Reading, math.
Academic advising: Provided by unit staff members, academic advisers. Students with LD may take up to 14 semester hours each term; most take 12 semester hours; 12 semester hours required to maintain full-time status.
Counseling services: Individual counseling.
Basic skills remediation: Offered in class-size groups by regular teachers. Available in reading, math, written language.
Subject-area tutoring: Offered one-on-one and in small groups by peer tutors. Available in most subjects.
Special courses: Reading, vocabulary development, composition, math. Most offered for credit; most enter into overall grade point average.
Auxiliary services: Alternative test arrangements, notetakers, priority registration.

GENERAL COLLEGE INFORMATION

Independent, 4-year, coed, affiliated with Church of God. Awards bachelor's degrees. Founded 1918. *Setting:* 45-acre small-town campus.

EXPENSES AND FINANCIAL AID

Expenses for 1996–97: *Application fee:* $25. Comprehensive fee of $8912 includes full-time tuition ($5232), mandatory fees ($140), and college room and board ($3540). College room only: $1780. Part-time tuition: $218 per semester hour. Part-time mandatory fees: $20 per semester.

Undergraduate Financial Aid: 70% of all full-time undergraduates enrolled in fall 1996 applied for aid; of these, 90% were judged to have need according to Federal Methodology, of whom 90% were aided. *Financial aid deadline (priority):* 4/15. *Financial aid forms:* FAFSA, institutional form required.
LD Services Contact: Dr. Ollie Lee, Academic Dean, Lee University, PO Box 3450, North Ocoee Street, Cleveland, TN 37320, 423-614-8115. Fax: 423-614-8533.

LIBERTY UNIVERSITY

Lynchburg, Virginia

LEARNING DISABILITIES SERVICES INFORMATION

Bruckner Learning Center began offering services in 1985. Currently the program serves 120 undergraduates with LD. Services are also available to graduate students. Students diagnosed with ADD/ADHD are eligible for the same services available to students with LD.
Staff: 7 full-time, 1 part-time staff members, including director, assistant director, tutoring center coordinator, faculty members. Services provided by remediation specialists, tutors.
Special Fees: No special fees are charged for services to students with LD.
Applications and admissions: *Required:* high school transcript, grade point average, autobiographical statement, letters of recommendation; *recommended:* high school class rank, IEP (Individualized Education Program), untimed or extended time SAT I or ACT, psychoeducational report. Students may begin taking classes in fall or spring. *Application deadline:* continuous.
Special policies: The college has written policies regarding grade forgiveness.

PROGRAM AND SERVICE COMPONENTS

Academic advising: Provided by unit staff members. Students with LD may take up to 18 semester hours each term; most take 12 semester hours; 12 semester hours required to maintain full-time status and be eligible for financial aid.
Basic skills remediation: Offered in small groups and in class-size groups by regular teachers. Available in reading, math, spelling, handwriting, written language, learning strategies, study skills, time management.
Subject-area tutoring: Offered one-on-one by peer tutors. Available in most subjects.
Special courses: Reading, composition, math, study skills. All offered for credit; all enter into overall grade point average.
Auxiliary aids: Typewriters, word-processors with spell-check.
Auxiliary services: Alternative test arrangements, priority registration, advocacy.

GENERAL COLLEGE INFORMATION

Independent nondenominational, comprehensive, coed. Awards associate, bachelor's, master's, doctoral, first professional degrees (also offers external degree program with significant enrollment not reflected in profile). Founded 1971. *Setting:* 160-acre suburban campus. *Total enrollment:* 5,581. *Faculty:* 244 (191 full-time, 49% with terminal degrees, 53 part-time); student–undergrad faculty ratio is 28:1.
Enrollment Profile: 5,314 students from 52 states and territories, 21 other countries. 51% women, 49% men, 4% part-time, 41% state residents, 70% live on campus, 11% transferred in, 4% international, 7% 25 or older, 1% Native American, 2% Hispanic, 8% black, 3% Asian or Pacific Islander. *Retention:* 65% of 1995 full-time freshmen returned. *Graduation:* 17% graduate in 4 years, 30% in 5 years, 35% in 6 years. *Most popular recent majors:* business administration/commerce/management, psychology, education.
First-Year Class: 1,192 total; 2,718 applied, 73% were accepted, 60% of whom enrolled.
Graduation Requirements: 64 semester hours for associate, 120 semester hours for bachelor's; 3 math/science courses including at least 1 lab science course; computer course for business, math, accounting, government majors; internship (some majors); senior project for honors program students.
Computers on Campus: 93 computers available on campus for general student use. A computer is recommended for all students. A campus-wide network can be accessed from student residence rooms and from off-campus. Students can contact faculty members and/or advisers through e-mail. Computers for student use in computer labs, learning resource center, library provide access to the Internet/World Wide Web, on- and off-campus e-mail addresses. Staffed computer lab on campus provides training in use of computers, software.

EXPENSES AND FINANCIAL AID

Expenses for 1996–97: *Application fee:* $35. Comprehensive fee of $12,480 includes full-time tuition ($7680) and college room and board ($4800). Part-time tuition: $256 per semester hour.
Undergraduate Financial Aid: *Financial aid deadline (priority):* 4/15. *Financial aid forms:* FAFSA required. State form required for some.
LD Services Contact: Mr. Denton McHaney, Faculty Advisor for Students with Learning Disabilities, Liberty University, 1971 University Boulevard, Lynchburg, VA 24502, 804-582-2226. Fax: 804-582-2554.

LINFIELD COLLEGE

McMinnville, Oregon

LEARNING DISABILITIES SERVICES INFORMATION

Learning Support Services began offering services in 1989. Currently the program serves 85 undergraduates with LD. Students diagnosed with ADD/ADHD are eligible for the same services available to students with LD.
Staff: 1 full-time staff member (director).
Special Fees: No special fees are charged for services to students with LD.
Applications and admissions: *Required:* high school transcript, grade point average, letters of recommendation, essay; *recommended:* high school class rank, courses completed, untimed or extended time SAT I, extended time ACT, personal interview, autobiographical statement, psychoeducational report completed within 5 years. Students may begin taking classes in fall only. *Application deadline:* 2/15.

PROGRAM AND SERVICE COMPONENTS

Academic advising: Provided by unit staff members, academic advisers. Students with LD may take up to 18 credit hours each term; most take 13 to 15 credit hours.
Counseling services: Individual counseling, small-group counseling, career counseling, self-advocacy training.
Basic skills remediation: Offered one-on-one, in small groups, and in class-size groups by regular teachers. Available in reading, math, written language, learning strategies, study skills, time management, social skills.
Subject-area tutoring: Offered one-on-one and in small groups by professional teachers, peer tutors, community volunteers. Available in all subjects.
Special courses: College survival skills, reading, learning strategies, study skills. All offered for credit; all enter into overall grade point average.
Auxiliary aids: Taped textbooks, tape recorders, calculators, typewriters, personal computers, optical character readers.
Auxiliary services: Alternative test arrangements, notetakers, priority registration, individual appointments with LD professional.

GENERAL COLLEGE INFORMATION

Independent American Baptist, 4-year, coed. Awards bachelor's degrees. Founded 1849. *Setting:* 110-acre small-town campus with easy access to Portland. *Endowment:* $31.7 million. *Educational spending 1995–96:* $8466 per undergrad. *Total enrollment:* 1,594. *Faculty:*; student–undergrad faculty ratio is 15:1.
Enrollment Profile: 1,582 students from 21 states and territories, 30 other countries. 55% women, 45% men, 5% part-time, 59% state residents, 66% live on campus, 10% transferred in, 5% international, 4% 25 or older, 1% Native American, 2% Hispanic, 1% black, 5% Asian or Pacific Islander. *Retention:* 84% of 1995 full-time freshmen returned. *Graduation:* 62% graduate in 4 years, 64% in 5 years. *Most popular recent majors:* business administration/commerce/management, elementary education, biology/biological sciences.
First-Year Class: 454 total; 1,727 applied, 88% were accepted, 30% of whom enrolled. 39% from top 10% of their high school class, 74% from top quarter, 96% from top half. 10 National Merit Scholars.
Graduation Requirements: 125 credit hours; math proficiency; computer course for business-related majors; internship (some majors); senior project for honors program students and some majors.
Computers on Campus: 150 computers available on campus for general student use. Computer purchase/lease plans available. A computer is recommended for all students. A campus-wide network can be accessed from student residence rooms and from off-campus. Students can con-

Linfield College (continued)

tact faculty members and/or advisers through e-mail. Computers for student use in computer center, computer labs, learning resource center, classrooms, library, dorms provide access to the Internet/World Wide Web, on- and off-campus e-mail addresses. Staffed computer lab on campus provides training in use of computers, software. *Academic computing expenditure 1995–96:* $346,657.

EXPENSES AND FINANCIAL AID

Expenses for 1997–98: *Application fee:* $40. Comprehensive fee of $21,304 includes full-time tuition ($15,874), mandatory fees ($139), and college room and board ($5291). College room only: $2254. Part-time mandatory fees per semester (6 to 9 credit hours): $40. One-time mandatory fee: $200. Part-time tuition (1 to 9 credit hours): $496 per credit hour.

Undergraduate Financial Aid: Of all full-time undergraduates enrolled in fall 1996, 77% of those who applied for aid were judged to have need according to Federal Methodology, of whom 100% were aided. On average, 84% of need was met. *Financial aid deadline (priority):* 2/1. *Financial aid forms:* FAFSA, institutional form required.

LD Services Contact: Dr. Judith L. Haynes, Director, Linfield College, 900 South Baker, McMinnville, OR 97128, 503-434-2444. Fax: 503-434-2215. Email: jhaynes@linfield.edu.

LONGWOOD COLLEGE

Farmville, Virginia

LEARNING DISABILITIES SERVICES INFORMATION

Learning Center began offering services in 1988. Currently the program serves 99 undergraduates with LD. Services are also available to graduate students. Students diagnosed with ADD/ADHD are eligible for the same services available to students with LD.

Staff: 1 full-time, 2 part-time staff members, including director, coordinator. Services provided by tutors, diagnostic specialists.

Special Fees: No special fees are charged for services to students with LD.

Applications and admissions: *Required:* high school transcript, grade point average, courses completed, untimed SAT I or ACT; *recommended:* high school extracurricular activities, IEP (Individualized Education Program), extended time SAT I, letters of recommendation, psychoeducational report completed within 3 years, accommodated admission review (may be requested if student does not meet standard admission criteria). Students may begin taking classes any term. *Application deadline:* continuous.

Special policies: The college has written policies regarding substitutions and waivers of admissions, graduation, and degree requirements.

PROGRAM AND SERVICE COMPONENTS

Diagnostic testing: Intelligence, reading, math, spelling, handwriting, spoken language, written language, perceptual skills, study skills, personality, social skills, psychoneurology, speech, hearing, learning strategies, memory/attention (cognitive assessment).

Academic advising: Provided by unit staff members, academic advisers. Students with LD may take up to 19 credit hours each term; most take 16 credit hours; 12 credit hours (fewer with special permission) required to maintain full-time status and be eligible for financial aid.

Counseling services: Individual counseling, small-group counseling, career counseling, self-advocacy training.

Basic skills remediation: Offered in class-size groups by regular teachers. Available in math, written language, study skills, time management.

Subject-area tutoring: Offered one-on-one and in small groups by peer tutors. Available in most subjects.

Auxiliary aids: Taped textbooks, typewriters, word-processors with spell-check, personal computers.

Auxiliary services: Alternative test arrangements, notetakers, priority registration, advocacy.

GENERAL COLLEGE INFORMATION

State-supported, comprehensive, coed. Part of Commonwealth of Virginia Council of Higher Education. Awards bachelor's, master's degrees. Founded 1839. *Setting:* 154-acre small-town campus with easy access to Richmond. *Endowment:* $8 million. *Research spending 1995–96:* $55,045. *Educational spending 1995–96:* $3410 per undergrad. *Total enrollment:* 3,023. *Faculty:* 222 (162 full-time, 92% with terminal degrees, 60 part-time); student–undergrad faculty ratio is 14:1.

Enrollment Profile: 2,891 students from 25 states and territories, 13 other countries. 67% women, 33% men, 13% part-time, 87% state residents, 24% transferred in, 1% international, 11% 25 or older, 1% Hispanic, 10% black, 1% Asian or Pacific Islander. *Retention:* 79% of 1995 full-time freshmen returned. *Graduation:* 42% graduate in 4 years, 57% in 5 years, 59% in 6 years. *Areas of study chosen:* 20% education, 16% business management and administrative services, 14% social sciences, 11% psychology, 10% liberal arts/general studies, 7% biological and life sciences, 6% English language/literature/letters, 6% performing arts, 5% health professions and related sciences, 4% premed, 3% physical sciences, 2% mathematics, 1% foreign language and literature. *Most popular recent majors:* business administration/commerce/management, education, psychology.

First-Year Class: 786 total; 2,358 applied, 76% were accepted, 44% of whom enrolled. 13% from top 10% of their high school class, 40% from top quarter, 82% from top half.

Graduation Requirements: 120 credit hours; 3 credit hours of math; 4 credit hours of science; computer course for math, science, business majors; internship (some majors); senior project (some majors).

Computers on Campus: 185 computers available on campus for general student use. A computer is strongly recommended for all students. A campus-wide network can be accessed from student residence rooms and from off-campus. Students can contact faculty members and/or advisers through e-mail. Computers for student use in computer center, computer labs, learning resource center, library, dorms, schools of business, art and education provide access to the Internet/World Wide Web, on- and off-campus e-mail addresses. Staffed computer lab on campus provides training in use of computers, software. *Academic computing expenditure 1995–96:* $613,785.

EXPENSES AND FINANCIAL AID

Expenses for 1997–98: *Application fee:* $25. State resident tuition: $2684 full-time, $112 per credit hour part-time. Nonresident tuition: $8156 full-time, $340 per credit hour part-time. Part-time mandatory fees: $25 per credit hour. Full-time mandatory fees: $1732. College room and board: $4204. College room only: $2506.

Undergraduate Financial Aid: Of all full-time undergraduates enrolled in fall 1996, 81% of those who applied for aid were judged to have need according to Federal Methodology, of whom 98% were aided. On average, 82% of need was met. *Financial aid deadline (priority):* 2/15. *Financial aid forms:* FAFSA required.

LD Services Contact: Mr. L. Scott Lissner, Director of Academic and Disability Support Services, Longwood College, 201 High Street, Farmville, VA 23909-1899, 804-395-2391. Fax: 804-395-2252.

LOUISIANA STATE UNIVERSITY AND AGRICULTURAL AND MECHANICAL COLLEGE

Baton Rouge, Louisiana

LEARNING DISABILITIES SERVICES INFORMATION

Disability Services began offering services in 1991. Currently the program serves 350 undergraduates with LD. Services are also available to graduate students. Students diagnosed with ADD/ADHD are eligible for the same services available to students with LD.

Staff: 5 full-time staff members, including director, coordinator, interpreter/program assistant, supported education adviser, administrative assistant. Services provided by tutors, counselors.

Special Fees: No special fees are charged for services to students with LD.

Applications and admissions: *Required:* high school transcript, grade point average, courses completed, untimed SAT I or ACT; *recommended:* high school class rank, extracurricular activities, extended time SAT I or ACT, personal interview, autobiographical statement, letters of recommendation, psychoeducational report completed within 3 years. Students may begin taking classes any term. *Application deadline:* continuous.

Special policies: The college has written policies regarding substitutions and waivers of admissions and degree requirements.

PROGRAM AND SERVICE COMPONENTS

Diagnostic testing: Intelligence, perceptual skills, personality.

Academic advising: Provided by academic advisers. Students with LD may take up to 18 semester hours each term; most take 12 semester hours; 12 semester hours required to maintain full-time status.

Counseling services: Individual counseling, career counseling.

Basic skills remediation: Offered in class-size groups by regular teachers. Available in reading, math, study skills.

Subject-area tutoring: Offered one-on-one by peer tutors. Available in most subjects.

Special courses: Math, Latin. All offered for credit; all enter into overall grade point average.

Auxiliary aids: Taped textbooks, typewriters, word-processors with spell-check, personal computers, optical character readers.

Auxiliary services: Alternative test arrangements, notetakers, priority registration.

Campus support group: A special student organization is available to students with LD.

GENERAL COLLEGE INFORMATION

State-supported, coed. Part of Louisiana State University System. Awards bachelor's, master's, doctoral, first professional degrees. Founded 1860. *Setting:* 2,000-acre urban campus with easy access to New Orleans. *Endowment:* $90.3 million. *Research spending 1995–96:* $63.2 million. *Educational spending 1995–96:* $4853 per undergrad. *Total enrollment:* 26,842. *Faculty:* 1,301 (1,206 full-time, 84% with terminal degrees, 95 part-time); student–undergrad faculty ratio is 18:1.

Enrollment Profile: 21,413 students from 52 states and territories, 102 other countries. 51% women, 49% men, 16% part-time, 87% state residents, 24% live on campus, 5% transferred in, 3% international, 17% 25 or older, 1% Native American, 3% Hispanic, 9% black, 4% Asian or Pacific Islander. *Retention:* 82% of 1995 full-time freshmen returned. *Graduation:* 16% graduate in 4 years, 40% in 5 years, 47% in 6 years. *Areas of study chosen:* 24% liberal arts/general studies, 12% business management and administrative services, 12% engineering and applied sciences, 9% health professions and related sciences, 7% education, 6% biological and life sciences, 6% social sciences, 4% agriculture, 4% psychology, 3% architecture, 3% communications and journalism, 2% English language/literature/letters, 2% physical sciences, 2% vocational and home economics, 1% computer and information sciences, 1% fine arts, 1% mathematics, 1% performing arts, 1% prelaw. *Most popular recent majors:* liberal arts/general studies, psychology, accounting.

First-Year Class: 4,025 total; 7,908 applied, 81% were accepted, 63% of whom enrolled. 26% from top 10% of their high school class, 51% from top quarter, 79% from top half. 37 National Merit Scholars, 91 valedictorians.

Graduation Requirements: 127 semester hours; 1 college algebra course; computer course for most majors; senior project for honors program students and some majors.

Computers on Campus: 5,000 computers available on campus for general student use. A computer is recommended for some students. A campus-wide network can be accessed from student residence rooms and from off-campus. Students can contact faculty members and/or advisers through e-mail. Computers for student use in computer center, computer labs, library, dorms, business, engineering colleges provide access to the Internet/World Wide Web, on- and off-campus e-mail addresses. Staffed computer lab on campus provides training in use of computers, software. *Academic computing expenditure 1995–96:* $6.6 million.

EXPENSES AND FINANCIAL AID

Expenses for 1996–97: *Application fee:* $25. State resident tuition: $2687 full-time. Nonresident tuition: $5987 full-time. Part-time tuition per semester ranges from $285 to $860 for state residents, $435 to $2215 for nonresidents. College room and board: $3570. College room only: $1920.

Undergraduate Financial Aid: 46% of all full-time undergraduates enrolled in fall 1996 applied for aid; of these, 81% were judged to have need according to Federal Methodology, of whom 100% were aided. *Financial aid deadline (priority):* 3/1. *Financial aid forms:* FAFSA required.

LD Services Contact: Ms. Traci Bryant, Director, Louisiana State University and Agricultural and Mechanical College, 122 Johnston Hall, Baton Rouge, LA 70803, 504-388-5919. Fax: 504-388-1413.

LOURDES COLLEGE

Sylvania, Ohio

LEARNING DISABILITIES SERVICES INFORMATION

Learning Resource Center began offering services in 1992. Currently the program serves 8 undergraduates with LD. Students diagnosed with ADD/ADHD are eligible for the same services available to students with LD, as well as distraction-free testing space.

Staff: Includes director, work study students. Services provided by remediation specialists, tutors, counselors, test takers.

Special Fees: No special fees are charged for services to students with LD.

Applications and admissions: *Required:* high school transcript, grade point average, courses completed, untimed ACT, psychoeducational report completed within 3 years; *recommended:* high school IEP (Individualized Education Program), extended time SAT I or ACT, personal interview. Students may begin taking classes in fall or winter. *Application deadline:* continuous.

PROGRAM AND SERVICE COMPONENTS

Academic advising: Provided by unit staff members, academic advisers. Students with LD may take up to 12 credit hours each term; most take 6 to 12 credit hours; 12 credit hours required to maintain full-time status; 6 credit hours required to be eligible for financial aid.

Counseling services: Individual counseling, career counseling, stress management, study skills.

Basic skills remediation: Offered in class-size groups by regular teachers. Available in reading, math, written language, learning strategies, study skills, time management.

Subject-area tutoring: Offered one-on-one by professional teachers, peer tutors. Available in all subjects.

Auxiliary aids: Taped textbooks, word-processors with spell-check, personal computers.

Auxiliary services: Alternative test arrangements, notetakers, advocacy.

GENERAL COLLEGE INFORMATION

Independent Roman Catholic, 4-year, coed. Awards associate, bachelor's degrees. Founded 1958. *Setting:* 90-acre suburban campus with easy access to Toledo. *Endowment:* $1 million. *Total enrollment:* 1,540. *Faculty:* 120 (72 full-time, 25% with terminal degrees, 48 part-time); student–undergrad faculty ratio is 14:1.

Enrollment Profile: 1,540 students from 5 states and territories, 7 other countries. 82% women, 18% men, 70% part-time, 91% state residents, 85% transferred in, 1% international, 70% 25 or older, 1% Native American, 1% Hispanic, 5% black, 1% Asian or Pacific Islander. *Graduation:* 37% graduate in 4 years, 42% in 5 years, 48% in 6 years. *Areas of study chosen:* 25% health professions and related sciences, 21% business management and administrative services, 10% interdisciplinary studies, 5% psychology, 2% premed, 2% theology/religion, 1% fine arts. *Most popular recent majors:* business administration/commerce/management, nursing, occupational therapy.

First-Year Class: 50 total; 77 applied, 86% were accepted, 76% of whom enrolled. 13% from top quarter of their high school class, 35% from top half.

Graduation Requirements: 64 credit hours for associate, 128 credit hours for bachelor's; 1 course each in math and science; computer course for business administration majors; internship (some majors); senior project (some majors).

Computers on Campus: 47 computers available on campus for general student use. A campus-wide network can be accessed. Computers for student use in computer center, learning resource center, library, nursing lab provide access to campus network. Staffed computer lab on campus provides training in use of computers, software. *Academic computing expenditure 1995–96:* $170,232.

EXPENSES AND FINANCIAL AID

Expenses for 1997–98: *Application fee:* $20. Tuition: $7860 full-time, $262 per credit hour part-time. Part-time mandatory fees per semester range from $12 to $120. Full-time mandatory fees: $240.

Undergraduate Financial Aid: 89% of all full-time undergraduates enrolled in fall 1996 applied for aid; of these, 81% were judged to have need according to Federal Methodology, of whom 97% were aided. *Financial aid deadline (priority):* 8/1. *Financial aid forms:* FAFSA, institutional form required.

Lourdes College (continued)

LD Services Contact: Ms. Kim Naumann, Director of Academic Services, Lourdes College, 6832 Convent Boulevard, Sylvania, OH 43560, 419-885-3211 Ext. 271. Fax: 419-882-3987. Email: k.naumann@lourdes.edu.

LOYOLA COLLEGE

Baltimore, Maryland

LEARNING DISABILITIES SERVICES INFORMATION

Disability Support Services Office/Advising Office began offering services in 1994. Currently the program serves 115 undergraduates with LD. Services are also available to graduate students. Students diagnosed with ADD/ADHD are eligible for the same services available to students with LD.

Staff: 1 full-time, 1 part-time staff members, including assistant director, coordinator. Services provided by counselors.

Special Fees: $150 for diagnostic testing.

Applications and admissions: *Required:* high school transcript, grade point average, courses completed, untimed SAT I; *recommended:* high school class rank, extracurricular activities, extended time SAT I or ACT, personal interview, autobiographical statement, letters of recommendation, psychoeducational report. Students may begin taking classes in fall only. *Application deadline:* 1/15 (fall term), 12/1 (spring term).

Special policies: The college has written policies regarding substitutions and waivers of graduation and degree requirements.

PROGRAM AND SERVICE COMPONENTS

Diagnostic testing: Reading, written language, hearing, Woodcock-Johnson.

Academic advising: Provided by academic advisers. Most students with LD take 12 to 15 credits each term; 12 credits required to maintain full-time status.

Counseling services: Individual counseling, LD peer support group.

Basic skills remediation: Offered one-on-one by Assistant Director of Advising. Available in learning strategies, study skills, time management.

Auxiliary aids: Taped textbooks, tape recorders, word-processors with spell-check, talking computers, optical character readers.

Auxiliary services: Alternative test arrangements, notetakers, advocacy.

GENERAL COLLEGE INFORMATION

Independent Roman Catholic (Jesuit), comprehensive, coed. Awards bachelor's, master's, doctoral degrees. Founded 1852. *Setting:* 65-acre suburban campus with easy access to Washington, DC. *Total enrollment:* 6,245. *Faculty:* 442 (218 full-time, 91% with terminal degrees, 224 part-time); student–undergrad faculty ratio is 14:1.

Enrollment Profile: 3,205 students from 33 states and territories, 12 other countries. 55% women, 45% men, 4% part-time, 31% state residents, 75% live on campus, 4% transferred in, 2% international, 4% 25 or older, 0% Native American, 2% Hispanic, 4% black, 2% Asian or Pacific Islander. *Retention:* 93% of 1995 full-time freshmen returned. *Graduation:* 71% graduate in 4 years, 77% in 5 years, 78% in 6 years. *Areas of study chosen:* 24% business management and administrative services, 10% biological and life sciences, 10% social sciences, 9% psychology, 8% communications and journalism, 8% English language/literature/letters, 5% education, 3% interdisciplinary studies, 2% computer and information sciences, 2% mathematics, 1% engineering and applied sciences, 1% fine arts, 1% foreign language and literature, 1% philosophy, 1% physical sciences, 1% theology/religion. *Most popular recent majors:* business administration/commerce/management, psychology, biology/biological sciences.

First-Year Class: 822 total; 4,978 applied, 71% were accepted, 23% of whom enrolled. 25% from top 10% of their high school class, 62% from top quarter, 92% from top half.

Graduation Requirements: 120 credits; 3 math/science courses; 2 courses in intermediate level foreign language; computer course for mathematical science, physics, engineering science, all business majors; senior project for honors program students and some majors.

Computers on Campus: 179 computers available on campus for general student use. Computer purchase/lease plans available. A campuswide network can be accessed from student residence rooms and from off-campus. Students can contact faculty members and/or advisers through e-mail. Computers for student use in computer center, dorms, student rooms, academic buildings provide access to the Internet/World Wide Web, on and off campus e-mail addresses. Staffed computer lab on campus (open 24 hours a day) provides training in use of computers, software.

EXPENSES AND FINANCIAL AID

Expenses for 1997–98: *Application fee:* $30. Comprehensive fee of $24,090 includes full-time tuition ($16,300), mandatory fees ($260), and college room and board ($7530). College room only: $4810. Part-time tuition: $320 per credit. Part-time mandatory fees: $25 per semester.

Undergraduate Financial Aid: Of all full-time undergraduates enrolled in fall 1996, 91% of those who applied for aid were judged to have need according to Federal Methodology, of whom 97% were aided. On average, 95% of need was met. *Financial aid deadline:* 2/1. *Financial aid forms:* FAFSA, CSS Financial Aid PROFILE required. State form required for some.

LD Services Contact: Ms. Katherine Milam, Assistant Director of Advising, Loyola College, Humanities 176, 4501 North Charles Street, Baltimore, MD 21210, 410-617-2663. Fax: 410-617-2034. Email: milam@loyola.edu.

LOYOLA UNIVERSITY NEW ORLEANS

New Orleans, Louisiana

LEARNING DISABILITIES SERVICES INFORMATION

Office of Academic Enrichment and Disability Services began offering services in 1988. Currently the program serves 100 undergraduates with LD. Services are also available to graduate students. Students diagnosed with ADD/ADHD are eligible for the same services available to students with LD.

Staff: 8 full-time, 2 part-time staff members, including director, administrative assistant. Services provided by tutors, counselors, diagnostic specialists.

Special Fees: No special fees are charged for services to students with LD.

Applications and admissions: *Required:* high school transcript, grade point average, courses completed, untimed SAT I or ACT, autobiographical statement, letters of recommendation; *recommended:* high school class rank, extracurricular activities, personal interview. Students may begin taking classes in fall, spring, or summer. *Application deadline:* 8/1 (fall term), 1/1 (spring term).

PROGRAM AND SERVICE COMPONENTS

Diagnostic testing: Reading, spelling, handwriting, spoken language, written language, motor abilities, perceptual skills, study skills, personality, social skills, learning strategies, math; test results are valid only for in-house purposes.

Academic advising: Provided by unit staff members, academic advisers. Most students with LD take 12 to 15 credit hours each term; 12 credit hours required to maintain full-time status and be eligible for financial aid.

Counseling services: Individual counseling, small-group counseling, career counseling, self-advocacy training, academic counseling.

Subject-area tutoring: Offered one-on-one by professional teachers, peer tutors. Available in most subjects.

Special courses: Study skills. All offered for credit; none enter into overall grade point average.

Auxiliary aids: Taped textbooks, tape recorders, word-processors with spell-check, personal computers, Dragon Dictate.

Auxiliary services: Alternative test arrangements, notetakers, priority registration, advocacy, scribes.

Campus support group: A special student organization is available to students with LD.

GENERAL COLLEGE INFORMATION

Independent Roman Catholic (Jesuit), comprehensive, coed. Awards bachelor's, master's, first professional degrees. Founded 1912. *Setting:* 26-acre urban campus. *Endowment:* $227.7 million. *Research spending 1995–96:* $367,277. *Total enrollment:* 5,203. *Faculty:* 414 (252 full-time, 89% with terminal degrees, 162 part-time); student–undergrad faculty ratio is 9:1.

Enrollment Profile: 3,375 students from 47 states and territories, 45 other countries. 62% women, 38% men, 22% part-time, 61% state residents, 28% live on campus, 7% transferred in, 6% international, 25% 25 or older, 1% Native American, 12% Hispanic, 14% black, 4% Asian or Pacific Islander. *Retention:* 75% of 1995 full-time freshmen returned. *Graduation:* 35% graduate in 4 years, 53% in 5 years, 56% in 6 years.

Areas of study chosen: 18% business management and administrative services, 14% communications and journalism, 10% social sciences, 9% biological and life sciences, 9% health professions and related sciences, 9% performing arts, 8% psychology, 6% liberal arts/general studies, 4% computer and information sciences, 4% education, 4% English language/literature/letters, 1% engineering and applied sciences, 1% fine arts, 1% foreign language and literature, 1% mathematics, 1% philosophy, 1% physical sciences, 1% theology/religion. *Most popular recent majors:* communication, psychology, accounting.
First-Year Class: 530 total; 1,697 applied, 88% were accepted, 35% of whom enrolled. 30% from top 10% of their high school class, 53% from top quarter, 80% from top half. 13 valedictorians.
Graduation Requirements: 120 credit hours; 1 course each in math and science; computer course for behavioral sciences, business, communication, math, radiological technology majors; internship (some majors); senior project (some majors).
Computers on Campus: 240 computers available on campus for general student use. A campus-wide network can be accessed from student residence rooms and from off-campus. Students can contact faculty members and/or advisers through e-mail. Computers for student use in computer center, computer labs, library, student center, dorms, academic buildings provide access to the Internet/World Wide Web, on- and off-campus e-mail addresses. Staffed computer lab on campus provides training in use of computers, software. *Academic computing expenditure 1995–96:* $511,675.

EXPENSES AND FINANCIAL AID

Expenses for 1997–98: *Application fee:* $20. Comprehensive fee of $19,096 includes full-time tuition ($12,950), mandatory fees ($316), and college room and board ($5830). College room only: $3260. Part-time tuition: $458 per credit hour. Part-time mandatory fees: $159 per year.
Undergraduate Financial Aid: 62% of all full-time undergraduates enrolled in fall 1996 applied for aid; of these, 66% were judged to have need according to Federal Methodology, of whom 98% were aided. On average, 95% of need was met. *Financial aid deadline (priority):* 5/1. *Financial aid forms:* FAFSA required; state form acceptable.
LD Services Contact: Ms. Sarah M. Smith, Director, Office of Academic Enrichment and Disability Services, Loyola University New Orleans, Box 41, 6363 St. Charles Avenue, New Orleans, LA 70118, 504-865-2990. Email: ssmith@beta.loyno.edu.

LUTHERAN BIBLE INSTITUTE OF SEATTLE

Issaquah, Washington

LEARNING DISABILITIES SERVICES INFORMATION

Student Services began offering services in 1991. Currently the program serves 6 undergraduates with LD. Students diagnosed with ADD/ADHD are eligible for the same services available to students with LD.
Staff: 1 part-time staff member (coordinator). Services provided by tutors.
Special Fees: No special fees are charged for services to students with LD.
Applications and admissions: *Required:* high school transcript, grade point average, autobiographical statement, letters of recommendation; *recommended:* high school class rank, untimed or extended time SAT I or ACT. Students may begin taking classes any term. *Application deadline:* continuous.

PROGRAM AND SERVICE COMPONENTS

Special preparation or orientation: Required orientation held before classes begin.
Academic advising: Provided by academic advisers. Students with LD may take up to 18 quarter hours each term; most take 16 quarter hours; 12 quarter hours required to maintain full-time status and be eligible for financial aid.
Basic skills remediation: Offered one-on-one and in small groups by regular teachers. Available in reading, spelling, written language, study skills, time management, social skills.
Subject-area tutoring: Offered one-on-one and in small groups by peer tutors, volunteer retired teachers. Available in most subjects.
Auxiliary aids: Taped textbooks, tape recorders, calculators, word-processors with spell-check, personal computers.
Auxiliary services: Alternative test arrangements, notetakers, priority registration, advocacy.

GENERAL COLLEGE INFORMATION

Independent Lutheran, 4-year, specialized, coed. Awards associate, bachelor's degrees. Founded 1944. *Setting:* 46-acre suburban campus with easy access to Seattle. *Educational spending 1995–96:* $4117 per undergrad. *Total enrollment:* 167. *Faculty:* 26 (11 full-time, 42% with terminal degrees, 15 part-time); student–undergrad faculty ratio is 13:1.
Enrollment Profile: 167 students from 18 states and territories, 12 other countries. 50% women, 50% men, 13% part-time, 50% state residents, 16% transferred in, 10% international, 31% 25 or older, 0% Native American, 4% Hispanic, 1% black, 5% Asian or Pacific Islander. *Retention:* 76% of 1995 full-time freshmen returned. *Graduation:* 75% graduate in 6 years. *Areas of study chosen:* 100% theology/religion. *Most popular recent majors:* biblical studies, ministries, religious education.
First-Year Class: 24 total; 107 applied, 48% were accepted, 47% of whom enrolled.
Graduation Requirements: 90 credits for associate, 180 credits for bachelor's; 3 credits each of math and science; internship (some majors); senior project (some majors).
Computers on Campus: 8 computers available on campus for general student use. A computer is strongly recommended for all students. Computers for student use in library, student center provide access to the Internet/World Wide Web. Staffed computer lab on campus provides training in use of computers, software.

EXPENSES AND FINANCIAL AID

Expenses for 1997–98: *Application fee:* $30. Comprehensive fee of $9655 includes full-time tuition ($4600), mandatory fees ($710), and college room and board ($4345). Part-time tuition: $132 per credit. Part-time mandatory fees: $22.50 per credit.
Undergraduate Financial Aid: 68% of all full-time undergraduates enrolled in fall 1996 applied for aid; of these, 65% were judged to have need according to Federal Methodology, of whom 92% were aided. On average, 75% of need was met. *Financial aid deadline (priority):* 5/1. *Financial aid forms:* institutional form required; FAFSA, CSS Financial Aid PROFILE acceptable.
LD Services Contact: Mr. Jerry Hekkel, Dean of Students, Lutheran Bible Institute of Seattle, 4221 228th Avenue, SE, Issaquah, WA 98027, 206-392-0400. Fax: 206-392-0404. Email: internet-admissn@lbi.edu.

MACALESTER COLLEGE

St. Paul, Minnesota

LEARNING DISABILITIES SERVICES INFORMATION

Learning Center began offering services in 1972. Currently the program serves 17 undergraduates with LD. Students diagnosed with ADD/ADHD are eligible for the same services available to students with LD.
Staff: 3 full-time staff members, including director. Services provided by counselors.
Special Fees: No special fees are charged for services to students with LD.
Applications and admissions: *Required:* high school transcript, untimed SAT I or ACT, letters of recommendation. Students may begin taking classes in fall only. *Application deadline:* 1/15.

PROGRAM AND SERVICE COMPONENTS

Diagnostic testing: Reading, math, spelling, written language, study skills, personality, learning strategies.
Academic advising: Provided by unit staff members, academic advisers. Students with LD may take up to 16 semester hours each term; most take 12 to 16 semester hours; 12 semester hours required to maintain full-time status and be eligible for financial aid.
Counseling services: Individual counseling, career counseling.
Subject-area tutoring: Offered one-on-one by professional teachers, peer tutors. Available in all subjects.
Auxiliary aids: Taped textbooks, tape recorders, word-processors with spell-check, personal computers.
Auxiliary services: Alternative test arrangements, notetakers, priority registration, advocacy.

GENERAL COLLEGE INFORMATION

Independent Presbyterian, 4-year, coed. Awards bachelor's degrees. Founded 1874. *Setting:* 53-acre urban campus. *Endowment:* $509.5 million. *Research spending 1995–96:* $1.2 million. *Educational spending 1995–*

Macalester College (continued)

96: $8792 per undergrad. *Total enrollment:* 1,797. *Faculty:* 210 (143 full-time, 92% with terminal degrees, 67 part-time); student–undergrad faculty ratio is 11:1.
Enrollment Profile: 1,797 students from 50 states and territories, 81 other countries. 57% women, 43% men, 5% part-time, 23% state residents, 70% live on campus, 2% transferred in, 10% international, 2% 25 or older, 1% Native American, 4% Hispanic, 4% black, 6% Asian or Pacific Islander. *Retention:* 89% of 1995 full-time freshmen returned. *Graduation:* 70% graduate in 4 years, 78% in 5 years, 80% in 6 years. *Areas of study chosen:* 32% social sciences, 10% physical sciences, 8% biological and life sciences, 8% English language/literature/letters, 8% foreign language and literature, 8% psychology, 5% communications and journalism, 5% interdisciplinary studies, 4% area and ethnic studies, 3% fine arts, 3% mathematics, 3% performing arts, 3% philosophy, 2% computer and information sciences, 2% theology/religion. *Most popular recent majors:* psychology, English, history.
First-Year Class: 491 total; 3,132 applied, 55% were accepted, 29% of whom enrolled. 57% from top 10% of their high school class, 91% from top quarter, 100% from top half. 50 National Merit Scholars.
Graduation Requirements: 128 semester hours; 8 semester hours of math/science; 4 semester hours of a foreign language; senior project.
Computers on Campus: 350 computers available on campus for general student use. Computer purchase/lease plans available. A campus-wide network can be accessed from student residence rooms and from off-campus. Students can contact faculty members and/or advisers through e-mail. Computers for student use in computer center, computer labs, library, dorms, student rooms, departmental labs provide access to the Internet/World Wide Web, on- and off-campus e-mail addresses. Staffed computer lab on campus provides training in use of computers, software.

EXPENSES AND FINANCIAL AID

Expenses for 1997–98: *Application fee:* $40. Comprehensive fee of $24,188 includes full-time tuition ($18,630), mandatory fees ($128), and college room and board ($5430).
Undergraduate Financial Aid: *Financial aid deadline (priority):* 2/8. *Financial aid forms:* FAFSA, CSS Financial Aid PROFILE, W-2 forms, federal income tax forms required.
LD Services Contact: Mr. Charles Norman, Director, Macalester College, 1600 Grand Avenue, St. Paul, MN 55105, 612-696-6146. Fax: 612-696-6428.

MACMURRAY COLLEGE

Jacksonville, Illinois

LEARNING DISABILITIES SERVICES INFORMATION

Office of Special Needs began offering services in 1989. Currently the program serves 15 undergraduates with LD. Students diagnosed with ADD/ADHD are eligible for the same services available to students with LD.
Staff: 1 full-time staff member (director). Services provided by remediation specialists, tutors, counselors.
Special Fees: No special fees are charged for services to students with LD.
Applications and admissions: *Recommended:* high school transcript, grade point average, class rank, courses completed, extracurricular activities, IEP (Individualized Education Program), untimed or extended time SAT I or ACT, personal interview, autobiographical statement, letters of recommendation, psychoeducational report. Students may begin taking classes any term. *Application deadline:* continuous.

PROGRAM AND SERVICE COMPONENTS

Academic advising: Provided by unit staff members, academic advisers. Students with LD may take up to 15 semester hours each term; most take 15 semester hours; 12 semester hours required to maintain full-time status and be eligible for financial aid.
Counseling services: Individual counseling, small-group counseling, career counseling, self-advocacy training.
Basic skills remediation: Offered one-on-one and in small groups by Director of Learning Center, Coordinator of Special Needs; computer-aided instruction also offered. Available in reading, math, spelling, spoken language, written language, learning strategies, study skills, time management.
Subject-area tutoring: Offered one-on-one and in small groups by professional teachers, peer tutors. Available in all subjects.
Auxiliary aids: Taped textbooks, tape recorders, optical character readers.
Auxiliary services: Alternative test arrangements, notetakers.

GENERAL COLLEGE INFORMATION

Independent United Methodist, 4-year, coed. Awards associate, bachelor's degrees. Founded 1846. *Setting:* 60-acre small-town campus. *Endowment:* $9.7 million. *Educational spending 1995–96:* $3948 per undergrad. *Total enrollment:* 669. *Faculty:* 72 (55 full-time, 55% with terminal degrees, 17 part-time); student–undergrad faculty ratio is 12:1.
Enrollment Profile: 669 students from 18 states and territories, 4 other countries. 58% women, 42% men, 7% part-time, 84% state residents, 66% live on campus, 8% transferred in, 1% international, 10% 25 or older, 1% Native American, 4% Hispanic, 6% black. *Retention:* 59% of 1995 full-time freshmen returned. *Graduation:* 45% graduate in 4 years, 50% in 5 years, 53% in 6 years. *Areas of study chosen:* 30% education, 19% social sciences, 12% business management and administrative services, 8% health professions and related sciences, 7% biological and life sciences, 6% psychology, 3% fine arts, 2% English language/literature/letters, 1% communications and journalism, 1% computer and information sciences, 1% mathematics, 1% physical sciences, 1% premed, 1% theology/religion. *Most popular recent majors:* special education, nursing, business administration/commerce/management.
First-Year Class: 158 total; 639 applied, 76% were accepted, 32% of whom enrolled. 9% from top 10% of their high school class, 35% from top quarter, 60% from top half. 5 class presidents, 3 valedictorians.
Graduation Requirements: 60 semester hours for associate, 120 semester hours for bachelor's; basic math proficiency; 1 natural science course; computer course for math, physics, business administration, biology, social work majors; internship (some majors); senior project for honors program students and some majors.
Computers on Campus: 50 computers available on campus for general student use. A campus-wide network can be accessed. Students can contact faculty members and/or advisers through e-mail. Computers for student use in computer center, computer labs, learning resource center, library, student center, dorms, nursing lab provide access to the Internet/World Wide Web, on- and off-campus e-mail addresses, various software packages. Staffed computer lab on campus provides training in use of computers, software. *Academic computing expenditure 1995–96:* $99,650.

EXPENSES AND FINANCIAL AID

Expenses for 1997–98: *Application fee:* $10. Comprehensive fee of $15,530 includes full-time tuition ($11,400) and college room and board ($4130). College room only: $1850. Part-time tuition: $345 per semester hour.
Undergraduate Financial Aid: 99% of all full-time undergraduates enrolled in fall 1996 applied for aid; of these, 93% were judged to have need according to Federal Methodology, of whom 100% were aided. On average, 65% of need was met. *Financial aid deadline (priority):* 5/1. *Financial aid forms:* FAFSA required.
Financial aid specifically for students with LD: Scholarship: Sunset Freesen Award; loans; work-study.
LD Services Contact: Ms. Karen Engebrecht, Director, Career Services/Coordinator, Special Needs, MacMurray College, 447 East College Avenue, Jacksonville, IL 62650, 217-479-7123. Fax: 217-479-7137. Email: career@mac.edu.

MANCHESTER COLLEGE

North Manchester, Indiana

LEARNING DISABILITIES SERVICES INFORMATION

Learning Support Services began offering services in 1985. Currently the program serves 15 undergraduates with LD. Services are also available to graduate students. Students diagnosed with ADD/ADHD are eligible for the same services available to students with LD.
Staff: 1 full-time staff member (coordinator).
Special Fees: No special fees are charged for services to students with LD.
Applications and admissions: *Required:* high school transcript, grade point average, class rank, courses completed, untimed SAT I or ACT, psychoeducational report completed within 3 years; *recommended:* extended time SAT I or ACT, personal interview, autobiographical statement, letters of recommendation. Students may begin taking classes in fall or spring. *Application deadline:* continuous.

PROGRAM AND SERVICE COMPONENTS

Academic advising: Provided by unit staff members, academic advisers. Students with LD may take up to 16 semester hours each term; most take 13 to 16 semester hours; 12 semester hours required to maintain full-time status and be eligible for financial aid.
Counseling services: Individual counseling, small-group counseling, career counseling, self-advocacy training.
Subject-area tutoring: Offered one-on-one, in small groups, and in class-size groups by peer tutors. Available in all subjects.
Auxiliary services: Alternative test arrangements, notetakers.
Campus support group: A special student organization is available to students with LD.

GENERAL COLLEGE INFORMATION

Independent, comprehensive, coed, affiliated with Church of the Brethren. Awards associate, bachelor's, master's degrees. Founded 1889. *Setting:* 125-acre small-town campus. *Endowment:* $23 million. *Research spending 1995–96:* $44,432. *Educational spending 1995–96:* $3708 per undergrad. *Total enrollment:* 1,054. *Faculty:* 104 (68 full-time, 78% with terminal degrees, 36 part-time); student–undergrad faculty ratio is 13:1.
Enrollment Profile: 1,035 students from 23 states and territories, 22 other countries. 48% women, 52% men, 4% part-time, 76% state residents, 75% live on campus, 4% transferred in, 4% international, 6% 25 or older, 1% Native American, 2% Hispanic, 3% black, 1% Asian or Pacific Islander. *Retention:* 75% of 1995 full-time freshmen returned. *Graduation:* 45% graduate in 4 years, 55% in 5 years, 56% in 6 years. *Areas of study chosen:* 23% education, 11% social sciences, 10% business management and administrative services, 7% health professions and related sciences, 7% premed, 4% communications and journalism, 4% psychology, 2% computer and information sciences, 2% fine arts, 2% interdisciplinary studies, 2% natural resource sciences, 1% engineering and applied sciences, 1% English language/literature/letters, 1% mathematics, 1% performing arts, 1% philosophy, 1% physical sciences, 1% theology/religion. *Most popular recent majors:* accounting, education, social work.
First-Year Class: 307 total; 1,009 applied, 81% were accepted, 38% of whom enrolled. 24% from top 10% of their high school class, 41% from top quarter, 78% from top half. 4 valedictorians.
Graduation Requirements: 64 semester hours for associate, 128 semester hours for bachelor's; 3 semester hours of math; 6 semester hours of natural science; computer course; internship (some majors); senior project (some majors).
Computers on Campus: 110 computers available on campus for general student use. A campus-wide network can be accessed from off-campus. Students can contact faculty members and/or advisers through e-mail. Computers for student use in computer center, computer labs, library, dorms, science hall provide access to the Internet/World Wide Web, on- and off-campus e-mail addresses. Staffed computer lab on campus (open 24 hours a day) provides training in use of computers, software. *Academic computing expenditure 1995–96:* $231,932.

EXPENSES AND FINANCIAL AID

Expenses for 1997–98: *Application fee:* $20. Comprehensive fee of $17,160 includes full-time tuition ($12,270), mandatory fees ($390), and college room and board ($4500). Part-time tuition: $420 per semester hour.
Undergraduate Financial Aid: 96% of all full-time undergraduates enrolled in fall 1996 applied for aid; of these, 97% were judged to have need according to Federal Methodology, of whom 97% were aided. On average, 77% of need was met. *Financial aid deadline (priority):* 3/1. *Financial aid forms:* FAFSA required; CSS Financial Aid PROFILE, state form acceptable. Institutional form required for some.
LD Services Contact: Ms. Denise L. S. Howe, Coordinator of Learning Support Services, Manchester College, Box 86, North Manchester, IN 46962, 219-982-5076. Fax: 219-982-5043.

MANKATO STATE UNIVERSITY

Mankato, Minnesota

LEARNING DISABILITIES SERVICES INFORMATION

Disability Services Office currently serves 200 undergraduates with LD. Services are also available to graduate students. Students diagnosed with ADD/ADHD are eligible for the same services available to students with LD, as well as coaching.
Staff: 1 full-time, 2 part-time staff members, including director, coordinators. Services provided by tutors.
Special Fees: No special fees are charged for services to students with LD.
Applications and admissions: *Required:* high school transcript, grade point average, class rank, courses completed, extended time SAT I; *recommended:* high school extracurricular activities, IEP (Individualized Education Program), untimed or extended time ACT. Students may begin taking classes any term. *Application deadline:* continuous.
Special policies: The college has written policies regarding grade forgiveness.

PROGRAM AND SERVICE COMPONENTS

Diagnostic testing: Reading, math, study skills, learning strategies.
Academic advising: Provided by unit staff members, academic advisers. Students with LD may take up to 20 quarter hours each term; most take 12 quarter hours; 8 quarter hours required to maintain full-time status; 15 quarter hours (state), 12 quarter hours (federal) required to be eligible for financial aid.
Counseling services: Career counseling, self-advocacy training.
Basic skills remediation: Offered one-on-one and in small groups by regular teachers, graduate assistants; computer-aided instruction also offered. Available in reading, math, spoken language, written language, learning strategies, study skills, time management, computer skills.
Subject-area tutoring: Offered one-on-one and in small groups by peer tutors. Available in most subjects.
Auxiliary aids: Taped textbooks, tape recorders, calculators, word-processors with spell-check, optical character readers.
Auxiliary services: Alternative test arrangements, notetakers, priority registration, advocacy.

GENERAL COLLEGE INFORMATION

State-supported, comprehensive, coed. Part of Minnesota State Colleges and Universities System. Awards associate, bachelor's, master's degrees. Founded 1868. *Setting:* 303-acre small-town campus with easy access to Minneapolis–St. Paul. *Total enrollment:* 12,695. *Faculty:* 715 (540 full-time, 63% with terminal degrees, 175 part-time).
Enrollment Profile: 10,652 students from 45 states and territories, 68 other countries. 52% women, 48% men, 16% part-time, 84% state residents, 25% live on campus, 39% transferred in, 4% international, 21% 25 or older, 1% Hispanic, 1% black, 2% Asian or Pacific Islander. *Retention:* 73% of 1995 full-time freshmen returned. *Graduation:* 14% graduate in 4 years, 34% in 5 years, 41% in 6 years. *Areas of study chosen:* 15% liberal arts/general studies, 14% social sciences, 10% education, 8% health professions and related sciences, 7% business management and administrative services, 5% computer and information sciences, 4% engineering and applied sciences, 4% fine arts, 3% biological and life sciences, 3% psychology, 2% communications and journalism, 2% vocational and home economics, 1% English language/literature/letters, 1% interdisciplinary studies. *Most popular recent majors:* business administration/commerce/management, education, accounting.
First-Year Class: 1,537 total; 3,429 applied, 87% were accepted, 51% of whom enrolled. 9% from top 10% of their high school class, 29% from top quarter, 70% from top half.
Graduation Requirements: 96 quarter hours for associate, 192 quarter hours for bachelor's; 12 quarter hours of math/science; computer course for business, engineering, nursing majors; internship (some majors); senior project for honors program students and some majors.
Computers on Campus: 525 computers available on campus for general student use. Computer purchase/lease plans available. A campus-wide network can be accessed from student residence rooms and from off-campus. Students can contact faculty members and/or advisers through e-mail. Computers for student use in computer center, computer labs, classrooms, library, dorms provide access to the Internet/World Wide Web, on- and off-campus e-mail addresses. Staffed computer lab on campus provides training in use of computers, software.

EXPENSES AND FINANCIAL AID

Expenses for 1996–97: *Application fee:* $20. State resident tuition: $2517 full-time, $52.45 per quarter hour part-time. Nonresident tuition: $5625 full-time, $117.20 per quarter hour part-time. Part-time mandatory fees: $10.52 per quarter hour. Full-time mandatory fees: $379. College room and board: $2965.
Undergraduate Financial Aid: On average, 70% of need was met. *Financial aid deadline (priority):* 3/15. *Financial aid forms:* FAFSA required.
LD Services Contact: Ms. Audrey Metro, Director, Mankato State University, PO Box 8400, Mankato, MN 56002-8400, 507-389-2825. Fax: 507-389-5751. Email: audrey.metro@mankato.msus.edu.

MANSFIELD UNIVERSITY OF PENNSYLVANIA

Mansfield, Pennsylvania

LEARNING DISABILITIES SERVICES INFORMATION

Services for Students with Disabilities began offering services in 1986. Currently the program serves 45 undergraduates with LD. Services are also available to graduate students. Students diagnosed with ADD/ADHD are eligible for the same services available to students with LD.
Staff: 5 part-time staff members, including director, coordinators. Services provided by graduate assistants.
Special Fees: No special fees are charged for services to students with LD.
Applications and admissions: *Required:* high school transcript, grade point average, courses completed, untimed SAT I, personal interview; *recommended:* high school class rank, extracurricular activities, IEP (Individualized Education Program), extended time SAT I or untimed ACT, autobiographical statement, psychoeducational report completed within 1 year (if needed). Students may begin taking classes in fall, spring, or summer. *Application deadline:* continuous.

PROGRAM AND SERVICE COMPONENTS

Diagnostic testing: Reading, math, written language, perceptual skills, study skills.
Academic advising: Provided by unit staff members, academic advisers. Students with LD may take up to 18 credits each term; most take 16 credits; 12 credits required to maintain full-time status and be eligible for financial aid.
Counseling services: Individual counseling, small-group counseling, career counseling.
Subject-area tutoring: Offered one-on-one and in small groups by professional teachers, peer tutors. Available in some subjects.
Auxiliary aids: Taped textbooks, tape recorders, typewriters, word-processors with spell-check.
Auxiliary services: Alternative test arrangements, notetakers, priority registration, advocacy.
Campus support group: A special student organization is available to students with LD.

GENERAL COLLEGE INFORMATION

State-supported, comprehensive, coed. Part of Pennsylvania State System of Higher Education. Awards associate, bachelor's, master's degrees. Founded 1857. *Setting:* 205-acre small-town campus. *Total enrollment:* 2,897. *Undergraduate faculty:* 201 (181 full-time, 16% with terminal degrees, 20 part-time).
Enrollment Profile: 2,691 students from 17 states and territories, 13 other countries. 58% women, 42% men, 16% part-time, 88% state residents, 18% transferred in, 1% international, 13% 25 or older, 1% Native American, 1% Hispanic, 4% black, 1% Asian or Pacific Islander. *Retention:* 70% of 1995 full-time freshmen returned. *Most popular recent majors:* criminal justice, elementary education, business administration/commerce/management.
First-Year Class: 595 total; 2,431 applied, 61% were accepted, 40% of whom enrolled. 11% from top 10% of their high school class, 37% from top quarter, 74% from top half.
Graduation Requirements: 64 credits for associate, 120 credits for bachelor's; computer course for math, physical science, business administration, social science, pre-engineering, education majors; internship (some majors); senior project for honors program students.
Computers on Campus: 700 computers available on campus for general student use. A campus-wide network can be accessed from student residence rooms. Students can contact faculty members and/or advisers through e-mail. Computers for student use in computer center, computer labs, learning resource center, classrooms, library, dorms, recreational center provide access to the Internet/World Wide Web, on- and off-campus e-mail addresses. Staffed computer lab on campus (open 24 hours a day) provides training in use of software.

EXPENSES AND FINANCIAL AID

Expenses for 1997–98: *Application fee:* $25. State resident tuition: $3468 full-time, $144 per credit part-time. Nonresident tuition: $8824 full-time, $368 per credit part-time. Part-time mandatory fees per semester range from $101.25 to $372.50. Full-time mandatory fees: $986. College room and board: $3694. College room only: $2080.
Undergraduate Financial Aid: Of all full-time undergraduates enrolled in fall 1996, 65% of those who applied for aid were judged to have need according to Federal Methodology, of whom 98% were aided. On average, 85% of need was met. *Financial aid deadline:* Applications processed continuously. *Financial aid forms:* FAFSA, institutional form required. State form required for some.
LD Services Contact: Dr. Celeste Burns Sexauer, Coordinator of Services for Students with Disabilities, Mansfield University of Pennsylvania, 110 Retan Center, Mansfield, PA 16933, 717-662-4564. Fax: 717-662-4364.

MARQUETTE UNIVERSITY

Milwaukee, Wisconsin

LEARNING DISABILITIES SERVICES INFORMATION

Disability Services began offering services in 1982. Currently the program serves 24 undergraduates with LD. Services are also available to graduate students. Students diagnosed with ADD/ADHD are eligible for the same services available to students with LD, as well as assistance with time management and study skills.
Staff: 1 full-time staff member (coordinator).
Special Fees: $500 to $1000 for diagnostic testing.
Applications and admissions: *Required:* high school transcript, courses completed, untimed SAT I or ACT; *recommended:* high school grade point average, class rank, extended time SAT I or ACT, letters of recommendation, psychoeducational report completed within 3 years. Students may begin taking classes in fall only. *Application deadline:* continuous.
Special policies: The college has written policies regarding substitutions and waivers of degree requirements.

PROGRAM AND SERVICE COMPONENTS

Diagnostic testing: Intelligence, reading, math, spelling, written language, perceptual skills, learning strategies.
Academic advising: Provided by academic advisers. Students with LD may take up to 18 credits each term; most take 12 to 18 credits; 12 credits required to maintain full-time status and be eligible for financial aid.
Counseling services: Individual counseling, career counseling.
Auxiliary aids: Taped textbooks, tape recorders, word-processors with spell-check, personal computers, optical character readers.
Auxiliary services: Alternative test arrangements, notetakers, priority registration, advocacy.

GENERAL COLLEGE INFORMATION

Independent Roman Catholic (Jesuit), coed. Awards associate, bachelor's, master's, doctoral, first professional degrees. Founded 1881. *Setting:* 80-acre urban campus. *Endowment:* $159.8 million. *Research spending 1995–96:* $10.8 million. *Educational spending 1995–96:* $6065 per undergrad. *Total enrollment:* 10,539. *Faculty:* 996 (550 full-time, 96% with terminal degrees, 446 part-time); student–undergrad faculty ratio is 15:1.
Enrollment Profile: 7,474 students from 55 states and territories, 77 other countries. 53% women, 47% men, 8% part-time, 49% state residents, 39% live on campus, 4% transferred in, 5% international, 1% Native American, 4% Hispanic, 4% black, 5% Asian or Pacific Islander. *Retention:* 86% of 1995 full-time freshmen returned. *Graduation:* 54% graduate in 4 years, 72% in 5 years, 75% in 6 years. *Areas of study chosen:* 23% liberal arts/general studies, 18% business management and administrative services, 18% engineering and applied sciences, 12% communications and journalism, 10% health professions and related sciences, 4% education, 4% social sciences, 3% biological and life sciences, 3% psychology, 1% computer and information sciences, 1% English language/literature/letters, 1% foreign language and literature, 1% interdisciplinary studies, 1% mathematics, 1% performing arts, 1% philosophy, 1% physical sciences, 1% theology/religion. *Most popular recent majors:* business administration/commerce/management, electrical engineering, civil engineering.
First-Year Class: 1,420 total; 5,323 applied. 33% from top 10% of their high school class, 64% from top quarter, 91% from top half. 5 National Merit Scholars, 61 valedictorians.
Graduation Requirements: 65 credits for associate, 128 credits for bachelor's; computer course for business administration, engineering, communication majors; senior project for honors program students and some majors.
Computers on Campus: 800 computers available on campus for general student use. Computer purchase/lease plans available. A campus-wide network can be accessed from student residence rooms and from

off-campus. Students can contact faculty members and/or advisers through e-mail. Computers for student use in computer center, computer labs, research center, learning resource center, classrooms, library, student center, dorms provide access to the Internet/World Wide Web, on- and off-campus e-mail addresses. Staffed computer lab on campus (open 24 hours a day) provides training in use of computers, software. *Academic computing expenditure 1995–96:* $2.7 million.

EXPENSES AND FINANCIAL AID

Expenses for 1997–98: *Application fee:* $30. Comprehensive fee of $18,420 includes full-time tuition ($13,840 minimum), mandatory fees ($224), and college room and board ($4356 minimum). Part-time tuition: $455 per credit. Full-time tuition ranges up to $16,000 according to program and class level. Tuition for Part-time Studies Program: $315 per credit.

Undergraduate Financial Aid: 66% of all full-time undergraduates enrolled in fall 1996 applied for aid; of these, 88% were judged to have need according to Federal Methodology, of whom 100% were aided. On average, 92% of need was met. *Financial aid deadline (priority):* 3/1. *Financial aid forms:* FAFSA required. Institutional form required for some.

LD Services Contact: Ms. Patricia Almon, Coordinator, Disability Services, Marquette University, 1324 West Wisconsin Avenue, Milwaukee, WI 53233, 414-224-1645. Fax: 414-224-5799. Email: almonp@vms.csd.mu.edu.

MARYMOUNT COLLEGE

Tarrytown, New York

LEARNING DISABILITIES SERVICES INFORMATION

Learning Services began offering services in 1990. Currently the program serves 20 undergraduates with LD. Students diagnosed with ADD/ADHD are eligible for the same services available to students with LD.

Staff: 1 part-time staff member (director). Services provided by tutors.

Special Fees: No special fees are charged for services to students with LD.

Applications and admissions: *Required:* high school transcript, courses completed, untimed SAT I, letters of recommendation; *recommended:* high school grade point average, class rank, extracurricular activities, IEP (Individualized Education Program), extended time SAT I, personal interview, psychoeducational report. Students may begin taking classes in fall only. *Application deadline:* continuous.

Special policies: The college has written policies regarding substitutions and waivers of graduation and degree requirements.

PROGRAM AND SERVICE COMPONENTS

Academic advising: Provided by unit staff members, academic advisers. Students with LD may take up to 15 semester hours each term; most take 12 semester hours; 12 semester hours required to maintain full-time status and be eligible for financial aid.

Counseling services: Individual counseling, small-group counseling, self-advocacy training, LD support group.

Subject-area tutoring: Offered one-on-one and in small groups by peer tutors. Available in most subjects.

Auxiliary aids: Tape recorders, calculators, word-processors with spell-check, personal computers.

Auxiliary services: Alternative test arrangements, notetakers, advocacy.

GENERAL COLLEGE INFORMATION

Independent, 4-year, primarily women. Awards bachelor's degrees. Founded 1907. *Setting:* 25-acre suburban campus with easy access to New York City. *Endowment:* $2.8 million. *Total enrollment:* 947. *Faculty:* 146 (56 full-time, 97% with terminal degrees, 90 part-time); student–undergrad faculty ratio is 12:1.

Enrollment Profile: 947 students from 15 states and territories, 11 other countries. 94% women, 6% men, 28% part-time, 80% state residents, 43% transferred in, 6% international, 47% 25 or older, 14% Hispanic, 16% black, 3% Asian or Pacific Islander. *Retention:* 75% of 1995 full-time freshmen returned. *Graduation:* 37% graduate in 4 years, 43% in 5 years, 45% in 6 years. *Areas of study chosen:* 15% education, 12% fine arts, 12% social sciences, 11% business management and administrative services, 11% health professions and related sciences, 8% vocational and home economics, 6% psychology, 5% biological and life sciences, 5% English language/literature/letters, 4% communications and journalism, 3% foreign language and literature, 3% performing arts, 2% computer and information sciences, 2% mathematics, 1% physical sciences. *Most popular recent majors:* business administration/commerce/management, education, nutrition.

First-Year Class: 131 total; 455 applied, 84% were accepted, 34% of whom enrolled. 9% from top 10% of their high school class, 35% from top quarter, 75% from top half. 1 class president.

Graduation Requirements: 120 semester hours; 2 courses each in math and science; 2 courses in a foreign language; computer course; internship (some majors); senior project (some majors).

Computers on Campus: 82 computers available on campus for general student use. A computer is recommended for all students. A campus-wide network can be accessed from student residence rooms and from off-campus. Students can contact faculty members and/or advisers through e-mail. Computers for student use in computer center, computer labs, classrooms, dorms provide access to the Internet/World Wide Web, on- and off-campus e-mail addresses. Staffed computer lab on campus (open 24 hours a day) provides training in use of computers, software. *Academic computing expenditure 1995–96:* $49,236.

EXPENSES AND FINANCIAL AID

Expenses for 1997–98: *Application fee:* $30. Comprehensive fee of $21,015 includes full-time tuition ($13,370), mandatory fees ($445), and college room and board ($7200). Part-time tuition: $430 per semester hour. Part-time mandatory fees per semester range from $107.50 to $215.

Undergraduate Financial Aid: On average, 84% of need was met. *Financial aid deadline (priority):* 4/15. *Financial aid forms:* FAFSA, institutional form required. State form required for some.

LD Services Contact: Mr. Jason Berner, Director of Learning Services, Marymount College, 100 Marymount Avenue, Tarrytown, NY 10591, 914-631-3200. Email: berner@mmc.marymt.edu.

MARY WASHINGTON COLLEGE

Fredericksburg, Virginia

LEARNING DISABILITIES SERVICES INFORMATION

The Learning Disabilities special services program began offering services in 1989. Currently the program serves 61 undergraduates with LD. Services are also available to graduate students. Students diagnosed with ADD/ADHD are eligible for the same services available to students with LD.

Staff: 1 full-time staff member (director). Services provided by diagnostic specialists.

Special Fees: No special fees are charged for services to students with LD.

Applications and admissions: *Required:* high school transcript, essay. Students may begin taking classes in fall only. *Application deadline:* 2/1.

Special policies: The college has written policies regarding substitutions and waivers of graduation requirements.

PROGRAM AND SERVICE COMPONENTS

Special preparation or orientation: Optional summer program offered prior to entering college. Optional orientation offered the week before classes begin.

Diagnostic testing: Intelligence, reading, math, spelling, written language, perceptual skills.

Academic advising: Provided by unit staff members, academic advisers. Most students with LD take 15 semester hours each term; 12 semester hours (fewer with special permission) required to maintain full-time status.

Counseling services: Individual counseling, career counseling.

Special courses: College survival skills, reading, time management, study skills. None offered for credit; none enter into overall grade point average.

Auxiliary aids: Taped textbooks, tape recorders, word-processors with spell-check, optical character readers.

Auxiliary services: Alternative test arrangements, notetakers, priority registration.

Campus support group: A special student organization is available to students with LD.

GENERAL COLLEGE INFORMATION

State-supported, comprehensive, coed. Awards bachelor's, master's degrees. Founded 1908. *Setting:* 176-acre small-town campus with easy access to Richmond and Washington, DC. *Endowment:* $14.3 million. *Research spending 1995–96:* $289,896. *Educational spending 1995–96:*

$3271 per undergrad. *Total enrollment:* 3,745. *Undergraduate faculty:* 243 (172 full-time, 88% with terminal degrees, 71 part-time); student–undergrad faculty ratio is 18:1.

Enrollment Profile: 3,694 students from 42 states and territories, 33 other countries. 65% women, 35% men, 15% part-time, 70% state residents, 8% transferred in, 1% international, 6% 25 or older, 0% Native American, 2% Hispanic, 6% black, 3% Asian or Pacific Islander. *Retention:* 90% of 1995 full-time freshmen returned. *Graduation:* 65% graduate in 4 years, 72% in 5 years. *Areas of study chosen:* 35% social sciences, 15% business management and administrative services, 11% English language/literature/letters, 10% psychology, 8% biological and life sciences, 3% computer and information sciences, 3% fine arts, 3% foreign language and literature, 3% mathematics, 3% natural resource sciences, 3% physical sciences, 1% performing arts, 1% philosophy, 1% theology/religion. *Most popular recent majors:* business administration/commerce/management, psychology, English.

First-Year Class: 736 total; 4,003 applied, 55% were accepted, 33% of whom enrolled. 35% from top 10% of their high school class, 79% from top quarter, 98% from top half. 2 National Merit Scholars.

Graduation Requirements: 122 semester hours; 1 math course; 2 lab science courses; 2 years of a foreign language or the equivalent; computer course for math majors; senior project (some majors).

Computers on Campus: 157 computers available on campus for general student use. Computer purchase/lease plans available. A computer is recommended for all students. A campus-wide network can be accessed from student residence rooms and from off-campus. Students can contact faculty members and/or advisers through e-mail. Computers for student use in computer center, computer labs, library provide access to the Internet/World Wide Web, on- and off-campus e-mail addresses. Staffed computer lab on campus (open 24 hours a day) provides training in use of computers, software. *Academic computing expenditure 1995–96:* $393,000.

EXPENSES AND FINANCIAL AID

Expenses for 1997–98: *Application fee:* $25. State resident tuition: $3556 full-time, $115 per semester hour part-time. Nonresident tuition: $8516 full-time, $279 per semester hour part-time. College room and board: $5080.

Undergraduate Financial Aid: 74% of all full-time undergraduates enrolled in fall 1996 applied for aid; of these, 65% were judged to have need according to Federal Methodology, of whom 99% were aided. *Financial aid deadline:* Applications processed continuously. *Financial aid forms:* FAFSA required.

LD Services Contact: Ms. Patricia B. Tracy, Coordinator of Special Academic Support Services/Director of Disability Services, Mary Washington College, 1301 College Avenue, Fredericksburg, VA 22401-5358, 540-654-1010. Fax: 540-654-1163. Email: ptracy@mwcgw.mwc.edu.

MARYWOOD UNIVERSITY

Scranton, Pennsylvania

LEARNING DISABILITIES SERVICES INFORMATION

Office of Special Services currently serves 18 undergraduates with LD. Services are also available to graduate students. Students diagnosed with ADD/ADHD are eligible for the same services available to students with LD.

Staff: 2 part-time staff members, including Advisor for Special Services, academic adviser for Special Services. Services provided by tutors, counselors.

Special Fees: No special fees are charged for services to students with LD.

Applications and admissions: *Required:* high school transcript, grade point average, class rank, courses completed, extracurricular activities, letters of recommendation, psychoeducational report completed within 4 years; *recommended:* high school IEP (Individualized Education Program), untimed or extended time SAT I, personal interview. Students may begin taking classes in fall or spring. *Application deadline:* continuous.

PROGRAM AND SERVICE COMPONENTS

Special preparation or orientation: Optional orientation offered during orientation for all students (July).

Academic advising: Provided by academic advisers. Students with LD may take up to 12 credits each term; most take 12 credits; 12 credits required to maintain full-time status and be eligible for financial aid.

Counseling services: Individual counseling, career counseling.

Basic skills remediation: Offered in class-size groups by regular teachers. Available in reading, learning strategies, study skills, time management.

Subject-area tutoring: Offered one-on-one by peer tutors. Available in all subjects.

Auxiliary aids: Taped textbooks, tape recorders, optical character readers.

Auxiliary services: Alternative test arrangements, notetakers, advocacy, readers.

GENERAL COLLEGE INFORMATION

Independent Roman Catholic, comprehensive, coed. Awards associate, bachelor's, master's, doctoral degrees. Founded 1915. *Setting:* 115-acre suburban campus. *Endowment:* $2.5 million. *Research spending 1995–96:* $1.4 million. *Educational spending 1995–96:* $5859 per undergrad. *Total enrollment:* 2,926. *Faculty:* 250 (130 full-time, 83% with terminal degrees, 120 part-time); student–undergrad faculty ratio is 12:1.

Enrollment Profile: 1,758 students from 26 states and territories, 16 other countries. 75% women, 25% men, 19% part-time, 77% state residents, 31% live on campus, 35% transferred in, 1% international, 26% 25 or older, 1% Native American, 2% Hispanic, 1% black, 1% Asian or Pacific Islander. *Retention:* 83% of 1995 full-time freshmen returned. *Graduation:* 41% graduate in 4 years, 58% in 5 years, 59% in 6 years. *Areas of study chosen:* 17% education, 17% health professions and related sciences, 15% business management and administrative services, 12% performing arts, 12% social sciences, 6% communications and journalism, 5% psychology, 4% vocational and home economics, 3% English language/literature/letters, 2% biological and life sciences, 2% computer and information sciences, 2% natural resource sciences, 1% foreign language and literature, 1% interdisciplinary studies, 1% mathematics. *Most popular recent majors:* elementary education, graphic arts, business administration/commerce/management.

First-Year Class: 273 total; 1,006 applied, 75% were accepted, 36% of whom enrolled. 21% from top 10% of their high school class, 51% from top quarter, 89% from top half.

Graduation Requirements: 63 credits for associate, 126 credits for bachelor's; 9 math/science courses; 6 credits of a foreign language; computer course for most majors; internship (some majors); senior project for honors program students and some majors.

Computers on Campus: 300 computers available on campus for general student use. Computer purchase/lease plans available. Computers for student use in computer center, computer labs, research center, learning resource center, classrooms, library, student center, dorms, student rooms provide access to the Internet/World Wide Web. Staffed computer lab on campus provides training in use of computers, software. *Academic computing expenditure 1995–96:* $322,468.

EXPENSES AND FINANCIAL AID

Expenses for 1997–98: *Application fee:* $20. Comprehensive fee of $19,349 includes full-time tuition ($12,989), mandatory fees ($660), and college room and board ($5700). Part-time tuition: $419 per credit. Part-time mandatory fees: $110 per semester.

Undergraduate Financial Aid: 97% of all full-time undergraduates enrolled in fall 1996 applied for aid; of these, 80% were judged to have need according to Federal Methodology, of whom 100% were aided. On average, 77% of need was met. *Financial aid deadline (priority):* 2/15. *Financial aid forms:* FAFSA, institutional form required.

LD Services Contact: Sr. Marian Denise Walsh, Advisor for Special Services, Marywood University, 2300 Adams Avenue, Scranton, PA 18509-1598, 717-348-6211. Fax: 717-348-1899.

MAYVILLE STATE UNIVERSITY

Mayville, North Dakota

LEARNING DISABILITIES SERVICES INFORMATION

Learning Services Center/Student Support Services began offering services in 1988. Currently the program serves 25 undergraduates with LD. Students diagnosed with ADD/ADHD are eligible for the same services available to students with LD.

Staff: 1 full-time staff member (director). Services provided by tutors.

Special Fees: No special fees are charged for services to students with LD.

Applications and admissions: *Recommended:* psychoeducational report completed within 3 years. Students may begin taking classes in fall only. *Application deadline:* continuous.

PROGRAM AND SERVICE COMPONENTS

Academic advising: Provided by unit staff members, academic advisers. Students with LD may take up to 8 semester hours each term; most take 8 semester hours; 8 semester hours required to maintain full-time status and be eligible for financial aid.
Counseling services: Individual counseling.
Subject-area tutoring: Offered one-on-one and in small groups by professional teachers, peer tutors. Available in most subjects.
Special courses: Math. All offered for credit.
Auxiliary aids: Taped textbooks, tape recorders, calculators, word-processors with spell-check.
Auxiliary services: Alternative test arrangements, notetakers.

GENERAL COLLEGE INFORMATION

State-supported, 4-year, coed. Part of North Dakota University System. Awards associate, bachelor's degrees. Founded 1889. *Setting:* 60-acre rural campus. *Total enrollment:* 680. *Faculty:* 62 (39 full-time, 57% with terminal degrees, 23 part-time).
Enrollment Profile: 680 students from 17 states and territories, 2 other countries. 49% women, 51% men, 6% part-time, 74% state residents, 10% transferred in, 8% international, 15% 25 or older, 1% Native American, 1% Hispanic, 1% black, 1% Asian or Pacific Islander. *Most popular recent majors:* elementary education, business administration/commerce/ management, computer information systems.
First-Year Class: 217 total; 265 applied, 100% were accepted, 82% of whom enrolled.
Graduation Requirements: 96 quarter hours for associate, 192 quarter hours for bachelor's; 4 quarter hours of math; 12 quarter hours of science for bachelor's degree; computer course.
Computers on Campus: 50 computers available on campus for general student use. Computers for student use in computer center, computer labs, library, business departmental lab, learning center.

EXPENSES AND FINANCIAL AID

Expenses for 1997–98: State resident tuition: $1680 full-time, $70 per quarter hour part-time. Nonresident tuition: $4486 full-time, $186.92 per quarter hour part-time. Part-time mandatory fees: $10 per quarter hour. Tuition for Minnesota residents: $1912 full-time, $79.67 per quarter hour part-time. Tuition for Manitoba, Montana, Saskatchewan, and South Dakota residents: $2100 full-time, $85.50 per quarter hour part-time. Tuition for students eligible for the Western Undergraduate Exchange Program: $2520 full-time. $105 per quarter hour part-time. Full-time mandatory fees: $240. College room and board: $2382.
Undergraduate Financial Aid: Of all full-time undergraduates enrolled in fall 1996, 65% of those who applied for aid were judged to have need according to Federal Methodology, of whom 99% were aided. On average, 80% of need was met. *Financial aid deadline:* continuous. *Financial aid forms:* FAFSA, institutional form required.
LD Services Contact: Ms. Shirley Tiokasin, Academic Resource Coordinator, Mayville State University, 330 North 3rd Street, Mayville, ND 58045, 701-786-4883. Fax: 701-786-4846. Email: tiokasin@badlands.nodak.edu.

MCGILL UNIVERSITY

Montréal, Quebec, Canada

LEARNING DISABILITIES SERVICES INFORMATION

Office for Students with Disabilities began offering services in 1988. Currently the program serves 83 undergraduates with LD. Services are also available to graduate students. Students diagnosed with ADD/ ADHD are eligible for the same services available to students with LD, as well as time extensions for assignments, referrals to personal coaches, peer support group.
Staff: 2 full-time staff members, including director, co-director.
Special Fees: No special fees are charged for services to students with LD.
Applications and admissions: *Required:* untimed SAT I, letters of recommendation. Students may begin taking classes in fall or winter. *Application deadline:* 1/15 (fall term), 1/11 (spring term).

PROGRAM AND SERVICE COMPONENTS

Academic advising: Provided by unit staff members, academic advisers. Students with LD may take up to 15 credits each term; most take 9 to 12 credits; 12 credits required to maintain full-time status and be eligible for financial aid.
Counseling services: Individual counseling, small-group counseling, career counseling.
Basic skills remediation: Offered one-on-one and in small groups by graduate students; computer-aided instruction also offered. Available in written language, learning strategies, computer skills.
Subject-area tutoring: Offered one-on-one and in small groups by graduate students. Available in most subjects.
Auxiliary aids: Taped textbooks, tape recorders, calculators, typewriters, word-processors with spell-check, personal computers, talking computers, optical character readers, word processors with voice recognition.
Auxiliary services: Alternative test arrangements, notetakers, advocacy.
Campus support group: A special student organization is available to students with LD.

GENERAL COLLEGE INFORMATION

Province-supported, coed. Awards bachelor's, master's, doctoral degrees. Founded 1821. *Setting:* 80-acre urban campus. *Total enrollment:* 30,945. *Faculty:* 2,704 (2,039 full-time, 93% with terminal degrees, 665 part-time).
Enrollment Profile: 23,488 students: 57% women, 43% men, 44% part-time, 58% province residents, 9% live on campus, 11% international. *Most popular recent majors:* English, psychology, political science/ government.
First-Year Class: 3,616 total; 11,823 applied, 60% were accepted, 51% of whom enrolled. 90% from top quarter of their high school class, 100% from top half.
Graduation Requirements: 120 credits; computer course for chemistry, math, engineering, commerce majors.
Computers on Campus: 500 computers available on campus for general student use. Computer purchase/lease plans available. A computer is recommended for some students. A campus-wide network can be accessed from student residence rooms and from off-campus. Students can contact faculty members and/or advisers through e-mail. Computers for student use in computer center, library, student center, various locations provide access to the Internet/World Wide Web, on- and off-campus e-mail addresses. Staffed computer lab on campus (open 24 hours a day) provides training in use of computers, software.

EXPENSES AND FINANCIAL AID

Estimated Expenses for 1997–98: *Application fee:* $60. Area resident tuition: $1668 full-time, $55.61 per credit part-time. Canadian resident tuition: $2868 full-time, $95.61 per credit part-time. Nonresident tuition: $8268 (minimum) full-time, $275.61 per credit part-time. Part-time mandatory fees: $305.61 per semester. (All figures are in Canadian dollars.). Full-time mandatory fees range from $693 to $1090. College room and board: $5070.
Undergraduate Financial Aid: *Financial aid deadline:* continuous. *Financial aid forms:* FAFSA, CSS Financial Aid PROFILE, state form, institutional form required for some.
LD Services Contact: Ms. Joan Wolforth, Coordinator, McGill University, Room 107, Burnside Hall, 805 Sherbrooke Street West, Montreal, PQ H3A 2K6, Canada, 514-398-6009. Fax: 514-398-3984. Email: joanw@stuserv.lan.mcgill.ca.

MCMASTER UNIVERSITY

Hamilton, Ontario, Canada

LEARNING DISABILITIES SERVICES INFORMATION

Centre for Student Development began offering services in 1988. Currently the program serves 80 undergraduates with LD. Services are also available to graduate students. Students diagnosed with ADD/ ADHD are eligible for the same services available to students with LD.
Staff: 4 full-time staff members, including coordinators, administrative assistant. Services provided by counselors, diagnostic specialists.
Special Fees: $200 to $950 for diagnostic testing.
Applications and admissions: *Required:* high school transcript, grade point average, courses completed, psychoeducational report completed within 3 years. Students may begin taking classes in fall or winter. *Application deadline:* continuous.

PROGRAM AND SERVICE COMPONENTS

Diagnostic testing: Intelligence, reading, math, spelling, handwriting, written language, motor abilities, perceptual skills, study skills, personality, social skills, learning strategies.
Academic advising: Provided by unit staff members, academic advisers. Students with LD may take up to 30 units each term; most take 3 to 30

McMaster University (continued)

units; 18 units required to maintain full-time status; source of aid determines number of units required to be eligible for financial aid.
Counseling services: Individual counseling, career counseling, self-advocacy training.
Basic skills remediation: Offered one-on-one and in small groups by Learning Specialist, academic counselors. Available in written language, learning strategies, study skills, time management.
Subject-area tutoring: Offered one-on-one by peer tutors. Available in most subjects.
Auxiliary aids: Taped textbooks, tape recorders, calculators, typewriters, word-processors with spell-check, personal computers, optical character readers, taped tests and exams.
Auxiliary services: Alternative test arrangements, notetakers, advocacy.

GENERAL COLLEGE INFORMATION

Province-supported, coed. Awards bachelor's, master's, doctoral degrees (also offers 3-year general bachelor's degree). Founded 1887. *Setting:* 300-acre suburban campus with easy access to Toronto. *Total enrollment:* 16,683. *Faculty:* 1,265 (1,040 full-time, 225 part-time); student–undergrad faculty ratio is 23:1.
Enrollment Profile: 14,568 students from 12 provinces and territories, 90 other countries. 18% part-time.
First-Year Class: 3,371 total; 19,127 applied, 55% were accepted, 32% of whom enrolled.
Graduation Requirements: 90 units for bachelor of general studies, 120 credits for bachelor of arts or bachelor of science; computer course for business, math, economics, engineering, statistics majors; senior project (some majors).
Computers on Campus: 400 computers available on campus for general student use. Computer purchase/lease plans available. A campus-wide network can be accessed from student residence rooms and from off-campus. Students can contact faculty members and/or advisers through e-mail. Computers for student use in computer center, computer labs, learning resource center, library, various locations provide access to the Internet/World Wide Web, on- and off-campus e-mail addresses. Staffed computer lab on campus provides training in use of computers, software.

EXPENSES AND FINANCIAL AID

Expenses for 1997–98: *Application fee:* $85. Part-time mandatory fees: $9.95 per unit. Full-time tuition and fees range from $3710 to $4016 for Canadian residents, $11,515 to $13,530 for nonresidents, according to program. Part-time tuition per course range from $106.23 to $114.45 for Canadian residents, $364 to $431 for nonresidents, according to course load and program. (All figures are in Canadian dollars.). College room and board: $5050 (minimum). College room only: $2825.
Undergraduate Financial Aid: *Financial aid deadline (priority):* 7/1. *Financial aid forms:* state form required.
LD Services Contact: Ms. Caroline Cayuga, Programme Coordinator-Learning Specialist, McMaster University, Hamilton Hall, Room 409, Hamilton, ON L8S 4M1, Canada, 905-525-9140. Fax: 905-528-3749.

MEDAILLE COLLEGE
Buffalo, New York

LEARNING DISABILITIES SERVICES INFORMATION

Learning Services Center began offering services in 1979. Currently the program serves 30 undergraduates with LD. Students diagnosed with ADD/ADHD are eligible for the same services available to students with LD.
Staff: Includes director, associate directors, study skills specialist, reading specialist, writing specialist. Services provided by remediation specialists, tutors, counselors.
Special Fees: No special fees are charged for services to students with LD.
Applications and admissions: *Required:* high school transcript, courses completed, personal interview; *recommended:* high school extracurricular activities, untimed or extended time SAT I, autobiographical statement, letters of recommendation, psychoeducational report. Students may begin taking classes in fall or spring. *Application deadline:* continuous.

PROGRAM AND SERVICE COMPONENTS

Academic advising: Provided by academic advisers. Students with LD may take up to 12 credit hours each term; most take 12 credit hours; 12 credit hours required to maintain full-time status and be eligible for financial aid.
Counseling services: Individual counseling, career counseling.
Basic skills remediation: Offered in small groups by regular teachers. Available in reading, math, spelling, learning strategies, study skills.
Subject-area tutoring: Offered one-on-one by professional teachers, peer tutors. Available in all subjects.
Special courses: College survival skills, reading, vocabulary development, composition, word processing, math, career planning, stress management. All offered for credit; all enter into overall grade point average.
Auxiliary aids: Tape recorders, calculators, typewriters, word-processors with spell-check.
Auxiliary services: Alternative test arrangements, notetakers, advocacy.

GENERAL COLLEGE INFORMATION

Independent, 4-year, coed. Awards associate, bachelor's degrees. Founded 1875. *Setting:* 13-acre urban campus. *Endowment:* $1.1 million. *Total enrollment:* 878. *Faculty:* 97 (41 full-time, 78% with terminal degrees, 56 part-time); student–undergrad faculty ratio is 17:1.
Enrollment Profile: 878 students from 4 states and territories, 2 other countries. 70% women, 30% men, 25% part-time, 92% state residents, 5% live on campus, 30% transferred in, 7% international, 57% 25 or older, 1% Native American, 2% Hispanic, 14% black, 0% Asian or Pacific Islander. *Retention:* 64% of 1995 full-time freshmen returned. *Graduation:* 13% graduate in 4 years, 20% in 5 years, 26% in 6 years. *Areas of study chosen:* 20% education, 19% social sciences, 17% interdisciplinary studies, 9% prevet, 5% communications and journalism. *Most popular recent majors:* elementary education, veterinary technology, liberal arts/general studies.
First-Year Class: 127 total; 319 applied, 67% were accepted, 59% of whom enrolled. 1 class president, 1 valedictorian.
Graduation Requirements: 60 credit hours for associate, 120 credit hours for bachelor's; 6 credit hours of math/science; computer course; internship (some majors); senior project (some majors).
Computers on Campus: 110 computers available on campus for general student use. A computer is required for some students. A campus-wide network can be accessed. Students can contact faculty members and/or advisers through e-mail. Computers for student use in computer center, computer labs, learning resource center provide access to the Internet/World Wide Web, on- and off-campus e-mail addresses. Staffed computer lab on campus provides training in use of computers, software. *Academic computing expenditure 1995–96:* $93,618.

EXPENSES AND FINANCIAL AID

Expenses for 1997–98: *Application fee:* $25. Comprehensive fee of $15,170 includes full-time tuition ($10,230), mandatory fees ($240), and college room and board ($4700 minimum). College room only: $3000 (minimum). Part-time tuition: $341 per credit hour. Part-time mandatory fees per semester range from $30 to $130.
Undergraduate Financial Aid: 75% of all full-time undergraduates enrolled in fall 1996 applied for aid; of these, 92% were judged to have need according to Federal Methodology, of whom 100% were aided. On average, 80% of need was met. *Financial aid deadline (priority):* 3/15. *Financial aid forms:* FAFSA, state form, institutional form required.
LD Services Contact: Ms. Jacqueline Matheny, Director of Enrollment Management, Medaille College, 18 Agassiz Circle, Buffalo, NY 14214-2695, 716-884-3281. Fax: 716-884-0291.

MESSIAH COLLEGE
Grantham, Pennsylvania

LEARNING DISABILITIES SERVICES INFORMATION

Disability Services began offering services in 1995. Currently the program serves 12 undergraduates with LD. Students diagnosed with ADD/ADHD are eligible for the same services available to students with LD, as well as on-campus assessment for eligibility.
Staff: 1 full-time, 1 part-time staff members, including director, secretary.
Special Fees: No special fees are charged for services to students with LD.
Applications and admissions: *Required:* high school transcript, grade point average, class rank, courses completed, extracurricular activities,

autobiographical statement, letters of recommendation, psychoeducational report completed within 3 years; *recommended:* high school IEP (Individualized Education Program), untimed or extended time SAT I, extended time ACT, personal interview. Students may begin taking classes in summer only. *Application deadline:* continuous.

PROGRAM AND SERVICE COMPONENTS

Special preparation or orientation: Summer program (required for some) held prior to entering college. Optional orientation offered before registration and during registration.
Academic advising: Provided by unit staff members, academic advisers. Most students with LD take 14 to 16 credits each term; 12 credits required to maintain full-time status and be eligible for financial aid.
Counseling services: Individual counseling.
Basic skills remediation: Offered one-on-one by peer tutors. Available in written language, learning strategies, study skills, time management.
Subject-area tutoring: Offered one-on-one by peer tutors. Available in most subjects.
Special courses: College survival skills, composition, learning strategies, time management, study skills, career planning. Some offered for credit; none enter into overall grade point average.
Auxiliary aids: Taped textbooks, typewriters, word-processors with spell-check, personal computers.
Auxiliary services: Alternative test arrangements, notetakers, priority registration, advocacy.

GENERAL COLLEGE INFORMATION

Independent, 4-year, coed, affiliated with Brethren in Christ Church. Awards bachelor's degrees. Founded 1909. *Setting:* 350-acre small-town campus. *Endowment:* $81 million. *Educational spending 1995–96:* $5456 per undergrad. *Total enrollment:* 2,517. *Faculty:* 211 (135 full-time, 70% with terminal degrees, 76 part-time); student–undergrad faculty ratio is 15:1.
Enrollment Profile: 2,517 students from 38 states and territories, 16 other countries. 61% women, 39% men, 4% part-time, 51% state residents, 90% live on campus, 3% transferred in, 1% international, 6% 25 or older, 1% Native American, 2% Hispanic, 1% black, 2% Asian or Pacific Islander. *Retention:* 81% of 1995 full-time freshmen returned. *Graduation:* 66% graduate in 4 years, 70% in 6 years. *Areas of study chosen:* 19% education, 11% business management and administrative services, 11% health professions and related sciences, 5% vocational and home economics, 4% biological and life sciences, 4% communications and journalism, 4% engineering and applied sciences, 4% premed, 4% psychology, 4% social sciences, 3% computer and information sciences, 3% English language/literature/letters, 3% fine arts, 3% theology/religion, 2% natural resource sciences, 1% foreign language and literature, 1% liberal arts/general studies, 1% mathematics, 1% performing arts, 1% philosophy, 1% physical sciences. *Most popular recent majors:* nursing, elementary education, biology/biological sciences.
First-Year Class: 672 total; 1,904 applied, 85% were accepted, 42% of whom enrolled. 33% from top 10% of their high school class, 66% from top quarter, 90% from top half. 9 National Merit Scholars, 22 valedictorians.
Graduation Requirements: 126 credits; 3 credits each of math and science; 6 credits of a foreign language for a bachelor of science degree, 9 credits of a foreign language for a bachelor of arts degree; computer course for business information systems, engineering, math majors; internship (some majors); senior project (some majors).
Computers on Campus: 310 computers available on campus for general student use. A computer is recommended for all students. A campus-wide network can be accessed from student residence rooms and from off-campus. Students can contact faculty members and/or advisers through e-mail. Computers for student use in computer center, computer labs, research center, learning resource center, classrooms, library, dorms provide access to the Internet/World Wide Web, on- and off-campus e-mail addresses. Staffed computer lab on campus provides training in use of computers, software. *Academic computing expenditure 1995–96:* $730,572.

EXPENSES AND FINANCIAL AID

Expenses for 1997–98: *Application fee:* $30. Comprehensive fee of $18,490 includes full-time tuition ($12,900), mandatory fees ($90), and college room and board ($5500). College room only: $2800. Part-time tuition: $540 per credit. Part-time mandatory fees: $3 per credit.
Undergraduate Financial Aid: 79% of all full-time undergraduates enrolled in fall 1996 applied for aid; of these, 92% were judged to have need according to Federal Methodology, of whom 97% were aided. On average, 80% of need was met. *Financial aid deadline (priority):* 4/1. *Financial aid forms:* FAFSA, institutional form required; CSS Financial Aid PROFILE acceptable. State form required for some.

LD Services Contact: Dr. Keith W. Drahn, Director, Disability Services, Messiah College, 1 College Avenue, Grantham, PA 17027, 717-766-2511 Ext. 7258. Fax: 717-796-5373. Email: kdrahn@messiah.edu.

MIAMI UNIVERSITY

Oxford, Ohio

LEARNING DISABILITIES SERVICES INFORMATION

Learning Disabilities Program began offering services in 1987. Currently the program serves 385 undergraduates with LD. Services are also available to graduate students. Students diagnosed with ADD/ADHD are eligible for the same services available to students with LD.
Staff: 1 full-time, 2 part-time staff members, including coordinator. Services provided by tutors, graduate assistants.
Special Fees: No special fees are charged for services to students with LD.
Applications and admissions: *Required:* high school transcript, grade point average, class rank, courses completed; *recommended:* autobiographical statement, letters of recommendation. Students may begin taking classes in fall or summer. *Application deadline:* 1/31.
Special policies: The college has written policies regarding substitutions and waivers of admissions, graduation, and degree requirements.

PROGRAM AND SERVICE COMPONENTS

Academic advising: Provided by unit staff members, academic advisers. Students with LD may take up to 18 credit hours each term; most take 14 to 15 credit hours; 12 credit hours required to maintain full-time status.
Counseling services: Individual counseling, small-group counseling, career counseling.
Basic skills remediation: Offered one-on-one by peer tutors. Available in reading, math, written language, learning strategies, study skills, time management.
Subject-area tutoring: Offered one-on-one and in small groups by peer tutors. Available in most subjects.
Special courses: College survival skills. All offered for credit; all enter into overall grade point average.
Auxiliary aids: Taped textbooks, word-processors with spell-check, optical character readers, Book Wise.
Auxiliary services: Alternative test arrangements, priority registration, advocacy.
Campus support group: A special student organization is available to students with LD.

GENERAL COLLEGE INFORMATION

State-related, coed. Part of Miami University System. Awards bachelor's, master's, doctoral degrees. Founded 1809. *Setting:* 1,900-acre small-town campus with easy access to Cincinnati. *Endowment:* $117.8 million. *Research spending 1995–96:* $4.9 million. *Educational spending 1995–96:* $6345 per undergrad. *Total enrollment:* 16,103. *Faculty:* 1,063 (763 full-time, 89% with terminal degrees, 300 part-time); student–undergrad faculty ratio is 17:1.
Enrollment Profile: 14,523 students from 49 states and territories, 42 other countries. 55% women, 45% men, 6% part-time, 73% state residents, 46% live on campus, 3% transferred in, 1% international, 4% 25 or older, 1% Native American, 1% Hispanic, 3% black, 2% Asian or Pacific Islander. *Retention:* 90% of 1995 full-time freshmen returned. *Graduation:* 73% graduate in 4 years, 80% in 5 years, 81% in 6 years. *Areas of study chosen:* 28% business management and administrative services, 12% education, 10% biological and life sciences, 9% social sciences, 6% communications and journalism, 5% psychology, 4% health professions and related sciences, 3% English language/literature/letters, 3% fine arts, 3% physical sciences, 2% architecture, 2% computer and information sciences, 2% engineering and applied sciences, 2% natural resource sciences, 2% performing arts, 2% vocational and home economics, 1% foreign language and literature, 1% interdisciplinary studies, 1% mathematics. *Most popular recent majors:* marketing/retailing/merchandising, elementary education, zoology.
First-Year Class: 3,383 total; 11,623 applied, 72% were accepted, 40% of whom enrolled. 38% from top 10% of their high school class, 81% from top quarter, 97% from top half. 74 class presidents, 232 valedictorians.
Graduation Requirements: 128 credit hours; 6 credit hours of science; 3 credit hours of math; computer course for business, applied science majors; internship (some majors); senior project.
Computers on Campus: 1,000 computers available on campus for general student use. Computer purchase/lease plans available. A computer is strongly recommended for all students. A campus-wide network

Miami University (continued)

can be accessed from student residence rooms and from off-campus. Students can contact faculty members and/or advisers through e-mail. Computers for student use in computer center, computer labs, learning resource center, classrooms, library, dorms, academic buildings provide access to the Internet/World Wide Web. Staffed computer lab on campus provides training in use of computers, software.

EXPENSES AND FINANCIAL AID

Expenses for 1997–98: *Application fee:* $35. State resident tuition: $4482 full-time, $187 per credit hour part-time. Nonresident tuition: $10,582 full-time, $441 per credit hour part-time. Part-time mandatory fees per semester range from $64.50 to $479.50. Full-time mandatory fees: $1030. College room and board: $4810. College room only: $2270 (minimum).

Undergraduate Financial Aid: Of all full-time undergraduates enrolled in fall 1996, 71% of those who applied for aid were judged to have need according to Federal Methodology, of whom 98% were aided. On average, 91% of need was met. *Financial aid deadline (priority):* 2/15. *Financial aid forms:* FAFSA required. State form required for some.

LD Services Contact: Ms. Lois G. Philips, Coordinator, Learning Disabilities Program, Miami University, 23 Campus Avenue Building, Oxford, OH 45056, 513-529-8741. Fax: 513-529-8799. Email: philiplg@muohio.edu.

MICHIGAN TECHNOLOGICAL UNIVERSITY

Houghton, Michigan

LEARNING DISABILITIES SERVICES INFORMATION

Students with Disabilities Services began offering services in 1982. Currently the program serves 15 undergraduates with LD. Services are also available to graduate students. Students diagnosed with ADD/ADHD are eligible for the same services available to students with LD.

Staff: 1 part-time staff member (coordinator). Services provided by tutors, counselors.

Special Fees: No special fees are charged for services to students with LD.

Applications and admissions: *Required:* high school transcript, class rank, courses completed, psychoeducational report completed within 3 years; *recommended:* extended time ACT, Michigan Rehabilitation Service Report (for Michigan residents). Students may begin taking classes any term. *Application deadline:* continuous.

PROGRAM AND SERVICE COMPONENTS

Diagnostic testing: Math.

Academic advising: Provided by unit staff members, academic advisers. Students with LD may take up to as many quarter hours as an individual can handle each term; most take 12 to 15 quarter hours; 12 quarter hours required to maintain full-time status; 6 quarter hours required to be eligible for financial aid.

Counseling services: Individual counseling, small-group counseling, career counseling.

Subject-area tutoring: Offered one-on-one and in small groups by professional teachers, peer tutors. Available in most subjects.

Special courses: College survival skills, time management, study skills, career planning. Some offered for credit; none enter into overall grade point average.

Auxiliary aids: Tape recorders.

Auxiliary services: Alternative test arrangements, notetakers, priority registration.

GENERAL COLLEGE INFORMATION

State-supported, coed. Awards associate, bachelor's, master's, doctoral degrees. Founded 1885. *Setting:* 240-acre small-town campus. *Endowment:* $1.7 million. *Research spending 1995–96:* $24 million. *Educational spending 1995–96:* $6800 per undergrad. *Total enrollment:* 6,195. *Faculty:* 407 (377 full-time, 89% with terminal degrees, 30 part-time); student–undergrad faculty ratio is 15:1.

Enrollment Profile: 5,541 students from 41 states and territories, 41 other countries. 26% women, 74% men, 8% part-time, 78% state residents, 40% live on campus, 23% transferred in, 4% international, 10% 25 or older, 1% Native American, 1% Hispanic, 2% black, 1% Asian or Pacific Islander. *Retention:* 83% of 1995 full-time freshmen returned. *Graduation:* 25% graduate in 4 years, 56% in 5 years, 62% in 6 years. *Areas of study chosen:* 73% engineering and applied sciences, 5% biological and life sciences, 5% computer and information sciences, 4% business management and administrative services, 2% communications and journalism, 2% health professions and related sciences, 2% natural resource sciences, 2% physical sciences, 1% liberal arts/general studies, 1% mathematics, 1% social sciences. *Most popular recent majors:* mechanical engineering, electrical engineering, civil engineering.

First-Year Class: 1,076 total; 2,449 applied, 94% were accepted, 47% of whom enrolled. 38% from top 10% of their high school class, 73% from top quarter, 94% from top half. 15 National Merit Scholars, 82 valedictorians.

Graduation Requirements: 98 credit hours for associate, 186 credit hours for bachelor's; 21 credit hours of math/science; computer course; internship (some majors); senior project (some majors).

Computers on Campus: 1,036 computers available on campus for general student use. Computer purchase/lease plans available. A computer is recommended for all students. A campus-wide network can be accessed from student residence rooms and from off-campus. Students can contact faculty members and/or advisers through e-mail. Computers for student use in computer center, computer labs, research center, learning resource center, classrooms, dorms provide access to the Internet/World Wide Web, on- and off-campus e-mail addresses. Staffed computer lab on campus provides training in use of computers, software. *Academic computing expenditure 1995–96:* $2.4 million.

EXPENSES AND FINANCIAL AID

Expenses for 1997–98: *Application fee:* $30. State resident tuition: $3936 full-time, $110 per credit hour part-time. Nonresident tuition: $9576 full-time, $266 per credit hour part-time. College room and board: $4236 (minimum).

Undergraduate Financial Aid: Of all full-time undergraduates enrolled in fall 1996, 53% of those who applied for aid were judged to have need according to Federal Methodology, of whom 97% were aided. On average, 78% of need was met. *Financial aid deadline (priority):* 3/1. *Financial aid forms:* FAFSA required. Institutional form required for some.

LD Services Contact: Dr. Gloria B. Melton, Associate Dean of Student Affairs, Michigan Technological University, 1400 Townsend Drive, Houghton, MI 49931-1295, 906-487-2212. Fax: 906-487-3343. Email: gbmelton@mtu.edu.

MIDAMERICA NAZARENE UNIVERSITY

Olathe, Kansas

LEARNING DISABILITIES SERVICES INFORMATION

Kresge Academic Support Center began offering services in 1987. Currently the program serves 12 undergraduates with LD. Services are also available to graduate students. Students diagnosed with ADD/ADHD are eligible for the same services available to students with LD.

Staff: 4 full-time, 1 part-time staff members, including director, office manager. Services provided by remediation specialists, tutors, counselors, diagnostic specialists.

Special Fees: No special fees are charged for services to students with LD.

Applications and admissions: *Required:* high school transcript, grade point average, class rank, courses completed, untimed SAT I or ACT, autobiographical statement, letters of recommendation. Students may begin taking classes in fall only. *Application deadline:* 8/1 (fall term), 1/1 (spring term).

PROGRAM AND SERVICE COMPONENTS

Special preparation or orientation: Required orientation held during registration, after classes begin, and individually by special arrangement.

Academic advising: Provided by academic advisers. Students with LD may take up to 17 semester hours each term; most take 15 to 17 semester hours; 12 semester hours required to maintain full-time status and be eligible for financial aid.

Counseling services: Individual counseling, career counseling.

Basic skills remediation: Offered one-on-one and in class-size groups by regular teachers, teacher trainees. Available in reading, math, spelling, written language, learning strategies, study skills, time management.

Subject-area tutoring: Offered one-on-one and in small groups by peer tutors. Available in all subjects.

Special courses: College survival skills, reading, vocabulary development, composition, learning strategies, time management, math, study skills, career planning. Some offered for credit; some enter into overall grade point average.

Auxiliary aids: Taped textbooks, tape recorders, calculators, typewriters, word-processors with spell-check.
Auxiliary services: Alternative test arrangements, notetakers, advocacy.

GENERAL COLLEGE INFORMATION

Independent, comprehensive, coed, affiliated with Church of the Nazarene. Awards associate, bachelor's, master's degrees (master's degree in education and business administration). Founded 1966. *Setting:* 112-acre suburban campus with easy access to Kansas City. *Endowment:* $4.4 million. *Educational spending 1995–96:* $3201 per undergrad. *Total enrollment:* 1,394. *Faculty:* 117 (67 full-time, 43% with terminal degrees, 50 part-time); student–undergrad faculty ratio is 17:1.
Enrollment Profile: 1,266 students from 32 states and territories, 16 other countries. 56% women, 44% men, 9% part-time, 61% state residents, 57% live on campus, 19% transferred in, 2% international, 33% 25 or older, 2% Native American, 3% Hispanic, 4% black, 1% Asian or Pacific Islander. *Retention:* 69% of 1995 full-time freshmen returned. *Graduation:* 31% graduate in 4 years, 38% in 5 years. *Areas of study chosen:* 26% education, 25% business management and administrative services, 11% health professions and related sciences, 7% theology/religion, 6% psychology, 4% biological and life sciences, 3% communications and journalism, 3% performing arts, 2% computer and information sciences, 2% physical sciences, 1% agriculture, 1% English language/literature/letters, 1% foreign language and literature, 1% mathematics, 1% social sciences. *Most popular recent majors:* human resources, elementary education, nursing.
First-Year Class: 240 total; 422 applied, 100% were accepted, 57% of whom enrolled. 18% from top 10% of their high school class, 35% from top quarter, 64% from top half.
Graduation Requirements: 63 semester hours for associate, 126 semester hours for bachelor's; 12 semester hours of math/science; computer course for business, education majors; internship (some majors); senior project (some majors).
Computers on Campus: 33 computers available on campus for general student use. Computer purchase/lease plans available. A campus-wide network can be accessed from student residence rooms and from off-campus. Students can contact faculty members and/or advisers through e-mail. Computers for student use in library provide access to the Internet/World Wide Web, on- and off-campus e-mail addresses. Staffed computer lab on campus provides training in use of computers, software. *Academic computing expenditure 1995–96:* $79,736.

EXPENSES AND FINANCIAL AID

Expenses for 1997–98: *Application fee:* $15. Comprehensive fee of $13,752 includes full-time tuition ($8790), mandatory fees ($466 minimum), and college room and board ($4496). College room only: $2258. Part-time tuition: $293 per semester hour. Full-time mandatory fees for campus residents: $708. Part-time mandatory fees per semester (6 to 11 semester hours): $466.
Undergraduate Financial Aid: 73% of all full-time undergraduates enrolled in fall 1996 applied for aid; of these, 96% were judged to have need according to Federal Methodology, of whom 99% were aided. On average, 51% of need was met. *Financial aid deadline (priority):* 3/1. *Financial aid forms:* FAFSA, institutional form required; CSS Financial Aid PROFILE acceptable. State form required for some.
LD Services Contact: Ms. Sue Moore, Director, Kresge Academic Support Center, MidAmerica Nazarene University, 2030 College Way, Olathe, KS 66062-1899, 913-782-3750 Ext. 182. Fax: 913-791-3285.

MIDDLE TENNESSEE STATE UNIVERSITY

Murfreesboro, Tennessee

LEARNING DISABILITIES SERVICES INFORMATION

Disabled Student Services began offering services in 1981. Currently the program serves 126 undergraduates with LD. Services are also available to graduate students. Students diagnosed with ADD/ADHD are eligible for the same services available to students with LD.
Staff: 1 full-time, 5 part-time staff members, including director, coordinator. Services provided by tutors, counselor, graduate assistants, student workers.
Special Fees: No special fees are charged for services to students with LD.
Applications and admissions: *Required:* high school transcript, grade point average, courses completed, untimed ACT; *recommended:* high school class rank, extracurricular activities, untimed SAT I or extended time ACT, personal interview, autobiographical statement, letters of recommendation, psychoeducational report. Students may begin taking classes any term. *Application deadline:* continuous.

PROGRAM AND SERVICE COMPONENTS

Special preparation or orientation: Orientation offered before classes begin.
Academic advising: Provided by unit staff members, academic advisers. Most students with LD take 12 to 15 semester hours each term; 12 semester hours required to maintain full-time status; 6 semester hours required to be eligible for financial aid.
Counseling services: Individual counseling, career counseling, self-advocacy training.
Subject-area tutoring: Offered one-on-one and in small groups by peer tutors. Available in most subjects.
Auxiliary aids: Tape recorders, calculators, typewriters, word-processors with spell-check, optical character readers, OSCAR.
Auxiliary services: Alternative test arrangements, notetakers, priority registration, advocacy.

GENERAL COLLEGE INFORMATION

State-supported, coed. Part of State University and Community College System of Tennessee. Awards associate, bachelor's, master's, doctoral degrees. Founded 1911. *Setting:* 500-acre urban campus with easy access to Nashville. *Endowment:* $893,000. *Research spending 1995–96:* $1.8 million. *Educational spending 1995–96:* $3714 per undergrad. *Total enrollment:* 17,924. *Faculty:* 972 (701 full-time, 70% with terminal degrees, 271 part-time); student–undergrad faculty ratio is 20:1.
Enrollment Profile: 15,890 students: 54% women, 46% men, 20% part-time, 94% state residents, 23% live on campus, 45% transferred in, 5% international, 27% 25 or older, 1% Native American, 1% Hispanic, 10% black, 1% Asian or Pacific Islander. *Areas of study chosen:* 10% business management and administrative services, 8% communications and journalism, 7% interdisciplinary studies, 6% health professions and related sciences, 4% psychology, 3% agriculture, 2% biological and life sciences, 2% computer and information sciences, 2% English language/literature/letters, 1% foreign language and literature, 1% mathematics. *Most popular recent majors:* business administration/commerce/management, communication.
First-Year Class: 2,292 total; 5,276 applied, 69% were accepted, 63% of whom enrolled.
Graduation Requirements: 65 semester hours for associate, 132 semester hours for bachelor's; 3 semester hours of math; 8 semester hours of science; computer course; internship (some majors); senior project for honors program students and some majors.
Computers on Campus: 200 computers available on campus for general student use. Computer purchase/lease plans available. A campus-wide network can be accessed. Computers for student use in computer center, computer labs, learning resource center, classrooms, library, dorms, academic building provide access to the Internet/World Wide Web. Staffed computer lab on campus provides training in use of computers, software. *Academic computing expenditure 1995–96:* $3 million.

EXPENSES AND FINANCIAL AID

Expenses for 1997–98: *Application fee:* $5. State resident tuition: $2126 full-time, $81 per semester hour part-time. Nonresident tuition: $6722 full-time, $282 per semester hour part-time. Part-time mandatory fees per semester range from $10 to $25. College room and board: $3343. College room only: $1692.
Undergraduate Financial Aid: 66% of all full-time undergraduates enrolled in fall 1996 applied for aid; of these, 82% were judged to have need according to Federal Methodology, of whom 96% were aided. On average, 60% of need was met. *Financial aid deadline (priority):* 3/15. *Financial aid forms:* FAFSA required. Institutional form required for some.
LD Services Contact: Ms. Melissa Smith, Learning Disabilities Coordinator, Middle Tennessee State University, Box 7, Murfreesboro, TN 37132, 615-904-8246. Email: mesmith@mtsu.edu.

MIDWESTERN STATE UNIVERSITY

Wichita Falls, Texas

LEARNING DISABILITIES SERVICES INFORMATION

Counseling Center began offering services in 1985. Currently the program serves 30 undergraduates with LD. Services are also available to graduate students. Students diagnosed with ADD/ADHD are eligible for the same services available to students with LD.

Midwestern State University (continued)

Staff: 3 full-time staff members, including director. Services provided by counselors.
Special Fees: No special fees are charged for services to students with LD.
Applications and admissions: *Required:* high school transcript, class rank, courses completed, extended time SAT I or ACT. Students may begin taking classes any term. *Application deadline:* 8/7 (fall term), 12/15 (spring term).
Special policies: The college has written policies regarding substitutions and waivers of admissions requirements.

PROGRAM AND SERVICE COMPONENTS

Special preparation or orientation: Optional orientation offered before registration.
Academic advising: Provided by unit staff members, academic advisers. Students with LD may take up to 18 semester hours (if GPA is maintained) each term; most take 12 semester hours; 12 semester hours required to maintain full-time status; 6 semester hours (part-time), 12 semester hours (full-time) required to be eligible for financial aid.
Counseling services: Individual counseling, career counseling.
Subject-area tutoring: Offered one-on-one and in class-size groups by professional teachers, peer tutors. Available in some subjects.
Auxiliary aids: Taped textbooks, tape recorders, calculators, typewriters, word-processors with spell-check, talking computers, optical character readers.
Auxiliary services: Alternative test arrangements, notetakers, priority registration, advocacy, priority seating, newsletter, readers, scribes.

GENERAL COLLEGE INFORMATION

State-supported, comprehensive, coed. Awards associate, bachelor's, master's degrees. Founded 1922. *Setting:* 172-acre urban campus. *Endowment:* $2.7 million. *Research spending 1995–96:* $61,773. *Educational spending 1995–96:* $3400 per undergrad. *Total enrollment:* 5,643. *Faculty:* 281 (180 full-time, 72% with terminal degrees, 101 part-time); student–undergrad faculty ratio is 20:1.
Enrollment Profile: 4,956 students from 48 states and territories. 56% women, 44% men, 33% part-time, 88% state residents, 12% live on campus, 10% transferred in, 4% international, 39% 25 or older, 1% Native American, 6% Hispanic, 6% black, 2% Asian or Pacific Islander. *Retention:* 69% of 1995 full-time freshmen returned. *Graduation:* 24% graduate in 6 years. *Areas of study chosen:* 19% health professions and related sciences, 17% business management and administrative services, 13% education, 5% interdisciplinary studies, 4% social sciences, 3% biological and life sciences, 3% engineering and applied sciences, 3% fine arts, 3% premed, 3% psychology, 2% communications and journalism, 2% computer and information sciences, 2% English language/literature/letters, 1% mathematics, 1% prelaw, 1% prevet. *Most popular recent majors:* business administration/commerce/management, nursing.
First-Year Class: 724 total; 1,442 applied, 77% were accepted, 65% of whom enrolled. 5% from top 10% of their high school class, 22% from top quarter, 52% from top half.
Graduation Requirements: 64 semester hours for associate, 124 semester hours for bachelor's; 2 lab science courses; 1 college math course; computer course; internship (some majors); senior project (some majors).
Computers on Campus: 220 computers available on campus for general student use. Computer purchase/lease plans available. A computer is recommended for all students. A campus-wide network can be accessed from student residence rooms and from off-campus. Students can contact faculty members and/or advisers through e-mail. Computers for student use in computer center, computer labs, library, dorms, departmental lab provide access to the Internet/World Wide Web. Staffed computer lab on campus (open 24 hours a day). *Academic computing expenditure 1995–96:* $731,115.

EXPENSES AND FINANCIAL AID

Expenses for 1997–98: State resident tuition: $1054 full-time. Nonresident tuition: $7688 full-time, $248 per semester hour part-time. State resident part-time tuition per semester ranges from $120 to $374. Part-time mandatory fees per semester range from $74.94 to $394.34. Full-time mandatory fees: $1037. College room and board: $3534 (minimum). College room only: $1768 (minimum).
Undergraduate Financial Aid: Of all full-time undergraduates enrolled in fall 1996, 74% of those who applied for aid were judged to have need according to Federal Methodology, of whom 100% were aided. On average, 100% of need was met. *Financial aid deadline (priority):* 4/4. *Financial aid forms:* FAFSA, CSS Financial Aid PROFILE, state form, SINGLEFILE Form of United Student Aid Funds acceptable. Institutional form required for some.

LD Services Contact: Ms. Debra J. Higginbotham, Director, Counseling Center, Midwestern State University, 3400 Taft Boulevard, HS 211, Wichita Falls, TX 76308-2096, 940-397-4618. Fax: 940-397-4814. Email: fhiggnbd@nexus.mwsu.edu.

MISSISSIPPI STATE UNIVERSITY

Mississippi State, Mississippi

LEARNING DISABILITIES SERVICES INFORMATION

Student Support Services began offering services in 1989. Currently the program serves 91 undergraduates with LD. Services are also available to graduate students. Students diagnosed with ADD/ADHD are eligible for the same services available to students with LD.
Staff: 7 full-time, 2 part-time staff members, including associate director, support staff. Services provided by counselors.
Special Fees: No special fees are charged for services to students with LD.
Applications and admissions: *Required:* high school transcript, grade point average, courses completed, untimed ACT, psychoeducational report completed within 3 years. Students may begin taking classes in fall, spring, or summer. *Application deadline:* continuous.
Special policies: The college has written policies regarding substitutions and waivers of graduation and degree requirements.

PROGRAM AND SERVICE COMPONENTS

Academic advising: Provided by unit staff members, academic advisers. Students with LD may take up to 19 credit hours each term; most take 12 to 15 credit hours; 12 credit hours required to maintain full-time status; 1 credit hour required to be eligible for financial aid.
Counseling services: Individual counseling, small-group counseling, career counseling, self-advocacy training.
Auxiliary aids: Taped textbooks, tape recorders, word-processors with spell-check, personal computers, talking computers, optical character readers.
Auxiliary services: Alternative test arrangements, notetakers, priority registration, advocacy.

GENERAL COLLEGE INFORMATION

State-supported, coed. Awards bachelor's, master's, doctoral, first professional degrees. Founded 1878. *Setting:* 4,200-acre small-town campus. *Endowment:* $91.5 million. *Research spending 1995–96:* $79.9 million. *Total enrollment:* 14,064. *Faculty:* 832 (828 full-time, 87% with terminal degrees, 4 part-time); student–undergrad faculty ratio is 17:1.
Enrollment Profile: 11,548 students from 50 states and territories, 73 other countries. 42% women, 58% men, 12% part-time, 81% state residents, 26% live on campus, 11% transferred in, 2% international, 20% 25 or older, 1% Native American, 1% Hispanic, 16% black, 1% Asian or Pacific Islander. *Retention:* 76% of 1995 full-time freshmen returned. *Graduation:* 18% graduate in 4 years, 38% in 5 years. *Areas of study chosen:* 18% business management and administrative services, 18% engineering and applied sciences, 15% education, 9% agriculture, 8% liberal arts/general studies, 6% biological and life sciences, 4% physical sciences, 3% architecture, 3% communications and journalism, 3% social sciences, 2% fine arts, 2% psychology, 2% vocational and home economics, 1% computer and information sciences, 1% English language/literature/letters, 1% foreign language and literature, 1% health professions and related sciences, 1% mathematics, 1% philosophy, 1% predentistry, 1% prelaw, 1% premed, 1% prevet. *Most popular recent majors:* elementary education, business administration/commerce/management, marketing/retailing/merchandising.
First-Year Class: 1,813 total; 5,126 applied, 83% were accepted, 43% of whom enrolled. 48 National Merit Scholars.
Graduation Requirements: 128 credit hours; 15 credit hours of math/science including at least 6 credit hours of lab science; computer course; internship (some majors); senior project (some majors).
Computers on Campus: 3,000 computers available on campus for general student use. Computer purchase/lease plans available. A computer is required for some students. A campus-wide network can be accessed from student residence rooms and from off-campus. Students can contact faculty members and/or advisers through e-mail. Computers for student use in computer center, computer labs, research center, learning resource center, classrooms, library, student center, dorms, student rooms, academic buildings provide access to the Internet/World Wide Web, on- and off-campus e-mail addresses. Staffed computer lab on campus provides training in use of computers, software. *Academic computing expenditure 1995–96:* $1.6 million.

EXPENSES AND FINANCIAL AID

Expenses for 1997–98: *Application fee:* $15. State resident tuition: $2731 full-time, $113.62 per credit hour part-time. Nonresident tuition: $5551 full-time, $231.12 per credit hour part-time. College room and board: $3415. College room only: $1600.
Undergraduate Financial Aid: 79% of all full-time undergraduates enrolled in fall 1996 applied for aid; of these, 64% were judged to have need according to Federal Methodology, of whom 96% were aided. On average, 87% of need was met. *Financial aid deadline (priority):* 4/1. *Financial aid forms:* FAFSA, institutional form required. State form, scholarship application required for some.
LD Services Contact: Dr. Debbie Ann Baker, Associate Director, Mississippi State University, PO Box 806, Mississippi State, MS 39762, 601-325-3335. Fax: 601-325-8190. Email: sssdabu@ra.mstate.edu.

MISSOURI SOUTHERN STATE COLLEGE

Joplin, Missouri

LEARNING DISABILITIES SERVICES INFORMATION

Learning Center began offering services in 1984. Currently the program serves 30 undergraduates with LD. Students diagnosed with ADD/ADHD are eligible for the same services available to students with LD.
Staff: 5 full-time staff members, including director, coordinator. Services provided by counselor, English instructor, reading instructor.
Special Fees: No special fees are charged for services to students with LD.
Applications and admissions: *Required:* high school transcript, grade point average, class rank, courses completed, psychoeducational report completed within 3 years; *recommended:* high school extracurricular activities, extended time SAT I or ACT. Students may begin taking classes in fall, spring, or summer. *Application deadline:* continuous.
Special policies: The college has written policies regarding substitutions and waivers of admissions, graduation, and degree requirements.

PROGRAM AND SERVICE COMPONENTS

Academic advising: Provided by unit staff members, academic advisers. Students with LD may take up to 18 credits each term; most take 12 credits; 12 credits required to maintain full-time status.
Counseling services: Individual counseling.
Basic skills remediation: Offered in class-size groups by regular teachers. Available in reading, math, written language, study skills.
Subject-area tutoring: Offered one-on-one and in small groups by peer tutors. Available in some subjects.
Auxiliary aids: Taped textbooks, tape recorders, typewriters, word-processors with spell-check, Franklin Spellers.

GENERAL COLLEGE INFORMATION

State-supported, 4-year, coed. Part of Missouri Coordinating Board for Higher Education. Awards associate, bachelor's degrees. Founded 1937. *Setting:* 350-acre small-town campus. *Total enrollment:* 5,258. *Faculty:* 283 (223 full-time, 65% with terminal degrees, 60 part-time); student–undergrad faculty ratio is 27:1.
Enrollment Profile: 5,258 students from 13 states and territories, 10 other countries. 56% women, 44% men, 35% part-time, 93% state residents, 9% live on campus, 13% transferred in, 1% international, 36% 25 or older, 3% Native American, 1% Hispanic, 1% black, 1% Asian or Pacific Islander. *Retention:* 58% of 1995 full-time freshmen returned. *Areas of study chosen:* 22% liberal arts/general studies, 21% business management and administrative services, 15% education, 8% communications and journalism, 6% computer and information sciences, 6% health professions and related sciences, 4% engineering and applied sciences, 3% fine arts, 3% social sciences, 2% English language/literature/letters, 1% foreign language and literature, 1% performing arts, 1% philosophy, 1% physical sciences, 1% predentistry, 1% prelaw, 1% premed, 1% prevet, 1% psychology. *Most popular recent majors:* business administration/commerce/management, education, law enforcement/police sciences.
First-Year Class: 746 total; 1,320 applied, 99% were accepted, 57% of whom enrolled. 20% from top 10% of their high school class, 48% from top quarter, 95% from top half. 13 class presidents, 28 valedictorians.
Graduation Requirements: 64 credits for associate, 128 credits for bachelor's; 3 credits of math; 6 credits of science; computer course; senior project for honors program students.
Computers on Campus: 360 computers available on campus for general student use. A computer is strongly recommended for all students. A campus-wide network can be accessed from student residence rooms and from off-campus. Students can contact faculty members and/or advisers through e-mail. Computers for student use in computer center, computer labs, research center, learning resource center, classrooms, library, student center, dorms provide access to the Internet/World Wide Web, on- and off-campus e-mail addresses. Staffed computer lab on campus provides training in use of computers, software.

EXPENSES AND FINANCIAL AID

Expenses for 1997–98: *Application fee:* $15. State resident tuition: $2304 full-time, $72 per credit part-time. Nonresident tuition: $4608 full-time, $144 per credit part-time. Part-time mandatory fees: $20 per semester. Full-time mandatory fees: $80. College room and board: $3240.
Undergraduate Financial Aid: On average, 100% of need was met. *Financial aid deadline (priority):* 2/15. *Financial aid forms:* FAFSA required; state form, institutional form, acceptable.
LD Services Contact: Ms. Melissa Anne Zenon, Disabilities Coordinator, Missouri Southern State College, 3950 East Newman Road, Joplin, MO 64801, 417-625-9373. Fax: 417-625-3070. Email: zenon@vm.mssc.edu.

MONTANA STATE UNIVERSITY–BILLINGS

Billings, Montana

LEARNING DISABILITIES SERVICES INFORMATION

Disability Support Services began offering services in 1971. Currently the program serves 59 undergraduates with LD. Students diagnosed with ADD/ADHD are eligible for the same services available to students with LD.
Staff: 1 full-time, 1 part-time staff members, including coordinator, administrative assistant. Services provided by counselor.
Special Fees: No special fees are charged for services to students with LD.
Applications and admissions: *Required:* high school transcript, grade point average, class rank, courses completed, untimed or extended time SAT I, untimed ACT, autobiographical statement, psychoeducational report completed within 3 years (if younger than 21), immunization records. Students may begin taking classes any term. *Application deadline:* continuous.
Special policies: The college has written policies regarding substitutions and waivers of degree requirements.

PROGRAM AND SERVICE COMPONENTS

Special preparation or orientation: Optional orientation offered before registration and as needed.
Diagnostic testing: Intelligence, reading, math, spelling, handwriting, spoken language, written language.
Academic advising: Provided by unit staff members, academic advisers. Students with LD may take up to 18 credit hours each term; most take 12 credit hours; 12 credit hours required to maintain full-time status and be eligible for financial aid.
Counseling services: Individual counseling, career counseling, self-advocacy training.
Basic skills remediation: Offered one-on-one and in small groups by teacher trainees. Available in learning strategies, study skills, time management, social skills.
Subject-area tutoring: Offered one-on-one and in small groups by peer tutors. Available in most subjects.
Special courses: College survival skills, reading, communication skills, learning strategies, study skills. Some offered for credit; none enter into overall grade point average.
Auxiliary aids: Taped textbooks, typewriters, word-processors with spell-check, talking computers, optical character readers, assistive reading technology.
Auxiliary services: Alternative test arrangements, notetakers, priority registration, advocacy.

GENERAL COLLEGE INFORMATION

State-supported, comprehensive, coed. Part of Montana University System. Awards associate, bachelor's, master's degrees. Founded 1927. *Setting:* 92-acre urban campus. *Research spending 1995–96:* $88,593. *Educational spending 1995–96:* $2739 per undergrad. *Total enrollment:* 4,006. *Faculty:* 224 (162 full-time, 86% with terminal degrees, 62 part-time); student–undergrad faculty ratio is 20:1.

Montana State University–Billings (continued)

Enrollment Profile: 3,624 students from 35 states and territories. 63% women, 37% men, 25% part-time, 93% state residents, 11% live on campus, 10% transferred in, 1% international, 36% 25 or older, 5% Native American, 2% Hispanic, 1% black, 1% Asian or Pacific Islander. *Graduation:* 6% graduate in 4 years, 24% in 5 years, 35% in 6 years. *Areas of study chosen:* 30% education, 22% business management and administrative services, 19% liberal arts/general studies, 6% health professions and related sciences, 4% biological and life sciences, 4% psychology, 3% communications and journalism, 3% social sciences, 2% fine arts, 1% English language/literature/letters, 1% foreign language and literature, 1% mathematics, 1% performing arts. *Most popular recent majors:* elementary education, secondary education, business administration/commerce/management.
First-Year Class: 690 total. 12% from top 10% of their high school class, 25% from top quarter, 59% from top half.
Graduation Requirements: 64 credit hours for associate, 128 credit hours for bachelor's; 1 math course; 2 science courses; computer course for business, economics, education majors.
Computers on Campus: 243 computers available on campus for general student use. Computer purchase/lease plans available. A computer is recommended for all students. A campus-wide network can be accessed from student residence rooms and from off-campus. Students can contact faculty members and/or advisers through e-mail. Computers for student use in computer center, classrooms, library, student center, dorms provide access to the Internet/World Wide Web, on- and off-campus e-mail addresses. Staffed computer lab on campus provides training in use of computers, software. *Academic computing expenditure 1995–96:* $1.4 million.

EXPENSES AND FINANCIAL AID

Expenses for 1996–97: *Application fee:* $30. State resident tuition: $2388 full-time. Nonresident tuition: $6559 full-time. Part-time tuition per semester ranges from $174.50 to $993 for state residents, $323.45 to $2632 for nonresidents. Tuition for nonresidents who are eligible for the Western Undergraduate Exchange: $3582 full-time, $261.75 to $1489.50 per semester part-time. College room and board: $3000 (minimum).
Undergraduate Financial Aid: On average, 72% of need was met. *Financial aid deadline (priority):* 3/1. *Financial aid forms:* FAFSA, institutional form required; CSS Financial Aid PROFILE acceptable. Federal income tax form required for some.
LD Services Contact: Ms. Sharon Yazak, Coordinator, Disability Support Services, Montana State University–Billings, LA 216, 1500 North 30th Street, Billings, MT 59101, 406-657-2283. Fax: 406-657-2037.

MONTANA STATE UNIVERSITY–NORTHERN

Havre, Montana

LEARNING DISABILITIES SERVICES INFORMATION

Student Support Services began offering services in 1987. Currently the program serves 32 undergraduates with LD. Services are also available to graduate students. Students diagnosed with ADD/ADHD are eligible for the same services available to students with LD.
Staff: 1 full-time, 4 part-time staff members, including director, tutoring coordinator. Services provided by remediation specialist, counselors, graduate assistant.
Special Fees: No special fees are charged for services to students with LD.
Applications and admissions: *Required:* high school transcript, grade point average, class rank, untimed ACT; *recommended:* psychoeducational report. Students may begin taking classes any term. *Application deadline:* continuous.
Special policies: The college has written policies regarding grade forgiveness.

PROGRAM AND SERVICE COMPONENTS

Diagnostic testing: Reading, math, spelling, perceptual skills, study skills, personality, learning strategies.
Academic advising: Provided by unit staff members, academic advisers. Most students with LD take 9 to 15 credits each term; 12 credits required to maintain full-time status; 6 credits (part-time) required to be eligible for financial aid.
Counseling services: Individual counseling, small-group counseling, career counseling.
Basic skills remediation: Offered one-on-one and in small groups by learning specialist. Available in reading, math, spelling, learning strategies, study skills, time management.
Subject-area tutoring: Offered one-on-one, in small groups, and in class-size groups by peer tutors. Available in most subjects.
Auxiliary aids: Taped textbooks, tape recorders, word-processors with spell-check, talking computers, optical character readers.
Auxiliary services: Alternative test arrangements, notetakers.

GENERAL COLLEGE INFORMATION

State-supported, comprehensive, coed. Part of Montana University System. Awards associate, bachelor's, master's degrees. Founded 1929. *Setting:* 105-acre small-town campus. *Endowment:* $100,858. *Educational spending 1995–96:* $3653 per undergrad. *Total enrollment:* 1,702. *Faculty:* 118 (71 full-time, 47% with terminal degrees, 47 part-time); student–undergrad faculty ratio is 19:1.
Enrollment Profile: 1,529 students from 24 states and territories, 5 other countries. 55% women, 45% men, 25% part-time, 95% state residents, 15% transferred in, 1% international, 47% 25 or older, 8% Native American, 1% Hispanic, 1% black, 1% Asian or Pacific Islander. *Retention:* 65% of 1995 full-time freshmen returned. *Graduation:* 12% graduate in 4 years, 21% in 5 years, 35% in 6 years. *Areas of study chosen:* 29% education, 15% business management and administrative services, 12% health professions and related sciences, 9% liberal arts/general studies, 8% interdisciplinary studies, 3% computer and information sciences, 2% agriculture, 2% architecture, 2% engineering and applied sciences. *Most popular recent majors:* education, business administration/commerce/management, nursing.
First-Year Class: 390 total. Of the students accepted, 57% enrolled.
Graduation Requirements: 64 credits for associate, 128 credits for bachelor's; 3 credits of math; computer course; internship (some majors); senior project (some majors).
Computers on Campus: 140 computers available on campus for general student use. A campus-wide network can be accessed from student residence rooms and from off-campus. Students can contact faculty members and/or advisers through e-mail. Computers for student use in computer center, computer labs, classrooms, library, dorms provide access to the Internet/World Wide Web, on- and off-campus e-mail addresses. Staffed computer lab on campus provides training in use of computers, software. *Academic computing expenditure 1995–96:* $84,155.

EXPENSES AND FINANCIAL AID

Expenses for 1996–97: *Application fee:* $30. State resident tuition: $2350 full-time. Nonresident tuition: $6662 full-time. Part-time tuition per semester ranges from $113.85 to $1191 for state residents, $267.85 to $2885 for nonresidents. Tuition for nonresidents who are eligible for the Western Undergraduate Exchange: $3304 full-time, $147.90 to $1349.40 per semester part-time. College room and board: $3600.
Undergraduate Financial Aid: 87% of all full-time undergraduates enrolled in fall 1996 applied for aid; of these, 81% were judged to have need according to Federal Methodology, of whom 96% were aided. On average, 65% of need was met. *Financial aid deadline (priority):* 3/1. *Financial aid forms:* FAFSA, institutional form required.
LD Services Contact: Ms. Linda Hoines, Learning Specialist, Montana State University–Northern, PO Box 7751, Havre, MT 59501, 406-265-3783. Fax: 406-265-3777.

MOORHEAD STATE UNIVERSITY

Moorhead, Minnesota

LEARNING DISABILITIES SERVICES INFORMATION

Disability Services began offering services in 1976. Currently the program serves 30 undergraduates with LD. Services are also available to graduate students. Students diagnosed with ADD/ADHD are eligible for the same services available to students with LD.
Staff: 1 full-time staff member (coordinator).
Special Fees: No special fees are charged for services to students with LD.
Applications and admissions: *Required:* high school transcript, class rank, courses completed; *recommended:* untimed or extended time SAT I or ACT, personal interview. Students may begin taking classes any term. *Application deadline:* 8/15 (fall term), 12/15 (spring term).
Special policies: The college has written policies regarding substitutions and waivers of admissions, graduation, and degree requirements.

PROGRAM AND SERVICE COMPONENTS

Academic advising: Provided by unit staff members, academic advisers. Students with LD may take up to 18 credits each term; most take 12 credits; 12 credits required to maintain full-time status; 12 credits for full-time assistance (under 12 is pro-rated) required to be eligible for financial aid.
Auxiliary aids: Taped textbooks, word-processors with spell-check, personal computers.
Auxiliary services: Alternative test arrangements, notetakers, priority registration, advocacy, typists.

GENERAL COLLEGE INFORMATION

State-supported, comprehensive, coed. Part of Minnesota State Colleges and Universities System. Awards associate, bachelor's, master's degrees. Founded 1885. *Setting:* 118-acre urban campus. *Research spending 1995–96:* $73,895. *Educational spending 1995–96:* $3514 per undergrad. *Total enrollment:* 6,194. *Faculty:* 340 (255 full-time, 75% with terminal degrees, 85 part-time); student–undergrad faculty ratio is 18:1.
Enrollment Profile: 5,917 students from 36 states and territories, 25 other countries. 62% women, 38% men, 20% part-time, 59% state residents, 27% live on campus, 31% transferred in, 2% international, 22% 25 or older, 1% Native American, 1% Hispanic, 1% black, 1% Asian or Pacific Islander. *Retention:* 68% of 1995 full-time freshmen returned. *Graduation:* 22% graduate in 4 years, 37% in 5 years. *Areas of study chosen:* 19% business management and administrative services, 14% education, 9% interdisciplinary studies, 7% communications and journalism, 6% social sciences, 5% biological and life sciences, 5% performing arts, 4% fine arts, 4% psychology, 3% English language/literature/letters, 3% health professions and related sciences, 2% computer and information sciences, 1% engineering and applied sciences, 1% mathematics. *Most popular recent majors:* education, business administration/commerce/management, accounting.
First-Year Class: 1,026 total; 1,961 applied, 96% were accepted, 55% of whom enrolled. 11% from top 10% of their high school class, 38% from top quarter, 85% from top half.
Graduation Requirements: 64 credits for associate, 128 credits for bachelor's; 3 credits of math; 6 credits of natural science including at least 1 lab science course; computer course for business, mass communication, accounting, technology majors; internship (some majors); senior project (some majors).
Computers on Campus: 450 computers available on campus for general student use. Computer purchase/lease plans available. A campus-wide network can be accessed from student residence rooms and from off-campus. Students can contact faculty members and/or advisers through e-mail. Computers for student use in computer center, computer labs, classrooms, library, dorms, student rooms, departmental labs provide access to the Internet/World Wide Web, on- and off-campus e-mail addresses. Staffed computer lab on campus (open 24 hours a day) provides training in use of computers, software. *Academic computing expenditure 1995–96:* $504,591.

EXPENSES AND FINANCIAL AID

Expenses for 1996–97: *Application fee:* $20. State resident tuition: $2474 full-time, $77.30 per credit part-time. Nonresident tuition: $5573 full-time, $174.15 per credit part-time. Part-time mandatory fees: $16.95 per credit. North Dakota, South Dakota and Wisconsin residents pay tuition at the rate they would pay if attending a ccomparable state-supported institution in their home state. Full-time mandatory fees: $407. College room and board: $3078. College room only: $2084.
Undergraduate Financial Aid: 73% of all full-time undergraduates enrolled in fall 1996 applied for aid; of these, 88% were judged to have need according to Federal Methodology, of whom 100% were aided. *Financial aid deadline (priority):* 6/15. *Financial aid forms:* FAFSA, institutional form required.
LD Services Contact: Ms. Paula Ahles, Coordinator, Disability Services, Moorhead State University, 222 Comstock Memorial Union, Moorhead, MN 56563, 218-299-5859. Fax: 218-287-5050. Email: ahles@mhd5.moorhead.msus.edu.

MOREHEAD STATE UNIVERSITY

Morehead, Kentucky

LEARNING DISABILITIES SERVICES INFORMATION

Special Services began offering services in 1985. Currently the program serves 50 undergraduates with LD. Services are also available to graduate students. Students diagnosed with ADD/ADHD are eligible for the same services available to students with LD.
Staff: 3 full-time staff members, including coordinator. Services provided by tutors, counselors, learning specialists.
Special Fees: No special fees are charged for services to students with LD.
Applications and admissions: *Required:* high school transcript, grade point average, untimed ACT; *recommended:* extended time ACT. Students may begin taking classes in fall, spring, or summer. *Application deadline:* continuous.
Special policies: The college has written policies regarding grade forgiveness.

PROGRAM AND SERVICE COMPONENTS

Academic advising: Provided by academic advisers. Students with LD may take up to 18 credit hours each term; most take 12 to 15 credit hours; 12 credit hours required to maintain full-time status.
Counseling services: Individual counseling, small-group counseling, career counseling.
Basic skills remediation: Offered in class-size groups by regular teachers. Available in reading, math, written language, learning strategies, study skills, time management.
Subject-area tutoring: Offered one-on-one and in small groups by peer tutors. Available in most subjects.
Auxiliary aids: Taped textbooks.
Auxiliary services: Alternative test arrangements.

GENERAL COLLEGE INFORMATION

State-supported, comprehensive, coed. Awards associate, bachelor's, master's degrees. Founded 1922. *Setting:* 809-acre small-town campus. *Research spending 1995–96:* $312,323. *Educational spending 1995–96:* $3485 per undergrad. *Total enrollment:* 8,344. *Faculty:* 429 (328 full-time, 63% with terminal degrees, 101 part-time); student–undergrad faculty ratio is 20:1.
Enrollment Profile: 6,823 students from 39 states and territories, 33 other countries. 60% women, 40% men, 14% part-time, 88% state residents, 8% transferred in, 1% international, 24% 25 or older, 1% Hispanic, 3% black. *Most popular recent majors:* elementary education, interdisciplinary studies, biology/biological sciences.
First-Year Class: 1,277 total; 2,784 applied, 89% were accepted, 51% of whom enrolled.
Graduation Requirements: 64 credit hours for associate, 128 credit hours for bachelor's; 12 credit hours of math/science including at least 3 credit hours of math and 6 credit hours of science; computer course for business, math majors.
Computers on Campus: 800 computers available on campus for general student use. Computer purchase/lease plans available. Students can contact faculty members and/or advisers through e-mail. Computers for student use in computer labs, library, dorms, academic buildings provide access to the Internet/World Wide Web, on- and off-campus e-mail addresses. Staffed computer lab on campus provides training in use of computers, software. *Academic computing expenditure 1995–96:* $962,435.

EXPENSES AND FINANCIAL AID

Expenses for 1997–98: State resident tuition: $2090 full-time, $88 per credit hour part-time. Nonresident tuition: $5570 full-time, $233 per credit hour part-time. College room and board: $2950. College room only: $1418 (minimum).
Undergraduate Financial Aid: Of all full-time undergraduates enrolled in fall 1996, 74% of those who applied for aid were judged to have need according to Federal Methodology, of whom 98% were aided. On average, 77% of need was met. *Financial aid deadline (priority):* 4/1. *Financial aid forms:* FAFSA, institutional form, financial aid transcript (for transfers) required.
LD Services Contact: Ms. Debra Reed, Counselor, Morehead State University, UPO 1228, Morehead, KY 40351, 606-783-2005. Fax: 606-783-5026.

MOREHOUSE COLLEGE

Atlanta, Georgia

LEARNING DISABILITIES SERVICES INFORMATION

Counseling Center, Disability Services Department began offering services in 1996. Currently the program serves 15 undergraduates with LD. Students diagnosed with ADD/ADHD are eligible for the same services available to students with LD, as well as psychiatric prescriptions and medication monitoring by licensed psychiatrists.

Staff: 1 full-time staff member (psychologist). Services provided by tutors, counselors, diagnostic specialists.

Special Fees: No special fees are charged for services to students with LD.

Applications and admissions: *Required:* personal interview, psychoeducational report completed within 3 years; *recommended:* high school transcript, grade point average, class rank, courses completed, extracurricular activities, IEP (Individualized Education Program), extended time SAT I. Students may begin taking classes in fall only. *Application deadline:* continuous.

Special policies: The college has written policies regarding grade forgiveness; substitutions and waivers of admissions, graduation, and degree requirements.

PROGRAM AND SERVICE COMPONENTS

Diagnostic testing: Intelligence, reading, math, spelling, spoken language, written language, motor abilities, perceptual skills, study skills, personality, social skills, psychoneurology, learning strategies.

Academic advising: Provided by unit staff members, academic advisers. Students with LD may take up to 15 semester hours each term; most take 12 semester hours; 12 semester hours required to maintain full-time status and be eligible for financial aid.

Counseling services: Individual counseling, small-group counseling, career counseling, self-advocacy training.

Basic skills remediation: Offered one-on-one and in small groups by regular teachers; computer-aided instruction also offered. Available in reading, math, spelling, written language, learning strategies, study skills, time management, social skills, computer skills.

Subject-area tutoring: Offered one-on-one and in small groups by professional teachers, peer tutors. Available in all subjects.

Special courses: College survival skills, reading, communication skills, composition, time management, math, study skills, career planning, stress management, social relationships. Some offered for credit.

Auxiliary aids: Taped textbooks, tape recorders, calculators, typewriters, word-processors with spell-check, personal computers.

Auxiliary services: Alternative test arrangements, notetakers, priority registration, advocacy.

GENERAL COLLEGE INFORMATION

Independent, 4-year, men only. Awards bachelor's degrees. Founded 1867. *Setting:* 61-acre urban campus. *Endowment:* $69.4 million. *Research spending 1995–96:* $1.1 million. *Educational spending 1995–96:* $5696 per undergrad. *Total enrollment:* 2,926. *Faculty:* 231 (161 full-time, 72% with terminal degrees, 70 part-time); student–undergrad faculty ratio is 17:1.

Enrollment Profile: 2,926 students from 42 states and territories, 18 other countries. 0% women, 4% part-time, 23% state residents, 50% live on campus, 5% transferred in, 3% international, 98% black. *Retention:* 72% of 1995 full-time freshmen returned. *Graduation:* 31% graduate in 4 years, 46% in 5 years, 51% in 6 years. *Areas of study chosen:* 26% business management and administrative services, 13% biological and life sciences, 11% engineering and applied sciences, 8% psychology, 6% computer and information sciences, 4% English language/literature/letters, 4% physical sciences, 2% fine arts, 2% mathematics, 2% social sciences, 1% communications and journalism, 1% education, 1% foreign language and literature, 1% health professions and related sciences, 1% interdisciplinary studies, 1% performing arts, 1% philosophy, 1% theology/religion. *Most popular recent majors:* business administration/commerce/management, engineering (general), biology/biological sciences.

First-Year Class: 771 total; 2,798 applied, 68% were accepted, 41% of whom enrolled. 28% from top 10% of their high school class, 69% from top quarter, 99% from top half. 27 valedictorians.

Graduation Requirements: 124 semester hours; 6 semester hours each of math and science; 12 semester hours of a foreign language or the equivalent; computer course for math, engineering, accounting, finance, management majors; internship (some majors); senior project for honors program students and some majors.

Computers on Campus: 325 computers available on campus for general student use. Computer purchase/lease plans available. A campus-wide network can be accessed from student residence rooms and from off-campus. Students can contact faculty members and/or advisers through e-mail. Computers for student use in computer center, library, dorms, science building, writing skills lab provide access to the Internet/World Wide Web, on- and off-campus e-mail addresses. Staffed computer lab on campus provides training in use of computers, software. *Academic computing expenditure 1995–96:* $391,295.

EXPENSES AND FINANCIAL AID

Expenses for 1997–98: *Application fee:* $35. Comprehensive fee of $15,938 includes full-time tuition ($8008), mandatory fees ($1716), and college room and board ($6214). College room only: $3554. Part-time tuition: $350 per semester hour. Part-time mandatory fees per semester (4 to 11 semester hours): $858.

Undergraduate Financial Aid: Of all full-time undergraduates enrolled in fall 1996, 100% of those judged to have need according to Federal Methodology were aided. On average, 65% of need was met. *Financial aid deadline:* 4/1. *Financial aid forms:* FAFSA, CSS Financial Aid PROFILE, state form, institutional form required.

LD Services Contact: Dr. I. Fidel Turner, Director, Disability Services, Morehouse College, 109 Gluster Hall, Atlanta, GA 30314, 404-215-2636. Fax: 404-522-6419.

MORGAN STATE UNIVERSITY

Baltimore, Maryland

LEARNING DISABILITIES SERVICES INFORMATION

Support Services for Students with Disabilities began offering services in 1990. Currently the program serves 10 undergraduates with LD. Services are also available to graduate students. Students diagnosed with ADD/ADHD are eligible for the same services available to students with LD.

Staff: Includes director, coordinators. Services provided by counselors.

Special Fees: $100 for diagnostic testing.

Applications and admissions: *Recommended:* high school transcript, grade point average, extended time SAT I. Students may begin taking classes any term. *Application deadline:* continuous.

Special policies: The college has written policies regarding substitutions and waivers of graduation and degree requirements.

PROGRAM AND SERVICE COMPONENTS

Special preparation or orientation: Summer program (required for some) held prior to entering college. Optional orientation offered individually by arrangement.

Diagnostic testing: Intelligence, reading, math, spelling.

Academic advising: Provided by unit staff members, academic advisers. Most students with LD take 16 semester hours each term; 12 semester hours required to maintain full-time status and be eligible for financial aid.

Counseling services: Individual counseling, small-group counseling, career counseling.

Subject-area tutoring: Offered one-on-one by peer tutors. Available in most subjects.

Auxiliary aids: Tape recorders, calculators, typewriters, word-processors with spell-check, talking computers, optical character readers.

Auxiliary services: Alternative test arrangements, notetakers, advocacy.

Campus support group: A special student organization is available to students with LD.

GENERAL COLLEGE INFORMATION

State-supported, coed. Awards bachelor's, master's, doctoral degrees. Founded 1867. *Setting:* 130-acre urban campus with easy access to Washington, DC. *Total enrollment:* 5,889. *Faculty:* 340 (240 full-time, 80% with terminal degrees, 100 part-time); student–undergrad faculty ratio is 18:1.

Enrollment Profile: 5,552 students from 47 states and territories, 30 other countries. 59% women, 41% men, 14% part-time, 61% state residents, 30% live on campus, 8% transferred in, 1% international, 27% 25 or older, 0% Native American, 2% Hispanic, 94% black, 2% Asian or Pacific Islander. *Retention:* 76% of 1995 full-time freshmen returned. *Most popular recent majors:* electrical engineering, accounting, biology/biological sciences.

First-Year Class: 1,089 total; 5,200 applied, 47% were accepted. 40% from top half of their high school class.

Graduation Requirements: 120 semester hours; 4 semester hours of math; 8 semester hours of science; computer course for business, economics, engineering, engineering physics, math, physics, psychology majors; internship (some majors); senior project (some majors).

Computers on Campus: 65 computers available on campus for general student use. A campus-wide network can be accessed from student residence rooms and from off-campus. Students can contact faculty members and/or advisers through e-mail. Computers for student use in computer center, computer labs, classrooms, library provide access to engineering labs supercomputer. Staffed computer lab on campus provides training in use of computers, software.

EXPENSES AND FINANCIAL AID

Expenses for 1997–98: *Application fee:* $25. State resident tuition: $3412 full-time, $115 per semester hour part-time. Nonresident tuition: $7992 full-time, $205 per semester hour part-time. Part-time mandatory fees: $151 per semester. College room and board: $5090. College room only: $3150.

Undergraduate Financial Aid: *Financial aid deadline (priority):* 4/1. *Financial aid forms:* FAFSA, CSS Financial Aid PROFILE, institutional form required.

LD Services Contact: Ms. Joanne Frederick-Parris, Counselor/Coordinator, Morgan State University, 1700 East Cold Spring Lane/Hillen Road, Baltimore, MD 21250, 410-319-3043. Fax: 410-319-3253.

MORNINGSIDE COLLEGE

Sioux City, Iowa

LEARNING DISABILITIES SERVICES INFORMATION

Learning Center currently serves 10 undergraduates with LD. Services are also available to graduate students. Students diagnosed with ADD/ADHD are eligible for the same services available to students with LD.

Staff: 1 full-time, 1 part-time staff members, including director. Services provided by tutors/counselors/writing specialists.

Special Fees: No special fees are charged for services to students with LD.

Applications and admissions: *Required:* high school transcript, grade point average, class rank, courses completed, untimed SAT I or ACT, autobiographical statement, letters of recommendation, psychoeducational report; *recommended:* high school extracurricular activities, extended time SAT I or ACT. Students may begin taking classes in fall or spring. *Application deadline:* continuous.

Special policies: The college has written policies regarding grade forgiveness.

PROGRAM AND SERVICE COMPONENTS

Diagnostic testing: Reading, spelling, written language, study skills.

Academic advising: Provided by academic advisers. Students with LD may take up to 18 semester hours each term; most take 12 to 15 semester hours; 12 semester hours required to maintain full-time status and be eligible for financial aid.

Counseling services: Individual counseling, career counseling.

Basic skills remediation: Offered in class-size groups by regular teachers. Available in reading, spelling, written language, study skills.

Subject-area tutoring: Offered one-on-one and in small groups by professional teachers, peer tutors. Available in most subjects.

Special courses: College survival skills, reading, vocabulary development, composition, study skills. Some offered for credit; some enter into overall grade point average.

Auxiliary aids: Tape recorders, typewriters, word-processors with spell-check, reading machines.

Auxiliary services: Alternative test arrangements, notetakers.

GENERAL COLLEGE INFORMATION

Independent United Methodist, comprehensive, coed. Awards associate, bachelor's, master's degrees. Founded 1894. *Setting:* 27-acre suburban campus. *Endowment:* $21.9 million. *Total enrollment:* 1,137. *Faculty:* 118 (72 full-time, 69% with terminal degrees, 46 part-time); student–undergrad faculty ratio is 14:1.

Enrollment Profile: 1,041 students from 26 states and territories, 10 other countries. 66% women, 34% men, 17% part-time, 77% state residents, 66% live on campus, 7% transferred in, 2% international, 25% 25 or older, 1% Native American, 1% Hispanic, 3% black, 4% Asian or Pacific Islander. *Retention:* 89% of 1995 full-time freshmen returned. *Areas of study chosen:* 21% business management and administrative services, 16% education, 12% health professions and related sciences, 10% biological and life sciences, 10% fine arts, 9% social sciences, 5% communications and journalism, 4% computer and information sciences, 4% psychology, 2% English language/literature/letters, 2% theology/religion, 1% engineering and applied sciences, 1% foreign language and literature, 1% mathematics, 1% performing arts, 1% physical sciences, 1% premed. *Most popular recent majors:* business administration/commerce/management, education, biology/biological sciences.

First-Year Class: 208 total; 541 applied, 94% were accepted, 41% of whom enrolled. 18% from top 10% of their high school class, 45% from top quarter, 75% from top half.

Graduation Requirements: 62 semester hours for associate, 124 semester hours for bachelor's; 1 course each in math and lab science; computer course for all BS degree students; internship (some majors); senior project (some majors).

Computers on Campus: 800 computers available on campus for general student use. Computer purchase/lease plans available. A computer is required for some students. A campus-wide network can be accessed from student residence rooms and from off-campus. Students can contact faculty members and/or advisers through e-mail. Computers for student use in computer center, computer labs, learning resource center, library, student center, dorms, student rooms provide access to the Internet/World Wide Web, on- and off-campus e-mail addresses. Staffed computer lab on campus provides training in use of computers, software. *Academic computing expenditure 1995–96:* $161,925.

EXPENSES AND FINANCIAL AID

Expenses for 1997–98: *Application fee:* $15. Comprehensive fee of $16,140 includes full-time tuition ($11,436), mandatory fees ($176), and college room and board ($4528). College room only: $2230. Part-time tuition per semester hour: $240 for the first 6 semester hours, $390 for the next 5 semester hours for day classes, $245 for evening classes.

Undergraduate Financial Aid: 89% of all full-time undergraduates enrolled in fall 1996 applied for aid; of these, 95% were judged to have need according to Federal Methodology, of whom 100% were aided. On average, 99% of need was met. *Financial aid deadline (priority):* 3/1. *Financial aid forms:* FAFSA required.

LD Services Contact: Mr. Tim Orwig, Director of The Learning Center, Morningside College, 1501 Morningside Avenue, Sioux City, IA 51106-1751, 712-274-5104. Fax: 712-274-5101.

MOUNT HOLYOKE COLLEGE

South Hadley, Massachusetts

LEARNING DISABILITIES SERVICES INFORMATION

Office of Learning Skills began offering services in 1990. Currently the program serves 100 undergraduates with LD. Services are also available to graduate students. Students diagnosed with ADD/ADHD are eligible for the same services available to students with LD, as well as one-on-one coaching.

Staff: 1 full-time, 1 part-time staff members, including director, graduate student.

Special Fees: No special fees are charged for services to students with LD.

Applications and admissions: *Required:* high school transcript, grade point average, class rank, courses completed, extracurricular activities; *recommended:* high school IEP (Individualized Education Program), extended time SAT I, personal interview, autobiographical statement, letters of recommendation, psychoeducational report completed within 3 to 5 years. Students may begin taking classes in fall or spring. *Application deadline:* 1/15.

Special policies: The college has written policies regarding grade forgiveness; substitutions and waivers of graduation and degree requirements.

PROGRAM AND SERVICE COMPONENTS

Special preparation or orientation: Optional orientation offered during registration and after classes begin.

Diagnostic testing: Intelligence, reading, math, spelling, handwriting, spoken language, written language, perceptual skills, study skills, learning strategies.

Academic advising: Provided by unit staff members, academic advisers. Students with LD may take up to 20 credit hours each term; most take 16 credit hours; 12 credit hours required to maintain full-time status and be eligible for financial aid.

Counseling services: Individual counseling.

Basic skills remediation: Offered one-on-one by LD teachers. Available in reading, written language, learning strategies, study skills, time management, social skills.

Auxiliary aids: Taped textbooks, tape recorders, computer lab.

Auxiliary services: Alternative test arrangements, notetakers, one-on-one case management.

Mount Holyoke College (continued)

GENERAL COLLEGE INFORMATION

Independent, comprehensive, women only. Awards bachelor's, master's degrees. Founded 1837. *Setting:* 800-acre small-town campus. *Endowment:* $265.8 million. *Research spending 1995–96:* $580,000. *Educational spending 1995–96:* $11,317 per undergrad. *Total enrollment:* 1,898. *Faculty:* 213 (181 full-time, 96% with terminal degrees, 32 part-time); student–undergrad faculty ratio is 10:1.

Enrollment Profile: 1,889 students from 49 states and territories, 60 other countries. 100% women, 1% part-time, 20% state residents, 96% live on campus, 5% transferred in, 13% international, 5% 25 or older, 1% Native American, 4% Hispanic, 4% black, 8% Asian or Pacific Islander. *Retention:* 94% of 1995 full-time freshmen returned. *Graduation:* 78% graduate in 4 years, 81% in 5 years, 82% in 6 years. *Most popular recent majors:* English, political science/government, biology/biological sciences.

First-Year Class: 482 total; 2,026 applied, 65% were accepted, 36% of whom enrolled. 50% from top 10% of their high school class, 92% from top quarter, 99% from top half.

Graduation Requirements: 128 credit hours; 2 math/science courses; 1 course in intermediate level foreign language or the equivalent; computer course for math majors.

Computers on Campus: 245 computers available on campus for general student use. Computer purchase/lease plans available. A computer is recommended for some students. A campus-wide network can be accessed from student residence rooms and from off-campus. Students can contact faculty members and/or advisers through e-mail. Computers for student use in computer center, computer labs, research center, learning resource center, library, dorms, academic buildings provide access to the Internet/World Wide Web, on- and off-campus e-mail addresses. Staffed computer lab on campus provides training in use of computers, software. *Academic computing expenditure 1995–96:* $1.5 million.

EXPENSES AND FINANCIAL AID

Expenses for 1997–98: *Application fee:* $50. Comprehensive fee of $28,865 includes full-time tuition ($22,200), mandatory fees ($140), and college room and board ($6525). Part-time tuition: $695 per credit hour.

Undergraduate Financial Aid: 84% of all full-time undergraduates enrolled in fall 1996 applied for aid; of these, 94% were judged to have need according to Federal Methodology, of whom 100% were aided. On average, 100% of need was met. *Financial aid deadline:* 2/1. *Financial aid forms:* FAFSA, CSS Financial Aid PROFILE required. Institutional form required for some.

LD Services Contact: Dr. John Body, Assistant Dean of Studies for Learning Skills, Mount Holyoke College, 110 Groves Health Center, South Hadley, MA 01075, 413-538-2504. Email: jbody@mhc.mtholyoke.edu.

MURRAY STATE UNIVERSITY

Murray, Kentucky

LEARNING DISABILITIES SERVICES INFORMATION

Services for Students with Learning Disabilities (SSLD) began offering services in 1980. Currently the program serves 135 undergraduates with LD. Services are also available to graduate students. Students diagnosed with ADD/ADHD are eligible for the same services available to students with LD, as well as support group.

Staff: 1 full-time, 1 part-time staff members, including director, co-director. Services provided by tutors.

Special Fees: No special fees are charged for services to students with LD.

Applications and admissions: *Required:* high school transcript, grade point average, class rank, courses completed; *recommended:* untimed or extended time ACT. Students may begin taking classes in fall only. *Application deadline:* 8/1 (fall term), 12/1 (spring term).

Special policies: The college has written policies regarding grade forgiveness; substitutions and waivers of admissions, graduation, and degree requirements.

PROGRAM AND SERVICE COMPONENTS

Special preparation or orientation: Required orientation held during registration.

Academic advising: Provided by unit staff members, academic advisers. Students with LD may take up to 18 credit hours each term; most take 12 to 15 credit hours; 12 credit hours required to maintain full-time status and be eligible for financial aid.

Subject-area tutoring: Offered one-on-one by graduate mentors. Available in all subjects.

Special courses: College survival skills, reading, vocabulary development, time management, personal psychology, study skills. All offered for credit; all enter into overall grade point average.

Auxiliary aids: Taped textbooks, word-processors with spell-check.

Auxiliary services: Alternative test arrangements.

Campus support group: A special student organization is available to students with LD.

GENERAL COLLEGE INFORMATION

State-supported, comprehensive, coed. Part of Kentucky Council on Higher Education. Awards associate, bachelor's, master's degrees. Founded 1922. *Setting:* 238-acre small-town campus. *Endowment:* $8.1 million. *Research spending 1995–96:* $1 million. *Educational spending 1995–96:* $3750 per undergrad. *Total enrollment:* 8,636. *Faculty:* 384 (356 full-time, 85% with terminal degrees, 28 part-time); student–undergrad faculty ratio is 16:1.

Enrollment Profile: 7,120 students from 45 states and territories, 52 other countries. 55% women, 45% men, 14% part-time, 75% state residents, 40% live on campus, 8% transferred in, 3% international, 22% 25 or older, 1% Native American, 1% Hispanic, 6% black, 1% Asian or Pacific Islander. *Retention:* 70% of 1995 full-time freshmen returned. *Graduation:* 40% graduate in 4 years, 44% in 5 years, 49% in 6 years. *Areas of study chosen:* 17% education, 16% business management and administrative services, 13% engineering and applied sciences, 11% health professions and related sciences, 9% liberal arts/general studies, 6% communications and journalism, 5% biological and life sciences, 4% fine arts, 4% social sciences, 3% agriculture, 2% English language/literature/letters, 2% physical sciences, 2% psychology, 2% vocational and home economics, 1% computer and information sciences, 1% foreign language and literature, 1% mathematics, 1% performing arts. *Most popular recent majors:* business administration/commerce/management, education, occupational safety and health.

First-Year Class: 1,496 total; 2,492 applied, 66% were accepted, 92% of whom enrolled. 30% from top 10% of their high school class, 64% from top quarter, 100% from top half. 22 National Merit Scholars, 48 valedictorians.

Graduation Requirements: 64 credit hours for associate, 128 credit hours for bachelor's; 12 credit hours of math/science including at least 8 credit hours of lab science; computer course for business-related, education, engineering technology, physics majors; internship (some majors); senior project for honors program students and some majors.

Computers on Campus: 450 computers available on campus for general student use. Computer purchase/lease plans available. A computer is strongly recommended for all students. A campus-wide network can be accessed from student residence rooms and from off-campus. Students can contact faculty members and/or advisers through e-mail. Computers for student use in computer center, computer labs, learning resource center, classrooms, library, student center, dorms, student rooms, departmental labs provide access to the Internet/World Wide Web, on- and off-campus e-mail addresses. Staffed computer lab on campus provides training in use of computers, software. *Academic computing expenditure 1995–96:* $300,000.

EXPENSES AND FINANCIAL AID

Expenses for 1997–98: *Application fee:* $20. State resident tuition: $1800 full-time, $80 per credit hour part-time. Nonresident tuition: $5400 full-time, $231 per credit hour part-time. Full-time mandatory fees: $320. College room and board: $3410. College room only: $1470.

Undergraduate Financial Aid: 79% of all full-time undergraduates enrolled in fall 1996 applied for aid; of these, 71% were judged to have need according to Federal Methodology, of whom 97% were aided. On average, 90% of need was met. *Financial aid deadline (priority):* 4/1. *Financial aid forms:* FAFSA, institutional form, financial aid transcript (for transfers) required.

LD Services Contact: Ms. Cindy Clemson, Coordinator, Services for Students with Learning Disabilities Program, Murray State University, PO Box 9, Murray, KY 42071-0009, 502-762-2018. Fax: 502-762-3972.

NATIONAL AMERICAN UNIVERSITY

Rapid City, South Dakota

LEARNING DISABILITIES SERVICES INFORMATION

Learning Center began offering services in 1981. Students diagnosed with ADD/ADHD are eligible for the same services available to students with LD.

Staff: 1 full-time, 1 part-time staff members, including director. Services provided by tutors.

Special Fees: No special fees are charged for services to students with LD.

Applications and admissions: *Required:* high school transcript, courses completed. Students may begin taking classes any term. *Application deadline:* continuous.

Special policies: The college has written policies regarding grade forgiveness.

PROGRAM AND SERVICE COMPONENTS

Academic advising: Provided by academic advisers. Students with LD may take up to 16 credit hours each term; most take 8 to 12 credit hours; 12 credit hours required to maintain full-time status; 8 credit hours required to be eligible for financial aid.

Counseling services: Individual counseling, career counseling.

Basic skills remediation: Offered in small groups by LD teachers. Available in reading, math, written language, learning strategies, study skills, time management.

Subject-area tutoring: Offered one-on-one and in small groups by peer tutors. Available in all subjects.

Auxiliary aids: Tape recorders, calculators, word-processors with spell-check, personal computers.

Auxiliary services: Alternative test arrangements, notetakers.

GENERAL COLLEGE INFORMATION

Proprietary, 4-year, coed. Part of National College. Awards associate, bachelor's degrees. Founded 1941. *Setting:* 8-acre urban campus. *Endowment:* $30,000. *Research spending 1995–96:* $35,000. *Educational spending 1995–96:* $3320 per undergrad. *Total enrollment:* 621. *Faculty:* 49 (19 full-time, 50% with terminal degrees, 30 part-time); student–undergrad faculty ratio is 20:1.

Enrollment Profile: 621 students from 25 states and territories, 8 other countries. 60% women, 40% men, 30% part-time, 75% state residents, 37% live on campus, 48% transferred in, 12% international, 48% 25 or older, 5% Native American, 1% Hispanic, 3% black, 7% Asian or Pacific Islander. *Retention:* 44% of 1995 full-time freshmen returned. *Areas of study chosen:* 24% business management and administrative services, 18% interdisciplinary studies, 12% health professions and related sciences, 12% prevet, 10% computer and information sciences, 7% liberal arts/general studies. *Most popular recent majors:* business administration/commerce/management, accounting, computer information systems.

First-Year Class: 240 total; 450 applied, 99% were accepted, 54% of whom enrolled.

Graduation Requirements: 97 credit hours for associate, 193 credit hours for bachelor's; 4 credit hours each of math and science for associate degree; 8 credit hours each of math and science for bachelor's degree; computer course; internship (some majors).

Computers on Campus: 50 computers available on campus for general student use. A campus-wide network can be accessed. Computers for student use in computer center, computer labs, classrooms, library provide access to the Internet/World Wide Web, on-campus e-mail addresses. Staffed computer lab on campus provides training in use of computers, software. *Academic computing expenditure 1995–96:* $221,000.

EXPENSES AND FINANCIAL AID

Expenses for 1997–98: *Application fee:* $25. Comprehensive fee of $11,835 includes full-time tuition ($8400), mandatory fees ($75), and college room and board ($3360). College room only: $1530. Part-time tuition: $175 per credit hour. One-time mandatory fee: $75.

Undergraduate Financial Aid: *Financial aid deadline (priority):* 4/15. *Financial aid forms:* FAFSA, institutional form required. State form required for some.

LD Services Contact: Mr. Blake Faulkner, Dean of Admissions, National American University, PO Box 1780, Rapid City, SD 57709-1780, 605-394-4830. Fax: 605-394-4871.

THE NATIONAL COLLEGE OF CHIROPRACTIC

Lombard, Illinois

LEARNING DISABILITIES SERVICES INFORMATION

Disabled Student Services began offering services in 1991. Currently the program serves 12 undergraduates with LD. Services are also available to graduate students. Students diagnosed with ADD/ADHD are eligible for the same services available to students with LD.

Staff: 3 part-time staff members, including director, assistant director, secretary/clerk. Services provided by counselors.

Special Fees: No special fees are charged for services to students with LD.

Applications and admissions: *Required:* letters of recommendation, psychoeducational report completed within 3 years. Students may begin taking classes any term. *Application deadline:* continuous.

PROGRAM AND SERVICE COMPONENTS

Special preparation or orientation: Optional orientation offered before registration.

Diagnostic testing: Study skills, personality, learning strategies.

Academic advising: Provided by unit staff members. Students with LD may take up to 26.5 credit hours each term; most take 16 to 26.5 credit hours; 10 credit hours (in no less than 2 of 3 trimesters within a fiscal year) required to maintain full-time status; 30 credit hours (through the first 3 consecutive trimesters of attendance) required to be eligible for financial aid.

Counseling services: Individual counseling, small-group counseling, self-advocacy training.

Basic skills remediation: Offered one-on-one by regular teachers, peer tutors; computer-aided instruction also offered. Available in reading, learning strategies, motor abilities, study skills, time management, social skills, computer skills.

Subject-area tutoring: Offered one-on-one by professional teachers, peer tutors. Available in all subjects.

Special courses: College survival skills, reading, learning strategies, time management, study skills, stress management. None offered for credit; none enter into overall grade point average.

Auxiliary services: Alternative test arrangements, notetakers, priority registration, advocacy.

GENERAL COLLEGE INFORMATION

Independent, upper-level, specialized, coed. Awards incidental bachelor's, first professional degrees. Founded 1906. *Setting:* 32-acre suburban campus with easy access to Chicago. *Research spending 1995–96:* $800,000. *Total enrollment:* 900. *Undergraduate faculty:* 95 (75 full-time, 20 part-time); student–undergrad faculty ratio is 8:1.

Enrollment Profile: 31% women, 69% men, 0% part-time, 27% state residents, 33% live on campus, 100% transferred in, 13% international, 39% 25 or older, 1% Native American, 2% Hispanic, 3% black, 5% Asian or Pacific Islander.

First-Year Class: 110 total; 301 applied, 71% were accepted, 52% of whom enrolled.

Graduation Requirements: 128.5 credit hours; 68 credit hours of science; internship.

Computers on Campus: 18 computers available on campus for general student use. A campus-wide network can be accessed from student residence rooms. Computers for student use in learning resource center. Staffed computer lab on campus provides training in use of computers, software.

EXPENSES AND FINANCIAL AID

Estimated Expenses for 1997–98: *Application fee:* $55. Tuition: $10,404 full-time. Full-time mandatory fees: $100. College room only: $2400 (minimum).

Undergraduate Financial Aid: On average, 0% of need was met. *Financial aid deadline:* continuous. *Financial aid forms:* FAFSA, institutional form, income tax forms required.

LD Services Contact: Dr. Daniel R. Driscoll, Dean of Student and Alumni Affairs, The National College of Chiropractic, 200 East Roosevelt Road, Lombard, IL 60148-4539, 630-889-6546. Fax: 630-889-6554.

NATIONAL-LOUIS UNIVERSITY

Evanston, Illinois

LEARNING DISABILITIES SERVICES INFORMATION

Center for Academic Development began offering services in 1982. Currently the program serves 5 undergraduates with LD. Services are also available to graduate students. Students diagnosed with ADD/ADHD are eligible for the same services available to students with LD.
Staff: 1 full-time, 4 part-time staff members, including coordinators. Services provided by remediation specialists, tutors, counselors.
Special Fees: No special fees are charged for services to students with LD.
Applications and admissions: *Required:* high school transcript, grade point average, courses completed, extended time SAT I, psychoeducational report completed within 5 years; *recommended:* personal interview. Students may begin taking classes any term. *Application deadline:* continuous.

PROGRAM AND SERVICE COMPONENTS

Special preparation or orientation: Optional summer program offered prior to entering college. Optional orientation offered before registration.
Academic advising: Provided by unit staff members, academic advisers. Students with LD may take up to 12 quarter hours each term; most take 12 quarter hours; 12 quarter hours required to maintain full-time status and be eligible for financial aid.
Counseling services: Individual counseling, small-group counseling, career counseling, self-advocacy training.
Basic skills remediation: Offered one-on-one, in small groups, and in class-size groups by learning specialists. Available in reading, math, spelling, spoken language, written language, learning strategies, study skills, time management, social skills.
Subject-area tutoring: Offered one-on-one and in small groups by professional teachers, peer tutors. Available in all subjects.
Special courses: College survival skills, reading, vocabulary development, communication skills, composition, learning strategies, word processing, time management, math, personal psychology, study skills, career planning, social relationships. Some offered for credit; some enter into overall grade point average.
Auxiliary aids: Taped textbooks, tape recorders, word-processors with spell-check.
Auxiliary services: Alternative test arrangements, notetakers, priority registration, advocacy.
Campus support group: A special student organization is available to students with LD.

GENERAL COLLEGE INFORMATION

Independent, coed. Awards bachelor's, master's, doctoral degrees. Founded 1886. *Setting:* 12-acre suburban campus with easy access to Chicago. *Endowment:* $16.9 million. *Research spending 1995–96:* $203,871. *Educational spending 1995–96:* $3874 per undergrad. *Total enrollment:* 7,430. *Faculty:* 287 (271 full-time, 65% with terminal degrees, 16 part-time); student–undergrad faculty ratio is 13:1.
Enrollment Profile: 3,076 students from 19 states and territories, 2 other countries. 72% women, 28% men, 17% part-time, 95% state residents, 5% live on campus, 17% transferred in, 1% international, 69% 25 or older, 1% Native American, 8% Hispanic, 18% black, 4% Asian or Pacific Islander. *Retention:* 64% of 1995 full-time freshmen returned. *Graduation:* 27% graduate in 4 years, 32% in 5 years, 41% in 6 years. *Areas of study chosen:* 35% business management and administrative services, 21% education, 13% social sciences, 12% health professions and related sciences, 8% computer and information sciences, 4% liberal arts/general studies, 2% psychology, 1% performing arts. *Most popular recent majors:* business administration/commerce/management, behavioral sciences, elementary education.
First-Year Class: 231 total; 407 applied, 76% were accepted, 75% of whom enrolled. 5% from top 10% of their high school class, 21% from top quarter, 59% from top half.
Graduation Requirements: 180 quarter hours; 5 quarter hours each of math and science; computer course for education, business administration, accounting majors; internship (some majors); senior project (some majors).
Computers on Campus: 300 computers available on campus for general student use. Computer purchase/lease plans available. A campuswide network can be accessed from off-campus. Students can contact faculty members and/or advisers through e-mail. Computers for student use in computer center, computer labs, learning resource center, classrooms, library, dorms provide access to the Internet/World Wide Web. Staffed computer lab on campus provides training in use of computers, software. *Academic computing expenditure 1995–96:* $222,308.

EXPENSES AND FINANCIAL AID

Expenses for 1996–97: *Application fee:* $25. Comprehensive fee of $15,990 includes full-time tuition ($11,250) and college room and board ($4740 minimum). Part-time tuition: $250 per quarter hour.
Undergraduate Financial Aid: On average, 88% of need was met. *Financial aid deadline (priority):* 7/15. *Financial aid forms:* FAFSA, institutional form, federal income tax forms required; CSS Financial Aid PROFILE acceptable. State form required for some.
LD Services Contact: Dr. Ann Kim, Coordinator, Learning Disabilities Program, National-Louis University, 2840 Sheridan Road, Evanston, IL 60201-1730, 708-475-1100 Ext. 2357.

NAZARETH COLLEGE OF ROCHESTER

Rochester, New York

LEARNING DISABILITIES SERVICES INFORMATION

Academic Advisement began offering services in 1992. Currently the program serves 34 undergraduates with LD. Services are also available to graduate students. Students diagnosed with ADD/ADHD are eligible for the same services available to students with LD.
Staff: 1 full-time staff member. Services provided by remediation specialists, counselors, peer tutors.
Special Fees: No special fees are charged for services to students with LD.
Applications and admissions: *Required:* high school transcript, courses completed, autobiographical statement, letters of recommendation; *recommended:* extended time SAT I or ACT, personal interview, psychoeducational report completed within 3 years. Students may begin taking classes in fall, spring, or summer. *Application deadline:* continuous.
Special policies: The college has written policies regarding substitutions and waivers of degree requirements.

PROGRAM AND SERVICE COMPONENTS

Special preparation or orientation: Optional orientation offered before registration.
Academic advising: Provided by academic advisers. Students with LD may take up to 17 credit hours each term; most take 15 credit hours; 12 credit hours required to maintain full-time status and be eligible for financial aid.
Counseling services: Individual counseling, small-group counseling, career counseling, self-advocacy training, personal stress management.
Subject-area tutoring: Offered one-on-one by peer tutors. Available in all subjects.
Special courses: College survival skills, reading, composition, time management, study skills. None offered for credit; none enter into overall grade point average.
Auxiliary aids: Taped textbooks, tape recorders, calculators, word-processors with spell-check, talking computers, optical character readers.
Auxiliary services: Alternative test arrangements, notetakers.

GENERAL COLLEGE INFORMATION

Independent, comprehensive, coed. Awards bachelor's, master's degrees. Founded 1924. *Setting:* 75-acre suburban campus. *Endowment:* $31.9 million. *Total enrollment:* 2,761. *Undergraduate faculty:* 178 (111 full-time, 94% with terminal degrees, 67 part-time); student–undergrad faculty ratio is 14:1.
Enrollment Profile: 1,764 students from 25 states and territories, 6 other countries. 76% women, 24% men, 24% part-time, 98% state residents, 27% transferred in, 1% international, 30% 25 or older, 1% Native American, 3% Hispanic, 4% black, 1% Asian or Pacific Islander. *Retention:* 51% of 1995 full-time freshmen returned. *Areas of study chosen:* 27% education, 14% business management and administrative services, 13% fine arts, 13% social sciences, 10% English language/literature/letters, 10% psychology, 4% biological and life sciences, 4% health professions and related sciences, 3% foreign language and literature, 2% mathematics. *Most popular recent majors:* business administration/commerce/management, psychology, social work.
First-Year Class: 337 total; 1,099 applied, 79% were accepted, 39% of whom enrolled. 20% from top 10% of their high school class, 50% from top quarter, 93% from top half. 6 valedictorians.

Graduation Requirements: 120 credit hours; 3 credit hours each of math and science; 6 credit hours of a foreign language; computer course; internship (some majors); senior project for honors program students and some majors.
Computers on Campus: 120 computers available on campus for general student use. A computer is recommended for all students. A campus-wide network can be accessed from student residence rooms and from off-campus. Students can contact faculty members and/or advisers through e-mail. Computers for student use in computer center, computer labs, classrooms, library, dorms provide access to the Internet/World Wide Web, on- and off-campus e-mail addresses. Staffed computer lab on campus (open 24 hours a day) provides training in use of computers, software. *Academic computing expenditure 1995–96:* $458,870.

EXPENSES AND FINANCIAL AID

Expenses for 1997–98: *Application fee:* $30. Comprehensive fee of $18,951 includes full-time tuition ($12,560), mandatory fees ($406), and college room and board ($5985). College room only: $3475. Part-time tuition: $362 per credit hour. Part-time mandatory fees: $20 per semester.
Undergraduate Financial Aid: Of all full-time undergraduates enrolled in fall 1996, 91% of those who applied for aid were judged to have need according to Federal Methodology, of whom 99% were aided. On average, 82% of need was met. *Financial aid deadline (priority):* 2/15. *Financial aid forms:* FAFSA, CSS Financial Aid PROFILE required. State form required for some.
LD Services Contact: Ms. Amy Vottis, Academic Counselor for Students with Disabilities, Nazareth College of Rochester, 4245 East Avenue, Rochester, NY 14618-3790, 716-389-2875. Fax: 716-586-2452. Email: amvottis@naz.edu.

NEW ENGLAND COLLEGE

Henniker, New Hampshire

LEARNING DISABILITIES SERVICES INFORMATION

College Skills Center began offering services in 1982. Currently the program serves 176 undergraduates with LD. Students diagnosed with ADD/ADHD are eligible for the same services available to students with LD.
Staff: 7 full-time, 4 part-time staff members, including director, associate director, coordinator. Services provided by tutors, counselors.
Special Fees: No special fees are charged for services to students with LD.
Applications and admissions: *Required:* high school transcript, letters of recommendation, psychoeducational report completed within 2 years; *recommended:* personal interview. Students may begin taking classes in fall, spring, or summer. *Application deadline:* continuous.

PROGRAM AND SERVICE COMPONENTS

Special preparation or orientation: Summer program (required for some) held prior to entering college.
Academic advising: Provided by academic advisers. Students with LD may take up to 15 credits each term; most take 9 to 12 credits; 12 credits required to be eligible for financial aid.
Counseling services: Individual counseling, small-group counseling, career counseling.
Subject-area tutoring: Offered one-on-one and in small groups by professional teachers, peer tutors. Available in all subjects.
Auxiliary aids: Calculators, word-processors with spell-check, optical character readers.
Auxiliary services: Alternative test arrangements.

GENERAL COLLEGE INFORMATION

Independent, comprehensive, coed. Awards bachelor's, master's degrees. Founded 1946. *Setting:* 212-acre small-town campus with easy access to Boston. *Total enrollment:* 800. *Undergraduate faculty:* 72 (50 full-time, 76% with terminal degrees, 22 part-time); student–undergrad faculty ratio is 12:1.
Enrollment Profile: 700 students from 35 states and territories, 25 other countries. 48% women, 52% men, 8% part-time, 15% state residents, 7% transferred in, 8% international, 3% 25 or older, 1% Hispanic, 3% black, 0% Asian or Pacific Islander. *Retention:* 78% of 1995 full-time freshmen returned. *Graduation:* 48% graduate in 4 years, 50% in 5 years. *Areas of study chosen:* 20% business management and administrative services, 18% education, 14% communications and journalism, 11% social sciences, 10% psychology, 8% biological and life sciences, 6% English language/literature/letters, 4% fine arts, 4% performing arts, 3% interdisciplinary studies, 2% philosophy. *Most popular recent majors:* business administration/commerce/management, education, communication.
First-Year Class: 200 total; 975 applied, 72% were accepted, 28% of whom enrolled. 10% from top 10% of their high school class, 30% from top quarter, 85% from top half. 4 class presidents, 2 valedictorians.
Graduation Requirements: 120 credits; 1 math course; 7 credits of natural science; computer course for business, environmental studies majors; internship (some majors).
Computers on Campus: 45 computers available on campus for general student use. Computers for student use in computer center, college skills center provide access to the Internet/World Wide Web, on- and off-campus e-mail addresses. Staffed computer lab on campus provides training in use of computers, software.

EXPENSES AND FINANCIAL AID

Expenses for 1997–98: *Application fee:* $30. Comprehensive fee of $21,704 includes full-time tuition ($15,784) and college room and board ($5920). Part-time tuition: $658 per credit.
Undergraduate Financial Aid: 70% of all full-time undergraduates enrolled in fall 1996 applied for aid; of these, 88% were judged to have need according to Federal Methodology, of whom 100% were aided. On average, 88% of need was met. *Financial aid deadline (priority):* 3/1. *Financial aid forms:* FAFSA, institutional form required.
LD Services Contact: Dr. Joanne MacEachran, Director, College Skills Center, New England College, 7 Main Street, Henniker, NH 03242-3293, 603-428-2218. Fax: 603-428-7230.

NEW JERSEY INSTITUTE OF TECHNOLOGY

Newark, New Jersey

LEARNING DISABILITIES SERVICES INFORMATION

Counseling Center began offering services in 1984. Currently the program serves 14 undergraduates with LD. Services are also available to graduate students. Students diagnosed with ADD/ADHD are eligible for the same services available to students with LD.
Staff: Includes coordinator. Services provided by counselor.
Special Fees: No special fees are charged for services to students with LD.
Applications and admissions: *Required:* high school transcript, grade point average, class rank, courses completed, untimed SAT I; *recommended:* high school extracurricular activities, personal interview, autobiographical statement, letters of recommendation. Students may begin taking classes in fall or spring. *Application deadline:* 4/1 (fall term), 11/1 (spring term).

PROGRAM AND SERVICE COMPONENTS

Academic advising: Provided by academic advisers. Students with LD may take up to 18 credits each term; most take 13 credits; 12 credits required to maintain full-time status; 6 credits required to be eligible for financial aid.
Counseling services: Individual counseling, career counseling.
Auxiliary aids: Taped textbooks, tape recorders, word-processors with spell-check, personal computers.
Auxiliary services: Alternative test arrangements, notetakers.

GENERAL COLLEGE INFORMATION

State-supported, coed. Awards bachelor's, master's, doctoral degrees. Founded 1881. *Setting:* 45-acre urban campus with easy access to New York City. *Endowment:* $13.6 million. *Research spending 1995–96:* $32 million. *Total enrollment:* 7,837. *Faculty:* 534 (354 full-time, 98% with terminal degrees, 180 part-time); student–undergrad faculty ratio is 14:1.
Enrollment Profile: 5,007 students from 19 states and territories, 66 other countries. 19% women, 81% men, 32% part-time, 90% state residents, 25% live on campus, 40% transferred in, 4% international, 35% 25 or older, 1% Native American, 13% Hispanic, 13% black, 18% Asian or Pacific Islander. *Retention:* 85% of 1995 full-time freshmen returned. *Graduation:* 55% graduate in 6 years. *Areas of study chosen:* 66% engineering and applied sciences, 15% computer and information sciences, 11% architecture, 5% business management and administrative services, 2% mathematics, 1% interdisciplinary studies. *Most popular recent majors:* engineering technology, electrical engineering, mechanical engineering.

New Jersey Institute of Technology (continued)

First-Year Class: 624 total; 2,017 applied, 67% were accepted, 46% of whom enrolled. 23% from top 10% of their high school class, 51% from top quarter, 87% from top half. 3 valedictorians.
Graduation Requirements: 124 credits; 6 credits of math; 7 credits of lab science; computer course; senior project for honors program students and some majors.
Computers on Campus: 1,200 computers available on campus for general student use. Computer purchase/lease plans available. A computer is required for all students. A campus-wide network can be accessed from student residence rooms and from off-campus. Students can contact faculty members and/or advisers through e-mail. Computers for student use in computer center, computer labs, research center, learning resource center, classrooms, library, student center, dorms, student rooms provide access to the Internet/World Wide Web, on- and off-campus e-mail addresses. Staffed computer lab on campus provides training in use of computers, software. *Academic computing expenditure 1995–96:* $7 million.

EXPENSES AND FINANCIAL AID

Estimated Expenses for 1997–98: *Application fee:* $35. State resident tuition: $4638 full-time, $172 per credit part-time. Nonresident tuition: $8982 full-time, $357 per credit part-time. Part-time mandatory fees per semester range from $104 to $444. Full-time mandatory fees: $828. College room and board: $5210 (minimum). College room only: $3550 (minimum).
Undergraduate Financial Aid: 76% of all full-time undergraduates enrolled in fall 1996 applied for aid; of these, 79% were judged to have need according to Federal Methodology, of whom 100% were aided. On average, 91% of need was met. *Financial aid deadline (priority):* 3/15. *Financial aid forms:* FAFSA required. State form, institutional form required for some.
LD Services Contact: Dr. Phyllis Bolling, Associate Director/Coordinator of Student Disability Services, New Jersey Institute of Technology, University Heights, Newark, NJ 07102, 973-596-3414. Fax: 973-596-3419. Email: bolling@admin.njit.edu.

NEW MEXICO STATE UNIVERSITY

Las Cruces, New Mexico

LEARNING DISABILITIES SERVICES INFORMATION

Disabled Student Programs, Office of Student Development began offering services in 1984. Currently the program serves 80 undergraduates with LD. Services are also available to graduate students. Students diagnosed with ADD/ADHD are eligible for the same services available to students with LD.
Staff: 2 full-time, 1 part-time staff members, including coordinators. Services provided by work-study students, interpreters.
Special Fees: No special fees are charged for services to students with LD.
Applications and admissions: *Required:* high school transcript, untimed ACT; *recommended:* extended time ACT. Students may begin taking classes any term. *Application deadline:* continuous.
Special policies: The college has written policies regarding grade forgiveness.

PROGRAM AND SERVICE COMPONENTS

Academic advising: Provided by academic advisers. Students with LD may take up to 18 credits each term; most take 12 credits; 12 credits required to maintain full-time status; 6 credits required to be eligible for financial aid.
Auxiliary services: Alternative test arrangements, notetakers, priority registration, advocacy, readers.

GENERAL COLLEGE INFORMATION

State-supported, coed. Part of New Mexico State University System. Awards associate, bachelor's, master's, doctoral degrees. Founded 1888. *Setting:* 5,800-acre suburban campus with easy access to El Paso. *Total enrollment:* 14,748. *Undergraduate faculty:* 664 (634 full-time, 80% with terminal degrees, 30 part-time).
Enrollment Profile: 11,872 students from 51 states and territories, 87 other countries. 51% women, 49% men, 25% part-time, 80% state residents, 22% live on campus, 5% transferred in, 2% international, 27% 25 or older, 3% Native American, 37% Hispanic, 2% black, 1% Asian or Pacific Islander. *Retention:* 75% of 1995 full-time freshmen returned. *Areas of study chosen:* 22% business management and administrative services, 18% engineering and applied sciences, 16% education, 10% social sciences, 5% agriculture, 4% biological and life sciences, 4% psychology, 3% communications and journalism, 3% health professions and related sciences, 2% computer and information sciences, 2% fine arts, 2% natural resource sciences, 2% physical sciences, 2% vocational and home economics, 1% English language/literature/letters, 1% foreign language and literature, 1% mathematics, 1% performing arts, 1% philosophy, 1% prevet. *Most popular recent majors:* marketing/retailing/merchandising, electrical engineering technology, education.
First-Year Class: 1,520 total; 4,168 applied, 80% were accepted, 46% of whom enrolled.
Graduation Requirements: 66 credits for associate, 128 credits for bachelor's; basic math proficiency; computer course for business, economics, engineering majors; internship (some majors).
Computers on Campus: 3,500 computers available on campus for general student use. Computer purchase/lease plans available. A campus-wide network can be accessed from student residence rooms. Computers for student use in computer center, computer labs, dorms, departmental labs provide access to the Internet/World Wide Web. Staffed computer lab on campus (open 24 hours a day) provides training in use of computers, software.

EXPENSES AND FINANCIAL AID

Estimated Expenses for 1997–98: *Application fee:* $15. State resident tuition: $2196 full-time, $91.50 per credit part-time. Nonresident tuition: $7152 full-time, $298 per credit part-time. Part-time mandatory fees: $15.50 per semester. College room and board: $3288 (minimum). College room only: $1650 (minimum).
Undergraduate Financial Aid: On average, 80% of need was met. *Financial aid deadline (priority):* 3/1. *Financial aid forms:* FAFSA, institutional form required.
LD Services Contact: Ms. Michele Reynolds-Jackson, Coordinator, Services for Students with disABILITIES, New Mexico State University, Box 30001, Department 4149, Las Cruces, NM 88003, 505-646-6840. Fax: 505-646-1975. Email: ssd@nmsu.edu.

NIAGARA UNIVERSITY

Niagara University, New York

LEARNING DISABILITIES SERVICES INFORMATION

Office of Academic Support began offering services in 1983. Currently the program serves 45 undergraduates with LD. Services are also available to graduate students. Students diagnosed with ADD/ADHD are eligible for the same services available to students with LD.
Staff: 1 full-time staff member (coordinator). Services provided by remediation specialist, tutors, counselor, diagnostic specialist, part-time instructors.
Special Fees: No special fees are charged for services to students with LD.
Applications and admissions: *Required:* high school transcript, grade point average, class rank, courses completed, psychoeducational report completed within 3 years; *recommended:* high school extracurricular activities, IEP (Individualized Education Program), untimed or extended time SAT I or ACT, personal interview, letters of recommendation. Students may begin taking classes in fall, spring, or summer. *Application deadline:* continuous.

PROGRAM AND SERVICE COMPONENTS

Diagnostic testing: Reading, math, written language.
Academic advising: Provided by unit staff members, academic advisers. Students with LD may take up to 15 credit hours each term; most take 12 to 15 credit hours; 12 credit hours required to maintain full-time status and be eligible for financial aid.
Counseling services: Individual counseling, career counseling.
Basic skills remediation: Offered in class-size groups by developmental and remedial specialists. Available in reading, math, written language, study skills.
Subject-area tutoring: Offered one-on-one and in small groups by peer tutors, professional tutor. Available in most subjects.
Special courses: Reading, vocabulary development, composition, math, study skills. None offered for credit; none enter into overall grade point average.
Auxiliary aids: Taped textbooks, calculators, word-processors with spell-check, spelling aids.
Auxiliary services: Alternative test arrangements, notetakers, advocacy.

GENERAL COLLEGE INFORMATION

Independent, comprehensive, coed. Awards associate, bachelor's, master's degrees. Founded 1856. *Setting:* 160-acre suburban campus with easy access to Buffalo and Toronto. *Endowment:* $27.9 million. *Total enrollment:* 2,935. *Undergraduate faculty:* 206 (111 full-time, 83% with terminal degrees, 95 part-time); student–undergrad faculty ratio is 15:1.
Enrollment Profile: 2,291 students from 19 states and territories, 16 other countries. 61% women, 39% men, 12% part-time, 88% state residents, 58% live on campus, 8% transferred in, 3% international, 17% 25 or older, 1% Native American, 2% Hispanic, 5% black, 1% Asian or Pacific Islander. *Retention:* 80% of 1995 full-time freshmen returned. *Areas of study chosen:* 28% business management and administrative services, 13% education, 11% health professions and related sciences, 7% social sciences, 6% biological and life sciences, 4% communications and journalism, 4% psychology, 3% performing arts, 2% computer and information sciences, 2% English language/literature/letters, 1% foreign language and literature, 1% theology/religion. *Most popular recent majors:* business administration/commerce/management, tourism and travel, social science.
First-Year Class: 557 total; 2,359 applied, 81% were accepted, 29% of whom enrolled. 20% from top 10% of their high school class, 42% from top quarter, 76% from top half.
Graduation Requirements: 60 credit hours for associate, 120 credit hours for bachelor's; 1 course each in natural science and math; computer course for life sciences, math, social work, accounting, commerce, engineering, biology, sociology, business education, criminology, criminal justice, social sciences, travel and tourism, hotel and restaurant management majors; internship (some majors); senior project for honors program students and some majors.
Computers on Campus: 150 computers available on campus for general student use. A campus-wide network can be accessed from student residence rooms. Students can contact faculty members and/or advisers through e-mail. Computers for student use in computer center, computer labs, learning resource center, library provide access to the Internet/World Wide Web, on- and off-campus e-mail addresses. Staffed computer lab on campus. *Academic computing expenditure 1995–96:* $244,470.

EXPENSES AND FINANCIAL AID

Expenses for 1997–98: *Application fee:* $25. Comprehensive fee of $18,548 includes full-time tuition ($12,390 minimum), mandatory fees ($500), and college room and board ($5658). College room only: $3094 (minimum). Part-time tuition: $375 per credit hour. Part-time mandatory fees: $10 per semester. Part-time tuition for nursing program: $218 per credit hour.
Undergraduate Financial Aid: 94% of all full-time undergraduates enrolled in fall 1996 applied for aid; of these, 98% were judged to have need according to Federal Methodology, of whom 100% were aided. On average, 99% of need was met. *Financial aid deadline (priority):* 2/15. *Financial aid forms:* FAFSA, state form required.
LD Services Contact: Ms. Diane Stoelting, Coordinator, Individualized Instruction, Niagara University, Room 104, St. Vincent's Hall, Niagara University, NY 14109, 716-286-8076. Fax: 716-286-8063. Email: ds@niagara.edu.

NORTH CAROLINA AGRICULTURAL AND TECHNICAL STATE UNIVERSITY

Greensboro, North Carolina

LEARNING DISABILITIES SERVICES INFORMATION

Office of Veteran and Disability Support Services began offering services in 1978. Currently the program serves 16 undergraduates with LD. Services are also available to graduate students. Students diagnosed with ADD/ADHD are eligible for the same services available to students with LD.
Staff: 2 full-time staff members, including director, secretary. Services provided by counselors, diagnostic specialists.
Special Fees: No special fees are charged for services to students with LD.
Applications and admissions: *Required:* high school transcript, grade point average, courses completed, untimed SAT I; *recommended:* high school class rank, extracurricular activities, extended time SAT I, personal interview, autobiographical statement, letters of recommendation. Students may begin taking classes in fall only. *Application deadline:* continuous.

PROGRAM AND SERVICE COMPONENTS

Special preparation or orientation: Optional orientation offered during registration.
Diagnostic testing: Intelligence, reading, math, spelling, written language, motor abilities, study skills, personality, social skills, learning strategies.
Academic advising: Provided by unit staff members, academic advisers. Students with LD may take up to 12 semester hours each term; most take 9 to 12 semester hours; 12 semester hours required to maintain full-time status and be eligible for financial aid.
Counseling services: Individual counseling, career counseling.
Subject-area tutoring: Offered one-on-one by peer tutors. Available in most subjects.
Auxiliary aids: Taped textbooks, tape recorders, typewriters, word-processors with spell-check, personal computers.
Auxiliary services: Alternative test arrangements, notetakers, priority registration, advocacy.

GENERAL COLLEGE INFORMATION

State-supported, coed. Part of University of North Carolina System. Awards bachelor's, master's, doctoral degrees. Founded 1891. *Setting:* 181-acre urban campus. *Endowment:* $4.9 million. *Research spending 1995–96:* $13.4 million. *Educational spending 1995–96:* $4963 per undergrad. *Total enrollment:* 7,533. *Faculty:* 516 (434 full-time, 66% with terminal degrees, 82 part-time); student–undergrad faculty ratio is 15:1.
Enrollment Profile: 6,598 students from 44 states and territories, 34 other countries. 52% women, 48% men, 10% part-time, 73% state residents, 5% transferred in, 1% international, 15% 25 or older, 1% Native American, 1% Hispanic, 92% black, 1% Asian or Pacific Islander. *Retention:* 74% of 1995 full-time freshmen returned. *Graduation:* 14% graduate in 4 years, 23% in 5 years. *Areas of study chosen:* 21% engineering and applied sciences, 16% business management and administrative services, 9% education, 4% biological and life sciences, 4% communications and journalism, 4% computer and information sciences, 4% health professions and related sciences, 3% psychology, 3% social sciences, 3% vocational and home economics, 2% fine arts, 1% agriculture, 1% architecture, 1% English language/literature/letters, 1% foreign language and literature, 1% interdisciplinary studies, 1% mathematics, 1% physical sciences. *Most popular recent majors:* nursing, electrical engineering, accounting.
First-Year Class: 1,324 total; 4,540 applied, 65% were accepted, 45% of whom enrolled. 8% from top 10% of their high school class, 22% from top quarter, 53% from top half. 7 National Merit Scholars.
Graduation Requirements: 124 semester hours; 6 semester hours each of math and science; computer course for engineering, business, sociology, economics, math, industrial technology, education majors; senior project (some majors).
Computers on Campus: 250 computers available on campus for general student use. A campus-wide network can be accessed from off-campus. Students can contact faculty members and/or advisers through e-mail. Computers for student use in computer center, computer labs, library, academic buildings provide access to the Internet/World Wide Web. Staffed computer lab on campus (open 24 hours a day) provides training in use of computers, software. *Academic computing expenditure 1995–96:* $373,806.

EXPENSES AND FINANCIAL AID

Expenses for 1997–98: *Application fee:* $25. State resident tuition: $1596 full-time. Nonresident tuition: $8750 full-time. Part-time tuition per semester ranges from $169.50 to $689 for state residents, $1064 to $3372 for nonresidents. College room and board: $3860.
Undergraduate Financial Aid: 72% of all full-time undergraduates enrolled in fall 1996 applied for aid; of these, 87% were judged to have need according to Federal Methodology, of whom 94% were aided. On average, 63% of need was met. *Financial aid deadline (priority):* 5/15. *Financial aid forms:* FAFSA required.
LD Services Contact: Ms. Peggy Oliphant, Director, Veteran and Disability Support Services, North Carolina Agricultural and Technical State University, 1601 East Market Street, Greensboro, NC 27411, 910-334-7765. Fax: 910-334-7333.

NORTH CAROLINA STATE UNIVERSITY

Raleigh, North Carolina

LEARNING DISABILITIES SERVICES INFORMATION

Disability Services for Students began offering services in 1985. Currently the program serves 350 undergraduates with LD. Services are also

available to graduate students. Students diagnosed with ADD/ADHD are eligible for the same services available to students with LD.

Staff: 3 full-time staff members, including coordinator, LD coordinator, learning skills specialist. Services provided by tutors.

Special Fees: No special fees are charged for services to students with LD.

Applications and admissions: *Required:* high school transcript, grade point average, class rank, courses completed, untimed SAT I, psychoeducational report completed within 3 years; *recommended:* extended time SAT I. Students may begin taking classes any term. *Application deadline:* 2/1.

Special policies: The college has written policies regarding grade forgiveness.

PROGRAM AND SERVICE COMPONENTS

Academic advising: Provided by unit staff members, academic advisers. Students with LD may take up to 21 semester hours each term; most take 12 to 15 semester hours; 12 semester hours required to maintain full-time status; 12 semester hours (full-time), 6 semester hours (summer session) required to be eligible for financial aid.

Subject-area tutoring: Offered one-on-one by peer tutors, graduate students. Available in most subjects.

Auxiliary aids: Taped textbooks, tape recorders, optical character readers.

Auxiliary services: Alternative test arrangements, notetakers, priority registration, advocacy.

GENERAL COLLEGE INFORMATION

State-supported, coed. Part of University of North Carolina System. Awards associate, bachelor's, master's, doctoral degrees. Founded 1887. *Setting:* 1,623-acre suburban campus. *Endowment:* $156.8 million. *Research spending 1995–96:* $139 million. *Educational spending 1995–96:* $7566 per undergrad. *Total enrollment:* 27,169. *Faculty:* 2,623 (2,382 full-time, 92% with terminal degrees, 241 part-time); student–undergrad faculty ratio is 14:1.

Enrollment Profile: 18,965 students from 52 states and territories, 99 other countries. 43% women, 57% men, 9% part-time, 82% state residents, 40% live on campus, 7% transferred in, 4% international, 9% 25 or older, 1% Native American, 2% Hispanic, 9% black, 4% Asian or Pacific Islander. *Retention:* 89% of 1995 full-time freshmen returned. *Graduation:* 36% graduate in 4 years, 60% in 5 years, 71% in 6 years. *Areas of study chosen:* 22% engineering and applied sciences, 11% social sciences, 10% business management and administrative services, 5% agriculture, 5% computer and information sciences, 4% communications and journalism, 3% architecture, 3% education, 3% premed, 3% prevet, 2% interdisciplinary studies, 2% natural resource sciences. *Most popular recent majors:* business administration/commerce/management, electrical engineering, mechanical engineering.

First-Year Class: 3,535 total; 10,727 applied, 66% were accepted, 50% of whom enrolled. 70% from top 10% of their high school class, 90% from top quarter, 99% from top half. 45 National Merit Scholars, 101 class presidents, 381 valedictorians.

Graduation Requirements: 64 semester hours for associate, 120 semester hours for bachelor's; 2 courses each in math and science; proficiency in a foreign language; computer course; internship (some majors); senior project (some majors).

Computers on Campus: 4,100 computers available on campus for general student use. Computer purchase/lease plans available. A computer is recommended for all students. A campus-wide network can be accessed from student residence rooms and from off-campus. Students can contact faculty members and/or advisers through e-mail. Computers for student use in computer center, computer labs, research center, learning resource center, classrooms, library, student center, dorms provide access to the Internet/World Wide Web, on- and off-campus e-mail addresses. Staffed computer lab on campus (open 24 hours a day) provides training in use of computers, software. *Academic computing expenditure 1995–96:* $13.1 million.

EXPENSES AND FINANCIAL AID

Estimated Expenses for 1997–98: *Application fee:* $55. State resident tuition: $2200 full-time. Nonresident tuition: $10,732 full-time. Part-time tuition per semester ranges from $309 to $927 for state residents, $1376 to $4126 for nonresidents. College room and board: $3350. College room only: $1850.

Undergraduate Financial Aid: Of all full-time undergraduates enrolled in fall 1996, 77% of those who applied for aid were judged to have need according to Federal Methodology, of whom 73% were aided. On average, 72% of need was met. *Financial aid deadline (priority):* 3/1. *Financial aid forms:* FAFSA, institutional form required.

LD Services Contact: Ms. Lelia S. Brettmann, Learning Disabilities Coordinator, North Carolina State University, Box 7312, Raleigh, NC 27695-7312, 919-515-7653. Fax: 919-515-2376. Email: lelia_brettmann@ncsu.edu.

NORTH CENTRAL COLLEGE

Naperville, Illinois

LEARNING DISABILITIES SERVICES INFORMATION

Academic Advising Center began offering services in 1988. Currently the program serves 37 undergraduates with LD. Services are also available to graduate students. Students diagnosed with ADD/ADHD are eligible for the same services available to students with LD.

Staff: 2 part-time staff members, including director, associate director. Services provided by remediation specialist, tutors.

Special Fees: No special fees are charged for services to students with LD.

Applications and admissions: *Required:* high school transcript, grade point average, class rank, courses completed, untimed ACT; *recommended:* high school extracurricular activities, letters of recommendation. Students may begin taking classes in fall only. *Application deadline:* continuous.

PROGRAM AND SERVICE COMPONENTS

Academic advising: Provided by academic advisers. Students with LD may take up to 3 courses each term; most take 2.5 to 3 courses; 2.5 courses required to maintain full-time status.

Counseling services: Individual counseling, small-group counseling, career counseling.

Basic skills remediation: Offered one-on-one by LD teachers, peer tutors. Available in reading, math, spelling, written language, learning strategies, study skills, time management.

Subject-area tutoring: Offered one-on-one by peer tutors. Available in most subjects.

Special courses: Learning strategies, math, study skills. None offered for credit; none enter into overall grade point average.

Auxiliary aids: Taped textbooks, tape recorders, calculators, word-processors with spell-check.

Auxiliary services: Alternative test arrangements, advocacy.

Campus support group: A special student organization is available to students with LD.

GENERAL COLLEGE INFORMATION

Independent United Methodist, comprehensive, coed. Awards bachelor's, master's degrees. Founded 1861. *Setting:* 56-acre suburban campus with easy access to Chicago. *Endowment:* $31.1 million. *Research spending 1995–96:* $131,711. *Educational spending 1995–96:* $4193 per undergrad. *Total enrollment:* 2,623. *Faculty:* 205 (105 full-time, 87% with terminal degrees, 100 part-time); student–undergrad faculty ratio is 14:1.

Enrollment Profile: 1,759 students from 20 states and territories, 26 other countries. 54% women, 46% men, 19% part-time, 87% state residents, 38% transferred in, 1% international, 27% 25 or older, 1% Native American, 3% Hispanic, 4% black, 3% Asian or Pacific Islander. *Retention:* 85% of 1995 full-time freshmen returned. *Graduation:* 52% graduate in 4 years, 59% in 5 years. *Areas of study chosen:* 30% business management and administrative services, 9% computer and information sciences, 9% social sciences, 8% education, 7% communications and journalism, 7% psychology, 6% biological and life sciences, 5% fine arts, 4% English language/literature/letters, 4% foreign language and literature, 3% mathematics, 2% physical sciences, 1% philosophy, 1% theology/religion. *Most popular recent majors:* business administration/commerce/management, psychology, communication.

First-Year Class: 314 total; 1,340 applied, 84% were accepted, 28% of whom enrolled. 21% from top 10% of their high school class, 51% from top quarter, 83% from top half. 8 valedictorians.

Graduation Requirements: 120 semester hours; 1 course each in math and science; computer course for all bachelor of science degree programs, accounting, business majors; senior project (some majors).

Computers on Campus: 125 computers available on campus for general student use. A computer is recommended for some students. A campus-wide network can be accessed from student residence rooms and from off-campus. Students can contact faculty members and/or advisers through e-mail. Computers for student use in computer center, computer labs, library, dorms, student rooms provide access to the Internet/World Wide Web, on- and off-campus e-mail addresses. Staffed computer lab on campus provides training in use of computers, software. *Academic computing expenditure 1995–96:* $295,539.

EXPENSES AND FINANCIAL AID

Expenses for 1997–98: *Application fee:* $20. Comprehensive fee of $18,915 includes full-time tuition ($13,725), mandatory fees ($120), and college room and board ($5070). Part-time tuition: $1284 per course. Part-time tuition for nonmatriculated students (1 to 7 courses): $1028 per course.
Undergraduate Financial Aid: 74% of all full-time undergraduates enrolled in fall 1996 applied for aid; of these, 92% were judged to have need according to Federal Methodology, of whom 99% were aided. On average, 85% of need was met. *Financial aid deadline:* continuous. *Financial aid forms:* FAFSA, institutional form, federal income tax forms (student and parent) required; CSS Financial Aid PROFILE, state form acceptable.
LD Services Contact: Dr. Mary Jean Lynch, Director of Advising Center/ Academic Support Center, North Central College, 30 North Brainard, Naperville, IL 60566, 630-637-5268. Fax: 630-637-5819.

NORTH DAKOTA STATE UNIVERSITY

Fargo, North Dakota

LEARNING DISABILITIES SERVICES INFORMATION

Disability Services began offering services in 1979. Currently the program serves 180 undergraduates with LD. Services are also available to graduate students. Students diagnosed with ADD/ADHD are eligible for the same services available to students with LD.
Staff: 2 full-time, 3 part-time staff members, including coordinator. Services provided by LD specialist, assistive technology specialist.
Special Fees: No special fees are charged for services to students with LD.
Applications and admissions: *Required:* untimed ACT; *recommended:* high school transcript, courses completed, extended time ACT, personal interview, autobiographical statement, letters of recommendation, psychoeducational report completed within 2 years. Students may begin taking classes any term. *Application deadline:* continuous.

PROGRAM AND SERVICE COMPONENTS

Special preparation or orientation: Orientation offered before registration, during registration, after classes begin.
Academic advising: Provided by unit staff members, academic advisers. Students with LD may take up to 14 credits each term; most take 12 credits; 12 credits required to maintain full-time status; 6 credits (part-time) required to be eligible for financial aid.
Counseling services: Individual counseling, small-group counseling, career counseling.
Basic skills remediation: Offered one-on-one and in small groups by LD teachers. Available in reading, spelling, learning strategies, study skills, time management, social skills.
Subject-area tutoring: Offered one-on-one and in small groups by professional teachers, peer tutors. Available in most subjects.
Special courses: College survival skills, reading, vocabulary development, composition, learning strategies, time management, study skills, career planning. Most offered for credit; most enter into overall grade point average.
Auxiliary aids: Taped textbooks, tape recorders, talking computers, Language Master, Franklin Speller.
Auxiliary services: Alternative test arrangements, notetakers, priority registration, advocacy.

GENERAL COLLEGE INFORMATION

State-supported, coed. Part of North Dakota University System. Awards bachelor's, master's, doctoral, first professional degrees. Founded 1890. *Setting:* 2,100-acre urban campus. *Total enrollment:* 9,688. *Faculty:* 497 (464 full-time, 87% with terminal degrees, 33 part-time); student–undergrad faculty ratio is 19:1.
Enrollment Profile: 8,627 students from 40 states and territories, 20 other countries. 42% women, 58% men, 14% part-time, 58% state residents, 9% transferred in, 1% international, 14% 25 or older, 1% Native American, 1% Hispanic, 1% black, 1% Asian or Pacific Islander. *Retention:* 77% of 1995 full-time freshmen returned. *Areas of study chosen:* 25% engineering and applied sciences, 11% social sciences, 7% interdisciplinary studies, 4% education, 3% psychology, 2% architecture, 2% communications and journalism, 2% natural resource sciences, 2% performing arts, 1% agriculture, 1% fine arts, 1% prelaw, 1% premed, 1% prevet. *Most popular recent majors:* business administration/commerce/ management, electrical engineering, pharmacy/pharmaceutical sciences.
First-Year Class: 1,643 total; 2,663 applied, 77% were accepted, 80% of whom enrolled. 53% from top quarter of their high school class, 85% from top half. 4 National Merit Scholars.
Graduation Requirements: 122 credits; 3 credits of math; 10 credits of science; computer course; internship (some majors); senior project for honors program students and some majors.
Computers on Campus: 272 computers available on campus for general student use. Computer purchase/lease plans available. A campus-wide network can be accessed from student residence rooms and from off-campus. Students can contact faculty members and/or advisers through e-mail. Computers for student use in computer center, computer labs, learning resource center, classrooms, library, student center, student rooms, academic buildings provide access to the Internet/World Wide Web. Staffed computer lab on campus (open 24 hours a day) provides training in use of computers, software.

EXPENSES AND FINANCIAL AID

Expenses for 1996–97: *Application fee:* $25. State resident tuition: $2110 full-time, $87.92 per credit part-time. Nonresident tuition: $5634 full-time, $234.75 per credit part-time. Part-time mandatory fees: $12.50 per credit. Tuition for nonresidents eligible for the Western Undergraduate Exchange and Western Interstate Commission for Higher Education programs, and residents of Manitoba, Montana, Saskatchewan and South Dakota: $3166 full-time, $131.92 per credit part-time. Minnesota resident tuition: $2356 full-time, $98.17 per credit part-time. Full-time mandatory fees: $300. College room and board: $2968. College room only: $1120.
Undergraduate Financial Aid: Of all full-time undergraduates enrolled in fall 1996, 59% of those who applied for aid were judged to have need according to Federal Methodology, of whom 98% were aided. On average, 85% of need was met. *Financial aid deadline:* Applications processed continuously. *Financial aid forms:* FAFSA required. Institutional form required for some.
LD Services Contact: Ms. Cathy Anderson, Coordinator, Disability Services, North Dakota State University, Ceres Hall 212, Fargo, ND 58105, 701-237-7198. Fax: 701-237-7671.

NORTHERN ARIZONA UNIVERSITY

Flagstaff, Arizona

LEARNING DISABILITIES SERVICES INFORMATION

Disability Support Services (DSS) began offering services in 1982. Currently the program serves 110 undergraduates with LD. Services are also available to graduate students. Students diagnosed with ADD/ ADHD are eligible for the same services available to students with LD, as well as private/quiet testing arrangements.
Staff: 5 full-time, 1 part-time staff members, including director, assistant director, coordinator. Services provided by remediation specialists, tutors, counselors.
Special Fees: No special fees are charged for services to students with LD.
Applications and admissions: *Required:* high school transcript, grade point average, class rank, courses completed, extracurricular activities, extended time SAT I or ACT, psychoeducational report completed within 3 years; *recommended:* high school IEP (Individualized Education Program). Students may begin taking classes in fall, spring, or summer. *Application deadline:* continuous.
Special policies: The college has written policies regarding substitutions and waivers of admissions, graduation, and degree requirements.

PROGRAM AND SERVICE COMPONENTS

Special preparation or orientation: Optional orientation offered during registration.
Academic advising: Provided by unit staff members, academic advisers. Students with LD may take up to 15 semester hours each term; most take 12 semester hours; 12 semester hours required to maintain full-time status and be eligible for financial aid.
Counseling services: Individual counseling, small-group counseling, career counseling, self-advocacy training.
Basic skills remediation: Offered one-on-one and in small groups by graduate assistants. Available in reading, math, spelling, handwriting, written language, learning strategies, study skills, time management, social skills, speech.

Northern Arizona University (continued)

Auxiliary aids: Taped textbooks, tape recorders, calculators, word-processors with spell-check, personal computers, optical character readers, Franklin Speller.
Auxiliary services: Alternative test arrangements, notetakers, priority registration.
Campus support group: A special student organization is available to students with LD.

GENERAL COLLEGE INFORMATION

State-supported, coed. Awards bachelor's, master's, doctoral degrees. Founded 1899. *Setting:* 730-acre small-town campus. *Total enrollment:* 19,605. *Faculty:* 935 (659 full-time, 86% with terminal degrees, 276 part-time); student–undergrad faculty ratio is 22:1.
Enrollment Profile: 14,250 students from 55 states and territories, 55 other countries. 56% women, 44% men, 15% part-time, 81% state residents, 53% live on campus, 49% transferred in, 2% international, 26% 25 or older, 7% Native American, 9% Hispanic, 1% black, 2% Asian or Pacific Islander. *Retention:* 69% of 1995 full-time freshmen returned. *Areas of study chosen:* 15% education, 10% business management and administrative services, 10% social sciences, 9% health professions and related sciences, 9% interdisciplinary studies, 8% engineering and applied sciences, 6% natural resource sciences, 5% biological and life sciences, 5% performing arts, 5% psychology, 4% physical sciences, 3% fine arts, 2% communications and journalism, 2% computer and information sciences, 2% prelaw, 2% premed, 1% English language/literature/letters, 1% foreign language and literature, 1% mathematics. *Most popular recent majors:* business administration/commerce/management, education, psychology.
First-Year Class: 2,262 total; 6,741 applied, 84% were accepted, 40% of whom enrolled. 26% from top 10% of their high school class, 47% from top quarter, 83% from top half. 1 National Merit Scholar.
Graduation Requirements: 120 semester hours; 1 college algebra course; 8 semester hours of science including at least 1 lab science course; computer course for business administration, engineering, forestry, math, education majors; internship (some majors); senior project for honors program students and some majors.
Computers on Campus: 500 computers available on campus for general student use. A campus-wide network can be accessed from student residence rooms and from off-campus. Students can contact faculty members and/or advisers through e-mail. Computers for student use in computer center, computer labs, learning resource center, library, student center, dorms, learning assistance center provide access to the Internet/World Wide Web. Staffed computer lab on campus (open 24 hours a day) provides training in use of computers, software.

EXPENSES AND FINANCIAL AID

Expenses for 1997–98: *Application fee:* $40. State resident tuition: $1988 full-time. Nonresident tuition: $7754 full-time. Nonresident part-time tuition per semester ranges from $323 to $3554. Part-time mandatory fees per semester range from $10 to $36. Part-time tuition for state residents: $105 per semester hour for 1 to 6 semester hours, $994 per semester hour for 7 or more semester hours. Full-time mandatory fees: $72. College room and board: $3350. College room only: $1670.
Undergraduate Financial Aid: 73% of all full-time undergraduates enrolled in fall 1996 applied for aid; of these, 82% were judged to have need according to Federal Methodology, of whom 95% were aided. On average, 84% of need was met. *Financial aid deadline (priority):* 4/15. *Financial aid forms:* proof of Selective Service registration (for men), Statement of Educational Purpose required; FAFSA acceptable. Institutional form required for some.
LD Services Contact: Dr. Marsha Fields, Director, Northern Arizona University, Box 6045, Flagstaff, AZ 86011, 520-523-2261. Fax: 520-523-9060. Email: marsha.fields@nau.edu.

NORTHERN ILLINOIS UNIVERSITY

De Kalb, Illinois

LEARNING DISABILITIES SERVICES INFORMATION

Center for Access-Ability Resources began offering services in 1980. Currently the program serves 183 undergraduates with LD. Services are also available to graduate students. Students diagnosed with ADD/ADHD are eligible for the same services available to students with LD, as well as one-on-one coaching for time management/study skills, free diagnostic evaluations (by specifically trained University Health Service physicians).
Staff: 6 full-time, 8 part-time staff members, including director, coordinators, secretary, graduate assistants, student workers. Services provided by student aides.
Special Fees: $160 for diagnostic testing.
Applications and admissions: *Required:* high school transcript, grade point average, class rank, courses completed, IEP (Individualized Education Program), autobiographical statement, letters of recommendation, psychoeducational report completed within 3 years, personal interview (for special admission); *recommended:* high school extracurricular activities, untimed or extended time ACT, extended time SAT I. Students may begin taking classes in fall, spring, or summer. *Application deadline:* 8/1 (fall term), 12/15 (spring term).
Special policies: The college has written policies regarding substitutions and waivers of admissions, graduation, and degree requirements.

PROGRAM AND SERVICE COMPONENTS

Special preparation or orientation: Optional orientation offered during registration.
Diagnostic testing: Intelligence, reading, math, spelling, spoken language, written language, perceptual skills, personality, speech, hearing, learning strategies.
Academic advising: Provided by unit staff members, academic advisers. Students with LD may take up to 18 credit hours each term; most take 12 credit hours; 12 credit hours required to maintain full-time status and be eligible for financial aid.
Counseling services: Individual counseling, small-group counseling, career counseling, self-advocacy training.
Subject-area tutoring: Offered one-on-one and in small groups by peer tutors. Available in some subjects.
Special courses: College Reading and Study Skills. All offered for credit; all enter into overall grade point average.
Auxiliary aids: Taped textbooks, tape recorders, typewriters, word-processors with spell-check, optical character readers.
Auxiliary services: Alternative test arrangements, notetakers, priority registration, advocacy, editors.
Campus support group: A special student organization is available to students with LD.

GENERAL COLLEGE INFORMATION

State-supported, coed. Awards bachelor's, master's, doctoral, first professional degrees. Founded 1895. *Setting:* 589-acre small-town campus with easy access to Chicago. *Research spending 1995–96:* $10.6 million. *Educational spending 1995–96:* $5385 per undergrad. *Total enrollment:* 21,609. *Faculty:* 1,208 (1,049 full-time, 80% with terminal degrees, 159 part-time); student–undergrad faculty ratio is 17:1.
Enrollment Profile: 15,387 students from 50 states and territories, 100 other countries. 54% women, 46% men, 12% part-time, 97% state residents, 13% transferred in, 2% international, 16% 25 or older, 5% Hispanic, 10% black, 7% Asian or Pacific Islander. *Retention:* 74% of 1995 full-time freshmen returned. *Graduation:* 28% graduate in 4 years, 49% in 5 years, 53% in 6 years. *Areas of study chosen:* 21% business management and administrative services, 13% education, 11% health professions and related sciences, 11% liberal arts/general studies, 7% fine arts, 6% engineering and applied sciences, 6% social sciences, 4% biological and life sciences, 4% communications and journalism, 4% computer and information sciences, 3% English language/literature/letters, 3% psychology, 3% vocational and home economics, 1% foreign language and literature, 1% mathematics, 1% performing arts, 1% physical sciences. *Most popular recent majors:* communication, education, accounting.
First-Year Class: 2,451 total; 10,406 applied, 74% were accepted, 32% of whom enrolled. 10% from top 10% of their high school class, 34% from top quarter, 76% from top half.
Graduation Requirements: 124 credit hours; 7 credit hours of math/science; computer course for business majors, all BS degree programs; internship (some majors); senior project for honors program students and some majors.
Computers on Campus: 1,200 computers available on campus for general student use. Computer purchase/lease plans available. A campus-wide network can be accessed from student residence rooms and from off-campus. Students can contact faculty members and/or advisers through e-mail. Computers for student use in computer center, computer labs, student center, dorms provide access to the Internet/World Wide Web. Staffed computer lab on campus provides training in use of computers, software. *Academic computing expenditure 1995–96:* $915,310.

EXPENSES AND FINANCIAL AID

Expenses for 1997–98: State resident tuition: $3050 (minimum) full-time, $98.40 per credit hour part-time. Nonresident tuition: $9151 (minimum) full-time, $295.20 per credit hour part-time. Part-time mandatory fees: $36.80 per credit hour. Full-time mandatory fees: $883. College room and board: $4000.
Undergraduate Financial Aid: 65% of all full-time undergraduates enrolled in fall 1996 applied for aid; of these, 79% were judged to have need according to Federal Methodology, of whom 92% were aided. On average, 72% of need was met. *Financial aid deadline (priority):* 3/1. *Financial aid forms:* FAFSA, institutional form required.
LD Services Contact: Ms. Sharon Wyland, LD Coordinator, Center for Access-Ability Resources, Northern Illinois University, University Health Service, De Kalb, IL 60115-2854, 815-753-1303. Fax: 815-753-9599.

NORTHERN KENTUCKY UNIVERSITY

Highland Heights, Kentucky

LEARNING DISABILITIES SERVICES INFORMATION

Disability Services currently serves 150 undergraduates with LD. Students diagnosed with ADD/ADHD are eligible for the same services available to students with LD.
Staff: 1 full-time staff member (coordinator). Services provided by tutor, counselors.
Special Fees: No special fees are charged for services to students with LD.
Applications and admissions: *Required:* high school transcript, courses completed, untimed ACT, psychoeducational report completed within 3 years; *recommended:* personal interview, bureau of vocational rehabilitation testing. Students may begin taking classes any term. *Application deadline:* continuous.
Special policies: The college has written policies regarding grade forgiveness.

PROGRAM AND SERVICE COMPONENTS

Special preparation or orientation: Orientation (required for some) held before registration.
Academic advising: Provided by unit staff members, academic advisers. Students with LD may take up to 18 semester hours each term; most take 12 semester hours; 12 semester hours required to maintain full-time status and be eligible for financial aid.
Counseling services: Individual counseling, small-group counseling, career counseling, self-advocacy training.
Basic skills remediation: Offered one-on-one, in small groups, and in class-size groups by regular teachers. Available in reading, math, spelling, handwriting, spoken language, written language, learning strategies, study skills, time management, speech.
Subject-area tutoring: Offered one-on-one and in small groups by professional teachers, peer tutors. Available in most subjects.
Auxiliary aids: Tape recorders, calculators, typewriters, word-processors with spell-check, personal computers.
Auxiliary services: Alternative test arrangements, notetakers, priority registration, advocacy.

GENERAL COLLEGE INFORMATION

State-supported, comprehensive, coed. Awards associate, bachelor's, master's, first professional degrees. Founded 1968. *Setting:* 300-acre suburban campus with easy access to Cincinnati. *Research spending 1995–96:* $284,000. *Total enrollment:* 11,505. *Undergraduate faculty:* 701 (378 full-time, 82% with terminal degrees, 323 part-time); student–undergrad faculty ratio is 17:1.
Enrollment Profile: 10,283 students from 32 states and territories, 45 other countries. 58% women, 42% men, 37% part-time, 75% state residents, 10% live on campus, 5% transferred in, 1% international, 40% 25 or older, 1% Native American, 1% Hispanic, 3% black, 1% Asian or Pacific Islander. *Retention:* 61% of 1995 full-time freshmen returned. *Graduation:* 12% graduate in 4 years, 38% in 5 years, 51% in 6 years. *Areas of study chosen:* 20% liberal arts/general studies, 19% business management and administrative services, 15% education, 6% biological and life sciences, 6% communications and journalism, 5% psychology, 4% English language/literature/letters, 4% social sciences, 3% computer and information sciences, 3% engineering and applied sciences, 3% fine arts, 3% health professions and related sciences, 3% performing arts, 3% physical sciences, 1% foreign language and literature, 1% mathematics, 1% philosophy. *Most popular recent majors:* education, nursing, psychology.
First-Year Class: 1,628 total; 2,203 applied, 100% were accepted, 74% of whom enrolled.
Graduation Requirements: 64 semester hours for associate, 128 semester hours for bachelor's; 9 semester hours of math/science; computer course for all business-related, education majors; internship (some majors); senior project for honors program students and some majors.
Computers on Campus: 400 computers available on campus for general student use. Computer purchase/lease plans available. A campuswide network can be accessed from student residence rooms and from off-campus. Students can contact faculty members and/or advisers through e-mail. Computers for student use in computer center, computer labs, classrooms, library, student center, dorms provide access to the Internet/World Wide Web, on- and off-campus e-mail addresses. Staffed computer lab on campus provides training in use of computers, software.

EXPENSES AND FINANCIAL AID

Expenses for 1997–98: *Application fee:* $25. State resident tuition: $2020 full-time, $86 per semester hour part-time. Nonresident tuition: $5500 full-time, $231 per semester hour part-time. College room and board: $3164 (minimum). College room only: $1530 (minimum).
Undergraduate Financial Aid: Of all full-time undergraduates enrolled in fall 1996, 89% of those who applied for aid were judged to have need according to Federal Methodology, of whom 97% were aided. On average, 80% of need was met. *Financial aid deadline (priority):* 4/1. *Financial aid forms:* FAFSA, institutional form required.
LD Services Contact: Mr. A. Dale Adams, Coordinator of Disability Services, Northern Kentucky University, Louie B Nunn Drive, Highland Heights, KY 41099, 606-572-5180.

NORTHERN STATE UNIVERSITY

Aberdeen, South Dakota

LEARNING DISABILITIES SERVICES INFORMATION

Learning Center began offering services in 1989. Currently the program serves 41 undergraduates with LD. Services are also available to graduate students. Students diagnosed with ADD/ADHD are eligible for the same services available to students with LD.
Staff: 1 full-time staff member (director). Services provided by remediation specialists, tutors, counselors.
Special Fees: No special fees are charged for services to students with LD.
Applications and admissions: *Required:* personal interview, documentation of learning disability; *recommended:* high school transcript, IEP (Individualized Education Program), extended time ACT. Students may begin taking classes any term. *Application deadline:* continuous.
Special policies: The college has written policies regarding grade forgiveness; substitutions and waivers of admissions, graduation, and degree requirements.

PROGRAM AND SERVICE COMPONENTS

Academic advising: Provided by unit staff members, academic advisers. Students with LD may take up to 15 credit hours each term; most take 9 to 12 credit hours; 12 credit hours required to maintain full-time status; 6 credit hours required to be eligible for financial aid.
Counseling services: Individual counseling, small-group counseling, career counseling.
Basic skills remediation: Offered one-on-one, in small groups, and in class-size groups by regular teachers, teacher trainees; computer-aided instruction also offered. Available in reading, math, written language, learning strategies, study skills, time management.
Subject-area tutoring: Offered one-on-one and in small groups by peer tutors. Available in most subjects.
Special courses: College survival skills, reading, learning strategies, time management, math, study skills, career planning, stress management. All offered for credit; all enter into overall grade point average.
Auxiliary aids: Taped textbooks, tape recorders, typewriters, word-processors with spell-check, personal computers, talking computers, optical character readers.
Auxiliary services: Alternative test arrangements, notetakers, priority registration, advocacy.

Northern State University (continued)

GENERAL COLLEGE INFORMATION

State-supported, comprehensive, coed. Part of South Dakota Board of Regents. Awards associate, bachelor's, master's degrees. Founded 1901. *Setting:* 52-acre small-town campus. *Total enrollment:* 2,634. *Faculty:* 135 (120 full-time, 80% with terminal degrees, 15 part-time); student–undergrad faculty ratio is 18:1.
Enrollment Profile: 2,496 students from 26 states and territories, 21 other countries. 64% women, 36% men, 18% part-time, 84% state residents, 5% transferred in, 2% international, 25% 25 or older, 2% Native American, 0% Hispanic, 1% black, 1% Asian or Pacific Islander. *Retention:* 62% of 1995 full-time freshmen returned. *Graduation:* 15% graduate in 4 years, 30% in 5 years, 34% in 6 years. *Areas of study chosen:* 28% business management and administrative services, 24% education, 15% mathematics, 4% social sciences, 3% fine arts. *Most popular recent majors:* business administration/commerce/management, elementary education, sociology.
First-Year Class: 571 total; 1,001 applied, 97% were accepted, 59% of whom enrolled. 8% from top 10% of their high school class, 26% from top quarter, 57% from top half. 15 valedictorians.
Graduation Requirements: 64 credit hours for associate, 128 credit hours for bachelor's; 12 credit hours of math/science; computer course for business administration majors; internship (some majors).
Computers on Campus: 500 computers available on campus for general student use. A computer is strongly recommended for all students. A campus-wide network can be accessed from student residence rooms and from off-campus. Students can contact faculty members and/or advisers through e-mail. Computers for student use in computer center, computer labs, classrooms, library, dorms provide access to the Internet/World Wide Web, on- and off-campus e-mail addresses. Staffed computer lab on campus provides training in use of computers, software.

EXPENSES AND FINANCIAL AID

Expenses for 1997–98: *Application fee:* $15. State resident tuition: $1728 full-time, $54 per credit hour part-time. Nonresident tuition: $5496 full-time, $171.75 per credit hour part-time. Part-time mandatory fees: $30.50 per credit hour. Minnesota residents pay state resident tuition rates. Tuition for nonresidents who are eligible for the Western Undergraduate Exchange: $2592 full-time, $81 per credit hour part-time. Full-time mandatory fees: $976. College room and board: $2408. College room only: $1232.
Undergraduate Financial Aid: Of all full-time undergraduates enrolled in fall 1996, 69% of those who applied for aid were judged to have need according to Federal Methodology, of whom 100% were aided. On average, 100% of need was met. *Financial aid deadline (priority):* 3/1. *Financial aid forms:* FAFSA required; CSS Financial Aid PROFILE acceptable.
LD Services Contact: Mr. Paul Kraft, Director of Learning Center, Northern State University, 1200 South Jay Street, Aberdeen, SD 57401, 605-626-2371. Fax: 605-626-2431. Email: lcenter@wolf.northern.edu.

NORWICH UNIVERSITY
Northfield, Vermont

LEARNING DISABILITIES SERVICES INFORMATION

Learning Support Center began offering services in 1980. Currently the program serves 110 undergraduates with LD. Services are also available to graduate students. Students diagnosed with ADD/ADHD are eligible for the same services available to students with LD.
Staff: 2 full-time, 8 part-time staff members, including director, coordinators. Services provided by LD specialist.
Special Fees: No special fees are charged for services to students with LD.
Applications and admissions: *Required:* high school transcript, grade point average, class rank, courses completed, untimed SAT I or ACT, autobiographical statement; *recommended:* high school extracurricular activities, extended time SAT I, personal interview, letters of recommendation, psychoeducational report completed within 3 years. Students may begin taking classes any term. *Application deadline:* continuous.
Special policies: The college has written policies regarding substitutions and waivers of graduation and degree requirements.

PROGRAM AND SERVICE COMPONENTS

Special preparation or orientation: Optional orientation offered after classes begin.
Academic advising: Provided by unit staff members, academic advisors. Most students with LD take 12 to 16 credits each term; 12 credits required to maintain full-time status; 12 credits (full-time) required to be eligible for financial aid.
Auxiliary aids: Word-processors with spell-check, print enlarger.
Auxiliary services: Alternative test arrangements, priority registration, advocacy.

GENERAL COLLEGE INFORMATION

Independent, comprehensive, coed. Awards associate, bachelor's, master's degrees. Founded 1819. *Setting:* 1,125-acre small-town campus. *Research spending 1995–96:* $160,946. *Educational spending 1995–96:* $4923 per undergrad. *Total enrollment:* 2,556. *Faculty:* 179 (141 full-time, 85% with terminal degrees, 38 part-time); student–undergrad faculty ratio is 14:1.
Enrollment Profile: 1,500 students from 50 states and territories, 13 other countries. 30% women, 70% men, 6% part-time, 22% state residents, 17% transferred in, 2% international, 10% 25 or older, 1% Native American, 5% Hispanic, 3% black, 3% Asian or Pacific Islander. *Retention:* 71% of 1995 full-time freshmen returned. *Areas of study chosen:* 16% health professions and related sciences, 10% engineering and applied sciences, 6% architecture, 6% social sciences, 5% business management and administrative services, 3% communications and journalism, 2% biological and life sciences, 2% computer and information sciences, 2% psychology, 1% English language/literature/letters, 1% mathematics, 1% military science, 1% physical sciences. *Most popular recent majors:* criminal justice, mechanical engineering, business administration/commerce/management.
First-Year Class: 524 total; 1,759 applied, 94% were accepted, 32% of whom enrolled. 8% from top 10% of their high school class, 21% from top quarter, 57% from top half.
Graduation Requirements: 114 credit hours for bachelor's; 2 semesters of math/science; computer course for engineering, business majors; internship (some majors); senior project (some majors).
Computers on Campus: 150 computers available on campus for general student use. A computer is recommended for all students. A campus-wide network can be accessed from student residence rooms and from off-campus. Students can contact faculty members and/or advisers through e-mail. Computers for student use in computer center, computer labs, classrooms, library provide access to the Internet/World Wide Web, on- and off-campus e-mail addresses. Staffed computer lab on campus. *Academic computing expenditure 1995–96:* $575,258.

EXPENSES AND FINANCIAL AID

Expenses for 1997–98: *Application fee:* $25. Comprehensive fee of $20,580 includes full-time tuition ($14,926), mandatory fees ($24), and college room and board ($5630). Part-time tuition: $425 per credit hour.
Undergraduate Financial Aid: *Financial aid deadline:* continuous. *Financial aid forms:* CSS Financial Aid PROFILE required; FAFSA acceptable. State form required for some.
LD Services Contact: Ms. Paula A. Gills, Director, Learning Support, Norwich University, Kreitzberg Library, Northfield, VT 05663, 802-485-2130. Fax: 802-485-2580.

OAKLAND CITY UNIVERSITY
Oakland City, Indiana

LEARNING DISABILITIES SERVICES INFORMATION

Student Support Services began offering services in 1978. Currently the program serves 20 undergraduates with LD. Services are also available to graduate students. Students diagnosed with ADD/ADHD are eligible for the same services available to students with LD.
Staff: 4 full-time, 1 part-time staff members, including director, coordinator. Services provided by remediation specialist, counselors.
Special Fees: No special fees are charged for services to students with LD.
Applications and admissions: *Required:* high school transcript, untimed SAT I or ACT, personal interview. Students may begin taking classes in fall, spring, or summer. *Application deadline:* continuous.
Special policies: The college has written policies regarding grade forgiveness; substitutions and waivers of admissions, graduation, and degree requirements.

PROGRAM AND SERVICE COMPONENTS

Diagnostic testing: Reading, math, written language, personality.

Academic advising: Provided by academic advisers. Students with LD may take up to 15 semester hours each term; 12 semester hours required to maintain full-time status and be eligible for financial aid.
Counseling services: Individual counseling, career counseling.
Basic skills remediation: Offered in small groups by regular teachers. Available in reading, learning strategies, study skills, time management, social skills.
Subject-area tutoring: Offered one-on-one and in small groups by peer tutors. Available in all subjects.
Special courses: College survival skills, reading, vocabulary development, communication skills, composition, learning strategies, time management, study skills, career planning. All offered for credit; all enter into overall grade point average.
Auxiliary aids: Taped textbooks, tape recorders, word-processors with spell-check, personal computers.
Auxiliary services: Notetakers.

GENERAL COLLEGE INFORMATION

Independent General Baptist, comprehensive, coed. Awards associate, bachelor's, master's degrees. Founded 1885. *Setting:* 20-acre rural campus. *Endowment:* $700,000. *Total enrollment:* 1,087. *Faculty:* 67 (35 full-time, 55% with terminal degrees, 32 part-time); student–undergrad faculty ratio is 15:1.
Enrollment Profile: 1,030 students from 15 states and territories, 3 other countries. 46% women, 54% men, 6% part-time, 85% state residents, 75% live on campus, 8% transferred in, 2% international, 1% Native American, 1% Hispanic, 2% black, 1% Asian or Pacific Islander. *Retention:* 91% of 1995 full-time freshmen returned. *Most popular recent majors:* education, interdisciplinary studies, business administration/commerce/management.
First-Year Class: 218 total; 411 applied, 96% were accepted, 55% of whom enrolled. 6% from top 10% of their high school class, 26% from top quarter, 76% from top half.
Graduation Requirements: 64 semester hours for associate, 128 semester hours for bachelor's; 12 semester hours of math/science for associate degree; 20 semester hours of math/science including at least 4 semester hours of math and 8 semester hours of science for bachelor's degree; computer course.
Computers on Campus: 70 computers available on campus for general student use. A computer is recommended for all students. Computers for student use in computer center, computer labs, learning resource center, classrooms, library provide access to the Internet/World Wide Web, on-campus e-mail addresses. Staffed computer lab on campus provides training in use of computers, software. *Academic computing expenditure 1995–96:* $215,000.

EXPENSES AND FINANCIAL AID

Expenses for 1996–97: *Application fee:* $25. Comprehensive fee of $11,112 includes full-time tuition ($7800), mandatory fees ($166), and college room and board ($3146). Part-time tuition: $260 per semester hour.
Undergraduate Financial Aid: 95% of all full-time undergraduates enrolled in fall 1996 applied for aid. On average, 95% of need was met. *Financial aid deadline (priority):* 4/1. *Financial aid forms:* FAFSA, institutional form required.
LD Services Contact: Mr. Ron Malin, Director, Oakland City University, 143 Lucretia Street, Oakland City, IN 47660, 812-749-1273. Fax: 812-749-1233.

OAKLAND UNIVERSITY

Rochester, Michigan

LEARNING DISABILITIES SERVICES INFORMATION

Disability Support Services currently serves 53 undergraduates with LD. Services are also available to graduate students. Students diagnosed with ADD/ADHD are eligible for the same services available to students with LD.
Staff: 1 part-time staff member (director).
Special Fees: $70 for diagnostic testing.
Applications and admissions: *Required:* high school transcript, grade point average, extended time SAT I or ACT. Students may begin taking classes any term. *Application deadline:* 8/15 (fall term), 12/1 (spring term).

PROGRAM AND SERVICE COMPONENTS

Special preparation or orientation: Optional summer program offered prior to entering college.

Diagnostic testing: Intelligence, reading, math, spelling, written language, motor abilities, perceptual skills, study skills, personality, social skills, learning strategies.

Academic advising: Provided by academic advisers. Students with LD may take up to 16 credits each term; most take 8 to 12 credits; 12 credits required to maintain full-time status and be eligible for financial aid.

Counseling services: Individual counseling, career counseling.

Auxiliary aids: Taped textbooks, tape recorders, word-processors with spell-check, talking computers, optical character readers.

Auxiliary services: Alternative test arrangements, notetakers, priority registration, advocacy.

GENERAL COLLEGE INFORMATION

State-supported, coed. Awards bachelor's, master's, doctoral degrees. Founded 1957. *Setting:* 1,444-acre suburban campus with easy access to Detroit. *Endowment:* $14.1 million. *Research spending 1995–96:* $5.3 million. *Educational spending 1995–96:* $2220 per undergrad. *Total enrollment:* 13,965. *Faculty:* 697 (380 full-time, 86% with terminal degrees, 317 part-time); student–undergrad faculty ratio is 18:1.

Enrollment Profile: 10,886 students from 36 states and territories, 42 other countries. 64% women, 36% men, 39% part-time, 96% state residents, 10% live on campus, 45% transferred in, 3% international, 27% 25 or older, 1% Native American, 1% Hispanic, 6% black, 2% Asian or Pacific Islander. *Retention:* 74% of 1995 full-time freshmen returned. *Graduation:* 10% graduate in 4 years, 33% in 5 years, 42% in 6 years. *Areas of study chosen:* 15% health professions and related sciences, 14% business management and administrative services, 11% education, 9% social sciences, 8% engineering and applied sciences, 6% psychology, 4% biological and life sciences, 4% communications and journalism, 3% computer and information sciences, 3% liberal arts/general studies, 2% English language/literature/letters, 1% fine arts, 1% foreign language and literature, 1% mathematics. *Most popular recent majors:* psychology, biology/biological sciences, nursing.

First-Year Class: 1,411 total; 3,644 applied, 84% were accepted, 46% of whom enrolled. 20% from top 10% of their high school class, 49% from top quarter, 92% from top half.

Graduation Requirements: 124 credits; 4 credits each of math and science; 4 credits of a foreign language; computer course for political science, sociology, economics, management, engineering majors; internship (some majors); senior project for honors program students and some majors.

Computers on Campus: 294 computers available on campus for general student use. A campus-wide network can be accessed from student residence rooms and from off-campus. Students can contact faculty members and/or advisers through e-mail. Computers for student use in computer center, computer labs, classrooms, library, dorms, academic buildings provide access to the Internet/World Wide Web, on- and off-campus e-mail addresses. Staffed computer lab on campus provides training in use of computers, software. *Academic computing expenditure 1995–96:* $1.3 million.

EXPENSES AND FINANCIAL AID

Expenses for 1997–98: *Application fee:* $25. State resident tuition: $3472 (minimum) full-time. Nonresident tuition: $10,227 (minimum) full-time. Part-time mandatory fees: $131 per semester. Full-time tuition ranges up to $3816 for state residents, $11,017 for nonresidents, according to class level. Part-time tuition per credit ranges from $112 to $123.10 for state residents, $329.90 to $355.40 for nonresidents, according to class level. Full-time mandatory fees: $262. College room and board: $4555.

Undergraduate Financial Aid: Of all full-time undergraduates enrolled in fall 1996, 81% of those who applied for aid were judged to have need according to Federal Methodology, of whom 98% were aided. On average, 74% of need was met. *Financial aid deadline (priority):* 4/1. *Financial aid forms:* FAFSA, institutional form required; CSS Financial Aid PROFILE acceptable.

LD Services Contact: Ms. Lisa E. McGill, Director, Disability Support Services, Oakland University, 157 North Foundation Hall, Rochester, MI 48309-4401, 810-370-3266. Fax: 810-370-3351. Email: mcgill@oakland.edu.

THE OHIO STATE UNIVERSITY AT LIMA

Lima, Ohio

LEARNING DISABILITIES SERVICES INFORMATION

Office for LD Services began offering services in 1985. Currently the program serves 15 undergraduates with LD. Services are also available to graduate students. Students diagnosed with ADD/ADHD are eligible for the same services available to students with LD.
Staff: 1 part-time staff member. Services provided by LD specialist.
Special Fees: $225 for diagnostic testing.
Applications and admissions: *Required:* high school transcript, grade point average; *recommended:* high school IEP (Individualized Education Program), psychoeducational report completed within 3 years. Students may begin taking classes in fall only. *Application deadline:* continuous.
Special policies: The college has written policies regarding grade forgiveness; substitutions and waivers of admissions, graduation, and degree requirements.

PROGRAM AND SERVICE COMPONENTS

Diagnostic testing: Intelligence, reading, math, spelling, written language, study skills, learning strategies.
Academic advising: Provided by unit staff members, academic advisers. Students with LD required to take 12 quarter hours each term to maintain full-time status; 8 quarter hours required to be eligible for financial aid.
Counseling services: Individual counseling, career counseling, self-advocacy training.
Basic skills remediation: Offered one-on-one by LD specialist. Available in learning strategies.
Special courses: Composition, study skills, career planning. All offered for credit; all enter into overall grade point average.
Auxiliary aids: Taped textbooks.
Auxiliary services: Alternative test arrangements, notetakers, priority registration.

GENERAL COLLEGE INFORMATION

State-supported, 4-year, coed. Part of Ohio State University. Awards associate, bachelor's degrees (also offers some graduate courses). Founded 1960. *Setting:* 565-acre small-town campus. *Total enrollment:* 1,281. *Faculty:*; student–undergrad faculty ratio is 18:1.
Enrollment Profile: 1,128 students from 6 states and territories, 1 other country. 54% women, 46% men, 23% part-time, 98% state residents, 10% transferred in, 1% international, 26% 25 or older, 1% Native American, 1% Hispanic, 3% black, 1% Asian or Pacific Islander. *Retention:* 57% of 1995 full-time freshmen returned. *Areas of study chosen:* 26% education.
First-Year Class: 363 total; 583 applied, 94% were accepted, 66% of whom enrolled. 7% from top 10% of their high school class, 27% from top quarter, 63% from top half.
Graduation Requirements: 90 quarter hours for associate, 196 quarter hours for bachelor's; senior project for honors program students.
Computers on Campus: 104 computers available on campus for general student use. Computers for student use in computer center, computer labs, library.

EXPENSES

Expenses for 1997–98: *Application fee:* $30. State resident tuition: $3570 full-time. Nonresident tuition: $10,653 full-time. Part-time tuition per quarter ranges from $98 to $1092 for state residents, $195 to $3256 for nonresidents.
LD Services Contact: Ms. Carol German, LD Specialist, The Ohio State University at Lima, 4240 Campus Drive, Lima, OH 45804, 419-995-8453. Fax: 419-221-1658.

THE OHIO STATE UNIVERSITY AT MARION

Marion, Ohio

LEARNING DISABILITIES SERVICES INFORMATION

Learning Disability Services began offering services in 1985. Currently the program serves 20 to 25 undergraduates with LD. Students diagnosed with ADD/ADHD are eligible for the same services available to students with LD.
Staff: 1 part-time staff member (LD specialist). Services provided by remediation specialists, tutors.
Special Fees: $100 for diagnostic testing.
Applications and admissions: *Recommended:* high school transcript, grade point average, class rank, courses completed, extracurricular activities, untimed or extended time SAT I or ACT, personal interview, autobiographical statement, letters of recommendation, psychoeducational report. Students may begin taking classes any term. *Application deadline:* continuous.
Special policies: The college has written policies regarding grade forgiveness; substitutions and waivers of admissions, graduation, and degree requirements.

PROGRAM AND SERVICE COMPONENTS

Special preparation or orientation: Optional orientation offered individually by arrangement.
Diagnostic testing: Intelligence, reading, math, spelling, written language, study skills.
Academic advising: Provided by unit staff members, academic advisers. Most students with LD take 12 to 14 quarter hours each term; 12 quarter hours required to maintain full-time status and be eligible for financial aid.
Counseling services: Individual counseling, small-group counseling, career counseling.
Basic skills remediation: Offered one-on-one and in small groups by regular teachers, work-study student. Available in reading, math, spelling, written language, learning strategies, study skills.
Subject-area tutoring: Offered one-on-one and in small groups by peer tutors, professional math tutor. Available in most subjects.
Auxiliary aids: Taped textbooks, tape recorders, typewriters, word-processors with spell-check.
Auxiliary services: Alternative test arrangements, notetakers, priority registration.

GENERAL COLLEGE INFORMATION

State-supported, 4-year, coed. Part of Ohio State University. Awards associate, bachelor's degrees (also offers some graduate courses). Founded 1958. *Setting:* 180-acre small-town campus with easy access to Columbus. *Total enrollment:* 1,312. *Faculty:*; student–undergrad faculty ratio is 16:1.
Enrollment Profile: 1,060 students from 6 states and territories, 1 other country. 55% women, 45% men, 30% part-time, 98% state residents, 13% transferred in, 1% international, 33% 25 or older, 1% Native American, 1% Hispanic, 6% black, 1% Asian or Pacific Islander. *Retention:* 53% of 1995 full-time freshmen returned. *Areas of study chosen:* 23% education.
First-Year Class: 275 total; 445 applied, 97% were accepted, 64% of whom enrolled. 11% from top 10% of their high school class, 32% from top quarter, 65% from top half.
Graduation Requirements: 90 quarter hours for associate, 196 quarter hours for bachelor's.
Computers on Campus: 174 computers available on campus for general student use. Computers for student use in computer center, computer labs.

EXPENSES

Expenses for 1997–98: *Application fee:* $30. State resident tuition: $3570 full-time. Nonresident tuition: $10,653 full-time. Part-time tuition per quarter ranges from $98 to $1092 for state residents, $195 to $3256 for nonresidents.
LD Services Contact: Ms. Margaret C. Hazelett, Learning Disability Specialist, The Ohio State University at Marion, 1465 Mount Vernon Avenue, Marion, OH 43302-5695, 614-389-6786 Ext. 6247. Fax: 614-389-6786.

OHIO STATE UNIVERSITY–MANSFIELD CAMPUS

Mansfield, Ohio

LEARNING DISABILITIES SERVICES INFORMATION

Office for LD Services began offering services in 1985. Currently the program serves 10 undergraduates with LD. Services are also available to graduate students. Students diagnosed with ADD/ADHD are eligible for the same services available to students with LD.
Staff: 1 part-time staff member. Services provided by LD specialist.
Special Fees: $225 for diagnostic testing.

Applications and admissions: *Required:* high school transcript, grade point average, IEP (Individualized Education Program), psychoeducational report completed within 3 years. Students may begin taking classes in fall only. *Application deadline:* continuous.
Special policies: The college has written policies regarding grade forgiveness; substitutions and waivers of admissions, graduation, and degree requirements.

PROGRAM AND SERVICE COMPONENTS

Diagnostic testing: Intelligence, reading, math, spelling, written language, study skills, learning strategies.
Academic advising: Provided by unit staff members, academic advisers. Students with LD required to take 12 quarter hours each term to maintain full-time status; 8 quarter hours required to be eligible for financial aid.
Counseling services: Individual counseling, career counseling, self-advocacy training.
Basic skills remediation: Offered one-on-one by LD specialist. Available in learning strategies.
Special courses: Composition, study skills, career planning. Most offered for credit; all enter into overall grade point average.
Auxiliary aids: Taped textbooks, word-processors with spell-check, optical character readers.
Auxiliary services: Alternative test arrangements, notetakers, priority registration.

GENERAL COLLEGE INFORMATION

State-supported, 4-year, coed. Part of Ohio State University. Awards associate, bachelor's degrees (also offers some graduate courses). Founded 1958. *Setting:* 593-acre small-town campus with easy access to Columbus and Cleveland. *Total enrollment:* 1,343. *Faculty:*; student–undergrad faculty ratio is 21:1.
Enrollment Profile: 1,225 students from 10 states and territories, 1 other country. 61% women, 39% men, 36% part-time, 98% state residents, 15% transferred in, 1% international, 24% 25 or older, 1% Native American, 1% Hispanic, 4% black, 1% Asian or Pacific Islander. *Retention:* 55% of 1995 full-time freshmen returned. *Areas of study chosen:* 19% education.
First-Year Class: 363 total; 621 applied, 94% were accepted, 62% of whom enrolled. 7% from top 10% of their high school class, 32% from top quarter, 66% from top half.
Graduation Requirements: 90 quarter hours for associate, 196 quarter hours for bachelor's; senior project for honors program students.
Computers on Campus: 103 computers available on campus for general student use. Computers for student use in computer center, computer labs, classrooms.

EXPENSES

Expenses for 1997–98: *Application fee:* $30. State resident tuition: $3570 full-time. Nonresident tuition: $10,653 full-time. Part-time tuition per quarter ranges from $98 to $1092 for state residents, $195 to $3256 for nonresidents.
LD Services Contact: Ms. Carol German, LD Specialist, Ohio State University–Mansfield Campus, 1680 University Drive, Mansfield, OH 44906, 419-755-4304. Fax: 419-755-4241. Email: german.16@osu.edu.

OHIO STATE UNIVERSITY–NEWARK CAMPUS

Newark, Ohio

LEARNING DISABILITIES SERVICES INFORMATION

Developmental Education/Disability Services began offering services in 1985. Currently the program serves 23 undergraduates with LD. Services are also available to graduate students. Students diagnosed with ADD/ADHD are eligible for the same services available to students with LD.
Staff: 2 full-time, 1 part-time staff members, including director. Services provided by remediation specialist, tutors, diagnostic specialist, peer tutors.
Special Fees: No special fees are charged for services to students with LD.
Applications and admissions: *Required:* high school transcript, grade point average, courses completed, IEP (Individualized Education Program), psychoeducational report completed within 3 years; *recommended:* high school class rank, personal interview. Students may begin taking classes any term. *Application deadline:* continuous.
Special policies: The college has written policies regarding grade forgiveness; substitutions and waivers of admissions, graduation, and degree requirements.

PROGRAM AND SERVICE COMPONENTS

Diagnostic testing: Intelligence, reading, math, spelling, handwriting, written language, perceptual skills, study skills, psychoneurology, hearing, learning strategies.
Academic advising: Provided by unit staff members, academic advisers. Students with LD may take up to 23 quarter hours each term; most take 12 quarter hours; 12 quarter hours required to maintain full-time status; 6 quarter hours required to be eligible for financial aid.
Counseling services: Individual counseling, small-group counseling.
Basic skills remediation: Offered one-on-one by regular teachers, study skills specialist. Available in reading, math, spelling, handwriting, written language, learning strategies, study skills, time management, speech.
Subject-area tutoring: Offered one-on-one by peer tutors. Available in most subjects.
Special courses: College survival skills, reading, vocabulary development, communication skills, composition, word processing, math, typing, career planning. Some offered for credit; some enter into overall grade point average.
Auxiliary aids: Taped textbooks, tape recorders, calculators, typewriters, word-processors with spell-check, personal computers, talking computers, optical character readers, Arkenstone Reader.
Auxiliary services: Alternative test arrangements, notetakers, priority registration, advocacy.

GENERAL COLLEGE INFORMATION

State-supported, 4-year, coed. Part of Ohio State University. Awards associate, bachelor's degrees (also offers some graduate courses). Founded 1957. *Setting:* 101-acre small-town campus with easy access to Columbus. *Total enrollment:* 1,611. *Faculty:*; student–undergrad faculty ratio is 18:1.
Enrollment Profile: 1,522 students from 14 states and territories, 1 other country. 59% women, 41% men, 29% part-time, 98% state residents, 10% transferred in, 1% international, 24% 25 or older, 1% Native American, 1% Hispanic, 2% black, 1% Asian or Pacific Islander. *Retention:* 58% of 1995 full-time freshmen returned. *Areas of study chosen:* 18% education.
First-Year Class: 468 total; 738 applied, 97% were accepted, 65% of whom enrolled. 9% from top 10% of their high school class, 24% from top quarter, 51% from top half.
Graduation Requirements: 90 quarter hours for associate, 196 quarter hours for bachelor's; computer course for business, engineering majors; senior project for honors program students.
Computers on Campus: 36 computers available on campus for general student use. Computers for student use in computer labs, classrooms, library.

EXPENSES

Expenses for 1997–98: *Application fee:* $30. State resident tuition: $3570 full-time. Nonresident tuition: $10,653 full-time. Part-time tuition per quarter ranges from $98 to $1092 for state residents, $195 to $3256 for nonresidents.
LD Services Contact: Dr. Phyllis E. Thompson, Director, Developmental Education/Disability Services, Ohio State University–Newark Campus, University Drive, Newark, OH 43055-1797, 614-366-9246. Fax: 614-366-5047.

OKLAHOMA STATE UNIVERSITY

Stillwater, Oklahoma

LEARNING DISABILITIES SERVICES INFORMATION

Student Disability Services began offering services in 1985. Currently the program serves 55 undergraduates with LD. Services are also available to graduate students. Students diagnosed with ADD/ADHD are eligible for the same services available to students with LD.
Staff: 1 full-time staff member (coordinator).
Special Fees: No special fees are charged for services to students with LD.
Applications and admissions: *Required:* high school transcript, grade point average, class rank, courses completed, untimed SAT I or ACT,

Oklahoma State University (continued)

psychoeducational report completed within 3 years. Students may begin taking classes any term. *Application deadline:* continuous.

Special policies: The college has written policies regarding grade forgiveness; substitutions and waivers of admissions, graduation, and degree requirements.

PROGRAM AND SERVICE COMPONENTS

Academic advising: Provided by unit staff members, academic advisers. Students with LD may take up to 18 credit hours each term; most take 12 credit hours; 12 credit hours (fewer with special permission) required to maintain full-time status; 12 credit hours required to be eligible for financial aid.

Counseling services: Individual counseling, small-group counseling, career counseling.

Auxiliary aids: Taped textbooks, tape recorders, word-processors with spell-check, optical character readers.

Auxiliary services: Alternative test arrangements, priority registration.

GENERAL COLLEGE INFORMATION

State-supported, coed. Part of Oklahoma State University. Awards bachelor's, master's, doctoral, first professional degrees. Founded 1890. *Setting:* 840-acre small-town campus with easy access to Oklahoma City and Tulsa. *Endowment:* $80 million. *Research spending 1995–96:* $49.9 million. *Educational spending 1995–96:* $3679 per undergrad. *Total enrollment:* 19,201. *Faculty:* 1,158 (1,053 full-time, 92% with terminal degrees, 105 part-time); student–undergrad faculty ratio is 22:1.

Enrollment Profile: 14,640 students from 50 states and territories, 100 other countries. 46% women, 54% men, 11% part-time, 82% state residents, 21% live on campus, 11% transferred in, 7% international, 16% 25 or older, 7% Native American, 2% Hispanic, 3% black, 2% Asian or Pacific Islander. *Retention:* 77% of 1995 full-time freshmen returned. *Graduation:* 19% graduate in 4 years, 41% in 5 years, 49% in 6 years. *Areas of study chosen:* 17% business management and administrative services, 13% engineering and applied sciences, 9% agriculture, 7% education, 7% social sciences, 7% vocational and home economics, 4% biological and life sciences, 4% computer and information sciences, 2% architecture, 2% health professions and related sciences, 2% natural resource sciences, 2% psychology, 1% communications and journalism, 1% English language/literature/letters, 1% fine arts, 1% foreign language and literature, 1% mathematics, 1% performing arts, 1% philosophy, 1% physical sciences, 1% predentistry, 1% prelaw, 1% premed, 1% prevet. *Most popular recent majors:* education, management information systems, marketing/retailing/merchandising.

First-Year Class: 2,442 total; 4,469 applied, 96% were accepted, 57% of whom enrolled. 30% from top 10% of their high school class, 60% from top quarter, 89% from top half. 20 National Merit Scholars, 360 valedictorians.

Graduation Requirements: 120 credit hours; 6 credit hours of math; 8 credit hours of science; computer course for business administration, accounting, engineering majors; internship (some majors); senior project for honors program students and some majors.

Computers on Campus: 2,000 computers available on campus for general student use. A computer is recommended for some students. A campus-wide network can be accessed from student residence rooms and from off-campus. Students can contact faculty members and/or advisers through e-mail. Computers for student use in computer center, computer labs, research center, learning resource center, classrooms, library, student center, dorms provide access to the Internet/World Wide Web, on- and off-campus e-mail addresses. Staffed computer lab on campus (open 24 hours a day) provides training in use of computers, software. *Academic computing expenditure 1995–96:* $2.7 million.

EXPENSES AND FINANCIAL AID

Expenses for 1996–97: *Application fee:* $15. Full-time tuition ranges from $1248 to $1332 for state residents, $4020 to $4464 for nonresidents, according to class level. Full-time mandatory fees range from $460 to $796 according to program. Part-time tuition per credit hour ranges from $52 to $55.50 for state residents, $167.50 to $186 for nonresidents, according to class level. Part-time mandatory fees per semester range from $28.76 to $369.36 according to course load and program. College room and board: $4160 (minimum). College room only: $1904 (minimum).

Undergraduate Financial Aid: Of all full-time undergraduates enrolled in fall 1996, 68% of those who applied for aid were judged to have need according to Federal Methodology, of whom 99% were aided. On average, 85% of need was met. *Financial aid deadline (priority):* 3/1. *Financial aid forms:* FAFSA required.

LD Services Contact: Coordinator, Student Disability Services, Oklahoma State University, 326 Student Union, Stillwater, OK 74078, 405-744-7116. Fax: 405-744-8380.

OLIVET COLLEGE

Olivet, Michigan

LEARNING DISABILITIES SERVICES INFORMATION

Academic Resource Center began offering services in 1993. Currently the program serves 15 undergraduates with LD. Students diagnosed with ADD/ADHD are eligible for the same services available to students with LD.

Staff: 2 part-time staff members, including director, assistant director. Services provided by tutors, graduate student intern, student employees.

Special Fees: No special fees are charged for services to students with LD.

Applications and admissions: *Required:* high school transcript, grade point average, courses completed, extracurricular activities, untimed ACT, letters of recommendation, psychoeducational report completed within 5 years; *recommended:* high school IEP (Individualized Education Program), personal interview, autobiographical statement. Students may begin taking classes any term. *Application deadline:* continuous.

Special policies: The college has written policies regarding substitutions and waivers of admissions requirements.

PROGRAM AND SERVICE COMPONENTS

Academic advising: Provided by unit staff members, academic advisers. Most students with LD take 9 to 12 semester hours each term; 12 semester hours required to maintain full-time status; 6 semester hours required to be eligible for financial aid.

Counseling services: Individual counseling.

Basic skills remediation: Offered one-on-one, in small groups, and in class-size groups by regular teachers; computer-aided instruction also offered. Available in reading, math, written language, study skills, time management.

Subject-area tutoring: Offered one-on-one and in small groups by peer tutors. Available in all subjects.

Special courses: College survival skills, reading, communication skills, composition, learning strategies, time management, math, study skills. Most offered for credit; some enter into overall grade point average.

Auxiliary aids: Taped textbooks, tape recorders, typewriters, word-processors with spell-check, personal computers.

Auxiliary services: Alternative test arrangements, notetakers.

GENERAL COLLEGE INFORMATION

Independent, 4-year, coed, affiliated with Congregational Christian Church. Awards bachelor's degrees. Founded 1844. *Setting:* 92-acre rural campus. *Endowment:* $8.2 million. *Educational spending 1995–96:* $2690 per undergrad. *Total enrollment:* 831. *Faculty:* 76 (34 full-time, 42 part-time); student–undergrad faculty ratio is 15:1.

Enrollment Profile: 831 students from 20 states and territories, 10 other countries. 42% women, 58% men, 7% part-time, 83% state residents, 66% live on campus, 20% transferred in, 4% international, 13% 25 or older, 1% Native American, 3% Hispanic, 12% black, 2% Asian or Pacific Islander. *Retention:* 59% of 1995 full-time freshmen returned. *Graduation:* 22% graduate in 4 years, 38% in 5 years, 39% in 6 years. *Areas of study chosen:* 19% education, 8% business management and administrative services, 4% health professions and related sciences, 4% liberal arts/general studies, 3% biological and life sciences, 3% communications and journalism, 3% psychology, 2% fine arts, 1% computer and information sciences, 1% interdisciplinary studies, 1% mathematics, 1% social sciences. *Most popular recent majors:* business administration/commerce/management, education, psychology.

First-Year Class: 241 total; 535 applied, 83% were accepted, 54% of whom enrolled.

Graduation Requirements: 120 semester hours; math proficiency; 6 semester hours of science; computer course for business administration, math majors; senior project.

Computers on Campus: 40 computers available on campus for general student use. Computer purchase/lease plans available. A campus-wide network can be accessed from off-campus. Students can contact faculty members and/or advisers through e-mail. Computers for student use in computer center, computer labs, learning resource center, library provide access to the Internet/World Wide Web, on-campus e-mail addresses. Staffed computer lab on campus provides training in use of computers, software. *Academic computing expenditure 1995–96:* $95,510.

EXPENSES AND FINANCIAL AID

Expenses for 1997–98: *Application fee:* $25. Comprehensive fee of $16,698 includes full-time tuition ($12,524), mandatory fees ($136), and college room and board ($4038). College room only: $2164. Part-time tuition: $440 per semester hour.

Undergraduate Financial Aid: 95% of all full-time undergraduates enrolled in fall 1996 applied for aid; of these, 98% were judged to have need according to Federal Methodology, of whom 100% were aided. On average, 93% of need was met. *Financial aid deadline (priority):* 3/15. *Financial aid forms:* FAFSA required.

LD Services Contact: Ms. Lisa A. Haston, Director, Olivet College, 202 Mott, Olivet, MI 49076, 616-749-7186. Fax: 616-749-7178.

OLIVET NAZARENE UNIVERSITY

Kankakee, Illinois

LEARNING DISABILITIES SERVICES INFORMATION

Academic Support began offering services in 1992. Currently the program serves 30 undergraduates with LD. Services are also available to graduate students. Students diagnosed with ADD/ADHD are eligible for the same services available to students with LD.

Staff: 1 full-time staff member (director).

Special Fees: No special fees are charged for services to students with LD.

Applications and admissions: *Required:* high school transcript, grade point average, class rank, courses completed, autobiographical statement, letters of recommendation; *recommended:* high school extracurricular activities, IEP (Individualized Education Program), untimed or extended time SAT I or ACT, personal interview, psychoeducational report. Students may begin taking classes in fall or spring. *Application deadline:* continuous.

PROGRAM AND SERVICE COMPONENTS

Academic advising: Provided by academic advisers. Students with LD may take up to 18 semester hours each term; most take 14 semester hours; 12 semester hours required to maintain full-time status and be eligible for financial aid.

Counseling services: Individual counseling, career counseling, self-advocacy training.

Basic skills remediation: Offered one-on-one and in class-size groups by LD teachers, peer tutors; computer-aided instruction also offered. Available in reading, math, spelling, written language, learning strategies, study skills, time management, social skills, computer skills.

Subject-area tutoring: Offered one-on-one by peer tutors, professional tutor trained in LD. Available in all subjects.

Special courses: College survival skills, composition, math. Most offered for credit; all enter into overall grade point average.

Auxiliary aids: Tape recorders, calculators, word-processors with spell-check, personal computers.

Auxiliary services: Alternative test arrangements, notetakers, advocacy.

GENERAL COLLEGE INFORMATION

Independent, comprehensive, coed, affiliated with Church of the Nazarene. Awards associate, bachelor's, master's degrees. Founded 1907. *Setting:* 168-acre suburban campus with easy access to Chicago. *Endowment:* $5.7 million. *Research spending 1995–96:* $51,111. *Total enrollment:* 2,256. *Undergraduate faculty:* 145 (100 full-time, 70% with terminal degrees, 45 part-time); student–undergrad faculty ratio is 16:1.

Enrollment Profile: 1,593 students from 40 states and territories, 19 other countries. 55% women, 45% men, 15% part-time, 40% state residents, 20% transferred in, 2% international, 10% 25 or older, 1% Native American, 1% Hispanic, 6% black, 1% Asian or Pacific Islander. *Retention:* 78% of 1995 full-time freshmen returned.

First-Year Class: 389 total; 724 applied, 99% were accepted, 54% of whom enrolled. 23% from top 10% of their high school class, 40% from top quarter, 71% from top half.

Graduation Requirements: 64 semester hours for associate, 128 semester hours for bachelor's; 7 semester hours of math/science; computer course for some business, science majors.

Computers on Campus: 100 computers available on campus for general student use. Computer purchase/lease plans available. Computers for student use in computer center, computer labs, learning resource center, classrooms, library, departmental labs provide access to the Internet/World Wide Web. Staffed computer lab on campus provides training in use of computers, software. *Academic computing expenditure 1995–96:* $970,843.

EXPENSES AND FINANCIAL AID

Expenses for 1996–97: Comprehensive fee of $14,626 includes full-time tuition ($10,026), mandatory fees ($140), and college room and board ($4460). College room only: $2230.

Undergraduate Financial Aid: Of all full-time undergraduates enrolled in fall 1996, 91% of those who applied for aid were judged to have need according to Federal Methodology, of whom 99% were aided. On average, 97% of need was met. *Financial aid deadline (priority):* 3/1. *Financial aid forms:* FAFSA, institutional form required.

LD Services Contact: Ms. Sue Rattin, Director, Academic Support, Olivet Nazarene University, PO Box 592, Kankakee, IL 60901-0592, 815-939-5150. Fax: 815-939-5169. Email: srattin@olivet.edu.

ORAL ROBERTS UNIVERSITY

Tulsa, Oklahoma

LEARNING DISABILITIES SERVICES INFORMATION

Disability Services began offering services in 1988. Currently the program serves 77 undergraduates with LD. Services are also available to graduate students. Students diagnosed with ADD/ADHD are eligible for the same services available to students with LD, as well as accountability guides.

Staff: 1 full-time, 30 part-time staff members, including coordinator. Services provided by counselor, peer tutors, readers, notetakers, writers.

Special Fees: No special fees are charged for services to students with LD.

Applications and admissions: *Required:* high school transcript, courses completed, autobiographical statement, letters of recommendation, psychoeducational report completed within 2 years; *recommended:* high school grade point average, class rank, IEP (Individualized Education Program), untimed or extended time SAT I or ACT, personal interview. Students may begin taking classes in fall, winter, or spring. *Application deadline:* continuous.

Special policies: The college has written policies regarding substitutions and waivers of admissions, graduation, and degree requirements.

PROGRAM AND SERVICE COMPONENTS

Academic advising: Provided by unit staff members, academic advisers. Students with LD may take up to 18 credit hours each term; most take 12 credit hours; 9 credit hours required to maintain full-time status; 9 to 12 credit hours required to be eligible for financial aid.

Counseling services: Individual counseling, career counseling.

Basic skills remediation: Offered in class-size groups by regular teachers. Available in reading, math, spelling, written language, learning strategies, study skills, time management.

Subject-area tutoring: Offered one-on-one by peer tutors. Available in all subjects.

Auxiliary aids: Taped textbooks, tape recorders.

Auxiliary services: Alternative test arrangements, notetakers, priority registration, advocacy, writers, interpreters for the deaf, transcribers.

GENERAL COLLEGE INFORMATION

Independent interdenominational, coed. Awards bachelor's, master's, doctoral degrees. Founded 1963. *Setting:* 500-acre urban campus. *Total enrollment:* 3,761. *Faculty:* 223 (187 full-time, 52% with terminal degrees, 36 part-time); student–undergrad faculty ratio is 16:1.

Enrollment Profile: 3,001 students from 52 states and territories, 54 other countries. 55% women, 45% men, 7% part-time, 14% state residents, 68% live on campus, 18% transferred in, 7% international, 19% 25 or older, 1% Native American, 6% Hispanic, 22% black, 3% Asian or Pacific Islander. *Retention:* 74% of 1995 full-time freshmen returned. *Most popular recent majors:* business administration/commerce/management, telecommunications, elementary education.

First-Year Class: 564 total; 1,512 applied, 53% were accepted, 70% of whom enrolled. 21% from top 10% of their high school class, 46% from top quarter, 74% from top half. 6 National Merit Scholars, 15 valedictorians.

Graduation Requirements: 128 credit hours; 3 credit hours of math; 8 credit hours of science; computer course for business, chemistry, physics, engineering, broadcast design majors.

Computers on Campus: 250 computers available on campus for general student use. A computer is recommended for all students. A campus-wide network can be accessed from student residence rooms and from off-campus. Students can contact faculty members and/or advisers through e-mail. Computers for student use in computer center, computer labs, learning resource center, classrooms, library, dorms provide access to the Internet/World Wide Web, on- and off-campus e-mail addresses. Staffed computer lab on campus provides training in use of computers, software.

EXPENSES AND FINANCIAL AID

Expenses for 1997–98: *Application fee:* $35. Comprehensive fee of $14,658 includes full-time tuition ($9674), mandatory fees ($260), and college room and board ($4724). College room only: $2208. Part-time tuition: $410 per credit hour.
Undergraduate Financial Aid: 72% of all full-time undergraduates enrolled in fall 1996 applied for aid; of these, 94% were judged to have need according to Federal Methodology, of whom 99% were aided. On average, 80% of need was met. *Financial aid deadline (priority):* 3/1. *Financial aid forms:* FAFSA required.
LD Services Contact: Mr. Don Roberson, Disability Services Coordinator, Oral Roberts University, 7777 South Lewis Avenue, Tulsa, OK 74171, 918-495-6912. Fax: 918-495-6033.

OREGON INSTITUTE OF TECHNOLOGY

Klamath Falls, Oregon

LEARNING DISABILITIES SERVICES INFORMATION

Services for Students with Disabilities began offering services in 1980. Currently the program serves 25 undergraduates with LD. Services are also available to graduate students. Students diagnosed with ADD/ADHD are eligible for the same services available to students with LD.
Staff: 2 part-time staff members, including director. Services provided by tutors, counselors.
Special Fees: No special fees are charged for services to students with LD.
Applications and admissions: *Required:* high school transcript, grade point average, courses completed, untimed or extended time SAT I or ACT, college transcripts (if applicable); *recommended:* high school class rank. Students may begin taking classes any term. *Application deadline:* continuous.

PROGRAM AND SERVICE COMPONENTS

Special preparation or orientation: Optional orientation offered during registration.
Academic advising: Provided by unit staff members, academic advisers. Students with LD may take up to 21 credit hours each term; most take 6 to 15 credit hours; 12 credit hours required to maintain full-time status; 6 credit hours required to be eligible for financial aid.
Counseling services: Individual counseling, career counseling.
Subject-area tutoring: Offered one-on-one by peer tutors. Available in some subjects.
Auxiliary aids: Taped textbooks, word-processors with spell-check, personal computers, optical character readers.
Auxiliary services: Alternative test arrangements, notetakers, priority registration.

GENERAL COLLEGE INFORMATION

State-supported, comprehensive, coed. Part of Oregon State System of Higher Education. Awards associate, bachelor's, master's degrees. Founded 1947. *Setting:* 173-acre small-town campus. *Endowment:* $173,440. *Research spending 1995–96:* $306,567. *Total enrollment:* 2,339. *Undergraduate faculty:* 162 (121 full-time, 27% with terminal degrees, 41 part-time); student–undergrad faculty ratio is 12:1.
Enrollment Profile: 2,339 students from 7 states and territories, 16 other countries. 42% women, 58% men, 34% part-time, 87% state residents, 17% live on campus, 35% transferred in, 1% international, 42% 25 or older, 3% Native American, 3% Hispanic, 1% black, 5% Asian or Pacific Islander. *Retention:* 65% of 1995 full-time freshmen returned. *Graduation:* 24% graduate in 4 years, 32% in 5 years, 34% in 6 years. *Areas of study chosen:* 38% engineering and applied sciences, 27% health professions and related sciences, 23% liberal arts/general studies, 12% business management and administrative services. *Most popular recent majors:* radiological technology, civil engineering technology, electronics engineering technology.
First-Year Class: 302 total; 872 applied, 63% were accepted, 55% of whom enrolled. 1 National Merit Scholar.
Graduation Requirements: 99 credit hours for associate, 200 credit hours for bachelor's; 36 credit hours of math/science for bachelor's degree; computer course; internship (some majors); senior project (some majors).
Computers on Campus: 1,000 computers available on campus for general student use. A computer is recommended for some students. A campus-wide network can be accessed from off-campus. Students can contact faculty members and/or advisers through e-mail. Computers for student use in computer center, computer labs, learning resource center, library, dorms, departmental labs provide access to the Internet/World Wide Web, on- and off-campus e-mail addresses. Staffed computer lab on campus provides training in use of computers, software. *Academic computing expenditure 1995–96:* $1.5 million.

EXPENSES AND FINANCIAL AID

Expenses for 1996–97: *Application fee:* $50. State resident tuition: $3144 full-time. Nonresident tuition: $10,083 full-time. Part-time tuition per quarter ranges from $233 to $968 for state residents, $426 to $3088 for nonresidents. College room and board: $3910.
Undergraduate Financial Aid: Of all full-time undergraduates enrolled in fall 1996, 96% of those who applied for aid were judged to have need according to Federal Methodology, of whom 75% were aided. On average, 92% of need was met. *Financial aid deadline (priority):* 3/1. *Financial aid forms:* FAFSA, CSS Financial Aid PROFILE acceptable. State form required for some.
LD Services Contact: Dr. John Hancock, Director of Counseling and Testing, Oregon Institute of Technology, 3201 Campus Drive, Klamath Falls, OR 97601-8801, 541-885-1015. Fax: 541-885-1823. Email: hancockj@oit.edu.

OREGON STATE UNIVERSITY

Corvallis, Oregon

LEARNING DISABILITIES SERVICES INFORMATION

Services for Students with Disabilities (SSD) began offering services in 1987. Currently the program serves 120 undergraduates with LD. Services are also available to graduate students. Students diagnosed with ADD/ADHD are eligible for the same services available to students with LD.
Staff: 2 full-time, 2 part-time staff members, including director, coordinator, support staff, interviewers. Services provided by counselors.
Special Fees: No special fees are charged for services to students with LD.
Applications and admissions: *Required:* high school transcript, grade point average, autobiographical statement, letters of recommendation, psychoeducational report completed within 3 years; *recommended:* high school IEP (Individualized Education Program), extended time SAT I or ACT. Students may begin taking classes any term (fall preferred). *Application deadline:* 3/1 (fall term), 2/28 (spring term).

PROGRAM AND SERVICE COMPONENTS

Special preparation or orientation: Required orientation held before registration.
Academic advising: Provided by unit staff members, academic advisers. Students with LD may take up to 18 quarter hours each term; most take 12 to 15 quarter hours; 9 quarter hours required to maintain full-time status; 9 quarter hours (part-time), 12 quarter hours (full-time) required to be eligible for financial aid.
Basic skills remediation: Offered by regular teachers. Tutoring and skills remediation are available to general university population; referrals can be obtained through SSD program. Available in reading, math, written language, learning strategies, study skills, time management.
Subject-area tutoring: Offered one-on-one and in small groups by peer tutors. Available in all subjects.
Special courses: College survival skills, study skills. None offered for credit; all enter into overall grade point average.
Auxiliary aids: Taped textbooks, tape recorders, typewriters, word-processors with spell-check, talking computers, optical character readers.
Auxiliary services: Alternative test arrangements, notetakers, priority registration, advocacy.

GENERAL COLLEGE INFORMATION

State-supported, coed. Part of Oregon State System of Higher Education. Awards bachelor's, master's, doctoral, first professional degrees. Founded 1868. *Setting:* 530-acre small-town campus. *Research spending 1995–*

96: $99.2 million. *Total enrollment:* 13,784. *Faculty:* 2,204 (1,597 full-time, 83% with terminal degrees, 607 part-time); student–undergrad faculty ratio is 8:1.
Enrollment Profile: 11,096 students from 50 states and territories, 100 other countries. 45% women, 55% men, 9% part-time, 82% state residents, 25% transferred in, 4% international, 12% 25 or older, 2% Native American, 3% Hispanic, 1% black, 8% Asian or Pacific Islander. *Retention:* 84% of 1995 full-time freshmen returned. *Graduation:* 28% graduate in 4 years, 57% in 5 years, 63% in 6 years. *Areas of study chosen:* 17% engineering and applied sciences, 14% business management and administrative services, 11% health professions and related sciences, 8% agriculture, 8% biological and life sciences, 8% liberal arts/general studies, 6% vocational and home economics, 5% natural resource sciences, 5% social sciences, 3% interdisciplinary studies, 3% psychology, 2% communications and journalism, 2% computer and information sciences, 2% fine arts, 2% physical sciences, 1% area and ethnic studies, 1% English language/literature/letters, 1% foreign language and literature, 1% mathematics. *Most popular recent majors:* business administration/commerce/management, mechanical engineering, communication.
First-Year Class: 1,975 total; 5,078 applied, 89% were accepted, 44% of whom enrolled.
Graduation Requirements: 180 quarter hours; 3 quarter hours of math; 12 quarter hours of physical and biological science; computer course for business, engineering, atmospheric sciences, microbiology, housing studies, nutrition, food management, mathematical sciences majors; internship (some majors); senior project for honors program students and some majors.
Computers on Campus: 1,000 computers available on campus for general student use. Computer purchase/lease plans available. A computer is recommended for all students. A campus-wide network can be accessed from student residence rooms and from off-campus. Students can contact faculty members and/or advisers through e-mail. Computers for student use in computer center, computer labs, library, dorms provide access to the Internet/World Wide Web, on- and off-campus e-mail addresses. Staffed computer lab on campus (open 24 hours a day) provides training in use of computers, software.

EXPENSES AND FINANCIAL AID

Expenses for 1997–98: *Application fee:* $50. State resident tuition: $2694 full-time. Nonresident tuition: $10,644 full-time. Part-time tuition per quarter ranges from $73 to $823 for state residents, $296 to $3256 for nonresidents. Part-time mandatory fees per quarter range from $173 to $263. One-time mandatory fee: $50. Full-time mandatory fees: $816. College room and board: $4886.
Undergraduate Financial Aid: *Financial aid deadline (priority):* 2/1. *Financial aid forms:* FAFSA required.
LD Services Contact: Ms. Tracy Bentley-Townlin, Director, Services for Students with Disabilities, Oregon State University, Dean of Students Office, Ads A200, Corvallis, OR 97331-2133, 541-737-3669. Fax: 541-737-2400.

PACIFIC UNION COLLEGE

Angwin, California

LEARNING DISABILITIES SERVICES INFORMATION

Counseling Center began offering services in 1994. Currently the program serves 80 undergraduates with LD. Services are also available to graduate students. Students diagnosed with ADD/ADHD are eligible for the same services available to students with LD.
Staff: 3 part-time staff members, including coordinator. Services provided by tutor, counselor, diagnostic specialist.
Special Fees: $200 to $400 for diagnostic testing.
Applications and admissions: Students may begin taking classes in fall or summer. *Application deadline:* continuous.
Special policies: The college has written policies regarding grade forgiveness.

PROGRAM AND SERVICE COMPONENTS

Special preparation or orientation: Optional orientation offered before registration.
Diagnostic testing: Intelligence, reading, math, spelling, study skills, personality.
Academic advising: Provided by unit staff members, academic advisers. Students with LD may take up to 17 quarter hours each term; most take 12 quarter hours; 12 quarter hours required to maintain full-time status and be eligible for financial aid.
Counseling services: Individual counseling.
Subject-area tutoring: Offered one-on-one and in small groups by peer tutors. Available in most subjects.
Auxiliary aids: Tape recorders, talking computers.
Auxiliary services: Alternative test arrangements, notetakers, priority registration, advocacy.

GENERAL COLLEGE INFORMATION

Independent Seventh-day Adventist, comprehensive, coed. Awards associate, bachelor's, master's degrees. Founded 1882. *Setting:* 200-acre rural campus with easy access to San Francisco. *Total enrollment:* 1,544. *Undergraduate faculty:* 125 (105 full-time, 45% with terminal degrees, 20 part-time); student–undergrad faculty ratio is 13:1.
Enrollment Profile: 1,445 students from 31 states and territories, 12 other countries. 55% women, 45% men, 10% part-time, 92% state residents, 9% transferred in, 6% international, 17% 25 or older, 1% Native American, 9% Hispanic, 3% black, 17% Asian or Pacific Islander. *Areas of study chosen:* 19% health professions and related sciences, 15% premed, 12% business management and administrative services, 9% biological and life sciences, 7% psychology, 4% education, 4% fine arts, 3% communications and journalism, 3% predentistry, 3% prelaw, 2% engineering and applied sciences, 2% English language/literature/letters, 2% social sciences, 2% theology/religion, 2% vocational and home economics, 1% computer and information sciences, 1% foreign language and literature, 1% liberal arts/general studies, 1% mathematics, 1% physical sciences, 1% prevet. *Most popular recent majors:* nursing, business administration/commerce/management, behavioral sciences.
First-Year Class: 364 total; 766 applied, 67% were accepted, 71% of whom enrolled. 52% from top quarter of their high school class, 90% from top half. 47 National Merit Scholars.
Graduation Requirements: 90 quarter hours for associate, 192 quarter hours for bachelor's; 14 quarter hours of math/science; computer course for business majors; senior project for honors program students and some majors.
Computers on Campus: 60 computers available on campus for general student use. Computers for student use in computer center, computer labs, learning resource center, classrooms, library, departmental labs provide access to the Internet/World Wide Web.

EXPENSES AND FINANCIAL AID

Expenses for 1997–98: Comprehensive fee of $17,715 includes full-time tuition ($13,530) and college room and board ($4185). College room only: $2505.
Undergraduate Financial Aid: *Financial aid deadline (priority):* 3/2. *Financial aid forms:* FAFSA, CSS Financial Aid PROFILE, state form, institutional form required.
LD Services Contact: Ms. Sharon Teruya, Coordinator of Learning Disabilities Services, Pacific Union College, Angwin, CA 94508, 707-965-7364. Fax: 707-965-6390. Email: steruy@puc.edu.

PENNSYLVANIA STATE UNIVERSITY ALTOONA COLLEGE

Altoona, Pennsylvania

LEARNING DISABILITIES SERVICES INFORMATION

Excell Program began offering services in 1996. Currently the program serves 40 undergraduates with LD. Students diagnosed with ADD/ADHD are eligible for the same services available to students with LD.
Staff: 1 full-time staff member. Services provided by counselor.
Special Fees: No special fees are charged for services to students with LD.
Applications and admissions: *Required:* documentation of disability. Students may begin taking classes in fall only. *Application deadline:* continuous.

PROGRAM AND SERVICE COMPONENTS

Special preparation or orientation: Required orientation held during registration.
Academic advising: Provided by academic advisers. Students with LD may take up to 12 credits each term; most take 12 credits; 12 credits required to maintain full-time status and be eligible for financial aid.
Counseling services: Individual counseling, small-group counseling, career counseling.
Basic skills remediation: Offered in class-size groups by regular teachers. Available in reading, written language, learning strategies, study skills.

Pennsylvania State University Altoona College (continued)

Subject-area tutoring: Offered one-on-one by professional teachers, peer tutors. Available in most subjects.
Auxiliary aids: Taped textbooks, tape recorders.
Auxiliary services: Alternative test arrangements, notetakers, priority registration, advocacy.

GENERAL COLLEGE INFORMATION

State-related, 4-year, coed. Part of Pennsylvania State University. Awards associate, bachelor's degrees. Founded 1929. *Setting:* 81-acre suburban campus. *Research spending 1995–96:* $48,582. *Total enrollment:* 3,475. *Faculty:* 192 (81 full-time, 84% with terminal degrees, 111 part-time).
Enrollment Profile: 3,463 students from 25 states and territories. 47% women, 53% men, 12% part-time, 91% state residents, 17% live on campus, 3% transferred in, 0% international, 10% 25 or older, 0% Native American, 2% Hispanic, 3% black, 1% Asian or Pacific Islander. *Retention:* 76% of 1995 full-time freshmen returned. *Areas of study chosen:* 20% liberal arts/general studies, 19% engineering and applied sciences, 15% business management and administrative services, 13% interdisciplinary studies, 8% education, 8% health professions and related sciences, 4% agriculture, 4% communications and journalism, 2% social sciences, 2% vocational and home economics, 1% computer and information sciences, 1% natural resource sciences, 1% performing arts, 1% physical sciences, 1% psychology.
First-Year Class: 1,463 total; 3,853 applied, 92% were accepted, 41% of whom enrolled. 8% from top 10% of their high school class, 56% from top quarter, 82% from top half.
Graduation Requirements: 60 credits for associate, 120 credits for bachelor's; computer course for engineering, technology, business, science majors; internship (some majors).
Computers on Campus: 130 computers available on campus for general student use. Computers for student use in computer labs.

EXPENSES AND FINANCIAL AID

Expenses for 1996–97: *Application fee:* $40. State resident tuition: $5262 full-time, $211 per credit part-time. Nonresident tuition: $8178 full-time, $341 per credit part-time. Part-time mandatory fees per semester range from $33 to $95. Full-time mandatory fees: $190. College room and board: $4170.
Undergraduate Financial Aid: *Financial aid deadline (priority):* 2/15. *Financial aid forms:* FAFSA required.
Financial aid specifically for students with LD: Scholarship: Newcombe Scholarship.
LD Services Contact: Ms. Joy Himmel, Disabilities Coordinator, Pennsylvania State University Altoona College, 117 SLEP Student Center, 3000 Ivyside Park, Altoona, PA 16601, 814-949-5540. Fax: 814-949-5805. Email: jyh-1@psu.edu.

PENNSYLVANIA STATE UNIVERSITY HARRISBURG CAMPUS OF THE CAPITAL COLLEGE

Middletown, Pennsylvania

LEARNING DISABILITIES SERVICES INFORMATION

Student Assistance Center currently serves 20 undergraduates with LD. Services are also available to graduate students. Students diagnosed with ADD/ADHD are eligible for the same services available to students with LD.
Staff: 1 full-time staff member (coordinator). Services provided by tutors, counselors.
Special Fees: No special fees are charged for services to students with LD.
Applications and admissions: Students may begin taking classes in fall, spring, or summer. *Application deadline:* 6/1 (fall term), 12/1 (spring term).

PROGRAM AND SERVICE COMPONENTS

Academic advising: Provided by academic advisers. Most students with LD take 9 to 12 credits each term; 12 credits required to maintain full-time status.
Counseling services: Individual counseling, small-group counseling, career counseling.
Basic skills remediation: Offered one-on-one by psychologists. Available in written language, study skills, time management, social skills.
Subject-area tutoring: Offered one-on-one and in small groups by peer tutors. Available in most subjects.
Auxiliary aids: Taped textbooks, tape recorders, word-processors with spell-check, talking computers, optical character readers.
Auxiliary services: Alternative test arrangements, notetakers.

GENERAL COLLEGE INFORMATION

State-related, comprehensive, coed. Part of Pennsylvania State University. Awards associate, bachelor's, master's, doctoral degrees. Founded 1966. *Setting:* 218-acre small-town campus. *Research spending 1995–96:* $1.8 million. *Total enrollment:* 3,417. *Faculty:* 227 (137 full-time, 90% with terminal degrees, 90 part-time); student–undergrad faculty ratio is 14:1.
Enrollment Profile: 2,069 students from 17 states and territories. 52% women, 48% men, 41% part-time, 98% state residents, 19% live on campus, 1% international, 35% 25 or older, 2% Hispanic, 3% black, 3% Asian or Pacific Islander. *Areas of study chosen:* 29% business management and administrative services, 21% engineering and applied sciences, 14% education, 12% social sciences, 5% health professions and related sciences, 5% liberal arts/general studies, 4% psychology, 3% communications and journalism, 3% computer and information sciences, 2% mathematics, 1% area and ethnic studies, 1% interdisciplinary studies.
First-Year Class: 373 total; 600 applied, 84% were accepted, 74% of whom enrolled.
Graduation Requirements: 60 credits for associate, 120 credits for bachelor's; computer course for some engineering majors; internship (some majors); senior project (some majors).
Computers on Campus: 127 computers available on campus for general student use. Computers for student use in computer center, computer labs.

EXPENSES AND FINANCIAL AID

Expenses for 1996–97: *Application fee:* $40. State resident tuition: $5434 full-time, $227 per credit part-time. Nonresident tuition: $11,774 full-time, $491 per credit part-time. Part-time mandatory fees per semester range from $33 to $95. A per semester surcharge ranging from $68 to $225 (according to course load) is applied to upper division students in various engineering and engineering technology programs. Full-time mandatory fees: $190. College room and board: $4170.
Undergraduate Financial Aid: *Financial aid deadline (priority):* 2/15. *Financial aid forms:* FAFSA required.
LD Services Contact: Ms. Donna Howard, Assistant Coordinator of Non-Traditional Student Affairs, Pennsylvania State University Harrisburg Campus of the Capital College, 777 West Harrisburg Pike, Middletown, PA 17057, 717-948-6025. Fax: 717-948-6261. Email: djhl@email.psu.edu.

PENNSYLVANIA STATE UNIVERSITY UNIVERSITY PARK CAMPUS

University Park, Pennsylvania

LEARNING DISABILITIES SERVICES INFORMATION

Office for Disability Services began offering services in 1979. Currently the program serves 305 undergraduates with LD. Services are also available to graduate students. Students diagnosed with ADD/ADHD are eligible for the same services available to students with LD.
Staff: 2 full-time, 1 part-time staff members, including director. Services provided by counselor, LD specialist, clinicians.
Special Fees: $300 to $500 for diagnostic testing.
Applications and admissions: *Required:* high school transcript, courses completed, untimed SAT I or ACT; *recommended:* high school grade point average, class rank, extended time SAT I or ACT. Students may begin taking classes in fall, spring, or summer. *Application deadline:* continuous.
Special policies: The college has written policies regarding grade forgiveness.

PROGRAM AND SERVICE COMPONENTS

Special preparation or orientation: Optional orientation offered before summer and fall semester classes begin.
Diagnostic testing: Intelligence, reading, math, spelling, spoken language, psychoneurology, speech, hearing, written language; variable fee for testing depending on needs of student.

Academic advising: Provided by unit staff members, academic advisers. Students with LD may take up to 19 credits each term; most take 12 to 15 credits; 12 credits required to maintain full-time status; 26 credits per year required to be eligible for financial aid.
Counseling services: Individual counseling, career counseling.
Auxiliary aids: Taped textbooks, tape recorders, word-processors with spell-check, talking computers, optical character readers.
Auxiliary services: Alternative test arrangements, notetakers, priority registration, advocacy, course substitutions (if essential requirements are not involved).

GENERAL COLLEGE INFORMATION

State-related, coed. Part of Pennsylvania State University. Awards associate, bachelor's, master's, doctoral degrees. Founded 1855. *Setting:* 5,448-acre small-town campus. *Endowment:* $426.6 million. *Research spending 1995–96:* $234.5 million. *Total enrollment:* 39,782. *Faculty:* 2,231 (1,841 full-time, 88% with terminal degrees, 390 part-time); student–undergrad faculty ratio is 19:1.
Enrollment Profile: 33,163 students from 54 states and territories. 45% women, 55% men, 6% part-time, 81% state residents, 36% live on campus, 2% transferred in, 1% international, 3% 25 or older, 1% Native American, 2% Hispanic, 3% black, 5% Asian or Pacific Islander. *Retention:* 93% of 1995 full-time freshmen returned. *Graduation:* 46% graduate in 4 years, 76% in 5 years, 79% in 6 years. *Areas of study chosen:* 18% business management and administrative services, 18% engineering and applied sciences, 10% interdisciplinary studies, 7% education, 6% communications and journalism, 5% agriculture, 5% health professions and related sciences, 5% social sciences, 4% liberal arts/general studies, 4% performing arts, 3% biological and life sciences, 3% psychology, 3% vocational and home economics, 2% natural resource sciences, 2% physical sciences, 1% architecture, 1% computer and information sciences, 1% English language/literature/letters, 1% foreign language and literature, 1% mathematics. *Most popular recent majors:* engineering (general), science, business administration/commerce/management.
First-Year Class: 3,535 total; 22,921 applied, 46% were accepted, 34% of whom enrolled. 51% from top 10% of their high school class, 90% from top quarter, 94% from top half.
Graduation Requirements: 60 credits for associate, 120 credits for bachelor's; computer course for some engineering majors; internship (some majors); senior project for honors program students and some majors.
Computers on Campus: 3,349 computers available on campus for general student use. A campus-wide network can be accessed from student residence rooms and from off-campus. Students can contact faculty members and/or advisers through e-mail. Computers for student use in computer center, computer labs, learning resource center, classrooms, library, dorms provide access to the Internet/World Wide Web. Staffed computer lab on campus (open 24 hours a day) provides training in use of computers, software. *Academic computing expenditure 1995–96:* $10.1 million.

EXPENSES AND FINANCIAL AID

Expenses for 1996–97: *Application fee:* $35. State resident tuition: $5434 full-time, $227 per credit part-time. Nonresident tuition: $11,774 full-time, $491 per credit part-time. Part-time mandatory fees per semester range from $33 to $95. A per semester surcharge ranging from $68 to $225 (according to course load) is applied to upper division students in various engineering and engineering technology programs. Full-time mandatory fees: $190. College room and board: $4170.
Undergraduate Financial Aid: *Financial aid deadline (priority):* 2/15. *Financial aid forms:* FAFSA required.
LD Services Contact: Ms. Marianne Karwacki, Learning Disability Specialist, Pennsylvania State University University Park Campus, 105 Boucke Building, University Park, PA 16802-1503, 814-863-2291. Fax: 814-863-3217.

PERU STATE COLLEGE

Peru, Nebraska

LEARNING DISABILITIES SERVICES INFORMATION

Student Support Services began offering services in 1991. Currently the program serves 25 undergraduates with LD. Students diagnosed with ADD/ADHD are not eligible for the same services available to students with LD.
Staff: 3 full-time, 2 part-time staff members, including director, co-director, coordinators. Services provided by tutors, counselors.
Special Fees: No special fees are charged for services to students with LD.
Applications and admissions: *Required:* high school transcript, grade point average, class rank, courses completed, untimed or extended time SAT I or ACT, letters of recommendation; *recommended:* personal interview. Students may begin taking classes in fall only. *Application deadline:* continuous.

PROGRAM AND SERVICE COMPONENTS

Special preparation or orientation: Optional summer program offered prior to entering college.
Academic advising: Provided by unit staff members. Most students with LD take 9 to 15 semester hours each term; 12 semester hours required to maintain full-time status and be eligible for financial aid.
Counseling services: Individual counseling, career counseling.
Basic skills remediation: Offered in small groups by regular teachers. Available in reading, math, written language, study skills, time management.
Subject-area tutoring: Offered one-on-one and in small groups by peer tutors. Available in most subjects.
Special courses: College survival skills. All offered for credit; all enter into overall grade point average.
Auxiliary aids: Taped textbooks, tape recorders, calculators, word-processors with spell-check, talking computers.
Auxiliary services: Alternative test arrangements, notetakers, priority registration, advocacy.
Campus support group: A special student organization is available to students with LD.

GENERAL COLLEGE INFORMATION

State-supported, comprehensive, coed. Part of Nebraska State College System. Awards bachelor's, master's degrees. Founded 1867. *Setting:* 103-acre rural campus. *Endowment:* $4.4 million. *Educational spending 1995–96:* $1953 per undergrad. *Total enrollment:* 1,800. *Undergraduate faculty:* 121 (46 full-time, 51% with terminal degrees, 75 part-time); student–undergrad faculty ratio is 16:1.
Enrollment Profile: 1,635 students from 28 states and territories, 1 other country. 50% women, 50% men, 31% part-time, 89% state residents, 1% international, 29% 25 or older, 1% Native American, 2% Hispanic, 2% black, 1% Asian or Pacific Islander. *Retention:* 54% of 1995 full-time freshmen returned. *Graduation:* 13% graduate in 4 years, 20% in 5 years, 23% in 6 years. *Most popular recent majors:* business administration/commerce/management, education, psychology.
First-Year Class: 229 total; 566 applied, 57% were accepted, 71% of whom enrolled.
Graduation Requirements: 125 semester hours; 5 semester hours of math; 6 semester hours of science; computer course; internship (some majors); senior project (some majors).
Computers on Campus: 120 computers available on campus for general student use. A campus-wide network can be accessed from student residence rooms. Students can contact faculty members and/or advisers through e-mail. Computers for student use in computer center, computer labs, learning resource center, classrooms, library, student center, dorms provide access to the Internet/World Wide Web, on- and off-campus e-mail addresses. Staffed computer lab on campus provides training in use of computers, software. *Academic computing expenditure 1995–96:* $106,764.

EXPENSES AND FINANCIAL AID

Expenses for 1996–97: *Application fee:* $10. State resident tuition: $1650 full-time, $55 per semester hour part-time. Nonresident tuition: $3300 full-time, $110 per semester hour part-time. Full-time mandatory fees: $286. College room and board: $2966. College room only: $1456.
Undergraduate Financial Aid: On average, 80% of need was met. *Financial aid deadline (priority):* 3/1. *Financial aid forms:* institutional form required; CSS Financial Aid PROFILE, state form acceptable. FAFSA required for some.
LD Services Contact: Ms. Pam Williams, Acting Director, Student Support Services, Peru State College, PO Box 5, Peru, NE 68421, 402-872-2438. Fax: 402-872-2375.

PHILLIPS UNIVERSITY

Enid, Oklahoma

LEARNING DISABILITIES SERVICES INFORMATION

Office of Disability Services currently serves undergraduate and graduate students with LD. Students diagnosed with ADD/ADHD are eligible for the same services available to students with LD.

Phillips University (continued)

Staff: 1 full-time, 1 part-time staff members. Services provided by remediation specialists, tutors, diagnostic specialists.

Special Fees: No special fees are charged for services to students with LD.

Applications and admissions: *Recommended:* untimed or extended time SAT I or ACT. Students may begin taking classes any term. *Application deadline:* continuous.

Special policies: The college has written policies regarding grade forgiveness.

PROGRAM AND SERVICE COMPONENTS

Special preparation or orientation: Orientation offered before the start of each semester.

Academic advising: Provided by academic advisers. Students with LD may take up to 21 credit hours (with special permission) each term; most take 6 to 12 credit hours; 9 credit hours required to maintain full-time status; 6 credit hours required to be eligible for financial aid.

Counseling services: Individual counseling, career counseling, self-advocacy training.

Auxiliary aids: Taped textbooks, calculators, typewriters.

Auxiliary services: Alternative test arrangements.

Campus support group: A special student organization is available to students with LD.

GENERAL COLLEGE INFORMATION

Independent, comprehensive, coed, affiliated with Christian Church (Disciples of Christ). Awards associate, bachelor's, master's degrees. Founded 1906. *Setting:* 35-acre small-town campus with easy access to Oklahoma City. *Endowment:* $8.3 million. *Total enrollment:* 613. *Faculty:* 67 (45 full-time, 75% with terminal degrees, 22 part-time); student–undergrad faculty ratio is 13:1.

Enrollment Profile: 519 students from 20 states and territories, 13 other countries. 51% women, 49% men, 22% part-time, 57% state residents, 20% transferred in, 6% international, 21% 25 or older, 2% Native American, 5% Hispanic, 7% black, 2% Asian or Pacific Islander. *Retention:* 40% of 1995 full-time freshmen returned. *Graduation:* 24% graduate in 4 years, 34% in 5 years. *Areas of study chosen:* 25% business management and administrative services, 16% education, 12% biological and life sciences, 10% psychology, 8% health professions and related sciences, 7% social sciences, 5% natural resource sciences, 5% prelaw, 3% communications and journalism, 2% English language/literature/letters, 2% interdisciplinary studies, 2% mathematics, 2% theology/religion, 1% engineering and applied sciences, 1% fine arts, 1% physical sciences. *Most popular recent majors:* business administration/commerce/management, education, health science.

First-Year Class: 162 total; 235 applied, 85% were accepted, 81% of whom enrolled. 28% from top 10% of their high school class, 58% from top quarter, 77% from top half.

Graduation Requirements: 64 credit hours for associate, 128 credit hours for bachelor's; 3 credit hours of math; 5 credit hours of science; computer course for education, business majors; internship (some majors); senior project.

Computers on Campus: 45 computers available on campus for general student use. A computer is recommended for some students. Computers for student use in computer labs, library, academic buildings provide access to the Internet/World Wide Web, academic research databases. Staffed computer lab on campus provides training in use of computers, software.

EXPENSES AND FINANCIAL AID

Expenses for 1997–98: *Application fee:* $20. Comprehensive fee of $11,009 includes full-time tuition ($6490), mandatory fees ($615), and college room and board ($3904). College room only: $1700. Part-time tuition: $216 per credit hour.

Undergraduate Financial Aid: Of all full-time undergraduates enrolled in fall 1996, 86% of those who applied for aid were judged to have need according to Federal Methodology, of whom 100% were aided. On average, 77% of need was met. *Financial aid deadline (priority):* 4/30. *Financial aid forms:* FAFSA required for some.

LD Services Contact: Ms. Kibby K. Rose, Coordinator, Phillips University, 100 South University Avenue, Enid, OK 73701, 405-548-2437. Fax: 405-237-1607.

PIEDMONT BIBLE COLLEGE

Winston-Salem, North Carolina

LEARNING DISABILITIES SERVICES INFORMATION

Learning Resource Center began offering services in 1994. Currently the program serves 2 undergraduates with LD. Students diagnosed with ADD/ADHD are eligible for the same services available to students with LD.

Staff: 1 full-time staff member (director). Services provided by remediation specialist, tutors, diagnostic specialist.

Special Fees: No special fees are charged for services to students with LD.

Applications and admissions: *Required:* high school transcript, grade point average, courses completed, untimed SAT I or ACT, autobiographical statement, letters of recommendation; *recommended:* high school class rank, extracurricular activities, personal interview. Students may begin taking classes in fall only. *Application deadline:* continuous.

Special policies: The college has written policies regarding substitutions and waivers of admissions requirements.

PROGRAM AND SERVICE COMPONENTS

Diagnostic testing: Reading, math, written language, study skills.

Academic advising: Provided by unit staff members, academic advisers. Students with LD may take up to 12 credit hours each term; most take 9 to 12 credit hours; 12 credit hours required to maintain full-time status and be eligible for financial aid.

Counseling services: Individual counseling.

Basic skills remediation: Offered one-on-one by LD teachers; computer-aided instruction also offered. Available in reading, math, learning strategies, study skills, time management.

Subject-area tutoring: Offered one-on-one by peer tutors. Available in all subjects.

Special courses: College survival skills, reading, vocabulary development, word processing, time management, math, study skills. Most offered for credit; most enter into overall grade point average.

Auxiliary aids: Tape recorders, word-processors with spell-check, personal computers.

Auxiliary services: Alternative test arrangements, advocacy.

GENERAL COLLEGE INFORMATION

Independent Baptist, comprehensive, coed. Awards associate, bachelor's, master's degrees. Founded 1947. *Setting:* 12-acre urban campus. *Total enrollment:* 270. *Faculty:* 39 (21 full-time, 66% with terminal degrees, 18 part-time); student–undergrad faculty ratio is 13:1.

Enrollment Profile: 249 students from 23 states and territories, 4 other countries. 41% women, 59% men, 26% part-time, 61% state residents, 31% live on campus, 25% transferred in, 1% international, 36% 25 or older, 0% Native American, 0% Hispanic, 5% black, 1% Asian or Pacific Islander. *Retention:* 80% of 1995 full-time freshmen returned. *Most popular recent majors:* aviation technology, elementary education, biblical studies.

First-Year Class: 63 total; 80 applied, 94% were accepted, 84% of whom enrolled. 13% from top 10% of their high school class, 33% from top quarter, 69% from top half.

Graduation Requirements: 69 credit hours for associate, 135 credit hours for bachelor's; 6 credit hours of science; 3 credit hours of math; computer course; internship (some majors).

Computers on Campus: 40 computers available on campus for general student use. A computer is strongly recommended for all students. A campus-wide network can be accessed. Students can contact faculty members and/or advisers through e-mail. Computers for student use in computer center, learning resource center, library provide access to the Internet/World Wide Web. Staffed computer lab on campus provides training in use of computers, software.

EXPENSES AND FINANCIAL AID

Expenses for 1997–98: *Application fee:* $30. Comprehensive fee of $8340 includes full-time tuition ($4790), mandatory fees ($460), and college room and board ($3090). Part-time tuition: $200 per credit hour. Part-time mandatory fees per semester (6 to 11 credit hours): $55 to $110.

Undergraduate Financial Aid: Of all full-time undergraduates enrolled in fall 1996, 92% of those judged to have need according to Federal Methodology were aided. On average, 49% of need was met. *Financial aid deadline (priority):* 5/15. *Financial aid forms:* FAFSA, institutional form required; CSS Financial Aid PROFILE acceptable.

LD Services Contact: Mr. Jeff McCann, Vice President of Academics, Piedmont Bible College, 716 Franklin Street, Winston-Salem, NC 27101, 910-725-8344. Fax: 910-725-5522. Email: mccannrj@infoave.net.

POLYTECHNIC UNIVERSITY OF PUERTO RICO

Hato Rey, Puerto Rico

LEARNING DISABILITIES SERVICES INFORMATION

Counseling Office began offering services in 1992. Currently the program serves 35 undergraduates with LD. Students diagnosed with ADD/ADHD are eligible for the same services available to students with LD.

Staff: 6 part-time staff members. Services provided by counselors.

Special Fees: No special fees are charged for services to students with LD.

Applications and admissions: *Required:* high school transcript, grade point average, courses completed, College Board Test. Students may begin taking classes any term. *Application deadline:* continuous.

PROGRAM AND SERVICE COMPONENTS

Academic advising: Provided by unit staff members. Students with LD may take up to 12 credit hours each term; most take 12 credit hours; 12 credit hours required to maintain full-time status; 6 credit hours required to be eligible for financial aid.

Counseling services: Individual counseling, small-group counseling.

Basic skills remediation: Offered in small groups by tutors. Available in math, spelling, spoken language, written language, learning strategies, study skills, time management, social skills, computer skills.

Auxiliary services: Alternative test arrangements, notetakers, priority registration.

Campus support group: A special student organization is available to students with LD.

GENERAL COLLEGE INFORMATION

Independent, comprehensive, specialized, coed. Awards bachelor's, master's degrees. Founded 1966. *Setting:* 8-acre urban campus with easy access to San Juan. *Endowment:* $2.4 million. *Research spending 1995–96:* $75,000. *Educational spending 1995–96:* $1219 per undergrad. *Total enrollment:* 4,461. *Faculty:* 249 (104 full-time, 11% with terminal degrees, 145 part-time); student–undergrad faculty ratio is 23:1.

Enrollment Profile: 4,338 students: 13% women, 87% men, 25% part-time, 98% commonwealth residents, 40% transferred in, 17% 25 or older, 99% Hispanic. *Retention:* 70% of 1995 full-time freshmen returned. *Areas of study chosen:* 89% engineering and applied sciences, 7% business management and administrative services, 4% architecture.

First-Year Class: 894 total; 1,216 applied, 90% were accepted, 82% of whom enrolled.

Graduation Requirements: 141 credit hours; 15 credit hours of math; 16 credit hours of science; computer course.

Computers on Campus: 180 computers available on campus for general student use. A campus-wide network can be accessed from off-campus. Students can contact faculty members and/or advisers through e-mail. Computers for student use in computer center, library, student center provide access to the Internet/World Wide Web, on- and off-campus e-mail addresses. Staffed computer lab on campus provides training in use of computers, software. *Academic computing expenditure 1995–96:* $663,874.

EXPENSES AND FINANCIAL AID

Expenses for 1996–97: Tuition: $3420 full-time, $95 per credit hour part-time. Part-time mandatory fees: $240 per trimester. Full-time mandatory fees: $720.

Undergraduate Financial Aid: Of all full-time undergraduates enrolled in fall 1996, 100% of those who applied for aid were judged to have need according to Federal Methodology, of whom 100% were aided. On average, 70% of need was met. *Financial aid deadline (priority):* 6/30. *Financial aid forms:* FAFSA, institutional form required. Territory of Puerto Rico income tax form required for some.

LD Services Contact: Mrs. Judith Negrón, Director, Counseling Office, Polytechnic University of Puerto Rico, PO Box 192017, Hato Rey, PR 00919-2017, 787-754-8000 Ext. 247. Fax: 787-754-5931.

PROVIDENCE COLLEGE

Providence, Rhode Island

LEARNING DISABILITIES SERVICES INFORMATION

Office of Academic Services began offering services in 1982. Currently the program serves 120 undergraduates with LD. Services are also available to graduate students. Students diagnosed with ADD/ADHD are not eligible for the same services available to students with LD.

Staff: 4 part-time staff members, including director, coordinators. Services provided by tutors, learning specialist.

Special Fees: No special fees are charged for services to students with LD.

Applications and admissions: *Required:* high school transcript, grade point average, class rank, courses completed, untimed SAT I, autobiographical statement, letters of recommendation; *recommended:* high school extracurricular activities, IEP (Individualized Education Program), extended time SAT I or ACT, personal interview, psychoeducational report completed within 3 years. Students may begin taking classes in fall, spring, or summer. *Application deadline:* 2/1 (fall term), 11/15 (spring term).

Special policies: The college has written policies regarding substitutions and waivers of admissions and degree requirements.

PROGRAM AND SERVICE COMPONENTS

Academic advising: Provided by unit staff members, academic advisers. Students with LD may take up to 15 credits each term; most take 12 to 15 credits; 12 credits required to maintain full-time status and be eligible for financial aid.

Counseling services: Individual counseling, career counseling.

Subject-area tutoring: Offered one-on-one and in small groups by peer tutors. Available in most subjects.

Auxiliary aids: Taped textbooks, tape recorders, calculators, word-processors with spell-check, personal computers, talking computers, optical character readers.

Auxiliary services: Alternative test arrangements, notetakers, priority registration, advocacy.

GENERAL COLLEGE INFORMATION

Independent Roman Catholic, comprehensive, coed. Awards associate, bachelor's, master's, doctoral degrees. Founded 1917. *Setting:* 105-acre suburban campus with easy access to Boston. *Endowment:* $47.5 million. *Research spending 1995–96:* $434,018. *Educational spending 1995–96:* $5705 per undergrad. *Total enrollment:* 5,621. *Faculty:* 391 (278 full-time, 87% with terminal degrees, 113 part-time); student–undergrad faculty ratio is 13:1.

Enrollment Profile: 3,589 students from 39 states and territories, 12 other countries. 58% women, 42% men, 30% part-time, 15% state residents, 2% transferred in, 1% international, 1% 25 or older, 0% Native American, 1% Hispanic, 3% black, 1% Asian or Pacific Islander. *Retention:* 96% of 1995 full-time freshmen returned. *Graduation:* 92% graduate in 4 years, 93% in 5 years. *Areas of study chosen:* 20% business management and administrative services, 13% social sciences, 11% education, 6% liberal arts/general studies, 5% biological and life sciences, 5% English language/literature/letters, 5% interdisciplinary studies, 4% mathematics, 4% psychology, 3% premed, 1% computer and information sciences, 1% engineering and applied sciences, 1% fine arts, 1% foreign language and literature, 1% performing arts, 1% physical sciences, 1% theology/religion. *Most popular recent majors:* business administration/commerce/management, education, English.

First-Year Class: 937 total; 4,354 applied, 71% were accepted, 30% of whom enrolled. 30% from top 10% of their high school class, 64% from top quarter, 94% from top half. 38 National Merit Scholars, 24 class presidents, 27 valedictorians.

Graduation Requirements: 60 credits for associate, 116 credits for bachelor's; 3 credits of math; 6 credits of science; computer course for engineering, health services, math, business-related majors; internship (some majors); senior project for honors program students.

Computers on Campus: 144 computers available on campus for general student use. Computer purchase/lease plans available. A computer is recommended for some students. A campus-wide network can be accessed from student residence rooms and from off-campus. Students can contact faculty members and/or advisers through e-mail. Computers for student use in computer center, computer labs, learning resource center, classrooms, library provide access to the Internet/World Wide

Providence College (continued)

Web, on- and off-campus e-mail addresses. Staffed computer lab on campus provides training in use of computers, software. *Academic computing expenditure 1995–96:* $801,213.

EXPENSES AND FINANCIAL AID

Expenses for 1997–98: *Application fee:* $40. Comprehensive fee of $23,574 includes full-time tuition ($16,350), mandatory fees ($220), and college room and board ($7004). College room only: $3485. Part-time tuition: $545 per credit. Part-time tuition for evening program: $154 per credit.

Undergraduate Financial Aid: Of all full-time undergraduates enrolled in fall 1996, 100% of those judged to have need according to Federal Methodology were aided. On average, 80% of need was met. *Financial aid deadline (priority):* 2/1. *Financial aid forms:* FAFSA, state form required. CSS Financial Aid PROFILE required for some.

LD Services Contact: Director of Academic Services, Providence College, Meagher Hall, River Avenue, Providence, RI 02918, 401-865-2494.

PURDUE UNIVERSITY

West Lafayette, Indiana

LEARNING DISABILITIES SERVICES INFORMATION

Dean of Students Office began offering services in 1988. Currently the program serves 350 undergraduates with LD. Services are also available to graduate students. Students diagnosed with ADD/ADHD are eligible for the same services available to students with LD.

Staff: 1 full-time, 2 part-time staff members, including coordinators, program specialists. Services provided by counselors, diagnostic specialists.

Special Fees: No special fees are charged for services to students with LD.

Applications and admissions: *Required:* high school transcript, untimed SAT I or ACT; *recommended:* extended time SAT I or ACT. Students may begin taking classes any term. *Application deadline:* continuous.

Special policies: The college has written policies regarding substitutions and waivers of graduation and degree requirements.

PROGRAM AND SERVICE COMPONENTS

Special preparation or orientation: Optional orientation offered after classes begin.

Diagnostic testing: Intelligence, reading, math, spelling, handwriting, spoken language, written language, motor abilities, perceptual skills, study skills, personality, social skills, psychoneurology, speech, hearing.

Academic advising: Provided by unit staff members, academic advisers. Most students with LD take 12 semester hours each term; 12 semester hours required to maintain full-time status and be eligible for financial aid.

Counseling services: Individual counseling, small-group counseling, career counseling.

Auxiliary aids: Taped textbooks, tape recorders, word-processors with spell-check, personal computers, talking computers, optical character readers.

Auxiliary services: Alternative test arrangements, notetakers, priority registration, readers.

GENERAL COLLEGE INFORMATION

State-supported, coed. Part of Purdue University System. Awards associate, bachelor's, master's, doctoral, first professional degrees. Founded 1869. *Setting:* 1,579-acre suburban campus with easy access to Indianapolis. *Endowment:* $338 million. *Total enrollment:* 35,156. *Faculty:* 2,204 (1,999 full-time, 82% with terminal degrees, 205 part-time); student–undergrad faculty ratio is 16:1.

Enrollment Profile: 28,567 students from 58 states and territories, 79 other countries. 43% women, 57% men, 8% part-time, 74% state residents, 36% live on campus, 4% transferred in, 3% international, 8% 25 or older, 0% Native American, 2% Hispanic, 4% black, 4% Asian or Pacific Islander. *Retention:* 85% of 1995 full-time freshmen returned. *Graduation:* 30% graduate in 4 years, 58% in 5 years, 64% in 6 years. *Areas of study chosen:* 29% engineering and applied sciences, 13% business management and administrative services, 9% health professions and related sciences, 7% education, 4% agriculture, 4% biological and life sciences, 4% communications and journalism, 4% liberal arts/general studies, 4% social sciences, 3% vocational and home economics, 2% computer and information sciences, 2% natural resource sciences, 2% performing arts, 2% physical sciences, 2% psychology, 1% architecture, 1% English language/literature/letters, 1% foreign language and literature, 1% interdisciplinary studies, 1% mathematics. *Most popular recent majors:* communication, mechanical engineering, civil engineering.

First-Year Class: 6,241 total; 16,908 applied, 90% were accepted, 41% of whom enrolled. 25% from top 10% of their high school class, 57% from top quarter, 89% from top half. 34 National Merit Scholars, 146 valedictorians.

Graduation Requirements: 63 semester hours for associate, 126 semester hours for bachelor's; math/science requirements vary according to program; computer course for engineering, science, technology, management, agriculture, consumer/family sciences majors; internship (some majors); senior project (some majors).

Computers on Campus: 2,100 computers available on campus for general student use. Computer purchase/lease plans available. A computer is recommended for some students. A campus-wide network can be accessed from student residence rooms and from off-campus. Students can contact faculty members and/or advisers through e-mail. Computers for student use in computer center, computer labs, student center, dorms, individual schools provide access to the Internet/World Wide Web, on- and off-campus e-mail addresses. Staffed computer lab on campus.

EXPENSES AND FINANCIAL AID

Expenses for 1997–98: *Application fee:* $30. State resident tuition: $3352 full-time, $120 per semester hour part-time. Nonresident tuition: $11,184 full-time, $369 per semester hour part-time. Part-time mandatory fees: $8 per semester. College room and board: $4800.

Undergraduate Financial Aid: Of all full-time undergraduates enrolled in fall 1996, 69% of those who applied for aid were judged to have need according to Federal Methodology, of whom 93% were aided. On average, 100% of need was met. *Financial aid deadline (priority):* 3/1. *Financial aid forms:* FAFSA required.

LD Services Contact: Ms. Paula J. Micka, Assistant Dean, Adaptive Programs, Purdue University, Dean of Students Office, Schleman Hall, West Lafayette, IN 47907-1096, 765-494-1245. Fax: 765-496-1550. Email: pjmick@delta.reg.purdue.edu.

PURDUE UNIVERSITY NORTH CENTRAL

Westville, Indiana

LEARNING DISABILITIES SERVICES INFORMATION

Student Support Services began offering services in 1984. Currently the program serves 22 undergraduates with LD. Students diagnosed with ADD/ADHD are eligible for the same services available to students with LD.

Staff: 2 full-time, 2 part-time staff members, including director. Services provided by tutors, counselor.

Special Fees: No special fees are charged for services to students with LD.

Applications and admissions: *Required:* high school transcript, grade point average, class rank, courses completed, psychoeducational report completed within 3 years, proof of income level, parents educational level. Students may begin taking classes in fall, spring, or summer. *Application deadline:* continuous.

Special policies: The college has written policies regarding grade forgiveness.

PROGRAM AND SERVICE COMPONENTS

Special preparation or orientation: Optional summer program offered prior to entering college.

Academic advising: Provided by unit staff members, academic advisers. Students with LD may take up to 18 credit hours each term; 12 credit hours required to maintain full-time status; source of aid determines number of credit hours required to be eligible for financial aid.

Auxiliary aids: Taped textbooks, word-processors with spell-check, personal computers, talking computers.

Auxiliary services: Alternative test arrangements, notetakers, advocacy.

GENERAL COLLEGE INFORMATION

State-supported, comprehensive, coed. Part of Purdue University System. Awards associate, bachelor's, master's degrees. Founded 1967. *Setting:* 264-acre rural campus with easy access to Chicago. *Endowment:* $120,332. *Research spending 1995–96:* $18,503. *Total enrollment:* 3,399. *Faculty:* 221 (86 full-time, 60% with terminal degrees, 135 part-time); student–undergrad faculty ratio is 14:1.

Enrollment Profile: 3,355 students from 2 states and territories. 62% women, 38% men, 57% part-time, 99% state residents, 16% transferred in, 52% 25 or older, 1% Native American, 2% Hispanic, 4% black, 1% Asian or Pacific Islander. *Retention:* 52% of 1995 full-time freshmen returned. *Graduation:* 10% graduate in 4 years, 15% in 5 years, 18% in 6 years. *Areas of study chosen:* 13% English language/literature/letters, 12% engineering and applied sciences, 10% business management and administrative services, 7% health professions and related sciences, 6% education, 6% interdisciplinary studies, 5% liberal arts/general studies, 3% computer and information sciences, 1% agriculture, 1% architecture, 1% biological and life sciences, 1% psychology, 1% vocational and home economics. *Most popular recent majors:* business administration/commerce/management, nursing, liberal arts/general studies.
First-Year Class: 1,046 total; 1,612 applied, 90% were accepted, 72% of whom enrolled. 13% from top 10% of their high school class, 41% from top quarter, 85% from top half.
Graduation Requirements: 60 credit hours for associate, 123 credit hours for bachelor's; computer course for liberal studies, business, engineering, technology majors; internship (some majors).
Computers on Campus: 250 computers available on campus for general student use. A campus-wide network can be accessed. Students can contact faculty members and/or advisers through e-mail. Computers for student use in computer center, computer labs, learning resource center, classrooms, library, student rooms, student activity room provide access to the Internet/World Wide Web, on- and off-campus e-mail addresses. Staffed computer lab on campus provides training in use of computers, software. *Academic computing expenditure 1995–96:* $573,096.

EXPENSES AND FINANCIAL AID

Expenses for 1997–98: State resident tuition: $2715 full-time, $90.50 per credit hour part-time. Nonresident tuition: $6899 full-time, $229.95 per credit hour part-time. Part-time mandatory fees: $8.80 per credit hour. Full-time mandatory fees: $264.
Undergraduate Financial Aid: Of all full-time undergraduates enrolled in fall 1996, 68% of those who applied for aid were judged to have need according to Federal Methodology, of whom 85% were aided. On average, 65% of need was met. *Financial aid deadline (priority):* 3/1. *Financial aid forms:* FAFSA, state form, institutional form required.
LD Services Contact: Mr. Tom Lucas, Counselor, Student Support Services/Coordinator, Services for Students with Disabilities, Purdue University North Central, 1401 South US Highway 421, Westville, IN 46391-9528, 219-785-5374. Fax: 219-785-5544. Email: tomlucas@purduenc.edu.

QUEENS COLLEGE OF THE CITY UNIVERSITY OF NEW YORK

Flushing, New York

LEARNING DISABILITIES SERVICES INFORMATION

Office of Special Services began offering services in 1979. Currently the program serves 100 undergraduates with LD. Services are also available to graduate students. Students diagnosed with ADD/ADHD are eligible for the same services available to students with LD, as well as workshops on time management and increasing attention span.
Staff: 4 full-time, 8 part-time staff members, including director, coordinators. Services provided by remediation specialist, counselor, diagnostic specialist, peer counselors, college assistants.
Special Fees: No special fees are charged for services to students with LD.
Applications and admissions: *Recommended:* high school grade point average, untimed or extended time SAT I. Students may begin taking classes any term.
Special policies: The college has written policies regarding substitutions and waivers of admissions, graduation, and degree requirements.

PROGRAM AND SERVICE COMPONENTS

Special preparation or orientation: Required orientation held after classes begin.
Diagnostic testing: Reading, math, spelling, handwriting, written language, perceptual skills, study skills, personality, social skills, speech, hearing, learning strategies.
Academic advising: Provided by unit staff members, academic advisers. Most students with LD take 6 to 12 credits each term; 12 credits required to maintain full-time status and be eligible for financial aid.
Counseling services: Individual counseling, small-group counseling, career counseling.
Basic skills remediation: Offered one-on-one, in small groups, and in class-size groups by LD teachers, lab assistants. Available in reading, math, spelling, written language, learning strategies, study skills, time management.
Subject-area tutoring: Offered one-on-one, in small groups, and in class-size groups by professional teachers, peer tutors, college assistants. Available in most subjects.
Special courses: College survival skills, reading, communication skills, learning strategies, word processing, time management, math, study skills, career planning. None offered for credit.
Auxiliary aids: Taped textbooks, tape recorders, calculators, typewriters, word-processors with spell-check, personal computers, optical character readers.
Auxiliary services: Alternative test arrangements, notetakers, priority registration, advocacy.
Campus support group: A special student organization is available to students with LD.

GENERAL COLLEGE INFORMATION

State and locally supported, comprehensive, coed. Part of City University of New York System. Awards bachelor's, master's degrees. Founded 1937. *Setting:* 76-acre urban campus. *Total enrollment:* 17,073. *Faculty:* 1,035 (517 full-time, 85% with terminal degrees, 518 part-time); student–undergrad faculty ratio is 19:1.
Enrollment Profile: 13,442 students from 10 states and territories, 40 other countries. 61% women, 39% men, 39% part-time, 96% state residents, 45% transferred in, 3% international, 25% 25 or older, 0% Native American, 15% Hispanic, 9% black, 16% Asian or Pacific Islander. *Retention:* 76% of 1995 full-time freshmen returned. *Most popular recent majors:* accounting, communication, elementary education.
First-Year Class: 1,183 total; 4,089 applied, 61% were accepted, 47% of whom enrolled. 19% from top 10% of their high school class, 60% from top quarter, 95% from top half.
Graduation Requirements: 120 credits; 1 semester each of algebra and trigonometry or the equivalent; 3 semesters of a foreign language or the equivalent; computer course for most science, some social science majors.
Computers on Campus: 450 computers available on campus for general student use. Computer purchase/lease plans available. A computer is strongly recommended for all students. A campus-wide network can be accessed. Students can contact faculty members and/or advisers through e-mail. Computers for student use in computer center, classrooms, library, student center, departmental labs provide access to the Internet/World Wide Web, on-campus e-mail addresses. Staffed computer lab on campus provides training in use of computers, software.

EXPENSES AND FINANCIAL AID

Expenses for 1996–97: *Application fee:* $40. State resident tuition: $3200 full-time, $135 per credit part-time. Nonresident tuition: $6800 full-time, $285 per credit part-time. Part-time mandatory fees: $93.25 per semester. Full-time mandatory fees: $187.
Undergraduate Financial Aid: On average, 80% of need was met. *Financial aid deadline (priority):* 5/31. *Financial aid forms:* FAFSA, institutional form required.
LD Services Contact: Ms. MaryEllen Rooney, Learning Disabilities Specialist, Queens College of the City University of New York, Kiely 171, Flushing, NY 11367-1597, 718-997-5870.

RAMAPO COLLEGE OF NEW JERSEY

Mahwah, New Jersey

LEARNING DISABILITIES SERVICES INFORMATION

Office of Specialized Services began offering services in 1987. Currently the program serves 80 undergraduates with LD. Students diagnosed with ADD/ADHD are eligible for the same services available to students with LD.
Staff: 5 full-time, 2 part-time staff members, including director, assistant director, administrative assistant. Services provided by counselors, learning specialist, career development specialist.
Special Fees: No special fees are charged for services to students with LD.
Applications and admissions: *Required:* high school transcript, grade point average, class rank, courses completed, untimed SAT I or ACT, autobiographical statement, letters of recommendation. Students may begin taking classes any term. *Application deadline:* 5/1 (fall term), 10/31 (spring term).

Ramapo College of New Jersey (continued)

PROGRAM AND SERVICE COMPONENTS

Special preparation or orientation: Required orientation held before registration.

Academic advising: Provided by unit staff members, academic advisers. Most students with LD take 9 to 16 credits each term; 12 credits required to maintain full-time status; source of aid determines number of credits required to be eligible for financial aid.

Counseling services: Individual counseling, small-group counseling, career counseling, self-advocacy training.

Subject-area tutoring: Offered one-on-one and in small groups by professional teachers, peer tutors. Available in most subjects.

Auxiliary aids: Taped textbooks, tape recorders, calculators, typewriters, word-processors with spell-check, personal computers, talking computers, optical character readers, services provided through Recordings for the Blind.

Auxiliary services: Alternative test arrangements, notetakers, priority registration.

GENERAL COLLEGE INFORMATION

State-supported, comprehensive, coed. Part of New Jersey State College System. Awards bachelor's, master's degrees. Founded 1969. *Setting:* 300-acre suburban campus with easy access to New York City. *Research spending 1995–96:* $75,000. *Educational spending 1995–96:* $3947 per undergrad. *Total enrollment:* 4,001. *Faculty:* 298 (153 full-time, 97% with terminal degrees, 145 part-time); student–undergrad faculty ratio is 17:1.

Enrollment Profile: 3,947 students from 18 states and territories, 51 other countries. 56% women, 44% men, 33% part-time, 81% state residents, 4% international, 40% 25 or older, 0% Native American, 6% Hispanic, 9% black, 3% Asian or Pacific Islander. *Retention:* 77% of 1995 full-time freshmen returned. *Graduation:* 16% graduate in 4 years, 33% in 5 years, 36% in 6 years. *Areas of study chosen:* 33% business management and administrative services, 14% social sciences, 10% biological and life sciences, 10% liberal arts/general studies, 9% communications and journalism, 9% psychology, 7% health professions and related sciences, 5% computer and information sciences, 3% performing arts, 2% area and ethnic studies, 1% physical sciences. *Most popular recent majors:* business administration/commerce/management, psychology, communication.

First-Year Class: 430 total; 1,911 applied, 50% were accepted, 45% of whom enrolled. 9% from top 10% of their high school class, 35% from top quarter, 87% from top half.

Graduation Requirements: 128 credits; 12 credits of math/science; computer course for math, business administration majors; internship (some majors); senior project for honors program students and some majors.

Computers on Campus: 283 computers available on campus for general student use. A campus-wide network can be accessed from student residence rooms and from off-campus. Students can contact faculty members and/or advisers through e-mail. Computers for student use in computer center, computer labs, learning resource center, classrooms, library, dorms, student rooms provide access to the Internet/World Wide Web, on- and off-campus e-mail addresses. Staffed computer lab on campus provides training in use of computers, software. *Academic computing expenditure 1995–96:* $219,810.

EXPENSES AND FINANCIAL AID

Expenses for 1997–98: *Application fee:* $35. State resident tuition: $4206 full-time, $136.20 per credit part-time. Nonresident tuition: $6576 full-time, $215.20 per credit part-time. College room and board: $5734. College room only: $4050.

Undergraduate Financial Aid: Of all full-time undergraduates enrolled in fall 1996, 84% of those who applied for aid were judged to have need according to Federal Methodology, of whom 72% were aided. On average, 41% of need was met. *Financial aid deadline (priority):* 3/15. *Financial aid forms:* FAFSA required.

LD Services Contact: Ms. Jean Balutanski, Director, Office of Specialized Services, Ramapo College of New Jersey, 505 Ramapo Valley Road, Mahwah, NJ 07430, 732-529-7514. Fax: 732-529-7508.

REDEEMER COLLEGE

Ancaster, Ontario, Canada

LEARNING DISABILITIES SERVICES INFORMATION

Office of Student Life Services began offering services in 1989. Currently the program serves 9 undergraduates with LD. Students diagnosed with ADD/ADHD are eligible for the same services available to students with LD.

Staff: Includes coordinators, Special Needs Coordinator, academic support counselor.

Special Fees: No special fees are charged for services to students with LD.

Applications and admissions: *Required:* high school transcript, grade point average, courses completed, letters of recommendation, psychoeducational report completed within 2 years; *recommended:* high school extracurricular activities, untimed ACT, personal interview. Students may begin taking classes in fall or winter. *Application deadline:* continuous.

Special policies: The college has written policies regarding substitutions and waivers of admissions, graduation, and degree requirements.

PROGRAM AND SERVICE COMPONENTS

Academic advising: Provided by academic advisers. Students with LD may take up to 4 courses each term; most take 3 to 4 courses; 3 courses required to maintain full-time status and be eligible for financial aid.

Counseling services: Individual counseling, career counseling.

Basic skills remediation: Offered in class-size groups by academic support coordinator. Available in math, written language, study skills, time management.

Subject-area tutoring: Offered one-on-one by peer tutors. Available in all subjects.

Auxiliary aids: Taped textbooks, word-processors with spell-check.

Auxiliary services: Alternative test arrangements, notetakers, proofreaders.

GENERAL COLLEGE INFORMATION

Independent interdenominational, 4-year, coed. Awards bachelor's degrees. Founded 1980. *Setting:* 78-acre small-town campus with easy access to Toronto. *Endowment:* $152,188. *Research spending 1995–96:* $158,300. *Educational spending 1995–96:* $8204 per undergrad. *Total enrollment:* 471. *Faculty:* 46 (31 full-time, 93% with terminal degrees, 15 part-time); student–undergrad faculty ratio is 14:1.

Enrollment Profile: 471 students from 8 provinces and territories, 5 other countries. 60% women, 40% men, 11% part-time, 95% province residents, 2% transferred in, 3% international, 11% 25 or older, 1% Hispanic, 1% black, 1% Asian or Pacific Islander. *Retention:* 76% of 1995 full-time freshmen returned. *Areas of study chosen:* 27% liberal arts/general studies, 13% education, 13% social sciences, 12% fine arts, 11% English language/literature/letters, 10% psychology, 6% business management and administrative services, 4% biological and life sciences, 4% theology/religion, 2% foreign language and literature, 1% mathematics, 1% philosophy, 1% premed, 1% prevet. *Most popular recent majors:* education, physical education, English.

First-Year Class: 156 total; 285 applied, 100% were accepted, 55% of whom enrolled.

Graduation Requirements: 40 courses; math proficiency; 1 course each in biology and physical science; 2 courses in a foreign language or proven competence; computer course for math, business majors; senior project for honors program students and some majors.

Computers on Campus: 15 computers available on campus for general student use. A computer is recommended for all students. A campus-wide network can be accessed from off-campus. Students can contact faculty members and/or advisers through e-mail. Computers for student use in computer center, dorms provide access to the Internet/World Wide Web, on- and off-campus e-mail addresses. Staffed computer lab on campus provides training in use of computers, software. *Academic computing expenditure 1995–96:* $72,400.

EXPENSES AND FINANCIAL AID

Expenses for 1997–98: *Application fee:* $30. Comprehensive fee of $12,493 includes full-time tuition ($7950), mandatory fees ($363), and college room and board ($4180). Part-time tuition per course: $445 for 1 course, $890 for 2 or more courses. (All figures are in Canadian dollars.).

Undergraduate Financial Aid: 75% of all full-time undergraduates enrolled in fall 1996 applied for aid; of these, 86% were judged to have need according to Federal Methodology, of whom 100% were aided. On

average, 87% of need was met. *Financial aid deadline (priority):* 6/30. *Financial aid forms:* state form required; CSS Financial Aid PROFILE acceptable. Institutional form required for some.

LD Services Contact: Ms. Nancy Hartholt, Special Needs Coordinator, Redeemer College, 777 Highway 53 East, Ancaster, ON L9K 1J4, Canada, 905-648-2131. Fax: 905-648-2134.

REED COLLEGE

Portland, Oregon

LEARNING DISABILITIES SERVICES INFORMATION

Student Services currently serves 25 undergraduates with LD. Students diagnosed with ADD/ADHD are eligible for the same services available to students with LD.

Staff: 1 full-time staff member (Associate Dean).

Special Fees: No special fees are charged for services to students with LD.

Applications and admissions: *Required:* high school transcript, untimed SAT I or ACT, writing samples; *recommended:* extended time SAT I or ACT. Students may begin taking classes in fall or spring. *Application deadline:* 2/1.

PROGRAM AND SERVICE COMPONENTS

Academic advising: Provided by unit staff members, academic advisers. Students with LD may take up to 4 units each term; 3 units required to maintain full-time status.

Counseling services: Individual counseling, career counseling.

Subject-area tutoring: Offered one-on-one by peer tutors. Available in most subjects.

Auxiliary services: Notetakers, readers.

GENERAL COLLEGE INFORMATION

Independent, comprehensive, coed. Awards bachelor's, master's degrees. Founded 1909. *Setting:* 98-acre suburban campus. *Endowment:* $176.5 million. *Educational spending 1995–96:* $9161 per undergrad. *Total enrollment:* 1,325. *Faculty:* 128 (116 full-time, 85% with terminal degrees, 12 part-time); student–undergrad faculty ratio is 10:1.

Enrollment Profile: 1,306 students from 50 states and territories, 8 other countries. 53% women, 47% men, 3% part-time, 15% state residents, 54% live on campus, 3% transferred in, 8% international, 2% 25 or older, 1% Native American, 4% Hispanic, 1% black, 9% Asian or Pacific Islander. *Retention:* 87% of 1995 full-time freshmen returned. *Graduation:* 48% graduate in 4 years, 65% in 5 years, 69% in 6 years. *Areas of study chosen:* 21% social sciences, 16% biological and life sciences, 11% English language/literature/letters, 9% interdisciplinary studies, 9% physical sciences, 8% psychology, 6% fine arts, 6% mathematics, 5% foreign language and literature, 5% philosophy, 4% theology/religion. *Most popular recent majors:* biology/biological sciences, history, English.

First-Year Class: 361 total; 2,086 applied, 76% were accepted, 23% of whom enrolled. 46% from top 10% of their high school class, 80% from top quarter, 96% from top half. 9 National Merit Scholars, 19 valedictorians.

Graduation Requirements: 120 semester hours; 1 year of science; computer course for physics, math, biology, psychology majors; senior project.

Computers on Campus: 140 computers available on campus for general student use. Computer purchase/lease plans available. A computer is recommended for all students. A campus-wide network can be accessed from student residence rooms and from off-campus. Students can contact faculty members and/or advisers through e-mail. Computers for student use in computer center, computer labs, library, dorms, student rooms, departmental labs provide access to the Internet/World Wide Web, on- and off-campus e-mail addresses. Staffed computer lab on campus (open 24 hours a day) provides training in use of computers, software.

EXPENSES AND FINANCIAL AID

Expenses for 1997–98: *Application fee:* $40. Comprehensive fee of $28,540 includes full-time tuition ($22,180), mandatory fees ($160), and college room and board ($6200). College room only: $3200.

Undergraduate Financial Aid: 54% of all full-time undergraduates enrolled in fall 1996 applied for aid; of these, 92% were judged to have need according to Federal Methodology, of whom 94% were aided. *Financial aid deadline:* 3/1. *Financial aid forms:* FAFSA, CSS Financial Aid PROFILE required. Institutional form required for some.

LD Services Contact: Ms. Lisa Pickert, Associate Dean, Reed College, 3203 Southeast Woodstock, Portland, OR 97202-8199, 503-777-7521. Fax: 503-777-7225.

RENSSELAER POLYTECHNIC INSTITUTE

Troy, New York

LEARNING DISABILITIES SERVICES INFORMATION

Disabled Student Services began offering services in 1978. Currently the program serves 56 undergraduates with LD. Services are also available to graduate students. Students diagnosed with ADD/ADHD are eligible for the same services available to students with LD.

Staff: 2 part-time staff members, including coordinator. Services provided by remediation specialist.

Special Fees: No special fees are charged for services to students with LD.

Applications and admissions: *Required:* high school transcript, grade point average, class rank, courses completed, extracurricular activities, untimed or extended time SAT I, autobiographical statement, letters of recommendation, psychoeducational report completed within 3 years. Students may begin taking classes any term. *Application deadline:* 1/1 (fall term), 11/1 (spring term).

PROGRAM AND SERVICE COMPONENTS

Academic advising: Provided by unit staff members, academic advisers. Students with LD may take up to 21 credit hours each term; most take 12 to 16 credit hours; 12 credit hours required to maintain full-time status.

Counseling services: Individual counseling, career counseling, peer counseling (for freshmen).

Basic skills remediation: Offered one-on-one and in small groups by LD specialist, peer tutors. Available in reading, written language, learning strategies, study skills, time management.

Subject-area tutoring: Offered one-on-one and in small groups by peer tutors. Available in most subjects.

Auxiliary aids: Taped textbooks, tape recorders, optical character readers.

Auxiliary services: Alternative test arrangements, notetakers, priority registration, advocacy.

GENERAL COLLEGE INFORMATION

Independent, coed. Awards bachelor's, master's, doctoral degrees. Founded 1824. *Setting:* 260-acre suburban campus with easy access to Albany. *Endowment:* $357.8 million. *Research spending 1995–96:* $29.2 million. *Total enrollment:* 6,250. *Faculty:* 342 (341 full-time, 99% with terminal degrees, 1 part-time); student–undergrad faculty ratio is 12:1.

Enrollment Profile: 4,149 students from 53 states and territories, 65 other countries. 25% women, 75% men, 0% part-time, 41% state residents, 3% transferred in, 6% international, 0% Native American, 4% Hispanic, 3% black, 14% Asian or Pacific Islander. *Retention:* 89% of 1995 full-time freshmen returned. *Graduation:* 46% graduate in 4 years, 66% in 5 years, 70% in 6 years. *Areas of study chosen:* 61% engineering and applied sciences, 9% biological and life sciences, 9% business management and administrative services, 7% computer and information sciences, 6% architecture, 3% physical sciences, 2% mathematics, 1% communications and journalism, 1% psychology, 1% social sciences. *Most popular recent majors:* mechanical engineering, electrical engineering, computer science.

First-Year Class: 899 total; 4,549 applied, 82% were accepted, 24% of whom enrolled. 50% from top 10% of their high school class, 81% from top quarter, 98% from top half. 20 National Merit Scholars, 41 valedictorians.

Graduation Requirements: 124 credit hours; 24 credit hours of math/science; computer course; senior project (some majors).

Computers on Campus: 618 computers available on campus for general student use. Computer purchase/lease plans available. A campus-wide network can be accessed from student residence rooms and from off-campus. Students can contact faculty members and/or advisers through e-mail. Computers for student use in computer center, computer labs, classrooms, library, dorms, academic buildings provide access to the Internet/World Wide Web, on- and off-campus e-mail addresses. Staffed computer lab on campus (open 24 hours a day) provides training in use of computers, software.

Rensselaer Polytechnic Institute (continued)

EXPENSES AND FINANCIAL AID

Expenses for 1997–98: *Application fee:* $45. Comprehensive fee of $27,386 includes full-time tuition ($20,030), mandatory fees ($570), and college room and board ($6786). Part-time tuition: $600 per credit hour. Part-time mandatory fees: $570 per year.
Undergraduate Financial Aid: *Financial aid deadline (priority):* 2/15. *Financial aid forms:* FAFSA required. State form, institutional form required for some.
LD Services Contact: Ms. Debra Hamilton, Coordinator, Disabled Student Services, Rensselaer Polytechnic Institute, Dean of Students Office, Troy, NY 12180-3590, 518-276-2746. Fax: 518-276-4839. Email: hamild@rpi.edu.

THE RICHARD STOCKTON COLLEGE OF NEW JERSEY

Pomona, New Jersey

LEARNING DISABILITIES SERVICES INFORMATION

Learning Access Program began offering services in 1987. Currently the program serves 71 undergraduates with LD. Students diagnosed with ADD/ADHD are eligible for the same services available to students with LD.
Staff: 2 full-time, 1 part-time staff members, including director, clerical support staff. Services provided by diagnostic specialist.
Special Fees: No special fees are charged for services to students with LD.
Applications and admissions: *Required:* high school transcript, grade point average, class rank, courses completed, autobiographical statement, letters of recommendation; *recommended:* high school extracurricular activities, untimed SAT I or extended time ACT, personal interview. Students may begin taking classes any term. *Application deadline:* continuous.

PROGRAM AND SERVICE COMPONENTS

Diagnostic testing: Intelligence, reading, math, spelling, handwriting, spoken language, written language, motor abilities, perceptual skills, study skills, personality, social skills, psychoneurology, speech, hearing, learning strategies, language disability.
Academic advising: Provided by academic advisers. Most students with LD take 12 credits each term; 12 credits required to maintain full-time status and be eligible for financial aid.
Counseling services: Individual counseling, career counseling, self-advocacy training.
Basic skills remediation: Offered in class-size groups by regular teachers. Available in reading, math, spelling, handwriting, spoken language, written language, learning strategies, study skills, time management, computer skills.
Subject-area tutoring: Offered in small groups by peer tutors. Available in all subjects.
Auxiliary aids: Taped textbooks, tape recorders, calculators, word-processors with spell-check, personal computers, talking computers.
Auxiliary services: Alternative test arrangements, notetakers, priority registration, advocacy.

GENERAL COLLEGE INFORMATION

State-supported, comprehensive, coed. Part of New Jersey State College System. Awards bachelor's, master's degrees. Founded 1971. *Setting:* 1,600-acre suburban campus with easy access to Philadelphia. *Endowment:* $1.3 million. *Research spending 1995–96:* $440,062. *Educational spending 1995–96:* $3769 per undergrad. *Total enrollment:* 5,512. *Undergraduate faculty:* 297 (197 full-time, 94% with terminal degrees, 100 part-time); student–undergrad faculty ratio is 18:1.
Enrollment Profile: 5,512 students from 25 states and territories, 23 other countries. 57% women, 43% men, 15% part-time, 96% state residents, 39% live on campus, 46% transferred in, 1% international, 24% 25 or older, 1% Native American, 4% Hispanic, 8% black, 3% Asian or Pacific Islander. *Retention:* 83% of 1995 full-time freshmen returned. *Graduation:* 31% graduate in 4 years, 48% in 5 years, 52% in 6 years. *Areas of study chosen:* 20% social sciences, 15% business management and administrative services, 15% health professions and related sciences, 10% natural resource sciences, 8% biological and life sciences, 5% English language/literature/letters, 5% psychology, 4% computer and information sciences, 4% physical sciences, 3% mathematics, 2% fine arts, 2% liberal arts/general studies, 1% communications and journalism, 1% education, 1% interdisciplinary studies, 1% performing arts, 1% philosophy. *Most popular recent majors:* business administration/commerce/management, environmental sciences, criminal justice.
First-Year Class: 742 total; 3,274 applied, 48% were accepted, 47% of whom enrolled. 27% from top 10% of their high school class, 64% from top quarter, 94% from top half. 1 National Merit Scholar, 38 class presidents, 6 valedictorians.
Graduation Requirements: 128 credit hours; quantitative reasoning proficiency; computer course (varies by major); internship (some majors); senior project for honors program students and some majors.
Computers on Campus: 398 computers available on campus for general student use. Computer purchase/lease plans available. A computer is recommended for some students. A campus-wide network can be accessed from student residence rooms and from off-campus. Students can contact faculty members and/or advisers through e-mail. Computers for student use in computer center, computer labs, learning resource center, classrooms, library, student center, dorms provide access to the Internet/World Wide Web, on- and off-campus e-mail addresses. Staffed computer lab on campus provides training in use of computers, software. *Academic computing expenditure 1995–96:* $1.1 million.

EXPENSES AND FINANCIAL AID

Expenses for 1997–98: *Application fee:* $35. State resident tuition: $2816 full-time, $88 per credit hour part-time. Nonresident tuition: $4544 full-time, $142 per credit hour part-time. Part-time mandatory fees: $30 per credit hour. Full-time mandatory fees: $960. College room and board: $4995. College room only: $3150.
Undergraduate Financial Aid: 63% of all full-time undergraduates enrolled in fall 1996 applied for aid; of these, 79% were judged to have need according to Federal Methodology, of whom 95% were aided. On average, 95% of need was met. *Financial aid deadline (priority):* 3/1. *Financial aid forms:* FAFSA required.
LD Services Contact: Ms. Thomasa Gonzalez, Director, Counseling Services, The Richard Stockton College of New Jersey, Jimmie Leeds Road, Pomona, NJ 08240, 609-652-4722. Fax: 609-748-5550. Email: iaprod238@pollux.stockton.edu.

RIDER UNIVERSITY

Lawrenceville, New Jersey

LEARNING DISABILITIES SERVICES INFORMATION

Education Enhancement Program/Rider Learning Center began offering services in 1990. Currently the program serves 50 undergraduates with LD. Services are also available to graduate students. Students diagnosed with ADD/ADHD are eligible for the same services available to students with LD.
Staff: 1 full-time, 4 part-time staff members, including director, associate director. Services provided by tutors, professional tutors.
Special Fees: No special fees are charged for services to students with LD.
Applications and admissions: *Required:* high school transcript, grade point average, class rank, untimed SAT I; *recommended:* extended time SAT I, personal interview, letters of recommendation, psychoeducational report completed most recently. Students may begin taking classes in fall or spring. *Application deadline:* continuous.
Special policies: The college has written policies regarding grade forgiveness; substitutions and waivers of graduation and degree requirements.

PROGRAM AND SERVICE COMPONENTS

Academic advising: Provided by unit staff members. Students with LD may take up to 17 semester hours each term; most take 12 semester hours; 12 semester hours required to maintain full-time status; 24 semester hours per year required to be eligible for financial aid.
Counseling services: Individual counseling, self-advocacy training.
Basic skills remediation: Offered one-on-one by professional tutors. Available in reading, math, written language, learning strategies, study skills, time management.
Subject-area tutoring: Offered one-on-one and in small groups by peer tutors. Available in most subjects.
Auxiliary aids: Taped textbooks, tape recorders, typewriters, word-processors with spell-check, personal computers.
Auxiliary services: Alternative test arrangements, priority registration, advocacy.

GENERAL COLLEGE INFORMATION

Independent, comprehensive, coed. Awards bachelor's, master's degrees. Founded 1865. *Setting:* 340-acre suburban campus with easy access to Philadelphia and New York City. *Endowment:* $44.1 million. *Research spending 1995–96:* $423,588. *Educational spending 1995–96:* $6891 per undergrad. *Total enrollment:* 4,640. *Faculty:* 369 (233 full-time, 86% with terminal degrees, 136 part-time); student–undergrad faculty ratio is 13:1.

Enrollment Profile: 3,633 students from 26 states and territories, 25 other countries. 59% women, 41% men, 30% part-time, 78% state residents, 48% live on campus, 25% transferred in, 1% international, 18% 25 or older, 1% Native American, 4% Hispanic, 6% black, 4% Asian or Pacific Islander. *Retention:* 76% of 1995 full-time freshmen returned. *Graduation:* 43% graduate in 4 years, 56% in 5 years, 58% in 6 years. *Areas of study chosen:* 35% business management and administrative services, 21% education, 9% liberal arts/general studies, 8% communications and journalism, 7% psychology, 5% social sciences, 4% biological and life sciences, 4% physical sciences, 3% computer and information sciences, 2% English language/literature/letters, 2% fine arts. *Most popular recent majors:* elementary education, accounting, business administration/commerce/management.

First-Year Class: 696 total; 3,161 applied, 85% were accepted, 26% of whom enrolled. 12% from top 10% of their high school class, 32% from top quarter, 61% from top half.

Graduation Requirements: 120 semester hours; 6 semester hours of science; computer course for business administration, math majors; senior project for honors program students and some majors.

Computers on Campus: 300 computers available on campus for general student use. Computer purchase/lease plans available. Computers for student use in computer center, computer labs, classrooms, library, student center, dorms, departmental labs provide access to the Internet/World Wide Web. Staffed computer lab on campus (open 24 hours a day) provides training in use of computers, software. *Academic computing expenditure 1995–96:* $551,465.

EXPENSES AND FINANCIAL AID

Expenses for 1997–98: *Application fee:* $35. Comprehensive fee of $21,680 includes full-time tuition ($15,120), mandatory fees ($290), and college room and board ($6270). College room only: $3370. Part-time tuition: $505 per semester hour. Part-time mandatory fees: $10 per course.

Undergraduate Financial Aid: Of all full-time undergraduates enrolled in fall 1996, 100% of those judged to have need according to Federal Methodology were aided. On average, 96% of need was met. *Financial aid deadline (priority):* 3/1. *Financial aid forms:* FAFSA required.

LD Services Contact: Dr. Barbara Blandford, Associate Director, Education Enhancement Program, Rider University, 2083 Lawrenceville Road, Academic Annex #3, Lawrenceville, NJ 08648-3099, 609-896-5000 Ext. 7365. Fax: 609-896-8029. Email: blandford@rider.edu.

RINGLING SCHOOL OF ART AND DESIGN

Sarasota, Florida

LEARNING DISABILITIES SERVICES INFORMATION

Office of Academic Advising and Disability Services began offering services in 1993. Currently the program serves 65 undergraduates with LD. Students diagnosed with ADD/ADHD are eligible for the same services available to students with LD.

Staff: 1 full-time staff member (director).

Special Fees: No special fees are charged for services to students with LD.

Applications and admissions: *Required:* high school transcript, grade point average, letters of recommendation, psychoeducational report completed within 3 years, portfolio. *Application deadline:* continuous.

PROGRAM AND SERVICE COMPONENTS

Academic advising: Provided by academic advisers. Students with LD may take up to 18 semester hours each term; most take 15 semester hours; 12 semester hours required to maintain full-time status and be eligible for financial aid.

Counseling services: Individual counseling, small-group counseling.

Auxiliary aids: Taped textbooks, tape recorders, word-processors with spell-check.

Auxiliary services: Alternative test arrangements, notetakers.

GENERAL COLLEGE INFORMATION

Independent, 4-year, specialized, coed. Awards bachelor's degrees. Founded 1931. *Setting:* 35-acre urban campus with easy access to Tampa–St. Petersburg. *Total enrollment:* 830. *Faculty:* 98 (80% of full-time faculty have terminal degrees); student–undergrad faculty ratio is 13:1.

Enrollment Profile: 830 students from 44 states and territories, 35 other countries. 40% women, 60% men, 5% part-time, 45% state residents, 40% transferred in, 7% international, 25% 25 or older, 1% Native American, 8% Hispanic, 3% black, 5% Asian or Pacific Islander. *Retention:* 80% of 1995 full-time freshmen returned. *Areas of study chosen:* 100% fine arts. *Most popular recent majors:* illustration, graphic arts.

First-Year Class: 218 total; 840 applied, 42% were accepted, 62% of whom enrolled.

Graduation Requirements: 124 semester hours; 1 math course; senior project (some majors).

Computers on Campus: 154 computers available on campus for general student use. A campus-wide network can be accessed from student residence rooms. Students can contact faculty members and/or advisers through e-mail. Computers for student use in computer center, computer labs, learning resource center, classrooms, library provide access to the Internet/World Wide Web, on- and off-campus e-mail addresses. Staffed computer lab on campus provides training in use of computers, software.

EXPENSES AND FINANCIAL AID

Expenses for 1997–98: *Application fee:* $30. Comprehensive fee of $19,942 includes full-time tuition ($13,050), mandatory fees ($200), and college room and board ($6692). Part-time tuition: $635 per semester hour. Part-time mandatory fees: $200 per year. Mandatory technology fee per course ranges from $300 to $1900.

Undergraduate Financial Aid: 87% of all full-time undergraduates enrolled in fall 1996 applied for aid; of these, 91% were judged to have need according to Federal Methodology, of whom 96% were aided. On average, 73% of need was met. *Financial aid deadline (priority):* 3/1. *Financial aid forms:* FAFSA, CSS Financial Aid PROFILE, institutional form required. State form required for some.

LD Services Contact: Ms. Donna Anderson, Academic Adviser and LD Coordinator, Ringling School of Art and Design, 2700 North Tamiami Trail, Sarasota, FL 34234, 941-351-5100. Fax: 941-359-7517. Email: danderson@rsad.edu.

RIPON COLLEGE

Ripon, Wisconsin

LEARNING DISABILITIES SERVICES INFORMATION

Student Support Services began offering services in 1987. Currently the program serves 13 undergraduates with LD. Students diagnosed with ADD/ADHD are eligible for the same services available to students with LD.

Staff: 2 full-time staff members, including director, assistant director. Services provided by tutors, counselors.

Special Fees: No special fees are charged for services to students with LD.

Applications and admissions: *Required:* high school transcript, grade point average, class rank, courses completed, extracurricular activities, untimed SAT I or ACT, personal interview, autobiographical statement, letters of recommendation, psychoeducational report completed within 3 years. Students may begin taking classes in fall only. *Application deadline:* continuous.

Special policies: The college has written policies regarding grade forgiveness; substitutions and waivers of admissions, graduation, and degree requirements.

PROGRAM AND SERVICE COMPONENTS

Special preparation or orientation: Optional orientation offered before registration, during registration, after classes begin.

Academic advising: Provided by unit staff members, academic advisers. Most students with LD take 16 credits each term; 12 credits required to maintain full-time status and be eligible for financial aid.

Counseling services: Individual counseling, career counseling, self-advocacy training.

Subject-area tutoring: Offered one-on-one and in small groups by peer tutors. Available in most subjects.

Ripon College (continued)

Special courses: College survival skills, reading, learning strategies, word processing, time management, career planning. None offered for credit; none enter into overall grade point average.
Auxiliary aids: Taped textbooks, tape recorders, calculators, typewriters, word-processors with spell-check, personal computers.
Auxiliary services: Alternative test arrangements, notetakers, advocacy.

GENERAL COLLEGE INFORMATION

Independent, 4-year, coed. Awards bachelor's degrees. Founded 1851. *Setting:* 250-acre small-town campus with easy access to Milwaukee. *Endowment:* $25 million. *Total enrollment:* 734. *Faculty:* 96 (62 full-time, 90% with terminal degrees, 34 part-time); student–undergrad faculty ratio is 10:1.
Enrollment Profile: 734 students from 36 states and territories, 17 other countries. 50% women, 50% men, 3% part-time, 61% state residents, 97% live on campus, 11% transferred in, 3% international, 1% 25 or older, 1% Native American, 2% Hispanic, 2% black, 2% Asian or Pacific Islander. *Retention:* 81% of 1995 full-time freshmen returned. *Most popular recent majors:* history, English, biology/biological sciences.
First-Year Class: 169 total; 473 applied, 88% were accepted, 41% of whom enrolled. 30% from top 10% of their high school class, 58% from top quarter, 85% from top half.
Graduation Requirements: 124 credits; 6 credits of math/science; 11 credits of a foreign language or proven competence; computer course for math, science, business majors; senior project.
Computers on Campus: 140 computers available on campus for general student use. A computer is recommended for all students. A campus-wide network can be accessed from student residence rooms and from off-campus. Students can contact faculty members and/or advisers through e-mail. Computers for student use in computer center, computer labs, classrooms, library, dorms provide access to the Internet/World Wide Web, on- and off-campus e-mail addresses. Staffed computer lab on campus provides training in use of computers, software.

EXPENSES AND FINANCIAL AID

Expenses for 1997–98: *Application fee:* $25. Comprehensive fee of $21,980 includes full-time tuition ($17,350), mandatory fees ($230), and college room and board ($4400). College room only: $2000. Part-time tuition: $745 per credit.
Undergraduate Financial Aid: 90% of all full-time undergraduates enrolled in fall 1996 applied for aid; of these, 98% were judged to have need according to Federal Methodology, of whom 100% were aided. On average, 96% of need was met. *Financial aid deadline (priority):* 3/1. *Financial aid forms:* FAFSA required. Institutional form required for some.
LD Services Contact: Mr. Dan Krhin, Director, Student Support Services, Ripon College, 300 Seward Street, PO Box 248, Ripon, WI 54971, 414-748-8107. Fax: 414-748-7243.

RIVIER COLLEGE

Nashua, New Hampshire

LEARNING DISABILITIES SERVICES INFORMATION

Academic Support Services began offering services in 1991. Currently the program serves 20 undergraduates with LD. Services are also available to graduate students. Students diagnosed with ADD/ADHD are eligible for the same services available to students with LD.
Staff: 1 part-time staff member (coordinator).
Special Fees: No special fees are charged for services to students with LD.
Applications and admissions: *Required:* high school transcript, grade point average, class rank, courses completed, untimed SAT I, autobiographical statement, letters of recommendation, psychoeducational report completed within 3 years; *recommended:* high school extracurricular activities, IEP (Individualized Education Program), extended time SAT I or ACT, personal interview. Students may begin taking classes in fall or spring. *Application deadline:* continuous.

PROGRAM AND SERVICE COMPONENTS

Academic advising: Provided by unit staff members, academic advisers. Students with LD may take up to 17 credits each term; most take 15 credits; 12 credits required to maintain full-time status; 6 credits required to be eligible for financial aid.
Counseling services: Individual counseling, small-group counseling, career counseling.
Basic skills remediation: Offered in class-size groups by regular teachers. Available in math, written language, study skills.
Subject-area tutoring: Offered one-on-one by professional teachers, peer tutors. Available in some subjects.
Special courses: College survival skills, composition, word processing, math, study skills, career planning. Most offered for credit; most enter into overall grade point average.
Auxiliary aids: Tape recorders, word-processors with spell-check, personal computers.
Auxiliary services: Alternative test arrangements, notetakers, priority registration, advocacy.

GENERAL COLLEGE INFORMATION

Independent Roman Catholic, comprehensive, coed. Awards associate, bachelor's, master's degrees. Founded 1933. *Setting:* 60-acre suburban campus with easy access to Boston. *Endowment:* $9.3 million. *Educational spending 1995–96:* $2856 per undergrad. *Total enrollment:* 2,798. *Faculty:* 190 (66 full-time, 56% with terminal degrees, 124 part-time); student–undergrad faculty ratio is 13:1.
Enrollment Profile: 1,726 students from 8 states and territories, 12 other countries. 83% women, 17% men, 63% part-time, 78% state residents, 52% transferred in, 2% international, 43% 25 or older, 1% Native American, 2% Hispanic, 1% black, 2% Asian or Pacific Islander. *Retention:* 63% of 1995 full-time freshmen returned. *Areas of study chosen:* 22% health professions and related sciences, 14% business management and administrative services, 13% education, 4% fine arts, 4% psychology, 2% biological and life sciences, 2% communications and journalism, 2% computer and information sciences, 2% liberal arts/general studies, 1% English language/literature/letters, 1% foreign language and literature, 1% interdisciplinary studies, 1% mathematics, 1% prelaw, 1% premed, 1% prevet, 1% social sciences. *Most popular recent majors:* business administration/commerce/management, education, behavioral sciences.
First-Year Class: 124 total; 559 applied, 78% were accepted, 28% of whom enrolled. 10% from top 10% of their high school class, 34% from top quarter, 71% from top half.
Graduation Requirements: 60 credits for associate, 120 credits for bachelor's; 1 math course; 2 science courses; 2 semesters of a foreign language; computer course for business, education, English, paralegal studies majors; internship (some majors).
Computers on Campus: 90 computers available on campus for general student use. Computer purchase/lease plans available. A campus-wide network can be accessed from student residence rooms. Computers for student use in computer center, computer labs, dorms, imaging lab provide access to the Internet/World Wide Web. Staffed computer lab on campus provides training in use of computers, software. *Academic computing expenditure 1995–96:* $144,100.

EXPENSES AND FINANCIAL AID

Expenses for 1997–98: *Application fee:* $25. Comprehensive fee of $17,880 includes full-time tuition ($12,300), mandatory fees ($200), and college room and board ($5380). Part-time mandatory fees: $50 per semester. Part-time tuition per credit: $410 for day division, $188 for evening division.
Undergraduate Financial Aid: On average, 85% of need was met. *Financial aid deadline (priority):* 4/1. *Financial aid forms:* FAFSA required. State form required for some.
LD Services Contact: Ms. Lisa Baroody, Coordinator of Special Needs Services, Rivier College, 420 Main Street, Nashua, NH 03060-5086, 603-888-1311 Ext. 8497. Fax: 603-888-4049. Email: lbaroody@rivier.edu.

ROBERTS WESLEYAN COLLEGE

Rochester, New York

LEARNING DISABILITIES SERVICES INFORMATION

Learning Center began offering services in 1983. Currently the program serves 30 undergraduates with LD. Services are also available to graduate students. Students diagnosed with ADD/ADHD are eligible for the same services available to students with LD, as well as quiet testing room.
Staff: 1 full-time, 2 part-time staff members, including director. Services provided by remediation specialists.
Special Fees: No special fees are charged for services to students with LD.

Applications and admissions: *Required:* high school transcript, courses completed, autobiographical statement, letters of recommendation, psychoeducational report completed within 4 years; *recommended:* high school grade point average, class rank, IEP (Individualized Education Program), extended time SAT I or ACT, personal interview. Students may begin taking classes in fall or spring. *Application deadline:* continuous.

Special policies: The college has written policies regarding substitutions and waivers of degree requirements.

PROGRAM AND SERVICE COMPONENTS

Academic advising: Provided by unit staff members, academic advisers. Students with LD may take up to 16 semester credits each term; most take 14 semester credits; 12 semester credits required to maintain full-time status and be eligible for financial aid.

Auxiliary aids: Taped textbooks, tape recorders, word-processors with spell-check.

Auxiliary services: Alternative test arrangements, notetakers, time extensions for course completion.

GENERAL COLLEGE INFORMATION

Independent, comprehensive, coed, affiliated with Free Methodist Church of North America. Awards associate, bachelor's, master's degrees. Founded 1866. *Setting:* 75-acre suburban campus. *Endowment:* $7.2 million. *Total enrollment:* 1,337. *Faculty:* 121 (66 full-time, 45% with terminal degrees, 55 part-time); student–undergrad faculty ratio is 14:1.

Enrollment Profile: 1,134 students from 23 states and territories, 16 other countries. 64% women, 36% men, 10% part-time, 81% state residents, 17% transferred in, 5% international, 27% 25 or older, 1% Native American, 2% Hispanic, 4% black, 1% Asian or Pacific Islander. *Retention:* 76% of 1995 full-time freshmen returned. *Areas of study chosen:* 17% business management and administrative services, 11% education, 10% fine arts, 10% health professions and related sciences, 7% social sciences, 5% theology/religion, 4% liberal arts/general studies, 3% communications and journalism, 3% psychology, 2% biological and life sciences, 2% computer and information sciences, 2% English language/literature/letters, 1% mathematics. *Most popular recent majors:* education, nursing, business administration/commerce/management.

First-Year Class: 173 total; 476 applied, 89% were accepted, 41% of whom enrolled. 16% from top 10% of their high school class, 44% from top quarter, 79% from top half. 2 valedictorians.

Graduation Requirements: 62 semester hours for associate, 124 semester hours for bachelor's; basic math proficiency; 1 science course; 9 semester hours of a foreign language or the equivalent; computer course for math, business administration, communication, physics, criminal justice majors; internship (some majors); senior project for honors program students and some majors.

Computers on Campus: 60 computers available on campus for general student use. A campus-wide network can be accessed. Students can contact faculty members and/or advisers through e-mail. Computers for student use in computer center, computer labs, learning resource center, library provide access to the Internet/World Wide Web, on- and off-campus e-mail addresses. Staffed computer lab on campus provides training in use of computers, software. *Academic computing expenditure 1995–96:* $150,000.

EXPENSES AND FINANCIAL AID

Expenses for 1997–98: *Application fee:* $35. Comprehensive fee of $16,570 includes full-time tuition ($11,930), mandatory fees ($470), and college room and board ($4170). College room only: $2890. Part-time tuition: $235 per semester hour for 1 to 6 semester hours, $497 per semester hour for 6.5 or more semester hours. One-time mandatory fee: $90.

Undergraduate Financial Aid: 79% of all full-time undergraduates enrolled in fall 1996 applied for aid; of these, 96% were judged to have need according to Federal Methodology, of whom 99% were aided. On average, 91% of need was met. *Financial aid deadline (priority):* 3/15. *Financial aid forms:* FAFSA, institutional form required; CSS Financial Aid PROFILE acceptable. State form required for some.

LD Services Contact: Ms. Carol Ernsthausen, Director of Learning Center, Roberts Wesleyan College, 2301 Westside Drive, Rochester, NY 14624-1997, 716-594-6270. Fax: 716-594-6543.

ROCKY MOUNTAIN COLLEGE

Billings, Montana

LEARNING DISABILITIES SERVICES INFORMATION

Services for Academic Success began offering services in 1984. Currently the program serves 30 undergraduates with LD. Students diagnosed with ADD/ADHD are eligible for the same services available to students with LD.

Staff: 4 full-time staff members, including director. Services provided by counselors.

Special Fees: No special fees are charged for services to students with LD.

Applications and admissions: *Required:* high school transcript, grade point average, class rank, letters of recommendation; *recommended:* high school extracurricular activities, untimed or extended time SAT I or ACT, personal interview, autobiographical statement, psychoeducational report completed within 3 years. Students may begin taking classes any term. *Application deadline:* continuous.

PROGRAM AND SERVICE COMPONENTS

Academic advising: Provided by unit staff members, academic advisers. Students with LD may take up to 19 semester hours each term; most take 9 to 12 semester hours; 12 semester hours required to maintain full-time status; 6 semester hours required to be eligible for financial aid.

Counseling services: Individual counseling, small-group counseling, career counseling, self-advocacy training.

Basic skills remediation: Offered in small groups by regular teachers. Available in reading, math, written language, learning strategies, study skills, time management.

Subject-area tutoring: Offered one-on-one and in small groups by professional teachers, peer tutors. Available in all subjects.

Special courses: College survival skills, reading, vocabulary development, composition, learning strategies, word processing, time management, math, typing, study skills, career planning. Most offered for credit; most enter into overall grade point average.

Auxiliary aids: Taped textbooks, tape recorders, typewriters, word-processors with spell-check, personal computers.

Auxiliary services: Alternative test arrangements, notetakers, advocacy.

GENERAL COLLEGE INFORMATION

Independent interdenominational, 4-year, coed. Awards associate, bachelor's degrees. Founded 1878. *Setting:* 60-acre suburban campus. *Endowment:* $5.7 million. *Educational spending 1995–96:* $3717 per undergrad. *Total enrollment:* 744. *Faculty:* 75 (43 full-time, 74% with terminal degrees, 32 part-time); student–undergrad faculty ratio is 15:1.

Enrollment Profile: 744 students from 44 states and territories, 15 other countries. 53% women, 47% men, 13% part-time, 67% state residents, 29% live on campus, 40% transferred in, 7% international, 29% 25 or older, 6% Native American, 2% Hispanic, 1% black, 1% Asian or Pacific Islander. *Retention:* 68% of 1995 full-time freshmen returned. *Graduation:* 22% graduate in 4 years, 29% in 5 years, 30% in 6 years. *Areas of study chosen:* 15% education, 10% biological and life sciences, 9% business management and administrative services, 7% psychology, 5% health professions and related sciences, 5% natural resource sciences, 5% social sciences, 3% fine arts, 2% computer and information sciences, 2% English language/literature/letters, 2% mathematics, 1% philosophy. *Most popular recent majors:* business administration/commerce/management, education, psychology.

First-Year Class: 122 total; 396 applied, 99% were accepted, 31% of whom enrolled. 13% from top 10% of their high school class, 36% from top quarter, 61% from top half.

Graduation Requirements: 62 semester hours for associate, 124 semester hours for bachelor's; 2 math/science courses; computer course; internship (some majors); senior project for honors program students and some majors.

Computers on Campus: 40 computers available on campus for general student use. A computer is recommended for all students. A campus-wide network can be accessed from student residence rooms and from off-campus. Students can contact faculty members and/or advisers through e-mail. Computers for student use in computer center, computer labs, classrooms, library provide access to the Internet/World Wide Web, on- and off-campus e-mail addresses. Staffed computer lab on campus provides training in use of computers, software. *Academic computing expenditure 1995–96:* $7679.

Rocky Mountain College (continued)

EXPENSES AND FINANCIAL AID

Expenses for 1996–97: *Application fee:* $25. Comprehensive fee of $13,921 includes full-time tuition ($9994), mandatory fees ($105), and college room and board ($3822). Part-time tuition: $417 per semester hour.
Undergraduate Financial Aid: 89% of all full-time undergraduates enrolled in fall 1996 applied for aid; of these, 78% were judged to have need according to Federal Methodology, of whom 100% were aided. On average, 87% of need was met. *Financial aid deadline (priority):* 4/1. *Financial aid forms:* FAFSA, state form, institutional form required; CSS Financial Aid PROFILE acceptable.
LD Services Contact: Dr. Jane Van Dyk, Director, Services for Academic Success, Rocky Mountain College, 1511 Poly Drive, Billings, MT 59102, 406-657-1128. Fax: 406-259-9751.

ROSEMONT COLLEGE
Rosemont, Pennsylvania

LEARNING DISABILITIES SERVICES INFORMATION

Learning Resources Center/Assistant Academic Dean's Office currently serves 5 to 15 undergraduates with LD. Services are also available to graduate students. Students diagnosed with ADD/ADHD are eligible for the same services available to students with LD.
Staff: 1 part-time staff member (coordinator).
Special Fees: No special fees are charged for services to students with LD.
Applications and admissions: *Required:* documentation of disability (for receipt of services). Students may begin taking classes in fall, spring, or summer. *Application deadline:* continuous.

PROGRAM AND SERVICE COMPONENTS

Academic advising: Provided by academic advisers. Students with LD may take up to 5 courses each term; most take 4 to 5 courses; 4 courses required to maintain full-time status and be eligible for financial aid.
Counseling services: Individual counseling, self-advocacy training.
Subject-area tutoring: Offered one-on-one by peer tutors. Available in all subjects.
Auxiliary aids: Individually arranged.
Auxiliary services: Individually arranged.

GENERAL COLLEGE INFORMATION

Independent Roman Catholic, comprehensive, women only. Awards bachelor's, master's degrees. Founded 1921. *Setting:* 56-acre suburban campus with easy access to Philadelphia. *Endowment:* $3.3 million. *Total enrollment:* 846. *Faculty:* 123 (35 full-time, 80% with terminal degrees, 88 part-time); student–undergrad faculty ratio is 8:1.
Enrollment Profile: 736 students: 100% women, 20% part-time, 56% state residents, 25% transferred in, 6% international, 6% 25 or older, 2% Hispanic, 7% black, 5% Asian or Pacific Islander. *Retention:* 75% of 1995 full-time freshmen returned. *Graduation:* 67% graduate in 4 years, 68% in 5 years. *Areas of study chosen:* 18% psychology, 15% English language/literature/letters, 12% fine arts, 9% business management and administrative services, 8% social sciences, 5% biological and life sciences, 5% foreign language and literature, 5% interdisciplinary studies, 3% liberal arts/general studies, 2% mathematics, 1% philosophy, 1% theology/religion. *Most popular recent majors:* psychology, English, political science/government.
First-Year Class: 110 total; 320 applied, 67% were accepted, 51% of whom enrolled. 27% from top 10% of their high school class, 55% from top quarter, 84% from top half.
Graduation Requirements: 39 units; 1 year of calculus/lab science; 1 year of a foreign language; computer course for business, business/accounting, math, political science majors; internship (some majors); senior project (some majors).
Computers on Campus: 58 computers available on campus for general student use. Students can contact faculty members and/or advisers through e-mail. Computers for student use in computer labs, library, language center provide access to the Internet/World Wide Web, on- and off-campus e-mail addresses. Staffed computer lab on campus provides training in use of computers, software. *Academic computing expenditure 1995–96:* $100,000.

EXPENSES AND FINANCIAL AID

Expenses for 1997–98: *Application fee:* $35. Comprehensive fee of $19,840 includes full-time tuition ($12,960), mandatory fees ($380), and college room and board ($6500). Part-time tuition: $1560 per course. Part-time mandatory fees: $190 per semester.
Undergraduate Financial Aid: 75% of all full-time undergraduates enrolled in fall 1996 applied for aid; of these, 96% were judged to have need according to Federal Methodology, of whom 100% were aided. On average, 80% of need was met. *Financial aid deadline (priority):* 3/15. *Financial aid forms:* FAFSA required. State form required for some.
LD Services Contact: Ms. Sandra Zerby, Dean of Enrollment, Rosemont College, 1400 Montgomery Avenue, Rosemont, PA 19010-1699, 610-527-0200 Ext. 2966.

RUTGERS, THE STATE UNIVERSITY OF NEW JERSEY, CAMDEN COLLEGE OF ARTS AND SCIENCES
Camden, New Jersey

LEARNING DISABILITIES SERVICES INFORMATION

Office of Student Life and Development currently serves undergraduate and graduate students with LD. Students diagnosed with ADD/ADHD are eligible for the same services available to students with LD.
Staff: Services provided by remediation specialists, tutors, counselors, diagnostic specialists.
Special Fees: $200 to $275 for diagnostic testing.
Applications and admissions: *Required:* high school transcript, courses completed, extended time SAT I or ACT; *recommended:* high school extracurricular activities, IEP (Individualized Education Program), letters of recommendation, high school GPA or class rank. Students may begin taking classes in fall, spring, or summer. *Application deadline:* 12/15 (fall term), 11/1 (spring term).
Special policies: The college has written policies regarding substitutions and waivers of admissions requirements.

PROGRAM AND SERVICE COMPONENTS

Special preparation or orientation: Orientation offered individually by appointment.
Diagnostic testing: Reading, math, spelling, perceptual skills, study skills, learning strategies.
Academic advising: Provided by academic advisers. Students with LD may take up to 12 credits each term; most take 12 credits; 12 credits required to maintain full-time status; 6 credits required to be eligible for financial aid.
Counseling services: Individual counseling, small-group counseling, career counseling, self-advocacy training.
Basic skills remediation: Offered one-on-one and in small groups by teacher trainees, learning specialist; computer-aided instruction also offered. Available in reading, math, spelling, spoken language, written language, learning strategies, perceptual skills, study skills, time management, computer skills.
Subject-area tutoring: Offered one-on-one and in small groups by professional teachers, peer tutors. Available in all subjects.
Special courses: Reading, communication skills, composition, learning strategies, Internet use, time management, math, personal psychology, study skills, career planning, stress management, health and nutrition. Some offered for credit; some enter into overall grade point average.
Auxiliary aids: Taped textbooks, tape recorders, calculators, word-processors with spell-check, personal computers.
Auxiliary services: Alternative test arrangements, notetakers, sign language interpreter.

GENERAL COLLEGE INFORMATION

State-supported, 4-year, coed. Part of Rutgers, The State University of New Jersey. Awards bachelor's degrees. Founded 1927. *Setting:* 25-acre urban campus with easy access to Philadelphia. *System endowment:* $232.7 million. *System-wide research spending 1995–96:* $127.6 million. *Total university enrollment:* 47,812. *Faculty:*; student–undergrad faculty ratio is 14:1.
Enrollment Profile: 2,223 students from 18 states and territories, 14 other countries. 61% women, 39% men, 21% part-time, 97% state residents, 9% live on campus, 17% transferred in, 1% international, 31% 25 or older, 1% Native American, 7% Hispanic, 15% black, 6% Asian or Pacific Islander. *Retention:* 78% of 1995 full-time freshmen returned.

Graduation: 21% graduate in 4 years, 47% in 5 years, 51% in 6 years. *Areas of study chosen:* 25% business management and administrative services, 22% social sciences, 13% psychology, 8% English language/literature/letters, 7% health professions and related sciences, 5% biological and life sciences, 3% computer and information sciences, 2% fine arts, 2% foreign language and literature, 2% mathematics, 2% physical sciences, 1% area and ethnic studies, 1% education, 1% performing arts. *Most popular recent majors:* psychology, accounting, sociology.
First-Year Class: 189 total; 2,913 applied, 57% were accepted, 11% of whom enrolled. 20% from top 10% of their high school class, 52% from top quarter, 91% from top half. 1 valedictorian.
Graduation Requirements: 120 credit hours; 12 credit hours of math/science; 3 credit hours of a foreign language; computer course for business, math, economics, physics, art majors; senior project for honors program students.
Computers on Campus: 195 computers available on campus for general student use. Computer purchase/lease plans available. A campus-wide network can be accessed from student residence rooms and from off-campus. Students can contact faculty members and/or advisers through e-mail. Computers for student use in computer center, computer labs, learning resource center, classrooms, library, student center, dorms, student rooms provide access to the Internet/World Wide Web, on- and off-campus e-mail addresses. Staffed computer lab on campus provides training in use of computers, software. *System-wide academic computing expenditure 1995–96:* $10.7 million.

EXPENSES AND FINANCIAL AID

Expenses for 1997–98: *Application fee:* $50. State resident tuition: $4262 full-time, $138 per credit hour part-time. Nonresident tuition: $8676 full-time, $281 per credit hour part-time. Part-time mandatory fees per semester range from $336 to $396. Full-time mandatory fees: $928. College room and board: $5478. College room only: $3276.
Undergraduate Financial Aid: Of all full-time undergraduates enrolled in fall 1996, 86% of those who applied for aid were judged to have need according to Federal Methodology, of whom 97% were aided. On average, 90% of need was met. *Financial aid deadline (priority):* 3/1. *Financial aid forms:* FAFSA, financial aid transcript (for transfers) required. State form required for some.
LD Services Contact: Mr. William Edwards, Assistant Dean of Students/Coordinator for Students with Disabilities, Rutgers, The State University of New Jersey, Camden College of Arts and Sciences, 311 North 5th Street, Camden, NJ 08102, 609-225-6043. Fax: 609-225-6049.

RUTGERS, THE STATE UNIVERSITY OF NEW JERSEY, COLLEGE OF ENGINEERING

Piscataway, New Jersey

LEARNING DISABILITIES SERVICES INFORMATION

Services for Students with Disabilities currently serves undergraduate and graduate students with LD. Students diagnosed with ADD/ADHD are eligible for the same services available to students with LD.
Special Fees: $500 to $800 for diagnostic testing.
Applications and admissions: *Required:* high school transcript, courses completed, extended time SAT I or ACT; *recommended:* high school extracurricular activities, IEP (Individualized Education Program), letters of recommendation, high school GPA or class rank. Students may begin taking classes in fall or summer. *Application deadline:* 12/15.
Special policies: The college has written policies regarding substitutions and waivers of admissions requirements.

PROGRAM AND SERVICE COMPONENTS

Special preparation or orientation: Optional orientation offered individually by special arrangement as well as in a group.
Diagnostic testing: Intelligence, reading, motor abilities, perceptual skills, psychoneurology.
Academic advising: Provided by unit staff members, academic advisers. Students with LD may take up to 18 credits each term; 12 credits required to maintain full-time status; 12 credits (unless accommodation is needed) required to be eligible for financial aid.
Counseling services: Individual counseling, small-group counseling, career counseling.
Basic skills remediation: Offered one-on-one and in small groups by teacher trainees, Basic Skills Program staff. Available in math, written language, learning strategies, perceptual skills, study skills, social skills.
Subject-area tutoring: Offered one-on-one and in small groups by peer tutors, learning specialists. Available in most subjects.
Auxiliary aids: Typewriters, word-processors with spell-check, optical character readers.
Auxiliary services: Alternative test arrangements, priority registration, advocacy.
Campus support group: A special student organization is available to students with LD.

GENERAL COLLEGE INFORMATION

State-supported, 4-year, specialized, coed. Part of Rutgers, The State University of New Jersey. Awards bachelor's degrees (master of science, master of philosophy, and doctor of philosophy degrees are offered through the Graduate School, New Brunswick). Founded 1864. *Setting:* 2,695-acre small-town campus with easy access to New York City and Philadelphia. *System endowment:* $232.7 million. *System-wide research spending 1995–96:* $127.6 million. *Total university enrollment:* 47,812. *Faculty:* 127 full-time, 98% with terminal degrees; student–undergrad faculty ratio is 10:1.
Enrollment Profile: 2,156 students from 23 states and territories, 35 other countries. 20% women, 80% men, 3% part-time, 87% state residents, 63% live on campus, 4% transferred in, 5% international, 7% 25 or older, 1% Native American, 7% Hispanic, 8% black, 24% Asian or Pacific Islander. *Retention:* 94% of 1995 full-time freshmen returned. *Graduation:* 35% graduate in 4 years, 65% in 5 years, 73% in 6 years. *Areas of study chosen:* 100% engineering and applied sciences. *Most popular recent majors:* mechanical engineering, electrical engineering, civil engineering.
First-Year Class: 497 total; 3,031 applied, 72% were accepted, 23% of whom enrolled. 30% from top 10% of their high school class, 70% from top quarter, 97% from top half. 3 National Merit Scholars, 7 valedictorians.
Graduation Requirements: 131 credit hours; 16 credit hours of math; 19 credit hours of pure science; computer course; senior project for honors program students.
Computers on Campus: 850 computers available on campus for general student use. Computer purchase/lease plans available. A campus-wide network can be accessed from student residence rooms and from off-campus. Students can contact faculty members and/or advisers through e-mail. Computers for student use in computer center, computer labs, research center, learning resource center, classrooms, library, student center, dorms, student rooms, various locations provide access to the Internet/World Wide Web, on- and off-campus e-mail addresses. Staffed computer lab on campus (open 24 hours a day) provides training in use of computers, software. *System-wide academic computing expenditure 1995–96:* $10.7 million.

EXPENSES AND FINANCIAL AID

Expenses for 1997–98: *Application fee:* $50. State resident tuition: $4732 full-time, $156 per semester part-time. Nonresident tuition: $9626 full-time, $320 per semester part-time. Mandatory fees range from $1085 to $1124 full-time, $203 to $314 per year part-time, according to college of affiliation. College room and board: $5494 (minimum). College room only: $3292 (minimum).
Undergraduate Financial Aid: Of all full-time undergraduates enrolled in fall 1996, 82% of those who applied for aid were judged to have need according to Federal Methodology, of whom 98% were aided. On average, 82% of need was met. *Financial aid deadline (priority):* 3/1. *Financial aid forms:* FAFSA, financial aid transcript (for transfers) required. State form required for some.
LD Services Contact: Mr. Don Brown, Acting Director, Special Programs, Rutgers, The State University of New Jersey, College of Engineering, Engineering Building, Piscataway, NJ 08854, 732-445-2687.

RUTGERS, THE STATE UNIVERSITY OF NEW JERSEY, COLLEGE OF PHARMACY

Piscataway, New Jersey

LEARNING DISABILITIES SERVICES INFORMATION

Services for Students with Disabilities currently serves undergraduate and graduate students with LD. Students diagnosed with ADD/ADHD are eligible for the same services available to students with LD.
Special Fees: $500 to $800 for diagnostic testing.
Applications and admissions: *Required:* high school transcript, courses completed, extended time SAT I or ACT; *recommended:* high school extracurricular activities, IEP (Individualized Education Program), letters

Rutgers, The State University of New Jersey, College of Pharmacy (continued)

of recommendation, high school GPA or class rank. Students may begin taking classes in fall or summer. *Application deadline:* 12/15.
Special policies: The college has written policies regarding substitutions and waivers of admissions requirements.

PROGRAM AND SERVICE COMPONENTS

Special preparation or orientation: Optional orientation offered individually by special arrangement as well as in a group.
Diagnostic testing: Intelligence, reading, motor abilities, perceptual skills, psychoneurology.
Academic advising: Provided by unit staff members, academic advisers. Students with LD may take up to 18 credits each term; 12 credits required to maintain full-time status; 12 credits (unless accommodation is needed) required to be eligible for financial aid.
Counseling services: Individual counseling, small-group counseling, career counseling.
Basic skills remediation: Offered one-on-one and in small groups by teacher trainees, Basic Skills Program staff. Available in math, written language, learning strategies, perceptual skills, study skills, social skills.
Subject-area tutoring: Offered one-on-one and in small groups by peer tutors, learning specialists. Available in most subjects.
Auxiliary aids: Typewriters, word-processors with spell-check, optical character readers.
Auxiliary services: Alternative test arrangements, priority registration, advocacy.
Campus support group: A special student organization is available to students with LD.

GENERAL COLLEGE INFORMATION

State-supported, comprehensive, specialized, coed. Part of Rutgers, The State University of New Jersey. Awards bachelor's, doctoral degrees (in addition to the master of science and doctor of philosophy degrees offered through the Graduate School, New Brunswick, a two year doctor of pharmacy degree (Pharm. D) is offered through the College of Pharmacy). Founded 1927. *Setting:* 2,695-acre small-town campus with easy access to New York City and Philadelphia. *System endowment:* $232.7 million. *System-wide research spending 1995–96:* $127.6 million. *Total university enrollment:* 47,812; total unit enrollment: 986. *Faculty:* 55 full-time, 98% with terminal degrees; student–undergrad faculty ratio is 16:1.
Enrollment Profile: 899 students from 19 states and territories, 11 other countries. 62% women, 38% men, 1% part-time, 84% state residents, 66% live on campus, 3% transferred in, 2% international, 8% 25 or older, 1% Native American, 6% Hispanic, 5% black, 43% Asian or Pacific Islander. *Retention:* 96% of 1995 full-time freshmen returned. *Graduation:* 62% graduate in 5 years, 79% in 6 years. *Areas of study chosen:* 100% health professions and related sciences.
First-Year Class: 187 total; 1,539 applied, 39% were accepted, 31% of whom enrolled. 71% from top 10% of their high school class, 97% from top quarter, 100% from top half. 3 National Merit Scholars, 4 valedictorians.
Graduation Requirements: 172 credit hours; 1 semester each of calculus and statistics; internship; senior project for honors program students.
Computers on Campus: 850 computers available on campus for general student use. Computer purchase/lease plans available. A campus-wide network can be accessed from student residence rooms and from off-campus. Students can contact faculty members and/or advisers through e-mail. Computers for student use in computer center, computer labs, research center, learning resource center, classrooms, library, student center, dorms, student rooms, various locations provide access to the Internet/World Wide Web, on- and off-campus e-mail addresses. Staffed computer lab on campus (open 24 hours a day) provides training in use of computers, software. *System-wide academic computing expenditure 1995–96:* $10.7 million.

EXPENSES AND FINANCIAL AID

Expenses for 1997–98: *Application fee:* $50. State resident tuition: $4732 full-time, $156 per semester part-time. Nonresident tuition: $9626 full-time, $320 per semester part-time. Mandatory fees range from $1085 to $1124 full-time, $203 to $314 per year part-time, according to college of affiliation. College room and board: $5494 (minimum). College room only: $3292 (minimum).
Undergraduate Financial Aid: 63% of all full-time undergraduates enrolled in fall 1996 applied for aid; of these, 85% were judged to have need according to Federal Methodology, of whom 99% were aided. On average, 81% of need was met. *Financial aid deadline (priority):* 3/1. *Financial aid forms:* FAFSA, financial aid transcript (for transfers) required. State form required for some.

LD Services Contact: Ms. Nancy Cintron-Budet, Associate Professor, Rutgers, The State University of New Jersey, College of Pharmacy, Pharmacy Building, Piscataway, NJ 08854, 732-445-2678.

RUTGERS, THE STATE UNIVERSITY OF NEW JERSEY, COOK COLLEGE

New Brunswick, New Jersey

LEARNING DISABILITIES SERVICES INFORMATION

Services for Students with Disabilities currently serves 50 undergraduates with LD. Services are also available to graduate students. Students diagnosed with ADD/ADHD are eligible for the same services available to students with LD.
Staff: Includes director.
Special Fees: $500 to $800 for diagnostic testing.
Applications and admissions: *Required:* high school transcript, courses completed, extended time SAT I or ACT; *recommended:* high school extracurricular activities, IEP (Individualized Education Program), letters of recommendation, high school GPA or class rank. Students may begin taking classes in fall or summer. *Application deadline:* 12/15.
Special policies: The college has written policies regarding substitutions and waivers of admissions requirements.

PROGRAM AND SERVICE COMPONENTS

Special preparation or orientation: Optional orientation offered after classes begin.
Diagnostic testing: Intelligence, reading, motor abilities, perceptual skills, psychoneurology.
Academic advising: Provided by unit staff members, academic advisers. Students with LD may take up to 18 credits each term; 12 credits required to maintain full-time status; 12 credits (unless accommodation is needed) required to be eligible for financial aid.
Counseling services: Individual counseling, small-group counseling, career counseling.
Basic skills remediation: Offered one-on-one and in small groups by regular teachers, Basic Skills Program staff. Available in math, written language, learning strategies, perceptual skills, study skills, social skills.
Subject-area tutoring: Offered one-on-one and in small groups by professional teachers, peer tutors, learning specialists. Available in all subjects.
Auxiliary aids: Taped textbooks, word-processors with spell-check, personal computers, talking computers, optical character readers.
Auxiliary services: Alternative test arrangements, notetakers, priority registration, advocacy.
Campus support group: A special student organization is available to students with LD.

GENERAL COLLEGE INFORMATION

State-supported, 4-year, coed. Part of Rutgers, The State University of New Jersey. Awards bachelor's degrees. Founded 1921. *Setting:* 2,695-acre small-town campus with easy access to New York City and Philadelphia. *System endowment:* $232.7 million. *System-wide research spending 1995–96:* $127.6 million. *Total university enrollment:* 47,812. *Faculty:* 93 full-time, 98% with terminal degrees; student–undergrad faculty ratio is 16:1.
Enrollment Profile: 3,160 students from 25 states and territories, 20 other countries. 50% women, 50% men, 10% part-time, 90% state residents, 59% live on campus, 6% transferred in, 1% international, 11% 25 or older, 1% Native American, 6% Hispanic, 5% black, 12% Asian or Pacific Islander. *Retention:* 88% of 1995 full-time freshmen returned. *Graduation:* 36% graduate in 4 years, 62% in 5 years, 68% in 6 years. *Areas of study chosen:* 29% natural resource sciences, 24% biological and life sciences, 10% agriculture, 9% social sciences, 6% health professions and related sciences, 5% interdisciplinary studies, 4% physical sciences, 3% communications and journalism, 2% computer and information sciences, 2% education, 1% engineering and applied sciences. *Most popular recent majors:* environmental sciences, biology/biological sciences, business economics.
First-Year Class: 629 total; 7,653 applied, 61% were accepted, 14% of whom enrolled. 30% from top 10% of their high school class, 77% from top quarter, 97% from top half. 1 National Merit Scholar, 6 valedictorians.
Graduation Requirements: 128 credit hours; math/science requirements vary according to program; computer course; internship; senior project for honors program students and some majors.

Computers on Campus: 850 computers available on campus for general student use. Computer purchase/lease plans available. A campus-wide network can be accessed from student residence rooms and from off-campus. Students can contact faculty members and/or advisers through e-mail. Computers for student use in computer center, computer labs, research center, learning resource center, classrooms, library, student center, dorms, student rooms, various locations provide access to the Internet/World Wide Web, on- and off-campus e-mail addresses. Staffed computer lab on campus (open 24 hours a day) provides training in use of computers, software. *System-wide academic computing expenditure 1995–96:* $10.7 million.

EXPENSES AND FINANCIAL AID

Expenses for 1997–98: *Application fee:* $50. State resident tuition: $4732 full-time, $156 per credit hour part-time. Nonresident tuition: $9626 full-time, $320 per credit hour part-time. Part-time mandatory fees per year range from $238 to $298. Full-time mandatory fees: $1085. College room and board: $5506. College room only: $3304.
Undergraduate Financial Aid: Of all full-time undergraduates enrolled in fall 1996, 83% of those who applied for aid were judged to have need according to Federal Methodology, of whom 98% were aided. On average, 85% of need was met. *Financial aid deadline (priority):* 3/1. *Financial aid forms:* FAFSA, financial aid transcript (for transfers) required. State form required for some.
LD Services Contact: Mr. Andrew Campbell, Director, Community Affairs and Special Services, Rutgers, The State University of New Jersey, Cook College, Cook Campus Center, New Brunswick, NJ 08903, 732-932-1424. Fax: 732-932-1755. Email: acampbell@aesop.rutgers.edu.

RUTGERS, THE STATE UNIVERSITY OF NEW JERSEY, DOUGLASS COLLEGE

New Brunswick, New Jersey

LEARNING DISABILITIES SERVICES INFORMATION

Services for Students with Disabilities currently serves undergraduate and graduate students with LD. Students diagnosed with ADD/ADHD are eligible for the same services available to students with LD.
Special Fees: $500 to $800 for diagnostic testing.
Applications and admissions: *Required:* high school transcript, courses completed, extended time SAT I or ACT; *recommended:* high school extracurricular activities, IEP (Individualized Education Program), letters of recommendation, high school GPA or class rank. Students may begin taking classes in fall or summer. *Application deadline:* 12/15.
Special policies: The college has written policies regarding substitutions and waivers of admissions requirements.

PROGRAM AND SERVICE COMPONENTS

Special preparation or orientation: Orientation offered individually by special arrangement.
Diagnostic testing: Intelligence, reading, motor abilities, perceptual skills, psychoneurology.
Academic advising: Provided by unit staff members, academic advisers. Students with LD may take up to 18 credits each term; 12 credits required to maintain full-time status; 12 credits (unless accommodation is needed) required to be eligible for financial aid.
Counseling services: Individual counseling, small-group counseling, career counseling.
Basic skills remediation: Offered one-on-one and in small groups by teacher trainees, Basic Skills Program staff. Available in math, written language, learning strategies, perceptual skills, study skills, social skills.
Subject-area tutoring: Offered one-on-one and in small groups by peer tutors, learning specialists. Available in most subjects.
Auxiliary aids: Typewriters, word-processors with spell-check, optical character readers.
Auxiliary services: Alternative test arrangements, priority registration, advocacy.
Campus support group: A special student organization is available to students with LD.

GENERAL COLLEGE INFORMATION

State-supported, 4-year, women only. Part of Rutgers, The State University of New Jersey. Awards bachelor's degrees. Founded 1918. *Setting:* 2,695-acre small-town campus with easy access to New York City and Philadelphia. *System endowment:* $232.7 million. *System-wide research spending 1995–96:* $127.6 million. *Total university enrollment:* 47,812. *Faculty* (shared by Douglass College, Livingston College, Rutgers College, University College-New Brunswick): 817 full-time, 98% with terminal degrees; student–undergrad faculty ratio is 17:1.
Enrollment Profile: 2,965 students from 25 states and territories, 23 other countries. 100% women, 6% part-time, 94% state residents, 53% live on campus, 7% transferred in, 1% international, 7% 25 or older, 1% Native American, 7% Hispanic, 12% black, 14% Asian or Pacific Islander. *Retention:* 88% of 1995 full-time freshmen returned. *Graduation:* 53% graduate in 4 years, 72% in 5 years, 76% in 6 years. *Areas of study chosen:* 23% social sciences, 16% psychology, 12% communications and journalism, 9% English language/literature/letters, 6% area and ethnic studies, 6% biological and life sciences, 6% business management and administrative services, 4% foreign language and literature, 3% fine arts, 3% health professions and related sciences, 2% computer and information sciences, 2% mathematics, 2% performing arts, 1% interdisciplinary studies, 1% philosophy, 1% physical sciences. *Most popular recent majors:* psychology, English, political science/government.
First-Year Class: 623 total; 5,436 applied, 71% were accepted, 16% of whom enrolled. 19% from top 10% of their high school class, 55% from top quarter, 96% from top half. 1 National Merit Scholar, 5 valedictorians.
Graduation Requirements: 120 credit hours; 9 credit hours of math/science; proven proficiency in a foreign language at the intermediate level; computer course for math, psychology, statistics, business, art majors; senior project for honors program students and some majors.
Computers on Campus: 850 computers available on campus for general student use. Computer purchase/lease plans available. A campus-wide network can be accessed from student residence rooms and from off-campus. Students can contact faculty members and/or advisers through e-mail. Computers for student use in computer center, computer labs, research center, learning resource center, classrooms, library, student center, dorms, student rooms provide access to the Internet/World Wide Web, on- and off-campus e-mail addresses. Staffed computer lab on campus (open 24 hours a day) provides training in use of computers, software. *System-wide academic computing expenditure 1995–96:* $10.7 million.

EXPENSES AND FINANCIAL AID

Expenses for 1997–98: *Application fee:* $50. State resident tuition: $4262 full-time, $138 per credit hour part-time. Nonresident tuition: $8676 full-time, $281 per credit hour part-time. Part-time mandatory fees per year range from $254 to $314. Full-time mandatory fees: $1087. College room and board: $5504. College room only: $3302.
Undergraduate Financial Aid: Of all full-time undergraduates enrolled in fall 1996, 84% of those who applied for aid were judged to have need according to Federal Methodology, of whom 98% were aided. On average, 85% of need was met. *Financial aid deadline (priority):* 3/1. *Financial aid forms:* FAFSA, financial aid transcript (for transfers) required. State form required for some.
LD Services Contact: Ms. Susan Armstrong-West, Assistant Dean of Students, Rutgers, The State University of New Jersey, Douglass College, College Hall, New Brunswick, NJ 08903, 732-932-9630.

RUTGERS, THE STATE UNIVERSITY OF NEW JERSEY, LIVINGSTON COLLEGE

New Brunswick, New Jersey

LEARNING DISABILITIES SERVICES INFORMATION

Services for Students with Disabilities currently serves undergraduate and graduate students with LD. Students diagnosed with ADD/ADHD are eligible for the same services available to students with LD.
Special Fees: $500 to $800 for diagnostic testing.
Applications and admissions: *Required:* high school transcript, courses completed, extended time SAT I or ACT; *recommended:* high school extracurricular activities, IEP (Individualized Education Program), letters of recommendation, high school GPA or class rank. Students may begin taking classes in fall or summer. *Application deadline:* 12/15.
Special policies: The college has written policies regarding substitutions and waivers of admissions requirements.

PROGRAM AND SERVICE COMPONENTS

Special preparation or orientation: Optional orientation offered individually by special arrangement.
Diagnostic testing: Intelligence, reading, motor abilities, perceptual skills, psychoneurology.

Rutgers, The State University of New Jersey, Livingston College (continued)

Academic advising: Provided by unit staff members, academic advisers. Students with LD may take up to 18 credits each term; 12 credits required to maintain full-time status; 12 credits (unless accommodation is needed) required to be eligible for financial aid.

Counseling services: Individual counseling, small-group counseling, career counseling.

Basic skills remediation: Offered one-on-one and in small groups by teacher trainees, Basic Skills Program staff. Available in math, written language, learning strategies, perceptual skills, study skills, social skills.

Subject-area tutoring: Offered one-on-one and in small groups by peer tutors, learning specialists. Available in most subjects.

Auxiliary aids: Typewriters, word-processors with spell-check, optical character readers.

Auxiliary services: Alternative test arrangements, priority registration, advocacy.

Campus support group: A special student organization is available to students with LD.

GENERAL COLLEGE INFORMATION

State-supported, 4-year, coed. Part of Rutgers, The State University of New Jersey. Awards bachelor's degrees. Founded 1969. *Setting:* 2,695-acre small-town campus with easy access to New York City and Philadelphia. *System endowment:* $232.7 million. *System-wide research spending 1995–96:* $127.6 million. *Total university enrollment:* 47,812. *Faculty* (shared by Douglass College, Livingston College, Rutgers College, University College-New Brunswick): 817 full-time, 98% with terminal degrees; student–undergrad faculty ratio is 17:1.

Enrollment Profile: 3,032 students from 23 states and territories, 25 other countries. 39% women, 61% men, 6% part-time, 90% state residents, 44% live on campus, 8% transferred in, 2% international, 6% 25 or older, 1% Native American, 8% Hispanic, 13% black, 16% Asian or Pacific Islander. *Retention:* 87% of 1995 full-time freshmen returned. *Graduation:* 39% graduate in 4 years, 60% in 5 years, 66% in 6 years. *Areas of study chosen:* 30% social sciences, 13% psychology, 11% communications and journalism, 9% business management and administrative services, 6% English language/literature/letters, 5% health professions and related sciences, 3% area and ethnic studies, 3% biological and life sciences, 2% computer and information sciences, 2% mathematics, 2% physical sciences, 1% fine arts, 1% foreign language and literature, 1% philosophy. *Most popular recent majors:* psychology, economics, criminal justice.

First-Year Class: 659 total; 11,759 applied, 60% were accepted, 9% of whom enrolled. 10% from top 10% of their high school class, 49% from top quarter, 93% from top half. 1 valedictorian.

Graduation Requirements: 120 credit hours; 1 course each in math and science; computer course for math, psychology, statistics, business, art majors; senior project for honors program students.

Computers on Campus: 850 computers available on campus for general student use. Computer purchase/lease plans available. A campus-wide network can be accessed from student residence rooms and from off-campus. Students can contact faculty members and/or advisers through e-mail. Computers for student use in computer center, computer labs, research center, learning resource center, classrooms, library, student center, dorms, student rooms provide access to the Internet/World Wide Web, on- and off-campus e-mail addresses. Staffed computer lab on campus (open 24 hours a day) provides training in use of computers, software. *System-wide academic computing expenditure 1995–96:* $10.7 million.

EXPENSES AND FINANCIAL AID

Expenses for 1997–98: *Application fee:* $50. State resident tuition: $4262 full-time, $138 per credit hour part-time. Nonresident tuition: $8676 full-time, $281 per credit hour part-time. Part-time mandatory fees per year range from $203 to $263. Full-time mandatory fees: $1120. College room and board: $5506. College room only: $3304.

Undergraduate Financial Aid: Of all full-time undergraduates enrolled in fall 1996, 84% of those who applied for aid were judged to have need according to Federal Methodology, of whom 98% were aided. On average, 76% of need was met. *Financial aid deadline (priority):* 3/1. *Financial aid forms:* FAFSA, financial aid transcript (for transfers) required. State form required for some.

LD Services Contact: Mr. John E. Leoniak, Assistant Director, Student Services, Rutgers, The State University of New Jersey, Livingston College, Lucy Stone Hall, Piscataway, NJ 08854, 732-445-2050.

RUTGERS, THE STATE UNIVERSITY OF NEW JERSEY, MASON GROSS SCHOOL OF THE ARTS

New Brunswick, New Jersey

LEARNING DISABILITIES SERVICES INFORMATION

Services for Students with Disabilities currently serves 8 undergraduates with LD. Services are also available to graduate students. Students diagnosed with ADD/ADHD are eligible for the same services available to students with LD.

Special Fees: $500 to $800 for diagnostic testing.

Applications and admissions: *Required:* high school transcript, courses completed, extended time SAT I or ACT, audition/portfolio review/interview (depending on major); *recommended:* high school IEP (Individualized Education Program), letters of recommendation, high school GPA or class rank. Students may begin taking classes in fall or summer. *Application deadline:* 12/15.

Special policies: The college has written policies regarding substitutions and waivers of admissions requirements.

PROGRAM AND SERVICE COMPONENTS

Diagnostic testing: Intelligence, reading, motor abilities, perceptual skills, psychoneurology.

Academic advising: Provided by unit staff members, academic advisers. Students with LD may take up to 18 credits each term; 12 credits required to maintain full-time status; 12 credits (unless accommodation is needed) required to be eligible for financial aid.

Counseling services: Individual counseling, small-group counseling, career counseling.

Basic skills remediation: Offered one-on-one and in small groups by teacher trainees, Basic Skills Program staff. Available in math, written language, learning strategies, perceptual skills, study skills, social skills.

Subject-area tutoring: Offered one-on-one and in small groups by professional teachers, peer tutors, learning specialists. Available in most subjects.

Auxiliary aids: Typewriters, word-processors with spell-check, optical character readers.

Auxiliary services: Alternative test arrangements, priority registration, advocacy.

Campus support group: A special student organization is available to students with LD.

GENERAL COLLEGE INFORMATION

State-supported, comprehensive, coed. Part of Rutgers, The State University of New Jersey. Awards bachelor's, master's, doctoral degrees (also offers artist diploma). Founded 1976. *Setting:* 2,695-acre small-town campus with easy access to New York City and Philadelphia. *System endowment:* $232.7 million. *System-wide research spending 1995–96:* $127.6 million. *Total university enrollment:* 47,812; total unit enrollment: 725. *Faculty:* 77 full-time, 98% with terminal degrees; student–undergrad faculty ratio is 11:1.

Enrollment Profile: 499 students from 22 states and territories, 3 other countries. 54% women, 46% men, 3% part-time, 84% state residents, 49% live on campus, 7% transferred in, 1% international, 8% 25 or older, 1% Native American, 6% Hispanic, 7% black, 8% Asian or Pacific Islander. *Retention:* 89% of 1995 full-time freshmen returned. *Graduation:* 33% graduate in 4 years, 49% in 5 years, 53% in 6 years. *Areas of study chosen:* 59% performing arts, 41% fine arts. *Most popular recent majors:* art/fine arts, music, theater arts/drama.

First-Year Class: 120 total; 1,081 applied, 23% were accepted, 47% of whom enrolled. 13% from top 10% of their high school class, 40% from top quarter, 79% from top half. 1 valedictorian.

Graduation Requirements: 120 credit hours; 6 credit hours of math/science.

Computers on Campus: 850 computers available on campus for general student use. Computer purchase/lease plans available. A campus-wide network can be accessed from student residence rooms and from off-campus. Students can contact faculty members and/or advisers through e-mail. Computers for student use in computer center, computer labs, research center, learning resource center, classrooms, library, student center, dorms, student rooms, various locations provide access to the Internet/World Wide Web, on- and off-campus e-mail addresses. Staffed computer lab on campus (open 24 hours a day) provides training in use of computers, software. *System-wide academic computing expenditure 1995–96:* $10.7 million.

EXPENSES AND FINANCIAL AID

Expenses for 1997–98: *Application fee:* $50. State resident tuition: $4262 full-time, $138 per credit hour part-time. Nonresident tuition: $8676 full-time, $281 per credit hour part-time. Mandatory fees range from $1085 to $1124 full-time, $203 to $314 per year part-time, according to college of affiliation. College room and board: $5494 (minimum). College room only: $3292 (minimum).
Undergraduate Financial Aid: Of all full-time undergraduates enrolled in fall 1996, 82% of those who applied for aid were judged to have need according to Federal Methodology, of whom 98% were aided. On average, 81% of need was met. *Financial aid deadline (priority):* 3/1. *Financial aid forms:* FAFSA, financial aid transcript (for transfers) required. State form required for some.
LD Services Contact: Ms. Catherine Charlton, Assistant Dean, Rutgers, The State University of New Jersey, Mason Gross School of the Arts, PO Box 270, New Brunswick, NJ 08903, 732-932-9360 Ext. 508. Fax: 732-932-8794.

RUTGERS, THE STATE UNIVERSITY OF NEW JERSEY, NEWARK COLLEGE OF ARTS AND SCIENCES

Newark, New Jersey

LEARNING DISABILITIES SERVICES INFORMATION

Services for Students with Disabilities currently serves undergraduate and graduate students with LD. Students diagnosed with ADD/ADHD are eligible for the same services available to students with LD.
Special Fees: No special fees are charged for services to students with LD.
Applications and admissions: *Required:* high school transcript, courses completed, extended time SAT I or ACT; *recommended:* high school extracurricular activities, IEP (Individualized Education Program), letters of recommendation, high school GPA or class rank. Students may begin taking classes in fall, spring, or summer. *Application deadline:* 12/15 (fall term), 11/1 (spring term).
Special policies: The college has written policies regarding substitutions and waivers of admissions requirements.

PROGRAM AND SERVICE COMPONENTS

Academic advising: Provided by unit staff members, academic advisers. Students with LD may take up to 12 credits each term; 12 credits required to maintain full-time status and be eligible for financial aid.
Counseling services: Individual counseling, career counseling.
Basic skills remediation: Offered in class-size groups by regular teachers. Available in reading, math.
Subject-area tutoring: Offered one-on-one and in small groups by professional teachers, peer tutors. Available in some subjects.
Special courses: Communication skills, composition, math.
Auxiliary aids: Tape recorders, calculators, typewriters, word-processors with spell-check, personal computers.
Auxiliary services: Alternative test arrangements, priority registration.

GENERAL COLLEGE INFORMATION

State-supported, 4-year, coed. Part of Rutgers, The State University of New Jersey. Awards bachelor's degrees. Founded 1946. *Setting:* 34-acre urban campus with easy access to New York City. *System endowment:* $232.7 million. *System-wide research spending 1995–96:* $127.6 million. *Total university enrollment:* 47,812. *Faculty:*; student–undergrad faculty ratio is 15:1.
Enrollment Profile: 3,684 students from 17 states and territories, 42 other countries. 53% women, 47% men, 16% part-time, 94% state residents, 13% live on campus, 13% transferred in, 4% international, 21% 25 or older, 1% Native American, 21% Hispanic, 18% black, 16% Asian or Pacific Islander. *Retention:* 90% of 1995 full-time freshmen returned. *Graduation:* 21% graduate in 4 years, 46% in 5 years, 52% in 6 years. *Areas of study chosen:* 36% business management and administrative services, 15% biological and life sciences, 12% psychology, 11% social sciences, 4% computer and information sciences, 4% physical sciences, 2% communications and journalism, 2% English language/literature/letters, 2% fine arts, 2% foreign language and literature, 2% performing arts, 1% area and ethnic studies, 1% mathematics, 1% philosophy. *Most popular recent majors:* accounting, biology/biological sciences, psychology.
First-Year Class: 454 total; 4,789 applied, 52% were accepted, 18% of whom enrolled. 22% from top 10% of their high school class, 56% from top quarter, 92% from top half. 5 valedictorians.
Graduation Requirements: 124 credit hours; 11 credit hours of math/natural science; computer course for chemistry, art, accounting, business, math, applied physics, science, technology, society majors; internship (some majors); senior project for honors program students and some majors.
Computers on Campus: 570 computers available on campus for general student use. Computer purchase/lease plans available. A campuswide network can be accessed from student residence rooms and from off-campus. Students can contact faculty members and/or advisers through e-mail. Computers for student use in computer center, computer labs, research center, learning resource center, classrooms, library, dorms, student rooms, various locations provide access to the Internet/World Wide Web, on- and off-campus e-mail addresses. Staffed computer lab on campus provides training in use of computers, software. *System-wide academic computing expenditure 1995–96:* $27.5 million.

EXPENSES AND FINANCIAL AID

Expenses for 1997–98: *Application fee:* $50. State resident tuition: $4262 full-time, $138 per credit hour part-time. Nonresident tuition: $8676 full-time, $281 per credit hour part-time. Part-time mandatory fees per year range from $237 to $297. Full-time mandatory fees: $889. College room and board: $5500. College room only: $3289.
Undergraduate Financial Aid: Of all full-time undergraduates enrolled in fall 1996, 91% of those who applied for aid were judged to have need according to Federal Methodology, of whom 96% were aided. On average, 76% of need was met. *Financial aid deadline (priority):* 3/1. *Financial aid forms:* FAFSA, financial aid transcript (for transfers) required. State form required for some.
LD Services Contact: Mr. James Credle, Assistant Dean, Rutgers, The State University of New Jersey, Newark College of Arts and Sciences, Campus Center, Newark, NJ 07102, 973-353-5300.

RUTGERS, THE STATE UNIVERSITY OF NEW JERSEY, RUTGERS COLLEGE

New Brunswick, New Jersey

LEARNING DISABILITIES SERVICES INFORMATION

Services for Students with Disabilities currently serves 38 undergraduates with LD. Services are also available to graduate students. Students diagnosed with ADD/ADHD are eligible for the same services available to students with LD.
Staff: Includes coordinator.
Special Fees: $500 to $800 for diagnostic testing.
Applications and admissions: *Required:* high school transcript, courses completed, extended time SAT I or ACT; *recommended:* high school extracurricular activities, IEP (Individualized Education Program), letters of recommendation, high school GPA or class rank. Students may begin taking classes in fall or summer. *Application deadline:* 12/15.
Special policies: The college has written policies regarding substitutions and waivers of admissions requirements.

PROGRAM AND SERVICE COMPONENTS

Special preparation or orientation: Optional orientation offered individually by special arrangement as well as in a group.
Diagnostic testing: Intelligence, reading, motor abilities, perceptual skills, psychoneurology.
Academic advising: Provided by unit staff members, academic advisers. Students with LD may take up to 18 credits each term; 12 credits required to maintain full-time status; 12 credits (unless accommodation is needed) required to be eligible for financial aid.
Counseling services: Individual counseling, small-group counseling, career counseling.
Basic skills remediation: Offered one-on-one and in small groups by teacher trainees, Basic Skills Program staff. Available in math, written language, learning strategies, perceptual skills, study skills, social skills.
Subject-area tutoring: Offered one-on-one and in small groups by peer tutors, learning specialists. Available in most subjects.
Auxiliary aids: Typewriters, word-processors with spell-check, optical character readers.
Auxiliary services: Alternative test arrangements, priority registration, advocacy.

Rutgers, The State University of New Jersey, Rutgers College (continued)

Campus support group: A special student organization is available to students with LD.

GENERAL COLLEGE INFORMATION

State-supported, 4-year, coed. Part of Rutgers, The State University of New Jersey. Awards bachelor's degrees. Founded 1766. *Setting:* 2,695-acre small-town campus with easy access to New York City and Philadelphia. *System endowment:* $232.7 million. *System-wide research spending 1995–96:* $127.6 million. *Total university enrollment:* 47,812. *Faculty* (shared by Douglass College, Livingston College, Rutgers College, University College-New Brunswick): 817 full-time, 98% with terminal degrees; student–undergrad faculty ratio is 17:1.

Enrollment Profile: 10,317 students from 43 states and territories, 52 other countries. 51% women, 49% men, 4% part-time, 88% state residents, 54% live on campus, 6% transferred in, 2% international, 3% 25 or older, 1% Native American, 10% Hispanic, 7% black, 19% Asian or Pacific Islander. *Retention:* 92% of 1995 full-time freshmen returned. *Graduation:* 57% graduate in 4 years, 76% in 5 years, 80% in 6 years. *Areas of study chosen:* 26% social sciences, 14% psychology, 9% biological and life sciences, 9% business management and administrative services, 8% communications and journalism, 7% English language/literature/letters, 4% computer and information sciences, 4% foreign language and literature, 3% area and ethnic studies, 3% mathematics, 3% physical sciences, 2% fine arts, 2% health professions and related sciences, 1% performing arts, 1% philosophy. *Most popular recent majors:* psychology, political science/government, biology/biological sciences.

First-Year Class: 2,273 total; 16,683 applied, 52% were accepted, 26% of whom enrolled. 35% from top 10% of their high school class, 80% from top quarter, 98% from top half. 18 National Merit Scholars, 29 valedictorians.

Graduation Requirements: 120 credit hours; 2 courses each in quantitative skills and natural science; computer course for math, business, art, psychology, statistics majors; internship (some majors); senior project for honors program students.

Computers on Campus: 690 computers available on campus for general student use. Computer purchase/lease plans available. A campus-wide network can be accessed from student residence rooms and from off-campus. Students can contact faculty members and/or advisers through e-mail. Computers for student use in computer center, computer labs, research center, learning resource center, classrooms, library, student center, dorms, student rooms, various locations provide access to the Internet/World Wide Web, on- and off-campus e-mail addresses. Staffed computer lab on campus (open 24 hours a day) provides training in use of computers, software. *System-wide academic computing expenditure 1995–96:* $10.7 million.

EXPENSES AND FINANCIAL AID

Expenses for 1997–98: *Application fee:* $50. State resident tuition: $4262 full-time, $138 per credit hour part-time. Nonresident tuition: $8676 full-time, $281 per credit hour part-time. Part-time mandatory fees per year range from $226 to $286. Full-time mandatory fees: $1124. College room and board: $5494. College room only: $3292.

Undergraduate Financial Aid: Of all full-time undergraduates enrolled in fall 1996, 82% of those who applied for aid were judged to have need according to Federal Methodology, of whom 98% were aided. On average, 84% of need was met. *Financial aid deadline (priority):* 3/1. *Financial aid forms:* FAFSA, financial aid transcript (for transfers) required. State form required for some.

LD Services Contact: Mr. Clarence Shive, Assistant Dean, Rutgers, The State University of New Jersey, Rutgers College, Bishop House, Room 107, New Brunswick, NJ 08903, 732-932-7109. Fax: 732-932-1507.

RUTGERS, THE STATE UNIVERSITY OF NEW JERSEY, UNIVERSITY COLLEGE–CAMDEN

Camden, New Jersey

LEARNING DISABILITIES SERVICES INFORMATION

Office of Student Life and Development currently serves 21 undergraduates with LD. Services are also available to graduate students. Students diagnosed with ADD/ADHD are eligible for the same services available to students with LD.

Staff: Services provided by remediation specialists, tutors, counselors, diagnostic specialists.

Special Fees: $200 to $275 for diagnostic testing.

Applications and admissions: *Required:* high school transcript, courses completed, extended time SAT I or ACT; *recommended:* high school extracurricular activities, IEP (Individualized Education Program), letters of recommendation, high school GPA or class rank. Students may begin taking classes in fall, spring, or summer. *Application deadline:* 12/15 (fall term), 11/1 (spring term).

Special policies: The college has written policies regarding substitutions and waivers of admissions requirements.

PROGRAM AND SERVICE COMPONENTS

Special preparation or orientation: Orientation offered individually by appointment.

Diagnostic testing: Reading, math, spelling, perceptual skills, study skills, learning strategies.

Academic advising: Provided by academic advisers. Students with LD may take up to 12 credits each term; most take 12 credits; 12 credits required to maintain full-time status; 6 credits required to be eligible for financial aid.

Counseling services: Individual counseling, small-group counseling, career counseling, self-advocacy training.

Basic skills remediation: Offered one-on-one and in small groups by teacher trainees, learning specialist; computer-aided instruction also offered. Available in reading, math, spelling, spoken language, written language, learning strategies, perceptual skills, study skills, time management, computer skills.

Subject-area tutoring: Offered one-on-one and in small groups by professional teachers, peer tutors. Available in all subjects.

Special courses: Reading, communication skills, composition, learning strategies, Internet use, time management, math, personal psychology, study skills, career planning, stress management, health and nutrition. Some offered for credit; some enter into overall grade point average.

Auxiliary aids: Taped textbooks, tape recorders, calculators, word-processors with spell-check, personal computers.

Auxiliary services: Alternative test arrangements, notetakers, sign language interpreter.

GENERAL COLLEGE INFORMATION

State-supported, 4-year, coed. Part of Rutgers, The State University of New Jersey. Awards bachelor's degrees (offers primarily part-time evening degree programs). Founded 1950. *Setting:* 25-acre urban campus with easy access to Philadelphia. *System endowment:* $232.7 million. *System-wide research spending 1995–96:* $127.6 million. *Total university enrollment:* 47,812. *Faculty:*; student–undergrad faculty ratio is 14:1.

Enrollment Profile: 714 students from 2 states and territories. 54% women, 46% men, 54% part-time, 98% state residents, 25% transferred in, 59% 25 or older, 1% Native American, 2% Hispanic, 16% black, 4% Asian or Pacific Islander. *Areas of study chosen:* 25% psychology, 23% English language/literature/letters, 21% social sciences, 15% computer and information sciences, 4% physical sciences, 2% biological and life sciences. *Most popular recent majors:* psychology, English, computer science.

First-Year Class: 64 total; 372 applied, 70% were accepted, 25% of whom enrolled.

Graduation Requirements: 120 credit hours; 12 credit hours of math/science; 3 credit hours of a foreign language; computer course for business, math, physics, economics, art majors; internship (some majors); senior project for honors program students and some majors.

Computers on Campus: 195 computers available on campus for general student use. Computer purchase/lease plans available. A campus-wide network can be accessed from off-campus. Students can contact faculty members and/or advisers through e-mail. Computers for student use in computer center, computer labs, learning resource center, classrooms, library, student center provide access to the Internet/World Wide Web, on- and off-campus e-mail addresses. Staffed computer lab on campus provides training in use of computers, software. *System-wide academic computing expenditure 1995–96:* $10.7 million.

EXPENSES AND FINANCIAL AID

Expenses for 1997–98: *Application fee:* $50. State resident tuition: $138 per credit hour part-time. Nonresident tuition: $281 per credit hour part-time. Part-time mandatory fees per semester range from $148 to $178.

Undergraduate Financial Aid: Of all full-time undergraduates enrolled in fall 1996, 82% of those who applied for aid were judged to have need according to Federal Methodology, of whom 98% were aided. On average, 94% of need was met. *Financial aid deadline (priority):* 3/1.

Financial aid forms: FAFSA, CSS Financial Aid PROFILE, financial aid transcript (for transfers) required. State form required for some.
LD Services Contact: Mr. William Edwards, Assistant Dean of Students/ Coordinator for Students with Disabilities, Rutgers, The State University of New Jersey, University College–Camden, 311 North 5th Street, Camden, NJ 08102, 609-225-6043. Fax: 609-225-6049.

RUTGERS, THE STATE UNIVERSITY OF NEW JERSEY, UNIVERSITY COLLEGE–NEWARK

Newark, New Jersey

LEARNING DISABILITIES SERVICES INFORMATION

Services for Students with Disabilities currently serves undergraduate and graduate students with LD. Students diagnosed with ADD/ ADHD are eligible for the same services available to students with LD.
Special Fees: No special fees are charged for services to students with LD.
Applications and admissions: *Required:* high school transcript, courses completed, extended time SAT I or ACT; *recommended:* high school extracurricular activities, IEP (Individualized Education Program), letters of recommendation, high school GPA or class rank. Students may begin taking classes in fall, spring, or summer. *Application deadline:* 12/15 (fall term), 11/1 (spring term).
Special policies: The college has written policies regarding substitutions and waivers of admissions requirements.

PROGRAM AND SERVICE COMPONENTS

Academic advising: Provided by unit staff members, academic advisers. Students with LD may take up to 12 credits each term; 12 credits required to maintain full-time status and be eligible for financial aid.
Counseling services: Individual counseling, career counseling.
Basic skills remediation: Offered in class-size groups by regular teachers. Available in reading, math.
Subject-area tutoring: Offered one-on-one and in small groups by professional teachers, peer tutors. Available in some subjects.
Special courses: Communication skills, composition, math.
Auxiliary aids: Tape recorders, calculators, typewriters, word-processors with spell-check, personal computers.
Auxiliary services: Alternative test arrangements, priority registration.

GENERAL COLLEGE INFORMATION

State-supported, 4-year, coed. Part of Rutgers, The State University of New Jersey. Awards bachelor's degrees (offers primarily part-time evening degree programs). Founded 1934. *Setting:* 34-acre urban campus with easy access to New York City. *System endowment:* $232.7 million. *System-wide research spending 1995–96:* $127.6 million. *Total university enrollment:* 47,812. *Faculty:*; student–undergrad faculty ratio is 15:1.
Enrollment Profile: 1,776 students from 5 states and territories. 54% women, 46% men, 62% part-time, 98% state residents, 16% transferred in, 1% international, 56% 25 or older, 1% Native American, 16% Hispanic, 32% black, 12% Asian or Pacific Islander. *Areas of study chosen:* 48% business management and administrative services, 10% psychology, 10% social sciences, 9% English language/literature/letters, 5% computer and information sciences, 1% philosophy. *Most popular recent majors:* accounting, criminal justice, business administration/commerce/ management.
First-Year Class: 101 total; 291 applied, 73% were accepted, 48% of whom enrolled.
Graduation Requirements: 124 credit hours; 3 math/science courses; computer course for business majors; internship (some majors); senior project for honors program students and some majors.
Computers on Campus: 570 computers available on campus for general student use. Computer purchase/lease plans available. A campus-wide network can be accessed from off-campus. Students can contact faculty members and/or advisers through e-mail. Computers for student use in computer center, computer labs, research center, learning resource center, classrooms, library provide access to the Internet/World Wide Web, on- and off-campus e-mail addresses. Staffed computer lab on campus provides training in use of computers, software. *System-wide academic computing expenditure 1995–96:* $10.7 million.

EXPENSES AND FINANCIAL AID

Expenses for 1997–98: *Application fee:* $50. State resident tuition: $138 per credit hour part-time. Nonresident tuition: $281 per credit hour part-time. Part-time mandatory fees per semester range from $121 to $151.
Undergraduate Financial Aid: Of all full-time undergraduates enrolled in fall 1996, 91% of those who applied for aid were judged to have need according to Federal Methodology, of whom 97% were aided. On average, 82% of need was met. *Financial aid deadline (priority):* 3/1. *Financial aid forms:* FAFSA, financial aid transcript (for transfers) required. State form required for some.
LD Services Contact: Mr. James Credle, Assistant Dean, Rutgers, The State University of New Jersey, University College–Newark, Campus Center, Newark, NJ 07102, 973-353-5300.

RUTGERS, THE STATE UNIVERSITY OF NEW JERSEY, UNIVERSITY COLLEGE–NEW BRUNSWICK

New Brunswick, New Jersey

LEARNING DISABILITIES SERVICES INFORMATION

University College Counseling Office currently serves 18 undergraduates with LD. Services are also available to graduate students. Students diagnosed with ADD/ADHD are eligible for the same services available to students with LD.
Staff: 1 full-time staff member (coordinator).
Special Fees: $200 to $300 for diagnostic testing.
Applications and admissions: *Required:* high school transcript, college transcripts (if transferring from another college), psychoeducational report (if accommodations are required). Students may begin taking classes in fall, spring, or summer. *Application deadline:* 7/15 (fall term), 12/2 (spring term).

PROGRAM AND SERVICE COMPONENTS

Diagnostic testing: Intelligence, reading, math, spelling, handwriting, spoken language, written language, motor abilities, perceptual skills, personality.
Academic advising: Provided by unit staff members, academic advisers. Students with LD may take up to 13 credits each term; most take 6 credits; 12 credits required to maintain full-time status; 6 credits (part-time), 12 credits (full-time) required to be eligible for financial aid.
Counseling services: Individual counseling.
Basic skills remediation: Offered one-on-one and in small groups by teacher trainees, Basic Skills Program staff. Available in math, written language, perceptual skills, study skills, social skills.
Subject-area tutoring: Offered one-on-one and in small groups by professional teachers, peer tutors. Available in some subjects.
Special courses: College survival skills, reading, composition, learning strategies, word processing, Internet use, time management, math, study skills, career planning, stress management, health and nutrition. None offered for credit.
Auxiliary services: Alternative test arrangements, notetakers.
Campus support group: A special student organization is available to students with LD.

GENERAL COLLEGE INFORMATION

State-supported, 4-year, coed. Part of Rutgers, The State University of New Jersey. Awards bachelor's degrees (offers primarily part-time degree programs). Founded 1934. *Setting:* 2,694-acre small-town campus with easy access to New York City and Philadelphia. *System endowment:* $232.7 million. *System-wide research spending 1995–96:* $127.6 million. *Total university enrollment:* 47,812. *Faculty* (shared by Douglass College, Livingston College, Rutgers College, University College-New Brunswick): 817 full-time, 98% with terminal degrees; student–undergrad faculty ratio is 17:1.
Enrollment Profile: 2,911 students from 4 states and territories, 3 other countries. 54% women, 46% men, 78% part-time, 99% state residents, 19% transferred in, 1% international, 71% 25 or older, 1% Native American, 5% Hispanic, 7% black, 8% Asian or Pacific Islander. *Areas of study chosen:* 27% social sciences, 12% business management and administrative services, 12% psychology, 10% English language/literature/letters, 9% communications and journalism, 8% computer and information sciences, 4% fine arts, 3% biological and life sciences, 3% physical sciences, 2% foreign language and literature, 2% mathematics, 1% area and

Rutgers, The State University of New Jersey, University College–New Brunswick (continued)

ethnic studies, 1% interdisciplinary studies, 1% performing arts, 1% philosophy. *Most popular recent majors:* psychology, English, computer science.

First-Year Class: 26 total; 50 applied, 64% were accepted, 81% of whom enrolled.

Graduation Requirements: 120 credit hours; 4 math/science courses; computer course for math majors; senior project for honors program students and some majors.

Computers on Campus: 850 computers available on campus for general student use. Computer purchase/lease plans available. A campus-wide network can be accessed from off-campus. Students can contact faculty members and/or advisers through e-mail. Computers for student use in computer center, computer labs, research center, learning resource center, classrooms, library, student center provide access to the Internet/World Wide Web, on- and off-campus e-mail addresses. Staffed computer lab on campus (open 24 hours a day) provides training in use of computers, software. *System-wide academic computing expenditure 1995–96:* $10.7 million.

EXPENSES AND FINANCIAL AID

Expenses for 1997–98: *Application fee:* $50. State resident tuition: $138 per credit hour part-time. Nonresident tuition: $281 per credit hour part-time. Part-time mandatory fees per semester range from $120 to $150.

Undergraduate Financial Aid: Of all full-time undergraduates enrolled in fall 1996, 90% of those who applied for aid were judged to have need according to Federal Methodology, of whom 98% were aided. On average, 87% of need was met. *Financial aid deadline (priority):* 3/1. *Financial aid forms:* FAFSA, financial aid transcript (for transfers) required. State form required for some.

LD Services Contact: Jean Romsted, Counselor/Coordinator for Students with Disabilities, Rutgers, The State University of New Jersey, University College–New Brunswick, 14 College Avenue, New Brunswick, NJ 08903, 732-932-8093. Fax: 732-932-1903. Email: jromsted@rci.rutgers.edu.

SAGINAW VALLEY STATE UNIVERSITY

University Center, Michigan

LEARNING DISABILITIES SERVICES INFORMATION

Disability Services currently serves 35 undergraduates with LD. Services are also available to graduate students. Students diagnosed with ADD/ADHD are eligible for the same services available to students with LD, as well as on-campus diagnostic testing.

Staff: 1 part-time staff member (coordinator).

Special Fees: No special fees are charged for services to students with LD.

Applications and admissions: *Recommended:* high school transcript, grade point average, courses completed, untimed or extended time ACT, letters of recommendation. Students may begin taking classes any term. *Application deadline:* continuous.

PROGRAM AND SERVICE COMPONENTS

Academic advising: Provided by academic advisers. Students with LD may take up to 15 credits each term; most take 9 to 12 credits; 12 credits required to maintain full-time status; 6 credits required to be eligible for financial aid.

Counseling services: Individual counseling, career counseling.

Special courses: Reading, vocabulary development, composition, learning strategies, time management, math, study skills, career planning. None offered for credit; none enter into overall grade point average.

Auxiliary aids: Tape recorders, word-processors with spell-check, talking computers, optical character readers.

Auxiliary services: Alternative test arrangements, notetakers, advocacy.

Campus support group: A special student organization is available to students with LD.

GENERAL COLLEGE INFORMATION

State-supported, comprehensive, coed. Part of Michigan Department of Education. Awards bachelor's, master's degrees. Founded 1963. *Setting:* 782-acre rural campus. *Research spending 1995–96:* $1.3 million. *Educational spending 1995–96:* $3029 per undergrad. *Total enrollment:* 7,338. *Undergraduate faculty:* 461 (186 full-time, 83% with terminal degrees, 275 part-time); student–undergrad faculty ratio is 34:1.

Enrollment Profile: 6,407 students from 14 states and territories, 31 other countries. 60% women, 40% men, 42% part-time, 99% state residents, 10% transferred in, 25% 25 or older, 1% Native American, 4% Hispanic, 6% black, 1% Asian or Pacific Islander. *Retention:* 68% of 1995 full-time freshmen returned. *Graduation:* 5% graduate in 4 years, 22% in 5 years, 31% in 6 years. *Areas of study chosen:* 25% education, 12% business management and administrative services, 12% health professions and related sciences, 6% engineering and applied sciences, 4% computer and information sciences, 4% psychology, 3% biological and life sciences, 3% social sciences, 2% English language/literature/letters, 2% performing arts, 1% communications and journalism, 1% foreign language and literature, 1% interdisciplinary studies, 1% mathematics, 1% physical sciences. *Most popular recent majors:* business administration/commerce/management, elementary education, criminal justice.

First-Year Class: 784 total; 1,681 applied, 92% were accepted, 51% of whom enrolled.

Graduation Requirements: 124 credit hours; 4 credit hours of math; 7 credit hours of natural science; computer course for business, engineering, chemistry majors; internship (some majors); senior project.

Computers on Campus: 340 computers available on campus for general student use. A campus-wide network can be accessed from off-campus. Students can contact faculty members and/or advisers through e-mail. Computers for student use in computer center, computer labs, research center, learning resource center, classrooms, library provide access to the Internet/World Wide Web. Staffed computer lab on campus provides training in use of computers, software. *Academic computing expenditure 1995–96:* $507,028.

EXPENSES AND FINANCIAL AID

Expenses for 1996–97: State resident tuition: $3092 full-time, $99.75 per credit hour part-time. Nonresident tuition: $6470 full-time, $208.70 per credit hour part-time. Part-time mandatory fees: $8.30 per credit hour. Full-time mandatory fees: $257. College room and board: $4140.

Undergraduate Financial Aid: 78% of all full-time undergraduates enrolled in fall 1996 applied for aid; of these, 70% were judged to have need according to Federal Methodology, of whom 100% were aided. On average, 91% of need was met. *Financial aid deadline:* continuous. *Financial aid forms:* FAFSA acceptable. CSS Financial Aid PROFILE required for some.

LD Services Contact: Ms. Cynthia Woiderski, Coordinator, Saginaw Valley State University, 173 Wickes Hall, 7400 Bay Road, University Center, MI 48710, 517-792-5600.

ST. AMBROSE UNIVERSITY

Davenport, Iowa

LEARNING DISABILITIES SERVICES INFORMATION

Services for Students with Disabilities began offering services in 1990. Currently the program serves 85 undergraduates with LD. Services are also available to graduate students. Students diagnosed with ADD/ADHD are eligible for the same services available to students with LD, as well as medication counseling.

Staff: 4 full-time staff members, including coordinator. Services provided by tutors, LD specialist, graduate assistants.

Special Fees: No special fees are charged for services to students with LD.

Applications and admissions: *Required:* high school transcript, grade point average, class rank, untimed ACT, psychoeducational report completed within 3 years; *recommended:* untimed or extended time SAT I, extended time ACT, letters of recommendation. Students may begin taking classes in fall, spring, or summer. *Application deadline:* continuous.

Special policies: The college has written policies regarding grade forgiveness.

PROGRAM AND SERVICE COMPONENTS

Special preparation or orientation: Optional summer program offered prior to entering college. Optional orientation offered before registration and during registration.

Academic advising: Provided by unit staff members, academic advisers. Students with LD may take up to 18 credit hours each term; most take 12 to 15 credit hours; 12 credit hours required to maintain full-time status; 6 credit hours (part-time), 12 credit hours (full-time) required to be eligible for financial aid.

Counseling services: Individual counseling, small-group counseling, career counseling, self-advocacy training.

Basic skills remediation: Offered one-on-one and in class-size groups by regular teachers, LD specialist. Available in reading, math, written language, learning strategies, study skills, time management.
Subject-area tutoring: Offered one-on-one and in small groups by peer tutors, LD specialist, graduate assistants. Available in all subjects.
Special courses: College survival skills, reading, vocabulary development, composition, learning strategies, word processing, math, personal psychology, study skills, career planning. All offered for credit; all enter into overall grade point average.
Auxiliary aids: Taped textbooks, tape recorders, word-processors with spell-check, personal computers, talking computers, optical character readers.
Auxiliary services: Alternative test arrangements, notetakers, advocacy.
Campus support group: A special student organization is available to students with LD.

GENERAL COLLEGE INFORMATION

Independent Roman Catholic, comprehensive, coed. Awards bachelor's, master's degrees. Founded 1882. *Setting:* 11-acre urban campus. *Endowment:* $15.5 million. *Educational spending 1995–96:* $3100 per undergrad. *Total enrollment:* 2,680. *Faculty:* 200 (118 full-time, 95% with terminal degrees, 82 part-time); student–undergrad faculty ratio is 16:1.
Enrollment Profile: 1,820 students from 19 states and territories, 9 other countries. 57% women, 43% men, 20% part-time, 69% state residents, 44% live on campus, 35% transferred in, 1% international, 36% 25 or older, 3% Hispanic, 4% black. *Retention:* 88% of 1995 full-time freshmen returned. *Areas of study chosen:* 22% health professions and related sciences, 18% communications and journalism, 16% business management and administrative services, 13% engineering and applied sciences, 12% computer and information sciences, 10% psychology, 5% fine arts, 4% social sciences. *Most popular recent majors:* business administration/commerce/management, biology/biological sciences, communication.
First-Year Class: 306 total; 913 applied, 85% were accepted, 39% of whom enrolled. 15% from top 10% of their high school class, 45% from top quarter, 85% from top half. 2 National Merit Scholars, 19 valedictorians.
Graduation Requirements: 120 credit hours; 9 credit hours of math/science; computer course for accounting, business administration, industrial engineering, natural science, math majors; internship (some majors); senior project (some majors).
Computers on Campus: 80 computers available on campus for general student use. Computer purchase/lease plans available. A campus-wide network can be accessed from student residence rooms. Computers for student use in computer center, library, Cosgrove, Hays Halls. Staffed computer lab on campus. *Academic computing expenditure 1995–96:* $232,880.

EXPENSES AND FINANCIAL AID

Estimated Expenses for 1997–98: *Application fee:* $15. Comprehensive fee of $16,700 includes full-time tuition ($12,300) and college room and board ($4400 minimum). Part-time tuition: $385 per credit hour.
Undergraduate Financial Aid: Of all full-time undergraduates enrolled in fall 1996, 89% of those who applied for aid were judged to have need according to Federal Methodology, of whom 100% were aided. On average, 90% of need was met. *Financial aid deadline (priority):* 3/15. *Financial aid forms:* FAFSA, institutional form required. State form required for some.
LD Services Contact: Mr. Andy Kaiser, Coordinator, St. Ambrose University, 518 West Locust Street, Davenport, IA 52803, 319-333-6275. Fax: 319-333-6243.

ST. BONAVENTURE UNIVERSITY

St. Bonaventure, New York

LEARNING DISABILITIES SERVICES INFORMATION

Services for Students with Disabilities began offering services in 1991. Currently the program serves 28 undergraduates with LD. Services are also available to graduate students. Students diagnosed with ADD/ADHD are eligible for the same services available to students with LD.
Staff: 1 full-time staff member (coordinator). Services provided by remediation specialists, tutors, counselors.
Special Fees: No special fees are charged for services to students with LD.
Applications and admissions: *Required:* high school transcript, courses completed, untimed SAT I or ACT, letters of recommendation; *recommended:* high school grade point average, class rank, extracurricular activities, personal interview, autobiographical statement. Students may begin taking classes any term. *Application deadline:* continuous.

Special policies: The college has written policies regarding substitutions and waivers of admissions, graduation, and degree requirements.

PROGRAM AND SERVICE COMPONENTS

Academic advising: Provided by unit staff members, academic advisers. Students with LD may take up to 18 credit hours each term; most take 12 credit hours during the first semester (15 credit hours thereafter); 12 credit hours (fewer than 12 requires a review) required to maintain full-time status and be eligible for financial aid.

Counseling services: Individual counseling, career counseling, self-advocacy training.

Basic skills remediation: Offered one-on-one by LD teachers, regular teachers, graduate teaching assistants. Available in reading, math, spelling, written language, learning strategies, time management, social skills.

Auxiliary aids: Taped textbooks, tape recorders, word-processors with spell-check, word processors with grammar check.

Auxiliary services: Alternative test arrangements, notetakers, advocacy, readers.

GENERAL COLLEGE INFORMATION

Independent, comprehensive, coed, affiliated with Roman Catholic Church. Awards bachelor's, master's degrees. Founded 1858. *Setting:* 600-acre small-town campus. *Endowment:* $9.7 million. *Research spending 1995–96:* $648,470. *Educational spending 1995–96:* $3919 per undergrad. *Total enrollment:* 2,723. *Faculty:* 117 (110 full-time, 93% with terminal degrees, 7 part-time); student–undergrad faculty ratio is 17:1.

Enrollment Profile: 2,045 students from 35 states and territories, 7 other countries. 52% women, 48% men, 5% part-time, 77% state residents, 72% live on campus, 12% transferred in, 2% international, 4% 25 or older, 0% Native American, 1% Hispanic, 1% black, 1% Asian or Pacific Islander. *Retention:* 83% of 1995 full-time freshmen returned. *Graduation:* 59% graduate in 4 years, 70% in 5 years, 72% in 6 years. *Areas of study chosen:* 22% business management and administrative services, 17% education, 11% communications and journalism, 7% biological and life sciences, 7% psychology, 6% social sciences, 3% English language/literature/letters, 2% computer and information sciences, 2% mathematics, 2% philosophy, 1% engineering and applied sciences, 1% fine arts, 1% health professions and related sciences, 1% physical sciences. *Most popular recent majors:* accounting, elementary education, communication.

First-Year Class: 590 total; 1,837 applied, 90% were accepted, 36% of whom enrolled. 15% from top 10% of their high school class, 42% from top quarter, 76% from top half.

Graduation Requirements: 129 credit hours; 12 credit hours of math/science; computer course for math, business, education, mass communication, chemistry, psychology majors; internship (some majors); senior project for honors program students and some majors.

Computers on Campus: 80 computers available on campus for general student use. A campus-wide network can be accessed from student residence rooms and from off-campus. Students can contact faculty members and/or advisers through e-mail. Computers for student use in computer center, computer labs, learning resource center, library, student center, dorms, academic buildings provide access to the Internet/World Wide Web, on- and off-campus e-mail addresses. Staffed computer lab on campus provides training in use of computers, software. *Academic computing expenditure 1995–96:* $587,587.

EXPENSES AND FINANCIAL AID

Expenses for 1997–98: *Application fee:* $30. Comprehensive fee of $18,478 includes full-time tuition ($12,580), mandatory fees ($520), and college room and board ($5378). Part-time tuition: $400 per credit hour.

Undergraduate Financial Aid: Of all full-time undergraduates enrolled in fall 1996, 89% of those who applied for aid were judged to have need according to Federal Methodology, of whom 99% were aided. On average, 84% of need was met. *Financial aid deadline (priority):* 2/1. *Financial aid forms:* FAFSA, institutional form required. State form required for some.

LD Services Contact: Ms. Debra Bookmiller, Coordinator, Services for Students with Disabilities, St. Bonaventure University, Teaching and Learning Center, Room 26, Doyle Hall, St. Bonaventure, NY 14778-2284, 716-375-2066. Fax: 716-375-2135. Email: dbookmil@sbu.edu.

ST. CLOUD STATE UNIVERSITY

St. Cloud, Minnesota

LEARNING DISABILITIES SERVICES INFORMATION

Student Disabilities Services began offering services in 1976. Currently the program serves 125 undergraduates with LD. Services are also available to graduate students. Students diagnosed with ADD/ADHD are eligible for the same services available to students with LD.

Staff: 5 full-time, 3 part-time staff members, including director, Office Manager. Services provided by graduate assistants, interpreters.

Special Fees: No special fees are charged for services to students with LD.

Applications and admissions: *Required:* high school transcript, grade point average, class rank, untimed ACT. Students may begin taking classes any term. *Application deadline:* continuous.

Special policies: The college has written policies regarding grade forgiveness; substitutions and waivers of admissions, graduation, and degree requirements.

PROGRAM AND SERVICE COMPONENTS

Academic advising: Provided by unit staff members, academic advisers. Most students with LD take 12 to 16 credits each term; 12 credits required to maintain full-time status; 12 credits (15 for state aid) required to be eligible for financial aid.

Counseling services: Individual counseling, small-group counseling, career counseling.

Basic skills remediation: Offered one-on-one and in class-size groups by regular teachers, peer tutors. Available in reading, math, written language, study skills.

Subject-area tutoring: Offered one-on-one and in small groups by professional teachers, peer tutors, graduate assistants. Available in some subjects.

Auxiliary services: Alternative test arrangements, notetakers, priority registration, advocacy.

GENERAL COLLEGE INFORMATION

State-supported, comprehensive, coed. Part of Minnesota State Colleges and Universities System. Awards associate, bachelor's, master's, doctoral degrees. Founded 1869. *Setting:* 82-acre suburban campus with easy access to Minneapolis–St. Paul. *Endowment:* $6.5 million. *Research spending 1995–96:* $500,000. *Educational spending 1995–96:* $4200 per undergrad. *Total enrollment:* 14,048. *Faculty:* 662 (582 full-time, 84% with terminal degrees, 80 part-time); student–undergrad faculty ratio is 22:1.

Enrollment Profile: 12,958 students from 48 states and territories, 52 other countries. 51% women, 49% men, 15% part-time, 90% state residents, 20% live on campus, 10% transferred in, 3% international, 16% 25 or older, 1% Native American, 1% Hispanic, 1% black, 1% Asian or Pacific Islander. *Retention:* 76% of 1995 full-time freshmen returned. *Graduation:* 41% graduate in 6 years. *Most popular recent majors:* elementary education, psychology, communication.

First-Year Class: 2,114 total; 4,368 applied, 87% were accepted, 56% of whom enrolled. 12% from top 10% of their high school class, 38% from top quarter, 87% from top half. 1 National Merit Scholar, 25 valedictorians.

Graduation Requirements: 96 quarter hours for associate, 192 quarter hours for bachelor's; 16 quarter hours of math/science; computer course for business, electrical engineering, engineering technology, geography, meteorology, statistics majors.

Computers on Campus: 2,400 computers available on campus for general student use. Computer purchase/lease plans available. A campus-wide network can be accessed from student residence rooms and from off-campus. Students can contact faculty members and/or advisers through e-mail. Computers for student use in computer center, computer labs, research center, learning resource center, classrooms, library, student center, dorms provide access to the Internet/World Wide Web, on- and off-campus e-mail addresses. Staffed computer lab on campus provides training in use of computers, software. *Academic computing expenditure 1995–96:* $1.7 million.

EXPENSES AND FINANCIAL AID

Expenses for 1996–97: *Application fee:* $20. State resident tuition: $2526 full-time, $52.50 per quarter hour part-time. Nonresident tuition: $5470 full-time, $113.95 per quarter hour part-time. Part-time mandatory fees: $10.10 per quarter hour. Full-time mandatory fees: $378. College room and board: $3027.

Undergraduate Financial Aid: 73% of all full-time undergraduates enrolled in fall 1996 applied for aid; of these, 80% were judged to have need according to Federal Methodology, of whom 100% were aided. On average, 95% of need was met. *Financial aid deadline (priority):* 4/20. *Financial aid forms:* FAFSA, institutional form required.

LD Services Contact: Ms. Joyce Koshuil, Office Manager, St. Cloud State University, Atwood Center, St. Cloud, MN 56301-4498, 320-255-4080.

ST. FRANCIS XAVIER UNIVERSITY

Antigonish, Nova Scotia, Canada

LEARNING DISABILITIES SERVICES INFORMATION

Program for Students with Disabilities currently serves 31 undergraduates with LD. Services are also available to graduate students. Students diagnosed with ADD/ADHD are eligible for the same services available to students with LD.

Staff: 1 full-time, 1 part-time staff members. Services provided by tutors, counselors.

Special Fees: No special fees are charged for services to students with LD.

Applications and admissions: *Required:* high school transcript, courses completed; *recommended:* autobiographical statement, psychoeducational report completed within 5 years. Students may begin taking classes in fall only. *Application deadline:* 8/31.

PROGRAM AND SERVICE COMPONENTS

Special preparation or orientation: Optional orientation offered before registration.

Academic advising: Provided by unit staff members, academic advisers. Students with LD may take up to 15 credits each term; most take 15 credits; 9 credits required to maintain full-time status and be eligible for financial aid.

Counseling services: Individual counseling.

Subject-area tutoring: Offered one-on-one by peer tutors. Available in most subjects.

Auxiliary aids: Taped textbooks, tape recorders, word-processors with spell-check.

Auxiliary services: Alternative test arrangements, notetakers, advocacy.

Campus support group: A special student organization is available to students with LD.

GENERAL COLLEGE INFORMATION

Independent Roman Catholic, comprehensive, coed. Awards bachelor's, master's degrees. Founded 1853. *Setting:* 60-acre small-town campus. *Endowment:* $19.5 million. *Research spending 1995–96:* $1.7 million. *Educational spending 1995–96:* $4663 per undergrad. *Total enrollment:* 3,801. *Undergraduate faculty:* 226 (184 full-time, 79% with terminal degrees, 42 part-time); student–undergrad faculty ratio is 17:1.

Enrollment Profile: 3,600 students from 12 provinces and territories, 18 other countries. 55% women, 45% men, 15% part-time, 67% province residents, 38% live on campus, 6% transferred in, 4% international, 7% 25 or older. *Retention:* 79% of 1995 full-time freshmen returned. *Graduation:* 57% graduate in 4 years, 64% in 5 years, 67% in 6 years. *Areas of study chosen:* 34% liberal arts/general studies, 18% business management and administrative services, 16% health professions and related sciences, 14% biological and life sciences, 6% physical sciences, 5% education, 4% computer and information sciences, 2% engineering and applied sciences, 2% performing arts. *Most popular recent majors:* business administration/commerce/management, English, psychology.

First-Year Class: 725 total; 1,798 applied, 89% were accepted, 45% of whom enrolled.

Graduation Requirements: 20 courses; computer course for math, physics, chemistry, geology, biology, business administration majors; internship (some majors); senior project for honors program students and some majors.

Computers on Campus: 180 computers available on campus for general student use. A campus-wide network can be accessed from student residence rooms and from off-campus. Students can contact faculty members and/or advisers through e-mail. Computers for student use in computer center, computer labs, classrooms, library provide access to the Internet/World Wide Web, on- and off-campus e-mail addresses. Staffed computer lab on campus provides training in use of computers, software. *Academic computing expenditure 1995–96:* $470,309.

EXPENSES AND FINANCIAL AID

Expenses for 1997–98: *Application fee:* $30. Canadian resident tuition: $3775 full-time, $810 per course part-time. Part-time mandatory fees: $13 per course. Tuition for nonresidents ranges from $5475 to $6775 full-time, $1150 to $1410 per course part-time, according to class level. (All figures in Canadian dollars.). Full-time mandatory fees: $123. College room and board: $4965.
Undergraduate Financial Aid: 75% of all full-time undergraduates enrolled in fall 1996 applied for aid; of these, 14% were judged to have need according to Federal Methodology, of whom 100% were aided. On average, 75% of need was met. *Financial aid deadline (priority):* 3/1. *Financial aid forms:* institutional form required.
LD Services Contact: Ms. Mary Ellen Clancy, Counsellor, St. Francis Xavier University, Box 5000, Antigonish, NS B2G 2W5, Canada, 902-867-2370. Fax: 902-867-2406. Email: mclancy@stfx.ca.

SAINT JOHN'S UNIVERSITY

Collegeville, Minnesota

LEARNING DISABILITIES SERVICES INFORMATION

Academic Advising Office began offering services in 1987. Currently the program serves 35 undergraduates with LD. Students diagnosed with ADD/ADHD are eligible for the same services available to students with LD.
Staff: 2 part-time staff members, including director, assistant director.
Special Fees: No special fees are charged for services to students with LD.
Applications and admissions: *Required:* essay; *recommended:* high school transcript, untimed or extended time SAT I or ACT. Students may begin taking classes in fall only. *Application deadline:* continuous.
Special policies: The college has written policies regarding substitutions and waivers of graduation and degree requirements.

PROGRAM AND SERVICE COMPONENTS

Academic advising: Provided by unit staff members, academic advisers. Students with LD may take up to 17 credits each term; most take 16 credits; 12 credits required to maintain full-time status and be eligible for financial aid.
Counseling services: Individual counseling, small-group counseling, career counseling.
Basic skills remediation: Offered one-on-one, in small groups, and in class-size groups by regular teachers. Available in reading, math, written language, study skills, time management, computer skills.
Auxiliary aids: Taped textbooks, tape recorders, word-processors with spell-check.
Auxiliary services: Alternative test arrangements, notetakers, priority registration, advocacy.

GENERAL COLLEGE INFORMATION

Independent Roman Catholic, comprehensive, men only, coordinate with College of Saint Benedict. Awards bachelor's, master's degrees. Founded 1857. *Setting:* 2,400-acre rural campus with easy access to Minneapolis–St. Paul. *Endowment:* $58.4 million. *Research spending 1995–96:* $49,412. *Total enrollment:* 1,796. *Faculty:* 172 (138 full-time, 85% with terminal degrees, 34 part-time); student–undergrad faculty ratio is 13:1.
Enrollment Profile: 1,687 students from 34 states and territories, 28 other countries. 100% men, 4% part-time, 82% state residents, 75% live on campus, 3% transferred in, 3% international, 3% 25 or older, 1% Native American, 1% Hispanic, 1% black, 2% Asian or Pacific Islander. *Retention:* 84% of 1995 full-time freshmen returned. *Graduation:* 56% graduate in 4 years, 66% in 5 years, 67% in 6 years. *Areas of study chosen:* 22% business management and administrative services, 15% social sciences, 11% biological and life sciences, 5% mathematics, 5% physical sciences, 5% psychology, 4% communications and journalism, 4% English language/literature/letters, 4% health professions and related sciences, 3% computer and information sciences, 3% education, 3% engineering and applied sciences, 3% premed, 2% foreign language and literature, 2% interdisciplinary studies, 2% performing arts, 1% fine arts, 1% philosophy, 1% predentistry, 1% prelaw, 1% prevet, 1% theology/religion. *Most popular recent majors:* business administration/commerce/management, biology/biological sciences, accounting.
First-Year Class: 426 total; 893 applied, 87% were accepted, 55% of whom enrolled. 21% from top 10% of their high school class, 50% from top quarter, 86% from top half.
Graduation Requirements: 124 credits; basic math proficiency; 1 semester of math; 2 semesters of natural science; 3 semesters of a foreign language or the equivalent; computer course for math, accounting, business administration, physics, political science majors; internship (some majors); senior project for honors program students and some majors.
Computers on Campus: 250 computers available on campus for general student use. Computer purchase/lease plans available. A campus-wide network can be accessed from student residence rooms and from off-campus. Students can contact faculty members and/or advisers through e-mail. Computers for student use in computer center, computer labs, classrooms, library, student center, dorms, academic buildings provide access to the Internet/World Wide Web, on- and off-campus e-mail addresses. Staffed computer lab on campus provides training in use of computers, software. *Academic computing expenditure 1995–96:* $712,133.

EXPENSES AND FINANCIAL AID

Expenses for 1997–98: *Application fee:* $25. Comprehensive fee of $19,332 includes full-time tuition ($14,620), mandatory fees ($138), and college room and board ($4574). College room only: $2179. Part-time tuition: $609 per credit.
Undergraduate Financial Aid: 85% of all full-time undergraduates enrolled in fall 1996 applied for aid; of these, 77% were judged to have need according to Federal Methodology, of whom 100% were aided. On average, 96% of need was met. *Financial aid deadline (priority):* 3/1. *Financial aid forms:* FAFSA required; CSS Financial Aid PROFILE acceptable. Institutional form required for some.
LD Services Contact: Fr. Thomas Andert or Mr. Mark Shimota, Academic Advisors, Saint John's University, Collegeville, MN 56321-2000, 320-363-2248. Above services are also available to students attending coordinate institution College of Saint Benedict in Saint Joseph, MN.

ST. LAWRENCE UNIVERSITY

Canton, New York

LEARNING DISABILITIES SERVICES INFORMATION

Office of Services for Students with Special Needs began offering services in 1985. Currently the program serves 125 to 135 undergraduates with LD. Services are also available to graduate students. Students diagnosed with ADD/ADHD are eligible for the same services available to students with LD.
Staff: 1 part-time staff member (director).
Special Fees: No special fees are charged for services to students with LD.
Applications and admissions: *Required:* high school transcript, courses completed, untimed SAT I or ACT, letters of recommendation, essay; *recommended:* personal interview. Students may begin taking classes in fall only. *Application deadline:* 2/15 (fall term), 12/1 (spring term).

PROGRAM AND SERVICE COMPONENTS

Academic advising: Provided by unit staff members, academic advisers. Students with LD may take up to 4 units each term; most take 3 to 4 units; 3.5 units required to maintain full-time status and be eligible for financial aid.
Counseling services: Individual counseling, career counseling, accommodation and accessibility awareness counseling.
Auxiliary aids: Taped textbooks, tape recorders, calculators, personal computers, talking computers, optical character readers.
Auxiliary services: Alternative test arrangements, notetakers, priority registration, advocacy.

GENERAL COLLEGE INFORMATION

Independent, comprehensive, coed. Awards bachelor's, master's degrees. Founded 1856. *Setting:* 1,000-acre small-town campus with easy access to Ottawa. *Endowment:* $146 million. *Total enrollment:* 2,096. *Undergraduate faculty:* 181 (152 full-time, 91% with terminal degrees, 29 part-time); student–undergrad faculty ratio is 12:1.
Enrollment Profile: 1,999 students from 39 states and territories, 25 other countries. 50% women, 50% men, 1% part-time, 47% state residents, 93% live on campus, 5% transferred in, 4% international, 2% 25 or older, 1% Native American, 2% Hispanic, 2% black, 2% Asian or Pacific Islander. *Retention:* 85% of 1995 full-time freshmen returned. *Graduation:* 73% graduate in 4 years, 79% in 5 years, 81% in 6 years. *Areas of study chosen:* 39% social sciences, 13% psychology, 11% English language/literature/letters, 10% area and ethnic studies, 9% biological and life sciences, 4% fine arts, 4% physical sciences, 3% foreign lan-

St. Lawrence University (continued)

guage and literature, 3% mathematics, 2% interdisciplinary studies, 2% performing arts, 1% philosophy, 1% theology/religion. *Most popular recent majors:* psychology, economics, political science/government.
First-Year Class: 593 total; 2,778 applied, 66% were accepted, 32% of whom enrolled. 29% from top 10% of their high school class, 51% from top quarter, 92% from top half. 8 valedictorians.
Graduation Requirements: 34 units; 1 course each in math and lab science; senior project for honors program students and some majors.
Computers on Campus: 600 computers available on campus for general student use. Computer purchase/lease plans available. A computer is recommended for all students. A campus-wide network can be accessed from student residence rooms and from off-campus. Students can contact faculty members and/or advisers through e-mail. Computers for student use in computer center, computer labs, classrooms, library, dorms provide access to the Internet/World Wide Web, on- and off-campus e-mail addresses. Staffed computer lab on campus (open 24 hours a day) provides training in use of computers, software.

EXPENSES AND FINANCIAL AID

Expenses for 1997–98: *Application fee:* $40. Comprehensive fee of $27,785 includes full-time tuition ($21,175), mandatory fees ($250), and college room and board ($6360). College room only: $3280.
Undergraduate Financial Aid: 70% of all full-time undergraduates enrolled in fall 1996 applied for aid; of these, 95% were judged to have need according to Federal Methodology, of whom 99% were aided. On average, 93% of need was met. *Financial aid deadline:* 2/15. *Financial aid forms:* FAFSA, CSS Financial Aid PROFILE, institutional form required. State form required for some.
LD Services Contact: Mr. John Meagher, Director, St. Lawrence University, Canton, NY 13617, 315-379-5104. Fax: 315-379-7424. Email: jmea@music.stlawu.edu.

SAINT MARTIN'S COLLEGE

Lacey, Washington

LEARNING DISABILITIES SERVICES INFORMATION

Disability Support Services began offering services in 1995. Currently the program serves 8 undergraduates with LD. Services are also available to graduate students. Students diagnosed with ADD/ADHD are eligible for the same services available to students with LD, as well as one-on-one assistance with organizational management and planning.
Staff: 1 part-time staff member (coordinator). Services provided by counseling services staff, Writing Skills Center staff.
Special Fees: No special fees are charged for services to students with LD.
Applications and admissions: *Required:* high school transcript, grade point average, courses completed, autobiographical statement, letters of recommendation; *recommended:* high school IEP (Individualized Education Program), untimed or extended time SAT I, extended time ACT, personal interview. Students may begin taking classes in fall only. *Application deadline:* continuous.

PROGRAM AND SERVICE COMPONENTS

Diagnostic testing: Study skills, learning strategies.
Academic advising: Provided by academic advisers. Students with LD may take up to 15 credit hours each term; most take 12 to 15 credit hours; 12 credit hours required to maintain full-time status and be eligible for financial aid.
Counseling services: Individual counseling, self-advocacy training.
Basic skills remediation: Offered one-on-one, in small groups, and in class-size groups by regular teachers, support staff. Available in written language, learning strategies, study skills, time management, social skills.
Subject-area tutoring: Offered one-on-one by peer tutors. Available in some subjects.
Special courses: College survival skills, communication skills, learning strategies, time management, study skills, career planning, stress management. Most offered for credit; most enter into overall grade point average.
Auxiliary aids: Taped textbooks, tape recorders, word-processors with spell-check, Franklin Spellers.
Auxiliary services: Alternative test arrangements, notetakers.

GENERAL COLLEGE INFORMATION

Independent Roman Catholic, comprehensive, coed. Awards associate, bachelor's, master's degrees. Founded 1895. *Setting:* 380-acre suburban campus with easy access to Tacoma. *Endowment:* $2.7 million. *Total enrollment:* 958. *Faculty:* 68 (55 full-time, 68% with terminal degrees, 13 part-time); student–undergrad faculty ratio is 12:1.
Enrollment Profile: 674 students from 14 states and territories, 4 other countries. 64% women, 36% men, 30% part-time, 81% state residents, 16% live on campus, 70% transferred in, 9% international, 65% 25 or older, 1% Native American, 5% Hispanic, 4% black, 7% Asian or Pacific Islander. *Retention:* 75% of 1995 full-time freshmen returned. *Graduation:* 43% graduate in 4 years, 45% in 5 years. *Areas of study chosen:* 31% education, 13% business management and administrative services, 11% engineering and applied sciences, 11% social sciences, 6% biological and life sciences, 6% psychology, 4% health professions and related sciences, 3% computer and information sciences, 2% English language/literature/letters, 1% mathematics, 1% physical sciences, 1% theology/religion. *Most popular recent majors:* education, business administration/commerce/management.
First-Year Class: 87 total; 181 applied, 65% were accepted, 74% of whom enrolled. 5% from top 10% of their high school class, 10% from top quarter, 70% from top half. 3 class presidents, 4 valedictorians.
Graduation Requirements: 64 credits for associate, 128 credits for bachelor's; 1 course each in pre-calculus and lab science; 2 years of a foreign language in high school or 1 year in college; computer course; internship (some majors); senior project.
Computers on Campus: 45 computers available on campus for general student use. Computer purchase/lease plans available. Students can contact faculty members and/or advisers through e-mail. Computers for student use in computer center, engineering departmental lab provide access to the Internet/World Wide Web. Staffed computer lab on campus provides training in use of computers, software. *Academic computing expenditure 1995–96:* $128,300.

EXPENSES AND FINANCIAL AID

Expenses for 1997–98: Comprehensive fee of $17,710 includes full-time tuition ($12,990), mandatory fees ($130), and college room and board ($4590). Part-time tuition: $433 per credit.
Undergraduate Financial Aid: On average, 90% of need was met. *Financial aid deadline (priority):* 3/1. *Financial aid forms:* FAFSA required; CSS Financial Aid PROFILE acceptable. Institutional form required for some.
LD Services Contact: Ms. Deborah DeBow, Coordinator, Saint Martin's College, 5300 Pacific Avenue SE, Lacey, WA 98503, 360-438-4580. Fax: 360-459-4124. Email: ddebow@crc.stmartin.edu.

SAINT XAVIER UNIVERSITY

Chicago, Illinois

LEARNING DISABILITIES SERVICES INFORMATION

Scholastic Teaching Assessment Resource Learning Academy (S.T.A.R.) currently serves 15 undergraduates with LD. Services are also available to graduate students. Students diagnosed with ADD/ADHD are eligible for the same services available to students with LD.
Staff: 1 full-time staff member (LD specialist). Services provided by diagnostic specialists.
Special Fees: $350 for diagnostic testing.
Applications and admissions: *Required:* high school transcript, grade point average, class rank, untimed or extended time ACT, autobiographical statement, letters of recommendation. Students may begin taking classes any term. *Application deadline:* continuous.

PROGRAM AND SERVICE COMPONENTS

Diagnostic testing: Intelligence, reading, math, spelling, handwriting, written language, study skills.
Academic advising: Provided by academic advisers. Most students with LD take 12 to 15 semester hours each term; 12 semester hours required to maintain full-time status and be eligible for financial aid.
Counseling services: Individual counseling, career counseling.
Basic skills remediation: Offered one-on-one by LD teachers. Available in reading, math, spelling, written language, learning strategies, time management.
Subject-area tutoring: Offered one-on-one by professional teachers. Available in some subjects.
Auxiliary aids: Taped textbooks, tape recorders, calculators, word-processors with spell-check.

Auxiliary services: Alternative test arrangements, notetakers, priority registration.

GENERAL COLLEGE INFORMATION

Independent Roman Catholic, comprehensive, coed. Awards bachelor's, master's degrees. Founded 1847. *Setting:* 55-acre urban campus. *Total enrollment:* 4,200. *Faculty:* 261 (142 full-time, 66% with terminal degrees, 119 part-time); student–undergrad faculty ratio is 16:1.
Enrollment Profile: 3,000 students: 73% women, 27% men, 43% part-time, 94% state residents, 40% transferred in, 1% international, 44% 25 or older, 8% Hispanic, 13% black, 1% Asian or Pacific Islander. *Retention:* 83% of 1995 full-time freshmen returned. *Most popular recent majors:* business administration/commerce/management, nursing, education.
First-Year Class: 237 total; 630 applied, 83% were accepted, 46% of whom enrolled. 18% from top 10% of their high school class, 42% from top quarter, 75% from top half.
Graduation Requirements: 120 semester hours; 1 math course; computer course for business administration, math, international business majors; internship (some majors); senior project (some majors).
Computers on Campus: 90 computers available on campus for general student use. Computer purchase/lease plans available. A campuswide network can be accessed. Students can contact faculty members and/or advisers through e-mail. Computers for student use in computer center, computer labs, learning resource center, dorms provide access to the Internet/World Wide Web, on- and off-campus e-mail addresses. Staffed computer lab on campus provides training in use of computers, software.

EXPENSES AND FINANCIAL AID

Expenses for 1997–98: *Application fee:* $25. Comprehensive fee of $17,744 includes full-time tuition ($12,450), mandatory fees ($110), and college room and board ($5184). Part-time tuition: $415 per semester hour. Part-time mandatory fees: $25 per semester. One-time mandatory fee: $30.
Undergraduate Financial Aid: On average, 100% of need was met. *Financial aid deadline (priority):* 3/1. *Financial aid forms:* FAFSA required.
LD Services Contact: Ms. Loretta Kucharczyk, Learning Disabilities Specialist, Saint Xavier University, 3700 West 103rd Street, Chicago, IL 60655, 773-298-3338. Fax: 773-298-3066.

SALVE REGINA UNIVERSITY

Newport, Rhode Island

LEARNING DISABILITIES SERVICES INFORMATION

Academic Development Center (ADC) began offering services in 1991. Currently the program serves 51 undergraduates with LD. Students diagnosed with ADD/ADHD are eligible for the same services available to students with LD.
Staff: Includes director, assistant director, coordinator. Services provided by tutors, counselors.
Special Fees: No special fees are charged for services to students with LD.
Applications and admissions: *Required:* high school transcript, grade point average, courses completed, extracurricular activities, autobiographical statement, letters of recommendation; *recommended:* high school class rank, untimed or extended time SAT I, personal interview. Students may begin taking classes in fall, spring, or summer. *Application deadline:* continuous.
Special policies: The college has written policies regarding substitutions and waivers of degree requirements.

PROGRAM AND SERVICE COMPONENTS

Academic advising: Provided by unit staff members, academic advisers. Students with LD may take up to 18 credit hours each term; most take 12 to 16 credit hours; 12 credit hours required to maintain full-time status and be eligible for financial aid.
Counseling services: Individual counseling, career counseling, self-advocacy training.
Basic skills remediation: Offered one-on-one and in small groups by peer tutors; computer-aided instruction also offered. Available in reading, math, written language, learning strategies, study skills, time management, computer skills.
Subject-area tutoring: Offered one-on-one and in small groups by peer tutors. Available in most subjects.
Auxiliary aids: Taped textbooks, tape recorders, calculators, word-processors with spell-check, personal computers.
Auxiliary services: Alternative test arrangements, notetakers.

GENERAL COLLEGE INFORMATION

Independent Roman Catholic, comprehensive, coed. Awards associate, bachelor's, master's, doctoral degrees. Founded 1934. *Setting:* 65-acre suburban campus with easy access to Boston. *Endowment:* $4.1 million. *Educational spending 1995–96:* $4951 per undergrad. *Total enrollment:* 1,844. *Faculty:* 197 (107 full-time, 68% with terminal degrees, 90 part-time); student–undergrad faculty ratio is 12:1.
Enrollment Profile: 1,433 students from 24 states and territories, 10 other countries. 66% women, 34% men, 9% part-time, 26% state residents, 57% live on campus, 17% transferred in, 2% international, 9% 25 or older, 0% Native American, 2% Hispanic, 2% black, 1% Asian or Pacific Islander. *Retention:* 79% of 1995 full-time freshmen returned. *Graduation:* 61% graduate in 4 years, 62% in 5 years, 63% in 6 years. *Areas of study chosen:* 24% social sciences, 19% education, 16% business management and administrative services, 11% health professions and related sciences, 6% biological and life sciences, 6% psychology, 3% English language/literature/letters, 3% fine arts, 1% liberal arts/general studies, 1% mathematics, 1% performing arts. *Most popular recent majors:* business administration/commerce/management, elementary education, nursing.
First-Year Class: 393 total; 1,627 applied, 88% were accepted, 27% of whom enrolled. 7% from top 10% of their high school class, 21% from top quarter, 52% from top half.
Graduation Requirements: 64 credit hours for associate, 128 credit hours for bachelor's; 1 math course; 2 science courses; 2 semesters of a foreign language; computer course for accounting, economics, art, management, business, math majors; senior project for honors program students and some majors.
Computers on Campus: 108 computers available on campus for general student use. Computer purchase/lease plans available. A campuswide network can be accessed from student residence rooms and from off-campus. Students can contact faculty members and/or advisers through e-mail. Computers for student use in computer center, computer labs, learning resource center, library, academic buildings provide access to the Internet/World Wide Web, on- and off-campus e-mail addresses. Staffed computer lab on campus provides training in use of computers, software. *Academic computing expenditure 1995–96:* $168,000.

EXPENSES AND FINANCIAL AID

Expenses for 1997–98: *Application fee:* $25. Comprehensive fee of $22,750 includes full-time tuition ($15,450), mandatory fees ($200), and college room and board ($7100). Part-time tuition: $515 per credit hour. Part-time mandatory fees: $35 per semester.
Undergraduate Financial Aid: 80% of all full-time undergraduates enrolled in fall 1996 applied for aid; of these, 89% were judged to have need according to Federal Methodology, of whom 100% were aided. *Financial aid deadline (priority):* 3/1. *Financial aid forms:* FAFSA, CSS Financial Aid PROFILE, state form, institutional form, affidavit of non-support required.
LD Services Contact: Ms. Kathryn Rok, Assistant Director, Salve Regina University, 100 Ochre Point Avenue, Newport, RI 02840, 401-847-6650 Ext. 3150. Fax: 401-847-5490.

SAN DIEGO STATE UNIVERSITY

San Diego, California

LEARNING DISABILITIES SERVICES INFORMATION

Disabled Student Services, Learning Disabilities Program began offering services in 1981. Currently the program serves 670 undergraduates with LD. Services are also available to graduate students. Students diagnosed with ADD/ADHD are eligible for the same services available to students with LD, as well as medication and student health monitoring.
Staff: Includes coordinator, LD assistant, LD assessment assistants. Services provided by remediation specialists, tutors, counselors, diagnostic specialists.
Special Fees: No special fees are charged for services to students with LD.
Applications and admissions: *Required:* high school transcript, untimed SAT I or ACT, psychoeducational report completed within 3 years, documentation of learning disability from a qualified professional; *recommended:* extended time SAT I or ACT. Students may begin taking classes in fall, spring, or summer. *Application deadline:* continuous.

San Diego State University (continued)

Special policies: The college has written policies regarding grade forgiveness.

PROGRAM AND SERVICE COMPONENTS

Special preparation or orientation: Required orientation held after classes begin.

Diagnostic testing: Intelligence, reading, math, spelling, handwriting, spoken language, written language, perceptual skills, speech, hearing.

Academic advising: Provided by unit staff members, academic advisers. Students with LD may take up to 12 units each term; most take 12 units; 12 units required to maintain full-time status.

Counseling services: Individual counseling, small-group counseling, career counseling.

Subject-area tutoring: Offered one-on-one and in small groups by professional teachers, peer tutors. Available in most subjects.

Special courses: Communication skills, composition, learning strategies, word processing, time management, math, study skills. Some offered for credit; none enter into overall grade point average.

Auxiliary aids: Taped textbooks, tape recorders, calculators, typewriters, word-processors with spell-check.

Auxiliary services: Alternative test arrangements, notetakers, priority registration, advocacy.

Campus support group: A special student organization is available to students with LD.

GENERAL COLLEGE INFORMATION

State-supported, coed. Part of California State University System. Awards bachelor's, master's, doctoral degrees. Founded 1897. *Setting:* 300-acre urban campus. *Endowment:* $84.2 million. *Research spending 1995–96:* $73.7 million. *Educational spending 1995–96:* $9141 per undergrad. *Total enrollment:* 29,331. *Faculty:* 2,264 (886 full-time, 1,378 part-time); student–undergrad faculty ratio is 13:1.

Enrollment Profile: 23,847 students: 55% women, 45% men, 18% part-time, 93% state residents, 10% live on campus, 11% transferred in, 2% international, 37% 25 or older, 1% Native American, 18% Hispanic, 5% black, 14% Asian or Pacific Islander. *Retention:* 71% of 1995 full-time freshmen returned. *Graduation:* 5% graduate in 4 years, 22% in 5 years, 36% in 6 years. *Areas of study chosen:* 23% business management and administrative services, 14% health professions and related sciences, 8% psychology, 8% social sciences, 7% biological and life sciences, 6% engineering and applied sciences, 4% communications and journalism, 4% computer and information sciences, 4% English language/literature/letters, 3% education, 2% fine arts, 2% performing arts, 2% physical sciences, 1% area and ethnic studies, 1% foreign language and literature, 1% mathematics. *Most popular recent majors:* business administration/commerce/management, psychology, biology/biological sciences.

First-Year Class: 3,254 total; 12,231 applied, 82% were accepted, 32% of whom enrolled.

Graduation Requirements: 124 units; math proficiency; internship (some majors); senior project (some majors).

Computers on Campus: 2,000 computers available on campus for general student use. Computer purchase/lease plans available. A campus-wide network can be accessed from student residence rooms and from off-campus. Students can contact faculty members and/or advisers through e-mail. Computers for student use in computer labs, research center, classrooms, library, student center provide access to the Internet/World Wide Web. Staffed computer lab on campus (open 24 hours a day) provides training in use of computers, software.

EXPENSES AND FINANCIAL AID

Expenses for 1997–98: *Application fee:* $55. State resident tuition: $0 full-time. Nonresident tuition: $7626 full-time, $246 per unit part-time. Part-time mandatory fees: $633 per semester. Full-time mandatory fees: $1932. College room and board: $6730.

Undergraduate Financial Aid: 63% of all full-time undergraduates enrolled in fall 1996 applied for aid; of these, 88% were judged to have need according to Federal Methodology, of whom 95% were aided. On average, 87% of need was met. *Financial aid deadline (priority):* 3/1. *Financial aid forms:* FAFSA, state form required; CSS Financial Aid PROFILE acceptable.

LD Services Contact: Dr. Frank Siehien, Coordinator, Learning Disabilities Program, San Diego State University, Disabled Student Services, San Diego, CA 92182, 619-594-6473.

SAN FRANCISCO STATE UNIVERSITY

San Francisco, California

LEARNING DISABILITIES SERVICES INFORMATION

Disability Resource Center began offering services in 1984. Currently the program serves 400 undergraduates with LD. Services are also available to graduate students. Students diagnosed with ADD/ADHD are eligible for the same services available to students with LD.

Staff: 3 part-time staff members, including coordinator. Services provided by tutors, counselors, diagnostic specialists.

Special Fees: No special fees are charged for services to students with LD.

Applications and admissions: *Required:* high school transcript, untimed SAT I or ACT; *recommended:* extended time SAT I or ACT, admissions consultation (if needed). Students may begin taking classes in fall or spring. *Application deadline:* continuous.

PROGRAM AND SERVICE COMPONENTS

Special preparation or orientation: Optional orientation offered before classes begin.

Diagnostic testing: Intelligence, reading, math, spelling, handwriting, spoken language, written language, perceptual skills.

Academic advising: Provided by unit staff members, academic advisers. Most students with LD take 12 units each term; 12 units required to maintain full-time status.

Counseling services: Individual counseling, career counseling.

Subject-area tutoring: Offered in small groups by peer tutors. Available in all subjects.

Auxiliary aids: Taped textbooks, calculators, word-processors with spell-check, personal computers, Franklin Speller.

Auxiliary services: Alternative test arrangements, notetakers, advocacy.

Campus support group: A special student organization is available to students with LD.

GENERAL COLLEGE INFORMATION

State-supported, comprehensive, coed. Part of California State University System. Awards bachelor's, master's degrees. Founded 1899. *Setting:* 90-acre urban campus. *Educational spending 1995–96:* $5264 per undergrad. *Total enrollment:* 27,420. *Faculty:* 1,546 (761 full-time, 77% with terminal degrees, 785 part-time); student–undergrad faculty ratio is 21:1.

Enrollment Profile: 21,049 students from 46 states and territories, 136 other countries. 58% women, 42% men, 30% part-time, 95% state residents, 10% live on campus, 16% transferred in, 35% 25 or older, 1% Native American, 13% Hispanic, 8% black, 26% Asian or Pacific Islander. *Retention:* 79% of 1995 full-time freshmen returned. *Graduation:* 6% graduate in 4 years, 22% in 5 years, 37% in 6 years. *Areas of study chosen:* 24% business management and administrative services, 11% social sciences, 10% health professions and related sciences, 8% fine arts, 8% performing arts, 8% psychology, 6% biological and life sciences, 5% computer and information sciences, 5% English language/literature/letters, 5% interdisciplinary studies, 4% engineering and applied sciences, 2% communications and journalism, 2% foreign language and literature, 2% vocational and home economics, 1% area and ethnic studies, 1% mathematics, 1% philosophy, 1% physical sciences, 1% theology/religion. *Most popular recent majors:* accounting, liberal arts/general studies, business administration/commerce/management.

First-Year Class: 1,960 total; 7,681 applied, 72% were accepted, 35% of whom enrolled.

Graduation Requirements: 124 units; 9 units of science; computer course for business, engineering majors; internship (some majors); senior project for honors program students.

Computers on Campus: 1,474 computers available on campus for general student use. A campus-wide network can be accessed from student residence rooms and from off-campus. Students can contact faculty members and/or advisers through e-mail. Computers for student use in computer center, computer labs, library provide access to the Internet/World Wide Web, on- and off-campus e-mail addresses. Staffed computer lab on campus (open 24 hours a day) provides training in use of computers, software. *Academic computing expenditure 1995–96:* $4.6 million.

EXPENSES AND FINANCIAL AID

Expenses for 1997–98: *Application fee:* $55. State resident tuition: $0 full-time. Nonresident tuition: $7626 full-time, $246 per unit part-time. Part-time mandatory fees: $658 per semester. Full-time mandatory fees: $1982. College room and board: $5935.
Undergraduate Financial Aid: 63% of all full-time undergraduates enrolled in fall 1996 applied for aid; of these, 93% were judged to have need according to Federal Methodology, of whom 99% were aided. On average, 80% of need was met. *Financial aid deadline (priority):* 3/1. *Financial aid forms:* FAFSA required.
LD Services Contact: Dr. Kimberly Bartlett, Director, Disability Resource Center, San Francisco State University, 1600 Holloway Avenue, TI-2, San Francisco, CA 94132, 415-338-2472. Fax: 415-338-1041.

SANTA CLARA UNIVERSITY

Santa Clara, California

LEARNING DISABILITIES SERVICES INFORMATION

Disabled Student Resources began offering services in 1985. Currently the program serves 89 undergraduates with LD. Services are also available to graduate students. Students diagnosed with ADD/ADHD are eligible for the same services available to students with LD.
Staff: 1 full-time staff member (director). Services provided by proctors, readers.
Special Fees: $600 to $800 for diagnostic testing.
Applications and admissions: *Required:* high school transcript, grade point average, class rank, courses completed, extracurricular activities, untimed SAT I, autobiographical statement, letters of recommendation; *recommended:* extended time SAT I or ACT, personal interview, psychoeducational report completed within 3 years. Students may begin taking classes any term. *Application deadline:* 2/1.

PROGRAM AND SERVICE COMPONENTS

Special preparation or orientation: Optional orientation offered before registration.
Diagnostic testing: Intelligence, reading, math, spelling, handwriting, written language, perceptual skills, social skills, learning strategies.
Academic advising: Provided by unit staff members, academic advisers. Students with LD may take up to 20 quarter hours each term; most take 12 to 16 quarter hours; 12 quarter hours (can vary according to individual needs) required to maintain full-time status and be eligible for financial aid.
Counseling services: Individual counseling, small-group counseling, career counseling, self-advocacy training.
Auxiliary aids: Taped textbooks, tape recorders, calculators, typewriters, word-processors with spell-check, personal computers, Arkenstone Reader.
Auxiliary services: Alternative test arrangements, notetakers, priority registration, advocacy, readers, proctors, scribes, proofreaders.

GENERAL COLLEGE INFORMATION

Independent Roman Catholic (Jesuit), comprehensive, coed. Awards bachelor's, master's, doctoral, first professional degrees. Founded 1851. *Setting:* 104-acre suburban campus with easy access to San Francisco and San Jose. *Endowment:* $225.7 million. *Research spending 1995–96:* $1.3 million. *Total enrollment:* 7,863. *Faculty:* 592 (367 full-time, 90% with terminal degrees, 225 part-time); student–undergrad faculty ratio is 10:1.
Enrollment Profile: 4,230 students from 46 states and territories, 71 other countries. 53% women, 47% men, 3% part-time, 67% state residents, 42% live on campus, 16% transferred in, 4% international, 5% 25 or older, 1% Native American, 14% Hispanic, 3% black, 22% Asian or Pacific Islander. *Retention:* 92% of 1995 full-time freshmen returned. *Graduation:* 70% graduate in 4 years, 78% in 5 years, 80% in 6 years. *Areas of study chosen:* 26% business management and administrative services, 14% engineering and applied sciences, 9% social sciences, 7% biological and life sciences, 6% psychology, 5% communications and journalism, 5% physical sciences, 4% English language/literature/letters, 2% computer and information sciences, 2% liberal arts/general studies, 2% performing arts, 1% fine arts, 1% foreign language and literature, 1% mathematics, 1% philosophy. *Most popular recent majors:* finance/banking, psychology, political science/government.
First-Year Class: 1,075 total; 4,940 applied, 74% were accepted, 29% of whom enrolled. 38% from top 10% of their high school class, 69% from top quarter, 94% from top half. 4 National Merit Scholars.
Graduation Requirements: 176 units; 3 math/science courses; computer course for business, engineering majors; senior project for honors program students and some majors.
Computers on Campus: 350 computers available on campus for general student use. Computer purchase/lease plans available. A campuswide network can be accessed from student residence rooms and from off-campus. Students can contact faculty members and/or advisers through e-mail. Computers for student use in computer center, computer labs, classrooms, library, student center provide access to the Internet/World Wide Web. Staffed computer lab on campus provides training in use of computers, software. *Academic computing expenditure 1995–96:* $1.3 million.

EXPENSES AND FINANCIAL AID

Expenses for 1997–98: *Application fee:* $40. Comprehensive fee of $23,661 includes full-time tuition ($16,455), mandatory fees ($180), and college room and board ($7026). College room only: $4446. Part-time tuition: $1850 per course.
Undergraduate Financial Aid: 71% of all full-time undergraduates enrolled in fall 1996 applied for aid; of these, 90% were judged to have need according to Federal Methodology, of whom 100% were aided. On average, 85% of need was met. *Financial aid deadline (priority):* 2/1. *Financial aid forms:* FAFSA, CSS Financial Aid PROFILE required.
LD Services Contact: Mr. Ramón A. Chacón, Assistant Director, Student Resource Center, Santa Clara University, Disabled Student Resources, Santa Clara, CA 95053-0001, 408-554-4109. Fax: 408-554-5136.

SAVANNAH STATE UNIVERSITY

Savannah, Georgia

LEARNING DISABILITIES SERVICES INFORMATION

Comprehensive Counseling Services currently serves 9 undergraduates with LD. Services are also available to graduate students. Students diagnosed with ADD/ADHD are eligible for the same services available to students with LD.
Staff: 2 full-time, 1 part-time staff members, including director, counselors. Services provided by tutors, counselors, diagnostic specialists.
Special Fees: No special fees are charged for services to students with LD.
Applications and admissions: *Required:* high school transcript, grade point average, class rank, courses completed, extracurricular activities, IEP (Individualized Education Program), untimed or extended time SAT I, letters of recommendation, psychoeducational report completed within 3 years; *recommended:* untimed or extended time ACT, autobiographical statement. Students may begin taking classes any term. *Application deadline:* continuous.
Special policies: The college has written policies regarding substitutions and waivers of admissions, graduation, and degree requirements.

PROGRAM AND SERVICE COMPONENTS

Special preparation or orientation: Optional summer program offered prior to entering college.
Academic advising: Provided by unit staff members. Students with LD may take up to 15 quarter hours each term; most take 15 quarter hours; 12 quarter hours required to maintain full-time status and be eligible for financial aid.
Counseling services: Individual counseling, small-group counseling, career counseling, self-advocacy training.
Basic skills remediation: Offered in class-size groups by regular teachers. Available in reading, math, spelling, handwriting, written language, learning strategies, study skills, time management, social skills, speech, computer skills.
Subject-area tutoring: Offered one-on-one by peer tutors. Available in most subjects.
Special courses: College survival skills, reading, vocabulary development, communication skills, composition, learning strategies, word processing, Internet use, time management, math, typing, personal psychology, study skills, career planning, stress management, social relationships. Some offered for credit; some enter into overall grade point average.
Auxiliary aids: Taped textbooks, tape recorders, calculators, typewriters, word-processors with spell-check.
Auxiliary services: Alternative test arrangements, notetakers, priority registration, advocacy.

Savannah State University (continued)

GENERAL COLLEGE INFORMATION

State-supported, 4-year, coed. Part of University System of Georgia. Awards bachelor's degrees. Founded 1890. *Setting:* 165-acre suburban campus. *Total enrollment:* 3,211. *Faculty:* 155 (135 full-time, 52% with terminal degrees, 20 part-time).
Enrollment Profile: 3,211 students from 28 states and territories, 18 other countries. 57% women, 43% men, 15% part-time, 80% state residents, 10% transferred in, 1% international, 9% 25 or older, 1% Hispanic, 86% black, 2% Asian or Pacific Islander.
First-Year Class: 660 total; 2,391 applied, 66% were accepted, 42% of whom enrolled. 15% from top 10% of their high school class, 25% from top quarter, 60% from top half. 1 class president, 1 valedictorian.
Graduation Requirements: 185 quarter hours; 3 years each of math and science; 2 years of a foreign language; computer course for math, engineering, business majors; internship (some majors); senior project (some majors).
Computers on Campus: 115 computers available on campus for general student use. Computers for student use in computer labs, classrooms, school of business, engineering, math buildings.

EXPENSES AND FINANCIAL AID

Expenses for 1996–97: *Application fee:* $10. State resident tuition: $2130 full-time. Nonresident tuition: $6009 full-time. Part-time tuition per quarter ranges from $186 to $666 for state residents, $294 to $1854 for nonresidents. Full-time mandatory fees: $426. College room and board: $2970.
Undergraduate Financial Aid: Of all full-time undergraduates enrolled in fall 1996, 91% of those who applied for aid were judged to have need according to Federal Methodology, of whom 100% were aided. On average, 82% of need was met. *Financial aid deadline (priority):* 9/1. *Financial aid forms:* CSS Financial Aid PROFILE, institutional form required. FAFSA required for some.
LD Services Contact: Mrs. Gail G. Brown, Disability Counselor, Savannah State University, 2319 Falligant Avenue, Savannah, GA 31404, 912-356-2202. Fax: 912-356-2464.

SCHOOL OF THE ART INSTITUTE OF CHICAGO

Chicago, Illinois

LEARNING DISABILITIES SERVICES INFORMATION

Office of Student Affairs, The Learning Center began offering services in 1986. Currently the program serves 65 undergraduates with LD. Services are also available to graduate students. Students diagnosed with ADD/ADHD are eligible for the same services available to students with LD.
Staff: 2 part-time staff members, including director, tutor. Services provided by remediation specialists, tutors, diagnostic specialists, LD specialists.
Special Fees: No special fees are charged for services to students with LD.
Applications and admissions: *Required:* high school transcript, courses completed, untimed SAT I or ACT, autobiographical statement, letters of recommendation, psychoeducational report completed within 3 years, portfolio, statement of purpose; *recommended:* high school grade point average, extracurricular activities, extended time SAT I or ACT, personal interview. Students may begin taking classes in fall only. *Application deadline:* continuous.
Special policies: The college has written policies regarding substitutions and waivers of admissions, graduation, and degree requirements.

PROGRAM AND SERVICE COMPONENTS

Diagnostic testing: Intelligence, reading, math, spelling, spoken language, written language, perceptual skills, learning strategies, thinking, reasoning, non-verbal abilities.
Academic advising: Provided by unit staff members, academic advisers. Students with LD may take up to 18 semester hours each term; most take 15 semester hours; 12 semester hours required to maintain full-time status; 9 semester hours required to be eligible for financial aid.
Counseling services: Individual counseling, small-group counseling, career counseling, self-advocacy training.
Basic skills remediation: Offered one on one by LD teachers. Available in reading, math, spelling, spoken language, written language, learning strategies, perceptual skills, study skills, time management, social skills, computer skills.
Subject-area tutoring: Offered one-on-one and in small groups by LD specialists. Available in most subjects.
Special courses: Reading, composition. All offered for credit; all enter into overall grade point average.
Auxiliary aids: Taped textbooks, tape recorders, word-processors with spell-check.
Auxiliary services: Alternative test arrangements, notetakers, priority registration, advocacy, support groups, special programs with guest speakers.

GENERAL COLLEGE INFORMATION

Independent, comprehensive, specialized, coed. Awards bachelor's, master's degrees. Founded 1866. *Setting:* 1-acre urban campus. *Endowment:* $148.9 million. *Educational spending 1995–96:* $5979 per undergrad. *Total enrollment:* 2,012. *Faculty:* 392 (99 full-time, 85% with terminal degrees, 293 part-time); student–undergrad faculty ratio is 12:1.
Enrollment Profile: 1,485 students from 50 states and territories, 20 other countries. 58% women, 42% men, 14% part-time, 32% state residents, 13% live on campus, 16% transferred in, 7% international, 24% 25 or older, 1% Native American, 7% Hispanic, 5% black, 7% Asian or Pacific Islander. *Retention:* 73% of 1995 full-time freshmen returned. *Areas of study chosen:* 100% fine arts.
First-Year Class: 945 applied, 76% were accepted, 32% of whom enrolled.
Graduation Requirements: 132 semester hours; 6 semester hours of natural science; internship (some majors); senior project (some majors).
Computers on Campus: 80 computers available on campus for general student use. Computer purchase/lease plans available. A campus-wide network can be accessed from off-campus. Students can contact faculty members and/or advisers through e-mail. Computers for student use in computer labs, learning resource center, library, dorms, art and technology lab, visual communications lab provide access to the Internet/World Wide Web, on- and off-campus e-mail addresses. Staffed computer lab on campus provides training in use of computers, software. *Academic computing expenditure 1995–96:* $58,919.

EXPENSES AND FINANCIAL AID

Expenses for 1997–98: *Application fee:* $45. Tuition: $17,160 full-time, $572 per semester hour part-time. College room only: $5150.
Undergraduate Financial Aid: 74% of all full-time undergraduates enrolled in fall 1996 applied for aid; of these, 95% were judged to have need according to Federal Methodology, of whom 100% were aided. *Financial aid deadline (priority):* 4/1. *Financial aid forms:* FAFSA, institutional form required; state form acceptable.
LD Services Contact: Ms. Judy Watson, Director of Learning Center, School of the Art Institute of Chicago, 112 South Michigan Avenue, Chicago, IL 60603, 312-345-3507. Fax: 312-541-8063. Email: jwatso@artic.edu.

SEATTLE PACIFIC UNIVERSITY

Seattle, Washington

LEARNING DISABILITIES SERVICES INFORMATION

Services for Students with Disabilities began offering services in 1979. Currently the program serves 83 undergraduates with LD. Services are also available to graduate students. Students diagnosed with ADD/ADHD are eligible for the same services available to students with LD.
Staff: 1 part-time staff member (coordinator). Services provided by tutors, readers.
Special Fees: No special fees are charged for services to students with LD.
Applications and admissions: *Required:* high school transcript, grade point average, courses completed, untimed or extended time ACT, untimed SAT I, letters of recommendation, psychoeducational report completed within 3 years; *recommended:* high school extracurricular activities, extended time SAT I, personal interview. Students may begin taking classes in fall only. *Application deadline:* continuous.
Special policies: The college has written policies regarding substitutions and waivers of graduation requirements.

PROGRAM AND SERVICE COMPONENTS

Special preparation or orientation: Optional orientation offered after classes begin.
Academic advising: Provided by academic advisers. Students with LD may take up to 17 quarter credits each term; most take 12 to 17 quarter credits; 12 quarter credits required to maintain full-time status; 6 quarter credits required to be eligible for financial aid.
Subject-area tutoring: Offered one-on-one by peer tutors. Available in some subjects.
Auxiliary aids: Taped textbooks, word-processors with spell-check, talking computers.
Auxiliary services: Alternative test arrangements, notetakers, priority registration, advocacy.

GENERAL COLLEGE INFORMATION

Independent Free Methodist, comprehensive, coed. Awards bachelor's, master's, doctoral degrees. Founded 1891. *Setting:* 35-acre urban campus. *Endowment:* $17.6 million. *Research spending 1995–96:* $255,000. *Educational spending 1995–96:* $5665 per undergrad. *Total enrollment:* 3,293. *Faculty:* 208 (159 full-time, 85% with terminal degrees, 49 part-time); student–undergrad faculty ratio is 15:1.
Enrollment Profile: 2,506 students from 36 states and territories, 51 other countries. 64% women, 36% men, 19% part-time, 64% state residents, 49% live on campus, 35% transferred in, 5% international, 19% 25 or older, 1% Native American, 2% Hispanic, 2% black, 5% Asian or Pacific Islander. *Retention:* 76% of 1995 full-time freshmen returned. *Areas of study chosen:* 13% health professions and related sciences, 9% business management and administrative services, 6% education, 6% psychology, 5% computer and information sciences, 5% engineering and applied sciences, 4% communications and journalism, 4% English language/literature/letters, 4% fine arts, 4% social sciences, 3% biological and life sciences, 3% vocational and home economics, 2% physical sciences, 2% prelaw, 2% premed, 2% theology/religion, 1% foreign language and literature, 1% interdisciplinary studies, 1% liberal arts/general studies, 1% mathematics, 1% performing arts, 1% philosophy. *Most popular recent majors:* education, nursing.
First-Year Class: 478 total; 1,364 applied, 91% were accepted, 38% of whom enrolled. 4 National Merit Scholars.
Graduation Requirements: 180 credits; 15 credits of math/science/quantitative reasoning; 15 credits of a foreign language; computer course for engineering science, electrical engineering, business, biology, math, economics majors; senior project for honors program students and some majors.
Computers on Campus: 150 computers available on campus for general student use. Computer purchase/lease plans available. A computer is recommended for all students. A campus-wide network can be accessed from student residence rooms and from off-campus. Students can contact faculty members and/or advisers through e-mail. Computers for student use in learning resource center, library, media center provide access to the Internet/World Wide Web, on- and off-campus e-mail addresses. Staffed computer lab on campus provides training in use of computers, software. *Academic computing expenditure 1995–96:* $459,000.

EXPENSES AND FINANCIAL AID

Expenses for 1997–98: *Application fee:* $35. Comprehensive fee of $19,548 includes full-time tuition ($14,130) and college room and board ($5418). Part-time tuition per credit ranges from $225 to $395.
Undergraduate Financial Aid: Of all full-time undergraduates enrolled in fall 1996, 91% of those who applied for aid were judged to have need according to Federal Methodology, of whom 99% were aided. On average, 89% of need was met. *Financial aid deadline (priority):* 1/1. *Financial aid forms:* FAFSA required.
LD Services Contact: Mr. Richard T. Okamoto, Coordinator of Academic Support Services, Seattle Pacific University, 3307 Third Avenue West, Seattle, WA 98119, 206-281-2272. Fax: 206-286-7348. Email: rokamoto@paul.spu.edu.

SHASTA BIBLE COLLEGE

Redding, California

LEARNING DISABILITIES SERVICES INFORMATION

Summer Opportunity for Academic Recovery (SOAR) began offering services in 1996. Currently the program serves 4 undergraduates with LD. Students diagnosed with ADD/ADHD are eligible for the same services available to students with LD.
Staff: 6 part-time staff members, including director. Services provided by tutors.
Special Fees: No special fees are charged for services to students with LD.
Applications and admissions: *Required:* personal interview, autobiographical statement, letters of recommendation; *recommended:* high school transcript. Students may begin taking classes any term. *Application deadline:* continuous.

PROGRAM AND SERVICE COMPONENTS

Special preparation or orientation: Optional summer program offered prior to entering college.
Diagnostic testing: Intelligence, reading, math, spelling, written language.
Academic advising: Provided by academic advisers. Most students with LD take 12 units each term; 12 units required to maintain full-time status.
Counseling services: Individual counseling, career counseling.
Basic skills remediation: Offered one-on-one by LD teachers, teacher trainees. Available in reading, math, spelling, spoken language, written language, learning strategies, study skills, time management, computer skills.
Subject-area tutoring: Offered one-on-one by professional teachers, peer tutors. Available in all subjects.
Auxiliary services: Alternative test arrangements, programmed English course.

GENERAL COLLEGE INFORMATION

Independent nondenominational, 4-year. Awards associate, bachelor's degrees. Founded 1971. *Total enrollment:* 175. *Faculty:* 26 (6 full-time, 20 part-time).
Enrollment Profile: 175 students.
First-Year Class: 25 total.
Graduation Requirements: 64 credit hours for associate, 128 credit hours for bachelor's.
Computers on Campus: 6 computers available on campus for general student use. Computer purchase/lease plans available. A computer is recommended for all students. Computers for student use in computer labs, library provide access to the Internet/World Wide Web, on- and off-campus e-mail addresses.

EXPENSES AND FINANCIAL AID

Expenses for 1996–97: Tuition: $3300 full-time, $125 per credit hour part-time. Full-time mandatory fees: $130. College room only: $1107 (minimum).
Undergraduate Financial Aid: *Financial aid deadline:* continuous. *Financial aid forms:* FAFSA required.
LD Services Contact: Dr. E. Gail Everett, Director, Shasta Bible College, 2980 Hartnell Road, Redding, CA 96002, 916-221-4275. Fax: 916-221-6929.

SHAWNEE STATE UNIVERSITY

Portsmouth, Ohio

LEARNING DISABILITIES SERVICES INFORMATION

Department of Educational Needs Services/Disability Services currently serves 25 undergraduates with LD. Students diagnosed with ADD/ADHD are eligible for the same services available to students with LD.
Staff: 1 full-time staff member (director). Services provided by counselor.
Special Fees: No special fees are charged for services to students with LD.
Applications and admissions: *Required:* high school transcript, grade point average, courses completed, extended time SAT I, psychoeducational report completed within 3 years; *recommended:* untimed or extended time ACT, untimed SAT I. Students may begin taking classes in fall or summer. *Application deadline:* continuous.

PROGRAM AND SERVICE COMPONENTS

Academic advising: Provided by unit staff members. Students with LD may take up to 16 quarter hours each term; most take 12 quarter hours; 12 quarter hours required to maintain full-time status and be eligible for financial aid.
Counseling services: Individual counseling.

Shawnee State University (continued)

Basic skills remediation: Offered in class-size groups by LD teachers, regular teachers; computer-aided instruction also offered. Available in reading, math, written language, learning strategies, study skills, time management, social skills, computer skills.
Subject-area tutoring: Offered one-on-one by professional teachers, peer tutors. Available in all subjects.
Auxiliary aids: Taped textbooks, tape recorders, calculators, word-processors with spell-check, talking computers, optical character readers.
Auxiliary services: Alternative test arrangements, notetakers, priority registration, advocacy.

GENERAL COLLEGE INFORMATION

State-supported, 4-year, coed. Part of Ohio Board of Regents. Awards associate, bachelor's degrees. Founded 1986. *Setting:* 500-acre small-town campus. *Total enrollment:* 3,505. *Faculty:* 239 (119 full-time, 50% with terminal degrees, 120 part-time); student–undergrad faculty ratio is 13:1.
Enrollment Profile: 3,505 students from 11 states and territories, 5 other countries. 63% women, 37% men, 24% part-time, 90% state residents, 4% live on campus, 5% transferred in, 1% international, 41% 25 or older, 1% Native American, 1% Hispanic, 4% black, 1% Asian or Pacific Islander. *Areas of study chosen:* 25% health professions and related sciences, 12% engineering and applied sciences, 12% social sciences, 10% business management and administrative services, 9% liberal arts/general studies, 2% biological and life sciences, 2% mathematics. *Most popular recent majors:* health science, elementary education, business administration/commerce/management.
First-Year Class: 1,083 total; 1,780 applied, 100% were accepted, 61% of whom enrolled. 20% from top 10% of their high school class, 60% from top half.
Graduation Requirements: 90 quarter hours for associate, 186 quarter hours for bachelor's; 4 quarter hours of math; computer course for accounting, arts and science, secretarial, engineering technologies, administration majors; senior project.
Computers on Campus: 200 computers available on campus for general student use. A campus-wide network can be accessed from off-campus. Computers for student use in computer labs, learning resource center, classrooms, library, student center provide access to the Internet/World Wide Web, on- and off-campus e-mail addresses. Staffed computer lab on campus provides training in use of computers, software.

EXPENSES AND FINANCIAL AID

Estimated Expenses for 1997–98: *Application fee:* $30. State resident tuition: $2532 full-time, $71 per quarter hour part-time. Nonresident tuition: $4785 full-time, $134 per quarter hour part-time. Part-time mandatory fees: $15 per quarter hour. Tuition for Kentucky residents of Boyd, Greenup, Lewis and Mason counties and West Virginia residents of Cabell and Wayne counties: $3381 full-time, $94 per quarter hour part-time. Full-time mandatory fees: $531. College room and board: $4077. College room only: $2841.
Undergraduate Financial Aid: 96% of all full-time undergraduates enrolled in fall 1996 applied for aid. *Financial aid deadline (priority):* 3/1. *Financial aid forms:* FAFSA required.
LD Services Contact: Mrs. Gloria Horsley, Secretary, Shawnee State University, 940 Second Street, Portsmouth, OH 45662-2416, 614-355-2442. Fax: 614-355-2416. Email: ghorsley@shawnee.edu.

SHELDON JACKSON COLLEGE
Sitka, Alaska

LEARNING DISABILITIES SERVICES INFORMATION

Learning Center began offering services in 1989. Currently the program serves 7 undergraduates with LD. Students diagnosed with ADD/ADHD are eligible for the same services available to students with LD.
Staff: 1 full-time, 1 part-time staff members, including director. Services provided by remediation specialist, tutors, diagnostic specialist.
Special Fees: No special fees are charged for services to students with LD.
Applications and admissions: *Required:* high school transcript, untimed ACT; *recommended:* personal interview, psychoeducational report completed within 3 years. Students may begin taking classes in fall, winter, or spring. *Application deadline:* continuous.
Special policies: The college has written policies regarding grade forgiveness.

PROGRAM AND SERVICE COMPONENTS

Special preparation or orientation: Optional orientation offered as needed.

Diagnostic testing: Intelligence, reading, math, written language, personality.

Academic advising: Provided by academic advisers. Students with LD may take up to 12 credits (first semester, 21 credits thereafter) each term; most take 12 to 15 credits; 12 credits required to maintain full-time status and be eligible for financial aid.

Counseling services: Individual counseling, career counseling.

Basic skills remediation: Offered one-on-one and in small groups by LD teachers, regular teachers. Available in reading, math, spelling, learning strategies, study skills, time management.

Subject-area tutoring: Offered one-on-one by professional teachers, peer tutors. Available in most subjects.

Special courses: Reading, vocabulary development, communication skills, composition, learning strategies, word processing, time management, math, typing, study skills, career planning. Most offered for credit; some enter into overall grade point average.

Auxiliary aids: Taped textbooks, tape recorders, typewriters, word-processors with spell-check, personal computers.

Auxiliary services: Alternative test arrangements, notetakers, advocacy.

Campus support group: A special student organization is available to students with LD.

GENERAL COLLEGE INFORMATION

Independent, 4-year, coed, affiliated with Presbyterian Church (U.S.A.). Awards associate, bachelor's degrees. Founded 1878. *Setting:* 320-acre small-town campus. *Total enrollment:* 223. *Faculty:* 32 (18 full-time, 62% with terminal degrees, 14 part-time); student–undergrad faculty ratio is 11:1.

Enrollment Profile: 223 students from 25 states and territories, 3 other countries. 51% women, 49% men, 15% part-time, 40% state residents, 45% live on campus, 38% transferred in, 1% international, 40% 25 or older, 25% Native American, 1% Hispanic, 1% black, 1% Asian or Pacific Islander. *Retention:* 60% of 1995 full-time freshmen returned. *Graduation:* 15% graduate in 4 years, 35% in 5 years, 50% in 6 years. *Areas of study chosen:* 38% natural resource sciences, 30% education, 10% biological and life sciences, 10% social sciences, 5% business management and administrative services, 4% liberal arts/general studies, 3% interdisciplinary studies. *Most popular recent majors:* natural resource management, fish and game management, education.

First-Year Class: 35 total; 71 applied, 100% were accepted, 49% of whom enrolled.

Graduation Requirements: 64 credits for associate, 130 credits for bachelor's; 3 math/science courses including at least 1 math course; computer course; internship (some majors); senior project (some majors).

Computers on Campus: 50 computers available on campus for general student use. Computer purchase/lease plans available. A campus-wide network can be accessed from student residence rooms and from off-campus. Students can contact faculty members and/or advisers through e-mail. Computers for student use in computer center, computer labs, research center, learning resource center, classrooms, library, student center, dorms provide access to the Internet/World Wide Web, on- and off-campus e-mail addresses. Staffed computer lab on campus provides training in use of computers, software.

EXPENSES AND FINANCIAL AID

Estimated Expenses for 1997–98: Comprehensive fee of $14,100 includes full-time tuition ($9000), mandatory fees ($300), and college room and board ($4800). College room only: $2100. Part-time tuition: $300 per credit. Part-time mandatory fees: $12 per term.

Undergraduate Financial Aid: Of all full-time undergraduates enrolled in fall 1996, 95% of those who applied for aid were judged to have need according to Federal Methodology, of whom 100% were aided. On average, 79% of need was met. *Financial aid deadline (priority):* 6/1. *Financial aid forms:* FAFSA, institutional form required; CSS Financial Aid PROFILE acceptable. State form required for some.

LD Services Contact: Ms. Alice Zellhuber, Learning Center Coordinator/Assistant Professor, Sheldon Jackson College, 801 Lincoln Street, Sitka, AK 99835-7699, 907-747-5235.

SIMON FRASER UNIVERSITY

Burnaby, British Columbia, Canada

LEARNING DISABILITIES SERVICES INFORMATION

Centre for Students with Disabilities began offering services in 1996. Currently the program serves 20 undergraduates with LD. Services are also available to graduate students. Students diagnosed with ADD/ADHD are eligible for the same services available to students with LD.
Staff: 1 full-time, 1 part-time staff members, including coordinators. Services provided by counselors, diagnostic specialists.
Special Fees: No special fees are charged for services to students with LD.
Applications and admissions: *Required:* high school transcript, grade point average, courses completed, extended time SAT I; *recommended:* high school class rank. Students may begin taking classes any term. *Application deadline:* 4/30 (fall term), 9/30 (spring term).

PROGRAM AND SERVICE COMPONENTS

Academic advising: Provided by academic advisers. Students with LD required to take 9 credit hours to maintain full-time status and be eligible for financial aid.
Counseling services: Individual counseling, small-group counseling, career counseling.
Subject-area tutoring: Offered one-on-one by peer tutors. Available in all subjects.
Auxiliary aids: Tape recorders, word-processors with spell-check, personal computers, optical character readers.

GENERAL COLLEGE INFORMATION

Province-supported, coed. Awards bachelor's, master's, doctoral degrees. Founded 1965. *Setting:* 1,200-acre suburban campus with easy access to Vancouver. *Total enrollment:* 19,000. *Undergraduate faculty:* 634 (616 full-time, 93% with terminal degrees, 18 part-time).
Enrollment Profile: 16,550 students: 56% women, 44% men, 46% part-time, 83% province residents, 8% live on campus, 40% transferred in, 3% international, 27% 25 or older. *Retention:* 80% of 1995 full-time freshmen returned. *Graduation:* 10% graduate in 4 years, 38% in 5 years, 53% in 6 years. *Areas of study chosen:* 24% social sciences, 19% business management and administrative services, 9% education, 8% psychology, 7% liberal arts/general studies, 6% English language/literature/letters, 5% biological and life sciences, 5% communications and journalism, 4% computer and information sciences, 4% health professions and related sciences, 2% engineering and applied sciences, 2% foreign language and literature, 2% mathematics, 2% performing arts, 1% philosophy, 1% physical sciences. *Most popular recent majors:* business administration/commerce/management, psychology, communication.
First-Year Class: 2,261 total; 7,591 applied, 68% were accepted, 44% of whom enrolled.
Graduation Requirements: 120 credit hours; computer course for kinesiology, cognitive science, business administration, chemistry, mathematical physics, engineering science, biochemistry majors; internship (some majors); senior project (some majors).
Computers on Campus: 900 computers available on campus for general student use. Computer purchase/lease plans available. A campuswide network can be accessed from off-campus. Students can contact faculty members and/or advisers through e-mail. Computers for student use in computer center, computer labs, research center, learning resource center, classrooms, library, student center provide access to the Internet/World Wide Web, on- and off-campus e-mail addresses. Staffed computer lab on campus provides training in use of computers, software.

EXPENSES AND FINANCIAL AID

Expenses for 1997–98: *Application fee:* $20. Canadian resident tuition: $2310 full-time, $77 per credit hour part-time. Nonresident tuition: $6930 full-time, $231 per credit hour part-time. Part-time mandatory fees: $120.26 per year. (All figures are in Canadian dollars.). Full-time mandatory fees: $205. College room only: $2800.
Undergraduate Financial Aid: Of all full-time undergraduates enrolled in fall 1996, 86% of those who applied for aid were judged to have need according to Federal Methodology, of whom 100% were aided. *Financial aid deadline (priority):* 9/1. *Financial aid forms:* FAFSA, institutional form required.
LD Services Contact: Ms. Eileen Lennox, Co-ordinator, Services–Centre for Students with Disabilities, Simon Fraser University, Burnaby, BC V5A 1S6, Canada, 604-291-3112. Fax: 604-291-5682. Email: eileen_lennox@sfu.ca.

SMITH COLLEGE

Northampton, Massachusetts

LEARNING DISABILITIES SERVICES INFORMATION

Office of Disability Services began offering services in 1986. Currently the program serves 54 undergraduates with LD. Services are also available to graduate students. Students diagnosed with ADD/ADHD are eligible for the same services available to students with LD.
Staff: 1 full-time staff member (coordinator). Services provided by remediation specialists, tutors, counselors.
Special Fees: No special fees are charged for services to students with LD.
Applications and admissions: *Required:* high school transcript, courses completed, untimed SAT I or ACT, letters of recommendation; *recommended:* high school grade point average, class rank, extracurricular activities, personal interview. Students may begin taking classes in fall only. *Application deadline:* 1/15.
Special policies: The college has written policies regarding substitutions and waivers of degree requirements.

PROGRAM AND SERVICE COMPONENTS

Special preparation or orientation: Orientation required.
Academic advising: Provided by academic advisers. Most students with LD take 16 credits each term; 12 credits required to maintain full-time status and be eligible for financial aid.
Counseling services: Individual counseling, small-group counseling, career counseling, self-advocacy training, peer support group (for students with LD or ADD).
Basic skills remediation: Offered one-on-one and in small groups by Coordinator of Disability Services, writing counselors, quantitative skills counselor. Available in reading, math, spelling, written language, learning strategies, study skills, time management, public speaking.
Subject-area tutoring: Offered one-on-one and in small groups by peer tutors. Available in most subjects.
Auxiliary aids: Taped textbooks, tape recorders, calculators, typewriters, word-processors with spell-check, personal computers, optical character readers, voice-synthesized computer, reading enlargers.
Auxiliary services: Alternative test arrangements, notetakers, priority registration, taping service, readers.

GENERAL COLLEGE INFORMATION

Independent, comprehensive, women only. Awards bachelor's, master's, doctoral degrees. Founded 1871. *Setting:* 125-acre urban campus with easy access to Hartford. *Endowment:* $583.2 million. *Research spending 1995–96:* $1.8 million. *Educational spending 1995–96:* $11,182 per undergrad. *Total enrollment:* 2,788. *Faculty:* 276 (257 full-time, 97% with terminal degrees, 19 part-time); student–undergrad faculty ratio is 10:1.
Enrollment Profile: 2,670 students from 54 states and territories, 62 other countries. 100% women, 3% part-time, 18% state residents, 87% live on campus, 3% transferred in, 7% international, 9% 25 or older, 1% Native American, 4% Hispanic, 4% black, 11% Asian or Pacific Islander. *Retention:* 89% of 1995 full-time freshmen returned. *Graduation:* 81% graduate in 4 years, 84% in 5 years, 85% in 6 years. *Areas of study chosen:* 28% social sciences, 11% area and ethnic studies, 10% biological and life sciences, 10% English language/literature/letters, 9% psychology, 7% fine arts, 5% foreign language and literature, 4% performing arts, 4% physical sciences, 3% mathematics, 2% computer and information sciences, 2% education, 2% philosophy, 2% theology/religion, 1% interdisciplinary studies. *Most popular recent majors:* political science/government, psychology, economics.
First-Year Class: 643 total; 3,131 applied, 52% were accepted, 39% of whom enrolled. 53% from top 10% of their high school class, 85% from top quarter, 97% from top half. 30 valedictorians.
Graduation Requirements: 128 credits; computer course (varies by major); senior project for honors program students and some majors.
Computers on Campus: 230 computers available on campus for general student use. Computer purchase/lease plans available. A campuswide network can be accessed from student residence rooms. Students can contact faculty members and/or advisers through e-mail. Computers for student use in computer center, computer labs, learning resource center, classrooms, library, special needs computer lab provide access to the Internet/World Wide Web, on- and off-campus e-mail addresses. Staffed computer lab on campus (open 24 hours a day) provides training in use of computers, software. *Academic computing expenditure 1995–96:* $1.1 million.

Smith College (continued)

EXPENSES AND FINANCIAL AID

Expenses for 1997–98: *Application fee:* $50. Comprehensive fee of $28,762 includes full-time tuition ($21,360), mandatory fees ($152), and college room and board ($7250). Part-time tuition for nontraditional students: $2680 per course.
Undergraduate Financial Aid: Of all full-time undergraduates enrolled in fall 1996, 92% of those who applied for aid were judged to have need according to Federal Methodology, of whom 100% were aided. On average, 100% of need was met. *Financial aid deadline:* 2/1. *Financial aid forms:* FAFSA, CSS Financial Aid PROFILE, institutional form required. State form required for some.
LD Services Contact: Ms. Belinda M. Rosin, Coordinator of Disability Services, Smith College, College Hall 7, Northampton, MA 01063, 413-585-2071. Fax: 413-585-2206. Email: brosin@eunice.smith.edu.

SONOMA STATE UNIVERSITY

Rohnert Park, California

LEARNING DISABILITIES SERVICES INFORMATION

Disability Resource Center began offering services in 1978. Currently the program serves 185 undergraduates with LD. Services are also available to graduate students. Students diagnosed with ADD/ADHD are eligible for the same services available to students with LD.
Staff: 2 full-time, 1 part-time staff members, including director, Disability Management Advisors. Services provided by counselor, student assistant, work-study students.
Special Fees: No special fees are charged for services to students with LD.
Applications and admissions: *Required:* high school transcript, grade point average, courses completed, extended time SAT I; *recommended:* personal interview, autobiographical statement, letters of recommendation, psychoeducational report completed within 3 years. Students may begin taking classes in fall or spring. *Application deadline:* 11/1 (fall term), 8/9 (spring term).
Special policies: The college has written policies regarding substitutions and waivers of admissions and degree requirements.

PROGRAM AND SERVICE COMPONENTS

Special preparation or orientation: Optional orientation offered individually by special arrangement.
Academic advising: Provided by unit staff members, academic advisers. Students with LD may take up to 19 units each term; most take 12 units; 12 units required to maintain full-time status and be eligible for financial aid.
Counseling services: Individual counseling, career counseling, self-advocacy training.
Auxiliary aids: Taped textbooks, tape recorders, typewriters, word-processors with spell-check, personal computers.
Auxiliary services: Alternative test arrangements, notetakers, priority registration, advocacy, TDD/(707)664-2958.

GENERAL COLLEGE INFORMATION

State-supported, comprehensive, coed. Part of California State University System. Awards bachelor's, master's degrees. Founded 1960. *Setting:* 220-acre small-town campus with easy access to San Francisco. *Endowment:* $12.8 million. *Research spending 1995–96:* $6.8 million. *Total enrollment:* 6,999. *Faculty:* 435 (247 full-time, 84% with terminal degrees, 188 part-time); student–undergrad faculty ratio is 19:1.
Enrollment Profile: 5,872 students from 30 states and territories, 74 other countries. 61% women, 39% men, 18% part-time, 96% state residents, 15% live on campus, 17% transferred in, 2% international, 30% 25 or older, 1% Native American, 10% Hispanic, 4% black, 6% Asian or Pacific Islander. *Retention:* 77% of 1995 full-time freshmen returned. *Graduation:* 16% graduate in 4 years, 30% in 5 years. *Areas of study chosen:* 18% social sciences, 17% business management and administrative services, 9% liberal arts/general studies, 8% psychology, 6% biological and life sciences, 6% English language/literature/letters, 4% education, 3% communications and journalism, 3% fine arts, 3% health professions and related sciences, 3% performing arts, 3% physical sciences, 2% computer and information sciences, 2% interdisciplinary studies, 2% mathematics, 1% area and ethnic studies, 1% foreign language and literature, 1% philosophy. *Most popular recent majors:* business administration/commerce/management, psychology, liberal arts/general studies.
First Year Class: 816 total, 3,722 applied, 83% were accepted, 27% of whom enrolled.
Graduation Requirements: 124 units; 3 units of math; 9 units of science including at least 3 units of lab science; computer course for management, psychology majors; senior project (some majors).
Computers on Campus: 300 computers available on campus for general student use. Computer purchase/lease plans available. A computer is required for all students. A campus-wide network can be accessed from student residence rooms and from off-campus. Students can contact faculty members and/or advisers through e-mail. Computers for student use in computer center, computer labs, library, student center provide access to the Internet/World Wide Web, on- and off-campus e-mail addresses. Staffed computer lab on campus provides training in use of computers, software. *Academic computing expenditure 1995–96:* $2.7 million.

EXPENSES AND FINANCIAL AID

Expenses for 1997–98: *Application fee:* $55. State resident tuition: $0 full-time. Nonresident tuition: $7626 full-time, $246 per unit part-time. Part-time mandatory fees: $732 per semester. Full-time mandatory fees: $2130. College room and board: $5869.
Undergraduate Financial Aid: 57% of all full-time undergraduates enrolled in fall 1996 applied for aid; of these, 83% were judged to have need according to Federal Methodology, of whom 99% were aided. On average, 79% of need was met. *Financial aid deadline (priority):* 3/2. *Financial aid forms:* FAFSA required.
LD Services Contact: Mr. Bill Clopton, Disability Management Advisor, Sonoma State University, 1801 East Cotati Avenue, Rohnert Park, CA 94928-3609, 707-664-2677. Fax: 707-664-2505.

SOUTHEASTERN BIBLE COLLEGE

Birmingham, Alabama

LEARNING DISABILITIES SERVICES INFORMATION

Education Department currently serves 3 undergraduates with LD. Students diagnosed with ADD/ADHD are eligible for the same services available to students with LD.
Staff: 1 part-time staff member.
Special Fees: No special fees are charged for services to students with LD.
Applications and admissions: *Required:* high school transcript, personal interview, psychoeducational report completed in 9th or 10th grade. Students may begin taking classes in fall or spring. *Application deadline:* continuous.
Special policies: The college has written policies regarding grade forgiveness.

PROGRAM AND SERVICE COMPONENTS

Diagnostic testing: Reading, math, study skills, personality.
Academic advising: Provided by academic advisers. Most students with LD take 12 semester hours each term; 12 semester hours required to maintain full-time status.
Counseling services: Individual counseling.
Basic skills remediation: Offered one-on-one and in class-size groups by regular teachers; computer-aided instruction also offered. Available in math, spoken language, written language, learning strategies, study skills, time management.
Subject-area tutoring: Offered one-on-one and in small groups by professional teachers. Available in all subjects.
Auxiliary aids: Tape recorders, word-processors with spell-check, personal computers.
Auxiliary services: Alternative test arrangements, notetakers.

GENERAL COLLEGE INFORMATION

Independent nondenominational, 4-year, coed. Awards associate, bachelor's degrees. Founded 1935. *Setting:* 10-acre suburban campus.

EXPENSES AND FINANCIAL AID

Expenses for 1996–97: *Application fee:* $20. Comprehensive fee of $7980 includes full-time tuition ($4640), mandatory fees ($400), and college room and board ($2940). Part-time tuition: $145 per semester hour. Part-time mandatory fees: $110 per semester.
Undergraduate Financial Aid: 84% of all full-time undergraduates enrolled in fall 1996 applied for aid; of these, 98% were judged to have need according to Federal Methodology, of whom 100% were aided. On

average, 85% of need was met. *Financial aid deadline (priority):* 5/1. *Financial aid forms:* FAFSA required. Institutional form required for some.
LD Services Contact: Dr. William Maynor, Supervisor, Church Education, Southeastern Bible College, 3001 Highway 280 East, Birmingham, AL 35243, 205-969-0880. Fax: 205-970-9207.

SOUTHEASTERN COLLEGE OF THE ASSEMBLIES OF GOD

Lakeland, Florida

LEARNING DISABILITIES SERVICES INFORMATION

Pastoral Care and Counseling Department currently serves 23 undergraduates with LD. Students diagnosed with ADD/ADHD are eligible for the same services available to students with LD.
Staff: 1 part-time staff member (director). Services provided by counselor.
Special Fees: No special fees are charged for services to students with LD.
Applications and admissions: *Required:* high school transcript, IEP (Individualized Education Program); *recommended:* untimed or extended time ACT, extended time SAT I, letters of recommendation, psychoeducational report completed within 4 years. Students may begin taking classes in fall or spring. *Application deadline:* continuous.

PROGRAM AND SERVICE COMPONENTS

Academic advising: Provided by unit staff members. Students with LD may take up to 12 credits (first semester, re-evaluated afterwards) each term; most take 12 to 14 credits; 12 credits required to maintain full-time status; source of aid determines number of credits required to be eligible for financial aid.
Counseling services: Individual counseling, career counseling.
Basic skills remediation: Offered in class-size groups by regular teachers. Available in reading, math, written language.
Subject-area tutoring: Offered one-on-one by professional teachers, peer tutors. Available in all subjects.
Auxiliary aids: Personal computers.
Auxiliary services: Alternative test arrangements, notetakers, priority registration, advocacy.

GENERAL COLLEGE INFORMATION

Independent, 4-year, coed, affiliated with Assemblies of God. Awards bachelor's degrees. Founded 1935. *Setting:* 62-acre small-town campus with easy access to Tampa and Orlando. *Endowment:* $736,202. *Educational spending 1995–96:* $2121 per undergrad. *Total enrollment:* 1,090. *Faculty:* 85 (57 full-time, 57% with terminal degrees, 28 part-time); student–undergrad faculty ratio is 20:1.
Enrollment Profile: 1,090 students from 41 states and territories, 9 other countries. 51% women, 49% men, 6% part-time, 46% state residents, 58% live on campus, 2% international, 15% 25 or older, 1% Native American, 10% Hispanic, 3% black, 1% Asian or Pacific Islander. *Retention:* 68% of 1995 full-time freshmen returned. *Areas of study chosen:* 55% theology/religion, 32% education, 13% psychology. *Most popular recent majors:* ministries, education, psychology.
First-Year Class: 194 total; 256 applied, 99% were accepted, 76% of whom enrolled.
Graduation Requirements: 130 credits; 6 credits of math/science; computer course for education majors; internship (some majors).
Computers on Campus: 44 computers available on campus for general student use. Computer purchase/lease plans available. A computer is recommended for all students. A campus-wide network can be accessed from student residence rooms and from off-campus. Students can contact faculty members and/or advisers through e-mail. Computers for student use in computer labs, library, multimedia lab provide access to the Internet/World Wide Web, on- and off-campus e-mail addresses, network programs. Staffed computer lab on campus provides training in use of computers, software. *Academic computing expenditure 1995–96:* $137,994.

EXPENSES AND FINANCIAL AID

Expenses for 1996–97: *Application fee:* $40. Comprehensive fee of $7850 includes full-time tuition ($4170), mandatory fees ($634), and college room and board ($3046). Part-time tuition: $139 per credit.
Undergraduate Financial Aid: 88% of all full-time undergraduates enrolled in fall 1996 applied for aid; of these, 85% were judged to have need according to Federal Methodology, of whom 94% were aided. *Financial aid deadline (priority):* 5/1. *Financial aid forms:* FAFSA, institutional form required. State form required for some.
LD Services Contact: Mr. Gary Yost, Director of Pastoral Care and Counseling, Southeastern College of the Assemblies of God, 1660 Longfellow Boulevard, Lakeland, FL 33801, 941-667-5075. Fax: 941-667-5200. Email: gyost@secollege.edu.

SOUTHEASTERN OKLAHOMA STATE UNIVERSITY

Durant, Oklahoma

LEARNING DISABILITIES SERVICES INFORMATION

Office for Student Disability Services currently serves 25 undergraduates with LD. Services are also available to graduate students. Students diagnosed with ADD/ADHD are eligible for the same services available to students with LD.
Staff: 2 full-time staff members, including director, academic counselor. Services provided by counselors.
Special Fees: No special fees are charged for services to students with LD.
Applications and admissions: *Required:* high school transcript, grade point average, class rank, courses completed, extended time ACT. *Application deadline:* continuous.
Special policies: The college has written policies regarding grade forgiveness; substitutions and waivers of admissions and degree requirements.

PROGRAM AND SERVICE COMPONENTS

Academic advising: Provided by academic advisers. Students with LD may take up to 18 credit hours (more with special permission) each term; most take 13 credit hours; 12 credit hours required to maintain full-time status; 6 credit hours (part-time), 12 credit hours (full-time) required to be eligible for financial aid.
Counseling services: Individual counseling, small-group counseling, career counseling.
Basic skills remediation: Offered in small groups by regular teachers; computer-aided instruction also offered. Available in reading, math, written language, learning strategies, study skills, time management.
Auxiliary aids: Taped textbooks, tape recorders.
Auxiliary services: Alternative test arrangements, notetakers.

GENERAL COLLEGE INFORMATION

State-supported, comprehensive, coed. Part of Oklahoma State Regents for Higher Education. Awards bachelor's, master's degrees. Founded 1909. *Setting:* 176-acre small-town campus. *Research spending 1995–96:* $272,881. *Total enrollment:* 3,831. *Undergraduate faculty:* 202 (153 full-time, 58% with terminal degrees, 49 part-time); student–undergrad faculty ratio is 20:1.
Enrollment Profile: 3,401 students from 37 states and territories, 17 other countries. 54% women, 46% men, 19% part-time, 83% state residents, 15% live on campus, 39% transferred in, 2% international, 30% 25 or older, 32% Native American, 1% Hispanic, 4% black, 1% Asian or Pacific Islander. *Retention:* 60% of 1995 full-time freshmen returned. *Graduation:* 12% graduate in 4 years, 28% in 5 years, 32% in 6 years. *Areas of study chosen:* 27% education, 15% business management and administrative services, 13% liberal arts/general studies, 6% biological and life sciences, 5% engineering and applied sciences, 5% psychology, 4% computer and information sciences, 4% physical sciences, 4% social sciences, 3% communications and journalism, 3% natural resource sciences, 1% fine arts, 1% mathematics, 1% performing arts. *Most popular recent majors:* elementary education, criminal justice, business administration/commerce/management.
First-Year Class: 562 total; 833 applied, 84% were accepted, 80% of whom enrolled. 16% from top 10% of their high school class, 42% from top quarter, 72% from top half. 20 valedictorians.
Graduation Requirements: 124 credit hours; 1 math/science course; computer course; internship (some majors).
Computers on Campus: 100 computers available on campus for general student use. A campus-wide network can be accessed. Students can contact faculty members and/or advisers through e-mail. Computers for student use in computer center, computer labs, dorms, business, education schools provide access to the Internet/World Wide Web, off-campus e-mail addresses. Staffed computer lab on campus. *Academic computing expenditure 1995–96:* $425,080.

Southeastern Oklahoma State University (continued)

EXPENSES AND FINANCIAL AID

Expenses for 1996–97: Part-time mandatory fees per semester range from $18.90 to $147.90. Full-time tuition ranges from $1290 to $1320 for state residents, $3495 to $3765 for nonresidents, according to class level. Part-time tuition per credit hour ranges from $43 to $44 for state residents, $116.50 to $125.50 for nonresidents, according to class level. Full-time mandatory fees: $419. College room and board: $2619. College room only: $888.
Undergraduate Financial Aid: *Financial aid deadline (priority):* 4/1. *Financial aid forms:* FAFSA, institutional form required; CSS Financial Aid PROFILE acceptable.
LD Services Contact: Jan Anderson, Director, Student Support Services, Southeastern Oklahoma State University, Box 4112, Durant, OK 74701, 405-924-0121 Ext. 2557. Fax: 405-920-7470.

SOUTHEAST MISSOURI STATE UNIVERSITY

Cape Girardeau, Missouri

LEARNING DISABILITIES SERVICES INFORMATION

Campus Assistance Center currently serves 55 undergraduates with LD. Services are also available to graduate students. Students diagnosed with ADD/ADHD are eligible for the same services available to students with LD, as well as an early intervention program.
Staff: 4 full-time, 3 part-time staff members, including director, assistant directors. Services provided by tutors, graduate assistants.
Special Fees: $3 per hour for tutorial services.
Applications and admissions: *Required:* high school transcript, grade point average, courses completed, untimed or extended time ACT. Students may begin taking classes any term. *Application deadline:* 7/1 (fall term), 12/1 (spring term).

PROGRAM AND SERVICE COMPONENTS

Academic advising: Provided by academic advisers. Students with LD may take up to 18 credit hours each term; 12 credit hours required to maintain full-time status and be eligible for financial aid.
Counseling services: Individual counseling, small-group counseling.
Auxiliary aids: Taped textbooks, calculators, talking computers.
Auxiliary services: Alternative test arrangements, notetakers, priority registration, advocacy.

GENERAL COLLEGE INFORMATION

State-supported, comprehensive, coed. Part of Missouri Coordinating Board for Higher Education. Awards associate, bachelor's, master's degrees. Founded 1873. *Setting:* 800-acre small-town campus with easy access to St. Louis. *Endowment:* $8.8 million. *Research spending 1995–96:* $468,000. *Educational spending 1995–96:* $3209 per undergrad. *Total enrollment:* 8,200. *Undergraduate faculty:* 436 (361 full-time, 88% with terminal degrees, 75 part-time); student–undergrad faculty ratio is 18:1.
Enrollment Profile: 7,400 students from 43 states and territories, 37 other countries. 56% women, 44% men, 19% part-time, 84% state residents, 25% live on campus, 25% transferred in, 4% international, 19% 25 or older, 1% Native American, 1% Hispanic, 5% black, 1% Asian or Pacific Islander. *Retention:* 74% of 1995 full-time freshmen returned. *Areas of study chosen:* 20% business management and administrative services, 20% health professions and related sciences, 18% education, 7% communications and journalism, 6% psychology, 4% computer and information sciences, 4% social sciences, 4% vocational and home economics, 3% agriculture, 2% biological and life sciences, 2% performing arts, 2% physical sciences, 1% English language/literature/letters, 1% fine arts, 1% foreign language and literature, 1% interdisciplinary studies, 1% mathematics, 1% philosophy, 1% prelaw, 1% premed, 1% prevet. *Most popular recent majors:* business administration/commerce/management, education, communication.
First-Year Class: 1,300 total; 2,700 applied, 90% were accepted, 58% of whom enrolled. 20% from top 10% of their high school class, 45% from top quarter, 80% from top half. 2 National Merit Scholars, 39 valedictorians.
Graduation Requirements: 64 credit hours for associate, 124 credit hours for bachelor's; 1 college algebra course or equivalent; internship (some majors); senior project (some majors).
Computers on Campus: 695 computers available on campus for general student use. A computer is recommended for some students. A campus-wide network can be accessed from student residence rooms and from off-campus. Students can contact faculty members and/or advisers through e-mail. Computers for student use in computer labs, classrooms, library, student center, dorms, academic buildings provide access to the Internet/World Wide Web, on- and off-campus e-mail addresses. Staffed computer lab on campus provides training in use of computers, software. *Academic computing expenditure 1995–96:* $1.8 million.

EXPENSES AND FINANCIAL AID

Expenses for 1997–98: State resident tuition: $2892 full-time, $93.30 per credit hour part-time. Nonresident tuition: $5372 full-time, $173.30 per credit hour part-time. Part-time mandatory fees: $6.70 per credit hour. Full-time mandatory fees: $208. College room and board: $4000 (minimum). College room only: $2500 (minimum).
Undergraduate Financial Aid: 74% of all full-time undergraduates enrolled in fall 1996 applied for aid; of these, 78% were judged to have need according to Federal Methodology, of whom 95% were aided. On average, 65% of need was met. *Financial aid deadline (priority):* 3/1. *Financial aid forms:* FAFSA required; CSS Financial Aid PROFILE, state form acceptable.
LD Services Contact: Dr. Kerry H. Wynn, Assistant Director, Campus Assistance Center, Southeast Missouri State University, One University Plaza, Cape Girardeau, MO 63701, 573-651-2273. Fax: 573-651-2272.

SOUTHERN ADVENTIST UNIVERSITY

Collegedale, Tennessee

LEARNING DISABILITIES SERVICES INFORMATION

Center for Learning Success began offering services in 1993. Currently the program serves 47 undergraduates with LD. Services are also available to graduate students. Students diagnosed with ADD/ADHD are eligible for the same services available to students with LD.
Staff: 1 full-time, 1 part-time staff members, including coordinator. Services provided by tutor, counselor.
Special Fees: No special fees are charged for services to students with LD.
Applications and admissions: *Required:* high school transcript, grade point average, courses completed, untimed SAT I or ACT, letters of recommendation; *recommended:* extended time SAT I or ACT. Students may begin taking classes in fall, spring, or summer. *Application deadline:* continuous.

PROGRAM AND SERVICE COMPONENTS

Diagnostic testing: Intelligence, reading, math, spelling, handwriting, spoken language, written language, perceptual skills, study skills, personality.
Academic advising: Provided by unit staff members, academic advisers. Students with LD may take up to 12 semester hours each term; most take 10 to 12 semester hours; 10 semester hours required to maintain full-time status; 12 semester hours required to be eligible for financial aid.
Counseling services: Individual counseling, small-group counseling, career counseling.
Basic skills remediation: Offered one-on-one by regular teachers, teacher trainees; computer-aided instruction also offered. Available in reading, math, spelling, handwriting, spoken language, written language, study skills, time management, social skills.
Subject-area tutoring: Offered one-on-one by professional teachers, peer tutors. Available in some subjects.
Special courses: College survival skills, reading, communication skills, composition, learning strategies, time management, math, study skills, career planning. Most offered for credit; most enter into overall grade point average.
Auxiliary aids: Tape recorders, calculators, typewriters, word-processors with spell-check, personal computers.
Auxiliary services: Individually arranged.

GENERAL COLLEGE INFORMATION

Independent Seventh-day Adventist, comprehensive, coed. Awards associate, bachelor's, master's degrees. Founded 1892. *Setting:* 1,000-acre small-town campus with easy access to Chattanooga. *Endowment:* $13.7 million. *Research spending 1995–96:* $200,450. *Educational spending 1995–96:* $4899 per undergrad. *Total enrollment:* 1,650. *Faculty:* 133 (84 full-time, 48% with terminal degrees, 49 part-time); student–undergrad faculty ratio is 13:1.

Enrollment Profile: 1,625 students from 48 states and territories, 49 other countries. 56% women, 44% men, 21% part-time, 23% state residents, 75% live on campus, 9% transferred in, 11% international, 16% 25 or older, 0% Native American, 8% Hispanic, 4% black, 6% Asian or Pacific Islander. *Retention:* 62% of 1995 full-time freshmen returned. *Graduation:* 43% graduate in 5 years, 48% in 6 years. *Areas of study chosen:* 28% health professions and related sciences, 13% business management and administrative services, 9% theology/religion, 8% premed, 7% biological and life sciences, 7% education, 6% social sciences, 5% psychology, 3% communications and journalism, 3% computer and information sciences, 2% English language/literature/letters, 2% fine arts, 2% prelaw, 1% engineering and applied sciences, 1% foreign language and literature, 1% mathematics, 1% physical sciences, 1% predentistry. *Most popular recent majors:* nursing, business administration/commerce/management, biology/biological sciences.
First-Year Class: 401 total; 813 applied, 98% were accepted, 50% of whom enrolled. 2 National Merit Scholars.
Graduation Requirements: 64 semester hours for associate, 124 semester hours for bachelor's; 3 semester hours of math; 6 semester hours of science; computer course for business, education, physics majors; internship (some majors); senior project for honors program students and some majors.
Computers on Campus: 136 computers available on campus for general student use. A campus-wide network can be accessed from student residence rooms and from off-campus. Students can contact faculty members and/or advisers through e-mail. Computers for student use in computer center, computer labs, classrooms, library, departmental labs provide access to the Internet/World Wide Web, on- and off-campus e-mail addresses. Staffed computer lab on campus provides training in use of computers, software. *Academic computing expenditure 1995–96:* $446,472.

EXPENSES AND FINANCIAL AID

Expenses for 1997–98: *Application fee:* $20. Comprehensive fee of $13,364 includes full-time tuition ($9476), mandatory fees ($260), and college room and board ($3628). College room only: $1678. Part-time tuition: $410 per semester hour. Part-time mandatory fees: $130 per semester.
Undergraduate Financial Aid: 52% of all full-time undergraduates enrolled in fall 1996 applied for aid; of these, 96% were judged to have need according to Federal Methodology, of whom 92% were aided. On average, 77% of need was met. *Financial aid deadline (priority):* 3/1. *Financial aid forms:* FAFSA, institutional form, federal income tax forms, W-2 forms, and supporting documents required; state form acceptable.
LD Services Contact: Ms. Sheila S. Smith, Director of the Center for Learning Success, Southern Adventist University, PO Box 370, Collegedale, TN 37315-0370, 423-238-2574. Fax: 423-238-2575. Email: sssmith@southern.edu.

SOUTHERN ARKANSAS UNIVERSITY–MAGNOLIA

Magnolia, Arkansas

LEARNING DISABILITIES SERVICES INFORMATION

Office of Disability Support Services began offering services in 1990. Currently the program serves 14 undergraduates with LD. Services are also available to graduate students. Students diagnosed with ADD/ADHD are eligible for the same services available to students with LD.
Staff: 1 part-time staff member (coordinator). Services provided by counselors.
Special Fees: No special fees are charged for services to students with LD.
Applications and admissions: *Required:* high school transcript, psychoeducational report completed within 3 years; *recommended:* high school IEP (Individualized Education Program). Students may begin taking classes in fall, spring, or summer. *Application deadline:* continuous.
Special policies: The college has written policies regarding grade forgiveness; substitutions and waivers of admissions requirements.

PROGRAM AND SERVICE COMPONENTS

Academic advising: Provided by unit staff members, academic advisers. Students with LD may take up to 15 semester hours each term; most take 15 semester hours; 12 semester hours required to maintain full-time status and be eligible for financial aid.
Counseling services: Individual counseling, career counseling.
Auxiliary aids: Taped textbooks, tape recorders, word-processors with spell-check, personal computers.
Auxiliary services: Alternative test arrangements, notetakers, advocacy.

GENERAL COLLEGE INFORMATION

State-supported, comprehensive, coed. Part of Southern Arkansas University System. Awards associate, bachelor's, master's degrees. Founded 1909. *Setting:* 781-acre small-town campus. *Endowment:* $9.8 million. *Research spending 1995–96:* $111,748. *Educational spending 1995–96:* $2721 per undergrad. *Total enrollment:* 2,592. *Faculty:* 154 (122 full-time, 32 part-time); student–undergrad faculty ratio is 18:1.
Enrollment Profile: 2,408 students from 25 states and territories, 22 other countries. 56% women, 44% men, 15% part-time, 77% state residents, 39% transferred in, 2% international, 33% 25 or older, 1% Native American, 1% Hispanic, 22% black, 1% Asian or Pacific Islander. *Retention:* 59% of 1995 full-time freshmen returned. *Areas of study chosen:* 19% education, 18% business management and administrative services, 13% health professions and related sciences, 7% biological and life sciences, 6% agriculture, 5% social sciences, 3% psychology, 2% communications and journalism, 2% fine arts, 1% English language/literature/letters, 1% performing arts, 1% physical sciences, 1% predentistry, 1% premed, 1% prevet. *Most popular recent majors:* nursing, elementary education, business administration/commerce/management.
First-Year Class: 483 total; 558 applied, 98% were accepted, 88% of whom enrolled. 3% from top 10% of their high school class, 18% from top quarter, 79% from top half.
Graduation Requirements: 65 semester hours for associate, 124 semester hours for bachelor's; 1 college algebra course; computer course for business, chemistry, engineering, industrial technology, math, nursing, physics, psychology majors; senior project (some majors).
Computers on Campus: 150 computers available on campus for general student use. Computer purchase/lease plans available. A campus-wide network can be accessed from off-campus. Students can contact faculty members and/or advisers through e-mail. Computers for student use in computer center, computer labs, classrooms, library provide access to the Internet/World Wide Web, on- and off-campus e-mail addresses. Staffed computer lab on campus provides training in use of computers, software. *Academic computing expenditure 1995–96:* $434,424.

EXPENSES AND FINANCIAL AID

Expenses for 1997–98: State resident tuition: $1848 full-time, $77 per semester hour part-time. Nonresident tuition: $2856 full-time, $119 per semester hour part-time. Part-time mandatory fees: $2 per semester hour. Full-time mandatory fees: $48. College room and board: $2530.
Undergraduate Financial Aid: 91% of all full-time undergraduates enrolled in fall 1996 applied for aid; of these, 91% were judged to have need according to Federal Methodology, of whom 100% were aided. On average, 100% of need was met. *Financial aid deadline (priority):* 7/1. *Financial aid forms:* FAFSA, institutional form required. State form required for some.
LD Services Contact: Ms. Paula Washington-Woods, Interim Director, Counseling and Testing, Southern Arkansas University–Magnolia, Box 9371, Magnolia, AR 71753, 501-235-4145. Fax: 501-235-5005. Email: pwwoods@saumag.edu.

SOUTHERN CONNECTICUT STATE UNIVERSITY

New Haven, Connecticut

LEARNING DISABILITIES SERVICES INFORMATION

Disability Resource Office began offering services in 1981. Currently the program serves 560 undergraduates with LD. Services are also available to graduate students. Students diagnosed with ADD/ADHD are eligible for the same services available to students with LD.
Staff: 2 full-time, 2 part-time staff members, including coordinator, assistant coordinator. Services provided by remediation specialists, tutors, peer assistants.
Special Fees: No special fees are charged for services to students with LD.
Applications and admissions: *Required:* high school transcript, grade point average, class rank, untimed or extended time SAT I or ACT, autobiographical statement, psychoeducational report completed within 3 years; *recommended:* high school courses completed, extracurricular

Southern Connecticut State University (continued)

activities, letters of recommendation. Students may begin taking classes in fall, spring, or summer. *Application deadline:* continuous.

Special policies: The college has written policies regarding grade forgiveness; substitutions and waivers of graduation requirements.

PROGRAM AND SERVICE COMPONENTS

Special preparation or orientation: Orientation (required for some) held after classes begin.

Academic advising: Provided by unit staff members, academic advisers. Students with LD may take up to as many semester hours as an individual can handle each term; most take 9 to 15 semester hours; 6 semester hours required to maintain full-time status; 24 semester hours (fewer with petition) required to be eligible for financial aid.

Counseling services: Small-group counseling, career counseling, self-advocacy training.

Basic skills remediation: Offered one-on-one, in small groups, and in class-size groups by LD teachers; computer-aided instruction also offered. Available in math, written language, learning strategies, study skills, time management, word processing.

Subject-area tutoring: Offered one-on-one by peer tutors. Available in some subjects.

Special courses: College survival skills, composition, learning strategies, math. Most offered for credit; most enter into overall grade point average.

Auxiliary aids: Taped textbooks, tape recorders, calculators, typewriters, word-processors with spell-check, personal computers, optical character readers, adaptive technology lab.

Auxiliary services: Alternative test arrangements, notetakers, priority registration, advocacy.

GENERAL COLLEGE INFORMATION

State-supported, comprehensive, coed. Part of Connecticut State University System. Awards associate, bachelor's, master's degrees. Founded 1893. *Setting:* 168-acre urban campus with easy access to New York City. *Total enrollment:* 11,412. *Faculty:* 719 (368 full-time, 72% with terminal degrees, 351 part-time); student–undergrad faculty ratio is 19:1.

Enrollment Profile: 7,568 students from 43 states and territories, 26 other countries. 56% women, 44% men, 29% part-time, 92% state residents, 8% transferred in, 1% international, 23% 25 or older, 1% Native American, 4% Hispanic, 10% black, 2% Asian or Pacific Islander. *Retention:* 70% of 1995 full-time freshmen returned. *Graduation:* 50% graduate in 4 years.

First-Year Class: 1,009 total; 3,532 applied, 71% were accepted, 40% of whom enrolled. 3% from top 10% of their high school class, 30% from top quarter, 41% from top half.

Graduation Requirements: 62 semester hours for associate, 120 semester hours for bachelor's; 1 semester of math; 2 semesters of science; 1 year of a foreign language for bachelor's degree; computer course for economics, business administration, physics, chemistry, math, biology majors; internship (some majors); senior project for honors program students.

Computers on Campus: 486 computers available on campus for general student use. Computer purchase/lease plans available. A computer is recommended for all students. A campus-wide network can be accessed from student residence rooms and from off-campus. Students can contact faculty members and/or advisers through e-mail. Computers for student use in computer center, computer labs, library provide access to the Internet/World Wide Web, on- and off-campus e-mail addresses. Staffed computer lab on campus provides training in use of computers, software.

EXPENSES AND FINANCIAL AID

Expenses for 1997–98: *Application fee:* $20. State resident tuition: $2062 full-time. Nonresident tuition: $6674 full-time. Full-time tuition for nonresidents who are eligible for the New England Regional Student Program: $3093. Full-time mandatory fees: $1506 for state residents and nonresidents who are eligible for the New England Regional Student Program, $2372 for other nonresidents. College room and board: $5366. College room only: $2774.

Undergraduate Financial Aid: On average, 70% of need was met. *Financial aid deadline:* Applications processed continuously. *Financial aid forms:* FAFSA, institutional form, parent and student federal income tax forms required.

LD Services Contact: Ms. Suzanne Tucker, Coordinator, Southern Connecticut State University, Engleman Hall-25, New Haven, CT 06515, 203-392-6828. Fax: 203-392-6813.

SOUTHERN ILLINOIS UNIVERSITY AT EDWARDSVILLE

Edwardsville, Illinois

LEARNING DISABILITIES SERVICES INFORMATION

Disabled Student Services began offering services in 1986. Currently the program serves 55 undergraduates with LD. Services are also available to graduate students. Students diagnosed with ADD/ADHD are eligible for the same services available to students with LD.

Staff: 1 full-time, 3 part-time staff members, including coordinator. Services provided by tutors, graduate assistant, student workers.

Special Fees: No special fees are charged for services to students with LD.

Applications and admissions: *Required:* high school transcript, grade point average, class rank, courses completed, IEP (Individualized Education Program), untimed or extended time ACT, untimed SAT I, psychoeducational report completed within 3 years. Students may begin taking classes any term. *Application deadline:* continuous.

Special policies: The college has written policies regarding substitutions and waivers of admissions, graduation, and degree requirements.

PROGRAM AND SERVICE COMPONENTS

Special preparation or orientation: Optional orientation offered during first week of fall semester.

Diagnostic testing: Reading, math, spelling, written language.

Academic advising: Provided by unit staff members, academic advisers. Students with LD may take up to 18 semester hours each term; most take 15 semester hours; 12 semester hours required to maintain full-time status; 6 semester hours (part-time), 12 semester hours (full-time) required to be eligible for financial aid.

Counseling services: Individual counseling, career counseling.

Basic skills remediation: Offered in class-size groups by regular teachers. Available in reading, math, spelling, written language, learning strategies, study skills, time management, social skills.

Subject-area tutoring: Offered one-on-one by peer tutors. Available in all subjects.

Special courses: College survival skills, reading, vocabulary development, composition, learning strategies, time management, math, study skills, career planning. All offered for credit; some enter into overall grade point average.

Auxiliary aids: Taped textbooks, tape recorders, calculators, typewriters, word-processors with spell-check, personal computers, talking computers, optical character readers, Spell Center software.

Auxiliary services: Alternative test arrangements, notetakers, priority registration, reader, writers.

Campus support group: A special student organization is available to students with LD.

GENERAL COLLEGE INFORMATION

State-supported, comprehensive, coed. Part of Southern Illinois University. Awards bachelor's, master's, first professional degrees. Founded 1957. *Setting:* 2,660-acre suburban campus with easy access to St. Louis. *Endowment:* $4.1 million. *Research spending 1995–96:* $2.7 million. *Educational spending 1995–96:* $4317 per undergrad. *Total enrollment:* 11,151. *Faculty:* 750 (550 full-time, 85% with terminal degrees, 200 part-time); student–undergrad faculty ratio is 15:1.

Enrollment Profile: 8,610 students from 41 states and territories, 59 other countries. 58% women, 42% men, 26% part-time, 87% state residents, 19% live on campus, 14% transferred in, 1% international, 31% 25 or older, 0% Native American, 1% Hispanic, 13% black, 2% Asian or Pacific Islander. *Retention:* 68% of 1995 full-time freshmen returned. *Graduation:* 10% graduate in 4 years, 25% in 5 years, 33% in 6 years. *Areas of study chosen:* 7% business management and administrative services, 6% education, 6% engineering and applied sciences, 6% social sciences, 4% biological and life sciences, 4% health professions and related sciences, 3% psychology, 2% fine arts, 2% performing arts, 1% communications and journalism, 1% computer and information sciences, 1% English language/literature/letters, 1% mathematics, 1% physical sciences. *Most popular recent majors:* business administration/commerce/management, nursing, elementary education.

First-Year Class: 1,274 total; 3,175 applied, 85% were accepted, 47% of whom enrolled. 13% from top 10% of their high school class, 39% from top quarter, 78% from top half.

Graduation Requirements: 124 semester hours; 9 semester hours of math/science; computer course for civil engineering, chemistry, math, accounting, business administration, economics, business education majors; internship (some majors); senior project.
Computers on Campus: 454 computers available on campus for general student use. Computer purchase/lease plans available. A campus-wide network can be accessed from student residence rooms. Students can contact faculty members and/or advisers through e-mail. Computers for student use in computer labs, learning resource center, classrooms, library, dorms provide access to the Internet/World Wide Web, on- and off-campus e-mail addresses. Staffed computer lab on campus (open 24 hours a day) provides training in use of computers, software. *Academic computing expenditure 1995–96:* $2.1 million.

EXPENSES AND FINANCIAL AID

Expenses for 1997–98: State resident tuition: $2020 full-time, $84.15 per semester hour part-time. Nonresident tuition: $6059 full-time, $252.45 per semester hour part-time. Part-time mandatory fees per semester range from $112.70 to $127.85. Full-time mandatory fees: $256. College room and board: $4160. College room only: $2300.
Undergraduate Financial Aid: Of all full-time undergraduates enrolled in fall 1996, 75% of those who applied for aid were judged to have need according to Federal Methodology, of whom 92% were aided. On average, 95% of need was met. *Financial aid deadline (priority):* 3/1. *Financial aid forms:* FAFSA required.
LD Services Contact: Ms. Jane Floyd-Hendey, Coordinator for Disability Support Services, Southern Illinois University at Edwardsville, Box 1611, Edwardsville, IL 62026-0001, 618-692-3782. Fax: 618-692-3388. Email: jfloydh@siue.edu.

SOUTHERN METHODIST UNIVERSITY

Dallas, Texas

LEARNING DISABILITIES SERVICES INFORMATION

Services for Students with Disabilities began offering services in 1980. Currently the program serves 300 undergraduates with LD. Services are also available to graduate students. Students diagnosed with ADD/ADHD are eligible for the same services available to students with LD, as well as psychiatric evaluation (for ADHD assessment).
Staff: 3 full-time staff members, including director. Services provided by remediation specialists, tutors, counselors, diagnostic specialists.
Special Fees: $100 for diagnostic testing.
Applications and admissions: *Required:* high school transcript, untimed SAT I or ACT, letters of recommendation, psychoeducational report completed within 3 years, essay; *recommended:* extended time SAT I or ACT. Students may begin taking classes in fall, spring, or summer. *Application deadline:* 4/1.

PROGRAM AND SERVICE COMPONENTS

Diagnostic testing: Intelligence, reading, math, spelling, written language, perceptual skills, study skills, personality, learning strategies.
Academic advising: Provided by academic advisers. Students with LD may take up to 18 credit hours each term; most take 12 credit hours; 12 credit hours required to maintain full-time status and be eligible for financial aid.
Counseling services: Individual counseling, career counseling.
Basic skills remediation: Offered in small groups and in class-size groups by professional staff. Available in reading, written language, learning strategies, study skills, time management.
Subject-area tutoring: Offered one-on-one and in small groups by professional teachers, peer tutors, graduate students. Available in all subjects.
Special courses: College survival skills, reading, vocabulary development, learning strategies, word processing, time management, typing, study skills, career planning. None offered for credit.
Auxiliary aids: Taped textbooks, tape recorders, personal computers, optical character readers, Optic 20/20.
Auxiliary services: Alternative test arrangements, notetakers, priority registration, advocacy.

GENERAL COLLEGE INFORMATION

Independent, coed, affiliated with United Methodist Church. Awards bachelor's, master's, doctoral, first professional degrees. Founded 1911. *Setting:* 163-acre suburban campus. *Endowment:* $562.8 million. *Research spending 1995–96:* $7.5 million. *Total enrollment:* 9,464. *Faculty:* 752 (493 full-time, 90% with terminal degrees, 259 part-time); student–undergrad faculty ratio is 12:1.
Enrollment Profile: 5,362 students from 50 states and territories, 66 other countries. 54% women, 46% men, 7% part-time, 60% state residents, 30% transferred in, 3% international, 8% 25 or older, 1% Native American, 9% Hispanic, 6% black, 6% Asian or Pacific Islander. *Retention:* 86% of 1995 full-time freshmen returned. *Graduation:* 57% graduate in 4 years, 71% in 5 years, 72% in 6 years. *Areas of study chosen:* 25% business management and administrative services, 16% communications and journalism, 10% social sciences, 8% engineering and applied sciences, 8% English language/literature/letters, 7% performing arts, 6% psychology, 4% biological and life sciences, 3% computer and information sciences, 3% fine arts, 3% foreign language and literature, 2% mathematics, 1% area and ethnic studies, 1% interdisciplinary studies, 1% philosophy, 1% physical sciences, 1% theology/religion. *Most popular recent majors:* finance/banking, psychology, advertising.
First-Year Class: 1,218 total; 3,924 applied, 90% were accepted, 35% of whom enrolled. 30% from top 10% of their high school class, 60% from top quarter, 90% from top half.
Graduation Requirements: 122 credit hours; 9 credit hours of math/science including at least 2 lab science courses; computer course for engineering, business majors.
Computers on Campus: 339 computers available on campus for general student use. Computer purchase/lease plans available. A computer is recommended for all students. A campus-wide network can be accessed from student residence rooms and from off-campus. Students can contact faculty members and/or advisers through e-mail. Computers for student use in computer center, computer labs, research center, learning resource center, classrooms, library, student center, dorms, various locations provide access to the Internet/World Wide Web, on- and off-campus e-mail addresses. Staffed computer lab on campus provides training in use of computers, software. *Academic computing expenditure 1995–96:* $545,000.

EXPENSES AND FINANCIAL AID

Expenses for 1997–98: *Application fee:* $40. Comprehensive fee of $26,926 includes full-time tuition ($16,790), mandatory fees ($2400), and college room and board ($7736 minimum). College room only: $3520 (minimum). Part-time tuition: $622 per credit hour. Part-time mandatory fees: $80 per credit hour.
Undergraduate Financial Aid: Of all full-time undergraduates enrolled in fall 1996, 90% of those who applied for aid were judged to have need according to Federal Methodology, of whom 100% were aided. On average, 40% of need was met. *Financial aid deadline (priority):* 1/15. *Financial aid forms:* FAFSA required.
LD Services Contact: Ms. Sandra Muskopf, Assistant Dean of Student Life, Southern Methodist University, Box 355, Dallas, TX 75275-0355, 214-768-4563.

SOUTHERN POLYTECHNIC STATE UNIVERSITY

Marietta, Georgia

LEARNING DISABILITIES SERVICES INFORMATION

Counseling Center began offering services in 1985. Currently the program serves 14 undergraduates with LD. Services are also available to graduate students. Students diagnosed with ADD/ADHD are eligible for the same services available to students with LD.
Staff: 1 part-time staff member (director). Services provided by remediation specialists, tutors, counselor.
Special Fees: No special fees are charged for services to students with LD.
Applications and admissions: *Required:* high school transcript, untimed SAT I; *recommended:* extended time SAT I. Students may begin taking classes any term. *Application deadline:* 8/31 (fall term), 3/10 (spring term).
Special policies: The college has written policies regarding grade forgiveness; substitutions and waivers of admissions, graduation, and degree requirements.

PROGRAM AND SERVICE COMPONENTS

Academic advising: Provided by unit staff members, academic advisers. Students with LD required to take 12 quarter hours each term to maintain full-time status; 4 quarter hours (Pell Grant), 6 quarter hours (all other aid) required to be eligible for financial aid.

Counseling services: Individual counseling, small-group counseling, career counseling.
Basic skills remediation: Offered one-on-one by regular teachers, teacher trainees, developmental studies department and Learning Resource Center staff; computer-aided instruction also offered. Available in reading, math, spelling, written language, study skills.
Subject-area tutoring: Offered one-on-one by peer tutors. Available in most subjects.
Auxiliary aids: Word-processors with spell-check.
Auxiliary services: Alternative test arrangements, notetakers, priority registration, advocacy.

GENERAL COLLEGE INFORMATION

State-supported, comprehensive, coed. Part of University System of Georgia. Awards associate, bachelor's, master's degrees. Founded 1948. *Setting:* 200-acre suburban campus with easy access to Atlanta. *Endowment:* $532,750. *Research spending 1995–96:* $139,459. *Total enrollment:* 3,871. *Faculty:* 203 (143 full-time, 55% with terminal degrees, 60 part-time); student–undergrad faculty ratio is 18:1.
Enrollment Profile: 3,296 students from 23 states and territories, 46 other countries. 17% women, 83% men, 37% part-time, 93% state residents, 12% live on campus, 61% transferred in, 4% international, 42% 25 or older, 1% Native American, 2% Hispanic, 17% black, 5% Asian or Pacific Islander. *Retention:* 65% of 1995 full-time freshmen returned. *Graduation:* 2% graduate in 4 years, 10% in 5 years, 19% in 6 years. *Areas of study chosen:* 71% engineering and applied sciences, 14% computer and information sciences, 10% architecture, 3% business management and administrative services, 1% mathematics, 1% physical sciences. *Most popular recent majors:* electrical engineering technology, civil engineering technology, industrial engineering technology.
First-Year Class: 375 total; 799 applied, 74% were accepted, 63% of whom enrolled.
Graduation Requirements: 95 quarter hours for associate, 196 quarter hours for bachelor's; 3 quarters each of math and science; computer course; senior project (some majors).
Computers on Campus: 500 computers available on campus for general student use. A computer is recommended for some students. A campus-wide network can be accessed from off-campus. Students can contact faculty members and/or advisers through e-mail. Computers for student use in computer center, computer labs, learning resource center, library, departmental labs provide access to the Internet/World Wide Web. Staffed computer lab on campus provides training in use of computers, software. *Academic computing expenditure 1995–96:* $600,000.

EXPENSES AND FINANCIAL AID

Expenses for 1996–97: State resident tuition: $1584 full-time, $44 per quarter hour part-time. Nonresident tuition: $5463 full-time, $152 per quarter hour part-time. Full-time mandatory fees: $267. College room and board: $3930. College room only: $1725 (minimum).
Undergraduate Financial Aid: Of all full-time undergraduates enrolled in fall 1996, 70% of those who applied for aid were judged to have need according to Federal Methodology, of whom 84% were aided. On average, 85% of need was met. *Financial aid deadline (priority):* 3/15. *Financial aid forms:* FAFSA, institutional form required; CSS Financial Aid PROFILE acceptable.
LD Services Contact: Ms. Mary Stoy, Director, Counseling Services, Southern Polytechnic State University, 1100 South Marietta Parkway, Marietta, GA 30060-2896, 404-528-7226. Fax: 404-528-7409.

SOUTHERN UTAH UNIVERSITY

Cedar City, Utah

LEARNING DISABILITIES SERVICES INFORMATION

Student Support Services began offering services in 1981. Currently the program serves 53 undergraduates with LD. Students diagnosed with ADD/ADHD are eligible for the same services available to students with LD.
Staff: 4 full-time, 2 part-time staff members, including director, coordinator, English instructors, math specialist, learning specialist. Services provided by remediation specialists, tutors, counselors.
Special Fees: No special fees are charged for services to students with LD.
Applications and admissions: *Required:* high school transcript, grade point average, courses completed, untimed or extended time ACT; *recommended:* untimed or extended time SAT I, psychoeducational report completed within 3 years. Students may begin taking classes in fall, winter, or spring. *Application deadline:* 7/1 (fall term), 3/1 (spring term).
Special policies: The college has written policies regarding grade forgiveness; substitutions and waivers of admissions, graduation, and degree requirements.

PROGRAM AND SERVICE COMPONENTS

Diagnostic testing: Reading, math, written language, study skills, personality, learning strategies.
Academic advising: Provided by unit staff members, academic advisers. Most students with LD take 12 to 15 quarter hours each term; 12 quarter hours required to maintain full-time status and be eligible for financial aid.
Counseling services: Individual counseling, small-group counseling, career counseling.
Basic skills remediation: Offered one-on-one, in small groups, and in class-size groups by regular teachers. Available in reading, math, spelling, written language, learning strategies, perceptual skills, study skills, time management.
Subject-area tutoring: Offered one-on-one and in small groups by professional teachers, peer tutors. Available in some subjects.
Special courses: College survival skills, reading, vocabulary development, communication skills, composition, learning strategies, time management, math, personal psychology, study skills, career planning, test anxiety. Some offered for credit; some enter into overall grade point average.
Auxiliary aids: Taped textbooks, tape recorders, calculators, word-processors with spell-check, personal computers, optical character readers.
Auxiliary services: Alternative test arrangements, notetakers, advocacy.

GENERAL COLLEGE INFORMATION

State-supported, comprehensive, coed. Part of Utah System of Higher Education. Awards associate, bachelor's, master's degrees. Founded 1897. *Setting:* 113-acre small-town campus. *Endowment:* $4.4 million. *Educational spending 1995–96:* $2620 per undergrad. *Total enrollment:* 5,640. *Faculty:* 217 (184 full-time, 65% with terminal degrees, 33 part-time); student–undergrad faculty ratio is 24:1.
Enrollment Profile: 5,426 students from 40 states and territories, 14 other countries. 57% women, 43% men, 25% part-time, 90% state residents, 11% transferred in, 1% international, 29% 25 or older, 1% Native American, 1% Hispanic, 1% black, 3% Asian or Pacific Islander. *Retention:* 60% of 1995 full-time freshmen returned. *Most popular recent majors:* elementary education, business administration/commerce/management, biology/biological sciences.
First-Year Class: 1,011 total; 1,959 applied, 99% were accepted, 52% of whom enrolled. 1% from top 10% of their high school class, 23% from top quarter, 57% from top half.
Graduation Requirements: 96 quarter hours for associate, 183 quarter hours for bachelor's; 1 course each in intermediate algebra and science; computer course for accounting, business administration, math majors; senior project (some majors).
Computers on Campus: 300 computers available on campus for general student use. Computer purchase/lease plans available. A campus-wide network can be accessed from student residence rooms and from off-campus. Students can contact faculty members and/or advisers through e-mail. Computers for student use in computer center, computer labs, classrooms, library, student center, dorms, student rooms, departmental labs provide access to the Internet/World Wide Web, on- and off-campus e-mail addresses. Staffed computer lab on campus provides training in use of computers, software. *Academic computing expenditure 1995–96:* $576,379.

EXPENSES AND FINANCIAL AID

Expenses for 1997–98: *Application fee:* $25. State resident tuition: $1440 full-time. Nonresident tuition: $5439 full-time. Part-time mandatory fees per quarter hour range from $20 to $127. Part-time tuition (1 to 9 quarter hours): $48 per quarter hour for state residents, $184 to $1632 per quarter for nonresidents. Full-time mandatory fees: $414. College room and board: $2502. College room only: $1077 (minimum).
Undergraduate Financial Aid: *Financial aid deadline (priority):* 8/10. *Financial aid forms:* FAFSA, institutional form required.
LD Services Contact: Ms. Cindi Klaus, Academic Coordinator, Student Support Services, Southern Utah University, 351 West Center, Cedar City, UT 84720, 801-586-7848. Fax: 801-586-7934. Email: klaus_c@suu.edu.

SOUTHERN VERMONT COLLEGE

Bennington, Vermont

LEARNING DISABILITIES SERVICES INFORMATION

Learning Disabilities Program began offering services in 1983. Currently the program serves 69 undergraduates with LD. Students diagnosed with ADD/ADHD are eligible for the same services available to students with LD, as well as assistance with organizational and time management skills.
Staff: 2 full-time staff members, including assistant director, coordinator. Services provided by tutors, diagnostic specialists, LD specialist.
Special Fees: No special fees are charged for services to students with LD.
Applications and admissions: *Required:* high school transcript, grade point average, class rank, courses completed, IEP (Individualized Education Program), letters of recommendation, psychoeducational report completed within 2 years, WISC-R or WAIS-R, Woodcock-Johnson Psychoeducational Battery or other cognitive achievement testing; *recommended:* high school extracurricular activities, extended time SAT I, personal interview, autobiographical statement. Students may begin taking classes in fall or summer. *Application deadline:* continuous.
Special policies: The college has written policies regarding substitutions and waivers of degree requirements.

PROGRAM AND SERVICE COMPONENTS

Special preparation or orientation: Optional summer program offered prior to entering college. Required orientation held before registration.
Diagnostic testing: Reading, math, spelling.
Academic advising: Provided by unit staff members, academic advisers. Students with LD may take up to 15 credits each term; most take 12 credits; 12 credits required to maintain full-time status; 6 credits required to be eligible for financial aid.
Subject-area tutoring: Offered one-on-one and in small groups by professional teachers, peer tutors, LD Coordinator. Available in most subjects.
Auxiliary aids: Taped textbooks.
Auxiliary services: Alternative test arrangements, advocacy.

GENERAL COLLEGE INFORMATION

Independent, 4-year, coed. Awards associate, bachelor's degrees. Founded 1926. *Setting:* 371-acre small-town campus. *Endowment:* $584,946. *Total enrollment:* 616. *Faculty:* 56 (27 full-time, 19% with terminal degrees, 29 part-time); student–undergrad faculty ratio is 18:1.
Enrollment Profile: 616 students from 16 states and territories, 6 other countries. 58% women, 42% men, 39% part-time, 43% state residents, 25% transferred in, 1% international, 38% 25 or older, 0% Native American, 1% Hispanic, 1% black, 1% Asian or Pacific Islander. *Areas of study chosen:* 39% social sciences, 26% business management and administrative services, 14% liberal arts/general studies, 8% natural resource sciences, 5% communications and journalism, 5% health professions and related sciences, 3% biological and life sciences. *Most popular recent majors:* criminal justice, business administration/commerce/management, liberal arts/general studies.
First-Year Class: 135 total; 321 applied, 86% were accepted, 49% of whom enrolled. 11% from top 10% of their high school class, 17% from top quarter, 62% from top half.
Graduation Requirements: 60 credits for associate, 120 credits for bachelor's; 1 course each in math and science for associate degree; 2 courses each in math and science for bachelor's degree; computer course for all bachelor's degree programs; internship (some majors); senior project for honors program students.
Computers on Campus: 30 computers available on campus for general student use. Computer purchase/lease plans available. A campuswide network can be accessed from student residence rooms and from off-campus. Students can contact faculty members and/or advisers through e-mail. Computers for student use in computer center, computer labs, library provide access to the Internet/World Wide Web, on- and off-campus e-mail addresses. Staffed computer lab on campus (open 24 hours a day) provides training in use of computers, software.

EXPENSES AND FINANCIAL AID

Expenses for 1997–98: *Application fee:* $25. Comprehensive fee of $16,234 includes full-time tuition ($11,130), mandatory fees ($170), and college room and board ($4934). College room only: $2394. Part-time tuition: $371 per credit. Part-time mandatory fees per semester range from $40 to $85.
Undergraduate Financial Aid: 87% of all full-time undergraduates enrolled in fall 1996 applied for aid; of these, 93% were judged to have need according to Federal Methodology, of whom 100% were aided. On average, 100% of need was met. *Financial aid deadline (priority):* 5/1. *Financial aid forms:* FAFSA, institutional form required; CSS Financial Aid PROFILE acceptable.
LD Services Contact: Ms. Linda Crowe, Learning Disabilities Coordinator, Southern Vermont College, Monument Avenue, Bennington, VT 05201-2128, 802-447-6360.

SOUTHWEST STATE UNIVERSITY

Marshall, Minnesota

LEARNING DISABILITIES SERVICES INFORMATION

Learning Resources began offering services in 1976. Currently the program serves 60 undergraduates with LD. Services are also available to graduate students. Students diagnosed with ADD/ADHD are eligible for the same services available to students with LD.
Staff: 3 full-time, 3 part-time staff members, including director, coordinators. Services provided by remediation specialist, tutors, diagnostic specialists.
Special Fees: No special fees are charged for services to students with LD.
Applications and admissions: *Required:* high school transcript, courses completed, extracurricular activities, extended time ACT; *recommended:* untimed ACT, personal interview, autobiographical statement, letters of recommendation, psychoeducational report completed within 2 years if traditional age High School graduate (adult diagnostic if non-traditional age). Students may begin taking classes in fall, spring, or summer. *Application deadline:* continuous.
Special policies: The college has written policies regarding grade forgiveness.

PROGRAM AND SERVICE COMPONENTS

Special preparation or orientation: Optional orientation offered the week before classes begin.
Diagnostic testing: Intelligence, reading, math, spelling, written language, perceptual skills, study skills, personality, speech, learning strategies, vocational aptitude.
Academic advising: Provided by unit staff members, academic advisers. Most students with LD take 16 credits each term; 16 credits required to maintain full-time status; 12 credits (16 for state aid) required to be eligible for financial aid.
Counseling services: Individual counseling, small-group counseling, career counseling, self-advocacy training.
Basic skills remediation: Offered one-on-one, in small groups, and in class-size groups by LD teachers, regular teachers; computer-aided instruction also offered. Available in reading, math, spelling, learning strategies, perceptual skills, time management, speech, computer skills, reasoning skills.
Subject-area tutoring: Offered one-on-one, in small groups, and in class-size groups by professional teachers, peer tutors. Available in most subjects.
Special courses: College survival skills, reading, vocabulary development, communication skills, composition, learning strategies, word processing, math, study skills, career planning, stress management, any recommended skill area according to individual need. All offered for credit; all enter into overall grade point average.
Auxiliary aids: Taped textbooks, tape recorders, word-processors with spell-check, personal computers, talking computers, optical character readers, speech screen reader on Mac computer.
Auxiliary services: Alternative test arrangements, notetakers, priority registration, advocacy.
Campus support group: A special student organization is available to students with LD.

GENERAL COLLEGE INFORMATION

State-supported, comprehensive, coed. Part of Minnesota Colleges and Universities System. Awards associate, bachelor's, master's degrees. Founded 1963. *Setting:* 216-acre small-town campus. *Endowment:* $83,000. *Research spending 1995–96:* $128,146. *Educational spending 1995–96:* $3373 per undergrad. *Total enrollment:* 2,900. *Faculty:* 124 (115 full-time, 86% with terminal degrees, 9 part-time); student–undergrad faculty ratio is 19:1.
Enrollment Profile: 2,798 students from 26 states and territories, 21 other countries. 56% women, 44% men, 40% part-time, 84% state resi-

Southwest State University (continued)

dents, 27% transferred in, 2% international, 10% 25 or older, 1% Native American, 1% Hispanic, 2% black, 1% Asian or Pacific Islander. *Retention:* 87% of 1995 full-time freshmen returned. *Areas of study chosen:* 40% business management and administrative services, 11% social sciences, 9% education, 6% health professions and related sciences, 5% English language/literature/letters, 5% interdisciplinary studies, 5% psychology, 3% computer and information sciences, 3% mathematics, 2% agriculture, 2% biological and life sciences, 2% communications and journalism, 2% engineering and applied sciences, 2% fine arts, 2% physical sciences, 1% performing arts. *Most popular recent majors:* business administration/commerce/management, education, accounting.

First-Year Class: 420 total; 858 applied, 90% were accepted, 54% of whom enrolled. 17% from top 10% of their high school class, 43% from top quarter, 82% from top half.

Graduation Requirements: 64 credit hours for associate, 128 credit hours for bachelor's; 3 credit hours of math; 12 credit hours of science; computer course for math, business majors; internship (some majors); senior project.

Computers on Campus: 225 computers available on campus for general student use. Computer purchase/lease plans available. A computer is recommended for all students. A campus-wide network can be accessed from student residence rooms and from off-campus. Students can contact faculty members and/or advisers through e-mail. Computers for student use in computer center, computer labs, research center, learning resource center, classrooms, library, dorms provide access to the Internet/World Wide Web, on- and off-campus e-mail addresses. Staffed computer lab on campus provides training in use of computers, software. *Academic computing expenditure 1995–96:* $368,895.

EXPENSES AND FINANCIAL AID

Expenses for 1996–97: *Application fee:* $20. State resident tuition: $2496 full-time, $78 per credit hour part-time. Nonresident tuition: $5624 full-time, $175.75 per credit hour part-time. Part-time mandatory fees: $19.41 per credit hour. North and South Dakota residents pay state resident tuition rates. Full-time mandatory fees: $484. College room and board: $2900. College room only: $2012.

Undergraduate Financial Aid: Of all full-time undergraduates enrolled in fall 1996, 86% of those who applied for aid were judged to have need according to Federal Methodology, of whom 98% were aided. On average, 92% of need was met. *Financial aid deadline (priority):* 4/1. *Financial aid forms:* FAFSA, institutional form required.

LD Services Contact: Ms. Lynn Monge, Coordinator for Academic Success, Southwest State University, 1501 State Street, Marshall, MN 56258, 507-537-7304. Fax: 507-537-6200. Email: monge@ssu.southwest.msus.edu.

SPRINGFIELD COLLEGE

Springfield, Massachusetts

LEARNING DISABILITIES SERVICES INFORMATION

Office of Student Support Services began offering services in 1993. Currently the program serves 100 undergraduates with LD. Services are also available to graduate students. Students diagnosed with ADD/ADHD are eligible for the same services available to students with LD, as well as distraction-free testing locations.

Staff: 1 full-time staff member (director). Services provided by tutors.

Special Fees: No special fees are charged for services to students with LD.

Applications and admissions: *Required:* high school transcript, grade point average, class rank, courses completed, personal interview, autobiographical statement, letters of recommendation; *recommended:* high school extracurricular activities, IEP (Individualized Education Program), untimed or extended time SAT I or ACT, psychoeducational report completed within 3 years. Students may begin taking classes in fall only. *Application deadline:* 4/1.

PROGRAM AND SERVICE COMPONENTS

Academic advising: Provided by unit staff members, academic advisers. Students with LD may take up to 18 credits each term; most take 12 to 15 credits; 12 credits required to maintain full-time status and be eligible for financial aid.

Counseling services: Individual counseling, career counseling, self-advocacy training.

Basic skills remediation: Offered one-on-one by Director. Available in learning strategies, study skills, time management, self-advocacy skills.

Subject area tutoring: Offered one on one by peer tutors. Available in all subjects.

Auxiliary aids: Taped textbooks, tape recorders, optical character readers, spell checkers (pocket-size).

Auxiliary services: Alternative test arrangements, notetakers.

GENERAL COLLEGE INFORMATION

Independent, comprehensive, coed. Awards bachelor's, master's, doctoral degrees. Founded 1885. *Setting:* 167-acre suburban campus. *Total enrollment:* 2,923. *Faculty:* 232 (174 full-time, 58 part-time); student–undergrad faculty ratio is 15:1.

Enrollment Profile: 2,011 students from 37 states and territories, 16 other countries. 49% women, 51% men, 3% part-time, 33% state residents, 16% transferred in, 3% international, 0% Native American, 1% Hispanic, 6% black, 1% Asian or Pacific Islander. *Retention:* 83% of 1995 full-time freshmen returned. *Graduation:* 68% graduate in 5 years.

First-Year Class: 482 total; 2,400 applied, 56% were accepted, 36% of whom enrolled. 17% from top 10% of their high school class, 36% from top quarter, 75% from top half.

Graduation Requirements: 130 credit hours; 1 math/science course; computer course.

Computers on Campus: 95 computers available on campus for general student use. Computer purchase/lease plans available. A computer is recommended for all students. A campus-wide network can be accessed from student residence rooms and from off-campus. Students can contact faculty members and/or advisers through e-mail. Computers for student use in computer center provide access to the Internet/World Wide Web, on- and off-campus e-mail addresses.

EXPENSES AND FINANCIAL AID

Expenses for 1996–97: *Application fee:* $30. Comprehensive fee of $18,500 includes full-time tuition ($12,700) and college room and board ($5800). College room only: $2716. Part-time tuition: $385 per credit hour.

Undergraduate Financial Aid: Of all full-time undergraduates enrolled in fall 1996, 93% of those who applied for aid were judged to have need according to Federal Methodology, of whom 100% were aided. On average, 80% of need was met. *Financial aid deadline (priority):* 3/15. *Financial aid forms:* FAFSA, federal income tax forms required. CSS Financial Aid PROFILE, institutional form required for some.

LD Services Contact: Ms. Deb Dickens, Director, Springfield College, 263 Alden Street, Springfield, MA 01109, 413-748-3768. Fax: 413-748-3509. Email: ddickens@spfldcol.edu.

STANFORD UNIVERSITY

Stanford, California

LEARNING DISABILITIES SERVICES INFORMATION

Disability Resource Center began offering services in 1987. Currently the program serves 65 undergraduates with LD. Services are also available to graduate students. Students diagnosed with ADD/ADHD are eligible for the same services available to students with LD, as well as distraction-free testing room.

Staff: 1 full-time staff member (coordinator). Services provided by tutors, accommodations coordinator.

Special Fees: No special fees are charged for services to students with LD.

Applications and admissions: *Required:* high school transcript, courses completed, untimed SAT I or ACT, letters of recommendation, essay. Students may begin taking classes in fall only. *Application deadline:* 12/15.

Special policies: The college has written policies regarding grade forgiveness; substitutions and waivers of graduation requirements.

PROGRAM AND SERVICE COMPONENTS

Special preparation or orientation: Optional orientation offered during registration.

Academic advising: Provided by unit staff members, academic advisers. Students with LD may take up to 20 quarter hours each term; most take 15 quarter hours; 12 quarter hours (fewer with special permission) required to maintain full-time status; 12 quarter hours (8 with special permission) required to be eligible for financial aid.

Counseling services: Individual counseling, small-group counseling, career counseling, self-advocacy training.

Auxiliary aids: Taped textbooks, word-processors with spell-check, personal computers, talking computers, optical character readers, Book Wise Reading System with DecTalk and Book Manager software programs.
Auxiliary services: Alternative test arrangements, notetakers, advocacy, scribes, readers.
Campus support group: A special student organization is available to students with LD.

GENERAL COLLEGE INFORMATION

Independent, coed. Awards bachelor's, master's, doctoral, first professional degrees. Founded 1891. *Setting:* 8,180-acre suburban campus with easy access to San Francisco. *Endowment:* $3.6 billion. *Research spending 1995–96:* $410.9 million. *Total enrollment:* 13,811. *Faculty:* 1,488 (1,469 full-time, 99% with terminal degrees, 19 part-time); student–undergrad faculty ratio is 10:1.
Enrollment Profile: 6,550 students from 52 states and territories, 62 other countries. 50% women, 50% men, 0% part-time, 46% state residents, 88% live on campus, 2% transferred in, 5% international, 2% Native American, 11% Hispanic, 8% black, 24% Asian or Pacific Islander. *Retention:* 97% of 1995 full-time freshmen returned. *Areas of study chosen:* 14% social sciences, 9% interdisciplinary studies, 8% engineering and applied sciences, 5% biological and life sciences, 5% psychology, 3% English language/literature/letters, 2% computer and information sciences, 1% area and ethnic studies, 1% communications and journalism, 1% fine arts, 1% foreign language and literature, 1% mathematics, 1% philosophy, 1% theology/religion. *Most popular recent majors:* engineering (general), economics.
First-Year Class: 1,614 total; 16,359 applied, 16% were accepted, 61% of whom enrolled. 87% from top 10% of their high school class, 95% from top half.
Graduation Requirements: 180 quarter hours; 1 course each in math, natural science, technology and applied science; 1 year of a foreign language or the equivalent; computer course for electrical engineering, math majors; senior project for honors program students.
Computers on Campus: 7,100 computers available on campus for general student use. A campus-wide network can be accessed. Students can contact faculty members and/or advisers through e-mail. Computers for student use in computer center, computer labs, classrooms, library, student center, dorms, clusters provide access to the Internet/World Wide Web, on-campus e-mail addresses.

EXPENSES AND FINANCIAL AID

Expenses for 1997–98: *Application fee:* $50. Comprehensive fee of $29,108 includes full-time tuition ($21,300), mandatory fees ($89), and college room and board ($7719).
Undergraduate Financial Aid: 48% of all full-time undergraduates enrolled in fall 1996 applied for aid; of these, 92% were judged to have need according to Federal Methodology, of whom 99% were aided. On average, 100% of need was met. *Financial aid deadline (priority):* 4/15. *Financial aid forms:* FAFSA, CSS Financial Aid PROFILE required.
LD Services Contact: Ms. Anne Peterson, Program Coordinator for Learning Disabilities, Stanford University, 123 Meyer Library, Stanford, CA 94305-3094, 415-725-2483. Fax: 415-725-5301. Email: anne.peterson@stanford.edu.

STATE UNIVERSITY OF NEW YORK AT BINGHAMTON

Binghamton, New York

LEARNING DISABILITIES SERVICES INFORMATION

Services for Students with Disabilities began offering services in 1984. Currently the program serves 65 undergraduates with LD. Services are also available to graduate students. Students diagnosed with ADD/ADHD are eligible for the same services available to students with LD.
Staff: 1 full-time, 1 part-time staff members, including director. Services provided by tutors, peer tutors, notetakers, readers, scribes, sign language interpreters.
Special Fees: No special fees are charged for services to students with LD.
Applications and admissions: *Required:* high school transcript, grade point average, class rank, courses completed, untimed SAT I or ACT, autobiographical statement; *recommended:* high school extracurricular activities, extended time SAT I or ACT, letters of recommendation, psychoeducational report completed in high school. Students may begin taking classes in fall, spring, or summer. *Application deadline:* continuous.

PROGRAM AND SERVICE COMPONENTS

Special preparation or orientation: Optional orientation offered before registration and after classes begin.
Academic advising: Provided by unit staff members, academic advisers. Most students with LD take 12 to 16 credits each term; 12 credits required to maintain full-time status; 6 credits (part-time), 12 credits (regular TAP) required to be eligible for financial aid.
Counseling services: Individual counseling, small-group counseling, career counseling, self-advocacy training.
Subject-area tutoring: Offered one-on-one and in small groups by peer tutors. Available in most subjects.
Auxiliary aids: Taped textbooks, tape recorders, calculators, word-processors with spell-check, personal computers, talking computers, optical character readers.
Auxiliary services: Alternative test arrangements, notetakers, priority registration, advocacy, readers, scribes.

GENERAL COLLEGE INFORMATION

State-supported, coed. Part of State University of New York System. Awards bachelor's, master's, doctoral degrees. Founded 1946. *Setting:* 606-acre suburban campus. *Endowment:* $13.8 million. *Research spending 1995–96:* $19.8 million. *Total enrollment:* 11,976. *Faculty:* 683 (451 full-time, 95% with terminal degrees, 232 part-time); student–undergrad faculty ratio is 21:1.
Enrollment Profile: 9,349 students from 33 states and territories, 47 other countries. 53% women, 47% men, 5% part-time, 95% state residents, 52% live on campus, 9% transferred in, 2% international, 8% 25 or older, 1% Native American, 6% Hispanic, 5% black, 14% Asian or Pacific Islander. *Retention:* 91% of 1995 full-time freshmen returned. *Graduation:* 66% graduate in 4 years, 77% in 5 years, 79% in 6 years. *Most popular recent majors:* English, psychology, biology/biological sciences.
First-Year Class: 1,804 total; 15,660 applied, 42% were accepted, 27% of whom enrolled. 52% from top 10% of their high school class, 94% from top quarter, 100% from top half. 15 valedictorians.
Graduation Requirements: 126 credits; 1 course in math, logic or computer science; 1 lab science course; computer course for management, math, accounting, engineering majors; senior project (some majors).
Computers on Campus: 1,200 computers available on campus for general student use. Computer purchase/lease plans available. A campus-wide network can be accessed from student residence rooms and from off-campus. Students can contact faculty members and/or advisers through e-mail. Computers for student use in computer center, computer labs, learning resource center, library, dorms provide access to the Internet/World Wide Web, on- and off-campus e-mail addresses. Staffed computer lab on campus provides training in use of computers, software. *Academic computing expenditure 1995–96:* $4.7 million.

EXPENSES AND FINANCIAL AID

Expenses for 1996–97: *Application fee:* $30. State resident tuition: $3400 full-time, $137 per credit part-time. Nonresident tuition: $8300 full-time, $346 per credit part-time. Part-time mandatory fees per semester range from $50.60 to $286.60. Full-time mandatory fees: $645. College room and board: $4814.
Undergraduate Financial Aid: 70% of all full-time undergraduates enrolled in fall 1996 applied for aid; of these, 92% were judged to have need according to Federal Methodology, of whom 92% were aided. On average, 63% of need was met. *Financial aid deadline (priority):* 3/1. *Financial aid forms:* FAFSA, state form required. CSS Financial Aid PROFILE required for some.
LD Services Contact: Ms. Barbara Jean Fairbairn, Director, Services for Students with Disabilities, State University of New York at Binghamton, PO Box 6000, Binghamton, NY 13902-6000, 607-777-2686. Fax: 607-777-6893.

STATE UNIVERSITY OF NEW YORK AT BUFFALO

Buffalo, New York

LEARNING DISABILITIES SERVICES INFORMATION

Office of Disability Services began offering services in 1976. Currently the program serves 108 undergraduates with LD. Services are also available to graduate students. Students diagnosed with ADD/ADHD are eligible for the same services available to students with LD.
Staff: 2 full-time, 2 part-time staff members, including director, assistant director, ADA assistant. Services provided by tutors, readers, notetakers.

Special Fees: No special fees are charged for services to students with LD.

Applications and admissions: *Required:* high school transcript, grade point average, class rank, untimed SAT I or ACT; *recommended:* high school courses completed, extended time SAT I or ACT, psychoeducational report completed within 1 year. Students may begin taking classes in fall, spring, or summer. *Application deadline:* 1/5 (fall term), 12/1 (spring term).

PROGRAM AND SERVICE COMPONENTS

Academic advising: Provided by academic advisers. Students with LD may take up to 18 credit hours each term; most take 9 to 12 credit hours; 12 credit hours required to maintain full-time status and be eligible for financial aid.

Counseling services: Individual counseling, small-group counseling, career counseling.

Basic skills remediation: Offered one-on-one and in small groups by Learning Center staff. Available in math, spelling, spoken language, written language, learning strategies, study skills, time management, speech.

Subject-area tutoring: Offered one-on-one and in small groups by peer tutors, graduate assistants. Available in all subjects.

Auxiliary aids: Tape recorders, word-processors with spell-check, personal computers, talking computers, optical character readers.

Auxiliary services: Alternative test arrangements, notetakers, advocacy.

GENERAL COLLEGE INFORMATION

State-supported, coed. Part of State University of New York System. Awards bachelor's, master's, doctoral, first professional degrees. Founded 1846. *Setting:* 1,350-acre suburban campus. *Endowment:* $245.3 million. *Research spending 1995–96:* $62 million. *Total enrollment:* 23,577. *Faculty:* 1,734 (1,251 full-time, 96% with terminal degrees, 483 part-time); student–undergrad faculty ratio is 13:1.

Enrollment Profile: 15,571 students from 34 states and territories, 56 other countries. 45% women, 55% men, 15% part-time, 96% state residents, 38% live on campus, 10% transferred in, 2% international, 19% 25 or older, 1% Native American, 3% Hispanic, 7% black, 12% Asian or Pacific Islander. *Retention:* 84% of 1995 full-time freshmen returned. *Graduation:* 30% graduate in 4 years, 55% in 5 years, 60% in 6 years. *Areas of study chosen:* 22% social sciences, 14% health professions and related sciences, 12% engineering and applied sciences, 11% business management and administrative services, 3% architecture, 3% interdisciplinary studies, 2% biological and life sciences, 2% fine arts, 2% performing arts, 1% communications and journalism, 1% computer and information sciences. *Most popular recent majors:* business administration/commerce/management, social science, psychology.

First-Year Class: 2,575 total; 14,143 applied, 71% were accepted, 26% of whom enrolled. 22% from top 10% of their high school class, 58% from top quarter, 97% from top half.

Graduation Requirements: 120 credit hours; math proficiency or 1 math course; computer course for management, engineering majors; internship (some majors); senior project for honors program students and some majors.

Computers on Campus: 750 computers available on campus for general student use. Computer purchase/lease plans available. A campus-wide network can be accessed from student residence rooms and from off-campus. Students can contact faculty members and/or advisers through e-mail. Computers for student use in computer center, computer labs, classrooms, library, dorms, academic buildings provide access to the Internet/World Wide Web, on- and off-campus e-mail addresses. Staffed computer lab on campus provides training in use of computers, software.

EXPENSES AND FINANCIAL AID

Expenses for 1996–97: *Application fee:* $30. State resident tuition: $3400 full-time, $137 per credit hour part-time. Nonresident tuition: $8300 full-time, $346 per credit hour part-time. Part-time mandatory fees: $32.55 per credit hour. Full-time mandatory fees: $790. College room and board: $5455. College room only: $3125.

Undergraduate Financial Aid: 70% of all full-time undergraduates enrolled in fall 1996 applied for aid; of these, 83% were judged to have need according to Federal Methodology, of whom 98% were aided. On average, 100% of need was met. *Financial aid deadline (priority):* 3/1. *Financial aid forms:* FAFSA required. State form required for some.

LD Services Contact: Ms. A. Schunke, Administrative Assistant, State University of New York at Buffalo, 25 Capen Hall, Box 601632, Buffalo, NY 14260-1632, 716-645-2608. Fax: 716-645-3116. Email: aschunke@acsu.buffalo.edu.

STATE UNIVERSITY OF NEW YORK AT NEW PALTZ

New Paltz, New York

LEARNING DISABILITIES SERVICES INFORMATION

Center for Academic Development and Learning began offering services in 1989. Currently the program serves 90 undergraduates with LD. Services are also available to graduate students. Students diagnosed with ADD/ADHD are eligible for the same services available to students with LD, as well as support group.

Staff: 6 full-time staff members, including director, coordinators. Services provided by learning specialist, writing specialist, critical thinking specialist.

Special Fees: No special fees are charged for services to students with LD.

Applications and admissions: *Required:* high school transcript, grade point average, untimed SAT I or ACT; *recommended:* high school courses completed, extracurricular activities, extended time SAT I or ACT, autobiographical statement, letters of recommendation. Students may begin taking classes any term. *Application deadline:* continuous.

Special policies: The college has written policies regarding substitutions and waivers of graduation requirements.

PROGRAM AND SERVICE COMPONENTS

Special preparation or orientation: Optional orientation offered before registration and after classes begin.

Academic advising: Provided by academic advisers. Students with LD may take up to 18 credits each term; most take 12 to 15 credits; 12 credits required to maintain full-time status; 12 credits (full-time) required to be eligible for financial aid.

Counseling services: Individual counseling, small-group counseling, career counseling.

Basic skills remediation: Offered one-on-one and in small groups by learning specialist. Available in reading, spelling, spoken language, written language, learning strategies, study skills, time management, social skills, computer skills.

Subject-area tutoring: Offered one-on-one by peer tutors. Available in most subjects.

Auxiliary aids: Taped textbooks, tape recorders, talking computers, optical character readers, carbonless copy paper.

Auxiliary services: Alternative test arrangements, notetakers, Disabled Student Services Mentor Program.

GENERAL COLLEGE INFORMATION

State-supported, comprehensive, coed. Part of State University of New York System. Awards bachelor's, master's degrees. Founded 1828. *Setting:* 216-acre small-town campus. *Endowment:* $2.3 million. *Research spending 1995–96:* $3.9 million. *Educational spending 1995–96:* $4612 per undergrad. *Total enrollment:* 7,539. *Faculty:* 555 (265 full-time, 85% with terminal degrees, 290 part-time); student–undergrad faculty ratio is 19:1.

Enrollment Profile: 6,029 students from 19 states and territories, 43 other countries. 62% women, 38% men, 22% part-time, 95% state residents, 52% live on campus, 51% transferred in, 4% international, 29% 25 or older, 1% Native American, 8% Hispanic, 7% black, 5% Asian or Pacific Islander. *Retention:* 79% of 1995 full-time freshmen returned. *Graduation:* 30% graduate in 4 years, 53% in 5 years, 58% in 6 years. *Areas of study chosen:* 14% education, 11% business management and administrative services, 10% social sciences, 7% communications and journalism, 7% fine arts, 4% psychology, 3% biological and life sciences, 3% engineering and applied sciences, 3% health professions and related sciences, 3% performing arts, 2% computer and information sciences, 2% English language/literature/letters, 2% liberal arts/general studies, 1% area and ethnic studies, 1% foreign language and literature, 1% interdisciplinary studies, 1% mathematics, 1% philosophy, 1% physical sciences, 1% predentistry, 1% prelaw, 1% premed. *Most popular recent majors:* elementary education, psychology, business administration/commerce/management.

First-Year Class: 886 total; 7,788 applied, 43% were accepted, 27% of whom enrolled. 21% from top 10% of their high school class, 45% from top quarter, 96% from top half. 1 National Merit Scholar, 2 valedictorians.

Graduation Requirements: 120 credits; 6 credits of math; 8 credits of science; 6 credits of a foreign language; computer course for business, education, engineering, communications majors; internship (some majors); senior project (some majors).

Computers on Campus: 260 computers available on campus for general student use. A computer is recommended for some students. A campus-wide network can be accessed from student residence rooms and from off-campus. Students can contact faculty members and/or advisers through e-mail. Computers for student use in computer center, computer labs, learning resource center, classrooms, library, dorms provide access to the Internet/World Wide Web, on- and off-campus e-mail addresses. Staffed computer lab on campus provides training in use of computers, software. *Academic computing expenditure 1995–96:* $398,079.

EXPENSES AND FINANCIAL AID

Expenses for 1996–97: *Application fee:* $30. State resident tuition: $3400 full-time, $137 per credit part-time. Nonresident tuition: $8300 full-time, $346 per credit part-time. Part-time mandatory fees per semester range from $40.60 to $148.60. Full-time mandatory fees: $425. College room and board: $5030. College room only: $2990.

Undergraduate Financial Aid: Of all full-time undergraduates enrolled in fall 1996, 80% of those who applied for aid were judged to have need according to Federal Methodology, of whom 96% were aided. On average, 75% of need was met. *Financial aid deadline (priority):* 3/15. *Financial aid forms:* FAFSA required. State form, institutional form required for some.

LD Services Contact: Mr. Ken Gilman, Director, Special Student Programs, State University of New York at New Paltz, 75 South Manheim Boulevard, New Paltz, NY 12561-2499, 914-257-3590. Fax: 914-257-3555.

STATE UNIVERSITY OF NEW YORK AT OSWEGO

Oswego, New York

LEARNING DISABILITIES SERVICES INFORMATION

Learning Enhancement Office (LEO) began offering services in 1989. Currently the program serves 170 undergraduates with LD. Services are also available to graduate students. Students diagnosed with ADD/ADHD are eligible for the same services available to students with LD, as well as distraction-free testing location.

Staff: Includes coordinators. Services provided by remediation specialists, tutors, counselors, graduate assistants, student workers.

Special Fees: No special fees are charged for services to students with LD.

Applications and admissions: *Required:* high school transcript, grade point average, courses completed, psychoeducational report completed within 3 years; *recommended:* untimed or extended time SAT I or ACT, personal interview, autobiographical statement, letters of recommendation. Students may begin taking classes in fall only. *Application deadline:* 3/15.

Special policies: The college has written policies regarding grade forgiveness; substitutions and waivers of graduation and degree requirements.

PROGRAM AND SERVICE COMPONENTS

Special preparation or orientation: Optional orientation offered before registration and during registration.

Academic advising: Provided by unit staff members, academic advisers. Students with LD may take up to 15 credit hours each term; most take 12 credit hours; 12 credit hours required to maintain full-time status and be eligible for financial aid.

Counseling services: Individual counseling, small-group counseling, career counseling, self-advocacy training.

Basic skills remediation: Offered in small groups and in class-size groups by regular teachers, graduate assistants. Available in reading, math, written language, learning strategies, study skills, time management.

Subject-area tutoring: Offered one-on-one, in small groups, and in class-size groups by professional teachers, peer tutors. Available in most subjects.

Special courses: College survival skills, reading, composition. All offered for credit; most enter into overall grade point average.

Auxiliary aids: Taped textbooks, tape recorders, calculators, typewriters, word-processors with spell-check, personal computers, talking computers, optical character readers, photocopier.

Auxiliary services: Alternative test arrangements, notetakers, priority registration, advocacy, readers, typists.

Campus support group: A special student organization is available to students with LD.

GENERAL COLLEGE INFORMATION

State-supported, comprehensive, coed. Part of State University of New York System. Awards bachelor's, master's degrees. Founded 1861. *Setting:* 696-acre small-town campus with easy access to Syracuse. *Endowment:* $760,000. *Research spending 1995–96:* $486,127. *Educational spending 1995–96:* $3042 per undergrad. *Total enrollment:* 8,264. *Faculty:* 391 (326 full-time, 72% with terminal degrees, 65 part-time); student–undergrad faculty ratio is 22:1.

Enrollment Profile: 7,090 students from 16 states and territories, 30 other countries. 53% women, 47% men, 15% part-time, 97% state residents, 36% transferred in, 1% international, 12% 25 or older, 1% Native American, 4% Hispanic, 4% black, 2% Asian or Pacific Islander. *Retention:* 80% of 1995 full-time freshmen returned. *Graduation:* 44% graduate in 4 years, 58% in 5 years, 61% in 6 years. *Areas of study chosen:* 17% business management and administrative services, 17% education, 11% social sciences, 8% communications and journalism, 8% psychology, 6% English language/literature/letters, 6% physical sciences, 5% fine arts, 4% performing arts, 4% prelaw, 3% biological and life sciences, 3% computer and information sciences, 2% mathematics, 2% natural resource sciences, 2% premed, 1% prevet. *Most popular recent majors:* business administration/commerce/management, elementary education, communication.

First-Year Class: 1,350 total; 7,000 applied, 57% were accepted, 34% of whom enrolled. 8% from top 10% of their high school class, 45% from top quarter, 85% from top half.

Graduation Requirements: 122 credit hours; 6 credit hours of math; 9 credit hours of science; computer course for business administration, math, economics, marketing, management, science, technology, broadcasting, meteorology majors; internship (some majors); senior project for honors program students and some majors.

Computers on Campus: 300 computers available on campus for general student use. Computer purchase/lease plans available. A computer is recommended for all students. A campus-wide network can be accessed from student residence rooms and from off-campus. Students can contact faculty members and/or advisers through e-mail. Computers for student use in computer center, learning resource center, library, dorms, academic buildings provide access to the Internet/World Wide Web, on- and off-campus e-mail addresses. Staffed computer lab on campus (open 24 hours a day) provides training in use of computers, software. *Academic computing expenditure 1995–96:* $383,273.

EXPENSES AND FINANCIAL AID

Expenses for 1996–97: *Application fee:* $30. State resident tuition: $3400 full-time, $137 per credit hour part-time. Nonresident tuition: $8300 full-time, $346 per credit hour part-time. Part-time mandatory fees: $13.59 per credit hour. Full-time mandatory fees: $487. College room and board: $5460. College room only: $3190.

Undergraduate Financial Aid: Of all full-time undergraduates enrolled in fall 1996, 84% of those who applied for aid were judged to have need according to Federal Methodology, of whom 95% were aided. On average, 75% of need was met. *Financial aid deadline (priority):* 4/1. *Financial aid forms:* FAFSA required; state form acceptable.

LD Services Contact: Mr. Bernardo DelSavio, Coordinator, Learning Enhancement Office, State University of New York at Oswego, 210 Swetman Hall, Oswego, NY 13126, 315-341-3358. Fax: 315-341-2854. Email: delsavio@oswego.edu.

STATE UNIVERSITY OF NEW YORK AT STONY BROOK

Stony Brook, New York

LEARNING DISABILITIES SERVICES INFORMATION

Support Services for Students with Learning Disabilities began offering services in 1985. Currently the program serves 85 undergraduates with LD. Services are also available to graduate students. Students diagnosed with ADD/ADHD are eligible for the same services available to students with LD.

Staff: 2 full-time, 1 part-time staff members, including director, coordinator. Services provided by social work intern, graduate students.

Special Fees: No special fees are charged for services to students with LD.

Applications and admissions: *Required:* high school transcript, grade point average, class rank, courses completed, letters of recommenda-

State University of New York at Stony Brook (continued)

tion; *recommended:* untimed or extended time SAT I, psychoeducational report. Students may begin taking classes any term. *Application deadline:* continuous.

Special policies: The college has written policies regarding substitutions and waivers of degree requirements.

PROGRAM AND SERVICE COMPONENTS

Special preparation or orientation: Optional orientation offered after classes begin.

Academic advising: Provided by unit staff members, academic advisers. Students with LD may take up to 19 credits each term; most take 12 credits; 12 credits required to maintain full-time status and be eligible for financial aid.

Counseling services: Individual counseling.

Auxiliary aids: Taped textbooks, tape recorders, calculators, typewriters, word-processors with spell-check, reading machine.

Auxiliary services: Alternative test arrangements, notetakers, priority registration, advocacy.

GENERAL COLLEGE INFORMATION

State-supported, coed. Part of State University of New York System. Awards bachelor's, master's, doctoral, first professional degrees. Founded 1957. *Setting:* 1,100-acre small-town campus with easy access to New York City. *Endowment:* $14.1 million. *Research spending 1995–96:* $78 million. *Total enrollment:* 17,309. *Faculty:* 1,610 (1,220 full-time, 95% with terminal degrees, 390 part-time); student–undergrad faculty ratio is 17:1.

Enrollment Profile: 11,265 students from 37 states and territories, 47 other countries. 52% women, 48% men, 11% part-time, 95% state residents, 45% live on campus, 14% transferred in, 3% international, 18% 25 or older, 0% Native American, 7% Hispanic, 10% black, 18% Asian or Pacific Islander. *Retention:* 81% of 1995 full-time freshmen returned. *Areas of study chosen:* 20% social sciences, 15% biological and life sciences, 14% psychology, 10% health professions and related sciences, 7% engineering and applied sciences, 6% business management and administrative services, 6% English language/literature/letters, 5% liberal arts/general studies, 4% computer and information sciences, 4% mathematics, 4% physical sciences, 2% foreign language and literature, 1% fine arts, 1% performing arts, 1% philosophy. *Most popular recent majors:* psychology, biology/biological sciences, business administration/commerce/management.

First-Year Class: 1,770 total; 12,725 applied, 58% were accepted, 24% of whom enrolled. 27% from top 10% of their high school class, 68% from top quarter, 97% from top half.

Graduation Requirements: 120 credits; basic math proficiency; proven proficiency in a foreign language; computer course for engineering majors; senior project for honors program students.

Computers on Campus: 390 computers available on campus for general student use. Computer purchase/lease plans available. A campus-wide network can be accessed from student residence rooms and from off-campus. Students can contact faculty members and/or advisers through e-mail. Computers for student use in computer center, computer labs, classrooms, library, dorms, student rooms, academic buildings provide access to the Internet/World Wide Web. Staffed computer lab on campus provides training in use of computers, software.

EXPENSES AND FINANCIAL AID

Expenses for 1996–97: *Application fee:* $30. State resident tuition: $3400 full-time, $137 per credit part-time. Nonresident tuition: $8300 full-time, $346 per credit part-time. Part-time mandatory fees: $15.35 per credit. Full-time mandatory fees: $479. College room and board: $5594. College room only: $3494.

Undergraduate Financial Aid: 70% of all full-time undergraduates enrolled in fall 1996 applied for aid; of these, 88% were judged to have need according to Federal Methodology, of whom 99% were aided. On average, 66% of need was met. *Financial aid deadline (priority):* 3/1. *Financial aid forms:* FAFSA, state form required.

LD Services Contact: Ms. Carol Dworkin, Learning Disabilities Specialist, State University of New York at Stony Brook, Room 133, Humanities Building, Stony Brook, NY 11794-5328, 516-632-6748. Fax: 516-632-6747.

STATE UNIVERSITY OF NEW YORK COLLEGE AT BROCKPORT

Brockport, New York

LEARNING DISABILITIES SERVICES INFORMATION

Center for Academic Improvement and Student Services Program began offering services in 1978. Currently the program serves 70 undergraduates with LD. Services are also available to graduate students. Students diagnosed with ADD/ADHD are eligible for the same services available to students with LD.

Staff: 5 full-time staff members, including director, academic coordinator. Services provided by tutors, counselors.

Special Fees: No special fees are charged for services to students with LD.

Applications and admissions: *Required:* high school transcript, grade point average, courses completed, untimed SAT I or ACT; *recommended:* high school class rank, extracurricular activities, extended time SAT I or ACT, psychoeducational report completed within 3 years. Students may begin taking classes in fall, spring, or summer. *Application deadline:* 3/1 (fall term), 12/1 (spring term).

PROGRAM AND SERVICE COMPONENTS

Special preparation or orientation: Required orientation held during first week of classes.

Academic advising: Provided by unit staff members, academic advisers. Students with LD may take up to 21 credit hours each term; most take 12 credit hours; 12 credit hours required to maintain full-time status; 6 to 11 credit hours (part-time) required to be eligible for financial aid.

Counseling services: Individual counseling, small-group counseling, career counseling.

Basic skills remediation: Offered one-on-one by peer teachers. Available in math, written language, learning strategies, study skills.

Subject-area tutoring: Offered one-on-one by peer tutors. Available in most subjects.

Auxiliary aids: Taped textbooks, tape recorders, word-processors with spell-check, personal computers, optical character readers.

Auxiliary services: Alternative test arrangements, notetakers, priority registration, advocacy.

Campus support group: A special student organization is available to students with LD.

GENERAL COLLEGE INFORMATION

State-supported, comprehensive, coed. Part of State University of New York System. Awards bachelor's, master's degrees. Founded 1867. *Setting:* 591-acre small-town campus with easy access to Rochester. *Research spending 1995–96:* $2.7 million. *Total enrollment:* 8,723. *Faculty:* 509 (88% of full-time faculty have terminal degrees); student–undergrad faculty ratio is 21:1.

Enrollment Profile: 6,854 students from 23 states and territories, 10 other countries. 54% women, 46% men, 18% part-time, 98% state residents, 15% transferred in, 1% international, 22% 25 or older, 1% Native American, 2% Hispanic, 7% black, 1% Asian or Pacific Islander. *Retention:* 75% of 1995 full-time freshmen returned. *Graduation:* 26% graduate in 4 years, 50% in 5 years, 52% in 6 years. *Areas of study chosen:* 22% social sciences, 16% business management and administrative services, 11% health professions and related sciences, 10% education, 9% psychology, 6% communications and journalism, 5% biological and life sciences, 5% English language/literature/letters, 3% computer and information sciences, 3% fine arts, 3% mathematics, 3% physical sciences, 1% area and ethnic studies, 1% foreign language and literature, 1% interdisciplinary studies, 1% performing arts. *Most popular recent majors:* business administration/commerce/management, psychology, criminal justice.

First-Year Class: 921 total; 5,659 applied, 55% were accepted, 29% of whom enrolled. 8% from top 10% of their high school class, 41% from top quarter, 87% from top half.

Graduation Requirements: 120 credit hours; math proficiency; computer course; internship (some majors); senior project for honors program students and some majors.

Computers on Campus: 400 computers available on campus for general student use. Computer purchase/lease plans available. A computer is recommended for all students. A campus-wide network can be accessed from student residence rooms and from off-campus. Students can contact faculty members and/or advisers through e-mail. Computers for student use in computer center, computer labs, learning resource center, library, dorms, academic buildings provide access to the Internet/World

Wide Web, on-campus e-mail addresses. Staffed computer lab on campus provides training in use of computers, software. *Academic computing expenditure 1995–96:* $361,200.

EXPENSES AND FINANCIAL AID

Expenses for 1996–97: *Application fee:* $25. State resident tuition: $3400 full-time, $137 per credit hour part-time. Nonresident tuition: $8300 full-time, $346 per credit hour part-time. Part-time mandatory fees: $21.60 per credit hour. Full-time mandatory fees: $515. College room and board: $4780. College room only: $2960.
Undergraduate Financial Aid: 80% of all full-time undergraduates enrolled in fall 1996 applied for aid; of these, 85% were judged to have need according to Federal Methodology, of whom 96% were aided. On average, 95% of need was met. *Financial aid deadline (priority):* 5/1. *Financial aid forms:* FAFSA, state form required; CSS Financial Aid PROFILE acceptable.
LD Services Contact: Ms. Karen A. Phelps, Coordinator, Disabled Student Services, State University of New York College at Brockport, Seymour College Union, Room 224, Brockport, NY 14420, 716-395-5409. Fax: 716-395-2567.

STATE UNIVERSITY OF NEW YORK COLLEGE AT OLD WESTBURY

Old Westbury, New York

LEARNING DISABILITIES SERVICES INFORMATION

Office of Services for Students with Disabilities (OSSD) began offering services in 1982. Currently the program serves 48 undergraduates with LD. Students diagnosed with ADD/ADHD are eligible for the same services available to students with LD.
Staff: 1 part-time staff member (coordinator). Services provided by tutors.
Special Fees: No special fees are charged for services to students with LD.
Applications and admissions: *Required:* high school transcript, grade point average, courses completed, psychoeducational report completed within 2 years; *recommended:* high school class rank, extracurricular activities, untimed or extended time SAT I, extended time ACT, personal interview, autobiographical statement, letters of recommendation. Students may begin taking classes in fall, spring, or summer. *Application deadline:* continuous.

PROGRAM AND SERVICE COMPONENTS

Special preparation or orientation: Optional orientation offered individually or in small groups by appointment.
Academic advising: Provided by unit staff members, academic advisers. Students with LD may take up to 16 credits each term; most take 12 credits; 12 credits required to maintain full-time status; 4 credits required to be eligible for financial aid.
Counseling services: Individual counseling, small-group counseling, career counseling, self-advocacy training.
Basic skills remediation: Offered in small groups and in class-size groups by regular teachers, teacher trainees. Available in reading, math, handwriting, written language, learning strategies, study skills, time management.
Subject-area tutoring: Offered one-on-one and in small groups by professional teachers, peer tutors. Available in most subjects.
Auxiliary aids: Taped textbooks, tape recorders, calculators, typewriters, word-processors with spell-check, personal computers, Visualtek print enlarger.
Auxiliary services: Alternative test arrangements, notetakers, priority registration, advocacy.

GENERAL COLLEGE INFORMATION

State-supported, 4-year, coed. Part of State University of New York System. Awards bachelor's degrees. Founded 1965. *Setting:* 605-acre suburban campus with easy access to New York City. *Total enrollment:* 3,790. *Faculty:* 233 (114 full-time, 75% with terminal degrees, 119 part-time); student–undergrad faculty ratio is 16:1.
Enrollment Profile: 3,790 students from 8 states and territories, 24 other countries. 57% women, 43% men, 26% part-time, 97% state residents, 20% live on campus, 16% transferred in, 2% international, 39% 25 or older, 1% Native American, 15% Hispanic, 29% black, 7% Asian or Pacific Islander. *Retention:* 64% of 1995 full-time freshmen returned. *Graduation:* 7% graduate in 4 years, 24% in 5 years, 29% in 6 years. *Areas of study chosen:* 36% business management and administrative services, 20% education, 9% computer and information sciences, 9% social sciences, 7% psychology, 6% biological and life sciences, 3% area and ethnic studies, 3% communications and journalism, 2% English language/literature/letters, 2% liberal arts/general studies, 1% fine arts, 1% foreign language and literature, 1% mathematics, 1% philosophy, 1% physical sciences.
First-Year Class: 467 total; 1,788 applied, 88% were accepted, 30% of whom enrolled. 4% from top 10% of their high school class, 15% from top quarter, 50% from top half.
Graduation Requirements: 120 credits; math proficiency; computer course for accounting, business education, finance, math majors; internship (some majors); senior project (some majors).
Computers on Campus: 200 computers available on campus for general student use. Computer purchase/lease plans available. Computers for student use in computer center, computer labs, classrooms, library, campus center provide access to the Internet/World Wide Web, on-campus e-mail addresses. Staffed computer lab on campus provides training in use of computers, software.

EXPENSES AND FINANCIAL AID

Expenses for 1996–97: *Application fee:* $30. State resident tuition: $3400 full-time, $137 per credit part-time. Nonresident tuition: $8300 full-time, $346 per credit part-time. Part-time mandatory fees per semester range from $81.90 to $115.85. Full-time mandatory fees: $331. College room and board: $5407. College room only: $3448.
Undergraduate Financial Aid: Of all full-time undergraduates enrolled in fall 1996, 70% of those who applied for aid were judged to have need according to Federal Methodology, of whom 89% were aided. On average, 70% of need was met. *Financial aid deadline (priority):* 4/23. *Financial aid forms:* FAFSA, state form, institutional form required; CSS Financial Aid PROFILE acceptable.
LD Services Contact: Mr. William Lupardo, Coordinator, Services for Students with Disabilities, State University of New York College at Old Westbury, PO Box 210, Old Westbury, NY 11568, 516-876-3009. Fax: 516-876-3353.

STATE UNIVERSITY OF NEW YORK COLLEGE AT ONEONTA

Oneonta, New York

LEARNING DISABILITIES SERVICES INFORMATION

Office of Services for Students with Disabilities currently serves 240 undergraduates with LD. Services are also available to graduate students. Students diagnosed with ADD/ADHD are eligible for the same services available to students with LD.
Staff: 1 full-time, 1 part-time staff members, including coordinator, graduate assistant. Services provided by remediation specialists, tutors, professional tutors.
Special Fees: No special fees are charged for services to students with LD.
Applications and admissions: *Required:* high school transcript, IEP (Individualized Education Program), untimed SAT I or ACT, psychoeducational report completed within 3 years; *recommended:* high school grade point average, courses completed, extended time SAT I or ACT. Students may begin taking classes any term. *Application deadline:* continuous.

PROGRAM AND SERVICE COMPONENTS

Academic advising: Provided by unit staff members, academic advisers. Students with LD may take up to 15 semester hours (12 recommended) each term; most take 12 semester hours first semester (15 semester hours thereafter); 12 semester hours required to maintain full-time status; 6 semester hours (part-time), 12 semester hours (full-time) required to be eligible for financial aid.
Counseling services: Individual counseling, small-group counseling, career counseling, self-advocacy training.
Basic skills remediation: Offered one-on-one, in small groups, and in class-size groups by regular teachers, learning laboratory personnel. Available in reading, math, spelling, written language, learning strategies, perceptual skills, study skills, time management, speech.
Subject-area tutoring: Offered one-on-one and in small groups by professional teachers, peer tutors, professional tutors. Available in most subjects.

State University of New York College at Oneonta (continued)

Special courses: College survival skills, reading, vocabulary development, communication skills, composition, learning strategies, word processing, time management, math, study skills. Some offered for credit; some enter into overall grade point average.
Auxiliary aids: Taped textbooks, word-processors with spell-check.
Auxiliary services: Alternative test arrangements, notetakers, priority registration, advocacy, scribes, readers, use of lab programs.

GENERAL COLLEGE INFORMATION

State-supported, comprehensive, coed. Part of State University of New York System. Awards bachelor's, master's degrees. Founded 1889. *Setting:* 251-acre small-town campus. *Endowment:* $6 million. *Total enrollment:* 5,616. *Faculty:* 325 (218 full-time, 71% with terminal degrees, 107 part-time); student–undergrad faculty ratio is 21:1.
Enrollment Profile: 5,171 students from 14 states and territories, 13 other countries. 59% women, 41% men, 8% part-time, 98% state residents, 1% international, 13% 25 or older, 4% Hispanic, 3% black, 1% Asian or Pacific Islander. *Graduation:* 42% graduate in 4 years, 53% in 5 years, 56% in 6 years. *Areas of study chosen:* 20% education, 11% business management and administrative services, 10% psychology, 7% computer and information sciences, 7% vocational and home economics, 4% communications and journalism, 4% fine arts, 3% biological and life sciences, 3% English language/literature/letters, 1% foreign language and literature, 1% mathematics, 1% natural resource sciences, 1% performing arts. *Most popular recent majors:* education, business economics, psychology.
First-Year Class: 1,160 total; 6,411 applied, 75% were accepted, 24% of whom enrolled.
Graduation Requirements: 122 semester hours; 3 semester hours of math; 6 semester hours of science; computer course for math, statistics, business economics majors.
Computers on Campus: 300 computers available on campus for general student use. A computer is recommended for all students. A campus-wide network can be accessed from student residence rooms and from off-campus. Students can contact faculty members and/or advisers through e-mail. Computers for student use in computer center, computer labs, learning resource center, library, student center, dorms, academic buildings provide access to the Internet/World Wide Web. Staffed computer lab on campus provides training in use of computers, software.

EXPENSES AND FINANCIAL AID

Expenses for 1996–97: *Application fee:* $35. State resident tuition: $3400 full-time, $137 per semester hour part-time. Nonresident tuition: $8300 full-time, $346 per semester hour part-time. Part-time mandatory fees per semester range from $8.85 to $223.35. Full-time mandatory fees range from $358 to $484. College room and board: $5590. College room only: $3000.
Undergraduate Financial Aid: Of all full-time undergraduates enrolled in fall 1996, 89% of those who applied for aid were judged to have need according to Federal Methodology, of whom 97% were aided. On average, 90% of need was met. *Financial aid deadline (priority):* 4/15. *Financial aid forms:* FAFSA required.
LD Services Contact: Ms. Sandra Denicore, Coordinator of Services for Students with Disabilities, State University of New York College at Oneonta, Alumni Hall, Oneonta, NY 13820, 607-436-2137. Fax: 607-436-2124.

STATE UNIVERSITY OF NEW YORK COLLEGE AT PLATTSBURGH

Plattsburgh, New York

LEARNING DISABILITIES SERVICES INFORMATION

Special Services Project began offering services in 1984. Currently the program serves 150 undergraduates with LD. Students diagnosed with ADD/ADHD are eligible for the same services available to students with LD.
Staff: 6 full-time, 3 part-time staff members, including director, administrative assistant. Services provided by remediation specialists, tutors, counselor.
Special Fees: A fee is charged for diagnostic testing.
Applications and admissions: *Required:* high school transcript, grade point average, courses completed, extended time SAT I, psychoeducational report completed within 3 years, personal interview (in some cases); *recommended:* high school class rank, extracurricular activities. Students may begin taking classes in fall only. *Application deadline:* 10/15.
Special policies: The college has written policies regarding grade forgiveness; substitutions and waivers of admissions, graduation, and degree requirements.

PROGRAM AND SERVICE COMPONENTS

Special preparation or orientation: Orientation (required for some) held before registration.
Diagnostic testing: Intelligence, reading, math, spelling, handwriting, spoken language, written language, motor abilities, perceptual skills, study skills, personality, social skills, speech, hearing.
Academic advising: Provided by unit staff members. Students with LD may take up to 18 credit hours each term; most take 12 credit hours; 12 credit hours required to maintain full-time status and be eligible for financial aid.
Counseling services: Individual counseling, small-group counseling, career counseling, self-advocacy training.
Basic skills remediation: Offered one-on-one, in small groups, and in class-size groups by skills specialists. Available in reading, math, spelling, spoken language, written language, learning strategies, study skills, time management, speech.
Subject-area tutoring: Offered one-on-one and in small groups by professional teachers, peer tutors. Available in most subjects.
Special courses: College survival skills, reading, composition, study skills. All offered for credit; most enter into overall grade point average.
Auxiliary aids: Taped textbooks, tape recorders, word-processors with spell-check, talking computers, optical character readers.
Auxiliary services: Alternative test arrangements, notetakers, advocacy, readers.

GENERAL COLLEGE INFORMATION

State-supported, comprehensive, coed. Part of State University of New York System. Awards bachelor's, master's degrees. Founded 1889. *Setting:* 265-acre small-town campus with easy access to Montreal. *Endowment:* $5.9 million. *Research spending 1995–96:* $968,600. *Educational spending 1995–96:* $4138 per undergrad. *Total enrollment:* 5,624. *Faculty:* 346 (237 full-time, 97% with terminal degrees, 109 part-time); student–undergrad faculty ratio is 21:1.
Enrollment Profile: 5,147 students from 20 states and territories, 13 other countries. 57% women, 43% men, 5% part-time, 98% state residents, 46% live on campus, 13% transferred in, 1% international, 12% 25 or older, 1% Native American, 2% Hispanic, 3% black, 1% Asian or Pacific Islander. *Retention:* 78% of 1995 full-time freshmen returned. *Graduation:* 51% graduate in 4 years, 61% in 5 years, 62% in 6 years. *Areas of study chosen:* 18% business management and administrative services, 17% education, 16% social sciences, 11% health professions and related sciences, 8% communications and journalism, 7% natural resource sciences, 7% psychology, 5% biological and life sciences, 4% vocational and home economics, 3% English language/literature/letters, 2% computer and information sciences, 1% foreign language and literature, 1% mathematics. *Most popular recent majors:* elementary education, nursing, psychology.
First-Year Class: 934 total; 4,621 applied, 69% were accepted, 29% of whom enrolled. 7% from top 10% of their high school class, 30% from top quarter, 76% from top half.
Graduation Requirements: 120 credit hours; 10 credit hours of math/science; computer course for accounting, math, management, marketing, environmental science, nutrition majors; senior project for honors program students and some majors.
Computers on Campus: 219 computers available on campus for general student use. Computer purchase/lease plans available. A computer is strongly recommended for all students. A campus-wide network can be accessed from student residence rooms and from off-campus. Students can contact faculty members and/or advisers through e-mail. Computers for student use in computer labs, learning resource center, classrooms, library, dorms, departmental labs provide access to the Internet/World Wide Web, on- and off-campus e-mail addresses. Staffed computer lab on campus provides training in use of computers, software. *Academic computing expenditure 1995–96:* $918,592.

EXPENSES AND FINANCIAL AID

Expenses for 1996–97: *Application fee:* $30. State resident tuition: $3400 full-time, $137 per credit hour part-time. Nonresident tuition: $8300 full-time, $346 per credit hour part-time. Part-time mandatory fees: $11.25 per credit hour. Full-time mandatory fees: $437. College room and board: $4250. College room only: $2620.

Undergraduate Financial Aid: 74% of all full-time undergraduates enrolled in fall 1996 applied for aid; of these, 83% were judged to have need according to Federal Methodology, of whom 97% were aided. On average, 60% of need was met. *Financial aid deadline (priority):* 4/15. *Financial aid forms:* FAFSA, state form required.
LD Services Contact: Ms. Cordelia Drake, Counselor, Special Services Project, State University of New York College at Plattsburgh, 101 Broad Steet, Plattsburgh, NY 12901, 518-564-2810. Fax: 518-564-2807.

STATE UNIVERSITY OF NEW YORK COLLEGE AT POTSDAM

Potsdam, New York

LEARNING DISABILITIES SERVICES INFORMATION

Disabled Student Services began offering services in 1984. Currently the program serves 32 undergraduates with LD. Services are also available to graduate students. Students diagnosed with ADD/ADHD are eligible for the same services available to students with LD.
Staff: 1 full-time staff member (coordinator).
Special Fees: No special fees are charged for services to students with LD.
Applications and admissions: *Required:* high school transcript, grade point average, class rank, courses completed, untimed SAT I or ACT; *recommended:* high school extracurricular activities, IEP (Individualized Education Program), extended time SAT I or ACT, personal interview, autobiographical statement, letters of recommendation, psychoeducational report completed within 3 years. Students may begin taking classes in fall or spring. *Application deadline:* continuous.

PROGRAM AND SERVICE COMPONENTS

Academic advising: Provided by unit staff members, academic advisers. Students with LD may take up to 17 credit hours each term; most take 12 credit hours; 12 credit hours required to maintain full-time status; source of aid determines number of credit hours required to be eligible for financial aid.
Counseling services: Individual counseling, career counseling.
Basic skills remediation: Offered one-on-one by tutoring coordinator, program counselor. Available in reading, learning strategies, study skills, time management.
Subject-area tutoring: Offered one-on-one and in small groups by peer tutors. Available in most subjects.
Special courses: Learning strategies. All offered for credit; all enter into overall grade point average.
Auxiliary aids: Taped textbooks, tape recorders, calculators, word-processors with spell-check, personal computers, optical character readers, spell checkers.
Auxiliary services: Alternative test arrangements, notetakers, priority registration, advocacy.

GENERAL COLLEGE INFORMATION

State-supported, comprehensive, coed. Part of State University of New York System. Awards bachelor's, master's degrees. Founded 1816. *Setting:* 240-acre small-town campus. *Endowment:* $6.8 million. *Total enrollment:* 4,073. *Faculty:* 272 (191 full-time, 81 part-time); student–undergrad faculty ratio is 20:1.
Enrollment Profile: 3,583 students from 18 states and territories, 7 other countries. 56% women, 44% men, 6% part-time, 94% state residents, 64% live on campus, 1% international, 11% 25 or older, 1% Native American, 2% Hispanic, 2% black, 1% Asian or Pacific Islander. *Retention:* 76% of 1995 full-time freshmen returned. *Graduation:* 30% graduate in 4 years, 51% in 5 years. *Areas of study chosen:* 27% education, 18% social sciences, 11% psychology, 9% English language/literature/letters, 4% biological and life sciences, 4% mathematics, 3% fine arts, 3% performing arts, 3% physical sciences, 2% foreign language and literature, 1% business management and administrative services, 1% computer and information sciences, 1% philosophy. *Most popular recent majors:* education, music education, psychology.
First-Year Class: 815 total; 3,078 applied, 84% were accepted, 32% of whom enrolled. 9% from top 10% of their high school class, 46% from top quarter, 69% from top half.
Graduation Requirements: 120 credit hours; 12 credit hours of math/science; competence in a foreign language; senior project (some majors).
Computers on Campus: 375 computers available on campus for general student use. Computer purchase/lease plans available. A computer is strongly recommended for all students. A campus-wide network can be accessed from student residence rooms and from off-campus. Students can contact faculty members and/or advisers through e-mail. Computers for student use in computer center, computer labs, learning resource center, classrooms, library, student center, dorms, education, music and science lab, writing center provide access to the Internet/World Wide Web, on- and off-campus e-mail addresses, IPX and Appletalk networks. Staffed computer lab on campus (open 24 hours a day) provides training in use of computers, software.

EXPENSES AND FINANCIAL AID

Expenses for 1996–97: *Application fee:* $30. State resident tuition: $3400 full-time, $137 per credit hour part-time. Nonresident tuition: $8300 full-time, $346 per credit hour part-time. Part-time mandatory fees: $12.85 per credit hour. Full-time mandatory fees: $339. College room and board: $4900 (minimum). College room only: $3000.
Undergraduate Financial Aid: 80% of all full-time undergraduates enrolled in fall 1996 applied for aid; of these, 87% were judged to have need according to Federal Methodology, of whom 96% were aided. On average, 98% of need was met. *Financial aid deadline:* continuous. *Financial aid forms:* FAFSA required. State form, institutional form required for some.
LD Services Contact: Ms. Tamara Durant, Academic Coordinator, Disabled Student Services, State University of New York College at Potsdam, 120 Sisson Hall, Potsdam, NY 13676, 315-267-3267. Fax: 315-267-3268.

STATE UNIVERSITY OF NEW YORK COLLEGE OF ENVIRONMENTAL SCIENCE AND FORESTRY

Syracuse, New York

LEARNING DISABILITIES SERVICES INFORMATION

Academic Support Center began offering services in 1984. Currently the program serves 19 undergraduates with LD. Services are also available to graduate students. Students diagnosed with ADD/ADHD are eligible for the same services available to students with LD.
Staff: 1 full-time, 1 part-time staff members, including director, associate director. Services provided by remediation specialists, tutors, counselors.
Special Fees: No special fees are charged for services to students with LD.
Applications and admissions: *Required:* high school transcript, courses completed; *recommended:* high school grade point average, psychoeducational report completed within 3 years. Students may begin taking classes in fall or spring. *Application deadline:* continuous.

PROGRAM AND SERVICE COMPONENTS

Academic advising: Provided by academic advisers. Students with LD may take up to 18 credit hours each term; most take 15 credit hours; 12 credit hours required to maintain full-time status and be eligible for financial aid.
Counseling services: Individual counseling, small-group counseling, career counseling, self-advocacy training.
Basic skills remediation: Offered one-on-one and in small groups by LD teachers, regular teachers. Available in reading, math, spelling, spoken language, written language, learning strategies, study skills, time management.
Subject-area tutoring: Offered one-on-one and in small groups by professional teachers, peer tutors. Available in most subjects.
Special courses: College survival skills, reading, communication skills, composition, math, study skills. Some offered for credit; none enter into overall grade point average.
Auxiliary aids: Taped textbooks, word-processors with spell-check, personal computers, talking computers, optical character readers.
Auxiliary services: Alternative test arrangements, notetakers, advocacy.
Campus support group: A special student organization is available to students with LD.

GENERAL COLLEGE INFORMATION

State-supported, coed. Part of State University of New York System. Awards bachelor's, master's, doctoral degrees. Founded 1911. *Setting:* 12-acre urban campus. *Endowment:* $7.5 million. *Total enrollment:* 1,740. *Faculty:* 120 full-time, 90% with terminal degrees.
Enrollment Profile: 1,187 students from 13 states and territories, 5 other countries. 37% women, 63% men, 7% part-time, 90% state residents, 33% live on campus, 85% transferred in, 1% international, 26% 25

State University of New York College of Environmental Science and Forestry (continued)

or older, 1% Native American, 2% Hispanic, 3% black, 2% Asian or Pacific Islander. *Retention:* 91% of 1995 full-time freshmen returned. *Graduation:* 59% graduate in 4 years, 79% in 5 years, 85% in 6 years. *Areas of study chosen:* 41% natural resource sciences, 30% biological and life sciences, 19% engineering and applied sciences, 10% architecture. *Most popular recent majors:* environmental biology, environmental engineering, environmental sciences.
First-Year Class: 116 total; 675 applied, 37% were accepted, 46% of whom enrolled. 24% from top 10% of their high school class, 62% from top quarter, 98% from top half.
Graduation Requirements: 125 credit hours; 2 courses each in math and science; computer course for forest engineering, paper science/engineering, forestry, landscape architecture, environmental sciences, natural resources management majors; internship (some majors); senior project (some majors).
Computers on Campus: 100 computers available on campus for general student use. Computers for student use in computer center, library, academic buildings. Staffed computer lab on campus provides training in use of computers, software.

EXPENSES AND FINANCIAL AID

Estimated Expenses for 1997–98: *Application fee:* $25. State resident tuition: $3400 full-time, $137 per credit hour part-time. Nonresident tuition: $8300 full-time, $346 per credit hour part-time. Part-time mandatory fees: $1 per credit hour. (Room and board are provided by Syracuse University.). Full-time mandatory fees: $13. College room and board: $6910. College room only: $3760.
Undergraduate Financial Aid: Of all full-time undergraduates enrolled in fall 1996, 100% of those judged to have need according to Federal Methodology were aided. On average, 80% of need was met. *Financial aid deadline (priority):* 3/1. *Financial aid forms:* FAFSA, state form required.
LD Services Contact: Mr. Thomas O. Slocum, Director of Counseling, Academic Support Center, State University of New York College of Environmental Science and Forestry, 110 Bray Hall, Syracuse, NY 13210-2779, 315-470-6660. Fax: 315-470-6693.

STATE UNIVERSITY OF WEST GEORGIA

Carrollton, Georgia

LEARNING DISABILITIES SERVICES INFORMATION

Disabled Student Services began offering services in 1975. Currently the program serves 53 undergraduates with LD. Services are also available to graduate students. Students diagnosed with ADD/ADHD are eligible for the same services available to students with LD.
Staff: 1 part-time staff member (coordinator). Services provided by graduate assistant.
Special Fees: No special fees are charged for services to students with LD.
Applications and admissions: *Required:* personal interview, psychoeducational report completed within 3 years; *recommended:* untimed or extended time SAT I or ACT. Students may begin taking classes any term. *Application deadline:* continuous.
Special policies: The college has written policies regarding grade forgiveness; substitutions and waivers of admissions requirements.

PROGRAM AND SERVICE COMPONENTS

Academic advising: Provided by unit staff members, academic advisers. Students with LD may take up to 18 quarter hours each term; most take 10 to 15 quarter hours; 12 quarter hours required to maintain full-time status; source of aid determines number of quarter hours required to be eligible for financial aid.
Special courses: Learning strategies, study skills. None offered for credit; none enter into overall grade point average.
Auxiliary aids: Taped textbooks, tape recorders, calculators, typewriters, word-processors with spell-check, talking computers, optical character readers.
Auxiliary services: Alternative test arrangements, notetakers, priority registration, advocacy, disability report for professors.

GENERAL COLLEGE INFORMATION

State-supported, comprehensive, coed. Part of University System of Georgia. Awards associate, bachelor's, master's degrees. Founded 1933. *Setting:* 400-acre small-town campus with easy access to Atlanta. *Endowment:* $3.1 million. *Research spending 1995–96:* $404,314. *Educational spending 1995–96:* $3177 per undergrad. *Total enrollment:* 8,560. *Faculty:* 375 (318 full-time, 78% with terminal degrees, 57 part-time); student–undergrad faculty ratio is 16:1.
Enrollment Profile: 6,189 students from 32 states and territories, 52 other countries. 61% women, 39% men, 20% part-time, 96% state residents, 33% live on campus, 7% transferred in, 1% international, 21% 25 or older, 0% Native American, 1% Hispanic, 16% black, 1% Asian or Pacific Islander. *Retention:* 63% of 1995 full-time freshmen returned. *Graduation:* 19% graduate in 4 years, 25% in 5 years, 29% in 6 years. *Areas of study chosen:* 26% education, 23% business management and administrative services, 9% social sciences, 7% psychology, 6% health professions and related sciences, 5% biological and life sciences, 5% premed, 4% communications and journalism, 3% computer and information sciences, 3% fine arts, 2% English language/literature/letters, 1% engineering and applied sciences, 1% foreign language and literature, 1% liberal arts/general studies, 1% mathematics, 1% natural resource sciences, 1% performing arts, 1% philosophy, 1% physical sciences, 1% prelaw. *Most popular recent majors:* early childhood education, nursing, psychology.
First-Year Class: 1,276 total; 3,628 applied, 65% were accepted, 54% of whom enrolled.
Graduation Requirements: 90 quarter hours for associate, 196 quarter hours for bachelor's; 5 quarter hours of math; 15 quarter hours of science; computer course for biology, chemistry, math, business education, economics majors; internship (some majors); senior project for honors program students and some majors.
Computers on Campus: 300 computers available on campus for general student use. A campus-wide network can be accessed from off-campus. Students can contact faculty members and/or advisers through e-mail. Computers for student use in computer center, computer labs, library, business, social science, math/computer science, mass communications schools provide access to the Internet/World Wide Web, on- and off-campus e-mail addresses. Staffed computer lab on campus provides training in use of computers, software. *Academic computing expenditure 1995–96:* $920,091.

EXPENSES AND FINANCIAL AID

Expenses for 1996–97: *Application fee:* $15. State resident tuition: $1584 full-time. Nonresident tuition: $5463 full-time. Part-time tuition per quarter ranges from $49 to $484 for state residents, $157 to $1672 for nonresidents. Part-time mandatory fees per quarter (6 to 11 credit hours): $135. Full-time mandatory fees: $405. College room and board: $3105. College room only: $1635.
Undergraduate Financial Aid: *Financial aid deadline (priority):* 3/15. *Financial aid forms:* FAFSA, institutional form required; CSS Financial Aid PROFILE acceptable.
LD Services Contact: Dr. Ann Phillips, Coordinator, Disabled Student Services, State University of West Georgia, 137 Parker Hall, Carrollton, GA 30118, 770-836-6428. Fax: 770-836-6638. Email: aphillip@westga.edu.

STONEHILL COLLEGE

Easton, Massachusetts

LEARNING DISABILITIES SERVICES INFORMATION

Office of Academic Services began offering services in 1986. Currently the program serves 75 undergraduates with LD. Students diagnosed with ADD/ADHD are eligible for the same services available to students with LD, as well as medication support by medical staff.
Staff: 2 full-time staff members, including director, coordinator. Services provided by tutors, counselor, faculty consultant.
Special Fees: No special fees are charged for services to students with LD.
Applications and admissions: *Required:* high school transcript, grade point average, courses completed, extracurricular activities, untimed or extended time SAT I or ACT, letters of recommendation, psychoeducational report completed within 3 years; *recommended:* high school class rank. Students may begin taking classes in summer only. *Application deadline:* 2/15 (fall term), 11/1 (spring term).
Special policies: The college has written policies regarding substitutions and waivers of graduation and degree requirements.

PROGRAM AND SERVICE COMPONENTS

Diagnostic testing: Intelligence, reading, math, spelling, handwriting, written language, motor abilities, perceptual skills, study skills, personality, social skills, psychoneurology, learning strategies.

Academic advising: Provided by unit staff members, academic advisers. Students with LD may take up to 17 credit hours each term; most take 15 credit hours; 12 credit hours required to maintain full-time status; 6 credit hours required to be eligible for financial aid.
Counseling services: Individual counseling, small-group counseling, career counseling.
Subject-area tutoring: Offered one-on-one and in small groups by professional teachers, peer tutors. Available in most subjects.
Special courses: College survival skills, reading, composition, learning strategies, time management, study skills. Some offered for credit; some enter into overall grade point average.
Auxiliary aids: Taped textbooks, tape recorders, calculators, typewriters, word-processors with spell-check, personal computers, optical character readers.
Auxiliary services: Alternative test arrangements, notetakers, advocacy.

GENERAL COLLEGE INFORMATION

Independent Roman Catholic, 4-year, coed. Awards bachelor's degrees. Founded 1948. *Setting:* 375-acre suburban campus with easy access to Boston. *Endowment:* $60.7 million. *Educational spending 1995–96:* $4917 per undergrad. *Total enrollment:* 2,041. *Faculty:* 195 (118 full-time, 80% with terminal degrees, 77 part-time); student–undergrad faculty ratio is 13:1.
Enrollment Profile: 2,041 students from 24 states and territories, 17 other countries. 57% women, 43% men, 1% part-time, 62% state residents, 80% live on campus, 8% transferred in, 3% international, 1% 25 or older, 0% Native American, 1% Hispanic, 2% black, 2% Asian or Pacific Islander. *Retention:* 90% of 1995 full-time freshmen returned. *Graduation:* 79% graduate in 4 years, 82% in 5 years. *Areas of study chosen:* 19% business management and administrative services, 19% social sciences, 12% biological and life sciences, 10% education, 10% liberal arts/general studies, 9% psychology, 7% communications and journalism, 4% English language/literature/letters, 4% health professions and related sciences, 2% computer and information sciences, 2% interdisciplinary studies, 1% foreign language and literature, 1% mathematics. *Most popular recent majors:* psychology, criminal justice, biology/biological sciences.
First-Year Class: 551 total; 4,193 applied, 54% were accepted, 24% of whom enrolled. 30% from top 10% of their high school class, 73% from top quarter, 98% from top half.
Graduation Requirements: 40 courses; 2 math/science courses; 1 year of a foreign language; computer course for accounting, finance, managerial economics, management, marketing, math, health care administration majors; internship (some majors); senior project for honors program students and some majors.
Computers on Campus: 100 computers available on campus for general student use. Computer purchase/lease plans available. A campus-wide network can be accessed from off-campus. Students can contact faculty members and/or advisers through e-mail. Computers for student use in computer center, computer labs, learning resource center, classrooms, library, science labs provide access to the Internet/World Wide Web, on- and off-campus e-mail addresses. Staffed computer lab on campus provides training in use of computers, software. *Academic computing expenditure 1995–96:* $431,000.

EXPENSES AND FINANCIAL AID

Expenses for 1997–98: *Application fee:* $45. Comprehensive fee of $21,852 includes full-time tuition ($14,406), mandatory fees ($450), and college room and board ($6996). Part-time tuition: $1440 per course. Part-time mandatory fees: $45 per course.
Undergraduate Financial Aid: 82% of all full-time undergraduates enrolled in fall 1996 applied for aid; of these, 86% were judged to have need according to Federal Methodology, of whom 99% were aided. On average, 86% of need was met. *Financial aid deadline (priority):* 2/1. *Financial aid forms:* FAFSA, CSS Financial Aid PROFILE required.
LD Services Contact: Mr. Richard Grant, Assistant Dean of Academic Services, Stonehill College, 320 Washington Street, North Easton, MA 02357, 508-565-1306. Fax: 508-565-1434.

SYRACUSE UNIVERSITY

Syracuse, New York

LEARNING DISABILITIES SERVICES INFORMATION

Learning Disability Services/Center for Academic Achievement began offering services in 1981. Currently the program serves 275 undergraduates with LD. Services are also available to graduate students. Students diagnosed with ADD/ADHD are eligible for the same services available to students with LD.
Staff: 2 full-time staff members, including director, assistant director. Services provided by counselors.
Special Fees: No special fees are charged for services to students with LD.
Applications and admissions: *Required:* high school transcript, grade point average, courses completed, untimed SAT I or ACT, letters of recommendation; *recommended:* high school IEP (Individualized Education Program), extended time SAT I, personal interview, psychoeducational report completed within 3 years, admissions consultation (if needed). Students may begin taking classes in summer only (before their first year). *Application deadline:* 2/1.
Special policies: The college has written policies regarding substitutions and waivers of degree requirements.

PROGRAM AND SERVICE COMPONENTS

Special preparation or orientation: Optional summer program offered prior to entering college. Optional orientation offered opening weekend.
Academic advising: Provided by unit staff members, academic advisers. Students with LD may take up to 18 credit hours each term; most take 12 to 15 credit hours; 12 credit hours (9 with special permission) required to maintain full-time status; 12 credit hours (fewer with special permission) required to be eligible for financial aid.
Counseling services: Individual counseling, small-group counseling, career counseling, self-advocacy training.
Subject-area tutoring: Offered one-on-one and in small groups by peer tutors. Available in most subjects.
Auxiliary aids: Taped textbooks, tape recorders, calculators, personal computers, optical character readers.
Auxiliary services: Alternative test arrangements, notetakers, priority registration, advocacy, proofreaders, readers.
Campus support group: A special student organization is available to students with LD.

GENERAL COLLEGE INFORMATION

Independent, coed. Awards bachelor's, master's, doctoral, first professional degrees. Founded 1870. *Setting:* 200-acre urban campus. *Endowment:* $322 million. *Research spending 1995–96:* $20.4 million. *Educational spending 1995–96:* $12,426 per undergrad. *Total enrollment:* 14,719. *Faculty:* 1,378 (807 full-time, 87% with terminal degrees, 571 part-time); student–undergrad faculty ratio is 12:1.
Enrollment Profile: 10,289 students from 54 states and territories, 68 other countries. 52% women, 48% men, 1% part-time, 42% state residents, 95% live on campus, 14% transferred in, 4% international, 3% 25 or older, 1% Native American, 5% Hispanic, 7% black, 5% Asian or Pacific Islander. *Retention:* 88% of 1995 full-time freshmen returned. *Graduation:* 68% graduate in 5 years. *Areas of study chosen:* 13% social sciences, 12% communications and journalism, 12% fine arts, 11% business management and administrative services, 7% engineering and applied sciences, 7% performing arts, 5% health professions and related sciences, 4% architecture, 4% biological and life sciences, 4% education, 4% library and information studies, 4% psychology, 2% English language/literature/letters, 1% computer and information sciences, 1% foreign language and literature, 1% mathematics, 1% philosophy, 1% physical sciences, 1% prelaw, 1% premed. *Most popular recent majors:* computer information systems, psychology, architecture.
First-Year Class: 2,665 total; 10,326 applied, 65% were accepted, 40% of whom enrolled. 33% from top 10% of their high school class, 77% from top quarter, 95% from top half. 28 valedictorians.
Graduation Requirements: 120 credit hours; computer course for engineering, management majors; internship (some majors); senior project for honors program students and some majors.
Computers on Campus: 1,200 computers available on campus for general student use. Computer purchase/lease plans available. A computer is strongly recommended for all students. A campus-wide network can be accessed from student residence rooms and from off-campus. Students can contact faculty members and/or advisers through e-mail. Computers for student use in computer center, computer labs, research center, learning resource center, classrooms, library, student center, dorms, academic buildings provide access to the Internet/World Wide Web, on- and off-campus e-mail addresses. Staffed computer lab on campus (open 24 hours a day) provides training in use of computers, software. *Academic computing expenditure 1995–96:* $11.9 million.

Syracuse University (continued)

EXPENSES AND FINANCIAL AID

Expenses for 1997–98: *Application fee:* $40. Comprehensive fee of $25,166 includes full-time tuition ($17,550), mandatory fees ($506), and college room and board ($7110). College room only: $3690. Part-time tuition: $765 per credit hour.

Undergraduate Financial Aid: 71% of all full-time undergraduates enrolled in fall 1996 applied for aid; of these, 89% were judged to have need according to Federal Methodology, of whom 100% were aided. *Financial aid deadline (priority):* 2/15. *Financial aid forms:* FAFSA, state form required.

LD Services Contact: Ms. Bethany Heaton Crawford, Assistant Director and Coordinator of LD Services, Syracuse University, 804 University Avenue, Syracuse, NY 13244, 315-443-4498. Fax: 315-443-5020. Email: bbheaton@summon.syr.edu.

TARLETON STATE UNIVERSITY

Stephenville, Texas

LEARNING DISABILITIES SERVICES INFORMATION

Academic Affairs, Compliance Office currently serves 80 undergraduates with LD. Services are also available to graduate students. Students diagnosed with ADD/ADHD are eligible for the same services available to students with LD.

Staff: 1 part-time staff member (director). Services provided by tutors, counselors.

Special Fees: No special fees are charged for services to students with LD.

Applications and admissions: *Required:* high school transcript, grade point average, class rank, courses completed, untimed SAT I or ACT; *recommended:* personal interview. Students may begin taking classes in fall, spring, or summer. *Application deadline:* continuous.

Special policies: The college has written policies regarding grade forgiveness.

PROGRAM AND SERVICE COMPONENTS

Academic advising: Provided by academic advisers. Students with LD may take up to 14 semester hours each term; most take 12 semester hours; 12 semester hours required to maintain full-time status and be eligible for financial aid.

Counseling services: Individual counseling, small-group counseling, career counseling.

Subject-area tutoring: Offered one-on-one by peer tutors. Available in all subjects.

Auxiliary aids: Taped textbooks, tape recorders, calculators, word-processors with spell-check, personal computers, talking computers, optical character readers, enlarged print computer screen (Magic).

Auxiliary services: Alternative test arrangements, notetakers, advocacy.

GENERAL COLLEGE INFORMATION

State-supported, comprehensive, coed. Part of Texas A&M University System. Awards associate, bachelor's, master's degrees. Founded 1899. *Setting:* 165-acre small-town campus with easy access to Dallas–Fort Worth. *Endowment:* $5.4 million. *Research spending 1995–96:* $2.3 million. *Total enrollment:* 6,369. *Faculty:* 332 (239 full-time, 60% with terminal degrees, 93 part-time); student–undergrad faculty ratio is 20:1.

Enrollment Profile: 5,551 students from 29 states and territories, 4 other countries. 52% women, 48% men, 6% part-time, 99% state residents, 22% live on campus, 13% transferred in, 1% international, 21% 25 or older, 1% Native American, 5% Hispanic, 3% black, 1% Asian or Pacific Islander. *Retention:* 58% of 1995 full-time freshmen returned. *Areas of study chosen:* 20% agriculture, 10% education, 10% interdisciplinary studies, 8% biological and life sciences, 7% business management and administrative services, 7% health professions and related sciences, 7% liberal arts/general studies, 3% computer and information sciences, 3% social sciences, 2% English language/literature/letters, 2% premed, 2% prevet, 2% psychology, 2% vocational and home economics, 1% communications and journalism, 1% engineering and applied sciences, 1% fine arts, 1% foreign language and literature, 1% mathematics, 1% performing arts, 1% physical sciences, 1% predentistry, 1% prelaw. *Most popular recent majors:* interdisciplinary studies, physical fitness/exercise science, agricultural education.

First-Year Class: 903 total; 1,588 applied, 74% were accepted, 77% of whom enrolled. 13% from top 10% of their high school class, 37% from top quarter, 75% from top half.

Graduation Requirements: 81 semester hours for associate, 128 semester hours for bachelor's; 3 semester hours of math; 8 semester hours of lab science; computer course; internship (some majors); senior project for honors program students.

Computers on Campus: 450 computers available on campus for general student use. Computer purchase/lease plans available. A computer is recommended for some students. A campus-wide network can be accessed from off-campus. Students can contact faculty members and/or advisers through e-mail. Computers for student use in computer center, computer labs, learning resource center, library, departmental labs provide access to the Internet/World Wide Web. Staffed computer lab on campus provides training in use of computers, software. *Academic computing expenditure 1995–96:* $199,661.

EXPENSES AND FINANCIAL AID

Expenses for 1996–97: *Application fee:* $20. State resident tuition: $960 full-time. Nonresident tuition: $7380 full-time, $246 per semester hour part-time. State resident part-time tuition per semester ranges from $120 to $352. Part-time mandatory fees per semester range from $41.25 to $405.25. Full-time mandatory fees: $978. College room and board: $2324 (minimum).

Undergraduate Financial Aid: On average, 90% of need was met. *Financial aid deadline (priority):* 5/1. *Financial aid forms:* FAFSA, institutional form acceptable.

LD Services Contact: Academic Affairs, Compliance Office, Tarleton State University, P.O. Box T-0010, Stephenville, TX 76401, 817-968-9103. Fax: 817-968-9707.

TAYLOR UNIVERSITY

Upland, Indiana

LEARNING DISABILITIES SERVICES INFORMATION

Academic Support Services currently serves 17 undergraduates with LD. Students diagnosed with ADD/ADHD are eligible for the same services available to students with LD.

Staff: 1 part-time staff member (coordinator).

Special Fees: No special fees are charged for services to students with LD.

Applications and admissions: *Required:* high school transcript, grade point average, class rank, courses completed, autobiographical statement, letters of recommendation, psychoeducational report completed within 3 years; *recommended:* high school extracurricular activities, IEP (Individualized Education Program), extended time SAT I or ACT, personal interview. Students may begin taking classes in fall only. *Application deadline:* continuous.

Special policies: The college has written policies regarding substitutions and waivers of degree requirements.

PROGRAM AND SERVICE COMPONENTS

Academic advising: Provided by academic advisers. Students with LD may take up to 17 credit hours each term; most take 12 to 15 credit hours; 12 credit hours required to maintain full-time status and be eligible for financial aid.

Counseling services: Individual counseling.

Basic skills remediation: Offered in small groups by regular teachers. Available in reading, math, written language, learning strategies, study skills, time management.

Subject-area tutoring: Offered one-on-one and in small groups by peer tutors. Available in most subjects.

Auxiliary aids: Taped textbooks, tape recorders, word-processors with spell-check.

Auxiliary services: Alternative test arrangements, notetakers, priority registration.

GENERAL COLLEGE INFORMATION

Independent interdenominational, 4-year, coed. Awards associate, bachelor's degrees. Founded 1846. *Setting:* 250-acre rural campus with easy access to Indianapolis. *Endowment:* $21.6 million. *Educational spending 1995–96:* $6935 per undergrad. *Total enrollment:* 1,866. *Faculty:* 144 (105 full-time, 68% with terminal degrees, 39 part-time); student–undergrad faculty ratio is 18:1.

Enrollment Profile: 1,866 students from 45 states and territories, 21 other countries. 52% women, 48% men, 2% part-time, 29% state residents, 76% live on campus, 11% transferred in, 3% international, 1% Native American, 1% Hispanic, 2% black, 2% Asian or Pacific Islander. *Retention:* 89% of 1995 full-time freshmen returned. *Graduation:* 55%

graduate in 4 years, 72% in 5 years, 75% in 6 years. *Areas of study chosen:* 18% education, 10% business management and administrative services, 10% liberal arts/general studies, 7% biological and life sciences, 7% communications and journalism, 7% psychology, 7% theology/religion, 6% social sciences, 5% computer and information sciences, 4% English language/literature/letters, 4% fine arts, 3% foreign language and literature, 3% premed, 2% interdisciplinary studies, 2% mathematics, 2% natural resource sciences, 2% physical sciences, 2% prelaw, 1% engineering and applied sciences, 1% health professions and related sciences, 1% performing arts, 1% philosophy. *Most popular recent majors:* business administration/commerce/management, elementary education, psychology.
First-Year Class: 489 total; 1,572 applied, 65% were accepted, 48% of whom enrolled. 44% from top 10% of their high school class, 74% from top quarter, 95% from top half. 42 valedictorians.
Graduation Requirements: 64 credit hours for associate, 128 credit hours for bachelor's; 1 course each in math and lab science or completion of a math proficiency test; computer course; internship (some majors); senior project.
Computers on Campus: 234 computers available on campus for general student use. Computer purchase/lease plans available. A computer is recommended for some students. A campus-wide network can be accessed from student residence rooms. Students can contact faculty members and/or advisers through e-mail. Computers for student use in computer labs, learning resource center, library, dorms provide access to the Internet/World Wide Web, on- and off-campus e-mail addresses. Staffed computer lab on campus provides training in use of computers, software. *Academic computing expenditure 1995–96:* $579,956.

EXPENSES AND FINANCIAL AID

Expenses for 1997–98: *Application fee:* $20. Comprehensive fee of $17,894 includes full-time tuition ($13,270), mandatory fees ($214), and college room and board ($4410). College room only: $2100. Part-time mandatory fees per semester (7 to 11 credit hours): $27. Part-time tuition: $380 per credit hour for 1 to 6 credit hours, $475 per credit hour for 7 or more credit hours.
Undergraduate Financial Aid: 66% of all full-time undergraduates enrolled in fall 1996 applied for aid; of these, 86% were judged to have need according to Federal Methodology, of whom 98% were aided. On average, 85% of need was met. *Financial aid deadline:* Applications processed continuously. *Financial aid forms:* FAFSA, institutional form required.
Financial aid specifically for students with LD: Scholarship: Dianne Newman Memorial Scholarship; loans; work-study.
LD Services Contact: Mr. R. Edwin Welch, Coordinator of Academic Support Services, Taylor University, 500 West Reade Avenue, Upland, IN 46989, 765-998-5523. Fax: 765-998-5569. Email: edwelch@tayloru.edu.

TEMPLE UNIVERSITY

Philadelphia, Pennsylvania

LEARNING DISABILITIES SERVICES INFORMATION

Disability Resources and Services began offering services in 1985. Currently the program serves 200 undergraduates with LD. Services are also available to graduate students. Students diagnosed with ADD/ADHD are eligible for the same services available to students with LD.
Staff: 4 full-time, 1 part-time staff members, including director, assistant director, LD adviser, secretary, graduate assistant. Services provided by tutors, counselors, test proctors, readers.
Special Fees: No special fees are charged for services to students with LD.
Applications and admissions: *Required:* high school transcript, grade point average, class rank, courses completed, autobiographical statement, SAT I (untimed) or extended time ACT; *recommended:* high school IEP (Individualized Education Program), extended time SAT I, personal interview, letters of recommendation, psychoeducational report. Students may begin taking classes in summer only. *Application deadline:* 5/1.

PROGRAM AND SERVICE COMPONENTS

Special preparation or orientation: Optional orientation offered after registration and before classes begin.
Academic advising: Provided by unit staff members, academic advisers. Students with LD may take up to 19 semester hours each term; most take 12 semester hours; 12 semester hours required to maintain full-time status; 6 semester hours (partial assistance) required to be eligible for financial aid.
Counseling services: Small-group counseling, career counseling.
Auxiliary aids: Taped textbooks, tape recorders, calculators, talking computers, optical character readers.
Auxiliary services: Alternative test arrangements, notetakers.

GENERAL COLLEGE INFORMATION

State-related, coed. Awards associate, bachelor's, master's, doctoral, first professional degrees. Founded 1884. *Setting:* 76-acre urban campus. *Endowment:* $89.8 million. *Research spending 1995–96:* $31.9 million. *Total enrollment:* 25,469. *Faculty:* 2,457 (1,596 full-time, 91% with terminal degrees, 861 part-time); student–undergrad faculty ratio is 24:1.
Enrollment Profile: 16,982 students from 44 states and territories, 79 other countries. 55% women, 45% men, 17% part-time, 83% state residents, 48% transferred in, 8% international, 28% 25 or older, 1% Native American, 3% Hispanic, 25% black, 12% Asian or Pacific Islander. *Graduation:* 49% graduate in 6 years. *Areas of study chosen:* 18% business management and administrative services, 12% education, 12% liberal arts/general studies, 7% communications and journalism, 7% health professions and related sciences, 7% performing arts, 6% psychology, 5% social sciences, 4% biological and life sciences, 4% engineering and applied sciences, 3% computer and information sciences, 2% architecture, 2% English language/literature/letters, 1% agriculture, 1% area and ethnic studies, 1% foreign language and literature, 1% mathematics, 1% philosophy, 1% physical sciences. *Most popular recent majors:* business administration/commerce/management, education.
First-Year Class: 2,321 total; 8,409 applied, 71% were accepted, 39% of whom enrolled. 14% from top 10% of their high school class, 39% from top quarter, 72% from top half.
Graduation Requirements: 64 semester hours for associate, 124 semester hours for bachelor's; 2 semesters of math/science; computer course for business, management, engineering, architecture majors.
Computers on Campus: 2,000 computers available on campus for general student use. Computer purchase/lease plans available. A computer is recommended for some students. A campus-wide network can be accessed from student residence rooms and from off-campus. Students can contact faculty members and/or advisers through e-mail. Computers for student use in computer center, computer labs, learning resource center, library, dorms provide access to the Internet/World Wide Web, on- and off-campus e-mail addresses. Staffed computer lab on campus provides training in use of computers, software.

EXPENSES AND FINANCIAL AID

Expenses for 1996–97: *Application fee:* $30. State resident tuition: $5628 full-time, $196 per semester hour part-time. Nonresident tuition: $10,510 full-time, $297 per semester hour part-time. Part-time mandatory fees per semester range from $22 to $85. Full-time mandatory fees: $220. College room and board: $5712.
Undergraduate Financial Aid: Of all full-time undergraduates enrolled in fall 1996, 87% of those who applied for aid were judged to have need according to Federal Methodology, of whom 96% were aided. On average, 70% of need was met. *Financial aid deadline (priority):* 3/31. *Financial aid forms:* FAFSA, state form required; CSS Financial Aid PROFILE acceptable.
LD Services Contact: Ms. Maryanne Ficker, Learning Disabilities Adviser, Temple University, 1301 C.B. Moore Avenue, Philadelphia, PA 19122, 215-204-1280. Fax: 215-204-6794.

TENNESSEE STATE UNIVERSITY

Nashville, Tennessee

LEARNING DISABILITIES SERVICES INFORMATION

Office of Disabled Student Services (ODSS) began offering services in 1996. Currently the program serves 25 undergraduates with LD. Services are also available to graduate students. Students diagnosed with ADD/ADHD are eligible for the same services available to students with LD.
Staff: 2 full-time, 6 part-time staff members, including director, coordinator. Services provided by remediation specialists, tutors, counselors.
Special Fees: No special fees are charged for services to students with LD.
Applications and admissions: *Required:* high school transcript, grade point average, courses completed, letters of recommendation; *recommended:* untimed or extended time SAT I, untimed ACT. Students may begin taking classes any term. *Application deadline:* continuous.

Tennessee State University (continued)

Special policies: The college has written policies regarding substitutions and waivers of admissions, graduation, and degree requirements.

PROGRAM AND SERVICE COMPONENTS

Special preparation or orientation: Optional orientation offered after classes begin.

Academic advising: Provided by unit staff members, academic advisers. Students with LD may take up to 15 semester hours each term; most take 12 semester hours; 12 semester hours required to maintain full-time status and be eligible for financial aid.

Basic skills remediation: Offered one-on-one, in small groups, and in class-size groups by regular teachers; computer-aided instruction also offered. Available in reading, math, learning strategies, study skills, time management.

Subject-area tutoring: Offered one-on-one and in small groups by peer tutors. Available in some subjects.

Special courses: College survival skills, learning strategies, time management, study skills. None offered for credit; none enter into overall grade point average.

Auxiliary aids: Taped textbooks, tape recorders, calculators, word-processors with spell-check, talking computers, optical character readers.

Auxiliary services: Alternative test arrangements, notetakers, priority registration, advocacy.

GENERAL COLLEGE INFORMATION

State-supported, comprehensive, coed. Part of State University and Community College System of Tennessee. Awards associate, bachelor's, master's, doctoral degrees. Founded 1912. *Setting:* 450-acre urban campus. *Total enrollment:* 8,643. *Faculty:* 473 (323 full-time, 77% with terminal degrees, 150 part-time).

Enrollment Profile: 7,013 students from 42 states and territories, 50 other countries. 61% women, 39% men, 20% part-time, 71% state residents, 7% transferred in, 1% international, 39% 25 or older, 1% Native American, 1% Hispanic, 75% black, 1% Asian or Pacific Islander. *Areas of study chosen:* 26% health professions and related sciences, 14% business management and administrative services, 12% engineering and applied sciences, 8% biological and life sciences, 8% liberal arts/general studies, 5% performing arts, 4% computer and information sciences, 4% interdisciplinary studies, 3% communications and journalism, 3% psychology, 3% social sciences, 2% education, 2% mathematics, 2% physical sciences, 1% agriculture, 1% area and ethnic studies, 1% English language/literature/letters, 1% foreign language and literature, 1% vocational and home economics. *Most popular recent majors:* nursing, elementary education, business administration/commerce/management.

First-Year Class: 1,095 total; 3,398 applied, 67% were accepted, 48% of whom enrolled.

Graduation Requirements: 65 semester hours for associate, 132 semester hours for bachelor's; 3 semester hours of math; 6 semester hours of science; computer course (varies by major); internship (some majors); senior project.

Computers on Campus: 300 computers available on campus for general student use. Computers for student use in computer labs, learning resource center, library provide access to the Internet/World Wide Web, on- and off-campus e-mail addresses. Staffed computer lab on campus provides training in use of computers, software.

EXPENSES AND FINANCIAL AID

Expenses for 1997–98: *Application fee:* $5. State resident tuition: $2118 full-time, $93 per semester hour part-time. Nonresident tuition: $6714 full-time, $294 per semester hour part-time. College room and board: $2770.

Undergraduate Financial Aid: On average, 77% of need was met. *Financial aid deadline (priority):* 4/1. *Financial aid forms:* FAFSA required.

LD Services Contact: Mrs. LeAnn Kelly, Coordinator, Tennessee State University, 3500 John A. Merritt Boulevard, Nashville, TN 37209-1561, 615-963-7872. Fax: 615-963-5054.

TENNESSEE TECHNOLOGICAL UNIVERSITY

Cookeville, Tennessee

LEARNING DISABILITIES SERVICES INFORMATION

Disability Services Office began offering services in 1996. Currently the program serves 40 undergraduates with LD. Services are also available to graduate students. Students diagnosed with ADD/ADHD are eligible for the same services available to students with LD.

Staff: 2 full-time staff members, including coordinator, secretary. Services provided by tutors, peer tutors.

Special Fees: No special fees are charged for services to students with LD.

Applications and admissions: *Required:* personal interview, autobiographical statement, psychoeducational report completed within 3 years, semester class schedule; *recommended:* high school transcript, grade point average, class rank, courses completed, IEP (Individualized Education Program), untimed or extended time SAT I or ACT. Students may begin taking classes any term. *Application deadline:* continuous.

PROGRAM AND SERVICE COMPONENTS

Special preparation or orientation: Optional orientation offered during registration and after classes begin.

Academic advising: Provided by academic advisers. Students with LD may take up to 16 semester hours each term; most take 15 semester hours; 12 semester hours required to maintain full-time status and be eligible for financial aid.

Counseling services: Individual counseling, small-group counseling, career counseling, self-advocacy training.

Subject-area tutoring: Offered one-on-one by professional teachers, peer tutors. Available in most subjects.

Auxiliary aids: Taped textbooks, tape recorders, calculators, typewriters, word-processors with spell-check, personal computers, talking computers, optical character readers.

Auxiliary services: Alternative test arrangements, notetakers, priority registration, advocacy, tutors, readers.

GENERAL COLLEGE INFORMATION

State-supported, coed. Part of State University and Community College System of Tennessee. Awards associate, bachelor's, master's, doctoral degrees. Founded 1915. *Setting:* 235-acre small-town campus. *Total enrollment:* 8,173. *Faculty:* 472 (371 full-time, 74% with terminal degrees, 101 part-time); student–undergrad faculty ratio is 18:1.

Enrollment Profile: 7,107 students from 40 states and territories, 38 other countries. 47% women, 53% men, 14% part-time, 93% state residents, 40% live on campus, 9% transferred in, 3% international, 20% 25 or older, 1% Native American, 1% Hispanic, 3% black, 2% Asian or Pacific Islander. *Retention:* 70% of 1995 full-time freshmen returned. *Graduation:* 12% graduate in 4 years, 31% in 5 years, 41% in 6 years. *Areas of study chosen:* 26% engineering and applied sciences, 16% business management and administrative services, 16% education, 7% health professions and related sciences, 5% biological and life sciences, 5% liberal arts/general studies, 5% social sciences, 3% agriculture, 3% psychology, 2% computer and information sciences, 2% mathematics, 2% premed, 2% vocational and home economics, 1% communications and journalism, 1% English language/literature/letters, 1% foreign language and literature, 1% physical sciences, 1% predentistry, 1% prelaw, 1% prevet. *Most popular recent majors:* mechanical engineering, business administration/commerce/management, elementary education.

First-Year Class: 1,162 total; 2,208 applied, 90% were accepted, 58% of whom enrolled. 38% from top 10% of their high school class, 69% from top quarter, 89% from top half. 6 National Merit Scholars, 65 valedictorians.

Graduation Requirements: 67 semester hours for associate, 132 semester hours for bachelor's; 3 semester hours of math; 8 semester hours of science; computer course for engineering, business, physics, agriculture, biology, geology, home economics, industrial technology majors; senior project (some majors).

Computers on Campus: 407 computers available on campus for general student use. Computers for student use in computer center, library, departmental labs provide access to the Internet/World Wide Web, on- and off-campus e-mail addresses. Staffed computer lab on campus provides training in use of computers.

EXPENSES AND FINANCIAL AID

Expenses for 1997–98: *Application fee:* $5. State resident tuition: $0 full-time. Nonresident tuition: $4824 full-time, $201 per semester hour part-time. Part-time mandatory fees: $95 per semester hour. Full-time mandatory fees: $2298. College room and board: $3260. College room only: $1700.

Undergraduate Financial Aid: 66% of all full-time undergraduates enrolled in fall 1996 applied for aid; of these, 84% were judged to have need according to Federal Methodology, of whom 82% were aided. On average, 98% of need was met. *Financial aid deadline (priority):* 3/15. *Financial aid forms:* FAFSA, student and parent tax returns required.

LD Services Contact: Leilani Gordon, Coordinator, Learning Disabilities Program, Tennessee Technological University, Box 5091, Cookeville, TN 38501, 615-372-6119. Fax: 615-372-6335.

TEXAS A&M UNIVERSITY

College Station, Texas

LEARNING DISABILITIES SERVICES INFORMATION

Department of Student Life, Services for Students with Disabilities began offering services in 1982. Currently the program serves 124 undergraduates with LD. Services are also available to graduate students. Students diagnosed with ADD/ADHD are eligible for the same services available to students with LD.

Staff: 6 full-time, 1 part-time staff members, including coordinator, accommodations coordinators, adaptive technology coordinator, secretary, testing supervisor, student assistants. Services provided by peer helpers.

Special Fees: No special fees are charged for services to students with LD.

Applications and admissions: *Required:* high school transcript, class rank, untimed SAT I or ACT, verification of disability; *recommended:* high school extracurricular activities, letters of recommendation. Students may begin taking classes any term. *Application deadline:* 3/1 (fall term), 10/15 (spring term).

Special policies: The college has written policies regarding grade forgiveness.

PROGRAM AND SERVICE COMPONENTS

Academic advising: Provided by academic advisers. Students with LD may take up to 12 semester hours each term; most take 9 to 12 semester hours; 12 semester hours required to maintain full-time status and be eligible for financial aid.

Counseling services: Individual counseling, small-group counseling, career counseling, self-advocacy training.

Special courses: College survival skills, composition, learning strategies, Internet use, time management, math, study skills. Some offered for credit; some enter into overall grade point average.

Auxiliary aids: Taped textbooks, tape recorders, calculators, word-processors with spell-check, personal computers, optical character readers.

Auxiliary services: Alternative test arrangements, notetakers, priority registration, advocacy.

Campus support group: A special student organization is available to students with LD.

GENERAL COLLEGE INFORMATION

State-supported, coed. Part of Texas A&M University System. Awards bachelor's, master's, doctoral, first professional degrees. Founded 1876. *Setting:* 5,142-acre suburban campus with easy access to Houston. *Endowment:* $2.4 billion. *Research spending 1995–96:* $355.8 million. *Total enrollment:* 41,892. *Faculty:* 2,307 (1,934 full-time, 90% with terminal degrees, 373 part-time); student–undergrad faculty ratio is 27:1.

Enrollment Profile: 34,342 students from 55 states and territories. 45% women, 55% men, 13% part-time, 86% state residents, 32% live on campus, 21% transferred in, 6% international, 4% 25 or older, 0% Native American, 10% Hispanic, 3% black, 4% Asian or Pacific Islander. *Retention:* 87% of 1995 full-time freshmen returned. *Graduation:* 68% graduate in 6 years. *Areas of study chosen:* 22% engineering and applied sciences, 16% business management and administrative services, 14% agriculture, 12% liberal arts/general studies, 9% education, 8% biological and life sciences, 8% health professions and related sciences, 4% architecture. *Most popular recent majors:* psychology, management information systems, accounting.

First-Year Class: 6,387 total; 15,973 applied, 69% were accepted, 58% of whom enrolled. 47% from top 10% of their high school class, 83% from top quarter, 98% from top half. 194 National Merit Scholars.

Graduation Requirements: 128 semester hours; 6 semester hours of math/logical reasoning; 8 semester hours of science; 2 years of a foreign language in high school or 1 year in college; computer course; internship (some majors).

Computers on Campus: 1,700 computers available on campus for general student use. Computer purchase/lease plans available. A campus-wide network can be accessed from student residence rooms and from off-campus. Students can contact faculty members and/or advisers through e-mail. Computers for student use in computer center, computer labs, research center, learning resource center, classrooms, library, student center, dorms, various locations. Staffed computer lab on campus (open 24 hours a day) provides training in use of computers, software. *Academic computing expenditure 1995–96:* $11 million.

EXPENSES AND FINANCIAL AID

Expenses for 1996–97: *Application fee:* $35. State resident tuition: $1024 full-time. Nonresident tuition: $7872 full-time, $246 per semester hour part-time. State resident part-time tuition per semester ranges from $120 to $352. Part-time mandatory fees per semester range from $69.25 to $566.75. Full-time mandatory fees: $1464. College room and board: $2496 (minimum). College room only: $1590.

Undergraduate Financial Aid: Of all full-time undergraduates enrolled in fall 1996, 78% of those who applied for aid were judged to have need according to Federal Methodology, of whom 93% were aided. On average, 70% of need was met. *Financial aid deadline (priority):* 4/1. *Financial aid forms:* FAFSA, institutional form, financial aid transcript (for transfers) required; CSS Financial Aid PROFILE acceptable.

LD Services Contact: Dr. Jo Hudson, Coordinator, Services for Students with Disabilities, Texas A&M University, Department of Student Life, College Station, TX 77843-1257, 409-845-1637. Fax: 409-862-1026. Email: 2ssd@ats.tamu.edu.

TEXAS A&M UNIVERSITY–KINGSVILLE

Kingsville, Texas

LEARNING DISABILITIES SERVICES INFORMATION

Services for Students with Disabilities began offering services in 1995. Currently the program serves 28 undergraduates with LD. Services are also available to graduate students. Students diagnosed with ADD/ADHD are eligible for the same services available to students with LD.

Staff: 4 part-time staff members, including Counselor. Services provided by tutors, counselors, diagnostic specialists, scribes, readers.

Special Fees: $30 for diagnostic testing.

Applications and admissions: *Required:* personal interview, documentation of disability (within 2 years). Students may begin taking classes any term. *Application deadline:* continuous.

PROGRAM AND SERVICE COMPONENTS

Special preparation or orientation: Optional orientation offered after classes begin.

Diagnostic testing: Intelligence, reading, math, spelling, handwriting, written language, motor abilities, perceptual skills, personality, memory; ADD testing also available.

Academic advising: Provided by academic advisers. Students with LD may take up to 15 credits (more with dean's permission) each term; most take 12 credits; 12 credits required to maintain full-time status; 6 credits required to be eligible for financial aid.

Counseling services: Individual counseling, career counseling.

Subject-area tutoring: Offered one-on-one by peer tutors, upper-level students. Available in all subjects.

Auxiliary aids: Taped textbooks, tape recorders.

Auxiliary services: Alternative test arrangements, notetakers, advocacy.

GENERAL COLLEGE INFORMATION

State-supported, coed. Part of Texas A&M University System. Awards bachelor's, master's, doctoral degrees. Founded 1925. *Setting:* 255-acre small-town campus. *Research spending 1995–96:* $5.8 million. *Total enrollment:* 6,113. *Faculty:* 337 (236 full-time, 90% with terminal degrees, 101 part-time).

Enrollment Profile: 5,021 students from 37 states and territories, 58 other countries. 49% women, 51% men, 18% part-time, 96% state residents, 20% live on campus, 32% transferred in, 2% international, 32% 25 or older, 60% Hispanic, 4% black, 1% Asian or Pacific Islander. *Retention:* 56% of 1995 full-time freshmen returned. *Graduation:* 18% graduate in 4 years, 20% in 5 years, 22% in 6 years. *Areas of study chosen:* 20% education, 13% engineering and applied sciences, 10% business management and administrative services, 8% agriculture, 8% liberal arts/general studies, 6% biological and life sciences, 6% social sciences, 5% psychology, 4% performing arts, 3% communications and journalism, 3% computer and information sciences, 3% natural resource sciences, 3% vocational and home economics, 1% English language/literature/letters, 1% fine arts, 1% foreign language and literature, 1% health professions and related sciences, 1% interdisciplinary studies, 1% mathematics, 1% physical sciences, 1% predentistry, 1% prelaw, 1% premed. *Most popular recent majors:* education, accounting, business administration/commerce/management.

Texas A&M University–Kingsville (continued)

First-Year Class: 886 total; 2,410 applied, 83% were accepted, 44% of whom enrolled. 4% from top 10% of their high school class, 32% from top quarter, 66% from top half.

Graduation Requirements: 124 credits; 6 credits of math/science; computer course for math, business, engineering majors; senior project (some majors).

Computers on Campus: 600 computers available on campus for general student use. Computer purchase/lease plans available. A campuswide network can be accessed from student residence rooms and from off-campus. Students can contact faculty members and/or advisers through e-mail. Computers for student use in computer center, library, academic offices provide access to the Internet/World Wide Web, on- and off-campus e-mail addresses. Staffed computer lab on campus.

EXPENSES AND FINANCIAL AID

Expenses for 1996–97: *Application fee:* $15. State resident tuition: $960 full-time. Nonresident tuition: $7380 full-time, $246 per credit part-time. State resident part-time tuition per semester ranges from $120 to $352. Part-time mandatory fees per semester range from $71.65 to $346. Full-time mandatory fees: $812. College room and board: $3484. College room only: $1784.

Undergraduate Financial Aid: On average, 62% of need was met. *Financial aid deadline (priority):* 4/15. *Financial aid forms:* FAFSA, CSS Financial Aid PROFILE, institutional form, financial aid transcript (for transfers) required.

LD Services Contact: Ms. Pat Bernsen, Counselor, Texas A&M University–Kingsville, Box 112, Kingsville, TX 78363, 512-593-3024. Fax: 512-593-2006.

TEXAS WESLEYAN UNIVERSITY

Fort Worth, Texas

LEARNING DISABILITIES SERVICES INFORMATION

Career, Counseling, and Testing Services began offering services in 1989. Currently the program serves 30 undergraduates with LD. Services are also available to graduate students. Students diagnosed with ADD/ADHD are eligible for the same services available to students with LD.

Staff: 1 full-time staff member (director). Services provided by counselor.

Special Fees: No special fees are charged for services to students with LD.

Applications and admissions: *Required:* high school transcript, grade point average, class rank, courses completed, letters of recommendation, psychoeducational report completed within 3 years; *recommended:* untimed SAT I or ACT. Students may begin taking classes any term. *Application deadline:* 8/1 (fall term), 11/1 (spring term).

Special policies: The college has written policies regarding grade forgiveness.

PROGRAM AND SERVICE COMPONENTS

Diagnostic testing: Intelligence, reading, math, spelling, handwriting, spoken language, written language, motor abilities, perceptual skills, personality, psychoneurology.

Academic advising: Provided by academic advisers. Students with LD may take up to 12 credit hours each term; most take 12 credit hours; 12 credit hours required to maintain full-time status and be eligible for financial aid.

Counseling services: Individual counseling, small-group counseling, career counseling.

Subject-area tutoring: Offered one-on-one by professional teachers, peer tutors. Available in most subjects.

Special courses: College survival skills, reading, composition, learning strategies, time management, study skills. All offered for credit; none enter into overall grade point average.

Auxiliary aids: Taped textbooks, word-processors with spell-check, personal computers.

Auxiliary services: Alternative test arrangements, notetakers, priority registration, advocacy.

GENERAL COLLEGE INFORMATION

Independent United Methodist, comprehensive, coed. Awards bachelor's, master's, first professional degrees. Founded 1890. *Setting:* 74-acre urban campus. *Endowment:* $33.1 million. *Research spending 1995–96:* $24,501. *Educational spending 1995–96:* $4017 per undergrad. *Total enrollment:* 2,966. *Faculty:* 245 (123 full-time, 67% with terminal degrees, 122 part-time); student–undergrad faculty ratio is 15:1.

Enrollment Profile: 1,871 students from 12 states and territories, 62 other countries. 65% women, 35% men, 32% part-time, 96% state residents, 18% transferred in, 1% international, 60% 25 or older, 2% Native American, 10% Hispanic, 13% black, 2% Asian or Pacific Islander. *Retention:* 61% of 1995 full-time freshmen returned. *Areas of study chosen:* 52% liberal arts/general studies, 20% business management and administrative services, 8% psychology, 5% biological and life sciences, 4% communications and journalism, 4% fine arts, 3% English language/literature/letters, 1% interdisciplinary studies, 1% mathematics, 1% pre-med, 1% theology/religion. *Most popular recent majors:* business administration/commerce/management, education, psychology.

First-Year Class: 273 total; 682 applied, 79% were accepted, 50% of whom enrolled. 21% from top 10% of their high school class, 48% from top quarter, 73% from top half.

Graduation Requirements: 124 credit hours; 3 credit hours of math; computer course for communication, business, education majors; senior project (some majors).

Computers on Campus: 134 computers available on campus for general student use. A computer is strongly recommended for all students. Computers for student use in computer labs, learning resource center, library. Staffed computer lab on campus provides training in use of computers, software. *Academic computing expenditure 1995–96:* $578,478.

EXPENSES AND FINANCIAL AID

Expenses for 1996–97: *Application fee:* $20. Comprehensive fee of $11,084 includes full-time tuition ($7200), mandatory fees ($400), and college room and board ($3484). Part-time tuition: $239 per credit hour. Part-time mandatory fees per semester range from $55 to $85.

Undergraduate Financial Aid: 99% of all full-time undergraduates enrolled in fall 1996 applied for aid; of these, 83% were judged to have need according to Federal Methodology, of whom 100% were aided. On average, 78% of need was met. *Financial aid deadline (priority):* 4/15. *Financial aid forms:* FAFSA, institutional form required; CSS Financial Aid PROFILE acceptable. State form required for some.

LD Services Contact: Dr. James Cannici, Director, Career, Counseling, and Testing Services, Texas Wesleyan University, 1201 Wesleyan, Ft. Worth, TX 76105, 817-531-4859. Fax: 817-531-4859.

THOMAS MORE COLLEGE

Crestview Hills, Kentucky

LEARNING DISABILITIES SERVICES INFORMATION

Student Support Services began offering services in 1982. Currently the program serves 120 undergraduates with LD. Services are also available to graduate students. Students diagnosed with ADD/ADHD are eligible for the same services available to students with LD.

Staff: 1 full-time, 2 part-time staff members, including director, assistant director, instructor. Services provided by remediation specialists, tutors, counselors.

Special Fees: No special fees are charged for services to students with LD.

Applications and admissions: *Required:* high school transcript, grade point average, class rank, courses completed, untimed or extended time ACT, psychoeducational report completed within 3 years; *recommended:* high school extracurricular activities, IEP (Individualized Education Program), extended time SAT I, personal interview, autobiographical statement, letters of recommendation. Students may begin taking classes in fall only. *Application deadline:* continuous.

Special policies: The college has written policies regarding grade forgiveness; substitutions and waivers of admissions, graduation, and degree requirements.

PROGRAM AND SERVICE COMPONENTS

Special preparation or orientation: Optional orientation offered on an individual basis.

Academic advising: Provided by unit staff members, academic advisers. Students with LD may take up to as many credit hours as an individual can handle each term; most take 12 to 15 credit hours; 12 credit hours required to maintain full-time status and be eligible for financial aid.

Counseling services: Individual counseling, small-group counseling, career counseling.

Auxiliary aids: Taped textbooks, tape recorders, typewriters, word-processors with spell-check.

Auxiliary services: Alternative test arrangements, notetakers, priority registration, advocacy.

GENERAL COLLEGE INFORMATION

Independent Roman Catholic, comprehensive, coed. Awards associate, bachelor's, master's degrees. Founded 1921. *Setting:* 120-acre suburban campus with easy access to Cincinnati. *Endowment:* $4.1 million. *Educational spending 1995–96:* $3189 per undergrad. *Total enrollment:* 1,345. *Undergraduate faculty:* 174 (76 full-time, 62% with terminal degrees, 98 part-time); student–undergrad faculty ratio is 12:1.

Enrollment Profile: 1,345 students from 13 states and territories, 7 other countries. 53% women, 47% men, 43% part-time, 68% state residents, 33% live on campus, 3% transferred in, 1% international, 36% 25 or older, 1% Native American, 1% Hispanic, 5% black, 1% Asian or Pacific Islander. *Retention:* 72% of 1995 full-time freshmen returned. *Areas of study chosen:* 36% business management and administrative services, 14% biological and life sciences, 8% health professions and related sciences, 6% social sciences, 5% computer and information sciences, 5% education, 4% English language/literature/letters, 4% psychology, 3% liberal arts/general studies, 2% communications and journalism, 2% fine arts, 1% interdisciplinary studies, 1% mathematics, 1% natural resource sciences, 1% performing arts, 1% philosophy, 1% physical sciences, 1% theology/religion. *Most popular recent majors:* business administration/commerce/management, biology/biological sciences, computer information systems.

First-Year Class: 263 total; 1,013 applied, 77% were accepted, 34% of whom enrolled. 18% from top 10% of their high school class, 42% from top quarter, 67% from top half. 5 valedictorians.

Graduation Requirements: 64 credit hours for associate, 128 credit hours for bachelor's; 9 credit hours of math/science; 6 credit hours of a foreign language; computer course for business, economics, math, chemistry, accounting majors; senior project.

Computers on Campus: 62 computers available on campus for general student use. A computer is recommended for some students. A campus-wide network can be accessed from student residence rooms and from off-campus. Students can contact faculty members and/or advisers through e-mail. Computers for student use in computer center, computer labs, classrooms, library provide access to the Internet/World Wide Web, on- and off-campus e-mail addresses. Staffed computer lab on campus provides training in use of computers, software. *Academic computing expenditure 1995–96:* $696,171.

EXPENSES AND FINANCIAL AID

Expenses for 1997–98: *Application fee:* $15. Comprehensive fee of $15,140 includes full-time tuition ($10,970), mandatory fees ($280), and college room and board ($3890 minimum). College room only: $1900 (minimum). Part-time mandatory fees per semester range from $20 to $90. Part-time tuition: $281 per credit hour for 1 to 7 credit hours, $315 per credit hour for 8 or more credit hours. Additional tuition for nursing courses: $30 per credit hour.

Undergraduate Financial Aid: Of all full-time undergraduates enrolled in fall 1996, 97% of those judged to have need according to Federal Methodology were aided. On average, 71% of need was met. *Financial aid deadline (priority):* 3/1. *Financial aid forms:* FAFSA, institutional form required; CSS Financial Aid PROFILE acceptable.

LD Services Contact: Mrs. Barbara S. Davis, Director, Student Support Services, Thomas More College, 333 Thomas More Parkway, Crestview Hills, KY 41017-3495, 606-344-3521. Fax: 606-344-3342. Email: davisb@thomasmore.edu.

TRENT UNIVERSITY

Peterborough, Ontario, Canada

LEARNING DISABILITIES SERVICES INFORMATION

Special Needs Office began offering services in 1989. Currently the program serves 160 undergraduates with LD. Services are also available to graduate students. Students diagnosed with ADD/ADHD are eligible for the same services available to students with LD.

Staff: 2 full-time, 1 part-time staff members, including coordinator. Services provided by counselor, diagnostic specialist.

Special Fees: No special fees are charged for services to students with LD.

Applications and admissions: *Required:* high school transcript; *recommended:* psychoeducational report completed within 3 years. Students may begin taking classes in fall only. *Application deadline:* 6/15.

PROGRAM AND SERVICE COMPONENTS

Special preparation or orientation: Optional orientation offered during registration.

Diagnostic testing: Reading, math, spelling, spoken language, written language, motor abilities, perceptual skills, learning strategies.

Academic advising: Provided by unit staff members, academic advisers. Students with LD may take up to 5 full courses each term; most take 4 full courses; 3.5 courses required to maintain full-time status; 3 full courses required to be eligible for financial aid.

Counseling services: Individual counseling.

Basic skills remediation: Offered one-on-one and in small groups by LD teachers. Available in reading, math, spelling, written language, study skills, time management.

Special courses: Reading, vocabulary development, composition, learning strategies, time management, study skills. None offered for credit; none enter into overall grade point average.

Auxiliary aids: Taped textbooks, tape recorders, calculators, word-processors with spell-check, personal computers, talking computers, optical character readers.

Auxiliary services: Alternative test arrangements, notetakers, advocacy.

Campus support group: A special student organization is available to students with LD.

GENERAL COLLEGE INFORMATION

Province-supported, comprehensive, coed. Awards bachelor's, master's, doctoral degrees. Founded 1963. *Setting:* 1,500-acre suburban campus with easy access to Toronto. *Total enrollment:* 5,450. *Undergraduate faculty:* 320 (212 full-time, 85% with terminal degrees, 108 part-time); student–undergrad faculty ratio is 17:1.

Enrollment Profile: 5,300 students from 12 provinces and territories, 52 other countries. 66% women, 34% men, 27% part-time, 85% province residents, 7% transferred in, 3% international. *Most popular recent majors:* psychology, English, history.

First-Year Class: 1,183 total; 5,582 applied, 74% were accepted, 29% of whom enrolled.

Graduation Requirements: 15 courses; internship (some majors); senior project (some majors).

Computers on Campus: 250 computers available on campus for general student use. Computer purchase/lease plans available. A computer is recommended for some students. A campus-wide network can be accessed from off-campus. Students can contact faculty members and/or advisers through e-mail. Computers for student use in computer center, classrooms, library, dorms, departmental labs provide access to the Internet/World Wide Web, on- and off-campus e-mail addresses. Staffed computer lab on campus provides training in use of computers, software.

EXPENSES AND FINANCIAL AID

Expenses for 1997–98: Canadian resident tuition: $3897 full-time, $715.75 per course part-time. Nonresident tuition: $10,462 full-time, $2029 per course part-time. Mandatory fee for nonresidents: $570.43 per year. (All figures are in Canadian dollars.). College room and board: $5571.

Undergraduate Financial Aid: Of all full-time undergraduates enrolled in fall 1996, 78% of those who applied for aid were judged to have need according to Federal Methodology, of whom 94% were aided. *Financial aid deadline (priority):* 7/31. *Financial aid forms:* institutional form, Canada Student Loan form required. State form required for some.

Financial aid specifically for students with LD: Scholarship: Bursaries for Students with Disabilities.

LD Services Contact: Ms. Eunice Lund-Lucas, Coordinator, Special Needs, Trent University, PO Box 4800, Peterborough, ON K9J 7B8, Canada, 705-748-1637. Fax: 705-748-1509. Email: specialneeds@trentu.ca.

TROY STATE UNIVERSITY

Troy, Alabama

LEARNING DISABILITIES SERVICES INFORMATION

Adaptive Needs Program currently serves 52 undergraduates with LD. Services are also available to graduate students. Students diagnosed with ADD/ADHD are eligible for the same services available to students with LD, as well as quiet testing area.

Staff: 1 full-time staff member (director). Services provided by tutors, counselor.

Troy State University (continued)

Special Fees: No special fees are charged for services to students with LD.

Applications and admissions: *Required:* high school transcript, grade point average, courses completed, untimed or extended time ACT, extended time SAT I, psychoeducational report completed within 3 years; *recommended:* high school IEP (Individualized Education Program). Students may begin taking classes in fall only. *Application deadline:* continuous.

PROGRAM AND SERVICE COMPONENTS

Special preparation or orientation: Optional orientation offered during registration.

Academic advising: Provided by unit staff members, academic advisers. Students with LD may take up to 19 quarter hours (depending upon GPA) each term; most take 12 to 15 quarter hours; 12 quarter hours required to maintain full-time status and be eligible for financial aid.

Counseling services: Individual counseling, career counseling.

Subject-area tutoring: Offered one-on-one by peer tutors. Available in some subjects.

Auxiliary aids: Tape recorders, calculators, Franklin Spellers, 4-track tape players.

Auxiliary services: Alternative test arrangements, notetakers, priority registration, advocacy, teacher notification.

GENERAL COLLEGE INFORMATION

State-supported, comprehensive, coed. Part of Troy State University System. Awards associate, bachelor's, master's degrees. Founded 1887. *Setting:* 500-acre small-town campus. *Endowment:* $10.6 million. *Research spending 1995–96:* $127,613. *Total enrollment:* 6,211. *Faculty:* 359 (221 full-time, 138 part-time); student–undergrad faculty ratio is 22:1.

Enrollment Profile: 5,126 students from 45 states and territories, 19 other countries. 62% women, 38% men, 25% part-time, 1% international, 1% Native American, 1% Hispanic, 20% black, 1% Asian or Pacific Islander. *Areas of study chosen:* 29% education, 16% business management and administrative services, 8% health professions and related sciences, 6% biological and life sciences, 3% communications and journalism, 3% computer and information sciences, 2% psychology, 2% social sciences, 1% English language/literature/letters, 1% fine arts, 1% foreign language and literature, 1% mathematics, 1% performing arts, 1% physical sciences, 1% prelaw, 1% premed. *Most popular recent majors:* education, business administration/commerce/management, nursing.

First-Year Class: 811 total; 1,784 applied, 78% were accepted, 59% of whom enrolled.

Graduation Requirements: 92 quarter hours for associate, 180 quarter hours for bachelor's; 5 quarter hours of algebra; 10 quarter hours of science; computer course for business administration majors; internship (some majors); senior project for honors program students and some majors.

Computers on Campus: 100 computers available on campus for general student use. Computers for student use in computer center, computer labs, library, student center. Staffed computer lab on campus provides training in use of computers, software.

EXPENSES AND FINANCIAL AID

Expenses for 1996–97: *Application fee:* $20. State resident tuition: $1980 full-time, $52.50 per quarter hour part-time. Nonresident tuition: $3960 full-time, $105 per quarter hour part-time. Part-time mandatory fees: $65 per quarter. Full-time mandatory fees: $195. College room and board: $3000. College room only: $1350.

Undergraduate Financial Aid: Of all full-time undergraduates enrolled in fall 1996, 58% of those who applied for aid were judged to have need according to Federal Methodology, of whom 100% were aided. On average, 68% of need was met. *Financial aid deadline (priority):* 5/1. *Financial aid forms:* FAFSA, institutional form required; CSS Financial Aid PROFILE acceptable.

LD Services Contact: Ms. Deborah G. Sellers, Adaptive Needs Coordinator, Troy State University, 226 Wright Hall, Troy, AL 36082, 334-670-3221. Fax: 334-670-3810.

TROY STATE UNIVERSITY DOTHAN

Dothan, Alabama

LEARNING DISABILITIES SERVICES INFORMATION

Counseling Center began offering services in 1988. Currently the program serves 8 undergraduates with LD. Services are also available to graduate students. Students diagnosed with ADD/ADHD are eligible for the same services available to students with LD.

Staff: 4 part-time staff members, including director. Services provided by tutors, counselor.

Special Fees: No special fees are charged for services to students with LD.

Applications and admissions: *Required:* high school transcript, grade point average, psychoeducational report completed within 2 years. Students may begin taking classes any term. *Application deadline:* continuous.

PROGRAM AND SERVICE COMPONENTS

Special preparation or orientation: Required orientation held during registration.

Academic advising: Provided by academic advisers. Students with LD may take up to 16 quarter hours each term; most take 15 quarter hours; 12 quarter hours required to maintain full-time status and be eligible for financial aid.

Counseling services: Individual counseling, small-group counseling, career counseling.

Basic skills remediation: Offered in small groups by regular teachers. Available in math, written language, study skills.

Subject-area tutoring: Offered one-on-one and in small groups by peer tutors. Available in most subjects.

Special courses: College survival skills, study skills, career planning. None offered for credit; none enter into overall grade point average.

Auxiliary aids: Tape recorders, typewriters, word-processors with spell-check, talking computers.

Auxiliary services: Alternative test arrangements, notetakers.

GENERAL COLLEGE INFORMATION

State-supported, comprehensive, coed. Part of Troy State University System. Awards associate, bachelor's, master's degrees. Founded 1961. *Setting:* 250-acre small-town campus. *Research spending 1995–96:* $2529. *Total enrollment:* 2,150. *Faculty:* 144 (65 full-time, 89% with terminal degrees, 79 part-time).

Enrollment Profile: 1,574 students from 13 states and territories, 14 other countries. 56% women, 44% men, 58% part-time, 81% state residents, 36% transferred in, 85% 25 or older, 1% Native American, 3% Hispanic, 12% black, 1% Asian or Pacific Islander. *Retention:* 65% of 1995 full-time freshmen returned. *Areas of study chosen:* 23% education, 20% business management and administrative services, 8% social sciences. *Most popular recent majors:* business administration/commerce/management, education, psychology.

First-Year Class: 34 total; 71 applied, 61% were accepted, 79% of whom enrolled.

Graduation Requirements: 90 quarter hours for associate, 180 quarter hours for bachelor's; 5 quarter hours of math; 10 quarter hours of science; computer course.

Computers on Campus: 67 computers available on campus for general student use. Computers for student use in computer center, Instructional Support Center provide access to the Internet/World Wide Web. Staffed computer lab on campus provides training in use of computers, software. *Academic computing expenditure 1995–96:* $173,365.

EXPENSES AND FINANCIAL AID

Expenses for 1997–98: *Application fee:* $15. State resident tuition: $2184 full-time, $62 per quarter hour part-time. Nonresident tuition: $4368 full-time, $124 per quarter hour part-time. Part-time mandatory fees: $1 per quarter hour. Full-time mandatory fees: $45.

Undergraduate Financial Aid: *Financial aid deadline (priority):* 5/1. *Financial aid forms:* FAFSA, institutional form required; CSS Financial Aid PROFILE acceptable.

LD Services Contact: Ms. Pamela Williamson, Director of Counseling Services, Troy State University Dothan, PO Box 8368, Dothan, AL 36304, 334-983-6556 Ext. 221. Fax: 334-983-6322.

TUFTS UNIVERSITY

Medford, Massachusetts

LEARNING DISABILITIES SERVICES INFORMATION

Academic Resource Center began offering services in 1986. Currently the program serves 10 undergraduates with LD. Services are also available to graduate students.

Staff: 1 full-time staff member (director).

Special Fees: No special fees are charged for services to students with LD.

Applications and admissions: *Required:* high school transcript, grade point average, class rank, courses completed, extracurricular activities, untimed SAT I, autobiographical statement, letters of recommendation; *recommended:* extended time SAT I, psychoeducational report completed within 3 years. Students may begin taking classes in fall or spring. *Application deadline:* 1/1 (fall term), 11/15 (spring term).

PROGRAM AND SERVICE COMPONENTS

Academic advising: Provided by academic advisers. Students with LD may take up to 5 courses each term; most take 4 to 5 courses; 3 courses required to maintain full-time status.

Counseling services: Individual counseling, career counseling.

Subject-area tutoring: Offered one-on-one by peer tutors. Available in all subjects.

Auxiliary aids: Taped textbooks, tape recorders, calculators, typewriters, optical character readers.

Auxiliary services: Alternative test arrangements, notetakers, advocacy.

GENERAL COLLEGE INFORMATION

Independent, coed. Awards bachelor's, master's, doctoral, first professional degrees. Founded 1852. *Setting:* 150-acre suburban campus with easy access to Boston. *Endowment:* $298 million. *Research spending 1995–96:* $32.3 million. *Total enrollment:* 8,183. *Faculty:* 1,084 (561 full-time, 99% with terminal degrees, 523 part-time); student–undergrad faculty ratio is 13:1.

Enrollment Profile: 4,504 students from 51 states and territories, 62 other countries. 52% women, 48% men, 0% part-time, 26% state residents, 80% live on campus, 6% transferred in, 7% international, 5% Hispanic, 4% black, 15% Asian or Pacific Islander. *Retention:* 98% of 1995 full-time freshmen returned. *Graduation:* 88% graduate in 4 years, 89% in 6 years. *Most popular recent majors:* biology/biological sciences, English, international relations.

First-Year Class: 1,181 total; 11,873 applied, 31% were accepted, 32% of whom enrolled. 63% from top 10% of their high school class, 91% from top quarter, 99% from top half. 22 National Merit Scholars.

Graduation Requirements: 34 courses; 2 courses each in math and science; computer course for engineering majors; senior project for honors program students.

Computers on Campus: 254 computers available on campus for general student use. Computer purchase/lease plans available. A campus-wide network can be accessed from student residence rooms and from off-campus. Students can contact faculty members and/or advisers through e-mail. Computers for student use in computer center, computer labs, library, student center, dorms, CAD lab provide access to the Internet/World Wide Web, on- and off-campus e-mail addresses. Staffed computer lab on campus provides training in use of computers, software.

EXPENSES AND FINANCIAL AID

Expenses for 1997–98: *Application fee:* $50. Comprehensive fee of $29,429 includes full-time tuition ($22,230), mandatory fees ($581), and college room and board ($6618). College room only: $3518.

Undergraduate Financial Aid: 42% of all full-time undergraduates enrolled in fall 1996 applied for aid; of these, 91% were judged to have need according to Federal Methodology, of whom 100% were aided. On average, 99% of need was met. *Financial aid deadline (priority):* 1/15. *Financial aid forms:* FAFSA, CSS Financial Aid PROFILE, parent and student federal tax forms required.

LD Services Contact: Ms. Nadia Medina, Director, Academic Resource Center, Tufts University, 72 Professors Row, Medford, MA 02155, 617-627-3724. Fax: 617-627-3647.

UNION UNIVERSITY

Jackson, Tennessee

LEARNING DISABILITIES SERVICES INFORMATION

Academic Services began offering services in 1991. Currently the program serves 6 undergraduates with LD. Services are also available to graduate students. Students diagnosed with ADD/ADHD are eligible for the same services available to students with LD.

Staff: 1 part-time staff member (coordinator). Services provided by counselor.

Special Fees: No special fees are charged for services to students with LD.

Applications and admissions: *Required:* high school transcript, grade point average, class rank, courses completed, untimed or extended time ACT, psychoeducational report completed within 3 years; *recommended:* high school extracurricular activities, untimed or extended time SAT I, autobiographical statement, letters of recommendation. Students may begin taking classes any term. *Application deadline:* continuous.

PROGRAM AND SERVICE COMPONENTS

Special preparation or orientation: Orientation offered during first 2 weeks of classes.

Academic advising: Provided by academic advisers. Most students with LD take 12 semester hours each term; 12 semester hours required to maintain full-time status and be eligible for financial aid.

Counseling services: Individual counseling, career counseling.

Subject-area tutoring: Offered one-on-one and in small groups by peer tutors. Available in most subjects.

Auxiliary services: Alternative test arrangements, notetakers, advocacy.

GENERAL COLLEGE INFORMATION

Independent Southern Baptist, comprehensive, coed. Awards bachelor's, master's degrees. Founded 1823. *Setting:* 290-acre small-town campus with easy access to Memphis. *Endowment:* $14 million. *Educational spending 1995–96:* $3899 per undergrad. *Total enrollment:* 1,975. *Faculty:* 157 (108 full-time, 56% with terminal degrees, 49 part-time); student–undergrad faculty ratio is 13:1.

Enrollment Profile: 1,832 students from 31 states and territories, 10 other countries. 63% women, 37% men, 13% part-time, 75% state residents, 53% live on campus, 13% transferred in, 1% international, 0% Native American, 0% Hispanic, 4% black, 0% Asian or Pacific Islander. *Retention:* 93% of 1995 full-time freshmen returned. *Graduation:* 29% graduate in 4 years, 42% in 5 years, 45% in 6 years. *Areas of study chosen:* 15% health professions and related sciences, 13% education, 12% business management and administrative services, 8% theology/religion, 6% fine arts, 6% social sciences, 5% communications and journalism, 5% psychology, 4% biological and life sciences, 3% English language/literature/letters, 3% predentistry, 3% prelaw, 3% premed, 3% prevet, 2% computer and information sciences, 2% mathematics, 2% physical sciences, 1% foreign language and literature. *Most popular recent majors:* nursing, education, business administration/commerce/management.

First-Year Class: 353 total; 875 applied, 80% were accepted, 50% of whom enrolled. 28 valedictorians.

Graduation Requirements: 128 semester hours; 3 semester hours of math; 8 semester hours of science; computer course for math, business, education majors; internship (some majors); senior project for honors program students and some majors.

Computers on Campus: 175 computers available on campus for general student use. Computer purchase/lease plans available. A computer is recommended for some students. A campus-wide network can be accessed. Students can contact faculty members and/or advisers through e-mail. Computers for student use in computer center, computer labs, classrooms, library, dorms provide access to the Internet/World Wide Web, on- and off-campus e-mail addresses. Staffed computer lab on campus (open 24 hours a day) provides training in use of computers, software. *Academic computing expenditure 1995–96:* $412,489.

EXPENSES AND FINANCIAL AID

Expenses for 1997–98: *Application fee:* $10. Comprehensive fee of $11,185 includes full-time tuition ($7990), mandatory fees ($190), and college room and board ($3005). Part-time tuition: $320 per semester hour. Part-time mandatory fees per term range from $50 to $75.

Undergraduate Financial Aid: 73% of all full-time undergraduates enrolled in fall 1996 applied for aid; of these, 76% were judged to have need according to Federal Methodology, of whom 100% were aided. On average, 80% of need was met. *Financial aid deadline (priority):* 2/1. *Financial aid forms:* FAFSA, institutional form required.

LD Services Contact: Dr. Margaret Lillard, Director of Counseling Services, Union University, 1050 Union University Drive, Jackson, TN 38305, 901-661-5322. Fax: 901-661-5017. Email: mlillard@buster.uu.edu.

UNIVERSITY AT ALBANY, STATE UNIVERSITY OF NEW YORK

Albany, New York

LEARNING DISABILITIES SERVICES INFORMATION

Disabled Student Services began offering services in 1973. Currently the program serves 150 undergraduates with LD. Services are also available to graduate students. Students diagnosed with ADD/ADHD are eligible for the same services available to students with LD.

Staff: 1 full-time, 1 part-time staff members, including director, graduate assistant. Services provided by tutors, diagnostic specialists, writing lab coordinator, graduate assistant.

Special Fees: $1300 per year.

Applications and admissions: *Required:* high school transcript, grade point average, class rank, untimed SAT I; *recommended:* high school extracurricular activities, extended time SAT I, autobiographical statement, letters of recommendation, psychoeducational report completed within 3 years. Students may begin taking classes any term. *Application deadline:* 3/1 (fall term), 9/1 (spring term).

PROGRAM AND SERVICE COMPONENTS

Special preparation or orientation: Optional orientation offered before registration.

Diagnostic testing: Intelligence, reading, math, spelling, written language, perceptual skills, psychoneurology.

Academic advising: Provided by unit staff members, academic advisers. Students with LD may take up to 18 credits each term; most take 12 credits; 12 credits required to maintain full-time status and be eligible for financial aid.

Counseling services: Individual counseling, small-group counseling, career counseling.

Subject-area tutoring: Offered one-on-one and in small groups by professional teachers, peer tutors. Available in most subjects.

Auxiliary aids: Taped textbooks, tape recorders, word-processors with spell-check, personal computers, optical character readers.

Auxiliary services: Alternative test arrangements, notetakers, priority registration, advocacy, pre-registration counseling.

Campus support group: A special student organization is available to students with LD.

GENERAL COLLEGE INFORMATION

State-supported, coed. Part of State University of New York System. Awards bachelor's, master's, doctoral degrees. Founded 1844. *Setting:* 560-acre suburban campus. *Endowment:* $8 million. *Research spending 1995–96:* $70 million. *Educational spending 1995–96:* $7435 per undergrad. *Total enrollment:* 14,215. *Faculty:* 835 (591 full-time, 96% with terminal degrees, 244 part-time); student–undergrad faculty ratio is 16:1.

Enrollment Profile: 10,027 students from 26 states and territories, 29 other countries. 48% women, 52% men, 6% part-time, 97% state residents, 54% live on campus, 33% transferred in, 1% international, 9% 25 or older, 1% Native American, 7% Hispanic, 8% black, 9% Asian or Pacific Islander. *Retention:* 81% of 1995 full-time freshmen returned. *Graduation:* 60% graduate in 4 years, 71% in 5 years, 72% in 6 years. *Areas of study chosen:* 18% social sciences, 10% English language/literature/letters, 7% biological and life sciences, 6% psychology, 4% business management and administrative services, 3% computer and information sciences, 2% area and ethnic studies, 2% communications and journalism, 2% foreign language and literature, 2% mathematics, 2% performing arts, 2% physical sciences, 1% education, 1% fine arts, 1% interdisciplinary studies, 1% natural resource sciences, 1% philosophy. *Most popular recent majors:* English, psychology, business administration/commerce/management.

First-Year Class: 2,008 total; 13,678 applied, 65% were accepted, 23% of whom enrolled. 14% from top 10% of their high school class, 52% from top quarter, 91% from top half. 18 valedictorians.

Graduation Requirements: 120 credits; 2 credits each of math and science; computer course for business administration, accounting, applied math, rhetoric and communications, information science, geology, teacher education, physics majors; internship (some majors); senior project for honors program students and some majors.

Computers on Campus: 500 computers available on campus for general student use. Computer purchase/lease plans available. A computer is recommended for some students. A campus-wide network can be accessed from student residence rooms and from off-campus. Students can contact faculty members and/or advisers through e-mail. Computers for student use in computer center, computer labs, research center, learning resource center, classrooms, library, dorms, special user labs provide access to the Internet/World Wide Web, on- and off-campus e-mail addresses. Staffed computer lab on campus (open 24 hours a day) provides training in use of computers, software.

EXPENSES AND FINANCIAL AID

Expenses for 1996–97: *Application fee:* $30. State resident tuition: $3400 full-time, $137 per credit part-time. Nonresident tuition: $8300 full-time, $346 per credit part-time. Part-time mandatory fees per semester range from $21 to $306. Full-time mandatory fees: $730. College room and board: $5050. College room only: $3412.

Undergraduate Financial Aid: Of all full-time undergraduates enrolled in fall 1996, 80% of those who applied for aid were judged to have need according to Federal Methodology, of whom 95% were aided. On average, 75% of need was met. *Financial aid deadline (priority):* 3/15. *Financial aid forms:* FAFSA required; CSS Financial Aid PROFILE acceptable.

Financial aid specifically for students with LD: Scholarship: Disabled Student Scholarship Fund.

LD Services Contact: Ms. Nancy Belowich-Negron, Director, Disabled Student Services, University at Albany, State University of New York, Campus Center 137, 1400 Washington Avenue, Albany, NY 12222, 518-442-5491.

THE UNIVERSITY OF AKRON

Akron, Ohio

LEARNING DISABILITIES SERVICES INFORMATION

Services for Students with Disabilities began offering services in 1985. Currently the program serves 150 undergraduates with LD. Services are also available to graduate students. Students diagnosed with ADD/ADHD are eligible for the same services available to students with LD, as well as isolated testing location.

Staff: 2 full-time, 1 part-time staff members, including director, secretary. Services provided by graduate assistant.

Special Fees: No special fees are charged for services to students with LD.

Applications and admissions: *Required:* high school transcript, grade point average, class rank, courses completed, untimed or extended time SAT I or ACT, separate application and interview for BS/MD; *recommended:* high school extracurricular activities. Students may begin taking classes any term. *Application deadline:* 8/12 (fall term), 12/31 (spring term).

Special policies: The college has written policies regarding grade forgiveness.

PROGRAM AND SERVICE COMPONENTS

Diagnostic testing: Intelligence, reading, math, spelling, spoken language, written language, motor abilities, perceptual skills, study skills, personality, social skills, psychoneurology, speech, hearing, learning strategies.

Academic advising: Provided by unit staff members, academic advisers. Most students with LD take 14 credits each term; 12 credits required to maintain full-time status; source of aid determines number of credits required to be eligible for financial aid.

Counseling services: Individual counseling, small-group counseling, career counseling.

Subject-area tutoring: Offered one-on-one and in small groups by peer tutors, graduate assistants in specific subjects. Available in all subjects.

Special courses: College survival skills, reading, vocabulary development, communication skills, composition, learning strategies, word processing, time management, math, typing, study skills, career planning. Some offered for credit; some enter into overall grade point average.

Auxiliary aids: Taped textbooks, tape recorders, typewriters, word-processors with spell-check, personal computers, optical character readers.

Auxiliary services: Alternative test arrangements, notetakers, priority registration, advocacy, test proctors, readers, library research assistants.

GENERAL COLLEGE INFORMATION

State-supported, coed. Awards associate, bachelor's, master's, doctoral, first professional degrees. Founded 1870. *Setting:* 170-acre urban campus with easy access to Cleveland. *Endowment:* $90.1 million. *Research spending 1995–96:* $9.8 million. *Educational spending 1995–96:* $2346 per undergrad. *Total enrollment:* 24,252. *Faculty:* 1,739 (718 full-time, 81% with terminal degrees, 1,021 part-time); student–undergrad faculty ratio is 20:1.

Enrollment Profile: 20,037 students from 25 states and territories, 55 other countries. 55% women, 45% men, 44% part-time, 98% state residents, 6% transferred in, 1% international, 37% 25 or older, 1% Native American, 1% Hispanic, 12% black, 2% Asian or Pacific Islander. *Retention:* 70% of 1995 full-time freshmen returned. *Graduation:* 13% graduate in 4 years, 29% in 5 years, 37% in 6 years. *Areas of study chosen:* 18% business management and administrative services, 12% engineering and applied sciences, 11% education, 10% liberal arts/general studies, 9% health professions and related sciences, 8% social sciences, 4% biological and life sciences, 3% communications and journalism, 3% mathematics, 3% psychology, 3% vocational and home economics, 2% computer and information sciences, 2% English language/literature/letters, 2% fine arts, 2% foreign language and literature, 2% natural resource sciences, 2% performing arts, 2% philosophy, 2% physical sciences. *Most popular recent majors:* elementary education, accounting, marketing/retailing/merchandising.

First-Year Class: 3,065 total; 5,558 applied, 100% were accepted, 55% of whom enrolled. 10% from top 10% of their high school class, 29% from top quarter, 60% from top half. 7 National Merit Scholars.

Graduation Requirements: 64 credits for associate, 128 credits for bachelor's; 1 semester of math; 2 semesters of science; computer course for business administration, engineering majors; internship (some majors); senior project for honors program students and some majors.

Computers on Campus: 850 computers available on campus for general student use. Computer purchase/lease plans available. A computer is recommended for all students. A campus-wide network can be accessed from student residence rooms and from off-campus. Students can contact faculty members and/or advisers through e-mail. Computers for student use in computer center, computer labs, research center, learning resource center, classrooms, library, dorms, departmental labs provide access to the Internet/World Wide Web, on- and off-campus e-mail addresses. Staffed computer lab on campus provides training in use of computers, software. *Academic computing expenditure 1995–96:* $4.2 million.

EXPENSES AND FINANCIAL AID

Expenses for 1997–98: *Application fee:* $25. State resident tuition: $3282 full-time, $136.85 per credit part-time. Nonresident tuition: $9051 full-time, $317.10 per credit part-time. Part-time mandatory fees: $14.45 per credit. Full-time mandatory fees: $343. College room and board: $4380. College room only: $2710 (minimum).

Undergraduate Financial Aid: 61% of all full-time undergraduates enrolled in fall 1996 applied for aid; of these, 84% were judged to have need according to Federal Methodology, of whom 100% were aided. On average, 100% of need was met. *Financial aid deadline (priority):* 3/1. *Financial aid forms:* FAFSA, state form required. Institutional form required for some.

LD Services Contact: Ms. Grace E. Olmstead, Director of Services for Students with Disabilities, The University of Akron, Spicer Hall 124, Akron, OH 44325, 330-972-7928. Fax: 330-972-6720.

THE UNIVERSITY OF ALABAMA

Tuscaloosa, Alabama

LEARNING DISABILITIES SERVICES INFORMATION

Office of Disability Services began offering services in 1987. Currently the program serves 235 undergraduates with LD. Services are also available to graduate students. Students diagnosed with ADD/ADHD are eligible for the same services available to students with LD, as well as support group.

Staff: 4 full-time, 6 part-time staff members, including associate director, coordinator, graduate teaching assistants, administrative assistants. Services provided by remediation specialist, tutors, counselors, diagnostic specialist.

Special Fees: $250 to $700 for diagnostic testing.

Applications and admissions: *Required:* high school transcript, grade point average, courses completed, untimed SAT I or ACT, psychoeducational report completed within 3 years; *recommended:* high school class rank, extracurricular activities, IEP (Individualized Education Program), extended time SAT I or ACT, personal interview, autobiographical statement, letters of recommendation. Students may begin taking classes any term. *Application deadline:* continuous.

Special policies: The college has written policies regarding grade forgiveness; substitutions and waivers of admissions and degree requirements.

PROGRAM AND SERVICE COMPONENTS

Special preparation or orientation: Optional orientation offered before registration.

Diagnostic testing: Intelligence, reading, math, spelling, handwriting, spoken language, written language, motor abilities, perceptual skills, study skills, personality, social skills, psychoneurology, speech, hearing, learning strategies, cognitive processing.

Academic advising: Provided by unit staff members, academic advisers. Students with LD may take up to 18 semester hours each term; most take 12 to 16 semester hours; 12 semester hours required to maintain full-time status; 12 semester hours (unless special conditions exist) required to be eligible for financial aid.

Counseling services: Individual counseling, small-group counseling, career counseling, self-advocacy training.

Basic skills remediation: Offered in small groups by remedial specialist; computer-aided instruction also offered. Available in reading, math, written language, learning strategies, study skills, time management, word processing.

Subject-area tutoring: Offered one-on-one and in small groups by professional teachers, peer tutors. Available in some subjects.

Special courses: College survival skills, learning strategies, word processing, time management, study skills, career planning. All offered for credit; all enter into overall grade point average.

Auxiliary aids: Taped textbooks, tape recorders, calculators, word-processors with spell-check, talking computers, optical character readers, videotaped course lectures, Dragon Dictate, Arkenstone Reader.

Auxiliary services: Alternative test arrangements, priority registration.

GENERAL COLLEGE INFORMATION

State-supported, coed. Part of University of Alabama System. Awards bachelor's, master's, doctoral, first professional degrees. Founded 1831. *Setting:* 1,000-acre suburban campus with easy access to Birmingham. *Endowment:* $226.2 million. *Research spending 1995–96:* $17.2 million. *Educational spending 1995–96:* $2573 per undergrad. *Total enrollment:* 17,565. *Faculty:* 1,011 (827 full-time, 97% with terminal degrees, 184 part-time); student–undergrad faculty ratio is 19:1.

Enrollment Profile: 14,087 students from 52 states and territories, 92 other countries. 53% women, 47% men, 11% part-time, 68% state residents, 8% transferred in, 3% international, 6% 25 or older, 1% Native American, 1% Hispanic, 12% black, 1% Asian or Pacific Islander. *Retention:* 80% of 1995 full-time freshmen returned. *Graduation:* 26% graduate in 4 years, 51% in 5 years, 57% in 6 years. *Areas of study chosen:* 22% business management and administrative services, 11% education, 9% communications and journalism, 9% engineering and applied sciences, 9% liberal arts/general studies, 6% social sciences, 5% interdisciplinary studies, 5% vocational and home economics, 3% biological and life sciences, 3% psychology, 2% English language/literature/letters, 2% premed, 1% area and ethnic studies, 1% computer and information sciences, 1% fine arts, 1% foreign language and literature, 1% health professions and related sciences, 1% mathematics, 1% natural resource sciences, 1% performing arts, 1% philosophy, 1% physical sciences, 1% predentistry, 1% prelaw, 1% theology/religion. *Most popular recent majors:* marketing/retailing/merchandising, elementary education, accounting.

First-Year Class: 2,120 total; 6,671 applied, 77% were accepted, 41% of whom enrolled. 21% from top 10% of their high school class, 61% from top quarter, 90% from top half. 40 National Merit Scholars.

Graduation Requirements: 128 semester hours; 1 year each of math and lab science; 1 year of a foreign language or proven competence; computer course for business, engineering, education, math, health care management, clothing, textile, interior design majors; internship (some majors); senior project (some majors).

Computers on Campus: 2,500 computers available on campus for general student use. Computer purchase/lease plans available. A computer is recommended for some students. A campus-wide network can be accessed from student residence rooms. Students can contact faculty members and/or advisers through e-mail. Computers for student use in computer center, computer labs, research center, learning resource center, classrooms, library, student center, dorms, departmental labs provide access to the Internet/World Wide Web, on- and off-campus e-mail addresses. Staffed computer lab on campus (open 24 hours a day) provides training in use of computers, software. *Academic computing expenditure 1995–96:* $2.1 million.

The University of Alabama (continued)

EXPENSES AND FINANCIAL AID

Expenses for 1997–98: *Application fee:* $25. State resident tuition: $2570 full-time. Nonresident tuition: $6746 full-time. Part-time tuition per semester ranges from $339 to $1194 for state residents, $519 to $3282 for nonresidents. College room and board: $3610. College room only: $2060.
Undergraduate Financial Aid: *Financial aid deadline (priority):* 3/1. *Financial aid forms:* institutional form required. FAFSA required for some.
LD Services Contact: Dr. Pat Friend NeSmith, Associate Director, Center for Teaching and Learning, The University of Alabama, PO Box 87304, Tuscaloosa, AL 35487-0304, 205-348-4285. Fax: 205-348-5291.

THE UNIVERSITY OF ALABAMA IN HUNTSVILLE

Huntsville, Alabama

LEARNING DISABILITIES SERVICES INFORMATION

Student Development Services currently serves 152 undergraduates with LD. Services are also available to graduate students. Students diagnosed with ADD/ADHD are eligible for the same services available to students with LD.
Staff: 4 full-time staff members, including director, coordinator. Services provided by tutors, counselors.
Special Fees: No special fees are charged for services to students with LD.
Applications and admissions: *Required:* high school transcript, grade point average, untimed SAT I or ACT. *Application deadline:* continuous.
Special policies: The college has written policies regarding grade forgiveness; substitutions and waivers of admissions, graduation, and degree requirements.

PROGRAM AND SERVICE COMPONENTS

Diagnostic testing: Personality.
Academic advising: Provided by academic advisers. Students with LD may take up to 13 semester hours each term; most take 6 to 9 semester hours; 8 semester hours required to maintain full-time status; 7 semester hours required to be eligible for financial aid.
Counseling services: Individual counseling, career counseling.
Basic skills remediation: Offered in class-size groups by regular teachers. Available in reading, math.
Subject-area tutoring: Offered one-on-one and in small groups by peer tutors. Available in most subjects.
Special courses: College survival skills, reading, math, study skills, career planning. Most offered for credit; most enter into overall grade point average.
Auxiliary aids: Taped textbooks, tape recorders, calculators, word-processors with spell-check.
Auxiliary services: Alternative test arrangements, notetakers, priority registration, advocacy.

GENERAL COLLEGE INFORMATION

State-supported, coed. Part of University of Alabama System. Awards bachelor's, master's, doctoral degrees. Founded 1950. *Setting:* 337-acre suburban campus. *Endowment:* $12 million. *Research spending 1995–96:* $31.8 million. *Total enrollment:* 4,982. *Faculty:* 421 (281 full-time, 93% with terminal degrees, 140 part-time); student–undergrad faculty ratio is 10:1.
Enrollment Profile: 3,881 students from 50 states and territories, 50 other countries. 51% women, 49% men, 37% part-time, 80% state residents, 10% live on campus, 7% transferred in, 3% international, 34% 25 or older, 2% Native American, 2% Hispanic, 14% black, 4% Asian or Pacific Islander. *Retention:* 71% of 1995 full-time freshmen returned. *Graduation:* 12% graduate in 4 years, 35% in 5 years, 46% in 6 years. *Areas of study chosen:* 32% engineering and applied sciences, 15% business management and administrative services, 15% health professions and related sciences, 8% biological and life sciences, 8% computer and information sciences, 3% education, 3% fine arts, 3% physical sciences, 3% psychology, 3% social sciences, 2% English language/literature/letters, 2% mathematics, 1% communications and journalism, 1% foreign language and literature, 1% philosophy. *Most popular recent majors:* nursing, electrical engineering, mechanical engineering.
First-Year Class: 442 total; 1,289 applied, 71% were accepted, 48% of whom enrolled. 27% from top 10% of their high school class, 63% from top quarter, 86% from top half. 4 National Merit Scholars, 3 valedictorians.
Graduation Requirements: 128 semester hours; 4 semester hours of math; 12 semester hours of science; computer course for engineering, business, math majors; senior project for honors program students and some majors.
Computers on Campus: 300 computers available on campus for general student use. A campus-wide network can be accessed from student residence rooms and from off-campus. Students can contact faculty members and/or advisers through e-mail. Computers for student use in computer center, computer labs, research center, learning resource center, library, student center, dorms provide access to the Internet/World Wide Web, on- and off-campus e-mail addresses. Staffed computer lab on campus (open 24 hours a day) provides training in use of computers, software. *Academic computing expenditure 1995–96:* $2.2 million.

EXPENSES AND FINANCIAL AID

Expenses for 1997–98: *Application fee:* $20. State resident tuition: $2948 full-time. Nonresident tuition: $6196 full-time. Part-time tuition per semester ranges from $131 to $1141 for state residents, $276 to $2386 for nonresidents. College room and board: $3650. College room only: $2650.
Undergraduate Financial Aid: *Financial aid deadline:* continuous. *Financial aid forms:* FAFSA, institutional form required.
LD Services Contact: Mr. Tom Caldwell, Counselor, The University of Alabama in Huntsville, University Center, Room 113, Huntsville, AL 35899, 205-890-6203. Fax: 205-890-6672.

UNIVERSITY OF ALASKA FAIRBANKS

Fairbanks, Alaska

LEARNING DISABILITIES SERVICES INFORMATION

Center for Health and Counseling, Disability Services began offering services in 1985. Currently the program serves 36 undergraduates with LD. Services are also available to graduate students. Students diagnosed with ADD/ADHD are eligible for the same services available to students with LD.
Staff: 1 full-time, 7 part-time staff members, including director, coordinator, student assistants. Services provided by tutors, readers, proctors.
Special Fees: No special fees are charged for services to students with LD.
Applications and admissions: *Required:* high school transcript, courses completed, untimed SAT I or ACT, professional verification of disability; *recommended:* extended time SAT I or ACT. Students may begin taking classes in fall, spring, or summer. *Application deadline:* 8/1 (fall term), 12/1 (spring term).

PROGRAM AND SERVICE COMPONENTS

Special preparation or orientation: Optional summer program offered prior to entering college. Optional orientation offered during registration.
Academic advising: Provided by unit staff members, academic advisers. Students with LD may take up to 18 credits (more with special permission) each term; most take 12 credits; 12 credits required to maintain full-time status; 6 credits (part-time), 12 credits (full-time) required to be eligible for financial aid.
Counseling services: Individual counseling, career counseling.
Basic skills remediation: Offered one-on-one and in class-size groups by regular teachers, Disability Services Coordinator, self-help labs. Available in reading, math, written language, study skills, time management.
Subject-area tutoring: Offered one-on-one by peer tutors. Available in most subjects.
Special courses: College survival skills, reading, vocabulary development, composition, word processing, time management, math, personal psychology, study skills. Most offered for credit; most enter into overall grade point average.
Auxiliary aids: Taped textbooks, typewriters, word-processors with spell-check, personal computers, talking computers, optical character readers.
Auxiliary services: Alternative test arrangements, notetakers, advocacy, readers.
Campus support group: A special student organization is available to students with LD.

GENERAL COLLEGE INFORMATION

State-supported, coed. Part of University of Alaska System. Awards associate, bachelor's, master's, doctoral degrees. Founded 1917. *Setting:* 2,250-acre small-town campus. *Research spending 1995–96:* $60.5 million. *Total enrollment:* 5,197. *Faculty:* 717 (524 full-time, 70% with terminal degrees, 193 part-time).
Enrollment Profile: 57% women, 43% men, 47% part-time, 85% state residents, 25% live on campus, 10% transferred in, 2% international, 57% 25 or older, 15% Native American, 2% Hispanic, 2% black, 2% Asian or Pacific Islander. *Retention:* 61% of 1995 full-time freshmen returned. *Areas of study chosen:* 16% business management and administrative services, 14% biological and life sciences, 14% education, 13% engineering and applied sciences, 9% social sciences, 5% natural resource sciences, 5% physical sciences, 4% communications and journalism, 4% English language/literature/letters, 4% psychology, 2% computer and information sciences, 2% fine arts, 2% mathematics, 2% performing arts, 1% area and ethnic studies, 1% foreign language and literature, 1% interdisciplinary studies, 1% liberal arts/general studies, 1% philosophy. *Most popular recent majors:* education, business administration/commerce/management, accounting.
First-Year Class: 739 total; 1,460 applied, 79% were accepted, 64% of whom enrolled. 5% from top 10% of their high school class, 13% from top quarter, 37% from top half. 8 National Merit Scholars.
Graduation Requirements: 60 credits for associate, 120 credits for bachelor's; 8 credits each of math and science; computer course for engineering, business, science, statistics majors; senior project for honors program students and some majors.
Computers on Campus: 500 computers available on campus for general student use. Computer purchase/lease plans available. A campuswide network can be accessed from student residence rooms and from off-campus. Students can contact faculty members and/or advisers through e-mail. Computers for student use in computer center, computer labs, research center, library, dorms, departmental labs. Staffed computer lab on campus provides training in use of computers, software. *Academic computing expenditure 1995–96:* $5.5 million.

EXPENSES AND FINANCIAL AID

Expenses for 1997–98: *Application fee:* $35. State resident tuition ranges from $2130 to $2370 full-time, $71 to $79 per credit part-time, according to class level. Nonresident tuition ranges from $6630 to $6870 full-time, $71 to $229 per credit part-time, according to course load and class level. Part-time mandatory fees per semester (8 to 11 credits): $105. Full-time mandatory fees: $340. College room and board: $3850 (minimum). College room only: $2110 (minimum).
Undergraduate Financial Aid: On average, 60% of need was met. *Financial aid deadline (priority):* 5/15. *Financial aid forms:* FAFSA required; CSS Financial Aid PROFILE acceptable.
LD Services Contact: Ms. Jan Ohmstede, Coordinator, Disability Services, University of Alaska Fairbanks, Box 755580, Fairbanks, AK 99775-5580, 907-474-7043. Fax: 907-474-5777. Email: fnjlo1@aurora.alaska.edu.

UNIVERSITY OF ARKANSAS

Fayetteville, Arkansas

LEARNING DISABILITIES SERVICES INFORMATION

Office for Campus Access currently serves 113 undergraduates with LD. Services are also available to graduate students. Students diagnosed with ADD/ADHD are eligible for the same services available to students with LD.
Staff: 4 full-time, 151 part-time staff members, including director, coordinator, administrative assistant. Services provided by counselors, diagnostic specialists, readers, scribes.
Special Fees: No special fees are charged for services to students with LD.
Applications and admissions: *Required:* high school transcript, courses completed, untimed ACT, psychoeducational report completed within 3 years; *recommended:* extended time ACT. Students may begin taking classes any term. *Application deadline:* continuous.
Special policies: The college has written policies regarding grade forgiveness; substitutions and waivers of admissions, graduation, and degree requirements.

PROGRAM AND SERVICE COMPONENTS

Special preparation or orientation: Required orientation held before registration.
Academic advising: Provided by unit staff members, academic advisers. Most students with LD take 12 semester hours each term; 12 semester hours required to maintain full-time status and be eligible for financial aid.
Counseling services: Individual counseling, career counseling.
Auxiliary services: Alternative test arrangements, notetakers, priority registration, advocacy, readers, scribes.
Campus support group: A special student organization is available to students with LD.

GENERAL COLLEGE INFORMATION

State-supported, coed. Part of University of Arkansas System. Awards associate, bachelor's, master's, doctoral, first professional degrees. Founded 1871. *Setting:* 420-acre small-town campus. *Endowment:* $85.4 million. *Research spending 1995–96:* $38 million. *Total enrollment:* 14,577. *Faculty:* 884 (808 full-time, 93% with terminal degrees, 76 part-time); student–undergrad faculty ratio is 14:1.
Enrollment Profile: 11,991 students from 49 states and territories, 70 other countries. 47% women, 53% men, 14% part-time, 87% state residents, 25% live on campus, 10% transferred in, 2% international, 15% 25 or older, 2% Native American, 1% Hispanic, 6% black, 2% Asian or Pacific Islander. *Areas of study chosen:* 13% business management and administrative services, 13% engineering and applied sciences, 11% education, 8% social sciences, 5% communications and journalism, 4% agriculture, 4% biological and life sciences, 4% psychology, 3% architecture, 3% computer and information sciences, 3% health professions and related sciences, 3% performing arts, 2% English language/literature/letters, 2% physical sciences, 2% vocational and home economics, 1% foreign language and literature, 1% mathematics. *Most popular recent majors:* elementary education, accounting, psychology.
First-Year Class: 2,313 total; 4,578 applied, 88% were accepted, 57% of whom enrolled. 24 National Merit Scholars.
Graduation Requirements: 62 credit hours for associate, 124 credit hours for bachelor's; computer course for business administration, math, geology, physics, engineering, education majors; internship (some majors); senior project for honors program students and some majors.
Computers on Campus: 300 computers available on campus for general student use. Computer purchase/lease plans available. A campuswide network can be accessed from student residence rooms and from off-campus. Students can contact faculty members and/or advisers through e-mail. Computers for student use in computer center, computer labs, classrooms, library, student center, dorms, business administration building, departmental labs provide access to the Internet/World Wide Web, on- and off-campus e-mail addresses. Staffed computer lab on campus (open 24 hours a day) provides training in use of computers, software. *Academic computing expenditure 1995–96:* $2 million.

EXPENSES AND FINANCIAL AID

Expenses for 1997–98: *Application fee:* $15. State resident tuition: $2470 full-time, $87.50 per credit hour part-time. Nonresident tuition: $6418 full-time, $228.50 per credit hour part-time. Part-time mandatory fees per semester range from $4.50 to $95.50. Mandatory fees for engineering program: $287. Full-time mandatory fees: $191. College room and board: $3736 (minimum).
Undergraduate Financial Aid: *Financial aid deadline (priority):* 4/1. *Financial aid forms:* FAFSA required.
LD Services Contact: Dr. Riqua Serebreni, Director, Office for Campus Access, University of Arkansas, 116 ARU, Fayetteville, AR 72701-1201, 501-575-3104. Fax: 501-575-7445.

UNIVERSITY OF BALTIMORE

Baltimore, Maryland

LEARNING DISABILITIES SERVICES INFORMATION

Disability Support Services began offering services in 1980. Currently the program serves 29 undergraduates with LD. Services are also available to graduate students. Students diagnosed with ADD/ADHD are eligible for the same services available to students with LD.
Staff: 1 part-time staff member (director). Services provided by tutors, notetakers, readers, interpreters.
Special Fees: No special fees are charged for services to students with LD.
Applications and admissions: *Required:* psychoeducational report completed within 3 years. Students may begin taking classes any term. *Application deadline:* continuous.

University of Baltimore (continued)

Special policies: The college has written policies regarding substitutions and waivers of admissions, graduation, and degree requirements.

PROGRAM AND SERVICE COMPONENTS

Academic advising: Provided by academic advisers. Students with LD may take up to 12 semester hours each term; most take 9 to 12 semester hours; 12 semester hours required to maintain full-time status; 6 semester hours required to be eligible for financial aid.
Counseling services: Individual counseling, career counseling.
Basic skills remediation: Offered in small groups by regular teachers. Available in math, written language.
Subject-area tutoring: Offered one-on-one, in small groups, and in class-size groups by professional teachers, peer tutors. Available in most subjects.
Special courses: Reading, time management, study skills, stress management, Student Success seminar. Some offered for credit; some enter into overall grade point average.
Auxiliary aids: Taped textbooks, tape recorders, calculators, typewriters, word-processors with spell-check, optical character readers.
Auxiliary services: Alternative test arrangements, notetakers, priority registration, advocacy.

GENERAL COLLEGE INFORMATION

State-supported, upper-level, coed. Part of University of Maryland System. Awards bachelor's, master's, first professional degrees. Founded 1925. *Setting:* 49-acre urban campus. *Endowment:* $10.4 million. *Research spending 1995–96:* $4.1 million. *Educational spending 1995–96:* $5727 per undergrad. *Total enrollment:* 4,361. *Faculty:* 273 (160 full-time, 93% with terminal degrees, 113 part-time); student–undergrad faculty ratio is 16:1.
Enrollment Profile: 1,830 students from 13 states and territories, 29 other countries. 54% women, 46% men, 58% part-time, 97% state residents, 100% transferred in, 2% international, 72% 25 or older, 3% Native American, 1% Hispanic, 26% black, 2% Asian or Pacific Islander. *Areas of study chosen:* 56% business management and administrative services, 14% social sciences, 10% interdisciplinary studies, 6% liberal arts/general studies, 5% communications and journalism, 4% English language/literature/letters, 4% psychology. *Most popular recent majors:* business administration/commerce/management, criminal justice, interdisciplinary studies.
First-Year Class: 408 total; 557 applied, 92% were accepted, 80% of whom enrolled.
Graduation Requirements: 120 semester hours; 3 semester hours each of algebra and lab science; computer course; internship (some majors).
Computers on Campus: 155 computers available on campus for general student use. A campus-wide network can be accessed. Students can contact faculty members and/or advisers through e-mail. Computers for student use in computer center, computer labs, research center, learning resource center, library, student center provide access to the Internet/World Wide Web. Staffed computer lab on campus provides training in use of computers, software. *Academic computing expenditure 1995–96:* $697,564.

EXPENSES AND FINANCIAL AID

Expenses for 1997–98: *Application fee:* $20. State resident tuition: $3274 full-time, $151 per semester hour part-time. Nonresident tuition: $8770 full-time, $328 per semester hour part-time. Part-time mandatory fees: $78 per semester. Full-time mandatory fees: $530.
Undergraduate Financial Aid: *Financial aid deadline (priority):* 4/1. *Financial aid forms:* FAFSA, institutional form required.
LD Services Contact: Ms. Jacquelyn Truelove-DeSimone, Director, Disability Support Services, University of Baltimore, 1420 North Charles Street, Baltimore, MD 21201-5779, 410-837-4775. Fax: 410-837-4820.

UNIVERSITY OF BRITISH COLUMBIA

Vancouver, British Columbia, Canada

LEARNING DISABILITIES SERVICES INFORMATION

Disability Resource Centre began offering services in 1988. Currently the program serves 103 undergraduates with LD. Services are also available to graduate students. Students diagnosed with ADD/ADHD are eligible for the same services available to students with LD, as well as distraction-free testing location.
Staff: 6 full time, 1 part time staff members, including director, associate director, coordinators, Coordinator of Student Assistants.
Special Fees: No special fees are charged for services to students with LD.
Applications and admissions: *Required:* high school transcript, psychoeducational report completed within 3 years; *recommended:* high school IEP (Individualized Education Program), letters of recommendation. *Application deadline:* 4/30.

PROGRAM AND SERVICE COMPONENTS

Academic advising: Provided by unit staff members. Most students with LD take 9 to 12 credits each term; 6 credits required to maintain full-time status and be eligible for financial aid.
Subject-area tutoring: Offered one-on-one by peer tutors. Available in most subjects.
Auxiliary aids: Taped textbooks, word-processors with spell-check, personal computers, talking computers, optical character readers.
Auxiliary services: Alternative test arrangements, notetakers, priority registration.

GENERAL COLLEGE INFORMATION

Province-supported, coed. Awards bachelor's, master's, doctoral degrees. Founded 1915. *Setting:* 1,000-acre urban campus. *Endowment:* $303.7 million. *Research spending 1995–96:* $134.6 million. *Total enrollment:* 32,181. *Faculty:* 1,847 full-time, 95% with terminal degrees.
Enrollment Profile: 26,053 students from 12 provinces and territories, 70 other countries. 56% women, 44% men, 36% part-time, 73% province residents, 23% live on campus, 35% transferred in, 3% international, 26% 25 or older. *Areas of study chosen:* 20% natural resource sciences, 12% education, 9% engineering and applied sciences, 4% agriculture, 2% performing arts, 1% architecture.
First-Year Class: 4,291 total; 17,800 applied, 45% were accepted, 53% of whom enrolled.
Graduation Requirements: 120 credits; computer course for math, statistics, engineering, geophysics, physical geography, atmospheric science, biochemistry majors; internship (some majors); senior project (some majors).
Computers on Campus: 600 computers available on campus for general student use. A campus-wide network can be accessed from student residence rooms. Computers for student use in library, academic buildings provide access to the Internet/World Wide Web. Staffed computer lab on campus.

EXPENSES AND FINANCIAL AID

Expenses for 1997–98: Canadian resident tuition: $2295 full-time, $76.50 per credit part-time. Nonresident tuition: $13,625 full-time, $454.17 per credit part-time. Part-time mandatory fees: $11.45 per credit. (All figures are in Canadian dollars.). Full-time mandatory fees: $210. College room and board: $4851 (minimum). College room only: $2562 (minimum).
Undergraduate Financial Aid: Of all full-time undergraduates enrolled in fall 1996, 90% of those who applied for aid were judged to have need according to Federal Methodology, of whom 100% were aided. On average, 94% of need was met. *Financial aid deadline:* Applications processed continuously. *Financial aid forms:* institutional form, Canada Student Loan form required. FAFSA, CSS Financial Aid PROFILE required for some.
LD Services Contact: Mr. Lawrie Williams, Liaison Officer, Disability Resource Centre, University of British Columbia, 1040-1874 East Mall, Vancouver, BC V6T 1Z1, Canada, 604-822-5844. Fax: 604-822-6655. Email: drc@unixg.abc.ca.

UNIVERSITY OF CALIFORNIA, BERKELEY

Berkeley, California

LEARNING DISABILITIES SERVICES INFORMATION

Disabled Students' Program began offering services in 1978. Currently the program serves 475 undergraduates with LD. Services are also available to graduate students. Students diagnosed with ADD/ADHD are eligible for the same services available to students with LD.
Staff: 2 full-time, 2 part-time staff members, including coordinator. Services provided by LD specialists.
Special Fees: No special fees are charged for services to students with LD.
Applications and admissions: *Required:* high school transcript, grade point average, courses completed, untimed or extended time ACT, untimed SAT I, autobiographical statement, psychoeducational report

completed within 3 years; *recommended:* extended time SAT I. Students may begin taking classes in fall or spring. *Application deadline:* 11/30.
Special policies: The college has written policies regarding grade forgiveness; substitutions and waivers of graduation requirements.

PROGRAM AND SERVICE COMPONENTS

Special preparation or orientation: Optional orientation offered during registration and individually by special arrangement.
Academic advising: Provided by unit staff members, academic advisers. Most students with LD take 13 to 15 credits each term; 12 credits required to maintain full-time status; 6.5 credits required to be eligible for financial aid.
Counseling services: Individual counseling, career counseling.
Subject-area tutoring: Offered one-on-one and in small groups by peer tutors, Student Learning Center staff. Available in most subjects.
Special courses: Understanding Learning Differences. All offered for credit; none enter into overall grade point average.
Auxiliary aids: Taped textbooks, tape recorders, word-processors with spell-check, personal computers, talking computers, optical character readers, Arkenstone Reader, Dragon Dictate, Inspiration software.
Auxiliary services: Alternative test arrangements, notetakers, priority registration, advocacy, proofreaders, typing service, readers.

GENERAL COLLEGE INFORMATION

State-supported, coed. Part of University of California System. Awards bachelor's, master's, doctoral, first professional degrees. Founded 1868. *Setting:* 1,232-acre urban campus with easy access to San Francisco. *Total enrollment:* 29,630. *Faculty:* 1,787 (95% of full-time faculty have terminal degrees); student–undergrad faculty ratio is 17:1.
Enrollment Profile: 21,189 students from 53 states and territories, 100 other countries. 48% women, 52% men, 0% part-time, 88% state residents, 25% live on campus, 7% transferred in, 4% international, 1% Native American, 13% Hispanic, 6% black, 40% Asian or Pacific Islander. *Retention:* 94% of 1995 full-time freshmen returned. *Most popular recent majors:* English, molecular biology, political science/government.
First-Year Class: 3,775 total; 25,111 applied, 36% were accepted, 42% of whom enrolled. 96% from top 10% of their high school class, 100% from top half.
Graduation Requirements: 120 credits; computer course for engineering, business majors.
Computers on Campus: Computer purchase/lease plans available. A campus-wide network can be accessed from student residence rooms and from off-campus. Students can contact faculty members and/or advisers through e-mail. Computers for student use in computer center, computer labs, learning resource center, classrooms, library, student center, dorms, student rooms, departmental labs provide access to the Internet/World Wide Web, on-campus e-mail addresses. Staffed computer lab on campus provides training in use of computers, software.

EXPENSES AND FINANCIAL AID

Expenses for 1997–98: *Application fee:* $40. State resident tuition: $0 full-time. Nonresident tuition: $8984 full-time. Full-time mandatory fees: $4355. College room and board: $7300.
Undergraduate Financial Aid: Of all full-time undergraduates enrolled in fall 1996, 82% of those who applied for aid were judged to have need according to Federal Methodology, of whom 100% were aided. On average, 100% of need was met. *Financial aid deadline (priority):* 3/2. *Financial aid forms:* FAFSA, state form required.
LD Services Contact: Ms. Constance Chiba, Disabilities Services Coordinator, University of California, Berkeley, 230 César Chavez Student Center, Berkeley, CA 94720-4250, 510-642-0518. Fax: 510-643-9686.

UNIVERSITY OF CALIFORNIA, LOS ANGELES

Los Angeles, California

LEARNING DISABILITIES SERVICES INFORMATION

Office for Students with Disabilities began offering services in 1960. Currently the program serves 206 undergraduates with LD. Services are also available to graduate students. Students diagnosed with ADD/ADHD are eligible for the same services available to students with LD.
Staff: 12 full-time staff members, including director, assistant director, coordinators. Services provided by tutors, counselors, notetakers, proctors, readers, transcribers, LD specialist.
Special Fees: No special fees are charged for services to students with LD.
Applications and admissions: *Required:* high school transcript, grade point average, courses completed, untimed SAT I or ACT; *recommended:* extended time SAT I or ACT. Students may begin taking classes any term. *Application deadline:* 11/30 (fall term), 10/31 (spring term).
Special policies: The college has written policies regarding substitutions and waivers of graduation and degree requirements.

PROGRAM AND SERVICE COMPONENTS

Special preparation or orientation: Optional orientation offered in the fall, prior to the onset of classes.
Academic advising: Provided by unit staff members, academic advisers. Students with LD may take up to 18 quarter credits each term; most take 8 to 12 quarter credits; 10 quarter credits (fewer with approval for reduced fee program) required to maintain full-time status; 10 quarter credits (fewer with approval from financial aid office) required to be eligible for financial aid.
Counseling services: Individual counseling, small-group counseling, career counseling, self-advocacy training, peer-mentor program.
Basic skills remediation: Offered one-on-one and in small groups by LD specialist, peer tutors. Available in reading, written language, learning strategies, study skills, time management.
Subject-area tutoring: Offered one-on-one and in small groups by peer tutors, graduate students. Available in most subjects.
Special courses: College survival skills, reading, learning strategies, word processing, time management, study skills, career planning. None offered for credit.
Auxiliary aids: Taped textbooks, tape recorders, typewriters, word-processors with spell-check, personal computers, optical character readers, voice recognition computer programs (Dragon Dictate), voice synthesis computer programs (Bookwise, Soundproof).
Auxiliary services: Alternative test arrangements, notetakers, priority registration, advocacy, readers, scribes, research assistants.
Campus support group: A special student organization is available to students with LD.

GENERAL COLLEGE INFORMATION

State-supported, coed. Part of University of California System. Awards bachelor's, master's, doctoral, first professional degrees. Founded 1919. *Setting:* 419-acre urban campus. *Endowment:* $685.4 million. *Research spending 1995–96:* $268.9 million. *Total enrollment:* 34,935. *Faculty:* 3,228 (100% of full-time faculty have terminal degrees); student–undergrad faculty ratio is 17:1.
Enrollment Profile: 23,914 students from 50 states and territories, 100 other countries. 52% women, 48% men, 0% part-time, 95% state residents, 9% transferred in, 3% international, 9% 25 or older, 1% Native American, 18% Hispanic, 6% black, 40% Asian or Pacific Islander. *Retention:* 94% of 1995 full-time freshmen returned. *Areas of study chosen:* 27% social sciences, 16% biological and life sciences, 16% interdisciplinary studies, 9% engineering and applied sciences, 9% psychology, 7% English language/literature/letters, 6% physical sciences, 3% fine arts, 3% mathematics, 2% foreign language and literature, 2% performing arts, 1% health professions and related sciences. *Most popular recent majors:* biology/biological sciences, psychology, economics.
First-Year Class: 3,821 total; 28,075 applied, 39% were accepted, 35% of whom enrolled. 73 National Merit Scholars.
Graduation Requirements: 180 quarter credits; computer course (varies by major).
Computers on Campus: Computer purchase/lease plans available. A campus-wide network can be accessed from student residence rooms and from off-campus. Students can contact faculty members and/or advisers through e-mail. Computers for student use in computer center, library, student center, dorms. Staffed computer lab on campus. *Academic computing expenditure 1995–96:* $14.9 million.

EXPENSES AND FINANCIAL AID

Expenses for 1997–98: *Application fee:* $40. State resident tuition: $0 full-time. Nonresident tuition: $8984 full-time. Full-time mandatory fees: $4050. College room and board: $6175.
Undergraduate Financial Aid: 65% of all full-time undergraduates enrolled in fall 1996 applied for aid; of these, 82% were judged to have need according to Federal Methodology, of whom 100% were aided. On average, 100% of need was met. *Financial aid deadline:* Applications processed continuously. *Financial aid forms:* FAFSA, institutional form required. CSS Financial Aid PROFILE, state form required for some.
LD Services Contact: Dr. Arline Halper, Learning Disability Specialist, University of California, Los Angeles, A-255 Murphy Hall, 405 Hilgard Avenue, Los Angeles, CA 90024-1426, 310-825-1501. Fax: 310-825-9656.

UNIVERSITY OF CALIFORNIA, RIVERSIDE

Riverside, California

LEARNING DISABILITIES SERVICES INFORMATION

Disabled Student Services began offering services in 1977. Currently the program serves 30 undergraduates with LD. Services are also available to graduate students. Students diagnosed with ADD/ADHD are eligible for the same services available to students with LD.

Staff: 4 full-time, 1 part-time staff members, including director, Assistant to the Director. Services provided by counselor, support services assistant.

Special Fees: No special fees are charged for services to students with LD.

Applications and admissions: *Required:* high school transcript, grade point average, courses completed, untimed SAT I, autobiographical statement, psychoeducational report completed within 3 years; *recommended:* extended time SAT I, letters of recommendation. Students may begin taking classes any term. *Application deadline:* 11/30 (fall term), 10/31 (spring term).

Special policies: The college has written policies regarding grade forgiveness.

PROGRAM AND SERVICE COMPONENTS

Academic advising: Provided by academic advisers. Students with LD may take up to 20 quarter hours each term; most take 12 quarter hours; 12 quarter hours required to maintain full-time status.

Counseling services: Individual counseling, small-group counseling, career counseling.

Subject-area tutoring: Offered one-on-one, in small groups, and in class-size groups by peer tutors. Available in some subjects.

Auxiliary aids: Taped textbooks, tape recorders, calculators, typewriters, word-processors with spell-check, personal computers, talking computers, optical character readers.

Auxiliary services: Alternative test arrangements, notetakers, priority registration, advocacy.

GENERAL COLLEGE INFORMATION

State-supported, coed. Part of University of California System. Awards bachelor's, master's, doctoral degrees. Founded 1954. *Setting:* 1,200-acre suburban campus with easy access to Los Angeles. *Endowment:* $19.9 million. *Research spending 1995–96:* $56.5 million. *Educational spending 1995–96:* $7728 per undergrad. *Total enrollment:* 9,063. *Faculty:* 430 (all full-time, 98% with terminal degrees); student–undergrad faculty ratio is 18:1.

Enrollment Profile: 7,665 students from 17 states and territories, 12 other countries. 52% women, 48% men, 2% part-time, 98% state residents, 10% transferred in, 1% international, 9% 25 or older, 1% Native American, 18% Hispanic, 5% black, 39% Asian or Pacific Islander. *Retention:* 85% of 1995 full-time freshmen returned. *Graduation:* 47% graduate in 4 years, 64% in 5 years, 67% in 6 years. *Areas of study chosen:* 22% biological and life sciences, 16% business management and administrative services, 15% social sciences, 10% psychology, 7% premed, 6% liberal arts/general studies, 4% engineering and applied sciences, 4% English language/literature/letters, 3% computer and information sciences, 3% physical sciences, 2% foreign language and literature, 2% mathematics, 2% natural resource sciences, 1% area and ethnic studies, 1% fine arts, 1% performing arts, 1% philosophy. *Most popular recent majors:* business administration/commerce/management, biology/biological sciences, psychology.

First-Year Class: 1,485 total; 10,199 applied, 78% were accepted, 19% of whom enrolled. 70% from top 10% of their high school class, 100% from top quarter.

Graduation Requirements: 180 quarter hours; 1 statistics or math course; 4 science courses; computer course for statistics, math, business administration, political science, environmental science, engineering majors; internship (some majors); senior project for honors program students and some majors.

Computers on Campus: 400 computers available on campus for general student use. Computer purchase/lease plans available. A campuswide network can be accessed from student residence rooms and from off-campus. Students can contact faculty members and/or advisers through e-mail. Computers for student use in computer center, computer labs, library, student center, dorms, various locations provide access to the Internet/World Wide Web, off-campus e-mail addresses. Staffed computer lab on campus provides training in use of computers, software. *Academic computing expenditure 1995–96:* $1.5 million.

EXPENSES AND FINANCIAL AID

Expenses for 1997–98: *Application fee:* $40. State resident tuition: $0 full-time. Nonresident tuition: $8984 full-time. Full-time mandatory fees: $4126. College room and board: $6000.

Undergraduate Financial Aid: 76% of all full-time undergraduates enrolled in fall 1996 applied for aid; of these, 87% were judged to have need according to Federal Methodology, of whom 96% were aided. On average, 86% of need was met. *Financial aid deadline (priority):* 3/2. *Financial aid forms:* FAFSA required. Institutional form, financial aid transcript (for transfers) required for some.

LD Services Contact: Ms. Marcia Theise Schiffer, Director, Disabled Student Services, University of California, Riverside, 125 Commons, Riverside, CA 92521, 909-787-4538. Fax: 909-787-4218.

UNIVERSITY OF CALIFORNIA, SAN DIEGO

La Jolla, California

LEARNING DISABILITIES SERVICES INFORMATION

Office for Students with Disabilities (OSD) began offering services in 1978. Currently the program serves 200 undergraduates with LD. Services are also available to graduate students. Students diagnosed with ADD/ADHD are eligible for the same services available to students with LD, as well as separate testing location.

Staff: 4 full-time, 6 part-time staff members, including director, program representatives. Services provided by remediation specialists, tutors, counselors, diagnostic specialists.

Special Fees: No special fees are charged for services to students with LD.

Applications and admissions: *Required:* high school transcript, grade point average, untimed SAT I, autobiographical statement; *recommended:* high school extracurricular activities, extended time SAT I. Students may begin taking classes in fall only. *Application deadline:* 11/30.

Special policies: The college has written policies regarding grade forgiveness; substitutions and waivers of admissions, graduation, and degree requirements.

PROGRAM AND SERVICE COMPONENTS

Special preparation or orientation: Required orientation held during regular fall orientation.

Academic advising: Provided by unit staff members, academic advisers. Students with LD may take up to 12 quarter hours each term; most take 8 to 12 quarter hours; 12 quarter hours required to maintain full-time status; minimum of 8 quarter hours required to be eligible for financial aid.

Counseling services: Individual counseling, small-group counseling, career counseling, self-advocacy training, disability management, ten-week peer-mentor support group.

Basic skills remediation: Offered one-on-one and in small groups by OSD staff, campus tutorial center staff, peer mentors. Available in reading, math, written language, learning strategies, study skills, time management, social skills, stress management.

Subject-area tutoring: Offered one-on-one and in small groups by peer tutors. Available in some subjects.

Auxiliary aids: Taped textbooks, tape recorders, calculators, word-processors with spell-check, personal computers, talking computers, optical character readers, Chroma print enlarger, Dragon Dictate.

Auxiliary services: Alternative test arrangements, notetakers, priority registration, advocacy, readers, writers.

Campus support group: A special student organization is available to students with LD.

GENERAL COLLEGE INFORMATION

State-supported, coed. Part of University of California System. Awards bachelor's, master's, doctoral degrees. Founded 1959. *Setting:* 1,976-acre suburban campus with easy access to San Diego. *Endowment:* $1.1 billion. *Research spending 1995–96:* $238.5 million. *Total enrollment:* 18,119. *Faculty:* 1,436 (1,280 full-time, 95% with terminal degrees, 156 part-time); student–undergrad faculty ratio is 10:1.

Enrollment Profile: 14,623 students: 50% women, 50% men, 1% part-time, 98% state residents, 29% live on campus, 26% transferred in, 1% international, 9% 25 or older, 1% Native American, 11% Hispanic, 2% black, 27% Asian or Pacific Islander. *Retention:* 74% of 1995 full-time freshmen returned. *Areas of study chosen:* 32% social sciences, 27%

biological and life sciences, 13% engineering and applied sciences, 7% psychology, 5% computer and information sciences, 4% communications and journalism, 3% English language/literature/letters, 3% performing arts, 2% fine arts, 1% mathematics. *Most popular recent majors:* biology/biological sciences, psychology, political science/government.
First-Year Class: 2,725 total; 23,685 applied, 50% were accepted, 23% of whom enrolled. 95% from top 10% of their high school class, 100% from top quarter.
Graduation Requirements: 45 courses; computer course for applied mechanics, engineering sciences, quantitative sciences, electrical engineering, psychology, economics majors; senior project for honors program students and some majors.
Computers on Campus: 1,020 computers available on campus for general student use. Computer purchase/lease plans available. A computer is recommended for all students. A campus-wide network can be accessed from student residence rooms and from off-campus. Students can contact faculty members and/or advisers through e-mail. Computers for student use in computer center, computer labs, library, student center, each academic college provide access to the Internet/World Wide Web, on- and off-campus e-mail addresses. Staffed computer lab on campus (open 24 hours a day) provides training in use of computers, software.

EXPENSES AND FINANCIAL AID

Expenses for 1997–98: *Application fee:* $40. State resident tuition: $0 full-time. Nonresident tuition: $8985 full-time, $1498 per quarter part-time. Part-time mandatory fees: $885.50 per quarter. Full-time mandatory fees: $4200. College room and board: $6682.
Undergraduate Financial Aid: Of all full-time undergraduates enrolled in fall 1996, 86% of those who applied for aid were judged to have need according to Federal Methodology, of whom 98% were aided. On average, 100% of need was met. *Financial aid deadline (priority):* 3/2. *Financial aid forms:* FAFSA, state form required.
Financial aid specifically for students with LD: Scholarship: Jane Bosworth Annual Scholarship.
LD Services Contact: Mr. Moshe Witztum, Outreach Assistant, University of California, San Diego, 9500 Gilman Drive, La Jolla, CA 92093-0019, 619-534-4382. Fax: 619-534-4650. Email: mwitztum@ucsd.edu.

UNIVERSITY OF CALIFORNIA, SANTA BARBARA

Santa Barbara, California

LEARNING DISABILITIES SERVICES INFORMATION

Disabled Students Program began offering services in 1990. Currently the program serves 200 undergraduates with LD. Services are also available to graduate students. Students diagnosed with ADD/ADHD are eligible for the same services available to students with LD.
Staff: 5 full-time, 1 part-time staff members, including director, LD specialist, administrative assistant, transportation and equipment supervisor. Services provided by readers, notetakers, scribes, proctors.
Special Fees: No special fees are charged for services to students with LD.
Applications and admissions: *Required:* high school transcript, grade point average, courses completed, untimed SAT I, autobiographical statement; *recommended:* high school extracurricular activities, extended time SAT I, letters of recommendation, psychoeducational report completed within 3 years. Students may begin taking classes any term. *Application deadline:* 11/30.
Special policies: The college has written policies regarding substitutions and waivers of admissions and graduation requirements.

PROGRAM AND SERVICE COMPONENTS

Special preparation or orientation: Required orientation held during registration.
Academic advising: Provided by academic advisers. Students with LD may take up to 16 units each term; most take 12 units; 12 units required to maintain full-time status; source of aid determines number of units required to be eligible for financial aid.
Counseling services: Individual counseling, small-group counseling, career counseling.
Auxiliary aids: Tape recorders, calculators, optical character readers, spell checkers.
Auxiliary services: Alternative test arrangements, notetakers, priority registration, advocacy, readers.

GENERAL COLLEGE INFORMATION

State-supported, coed. Part of University of California System. Awards bachelor's, master's, doctoral degrees. Founded 1909. *Setting:* 989-acre suburban campus. *Research spending 1995–96:* $70.3 million. *Total enrollment:* 18,531. *Faculty:* 849 (684 full-time, 99% with terminal degrees, 165 part-time); student–undergrad faculty ratio is 19:1.
Enrollment Profile: 16,281 students from 49 states and territories, 50 other countries. 53% women, 47% men, 4% part-time, 95% state residents, 16% live on campus, 25% transferred in, 2% international, 6% 25 or older, 1% Native American, 13% Hispanic, 3% black, 17% Asian or Pacific Islander. *Retention:* 86% of 1995 full-time freshmen returned. *Graduation:* 44% graduate in 4 years, 65% in 5 years, 69% in 6 years. *Areas of study chosen:* 14% biological and life sciences, 13% social sciences, 11% business management and administrative services, 11% English language/literature/letters, 7% interdisciplinary studies, 7% psychology, 6% fine arts, 5% engineering and applied sciences, 2% foreign language and literature, 2% physical sciences, 1% area and ethnic studies, 1% mathematics. *Most popular recent majors:* business economics, biology/biological sciences, psychology.
First-Year Class: 3,464 total; 19,232 applied, 78% were accepted, 23% of whom enrolled. 100% from top quarter of their high school class.
Graduation Requirements: 180 quarter units; computer course for engineering, math, statistical science, geophysics majors; senior project (some majors).
Computers on Campus: 3,000 computers available on campus for general student use. Computer purchase/lease plans available. A campus-wide network can be accessed from off-campus. Students can contact faculty members and/or advisers through e-mail. Computers for student use in computer center, computer labs, library, student center, dorms, departmental labs provide access to the Internet/World Wide Web, on- and off-campus e-mail addresses. Staffed computer lab on campus provides training in use of computers, software.

EXPENSES AND FINANCIAL AID

Expenses for 1997–98: *Application fee:* $40. State resident tuition: $0 full-time. Nonresident tuition: $8985 full-time. Full-time mandatory fees: $4105. College room and board: $6560.
Undergraduate Financial Aid: *Financial aid deadline (priority):* 3/2. *Financial aid forms:* FAFSA required. State form, institutional form required for some.
LD Services Contact: Ms. Claudia Nicastro-Batty, Learning Disability Specialist, University of California, Santa Barbara, Santa Barbara, CA 93106, 805-893-8897. Fax: 805-893-7127. Email: batty-c@sa.ucsb.edu.

UNIVERSITY OF CINCINNATI

Cincinnati, Ohio

LEARNING DISABILITIES SERVICES INFORMATION

Disability Services began offering services in 1980. Currently the program serves 259 undergraduates with LD. Services are also available to graduate students. Students diagnosed with ADD/ADHD are eligible for the same services available to students with LD, as well as isolated testing.
Staff: Includes coordinator, student assistants. Services provided by tutors, counselors, readers, scribes, test proctors, transcribers, notetakers.
Special Fees: No special fees are charged for services to students with LD.
Applications and admissions: *Required:* high school transcript, grade point average, courses completed, untimed SAT I or ACT, high school diploma or GED (for Associate's degree); *recommended:* high school class rank, extracurricular activities, IEP (Individualized Education Program), extended time SAT I or ACT, personal interview, autobiographical statement, letters of recommendation, psychoeducational report completed within 3 years. Students may begin taking classes any term. *Application deadline:* continuous.

PROGRAM AND SERVICE COMPONENTS

Special preparation or orientation: Required orientation held before classes begin.
Academic advising: Provided by unit staff members, academic advisers. Students with LD may take up to 19 credit hours each term; most take 12 credit hours; 12 credit hours required to maintain full-time status and be eligible for financial aid.
Counseling services: Individual counseling, small-group counseling, career counseling.

University of Cincinnati (continued)

Basic skills remediation: Offered in small groups and in class-size groups by regular teachers. Available in reading, math, written language, study skills.
Subject-area tutoring: Offered one-on-one and in small groups by peer tutors. Available in all subjects.
Auxiliary aids: Taped textbooks, tape recorders, calculators, typewriters, word-processors with spell-check, personal computers, Reading Edge, voice synthesizer.
Auxiliary services: Alternative test arrangements, notetakers, priority registration, advocacy, readers, scribes, transcribers.

GENERAL COLLEGE INFORMATION

State-supported, coed. Part of University of Cincinnati System. Awards associate, bachelor's, master's, doctoral, first professional degrees. Founded 1819. *Setting:* 137-acre urban campus. *Endowment:* $496.6 million. *Research spending 1995–96:* $62.1 million. *Total enrollment:* 19,139. *Faculty:* 953 (all full-time, 86% with terminal degrees); student–undergrad faculty ratio is 19:1.
Enrollment Profile: 13,730 students from 46 states and territories, 50 other countries. 48% women, 52% men, 17% part-time, 93% state residents, 18% live on campus, 5% transferred in, 1% international, 16% 25 or older, 0% Native American, 1% Hispanic, 9% black, 4% Asian or Pacific Islander. *Retention:* 75% of 1995 full-time freshmen returned. *Graduation:* 40% graduate in 5 years, 48% in 6 years. *Areas of study chosen:* 23% business management and administrative services, 15% social sciences, 14% engineering and applied sciences, 8% health professions and related sciences, 7% performing arts, 6% education, 6% liberal arts/general studies, 4% biological and life sciences, 4% communications and journalism, 3% architecture, 2% computer and information sciences, 2% English language/literature/letters, 2% interdisciplinary studies, 2% vocational and home economics, 1% foreign language and literature, 1% mathematics. *Most popular recent majors:* business administration/commerce/management, engineering and applied sciences, education.
First-Year Class: 2,444 total; 6,270 applied, 85% were accepted, 46% of whom enrolled. 28% from top 10% of their high school class, 51% from top quarter, 85% from top half.
Graduation Requirements: 90 credit hours for associate, 185 credit hours for bachelor's; computer course for business, engineering majors.
Computers on Campus: 325 computers available on campus for general student use. A computer is recommended for some students. A campus-wide network can be accessed from off-campus. Students can contact faculty members and/or advisers through e-mail. Computers for student use in computer labs, library, University College Medical Sciences Building provide access to the Internet/World Wide Web. Staffed computer lab on campus (open 24 hours a day) provides training in use of computers, software.

EXPENSES AND FINANCIAL AID

Expenses for 1997–98: *Application fee:* $30. State resident tuition: $3879 full-time, $121 per credit hour part-time. Nonresident tuition: $10,986 full-time, $305 per credit hour part-time. Full-time mandatory fees: $480. College room and board: $5253.
Undergraduate Financial Aid: 60% of all full-time undergraduates enrolled in fall 1996 applied for aid; of these, 84% were judged to have need according to Federal Methodology, of whom 96% were aided. On average, 61% of need was met. *Financial aid deadline:* continuous. *Financial aid forms:* FAFSA required.
LD Services Contact: Mr. Stanley Henderson, Vice President, Enrollment Management, University of Cincinnati, 350 Tangeman University Center, Cincinnati, OH 45221-0090, 513-556-3379.

UNIVERSITY OF EVANSVILLE

Evansville, Indiana

LEARNING DISABILITIES SERVICES INFORMATION

Counseling and Testing currently serves 30 undergraduates with LD. Services are also available to graduate students. Students diagnosed with ADD/ADHD are eligible for the same services available to students with LD.
Staff: 2 full-time, 1 part-time staff members, including director, counselor. Services provided by tutors, counselors.
Special Fees: No special fees are charged for services to students with LD.
Applications and admissions: *Required:* high school transcript, grade point average, class rank, untimed SAT I or ACT, documentation of disability; *recommended:* high school courses completed, personal interview, letters of recommendation, psychoeducational report. Students may begin taking classes in fall only. *Application deadline:* continuous.

PROGRAM AND SERVICE COMPONENTS

Diagnostic testing: Intelligence, reading, math, written language, personality, learning strategies.
Academic advising: Provided by academic advisers. Students with LD may take up to 18 semester hours each term; most take 12 to 15 semester hours; 12 semester hours required to maintain full-time status; 24 semester hours (each 12 months) required to be eligible for financial aid.
Counseling services: Individual counseling, career counseling.
Subject-area tutoring: Offered one-on-one and in small groups by peer tutors. Available in most subjects.
Auxiliary aids: Taped textbooks, tape recorders, word-processors with spell-check, personal computers.
Auxiliary services: Alternative test arrangements, advocacy, readers.

GENERAL COLLEGE INFORMATION

Independent, comprehensive, coed, affiliated with United Methodist Church. Awards associate, bachelor's, master's degrees. Founded 1854. *Setting:* 75-acre suburban campus. *Endowment:* $27.7 million. *Research spending 1995–96:* $68,142. *Educational spending 1995–96:* $4275 per undergrad. *Total enrollment:* 3,185. *Faculty:* 183 (176 full-time, 83% with terminal degrees, 7 part-time); student–undergrad faculty ratio is 13:1.
Enrollment Profile: 3,091 students from 48 states and territories, 52 other countries. 53% women, 47% men, 9% part-time, 55% state residents, 68% live on campus, 3% transferred in, 5% international, 2% 25 or older, 0% Native American, 1% Hispanic, 3% black, 1% Asian or Pacific Islander. *Areas of study chosen:* 16% biological and life sciences, 13% social sciences, 12% interdisciplinary studies, 11% business management and administrative services, 9% engineering and applied sciences, 9% health professions and related sciences, 8% education, 8% natural resource sciences, 7% liberal arts/general studies, 5% physical sciences, 2% computer and information sciences. *Most popular recent majors:* accounting, electrical engineering, elementary education.
First-Year Class: 675 total; 2,214 applied, 91% were accepted, 34% of whom enrolled. 35% from top 10% of their high school class, 80% from top quarter, 89% from top half. 4 National Merit Scholars, 39 valedictorians.
Graduation Requirements: 60 semester hours for associate, 124 semester hours for bachelor's; 3 semester hours of math; 7 semester hours of natural science; 1 year of a foreign language; computer course for business, engineering majors; senior project for honors program students and some majors.
Computers on Campus: 300 computers available on campus for general student use. Computer purchase/lease plans available. Computers for student use in computer labs, classrooms, library provide access to the Internet/World Wide Web. Staffed computer lab on campus provides training in use of computers, software. *Academic computing expenditure 1995–96:* $507,993.

EXPENSES AND FINANCIAL AID

Expenses for 1997–98: *Application fee:* $30. Comprehensive fee of $18,400 includes full-time tuition ($13,600), mandatory fees ($280), and college room and board ($4520). College room only: $2060. Part-time tuition: $395 per semester hour. Part-time mandatory fees: $15 per semester.
Undergraduate Financial Aid: 80% of all full-time undergraduates enrolled in fall 1996 applied for aid; of these, 79% were judged to have need according to Federal Methodology, of whom 100% were aided. On average, 82% of need was met. *Financial aid deadline (priority):* 3/1. *Financial aid forms:* FAFSA, institutional form required; CSS Financial Aid PROFILE acceptable. State form required for some.
LD Services Contact: Dr. Francis Segedin, Director of Counseling and Testing, University of Evansville, 1800 Lincoln Avenue, Evansville, IN 47722-0002, 812-479-2720. Fax: 812-479-2156.

THE UNIVERSITY OF FINDLAY

Findlay, Ohio

LEARNING DISABILITIES SERVICES INFORMATION

Office of Disability Services (ODS) began offering services in 1980. Currently the program serves 37 undergraduates with LD. Services are

also available to graduate students. Students diagnosed with ADD/ADHD are eligible for the same services available to students with LD.
Staff: 1 full-time, 2 part-time staff members, including director, disability specialist. Services provided by remediation specialist, counselors.
Special Fees: No special fees are charged for services to students with LD.
Applications and admissions: *Required:* high school transcript, grade point average, class rank, courses completed, untimed ACT, psychoeducational report completed within 3 years; *recommended:* high school extracurricular activities, IEP (Individualized Education Program), untimed or extended time SAT I, extended time ACT, personal interview, autobiographical statement, letters of recommendation. Students may begin taking classes in fall only. *Application deadline:* continuous.
Special policies: The college has written policies regarding grade forgiveness.

PROGRAM AND SERVICE COMPONENTS

Academic advising: Provided by unit staff members, academic advisers. Students with LD may take up to 16 semester hours each term; most take 12 to 15 semester hours; 12 semester hours required to maintain full-time status and be eligible for financial aid.
Counseling services: Individual counseling, career counseling.
Basic skills remediation: Offered in class-size groups by regular teachers. Available in reading, math, spelling, learning strategies, study skills.
Subject-area tutoring: Offered one-on-one and in small groups by professional teachers, peer tutors. Available in most subjects.
Special courses: College survival skills, reading, vocabulary development, composition, learning strategies, time management, math, study skills, career planning, stress management. Some offered for credit; all enter into overall grade point average.
Auxiliary aids: Taped textbooks, tape recorders, typewriters, word-processors with spell-check, personal computers.
Auxiliary services: Alternative test arrangements, notetakers, priority registration, advocacy.

GENERAL COLLEGE INFORMATION

Independent, comprehensive, coed, affiliated with Church of God. Awards associate, bachelor's, master's degrees. Founded 1882. *Setting:* small-town campus with easy access to Toledo. *Endowment:* $10.6 million. *Educational spending 1995–96:* $4253 per undergrad. *Total enrollment:* 3,743. *Faculty:* 267 (117 full-time, 47% with terminal degrees, 150 part-time); student–undergrad faculty ratio is 19:1.
Enrollment Profile: 3,160 students from 35 states and territories, 20 other countries. 53% women, 47% men, 22% part-time, 79% state residents, 38% live on campus, 5% transferred in, 7% international, 31% 25 or older, 1% Native American, 4% Hispanic, 9% black, 3% Asian or Pacific Islander. *Retention:* 89% of 1995 full-time freshmen returned. *Areas of study chosen:* 25% business management and administrative services, 15% education, 12% physical sciences, 10% communications and journalism, 10% prevet, 8% social sciences, 1% computer and information sciences, 1% fine arts, 1% foreign language and literature, 1% mathematics, 1% performing arts, 1% premed. *Most popular recent majors:* business administration/commerce/management, (pre)veterinary medicine sequence, environmental sciences.
First-Year Class: 583 total; 2,216 applied, 78% were accepted, 34% of whom enrolled. 8% from top 10% of their high school class, 30% from top quarter, 80% from top half.
Graduation Requirements: 62 semester hours for associate, 124 semester hours for bachelor's; 3 semester hours of math/science; 1 course in foreign language or equivalent; computer course; senior project for honors program students.
Computers on Campus: 250 computers available on campus for general student use. Computer purchase/lease plans available. A computer is recommended for all students. A campus-wide network can be accessed from student residence rooms and from off-campus. Students can contact faculty members and/or advisers through e-mail. Computers for student use in computer center, computer labs, library provide access to the Internet/World Wide Web. Staffed computer lab on campus provides training in use of computers, software. *Academic computing expenditure 1995–96:* $123,942.

EXPENSES AND FINANCIAL AID

Expenses for 1996–97: Comprehensive fee of $18,322 includes full-time tuition ($13,000), mandatory fees ($112), and college room and board ($5210). College room only: $2550. Part-time tuition: $290 per semester hour. Part-time mandatory fees: $30 per semester.
Undergraduate Financial Aid: Of all full-time undergraduates enrolled in fall 1996, 100% of those judged to have need according to Federal Methodology were aided. On average, 90% of need was met. *Financial aid deadline (priority):* 6/1. *Financial aid forms:* FAFSA required; CSS Financial Aid PROFILE acceptable. State form required for some.
LD Services Contact: Mrs. Susan Rood, Director, Disability Services, The University of Findlay, 1000 North Main Street, Findlay, OH 45840-3653, 419-424-5532. Fax: 419-424-4822. Email: rood@lucy.findlay.edu.

UNIVERSITY OF FLORIDA

Gainesville, Florida

LEARNING DISABILITIES SERVICES INFORMATION

Office for Students with Disabilities began offering services in 1987. Currently the program serves 367 undergraduates with LD. Services are also available to graduate students. Students diagnosed with ADD/ADHD are eligible for the same services available to students with LD, as well as success/support group.
Staff: 5 full-time, 4 part-time staff members, including director, coordinators.
Special Fees: $500 to $1400 for diagnostic testing.
Applications and admissions: *Required:* high school transcript, grade point average, untimed SAT I, psychoeducational report completed within 4 years, recent professional documentation of learning disability; *recommended:* high school courses completed, untimed or extended time ACT, extended time SAT I. Students may begin taking classes in fall or summer. *Application deadline:* continuous.
Special policies: The college has written policies regarding substitutions and waivers of admissions, graduation, and degree requirements.

PROGRAM AND SERVICE COMPONENTS

Special preparation or orientation: Optional summer program offered prior to entering college.
Diagnostic testing: Intelligence, reading, math, spelling, written language, perceptual skills, personality, speech, hearing.
Academic advising: Provided by academic advisers. Students with LD may take up to as many semester hours as an individual can handle each term; most take 6 to 14 semester hours; 6 semester hours required to maintain full-time status; 12 semester hours required to be eligible for financial aid.
Counseling services: Individual counseling, small-group counseling, career counseling.
Subject-area tutoring: Offered one-on-one and in small groups by peer tutors. Available in all subjects.
Special courses: College survival skills, reading, word processing, time management, study skills, career planning. Some offered for credit; some enter into overall grade point average.
Auxiliary aids: Taped textbooks, tape recorders, calculators, typewriters, word-processors with spell-check, personal computers, talking computers, optical character readers, computer with voice recognition.
Auxiliary services: Alternative test arrangements, notetakers, priority registration, advocacy.
Campus support group: A special student organization is available to students with LD.

GENERAL COLLEGE INFORMATION

State-supported, coed. Part of State University System of Florida. Awards bachelor's, master's, doctoral, first professional degrees. Founded 1853. *Setting:* 2,000-acre suburban campus with easy access to Jacksonville. *Endowment:* $334.8 million. *Research spending 1995–96:* $244.8 million. *Total enrollment:* 39,932. *Faculty:* 2,225 (all full-time, 97% with terminal degrees); student–undergrad faculty ratio is 17:1.
Enrollment Profile: 30,711 students from 52 states and territories, 114 other countries. 53% women, 47% men, 12% part-time, 92% state residents, 21% live on campus, 40% transferred in, 22% 25 or older, 9% Hispanic, 6% black, 6% Asian or Pacific Islander. *Retention:* 90% of 1995 full-time freshmen returned. *Areas of study chosen:* 12% engineering and applied sciences, 10% business management and administrative services, 8% communications and journalism, 7% social sciences, 6% education, 5% biological and life sciences, 5% psychology, 4% agriculture, 4% English language/literature/letters, 3% architecture, 2% computer and information sciences, 2% performing arts, 2% physical sciences, 1% area and ethnic studies, 1% fine arts, 1% foreign language and literature, 1% health professions and related sciences, 1% interdisciplinary studies, 1% mathematics, 1% natural resource sciences, 1% philosophy. *Most popular recent majors:* psychology, finance/banking, English.

University of Florida (continued)

First-Year Class: 3,318 total; 12,901 applied, 59% were accepted, 44% of whom enrolled. 50% from top 10% of their high school class, 85% from top quarter, 97% from top half. 127 National Merit Scholars.
Graduation Requirements: 120 semester hours; 6 semester hours of math; 9 semester hours of physical science/biological science; computer course for business-related, insurance, nutrition, building construction, poultry science, physical education, engineering, physics majors; internship (some majors); senior project for honors program students and some majors.
Computers on Campus: 575 computers available on campus for general student use. Computer purchase/lease plans available. A computer is required for some students. A campus-wide network can be accessed from student residence rooms and from off-campus. Students can contact faculty members and/or advisers through e-mail. Computers for student use in computer center, computer labs, research center, learning resource center, classrooms, library, student center, dorms, student rooms provide access to the Internet/World Wide Web, on- and off-campus e-mail addresses. Staffed computer lab on campus (open 24 hours a day) provides training in use of computers, software. *Academic computing expenditure 1995–96:* $17.4 million.

EXPENSES AND FINANCIAL AID

Expenses for 1996–97: *Application fee:* $20. State resident tuition: $1793 full-time, $59.77 per semester hour part-time. Nonresident tuition: $7038 full-time, $234.61 per semester hour part-time. College room and board: $4500. College room only: $2200.
Undergraduate Financial Aid: 66% of all full-time undergraduates enrolled in fall 1996 applied for aid; of these, 58% were judged to have need according to Federal Methodology, of whom 99% were aided. On average, 88% of need was met. *Financial aid deadline (priority):* 4/15. *Financial aid forms:* FAFSA, institutional form required; CSS Financial Aid PROFILE acceptable.
Financial aid specifically for students with LD: Scholarships: University Women's Club Scholarship, Theodore and Vivian Johnson Scholarship, Christopher M. Squitieri Scholarship; loans; work-study.
LD Services Contact: Mr. James Costello, Assistant Dean for Student Services, University of Florida, 205 Peabody Hall, Gainesville, FL 32611-4075, 352-392-1261. Fax: 352-392-5566. Email: james_costello@sfa.ufl.edu.

UNIVERSITY OF GUELPH

Guelph, Ontario, Canada

LEARNING DISABILITIES SERVICES INFORMATION

Centre for Students with Disabilities began offering services in 1990. Currently the program serves 150 undergraduates with LD. Services are also available to graduate students. Students diagnosed with ADD/ADHD are eligible for the same services available to students with LD.
Staff: 1 full-time, 2 part-time staff members, including director. Services provided by counselors, diagnostic specialists.
Special Fees: No special fees are charged for services to students with LD.
Applications and admissions: *Required:* high school transcript, courses completed; *recommended:* high school extracurricular activities, letters of recommendation. Students may begin taking classes in fall, winter, or spring. *Application deadline:* continuous.

PROGRAM AND SERVICE COMPONENTS

Special preparation or orientation: Optional orientation offered before registration, during registration, after classes begin.
Diagnostic testing: Intelligence, reading, math, spelling, spoken language, written language, perceptual skills, personality, learning strategies.
Academic advising: Provided by unit staff members, academic advisers. Students with LD may take up to 5 courses each term; most take 3 courses; 4 courses required to maintain full-time status; 1 course required to be eligible for financial aid.
Counseling services: Individual counseling, small-group counseling, career counseling, self-advocacy training.
Subject-area tutoring: Offered one-on-one by peer tutors. Available in all subjects.
Auxiliary aids: Taped textbooks, tape recorders, calculators, typewriters, word-processors with spell-check, personal computers, optical character readers.
Auxiliary services: Alternative test arrangements, notetakers, priority registration, advocacy.

GENERAL COLLEGE INFORMATION

Province-supported, coed. Awards bachelor's, master's, doctoral, first professional degrees. Founded 1964. *Setting:* 817-acre urban campus with easy access to Toronto. *Total enrollment:* 13,512. *Faculty:* 738 (610 full-time, 93% with terminal degrees, 128 part-time); student–undergrad faculty ratio is 17:1.
Enrollment Profile: 11,892 students from 12 provinces and territories, 85 other countries. 63% women, 37% men, 14% part-time, 95% province residents, 36% live on campus, 5% transferred in, 3% international, 15% 25 or older. *Retention:* 88% of 1995 full-time freshmen returned. *Graduation:* 48% graduate in 4 years, 65% in 5 years, 72% in 6 years. *Areas of study chosen:* 18% biological and life sciences, 17% health professions and related sciences, 11% business management and administrative services, 9% liberal arts/general studies, 7% agriculture, 7% natural resource sciences, 7% physical sciences, 4% engineering and applied sciences, 4% psychology, 4% social sciences, 3% computer and information sciences, 3% English language/literature/letters, 2% area and ethnic studies, 2% fine arts, 1% foreign language and literature.
First-Year Class: 2,614 total; 10,157 applied, 67% were accepted, 39% of whom enrolled.
Graduation Requirements: 30 courses; computer course for nutrition, management, economics, math, applied math, statistics, biochemistry, ecology, gerontology, marketing management, engineering; internship (some majors); senior project for honors program students and some majors.
Computers on Campus: 1,000 computers available on campus for general student use. A campus-wide network can be accessed from student residence rooms and from off-campus. Students can contact faculty members and/or advisers through e-mail. Computers for student use in computer center, computer labs, learning resource center, classrooms, library, student center, dorms, academic buildings provide access to the Internet/World Wide Web, on- and off-campus e-mail addresses. Staffed computer lab on campus provides training in use of computers, software.

EXPENSES AND FINANCIAL AID

Expenses for 1997–98: *Application fee:* $75. Canadian resident tuition: $334.66 per course part-time. Part-time mandatory fees: $68.05 per trimester. Full-time tuition ranges from $3222 to $3500 for Canadian residents. Tuition for nonresidents ranges from $10,280 to $16,760 full-time, $1041 to $1689 per course part-time, according to program. Full-time mandatory fees range from $477 to $486. College room and board: $5082 (minimum). College room only: $3272 (minimum).
Undergraduate Financial Aid: *Financial aid deadline (priority):* 6/30. *Financial aid forms:* institutional form required.
LD Services Contact: Mr. Bruno Mancini, Coordinator, University of Guelph, Guelph, ON N1G 2W1, Canada, 519-824-4120 Ext. 6208. Fax: 519-763-5244.

UNIVERSITY OF HAWAII AT HILO

Hilo, Hawaii

LEARNING DISABILITIES SERVICES INFORMATION

Student Support Services Program began offering services in 1987. Currently the program serves 10 undergraduates with LD. Students diagnosed with ADD/ADHD are eligible for the same services available to students with LD.
Staff: 2 full-time, 1 part-time staff members, including director. Services provided by tutors, counselors.
Special Fees: No special fees are charged for services to students with LD.
Applications and admissions: *Required:* high school transcript, grade point average, courses completed, extended time SAT I; *recommended:* untimed or extended time ACT, untimed SAT I, psychoeducational report. Students may begin taking classes in fall, spring, or summer. *Application deadline:* 5/15 (fall term), 10/15 (spring term).

PROGRAM AND SERVICE COMPONENTS

Academic advising: Provided by unit staff members, academic advisers. Students with LD may take up to 18 semester hours each term; most take 9 to 12 semester hours; 12 semester hours required to maintain full-time status; 6 semester hours (part-time), 12 semester hours (full-time) required to be eligible for financial aid.

Counseling services: Individual counseling, career counseling, self-advocacy training.
Subject-area tutoring: Offered one-on-one and in small groups by peer tutors. Available in some subjects.
Auxiliary aids: Taped textbooks, tape recorders, calculators, typewriters, word-processors with spell-check, personal computers.
Auxiliary services: Alternative test arrangements, notetakers, advocacy.

GENERAL COLLEGE INFORMATION

State-supported, 4-year, coed. Part of University of Hawaii System. Awards bachelor's degrees. Founded 1970. *Setting:* 115-acre small-town campus. *Total enrollment:* 2,870. *Faculty:* 281 (206 full-time, 87% with terminal degrees, 75 part-time); student–undergrad faculty ratio is 11:1.
Enrollment Profile: 2,870 students: 59% women, 41% men, 25% part-time, 82% state residents, 29% live on campus, 13% transferred in, 6% international, 41% 25 or older, 19% Native American, 2% Hispanic, 1% black, 35% Asian or Pacific Islander. *Areas of study chosen:* 27% social sciences, 23% business management and administrative services, 13% interdisciplinary studies, 8% biological and life sciences, 8% physical sciences, 7% English language/literature/letters, 6% agriculture, 6% fine arts, 2% education, 1% premed. *Most popular recent majors:* business administration/commerce/management, psychology, English.
First-Year Class: 445 total; 1,275 applied, 62% were accepted, 57% of whom enrolled. 18% from top 10% of their high school class, 47% from top quarter, 81% from top half.
Graduation Requirements: 120 semester hours; 6 semester hours of quantitative/logical reasoning; computer course for business administration, agriculture, economics majors; senior project for honors program students.
Computers on Campus: 136 computers available on campus for general student use. Computer purchase/lease plans available. Computers for student use in computer center, library, dorms, departmental labs provide access to PC applications. Staffed computer lab on campus provides training in use of computers, software.

EXPENSES AND FINANCIAL AID

Estimated Expenses for 1997–98: *Application fee:* $10. Part-time mandatory fees: $15 per semester. Full-time tuition ranges from $1272 to $2136 for state residents, $6888 to $7704 for nonresidents, according to class level. Part-time tuition per semester hour ranges from $53 to $89 for state residents, $287 to $321 for nonresidents, according to class level. Full-time mandatory fees: $50. College room and board: $3480 (minimum). College room only: $1382.
Undergraduate Financial Aid: Of all full-time undergraduates enrolled in fall 1996, 100% of those who applied for aid were judged to have need according to Federal Methodology, of whom 100% were aided. On average, 74% of need was met. *Financial aid deadline (priority):* 3/1. *Financial aid forms:* FAFSA, institutional form required.
LD Services Contact: Ms. Barbara Lee, Coordinator for Students with Disabilities, University of Hawaii at Hilo, 200 West Kawili Street, Hilo, HI 96720-4091, 808-974-7616. Fax: 808-974-7691. Email: barblee@hawaii.edu.

UNIVERSITY OF HOUSTON

Houston, Texas

LEARNING DISABILITIES SERVICES INFORMATION

Center for Students with Disabilities (CSD) began offering services in 1981. Currently the program serves 150 undergraduates with LD. Services are also available to graduate students. Students diagnosed with ADD/ADHD are eligible for the same services available to students with LD.
Staff: 4 full-time, 7 part-time staff members, including director, assistant director, coordinators. Services provided by remediation specialists, counselor, diagnostic specialist, proctors, accommodation assistants.
Special Fees: No special fees are charged for services to students with LD.
Applications and admissions: *Required:* high school transcript, grade point average, class rank, courses completed, untimed SAT I or ACT; *recommended:* high school extracurricular activities. Students may begin taking classes any term. *Application deadline:* 7/15 (fall term), 11/21 (spring term).
Special policies: The college has written policies regarding substitutions and waivers of admissions, graduation, and degree requirements.

PROGRAM AND SERVICE COMPONENTS

Academic advising: Provided by academic advisers. Students with LD may take up to 18 semester hours each term; most take 12 to 15 semester hours; 12 semester hours required to maintain full-time status; 12 semester hours (9 as individually determined appropriate) required to be eligible for financial aid.
Counseling services: Individual counseling, small-group counseling, career counseling, self-advocacy training.
Basic skills remediation: Offered one-on-one by LD specialist. Available in spoken language, learning strategies, study skills, time management, computer skills.
Special courses: College survival skills, reading, vocabulary development, communication skills, composition, learning strategies, word processing, time management, math, typing, personal psychology, study skills, career planning. None offered for credit.
Auxiliary aids: Taped textbooks, calculators, typewriters, word-processors with spell-check, optical character readers, carbonized notepaper.
Auxiliary services: Alternative test arrangements, priority registration, advocacy.
Campus support group: A special student organization is available to students with LD.

GENERAL COLLEGE INFORMATION

State-supported, coed. Part of University of Houston System. Awards bachelor's, master's, doctoral, first professional degrees. Founded 1927. *Setting:* 557-acre urban campus. *Endowment:* $162.2 million. *Research spending 1995–96:* $38.8 million. *Educational spending 1995–96:* $4903 per undergrad. *Total enrollment:* 30,774. *Faculty:* 1,927 (1,005 full-time, 85% with terminal degrees, 922 part-time); student–undergrad faculty ratio is 18:1.
Enrollment Profile: 21,522 students from 44 states and territories, 96 other countries. 52% women, 48% men, 31% part-time, 93% state residents, 8% live on campus, 13% transferred in, 4% international, 30% 25 or older, 1% Native American, 17% Hispanic, 12% black, 18% Asian or Pacific Islander. *Retention:* 72% of 1995 full-time freshmen returned. *Graduation:* 10% graduate in 4 years, 27% in 5 years, 35% in 6 years. *Areas of study chosen:* 25% business management and administrative services, 12% engineering and applied sciences, 11% biological and life sciences, 9% social sciences, 8% psychology, 7% health professions and related sciences, 6% education, 5% performing arts, 3% architecture, 3% English language/literature/letters, 2% computer and information sciences, 2% physical sciences, 2% vocational and home economics, 1% area and ethnic studies, 1% communications and journalism, 1% fine arts, 1% foreign language and literature, 1% mathematics. *Most popular recent majors:* business administration/commerce/management, engineering (general), biology/biological sciences.
First-Year Class: 2,433 total; 6,681 applied, 62% were accepted, 59% of whom enrolled. 27% from top 10% of their high school class, 57% from top quarter, 87% from top half. 21 National Merit Scholars.
Graduation Requirements: 122 semester hours; 6 semester hours each of math and science; computer course (varies by major); internship (some majors); senior project for honors program students and some majors.
Computers on Campus: 850 computers available on campus for general student use. A campus-wide network can be accessed from student residence rooms and from off-campus. Students can contact faculty members and/or advisers through e-mail. Computers for student use in computer center, computer labs, library, dorms provide access to the Internet/World Wide Web, on- and off-campus e-mail addresses. Staffed computer lab on campus (open 24 hours a day) provides training in use of computers, software. *Academic computing expenditure 1995–96:* $7.8 million.

EXPENSES AND FINANCIAL AID

Expenses for 1996–97: *Application fee:* $30. State resident tuition: $960 full-time. Nonresident tuition: $7300 full-time, $222 per semester hour part-time. State resident part-time tuition per semester ranges from $100 to $308. Part-time mandatory fees per semester range from $93 to $333. Full-time mandatory fees: $766. College room and board: $4405. College room only: $2445.
Undergraduate Financial Aid: 77% of all full-time undergraduates enrolled in fall 1996 applied for aid; of these, 87% were judged to have need according to Federal Methodology, of whom 93% were aided. On average, 75% of need was met. *Financial aid deadline (priority):* 4/1. *Financial aid forms:* FAFSA, institutional form required.

University of Houston (continued)

LD Services Contact: Mr. David Genac, Learning Disability Specialist, University of Houston, CSD, 303 SSC, Houston, TX 77204-3243, 713-743-5400. Fax: 713-743-5396. Email: genac@uh.edu.

UNIVERSITY OF HOUSTON–DOWNTOWN

Houston, Texas

LEARNING DISABILITIES SERVICES INFORMATION

Disabled Student Services began offering services in 1975. Currently the program serves 18 undergraduates with LD. Students diagnosed with ADD/ADHD are eligible for the same services available to students with LD.

Staff: 1 full-time staff member (coordinator). Services provided by counselors.

Special Fees: No special fees are charged for services to students with LD.

Applications and admissions: *Required:* high school transcript, psychoeducational report, state-mandated high school exit exam. Students may begin taking classes in fall, spring, or summer. *Application deadline:* continuous.

Special policies: The college has written policies regarding grade forgiveness.

PROGRAM AND SERVICE COMPONENTS

Special preparation or orientation: Required orientation held after classes begin and upon request of the student.

Academic advising: Provided by unit staff members, academic advisers. Students with LD may take up to 18 credit hours each term; most take 12 credit hours; 12 credit hours required to maintain full-time status; 6 credit hours required to be eligible for financial aid.

Counseling services: Individual counseling, career counseling, self-advocacy training.

Auxiliary aids: Taped textbooks, calculators, typewriters, word-processors with spell-check, personal computers, talking computers, optical character readers, word processor with speech output.

Auxiliary services: Alternative test arrangements, priority registration, advocacy, assistance in finding tutors and notetakers.

Campus support group: A special student organization is available to students with LD.

GENERAL COLLEGE INFORMATION

State-supported, 4-year, coed. Part of University of Houston System. Awards bachelor's degrees. Founded 1974. *Setting:* 20-acre urban campus. *Total enrollment:* 7,947. *Faculty:* 394 (146 full-time, 248 part-time).

Enrollment Profile: 7,947 students from 20 states and territories, 79 other countries. 54% women, 46% men, 54% part-time, 95% state residents, 16% transferred in, 4% international, 52% 25 or older, 1% Native American, 31% Hispanic, 25% black, 11% Asian or Pacific Islander. *Most popular recent majors:* criminal justice, interdisciplinary studies, accounting.

First-Year Class: 927 total; 1,355 applied, 100% were accepted, 68% of whom enrolled.

Graduation Requirements: 126 credit hours; 3 credit hours of math; 8 credit hours of science; computer course.

Computers on Campus: 350 computers available on campus for general student use. A campus-wide network can be accessed from off-campus. Students can contact faculty members and/or advisers through e-mail. Computers for student use in computer center, computer labs, learning resource center, classrooms, library, departmental labs provide access to the Internet/World Wide Web, on- and off-campus e-mail addresses. Staffed computer lab on campus provides training in use of computers, software.

EXPENSES AND FINANCIAL AID

Expenses for 1997–98: State resident tuition: $1071 full-time. Nonresident tuition: $7812 full-time, $248 per credit hour part-time. State resident part-time tuition per semester ranges from $120 to $374. Part-time mandatory fees per semester range from $56 to $369. Full-time mandatory fees: $906.

Undergraduate Financial Aid: Of all full-time undergraduates enrolled in fall 1996, 100% of those judged to have need according to Federal Methodology were aided. On average, 85% of need was met. *Financial aid deadline (priority):* 4/1. *Financial aid forms:* FAFSA, institutional form required.

LD Services Contact: Ms. Duraesé Hall, Coordinator, Disabled Student Services, University of Houston–Downtown, One Main Street, Room 903-S, Houston, TX 77002-1001, 713-226-5227. Fax: 713-221-8496.

UNIVERSITY OF IDAHO

Moscow, Idaho

LEARNING DISABILITIES SERVICES INFORMATION

Student Support Services currently serves 100 undergraduates with LD. Services are also available to graduate students. Students diagnosed with ADD/ADHD are eligible for the same services available to students with LD.

Staff: 2 full-time, 2 part-time staff members, including director. Services provided by tutors, counselors, math specialist.

Special Fees: $100 for diagnostic testing.

Applications and admissions: *Required:* high school transcript, grade point average, courses completed, untimed SAT I or ACT, psychoeducational report completed within 3 years; *recommended:* extended time SAT I or ACT, autobiographical statement, letters of recommendation. Students may begin taking classes any term. *Application deadline:* continuous.

PROGRAM AND SERVICE COMPONENTS

Special preparation or orientation: Optional orientation offered individually by special arrangement.

Diagnostic testing: Intelligence, reading, math, spelling, written language, perceptual skills, study skills, personality, learning strategies.

Academic advising: Provided by unit staff members. Most students with LD take 12 to 15 credits each term; 12 credits required to maintain full-time status and be eligible for financial aid.

Counseling services: Individual counseling, small-group counseling, career counseling, self-advocacy training.

Subject-area tutoring: Offered one-on-one by peer tutors. Available in most subjects.

Auxiliary aids: Taped textbooks, carbonless notepaper.

Auxiliary services: Alternative test arrangements, notetakers, advocacy.

GENERAL COLLEGE INFORMATION

State-supported, coed. Awards bachelor's, master's, doctoral, first professional degrees. Founded 1889. *Setting:* 1,450-acre small-town campus. *Endowment:* $49.4 million. *Research spending 1995–96:* $46.3 million. *Educational spending 1995–96:* $6872 per undergrad. *Total enrollment:* 11,727. *Faculty:* 625 (549 full-time, 82% with terminal degrees, 76 part-time); student–undergrad faculty ratio is 17:1.

Enrollment Profile: 8,103 students from 52 states and territories, 40 other countries. 43% women, 57% men, 10% part-time, 77% state residents, 11% transferred in, 2% international, 24% 25 or older, 1% Native American, 2% Hispanic, 1% black, 2% Asian or Pacific Islander. *Retention:* 76% of 1995 full-time freshmen returned. *Most popular recent majors:* communication, engineering (general), biology/biological sciences.

First-Year Class: 1,260 total; 3,200 applied, 85% were accepted, 46% of whom enrolled. 21% from top 10% of their high school class, 47% from top quarter, 83% from top half.

Graduation Requirements: 128 credits; 3 credits of math/statistics; computer course for business, engineering, agriculture, psychology majors; internship (some majors); senior project (some majors).

Computers on Campus: 500 computers available on campus for general student use. Computer purchase/lease plans available. A campus-wide network can be accessed from student residence rooms. Computers for student use in computer center, library, student center, dorms provide access to the Internet/World Wide Web. Staffed computer lab on campus (open 24 hours a day) provides training in use of computers, software. *Academic computing expenditure 1995–96:* $2.5 million.

EXPENSES AND FINANCIAL AID

Expenses for 1997–98: *Application fee:* $30. State resident tuition: $0 full-time. Nonresident tuition: $5800 full-time, $95 per credit part-time. Part-time mandatory fees: $97 per credit. Full-time mandatory fees: $1942. College room and board: $3680.

Undergraduate Financial Aid: 64% of all full-time undergraduates enrolled in fall 1996 applied for aid; of these, 84% were judged to have need according to Federal Methodology, of whom 100% were aided. On average, 80% of need was met. *Financial aid deadline (priority):* 2/15. *Financial aid forms:* FAFSA required.

LD Services Contact: Ms. Meredyth Goodwin, Director, Student Support Services, University of Idaho, Continuing Education, 106, Moscow, ID 83844-3230, 208-885-6746.

UNIVERSITY OF ILLINOIS AT CHICAGO

Chicago, Illinois

LEARNING DISABILITIES SERVICES INFORMATION

Disability Services began offering services in 1973. Currently the program serves 60 undergraduates with LD. Services are also available to graduate students. Students diagnosed with ADD/ADHD are eligible for the same services available to students with LD.

Staff: 1 part-time staff member. Services provided by graduate assistant, student worker.

Special Fees: $800 for diagnostic testing.

Applications and admissions: *Required:* high school transcript, courses completed, untimed SAT I or ACT, psychoeducational report completed within 3 years; *recommended:* extended time SAT I or ACT, letters of recommendation. Students may begin taking classes in fall, spring, or summer. *Application deadline:* 6/7 (fall term), 10/28 (spring term).

PROGRAM AND SERVICE COMPONENTS

Diagnostic testing: Intelligence, reading, math, spelling, written language, motor abilities, perceptual skills, study skills, personality, psychoneurology.

Academic advising: Provided by academic advisers. Students with LD may take up to as many semester hours as an individual can handle each term; 12 semester hours required to maintain full-time status and be eligible for financial aid.

Counseling services: Individual counseling, small-group counseling, career counseling, self-advocacy training (available individually by special arrangement), peer support groups.

Basic skills remediation: Offered one-on-one and in class-size groups by regular teachers. Available in reading, math, spoken language, study skills, time management, learning strategies; supplemental instruction and study skills for some specific classes.

Auxiliary aids: Taped textbooks, tape recorders, calculators, word-processors with spell-check, personal computers, V-tek, Dragon Dictate, screen magnification, optical scanner.

Auxiliary services: Alternative test arrangements, priority registration, advocacy, volunteer notetakers, phone registration, TDD/(312)413-2183.

GENERAL COLLEGE INFORMATION

State-supported, coed. Part of University of Illinois System. Awards bachelor's, master's, doctoral, first professional degrees. Founded 1946. *Setting:* 200-acre urban campus. *Endowment:* $16.9 million. *Research spending 1995–96:* $86.4 million. *Educational spending 1995–96:* $10,650 per undergrad. *Total enrollment:* 24,583. *Faculty:* 2,723 (1,931 full-time, 88% with terminal degrees, 792 part-time); student–undergrad faculty ratio is 14:1.

Enrollment Profile: 16,190 students from 44 states and territories, 46 other countries. 54% women, 46% men, 16% part-time, 96% state residents, 10% live on campus, 39% transferred in, 2% international, 20% 25 or older, 1% Native American, 17% Hispanic, 10% black, 20% Asian or Pacific Islander. *Retention:* 73% of 1995 full-time freshmen returned. *Graduation:* 9% graduate in 4 years, 26% in 5 years, 35% in 6 years. *Areas of study chosen:* 14% health professions and related sciences, 12% business management and administrative services, 12% engineering and applied sciences, 11% liberal arts/general studies, 8% social sciences, 6% biological and life sciences, 6% psychology, 4% prelaw, 3% architecture, 3% education, 3% English language/literature/letters, 3% fine arts, 3% premed, 2% communications and journalism, 2% physical sciences, 1% computer and information sciences, 1% foreign language and literature. *Most popular recent majors:* psychology, accounting, nursing.

First-Year Class: 2,807 total; 9,304 applied, 63% were accepted, 48% of whom enrolled. 23% from top 10% of their high school class, 56% from top quarter, 91% from top half.

Graduation Requirements: 120 semester hours; 6 semester hours of science; computer course for business, engineering, health information management, geography, statistics, operations research majors; internship (some majors); senior project (some majors).

Computers on Campus: 1,125 computers available on campus for general student use. Computer purchase/lease plans available. A computer is recommended for some students. A campus-wide network can be accessed from student residence rooms and from off-campus. Students can contact faculty members and/or advisers through e-mail. Computers for student use in computer center, computer labs, library, dorms, career placement center, client services offices provide access to the Internet/World Wide Web, super computer on Urbana campus with professors approval. Staffed computer lab on campus (open 24 hours a day) provides training in use of computers, software. *Academic computing expenditure 1995–96:* $4.9 million.

EXPENSES AND FINANCIAL AID

Expenses for 1996–97: *Application fee:* $30. Part-time mandatory fees: $453 per semester. Full-time tuition ranges from $2870 to $3270 for state residents, $8610 to $8614 for nonresidents, according to program. Part-time tuition per semester ranges from $478 to $957 for state residents, $1435 to $2870 for nonresidents, according to program and course load. Full-time mandatory fees: $906. College room and board: $5188. College room only: $3112.

Undergraduate Financial Aid: Of all full-time undergraduates enrolled in fall 1996, 96% of those who applied for aid were judged to have need according to Federal Methodology, of whom 100% were aided. On average, 65% of need was met. *Financial aid deadline (priority):* 3/1. *Financial aid forms:* FAFSA, financial aid transcript (for transfers) required. Institutional form required for some.

LD Services Contact: Ms. Mary Stainton, Program Services Aide, University of Illinois at Chicago, 1200 West Harrison, Room 1190, Chicago, IL 60607, 312-413-2183. Fax: 312-413-7781.

UNIVERSITY OF ILLINOIS AT URBANA–CHAMPAIGN

Champaign, Illinois

LEARNING DISABILITIES SERVICES INFORMATION

Services for Sensory Accommodations, Division of Rehabilitation Education Services began offering services in 1988. Currently the program serves 96 undergraduates with LD. Services are also available to graduate students. Students diagnosed with ADD/ADHD are eligible for the same services available to students with LD.

Staff: 5 full-time, 2 part-time staff members, including director, coordinators. Services provided by counselors.

Special Fees: $300 to $1000 for diagnostic testing.

Applications and admissions: *Required:* high school transcript, class rank, personal interview, psychoeducational report completed within 3 years; *recommended:* extended time SAT I or ACT. Students may begin taking classes any term. *Application deadline:* 1/2 (fall term), 11/1 (spring term).

PROGRAM AND SERVICE COMPONENTS

Diagnostic testing: Intelligence, psychoneurology.

Academic advising: Provided by academic advisers. Most students with LD take 12 to 14 semester hours each term; 12 semester hours required to maintain full-time status; 6 semester hours required to be eligible for financial aid.

Counseling services: Individual counseling, career counseling, self-advocacy training, mental health counseling.

Auxiliary aids: Taped textbooks, tape recorders, word-processors with spell-check, personal computers, talking computers, optical character readers.

Auxiliary services: Alternative test arrangements, notetakers, priority registration, advocacy.

GENERAL COLLEGE INFORMATION

State-supported, coed. Part of University of Illinois System. Awards bachelor's, master's, doctoral, first professional degrees. Founded 1867. *Setting:* 1,470-acre small-town campus. *Endowment:* $454.4 million. *Research spending 1995–96:* $208.2 million. *Educational spending 1995–96:* $5455 per undergrad. *Total enrollment:* 36,164. *Faculty:* 1,843 (1,818 full-time, 91% with terminal degrees, 25 part-time); student–undergrad faculty ratio is 14:1.

Enrollment Profile: 26,738 students from 52 states and territories, 48 other countries. 46% women, 54% men, 3% part-time, 90% state residents, 33% live on campus, 16% transferred in, 2% international, 4% 25 or older, 1% Native American, 5% Hispanic, 7% black, 13% Asian or Pacific Islander. *Retention:* 91% of 1995 full-time freshmen returned. *Graduation:* 53% graduate in 4 years. *Areas of study chosen:* 47% liberal arts/general studies, 19% engineering and applied sciences, 11% business management and administrative services, 8% agriculture, 8% fine

University of Illinois at Urbana Champaign (continued)

arts, 4% biological and life sciences, 3% education, 2% communications and journalism. *Most popular recent majors:* biology/biological sciences, psychology, electrical engineering.

First-Year Class: 5,946 total; 17,250 applied, 70% were accepted, 49% of whom enrolled. 51% from top 10% of their high school class, 86% from top quarter, 99% from top half. 74 National Merit Scholars.

Graduation Requirements: 120 semester hours; computer course for all science, engineering, commerce majors; internship (some majors); senior project (some majors).

Computers on Campus: 3,000 computers available on campus for general student use. Computer purchase/lease plans available. A computer is strongly recommended for all students. A campus-wide network can be accessed from student residence rooms and from off-campus. Students can contact faculty members and/or advisers through e-mail. Computers for student use in computer center, computer labs, library, student center, dorms provide access to the Internet/World Wide Web, on- and off-campus e-mail addresses. Staffed computer lab on campus (open 24 hours a day) provides training in use of computers, software. *Academic computing expenditure 1995–96:* $6.3 million.

EXPENSES AND FINANCIAL AID

Expenses for 1996–97: *Application fee:* $30. Part-time mandatory fees per semester range from $216 to $518. Full-time tuition ranges from $3150 to $3650 for state residents, $8580 to $9080 for nonresidents, according to class level. Part-time tuition per semester ranges from $525 to $1217 for state residents, $1430 to $3027 for nonresidents, according to class level and course load. Full-time mandatory fees: $1036. College room and board: $4560.

Undergraduate Financial Aid: Of all full-time undergraduates enrolled in fall 1996, 76% of those who applied for aid were judged to have need according to Federal Methodology, of whom 95% were aided. On average, 75% of need was met. *Financial aid deadline (priority):* 3/15. *Financial aid forms:* FAFSA required.

LD Services Contact: Dr. Janet A. Macomber, Learning Disabilities Specialist, University of Illinois at Urbana–Champaign, 1207 South Oak Street, Champaign, IL 61820-5711, 217-333-8705. Fax: 217-333-0248. Email: macomber@uiuc.edu.

THE UNIVERSITY OF IOWA

Iowa City, Iowa

LEARNING DISABILITIES SERVICES INFORMATION

Student Disability Services began offering services in 1980. Currently the program serves 505 undergraduates with LD. Services are also available to graduate students. Students diagnosed with ADD/ADHD are eligible for the same services available to students with LD, as well as support groups.

Staff: 4 full-time, 5 part-time staff members, including director, coordinators. Services provided by counselors, diagnostic specialist.

Special Fees: A fee is charged for diagnostic testing.

Applications and admissions: *Required:* high school transcript, grade point average, class rank, courses completed, untimed or extended time SAT I or ACT, psychoeducational report completed within 3 years; *recommended:* high school extracurricular activities. Students may begin taking classes in fall, spring, or summer. *Application deadline:* continuous.

Special policies: The college has written policies regarding grade forgiveness; substitutions and waivers of admissions requirements.

PROGRAM AND SERVICE COMPONENTS

Special preparation or orientation: Optional summer program offered prior to entering college. Optional orientation offered before registration and after classes begin.

Diagnostic testing: Intelligence, reading, math, spelling, spoken language, written language, perceptual skills, study skills, psychoneurology, speech, hearing, learning strategies.

Academic advising: Provided by unit staff members, academic advisers. Students with LD may take up to 18 semester hours each term; most take 12 to 14 semester hours; 22 semester hours (per year in any combination) required to maintain full-time status; 12 semester hours required to be eligible for financial aid.

Counseling services: Individual counseling, small-group counseling, career counseling, self-advocacy training.

Subject-area tutoring: Offered one-on-one and in small groups by peer tutors. Available in most subjects.

Auxiliary aids: Taped textbooks, word-processors with spell-check, talking computers, optical character readers.

Auxiliary services: Alternative test arrangements, notetakers, priority registration, advocacy.

Campus support group: A special student organization is available to students with LD.

GENERAL COLLEGE INFORMATION

State-supported, coed. Awards bachelor's, master's, doctoral, first professional degrees. Founded 1847. *Setting:* 1,900-acre small-town campus. *Endowment:* $265 million. *Total enrollment:* 27,921. *Faculty:* 1,803 (1,747 full-time, 99% with terminal degrees, 56 part-time); student–undergrad faculty ratio is 15:1.

Enrollment Profile: 16,566 students from 54 states and territories, 61 other countries. 54% women, 46% men, 15% part-time, 69% state residents, 35% live on campus, 17% transferred in, 2% international, 13% 25 or older, 1% Native American, 2% Hispanic, 2% black, 4% Asian or Pacific Islander. *Retention:* 83% of 1995 full-time freshmen returned. *Graduation:* 33% graduate in 4 years, 57% in 5 years, 63% in 6 years. *Areas of study chosen:* 17% liberal arts/general studies, 15% business management and administrative services, 14% health professions and related sciences, 8% social sciences, 7% engineering and applied sciences, 6% communications and journalism, 5% English language/literature/letters, 5% psychology, 4% biological and life sciences, 4% education, 3% fine arts, 3% premed, 2% performing arts, 1% area and ethnic studies, 1% computer and information sciences, 1% foreign language and literature, 1% mathematics, 1% physical sciences, 1% predentistry, 1% prelaw. *Most popular recent majors:* psychology, English, finance/banking.

First-Year Class: 3,535 total; 9,847 applied, 86% were accepted, 42% of whom enrolled. 22% from top 10% of their high school class, 52% from top quarter, 90% from top half. 21 National Merit Scholars, 140 valedictorians.

Graduation Requirements: 124 semester hours; 2 years of algebra, 1 year of geometry; 7 semester hours of science; computer course for business administration, geography, engineering, education, nursing, exercise science majors; internship (some majors); senior project for honors program students.

Computers on Campus: 1,200 computers available on campus for general student use. Computer purchase/lease plans available. A campus-wide network can be accessed from off-campus. Students can contact faculty members and/or advisers through e-mail. Computers for student use in computer center, computer labs, research center, classrooms, library, student center, dorms, academic buildings provide access to the Internet/World Wide Web, on- and off-campus e-mail addresses. Staffed computer lab on campus (open 24 hours a day) provides training in use of computers, software.

EXPENSES AND FINANCIAL AID

Expenses for 1997–98: *Application fee:* $20. State resident tuition: $2566 full-time. Nonresident tuition: $9422 full-time. Part-time tuition per semester ranges from $214 to $1177 for state residents, $214 to $4323 for nonresidents. Part-time mandatory fees per semester range from $25 to $85. Full-time mandatory fees: $194. College room and board: $3992.

Undergraduate Financial Aid: Of all full-time undergraduates enrolled in fall 1996, 90% of those who applied for aid were judged to have need according to Federal Methodology, of whom 94% were aided. *Financial aid deadline:* Applications processed continuously. *Financial aid forms:* FAFSA, institutional form required.

LD Services Contact: Ms. Donna Chandler, Director, The University of Iowa, 3101 Burge Hall, Iowa City, IA 52242, 319-335-1462. Fax: 319-335-3973. Email: sds-test@uiowa.edu.

UNIVERSITY OF KANSAS

Lawrence, Kansas

LEARNING DISABILITIES SERVICES INFORMATION

Student Assistance Center began offering services in 1978. Currently the program serves 160 undergraduates with LD. Services are also available to graduate students. Students diagnosed with ADD/ADHD are eligible for the same services available to students with LD.

Staff: 1 full-time, 1 part-time staff members, including assistant director, graduate assistant. Services provided by readers, scribes, typists.

Special Fees: $100 to $300 for diagnostic testing.

Applications and admissions: *Required:* high school transcript, grade point average, class rank, courses completed, letters of recommendation, psychoeducational report; *recommended:* high school extracurricular activities, IEP (Individualized Education Program), extended time SAT I or ACT, autobiographical statement. Students may begin taking classes in fall, winter, or summer.

Special policies: The college has written policies regarding grade forgiveness.

PROGRAM AND SERVICE COMPONENTS

Diagnostic testing: Intelligence, reading, math, spelling, spoken language, written language, motor abilities, perceptual skills, personality, speech, hearing.

Academic advising: Provided by unit staff members, academic advisers. Students with LD may take up to 18 credits each term; most take 12 credits; 12 credits (as defined by financial aid and Health Insurance agencies) required to maintain full-time status; 6 to 12 credits required to be eligible for financial aid.

Counseling services: Individual counseling.

Subject-area tutoring: Offered one-on-one by peer tutors. Available in most subjects.

Auxiliary aids: Taped textbooks, tape recorders, typewriters, talking computers, optical character readers, voice recognition computer programs (Dragon Dictate).

Auxiliary services: Alternative test arrangements, notetakers, advocacy.

GENERAL COLLEGE INFORMATION

State-supported, coed. Awards bachelor's, master's, doctoral, first professional degrees (University of Kansas is a single institution with academic programs and facilities at two primary locations: Lawrence and Kansas City. Undergraduate, graduate, and professional education are the principal missions of the Lawrence campus, with medicine and related professional education the focus of the Kansas City campus). Founded 1866. *Setting:* 1,000-acre suburban campus with easy access to Kansas City. *Endowment:* $519.4 million. *Research spending 1995–96:* $87.4 million. *Total enrollment:* 27,407. *Faculty:* 2,084 (1,704 full-time, 96% with terminal degrees, 380 part-time); student–undergrad faculty ratio is 14:1.

Enrollment Profile: 18,652 students from 53 states and territories, 108 other countries. 51% women, 49% men, 11% part-time, 70% state residents, 22% live on campus, 8% transferred in, 5% international, 11% 25 or older, 1% Native American, 2% Hispanic, 3% black, 3% Asian or Pacific Islander. *Areas of study chosen:* 14% business management and administrative services, 11% health professions and related sciences, 8% social sciences, 7% biological and life sciences, 7% communications and journalism, 7% engineering and applied sciences, 6% education, 6% fine arts, 6% psychology, 5% performing arts, 4% English language/literature/letters, 4% premed, 3% foreign language and literature, 2% architecture, 2% interdisciplinary studies, 2% physical sciences, 2% prelaw, 1% area and ethnic studies, 1% computer and information sciences, 1% mathematics, 1% philosophy. *Most popular recent majors:* journalism, psychology, biology/biological sciences.

First-Year Class: 3,644 total; 8,041 applied, 62% were accepted, 73% of whom enrolled. 55% from top quarter of their high school class, 84% from top half. 59 National Merit Scholars.

Graduation Requirements: 124 credit hours; algebra proficiency; computer course for business, math, physics, geology, most engineering majors; internship (some majors); senior project (some majors).

Computers on Campus: 550 computers available on campus for general student use. A campus-wide network can be accessed from student residence rooms and from off-campus. Students can contact faculty members and/or advisers through e-mail. Computers for student use in computer center, computer labs, classrooms, library, dorms provide access to the Internet/World Wide Web, on- and off-campus e-mail addresses. Staffed computer lab on campus (open 24 hours a day) provides training in use of computers, software. *Academic computing expenditure 1995–96:* $3.6 million.

EXPENSES AND FINANCIAL AID

Expenses for 1997–98: *Application fee:* $15. State resident tuition: $2031 full-time, $65.50 per credit hour part-time. Nonresident tuition: $8545 full-time, $275.65 per credit hour part-time. Part-time mandatory fees: $30 per credit hour for 1 to 7 credit hours, $210 per semester for 8 or more credit hours. Full-time mandatory fees: $420. College room and board: $3736.

Undergraduate Financial Aid: 48% of all full-time undergraduates enrolled in fall 1996 applied for aid; of these, 81% were judged to have need according to Federal Methodology, of whom 82% were aided. On average, 65% of need was met. *Financial aid deadline (priority):* 3/1. *Financial aid forms:* FAFSA required. State form required for some.

LD Services Contact: Mr. Mike Shuttic, Assistant Director/Coordinator of Disability Services, University of Kansas, 22 Strong Hall, Student Assistance Center, Lawrence, KS 66045, 913-864-4064. Fax: 913-864-4050. Email: mshuttic@ukans.edu.

UNIVERSITY OF MAINE

Orono, Maine

LEARNING DISABILITIES SERVICES INFORMATION

Services for Students with Disabilities, Onward Program currently serves 225 undergraduates with LD. Services are also available to graduate students. Students diagnosed with ADD/ADHD are eligible for the same services available to students with LD.

Staff: 2 full-time staff members, including coordinator.

Special Fees: No special fees are charged for services to students with LD.

Applications and admissions: *Required:* high school transcript, untimed SAT I or ACT, letters of recommendation; *recommended:* extended time SAT I or ACT. Students may begin taking classes in fall or spring. *Application deadline:* 2/1 (fall term), 11/1 (spring term).

PROGRAM AND SERVICE COMPONENTS

Academic advising: Provided by academic advisers. Most students with LD take 12 to 15 credit hours each term; 12 credit hours (fewer with documentation) required to maintain full-time status; 12 credit hours required to be eligible for financial aid.

Counseling services: Individual counseling.

Basic skills remediation: Offered in class-size groups by regular teachers. Available in reading, math, written language.

Subject-area tutoring: Offered in small groups by peer tutors. Available in some subjects.

Auxiliary aids: Taped textbooks, tape recorders.

Auxiliary services: Alternative test arrangements, notetakers, priority registration, advocacy.

GENERAL COLLEGE INFORMATION

State-supported, coed. Part of University of Maine System. Awards associate, bachelor's, master's, doctoral degrees. Founded 1865. *Setting:* 3,298-acre small-town campus. *Endowment:* $88 million. *Research spending 1995–96:* $24.5 million. *Total enrollment:* 9,928. *Faculty:* 634 (486 full-time, 82% with terminal degrees, 148 part-time); student–undergrad faculty ratio is 14:1.

Enrollment Profile: 7,850 students from 44 states and territories, 69 other countries. 52% women, 48% men, 24% part-time, 82% state residents, 52% live on campus, 4% transferred in, 4% international, 34% 25 or older, 2% Native American, 1% Hispanic, 1% black, 2% Asian or Pacific Islander. *Retention:* 79% of 1995 full-time freshmen returned. *Areas of study chosen:* 10% education, 10% engineering and applied sciences, 9% natural resource sciences, 8% business management and administrative services, 6% health professions and related sciences, 6% liberal arts/general studies, 4% social sciences, 3% biological and life sciences, 2% communications and journalism, 2% English language/literature/letters, 2% physical sciences, 2% psychology, 1% agriculture, 1% computer and information sciences, 1% fine arts, 1% foreign language and literature, 1% mathematics, 1% performing arts, 1% philosophy. *Most popular recent majors:* business administration/commerce/management, elementary education, nursing.

First-Year Class: 1,779 total; 4,399 applied, 77% were accepted, 53% of whom enrolled. 17% from top 10% of their high school class, 37% from top quarter, 84% from top half. 7 National Merit Scholars, 11 valedictorians.

Graduation Requirements: 60 credit hours for associate, 120 credit hours for bachelor's; computer course for engineering, economics, business administration majors; senior project for honors program students and some majors.

Computers on Campus: 250 computers available on campus for general student use. Computer purchase/lease plans available. A computer is recommended for some students. A campus-wide network can be accessed from student residence rooms and from off-campus. Students can contact faculty members and/or advisers through e-mail. Computers for student use in computer center, computer labs, library, student center, dorms, student rooms, departmental labs provide access to the Internet/World Wide Web, on- and off-campus e-mail addresses. Staffed computer lab on campus provides training in use of computers, software. *Academic computing expenditure 1995–96:* $774,668.

University of Maine (continued)

EXPENSES AND FINANCIAL AID

Expenses for 1997–98: *Application fee:* $25. State resident tuition: $3750 full-time, $125 per credit hour part-time. Nonresident tuition: $10,620 full-time, $354 per credit hour part-time. Part-time mandatory fees per semester range from $3 to $181.50. Tuition for nonresidents who are eligible for the New England Regional Student Program: $5625 full-time, $187.50 per credit hour part-time. Full-time mandatory fees: $589. College room and board: $4906.
Undergraduate Financial Aid: *Financial aid deadline (priority):* 3/1. *Financial aid forms:* FAFSA, CSS Financial Aid PROFILE required.
LD Services Contact: Ms. Ann Smith, Counselor/Coordinator of Services for Students with Disabilities, Onward Program, University of Maine, Onward Building, Orono, ME 04469, 207-581-2319. Fax: 207-581-4252.

UNIVERSITY OF MAINE AT FARMINGTON

Farmington, Maine

LEARNING DISABILITIES SERVICES INFORMATION

Learning Assistance Center began offering services in 1993. Currently the program serves 27 undergraduates with LD. Students diagnosed with ADD/ADHD are eligible for the same services available to students with LD.
Staff: 1 part-time staff member (coordinator).
Special Fees: No special fees are charged for services to students with LD.
Applications and admissions: *Required:* high school transcript, grade point average, class rank, courses completed, letters of recommendation; *recommended:* personal interview. *Application deadline:* continuous.
Special policies: The college has written policies regarding substitutions and waivers of graduation and degree requirements.

PROGRAM AND SERVICE COMPONENTS

Academic advising: Provided by academic advisers. Most students with LD take 12 to 15 credit hours each term; 12 credit hours required to maintain full-time status and be eligible for financial aid.
Auxiliary aids: Taped textbooks, tape recorders, calculators, word-processors with spell-check.
Auxiliary services: Alternative test arrangements, notetakers.

GENERAL COLLEGE INFORMATION

State-supported, 4-year, coed. Part of University of Maine System. Awards bachelor's degrees. Founded 1863. *Setting:* 50-acre small-town campus. *Endowment:* $3.3 million. *Research spending 1995–96:* $539,843. *Educational spending 1995–96:* $4091 per undergrad. *Total enrollment:* 2,391. *Faculty:* 156 (109 full-time, 83% with terminal degrees, 47 part-time); student–undergrad faculty ratio is 16:1.
Enrollment Profile: 2,391 students from 26 states and territories, 17 other countries. 69% women, 31% men, 11% part-time, 87% state residents, 43% live on campus, 7% transferred in, 2% international, 21% 25 or older, 1% Native American, 1% Hispanic, 1% black, 1% Asian or Pacific Islander. *Retention:* 72% of 1995 full-time freshmen returned. *Graduation:* 40% graduate in 4 years, 60% in 5 years, 62% in 6 years. *Areas of study chosen:* 38% education, 14% interdisciplinary studies, 8% health professions and related sciences, 7% liberal arts/general studies, 7% psychology, 3% biological and life sciences, 3% English language/literature/letters, 2% fine arts, 1% mathematics, 1% social sciences. *Most popular recent majors:* elementary education, interdisciplinary studies, secondary education.
First-Year Class: 489 total; 1,189 applied, 74% were accepted, 55% of whom enrolled. 18% from top 10% of their high school class, 36% from top quarter, 77% from top half. 20 class presidents, 3 valedictorians.
Graduation Requirements: 120 credit hours; 3 credit hours of math; 8 credit hours of lab science; computer course for elementary education majors; internship (some majors); senior project (some majors).
Computers on Campus: 130 computers available on campus for general student use. A campus-wide network can be accessed from student residence rooms and from off-campus. Students can contact faculty members and/or advisers through e-mail. Computers for student use in computer center, computer labs, classrooms provide access to the Internet/World Wide Web, on- and off-campus e-mail addresses. Staffed computer lab on campus (open 24 hours a day) provides training in use of computers, software. *Academic computing expenditure 1995–96:* $216,551.

EXPENSES AND FINANCIAL AID

Expenses for 1997–98: *Application fee:* $25. State resident tuition: $3210 full-time, $107 per credit hour part-time. Nonresident tuition: $7830 full-time, $266 per credit hour part-time. Part-time mandatory fees per semester range from $3 to $143. Tuition for nonresidents who are eligible for the New England Regional Student Program: $4815 full-time, $160.50 per credit hour part-time. Full-time mandatory fees: $310. College room and board: $4406. College room only: $2276.
Undergraduate Financial Aid: *Financial aid deadline (priority):* 3/1. *Financial aid forms:* FAFSA, financial aid transcript (for transfers) required.
LD Services Contact: Ms. Claire Nelson, Coordinator of Academic Services for Students with Disabilities, University of Maine at Farmington, 86 Main Street, Farmington, ME 04911, 207-778-7295. Fax: 207-778-7247.

UNIVERSITY OF MAINE AT FORT KENT

Fort Kent, Maine

LEARNING DISABILITIES SERVICES INFORMATION

Academic and Counseling Services began offering services in 1983. Currently the program serves 10 undergraduates with LD. Students diagnosed with ADD/ADHD are eligible for the same services available to students with LD.
Staff: 3 full-time, 4 part-time staff members, including director, coordinator, administrative assistant. Services provided by tutors, counselors, learning specialist.
Special Fees: No special fees are charged for services to students with LD.
Applications and admissions: *Required:* high school transcript, psychoeducational report completed within 3 years, documentation of disability (within 3 years); *recommended:* untimed SAT I. Students may begin taking classes in fall, spring, or summer. *Application deadline:* continuous.
Special policies: The college has written policies regarding grade forgiveness.

PROGRAM AND SERVICE COMPONENTS

Academic advising: Provided by academic advisers. Students with LD may take up to 12 credit hours each term; most take 12 credit hours; 12 credit hours required to maintain full-time status; 6 credit hours required to be eligible for financial aid.
Counseling services: Individual counseling, small-group counseling, career counseling.
Basic skills remediation: Offered one-on-one and in class-size groups by regular teachers. Available in reading, math, written language, learning strategies.
Subject-area tutoring: Offered one-on-one and in small groups by professional teachers, peer tutors. Available in all subjects.
Special courses: College survival skills, reading, vocabulary development, learning strategies, word processing, math, study skills. All offered for credit; some enter into overall grade point average.
Auxiliary aids: Taped textbooks, tape recorders, calculators, typewriters, word-processors with spell-check, personal computers.
Auxiliary services: Alternative test arrangements, notetakers, advocacy.

GENERAL COLLEGE INFORMATION

State-supported, 4-year, coed. Part of University of Maine System. Awards associate, bachelor's degrees. Founded 1878. *Setting:* 52-acre rural campus. *Endowment:* $3.8 million. *Total enrollment:* 767. *Faculty:* 31 (all full-time, 52% with terminal degrees).
Enrollment Profile: 767 students from 13 states and territories, 8 other countries. 61% women, 39% men, 42% part-time, 77% state residents, 53% transferred in, 33% 25 or older, 1% Native American, 0% Hispanic, 1% black, 1% Asian or Pacific Islander. *Retention:* 54% of 1995 full-time freshmen returned. *Graduation:* 48% graduate in 4 years, 56% in 5 years, 60% in 6 years. *Areas of study chosen:* 45% education, 21% English language/literature/letters, 18% health professions and related sciences, 7% business management and administrative services, 6% social sciences, 2% computer and information sciences, 1% foreign language and literature. *Most popular recent majors:* nursing, education, social science.

First-Year Class: 94 total; 181 applied, 96% were accepted, 54% of whom enrolled. 8% from top 10% of their high school class, 30% from top quarter, 54% from top half.
Graduation Requirements: 60 credit hours for associate, 120 credit hours for bachelor's; computer course for education, behavioral science, nursing, business management majors; internship (some majors); senior project for honors program students and some majors.
Computers on Campus: 50 computers available on campus for general student use. A computer is recommended for all students. A campus-wide network can be accessed from student residence rooms and from off-campus. Students can contact faculty members and/or advisers through e-mail. Computers for student use in computer center, computer labs, research center, learning resource center, library, dorms provide access to the Internet/World Wide Web, on- and off-campus e-mail addresses. Staffed computer lab on campus provides training in use of computers, software.

EXPENSES AND FINANCIAL AID

Expenses for 1997–98: *Application fee:* $25. State resident tuition: $2940 full-time, $98 per credit hour part-time. Nonresident tuition: $7200 full-time, $240 per credit hour part-time. Part-time mandatory fees per semester range from $4 to $71.50. Tuition for nonresidents who are eligible for the New England Regional Student Program: $4410 full-time, $147 per credit hour part-time. One-time mandatory fee: $15. Full-time mandatory fees: $200. College room and board: $3750 (minimum). College room only: $1925.
Undergraduate Financial Aid: 80% of all full-time undergraduates enrolled in fall 1996 applied for aid; of these, 88% were judged to have need according to Federal Methodology, of whom 99% were aided. On average, 81% of need was met. *Financial aid deadline (priority):* 3/15. *Financial aid forms:* FAFSA required.
LD Services Contact: Mr. George Diaz, Academic Counselor, Academic and Counseling Services, University of Maine at Fort Kent, Pleasant Street, Fort Kent, ME 04743, 207-834-7532. Fax: 207-834-7503.

UNIVERSITY OF MAINE AT MACHIAS

Machias, Maine

LEARNING DISABILITIES SERVICES INFORMATION

Student Resources began offering services in 1983. Currently the program serves 39 undergraduates with LD. Students diagnosed with ADD/ADHD are eligible for the same services available to students with LD.
Staff: Includes coordinator, psychologist. Services provided by remediation specialists, tutors, counselors.
Special Fees: No special fees are charged for services to students with LD.
Applications and admissions: *Required:* high school transcript, letters of recommendation, essay. Students may begin taking classes any term. *Application deadline:* continuous.
Special policies: The college has written policies regarding grade forgiveness.

PROGRAM AND SERVICE COMPONENTS

Academic advising: Provided by academic advisers. Students with LD may take up to 15 credits each term; most take 12 credits; 12 credits required to maintain full-time status.
Counseling services: Individual counseling, small-group counseling, career counseling.
Basic skills remediation: Offered one-on-one and in class-size groups by regular teachers. Available in reading, math, written language.
Special courses: College survival skills, reading, vocabulary development, composition, math, career planning. Some offered for credit; some enter into overall grade point average.
Auxiliary aids: Taped textbooks, tape recorders, personal computers.
Auxiliary services: Alternative test arrangements, notetakers, advocacy, time management, paper writing assistance.

GENERAL COLLEGE INFORMATION

State-supported, 4-year, coed. Part of University of Maine System. Awards associate, bachelor's degrees. Founded 1909. *Setting:* 42-acre rural campus. *Endowment:* $845,840. *Research spending 1995–96:* $97,111. *Educational spending 1995–96:* $3718 per undergrad. *Total enrollment:* 915. *Faculty:* 64 (37 full-time, 52% with terminal degrees, 27 part-time); student–undergrad faculty ratio is 16:1.
Enrollment Profile: 915 students from 21 states and territories, 18 other countries. 63% women, 37% men, 40% part-time, 80% state residents, 30% live on campus, 9% transferred in, 4% international, 3% Native American, 0% Hispanic, 1% black. *Retention:* 68% of 1995 full-time freshmen returned. *Most popular recent majors:* business administration/commerce/management, environmental studies, behavioral sciences.
First-Year Class: 181 total; 521 applied, 83% were accepted, 42% of whom enrolled. 25% from top 10% of their high school class, 25% from top quarter, 90% from top half.
Graduation Requirements: 60 credits for associate, 120 credits for bachelor's; 1 course each in math and lab science; computer course for business majors; internship (some majors); senior project (some majors).
Computers on Campus: 175 computers available on campus for general student use. Computer purchase/lease plans available. A campus-wide network can be accessed from student residence rooms and from off-campus. Students can contact faculty members and/or advisers through e-mail. Computers for student use in computer center, computer labs, learning resource center, library, student center, dorms provide access to the Internet/World Wide Web, on- and off-campus e-mail addresses. Staffed computer lab on campus provides training in use of computers, software. *Academic computing expenditure 1995–96:* $33,458.

EXPENSES AND FINANCIAL AID

Expenses for 1996–97: *Application fee:* $25. State resident tuition: $2820 full-time, $94 per credit part-time. Nonresident tuition: $6870 full-time, $229 per credit part-time. Part-time mandatory fees: $6.50 per credit. Tuition for nonresidents who are eligible for the New England Regional Student Program: $4230 full-time, $141 per credit part-time. Full-time mandatory fees: $175. College room and board: $3895 (minimum).
Undergraduate Financial Aid: 79% of all full-time undergraduates enrolled in fall 1996 applied for aid; of these, 89% were judged to have need according to Federal Methodology, of whom 96% were aided. On average, 80% of need was met. *Financial aid deadline (priority):* 3/1. *Financial aid forms:* FAFSA required.
LD Services Contact: Mr. Dave Baldwin, Director of Admissions, University of Maine at Machias, 9 O'Brien Avenue, Machias, ME 04654-1321, 207-255-3318. Fax: 207-255-4864. Email: dbaldwin@acad.umm.maine.edu.

UNIVERSITY OF MARYLAND, BALTIMORE COUNTY

Baltimore, Maryland

LEARNING DISABILITIES SERVICES INFORMATION

Student Support Services Department began offering services in 1980. Currently the program serves 77 undergraduates with LD. Services are also available to graduate students. Students diagnosed with ADD/ADHD are eligible for the same services available to students with LD.
Staff: 4 full-time, 4 part-time staff members, including director, graduate assistants. Services provided by remediation specialists, tutors, counselors.
Special Fees: No special fees are charged for services to students with LD.
Applications and admissions: *Required:* high school transcript, grade point average, courses completed, untimed SAT I, autobiographical statement; *recommended:* high school class rank, extracurricular activities, untimed or extended time ACT, extended time SAT I, letters of recommendation, psychoeducational report. Students may begin taking classes any term. *Application deadline:* 3/15 (fall term), 12/15 (spring term).
Special policies: The college has written policies regarding grade forgiveness.

PROGRAM AND SERVICE COMPONENTS

Special preparation or orientation: Optional orientation offered on an individual basis.
Academic advising: Provided by unit staff members, academic advisers. Most students with LD take 12 to 18 credit hours each term; 12 credit hours required to maintain full-time status and be eligible for financial aid.
Counseling services: Individual counseling, career counseling, self-advocacy training.
Basic skills remediation: Offered one-on-one by academic skills specialists; computer-aided instruction also offered. Available in reading, math, written language, learning strategies, study skills, time management, social skills.
Subject-area tutoring: Offered one-on-one by peer tutors, academic skills specialists. Available in most subjects.

University of Maryland, Baltimore County (continued)

Auxiliary aids: Taped textbooks, tape recorders, calculators, typewriters, word-processors with spell-check, personal computers, talking computers.

Auxiliary services: Alternative test arrangements, notetakers, advocacy, scribes, readers.

GENERAL COLLEGE INFORMATION

State-supported, coed. Part of University of Maryland System. Awards bachelor's, master's, doctoral degrees. Founded 1963. *Setting:* 500-acre suburban campus. *Endowment:* $2.4 million. *Research spending 1995–96:* $12.4 million. *Educational spending 1995–96:* $5969 per undergrad. *Total enrollment:* 9,932. *Faculty:* 664 (431 full-time, 85% with terminal degrees, 233 part-time); student–undergrad faculty ratio is 14:1.

Enrollment Profile: 8,475 students from 37 states and territories, 52 other countries. 51% women, 49% men, 27% part-time, 92% state residents, 25% live on campus, 13% transferred in, 3% international, 27% 25 or older, 1% Native American, 2% Hispanic, 15% black, 13% Asian or Pacific Islander. *Retention:* 83% of 1995 full-time freshmen returned. *Graduation:* 17% graduate in 4 years, 37% in 5 years, 44% in 6 years. *Areas of study chosen:* 18% computer and information sciences, 13% social sciences, 12% biological and life sciences, 9% psychology, 8% fine arts, 4% engineering and applied sciences, 4% English language/literature/letters, 3% health professions and related sciences, 2% interdisciplinary studies, 2% mathematics, 2% physical sciences, 1% area and ethnic studies, 1% foreign language and literature, 1% performing arts, 1% premed. *Most popular recent majors:* psychology, computer information systems.

First-Year Class: 1,023 total; 4,536 applied, 61% were accepted, 37% of whom enrolled. 26% from top 10% of their high school class, 57% from top quarter, 87% from top half. 3 National Merit Scholars.

Graduation Requirements: 120 credit hours; 3 math/science courses; intermediate level competence in a foreign language; computer course for chemistry, health science, math, physics majors; internship (some majors); senior project (some majors).

Computers on Campus: 400 computers available on campus for general student use. A campus-wide network can be accessed from student residence rooms and from off-campus. Students can contact faculty members and/or advisers through e-mail. Computers for student use in computer center, computer labs, learning resource center, classrooms, library, student center, dorms, student rooms, academic buildings provide access to the Internet/World Wide Web, on- and off-campus e-mail addresses. Staffed computer lab on campus (open 24 hours a day).

EXPENSES AND FINANCIAL AID

Expenses for 1997–98: *Application fee:* $25. State resident tuition: $3740 full-time, $158 per credit hour part-time. Nonresident tuition: $8192 full-time, $351 per credit hour part-time. Part-time mandatory fees: $36 per credit hour. Full-time mandatory fees: $830. College room and board: $4992. College room only: $2902.

Undergraduate Financial Aid: Of all full-time undergraduates enrolled in fall 1996, 84% of those who applied for aid were judged to have need according to Federal Methodology, of whom 74% were aided. On average, 75% of need was met. *Financial aid deadline (priority):* 3/1. *Financial aid forms:* FAFSA required.

LD Services Contact: Ms. Cynthia M. Hill, Assistant Vice Provost, University of Maryland, Baltimore County, Math/Psychology Building, Room 211, Baltimore, MD 21250, 410-455-2459. Fax: 410-455-1028. Email: chill@umbc.edu.

UNIVERSITY OF MARYLAND, COLLEGE PARK

College Park, Maryland

LEARNING DISABILITIES SERVICES INFORMATION

Disability Support Service/Learning Assistance Service began offering services in 1982. Currently the program serves 350 undergraduates with LD. Services are also available to graduate students. Students diagnosed with ADD/ADHD are eligible for the same services available to students with LD, as well as support group, peer mentoring.

Staff: 3 full-time, 3 part-time staff members, including director, coordinator, counselor, graduate students. Services provided by counselors, graduate assistant.

Special Fees: No special fees are charged for services to students with LD.

Applications and admissions: *Required:* high school transcript, grade point average, class rank, courses completed; *recommended:* high school extracurricular activities, untimed or extended time SAT I or ACT, personal interview, autobiographical statement, letters of recommendation, psychoeducational report completed within 3 years. Students may begin taking classes any term. *Application deadline:* continuous.

PROGRAM AND SERVICE COMPONENTS

Special preparation or orientation: Optional orientation offered before classes begin.

Diagnostic testing: Reading, math, spelling, study skills, foreign language.

Academic advising: Provided by academic advisers. Most students with LD take 12 to 15 semester hours each term; 9 semester hours required to maintain full-time status; 12 semester hours required to be eligible for financial aid.

Counseling services: Individual counseling, small-group counseling, career counseling, self-advocacy training.

Basic skills remediation: Offered one-on-one by regular teachers; computer-aided instruction also offered. Available in reading, math, spelling, written language, study skills, time management.

Auxiliary aids: Taped textbooks, tape recorders, typewriters, word-processors with spell-check, personal computers, talking computers, optical character readers.

Auxiliary services: Alternative test arrangements, notetakers, priority registration, advocacy.

GENERAL COLLEGE INFORMATION

State-supported, coed. Part of University of Maryland System. Awards bachelor's, master's, doctoral degrees. Founded 1856. *Setting:* 3,773-acre suburban campus with easy access to Baltimore and Washington, DC. *Endowment:* $116 million. *Research spending 1995–96:* $148.6 million. *Educational spending 1995–96:* $7062 per undergrad. *Total enrollment:* 31,471. *Faculty:* 1,849 (1,496 full-time, 94% with terminal degrees, 353 part-time).

Enrollment Profile: 23,758 students from 52 states and territories, 129 other countries. 48% women, 52% men, 12% part-time, 74% state residents, 33% live on campus, 10% transferred in, 3% international, 16% 25 or older, 1% Native American, 5% Hispanic, 14% black, 14% Asian or Pacific Islander. *Retention:* 87% of 1995 full-time freshmen returned. *Graduation:* 31% graduate in 4 years, 55% in 5 years, 61% in 6 years. *Areas of study chosen:* 15% business management and administrative services, 15% liberal arts/general studies, 12% engineering and applied sciences, 12% social sciences, 10% biological and life sciences, 6% education, 5% computer and information sciences, 4% psychology, 3% agriculture, 3% communications and journalism, 3% English language/literature/letters, 3% health professions and related sciences, 2% performing arts, 1% architecture, 1% area and ethnic studies, 1% fine arts, 1% foreign language and literature, 1% mathematics, 1% physical sciences, 1% vocational and home economics. *Most popular recent majors:* criminal justice, psychology, political science/government.

First-Year Class: 3,638 total; 17,118 applied, 61% were accepted, 35% of whom enrolled. 26% from top 10% of their high school class, 61% from top quarter, 92% from top half. 28 National Merit Scholars.

Graduation Requirements: 120 semester hours; 1 course each in math and lab science; computer course for accounting, finance, education majors; senior project for honors program students and some majors.

Computers on Campus: 3,470 computers available on campus for general student use. Computer purchase/lease plans available. A computer is recommended for some students. A campus-wide network can be accessed from student residence rooms and from off-campus. Students can contact faculty members and/or advisers through e-mail. Computers for student use in computer center, computer labs, library, dorms, academic buildings provide access to the Internet/World Wide Web, on- and off-campus e-mail addresses. Staffed computer lab on campus (open 24 hours a day) provides training in use of computers, software. *Academic computing expenditure 1995–96:* $9 million.

EXPENSES AND FINANCIAL AID

Expenses for 1997–98: *Application fee:* $45. State resident tuition: $3744 full-time, $170 per semester hour part-time. Nonresident tuition: $9873 full-time, $424 per semester hour part-time. Part-time mandatory fees: $156 per semester. Full-time mandatory fees: $716. College room and board: $5807. College room only: $3358.

Undergraduate Financial Aid: *Financial aid deadline (priority):* 2/15. *Financial aid forms:* FAFSA required.

LD Services Contact: Ms. Peggy Hayeslip, Learning Disabilities Coordinator, University of Maryland, College Park, 2201 A Shoemaker, College Park, MD 20742, 301-314-9969. Fax: 301-314-9011. Email: mh@umail.umd.edu.

UNIVERSITY OF MIAMI

Coral Gables, Florida

LEARNING DISABILITIES SERVICES INFORMATION

Office of Disability Services currently serves 92 undergraduates with LD. Services are also available to graduate students. Students diagnosed with ADD/ADHD are eligible for the same services available to students with LD, as well as quiet testing location, referrals for ADD coaching.
Staff: 2 full-time, 2 part-time staff members, including coordinator, Staff Associate. Services provided by tutors, counselors, diagnostic specialists.
Special Fees: No special fees are charged for services to students with LD.
Applications and admissions: *Required:* high school transcript, untimed SAT I or ACT, essay; *recommended:* high school grade point average, class rank, courses completed, extracurricular activities, extended time SAT I or ACT, personal interview, autobiographical statement, letters of recommendation. Students may begin taking classes any term. *Application deadline:* 3/1 (fall term), 10/30 (spring term).
Special policies: The college has written policies regarding grade forgiveness.

PROGRAM AND SERVICE COMPONENTS

Special preparation or orientation: Optional orientation offered before classes begin.
Academic advising: Provided by academic advisers. Students with LD may take up to as many credits as an individual can handle each term; most take 9 to 15 credits; 9 credits required to maintain full-time status; 12 credits (fewer with special permission) required to be eligible for financial aid.
Auxiliary aids: Taped textbooks, tape recorders, calculators, word-processors with spell-check, personal computers, talking computers, optical character readers.
Auxiliary services: Alternative test arrangements, notetakers, priority registration, advocates; other arrangements as needed.

GENERAL COLLEGE INFORMATION

Independent, coed. Awards bachelor's, master's, doctoral, first professional degrees. Founded 1925. *Setting:* 260-acre suburban campus with easy access to Miami. *Endowment:* $310 million. *Research spending 1995–96:* $87.5 million. *Educational spending 1995–96:* $13,435 per undergrad. *Total enrollment:* 13,677. *Faculty:* 2,370 (1,892 full-time, 97% with terminal degrees, 478 part-time); student–undergrad faculty ratio is 13:1.
Enrollment Profile: 8,377 students from 51 states and territories, 89 other countries. 53% women, 47% men, 12% part-time, 58% state residents, 36% live on campus, 10% international, 14% 25 or older, 0% Native American, 28% Hispanic, 11% black, 5% Asian or Pacific Islander. *Retention:* 80% of 1995 full-time freshmen returned. *Graduation:* 42% graduate in 4 years, 55% in 5 years, 58% in 6 years. *Areas of study chosen:* 18% business management and administrative services, 11% biological and life sciences, 11% liberal arts/general studies, 11% performing arts, 9% engineering and applied sciences, 8% health professions and related sciences, 7% communications and journalism, 7% social sciences, 6% psychology, 3% architecture, 2% computer and information sciences, 2% education, 2% English language/literature/letters, 2% physical sciences, 1% prelaw. *Most popular recent majors:* psychology, biology/biological sciences, nursing.
First-Year Class: 1,708 total; 10,112 applied, 60% were accepted, 28% of whom enrolled. 42% from top 10% of their high school class, 71% from top quarter, 93% from top half. 18 National Merit Scholars.
Graduation Requirements: 120 credits; math/science requirements vary according to program; computer course for business, engineering majors; internship (some majors); senior project (some majors).
Computers on Campus: 2,000 computers available on campus for general student use. Computer purchase/lease plans available. A campus-wide network can be accessed from student residence rooms and from off-campus. Students can contact faculty members and/or advisers through e-mail. Computers for student use in computer center, computer labs, research center, learning resource center, classrooms, library, student center, dorms, departmental labs provide access to the Internet/World Wide Web, on- and off-campus e-mail addresses. Staffed computer lab on campus provides training in use of computers, software.

EXPENSES AND FINANCIAL AID

Estimated Expenses for 1997–98: *Application fee:* $35. Comprehensive fee of $26,865 includes full-time tuition ($19,140), mandatory fees ($373), and college room and board ($7352). College room only: $4194. Part-time tuition: $779 per credit.
Undergraduate Financial Aid: 64% of all full-time undergraduates enrolled in fall 1996 applied for aid; of these, 94% were judged to have need according to Federal Methodology, of whom 98% were aided. On average, 90% of need was met. *Financial aid deadline (priority):* 2/15. *Financial aid forms:* FAFSA required; CSS Financial Aid PROFILE acceptable. State form required for some.
LD Services Contact: Ms. Jennifer Lenoir, Staff Associate, Office of Disability Services, University of Miami, PO Box 248106 (Panhellenic 108), Coral Gables, FL 33124, 305-284-6434. Fax: 305-284-1999.

UNIVERSITY OF MICHIGAN–DEARBORN

Dearborn, Michigan

LEARNING DISABILITIES SERVICES INFORMATION

Counseling and Support Services currently serves 72 undergraduates with LD. Services are also available to graduate students. Students diagnosed with ADD/ADHD are eligible for the same services available to students with LD.
Staff: 3 full-time, 2 part-time staff members, including director. Services provided by tutors, counselors, mentor coordinator, special needs assistant.
Special Fees: $75 for diagnostic testing.
Applications and admissions: *Required:* high school transcript, grade point average, untimed SAT I or ACT, psychoeducational report completed within 5 years; *recommended:* extended time SAT I or ACT, personal interview. Students may begin taking classes any term. *Application deadline:* continuous.

PROGRAM AND SERVICE COMPONENTS

Diagnostic testing: Intelligence, reading, math, spelling.
Academic advising: Provided by academic advisers. Students with LD may take up to 18 credit hours each term; most take 8 to 12 credit hours; 12 credit hours required to maintain full-time status and be eligible for financial aid.
Counseling services: Individual counseling, career counseling, self-advocacy training.
Basic skills remediation: Offered in class-size groups by tutors. Available in reading, math, learning strategies, study skills, time management.
Subject-area tutoring: Offered in class-size groups by peer tutors, professional tutors. Available in all subjects.
Special courses: College survival skills, composition, learning strategies, time management, math, study skills, career planning. Some offered for credit; some enter into overall grade point average.
Auxiliary aids: Taped textbooks, tape recorders, word-processors with spell-check, talking computers, optical character readers.
Auxiliary services: Alternative test arrangements, notetakers, priority registration, advocacy.

GENERAL COLLEGE INFORMATION

State-supported, comprehensive, coed. Part of University of Michigan System. Awards bachelor's, master's degrees. Founded 1959. *Setting:* 210-acre suburban campus with easy access to Detroit. *Research spending 1995–96:* $1.4 million. *Total enrollment:* 8,324. *Undergraduate faculty:* 383 (219 full-time, 84% with terminal degrees, 164 part-time); student–undergrad faculty ratio is 21:1.
Enrollment Profile: 6,744 students from 7 states and territories. 54% women, 46% men, 44% part-time, 99% state residents, 53% transferred in, 31% 25 or older, 1% Native American, 2% Hispanic, 7% black, 4% Asian or Pacific Islander. *Areas of study chosen:* 24% social sciences, 16% engineering and applied sciences, 6% biological and life sciences, 6% education, 2% library and information studies, 2% physical sciences, 1% performing arts. *Most popular recent majors:* mechanical engineering, electrical engineering, psychology.
First-Year Class: 792 total; 1,856 applied, 77% were accepted, 55% of whom enrolled.
Graduation Requirements: 120 credit hours; 1 math course or the equivalent; 1 lab science course; computer course for business administration, engineering majors.

University of Michigan Dearborn (continued)

Computers on Campus: 350 computers available on campus for general student use. Computer purchase/lease plans available. A campus-wide network can be accessed from off-campus. Students can contact faculty members and/or advisers through e-mail. Computers for student use in computer center, computer labs, engineering and writing labs. Staffed computer lab on campus provides training in use of computers, software. *Academic computing expenditure 1995–96:* $769,929.

EXPENSES AND FINANCIAL AID

Expenses for 1996–97: *Application fee:* $30. Part-time tuition per credit hour ranges from $145 to $148 for state residents, $427 to $435 for nonresidents. Part-time mandatory fees per semester range from $35 to $470. Full-time tuition ranges from $3820 to $3892 for state residents, $10,450 to $10,688 for nonresidents, according to class level. Fees vary according to program and class level. Full-time mandatory fees range from $220 to $1180.

Undergraduate Financial Aid: Of all full-time undergraduates enrolled in fall 1996, 100% of those judged to have need according to Federal Methodology were aided. On average, 80% of need was met. *Financial aid deadline (priority):* 4/1. *Financial aid forms:* FAFSA required; CSS Financial Aid PROFILE, institutional form acceptable.

LD Services Contact: Mr. Dennis Underwood, Coordinator, Disability Resource Services, University of Michigan–Dearborn, 4901 Evergreen Road, Dearborn, MI 48128-1491, 313-593-5430. Fax: 313-593-5604.

UNIVERSITY OF MINNESOTA, DULUTH

Duluth, Minnesota

LEARNING DISABILITIES SERVICES INFORMATION

Access Center/Learning Disabilities Program began offering services in 1980. Currently the program serves 121 undergraduates with LD. Services are also available to graduate students. Students diagnosed with ADD/ADHD are eligible for the same services available to students with LD, as well as support group.

Staff: 2 full-time staff members, including director, coordinator. Services provided by tutors, diagnostic specialists.

Special Fees: No special fees are charged for services to students with LD.

Applications and admissions: *Required:* high school transcript, class rank, courses completed, untimed ACT, psychoeducational report completed within 3 years; *recommended:* high school extracurricular activities, IEP (Individualized Education Program), extended time ACT, personal interview, letters of recommendation. Students may begin taking classes any term. *Application deadline:* 2/1 (fall term), 1/15 (spring term).

Special policies: The college has written policies regarding grade forgiveness.

PROGRAM AND SERVICE COMPONENTS

Diagnostic testing: Intelligence, reading, math, spelling, spoken language, written language, study skills, speech, hearing, cognition, academic skills (Woodcock-Johnson).

Academic advising: Provided by unit staff members, academic advisers. Students with LD may take up to 20 credits each term; most take 12 credits; 12 credits required to maintain full-time status and be eligible for financial aid.

Counseling services: Individual counseling, career counseling.

Basic skills remediation: Offered in class-size groups by regular teachers. Available in math, written language, study skills.

Subject-area tutoring: Offered one-on-one by peer tutors. Available in most subjects.

Auxiliary aids: Taped textbooks, tape recorders, word-processors with spell-check, personal computers, talking computers, optical character readers.

Auxiliary services: Alternative test arrangements, notetakers, priority registration.

Campus support group: A special student organization is available to students with LD.

GENERAL COLLEGE INFORMATION

State-supported, comprehensive, coed. Part of University of Minnesota System. Awards bachelor's, master's degrees. Founded 1947. *Setting:* 250-acre suburban campus. *Endowment:* $23 million. *Research spending 1995–96:* $9.9 million. *Educational spending 1995–96:* $3891 per undergrad. *Total enrollment:* 7,501. *Faculty:* 400 (330 full-time, 85% with terminal degrees, 70 part-time); student–undergrad faculty ratio is 19:1.

Enrollment Profile: 7,023 students from 31 states and territories, 30 other countries. 48% women, 52% men, 8% part-time, 87% state residents, 37% live on campus, 20% transferred in, 1% international, 11% 25 or older, 1% Native American, 1% Hispanic, 1% black, 2% Asian or Pacific Islander. *Retention:* 77% of 1995 full-time freshmen returned. *Graduation:* 19% graduate in 4 years, 40% in 5 years. *Areas of study chosen:* 17% business management and administrative services, 16% education, 10% social sciences, 9% engineering and applied sciences, 8% biological and life sciences, 5% fine arts, 5% psychology, 4% communications and journalism, 4% premed, 3% computer and information sciences, 3% physical sciences, 2% health professions and related sciences, 2% performing arts, 1% area and ethnic studies, 1% English language/literature/letters, 1% foreign language and literature, 1% interdisciplinary studies, 1% liberal arts/general studies, 1% mathematics, 1% natural resource sciences, 1% philosophy, 1% predentistry, 1% prelaw, 1% prevet, 1% vocational and home economics. *Most popular recent majors:* business administration/commerce/management, criminology, biology/biological sciences.

First-Year Class: 1,794 total; 4,444 applied, 85% were accepted, 48% of whom enrolled. 16% from top 10% of their high school class, 46% from top quarter, 85% from top half. 4 National Merit Scholars, 29 valedictorians.

Graduation Requirements: 180 credits; 2 science courses; computer course for business, accounting, science majors; internship (some majors); senior project (some majors).

Computers on Campus: 212 computers available on campus for general student use. Computer purchase/lease plans available. A campus-wide network can be accessed from student residence rooms and from off-campus. Students can contact faculty members and/or advisers through e-mail. Computers for student use in computer center, learning resource center, library, student center, dorms provide access to the Internet/World Wide Web, on- and off-campus e-mail addresses. Staffed computer lab on campus provides training in use of computers, software.

EXPENSES AND FINANCIAL AID

Expenses for 1996–97: *Application fee:* $25. State resident tuition: $3850 full-time, $76.45 per credit part-time. Nonresident tuition: $11,004 full-time, $225.50 per credit part-time. Part-time mandatory fees per quarter (6 to 11 credits): $112.30. Full-time mandatory fees: $337. College room and board: $3774.

Undergraduate Financial Aid: Of all full-time undergraduates enrolled in fall 1996, 82% of those who applied for aid were judged to have need according to Federal Methodology, of whom 99% were aided. On average, 96% of need was met. *Financial aid deadline:* continuous. *Financial aid forms:* FAFSA required.

LD Services Contact: Ms. Judy Bromen, Program Coordinator, University of Minnesota, Duluth, 10 University Drive, Duluth, MN 55812-2496, 218-726-7965. Fax: 218-726-6244.

THE UNIVERSITY OF MONTANA–MISSOULA

Missoula, Montana

LEARNING DISABILITIES SERVICES INFORMATION

Disability Services for Students (DSS) began offering services in 1991. Currently the program serves 150 undergraduates with LD. Services are also available to graduate students. Students diagnosed with ADD/ADHD are eligible for the same services available to students with LD.

Staff: 1 full-time staff member (director). Services provided by LD specialist.

Special Fees: No special fees are charged for services to students with LD.

Applications and admissions: *Required:* high school transcript, grade point average, courses completed, untimed SAT I or ACT, psychoeducational report completed within 3 years; *recommended:* high school class rank, extracurricular activities, extended time SAT I or ACT, personal interview, autobiographical statement, letters of recommendation. Students may begin taking classes in fall only. *Application deadline:* continuous.

Special policies: The college has written policies regarding substitutions and waivers of graduation and degree requirements.

PROGRAM AND SERVICE COMPONENTS

Academic advising: Provided by unit staff members, academic advisers. Most students with LD take 3 to 18 credits each term; 12 credits required to maintain full-time status; 12 credits (fewer in special cases) required to be eligible for financial aid.

Counseling services: Individual counseling, small-group counseling, career counseling, self-advocacy training.

Subject-area tutoring: Offered one-on-one and in small groups by peer tutors, tutors assigned by DSS. Available in all subjects.

Special courses: Learning strategies, study skills. All offered for credit; all enter into overall grade point average.

Auxiliary aids: Taped textbooks, tape recorders, calculators, word-processors with spell-check, Arkenstone Reader, word processor with voice synthesizers.

Auxiliary services: Alternative test arrangements, notetakers, priority registration, advocacy.

Campus support group: A special student organization is available to students with LD.

GENERAL COLLEGE INFORMATION

State-supported, coed. Part of Montana University System. Awards associate, bachelor's, master's, doctoral, first professional degrees. Founded 1893. *Setting:* 220-acre urban campus. *Research spending 1995–96:* $13.9 million. *Total enrollment:* 11,886. *Faculty:* 635 (481 full-time, 85% with terminal degrees, 154 part-time); student–undergrad faculty ratio is 19:1.

Enrollment Profile: 9,853 students from 55 states and territories, 67 other countries. 51% women, 49% men, 18% part-time, 65% state residents, 30% live on campus, 9% transferred in, 3% international, 24% 25 or older, 3% Native American, 1% Hispanic, 1% black, 1% Asian or Pacific Islander. *Retention:* 66% of 1995 full-time freshmen returned. *Graduation:* 32% graduate in 4 years, 57% in 5 years, 66% in 6 years. *Areas of study chosen:* 12% business management and administrative services, 12% social sciences, 9% health professions and related sciences, 8% biological and life sciences, 7% vocational and home economics, 6% natural resource sciences, 5% communications and journalism, 5% education, 4% English language/literature/letters, 4% fine arts, 4% foreign language and literature, 4% psychology, 3% performing arts, 2% computer and information sciences, 2% interdisciplinary studies, 2% liberal arts/general studies, 2% mathematics, 2% physical sciences, 2% prelaw, 2% premed, 1% philosophy, 1% predentistry, 1% prevet. *Most popular recent majors:* business administration/commerce/management, education, forestry.

First-Year Class: 2,009 total; 3,784 applied, 83% were accepted, 57% of whom enrolled. 16% from top 10% of their high school class, 33% from top quarter, 98% from top half. 15 National Merit Scholars, 51 valedictorians.

Graduation Requirements: 65 credits for associate, 130 credits for bachelor's; 1 math course; 3 natural science courses including 1 lab science; 1 year of a foreign language; computer course for business administration, geology, economics, chemistry, geography, math, physics, psychology majors; internship (some majors); senior project for honors program students and some majors.

Computers on Campus: 375 computers available on campus for general student use. Computer purchase/lease plans available. A computer is strongly recommended for all students. A campus-wide network can be accessed from student residence rooms and from off-campus. Students can contact faculty members and/or advisers through e-mail. Computers for student use in computer center, computer labs, learning resource center, classrooms, library, student center, dorms provide access to the Internet/World Wide Web, on- and off-campus e-mail addresses. Staffed computer lab on campus provides training in use of computers, software. *Academic computing expenditure 1995–96:* $3 million.

EXPENSES AND FINANCIAL AID

Expenses for 1996–97: *Application fee:* $30. State resident tuition: $2484 full-time, $119 per credit part-time. Nonresident tuition: $6733 full-time, $296 per credit part-time. College room and board: $3962.

Undergraduate Financial Aid: Of all full-time undergraduates enrolled in fall 1996, 87% of those who applied for aid were judged to have need according to Federal Methodology, of whom 92% were aided. On average, 90% of need was met. *Financial aid deadline (priority):* 3/1. *Financial aid forms:* FAFSA, CSS Financial Aid PROFILE, institutional form required.

LD Services Contact: Ms. Kristie Mudsen, LD Specialist, The University of Montana–Missoula, Corbin 33, Missoula, MT 59812, 406-243-5306. Fax: 406-243-5330. Email: vangen@selway.umt.edu.

UNIVERSITY OF MONTEVALLO

Montevallo, Alabama

LEARNING DISABILITIES SERVICES INFORMATION

Office for Services for Students with Disabilities began offering services in 1988. Currently the program serves 60 undergraduates with LD. Services are also available to graduate students. Students diagnosed with ADD/ADHD are eligible for the same services available to students with LD.

Staff: 1 full-time staff member (coordinator). Services provided by tutors, counselors, notetakers.

Special Fees: No special fees are charged for services to students with LD.

Applications and admissions: *Required:* high school transcript, grade point average, courses completed, extended time ACT; *recommended:* high school class rank. Students may begin taking classes in fall, spring, or summer. *Application deadline:* continuous.

Special policies: The college has written policies regarding grade forgiveness.

PROGRAM AND SERVICE COMPONENTS

Special preparation or orientation: Summer program (required for some) held prior to entering college.

Academic advising: Provided by unit staff members, academic advisers. Students with LD may take up to 18 semester hours (more with Dean's permission) each term; most take 12 semester hours; 12 semester hours required to maintain full-time status and be eligible for financial aid.

Basic skills remediation: Offered one-on-one and in small groups by regular teachers, Services for Students with Disabilities staff. Available in math, learning strategies, study skills, time management.

Subject-area tutoring: Offered one-on-one, in small groups, and in class-size groups by professional teachers, peer tutors. Available in most subjects.

Special courses: Math. None offered for credit; none enter into overall grade point average.

Auxiliary aids: Taped textbooks, tape recorders, calculators, typewriters, word-processors with spell-check, personal computers.

Auxiliary services: Alternative test arrangements, notetakers, priority registration, advocacy.

GENERAL COLLEGE INFORMATION

State-supported, comprehensive, coed. Awards bachelor's, master's degrees. Founded 1896. *Setting:* 106-acre small-town campus with easy access to Birmingham. *Endowment:* $1.9 million. *Research spending 1995–96:* $6642. *Total enrollment:* 3,206. *Faculty:* 202 (137 full-time, 77% with terminal degrees, 65 part-time); student–undergrad faculty ratio is 19:1.

Enrollment Profile: 2,702 students from 21 states and territories, 26 other countries. 68% women, 32% men, 12% part-time, 95% state residents, 36% live on campus, 30% transferred in, 2% international, 12% 25 or older, 1% Native American, 0% Hispanic, 11% black, 0% Asian or Pacific Islander. *Retention:* 71% of 1995 full-time freshmen returned. *Areas of study chosen:* 18% education, 17% liberal arts/general studies, 13% business management and administrative services, 9% social sciences, 6% communications and journalism, 6% fine arts, 6% health professions and related sciences, 5% biological and life sciences, 5% English language/literature/letters, 4% vocational and home economics, 3% mathematics, 3% performing arts, 3% psychology, 1% foreign language and literature, 1% physical sciences. *Most popular recent majors:* elementary education, speech pathology and audiology, communication.

First-Year Class: 505 total; 1,218 applied, 76% were accepted, 55% of whom enrolled. 20% from top 10% of their high school class, 53% from top quarter, 89% from top half. 56 valedictorians.

Graduation Requirements: 130 semester hours; 3 semester hours of math; 7 semester hours of science; computer course; internship (some majors); senior project (some majors).

Computers on Campus: 185 computers available on campus for general student use. A computer is recommended for all students. A campus-wide network can be accessed from student residence rooms and from off-campus. Students can contact faculty members and/or advisers through e-mail. Computers for student use in computer center, computer labs, classrooms, library, dorms provide access to the Internet/World Wide Web, on- and off-campus e-mail addresses. Staffed computer lab on campus. *Academic computing expenditure 1995–96:* $697,411.

University of Montevallo (continued)

EXPENSES AND FINANCIAL AID

Expenses for 1997–98: *Application fee:* $25. State resident tuition: $3040 full-time, $95 per semester hour part-time. Nonresident tuition: $6080 full-time, $190 per semester hour part-time. Part-time mandatory fees: $35 per semester. Full-time mandatory fees: $140. College room and board: $3116 (minimum).
Undergraduate Financial Aid: Of all full-time undergraduates enrolled in fall 1996, 57% of those who applied for aid were judged to have need according to Federal Methodology, of whom 89% were aided. On average, 87% of need was met. *Financial aid deadline (priority):* 4/1. *Financial aid forms:* FAFSA, institutional form required for some.
LD Services Contact: Ms. Deborah McCune, Coordinator of Services for Students with Disabilities, University of Montevallo, Station 6250, Montevallo, AL 35115, 205-665-6250. Fax: 205-665-6255. Email: mccuned@um.montevallo.edu.

UNIVERSITY OF NEW HAVEN

West Haven, Connecticut

LEARNING DISABILITIES SERVICES INFORMATION

Office for Students with Disabilities began offering services in 1986. Currently the program serves 59 undergraduates with LD. Services are also available to graduate students. Students diagnosed with ADD/ADHD are eligible for the same services available to students with LD, as well as distraction-free testing environment, assistance with organizational skills.
Staff: 1 full-time, 1 part-time staff members, including director, learning assistant. Services provided by tutors, counselors.
Special Fees: No special fees are charged for services to students with LD.
Applications and admissions: *Required:* high school transcript, grade point average, class rank, courses completed, extracurricular activities, untimed or extended time SAT I, autobiographical statement, letters of recommendation; *recommended:* high school IEP (Individualized Education Program). Students may begin taking classes any term. *Application deadline:* continuous.

PROGRAM AND SERVICE COMPONENTS

Academic advising: Provided by unit staff members, academic advisers. Students with LD may take up to 15 credit hours each term; most take 12 to 15 credit hours; 12 credit hours required to maintain full-time status; 9 credit hours required to be eligible for financial aid.
Counseling services: Individual counseling, career counseling.
Basic skills remediation: Offered in class-size groups by regular teachers. Available in reading, math, spelling, spoken language, written language, learning strategies, study skills, time management, speech.
Subject-area tutoring: Offered one-on-one by professional teachers, peer tutors. Available in most subjects.
Auxiliary aids: Taped textbooks, tape recorders, word-processors with spell-check, talking computers.
Auxiliary services: Alternative test arrangements, notetakers, advocacy.

GENERAL COLLEGE INFORMATION

Independent, comprehensive, coed. Awards associate, bachelor's, master's, doctoral degrees. Founded 1920. *Setting:* 78-acre suburban campus with easy access to Hartford. *Endowment:* $2.4 million. *Educational spending 1995–96:* $2993 per undergrad. *Total enrollment:* 5,438. *Faculty:* 546 (156 full-time, 90% with terminal degrees, 390 part-time); student–undergrad faculty ratio is 11:1.
Enrollment Profile: 3,004 students from 34 states and territories, 24 other countries. 37% women, 63% men, 47% part-time, 74% state residents, 26% transferred in, 5% international, 1% Native American, 4% Hispanic, 8% black, 2% Asian or Pacific Islander. *Retention:* 67% of 1995 full-time freshmen returned. *Graduation:* 18% graduate in 4 years, 30% in 5 years, 33% in 6 years. *Areas of study chosen:* 16% business management and administrative services, 16% engineering and applied sciences, 4% computer and information sciences, 3% biological and life sciences, 3% liberal arts/general studies, 2% communications and journalism, 2% fine arts, 2% psychology, 1% English language/literature/letters, 1% mathematics, 1% physical sciences. *Most popular recent majors:* business administration/commerce/management, mechanical engineering, criminal justice.
First-Year Class: 411 total. Of the students who applied, 84% were accepted, 25% of whom enrolled. 6% from top 10% of their high school class, 22% from top quarter, 56% from top half.
Graduation Requirements: 60 credit hours for associate, 120 credit hours for bachelor's; 1 course each in math and lab science; computer course; senior project for honors program students.
Computers on Campus: 200 computers available on campus for general student use. A computer is recommended for all students. A campus-wide network can be accessed from student residence rooms and from off-campus. Students can contact faculty members and/or advisers through e-mail. Computers for student use in computer center, computer labs, learning resource center, library, academic/administrative buildings provide access to the Internet/World Wide Web. Staffed computer lab on campus (open 24 hours a day) provides training in use of computers, software. *Academic computing expenditure 1995–96:* $373,259.

EXPENSES AND FINANCIAL AID

Expenses for 1997–98: *Application fee:* $25. Comprehensive fee of $18,800 includes full-time tuition ($12,800), mandatory fees ($300), and college room and board ($5700 minimum). College room only: $3600. Part-time tuition: $427 per credit hour. Part-time mandatory fees: $8 per course. Part-time tuition for evening classes: $245 per credit hour. Mandatory fee for engineering program: $75 per course.
Undergraduate Financial Aid: 71% of all full-time undergraduates enrolled in fall 1996 applied for aid. *Financial aid deadline (priority):* 3/15. *Financial aid forms:* FAFSA, CSS Financial Aid PROFILE, institutional form required.
LD Services Contact: Ms. Linda Copney-Okeke, Director, Disability Services and Resources, University of New Haven, 300 Orange Avenue, West Haven, CT 06516-1916, 203-932-7331. Fax: 203-932-7178.

UNIVERSITY OF NORTH CAROLINA AT CHARLOTTE

Charlotte, North Carolina

LEARNING DISABILITIES SERVICES INFORMATION

Disability Services began offering services in 1986. Currently the program serves 104 undergraduates with LD. Services are also available to graduate students. Students diagnosed with ADD/ADHD are eligible for the same services available to students with LD.
Staff: 4 full-time staff members, including director. Services provided by counselors, program assistant.
Special Fees: No special fees are charged for services to students with LD.
Applications and admissions: *Required:* high school transcript, grade point average, courses completed, untimed SAT I or ACT, letters of recommendation. Students may begin taking classes any term. *Application deadline:* 7/1 (fall term), 11/15 (spring term).
Special policies: The college has written policies regarding substitutions and waivers of graduation and degree requirements.

PROGRAM AND SERVICE COMPONENTS

Academic advising: Provided by unit staff members, academic advisers. Most students with LD take 9 to 12 semester hours each term; 12 semester hours required to maintain full-time status; 6 semester hours required to be eligible for financial aid.
Counseling services: Individual counseling, career counseling.
Basic skills remediation: Offered one-on-one by Learning Assistance Center staff, Writing Resource Center staff, tutors. Available in math, written language, learning strategies, study skills, time management.
Subject-area tutoring: Offered one-on-one and in small groups by students recommended by University tutorial services. Available in most subjects.
Special courses: Learning strategies, study skills. None offered for credit; none enter into overall grade point average.
Auxiliary aids: Taped textbooks, tape recorders, calculators, typewriters, word-processors with spell-check, optical character readers, FM equipment, Visualtek machine, Franklin Speller.
Auxiliary services: Alternative test arrangements, notetakers, priority registration, advocacy.

GENERAL COLLEGE INFORMATION

State-supported, coed. Part of University of North Carolina System. Awards bachelor's, master's, doctoral degrees. Founded 1946. *Setting:* 1,000-acre urban campus. *Endowment:* $52.3 million. *Research spending 1995–96:*

$5.5 million. *Total enrollment:* 15,795. *Faculty:* 911 (636 full-time, 90% with terminal degrees, 275 part-time); student–undergrad faculty ratio is 16:1.

Enrollment Profile: 13,147 students from 47 states and territories, 64 other countries. 52% women, 48% men, 26% part-time, 88% state residents, 27% live on campus, 11% transferred in, 2% international, 28% 25 or older, 1% Native American, 1% Hispanic, 16% black, 4% Asian or Pacific Islander. *Retention:* 79% of 1995 full-time freshmen returned. *Graduation:* 23% graduate in 4 years, 46% in 5 years, 54% in 6 years. *Areas of study chosen:* 18% business management and administrative services, 13% social sciences, 9% education, 8% engineering and applied sciences, 6% psychology, 5% biological and life sciences, 5% health professions and related sciences, 4% English language/literature/letters, 3% computer and information sciences, 3% fine arts, 2% architecture, 2% physical sciences, 1% foreign language and literature, 1% mathematics, 1% performing arts, 1% philosophy. *Most popular recent majors:* psychology, English, criminal justice.

First-Year Class: 1,719 total; 6,053 applied, 72% were accepted, 39% of whom enrolled. 16% from top 10% of their high school class, 51% from top quarter, 96% from top half.

Graduation Requirements: 120 semester hours; 8 semester hours of science; 2 semesters of a foreign language or proven proficiency; computer course for accounting, business administration, economics, engineering, math, geography, physics majors; senior project for honors program students and some majors.

Computers on Campus: 700 computers available on campus for general student use. A campus-wide network can be accessed from student residence rooms and from off-campus. Students can contact faculty members and/or advisers through e-mail. Computers for student use in computer center, computer labs, research center, learning resource center, library, student center, dorms, student labs provide access to the Internet/World Wide Web, on- and off-campus e-mail addresses. Staffed computer lab on campus (open 24 hours a day) provides training in use of computers, software. *Academic computing expenditure 1995–96:* $5 million.

EXPENSES AND FINANCIAL AID

Estimated Expenses for 1997–98: *Application fee:* $35. State resident tuition: $874 full-time. Nonresident tuition: $8028 full-time. Part-time tuition per semester ranges from $109 to $328 for state residents, $1004 to $3011 for nonresidents. Part-time mandatory fees per semester range from $106.50 to $422. Full-time mandatory fees: $844. College room and board: $3446. College room only: $1796 (minimum).

Undergraduate Financial Aid: Of all full-time undergraduates enrolled in fall 1996, 86% of those who applied for aid were judged to have need according to Federal Methodology, of whom 95% were aided. On average, 76% of need was met. *Financial aid deadline (priority):* 4/1. *Financial aid forms:* FAFSA required.

LD Services Contact: Ms. Jane Rochester, Director, University of North Carolina at Charlotte, 230 Fretwell, Charlotte, NC 28223, 704-547-4355. Fax: 704-547-3226.

UNIVERSITY OF NORTH CAROLINA AT GREENSBORO

Greensboro, North Carolina

LEARNING DISABILITIES SERVICES INFORMATION

Disabled Student Services began offering services in 1984. Currently the program serves 200 undergraduates with LD. Services are also available to graduate students. Students diagnosed with ADD/ADHD are eligible for the same services available to students with LD, as well as support group.

Staff: 4 full-time staff members, including director, assistant directors, academic assistants. Services provided by tutors, counselors, diagnostic specialists.

Special Fees: No special fees are charged for services to students with LD.

Applications and admissions: *Required:* high school transcript, courses completed, untimed SAT I or ACT; *recommended:* psychoeducational report completed within 3 years. Students may begin taking classes any term. *Application deadline:* 8/1 (fall term), 12/10 (spring term).

Special policies: The college has written policies regarding substitutions and waivers of admissions, graduation, and degree requirements.

PROGRAM AND SERVICE COMPONENTS

Special preparation or orientation: Optional orientation offered before registration.

Diagnostic testing: Intelligence, reading, math, spelling, handwriting, spoken language, written language, motor abilities, perceptual skills, study skills, personality, social skills, psychoneurology, speech, hearing, various other areas as appropriate.

Academic advising: Provided by academic advisers. Students with LD may take up to 18 semester hours each term; most take 12 to 15 semester hours; 12 semester hours required to maintain full-time status; 6 semester hours required to be eligible for financial aid.

Counseling services: Individual counseling, small-group counseling, career counseling.

Subject-area tutoring: Offered one-on-one and in small groups by peer tutors, graduate assistants. Available in most subjects.

Special courses: Learning strategies. All offered for credit; all enter into overall grade point average.

Auxiliary aids: Taped textbooks, tape recorders, calculators, typewriters, word-processors with spell-check, optical character readers.

Auxiliary services: Alternative test arrangements, notetakers, priority registration, advocacy, computer training.

GENERAL COLLEGE INFORMATION

State-supported, coed. Part of University of North Carolina System. Awards bachelor's, master's, doctoral degrees. Founded 1891. *Setting:* 190-acre urban campus. *Endowment:* $60.1 million. *Research spending 1995–96:* $11.3 million. *Total enrollment:* 12,323. *Faculty:* 718 (573 full-time, 94% with terminal degrees, 145 part-time); student–undergrad faculty ratio is 15:1.

Enrollment Profile: 9,694 students from 41 states and territories, 27 other countries. 66% women, 34% men, 19% part-time, 90% state residents, 33% live on campus, 10% transferred in, 1% international, 27% 25 or older, 1% Native American, 1% Hispanic, 15% black, 2% Asian or Pacific Islander. *Retention:* 76% of 1995 full-time freshmen returned. *Areas of study chosen:* 15% business management and administrative services, 8% health professions and related sciences, 7% education, 7% vocational and home economics, 6% biological and life sciences, 6% fine arts, 6% psychology, 6% social sciences, 5% communications and journalism, 4% computer and information sciences, 4% English language/literature/letters, 2% mathematics, 1% foreign language and literature, 1% interdisciplinary studies, 1% physical sciences. *Most popular recent majors:* business administration/commerce/management, nursing, psychology.

First-Year Class: 1,567 total; 5,190 applied, 80% were accepted, 38% of whom enrolled. 13% from top 10% of their high school class, 41% from top quarter, 83% from top half.

Graduation Requirements: 122 semester hours; 2 semesters of math/science including at least 1 semester of math; computer course for business majors; internship (some majors); senior project for honors program students and some majors.

Computers on Campus: 400 computers available on campus for general student use. Computer purchase/lease plans available. A campus-wide network can be accessed from student residence rooms and from off-campus. Students can contact faculty members and/or advisers through e-mail. Computers for student use in computer center, computer labs, research center, learning resource center, classrooms, library, student center, dorms, academic buildings provide access to the Internet/World Wide Web, on- and off-campus e-mail addresses. Staffed computer lab on campus (open 24 hours a day) provides training in use of computers, software.

EXPENSES AND FINANCIAL AID

Estimated Expenses for 1997–98: *Application fee:* $35. State resident tuition: $1006 full-time. Nonresident tuition: $9768 full-time. Part-time tuition per semester ranges from $130 to $390 for state residents, $1220 to $3670 for nonresidents. Part-time mandatory fees per semester range from $38 to $429. Full-time mandatory fees: $1015. College room and board: $3505. College room only: $1715.

Undergraduate Financial Aid: Of all full-time undergraduates enrolled in fall 1996, 81% of those who applied for aid were judged to have need according to Federal Methodology, of whom 96% were aided. On average, 67% of need was met. *Financial aid deadline (priority):* 3/1. *Financial aid forms:* FAFSA required.

LD Services Contact: Dr. Patricia L. Bailey, Director, Disability Services, University of North Carolina at Greensboro, 157 Elliott University Center, Greensboro, NC 27412-5001, 910-334-5440. Fax: 910-334-4412.

UNIVERSITY OF NORTH CAROLINA AT PEMBROKE

Pembroke, North Carolina

LEARNING DISABILITIES SERVICES INFORMATION

ADA Office currently serves 34 undergraduates with LD. Services are also available to graduate students. Students diagnosed with ADD/ADHD are eligible for the same services available to students with LD.

Staff: 1 part-time staff member (coordinator).

Special Fees: No special fees are charged for services to students with LD.

Applications and admissions: *Required:* high school transcript, grade point average, class rank, courses completed, untimed or extended time SAT I. *Application deadline:* 7/15 (fall term), 12/1 (spring term).

PROGRAM AND SERVICE COMPONENTS

Academic advising: Provided by academic advisers. Students with LD may take up to 18 semester hours each term; most take 12 to 18 semester hours; 12 semester hours required to maintain full-time status and be eligible for financial aid.

Counseling services: Individual counseling, career counseling.

Subject-area tutoring: Offered one-on-one and in small groups by peer tutors, professional tutors. Available in all subjects.

Auxiliary aids: Taped textbooks, tape recorders, calculators, typewriters, word-processors with spell-check, personal computers.

Auxiliary services: Alternative test arrangements, notetakers.

GENERAL COLLEGE INFORMATION

State-supported, comprehensive, coed. Part of University of North Carolina System. Awards bachelor's, master's degrees. Founded 1887. *Setting:* 108-acre rural campus. *Endowment:* $2.5 million. *Research spending 1995–96:* $183,075. *Educational spending 1995–96:* $4060 per undergrad. *Total enrollment:* 3,006. *Faculty:* 211 (146 full-time, 77% with terminal degrees, 65 part-time); student–undergrad faculty ratio is 18:1.

Enrollment Profile: 2,690 students from 20 states and territories, 6 other countries. 60% women, 40% men, 20% part-time, 98% state residents, 23% live on campus, 11% transferred in, 1% international, 41% 25 or older, 25% Native American, 1% Hispanic, 14% black, 1% Asian or Pacific Islander. *Retention:* 65% of 1995 full-time freshmen returned. *Most popular recent majors:* education, business administration/commerce/management, sociology.

First-Year Class: 465 total; 831 applied, 91% were accepted, 62% of whom enrolled. 11% from top 10% of their high school class, 33% from top quarter, 65% from top half.

Graduation Requirements: 128 semester hours; 3 semester hours each of math and science; computer course for business administration, math majors.

Computers on Campus: 250 computers available on campus for general student use. A campus-wide network can be accessed from student residence rooms and from off-campus. Students can contact faculty members and/or advisers through e-mail. Computers for student use in computer center, computer labs, library, study lab provide access to the Internet/World Wide Web, on- and off-campus e-mail addresses. Staffed computer lab on campus provides training in use of computers, software. *Academic computing expenditure 1995–96:* $404,555.

EXPENSES AND FINANCIAL AID

Expenses for 1997–98: *Application fee:* $25. State resident tuition: $1510 full-time. Nonresident tuition: $8664 full-time. Part-time tuition per semester ranges from $177 to $582 for state residents, $1072 to $3265 for nonresidents. College room and board: $2910 (minimum).

Undergraduate Financial Aid: 89% of all full-time undergraduates enrolled in fall 1996 applied for aid; of these, 79% were judged to have need according to Federal Methodology, of whom 91% were aided. On average, 77% of need was met. *Financial aid deadline (priority):* 3/15. *Financial aid forms:* FAFSA, institutional form required.

LD Services Contact: Danford Groves, ADA Coordinator, University of North Carolina at Pembroke, PO Box 1510, Pembroke, NC 28372-1510, 910-521-6242. Fax: 910-521-6496.

UNIVERSITY OF NORTH CAROLINA AT WILMINGTON

Wilmington, North Carolina

LEARNING DISABILITIES SERVICES INFORMATION

Disability Services began offering services in 1983. Currently the program serves 100 undergraduates with LD. Services are also available to graduate students. Students diagnosed with ADD/ADHD are eligible for the same services available to students with LD.

Staff: 1 full-time, 1 part-time staff members, including coordinator, program assistant. Services provided by counselors.

Special Fees: No special fees are charged for services to students with LD.

Applications and admissions: *Required:* high school transcript; *recommended:* untimed or extended time SAT I or ACT, psychoeducational report completed within 3 years. Students may begin taking classes in fall or summer. *Application deadline:* 2/1.

Special policies: The college has written policies regarding substitutions and waivers of admissions, graduation, and degree requirements.

PROGRAM AND SERVICE COMPONENTS

Special preparation or orientation: Required orientation held prior to or during the first weeks of classes.

Academic advising: Provided by academic advisers. Students with LD may take up to 18 semester hours each term; most take 12 semester hours; 12 semester hours required to maintain full-time status and be eligible for financial aid.

Counseling services: Individual counseling, small-group counseling, career counseling, emergency intervention.

Subject-area tutoring: Offered one-on-one and in small groups by peer tutors. Available in most subjects.

Auxiliary aids: Taped textbooks, word-processors with spell-check, optical character readers, enlarger.

Auxiliary services: Alternative test arrangements, notetakers, advocacy, readers.

GENERAL COLLEGE INFORMATION

State-supported, comprehensive, coed. Part of University of North Carolina System. Awards bachelor's, master's degrees. Founded 1947. *Setting:* 650-acre urban campus. *Endowment:* $10.8 million. *Research spending 1995–96:* $5.9 million. *Educational spending 1995–96:* $4176 per undergrad. *Total enrollment:* 9,077. *Faculty:* 512 (369 full-time, 90% with terminal degrees, 143 part-time); student–undergrad faculty ratio is 16:1.

Enrollment Profile: 8,584 students from 37 states and territories, 40 other countries. 60% women, 40% men, 16% part-time, 87% state residents, 22% live on campus, 10% transferred in, 1% international, 16% 25 or older, 1% Native American, 1% Hispanic, 6% black, 1% Asian or Pacific Islander. *Retention:* 78% of 1995 full-time freshmen returned. *Graduation:* 29% graduate in 4 years, 52% in 5 years, 57% in 6 years. *Areas of study chosen:* 12% business management and administrative services, 10% education, 10% social sciences, 6% biological and life sciences, 4% English language/literature/letters, 3% communications and journalism, 3% health professions and related sciences, 3% physical sciences, 3% psychology, 2% computer and information sciences, 2% fine arts, 2% interdisciplinary studies, 1% foreign language and literature, 1% mathematics. *Most popular recent majors:* psychology, marine biology, English.

First-Year Class: 1,670 total; 6,906 applied, 63% were accepted, 38% of whom enrolled. 16% from top 10% of their high school class, 58% from top quarter, 90% from top half.

Graduation Requirements: 124 semester hours; 3 semester hours of math; 2 semesters of a foreign language or the equivalent; computer course for earth science, math, environmental science majors.

Computers on Campus: 200 computers available on campus for general student use. Computer purchase/lease plans available. A campus-wide network can be accessed from student residence rooms and from off-campus. Students can contact faculty members and/or advisers through e-mail. Computers for student use in computer labs, library, student center, dorms provide access to the Internet/World Wide Web. Staffed computer lab on campus provides training in use of computers, software. *Academic computing expenditure 1995–96:* $1.9 million.

EXPENSES AND FINANCIAL AID

Expenses for 1996–97: *Application fee:* $35. State resident tuition: $874 full-time. Nonresident tuition: $8028 full-time. Part-time tuition per semester ranges from $109 to $328 for state residents, $1004 to $3011 for nonresidents. Part-time mandatory fees per semester range from $72 to $437. Full-time mandatory fees: $874. College room and board: $3900 (minimum).

Undergraduate Financial Aid: Of all full-time undergraduates enrolled in fall 1996, 79% of those who applied for aid were judged to have need according to Federal Methodology, of whom 84% were aided. On average, 97% of need was met. *Financial aid deadline (priority):* 3/15. *Financial aid forms:* FAFSA, financial aid transcript (for transfers) required; state form acceptable.

LD Services Contact: Dr. Margaret Turner, Coordinator of Disability Services, University of North Carolina at Wilmington, Student Development Center, Wilmington, NC 28403-3201, 910-962-3746.

UNIVERSITY OF NORTH DAKOTA

Grand Forks, North Dakota

LEARNING DISABILITIES SERVICES INFORMATION

Disability Support Services (DSS) currently serves 215 undergraduates with LD. Services are also available to graduate students. Students diagnosed with ADD/ADHD are eligible for the same services available to students with LD, as well as student health referrals for medication on a trial basis, referrals for LD/ADHD assessment, information sheets about ADHD, academic counseling for ADHD issues in higher education.

Staff: 8 full-time, 200 part-time staff members, including director, assistant director. Services provided by remediation specialist, tutors, counselors, diagnostic specialist, notetakers, interpreters, test readers.

Special Fees: No special fees are charged for services to students with LD.

Applications and admissions: *Required:* high school transcript, grade point average, courses completed, IEP (Individualized Education Program), extended time ACT, personal interview, autobiographical statement, psychoeducational report completed within 3 years; *recommended:* high school class rank, extracurricular activities, untimed or extended time SAT I, untimed ACT, letters of recommendation. Students may begin taking classes any term. *Application deadline:* continuous.

Special policies: The college has written policies regarding grade forgiveness; substitutions and waivers of admissions, graduation, and degree requirements.

PROGRAM AND SERVICE COMPONENTS

Academic advising: Provided by unit staff members, academic advisers. Students with LD may take up to 18 credit hours each term; most take 12 to 15 credit hours; 12 credit hours required to maintain full-time status; 12 credit hours (unless waiver is requested and granted) required to be eligible for financial aid.

Counseling services: Individual counseling, career counseling, self-advocacy training.

Subject-area tutoring: Offered one-on-one and in small groups by peer tutors. Available in all subjects.

Special courses: Learning strategies, time management, study skills. Most offered for credit; none enter into overall grade point average.

Auxiliary aids: Taped textbooks, tape recorders, typewriters, word-processors with spell-check, optical character readers.

Auxiliary services: Alternative test arrangements, notetakers, priority registration, advocacy.

Campus support group: A special student organization is available to students with LD.

GENERAL COLLEGE INFORMATION

State-supported, coed. Part of North Dakota University System. Awards bachelor's, master's, doctoral, first professional degrees. Founded 1883. *Setting:* 570-acre small-town campus. *Endowment:* $8.1 million. *Research spending 1995–96:* $28.2 million. *Total enrollment:* 11,300. *Faculty:* 720 (592 full-time, 80% with terminal degrees, 128 part-time); student–undergrad faculty ratio is 15:1.

Enrollment Profile: 9,351 students from 50 states and territories, 55 other countries. 49% women, 51% men, 12% part-time, 56% state residents, 32% live on campus, 7% transferred in, 4% international, 29% 25 or older, 3% Native American, 1% Hispanic, 1% black, 1% Asian or Pacific Islander. *Retention:* 75% of 1995 full-time freshmen returned. *Graduation:* 25% graduate in 4 years, 38% in 5 years, 46% in 6 years. *Areas of study chosen:* 19% engineering and applied sciences, 18% health professions and related sciences, 15% business management and administrative services, 7% education, 6% social sciences, 4% communications and journalism, 4% psychology, 3% biological and life sciences, 3% computer and information sciences, 2% English language/literature/letters, 2% physical sciences, 1% fine arts, 1% foreign language and literature, 1% library and information studies, 1% mathematics, 1% natural resource sciences, 1% performing arts, 1% theology/religion. *Most popular recent majors:* aerospace sciences, accounting, business administration/commerce/management.

First-Year Class: 1,654 total; 2,741 applied, 73% were accepted, 83% of whom enrolled. 23% from top 10% of their high school class, 57% from top quarter, 88% from top half. 3 National Merit Scholars.

Graduation Requirements: 125 credit hours; computer course for aeronautical studies, airway science, engineering majors; internship (some majors); senior project for honors program students and some majors.

Computers on Campus: 3,500 computers available on campus for general student use. Computer purchase/lease plans available. A computer is required for some students. A campus-wide network can be accessed from student residence rooms and from off-campus. Students can contact faculty members and/or advisers through e-mail. Computers for student use in computer center, computer labs, learning resource center, library, student center, dorms, academic buildings provide access to the Internet/World Wide Web, on- and off-campus e-mail addresses. Staffed computer lab on campus provides training in use of computers, software.

EXPENSES AND FINANCIAL AID

Expenses for 1996–97: *Application fee:* $25. State resident tuition: $2528 full-time, $87.92 per credit hour part-time. Nonresident tuition: $6052 full-time, $234.75 per credit hour part-time. Part-time mandatory fees: $13.67 per credit hour. Full-time mandatory fees: $418. College room and board: $2910. College room only: $1122.

Undergraduate Financial Aid: 64% of all full-time undergraduates enrolled in fall 1996 applied for aid; of these, 56% were judged to have need according to Federal Methodology, of whom 100% were aided. On average, 70% of need was met. *Financial aid deadline (priority):* 4/15. *Financial aid forms:* FAFSA required. Institutional form required for some.

LD Services Contact: Ms. Debra Glennen, Disability Specialist/Interim Director, DSS, University of North Dakota, Box 9040, Grand Forks, ND 58202, 701-777-3425. Fax: 701-777-6121. Email: deb_glennen@mail.und.nodak.edu.

UNIVERSITY OF NORTH TEXAS

Denton, Texas

LEARNING DISABILITIES SERVICES INFORMATION

Office of Disability Accommodation began offering services in 1972. Currently the program serves 200 undergraduates with LD. Services are also available to graduate students. Students diagnosed with ADD/ADHD are eligible for the same services available to students with LD.

Staff: 2 full-time, 8 part-time staff members, including director, assistant director. Services provided by tutors, counselors.

Special Fees: A fee is charged for diagnostic testing.

Applications and admissions: *Required:* high school transcript, grade point average, class rank, untimed SAT I or ACT, psychoeducational report completed within 3 years, documentation of disability; *recommended:* high school courses completed, extended time SAT I or ACT. Students may begin taking classes any term. *Application deadline:* 5/1 (fall term), 12/1 (spring term).

Special policies: The college has written policies regarding grade forgiveness; substitutions and waivers of admissions, graduation, and degree requirements.

PROGRAM AND SERVICE COMPONENTS

Special preparation or orientation: Optional orientation offered after classes begin.

Diagnostic testing: Intelligence, reading, math, spelling, handwriting, spoken language, written language, motor abilities, perceptual skills, study skills, personality, social skills, psychoneurology, speech, hearing, learning strategies.

Academic advising: Provided by unit staff members, academic advisers. Students with LD may take up to as many credit hours as an individual can handle each term; most take 12 to 15 credit hours; 12 credit hours required to maintain full-time status; source of aid determines number of credit hours required to be eligible for financial aid.

Counseling services: Individual counseling, small-group counseling, career counseling, self-advocacy training.

Special courses: College survival skills, reading, vocabulary development, communication skills, composition, learning strategies, word pro-

University of North Texas (continued)

cessing, time management, study skills, career planning, stress management. Some offered for credit; some enter into overall grade point average.
Auxiliary aids: Taped textbooks, tape recorders, calculators, typewriters, word-processors with spell-check, personal computers, talking computers, optical character readers, talking calculators, Visualtek machine, carbonless notepaper.
Auxiliary services: Alternative test arrangements, notetakers, priority registration.

GENERAL COLLEGE INFORMATION

State-supported, coed. Awards bachelor's, master's, doctoral degrees. Founded 1890. *Setting:* 456-acre urban campus with easy access to Dallas–Fort Worth. *Endowment:* $5.2 million. *Research spending 1995–96:* $13.9 million. *Total enrollment:* 24,957. *Faculty:* 994 (747 full-time, 82% with terminal degrees, 247 part-time); student–undergrad faculty ratio is 20:1.
Enrollment Profile: 18,665 students from 49 states and territories, 105 other countries. 52% women, 48% men, 32% part-time, 91% state residents, 13% transferred in, 4% international, 14% 25 or older, 1% Native American, 7% Hispanic, 8% black, 3% Asian or Pacific Islander. *Retention:* 69% of 1995 full-time freshmen returned. *Graduation:* 10% graduate in 4 years, 19% in 5 years, 37% in 6 years. *Areas of study chosen:* 28% business management and administrative services, 14% education, 11% social sciences, 9% fine arts, 7% communications and journalism, 7% performing arts, 6% biological and life sciences, 5% computer and information sciences, 4% psychology, 3% engineering and applied sciences, 2% English language/literature/letters, 1% foreign language and literature, 1% health professions and related sciences, 1% mathematics, 1% physical sciences. *Most popular recent majors:* biology/biological sciences, psychology, accounting.
First-Year Class: 2,288 total; 5,494 applied, 76% were accepted, 55% of whom enrolled. 22% from top 10% of their high school class, 49% from top quarter, 84% from top half. 10 National Merit Scholars.
Graduation Requirements: 124 semester hours; 6 semester hours of science; computer course (varies by major); internship (some majors); senior project for honors program students and some majors.
Computers on Campus: 575 computers available on campus for general student use. A computer is recommended for all students. A campus-wide network can be accessed from student residence rooms and from off-campus. Students can contact faculty members and/or advisers through e-mail. Computers for student use in computer labs, classrooms, library provide access to the Internet/World Wide Web, on- and off-campus e-mail addresses. Staffed computer lab on campus provides training in use of computers, software.

EXPENSES AND FINANCIAL AID

Expenses for 1997–98: *Application fee:* $25. State resident tuition: $1666 full-time. Nonresident tuition: $8300 full-time, $267.75 per semester hour part-time. State resident part-time tuition per semester ranges from $139.75 to $591.25. Part-time mandatory fees per semester range from $88.10 to $229.10. Full-time mandatory fees: $521. College room and board: $3575 (minimum).
Undergraduate Financial Aid: *Financial aid deadline (priority):* 6/1. *Financial aid forms:* FAFSA required. Financial aid transcript (for transfers) required for some.
LD Services Contact: Mr. Steve Pickett, Director, Office of Disability Accommodation, University of North Texas, NT Box 305358, Denton, TX 76203-5358, 940-565-4323. Fax: 940-565-4376. Email: steve@dsa.admin.unt.edu.

UNIVERSITY OF OKLAHOMA

Norman, Oklahoma

LEARNING DISABILITIES SERVICES INFORMATION

Disabled Student Services began offering services in 1978. Currently the program serves 120 undergraduates with LD. Services are also available to graduate students. Students diagnosed with ADD/ADHD are eligible for the same services available to students with LD.
Staff: 1 full-time, 1 part-time staff members, including assistant director, graduate assistants.
Special Fees: No special fees are charged for services to students with LD.
Applications and admissions: *Required:* high school transcript, grade point average, class rank, untimed or extended time SAT I, extended time ACT, psychoeducational report completed within 3 years. Students may begin taking classes in fall, spring, or summer. *Application deadline:* continuous.

PROGRAM AND SERVICE COMPONENTS

Special preparation or orientation: Optional orientation offered individually by special arrangement.
Academic advising: Provided by unit staff members, academic advisers. Most students with LD take 12 credit hours each term; 12 credit hours required to maintain full-time status and be eligible for financial aid.
Counseling services: Individual counseling, small-group counseling, career counseling.
Basic skills remediation: Offered one-on-one by graduate assistants. Available in learning strategies, study skills, time management.
Auxiliary aids: Taped textbooks, tape recorders, word-processors with spell-check, talking computers, optical character readers, Dragon Dictate (voice recognition).
Auxiliary services: Alternative test arrangements, notetakers, priority registration, advocacy.
Campus support group: A special student organization is available to students with LD.

GENERAL COLLEGE INFORMATION

State-supported, coed. Awards bachelor's, master's, doctoral, first professional degrees. Founded 1890. *Setting:* 3,200-acre suburban campus with easy access to Oklahoma City. *Endowment:* $278.2 million. *Research spending 1995–96:* $35.5 million. *Educational spending 1995–96:* $5460 per undergrad. *Total enrollment:* 20,026. *Faculty:* 1,037 (848 full-time, 85% with terminal degrees, 189 part-time).
Enrollment Profile: 15,732 students from 51 states and territories, 89 other countries. 45% women, 55% men, 16% part-time, 78% state residents, 16% live on campus, 12% transferred in, 7% international, 16% 25 or older, 7% Native American, 3% Hispanic, 7% black, 5% Asian or Pacific Islander. *Retention:* 79% of 1995 full-time freshmen returned. *Graduation:* 16% graduate in 4 years, 37% in 5 years, 44% in 6 years. *Areas of study chosen:* 20% business management and administrative services, 11% engineering and applied sciences, 10% social sciences, 7% English language/literature/letters, 5% biological and life sciences, 5% education, 5% fine arts, 4% communications and journalism, 4% physical sciences, 4% psychology, 3% architecture, 2% computer and information sciences, 1% area and ethnic studies, 1% foreign language and literature, 1% mathematics. *Most popular recent majors:* management information systems, accounting, psychology.
First-Year Class: 2,645 total; 5,172 applied, 88% were accepted, 58% of whom enrolled. 31% from top 10% of their high school class, 61% from top quarter, 87% from top half. 163 National Merit Scholars.
Graduation Requirements: 124 credit hours; 1 math course; 2 science courses; 2 semesters of a foreign language; computer course for engineering, business majors; internship (some majors); senior project.
Computers on Campus: 600 computers available on campus for general student use. Computer purchase/lease plans available. A computer is strongly recommended for all students. A campus-wide network can be accessed from student residence rooms and from off-campus. Students can contact faculty members and/or advisers through e-mail. Computers for student use in computer center, computer labs, research center, classrooms, library, student center, dorms, student rooms, academic buildings provide access to the Internet/World Wide Web. Staffed computer lab on campus (open 24 hours a day) provides training in use of computers, software. *Academic computing expenditure 1995–96:* $4.7 million.

EXPENSES AND FINANCIAL AID

Expenses for 1996–97: *Application fee:* $25. Part-time mandatory fees: $93 per semester. Full-time tuition ranges from $1940 to $2046 for state residents, $5405 to $5886 for nonresidents, according to class level. Part-time tuition per credit hour ranges from $64.65 to $68.15 for state residents, $180.15 to $198.65 for nonresidents, according to class level. Full-time mandatory fees: $186. College room and board: $3904.
Undergraduate Financial Aid: Of all full-time undergraduates enrolled in fall 1996, 90% of those who applied for aid were judged to have need according to Federal Methodology, of whom 90% were aided. On average, 92% of need was met. *Financial aid deadline (priority):* 3/1. *Financial aid forms:* FAFSA required.
LD Services Contact: Ms. Suzette Dyer, Assistant Director, Center for Student Life, University of Oklahoma, 900 Asp Avenue, Room 397, OK Memorial Union, Norman, OK 73019-0230, 405-325-3163. Fax: 405-325-7493. Email: sdyer@ou.edu.

UNIVERSITY OF PENNSYLVANIA

Philadelphia, Pennsylvania

LEARNING DISABILITIES SERVICES INFORMATION

Programs for People with Disabilities began offering services in 1982. Currently the program serves 250 undergraduates with LD. Services are also available to graduate students. Students diagnosed with ADD/ADHD are eligible for the same services available to students with LD.
Staff: Includes director, assistant director, coordinator, administrative assistant, LD specialist. Services provided by tutors, counselors.
Special Fees: A fee is charged for diagnostic testing.
Applications and admissions: *Required:* high school transcript, grade point average, class rank, courses completed, untimed SAT I or ACT, autobiographical statement, letters of recommendation, essays, work experience, 3 achievement tests; *recommended:* high school extracurricular activities, extended time SAT I or ACT, personal interview. Students may begin taking classes any term. *Application deadline:* 1/1.

PROGRAM AND SERVICE COMPONENTS

Special preparation or orientation: Optional orientation offered before registration, during registration, after classes begin, at time of disclosure.
Diagnostic testing: Foreign language; other areas by referral.
Academic advising: Provided by unit staff members, academic advisers. Students with LD may take up to 5 courses each term; most take 3 to 4 courses; 3 courses required to maintain full-time status and be eligible for financial aid.
Counseling services: Individual counseling, small-group counseling, career counseling, student support group.
Subject-area tutoring: Offered one-on-one and in small groups by peer tutors, graduate students. Available in all subjects.
Special courses: College survival skills, reading, composition, learning strategies, time management, study skills, career planning. None offered for credit; none enter into overall grade point average.
Auxiliary aids: Taped textbooks, tape recorders, word-processors with spell-check, personal computers, talking computers, optical character readers.
Auxiliary services: Alternative test arrangements, notetakers, priority registration, advocacy, readers, library and editorial assistants.

GENERAL COLLEGE INFORMATION

Independent, coed. Awards associate, bachelor's, master's, doctoral, first professional degrees. Founded 1740. *Setting:* 260-acre urban campus. *Endowment:* $1.7 billion. *Research spending 1995–96:* $143.8 million. *Total enrollment:* 21,171. *Faculty:* 3,853 (2,174 full-time, 99% with terminal degrees, 1,679 part-time); student–undergrad faculty ratio is 5:1.
Enrollment Profile: 11,024 students: 50% women, 50% men, 7% part-time, 21% state residents, 2% transferred in, 8% international, 11% 25 or older, 1% Native American, 4% Hispanic, 6% black, 17% Asian or Pacific Islander. *Retention:* 94% of 1995 full-time freshmen returned. *Graduation:* 80% graduate in 4 years, 87% in 5 years. *Areas of study chosen:* 15% social sciences, 14% business management and administrative services, 9% engineering and applied sciences, 7% biological and life sciences, 4% health professions and related sciences, 4% liberal arts/general studies, 2% area and ethnic studies, 2% communications and journalism, 1% fine arts, 1% mathematics. *Most popular recent majors:* finance/banking, history, communication.
First-Year Class: 2,331 total; 15,862 applied, 30% were accepted, 49% of whom enrolled. 86% from top 10% of their high school class. 71 class presidents, 159 valedictorians.
Graduation Requirements: 32 courses for bachelor's; proven competence in a foreign language; computer course for some math, business, engineering majors; senior project for honors program students and some majors.
Computers on Campus: 555 computers available on campus for general student use. Computer purchase/lease plans available. A campus-wide network can be accessed from student residence rooms and from off-campus. Students can contact faculty members and/or advisers through e-mail. Computers for student use in computer center, computer labs, research center, classrooms, library, student center, dorms, academic buildings. Staffed computer lab on campus (open 24 hours a day) provides training in use of computers, software.

EXPENSES AND FINANCIAL AID

Expenses for 1997–98: *Application fee:* $55. Comprehensive fee of $29,680 includes full-time tuition ($19,970), mandatory fees ($2280), and college room and board ($7430). College room only: $4230. Part-time tuition: $2551 per course. Part-time mandatory fees: $221 per course.
Undergraduate Financial Aid: 53% of all full-time undergraduates enrolled in fall 1996 applied for aid. On average, 100% of need was met. *Financial aid deadline (priority):* 2/15. *Financial aid forms:* FAFSA, CSS Financial Aid PROFILE, state form, institutional form required.
LD Services Contact: Ms. Alice Nagle, Coordinator, Programs for People with Disabilities, University of Pennsylvania, 1133 Blockley Hall, 6021, Philadelphia, PA 19104-6021, 215-898-6993. Fax: 215-662-7862. Email: anagle@pobox.upenn.edu.

UNIVERSITY OF PITTSBURGH AT GREENSBURG

Greensburg, Pennsylvania

LEARNING DISABILITIES SERVICES INFORMATION

Counseling Center began offering services in 1988. Currently the program serves 3 undergraduates with LD. Students diagnosed with ADD/ADHD are eligible for the same services available to students with LD.
Staff: 1 full-time staff member (coordinator). Services provided by tutor, counselor, diagnostic specialist.
Special Fees: No special fees are charged for services to students with LD.
Applications and admissions: *Required:* high school transcript, untimed SAT I or ACT, psychoeducational report completed within 3 years; *recommended:* extended time SAT I or ACT, personal interview, letters of recommendation. Students may begin taking classes in fall or spring. *Application deadline:* continuous.

PROGRAM AND SERVICE COMPONENTS

Diagnostic testing: Intelligence, reading, math, spelling, study skills, personality, learning strategies.
Academic advising: Provided by academic advisers. Students with LD required to take 12 credits each term to maintain full-time status; 6 credits required to be eligible for financial aid.
Counseling services: Individual counseling, career counseling.
Basic skills remediation: Offered one-on-one and in class-size groups by regular teachers, counselor. Available in reading, math, spelling, learning strategies, study skills, time management, social skills.
Subject-area tutoring: Offered one-on-one and in small groups by peer tutors. Available in some subjects.
Special courses: Learning strategies, time management, study skills, career planning. None offered for credit.
Auxiliary aids: Tape recorders, typewriters, word-processors with spell-check, personal computers.
Auxiliary services: Alternative test arrangements, notetakers, advocacy.

GENERAL COLLEGE INFORMATION

State-related, 4-year, coed. Part of University of Pittsburgh System. Awards bachelor's degrees. Founded 1963. *Setting:* 165-acre small-town campus with easy access to Pittsburgh. *Research spending 1995–96:* $21,391. *Educational spending 1995–96:* $2313 per undergrad. *Total enrollment:* 1,381. *Faculty:* 90 (60 full-time, 76% with terminal degrees, 30 part-time); student–undergrad faculty ratio is 18:1.
Enrollment Profile: 1,381 students from 5 states and territories, 2 other countries. 50% women, 50% men, 21% part-time, 98% state residents, 45% live on campus, 19% transferred in, 1% international, 30% 25 or older, 0% Native American, 0% Hispanic, 1% black, 1% Asian or Pacific Islander. *Retention:* 75% of 1995 full-time freshmen returned. *Areas of study chosen:* 30% business management and administrative services, 18% psychology, 14% social sciences, 10% health professions and related sciences, 6% biological and life sciences, 6% communications and journalism, 6% mathematics, 4% engineering and applied sciences, 2% computer and information sciences, 2% education, 2% library and information studies. *Most popular recent majors:* business administration/commerce/management, psychology, accounting.
First-Year Class: 326 total; 662 applied, 74% were accepted, 66% of whom enrolled. 11% from top 10% of their high school class, 35% from top quarter, 70% from top half. 1 valedictorian.
Graduation Requirements: 120 credits; algebra proficiency; 5 natural science courses; 1 year of a foreign language in high school or 1 year in college; computer course for business administration, information science, engineering, math majors; internship (some majors); senior project (some majors).

Computers on Campus: 50 computers available on campus for general student use. Computer purchase/lease plans available. A campus-wide network can be accessed from student residence rooms and from off-campus. Students can contact faculty members and/or advisers through e-mail. Computers for student use in computer center provide access to the Internet/World Wide Web. Staffed computer lab on campus provides training in use of computers, software.

EXPENSES AND FINANCIAL AID

Expenses for 1997–98: *Application fee:* $35. State resident tuition: $5658 full-time, $197 per credit part-time. Nonresident tuition: $12,422 full-time, $425 per credit part-time. Part-time mandatory fees: $55 per semester. Full-time mandatory fees: $416. College room and board: $4280.
Undergraduate Financial Aid: 78% of all full-time undergraduates enrolled in fall 1996 applied for aid; of these, 91% were judged to have need according to Federal Methodology, of whom 93% were aided. On average, 84% of need was met. *Financial aid deadline:* Applications processed continuously. *Financial aid forms:* FAFSA, state form, institutional form required.
Financial aid specifically for students with LD: Scholarships.
LD Services Contact: Ms. Helen M. Connors, Psychologist, University of Pittsburgh at Greensburg, 1150 Mount Pleasant Road, Greensburg, PA 15601-5860, 412-836-9870. Fax: 412-836-7134.

UNIVERSITY OF PUERTO RICO, HUMACAO UNIVERSITY COLLEGE

Humacao, Puerto Rico

LEARNING DISABILITIES SERVICES INFORMATION

Student Support Services Program began offering services in 1992. Currently the program serves 4 undergraduates with LD. Students diagnosed with ADD/ADHD are not eligible for the same services available to students with LD.
Staff: 6 full-time, 25 part-time staff members, including director, coordinator. Services provided by tutors, counselors.
Special Fees: No special fees are charged for services to students with LD.
Applications and admissions: *Required:* high school transcript, grade point average, courses completed, medical history; *recommended:* personal interview. Students may begin taking classes in summer only. *Application deadline:* 12/17.

PROGRAM AND SERVICE COMPONENTS

Special preparation or orientation: Required orientation held before registration and after classes begin.
Academic advising: Provided by unit staff members, academic advisers. Students with LD may take up to 12 credits each term; most take 12 credits; 12 credits required to maintain full-time status; 6 credits required to be eligible for financial aid.
Counseling services: Individual counseling, career counseling.
Subject-area tutoring: Offered one-on-one and in small groups by peer tutors. Available in most subjects.
Special courses: College survival skills, learning strategies, word processing, time management, study skills. None offered for credit.
Auxiliary aids: Tape recorders, calculators, word-processors with spell-check, personal computers.
Auxiliary services: Notetakers.

GENERAL COLLEGE INFORMATION

Commonwealth-supported, 4-year, coed. Part of University of Puerto Rico System. Awards associate, bachelor's degrees. Founded 1962. *Setting:* 62-acre suburban campus with easy access to San Juan. *Research spending 1995–96:* $652,465. *Educational spending 1995–96:* $3676 per undergrad. *Total enrollment:* 4,294. *Faculty:* 265 (248 full-time, 32% with terminal degrees, 17 part-time); student–undergrad faculty ratio is 16:1.
Enrollment Profile: 4,294 students: 68% women, 32% men, 18% part-time, 100% commonwealth residents, 1% transferred in, 0% international, 9% 25 or older, 0% Native American, 100% Hispanic, 0% black, 0% Asian or Pacific Islander. *Retention:* 84% of 1995 full-time freshmen returned. *Graduation:* 14% graduate in 4 years, 38% in 5 years, 46% in 6 years. *Areas of study chosen:* 34% business management and administrative services, 13% education, 10% physical sciences, 9% biological and life sciences, 9% health professions and related sciences, 5% agriculture, 3% liberal arts/general studies, 2% communications and journalism, 2% interdisciplinary studies, 2% mathematics, 2% social sciences. *Most popular recent majors:* accounting, business administration/commerce/management, elementary education.
First-Year Class: 945 total; 1,598 applied, 62% were accepted, 95% of whom enrolled.
Graduation Requirements: 65 credits for associate, 128 credits for bachelor's; 3 credits of math; 6 credits of science; computer course for business administration, math, science majors; internship (some majors); senior project for honors program students.
Computers on Campus: 272 computers available on campus for general student use. A computer is recommended for some students. A campus-wide network can be accessed from off-campus. Students can contact faculty members and/or advisers through e-mail. Computers for student use in computer center, computer labs, research center, library, business administration, math labs provide access to the Internet/World Wide Web, on- and off-campus e-mail addresses. Staffed computer lab on campus provides training in use of computers, software. *Academic computing expenditure 1995–96:* $689,608.

EXPENSES AND FINANCIAL AID

Expenses for 1996–97: *Application fee:* $15. Commonwealth resident tuition: $1020 full-time, $30 per credit part-time. Nonresidents who are U.S. citizens pay an amount equal to the rate for nonresidents at a state university in their home state. Full-time tuition for international students: $2400. Full-time mandatory fees: $70 (minimum).
Undergraduate Financial Aid: Of all full-time undergraduates enrolled in fall 1996, 86% of those who applied for aid were judged to have need according to Federal Methodology, of whom 100% were aided. On average, 47% of need was met. *Financial aid deadline:* Applications processed continuously. *Financial aid forms:* FAFSA, institutional form required.
LD Services Contact: Mrs. María V. Ortiz, Counselor, University of Puerto Rico, Humacao University College, CUH Station, Humacao, PR 00791, 787-850-9340. Fax: 787-852-0549.

UNIVERSITY OF PUERTO RICO, RÍO PIEDRAS

San Juan, Puerto Rico

LEARNING DISABILITIES SERVICES INFORMATION

Disable Students Support Services Program began offering services in 1981. Currently the program serves 34 undergraduates with LD. Services are also available to graduate students. Students diagnosed with ADD/ADHD are eligible for the same services available to students with LD.
Staff: 2 full-time, 2 part-time staff members, including director, assistant director, coordinator. Services provided by tutors, counselors.
Special Fees: No special fees are charged for services to students with LD.
Applications and admissions: *Required:* high school transcript, grade point average. Students may begin taking classes in summer only. *Application deadline:* 2/21.
Special policies: The college has written policies regarding substitutions and waivers of admissions, graduation, and degree requirements.

PROGRAM AND SERVICE COMPONENTS

Special preparation or orientation: Optional summer program offered prior to entering college. Optional orientation offered before registration, during registration, after classes begin.
Academic advising: Provided by academic advisers. Students with LD may take up to 15 credits each term; most take 9 to 12 credits; 18 credits per year required to maintain full-time status and be eligible for financial aid.
Counseling services: Individual counseling, career counseling, self-advocacy training.
Basic skills remediation: Offered one-on-one. Available in computer skills.
Subject-area tutoring: Offered one-on-one by peer tutors. Available in most subjects.
Auxiliary aids: Taped textbooks, tape recorders, calculators, typewriters, word-processors with spell-check, personal computers, talking computers, optical character readers.

Auxiliary services: Alternative test arrangements, notetakers, priority registration, advocacy.

GENERAL COLLEGE INFORMATION

Commonwealth-supported, coed. Part of University of Puerto Rico System. Awards associate, bachelor's, master's, doctoral, first professional degrees. Founded 1903. *Setting:* 281-acre urban campus with easy access to San Juan. *Total enrollment:* 19,234. *Faculty:* 1,476 (1,292 full-time, 184 part-time); student–undergrad faculty ratio is 15:1.
Enrollment Profile: 15,738 students from 11 states and territories, 23 other countries. 63% women, 37% men, 15% part-time, 99% commonwealth residents, 99% Hispanic. *Most popular recent majors:* accounting, secondary education, business administration/commerce/management.
First-Year Class: 3,071 total. Of the students accepted, 85% enrolled.
Graduation Requirements: 77 credits for associate, 120 credits for bachelor's; 6 credits each of math and science; computer course for business administration, natural science majors.
Computers on Campus: 170 computers available on campus for general student use. Computer purchase/lease plans available. A campus-wide network can be accessed from student residence rooms. Computers for student use in computer center, dorms, academic buildings. Staffed computer lab on campus provides training in use of computers, software.

FINANCIAL AID

Undergraduate Financial Aid: Of all full-time undergraduates enrolled in fall 1996, 38% of those who applied for aid were judged to have need according to Federal Methodology, of whom 50% were aided. On average, 100% of need was met. *Financial aid deadline (priority):* 6/30. *Financial aid forms:* FAFSA, institutional form required.
LD Services Contact: José R. Ocasio, Director, University of Puerto Rico, Río Piedras, Box 23336, Río Piedras, PR 00931-3336, 787-764-0000 Ext. 3450. Fax: 787-763-5722.

UNIVERSITY OF REDLANDS

Redlands, California

LEARNING DISABILITIES SERVICES INFORMATION

Academic Support Services began offering services in 1989. Currently the program serves 80 undergraduates with LD. Students diagnosed with ADD/ADHD are eligible for the same services available to students with LD.
Staff: 1 full-time staff member (director). Services provided by tutors, counselors.
Special Fees: No special fees are charged for services to students with LD.
Applications and admissions: *Required:* high school transcript, grade point average, courses completed; *recommended:* high school class rank, extracurricular activities, untimed or extended time SAT I or ACT, personal interview, autobiographical statement, letters of recommendation, psychoeducational report completed within 5 years. Students may begin taking classes in fall only. *Application deadline:* continuous.
Special policies: The college has written policies regarding substitutions and waivers of graduation requirements.

PROGRAM AND SERVICE COMPONENTS

Academic advising: Provided by unit staff members, academic advisers. Students with LD may take up to 16 units each term; most take 12 to 16 units; 12 units required to maintain full-time status and be eligible for financial aid.
Counseling services: Individual counseling, small-group counseling, career counseling.
Basic skills remediation: Offered in class-size groups by regular teachers. Available in math, written language, learning strategies, study skills, time management.
Special courses: Study skills, career planning. All offered for credit; none enter into overall grade point average.
Auxiliary aids: Word-processors with spell-check, personal computers.
Auxiliary services: Alternative test arrangements, notetakers.
Campus support group: A special student organization is available to students with LD.

GENERAL COLLEGE INFORMATION

Independent, comprehensive, coed. Awards bachelor's, master's degrees. Founded 1907. *Setting:* 140-acre small-town campus with easy access to Los Angeles. *Endowment:* $57.2 million. *Educational spending 1995–96:* $4100 per undergrad. *Total enrollment:* 3,584. *Undergraduate faculty:* 661 (176 full-time, 90% with terminal degrees, 485 part-time); student–undergrad faculty ratio is 12:1.
Enrollment Profile: 2,636 students from 44 states and territories, 35 other countries. 51% women, 49% men, 5% part-time, 61% state residents, 24% transferred in, 5% international, 1% 25 or older, 1% Native American, 14% Hispanic, 4% black, 8% Asian or Pacific Islander. *Retention:* 77% of 1995 full-time freshmen returned. *Areas of study chosen:* 11% performing arts, 10% psychology, 10% social sciences, 9% interdisciplinary studies, 8% English language/literature/letters, 7% business management and administrative services, 7% health professions and related sciences, 7% physical sciences, 6% education. *Most popular recent majors:* liberal arts/general studies, social science, business administration/commerce/management.
First-Year Class: 383 total; 1,788 applied, 83% were accepted, 26% of whom enrolled. 36% from top 10% of their high school class, 56% from top quarter, 78% from top half. 6 National Merit Scholars, 6 class presidents.
Graduation Requirements: 132 units; 1 course each in math and lab science; 2 years of a foreign language or the equivalent; computer course for business, education, math, environmental studies majors; internship (some majors); senior project.
Computers on Campus: 300 computers available on campus for general student use. Computer purchase/lease plans available. A campus-wide network can be accessed from student residence rooms. Computers for student use in computer center, computer labs, learning resource center, classrooms, library, departmental labs provide access to the Internet/World Wide Web. Staffed computer lab on campus provides training in use of computers, software. *Academic computing expenditure 1995–96:* $369,388.

EXPENSES AND FINANCIAL AID

Expenses for 1997–98: *Application fee:* $40. Comprehensive fee of $25,859 includes full-time tuition ($18,300), mandatory fees ($245), and college room and board ($7314). College room only: $3954. Part-time mandatory fees: $76 per year. Part-time tuition (1 to 8 units): $572 per unit.
Undergraduate Financial Aid: 80% of all full-time undergraduates enrolled in fall 1996 applied for aid; of these, 94% were judged to have need according to Federal Methodology, of whom 100% were aided. On average, 93% of need was met. *Financial aid deadline (priority):* 2/15. *Financial aid forms:* FAFSA required.
LD Services Contact: Mrs. Judy Bowman, Director, Academic Support Services, University of Redlands, PO Box 3080, Redlands, CA 92373-0999, 909-335-4079. Fax: 909-793-2029.

UNIVERSITY OF RHODE ISLAND

Kingston, Rhode Island

LEARNING DISABILITIES SERVICES INFORMATION

Disability Services for Students began offering services in 1981. Currently the program serves 250 undergraduates with LD. Services are also available to graduate students. Students diagnosed with ADD/ADHD are eligible for the same services available to students with LD, as well as private testing space.
Staff: 2 full-time, 1 part-time staff members, including director, coordinator, graduate assistant.
Special Fees: No special fees are charged for services to students with LD.
Applications and admissions: *Required:* high school transcript, grade point average, class rank, courses completed, untimed SAT I, letters of recommendation; *recommended:* high school extracurricular activities, IEP (Individualized Education Program), extended time SAT I or ACT, personal interview, autobiographical statement, psychoeducational report completed within 3 to 5 years. Students may begin taking classes any term. *Application deadline:* 3/1.
Special policies: The college has written policies regarding substitutions and waivers of admissions and graduation requirements.

PROGRAM AND SERVICE COMPONENTS

Special preparation or orientation: Optional orientation offered during general orientation.
Academic advising: Provided by unit staff members, academic advisers. Students with LD may take up to 18 credits each term; most take 12 to 15 credits; 12 credits (fewer with special permission) required to maintain full-time status.

University of Rhode Island (continued)

Counseling services: Individual counseling, career counseling, self-advocacy training.

Basic skills remediation: Offered one-on-one by Disability Services staff. Available in learning strategies, study skills, time management.

Auxiliary aids: Taped textbooks, tape recorders, calculators, word-processors with spell-check, talking computers, optical character readers, assistive listening systems.

Auxiliary services: Alternative test arrangements, notetakers, priority registration, advocacy, foreign language course substitution, time extensions for assignments.

GENERAL COLLEGE INFORMATION

State-supported, coed. Part of Rhode Island State System of Higher Education. Awards bachelor's, master's, doctoral, first professional degrees. Founded 1892. *Setting:* 1,200-acre small-town campus. *Endowment:* $30.2 million. *Research spending 1995–96:* $41 million. *Educational spending 1995–96:* $5654 per undergrad. *Total enrollment:* 13,261. *Faculty:* 642 (620 full-time, 91% with terminal degrees, 22 part-time); student–undergrad faculty ratio is 15:1.

Enrollment Profile: 10,136 students from 50 states and territories, 74 other countries. 55% women, 45% men, 19% part-time, 63% state residents, 5% transferred in, 1% international, 19% 25 or older, 1% Native American, 3% Hispanic, 3% black, 3% Asian or Pacific Islander. *Retention:* 77% of 1995 full-time freshmen returned. *Areas of study chosen:* 15% health professions and related sciences, 13% business management and administrative services, 12% social sciences, 11% engineering and applied sciences, 8% natural resource sciences, 7% education, 6% biological and life sciences, 6% interdisciplinary studies, 6% psychology, 5% communications and journalism, 3% English language/literature/letters, 2% liberal arts/general studies, 1% agriculture, 1% computer and information sciences, 1% fine arts, 1% foreign language and literature, 1% performing arts, 1% physical sciences. *Most popular recent majors:* psychology, pharmacy/pharmaceutical sciences, human development.

First-Year Class: 1,968 total; 7,858 applied, 81% were accepted, 31% of whom enrolled. 20% from top 10% of their high school class, 51% from top quarter, 85% from top half.

Graduation Requirements: 120 credits; 3 credits of math; 4 credits of science; computer course for engineering, some business, textile marketing majors; internship (some majors); senior project for honors program students and some majors.

Computers on Campus: 552 computers available on campus for general student use. Computer purchase/lease plans available. A computer is recommended for some students. A campus-wide network can be accessed from off-campus. Students can contact faculty members and/or advisers through e-mail. Computers for student use in computer center, computer labs, classrooms, library, student center, dorms, academic buildings provide access to the Internet/World Wide Web, on- and off-campus e-mail addresses. Staffed computer lab on campus provides training in use of computers, software. *Academic computing expenditure 1995–96:* $2.1 million.

EXPENSES AND FINANCIAL AID

Expenses for 1996–97: *Application fee:* $30. State resident tuition: $3154 full-time, $131 per credit part-time. Nonresident tuition: $10,846 full-time, $452 per credit part-time. Part-time mandatory fees: $70 per year. Tuition for nonresidents who are eligible for the New England Regional Student Program: $4732 full-time, $197 per credit part-time. Full-time mandatory fees: $1306. College room and board: $5824 (minimum). College room only: $3276.

Undergraduate Financial Aid: Of all full-time undergraduates enrolled in fall 1996, 91% of those who applied for aid were judged to have need according to Federal Methodology, of whom 100% were aided. On average, 72% of need was met. *Financial aid deadline (priority):* 3/1. *Financial aid forms:* FAFSA required.

LD Services Contact: Ms. Pamela A. Rohland, Assistant Director, Student Life/Disability Services for Students, University of Rhode Island, 330 Memorial Union, Kingston, RI 02881, 401-874-2098. Fax: 401-874-5574. Email: prohl@uriacc.uri.edu.

UNIVERSITY OF ROCHESTER

Rochester, New York

LEARNING DISABILITIES SERVICES INFORMATION

Learning Assistance Services began offering services in 1990. Currently the program serves 99 undergraduates with LD. Services are also available to graduate students. Students diagnosed with ADD/ADHD are eligible for the same services available to students with LD.

Staff: 1 full-time, 1 part-time staff members, including coordinator, Assistant Dean. Services provided by tutors, counselors.

Special Fees: No special fees are charged for services to students with LD.

Applications and admissions: *Required:* high school transcript, grade point average, courses completed, extracurricular activities, extended time SAT I or ACT, letters of recommendation; *recommended:* high school class rank, personal interview, autobiographical statement. Students may begin taking classes in fall, spring, or summer. *Application deadline:* 1/31 (fall term), 11/30 (spring term).

Special policies: The college has written policies regarding substitutions and waivers of graduation and degree requirements.

PROGRAM AND SERVICE COMPONENTS

Special preparation or orientation: Optional orientation offered before registration and as needed.

Diagnostic testing: Reading.

Academic advising: Provided by unit staff members, academic advisers. Most students with LD take 16 credit hours each term; 12 credit hours required to maintain full-time status; 12 credit hours (fewer as individually determined) required to be eligible for financial aid.

Counseling services: Individual counseling, small-group counseling, self-advocacy training.

Subject-area tutoring: Offered one-on-one and in small groups by peer tutors, graduate students. Available in most subjects.

Auxiliary aids: Taped textbooks, tape recorders, typewriters, optical character readers.

Auxiliary services: Alternative test arrangements, notetakers, advocacy, scribes.

Campus support group: A special student organization is available to students with LD.

GENERAL COLLEGE INFORMATION

Independent, coed. Awards bachelor's, master's, doctoral degrees. Founded 1850. *Setting:* 534-acre suburban campus. *Endowment:* $706 million. *Total enrollment:* 8,172. *Faculty:* 1,295 (1,183 full-time, 99% with terminal degrees, 112 part-time); student–undergrad faculty ratio is 12:1.

Enrollment Profile: 4,885 students from 52 states and territories, 75 other countries. 50% women, 50% men, 3% part-time, 49% state residents, 5% transferred in, 5% international, 0% Native American, 5% Hispanic, 8% black, 11% Asian or Pacific Islander. *Retention:* 93% of 1995 full-time freshmen returned. *Graduation:* 69% graduate in 4 years, 77% in 5 years, 79% in 6 years. *Most popular recent majors:* psychology, political science/government, economics.

First-Year Class: 1,042 total; 9,884 applied, 52% were accepted, 20% of whom enrolled. 66% from top 10% of their high school class, 88% from top quarter, 98% from top half. 10 National Merit Scholars.

Graduation Requirements: 128 credit hours; math/science requirements vary according to program; internship (some majors).

Computers on Campus: 260 computers available on campus for general student use. Computer purchase/lease plans available. A campus-wide network can be accessed from student residence rooms and from off-campus. Students can contact faculty members and/or advisers through e-mail. Computers for student use in computer center, library, dorms, academic buildings. Staffed computer lab on campus (open 24 hours a day) provides training in use of computers, software.

EXPENSES AND FINANCIAL AID

Expenses for 1996–97: *Application fee:* $50. Comprehensive fee of $27,010 includes full-time tuition ($19,630), mandatory fees ($450), and college room and board ($6930 minimum). College room only: $4180. Part-time tuition: $615 per credit hour.

Undergraduate Financial Aid: 86% of all full-time undergraduates enrolled in fall 1996 applied for aid; of these, 81% were judged to have need according to Federal Methodology, of whom 98% were aided. On average, 86% of need was met. *Financial aid deadline (priority):* 2/1. *Financial aid forms:* FAFSA required. CSS Financial Aid PROFILE, state form, institutional form required for some.

LD Services Contact: Ms. Vicki Roth, Assistant Dean, University of Rochester, Lattimore 107, Rochester, NY 14627, 716-275-9049. Fax: 716-273-1116. Email: vrth@uhura.cc.rochester.edu.

UNIVERSITY OF ST. THOMAS

St. Paul, Minnesota

LEARNING DISABILITIES SERVICES INFORMATION

Enhancement Program began offering services in 1985. Currently the program serves 140 undergraduates with LD. Services are also available to graduate students. Students diagnosed with ADD/ADHD are eligible for the same services available to students with LD.
Staff: 2 full-time, 1 part-time staff members, including coordinators. Services provided by tutors, counselors, work-study students, graduate assistant.
Special Fees: No special fees are charged for services to students with LD.
Applications and admissions: *Required:* high school transcript, grade point average, class rank, autobiographical statement, letters of recommendation, psychoeducational report completed within 3 years; *recommended:* high school courses completed, extracurricular activities, IEP (Individualized Education Program), untimed SAT I or ACT, personal interview. Students may begin taking classes any term. *Application deadline:* continuous.
Special policies: The college has written policies regarding substitutions and waivers of degree requirements.

PROGRAM AND SERVICE COMPONENTS

Special preparation or orientation: Optional orientation offered during interview with coordinator.
Academic advising: Provided by unit staff members, academic advisers. Students with LD may take up to 16 semester credits each term; most take 12 to 16 semester credits; 12 semester credits required to maintain full-time status; source of aid determines number of semester credits required to be eligible for financial aid.
Counseling services: Individual counseling, small-group counseling, career counseling, self-advocacy training, referrals to other campus resources.
Basic skills remediation: Offered one-on-one, in small groups, and in class-size groups by LD teachers, regular teachers, work-study students, graduate assistant. Available in reading, math, spelling, written language, learning strategies, study skills, time management, social skills.
Subject-area tutoring: Offered one-on-one and in small groups by professional teachers, peer tutors. Available in some subjects.
Auxiliary aids: Taped textbooks, tape recorders, typewriters, word-processors with spell-check, personal computers, optical character readers.
Auxiliary services: Alternative test arrangements, notetakers, advocacy.

GENERAL COLLEGE INFORMATION

Independent Roman Catholic, coed. Awards bachelor's, master's, doctoral, first professional degrees. Founded 1885. *Setting:* 78-acre urban campus. *Endowment:* $151.6 million. *Research spending 1995–96:* $566,214. *Total enrollment:* 10,324. *Faculty:* 694 (319 full-time, 83% with terminal degrees, 375 part-time); student–undergrad faculty ratio is 17:1.
Enrollment Profile: 5,066 students from 42 states and territories, 21 other countries. 52% women, 48% men, 17% part-time, 84% state residents, 37% live on campus, 38% transferred in, 1% international, 17% 25 or older, 0% Native American, 2% Hispanic, 3% black, 4% Asian or Pacific Islander. *Retention:* 83% of 1995 full-time freshmen returned. *Graduation:* 45% graduate in 4 years, 64% in 5 years, 66% in 6 years. *Areas of study chosen:* 37% business management and administrative services, 12% social sciences, 9% communications and journalism, 7% biological and life sciences, 7% education, 6% psychology, 3% computer and information sciences, 3% English language/literature/letters, 3% foreign language and literature, 2% engineering and applied sciences, 2% fine arts, 2% interdisciplinary studies, 2% natural resource sciences, 2% physical sciences, 2% theology/religion, 1% mathematics, 1% philosophy. *Most popular recent majors:* business administration/commerce/management, sociology, communication.
First-Year Class: 997 total; 2,199 applied, 91% were accepted, 50% of whom enrolled. 23% from top 10% of their high school class, 52% from top quarter, 83% from top half. 6 National Merit Scholars.
Graduation Requirements: 33 courses; 3 math/science courses including at least 1 science course; proven competence in a foreign language; computer course; internship (some majors); senior project (some majors).
Computers on Campus: 350 computers available on campus for general student use. Computer purchase/lease plans available. A campus-wide network can be accessed from student residence rooms and from off-campus. Students can contact faculty members and/or advisers through e-mail. Computers for student use in computer center, computer labs, learning resource center, classrooms, library, student center, dorms provide access to the Internet/World Wide Web, on- and off-campus e-mail addresses. Staffed computer lab on campus provides training in use of computers, software.

EXPENSES AND FINANCIAL AID

Expenses for 1997–98: *Application fee:* $25. Comprehensive fee of $19,429 includes full-time tuition ($14,560), mandatory fees ($100), and college room and board ($4769). College room only: $2769. Part-time tuition: $455 per credit. Part-time mandatory fees: $25 per year.
Undergraduate Financial Aid: 73% of all full-time undergraduates enrolled in fall 1996 applied for aid; of these, 89% were judged to have need according to Federal Methodology, of whom 99% were aided. On average, 86% of need was met. *Financial aid deadline (priority):* 4/1. *Financial aid forms:* FAFSA required; CSS Financial Aid PROFILE acceptable.
LD Services Contact: The Enhancement Program, University of St. Thomas, 2115 Summit Avenue, AQU110, St. Paul, MN 55105-1096, 612-962-6315. Fax: 612-962-6110.

UNIVERSITY OF SIOUX FALLS

Sioux Falls, South Dakota

LEARNING DISABILITIES SERVICES INFORMATION

Career Services Center currently serves 5 undergraduates with LD. Students diagnosed with ADD/ADHD are eligible for the same services available to students with LD.
Staff: 1 part-time staff member (coordinator). Services provided by tutors, counselors.
Special Fees: No special fees are charged for services to students with LD.
Applications and admissions: *Required:* personal interview, documentation of disability. Students may begin taking classes any term. *Application deadline:* continuous.
Special policies: The college has written policies regarding substitutions and waivers of admissions, graduation, and degree requirements.

PROGRAM AND SERVICE COMPONENTS

Special preparation or orientation: Optional orientation offered before classes begin.
Academic advising: Provided by academic advisers. Students with LD required to take 12 semester hours each term to maintain full-time status; 6 semester hours (federal assistance) required to be eligible for financial aid.
Counseling services: Individual counseling, career counseling.
Basic skills remediation: Offered one-on-one by regular teachers, peer counselors. Available in reading.
Subject-area tutoring: Offered one-on-one by professional teachers, peer tutors. Available in some subjects.
Special courses: Reading. All offered for credit; all enter into overall grade point average.
Auxiliary aids: Taped textbooks, tape recorders, calculators, typewriters, word-processors with spell-check, personal computers.
Auxiliary services: Alternative test arrangements, notetakers, priority registration, advocacy.

GENERAL COLLEGE INFORMATION

Independent American Baptist, comprehensive, coed. Awards associate, bachelor's, master's degrees. Founded 1883. *Setting:* 22-acre suburban campus. *Endowment:* $4.8 million. *Total enrollment:* 947. *Faculty:* 71 (39 full-time, 72% with terminal degrees, 32 part-time); student–undergrad faculty ratio is 14:1.
Enrollment Profile: 829 students from 19 states and territories, 6 other countries. 56% women, 44% men, 29% part-time, 64% state residents, 28% live on campus, 10% transferred in, 1% international, 40% 25 or older, 1% Native American, 1% Hispanic, 2% black, 1% Asian or Pacific Islander. *Retention:* 65% of 1995 full-time freshmen returned. *Areas of study chosen:* 32% business management and administrative services, 18% social sciences, 15% education, 10% fine arts, 8% biological and life sciences, 7% interdisciplinary studies, 6% communications and journalism, 3% mathematics, 1% premed. *Most popular recent majors:* business administration/commerce/management, education, behavioral sciences.
First-Year Class: 140 total; 495 applied, 92% were accepted, 31% of whom enrolled. 13% from top 10% of their high school class, 29% from top quarter, 54% from top half.

University of Sioux Falls (continued)

Graduation Requirements: 64 semester hours for associate, 128 semester hours for bachelor's; 1 semester each of math and lab science; computer course; internship (some majors); senior project for honors program students and some majors.

Computers on Campus: 44 computers available on campus for general student use. A campus-wide network can be accessed. Students can contact faculty members and/or advisers through e-mail. Computers for student use in computer center, computer labs, library provide access to the Internet/World Wide Web, on-campus e-mail addresses. Staffed computer lab on campus provides training in use of computers, software. *Academic computing expenditure 1995–96:* $114,747.

EXPENSES AND FINANCIAL AID

Expenses for 1997–98: *Application fee:* $25. Comprehensive fee of $14,200 includes full-time tuition ($10,750) and college room and board ($3450). Part-time tuition: $190 per semester hour.

Undergraduate Financial Aid: 89% of all full-time undergraduates enrolled in fall 1996 applied for aid; of these, 89% were judged to have need according to Federal Methodology, of whom 100% were aided. On average, 75% of need was met. *Financial aid deadline (priority):* 4/1. *Financial aid forms:* FAFSA, institutional form required; CSS Financial Aid PROFILE acceptable. State form required for some.

LD Services Contact: Mr. William C. Minnick, Academic/Career Counselor, University of Sioux Falls, 1101 West 22nd Street, Sioux Falls, SD 57105, 605-331-6740. Fax: 605-331-6615. Email: william.minnick@thecoo.edu.

UNIVERSITY OF SOUTH ALABAMA

Mobile, Alabama

LEARNING DISABILITIES SERVICES INFORMATION

Special Student Services began offering services in 1986. Currently the program serves 310 undergraduates with LD. Services are also available to graduate students. Students diagnosed with ADD/ADHD are eligible for the same services available to students with LD.

Staff: 4 full-time staff members, including director, coordinators, secretary. Services provided by tutors.

Special Fees: $80 for diagnostic testing.

Applications and admissions: *Required:* high school transcript, extended time ACT, psychoeducational report completed within 3 years. Students may begin taking classes any term. *Application deadline:* continuous.

Special policies: The college has written policies regarding grade forgiveness.

PROGRAM AND SERVICE COMPONENTS

Diagnostic testing: Intelligence, reading, math, spelling, handwriting, spoken language, written language, motor abilities, perceptual skills, personality, hearing, learning strategies.

Academic advising: Provided by unit staff members, academic advisers. Students with LD may take up to 16 quarter hours each term; most take 12 quarter hours; 12 quarter hours required to maintain full-time status; 8 to 12 quarter hours required to be eligible for financial aid.

Counseling services: Individual counseling.

Basic skills remediation: Offered in small groups by peer tutors. Available in study skills, time management.

Subject-area tutoring: Offered one-on-one and in small groups by peer tutors. Available in most subjects.

Auxiliary aids: Taped textbooks, tape recorders, calculators, typewriters, word-processors with spell-check, optical character readers.

Auxiliary services: Alternative test arrangements, notetakers, priority registration, advocacy, readers, writers.

GENERAL COLLEGE INFORMATION

State-supported, coed. Awards bachelor's, master's, doctoral, first professional degrees. Founded 1963. *Setting:* 1,215-acre suburban campus. *Endowment:* $224.4 million. *Research spending 1995–96:* $12.3 million. *Educational spending 1995–96:* $7003 per undergrad. *Total enrollment:* 12,041. *Faculty:* 844 (689 full-time, 84% with terminal degrees, 155 part-time); student–undergrad faculty ratio is 16:1.

Enrollment Profile: 9,800 students from 47 states and territories, 90 other countries. 55% women, 45% men, 27% part-time, 71% state residents, 16% live on campus, 60% transferred in, 6% international, 1% Native American, 1% Hispanic, 11% black, 3% Asian or Pacific Islander. *Retention:* 73% of 1995 full-time freshmen returned. *Graduation:* 10% graduate in 4 years, 24% in 5 years. *Areas of study chosen:* 25% health professions and related sciences, 16% business management and administrative services, 10% education, 8% engineering and applied sciences, 7% social sciences, 4% computer and information sciences, 4% psychology, 3% biological and life sciences, 3% communications and journalism, 3% liberal arts/general studies, 3% premed, 2% fine arts, 1% English language/literature/letters, 1% physical sciences. *Most popular recent majors:* nursing, liberal arts/general studies, finance/banking.

First-Year Class: 1,200 total; 2,688 applied, 93% were accepted, 48% of whom enrolled.

Graduation Requirements: 192 quarter hours; 2 math/science courses; computer course for business, engineering, math, statistics, nursing, allied health majors; internship (some majors); senior project (some majors).

Computers on Campus: 325 computers available on campus for general student use. Computer purchase/lease plans available. A campus-wide network can be accessed from student residence rooms and from off-campus. Students can contact faculty members and/or advisers through e-mail. Computers for student use in computer center, computer labs, learning resource center, classrooms, library, student center, academic buildings provide access to the Internet/World Wide Web, on- and off-campus e-mail addresses. Staffed computer lab on campus provides training in use of computers, software.

EXPENSES AND FINANCIAL AID

Expenses for 1997–98: *Application fee:* $25. State resident tuition: $2640 full-time, $55 per quarter hour part-time. Nonresident tuition: $5280 full-time, $110 per quarter hour part-time. Part-time mandatory fees: $44 per quarter for 1 to 5 quarter hours, $52 per quarter for 6 or more quarter hours. Full-time mandatory fees: $198. College room and board: $3375 (minimum). College room only: $1275 (minimum).

Undergraduate Financial Aid: Of all full-time undergraduates enrolled in fall 1996, 79% of those who applied for aid were judged to have need according to Federal Methodology, of whom 100% were aided. On average, 76% of need was met. *Financial aid deadline (priority):* 5/1. *Financial aid forms:* FAFSA, institutional form required.

LD Services Contact: Ms. Bernita Pulmas, Director, University of South Alabama, UC-Room 270, Mobile, AL 36688-0002, 334-460-7212. Fax: 334-460-6157.

UNIVERSITY OF SOUTH CAROLINA

Columbia, South Carolina

LEARNING DISABILITIES SERVICES INFORMATION

Academic Support Services began offering services in 1990. Currently the program serves 250 undergraduates with LD. Services are also available to graduate students. Students diagnosed with ADD/ADHD are eligible for the same services available to students with LD.

Staff: 1 full-time, 2 part-time staff members, including director, graduate assistants. Services provided by counselors, readers, notetakers, graduate assistants.

Special Fees: No special fees are charged for services to students with LD.

Applications and admissions: *Required:* high school transcript, grade point average, class rank, courses completed, untimed SAT I or ACT; *recommended:* extended time SAT I or ACT. Students may begin taking classes in fall, spring, or summer. *Application deadline:* continuous.

Special policies: The college has written policies regarding substitutions and waivers of admissions, graduation, and degree requirements.

PROGRAM AND SERVICE COMPONENTS

Special preparation or orientation: Optional orientation offered before registration.

Academic advising: Provided by unit staff members, academic advisers. Students with LD may take up to 18 credit hours each term; most take 12 to 15 credit hours; 9 credit hours required to maintain full-time status; source of aid determines number of credit hours required to be eligible for financial aid.

Counseling services: Individual counseling, career counseling.

Basic skills remediation: Offered one-on-one by program staff members; computer-aided instruction also offered. Available in reading, learning strategies, study skills, time management.

Auxiliary aids: Taped textbooks, optical character readers.

Auxiliary services: Alternative test arrangements, notetakers, priority registration, advocacy, readers, textbook reservations.

GENERAL COLLEGE INFORMATION

State-supported, coed. Part of University of South Carolina System. Awards bachelor's, master's, doctoral, first professional degrees. Founded 1801. *Setting:* 242-acre urban campus. *Research spending 1995–96:* $46 million. *Total enrollment:* 25,489. *Faculty:* 1,379 (all full-time, 85% with terminal degrees); student–undergrad faculty ratio is 17:1.
Enrollment Profile: 15,747 students from 52 states and territories, 114 other countries. 55% women, 45% men, 21% part-time, 87% state residents, 38% live on campus, 8% transferred in, 2% international, 20% 25 or older, 1% Native American, 1% Hispanic, 19% black, 3% Asian or Pacific Islander. *Graduation:* 30% graduate in 4 years, 56% in 5 years, 63% in 6 years. *Areas of study chosen:* 16% engineering and applied sciences, 10% biological and life sciences, 10% social sciences, 7% psychology, 6% English language/literature/letters, 5% communications and journalism, 2% performing arts, 1% education.
First-Year Class: 2,703 total; 9,029 applied, 78% were accepted, 38% of whom enrolled. 28% from top 10% of their high school class, 62% from top quarter, 92% from top half. 27 National Merit Scholars, 40 valedictorians.
Graduation Requirements: 120 credit hours; 2 courses each in math and science; proven competence in a foreign language; computer course for business, engineering, math, science, criminal justice, news-editorial, pharmacy, broadcasting, hotel and restaurant management, tourism majors.
Computers on Campus: 2,000 computers available on campus for general student use. Computer purchase/lease plans available. A campus-wide network can be accessed from student residence rooms and from off-campus. Students can contact faculty members and/or advisers through e-mail. Computers for student use in computer center, computer labs, library, various locations provide access to the Internet/World Wide Web. Staffed computer lab on campus provides training in use of computers, software. *Academic computing expenditure 1995–96:* $7.2 million.

EXPENSES AND FINANCIAL AID

Expenses for 1997–98: *Application fee:* $35. State resident tuition: $3434 full-time, $160 per credit hour part-time. Nonresident tuition: $8840 full-time, $400 per credit hour part-time. College room and board: $3690.
Undergraduate Financial Aid: 35% of all full-time undergraduates enrolled in fall 1996 applied for aid; of these, 82% were judged to have need according to Federal Methodology, of whom 96% were aided. On average, 76% of need was met. *Financial aid deadline (priority):* 4/15. *Financial aid forms:* FAFSA, institutional form required; CSS Financial Aid PROFILE acceptable.
LD Services Contact: Ms. Joyce Haddock, Director, Academic Support Services, University of South Carolina, Room 106 LeConte, Columbia, SC 29208, 803-777-6142. Fax: 803-777-6741. Email: debbie@studaff.sa.sc.edu.

UNIVERSITY OF SOUTH CAROLINA–AIKEN

Aiken, South Carolina

LEARNING DISABILITIES SERVICES INFORMATION

Disabled Student Services began offering services in 1991. Currently the program serves 5 undergraduates with LD. Services are also available to graduate students. Students diagnosed with ADD/ADHD are eligible for the same services available to students with LD.
Staff: Includes director, administrative assistant. Services provided by counselors.
Special Fees: No special fees are charged for services to students with LD.
Applications and admissions: *Required:* high school transcript, courses completed, untimed SAT I or ACT, psychoeducational report completed within 3 years; *recommended:* extended time SAT I or ACT, personal interview, autobiographical statement. Students may begin taking classes any term. *Application deadline:* 8/1 (fall term), 12/1 (spring term).
Special policies: The college has written policies regarding grade forgiveness; substitutions and waivers of admissions, graduation, and degree requirements.

PROGRAM AND SERVICE COMPONENTS

Special preparation or orientation: Optional orientation offered upon request of the student.
Academic advising: Provided by academic advisers. Students with LD may take up to 15 semester hours each term; most take 11 semester hours; 12 semester hours required to maintain full-time status; 6 semester hours required to be eligible for financial aid.
Counseling services: Individual counseling, small-group counseling.
Auxiliary aids: Taped textbooks, tape recorders.
Auxiliary services: Alternative test arrangements, notetakers, priority registration.

GENERAL COLLEGE INFORMATION

State-supported, comprehensive, coed. Part of University of South Carolina System. Awards associate, bachelor's, master's degrees. Founded 1961. *Setting:* 144-acre small-town campus with easy access to Columbia. *Endowment:* $7 million. *Research spending 1995–96:* $481,812. *Educational spending 1995–96:* $3822 per undergrad. *Total enrollment:* 3,027. *Faculty:* 205 (106 full-time, 75% with terminal degrees, 99 part-time); student–undergrad faculty ratio is 12:1.
Enrollment Profile: 2,981 students from 34 states and territories, 12 other countries. 65% women, 35% men, 38% part-time, 85% state residents, 11% live on campus, 29% transferred in, 1% international, 37% 25 or older, 1% Native American, 1% Hispanic, 18% black, 1% Asian or Pacific Islander. *Retention:* 66% of 1995 full-time freshmen returned. *Graduation:* 15% graduate in 4 years, 34% in 5 years. *Areas of study chosen:* 21% education, 18% business management and administrative services, 14% health professions and related sciences, 7% social sciences, 6% biological and life sciences, 4% engineering and applied sciences, 3% computer and information sciences, 3% psychology, 2% English language/literature/letters, 2% fine arts, 2% interdisciplinary studies, 1% communications and journalism, 1% mathematics, 1% physical sciences. *Most popular recent majors:* business administration/commerce/management, education, nursing.
First-Year Class: 445 total; 853 applied, 77% were accepted, 68% of whom enrolled. 15% from top 10% of their high school class, 36% from top quarter, 68% from top half. 7 valedictorians.
Graduation Requirements: 60 semester hours for associate, 120 semester hours for bachelor's; 6 semester hours of math; 2 years of lab science; computer course for math, business administration, education, chemistry majors; senior project (some majors).
Computers on Campus: 220 computers available on campus for general student use. A campus-wide network can be accessed. Students can contact faculty members and/or advisers through e-mail. Computers for student use in computer center, computer labs, learning resource center, classrooms, library, academic buildings provide access to the Internet/World Wide Web, on- and off-campus e-mail addresses. Staffed computer lab on campus (open 24 hours a day) provides training in use of computers, software. *Academic computing expenditure 1995–96:* $299,006.

EXPENSES AND FINANCIAL AID

Expenses for 1997–98: *Application fee:* $25. State resident tuition: $2874 full-time, $126 per semester hour part-time. Nonresident tuition: $7184 full-time, $316 per semester hour part-time. Part-time mandatory fees per semester range from $15 to $65. One-time mandatory fee: $50. Full-time mandatory fees: $140. College room and board: $3576. College room only: $2110.
Undergraduate Financial Aid: *Financial aid deadline (priority):* 3/15. *Financial aid forms:* institutional form required; FAFSA, CSS Financial Aid PROFILE acceptable.
LD Services Contact: Dr. Linda P. Matthews, Director, Counseling Services, University of South Carolina–Aiken, 171 University Parkway, Aiken, SC 29801, 803-648-6851 Ext. 3317.

UNIVERSITY OF SOUTH CAROLINA–SPARTANBURG

Spartanburg, South Carolina

LEARNING DISABILITIES SERVICES INFORMATION

Office of Disability Services began offering services in 1992. Currently the program serves 100 undergraduates with LD. Services are also available to graduate students. Students diagnosed with ADD/ADHD are eligible for the same services available to students with LD.
Staff: 1 full-time, 1 part-time staff members, including coordinator, Administrative Assistant. Services provided by counselors.
Special Fees: No special fees are charged for services to students with LD.

University of South Carolina–Spartanburg (continued)

Applications and admissions: *Required:* high school transcript, grade point average, courses completed, psychoeducational report completed within 3 years, IEP (if requesting accommodations); *recommended:* high school class rank, extracurricular activities, untimed or extended time SAT I or ACT, personal interview, autobiographical statement, letters of recommendation. *Application deadline:* continuous.

Special policies: The college has written policies regarding grade forgiveness; substitutions and waivers of graduation and degree requirements.

PROGRAM AND SERVICE COMPONENTS

Academic advising: Provided by unit staff members, academic advisers. Most students with LD take 9 to 15 semester hours each term.

Counseling services: Individual counseling, career counseling.

Basic skills remediation: Offered in class-size groups by trained university personnel. Available in reading, math, learning strategies, study skills, time management, foreign language, notetaking.

Auxiliary aids: Taped textbooks, tape recorders, word-processors with spell-check.

Auxiliary services: Alternative test arrangements, notetakers, priority registration, advocacy.

GENERAL COLLEGE INFORMATION

State-supported, comprehensive, coed. Part of University of South Carolina System. Awards associate, bachelor's, master's degrees. Founded 1967. *Setting:* 298-acre urban campus. *Endowment:* $1.9 million. *Research spending 1995–96:* $277,940. *Educational spending 1995–96:* $3723 per undergrad. *Total enrollment:* 3,549. *Undergraduate faculty:* 214 (134 full-time, 71% with terminal degrees, 80 part-time); student–undergrad faculty ratio is 16:1.

Enrollment Profile: 3,285 students from 30 states and territories, 16 other countries. 63% women, 37% men, 30% part-time, 94% state residents, 36% transferred in, 1% international, 32% 25 or older, 0% Native American, 1% Hispanic, 16% black, 2% Asian or Pacific Islander. *Retention:* 64% of 1995 full-time freshmen returned. *Graduation:* 17% graduate in 4 years, 31% in 5 years, 37% in 6 years. *Areas of study chosen:* 17% education, 16% business management and administrative services, 15% health professions and related sciences, 9% social sciences, 7% interdisciplinary studies, 6% psychology, 5% computer and information sciences, 3% biological and life sciences, 3% liberal arts/general studies, 1% communications and journalism, 1% engineering and applied sciences, 1% English language/literature/letters, 1% foreign language and literature, 1% mathematics, 1% prelaw, 1% premed. *Most popular recent majors:* business administration/commerce/management, psychology, nursing.

First-Year Class: 466 total; 1,129 applied, 61% were accepted, 68% of whom enrolled. 14% from top 10% of their high school class, 41% from top quarter, 81% from top half.

Graduation Requirements: 65 semester hours for associate, 120 semester hours for bachelor's; 6 semester hours of math/science; computer course; internship (some majors); senior project.

Computers on Campus: 170 computers available on campus for general student use. Computer purchase/lease plans available. A computer is recommended for some students. A campus-wide network can be accessed from off-campus. Students can contact faculty members and/or advisers through e-mail. Computers for student use in computer center, computer labs, library, various locations provide access to the Internet/World Wide Web, on- and off-campus e-mail addresses. Staffed computer lab on campus provides training in use of computers, software. *Academic computing expenditure 1995–96:* $500,000.

EXPENSES AND FINANCIAL AID

Expenses for 1997–98: *Application fee:* $25. State resident tuition: $2874 full-time, $126 per semester hour part-time. Nonresident tuition: $7184 full-time, $316 per semester hour part-time. Part-time mandatory fees per semester range from $15 to $65. One-time mandatory fee: $50. Full-time mandatory fees: $140.

Undergraduate Financial Aid: *Financial aid deadline (priority):* 5/1. *Financial aid forms:* FAFSA required.

LD Services Contact: Ms. Mary Hoey, Administrative Assistant, Disability Services, University of South Carolina–Spartanburg, 800 University Way, Spartanburg, SC 29303, 864-503-5123. Fax: 864-503-5100. Email: mhoey@sc.edu.

UNIVERSITY OF SOUTH DAKOTA

Vermillion, South Dakota

LEARNING DISABILITIES SERVICES INFORMATION

Disability Services began offering services in 1990. Currently the program serves undergraduate and graduate students with LD. Students diagnosed with ADD/ADHD are eligible for the same services available to students with LD.

Staff: 8 part-time staff members, including coordinator, graduate assistants.

Special Fees: No special fees are charged for services to students with LD.

Applications and admissions: *Required:* high school transcript, grade point average, class rank, courses completed. Students may begin taking classes any term. *Application deadline:* continuous.

Special policies: The college has written policies regarding substitutions and waivers of graduation and degree requirements.

PROGRAM AND SERVICE COMPONENTS

Diagnostic testing: Intelligence, reading, math, spelling, handwriting, spoken language, written language, motor abilities, perceptual skills, study skills, personality, social skills, psychoneurology, speech, hearing, learning strategies.

Academic advising: Provided by unit staff members, academic advisers. Most students with LD take 12 credit hours each term; 9 credit hours required to maintain full-time status.

Counseling services: Individual counseling, small-group counseling, career counseling, self-advocacy training.

Auxiliary aids: Taped textbooks, tape recorders, word-processors with spell-check, optical character readers.

Auxiliary services: Alternative test arrangements, priority registration, advocacy, classroom modifications as needed.

Campus support group: A special student organization is available to students with LD.

GENERAL COLLEGE INFORMATION

State-supported, coed. Awards associate, bachelor's, master's, doctoral, first professional degrees. Founded 1862. *Setting:* 216-acre small-town campus. *Endowment:* $20.8 million. *Research spending 1995–96:* $5.5 million. *Educational spending 1995–96:* $5146 per undergrad. *Total enrollment:* 7,028. *Faculty:* 456 (433 full-time, 75% with terminal degrees, 23 part-time); student–undergrad faculty ratio is 15:1.

Enrollment Profile: 5,215 students from 47 states and territories, 47 other countries. 56% women, 44% men, 2% part-time, 66% state residents, 34% live on campus, 3% international, 3% Native American, 1% Hispanic, 1% black, 1% Asian or Pacific Islander. *Retention:* 69% of 1995 full-time freshmen returned. *Areas of study chosen:* 19% social sciences, 16% business management and administrative services, 16% liberal arts/general studies, 13% education, 12% biological and life sciences, 11% health professions and related sciences, 3% communications and journalism, 3% English language/literature/letters, 2% computer and information sciences, 1% fine arts, 1% foreign language and literature, 1% mathematics, 1% performing arts, 1% philosophy. *Most popular recent majors:* business administration/commerce/management, biology/biological sciences, psychology.

First-Year Class: 899 total; 1,913 applied, 98% were accepted, 48% of whom enrolled. 12% from top 10% of their high school class, 22% from top quarter, 56% from top half. 5 National Merit Scholars, 40 valedictorians.

Graduation Requirements: 66 credit hours for associate, 128 credit hours for bachelor's; 12 credit hours of math/science; computer course for mass communication, chemistry, math, business, physics majors; internship (some majors); senior project (some majors).

Computers on Campus: 1,500 computers available on campus for general student use. A computer is recommended for all students. A campus-wide network can be accessed from student residence rooms and from off-campus. Students can contact faculty members and/or advisers through e-mail. Computers for student use in computer labs, classrooms, library, student center, dorms provide access to the Internet/World Wide Web, on- and off-campus e-mail addresses. Staffed computer lab on campus provides training in use of computers, software. *Academic computing expenditure 1995–96:* $329,836.

EXPENSES AND FINANCIAL AID

Expenses for 1997–98: *Application fee:* $15. State resident tuition: $1728 full-time, $54 per credit hour part-time. Nonresident tuition: $5496 full-time, $171.75 per credit hour part-time. Part-time mandatory fees: $40.14 per credit hour. Tuition for nonresidents who are eligible for the

Western Undergraduate Exchange: $2592 full-time, $81 percredit hour part-time. Tuition for Minnesota residents: $1886 full-time, $58.93 per credit hour part-time. Full-time mandatory fees: $1284. College room and board: $2912. College room only: $1322.
Undergraduate Financial Aid: Of all full-time undergraduates enrolled in fall 1996, 80% of those who applied for aid were judged to have need according to Federal Methodology, of whom 100% were aided. On average, 68% of need was met. *Financial aid deadline (priority):* 3/1. *Financial aid forms:* FAFSA, state form required; CSS Financial Aid PROFILE acceptable. Institutional form required for some.
LD Services Contact: Dr. Elaine Pearson, Coordinator, University of South Dakota, Room 119B, Vermillion, SD 57069, 605-677-6389. Fax: 605-677-6752. Email: epearson@sundance.usd.edu.

UNIVERSITY OF SOUTHERN CALIFORNIA

Los Angeles, California

LEARNING DISABILITIES SERVICES INFORMATION

Disability Services and Programs began offering services in 1984. Currently the program serves 230 undergraduates with LD. Services are also available to graduate students. Students diagnosed with ADD/ADHD are eligible for the same services available to students with LD, as well as support group.
Staff: 3 full-time, 27 part-time staff members, including director, associate director, administrative assistant. Services provided by tutors, counselors, diagnostic specialists, learning assistants, graduate assistants.
Special Fees: No special fees are charged for services to students with LD.
Applications and admissions: *Required:* high school transcript, grade point average, class rank, courses completed, untimed SAT I or ACT, autobiographical statement; *recommended:* extended time SAT I or ACT, letters of recommendation, psychoeducational report completed within 3 years. Students may begin taking classes in fall or spring. *Application deadline:* 2/1 (fall term), 9/15 (spring term).
Special policies: The college has written policies regarding substitutions and waivers of graduation requirements.

PROGRAM AND SERVICE COMPONENTS

Special preparation or orientation: Optional orientation offered during registration and during summer prior to enrollment.
Academic advising: Provided by unit staff members, academic advisers. Most students with LD take 12 units each term; 12 units required to maintain full-time status and be eligible for financial aid.
Counseling services: Individual counseling, small-group counseling, career counseling.
Basic skills remediation: Offered one-on-one by learning assistants. Available in reading, math, spelling, handwriting, spoken language, written language, learning strategies, study skills, time management.
Subject-area tutoring: Offered one-on-one and in small groups by paraprofessionals, graduate students. Available in most subjects.
Auxiliary aids: Taped textbooks, tape recorders, word-processors with spell-check.
Auxiliary services: Alternative test arrangements, notetakers, advocacy.
Campus support group: A special student organization is available to students with LD.

GENERAL COLLEGE INFORMATION

Independent, coed. Awards bachelor's, master's, doctoral, first professional degrees. Founded 1880. *Setting:* 150-acre urban campus. *Endowment:* $791.4 million. *Research spending 1995–96:* $129.3 million. *Total enrollment:* 27,558. *Faculty:* 2,601 (1,629 full-time, 94% with terminal degrees, 972 part-time); student–undergrad faculty ratio is 14:1.
Enrollment Profile: 14,631 students from 52 states and territories, 109 other countries. 48% women, 52% men, 9% part-time, 69% state residents, 36% transferred in, 9% international, 11% 25 or older, 1% Native American, 14% Hispanic, 7% black, 23% Asian or Pacific Islander. *Areas of study chosen:* 23% business management and administrative services, 13% social sciences, 11% engineering and applied sciences, 10% physical sciences, 8% liberal arts/general studies, 5% performing arts, 4% communications and journalism, 3% architecture, 3% English language/literature/letters, 3% health professions and related sciences, 1% education, 1% fine arts. *Most popular recent majors:* business administration/commerce/management, communication, political science/government.
First-Year Class: 2,843 total; 12,790 applied, 72% were accepted, 31% of whom enrolled. 44% from top 10% of their high school class, 74% from top quarter, 94% from top half. 100 National Merit Scholars.
Graduation Requirements: 128 units; algebra proficiency; science requirements vary according to program; computer course for business administration, some engineering majors; internship (some majors); senior project for honors program students and some majors.
Computers on Campus: 5,000 computers available on campus for general student use. A campus-wide network can be accessed from student residence rooms and from off-campus. Students can contact faculty members and/or advisers through e-mail. Computers for student use in computer center, computer labs, classrooms, library, student center provide access to the Internet/World Wide Web, on- and off-campus e-mail addresses. Staffed computer lab on campus (open 24 hours a day) provides training in use of computers, software. *Academic computing expenditure 1995–96:* $10.2 million.

EXPENSES AND FINANCIAL AID

Expenses for 1996–97: *Application fee:* $55. Comprehensive fee of $26,228 includes full-time tuition ($19,140), mandatory fees ($376), and college room and board ($6712). College room only: $3672. Part-time tuition: $645 per unit. Part-time mandatory fees: $188 per semester.
Undergraduate Financial Aid: *Financial aid deadline:* Applications processed continuously. *Financial aid forms:* FAFSA, CSS Financial Aid PROFILE, state form, institutional form required.
LD Services Contact: Dr. Janet Eddy, Director, Disability Services and Programs, University of Southern California, University Park, STU 301, Los Angeles, CA 90089-0896, 213-740-0776. Fax: 213-740-8216.

UNIVERSITY OF SOUTHERN INDIANA

Evansville, Indiana

LEARNING DISABILITIES SERVICES INFORMATION

Counseling Center began offering services in 1982. Currently the program serves 51 undergraduates with LD. Services are also available to graduate students. Students diagnosed with ADD/ADHD are eligible for the same services available to students with LD.
Staff: 2 full-time staff members, including director, Counselor. Services provided by tutors, counselor, readers.
Special Fees: No special fees are charged for services to students with LD.
Applications and admissions: *Required:* high school transcript, courses completed, personal interview, psychoeducational report completed within 3 years; *recommended:* extended time SAT I or ACT. Students may begin taking classes any term. *Application deadline:* continuous.

PROGRAM AND SERVICE COMPONENTS

Academic advising: Provided by academic advisers. Most students with LD take 9 to 12 semester hours each term; 12 semester hours required to maintain full-time status; 6 semester hours required to be eligible for financial aid.
Counseling services: Individual counseling, small-group counseling, career counseling.
Auxiliary aids: Taped textbooks, typewriters, word-processors with spell-check, optical character readers, Dragon Dictate.
Auxiliary services: Alternative test arrangements, notetakers, priority registration, advocacy, readers.
Campus support group: A special student organization is available to students with LD.

GENERAL COLLEGE INFORMATION

State-supported, comprehensive, coed. Part of Indiana Commission for Higher Education. Awards associate, bachelor's, master's degrees. Founded 1965. *Setting:* 300-acre suburban campus. *Research spending 1995–96:* $111,993. *Educational spending 1995–96:* $3035 per undergrad. *Total enrollment:* 7,763. *Faculty:* 416 (209 full-time, 65% with terminal degrees, 207 part-time); student–undergrad faculty ratio is 18:1.
Enrollment Profile: 7,295 students from 33 states and territories, 30 other countries. 60% women, 40% men, 32% part-time, 92% state residents, 22% live on campus, 37% transferred in, 1% international, 34% 25 or older, 1% Native American, 1% Hispanic, 3% black, 1% Asian or Pacific Islander. *Retention:* 58% of 1995 full-time freshmen returned. *Graduation:* 18% graduate in 4 years, 27% in 5 years, 31% in 6 years. *Areas of study chosen:* 23% business management and administrative services, 19% health professions and related sciences, 15% education, 10% social sciences, 7% biological and life sciences, 7% communications and journalism, 5% psychology, 4% engineering and applied sciences, 2% computer and information sciences, 2% English language/literature/letters, 2% fine arts, 1% foreign language and literature, 1% mathematics,

University of Southern Indiana (continued)

1% philosophy, 1% physical sciences. *Most popular recent majors:* business administration/commerce/management, elementary education.
First-Year Class: 1,721 total; 4,011 applied, 98% were accepted, 43% of whom enrolled. 10% from top 10% of their high school class, 28% from top quarter, 58% from top half.
Graduation Requirements: 62 semester hours for associate, 124 semester hours for bachelor's; 10 semester hours of math/science; computer course for business, engineering technology, elementary education majors; internship (some majors); senior project (some majors).
Computers on Campus: 345 computers available on campus for general student use. A computer is recommended for all students. A campus-wide network can be accessed from student residence rooms and from off-campus. Students can contact faculty members and/or advisers through e-mail. Computers for student use in computer center, computer labs, research center, learning resource center, library, student center, dorms provide access to the Internet/World Wide Web. Staffed computer lab on campus provides training in use of computers, software. *Academic computing expenditure 1995–96:* $710,053.

EXPENSES AND FINANCIAL AID

Estimated Expenses for 1997–98: *Application fee:* $25. State resident tuition: $2651 full-time, $85.50 per semester hour part-time. Nonresident tuition: $6417 full-time, $207 per semester hour part-time. Part-time mandatory fees: $27 per semester. Full-time mandatory fees: $54. College room only: $2200.
Undergraduate Financial Aid: Of all full-time undergraduates enrolled in fall 1996, 77% of those who applied for aid were judged to have need according to Federal Methodology, of whom 92% were aided. On average, 67% of need was met. *Financial aid deadline (priority):* 3/1. *Financial aid forms:* FAFSA, CSS Financial Aid PROFILE, institutional form required.
LD Services Contact: Ms. Leslie M. Swanson, Counselor, University of Southern Indiana, 8600 University Boulevard, Evansville, IN 47712, 812-464-1867. Fax: 812-464-1960.

UNIVERSITY OF SOUTHWESTERN LOUISIANA

Lafayette, Louisiana

LEARNING DISABILITIES SERVICES INFORMATION

Services for Students with Disabilities (SSD) began offering services in 1970. Currently the program serves 128 undergraduates with LD. Services are also available to graduate students. Students diagnosed with ADD/ADHD are eligible for the same services available to students with LD, as well as support group.
Staff: 1 full-time, 5 part-time staff members, including coordinator. Services provided by tutors, counselors.
Special Fees: No special fees are charged for services to students with LD.
Applications and admissions: *Required:* high school transcript, untimed SAT I or ACT, LD criteria testing; *recommended:* extended time SAT I or ACT. Students may begin taking classes in fall, spring, or summer. *Application deadline:* continuous.

PROGRAM AND SERVICE COMPONENTS

Academic advising: Provided by academic advisers. Most students with LD take 12 semester hours each term; 12 semester hours required to maintain full-time status and be eligible for financial aid.
Counseling services: Individual counseling, career counseling.
Basic skills remediation: Offered in class-size groups by regular teachers, counselors. Available in reading, math, spelling, written language, learning strategies, study skills, time management, social skills.
Subject-area tutoring: Offered one-on-one and in small groups by professional teachers, peer tutors. Available in most subjects.
Auxiliary aids: Tape recorders, word-processors with spell-check, optical character readers.
Auxiliary services: Alternative test arrangements, notetakers, priority registration, advocacy.
Campus support group: A special student organization is available to students with LD.

GENERAL COLLEGE INFORMATION

State-supported, coed. Awards associate, bachelor's, master's, doctoral degrees. Founded 1898. *Setting:* 1,375-acre urban campus. *Research spending 1995–96:* $24.2 million. *Total enrollment:* 16,742. *Faculty:* 670 (578 full-time, 70% with terminal degrees, 92 part-time); student–undergrad faculty ratio is 23:1.
Enrollment Profile: 15,281 students from 46 states and territories, 77 other countries. 57% women, 43% men, 22% part-time, 97% state residents, 13% live on campus, 6% transferred in, 2% international, 29% 25 or older, 1% Native American, 1% Hispanic, 20% black, 1% Asian or Pacific Islander. *Retention:* 62% of 1995 full-time freshmen returned. *Graduation:* 5% graduate in 4 years, 18% in 5 years, 27% in 6 years. *Areas of study chosen:* 23% architecture, 16% education, 14% business management and administrative services, 10% health professions and related sciences, 8% engineering and applied sciences, 7% interdisciplinary studies, 5% agriculture, 5% biological and life sciences, 4% communications and journalism, 3% psychology, 3% social sciences, 2% computer and information sciences, 1% English language/literature/letters, 1% fine arts, 1% foreign language and literature, 1% mathematics, 1% performing arts, 1% physical sciences.
First-Year Class: 3,015 total; 4,424 applied, 99% were accepted, 62% of whom enrolled. 3 National Merit Scholars.
Graduation Requirements: 64 semester hours for associate, 132 semester hours for bachelor's; 6 semester hours of math; 9 semester hours of science; computer course; senior project for honors program students.
Computers on Campus: 600 computers available on campus for general student use. Computer purchase/lease plans available. A campus-wide network can be accessed from off-campus. Students can contact faculty members and/or advisers through e-mail. Computers for student use in computer center, computer labs, research center, learning resource center, dorms, departmental labs provide access to the Internet/World Wide Web, on- and off-campus e-mail addresses. Staffed computer lab on campus (open 24 hours a day) provides training in use of computers, software. *Academic computing expenditure 1995–96:* $1.8 million.

EXPENSES AND FINANCIAL AID

Expenses for 1996–97: *Application fee:* $5. State resident tuition: $1897 full-time. Nonresident tuition: $5633 full-time. Part-time tuition per semester ranges from $273.50 to $844.50 for state residents, $363.50 to $2585 for nonresidents. College room and board: $2350 (minimum).
Undergraduate Financial Aid: Of all full-time undergraduates enrolled in fall 1996, 64% of those who applied for aid were judged to have need according to Federal Methodology, of whom 91% were aided. On average, 90% of need was met. *Financial aid deadline (priority):* 3/1. *Financial aid forms:* FAFSA, institutional form required; CSS Financial Aid PROFILE, state form acceptable.
LD Services Contact: Ms. Page T. Salley, Coordinator, Services for Students with Disabilities, University of Southwestern Louisiana, Drawer 41650, Lafayette, LA 70504, 318-231-5252. Fax: 318-231-6195.

UNIVERSITY OF TENNESSEE, KNOXVILLE

Knoxville, Tennessee

LEARNING DISABILITIES SERVICES INFORMATION

Disability Services began offering services in 1985. Currently the program serves 100 undergraduates with LD. Services are also available to graduate students. Students diagnosed with ADD/ADHD are eligible for the same services available to students with LD, as well as medication monitoring (through Student Health Center).
Staff: 8 full-time staff members, including director, interpreters, lead interpreter, administrative assistant, principal secretary. Services provided by diagnostic specialists.
Special Fees: A fee is charged for diagnostic testing.
Applications and admissions: *Required:* high school transcript, courses completed, psychoeducational report completed within 3 years, documentation from LD specialist or psychologist; *recommended:* untimed or extended time SAT I or ACT, personal interview, letters of recommendation. Students may begin taking classes any term. *Application deadline:* 7/1 (fall term), 11/1 (spring term).
Special policies: The college has written policies regarding grade forgiveness; substitutions and waivers of admissions, graduation, and degree requirements.

PROGRAM AND SERVICE COMPONENTS

Special preparation or orientation: Orientation optional.
Diagnostic testing: Intelligence, reading, math, written language.
Academic advising: Provided by academic advisers. Students with LD may take up to 15 semester hours each term; most take 12 semester

hours; 12 semester hours required to maintain full-time status; 15 semester hours for Vocational Rehabilitation (fewer with special permission) required to be eligible for financial aid.

Counseling services: Individual counseling, career counseling.

Special courses: College survival skills, time management, math, study skills, career planning, biology. All offered for credit; all enter into overall grade point average.

Auxiliary aids: Tape recorders, word-processors with spell-check, optical character readers.

Auxiliary services: Alternative test arrangements, notetakers, advocacy.

GENERAL COLLEGE INFORMATION

State-supported, coed. Part of University of Tennessee System. Awards bachelor's, master's, doctoral, first professional degrees. Founded 1794. *Setting:* 511-acre urban campus. *Endowment:* $140 million. *Research spending 1995–96:* $87.6 million. *Educational spending 1995–96:* $5864 per undergrad. *Total enrollment:* 25,517. *Faculty:* 1,517 (1,458 full-time, 85% with terminal degrees, 59 part-time); student–undergrad faculty ratio is 17:1.

Enrollment Profile: 18,825 students from 49 states and territories, 72 other countries. 50% women, 50% men, 14% part-time, 85% state residents, 35% live on campus, 8% transferred in, 2% international, 18% 25 or older, 1% Native American, 1% Hispanic, 5% black, 3% Asian or Pacific Islander. *Retention:* 76% of 1995 full-time freshmen returned. *Graduation:* 24% graduate in 4 years, 49% in 5 years, 55% in 6 years. *Areas of study chosen:* 15% engineering and applied sciences, 11% business management and administrative services, 10% interdisciplinary studies, 9% agriculture, 7% biological and life sciences, 6% performing arts, 6% social sciences, 5% vocational and home economics, 4% communications and journalism, 4% English language/literature/letters, 4% psychology, 3% architecture, 3% education, 3% health professions and related sciences, 1% area and ethnic studies, 1% computer and information sciences, 1% foreign language and literature, 1% mathematics, 1% philosophy, 1% physical sciences. *Most popular recent majors:* psychology, English, accounting.

First-Year Class: 3,692 total; 8,630 applied, 75% were accepted, 57% of whom enrolled. 22% from top 10% of their high school class, 52% from top quarter, 82% from top half. 37 National Merit Scholars.

Graduation Requirements: 120 semester hours; 2 courses each in math and natural science; computer course for agricultural economics, agricultural education, animal sciences, food sciences, forestry, ornamental horticulture, business, advertising, child and family studies, adult and continuing education majors; internship (some majors); senior project for honors program students and some majors.

Computers on Campus: 260 computers available on campus for general student use. Computer purchase/lease plans available. A computer is required for some students. A campus-wide network can be accessed from student residence rooms and from off-campus. Students can contact faculty members and/or advisers through e-mail. Computers for student use in computer center, computer labs, classrooms, library, student center, dorms provide access to the Internet/World Wide Web, on- and off-campus e-mail addresses. Staffed computer lab on campus (open 24 hours a day) provides training in use of computers, software. *Academic computing expenditure 1995–96:* $5.8 million.

EXPENSES AND FINANCIAL AID

Expenses for 1997–98: *Application fee:* $25. State resident tuition: $2096 full-time, $90 per semester hour part-time. Nonresident tuition: $6778 full-time, $285 per semester hour part-time. Part-time mandatory fees: $21 per semester hour. Full-time mandatory fees: $480. College room and board: $3580 (minimum).

Undergraduate Financial Aid: 63% of all full-time undergraduates enrolled in fall 1996 applied for aid; of these, 83% were judged to have need according to Federal Methodology, of whom 77% were aided. On average, 60% of need was met. *Financial aid deadline (priority):* 2/15. *Financial aid forms:* FAFSA required; CSS Financial Aid PROFILE acceptable.

LD Services Contact: Ms. Jan Howard, Director, Disability Services, University of Tennessee, Knoxville, 191 Hoskins Library, Knoxville, TN 37996-4250, 423-974-6087. Fax: 423-974-9552. Email: jhoward5@utk.edu.

THE UNIVERSITY OF TEXAS AT ARLINGTON

Arlington, Texas

LEARNING DISABILITIES SERVICES INFORMATION

Office of Counseling and Career Development currently serves 150 undergraduates with LD. Services are also available to graduate students. Students diagnosed with ADD/ADHD are eligible for the same services available to students with LD.

Staff: 1 full-time staff member (Counseling/Learning Specialist). Services provided by tutors, counselors, ADA coordinator, special services testing coordinator.

Special Fees: No special fees are charged for services to students with LD.

Applications and admissions: *Required:* high school transcript, class rank, courses completed, untimed SAT I or ACT; *recommended:* extended time SAT I or ACT, personal interview. Students may begin taking classes any term. *Application deadline:* 8/1 (fall term), 12/15 (spring term).

Special policies: The college has written policies regarding grade forgiveness.

PROGRAM AND SERVICE COMPONENTS

Academic advising: Provided by unit staff members, academic advisers. Students with LD may take up to 19 semester hours each term; most take 12 semester hours; 9 semester hours required to maintain full-time status; 6 semester hours (part-time), 12 semester hours (full-time) required to be eligible for financial aid.

Counseling services: Individual counseling, career counseling.

Subject-area tutoring: Offered one-on-one, in small groups, and in class-size groups by professional teachers, peer tutors, counselors. Available in most subjects.

Auxiliary aids: Taped textbooks, optical character readers, Arkenstone Reader/Scanner.

Auxiliary services: Alternative test arrangements, advocacy.

GENERAL COLLEGE INFORMATION

State-supported, coed. Part of University of Texas System. Awards bachelor's, master's, doctoral degrees. Founded 1895. *Setting:* 395-acre suburban campus with easy access to Dallas–Fort Worth. *Endowment:* $17.4 million. *Research spending 1995–96:* $22.4 million. *Educational spending 1995–96:* $3429 per undergrad. *Total enrollment:* 20,544. *Faculty:* 1,215 (664 full-time, 88% with terminal degrees, 551 part-time).

Enrollment Profile: 16,575 students from 47 states and territories, 100 other countries. 51% women, 49% men, 42% part-time, 95% state residents, 9% live on campus, 64% transferred in, 3% international, 41% 25 or older, 1% Native American, 9% Hispanic, 10% black, 11% Asian or Pacific Islander. *Retention:* 67% of 1995 full-time freshmen returned. *Graduation:* 7% graduate in 4 years, 20% in 5 years, 27% in 6 years. *Areas of study chosen:* 26% liberal arts/general studies, 20% business management and administrative services, 8% biological and life sciences, 8% engineering and applied sciences, 5% communications and journalism, 5% health professions and related sciences, 4% computer and information sciences, 4% psychology, 3% architecture, 3% English language/literature/letters, 3% fine arts, 3% social sciences, 2% interdisciplinary studies, 1% education, 1% foreign language and literature, 1% mathematics, 1% physical sciences. *Most popular recent majors:* interdisciplinary studies, business administration/commerce/management, accounting.

First-Year Class: 1,424 total; 2,416 applied, 88% were accepted, 67% of whom enrolled. 40% from top quarter of their high school class, 71% from top half.

Graduation Requirements: 124 semester hours; 6 semester hours of math; 11 semester hours of science; computer course; senior project (some majors).

Computers on Campus: 300 computers available on campus for general student use. Computer purchase/lease plans available. A campus-wide network can be accessed from student residence rooms and from off-campus. Students can contact faculty members and/or advisers through e-mail. Computers for student use in computer center, computer labs, library, student rooms provide access to the Internet/World Wide Web, on- and off-campus e-mail addresses. Staffed computer lab on campus provides training in use of computers, software. *Academic computing expenditure 1995–96:* $4.5 million.

The University of Texas at Arlington (continued)

EXPENSES AND FINANCIAL AID

Expenses for 1996–97: *Application fee:* $25. State resident tuition: $960 full-time. Nonresident tuition: $7380 full-time, $246 per semester hour part-time. State resident part-time tuition per semester ranges from $120 to $352. Part-time mandatory fees per semester range from $116.95 to $506.45. Full-time mandatory fees: $1261. College room and board: $2900. College room only: $1500.

Undergraduate Financial Aid: Of all full-time undergraduates enrolled in fall 1996, 72% of those who applied for aid were judged to have need according to Federal Methodology, of whom 89% were aided. On average, 100% of need was met. *Financial aid deadline (priority):* 6/1. *Financial aid forms:* FAFSA, institutional form required.

LD Services Contact: Dr. Cheryl D. Cardell, Counseling/Learning Specialist, The University of Texas at Arlington, Box 19156, Arlington, TX 76019-0407, 817-272-3670. Fax: 817-794-5792.

THE UNIVERSITY OF TEXAS AT AUSTIN

Austin, Texas

LEARNING DISABILITIES SERVICES INFORMATION

Services for Students with Disabilities, Office of the Dean of Students began offering services in 1980. Currently the program serves 400 undergraduates with LD. Services are also available to graduate students. Students diagnosed with ADD/ADHD are eligible for the same services available to students with LD.

Staff: 7 full-time, 1 part-time staff members, including director, support staff. Services provided by counselors.

Special Fees: No special fees are charged for services to students with LD.

Applications and admissions: *Required:* personal interview, psychoeducational report. Students may begin taking classes any term. *Application deadline:* continuous.

Special policies: The college has written policies regarding substitutions and waivers of degree requirements.

PROGRAM AND SERVICE COMPONENTS

Academic advising: Provided by unit staff members, academic advisers. Students with LD may take up to 21 semester hours (with permission of academic dean) each term; most take 12 to 14 semester hours; 12 semester hours (or as arranged on an individual basis) required to maintain full-time status; 12 semester hours (may be eligible for reduced package with reduced course load) required to be eligible for financial aid.

Counseling services: Individual counseling, small-group counseling, self-advocacy training.

Auxiliary aids: Taped textbooks, tape recorders, word-processors with spell-check, personal computers, talking computers, optical character readers.

Auxiliary services: Alternative test arrangements, notetakers, priority registration, advocacy.

Campus support group: A special student organization is available to students with LD.

GENERAL COLLEGE INFORMATION

State-supported, coed. Part of University of Texas System. Awards bachelor's, master's, doctoral, first professional degrees. Founded 1883. *Setting:* 350-acre urban campus with easy access to San Antonio. *Endowment:* $831.7 million. *Research spending 1995–96:* $210.7 million. *Educational spending 1995–96:* $6908 per undergrad. *Total enrollment:* 48,008. *Faculty:* 2,431 (2,239 full-time, 91% with terminal degrees, 192 part-time); student–undergrad faculty ratio is 19:1.

Enrollment Profile: 35,789 students from 52 states and territories, 115 other countries. 49% women, 51% men, 13% part-time, 91% state residents, 22% live on campus, 6% transferred in, 3% international, 11% 25 or older, 1% Native American, 15% Hispanic, 4% black, 13% Asian or Pacific Islander. *Retention:* 59% of 1995 full-time freshmen returned. *Graduation:* 28% graduate in 4 years, 56% in 5 years, 63% in 6 years. *Areas of study chosen:* 12% business management and administrative services, 12% engineering and applied sciences, 11% communications and journalism, 10% liberal arts/general studies, 9% social sciences, 8% biological and life sciences, 6% physical sciences, 5% computer and information sciences, 5% education, 5% psychology, 3% English language/literature/letters, 3% health professions and related sciences, 2% fine arts, 2% performing arts, 2% vocational and home economics, 1% architecture, 1% area and ethnic studies, 1% foreign language and literature, 1% mathematics, 1% philosophy.

First-Year Class: 6,430 total; 17,263 applied, 61% were accepted, 61% of whom enrolled. 46% from top 10% of their high school class, 83% from top quarter, 98% from top half. 299 National Merit Scholars.

Graduation Requirements: 120 semester hours; 3 semester hours of math; 6 semester hours of science; 2 semesters of a foreign language; computer course for engineering, business, education majors; internship (some majors); senior project for honors program students and some majors.

Computers on Campus: 500 computers available on campus for general student use. Computer purchase/lease plans available. A campuswide network can be accessed from student residence rooms and from off-campus. Students can contact faculty members and/or advisers through e-mail. Computers for student use in computer center, computer labs, classrooms, library, student center, dorms provide access to the Internet/World Wide Web, on- and off-campus e-mail addresses. Staffed computer lab on campus (open 24 hours a day) provides training in use of computers, software. *Academic computing expenditure 1995–96:* $7.7 million.

EXPENSES AND FINANCIAL AID

Expenses for 1996–97: *Application fee:* $40. State resident tuition: $960 full-time. Nonresident tuition: $7380 full-time, $246 per semester hour part-time. State resident part-time tuition per semester ranges from $120 to $352. Part-time mandatory fees per semester range from $184.44 to $672.24. Full-time mandatory fees: $1652. College room and board: $4550.

Undergraduate Financial Aid: Of all full-time undergraduates enrolled in fall 1996, 78% of those who applied for aid were judged to have need according to Federal Methodology, of whom 95% were aided. On average, 90% of need was met. *Financial aid deadline (priority):* 4/1. *Financial aid forms:* FAFSA required.

LD Services Contact: Mr. Matthew F. Tominey, Student Affairs Administrator, The University of Texas at Austin, PO Box 7849, Austin, TX 78712, 512-471-6259. Fax: 512-471-7833. Email: m.tominey@mail.utexas.edu.

THE UNIVERSITY OF TEXAS AT EL PASO

El Paso, Texas

LEARNING DISABILITIES SERVICES INFORMATION

Disabled Student Services Office began offering services in 1995. Currently the program serves 30 undergraduates with LD. Services are also available to graduate students. Students diagnosed with ADD/ADHD are eligible for the same services available to students with LD, as well as quiet testing location.

Staff: 4 full-time staff members, including director, administrative assistant, senior administrative clerk, learning specialist. Services provided by learning specialist.

Special Fees: No special fees are charged for services to students with LD.

Applications and admissions: *Required:* high school transcript, grade point average, class rank, courses completed, untimed SAT I or ACT; *recommended:* psychoeducational report completed within 3 years. Students may begin taking classes any term. *Application deadline:* continuous.

PROGRAM AND SERVICE COMPONENTS

Diagnostic testing: Intelligence, reading, math, spelling.

Academic advising: Provided by academic advisers. Students with LD may take up to 21 semester hours each term; most take 12 semester hours; 9 semester hours required to maintain full-time status; 12 semester hours required to be eligible for financial aid.

Counseling services: Guidance counseling.

Basic skills remediation: Offered one-on-one, in small groups, and in class-size groups by regular teachers; computer-aided instruction also offered. Available in reading, math, spelling, learning strategies, study skills, time management.

Subject-area tutoring: Offered one-on-one by learning specialist. Available in all subjects.

Special courses: College survival skills, reading, study skills. Some offered for credit; none enter into overall grade point average.

Auxiliary aids: Taped textbooks, word-processors with spell-check, personal computers, optical character readers, closed circuit television, talking calculator, 4-track tape player.

Auxiliary services: Alternative test arrangements, notetakers, advocacy, readers.
Campus support group: A special student organization is available to students with LD.

GENERAL COLLEGE INFORMATION

State-supported, coed. Part of University of Texas System. Awards bachelor's, master's, doctoral degrees. Founded 1913. *Setting:* 360-acre urban campus. *Research spending 1995–96:* $11.8 million. *Total enrollment:* 15,386. *Faculty:* 799 (472 full-time, 82% with terminal degrees, 327 part-time); student–undergrad faculty ratio is 17:1.
Enrollment Profile: 13,159 students from 47 states and territories, 67 other countries. 54% women, 46% men, 34% part-time, 88% state residents, 2% live on campus, 35% transferred in, 8% international, 29% 25 or older, 1% Native American, 68% Hispanic, 3% black, 2% Asian or Pacific Islander. *Retention:* 63% of 1995 full-time freshmen returned. *Graduation:* 28% graduate in 6 years. *Areas of study chosen:* 12% business management and administrative services, 12% education, 12% engineering and applied sciences, 10% health professions and related sciences, 8% interdisciplinary studies, 6% liberal arts/general studies, 5% psychology, 4% biological and life sciences, 3% communications and journalism, 2% social sciences, 1% computer and information sciences, 1% English language/literature/letters, 1% mathematics, 1% performing arts, 1% philosophy, 1% physical sciences. *Most popular recent majors:* interdisciplinary studies, criminal justice, psychology.
First-Year Class: 1,617 total; 3,097 applied, 79% were accepted, 66% of whom enrolled. 41% from top quarter of their high school class, 70% from top half.
Graduation Requirements: 123 semester hours; 9 semester hours of science; computer course for business, engineering majors.
Computers on Campus: A campus-wide network can be accessed from student residence rooms and from off-campus. Students can contact faculty members and/or advisers through e-mail. Computers for student use in computer center, computer labs, research center, learning resource center, library provide access to the Internet/World Wide Web, on- and off-campus e-mail addresses. Staffed computer lab on campus provides training in use of computers, software. *Academic computing expenditure 1995–96:* $7 million.

EXPENSES AND FINANCIAL AID

Expenses for 1996–97: State resident tuition: $960 full-time. Nonresident tuition: $7380 full-time. Students who are Mexican nationals and able to demonstrate financial need pay state resident tuition rates. Full-time mandatory fees: $1096. College room only: $1850 (minimum).
Undergraduate Financial Aid: 62% of all full-time undergraduates enrolled in fall 1996 applied for aid; of these, 84% were judged to have need according to Federal Methodology, of whom 80% were aided. On average, 55% of need was met. *Financial aid deadline (priority):* 3/15. *Financial aid forms:* FAFSA, institutional form required; CSS Financial Aid PROFILE acceptable.
LD Services Contact: Ms. Susan J. López, Director, Disabled Student Services Office, The University of Texas at El Paso, 500 West University Avenue, El Paso, TX 79968, 915-747-5148. Fax: 915-747-8712. Email: sulopez@utep.edu.

THE UNIVERSITY OF TEXAS AT SAN ANTONIO

San Antonio, Texas

LEARNING DISABILITIES SERVICES INFORMATION

Office of Disabled Student Services began offering services in 1979. Currently the program serves 50 undergraduates with LD. Services are also available to graduate students. Students diagnosed with ADD/ADHD are eligible for the same services available to students with LD.
Staff: 2 full-time, 9 part-time staff members, including director. Services provided by work-study students, student development specialist.
Special Fees: $50 for diagnostic testing.
Applications and admissions: *Required:* high school transcript, class rank, courses completed, untimed SAT I or ACT; *recommended:* extended time SAT I or ACT, Texas Rehabilitation Commission referral (for receipt of services). Students may begin taking classes any term. *Application deadline:* 7/1 (fall term), 12/1 (spring term).

PROGRAM AND SERVICE COMPONENTS

Diagnostic testing: Intelligence, reading, math, spelling, written language, study skills, personality.
Academic advising: Provided by academic advisers. Students with LD may take up to 18 semester hours each term; most take 9 to 12 semester hours; 9 semester hours required to maintain full-time status; 6 semester hours required to be eligible for financial aid.
Counseling services: Individual counseling, small-group counseling, career counseling, self-advocacy training, support group.
Basic skills remediation: Offered in small groups by regular teachers, peer teachers. Available in reading, math, written language, study skills.
Subject-area tutoring: Offered one-on-one and in small groups by peer tutors. Available in some subjects.
Auxiliary aids: Taped textbooks, tape recorders, typewriters, word-processors with spell-check, personal computers, optical character readers, scanner with DecTalk and Vocal Eyes.
Auxiliary services: Alternative test arrangements, notetakers, advocacy, reading services.

GENERAL COLLEGE INFORMATION

State-supported, comprehensive, coed. Part of University of Texas System. Awards bachelor's, master's, doctoral degrees. Founded 1969. *Setting:* 600-acre suburban campus. *Endowment:* $9.1 million. *Research spending 1995–96:* $3.9 million. *Educational spending 1995–96:* $1137 per undergrad. *Total enrollment:* 17,547. *Faculty:* 783 (350 full-time, 99% with terminal degrees, 433 part-time); student–undergrad faculty ratio is 22:1.
Enrollment Profile: 53% women, 47% men, 36% part-time, 95% state residents, 9% live on campus, 16% transferred in, 2% international, 41% 25 or older, 1% Native American, 37% Hispanic, 4% black, 1% Asian or Pacific Islander. *Areas of study chosen:* 24% business management and administrative services, 14% social sciences, 11% biological and life sciences, 10% interdisciplinary studies, 8% engineering and applied sciences, 6% psychology, 5% fine arts, 5% liberal arts/general studies, 4% computer and information sciences, 4% health professions and related sciences, 3% English language/literature/letters, 3% physical sciences, 1% architecture, 1% communications and journalism, 1% foreign language and literature, 1% mathematics. *Most popular recent majors:* accounting, business administration/commerce/management, interdisciplinary studies.
First-Year Class: Of the students who applied, 80% were accepted. 15% from top 10% of their high school class, 42% from top quarter, 74% from top half.
Graduation Requirements: 120 semester hours; 3 semester hours of math; 3 semester hours of a foreign language; computer course.
Computers on Campus: 550 computers available on campus for general student use. A campus-wide network can be accessed from off-campus. Students can contact faculty members and/or advisers through e-mail. Computers for student use in computer center, computer labs, library, student center, dorms provide access to the Internet/World Wide Web. Staffed computer lab on campus (open 24 hours a day).

EXPENSES AND FINANCIAL AID

Expenses for 1996–97: *Application fee:* $20. State resident tuition: $960 full-time. Nonresident tuition: $7380 full-time, $246 per semester hour part-time. State resident part-time tuition per semester ranges from $120 to $352. Part-time mandatory fees per semester range from $132 to $588. Full-time mandatory fees: $1234. College room only: $2833.
Undergraduate Financial Aid: 62% of all full-time undergraduates enrolled in fall 1996 applied for aid; of these, 57% were judged to have need according to Federal Methodology, of whom 91% were aided. On average, 73% of need was met. *Financial aid deadline (priority):* 3/31. *Financial aid forms:* FAFSA required; CSS Financial Aid PROFILE acceptable.
LD Services Contact: Ms. Lorraine Donham, Director, Disability Services, The University of Texas at San Antonio, 6900 North Loop 1604 West, San Antonio, TX 78249, 210-458-4157. Fax: 210-458-4980. Email: ldonham@lonestar.utsa.edu.

UNIVERSITY OF THE PACIFIC

Stockton, California

LEARNING DISABILITIES SERVICES INFORMATION

Learning Disabilities Support Program began offering services in 1990. Currently the program serves 150 undergraduates with LD. Ser-

University of the Pacific (continued)

vices are also available to graduate students. Students diagnosed with ADD/ADHD are eligible for the same services available to students with LD, as well as soundproof booths.
Staff: 4 part-time staff members, including coordinator. Services provided by tutors, aides, clerk.
Special Fees: $300 for diagnostic testing.
Applications and admissions: *Required:* high school transcript, grade point average, courses completed, untimed SAT I or ACT, letters of recommendation; *recommended:* extended time SAT I or ACT. Students may begin taking classes in fall or spring. *Application deadline:* continuous.

PROGRAM AND SERVICE COMPONENTS

Special preparation or orientation: Optional summer program offered prior to entering college.
Diagnostic testing: Intelligence, reading, math, spelling, spoken language, written language, perceptual skills, personality, speech, hearing.
Academic advising: Provided by academic advisers. Students with LD may take up to 14 units each term; most take 12 to 14 units; 12 units (waivers may be requested) required to maintain full-time status; 12 units (assistance can be prorated for fewer than 12 units) required to be eligible for financial aid.
Counseling services: Individual counseling, career counseling.
Subject-area tutoring: Offered one-on-one by peer tutors. Available in most subjects.
Special courses: Reading, composition, learning strategies, math, study skills. Most offered for credit.
Auxiliary aids: Taped textbooks, tape recorders, word-processors with spell-check, personal computers, talking computers, optical character readers.
Auxiliary services: Alternative test arrangements, notetakers, priority registration, advocacy.
Campus support group: A special student organization is available to students with LD.

GENERAL COLLEGE INFORMATION

Independent, coed. Awards bachelor's, master's, doctoral, first professional degrees. Founded 1851. *Setting:* 175-acre suburban campus with easy access to Sacramento. *Endowment:* $73.3 million. *Research spending 1995–96:* $5.4 million. *Total enrollment:* 4,785. *Faculty:* 614 (390 full-time, 94% with terminal degrees, 224 part-time); student–undergrad faculty ratio is 15:1.
Enrollment Profile: 3,368 students from 45 states and territories, 50 other countries. 55% women, 45% men, 5% part-time, 80% state residents, 50% live on campus, 46% transferred in, 6% international, 5% 25 or older, 1% Native American, 8% Hispanic, 4% black, 23% Asian or Pacific Islander. *Retention:* 82% of 1995 full-time freshmen returned. *Most popular recent majors:* liberal arts/general studies, pharmacy/pharmaceutical sciences, business administration/commerce/management.
First-Year Class: 568 total; 2,090 applied, 85% were accepted, 32% of whom enrolled. 38% from top 10% of their high school class, 74% from top quarter, 90% from top half.
Graduation Requirements: 124 units; math proficiency; computer course for engineering, math, geophysics, business majors; internship (some majors); senior project (some majors).
Computers on Campus: 185 computers available on campus for general student use. Computer purchase/lease plans available. A computer is recommended for all students. A campus-wide network can be accessed from student residence rooms and from off-campus. Students can contact faculty members and/or advisers through e-mail. Computers for student use in computer center, computer labs, library, dorms provide access to the Internet/World Wide Web, on- and off-campus e-mail addresses. Staffed computer lab on campus provides training in use of computers, software.

EXPENSES AND FINANCIAL AID

Expenses for 1997–98: *Application fee:* $50. Comprehensive fee of $24,436 includes full-time tuition ($18,450 minimum), mandatory fees ($350), and college room and board ($5636). Full-time tuition for pharmacy program: $27,675.
Undergraduate Financial Aid: 75% of all full-time undergraduates enrolled in fall 1996 applied for aid; of these, 96% were judged to have need according to Federal Methodology, of whom 100% were aided. On average, 86% of need was met. *Financial aid deadline (priority):* 3/2. *Financial aid forms:* FAFSA required. State form required for some.

LD Services Contact: Mr. Howard Houck, Coordinator, LD Program, University of the Pacific, 3601 Pacific Avenue, Bannister Hall, Stockton, CA 95211, 209-946-2458.

UNIVERSITY OF UTAH

Salt Lake City, Utah

LEARNING DISABILITIES SERVICES INFORMATION

Center for Disabled Student Services began offering services in 1983. Currently the program serves 317 undergraduates with LD. Services are also available to graduate students. Students diagnosed with ADD/ADHD are eligible for the same services available to students with LD.
Staff: 5 full-time, 4 part-time staff members, including director, LD counselors. Services provided by tutors, counselors, diagnostic specialists.
Special Fees: No special fees are charged for services to students with LD.
Applications and admissions: *Required:* high school transcript, grade point average, courses completed, untimed SAT I or ACT; *recommended:* extended time SAT I or ACT, psychoeducational report completed within 3 years. Students may begin taking classes any term. *Application deadline:* 7/1 (fall term), 2/15 (spring term).
Special policies: The college has written policies regarding substitutions and waivers of admissions, graduation, and degree requirements.

PROGRAM AND SERVICE COMPONENTS

Special preparation or orientation: Optional orientation offered during summer prior to autumn enrollment.
Diagnostic testing: Intelligence, reading, math, spelling, handwriting, spoken language, written language, perceptual skills, study skills, personality, social skills, psychoneurology, speech, hearing, learning strategies.
Academic advising: Provided by unit staff members, academic advisers. Students with LD may take up to 18 semester hours each term; most take 12 semester hours; 12 semester hours required to maintain full-time status and be eligible for financial aid.
Counseling services: Individual counseling, small-group counseling, career counseling.
Basic skills remediation: Offered one-on-one, in small groups, and in class-size groups by student support services teachers, communication disorders teachers. Available in reading, math, spelling, written language, learning strategies, study skills, time management, speech.
Subject-area tutoring: Offered one-on-one and in small groups by peer tutors. Available in all subjects.
Special courses: College survival skills, reading, composition, learning strategies, word processing, time management, math, typing, personal psychology, study skills, career planning. Most offered for credit; most enter into overall grade point average.
Auxiliary aids: Taped textbooks, tape recorders, calculators, typewriters, word-processors with spell-check, talking computer terminal.
Auxiliary services: Alternative test arrangements, notetakers, priority registration, advocacy, scribes, readers.
Campus support group: A special student organization is available to students with LD.

GENERAL COLLEGE INFORMATION

State-supported, coed. Part of Utah System of Higher Education. Awards bachelor's, master's, doctoral, first professional degrees. Founded 1850. *Setting:* 1,500-acre urban campus. *Endowment:* $128.8 million. *Research spending 1995–96:* $98.7 million. *Total enrollment:* 24,930. *Faculty:* 1,454 (all full-time, 97% with terminal degrees); student–undergrad faculty ratio is 23:1.
Enrollment Profile: 19,979 students from 54 states and territories, 93 other countries. 46% women, 54% men, 32% part-time, 90% state residents, 10% live on campus, 39% transferred in, 3% international, 32% 25 or older, 1% Native American, 3% Hispanic, 1% black, 3% Asian or Pacific Islander. *Retention:* 59% of 1995 full-time freshmen returned. *Areas of study chosen:* 13% business management and administrative services, 13% social sciences, 8% health professions and related sciences, 7% engineering and applied sciences, 6% biological and life sciences, 5% communications and journalism, 5% education, 3% computer and information sciences, 3% English language/literature/letters, 3% fine arts, 3% performing arts, 3% physical sciences, 2% architecture, 2% foreign language and literature, 2% premed, 2% psychology, 1% area and ethnic studies, 1% mathematics, 1% natural resource sciences, 1%

philosophy, 1% predentistry, 1% prelaw, 1% vocational and home economics. *Most popular recent majors:* sociology, psychology, political science/government.
First-Year Class: 2,379 total; 5,431 applied, 91% were accepted, 48% of whom enrolled. 27% from top 10% of their high school class, 54% from top quarter, 80% from top half. 40 National Merit Scholars, 30 class presidents, 40 valedictorians.
Graduation Requirements: 183 credit hours; computer course for business, math, engineering majors.
Computers on Campus: 5,000 computers available on campus for general student use. Computer purchase/lease plans available. A computer is recommended for all students. A campus-wide network can be accessed from student residence rooms and from off-campus. Students can contact faculty members and/or advisers through e-mail. Computers for student use in computer center, computer labs, research center, learning resource center, library, student center, dorms, departmental labs provide access to the Internet/World Wide Web. Staffed computer lab on campus provides training in use of computers, software. *Academic computing expenditure 1995–96:* $25 million.

EXPENSES AND FINANCIAL AID

Expenses for 1997–98: *Application fee:* $30. State resident tuition: $2601 full-time. Nonresident tuition: $7998 full-time. Part-time tuition per quarter ranges from $227.30 to $684.30 for state residents, $645.90 to $2089 for nonresidents. College room and board: $4400. College room only: $1700.
Undergraduate Financial Aid: 47% of all full-time undergraduates enrolled in fall 1996 applied for aid; of these, 96% were judged to have need according to Federal Methodology, of whom 84% were aided. On average, 54% of need was met. *Financial aid deadline (priority):* 3/1. *Financial aid forms:* FAFSA, institutional form required; state form acceptable.
Financial aid specifically for students with LD: Scholarship: Louise J. Snow Scholarship.
LD Services Contact: Ms. Olga Nadeau, Director, Center for Disabled Student Services, University of Utah, 160 Union, Salt Lake City, UT 84112, 801-581-5020. Fax: 801-581-6652.

UNIVERSITY OF VIRGINIA

Charlottesville, Virginia

LEARNING DISABILITIES SERVICES INFORMATION

Learning Needs and Evaluation Center began offering services in 1979. Currently the program serves 200 undergraduates with LD. Students diagnosed with ADD/ADHD are eligible for the same services available to students with LD.
Staff: 4 full-time, 7 part-time staff members, including director, coordinators. Services provided by remediation specialist, counselors, diagnostic specialist, office services specialists, transcribers, monitors.
Special Fees: No special fees are charged for services to students with LD.
Applications and admissions: *Required:* high school transcript, courses completed, untimed SAT I, autobiographical statement, letters of recommendation. Students may begin taking classes in fall only. *Application deadline:* 1/1.
Special policies: The college has written policies regarding substitutions and waivers of degree requirements.

PROGRAM AND SERVICE COMPONENTS

Special preparation or orientation: Optional orientation offered before classes begin.
Academic advising: Provided by academic advisers. Students with LD may take up to 18 semester hours each term; most take 15 semester hours; 12 semester hours required to maintain full-time status and be eligible for financial aid.
Counseling services: Individual counseling.
Auxiliary aids: Taped textbooks, tape recorders, typewriters, word-processors with spell-check, talking computers, optical character readers.
Auxiliary services: Alternative test arrangements, notetakers, advocacy.

GENERAL COLLEGE INFORMATION

State-supported, coed. Awards bachelor's, master's, doctoral, first professional degrees. Founded 1819. *Setting:* 1,136-acre suburban campus with easy access to Richmond. *Endowment:* $823.3 million. *Research spending 1995–96:* $106.7 million. *Total enrollment:* 17,959. *Faculty:* 2,095 (1,795 full-time, 90% with terminal degrees, 300 part-time); student–undergrad faculty ratio is 14:1.
Enrollment Profile: 12,040 students from 53 states and territories, 91 other countries. 53% women, 47% men, 1% part-time, 66% state residents, 49% live on campus, 11% transferred in, 2% international, 2% 25 or older, 0% Native American, 2% Hispanic, 11% black, 10% Asian or Pacific Islander. *Retention:* 97% of 1995 full-time freshmen returned. *Graduation:* 81% graduate in 4 years, 91% in 5 years. *Areas of study chosen:* 21% engineering and applied sciences, 19% social sciences, 9% business management and administrative services, 8% interdisciplinary studies, 7% biological and life sciences, 6% English language/literature/letters, 6% psychology, 5% architecture, 4% health professions and related sciences, 3% foreign language and literature, 3% natural resource sciences, 3% physical sciences, 2% computer and information sciences, 1% area and ethnic studies, 1% fine arts, 1% mathematics, 1% performing arts, 1% theology/religion. *Most popular recent majors:* business administration/commerce/management, biology/biological sciences, psychology.
First-Year Class: 2,827 total; 17,338 applied, 33% were accepted, 50% of whom enrolled. 79% from top 10% of their high school class, 96% from top quarter, 99% from top half. 1 Westinghouse recipient, 175 valedictorians.
Graduation Requirements: 120 semester hours; 12 semester hours of math/natural science; computer course for engineering, commerce majors; internship (some majors); senior project for honors program students and some majors.
Computers on Campus: 1,745 computers available on campus for general student use. A computer is strongly recommended for all students. A campus-wide network can be accessed from student residence rooms and from off-campus. Students can contact faculty members and/or advisers through e-mail. Computers for student use in computer center, computer labs, library, dorms provide access to the Internet/World Wide Web, on- and off-campus e-mail addresses. Staffed computer lab on campus (open 24 hours a day) provides training in use of computers, software.

EXPENSES AND FINANCIAL AID

Expenses for 1997–98: *Application fee:* $40. State resident tuition: $4790 full-time. Nonresident tuition: $15,034 full-time. Part-time tuition (1 to 8 semester hours): $918 per semester for 1 to 3 semester hours, $1766 per semester for 4 or more semester hours for state residents; $2612 per semester for 1 to 3 semester hours, $5191 per semester for 4 or more semester hours for nonresidents. College room and board: $2700 (minimum). College room only: $1800 (minimum).
Undergraduate Financial Aid: Of all full-time undergraduates enrolled in fall 1996, 91% of those who applied for aid were judged to have need according to Federal Methodology, of whom 96% were aided. On average, 90% of need was met. *Financial aid deadline (priority):* 3/1. *Financial aid forms:* FAFSA, institutional form required.
LD Services Contact: Ms. Valerie Schoolcraft, Administrative Assistant, University of Virginia, 530 McCormick Road, Charlottesville, VA 22903, 804-243-5180. Fax: 804-243-5188.

UNIVERSITY OF WATERLOO

Waterloo, Ontario, Canada

LEARNING DISABILITIES SERVICES INFORMATION

Services for Persons with Disabilities currently serves 160 undergraduates with LD. Services are also available to graduate students. Students diagnosed with ADD/ADHD are eligible for the same services available to students with LD.
Staff: 3 full-time, 3 part-time staff members, including co-director, administrative assistants. Services provided by counselor, learning specialist.
Special Fees: No special fees are charged for services to students with LD.
Applications and admissions: *Required:* high school transcript, grade point average, courses completed; *recommended:* personal interview, letters of recommendation, psychoeducational report. Students may begin taking classes in fall, winter, or spring. *Application deadline:* 5/1 (fall term), 3/1 (spring term).

PROGRAM AND SERVICE COMPONENTS

Special preparation or orientation: Optional orientation offered during registration.

Diagnostic testing: Intelligence, reading, math, spelling, handwriting, spoken language, written language, study skills, personality, learning strategies, career counselling.
Academic advising: Provided by unit staff members, academic advisers. Students with LD may take up to 5.5 credit courses each term; most take 2 to 5.5 credit courses; 3.5 credit courses required to maintain full-time status.
Counseling services: Individual counseling, career counseling, anxiety and stress management.
Subject-area tutoring: Offered one-on-one by peer tutors. Available in some subjects.
Special courses: College survival skills, reading, vocabulary development, composition, learning strategies, time management, math, study skills, career planning, stress management. None offered for credit.
Auxiliary aids: Taped textbooks, tape recorders, calculators, word-processors with spell-check, personal computers, talking computers, optical character readers, laptop computers.
Auxiliary services: Alternative test arrangements, notetakers, advocacy, priority in residence placement.

GENERAL COLLEGE INFORMATION

Province-supported, coed. Awards bachelor's, master's, doctoral, first professional degrees. Founded 1957. *Setting:* 900-acre suburban campus with easy access to Toronto. *Total enrollment:* 21,903. *Faculty:* 969 (829 full-time, 95% with terminal degrees, 140 part-time); student–undergrad faculty ratio is 17:1.
Enrollment Profile: 20,116 students from 12 provinces and territories, 69 other countries. 50% women, 50% men, 26% part-time, 91% province residents, 4% transferred in. *Most popular recent majors:* art/fine arts, science, mathematics.
First-Year Class: 3,501 total; 17,684 applied, 57% were accepted, 35% of whom enrolled.
Graduation Requirements: 30 term courses; computer course for most co-op, most honors programs; senior project (some majors).
Computers on Campus: 4,000 computers available on campus for general student use. Computer purchase/lease plans available. Computers for student use in computer center, computer labs, research center, various locations.

EXPENSES AND FINANCIAL AID

Expenses for 1996–97: *Application fee:* $85. Canadian resident tuition: $330 per course part-time. Part-time mandatory fees: $394 per year (minimum). Canadian resident full-time tuition ranges from $2936 to $3216 according to program. Nonresident tuition ranges from $11,068 to $18,894 full-time, $2214 to $3608 per course part-time, according to program. (All figures are in Canadian dollars.). Full-time mandatory fees: $487 (minimum). College room and board: $5652 (minimum). College room only: $3662.
Undergraduate Financial Aid: 42% of all full-time undergraduates enrolled in fall 1996 applied for aid; of these,100% were judged to have need according to Federal Methodology, of whom 85% were aided. *Financial aid deadline (priority):* 8/31. *Financial aid forms:* student budget, Canadian Student Aid form, Free Application for Federal Student Aid (FAFSA) (for American students) required; CSS Financial Aid PROFILE acceptable.
Financial aid specifically for students with LD: Scholarship: Special Achievement Bursary for Students with Disabilities.
LD Services Contact: Ms. Virginia Nusca, Learning Specialist, University of Waterloo, 200 University Avenue West, Waterloo, ON N2C 3G1, 519-885-1211. Fax: 519-746-2401. Email: vnusca@nh3adm.uwaterloo.ca.

THE UNIVERSITY OF WESTERN ONTARIO

London, Ontario, Canada

LEARNING DISABILITIES SERVICES INFORMATION

Services for Students with Disabilities began offering services in 1980. Currently the program serves 253 undergraduates with LD. Services are also available to graduate students. Students diagnosed with ADD/ADHD are eligible for the same services available to students with LD.
Staff: 2 full-time, 3 part-time staff members, including coordinator, administrative assistant. Services provided by remediation specialists, counselors.
Special Fees: No special fees are charged for services to students with LD.
Applications and admissions: *Required:* high school transcript, grade point average, courses completed, psychoeducational report completed within 3 years; *recommended:* letters of recommendation. Students may begin taking classes any term. *Application deadline:* 6/1.

PROGRAM AND SERVICE COMPONENTS

Academic advising: Provided by academic advisers. Students with LD may take up to 6 courses each term; most take 4 to 5 courses; 3.5 courses required to maintain full-time status.
Counseling services: Individual counseling, career counseling.
Basic skills remediation: Offered one-on-one and in small groups by learning skills counselors. Available in reading, math, spelling, written language, learning strategies, study skills, time management.
Auxiliary aids: Taped textbooks, tape recorders, word-processors with spell-check, personal computers, talking computers, optical character readers.
Auxiliary services: Alternative test arrangements, advocacy.

GENERAL COLLEGE INFORMATION

Province-supported, coed. Awards bachelor's, master's, doctoral degrees. Founded 1878. *Setting:* 402-acre suburban campus. *Endowment:* $40 million. *Research spending 1995–96:* $41.6 million. *Educational spending 1995–96:* $6995 per undergrad. *Total enrollment:* 27,722. *Faculty:* 1,577 (1,402 full-time, 55% with terminal degrees, 175 part-time); student–undergrad faculty ratio is 16:1.
Enrollment Profile: 24,977 students from 12 provinces and territories, 71 other countries. 55% women, 45% men, 21% part-time, 90% province residents, 13% live on campus, 4% transferred in, 2% international, 26% 25 or older. *Retention:* 93% of 1995 full-time freshmen returned. *Areas of study chosen:* 42% social sciences, 20% biological and life sciences, 12% fine arts, 12% health professions and related sciences, 5% engineering and applied sciences, 3% education, 2% business management and administrative services, 2% performing arts, 2% prelaw. *Most popular recent majors:* sociology, political science/government, psychology.
First-Year Class: 4,937 total; 23,503 applied, 54% were accepted, 39% of whom enrolled.
Graduation Requirements: 15 courses; computer course for engineering science majors; internship (some majors); senior project (some majors).
Computers on Campus: 100 computers available on campus for general student use. Computer purchase/lease plans available. A computer is recommended for some students. A campus-wide network can be accessed from student residence rooms and from off-campus. Students can contact faculty members and/or advisers through e-mail. Computers for student use in computer center, computer labs, library, student center provide access to the Internet/World Wide Web, on- and off-campus e-mail addresses. Staffed computer lab on campus provides training in use of computers, software. *Academic computing expenditure 1995–96:* $3.4 million.

EXPENSES AND FINANCIAL AID

Expenses for 1997–98: *Application fee:* $75. Canadian resident tuition: $3217 (minimum) full-time, $643.40 per course part-time. Nonresident tuition: $8217 (minimum) full-time. Part-time mandatory fees: $111.86 per course. Full-time tuition ranges up to $3808 for Canadian residents, $11,217 for nonresidents, according to program. Part-time tuition for nonresidents ranges from $1643 to $2362 per course according to program. (All figures are in Canadian dollars.). Full-time mandatory fees: $644. College room and board: $5591. College room only: $3106.
Undergraduate Financial Aid: *Financial aid deadline:* Applications processed continuously. *Financial aid forms:* state form, institutional form required.
LD Services Contact: Dr. Susan M. Weaver, Coordinator, The University of Western Ontario, Room 210, UCC, London, ON N6A 3K7, Canada, 519-661-2147. Fax: 519-661-3949. Email: sue@sdc.uwo.ca.

THE UNIVERSITY OF WINNIPEG

Winnipeg, Manitoba, Canada

LEARNING DISABILITIES SERVICES INFORMATION

Special Needs Program began offering services in 1993. Currently the program serves 40 undergraduates with LD. Services are also available to graduate students. Students diagnosed with ADD/ADHD are eligible for the same services available to students with LD.

Staff: 1 full-time, 1 part-time staff members, including coordinator. Services provided by remediation specialists.
Special Fees: No special fees are charged for services to students with LD.
Applications and admissions: *Required:* high school courses completed; *recommended:* psychoeducational report completed within 3 years. Students may begin taking classes in fall, winter, or spring. *Application deadline:* continuous.
Special policies: The college has written policies regarding grade forgiveness; substitutions and waivers of admissions, graduation, and degree requirements.

PROGRAM AND SERVICE COMPONENTS

Special preparation or orientation: Optional orientation offered at the end of August before classes begin.
Academic advising: Provided by academic advisers. Students with LD may take up to 30 credit hours each term; most take 18 credit hours; 18 credit hours required to maintain full-time status and be eligible for financial aid.
Counseling services: Individual counseling, career counseling.
Basic skills remediation: Offered one-on-one and in class-size groups by learning specialist/resource coordinator. Available in reading, spelling, written language, learning strategies, perceptual skills, study skills, time management, social skills.
Auxiliary aids: Taped textbooks, word-processors with spell-check, personal computers, talking computers, optical character readers.
Auxiliary services: Alternative test arrangements, notetakers, priority registration, advocacy.

GENERAL COLLEGE INFORMATION

Province-supported, comprehensive, coed. Awards bachelor's, master's degrees. Founded 1967. *Setting:* 2-acre urban campus. *Total enrollment:* 7,887. *Faculty:* 378 (240 full-time, 138 part-time).
Enrollment Profile: 58% women, 42% men, 57% part-time, 82% province residents, 10% transferred in, 7% international. *Most popular recent majors:* psychology, sociology, mathematics.
First-Year Class: 2,474 applied, 86% were accepted.
Graduation Requirements: 15 full-year courses; 1 science course; senior project (some majors).
Computers on Campus: 175 computers available on campus for general student use. A campus-wide network can be accessed from off-campus. Students can contact faculty members and/or advisers through e-mail. Computers for student use in computer center, computer labs, learning resource center, library, student center provide access to the Internet/World Wide Web, on- and off-campus e-mail addresses. Staffed computer lab on campus.

EXPENSES AND FINANCIAL AID

Expenses for 1997–98: *Application fee:* $30. Part-time mandatory fees: $48 per course. Tuition ranges from $2631 to $3050 full-time, $526.28 to $610.04 per course part-time for Canadian residents; $4694 to $5430 full-time, $938.88 to $1086 per course part-time for nonresidents, according to program. One-time mandatory fee: $13.30. (All figures are in Canadian dollars.). Full-time mandatory fees: $240.
Undergraduate Financial Aid: *Financial aid deadline (priority):* 6/30. *Financial aid forms:* FAFSA, state form, institutional form required for some.
LD Services Contact: Ms. Carlene Besner, Coordinator of Special Needs, The University of Winnipeg, 515 Portage Avenue, Winnipeg, MB R3B 2E9, Canada, 204-786-9771. Fax: 204-783-7981. Email: cbesner@uwinnipeg.ca.

UNIVERSITY OF WISCONSIN–EAU CLAIRE

Eau Claire, Wisconsin

LEARNING DISABILITIES SERVICES INFORMATION

Services for Students with Disabilities began offering services in 1982. Currently the program serves 40 undergraduates with LD. Services are also available to graduate students. Students diagnosed with ADD/ADHD are eligible for the same services available to students with LD.
Staff: Includes director, coordinators, program assistant. Services provided by remediation specialists, tutors, counselors.
Special Fees: No special fees are charged for services to students with LD.
Applications and admissions: *Required:* high school transcript, class rank; *recommended:* extended time ACT. Students may begin taking classes any term. *Application deadline:* continuous.
Special policies: The college has written policies regarding substitutions and waivers of graduation and degree requirements.

PROGRAM AND SERVICE COMPONENTS

Academic advising: Provided by unit staff members, academic advisers. Students with LD may take up to 18 credits each term; most take 12 to 14 credits; 12 credits required to maintain full-time status and be eligible for financial aid.
Counseling services: Individual counseling, career counseling.
Basic skills remediation: Offered in class-size groups by regular teachers. Available in reading, math, written language, study skills, time management, speech.
Subject-area tutoring: Offered one-on-one and in small groups by peer tutors. Available in most subjects.
Special courses: Reading, communication skills, composition. All offered for credit; all enter into overall grade point average.
Auxiliary aids: Taped textbooks, word-processors with spell-check.
Auxiliary services: Alternative test arrangements, notetakers, priority registration, advocacy.
Campus support group: A special student organization is available to students with LD.

GENERAL COLLEGE INFORMATION

State-supported, comprehensive, coed. Part of University of Wisconsin System. Awards associate, bachelor's, master's degrees. Founded 1916. *Setting:* 333-acre urban campus. *Endowment:* $8.9 million. *Research spending 1995–96:* $390,000. *Total enrollment:* 10,503. *Faculty:* 515 (417 full-time, 91% with terminal degrees, 98 part-time); student–undergrad faculty ratio is 19:1.
Enrollment Profile: 10,023 students from 28 states and territories, 46 other countries. 60% women, 40% men, 13% part-time, 80% state residents, 35% live on campus, 7% transferred in, 2% international, 11% 25 or older, 1% Native American, 1% Hispanic, 1% black, 2% Asian or Pacific Islander. *Retention:* 77% of 1995 full-time freshmen returned. *Graduation:* 14% graduate in 4 years, 46% in 5 years, 55% in 6 years. *Areas of study chosen:* 21% education, 17% business management and administrative services, 9% health professions and related sciences, 9% social sciences, 5% biological and life sciences, 5% communications and journalism, 5% computer and information sciences, 4% psychology, 3% fine arts, 3% physical sciences, 2% English language/literature/letters, 1% foreign language and literature, 1% mathematics, 1% premed. *Most popular recent majors:* nursing, elementary education, accounting.
First-Year Class: 2,048 total; 4,986 applied, 85% were accepted, 48% of whom enrolled. 15% from top 10% of their high school class, 46% from top quarter, 86% from top half. 1 National Merit Scholar, 49 valedictorians.
Graduation Requirements: 60 credits for associate, 120 credits for bachelor's; 11 credits of science; computer course for business majors.
Computers on Campus: 878 computers available on campus for general student use. Computer purchase/lease plans available. A campus-wide network can be accessed from student residence rooms and from off-campus. Students can contact faculty members and/or advisers through e-mail. Computers for student use in academic/administrative buildings provide access to the Internet/World Wide Web, on- and off-campus e-mail addresses. Staffed computer lab on campus (open 24 hours a day) provides training in use of computers, software.

EXPENSES AND FINANCIAL AID

Expenses for 1996–97: *Application fee:* $28. State resident tuition: $2572 full-time, $107.13 per credit part-time. Nonresident tuition: $8036 full-time, $334.88 per credit part-time. Minnesota residents pay tuition at the rate they would pay if attending a comparable state-supported institution in Minnesota. Full-time mandatory fees: $2. College room and board: $2904 (minimum). College room only: $1670.
Undergraduate Financial Aid: Of all full-time undergraduates enrolled in fall 1996, 78% of those who applied for aid were judged to have need according to Federal Methodology, of whom 98% were aided. On average, 98% of need was met. *Financial aid deadline (priority):* 4/15. *Financial aid forms:* FAFSA, CSS Financial Aid PROFILE acceptable.
LD Services Contact: Mr. Joseph C. Hisrich, Director, Services for Students with Disabilities, University of Wisconsin–Eau Claire, PO Box 4004, Eau Claire, WI 54702-4004, 715-836-4542. Fax: 715-836-2380.

UNIVERSITY OF WISCONSIN–GREEN BAY

Green Bay, Wisconsin

LEARNING DISABILITIES SERVICES INFORMATION

Services for Students with Disabilities (SSD) began offering services in 1992. Currently the program serves 20 undergraduates with LD. Services are also available to graduate students. Students diagnosed with ADD/ADHD are eligible for the same services available to students with LD, as well as special counseling and advocacy.
Staff: 1 full-time, 1 part-time staff members, including coordinator, program assistant. Services provided by remediation specialists, tutors, counselors.
Special Fees: No special fees are charged for services to students with LD.
Applications and admissions: *Required:* high school transcript, grade point average, courses completed, untimed or extended time ACT; *recommended:* high school class rank, autobiographical statement, letters of recommendation. Students may begin taking classes in fall, spring, or summer. *Application deadline:* continuous.

PROGRAM AND SERVICE COMPONENTS

Academic advising: Provided by unit staff members, academic advisers. Most students with LD take 9 to 12 credits each term; 12 credits required to maintain full-time status; 6 credits required to be eligible for financial aid.
Auxiliary aids: Taped textbooks, tape recorders, calculators, typewriters, word-processors with spell-check, talking computers.
Auxiliary services: Alternative test arrangements, notetakers, priority registration, advocacy, typing and library assistance.

GENERAL COLLEGE INFORMATION

State-supported, comprehensive, coed. Part of University of Wisconsin System. Awards associate, bachelor's, master's degrees. Founded 1968. *Setting:* 700-acre suburban campus. *Endowment:* $3.2 million. *Research spending 1995–96:* $446,015. *Educational spending 1995–96:* $3412 per undergrad. *Total enrollment:* 5,220. *Faculty:* 274 (157 full-time, 86% with terminal degrees, 117 part-time); student–undergrad faculty ratio is 19:1.
Enrollment Profile: 5,112 students from 30 states and territories, 30 other countries. 63% women, 37% men, 18% part-time, 95% state residents, 26% live on campus, 25% transferred in, 1% international, 22% 25 or older, 2% Native American, 1% Hispanic, 1% black, 2% Asian or Pacific Islander. *Retention:* 73% of 1995 full-time freshmen returned. *Graduation:* 10% graduate in 4 years, 34% in 5 years, 41% in 6 years. *Areas of study chosen:* 16% business management and administrative services, 12% biological and life sciences, 10% psychology, 9% social sciences, 8% communications and journalism, 8% liberal arts/general studies, 6% natural resource sciences, 4% education, 4% English language/literature/letters, 4% foreign language and literature, 4% performing arts, 3% computer and information sciences, 3% fine arts, 2% health professions and related sciences, 2% interdisciplinary studies, 2% mathematics, 2% physical sciences, 1% philosophy. *Most popular recent majors:* business administration/commerce/management, human development, psychology.
First-Year Class: 1,018 total; 2,387 applied, 89% were accepted, 48% of whom enrolled. 16% from top 10% of their high school class, 47% from top quarter, 88% from top half. 15 valedictorians.
Graduation Requirements: 60 credits for associate, 120 credits for bachelor's; 9 credits of math/science; computer course for math, business, accounting, communication, economics, environmental science, nutrition majors; internship (some majors); senior project (some majors).
Computers on Campus: 200 computers available on campus for general student use. Computer purchase/lease plans available. A campuswide network can be accessed from student residence rooms and from off-campus. Students can contact faculty members and/or advisers through e-mail. Computers for student use in computer center, computer labs, learning resource center, classrooms, library, student center, dorms, advising center provide access to the Internet/World Wide Web, on- and off-campus e-mail addresses. Staffed computer lab on campus provides training in use of computers, software. *Academic computing expenditure 1995–96:* $1.4 million.

EXPENSES AND FINANCIAL AID

Expenses for 1996–97: *Application fee:* $28. State resident tuition: $2545 full-time. Nonresident tuition: $8009 full-time. Part-time tuition per semester ranges from $107 to $1177 for state residents, $335 to $3685 for nonresidents. Minnesota residents pay tuition at the rate they would pay if attending a comparable state-supported institution in Minnesota. College room and board: $2550 (minimum). College room only: $1650.
Undergraduate Financial Aid: 59% of all full-time undergraduates enrolled in fall 1996 applied for aid; of these, 98% were judged to have need according to Federal Methodology, of whom 93% were aided. On average, 99% of need was met. *Financial aid deadline (priority):* 4/15. *Financial aid forms:* FAFSA required; CSS Financial Aid PROFILE acceptable. Institutional form required for some.
LD Services Contact: Ms. Elizabeth MacNeille, Coordinator, Services for Students with Disabilities, University of Wisconsin–Green Bay, 2420 Nicolet Drive, Green Bay, WI 54311, 414-465-2849. Fax: 414-465-2954.

UNIVERSITY OF WISCONSIN–LA CROSSE

La Crosse, Wisconsin

LEARNING DISABILITIES SERVICES INFORMATION

Services for Students with Special Needs began offering services in 1982. Currently the program serves 129 undergraduates with LD. Services are also available to graduate students. Students diagnosed with ADD/ADHD are eligible for the same services available to students with LD.
Staff: 4 full-time, 1 part-time staff members, including director. Services provided by counselors.
Special Fees: No special fees are charged for services to students with LD.
Applications and admissions: *Required:* high school transcript, class rank, courses completed, extended time ACT, psychoeducational report completed within 3 years; *recommended:* personal interview, letters of recommendation. Students may begin taking classes in fall, winter, or summer. *Application deadline:* 1/1.

PROGRAM AND SERVICE COMPONENTS

Special preparation or orientation: Required orientation held during registration.
Academic advising: Provided by unit staff members, academic advisers. Students with LD may take up to 18 credits each term; most take 12 credits; 12 credits required to maintain full-time status and be eligible for financial aid.
Counseling services: Individual counseling, small-group counseling, career counseling.
Auxiliary aids: Taped textbooks, word-processors with spell-check, talking computers, optical character readers.
Auxiliary services: Alternative test arrangements, notetakers, priority registration, advocacy.

GENERAL COLLEGE INFORMATION

State-supported, comprehensive, coed. Part of University of Wisconsin System. Awards associate, bachelor's, master's degrees. Founded 1909. *Setting:* 119-acre suburban campus. *Research spending 1995–96:* $1.6 million. *Total enrollment:* 9,046. *Faculty:* 449 (350 full-time, 81% with terminal degrees, 99 part-time); student–undergrad faculty ratio is 20:1.
Enrollment Profile: 8,471 students from 34 states and territories, 37 other countries. 57% women, 43% men, 9% part-time, 82% state residents, 33% live on campus, 6% transferred in, 2% international, 13% 25 or older, 1% Native American, 1% Hispanic, 1% black, 1% Asian or Pacific Islander. *Retention:* 78% of 1995 full-time freshmen returned. *Graduation:* 10% graduate in 4 years, 39% in 5 years, 50% in 6 years. *Areas of study chosen:* 20% education, 18% business management and administrative services, 11% biological and life sciences, 7% health professions and related sciences, 5% psychology, 5% social sciences, 2% communications and journalism, 2% computer and information sciences, 2% English language/literature/letters, 2% physical sciences, 1% fine arts, 1% foreign language and literature, 1% mathematics, 1% performing arts. *Most popular recent majors:* biology/biological sciences, business administration/commerce/management, elementary education.
First-Year Class: 1,735 total; 4,555 applied, 81% were accepted, 47% of whom enrolled. 21% from top 10% of their high school class, 57% from top quarter, 94% from top half. 34 valedictorians.
Graduation Requirements: 64 credits for associate, 120 credits for bachelor's; 12 credits of math/science; computer course for math, business majors; internship (some majors).
Computers on Campus: 350 computers available on campus for general student use. Computer purchase/lease plans available. A campus-

wide network can be accessed from student residence rooms and from off-campus. Students can contact faculty members and/or advisers through e-mail. Computers for student use in computer center, computer labs, learning resource center, library, student center, dorms provide access to the Internet/World Wide Web, on- and off-campus e-mail addresses. Staffed computer lab on campus provides training in use of computers, software. *Academic computing expenditure 1995–96:* $644,009.

EXPENSES AND FINANCIAL AID

Expenses for 1996–97: *Application fee:* $28. State resident tuition: $2633 full-time. Nonresident tuition: $8097 full-time. Full-time tuition for Minnesota residents: $2952. Full-time mandatory fees: $2. College room and board: $2800. College room only: $1400.
Undergraduate Financial Aid: Of all full-time undergraduates enrolled in fall 1996, 90% of those who applied for aid were judged to have need according to Federal Methodology, of whom 100% were aided. On average, 96% of need was met. *Financial aid deadline (priority):* 3/15. *Financial aid forms:* FAFSA, institutional form, federal income tax form required.
LD Services Contact: Ms. June Reinert, Coordinator of Disability Resource Services, University of Wisconsin–La Crosse, 165 Murphy Library, 1725 State Street, La Crosse, WI 54601, 608-785-6900. Fax: 608-785-6910.

UNIVERSITY OF WISCONSIN–MADISON

Madison, Wisconsin

LEARNING DISABILITIES SERVICES INFORMATION

McBurney Disability Resource Center began offering services in 1981. Currently the program serves 300 undergraduates with LD. Services are also available to graduate students. Students diagnosed with ADD/ADHD are eligible for the same services available to students with LD, as well as medication management (through University psychiatric staff).
Staff: 2 part-time staff members, including coordinator, LD specialist. Services provided by counselors, Learning Specialist.
Special Fees: $150 for diagnostic testing.
Applications and admissions: *Required:* high school transcript, grade point average, class rank, courses completed; *recommended:* high school IEP (Individualized Education Program), extended time SAT I or ACT, autobiographical statement, letters of recommendation, psychoeducational report. Students may begin taking classes any term. *Application deadline:* 2/1 (fall term), 11/15 (spring term).
Special policies: The college has written policies regarding substitutions and waivers of admissions and graduation requirements.

PROGRAM AND SERVICE COMPONENTS

Special preparation or orientation: Orientation (required for some) held during Wisconsin Welcome prior to beginning of semester.
Diagnostic testing: Intelligence, reading, math, spelling, spoken language, written language, perceptual skills, study skills, personality, social skills, speech, hearing.
Academic advising: Provided by academic advisers. Students with LD may take up to 18 credits each term; most take 12 to 15 credits; 12 credits (fewer as recommended for accommodation) required to maintain full-time status.
Counseling services: Individual counseling, small-group counseling, career counseling, self-advocacy training.
Special courses: College survival skills, learning strategies, study skills. None offered for credit.
Auxiliary aids: Taped textbooks, tape recorders, calculators, word-processors with spell-check, personal computers, optical character readers.
Auxiliary services: Alternative test arrangements, notetakers, priority registration, advocacy, peer mentor program.
Campus support group: A special student organization is available to students with LD.

GENERAL COLLEGE INFORMATION

State-supported, coed. Part of University of Wisconsin System. Awards bachelor's, master's, doctoral, first professional degrees. Founded 1848. *Setting:* 1,050-acre urban campus. *Research spending 1995–96:* $450 million. *Total enrollment:* 39,826. *Undergraduate faculty:* 2,545 (2,419 full-time, 96% with terminal degrees, 126 part-time); student–undergrad faculty ratio is 12:1.
Enrollment Profile: 26,910 students from 53 states and territories, 82 other countries. 51% women, 49% men, 3% part-time, 64% state residents, 5% transferred in, 6% international, 4% 25 or older, 1% Native American, 4% Hispanic, 4% black, 5% Asian or Pacific Islander. *Retention:* 97% of 1995 full-time freshmen returned. *Graduation:* 80% graduate in 5 years, 90% in 6 years. *Most popular recent majors:* political science/government, mechanical engineering, history.
First-Year Class: 5,455 total; 15,250 applied, 78% were accepted, 46% of whom enrolled. 42% from top 10% of their high school class, 88% from top quarter, 99% from top half. 344 valedictorians.
Graduation Requirements: 120 semester hours; 6 semester hours of quantitative reasoning; computer course for business, engineering, education, some science majors; internship (some majors); senior project for honors program students and some majors.
Computers on Campus: 2,800 computers available on campus for general student use. Computer purchase/lease plans available. A campus-wide network can be accessed from student residence rooms and from off-campus. Students can contact faculty members and/or advisers through e-mail. Computers for student use in computer center, computer labs, research center, learning resource center, classrooms, library, student center, dorms provide access to the Internet/World Wide Web, on- and off-campus e-mail addresses. Staffed computer lab on campus provides training in use of computers, software.

EXPENSES AND FINANCIAL AID

Expenses for 1996–97: *Application fee:* $28. State resident tuition: $3040 full-time, $127.20 per semester hour part-time. Nonresident tuition: $10,210 full-time, $423.70 per semester hour part-time. Tuition for Minnesota residents: $4024 full-time, $168.50 per semester hour part-time. College room and board: $4650.
Undergraduate Financial Aid: *Financial aid deadline (priority):* 3/1. *Financial aid forms:* FAFSA, institutional form required; CSS Financial Aid PROFILE acceptable.
LD Services Contact: Ms. Cathleen Trueba, Learning Disability Services Coordinator, University of Wisconsin–Madison, 905 University Avenue, Madison, WI 53706-1380, 608-263-2741. Fax: 608-265-2998. Email: cmtrueba@facstaff.wisc.edu.

UNIVERSITY OF WISCONSIN–MILWAUKEE

Milwaukee, Wisconsin

LEARNING DISABILITIES SERVICES INFORMATION

Learning Disabilities Program of the Student Accessibility Center began offering services in 1987. Currently the program serves 230 undergraduates with LD. Services are also available to graduate students. Students diagnosed with ADD/ADHD are eligible for the same services available to students with LD.
Staff: 1 full-time staff member (director). Services provided by tutors.
Special Fees: $150 to $500 for diagnostic testing.
Applications and admissions: *Required:* high school transcript, grade point average, class rank, courses completed, psychoeducational report completed within 3 years (preferably senior year of high school); *recommended:* high school extracurricular activities, IEP (Individualized Education Program), untimed or extended time SAT I or ACT, personal interview, autobiographical statement, letters of recommendation. Students may begin taking classes in fall or summer. *Application deadline:* 6/30 (fall term), 11/30 (spring term).

PROGRAM AND SERVICE COMPONENTS

Diagnostic testing: Intelligence, reading, math, spelling, handwriting, spoken language, written language, motor abilities, perceptual skills, personality, psychoneurology, speech, hearing.
Academic advising: Provided by unit staff members, academic advisers. Most students with LD take 9 to 12 credit hours each term; 12 credit hours required to maintain full-time status; 12 credit hours (can be prorated) required to be eligible for financial aid.
Counseling services: Individual counseling, small-group counseling, career counseling, self-advocacy training.
Basic skills remediation: Offered one-on-one, in small groups, and in class-size groups by regular teachers, peer tutors. Available in reading, math, written language, learning strategies, study skills, time management, speech, computer skills.
Subject-area tutoring: Offered one-on-one and in small groups by peer tutors. Available in most subjects.
Special courses: Reading, composition, word processing, time management, math, study skills, career planning, stress management. Most offered for credit; most enter into overall grade point average.

University of Wisconsin–Milwaukee (continued)

Auxiliary aids: Taped textbooks, tape recorders, typewriters, word-processors with spell-check, personal computers, optical character readers.
Auxiliary services: Alternative test arrangements, notetakers, priority registration, advocacy, progress reports.

GENERAL COLLEGE INFORMATION

State-supported, coed. Part of University of Wisconsin System. Awards bachelor's, master's, doctoral degrees. Founded 1956. *Setting:* 90-acre urban campus. *Endowment:* $982,640. *Research spending 1995–96:* $12 million. *Total enrollment:* 21,877. *Faculty:* 1,354 (825 full-time, 87% with terminal degrees, 529 part-time).
Enrollment Profile: 15,272 students from 53 states and territories, 61 other countries. 55% women, 45% men, 32% part-time, 96% state residents, 9% transferred in, 3% international, 36% 25 or older, 1% Native American, 3% Hispanic, 8% black, 3% Asian or Pacific Islander. *Retention:* 69% of 1995 full-time freshmen returned. *Graduation:* 8% graduate in 4 years, 25% in 5 years, 37% in 6 years. *Areas of study chosen:* 18% social sciences, 9% education, 7% engineering and applied sciences, 6% fine arts, 5% communications and journalism, 4% architecture, 1% interdisciplinary studies.
First-Year Class: 2,253 total; 5,034 applied, 81% were accepted, 55% of whom enrolled. 8% from top 10% of their high school class, 28% from top quarter, 67% from top half.
Graduation Requirements: 120 credit hours; math proficiency; computer course for architecture, medical records administration, engineering, some business and math majors; internship (some majors).
Computers on Campus: 310 computers available on campus for general student use. A campus-wide network can be accessed from off-campus. Students can contact faculty members and/or advisers through e-mail. Computers for student use in computer center, library, student center, dorms provide access to the Internet/World Wide Web. Staffed computer lab on campus (open 24 hours a day).

EXPENSES AND FINANCIAL AID

Expenses for 1996–97: *Application fee:* $28. State resident tuition: $3102 full-time. Nonresident tuition: $9965 full-time. Part-time tuition per semester ranges from $247.85 to $1441 for state residents, $533.85 to $4587 for nonresidents. Minnesota residents pay tuition at the rate they would pay if attending a comparable state-supported institution in Minnesota. Full-time mandatory fees: $2. College room and board: $2912 (minimum).
Undergraduate Financial Aid: Of all full-time undergraduates enrolled in fall 1996, 85% of those who applied for aid were judged to have need according to Federal Methodology, of whom 94% were aided. On average, 77% of need was met. *Financial aid deadline (priority):* 3/1. *Financial aid forms:* FAFSA required.
LD Services Contact: Ms. Laurie Petersen, Learning Disabilities Program Manager, University of Wisconsin–Milwaukee, Student Accessibility Center, PO Box 413, Milwaukee, WI 53201, 414-229-6239. Fax: 414-229-2237. Email: laurieg@csd.uwm.edu.

UNIVERSITY OF WISCONSIN–STOUT

Menomonie, Wisconsin

LEARNING DISABILITIES SERVICES INFORMATION

Student Services: Services for Students with Disabilities began offering services in 1981. Currently the program serves 160 undergraduates with LD. Services are also available to graduate students. Students diagnosed with ADD/ADHD are eligible for the same services available to students with LD.
Staff: 1 full-time, 3 part-time staff members, including director, coordinator. Services provided by test accommodation coordinator, reader, taping coordinator.
Special Fees: $75 to $125 for diagnostic testing.
Applications and admissions: *Required:* high school transcript, class rank, courses completed, untimed ACT, psychoeducational report; *recommended:* high school IEP (Individualized Education Program), personal interview, letters of recommendation. Students may begin taking classes in fall, winter, or summer. *Application deadline:* continuous.

PROGRAM AND SERVICE COMPONENTS

Special preparation or orientation: Optional orientation offered after classes begin.
Diagnostic testing: Intelligence, reading, math, spelling, written language, motor abilities, personality.
Academic advising: Provided by unit staff members, academic advisers. Students with LD may take up to as many credits as an individual can handle (with permission of Program Director) each term; most take 13 to 17 credits; 12 credits required to maintain full-time status; 6 credits required to be eligible for financial aid.
Counseling services: Individual counseling, career counseling, self-advocacy training.
Special courses: College survival skills, composition, time management, study skills. All offered for credit; all enter into overall grade point average.
Auxiliary aids: Taped textbooks, word-processors with spell-check, talking computers, optical character readers.
Auxiliary services: Alternative test arrangements, notetakers, priority registration, advocacy.

GENERAL COLLEGE INFORMATION

State-supported, comprehensive, coed. Part of University of Wisconsin System. Awards bachelor's, master's degrees. Founded 1891. *Setting:* 120-acre small-town campus with easy access to Minneapolis–St. Paul. *Endowment:* $296,578. *Research spending 1995–96:* $1.3 million. *Total enrollment:* 7,322. *Faculty:* 364 (321 full-time, 76% with terminal degrees, 43 part-time); student–undergrad faculty ratio is 21:1.
Enrollment Profile: 6,701 students from 27 states and territories, 32 other countries. 48% women, 52% men, 11% part-time, 73% state residents, 35% live on campus, 9% transferred in, 2% international, 17% 25 or older, 1% Native American, 1% Hispanic, 1% black, 2% Asian or Pacific Islander. *Retention:* 79% of 1995 full-time freshmen returned. *Graduation:* 38% graduate in 5 years, 51% in 6 years. *Areas of study chosen:* 29% business management and administrative services, 24% engineering and applied sciences, 17% education, 10% fine arts, 8% vocational and home economics, 5% psychology, 4% health professions and related sciences, 3% mathematics. *Most popular recent majors:* hotel and restaurant management, industrial engineering technology, business administration/commerce/management.
First-Year Class: 1,471 total; 2,224 applied, 94% were accepted, 70% of whom enrolled. 7% from top 10% of their high school class, 27% from top quarter, 45% from top half.
Graduation Requirements: 124 credits; 6 credits of analytic reasoning; 4 credits of natural science; computer course for applied math, applied technology, business administration, dietetics, fashion merchandising, food service administration, industrial technology majors; internship (some majors); senior project (some majors).
Computers on Campus: 470 computers available on campus for general student use. Computer purchase/lease plans available. A campus-wide network can be accessed from student residence rooms and from off-campus. Students can contact faculty members and/or advisers through e-mail. Computers for student use in computer labs, library, dorms provide access to the Internet/World Wide Web, on- and off-campus e-mail addresses. Staffed computer lab on campus provides training in use of computers, software. *Academic computing expenditure 1995–96:* $193,345.

EXPENSES AND FINANCIAL AID

Expenses for 1996–97: *Application fee:* $28. State resident tuition: $2619 full-time, $109.95 per credit part-time. Nonresident tuition: $8083 full-time, $337.70 per credit part-time. Tuition for Minnesota residents: $2938 full-time, $123.70 per credit part-time. College room and board: $2922. College room only: $1526.
Undergraduate Financial Aid: 65% of all full-time undergraduates enrolled in fall 1996 applied for aid; of these, 83% were judged to have need according to Federal Methodology, of whom 98% were aided. On average, 78% of need was met. *Financial aid deadline (priority):* 4/1. *Financial aid forms:* FAFSA required.
LD Services Contact: Mr. M. Scott Bay, Director, Disability Services, University of Wisconsin–Stout, 206 Bowman Hall, Menomonie, WI 54751, 715-232-2995. Fax: 715-232-2996. Email: bays@uwstout.edu.

UNIVERSITY OF WISCONSIN–SUPERIOR

Superior, Wisconsin

LEARNING DISABILITIES SERVICES INFORMATION

Student Support Services currently serves 25 undergraduates with LD. Services are also available to graduate students. Students diagnosed with ADD/ADHD are eligible for the same services available to students with LD.

Staff: 5 full-time staff members, including director, program assistant. Services provided by remediation specialists, tutors, LD specialist, writing specialist, math specialist.

Special Fees: No special fees are charged for services to students with LD.

Applications and admissions: *Required:* high school transcript, class rank, untimed SAT I or ACT, psychoeducational report completed within 3 years; *recommended:* high school grade point average, courses completed. Students may begin taking classes in fall, spring, or summer. *Application deadline:* continuous.

Special policies: The college has written policies regarding grade forgiveness; substitutions and waivers of degree requirements.

PROGRAM AND SERVICE COMPONENTS

Special preparation or orientation: Optional orientation offered individually by special arrangement.

Diagnostic testing: Intelligence, reading, math, spelling, handwriting, written language, study skills, learning strategies.

Academic advising: Provided by unit staff members, academic advisers. Most students with LD take 12 to 14 credits each term; 12 credits required to maintain full-time status; 12 credits (full-time), 6 credits (part-time) required to be eligible for financial aid.

Counseling services: Individual counseling, small-group counseling, career counseling, self-advocacy training, support group.

Basic skills remediation: Offered one-on-one, in small groups, and in class-size groups by LD teachers, math specialist, English specialist. Available in reading, math, written language, learning strategies, study skills, time management.

Subject-area tutoring: Offered one-on-one and in small groups by peer tutors, Student Support Services professional staff. Available in all subjects.

Special courses: College survival skills, reading, vocabulary development, composition, learning strategies, word processing, time management, math, study skills, career planning. All offered for credit; all enter into overall grade point average.

Auxiliary aids: Taped textbooks, tape recorders, typewriters, word-processors with spell-check, Arkenstone Reader.

Auxiliary services: Alternative test arrangements, notetakers, priority registration, advocacy.

GENERAL COLLEGE INFORMATION

State-supported, comprehensive, coed. Part of University of Wisconsin System. Awards associate, bachelor's, master's degrees. Founded 1893. *Setting:* 230-acre small-town campus. *Endowment:* $5.5 million. *Research spending 1995–96:* $1.9 million. *Total enrollment:* 2,647. *Undergraduate faculty:* 160 (110 full-time, 50 part-time); student–undergrad faculty ratio is 12:1.

Enrollment Profile: 2,117 students from 26 states and territories, 17 other countries. 51% women, 49% men, 26% part-time, 61% state residents, 8% transferred in, 3% international, 21% 25 or older, 2% Native American, 1% Hispanic, 1% black, 3% Asian or Pacific Islander. *Retention:* 66% of 1995 full-time freshmen returned. *Areas of study chosen:* 31% education, 14% business management and administrative services, 14% social sciences, 11% biological and life sciences, 7% liberal arts/general studies, 6% fine arts, 5% communications and journalism, 5% psychology, 2% computer and information sciences, 2% English language/literature/letters, 1% engineering and applied sciences, 1% interdisciplinary studies, 1% mathematics. *Most popular recent majors:* business administration/commerce/management, education, art/fine arts.

First-Year Class: 321 total; 760 applied, 84% were accepted, 50% of whom enrolled. 12% from top 10% of their high school class, 35% from top quarter, 81% from top half. 3 National Merit Scholars, 11 class presidents, 11 valedictorians.

Graduation Requirements: 64 credits for associate, 120 credits for bachelor's; 9 credits of math; 6 credits of science; computer course for math, business majors; internship (some majors); senior project.

Computers on Campus: 125 computers available on campus for general student use. Computer purchase/lease plans available. A computer is recommended for all students. A campus-wide network can be accessed from student residence rooms and from off-campus. Students can contact faculty members and/or advisers through e-mail. Computers for student use in computer center, computer labs, learning resource center, classrooms, library, student center, dorms, business lab, education departmental lab provide access to the Internet/World Wide Web, on- and off-campus e-mail addresses. Staffed computer lab on campus (open 24 hours a day) provides training in use of computers, software. *Academic computing expenditure 1995–96:* $220,000.

EXPENSES AND FINANCIAL AID

Expenses for 1996–97: *Application fee:* $28. State resident tuition: $2463 full-time. Nonresident tuition: $7927 full-time. Part-time tuition per semester ranges from $117.43 to $1136 for state residents, $345.18 to $3803 for nonresidents. Tuition for Minnesota residents: $2782 full-time, $131.18 to $1287 per semester part-time. Full-time mandatory fees: $2. College room and board: $3100. College room only: $1506.

Undergraduate Financial Aid: 100% of all full-time undergraduates enrolled in fall 1996 applied for aid; of these, 83% were judged to have need according to Federal Methodology, of whom 98% were aided. On average, 93% of need was met. *Financial aid deadline (priority):* 4/15. *Financial aid forms:* FAFSA required. State form required for some.

LD Services Contact: Ms. Eloise Lozar, Learning Disabilities Specialist and Reading/Study Skills Specialist, University of Wisconsin–Superior, 1800 Grand Avenue, Superior, WI 54880, 715-394-8288. Fax: 715-394-8107.

UNIVERSITY OF WYOMING

Laramie, Wyoming

LEARNING DISABILITIES SERVICES INFORMATION

University Disability Support Services began offering services in 1985. Currently the program serves 75 undergraduates with LD. Services are also available to graduate students. Students diagnosed with ADD/ADHD are eligible for the same services available to students with LD.

Staff: 3 full-time staff members, including director, coordinators. Services provided by tutors, readers, interpreters.

Special Fees: No special fees are charged for services to students with LD.

Applications and admissions: *Required:* high school transcript, grade point average, courses completed, untimed or extended time SAT I or ACT. Students may begin taking classes in fall, spring, or summer. *Application deadline:* 8/10 (fall term), 1/3 (spring term).

PROGRAM AND SERVICE COMPONENTS

Special preparation or orientation: Optional orientation offered during registration.

Academic advising: Provided by unit staff members, academic advisers. Most students with LD take 12 semester hours each term; 12 semester hours required to maintain full-time status; source of aid determines number of semester hours required to be eligible for financial aid.

Counseling services: Individual counseling, small-group counseling, career counseling, self-advocacy training.

Basic skills remediation: Offered in class-size groups by regular teachers. Available in reading, math, written language, learning strategies, study skills.

Subject-area tutoring: Offered one-on-one and in small groups by peer tutors. Available in all subjects.

Special courses: College survival skills, reading, composition, math, typing, study skills, career planning. Some offered for credit; some enter into overall grade point average.

Auxiliary aids: Taped textbooks, tape recorders, calculators, typewriters, word-processors with spell-check, personal computers, talking computers, optical character readers, screen reading software with voice synthesizers, voice recognition system.

Auxiliary services: Alternative test arrangements, notetakers, priority registration, advocacy.

GENERAL COLLEGE INFORMATION

State-supported, coed. Awards bachelor's, master's, doctoral, first professional degrees. Founded 1886. *Setting:* 785-acre small-town campus. *Endowment:* $89.5 million. *Research spending 1995–96:* $38.2 million. *Educational spending 1995–96:* $6692 per undergrad. *Total enrollment:* 11,251. *Faculty:* 720 (620 full-time, 90% with terminal degrees, 100 part-time); student–undergrad faculty ratio is 15:1.

Enrollment Profile: 8,820 students from 56 states and territories, 42 other countries. 51% women, 49% men, 14% part-time, 77% state residents, 25% live on campus, 36% transferred in, 3% international, 24% 25 or older, 1% Native American, 5% Hispanic, 1% black, 1% Asian or Pacific Islander. *Retention:* 73% of 1995 full-time freshmen returned. *Graduation:* 16% graduate in 4 years, 36% in 5 years, 45% in 6 years. *Areas of study chosen:* 13% education, 13% liberal arts/general studies, 11% business management and administrative services, 11% engineering and applied sciences, 11% social sciences, 10% health professions and related sciences, 5% agriculture, 5% biological and life sciences, 4%

University of Wyoming (continued)

psychology, 3% communications and journalism, 3% fine arts, 2% computer and information sciences, 2% English language/literature/letters, 2% natural resource sciences, 2% physical sciences, 2% vocational and home economics, 1% mathematics. *Most popular recent majors:* elementary education, psychology, nursing.
First-Year Class: 1,239 total; 2,331 applied, 96% were accepted, 55% of whom enrolled. 27% from top 10% of their high school class, 53% from top quarter, 82% from top half. 10 National Merit Scholars.
Graduation Requirements: 120 semester hours; 5 math/science courses; computer course for most majors; internship (some majors); senior project for honors program students and some majors.
Computers on Campus: 550 computers available on campus for general student use. Computer purchase/lease plans available. A campus-wide network can be accessed from student residence rooms and from off-campus. Students can contact faculty members and/or advisers through e-mail. Computers for student use in computer center, computer labs, classrooms, library, student center, dorms, academic buildings provide access to the Internet/World Wide Web, on- and off-campus e-mail addresses. Staffed computer lab on campus provides training in use of computers, software. *Academic computing expenditure 1995–96:* $886,537.

EXPENSES AND FINANCIAL AID

Expenses for 1997–98: *Application fee:* $30. State resident tuition: $1944 full-time, $81 per semester hour part-time. Nonresident tuition: $7032 full-time, $293 per semester hour part-time. Part-time mandatory fees: $6.75 per semester hour. Full-time mandatory fees: $382. College room and board: $4245. College room only: $1724.
Undergraduate Financial Aid: Of all full-time undergraduates enrolled in fall 1996, 79% of those who applied for aid were judged to have need according to Federal Methodology, of whom 98% were aided. On average, 77% of need was met. *Financial aid deadline (priority):* 3/1. *Financial aid forms:* institutional form required. FAFSA required for some.
LD Services Contact: Ms. Chris Primus, Project Director of Disability Services, University of Wyoming, Box 3808, University Station, Laramie, WY 82071, 307-766-6189. Fax: 307-766-4010.

URBANA UNIVERSITY

Urbana, Ohio

LEARNING DISABILITIES SERVICES INFORMATION

Student Support Services Program began offering services in 1984. Currently the program serves 10 undergraduates with LD. Students diagnosed with ADD/ADHD are eligible for the same services available to students with LD.
Staff: 2 full-time staff members, including director, instructor. Services provided by remediation specialists, tutors, counselors.
Special Fees: No special fees are charged for services to students with LD.
Applications and admissions: *Required:* high school transcript, grade point average, class rank, courses completed, psychoeducational report; *recommended:* untimed or extended time SAT I or ACT. Students may begin taking classes any term. *Application deadline:* continuous.

PROGRAM AND SERVICE COMPONENTS

Special preparation or orientation: Optional orientation offered during first week of classes.
Diagnostic testing: Reading, math, written language, perceptual skills, study skills, personality, learning strategies.
Academic advising: Provided by unit staff members, academic advisers. Students with LD may take up to 18 semester hours each term; most take 12 to 16 semester hours; 12 semester hours required to maintain full-time status and be eligible for financial aid.
Counseling services: Individual counseling, career counseling.
Basic skills remediation: Offered in class-size groups by regular teachers. Available in reading, math, written language, learning strategies, study skills, time management, social skills.
Subject-area tutoring: Offered one-on-one by peer tutors. Available in all subjects.
Auxiliary aids: Taped textbooks, tape recorders, typewriters, personal computers, Recordings for the Blind, computer lab.
Auxiliary services: Alternative test arrangements, notetakers, advocacy.

GENERAL COLLEGE INFORMATION

Independent Swedenborgian, 4-year, coed. Awards associate, bachelor's degrees. Founded 1850. *Setting:* 128-acre small-town campus with easy access to Columbus and Dayton. *Educational spending 1995–96:* $2070 per undergrad. *Total enrollment:* 1,179. *Faculty:* 75 (36 full-time, 60% with terminal degrees, 39 part-time); student–undergrad faculty ratio is 16:1.
Enrollment Profile: 1,179 students from 7 states and territories, 3 other countries. 49% women, 51% men, 19% part-time, 96% state residents, 12% transferred in, 1% international, 20% 25 or older, 1% Native American, 1% Hispanic, 25% black. *Areas of study chosen:* 34% business management and administrative services, 26% social sciences, 20% education, 11% liberal arts/general studies, 4% biological and life sciences, 4% health professions and related sciences, 1% physical sciences. *Most popular recent majors:* business administration/commerce/management, education, liberal arts/general studies.
First-Year Class: 150 total; 354 applied, 79% were accepted, 54% of whom enrolled. 15% from top 10% of their high school class, 34% from top quarter, 66% from top half. 5 valedictorians.
Graduation Requirements: 63 credit hours for associate, 126 credit hours for bachelor's; 10 credit hours of math/science; computer course.
Computers on Campus: 30 computers available on campus for general student use. Computers for student use in computer center, computer labs, classrooms, library. Staffed computer lab on campus provides training in use of computers, software. *Academic computing expenditure 1995–96:* $44,031.

EXPENSES AND FINANCIAL AID

Estimated Expenses for 1997–98: *Application fee:* $25. Comprehensive fee of $14,880 includes full-time tuition ($10,530) and college room and board ($4350 minimum). College room only: $1900. Part-time tuition: $226 per credit hour.
Undergraduate Financial Aid: On average, 100% of need was met. *Financial aid deadline (priority):* 6/1. *Financial aid forms:* FAFSA, institutional form required; state form acceptable.
LD Services Contact: Ms. Sheri Haines, Director, Student Support Services, Urbana University, 597 College Way, Urbana, OH 43078, 937-484-1398.

UTAH STATE UNIVERSITY

Logan, Utah

LEARNING DISABILITIES SERVICES INFORMATION

Disability Resource Center began offering services in 1975. Currently the program serves 420 undergraduates with LD. Services are also available to graduate students. Students diagnosed with ADD/ADHD are eligible for the same services available to students with LD.
Staff: 9 full-time, 90 part-time staff members, including director, assistant director, coordinator, LD specialist, deaf specialist, staff assistants. Services provided by tutors, interpreters, notetakers, proctors.
Special Fees: $50 for diagnostic testing.
Applications and admissions: *Required:* high school transcript, untimed SAT I or ACT, psychoeducational report completed within 3 years; *recommended:* high school grade point average, courses completed. Students may begin taking classes any term. *Application deadline:* continuous.

PROGRAM AND SERVICE COMPONENTS

Special preparation or orientation: Summer program (required for some) held prior to entering college. Optional orientation offered before registration.
Diagnostic testing: Intelligence, math, speech, hearing, learning strategies.
Academic advising: Provided by unit staff members, academic advisers. Students with LD may take up to 15 credit hours each term; most take 12 to 15 credit hours; 12 credit hours required to maintain full-time status and be eligible for financial aid.
Counseling services: Individual counseling, small-group counseling, career counseling.
Basic skills remediation: Offered in class-size groups by regular teachers. Available in reading, math, learning strategies, study skills, time management, social skills.
Subject-area tutoring: Offered one-on-one and in small groups by peer tutors. Available in all subjects.

Special courses: College survival skills, reading, communication skills, learning strategies, time management, math, study skills, career planning. Most offered for credit; most enter into overall grade point average.
Auxiliary aids: Taped textbooks, tape recorders, calculators, word-processors with spell-check, personal computers, optical character readers.
Auxiliary services: Alternative test arrangements, notetakers, priority registration, advocacy.
Campus support group: A special student organization is available to students with LD.

GENERAL COLLEGE INFORMATION

State-supported, coed. Part of Utah System of Higher Education. Awards associate, bachelor's, master's, doctoral degrees. Founded 1888. *Setting:* 456-acre urban campus. *Endowment:* $34.8 million. *Research spending 1995–96:* $65.5 million. *Educational spending 1995–96:* $2871 per undergrad. *Total enrollment:* 20,808. *Faculty:* 780 (751 full-time, 29 part-time); student–undergrad faculty ratio is 22:1.
Enrollment Profile: 16,703 students from 52 states and territories, 63 other countries. 53% women, 47% men, 32% part-time, 88% state residents, 3% international, 24% 25 or older, 1% Native American, 2% Hispanic, 1% black, 1% Asian or Pacific Islander. *Areas of study chosen:* 19% liberal arts/general studies, 14% education, 11% business management and administrative services, 9% engineering and applied sciences, 6% social sciences, 5% performing arts, 4% agriculture, 4% computer and information sciences, 4% vocational and home economics, 3% health professions and related sciences, 3% natural resource sciences, 3% psychology, 2% biological and life sciences, 2% English language/literature/letters, 2% physical sciences, 2% premed, 1% architecture, 1% communications and journalism, 1% fine arts, 1% foreign language and literature, 1% mathematics, 1% predentistry, 1% prevet. *Most popular recent majors:* elementary education, family services, accounting.
First-Year Class: 2,442 total; 4,529 applied, 99% were accepted, 55% of whom enrolled. 17% from top 10% of their high school class, 65% from top quarter, 100% from top half. 18 National Merit Scholars.
Graduation Requirements: 96 credit hours for associate, 186 credit hours for bachelor's; math/science requirements vary according to program; computer course for engineering, math, business-related, some science, some education majors; internship (some majors); senior project for honors program students and some majors.
Computers on Campus: 712 computers available on campus for general student use. A campus-wide network can be accessed from student residence rooms and from off-campus. Students can contact faculty members and/or advisers through e-mail. Computers for student use in computer center, computer labs, learning resource center, library, student center, dorms, academic buildings provide access to the Internet/World Wide Web, on- and off-campus e-mail addresses. Staffed computer lab on campus provides training in use of computers, software.

EXPENSES AND FINANCIAL AID

Expenses for 1997–98: *Application fee:* $35. State resident tuition: $1767 full-time. Nonresident tuition: $6207 full-time. Part-time tuition per quarter ranges from $103.16 to $507.96 for state residents, $362.46 to $1785 for nonresidents. Part-time mandatory fees per quarter range from $46 to $136. Full-time mandatory fees: $408. College room and board: $2985.
Undergraduate Financial Aid: *Financial aid deadline:* continuous. *Financial aid forms:* FAFSA, institutional form, federal income tax form required; CSS Financial Aid PROFILE acceptable.
Financial aid specifically for students with LD: Scholarship: Disability Resource Center Scholarships; work-study.
LD Services Contact: Ms. Diane Craig Baum, Director, Disability Resource Center, Utah State University, University Hill, Logan, UT 84322-0101, 801-797-2444. Fax: 801-797-0130.

UTICA COLLEGE OF SYRACUSE UNIVERSITY

Utica, New York

LEARNING DISABILITIES SERVICES INFORMATION

Academic Support Services began offering services in 1983. Currently the program serves 44 undergraduates with LD. Students diagnosed with ADD/ADHD are eligible for the same services available to students with LD.
Staff: 3 full-time staff members, including director. Services provided by counselors, diagnostic specialists.
Special Fees: $100 for diagnostic testing.
Applications and admissions: *Required:* high school transcript, grade point average, letters of recommendation; *recommended:* high school class rank, untimed or extended time SAT I, extended time ACT, personal interview, autobiographical statement. Students may begin taking classes in fall only. *Application deadline:* continuous.

PROGRAM AND SERVICE COMPONENTS

Diagnostic testing: Intelligence, reading, math, spelling, handwriting, spoken language, written language, perceptual skills, learning strategies.
Academic advising: Provided by unit staff members, academic advisers. Students with LD may take up to 17 credit hours each term; most take 12 to 15 credit hours; 12 credit hours required to maintain full-time status and be eligible for financial aid.
Counseling services: Individual counseling, career counseling.
Basic skills remediation: Offered one-on-one and in class-size groups by regular teachers, counselors. Available in reading, math, learning strategies, study skills.
Subject-area tutoring: Offered one-on-one by peer tutors. Available in most subjects.
Auxiliary aids: Taped textbooks, word-processors with spell-check.
Auxiliary services: Alternative test arrangements, notetakers, priority registration, advocacy.

GENERAL COLLEGE INFORMATION

Independent, 4-year, coed. Part of Syracuse University. Awards bachelor's degrees. Founded 1946. *Setting:* 132-acre suburban campus. *Endowment:* $6 million. *Research spending 1995–96:* $175,934. *Educational spending 1995–96:* $4649 per undergrad. *Total enrollment:* 1,748. *Faculty:* 168 (100 full-time, 92% with terminal degrees, 68 part-time); student–undergrad faculty ratio is 17:1.
Enrollment Profile: 1,748 students from 29 states and territories, 9 other countries. 63% women, 37% men, 17% part-time, 87% state residents, 38% live on campus, 53% transferred in, 2% international, 31% 25 or older, 0% Native American, 3% Hispanic, 7% black, 2% Asian or Pacific Islander. *Retention:* 77% of 1995 full-time freshmen returned. *Graduation:* 27% graduate in 4 years, 43% in 5 years, 46% in 6 years. *Areas of study chosen:* 31% health professions and related sciences, 15% business management and administrative services, 13% social sciences, 10% liberal arts/general studies, 10% psychology, 6% biological and life sciences, 6% communications and journalism, 3% English language/literature/letters, 2% computer and information sciences, 1% education, 1% fine arts, 1% mathematics, 1% physical sciences. *Most popular recent majors:* business administration/commerce/management, criminal justice, occupational therapy.
First-Year Class: 337 total; 1,356 applied, 85% were accepted, 29% of whom enrolled. 15% from top 10% of their high school class, 38% from top quarter, 64% from top half. 2 valedictorians.
Graduation Requirements: 120 credit hours; 10 credit hours of math/science; competence in a foreign language; computer course for accounting, business administration, biology, public relations majors; internship (some majors); senior project for honors program students.
Computers on Campus: 127 computers available on campus for general student use. A campus-wide network can be accessed. Students can contact faculty members and/or advisers through e-mail. Computers for student use in computer center, computer labs, library, academic buildings provide access to the Internet/World Wide Web, on- and off-campus e-mail addresses. Staffed computer lab on campus provides training in use of computers, software. *Academic computing expenditure 1995–96:* $155,000.

EXPENSES AND FINANCIAL AID

Expenses for 1997–98: *Application fee:* $25. Comprehensive fee of $20,562 includes full-time tuition ($14,822), mandatory fees ($90), and college room and board ($5650). College room only: $2794. Part-time tuition for day classes (1 to 9 credit hours): $497 per credit hour. Part-time tuition for evening classes (1 to 9 credit hours): $152 per credit hour for 1 to 6 credit hours, $223 per credit hour for 7 or more credit hours.
Undergraduate Financial Aid: 94% of all full-time undergraduates enrolled in fall 1996 applied for aid; of these, 92% were judged to have need according to Federal Methodology, of whom 99% were aided. *Financial aid deadline (priority):* 2/15. *Financial aid forms:* FAFSA required. State form required for some.
LD Services Contact: Mr. Stephen M. Pattarini, Director of Student Development, Utica College of Syracuse University, 1600 Burrstone Road, Utica, NY 13502-4892, 315-792-3032.

VALDOSTA STATE UNIVERSITY

Valdosta, Georgia

LEARNING DISABILITIES SERVICES INFORMATION

Special Services Program began offering services in 1991. Currently the program serves 70 undergraduates with LD. Services are also available to graduate students. Students diagnosed with ADD/ADHD are eligible for the same services available to students with LD, as well as support group.
Staff: 4 full-time, 3 part-time staff members, including director, assistant director. Services provided by tutors, diagnostic specialists.
Special Fees: No special fees are charged for services to students with LD.
Applications and admissions: *Required:* high school transcript, grade point average, psychoeducational report completed within 3 years; *recommended:* extended time SAT I. Students may begin taking classes any term. *Application deadline:* continuous.
Special policies: The college has written policies regarding substitutions and waivers of admissions, graduation, and degree requirements.

PROGRAM AND SERVICE COMPONENTS

Special preparation or orientation: Optional orientation offered before registration and during registration.
Diagnostic testing: Intelligence, reading, math, spelling, spoken language, written language, perceptual skills, speech, hearing, learning strategies.
Academic advising: Provided by unit staff members, academic advisers. Students with LD may take up to 15 quarter hours each term; most take 12 quarter hours; 12 quarter hours required to maintain full-time status; source of aid determines number of quarter hours required to be eligible for financial aid.
Counseling services: Individual counseling, small-group counseling, career counseling, self-advocacy training.
Basic skills remediation: Offered one-on-one by LD teachers, graduate assistants. Available in reading, math, spelling, written language, learning strategies, study skills, time management.
Subject-area tutoring: Offered one-on-one by professional teachers, peer tutors. Available in most subjects.
Auxiliary aids: Taped textbooks, tape recorders, word-processors with spell-check, assistive listening devices, Dragon Dictate.
Auxiliary services: Alternative test arrangements, notetakers, advocacy.
Campus support group: A special student organization is available to students with LD.

GENERAL COLLEGE INFORMATION

State-supported, coed. Part of University System of Georgia. Awards associate, bachelor's, master's, doctoral degrees. Founded 1906. *Setting:* 168-acre small-town campus with easy access to Jacksonville. *Endowment:* $105.7 million. *Total enrollment:* 9,810. *Undergraduate faculty:* 472 (392 full-time, 70% with terminal degrees, 80 part-time); student–undergrad faculty ratio is 22:1.
Enrollment Profile: 8,338 students from 47 states and territories, 48 other countries. 61% women, 39% men, 17% part-time, 87% state residents, 30% live on campus, 9% transferred in, 1% international, 22% 25 or older, 1% Native American, 1% Hispanic, 19% black, 1% Asian or Pacific Islander. *Retention:* 68% of 1995 full-time freshmen returned. *Graduation:* 37% graduate in 4 years, 38% in 5 years. *Areas of study chosen:* 30% education, 12% social sciences, 10% business management and administrative services, 8% health professions and related sciences, 8% liberal arts/general studies, 6% biological and life sciences, 4% fine arts, 3% computer and information sciences, 3% physical sciences, 3% psychology, 2% communications and journalism, 2% English language/literature/letters, 1% engineering and applied sciences, 1% foreign language and literature, 1% mathematics, 1% natural resource sciences, 1% performing arts, 1% philosophy, 1% predentistry, 1% prelaw, 1% premed. *Most popular recent majors:* biology/biological sciences, business administration/commerce/management, early childhood education.
First-Year Class: 2,520 total; 6,413 applied, 73% were accepted, 54% of whom enrolled.
Graduation Requirements: 93 quarter hours for associate, 183 quarter hours for bachelor's; 1 math course; 2 science courses; computer course for math, business administration, education majors; internship (some majors).
Computers on Campus: 400 computers available on campus for general student use. Computer purchase/lease plans available. A campuswide network can be accessed from student residence rooms and from off-campus. Students can contact faculty members and/or advisers through e-mail. Computers for student use in computer center, computer labs, learning resource center, classrooms, library, student center provide access to the Internet/World Wide Web, on- and off-campus e-mail addresses. Staffed computer lab on campus provides training in use of computers, software. *Academic computing expenditure 1995–96:* $2.5 million.

EXPENSES AND FINANCIAL AID

Expenses for 1996–97: *Application fee:* $10. State resident tuition: $2043 full-time, $44 per quarter hour part-time. Nonresident tuition: $5922 full-time, $152 per quarter hour part-time. College room and board: $3300. College room only: $1515.
Undergraduate Financial Aid: On average, 80% of need was met. *Financial aid deadline (priority):* 4/15. *Financial aid forms:* FAFSA, state form, institutional form required. CSS Financial Aid PROFILE required for some.
LD Services Contact: Ms. Maggie Viverette, Special Services Coordinator, Valdosta State University, Valdosta, GA 31698, 912-245-2498. Fax: 912-245-3788. Email: mviveret@valdosta.edu.

VALLEY CITY STATE UNIVERSITY

Valley City, North Dakota

LEARNING DISABILITIES SERVICES INFORMATION

Academic Services currently serves 10 undergraduates with LD. Students diagnosed with ADD/ADHD are eligible for the same services available to students with LD.
Staff: 2 full-time staff members, including coordinators. Services provided by remediation specialists, tutors, peer tutors.
Special Fees: No special fees are charged for services to students with LD.
Applications and admissions: *Required:* high school transcript, untimed ACT; *recommended:* high school grade point average, class rank, courses completed, letters of recommendation. Students may begin taking classes in fall, spring, or summer. *Application deadline:* continuous.
Special policies: The college has written policies regarding grade forgiveness.

PROGRAM AND SERVICE COMPONENTS

Academic advising: Provided by unit staff members, academic advisers. Students with LD may take up to 19 semester hours each term; most take 15 semester hours; 12 semester hours required to maintain full-time status and be eligible for financial aid.
Counseling services: Individual counseling, career counseling.
Subject-area tutoring: Offered one-on-one, in small groups, and in class-size groups by peer tutors. Available in most subjects.
Auxiliary aids: Taped textbooks, word-processors with spell-check, notebook computers.
Auxiliary services: Alternative test arrangements, notetakers, priority registration, advocacy.

GENERAL COLLEGE INFORMATION

State-supported, 4-year, coed. Part of North Dakota University System. Awards bachelor's degrees. Founded 1890. *Setting:* 55-acre small-town campus. *Endowment:* $585,341. *Total enrollment:* 1,121. *Faculty:* 89 (51 full-time, 52% with terminal degrees, 38 part-time); student–undergrad faculty ratio is 15:1.
Enrollment Profile: 1,121 students from 30 states and territories, 4 other countries. 48% women, 52% men, 25% part-time, 80% state residents, 35% live on campus, 8% transferred in, 5% international, 25% 25 or older, 2% Native American, 1% Hispanic, 1% black, 1% Asian or Pacific Islander. *Retention:* 71% of 1995 full-time freshmen returned. *Areas of study chosen:* 58% education, 22% business management and administrative services, 7% liberal arts/general studies, 5% interdisciplinary studies, 4% biological and life sciences, 3% computer and information sciences, 1% English language/literature/letters. *Most popular recent majors:* elementary education, business administration/commerce/management, human resources.
First-Year Class: 183 total; 285 applied, 94% were accepted, 69% of whom enrolled. 6% from top 10% of their high school class, 19% from top quarter, 51% from top half.
Graduation Requirements: 128 semester hours; 1 math course; 2 science courses; computer course; senior project (some majors).
Computers on Campus: 335 computers available on campus for general student use. Computer purchase/lease plans available. A campuswide network can be accessed from off-campus. Students can contact faculty members and/or advisers through e-mail. Computers for student use in computer center, computer labs, classrooms, library, student rooms provide access to the Internet/World Wide Web, on- and off-

campus e-mail addresses. Staffed computer lab on campus provides training in use of computers, software. *Academic computing expenditure 1995–96:* $146,130.

EXPENSES AND FINANCIAL AID

Expenses for 1996–97: *Application fee:* $25. State resident tuition: $1680 full-time, $70 per semester hour part-time. Nonresident tuition: $4486 full-time, $186.92 per semester hour part-time. Part-time mandatory fees: $8.88 per semester hour. Tuition for Minnesota residents: $1882 full-time, $78.42 per semester hour part-time. Tuition for Manitoba, Montana, Saskatchewan and South Dakota residents: $2100 full-time, $87.50 per semester hour part-time. Tuition for students who are eligible for the Western Interstate Commission of Higher Education program: $2520 full-time, $105 per semester hour part-time. Full-time mandatory fees: $213. College room and board: $2770 (minimum). College room only: $880.
Undergraduate Financial Aid: 75% of all full-time undergraduates enrolled in fall 1996 applied for aid; of these, 94% were judged to have need according to Federal Methodology, of whom 96% were aided. On average, 89% of need was met. *Financial aid deadline (priority):* 4/15. *Financial aid forms:* FAFSA required; CSS Financial Aid PROFILE, state form, institutional form acceptable.
LD Services Contact: Ms. Jan Drake, Director of Student Academic Services, Valley City State University, 101 College Street, SW, Valley City, ND 58072, 701-845-7302. Fax: 701-845-7245.

VIRGINIA COMMONWEALTH UNIVERSITY

Richmond, Virginia

LEARNING DISABILITIES SERVICES INFORMATION

Student Affairs, Services for Students with Disabilities began offering services in 1986. Currently the program serves 273 undergraduates with LD. Services are also available to graduate students. Students diagnosed with ADD/ADHD are eligible for the same services available to students with LD, as well as medical services follow-up, screening interview.
Staff: Includes coordinators, graduate assistants, student workers. Services provided by remediation specialists, tutors, counselors, diagnostic specialists.
Special Fees: No special fees are charged for services to students with LD.
Applications and admissions: *Required:* high school transcript, grade point average, class rank, untimed or extended time SAT I or ACT; *recommended:* high school courses completed, extracurricular activities, personal interview, letters of recommendation, psychoeducational report, letter from student explaining disability and its effect on academic performance, interview with Coordinator. Students may begin taking classes the first session following admission. *Application deadline:* continuous.
Special policies: The college has written policies regarding grade forgiveness.

PROGRAM AND SERVICE COMPONENTS

Academic advising: Provided by unit staff members, academic advisers. Most students with LD take 12 to 15 credits each term; 12 credits required to maintain full-time status; 6 credits required to be eligible for financial aid.
Counseling services: Career counseling.
Subject-area tutoring: Offered one-on-one by peer tutors. Available in most subjects.
Auxiliary aids: Taped textbooks.
Auxiliary services: Alternative test arrangements, notetakers, priority registration, advocacy.

GENERAL COLLEGE INFORMATION

State-supported, coed. Awards bachelor's, master's, doctoral, first professional degrees. Founded 1838. *Setting:* 101-acre urban campus. *Endowment:* $130.8 million. *Research spending 1995–96:* $63.5 million. *Total enrollment:* 21,681. *Faculty:* 2,502 (1,498 full-time, 84% with terminal degrees, 1,004 part-time).
Enrollment Profile: 12,527 students from 35 states and territories, 55 other countries. 59% women, 41% men, 21% part-time, 95% state residents, 17% live on campus, 13% transferred in, 2% international, 27% 25 or older, 1% Native American, 2% Hispanic, 21% black, 8% Asian or Pacific Islander. *Retention:* 76% of 1995 full-time freshmen returned. *Graduation:* 20% graduate in 4 years, 37% in 5 years, 43% in 6 years. *Areas of study chosen:* 18% business management and administrative services, 14% health professions and related sciences, 11% fine arts, 9% psychology, 8% biological and life sciences, 6% communications and journalism, 6% social sciences, 4% computer and information sciences, 4% education, 4% English language/literature/letters, 3% performing arts, 3% physical sciences, 1% engineering and applied sciences, 1% foreign language and literature, 1% liberal arts/general studies, 1% mathematics, 1% philosophy. *Most popular recent majors:* psychology, nursing, English.
First-Year Class: 1,928 total; 4,762 applied, 82% were accepted, 49% of whom enrolled. 15% from top 10% of their high school class, 39% from top quarter, 74% from top half.
Graduation Requirements: 126 credits; computer course for business, math majors; internship (some majors); senior project (some majors).
Computers on Campus: 500 computers available on campus for general student use. Computer purchase/lease plans available. A computer is required for some students. A campus-wide network can be accessed from student residence rooms and from off-campus. Students can contact faculty members and/or advisers through e-mail. Computers for student use in computer center, computer labs, learning resource center, classrooms, library, student center, dorms, student rooms provide access to the Internet/World Wide Web, on- and off-campus e-mail addresses. Staffed computer lab on campus (open 24 hours a day) provides training in use of computers, software. *Academic computing expenditure 1995–96:* $3.8 million.

EXPENSES AND FINANCIAL AID

Expenses for 1997–98: *Application fee:* $25. State resident tuition: $3125 full-time, $130 per credit part-time. Nonresident tuition: $11,293 full-time, $471 per credit part-time. Part-time mandatory fees: $84 per credit. Full-time mandatory fees: $986. College room and board: $4352. College room only: $1690 (minimum).
Undergraduate Financial Aid: Of all full-time undergraduates enrolled in fall 1996, 91% of those who applied for aid were judged to have need according to Federal Methodology, of whom 96% were aided. On average, 64% of need was met. *Financial aid deadline (priority):* 3/15. *Financial aid forms:* FAFSA required.
LD Services Contact: Dr. Shyla M. Ipsen, Coordinator, Services for Students with Disabilities, Virginia Commonwealth University, 109 North Harrison Street, Richmond, VA 23284-2500, 804-VCU-ABLE. Fax: 804-828-1944. Email: sipsen@saturn.vcu.edu.

VIRGINIA INTERMONT COLLEGE

Bristol, Virginia

LEARNING DISABILITIES SERVICES INFORMATION

Student Support Services began offering services in 1987. Currently the program serves 33 undergraduates with LD. Students diagnosed with ADD/ADHD are eligible for the same services available to students with LD.
Staff: 3 full-time staff members, including director, psychologist, secretary. Services provided by remediation specialists, tutors, counselors, diagnostic specialists.
Special Fees: No special fees are charged for services to students with LD.
Applications and admissions: *Required:* high school transcript, grade point average, class rank, untimed SAT I or ACT; *recommended:* high school extracurricular activities, extended time SAT I or ACT, personal interview, letters of recommendation, psychoeducational report completed within 3 years, essay. Students may begin taking classes in fall or spring. *Application deadline:* continuous.

PROGRAM AND SERVICE COMPONENTS

Diagnostic testing: Intelligence, reading, math, spelling, handwriting, spoken language, written language, motor abilities, perceptual skills, study skills, learning strategies.
Academic advising: Provided by unit staff members, academic advisers. Students with LD may take up to 18 semester hours each term; most take 12 semester hours; 12 semester hours required to maintain full-time status and be eligible for financial aid.
Counseling services: Individual counseling, small-group counseling, career counseling, self-advocacy training.
Basic skills remediation: Offered one-on-one, in small groups, and in class-size groups by regular teachers; computer-aided instruction also offered. Available in reading, math, written language, learning strategies, study skills, time management, social skills, computer skills.
Subject-area tutoring: Offered one-on-one and in small groups by professional teachers, peer tutors, LD specialist. Available in all subjects.

Virginia Intermont College (continued)

Special courses: Study skills. All offered for credit; all enter into overall grade point average.
Auxiliary aids: Taped textbooks, tape recorders, calculators, personal computers, talking computers, optical character readers.
Auxiliary services: Alternative test arrangements, notetakers, advocacy, transcribers.

GENERAL COLLEGE INFORMATION

Independent, 4-year, coed, affiliated with Baptist Church. Awards associate, bachelor's degrees. Founded 1884. *Setting:* 27-acre small-town campus. *Endowment:* $1.6 million. *Total enrollment:* 769. *Faculty:* 101 (39 full-time, 79% with terminal degrees, 62 part-time); student–undergrad faculty ratio is 12:1.
Enrollment Profile: 769 students from 31 states and territories, 11 other countries. 73% women, 27% men, 19% part-time, 72% state residents, 31% live on campus, 21% transferred in, 3% international, 52% 25 or older, 1% Native American, 1% Hispanic, 2% black, 1% Asian or Pacific Islander. *Retention:* 46% of 1995 full-time freshmen returned. *Graduation:* 36% graduate in 4 years, 39% in 5 years, 42% in 6 years. *Areas of study chosen:* 19% fine arts, 17% education, 11% business management and administrative services, 6% liberal arts/general studies, 4% biological and life sciences, 4% performing arts, 3% English language/literature/letters, 3% psychology, 1% health professions and related sciences. *Most popular recent majors:* business administration/commerce/management, social work, photography.
First-Year Class: 160 total; 531 applied, 81% were accepted, 37% of whom enrolled. 11% from top 10% of their high school class, 26% from top quarter, 66% from top half.
Graduation Requirements: 64 semester hours for associate, 124 semester hours for bachelor's; 4 semester hours of science; 3 semester hours of math; computer course; internship (some majors); senior project (some majors).
Computers on Campus: 64 computers available on campus for general student use. Computer purchase/lease plans available. Computers for student use in computer center, computer labs, library provide access to the Internet/World Wide Web. Staffed computer lab on campus provides training in use of computers, software. *Academic computing expenditure 1995–96:* $5067.

EXPENSES AND FINANCIAL AID

Expenses for 1997–98: *Application fee:* $15. Comprehensive fee of $15,550 includes full-time tuition ($10,650), mandatory fees ($200), and college room and board ($4700). College room only: $2400. Part-time mandatory fees: $25 per semester. Part-time tuition: $125 per semester for 1 to 6 semester hours, $300 per semester hour for 7 or more semester hours.
Undergraduate Financial Aid: 96% of all full-time undergraduates enrolled in fall 1996 applied for aid; of these, 80% were judged to have need according to Federal Methodology, of whom 99% were aided. On average, 80% of need was met. *Financial aid deadline (priority):* 4/15. *Financial aid forms:* FAFSA required. State form, institutional form required for some.
LD Services Contact: Ms. Barbara Holbrook, School Psychologist/Learning Disabilities Specialist, Student Support Services, Virginia Intermont College, 1013 Moore Street, Bristol, VA 24201-4298, 540-669-6101 Ext. 217. Fax: 540-669-5763.

VIRGINIA POLYTECHNIC INSTITUTE AND STATE UNIVERSITY

Blacksburg, Virginia

LEARNING DISABILITIES SERVICES INFORMATION

Dean of Students Office, Services for Students with Disabilities began offering services in 1978. Currently the program serves 210 undergraduates with LD. Services are also available to graduate students. Students diagnosed with ADD/ADHD are eligible for the same services available to students with LD, as well as support group.
Staff: 2 full-time, 2 part-time staff members, including coordinators, associate dean.
Special Fees: No special fees are charged for services to students with LD.
Applications and admissions: *Required:* high school transcript, courses completed, untimed SAT I, 2 achievement tests, English composition; *recommended:* extended time SAT I, autobiographical statement, letters of recommendation, psychoeducational report completed within 3 years. Students may begin taking classes any term. *Application deadline:* 2/1 (fall term), 10/1 (spring term).
Special policies: The college has written policies regarding substitutions and waivers of admissions and degree requirements.

PROGRAM AND SERVICE COMPONENTS

Diagnostic testing: Intelligence, reading, math, spelling, written language.
Academic advising: Provided by academic advisers. Students with LD may take up to 15 semester hours each term; most take 12 to 14 semester hours; 12 semester hours required to maintain full-time status.
Counseling services: Individual counseling, small-group counseling, career counseling.
Basic skills remediation: Offered one-on-one by peer tutors, graduate assistants. Available in learning strategies, study skills, time management.
Subject-area tutoring: Offered one-on-one by Academic Enrichment Center staff. Available in some subjects.
Auxiliary aids: Taped textbooks, word-processors with spell-check, optical character readers.
Auxiliary services: Alternative test arrangements, notetakers, priority registration.
Campus support group: A special student organization is available to students with LD.

GENERAL COLLEGE INFORMATION

State-supported, coed. Awards associate, bachelor's, master's, doctoral degrees. Founded 1872. *Setting:* 2,600-acre small-town campus. *Endowment:* $244.5 million. *Research spending 1995–96:* $92.2 million. *Total enrollment:* 24,812. *Faculty:* 1,574 (1,410 full-time, 84% with terminal degrees, 164 part-time); student–undergrad faculty ratio is 17:1.
Enrollment Profile: 20,525 students from 50 states and territories, 100 other countries. 41% women, 59% men, 3% part-time, 79% state residents, 44% live on campus, 4% transferred in, 1% international, 3% 25 or older, 0% Native American, 1% Hispanic, 5% black, 6% Asian or Pacific Islander. *Retention:* 89% of 1995 full-time freshmen returned. *Graduation:* 40% graduate in 4 years, 69% in 5 years, 73% in 6 years. *Areas of study chosen:* 19% engineering and applied sciences, 11% business management and administrative services, 9% biological and life sciences, 7% social sciences, 4% psychology, 3% architecture, 3% communications and journalism, 3% natural resource sciences, 2% computer and information sciences, 2% education, 2% English language/literature/letters, 2% interdisciplinary studies, 1% agriculture, 1% fine arts, 1% mathematics, 1% performing arts, 1% physical sciences. *Most popular recent majors:* psychology, mechanical engineering, marketing/retailing/merchandising.
First-Year Class: 4,976 total; 16,285 applied, 81% were accepted, 38% of whom enrolled. 30% from top 10% of their high school class, 69% from top quarter, 99% from top half. 39 National Merit Scholars.
Graduation Requirements: 72 credit hours for associate, 126 credit hours for bachelor's; 6 credit hours of math; 8 credit hours of science; proven competence in a foreign language; computer course for engineering, business, chemistry, physics, economics, geophysics, forestry, wildlife, crop soil/environmental sciences, poultry sciences, math education, business education, nuclear science, statistics, clothing/textiles majors; internship (some majors); senior project for honors program students and some majors.
Computers on Campus: 2,000 computers available on campus for general student use. Computer purchase/lease plans available. A computer is required for some students. A campus-wide network can be accessed from student residence rooms and from off-campus. Students can contact faculty members and/or advisers through e-mail. Computers for student use in computer labs, classrooms, library, dorms, academic buildings provide access to the Internet/World Wide Web, on- and off-campus e-mail addresses. Staffed computer lab on campus provides training in use of computers, software.

EXPENSES AND FINANCIAL AID

Expenses for 1997–98: *Application fee:* $20. State resident tuition: $3500 full-time, $145.85 per credit hour part-time. Nonresident tuition: $10,464 full-time, $436 per credit hour part-time. Part-time mandatory fees: $70 per semester. Full-time mandatory fees: $647. College room and board: $3420. College room only: $1568.
Undergraduate Financial Aid: Of all full-time undergraduates enrolled in fall 1996, 78% of those who applied for aid were judged to have need according to Federal Methodology, of whom 100% were aided. *Financial aid deadline (priority):* 3/1. *Financial aid forms:* FAFSA required. Institutional form required for some.
LD Services Contact: Ms. Patricia Roth or Ms. Susan Angle, Coordinators, Services for Students with Disabilities, Virginia Polytechnic Institute and State University, 105 Brodie Hall, Blacksburg, VA 24061-0255, 540-231-3787. Fax: 540-231-4035.

VITERBO COLLEGE

La Crosse, Wisconsin

LEARNING DISABILITIES SERVICES INFORMATION

Learning Center began offering services in 1990. Currently the program serves 30 undergraduates with LD. Students diagnosed with ADD/ADHD are eligible for the same services available to students with LD.

Staff: 5 full-time staff members, including director. Services provided by tutors, counselor, reading, writing, and math specialists, peer tutors.

Special Fees: No special fees are charged for services to students with LD.

Applications and admissions: *Required:* high school transcript, grade point average, class rank, courses completed, extended time ACT, personal interview, letters of recommendation, psychoeducational report completed within 3 years; *recommended:* high school IEP (Individualized Education Program). Students may begin taking classes in fall only. *Application deadline:* continuous.

PROGRAM AND SERVICE COMPONENTS

Academic advising: Provided by academic advisers. Students with LD may take up to 16 credits each term; most take 12 to 16 credits; 12 credits required to maintain full-time status; 6 credits required to be eligible for financial aid.

Counseling services: Individual counseling, career counseling.

Subject-area tutoring: Offered one-on-one and in small groups by peer tutors. Available in all subjects.

Auxiliary aids: Word-processors with spell-check, optical character readers.

Auxiliary services: Alternative test arrangements.

GENERAL COLLEGE INFORMATION

Independent Roman Catholic, comprehensive, coed. Awards bachelor's, master's degrees. Founded 1890. *Setting:* 5-acre urban campus. *Total enrollment:* 1,914. *Faculty:* 173 (105 full-time, 85% with terminal degrees, 68 part-time); student–undergrad faculty ratio is 14:1.

Enrollment Profile: 1,637 students from 21 states and territories, 8 other countries. 74% women, 26% men, 23% part-time, 76% state residents, 33% live on campus, 10% transferred in, 1% international, 32% 25 or older, 1% Native American, 1% Hispanic, 1% black, 2% Asian or Pacific Islander. *Retention:* 79% of 1995 full-time freshmen returned. *Most popular recent majors:* nursing, business administration/commerce/management, elementary education.

First-Year Class: 292 total; 962 applied, 90% were accepted, 34% of whom enrolled. 15% from top 10% of their high school class, 69% from top quarter, 98% from top half.

Graduation Requirements: 128 credits; 8 credits of science; computer course for business, accounting, dietetics, nursing majors; internship (some majors); senior project (some majors).

Computers on Campus: 102 computers available on campus for general student use. A campus-wide network can be accessed from off-campus. Students can contact faculty members and/or advisers through e-mail. Computers for student use in computer center, computer labs, learning resource center, classrooms, library, student center, academic offices provide access to the Internet/World Wide Web, on- and off-campus e-mail addresses. Staffed computer lab on campus provides training in use of computers, software.

EXPENSES AND FINANCIAL AID

Expenses for 1997–98: *Application fee:* $15. Comprehensive fee of $15,200 includes full-time tuition ($10,880), mandatory fees ($270), and college room and board ($4050). College room only: $1770. Part-time mandatory fees per semester range from $14 to $76. Part-time tuition per semester ranges from $315 to $4955 according to course load.

Undergraduate Financial Aid: 91% of all full-time undergraduates enrolled in fall 1996 applied for aid; of these, 94% were judged to have need according to Federal Methodology, of whom 100% were aided. On average, 81% of need was met. *Financial aid deadline (priority):* 3/15. *Financial aid forms:* FAFSA, institutional form required. State form required for some.

LD Services Contact: Mr. Wayne Wojciechowski, Assistant to the Academic Vice President/ADA Coordinator, Viterbo College, 815 South Ninth Street, La Crosse, WI 54601, 608-796-3085. Fax: 608-796-3050. Email: reg_wayne@viterbo.edu.

WALLA WALLA COLLEGE

College Place, Washington

LEARNING DISABILITIES SERVICES INFORMATION

Teaching Learning Center (TLC) began offering services in 1995. Currently the program serves 50 undergraduates with LD. Services are also available to graduate students. Students diagnosed with ADD/ADHD are eligible for the same services available to students with LD.

Staff: 2 full-time staff members, including director, coordinator. Services provided by remediation specialist, tutors, counselor.

Special Fees: No special fees are charged for services to students with LD.

Applications and admissions: *Required:* high school transcript, grade point average, courses completed, psychoeducational report completed within 3 years; *recommended:* high school IEP (Individualized Education Program), extended time ACT. Students may begin taking classes any term. *Application deadline:* continuous.

Special policies: The college has written policies regarding substitutions and waivers of admissions and degree requirements.

PROGRAM AND SERVICE COMPONENTS

Academic advising: Provided by unit staff members, academic advisers. Students with LD may take up to 17 quarter hours each term; most take 12 to 14 quarter hours; 12 quarter hours (fewer with petition) required to maintain full-time status and be eligible for financial aid.

Basic skills remediation: Offered in small groups by regular teachers, reading specialist. Available in reading, written language, learning strategies, study skills, time management.

Subject-area tutoring: Offered one-on-one and in small groups by peer tutors. Available in most subjects.

Auxiliary aids: Taped textbooks, tape recorders, word-processors with spell-check, optical character readers.

Auxiliary services: Alternative test arrangements, notetakers, priority registration, advocacy.

GENERAL COLLEGE INFORMATION

Independent Seventh-day Adventist, comprehensive, coed. Awards associate, bachelor's, master's degrees. Founded 1892. *Setting:* 77-acre small-town campus. *Endowment:* $6.5 million. *Research spending 1995–96:* $14,598. *Educational spending 1995–96:* $4355 per undergrad. *Total enrollment:* 1,763. *Faculty:* 193 (126 full-time, 60% with terminal degrees, 67 part-time); student–undergrad faculty ratio is 12:1.

Enrollment Profile: 1,606 students from 52 states and territories, 28 other countries. 49% women, 51% men, 14% part-time, 39% state residents, 5% international, 14% 25 or older, 1% Native American, 5% Hispanic, 1% black, 4% Asian or Pacific Islander. *Retention:* 69% of 1995 full-time freshmen returned. *Graduation:* 23% graduate in 4 years, 37% in 5 years, 40% in 6 years. *Areas of study chosen:* 18% health professions and related sciences, 13% engineering and applied sciences, 11% business management and administrative services, 8% education, 7% social sciences, 5% biological and life sciences, 4% vocational and home economics, 3% communications and journalism, 3% English language/literature/letters, 3% theology/religion, 2% computer and information sciences, 2% foreign language and literature, 2% psychology, 1% fine arts, 1% interdisciplinary studies, 1% liberal arts/general studies, 1% mathematics, 1% natural resource sciences, 1% performing arts, 1% physical sciences, 1% predentistry, 1% premed. *Most popular recent majors:* engineering (general), nursing, business administration/commerce/management.

First-Year Class: 300 total; 367 applied.

Graduation Requirements: 96 quarter hours for associate, 192 quarter hours for bachelor's; 4 quarter hours of math; 8 quarter hours of science; computer course for art, education, engineering, business, chemistry, communications, psychology, industrial technology, math, nursing, physics majors; internship (some majors); senior project (some majors).

Computers on Campus: 92 computers available on campus for general student use. A campus-wide network can be accessed from student residence rooms and from off-campus. Students can contact faculty members and/or advisers through e-mail. Computers for student use in computer center, computer labs, library, departmental labs provide access to the Internet/World Wide Web, on- and off-campus e-mail addresses. Staffed computer lab on campus. *Academic computing expenditure 1995–96:* $239,841.

EXPENSES AND FINANCIAL AID

Expenses for 1997–98: *Application fee:* $30. Comprehensive fee of $16,073 includes full-time tuition ($12,570), mandatory fees ($123), and college room and board ($3380). College room only: $1836. Part-time tuition: $333 per quarter hour. Part-time mandatory fees: $123 per year.

Walla Walla College (continued)

Undergraduate Financial Aid: Of all full-time undergraduates enrolled in fall 1996, 94% of those who applied for aid were judged to have need according to Federal Methodology, of whom 100% were aided. On average, 87% of need was met. *Financial aid deadline (priority):* 4/1. *Financial aid forms:* FAFSA, institutional form required; CSS Financial Aid PROFILE acceptable. Verification worksheet required for some.

LD Services Contact: Ms. Sue Hultt, Disability Support Service Coordinator, Walla Walla College, 204 South College Avenue, College Place, WA 99324, 509-527-2366. Email: hultsu@wwc.edu.

WASHINGTON AND JEFFERSON COLLEGE

Washington, Pennsylvania

LEARNING DISABILITIES SERVICES INFORMATION

Student Resource Center began offering services in 1984. Currently the program serves 6 undergraduates with LD. Students diagnosed with ADD/ADHD are eligible for the same services available to students with LD.

Staff: 1 full-time, 5 part-time staff members, including director. Services provided by peer counselors.

Special Fees: No special fees are charged for services to students with LD.

Applications and admissions: *Required:* high school transcript, class rank, courses completed, untimed SAT I or ACT, essay; *recommended:* high school extracurricular activities, IEP (Individualized Education Program), extended time SAT I or ACT, autobiographical statement, letters of recommendation, psychoeducational report completed within 3 to 5 years. Students may begin taking classes in summer only. *Application deadline:* 3/1.

PROGRAM AND SERVICE COMPONENTS

Diagnostic testing: Study skills, personality, learning strategies.

Academic advising: Provided by academic advisers. Students with LD may take up to 5 courses each term; most take 4 courses; 3 courses required to maintain full-time status and be eligible for financial aid.

Counseling services: Individual counseling, small-group counseling, career counseling.

Basic skills remediation: Offered one-on-one and in small groups by Director, peer counselors. Available in math, written language, learning strategies, study skills, time management.

Subject-area tutoring: Offered one-on-one and in small groups by peer tutors. Available in most subjects.

Auxiliary aids: Taped textbooks, word-processors with spell-check, personal computers.

Auxiliary services: Alternative test arrangements, advocacy.

GENERAL COLLEGE INFORMATION

Independent, 4-year, coed. Awards bachelor's degrees. Founded 1781. *Setting:* 40-acre small-town campus with easy access to Pittsburgh. *Endowment:* $71 million. *Total enrollment:* 1,128. *Faculty:* 101 (89 full-time, 92% with terminal degrees, 12 part-time); student–undergrad faculty ratio is 11:1.

Enrollment Profile: 1,128 students from 30 states and territories, 3 other countries. 46% women, 54% men, 1% part-time, 70% state residents, 95% live on campus, 9% transferred in, 1% international, 1% Native American, 1% Hispanic, 3% black, 2% Asian or Pacific Islander. *Retention:* 93% of 1995 full-time freshmen returned. *Graduation:* 76% graduate in 4 years, 77% in 5 years, 78% in 6 years. *Areas of study chosen:* 22% biological and life sciences, 19% business management and administrative services, 16% social sciences, 10% premed, 10% psychology, 9% prelaw, 6% English language/literature/letters, 6% physical sciences, 2% mathematics, 1% philosophy, 1% predentistry.

First-Year Class: 321 total; 1,227 applied, 86% were accepted, 31% of whom enrolled. 40% from top 10% of their high school class, 87% from top quarter, 98% from top half.

Graduation Requirements: 36 courses; 4 math/science courses.

Computers on Campus: 205 computers available on campus for general student use. Computer purchase/lease plans available. A campus-wide network can be accessed from student residence rooms and from off-campus. Students can contact faculty members and/or advisers through e-mail. Computers for student use in computer center, computer labs, learning resource center, classrooms, library, student center provide access to the Internet/World Wide Web, on- and off-campus e-mail addresses. Staffed computer lab on campus provides training in use of computers, software. *Academic computing expenditure 1995–96:* $255,313.

EXPENSES AND FINANCIAL AID

Expenses for 1996–97: *Application fee:* $25. Comprehensive fee of $21,675 includes full-time tuition ($17,190), mandatory fees ($280), and college room and board ($4205). College room only: $2035. Part-time tuition: $1700 per course.

Undergraduate Financial Aid: 85% of all full-time undergraduates enrolled in fall 1996 applied for aid; of these, 94% were judged to have need according to Federal Methodology, of whom 99% were aided. On average, 92% of need was met. *Financial aid deadline (priority):* 3/15. *Financial aid forms:* FAFSA, state form required.

LD Services Contact: Ms. Patricia D. Bright, Director, Washington and Jefferson College, 60 South Lincoln Street, Washington, PA 15301-4801, 412-223-5279. Fax: 412-223-5271.

WASHINGTON COLLEGE

Chestertown, Maryland

LEARNING DISABILITIES SERVICES INFORMATION

Office for Students with Special Needs began offering services in 1995. Currently the program serves 25 undergraduates with LD. Services are also available to graduate students. Students diagnosed with ADD/ADHD are eligible for the same services available to students with LD.

Staff: 1 part-time staff member (director). Services provided by tutors, counselors, diagnostic specialists.

Special Fees: No special fees are charged for services to students with LD.

Applications and admissions: *Required:* documentation of learning disability. Students may begin taking classes in fall only.

PROGRAM AND SERVICE COMPONENTS

Academic advising: Provided by unit staff members, academic advisers. Students with LD may take up to 20 credits each term; most take 16 credits; 12 credits required to maintain full-time status and be eligible for financial aid.

Auxiliary aids: Laptop computer.

Campus support group: A special student organization is available to students with LD.

GENERAL COLLEGE INFORMATION

Independent, comprehensive, coed. Awards bachelor's, master's degrees. Founded 1782. *Setting:* 120-acre small-town campus with easy access to Baltimore and Washington, DC. *Endowment:* $37.8 million. *Educational spending 1995–96:* $6480 per undergrad. *Total enrollment:* 1,009. *Faculty:* 93 (61 full-time, 93% with terminal degrees, 32 part-time); student–undergrad faculty ratio is 12:1.

Enrollment Profile: 952 students from 31 states and territories, 39 other countries. 57% women, 43% men, 1% part-time, 55% state residents, 80% live on campus, 3% transferred in, 8% international, 3% 25 or older, 1% Native American, 2% Hispanic, 5% black, 2% Asian or Pacific Islander. *Retention:* 91% of 1995 full-time freshmen returned. *Graduation:* 56% graduate in 4 years, 66% in 5 years, 67% in 6 years. *Areas of study chosen:* 8% social sciences, 6% psychology, 5% business management and administrative services, 4% biological and life sciences, 4% English language/literature/letters, 4% liberal arts/general studies, 4% physical sciences, 2% area and ethnic studies, 1% fine arts, 1% foreign language and literature, 1% mathematics, 1% natural resource sciences. *Most popular recent majors:* English, psychology, business administration/commerce/management.

First-Year Class: 312 total; 1,540 applied, 84% were accepted, 24% of whom enrolled. 33% from top 10% of their high school class, 71% from top quarter, 93% from top half.

Graduation Requirements: 32 courses; 2 science courses; computer course for math, economics, business management majors; senior project.

Computers on Campus: 80 computers available on campus for general student use. Computer purchase/lease plans available. A campus-wide network can be accessed from student residence rooms and from off-campus. Students can contact faculty members and/or advisers through e-mail. Computers for student use in computer center, computer labs, library, dorms, study center provide access to the Internet/World Wide Web, on- and off-campus e-mail addresses. Staffed computer lab on campus provides training in use of computers, software.

EXPENSES AND FINANCIAL AID

Expenses for 1997–98: *Application fee:* $35. Comprehensive fee of $23,990 includes full-time tuition ($17,800), mandatory fees ($450), and college room and board ($5740). Part-time tuition: $2967 per course. Part-time mandatory fees: $75 per semester.
Undergraduate Financial Aid: 85% of all full-time undergraduates enrolled in fall 1996 applied for aid; of these,100% were judged to have need according to Federal Methodology, of whom 100% were aided. On average, 85% of need was met. *Financial aid deadline (priority):* 2/15. *Financial aid forms:* FAFSA, CSS Financial Aid PROFILE, federal income tax form required.
LD Services Contact: Ms. Beverly A. Wolff, Assistant Dean, Washington College, 300 Washington Avenue, Chestertown, MD 21620, 410-778-7206. Fax: 410-778-7850.

WASHINGTON STATE UNIVERSITY

Pullman, Washington

LEARNING DISABILITIES SERVICES INFORMATION

Disability Resource Center began offering services in 1986. Currently the program serves 250 undergraduates with LD. Services are also available to graduate students. Students diagnosed with ADD/ADHD are eligible for the same services available to students with LD.
Staff: 5 full-time staff members, including director, taping and testing coordinator. Services provided by remediation specialist, counselors.
Special Fees: No special fees are charged for services to students with LD.
Applications and admissions: *Required:* high school transcript, grade point average, courses completed, untimed SAT I, psychoeducational report completed within 5 years; *recommended:* high school extracurricular activities, extended time SAT I or ACT, autobiographical statement, letters of recommendation. Students may begin taking classes in fall, spring, or summer. *Application deadline:* 5/1.
Special policies: The college has written policies regarding grade forgiveness; substitutions and waivers of admissions and graduation requirements.

PROGRAM AND SERVICE COMPONENTS

Special preparation or orientation: Optional orientation offered before registration.
Academic advising: Provided by unit staff members, academic advisers. Most students with LD take 12 to 15 credits each term; 10 credits required to maintain full-time status; 12 credits required to be eligible for financial aid.
Counseling services: Individual counseling, small-group counseling, career counseling, self-advocacy training.
Basic skills remediation: Offered one-on-one and in small groups by LD teachers. Available in learning strategies, study skills, time management.
Auxiliary aids: Taped textbooks, word-processors with spell-check, personal computers, talking computers, optical character readers, FM systems.
Auxiliary services: Alternative test arrangements, notetakers, priority registration, advocacy.
Campus support group: A special student organization is available to students with LD.

GENERAL COLLEGE INFORMATION

State-supported, coed. Awards bachelor's, master's, doctoral, first professional degrees. Founded 1890. *Setting:* 620-acre rural campus. *Endowment:* $289.8 million. *Research spending 1995–96:* $60 million. *Total enrollment:* 20,121. *Faculty:* 1,234 (1,040 full-time, 89% with terminal degrees, 194 part-time); student–undergrad faculty ratio is 12:1.
Enrollment Profile: 16,686 students from 50 states and territories, 72 other countries. 50% women, 50% men, 11% part-time, 85% state residents, 12% transferred in, 5% international, 17% 25 or older, 2% Native American, 3% Hispanic, 2% black, 5% Asian or Pacific Islander. *Retention:* 82% of 1995 full-time freshmen returned. *Graduation:* 31% graduate in 4 years, 57% in 5 years, 63% in 6 years. *Areas of study chosen:* 10% business management and administrative services, 7% social sciences, 5% education, 5% engineering and applied sciences, 4% agriculture, 4% health professions and related sciences, 3% biological and life sciences, 2% communications and journalism, 2% liberal arts/general studies, 1% architecture, 1% computer and information sciences, 1% English language/literature/letters, 1% foreign language and literature, 1% mathematics, 1% natural resource sciences, 1% physical sciences, 1% vocational and home economics. *Most popular recent majors:* business administration/commerce/management, communication, social science.
First-Year Class: 2,280 total; 6,543 applied, 89% were accepted, 39% of whom enrolled.
Graduation Requirements: 120 credits; 10 credits of science including at least 1 lab science course; computer course for business, communication, engineering, construction management, zoology, mathematics, English majors; internship (some majors); senior project (some majors).
Computers on Campus: 5,600 computers available on campus for general student use. Computer purchase/lease plans available. A campuswide network can be accessed from student residence rooms and from off-campus. Students can contact faculty members and/or advisers through e-mail. Computers for student use in computer center, student center, dorms, departmental labs provide access to the Internet/World Wide Web. Staffed computer lab on campus (open 24 hours a day) provides training in use of computers, software.

EXPENSES AND FINANCIAL AID

Expenses for 1996–97: *Application fee:* $35. State resident tuition: $3142 full-time, $157 per credit part-time. Nonresident tuition: $9758 full-time, $488 per credit part-time. Full-time mandatory fees: $128. College room and board: $4150.
Undergraduate Financial Aid: Of all full-time undergraduates enrolled in fall 1996, 74% of those who applied for aid were judged to have need according to Federal Methodology, of whom 100% were aided. On average, 98% of need was met. *Financial aid deadline (priority):* 3/1. *Financial aid forms:* FAFSA required; CSS Financial Aid PROFILE acceptable. State form, institutional form required for some.
LD Services Contact: Mr. Marshall Mitchell, Director, Disability Resource Center, Washington State University, Administration Annex 206, Pullman, WA 99164-4122, 509-335-1566. Fax: 509-335-8511.

WASHINGTON UNIVERSITY

St. Louis, Missouri

LEARNING DISABILITIES SERVICES INFORMATION

Disabled Student Services began offering services in 1979. Currently the program serves 117 undergraduates with LD. Services are also available to graduate students. Students diagnosed with ADD/ADHD are eligible for the same services available to students with LD.
Staff: 2 full-time staff members, including coordinator, assistant coordinator. Services provided by tutors, counselors, student educational services staff.
Special Fees: No special fees are charged for services to students with LD.
Applications and admissions: *Required:* high school transcript, class rank, untimed SAT I or ACT, autobiographical statement, letters of recommendation; *recommended:* high school extracurricular activities, extended time SAT I or ACT, personal interview, psychoeducational report completed within 3 years. Students may begin taking classes in fall only. *Application deadline:* 1/15.
Special policies: The college has written policies regarding grade forgiveness.

PROGRAM AND SERVICE COMPONENTS

Academic advising: Provided by unit staff members, academic advisers. Students with LD may take up to 18 semester hours each term; most take 15 semester hours; 12 semester hours required to maintain full-time status and be eligible for financial aid.
Counseling services: Individual counseling, career counseling, self-advocacy training.
Subject-area tutoring: Offered one-on-one and in small groups by peer tutors. Available in most subjects.
Special courses: College survival skills, reading, composition, learning strategies, word processing, time management, math, study skills, career planning. None offered for credit.
Auxiliary aids: Taped textbooks, tape recorders, typewriters.
Auxiliary services: Alternative test arrangements, notetakers, advocacy.

GENERAL COLLEGE INFORMATION

Independent, coed. Awards bachelor's, master's, doctoral, first professional degrees. Founded 1853. *Setting:* 169-acre suburban campus. *Endowment:* $2.3 billion. *Total enrollment:* 10,767. *Faculty:* 2,354 (1,967 full-time, 98% with terminal degrees, 387 part-time); student–undergrad faculty ratio is 7:1.
Enrollment Profile: 5,443 students from 52 states and territories, 89 other countries. 49% women, 51% men, 8% part-time, 14% state residents, 60% live on campus, 11% transferred in, 6% international, 2% 25 or older, 1% Native American, 2% Hispanic, 6% black, 12% Asian or Pacific Islander. *Retention:* 95% of 1995 full-time freshmen returned.

Washington University (continued)

Graduation: 74% graduate in 4 years, 82% in 5 years, 86% in 6 years. *Areas of study chosen:* 17% engineering and applied sciences, 16% social sciences, 12% business management and administrative services, 11% psychology, 9% biological and life sciences, 6% fine arts, 5% computer and information sciences, 5% English language/literature/letters, 5% foreign language and literature, 3% architecture, 2% education, 2% physical sciences, 1% area and ethnic studies, 1% communications and journalism, 1% health professions and related sciences, 1% interdisciplinary studies, 1% mathematics, 1% performing arts, 1% philosophy. *Most popular recent majors:* engineering (general), psychology, business administration/commerce/management.
First-Year Class: 1,296 total; 11,276 applied, 51% were accepted, 23% of whom enrolled. 66% from top 10% of their high school class, 92% from top quarter, 99% from top half. 92 National Merit Scholars, 25 class presidents, 81 valedictorians.
Graduation Requirements: 120 semester hours; computer course for business, engineering majors.
Computers on Campus: 1,000 computers available on campus for general student use. Computer purchase/lease plans available. A campus-wide network can be accessed from student residence rooms and from off-campus. Students can contact faculty members and/or advisers through e-mail. Computers for student use in computer center, computer labs, research center, classrooms, library, dorms, every school provide access to the Internet/World Wide Web. Staffed computer lab on campus (open 24 hours a day) provides training in use of computers, software.

EXPENSES AND FINANCIAL AID

Expenses for 1997–98: *Application fee:* $50. Comprehensive fee of $27,803 includes full-time tuition ($21,000), mandatory fees ($210), and college room and board ($6593). College room only: $3948. Part-time tuition: $875 per semester hour.
Undergraduate Financial Aid: Of all full-time undergraduates enrolled in fall 1996, 89% of those who applied for aid were judged to have need according to Federal Methodology, of whom 98% were aided. On average, 94% of need was met. *Financial aid deadline:* 2/15. *Financial aid forms:* FAFSA, Divorced/Separated Parents' Statement required. CSS Financial Aid PROFILE, institutional form required for some.
LD Services Contact: Mr. Daniel R . Herbst, Interim Coordinator of Disabled Student Services, Washington University, Campus Box 1136, St. Louis, MO 63130, 314-935-4062. Fax: 314-935-8516. Email: herbst@dosa.wustl.edu.

WAYNE STATE COLLEGE

Wayne, Nebraska

LEARNING DISABILITIES SERVICES INFORMATION

Stride: Student Support Services began offering services in 1979. Currently the program serves 44 undergraduates with LD. Services are also available to graduate students. Students diagnosed with ADD/ADHD are eligible for the same services available to students with LD.
Staff: 4 full-time, 1 part-time staff members, including director, coordinators, learning skills specialist. Services provided by tutors.
Special Fees: No special fees are charged for services to students with LD.
Applications and admissions: *Required:* psychoeducational report completed within 3 years; *recommended:* high school transcript, grade point average, class rank, courses completed, untimed SAT I or ACT, personal interview. Students may begin taking classes any term. *Application deadline:* continuous.

PROGRAM AND SERVICE COMPONENTS

Special preparation or orientation: Optional orientation offered before registration.
Diagnostic testing: Intelligence, reading, math, written language, motor abilities, perceptual skills, study skills, personality, learning strategies.
Academic advising: Provided by unit staff members, academic advisers. Students with LD may take up to 15 semester hours each term; most take 12 to 14 semester hours; 12 semester hours required to maintain full-time status and be eligible for financial aid.
Counseling services: Individual counseling, small-group counseling, career counseling.
Basic skills remediation: Offered one-on-one and in small groups by Student Support Services staff. Available in reading, math, spelling, learning strategies, study skills, time management.
Subject-area tutoring: Offered one-on-one and in small groups by professional teachers, peer tutors. Available in most subjects.
Special courses: College survival skills, vocabulary development, learning strategies, word processing, time management, personal psychology, study skills, career planning. Most offered for credit; most enter into overall grade point average.
Auxiliary aids: Taped textbooks, tape recorders, calculators, typewriters, word-processors with spell-check, personal computers.
Auxiliary services: Alternative test arrangements, notetakers, priority registration.

GENERAL COLLEGE INFORMATION

State-supported, comprehensive, coed. Part of Nebraska State College System. Awards bachelor's, master's degrees. Founded 1910. *Setting:* 128-acre small-town campus. *Total enrollment:* 3,828. *Faculty:* 228 (123 full-time, 72% with terminal degrees, 105 part-time); student–undergrad faculty ratio is 23:1.
Enrollment Profile: 3,141 students from 25 states and territories, 11 other countries. 57% women, 43% men, 12% part-time, 82% state residents, 45% live on campus, 9% transferred in, 1% international, 14% 25 or older, 3% Native American, 1% Hispanic, 2% black, 1% Asian or Pacific Islander. *Retention:* 61% of 1995 full-time freshmen returned. *Graduation:* 16% graduate in 4 years, 35% in 5 years, 40% in 6 years. *Areas of study chosen:* 19% business management and administrative services, 14% education, 9% social sciences, 7% health professions and related sciences, 5% psychology, 4% communications and journalism, 4% fine arts, 3% biological and life sciences, 3% computer and information sciences, 3% vocational and home economics, 2% engineering and applied sciences, 2% English language/literature/letters, 2% mathematics, 2% physical sciences, 1% foreign language and literature, 1% premed. *Most popular recent majors:* business administration/commerce/management, education, criminal justice.
First-Year Class: 708 total; 1,450 applied, 99% were accepted, 49% of whom enrolled. 8% from top 10% of their high school class, 25% from top quarter, 58% from top half.
Graduation Requirements: 125 semester hours; 3 semester hours of math; 6 semester hours of science; computer course for business majors; internship (some majors); senior project for honors program students and some majors.
Computers on Campus: 200 computers available on campus for general student use. A computer is recommended for some students. A campus-wide network can be accessed. Computers for student use in computer labs, library, academic buildings provide access to the Internet/World Wide Web. Staffed computer lab on campus provides training in use of computers, software.

EXPENSES AND FINANCIAL AID

Expenses for 1996–97: *Application fee:* $10. State resident tuition: $1650 full-time, $55 per semester hour part-time. Nonresident tuition: $3300 full-time, $110 per semester hour part-time. Part-time mandatory fees: $12 per semester hour. Full-time mandatory fees: $288. College room and board: $2870. College room only: $1350.
Undergraduate Financial Aid: 76% of all full-time undergraduates enrolled in fall 1996 applied for aid; of these, 86% were judged to have need according to Federal Methodology, of whom 97% were aided. On average, 91% of need was met. *Financial aid deadline:* continuous. *Financial aid forms:* FAFSA, institutional form required.
LD Services Contact: Mr. Jeff Carstens, Acting Director, Student Support Services, Wayne State College, 200 East 10th, Wayne, NE 68787, 402-375-7500. Fax: 402-375-7204.

WAYNE STATE UNIVERSITY

Detroit, Michigan

LEARNING DISABILITIES SERVICES INFORMATION

Handicapper Educational Services began offering services in 1994. Currently the program serves 51 undergraduates with LD. Services are also available to graduate students. Students diagnosed with ADD/ADHD are eligible for the same services available to students with LD.
Staff: 3 full-time, 7 part-time staff members, including supervisor/LD specialist. Services provided by student workers.
Special Fees: A fee is charged for diagnostic testing.
Applications and admissions: *Required:* high school transcript, grade point average, untimed ACT. Students may begin taking classes any term. *Application deadline:* 8/1.
Special policies: The college has written policies regarding substitutions and waivers of admissions, graduation, and degree requirements.

PROGRAM AND SERVICE COMPONENTS

Special preparation or orientation: Optional orientation offered during registration.
Diagnostic testing: Intelligence, reading, math, spelling, handwriting, written language, study skills, personality, speech, hearing, learning strategies.
Academic advising: Provided by academic advisers. Most students with LD take 9 to 15 semester hours each term; 12 semester hours required to maintain full-time status and be eligible for financial aid.
Counseling services: Individual counseling, small-group counseling, career counseling.
Basic skills remediation: Offered one-on-one and in class-size groups by regular teachers; computer-aided instruction also offered. Available in reading, math, spelling, learning strategies, study skills, time management.
Special courses: College survival skills, reading, vocabulary development, learning strategies, time management, study skills, career planning. Some offered for credit; some enter into overall grade point average.
Auxiliary aids: Taped textbooks, tape recorders, calculators, typewriters, word-processors with spell-check, personal computers, talking computers, optical character readers, Frankin Speller, Dragon Dictate.
Auxiliary services: Alternative test arrangements, priority registration, advocacy, TDD/(313)577-3365.
Campus support group: A special student organization is available to students with LD.

GENERAL COLLEGE INFORMATION

State-supported, coed. Awards bachelor's, master's, doctoral, first professional degrees. Founded 1868. *Setting:* 203-acre urban campus. *Endowment:* $90 million. *Research spending 1995–96:* $78.8 million. *Educational spending 1995–96:* $6898 per undergrad. *Total enrollment:* 31,185. *Faculty:* 2,701 (1,708 full-time, 85% with terminal degrees, 993 part-time).
Enrollment Profile: 18,200 students from 33 states and territories, 35 other countries. 60% women, 40% men, 51% part-time, 97% state residents, 61% transferred in, 2% international, 43% 25 or older, 1% Native American, 2% Hispanic, 28% black, 5% Asian or Pacific Islander. *Retention:* 62% of 1995 full-time freshmen returned. *Most popular recent majors:* psychology, elementary education, accounting.
First-Year Class: 1,970 total; 4,733 applied, 81% were accepted, 51% of whom enrolled. 47% from top quarter of their high school class, 78% from top half.
Graduation Requirements: 120 credit hours; math proficiency; computer course; internship (some majors); senior project (some majors).
Computers on Campus: 800 computers available on campus for general student use. Computer purchase/lease plans available. A campus-wide network can be accessed from student residence rooms and from off-campus. Students can contact faculty members and/or advisers through e-mail. Computers for student use in computer center, computer labs, research center, library, student center, departmental labs, off-campus centers provide access to the Internet/World Wide Web, on- and off-campus e-mail addresses. Staffed computer lab on campus provides training in use of computers, software.

EXPENSES AND FINANCIAL AID

Expenses for 1996–97: *Application fee:* $20. Part-time mandatory fees: $72 per semester. Full-time tuition ranges from $3255 to $3844 for state residents, $7254 to $8618 for nonresidents, according to class level. Part-time tuition per credit hour ranges from $105 to $124 for state residents, $234 to $278 for nonresidents, according to class level. Full-time mandatory fees: $144. College room only: $3880 (minimum).
Undergraduate Financial Aid: 66% of all full-time undergraduates enrolled in fall 1996 applied for aid; of these, 93% were judged to have need according to Federal Methodology, of whom 92% were aided. On average, 53% of need was met. *Financial aid deadline:* Applications processed continuously. *Financial aid forms:* FAFSA required.
LD Services Contact: Mr. Don Anderson, University Counselor, Wayne State University, 583 Student Center Building, Detroit, MI 48202, 313-577-1851. Fax: 313-577-0617. Email: danderso@cms.cc.wayne.edu.

WEBER STATE UNIVERSITY

Ogden, Utah

LEARNING DISABILITIES SERVICES INFORMATION

Services for Students with Disabilities began offering services in 1976. Currently the program serves 92 undergraduates with LD. Services are also available to graduate students. Students diagnosed with ADD/ADHD are eligible for the same services available to students with LD.
Staff: 4 full-time, 28 part-time staff members, including director, coordinator. Services provided by tutors, counselor, office specialist, vocational specialist, interpreters.
Special Fees: No special fees are charged for services to students with LD.
Applications and admissions: *Required:* high school transcript, grade point average, untimed ACT; *recommended:* extended time ACT. Students may begin taking classes any term. *Application deadline:* 7/1 (fall term), 4/1 (spring term).

PROGRAM AND SERVICE COMPONENTS

Special preparation or orientation: Optional orientation offered before registration.
Academic advising: Provided by unit staff members, academic advisers. Students with LD may take up to 18 credit hours each term; most take 12 credit hours; 12 credit hours required to maintain full-time status; 6 credit hours (part-time), 12 credit hours (full-time) required to be eligible for financial aid.
Counseling services: Individual counseling, small-group counseling, career counseling, self-advocacy training.
Basic skills remediation: Offered one-on-one, in small groups, and in class-size groups by academic departments. Available in reading, math.
Subject-area tutoring: Offered one-on-one by peer tutors. Available in most subjects.
Auxiliary aids: Taped textbooks, tape recorders, word-processors with spell-check, optical character readers.
Auxiliary services: Alternative test arrangements, notetakers, priority registration, advocacy, proofreading.
Campus support group: A special student organization is available to students with LD.

GENERAL COLLEGE INFORMATION

State-supported, comprehensive, coed. Part of Utah System of Higher Education. Awards associate, bachelor's, master's degrees. Founded 1889. *Setting:* 422-acre urban campus with easy access to Salt Lake City. *Endowment:* $9.5 million. *Research spending 1995–96:* $773,366. *Educational spending 1995–96:* $3554 per undergrad. *Total enrollment:* 13,906. *Faculty:* 487 (417 full-time, 69% with terminal degrees, 70 part-time); student–undergrad faculty ratio is 19:1.
Enrollment Profile: 13,728 students from 48 states and territories, 35 other countries. 53% women, 47% men, 39% part-time, 94% state residents, 4% live on campus, 10% transferred in, 2% international, 38% 25 or older, 1% Native American, 3% Hispanic, 1% black, 2% Asian or Pacific Islander. *Retention:* 63% of 1995 full-time freshmen returned. *Graduation:* 10% graduate in 4 years, 19% in 5 years, 27% in 6 years. *Areas of study chosen:* 29% interdisciplinary studies, 10% education, 10% social sciences, 9% engineering and applied sciences, 2% communications and journalism, 2% fine arts, 2% premed. *Most popular recent majors:* nursing, education, business administration/commerce/management.
First-Year Class: 2,199 total; 3,584 applied, 61% of whom enrolled. 48% from top quarter of their high school class, 86% from top half. 2 National Merit Scholars.
Graduation Requirements: 93 credit hours for associate, 183 credit hours for bachelor's; 18 credit hours of natural science; 5 credit hours of math or completion of proficiency test; computer course for business, economics majors; internship (some majors); senior project (some majors).
Computers on Campus: 558 computers available on campus for general student use. Computer purchase/lease plans available. A computer is recommended for some students. A campus-wide network can be accessed from student residence rooms and from off-campus. Students can contact faculty members and/or advisers through e-mail. Computers for student use in computer center, computer labs, research center, learning resource center, classrooms, library, student center, writing lab provide access to the Internet/World Wide Web, on- and off-campus e-mail addresses. Staffed computer lab on campus provides training in use of computers, software. *Academic computing expenditure 1995–96:* $439,665.

EXPENSES AND FINANCIAL AID

Expenses for 1997–98: *Application fee:* $30. State resident tuition: $1935 full-time. Nonresident tuition: $5730 full-time. Part-time tuition per quarter ranges from $118 to $633 for state residents, $331 to $1871 for nonresidents. College room and board: $2955 (minimum). College room only: $1500 (minimum).
Undergraduate Financial Aid: Of all full-time undergraduates enrolled in fall 1996, 75% of those judged to have need according to Federal Methodology were aided. On average, 82% of need was met. *Financial aid deadline (priority):* 4/1. *Financial aid forms:* FAFSA, institutional form required.

Weber State University (continued)

LD Services Contact: Mr. Jeff Morris, Coordinator, Weber State University, 1129 University Circle, Ogden, UT 84408-1129, 801-626-6413. Fax: 801-626-6620.

WELLESLEY COLLEGE

Wellesley, Massachusetts

LEARNING DISABILITIES SERVICES INFORMATION

Learning and Teaching Center currently serves 65 undergraduates with LD. Students diagnosed with ADD/ADHD are eligible for the same services available to students with LD.
Staff: 2 full-time, 1 part-time staff members, including director. Services provided by tutors.
Special Fees: No special fees are charged for services to students with LD.
Applications and admissions: *Required:* high school transcript, untimed SAT I, letters of recommendation, 3 achievement tests, English composition test; *recommended:* high school courses completed, personal interview. Students may begin taking classes in fall only. *Application deadline:* 1/15.
Special policies: The college has written policies regarding substitutions and waivers of graduation requirements.

PROGRAM AND SERVICE COMPONENTS

Academic advising: Provided by academic advisers. Students with LD may take up to 5 courses each term; most take 4 courses; 3 courses required to maintain full-time status.
Counseling services: Individual counseling, small-group counseling, career counseling.
Basic skills remediation: Offered one-on-one by Learning and Teaching Center staff. Available in various areas as appropriate.
Subject-area tutoring: Offered one-on-one and in small groups by peer tutors. Available in all subjects.
Auxiliary aids: Taped textbooks, tape recorders, calculators, typewriters, word-processors with spell-check, personal computers.
Auxiliary services: Alternative test arrangements, notetakers, advocacy.

GENERAL COLLEGE INFORMATION

Independent, 4-year, women only. Awards bachelor's degrees (double bachelor's degree with Massachusetts Institute of Technology). Founded 1870. *Setting:* 500-acre suburban campus with easy access to Boston. *Endowment:* $605.5 million. *Research spending 1995–96:* $6.4 million. *Total enrollment:* 2,319. *Faculty:* 320 (237 full-time, 97% with terminal degrees, 83 part-time); student–undergrad faculty ratio is 9:1.
Enrollment Profile: 2,319 students from 53 states and territories, 70 other countries. 100% women, 6% part-time, 22% state residents, 97% live on campus, 10% transferred in, 6% international, 2% 25 or older, 1% Native American, 7% Hispanic, 7% black, 30% Asian or Pacific Islander. *Retention:* 97% of 1995 full-time freshmen returned. *Graduation:* 82% graduate in 4 years, 85% in 5 years, 86% in 6 years. *Most popular recent majors:* psychology, economics, English.
First-Year Class: 597 total; 3,310 applied, 40% were accepted, 45% of whom enrolled. 75% from top 10% of their high school class, 93% from top quarter, 100% from top half.
Graduation Requirements: 32 courses; 3 math/science courses including at least 1 lab science course; 2 years of a foreign language or the equivalent.
Computers on Campus: 200 computers available on campus for general student use. Computer purchase/lease plans available. A campus-wide network can be accessed from student residence rooms and from off-campus. Students can contact faculty members and/or advisers through e-mail. Computers for student use in computer center, computer labs, research center, learning resource center, classrooms, library, dorms, science center, social science building provide access to the Internet/World Wide Web, on- and off-campus e-mail addresses, electronic bulletin boards. Staffed computer lab on campus (open 24 hours a day) provides training in use of computers, software.

EXPENSES AND FINANCIAL AID

Expenses for 1997–98: *Application fee:* $50. Comprehensive fee of $28,332 includes full-time tuition ($21,256), mandatory fees ($406), and college room and board ($6670). College room only: $3400. Part-time tuition: $2657 per course. Part-time mandatory fees: $51 per course.
Undergraduate Financial Aid: Of all full-time undergraduates enrolled in fall 1996, 100% of those judged to have need according to Federal Methodology were aided. On average, 100% of need was met. *Financial aid deadline:* 1/15. *Financial aid forms:* FAFSA, CSS Financial Aid PROFILE, institutional form, federal income tax forms required.
LD Services Contact: Dr. Barbara C. Boger, Director of Programs, Learning and Teaching Center, Wellesley College, 106 Central Street, Wellesley, MA 02181, 617-283-2641.

WEST CHESTER UNIVERSITY OF PENNSYLVANIA

West Chester, Pennsylvania

LEARNING DISABILITIES SERVICES INFORMATION

Office of Services for Students with Disabilities (OSSD) currently serves 280 undergraduates with LD. Services are also available to graduate students. Students diagnosed with ADD/ADHD are eligible for the same services available to students with LD, as well as coaching.
Staff: Includes director, assistant director, graduate assistant. Services provided by remediation specialists, counselors, diagnostic specialists.
Special Fees: No special fees are charged for services to students with LD.
Applications and admissions: *Required:* high school transcript, grade point average, psychoeducational report completed within 3 years; *recommended:* extended time SAT I, personal interview. Students may begin taking classes in fall only. *Application deadline:* continuous.
Special policies: The college has written policies regarding substitutions and waivers of admissions, graduation, and degree requirements.

PROGRAM AND SERVICE COMPONENTS

Special preparation or orientation: Optional orientation offered during registration.
Diagnostic testing: Study skills, learning strategies.
Academic advising: Provided by unit staff members, academic advisers. Most students with LD take 12 credits each term; 12 credits required to maintain full-time status; 6 credits required to be eligible for financial aid.
Basic skills remediation: Offered one-on-one by assistant director, graduate assistant. Available in written language, learning strategies, study skills, time management.
Subject-area tutoring: Offered one-on-one and in small groups by graduate students. Available in some subjects.
Special courses: Math. All offered for credit; all enter into overall grade point average.
Auxiliary aids: Taped textbooks, tape recorders, calculators, word-processors with spell-check, personal computers, talking computers, optical character readers, voice-activated computers.
Auxiliary services: Alternative test arrangements, priority registration, advocacy.
Campus support group: A special student organization is available to students with LD.

GENERAL COLLEGE INFORMATION

State-supported, comprehensive, coed. Part of Pennsylvania State System of Higher Education. Awards associate, bachelor's, master's degrees. Founded 1871. *Setting:* 547-acre small-town campus with easy access to Philadelphia. *Endowment:* $3.6 million. *Total enrollment:* 11,261. *Faculty:* 706 (530 full-time, 176 part-time); student–undergrad faculty ratio is 17:1.
Enrollment Profile: 9,422 students from 29 states and territories, 6 other countries. 59% women, 41% men, 18% part-time, 89% state residents, 36% live on campus, 36% transferred in, 19% 25 or older, 1% Native American, 2% Hispanic, 8% black, 2% Asian or Pacific Islander. *Retention:* 82% of 1995 full-time freshmen returned. *Graduation:* 28% graduate in 4 years, 53% in 5 years, 59% in 6 years. *Areas of study chosen:* 25% liberal arts/general studies, 18% education, 11% social sciences, 9% business management and administrative services, 7% health professions and related sciences, 6% English language/literature/letters, 6% natural resource sciences, 5% psychology, 4% biological and life sciences, 3% fine arts, 2% computer and information sciences, 2% physical sciences, 1% foreign language and literature, 1% mathematics. *Most popular recent majors:* education, marketing/retailing/merchandising, criminal justice.
First-Year Class: 1,460 total; 6,296 applied, 61% were accepted, 38% of whom enrolled. 10% from top 10% of their high school class, 83% from top half.
Graduation Requirements: 64 credits for associate, 128 credits for bachelor's; 3 credits of math; 9 credits of science; computer course for

business administration, geography, planning, applied media technology majors; internship (some majors); senior project for honors program students and some majors.
Computers on Campus: 400 computers available on campus for general student use. A computer is recommended for some students. A campus-wide network can be accessed from student residence rooms and from off-campus. Students can contact faculty members and/or advisers through e-mail. Computers for student use in computer center, computer labs, library, student center, dorms provide access to the Internet/World Wide Web. Staffed computer lab on campus provides training in use of computers, software.

EXPENSES AND FINANCIAL AID

Expenses for 1997–98: *Application fee:* $25. State resident tuition: $3468 full-time, $144 per credit part-time. Nonresident tuition: $8824 full-time, $368 per credit part-time. Part-time mandatory fees: $30 per credit. Full-time mandatory fees: $694. College room and board: $4376. College room only: $2776.
Undergraduate Financial Aid: 63% of all full-time undergraduates enrolled in fall 1996 applied for aid; of these, 96% were judged to have need according to Federal Methodology, of whom 87% were aided. *Financial aid deadline (priority):* 3/1. *Financial aid forms:* FAFSA required. State form required for some.
LD Services Contact: Dr. Martin Patwell, Director, West Chester University of Pennsylvania, University Avenue and High Street, West Chester, PA 19383, 610-436-3217. Fax: 610-436-2600. Email: mpatwell@wcupa.edu.

WESTERN BAPTIST COLLEGE

Salem, Oregon

LEARNING DISABILITIES SERVICES INFORMATION

Academic Services began offering services in 1995. Currently the program serves 3 undergraduates with LD. Students diagnosed with ADD/ADHD are eligible for the same services available to students with LD.
Staff: 1 part-time staff member (coordinator). Services provided by tutors, counselors.
Special Fees: No special fees are charged for services to students with LD.
Applications and admissions: *Required:* high school transcript, grade point average, courses completed, extended time SAT I, personal interview, autobiographical statement, letters of recommendation, psychoeducational report completed within 3 years (if requesting accommodations); *recommended:* extended time ACT. Students may begin taking classes in fall only. *Application deadline:* continuous.
Special policies: The college has written policies regarding substitutions and waivers of admissions, graduation, and degree requirements.

PROGRAM AND SERVICE COMPONENTS

Academic advising: Provided by unit staff members, academic advisers. Most students with LD take 12 to 13 credit hours each term; 12 credit hours required to maintain full-time status and be eligible for financial aid.
Counseling services: Individual counseling, career counseling, self-advocacy training.
Subject-area tutoring: Offered one-on-one, in small groups, and in class-size groups by professional teachers, peer tutors. Available in all subjects.
Auxiliary aids: Taped textbooks, tape recorders, word-processors with spell-check.
Auxiliary services: Alternative test arrangements, notetakers, priority registration, advocacy.

GENERAL COLLEGE INFORMATION

Independent-religious, 4-year, coed. Awards associate, bachelor's degrees. Founded 1935. *Setting:* 107-acre suburban campus with easy access to Portland. *Endowment:* $301,295. *Educational spending 1995–96:* $2018 per undergrad. *Total enrollment:* 720. *Faculty:* 52 (20 full-time, 30% with terminal degrees, 32 part-time); student–undergrad faculty ratio is 12:1.
Enrollment Profile: 720 students from 11 states and territories, 2 other countries. 59% women, 41% men, 22% part-time, 71% state residents, 49% live on campus, 17% transferred in, 1% international, 25% 25 or older, 2% Native American, 2% Hispanic, 1% black, 1% Asian or Pacific Islander. *Retention:* 86% of 1995 full-time freshmen returned. *Graduation:* 39% graduate in 4 years, 52% in 5 years. *Areas of study chosen:* 32% education, 19% business management and administrative services, 14% psychology, 3% English language/literature/letters, 2% fine arts, 2% theology/religion, 1% prelaw. *Most popular recent majors:* business administration/commerce/management, education, psychology.
First-Year Class: 160 total; 290 applied, 91% were accepted, 61% of whom enrolled. 29% from top 10% of their high school class, 38% from top quarter, 90% from top half. 10 valedictorians.
Graduation Requirements: 64 credit hours for associate, 128 credit hours for bachelor's; 4 credit hours each of math and lab science; computer course; senior project (some majors).
Computers on Campus: 22 computers available on campus for general student use. A computer is strongly recommended for all students. A campus-wide network can be accessed from student residence rooms and from off-campus. Students can contact faculty members and/or advisers through e-mail. Computers for student use in computer labs, dorms provide access to the Internet/World Wide Web, on- and off-campus e-mail addresses. Staffed computer lab on campus provides training in use of computers, software. *Academic computing expenditure 1995–96:* $126,860.

EXPENSES AND FINANCIAL AID

Expenses for 1997–98: *Application fee:* $25. Comprehensive fee of $17,170 includes full-time tuition ($11,900), mandatory fees ($450), and college room and board ($4820). Part-time tuition: $495 per credit hour.
Undergraduate Financial Aid: On average, 60% of need was met. *Financial aid deadline (priority):* 2/15. *Financial aid forms:* FAFSA required; CSS Financial Aid PROFILE, state form acceptable. Institutional form required for some.
LD Services Contact: Mrs. Faythe Moore, Learning Services Coordinator, Western Baptist College, 5000 Deer Park Drive SE, Salem, OR 97301-9392, 503-375-7015. Fax: 503-585-4316. Email: fmoore@wbc.edu.

WESTERN CAROLINA UNIVERSITY

Cullowhee, North Carolina

LEARNING DISABILITIES SERVICES INFORMATION

Student Support Services began offering services in 1983. Currently the program serves undergraduate and graduate students with LD. Students diagnosed with ADD/ADHD are eligible for the same services available to students with LD.
Staff: 5 full-time staff members, including director, coordinator. Services provided by remediation specialists, tutors, counselors, notetakers, readers.
Special Fees: No special fees are charged for services to students with LD.
Applications and admissions: *Required:* high school transcript, grade point average, courses completed, untimed SAT I. Students may begin taking classes any term. *Application deadline:* 5/1.
Special policies: The college has written policies regarding grade forgiveness.

PROGRAM AND SERVICE COMPONENTS

Diagnostic testing: Intelligence, reading, perceptual skills, personality, speech, hearing, written language; testing done on a case-by-case basis.
Academic advising: Provided by unit staff members. Students with LD may take up to 19 credit hours each term; most take 12 to 15 credit hours; 12 credit hours required to maintain full-time status and be eligible for financial aid.
Counseling services: Individual counseling, small-group counseling, career counseling.
Basic skills remediation: Offered one-on-one, in small groups, and in class-size groups by regular teachers. Available in reading, math, spelling, written language, study skills, time management, speech.
Subject-area tutoring: Offered one-on-one by peer tutors. Available in all subjects.
Special courses: College survival skills, study skills, career planning. All offered for credit; all enter into overall grade point average.
Auxiliary aids: Taped textbooks, tape recorders, calculators, word-processors with spell-check, talking computers, optical character readers.
Auxiliary services: Alternative test arrangements, notetakers, priority registration, readers.

GENERAL COLLEGE INFORMATION

State-supported, comprehensive, coed. Part of University of North Carolina System. Awards bachelor's, master's, doctoral degrees. Founded 1889. *Setting:* 260-acre rural campus. *Endowment:* $11.2 million. *Research spending 1995–96:* $1.2 million. *Total enrollment:* 6,511. *Faculty:* 508 (349 full-time, 84% with terminal degrees, 159 part-time); student–undergrad faculty ratio is 18:1.

Western Carolina University (continued)

Enrollment Profile: 5,674 students from 33 states and territories, 25 other countries. 51% women, 49% men, 10% part-time, 93% state residents, 50% live on campus, 30% transferred in, 1% international, 16% 25 or older, 2% Native American, 1% Hispanic, 4% black, 1% Asian or Pacific Islander. *Retention:* 71% of 1995 full-time freshmen returned. *Graduation:* 18% graduate in 4 years, 43% in 5 years, 48% in 6 years. *Areas of study chosen:* 19% education, 16% social sciences, 14% business management and administrative services, 12% health professions and related sciences, 8% vocational and home economics, 4% biological and life sciences, 4% computer and information sciences, 3% communications and journalism, 3% engineering and applied sciences, 3% English language/literature/letters, 3% fine arts, 3% performing arts, 3% psychology, 2% natural resource sciences, 2% physical sciences, 1% foreign language and literature, 1% mathematics, 1% philosophy. *Most popular recent majors:* criminal justice, marketing/retailing/merchandising, nursing.

First-Year Class: 1,182 total; 3,192 applied, 85% were accepted, 43% of whom enrolled. 9% from top 10% of their high school class, 27% from top quarter, 66% from top half. 10 National Merit Scholars, 3 valedictorians.

Graduation Requirements: 128 credit hours; 3 credit hours of math; 6 credit hours of science; computer course; internship (some majors); senior project (some majors).

Computers on Campus: 400 computers available on campus for general student use. A computer is recommended for all students. A campus-wide network can be accessed from student residence rooms and from off-campus. Students can contact faculty members and/or advisers through e-mail. Computers for student use in computer center, computer labs, classrooms, library provide access to the Internet/World Wide Web, on- and off-campus e-mail addresses. Staffed computer lab on campus provides training in use of computers, software.

EXPENSES AND FINANCIAL AID

Estimated Expenses for 1997–98: *Application fee:* $25. State resident tuition: $874 full-time. Nonresident tuition: $8028 full-time. Part-time tuition per semester ranges from $109 to $328 for state residents, $1004 to $3011 for nonresidents. Part-time mandatory fees per semester range from $37.80 to $415.80. Full-time mandatory fees: $965. College room and board: $2800. College room only: $1410.

Undergraduate Financial Aid: Of all full-time undergraduates enrolled in fall 1996, 75% of those who applied for aid were judged to have need according to Federal Methodology, of whom 95% were aided. On average, 95% of need was met. *Financial aid deadline (priority):* 3/31. *Financial aid forms:* FAFSA, institutional form required.

LD Services Contact: Dr. Bonita Jacobs, Dean for Student Development, Western Carolina University, H. F. Robinson Administration Building, Cullowhee, NC 28723, 704-227-7234.

WESTERN ILLINOIS UNIVERSITY

Macomb, Illinois

LEARNING DISABILITIES SERVICES INFORMATION

Disability Support Services began offering services in 1982. Currently the program serves 103 undergraduates with LD. Services are also available to graduate students. Students diagnosed with ADD/ADHD are eligible for the same services available to students with LD.

Staff: 1 full-time, 3 part-time staff members, including coordinator.

Special Fees: No special fees are charged for services to students with LD.

Applications and admissions: *Required:* high school transcript, grade point average, class rank, courses completed, psychoeducational report completed within 3 years; *recommended:* high school extracurricular activities, untimed or extended time ACT, extended time SAT I. Students may begin taking classes in fall, spring, or summer. *Application deadline:* continuous.

PROGRAM AND SERVICE COMPONENTS

Special preparation or orientation: Optional orientation offered prior to start of Fall semester.

Academic advising: Provided by unit staff members, academic advisers. Most students with LD take 12 to 15 credit hours each term; 12 credit hours required to maintain full-time status and be eligible for financial aid.

Auxiliary aids: Taped textbooks, tape recorders, calculators, typewriters, word-processors with spell-check, personal computers, talking computers, optical character readers, Soundproof software, Kurzweil voice-activated software.

Auxiliary services: Alternative test arrangements, notetakers, priority registration, advocacy.

GENERAL COLLEGE INFORMATION

State-supported, comprehensive, coed. Awards bachelor's, master's degrees. Founded 1899. *Setting:* 1,050-acre small-town campus. *Endowment:* $7.8 million. *Research spending 1995–96:* $1.9 million. *Educational spending 1995–96:* $4745 per undergrad. *Total enrollment:* 12,184. *Faculty:* 659 (605 full-time, 72% with terminal degrees, 54 part-time); student–undergrad faculty ratio is 15:1.

Enrollment Profile: 9,644 students from 19 states and territories, 34 other countries. 49% women, 51% men, 16% part-time, 92% state residents, 44% live on campus, 14% transferred in, 4% international, 21% 25 or older, 1% Native American, 3% Hispanic, 7% black, 1% Asian or Pacific Islander. *Retention:* 70% of 1995 full-time freshmen returned. *Graduation:* 22% graduate in 4 years, 43% in 5 years, 48% in 6 years. *Areas of study chosen:* 16% social sciences, 14% education, 9% business management and administrative services, 9% interdisciplinary studies, 6% communications and journalism, 3% agriculture, 3% biological and life sciences, 3% computer and information sciences, 3% engineering and applied sciences, 3% performing arts, 3% psychology, 2% English language/literature/letters, 2% fine arts, 2% health professions and related sciences, 2% vocational and home economics, 1% architecture, 1% foreign language and literature, 1% mathematics, 1% philosophy, 1% physical sciences, 1% predentistry, 1% premed, 1% prevet. *Most popular recent majors:* law enforcement/police sciences, elementary education, communication.

First-Year Class: 1,506 total; 6,614 applied, 69% were accepted, 33% of whom enrolled. 8% from top 10% of their high school class, 26% from top quarter, 63% from top half.

Graduation Requirements: 120 credit hours; 9 credit hours of math/science; computer course for math, business, home economics, some agriculture majors; internship (some majors); senior project for honors program students.

Computers on Campus: 700 computers available on campus for general student use. A computer is recommended for all students. A campus-wide network can be accessed from off-campus. Students can contact faculty members and/or advisers through e-mail. Computers for student use in computer center, computer labs, classrooms, library, dorms, academic buildings provide access to the Internet/World Wide Web, on- and off-campus e-mail addresses, course registration. Staffed computer lab on campus provides training in use of computers, software. *Academic computing expenditure 1995–96:* $1.9 million.

EXPENSES AND FINANCIAL AID

Expenses for 1997–98: State resident tuition: $2119 full-time, $88.30 per credit hour part-time. Nonresident tuition: $6358 full-time, $264.90 per credit hour part-time. Part-time mandatory fees: $31.90 per credit hour. Full-time mandatory fees: $766. College room and board: $3838.

Undergraduate Financial Aid: 86% of all full-time undergraduates enrolled in fall 1996 applied for aid; of these, 65% were judged to have need according to Federal Methodology, of whom 98% were aided. On average, 84% of need was met. *Financial aid deadline (priority):* 3/1. *Financial aid forms:* FAFSA required.

LD Services Contact: Ms. Joan Green, Coordinator, Western Illinois University, 1 University Circle, Macomb, IL 61455-1396, 309-298-2512. Fax: 309-298-2361. Email: joan_green@ccmail.wiu.edu.

WESTERN KENTUCKY UNIVERSITY

Bowling Green, Kentucky

LEARNING DISABILITIES SERVICES INFORMATION

Disabled Student Services currently serves 50 undergraduates with LD. Students diagnosed with ADD/ADHD are eligible for the same services available to students with LD.

Staff: 2 full-time staff members, including director, secretary. Services provided by counselors.

Special Fees: A fee is charged for diagnostic testing.

Applications and admissions: *Required:* high school transcript, grade point average, personal interview, psychoeducational report. Students may begin taking classes in fall only. *Application deadline:* continuous.

Special policies: The college has written policies regarding substitutions and waivers of admissions and graduation requirements.

PROGRAM AND SERVICE COMPONENTS

Diagnostic testing: Intelligence, spoken language, speech.

Academic advising: Provided by unit staff members, academic advisers. Students with LD may take up to 21 semester hours each term; 12 semester hours required to maintain full-time status and be eligible for financial aid.
Subject-area tutoring: Offered one-on-one by professional teachers, peer tutors, graduate assistant. Available in some subjects.
Auxiliary aids: Calculators, typewriters, word-processors with spell-check.
Auxiliary services: Alternative test arrangements, notetakers.

GENERAL COLLEGE INFORMATION

State-supported, comprehensive, coed. Awards associate, bachelor's, master's degrees. Founded 1906. *Setting:* 223-acre suburban campus with easy access to Nashville. *Research spending 1995–96:* $2.3 million. *Total enrollment:* 14,613. *Faculty:* 867 (546 full-time, 321 part-time).
Enrollment Profile: 12,475 students: 57% women, 43% men, 21% part-time, 83% state residents, 7% transferred in, 23% 25 or older, 1% Hispanic, 7% black, 1% Asian or Pacific Islander. *Most popular recent majors:* elementary education, liberal arts/general studies, nursing.
First-Year Class: 2,338 total; 4,283 applied, 97% were accepted, 56% of whom enrolled.
Graduation Requirements: 64 semester hours for associate, 128 semester hours for bachelor's; 3 semester hours of math; 9 semester hours of science; computer course for business, industrial technology, engineering technology, math majors; internship (some majors); senior project (some majors).
Computers on Campus: 750 computers available on campus for general student use. Computer purchase/lease plans available. A campus-wide network can be accessed from student residence rooms and from off-campus. Students can contact faculty members and/or advisers through e-mail. Computers for student use in computer center, computer labs, research center, learning resource center, classrooms, library, student center, dorms, student rooms provide access to the Internet/World Wide Web. Staffed computer lab on campus provides training in use of computers. *Academic computing expenditure 1995–96:* $1.1 million.

EXPENSES AND FINANCIAL AID

Expenses for 1997–98: *Application fee:* $15. State resident tuition: $1800 full-time, $87 per semester hour part-time. Nonresident tuition: $5400 full-time, $237 per semester hour part-time. Part-time mandatory fees: $9 per semester hour. Full-time mandatory fees: $340. College room and board: $2700. College room only: $1430 (minimum).
Undergraduate Financial Aid: 76% of all full-time undergraduates enrolled in fall 1996 applied for aid; of these, 65% were judged to have need according to Federal Methodology, of whom 94% were aided. On average, 95% of need was met. *Financial aid deadline (priority):* 4/1. *Financial aid forms:* FAFSA required; CSS Financial Aid PROFILE acceptable. Proof of Selective Service registration (for men) required for some.
LD Services Contact: Mr. Howard E. Bailey, Dean of Student Life, Western Kentucky University, 442 Potter Hall, Bowling Green, KY 42101, 502-745-2791. Fax: 502-745-6582. Email: howard.bailey@wku.edu.

WESTERN MONTANA COLLEGE OF THE UNIVERSITY OF MONTANA

Dillon, Montana

LEARNING DISABILITIES SERVICES INFORMATION

Learning Center began offering services in 1985. Currently the program serves 21 undergraduates with LD. Students diagnosed with ADD/ADHD are eligible for the same services available to students with LD.
Staff: 1 full-time, 3 part-time staff members, including director, assistant director, Learning Center assistants. Services provided by remediation specialists, tutors, counselors.
Special Fees: No special fees are charged for services to students with LD.
Applications and admissions: *Required:* high school transcript, courses completed, extended time ACT; *recommended:* high school grade point average, class rank, extended time SAT I, personal interview, autobiographical statement, letters of recommendation. Students may begin taking classes any term. *Application deadline:* continuous.
Special policies: The college has written policies regarding grade forgiveness.

PROGRAM AND SERVICE COMPONENTS

Diagnostic testing: Reading, math, written language, study skills.
Academic advising: Provided by unit staff members, academic advisers. Students with LD may take up to 16 credits each term; most take 12 credits; 12 credits required to maintain full-time status and be eligible for financial aid.
Counseling services: Individual counseling, small-group counseling, career counseling.
Basic skills remediation: Offered one-on-one, in small groups, and in class-size groups by LD teachers, regular teachers. Available in reading, math, spelling, written language, learning strategies, study skills, time management.
Subject-area tutoring: Offered one-on-one, in small groups, and in class-size groups by professional teachers, peer tutors. Available in all subjects.
Special courses: College survival skills, reading, vocabulary development, composition, learning strategies, Internet use, time management, math, personal psychology, study skills, career planning, health and nutrition. All offered for credit; all enter into overall grade point average.
Auxiliary aids: Taped textbooks, tape recorders, calculators, typewriters, word-processors with spell-check, personal computers.
Auxiliary services: Alternative test arrangements, notetakers, priority registration, advocacy, signing for the hearing impaired.

GENERAL COLLEGE INFORMATION

State-supported, 4-year, coed. Part of Montana University System. Awards associate, bachelor's degrees. Founded 1893. *Setting:* 36-acre small-town campus. *Endowment:* $2.5 million. *Research spending 1995–96:* $23,335. *Educational spending 1995–96:* $3651 per undergrad. *Total enrollment:* 1,115. *Faculty:* 75 (50 full-time, 70% with terminal degrees, 25 part-time); student–undergrad faculty ratio is 20:1.
Enrollment Profile: 1,115 students from 20 states and territories, 2 other countries. 56% women, 44% men, 15% part-time, 91% state residents, 15% transferred in, 2% international, 20% 25 or older, 1% Native American, 0% Hispanic, 2% black. *Retention:* 50% of 1995 full-time freshmen returned. *Areas of study chosen:* 58% education, 42% liberal arts/general studies. *Most popular recent majors:* elementary education, liberal arts/general studies, physical education.
First-Year Class: 219 total; 307 applied, 95% were accepted, 75% of whom enrolled.
Graduation Requirements: 64 credits for associate, 128 credits for bachelor's; 1 course each in math and science; computer course; internship (some majors); senior project (some majors).
Computers on Campus: 75 computers available on campus for general student use. A computer is recommended for all students. A campus-wide network can be accessed from off-campus. Students can contact faculty members and/or advisers through e-mail. Computers for student use in computer center, computer labs, learning resource center, classrooms, library, dorms, Office Simulation Center provide access to the Internet/World Wide Web, on- and off-campus e-mail addresses. Staffed computer lab on campus provides training in use of computers, software. *Academic computing expenditure 1995–96:* $165,200.

EXPENSES AND FINANCIAL AID

Expenses for 1996–97: *Application fee:* $30. State resident tuition: $2162 full-time. Nonresident tuition: $6154 full-time. Part-time tuition per semester ranges from $126 to $1006 for state residents, $293 to $2836 for nonresidents. College room and board: $3524. College room only: $1450.
Undergraduate Financial Aid: 90% of all full-time undergraduates enrolled in fall 1996 applied for aid; of these, 94% were judged to have need according to Federal Methodology, of whom 100% were aided. On average, 64% of need was met. *Financial aid deadline (priority):* 3/1. *Financial aid forms:* FAFSA, CSS Financial Aid PROFILE required.
LD Services Contact: Mr. Clarence Kostelecky, Director, Learning Center, Western Montana College of The University of Montana, 710 South Atlantic, Dillon, MT 59725-3598, 406-683-7330. Fax: 406-683-7493. Email: c_kostelecky@wmc.edu.

WESTERN OREGON UNIVERSITY

Monmouth, Oregon

LEARNING DISABILITIES SERVICES INFORMATION

Office of Disability Services began offering services in 1984. Currently the program serves 35 undergraduates with LD. Services are also available to graduate students. Students diagnosed with ADD/ADHD are eligible for the same services available to students with LD.
Staff: 1 full-time staff member (director). Services provided by interpreters, notetakers, readers.

Western Oregon University (continued)

Special Fees: No special fees are charged for services to students with LD.

Applications and admissions: *Required:* high school transcript, grade point average, courses completed, untimed SAT I or ACT; *recommended:* extended time SAT I or ACT, personal interview, autobiographical statement, letters of recommendation, psychoeducational report completed within 3 years. Students may begin taking classes any term. *Application deadline:* continuous.

Special policies: The college has written policies regarding substitutions and waivers of admissions requirements.

PROGRAM AND SERVICE COMPONENTS

Special preparation or orientation: Optional orientation offered before registration and during registration.

Academic advising: Provided by unit staff members, academic advisers. Students with LD may take up to 18 credit hours each term; most take 9 to 12 credit hours; 12 credit hours required to maintain full-time status; 6 credit hours required to be eligible for financial aid.

Counseling services: Individual counseling, small-group counseling, career counseling.

Basic skills remediation: Offered one-on-one, in small groups, and in class-size groups by college enrichment program staff. Available in math, written language, learning strategies, study skills, time management, critical thinking.

Special courses: College survival skills, composition, time management, math, study skills, critical thinking. Some offered for credit; some enter into overall grade point average.

Auxiliary aids: Taped textbooks, tape recorders, calculators, typewriters, word-processors with spell-check, optical character readers, computer station with voice output.

Auxiliary services: Alternative test arrangements, notetakers, advocacy, readers, transcribers.

GENERAL COLLEGE INFORMATION

State-supported, comprehensive, coed. Part of Oregon State System of Higher Education. Awards associate, bachelor's, master's degrees. Founded 1856. *Setting:* 134-acre rural campus with easy access to Portland. *Total enrollment:* 4,030. *Faculty:* 261 (129 full-time, 87% with terminal degrees, 132 part-time); student–undergrad faculty ratio is 15:1.

Enrollment Profile: 3,798 students from 20 states and territories, 21 other countries. 58% women, 42% men, 9% part-time, 92% state residents, 26% live on campus, 15% transferred in, 3% international, 23% 25 or older, 2% Native American, 4% Hispanic, 1% black, 5% Asian or Pacific Islander. *Retention:* 63% of 1995 full-time freshmen returned. *Graduation:* 16% graduate in 4 years, 32% in 5 years, 35% in 6 years.

First-Year Class: 742 total; 1,475 applied, 56% were accepted, 90% of whom enrolled. 18% from top 10% of their high school class, 46% from top quarter, 83% from top half.

Graduation Requirements: 93 credit hours for associate, 192 credit hours for bachelor's; 16 credit hours of math/science including at least 4 credit hours of math; computer course; internship (some majors); senior project for honors program students and some majors.

Computers on Campus: 150 computers available on campus for general student use. Computer purchase/lease plans available. A campus-wide network can be accessed from student residence rooms and from off-campus. Students can contact faculty members and/or advisers through e-mail. Computers for student use in computer center, computer labs, classrooms, library, dorms provide access to the Internet/World Wide Web, on- and off-campus e-mail addresses. Staffed computer lab on campus provides training in use of computers, software.

EXPENSES AND FINANCIAL AID

Estimated Expenses for 1997–98: *Application fee:* $50. State resident tuition: $3153 full-time. Nonresident tuition: $9429 full-time. Part-time tuition per quarter ranges from $121 to $952 for state residents, $121 to $2870 for nonresidents. College room and board: $4013.

Undergraduate Financial Aid: 70% of all full-time undergraduates enrolled in fall 1996 applied for aid; of these, 84% were judged to have need according to Federal Methodology, of whom 100% were aided. On average, 65% of need was met. *Financial aid deadline (priority):* 3/1. *Financial aid forms:* FAFSA required.

LD Services Contact: Ms. Martha R. Smith, Director, Disability Services, Western Oregon University, 345 North Monmouth Avenue, Monmouth, OR 97361, 503-838-8250. Fax: 503-838-8511.

WESTERN WASHINGTON UNIVERSITY

Bellingham, Washington

LEARNING DISABILITIES SERVICES INFORMATION

Disabled Student Services currently serves 185 undergraduates with LD. Services are also available to graduate students. Students diagnosed with ADD/ADHD are eligible for the same services available to students with LD.

Staff: 2 full-time staff members, including coordinator. Services provided by counselors.

Special Fees: No special fees are charged for services to students with LD.

Applications and admissions: *Required:* high school transcript, grade point average, courses completed, untimed SAT I, autobiographical statement; *recommended:* high school extracurricular activities, untimed or extended time ACT, extended time SAT I, letters of recommendation, psychoeducational report completed within 3 years. Students may begin taking classes any term. *Application deadline:* continuous.

Special policies: The college has written policies regarding grade forgiveness.

PROGRAM AND SERVICE COMPONENTS

Special preparation or orientation: Optional summer program offered prior to entering college.

Academic advising: Provided by unit staff members, academic advisers. Students with LD may take up to 20 credits each term; most take 12 to 16 credits; 12 credits required to maintain full-time status and be eligible for financial aid.

Counseling services: Individual counseling, small-group counseling, career counseling, self-advocacy training, disability management.

Subject-area tutoring: Offered one-on-one, in small groups, and in class-size groups by peer tutors, tutorial center staff. Available in some subjects.

Auxiliary aids: Taped textbooks, typewriters, word-processors with spell-check, personal computers, optical character readers, copies of class notes.

Auxiliary services: Alternative test arrangements, notetakers, priority registration, advocacy.

GENERAL COLLEGE INFORMATION

State-supported, comprehensive, coed. Awards bachelor's, master's degrees. Founded 1893. *Setting:* 223-acre small-town campus with easy access to Seattle and Vancouver. *Endowment:* $3 million. *Research spending 1995–96:* $2.4 million. *Educational spending 1995–96:* $4969 per undergrad. *Total enrollment:* 11,039. *Undergraduate faculty:* 523 (398 full-time, 89% with terminal degrees, 125 part-time); student–undergrad faculty ratio is 21:1.

Enrollment Profile: 10,252 students from 46 states and territories, 32 other countries. 56% women, 44% men, 5% part-time, 92% state residents, 34% live on campus, 57% transferred in, 1% international, 12% 25 or older, 2% Native American, 3% Hispanic, 2% black, 7% Asian or Pacific Islander. *Retention:* 84% of 1995 full-time freshmen returned. *Graduation:* 20% graduate in 4 years, 51% in 5 years, 60% in 6 years. *Areas of study chosen:* 13% social sciences, 12% business management and administrative services, 10% education, 6% English language/literature/letters, 6% natural resource sciences, 4% biological and life sciences, 4% communications and journalism, 4% engineering and applied sciences, 4% psychology, 3% fine arts, 3% performing arts, 3% physical sciences, 2% computer and information sciences, 1% foreign language and literature, 1% interdisciplinary studies, 1% mathematics, 1% premed. *Most popular recent majors:* business administration/commerce/management, English.

First-Year Class: 2,082 total; 6,014 applied, 83% were accepted, 42% of whom enrolled. 25% from top 10% of their high school class, 60% from top quarter, 92% from top half. 15 National Merit Scholars, 30 valedictorians.

Graduation Requirements: 180 quarter hours; 1 math course beyond intermediate algebra; 4 natural science courses; computer course for science, technology, business administration, education, math majors; internship (some majors); senior project (some majors).

Computers on Campus: 500 computers available on campus for general student use. Computer purchase/lease plans available. A campus-wide network can be accessed from student residence rooms and from off-campus. Students can contact faculty members and/or advisers through e-mail. Computers for student use in computer center, computer labs, learning resource center, library, student center, dorms provide access to the Internet/World Wide Web. Staffed computer lab on campus (open

24 hours a day) provides training in use of computers, software. *Academic computing expenditure 1995–96:* $1.3 million.

EXPENSES AND FINANCIAL AID

Expenses for 1996–97: *Application fee:* $35. State resident tuition: $2433 full-time, $81 per quarter hour part-time. Nonresident tuition: $8616 full-time, $287 per quarter hour part-time. Part-time mandatory fees per quarter (6 to 11 quarter hours): $60. Full-time mandatory fees: $180. College room and board: $4478.
Undergraduate Financial Aid: Of all full-time undergraduates enrolled in fall 1996, 77% of those who applied for aid were judged to have need according to Federal Methodology, of whom 94% were aided. On average, 81% of need was met. *Financial aid deadline (priority):* 2/15. *Financial aid forms:* FAFSA required.
LD Services Contact: Mr. David Brunnemer, Coordinator, Western Washington University, Old Main 110, MS 9019, Bellingham, WA 98225-9003, 206-650-3083. Fax: 206-650-6504.

WEST LIBERTY STATE COLLEGE

West Liberty, West Virginia

LEARNING DISABILITIES SERVICES INFORMATION

Counseling Services Office began offering services in 1993. Currently the program serves 10 undergraduates with LD. Students diagnosed with ADD/ADHD are eligible for the same services available to students with LD, as well as special housing arrangements.
Staff: 1 full-time, 3 part-time staff members, including director, counselor, tutoring program coordinator. Services provided by remediation specialists, tutors, counselors, diagnostic specialist.
Special Fees: No special fees are charged for services to students with LD.
Applications and admissions: *Required:* high school transcript, grade point average, class rank, courses completed; *recommended:* high school IEP (Individualized Education Program), psychoeducational report. Students may begin taking classes any term. *Application deadline:* 8/26 (fall term), 1/13 (spring term).
Special policies: The college has written policies regarding grade forgiveness; substitutions and waivers of admissions requirements.

PROGRAM AND SERVICE COMPONENTS

Academic advising: Provided by unit staff members, academic advisers. Students with LD may take up to 17 semester hours (up to 23 with special permission) each term; most take 14 to 16 semester hours; 12 semester hours required to maintain full-time status; 22 semester hours per year required to be eligible for financial aid.
Counseling services: Individual counseling, career counseling.
Basic skills remediation: Offered in class-size groups by regular teachers. Available in math, written language.
Subject-area tutoring: Offered one-on-one and in small groups by professional teachers, peer tutors. Available in all subjects.
Auxiliary aids: Taped textbooks, optical character readers.
Auxiliary services: Alternative test arrangements, notetakers, priority registration, advocacy, campus orientation for the visually challenged.

GENERAL COLLEGE INFORMATION

State-supported, 4-year, coed. Part of State College System of West Virginia. Awards associate, bachelor's degrees. Founded 1837. *Setting:* 290-acre rural campus with easy access to Pittsburgh. *Educational spending 1995–96:* $2751 per undergrad. *Total enrollment:* 2,412. *Faculty:* 142 (127 full-time, 39% with terminal degrees, 15 part-time); student–undergrad faculty ratio is 18:1.
Enrollment Profile: 2,412 students from 22 states and territories, 8 other countries. 55% women, 45% men, 11% part-time, 70% state residents, 56% live on campus, 35% transferred in, 1% international, 16% 25 or older, 1% Hispanic, 3% black. *Retention:* 68% of 1995 full-time freshmen returned. *Graduation:* 21% graduate in 4 years, 41% in 5 years, 45% in 6 years. *Areas of study chosen:* 24% education, 23% business management and administrative services, 12% health professions and related sciences, 4% communications and journalism, 4% psychology, 3% biological and life sciences, 3% interdisciplinary studies, 2% social sciences, 1% English language/literature/letters. *Most popular recent majors:* business administration/commerce/management, education, criminal justice.
First-Year Class: 468 total; 1,068 applied, 95% were accepted, 46% of whom enrolled. 12% from top 10% of their high school class, 25% from top quarter, 60% from top half.
Graduation Requirements: 64 semester hours for associate, 128 semester hours for bachelor's; 3 semester hours of math; 8 semester hours of science; computer course for business majors; internship (some majors); senior project for honors program students and some majors.
Computers on Campus: 200 computers available on campus for general student use. A campus-wide network can be accessed from off-campus. Students can contact faculty members and/or advisers through e-mail. Computers for student use in computer center, computer labs, classrooms, library provide access to the Internet/World Wide Web, on- and off-campus e-mail addresses. Staffed computer lab on campus. *Academic computing expenditure 1995–96:* $78,913.

EXPENSES AND FINANCIAL AID

Expenses for 1997–98: State resident tuition: $2120 full-time, $88.33 per semester hour part-time. Nonresident tuition: $5560 full-time, $231.67 per semester hour part-time. College room and board: $3100.
Undergraduate Financial Aid: 65% of all full-time undergraduates enrolled in fall 1996 applied for aid; of these, 90% were judged to have need according to Federal Methodology, of whom 100% were aided. On average, 85% of need was met. *Financial aid deadline (priority):* 3/1. *Financial aid forms:* FAFSA required. State form required for some.
LD Services Contact: Mr. Walter T. Austin, A.D.A. Coordinator, West Liberty State College, PO Box 295, West Liberty, WV 26074, 304-336-8018.

WESTMINSTER COLLEGE

New Wilmington, Pennsylvania

LEARNING DISABILITIES SERVICES INFORMATION

Learning Center began offering services in 1996. Currently the program serves 11 undergraduates with LD. Students diagnosed with ADD/ADHD are eligible for the same services available to students with LD.
Staff: Includes director, writing skills/LD consultants. Services provided by remediation specialists, tutors, counselors.
Special Fees: No special fees are charged for services to students with LD.
Applications and admissions: *Required:* high school transcript, grade point average, class rank, courses completed, untimed or extended time SAT I or ACT; *recommended:* personal interview, letters of recommendation, psychoeducational report. Students may begin taking classes in fall only. *Application deadline:* continuous.

PROGRAM AND SERVICE COMPONENTS

Academic advising: Provided by academic advisers. Students with LD may take up to 16 semester hours each term; most take 16 semester hours; 12 semester hours required to maintain full-time status and be eligible for financial aid.
Basic skills remediation: Offered one-on-one and in class-size groups by LD teachers, regular teachers. Available in reading, written language, learning strategies, time management, social skills, computer skills.
Subject-area tutoring: Offered one-on-one by professional teachers, peer tutors, remediation specialist. Available in most subjects.
Special courses: Reading, composition. Some offered for credit; some enter into overall grade point average.
Auxiliary services: Alternative test arrangements, notetakers, advocacy.

GENERAL COLLEGE INFORMATION

Independent, comprehensive, coed, affiliated with Presbyterian Church (U.S.A.). Awards bachelor's, master's degrees. Founded 1852. *Setting:* 300-acre small-town campus with easy access to Pittsburgh. *Endowment:* $46.2 million. *Educational spending 1995–96:* $4600 per undergrad. *Total enrollment:* 1,584. *Faculty:* 122 (98 full-time, 77% with terminal degrees, 24 part-time); student–undergrad faculty ratio is 16:1.
Enrollment Profile: 1,469 students from 23 states and territories, 3 other countries. 60% women, 40% men, 10% part-time, 76% state residents, 7% transferred in, 1% international, 1% 25 or older, 1% Native American, 1% Hispanic, 2% black, 1% Asian or Pacific Islander. *Retention:* 87% of 1995 full-time freshmen returned. *Graduation:* 64% graduate in 4 years, 73% in 5 years, 75% in 6 years. *Areas of study chosen:* 19% business management and administrative services, 10% biological and life sciences, 8% education, 7% social sciences, 6% English language/literature/letters, 5% psychology, 4% communications and journalism, 4% mathematics, 3% natural resource sciences, 3% physical sciences, 2% computer and information sciences, 2% fine arts, 2% performing arts, 1% foreign language and literature, 1% interdisciplinary studies, 1% theology/religion. *Most popular recent majors:* business administration/commerce/management, elementary education, history.
First-Year Class: 301 total; 857 applied, 88% were accepted, 40% of whom enrolled. 22% from top 10% of their high school class, 70% from top quarter, 90% from top half.

Westminster College (continued)

Graduation Requirements: 2 math/science courses including at least 1 lab science course; 2 courses in a foreign language or the equivalent; computer course.

Computers on Campus: 158 computers available on campus for general student use. A computer is strongly recommended for all students. A campus-wide network can be accessed from student residence rooms and from off-campus. Students can contact faculty members and/or advisers through e-mail. Computers for student use in computer center, library, departmental labs provide access to the Internet/World Wide Web, on- and off-campus e-mail addresses. Staffed computer lab on campus provides training in use of computers, software. *Academic computing expenditure 1995–96:* $537,722.

EXPENSES AND FINANCIAL AID

Expenses for 1997–98: *Application fee:* $20. Comprehensive fee of $18,930 includes full-time tuition ($14,650) and college room and board ($4280). Part-time tuition: $434 per semester hour.

Undergraduate Financial Aid: Of all full-time undergraduates enrolled in fall 1996, 91% of those who applied for aid were judged to have need according to Federal Methodology, of whom 99% were aided. On average, 95% of need was met. *Financial aid deadline (priority):* 5/1. *Financial aid forms:* FAFSA, institutional form, federal income tax forms required; CSS Financial Aid PROFILE, state form acceptable.

LD Services Contact: Ms. Linda P. Domanski, Learning Center Consultant/Liaison for Students with Disabilities, Westminster College, Box 115, New Wilmington, PA 16142, 412-946-6035. Fax: 412-946-7171. Email: domanslp@westminster.edu.

WEST VIRGINIA STATE COLLEGE

Institute, West Virginia

LEARNING DISABILITIES SERVICES INFORMATION

Collegiate Support and Counseling Office currently serves 75 undergraduates with LD. Students diagnosed with ADD/ADHD are eligible for the same services available to students with LD.

Staff: 1 full-time staff member (coordinator). Services provided by tutors, counselors.

Special Fees: No special fees are charged for services to students with LD.

Applications and admissions: *Required:* high school transcript, untimed ACT. Students may begin taking classes in fall, spring, or summer. *Application deadline:* continuous.

Special policies: The college has written policies regarding grade forgiveness.

PROGRAM AND SERVICE COMPONENTS

Academic advising: Provided by unit staff members, academic advisers. Students with LD may take up to 18 semester hours each term; most take 12 semester hours; 12 semester hours required to maintain full-time status; 6 semester hours required to be eligible for financial aid.

Counseling services: Individual counseling, career counseling, self-advocacy training.

Subject-area tutoring: Offered one-on-one and in small groups by peer tutors. Available in most subjects.

Auxiliary aids: Taped textbooks, tape recorders, calculators, typewriters, word-processors with spell-check, talking computers, optical character readers.

Auxiliary services: Alternative test arrangements, notetakers, priority registration, advocacy.

Campus support group: A special student organization is available to students with LD.

GENERAL COLLEGE INFORMATION

State-supported, 4-year, coed. Part of State College System of West Virginia. Awards associate, bachelor's degrees. Founded 1891. *Setting:* 90-acre suburban campus. *Endowment:* $94,134. *Research spending 1995–96:* $9666. *Total enrollment:* 4,545. *Faculty:* 253 (137 full-time, 55% with terminal degrees, 116 part-time); student–undergrad faculty ratio is 18:1.

Enrollment Profile: 4,545 students from 25 states and territories, 4 other countries. 55% women, 45% men, 39% part-time, 93% state residents, 8% live on campus, 7% transferred in, 1% international, 40% 25 or older, 0% Native American, 1% Hispanic, 13% black, 1% Asian or Pacific Islander. *Areas of study chosen:* 22% business management and administrative services, 12% education, 5% biological and life sciences, 4% communications and journalism, 3% computer and information sciences, 3% interdisciplinary studies, 2% health professions and related sciences, 1% engineering and applied sciences, 1% English language/literature/letters, 1% fine arts, 1% liberal arts/general studies, 1% psychology, 1% social sciences. *Most popular recent majors:* business administration/commerce/management, elementary education, criminal justice.

First-Year Class: 729 total; 2,317 applied, 99% were accepted, 31% of whom enrolled.

Graduation Requirements: 61 semester hours for associate, 121 semester hours for bachelor's; 12 semester hours of math/science; computer course; internship (some majors).

Computers on Campus: 111 computers available on campus for general student use. A computer is recommended for all students. A campus-wide network can be accessed from student residence rooms and from off-campus. Students can contact faculty members and/or advisers through e-mail. Computers for student use in computer center, computer labs, library, dorms provide access to the Internet/World Wide Web, on- and off-campus e-mail addresses. Staffed computer lab on campus provides training in use of computers, software.

EXPENSES AND FINANCIAL AID

Expenses for 1997–98: State resident tuition: $2184 full-time, $91 per semester hour part-time. Nonresident tuition: $5386 full-time, $225 per semester hour part-time. College room and board: $3450. College room only: $1650.

Undergraduate Financial Aid: Of all full-time undergraduates enrolled in fall 1996, 82% of those who applied for aid were judged to have need according to Federal Methodology, of whom 100% were aided. On average, 100% of need was met. *Financial aid deadline:* Applications processed continuously. *Financial aid forms:* FAFSA, CSS Financial Aid PROFILE, institutional form required. Financial aid transcript (for transfers) required for some.

LD Services Contact: Ms. Kellie Dunlap, Disability Services Counselor, West Virginia State College, Campus Box 178, PO Box 1000, Institute, WV 25112, 304-766-3083. Fax: 304-766-4158.

WEST VIRGINIA UNIVERSITY

Morgantown, West Virginia

LEARNING DISABILITIES SERVICES INFORMATION

Disability Services began offering services in 1983. Currently the program serves 320 undergraduates with LD. Services are also available to graduate students. Students diagnosed with ADD/ADHD are eligible for the same services available to students with LD.

Staff: 6 full-time staff members, including director. Services provided by counselors.

Special Fees: $100 to $1000 for diagnostic testing.

Applications and admissions: *Required:* high school transcript, grade point average, courses completed, extended time SAT I or ACT, psychoeducational report completed within 2 years. Students may begin taking classes any term. *Application deadline:* continuous.

PROGRAM AND SERVICE COMPONENTS

Diagnostic testing: Intelligence, reading, math, spelling, motor abilities, perceptual skills, psychoneurology, speech, hearing.

Academic advising: Provided by unit staff members, academic advisers. Students with LD may take up to 22 credit hours each term; most take 12 to 15 credit hours; 12 credit hours required to maintain full-time status; 24 credit hours per year required to be eligible for financial aid.

GENERAL COLLEGE INFORMATION

State-supported, coed. Part of University of West Virginia System. Awards bachelor's, master's, doctoral, first professional degrees. Founded 1867. *Setting:* 541-acre small-town campus with easy access to Pittsburgh. *Endowment:* $160 million. *Research spending 1995–96:* $52.3 million. *Educational spending 1995–96:* $5202 per undergrad. *Total enrollment:* 21,743. *Faculty:* 1,592 (1,380 full-time, 86% with terminal degrees, 212 part-time); student–undergrad faculty ratio is 17:1.

Enrollment Profile: 14,897 students from 46 states and territories, 59 other countries. 47% women, 53% men, 7% part-time, 59% state residents, 5% transferred in, 2% international, 9% 25 or older, 1% Native American, 1% Hispanic, 4% black, 2% Asian or Pacific Islander. *Retention:* 78% of 1995 full-time freshmen returned. *Graduation:* 26% graduate in 4 years, 49% in 5 years, 56% in 6 years. *Areas of study chosen:* 14% health professions and related sciences, 12% business management and administrative services, 12% social sciences, 8% engineering and applied sciences, 6% education, 5% biological and life sciences, 5% communications and journalism, 5% natural resource sciences, 3% agriculture, 3% fine arts, 3% interdisciplinary studies, 3% vocational and home economics, 2% physical sciences, 1% architecture, 1% computer and information

sciences, 1% English language/literature/letters, 1% foreign language and literature. *Most popular recent majors:* accounting, journalism.
First-Year Class: 3,151 total; 8,676 applied, 89% were accepted, 41% of whom enrolled. 13 National Merit Scholars.
Graduation Requirements: 128 credit hours; 12 credit hours of math/science; computer course for most majors; internship (some majors); senior project for honors program students and some majors.
Computers on Campus: 6,000 computers available on campus for general student use. Computer purchase/lease plans available. A campus-wide network can be accessed from off-campus. Students can contact faculty members and/or advisers through e-mail. Computers for student use in computer center, computer labs, research center, learning resource center, classrooms, library, student center, dorms, departmental labs provide access to the Internet/World Wide Web, on- and off-campus e-mail addresses. Staffed computer lab on campus provides training in use of computers, software.

EXPENSES AND FINANCIAL AID

Expenses for 1997–98: *Application fee:* $15. State resident tuition: $2336 full-time, $100 per credit hour part-time. Nonresident tuition: $7356 full-time, $309 per credit hour part-time. College room and board: $4832.
Undergraduate Financial Aid: Of all full-time undergraduates enrolled in fall 1996, 62% of those who applied for aid were judged to have need according to Federal Methodology, of whom 99% were aided. On average, 94% of need was met. *Financial aid deadline:* Applications processed continuously. *Financial aid forms:* institutional form required. FAFSA, state form required for some.
LD Services Contact: Dr. Gordon R. Kent, Associate Director for Disability Services, West Virginia University, 215 Student Services Center, PO Box 6423, Morgantown, WV 26506-6423, 304-293-6700. Fax: 304-293-3861.

WHEELOCK COLLEGE

Boston, Massachusetts

LEARNING DISABILITIES SERVICES INFORMATION

Office of Academic Advising and Assistance currently serves 45 undergraduates with LD. Students diagnosed with ADD/ADHD are eligible for the same services available to students with LD.
Staff: 1 full-time, 2 part-time staff members, including director. Services provided by remediation specialists, tutors.
Special Fees: No special fees are charged for services to students with LD.
Applications and admissions: *Required:* high school transcript, grade point average, class rank, courses completed, extracurricular activities, personal interview, autobiographical statement, letters of recommendation; *recommended:* psychoeducational report completed within 3 years, interview with Office of Academic Advising/Assistance.
Special policies: The college has written policies regarding substitutions and waivers of admissions, graduation, and degree requirements.

PROGRAM AND SERVICE COMPONENTS

Academic advising: Provided by unit staff members, academic advisers. Students with LD may take up to 20 credits each term; most take 12 to 16 credits; 12 credits required to maintain full-time status; 6 credits (part-time) required to be eligible for financial aid.
Counseling services: Individual counseling, career counseling, self-advocacy training.
Basic skills remediation: Offered one-on-one by professional tutors. Available in reading, math, spelling, written language, learning strategies, study skills, time management, social skills.
Subject-area tutoring: Offered one-on-one and in small groups by professional teachers, peer tutors, professional tutors. Available in all subjects.
Auxiliary aids: Taped textbooks, tape recorders, calculators, word-processors with spell-check.
Auxiliary services: Alternative test arrangements, notetakers, priority registration, advocacy.

GENERAL COLLEGE INFORMATION

Independent, comprehensive, primarily women. Awards bachelor's, master's degrees. Founded 1888. *Setting:* 5-acre urban campus. *Endowment:* $15.7 million. *Research spending 1995–96:* $3 million. *Total enrollment:* 1,369. *Faculty:* 183 (67 full-time, 76% with terminal degrees, 116 part-time); student–undergrad faculty ratio is 11:1.
Enrollment Profile: 682 students from 17 states and territories, 6 other countries. 96% women, 4% men, 12% part-time, 54% state residents, 69% live on campus, 28% transferred in, 2% international, 8% 25 or older, 0% Native American, 1% Hispanic, 4% black, 2% Asian or Pacific Islander. *Retention:* 82% of 1995 full-time freshmen returned. *Areas of study chosen:* 65% education, 35% social sciences. *Most popular recent majors:* education, social work, child care/child and family studies.
First-Year Class: 135 total; 397 applied, 78% were accepted, 43% of whom enrolled. 26% from top quarter of their high school class, 57% from top half.
Graduation Requirements: 134 credits; 8 credits of math/science; internship; senior project for honors program students and some majors.
Computers on Campus: 116 computers available on campus for general student use. A campus-wide network can be accessed. Students can contact faculty members and/or advisers through e-mail. Computers for student use in computer center, dorms. Staffed computer lab on campus. *Academic computing expenditure 1995–96:* $259,906.

EXPENSES AND FINANCIAL AID

Expenses for 1997–98: *Application fee:* $30. Comprehensive fee of $21,520 includes full-time tuition ($15,520) and college room and board ($6000). Part-time tuition: $485 per credit.
Undergraduate Financial Aid: Of all full-time undergraduates enrolled in fall 1996, 100% of those who applied for aid were judged to have need according to Federal Methodology, of whom 100% were aided. On average, 100% of need was met. *Financial aid deadline:* Applications processed continuously. *Financial aid forms:* FAFSA, CSS Financial Aid PROFILE, verification worksheet required. State form required for some.
LD Services Contact: Ms. Mary McCormack, Director, Wheelock College, 200 The Riverway, Boston, MA 02215, 617-734-5200 Ext. 276. Fax: 617-734-7103. Email: mmccormack@wheelock.edu.

WHITMAN COLLEGE

Walla Walla, Washington

LEARNING DISABILITIES SERVICES INFORMATION

Study Resources Center began offering services in 1989. Currently the program serves 33 undergraduates with LD. Students diagnosed with ADD/ADHD are eligible for the same services available to students with LD.
Staff: 1 full-time, 17 part-time staff members, including director, student assistant, academic advisers. Services provided by tutors, counselors, diagnostic specialists.
Special Fees: No special fees are charged for services to students with LD.
Applications and admissions: *Required:* high school transcript, grade point average, courses completed, extracurricular activities, untimed or extended time SAT I, untimed ACT, autobiographical statement, letters of recommendation; *recommended:* high school class rank, personal interview, psychoeducational report completed within 3 years. Students may begin taking classes in fall only. *Application deadline:* 2/15.

PROGRAM AND SERVICE COMPONENTS

Diagnostic testing: Intelligence, reading, math, spelling, spoken language, written language, perceptual skills, study skills, learning strategies, cognition, academic skills (Woodcock-Johnson).
Academic advising: Provided by academic advisers. Students with LD may take up to 18 credits each term; most take 13 credits; 12 credits required to maintain full-time status and be eligible for financial aid.
Counseling services: Individual counseling, small-group counseling, career counseling.
Basic skills remediation: Offered one-on-one and in small groups by Director of Study Resources Center. Available in learning strategies, perceptual skills, study skills, time management, notetaking.
Subject-area tutoring: Offered one-on-one and in small groups by peer tutors. Available in most subjects.
Auxiliary aids: Taped textbooks, tape recorders, word-processors with spell-check, talking computers, optical character readers.
Auxiliary services: Alternative test arrangements, notetakers, advocacy.

GENERAL COLLEGE INFORMATION

Independent, 4-year, coed. Awards bachelor's degrees. Founded 1859. *Setting:* 55-acre small-town campus. *Endowment:* $172.9 million. *Research spending 1995–96:* $193,040. *Educational spending 1995–96:* $6787 per undergrad. *Total enrollment:* 1,309. *Faculty:* 174 (96 full-time, 86% with terminal degrees, 78 part-time); student–undergrad faculty ratio is 11:1.
Enrollment Profile: 1,309 students from 26 states and territories, 9 other countries. 54% women, 46% men, 3% part-time, 45% state residents, 59% live on campus, 1% transferred in, 2% international, 2% 25 or

Whitman College (continued)

older, 1% Native American, 2% Hispanic, 2% black, 7% Asian or Pacific Islander. *Retention:* 86% of 1995 full-time freshmen returned. *Graduation:* 64% graduate in 4 years, 73% in 5 years, 75% in 6 years. *Areas of study chosen:* 13% English language/literature/letters, 11% fine arts, 11% psychology, 10% biological and life sciences, 9% physical sciences, 8% social sciences, 6% performing arts, 4% mathematics, 4% philosophy, 2% foreign language and literature. *Most popular recent majors:* history, psychology, English.

First-Year Class: 357 total; 1,948 applied, 54% were accepted, 34% of whom enrolled. 59% from top 10% of their high school class, 86% from top quarter, 99% from top half. 24 National Merit Scholars, 52 valedictorians.

Graduation Requirements: 124 credits; 6 credits of math; 6 credits of physical or descriptive science; senior project for honors program students and some majors.

Computers on Campus: 134 computers available on campus for general student use. A campus-wide network can be accessed from student residence rooms and from off-campus. Students can contact faculty members and/or advisers through e-mail. Computers for student use in computer labs, learning resource center, library, academic buildings provide access to the Internet/World Wide Web, on- and off-campus e-mail addresses, course registration information. Staffed computer lab on campus provides training in use of computers, software. *Academic computing expenditure 1995–96:* $669,216.

EXPENSES AND FINANCIAL AID

Expenses for 1997–98: Comprehensive fee of $25,396 includes full-time tuition ($19,580), mandatory fees ($176), and college room and board ($5640). College room only: $2580. Part-time tuition: $816 per credit.

Undergraduate Financial Aid: Of all full-time undergraduates enrolled in fall 1996, 92% of those who applied for aid were judged to have need according to Federal Methodology, of whom 91% were aided. On average, 80% of need was met. *Financial aid deadline:* 2/1. *Financial aid forms:* FAFSA, CSS Financial Aid PROFILE required. Parent and student tax returns required for some.

LD Services Contact: Ms. Clare Carson, Director of the Study Resources Center, Whitman College, 345 Boyer Avenue, Walla Walla, WA 99362, 509-527-5213. Fax: 509-527-5859. Email: carsonc@whitman.edu.

WICHITA STATE UNIVERSITY

Wichita, Kansas

LEARNING DISABILITIES SERVICES INFORMATION

Office of Disability Services began offering services in 1985. Currently the program serves 25 undergraduates with LD. Services are also available to graduate students. Students diagnosed with ADD/ADHD are eligible for the same services available to students with LD.

Staff: 5 full-time staff members, including director, braillist. Services provided by tutors, study partners.

Special Fees: No special fees are charged for services to students with LD.

Applications and admissions: Open admissions. Students may begin taking classes any term. *Application deadline:* continuous.

Special policies: The college has written policies regarding substitutions and waivers of admissions and graduation requirements.

PROGRAM AND SERVICE COMPONENTS

Diagnostic testing: Spoken language, written language.

Academic advising: Provided by academic advisers. Students with LD may take up to 12 credit hours each term; most take 6 credit hours; 6 credit hours required to maintain full-time status and be eligible for financial aid.

Counseling services: Individual counseling, career counseling, self-advocacy training.

Basic skills remediation: Offered in small groups by reading and study skills specialist. Available in reading, math, written language.

Subject-area tutoring: Offered one-on-one and in small groups by peer tutors. Available in most subjects.

Auxiliary aids: Taped textbooks, tape recorders, calculators, typewriters, word-processors with spell-check, personal computers, talking computers, optical character readers.

Auxiliary services: Alternative test arrangements, notetakers.

GENERAL COLLEGE INFORMATION

State-supported, coed. Awards associate, bachelor's, master's, doctoral degrees. Founded 1895. *Setting:* 335-acre urban campus. *Endowment:* $81.4 million. *Research spending 1995–96:* $7.6 million. *Total enrollment:* 14,264. *Faculty:* 758 (445 full-time, 87% with terminal degrees, 313 part-time); student–undergrad faculty ratio is 15:1.

Enrollment Profile: 11,280 students from 54 states and territories, 93 other countries. 53% women, 47% men, 52% part-time, 87% state residents, 6% live on campus, 7% transferred in, 9% international, 40% 25 or older, 1% Native American, 3% Hispanic, 7% black, 5% Asian or Pacific Islander. *Retention:* 64% of 1995 full-time freshmen returned. *Graduation:* 8% graduate in 4 years, 21% in 5 years, 26% in 6 years. *Areas of study chosen:* 17% business management and administrative services, 11% health professions and related sciences, 9% engineering and applied sciences, 5% fine arts, 5% performing arts, 3% communications and journalism, 3% computer and information sciences, 3% liberal arts/general studies, 3% psychology, 3% social sciences, 2% biological and life sciences, 1% area and ethnic studies, 1% English language/literature/letters, 1% foreign language and literature, 1% mathematics, 1% philosophy, 1% physical sciences. *Most popular recent major:* business administration/commerce/management.

First-Year Class: 1,061 total; 2,553 applied, 76% were accepted, 55% of whom enrolled. 15% from top 10% of their high school class, 40% from top quarter, 69% from top half. 14 National Merit Scholars.

Graduation Requirements: 64 credit hours for associate, 124 credit hours for bachelor's; 3 credit hours of algebra; computer course for engineering, business majors; internship (some majors); senior project (some majors).

Computers on Campus: 1,500 computers available on campus for general student use. Computer purchase/lease plans available. A campus-wide network can be accessed from student residence rooms and from off-campus. Students can contact faculty members and/or advisers through e-mail. Computers for student use in computer center, classrooms, library, dorms provide access to the Internet/World Wide Web. Staffed computer lab on campus provides training in use of computers, software. *Academic computing expenditure 1995–96:* $1.3 million.

EXPENSES AND FINANCIAL AID

Estimated Expenses for 1997–98: *Application fee:* $15. State resident tuition: $1845 full-time, $59.50 per credit hour part-time. Nonresident tuition: $7965 full-time, $256.95 per credit hour part-time. Part-time mandatory fees per semester range from $38.40 to $232.80. Full-time mandatory fees: $644. College room and board: $3639 (minimum).

Undergraduate Financial Aid: Of all full-time undergraduates enrolled in fall 1996, 79% of those who applied for aid were judged to have need according to Federal Methodology, of whom 70% were aided. On average, 54% of need was met. *Financial aid deadline (priority):* 3/15. *Financial aid forms:* FAFSA required.

LD Services Contact: Mr. Grady L. Landrum, Director, Wichita State University, 1845 Fairmount, Wichita, KS 67260, 316-978-3309. Fax: 316-978-3002.

WIDENER UNIVERSITY

Chester, Pennsylvania

LEARNING DISABILITIES SERVICES INFORMATION

Enable began offering services in 1987. Currently the program serves 97 undergraduates with LD. Services are also available to graduate students. Students diagnosed with ADD/ADHD are eligible for the same services available to students with LD, as well as specific group counseling.

Staff: 1 full-time, 4 part-time staff members, including director, clinical psychology interns. Services provided by remediation specialists, tutors, counselors, diagnostic specialists, psychologist.

Special Fees: No special fees are charged for services to students with LD.

Applications and admissions: *Required:* high school transcript, grade point average, class rank, courses completed, untimed SAT I, psychoeducational report completed within 3 years; *recommended:* high school extracurricular activities, extended time SAT I or ACT, personal interview, autobiographical statement, letters of recommendation. Students may begin taking classes in fall or spring. *Application deadline:* continuous.

Special policies: The college has written policies regarding grade forgiveness.

PROGRAM AND SERVICE COMPONENTS

Special preparation or orientation: Optional orientation offered during registration.

Diagnostic testing: Intelligence, reading, math, spelling, handwriting, spoken language, written language, motor abilities, perceptual skills, study skills, personality, social skills, hearing, learning strategies, vision.

Academic advising: Provided by unit staff members, academic advisers. Students with LD may take up to 16 credits each term; most take 12 credits; 12 credits required to maintain full-time status and be eligible for financial aid.
Counseling services: Individual counseling, small-group counseling, career counseling, self-advocacy training.
Basic skills remediation: Offered in class-size groups by regular teachers. Available in reading, math, written language, learning strategies, study skills, time management.
Subject-area tutoring: Offered one-on-one, in small groups, and in class-size groups by professional teachers, peer tutors, doctoral psychology interns. Available in most subjects.
Special courses: College survival skills, reading, composition, math, study skills. Some offered for credit; some enter into overall grade point average.
Auxiliary aids: Taped textbooks, tape recorders, calculators, typewriters, word-processors with spell-check, personal computers, optical character readers.
Auxiliary services: Alternative test arrangements, notetakers, advocacy.

GENERAL COLLEGE INFORMATION

Independent, comprehensive, coed. Awards associate, bachelor's, master's, doctoral, first professional degrees. Founded 1821. *Setting:* 110-acre suburban campus with easy access to Philadelphia. *Endowment:* $19.5 million. *Research spending 1995–96:* $57,433. *Total enrollment:* 8,150. *Faculty:* 435 (241 full-time, 92% with terminal degrees, 194 part-time); student–undergrad faculty ratio is 12:1.
Enrollment Profile: 3,850 students from 22 states and territories, 34 other countries. 48% women, 52% men, 40% part-time, 55% state residents, 25% transferred in, 6% international, 16% 25 or older, 1% Native American, 2% Hispanic, 14% black, 4% Asian or Pacific Islander. *Retention:* 80% of 1995 full-time freshmen returned. *Graduation:* 50% graduate in 4 years, 57% in 5 years. *Areas of study chosen:* 14% social sciences, 11% biological and life sciences, 11% business management and administrative services, 8% engineering and applied sciences, 8% liberal arts/general studies, 7% education, 7% health professions and related sciences, 6% premed, 6% psychology, 5% interdisciplinary studies, 4% prelaw, 3% communications and journalism, 3% English language/literature/letters, 2% foreign language and literature, 1% computer and information sciences, 1% mathematics, 1% military science, 1% physical sciences, 1% prevet.
First-Year Class: 527 total; 2,180 applied, 83% were accepted, 29% of whom enrolled. 27% from top 10% of their high school class, 45% from top quarter, 85% from top half.
Graduation Requirements: 60 credits for associate, 121 credits for bachelor's; math proficiency; computer course for engineering, accounting, economics, management majors.
Computers on Campus: 110 computers available on campus for general student use. A campus-wide network can be accessed from off-campus. Students can contact faculty members and/or advisers through e-mail. Computers for student use in computer center, learning resource center, library, engineering/science center, academic center provide access to the Internet/World Wide Web, on- and off-campus e-mail addresses. Staffed computer lab on campus provides training in use of computers, software. *Academic computing expenditure 1995–96:* $2 million.

EXPENSES AND FINANCIAL AID

Expenses for 1997–98: *Application fee:* $25. Comprehensive fee of $20,580 includes full-time tuition ($14,380 minimum) and college room and board ($6200 minimum). Part-time mandatory fees: $15 per semester. Full-time tuition ranges up to $15,260 according to program. Part-time tuition per credit ranges from $480 to $510 according to program.
Undergraduate Financial Aid: 71% of all full-time undergraduates enrolled in fall 1996 applied for aid; of these, 91% were judged to have need according to Federal Methodology, of whom 97% were aided. On average, 77% of need was met. *Financial aid deadline (priority):* 4/1. *Financial aid forms:* FAFSA, state form, institutional form required; CSS Financial Aid PROFILE acceptable.
LD Services Contact: Dr. LaVerne R. Ziegenfuss, Director, Enable, Widener University, One University Place, Chester, PA 19013, 610-499-1270. Fax: 610-499-1279. Email: laverne@ibm.net.

WILFRID LAURIER UNIVERSITY

Waterloo, Ontario, Canada

LEARNING DISABILITIES SERVICES INFORMATION

Special Needs Office began offering services in 1990. Currently the program serves 130 undergraduates with LD. Services are also available to graduate students. Students diagnosed with ADD/ADHD are eligible for the same services available to students with LD.
Staff: 2 full-time, 1 part-time staff members, including coordinator. Services provided by Learning Resource Consultant.
Special Fees: $800 to $1200 for diagnostic testing.
Applications and admissions: *Required:* high school transcript, grade point average, class rank, courses completed, untimed SAT I, autobiographical statement, letters of recommendation, psychoeducational report; *recommended:* high school extracurricular activities, personal interview. Students may begin taking classes in fall only. *Application deadline:* 5/1.
Special policies: The college has written policies regarding substitutions and waivers of admissions requirements.

PROGRAM AND SERVICE COMPONENTS

Special preparation or orientation: Optional orientation offered in early September.
Diagnostic testing: Intelligence, reading, math, spelling, handwriting, spoken language, written language, study skills, personality, learning strategies.
Academic advising: Provided by academic advisers. Students with LD may take up to 6 half credits each term; most take 5 half credits; 4 half credits required to maintain full-time status; 1 full credit over 8 months required to be eligible for financial aid.
Counseling services: Individual counseling, career counseling.
Subject-area tutoring: Offered one-on-one by peer tutors. Available in most subjects.
Auxiliary aids: Taped textbooks, tape recorders, typewriters, word-processors with spell-check, optical character readers.
Auxiliary services: Alternative test arrangements, notetakers, priority registration.
Campus support group: A special student organization is available to students with LD.

GENERAL COLLEGE INFORMATION

Province-supported, comprehensive, coed. Awards bachelor's, master's, doctoral degrees. Founded 1911. *Setting:* 40-acre urban campus with easy access to Toronto. *Total enrollment:* 7,802. *Faculty:* 607 (329 full-time, 88% with terminal degrees, 278 part-time); student–undergrad faculty ratio is 15:1.
Enrollment Profile: 6,982 students from 10 provinces and territories, 25 other countries. 54% women, 46% men, 31% part-time, 98% province residents, 20% transferred in, 1% international, 22% 25 or older. *Most popular recent majors:* business administration/commerce/management, psychology, economics.
First-Year Class: 1,673 total; 8,227 applied, 45% were accepted, 46% of whom enrolled.
Graduation Requirements: 15 courses; computer course for business, biology, economics majors; internship (some majors); senior project (some majors).
Computers on Campus: 450 computers available on campus for general student use. A computer is recommended for some students. A campus-wide network can be accessed from off-campus. Students can contact faculty members and/or advisers through e-mail. Computers for student use in computer labs, library, student center, dorms, various locations provide access to the Internet/World Wide Web, on- and off-campus e-mail addresses, microcomputer network.

EXPENSES AND FINANCIAL AID

Expenses for 1997–98: *Application fee:* $75. Canadian resident tuition: $3228 full-time, $724 per course part-time. Nonresident tuition: $7000 full-time, $1400 per course part-time. Part-time mandatory fees: $44.50 per course. (All figures are in Canadian dollars.). Full-time mandatory fees: $260. College room and board: $5300. College room only: $3000.
Undergraduate Financial Aid: *Financial aid deadline (priority):* 6/30. *Financial aid forms:* FAFSA, CSS Financial Aid PROFILE, state form required.
LD Services Contact: Ms. Kelly Nixon, Learning Resource Consultant, Special Needs Office, Wilfrid Laurier University, 75 University Avenue, West, Waterloo, ON N2L 3C5, Canada, 519-884-1970 Ext. 2739. Fax: 519-886-9351. Email: knixon@mach2.wlu.ca.

WILLIAM CAREY COLLEGE

Hattiesburg, Mississippi

LEARNING DISABILITIES SERVICES INFORMATION

Student Support Services began offering services in 1991. Currently the program serves 15 undergraduates with LD. Services are also avail-

William Carey College (continued)

able to graduate students. Students diagnosed with ADD/ADHD are eligible for the same services available to students with LD.

Staff: 4 full-time staff members, including director, administrative assistant. Services provided by remediation specialist, counselor.

Special Fees: No special fees are charged for services to students with LD.

Applications and admissions: *Required:* high school transcript, grade point average, class rank, courses completed, untimed or extended time SAT I or ACT, psychoeducational report completed within 5 years; *recommended:* personal interview. Students may begin taking classes any term. *Application deadline:* continuous.

PROGRAM AND SERVICE COMPONENTS

Academic advising: Provided by unit staff members, academic advisers. Students with LD may take up to 13 semester hours each term; most take 9 semester hours; 9 semester hours required to maintain full-time status and be eligible for financial aid.

Basic skills remediation: Offered in small groups by regular teachers. Available in reading, math, written language, learning strategies, study skills, time management.

Subject-area tutoring: Offered one-on-one and in small groups by peer tutors. Available in all subjects.

Special courses: College survival skills, learning strategies, time management, math, study skills. All offered for credit; some enter into overall grade point average.

Auxiliary aids: Taped textbooks, tape recorders, calculators, word-processors with spell-check, personal computers.

Auxiliary services: Alternative test arrangements, notetakers.

GENERAL COLLEGE INFORMATION

Independent Southern Baptist, comprehensive, coed. Awards bachelor's, master's degrees. Founded 1906. *Setting:* 64-acre small-town campus with easy access to New Orleans. *Endowment:* $4.4 million. *Educational spending 1995–96:* $3044 per undergrad. *Total enrollment:* 2,254. *Faculty:* 172 (80 full-time, 54% with terminal degrees, 92 part-time); student–undergrad faculty ratio is 17:1.

Enrollment Profile: 1,902 students from 30 states and territories, 21 other countries. 66% women, 34% men, 25% part-time, 68% state residents, 35% live on campus, 66% transferred in, 1% international, 46% 25 or older, 1% Native American, 1% Hispanic, 24% black, 2% Asian or Pacific Islander. *Retention:* 64% of 1995 full-time freshmen returned. *Areas of study chosen:* 36% health professions and related sciences, 15% education, 14% business management and administrative services, 8% psychology, 6% theology/religion, 5% interdisciplinary studies, 5% liberal arts/general studies, 3% biological and life sciences, 3% fine arts, 1% communications and journalism, 1% computer and information sciences, 1% English language/literature/letters, 1% foreign language and literature, 1% mathematics, 1% performing arts, 1% physical sciences, 1% predentistry, 1% prelaw, 1% premed, 1% social sciences.

First-Year Class: 155 total; 409 applied, 52% were accepted, 73% of whom enrolled.

Graduation Requirements: 128 credit hours; 3 credit hours each of math and science; computer course for business, nursing, elementary education majors; senior project (some majors).

Computers on Campus: 30 computers available on campus for general student use. Computers for student use in computer labs, library provide access to the Internet/World Wide Web. Staffed computer lab on campus provides training in use of computers, software. *Academic computing expenditure 1995–96:* $144,319.

EXPENSES AND FINANCIAL AID

Expenses for 1997–98: *Application fee:* $10. Comprehensive fee of $8340 includes full-time tuition ($6624) and college room and board ($1716 minimum). Part-time tuition: $207 per semester hour.

Undergraduate Financial Aid: On average, 76% of need was met. *Financial aid deadline (priority):* 4/1. *Financial aid forms:* FAFSA, institutional form required; CSS Financial Aid PROFILE acceptable.

LD Services Contact: Ms. Wynde Fitts, Counselor, Student Support Services, William Carey College, Box 181, Hattiesburg, MS 39401, 601-582-6212. Fax: 601-582-6208.

WINGATE UNIVERSITY

Wingate, North Carolina

LEARNING DISABILITIES SERVICES INFORMATION

Specific Learning Disability-Dyslexia Program began offering services in 1988. Currently the program serves 50 undergraduates with LD. Students diagnosed with ADD/ADHD are eligible for the same services available to students with LD.

Staff: Includes director, coordinator. Services provided by counselor.

Special Fees: No special fees are charged for services to students with LD.

Applications and admissions: *Required:* high school transcript, grade point average, class rank, courses completed; *recommended:* personal interview, letters of recommendation, psychoeducational report completed within 4 years. Students may begin taking classes in fall, winter, or spring. *Application deadline:* continuous.

Special policies: The college has written policies regarding grade forgiveness; substitutions and waivers of admissions, graduation, and degree requirements.

PROGRAM AND SERVICE COMPONENTS

Academic advising: Provided by unit staff members, academic advisers. Students with LD may take up to 16 credit hours each term; most take 12 credit hours; 12 credit hours required to maintain full-time status and be eligible for financial aid.

Counseling services: Individual counseling, career counseling.

Subject-area tutoring: Offered one-on-one and in small groups by peer tutors. Available in all subjects.

Special courses: College survival skills. All offered for credit; none enter into overall grade point average.

Auxiliary aids: Taped textbooks, word-processors with spell-check, personal computers.

Auxiliary services: Alternative test arrangements, notetakers.

GENERAL COLLEGE INFORMATION

Independent Baptist, comprehensive, coed. Awards bachelor's, master's degrees. Founded 1896. *Setting:* 330-acre small-town campus with easy access to Charlotte. *Endowment:* $18.1 million. *Research spending 1995–96:* $67,000. *Educational spending 1995–96:* $4116 per undergrad. *Total enrollment:* 1,275. *Faculty:* 105 (85 full-time, 81% with terminal degrees, 20 part-time); student–undergrad faculty ratio is 13:1.

Enrollment Profile: 1,185 students from 31 states and territories, 12 other countries. 48% women, 52% men, 8% part-time, 55% state residents, 15% transferred in, 2% international, 9% 25 or older, 1% Native American, 1% Hispanic, 10% black, 1% Asian or Pacific Islander. *Retention:* 62% of 1995 full-time freshmen returned. *Areas of study chosen:* 26% liberal arts/general studies, 17% business management and administrative services, 13% education, 10% social sciences, 8% communications and journalism, 5% biological and life sciences, 4% health professions and related sciences, 4% psychology, 3% fine arts, 2% English language/literature/letters, 2% premed, 2% theology/religion, 1% computer and information sciences, 1% mathematics, 1% physical sciences, 1% prelaw. *Most popular recent majors:* business administration/commerce/management, communication, education.

First-Year Class: 331 total; 1,231 applied, 79% were accepted, 34% of whom enrolled. 16% from top 10% of their high school class, 39% from top quarter, 70% from top half. 6 class presidents, 6 valedictorians.

Graduation Requirements: 125 credit hours; 3 credit hours of math; 4 credit hours of science; 6 credit hours of a foreign language for bachelor of science degree; 12 credit hours of a foreign language for bachelor of arts degree; computer course for business, math majors; internship (some majors); senior project for honors program students and some majors.

Computers on Campus: 75 computers available on campus for general student use. A computer is recommended for all students. A campus-wide network can be accessed from student residence rooms and from off-campus. Students can contact faculty members and/or advisers through e-mail. Computers for student use in computer center, computer labs, learning resource center, classrooms, library provide access to the Internet/World Wide Web, on- and off-campus e-mail addresses. Staffed computer lab on campus provides training in use of computers, software. *Academic computing expenditure 1995–96:* $26,852.

EXPENSES AND FINANCIAL AID

Expenses for 1997–98: *Application fee:* $25. Comprehensive fee of $15,790 includes full-time tuition ($11,250), mandatory fees ($440), and college room and board ($4100). College room only: $2000. Part-time tuition: $375 per credit hour. Part-time mandatory fees: $75 per semester.

Undergraduate Financial Aid: Of all full-time undergraduates enrolled in fall 1996, 95% of those who applied for aid were judged to have need according to Federal Methodology, of whom 100% were aided. On average, 78% of need was met. *Financial aid deadline (priority):* 3/1. *Financial aid forms:* FAFSA, institutional form required. State form required for some.
LD Services Contact: Mrs. Linda E. Stedje-Larsen, Coordinator, Support Services, Wingate University, Wingate, NC 28174, 704-233-8269.

XAVIER UNIVERSITY

Cincinnati, Ohio

LEARNING DISABILITIES SERVICES INFORMATION

Learning Assistance Program began offering services in 1982. Currently the program serves 156 undergraduates with LD. Services are also available to graduate students. Students diagnosed with ADD/ADHD are eligible for the same services available to students with LD, as well as mentoring programs.
Staff: 1 full-time, 1 part-time staff members, including director, graduate assistant. Services provided by tutors, counselors, diagnostic specialists.
Special Fees: No special fees are charged for services to students with LD.
Applications and admissions: *Required:* high school transcript, grade point average, class rank, courses completed, extracurricular activities; *recommended:* high school IEP (Individualized Education Program), extended time SAT I, personal interview, autobiographical statement, letters of recommendation, psychoeducational report completed within 3 years. Students may begin taking classes in fall, spring, or summer. *Application deadline:* continuous.
Special policies: The college has written policies regarding substitutions and waivers of admissions and graduation requirements.

PROGRAM AND SERVICE COMPONENTS

Diagnostic testing: Intelligence, reading, math, written language, study skills, speech, hearing, learning strategies.
Academic advising: Provided by academic advisers. Students with LD may take up to 15 semester hours each term; most take 12 to 15 semester hours; 12 semester hours required to maintain full-time status.
Counseling services: Individual counseling, small-group counseling, self-advocacy training, support groups.
Subject-area tutoring: Offered one-on-one by peer tutors. Available in most subjects.
Auxiliary aids: Taped textbooks, tape recorders, calculators, word-processors with spell-check.
Auxiliary services: Alternative test arrangements.
Campus support group: A special student organization is available to students with LD.

GENERAL COLLEGE INFORMATION

Independent Roman Catholic, comprehensive, coed. Awards associate, bachelor's, master's, doctoral degrees. Founded 1831. *Setting:* 100-acre suburban campus. *Endowment:* $46 million. *Total enrollment:* 6,423. *Faculty:* 490 (235 full-time, 80% with terminal degrees, 255 part-time); student–undergrad faculty ratio is 14:1.

Enrollment Profile: 3,864 students from 41 states and territories, 40 other countries. 59% women, 41% men, 22% part-time, 68% state residents, 50% live on campus, 5% transferred in, 3% international, 0% Native American, 1% Hispanic, 8% black, 2% Asian or Pacific Islander. *Retention:* 87% of 1995 full-time freshmen returned. *Areas of study chosen:* 20% business management and administrative services, 14% social sciences, 11% education, 10% communications and journalism, 10% health professions and related sciences, 6% liberal arts/general studies, 5% biological and life sciences, 5% interdisciplinary studies, 5% premed, 4% psychology, 3% English language/literature/letters, 2% fine arts, 2% physical sciences, 1% foreign language and literature, 1% mathematics, 1% theology/religion. *Most popular recent majors:* business administration/commerce/management, education, communication.

First-Year Class: 787 total; 2,456 applied, 95% were accepted, 34% of whom enrolled. 28% from top 10% of their high school class, 55% from top quarter, 79% from top half. 6 National Merit Scholars, 14 valedictorians.

Graduation Requirements: 60 semester hours for associate, 120 semester hours for bachelor's; 6 semester hours of math; 9 semester hours of science; 6 semester hours of a modern foreign language or proven competence; computer course for business, math, physics majors; senior project (some majors).

Computers on Campus: 425 computers available on campus for general student use. Computer purchase/lease plans available. A computer is recommended for some students. A campus-wide network can be accessed from student residence rooms and from off-campus. Students can contact faculty members and/or advisers through e-mail. Computers for student use in computer center, library, dorms, academic buildings provide access to the Internet/World Wide Web, on- and off-campus e-mail addresses. Staffed computer lab on campus provides training in use of computers, software. *Academic computing expenditure 1995–96:* $675,000.

EXPENSES AND FINANCIAL AID

Expenses for 1997–98: *Application fee:* $25. Comprehensive fee of $19,090 includes full-time tuition ($13,650) and college room and board ($5440 minimum). College room only: $3020. Part-time tuition per semester ranges from $335 to $4950.

Undergraduate Financial Aid: 67% of all full-time undergraduates enrolled in fall 1996 applied for aid; of these, 87% were judged to have need according to Federal Methodology, of whom 100% were aided. *Financial aid deadline (priority):* 2/15. *Financial aid forms:* FAFSA, financial aid transcript (for transfers) required.

LD Services Contact: Ms. Sarah M. Kelly, Director, Xavier University, 3800 Victory Parkway, Cincinnati, OH 45207-2612, 513-745-3280. Fax: 513-745-3563. Email: kellys@admin.xu.edu.

▸ TWO-YEAR COLLEGES ◂

WITH COMPREHENSIVE PROGRAMS

AMERICAN RIVER COLLEGE

Sacramento, California

Students with LD	500	Subject-Area Tutoring	✓
ADD services		Special Courses	✓
Staff	6 full-, 2 part-time	Taped Textbooks	✓
Special Fee	None	Alternative Test Arrang.	✓
Diagnostic Testing	✓	Notetakers	✓
Basic Skills Remediation	✓	LD Student Organization	✓

LEARNING DISABILITIES PROGRAM INFORMATION

The Learning Disabilities Program began offering services in 1987. Currently the program serves 500 undergraduates with LD. Students diagnosed with ADD/ADHD are not eligible for the same services available to students with LD.

Staff: 6 full-time, 2 part-time staff members, including director. Services provided by remediation specialist, tutor, counselors, diagnostic specialist, learning specialists.

Special Fees: No special fees are charged for services to students with LD.

Applications and admissions: *Recommended:* psychoeducational report completed within 3 years. Students may begin taking classes any term. *Application deadline:* continuous.

Special policies: The college has written policies regarding grade forgiveness.

PROGRAM AND SERVICE COMPONENTS

Special preparation or orientation: Optional orientation offered after classes begin.

Diagnostic testing: Intelligence, reading, math, spelling, written language, perceptual skills, study skills, personality, hearing, learning strategies.

Academic advising: Provided by LD staff members, academic advisers. Most students with LD take 12 units each term; 12 units (fewer with special permission) required to maintain full-time status; 12 units required to be eligible for financial aid.

Counseling services: Individual counseling, career counseling.

Basic skills remediation: Offered by regular teachers. Available in reading, math, spelling, written language, learning strategies, study skills, time management.

Subject-area tutoring: Offered one-on-one by peer tutors, LD staff. Available in all subjects.

Special courses: College survival skills, learning strategies, word processing, time management, study skills. All offered for credit; none enter into overall grade point average.

Auxiliary aids: Taped textbooks, tape recorders, word-processors with spell-check, personal computers, optical character readers.

Auxiliary services: Alternative test arrangements, notetakers, priority registration, advocacy.

Campus support group: A special student organization is available to students with LD.

GENERAL COLLEGE INFORMATION

District-supported, 2-year, coed. Part of Los Rios Community College District System. Awards associate degrees. Founded 1955. *Setting:* 153-acre suburban campus. *Total enrollment:* 19,854. *Faculty:* 790 (415 full-time, 375 part-time).

Enrollment Profile: 19,854 students: 53% women, 47% men, 75% part-time, 99% state residents, 18% transferred in, 1% international, 52% 25 or older, 2% Native American, 8% Hispanic, 8% black, 8% Asian or Pacific Islander.

First-Year Class: 4,087 total. Of the students who applied, 100% were accepted.

Graduation Requirements: 60 units; math proficiency; internship (some majors).

Computers on Campus: Computers for student use in learning resource center, library.

EXPENSES

Expenses for 1997–98: State resident tuition: $0 full-time. Nonresident tuition: $3750 full-time, $125 per unit part-time. Part-time mandatory fees: $13 per unit. Full-time mandatory fees: $390.

LD Program Contact: Ms. Regena Tiner, Program Assistant, American River College, 4700 College Oak Drive, Sacramento, CA 95841, 916-484-8487. Fax: 916-484-8674.

ANOKA-RAMSEY COMMUNITY COLLEGE

Coon Rapids, Minnesota

Students with LD	125	Subject-Area Tutoring	✓
ADD services	✓	Special Courses	✓
Staff	1 full-, 3 part-time	Taped Textbooks	✓
Special Fee	None	Alternative Test Arrang.	✓
Diagnostic Testing	✓	Notetakers	✓
Basic Skills Remediation	✓	LD Student Organization	

LEARNING DISABILITIES PROGRAM INFORMATION

The Access Services began offering services in 1985. Currently the program serves 125 undergraduates with LD. Students diagnosed with ADD/ADHD are eligible for the same services available to students with LD.

Staff: 1 full-time, 3 part-time staff members, including director, LD instructor. Services provided by remediation specialist, tutors, counselors.

Special Fees: No special fees are charged for services to students with LD.

Applications and admissions: *Required:* high school transcript, IEP or other documentation of disability; *recommended:* personal interview, psychoeducational report completed within 3 years. Students may begin taking classes any term. *Application deadline:* continuous.

Special policies: The college has written policies regarding grade forgiveness; substitutions and waivers of admissions, graduation, and degree requirements.

PROGRAM AND SERVICE COMPONENTS

Special preparation or orientation: Optional summer program offered prior to entering college. Required orientation held before registration.

Diagnostic testing: Reading, math, written language, study skills, personality, learning strategies.

Academic advising: Provided by LD staff members, academic advisers. Students with LD may take up to 18 quarter credits (more with counselor's approval) each term; most take 9 to 12 quarter credits; 12 quarter credits required to maintain full-time status; 6 quarter credits (part-time), 12 quarter credits (full-time) required to be eligible for financial aid.

Counseling services: Individual counseling, small-group counseling, career counseling, self-advocacy training.

Basic skills remediation: Offered one-on-one and in class-size groups by LD teachers, regular teachers, Adult Basic Education teachers. Available in reading, math, spelling, written language, learning strategies, perceptual skills, study skills, time management, social skills.

Subject-area tutoring: Offered one-on-one and in small groups by professional teachers, peer tutors, local volunteers, work-study students. Available in all subjects.

Special courses: College survival skills, reading, vocabulary development, composition, learning strategies, word processing, time management, math, typing, personal psychology, study skills, career planning. Some offered for credit; all enter into overall grade point average.
Auxiliary aids: Taped textbooks, tape recorders, typewriters, word-processors with spell-check, personal computers, Arkenstone Open Book Reading Computers, Jaws for Windows, Dragon Dictate.
Auxiliary services: Alternative test arrangements, notetakers, priority registration, advocacy, scheduling assistance.

GENERAL COLLEGE INFORMATION

State-supported, 2-year, coed. Part of Minnesota State Colleges and Universities System. Awards associate degrees. Founded 1965. *Setting:* 100-acre suburban campus with easy access to Minneapolis–St. Paul. *Total enrollment:* 4,510. *Faculty:* 170 (95 full-time, 100% with terminal degrees, 75 part-time); student–undergrad faculty ratio is 26:1.
Enrollment Profile: 4,510 students: 66% women, 34% men, 59% part-time, 98% state residents, 10% transferred in, 1% international, 36% 25 or older, 1% Native American, 1% Hispanic, 1% black, 2% Asian or Pacific Islander. *Areas of study chosen:* 63% liberal arts/general studies, 7% health professions and related sciences, 6% business management and administrative services, 3% social sciences, 2% engineering and applied sciences, 1% agriculture, 1% architecture, 1% biological and life sciences, 1% communications and journalism, 1% computer and information sciences, 1% education, 1% English language/literature/letters, 1% fine arts, 1% library and information studies, 1% mathematics, 1% natural resource sciences, 1% performing arts, 1% physical sciences, 1% prelaw, 1% premed, 1% prevet, 1% psychology, 1% theology/religion, 1% vocational and home economics. *Most popular recent majors:* liberal arts/general studies, business administration/commerce/management, nursing.
First-Year Class: 1,761 total; 2,160 applied, 99% were accepted, 82% of whom enrolled.
Graduation Requirements: 96 quarter credits; computer course for business majors.
Computers on Campus: 200 computers available on campus for general student use. A campus-wide network can be accessed from off-campus. Students can contact faculty members and/or advisers through e-mail. Computers for student use in computer center, computer labs, learning resource center, classrooms, library provide access to the Internet/World Wide Web, on- and off-campus e-mail addresses. Staffed computer lab on campus provides training in use of computers, software. *Academic computing expenditure 1995–96:* $1.1 million.

EXPENSES AND FINANCIAL AID

Expenses for 1996–97: *Application fee:* $20. State resident tuition: $2143 full-time, $44.65 per credit part-time. Nonresident tuition: $4178 full-time, $87.05 per credit part-time. Part-time mandatory fees: $3.17 per credit. North Dakota, South Dakota and Wisconsin residents pay tuition at the rate they would pay if attending a comparable state-supported institution in their home state. Full-time mandatory fees: $152.
Financial aid specifically for students with LD: Scholarship: Students with Disabilities Scholarship.
LD Program Contact: Mr. Eric Sime, Director of Access Services, Anoka-Ramsey Community College, 11200 Mississippi Boulevard, Coon Rapids, MN 55433-3470, 612-422-3459. Fax: 612-422-3341.

BLINN COLLEGE

Brenham, Texas

Students with LD	250	Subject-Area Tutoring	✓
ADD services	✓	Special Courses	
Staff	1 full-time	Taped Textbooks	✓
Special Fee	None	Alternative Test Arrang.	✓
Diagnostic Testing		Notetakers	✓
Basic Skills Remediation		LD Student Organization	

LEARNING DISABILITIES PROGRAM INFORMATION

The Office of Disability Services began offering services in 1994. Currently the program serves 250 undergraduates with LD. Students diagnosed with ADD/ADHD are eligible for the same services available to students with LD.
Staff: 1 full-time staff member (coordinator).
Special Fees: No special fees are charged for services to students with LD.
Applications and admissions: *Required:* high school transcript, psychoeducational report. Students may begin taking classes in fall, spring, or summer. *Application deadline:* continuous.
Special policies: The college has written policies regarding grade forgiveness; substitutions and waivers of admissions, graduation, and degree requirements.

PROGRAM AND SERVICE COMPONENTS

Special preparation or orientation: Optional orientation offered before registration and prior to high school graduation.
Academic advising: Provided by LD staff members. Students with LD may take up to 18 credit hours each term; most take 12 credit hours; 12 credit hours required to maintain full-time status and be eligible for financial aid.
Counseling services: Individual counseling, self-advocacy training.
Subject-area tutoring: Offered one-on-one by peer tutors, Coordinator. Available in some subjects.
Auxiliary aids: Taped textbooks, tape recorders.
Auxiliary services: Alternative test arrangements, notetakers, priority registration, advocacy, readers, scribes, oral exams, time extensions for writing assignments.

GENERAL COLLEGE INFORMATION

State and locally supported, 2-year, coed. Part of Texas Higher Education Coordinating Board. Awards associate degrees. Founded 1883. *Setting:* 100-acre small-town campus with easy access to Houston. *Endowment:* $29.8 million. *Total enrollment:* 9,209. *Faculty:* 376 (16% of full-time faculty have terminal degrees); student–undergrad faculty ratio is 25:1.
Enrollment Profile: 9,209 students from 36 states and territories, 57 other countries. 49% women, 51% men, 48% part-time, 96% state residents, 9% live on campus, 38% transferred in, 2% international, 18% 25 or older, 1% Native American, 10% Hispanic, 7% black, 2% Asian or Pacific Islander. *Retention:* 34% of 1995 full-time freshmen returned.
Graduation Requirements: 62 credit hours; 1 college algebra course; 4 credit hours of science; computer course for accounting, biology, business, agriculture, math, physics, chemistry majors.
Computers on Campus: 420 computers available on campus for general student use. Computers for student use in computer center, computer labs, classrooms provide access to the Internet/World Wide Web. Staffed computer lab on campus provides training in use of computers, software.

Blinn College (continued)

EXPENSES AND FINANCIAL AID

Expenses for 1997–98: Area resident tuition: $558 full-time. State resident tuition: $837 full-time. Nonresident tuition: $2790 full-time. Part-time tuition per credit ranges from $18 to $198 for area residents, $27 to $297 for state residents, $300 to $990 for nonresidents. Part-time mandatory fees per semester range from $69 to $110. Full-time mandatory fees: $248. College room and board: $2843. College room only: $1100.

Financial aid specifically for students with LD: Scholarships.

LD Program Contact: Ms. Patricia E. Moran, Coordinator, Blinn College, 902 College Avenue, Brenham, TX 77833, 409-830-4157. Fax: 409-830-4110.

BLUE MOUNTAIN COMMUNITY COLLEGE

Pendleton, Oregon

Students with LD	60	Subject-Area Tutoring	✓
ADD services	✓	Special Courses	
Staff	1 part-time	Taped Textbooks	✓
Special Fee	None	Alternative Test Arrang.	✓
Diagnostic Testing	✓	Notetakers	✓
Basic Skills Remediation	✓	LD Student Organization	✓

LEARNING DISABILITIES PROGRAM INFORMATION

The Services for Students with Disabilities began offering services in 1988. Currently the program serves 60 undergraduates with LD. Students diagnosed with ADD/ADHD are eligible for the same services available to students with LD.

Staff: 1 part-time staff member (coordinator). Services provided by tutors, diagnostic specialist.

Special Fees: No special fees are charged for services to students with LD.

Applications and admissions: *Required:* psychoeducational report completed within 3 years, IQ scores; *recommended:* high school transcript, courses completed, IEP (Individualized Education Program), personal interview. Students may begin taking classes any term. *Application deadline:* continuous.

PROGRAM AND SERVICE COMPONENTS

Special preparation or orientation: Optional orientation offered before registration and after classes begin.

Diagnostic testing: Intelligence, reading, math, spelling, spoken language, written language, motor abilities, perceptual skills, study skills, learning strategies.

Academic advising: Provided by LD staff members, academic advisers. Students with LD may take up to 12 credit hours each term; most take 9 credit hours; 12 credit hours required to maintain full-time status and be eligible for financial aid.

Counseling services: Individual counseling, self-advocacy training.

Basic skills remediation: Offered one-on-one, in small groups, and in class-size groups by regular teachers; computer-aided instruction also offered. Available in reading, math, spelling, written language, learning strategies, study skills, time management.

Subject-area tutoring: Offered one-on-one, in small groups, and in class-size groups by professional teachers, peer tutors. Available in all subjects.

Auxiliary aids: Taped textbooks, tape recorders, calculators, typewriters, word-processors with spell-check, personal computers, optical character readers.

Auxiliary services: Alternative test arrangements, notetakers, advocacy.

Campus support group: A special student organization is available to students with LD.

GENERAL COLLEGE INFORMATION

State and locally supported, 2-year, coed. Awards associate degrees. Founded 1962. *Setting:* 170-acre rural campus. *Total enrollment:* 2,754. *Faculty:* 256 (74 full-time, 182 part-time); student–undergrad faculty ratio is 15:1.

Enrollment Profile: 2,754 students from 11 states and territories, 3 other countries. 50% women, 50% men, 73% part-time, 96% state residents, 10% transferred in, 1% international, 59% 25 or older, 2% Native American, 6% Hispanic, 1% black, 1% Asian or Pacific Islander. *Areas of study chosen:* 29% liberal arts/general studies, 24% business management and administrative services, 16% social sciences, 12% health professions and related sciences, 9% engineering and applied sciences, 7% vocational and home economics, 3% agriculture.

First-Year Class: 392 total. Of the students who applied, 100% were accepted, 80% of whom enrolled.

Graduation Requirements: 90 credit hours; math/science requirements vary according to program.

Computers on Campus: 180 computers available on campus for general student use. Students can contact faculty members and/or advisers through e-mail. Computers for student use in computer center, academic buildings. Staffed computer lab on campus.

EXPENSES

Expenses for 1997–98: State resident tuition: $1575 full-time, $35 per credit hour part-time. Nonresident tuition: $4725 full-time, $35 per credit hour (minimum) part-time. Full-time mandatory fees: $27.

LD Program Contact: Ms. Cynthia A. Hilden, Special Services Provider, Blue Mountain Community College, Box 100, Pendleton, OR 97801-1000, 541-278-5796. Fax: 541-276-7119. Email: childen@bmcc.cc.or.us.

BLUE RIDGE COMMUNITY COLLEGE

Flat Rock, North Carolina

Students with LD	100	Subject-Area Tutoring	✓
ADD services	✓	Special Courses	✓
Staff	1 full-, 1 part-time	Taped Textbooks	✓
Special Fee	None	Alternative Test Arrang.	✓
Diagnostic Testing	✓	Notetakers	✓
Basic Skills Remediation	✓	LD Student Organization	✓

LEARNING DISABILITIES PROGRAM INFORMATION

The Special Populations Office began offering services in 1991. Currently the program serves 100 undergraduates with LD. Students diagnosed with ADD/ADHD are eligible for the same services available to students with LD.

Staff: 1 full-time, 1 part-time staff members, including coordinator, assistant. Services provided by tutors, mentors.

Special Fees: No special fees are charged for services to students with LD.

Applications and admissions: *Required:* high school transcript, personal interview; *recommended:* psychoeducational report completed within 3 years. Students may begin taking classes in fall, spring, or summer. *Application deadline:* continuous.

Special policies: The college has written policies regarding grade forgiveness; substitutions and waivers of admissions requirements.

PROGRAM AND SERVICE COMPONENTS

Special preparation or orientation: Required orientation held before registration, during registration, after classes begin.
Diagnostic testing: Intelligence, reading, math, spelling, handwriting, spoken language, written language, motor abilities, perceptual skills, study skills, social skills, psychoneurology, learning strategies.
Academic advising: Provided by LD staff members, academic advisers. Most students with LD take 6 to 12 semester hours each term; 12 semester hours required to maintain full-time status; 6 semester hours required to be eligible for financial aid.
Counseling services: Individual counseling, small-group counseling, career counseling, self-advocacy training.
Basic skills remediation: Offered one-on-one, in small groups, and in class-size groups by LD teachers, regular teachers, Coordinator of Special Populations Office. Available in reading, math, spelling, handwriting, spoken language, written language, learning strategies, perceptual skills, study skills, time management, social skills.
Subject-area tutoring: Offered one-on-one and in small groups by peer tutors, volunteer retirees. Available in all subjects.
Special courses: College survival skills, reading, vocabulary development, communication skills, composition, learning strategies, word processing, time management, math, personal psychology, study skills, career planning. All offered for credit; all enter into overall grade point average.
Auxiliary aids: Taped textbooks, tape recorders, calculators, word-processors with spell-check, optical character readers, spell checkers.
Auxiliary services: Alternative test arrangements, notetakers, priority registration, advocacy, readers, study partners, research assistants.
Campus support group: A special student organization is available to students with LD.

GENERAL COLLEGE INFORMATION

State and locally supported, 2-year, coed. Part of North Carolina Community College System. Awards associate degrees. Founded 1969. *Setting:* 109-acre small-town campus. *Total enrollment:* 2,496. *Faculty:* 176 (44 full-time, 66% with terminal degrees, 132 part-time); student–undergrad faculty ratio is 19:1.
Enrollment Profile: 2,496 students: 64% women, 36% men, 74% part-time, 99% state residents, 3% transferred in, 61% 25 or older, 1% Native American, 1% Hispanic, 3% black, 1% Asian or Pacific Islander. *Areas of study chosen:* 17% liberal arts/general studies, 12% business management and administrative services, 6% engineering and applied sciences, 3% education, 2% health professions and related sciences, 1% agriculture, 1% fine arts. *Most popular recent majors:* business administration/commerce/management, liberal arts/general studies, computer programming.
First-Year Class: 724 total. Of the students who applied, 100% were accepted.
Graduation Requirements: 1 math course; computer course for business majors.
Computers on Campus: 100 computers available on campus for general student use. A campus-wide network can be accessed from off-campus. Students can contact faculty members and/or advisers through e-mail. Computers for student use in computer labs, learning resource center, library provide access to the Internet/World Wide Web. Staffed computer lab on campus provides training in use of computers, software.

EXPENSES AND FINANCIAL AID

Expenses for 1997–98: State resident tuition: $560 full-time, $20 per credit hour part-time. Nonresident tuition: $4564 full-time, $163 per credit hour part-time. Part-time mandatory fees per semester range from $2.35 to $10.35. Full-time mandatory fees: $21.
Financial aid specifically for students with LD: Scholarships: Mayor's Committee Scholarship, Yehling Scholarship, Ora Treutt Scholarship.
LD Program Contact: Ms. Linda K. Holt, Coordinator, Blue Ridge Community College, College Drive, Flat Rock, NC 28731-9624, 704-692-3572 Ext. 290. Fax: 704-692-2441. Email: lindah@blueridge.cc.nc.us.

BROOKDALE COMMUNITY COLLEGE

Lincroft, New Jersey

Students with LD	250	Subject-Area Tutoring	✓
ADD services	✓	Special Courses	✓
Staff	2 full-, 21 part-time	Taped Textbooks	
Special Fee	✓	Alternative Test Arrang.	✓
Diagnostic Testing		Notetakers	
Basic Skills Remediation	✓	LD Student Organization	

LEARNING DISABILITIES PROGRAM INFORMATION

The Academic Skills Workshops began offering services in 1985. Currently the program serves 250 undergraduates with LD. Students diagnosed with ADD/ADHD are eligible for the same services available to students with LD.
Staff: 2 full-time, 21 part-time staff members, including director, coordinator. Services provided by tutors, counselor, faculty members.
Special Fees: $80 per year (lab fee with courses).
Applications and admissions: *Required:* high school transcript, formal documentation of LD and necessary accommodations. Students may begin taking classes in fall, winter, or summer. *Application deadline:* continuous.

PROGRAM AND SERVICE COMPONENTS

Special preparation or orientation: Optional summer program offered prior to entering college. Optional orientation offered during 6-week summer course.
Academic advising: Provided by academic advisers. Students with LD may take up to 15 credits each term; most take 8 to 12 credits; 12 credits required to maintain full-time status and be eligible for financial aid.
Counseling services: Individual counseling.
Basic skills remediation: Offered in class-size groups by LD teachers, regular teachers. Available in reading, math, spelling, spoken language, written language, learning strategies.
Subject-area tutoring: Offered one-on-one by reading or subject area specialists. Available in most subjects.
Special courses: College survival skills, reading, vocabulary development, communication skills, composition, learning strategies, word processing, math, typing. None offered for credit; none enter into overall grade point average.
Auxiliary aids: Personal computers, optical character readers.
Auxiliary services: Alternative test arrangements.

GENERAL COLLEGE INFORMATION

County-supported, 2-year, coed. Part of New Jersey Commission on Higher Education. Awards associate degrees. Founded 1967. *Setting:* 221-acre small-town campus with easy access to New York City. *Total enrollment:* 11,868. *Faculty:* 443 (193 full-time, 250 part-time); student–undergrad faculty ratio is 22:1.

Brookdale Community College (continued)

Enrollment Profile: 11,868 students from 6 states and territories, 37 other countries. 59% women, 41% men, 62% part-time, 98% state residents, 5% transferred in, 48% 25 or older, 4% Hispanic, 8% black, 4% Asian or Pacific Islander. *Retention:* 61% of 1995 full-time freshmen returned. *Areas of study chosen:* 21% business management and administrative services, 15% biological and life sciences, 12% liberal arts/general studies, 9% education, 7% social sciences, 5% health professions and related sciences, 4% communications and journalism, 4% computer and information sciences, 4% vocational and home economics, 3% engineering and applied sciences, 2% fine arts, 1% agriculture, 1% architecture, 1% English language/literature/letters, 1% library and information studies, 1% mathematics, 1% performing arts, 1% physical sciences. *Most popular recent majors:* business administration/commerce/management, humanities, social science.
First-Year Class: 4,185 applied, 100% were accepted, 75% of whom enrolled.
Graduation Requirements: 60 credits; math proficiency.
Computers on Campus: 700 computers available on campus for general student use. Computers for student use in computer center, computer labs, library. Staffed computer lab on campus.

EXPENSES

Expenses for 1997–98: Area resident tuition: $2168 full-time, $72.25 per credit part-time. State resident tuition: $4335 full-time, $144.50 per credit part-time. Nonresident tuition: $8670 full-time, $289 per credit part-time. Part-time mandatory fees: $13 per credit. Full-time mandatory fees: $390.
LD Program Contact: Ms. Sally Sorrell, Professor of Reading/Learning Disabilities Specialist, Brookdale Community College, Applied Humanities, Lincroft, NJ 07738-1597, 732-224-2786.

BUTTE COLLEGE

Oroville, California

Students with LD	350	Subject-Area Tutoring	✓
ADD services		Special Courses	✓
Staff	7 full-, 2 part-time	Taped Textbooks	✓
Special Fee	None	Alternative Test Arrang.	✓
Diagnostic Testing	✓	Notetakers	
Basic Skills Remediation	✓	LD Student Organization	

LEARNING DISABILITIES PROGRAM INFORMATION

The Disabled Student Programs and Services began offering services in 1981. Currently the program serves 350 undergraduates with LD. Students diagnosed with ADD/ADHD are not eligible for the same services available to students with LD.
Staff: 7 full-time, 2 part-time staff members, including director, coordinators. Services provided by remediation specialists, tutors, counselor, diagnostic specialist.
Special Fees: No special fees are charged for services to students with LD.
Applications and admissions: *Required:* California Assessment System for Adults with Learning Disabilities; *recommended:* psychoeducational report. Students may begin taking classes in fall only. *Application deadline:* continuous.
Special policies: The college has written policies regarding grade forgiveness.

PROGRAM AND SERVICE COMPONENTS

Special preparation or orientation: Optional orientation offered before registration, during registration, after classes begin.
Diagnostic testing: Reading, math, spelling, spoken language, written language, motor abilities, perceptual skills, study skills, personality, social skills, hearing.
Academic advising: Provided by LD staff members, academic advisers. Students with LD may take up to 18 units each term; most take 12 units; 12 units required to maintain full-time status; 9 units required to be eligible for financial aid.
Counseling services: Individual counseling, career counseling.
Basic skills remediation: Offered one-on-one and in small groups by LD teachers, regular teachers; computer-aided instruction also offered. Available in reading, math, spelling, spoken language, written language, learning strategies, perceptual skills, study skills, social skills.
Subject-area tutoring: Offered one-on-one by peer tutors. Available in some subjects.
Special courses: Learning strategies, word processing, personal psychology. All offered for credit; all enter into overall grade point average.
Auxiliary aids: Taped textbooks, tape recorders, calculators, typewriters, word-processors with spell-check, personal computers, optical character readers.
Auxiliary services: Alternative test arrangements, priority registration, advocacy.

GENERAL COLLEGE INFORMATION

District-supported, 2-year, coed. Part of California Community Colleges System. Awards associate degrees. Founded 1966. *Setting:* 900-acre rural campus. *Total enrollment:* 12,300. *Faculty:* 561 (123 full-time, 10% with terminal degrees, 438 part-time).
Enrollment Profile: 12,300 students from 19 states and territories, 25 other countries. 55% women, 45% men, 60% part-time, 86% state residents, 15% transferred in, 1% international, 53% 25 or older, 3% Native American, 5% Hispanic, 1% black, 3% Asian or Pacific Islander.
First-Year Class: 4,500 total. Of the students who applied, 100% were accepted. 5% from top 10% of their high school class, 60% from top half.
Graduation Requirements: 60 semester units; 1 course each in math and lab science; internship (some majors).
Computers on Campus: 65 computers available on campus for general student use. A campus-wide network can be accessed from off-campus. Computers for student use in computer labs, library. Staffed computer lab on campus provides training in use of computers, software.

EXPENSES

Expenses for 1997–98: State resident tuition: $0 full-time. Nonresident tuition: $3750 full-time, $125 per unit part-time. Part-time mandatory fees per semester range from $67.50 to $215. Full-time mandatory fees: $534.
LD Program Contact: Mr. Richard L. Dunn, Learning Disabilities Specialist/Program Director, Butte College, 3536 Butte Campus Drive, Oroville, CA 95965, 916-895-2455. Fax: 916-895-2235.

CABRILLO COLLEGE

Aptos, California

Students with LD	300	Subject-Area Tutoring	✓
ADD services	✓	Special Courses	✓
Staff	3 full-, 4 part-time	Taped Textbooks	✓
Special Fee	None	Alternative Test Arrang.	✓
Diagnostic Testing	✓	Notetakers	✓
Basic Skills Remediation	✓	LD Student Organization	

LEARNING DISABILITIES PROGRAM INFORMATION

The Learning Skills Program began offering services in 1977. Currently the program serves 300 undergraduates with LD. Students diagnosed with ADD/ADHD are eligible for the same services available to students with LD.

Staff: 3 full-time, 4 part-time staff members, including coordinator, LD specialists, program assistants. Services provided by remediation specialists, counselors, diagnostic specialists.
Special Fees: $45.50 to $163.50 for diagnostic testing.
Applications and admissions: *Recommended:* psychoeducational report completed within 3 years. Students may begin taking classes in fall, spring, or summer. *Application deadline:* continuous.
Special policies: The college has written policies regarding substitutions and waivers of graduation requirements.

PROGRAM AND SERVICE COMPONENTS

Diagnostic testing: Intelligence, reading, math, spelling, written language, perceptual skills, cognitive abilities.
Academic advising: Provided by LD staff members. Most students with LD take 6 to 15 semester units each term; 12 semester units required to maintain full-time status and be eligible for financial aid.
Counseling services: Individual counseling.
Basic skills remediation: Offered in class-size groups by LD teachers, regular teachers. Available in reading, math, written language, learning strategies, study skills, time management.
Subject-area tutoring: Offered one-on-one and in small groups by peer tutors. Available in most subjects.
Special courses: College survival skills, word processing, time management, study skills, Strategies for Success (for LD and ADD students). All offered for credit; all enter into overall grade point average.
Auxiliary aids: Taped textbooks, tape recorders, calculators, word-processors with spell-check, personal computers.
Auxiliary services: Alternative test arrangements, notetakers, priority registration.

GENERAL COLLEGE INFORMATION

District-supported, 2-year, coed. Part of California Community Colleges System. Awards associate degrees. Founded 1959. *Setting:* 120-acre small-town campus with easy access to San Jose. *Total enrollment:* 11,805. *Faculty:* 552 (207 full-time, 345 part-time).
Enrollment Profile: 11,805 students: 58% women, 42% men, 72% part-time, 98% state residents, 16% transferred in, 1% international, 50% 25 or older, 1% Native American, 14% Hispanic, 1% black, 3% Asian or Pacific Islander.
First-Year Class: 2,040 total. Of the students who applied, 100% were accepted, 70% of whom enrolled.
Graduation Requirements: 60 semester units; math proficiency; 1 science course; computer course for physical science majors.

EXPENSES

Expenses for 1997–98: State resident tuition: $0 full-time. Nonresident tuition: $3540 full-time, $118 per unit part-time. Part-time mandatory fees per semester range from $24 to $158. Full-time mandatory fees: $420.
LD Program Contact: Ms. Deborah Shulman, Learning Disabilities Specialist, Cabrillo College, 6500 Soquel Drive, Aptos, CA 95003, 408-479-6566. Fax: 408-479-6393.

CAÑADA COLLEGE

Redwood City, California

Students with LD	50	Subject-Area Tutoring	✓
ADD services	✓	Special Courses	✓
Staff	1 full-, 3 part-time	Taped Textbooks	✓
Special Fee	None	Alternative Test Arrang.	✓
Diagnostic Testing	✓	Notetakers	✓
Basic Skills Remediation	✓	LD Student Organization	✓

LEARNING DISABILITIES PROGRAM INFORMATION

The Learning Disabilities Program began offering services in 1968. Students diagnosed with ADD/ADHD are eligible for the same services available to students with LD.
Staff: 1 full-time, 3 part-time staff members, including coordinator, supervisor, Humanities Dean. Services provided by tutors, counselors, diagnostic specialists, LD specialists.
Special Fees: No special fees are charged for services to students with LD.
Applications and admissions: Open admissions. Students may begin taking classes in fall, spring, or summer. *Application deadline:* 8/1 (fall term), 1/1 (spring term).
Special policies: The college has written policies regarding grade forgiveness; substitutions and waivers of graduation and degree requirements.

PROGRAM AND SERVICE COMPONENTS

Special preparation or orientation: Required orientation held before registration and during registration.
Diagnostic testing: Intelligence, reading, math, spelling, handwriting, spoken language, written language, perceptual skills.
Academic advising: Provided by LD staff members, academic advisers. Students with LD may take up to 18 units each term; most take 12 units (4 in program); 12 units required to maintain full-time status and be eligible for financial aid.
Counseling services: Individual counseling, small-group counseling, career counseling.
Basic skills remediation: Offered in small groups by LD teachers; computer-aided instruction also offered. Available in reading, math, spelling, handwriting, spoken language, written language, learning strategies, perceptual skills, study skills, social skills, computer skills.
Subject-area tutoring: Offered one-on-one, in small groups, and in class-size groups by professional teachers, peer tutors. Available in most subjects.
Special courses: College survival skills, reading, vocabulary development, math, study skills. All offered for credit; some enter into overall grade point average.
Auxiliary aids: Taped textbooks, tape recorders, typewriters, word-processors with spell-check, personal computers.
Auxiliary services: Alternative test arrangements, notetakers, priority registration, advocacy.
Campus support group: A special student organization is available to students with LD.

GENERAL COLLEGE INFORMATION

District-supported, 2-year, coed. Part of San Mateo County Community College District System. Awards associate degrees. Founded 1968. *Setting:* 131-acre suburban campus with easy access to San Francisco and San Jose. *Total enrollment:* 5,640. *Faculty:* 231 (77 full-time, 26% with terminal degrees, 154 part-time); student–undergrad faculty ratio is 24:1.
Enrollment Profile: 5,640 students: 65% women, 35% men, 79% part-time, 97% state residents, 13% transferred in, 3% international, 65% 25 or older, 1% Native American, 23% Hispanic, 5% black, 8% Asian or Pacific Islander.
First-Year Class: 730 total. Of the students who applied, 100% were accepted, 100% of whom enrolled.
Graduation Requirements: 60 credits; computer course.

Cañada College (continued)

Computers on Campus: 55 computers available on campus for general student use. Computer purchase/lease plans available. Computers for student use in computer center, computer labs, classrooms, library provide access to the Internet/World Wide Web. Staffed computer lab on campus provides training in use of computers, software.

EXPENSES

Expenses for 1997–98: State resident tuition: $0 full-time. Nonresident tuition: $3780 full-time, $126 per unit part-time. Part-time mandatory fees per semester range from $29 to $159. Full-time mandatory fees: $422.

LD Program Contact: Ms. Kathleen Shiels, Learning Disabilities Specialist, Cañada College, Building 3, Room 117, Redwood City, CA 94061-1099, 415-306-3423. Fax: 415-306-3176.

CAPE COD COMMUNITY COLLEGE

West Barnstable, Massachusetts

Students with LD	150	Subject-Area Tutoring	✓
ADD services	✓	Special Courses	
Staff	1 full-, 1 part-time	Taped Textbooks	✓
Special Fee	None	Alternative Test Arrang.	✓
Diagnostic Testing		Notetakers	
Basic Skills Remediation	✓	LD Student Organization	✓

LEARNING DISABILITIES PROGRAM INFORMATION

The Learning Disabilities Supportive Services (Student Services) began offering services in 1987. Currently the program serves 150 undergraduates with LD. Students diagnosed with ADD/ADHD are eligible for the same services available to students with LD.

Staff: 1 full-time, 1 part-time staff members, including director, coordinator. Services provided by tutors, diagnostic specialist.

Special Fees: No special fees are charged for services to students with LD.

Applications and admissions: *Required:* high school transcript, psychoeducational report completed within 4 years. Students may begin taking classes in fall, spring, or summer. *Application deadline:* continuous.

Special policies: The college has written policies regarding grade forgiveness; substitutions and waivers of graduation and degree requirements.

PROGRAM AND SERVICE COMPONENTS

Special preparation or orientation: Required orientation held during registration.

Academic advising: Provided by academic advisers. Students with LD may take up to 15 credit hours each term; most take 9 credit hours; 12 credit hours required to maintain full-time status; 6 credit hours required to be eligible for financial aid.

Counseling services: Individual counseling, small-group counseling, career counseling.

Basic skills remediation: Offered one-on-one, in small groups, and in class-size groups by regular teachers. Available in reading, math, spelling, written language, learning strategies, study skills.

Subject-area tutoring: Offered one-on-one by professional teachers, peer tutors. Available in all subjects.

Auxiliary aids: Taped textbooks, tape recorders, calculators, word-processors with spell-check, optical character readers.

Auxiliary services: Alternative test arrangements, priority registration, advocacy.

Campus support group: A special student organization is available to students with LD.

GENERAL COLLEGE INFORMATION

State-supported, 2-year, coed. Part of Massachusetts Public Higher Education System. Awards associate degrees. Founded 1961. *Setting:* 120-acre rural campus with easy access to Boston. *Endowment:* $1.5 million. *Total enrollment:* 3,630. *Faculty:* 256 (81 full-time, 175 part-time); student–undergrad faculty ratio is 16:1.

Enrollment Profile: 3,630 students: 64% women, 36% men, 53% part-time, 99% state residents, 9% transferred in, 51% 25 or older, 1% Hispanic, 2% black, 1% Asian or Pacific Islander. *Areas of study chosen:* 27% liberal arts/general studies, 26% health professions and related sciences, 7% education, 3% computer and information sciences, 3% fine arts, 3% social sciences, 1% communications and journalism, 1% engineering and applied sciences. *Most popular recent majors:* liberal arts/general studies, nursing.

First-Year Class: 1,140 total; 1,744 applied, 96% were accepted, 68% of whom enrolled. 9% from top quarter of their high school class, 31% from top half.

Graduation Requirements: 60 credit hours; 8 credit hours science, 3 credit hours of math for associate of arts degree; 3 credit hours of math/science for associate of science degree; internship (some majors).

Computers on Campus: 125 computers available on campus for general student use. Computers for student use in computer center, Assessment Center. Staffed computer lab on campus provides training in use of computers. *Academic computing expenditure 1995–96:* $310,000.

EXPENSES

Expenses for 1997–98: *Application fee:* $10. State resident tuition: $1020 full-time, $34 per credit hour part-time. Nonresident tuition: $6120 full-time, $204 per credit hour part-time. Part-time mandatory fees: $50.50 per credit hour. Full-time mandatory fees: $1515.

LD Program Contact: Dr. Richard H. Sommers, Learning Disabilities Specialist, Cape Cod Community College, 2240 Iyanough Road, West Barnstable, MA 02668-1599, 508-362-2131. Fax: 508-362-3988.

CATAWBA VALLEY COMMUNITY COLLEGE

Hickory, North Carolina

Students with LD	16	Subject-Area Tutoring	✓
ADD services	✓	Special Courses	✓
Staff		Taped Textbooks	✓
Special Fee	None	Alternative Test Arrang.	✓
Diagnostic Testing	✓	Notetakers	✓
Basic Skills Remediation	✓	LD Student Organization	

LEARNING DISABILITIES PROGRAM INFORMATION

The Learning Assistance Center began offering services in 1970. Currently the program serves 16 undergraduates with LD. Students diagnosed with ADD/ADHD are eligible for the same services available to students with LD.

Staff: Includes director, co-directors, Dean of Student Services, Chairman of Arts and Sciences Division. Services provided by remediation specialists, tutors, counselors, diagnostic specialist.

Special Fees: No special fees are charged for services to students with LD.

Applications and admissions: *Required:* high school transcript, ACT ASSET; *recommended:* high school grade point average, courses completed, untimed SAT I, personal interview. Students may begin taking classes in fall, spring, or summer. *Application deadline:* continuous.
Special policies: The college has written policies regarding grade forgiveness.

PROGRAM AND SERVICE COMPONENTS

Special preparation or orientation: Optional orientation offered before registration.
Diagnostic testing: Intelligence, reading, math, spelling, written language, study skills, personality.
Academic advising: Provided by LD staff members, academic advisers. Students with LD may take up to 12 semester hours each term; most take 9 to 12 semester hours; 12 semester hours required to maintain full-time status; 6 semester hours required to be eligible for financial aid.
Counseling services: Individual counseling, small-group counseling, career counseling.
Basic skills remediation: Offered one-on-one and in class-size groups by LD teachers, regular teachers; computer-aided instruction also offered. Available in reading, math, spelling, spoken language, written language, learning strategies, study skills, time management, social skills.
Subject-area tutoring: Offered one-on-one by professional teachers, peer tutors. Available in all subjects.
Special courses: College survival skills, reading, vocabulary development, composition, time management, math, personal psychology, study skills, career planning. Some offered for credit; some enter into overall grade point average.
Auxiliary aids: Taped textbooks, tape recorders, calculators, typewriters, word-processors with spell-check, personal computers.
Auxiliary services: Alternative test arrangements, notetakers, readers, interpreters.

GENERAL COLLEGE INFORMATION

State and locally supported, 2-year, coed. Part of North Carolina Community College System. Awards associate degrees. Founded 1960. *Setting:* 50-acre small-town campus with easy access to Charlotte. *Total enrollment:* 3,401. *Faculty:* 250 (100 full-time, 150 part-time); student–undergrad faculty ratio is 19:1.
Enrollment Profile: 3,401 students from 10 states and territories, 4 other countries. 60% women, 40% men, 74% part-time, 98% state residents, 10% transferred in, 54% 25 or older, 1% Native American, 1% Hispanic, 6% black, 1% Asian or Pacific Islander. *Most popular recent majors:* nursing, electronics engineering technology, accounting.
First-Year Class: 825 total; 2,000 applied, 100% were accepted, 41% of whom enrolled.
Graduation Requirements: 1 course each in math and lab science; computer course for students without computer competency; internship (some majors).
Computers on Campus: A campus-wide network can be accessed from off-campus. Students can contact faculty members and/or advisers through e-mail. Computers for student use in computer center, computer labs, learning resource center, classrooms, library provide access to the Internet/World Wide Web. Staffed computer lab on campus provides training in use of computers, software.

EXPENSES

Expenses for 1997–98: State resident tuition: $560 full-time, $20 per semester hour part-time. Nonresident tuition: $4564 full-time, $163 per semester hour part-time. Part-time mandatory fees: $2 per semester hour. Full-time mandatory fees: $56.

LD Program Contact: Dr. Janette Sims, Director of Developmental Studies, Catawba Valley Community College, 2550 Highway 70, SE, Hickory, NC 28602-9699, 704-327-7000 Ext. 383. Fax: 704-327-7000 Ext. 400.

CENTRAL OHIO TECHNICAL COLLEGE
Newark, Ohio

Students with LD	60	Subject-Area Tutoring	✓
ADD services	✓	Special Courses	
Staff	2 full-, 1 part-time	Taped Textbooks	✓
Special Fee	None	Alternative Test Arrang.	✓
Diagnostic Testing	✓	Notetakers	✓
Basic Skills Remediation	✓	LD Student Organization	

LEARNING DISABILITIES PROGRAM INFORMATION

The Developmental Education/Disability Services began offering services in 1985. Currently the program serves 60 undergraduates with LD. Students diagnosed with ADD/ADHD are eligible for the same services available to students with LD.
Staff: 2 full-time, 1 part-time staff members, including director. Services provided by remediation specialist, tutors, diagnostic specialist.
Special Fees: No special fees are charged for services to students with LD.
Applications and admissions: *Required:* high school transcript, psychoeducational report completed within 3 years; *recommended:* high school IEP (Individualized Education Program). Students may begin taking classes any term. *Application deadline:* continuous.
Special policies: The college has written policies regarding grade forgiveness.

PROGRAM AND SERVICE COMPONENTS

Diagnostic testing: Intelligence, reading, math, spelling, handwriting, written language, motor abilities, perceptual skills, study skills, hearing, learning strategies.
Academic advising: Provided by LD staff members, academic advisers. Students with LD may take up to 23 quarter credit hours each term; most take 10 quarter credit hours; 12 quarter credit hours required to maintain full-time status; 6 quarter credit hours required to be eligible for financial aid.
Counseling services: Individual counseling, small-group counseling.
Basic skills remediation: Offered one-on-one by regular teachers, study skills specialist. Available in reading, math, spelling, handwriting, written language, learning strategies, study skills, time management, speech.
Subject-area tutoring: Offered one-on-one by peer tutors. Available in most subjects.
Auxiliary aids: Taped textbooks, tape recorders, calculators, typewriters, word-processors with spell-check, personal computers, talking computers, Arkenstone Reader, Book Wise.
Auxiliary services: Alternative test arrangements, notetakers, priority registration, advocacy.

GENERAL COLLEGE INFORMATION

State-supported, 2-year, coed. Part of Ohio Board of Regents. Awards associate degrees. Founded 1971. *Setting:* 155-acre small-town campus with easy access to Columbus. *Total enrollment:* 1,636. *Faculty:* 149 (51 full-time, 7% with terminal degrees, 98 part-time); student–undergrad faculty ratio is 15:1.
Enrollment Profile: 1,636 students: 71% women, 29% men, 58% part-time, 99% state residents, 8% transferred in, 1% international, 76% 25 or older, 1% Native American, 1% Hispanic, 3%

Central Ohio Technical College (continued)

black, 1% Asian or Pacific Islander. *Retention:* 65% of 1995 full-time freshmen returned. *Areas of study chosen:* 39% health professions and related sciences, 31% business management and administrative services, 12% engineering and applied sciences, 10% social sciences, 8% computer and information sciences. *Most popular recent majors:* nursing, business administration/commerce/management, accounting.
First-Year Class: 468 total; 747 applied, 100% were accepted, 63% of whom enrolled.
Graduation Requirements: 101 quarter credit hours; computer course for business, accounting, engineering, criminal justice, secretarial science, nursing majors.
Computers on Campus: 300 computers available on campus for general student use. Computers for student use in computer center, computer labs, learning resource center provide access to the Internet/World Wide Web. Staffed computer lab on campus provides training in use of computers, software.

EXPENSES

Expenses for 1997–98: *Application fee:* $15. State resident tuition: $2466 full-time, $68 per quarter hour part-time. Nonresident tuition: $4620 full-time, $128 per quarter hour part-time. Part-time mandatory fees: $6 per quarter. Full-time mandatory fees: $18.
LD Program Contact: Dr. Phyllis E. Thompsen, Coordinator, Developmental Education, Central Ohio Technical College, University Drive, Newark, OH 43055-1767, 614-366-9246. Fax: 614-366-5047.

CENTRAL PIEDMONT COMMUNITY COLLEGE

Charlotte, North Carolina

Students with LD	130	Subject-Area Tutoring	✓
ADD services	✓	Special Courses	✓
Staff	2 full-time	Taped Textbooks	✓
Special Fee	None	Alternative Test Arrang.	✓
Diagnostic Testing	✓	Notetakers	✓
Basic Skills Remediation	✓	LD Student Organization	✓

LEARNING DISABILITIES PROGRAM INFORMATION

The Support Services for Students with Learning Disabilities began offering services in 1981. Currently the program serves 130 undergraduates with LD. Students diagnosed with ADD/ADHD are eligible for the same services available to students with LD.
Staff: 2 full-time staff members, including director, LD counselor. Services provided by remediation specialists, tutors, counselor.
Special Fees: No special fees are charged for services to students with LD.
Applications and admissions: *Required:* high school transcript, extended time SAT I, personal interview, psychoeducational report completed within 3 years. Students may begin taking classes any term. *Application deadline:* continuous.
Special policies: The college has written policies regarding substitutions and waivers of degree requirements.

PROGRAM AND SERVICE COMPONENTS

Special preparation or orientation: Optional orientation offered after classes begin.
Diagnostic testing: Reading, math, spelling, career aptitude/interests.
Academic advising: Provided by LD staff members, academic advisers. Students with LD may take up to 15 semester hours each term; most take 12 semester hours; 12 semester hours required to maintain full-time status; 6 semester hours (part-time), 12 semester hours (full-time) required to be eligible for financial aid.
Counseling services: Individual counseling, career counseling.
Basic skills remediation: Offered one-on-one by retired teachers, part-time teachers. Available in reading, math, spelling, written language, learning strategies, study skills, time management, social skills.
Subject-area tutoring: Offered one-on-one by peer tutors, retired teachers, part-time teachers. Available in all subjects.
Special courses: Reading, time management, study skills. All offered for credit; all enter into overall grade point average.
Auxiliary aids: Taped textbooks, tape recorders, calculators, typewriters, word-processors with spell-check, personal computers, optical character readers.
Auxiliary services: Alternative test arrangements, notetakers, priority registration, advocacy.
Campus support group: A special student organization is available to students with LD.

GENERAL COLLEGE INFORMATION

State and locally supported, 2-year, coed. Part of North Carolina Community College System. Awards associate degrees. Founded 1963. *Setting:* 37-acre urban campus. *Endowment:* $4.4 million. *Total enrollment:* 15,420. *Faculty:* 1,877 (677 full-time, 1,200 part-time); student–undergrad faculty ratio is 10:1.
Enrollment Profile: 15,420 students from 21 states and territories, 14 other countries. 57% women, 43% men, 70% part-time, 85% state residents, 1% transferred in, 2% international, 62% 25 or older, 1% Native American, 1% Hispanic, 22% black, 2% Asian or Pacific Islander. *Most popular recent majors:* nursing, medical assistant technologies.
First-Year Class: 1,646 total. Of the students who applied, 100% were accepted.
Graduation Requirements: course each in math and science.
Computers on Campus: Computers for student use in computer center, learning resource center, library, student center provide access to the Internet/World Wide Web. Staffed computer lab on campus provides training in use of computers, software.

EXPENSES AND FINANCIAL AID

Expenses for 1997–98: State resident tuition: $560 full-time, $20 per semester hour part-time. Nonresident tuition: $4564 full-time, $163 per semester hour part-time.
Financial aid specifically for students with LD: Scholarship: The Fontes Scholarship.
LD Program Contact: Ms. Pat Adams, Learning Disabilities Counselor, Central Piedmont Community College, PO Box 35009, Charlotte, NC 28235-5009, 704-330-6556. Fax: 704-330-4020. Email: patricia_adams@cpcc.cc.nc.us.

CERRITOS COLLEGE

Norwalk, California

Students with LD	100	Subject-Area Tutoring	✓
ADD services	✓	Special Courses	✓
Staff	2 part-time	Taped Textbooks	✓
Special Fee	None	Alternative Test Arrang.	✓
Diagnostic Testing	✓	Notetakers	✓
Basic Skills Remediation	✓	LD Student Organization	✓

LEARNING DISABILITIES PROGRAM INFORMATION

The Instructional Support Center began offering services in 1982. Currently the program serves 100 undergraduates with LD. Students diagnosed with ADD/ADHD are eligible for the same services available to students with LD.
Staff: 2 part-time staff members, including Program Specialist. Services provided by counselor, LD specialists, instructional aides.
Special Fees: No special fees are charged for services to students with LD.
Applications and admissions: *Required:* psychoeducational report completed within 3 years, California Learning Disabilities Eligibility Criteria. Students may begin taking classes any term. *Application deadline:* continuous.
Special policies: The college has written policies regarding grade forgiveness; substitutions and waivers of graduation and degree requirements.

PROGRAM AND SERVICE COMPONENTS

Special preparation or orientation: Optional orientation offered before registration, during registration, after classes begin.
Diagnostic testing: Reading, math, spelling, spoken language, written language, perceptual skills.
Academic advising: Provided by LD staff members, academic advisers. Students with LD may take up to 12 units each term; most take 6 to 8 units; 12 units required to maintain full-time status; 9 to 10 units required to be eligible for financial aid.
Counseling services: Individual counseling, career counseling.
Basic skills remediation: Offered one-on-one, in small groups, and in class-size groups by LD teachers, instructional aides. Available in reading, math, spelling, written language, learning strategies, perceptual skills, study skills, time management.
Subject-area tutoring: Offered one-on-one, in small groups, and in class-size groups by professional teachers, instructional aides. Available in most subjects.
Special courses: Reading, vocabulary development, composition, learning strategies, word processing, time management, math, study skills, career planning. None offered for credit.
Auxiliary aids: Taped textbooks, tape recorders, calculators, word-processors with spell-check, optical character readers.
Auxiliary services: Alternative test arrangements, notetakers, priority registration, advocacy.
Campus support group: A special student organization is available to students with LD.

GENERAL COLLEGE INFORMATION

State and locally supported, 2-year, coed. Part of California Community Colleges System. Awards associate degrees. Founded 1956. *Setting:* 140-acre suburban campus with easy access to Los Angeles. *Total enrollment:* 20,717. *Faculty:* 690 (250 full-time, 440 part-time).
Enrollment Profile: 20,717 students: 56% women, 44% men, 77% part-time, 95% state residents, 7% transferred in, 1% international, 46% 25 or older, 2% Native American, 31% Hispanic, 6% black, 14% Asian or Pacific Islander. *Most popular recent majors:* liberal arts/general studies, business administration/commerce/management, nursing.
First-Year Class: 3,245 total. Of the students who applied, 100% were accepted.
Graduation Requirements: 64 units; math proficiency; 2 science courses; computer course for engineering, business-related majors.
Computers on Campus: 400 computers available on campus for general student use. A campus-wide network can be accessed from off-campus. Students can contact faculty members and/or advisers through e-mail. Computers for student use in computer center, classrooms, library provide access to the Internet/World Wide Web, on- and off-campus e-mail addresses.

EXPENSES

Expenses for 1997–98: State resident tuition: $0 full-time. Nonresident tuition: $3776 full-time, $118 per unit part-time. Part-time mandatory fees per semester range from $33 to $163. Full-time mandatory fees: $456.
LD Program Contact: Mr. Al Spetrino, Program Specialist, Cerritos College, 11110 Alondra Boulevard, Norwalk, CA 90650, 562-860-2451 Ext. 2347. Fax: 562-467-5006. Email: spetrino@cerritos.edu.

CERRO COSO COMMUNITY COLLEGE

Ridgecrest, California

Students with LD	130	Subject-Area Tutoring	✓
ADD services	✓	Special Courses	✓
Staff	1 full-, 25 part-time	Taped Textbooks	✓
Special Fee	None	Alternative Test Arrang.	✓
Diagnostic Testing	✓	Notetakers	✓
Basic Skills Remediation	✓	LD Student Organization	✓

LEARNING DISABILITIES PROGRAM INFORMATION

The Special Services Program, Learning Skills began offering services in 1981. Currently the program serves 130 undergraduates with LD. Students diagnosed with ADD/ADHD are eligible for the same services available to students with LD.
Staff: 1 full-time, 25 part-time staff members, including director, coordinator. Services provided by remediation specialist, tutors, counselor, diagnostic specialist.
Special Fees: No special fees are charged for services to students with LD.
Applications and admissions: *Required:* personal interview, psychoeducational report completed within 3 years, LD assessment; *recommended:* high school transcript. Students may begin taking classes any term. *Application deadline:* continuous.
Special policies: The college has written policies regarding grade forgiveness; substitutions and waivers of admissions, graduation, and degree requirements.

PROGRAM AND SERVICE COMPONENTS

Special preparation or orientation: Required orientation held before registration, during registration, after classes begin.
Diagnostic testing: Intelligence, reading, math, spelling, spoken language, written language, perceptual skills, study skills, personality, social skills, learning strategies.
Academic advising: Provided by LD staff members. Students with LD may take up to 15 semester units each term; most take 10 semester units; 9 semester units required to maintain full-time status; 9 to 12 semester units required to be eligible for financial aid.
Counseling services: Individual counseling, small-group counseling, career counseling, self-advocacy training.
Basic skills remediation: Offered one-on-one, in small groups, and in class-size groups by LD teachers, regular teachers, teacher trainees; computer-aided instruction also offered. Available in reading, math, spelling, handwriting, written language, learning strategies, motor abilities, perceptual skills, study skills, time management, social skills, computer skills.
Subject-area tutoring: Offered one-on-one and in small groups by professional teachers, peer tutors. Available in all subjects.
Special courses: College survival skills, communication skills, learning strategies, word processing, time management, study skills, career planning. All offered for credit; all enter into overall grade point average.

Auxiliary aids: Taped textbooks, tape recorders, calculators, typewriters, word-processors with spell-check, talking computers, optical character readers, Arkenstone Reader, laptop computers.
Auxiliary services: Alternative test arrangements, notetakers, priority registration, advocacy.
Campus support group: A special student organization is available to students with LD.

GENERAL COLLEGE INFORMATION

State-supported, 2-year, coed. Part of Kern Community College District System. Awards associate degrees. Founded 1973. *Setting:* 320-acre small-town campus. *Total enrollment:* 3,855. *Faculty:* 262 (37 full-time, 225 part-time).
Enrollment Profile: 3,855 students: 62% women, 38% men, 84% part-time, 96% state residents, 12% transferred in, 70% 25 or older, 3% Native American, 8% Hispanic, 5% black, 9% Asian or Pacific Islander.
First-Year Class: 622 total; 622 applied, 100% were accepted, 100% of whom enrolled.
Graduation Requirements: 60 semester units; algebra proficiency; 1 course each in natural and physical science.
Computers on Campus: 80 computers available on campus for general student use. A campus-wide network can be accessed from off-campus. Students can contact faculty members and/or advisers through e-mail. Computers for student use in computer center, library, business skills lab, learning center. Staffed computer lab on campus provides training in use of computers, software.

EXPENSES

Expenses for 1996–97: State resident tuition: $0 full-time. Nonresident tuition: $3600 full-time, $120 per unit part-time. Part-time mandatory fees: $13 per unit. Full-time mandatory fees: $390.
LD Program Contact: Ms. Susan Smith, Director of Special Services, Cerro Coso Community College, 3000 College Heights Boulevard, Ridgecrest, CA 93555-9571, 760-384-6248. Fax: 760-375-4776.

CHAFFEY COLLEGE

Rancho Cucamonga, California

Students with LD	380	Subject-Area Tutoring	✓
ADD services	✓	Special Courses	✓
Staff	5 full-, 11 part-time	Taped Textbooks	✓
Special Fee	None	Alternative Test Arrang.	✓
Diagnostic Testing	✓	Notetakers	✓
Basic Skills Remediation	✓	LD Student Organization	✓

LEARNING DISABILITIES PROGRAM INFORMATION

The Basic Skills Program began offering services in 1975. Currently the program serves 380 undergraduates with LD. Students diagnosed with ADD/ADHD are eligible for the same services available to students with LD.
Staff: 5 full-time, 11 part-time staff members, including director, secretary. Services provided by remediation specialists, tutors, instructors, instructional assistants.
Special Fees: No special fees are charged for services to students with LD.
Applications and admissions: *Required:* psychoeducational report completed within 3 years. Students may begin taking classes in fall, spring, or summer. *Application deadline:* continuous.

PROGRAM AND SERVICE COMPONENTS

Diagnostic testing: Intelligence, reading, math, spelling, Woodcock-Johnson.
Academic advising: Provided by LD staff members. Most students with LD take 12 units each term; 12 units required to maintain full-time status and be eligible for financial aid.
Counseling services: Individual counseling, career counseling.
Basic skills remediation: Offered one-on-one and in small groups by LD teachers. Available in reading, math, spelling, handwriting, spoken language, written language, learning strategies, perceptual skills, study skills, time management, social skills, computer skills.
Subject-area tutoring: Offered one-on-one and in small groups by professional teachers, peer tutors. Available in all subjects.
Special courses: College survival skills, reading, vocabulary development, communication skills, composition, learning strategies, word processing, time management, math, study skills, career planning. All offered for credit; none enter into overall grade point average.
Auxiliary aids: Taped textbooks, tape recorders, calculators, word-processors with spell-check, personal computers.
Auxiliary services: Alternative test arrangements, notetakers, priority registration, advocacy.
Campus support group: A special student organization is available to students with LD.

GENERAL COLLEGE INFORMATION

District-supported, 2-year, coed. Part of California Community Colleges System. Awards associate degrees. Founded 1883. *Setting:* 200-acre suburban campus with easy access to Los Angeles. *Total enrollment:* 12,651. *Faculty:* 540 (190 full-time, 350 part-time); student–undergrad faculty ratio is 27:1.
Enrollment Profile: 12,651 students: 60% women, 40% men, 72% part-time, 97% state residents, 10% transferred in, 2% international, 42% 25 or older, 1% Native American, 29% Hispanic, 11% black, 7% Asian or Pacific Islander. *Most popular recent majors:* business administration/commerce/management, nursing, liberal arts/general studies.
First-Year Class: 8,000 total; 8,000 applied, 100% were accepted, 100% of whom enrolled.
Graduation Requirements: 60 units; computer course (varies by major).
Computers on Campus: 150 computers available on campus for general student use. Computer purchase/lease plans available. Computers for student use in computer center, computer labs, learning resource center, classrooms, library.

EXPENSES

Expenses for 1997–98: State resident tuition: $0 full-time. Nonresident tuition: $3810 full-time, $127 per unit part-time. Part-time mandatory fees per semester range from $23 to $153. Full-time mandatory fees: $410.
LD Program Contact: Ms. Danile Brookins, Secretary, Learning Resource Center, Chaffey College, 5885 Haven Avenue, Rancho Cucamonga, CA 91737-3002, 909-941-2332. Fax: 909-941-2783.

CHIPPEWA VALLEY TECHNICAL COLLEGE

Eau Claire, Wisconsin

Students with LD	140	Subject-Area Tutoring	✓
ADD services	✓	Special Courses	✓
Staff	2 full-, 1 part-time	Taped Textbooks	✓
Special Fee	None	Alternative Test Arrang.	✓

Diagnostic Testing		Notetakers	✓
Basic Skills Remediation	✓	LD Student Organization	

LEARNING DISABILITIES PROGRAM INFORMATION

The Serve Lab currently serves 140 undergraduates with LD. Students diagnosed with ADD/ADHD are eligible for the same services available to students with LD.

Staff: 2 full-time, 1 part-time staff members. Services provided by counselor, transition specialist, certified instructors.

Special Fees: No special fees are charged for services to students with LD.

Applications and admissions: *Required:* high school transcript, documentation of disability; *recommended:* vocational evaluation. Students may begin taking classes any term. *Application deadline:* continuous.

Special policies: The college has written policies regarding grade forgiveness.

PROGRAM AND SERVICE COMPONENTS

Special preparation or orientation: Optional orientation offered individually by arrangement with transition specialist.

Academic advising: Provided by LD staff members, academic advisers. Students with LD may take up to as many credits as an individual can handle each term; most take 12 to 16 credits; 12 credits required to maintain full-time status; 6 credits (part-time), 12 credits (full-time) required to be eligible for financial aid.

Counseling services: Individual counseling, career counseling.

Basic skills remediation: Offered one-on-one by LD teachers, basic skills specialists. Available in reading, math, spelling, handwriting, spoken language, written language, learning strategies, perceptual skills, study skills, time management, social skills.

Subject-area tutoring: Offered one-on-one and in small groups by professional teachers, peer tutors. Available in all subjects.

Special courses: College Success. All offered for credit; all enter into overall grade point average.

Auxiliary aids: Taped textbooks, tape recorders, calculators, typewriters, word-processors with spell-check, personal computers, FM system.

Auxiliary services: Alternative test arrangements, notetakers, priority registration, advocacy, oral and sign interpreters.

GENERAL COLLEGE INFORMATION

District-supported, 2-year, coed. Part of Wisconsin Technical College System. Awards associate degrees. Founded 1912. *Setting:* 160-acre urban campus. *Total enrollment:* 3,800. *Faculty:* 400 (350 full-time, 50% with terminal degrees, 50 part-time); student–undergrad faculty ratio is 9:1.

Enrollment Profile: 3,800 students from 20 states and territories, 7 other countries. 50% women, 50% men, 10% part-time, 98% state residents, 10% transferred in, 1% international, 50% 25 or older, 1% Native American, 1% Hispanic, 1% black, 5% Asian or Pacific Islander. *Areas of study chosen:* 15% engineering and applied sciences, 7% architecture, 5% agriculture. *Most popular recent majors:* radiological technology, nursing, laboratory technologies.

First-Year Class: 2,350 total; 4,600 applied, 67% of whom enrolled. 10% from top 10% of their high school class, 15% from top quarter, 25% from top half.

Graduation Requirements: 70 credits; math/science requirements vary according to program; computer course; internship (some majors).

Computers on Campus: 600 computers available on campus for general student use. Computers for student use in computer center, library.

EXPENSES

Expenses for 1997–98: *Application fee:* $25. State resident tuition: $1897 full-time, $54.20 per credit part-time. Nonresident tuition: $14,952 full-time, $427.20 per credit part-time.

LD Program Contact: Ms. Carolyn Dunning, Manager of Special Services, Chippewa Valley Technical College, 620 West Clairemont Avenue, Eau Claire, WI 54701, 715-833-6280. Fax: 715-833-6470.

CITRUS COLLEGE

Glendora, California

Students with LD	180	Subject-Area Tutoring	✓
ADD services	✓	Special Courses	✓
Staff	1 full-, 3 part-time	Taped Textbooks	✓
Special Fee	None	Alternative Test Arrang.	✓
Diagnostic Testing	✓	Notetakers	✓
Basic Skills Remediation	✓	LD Student Organization	✓

LEARNING DISABILITIES PROGRAM INFORMATION

The Disabled Student Programs & Services (DSP&S) began offering services in 1972. Currently the program serves 180 undergraduates with LD. Students diagnosed with ADD/ADHD are eligible for the same services available to students with LD.

Staff: 1 full-time, 3 part-time staff members, including coordinator. Services provided by tutors, counselors, diagnostic specialist.

Special Fees: No special fees are charged for services to students with LD.

Applications and admissions: *Required:* personal interview; *recommended:* high school transcript, psychoeducational report completed within 3 years. Students may begin taking classes in fall, spring, or summer. *Application deadline:* continuous.

Special policies: The college has written policies regarding grade forgiveness; substitutions and waivers of graduation requirements.

PROGRAM AND SERVICE COMPONENTS

Diagnostic testing: Intelligence, reading, math, spelling, spoken language, written language, motor abilities, perceptual skills, study skills, learning strategies.

Academic advising: Provided by LD staff members, academic advisers. Students with LD may take up to 18 units (more with Dean's permission) each term; 12 units required to maintain full-time status; 6 units required to be eligible for financial aid.

Counseling services: Individual counseling, career counseling, self-advocacy training.

Basic skills remediation: Offered in class-size groups by regular teachers. Available in reading, math, spelling, spoken language, written language, learning strategies, study skills, time management.

Subject-area tutoring: Offered one-on-one and in small groups by peer tutors, instructional assistants. Available in most subjects.

Special courses: College survival skills, word processing. All offered for credit; all enter into overall grade point average.

Auxiliary aids: Taped textbooks, tape recorders, calculators, word-processors with spell-check, personal computers, talking computers, optical character readers.

Auxiliary services: Alternative test arrangements, notetakers, priority registration, advocacy.

Campus support group: A special student organization is available to students with LD.

Citrus College (continued)

GENERAL COLLEGE INFORMATION

State and locally supported, 2-year, coed. Part of California Community Colleges System. Awards associate degrees. Founded 1915. *Setting:* 104-acre small-town campus with easy access to Los Angeles. *Total enrollment:* 10,448. *Faculty:* 392 (132 full-time, 10% with terminal degrees, 260 part-time); student–undergrad faculty ratio is 22:1.

Enrollment Profile: 10,448 students: 56% women, 44% men, 71% part-time, 95% state residents, 2% international, 45% 25 or older, 1% Native American, 32% Hispanic, 7% black, 10% Asian or Pacific Islander. *Areas of study chosen:* 10% business management and administrative services, 5% health professions and related sciences, 4% engineering and applied sciences, 3% psychology, 2% fine arts, 1% agriculture, 1% architecture, 1% biological and life sciences, 1% communications and journalism, 1% computer and information sciences, 1% English language/literature/letters, 1% foreign language and literature, 1% library and information studies, 1% mathematics, 1% philosophy, 1% physical sciences, 1% social sciences. *Most popular recent major:* business administration/commerce/management.

First-Year Class: 1,900 total. Of the students who applied, 100% were accepted.

Graduation Requirements: 60 units; math proficiency; computer course (varies by major).

Computers on Campus: 250 computers available on campus for general student use. Computers for student use in various locations.

EXPENSES

Expenses for 1997–98: State resident tuition: $0 full-time. Nonresident tuition: $4260 full-time, $142 per unit part-time. Part-time mandatory fees per semester range from $32 to $169. Full-time mandatory fees: $442.

LD Program Contact: Ms. Audrey Abas, Learning Disabilities Specialist, Citrus College, 1000 West Foothill Boulevard, Glendora, CA 91741, 818-914-8573. Fax: 818-857-0687.

CITY COLLEGES OF CHICAGO, MALCOLM X COLLEGE

Chicago, Illinois

Students with LD	1	Subject-Area Tutoring	✓
ADD services	✓	Special Courses	✓
Staff	2 part-time	Taped Textbooks	✓
Special Fee	None	Alternative Test Arrang.	✓
Diagnostic Testing		Notetakers	✓
Basic Skills Remediation	✓	LD Student Organization	

LEARNING DISABILITIES PROGRAM INFORMATION

The Special Populations Program began offering services in 1984. Currently the program serves 1 undergraduate with LD. Students diagnosed with ADD/ADHD are eligible for the same services available to students with LD.

Staff: 2 part-time staff members, including coordinator. Services provided by remediation specialists, tutors, counselors.

Special Fees: No special fees are charged for services to students with LD.

Applications and admissions: *Required:* high school transcript, grade point average, courses completed, IEP (Individualized Education Program), untimed or extended time SAT I or ACT, personal interview, letters of recommendation, psychoeducational report completed within 6 to 12 months. Students may begin taking classes any term. *Application deadline:* continuous.

PROGRAM AND SERVICE COMPONENTS

Special preparation or orientation: Required orientation held before registration and during registration.

Academic advising: Provided by academic advisers. Most students with LD take 9 to 12 credit hours each term; 12 credit hours required to maintain full-time status; 3 credit hours required to be eligible for financial aid.

Counseling services: Individual counseling, career counseling.

Basic skills remediation: Offered one-on-one by hired tutors with qualifications in specific areas; computer-aided instruction also offered. Available in reading, math, spelling, learning strategies, study skills, time management.

Subject-area tutoring: Offered one-on-one by peer tutors, hired tutors with qualifications in specific areas. Available in all subjects.

Special courses: Reading, vocabulary development, communication skills. Some offered for credit; some enter into overall grade point average.

Auxiliary aids: Taped textbooks, tape recorders, calculators, typewriters, personal computers, talking computers, optical character readers.

Auxiliary services: Alternative test arrangements, notetakers, priority registration, advocacy.

GENERAL COLLEGE INFORMATION

State and locally supported, 2-year, coed. Part of City Colleges of Chicago System. Awards associate degrees. Founded 1911. *Setting:* 20-acre urban campus. *Endowment:* $400,000. *Educational spending 1995–96:* $2561 per undergrad. *Total enrollment:* 3,480. *Faculty:* 93 (83 full-time, 100% with terminal degrees, 10 part-time); student–undergrad faculty ratio is 33:1.

Enrollment Profile: 3,480 students: 54% men, 69% part-time, 99% state residents, 24% transferred in, 1% international, 41% 25 or older, 1% Native American, 9% Hispanic, 74% black, 6% Asian or Pacific Islander. *Retention:* 80% of 1995 full-time freshmen returned. *Areas of study chosen:* 45% health professions and related sciences, 44% liberal arts/general studies, 9% business management and administrative services, 1% computer and information sciences, 1% education. *Most popular recent majors:* nursing, liberal arts/general studies, radiological technology.

First-Year Class: 1,006 total; 1,500 applied, 100% were accepted, 67% of whom enrolled. 10% from top 10% of their high school class, 25% from top quarter, 35% from top half.

Graduation Requirements: 60 credit hours; 1 course each in biology and algebra; computer course for respiratory therapy, mortuary science majors.

Computers on Campus: 75 computers available on campus for general student use. A campus-wide network can be accessed from off-campus. Students can contact faculty members and/or advisers through e-mail. Computers for student use in computer center, computer labs, learning resource center, library provide access to the Internet/World Wide Web, on- and off-campus e-mail addresses. Staffed computer lab on campus provides training in use of computers, software. *Academic computing expenditure 1995–96:* $304,402.

EXPENSES

Expenses for 1997–98: Area resident tuition: $1350 full-time, $45 per credit hour part-time. State resident tuition: $4289 full-time, $142.98 per credit hour part-time. Nonresident tuition: $6055 full-time, $201.84 per credit hour part-time. Part-time mandatory fees: $25 per semester. Full-time mandatory fees: $50.

LD Program Contact: Ms. Rita Rivers, Special Populations Coordinator, City Colleges of Chicago, Malcolm X College, 1900 West Van Buren Street, Chicago, IL 60612, 312-850-7342. Fax: 312-942-2470.

COLLEGE OF ALAMEDA

Alameda, California

Students with LD	120	Subject-Area Tutoring	✓
ADD services	✓	Special Courses	✓
Staff	1 full-, 2 part-time	Taped Textbooks	✓
Special Fee	None	Alternative Test Arrang.	✓
Diagnostic Testing	✓	Notetakers	✓
Basic Skills Remediation	✓	LD Student Organization	✓

LEARNING DISABILITIES PROGRAM INFORMATION

The Learning Disabilities Program began offering services in 1978. Currently the program serves 120 undergraduates with LD. Students diagnosed with ADD/ADHD are eligible for the same services available to students with LD.

Staff: 1 full-time, 2 part-time staff members, including LD specialists. Services provided by tutors, instructional aides.

Special Fees: No special fees are charged for services to students with LD.

Applications and admissions: *Required:* California Assessment System for Adults with Learning Disabilities. Students may begin taking classes in fall or spring. *Application deadline:* continuous.

PROGRAM AND SERVICE COMPONENTS

Diagnostic testing: Intelligence, reading, math, spelling, spoken language, written language, motor abilities, perceptual skills, study skills, social skills, hearing.

Academic advising: Provided by LD staff members, academic advisers. Students with LD may take up to 14 semester hours each term; most take 12 semester hours; 12 semester hours required to maintain full-time status.

Counseling services: Individual counseling, career counseling.

Basic skills remediation: Offered one-on-one, in small groups, and in class-size groups by LD teachers. Available in reading, math, spelling, written language, learning strategies, perceptual skills, study skills, social skills.

Subject-area tutoring: Offered one-on-one by peer tutors, instructional aides. Available in all subjects.

Special courses: Reading, vocabulary development, communication skills, composition, learning strategies, word processing, math, career planning, memory, concentration, thinking. All offered for credit; none enter into overall grade point average.

Auxiliary aids: Taped textbooks, tape recorders, calculators, typewriters, word-processors with spell-check, personal computers.

Auxiliary services: Alternative test arrangements, notetakers, priority registration.

Campus support group: A special student organization is available to students with LD.

GENERAL COLLEGE INFORMATION

State and locally supported, 2-year, coed. Part of Peralta Community College District System. Awards associate degrees. Founded 1970. *Setting:* 62-acre urban campus with easy access to San Francisco. *Research spending 1995–96:* $37,247. *Educational spending 1995–96:* $953 per undergrad. *Total enrollment:* 5,030. *Faculty:* 166 (80 full-time, 14% with terminal degrees, 86 part-time); student–undergrad faculty ratio is 24:1.

Enrollment Profile: 5,030 students from 18 states and territories, 9 other countries. 56% women, 44% men, 73% part-time, 97% state residents, 11% transferred in, 1% international, 44% 25 or older, 1% Native American, 9% Hispanic, 30% black, 32% Asian or Pacific Islander. *Retention:* 61% of 1995 full-time freshmen returned. *Areas of study chosen:* 10% business management and administrative services, 9% engineering and applied sciences, 6% health professions and related sciences, 4% interdisciplinary studies, 3% computer and information sciences, 3% psychology, 3% social sciences, 3% vocational and home economics, 2% biological and life sciences, 2% fine arts, 2% liberal arts/general studies, 1% architecture, 1% communications and journalism, 1% education, 1% mathematics.

First-Year Class: 1,153 total. Of the students who applied, 100% were accepted, 90% of whom enrolled.

Graduation Requirements: 60 semester hours; 3 semester hours of math; computer course.

Computers on Campus: 20 computers available on campus for general student use. Computers for student use in computer labs.

EXPENSES

Expenses for 1997–98: State resident tuition: $0 full-time. Nonresident tuition: $4050 full-time, $135 per semester hour part-time. Part-time mandatory fees per semester range from $15 to $145. Full-time mandatory fees: $394.

LD Program Contact: Ms. Judy Merrill, Learning Disabilities Specialist, College of Alameda, 555 Atlantic Avenue, Alameda, CA 94501-2109, 510-748-2388. Fax: 510-769-6019.

COLLEGE OF MARIN

Kentfield, California

Students with LD		Subject-Area Tutoring	
ADD services	✓	Special Courses	✓
Staff		Taped Textbooks	
Special Fee	None	Alternative Test Arrang.	✓
Diagnostic Testing	✓	Notetakers	
Basic Skills Remediation	✓	LD Student Organization	✓

LEARNING DISABILITIES PROGRAM INFORMATION

The Study Skills 70-77 began offering services in 1974. Students diagnosed with ADD/ADHD are eligible for the same services available to students with LD.

Staff: Includes coordinator. Services provided by counselors, LD instructors.

Special Fees: No special fees are charged for services to students with LD.

Applications and admissions: *Required:* California Assessment System for Adults with Learning Disabilities. Students may begin taking classes any term. *Application deadline:* continuous.

PROGRAM AND SERVICE COMPONENTS

Special preparation or orientation: Optional summer program offered prior to entering college. Optional orientation offered individually by arrangement.

Diagnostic testing: Intelligence, reading, math, spelling, handwriting, spoken language, written language, motor abilities, perceptual skills, study skills, personality, social skills.

Academic advising: Provided by academic advisers. Students with LD required to take 6 units each term to maintain full-time status; 10 units required to be eligible for financial aid.

Counseling services: Individual counseling, small-group counseling, career counseling.

Basic skills remediation: Offered one-on-one and in small groups by LD teachers. Available in reading, math, spelling, handwriting, spoken language, written language, learning strategies, motor abilities, perceptual skills, study skills, social skills.

Special courses: College survival skills, reading, vocabulary development, communication skills, composition, learning strategies, word processing, math, personal psychology, study skills, career planning. All offered for credit; all enter into overall grade point average.

College of Marin (continued)

Auxiliary services: Alternative test arrangements, advocacy.
Campus support group: A special student organization is available to students with LD.

GENERAL COLLEGE INFORMATION

State and locally supported, 2-year, coed. Part of California Community Colleges System. Awards associate degrees. Founded 1926. *Setting:* 410-acre small-town campus with easy access to San Francisco. *Total enrollment:* 8,845. *Faculty:* 464 (161 full-time, 303 part-time).
Enrollment Profile: 8,845 students: 62% women, 38% men, 77% part-time, 92% state residents, 15% transferred in, 1% international, 50% 25 or older, 1% Native American, 7% Hispanic, 3% black, 8% Asian or Pacific Islander.
First-Year Class: 1,923 total. Of the students who applied, 100% were accepted, 99% of whom enrolled.
Graduation Requirements: 60 units; 4 units of intermediate college algebra or demonstrated proficiency; 3 units of natural science.
Computers on Campus: 25 computers available on campus for general student use. Computers for student use in computer center, computer labs, learning resource center, classrooms provide access to the Internet/World Wide Web. Staffed computer lab on campus provides training in use of computers, software.

EXPENSES

Estimated Expenses for 1997–98: State resident tuition: $0 full-time. Nonresident tuition: $4470 full-time, $149 per unit part-time. Part-time mandatory fees per semester range from $24 to $154. Full-time mandatory fees: $412.
LD Program Contact: Ms. Milo Mayo, Department Secretary, College of Marin, 835 College Avenue, Kentfield, CA 94904, 415-485-9406. Fax: 415-457-4791.

COLLEGE OF SAN MATEO

San Mateo, California

Students with LD	130	Subject-Area Tutoring	✓
ADD services	✓	Special Courses	✓
Staff	1 full-, 2 part-time	Taped Textbooks	✓
Special Fee	None	Alternative Test Arrang.	✓
Diagnostic Testing	✓	Notetakers	✓
Basic Skills Remediation		LD Student Organization	

LEARNING DISABILITIES PROGRAM INFORMATION

The Learning Disabilities Program began offering services in 1978. Currently the program serves 130 undergraduates with LD. Students diagnosed with ADD/ADHD are eligible for the same services available to students with LD.
Staff: 1 full-time, 2 part-time staff members, including coordinator, LD specialist, staff assistant. Services provided by tutors, diagnostic specialists, program assistant, peer tutors.
Special Fees: No special fees are charged for services to students with LD.
Applications and admissions: *Required:* high school transcript, California Assessment System for Adults with Learning Disabilities; *recommended:* high school IEP (Individualized Education Program), psychoeducational report completed within 3 years. Students may begin taking classes in fall, spring, or summer. *Application deadline:* continuous.
Special policies: The college has written policies regarding grade forgiveness.

PROGRAM AND SERVICE COMPONENTS

Diagnostic testing: Intelligence, reading, math, spelling, written language, perceptual skills, learning strategies.
Academic advising: Provided by academic advisers. Students with LD may take up to 15 credits each term; most take 9 credits; 12 credits required to maintain full-time status; 6 credits required to be eligible for financial aid.
Counseling services: Referrals made for psychological, career, and academic counseling.
Subject-area tutoring: Offered one-on-one and in small groups by peer tutors, College Tutoring Center staff. Available in most subjects.
Special courses: Learning strategies, word processing, study skills, adaptive physical education. All offered for credit; all enter into overall grade point average.
Auxiliary aids: Taped textbooks, tape recorders, calculators, word-processors with spell-check, High Tech Center computers.
Auxiliary services: Alternative test arrangements, notetakers, priority registration.

GENERAL COLLEGE INFORMATION

State and locally supported, 2-year, coed. Part of California Community Colleges System. Awards associate degrees. Founded 1922. *Setting:* 150-acre suburban campus. *Total enrollment:* 11,506. *Faculty:* 476 (184 full-time, 292 part-time).
Enrollment Profile: 11,506 students: 51% women, 49% men, 71% part-time, 98% state residents, 21% transferred in, 1% international, 51% 25 or older, 1% Native American, 15% Hispanic, 4% black, 15% Asian or Pacific Islander. *Most popular recent majors:* business administration/commerce/management, computer science, liberal arts/general studies.
First-Year Class: 3,408 total; 3,408 applied, 100% were accepted, 100% of whom enrolled.
Graduation Requirements: 60 semester units; math proficiency; computer course for business, math, science majors.
Computers on Campus: 150 computers available on campus for general student use. A campus-wide network can be accessed from off-campus. Students can contact faculty members and/or advisers through e-mail. Computers for student use in computer center, computer labs, learning resource center, library, student center provide access to the Internet/World Wide Web. Staffed computer lab on campus provides training in use of computers, software.

EXPENSES AND FINANCIAL AID

Expenses for 1997–98: State resident tuition: $0 full-time. Nonresident tuition: $3780 full-time, $126 per unit part-time. Part-time mandatory fees per semester range from $23 to $153. Full-time mandatory fees: $410.
Financial aid specifically for students with LD: Scholarship: The Patty Ramos Scholarship for Students with Learning Disabilities.
LD Program Contact: Ms. Marie Paparelli, Learning Disabilities Specialist, College of San Mateo, 1700 West Hillsdale Boulevard, Building 18-193, San Mateo, CA 94402-3784, 415-574-6433. Fax: 415-574-6680.

COLLEGE OF THE REDWOODS

Eureka, California

Students with LD	360	Subject-Area Tutoring	✓
ADD services	✓	Special Courses	✓
Staff	2 full-, 13 part-time	Taped Textbooks	✓
Special Fee	None	Alternative Test Arrang.	✓

Diagnostic Testing	✓	Notetakers	✓
Basic Skills Remediation	✓	LD Student Organization	

LEARNING DISABILITIES PROGRAM INFORMATION

The CR LIGHT Center began offering services in 1980. Currently the program serves 360 undergraduates with LD. Students diagnosed with ADD/ADHD are eligible for the same services available to students with LD.

Staff: 2 full-time, 13 part-time staff members, including coordinator, LD specialist. Services provided by diagnostic specialists, instructional assistants, computer specialist, office staff.

Special Fees: No special fees are charged for services to students with LD.

Applications and admissions: *Recommended:* high school transcript, grade point average, courses completed. Students may begin taking classes any term. *Application deadline:* continuous.

Special policies: The college has written policies regarding grade forgiveness.

PROGRAM AND SERVICE COMPONENTS

Special preparation or orientation: Optional summer program offered prior to entering college. Required orientation held after classes begin during a Guidance Class.

Diagnostic testing: Intelligence, reading, math, spelling, spoken language, written language, motor abilities, perceptual skills.

Academic advising: Provided by academic advisers. Most students with LD take 12 units each term; 12 units required to maintain full-time status and be eligible for financial aid.

Counseling services: Individual counseling, self-advocacy training.

Basic skills remediation: Offered one-on-one and in small groups by LD teachers, instructional assistants; computer-aided instruction also offered. Available in reading, math, spelling, written language, learning strategies, motor abilities, perceptual skills, study skills, time management, computer skills.

Subject-area tutoring: Offered one-on-one and in small groups by professional teachers, instructional assistants. Available in most subjects.

Special courses: College survival skills, reading, learning strategies, word processing, study skills. Some offered for credit; none enter into overall grade point average.

Auxiliary aids: Taped textbooks, tape recorders, calculators, word-processors with spell-check, personal computers, talking computers, optical character readers.

Auxiliary services: Alternative test arrangements, notetakers, priority registration.

GENERAL COLLEGE INFORMATION

State and locally supported, 2-year, coed. Part of California Community Colleges System. Awards associate degrees. Founded 1964. *Setting:* 322-acre small-town campus. *Endowment:* $629,806. *Total enrollment:* 6,968. *Faculty:* 376 (116 full-time, 260 part-time).

Enrollment Profile: 6,968 students from 52 states and territories, 32 other countries. 57% women, 43% men, 67% part-time, 96% state residents, 2% live on campus, 12% transferred in, 1% international, 52% 25 or older, 6% Native American, 6% Hispanic, 1% black, 3% Asian or Pacific Islander. *Most popular recent majors:* business administration/commerce/management, nursing.

First-Year Class: 1,384 total. Of the students who applied, 100% were accepted.

Graduation Requirements: 60 units; 3 units each of math and biological/physical science; computer course (varies by major).

Computers on Campus: 387 computers available on campus for general student use. Computers for student use in computer labs, learning resource center, classrooms, dorms. Staffed computer lab on campus.

EXPENSES

Expenses for 1997–98: State resident tuition: $0 full-time. Nonresident tuition: $3840 full-time, $128 per unit part-time. Part-time mandatory fees per semester range from $23 to $153. Full-time mandatory fees: $410. College room and board: $4971.

LD Program Contact: Ms. Sonja Roseth, Lead Learning Disabilities Specialist, College of the Redwoods, 7351 Tompkins Hill Road, Eureka, CA 95501-9300, 707-445-6812. Fax: 707-445-6990.

COLLIN COUNTY COMMUNITY COLLEGE

McKinney, Texas

Students with LD	108	Subject-Area Tutoring	✓
ADD services	✓	Special Courses	
Staff	4 full-time	Taped Textbooks	
Special Fee	None	Alternative Test Arrang.	✓
Diagnostic Testing	✓	Notetakers	✓
Basic Skills Remediation		LD Student Organization	

LEARNING DISABILITIES PROGRAM INFORMATION

The ACCESS began offering services in 1988. Currently the program serves 108 undergraduates with LD. Students diagnosed with ADD/ADHD are eligible for the same services available to students with LD, as well as screenings.

Staff: 4 full-time staff members, including coordinator, disabilities adviser, LD specialist/adviser. Services provided by remediation specialists, tutors, diagnostic specialist, tutor coordinator.

Special Fees: No special fees are charged for services to students with LD.

Applications and admissions: *Required:* psychoeducational report completed within 3 years. Students may begin taking classes any term. *Application deadline:* continuous.

PROGRAM AND SERVICE COMPONENTS

Diagnostic testing: Intelligence, reading, math, written language, learning strategies.

Academic advising: Provided by LD staff members, academic advisers. Students with LD may take up to 18 credits (without special permission) each term; most take 6 to 12 credits; 12 credits (fewer with special permission) required to maintain full-time status; 12 credits required to be eligible for financial aid.

Subject-area tutoring: Offered one-on-one by professional teachers, peer tutors. Available in all subjects.

Auxiliary aids: Calculators, word-processors with spell-check, optical character readers.

Auxiliary services: Alternative test arrangements, notetakers, advocacy, scribes, readers.

GENERAL COLLEGE INFORMATION

State and locally supported, 2-year, coed. Part of Texas Higher Education Coordinating Board. Awards associate degrees. Founded 1985. *Setting:* 100-acre suburban campus with easy access to Dallas–Fort Worth. *Total enrollment:* 10,580. *Faculty:* 613 (123 full-time, 92% with terminal degrees, 490 part-time); student–undergrad faculty ratio is 25:1.

Enrollment Profile: 10,580 students from 21 states and territories, 46 other countries. 56% women, 44% men, 69% part-time, 95% state residents, 15% transferred in, 1% international, 54% 25 or older, 1% Native American, 6% Hispanic, 4% black, 5% Asian

Collin County Community College (continued)

or Pacific Islander. *Areas of study chosen:* 31% interdisciplinary studies, 22% vocational and home economics. *Most popular recent majors:* liberal arts/general studies, nursing, data processing.
First-Year Class: 2,049 total; 2,157 applied, 100% were accepted, 95% of whom enrolled.
Graduation Requirements: 60 credit hours; math/science requirements vary according to program; computer course.
Computers on Campus: 1,000 computers available on campus for general student use. A campus-wide network can be accessed from off-campus. Computers for student use in computer center, computer labs, learning resource center, classrooms, library, student center provide access to the Internet/World Wide Web. Staffed computer lab on campus provides training in use of computers, software.

EXPENSES AND FINANCIAL AID

Expenses for 1996–97: Area resident tuition: $435 full-time. State resident tuition: $645 full-time. Nonresident tuition: $1695 full-time. Part-time tuition per credit hour ranges from $25 to $159.50 for area residents, $25 to $236.50 for state residents, $200 to $621.50 for nonresidents. Part-time mandatory fees per semester range from $11.50 to $106.50. Full-time mandatory fees: $289.
Financial aid specifically for students with LD: Scholarship: Jacqueline Dooley Memorial Scholarship.
LD Program Contact: Ms. Marjorie Ramsey, Learning Disabilities Specialist, Collin County Community College, 2800 East Spring Creek Parkway, Plano, TX 75074, 972-881-5109. Fax: 972-881-5619.

COMMUNITY COLLEGE OF ALLEGHENY COUNTY

Pittsburgh, Pennsylvania

Students with LD	250	Subject-Area Tutoring	✓
ADD services	✓	Special Courses	✓
Staff	4 full-, 2 part-time	Taped Textbooks	✓
Special Fee	None	Alternative Test Arrang.	✓
Diagnostic Testing		Notetakers	✓
Basic Skills Remediation	✓	LD Student Organization	✓

LEARNING DISABILITIES PROGRAM INFORMATION

The Special Services for Disabled Students began offering services in 1979. Currently the program serves 250 undergraduates with LD. Students diagnosed with ADD/ADHD are eligible for the same services available to students with LD.
Staff: 4 full-time, 2 part-time staff members, including director, assistant director, coordinator, administrative assistant. Services provided by tutors, computer instructor.
Special Fees: No special fees are charged for services to students with LD.
Applications and admissions: *Required:* high school transcript, psychoeducational report completed within 3 years, college placement test. Students may begin taking classes in fall or winter. *Application deadline:* continuous.
Special policies: The college has written policies regarding grade forgiveness.

PROGRAM AND SERVICE COMPONENTS

Special preparation or orientation: Optional summer program offered prior to entering college.
Academic advising: Provided by LD staff members, academic advisers. Students with LD may take up to 16 credits each term; most take 12 credits; 12 credits required to maintain full-time status; no minimum number of credits required to be eligible for financial aid.
Counseling services: Individual counseling, career counseling.
Basic skills remediation: Offered in class-size groups by regular teachers. Available in reading, math, written language, learning strategies, study skills, time management.
Subject-area tutoring: Offered one-on-one and in small groups by professional teachers, peer tutors. Available in some subjects.
Special courses: College survival skills, reading, composition, learning strategies, word processing, time management, math, study skills. All offered for credit; all enter into overall grade point average.
Auxiliary aids: Taped textbooks, tape recorders, calculators, typewriters, word-processors with spell-check.
Auxiliary services: Alternative test arrangements, notetakers, priority registration, advocacy.
Campus support group: A special student organization is available to students with LD.

GENERAL COLLEGE INFORMATION

County-supported, 2-year, coed. Awards associate degrees. Founded 1966. *Setting:* 242-acre urban campus. *Endowment:* $264,000. *Total enrollment:* 16,984. *Faculty:* 3,436 (315 full-time, 83% with terminal degrees, 3,121 part-time); student–undergrad faculty ratio is 5:1.
Enrollment Profile: 16,984 students: 59% women, 41% men, 59% part-time, 95% state residents, 9% transferred in, 1% international, 40% 25 or older, 1% Native American, 1% Hispanic, 14% black, 1% Asian or Pacific Islander. *Retention:* 55% of 1995 full-time freshmen returned. *Areas of study chosen:* 24% liberal arts/general studies, 22% health professions and related sciences, 20% business management and administrative services, 5% computer and information sciences, 5% education, 5% engineering and applied sciences, 5% social sciences, 5% vocational and home economics, 1% agriculture, 1% biological and life sciences, 1% communications and journalism, 1% English language/literature/letters, 1% fine arts, 1% mathematics, 1% performing arts, 1% physical sciences, 1% psychology. *Most popular recent majors:* liberal arts/general studies, business administration/commerce/management.
First-Year Class: Of the students who applied, 94% were accepted, 54% of whom enrolled.
Graduation Requirements: 60 credits.
Computers on Campus: 1,625 computers available on campus for general student use. A campus-wide network can be accessed. Students can contact faculty members and/or advisers through e-mail. Computers for student use in computer center, computer labs, learning resource center, classrooms, library, departmental labs. Staffed computer lab on campus provides training in use of computers, software. *Academic computing expenditure 1995–96:* $3.5 million.

EXPENSES

Estimated Expenses for 1997–98: Area resident tuition: $2040 full-time, $68 per credit part-time. State resident tuition: $4080 full-time, $136 per credit part-time. Nonresident tuition: $6120 full-time, $204 per credit part-time. Part-time mandatory fees per semester range from $52.40 to $72.40. Full-time mandatory fees: $161.
LD Program Contact: Ms. Lisa Antoun, Learning Disabilities Coordinator, Community College of Allegheny County, 808 Ridge Avenue, Pittsburgh, PA 15233, 412-237-4612. Fax: 412-237-4678.

COMMUNITY COLLEGE OF DENVER

Denver, Colorado

Students with LD	250	Subject-Area Tutoring	✓
ADD services	✓	Special Courses	✓
Staff	1 full-, 5 part-time	Taped Textbooks	✓
Special Fee	✓	Alternative Test Arrang.	✓
Diagnostic Testing	✓	Notetakers	✓
Basic Skills Remediation	✓	LD Student Organization	✓

LEARNING DISABILITIES PROGRAM INFORMATION

The Special Learning Support Program began offering services in 1981. Currently the program serves 250 undergraduates with LD. Services are also available to graduate students. Students diagnosed with ADD/ADHD are eligible for the same services available to students with LD.
Staff: 1 full-time, 5 part-time staff members, including coordinator, career guidance and placement specialist. Services provided by remediation specialists, tutors, counselor, diagnostic specialist, administrative assistant.
Special Fees: $49.50 per year.
Applications and admissions: *Required:* psychoeducational report completed within 3 years. Students may begin taking classes any term. *Application deadline:* continuous.
Special policies: The college has written policies regarding substitutions and waivers of degree requirements.

PROGRAM AND SERVICE COMPONENTS

Special preparation or orientation: Optional summer program offered prior to entering college.
Diagnostic testing: Reading, math, spelling, written language.
Academic advising: Provided by LD staff members, academic advisers. Most students with LD take 12 credit hours each term; 12 credit hours required to maintain full-time status; 6 credit hours (part-time), 12 credit hours (full-time) required to be eligible for financial aid.
Counseling services: Individual counseling, small-group counseling, career counseling, self-advocacy training.
Basic skills remediation: Offered in small groups by LD teachers. Available in reading, math, spelling, written language, learning strategies, study skills, time management, computer skills.
Subject-area tutoring: Offered one-on-one, in small groups, and in class-size groups by professional teachers, peer tutors. Available in most subjects.
Special courses: Reading, learning strategies, math, study skills, spelling strategies. None offered for credit; all enter into overall grade point average.
Auxiliary aids: Taped textbooks, tape recorders, calculators, typewriters, word-processors with spell-check, personal computers, talking computers.
Auxiliary services: Alternative test arrangements, notetakers, priority registration, advocacy.
Campus support group: A special student organization is available to students with LD.

GENERAL COLLEGE INFORMATION

State-supported, 2-year, coed. Awards associate degrees. Founded 1970. *Setting:* urban campus. *Total enrollment:* 11,897. *Faculty:* 596 (96 full-time, 500 part-time); student–undergrad faculty ratio is 25:1.
Enrollment Profile: 11,897 students from 3 states and territories, 42 other countries. 58% women, 42% men, 68% part-time, 95% state residents, 8% transferred in, 3% international, 51% 25 or older, 2% Native American, 24% Hispanic, 12% black, 5% Asian or Pacific Islander. *Most popular recent majors:* liberal arts/general studies, business administration/commerce/management, nursing.
First-Year Class: 5,405 total. Of the students who applied, 100% were accepted.
Graduation Requirements: 60 credit hours; math/science requirements vary according to program.
Computers on Campus: 250 computers available on campus for general student use. A campus-wide network can be accessed from off-campus. Computers for student use in computer labs, media lab. Staffed computer lab on campus provides training in use of computers, software.

EXPENSES

Expenses for 1997–98: State resident tuition: $1629 full-time, $54.30 per credit hour part-time. Nonresident tuition: $7568 full-time, $252.25 per credit hour part-time. Part-time mandatory fees per semester range from $36.20 to $141.20. Full-time mandatory fees: $315.
LD Program Contact: Ms. Sharon Walton-Hunt, Coordinator, Special Learning Support Program, Community College of Denver, Campus Box 600, PO Box 173363, Denver, CO 80217-3363, 303-556-3406. Fax: 303-556-4705.

CONTRA COSTA COLLEGE

San Pablo, California

Students with LD	178	Subject-Area Tutoring	✓
ADD services	✓	Special Courses	✓
Staff	4 full-, 12 part-time	Taped Textbooks	✓
Special Fee	None	Alternative Test Arrang.	✓
Diagnostic Testing	✓	Notetakers	✓
Basic Skills Remediation	✓	LD Student Organization	

LEARNING DISABILITIES PROGRAM INFORMATION

The Learning Specialist Program began offering services in 1979. Currently the program serves 178 undergraduates with LD. Students diagnosed with ADD/ADHD are eligible for the same services available to students with LD.
Staff: 4 full-time, 12 part-time staff members, including director, instructors, office assistants. Services provided by tutors, counselors, diagnostic specialists.
Special Fees: No special fees are charged for services to students with LD.
Applications and admissions: Students may begin taking classes in fall, spring, or summer. *Application deadline:* continuous.
Special policies: The college has written policies regarding grade forgiveness; substitutions and waivers of graduation and degree requirements.

PROGRAM AND SERVICE COMPONENTS

Special preparation or orientation: Optional orientation offered before registration, during registration, after classes begin.
Diagnostic testing: Intelligence, reading, math, spelling, spoken language, written language, perceptual skills, study skills, psychoneurology, speech, hearing, learning strategies.
Academic advising: Provided by LD staff members. Students with LD may take up to 22 units each term; most take 9 to 12 units; 9 units required to maintain full-time status; 12 units required to be eligible for financial aid.
Counseling services: Individual counseling, career counseling, self-advocacy training.
Basic skills remediation: Offered in class-size groups by LD teachers. Available in reading, math, spelling, written language, learning strategies, perceptual skills, speech.

Contra Costa College (continued)

Subject-area tutoring: Offered one-on-one and in small groups by professional teachers, peer tutors. Available in all subjects.
Special courses: College survival skills, reading, vocabulary development, composition, learning strategies, word processing, math, study skills. All offered for credit; all enter into overall grade point average.
Auxiliary aids: Taped textbooks, tape recorders, calculators, word-processors with spell-check, personal computers, optical character readers.
Auxiliary services: Alternative test arrangements, notetakers, priority registration, advocacy.

GENERAL COLLEGE INFORMATION

State and locally supported, 2-year, coed. Part of Contra Costa Community College District System. Awards associate degrees. Founded 1948. *Setting:* 83-acre small-town campus with easy access to San Francisco. *Total enrollment:* 3,000. *Faculty:* 222 (117 full-time, 105 part-time).
Enrollment Profile: 3,000 students from 5 states and territories, 16 other countries. 62% women, 38% men, 79% part-time, 98% state residents, 11% transferred in, 54% 25 or older, 1% Native American, 16% Hispanic, 28% black, 14% Asian or Pacific Islander. *Most popular recent majors:* nursing, liberal arts/general studies, business administration/commerce/management.
First-Year Class: 1,650 total. Of the students who applied, 100% were accepted, 90% of whom enrolled.
Graduation Requirements: 60 units; 3 units of math; 6 units of science; computer course.
Computers on Campus: 180 computers available on campus for general student use. Staffed computer lab on campus.

EXPENSES

Expenses for 1997–98: State resident tuition: $0 full-time. Nonresident tuition: $3750 full-time, $125 per unit part-time. Part-time mandatory fees: $13 per unit. Full-time mandatory fees: $390.
LD Program Contact: Ms. Alyssa Scanlin, Learning Disability Specialist, Contra Costa College, 2600 Mission Bell Drive, San Pablo, CA 94806-3195, 510-235-7800. Fax: 510-236-6768.

COUNTY COLLEGE OF MORRIS

Randolph, New Jersey

Students with LD	500	Subject-Area Tutoring	✓
ADD services	✓	Special Courses	✓
Staff	3 full-, 16 part-time	Taped Textbooks	✓
Special Fee	None	Alternative Test Arrang.	✓
Diagnostic Testing		Notetakers	
Basic Skills Remediation	✓	LD Student Organization	

LEARNING DISABILITIES PROGRAM INFORMATION

The Horizons began offering services in 1989. Currently the program serves 500 undergraduates with LD. Students diagnosed with ADD/ADHD are eligible for the same services available to students with LD, as well as academic adjustments (arranged through the Counseling Services Office).
Staff: 3 full-time, 16 part-time staff members, including coordinator. Services provided by tutors, diagnostic specialists.
Special Fees: No special fees are charged for services to students with LD.
Applications and admissions: *Required:* high school transcript, letters of recommendation, psychoeducational report completed within 3 years, IEP (if exempt from all or part of HSPT), attendance at information meeting, neurological or psychiatric evaluation (if applicable). Students may begin taking classes in fall or spring. *Application deadline:* 4/1 (fall term), 6/1 (spring term).

PROGRAM AND SERVICE COMPONENTS

Special preparation or orientation: Orientation (required for some) held the week before classes begin.
Academic advising: Provided by LD staff members. Students with LD may take up to 18 credits (more with dean's permission) each term; most take 12 credits; 12 credits required to maintain full-time status; source of aid determines number of credits required to be eligible for financial aid.
Counseling services: Individual counseling, small-group counseling, career counseling, self-advocacy training.
Basic skills remediation: Offered in small groups by regular teachers. Available in reading, math, spelling, written language, learning strategies, study skills, time management.
Subject-area tutoring: Offered in small groups by professional teachers. Available in some subjects.
Special courses: Learning strategies. Some offered for credit; all enter into overall grade point average.
Auxiliary aids: Taped textbooks, tape recorders, calculators, word-processors with spell-check, optical character readers.
Auxiliary services: Alternative test arrangements, advocacy.

GENERAL COLLEGE INFORMATION

County-supported, 2-year, coed. Part of New Jersey Commission on Higher Education. Awards associate degrees. Founded 1966. *Setting:* 218-acre rural campus with easy access to New York City. *Total enrollment:* 8,910. *Faculty:* 517 (192 full-time, 27% with terminal degrees, 325 part-time); student–undergrad faculty ratio is 21:1.
Enrollment Profile: 8,910 students: 53% women, 47% men, 55% part-time, 99% state residents, 2% transferred in, 1% international, 41% 25 or older, 1% Native American, 8% Hispanic, 4% black, 6% Asian or Pacific Islander. *Retention:* 59% of 1995 full-time freshmen returned. *Areas of study chosen:* 23% liberal arts/general studies, 17% business management and administrative services, 7% health professions and related sciences, 4% computer and information sciences, 3% biological and life sciences, 3% engineering and applied sciences, 2% communications and journalism, 1% agriculture, 1% fine arts, 1% mathematics, 1% performing arts, 1% physical sciences. *Most popular recent majors:* liberal arts/general studies, business administration/commerce/management, nursing.
First-Year Class: 2,927 total; 4,173 applied, 100% were accepted, 70% of whom enrolled.
Graduation Requirements: 62 credits; 6 credits of math/science; computer course for electronic engineering technology, business telecommunications majors; internship (some majors).
Computers on Campus: 41 computers available on campus for general student use. A campus-wide network can be accessed from off-campus. Students can contact faculty members and/or advisers through e-mail. Computers for student use in library. Staffed computer lab on campus provides training in use of computers, software.

EXPENSES

Expenses for 1997–98: *Application fee:* $25. Area resident tuition: $2077 full-time, $67 per credit part-time. State resident tuition: $4154 full-time, $134 per credit part-time. Nonresident tuition: $5704 full-time, $184 per credit part-time. Part-time mandatory fees: $10 per credit. Full-time mandatory fees: $310.
LD Program Contact: Coordinator, Horizons, County College of Morris, 214 Center Grove Road, Randolph, NJ 07869-2086, 201-328-5284.

CRAFTON HILLS COLLEGE

Yucaipa, California

Students with LD	100	Subject-Area Tutoring	✓
ADD services	✓	Special Courses	✓
Staff	4 full-time	Taped Textbooks	✓
Special Fee	None	Alternative Test Arrang.	✓
Diagnostic Testing	✓	Notetakers	✓
Basic Skills Remediation	✓	LD Student Organization	

LEARNING DISABILITIES PROGRAM INFORMATION

The Program for the Learning Disabled Student began offering services in 1981. Currently the program serves 100 undergraduates with LD. Students diagnosed with ADD/ADHD are eligible for the same services available to students with LD.

Staff: 4 full-time staff members, including coordinator, LD specialist. Services provided by tutors, LD paraprofessional.

Special Fees: No special fees are charged for services to students with LD.

Applications and admissions: *Recommended:* psychoeducational report completed within 3 years, Department of Rehabilitation plan (if applicable). Students may begin taking classes in fall, winter, or spring. *Application deadline:* continuous.

PROGRAM AND SERVICE COMPONENTS

Special preparation or orientation: Required orientation held before registration.

Diagnostic testing: Intelligence, reading, math, spelling, written language, perceptual skills, social skills.

Academic advising: Provided by LD staff members. Students with LD may take up to 12 credits each term; most take 9 or fewer credits; 12 credits required to maintain full-time status; 6 credits required to be eligible for financial aid.

Counseling services: Individual counseling.

Basic skills remediation: Offered one-on-one and in small groups by LD teachers. Available in reading, math, spelling, learning strategies, study skills.

Subject-area tutoring: Offered one-on-one and in small groups by professional teachers, peer tutors. Available in most subjects.

Special courses: Reading, math. Most offered for credit; most enter into overall grade point average.

Auxiliary aids: Taped textbooks, tape recorders, calculators, typewriters, word-processors with spell-check.

Auxiliary services: Alternative test arrangements, notetakers, priority registration, advocacy.

GENERAL COLLEGE INFORMATION

State and locally supported, 2-year, coed. Part of California Community Colleges System. Awards associate degrees. Founded 1972. *Setting:* 526-acre small-town campus with easy access to Los Angeles. *Total enrollment:* 5,103. *Faculty:* 184 (64 full-time, 14% with terminal degrees, 120 part-time); student–undergrad faculty ratio is 35:1.

Enrollment Profile: 5,103 students from 19 states and territories, 12 other countries. 55% women, 45% men, 71% part-time, 95% state residents, 15% transferred in, 1% international, 47% 25 or older, 1% Native American, 17% Hispanic, 4% black, 1% Asian or Pacific Islander. *Most popular recent major:* liberal arts/general studies.

First-Year Class: 2,013 total; 2,881 applied, 100% were accepted, 70% of whom enrolled.

Graduation Requirements: 60 credits; 1 course each in math and science.

Computers on Campus: 52 computers available on campus for general student use. A campus-wide network can be accessed from off-campus. Students can contact faculty members and/or advisers through e-mail. Computers for student use in computer center, computer labs, learning resource center, classrooms. Staffed computer lab on campus.

EXPENSES

Expenses for 1997–98: State resident tuition: $0 full-time. Nonresident tuition: $3540 full-time, $118 per unit part-time. Part-time mandatory fees per semester range from $25 to $165. Full-time mandatory fees: $442.

LD Program Contact: Mrs. Kirsten S. Colvey, Learning Disabilities Specialist, Crafton Hills College, 11711 Sand Canyon Road, Yucaipa, CA 92399-1799, 909-389-3325. Fax: 909-794-3684.

CUESTA COLLEGE

San Luis Obispo, California

Students with LD	342	Subject-Area Tutoring	✓
ADD services	✓	Special Courses	✓
Staff	6 full-, 7 part-time	Taped Textbooks	✓
Special Fee	None	Alternative Test Arrang.	✓
Diagnostic Testing	✓	Notetakers	✓
Basic Skills Remediation	✓	LD Student Organization	

LEARNING DISABILITIES PROGRAM INFORMATION

The Disabled Student Programs and Services (DSPS) began offering services in 1973. Currently the program serves 342 undergraduates with LD. Students diagnosed with ADD/ADHD are eligible for the same services available to students with LD.

Staff: 6 full-time, 7 part-time staff members, including director, LD specialists. Services provided by remediation specialists, tutors, counselor, diagnostic specialists, teaching assistants, support services coordinator, student assistants, volunteers.

Special Fees: No special fees are charged for services to students with LD.

Applications and admissions: *Required:* psychoeducational report completed within 3 years, Assessment and Eligibility Process for California Community Colleges; *recommended:* high school IEP (Individualized Education Program). Students may begin taking classes in fall, spring, or summer. *Application deadline:* continuous.

Special policies: The college has written policies regarding substitutions and waivers of graduation and degree requirements.

PROGRAM AND SERVICE COMPONENTS

Special preparation or orientation: Optional orientation offered before classes begin.

Diagnostic testing: Intelligence, reading, math, spelling, written language, perceptual skills.

Academic advising: Provided by LD staff members, academic advisers. Most students with LD take 9 to 12 units each term; 12 units required to maintain full-time status; 6 to 12 units required to be eligible for financial aid.

Counseling services: Individual counseling, career counseling, self-advocacy training, LD support group.

Basic skills remediation: Offered one-on-one, in small groups, and in class-size groups by LD teachers, regular teachers, instructional aides; computer-aided instruction also offered. Available in reading, math, spelling, written language, learning strategies, perceptual skills, study skills, time management, social skills, computer skills.

Subject-area tutoring: Offered one-on-one and in small groups by professional teachers, peer tutors, paraprofessional aides. Available in most subjects.

Special courses: College survival skills, reading, vocabulary development, composition, learning strategies, word processing, time management, math, typing, study skills, career planning, Introduction to Learning Disabilities. Some enter into overall grade point average.
Auxiliary aids: Taped textbooks, tape recorders, calculators, typewriters, word-processors with spell-check, personal computers, optical character readers, spell checkers (hand-held).
Auxiliary services: Alternative test arrangements, notetakers, priority registration.

GENERAL COLLEGE INFORMATION

District-supported, 2-year, coed. Part of California Community Colleges System. Awards associate degrees. Founded 1964. *Setting:* 129-acre rural campus. *Research spending 1995–96:* $40,102. *Educational spending 1995–96:* $1303 per undergrad. *Total enrollment:* 8,126. *Faculty:* 309 (106 full-time, 203 part-time).
Enrollment Profile: 8,126 students: 54% women, 46% men, 56% part-time, 98% state residents, 15% transferred in, 1% international, 33% 25 or older, 1% Native American, 13% Hispanic, 2% black, 43% Asian or Pacific Islander. *Most popular recent majors:* liberal arts/general studies, nursing, business administration/commerce/management.
First-Year Class: 1,632 total. Of the students who applied, 100% were accepted, 40% of whom enrolled.
Graduation Requirements: 60 units; math proficiency; 1 course of biological/physical science; computer course (varies by major).
Computers on Campus: 400 computers available on campus for general student use. Computer purchase/lease plans available. A computer is recommended for all students. A campus-wide network can be accessed from off-campus. Computers for student use in computer center, computer labs, learning resource center, classrooms, library provide access to the Internet/World Wide Web. Staffed computer lab on campus. *Academic computing expenditure 1995–96:* $217,887.

EXPENSES

Expenses for 1997–98: State resident tuition: $0 full-time. Nonresident tuition: $3540 full-time, $118 per unit part-time. Part-time mandatory fees per semester range from $24 to $163. Full-time mandatory fees: $430.
LD Program Contact: Dr. Lynn Frady, Director, Disabled Student Programs and Services (DSPS), Cuesta College, PO Box 8106, San Luis Obispo, CA 93403-8106, 805-546-3148. Fax: 805-546-3930. Email: lfrady@bass.cuesta.cc.ca.us.

CUMBERLAND COUNTY COLLEGE

Vineland, New Jersey

Students with LD	80	Subject-Area Tutoring	✓
ADD services	✓	Special Courses	✓
Staff	1 full-, 6 part-time	Taped Textbooks	✓
Special Fee	None	Alternative Test Arrang.	✓
Diagnostic Testing	✓	Notetakers	✓
Basic Skills Remediation	✓	LD Student Organization	✓

LEARNING DISABILITIES PROGRAM INFORMATION

The Project Assist began offering services in 1987. Currently the program serves 80 undergraduates with LD. Students diagnosed with ADD/ADHD are eligible for the same services available to students with LD.
Staff: 1 full-time, 6 part-time staff members, including director. Services provided by remediation specialists, tutors, counselors, diagnostic specialists.
Special Fees: No special fees are charged for services to students with LD.
Applications and admissions: *Required:* high school courses completed, personal interview, psychoeducational report completed within 2 years; *recommended:* high school transcript. Students may begin taking classes any term. *Application deadline:* continuous.

PROGRAM AND SERVICE COMPONENTS

Special preparation or orientation: Orientation (required for some) held before registration.
Diagnostic testing: Intelligence, reading, math, spelling, handwriting, spoken language, written language, motor abilities, perceptual skills, study skills, learning strategies.
Academic advising: Provided by LD staff members, academic advisers. Students with LD may take up to 12 credits each term; most take 9 credits; 12 credits required to maintain full-time status; 6 to 12 credits required to be eligible for financial aid.
Counseling services: Individual counseling, small-group counseling, career counseling, self-advocacy training.
Basic skills remediation: Offered in class-size groups by LD teachers, regular teachers; computer-aided instruction also offered. Available in reading, math, spelling, handwriting, spoken language, written language, learning strategies, perceptual skills, study skills, time management, social skills, speech.
Subject-area tutoring: Offered one-on-one by professional teachers, peer tutors. Available in all subjects.
Special courses: Learning strategies. All offered for credit; all enter into overall grade point average.
Auxiliary aids: Taped textbooks, tape recorders, calculators, typewriters, word-processors with spell-check, personal computers, talking computers, optical character readers, Language Master 4000.
Auxiliary services: Alternative test arrangements, notetakers, priority registration, advocacy.
Campus support group: A special student organization is available to students with LD.

GENERAL COLLEGE INFORMATION

State and locally supported, 2-year, coed. Part of New Jersey Commission on Higher Education. Awards associate degrees. Founded 1963. *Setting:* 100-acre small-town campus with easy access to Philadelphia. *Total enrollment:* 2,460. *Faculty:* 118 (41 full-time, 77 part-time).
Enrollment Profile: 2,460 students: 64% women, 36% men, 58% part-time, 99% state residents, 3% transferred in, 1% international, 50% 25 or older, 1% Native American, 9% Hispanic, 11% black, 1% Asian or Pacific Islander. *Most popular recent majors:* liberal arts/general studies, nursing.
First-Year Class: 650 total. Of the students who applied, 100% were accepted, 62% of whom enrolled.
Graduation Requirements: 64 credits; math proficiency or 1 math course; 1 science course; computer course.
Computers on Campus: 115 computers available on campus for general student use. Computers for student use in computer center. Staffed computer lab on campus provides training in use of computers, software.

EXPENSES

Expenses for 1997–98: *Application fee:* $15. Area resident tuition: $2248 full-time, $70.25 per credit part-time. State resident tuition: $4496 full-time, $140.50 per credit part-time. Nonresident tuition: $8992 full-time, $281 per credit part-time. Part-time mandatory fees: $14 per credit. Full-time mandatory fees: $448.
LD Program Contact: Ms. Heidi McGarvey, Director of Project Assist, Cumberland County College, PO Box 517, College Drive, Vineland, NJ 08360, 609-691-8600 Ext. 282. Fax: 609-691-6157.

DE ANZA COLLEGE
Cupertino, California

Students with LD	500	Subject-Area Tutoring	✓
ADD services	✓	Special Courses	✓
Staff	5 full-, 2 part-time	Taped Textbooks	✓
Special Fee	None	Alternative Test Arrang.	✓
Diagnostic Testing	✓	Notetakers	
Basic Skills Remediation	✓	LD Student Organization	✓

LEARNING DISABILITIES PROGRAM INFORMATION

The Educational Diagnostic Center (EDC) began offering services in 1973. Currently the program serves 500 undergraduates with LD. Students diagnosed with ADD/ADHD are eligible for the same services available to students with LD.
Staff: 5 full-time, 2 part-time staff members, including director. Services provided by remediation specialists, tutors, counselors, diagnostic specialists.
Special Fees: No special fees are charged for services to students with LD.
Applications and admissions: *Recommended:* high school transcript, IEP (Individualized Education Program). Students may begin taking classes any term. *Application deadline:* continuous.
Special policies: The college has written policies regarding substitutions and waivers of graduation requirements.

PROGRAM AND SERVICE COMPONENTS

Special preparation or orientation: Optional summer program offered prior to entering college. Optional orientation offered before registration and after classes begin.
Diagnostic testing: Reading, math, spelling, written language, perceptual skills.
Academic advising: Provided by LD staff members, academic advisers. Students with LD may take up to 12 units each term; most take 9 to 12 units; 12 units required to maintain full-time status; 12 units for full-time assistance required to be eligible for financial aid.
Counseling services: Individual counseling, career counseling, self-advocacy training.
Basic skills remediation: Offered one-on-one, in small groups, and in class-size groups by LD teachers. Available in reading, math, spelling, written language, learning strategies, study skills, computer skills.
Subject-area tutoring: Offered one-on-one and in small groups by part-time professionals. Available in some subjects.
Special courses: College survival skills, reading, vocabulary development, composition, learning strategies, word processing, Internet use, math, study skills, career planning, assistive technology. All offered for credit; some enter into overall grade point average.
Auxiliary aids: Taped textbooks, tape recorders, word-processors with spell-check, talking computers, optical character readers.
Auxiliary services: Alternative test arrangements, priority registration.
Campus support group: A special student organization is available to students with LD.

GENERAL COLLEGE INFORMATION

State and locally supported, 2-year, coed. Part of California Community Colleges System. Awards associate degrees. Founded 1967. *Setting:* 112-acre small-town campus with easy access to San Francisco and San Jose. *Total enrollment:* 24,721. *Faculty:* 945 (345 full-time, 600 part-time).
Enrollment Profile: 24,721 students from 48 states and territories, 79 other countries. 54% women, 46% men, 70% part-time, 93% state residents, 28% transferred in, 1% international, 52% 25 or older, 1% Native American, 12% Hispanic, 4% black, 35% Asian or Pacific Islander. *Retention:* 32% of 1995 full-time freshmen returned.
First-Year Class: 8,742 total; 9,800 applied, 89% were accepted, 100% of whom enrolled.
Graduation Requirements: 90 units; 1 course each in elementary algebra and science; computer course.
Computers on Campus: 800 computers available on campus for general student use. Computer purchase/lease plans available. A campus-wide network can be accessed from off-campus. Students can contact faculty members and/or advisers through e-mail. Computers for student use in computer center, computer labs, library. Staffed computer lab on campus provides training in use of computers, software.

EXPENSES AND FINANCIAL AID

Expenses for 1997–98: *Application fee:* $22. State resident tuition: $0 full-time. Nonresident tuition: $3645 full-time, $81 per unit part-time. Part-time mandatory fees per quarter range from $32 to $122. Tuition for international students: $3870 full-time, $86 per unit part-time. Full-time mandatory fees: $474.
Financial aid specifically for students with LD: Scholarships: Seth Stauffer Memorial Scholarship, Barbara Mariques Memorial Scholarship.
LD Program Contact: Ms. Pauline Waathiq, Director/Learning Disabilities Specialist, De Anza College, 21250 Stevens Creek, Cupertino, CA 95014-5793, 408-996-4838. Fax: 408-864-5492. Email: pew2305@mercury.fhda.edu.

DELAWARE COUNTY COMMUNITY COLLEGE
Media, Pennsylvania

Students with LD	175	Subject-Area Tutoring	✓
ADD services	✓	Special Courses	✓
Staff	1 full-, 1 part-time	Taped Textbooks	✓
Special Fee	None	Alternative Test Arrang.	✓
Diagnostic Testing	✓	Notetakers	✓
Basic Skills Remediation	✓	LD Student Organization	

LEARNING DISABILITIES PROGRAM INFORMATION

The Career and Counseling Center began offering services in 1977. Currently the program serves 175 undergraduates with LD. Students diagnosed with ADD/ADHD are eligible for the same services available to students with LD.
Staff: 1 full-time, 1 part-time staff members, including director. Services provided by counselor.
Special Fees: No special fees are charged for services to students with LD.
Applications and admissions: *Required:* documentation of LD (for receipt of services; e.g., psychoeducational report, IEP, school records). Students may begin taking classes any term. *Application deadline:* continuous.
Special policies: The college has written policies regarding grade forgiveness; substitutions and waivers of graduation and degree requirements.

PROGRAM AND SERVICE COMPONENTS

Diagnostic testing: Reading, math, written language.
Academic advising: Provided by LD staff members. Students with LD may take up to 18 credit hours each term; most take 9 to 12 credit hours; 12 credit hours required to maintain full-time status; 6 credit hours required to be eligible for financial aid.

Delaware County Community College (continued)

Counseling services: Individual counseling, career counseling.
Basic skills remediation: Offered in class-size groups by LD teachers, regular teachers. Available in reading, math, spelling, written language, learning strategies, speech.
Subject-area tutoring: Offered one-on-one and in small groups by professional teachers, peer tutors. Available in most subjects.
Special courses: College survival skills, reading, vocabulary development, communication skills, composition, word processing, time management, math, typing, personal psychology, study skills, career planning. Some offered for credit; some enter into overall grade point average.
Auxiliary aids: Taped textbooks, tape recorders, calculators, typewriters, word-processors with spell-check, talking computers, optical character readers.
Auxiliary services: Alternative test arrangements, notetakers, priority registration, advocacy.

GENERAL COLLEGE INFORMATION

State and locally supported, 2-year, coed. Awards associate degrees. Founded 1967. *Setting:* 125-acre suburban campus with easy access to Philadelphia. *Total enrollment:* 9,807. *Faculty:* 438 (123 full-time, 14% with terminal degrees, 315 part-time); student–undergrad faculty ratio is 24:1.
Enrollment Profile: 9,807 students: 54% women, 46% men, 68% part-time, 99% state residents, 1% international, 48% 25 or older, 1% Native American, 1% Hispanic, 9% black, 3% Asian or Pacific Islander. *Retention:* 54% of 1995 full-time freshmen returned. *Most popular recent majors:* liberal arts/general studies, business administration/commerce/management, nursing.
First-Year Class: 3,046 total; 4,029 applied, 100% were accepted, 76% of whom enrolled.
Graduation Requirements: 60 credit hours.
Computers on Campus: 250 computers available on campus for general student use. Computer purchase/lease plans available. A campus-wide network can be accessed. Students can contact faculty members and/or advisers through e-mail. Computers for student use in computer center, computer labs, learning resource center, classrooms, library provide access to the Internet/World Wide Web. Staffed computer lab on campus provides training in use of computers, software. *Academic computing expenditure 1995–96:* $452,869.

EXPENSES

Expenses for 1997–98: *Application fee:* $20. Area resident tuition: $1785 full-time, $59.50 per credit hour part-time. State resident tuition: $3570 full-time, $119 per credit hour part-time. Nonresident tuition: $5355 full-time, $178.50 per credit hour part-time. Part-time mandatory fees per semester range from $21.50 to $196.50. Full-time mandatory fees range from $225 to $525.
LD Program Contact: Mrs. Ann Binder, Special Services Counselor, Delaware County Community College, 901 South Media Line Road, Media, PA 19063-1094, 610-325-2748. Fax: 610-359-5343.

DIABLO VALLEY COLLEGE

Pleasant Hill, California

Students with LD	500	Subject-Area Tutoring	✓
ADD services	✓	Special Courses	✓
Staff	5 full-time	Taped Textbooks	✓
Special Fee	None	Alternative Test Arrang.	✓
Diagnostic Testing	✓	Notetakers	✓
Basic Skills Remediation	✓	LD Student Organization	

LEARNING DISABILITIES PROGRAM INFORMATION

The Disabled Student Programs and Services currently serves 500 undergraduates with LD. Students diagnosed with ADD/ADHD are eligible for the same services available to students with LD.
Staff: 5 full-time staff members, including Program Manager. Services provided by diagnostic specialist, LD specialists.
Special Fees: No special fees are charged for services to students with LD.
Applications and admissions: *Recommended:* psychoeducational report completed within 2 years. *Application deadline:* continuous.

PROGRAM AND SERVICE COMPONENTS

Special preparation or orientation: Required orientation held before registration.
Diagnostic testing: Intelligence, reading, math, spelling.
Academic advising: Provided by LD staff members, academic advisers. Students with LD may take up to 17 semester hours each term; most take 9 to 10 semester hours; 9 semester hours required to maintain full-time status; 12 semester hours required to be eligible for financial aid.
Counseling services: Individual counseling, career counseling.
Basic skills remediation: Offered in class-size groups by LD teachers. Available in reading, math, spelling, learning strategies, study skills.
Subject-area tutoring: Offered one-on-one and in small groups by paraprofessional tutors. Available in most subjects.
Special courses: College survival skills, reading, vocabulary development, composition, learning strategies, word processing, math, typing, study skills. Most offered for credit; most enter into overall grade point average.
Auxiliary aids: Taped textbooks, tape recorders, personal computers, optical character readers, Book Wise.
Auxiliary services: Alternative test arrangements, notetakers, priority registration, advocacy.

GENERAL COLLEGE INFORMATION

State and locally supported, 2-year, coed. Part of Contra Costa Community College District System. Awards associate degrees. Founded 1949. *Setting:* 100-acre small-town campus with easy access to San Francisco.

EXPENSES

Expenses for 1996–97: State resident tuition: $0 full-time. Nonresident tuition: $4050 full-time, $135 per unit part-time. Part-time mandatory fees: $13 per unit. Full-time mandatory fees: $390.
LD Program Contact: Ms. Sue Garcia, Disabled Student Programs and Services Specialist, Diablo Valley College, 1321 Golf Club Road, Pleasant Hill, CA 94523, 510-685-1230 Ext. 546.

ELLSWORTH COMMUNITY COLLEGE

Iowa Falls, Iowa

Students with LD	18	Subject-Area Tutoring	✓
ADD services	✓	Special Courses	
Staff	2 full-time	Taped Textbooks	✓
Special Fee	None	Alternative Test Arrang.	✓
Diagnostic Testing	✓	Notetakers	✓
Basic Skills Remediation	✓	LD Student Organization	

LEARNING DISABILITIES PROGRAM INFORMATION

The Community Based Vocational Training Program (CBVT) began offering services in 1986. Currently the program serves 18 undergraduates with LD. Students diagnosed with ADD/ADHD are eligible for the same services available to students with LD.
Staff: 2 full-time staff members, including assistant director, coordinator.
Special Fees: A fee is charged for diagnostic testing.
Applications and admissions: *Required:* high school transcript, IEP (Individualized Education Program), personal interview. Students may begin taking classes in fall only. *Application deadline:* 7/1.

PROGRAM AND SERVICE COMPONENTS

Diagnostic testing: Reading, math, spelling, written language.
Academic advising: Provided by LD staff members. Students with LD may take up to 12 semester hours each term; most take 8 to 10 semester hours; 12 semester hours required to maintain full-time status; 6 to 12 semester hours required to be eligible for financial aid.
Counseling services: Individual counseling, career counseling.
Basic skills remediation: Offered in class-size groups by regular teachers. Available in reading, math, written language, study skills.
Subject-area tutoring: Offered in small groups by professional teachers. Available in most subjects.
Auxiliary aids: Taped textbooks, tape recorders, calculators, typewriters, word-processors with spell-check.
Auxiliary services: Alternative test arrangements, notetakers.

GENERAL COLLEGE INFORMATION

State and locally supported, 2-year, coed. Part of Iowa Valley Community College District System. Awards associate degrees. Founded 1890. *Setting:* 10-acre small-town campus. *Total enrollment:* 850. *Faculty:* 50 (41 full-time, 9 part-time); student–undergrad faculty ratio is 15:1.
Enrollment Profile: 850 students: 49% women, 51% men, 21% part-time, 94% state residents, 34% live on campus, 15% transferred in, 1% international, 30% 25 or older, 5% black. *Retention:* 55% of 1995 full-time freshmen returned. *Areas of study chosen:* 20% liberal arts/general studies, 20% vocational and home economics, 16% business management and administrative services, 13% social sciences, 10% biological and life sciences, 10% health professions and related sciences, 9% agriculture, 2% fine arts. *Most popular recent majors:* business administration/commerce/management, education, liberal arts/general studies.
First-Year Class: 450 total; 630 applied, 98% were accepted, 73% of whom enrolled. 5% from top 10% of their high school class, 40% from top half.
Graduation Requirements: 64 semester hours; 7 semester hours of math/science for associate of science degree; 8 semester hours of math/science for associate of arts degree; computer course; internship (some majors).
Computers on Campus: 50 computers available on campus for general student use. Computers for student use in computer center, classrooms, library, academic buildings. Staffed computer lab on campus provides training in use of computers, software. *Academic computing expenditure 1995–96:* $64,589.

EXPENSES

Expenses for 1997–98: *Application fee:* $25. State resident tuition: $1856 full-time, $58 per semester hour part-time. Nonresident tuition: $3712 full-time, $116 per semester hour part-time. Part-time mandatory fees per semester range from $8 to $189.50. Full-time mandatory fees: $524. College room and board: $3164.

LD Program Contact: Ms. Lori Mulford, Coordinator, Ellsworth Community College, 1100 College Avenue, Iowa Falls, IA 50126-1199, 515-648-4611. Fax: 515-648-3128. The Community Based Vocational Training Program is also available to students with LD who are enrolled in either full-time vocational or arts and sciences programs.

FEATHER RIVER COMMUNITY COLLEGE DISTRICT

Quincy, California

Students with LD	85	Subject-Area Tutoring	✓
ADD services	✓	Special Courses	✓
Staff	3 full-time	Taped Textbooks	✓
Special Fee	None	Alternative Test Arrang.	✓
Diagnostic Testing	✓	Notetakers	✓
Basic Skills Remediation	✓	LD Student Organization	

LEARNING DISABILITIES PROGRAM INFORMATION

The Disabled Students Program and Services (DSPS) began offering services in 1986. Currently the program serves 85 undergraduates with LD. Students diagnosed with ADD/ADHD are eligible for the same services available to students with LD.
Staff: 3 full-time staff members, including coordinator. Services provided by tutors, counselor, diagnostic specialist, LD instructional assistant/program specialist.
Special Fees: No special fees are charged for services to students with LD.
Applications and admissions: *Required:* high school IEP (Individualized Education Program), personal interview, California Assessment System for Adults with Learning Disabilities; *recommended:* high school transcript, courses completed, psychoeducational report completed within 3 years. Students may begin taking classes in fall or spring. *Application deadline:* continuous.

PROGRAM AND SERVICE COMPONENTS

Special preparation or orientation: Required orientation held during registration and throughout the year.
Diagnostic testing: Intelligence, reading, math, spelling, written language, perceptual skills, study skills, personality, social skills, learning strategies.
Academic advising: Provided by LD staff members, academic advisers. Students with LD may take up to 12 units each term; most take 12 units; 12 units required to maintain full-time status and be eligible for financial aid.
Counseling services: Individual counseling, small-group counseling, career counseling.
Basic skills remediation: Offered one-on-one, in small groups, and in class-size groups by LD teachers, regular teachers, LD instructional assistant; computer-aided instruction also offered. Available in reading, math, spelling, written language, learning strategies, motor abilities, perceptual skills, study skills, time management, computer skills.
Subject-area tutoring: Offered one-on-one and in small groups by professional teachers, peer tutors, LD Instructional Assistant. Available in all subjects.
Special courses: College survival skills, reading, vocabulary development, composition, learning strategies, word processing, Internet use, time management, math, typing, study skills, career planning, introduction to learning disabilities, writing skills (lab). All offered for credit; all enter into overall grade point average.
Auxiliary aids: Taped textbooks, tape recorders, calculators, typewriters, word-processors with spell-check, talking computers, optical character readers, computer software.

Feather River Community College District (continued)

Auxiliary services: Alternative test arrangements, notetakers, priority registration, advocacy.

GENERAL COLLEGE INFORMATION

State and locally supported, 2-year, coed. Awards associate degrees. Founded 1968. *Setting:* 150-acre rural campus. *Total enrollment:* 1,200. *Faculty:* 95 (20 full-time, 75 part-time).
Enrollment Profile: 1,200 students from 4 states and territories. 60% women, 40% men, 74% part-time, 96% state residents, 24% transferred in, 3% Hispanic, 1% black, 1% Asian or Pacific Islander. *Most popular recent majors:* forest technology, wildlife biology, recreation and leisure services.
First-Year Class: Of the students who applied, 100% were accepted, 100% of whom enrolled.
Graduation Requirements: 60 units; 1 course each in math and science; computer course.
Computers on Campus: 25 computers available on campus for general student use. A campus-wide network can be accessed from off-campus. Computers for student use in computer center, learning center provide access to the Internet/World Wide Web. Staffed computer lab on campus.

EXPENSES

Expenses for 1996–97: State resident tuition: $0 full-time. Nonresident tuition: $3750 full-time, $125 per unit part-time. Part-time mandatory fees: $13 per semester. Tuition for Nevada residents who are eligible for the Good Neighbor Program: $1260 full-time, $42 per unitpart-time. Full-time mandatory fees: $390.
LD Program Contact: Ms. Maureen McPhee, Disabled Students Programs and Services Coordinator/LD Specialist, Feather River Community College District, PO Box 1110, Quincy, CA 95971-6023, 916-283-0202. Fax: 916-283-3757. Email: mcphee@frcc.cc.ca.us.

FOOTHILL COLLEGE

Los Altos Hills, California

Students with LD	100	Subject-Area Tutoring	✓
ADD services	✓	Special Courses	✓
Staff	1 full-, 10 part-time	Taped Textbooks	
Special Fee	None	Alternative Test Arrang.	✓
Diagnostic Testing	✓	Notetakers	✓
Basic Skills Remediation	✓	LD Student Organization	

LEARNING DISABILITIES PROGRAM INFORMATION

The Student Tutorial Evaluation Program (STEP) began offering services in 1986. Currently the program serves 100 undergraduates with LD. Students diagnosed with ADD/ADHD are eligible for the same services available to students with LD.
Staff: 1 full-time, 10 part-time staff members, including director. Services provided by tutors, counselors, diagnostic specialists.
Special Fees: No special fees are charged for services to students with LD.
Applications and admissions: *Required:* Assessment and Eligibility Process for California Community Colleges. Students may begin taking classes in fall, winter, or spring. *Application deadline:* continuous.

PROGRAM AND SERVICE COMPONENTS

Diagnostic testing: Reading, math, spelling, spoken language, written language.
Academic advising: Provided by LD staff members, academic advisers. Students with LD may take up to 20 quarter units (more with academic counselor's approval) each term; most take 12 quarter units; 6 quarter units required to be eligible for financial aid.
Counseling services: Individual counseling, career counseling.
Basic skills remediation: Offered one-on-one, in small groups, and in class-size groups by LD teachers, local college graduates, retired professional personnel; computer-aided instruction also offered. Available in reading, math, spelling, written language.
Subject-area tutoring: Offered one-on-one and in small groups by local college graduates, retired professional personnel. Available in some subjects.
Special courses: Reading, vocabulary development, word processing, math. All offered for credit; none enter into overall grade point average.
Auxiliary aids: Tape recorders, calculators, word-processors with spell-check, personal computers.
Auxiliary services: Alternative test arrangements, notetakers, priority registration, advocacy.

GENERAL COLLEGE INFORMATION

State and locally supported, 2-year, coed. Part of Foothill/DeAnza Community College District System. Awards associate degrees. Founded 1958. *Setting:* 122-acre suburban campus with easy access to San Jose. *Total enrollment:* 15,500. *Faculty:* 578 (238 full-time, 340 part-time).
Enrollment Profile: 15,500 students from 51 states and territories, 45 other countries. 49% women, 51% men, 78% part-time, 98% state residents, 22% transferred in, 1% international, 67% 25 or older, 1% Native American, 6% Hispanic, 3% black, 9% Asian or Pacific Islander. *Most popular recent majors:* liberal arts/general studies, radiological technology, business administration/commerce/management.
First-Year Class: 3,000 total; 9,000 applied, 100% were accepted, 33% of whom enrolled. 10% from top 10% of their high school class, 35% from top quarter, 50% from top half.
Graduation Requirements: 90 quarter units; 1 math course.
Computers on Campus: 200 computers available on campus for general student use. Computer purchase/lease plans available. Computers for student use in computer center.

EXPENSES

Expenses for 1996–97: *Application fee:* $22. State resident tuition: $0 full-time. Nonresident tuition: $3510 full-time, $78 per unit part-time. Part-time mandatory fees per quarter range from $23 to $113. Full-time mandatory fees: $447.
LD Program Contact: Ms. Diana Lydgate, Director, Student Tutorial Evaluation Program, Foothill College, 12345 El Monte Road, Los Altos Hills, CA 94022-4599, 415-949-7377. Fax: 415-941-3767.

GAVILAN COLLEGE

Gilroy, California

Students with LD	250	Subject-Area Tutoring	✓
ADD services	✓	Special Courses	✓
Staff	6 full-, 1 part-time	Taped Textbooks	✓
Special Fee		Alternative Test Arrang.	✓
Diagnostic Testing	✓	Notetakers	✓
Basic Skills Remediation	✓	LD Student Organization	

LEARNING DISABILITIES PROGRAM INFORMATION

The Disabled Students Programs and Services Learning Skills Lab began offering services in 1978. Currently the program serves 250 undergraduates with LD. Students diagnosed with ADD/ADHD are eligible for the same services available to students with LD.
Staff: 6 full-time, 1 part-time staff members, including coordinator, instructors/specialists, instructional assistants. Services provided by tutors, counselor, instructional assistants.
Special Fees: A fee is charged for diagnostic testing.
Applications and admissions: Students may begin taking classes any term. *Application deadline:* continuous.

PROGRAM AND SERVICE COMPONENTS

Special preparation or orientation: Optional summer program offered prior to entering college. Orientation (required for some) held during registration and after classes begin.
Diagnostic testing: Intelligence, reading, math, spelling, written language, perceptual skills, social skills, speech, hearing, learning strategies.
Academic advising: Provided by LD staff members, academic advisers. Students with LD may take up to 18 units each term; most take 9 to 12 units; 12 units required to maintain full-time status; 6 units required to be eligible for financial aid.
Counseling services: Individual counseling, career counseling.
Basic skills remediation: Offered one-on-one, in small groups, and in class-size groups by LD teachers; computer-aided instruction also offered. Available in math, written language, learning strategies, speech.
Subject-area tutoring: Offered one-on-one, in small groups, and in class-size groups by professional teachers, peer tutors, instructional assistants. Available in most subjects.
Special courses: College survival skills, composition, learning strategies, word processing, math, study skills, career planning. All offered for credit.
Auxiliary aids: Taped textbooks, tape recorders, calculators, typewriters, word-processors with spell-check, personal computers, talking computers, optical character readers.
Auxiliary services: Alternative test arrangements, notetakers, priority registration, readers.

GENERAL COLLEGE INFORMATION

State and locally supported, 2-year, coed. Part of California Community Colleges System. Awards associate degrees. Founded 1919. *Setting:* 150-acre rural campus with easy access to San Jose. *Total enrollment:* 4,029. *Faculty:* 164 (74 full-time, 90 part-time); student–undergrad faculty ratio is 30:1.
Enrollment Profile: 4,029 students from 7 states and territories, 16 other countries. 52% women, 48% men, 63% part-time, 96% state residents, 17% transferred in, 1% international, 40% 25 or older, 1% Native American, 35% Hispanic, 2% black, 4% Asian or Pacific Islander. *Areas of study chosen:* 70% liberal arts/general studies, 8% fine arts, 6% business management and administrative services, 5% health professions and related sciences, 4% vocational and home economics, 3% education, 1% biological and life sciences, 1% computer and information sciences, 1% English language/literature/letters, 1% social sciences.
First-Year Class: 921 total; 1,200 applied, 100% were accepted, 77% of whom enrolled.
Graduation Requirements: 60 units; 9 units of math/science; computer course.
Computers on Campus: 31 computers available on campus for general student use. Computers for student use in learning resource center.

EXPENSES

Expenses for 1997–98: State resident tuition: $0 full-time. Nonresident tuition: $3840 full-time, $128 per unit part-time. Part-time mandatory fees per semester range from $29 to $159. Part-time tuition for international students: $136 per unit. Full-time mandatory fees: $422.
LD Program Contact: Ms. Sherrean Carr, Coordinator, Disabled Students Programs and Services, Gavilan College, 5055 Santa Teresa Boulevard, Gilroy, CA 95020-9599, 408-848-4871. Fax: 408-848-4865.

GLENDALE COMMUNITY COLLEGE

Glendale, California

Students with LD	280	Subject-Area Tutoring	✓
ADD services	✓	Special Courses	✓
Staff	4 full-, 2 part-time	Taped Textbooks	✓
Special Fee	None	Alternative Test Arrang.	✓
Diagnostic Testing	✓	Notetakers	✓
Basic Skills Remediation	✓	LD Student Organization	✓

LEARNING DISABILITIES PROGRAM INFORMATION

The Disabled Students' Program began offering services in 1980. Currently the program serves 280 undergraduates with LD. Students diagnosed with ADD/ADHD are eligible for the same services available to students with LD.
Staff: 4 full-time, 2 part-time staff members. Services provided by remediation specialists, tutors, counselors, diagnostic specialists.
Special Fees: $13 for diagnostic testing.
Applications and admissions: *Required:* Woodcock-Johnson Revised or WAIS-R; *recommended:* high school transcript, grade point average, courses completed, IEP (Individualized Education Program), psychoeducational report completed within 3 years. Students may begin taking classes in fall or spring. *Application deadline:* continuous.
Special policies: The college has written policies regarding grade forgiveness; substitutions and waivers of admissions and degree requirements.

PROGRAM AND SERVICE COMPONENTS

Special preparation or orientation: Optional orientation offered after classes begin.
Diagnostic testing: Reading, math, spelling, spoken language, written language, perceptual skills, study skills, learning strategies.
Academic advising: Provided by academic advisers. Students with LD may take up to 12 units (more with special permission) each term; most take 9 to 12 units; 12 units required to maintain full-time status; 6 units required to be eligible for financial aid.
Counseling services: Individual counseling, career counseling.
Basic skills remediation: Offered one-on-one, in small groups, and in class-size groups by LD teachers, regular teachers. Available in reading, math, spelling, spoken language, written language, learning strategies, study skills, vocabulary.
Subject-area tutoring: Offered one-on-one and in small groups by professional teachers, peer tutors, instructional aides. Available in most subjects.
Special courses: College survival skills, reading, vocabulary development, communication skills, composition, learning strategies, word processing, study skills, career planning. All offered for credit; some enter into overall grade point average.
Auxiliary aids: Taped textbooks, tape recorders, calculators, typewriters, word-processors with spell-check, personal computers, talking computers, optical character readers.
Auxiliary services: Alternative test arrangements, notetakers, priority registration, advocacy.

Glendale Community College (continued)

Campus support group: A special student organization is available to students with LD.

GENERAL COLLEGE INFORMATION

State and locally supported, 2-year, coed. Part of California Community Colleges System. Awards associate degrees. Founded 1927. *Setting:* 119-acre urban campus with easy access to Los Angeles. *Total enrollment:* 15,337. *Faculty:* 345.

Enrollment Profile: 15,337 students from 21 states and territories, 53 other countries. 57% women, 43% men, 74% part-time, 96% state residents, 6% transferred in, 3% international, 49% 25 or older, 1% Native American, 22% Hispanic, 2% black, 13% Asian or Pacific Islander. *Most popular recent majors:* humanities, applied art, science.

First-Year Class: 3,997 total; 19,051 applied, 99% were accepted, 21% of whom enrolled.

Graduation Requirements: 60 units; math proficiency; computer course (varies by major).

Computers on Campus: 140 computers available on campus for general student use.

EXPENSES

Expenses for 1997–98: State resident tuition: $0 full-time. Nonresident tuition: $3900 full-time, $130 per unit part-time. Part-time mandatory fees per semester range from $36 to $166. Full-time mandatory fees: $436.

LD Program Contact: Ms. Ellen Oppenberg, Learning Disabilities Specialist, Glendale Community College, 1500 North Verdugo Road, Glendale, CA 91208-2894, 818-240-1000 Ext. 5530. Fax: 818-549-9436.

GROSSMONT COLLEGE

El Cajon, California

Students with LD	240	Subject-Area Tutoring	✓
ADD services	✓	Special Courses	✓
Staff	3 full-, 5 part-time	Taped Textbooks	✓
Special Fee	None	Alternative Test Arrang.	✓
Diagnostic Testing	✓	Notetakers	✓
Basic Skills Remediation	✓	LD Student Organization	

LEARNING DISABILITIES PROGRAM INFORMATION

The Disabled Student Services, Learning Development Center began offering services in 1974. Currently the program serves 240 undergraduates with LD. Students diagnosed with ADD/ADHD are eligible for the same services available to students with LD.

Staff: 3 full-time, 5 part-time staff members, including coordinator, speech/language specialists, LD specialist. Services provided by remediation specialists, tutors, counselors, diagnostic specialists.

Special Fees: No special fees are charged for services to students with LD.

Applications and admissions: *Required:* psychoeducational report completed within 3 years; *recommended:* personal interview. Students may begin taking classes in fall, spring, or summer. *Application deadline:* 8/15 (fall term), 1/15 (spring term).

Special policies: The college has written policies regarding grade forgiveness; substitutions and waivers of graduation and degree requirements.

PROGRAM AND SERVICE COMPONENTS

Special preparation or orientation: Optional orientation offered before registration.

Diagnostic testing: Intelligence, reading, math, spelling, written language, speech, hearing, learning strategies.

Academic advising: Provided by LD staff members, academic advisers. Students with LD may take up to 12 units each term; most take 6 to 12 units; 12 units required to maintain full-time status; 6 units required to be eligible for financial aid.

Counseling services: Individual counseling, career counseling.

Basic skills remediation: Offered in small groups by LD teachers, tutors; computer-aided instruction also offered. Available in reading, math, spelling, spoken language, written language, learning strategies, perceptual skills, study skills, time management, speech.

Subject-area tutoring: Offered in small groups by peer tutors. Available in most subjects.

Special courses: Reading, vocabulary development, communication skills, composition, learning strategies, word processing, math, study skills. All offered for credit; none enter into overall grade point average.

Auxiliary aids: Taped textbooks, tape recorders, calculators, word-processors with spell-check, optical character readers.

Auxiliary services: Alternative test arrangements, notetakers, priority registration, advocacy.

GENERAL COLLEGE INFORMATION

State and locally supported, 2-year, coed. Part of California Community Colleges System. Awards associate degrees. Founded 1961. *Setting:* 135-acre suburban campus with easy access to San Diego. *Total enrollment:* 15,000. *Faculty:* 653 (203 full-time, 450 part-time); student–undergrad faculty ratio is 25:1.

Enrollment Profile: 15,000 students: 57% women, 43% men, 64% part-time, 97% state residents, 21% transferred in, 1% international, 38% 25 or older, 1% Native American, 10% Hispanic, 3% black, 5% Asian or Pacific Islander. *Most popular recent majors:* liberal arts/general studies, business administration/commerce/management, nursing.

First-Year Class: 2,400 total. Of the students who applied, 100% were accepted.

Graduation Requirements: 60 units; 1 course each in math and lab science; computer course for business majors; internship (some majors).

Computers on Campus: 300 computers available on campus for general student use. Computer purchase/lease plans available. Computers for student use in computer center, computer labs, learning resource center, library. Staffed computer lab on campus provides training in use of computers, software.

EXPENSES AND FINANCIAL AID

Expenses for 1997–98: State resident tuition: $0 full-time. Nonresident tuition: $3420 full-time, $114 per unit part-time. Part-time mandatory fees per semester range from $23 to $153. Full-time mandatory fees: $410.

Financial aid specifically for students with LD: Scholarship: College Disabled Student Scholarship.

LD Program Contact: Ms. Mary Paschke, Learning Disabilities Specialist, Grossmont College, 8800 Grossmont College Drive, El Cajon, CA 92020, 619-465-1700 Ext. 112. Fax: 619-461-3396.

HARCUM COLLEGE

Bryn Mawr, Pennsylvania

Students with LD	30	Subject-Area Tutoring	✓
ADD services	✓	Special Courses	✓

Staff	2 full-, 3 part-time	Taped Textbooks	✓
Special Fee	✓	Alternative Test Arrang.	✓
Diagnostic Testing		Notetakers	✓
Basic Skills Remediation	✓	LD Student Organization	✓

LEARNING DISABILITIES PROGRAM INFORMATION

The PLUS Program currently serves 30 undergraduates with LD. Students diagnosed with ADD/ADHD are eligible for the same services available to students with LD.

Staff: 2 full-time, 3 part-time staff members, including director. Services provided by tutors, counselors.

Special Fees: $2600 per year.

Applications and admissions: *Recommended:* high school transcript, courses completed, personal interview, autobiographical statement, letters of recommendation, psychoeducational report completed within 2 years. Students may begin taking classes in summer only. *Application deadline:* continuous.

Special policies: The college has written policies regarding substitutions and waivers of graduation and degree requirements.

PROGRAM AND SERVICE COMPONENTS

Special preparation or orientation: Required orientation held before registration, during registration, after classes begin.

Academic advising: Provided by LD staff members, academic advisers. Most students with LD take 12 to 15 credits each term; 12 credits required to maintain full-time status and be eligible for financial aid.

Counseling services: Individual counseling, small-group counseling, career counseling.

Basic skills remediation: Offered in small groups and in class-size groups by regular teachers; computer-aided instruction also offered. Available in reading, math, spoken language, written language, learning strategies, study skills, time management, social skills.

Subject-area tutoring: Offered one-on-one and in small groups by professional teachers, peer tutors. Available in most subjects.

Special courses: College survival skills, vocabulary development, communication skills, composition, learning strategies, word processing, time management, personal psychology, study skills, career planning. Most offered for credit; most enter into overall grade point average.

Auxiliary aids: Taped textbooks, tape recorders, calculators, word-processors with spell-check, personal computers, talking computers, Dragon Dictate.

Auxiliary services: Alternative test arrangements, notetakers, priority registration, advocacy.

Campus support group: A special student organization is available to students with LD.

GENERAL COLLEGE INFORMATION

Independent, 2-year, primarily women. Awards associate degrees. Founded 1915. *Setting:* 12-acre suburban campus with easy access to Philadelphia. *Endowment:* $6.2 million. *Research spending 1995–96:* $14,624. *Total enrollment:* 654. *Faculty:* 85 (40 full-time, 100% with terminal degrees, 45 part-time); student–undergrad faculty ratio is 9:1.

Enrollment Profile: 654 students from 9 states and territories, 10 other countries. 89% women, 11% men, 29% part-time, 78% state residents, 30% live on campus, 15% transferred in, 6% international, 23% 25 or older, 0% Native American, 1% Hispanic, 9% black, 2% Asian or Pacific Islander. *Areas of study chosen:* 59% health professions and related sciences, 20% interdisciplinary studies, 7% liberal arts/general studies, 6% education, 3% business management and administrative services, 3% fine arts, 1% communications and journalism, 1% computer and information sciences. *Most popular recent majors:* veterinary technology, physical therapy, occupational therapy.

First-Year Class: 110 total; 828 applied, 41% were accepted, 33% of whom enrolled. 40% from top half of their high school class.

Graduation Requirements: 60 credits; 1 course each in math and science; computer course; internship (some majors).

Computers on Campus: 65 computers available on campus for general student use. Computers for student use in computer center, classrooms, library provide access to the Internet/World Wide Web. Staffed computer lab on campus. *Academic computing expenditure 1995–96:* $76,481.

EXPENSES

Expenses for 1997–98: *Application fee:* $25. Comprehensive fee of $14,582 includes full-time tuition ($8642), mandatory fees ($518), and college room and board ($5422). Part-time tuition: $288 per credit. Part-time mandatory fees: $28 per credit.

LD Program Contact: Ms. Nancy O'Connor, Director, PLUS Program, Harcum College, Montgomery Avenue, Bryn Mawr, PA 19010-3476, 610-526-6027. Fax: 610-526-6086.

HOUSATONIC COMMUNITY-TECHNICAL COLLEGE

Bridgeport, Connecticut

Students with LD	80	Subject-Area Tutoring	✓
ADD services	✓	Special Courses	
Staff	2 full-, 2 part-time	Taped Textbooks	✓
Special Fee	None	Alternative Test Arrang.	✓
Diagnostic Testing		Notetakers	✓
Basic Skills Remediation	✓	LD Student Organization	

LEARNING DISABILITIES PROGRAM INFORMATION

The Disabilities Support Services began offering services in 1982. Currently the program serves 80 undergraduates with LD. Students diagnosed with ADD/ADHD are eligible for the same services available to students with LD.

Staff: 2 full-time, 2 part-time staff members, including director. Services provided by remediation specialists, tutors, counselors.

Special Fees: No special fees are charged for services to students with LD.

Applications and admissions: *Required:* high school transcript, GED (in lieu of high school diploma), placement testing. Students may begin taking classes in fall, spring, or summer. *Application deadline:* continuous.

Special policies: The college has written policies regarding substitutions and waivers of graduation and degree requirements.

PROGRAM AND SERVICE COMPONENTS

Special preparation or orientation: Optional orientation offered before registration and during registration.

Academic advising: Provided by LD staff members, academic advisers. Students with LD may take up to 18 credits each term; most take 6 to 9 credits; 12 credits required to maintain full-time status; 6 credits required to be eligible for financial aid.

Counseling services: Individual counseling, small-group counseling.

Basic skills remediation: Offered one-on-one and in small groups by LD teachers. Available in reading, math, written language, learning strategies, study skills, social skills.

Subject-area tutoring: Offered one-on-one and in small groups by professional teachers, peer tutors. Available in some subjects.

Auxiliary aids: Taped textbooks, tape recorders, calculators, word-processors with spell-check, talking computers, optical character readers.

Housatonic Community-Technical College (continued)

Auxiliary services: Alternative test arrangements, notetakers, priority registration, advocacy, readers, writers.

GENERAL COLLEGE INFORMATION

State-supported, 2-year, coed. Part of Connecticut Community–Technical College System. Awards associate degrees. Founded 1965. *Setting:* 4-acre urban campus with easy access to New York City. *Total enrollment:* 2,654. *Faculty:* 137 (45 full-time, 12% with terminal degrees, 92 part-time); student–undergrad faculty ratio is 18:1.

Enrollment Profile: 2,654 students: 70% women, 30% men, 84% part-time, 99% state residents, 5% transferred in, 1% international, 54% 25 or older, 0% Native American, 20% Hispanic, 28% black, 3% Asian or Pacific Islander. *Areas of study chosen:* 15% business management and administrative services, 6% health professions and related sciences, 2% liberal arts/general studies, 1% fine arts.

First-Year Class: 663 total; 2,182 applied, 99% were accepted.

Graduation Requirements: 60 credits; 3 credits of math; 3 credits of science.

Computers on Campus: 100 computers available on campus for general student use. Computers for student use in computer labs, library. Staffed computer lab on campus.

EXPENSES

Expenses for 1997–98: *Application fee:* $20. State resident tuition: $1608 full-time, $67 per credit part-time. Nonresident tuition: $5232 full-time, $218 per credit part-time. Part-time mandatory fees per semester range from $42 to $103. Tuition for nonresidents who are eligible for the New England Regional Student Program: $2412 full-time, $100.50 per credit part-time. Full-time mandatory fees: $206.

LD Program Contact: Mr. Peter G. Anderheggen, Director, Disabilities Support Services, Housatonic Community-Technical College, 900 Lafayette Boulevard, Bridgeport, CT 06604-4704, 203-332-5018. Fax: 203-332-5123. Email: ho_ander@comment.edu.

HOWARD COMMUNITY COLLEGE

Columbia, Maryland

Students with LD	175	Subject-Area Tutoring	✓
ADD services	✓	Special Courses	✓
Staff	5 full-time	Taped Textbooks	✓
Special Fee	None	Alternative Test Arrang.	✓
Diagnostic Testing		Notetakers	✓
Basic Skills Remediation	✓	LD Student Organization	

LEARNING DISABILITIES PROGRAM INFORMATION

The Student Support Services began offering services in 1979. Currently the program serves 175 undergraduates with LD. Students diagnosed with ADD/ADHD are eligible for the same services available to students with LD.

Staff: 5 full-time staff members, including director, co-director, coordinator, administrative assistant. Services provided by remediation specialists, tutors, counselors.

Special Fees: No special fees are charged for services to students with LD.

Applications and admissions: *Required:* psychoeducational report; *recommended:* high school IEP (Individualized Education Program), referrals from other agencies. Students may begin taking classes in fall or spring. *Application deadline:* continuous.

Special policies: The college has written policies regarding substitutions and waivers of admissions, graduation, and degree requirements.

PROGRAM AND SERVICE COMPONENTS

Special preparation or orientation: Optional summer program offered prior to entering college. Optional orientation offered either the week before or right after classes begin.

Academic advising: Provided by LD staff members. Students with LD may take up to 15 credit hours (more with dean's permission) each term; most take 6 to 12 credit hours; 12 credit hours required to maintain full-time status; 3 credit hours (institutional assistance), 6 credit hours (federal assistance) required to be eligible for financial aid.

Counseling services: Individual counseling, small-group counseling, career counseling, self-advocacy training.

Basic skills remediation: Offered one-on-one by LD teachers, instructional specialists. Available in reading, math, spelling, written language, learning strategies, study skills, time management, social skills, ESL.

Subject-area tutoring: Offered one-on-one and in small groups by professional teachers, peer tutors, LD specialists. Available in all subjects.

Special courses: Learning strategies. All offered for credit; all enter into overall grade point average.

Auxiliary aids: Taped textbooks, tape recorders, calculators, typewriters, word-processors with spell-check, personal computers, talking computers, optical character readers, Dragon Dictate (voice recognition computer program).

Auxiliary services: Alternative test arrangements, notetakers, priority registration, advocacy, readers.

GENERAL COLLEGE INFORMATION

State and locally supported, 2-year, coed. Awards associate degrees. Founded 1966. *Setting:* 122-acre suburban campus with easy access to Baltimore and Washington, DC. *Endowment:* $1.6 million. *Total enrollment:* 4,954. *Faculty:* 318 (89 full-time, 18% with terminal degrees, 229 part-time); student–undergrad faculty ratio is 20:1.

Enrollment Profile: 4,954 students: 60% women, 40% men, 72% part-time, 99% state residents, 13% transferred in, 54% 25 or older, 1% Native American, 2% Hispanic, 18% black, 7% Asian or Pacific Islander. *Retention:* 60% of 1995 full-time freshmen returned. *Most popular recent majors:* nursing, business administration/commerce/management.

First-Year Class: 834 total; 1,336 applied, 100% were accepted, 62% of whom enrolled.

Graduation Requirements: 60 credit hours; math/science requirements vary according to program; computer course for business administration, engineering majors.

Computers on Campus: 750 computers available on campus for general student use. Computers for student use in computer labs, learning resource center, classrooms, library provide access to the Internet/World Wide Web. Staffed computer lab on campus provides training in use of computers, software.

EXPENSES

Expenses for 1997–98: *Application fee:* $10. Area resident tuition: $2370 full-time, $79 per credit hour part-time. State resident tuition: $4020 full-time, $134 per credit hour part-time. Nonresident tuition: $6540 full-time, $218 per credit hour part-time. Part-time mandatory fees: $7.90 per credit hour. Full-time mandatory fees: $237.

LD Program Contact: Ms. Janice Marks, Director, Learning Assistance Center, Howard Community College, Little Patuxent Parkway, Columbia, MD 21044, 410-772-4822.

KINGS RIVER COMMUNITY COLLEGE

Reedley, California

Students with LD		Subject-Area Tutoring	
ADD services	✓	Special Courses	
Staff	5 full-time	Taped Textbooks	✓
Special Fee	None	Alternative Test Arrang.	✓
Diagnostic Testing	✓	Notetakers	✓
Basic Skills Remediation	✓	LD Student Organization	

LEARNING DISABILITIES PROGRAM INFORMATION

The Disabled Student Services currently serves undergraduate students with LD. Students diagnosed with ADD/ADHD are eligible for the same services available to students with LD.
Staff: 5 full-time staff members, including director. Services provided by counselors, diagnostic specialist.
Special Fees: No special fees are charged for services to students with LD.
Applications and admissions: Open admissions. Students may begin taking classes any term. *Application deadline:* continuous.
Special policies: The college has written policies regarding substitutions and waivers of admissions, graduation, and degree requirements.

PROGRAM AND SERVICE COMPONENTS

Special preparation or orientation: Optional orientation offered before classes begin in the Fall.
Diagnostic testing: Intelligence, reading, math, spoken language, written language, perceptual skills, personality, social skills.
Academic advising: Provided by LD staff members. Students with LD may take up to 15 units each term; most take 9 to 12 units; 12 units (fewer with waiver) required to maintain full-time status; 6 units (part-time), 12 units (full-time) required to be eligible for financial aid.
Counseling services: Individual counseling, career counseling.
Basic skills remediation: Offered in small groups and in class-size groups by regular teachers. Available in reading, math, spelling, written language, learning strategies, study skills, computer skills.
Auxiliary aids: Taped textbooks, tape recorders, calculators, typewriters, word-processors with spell-check, talking computers, optical character readers, readers, writers.
Auxiliary services: Alternative test arrangements, notetakers, priority registration, advocacy, transcribers.

GENERAL COLLEGE INFORMATION

State and locally supported, 2-year, coed. Part of State Center Community College District System. Awards associate degrees. Founded 1926. *Setting:* 350-acre rural campus. *Total enrollment:* 6,704. *Faculty:* 221 (76 full-time, 145 part-time).
Enrollment Profile: 6,704 students from 15 states and territories, 7 other countries. 63% women, 37% men, 56% part-time, 98% state residents, 16% transferred in, 1% international, 53% 25 or older, 2% Native American, 40% Hispanic, 2% black, 3% Asian or Pacific Islander. *Most popular recent majors:* liberal arts/general studies, aviation technology, agricultural sciences.
First-Year Class: 1,600 total. Of the students who applied, 100% were accepted, 89% of whom enrolled.
Graduation Requirements: 60 units; 1 college algebra course; computer course.
Computers on Campus: 90 computers available on campus for general student use. Computers for student use in computer center, library, agriculture, business, English departmental labs. Staffed computer lab on campus.

EXPENSES

Expenses for 1997–98: State resident tuition: $0 full-time. Nonresident tuition: $3900 full-time, $130 per unit part-time. Part-time mandatory fees: $13 per unit. Full-time mandatory fees: $390. College room only: $1500.
LD Program Contact: Ms. Liz Hubert, Department Secretary, Kings River Community College, 995 North Reed Avenue, Reedley, CA 93654-2099, 209-638-3641. Fax: 209-638-7031.

LANDMARK COLLEGE

Putney, Vermont

Students with LD	260	Subject-Area Tutoring	✓
ADD services	✓	Special Courses	✓
Staff	88 full-, 20 part-time	Taped Textbooks	
Special Fee	None	Alternative Test Arrang.	✓
Diagnostic Testing	✓	Notetakers	
Basic Skills Remediation	✓	LD Student Organization	✓

LEARNING DISABILITIES PROGRAM INFORMATION

The Landmark College began offering services in 1985. Currently the program serves 260 undergraduates with LD. Students diagnosed with ADD/ADHD are eligible for the same services available to students with LD.
Staff: 88 full-time, 20 part-time staff members, including director, Dean of Students, Director of Admissions, Academic Dean. Services provided by remediation specialists, tutors, counselors, diagnostic specialists.
Special Fees: No special fees are charged for services to students with LD.
Applications and admissions: *Required:* high school transcript, personal interview, autobiographical statement, letters of recommendation, psychoeducational report completed within 2 years, WAIS-R. Students may begin taking classes in fall, spring, or summer. *Application deadline:* 7/15 (fall term), 12/15 (spring term).

PROGRAM AND SERVICE COMPONENTS

Special preparation or orientation: Required orientation held before classes begin.
Diagnostic testing: Intelligence, reading, math, spelling, handwriting, spoken language, written language, motor abilities, perceptual skills, study skills, social skills.
Academic advising: Provided by LD staff members, academic advisers. Students with LD may take up to 16 credits each term; most take 9 to 12 credits; 3 courses (may be non-credit) required to maintain full-time status; 3 courses (and at least 3 credits) required to be eligible for financial aid.
Counseling services: Individual counseling, small-group counseling, career counseling.
Basic skills remediation: Offered one-on-one, in small groups, and in class-size groups by LD teachers. Available in reading, math, spelling, handwriting, spoken language, written language, learning strategies, perceptual skills, study skills, time management, social skills, speech, computer skills.
Subject-area tutoring: Offered one-on-one by professional teachers. Available in all subjects.
Special courses: College survival skills, reading, vocabulary development, communication skills, composition, learning strategies, word processing, Internet use, time management, math, typing, personal psychology, study skills, career planning, stress management, health and nutrition. Most offered for credit; most enter into overall grade point average.
Auxiliary aids: Calculators, word-processors with spell-check.
Auxiliary services: Alternative test arrangements, advocacy.

Landmark College (continued)

Campus support group: A special student organization is available to students with LD.

GENERAL COLLEGE INFORMATION

Independent, 2-year, coed. Awards associate degrees (offers degree program for high-potential students with dyslexia, ADHD, or specific learning disabilities). Founded 1983. *Setting:* 125-acre rural campus. *Endowment:* $21,061. *Educational spending 1995–96:* $14,435 per undergrad. *Total enrollment:* 260. *Faculty:* 118 (80 full-time, 38 part-time); student–undergrad faculty ratio is 3:1.

Enrollment Profile: 260 students from 44 states and territories, 10 other countries. 30% women, 70% men, 0% part-time, 2% state residents, 50% transferred in, 5% international, 14% 25 or older, 0% Native American, 2% Hispanic, 3% black, 2% Asian or Pacific Islander.

First-Year Class: 99 total.

Graduation Requirements: 60 credits; 3 credits of math; 8 credits of science.

Computers on Campus: 28 computers available on campus for general student use. Computer purchase/lease plans available. A computer is strongly recommended for all students. Students can contact faculty members and/or advisers through e-mail. Computers for student use in computer center, computer labs, classrooms, library, dorms provide access to the Internet/World Wide Web, on- and off-campus e-mail addresses. Staffed computer lab on campus provides training in use of computers, software. *Academic computing expenditure 1995–96:* $161,311.

EXPENSES AND FINANCIAL AID

Expenses for 1996–97: *Application fee:* $50. Comprehensive fee of $31,350 includes full-time tuition ($25,200), mandatory fees ($550), and college room and board ($5600). Because Landmark College serves only diagnosed learning disabled or ADHD students, tuition, fees, and related expenses may be deductible as a medical expense for federal income tax purposes.

Financial aid specifically for students with LD: Scholarships: Arellano Scholarship, Landmark College Scholarships; loans; work-study.

LD Program Contact: Mr. Frank Sopper, Director of Admissions, Landmark College, River Road, RR 1, Box 1000, Putney, VT 05346, 802-387-4767. Fax: 802-387-4779.

LANEY COLLEGE

Oakland, California

Students with LD	160	Subject-Area Tutoring	✓
ADD services	✓	Special Courses	✓
Staff	1 full-, 10 part-time	Taped Textbooks	✓
Special Fee	None	Alternative Test Arrang.	✓
Diagnostic Testing	✓	Notetakers	✓
Basic Skills Remediation	✓	LD Student Organization	✓

LEARNING DISABILITIES PROGRAM INFORMATION

The Learning Skills Program began offering services in 1982. Currently the program serves 160 undergraduates with LD. Students diagnosed with ADD/ADHD are eligible for the same services available to students with LD.

Staff: 1 full-time, 10 part-time staff members, including director. Services provided by tutors, diagnostic specialist, instructional assistants.

Special Fees: No special fees are charged for services to students with LD.

Applications and admissions: *Required:* personal interview; *recommended:* high school transcript, grade point average, courses completed, extracurricular activities, IEP (Individualized Education Program), extended time SAT I, psychoeducational report completed within 3 years. Students may begin taking classes in fall or spring. *Application deadline:* continuous.

Special policies: The college has written policies regarding grade forgiveness; substitutions and waivers of admissions requirements.

PROGRAM AND SERVICE COMPONENTS

Special preparation or orientation: Required orientation held after classes begin.

Diagnostic testing: Intelligence, reading, math, spelling, handwriting, spoken language, written language, motor abilities, perceptual skills, study skills, social skills.

Academic advising: Provided by LD staff members, academic advisers. Students with LD may take up to 18 semester hours each term; most take 12 semester hours; 12 semester hours required to maintain full-time status and be eligible for financial aid.

Counseling services: Individual counseling, small-group counseling, career counseling.

Basic skills remediation: Offered in small groups and in class-size groups by LD teachers, instructional aides, peer teachers; computer-aided instruction also offered. Available in reading, math, spelling, written language, learning strategies, study skills, time management, social skills, computer skills.

Subject-area tutoring: Offered one-on-one, in small groups, and in class-size groups by professional teachers, peer tutors, instructional assistants. Available in most subjects.

Special courses: College survival skills, reading, vocabulary development, communication skills, composition, word processing, math, study skills. All offered for credit; all enter into overall grade point average.

Auxiliary aids: Taped textbooks, tape recorders, calculators, word-processors with spell-check, personal computers.

Auxiliary services: Alternative test arrangements, notetakers, priority registration, advocacy, time extensions for writing assignments.

Campus support group: A special student organization is available to students with LD.

GENERAL COLLEGE INFORMATION

State and locally supported, 2-year, coed. Part of Peralta Community College District System. Awards associate degrees. Founded 1953. *Setting:* urban campus with easy access to San Francisco. *Research spending 1995–96:* $68,724. *Educational spending 1995–96:* $824 per undergrad. *Total enrollment:* 10,454. *Faculty:* 315 (130 full-time, 185 part-time); student–undergrad faculty ratio is 33:1.

Enrollment Profile: 10,454 students: 57% women, 43% men, 71% part-time, 98% state residents, 10% transferred in, 1% international, 57% 25 or older, 1% Native American, 10% Hispanic, 39% black, 30% Asian or Pacific Islander. *Retention:* 71% of 1995 full-time freshmen returned. *Areas of study chosen:* 9% business management and administrative services, 9% engineering and applied sciences, 5% fine arts, 5% health professions and related sciences, 4% computer and information sciences, 4% interdisciplinary studies, 3% liberal arts/general studies, 3% social sciences, 2% biological and life sciences, 2% psychology, 1% architecture, 1% communications and journalism, 1% education, 1% mathematics.

First-Year Class: 2,313 total. Of the students who applied, 98% were accepted.

Graduation Requirements: 60 semester hours; 3 semester hours of math; computer course.

Computers on Campus: 30 computers available on campus for general student use. Computers for student use in computer labs.

EXPENSES

Expenses for 1997–98: State resident tuition: $0 full-time. Nonresident tuition: $3420 full-time, $114 per semester hour part-time. Part-time mandatory fees per semester range from $15 to $145. Full-time mandatory fees: $394.

LD Program Contact: Ms. Sondra Neiman, Learning Disabilities Specialist, Laney College, 900 Fallon Street, Oakland, CA 94607-4893, 510-464-3534.

LONG BEACH CITY COLLEGE

Long Beach, California

Students with LD	100	Subject-Area Tutoring	✓
ADD services	✓	Special Courses	
Staff	2 full-, 2 part-time	Taped Textbooks	✓
Special Fee	None	Alternative Test Arrang.	✓
Diagnostic Testing	✓	Notetakers	✓
Basic Skills Remediation	✓	LD Student Organization	

LEARNING DISABILITIES PROGRAM INFORMATION

The Learning Disabilities Program began offering services in 1979. Currently the program serves 100 undergraduates with LD. Students diagnosed with ADD/ADHD are eligible for the same services available to students with LD, as well as ADD screening (information, counseling and referral services).

Staff: 2 full-time, 2 part-time staff members, including coordinator. Services provided by remediation specialists, tutors, counselor, diagnostic specialists.

Special Fees: No special fees are charged for services to students with LD.

Applications and admissions: *Required:* psychoeducational report completed within 3 years, California Assessment System for Adults with Learning Disabilities. Students may begin taking classes any term. *Application deadline:* continuous.

Special policies: The college has written policies regarding grade forgiveness; substitutions and waivers of graduation requirements.

PROGRAM AND SERVICE COMPONENTS

Special preparation or orientation: Optional orientation offered individually by special arrangement.

Diagnostic testing: Intelligence, reading, math, spelling, spoken language, written language, perceptual skills, speech, hearing.

Academic advising: Provided by LD staff members, academic advisers. Students with LD may take up to 18 units each term; most take 9 to 12 units; 12 units required to maintain full-time status; .5 units required to be eligible for financial aid.

Counseling services: Individual counseling, career counseling.

Basic skills remediation: Offered one-on-one by LD teachers. Available in reading, math, spelling, handwriting, spoken language, written language, learning strategies.

Subject-area tutoring: Offered one-on-one by peer tutors. Available in most subjects.

Auxiliary aids: Taped textbooks, tape recorders, calculators, typewriters, word-processors with spell-check, personal computers, talking computers, optical character readers.

Auxiliary services: Alternative test arrangements, notetakers, priority registration, advocacy.

GENERAL COLLEGE INFORMATION

State-supported, 2-year, coed. Part of California Community Colleges System. Awards associate degrees. Founded 1927. *Setting:* 40-acre urban campus with easy access to Los Angeles. *Research spending 1995–96:* $30,000. *Total enrollment:* 25,100. *Faculty:* 900 (300 full-time, 21% with terminal degrees, 600 part-time); student–undergrad faculty ratio is 32:1.

Enrollment Profile: 25,100 students: 56% women, 44% men, 64% part-time, 96% state residents, 5% transferred in, 3% international, 51% 25 or older, 1% Native American, 22% Hispanic, 15% black, 11% Asian or Pacific Islander. *Areas of study chosen:* 36% liberal arts/general studies, 17% health professions and related sciences, 11% business management and administrative services, 8% engineering and applied sciences, 5% computer and information sciences, 5% social sciences, 4% education, 4% vocational and home economics, 1% biological and life sciences, 1% physical sciences. *Most popular recent majors:* liberal arts/general studies, nursing, electrical and electronics technologies.

First-Year Class: 4,600 total. Of the students who applied, 100% were accepted.

Graduation Requirements: 60 units; 1 natural science course; computer course.

Computers on Campus: 200 computers available on campus for general student use. Computer purchase/lease plans available. Computers for student use in computer center, computer labs, library. Staffed computer lab on campus provides training in use of computers, software. *Academic computing expenditure 1995–96:* $1 million.

EXPENSES

Expenses for 1997–98: State resident tuition: $0 full-time. Nonresident tuition: $3540 full-time, $118 per unit part-time. Part-time mandatory fees per semester range from $23 to $153. Tuition for international students: $3750 full-time, $125 per unit part-time. Full-time mandatory fees: $410.

LD Program Contact: Mr. Marvin Mastros, Learning Disabilities Specialist, Long Beach City College, 1305 East Pacific Coast Highway, Long Beach, CA 90806, 562-938-3926. Fax: 562-938-3912. Email: mmastros@lbcc.cc.ca.us.

LONGVIEW COMMUNITY COLLEGE

Lee's Summit, Missouri

Students with LD	99	Subject-Area Tutoring	✓
ADD services	✓	Special Courses	✓
Staff	2 full-, 3 part-time	Taped Textbooks	✓
Special Fee	✓	Alternative Test Arrang.	✓
Diagnostic Testing	✓	Notetakers	✓
Basic Skills Remediation	✓	LD Student Organization	

LEARNING DISABILITIES PROGRAM INFORMATION

The Academic Bridges to Learning Effectiveness (ABLE) began offering services in 1991. Currently the program serves 99 undergraduates with LD. Students diagnosed with ADD/ADHD are eligible for the same services available to students with LD.

Staff: 2 full-time, 3 part-time staff members, including director, secretary. Services provided by tutors, counselors, LD specialist.

Special Fees: $35 per credit hour, plus $15 program fee for the first semester.

Applications and admissions: *Required:* high school transcript, personal interview, psychoeducational report completed within 5 years, Reading and Study Skills Survey, college transcript, ACT ASSET, reading/auditory discrimination screening tests; *recommended:* high school courses completed, extended time ACT. Students may begin taking classes in fall, spring, or summer. *Application deadline:* continuous.

PROGRAM AND SERVICE COMPONENTS

Special preparation or orientation: Required orientation held during first semester.

Longview Community College (continued)

Diagnostic testing: Intelligence, reading, math, spelling, written language, motor abilities, study skills, personality, self-esteem, locus of control, critical thinking skills.

Academic advising: Provided by LD staff members. Students with LD may take up to 13 credit hours each term; most take 9 credit hours; 6 credit hours required to maintain full-time status.

Counseling services: Individual counseling, small-group counseling, career counseling, self-advocacy training.

Basic skills remediation: Offered in class-size groups by LD teachers, regular teachers. Available in reading, math, spelling, written language, learning strategies, study skills, time management, social skills.

Subject-area tutoring: Offered in small groups by professional teachers, peer tutors. Available in all subjects.

Special courses: College survival skills, reading, vocabulary development, communication skills, composition, learning strategies, time management, math, typing, personal psychology, study skills, career planning, self-advocacy. Most offered for credit; all enter into overall grade point average.

Auxiliary aids: Taped textbooks, tape recorders, spell checkers.

Auxiliary services: Alternative test arrangements, notetakers, priority registration, advocacy.

GENERAL COLLEGE INFORMATION

State and locally supported, 2-year, coed. Part of Metropolitan Community Colleges System. Awards associate degrees. Founded 1969. *Setting:* 147-acre suburban campus with easy access to Kansas City. *Educational spending 1995–96:* $2308 per undergrad. *Total enrollment:* 6,079. *Faculty:* 268 (78 full-time, 98% with terminal degrees, 190 part-time); student–undergrad faculty ratio is 23:1.

Enrollment Profile: 6,079 students: 60% women, 40% men, 69% part-time, 99% state residents, 7% transferred in, 1% international, 50% 25 or older, 0% Native American, 2% Hispanic, 11% black, 1% Asian or Pacific Islander. *Retention:* 45% of 1995 full-time freshmen returned. *Areas of study chosen:* 61% liberal arts/general studies, 17% vocational and home economics, 8% business management and administrative services, 8% health professions and related sciences, 3% computer and information sciences, 3% engineering and applied sciences. *Most popular recent majors:* liberal arts/general studies, automotive technologies, business administration/commerce/management.

First-Year Class: 1,242 total. Of the students who applied, 100% were accepted.

Graduation Requirements: 62 credit hours; 9 credit hours of math/science including at least 1 lab science course; computer course for business administration, most vocational majors; internship (some majors).

Computers on Campus: 497 computers available on campus for general student use. A campus-wide network can be accessed from off-campus. Students can contact faculty members and/or advisers through e-mail. Computers for student use in computer center, computer labs, classrooms, library, student center, departmental labs provide access to the Internet/World Wide Web. Staffed computer lab on campus provides training in use of computers, software. *Academic computing expenditure 1995–96:* $665,082.

EXPENSES AND FINANCIAL AID

Expenses for 1997–98: Area resident tuition: $1457 full-time, $47 per credit hour part-time. State resident tuition: $2449 full-time, $79 per credit hour part-time. Nonresident tuition: $3472 full-time, $112 per credit hour part-time.

Financial aid specifically for students with LD: Scholarships: LDA of Greater Kansas City (MO) Scholarship, Pilot Club of Blue Springs; work-study.

LD Program Contact: Ms. Mary Ellen Jenison, ABLE Program Director, Longview Community College, 500 Southwest Longview Road, Lee's Summit, MO 64081-2105, 816-672-2366. Fax: 816-672-2025. Email: jenison@longview.cc.mo.us.

LOS ANGELES PIERCE COLLEGE

Woodland Hills, California

Students with LD	250	Subject-Area Tutoring	✓
ADD services	✓	Special Courses	✓
Staff	1 full-, 1 part-time	Taped Textbooks	
Special Fee	✓	Alternative Test Arrang.	✓
Diagnostic Testing	✓	Notetakers	✓
Basic Skills Remediation	✓	LD Student Organization	

LEARNING DISABILITIES PROGRAM INFORMATION

The Learning Disabilities Program of Pierce College began offering services in 1984. Currently the program serves 250 undergraduates with LD. Students diagnosed with ADD/ADHD are eligible for the same services available to students with LD.

Staff: 1 full-time, 1 part-time staff members, including director, assistant director. Services provided by tutors, counselor, diagnostic specialist.

Special Fees: $15 per year.

Applications and admissions: *Required:* high school transcript, personal interview; *recommended:* letters of recommendation, psychoeducational report completed within 1 year. Students may begin taking classes in fall or spring. *Application deadline:* continuous.

Special policies: The college has written policies regarding substitutions and waivers of admissions, graduation, and degree requirements.

PROGRAM AND SERVICE COMPONENTS

Special preparation or orientation: Optional summer program offered prior to entering college. Optional orientation offered before registration.

Diagnostic testing: Intelligence, reading, math, spelling, written language, perceptual skills, study skills, learning strategies.

Academic advising: Provided by LD staff members, academic advisers. Most students with LD take 12 to 15 units each term; 12 units required to maintain full-time status and be eligible for financial aid.

Counseling services: Individual counseling, small-group counseling, career counseling.

Basic skills remediation: Offered one-on-one, in small groups, and in class-size groups by LD teachers, teacher trainees. Available in reading, math, spelling, written language, learning strategies, study skills, time management, computer skills.

Subject-area tutoring: Offered one-on-one and in small groups by professional teachers, peer tutors. Available in most subjects.

Special courses: College survival skills, reading, vocabulary development, communication skills, composition, learning strategies, word processing, time management, math, personal psychology, study skills, career planning. All offered for credit; all enter into overall grade point average.

Auxiliary aids: Word-processors with spell-check, optical character readers, high-tech center computers.

Auxiliary services: Alternative test arrangements, notetakers, priority registration, advocacy.

GENERAL COLLEGE INFORMATION

State and locally supported, 2-year, coed. Part of Los Angeles Community College District System. Awards associate degrees. Founded 1947. *Setting:* 425-acre suburban campus with easy access to Los Angeles. *Total enrollment:* 18,212. *Faculty:* 519 (288 full-time, 40% with terminal degrees, 231 part-time).

Enrollment Profile: 18,212 students from 2 states and territories, 48 other countries. 54% women, 46% men, 70% part-time, 98% state residents, 48% 25 or older, 1% Native American, 13% Hispanic, 4% black, 17% Asian or Pacific Islander. *Areas of study chosen:* 71% liberal arts/general studies, 9% health professions and related sciences, 5% vocational and home economics, 4% agriculture, 3% business management and administrative services, 2% computer and information sciences, 2% engineering and applied sciences, 2% performing arts, 1% architecture, 1% foreign language and literature. *Most popular recent majors:* liberal arts/general studies, nursing, (pre)engineering sequence.

First-Year Class: 2,425 total. Of the students who applied, 100% were accepted.

Graduation Requirements: 60 credits; 1 math course; internship (some majors).

Computers on Campus: 60 computers available on campus for general student use. Computers for student use in computer center, learning resource center. Staffed computer lab on campus provides training in use of computers, software. *Academic computing expenditure 1995–96:* $169,525.

EXPENSES

Expenses for 1996–97: State resident tuition: $0 full-time. Nonresident tuition: $3750 full-time, $125 per unit part-time. Part-time mandatory fees per semester range from $21.50 to $161.50. Full-time mandatory fees: $435.

LD Program Contact: Prof. David Phoenix, Professor of Special Education/Learning Specialist/Certified Educational Therapist, Los Angeles Pierce College, 6201 Winnetka Avenue, Woodland Hills, CA 91371-0001, 818-719-6430.

LOS MEDANOS COLLEGE

Pittsburg, California

Students with LD	433	Subject-Area Tutoring	✓
ADD services	✓	Special Courses	✓
Staff	5 full-, 5 part-time	Taped Textbooks	✓
Special Fee	None	Alternative Test Arrang.	✓
Diagnostic Testing	✓	Notetakers	✓
Basic Skills Remediation	✓	LD Student Organization	

LEARNING DISABILITIES PROGRAM INFORMATION

The Disabled Students Programs and Services began offering services in 1974. Currently the program serves 433 undergraduates with LD. Students diagnosed with ADD/ADHD are eligible for the same services available to students with LD.

Staff: 5 full-time, 5 part-time staff members, including director, coordinator. Services provided by remediation specialists, tutors, counselors, diagnostic specialists.

Special Fees: No special fees are charged for services to students with LD.

Applications and admissions: *Required:* high school IEP (Individualized Education Program), psychoeducational report completed within 3 years. Students may begin taking classes any term.

PROGRAM AND SERVICE COMPONENTS

Special preparation or orientation: Optional orientation offered before registration.

Diagnostic testing: Intelligence, reading, math, spelling, handwriting, perceptual skills, study skills, learning strategies.

Academic advising: Provided by LD staff members, academic advisers. Students with LD may take up to 12 units each term; most take 9 to 12 units; 12 units (9 with waiver) required to maintain full-time status; 12 units required to be eligible for financial aid.

Counseling services: Individual counseling, career counseling.

Basic skills remediation: Offered one-on-one and in small groups by LD teachers. Available in reading, math, spelling, written language, learning strategies.

Subject-area tutoring: Offered one-on-one and in small groups by professional teachers, peer tutors. Available in most subjects.

Special courses: Reading, vocabulary development, composition, learning strategies, math. All offered for credit; all enter into overall grade point average.

Auxiliary aids: Taped textbooks, tape recorders, calculators, typewriters, word-processors with spell-check, personal computers, talking computers, optical character readers.

Auxiliary services: Alternative test arrangements, notetakers, priority registration.

GENERAL COLLEGE INFORMATION

District-supported, 2-year, coed. Part of California Community Colleges System. Awards associate degrees. Founded 1970. *Setting:* 120-acre suburban campus with easy access to San Francisco. *Total enrollment:* 7,311. *Faculty:* 236 (94 full-time, 142 part-time); student–undergrad faculty ratio is 30:1.

Enrollment Profile: 7,311 students: 61% women, 39% men, 76% part-time, 99% state residents, 15% transferred in, 1% international, 53% 25 or older, 1% Native American, 18% Hispanic, 10% black, 5% Asian or Pacific Islander. *Most popular recent majors:* liberal arts/general studies, nursing, accounting.

First-Year Class: 1,768 total; 1,768 applied, 100% were accepted, 100% of whom enrolled.

Graduation Requirements: 57 units; math proficiency; 1 course each in biological science and physical science; computer course.

Computers on Campus: 200 computers available on campus for general student use. Computers for student use in computer center, computer labs, learning resource center, classrooms. Staffed computer lab on campus.

EXPENSES

Expenses for 1997–98: State resident tuition: $0 full-time. Nonresident tuition: $3750 full-time, $125 per unit part-time. Part-time mandatory fees: $13 per unit. Full-time mandatory fees: $390.

LD Program Contact: Ms. Dorrie Fisher, Coordinator, Disabled Students Programs and Services, Los Medanos College, 2700 East Leland Road, Pittsburg, CA 94565-5197, 510-439-2181 Ext. 353. Fax: 510-427-1599.

MENDOCINO COLLEGE

Ukiah, California

Students with LD	75 to 90	Subject-Area Tutoring	✓
ADD services		Special Courses	✓
Staff	3 full-time	Taped Textbooks	✓
Special Fee	None	Alternative Test Arrang.	✓
Diagnostic Testing	✓	Notetakers	✓
Basic Skills Remediation	✓	LD Student Organization	

LEARNING DISABILITIES PROGRAM INFORMATION

The Disabled Student Program and Services began offering services in 1982. Currently the program serves 75 to 90 undergraduates with LD.

Mendocino College (continued)

Staff: 3 full-time staff members, including director. Services provided by remediation specialist, counselor, diagnostic specialist.
Special Fees: No special fees are charged for services to students with LD.
Applications and admissions: *Recommended:* high school transcript, grade point average, courses completed, psychoeducational report completed within 3 years, Community College Placement Test, appointment with counselor. Students may begin taking classes any term. *Application deadline:* continuous.
Special policies: The college has written policies regarding grade forgiveness.

PROGRAM AND SERVICE COMPONENTS

Special preparation or orientation: Optional orientation offered before registration, during registration, after classes begin.
Diagnostic testing: Reading, math, spelling, written language, perceptual skills, study skills, learning strategies.
Academic advising: Provided by LD staff members. Most students with LD take 6 to 12 units each term; 9 units required to maintain full-time status; 12 units (full assistance), 6 to 9 units (partial assistance) required to be eligible for financial aid.
Counseling services: Individual counseling, career counseling, self-advocacy training, disability management.
Basic skills remediation: Offered one-on-one and in small groups by LD teachers, regular teachers, instructional assistants. Available in reading, math, spelling, written language, learning strategies, perceptual skills, study skills, time management, computer skills.
Subject-area tutoring: Offered one-on-one and in small groups by professional teachers, peer tutors. Available in all subjects.
Special courses: College survival skills, reading, vocabulary development, composition, learning strategies, word processing, time management, math, typing, study skills, career planning, mainstream support. All offered for credit; all enter into overall grade point average.
Auxiliary aids: Taped textbooks, tape recorders, calculators, word-processors with spell-check, personal computers.
Auxiliary services: Alternative test arrangements, notetakers, priority registration, advocacy, scribes.

GENERAL COLLEGE INFORMATION

State and locally supported, 2-year, coed. Part of California Community Colleges System. Awards associate degrees. Founded 1973. *Setting:* 127-acre rural campus. *Total enrollment:* 3,823. *Faculty:* 193 (53 full-time, 11% with terminal degrees, 140 part-time); student–undergrad faculty ratio is 25:1.
Enrollment Profile: 3,823 students from 16 states and territories, 5 other countries. 60% women, 40% men, 72% part-time, 97% state residents, 7% transferred in, 1% international, 65% 25 or older, 4% Native American, 8% Hispanic, 2% black, 1% Asian or Pacific Islander. *Most popular recent majors:* computer information systems, secretarial studies/office management, liberal arts/general studies.
First-Year Class: 534 total; 600 applied, 100% were accepted, 89% of whom enrolled.
Graduation Requirements: 60 units; 3 units of math; computer course for business administration majors; internship (some majors).
Computers on Campus: 90 computers available on campus for general student use. A computer is strongly recommended for all students. A campus-wide network can be accessed from off-campus. Students can contact faculty members and/or advisers through e-mail. Computers for student use in computer labs provide access to the Internet/World Wide Web. Staffed computer lab on campus provides training in use of computers, software.

EXPENSES

Expenses for 1997–98: State resident tuition: $0 full-time. Nonresident tuition: $3540 full-time, $118 per unit part-time. Part-time mandatory fees per semester range from $24 to $154. Full-time mandatory fees: $412.
LD Program Contact: Ms. Kathleen Daigle, Learning Disabilities Specialist, Mendocino College, PO Box 3000, Ukiah, CA 95482, 707-468-3151. Fax: 707-468-3120.

MIDDLESEX COMMUNITY COLLEGE

Bedford, Massachusetts

Students with LD	298	Subject-Area Tutoring	✓
ADD services	✓	Special Courses	
Staff	1 full-, 5 part-time	Taped Textbooks	✓
Special Fee	None	Alternative Test Arrang.	✓
Diagnostic Testing	✓	Notetakers	✓
Basic Skills Remediation	✓	LD Student Organization	

LEARNING DISABILITIES PROGRAM INFORMATION

The Disability Support Services began offering services in 1985. Currently the program serves 298 undergraduates with LD. Students diagnosed with ADD/ADHD are eligible for the same services available to students with LD.
Staff: 1 full-time, 5 part-time staff members, including director. Services provided by tutors.
Special Fees: No special fees are charged for services to students with LD.
Applications and admissions: Open admissions. Students may begin taking classes in fall, spring, or summer. *Application deadline:* continuous.

PROGRAM AND SERVICE COMPONENTS

Special preparation or orientation: Optional orientation offered before classes begin.
Diagnostic testing: Intelligence, reading, math, spelling, written language.
Academic advising: Provided by LD staff members, academic advisers. Most students with LD take 6 to 12 credits each term; 12 credits required to maintain full-time status; 6 credits required to be eligible for financial aid.
Counseling services: Individual counseling, career counseling.
Basic skills remediation: Offered in small groups and in class-size groups by regular teachers; computer-aided instruction also offered. Available in reading, math, written language, learning strategies, study skills, time management.
Subject-area tutoring: Offered one-on-one and in small groups by professional teachers. Available in most subjects.
Auxiliary aids: Taped textbooks, tape recorders, calculators, typewriters, word-processors with spell-check, personal computers, optical character readers.
Auxiliary services: Alternative test arrangements, notetakers, scribes.

GENERAL COLLEGE INFORMATION

State-supported, 2-year, coed. Part of Massachusetts Public Higher Education System. Awards associate degrees. Founded 1970. *Setting:* 200-acre campus with easy access to Boston. *Total enrollment:* 5,945. *Faculty:* 377 (124 full-time, 94% with terminal degrees, 253 part-time); student–undergrad faculty ratio is 18:1.
Enrollment Profile: 5,945 students from 2 states and territories, 20 other countries. 62% women, 38% men, 58% part-time, 97% state residents, 11% transferred in, 1% international, 49% 25 or older, 1% Native American, 6% Hispanic, 3% black, 6% Asian or Pacific Islander. *Retention:* 50% of 1995 full-time freshmen

returned. *Areas of study chosen:* 36% liberal arts/general studies, 15% business management and administrative services, 11% social sciences, 5% health professions and related sciences. *Most popular recent majors:* liberal arts/general studies, business administration/commerce/management.
First-Year Class: 1,268 total; 3,547 applied, 75% were accepted, 75% of whom enrolled.
Graduation Requirements: 60 credits; 1 math course; computer course for most majors; internship (some majors).
Computers on Campus: 100 computers available on campus for general student use. Computer purchase/lease plans available. A campus-wide network can be accessed from off-campus. Students can contact faculty members and/or advisers through e-mail. Computers for student use in computer center, computer labs, learning resource center, classrooms, library provide access to on- and off-campus e-mail addresses, word processing, software, graphics programs. Staffed computer lab on campus provides training in use of computers, software.

EXPENSES

Expenses for 1997–98: State resident tuition: $1020 full-time, $34 per credit part-time. Nonresident tuition: $6120 full-time, $204 per credit part-time. Part-time mandatory fees per semester range from $52 to $597. Tuition for nonresidents who are eligible for the New England Regional Student Program: $1275 full-time, $42.50 per credit part-time. Full-time mandatory fees: $1610.
LD Program Contact: Ms. Kathleen Monagle, Director, Disability Support Services, Middlesex Community College, Springs Road, Bedford, MA 01730, 617-280-3631. Fax: 617-275-7126. Email: monaglek@admin.mcc.mass.edu.

MIDDLESEX COUNTY COLLEGE

Edison, New Jersey

Students with LD	160	Subject-Area Tutoring	✓
ADD services		Special Courses	✓
Staff	5 full-, 11 part-time	Taped Textbooks	✓
Special Fee	None	Alternative Test Arrang.	✓
Diagnostic Testing	✓	Notetakers	✓
Basic Skills Remediation	✓	LD Student Organization	✓

LEARNING DISABILITIES PROGRAM INFORMATION

The Project Connections began offering services in 1984. Currently the program serves 160 undergraduates with LD.
Staff: 5 full-time, 11 part-time staff members, including director. Services provided by tutors, counselors, diagnostic specialists.
Special Fees: No special fees are charged for services to students with LD.
Applications and admissions: *Required:* personal interview, psychoeducational report completed within 2 years. Students may begin taking classes any term. *Application deadline:* 2/15.
Special policies: The college has written policies regarding grade forgiveness.

PROGRAM AND SERVICE COMPONENTS

Special preparation or orientation: Required orientation held after registration and before classes begin.
Diagnostic testing: Intelligence, reading, math, spelling, handwriting, spoken language, written language, motor abilities, perceptual skills, study skills, personality, social skills, learning strategies.
Academic advising: Provided by LD staff members. Students with LD may take up to as many credits as an individual can handle each term; most take 12 credits; 12 credits required to maintain full-time status and be eligible for financial aid.
Counseling services: Individual counseling, small-group counseling, career counseling, self-advocacy training.
Basic skills remediation: Offered in class-size groups by LD teachers, regular teachers. Available in reading, math, written language, learning strategies, time management.
Subject-area tutoring: Offered one-on-one and in small groups by professional teachers. Available in most subjects.
Special courses: College survival skills, learning strategies, time management, study skills, career planning. None offered for credit.
Auxiliary aids: Taped textbooks, tape recorders, calculators, typewriters, word-processors with spell-check, personal computers, Franklin Speller.
Auxiliary services: Alternative test arrangements, notetakers, priority registration, advocacy.
Campus support group: A special student organization is available to students with LD.

GENERAL COLLEGE INFORMATION

County-supported, 2-year, coed. Awards associate degrees. Founded 1964. *Setting:* 200-acre suburban campus with easy access to New York City. *Total enrollment:* 11,000. *Faculty:* 552 (206 full-time, 346 part-time); student–undergrad faculty ratio is 21:1.
Enrollment Profile: 11,000 students from 4 states and territories, 60 other countries. 56% women, 44% men, 55% part-time, 92% state residents, 3% international, 44% 25 or older, 1% Native American, 13% Hispanic, 9% black, 15% Asian or Pacific Islander.
First-Year Class: 5,000 total. Of the students who applied, 94% were accepted, 70% of whom enrolled.
Graduation Requirements: 64 credits; 1 algebra course; computer course for business majors; internship (some majors).
Computers on Campus: A campus-wide network can be accessed from off-campus. Computers for student use in computer center, computer labs, library provide access to the Internet/World Wide Web. Staffed computer lab on campus.

EXPENSES

Expenses for 1996–97: *Application fee:* $25. Area resident tuition: $2098 full-time, $65.55 per credit part-time. Nonresident tuition: $4195 full-time, $131.10 per credit part-time. Part-time mandatory fees: $25 per semester. Full-time mandatory fees: $50.
LD Program Contact: Ms. Joan Ikle, Director, Learning Disabilities Services, Middlesex County College, Mill Road, Edison, NJ 08818-3050, 732-906-2507. Fax: 732-906-4655.

MILWAUKEE AREA TECHNICAL COLLEGE

Milwaukee, Wisconsin

Students with LD	380	Subject-Area Tutoring	✓
ADD services		Special Courses	✓
Staff	10 full-, 2 part-time	Taped Textbooks	✓
Special Fee	None	Alternative Test Arrang.	✓
Diagnostic Testing	✓	Notetakers	✓
Basic Skills Remediation	✓	LD Student Organization	✓

LEARNING DISABILITIES PROGRAM INFORMATION

The Learning Impaired Program began offering services in 1985. Currently the program serves 380 undergraduates with LD. Students diagnosed with ADD/ADHD are not eligible for the same services available to students with LD.

Staff: 10 full-time, 2 part-time staff members, including associate director, learning center instructors, educational assistants. Services provided by tutors, counselor, diagnostic specialist, LD specialists.
Special Fees: No special fees are charged for services to students with LD.
Applications and admissions: *Required:* high school transcript, multidisciplinary team report, evaluations from high school counselors, ACT ASSET. Students may begin taking classes any term. *Application deadline:* continuous.

PROGRAM AND SERVICE COMPONENTS

Special preparation or orientation: Optional orientation offered before registration, during registration, after classes begin.
Diagnostic testing: Intelligence, reading, math, spelling, handwriting, spoken language, written language, perceptual skills, social skills.
Academic advising: Provided by academic advisers. Students with LD may take up to 12 credits each term; most take 9 to 12 credits; 12 credits required to maintain full-time status; 6 credits required to be eligible for financial aid.
Counseling services: Individual counseling, career counseling.
Basic skills remediation: Offered one-on-one and in class-size groups by LD teachers, regular teachers. Available in reading, math, spoken language, written language.
Subject-area tutoring: Offered one-on-one and in small groups by professional teachers, peer tutors, LD specialists. Available in all subjects.
Special courses: College survival skills. All offered for credit; all enter into overall grade point average.
Auxiliary aids: Taped textbooks, tape recorders, calculators, typewriters, word-processors with spell-check, personal computers, talking computers, optical character readers, personal FM systems, talking dictionaries, other equipment upon request.
Auxiliary services: Alternative test arrangements, notetakers.
Campus support group: A special student organization is available to students with LD.

GENERAL COLLEGE INFORMATION

District-supported, 2-year, coed. Part of Wisconsin Technical College System. Awards associate degrees. Founded 1912. *Setting:* urban campus. *Total enrollment:* 23,099. *Faculty:* 1,759 (603 full-time, 100% with terminal degrees, 1,156 part-time).
Enrollment Profile: 23,099 students from 8 states and territories. 56% women, 44% men, 74% part-time, 98% state residents, 4% transferred in, 1% international, 61% 25 or older, 1% Native American, 4% Hispanic, 19% black, 2% Asian or Pacific Islander. *Most popular recent majors:* liberal arts/general studies, human services, nursing.
First-Year Class: 15,000 applied, 100% were accepted, 33% of whom enrolled.
Graduation Requirements: 64 credits; math/science requirements vary according to program; computer course for business majors; internship (some majors).
Computers on Campus: 1,000 computers available on campus for general student use. Computers for student use in classrooms. Staffed computer lab on campus (open 24 hours a day) provides training in use of computers, software.

EXPENSES

Expenses for 1996–97: *Application fee:* $25. Part-time mandatory fees: $2.50 per credit. Full-time tuition ranges from $1638 to $2059 for state residents, $6694 to $12,640 for nonresidents, according to program. Part-time tuition per credit ranges from $51.20 to $64.35 for state residents, $209.20 to $395 for nonresidents, according to program. Full-time mandatory fees: $80.

LD Program Contact: Ms. Brenda H. Benton, Guidance Counselor, Milwaukee Area Technical College, 700 West State Street, Milwaukee, WI 53233-1419, 414-297-6594.

MITCHELL COLLEGE

New London, Connecticut

Students with LD	125	Subject-Area Tutoring	✓
ADD services	✓	Special Courses	
Staff	6 full-, 13 part-time	Taped Textbooks	
Special Fee	✓	Alternative Test Arrang.	✓
Diagnostic Testing		Notetakers	✓
Basic Skills Remediation		LD Student Organization	

LEARNING DISABILITIES PROGRAM INFORMATION

The Learning Resource Center began offering services in 1981. Currently the program serves 125 undergraduates with LD. Students diagnosed with ADD/ADHD are eligible for the same services available to students with LD.
Staff: 6 full-time, 13 part-time staff members, including director, coordinators. Services provided by tutors, LD specialists, proctors.
Special Fees: $3900 per year.
Applications and admissions: *Required:* high school transcript, grade point average, courses completed, letters of recommendation, psychoeducational report completed within 3 years, high school LD specialist's report, achievement tests, writing sample, WAIS-R, Woodcock-Johnson; *recommended:* high school extracurricular activities, untimed or extended time SAT I, personal interview. Students may begin taking classes in fall, spring, or summer. *Application deadline:* continuous.
Special policies: The college has written policies regarding substitutions and waivers of graduation and degree requirements.

PROGRAM AND SERVICE COMPONENTS

Special preparation or orientation: Summer program (required for some) held prior to entering college. Orientation (required for some) held during registration.
Academic advising: Provided by LD staff members, academic advisers. Students with LD may take up to 19 credit hours (freshman year) each term; most take 12 to 19 credit hours; 12 credit hours required to maintain full-time status and be eligible for financial aid.
Subject-area tutoring: Offered one-on-one and in small groups by professional teachers, professional tutors, learning specialists. Available in most subjects.
Auxiliary aids: Word-processors with spell-check.
Auxiliary services: Alternative test arrangements, notetakers, priority registration.

GENERAL COLLEGE INFORMATION

Independent, 2-year, coed. Awards associate degrees. Founded 1938. *Setting:* 67-acre suburban campus with easy access to Hartford and Providence. *Total enrollment:* 528. *Faculty:* 75 (25 full-time, 50 part-time); student–undergrad faculty ratio is 12:1.
Enrollment Profile: 528 students from 28 states and territories, 12 other countries. 47% women, 53% men, 16% part-time, 50% state residents, 90% live on campus, 8% transferred in, 6% international, 4% 25 or older, 1% Native American, 3% Hispanic, 8% black, 1% Asian or Pacific Islander. *Retention:* 66% of 1995 full-time freshmen returned. *Areas of study chosen:* 40% liberal arts/general studies, 15% business management and administrative services, 15% education, 5% biological and life sciences, 5% computer and information sciences, 5% engineering and applied

sciences, 5% health professions and related sciences, 5% psychology, 5% social sciences. *Most popular recent majors:* liberal arts/general studies, business administration/commerce/management, criminal justice.
First-Year Class: 291 total; 742 applied, 88% were accepted, 44% of whom enrolled. 1% from top 10% of their high school class, 12% from top quarter, 31% from top half.
Graduation Requirements: 60 credit hours; 1 course each in math and science; computer course; internship (some majors).
Computers on Campus: 60 computers available on campus for general student use. A computer is recommended for all students. Computers for student use in computer center, computer labs, learning resource center, classrooms, library, graphic design classroom provide access to the Internet/World Wide Web, off-campus e-mail addresses. Staffed computer lab on campus provides training in use of computers, software.

EXPENSES

Expenses for 1997–98: *Application fee:* $30. Comprehensive fee of $19,350 includes full-time tuition ($12,700), mandatory fees ($630), and college room and board ($6020). Part-time tuition: $160 per credit hour. Part-time mandatory fees: $25 per semester.
LD Program Contact: Dr. Joseph W. Madaus, Director, Mitchell College, 437 Pequot Avenue, New London, CT 06320, 860-701-5142. Fax: 860-437-0632.

MODESTO JUNIOR COLLEGE

Modesto, California

Students with LD	225	Subject-Area Tutoring	✓
ADD services	✓	Special Courses	✓
Staff	1 full-, 7 part-time	Taped Textbooks	✓
Special Fee	None	Alternative Test Arrang.	✓
Diagnostic Testing	✓	Notetakers	✓
Basic Skills Remediation	✓	LD Student Organization	✓

LEARNING DISABILITIES PROGRAM INFORMATION

The Learning Disabilities Program began offering services in 1979. Currently the program serves 225 undergraduates with LD. Students diagnosed with ADD/ADHD are eligible for the same services available to students with LD.
Staff: 1 full-time, 7 part-time staff members, including coordinator. Services provided by tutor, counselor, diagnostic specialist, instructional aides.
Special Fees: No special fees are charged for services to students with LD.
Applications and admissions: *Required:* high school transcript, California Assessment System for Adults with Learning Disabilities. Students may begin taking classes in fall, spring, or summer. *Application deadline:* continuous.
Special policies: The college has written policies regarding grade forgiveness; substitutions and waivers of graduation requirements.

PROGRAM AND SERVICE COMPONENTS

Special preparation or orientation: Optional orientation offered before registration and after classes begin.
Diagnostic testing: Intelligence, reading, math, spelling, spoken language, written language, perceptual skills, personality, social skills.
Academic advising: Provided by LD staff members. Students with LD may take up to 16 units each term; most take 12 units; 12 units required to maintain full-time status and be eligible for financial aid.
Counseling services: Individual counseling, career counseling, self-advocacy training.
Basic skills remediation: Offered in small groups and in class-size groups by LD teachers, regular teachers; computer-aided instruction also offered. Available in reading, math, spelling, written language, learning strategies, study skills, time management, social skills.
Subject-area tutoring: Offered one-on-one and in small groups by professional teachers, peer tutors. Available in most subjects.
Special courses: College survival skills, reading, vocabulary development, composition, learning strategies, word processing, time management, math, study skills, career planning. All offered for credit; all enter into overall grade point average.
Auxiliary aids: Taped textbooks, tape recorders, calculators, typewriters, word-processors with spell-check, personal computers, optical character readers, electronic spellers.
Auxiliary services: Alternative test arrangements, notetakers, priority registration, advocacy.
Campus support group: A special student organization is available to students with LD.

GENERAL COLLEGE INFORMATION

State and locally supported, 2-year, coed. Part of Yosemite Community College District System. Awards associate degrees. Founded 1921. *Setting:* 229-acre urban campus. *Endowment:* $1.1 million. *Research spending 1995–96:* $125,072. *Total enrollment:* 14,148. *Faculty:* 470 (225 full-time, 245 part-time).
Enrollment Profile: 14,148 students: 56% women, 44% men, 69% part-time, 93% state residents, 5% transferred in, 1% international, 53% 25 or older, 1% Native American, 22% Hispanic, 6% black, 8% Asian or Pacific Islander.
First-Year Class: 3,794 total; 8,220 applied, 100% were accepted, 46% of whom enrolled.
Graduation Requirements: 62 units; math proficiency.
Computers on Campus: 95 computers available on campus for general student use. Computer purchase/lease plans available. A campus-wide network can be accessed from off-campus. Students can contact faculty members and/or advisers through e-mail. Computers for student use in computer center, computer labs, learning resource center, classrooms, library, West Campus Study Center provide access to the Internet/World Wide Web, on-campus e-mail addresses. Staffed computer lab on campus provides training in use of computers, software. *Academic computing expenditure 1995–96:* $130,835.

EXPENSES

Expenses for 1997–98: State resident tuition: $0 full-time. Nonresident tuition: $3658 full-time, $118 per unit part-time. Part-time mandatory fees per semester range from $24 to $154. Full-time mandatory fees: $425.
LD Program Contact: Ms. Alysa Pearson, Learning Disabilities Specialist, Modesto Junior College, 435 College Avenue, Modesto, CA 95350-5800, 209-575-6181.

MONTEREY PENINSULA COLLEGE

Monterey, California

Students with LD	360	Subject-Area Tutoring	✓
ADD services	✓	Special Courses	✓
Staff	2 full-, 2 part-time	Taped Textbooks	✓
Special Fee	None	Alternative Test Arrang.	✓
Diagnostic Testing	✓	Notetakers	
Basic Skills Remediation	✓	LD Student Organization	✓

LEARNING DISABILITIES PROGRAM INFORMATION

The Learning Skills Program began offering services in 1977. Currently the program serves 360 undergraduates with LD. Students diagnosed with ADD/ADHD are eligible for the same services available to students with LD.

Staff: 2 full-time, 2 part-time staff members, including director, instructors. Services provided by remediation specialists, tutors, counselors, diagnostic specialists.

Special Fees: No special fees are charged for services to students with LD.

Applications and admissions: *Recommended:* California Assessment System for Adults with Learning Disabilities. Students may begin taking classes any term. *Application deadline:* continuous.

PROGRAM AND SERVICE COMPONENTS

Special preparation or orientation: Orientation (required for some) held before registration and after classes begin.

Diagnostic testing: Intelligence, reading, math, spelling, handwriting, spoken language, written language, motor abilities, perceptual skills, study skills, personality, social skills, psychoneurology, speech, hearing, learning strategies.

Academic advising: Provided by LD staff members, academic advisers. Students with LD may take up to 14 credits each term; most take 12 credits; 12 credits required to maintain full-time status and be eligible for financial aid.

Counseling services: Individual counseling, small-group counseling, career counseling.

Basic skills remediation: Offered one-on-one and in small groups by LD teachers, regular teachers, aides; computer-aided instruction also offered. Available in reading, math, spelling, handwriting, spoken language, written language, learning strategies, motor abilities, perceptual skills, study skills, social skills, speech, computer skills.

Subject-area tutoring: Offered one-on-one and in small groups by professional teachers, peer tutors, aides. Available in some subjects.

Special courses: College survival skills, reading, vocabulary development, communication skills, composition, learning strategies, word processing, math, typing, personal psychology, study skills, career planning. Most offered for credit; some enter into overall grade point average.

Auxiliary aids: Taped textbooks, tape recorders, calculators, typewriters, word-processors with spell-check.

Auxiliary services: Alternative test arrangements, advocacy.

Campus support group: A special student organization is available to students with LD.

GENERAL COLLEGE INFORMATION

State-supported, 2-year, coed. Part of California Community Colleges System. Awards associate degrees. Founded 1947. *Setting:* 87-acre small-town campus. *Total enrollment:* 8,300. *Faculty:* 388 (138 full-time, 250 part-time).

Enrollment Profile: 8,300 students from 29 states and territories, 47 other countries. 60% women, 40% men, 82% part-time, 97% state residents, 13% transferred in, 2% international, 1% Native American, 8% Hispanic, 6% black, 10% Asian or Pacific Islander. *Most popular recent majors:* liberal arts/general studies, business administration/commerce/management.

First-Year Class: 3,200 total; 3,200 applied, 100% were accepted, 100% of whom enrolled.

Graduation Requirements: 60 credits.

Computers on Campus: 120 computers available on campus for general student use. Computers for student use in library, departmental labs.

EXPENSES

Expenses for 1997–98: State resident tuition: $0 full-time. Nonresident tuition: $3270 full-time, $109 per unit part-time. Part-time mandatory fees per semester range from $33 to $163. Full-time mandatory fees: $430.

LD Program Contact: Mr. Bill Jones or Ms. Kathleen Rozman, Learning Disabilities Specialists, Monterey Peninsula College, 980 Fremont Street, Monterey, CA 93940-4799, 408-646-4070. Fax: 408-646-4171.

MONTGOMERY COLLEGE–ROCKVILLE CAMPUS

Rockville, Maryland

Students with LD	200	Subject-Area Tutoring	✓
ADD services		Special Courses	✓
Staff	6 full-, 2 part-time	Taped Textbooks	✓
Special Fee	None	Alternative Test Arrang.	✓
Diagnostic Testing	✓	Notetakers	✓
Basic Skills Remediation	✓	LD Student Organization	

LEARNING DISABILITIES PROGRAM INFORMATION

The Learning Center Program began offering services in 1978. Currently the program serves 200 undergraduates with LD.

Staff: 6 full-time, 2 part-time staff members, including director. Services provided by remediation specialists, tutors, counselors, diagnostic specialist, computer instructional assistant, disability services coordinator.

Special Fees: No special fees are charged for services to students with LD.

Applications and admissions: *Required:* personal interview, psychoeducational report completed within 3 years, writing sample, Woodcock-Johnson reading tests; *recommended:* high school transcript, IEP (Individualized Education Program). Students may begin taking classes in fall or spring. *Application deadline:* continuous.

Special policies: The college has written policies regarding substitutions and waivers of graduation and degree requirements.

PROGRAM AND SERVICE COMPONENTS

Special preparation or orientation: Required orientation held during registration and after classes begin.

Diagnostic testing: Reading, spelling, written language, learning strategies, learning styles.

Academic advising: Provided by LD staff members, academic advisers. Most students with LD take 7 to 10 semester hours each term; 12 semester hours (fewer with special permission) required to maintain full-time status; 3 semester hours required to be eligible for financial aid.

Counseling services: Individual counseling, career counseling.

Basic skills remediation: Offered one-on-one and in class-size groups by LD teachers, peer tutors; computer-aided instruction also offered. Available in reading, math, spelling, written language, learning strategies, study skills, time management.

Subject-area tutoring: Offered one-on-one by professional teachers, peer tutors. Available in some subjects.

Special courses: College survival skills, reading, vocabulary development, composition, learning strategies, time management, math, study skills. Some offered for credit; some enter into overall grade point average.

Auxiliary aids: Taped textbooks, calculators, word-processors with spell-check, personal computers, talking computers, optical character readers.

Auxiliary services: Alternative test arrangements, notetakers, priority registration, advocacy.

GENERAL COLLEGE INFORMATION

State and locally supported, 2-year, coed. Part of Montgomery College. Awards associate degrees. Founded 1965. *Setting:* 88-acre suburban campus with easy access to Washington, DC. *Total enrollment:* 13,144. *Faculty:* 698 (247 full-time, 451 part-time); student–undergrad faculty ratio is 21:1.

Enrollment Profile: 13,144 students: 53% women, 47% men, 66% part-time, 95% state residents, 5% transferred in, 43% 25 or older, 1% Native American, 9% Hispanic, 17% black, 18% Asian or Pacific Islander. *Retention:* 62% of 1995 full-time freshmen returned.

First-Year Class: 8,445 total; 8,700 applied, 100% were accepted, 97% of whom enrolled.

Graduation Requirements: 62 credit hours; math/science requirements vary according to program.

Computers on Campus: 260 computers available on campus for general student use. Computer purchase/lease plans available. Computers for student use in computer center. Staffed computer lab on campus provides training in use of computers, software.

EXPENSES

Expenses for 1997–98: *Application fee:* $25. Area resident tuition: $2077 full-time, $67 per credit hour part-time. State resident tuition: $4061 full-time, $131 per credit hour part-time. Nonresident tuition: $5673 full-time, $183 per credit hour part-time. Full-time mandatory fees: $374 for area residents, $731 for state residents, $1021 for nonresidents. Part-time mandatory fees per semester range from $51 to $132.66 for area residents, $51 to $259.38 for state residents, $51 to $362.34 for nonresidents.

LD Program Contact: Ms. Janet Merrick, Director, Disability Services, Montgomery College–Rockville Campus, 51 Mannakee Street, Rockville, MD 20850-1196, 301-279-5058. Fax: 301-279-5089. Email: jmerrick@mc.cc.md.us.

MOORPARK COLLEGE

Moorpark, California

Students with LD	400	Subject-Area Tutoring	✓
ADD services	✓	Special Courses	✓
Staff	6 full-time	Taped Textbooks	✓
Special Fee	None	Alternative Test Arrang.	✓
Diagnostic Testing	✓	Notetakers	✓
Basic Skills Remediation	✓	LD Student Organization	

LEARNING DISABILITIES PROGRAM INFORMATION

The Student Support Center began offering services in 1978. Currently the program serves 400 undergraduates with LD. Students diagnosed with ADD/ADHD are eligible for the same services available to students with LD.

Staff: 6 full-time staff members, including coordinator, instructors, job developer. Services provided by remediation specialists, tutors, counselor, diagnostic specialists.

Special Fees: No special fees are charged for services to students with LD.

Applications and admissions: *Recommended:* psychoeducational report completed within 3 years. Students may begin taking classes any term. *Application deadline:* continuous.

Special policies: The college has written policies regarding grade forgiveness; substitutions and waivers of graduation and degree requirements.

PROGRAM AND SERVICE COMPONENTS

Special preparation or orientation: Optional orientation offered before registration, during registration, after classes begin.

Diagnostic testing: Intelligence, reading, math, spelling, spoken language, written language, motor abilities, perceptual skills.

Academic advising: Provided by LD staff members, academic advisers. Most students with LD take 12 units each term; 12 units required to maintain full-time status; 6 units (part-time), 12 units (full-time) required to be eligible for financial aid.

Counseling services: Individual counseling.

Basic skills remediation: Offered in class-size groups by LD teachers; computer-aided instruction also offered. Available in reading, math, spelling, spoken language, written language, learning strategies, study skills, time management.

Subject-area tutoring: Offered one-on-one by peer tutors. Available in most subjects.

Special courses: Reading, composition, learning strategies, word processing, time management, math, study skills. All offered for credit; all enter into overall grade point average.

Auxiliary aids: Taped textbooks, tape recorders, word-processors with spell-check, personal computers, talking computers, optical character readers.

Auxiliary services: Alternative test arrangements, notetakers, priority registration, advocacy.

GENERAL COLLEGE INFORMATION

County-supported, 2-year, coed. Part of Ventura County Community College District System. Awards associate degrees. Founded 1967. *Setting:* 121-acre small-town campus with easy access to Los Angeles. *Total enrollment:* 11,780. *Faculty:* 450 (150 full-time, 300 part-time); student–undergrad faculty ratio is 26:1.

Enrollment Profile: 11,780 students from 45 states and territories, 20 other countries. 55% women, 45% men, 60% part-time, 98% state residents, 15% transferred in, 1% international, 42% 25 or older, 2% Native American, 13% Hispanic, 2% black, 9% Asian or Pacific Islander. *Areas of study chosen:* 85% liberal arts/general studies, 5% business management and administrative services, 5% health professions and related sciences, 2% biological and life sciences, 1% computer and information sciences. *Most popular recent majors:* liberal arts/general studies, business administration/commerce/management, wildlife management.

First-Year Class: 3,720 total; 4,100 applied, 100% were accepted, 91% of whom enrolled.

Graduation Requirements: 60 units; 1 course each in college algebra and natural science.

Computers on Campus: 80 computers available on campus for general student use. Computers for student use in learning resource center, library, student center provide access to the Internet/World Wide Web. Staffed computer lab on campus provides training in use of computers, software.

EXPENSES AND FINANCIAL AID

Expenses for 1997–98: State resident tuition: $0 full-time. Nonresident tuition: $3510 full-time, $117 per unit part-time. Part-time mandatory fees per semester range from $25 to $165. Full-time mandatory fees: $442.

Financial aid specifically for students with LD: Scholarship: DSPS Scholarship.

LD Program Contact: Ms. Sherry D'Attile, Learning Disabilities Specialist, Moorpark College, 7075 Campus Road, Moorpark, CA 93021-1695, 805-378-1461. Fax: 805-378-1594.

MOUNT IDA COLLEGE

Newton Centre, Massachusetts

Students with LD	120	Subject-Area Tutoring	✓
ADD services	✓	Special Courses	✓
Staff	12 part-time	Taped Textbooks	✓
Special Fee	✓	Alternative Test Arrang.	✓
Diagnostic Testing	✓	Notetakers	✓
Basic Skills Remediation	✓	LD Student Organization	✓

LEARNING DISABILITIES PROGRAM INFORMATION

The Learning Opportunities Program (LOP) began offering services in 1987. Currently the program serves 120 undergraduates with LD. Students diagnosed with ADD/ADHD are eligible for the same services available to students with LD.
Staff: 12 part-time staff members, including director. Services provided by tutors, counselor, tutor/academic counselor.
Special Fees: $2600 per year.
Applications and admissions: *Required:* high school transcript, grade point average, courses completed, psychoeducational report completed within 3 years, WAIS-R or WISC-R results, reading comprehension at grade level; *recommended:* high school extracurricular activities, IEP (Individualized Education Program), untimed or extended time SAT I or ACT, personal interview, autobiographical statement, letters of recommendation. Students may begin taking classes in fall only. *Application deadline:* continuous.

PROGRAM AND SERVICE COMPONENTS

Special preparation or orientation: Orientation (required for some) held before registration and during registration.
Diagnostic testing: Reading, study skills, learning strategies.
Academic advising: Provided by LD staff members, academic advisers. Students with LD may take up to 20 credit hours each term; most take 12 to 16 credit hours; 12 credit hours required to maintain full-time status and be eligible for financial aid.
Counseling services: Individual counseling, small-group counseling.
Basic skills remediation: Offered one-on-one by LD teachers, regular teachers. Available in reading, math, written language, learning strategies, study skills, time management.
Subject-area tutoring: Offered one-on-one by peer tutors, LD specialists. Available in all subjects.
Special courses: College survival skills, learning strategies, time management, study skills. All offered for credit; most enter into overall grade point average.
Auxiliary aids: Taped textbooks, tape recorders, word-processors with spell-check.
Auxiliary services: Alternative test arrangements, notetakers, priority registration, advocacy.
Campus support group: A special student organization is available to students with LD.

GENERAL COLLEGE INFORMATION

Independent, primarily 2-year, coed. Awards associate, bachelor's degrees. Founded 1899. *Setting:* 85-acre suburban campus with easy access to Boston. *Endowment:* $6.9 million. *Educational spending 1995–96:* $3908 per undergrad. *Total enrollment:* 2,009. *Faculty:* 222 (64 full-time, 25% with terminal degrees, 158 part-time); student–undergrad faculty ratio is 9:1.
Enrollment Profile: 2,009 students from 29 states and territories, 50 other countries. 63% women, 37% men, 21% part-time, 64% state residents, 38% live on campus, 10% transferred in, 12% international, 8% 25 or older, 3% Native American, 3% Hispanic, 11% black, 6% Asian or Pacific Islander. *Retention:* 94% of 1995 full-time freshmen returned. *Areas of study chosen:* 17% business management and administrative services, 17% health professions and related sciences, 9% engineering and applied sciences, 7% liberal arts/general studies, 5% education, 4% communications and journalism, 1% computer and information sciences. *Most popular recent majors:* occupational therapy, liberal arts/general studies, veterinary technology.
First-Year Class: 911 total; 4,335 applied, 80% were accepted, 26% of whom enrolled.
Graduation Requirements: 60 credit hours for associate, 120 credit hours for bachelor's; math/science requirements vary according to program; computer course for most majors; internship (some majors).
Computers on Campus: 101 computers available on campus for general student use. A computer is recommended for all students. A campus-wide network can be accessed. Computers for student use in computer center, computer labs, research center, learning resource center, library provide access to the Internet/World Wide Web. Staffed computer lab on campus provides training in use of computers, software. *Academic computing expenditure 1995–96:* $195,000.

EXPENSES

Expenses for 1997–98: *Application fee:* $25. Comprehensive fee of $21,096 includes full-time tuition ($12,396), mandatory fees ($166), and college room and board ($8534). Part-time tuition per course ranges from $630 to $930.
LD Program Contact: Mr. Harold Duvall III, Dean of Enrollment Management, Mount Ida College, 777 Dedham Street, Newton Centre, MA 02159, 617-928-4553. Fax: 617-928-4507.

MT. SAN ANTONIO COLLEGE

Walnut, California

Students with LD	461	Subject-Area Tutoring	✓
ADD services	✓	Special Courses	✓
Staff	3 full-, 3 part-time	Taped Textbooks	✓
Special Fee	None	Alternative Test Arrang.	✓
Diagnostic Testing	✓	Notetakers	✓
Basic Skills Remediation	✓	LD Student Organization	

LEARNING DISABILITIES PROGRAM INFORMATION

The Disabled Students Programs and Services began offering services in 1980. Currently the program serves 461 undergraduates with LD. Students diagnosed with ADD/ADHD are eligible for the same services available to students with LD.
Staff: 3 full-time, 3 part-time staff members, including director, instructor. Services provided by remediation specialist, tutors, counselor, educational adviser, speech pathologist, teaching assistant.
Special Fees: No special fees are charged for services to students with LD.
Applications and admissions: *Required:* psychoeducational report completed within 3 years. Students may begin taking classes in fall, spring, or summer. *Application deadline:* continuous.
Special policies: The college has written policies regarding grade forgiveness.

PROGRAM AND SERVICE COMPONENTS

Special preparation or orientation: Required orientation held before registration and during registration.
Diagnostic testing: Intelligence, reading, math, spelling, handwriting, written language, perceptual skills, speech, vision.

Academic advising: Provided by LD staff members, academic advisers. Students with LD may take up to 12 units each term; most take 9 to 12 units; 12 units required to maintain full-time status; source of aid determines number of units required to be eligible for financial aid.
Counseling services: Individual counseling, small-group counseling, career counseling.
Basic skills remediation: Offered one-on-one and in small groups by LD teachers, teaching assistants; computer-aided instruction also offered. Available in reading, math, spelling, handwriting, spoken language, written language, learning strategies, motor abilities, perceptual skills, study skills, speech.
Subject-area tutoring: Offered one-on-one and in small groups by peer tutors. Available in most subjects.
Special courses: College survival skills, reading, vocabulary development, communication skills, composition, learning strategies, word processing, math, study skills, career planning. All offered for credit; none enter into overall grade point average.
Auxiliary aids: Taped textbooks, typewriters, word-processors with spell-check, personal computers.
Auxiliary services: Alternative test arrangements, notetakers, priority registration, advocacy.

GENERAL COLLEGE INFORMATION

District-supported, 2-year, coed. Part of California Community Colleges System. Awards associate degrees. Founded 1946. *Setting:* 433-acre small-town campus with easy access to Los Angeles. *Total enrollment:* 32,000. *Faculty:* 799 (278 full-time, 521 part-time).
Enrollment Profile: 32,000 students from 51 states and territories. 54% women, 46% men, 67% part-time, 94% state residents, 9% transferred in, 2% international, 38% 25 or older, 1% Native American, 35% Hispanic, 7% black, 17% Asian or Pacific Islander. *Most popular recent majors:* liberal arts/general studies, nursing, business administration/commerce/management.
First-Year Class: Of the students who applied, 100% were accepted.
Graduation Requirements: 60 units; math/science requirements vary according to program; computer course (varies by major).
Computers on Campus: 162 computers available on campus for general student use. Computers for student use in computer center, library.

EXPENSES

Expenses for 1997–98: State resident tuition: $0 full-time. Nonresident tuition: $3540 full-time, $118 per unit part-time. Part-time mandatory fees per semester range from $33 to $163. Full-time mandatory fees: $430.
LD Program Contact: Ms. Grace Hanson, Director, Disabled Students Programs and Services, Mt. San Antonio College, 1100 North Grand Avenue, Walnut, CA 91789-1399, 909-594-5611 Ext. 4290. Fax: 909-468-3943. Email: ghanson@ibm.mtsac.edu.

MT. SAN JACINTO COLLEGE

San Jacinto, California

Students with LD	92	Subject-Area Tutoring	✓
ADD services		Special Courses	✓
Staff	1 full-, 3 part-time	Taped Textbooks	✓
Special Fee	None	Alternative Test Arrang.	✓
Diagnostic Testing	✓	Notetakers	✓
Basic Skills Remediation	✓	LD Student Organization	✓

LEARNING DISABILITIES PROGRAM INFORMATION

The Learning Skills Program began offering services in 1981. Currently the program serves 92 undergraduates with LD.
Staff: 1 full-time, 3 part-time staff members, including LD specialist/professor. Services provided by instructional assistants, assessment technician.
Special Fees: No special fees are charged for services to students with LD.
Applications and admissions: *Required:* Assessment and Eligibility Process for California Community Colleges; *recommended:* psychoeducational report completed within 3 years. Students may begin taking classes in fall or spring. *Application deadline:* 8/18 (fall term), 1/26 (spring term).

PROGRAM AND SERVICE COMPONENTS

Special preparation or orientation: Orientation (required for some) held after classes begin.
Diagnostic testing: Intelligence, reading, math, spelling, written language, perceptual skills, hearing, vision.
Academic advising: Provided by LD staff members, academic advisers. Students with LD may take up to 18 units each term; most take 9 to 12 units; 12 units required to maintain full-time status; 6 to 12 units required to be eligible for financial aid.
Counseling services: Individual counseling, career counseling.
Basic skills remediation: Offered in small groups and in class-size groups by LD teachers, instructional assistants; computer-aided instruction also offered. Available in reading, math, spelling, handwriting, spoken language, written language, learning strategies, study skills, time management, computer skills.
Subject-area tutoring: Offered in small groups by professional teachers, instructional assistants. Available in some subjects.
Special courses: Math, study skills, language arts. All offered for credit; none enter into overall grade point average.
Auxiliary aids: Taped textbooks, tape recorders, calculators, typewriters, word-processors with spell-check, personal computers, spellcheckers.
Auxiliary services: Alternative test arrangements, notetakers, priority registration, advocacy, readers.
Campus support group: A special student organization is available to students with LD.

GENERAL COLLEGE INFORMATION

State and locally supported, 2-year, coed. Part of California Community Colleges System. Awards associate degrees. Founded 1963. *Setting:* 180-acre suburban campus with easy access to San Diego. *Total enrollment:* 5,627. *Faculty:* 215 (70 full-time, 1% with terminal degrees, 145 part-time).
Enrollment Profile: 5,627 students from 14 states and territories, 10 other countries. 59% women, 41% men, 74% part-time, 0% transferred in, 1% international, 46% 25 or older, 3% Native American, 19% Hispanic, 4% black, 3% Asian or Pacific Islander. *Most popular recent majors:* humanities, social science, interdisciplinary studies.
First-Year Class: 4,134 total; 4,134 applied, 100% were accepted, 100% of whom enrolled.
Graduation Requirements: 60 units; 1 math course; 6 units of natural/physical science.
Computers on Campus: 35 computers available on campus for general student use. Computers for student use in classrooms, library.

EXPENSES

Expenses for 1997–98: State resident tuition: $0 full-time. Nonresident tuition: $3750 full-time, $125 per unit part-time. Part-time mandatory fees per semester range from $22 to $152. Full-time mandatory fees: $408.

Mt. San Jacinto College (continued)

LD Program Contact: Ms. Milly Douthit, Learning Disabilities Specialist, Mt. San Jacinto College, 1499 North State Street, San Jacinto, CA 92583-2399, 909-487-6752. Fax: 909-654-8387.

MUSCATINE COMMUNITY COLLEGE

Muscatine, Iowa

Students with LD	25	Subject-Area Tutoring	✓
ADD services	✓	Special Courses	✓
Staff		Taped Textbooks	✓
Special Fee	None	Alternative Test Arrang.	✓
Diagnostic Testing		Notetakers	✓
Basic Skills Remediation	✓	LD Student Organization	

LEARNING DISABILITIES PROGRAM INFORMATION

The Special Needs began offering services in 1990. Currently the program serves 25 undergraduates with LD. Students diagnosed with ADD/ADHD are eligible for the same services available to students with LD.

Staff: Includes coordinator, specialist/instructor. Services provided by tutors, counselors.

Special Fees: No special fees are charged for services to students with LD.

Applications and admissions: *Required:* high school transcript, ACT ASSET; *recommended:* high school IEP (Individualized Education Program), personal interview, psychoeducational report. Students may begin taking classes any term. *Application deadline:* continuous.

PROGRAM AND SERVICE COMPONENTS

Academic advising: Provided by LD staff members, academic advisers, vocational rehabilitation counselor. Students with LD may take up to as many credits as an individual can handle each term; most take 6 to 9 credits; 12 credits required to maintain full-time status; 6 credits required to be eligible for financial aid.

Counseling services: Individual counseling, small-group counseling, career counseling.

Basic skills remediation: Offered one-on-one and in class-size groups by LD teachers, regular teachers. Available in reading, math, spelling, handwriting, spoken language, written language, learning strategies, study skills, time management.

Subject-area tutoring: Offered one-on-one and in small groups by peer tutors, LD instructor. Available in most subjects.

Special courses: College survival skills, reading, vocabulary development, communication skills, composition, learning strategies, time management, math, study skills, career planning. Some offered for credit; all enter into overall grade point average.

Auxiliary aids: Taped textbooks, tape recorders, calculators, typewriters, word-processors with spell-check.

Auxiliary services: Alternative test arrangements, notetakers, mentors.

GENERAL COLLEGE INFORMATION

State supported, 2 year, coed. Part of Eastern Iowa Community College District System. Awards associate degrees. Founded 1929. *Setting:* 25-acre small-town campus. *Total enrollment:* 1,262. *Faculty:* 95 (36 full-time, 30% with terminal degrees, 59 part-time); student–undergrad faculty ratio is 17:1.

Enrollment Profile: 1,262 students from 6 states and territories. 58% women, 42% men, 54% part-time, 93% state residents, 1% transferred in, 0% international, 48% 25 or older, 1% Native American, 7% Hispanic, 1% black, 1% Asian or Pacific Islander. *Retention:* 50% of 1995 full-time freshmen returned.

First-Year Class: 405 total. Of the students who applied, 100% were accepted, 93% of whom enrolled.

Graduation Requirements: 64 credits; 3 credits of math; 8 credits of science; computer course; internship (some majors).

Computers on Campus: 57 computers available on campus for general student use. Computers for student use in computer center, library. Staffed computer lab on campus.

EXPENSES

Expenses for 1997–98: *Application fee:* $20. State resident tuition: $1696 full-time, $53 per credit hour part-time. Nonresident tuition: $2544 full-time, $79.50 per credit hour part-time. Part-time mandatory fees: $5.50 per credit hour. Full-time mandatory fees: $176.

LD Program Contact: Ms. Kathy Trosen, Director, Special Needs, Muscatine Community College, 152 Colorado Street, Muscatine, IA 52761, 319-263-8250 Ext. 182. Fax: 319-264-8341.

NAPA VALLEY COLLEGE

Napa, California

Students with LD	200	Subject-Area Tutoring	✓
ADD services		Special Courses	✓
Staff	3 full-time	Taped Textbooks	✓
Special Fee	None	Alternative Test Arrang.	✓
Diagnostic Testing	✓	Notetakers	✓
Basic Skills Remediation		LD Student Organization	

LEARNING DISABILITIES PROGRAM INFORMATION

The Diagnostic Learning Service currently serves 200 undergraduates with LD.

Staff: 3 full-time staff members, including coordinator. Services provided by remediation specialists.

Special Fees: $6.50 for diagnostic testing.

Applications and admissions: Students may begin taking classes any term. *Application deadline:* continuous.

PROGRAM AND SERVICE COMPONENTS

Diagnostic testing: Intelligence, reading, math, spelling, learning strategies.

Academic advising: Provided by LD staff members, academic advisers. Most students with LD take 12 units each term; 12 units required to maintain full-time status.

Counseling services: Individual counseling.

Subject-area tutoring: Offered one-on-one and in small groups by peer tutors, instructional assistants. Available in some subjects.

Special courses: Computer composition. All offered for credit; all enter into overall grade point average.

Auxiliary aids: Taped textbooks, tape recorders, word-processors with spell-check.

Auxiliary services: Alternative test arrangements, notetakers, priority registration.

GENERAL COLLEGE INFORMATION

State and locally supported, 2 year, coed. Part of California Community Colleges System. Awards associate degrees. Founded 1942. *Setting:* 188-acre suburban campus with easy access to San Francisco. *Total enrollment:* 7,000. *Faculty:* 304 (104 full-time, 200 part-time); student–undergrad faculty ratio is 23:1.

Enrollment Profile: 7,000 students from 12 states and territories, 21 other countries. 58% women, 42% men, 72% part-time, 92% state residents, 67% transferred in, 2% international, 44% 25 or older, 2% Native American, 16% Hispanic, 5% black, 9% Asian or Pacific Islander.

First-Year Class: 1,217 total; 1,350 applied, 100% were accepted, 90% of whom enrolled.
Graduation Requirements: 60 units; 1 math course; internship (some majors).
Computers on Campus: 30 computers available on campus for general student use. Computers for student use in computer center, library. Staffed computer lab on campus provides training in use of computers.

EXPENSES

Expenses for 1997–98: State resident tuition: $0 full-time. Nonresident tuition: $3780 full-time, $126 per unit part-time. Part-time mandatory fees: $14 per unit. Full-time mandatory fees: $420.
LD Program Contact: Dr. Gwynne Pacheco, Learning Disabilities Specialist, Napa Valley College, 2277 Napa-Vallejo Highway, Napa, CA 94558-6236, 707-253-3281.

NEW RIVER COMMUNITY COLLEGE

Dublin, Virginia

Students with LD	130	Subject-Area Tutoring	✓
ADD services	✓	Special Courses	✓
Staff		Taped Textbooks	✓
Special Fee	None	Alternative Test Arrang.	✓
Diagnostic Testing		Notetakers	✓
Basic Skills Remediation	✓	LD Student Organization	✓

LEARNING DISABILITIES PROGRAM INFORMATION

The Southwest Virginia Regional Center for the Learning Disabled began offering services in 1985. Currently the program serves 130 undergraduates with LD. Students diagnosed with ADD/ADHD are eligible for the same services available to students with LD, as well as special counseling.
Staff: Includes coordinator, LD specialist, counselor, graduate assistant. Services provided by remediation specialists, tutors, counselor.
Special Fees: No special fees are charged for services to students with LD.
Applications and admissions: *Required:* documentation of LD. Students may begin taking classes any term. *Application deadline:* continuous.

PROGRAM AND SERVICE COMPONENTS

Special preparation or orientation: Optional summer program offered prior to entering college. Optional orientation offered during summer prior to enrollment.
Academic advising: Provided by LD staff members, academic advisers. Students with LD may take up to 16 semester hours each term; most take 10 to 12 semester hours; 12 semester hours required to maintain full-time status.
Counseling services: Individual counseling, small-group counseling, career counseling, self-advocacy training.
Basic skills remediation: Offered in small groups and in class-size groups by LD teachers, regular teachers. Available in reading, math, learning strategies, study skills, time management.
Subject-area tutoring: Offered one-on-one by professional teachers, peer tutors. Available in all subjects.
Special courses: College survival skills, learning strategies, study skills, career planning. Some offered for credit; some enter into overall grade point average.
Auxiliary aids: Taped textbooks, tape recorders, calculators, typewriters, word-processors with spell-check, talking computers.
Auxiliary services: Alternative test arrangements, notetakers, advocacy.
Campus support group: A special student organization is available to students with LD.

GENERAL COLLEGE INFORMATION

State-supported, 2-year, coed. Part of Virginia Community College System. Awards associate degrees. Founded 1969. *Setting:* 100-acre rural campus. *Total enrollment:* 1,577. *Faculty:* 170 (60 full-time, 12% with terminal degrees, 110 part-time).
Enrollment Profile: 1,577 students from 24 states and territories, 12 other countries. 54% women, 46% men, 60% part-time, 97% state residents, 14% transferred in, 44% 25 or older, 0% Native American, 1% Hispanic, 4% black, 2% Asian or Pacific Islander. *Areas of study chosen:* 13% liberal arts/general studies, 7% engineering and applied sciences, 4% business management and administrative services, 3% computer and information sciences, 2% biological and life sciences, 2% education. *Most popular recent majors:* instrumentation technology, liberal arts/general studies, word processing.
First-Year Class: 332 total; 600 applied, 100% were accepted, 55% of whom enrolled.
Graduation Requirements: 62 semester hours; math/science requirements vary according to program; computer course; internship (some majors).
Computers on Campus: 120 computers available on campus for general student use. A campus-wide network can be accessed. Students can contact faculty members and/or advisers through e-mail. Computers for student use in computer center, learning resource center. Staffed computer lab on campus provides training in use of computers, software.

EXPENSES

Expenses for 1997–98: State resident tuition: $1446 full-time, $46.65 per semester hour part-time. Nonresident tuition: $4836 full-time, $156 per semester hour part-time. Part-time mandatory fees per semester range from $7 to $23. Full-time mandatory fees: $55.
LD Program Contact: Ms. Jeananne Dixon, Coordinator, Southwest Virginia Regional Center for the Learning Disabled, New River Community College, Box 1127, Dublin, VA 24084-1127, 540-674-3600 Ext. 358. Fax: 540-674-3642. Email: nrdixoj@nrcc.va.us.

NORTHEAST WISCONSIN TECHNICAL COLLEGE

Green Bay, Wisconsin

Students with LD	80	Subject-Area Tutoring	✓
ADD services	✓	Special Courses	✓
Staff	1 full-, 6 part-time	Taped Textbooks	✓
Special Fee	None	Alternative Test Arrang.	✓
Diagnostic Testing	✓	Notetakers	✓
Basic Skills Remediation	✓	LD Student Organization	

LEARNING DISABILITIES PROGRAM INFORMATION

The Special Needs Service Program began offering services in 1986. Currently the program serves 80 undergraduates with LD. Students diagnosed with ADD/ADHD are eligible for the same services available to students with LD.
Staff: 1 full-time, 6 part-time staff members, including coordinator. Services provided by remediation specialists, tutors, counselor, diagnostic specialist, LD specialist, special needs aide.
Special Fees: No special fees are charged for services to students with LD.

Northeast Wisconsin Technical College (continued)

Applications and admissions: *Recommended:* high school transcript, IEP (Individualized Education Program), personal interview, psychoeducational report, diagnostic evaluation. Students may begin taking classes in fall, winter, or summer. *Application deadline:* continuous.

PROGRAM AND SERVICE COMPONENTS

Special preparation or orientation: Optional summer program offered prior to entering college. Optional orientation offered individually before registration.
Diagnostic testing: Reading, math, spelling, spoken language, written language, motor abilities, perceptual skills, study skills, personality, learning strategies.
Academic advising: Provided by LD staff members. Students with LD may take up to 16 credits each term; most take 12 to 16 credits; 12 credits required to maintain full-time status; 6 to 9 credits (part-time), 12 credits (full-time) required to be eligible for financial aid.
Counseling services: Individual counseling, career counseling.
Basic skills remediation: Offered in class-size groups by regular teachers. Available in reading, math, spelling, written language, learning strategies, study skills.
Subject-area tutoring: Offered one-on-one by peer tutors, lab aides. Available in all subjects.
Special courses: College survival skills, vocabulary development, learning strategies, prevocational preparation. None offered for credit; none enter into overall grade point average.
Auxiliary aids: Taped textbooks, tape recorders, calculators, typewriters, personal computers, optical character readers.
Auxiliary services: Alternative test arrangements, notetakers, advocacy, readers.

GENERAL COLLEGE INFORMATION

State and locally supported, 2-year, coed. Part of Wisconsin Technical College System. Awards associate degrees. Founded 1913. *Setting:* suburban campus. *Total enrollment:* 7,187. *Faculty:* 215 (all full-time).
Enrollment Profile: 7,187 students from 9 states and territories. 52% women, 48% men, 70% part-time, 95% state residents, 0% international, 75% 25 or older, 2% Native American, 1% Hispanic, 1% Asian or Pacific Islander. *Areas of study chosen:* 28% health professions and related sciences, 24% business management and administrative services, 18% vocational and home economics, 8% engineering and applied sciences, 5% computer and information sciences.
First-Year Class: 771 total.
Graduation Requirements: 64 credits.
Computers on Campus: 395 computers available on campus for general student use. Computers for student use in computer labs, classrooms, library. Staffed computer lab on campus provides training in use of computers.

EXPENSES

Expenses for 1996–97: *Application fee:* $25. State resident tuition: $1638 full-time, $51.20 per credit part-time. Nonresident tuition: $11,854 full-time, $370.45 per credit part-time. Part-time mandatory fees: $5.25 per credit. Full-time mandatory fees: $168.
LD Program Contact: Mrs. Patty Wouters, Associate Dean, Northeast Wisconsin Technical College, 2740 W Mason Street, PO Box 19042, Green Bay, WI 54307-9042, 414-498-5613. Fax: 414-498-6260.

NORTHERN NEW MEXICO COMMUNITY COLLEGE

Española, New Mexico

Students with LD	400	Subject-Area Tutoring	✓
ADD services	✓	Special Courses	✓
Staff	1 full-time	Taped Textbooks	✓
Special Fee	None	Alternative Test Arrang.	✓
Diagnostic Testing	✓	Notetakers	✓
Basic Skills Remediation	✓	LD Student Organization	

LEARNING DISABILITIES PROGRAM INFORMATION

The Special Needs began offering services in 1987. Currently the program serves 400 undergraduates with LD. Students diagnosed with ADD/ADHD are eligible for the same services available to students with LD.
Staff: 1 full-time staff member (coordinator). Services provided by remediation specialists, tutors, counselors, diagnostic specialists, readers.
Special Fees: No special fees are charged for services to students with LD.
Applications and admissions: *Required:* personal interview, psychoeducational report completed within 5 years; *recommended:* high school transcript. Students may begin taking classes any term. *Application deadline:* continuous.
Special policies: The college has written policies regarding substitutions and waivers of admissions and degree requirements.

PROGRAM AND SERVICE COMPONENTS

Special preparation or orientation: Optional orientation offered during registration and after classes begin.
Diagnostic testing: Intelligence, reading, math, spelling, handwriting, spoken language, written language, motor abilities, perceptual skills, study skills, learning strategies, learning styles.
Academic advising: Provided by LD staff members, academic advisers. Students with LD may take up to 15 credits each term; most take 12 to 15 credits; 12 credits required to maintain full-time status and be eligible for financial aid.
Counseling services: Individual counseling, career counseling, self-advocacy training.
Basic skills remediation: Offered one-on-one, in small groups, and in class-size groups by regular teachers; computer-aided instruction also offered. Available in reading, math, spelling, handwriting, written language, learning strategies, perceptual skills, study skills, time management, social skills, computer skills.
Subject-area tutoring: Offered one-on-one and in small groups by peer tutors, professional tutors. Available in most subjects.
Special courses: College survival skills, reading, vocabulary development, communication skills, composition, learning strategies, Internet use, time management, math, study skills, career planning. All offered for credit; some enter into overall grade point average.
Auxiliary aids: Taped textbooks, tape recorders, word-processors with spell-check, personal computers, optical character readers.
Auxiliary services: Alternative test arrangements, notetakers, priority registration, advocacy.

GENERAL COLLEGE INFORMATION

State-supported, 2-year, coed. Part of New Mexico Commission on Higher Education. Awards associate degrees. Founded 1909. *Setting:* 35-acre rural campus. *Endowment:* $829,791. *Educa-*

tional spending 1995–96: $1661 per undergrad. *Total enrollment:* 1,652. *Faculty:* 160 (40 full-time, 5% with terminal degrees, 120 part-time); student–undergrad faculty ratio is 15:1.
Enrollment Profile: 1,652 students from 5 states and territories. 64% women, 36% men, 52% part-time, 99% state residents, 1% live on campus, 11% transferred in, 0% international, 53% 25 or older, 8% Native American, 74% Hispanic, 1% black, 1% Asian or Pacific Islander. *Areas of study chosen:* 30% business management and administrative services, 22% health professions and related sciences, 17% vocational and home economics, 6% liberal arts/general studies, 5% education, 5% engineering and applied sciences, 3% computer and information sciences, 2% agriculture, 2% natural resource sciences, 2% social sciences, 1% fine arts. *Most popular recent majors:* nursing, business administration/commerce/management, education.
First-Year Class: 169 total; 170 applied, 99% were accepted, 100% of whom enrolled.
Graduation Requirements: 64 credits; math requirement varies according to program; computer course for business, office administration, and social science majors.
Computers on Campus: 12 computers available on campus for general student use. A campus-wide network can be accessed from off-campus. Students can contact faculty members and/or advisers through e-mail. Computers for student use in developmental studies departmental lab provide access to the Internet/World Wide Web, on- and off-campus e-mail addresses. Staffed computer lab on campus. *Academic computing expenditure 1995–96:* $177,477.

EXPENSES

Expenses for 1996–97: State resident tuition: $492 full-time, $20.50 per credit hour part-time. Nonresident tuition: $1392 full-time, $58 per credit hour part-time. Part-time mandatory fees: $14 per semester. Full-time mandatory fees: $28. College room and board: $3096.
LD Program Contact: Ms. Carol Maestas, Special Needs Coordinator, Northern New Mexico Community College, 921 Paseo de Oñate, Española, NM 87532, 505-747-2163. Fax: 505-747-2180.

NORTHWEST COLLEGE

Powell, Wyoming

Students with LD	25	Subject-Area Tutoring	✓
ADD services	✓	Special Courses	✓
Staff	2 full-time	Taped Textbooks	✓
Special Fee	None	Alternative Test Arrang.	✓
Diagnostic Testing		Notetakers	✓
Basic Skills Remediation	✓	LD Student Organization	

LEARNING DISABILITIES PROGRAM INFORMATION

The Learning Skills Center began offering services in 1990. Currently the program serves 25 undergraduates with LD. Students diagnosed with ADD/ADHD are eligible for the same services available to students with LD.
Staff: 2 full-time staff members, including director. Services provided by remediation specialists, tutors.
Special Fees: No special fees are charged for services to students with LD.
Applications and admissions: *Required:* high school transcript, extended time ACT; *recommended:* high school IEP (Individualized Education Program). Students may begin taking classes in fall only. *Application deadline:* continuous.

PROGRAM AND SERVICE COMPONENTS

Special preparation or orientation: Optional orientation offered during registration.
Academic advising: Provided by LD staff members. Most students with LD take 12 credits each term; 12 credits required to maintain full-time status; 9 credits required to be eligible for financial aid.
Counseling services: Individual counseling.
Basic skills remediation: Offered one-on-one and in class-size groups by LD teachers, regular teachers. Available in reading, math, written language, learning strategies, study skills, time management, social skills, computer skills.
Subject-area tutoring: Offered one-on-one by professional teachers, peer tutors. Available in all subjects.
Special courses: College survival skills, reading, word processing, Internet use, math, study skills. All offered for credit; all enter into overall grade point average.
Auxiliary aids: Taped textbooks, tape recorders, calculators, word-processors with spell-check, personal computers, talking computers.
Auxiliary services: Alternative test arrangements, notetakers, priority registration.

GENERAL COLLEGE INFORMATION

State and locally supported, 2-year, coed. Part of Wyoming Community College Commission. Awards associate degrees. Founded 1946. *Setting:* 75-acre rural campus. *Educational spending 1995–96:* $2675 per undergrad. *Total enrollment:* 1,906. *Faculty:* 181 (94 full-time, 29% with terminal degrees, 87 part-time); student–undergrad faculty ratio is 12:1.
Enrollment Profile: 1,906 students from 28 states and territories, 10 other countries. 61% women, 39% men, 30% part-time, 75% state residents, 10% transferred in, 1% international, 29% 25 or older, 1% Native American, 3% Hispanic, 1% black, 1% Asian or Pacific Islander. *Areas of study chosen:* 20% education, 8% agriculture, 8% interdisciplinary studies, 7% engineering and applied sciences, 6% social sciences, 4% fine arts. *Most popular recent majors:* business administration/commerce/management, elementary education.
First-Year Class: 659 total; 1,200 applied, 99% were accepted, 55% of whom enrolled. 15% from top 10% of their high school class, 45% from top quarter, 60% from top half. 2 class presidents, 4 valedictorians.
Graduation Requirements: 64 credits; 1 math course.
Computers on Campus: 300 computers available on campus for general student use. Students can contact faculty members and/or advisers through e-mail. Computers for student use in computer center, computer labs, learning resource center, library, student center, dorms provide access to the Internet/World Wide Web, on-campus e-mail addresses. Staffed computer lab on campus provides training in use of computers, software. *Academic computing expenditure 1995–96:* $187,912.

EXPENSES AND FINANCIAL AID

Expenses for 1997–98: *Application fee:* $10. State resident tuition: $894 full-time, $39 per credit part-time. Nonresident tuition: $2682 full-time, $117 per credit part-time. Part-time mandatory fees: $18 per credit. Tuition for nonresidents who are eligible for the Western Undergraduate Exchange: $1350 full-time, $59 per credit part-time. Full-time mandatory fees: $432. College room and board: $2842.
Financial aid specifically for students with LD: Scholarships; loans; work-study.
LD Program Contact: Lyn Pizor, Director, Learning Skills Center, Northwest College, 231 West Sixth Street, Powell, WY 82435, 307-754-6695. Fax: 307-754-6700. Email: pizorl@mail.nwc.whecn.edu.

NORWALK COMMUNITY-TECHNICAL COLLEGE

Norwalk, Connecticut

Students with LD	94	Subject-Area Tutoring	✓
ADD services	✓	Special Courses	
Staff	1 full-time	Taped Textbooks	✓
Special Fee	None	Alternative Test Arrang.	✓
Diagnostic Testing		Notetakers	✓
Basic Skills Remediation		LD Student Organization	

LEARNING DISABILITIES PROGRAM INFORMATION

The Services for Students with Disabilities began offering services in 1987. Currently the program serves 94 undergraduates with LD. Students diagnosed with ADD/ADHD are eligible for the same services available to students with LD.

Staff: 1 full-time staff member (coordinator). Services provided by tutors, counselors.

Special Fees: No special fees are charged for services to students with LD.

Applications and admissions: *Required:* high school transcript, psychoeducational report completed most recently; *recommended:* high school IEP (Individualized Education Program). Students may begin taking classes any term. *Application deadline:* continuous.

PROGRAM AND SERVICE COMPONENTS

Academic advising: Provided by LD staff members, academic advisers. Students with LD may take up to 15 semester hours each term; most take 6 semester hours; 12 semester hours required to maintain full-time status; 6 semester hours required to be eligible for financial aid.

Counseling services: Individual counseling, career counseling, self-advocacy training, educational counseling.

Subject-area tutoring: Offered one-on-one and in small groups by professional teachers, peer tutors. Available in most subjects.

Auxiliary aids: Taped textbooks, tape recorders, calculators, typewriters, word-processors with spell-check, talking computers, optical character readers.

Auxiliary services: Alternative test arrangements, notetakers.

GENERAL COLLEGE INFORMATION

State-supported, 2-year, coed. Part of Connecticut Community–Technical College System. Awards associate degrees. Founded 1961. *Setting:* 30-acre urban campus with easy access to New York City. *Total enrollment:* 5,357. *Faculty:* 302 (87 full-time, 10% with terminal degrees, 215 part-time); student–undergrad faculty ratio is 24:1.

Enrollment Profile: 5,357 students from 4 states and territories, 17 other countries. 59% women, 41% men, 77% part-time, 95% state residents, 16% transferred in, 4% international, 54% 25 or older, 1% Native American, 11% Hispanic, 15% black, 4% Asian or Pacific Islander. *Areas of study chosen:* 57% liberal arts/general studies, 13% business management and administrative services, 9% engineering and applied sciences, 5% English language/literature/letters, 4% computer and information sciences, 4% education, 3% health professions and related sciences, 1% architecture, 1% communications and journalism, 1% fine arts, 1% mathematics. *Most popular recent majors:* liberal arts/general studies, business administration/commerce/management.

First-Year Class: 623 total; 999 applied, 100% were accepted, 62% of whom enrolled.

Graduation Requirements: 60 credits; computer course for some majors; internship (some majors).

Computers on Campus: 300 computers available on campus for general student use. A campus-wide network can be accessed from off-campus. Students can contact faculty members and/or advisers through e-mail. Computers for student use in computer center, computer labs, learning resource center, library, ESL, nursing labs provide access to the Internet/World Wide Web. Staffed computer lab on campus provides training in use of computers, software. *Academic computing expenditure 1995–96:* $483,270.

EXPENSES

Expenses for 1997–98: *Application fee:* $20. State resident tuition: $1608 full-time, $67 per credit part-time. Nonresident tuition: $5232 full-time, $218 per credit part-time. Part-time mandatory fees per semester range from $42 to $91. Tuition for nonresidents who are eligible for the New England Regional Student Program: $2412 full-time, $100.50 per credit part-time. Full-time mandatory fees: $206.

LD Program Contact: Ms. Lori Orvetti, Developmental Studies Counselor, Norwalk Community-Technical College, 188 Richards Avenue, Norwalk, CT 06854-1655, 203-857-7192. Fax: 203-857-7297.

OAKLAND COMMUNITY COLLEGE

Bloomfield Hills, Michigan

Students with LD	500	Subject-Area Tutoring	✓
ADD services	✓	Special Courses	
Staff	10 full-time	Taped Textbooks	✓
Special Fee	None	Alternative Test Arrang.	✓
Diagnostic Testing		Notetakers	✓
Basic Skills Remediation		LD Student Organization	

LEARNING DISABILITIES PROGRAM INFORMATION

The Program for Academic Support Services began offering services in 1982. Currently the program serves 500 undergraduates with LD. Students diagnosed with ADD/ADHD are eligible for the same services available to students with LD.

Staff: 10 full-time staff members, including coordinators. Services provided by remediation specialists, tutors, counselors.

Special Fees: No special fees are charged for services to students with LD.

Applications and admissions: *Required:* high school transcript; *recommended:* high school IEP (Individualized Education Program), psychoeducational report completed within 4 years. Students may begin taking classes any term. *Application deadline:* continuous.

Special policies: The college has written policies regarding grade forgiveness.

PROGRAM AND SERVICE COMPONENTS

Special preparation or orientation: Optional orientation offered before registration and during registration.

Academic advising: Provided by academic advisers. Students with LD may take up to 18 credit hours (more with special permission) each term; most take 8 credit hours; 12 credit hours required to maintain full-time status.

Counseling services: Career counseling, academic counseling.

Subject-area tutoring: Offered one-on-one and in small groups by peer tutors, professional tutors. Available in most subjects.

Auxiliary aids: Taped textbooks, tape recorders, calculators, personal computers, talking computers, optical character readers.

Auxiliary services: Alternative test arrangements, notetakers, reader/scribe.

GENERAL COLLEGE INFORMATION

State and locally supported, 2-year, coed. Part of Michigan Department of Education. Awards associate degrees. Founded 1964. *Setting:* 540-acre suburban campus with easy access to Detroit. *Total enrollment:* 24,941. *Faculty:* 788 (290 full-time, 498 part-time).

Enrollment Profile: 24,941 students: 60% women, 40% men, 80% part-time, 87% state residents, 7% transferred in, 1% international, 51% 25 or older, 1% Native American, 2% Hispanic, 13% black, 4% Asian or Pacific Islander. *Areas of study chosen:* 51% vocational and home economics, 15% health professions and related sciences, 14% liberal arts/general studies, 10% business management and administrative services, 3% engineering and applied sciences, 2% computer and information sciences, 2% library and information studies, 1% fine arts, 1% natural resource sciences. *Most popular recent majors:* liberal arts/general studies, business administration/commerce/management.

First-Year Class: 7,456 applied.

Graduation Requirements: 62 credit hours; computer course (varies by major); internship (some majors).

Computers on Campus: 60 computers available on campus for general student use. Computers for student use in computer labs, library. Staffed computer lab on campus provides training in use of computers, software.

EXPENSES

Expenses for 1997–98: Area resident tuition: $1426 full-time, $46 per credit hour part-time. State resident tuition: $2418 full-time, $78 per credit hour part-time. Nonresident tuition: $3379 full-time, $109 per credit hour part-time. Part-time mandatory fees: $35 per semester. Full-time mandatory fees: $70.

LD Program Contact: Ms. Mary Jo Lord, Coordinator, Oakland Community College, 2900 Featherstone, Auburn Hills, MI 48326, 810-340-6512. Email: mxlord@occ.cc.mi.us.

OCEAN COUNTY COLLEGE

Toms River, New Jersey

Students with LD	250	Subject-Area Tutoring	✓
ADD services	✓	Special Courses	✓
Staff	5 full-, 7 part-time	Taped Textbooks	✓
Special Fee	None	Alternative Test Arrang.	✓
Diagnostic Testing	✓	Notetakers	✓
Basic Skills Remediation	✓	LD Student Organization	✓

LEARNING DISABILITIES PROGRAM INFORMATION

The Project Academic Skills Support began offering services in 1985. Currently the program serves 250 undergraduates with LD. Students diagnosed with ADD/ADHD are eligible for the same services available to students with LD.

Staff: 5 full-time, 7 part-time staff members, including director. Services provided by tutors, counselor, diagnostic specialists, career specialists.

Special Fees: No special fees are charged for services to students with LD.

Applications and admissions: *Required:* personal interview, psychoeducational report completed within 3 years, current learning evaluation results, New Jersey College Basic Skills Test; *recommended:* high school transcript. Students may begin taking classes in fall or spring. *Application deadline:* continuous.

PROGRAM AND SERVICE COMPONENTS

Special preparation or orientation: Required orientation held during summer prior to enrollment.

Diagnostic testing: Intelligence, reading, math, spelling, spoken language, written language, perceptual skills, study skills, personality, learning styles.

Academic advising: Provided by LD staff members. Students with LD may take up to 15 semester hours each term; most take 9 to 12 semester hours; 12 semester hours required to maintain full-time status and be eligible for financial aid.

Counseling services: Individual counseling, small-group counseling, career counseling.

Basic skills remediation: Offered in class-size groups by regular teachers, teachers with LD experience. Available in reading, math, written language, learning strategies, study skills, time management, social skills.

Subject-area tutoring: Offered one-on-one and in small groups by professionally trained tutors. Available in most subjects.

Special courses: College survival skills, communication skills, learning strategies, typing, personal psychology, study skills, career planning, learning strategies from the University of Kansas Model. Some offered for credit; all enter into overall grade point average.

Auxiliary aids: Taped textbooks, tape recorders, calculators, typewriters, word-processors with spell-check, talking computers, optical character readers.

Auxiliary services: Alternative test arrangements, notetakers, time extensions for course completion.

Campus support group: A special student organization is available to students with LD.

GENERAL COLLEGE INFORMATION

County-supported, 2-year, coed. Part of New Jersey Commission on Higher Education. Awards associate degrees. Founded 1964. *Setting:* 275-acre small-town campus with easy access to Philadelphia. *Total enrollment:* 7,704. *Faculty:* 349 (129 full-time, 220 part-time); student–undergrad faculty ratio is 25:1.

Enrollment Profile: 7,704 students: 59% women, 41% men, 54% part-time, 96% state residents, 4% transferred in, 1% international, 39% 25 or older, 1% Native American, 2% Hispanic, 3% black, 2% Asian or Pacific Islander. *Most popular recent majors:* liberal arts/general studies, business administration/commerce/management.

First-Year Class: 1,938 total; 2,636 applied, 100% were accepted, 74% of whom enrolled.

Graduation Requirements: 64 semester hours; 1 course each in math and science.

Computers on Campus: 100 computers available on campus for general student use. Computers for student use in computer center, computer labs, academic buildings. Staffed computer lab on campus.

EXPENSES

Expenses for 1997–98: *Application fee:* $15. Area resident tuition: $1826 full-time, $57.05 per semester hour part-time. State resident tuition: $2162 full-time, $67.55 per semester hour part-time. Nonresident tuition: $3651 full-time, $114.10 per semester hour part-time. Part-time mandatory fees: $10.55 per semester hour. Full-time mandatory fees: $338.

LD Program Contact: Mrs. Anne Hammond, Counselor, Project Academic Skills Support, Ocean County College, College Drive, PO Box 2001, Toms River, NJ 08754-2001, 732-255-0456. Fax: 732-255-0444.

ORANGE COAST COLLEGE

Costa Mesa, California

Students with LD	350	Subject-Area Tutoring	✓
ADD services		Special Courses	
Staff	2 full-, 15 part-time	Taped Textbooks	
Special Fee	None	Alternative Test Arrang.	
Diagnostic Testing	✓	Notetakers	
Basic Skills Remediation	✓	LD Student Organization	

LEARNING DISABILITIES PROGRAM INFORMATION

The Learning Center began offering services in 1975. Currently the program serves 350 undergraduates with LD. Students diagnosed with ADD/ADHD are not eligible for the same services available to students with LD.

Staff: 2 full-time, 15 part-time staff members, including director. Services provided by remediation specialists, tutors, counselors, diagnostic specialists.

Special Fees: No special fees are charged for services to students with LD.

Applications and admissions: *Recommended:* high school transcript. Students may begin taking classes in fall, spring, or summer. *Application deadline:* continuous.

PROGRAM AND SERVICE COMPONENTS

Special preparation or orientation: Optional orientation offered before registration.

Diagnostic testing: Intelligence, reading, math, spelling, written language, perceptual skills.

Academic advising: Provided by LD staff members, academic advisers. Most students with LD take 6 to 10 units each term; 12 units required to maintain full-time status and be eligible for financial aid.

Counseling services: Individual counseling.

Basic skills remediation: Offered one-on-one and in small groups by LD teachers, specialist aides. Available in reading, math, spelling, written language.

Subject-area tutoring: Offered one-on-one by professional teachers, peer tutors. Available in most subjects.

GENERAL COLLEGE INFORMATION

State and locally supported, 2-year, coed. Part of Coast Community College District System. Awards associate degrees. Founded 1947. *Setting:* 200-acre suburban campus with easy access to Los Angeles. *Endowment:* $3 million. *Research spending 1995–96:* $90,000. *Educational spending 1995–96:* $1313 per undergrad. *Total enrollment:* 22,392. *Faculty:* 813 (293 full-time, 25% with terminal degrees, 520 part-time); student–undergrad faculty ratio is 30:1.

Enrollment Profile: 22,392 students from 52 states and territories, 76 other countries. 51% women, 49% men, 66% part-time, 97% state residents, 4% transferred in, 1% international, 42% 25 or older, 1% Native American, 13% Hispanic, 2% black, 24% Asian or Pacific Islander. *Areas of study chosen:* 7% business management and administrative services, 5% engineering and applied sciences, 5% health professions and related sciences, 5% liberal arts/general studies, 4% psychology, 3% biological and life sciences, 3% education, 2% architecture, 2% fine arts, 1% area and ethnic studies, 1% computer and information sciences, 1% English language/literature/letters, 1% foreign language and literature, 1% mathematics, 1% performing arts, 1% philosophy, 1% physical sciences, 1% predentistry, 1% social sciences, 1% theology/religion.

First-Year Class: 7,057 total. Of the students who applied, 100% were accepted, 67% of whom enrolled.

Graduation Requirements: 60 units; 1 math course; computer course for accounting majors; internship (some majors).

Computers on Campus: 1,200 computers available on campus for general student use. Computer purchase/lease plans available. Computers for student use in computer center, computer labs, classrooms, library provide access to the Internet/World Wide Web, on-campus e-mail addresses. Staffed computer lab on campus provides training in use of computers, software. *Academic computing expenditure 1995–96:* $1.3 million.

EXPENSES

Expenses for 1997–98: State resident tuition: $0 full-time. Nonresident tuition: $3540 full-time, $118 per unit part-time. Part-time mandatory fees per semester range from $33 to $163. Full-time mandatory fees: $430.

LD Program Contact: Dr. Ken Ortiz, Dean, Orange Coast College, 2701 Fairview Road, Costa Mesa, CA 92628-5005, 714-457-5042. Fax: 714-432-5557.

PARKLAND COLLEGE

Champaign, Illinois

Students with LD	200	Subject-Area Tutoring	✓
ADD services	✓	Special Courses	✓
Staff	2 full-, 1 part-time	Taped Textbooks	✓
Special Fee	None	Alternative Test Arrang.	✓
Diagnostic Testing		Notetakers	✓
Basic Skills Remediation	✓	LD Student Organization	

LEARNING DISABILITIES PROGRAM INFORMATION

The Learning Resource Services began offering services in 1980. Currently the program serves 200 undergraduates with LD. Students diagnosed with ADD/ADHD are eligible for the same services available to students with LD, as well as individual sessions to discuss strategies for success.

Staff: 2 full-time, 1 part-time staff members, including coordinator, LD specialist, testing assistant. Services provided by tutor, counselors.

Special Fees: No special fees are charged for services to students with LD.

Applications and admissions: *Required:* high school transcript, psychoeducational report completed within 3 years. Students may begin taking classes in fall, spring, or summer. *Application deadline:* continuous.

Special policies: The college has written policies regarding grade forgiveness.

PROGRAM AND SERVICE COMPONENTS

Academic advising: Provided by LD staff members, academic advisers. Students with LD may take up to 18 semester hours each term; most take 12 semester hours; 12 semester hours (may be less for insurance purposes) required to maintain full-time status; 6 semester hours required to be eligible for financial aid.

Counseling services: Individual counseling, small-group counseling, career counseling, self-advocacy training.

Basic skills remediation: Offered in class-size groups by LD teachers, regular teachers. Available in reading, math, spelling, written language, learning strategies, study skills, time management.

Subject-area tutoring: Offered one-on-one and in small groups by peer tutors, professional tutors. Available in most subjects.

Special courses: College survival skills, communication skills, learning strategies, time management, study skills. All offered for credit; all enter into overall grade point average.

Auxiliary aids: Taped textbooks, tape recorders, calculators, typewriters, word-processors with spell-check, personal computers, talking computers, optical character readers.

Auxiliary services: Alternative test arrangements, notetakers, Scotopic Syndrome screening.

GENERAL COLLEGE INFORMATION

District-supported, 2-year, coed. Part of Illinois Community College System. Awards associate degrees. Founded 1967. *Setting:* 233-acre suburban campus. *Total enrollment:* 8,074. *Faculty:* 466 (151 full-time, 100% with terminal degrees, 315 part-time); student–undergrad faculty ratio is 18:1.

Enrollment Profile: 8,074 students from 24 states and territories, 58 other countries. 57% women, 43% men, 55% part-time, 4% transferred in, 4% international, 43% 25 or older, 1% Native American, 2% Hispanic, 10% black, 4% Asian or Pacific Islander. *Areas of study chosen:* 21% business management and administrative services, 20% health professions and related sciences, 14% liberal arts/general studies, 10% education, 5% communications and journalism, 4% engineering and applied sciences, 3% computer and information sciences, 2% fine arts, 2% mathematics, 1% agriculture, 1% architecture, 1% area and ethnic studies, 1% biological and life sciences, 1% English language/literature/letters, 1% interdisciplinary studies, 1% performing arts, 1% physical sciences. *Most popular recent majors:* nursing, business administration/commerce/management, liberal arts/general studies.

First-Year Class: 2,701 applied, 100% were accepted.

Graduation Requirements: 60 semester hours; math/science requirements vary according to program; internship (some majors).

Computers on Campus: 500 computers available on campus for general student use. Computer purchase/lease plans available. Computers for student use in computer center, computer labs, learning resource center, classrooms, library. *Academic computing expenditure 1995–96:* $800,000.

EXPENSES

Expenses for 1997–98: Area resident tuition: $1410 full-time, $47 per semester hour part-time. State resident tuition: $4758 full-time, $158.61 per semester hour part-time. Nonresident tuition: $6259 full-time, $208.64 per semester hour part-time.

LD Program Contact: Ms. Evelyn Brown, LD Specialist, Parkland College, 2400 West Bradley Avenue, Champaign, IL 61821-1899, 217-351-2587. Fax: 217-351-2581.

PELLISSIPPI STATE TECHNICAL COMMUNITY COLLEGE

Knoxville, Tennessee

Students with LD	125	Subject-Area Tutoring	✓
ADD services	✓	Special Courses	
Staff	1 full-, 1 part-time	Taped Textbooks	✓
Special Fee	None	Alternative Test Arrang.	✓
Diagnostic Testing		Notetakers	✓
Basic Skills Remediation	✓	LD Student Organization	

LEARNING DISABILITIES PROGRAM INFORMATION

The Services for Students with Disabilities began offering services in 1991. Currently the program serves 125 undergraduates with LD. Students diagnosed with ADD/ADHD are eligible for the same services available to students with LD.

Staff: 1 full-time, 1 part-time staff members, including coordinator, Assistant Coordinator (LD specialist). Services provided by tutors, peer tutors.

Special Fees: No special fees are charged for services to students with LD.

Applications and admissions: *Required:* high school transcript, courses completed, untimed SAT I or ACT, psychoeducational report completed within 3 years, extended time exam (Academic and Placement Program); *recommended:* extended time SAT I or ACT. Students may begin taking classes in fall, spring, or summer. *Application deadline:* continuous.

Special policies: The college has written policies regarding grade forgiveness.

PROGRAM AND SERVICE COMPONENTS

Special preparation or orientation: Optional orientation offered before registration.

Academic advising: Provided by LD staff members, academic advisers. Students with LD may take up to 19 credit hours each term; most take 12 credit hours; 12 credit hours required to maintain full-time status; 6 to 12 credit hours required to be eligible for financial aid.

Counseling services: Individual counseling, career counseling.

Basic skills remediation: Offered in class-size groups by regular teachers. Available in reading, math, written language, study skills, time management.

Subject-area tutoring: Offered one-on-one and in small groups by professional teachers, peer tutors. Available in most subjects.

Auxiliary aids: Taped textbooks, tape recorders, talking computers, optical character readers.

Auxiliary services: Alternative test arrangements, notetakers, priority registration, advocacy, scribes.

GENERAL COLLEGE INFORMATION

State-supported, 2-year, coed. Part of State University and Community College System of Tennessee. Awards associate degrees. Founded 1974. *Setting:* 144-acre suburban campus. *Endowment:* $838,685. *Total enrollment:* 7,794. *Faculty:* 412 (169 full-time, 243 part-time); student–undergrad faculty ratio is 19:1.

Enrollment Profile: 7,794 students from 17 states and territories, 37 other countries. 55% women, 45% men, 51% part-time, 98% state residents, 9% transferred in, 1% international, 40% 25 or older, 1% Native American, 1% Hispanic, 6% black, 2% Asian or Pacific Islander.

First-Year Class: 1,303 total; 1,400 applied, 100% were accepted, 93% of whom enrolled.

Graduation Requirements: 64 credit hours; computer course; internship (some majors).

Computers on Campus: 1,200 computers available on campus for general student use. A computer is recommended for some students. A campus-wide network can be accessed from off-campus. Students can contact faculty members and/or advisers through e-mail. Computers for student use in computer center, computer labs, learning resource center, classrooms, library provide access to the Internet/World Wide Web, on- and off-campus e-mail addresses. Staffed computer lab on campus provides training in use of computers.

EXPENSES

Expenses for 1997–98: *Application fee:* $5. State resident tuition: $1086 full-time, $48 per credit hour part-time. Nonresident tuition: $4342 full-time, $190 per credit hour part-time. Part-time mandatory fees per semester range from $21 to $43. Full-time mandatory fees: $86.

LD Program Contact: Ms. Judy Fischer Mathis, Coordinator, Services for Students with Disabilities, Pellissippi State Technical Community College, 10915 Hardin Valley Road, Knoxville, TN 37933-0990, 423-694-6751. Fax: 423-539-7094.

PENNSYLVANIA STATE UNIVERSITY DELAWARE COUNTY CAMPUS OF THE COMMONWEALTH COLLEGE

Media, Pennsylvania

Students with LD	34	Subject-Area Tutoring	✓
ADD services	✓	Special Courses	
Staff	2 part-time	Taped Textbooks	✓
Special Fee	None	Alternative Test Arrang.	✓
Diagnostic Testing	✓	Notetakers	✓
Basic Skills Remediation	✓	LD Student Organization	

LEARNING DISABILITIES PROGRAM INFORMATION

The Success from the Start began offering services in 1994. Currently the program serves 34 undergraduates with LD. Students diagnosed with ADD/ADHD are eligible for the same services available to students with LD.

Staff: 2 part-time staff members, including director, associate director. Services provided by remediation specialists, tutors, counselors.

Special Fees: No special fees are charged for services to students with LD.

Applications and admissions: *Required:* high school transcript, grade point average, class rank, courses completed; *recommended:* high school IEP (Individualized Education Program), untimed or extended time SAT I, extended time ACT, personal interview, psychoeducational report completed within 2 years. Students may begin taking classes in fall only. *Application deadline:* continuous.

Special policies: The college has written policies regarding grade forgiveness; substitutions and waivers of admissions, graduation, and degree requirements.

PROGRAM AND SERVICE COMPONENTS

Special preparation or orientation: Summer program (required for some) held prior to entering college. Optional orientation offered after classes begin.

Diagnostic testing: Reading, math, study skills, learning strategies.

Academic advising: Provided by LD staff members, academic advisers. Most students with LD take 12 credits each term; 12 credits required to maintain full-time status and be eligible for financial aid.

Counseling services: Individual counseling, career counseling.

Basic skills remediation: Offered one-on-one and in class-size groups by LD teachers, regular teachers. Available in reading, math, written language, learning strategies, study skills, time management.

Subject-area tutoring: Offered one-on-one and in small groups by professional teachers, peer tutors. Available in most subjects.

Auxiliary aids: Taped textbooks, calculators, word-processors with spell-check, personal computers.

Auxiliary services: Alternative test arrangements, notetakers, priority registration, advocacy, course substitutions (in special instances).

GENERAL COLLEGE INFORMATION

State-related, primarily 2-year, coed. Part of Pennsylvania State University. Awards associate, bachelor's degrees (also offers up to 2 years of most bachelor's degree programs offered at University Park campus; of students entering the associate degree program, 25% complete the degree and an additional 35% change to a bachelor's degree program). Founded 1966. *Setting:* 87-acre small-town campus with easy access to Philadelphia. *Research spending 1995–96:* $126,511. *Total enrollment:* 1,567. *Faculty:* 96 (51 full-time, 95% with terminal degrees, 45 part-time); student–undergrad faculty ratio is 23:1.

Enrollment Profile: 1,567 students from 8 states and territories. 46% women, 54% men, 24% part-time, 98% state residents, 3% transferred in, 0% international, 13% 25 or older, 0% Native American, 1% Hispanic, 11% black, 4% Asian or Pacific Islander. *Retention:* 76% of 1995 full-time freshmen returned. *Areas of study chosen:* 20% liberal arts/general studies, 19% engineering and applied sciences, 15% business management and administrative services, 13% interdisciplinary studies, 8% education, 8% health professions and related sciences, 4% agriculture, 4% communications and journalism, 2% social sciences, 2% vocational and home economics, 1% computer and information sciences, 1% natural resource sciences, 1% performing arts, 1% physical sciences, 1% psychology.

First-Year Class: 503 total; 1,334 applied, 84% were accepted, 45% of whom enrolled. 8% from top 10% of their high school class, 56% from top quarter, 82% from top half.

Graduation Requirements: 60 credits for associate, 120 credits for bachelor's; computer course for some engineering majors; internship (some majors).

Computers on Campus: 94 computers available on campus for general student use. Computers for student use in computer labs.

EXPENSES AND FINANCIAL AID

Expenses for 1996–97: *Application fee:* $35. State resident tuition: $5262 full-time, $211 per credit part-time. Nonresident tuition: $8178 full-time, $341 per credit part-time. Part-time mandatory fees per semester range from $33 to $95. Full-time mandatory fees: $190.

Financial aid specifically for students with LD: Scholarships.

LD Program Contact: Ms. Norma Notzold, Director, Success from the Start, Pennsylvania State University Delaware County Campus of the Commonwealth College, 25 Yearsley Mill Road, Media, PA 19063, 610-892-1460. Fax: 610-892-1359. Email: non1@psu.edu.

PIKES PEAK COMMUNITY COLLEGE

Colorado Springs, Colorado

Students with LD	40	Subject-Area Tutoring	✓
ADD services	✓	Special Courses	✓
Staff	5 full-, 1 part-time	Taped Textbooks	✓
Special Fee	None	Alternative Test Arrang.	✓
Diagnostic Testing		Notetakers	✓
Basic Skills Remediation	✓	LD Student Organization	

LEARNING DISABILITIES PROGRAM INFORMATION

The Disabled Student Adaptive Center (DSAC) began offering services in 1972. Currently the program serves 40 undergraduates with LD. Students diagnosed with ADD/ADHD are eligible for the same services available to students with LD.

Staff: 5 full-time, 1 part-time staff members, including director, coordinator, interpreter, computer technician. Services provided by tutors, LD specialist.

Special Fees: No special fees are charged for services to students with LD.

Applications and admissions: *Recommended:* high school transcript, courses completed, extracurricular activities, IEP (Individualized Education Program), personal interview, psychoeducational report completed within 1 year. Students may begin taking classes any term. *Application deadline:* 8/1 (fall term), 1/1 (spring term).

Special policies: The college has written policies regarding grade forgiveness; substitutions and waivers of admissions requirements.

PROGRAM AND SERVICE COMPONENTS

Special preparation or orientation: Optional orientation offered during registration.
Academic advising: Provided by LD staff members, academic advisers. Students with LD may take up to 18 credit hours each term; most take 12 credit hours; 12 credit hours required to maintain full-time status; 6 credit hours required to be eligible for financial aid.
Counseling services: Individual counseling, career counseling.
Basic skills remediation: Offered in class-size groups by regular teachers. Available in reading, math, spelling, spoken language, written language, learning strategies, study skills, time management.
Subject-area tutoring: Offered one-on-one by peer tutors. Available in all subjects.
Special courses: Learning Disabilities Strategies. All offered for credit; all enter into overall grade point average.
Auxiliary aids: Taped textbooks, tape recorders, calculators, typewriters, word-processors with spell-check, optical character readers.
Auxiliary services: Alternative test arrangements, notetakers, priority registration.

GENERAL COLLEGE INFORMATION

State-supported, 2-year, coed. Part of Colorado Community Colleges and Occupational Education System. Awards associate degrees. Founded 1968. *Setting:* 212-acre urban campus. *Total enrollment:* 6,626. *Faculty:* 498 (118 full-time, 12% with terminal degrees, 380 part-time); student–undergrad faculty ratio is 16:1.
Enrollment Profile: 6,626 students from 47 states and territories, 13 other countries. 58% women, 42% men, 65% part-time, 97% state residents, 14% transferred in, 1% international, 58% 25 or older, 2% Native American, 9% Hispanic, 9% black, 5% Asian or Pacific Islander.
First-Year Class: 3,324 total; 5,030 applied, 100% were accepted, 66% of whom enrolled.
Graduation Requirements: 60 credit hours; 1 course each in math and science; computer course.
Computers on Campus: 120 computers available on campus for general student use. A campus-wide network can be accessed from off-campus. Students can contact faculty members and/or advisers through e-mail. Computers for student use in computer labs, library provide access to the Internet/World Wide Web. Staffed computer lab on campus provides training in use of computers, software.

EXPENSES

Expenses for 1997–98: State resident tuition: $1629 full-time, $54.30 per credit hour part-time. Nonresident tuition: $7568 full-time, $252.25 per credit hour part-time. Part-time mandatory fees per semester range from $35 to $55.50. Full-time mandatory fees: $111.
LD Program Contact: Ms. Sheila Blackwell, Learning Disabilities Instructor/Coordinator, Pikes Peak Community College, 5675 South Academy Boulevard, Colorado Springs, CO 80906-5498, 719-540-7135.

PORTERVILLE COLLEGE

Porterville, California

Students with LD	104	Subject-Area Tutoring	✓
ADD services	✓	Special Courses	
Staff	4 full-time	Taped Textbooks	✓
Special Fee	None	Alternative Test Arrang.	✓
Diagnostic Testing	✓	Notetakers	✓
Basic Skills Remediation	✓	LD Student Organization	✓

LEARNING DISABILITIES PROGRAM INFORMATION

The Disabled Student Services began offering services in 1983. Currently the program serves 104 undergraduates with LD. Students diagnosed with ADD/ADHD are eligible for the same services available to students with LD.
Staff: 4 full-time staff members, including director, LD specialist, administrative assistants. Services provided by tutors.
Special Fees: No special fees are charged for services to students with LD.
Applications and admissions: *Required:* California Community College Assessment for Eligibility in Learning Disabilities Program; *recommended:* psychoeducational report. Students may begin taking classes in fall, spring, or summer. *Application deadline:* continuous.
Special policies: The college has written policies regarding grade forgiveness.

PROGRAM AND SERVICE COMPONENTS

Special preparation or orientation: Optional orientation offered individually by special arrangement.
Diagnostic testing: Intelligence, reading, math, spelling, handwriting, written language.
Academic advising: Provided by LD staff members. Most students with LD take 12 units each term; 12 units required to maintain full-time status; 6 to 12 units (depending on assistance package) required to be eligible for financial aid.
Counseling services: Individual counseling, small-group counseling, career counseling.
Basic skills remediation: Offered in class-size groups by regular teachers, reading specialists. Available in reading, math, handwriting, learning strategies, study skills.
Subject-area tutoring: Offered one-on-one by peer tutors. Available in most subjects.
Auxiliary aids: Taped textbooks, tape recorders, calculators, typewriters, word-processors with spell-check, personal computers.
Auxiliary services: Alternative test arrangements, notetakers, priority registration, advocacy.
Campus support group: A special student organization is available to students with LD.

GENERAL COLLEGE INFORMATION

State-supported, 2-year, coed. Part of Kern Community College District System. Awards associate degrees. Founded 1927. *Setting:* 60-acre rural campus. *Total enrollment:* 2,778. *Faculty:* 140 (60 full-time, 10% with terminal degrees, 80 part-time); student–undergrad faculty ratio is 14:1.
Enrollment Profile: 2,778 students: 63% women, 37% men, 58% part-time, 99% state residents, 7% transferred in, 1% international, 2% Native American, 1% black, 6% Asian or Pacific Islander. *Most popular recent majors:* education, business administration/commerce/management, science.
First-Year Class: 494 total; 494 applied, 100% were accepted, 100% of whom enrolled.
Graduation Requirements: 60 units; computer course for business, information science majors.
Computers on Campus: 350 computers available on campus for general student use. A campus-wide network can be accessed. Computers for student use in computer center, learning resource center, library provide access to the Internet/World Wide Web. Staffed computer lab on campus provides training in use of computers, software.

Porterville College (continued)

EXPENSES

Expenses for 1997–98: State resident tuition: $0 full-time. Nonresident tuition: $3450 full-time, $115 per unit part-time. Part-time mandatory fees per semester range from $33 to $163. Full-time mandatory fees: $430.

LD Program Contact: Ms. Diane Allen, Learning Disabilities Specialist, Porterville College, 100 East College Avenue, Porterville, CA 93257-6058, 209-791-2326. Fax: 209-784-4779. Email: dallen@pc.cc.ca.us.

RANCHO SANTIAGO COLLEGE

Santa Ana, California

Students with LD	340	Subject-Area Tutoring	✓
ADD services	✓	Special Courses	✓
Staff	5 full-, 17 part-time	Taped Textbooks	✓
Special Fee	None	Alternative Test Arrang.	✓
Diagnostic Testing	✓	Notetakers	✓
Basic Skills Remediation	✓	LD Student Organization	

LEARNING DISABILITIES PROGRAM INFORMATION

The Learning Disabilities Program began offering services in 1977. Currently the program serves 340 undergraduates with LD. Students diagnosed with ADD/ADHD are eligible for the same services available to students with LD.

Staff: 5 full-time, 17 part-time staff members, including coordinator. Services provided by remediation specialists, tutors, diagnostic specialists, psychologist.

Special Fees: No special fees are charged for services to students with LD.

Applications and admissions: *Required:* personal interview, psychoeducational report, California Assessment System for Adults with Learning Disabilities; *recommended:* high school transcript, grade point average, courses completed, extracurricular activities, extended time SAT I. Students may begin taking classes in fall, spring, or summer. *Application deadline:* continuous.

Special policies: The college has written policies regarding grade forgiveness; substitutions and waivers of admissions requirements.

PROGRAM AND SERVICE COMPONENTS

Diagnostic testing: Intelligence, reading, math, spelling, handwriting, spoken language, written language, perceptual skills, study skills, personality, social skills, psychoneurology, speech, hearing, learning strategies.

Academic advising: Provided by LD staff members, academic advisers. Most students with LD take 8 units each term; 12 units required to maintain full-time status; 12 units (fewer with approval) required to be eligible for financial aid.

Counseling services: Individual counseling, career counseling.

Basic skills remediation: Offered one-on-one, in small groups, and in class-size groups by LD teachers, teacher trainees, paraprofessionals; computer-aided instruction also offered. Available in reading, math, spelling, handwriting, spoken language, written language, learning strategies, perceptual skills, study skills, time management, social skills, speech.

Subject-area tutoring: Offered one-on-one, in small groups, and in class-size groups by paraprofessionals. Available in some subjects.

Special courses: Communication skills, learning strategies, word processing, personal psychology, study skills, career planning, adapted exercise science. Some offered for credit; some enter into overall grade point average.

Auxiliary aids: Taped textbooks, tape recorders, calculators, typewriters, word-processors with spell-check, personal computers, talking computers, optical character readers, assistive technology center.

Auxiliary services: Alternative test arrangements, notetakers, priority registration, reader.

GENERAL COLLEGE INFORMATION

State-supported, 2-year, coed. Part of California Community Colleges System. Awards associate degrees. Founded 1915. *Setting:* 58-acre urban campus with easy access to Los Angeles. *Total enrollment:* 20,714. *Faculty:* 1,799 (299 full-time, 1,500 part-time); student–undergrad faculty ratio is 15:1.

Enrollment Profile: 20,714 students from 50 states and territories, 50 other countries. 48% women, 52% men, 81% part-time, 97% state residents, 17% transferred in, 2% international, 63% 25 or older, 2% Native American, 24% Hispanic, 3% black, 17% Asian or Pacific Islander. *Most popular recent majors:* liberal arts/general studies, business administration/commerce/management, nursing.

First-Year Class: 14,025 total. Of the students who applied, 100% were accepted.

Graduation Requirements: 60 credits; math requirement varies according to program.

Computers on Campus: 100 computers available on campus for general student use. Computers for student use in computer labs.

EXPENSES

Expenses for 1997–98: State resident tuition: $0 full-time. Nonresident tuition: $3720 full-time, $124 per unit part-time. Part-time mandatory fees per semester range from $30.50 to $160.50. Full-time mandatory fees: $425.

LD Program Contact: Dr. Cheryl Dunn, Coordinator of Special Services, Rancho Santiago College, 1530 West 17th Street, Santa Ana, CA 92706-3398, 714-564-6260. Fax: 714-285-9619.

RIO HONDO COLLEGE

Whittier, California

Students with LD	130	Subject-Area Tutoring	✓
ADD services	✓	Special Courses	✓
Staff	2 full-time	Taped Textbooks	✓
Special Fee	None	Alternative Test Arrang.	✓
Diagnostic Testing	✓	Notetakers	
Basic Skills Remediation	✓	LD Student Organization	✓

LEARNING DISABILITIES PROGRAM INFORMATION

The Disabled Students Programs and Services began offering services in 1981. Currently the program serves 130 undergraduates with LD. Students diagnosed with ADD/ADHD are eligible for the same services available to students with LD.

Staff: 2 full-time staff members, including director. Services provided by remediation specialists, tutors, counselors, diagnostic specialists.

Special Fees: No special fees are charged for services to students with LD.

Applications and admissions: *Required:* verification of disability; *recommended:* high school transcript, psychoeducational report. Students may begin taking classes any term. *Application deadline:* continuous.

Special policies: The college has written policies regarding grade forgiveness; substitutions and waivers of admissions, graduation, and degree requirements.

PROGRAM AND SERVICE COMPONENTS

Special preparation or orientation: Optional orientation offered before registration and during registration.
Diagnostic testing: Reading, math, spelling, spoken language.
Academic advising: Provided by LD staff members. Students with LD may take up to 18 units (more with special permission) each term; most take 12 units; 12 units required to maintain full-time status; 6 to 12 units required to be eligible for financial aid.
Counseling services: Individual counseling, career counseling.
Basic skills remediation: Offered one-on-one, in small groups, and in class-size groups by LD teachers, regular teachers, paraprofessionals. Available in reading, math, spelling, spoken language, written language, learning strategies, time management.
Subject-area tutoring: Offered one-on-one and in small groups by professional teachers, paraprofessionals. Available in most subjects.
Special courses: Reading, communication skills, composition, learning strategies, word processing, time management, math. Some offered for credit; some enter into overall grade point average.
Auxiliary aids: Taped textbooks, tape recorders, calculators, typewriters, word-processors with spell-check, personal computers, Arkenstone System, copy machine (for notes).
Auxiliary services: Alternative test arrangements, priority registration, advocacy.
Campus support group: A special student organization is available to students with LD.

GENERAL COLLEGE INFORMATION

State and locally supported, 2-year, coed. Part of California Community Colleges System. Awards associate degrees. Founded 1960. *Setting:* 128-acre suburban campus with easy access to Los Angeles. *Total enrollment:* 14,500. *Faculty:* 710 (210 full-time, 500 part-time).
Enrollment Profile: 14,500 students from 5 states and territories, 40 other countries. 52% women, 48% men, 78% part-time, 96% state residents, 11% transferred in, 1% international, 40% 25 or older, 2% Native American, 58% Hispanic, 6% black, 11% Asian or Pacific Islander.
First-Year Class: 3,500 total; 3,500 applied, 100% were accepted, 100% of whom enrolled.
Graduation Requirements: 62 units; math proficiency; computer course for business education majors.
Computers on Campus: 150 computers available on campus for general student use. Computer purchase/lease plans available. A computer is strongly recommended for all students. Computers for student use in academic buildings provide access to the Internet/World Wide Web.

EXPENSES

Expenses for 1997–98: State resident tuition: $0 full-time. Nonresident tuition: $3379 full-time, $109 per unit part-time. Part-time mandatory fees per semester range from $24 to $164. One-time mandatory fee: $5. Full-time mandatory fees: $454.
LD Program Contact: Ms. Judy I. Marks or Mr. Patrick McConnell, Learning Disability Specialists, Rio Hondo College, 3600 Workman Mill Road, Whittier, CA 90601, 562-908-3420.

SACRAMENTO CITY COLLEGE

Sacramento, California

Students with LD	403	Subject-Area Tutoring	
ADD services	✓	Special Courses	✓
Staff	2 full-, 14 part-time	Taped Textbooks	✓
Special Fee	None	Alternative Test Arrang.	✓
Diagnostic Testing	✓	Notetakers	✓
Basic Skills Remediation	✓	LD Student Organization	

LEARNING DISABILITIES PROGRAM INFORMATION

The Diagnostic Learning Center began offering services in 1987. Currently the program serves 403 undergraduates with LD. Students diagnosed with ADD/ADHD are eligible for the same services available to students with LD.
Staff: 2 full-time, 14 part-time staff members, including coordinators. Services provided by counselors, instructors, aides, counseling clerk.
Special Fees: A fee is charged for diagnostic testing.
Applications and admissions: *Required:* California Community College Eligibility guidelines; *recommended:* high school transcript, IEP (Individualized Education Program), psychoeducational report completed within 3 years. Students may begin taking classes any term. *Application deadline:* continuous.
Special policies: The college has written policies regarding grade forgiveness.

PROGRAM AND SERVICE COMPONENTS

Special preparation or orientation: Required orientation held throughout the year.
Diagnostic testing: Intelligence, reading, math, spelling, handwriting, spoken language, written language, perceptual skills, study skills, personality, learning strategies.
Academic advising: Provided by LD staff members, academic advisers. Students with LD may take up to 20 units each term; most take 9 to 15 units; 12 units required to maintain full-time status and be eligible for financial aid.
Counseling services: Individual counseling, career counseling, self-advocacy training.
Basic skills remediation: Offered in small groups by LD teachers. Available in reading, math, spelling, spoken language, written language, learning strategies, perceptual skills, study skills, time management, social skills, computer skills.
Special courses: Reading, vocabulary development, composition, learning strategies, math. All offered for credit; all enter into overall grade point average.
Auxiliary aids: Taped textbooks, typewriters, word-processors with spell-check, talking computers, optical character readers.
Auxiliary services: Alternative test arrangements, notetakers, priority registration, advocacy.

GENERAL COLLEGE INFORMATION

State and locally supported, 2-year, coed. Part of California Community Colleges System. Awards associate degrees. Founded 1916. *Setting:* 60-acre urban campus. *Educational spending 1995–96:* $828 per undergrad. *Total enrollment:* 16,345. *Faculty:* 375 (250 full-time, 11% with terminal degrees, 125 part-time).
Enrollment Profile: 16,345 students from 37 states and territories, 58 other countries. 58% women, 42% men, 68% part-time, 96% state residents, 21% transferred in, 3% international, 50% 25 or older, 2% Native American, 14% Hispanic, 13% black, 23% Asian or Pacific Islander. *Most popular recent major:* business administration/commerce/management.
First-Year Class: 2,571 total; 3,100 applied, 100% were accepted, 83% of whom enrolled. 5% from top 10% of their high school class, 10% from top quarter, 25% from top half.
Graduation Requirements: 60 units; completion of math proficiency exam or 1 math course; 1 science course.
Computers on Campus: 450 computers available on campus for general student use. Computer purchase/lease plans available. A computer is strongly recommended for all students. Comput-

Sacramento City College (continued)

ers for student use in computer center, computer labs, learning resource center, classrooms, library provide access to the Internet/World Wide Web. Staffed computer lab on campus provides training in use of computers, software.

EXPENSES

Expenses for 1997–98: State resident tuition: $0 full-time. Nonresident tuition: $3750 full-time, $125 per unit part-time. Part-time mandatory fees: $13 per unit. Full-time mandatory fees: $390.

LD Program Contact: Dr. Ann K. Schafer, Program Coordinator, Sacramento City College, 3835 Freeport Boulevard, Sacramento, CA 95822, 916-558-2454. Fax: 916-558-2670.

SALT LAKE COMMUNITY COLLEGE

Salt Lake City, Utah

Students with LD	250 to 700	Subject-Area Tutoring	✓
ADD services	✓	Special Courses	✓
Staff	1 full-, 12 part-time	Taped Textbooks	✓
Special Fee	None	Alternative Test Arrang.	✓
Diagnostic Testing		Notetakers	✓
Basic Skills Remediation	✓	LD Student Organization	

LEARNING DISABILITIES PROGRAM INFORMATION

The Disability Resource Center began offering services in 1994. Currently the program serves 250 to 700 undergraduates with LD. Students diagnosed with ADD/ADHD are eligible for the same services available to students with LD.

Staff: 1 full-time, 12 part-time staff members, including coordinator, Learning Specialist. Services provided by remediation specialists, tutors, counselor.

Special Fees: No special fees are charged for services to students with LD.

Applications and admissions: *Required:* psychoeducational report completed within 3 years; *recommended:* high school IEP (Individualized Education Program). Students may begin taking classes any term. *Application deadline:* continuous.

Special policies: The college has written policies regarding substitutions and waivers of admissions, graduation, and degree requirements.

PROGRAM AND SERVICE COMPONENTS

Special preparation or orientation: Required orientation held before registration, during registration, after classes begin.

Academic advising: Provided by LD staff members. Most students with LD take 10 credits each term.

Counseling services: Career counseling, self-advocacy training.

Basic skills remediation: Offered in class-size groups by LD teachers; computer-aided instruction also offered. Available in reading, math, spoken language, written language, learning strategies, study skills, time management, social skills.

Subject-area tutoring: Offered one-on-one and in small groups by peer tutors, learning strategists. Available in all subjects.

Special courses: Learning strategies, time management, study skills. None offered for credit; none enter into overall grade point average.

Auxiliary aids: Taped textbooks, tape recorders, calculators, word-processors with spell-check, personal computers, talking computers, optical character readers, voice-activated computers, videos.

Auxiliary services: Alternative test arrangements, notetakers, priority registration, advocacy, tutors, learning strategy training.

GENERAL COLLEGE INFORMATION

State-supported, 2-year, coed. Part of Utah System of Higher Education. Awards associate degrees. Founded 1948. *Setting:* 114-acre urban campus. *Endowment:* $628,373. *Educational spending 1995–96:* $2556 per undergrad. *Total enrollment:* 21,348. *Faculty:* 1,148 (316 full-time, 20% with terminal degrees, 832 part-time); student–undergrad faculty ratio is 20:1.

Enrollment Profile: 21,348 students from 44 states and territories, 44 other countries. 48% women, 52% men, 66% part-time, 97% state residents, 5% transferred in, 2% international, 39% 25 or older, 1% Native American, 5% Hispanic, 1% black, 3% Asian or Pacific Islander. *Retention:* 36% of 1995 full-time freshmen returned. *Areas of study chosen:* 42% liberal arts/general studies, 15% business management and administrative services, 15% vocational and home economics, 10% health professions and related sciences, 6% engineering and applied sciences, 4% education, 2% biological and life sciences, 2% computer and information sciences, 2% social sciences, 1% architecture, 1% communications and journalism, 1% English language/literature/letters. *Most popular recent majors:* liberal arts/general studies, business administration/commerce/management.

First-Year Class: 3,796 total; 5,036 applied, 100% were accepted, 75% of whom enrolled.

Graduation Requirements: 96 credits; math/science requirements vary according to program; computer course for most majors; internship (some majors).

Computers on Campus: 100 computers available on campus for general student use. Computer purchase/lease plans available. A campus-wide network can be accessed from off-campus. Students can contact faculty members and/or advisers through e-mail. Computers for student use in computer labs, learning resource center, library, student center, various buildings provide access to the Internet/World Wide Web, on- and off-campus e-mail addresses. Staffed computer lab on campus provides training in use of computers, software. *Academic computing expenditure 1995–96:* $2.3 million.

EXPENSES

Expenses for 1997–98: *Application fee:* $20. State resident tuition: $1239 full-time. Nonresident tuition: $4416 full-time. Part-time tuition per quarter ranges from $50 to $380 for state residents, $185 to $1355 for nonresidents. Part-time mandatory fees: $38 per quarter for 1 to 10 credits, $88 per quarter for 11 credits. Full-time mandatory fees: $264.

LD Program Contact: Mr. Steven P. Lewis, Learning Specialist, Salt Lake Community College, CC008, 4600 South Redwood Road, Salt Lake City, UT 84130-0808, 801-957-4736. Fax: 801-957-4958. Email: lewisst@slcc.edu.

SAN ANTONIO COLLEGE

San Antonio, Texas

Students with LD	295	Subject-Area Tutoring	✓
ADD services	✓	Special Courses	✓
Staff	10 full-time	Taped Textbooks	✓
Special Fee	None	Alternative Test Arrang.	✓
Diagnostic Testing	✓	Notetakers	✓
Basic Skills Remediation	✓	LD Student Organization	

LEARNING DISABILITIES PROGRAM INFORMATION

The Disabled Student Services began offering services in 1983. Currently the program serves 295 undergraduates with LD. Students diagnosed with ADD/ADHD are eligible for the same services available to students with LD.

Staff: 10 full-time staff members, including coordinator. Services provided by tutors, counselors, diagnostic specialists, student support assistants.
Special Fees: No special fees are charged for services to students with LD.
Applications and admissions: *Required:* high school transcript; *recommended:* personal interview, psychoeducational report completed within 3 years, any verification or assessment of LD. Students may begin taking classes any term. *Application deadline:* continuous.

PROGRAM AND SERVICE COMPONENTS

Special preparation or orientation: Required orientation held before classes begin.
Diagnostic testing: Intelligence, reading, math, spelling, handwriting, written language, motor abilities, perceptual skills, study skills, personality, social skills, learning strategies.
Academic advising: Provided by LD staff members. Students with LD may take up to 18 credits each term; most take 12 credits; 12 credits required to maintain full-time status; 6 credits required to be eligible for financial aid.
Counseling services: Individual counseling, small-group counseling, career counseling.
Basic skills remediation: Offered in class-size groups by regular teachers. Available in reading, math, spelling, handwriting, spoken language, written language, study skills, speech, science.
Subject-area tutoring: Offered one-on-one and in small groups by peer tutors. Available in most subjects.
Special courses: College survival skills, word processing, time management, study skills. None offered for credit.
Auxiliary aids: Taped textbooks, tape recorders, calculators, typewriters, word-processors with spell-check, personal computers, optical character readers, talking computer terminal.
Auxiliary services: Alternative test arrangements, notetakers, priority registration, advocacy, readers, writers.

GENERAL COLLEGE INFORMATION

State and locally supported, 2-year, coed. Part of Alamo Community College District System. Awards associate degrees. Founded 1925. *Setting:* 45-acre urban campus.

EXPENSES

Expenses for 1996–97: Area resident tuition: $792 full-time. State resident tuition: $1518 full-time. Nonresident tuition: $3036 full-time. Part-time tuition per semester ranges from $120 to $264 for area residents, $230 to $506 for state residents, $460 to $1012 for nonresidents. Part-time mandatory fees: $75 per semester. Full-time mandatory fees: $150.
LD Program Contact: Ms. Maria T. Gomez, Counselor/Coordinator, Disabled Student Services, San Antonio College, 1300 San Pedro, San Antonio, TX 78212-4299, 210-733-2350. Fax: 210-733-2242.

SANTA MONICA COLLEGE

Santa Monica, California

Students with LD	300	Subject-Area Tutoring	✓
ADD services	✓	Special Courses	✓
Staff	1 full-, 8 part-time	Taped Textbooks	✓
Special Fee	None	Alternative Test Arrang.	✓
Diagnostic Testing	✓	Notetakers	
Basic Skills Remediation	✓	LD Student Organization	

LEARNING DISABILITIES PROGRAM INFORMATION

The Learning Disabilities Program began offering services in 1977. Currently the program serves 300 undergraduates with LD. Students diagnosed with ADD/ADHD are eligible for the same services available to students with LD.
Staff: 1 full-time, 8 part-time staff members, including coordinator. Services provided by tutors, diagnostic specialists, paraprofessional aides.
Special Fees: No special fees are charged for services to students with LD.
Applications and admissions: *Required:* California Assessment System for Adults with Learning Disabilities. Students may begin taking classes in fall, spring, or summer. *Application deadline:* continuous.

PROGRAM AND SERVICE COMPONENTS

Special preparation or orientation: Optional summer program offered prior to entering college. Optional orientation offered before registration and after classes begin.
Diagnostic testing: Intelligence, reading, math, spelling, written language, perceptual skills, study skills, social skills, learning strategies.
Academic advising: Provided by LD staff members. Students with LD may take up to 15 units each term; most take 6 to 9 units; 12 units required to maintain full-time status; 6 to 12 units required to be eligible for financial aid.
Counseling services: Individual counseling, career counseling, self-advocacy training.
Basic skills remediation: Offered in class-size groups by regular teachers. Available in math, English.
Subject-area tutoring: Offered one-on-one and in small groups by peer tutors, paraprofessional aides. Available in most subjects.
Special courses: College survival skills, learning strategies, time management, study skills. All offered for credit; some enter into overall grade point average.
Auxiliary aids: Taped textbooks, tape recorders, calculators, word-processors with spell-check, personal computers, talking computers, optical character readers.
Auxiliary services: Alternative test arrangements, priority registration, instructor conferences.

GENERAL COLLEGE INFORMATION

State and locally supported, 2-year, coed. Part of California Community Colleges System. Awards associate degrees. Founded 1929. *Setting:* 40-acre urban campus with easy access to Los Angeles. *Total enrollment:* 22,127. *Faculty:* 664 (277 full-time, 387 part-time).
Enrollment Profile: 22,127 students from 20 states and territories, 103 other countries. 56% women, 44% men, 70% part-time, 89% state residents, 16% transferred in, 9% international, 41% 25 or older, 1% Native American, 18% Hispanic, 11% black, 20% Asian or Pacific Islander. *Areas of study chosen:* 26% liberal arts/general studies, 15% business management and administrative services, 6% fine arts, 5% engineering and applied sciences, 5% psychology, 3% communications and journalism, 3% health professions and related sciences, 2% architecture, 2% biological and life sciences, 2% education, 2% performing arts. *Most popular recent majors:* business administration/commerce/management, liberal arts/general studies, nursing.
First-Year Class: 3,103 total; 5,000 applied, 100% were accepted, 62% of whom enrolled.
Graduation Requirements: 60 units; 1 college algebra course.
Computers on Campus: 360 computers available on campus for general student use. Computer purchase/lease plans available. A campus-wide network can be accessed from off-campus. Students can contact faculty members and/or advisers through

Santa Monica College (continued)

e-mail. Computers for student use in computer labs, learning resource center, classrooms, library, various locations. Staffed computer lab on campus. *Academic computing expenditure 1995–96:* $705,864.

EXPENSES AND FINANCIAL AID

Expenses for 1997–98: State resident tuition: $0 full-time. Nonresident tuition: $3750 full-time, $125 per unit part-time. Part-time mandatory fees per semester range from $41 to $171. Tuition for international students: $4200 full-time, $140 per unit part-time. Full-time mandatory fees: $446.

Financial aid specifically for students with LD: Scholarships.

LD Program Contact: Ms. Mary Weil, Counselor, Santa Monica College, 1900 Pico Boulevard, Santa Monica, CA 90405-1628, 310-452-9265. Fax: 310-452-9272.

SIERRA COLLEGE

Rocklin, California

Students with LD	350	Subject-Area Tutoring	✓
ADD services		Special Courses	✓
Staff	5 full-time	Taped Textbooks	✓
Special Fee	None	Alternative Test Arrang.	✓
Diagnostic Testing	✓	Notetakers	✓
Basic Skills Remediation	✓	LD Student Organization	✓

LEARNING DISABILITIES PROGRAM INFORMATION

The Learning Opportunities Center began offering services in 1978. Currently the program serves 350 undergraduates with LD. Students diagnosed with ADD/ADHD are not eligible for the same services available to students with LD.

Staff: 5 full-time staff members, including LD specialists. Services provided by tutors, diagnostic specialists, instructional assistant.

Special Fees: No special fees are charged for services to students with LD.

Applications and admissions: *Required:* California Assessment Process for Adults with Learning Disabilities. Students may begin taking classes in fall or spring. *Application deadline:* continuous.

PROGRAM AND SERVICE COMPONENTS

Special preparation or orientation: Optional orientation offered after classes begin.

Diagnostic testing: Reading, math, spelling, written language, perceptual skills, learning strategies.

Academic advising: Provided by LD staff members, academic advisers. Students with LD may take up to 18 units each term; most take 12 units; 12 units required to maintain full-time status and be eligible for financial aid.

Counseling services: Individual counseling, small-group counseling, career counseling.

Basic skills remediation: Offered one-on-one, in small groups, and in class-size groups by LD teachers, regular teachers, instructional assistant, tutors. Available in reading, math, spelling, written language, learning strategies, perceptual skills, study skills, time management.

Subject-area tutoring: Offered one-on-one and in small groups by professional teachers, peer tutors, instructional assistant. Available in all subjects.

Special courses: College survival skills, reading, vocabulary development, composition, learning strategies, math, study skills, career planning. Most offered for credit.

Auxiliary aids: Taped textbooks, tape recorders, calculators, typewriters, word-processors with spell-check.

Auxiliary services: Alternative test arrangements, notetakers, priority registration, advocacy.

Campus support group: A special student organization is available to students with LD.

GENERAL COLLEGE INFORMATION

State-supported, 2-year, coed. Part of California Community Colleges System. Awards associate degrees. Founded 1936. *Setting:* 327-acre rural campus with easy access to Sacramento. *Research spending 1995–96:* $192,586. *Total enrollment:* 13,567. *Faculty:* 518 (143 full-time, 100% with terminal degrees, 375 part-time); student–undergrad faculty ratio is 27:1.

Enrollment Profile: 13,567 students: 55% women, 45% men, 71% part-time, 99% state residents, 1% live on campus, 12% transferred in, 1% international, 46% 25 or older, 3% Native American, 6% Hispanic, 1% black, 2% Asian or Pacific Islander. *Retention:* 14% of 1995 full-time freshmen returned. *Most popular recent majors:* liberal arts/general studies, business administration/commerce/management.

First-Year Class: 2,888 total; 7,181 applied, 100% were accepted, 40% of whom enrolled.

Graduation Requirements: 60 units; math proficiency; computer course for accounting, business, communication majors.

Computers on Campus: 430 computers available on campus for general student use. Computer purchase/lease plans available. A computer is recommended for all students. A campus-wide network can be accessed from off-campus. Students can contact faculty members and/or advisers through e-mail. Computers for student use in computer labs, learning resource center, library, student center provide access to the Internet/World Wide Web, on- and off-campus e-mail addresses. Staffed computer lab on campus provides training in use of computers, software. *Academic computing expenditure 1995–96:* $719,802.

EXPENSES

Expenses for 1997–98: State resident tuition: $0 full-time. Nonresident tuition: $3750 full-time, $125 per unit part-time. Part-time mandatory fees per semester range from $23 to $153. Full-time mandatory fees: $410. College room and board: $4230.

LD Program Contact: Ms. Denise Stone, Learning Disabilities Specialist, Sierra College, 5000 Rocklin Road, Rocklin, CA 95677-3397, 916-789-2697.

SKYLINE COLLEGE

San Bruno, California

Students with LD	100	Subject-Area Tutoring	✓
ADD services	✓	Special Courses	✓
Staff	1 full-, 2 part-time	Taped Textbooks	✓
Special Fee	None	Alternative Test Arrang.	✓
Diagnostic Testing	✓	Notetakers	✓
Basic Skills Remediation	✓	LD Student Organization	

LEARNING DISABILITIES PROGRAM INFORMATION

The Developmental Skills Program began offering services in 1975. Currently the program serves 100 undergraduates with LD. Students diagnosed with ADD/ADHD are eligible for the same services available to students with LD.

Staff: 1 full-time, 2 part-time staff members, including coordinator. Services provided by remediation specialists, tutors, counselors, diagnostic specialists.

Special Fees: No special fees are charged for services to students with LD.

Applications and admissions: Open admissions (must be 18 years of age). Students may begin taking classes in fall, spring, or summer. *Application deadline:* 8/30 (fall term), 1/15 (spring term).
Special policies: The college has written policies regarding grade forgiveness.

PROGRAM AND SERVICE COMPONENTS

Special preparation or orientation: Optional summer program offered prior to entering college. Required orientation held during registration and after classes begin.
Diagnostic testing: Intelligence, reading, math, spelling, spoken language, written language, motor abilities, perceptual skills, study skills, hearing, learning strategies, vision.
Academic advising: Provided by LD staff members, academic advisers, academic counselors. Students with LD may take up to 15 units each term; most take 9 units; 9 units required to maintain full-time status; 6 units required to be eligible for financial aid.
Counseling services: Individual counseling, career counseling.
Basic skills remediation: Offered in small groups and in class-size groups by LD teachers, regular teachers, teacher trainees; computer-aided instruction also offered. Available in reading, math, spelling, learning strategies, perceptual skills, study skills, time management, computer skills.
Subject-area tutoring: Offered one-on-one and in small groups by professional teachers, peer tutors. Available in most subjects.
Special courses: College survival skills, reading, vocabulary development, composition, learning strategies, math, study skills, career planning. All offered for credit; some enter into overall grade point average.
Auxiliary aids: Taped textbooks, tape recorders, calculators, typewriters, word-processors with spell-check, talking computers, optical character readers.
Auxiliary services: Alternative test arrangements, notetakers, priority registration, advocacy.

GENERAL COLLEGE INFORMATION

County-supported, 2-year, coed. Part of San Mateo County Community College District System. Awards associate degrees. Founded 1969. *Setting:* 125-acre suburban campus with easy access to San Francisco. *Total enrollment:* 8,104. *Faculty:* 268 (121 full-time, 147 part-time).
Enrollment Profile: 8,104 students: 55% women, 45% men, 75% part-time, 99% state residents, 21% transferred in, 1% international, 50% 25 or older, 1% Native American, 21% Hispanic, 5% black, 36% Asian or Pacific Islander. *Most popular recent majors:* business administration/commerce/management, computer science, art/fine arts.
First-Year Class: 1,974 applied, 100% were accepted, 63% of whom enrolled.
Graduation Requirements: 60 credits.
Computers on Campus: 220 computers available on campus for general student use. Computers for student use in computer labs, learning resource center, classrooms, library, student center provide access to the Internet/World Wide Web. Staffed computer lab on campus.

EXPENSES

Expenses for 1997–98: State resident tuition: $0 full-time. Nonresident tuition: $3780 full-time, $126 per unit part-time. Part-time mandatory fees per semester range from $24 to $154. Full-time mandatory fees: $412.
LD Program Contact: Ms. Linda Van Sciver, Counselor, Skyline College, 3300 College Drive, San Bruno, CA 94066-1698, 415-738-4280.

SOLANO COMMUNITY COLLEGE
Suisun City, California

Students with LD	90 to 110	Subject-Area Tutoring	
ADD services	✓	Special Courses	✓
Staff	1 full-, 1 part-time	Taped Textbooks	✓
Special Fee	None	Alternative Test Arrang.	✓
Diagnostic Testing	✓	Notetakers	✓
Basic Skills Remediation	✓	LD Student Organization	

LEARNING DISABILITIES PROGRAM INFORMATION

The LD Center began offering services in 1984. Currently the program serves 90 to 110 undergraduates with LD. Students diagnosed with ADD/ADHD are eligible for the same services available to students with LD, as well as verification of disorder from medical/psychological professionals.
Staff: 1 full-time, 1 part-time staff members, including coordinator. Services provided by strategics intervention instructor.
Special Fees: No special fees are charged for services to students with LD.
Applications and admissions: *Required:* verification of learning disability (or assessment by LD specialist or service if requirements of ADA are met). Students may begin taking classes any term. *Application deadline:* continuous.
Special policies: The college has written policies regarding substitutions and waivers of graduation and degree requirements.

PROGRAM AND SERVICE COMPONENTS

Diagnostic testing: Intelligence, reading, math, spelling, written language, learning strategies, academic attributes (self-survey).
Academic advising: Provided by LD staff members, academic advisers. Most students with LD take 12 credits each term; 12 credits required to maintain full-time status; 6 credits (12 for full assistance) required to be eligible for financial aid.
Counseling services: Individual counseling, career counseling, self-advocacy training.
Basic skills remediation: Offered in class-size groups by LD teachers. Available in reading, math, spelling, learning strategies, time management, social skills, computer skills.
Special courses: Learning strategies, word processing, time management, typing, study skills, social relationships. All offered for credit; some enter into overall grade point average.
Auxiliary aids: Taped textbooks, tape recorders, calculators, typewriters, word-processors with spell-check, talking computers, optical character readers.
Auxiliary services: Alternative test arrangements, notetakers, priority registration.

GENERAL COLLEGE INFORMATION

State and locally supported, 2-year, coed. Part of California Community Colleges System. Awards associate degrees. Founded 1945. *Setting:* 192-acre small-town campus with easy access to Sacramento and San Francisco. *Total enrollment:* 9,909. *Faculty:* 374 (147 full-time, 227 part-time); student–undergrad faculty ratio is 30:1.
Enrollment Profile: 9,909 students from 43 states and territories, 6 other countries. 58% women, 42% men, 72% part-time, 98% state residents, 9% transferred in, 1% international, 51% 25 or older, 1% Native American, 10% Hispanic, 15% black, 6% Asian or Pacific Islander.
First-Year Class: 2,000 total. Of the students who applied, 100% were accepted.
Graduation Requirements: 60 credits; 1 math course; 1 course each in physical science and natural science, including at least 1 lab science course.

Solano Community College (continued)

Computers on Campus: 150 computers available on campus for general student use. Computers for student use in learning resource center.

EXPENSES AND FINANCIAL AID

Expenses for 1997–98: State resident tuition: $0 full-time. Nonresident tuition: $3750 full-time, $125 per unit part-time. Part-time mandatory fees per semester range from $21.50 to $151.50. Full-time mandatory fees: $407.

Financial aid specifically for students with LD: Scholarships.

LD Program Contact: Ms. Ruth Miller, LD Specialist/Coordinator, Solano Community College, 4000 Suisun Valley Road, Suisun City, CA 94585, 707-864-7234. Fax: 707-864-7270. Email: rmiller@solano.cc.ca.us.

SUOMI COLLEGE

Hancock, Michigan

Students with LD	38	Subject-Area Tutoring	
ADD services	✓	Special Courses	
Staff	1 full-time	Taped Textbooks	✓
Special Fee	None	Alternative Test Arrang.	✓
Diagnostic Testing	✓	Notetakers	✓
Basic Skills Remediation		LD Student Organization	

LEARNING DISABILITIES PROGRAM INFORMATION

The Learning Disabilities Program began offering services in 1990. Currently the program serves 38 undergraduates with LD. Students diagnosed with ADD/ADHD are eligible for the same services available to students with LD, as well as assistance with organizational and time management skills.

Staff: 1 full-time staff member (director). Services provided by tutors.

Special Fees: No special fees are charged for services to students with LD.

Applications and admissions: *Required:* high school transcript, grade point average, courses completed, psychoeducational report completed within 3 years; *recommended:* high school extracurricular activities, IEP (Individualized Education Program), untimed or extended time ACT, letters of recommendation. Students may begin taking classes in fall only. *Application deadline:* continuous.

Special policies: The college has written policies regarding grade forgiveness.

PROGRAM AND SERVICE COMPONENTS

Special preparation or orientation: Required orientation held before registration.

Diagnostic testing: Reading, math, study skills, learning strategies.

Academic advising: Provided by LD staff members. Students with LD may take up to 18 credits each term; most take 12 to 14 credits; 12 credits required to maintain full-time status; 6 credits required to be eligible for financial aid.

Auxiliary aids: Taped textbooks, tape recorders, calculators, word-processors with spell-check, personal computers, optical character readers.

Auxiliary services: Alternative test arrangements, notetakers, priority registration, advocacy.

GENERAL COLLEGE INFORMATION

Independent, primarily 2-year, coed, affiliated with Evangelical Lutheran Church in America. Awards associate, bachelor's degrees. Founded 1896. *Setting:* 25-acre small-town campus. *Total enrollment:* 363. *Faculty:* 30 (19 full-time, 16% with terminal degrees, 11 part-time); student–undergrad faculty ratio is 14:1.

Enrollment Profile: 363 students from 8 states and territories, 4 other countries. 68% women, 32% men, 13% part-time, 79% state residents, 30% live on campus, 12% transferred in, 8% international, 37% 25 or older, 4% Native American, 1% Hispanic, 7% black, 0% Asian or Pacific Islander. *Retention:* 51% of 1995 full-time freshmen returned. *Areas of study chosen:* 43% health professions and related sciences, 17% liberal arts/general studies, 13% business management and administrative services, 11% vocational and home economics, 6% fine arts, 5% education, 2% social sciences, 1% engineering and applied sciences, 1% English language/literature/letters, 1% foreign language and literature, 1% prelaw. *Most popular recent major:* business administration/commerce/management.

First-Year Class: 174 total; 349 applied, 77% were accepted, 64% of whom enrolled. 9% from top 10% of their high school class, 13% from top quarter.

Graduation Requirements: 60 credits for associate, 129 credits for bachelor's; 1 semester each of math and science; internship (some majors).

Computers on Campus: 65 computers available on campus for general student use. A computer is strongly recommended for all students. Computers for student use in computer center, computer labs, teacher learning center provide access to the Internet/World Wide Web, on-campus e-mail addresses. Staffed computer lab on campus provides training in use of computers, software. *Academic computing expenditure 1995–96:* $60,909.

EXPENSES

Expenses for 1997–98: *Application fee:* $20. Comprehensive fee of $14,300 includes full-time tuition ($9880 minimum), mandatory fees ($520), and college room and board ($3900). Part-time tuition per semester ranges from $2080 to $4576. Part-time mandatory fees: $260 per semester. Full-time tuition ranges up to $14,820 according to program for bachelor's degree.

LD Program Contact: Ms. Carol Bates, Director, Learning Disabilities Program, Suomi College, 601 Quincy Street, Hancock, MI 49930, 906-487-7258. Fax: 906-487-7300. Email: cabates@up.net.

SUSSEX COUNTY COMMUNITY COLLEGE

Newton, New Jersey

Students with LD	105	Subject-Area Tutoring	✓
ADD services	✓	Special Courses	
Staff	1 full-, 9 part-time	Taped Textbooks	✓
Special Fee	None	Alternative Test Arrang.	✓
Diagnostic Testing	✓	Notetakers	
Basic Skills Remediation		LD Student Organization	

LEARNING DISABILITIES PROGRAM INFORMATION

The Project Success began offering services in 1988. Currently the program serves 105 undergraduates with LD. Students diagnosed with ADD/ADHD are eligible for the same services available to students with LD.

Staff: 1 full-time, 9 part-time staff members, including coordinator, Coordinating Assistant. Services provided by tutors, counselor, diagnostic specialist.

Special Fees: No special fees are charged for services to students with LD.
Applications and admissions: *Required:* personal interview. Students may begin taking classes in fall, spring, or summer. *Application deadline:* continuous.

PROGRAM AND SERVICE COMPONENTS

Diagnostic testing: Intelligence, reading, math, written language.
Academic advising: Provided by LD staff members, academic advisers. Students with LD may take up to 12 credits each term; most take 9 to 12 credits; 9 credits required to maintain full-time status; 12 credits required to be eligible for financial aid.
Counseling services: Individual counseling, small-group counseling, career counseling.
Subject-area tutoring: Offered one-on-one and in small groups by professional teachers, peer tutors. Available in all subjects.
Auxiliary aids: Taped textbooks, tape recorders, word-processors with spell-check, personal computers.
Auxiliary services: Alternative test arrangements, advocacy.

GENERAL COLLEGE INFORMATION

State and locally supported, 2-year, coed. Part of New Jersey Commission on Higher Education. Awards associate degrees. Founded 1981. *Setting:* 130-acre small-town campus with easy access to New York City. *Endowment:* $75,000. *Educational spending 1995–96:* $1737 per undergrad. *Total enrollment:* 2,376. *Faculty:* 188 (38 full-time, 39% with terminal degrees, 150 part-time); student–undergrad faculty ratio is 18:1.
Enrollment Profile: 2,376 students: 63% women, 37% men, 62% part-time, 95% state residents, 9% transferred in, 48% 25 or older, 0% Native American, 3% Hispanic, 1% black, 1% Asian or Pacific Islander. *Retention:* 56% of 1995 full-time freshmen returned. *Areas of study chosen:* 41% liberal arts/general studies, 9% business management and administrative services, 4% health professions and related sciences, 3% education, 1% communications and journalism, 1% computer and information sciences, 1% English language/literature/letters, 1% fine arts, 1% psychology, 1% social sciences. *Most popular recent majors:* liberal arts/general studies, business administration/commerce/management.
First-Year Class: 741 total; 860 applied, 100% were accepted, 86% of whom enrolled.
Graduation Requirements: 60 credits; 6 credits of math; 4 credits of science; computer course; internship (some majors).
Computers on Campus: A campus-wide network can be accessed. Students can contact faculty members and/or advisers through e-mail. Computers for student use in computer labs, learning resource center, classrooms, library provide access to the Internet/World Wide Web. Staffed computer lab on campus provides training in use of computers, software. *Academic computing expenditure 1995–96:* $200,000.

EXPENSES

Expenses for 1997–98: *Application fee:* $15. Area resident tuition: $2040 full-time, $68 per credit part-time. State resident tuition: $4080 full-time, $136 per credit part-time. Nonresident tuition: $6120 full-time, $204 per credit part-time. Part-time mandatory fees: $9 per credit. Full-time mandatory fees: $270.
LD Program Contact: Jean L. Coen, Coordinator, Disabilities Assistance Program, Sussex County Community College, 1 College Hill, Newton, NJ 07860, 201-300-2153. Fax: 201-300-2277. Email: jlcoen@planet.net.

TAFT COLLEGE
Taft, California

Students with LD	54	Subject-Area Tutoring	✓
ADD services	✓	Special Courses	
Staff	3 full-, 1 part-time	Taped Textbooks	✓
Special Fee	None	Alternative Test Arrang.	✓
Diagnostic Testing	✓	Notetakers	✓
Basic Skills Remediation	✓	LD Student Organization	

LEARNING DISABILITIES PROGRAM INFORMATION

The Learning Assistance Program began offering services in 1984. Currently the program serves 54 undergraduates with LD. Students diagnosed with ADD/ADHD are eligible for the same services available to students with LD.
Staff: 3 full-time, 1 part-time staff members, including director, coordinator. Services provided by remediation specialist, instructional aide.
Special Fees: No special fees are charged for services to students with LD.
Applications and admissions: *Required:* high school transcript, courses completed, Woodcock-Johnson Revised or WAIS-R; *recommended:* untimed SAT I, psychoeducational report completed within 2 years. Students may begin taking classes in fall only. *Application deadline:* continuous.

PROGRAM AND SERVICE COMPONENTS

Special preparation or orientation: Required orientation held during registration.
Diagnostic testing: Intelligence, reading, math, spelling, spoken language, written language, motor abilities, perceptual skills, personality, social skills, speech, hearing.
Academic advising: Provided by LD staff members. Most students with LD take 12 units each term; 12 units required to maintain full-time status and be eligible for financial aid.
Counseling services: Individual counseling.
Basic skills remediation: Offered one-on-one, in small groups, and in class-size groups by LD teachers, regular teachers. Available in reading, math, spelling, handwriting, spoken language, written language, learning strategies, motor abilities, perceptual skills, study skills, social skills, speech.
Subject-area tutoring: Offered one-on-one by professional teachers, peer tutors. Available in all subjects.
Auxiliary aids: Taped textbooks, tape recorders, calculators, typewriters, word-processors with spell-check.
Auxiliary services: Alternative test arrangements, notetakers, advocacy.

GENERAL COLLEGE INFORMATION

State and locally supported, 2-year, coed. Part of California Community Colleges System. Awards associate degrees. Founded 1922. *Setting:* 15-acre small-town campus. *Research spending 1995–96:* $5000. *Total enrollment:* 532. *Faculty:* 64 (24 full-time, 100% with terminal degrees, 40 part-time).
Enrollment Profile: 532 students from 9 states and territories, 4 other countries. 69% women, 31% men, 40% part-time, 98% state residents, 6% live on campus, 12% transferred in, 47% 25 or older, 3% Native American, 9% Hispanic, 11% black, 2% Asian or Pacific Islander. *Areas of study chosen:* 16% liberal arts/general studies, 6% business management and administrative services, 5% health professions and related sciences, 5% vocational and home economics, 4% interdisciplinary studies, 3% biological and life sciences, 1% communications and journalism, 1% computer and information sciences, 1% education, 1% engineering and applied sciences, 1% fine arts, 1% physical sciences, 1% social sciences.

Taft College (continued)

First-Year Class: 99 total. Of the students who applied, 100% were accepted, 85% of whom enrolled.
Graduation Requirements: 60 units.
Computers on Campus: 91 computers available on campus for general student use. Computers for student use in computer center, computer labs, learning resource center, classrooms, career center provide access to the Internet/World Wide Web, on- and off-campus e-mail addresses. Staffed computer lab on campus provides training in use of computers, software. *Academic computing expenditure 1995–96:* $214,000.

EXPENSES

Expenses for 1997–98: State resident tuition: $0 full-time. Nonresident tuition: $3420 full-time, $114 per unit part-time. Part-time mandatory fees per semester range from $28 to $158. Full-time mandatory fees: $405. College room and board: $2660 (minimum).
LD Program Contact: Mr. Jeff Ross, Coordinator, Disabled Student Services/Learning Assistance Program, Taft College, 29 Emmons Park Drive, Taft, CA 93268, 805-763-4282. Fax: 805-763-1038. Email: dsps@taft.cc.ca.us.

TRUCKEE MEADOWS COMMUNITY COLLEGE

Reno, Nevada

Students with LD	80	Subject-Area Tutoring	✓
ADD services	✓	Special Courses	✓
Staff		Taped Textbooks	✓
Special Fee	✓	Alternative Test Arrang.	✓
Diagnostic Testing	✓	Notetakers	✓
Basic Skills Remediation	✓	LD Student Organization	

LEARNING DISABILITIES PROGRAM INFORMATION

The Student Support Services began offering services in 1988. Currently the program serves 80 undergraduates with LD. Students diagnosed with ADD/ADHD are eligible for the same services available to students with LD.
Staff: Includes director, coordinator, counselor. Services provided by tutors, counselor.
Special Fees: $2500 per year.
Applications and admissions: *Required:* high school transcript, grade point average, courses completed, IEP (Individualized Education Program), personal interview, psychoeducational report completed within 5 years; *recommended:* high school class rank. Students may begin taking classes in fall, spring, or summer. *Application deadline:* continuous.
Special policies: The college has written policies regarding grade forgiveness; substitutions and waivers of degree requirements.

PROGRAM AND SERVICE COMPONENTS

Special preparation or orientation: Orientation (required for some) held before registration.
Diagnostic testing: Reading, math, personality, learning strategies.
Academic advising: Provided by LD staff members, academic advisers. Students with LD may take up to as many credits as an individual can handle each term; most take 12 credits; 12 credits required to maintain full-time status; 6 credits (part-time) required to be eligible for financial aid.
Counseling services: Individual counseling, career counseling.
Basic skills remediation: Offered one-on-one and in small groups by study skills teachers. Available in reading, math, spelling, written language, learning strategies, speech.
Subject area tutoring: Offered one on one, in small groups, and in class-size groups by peer tutors, community members. Available in most subjects.
Special courses: College survival skills, reading, composition, learning strategies, math, typing, study skills, career planning. Most offered for credit; most enter into overall grade point average.
Auxiliary aids: Taped textbooks, tape recorders, calculators, optical character readers.
Auxiliary services: Alternative test arrangements, notetakers, priority registration, advocacy.

GENERAL COLLEGE INFORMATION

State-supported, 2-year, coed. Part of University and Community College System of Nevada. Awards associate degrees. Founded 1971. *Setting:* 63-acre suburban campus. *Endowment:* $3.5 million. *Educational spending 1995–96:* $1163 per undergrad. *Total enrollment:* 9,338. *Faculty:* 464 (111 full-time, 95% with terminal degrees, 353 part-time); student–undergrad faculty ratio is 18:1.
Enrollment Profile: 9,338 students from 15 states and territories, 2 other countries. 56% women, 44% men, 84% part-time, 89% state residents, 10% live on campus, 14% transferred in, 2% international, 64% 25 or older, 3% Native American, 6% Hispanic, 2% black, 5% Asian or Pacific Islander. *Retention:* 50% of 1995 full-time freshmen returned. *Most popular recent majors:* nursing, business administration/commerce/management, fire science.
First-Year Class: 2,808 total; 2,808 applied, 100% were accepted, 100% of whom enrolled.
Graduation Requirements: 60 credits; computer course for legal assistant, general studies majors; internship (some majors).
Computers on Campus: 210 computers available on campus for general student use. A campus-wide network can be accessed from off-campus. Students can contact faculty members and/or advisers through e-mail. Computers for student use in computer center, computer labs, library, departmental labs provide access to the Internet/World Wide Web. Staffed computer lab on campus provides training in use of computers, software. *Academic computing expenditure 1995–96:* $80,980.

EXPENSES

Expenses for 1997–98: *Application fee:* $5. State resident tuition: $1140 full-time, $38 per credit part-time. Nonresident tuition: $4658 full-time. Nonresident part-time tuition per semester ranges from $57 to $2177. Tuition for California residents who are eligible for the Good Neighbor Program: $1710 full-time, $57 per credit part-time.
LD Program Contact: Mr. Harry Heiser, Director, Learning Support Services Program, Truckee Meadows Community College, 7000 Dandini Boulevard, Reno, NV 89512-3901, 702-673-7285. Fax: 702-673-7108. Email: hfh@scs.unr.edu.

UNIVERSITY OF HAWAII–LEEWARD COMMUNITY COLLEGE

Pearl City, Hawaii

Students with LD	130	Subject-Area Tutoring	✓
ADD services	✓	Special Courses	✓
Staff	1 full-, 1 part-time	Taped Textbooks	✓
Special Fee	None	Alternative Test Arrang.	✓
Diagnostic Testing	✓	Notetakers	✓
Basic Skills Remediation	✓	LD Student Organization	✓

LEARNING DISABILITIES PROGRAM INFORMATION

The Program for Adult Achievement began offering services in 1981. Currently the program serves 130 undergraduates with LD. Students diagnosed with ADD/ADHD are eligible for the same services available to students with LD.

Staff: 1 full-time, 1 part-time staff members, including coordinator. Services provided by tutors, counselor, remediation/diagnostic specialist.

Special Fees: No special fees are charged for services to students with LD.

Applications and admissions: *Required:* psychoeducational report; *recommended:* personal interview. Students may begin taking classes in fall, spring, or summer. *Application deadline:* continuous.

PROGRAM AND SERVICE COMPONENTS

Special preparation or orientation: Optional orientation offered after classes begin and before classes begin.

Diagnostic testing: Intelligence, reading, math, spelling, handwriting, spoken language, written language, perceptual skills, study skills, social skills, learning strategies.

Academic advising: Provided by LD staff members. Most students with LD take 9 to 12 credits each term; status of student determines the number of credits required to be eligible for financial aid.

Counseling services: Individual counseling, small-group counseling, career counseling.

Basic skills remediation: Offered one-on-one and in small groups by regular teachers, peer teachers, LD specialist. Available in reading, math, spelling, written language, learning strategies, study skills, time management.

Subject-area tutoring: Offered one-on-one and in small groups by peer tutors. Available in most subjects.

Special courses: Study skills, career planning. All offered for credit; all enter into overall grade point average.

Auxiliary aids: Taped textbooks, tape recorders, calculators, word-processors with spell-check.

Auxiliary services: Alternative test arrangements, notetakers, priority registration, advocacy, readers.

Campus support group: A special student organization is available to students with LD.

GENERAL COLLEGE INFORMATION

State-supported, 2-year, coed. Part of University of Hawaii System. Awards associate degrees. Founded 1968. *Setting:* 49-acre suburban campus with easy access to Honolulu. *Total enrollment:* 5,987. *Faculty:* 243 (172 full-time, 15% with terminal degrees, 71 part-time).

Enrollment Profile: 5,987 students from 25 states and territories. 58% women, 42% men, 54% part-time, 89% state residents, 11% transferred in, 35% 25 or older, 1% Native American, 3% Hispanic, 2% black, 64% Asian or Pacific Islander.

First-Year Class: 1,308 total. Of the students who applied, 100% were accepted.

Graduation Requirements: 60 credits; computer course for management majors; internship (some majors).

Computers on Campus: 162 computers available on campus for general student use. Computer purchase/lease plans available. A campus-wide network can be accessed from off-campus. Students can contact faculty members and/or advisers through e-mail. Computers for student use in computer center, computer labs, learning resource center, departmental labs provide access to the Internet/World Wide Web, on-campus e-mail addresses. Staffed computer lab on campus provides training in use of computers, software.

EXPENSES

Estimated Expenses for 1997–98: *Application fee:* $25. State resident tuition: $936 full-time, $39 per semester part-time. Nonresident tuition: $5712 full-time, $238 per semester part-time. Part-time mandatory fees per semester range from $3 to $7.50. Full-time mandatory fees: $15.

LD Program Contact: Ms. C. Lynne Douglas, Learning Disabilities Specialist, University of Hawaii–Leeward Community College, 96-045 Ala Ike, Pearl City, HI 96782-3366, 808-455-0421. Fax: 808-455-0471.

UTAH VALLEY STATE COLLEGE

Orem, Utah

Students with LD	600	Subject-Area Tutoring	✓
ADD services	✓	Special Courses	✓
Staff	6 full-, 37 part-time	Taped Textbooks	✓
Special Fee	None	Alternative Test Arrang.	✓
Diagnostic Testing	✓	Notetakers	✓
Basic Skills Remediation	✓	LD Student Organization	

LEARNING DISABILITIES PROGRAM INFORMATION

The Services for Students with Disabilities began offering services in 1983. Currently the program serves 600 undergraduates with LD. Students diagnosed with ADD/ADHD are eligible for the same services available to students with LD.

Staff: 6 full-time, 37 part-time staff members, including director, coordinators. Services provided by remediation specialists, counselors, diagnostic specialists.

Special Fees: No special fees are charged for services to students with LD.

Applications and admissions: *Recommended:* high school transcript. Students may begin taking classes any term. *Application deadline:* continuous.

Special policies: The college has written policies regarding substitutions and waivers of admissions, graduation, and degree requirements.

PROGRAM AND SERVICE COMPONENTS

Special preparation or orientation: Optional orientation offered individually by special arrangement.

Diagnostic testing: Intelligence, reading, math, spelling, handwriting, spoken language, written language, motor abilities, perceptual skills, study skills, personality, social skills, learning strategies, vocational and career aptitude.

Academic advising: Provided by LD staff members, academic advisers. Students with LD may take up to as many semester hours as they can handle provided they maintain a GPA of 2.0 each term; most take 6 to 12 semester hours; 12 semester hours required to maintain full-time status; 6 semester hours required to be eligible for financial aid.

Counseling services: Individual counseling, small-group counseling, career counseling, self-advocacy training, interagency coordination of services, pre-employment and job search skills training, job maintenance and enhancement training, work co-op and job placement counseling, academic program guidance and registration assistance.

Basic skills remediation: Offered one-on-one, in small groups, and in class-size groups by LD teachers, regular teachers; computer-aided instruction also offered. Available in reading, math, spelling, handwriting, spoken language, written language, learning strategies, study skills, time management, social skills.

Subject-area tutoring: Offered one-on-one and in small groups by peer tutors, trained teachers, counselors. Available in most subjects.

Utah Valley State College (continued)

Special courses: College survival skills, reading, vocabulary development, communication skills, composition, learning strategies, word processing, time management, math, typing, personal psychology, study skills, career planning. Most offered for credit; most enter into overall grade point average.

Auxiliary aids: Taped textbooks, tape recorders, typewriters, word-processors with spell-check, personal computers, FM auditory trainers, high speed scanner system with voice synthesizer, screen reading system (in computer lab), closed-captioned machines, print enlargers, bookcarts, laptop computers, scooters, adaptive software.

Auxiliary services: Alternative test arrangements, notetakers, advocacy, readers, scribes, accommodative testing proctors, interpreters.

GENERAL COLLEGE INFORMATION

State-supported, primarily 2-year, coed. Part of Utah System of Higher Education. Awards associate, bachelor's degrees. Founded 1941. *Setting:* 200-acre suburban campus with easy access to Salt Lake City. *Endowment:* $1.7 million. *Total enrollment:* 14,756. *Faculty:* 607 (229 full-time, 378 part-time); student–undergrad faculty ratio is 22:1.

Enrollment Profile: 14,756 students from 51 states and territories, 60 other countries. 47% women, 53% men, 55% part-time, 90% state residents, 7% transferred in, 2% international, 23% 25 or older, 1% Native American, 3% Hispanic, 0% black, 2% Asian or Pacific Islander. *Retention:* 45% of 1995 full-time freshmen returned. *Areas of study chosen:* 35% interdisciplinary studies, 20% business management and administrative services, 10% engineering and applied sciences, 7% health professions and related sciences, 6% education, 5% computer and information sciences, 5% fine arts, 2% biological and life sciences, 2% mathematics, 1% performing arts, 1% social sciences.

First-Year Class: 5,349 total; 7,366 applied, 100% were accepted, 73% of whom enrolled.

Graduation Requirements: 64 semester hours for associate, 128 semester hours for bachelor's; computer course for business management majors.

Computers on Campus: Computer purchase/lease plans available. A computer is recommended for all students. A campus-wide network can be accessed from off-campus. Students can contact faculty members and/or advisers through e-mail. Computers for student use in computer labs, learning resource center, classrooms, library, student center provide access to the Internet/World Wide Web, on- and off-campus e-mail addresses. Staffed computer lab on campus provides training in use of computers, software. *Academic computing expenditure 1995–96:* $973,664.

EXPENSES

Expenses for 1997–98: *Application fee:* $20. State resident tuition: $1239 (minimum) full-time. Nonresident tuition: $4493 (minimum) full-time. Minimum part-time tuition per semester ranges from $67.50 to $595.50 for state residents, $222.50 to $2159 for nonresidents. Part-time mandatory fees per semester range from $10 to $140. Full-time tuition ranges up to$1685 for state residents, $6111 for nonresidents, according to class level. Part-time tuition per semester ranges up to $76.80 to $809.40 for state residents, $256.20 to $2899.90 for nonresidents, according to class level. Full-time mandatory fees: $280.

LD Program Contact: Ms. Michelle Lundell, Director, Accessibility Services, Utah Valley State College, 800 West 1200 South Street, BU 145, Mail Stop 190, Orem, UT 84058-5999, 801-222-8000 Ext. 8404. Fax: 801-226-5207. Email: lundelmi@uvsc.edu.

VINCENNES UNIVERSITY

Vincennes, Indiana

Students with LD	105	Subject-Area Tutoring	✓
ADD services	✓	Special Courses	✓
Staff	3 full-, 12 part-time	Taped Textbooks	
Special Fee	✓	Alternative Test Arrang.	✓
Diagnostic Testing		Notetakers	
Basic Skills Remediation	✓	LD Student Organization	

LEARNING DISABILITIES PROGRAM INFORMATION

The Student Transition into Education Program (STEP) began offering services in 1990. Currently the program serves 105 undergraduates with LD. Students diagnosed with ADD/ADHD are eligible for the same services available to students with LD.

Staff: 3 full-time, 12 part-time staff members, including co-directors, professional tutors. Services provided by remediation specialists, tutors, counselors.

Special Fees: $600 per year.

Applications and admissions: *Required:* letters of recommendation, psychoeducational report completed within 3 years. Students may begin taking classes in fall only. *Application deadline:* continuous.

Special policies: The college has written policies regarding grade forgiveness.

PROGRAM AND SERVICE COMPONENTS

Special preparation or orientation: Required orientation held during registration.

Academic advising: Provided by LD staff members. Most students with LD take 12 to 15 credits each term; 12 credits required to maintain full-time status and be eligible for financial aid.

Counseling services: Individual counseling, career counseling, campus ministries.

Basic skills remediation: Offered one-on-one, in small groups, and in class-size groups by LD teachers, regular teachers. Available in reading, math, spelling, spoken language, written language, learning strategies, study skills, time management, social skills, computer skills.

Subject-area tutoring: Offered one-on-one and in small groups by professional teachers, peer tutors, Master's and Bachelor's level area professionals. Available in most subjects.

Special courses: College survival skills, communication skills, learning strategies, word processing, time management, typing, personal psychology, study skills, career planning, stress management. Most offered for credit; all enter into overall grade point average.

Auxiliary aids: Word-processors with spell-check, Franklin Spellers.

Auxiliary services: Alternative test arrangements, priority registration, advocacy.

GENERAL COLLEGE INFORMATION

State-supported, 2-year, coed. Awards associate degrees. Founded 1801. *Setting:* 95-acre small-town campus. *Total enrollment:* 6,500. *Faculty:* 400 (395 full-time, 5 part-time).

Enrollment Profile: 6,500 students from 25 states and territories, 30 other countries. 43% women, 57% men, 25% part-time, 91% state residents, 6% transferred in, 5% 25 or older, 1% Native American, 3% Hispanic, 6% black. *Most popular recent majors:* nursing, business administration/commerce/management, law enforcement/police sciences.

First-Year Class: 2,210 total; 5,140 applied, 98% were accepted. 5% from top 10% of their high school class, 10% from top quarter, 75% from top half.

Graduation Requirements: 64 credits; math/science requirements vary according to program; computer course.
Computers on Campus: 200 computers available on campus for general student use. A computer is recommended for all students. A campus-wide network can be accessed from student residence rooms and from off-campus. Students can contact faculty members and/or advisers through e-mail. Computers for student use in computer center, computer labs, learning resource center, classrooms, library, student center, dorms provide access to the Internet/World Wide Web, on- and off-campus e-mail addresses. Staffed computer lab on campus provides training in use of computers, software.

EXPENSES

Expenses for 1997–98: *Application fee:* $20. State resident tuition: $2576 full-time, $80.50 per credit part-time. Nonresident tuition: $6256 full-time, $195.50 per credit part-time. Tuition for Illinois residents of Crawford, Lawrence, Richland, and Wabash counties: $3936 full-time, $123 per credit part-time. Part-time mandatory fees per semester (7 to 11 credits): $20. Full-time mandatory fees: $40. College room and board: $4072.
LD Program Contact: Ms. Susan Lave, STEP Co-Director, Vincennes University, 1002 North First Street, Vincennes, IN 47591, 812-888-4212. Fax: 812-888-5531. Email: slave@vunet.vinu.edu.

WAKE TECHNICAL COMMUNITY COLLEGE

Raleigh, North Carolina

Students with LD	400	Subject-Area Tutoring	✓
ADD services	✓	Special Courses	
Staff	1 full-, 4 part-time	Taped Textbooks	✓
Special Fee	None	Alternative Test Arrang.	✓
Diagnostic Testing	✓	Notetakers	✓
Basic Skills Remediation	✓	LD Student Organization	✓

LEARNING DISABILITIES PROGRAM INFORMATION

The Office for Special Populations began offering services in 1988. Currently the program serves 400 undergraduates with LD. Students diagnosed with ADD/ADHD are eligible for the same services available to students with LD.
Staff: 1 full-time, 4 part-time staff members, including director, coordinator. Services provided by remediation specialists, LD specialist.
Special Fees: No special fees are charged for services to students with LD.
Applications and admissions: *Required:* high school transcript, courses completed, personal interview, psychoeducational report completed within 3 years, disability verification. Students may begin taking classes any term. *Application deadline:* continuous.
Special policies: The college has written policies regarding substitutions and waivers of admissions requirements.

PROGRAM AND SERVICE COMPONENTS

Special preparation or orientation: Required orientation held before registration.
Diagnostic testing: Reading, math, spelling, written language, personality, learning strategies.
Academic advising: Provided by LD staff members, academic advisers. Students with LD may take up to 15 semester hours each term; most take 6 to 9 semester hours; 6 semester hours required to maintain full-time status; 12 semester hours required to be eligible for financial aid.
Counseling services: Individual counseling, small-group counseling, career counseling, self-advocacy training.
Basic skills remediation: Offered one-on-one by regular teachers, LD specialists. Available in reading, math, spelling, written language, learning strategies, study skills, time management.
Subject-area tutoring: Offered one-on-one and in small groups by professional teachers, LD specialist. Available in most subjects.
Auxiliary aids: Taped textbooks, tape recorders, calculators, word-processors with spell-check, Franklin Speller.
Auxiliary services: Alternative test arrangements, notetakers, priority registration, advocacy.
Campus support group: A special student organization is available to students with LD.

GENERAL COLLEGE INFORMATION

State and locally supported, 2-year, coed. Part of North Carolina Community College System. Awards associate degrees. Founded 1958. *Setting:* 79-acre suburban campus. *Total enrollment:* 7,330. *Faculty:* 423 (202 full-time, 221 part-time).
Enrollment Profile: 7,330 students: 55% women, 45% men, 63% part-time, 98% state residents, 59% transferred in, 1% international, 56% 25 or older, 0% Native American, 1% Hispanic, 17% black, 3% Asian or Pacific Islander. *Areas of study chosen:* 36% business management and administrative services, 25% liberal arts/general studies, 16% engineering and applied sciences, 13% health professions and related sciences, 7% vocational and home economics, 3% computer and information sciences. *Most popular recent majors:* nursing, civil engineering technology, criminal justice.
First-Year Class: 507 total; 1,020 applied, 100% were accepted, 50% of whom enrolled. 4% from top 10% of their high school class, 22% from top quarter, 47% from top half.
Graduation Requirements: Math/science requirements vary according to program; computer course.
Computers on Campus: 675 computers available on campus for general student use. Computer purchase/lease plans available. Computers for student use in computer center, learning resource center, classrooms provide access to the Internet/World Wide Web. Staffed computer lab on campus provides training in use of computers, software.

EXPENSES

Expenses for 1997–98: State resident tuition: $560 full-time, $20 per semester hour part-time. Nonresident tuition: $4564 full-time, $163 per semester hour part-time. Part-time mandatory fees: $8 per semester. Full-time mandatory fees: $16.
LD Program Contact: Dr. Stephen Schulte, Director, Office for Special Populations, Wake Technical Community College, 9101 Fayetteville Road, Raleigh, NC 27603-5696, 919-662-3615. Fax: 919-779-3360.

WALDORF COLLEGE

Forest City, Iowa

Students with LD	32	Subject-Area Tutoring	✓
ADD services	✓	Special Courses	✓
Staff	3 full-, 25 part-time	Taped Textbooks	✓
Special Fee	✓	Alternative Test Arrang.	✓
Diagnostic Testing	✓	Notetakers	✓
Basic Skills Remediation	✓	LD Student Organization	

LEARNING DISABILITIES PROGRAM INFORMATION

The Learning Disabilities Program began offering services in 1989. Currently the program serves 32 undergraduates with LD. Students diagnosed with ADD/ADHD are eligible for the same services available to students with LD.

Waldorf College (continued)

Staff: 3 full-time, 25 part-time staff members, including director, coordinator. Services provided by tutors, counselors.
Special Fees: $800 per year for freshmen, $600 per year for sophomores.
Applications and admissions: *Required:* high school transcript, grade point average, courses completed, untimed or extended time ACT, letters of recommendation, psychoeducational report completed within 3 years; *recommended:* high school class rank, extracurricular activities, IEP (Individualized Education Program), personal interview. Students may begin taking classes in fall, winter, or summer. *Application deadline:* continuous.
Special policies: The college has written policies regarding substitutions and waivers of admissions requirements.

PROGRAM AND SERVICE COMPONENTS

Special preparation or orientation: Required orientation held before classes begin.
Diagnostic testing: Intelligence, reading, math, written language, perceptual skills, study skills, personality, social skills, learning strategies.
Academic advising: Provided by LD staff members, academic advisers. Students with LD may take up to 20 semester hours (with permission) each term; most take 14 to 17 semester hours; 12 semester hours required to maintain full-time status and be eligible for financial aid.
Counseling services: Individual counseling, small-group counseling, career counseling.
Basic skills remediation: Offered one-on-one, in small groups, and in class-size groups by LD teachers, academic support program director; computer-aided instruction also offered. Available in reading, math, written language, learning strategies, study skills, time management.
Subject-area tutoring: Offered one-on-one and in small groups by professional teachers, peer tutors. Available in most subjects.
Special courses: College survival skills, reading, vocabulary development, composition, word processing, math, typing, study skills, career planning. Most offered for credit; most enter into overall grade point average.
Auxiliary aids: Taped textbooks, tape recorders, calculators, typewriters, word-processors with spell-check, personal computers.
Auxiliary services: Alternative test arrangements, notetakers, advocacy.

GENERAL COLLEGE INFORMATION

Independent Lutheran, primarily 2-year, coed. Awards associate, bachelor's degrees. Founded 1903. *Setting:* 29-acre small-town campus. *Total enrollment:* 635. *Faculty:* 51 (36 full-time, 30% with terminal degrees, 15 part-time); student–undergrad faculty ratio is 13:1.
Enrollment Profile: 635 students from 21 states and territories, 22 other countries. 45% women, 55% men, 14% part-time, 62% state residents, 95% live on campus, 2% transferred in, 13% international, 10% 25 or older, 1% Native American, 1% Hispanic, 2% black, 1% Asian or Pacific Islander. *Retention:* 69% of 1995 full-time freshmen returned. *Most popular recent majors:* business administration/commerce/management, education, communication.
First-Year Class: 292 total; 813 applied, 75% were accepted, 48% of whom enrolled. 10% from top 10% of their high school class, 20% from top quarter, 52% from top half.
Graduation Requirements: 64 semester hours for associate, 124 semester hours for bachelor's; 4 semester hours each of math and lab science; internship (some majors).
Computers on Campus: Computer purchase/lease plans available. A computer is strongly recommended for all students. A campus-wide network can be accessed from student residence rooms. Students can contact faculty members and/or advisers through e-mail. Computers for student use in computer center, computer labs, library, Academic Achievement Center provide access to the Internet/World Wide Web, on- and off-campus e-mail addresses. Staffed computer lab on campus provides training in use of computers, software.

EXPENSES AND FINANCIAL AID

Expenses for 1997–98: *Application fee:* $20. Comprehensive fee of $15,450 includes full-time tuition ($11,050), mandatory fees ($200), and college room and board ($4200). Part-time tuition: $115 per semester hour. Tuition guaranteed not to increase for student's term of enrollment.
Financial aid specifically for students with LD: Scholarship: Philip Sigmond Memorial Scholarship.
LD Program Contact: Ms. Rebecca S. Hill, Learning Disabilities Program Director, Waldorf College, 106 South 6th Street, Forest City, IA 50436-1713, 515-582-8207. Fax: 515-582-8194. Email: hillb@waldorf.edu.

WAUBONSEE COMMUNITY COLLEGE

Sugar Grove, Illinois

Students with LD	200	Subject-Area Tutoring	✓
ADD services	✓	Special Courses	✓
Staff	8 full-, 14 part-time	Taped Textbooks	✓
Special Fee	None	Alternative Test Arrang.	✓
Diagnostic Testing	✓	Notetakers	✓
Basic Skills Remediation	✓	LD Student Organization	✓

LEARNING DISABILITIES PROGRAM INFORMATION

The Access Center for Students with Disabilities began offering services in 1986. Currently the program serves 200 undergraduates with LD. Students diagnosed with ADD/ADHD are eligible for the same services available to students with LD.
Staff: 8 full-time, 14 part-time staff members, including dean. Services provided by remediation specialists, tutors, counselor, diagnostic specialist, Manager.
Special Fees: $25 for diagnostic testing.
Applications and admissions: *Required:* autobiographical statement; *recommended:* high school transcript, IEP (Individualized Education Program), personal interview, letters of recommendation, psychoeducational report completed within 3 years. Students may begin taking classes in fall, winter, or summer. *Application deadline:* continuous.
Special policies: The college has written policies regarding grade forgiveness.

PROGRAM AND SERVICE COMPONENTS

Special preparation or orientation: Optional summer program offered prior to entering college. Optional orientation offered before registration and during registration.
Diagnostic testing: Intelligence, reading, math, spelling, handwriting, spoken language, written language, motor abilities, perceptual skills, study skills, psychoneurology, learning strategies.
Academic advising: Provided by LD staff members, academic advisers. Students with LD may take up to 21 semester hours each term; most take 9 to 12 semester hours; 12 semester hours required to maintain full-time status; 6 semester hours (state assistance), 2 semester hours (WCC/special needs assistance program) required to be eligible for financial aid.
Counseling services: Individual counseling, career counseling.

Basic skills remediation: Offered one-on-one, in small groups, and in class-size groups by LD teachers, regular teachers, tutors; computer-aided instruction also offered. Available in reading, math, spelling, written language, learning strategies, study skills, time management, social skills, computer skills.
Subject-area tutoring: Offered one-on-one and in small groups by professional teachers, peer tutors. Available in all subjects.
Special courses: College survival skills, reading, vocabulary development, communication skills, composition, learning strategies, word processing, time management, math, typing, study skills, career planning. Some offered for credit.
Auxiliary aids: Taped textbooks, tape recorders, calculators, typewriters, word-processors with spell-check, personal computers.
Auxiliary services: Alternative test arrangements, notetakers, advocacy, readers.
Campus support group: A special student organization is available to students with LD.

GENERAL COLLEGE INFORMATION

District-supported, 2-year, coed. Part of Illinois Community College System. Awards associate degrees. Founded 1966. *Setting:* 243-acre rural campus with easy access to Chicago. *Educational spending 1995–96:* $1003 per undergrad. *Total enrollment:* 7,666. *Faculty:* 501 (71 full-time, 13% with terminal degrees, 430 part-time); student–undergrad faculty ratio is 16:1.
Enrollment Profile: 7,666 students: 59% women, 41% men, 79% part-time, 100% state residents, 15% transferred in, 0% international, 54% 25 or older, 1% Native American, 22% Hispanic, 4% black, 1% Asian or Pacific Islander. *Retention:* 70% of 1995 full-time freshmen returned. *Areas of study chosen:* 37% vocational and home economics, 22% social sciences, 20% liberal arts/general studies, 10% health professions and related sciences, 6% physical sciences, 3% computer and information sciences, 2% engineering and applied sciences. *Most popular recent major:* nursing.
First-Year Class: 1,111 total; 1,272 applied, 100% were accepted, 87% of whom enrolled. 10% from top 10% of their high school class, 40% from top half.
Graduation Requirements: 64 semester hours; math/science requirements vary according to program.
Computers on Campus: 120 computers available on campus for general student use. A campus-wide network can be accessed. Students can contact faculty members and/or advisers through e-mail. Computers for student use in computer center. Staffed computer lab on campus. *Academic computing expenditure 1995–96:* $709,089.

EXPENSES AND FINANCIAL AID

Expenses for 1997–98: *Application fee:* $10. Area resident tuition: $1312 full-time, $41 per semester hour part-time. State resident tuition: $6074 full-time, $189.82 per semester hour part-time. Nonresident tuition: $7149 full-time, $223.41 per semester hour part-time. Part-time mandatory fees per semester range from $2 to $13. Full-time mandatory fees: $28.
Financial aid specifically for students with LD: Scholarship: Kufta Scholarship; work-study.
LD Program Contact: Ms. Iris Jorstad, Manager, Access Center for Students with Disabilities, Waubonsee Community College, Route 47 at Harter Road, Sugar Grove, IL 60554, 708-466-4811 Ext. 602. Fax: 708-466-7799. Email: irisj@wccg.wcc.cc.il.us.

WAUKESHA COUNTY TECHNICAL COLLEGE

Pewaukee, Wisconsin

Students with LD	100	Subject-Area Tutoring	✓
ADD services	✓	Special Courses	
Staff	3 full-, 3 part-time	Taped Textbooks	✓
Special Fee	None	Alternative Test Arrang.	✓
Diagnostic Testing	✓	Notetakers	✓
Basic Skills Remediation	✓	LD Student Organization	

LEARNING DISABILITIES PROGRAM INFORMATION

The Special Needs began offering services in 1977. Currently the program serves 100 undergraduates with LD. Students diagnosed with ADD/ADHD are eligible for the same services available to students with LD.
Staff: 3 full-time, 3 part-time staff members, including director, associate director. Services provided by remediation specialists, counselor, Transition Specialist.
Special Fees: $3.50 for diagnostic testing.
Applications and admissions: *Required:* high school transcript, grade point average, courses completed, IEP (Individualized Education Program), personal interview, psychoeducational report completed within 1 year, vocational rehabilitation evaluation; *recommended:* high school extracurricular activities. Students may begin taking classes in fall, spring, or summer. *Application deadline:* continuous.
Special policies: The college has written policies regarding substitutions and waivers of admissions, graduation, and degree requirements.

PROGRAM AND SERVICE COMPONENTS

Special preparation or orientation: Optional summer program offered prior to entering college. Orientation (required for some) held during summer transition program.
Diagnostic testing: Intelligence, reading, math, written language, motor abilities, perceptual skills, study skills.
Academic advising: Provided by LD staff members. Students with LD may take up to 18 credits each term; most take 12 credits; 12 credits required to maintain full-time status; 6 credits required to be eligible for financial aid.
Counseling services: Individual counseling, career counseling.
Basic skills remediation: Offered one-on-one by LD teachers, regular teachers. Available in reading, math, spelling, written language.
Subject-area tutoring: Offered one-on-one and in small groups by professional teachers, peer tutors. Available in most subjects.
Auxiliary aids: Taped textbooks, tape recorders, calculators.
Auxiliary services: Alternative test arrangements, notetakers.

GENERAL COLLEGE INFORMATION

State and locally supported, 2-year, coed. Part of Wisconsin Technical College System. Awards associate degrees. Founded 1923. *Setting:* 137-acre small-town campus with easy access to Milwaukee. *Total enrollment:* 4,700. *Faculty:* 520 (145 full-time, 375 part-time).
Enrollment Profile: 4,700 students: 65% part-time, 99% state residents, 20% transferred in, 90% 25 or older, 0% Native American, 1% Hispanic, 1% black, 1% Asian or Pacific Islander. *Most popular recent majors:* law enforcement/police sciences, marketing/retailing/merchandising, nursing.
First-Year Class: 1,150 total; 2,100 applied, 100% were accepted, 55% of whom enrolled.
Graduation Requirements: 66 credits; math/science requirements vary according to program.

Waukesha County Technical College (continued)

Computers on Campus: 50 computers available on campus for general student use. Computers for student use in classrooms, library.

EXPENSES

Expenses for 1997–98: *Application fee:* $25. State resident tuition: $1789 full-time, $54.20 per credit part-time. Nonresident tuition: $14,098 full-time, $427.20 per credit part-time. Part-time mandatory fees: $3.50 per credit. Full-time mandatory fees: $116.

LD Program Contact: Ms. Deb Jilbert, Transition Specialist, Waukesha County Technical College, 800 Main Street, Pewaukee, WI 53072, 414-691-5210. Fax: 414-691-5089. Email: djilbert@waukesha.tec.wi.us.

WEST LOS ANGELES COLLEGE

Culver City, California

Students with LD	125	Subject-Area Tutoring	✓
ADD services	✓	Special Courses	✓
Staff	1 full-, 1 part-time	Taped Textbooks	✓
Special Fee	None	Alternative Test Arrang.	✓
Diagnostic Testing	✓	Notetakers	
Basic Skills Remediation	✓	LD Student Organization	

LEARNING DISABILITIES PROGRAM INFORMATION

The Learning Specialist Program began offering services in 1980. Currently the program serves 125 undergraduates with LD. Students diagnosed with ADD/ADHD are eligible for the same services available to students with LD.

Staff: 1 full-time, 1 part-time staff members, including coordinator. Services provided by remediation specialist, tutors, counselor.

Special Fees: No special fees are charged for services to students with LD.

Applications and admissions: *Recommended:* high school transcript, IEP (Individualized Education Program), personal interview, psychoeducational report completed within 2 years. Students may begin taking classes in fall, spring, or summer. *Application deadline:* continuous.

Special policies: The college has written policies regarding grade forgiveness; substitutions and waivers of graduation requirements.

PROGRAM AND SERVICE COMPONENTS

Special preparation or orientation: Required orientation held after classes begin.

Diagnostic testing: Intelligence, reading, math, spelling, written language, study skills, learning strategies.

Academic advising: Provided by LD staff members. Students with LD may take up to 12 units each term; most take 9 to 12 units; 12 units required to maintain full-time status; 12 units (9 with special permission) required to be eligible for financial aid.

Counseling services: Individual counseling, career counseling.

Basic skills remediation: Offered by supervised computer-assisted instruction. Available in reading, math, spelling, written language.

Subject-area tutoring: Offered one-on-one, in small groups, and in class-size groups by professional teachers, peer tutors. Available in most subjects.

Special courses: College survival skills, communication skills, learning strategies, time management, study skills, career planning. Most offered for credit; none enter into overall grade point average.

Auxiliary aids: Taped textbooks, tape recorders, word-processors with spell-check, personal computers, talking computers, optical character readers, scanners, screen readers.

Auxiliary services: Alternative test arrangements, priority registration.

GENERAL COLLEGE INFORMATION

State and locally supported, 2-year, coed. Part of Los Angeles Community College District System. Awards associate degrees. Founded 1969. *Setting:* 69-acre urban campus with easy access to Los Angeles. *Total enrollment:* 7,400. *Faculty:* 320 (120 full-time, 200 part-time).

Enrollment Profile: 7,400 students from 20 states and territories. 64% women, 36% men, 78% part-time, 99% state residents, 17% transferred in, 76% 25 or older, 1% Native American, 11% Hispanic, 48% black, 9% Asian or Pacific Islander.

First-Year Class: 3,500 total; 8,000 applied, 100% were accepted, 44% of whom enrolled.

Graduation Requirements: 60 units; 1 college algebra course.

Computers on Campus: Computers for student use in learning resource center, classrooms.

EXPENSES

Expenses for 1996–97: State resident tuition: $0 full-time. Nonresident tuition: $3750 full-time, $125 per unit part-time. Part-time mandatory fees per semester range from $20.50 to $150.50. Full-time mandatory fees: $405.

LD Program Contact: Ms. Frances S. Israel, Learning Skills Specialist, West Los Angeles College, 4800 Freshman Drive, Culver City, CA 90230-3500, 310-287-4423. Fax: 310-841-0396. Email: israelf@laccd.cc.ca.us.

WEST VALLEY COLLEGE

Saratoga, California

Students with LD	400	Subject-Area Tutoring	✓
ADD services	✓	Special Courses	✓
Staff	13 full-, 11 part-time	Taped Textbooks	✓
Special Fee	None	Alternative Test Arrang.	✓
Diagnostic Testing	✓	Notetakers	✓
Basic Skills Remediation	✓	LD Student Organization	✓

LEARNING DISABILITIES PROGRAM INFORMATION

The Learning Efficiency Assistance Program (LEAP) began offering services in 1975. Currently the program serves 400 undergraduates with LD. Students diagnosed with ADD/ADHD are eligible for the same services available to students with LD.

Staff: 13 full-time, 11 part-time staff members, including coordinator. Services provided by remediation specialists, tutors, counselors, diagnostic specialists.

Special Fees: No special fees are charged for services to students with LD.

Applications and admissions: *Recommended:* high school transcript. Students may begin taking classes any term. *Application deadline:* continuous.

Special policies: The college has written policies regarding grade forgiveness; substitutions and waivers of graduation and degree requirements.

PROGRAM AND SERVICE COMPONENTS

Special preparation or orientation: Optional summer program offered prior to entering college. Required orientation held during registration.

Diagnostic testing: Intelligence, reading, math, spelling, handwriting, spoken language, written language, perceptual skills, study skills, speech, hearing.

Academic advising: Provided by LD staff members, academic advisers. Students with LD may take up to 15 units each term; most take 9 to 12 units; 9 units required to maintain full-time status; 6 to 12 units (depending on assistance package) required to be eligible for financial aid.
Counseling services: Individual counseling, small-group counseling, career counseling, self-advocacy training.
Basic skills remediation: Offered in small groups and in class-size groups by LD teachers, regular teachers. Available in reading, math, spelling, written language, learning strategies, study skills, time management, speech, computer skills.
Subject-area tutoring: Offered one-on-one, in small groups, and in class-size groups by professional teachers, peer tutors. Available in all subjects.
Special courses: College survival skills, reading, vocabulary development, communication skills, composition, learning strategies, word processing, time management, math, typing, personal psychology, study skills, career planning. All offered for credit; some enter into overall grade point average.
Auxiliary aids: Taped textbooks, tape recorders, calculators, word-processors with spell-check, personal computers, talking computers, optical character readers, optical scanner.
Auxiliary services: Alternative test arrangements, notetakers, priority registration, advocacy, readers.
Campus support group: A special student organization is available to students with LD.

GENERAL COLLEGE INFORMATION

State and locally supported, 2-year, coed. Part of California Community Colleges System. Awards associate degrees. Founded 1963. *Setting:* 143-acre small-town campus with easy access to San Francisco and San Jose. *Total enrollment:* 14,224. *Faculty:* 560 (210 full-time, 350 part-time); student–undergrad faculty ratio is 26:1.
Enrollment Profile: 14,224 students from 2 states and territories, 20 other countries. 60% women, 40% men, 69% part-time, 89% state residents, 19% transferred in, 3% international, 58% 25 or older, 1% Native American, 9% Hispanic, 3% black, 10% Asian or Pacific Islander.
First-Year Class: 2,434 total. Of the students who applied, 100% were accepted.
Graduation Requirements: 60 units; algebra or geometry proficiency; computer course for business, engineering, management, marketing majors.
Computers on Campus: 200 computers available on campus for general student use. Computers for student use in library, departmental labs.

EXPENSES

Expenses for 1997–98: State resident tuition: $0 full-time. Nonresident tuition: $3600 full-time, $120 per unit part-time. Part-time mandatory fees per semester range from $30 to $160. Full-time mandatory fees: $444.
LD Program Contact: Ms. Judith Colson, Learning Disabilities Specialist, West Valley College, 14000 Fruitvale Avenue, Saratoga, CA 95070-5698, 408-741-2450. Fax: 408-867-4882.

WILLIAM RAINEY HARPER COLLEGE
Palatine, Illinois

Students with LD	200	Subject-Area Tutoring	✓
ADD services	✓	Special Courses	✓
Staff	2 full-, 6 part-time	Taped Textbooks	✓
Special Fee	✓	Alternative Test Arrang.	✓
Diagnostic Testing	✓	Notetakers	✓
Basic Skills Remediation	✓	LD Student Organization	✓

LEARNING DISABILITIES PROGRAM INFORMATION

The Center for Students with Disabilities began offering services in 1981. Currently the program serves 200 undergraduates with LD. Students diagnosed with ADD/ADHD are eligible for the same services available to students with LD.
Staff: 2 full-time, 6 part-time staff members, including director. Services provided by tutors, counselor, diagnostic specialist, LD specialists.
Special Fees: $350 per year. $200 for diagnostic testing.
Applications and admissions: *Required:* high school transcript, untimed ACT, psychoeducational report completed within 3 years. Students may begin taking classes in fall or spring. *Application deadline:* continuous.
Special policies: The college has written policies regarding grade forgiveness; substitutions and waivers of admissions requirements.

PROGRAM AND SERVICE COMPONENTS

Special preparation or orientation: Required orientation held before registration and during registration.
Diagnostic testing: Intelligence, reading, math, spelling, perceptual skills, study skills.
Academic advising: Provided by LD staff members, academic advisers. Students with LD may take up to 12 semester hours each term; most take 9 to 10 semester hours; 12 semester hours required to maintain full-time status and be eligible for financial aid.
Counseling services: Individual counseling, career counseling.
Basic skills remediation: Offered one-on-one by LD teachers. Available in reading, math, spelling, written language, learning strategies, perceptual skills, study skills, time management, social skills, computer skills.
Subject-area tutoring: Offered one-on-one and in small groups by professional teachers. Available in most subjects.
Special courses: Composition, personal psychology, study skills, career planning. All offered for credit; some enter into overall grade point average.
Auxiliary aids: Taped textbooks, tape recorders, calculators, typewriters, word-processors with spell-check, personal computers.
Auxiliary services: Alternative test arrangements, notetakers, advocacy.
Campus support group: A special student organization is available to students with LD.

GENERAL COLLEGE INFORMATION

State and locally supported, 2-year, coed. Part of Illinois Community College System. Awards associate degrees. Founded 1965. *Setting:* 200-acre suburban campus with easy access to Chicago. *Endowment:* $1.1 million. *Research spending 1995–96:* $252,671. *Total enrollment:* 14,000. *Faculty:* 1,018 (218 full-time, 20% with terminal degrees, 800 part-time); student–undergrad faculty ratio is 25:1.
Enrollment Profile: 14,000 students: 58% women, 42% men, 69% part-time, 99% state residents, 34% transferred in, 1% international, 49% 25 or older, 0% Native American, 7% Hispanic, 3% black, 10% Asian or Pacific Islander. *Retention:* 63% of 1995 full-time freshmen returned. *Areas of study chosen:* 41% liberal arts/general studies, 13% business management and administrative services, 10% health professions and related sciences, 8% education, 7% engineering and applied sciences, 6% computer and information sciences, 3% physical sciences, 3% social sciences, 2% biological and life sciences, 2% vocational and home economics, 1% agriculture, 1% architecture, 1% fine arts, 1% foreign language and literature, 1% performing arts.

William Rainey Harper College (continued)

First-Year Class: 4,100 total; 4,839 applied, 100% were accepted, 85% of whom enrolled. 34% from top quarter of their high school class, 50% from top half.
Graduation Requirements: 60 semester hours; internship (some majors).
Computers on Campus: 206 computers available on campus for general student use. Computer purchase/lease plans available. A campus-wide network can be accessed from off-campus. Students can contact faculty members and/or advisers through e-mail. Computers for student use in computer center, computer labs, learning resource center, library provide access to the Internet/World Wide Web. Staffed computer lab on campus provides training in use of computers, software. *Academic computing expenditure 1995–96:* $3.5 million.

EXPENSES

Expenses for 1997–98: *Application fee:* $20. Area resident tuition: $1380 full-time, $46 per semester hour part-time. State resident tuition: $6170 full-time, $205.65 per semester hour part-time. Nonresident tuition: $7197 full-time, $239.91 per semester hour part-time. Part-time mandatory fees: $16.50 per semester. Full-time mandatory fees: $58.
LD Program Contact: Ms. Pascuala Herrera, LD Specialist, William Rainey Harper College, 1200 West Algonquin Road, Palatine, IL 60067-7398, 847-925-6266. Fax: 847-925-6036.

WISCONSIN INDIANHEAD TECHNICAL COLLEGE, ASHLAND CAMPUS

Ashland, Wisconsin

Students with LD	60	Subject-Area Tutoring	✓
ADD services	✓	Special Courses	✓
Staff	1 full-, 1 part-time	Taped Textbooks	✓
Special Fee	None	Alternative Test Arrang.	✓
Diagnostic Testing	✓	Notetakers	
Basic Skills Remediation	✓	LD Student Organization	

LEARNING DISABILITIES PROGRAM INFORMATION

The Special Needs Program began offering services in 1982. Currently the program serves 60 undergraduates with LD. Students diagnosed with ADD/ADHD are eligible for the same services available to students with LD, as well as individualized programming allowing for frequent breaks, follow-through on recommendations from medical doctors.
Staff: 1 full-time, 1 part-time staff members, including director, coordinator. Services provided by remediation specialists, tutors, counselors, diagnostic specialists.
Special Fees: No special fees are charged for services to students with LD.
Applications and admissions: *Required:* personal interview; *recommended:* psychoeducational report completed within 3 years, placement testing, ACT ASSET, Woodcock-Johnson (on an individual basis). Students may begin taking classes any term. *Application deadline:* continuous.

PROGRAM AND SERVICE COMPONENTS

Special preparation or orientation: Orientation (required for some) held before registration.
Diagnostic testing: Reading, math, spelling, written language, perceptual skills, learning strategies.
Academic advising: Provided by LD staff members. Students with LD may take up to 18 credits each term; most take 12 to 16 credits; 12 credits required to maintain full-time status and be eligible for financial aid.
Counseling services: Individual counseling, small-group counseling, career counseling.
Basic skills remediation: Offered one-on-one, in small groups, and in class-size groups by LD teachers. Available in reading, math, spelling, written language, learning strategies, study skills.
Subject-area tutoring: Offered one-on-one, in small groups, and in class-size groups by professional teachers, peer tutors. Available in most subjects.
Special courses: College survival skills, reading, vocabulary development, communication skills, composition, learning strategies, word processing, time management, math, typing, personal psychology, study skills, career planning. Some offered for credit; some enter into overall grade point average.
Auxiliary aids: Taped textbooks, tape recorders, calculators, typewriters, word-processors with spell-check, talking computers, Dragon Dictate.
Auxiliary services: Alternative test arrangements.

GENERAL COLLEGE INFORMATION

District-supported, 2-year, coed. Part of Wisconsin Technical College System. Awards associate degrees. Founded 1920. *Setting:* 40-acre small-town campus. *Total enrollment:* 474. *Faculty:* 28 (21 full-time, 7 part-time); student–undergrad faculty ratio is 18:1.
Enrollment Profile: 474 students: 65% women, 35% men, 30% part-time, 99% state residents, 3% transferred in, 50% 25 or older, 14% Native American.
First-Year Class: 191 total.
Graduation Requirements: 62 credits; computer course for business majors.
Computers on Campus: 73 computers available on campus for general student use. Staffed computer lab on campus.

EXPENSES

Expenses for 1997–98: *Application fee:* $10. State resident tuition: $1680 full-time, $54.20 per credit part-time. Nonresident tuition: $13,243 full-time, $427.20 per credit part-time.
LD Program Contact: Ms. Cindy Utities-Heart, Special Needs Instructor, Wisconsin Indianhead Technical College, Ashland Campus, 2100 Beaser Avenue, Ashland, WI 54806, 715-682-4591. Fax: 715-682-8040.

YORK TECHNICAL COLLEGE

Rock Hill, South Carolina

Students with LD	100	Subject-Area Tutoring	✓
ADD services	✓	Special Courses	
Staff	4 full-, 3 part-time	Taped Textbooks	✓
Special Fee	None	Alternative Test Arrang.	✓
Diagnostic Testing	✓	Notetakers	✓
Basic Skills Remediation	✓	LD Student Organization	

LEARNING DISABILITIES PROGRAM INFORMATION

The Learning Enhanced Achievement Program (LEAP) began offering services in 1987. Currently the program serves 100 undergraduates with LD. Students diagnosed with ADD/ADHD are eligible for the same services available to students with LD.
Staff: 4 full-time, 3 part-time staff members, including director. Services provided by remediation specialist, tutors, counselor.
Special Fees: No special fees are charged for services to students with LD.

Applications and admissions: *Required:* psychoeducational report completed within 3 years; *recommended:* personal interview. Students may begin taking classes any term. *Application deadline:* continuous.

PROGRAM AND SERVICE COMPONENTS

Special preparation or orientation: Optional summer program offered prior to entering college. Orientation (required for some) held before registration.
Diagnostic testing: Intelligence, reading, math, spelling, handwriting, spoken language, written language, motor abilities, perceptual skills, hearing, learning strategies.
Academic advising: Provided by academic advisers. Most students with LD take 12 semester hours each term; 12 semester hours required to maintain full-time status; no minimum number of semester hours required to be eligible for financial aid.
Counseling services: Individual counseling, small-group counseling, career counseling, self-advocacy training.
Basic skills remediation: Offered one-on-one and in small groups by regular teachers; computer-aided instruction also offered. Available in reading, math, written language, learning strategies, study skills, time management, social skills.
Subject-area tutoring: Offered one-on-one by professional teachers, peer tutors. Available in most subjects.
Auxiliary aids: Taped textbooks, tape recorders, calculators, word-processors with spell-check, optical character readers.
Auxiliary services: Alternative test arrangements, notetakers.

GENERAL COLLEGE INFORMATION

State-supported, 2-year, coed. Part of South Carolina State Board for Technical and Comprehensive Education. Awards associate degrees. Founded 1961. *Setting:* 110-acre small-town campus. *Total enrollment:* 3,528. *Faculty:* 236 (93 full-time, 98% with terminal degrees, 143 parttime).
Enrollment Profile: 3,528 students: 61% women, 39% men, 59% part-time, 99% state residents, 9% transferred in, 0% international, 47% 25 or older, 1% Native American, 1% Hispanic, 20% black, 1% Asian or Pacific Islander.
First-Year Class: 788 total.
Graduation Requirements: 62 semester hours; 3 semester hours of math; computer course for most majors.
Computers on Campus: 180 computers available on campus for general student use. Computers for student use in computer center, computer labs, learning resource center, library provide access to the Internet/World Wide Web. Staffed computer lab on campus provides training in use of computers, software.

EXPENSES

Expenses for 1997–98: *Application fee:* $10. Area resident tuition: $936 full-time, $39 per semester hour part-time. State resident tuition: $1224 full-time, $51 per semester hour part-time. Nonresident tuition: $3072 full-time, $128 per semester hour part-time. Part-time mandatory fees: $6 per semester. Full-time mandatory fees: $12.
LD Program Contact: Ms. Deborah Gladden, Director, York Technical College, 452 South Anderson Road, Rock Hill, SC 29730, 803-325-2876. Fax: 803-981-7237. Email: gladden@al.york.tec.sc.us.

▸ TWO-YEAR COLLEGES ◂

WITH SPECIAL SERVICES

ADIRONDACK COMMUNITY COLLEGE

Queensbury, New York

LEARNING DISABILITIES SERVICES INFORMATION

Special Services Office and Learning Disability Specialist Office began offering services in 1986. Currently the program serves 75 undergraduates with LD. Students diagnosed with ADD/ADHD are eligible for the same services available to students with LD.

Staff: 1 full-time, 1 part-time staff members, including director. Services provided by remediation specialist.

Special Fees: No special fees are charged for services to students with LD.

Applications and admissions: *Required:* high school transcript, grade point average, courses completed, IEP (Individualized Education Program), psychoeducational report completed within 3 years; *recommended:* high school extracurricular activities, untimed or extended time SAT I or ACT, personal interview, letters of recommendation. Students may begin taking classes in fall, spring, or summer. *Application deadline:* 8/30 (fall term), 1/15 (spring term).

Special policies: The college has written policies regarding grade forgiveness; substitutions and waivers of graduation and degree requirements.

PROGRAM AND SERVICE COMPONENTS

Academic advising: Provided by unit staff members, academic advisers. Students with LD may take up to 18 credit hours each term; most take 12 to 14 credit hours; 12 credit hours required to maintain full-time status; 3 to 12 credit hours required to be eligible for financial aid.

Counseling services: Individual counseling, career counseling, self-advocacy training.

Subject-area tutoring: Offered one-on-one and in small groups by peer tutors, LD specialist. Available in most subjects.

Auxiliary aids: Taped textbooks, tape recorders, typewriters, word-processors with spell-check, personal computers, talking computers, optical character readers.

Auxiliary services: Alternative test arrangements, notetakers, advocacy.

GENERAL COLLEGE INFORMATION

State and locally supported, 2-year, coed. Part of State University of New York System. Awards associate degrees. Founded 1960. *Setting:* 141-acre small-town campus. *Endowment:* $901,000. *Total enrollment:* 3,487. *Faculty:* 240 (100 full-time, 25% with terminal degrees, 140 part-time); student–undergrad faculty ratio is 17:1.

Enrollment Profile: 3,487 students from 5 states and territories, 6 other countries. 63% women, 37% men, 51% part-time, 98% state residents, 6% transferred in, 1% international, 46% 25 or older, 1% Native American, 1% Hispanic, 1% black, 1% Asian or Pacific Islander. *Retention:* 74% of 1995 full-time freshmen returned. *Areas of study chosen:* 39% liberal arts/general studies, 20% business management and administrative services, 10% health professions and related sciences, 7% mathematics, 6% engineering and applied sciences, 6% social sciences, 5% biological and life sciences, 3% physical sciences, 2% communications and journalism, 1% computer and information sciences, 1% vocational and home economics. *Most popular recent majors:* liberal arts/general studies, business administration/commerce/management, nursing.

First-Year Class: 901 total; 1,209 applied, 98% were accepted, 76% of whom enrolled. 7% from top 10% of their high school class, 29% from top quarter, 52% from top half.

Graduation Requirements: 64 credit hours; 3 credit hours each of math and science; computer course for most majors.

Computers on Campus: 150 computers available on campus for general student use. A campus-wide network can be accessed. Computers for student use in computer labs, classrooms, library. Staffed computer lab on campus provides training in use of computers, software. *Academic computing expenditure 1995–96:* $107,656.

EXPENSES

Expenses for 1996–97: *Application fee:* $30. State resident tuition: $2050 full-time, $73 per credit hour part-time. Nonresident tuition: $4100 full-time, $146 per credit hour part-time. Part-time mandatory fees: $3 per credit hour. Full-time mandatory fees: $150.

LD Services Contact: Ms. Ursula Woodfield, Learning Disability Specialist, Adirondack Community College, Bay Road, Queensbury, NY 12804, 518-743-2307. Fax: 518-745-1433. Email: woodfieu@acc.sunyacc.edu.

AIKEN TECHNICAL COLLEGE

Aiken, South Carolina

LEARNING DISABILITIES SERVICES INFORMATION

Counseling Services began offering services in 1989. Currently the program serves 90 undergraduates with LD. Students diagnosed with ADD/ADHD are eligible for the same services available to students with LD.

Staff: 1 full-time staff member (coordinator). Services provided by remediation specialists, tutors, counselors.

Special Fees: No special fees are charged for services to students with LD.

Applications and admissions: *Required:* psychoeducational report completed within 3 years, ACT ASSET; *recommended:* high school transcript, grade point average, class rank, courses completed, extracurricular activities, IEP (Individualized Education Program), untimed or extended time SAT I or ACT, personal interview. Students may begin taking classes in fall, spring, or summer. *Application deadline:* continuous.

PROGRAM AND SERVICE COMPONENTS

Special preparation or orientation: Optional orientation offered before registration.

Academic advising: Provided by unit staff members, academic advisers. Students with LD may take up to 18 semester hours each term; most take 9 semester hours; 12 semester hours (fall and spring), 9 semester hours (summer) required to maintain full-time status; 6 semester hours required to be eligible for financial aid.

Counseling services: Individual counseling, small-group counseling, career counseling, self-advocacy training, family counseling.

Basic skills remediation: Offered one-on-one and in small groups by regular teachers; computer-aided instruction also offered. Available in reading, math, written language, learning strategies, study skills, time management.

Subject-area tutoring: Offered one-on-one and in small groups by professional teachers, peer tutors. Available in most subjects.

Special courses: College survival skills, reading, vocabulary development, word processing, time management, study skills, career planning, stress management, resume writing and interviewing skills. Most offered for credit; some enter into overall grade point average.

Auxiliary aids: Taped textbooks, tape recorders, calculators, typewriters, word-processors with spell-check, personal computers.

Auxiliary services: Alternative test arrangements, notetakers, priority registration, advocacy.

GENERAL COLLEGE INFORMATION

State and locally supported, 2-year, coed. Part of South Carolina State Board for Technical and Comprehensive Education. Awards associate degrees. Founded 1972. *Setting:* 88-acre rural campus. *Endowment:* $539,800. *Educational spending 1995–96:* $1971 per undergrad. *Total enrollment:* 2,143. *Faculty:* 119 (50 full-time, 100% with terminal degrees, 69 part-time); student–undergrad faculty ratio is 19:1.

Enrollment Profile: 2,143 students: 56% women, 44% men, 60% part-time, 88% state residents, 9% transferred in, 49% 25 or older, 1% Native American, 1% Hispanic, 30% black, 1% Asian or Pacific Islander. *Retention:* 47% of 1995 full-time freshmen returned. *Areas of study chosen:* 22% engineering and applied sciences, 20% business management and administrative services, 17% liberal arts/general studies, 13% health professions and related sciences, 9% interdisciplinary studies, 8% computer and information sciences, 6% social sciences, 3% vocational and home economics. *Most popular recent majors:* computer technologies, nuclear technology.

First-Year Class: 493 total; 850 applied, 100% were accepted, 63% of whom enrolled. 3% from top 10% of their high school class, 12% from top quarter, 39% from top half.

Graduation Requirements: 64 semester hours; computer course (varies by major).

Computers on Campus: 140 computers available on campus for general student use. A campus-wide network can be accessed. Students can contact faculty members and/or advisers through e-mail. Computers for student use in computer labs, classrooms, library provide access to the Internet/World Wide Web. Staffed computer lab on campus provides training in use of computers, software.

EXPENSES

Expenses for 1996–97: *Application fee:* $15. State resident tuition: $912 full-time, $38 per semester hour part-time. Nonresident tuition:

$1248 full-time, $52 per semester hour part-time. Tuition for Georgia residents of Columbia and Richmond counties: $942 full-time, $38 per semester hour part-time. Full-time mandatory fees: $29.
LD Services Contact: Mr. Richard M. Weldon, Counselor, Aiken Technical College, PO Drawer 696, Aiken, SC 29802-0696, 803-593-9231 Ext. 1520. Fax: 803-593-6641. Email: weldon@aik.tec.sc.us.

ALAMANCE COMMUNITY COLLEGE

Graham, North Carolina

LEARNING DISABILITIES SERVICES INFORMATION

Special Needs Program currently serves 39 undergraduates with LD. Students diagnosed with ADD/ADHD are eligible for the same services available to students with LD.
Staff: 11 full-time staff members, including coordinator. Services provided by remediation specialist, tutors, counselors.
Special Fees: No special fees are charged for services to students with LD.
Applications and admissions: *Required:* high school transcript, IEP (Individualized Education Program), psychoeducational report completed within 5 years. Students may begin taking classes any term. *Application deadline:* continuous.

PROGRAM AND SERVICE COMPONENTS

Special preparation or orientation: Optional orientation offered before registration.
Academic advising: Provided by academic advisers. Most students with LD take 6 to 14 semester hours each term; 12 semester hours required to maintain full-time status; 6 semester hours required to be eligible for financial aid.
Counseling services: Individual counseling, small-group counseling, career counseling, self-advocacy training.
Basic skills remediation: Offered one-on-one, in small groups, and in class-size groups by skills lab. Available in reading, math, spelling, study skills, time management, social skills.
Subject-area tutoring: Offered one-on-one by professional teachers, peer tutors. Available in all subjects.
Special courses: College survival skills, reading, communication skills, time management, math, personal psychology, study skills, stress management. Some offered for credit; most enter into overall grade point average.
Auxiliary services: Advocacy.

GENERAL COLLEGE INFORMATION

State-supported, 2-year, coed. Part of North Carolina Community College System. Awards associate degrees. Founded 1959. *Setting:* 48-acre small-town campus. *Endowment:* $379,042. *Total enrollment:* 3,340. *Faculty:* 145 (65 full-time, 80 part-time); student–undergrad faculty ratio is 22:1.
Enrollment Profile: 3,340 students from 11 states and territories, 11 other countries. 60% women, 40% men, 64% part-time, 98% state residents, 6% transferred in, 1% international, 50% 25 or older, 17% black. *Retention:* 63% of 1995 full-time freshmen returned. *Areas of study chosen:* 32% business management and administrative services, 18% engineering and applied sciences, 15% health professions and related sciences, 9% social sciences, 7% computer and information sciences, 6% vocational and home economics, 4% performing arts, 3% biological and life sciences, 2% agriculture, 2% education. *Most popular recent majors:* nursing, business administration/commerce/management, accounting.
First-Year Class: 1,127 total; 2,747 applied, 100% were accepted, 41% of whom enrolled.
Graduation Requirements: omputer course (varies by major).
Computers on Campus: 100 computers available on campus for general student use. A campus-wide network can be accessed. Computers for student use in computer center, computer labs, classrooms, library. Staffed computer lab on campus provides training in use of computers, software. *Academic computing expenditure 1995–96:* $120,050.

EXPENSES

Expenses for 1997–98: State resident tuition: $560 full-time, $20 per semester hour part-time. Nonresident tuition: $4564 full-time, $163 per semester hour part-time. Part-time mandatory fees per semester range from $3 to $6.35. Full-time mandatory fees: $31.
LD Services Contact: Ms. Janice Reaves, Coordinator, Counseling Services, Alamance Community College, PO Box 8000, Graham, NC 27253, 910-578-2002. Fax: 910-578-1987.

ALBUQUERQUE TECHNICAL VOCATIONAL INSTITUTE

Albuquerque, New Mexico

LEARNING DISABILITIES SERVICES INFORMATION

Special Services currently serves over 100 undergraduates with LD. Students diagnosed with ADD/ADHD are eligible for the same services available to students with LD.
Staff: 5 full-time, 25 part-time staff members, including director. Services provided by counselors, diagnostic specialists, readers, writers.
Special Fees: No special fees are charged for services to students with LD.
Applications and admissions: Open admissions. Students may begin taking classes any term. *Application deadline:* continuous.

PROGRAM AND SERVICE COMPONENTS

Diagnostic testing: Intelligence, reading, math, spelling, written language, motor abilities, perceptual skills.
Academic advising: Provided by unit staff members. Students with LD may take up to as many credit hours as an individual can handle each term; 12 credit hours required to maintain full-time status; 6 credit hours (part-time), 12 credit hours (full-time) required to be eligible for financial aid.
Counseling services: Individual counseling, career counseling.
Auxiliary aids: Taped textbooks, tape recorders, calculators.
Auxiliary services: Alternative test arrangements, notetakers.
Campus support group: A special student organization is available to students with LD.

GENERAL COLLEGE INFORMATION

State-supported, 2-year, coed. Part of New Mexico Commission on Higher Education. Awards associate degrees. Founded 1965. *Setting:* urban campus. *Endowment:* $1 million. *Total enrollment:* 15,555. *Faculty:* 601 (302 full-time, 299 part-time); student–undergrad faculty ratio is 25:1.
Enrollment Profile: 15,555 students from 46 states and territories. 58% women, 42% men, 73% part-time, 97% state residents, 30% transferred in, 57% 25 or older, 5% Native American, 37% Hispanic, 3% black, 2% Asian or Pacific Islander. *Areas of study chosen:* 18% liberal arts/general studies, 15% business management and administrative services, 13% vocational and home economics, 9% health professions and related sciences. *Most popular recent majors:* liberal arts/general studies, nursing, paralegal studies.
First-Year Class: Of the students who applied, 100% were accepted.
Graduation Requirements: 64 credit hours; 1 college math course; computer course; internship (some majors).
Computers on Campus: 1,200 computers available on campus for general student use. Computer purchase/lease plans available. A computer is recommended for all students. A campus-wide network can be accessed from off-campus. Students can contact faculty members and/or advisers through e-mail. Computers for student use in computer labs, learning resource center, classrooms, library provide access to the Internet/World Wide Web, on- and off-campus e-mail addresses. Staffed computer lab on campus provides training in use of computers, software. *Academic computing expenditure 1995–96:* $1.5 million.

EXPENSES

Expenses for 1996–97: *Application fee:* $20. State resident tuition: $655 full-time, $27.30 per credit hour part-time. Nonresident tuition: $1823 full-time, $75.96 per credit hour part-time. Part-time mandatory fees: $21 per trimester. Full-time mandatory fees: $42.
LD Services Contact: Mr. A. Paul Smarrella, Director, Special Services, Albuquerque Technical Vocational Institute, 525 Buena Vista, SE, Albuquerque, NM 87106-4096, 505-224-3259.

ALEXANDRIA TECHNICAL COLLEGE

Alexandria, Minnesota

LEARNING DISABILITIES SERVICES INFORMATION

Support Services began offering services in 1975. Currently the program serves 60 undergraduates with LD. Students diagnosed with ADD/ADHD are eligible for the same services available to students with LD.

Alexandria Technical College (continued)

Staff: 3 part-time staff members, including coordinator. Services provided by tutors.
Special Fees: No special fees are charged for services to students with LD.
Applications and admissions: *Required:* high school transcript, grade point average, class rank, courses completed, personal interview; *recommended:* high school IEP (Individualized Education Program), untimed ACT. Students may begin taking classes in fall only. *Application deadline:* continuous.

PROGRAM AND SERVICE COMPONENTS

Academic advising: Provided by academic advisers. 12 credits (federal aid), 15 credits (state aid) are required each term to be eligible for financial aid.
Counseling services: Individual counseling, career counseling.
Basic skills remediation: Offered one-on-one by regular teachers; computer-aided instruction also offered. Available in math, spelling, written language, learning strategies, study skills, time management, speech, computer skills.
Subject-area tutoring: Offered one-on-one and in small groups by professional teachers, peer tutors. Available in most subjects.
Auxiliary aids: Taped textbooks, tape recorders, calculators, typewriters, word-processors with spell-check, personal computers, talking computers, FM system, enlarged computer screen.
Auxiliary services: Alternative test arrangements, notetakers.

GENERAL COLLEGE INFORMATION

State-supported, 2-year, coed. Part of Minnesota State Colleges and Universities System. Awards associate degrees. Founded 1961. *Setting:* 40-acre small-town campus. *Total enrollment:* 1,705. *Faculty:* 89 (79 full-time, 10 part-time).
Enrollment Profile: 1,705 students from 11 states and territories, 1 other country. 38% women, 62% men, 11% part-time, 94% state residents, 4% transferred in, 1% international, 23% 25 or older, 1% Native American, 1% Hispanic, 1% black, 1% Asian or Pacific Islander. *Retention:* 68% of 1995 full-time freshmen returned. *Most popular recent majors:* law enforcement/police sciences, practical nursing, robotics.
First-Year Class: 669 total; 1,958 applied, 69% were accepted.
Graduation Requirements: 96 credits; internship (some majors).
Computers on Campus: 450 computers available on campus for general student use. Computer purchase/lease plans available. A computer is required for some students. A campus-wide network can be accessed from off-campus. Students can contact faculty members and/or advisers through e-mail. Computers for student use in computer center, library provide access to the Internet/World Wide Web, on- and off-campus e-mail addresses. Staffed computer lab on campus.

EXPENSES

Expenses for 1996–97: *Application fee:* $20. State resident tuition: $1997 full-time, $41.60 per credit part-time. Nonresident tuition: $3994 full-time, $83.20 per credit part-time. Part-time mandatory fees per quarter range from $2.60 to $37.60. Manitoba, North Dakota, South Dakota, and Wisconsin residents pay state resident tuition rates. Missouri residents pay 150% of state resident tuition. Kansas and Nebraska residents pay 150% of state resident tuition for associate of applied science program only. Full-time mandatory fees: $155.
LD Services Contact: Ms. Mary Ackerman, Support Services Coordinator, Alexandria Technical College, 1601 Jefferson Street, Alexandria, MN 56308, 320-762-0221. Fax: 320-762-4501. Email: marya@alx.tec.mn.us.

ALLAN HANCOCK COLLEGE

Santa Maria, California

LEARNING DISABILITIES SERVICES INFORMATION

Learning Assistance Program began offering services in 1981. Currently the program serves 252 undergraduates with LD. Students diagnosed with ADD/ADHD are eligible for the same services available to students with LD.
Staff: 3 full-time, 3 part-time staff members, including director, LD specialist, technologies/adaptive needs specialist. Services provided by counselors, instructional assistant, aides, student workers, interpreter.
Special Fees: No special fees are charged for services to students with LD.
Applications and admissions: *Required.* California Assessment System for Adults with Learning Disabilities. Students may begin taking classes in fall, spring, or summer. *Application deadline:* continuous.
Special policies: The college has written policies regarding substitutions and waivers of graduation and degree requirements.

PROGRAM AND SERVICE COMPONENTS

Special preparation or orientation: Optional orientation offered before registration and during registration.
Diagnostic testing: Intelligence, reading, math, spelling, spoken language, written language, perceptual skills, social skills, learning strategies.
Academic advising: Provided by unit staff members. Most students with LD take 9 to 12 units each term; 12 units required to maintain full-time status and be eligible for financial aid.
Counseling services: Individual counseling, career counseling, self-advocacy training.
Basic skills remediation: Offered in small groups by LD teachers, instructional aides. Available in reading, spelling, learning strategies, study skills, time management, computer skills.
Subject-area tutoring: Offered one-on-one by peer tutors through Tutorial Center with an LD liaison. Available in most subjects.
Special courses: Learning strategies, word processing, time management, study skills, learning styles and strategies, assessment, specific skills, computer skills. All offered for credit; some enter into overall grade point average.
Auxiliary aids: Taped textbooks, tape recorders, calculators, typewriters, word-processors with spell-check, personal computers, talking computers, optical character readers, Franklin Speller.
Auxiliary services: Alternative test arrangements, notetakers, priority registration, advocacy, readers, tutors.
Campus support group: A special student organization is available to students with LD.

GENERAL COLLEGE INFORMATION

State and locally supported, 2-year, coed. Part of California Community Colleges System. Awards associate degrees. Founded 1920. *Setting:* 10-acre small-town campus. *Endowment:* $128,575. *Research spending 1995–96:* $53,396. *Educational spending 1995–96:* $1860 per undergrad. *Total enrollment:* 7,403. *Faculty:* 404 (124 full-time, 10% with terminal degrees, 280 part-time); student–undergrad faculty ratio is 19:1.
Enrollment Profile: 7,403 students from 24 states and territories, 6 other countries. 57% women, 43% men, 71% part-time, 96% state residents, 5% transferred in, 2% international, 51% 25 or older, 1% Native American, 25% Hispanic, 5% black, 3% Asian or Pacific Islander. *Most popular recent majors:* liberal arts/general studies, nursing, accounting.
First-Year Class: 532 total. Of the students who applied, 100% were accepted.
Graduation Requirements: 60 units.
Computers on Campus: 130 computers available on campus for general student use. Computers for student use in computer center, learning resource center, library, departmental labs provide access to the Internet/World Wide Web. Staffed computer lab on campus provides training in use of computers, software. *Academic computing expenditure 1995–96:* $504,711.

EXPENSES

Estimated Expenses for 1997–98: State resident tuition: $0 full-time. Nonresident tuition: $3540 full-time, $118 per unit part-time. Part-time mandatory fees: $13 per unit. Full-time mandatory fees: $416.
LD Services Contact: Ms. Dolores Pelton, Administrative Secretary, Allan Hancock College, 800 South College Drive, Santa Maria, CA 93454, 805-922-6966.

ANDREW COLLEGE

Cuthbert, Georgia

LEARNING DISABILITIES SERVICES INFORMATION

Learning Disabilities Support Services began offering services in 1994. Currently the program serves 25 undergraduates with LD. Students diagnosed with ADD/ADHD are eligible for the same services available to students with LD.
Staff: 1 full-time, 4 part-time staff members, including director. Services provided by tutor, peer tutors.
Special Fees: $5000 per year.
Applications and admissions: *Required:* high school transcript, grade point average, class rank, courses completed, extracurricular activities,

untimed SAT I, personal interview, autobiographical statement, psychoeducational report completed within 3 years; *recommended:* high school IEP (Individualized Education Program), untimed or extended time ACT, extended time SAT I, letters of recommendation. Students may begin taking classes any term. *Application deadline:* continuous.
Special policies: The college has written policies regarding grade forgiveness; substitutions and waivers of admissions, graduation, and degree requirements.

PROGRAM AND SERVICE COMPONENTS

Special preparation or orientation: Required orientation held during freshman orientation.
Academic advising: Provided by unit staff members, academic advisers. Students with LD may take up to 17 quarter hours each term; most take 15 quarter hours; 12 quarter hours required to maintain full-time status and be eligible for financial aid.
Basic skills remediation: Offered in class-size groups by regular teachers; computer-aided instruction also offered. Available in reading, math, written language, learning strategies, study skills.
Subject-area tutoring: Offered one-on-one and in small groups by professional teachers, peer tutors, professional tutors. Available in all subjects.
Auxiliary aids: Taped textbooks, tape recorders, calculators, word-processors with spell-check, personal computers.
Auxiliary services: Alternative test arrangements, notetakers, priority registration, advocacy.

GENERAL COLLEGE INFORMATION

Independent United Methodist, 2-year, coed. Awards associate degrees. Founded 1854. *Setting:* 40-acre small-town campus. *Endowment:* $2.7 million. *Educational spending 1995–96:* $3926 per undergrad. *Total enrollment:* 310. *Faculty:* 36 (20 full-time, 35% with terminal degrees, 16 part-time).
Enrollment Profile: 310 students from 8 states and territories, 10 other countries. 51% women, 49% men, 4% part-time, 74% state residents, 74% live on campus, 3% transferred in, 14% international, 5% 25 or older, 0% Native American, 0% Hispanic, 27% black, 0% Asian or Pacific Islander. *Areas of study chosen:* 18% health professions and related sciences, 11% business management and administrative services, 9% education, 9% premed, 8% performing arts, 4% engineering and applied sciences, 4% fine arts, 4% prelaw, 2% biological and life sciences, 2% communications and journalism, 2% English language/literature/letters, 1% agriculture, 1% liberal arts/general studies, 1% prevet, 1% theology/religion. *Most popular recent majors:* education, music.
First-Year Class: 175 total; 450 applied, 55% were accepted, 70% of whom enrolled.
Graduation Requirements: 100 quarter hours; 20 quarter hours of math/science.
Computers on Campus: 30 computers available on campus for general student use. Computers for student use in computer center, learning resource center, library, dorms. Staffed computer lab on campus provides training in use of computers, software.

EXPENSES

Expenses for 1997–98: *Application fee:* $15. Comprehensive fee of $10,431 includes full-time tuition ($6327) and college room and board ($4104). College room only: $1941. Part-time tuition: $120 per quarter hour.
LD Services Contact: Ms. Joy Sammons, Director of Admission, Andrew College, 413 College Street, Cuthbert, GA 31740-1395, 912-732-2171. Fax: 912-732-2176.

ANGELINA COLLEGE

Lufkin, Texas

LEARNING DISABILITIES SERVICES INFORMATION

Student Special Services currently serves undergraduate students with LD. Students diagnosed with ADD/ADHD are eligible for the same services available to students with LD.
Staff: 1 full-time, 2 part-time staff members, including teachers. Services provided by tutors, counselor.
Special Fees: No special fees are charged for services to students with LD.
Applications and admissions: *Required:* high school transcript, IEP (Individualized Education Program), personal interview; *recommended:* letters of recommendation, psychoeducational report completed within 5 years.
Special policies: The college has written policies regarding substitutions and waivers of graduation and degree requirements.

PROGRAM AND SERVICE COMPONENTS

Diagnostic testing: Intelligence, reading, math, perceptual skills, study skills, personality, learning strategies.
Academic advising: Provided by academic advisers.
Counseling services: Individual counseling, career counseling.
Basic skills remediation: Offered one-on-one and in small groups by regular teachers. Available in reading, math, written language, learning strategies, study skills, time management.
Subject-area tutoring: Offered one-on-one and in small groups by professional teachers, peer tutors. Available in most subjects.
Special courses: College survival skills, reading, vocabulary development, composition, learning strategies, time management, math, study skills. All offered for credit; none enter into overall grade point average.
Auxiliary aids: Taped textbooks, tape recorders, word-processors with spell-check, talking computers, large print readers.
Auxiliary services: Alternative test arrangements, notetakers, interpreters for the deaf.

GENERAL COLLEGE INFORMATION

State and locally supported, 2-year, coed. Part of Texas Higher Education Coordinating Board. Awards associate degrees. Founded 1968. *Setting:* 140-acre small-town campus. *Educational spending 1995–96:* $1296 per undergrad. *Total enrollment:* 3,984. *Faculty:* 201 (98 full-time, 7% with terminal degrees, 103 part-time); student–undergrad faculty ratio is 23:1.
Enrollment Profile: 3,984 students from 15 states and territories. 61% women, 39% men, 50% part-time, 99% state residents, 1% live on campus, 16% transferred in, 0% international, 58% 25 or older, 1% Native American, 4% Hispanic, 16% black, 1% Asian or Pacific Islander. *Retention:* 35% of 1995 full-time freshmen returned. *Areas of study chosen:* 13% social sciences, 7% education, 2% fine arts, 1% agriculture, 1% communications and journalism, 1% engineering and applied sciences. *Most popular recent majors:* nursing, criminal justice, liberal arts/general studies.
First-Year Class: 1,370 total; 1,924 applied, 100% were accepted, 71% of whom enrolled. 6% from top 10% of their high school class, 20% from top quarter, 40% from top half.
Graduation Requirements: 70 semester hours; computer course for drafting majors; internship (some majors).
Computers on Campus: 200 computers available on campus for general student use. Computers for student use in computer center, library, student center. Staffed computer lab on campus provides training in use of computers, software. *Academic computing expenditure 1995–96:* $400,000.

EXPENSES

Expenses for 1997–98: Area resident tuition: $525 full-time. State resident tuition: $735 full-time. Nonresident tuition: $1050 full-time. Part-time tuition per quarter hour ranges from $70 to $165 for area residents, $70 to $231 for state residents, $200 to $330 for nonresidents. Part-time mandatory fees per semester range from $9 to $66. Full-time mandatory fees: $132. College room and board: $2550.
LD Services Contact: Mr. Bill Berry, Vocational Counselor, Angelina College, PO Box 1768, Lufkin, TX 75902-1768, 409-639-1301.

ANTELOPE VALLEY COLLEGE

Lancaster, California

LEARNING DISABILITIES SERVICES INFORMATION

Learning Disability Program began offering services in 1980. Currently the program serves 250 undergraduates with LD. Students diagnosed with ADD/ADHD are eligible for the same services available to students with LD.
Staff: 1 full-time staff member (director).
Special Fees: No special fees are charged for services to students with LD.
Applications and admissions: *Recommended:* psychoeducational report. Students may begin taking classes any term. *Application deadline:* continuous.

Antelope Valley College (continued)

Special policies: The college has written policies regarding substitutions and waivers of admissions, graduation, and degree requirements.

PROGRAM AND SERVICE COMPONENTS

Special preparation or orientation: Optional orientation offered before registration.
Diagnostic testing: Intelligence, reading, math, spelling, written language.
Academic advising: Provided by unit staff members. Students with LD may take up to 18 units each term; most take 9 units; 12 units required to maintain full-time status; 6 to 12 units required to be eligible for financial aid.
Basic skills remediation: Offered in class-size groups by regular teachers; computer-aided instruction also offered. Available in reading, math, spelling, written language, learning strategies, computer skills.
Subject-area tutoring: Offered one-on-one and in small groups by peer tutors. Available in most subjects.
Auxiliary aids: Taped textbooks, tape recorders, calculators, typewriters, word-processors with spell-check, talking computers, optical character readers.
Auxiliary services: Alternative test arrangements, notetakers, priority registration.

GENERAL COLLEGE INFORMATION

State and locally supported, 2-year, coed. Part of California Community Colleges System. Awards associate degrees. Founded 1929. *Setting:* 160-acre suburban campus with easy access to Los Angeles. *Total enrollment:* 9,027. *Faculty:* 400 (115 full-time, 285 part-time).
Enrollment Profile: 9,027 students: 60% women, 40% men, 75% part-time, 98% state residents, 12% transferred in, 1% international, 53% 25 or older, 2% Native American, 14% Hispanic, 8% black, 7% Asian or Pacific Islander.
First-Year Class: Of the students who applied, 100% were accepted, 100% of whom enrolled.
Graduation Requirements: 60 units; 1 intermediate algebra course.
Computers on Campus: Computers for student use in computer center.

EXPENSES

Expenses for 1997–98: State resident tuition: $0 full-time. Nonresident tuition: $3450 full-time, $115 per unit part-time. Part-time mandatory fees: $13 per unit. Full-time mandatory fees: $390.
LD Services Contact: Mr. David W. Greenleaf, Learning Disability Specialist, Antelope Valley College, 3041 West Avenue K, Lancaster, CA 93551, 805-943-3241 Ext. 278. Fax: 805-722-2391. Email: greenleaf@hal.avc.cc.ca.us.

AQUINAS COLLEGE AT NEWTON

Newton, Massachusetts

LEARNING DISABILITIES SERVICES INFORMATION

Academic Success Center began offering services in 1980. Currently the program serves 7 undergraduates with LD. Students diagnosed with ADD/ADHD are eligible for the same services available to students with LD.
Staff: 1 full-time, 3 part-time staff members, including director. Services provided by tutors, counselor, instructor.
Special Fees: No special fees are charged for services to students with LD.
Applications and admissions: *Required:* high school transcript, grade point average, class rank, courses completed, personal interview; *recommended:* high school extracurricular activities, untimed or extended time SAT I, letters of recommendation, high school LD specialist's report. Students may begin taking classes in fall, winter, or spring. *Application deadline:* continuous.

PROGRAM AND SERVICE COMPONENTS

Special preparation or orientation: Optional orientation offered during registration and after classes begin.
Diagnostic testing: Intelligence, reading, spelling, spoken language, written language.
Academic advising: Provided by unit staff members, academic advisers. Students with LD may take up to 12 credits each term; most take 9 credits.
Counseling services: Individual counseling, career counseling.
Subject-area tutoring: Offered one-on-one and in small groups by professional teachers, peer tutors. Available in all subjects.
Auxiliary aids: Tape recorders, calculators, typewriters, word-processors with spell-check, personal computers, talking computers, supplementary texts/tapes.
Auxiliary services: Alternative test arrangements, notetakers, priority registration, advocacy.

GENERAL COLLEGE INFORMATION

Independent Roman Catholic, 2-year, women only. Awards associate degrees. Founded 1961. *Setting:* 14-acre suburban campus with easy access to Boston. *Total enrollment:* 225. *Faculty:* 22 (12 full-time, 8% with terminal degrees, 10 part-time); student–undergrad faculty ratio is 14:1.
Enrollment Profile: 225 students: 100% women, 8% part-time, 96% state residents, 13% transferred in, 4% international, 4% black, 2% Asian or Pacific Islander. *Most popular recent majors:* early childhood education, business administration/commerce/management, medical assistant technologies.
First-Year Class: 100 total; 195 applied, 56% were accepted, 91% of whom enrolled. 10% from top 10% of their high school class, 30% from top quarter, 60% from top half.
Graduation Requirements: 60 credits; 3 math/science courses.
Computers on Campus: 40 computers available on campus for general student use. A campus-wide network can be accessed. Computers for student use in computer center provide access to the Internet/World Wide Web. Staffed computer lab on campus.

EXPENSES

Expenses for 1996–97: *Application fee:* $15. Tuition: $7250 full-time, $233 per credit part-time. Full-time mandatory fees: $300.
LD Services Contact: Ms. Louise M. Silva, Director, Academic Success Center, Aquinas College at Newton, 15 Walnut Park, Newton, MA 02158-9928, 617-969-4400. Fax: 617-965-9363.

ARAPAHOE COMMUNITY COLLEGE

Littleton, Colorado

LEARNING DISABILITIES SERVICES INFORMATION

Disability Services began offering services in 1985. Currently the program serves 200 undergraduates with LD. Students diagnosed with ADD/ADHD are eligible for the same services available to students with LD.
Staff: 1 full-time, 1 part-time staff members, including coordinator, office manager. Services provided by tutors, counselors, diagnostic specialists.
Special Fees: $40 for diagnostic testing.
Applications and admissions: *Required:* personal interview, psychoeducational report completed within 3 years; *recommended:* high school transcript, courses completed, extracurricular activities, IEP (Individualized Education Program), untimed or extended time SAT I, extended time ACT, special education records from high school, ACT, computerized placement test. Students may begin taking classes in fall, spring, or summer. *Application deadline:* continuous.
Special policies: The college has written policies regarding grade forgiveness.

PROGRAM AND SERVICE COMPONENTS

Special preparation or orientation: Optional orientation offered throughout the year.
Diagnostic testing: Reading, math, written language.
Academic advising: Provided by unit staff members, academic advisers. Most students with LD take 3 to 11 credit hours each term; 12 credit hours required to maintain full-time status; 3 to 6 credit hours required to be eligible for financial aid.
Counseling services: Individual counseling, career counseling, self-advocacy training.
Basic skills remediation: Offered in small groups and in class-size groups by regular teachers, developmental studies specialists; computer-aided instruction also offered. Available in reading, math, spelling, spoken language, written language, learning strategies, study skills, time management, speech, computer skills.
Subject-area tutoring: Offered one-on-one and in small groups by professional teachers, peer tutors. Available in most subjects.
Special courses: College survival skills, reading, communication skills, composition, learning strategies, word processing, Internet use, time management, math, typing, study skills, career planning, spelling. All offered for credit; all enter into overall grade point average.

Auxiliary aids: Taped textbooks, tape recorders, word-processors with spell-check, talking computers, optical character readers.
Auxiliary services: Alternative test arrangements, notetakers.

GENERAL COLLEGE INFORMATION

State-supported, 2-year, coed. Part of Colorado Community College and Occupational Education System. Awards associate degrees. Founded 1965. *Setting:* 52-acre suburban campus with easy access to Denver. *Total enrollment:* 7,346. *Faculty:* 298 (98 full-time, 21% with terminal degrees, 200 part-time); student–undergrad faculty ratio is 19:1.
Enrollment Profile: 7,346 students from 42 states and territories, 35 other countries. 61% women, 39% men, 75% part-time, 95% state residents, 35% transferred in, 2% international, 61% 25 or older, 1% Native American, 6% Hispanic, 1% black, 2% Asian or Pacific Islander. *Most popular recent majors:* nursing, business administration/commerce/management, computer information systems.
First-Year Class: 3,634 total. Of the students who applied, 98% were accepted, 59% of whom enrolled.
Graduation Requirements: 61 credit hours; computer course for most majors; internship (some majors).
Computers on Campus: 200 computers available on campus for general student use. A computer is recommended for all students. A campus-wide network can be accessed from off-campus. Students can contact faculty members and/or advisers through e-mail. Computers for student use in computer center, computer labs, library, student center, instructional labs provide access to the Internet/World Wide Web, on- and off-campus e-mail addresses. Staffed computer lab on campus.

EXPENSES

Expenses for 1997–98: State resident tuition: $1629 full-time, $54.30 per credit hour part-time. Nonresident tuition: $7568 full-time, $252.25 per credit hour part-time. Part-time mandatory fees per semester range from $13.55 to $59.05. Full-time mandatory fees: $155.
LD Services Contact: Ms. Linda MacMackin, Office Manager, LD Program, Arapahoe Community College, 2500 West College Drive, Room 130, Littleton, CO 80160-9002, 303-797-5937.

THE ART INSTITUTE OF HOUSTON

Houston, Texas

LEARNING DISABILITIES SERVICES INFORMATION

Accelerated Learning Department began offering services in 1995. Currently the program serves 200 undergraduates with LD. Students diagnosed with ADD/ADHD are eligible for the same services available to students with LD, as well as counseling.
Staff: 1 full-time, 3 part-time staff members, including director. Services provided by remediation specialist, tutors, counselor.
Special Fees: No special fees are charged for services to students with LD.
Applications and admissions: *Required:* high school transcript, grade point average, ASSET; *recommended:* high school IEP (Individualized Education Program), personal interview, autobiographical statement. Students may begin taking classes any term. *Application deadline:* continuous.
Special policies: The college has written policies regarding grade forgiveness.

PROGRAM AND SERVICE COMPONENTS

Academic advising: Provided by unit staff members. Students with LD may take up to 18 credits each term; 12 credits required to maintain full-time status; 6 to 12 credits for loans (fewer than 6 for Pell Grant) required to be eligible for financial aid.
Basic skills remediation: Offered one-on-one, in small groups, and in class-size groups by Accelerated Learning Specialist, instructors. Available in math, spoken language, written language, learning strategies, study skills, time management, social skills, computer skills.
Subject-area tutoring: Offered one-on-one, in small groups, and in class-size groups by professional teachers. Available in some subjects.
Special courses: Composition, math. None offered for credit; none enter into overall grade point average.
Auxiliary aids: Taped textbooks, tape recorders, word-processors with spell-check, personal computers.
Auxiliary services: Alternative test arrangements, notetakers, advocacy.

GENERAL COLLEGE INFORMATION

Proprietary, 2-year, coed. Awards associate degrees. Founded 1978. *Setting:* urban campus. *Educational spending 1995–96:* $2975 per undergrad. *Total enrollment:* 1,111. *Faculty:* 78 (20 full-time, 58 part-time).
Enrollment Profile: 1,111 students: 38% women, 62% men, 36% part-time, 90% state residents, 17% transferred in, 0% 25 or older, 0% Native American, 21% Hispanic, 12% black, 6% Asian or Pacific Islander. *Retention:* 49% of 1995 full-time freshmen returned. *Most popular recent majors:* commercial art, culinary arts.
First-Year Class: 385 total. Of the students who applied, 95% were accepted.
Graduation Requirements: 90 credits; 1 course each in math and science; computer course; internship (some majors).
Computers on Campus: 194 computers available on campus for general student use. Students can contact faculty members and/or advisers through e-mail. Computers for student use in computer center, computer labs, learning resource center provide access to the Internet/World Wide Web. Staffed computer lab on campus provides training in use of computers, software. *Academic computing expenditure 1995–96:* $776,353.

EXPENSES AND FINANCIAL AID

Expenses for 1996–97: *Application fee:* $50. Tuition: $9855 full-time, $219 per credit part-time. College room only: $3495.
Financial aid specifically for students with LD: Scholarships; work-study.
LD Services Contact: Mr. Steve R. Gregg, President, The Art Institute of Houston, 1900 Yorktown, Houston, TX 77056, 713-623-2040. Fax: 713-966-2700.

ASHEVILLE-BUNCOMBE TECHNICAL COMMUNITY COLLEGE

Asheville, North Carolina

LEARNING DISABILITIES SERVICES INFORMATION

Special Needs began offering services in 1991. Currently the program serves 90 undergraduates with LD. Students diagnosed with ADD/ADHD are eligible for the same services available to students with LD.
Staff: 1 full-time staff member (director).
Special Fees: No special fees are charged for services to students with LD.
Applications and admissions: *Required:* high school transcript, courses completed; *recommended:* high school IEP (Individualized Education Program), personal interview, psychoeducational report completed within 3 years. Students may begin taking classes any term. *Application deadline:* continuous.
Special policies: The college has written policies regarding grade forgiveness.

PROGRAM AND SERVICE COMPONENTS

Special preparation or orientation: Optional orientation offered before registration.
Academic advising: Provided by unit staff members, academic advisers. Students with LD may take up to as many semester hours per a student's individual needs each term; most take 12 semester hours; 12 semester hours required to maintain full-time status; 6 semester hours required to be eligible for financial aid.
Counseling services: Individual counseling, career counseling, self-advocacy training.
Basic skills remediation: Offered in class-size groups by regular teachers; computer-aided instruction also offered. Available in reading, math, spelling, written language, learning strategies, study skills, time management.
Subject-area tutoring: Offered one-on-one and in class-size groups by professional teachers, peer tutors. Available in all subjects.
Special courses: College survival skills, reading, vocabulary development, composition, learning strategies, time management, math, study skills, career planning. All offered for credit; all enter into overall grade point average.
Auxiliary aids: Taped textbooks, tape recorders, calculators, word-processors with spell-check, personal computers, talking computers, optical character readers.
Auxiliary services: Alternative test arrangements, notetakers, priority registration.

Asheville-Buncombe Technical Community College (continued)

GENERAL COLLEGE INFORMATION

State-supported, 2-year, coed. Part of North Carolina Community College System. Awards associate degrees. Founded 1959. *Setting:* 126-acre urban campus. *Total enrollment:* 4,058. *Faculty:* 434 (94 full-time, 340 part-time).

Enrollment Profile: 4,058 students from 27 states and territories, 14 other countries. 57% women, 43% men, 64% part-time, 98% state residents, 36% transferred in, 83% 25 or older, 1% Native American, 2% Hispanic, 10% black, 1% Asian or Pacific Islander. *Areas of study chosen:* 38% liberal arts/general studies, 20% interdisciplinary studies, 15% business management and administrative services, 12% health professions and related sciences, 7% engineering and applied sciences, 4% vocational and home economics, 2% agriculture, 2% computer and information sciences. *Most popular recent majors:* business administration/commerce/management, nursing, law enforcement/police sciences.

First-Year Class: 1,516 total.

Graduation Requirements: 64 semester hours; math/science requirements vary according to program; computer course for most majors.

Computers on Campus: 414 computers available on campus for general student use. Computers for student use in computer center, computer labs, classrooms, library. Staffed computer lab on campus provides training in use of computers, software.

EXPENSES

Expenses for 1997–98: State resident tuition: $560 full-time, $20 per semester hour part-time. Nonresident tuition: $4564 full-time, $163 per semester hour part-time. Part-time mandatory fees: $8 per semester. Full-time mandatory fees: $26.

LD Services Contact: Ms. Deborah Harmon, Special Needs Coordinator/Counselor, Asheville-Buncombe Technical Community College, 301 Victoria Road, Asheville, NC 28801, 704-254-1921 Ext. 141. Email: harmond@ncccs.cc.nc.us.

ATLANTA METROPOLITAN COLLEGE

Atlanta, Georgia

LEARNING DISABILITIES SERVICES INFORMATION

Counseling Services began offering services in 1977. Currently the program serves 7 undergraduates with LD. Students diagnosed with ADD/ADHD are eligible for the same services available to students with LD.

Staff: 6 full-time, 12 part-time staff members, including director, coordinator, clerk-typist, secretary. Services provided by remediation specialist, tutors, counselors.

Special Fees: No special fees are charged for services to students with LD.

Applications and admissions: *Required:* high school transcript, grade point average, courses completed, psychoeducational report completed within 3 years, immunization form. Students may begin taking classes any term. *Application deadline:* 8/18 (fall term), 2/26 (spring term).

Special policies: The college has written policies regarding grade forgiveness; substitutions and waivers of admissions, graduation, and degree requirements.

PROGRAM AND SERVICE COMPONENTS

Special preparation or orientation: Required orientation held before registration and after classes begin.

Academic advising: Provided by unit staff members, academic advisers. Students with LD may take up to 15 credit hours each term; most take 12 to 15 credit hours; 12 credit hours required to maintain full-time status; 10 credit hours required to be eligible for financial aid.

Counseling services: Individual counseling, small-group counseling, career counseling, self-advocacy training.

Basic skills remediation: Offered one-on-one, in small groups, and in class-size groups by regular teachers; computer-aided instruction also offered. Available in reading, math, spelling, handwriting, spoken language, written language, learning strategies, study skills, time management, social skills, speech, computer skills.

Subject-area tutoring: Offered one-on-one, in small groups, and in class-size groups by professional teachers, peer tutors. Available in all subjects.

Special courses: College survival skills, learning strategies, Internet use, time management, study skills, career planning, stress management, health and nutrition, social relationships. None offered for credit; none enter into overall grade point average.

Auxiliary aids: Tape recorders, calculators, typewriters, word-processors with spell-check, personal computers, talking computers, optical character readers.

Auxiliary services: Alternative test arrangements, notetakers, priority registration, advocacy.

GENERAL COLLEGE INFORMATION

State-supported, 2-year, coed. Part of University System of Georgia. Awards associate degrees. Founded 1974. *Setting:* 83-acre urban campus. *Educational spending 1995–96:* $2087 per undergrad. *Total enrollment:* 1,992. *Faculty:* 73 (52 full-time, 38% with terminal degrees, 21 part-time); student–undergrad faculty ratio is 25:1.

Enrollment Profile: 1,992 students from 13 states and territories, 20 other countries. 62% women, 38% men, 48% part-time, 95% state residents, 13% transferred in, 38% 25 or older, 0% Native American, 0% Hispanic, 97% black, 1% Asian or Pacific Islander. *Retention:* 23% of 1995 full-time freshmen returned. *Areas of study chosen:* 24% business management and administrative services, 20% health professions and related sciences, 13% social sciences, 9% education, 7% communications and journalism, 7% computer and information sciences, 4% biological and life sciences, 4% fine arts, 4% psychology, 3% engineering and applied sciences, 1% mathematics, 1% physical sciences. *Most popular recent majors:* business administration/commerce/management, criminal justice.

First-Year Class: 311 total; 723 applied, 59% were accepted, 73% of whom enrolled.

Graduation Requirements: 1 math course; computer course for secretarial science, business administration majors.

Computers on Campus: 150 computers available on campus for general student use. A campus-wide network can be accessed from off-campus. Students can contact faculty members and/or advisers through e-mail. Computers for student use in learning resource center, library provide access to the Internet/World Wide Web, on- and off-campus e-mail addresses. Staffed computer lab on campus provides training in use of computers. *Academic computing expenditure 1995–96:* $28,111.

EXPENSES

Expenses for 1996–97: *Application fee:* $10. State resident tuition: $1080 full-time, $30 per quarter hour part-time. Nonresident tuition: $3984 full-time, $111 per quarter hour part-time. Part-time mandatory fees per quarter (6 to 11 quarter hours): $40. Full-time mandatory fees: $120.

LD Services Contact: Ms. Carolyn S. Walker, Director of Counseling Services, Atlanta Metropolitan College, 1630 Stewart Avenue, SW, Atlanta, GA 30310, 404-756-4055. Fax: 404-756-5686.

ATLANTIC COMMUNITY COLLEGE

Mays Landing, New Jersey

LEARNING DISABILITIES SERVICES INFORMATION

Special Needs Services, Counseling Unit began offering services in 1988. Currently the program serves 200 undergraduates with LD. Students diagnosed with ADD/ADHD are eligible for the same services available to students with LD.

Staff: 1 full-time, 1 part-time staff members, including coordinator. Services provided by diagnostic specialist.

Special Fees: $150 for diagnostic testing.

Applications and admissions: *Required:* high school transcript, learning evaluation. Students may begin taking classes after they have taken the New Jersey Basic Skills Placement Exam. *Application deadline:* continuous.

PROGRAM AND SERVICE COMPONENTS

Diagnostic testing: Intelligence, reading, math, spelling, handwriting, spoken language, written language, motor abilities, perceptual skills, study skills, learning strategies.

Academic advising: Provided by unit staff members. Students with LD may take up to as many credit hours as an individual can handle each term; most take 12 credit hours; 12 credit hours required to maintain full-time status; source of aid determines number of credit hours required to be eligible for financial aid.

Counseling services: Individual counseling, small-group counseling, career counseling, academic counseling.
Subject-area tutoring: Offered one-on-one and in small groups by peer tutors. Available in most subjects.
Special courses: College survival skills, time management, study skills, career planning. Some offered for credit; some enter into overall grade point average.
Auxiliary aids: Taped textbooks, tape recorders, calculators, optical character readers, Franklin Speller.
Auxiliary services: Alternative test arrangements, notetakers, advocacy, interpreters, readers.

GENERAL COLLEGE INFORMATION

County-supported, 2-year, coed. Awards associate degrees. Founded 1966. *Setting:* 546-acre small-town campus with easy access to Philadelphia. *Total enrollment:* 5,682. *Faculty:* 310 (65 full-time, 25% with terminal degrees, 245 part-time); student–undergrad faculty ratio is 20:1.
Enrollment Profile: 5,682 students from 6 states and territories, 5 other countries. 62% women, 38% men, 63% part-time, 77% state residents, 17% transferred in, 2% international, 49% 25 or older, 1% Native American, 7% Hispanic, 11% black, 6% Asian or Pacific Islander. *Most popular recent majors:* nursing, liberal arts/general studies, business administration/commerce/management.
First-Year Class: 1,783 total; 2,876 applied, 100% were accepted, 62% of whom enrolled. 5% from top 10% of their high school class, 15% from top quarter, 45% from top half.
Graduation Requirements: 64 credits; math/science requirements vary according to program; computer course for most majors.
Computers on Campus: 800 computers available on campus for general student use. Computer purchase/lease plans available. A computer is recommended for some students. A campus-wide network can be accessed from off-campus. Students can contact faculty members and/or advisers through e-mail. Computers for student use in computer center, computer labs, learning resource center, classrooms, library provide access to the Internet/World Wide Web, on-campus e-mail addresses. Staffed computer lab on campus provides training in use of computers, software.

EXPENSES

Expenses for 1997–98: *Application fee:* $30. Area resident tuition: $1786 full-time, $55.80 per credit part-time. State resident tuition: $3571 full-time, $111.60 per credit part-time. Nonresident tuition: $6227 full-time, $194.60 per credit part-time. Part-time mandatory fees per semester range from $11.70 to $98.70. Full-time mandatory fees: $284.
LD Services Contact: Ms. Electra S. Stulak, Coordinator, Special Needs, Atlantic Community College, 5100 Black Horse Pike, Mays Landing, NJ 08330, 609-343-5090. Fax: 609-343-4926. Email: stulak@nsvm.atlantic.edu.

BAINBRIDGE COLLEGE

Bainbridge, Georgia

LEARNING DISABILITIES SERVICES INFORMATION

Career Development and Counseling Center began offering services in 1982. Currently the program serves 25 undergraduates with LD. Students diagnosed with ADD/ADHD are eligible for the same services available to students with LD.
Staff: 1 full-time staff member (coordinator). Services provided by counselor.
Special Fees: No special fees are charged for services to students with LD.
Applications and admissions: *Required:* high school transcript, grade point average, courses completed, IEP (Individualized Education Program), untimed SAT I, autobiographical statement, psychoeducational report completed within 3 years. Students may begin taking classes any term. *Application deadline:* continuous.
Special policies: The college has written policies regarding grade forgiveness; substitutions and waivers of admissions, graduation, and degree requirements.

PROGRAM AND SERVICE COMPONENTS

Special preparation or orientation: Optional orientation offered before registration.
Academic advising: Provided by academic advisers. Students with LD may take up to as many quarter hours per student's need and request each term; 12 quarter hours required to maintain full-time status; 7 quarter hours required to be eligible for financial aid.
Counseling services: Individual counseling, small-group counseling, career counseling, self-advocacy training.
Basic skills remediation: Offered in class-size groups by regular teachers. Available in reading, math, written language.
Subject-area tutoring: Offered one-on-one, in small groups, and in class-size groups by peer tutors. Available in most subjects.
Auxiliary aids: Taped textbooks, typewriters, word-processors with spell-check, personal computers.
Auxiliary services: Alternative test arrangements, notetakers, priority registration.

GENERAL COLLEGE INFORMATION

State-supported, 2-year, coed. Part of University System of Georgia. Awards associate degrees. Founded 1972. *Setting:* 160-acre small-town campus. *Total enrollment:* 1,031. *Faculty:* 47 (32 full-time, 15 part-time); student–undergrad faculty ratio is 20:1.
Enrollment Profile: 1,031 students from 3 states and territories. 67% women, 33% men, 57% part-time, 98% state residents, 2% transferred in, 1% international, 41% 25 or older, 0% Native American, 1% Hispanic, 27% black, 1% Asian or Pacific Islander. *Retention:* 70% of 1995 full-time freshmen returned. *Areas of study chosen:* 34% vocational and home economics, 18% health professions and related sciences, 14% business management and administrative services, 10% education, 9% liberal arts/general studies, 7% social sciences, 2% English language/literature/letters, 2% mathematics, 2% physical sciences, 1% biological and life sciences, 1% fine arts. *Most popular recent majors:* education, nursing, business administration/commerce/management.
First-Year Class: Of the students who applied, 100% were accepted, 83% of whom enrolled. 15% from top 10% of their high school class, 20% from top quarter, 61% from top half. 3 valedictorians.
Graduation Requirements: 96 quarter hours; computer course for business administration, accounting majors.
Computers on Campus: 75 computers available on campus for general student use. A computer is recommended for some students. A campus-wide network can be accessed. Students can contact faculty members and/or advisers through e-mail. Computers for student use in computer center, computer labs. Staffed computer lab on campus provides training in use of computers, software.

EXPENSES

Expenses for 1996–97: State resident tuition: $1080 full-time, $30 per quarter hour part-time. Nonresident tuition: $3132 full-time, $87 per quarter hour part-time. Part-time mandatory fees per quarter (6 to 11 quarter hours): $15. Full-time mandatory fees: $45.
LD Services Contact: Ms. Joan Fryer, Counselor, Bainbridge College, 2500 East Shotwell Street, Bainbridge, GA 31717, 912-248-2560. Fax: 912-248-2589. Email: jfryer@catfish.bbc.peachnet.edu.

BAKER COLLEGE OF JACKSON

Jackson, Michigan

LEARNING DISABILITIES SERVICES INFORMATION

Learning Resource Center (LRC) began offering services in 1996. Currently the program serves 49 undergraduates with LD. Services are also available to graduate students. Students diagnosed with ADD/ADHD are eligible for the same services available to students with LD, as well as flexible testing schedules, focusing strategies.
Staff: 7 part-time staff members. Services provided by remediation specialists, tutors, counselors.
Special Fees: No special fees are charged for services to students with LD.
Applications and admissions: *Required:* high school transcript, grade point average, courses completed, personal interview, ASSET. Students may begin taking classes in fall, winter, or spring. *Application deadline:* continuous.
Special policies: The college has written policies regarding grade forgiveness; substitutions and waivers of admissions, graduation, and degree requirements.

PROGRAM AND SERVICE COMPONENTS

Diagnostic testing: Reading, math, written language.

Baker College of Jackson (continued)

Academic advising: Provided by academic advisers. Most students with LD take 12 credit hours each term; 12 credit hours required to maintain full-time status; 6 to 14 credit hours required to be eligible for financial aid.
Counseling services: Individual counseling, career counseling.
Basic skills remediation: Offered one-on-one by regular teachers, peer tutors; computer-aided instruction also offered. Available in reading, math, spelling, handwriting, written language, learning strategies, study skills, time management.
Subject-area tutoring: Offered one-on-one and in small groups by professional teachers, peer tutors. Available in all subjects.

GENERAL COLLEGE INFORMATION

Independent, 2-year, coed. Part of Baker College System. Awards associate degrees (also offers some bachelor's programs). Founded 1994. *Setting:* 42-acre urban campus. *Total enrollment:* 665. *Faculty:* 62 (3 full-time, 59 part-time); student–undergrad faculty ratio is 16:1.
Enrollment Profile: 665 students: 82% women, 18% men, 38% part-time, 100% state residents, 26% 25 or older, 0% Native American, 2% Hispanic, 9% black, 1% Asian or Pacific Islander. *Areas of study chosen:* 83% business management and administrative services, 8% computer and information sciences, 7% health professions and related sciences, 2% communications and journalism.
First-Year Class: 306 total; 408 applied, 100% were accepted, 75% of whom enrolled.
Graduation Requirements: 90 credits, 180 credits for bachelor's; 1 math course; computer course; internship.
Computers on Campus: 74 computers available on campus for general student use. A computer is recommended for some students. A campus-wide network can be accessed from off-campus. Students can contact faculty members and/or advisers through e-mail. Computers for student use in computer labs, classrooms, library provide access to the Internet/World Wide Web, on- and off-campus e-mail addresses. Staffed computer lab on campus provides training in use of computers, software.

EXPENSES

Expenses for 1996–97: *Application fee:* $20. Tuition: $5850 full-time, $130 per credit part-time.
LD Services Contact: Mr. Steve Kim, Director of Admissions, Baker College of Jackson, 2800 Springport Road, Jackson, MI 49202, 517-789-6123. Fax: 517-789-7331.

BAKERSFIELD COLLEGE

Bakersfield, California

LEARNING DISABILITIES SERVICES INFORMATION

Learning Disabilities Program began offering services in 1987. Currently the program serves 200 undergraduates with LD. Students diagnosed with ADD/ADHD are not eligible for the same services available to students with LD.
Staff: 2 full-time, 9 part-time staff members, including director, study skills instructor, LD specialist. Services provided by tutors, counselors, testing technicians.
Special Fees: No special fees are charged for services to students with LD.
Applications and admissions: Students may begin taking classes in fall, spring, or summer. *Application deadline:* continuous.

PROGRAM AND SERVICE COMPONENTS

Diagnostic testing: Intelligence, reading, math, spelling, written language, perceptual skills.
Academic advising: Provided by unit staff members. Students with LD may take up to 18 credits each term; most take 12 to 18 credits; 12 credits required to maintain full-time status; 9 credits required to be eligible for financial aid.
Counseling services: Individual counseling, referrals to community agencies.
Basic skills remediation: Offered in small groups and in class-size groups by LD teachers, regular teachers, adaptive computers. Available in reading, math, written language, learning strategies, study skills, computer skills.
Subject-area tutoring: Offered one-on-one and in small groups by peer tutors. Available in most subjects.
Special courses: Reading, vocabulary development, composition, learning strategies, word processing, math, study skills. All offered for credit; some enter into overall grade point average.
Auxiliary aids: Taped textbooks, tape recorders, typewriters, word-processors with spell-check, personal computers, optical character readers, Phonic Ears, electronic spellers.
Auxiliary services: Alternative test arrangements, notetakers, priority registration.

GENERAL COLLEGE INFORMATION

State and locally supported, 2-year, coed. Part of California Community Colleges System. Awards associate degrees. Founded 1913. *Setting:* 175-acre urban campus. *Total enrollment:* 12,000. *Faculty:* 496 (237 full-time, 87% with terminal degrees, 259 part-time).
Enrollment Profile: 12,000 students: 58% women, 42% men, 74% part-time, 99% state residents, 50% 25 or older, 2% Native American, 29% Hispanic, 7% black, 6% Asian or Pacific Islander. *Areas of study chosen:* 22% liberal arts/general studies, 13% social sciences, 10% education, 8% mathematics, 5% business management and administrative services, 5% fine arts, 5% vocational and home economics, 4% computer and information sciences, 4% engineering and applied sciences, 4% psychology, 3% foreign language and literature, 3% health professions and related sciences, 2% agriculture, 2% biological and life sciences, 2% physical sciences, 1% architecture, 1% communications and journalism. *Most popular recent major:* liberal arts/general studies.
First-Year Class: 7,000 total. Of the students who applied, 100% were accepted, 60% of whom enrolled.
Graduation Requirements: 60 units; math/science requirements vary according to program; internship (some majors).
Computers on Campus: 650 computers available on campus for general student use. A campus-wide network can be accessed. Students can contact faculty members and/or advisers through e-mail. Computers for student use in computer center, computer labs, classrooms, library, student center provide access to the Internet/World Wide Web, on- and off-campus e-mail addresses. Staffed computer lab on campus provides training in use of computers, software.

EXPENSES

Expenses for 1997–98: State resident tuition: $0 full-time. Nonresident tuition: $3450 full-time, $115 per unit part-time. Part-time mandatory fees per semester range from $28 to $158. Full-time mandatory fees: $420.
LD Services Contact: Ms. Joyce Kirst, Learning Disabilities Specialist, Bakersfield College, 1801 Panorama Drive, Bakersfield, CA 93305-1299, 805-395-4557.

BALTIMORE CITY COMMUNITY COLLEGE

Baltimore, Maryland

LEARNING DISABILITIES SERVICES INFORMATION

Disabled Student Services currently serves undergraduate students with LD. Students diagnosed with ADD/ADHD are eligible for the same services available to students with LD.
Staff: 2 full-time, 1 part-time staff members, including coordinator. Services provided by counselor.
Special Fees: No special fees are charged for services to students with LD.
Applications and admissions: *Required:* psychoeducational report completed within 3 years; *recommended:* high school transcript, grade point average, class rank, courses completed, extracurricular activities, extended time SAT I. Students may begin taking classes in fall, spring, or summer. *Application deadline:* continuous.

PROGRAM AND SERVICE COMPONENTS

Diagnostic testing: Psychoneurology.
Academic advising: Provided by unit staff members. Most students with LD take 9 to 11 credits each term; 12 credits required to maintain full-time status; 6 credits required to be eligible for financial aid.
Counseling services: Individual counseling, small-group counseling, career counseling, self-advocacy training.
Basic skills remediation: Offered in class-size groups by regular teachers; computer-aided instruction also offered. Available in reading, math, spelling, handwriting.

Subject-area tutoring: Offered one-on-one and in small groups by professional teachers, professional tutors. Available in some subjects.
Auxiliary aids: Taped textbooks, tape recorders, calculators, typewriters, word-processors with spell-check, personal computers, optical character readers.
Auxiliary services: Alternative test arrangements, notetakers, advocacy.
Campus support group: A special student organization is available to students with LD.

GENERAL COLLEGE INFORMATION

State-supported, 2-year, coed. Awards associate degrees. Founded 1947. *Setting:* 19-acre suburban campus. *Total enrollment:* 5,970. *Faculty:* 493 (143 full-time, 350 part-time).
Enrollment Profile: 5,970 students from 5 states and territories. 70% part-time, 98% state residents, 10% transferred in, 70% 25 or older, 2% Native American, 1% Hispanic, 74% black, 1% Asian or Pacific Islander. *Most popular recent majors:* liberal arts/general studies, accounting.
First-Year Class: 1,515 total. Of the students who applied, 100% were accepted, 50% of whom enrolled.
Graduation Requirements: 62 credits; math/science requirements vary according to program; computer course for students without computer competency.
Computers on Campus: 57 computers available on campus for general student use. Computers for student use in computer center.

EXPENSES

Expenses for 1997–98: State resident tuition: $1860 full-time, $60 per credit part-time. Nonresident tuition: $6355 full-time, $205 per credit part-time. Part-time mandatory fees per semester range from $19.50 to $64.50. Full-time mandatory fees: $170.
LD Services Contact: Ms. A. Quismat Gorham, Coordinator, Baltimore City Community College, 2901 Liberty Heights Avenue, Baltimore, MD 21215-7893, 410-462-8585. Fax: 410-333-5054.

BARTON COUNTY COMMUNITY COLLEGE

Great Bend, Kansas

LEARNING DISABILITIES SERVICES INFORMATION

Title IV Support Services, The Center for Learning Achievement began offering services in 1990. Currently the program serves 10 undergraduates with LD. Students diagnosed with ADD/ADHD are eligible for the same services available to students with LD.
Staff: 4 full-time, 2 part-time staff members, including director. Services provided by remediation specialist, tutors, counselors.
Special Fees: No special fees are charged for services to students with LD.
Applications and admissions: *Required:* high school IEP (Individualized Education Program), personal interview; *recommended:* high school transcript, all high school or other agency records. Students may begin taking classes in fall or summer. *Application deadline:* continuous.

PROGRAM AND SERVICE COMPONENTS

Special preparation or orientation: Orientation offered.
Diagnostic testing: Reading, math, written language, motor abilities, perceptual skills, study skills, personality, social skills, learning strategies, ACT ASSET.
Academic advising: Provided by unit staff members, academic advisers. Students with LD may take up to 12 credit hours (dependent upon student's assessed abilities) each term; most take 12 credit hours (3 to 6 during first semester); 12 credit hours required to maintain full-time status; 6 credit hours required to be eligible for financial aid.
Counseling services: Individual counseling, career counseling, self-advocacy training.
Basic skills remediation: Offered one-on-one, in small groups, and in class-size groups by LD teachers, regular teachers. Available in reading, math, spelling, spoken language, written language, learning strategies, study skills, time management, social skills, computer skills.
Subject-area tutoring: Offered one-on-one and in small groups by professional teachers, peer tutors. Available in most subjects.
Special courses: College survival skills, reading, vocabulary development, communication skills, composition, learning strategies, word processing, time management, math, typing, study skills, career planning, stress management, health and nutrition. Most offered for credit; some enter into overall grade point average.
Auxiliary aids: Taped textbooks, tape recorders, calculators, typewriters, word-processors with spell-check, personal computers, talking computers, optical character readers.
Auxiliary services: Alternative test arrangements, notetakers.

GENERAL COLLEGE INFORMATION

State and locally supported, 2-year, coed. Part of Kansas State Board of Education. Awards associate degrees. Founded 1969. *Setting:* 140-acre rural campus. *Total enrollment:* 10,000. *Faculty:* 292 (63 full-time, 12% with terminal degrees, 229 part-time); student–undergrad faculty ratio is 20:1.
Enrollment Profile: 10,000 students from 23 states and territories, 7 other countries. 56% women, 44% men, 80% part-time, 98% state residents, 10% live on campus, 30% transferred in, 1% international, 65% 25 or older, 1% Native American, 4% Hispanic, 12% black, 2% Asian or Pacific Islander. *Most popular recent major:* business administration/commerce/management.
First-Year Class: 2,600 total; 3,000 applied, 100% were accepted, 87% of whom enrolled. 13% from top 10% of their high school class, 40% from top quarter, 85% from top half.
Graduation Requirements: 64 credit hours; 3 credit hours of math/science; computer course (varies by major); internship (some majors).
Computers on Campus: 150 computers available on campus for general student use. A computer is recommended for some students. A campus-wide network can be accessed from off-campus. Students can contact faculty members and/or advisers through e-mail. Computers for student use in computer center, computer labs, learning resource center, library provide access to the Internet/World Wide Web, on- and off-campus e-mail addresses. Staffed computer lab on campus provides training in use of computers, software.

EXPENSES

Expenses for 1997–98: State resident tuition: $832 full-time, $26 per credit hour part-time. Nonresident tuition: $1664 full-time, $52 per credit hour part-time. Part-time mandatory fees: $18 per credit hour. Full-time mandatory fees: $576. College room and board: $2650 (minimum).
LD Services Contact: Ms. Jackie Elliott, Director, Barton County Community College, 245 Northeast 30th Road, Great Bend, KS 67530-9283, 316-792-2701. Fax: 316-792-3238. Email: elliottj@cougar.barton.cc.ks.us.

BEE COUNTY COLLEGE

Beeville, Texas

LEARNING DISABILITIES SERVICES INFORMATION

Counseling Center began offering services in 1980. Currently the program serves 101 undergraduates with LD. Students diagnosed with ADD/ADHD are eligible for the same services available to students with LD.
Staff: 1 full-time, 1 part-time staff members, including director. Services provided by remediation specialists, tutors, counselor.
Special Fees: No special fees are charged for services to students with LD.
Applications and admissions: *Required:* high school transcript. Students may begin taking classes any term. *Application deadline:* continuous.

PROGRAM AND SERVICE COMPONENTS

Academic advising: Provided by academic advisers. Students with LD may take up to 16 semester hours each term; most take 12 semester hours; 12 semester hours required to maintain full-time status; 6 semester hours required to be eligible for financial aid.
Counseling services: Individual counseling, small-group counseling, career counseling.
Basic skills remediation: Offered in class-size groups by regular teachers. Available in reading, math, spelling, written language, study skills.
Subject-area tutoring: Offered one-on-one and in small groups by professional teachers, peer tutors. Available in most subjects.
Special courses: College survival skills, reading, communication skills, personal psychology. Some offered for credit.
Auxiliary aids: Taped textbooks, tape recorders, calculators, typewriters, word-processors with spell-check, personal computers.
Auxiliary services: Alternative test arrangements, notetakers, priority registration.

Bee County College (continued)

GENERAL COLLEGE INFORMATION

County-supported, 2-year, coed. Part of Texas Higher Education Coordinating Board. Awards associate degrees. Founded 1965. *Setting:* 100-acre rural campus. *Total enrollment:* 2,734. *Faculty:* 140 (91 full-time, 11% with terminal degrees, 49 part-time); student–undergrad faculty ratio is 19:1.
Enrollment Profile: 2,734 students: 58% women, 42% men, 44% part-time, 99% state residents, 21% transferred in, 1% international, 59% 25 or older, 0% Native American, 56% Hispanic, 5% black, 1% Asian or Pacific Islander. *Areas of study chosen:* 62% vocational and home economics, 13% health professions and related sciences, 4% liberal arts/general studies, 3% business management and administrative services, 3% education, 2% agriculture, 2% interdisciplinary studies, 2% psychology, 2% social sciences, 1% biological and life sciences, 1% communications and journalism, 1% computer and information sciences, 1% engineering and applied sciences, 1% English language/literature/letters, 1% fine arts, 1% mathematics, 1% natural resource sciences, 1% performing arts, 1% predentistry, 1% prelaw, 1% premed, 1% prevet. *Most popular recent majors:* nursing, dental services, child care/child and family studies.
First-Year Class: 816 total; 816 applied, 100% were accepted, 100% of whom enrolled. 5% from top 10% of their high school class, 40% from top half.
Graduation Requirements: 62 semester hours; math/science requirements vary according to program; computer course; internship (some majors).
Computers on Campus: 300 computers available on campus for general student use. A campus-wide network can be accessed. Computers for student use in computer center, computer labs, learning resource center, classrooms, library, learning assistance center. Staffed computer lab on campus provides training in use of computers, software.

EXPENSES

Expenses for 1997–98: Area resident tuition: $496 full-time. State resident tuition: $868 full-time. Nonresident tuition: $1240 full-time. Part-time tuition per credit hour ranges from $75 to $176 for area residents, $87 to $308 for state residents, $200 to $440 for nonresidents. Part-time mandatory fees per semester range from $23 to $53. Full-time mandatory fees: $133. College room and board: $2220. College room only: $1255.
LD Services Contact: Mrs. Patsy Freeman, Special Needs Counselor, Bee County College, 3800 Charco Road, Beeville, TX 78102-2197, 512-358-3130 Ext. 2726. Fax: 512-358-3971.

BELLEVILLE AREA COLLEGE

Belleville, Illinois

LEARNING DISABILITIES SERVICES INFORMATION

Special Services Center began offering services in 1980. Currently the program serves 119 undergraduates with LD. Students diagnosed with ADD/ADHD are eligible for the same services available to students with LD.
Staff: 3 full-time, 8 part-time staff members, including director, assistant director, coordinators. Services provided by tutors, LD specialist, accommodation specialist.
Special Fees: No special fees are charged for services to students with LD.
Applications and admissions: *Required:* high school transcript, IEP (Individualized Education Program), ACT ASSET, Department of Rehabilitative Services assessment. Students may begin taking classes in fall, spring, or summer. *Application deadline:* continuous.
Special policies: The college has written policies regarding grade forgiveness.

PROGRAM AND SERVICE COMPONENTS

Special preparation or orientation: Optional orientation offered before registration.
Diagnostic testing: Intelligence, reading, math, spelling.
Academic advising: Provided by unit staff members, academic advisers. Most students with LD take 12 credit hours each term; 12 credit hours required to maintain full-time status; 6 credit hours required to be eligible for financial aid.
Counseling services: Individual counseling, career counseling.
Basic skills remediation: Offered in class-size groups by regular teachers. Available in reading, math, written language, study skills, time management.
Subject-area tutoring: Offered one-on-one and in small groups by professional teachers, peer tutors. Available in some subjects.
Auxiliary aids: Taped textbooks, tape recorders, calculators, typewriters, word-processors with spell-check, personal computers, talking computers, optical character readers, spell check calculators.
Auxiliary services: Alternative test arrangements, notetakers, priority registration, advocacy, interpreters.
Campus support group: A special student organization is available to students with LD.

GENERAL COLLEGE INFORMATION

District-supported, 2-year, coed. Part of Illinois Community College System. Awards associate degrees. Founded 1946. *Setting:* 150-acre suburban campus with easy access to St. Louis. *Research spending 1995–96:* $60,507. *Total enrollment:* 14,646. *Faculty:* 123 full-time, 18% with terminal degrees, 766 part-time; student–undergrad faculty ratio is 16:1.
Enrollment Profile: 14,646 students from 4 states and territories, 16 other countries. 58% women, 42% men, 73% part-time, 98% state residents, 4% transferred in, 60% 25 or older, 1% Native American, 2% Hispanic, 9% black, 2% Asian or Pacific Islander. *Most popular recent major:* liberal arts/general studies.
First-Year Class: 3,334 total; 3,334 applied, 100% were accepted, 100% of whom enrolled.
Graduation Requirements: 64 credit hours; 8 credit hours of math/science; computer course for some majors; internship (some majors).
Computers on Campus: 20 computers available on campus for general student use. Computer purchase/lease plans available. A campus-wide network can be accessed. Computers for student use in computer center, computer labs, learning resource center, classrooms, library. Staffed computer lab on campus provides training in use of computers, software. *Academic computing expenditure 1995–96:* $558,898.

EXPENSES

Expenses for 1997–98: *Application fee:* $10. Area resident tuition: $1360 full-time, $42.50 per credit hour part-time. State resident tuition: $2912 full-time, $91 per credit hour part-time. Nonresident tuition: $5088 full-time, $159 per credit hour part-time.
LD Services Contact: Ms. Patricia Brian, Director, Special Services Center, Belleville Area College, 2500 Carlyle Road, Belleville, IL 62221-5899, 618-235-2700 Ext. 333. Fax: 618-235-1578.

BERGEN COMMUNITY COLLEGE

Paramus, New Jersey

LEARNING DISABILITIES SERVICES INFORMATION

Office of Specialized Services began offering services in 1991. Currently the program serves 300 undergraduates with LD. Students diagnosed with ADD/ADHD are eligible for the same services available to students with LD.
Staff: 1 full-time, 6 part-time staff members, including director, coordinator. Services provided by tutors, counselors, adaptive technology specialist, academic counselors.
Special Fees: No special fees are charged for services to students with LD.
Applications and admissions: *Required:* high school transcript, IEP (Individualized Education Program), psychoeducational report completed within 3 years; *recommended:* high school grade point average, class rank, courses completed. Students may begin taking classes any term. *Application deadline:* continuous.

PROGRAM AND SERVICE COMPONENTS

Special preparation or orientation: Optional orientation offered before registration.
Academic advising: Provided by academic advisers. Students with LD may take up to 18 credits each term; most take 12 credits; 12 credits required to maintain full-time status and be eligible for financial aid.
Counseling services: Individual counseling, self-advocacy training.
Subject-area tutoring: Offered one-on-one by peer tutors. Available in all subjects.
Auxiliary aids: Taped textbooks, tape recorders, calculators, word-processors with spell-check, talking computers, optical character readers, adaptive technology.

Auxiliary services: Alternative test arrangements, notetakers, priority registration, advocacy.
Campus support group: A special student organization is available to students with LD.

GENERAL COLLEGE INFORMATION

County-supported, 2-year, coed. Awards associate degrees. Founded 1965. *Setting:* 167-acre suburban campus with easy access to New York City. *Research spending 1995–96:* $241,540. *Total enrollment:* 12,296. *Faculty:* 657 (221 full-time, 35% with terminal degrees, 436 part-time); student–undergrad faculty ratio is 20:1.
Enrollment Profile: 12,296 students: 57% women, 43% men, 59% part-time, 7% transferred in, 5% international, 44% 25 or older, 1% Native American, 14% Hispanic, 5% black, 9% Asian or Pacific Islander. *Retention:* 80% of 1995 full-time freshmen returned. *Areas of study chosen:* 32% liberal arts/general studies, 16% business management and administrative services, 8% health professions and related sciences, 7% education, 4% computer and information sciences, 3% psychology, 2% biological and life sciences, 2% communications and journalism, 2% engineering and applied sciences, 2% social sciences, 1% fine arts. *Most popular recent majors:* liberal arts/general studies, business administration/ commerce/management, nursing.
First-Year Class: 1,749 total; 3,002 applied, 94% were accepted, 62% of whom enrolled.
Graduation Requirements: 64 credits; internship (some majors).
Computers on Campus: 225 computers available on campus for general student use. Computers for student use in computer center, computer labs, library, student center. Staffed computer lab on campus.

EXPENSES

Expenses for 1997–98: *Application fee:* $20. Area resident tuition: $2133 full-time, $66.65 per credit part-time. State resident tuition: $4435 full-time, $138.60 per credit part-time. Nonresident tuition: $4755 full-time, $148.60 per credit part-time. Part-time mandatory fees: $13.20 per credit. Full-time mandatory fees: $422.
LD Services Contact: Ms. Merry Regenstreich, Learning Disabilities Specialist, Bergen Community College, 400 Paramus Road, Paramus, NJ 07652, 201-612-5270. Fax: 201-444-7036.

BERKSHIRE COMMUNITY COLLEGE

Pittsfield, Massachusetts

LEARNING DISABILITIES SERVICES INFORMATION

Services for Students with Disabilities began offering services in 1980. Currently the program serves 70 undergraduates with LD. Students diagnosed with ADD/ADHD are eligible for the same services available to students with LD.
Staff: 1 full-time, 1 part-time staff members, including coordinators.
Special Fees: No special fees are charged for services to students with LD.
Applications and admissions: *Required:* high school transcript, psychoeducational report completed within 5 years; *recommended:* high school IEP (Individualized Education Program). Students may begin taking classes any term. *Application deadline:* continuous.
Special policies: The college has written policies regarding grade forgiveness; substitutions and waivers of admissions, graduation, and degree requirements.

PROGRAM AND SERVICE COMPONENTS

Academic advising: Provided by unit staff members, academic advisers. Students with LD may take up to 15 credits each term; most take 12 credits; 12 credits required to maintain full-time status; 9 credits required to be eligible for financial aid.
Counseling services: Individual counseling, career counseling, self-advocacy training.
Auxiliary aids: Taped textbooks, tape recorders, calculators, word-processors with spell-check, personal computers, optical character readers.
Auxiliary services: Alternative test arrangements, notetakers, priority registration, advocacy.

GENERAL COLLEGE INFORMATION

State-supported, 2-year, coed. Part of Massachusetts Public Higher Education System. Awards associate degrees. Founded 1960. *Setting:* 100-acre suburban campus. *Total enrollment:* 2,351. *Faculty:* 180 (75 full-time, 105 part-time); student–undergrad faculty ratio is 17:1.
Enrollment Profile: 2,351 students from 10 states and territories, 19 other countries. 62% women, 38% men, 62% part-time, 97% state residents, 20% transferred in, 2% international, 55% 25 or older, 1% Hispanic, 3% black, 1% Asian or Pacific Islander. *Areas of study chosen:* 23% health professions and related sciences, 21% liberal arts/general studies, 17% business management and administrative services, 12% social sciences, 10% engineering and applied sciences, 6% computer and information sciences, 4% natural resource sciences, 3% fine arts, 2% biological and life sciences, 2% performing arts. *Most popular recent majors:* liberal arts/general studies, nursing, business administration/ commerce/management.
First-Year Class: 410 total; 642 applied, 100% were accepted, 64% of whom enrolled.
Graduation Requirements: 60 credits; math/science requirements vary according to program; internship (some majors).
Computers on Campus: 100 computers available on campus for general student use. A campus-wide network can be accessed from off-campus. Computers for student use in computer center, computer labs, classrooms, library provide access to the Internet/World Wide Web. Staffed computer lab on campus provides training in use of computers, software.

EXPENSES

Expenses for 1997–98: *Application fee:* $10. State resident tuition: $1020 full-time, $34 per credit part-time. Nonresident tuition: $6120 full-time, $204 per credit part-time. Part-time mandatory fees: $54 per credit. Tuition for nonresidents who are eligible for the New England Regional Student Program: $1530 full-time, $51 per credit part-time. Full-time mandatory fees: $1620.
LD Services Contact: Ms. Pamela A. Farron, Coordinator, Services for Students with Disabilities, Berkshire Community College, 1350 West Street, Pittsfield, MA 01201-5786, 413-499-4660 Ext. 220. Fax: 413-447-7840.

BISHOP STATE COMMUNITY COLLEGE

Mobile, Alabama

LEARNING DISABILITIES SERVICES INFORMATION

Disabled Student Services began offering services in 1978. Currently the program serves 87 undergraduates with LD. Students diagnosed with ADD/ADHD are eligible for the same services available to students with LD.
Staff: 2 full-time, 11 part-time staff members, including director. Services provided by tutors, counselors, interpreters.
Special Fees: No special fees are charged for services to students with LD.
Applications and admissions: *Required:* high school transcript; *recommended:* high school IEP (Individualized Education Program), untimed or extended time SAT I or ACT, psychoeducational report completed within 3 years. Students may begin taking classes any term. *Application deadline:* continuous.

PROGRAM AND SERVICE COMPONENTS

Academic advising: Provided by unit staff members. Students with LD may take up to 18 quarter hours each term; most take 12 to 15 quarter hours; 12 quarter hours required to maintain full-time status and be eligible for financial aid.
Counseling services: Individual counseling, small-group counseling, career counseling, self-advocacy training.
Basic skills remediation: Offered one-on-one, in small groups, and in class-size groups by regular teachers, paraprofessionals, peer tutors. Available in reading, math, spelling, spoken language, written language, learning strategies, study skills, time management, speech, computer skills.
Subject-area tutoring: Offered one-on-one and in small groups by peer tutors, paraprofessionals with associate degrees. Available in all subjects.
Auxiliary aids: Tape recorders, calculators, typewriters, word-processors with spell-check, personal computers, talking computers, optical character readers, DecTalk, Zoom (enlarger), talking calculator.
Auxiliary services: Alternative test arrangements, notetakers, advocacy, interpreters.
Campus support group: A special student organization is available to students with LD.

Bishop State Community College (continued)

GENERAL COLLEGE INFORMATION

State-supported, 2-year, coed. Part of Alabama College System. Awards associate degrees. Founded 1965. *Setting:* 9-acre urban campus. *Endowment:* $406,471. *Total enrollment:* 3,661. *Faculty:* 249 (139 full-time, 1% with terminal degrees, 110 part-time); student–undergrad faculty ratio is 19:1.

Enrollment Profile: 3,661 students: 62% women, 38% men, 45% part-time, 48% state residents, 2% transferred in, 1% international, 56% 25 or older, 1% Native American, 1% Hispanic, 53% black, 1% Asian or Pacific Islander. *Areas of study chosen:* 43% health professions and related sciences, 25% vocational and home economics, 20% education, 2% computer and information sciences. *Most popular recent major:* nursing.

First-Year Class: 857 total; 1,210 applied, 97% were accepted, 73% of whom enrolled.

Graduation Requirements: 96 credit hours; math/science requirements vary according to program; internship (some majors).

Computers on Campus: 96 computers available on campus for general student use. Computers for student use in computer center, computer labs, learning resource center, library. Staffed computer lab on campus provides training in use of computers, software.

EXPENSES

Expenses for 1996–97: State resident tuition: $1200 full-time, $25 per credit hour part-time. Nonresident tuition: $2400 full-time, $50 per credit hour part-time. Part-time mandatory fees per quarter range from $14 to $54. Full-time mandatory fees: $174.

LD Services Contact: Dr. Arvin F. Trotter, Disabled Student Services Coordinator/Peer Tutoring Coordinator, Bishop State Community College, 351 North Broad Street, Mobile, AL 36603-5898, 334-690-6449. Fax: 334-438-5403.

BISMARCK STATE COLLEGE

Bismarck, North Dakota

LEARNING DISABILITIES SERVICES INFORMATION

Disabled Student Services began offering services in 1974. Currently the program serves 35 undergraduates with LD. Students diagnosed with ADD/ADHD are eligible for the same services available to students with LD.

Staff: 1 full-time, 1 part-time staff members, including director, coordinator. Services provided by tutors.

Special Fees: No special fees are charged for services to students with LD.

Applications and admissions: *Required:* high school transcript, extended time ACT, psychoeducational report completed within 3 years, ACT Assessment scores (if 24 years old or younger); *recommended:* personal interview. Students may begin taking classes in fall, spring, or summer. *Application deadline:* 8/1 (fall term), 12/15 (spring term).

Special policies: The college has written policies regarding grade forgiveness.

PROGRAM AND SERVICE COMPONENTS

Academic advising: Provided by academic advisers. Students with LD may take up to 20 semester hours each term; most take 12 semester hours; 12 semester hours required to maintain full-time status; 6 semester hours required to be eligible for financial aid.

Auxiliary services: Alternative test arrangements, notetakers.

GENERAL COLLEGE INFORMATION

State-supported, 2-year, coed. Part of North Dakota University System. Awards associate degrees. Founded 1939. *Setting:* 100-acre suburban campus. *Total enrollment:* 2,406. *Faculty:* 117 (82 full-time, 35 part-time); student–undergrad faculty ratio is 22:1.

Enrollment Profile: 2,406 students from 10 states and territories, 3 other countries. 51% women, 49% men, 27% part-time, 97% state residents, 10% live on campus, 10% transferred in, 1% international, 26% 25 or older, 3% Native American. *Areas of study chosen:* 42% liberal arts/general studies, 17% business management and administrative services, 11% health professions and related sciences, 8% social sciences, 5% agriculture, 3% education, 3% engineering and applied sciences, 2% mathematics, 1% computer and information sciences. *Most popular recent major:* business administration/commerce/management.

First-Year Class: 792 total. Of the students who applied, 100% were accepted, 85% of whom enrolled.

Graduation Requirements: 60 credits; 1 course each in math and science.

Computers on Campus: 90 computers available on campus for general student use. Computer purchase/lease plans available. A campus-wide network can be accessed from student residence rooms and from off-campus. Students can contact faculty members and/or advisers through e-mail. Computers for student use in computer labs, library, student center, academic offices provide access to the Internet/World Wide Web, on- and off-campus e-mail addresses. Staffed computer lab on campus provides training in use of software.

EXPENSES

Expenses for 1996–97: *Application fee:* $25. State resident tuition: $1552 full-time, $64.66 per credit part-time. Nonresident tuition: $4143 full-time, $172.64 per credit part-time. Part-time mandatory fees: $10.70 per credit. Tuition for Minnesota residents: $1800 full-time, $75 per credit part-time. Tuition for Manitoba, Montana, Saskatchewan and South Dakota residents: $1940 full-time, $80.83 per credit part-time. Tuition for students eligible for the Western Undergraduate Exchange: $2328 full-time, $97 per credit part-time. Full-time mandatory fees: $257. College room and board: $2410.

LD Services Contact: Gerrie Hase, Director of Student Success Center, Bismarck State College, 1500 Edwards Avenue, Bismarck, ND 58501, 701-224-5468. Email: hase@gwmail.nodak.edu.

BLACK HAWK COLLEGE

Moline, Illinois

LEARNING DISABILITIES SERVICES INFORMATION

Student Services/Educational Service Center began offering services in 1990. Currently the program serves 65 undergraduates with LD. Students diagnosed with ADD/ADHD are eligible for the same services available to students with LD.

Staff: 2 part-time staff members, including coordinator, assistant to coordinator. Services provided by remediation specialists, tutors, counselors.

Special Fees: No special fees are charged for services to students with LD.

Applications and admissions: *Required:* high school transcript. Students may begin taking classes in fall, spring, or summer. *Application deadline:* continuous.

PROGRAM AND SERVICE COMPONENTS

Academic advising: Provided by unit staff members, academic advisers. Students with LD may take up to 18 semester hours each term; most take 6 to 12 semester hours; 12 semester hours required to maintain full-time status; need determines number of semester hours required to be eligible for financial aid.

Counseling services: Individual counseling, career counseling, self-advocacy training.

Basic skills remediation: Offered in class-size groups by regular teachers. Available in reading, math, written language, learning strategies, study skills, time management.

Subject-area tutoring: Offered one-on-one and in small groups by peer tutors. Available in most subjects.

Special courses: College survival skills, learning strategies, time management, study skills. All offered for credit; all enter into overall grade point average.

Auxiliary aids: Taped textbooks, tape recorders, word-processors with spell-check, personal computers, talking computers, optical character readers.

Auxiliary services: Alternative test arrangements, notetakers, priority registration, advocacy.

Campus support group: A special student organization is available to students with LD.

GENERAL COLLEGE INFORMATION

State and locally supported, 2-year, coed. Part of Black Hawk College District System. Awards associate degrees. Founded 1946. *Setting:* 149-acre suburban campus. *Total enrollment:* 6,335. *Faculty:* 488 (153 full-time, 335 part-time).

Enrollment Profile: 6,335 students: 62% women, 38% men, 57% part-time, 95% state residents, 21% transferred in, 0% international, 63% 25 or older, 0% Native American, 5% Hispanic, 5% black, 1% Asian or Pacific Islander. *Most popular recent majors:* liberal arts/general studies, business administration/commerce/management, elementary education.

First-Year Class: Of the students who applied, 100% were accepted.
Graduation Requirements: 64 semester hours; math/science requirements vary according to program.
Computers on Campus: 130 computers available on campus for general student use. Computers for student use in library.

EXPENSES

Expenses for 1997–98: Area resident tuition: $1696 full-time, $53 per semester hour part-time. State resident tuition: $4160 full-time, $130 per semester hour part-time. Nonresident tuition: $7296 full-time, $228 per semester hour part-time.
LD Services Contact: Ms. Cathy Langdon, Coordinator of Student Accommodations, Black Hawk College, 6600 34th Avenue, Moline, IL 61265, 309-796-1311 Ext. 1239. Fax: 309-792-5976. Email: langdonc@bhc1.bhc.edu.

BLACKHAWK TECHNICAL COLLEGE

Janesville, Wisconsin

LEARNING DISABILITIES SERVICES INFORMATION

Services to Students with Disabilities began offering services in 1985. Currently the program serves 50 undergraduates with LD. Students diagnosed with ADD/ADHD are eligible for the same services available to students with LD.
Staff: 2 full-time, 3 part-time staff members, including coordinator. Services provided by counselor, instructors, interpreter, aide.
Special Fees: No special fees are charged for services to students with LD.
Applications and admissions: *Required:* high school transcript, courses completed; *recommended:* high school IEP (Individualized Education Program), psychoeducational report, multidisciplinary team report. Students may begin taking classes in fall, spring, or summer. *Application deadline:* continuous.

PROGRAM AND SERVICE COMPONENTS

Special preparation or orientation: Optional summer program offered prior to entering college. Optional orientation offered before registration and during registration.
Diagnostic testing: Reading, math, spelling, written language, perceptual skills.
Academic advising: Provided by unit staff members, academic advisers. Most students with LD take 9 to 12 credits each term; 12 credits required to maintain full-time status; 6 credits required to be eligible for financial aid.
Counseling services: Individual counseling, career counseling.
Basic skills remediation: Offered one-on-one, in small groups, and in class-size groups by LD teachers, regular teachers. Available in reading, math, spelling, written language, learning strategies, study skills, time management, social skills, speech.
Subject-area tutoring: Offered one-on-one and in small groups by professional teachers, peer tutors. Available in all subjects.
Special courses: College survival skills, reading, vocabulary development, communication skills, composition, learning strategies, word processing, time management, math, study skills, career planning. Some offered for credit; none enter into overall grade point average.
Auxiliary aids: Taped textbooks, tape recorders, calculators, typewriters, word-processors with spell-check, personal computers, talking computers, optical character readers.
Auxiliary services: Alternative test arrangements, notetakers, priority registration, advocacy.

GENERAL COLLEGE INFORMATION

District-supported, 2-year, coed. Part of Wisconsin Technical College System. Awards associate degrees. Founded 1968. *Setting:* 84-acre rural campus. *Research spending 1995–96:* $119,401. *Total enrollment:* 3,000. *Faculty:* 293 (91 full-time, 2% with terminal degrees, 202 part-time).
Enrollment Profile: 3,000 students from 4 states and territories. 60% women, 40% men, 61% part-time, 98% state residents, 1% transferred in, 0% international, 60% 25 or older, 1% Native American, 1% Hispanic, 3% black, 1% Asian or Pacific Islander. *Areas of study chosen:* 22% engineering and applied sciences, 8% social sciences, 7% agriculture.
First-Year Class: 1,550 applied, 98% were accepted, 65% of whom enrolled.
Graduation Requirements: 65 credits; computer course for industrial management, marketing majors; internship (some majors).
Computers on Campus: 180 computers available on campus for general student use. A campus-wide network can be accessed. Computers for student use in computer center, computer labs, library provide access to the Internet/World Wide Web. Staffed computer lab on campus provides training in use of computers, software. *Academic computing expenditure 1995–96:* $300,000.

EXPENSES

Expenses for 1997–98: *Application fee:* $25. State resident tuition: $1734 full-time, $54.20 per credit part-time. Nonresident tuition: $13,670 full-time, $427.20 per credit part-time. Part-time mandatory fees: $2 per credit. Full-time mandatory fees: $64.
LD Services Contact: Ms. Christine Flottum, Special Populations Instructor, Blackhawk Technical College, 6004 Prairie Road, PO Box 5009, Janesville, WI 53547, 608-756-4121.

BREVARD COLLEGE

Brevard, North Carolina

LEARNING DISABILITIES SERVICES INFORMATION

Office for Students with Special Needs and Disabilities began offering services in 1987. Currently the program serves 46 undergraduates with LD. Students diagnosed with ADD/ADHD are eligible for the same services available to students with LD, as well as professional ADD/ADHD coach referrals (at student's expense).
Staff: 2 full-time, 1 part-time staff members, including director, assistant. Services provided by remediation specialist, tutors, counselor.
Special Fees: No special fees are charged for services to students with LD.
Applications and admissions: *Required:* high school transcript, grade point average, class rank, courses completed, untimed or extended time SAT I or ACT, autobiographical statement; *recommended:* high school extracurricular activities, personal interview, letters of recommendation, psychoeducational report completed within 3 years. Students may begin taking classes in summer only. *Application deadline:* continuous.
Special policies: The college has written policies regarding grade forgiveness.

PROGRAM AND SERVICE COMPONENTS

Special preparation or orientation: Optional orientation offered before registration, during registration, after classes begin.
Academic advising: Provided by unit staff members, academic advisers. Students with LD may take up to 16 semester hours each term; most take 9 to 16 semester hours; 12 semester hours required to maintain full-time status and be eligible for financial aid.
Counseling services: Individual counseling, small-group counseling, career counseling, self-advocacy training, academic counseling.
Basic skills remediation: Offered one-on-one, in small groups, and in class-size groups by regular teachers, counselors, tutors; computer-aided instruction also offered. Available in reading, math, spelling, handwriting, written language, learning strategies, perceptual skills, study skills, time management, social skills.
Subject-area tutoring: Offered one-on-one and in small groups by professional teachers, peer tutors, professional tutors, volunteer tutors. Available in most subjects.
Special courses: College survival skills, reading, vocabulary development, communication skills, composition, learning strategies, time management, math, personal psychology, study skills, career planning, stress management, health and nutrition, social relationships. All offered for credit; all enter into overall grade point average.
Auxiliary aids: Tape recorders, word-processors with spell-check, personal computers, word processors with grammar check.
Auxiliary services: Alternative test arrangements, notetakers, priority registration, advocacy.
Campus support group: A special student organization is available to students with LD.

GENERAL COLLEGE INFORMATION

Independent Methodist, primarily 2-year, coed. Awards associate, bachelor's degrees. Founded 1853. *Setting:* 140-acre small-town campus. *Endowment:* $16 million. *Educational spending 1995–96:* $14,947 per undergrad. *Total enrollment:* 655. *Faculty:* 82 (53 full-time, 45% with terminal degrees, 29 part-time); student–undergrad faculty ratio is 8:1.
Enrollment Profile: 655 students from 29 states and territories, 13 other countries. 42% women, 58% men, 8% part-time, 48% state residents, 75% live on campus, 5% transferred in, 7% international, 4% 25 or

Brevard College (continued)

older, 0% Native American, 1% Hispanic, 8% black, 1% Asian or Pacific Islander. *Retention:* 43% of 1995 full-time freshmen returned. *Areas of study chosen:* 77% liberal arts/general studies, 12% performing arts, 7% fine arts, 4% interdisciplinary studies. *Most popular recent majors:* music, art/fine arts, environmental studies.
First-Year Class: 320 total; 722 applied, 92% were accepted, 48% of whom enrolled.
Graduation Requirements: 66 semester hours for associate, 124 semester hours for bachelor's; 1 math course; computer course for students without computer competency; internship (some majors).
Computers on Campus: 66 computers available on campus for general student use. A computer is strongly recommended for all students. A campus-wide network can be accessed. Students can contact faculty members and/or advisers through e-mail. Computers for student use in computer center, computer labs, classrooms, library, student center provide access to the Internet/World Wide Web, on- and off-campus e-mail addresses. Staffed computer lab on campus (open 24 hours a day) provides training in use of computers, software. *Academic computing expenditure 1995–96:* $361,413.

EXPENSES

Expenses for 1997–98: *Application fee:* $20. Comprehensive fee of $13,970 includes full-time tuition ($8950), mandatory fees ($700), and college room and board ($4320). College room only: $1800. Part-time tuition: $280 per semester hour.
LD Services Contact: Ms. Susan Kuehn, Director, Brevard College, 400 North Broad Street, Brevard, NC 28712-3306, 704-883-8292. Fax: 704-884-3790. Email: skuehn@brevard.edu.

BREVARD COMMUNITY COLLEGE

Cocoa, Florida

LEARNING DISABILITIES SERVICES INFORMATION

Office of Disabled Student Services began offering services in 1981. Currently the program serves 240 undergraduates with LD. Students diagnosed with ADD/ADHD are eligible for the same services available to students with LD, as well as support group.
Staff: 2 full-time, 11 part-time staff members, including director. Services provided by tutors, diagnostic specialists, learning assistant, LD specialists.
Special Fees: No special fees are charged for services to students with LD.
Applications and admissions: Open admissions. Students may begin taking classes any term. *Application deadline:* continuous.
Special policies: The college has written policies regarding grade forgiveness; substitutions and waivers of admissions, graduation, and degree requirements.

PROGRAM AND SERVICE COMPONENTS

Diagnostic testing: Intelligence, reading, math, spelling, handwriting, written language.
Academic advising: Provided by unit staff members. Students with LD may take up to 18 credit hours each term; most take 12 credit hours; 12 credit hours required to maintain full-time status; 6 credit hours (part-time), 12 credit hours (full-time) required to be eligible for financial aid.
Counseling services: Individual counseling, career counseling.
Subject-area tutoring: Offered one-on-one by peer tutors, staff members. Available in some subjects.
Auxiliary aids: Taped textbooks, typewriters, word-processors with spell-check, personal computers.
Auxiliary services: Alternative test arrangements, priority registration.

GENERAL COLLEGE INFORMATION

State-supported, 2-year, coed. Part of Florida Community Colleges System. Awards associate degrees. Founded 1960. *Setting:* 100-acre suburban campus. *Total enrollment:* 14,557. *Faculty:* 1,468 (228 full-time, 1,240 part-time); student–undergrad faculty ratio is 17:1.
Enrollment Profile: 14,557 students from 50 states and territories, 78 other countries. 58% women, 42% men, 70% part-time, 96% state residents, 23% transferred in, 1% international, 53% 25 or older, 1% Native American, 5% Hispanic, 7% black, 3% Asian or Pacific Islander. *Retention:* 54% of 1995 full-time freshmen returned. *Most popular recent major:* liberal arts/general studies.
First-Year Class: 2,819 total; 3,453 applied, 100% were accepted, 82% of whom enrolled.
Graduation Requirements: 60 credit hours; math/science requirements vary according to program; computer course for business-related majors; internship (some majors).
Computers on Campus: A computer is required for some students. A campus-wide network can be accessed from off-campus. Computers for student use in computer labs, learning resource center, library, Disabled Student Center provide access to the Internet/World Wide Web. Staffed computer lab on campus provides training in use of computers, software.

EXPENSES

Expenses for 1997–98: *Application fee:* $25. State resident tuition: $1170 full-time, $39 per credit hour part-time. Nonresident tuition: $4200 full-time, $140 per credit hour part-time.
LD Services Contact: Ms. Brenda Fettrow, Director, The Office for Students with Disabilities, Brevard Community College, 1519 Clearlake Road, Cocoa, FL 32922-6597, 407-632-1111. Fax: 407-633-4565. Email: fettrow.b@a1.brevard.cc.fl.us.

BRIARWOOD COLLEGE

Southington, Connecticut

LEARNING DISABILITIES SERVICES INFORMATION

Office of the Coordinator of Students with Disabilities began offering services in 1989. Currently the program serves 37 undergraduates with LD. Students diagnosed with ADD/ADHD are eligible for the same services available to students with LD, as well as distraction-reduced testing area.
Staff: 3 part-time staff members, including coordinator. Services provided by tutors, counselor.
Special Fees: No special fees are charged for services to students with LD.
Applications and admissions: *Required:* high school transcript, personal interview, math and English tests, documentation of LD; *recommended:* letters of recommendation, psychoeducational report. Students may begin taking classes in fall, spring, or summer. *Application deadline:* continuous.

PROGRAM AND SERVICE COMPONENTS

Special preparation or orientation: Required orientation held either prior to or during registration.
Academic advising: Provided by academic advisers. Students with LD may take up to 18 credit hours each term; most take 12 credit hours; 12 credit hours required to maintain full-time status; 6 credit hours (part-time), 12 credit hours (full-time) required to be eligible for financial aid.
Counseling services: Individual counseling, career counseling.
Basic skills remediation: Offered one-on-one, in small groups, and in class-size groups by regular teachers; computer-aided instruction also offered. Available in math, spelling, learning strategies, study skills, time management, social skills, English.
Subject-area tutoring: Offered one-on-one and in small groups by professional teachers, peer tutors. Available in most subjects.
Special courses: College survival skills, math, remedial English. All offered for credit; some enter into overall grade point average.
Auxiliary aids: Tape recorders, typewriters, word-processors with spell-check.
Auxiliary services: Alternative test arrangements, notetakers, priority registration, advocacy, enlargement of textbook pages.

GENERAL COLLEGE INFORMATION

Proprietary, 2-year, coed. Awards associate degrees. Founded 1966. *Setting:* 32-acre small-town campus with easy access to Boston and Hartford. *Endowment:* $12,700. *Total enrollment:* 568. *Faculty:* 78 (26 full-time, 100% with terminal degrees, 52 part-time); student–undergrad faculty ratio is 12:1.
Enrollment Profile: 568 students from 6 states and territories, 4 other countries. 81% women, 19% men, 48% part-time, 95% state residents, 17% live on campus, 30% transferred in, 1% international, 45% 25 or older, 1% Native American, 6% Hispanic, 8% black, 1% Asian or Pacific Islander. *Retention:* 67% of 1995 full-time freshmen returned. *Areas of study chosen:* 52% health professions and related sciences, 9% business management and administrative services, 5% vocational and home economics, 3% communications and journalism, 3% computer and information sciences, 3% liberal arts/general studies. *Most popular recent majors:* child care/child and family studies, paralegal studies, medical records services.

First-Year Class: 174 total; 405 applied, 100% were accepted, 43% of whom enrolled. 2% from top 10% of their high school class, 17% from top quarter, 50% from top half.
Graduation Requirements: 65 credit hours; computer course; internship.
Computers on Campus: 52 computers available on campus for general student use. Computers for student use in computer labs, learning resource center, classrooms, library. Staffed computer lab on campus. *Academic computing expenditure 1995–96:* $100,000.

EXPENSES

Expenses for 1997–98: *Application fee:* $25. Tuition: $10,195 full-time, $150 per credit hour part-time. Full-time mandatory fees: $215. College room only: $2296. Tuition guaranteed not to increase for student's term of enrollment.
LD Services Contact: Mrs. Barbara R. Mackay, Registrar/Dean of Enrollment Management, Briarwood College, 2279 Mt. Vernon Road, Southington, CT 06489, 203-628-4751 Ext. 22. Fax: 203-628-6444.

BRISTOL COMMUNITY COLLEGE

Fall River, Massachusetts

LEARNING DISABILITIES SERVICES INFORMATION

Center for Developmental Education/Quest Project began offering services in 1986. Currently the program serves 134 undergraduates with LD. Students diagnosed with ADD/ADHD are eligible for the same services available to students with LD.
Staff: 1 full-time, 3 part-time staff members, including coordinator. Services provided by remediation specialists, diagnostic specialist.
Special Fees: No special fees are charged for services to students with LD.
Applications and admissions: *Required:* high school transcript; *recommended:* high school grade point average, class rank, courses completed, autobiographical statement, letters of recommendation, psychoeducational report completed within 3 years. Students may begin taking classes in fall, spring, or summer. *Application deadline:* continuous.
Special policies: The college has written policies regarding substitutions and waivers of admissions, graduation, and degree requirements.

PROGRAM AND SERVICE COMPONENTS

Special preparation or orientation: Orientation (required for some) held before registration and during registration.
Academic advising: Provided by unit staff members, academic advisers. Students with LD may take up to 15 credit hours each term; most take 12 credit hours; 9 credit hours required to maintain full-time status; 3 credit hours required to be eligible for financial aid.
Auxiliary aids: Taped textbooks, tape recorders, word-processors with spell-check, personal computers, talking computers, optical character readers, Franklin Speller, closed-captioned device/enlarger.
Auxiliary services: Alternative test arrangements, notetakers, advocacy, registration assistance.

GENERAL COLLEGE INFORMATION

State-supported, 2-year, coed. Awards associate degrees. Founded 1965. *Setting:* 105-acre urban campus with easy access to Boston. *Total enrollment:* 5,075. *Faculty:* 256 (96 full-time, 160 part-time).
Enrollment Profile: 5,075 students: 61% women, 39% men, 26% part-time, 91% state residents, 3% transferred in, 1% international, 1% Native American, 2% Hispanic, 4% black, 1% Asian or Pacific Islander. *Retention:* 33% of 1995 full-time freshmen returned. *Most popular recent majors:* business administration/commerce/management, nursing, elementary education.
First-Year Class: 1,507 total; 2,355 applied, 95% were accepted, 67% of whom enrolled.
Graduation Requirements: 60 credits.
Computers on Campus: 150 computers available on campus for general student use. A campus-wide network can be accessed from off-campus. Computers for student use in computer center, computer labs, learning resource center, library provide access to the Internet/World Wide Web, on- and off-campus e-mail addresses. Staffed computer lab on campus provides training in use of computers.

EXPENSES

Expenses for 1997–98: *Application fee:* $10. State resident tuition: $1020 full-time, $34 per credit part-time. Nonresident tuition: $6120 full-time, $204 per credit part-time. Part-time mandatory fees: $44 per credit. Full-time mandatory fees: $1320.
LD Services Contact: Ms. Sue Boissoneault, Learning Specialist, Bristol Community College, 777 Elsbree Street, Fall River, MA 02720-7395, 508-678-2811 Ext. 2318. Fax: 508-678-2811 Ext. 2470.

BROOKHAVEN COLLEGE

Farmers Branch, Texas

LEARNING DISABILITIES SERVICES INFORMATION

Special Services began offering services in 1980. Currently the program serves 350 undergraduates with LD. Students diagnosed with ADD/ADHD are eligible for the same services available to students with LD, as well as distraction-free testing environment.
Staff: 5 full-time, 15 part-time staff members, including director, Disabled Student Specialist. Services provided by tutors, counselors, diagnostic specialists.
Special Fees: A fee is charged for diagnostic testing.
Applications and admissions: *Required:* psychoeducational report completed within 5 years; *recommended:* high school transcript, IEP (Individualized Education Program), untimed SAT I or ACT, personal interview. Students may begin taking classes any term. *Application deadline:* continuous.

PROGRAM AND SERVICE COMPONENTS

Diagnostic testing: Intelligence, reading, math, spelling, spoken language, perceptual skills.
Academic advising: Provided by unit staff members, academic advisers. Students with LD may take up to 12 semester hours each term; most take 9 semester hours; 12 semester hours required to maintain full-time status; 6 semester hours required to be eligible for financial aid.
Counseling services: Individual counseling, career counseling.
Basic skills remediation: Offered one-on-one, in small groups, and in class-size groups by regular teachers; computer-aided instruction also offered. Available in reading, math, written language.
Subject-area tutoring: Offered one-on-one and in small groups by professional teachers, peer tutors. Available in most subjects.
Special courses: Math. All offered for credit; all enter into overall grade point average.
Auxiliary aids: Taped textbooks, tape recorders, word-processors with spell-check, optical character readers, talking calculators.
Auxiliary services: Alternative test arrangements, notetakers, priority registration, advocacy.

GENERAL COLLEGE INFORMATION

County-supported, 2-year, coed. Part of Dallas County Community College District System. Awards associate degrees. Founded 1978. *Setting:* 200-acre small-town campus with easy access to Dallas–Fort Worth. *Total enrollment:* 9,060. *Faculty:* 525 (100 full-time, 24% with terminal degrees, 425 part-time).
Enrollment Profile: 9,060 students: 56% women, 44% men, 75% part-time, 96% state residents, 41% transferred in, 1% international, 52% 25 or older, 1% Native American, 10% Hispanic, 8% black, 7% Asian or Pacific Islander. *Most popular recent major:* liberal arts/general studies.
First-Year Class: 4,042 total. Of the students who applied, 100% were accepted.
Graduation Requirements: 60 semester hours; computer course for accounting, automotive technologies, fashion merchandising, secretarial science, administrative management majors; internship (some majors).
Computers on Campus: 250 computers available on campus for general student use. Computers for student use in computer center, computer labs, learning resource center, classrooms, library.

EXPENSES

Expenses for 1997–98: Area resident tuition: $650 full-time. State resident tuition: $1030 full-time. Nonresident tuition: $2140 full-time. Part-time tuition per credit ranges from $79 to $245 for area residents, $135 to $435 for state residents, $225 to $786 for nonresidents.
LD Services Contact: Ms. Aliene Pylant, Disabled Student Specialist, Brookhaven College, 3939 Valley View Lane, Farmers Branch, TX 75244, 972-860-4196. Fax: 972-860-4129.

BROOME COMMUNITY COLLEGE

Binghamton, New York

LEARNING DISABILITIES SERVICES INFORMATION

Learning Assistance Center began offering services in 1980. Currently the program serves 72 undergraduates with LD. Students diagnosed with ADD/ADHD are eligible for the same services available to students with LD.
Staff: 11 full-time, 7 part-time staff members, including director, associate director, coordinator. Services provided by remediation specialists, diagnostic specialist, basic skills instructors.
Special Fees: No special fees are charged for services to students with LD.
Applications and admissions: *Required:* high school transcript; *recommended:* high school IEP (Individualized Education Program), personal interview, autobiographical statement, letters of recommendation. Students may begin taking classes in fall, spring, or summer. *Application deadline:* continuous.
Special policies: The college has written policies regarding grade forgiveness; substitutions and waivers of admissions, graduation, and degree requirements.

PROGRAM AND SERVICE COMPONENTS

Special preparation or orientation: Required orientation held before registration and individually by special arrangement.
Diagnostic testing: Reading, math, spelling, spoken language, written language, study skills, social skills, learning strategies, cognitive skills.
Academic advising: Provided by unit staff members. Most students with LD take 12 to 15 credit hours each term; 12 credit hours required to maintain full-time status; 6 credit hours required to be eligible for financial aid.
Counseling services: Individual counseling, small-group counseling, career counseling, self-advocacy training.
Basic skills remediation: Offered one-on-one, in small groups, and in class-size groups by regular teachers; computer-aided instruction also offered. Available in reading, math, spelling, spoken language, written language, learning strategies, study skills, time management, social skills, speech, computer skills.
Subject-area tutoring: Offered one-on-one, in small groups, and in class-size groups by professional teachers, peer tutors, Learning Assistance Center staff, LD Coordinator. Available in all subjects.
Special courses: College survival skills, reading, vocabulary development, composition, learning strategies, Internet use, time management, math, study skills. Some offered for credit; some enter into overall grade point average.
Auxiliary aids: Taped textbooks, tape recorders, calculators, typewriters, word-processors with spell-check, personal computers, optical character readers, Visualtek machine, voice-synthesized computer.
Auxiliary services: Alternative test arrangements, notetakers, priority registration, advocacy, scribes, test assistants, equipment trainers.
Campus support group: A special student organization is available to students with LD.

GENERAL COLLEGE INFORMATION

State and locally supported, 2-year, coed. Part of State University of New York System. Awards associate degrees. Founded 1946. *Setting:* 223-acre suburban campus. *Total enrollment:* 5,402. *Faculty:* 344 (159 full-time, 17% with terminal degrees, 185 part-time); student–undergrad faculty ratio is 16:1.
Enrollment Profile: 5,402 students from 8 states and territories, 34 other countries. 57% women, 2% men, 38% part-time, 95% state residents, 6% transferred in, 1% international, 46% 25 or older, 0% Native American, 1% Hispanic, 2% black, 2% Asian or Pacific Islander. *Areas of study chosen:* 43% liberal arts/general studies, 15% business management and administrative services, 10% health professions and related sciences, 7% engineering and applied sciences, 4% computer and information sciences, 2% communications and journalism. *Most popular recent majors:* liberal arts/general studies, business administration/commerce/management.
First-Year Class: 1,413 total; 3,450 applied, 95% were accepted, 43% of whom enrolled. 3% from top 10% of their high school class, 29% from top quarter, 68% from top half.
Graduation Requirements: 62 credit hours; math/science requirements vary according to program.
Computers on Campus: 400 computers available on campus for general student use. Computers for student use in computer center, computer labs, research center, learning resource center, classrooms, library, student center, applied technology, business buildings provide access to the Internet/World Wide Web. Staffed computer lab on campus provides training in use of computers, software.

EXPENSES

Expenses for 1996–97: State resident tuition: $2168 full-time, $91 per credit hour part-time. Nonresident tuition: $4336 full-time, $182 per credit hour part-time. Part-time mandatory fees: $5 per credit hour. One-time mandatory fee: $40. Full-time mandatory fees: $111.
LD Services Contact: Mr. Bruce Pomeroy, Director, Student Support Services, Broome Community College, PO Box 1017, Binghamton, NY 13902-1017, 607-778-5150. Fax: 607-778-5310. Email: pomeroy_b@sunybroome.edu.

BRYANT AND STRATTON BUSINESS INSTITUTE

Rochester, New York

LEARNING DISABILITIES SERVICES INFORMATION

Academic Center began offering services in 1985. Currently the program serves 18 undergraduates with LD. Students diagnosed with ADD/ADHD are eligible for the same services available to students with LD.
Staff: 1 full-time staff member (academic adviser). Services provided by remediation specialists, tutors, counselors, notetakers, interpreters.
Special Fees: No special fees are charged for services to students with LD.
Applications and admissions: *Required:* high school transcript, grade point average, class rank, courses completed, personal interview, autobiographical statement, letters of recommendation; *recommended:* high school extracurricular activities. Students may begin taking classes any term. *Application deadline:* continuous.
Special policies: The college has written policies regarding substitutions and waivers of admissions, graduation, and degree requirements.

PROGRAM AND SERVICE COMPONENTS

Academic advising: Provided by unit staff members, academic advisers. Students with LD may take up to 18 credit hours each term; most take 6 to 18 credit hours; 12 credit hours required to maintain full-time status and be eligible for financial aid.
Counseling services: Individual counseling, small-group counseling, career counseling.
Basic skills remediation: Offered one-on-one and in small groups by regular teachers; computer-aided instruction also offered. Available in reading, math, written language.
Subject-area tutoring: Offered one-on-one by professional teachers, peer tutors. Available in all subjects.
Auxiliary services: Alternative test arrangements, notetakers, interpreters.

GENERAL COLLEGE INFORMATION

Proprietary, 2-year, coed. Part of Bryant and Stratton Business Institute, Inc. Awards associate degrees. Founded 1985. *Setting:* 1-acre suburban campus. *Total enrollment:* 571. *Faculty:* 58 (15 full-time, 43 part-time).
Enrollment Profile: 571 students: 80% women, 20% men, 25% part-time, 100% state residents, 32% transferred in, 0% international, 68% 25 or older, 0% Native American, 2% Hispanic, 2% black, 1% Asian or Pacific Islander.
First-Year Class: 163 total. Of the students who applied, 80% were accepted, 80% of whom enrolled.
Graduation Requirements: 90 credit hours; 1 math course; computer course; internship (some majors).
Computers on Campus: 180 computers available on campus for general student use. A computer is recommended for all students. Computers for student use in computer center, computer labs, research center, learning resource center, classrooms, library provide access to the Internet/World Wide Web. Staffed computer lab on campus provides training in use of computers, software.

EXPENSES

Expenses for 1996–97: *Application fee:* $25. Tuition: $6720 full-time, $140 per credit hour part-time.
LD Services Contact: Ms. Mary Lanzafame, Academic Counselor, Bryant and Stratton Business Institute, 1225 Jefferson Road, Rochester, NY 14623-3136, 716-292-5627. Fax: 716-292-6015.

BRYANT AND STRATTON BUSINESS INSTITUTE

Syracuse, New York

LEARNING DISABILITIES SERVICES INFORMATION

Academic Center began offering services in 1988. Currently the program serves 22 undergraduates with LD. Students diagnosed with ADD/ADHD are eligible for the same services available to students with LD.
Staff: Includes director, coordinators. Services provided by counselors.
Special Fees: No special fees are charged for services to students with LD.
Applications and admissions: *Required:* high school transcript, courses completed, personal interview, autobiographical statement; *recommended:* letters of recommendation, psychoeducational report completed within 5 years. Students may begin taking classes any term. *Application deadline:* continuous.

PROGRAM AND SERVICE COMPONENTS

Special preparation or orientation: Required orientation held before registration.
Diagnostic testing: Reading, math, spelling, study skills, learning strategies.
Academic advising: Provided by unit staff members, academic advisers. Students with LD may take up to 18 credits each term; most take 15 credits; 12 credits required to maintain full-time status; 6 credits required to be eligible for financial aid.
Counseling services: Individual counseling, career counseling, self-advocacy training.
Basic skills remediation: Offered one-on-one by regular teachers; computer-aided instruction also offered. Available in reading, math, spelling, written language.
Subject-area tutoring: Offered one-on-one and in small groups by professional teachers, peer tutors. Available in all subjects.
Auxiliary aids: Taped textbooks, tape recorders, calculators, typewriters, word-processors with spell-check, personal computers.
Auxiliary services: Alternative test arrangements, notetakers, advocacy.

GENERAL COLLEGE INFORMATION

Proprietary, 2-year, coed. Part of Bryant and Stratton Business Institute, Inc. Awards associate degrees. Founded 1854. *Setting:* urban campus. *Total enrollment:* 596. *Faculty:* 49 (12 full-time, 100% with terminal degrees, 37 part-time).
Enrollment Profile: 596 students: 80% women, 20% men, 13% part-time, 100% state residents, 7% live on campus, 8% transferred in, 0% international, 60% 25 or older, 3% Native American, 2% Hispanic, 18% black, 1% Asian or Pacific Islander. *Retention:* 60% of 1995 full-time freshmen returned.
First-Year Class: 155 total. 2% from top 10% of their high school class, 8% from top quarter, 90% from top half.
Graduation Requirements: 90 credits; 1 math course; computer course; internship (some majors).
Computers on Campus: 114 computers available on campus for general student use. A computer is recommended for all students. Computers for student use in computer labs, learning resource center.

EXPENSES

Expenses for 1996–97: *Application fee:* $25. Comprehensive fee of $10,520 includes full-time tuition ($6720) and college room and board ($3800). College room only: $2400. Part-time tuition: $140 per credit.
LD Services Contact: Ms. Christine M. Rydelek, Academic Advisor, Bryant and Stratton Business Institute, 953 James Street, Syracuse, NY 13203-2502, 315-472-6603. Fax: 315-474-4383.

BUCKS COUNTY COMMUNITY COLLEGE

Newtown, Pennsylvania

LEARNING DISABILITIES SERVICES INFORMATION

Office for Students with Disabilities began offering services in 1981. Currently the program serves 125 undergraduates with LD. Students diagnosed with ADD/ADHD are eligible for the same services available to students with LD, as well as distraction-free testing environment.
Staff: 1 full-time, 1 part-time staff members, including coordinator. Services provided by tutor.
Special Fees: No special fees are charged for services to students with LD.
Applications and admissions: Students may begin taking classes in fall, winter, or spring. *Application deadline:* continuous.

PROGRAM AND SERVICE COMPONENTS

Special preparation or orientation: Optional orientation offered during registration and the week before classes begin (fall semester only).
Academic advising: Provided by unit staff members, academic advisers. Most students with LD take 6 to 9 credits each term; individual arrangement determines the number of credits required to maintain full-time status; source of aid determines number of credits required to be eligible for financial aid.
Subject-area tutoring: Offered one-on-one and in small groups by professional teachers, professional tutor. Available in some subjects.
Auxiliary aids: Taped textbooks, word-processors with spell-check, talking computers, optical character readers.
Auxiliary services: Alternative test arrangements, notetakers, priority registration, advocacy.

GENERAL COLLEGE INFORMATION

County-supported, 2-year, coed. Awards associate degrees. Founded 1964. *Setting:* 200-acre small-town campus with easy access to Philadelphia. *Total enrollment:* 9,204. *Faculty:* 452 (184 full-time, 268 part-time); student–undergrad faculty ratio is 25:1.
Enrollment Profile: 9,204 students from 2 states and territories. 59% women, 41% men, 70% part-time, 99% state residents, 15% transferred in, 0% international, 50% 25 or older, 1% Native American, 2% Hispanic, 2% black, 2% Asian or Pacific Islander. *Retention:* 46% of 1995 full-time freshmen returned. *Areas of study chosen:* 29% liberal arts/general studies, 25% business management and administrative services, 7% education, 6% fine arts, 6% health professions and related sciences, 5% social sciences, 4% computer and information sciences, 4% engineering and applied sciences, 4% psychology, 3% biological and life sciences, 2% communications and journalism, 2% performing arts, 1% English language/literature/letters, 1% mathematics, 1% prelaw. *Most popular recent majors:* business administration/commerce/management, liberal arts/general studies.
First-Year Class: 1,887 total. Of the students who applied, 100% were accepted.
Graduation Requirements: 60 credits; 1 math/science course; computer course for business, math, graphic arts majors; internship (some majors).
Computers on Campus: 275 computers available on campus for general student use. Computer purchase/lease plans available. Computers for student use in computer center, classrooms, library provide access to the Internet/World Wide Web, on- and off-campus e-mail addresses. Staffed computer lab on campus provides training in use of computers, software.

EXPENSES

Expenses for 1997–98: *Application fee:* $30. Area resident tuition: $2130 full-time, $71 per credit part-time. State resident tuition: $4260 full-time, $142 per credit part-time. Nonresident tuition: $6390 full-time, $213 per credit part-time. Full-time mandatory fees: $200 for area residents, $500 for state residents, $800 for nonresidents. Part-time mandatory fees per semester range from $30 to $80 for area residents, $40 to $190 for state residents, $50 to $300 for nonresidents, according to course load.
LD Services Contact: Ms. Marie Stevens Cooper, Coordinator for Students with Disabilities, Bucks County Community College, Swamp Road, Newtown, PA 18940, 215-968-8463. Fax: 215-968-8464. Email: cooperm@bucks.edu.

BUTLER COUNTY COMMUNITY COLLEGE

El Dorado, Kansas

LEARNING DISABILITIES SERVICES INFORMATION

Office of Special Needs began offering services in 1980. Currently the program serves 300 undergraduates with LD. Students diagnosed with ADD/ADHD are eligible for the same services available to students with LD.

Butler County Community College (continued)

Staff: 1 full-time, 10 part-time staff members, including director, coordinator. Services provided by tutors, counselor, paraprofessional, student tutors.
Special Fees: No special fees are charged for services to students with LD.
Applications and admissions: *Required:* high school transcript, IEP (Individualized Education Program), psychoeducational report completed within 2 to 3 years, vocational rehabilitation report; *recommended:* untimed SAT I or ACT. Students may begin taking classes in fall, spring, or summer. *Application deadline:* continuous.

PROGRAM AND SERVICE COMPONENTS

Special preparation or orientation: Optional orientation offered before registration.
Academic advising: Provided by unit staff members. Most students with LD take 12 credit hours each term; 12 credit hours required to maintain full-time status; 6 credit hours (part-time), 12 credit hours (full-time) required to be eligible for financial aid.
Counseling services: Individual counseling, small-group counseling, career counseling.
Basic skills remediation: Offered one-on-one and in small groups by LD teachers, regular teachers, developmental skills teachers. Available in reading, math, spelling, written language, learning strategies, study skills, time management, stress management.
Subject-area tutoring: Offered one-on-one and in small groups by professional teachers, peer tutors, paraprofessionals. Available in all subjects.
Special courses: College survival skills, reading, vocabulary development, communication skills, study skills, career planning, stress management. All offered for credit; all enter into overall grade point average.
Auxiliary aids: Taped textbooks, tape recorders, word-processors with spell-check, optical character readers, brailler.
Auxiliary services: Alternative test arrangements, notetakers, advocacy.

GENERAL COLLEGE INFORMATION

State and locally supported, 2-year, coed. Part of Kansas State Board of Education. Awards associate degrees. Founded 1927. *Setting:* 80-acre small-town campus. *Total enrollment:* 7,506. *Faculty:* 573.
Enrollment Profile: 7,506 students from 18 states and territories, 21 other countries. 60% women, 40% men, 70% part-time, 97% state residents, 20% transferred in, 50% 25 or older, 2% Native American, 2% Hispanic, 6% black, 3% Asian or Pacific Islander.
First-Year Class: 1,730 total. Of the students who applied, 100% were accepted, 83% of whom enrolled.
Graduation Requirements: 62 credit hours; math/science requirements vary according to program; computer course for all associate of science degree programs.
Computers on Campus: 90 computers available on campus for general student use. Computers for student use in computer center, classrooms, library.

EXPENSES

Expenses for 1996–97: State resident tuition: $1271 full-time, $41 per credit hour part-time. Nonresident tuition: $2976 full-time, $96 per credit hour part-time. College room and board: $3100 (minimum).
LD Services Contact: Ms. Liane R. Fowler, Coordinator, Special Needs, Butler County Community College, 901 South Haverhill Road, El Dorado, KS 67042-3280, 316-322-3166. Fax: 316-322-3316.

CALDWELL COMMUNITY COLLEGE AND TECHNICAL INSTITUTE

Hudson, North Carolina

LEARNING DISABILITIES SERVICES INFORMATION

Academic Support currently serves 10 undergraduates with LD. Students diagnosed with ADD/ADHD are eligible for the same services available to students with LD.
Staff: 1 full-time, 2 part-time staff members, including director. Services provided by tutors, learning and reading center technicians.
Special Fees: No special fees are charged for services to students with LD.
Applications and admissions: *Required:* high school transcript, psychoeducational report completed within 3 years. Students may begin taking classes any term. *Application deadline:* continuous.

PROGRAM AND SERVICE COMPONENTS

Special preparation or orientation: Optional orientation offered after classes begin.
Diagnostic testing: Reading, math, written language.
Academic advising: Provided by academic advisers. Most students with LD take 12 semester hours each term; 12 semester hours required to maintain full-time status; 6 semester hours required to be eligible for financial aid.
Counseling services: Individual counseling, career counseling.
Basic skills remediation: Offered one-on-one and in class-size groups by regular teachers; computer-aided instruction also offered. Available in reading, math, written language, study skills.
Subject-area tutoring: Offered one-on-one by peer tutors. Available in most subjects.
Special courses: College survival skills, reading, communication skills, word processing, math, typing, career planning. Some offered for credit.
Auxiliary aids: Taped textbooks, tape recorders, calculators, typewriters, word-processors with spell-check, personal computers, reading machines.
Auxiliary services: Alternative test arrangements, notetakers.

GENERAL COLLEGE INFORMATION

State-supported, 2-year, coed. Part of North Carolina Community College System. Awards associate degrees. Founded 1964. *Setting:* 50-acre small-town campus. *Total enrollment:* 3,127. *Faculty:* 225 (85 full-time, 7% with terminal degrees, 140 part-time); student–undergrad faculty ratio is 14:1.
Enrollment Profile: 3,127 students from 15 states and territories. 63% women, 37% men, 60% part-time, 98% state residents, 31% transferred in, 0% international, 48% 25 or older, 1% Hispanic, 4% black. *Retention:* 34% of 1995 full-time freshmen returned.
First-Year Class: 1,071 total; 1,757 applied, 61% of whom enrolled.
Graduation Requirements: Math/science requirements vary according to program; computer course for most majors.
Computers on Campus: 100 computers available on campus for general student use. Computers for student use in computer labs provide access to the Internet/World Wide Web. Staffed computer lab on campus provides training in use of computers, software.

EXPENSES

Expenses for 1997–98: State resident tuition: $560 full-time, $20 per semester hour part-time. Nonresident tuition: $4564 full-time, $163 per semester hour part-time. Part-time mandatory fees per semester range from $2.25 to $9. Full-time mandatory fees: $18.
LD Services Contact: Ms. Teena McRary, Coordinator, Academic Support, Caldwell Community College and Technical Institute, 1000 Hickory Boulevard, Hudson, NC 28638-2397, 704-726-2238. Fax: 704-726-2216.

CAMDEN COUNTY COLLEGE

Blackwood, New Jersey

LEARNING DISABILITIES SERVICES INFORMATION

Program for the Academically Challenged Student (PACS) began offering services in 1988. Currently the program serves 460 undergraduates with LD. Students diagnosed with ADD/ADHD are eligible for the same services available to students with LD.
Staff: 3 full-time, 15 part-time staff members, including director, learning specialist, program specialist. Services provided by tutors, counselor, instructors.
Special Fees: No special fees are charged for services to students with LD.
Applications and admissions: *Required:* high school IEP (Individualized Education Program), psychoeducational report completed within 3 years, New Jersey Basic Skills College Placement Test, psychological and educational evaluations. Students may begin taking classes in fall, spring, or summer. *Application deadline:* continuous.
Special policies: The college has written policies regarding grade forgiveness; substitutions and waivers of admissions, graduation, and degree requirements.

PROGRAM AND SERVICE COMPONENTS

Special preparation or orientation: Required summer program offered prior to entering college. Required orientation held before classes begin.

Academic advising: Provided by unit staff members. Students with LD may take up to 15 credits each term; most take 12 credits; 12 credits required to maintain full-time status; 6 credits (part-time), 12 credits (full-time) required to be eligible for financial aid.
Counseling services: Individual counseling, small-group counseling, career counseling.
Basic skills remediation: Offered in small groups and in class-size groups by LD teachers, regular teachers, professional tutors. Available in reading, math, spelling, spoken language, written language, learning strategies, study skills, time management, social skills.
Subject-area tutoring: Offered in small groups by professional teachers, peer tutors. Available in most subjects.
Special courses: College survival skills, reading, vocabulary development, communication skills, composition, learning strategies, word processing, time management, math, typing, study skills, career planning. Some offered for credit; some enter into overall grade point average.
Auxiliary aids: Taped textbooks, tape recorders, calculators, typewriters, word-processors with spell-check, personal computers, optical character readers.
Auxiliary services: Alternative test arrangements, notetakers, priority registration, advocacy.

GENERAL COLLEGE INFORMATION

State and locally supported, 2-year, coed. Part of New Jersey Commission on Higher Education. Awards associate degrees. Founded 1967. *Setting:* 320-acre suburban campus with easy access to Philadelphia. *Educational spending 1995–96:* $1063 per undergrad. *Total enrollment:* 12,669. *Faculty:* 627 (123 full-time, 21% with terminal degrees, 504 part-time).
Enrollment Profile: 12,669 students from 2 states and territories, 21 other countries. 60% women, 40% men, 61% part-time, 98% state residents, 22% transferred in, 1% international, 39% 25 or older, 0% Native American, 4% Hispanic, 14% black, 5% Asian or Pacific Islander. *Retention:* 60% of 1995 full-time freshmen returned. *Areas of study chosen:* 30% liberal arts/general studies, 25% health professions and related sciences, 13% business management and administrative services, 10% engineering and applied sciences. *Most popular recent majors:* liberal arts/general studies, nursing, criminal justice.
First-Year Class: 2,732 total. Of the students who applied, 100% were accepted.
Graduation Requirements: 64 credits; 1 math course.
Computers on Campus: 700 computers available on campus for general student use. Computers for student use in computer labs, classrooms, library provide access to the Internet/World Wide Web. Staffed computer lab on campus.

EXPENSES

Expenses for 1997–98: *Application fee:* $15. Area resident tuition: $1824 full-time, $57 per credit part-time. Nonresident tuition: $1952 full-time, $61 per credit part-time. Part-time mandatory fees: $21 per semester. Tuition for international students: $3488 full-time, $109 per credit part-time. Full-time mandatory fees: $48.
LD Services Contact: Ms. Joanne Kinzy, Director, Camden County College, PO Box 200, College Drive, Blackwood, NJ 08012-0200, 609-227-7200 Ext. 4430. Fax: 609-374-4981.

CARL SANDBURG COLLEGE
Galesburg, Illinois

LEARNING DISABILITIES SERVICES INFORMATION

Special Populations Office began offering services in 1989. Currently the program serves 28 undergraduates with LD. Students diagnosed with ADD/ADHD are eligible for the same services available to students with LD.
Staff: 1 full-time, 2 part-time staff members, including coordinator. Services provided by peer and professional tutors.
Special Fees: No special fees are charged for services to students with LD.
Applications and admissions: Open admissions. Students may begin taking classes any term. *Application deadline:* continuous.
Special policies: The college has written policies regarding substitutions and waivers of admissions, graduation, and degree requirements.

PROGRAM AND SERVICE COMPONENTS

Academic advising: Provided by unit staff members, academic advisers. Students with LD required to take 12 credit hours to maintain full-time status and be eligible for financial aid.
Counseling services: Individual counseling, small-group counseling, career counseling.
Basic skills remediation: Offered one-on-one, in small groups, and in class-size groups by regular teachers. Available in reading, math, written language, study skills.
Subject-area tutoring: Offered one-on-one, in small groups, and in class-size groups by professional teachers, peer tutors. Available in all subjects.
Auxiliary aids: Taped textbooks, tape recorders, calculators, typewriters, word-processors with spell-check, personal computers, talking computers, optical character readers, brailler.
Auxiliary services: Alternative test arrangements, notetakers, advocacy.

GENERAL COLLEGE INFORMATION

State and locally supported, 2-year, coed. Part of Illinois Community College System. Awards associate degrees. Founded 1967. *Setting:* 105-acre small-town campus. *Educational spending 1995–96:* $1150 per undergrad. *Total enrollment:* 3,000. *Faculty:* 208 (58 full-time, 5% with terminal degrees, 150 part-time); student–undergrad faculty ratio is 12:1.
Enrollment Profile: 3,000 students from 5 states and territories, 2 other countries. 54% women, 46% men, 78% part-time, 80% state residents, 14% transferred in, 1% international, 1% Native American, 3% Hispanic, 8% black, 1% Asian or Pacific Islander. *Most popular recent majors:* liberal arts/general studies, nursing.
First-Year Class: Of the students who applied, 100% were accepted, 95% of whom enrolled.
Graduation Requirements: 64 semester hours; 8 semester hours of math; 6 semester hours of lab science; computer course for all associate of science degree programs; internship (some majors).
Computers on Campus: 110 computers available on campus for general student use. Computers for student use in computer labs. Staffed computer lab on campus provides training in use of computers, software.

EXPENSES

Expenses for 1997–98: Area resident tuition: $1568 full-time, $49 per semester hour part-time. State resident tuition: $3897 full-time, $121.78 per semester hour part-time. Nonresident tuition: $6916 full-time, $216.11 per semester hour part-time. Part-time mandatory fees: $7 per semester hour. Full-time mandatory fees: $224.
LD Services Contact: Mr. John Larson, Assistant Coordinator of Special Populations, Carl Sandburg College, 2232 South Lake Storey Road, Galesburg, IL 61401-9576, 309-344-2518 Ext. 5323. Fax: 309-344-3526.

CARROLL COMMUNITY COLLEGE
Westminster, Maryland

LEARNING DISABILITIES SERVICES INFORMATION

Office of Student Support Services currently serves 41 undergraduates with LD. Students diagnosed with ADD/ADHD are eligible for the same services available to students with LD.
Staff: 1 full-time staff member (director). Services provided by tutors.
Special Fees: No special fees are charged for services to students with LD.
Applications and admissions: *Required:* high school IEP (Individualized Education Program), psychoeducational report completed within 3 years; *recommended:* personal interview. Students may begin taking classes in fall only. *Application deadline:* continuous.

PROGRAM AND SERVICE COMPONENTS

Academic advising: Provided by unit staff members, academic advisers. Most students with LD take 12 credits each term; 12 credits required to maintain full-time status; 6 credits required to be eligible for financial aid.
Subject-area tutoring: Offered one-on-one by professional teachers, peer tutors. Available in most subjects.
Auxiliary aids: Taped textbooks, tape recorders, word-processors with spell-check, talking computers, optical character readers.
Auxiliary services: Alternative test arrangements, notetakers, scribes.

Carroll Community College (continued)

GENERAL COLLEGE INFORMATION

State and locally supported, 2-year, coed. Part of Maryland Higher Education Commission. Awards associate degrees. Founded 1996. *Setting:* 80-acre small-town campus with easy access to Baltimore. *Total enrollment:* 2,532. *Faculty:* 210 (60 full-time, 150 part-time).
Enrollment Profile: 2,532 students from 2 states and territories, 4 other countries. 63% women, 37% men, 67% part-time, 98% state residents, 10% transferred in, 1% international, 32% 25 or older, 1% Native American, 3% Hispanic, 2% black, 1% Asian or Pacific Islander.
First-Year Class: 350 total. Of the students who applied, 100% were accepted, 100% of whom enrolled.
Graduation Requirements: 62 credits; 1 math course; 2 natural science courses; computer course.
Computers on Campus: 250 computers available on campus for general student use. Computers for student use in computer center, computer labs, classrooms, library, student rooms, career center provide access to the Internet/World Wide Web. Staffed computer lab on campus provides training in use of computers, software.

EXPENSES

Expenses for 1997–98: Area resident tuition: $1953 full-time, $63 per credit part-time. State resident tuition: $3863 full-time, $124.60 per credit part-time. Nonresident tuition: $6113 full-time, $197.20 per credit part-time. Part-time mandatory fees: $8.30 per credit. Full-time mandatory fees: $257.
LD Services Contact: Ms. Sherry Glass, Director, Student Support Services, Carroll Community College, 1601 Washington Road, Westminster, MD 21157, 410-876-9600. Fax: 410-876-8855.

CARTERET COMMUNITY COLLEGE

Morehead City, North Carolina

LEARNING DISABILITIES SERVICES INFORMATION

Academic Support Services began offering services in 1993. Currently the program serves 41 undergraduates with LD. Students diagnosed with ADD/ADHD are eligible for the same services available to students with LD.
Staff: 2 full-time, 2 part-time staff members, including coordinator. Services provided by tutors.
Special Fees: No special fees are charged for services to students with LD.
Applications and admissions: *Required:* high school transcript, placement test (ASSET); *recommended:* psychoeducational report completed within 3 to 5 years. Students may begin taking classes in fall, spring, or summer. *Application deadline:* continuous.
Special policies: The college has written policies regarding grade forgiveness.

PROGRAM AND SERVICE COMPONENTS

Diagnostic testing: Intelligence, reading, math, written language, perceptual skills.
Academic advising: Provided by unit staff members, academic advisers. Students with LD may take up to as many semester hours as an individual can handle each term; most take 12 semester hours; 12 semester hours required to maintain full-time status; 1 semester hour required to be eligible for financial aid.
Counseling services: Individual counseling.
Basic skills remediation: Offered one-on-one by regular teachers; computer-aided instruction also offered. Available in reading, math, written language.
Subject-area tutoring: Offered one-on-one and in small groups by professional teachers. Available in some subjects.
Special courses: College survival skills, reading, vocabulary development, word processing, study skills. Some offered for credit.
Auxiliary aids: Tape recorders, calculators.
Auxiliary services: Alternative test arrangements, notetakers.

GENERAL COLLEGE INFORMATION

State-supported, 2-year, coed. Part of North Carolina Community College System. Awards associate degrees. Founded 1963. *Setting:* 25-acre small-town campus.

EXPENSES

Expenses for 1996–97: State resident tuition: $557 full-time, $13.25 per quarter hour part-time. Nonresident tuition: $4515 full-time, $107.50 per quarter hour part-time. Part-time mandatory fees per quarter range from $4 to $7. Full-time mandatory fees: $21.
LD Services Contact: Ms. Gale Swann, Coordinator, Academic Support, Carteret Community College, 3505 Arendell Street, Morehead City, NC 28557, 919-247-6000 Ext. 218.

CASPER COLLEGE

Casper, Wyoming

LEARNING DISABILITIES SERVICES INFORMATION

Vocational Spectrum began offering services in 1988. Currently the program serves 30 undergraduates with LD. Students diagnosed with ADD/ADHD are eligible for the same services available to students with LD.
Staff: 2 full-time staff members, including director, learning specialist. Services provided by remediation specialist, tutors, counselors, diagnostic specialist.
Special Fees: No special fees are charged for services to students with LD.
Applications and admissions: *Required:* high school transcript, grade point average, class rank, courses completed, high school diploma or GED; *recommended:* untimed or extended time ACT, psychoeducational report completed within 2 years. Students may begin taking classes any term. *Application deadline:* continuous.
Special policies: The college has written policies regarding grade forgiveness; substitutions and waivers of graduation and degree requirements.

PROGRAM AND SERVICE COMPONENTS

Diagnostic testing: Intelligence, reading, math, spelling, handwriting, written language, motor abilities, perceptual skills, study skills, personality, hearing, learning strategies.
Academic advising: Provided by unit staff members, academic advisers. Most students with LD take 12 credit hours each term; 12 credit hours required to maintain full-time status; 6 credit hours required to be eligible for financial aid.
Counseling services: Individual counseling, small-group counseling, career counseling.
Basic skills remediation: Offered one-on-one and in class-size groups by regular teachers; computer-aided instruction also offered. Available in reading, math, spelling, spoken language, written language, learning strategies, perceptual skills, study skills.
Subject-area tutoring: Offered one-on-one and in small groups by peer tutors. Available in most subjects.
Auxiliary aids: Taped textbooks, tape recorders, calculators, word-processors with spell-check, optical character readers.
Auxiliary services: Alternative test arrangements, notetakers, priority registration, advocacy.

GENERAL COLLEGE INFORMATION

District-supported, 2-year, coed. Part of Wyoming Community College Commission. Awards associate degrees. Founded 1945. *Setting:* 175-acre small-town campus. *Endowment:* $50,000. *Educational spending 1995–96:* $2487 per undergrad. *Total enrollment:* 3,960. *Faculty:* 185 (132 full-time, 50% with terminal degrees, 53 part-time); student–undergrad faculty ratio is 24:1.
Enrollment Profile: 3,960 students from 43 states and territories, 10 other countries. 61% women, 39% men, 20% part-time, 95% state residents, 16% live on campus, 12% transferred in, 1% international, 38% 25 or older, 1% Native American, 1% Hispanic, 1% black, 1% Asian or Pacific Islander. *Retention:* 50% of 1995 full-time freshmen returned. *Most popular recent majors:* business administration/commerce/management, elementary education, nursing.
First-Year Class: 720 total; 960 applied, 99% were accepted, 66% of whom enrolled. 16% from top 10% of their high school class, 37% from top quarter, 68% from top half.
Graduation Requirements: 64 credit hours; computer course for most majors.
Computers on Campus: 130 computers available on campus for general student use. A campus-wide network can be accessed. Students can contact faculty members and/or advisers through e-mail. Computers for student use in computer center, computer labs, classrooms, library provide access to the Internet/World Wide Web, on- and off-campus e-mail

addresses. Staffed computer lab on campus provides training in use of computers, software. *Academic computing expenditure 1995–96:* $210,000.

EXPENSES

Expenses for 1996–97: State resident tuition: $1248 full-time, $39 per credit hour part-time. Nonresident tuition: $3744 full-time, $117 per credit hour part-time. Part-time mandatory fees: $5 per credit hour. Full-time mandatory fees: $120. College room and board: $2260 (minimum).
LD Services Contact: Ms. Ann Loader, Individual Learning Specialist, Casper College, 125 College Drive, AD 113B, Casper, WY 82601-4699, 307-268-2557. Fax: 307-235-1461. Email: aloader@admin.cc.whecn.edu.

CEDAR VALLEY COLLEGE

Lancaster, Texas

LEARNING DISABILITIES SERVICES INFORMATION

Special Services began offering services in 1978. Currently the program serves 30 undergraduates with LD. Students diagnosed with ADD/ADHD are eligible for the same services available to students with LD.
Staff: 2 full-time, 3 part-time staff members, including director. Services provided by remediation specialists, tutors, counselors.
Special Fees: No special fees are charged for services to students with LD.
Applications and admissions: *Required:* high school transcript, courses completed, personal interview, autobiographical statement, psychoeducational report completed within 2 years, in-house assessment test. Students may begin taking classes any term. *Application deadline:* continuous.

PROGRAM AND SERVICE COMPONENTS

Special preparation or orientation: Optional orientation offered before registration.
Academic advising: Provided by unit staff members. Most students with LD take 9 to 12 credit hours each term; 12 credit hours required to maintain full-time status and be eligible for financial aid.
Counseling services: Individual counseling, career counseling, self-advocacy training.
Basic skills remediation: Offered one-on-one by LD teachers; computer-aided instruction also offered. Available in reading, math, written language, learning strategies.
Subject-area tutoring: Offered one-on-one and in small groups by professional teachers, peer tutors. Available in all subjects.
Auxiliary aids: Taped textbooks, tape recorders, calculators, typewriters, personal computers.
Auxiliary services: Alternative test arrangements, notetakers, priority registration, advocacy.
Campus support group: A special student organization is available to students with LD.

GENERAL COLLEGE INFORMATION

State-supported, 2-year, coed. Part of Dallas County Community College District System. Awards associate degrees. Founded 1977. *Setting:* 353-acre small-town campus with easy access to Dallas–Fort Worth. *Total enrollment:* 3,136. *Faculty:* 130 (57 full-time, 73 part-time); student–undergrad faculty ratio is 25:1.
Enrollment Profile: 3,136 students from 2 states and territories, 1 other country. 57% women, 43% men, 74% part-time, 98% state residents, 32% transferred in, 1% international, 1% Native American, 7% Hispanic, 42% black, 1% Asian or Pacific Islander. *Most popular recent majors:* liberal arts/general studies, veterinary technology, automotive technologies.
First-Year Class: 2,314 total. Of the students who applied, 100% were accepted.
Graduation Requirements: 61 semester hours; 3 semester hours of college math; 8 semester hours of lab science.
Computers on Campus: 50 computers available on campus for general student use. Computers for student use in computer labs.

EXPENSES AND FINANCIAL AID

Expenses for 1997–98: Area resident tuition: $650 full-time. State resident tuition: $1030 full-time. Nonresident tuition: $2140 full-time. Part-time tuition per credit ranges from $79 to $245 for area residents, $136 to $435 for state residents, $226 to $786 for nonresidents.
Financial aid specifically for students with LD: Scholarships; loans.
LD Services Contact: Ms. Pamela Gist, Director of Special Populations, Cedar Valley College, 3030 North Dallas Avenue, Lancaster, TX 75134, 972-860-8119. Fax: 972-860-8014.

CENTRAL COMMUNITY COLLEGE–HASTINGS CAMPUS

Hastings, Nebraska

LEARNING DISABILITIES SERVICES INFORMATION

Coordinated Learning Assistance for Student Success (CLASS) began offering services in 1991. Currently the program serves 31 undergraduates with LD. Students diagnosed with ADD/ADHD are eligible for the same services available to students with LD.
Staff: Includes director, coordinators. Services provided by remediation specialists, tutors, counselors.
Special Fees: No special fees are charged for services to students with LD.
Applications and admissions: *Required:* high school transcript; *recommended:* high school IEP (Individualized Education Program), personal interview, psychoeducational report completed within 3 years. Students may begin taking classes in fall, spring, or summer. *Application deadline:* continuous.
Special policies: The college has written policies regarding grade forgiveness; substitutions and waivers of admissions, graduation, and degree requirements.

PROGRAM AND SERVICE COMPONENTS

Special preparation or orientation: Optional summer program offered prior to entering college.
Diagnostic testing: Reading, math, spelling, handwriting, spoken language, written language, study skills, learning strategies.
Academic advising: Provided by unit staff members, academic advisers. Students with LD may take up to 16 credits each term; most take 6 to 12 credits; 12 credits required to maintain full-time status; 6 credits required to be eligible for financial aid.
Counseling services: Individual counseling, career counseling, self-advocacy training.
Basic skills remediation: Offered one-on-one, in small groups, and in class-size groups by regular teachers, prescriptive instructors. Available in reading, math, written language, learning strategies, study skills.
Subject-area tutoring: Offered one-on-one and in small groups by peer tutors. Available in most subjects.
Special courses: College survival skills, reading, vocabulary development, communication skills, math, study skills, career planning. Most offered for credit; some enter into overall grade point average.
Auxiliary aids: Taped textbooks, typewriters, word-processors with spell-check, personal computers.
Auxiliary services: Alternative test arrangements.

GENERAL COLLEGE INFORMATION

State and locally supported, 2-year, coed. Part of Central Community College. Awards associate degrees. Founded 1966. *Setting:* 600-acre small-town campus. *Educational spending 1995–96:* $1397 per undergrad. *Total enrollment:* 2,812. *Faculty:* 111 (60 full-time, 2% with terminal degrees, 51 part-time); student–undergrad faculty ratio is 15:1.
Enrollment Profile: 2,812 students from 17 states and territories, 2 other countries. 53% women, 47% men, 63% part-time, 99% state residents, 26% live on campus, 6% transferred in, 82% 25 or older, 1% Native American, 1% Hispanic, 1% black, 1% Asian or Pacific Islander. *Areas of study chosen:* 28% engineering and applied sciences, 23% business management and administrative services, 16% interdisciplinary studies, 15% health professions and related sciences, 6% agriculture, 6% computer and information sciences, 2% biological and life sciences, 2% communications and journalism, 2% vocational and home economics. *Most popular recent majors:* heating/refrigeration/air conditioning, business administration/commerce/management, horticulture.
First-Year Class: 585 total; 1,286 applied, 93% were accepted. 3% from top 10% of their high school class, 13% from top quarter, 38% from top half.
Graduation Requirements: 64 credits; computer course for accounting, office technology, business administration, electronics majors; internship (some majors).
Computers on Campus: 190 computers available on campus for general student use. A campus-wide network can be accessed from off-campus. Students can contact faculty members and/or advisers through

Central Community College–Hastings Campus (continued)

e-mail. Computers for student use in computer center, computer labs, learning resource center, classrooms, library provide access to the Internet/World Wide Web. Staffed computer lab on campus provides training in use of computers, software.

EXPENSES

Expenses for 1997–98: State resident tuition: $1197 full-time, $38.60 per credit part-time. Nonresident tuition: $1795 full-time, $57.90 per credit part-time. Part-time mandatory fees: $4 per credit. Full-time mandatory fees: $128. College room and board: $2400.

LD Services Contact: Mr. Robert Shields, Counselor, Central Community College–Hastings Campus, PO Box 1024, Hastings, NE 68902, 402-461-2423. Fax: 402-461-2454.

CENTRAL COMMUNITY COLLEGE–PLATTE CAMPUS

Columbus, Nebraska

LEARNING DISABILITIES SERVICES INFORMATION

Special Populations Office began offering services in 1992. Currently the program serves 12 undergraduates with LD. Students diagnosed with ADD/ADHD are eligible for the same services available to students with LD.

Staff: 1 full-time, 1 part-time staff members, including director, staff assistant/secretary. Services provided by remediation specialists, tutors, counselor.

Special Fees: No special fees are charged for services to students with LD.

Applications and admissions: *Required:* high school transcript, grade point average, class rank, courses completed; *recommended:* untimed ACT. Students may begin taking classes in fall, winter, or summer. *Application deadline:* continuous.

Special policies: The college has written policies regarding grade forgiveness.

PROGRAM AND SERVICE COMPONENTS

Special preparation or orientation: Optional summer program offered prior to entering college.

Diagnostic testing: Reading, math, spelling, written language, study skills, learning strategies.

Academic advising: Provided by unit staff members. Students with LD may take up to 12 credit hours each term; most take 6 to 9 credit hours; 12 credit hours required to maintain full-time status; 6 credit hours required to be eligible for financial aid.

Counseling services: Individual counseling, career counseling, self-advocacy training.

Basic skills remediation: Offered in small groups and in class-size groups by regular teachers, lab assistants/tutors; computer-aided instruction also offered. Available in reading, math, spelling, learning strategies, study skills, time management.

Subject-area tutoring: Offered one-on-one and in small groups by professional teachers, peer tutors. Available in most subjects.

Special courses: Learning strategies, time management, study skills, career planning. None offered for credit.

Auxiliary aids: Taped textbooks, tape recorders, calculators, typewriters, word-processors with spell-check, personal computers, Language Masters, Arkenstone Reader.

Auxiliary services: Alternative test arrangements, notetakers, advocacy.

GENERAL COLLEGE INFORMATION

State and locally supported, 2-year, coed. Part of Central Community College. Awards associate degrees. Founded 1968. *Setting:* 90-acre rural campus. *Educational spending 1995–96:* $737 per undergrad. *Total enrollment:* 2,154. *Faculty:* 100 (36 full-time, 6% with terminal degrees, 64 part-time); student–undergrad faculty ratio is 15:1.

Enrollment Profile: 2,154 students from 9 states and territories. 59% women, 41% men, 66% part-time, 98% state residents, 17% live on campus, 10% transferred in, 1% international, 82% 25 or older, 1% Native American, 1% Hispanic, 1% black, 1% Asian or Pacific Islander. *Areas of study chosen:* 25% business management and administrative services, 20% engineering and applied sciences, 12% interdisciplinary studies, 10% agriculture, 9% education, 5% health professions and related sciences, 4% architecture, 4% fine arts, 3% computer and information sciences, 2% psychology, 2% social sciences, 2% vocational and home economics, 1% biological and life sciences, 1% communications and journalism, 1% mathematics, 1% physical sciences. *Most popular recent majors:* business administration/commerce/management, agricultural business, data processing.

First-Year Class: 341 total; 524 applied, 95% were accepted. 3% from top 10% of their high school class, 13% from top quarter, 38% from top half.

Graduation Requirements: 64 credits; computer course for accounting, office technology, business administration, electronics majors; internship (some majors).

Computers on Campus: 100 computers available on campus for general student use. A campus-wide network can be accessed from student residence rooms and from off-campus. Students can contact faculty members and/or advisers through e-mail. Computers for student use in computer center, computer labs, research center, learning resource center, classrooms, library, student rooms provide access to the Internet/World Wide Web. Staffed computer lab on campus provides training in use of computers, software.

EXPENSES

Expenses for 1997–98: State resident tuition: $1197 full-time, $38.60 per credit part-time. Nonresident tuition: $1795 full-time, $57.90 per credit part-time. Part-time mandatory fees: $4 per credit. Full-time mandatory fees: $128. College room and board: $2400.

LD Services Contact: Ms. Michele Lutz, Special Populations Director, Central Community College–Platte Campus, 4500 63rd Street, Columbus, NE 68601, 402-564-7132 Ext. 240. Fax: 402-562-1201. Email: lutpsts@cccadm.gi.cccneb.edu.

CENTRAL FLORIDA COMMUNITY COLLEGE

Ocala, Florida

LEARNING DISABILITIES SERVICES INFORMATION

Disabled Student Services, System for Applied Individualized Learning (SAIL) began offering services in 1982. Currently the program serves 95 undergraduates with LD. Students diagnosed with ADD/ADHD are eligible for the same services available to students with LD.

Staff: 4 full-time, 12 part-time staff members, including director, coordinator, staff assistants. Services provided by tutors, counselor, notetakers, readers, scribes, lab assistants, interpreters.

Special Fees: No special fees are charged for services to students with LD.

Applications and admissions: *Required:* high school transcript; *recommended:* high school IEP (Individualized Education Program), psychoeducational report. Students may begin taking classes any term. *Application deadline:* continuous.

Special policies: The college has written policies regarding grade forgiveness; substitutions and waivers of admissions, graduation, and degree requirements.

PROGRAM AND SERVICE COMPONENTS

Diagnostic testing: Intelligence, reading, math, written language, motor abilities, perceptual skills, study skills, personality, learning strategies.

Academic advising: Provided by unit staff members, academic advisers. Students with LD may take up to 18 credit hours each term; most take 6 to 12 credit hours; 12 credit hours required to maintain full-time status; 9 credit hours required to be eligible for financial aid.

Counseling services: Individual counseling, small-group counseling, career counseling, self-advocacy training.

Basic skills remediation: Offered one-on-one, in small groups, and in class-size groups by regular teachers, teacher trainees, honor students, paraprofessionals; computer-aided instruction also offered. Available in reading, math, spelling, written language, learning strategies, motor abilities, perceptual skills, study skills, time management.

Subject-area tutoring: Offered one-on-one and in small groups by peer tutors, honor students, selected paraprofessionals. Available in all subjects.

Auxiliary aids: Taped textbooks, tape recorders, typewriters, word-processors with spell-check, personal computers, optical character readers.

Auxiliary services: Alternative test arrangements, notetakers, priority registration, advocacy, scribes.

Campus support group: A special student organization is available to students with LD.

GENERAL COLLEGE INFORMATION

State and locally supported, 2-year, coed. Part of Florida Community Colleges System. Awards associate degrees. Founded 1957. *Setting:* 120-acre small-town campus. *Endowment:* $4.1 million. *Total enrollment:* 6,010. *Faculty:* 213 (92 full-time, 17% with terminal degrees, 121 part-time).

Enrollment Profile: 6,010 students: 62% women, 38% men, 61% part-time, 97% state residents, 15% transferred in, 1% international, 1% Native American, 5% Hispanic, 10% black, 2% Asian or Pacific Islander. *Areas of study chosen:* 20% vocational and home economics, 19% business management and administrative services, 15% education, 12% liberal arts/general studies, 10% health professions and related sciences, 2% engineering and applied sciences, 2% physical sciences, 1% interdisciplinary studies. *Most popular recent majors:* business administration/commerce/management, education, liberal arts/general studies.

First-Year Class: 734 total; 1,900 applied, 100% were accepted, 39% of whom enrolled.

Graduation Requirements: 60 credit hours; internship (some majors).

Computers on Campus: 175 computers available on campus for general student use. Computers for student use in computer labs, classrooms, skills lab provide access to the Internet/World Wide Web. Staffed computer lab on campus provides training in use of computers, software. *Academic computing expenditure 1995–96:* $462,418.

EXPENSES

Estimated Expenses for 1997–98: *Application fee:* $20. State resident tuition: $1228 full-time, $40.92 per credit hour part-time. Nonresident tuition: $4408 full-time, $146.94 per credit hour part-time.

LD Services Contact: Ms. Gina McGrath, Student Support Specialist, Central Florida Community College, PO Box 1388, Ocala, FL 34478, 352-237-2111 Ext. 246. Fax: 352-237-3747.

CENTRALIA COLLEGE

Centralia, Washington

LEARNING DISABILITIES SERVICES INFORMATION

Special Needs Office began offering services in 1982. Currently the program serves 48 undergraduates with LD. Students diagnosed with ADD/ADHD are eligible for the same services available to students with LD, as well as closed-circuit radio broadcasting (between lecturer and student).

Staff: 1 part-time staff member (coordinator). Services provided by remediation specialists, tutors, counselors, computer technician, readers, writers, sign language interpreters.

Special Fees: No special fees are charged for services to students with LD.

Applications and admissions: *Required:* high school transcript, psychoeducational report completed within 3 years, high school LD specialist's report, untimed ASSET test; *recommended:* high school IEP (Individualized Education Program). Students may begin taking classes any term. *Application deadline:* continuous.

Special policies: The college has written policies regarding grade forgiveness; substitutions and waivers of graduation and degree requirements.

PROGRAM AND SERVICE COMPONENTS

Special preparation or orientation: Optional orientation offered before registration and individually by special arrangement.

Academic advising: Provided by unit staff members, academic advisers. Students with LD may take up to as many credits as an individual can handle each term; most take 6 to 12 credits; 10 credits required to maintain full-time status; 6 credits required to be eligible for financial aid.

Counseling services: Individual counseling, small-group counseling, career counseling, self-advocacy training.

Basic skills remediation: Offered one-on-one, in small groups, and in class-size groups by LD teachers, regular teachers, teacher aides; computer-aided instruction also offered. Available in reading, math, spelling, handwriting, written language, learning strategies, study skills, time management, social skills.

Subject-area tutoring: Offered one-on-one and in small groups by professional teachers, peer tutors. Available in all subjects.

Auxiliary aids: Taped textbooks, tape recorders, calculators, typewriters, word-processors with spell-check, personal computers, optical character readers, spell checkers, voice-activated computer.

Auxiliary services: Alternative test arrangements, notetakers, priority registration, advocacy, readers, scribes.

GENERAL COLLEGE INFORMATION

State-supported, 2-year, coed. Part of Washington State Board for Community and Technical Colleges. Awards associate degrees. Founded 1925. *Setting:* 12-acre small-town campus. *Total enrollment:* 1,800. *Faculty:* 121 (56 full-time, 65 part-time); student–undergrad faculty ratio is 20:1.

Enrollment Profile: 1,800 students from 12 states and territories, 7 other countries. 60% women, 40% men, 5% part-time, 98% state residents, 2% transferred in, 1% international, 69% 25 or older, 1% Native American, 1% Hispanic, 1% black, 1% Asian or Pacific Islander.

First-Year Class: 960 total; 1,050 applied, 100% were accepted, 91% of whom enrolled.

Graduation Requirements: 93 credits; 1 math course; computer course for engineering majors.

Computers on Campus: 35 computers available on campus for general student use. Computer purchase/lease plans available. A campus-wide network can be accessed from off-campus. Students can contact faculty members and/or advisers through e-mail. Computers for student use in library, instructional labs, learning skills center provide access to the Internet/World Wide Web, on- and off-campus e-mail addresses. Staffed computer lab on campus provides training in use of computers, software.

EXPENSES

Expenses for 1996–97: State resident tuition: $1401 full-time, $46.70 per credit part-time. Nonresident tuition: $5511 full-time, $183.70 per credit part-time. Part-time mandatory fees: $5 per quarter. Full-time mandatory fees: $15.

LD Services Contact: Ms. Kay Odegaard, Coordinator, Special Needs Office, Centralia College, 600 West Locust, Centralia, WA 98531, 360-736-9391 Ext. 320. Fax: 360-330-7503.

CENTRAL LAKES COLLEGE

Brainerd, Minnesota

LEARNING DISABILITIES SERVICES INFORMATION

Academic Center for Enrichment (ACE) began offering services in 1989. Currently the program serves 80 undergraduates with LD. Students diagnosed with ADD/ADHD are eligible for the same services available to students with LD.

Staff: 7 full-time, 3 part-time staff members, including director, coordinators, technical tutors, secretary. Services provided by remediation specialists, tutors, counselors.

Special Fees: No special fees are charged for services to students with LD.

Applications and admissions: *Required:* high school transcript, psychoeducational report completed within 3 years; *recommended:* high school grade point average, class rank, courses completed, extracurricular activities, IEP (Individualized Education Program), untimed or extended time SAT I or ACT, personal interview, autobiographical statement, letters of recommendation. Students may begin taking classes any term. *Application deadline:* continuous.

PROGRAM AND SERVICE COMPONENTS

Academic advising: Provided by unit staff members. Students with LD may take up to 16 credits each term; most take 12 credits; 12 credits required to maintain full-time status and be eligible for financial aid.

Counseling services: Individual counseling, career counseling.

Basic skills remediation: Offered one-on-one by regular teachers; computer-aided instruction also offered. Available in reading, math, spelling, written language, learning strategies, study skills, time management, computer skills.

Subject-area tutoring: Offered one-on-one by professional teachers, peer tutors, technical tutors. Available in some subjects.

Auxiliary aids: Taped textbooks, tape recorders, word-processors with spell-check, talking computers, optical character readers.

Auxiliary services: Alternative test arrangements, notetakers, priority registration.

Central Lakes College (continued)

GENERAL COLLEGE INFORMATION

State-supported, 2-year, coed. Part of Minnesota State Colleges and Universities System. Awards associate degrees. Founded 1938. *Setting:* 1-acre small-town campus. *Total enrollment:* 3,300. *Faculty:* 140 (1% of full-time faculty have terminal degrees).
Enrollment Profile: 3,300 students: 62% women, 38% men, 52% part-time, 99% state residents, 20% transferred in, 45% 25 or older, 1% Native American, 1% Hispanic, 1% black, 1% Asian or Pacific Islander.
First-Year Class: 1,679 total. Of the students who applied, 100% were accepted, 93% of whom enrolled.
Graduation Requirements: 96 credits; 4 credits of math.
Computers on Campus: 100 computers available on campus for general student use. A campus-wide network can be accessed. Students can contact faculty members and/or advisers through e-mail. Computers for student use in computer center provide access to the Internet/World Wide Web, on- and off-campus e-mail addresses. Staffed computer lab on campus provides training in use of computers, software.

EXPENSES

Expenses for 1996–97: *Application fee:* $20. State resident tuition: $1997 full-time, $41.60 per credit part-time. Nonresident tuition: $3994 full-time, $83.20 per credit part-time. Part-time mandatory fees: $4.42 per credit. North Dakota, South Dakota and Wisconsin residents pay tuition at the rate they would pay if attending a comparable state-supported institution in their home state. Full-time mandatory fees: $212.
LD Services Contact: Ms. Karen Tharson, Disabilities Coordinator, Central Lakes College, 501 West College Drive, Brainerd, MN 56401, 218-828-2508. Fax: 218-828-2710.

CENTRAL TEXAS COLLEGE

Killeen, Texas

LEARNING DISABILITIES SERVICES INFORMATION

Disability Support Services currently serves 400 undergraduates with LD. Students diagnosed with ADD/ADHD are eligible for the same services available to students with LD.
Staff: 3 full-time, 5 part-time staff members, including coordinators. Services provided by remediation specialists, counselors.
Special Fees: No special fees are charged for services to students with LD.
Applications and admissions: *Required:* high school transcript, psychoeducational report completed within 5 years. Students may begin taking classes in fall, spring, or summer. *Application deadline:* continuous.
Special policies: The college has written policies regarding grade forgiveness; substitutions and waivers of admissions, graduation, and degree requirements.

PROGRAM AND SERVICE COMPONENTS

Special preparation or orientation: Required orientation held on an individual basis.
Academic advising: Provided by unit staff members, academic advisers. Students with LD may take up to 12 semester hours each term; most take 6 to 9 semester hours; 12 semester hours (full-time), 8 semester hours (summer session) required to be eligible for financial aid.
Counseling services: Individual counseling, small-group counseling, career counseling.
Auxiliary aids: Taped textbooks, tape recorders, calculators, word-processors with spell-check, personal computers, Book Wise.
Auxiliary services: Alternative test arrangements, notetakers, priority registration, advocacy.

GENERAL COLLEGE INFORMATION

State and locally supported, 2-year, coed. Part of Texas Higher Education Coordinating Board. Awards associate degrees. Founded 1967. *Setting:* 500-acre suburban campus with easy access to Austin. *Total enrollment:* 8,600. *Faculty:* 328 (120 full-time, 20% with terminal degrees, 208 part-time); student–undergrad faculty ratio is 27:1.
Enrollment Profile: 8,600 students from 48 states and territories, 19 other countries. 48% women, 52% men, 70% part-time, 77% state residents, 1% live on campus, 17% transferred in, 2% international, 55% 25 or older, 1% Native American, 11% Hispanic, 27% black, 4% Asian or Pacific Islander. *Areas of study chosen:* 36% liberal arts/general studies, 20% business management and administrative services, 9% health professions and related sciences, 5% social sciences, 4% computer and information sciences, 2% education, 2% engineering and applied sciences, 1% agriculture, 1% communications and journalism.
First-Year Class: 1,043 total. Of the students who applied, 100% were accepted, 75% of whom enrolled.
Graduation Requirements: 64 semester hours; 1 college algebra course; computer course; internship (some majors).
Computers on Campus: 120 computers available on campus for general student use. A campus-wide network can be accessed from student residence rooms and from off-campus. Students can contact faculty members and/or advisers through e-mail. Computers for student use in computer center, computer labs, learning resource center, classrooms, library provide access to the Internet/World Wide Web. Staffed computer lab on campus provides training in use of computers, software.

EXPENSES

Expenses for 1996–97: State resident tuition: $640 full-time. Nonresident tuition: $1600 full-time. Part-time tuition per semester ranges from $60 to $220 for state residents, $250 to $550 for nonresidents. Part-time mandatory fees: $8 per semester hour. Full-time mandatory fees: $256. College room and board: $3252.
LD Services Contact: Mr. José R. Aponte, Counselor/Coordinator of Disability Support Services, Central Texas College, PO Box 1800, Killeen, TX 76540-9990, 254-526-1339. Fax: 254-526-0817.

CENTURY COMMUNITY AND TECHNICAL COLLEGE

White Bear Lake, Minnesota

LEARNING DISABILITIES SERVICES INFORMATION

Access Center/Learning Skills Center began offering services in 1992. Currently the program serves 150 undergraduates with LD. Students diagnosed with ADD/ADHD are eligible for the same services available to students with LD.
Staff: 6 full-time, 2 part-time staff members, including director, assistant director, college lab assistants, secretary. Services provided by remediation specialists, counselor, lab assistant.
Special Fees: No special fees are charged for services to students with LD.
Applications and admissions: *Required:* high school transcript; *recommended:* high school IEP (Individualized Education Program), psychoeducational report. Students may begin taking classes in fall only. *Application deadline:* continuous.
Special policies: The college has written policies regarding grade forgiveness; substitutions and waivers of admissions, graduation, and degree requirements.

PROGRAM AND SERVICE COMPONENTS

Special preparation or orientation: Orientation (required for some) held before registration.
Academic advising: Provided by unit staff members, academic advisers. Most students with LD take 10 to 12 credits each term; 12 credits required to maintain full-time status; source of aid determines number of credits required to be eligible for financial aid.
Counseling services: Career counseling, academic counseling.
Basic skills remediation: Offered one-on-one and in small groups by regular teachers, supplemental resource instructors, lab assistants; computer-aided instruction also offered. Available in reading, math, spelling, written language, learning strategies, study skills, time management, computer skills.
Subject-area tutoring: Offered one-on-one and in small groups by professional teachers, lab assistants. Available in most subjects.
Special courses: College survival skills, reading, learning strategies, Internet use, time management, math, study skills, career planning. Some offered for credit; some enter into overall grade point average.
Auxiliary aids: Taped textbooks, tape recorders, calculators, word-processors with spell-check, talking computers, optical character readers.
Auxiliary services: Alternative test arrangements, notetakers, priority registration, advocacy.
Campus support group: A special student organization is available to students with LD.

GENERAL COLLEGE INFORMATION

State-supported, 2-year, coed. Part of Minnesota State Colleges and Universities System. Awards associate degrees. Founded 1970. *Setting:*

150-acre suburban campus with easy access to Minneapolis–St. Paul. *Total enrollment:* 7,000. *Faculty:* 280 (180 full-time, 20% with terminal degrees, 100 part-time); student–undergrad faculty ratio is 18:1.
Enrollment Profile: 7,000 students: 55% women, 45% men, 60% part-time, 90% state residents, 1% international, 65% 25 or older, 1% Native American, 1% Hispanic, 3% black, 5% Asian or Pacific Islander. *Retention:* 51% of 1995 full-time freshmen returned.
First-Year Class: 2,200 total; 3,500 applied, 100% were accepted, 63% of whom enrolled.
Graduation Requirements: 96 credits; internship (some majors).
Computers on Campus: 180 computers available on campus for general student use. A computer is recommended for all students. Computers for student use in computer center, classrooms, student rooms provide access to the Internet/World Wide Web, on-campus e-mail addresses. Staffed computer lab on campus provides training in use of computers, software.

EXPENSES

Expenses for 1996–97: *Application fee:* $20. Full-time tuition ranges from $2273 to $2276 for state residents, $4248 to $4292 for nonresidents, according to program. Part-time tuition per credit ranges from $47.35 to $47.42 for state residents, $88.50 to $89.42 for nonresidents, according to program.
LD Services Contact: Ms. Mary C. Bataglia, Director, Century Community and Technical College, 3300 Century Avenue North, White Bear Lake, MN 55110, 612-779-3355. Fax: 612-773-1746. Email: m.bataglia@cctc.mn.us.

CHARLES COUNTY COMMUNITY COLLEGE

La Plata, Maryland

LEARNING DISABILITIES SERVICES INFORMATION

Learning Assistance Center currently serves undergraduate students with LD. Students diagnosed with ADD/ADHD are eligible for the same services available to students with LD.
Staff: 3 full-time, 1 part-time staff members, including director, coordinator, office manager. Services provided by remediation specialist, tutors, diagnostic specialist, learning assistant.
Special Fees: No special fees are charged for services to students with LD.
Applications and admissions: *Recommended:* high school transcript, grade point average, courses completed, extracurricular activities, IEP (Individualized Education Program), untimed SAT I or extended time ACT, personal interview, psychoeducational report completed within 3 years. Students may begin taking classes in fall, spring, or summer. *Application deadline:* continuous.
Special policies: The college has written policies regarding grade forgiveness; substitutions and waivers of admissions, graduation, and degree requirements.

PROGRAM AND SERVICE COMPONENTS

Academic advising: Provided by unit staff members, academic advisers. Students with LD may take up to 18 credits each term.
Counseling services: Individual counseling, career counseling.
Auxiliary aids: Taped textbooks, tape recorders, calculators, typewriters, word-processors with spell-check, optical character readers, laptop computers, Dragon Dictate, Soundproof software, Magic Deluxe software.
Auxiliary services: Alternative test arrangements, notetakers, advocacy, advanced registration.

GENERAL COLLEGE INFORMATION

State and locally supported, 2-year, coed. Awards associate degrees. Founded 1958. *Setting:* 175-acre rural campus with easy access to Washington, DC. *Total enrollment:* 5,879. *Faculty:* 355 (76 full-time, 279 part-time).
Enrollment Profile: 5,879 students: 66% women, 34% men, 73% part-time, 98% state residents, 2% international, 60% 25 or older, 1% Native American, 1% Hispanic, 11% black, 2% Asian or Pacific Islander. *Retention:* 44% of 1995 full-time freshmen returned. *Most popular recent majors:* liberal arts/general studies, business administration/commerce/management, nursing.
First-Year Class: 1,751 total.
Graduation Requirements: 62 credits; 1 math course.
Computers on Campus: 130 computers available on campus for general student use. Computer purchase/lease plans available. A campus-wide network can be accessed. Computers for student use in computer labs, learning resource center, library. Staffed computer lab on campus provides training in use of computers, software.

EXPENSES

Expenses for 1997–98: *Application fee:* $20. Area resident tuition: $2015 full-time, $65 per credit part-time. State resident tuition: $4433 full-time, $143 per credit part-time. Nonresident tuition: $6851 full-time, $221 per credit part-time. Part-time mandatory fees: $13 per credit. Full-time mandatory fees: $403.
LD Services Contact: Dr. Jay Marciano, Learning Specialist, Charles County Community College, Mitchell Road, PO Box 910, La Plata, MD 20646-0910, 301-934-2251 Ext. 7614. Fax: 301-934-0779.

CHARLES STEWART MOTT COMMUNITY COLLEGE

Flint, Michigan

LEARNING DISABILITIES SERVICES INFORMATION

Disability Services for Students began offering services in 1980. Currently the program serves 60 undergraduates with LD. Students diagnosed with ADD/ADHD are eligible for the same services available to students with LD.
Staff: 3 full-time, 2 part-time staff members, including director, coordinators. Services provided by tutors, advisers, special needs counselors.
Special Fees: No special fees are charged for services to students with LD.
Applications and admissions: *Required:* psychoeducational report; *recommended:* high school transcript, IEP (Individualized Education Program). Students may begin taking classes any term. *Application deadline:* continuous.
Special policies: The college has written policies regarding grade forgiveness.

PROGRAM AND SERVICE COMPONENTS

Special preparation or orientation: Optional orientation offered before registration.
Academic advising: Provided by unit staff members, academic advisers. Students with LD may take up to 12 credit hours each term; most take 6 credit hours; 12 credit hours required to maintain full-time status; 6 credit hours required to be eligible for financial aid.
Counseling services: Individual counseling, self-advocacy training.
Basic skills remediation: Offered in class-size groups by regular teachers; computer-aided instruction also offered. Available in reading, math, spelling, written language, study skills.
Subject-area tutoring: Offered one-on-one by peer tutors, professional tutors. Available in some subjects.
Auxiliary aids: Taped textbooks, tape recorders, word-processors with spell-check, personal computers, talking computers, optical character readers, spell checkers, personal FM system.
Auxiliary services: Alternative test arrangements, notetakers, advocacy.

GENERAL COLLEGE INFORMATION

District-supported, 2-year, coed. Part of Michigan Department of Education. Awards associate degrees. Founded 1923. *Setting:* 20-acre urban campus with easy access to Detroit. *Endowment:* $22.5 million. *Educational spending 1995–96:* $1609 per undergrad. *Total enrollment:* 9,009. *Faculty:* 420 (157 full-time, 14% with terminal degrees, 263 part-time); student–undergrad faculty ratio is 24:1.
Enrollment Profile: 9,009 students: 61% women, 39% men, 73% part-time, 99% state residents, 3% transferred in, 1% international, 49% 25 or older, 2% Native American, 2% Hispanic, 16% black, 1% Asian or Pacific Islander.
First-Year Class: 1,916 total; 4,222 applied, 100% were accepted, 45% of whom enrolled.
Graduation Requirements: 62 credit hours; math/science requirements vary according to program; computer course (varies by major).
Computers on Campus: 250 computers available on campus for general student use. A campus-wide network can be accessed from off-campus. Students can contact faculty members and/or advisers through e-mail. Computers for student use in computer center, computer labs, classrooms, library provide access to the Internet/World Wide Web, on-

Charles Stewart Mott Community College (continued)

and off-campus e-mail addresses. Staffed computer lab on campus provides training in use of computers, software. *Academic computing expenditure 1995–96:* $926,163.

EXPENSES

Expenses for 1997–98: Area resident tuition: $1752 full-time, $56.50 per credit hour part-time. State resident tuition: $2527 full-time, $81.50 per credit hour part-time. Nonresident tuition: $3368 full-time, $108.65 per credit hour part-time. Part-time mandatory fees: $41.75 per semester. Full-time mandatory fees: $84.

LD Services Contact: Mr. Michael Littlejohn, Support Service Coordinator, Charles Stewart Mott Community College, 1401 East Court Street, Flint, MI 48503-2089, 810-762-0399. Fax: 810-762-0407.

CHEMEKETA COMMUNITY COLLEGE

Salem, Oregon

LEARNING DISABILITIES SERVICES INFORMATION

Services for Students with Disabilities began offering services in 1974. Currently the program serves 100 undergraduates with LD. Students diagnosed with ADD/ADHD are eligible for the same services available to students with LD.

Staff: 1 full-time, 1 part-time staff members, including director, coordinator. Services provided by tutors, counselors, diagnostic specialist.

Special Fees: No special fees are charged for services to students with LD.

Applications and admissions: *Required:* high school transcript, courses completed, IEP (Individualized Education Program); *recommended:* personal interview, psychoeducational report completed within 2 years, transition plan. Students may begin taking classes any term. *Application deadline:* continuous.

Special policies: The college has written policies regarding grade forgiveness; substitutions and waivers of admissions, graduation, and degree requirements.

PROGRAM AND SERVICE COMPONENTS

Special preparation or orientation: Optional orientation offered before registration and during registration.

Diagnostic testing: Intelligence, reading, math, spelling, handwriting, spoken language, written language, motor abilities, perceptual skills, study skills, hearing, learning strategies.

Academic advising: Provided by academic advisers. Students with LD may take up to 12 hours each term; most take 6 to 12 hours; 12 hours required to maintain full-time status; 6 hours required to be eligible for financial aid.

Counseling services: Individual counseling, career counseling, self-advocacy training.

Basic skills remediation: Offered one-on-one and in small groups by regular teachers; computer-aided instruction also offered. Available in reading, math, spelling, written language, learning strategies, study skills.

Subject-area tutoring: Offered one-on-one by professional teachers, professional tutors. Available in most subjects.

Special courses: College survival skills, reading, vocabulary development, communication skills, composition, learning strategies, word processing, time management, math, study skills, career planning, stress management. Most offered for credit; all enter into overall grade point average.

Auxiliary aids: Taped textbooks, tape recorders, calculators, typewriters, word-processors with spell-check, personal computers, talking computers, optical character readers.

Auxiliary services: Alternative test arrangements, notetakers, priority registration, advocacy.

GENERAL COLLEGE INFORMATION

State and locally supported, 2-year, coed. Awards associate degrees. Founded 1955. *Setting:* 72-acre urban campus with easy access to Portland. *Total enrollment:* 9,033. *Faculty:* 685 (240 full-time, 445 part-time); student–undergrad faculty ratio is 15:1.

Enrollment Profile: 9,033 students from 5 states and territories, 17 other countries. 57% women, 43% men, 80% part-time, 98% state residents, 2% international, 61% 25 or older, 2% Native American, 11% Hispanic, 1% black, 3% Asian or Pacific Islander. *Areas of study chosen:* 42% liberal arts/general studies, 10% business management and administrative services, 10% vocational and home economics, 9% health professions and related sciences, 6% social sciences, 4% computer and information sciences, 4% education, 3% engineering and applied sciences, 2% communications and journalism, 1% natural resource sciences, 1% physical sciences. *Most popular recent majors:* liberal arts/general studies, nursing, practical nursing.

First-Year Class: 5,871 total; 11,233 applied, 100% were accepted, 52% of whom enrolled.

Graduation Requirements: 90 credit hours; 1 math course; computer course; internship (some majors).

Computers on Campus: 325 computers available on campus for general student use. Computer purchase/lease plans available. A campus-wide network can be accessed from off-campus. Computers for student use in computer center, computer labs, classrooms, library provide access to the Internet/World Wide Web. Staffed computer lab on campus provides training in use of computers, software.

EXPENSES

Expenses for 1997–98: State resident tuition: $1530 full-time, $34 per credit hour part-time. Nonresident tuition: $5400 full-time, $120 per credit hour part-time.

LD Services Contact: Mr. Michael Duggan, Disabilities Specialist, Chemeketa Community College, PO Box 14007, Salem, OR 97309-7070, 503-399-5192. Fax: 503-399-2519. Email: dugm@chemek.cc.or.us.

CHIPOLA JUNIOR COLLEGE

Marianna, Florida

LEARNING DISABILITIES SERVICES INFORMATION

Disabled Student Services began offering services in 1985. Currently the program serves 29 undergraduates with LD. Students diagnosed with ADD/ADHD are eligible for the same services available to students with LD.

Staff: 2 full-time staff members, including Dean. Services provided by counselor, instructional aide.

Special Fees: No special fees are charged for services to students with LD.

Applications and admissions: *Required:* high school transcript, untimed SAT I or ACT, psychoeducational report completed within 2 years; *recommended:* high school grade point average, courses completed, extracurricular activities, extended time SAT I or ACT, personal interview. Students may begin taking classes any term. *Application deadline:* 8/5 (fall term), 12/7 (spring term).

Special policies: The college has written policies regarding grade forgiveness; substitutions and waivers of admissions, graduation, and degree requirements.

PROGRAM AND SERVICE COMPONENTS

Academic advising: Provided by unit staff members, academic advisers. Most students with LD take 9 to 12 semester hours each term; 12 semester hours required to maintain full-time status and be eligible for financial aid.

Counseling services: Individual counseling, career counseling.

Basic skills remediation: Offered one-on-one and in small groups by regular teachers, reading specialist. Available in reading, math, spelling, written language, study skills, time management.

Subject-area tutoring: Offered one-on-one by peer tutors. Available in all subjects.

Special courses: Reading, communication skills, word processing, math, typing, study skills. All offered for credit; all enter into overall grade point average.

Auxiliary aids: Taped textbooks, tape recorders, calculators, word-processors with spell-check, spell checkers, copy machines.

Auxiliary services: Alternative test arrangements, notetakers, registration assistance.

GENERAL COLLEGE INFORMATION

State-supported, 2-year, coed. Awards associate degrees. Founded 1947. *Setting:* 105-acre small-town campus. *Total enrollment:* 2,357. *Faculty:* 142 (79 full-time, 2% with terminal degrees, 63 part-time); student–undergrad faculty ratio is 22:1.

Enrollment Profile: 2,357 students from 9 states and territories, 6 other countries. 52% women, 48% men, 69% part-time, 95% state residents, 3% transferred in, 1% international, 1% Hispanic, 16% black, 1% Asian or Pacific Islander. *Retention:* 59% of 1995 full-time freshmen returned. *Most popular recent majors:* business administration/commerce/management, nursing, education.

First-Year Class: 560 total; 625 applied, 100% were accepted, 90% of whom enrolled.
Graduation Requirements: 60 semester hours; 6 semester hours each of math and science.
Computers on Campus: 80 computers available on campus for general student use. Computers for student use in computer labs, library.

EXPENSES

Expenses for 1996–97: State resident tuition: $1120 full-time, $37.34 per semester hour part-time. Nonresident tuition: $4301 full-time, $143.38 per semester hour part-time. College room and board: $2464. College room only: $1100.
LD Services Contact: Mr. Alfonsa James, Disabled Student Services Counselor, Chipola Junior College, 3094 Indian Circle, Marianna, FL 32446-2053, 904-718-2215. Fax: 904-718-2255. Email: james_a@popmail.firn.edu.

CISCO JUNIOR COLLEGE

Cisco, Texas

LEARNING DISABILITIES SERVICES INFORMATION

Student Services began offering services in 1978. Currently the program serves 12 undergraduates with LD. Students diagnosed with ADD/ADHD are eligible for the same services available to students with LD.
Staff: 6 full-time, 10 part-time staff members, including co-directors. Services provided by tutors, counselors.
Special Fees: No special fees are charged for services to students with LD.
Applications and admissions: *Required:* high school transcript. Students may begin taking classes in fall, spring, or summer. *Application deadline:* continuous.
Special policies: The college has written policies regarding substitutions and waivers of admissions requirements.

PROGRAM AND SERVICE COMPONENTS

Academic advising: Provided by unit staff members, academic advisers. Students with LD may take up to 18 credit hours each term; most take 12 credit hours; 12 credit hours required to maintain full-time status; 6 credit hours required to be eligible for financial aid.
Counseling services: Individual counseling, small-group counseling, career counseling.
Basic skills remediation: Offered one-on-one, in small groups, and in class-size groups by regular teachers. Available in reading, math, spelling, learning strategies.
Subject-area tutoring: Offered one-on-one and in small groups by peer tutors. Available in all subjects.
Special courses: College survival skills, reading, vocabulary development, composition, learning strategies. Some offered for credit; some enter into overall grade point average.
Auxiliary aids: Tape recorders, calculators, typewriters, word-processors with spell-check.
Auxiliary services: Alternative test arrangements, notetakers, priority registration.

GENERAL COLLEGE INFORMATION

State and locally supported, 2-year, coed. Part of Texas Higher Education Coordinating Board. Awards associate degrees. Founded 1940. *Setting:* 40-acre rural campus. *Total enrollment:* 2,553. *Faculty:* 98 (55 full-time, 43 part-time).
Enrollment Profile: 2,553 students from 21 states and territories. 54% women, 46% men, 44% part-time, 99% state residents, 12% live on campus, 15% transferred in, 0% international, 45% 25 or older, 1% Native American, 9% Hispanic, 9% black, 2% Asian or Pacific Islander. *Retention:* 45% of 1995 full-time freshmen returned. *Most popular recent majors:* law enforcement/police sciences, education, nursing.
First-Year Class: 847 total; 847 applied, 100% were accepted, 100% of whom enrolled. 20% from top quarter of their high school class, 40% from top half.
Graduation Requirements: 63 credit hours; computer course.
Computers on Campus: 36 computers available on campus for general student use. Computers for student use in computer center, computer labs, learning resource center, library provide access to the Internet/World Wide Web. Staffed computer lab on campus provides training in use of computers.

EXPENSES

Expenses for 1996–97: Area resident tuition: $858 full-time. State resident tuition: $986 full-time. Nonresident tuition: $1292 full-time. Part-time tuition per credit ranges from $69 to $329 for area residents, $73 to $373 for state residents, $226 to $526 for nonresidents. Room and board per year: $2250 for men, $2450 for women. Full-time mandatory fees: $20.
LD Services Contact: Randy Leath, Assistant Dean of Counseling (Abilene), Cisco Junior College, 841 North Judge Ely, Abilene, TX 79601, 915-673-4567. Fax: 915-673-4575.

CITY COLLEGE OF SAN FRANCISCO

San Francisco, California

LEARNING DISABILITIES SERVICES INFORMATION

Disabled Students Program and Services began offering services in 1977. Currently the program serves 200 undergraduates with LD. Students diagnosed with ADD/ADHD are eligible for the same services available to students with LD.
Staff: 20 full-time, 40 part-time staff members, including director, coordinators. Services provided by remediation specialists, tutors, counselors, diagnostic specialists.
Special Fees: No special fees are charged for services to students with LD.
Applications and admissions: *Required:* high school IEP (Individualized Education Program), high school reports. Students may begin taking classes any term. *Application deadline:* continuous.
Special policies: The college has written policies regarding substitutions and waivers of admissions, graduation, and degree requirements.

PROGRAM AND SERVICE COMPONENTS

Special preparation or orientation: Optional orientation offered before registration and during registration.
Diagnostic testing: Intelligence, reading, math, spelling, handwriting, written language, perceptual skills, learning strategies.
Academic advising: Provided by unit staff members. Most students with LD take 12 units each term; 12 units required to maintain full-time status; 12 units (pro-rated for less) required to be eligible for financial aid.
Counseling services: Individual counseling, small-group counseling, career counseling.
Basic skills remediation: Offered in small groups by LD teachers, tutors; computer-aided instruction also offered. Available in reading, math, spelling, written language, learning strategies, study skills, time management, social skills, speech.
Subject-area tutoring: Offered in small groups by professional tutors. Available in some subjects.
Special courses: College survival skills, reading, vocabulary development, communication skills, composition, learning strategies, word processing, Internet use, typing, study skills, career planning, disability law. Some offered for credit.
Auxiliary aids: Taped textbooks, tape recorders, calculators, word-processors with spell-check, personal computers, talking computers, optical character readers.
Auxiliary services: Alternative test arrangements, notetakers, priority registration, advocacy.

GENERAL COLLEGE INFORMATION

State and locally supported, 2-year, coed. Part of California Community Colleges System. Awards associate degrees. Founded 1935. *Setting:* 56-acre urban campus. *Faculty:* 1,117 (479 full-time, 638 part-time).
Enrollment Profile: 57% women, 43% men, 76% part-time, 94% state residents, 16% transferred in, 4% international, 56% 25 or older, 1% Native American, 14% Hispanic, 7% black, 49% Asian or Pacific Islander.
First-Year Class: Of the students who applied, 100% were accepted.
Graduation Requirements: 60 units; math proficiency; computer course for science majors.
Computers on Campus: Computers for student use in computer labs, departmental labs. Staffed computer lab on campus.

EXPENSES

Expenses for 1997–98: State resident tuition: $0 full-time. Nonresident tuition: $3900 full-time, $130 per unit part-time. Part-time mandatory fees per semester range from $23 to $153. Full-time mandatory fees: $410.

City College of San Francisco (continued)

LD Services Contact: Ms. Doreen Cotter and Ms. Kathy Kerr-Schochet, Department Chair and Coordinator of Disabled Students Program and Services, City College of San Francisco, 50 Phelan R323, San Francisco, CA 94112, 415-452-5481. Fax: 415-452-5565.

CITY COLLEGES OF CHICAGO, HARRY S TRUMAN COLLEGE

Chicago, Illinois

LEARNING DISABILITIES SERVICES INFORMATION

Special Needs Office began offering services in 1985. Currently the program serves 250 undergraduates with LD. Students diagnosed with ADD/ADHD are eligible for the same services available to students with LD.

Staff: 1 full-time, 4 part-time staff members, including coordinator. Services provided by tutors, counselors, diagnostic specialists, notetakers.

Special Fees: Special fees are charged for services to students with LD.

Applications and admissions: *Required:* documentation of disability. Students may begin taking classes any term. *Application deadline:* continuous.

PROGRAM AND SERVICE COMPONENTS

Special preparation or orientation: Required orientation held before registration.

Academic advising: Provided by unit staff members. Students with LD may take up to 12 credits each term; most take 9 credits; 12 credits required to maintain full-time status and be eligible for financial aid.

Counseling services: Individual counseling, small-group counseling, career counseling.

Basic skills remediation: Offered one-on-one, in small groups, and in class-size groups by LD teachers; computer-aided instruction also offered. Available in reading, math, spelling, learning strategies, study skills, time management, computer skills.

Subject-area tutoring: Offered one-on-one, in small groups, and in class-size groups by peer tutors. Available in all subjects.

Special courses: College survival skills, reading, vocabulary development, learning strategies, time management, study skills, career planning. Most offered for credit.

Auxiliary aids: Taped textbooks, tape recorders, calculators, typewriters.

Auxiliary services: Alternative test arrangements, notetakers, priority registration.

Campus support group: A special student organization is available to students with LD.

GENERAL COLLEGE INFORMATION

State and locally supported, 2-year, coed. Part of City Colleges of Chicago System. Awards associate degrees. Founded 1956. *Setting:* 5-acre urban campus. *Total enrollment:* 4,620. *Faculty:* 160 (70% of full-time faculty have terminal degrees); student–undergrad faculty ratio is 25:1.

Enrollment Profile: 4,620 students: 55% women, 45% men, 64% part-time, 98% state residents, 4% transferred in, 2% international, 70% 25 or older, 1% Native American, 13% Hispanic, 20% black, 24% Asian or Pacific Islander. *Most popular recent majors:* nursing, medical records services, computer information systems.

First-Year Class: 1,092 total; 1,092 applied, 100% were accepted, 100% of whom enrolled.

Graduation Requirements: 60 semester hours; 3 semester hours of math/science; internship (some majors).

Computers on Campus: 150 computers available on campus for general student use. Computers for student use in computer center, computer labs provide access to the Internet/World Wide Web. Staffed computer lab on campus provides training in use of computers, software.

EXPENSES

Expenses for 1997–98: Area resident tuition: $1350 full-time, $45 per semester hour part-time. State resident tuition: $4289 full-time, $142.98 per semester hour part-time. Nonresident tuition: $6055 full-time, $201.84 per semester hour part-time. Part-time mandatory fees: $25 per semester. Full-time mandatory fees: $50.

LD Services Contact: Mrs. Linda Ford, Director, Special Needs Office, City Colleges of Chicago, Harry S Truman College, 1145 West Wilson, Chicago, IL 60640-5616, 773-907-4725. Fax: 773-907-4725.

CLACKAMAS COMMUNITY COLLEGE

Oregon City, Oregon

LEARNING DISABILITIES SERVICES INFORMATION

Developmental Education began offering services in 1978. Currently the program serves 65 undergraduates with LD. Students diagnosed with ADD/ADHD are eligible for the same services available to students with LD.

Staff: 4 full-time, 6 part-time staff members, including coordinator. Services provided by tutors, counselors.

Special Fees: No special fees are charged for services to students with LD.

Applications and admissions: Open admissions. Students may begin taking classes any term. *Application deadline:* continuous.

PROGRAM AND SERVICE COMPONENTS

Academic advising: Provided by unit staff members. Most students with LD take 12 to 15 credit hours each term; 12 credit hours required to maintain full-time status; 6 credit hours (part-time), 12 credit hours (full-time) required to be eligible for financial aid.

Counseling services: Individual counseling, career counseling.

Basic skills remediation: Offered one-on-one and in small groups by regular teachers. Available in reading, math, spelling, spoken language, written language, learning strategies, study skills, speech.

Subject-area tutoring: Offered one-on-one and in small groups by professional teachers, peer tutors, professional tutors. Available in all subjects.

Special courses: College survival skills, word processing. All offered for credit; all enter into overall grade point average.

Auxiliary aids: Taped textbooks, tape recorders, word-processors with spell-check.

Auxiliary services: Alternative test arrangements, notetakers, priority registration, advocacy.

GENERAL COLLEGE INFORMATION

District-supported, 2-year, coed. Awards associate degrees. Founded 1966. *Setting:* 175-acre suburban campus with easy access to Portland. *Endowment:* $1.3 million. *Total enrollment:* 8,694. *Faculty:* 524 (153 full-time, 10% with terminal degrees, 371 part-time); student–undergrad faculty ratio is 17:1.

Enrollment Profile: 8,694 students from 4 states and territories, 5 other countries. 51% women, 49% men, 52% part-time, 97% state residents, 22% transferred in, 1% international, 43% 25 or older, 1% Native American, 4% Hispanic, 1% black, 3% Asian or Pacific Islander. *Retention:* 50% of 1995 full-time freshmen returned. *Areas of study chosen:* 40% liberal arts/general studies, 15% business management and administrative services, 12% biological and life sciences, 10% social sciences, 7% education, 7% mathematics, 5% English language/literature/letters, 4% fine arts. *Most popular recent majors:* business administration/commerce/management, science, social science.

First-Year Class: 1,137 total; 1,137 applied, 100% were accepted, 100% of whom enrolled.

Graduation Requirements: 93 credit hours; math/science requirements vary according to program; computer course; internship (some majors).

Computers on Campus: 450 computers available on campus for general student use. A campus-wide network can be accessed. Students can contact faculty members and/or advisers through e-mail. Computers for student use in computer labs, learning resource center, classrooms, library provide access to the Internet/World Wide Web, on- and off-campus e-mail addresses. Staffed computer lab on campus provides training in use of computers, software.

EXPENSES

Expenses for 1997–98: State resident tuition: $1428 full-time, $34 per credit hour part-time. Nonresident tuition: $4998 full-time, $119 per credit hour part-time. Part-time mandatory fees: $2 per credit hour. Full-time mandatory fees: $84. Tuition guaranteed not to increase for student's term of enrollment.

LD Services Contact: Ms. Cindi Andrews, Department Chairperson, Developmental Education, Clackamas Community College, 19600 South Molalla Avenue, Oregon City, OR 97045-7998, 503-657-6958 Ext. 2417.

CLINTON COMMUNITY COLLEGE

Clinton, Iowa

LEARNING DISABILITIES SERVICES INFORMATION

Developmental Education Department began offering services in 1968. Currently the program serves 25 undergraduates with LD. Students diagnosed with ADD/ADHD are eligible for the same services available to students with LD.
Staff: 3 full-time, 3 part-time staff members, including coordinator. Services provided by tutors, counselors, developmental instructors.
Special Fees: No special fees are charged for services to students with LD.
Applications and admissions: Open admissions. Students may begin taking classes in fall or spring. *Application deadline:* continuous.

PROGRAM AND SERVICE COMPONENTS

Diagnostic testing: Reading, math, written language.
Academic advising: Provided by academic advisers. Students with LD may take up to 12 semester hours each term; most take 6 to 12 semester hours; 12 semester hours required to maintain full-time status; 6 to 12 semester hours required to be eligible for financial aid.
Counseling services: Individual counseling, career counseling.
Basic skills remediation: Offered one-on-one, in small groups, and in class-size groups by regular teachers, developmental specialists. Available in reading, math, written language, learning strategies, study skills, time management.
Subject-area tutoring: Offered one-on-one and in class-size groups by professional teachers, peer tutors. Available in all subjects.
Special courses: College survival skills, reading, vocabulary development, composition, learning strategies, word processing, time management, math, study skills, career planning. All offered for credit; all enter into overall grade point average.
Auxiliary aids: Calculators, typewriters, word-processors with spell-check.
Auxiliary services: Alternative test arrangements, advocacy.

GENERAL COLLEGE INFORMATION

State-supported, 2-year, coed. Part of Eastern Iowa Community College District System. Awards associate degrees. Founded 1946. *Setting:* 20-acre small-town campus. *Total enrollment:* 1,161. *Faculty:* 75 (35 full-time, 40 part-time).
Enrollment Profile: 1,161 students from 9 states and territories. 66% women, 34% men, 48% part-time, 88% state residents, 5% transferred in, 0% international, 43% 25 or older, 1% Native American, 1% Hispanic, 2% black, 1% Asian or Pacific Islander. *Retention:* 42% of 1995 full-time freshmen returned.
First-Year Class: 461 total. Of the students who applied, 100% were accepted, 82% of whom enrolled. 12% from top 10% of their high school class, 17% from top quarter, 55% from top half.
Graduation Requirements: 64 semester hours; 3 semester hours of math, 8 semester hours of science for associate of arts degree; 6 semester hours of math, 12 semester hours of science for associate of science degree; computer course.
Computers on Campus: 37 computers available on campus for general student use. Computers for student use in computer labs. Staffed computer lab on campus.

EXPENSES

Expenses for 1997–98: *Application fee:* $20. State resident tuition: $1696 full-time, $53 per semester hour part-time. Nonresident tuition: $2544 full-time, $79.50 per semester hour part-time. Part-time mandatory fees: $5.50 per semester hour. Full-time mandatory fees: $176.
LD Services Contact: Ms. Marilyn Lyons, Developmental Education Department Coordinator, Clinton Community College, 1000 Lincoln Boulevard, Clinton, IA 52732-6299, 319-242-6841.

CLINTON COMMUNITY COLLEGE

Plattsburgh, New York

LEARNING DISABILITIES SERVICES INFORMATION

Learning Disabilities Specialist's Office currently serves 80 undergraduates with LD. Students diagnosed with ADD/ADHD are eligible for the same services available to students with LD.
Staff: 2 full-time staff members, including director. Services provided by remediation specialists, tutors, counselor.
Special Fees: No special fees are charged for services to students with LD.
Applications and admissions: *Required:* high school transcript, psychoeducational report completed most recently; *recommended:* personal interview. Students may begin taking classes any term. *Application deadline:* continuous.
Special policies: The college has written policies regarding substitutions and waivers of graduation and degree requirements.

PROGRAM AND SERVICE COMPONENTS

Diagnostic testing: Reading, math, written language.
Academic advising: Provided by unit staff members, academic advisers. Most students with LD take 12 credits each term; 12 credits required to maintain full-time status; 9 credits required to be eligible for financial aid.
Counseling services: Individual counseling, small-group counseling, career counseling, self-advocacy training.
Basic skills remediation: Offered in small groups and in class-size groups by regular teachers. Available in reading, math, written language, learning strategies.
Subject-area tutoring: Offered one-on-one and in small groups by professional teachers, peer tutors. Available in most subjects.
Auxiliary aids: Taped textbooks, tape recorders, calculators, word-processors with spell-check, personal computers, optical character readers, Arkenstone Reader.
Auxiliary services: Alternative test arrangements, notetakers, priority registration, advocacy.
Campus support group: A special student organization is available to students with LD.

GENERAL COLLEGE INFORMATION

State and locally supported, 2-year, coed. Part of State University of New York System. Awards associate degrees. Founded 1969. *Setting:* 100-acre small-town campus. *Total enrollment:* 1,644. *Faculty:* 179 (43 full-time, 136 part-time); student–undergrad faculty ratio is 18:1.
Enrollment Profile: 1,644 students from 7 states and territories, 4 other countries. 59% women, 41% men, 42% part-time, 82% state residents, 17% transferred in, 1% international, 36% 25 or older, 2% Native American, 2% Hispanic, 3% black, 2% Asian or Pacific Islander. *Areas of study chosen:* 33% liberal arts/general studies, 18% business management and administrative services, 8% health professions and related sciences, 3% education, 3% interdisciplinary studies. *Most popular recent majors:* liberal arts/general studies, business administration/commerce/management.
First-Year Class: 547 total; 898 applied, 81% of whom enrolled. 5% from top 10% of their high school class, 20% from top quarter, 75% from top half.
Graduation Requirements: 63 credits; math/science requirements vary according to program; computer course for business majors.
Computers on Campus: 60 computers available on campus for general student use. Computer purchase/lease plans available. Computers for student use in computer center, library, tutorial labs. Staffed computer lab on campus provides training in use of computers, software.

EXPENSES

Expenses for 1996–97: *Application fee:* $30. State resident tuition: $2275 full-time, $94 per credit part-time. Nonresident tuition: $4550 full-time, $188 per credit part-time. Part-time mandatory fees: $1.75 per credit. Full-time mandatory fees: $121.
LD Services Contact: Ms. Lisa Crain, Learning Disabilities Specialist, Clinton Community College, 136 Clinton Point Drive, Plattsburgh, NY 12901, 518-562-4299. Fax: 518-561-8621.

CLOUD COUNTY COMMUNITY COLLEGE

Concordia, Kansas

LEARNING DISABILITIES SERVICES INFORMATION

Learning Skills Center began offering services in 1986. Currently the program serves 20 undergraduates with LD. Students diagnosed with ADD/ADHD are eligible for the same services available to students with LD.
Staff: 2 full-time, 2 part-time staff members, including director, assistant director. Services provided by remediation specialists, tutors.

Cloud County Community College (continued)

Special Fees: No special fees are charged for services to students with LD.
Applications and admissions: *Required:* high school transcript, grade point average, class rank, courses completed, personal interview, psychoeducational report completed within 3 years; *recommended:* high school IEP (Individualized Education Program), untimed ACT. Students may begin taking classes any term. *Application deadline:* continuous.

PROGRAM AND SERVICE COMPONENTS

Diagnostic testing: Reading, math, spelling, study skills, learning strategies.
Academic advising: Provided by academic advisers. Students with LD may take up to 15 credit hours each term; most take 12 to 15 credit hours; 12 credit hours required to maintain full-time status; 6 credit hours (part-time), 12 credit hours (full-time) required to be eligible for financial aid.
Counseling services: Individual counseling, career counseling.
Basic skills remediation: Offered one-on-one, in small groups, and in class-size groups by regular teachers, reading specialist; computer-aided instruction also offered. Available in reading, math, spelling, written language, learning strategies, study skills.
Subject-area tutoring: Offered one-on-one and in small groups by professional teachers, peer tutors. Available in most subjects.
Special courses: College survival skills, reading, vocabulary development, composition, learning strategies, word processing, math, typing, study skills, career planning. Most offered for credit; most enter into overall grade point average.
Auxiliary aids: Taped textbooks, tape recorders, typewriters, word-processors with spell-check, personal computers.
Auxiliary services: Alternative test arrangements, notetakers.

GENERAL COLLEGE INFORMATION

State and locally supported, 2-year, coed. Part of Kansas Community College System. Awards associate degrees. Founded 1965. *Setting:* 35-acre rural campus. *Total enrollment:* 3,112. *Faculty:* 218 (38 full-time, 8% with terminal degrees, 180 part-time); student–undergrad faculty ratio is 15:1.
Enrollment Profile: 3,112 students from 12 states and territories, 2 other countries. 73% women, 27% men, 78% part-time, 98% state residents, 35% transferred in, 67% 25 or older, 1% Native American, 2% black, 1% Asian or Pacific Islander.
First-Year Class: 1,250 total. Of the students who applied, 100% were accepted, 91% of whom enrolled.
Graduation Requirements: 64 credit hours; 6 credit hours of math; 8 credit hours of science; internship (some majors).
Computers on Campus: 57 computers available on campus for general student use. Computers for student use in computer labs, learning resource center, science lab provide access to the Internet/World Wide Web, on- and off-campus e-mail addresses. Staffed computer lab on campus provides training in use of computers, software.

EXPENSES

Expenses for 1997–98: State resident tuition: $960 full-time, $30 per credit hour part-time. Nonresident tuition: $2480 full-time, $77.50 per credit hour part-time. Part-time mandatory fees per credit hour range from $7.50 to $12.50. Full-time mandatory fees range from $240 to $400. College room and board: $2700. College room only: $1755.
LD Services Contact: Ms. Sue Regan, Director, Cloud County Community College, PO Box 1002, Concordia, KS 66901-1002, 913-243-1435 Ext. 214. Fax: 913-243-1043.

CLOVIS COMMUNITY COLLEGE

Clovis, New Mexico

LEARNING DISABILITIES SERVICES INFORMATION

Expanding Visions and Opportunities for Learning in Vocational Education (EVOLVE) began offering services in 1990. Currently the program serves 62 undergraduates with LD. Students diagnosed with ADD/ADHD are eligible for the same services available to students with LD, as well as IVACPT assessment and treatment referral.
Staff: 2 full-time, 6 part-time staff members, including coordinators, lab assistant/secretary. Services provided by remediation specialist, tutors, diagnostic specialist.
Special Fees: No special fees are charged for services to students with LD.
Applications and admissions: *Required:* high school transcript; *recommended:* high school IEP (Individualized Education Program), personal interview, psychoeducational report completed within 3 years. Students may begin taking classes in fall, spring, or summer. *Application deadline:* continuous.
Special policies: The college has written policies regarding substitutions and waivers of admissions, graduation, and degree requirements.

PROGRAM AND SERVICE COMPONENTS

Diagnostic testing: Intelligence, reading, math, spelling, perceptual skills, learning strategies.
Academic advising: Provided by unit staff members, academic advisers. Students with LD may take up to 18 credit hours (without Dean's approval) each term; most take 6 to 12 credit hours; 12 credit hours required to maintain full-time status; 6 credit hours required to be eligible for financial aid.
Counseling services: Individual counseling, small-group counseling, career counseling, support group.
Basic skills remediation: Offered one-on-one and in small groups by regular teachers, teacher trainees; computer-aided instruction also offered. Available in reading, math, spelling, written language, learning strategies, study skills, time management.
Subject-area tutoring: Offered one-on-one by peer tutors. Available in most subjects.
Auxiliary aids: Taped textbooks, tape recorders, typewriters, word-processors with spell-check, personal computers, optical character readers, Phonic Ear, voice-activated word processors.
Auxiliary services: Alternative test arrangements, notetakers, advocacy.

GENERAL COLLEGE INFORMATION

State-supported, 2-year, coed. Awards associate degrees. Founded 1971. *Setting:* small-town campus. *Total enrollment:* 3,964. *Faculty:* 209 (49 full-time, 160 part-time).
Enrollment Profile: 3,964 students: 63% women, 37% men, 79% part-time, 11% transferred in, 1% international, 67% 25 or older, 1% Native American, 19% Hispanic, 5% black, 2% Asian or Pacific Islander. *Areas of study chosen:* 11% health professions and related sciences, 4% business management and administrative services, 4% liberal arts/general studies, 3% computer and information sciences, 2% psychology, 1% agriculture, 1% education, 1% fine arts, 1% library and information studies, 1% mathematics, 1% military science.
First-Year Class: 613 total; 613 applied, 100% were accepted, 100% of whom enrolled.
Graduation Requirements: 64 credit hours; computer course for business administration, occupation technology majors.
Computers on Campus: 250 computers available on campus for general student use. A campus-wide network can be accessed. Students can contact faculty members and/or advisers through e-mail. Computers for student use in computer center, computer labs, learning resource center, classrooms, library provide access to the Internet/World Wide Web. Staffed computer lab on campus provides training in use of computers, software. *Academic computing expenditure 1995–96:* $434,772.

EXPENSES

Expenses for 1997–98: Area resident tuition: $528 full-time, $22 per credit hour part-time. State resident tuition: $552 full-time, $23 per credit hour part-time. Nonresident tuition: $720 full-time, $30 per credit hour part-time. Part-time mandatory fees: $10 per semester. Full-time mandatory fees: $20.
LD Services Contact: Ms. Rosalie Richards, Coordinator, Clovis Community College, 417 Schepps Boulevard, Clovis, MN 88101, 505-769-4099. Fax: 505-769-4190. Email: richardsr@clovis.cc.nm.us.

COLBY COMMUNITY COLLEGE

Colby, Kansas

LEARNING DISABILITIES SERVICES INFORMATION

Comprehensive Learning Center currently serves 20 undergraduates with LD. Students diagnosed with ADD/ADHD are eligible for the same services available to students with LD.
Staff: Includes director, instructors. Services provided by remediation specialists, tutors, paraprofessional.
Special Fees: No special fees are charged for services to students with LD.

Applications and admissions: *Required:* high school transcript, grade point average, class rank, courses completed, ASSET; *recommended:* high school extracurricular activities, IEP (Individualized Education Program). Students may begin taking classes in fall only. *Application deadline:* continuous.

PROGRAM AND SERVICE COMPONENTS

Diagnostic testing: Reading, math, spelling, written language, study skills, learning strategies.

Academic advising: Provided by academic advisers. Students with LD may take up to 19 credit hours each term; most take 12 credit hours; 12 credit hours required to maintain full-time status; 3 credit hours required to be eligible for financial aid.

Counseling services: Individual counseling, career counseling.

Basic skills remediation: Offered in small groups and in class-size groups by regular teachers. Available in reading, math, spelling, written language, learning strategies, study skills, time management.

Subject-area tutoring: Offered one-on-one, in small groups, and in class-size groups by peer tutors. Available in all subjects.

Special courses: College survival skills, reading, vocabulary development, composition, learning strategies, time management, math, study skills, career planning. Most offered for credit; all enter into overall grade point average.

Auxiliary aids: Taped textbooks, tape recorders, calculators, typewriters, personal computers, optical character readers.

Auxiliary services: Alternative test arrangements, notetakers.

GENERAL COLLEGE INFORMATION

State and locally supported, 2-year, coed. Awards associate degrees. Founded 1964. *Setting:* 80-acre small-town campus. *Endowment:* $1.4 million. *Educational spending 1995–96:* $2426 per undergrad. *Total enrollment:* 1,138. *Faculty:* 63 (59 full-time, 20% with terminal degrees, 4 part-time); student–undergrad faculty ratio is 16:1.

Enrollment Profile: 1,138 students from 11 states and territories, 6 other countries. 51% women, 49% men, 30% part-time, 73% state residents, 5% transferred in, 2% international, 9% 25 or older, 1% Native American, 2% Hispanic, 5% black, 1% Asian or Pacific Islander. *Retention:* 83% of 1995 full-time freshmen returned. *Areas of study chosen:* 20% health professions and related sciences, 15% agriculture, 6% education, 5% communications and journalism, 5% computer and information sciences, 5% English language/literature/letters, 5% liberal arts/general studies, 5% physical sciences, 4% business management and administrative services, 4% engineering and applied sciences, 3% biological and life sciences, 3% fine arts, 3% interdisciplinary studies, 3% psychology, 2% mathematics, 2% natural resource sciences, 2% social sciences, 1% library and information studies, 1% performing arts, 1% philosophy, 1% predentistry, 1% prelaw, 1% premed, 1% prevet, 1% vocational and home economics.

First-Year Class: 324 total; 767 applied, 100% of whom enrolled. 12% from top 10% of their high school class, 25% from top quarter, 66% from top half. 10 class presidents, 8 valedictorians.

Graduation Requirements: 62 semester hours; 3 semester hours of math; computer course for business majors; internship (some majors).

Computers on Campus: 37 computers available on campus for general student use. A campus-wide network can be accessed. Computers for student use in computer center, computer labs, library, Comprehensive Learning Center provide access to the Internet/World Wide Web, on-campus e-mail addresses. Staffed computer lab on campus provides training in use of computers, software. *Academic computing expenditure 1995–96:* $32,000.

EXPENSES

Expenses for 1996–97: *Application fee:* $10. State resident tuition: $868 full-time, $28 per semester hour part-time. Nonresident tuition: $2170 full-time, $70 per semester hour part-time. Part-time mandatory fees: $9 per semester hour. Full-time mandatory fees: $279. College room and board: $2976.

LD Services Contact: Ms. Joyce Washburn, Director of Academic Services, Colby Community College, 1255 South Range, Colby, KS 67701-4099, 913-462-3984. Fax: 913-462-4600. Email: joyce@katie.colby.cc.ks.us.

COLLEGE OF EASTERN UTAH

Price, Utah

LEARNING DISABILITIES SERVICES INFORMATION

Resource Center for Students with Disabilities began offering services in 1983. Currently the program serves 50 undergraduates with LD. Students diagnosed with ADD/ADHD are eligible for the same services available to students with LD.

Staff: 1 full-time, 2 part-time staff members, including director, coordinator. Services provided by counselors, student helpers, interpreters.

Special Fees: No special fees are charged for services to students with LD.

Applications and admissions: *Required:* personal interview, ACT ASSET; *recommended:* high school transcript, psychoeducational report completed within 3 years. Students may begin taking classes any term. *Application deadline:* continuous.

Special policies: The college has written policies regarding grade forgiveness; substitutions and waivers of admissions, graduation, and degree requirements.

PROGRAM AND SERVICE COMPONENTS

Academic advising: Provided by academic advisers. Most students with LD take 12 credit hours each term; 12 credit hours required to maintain full-time status; 6 credit hours required to be eligible for financial aid.

Counseling services: Individual counseling, career counseling.

Auxiliary aids: Taped textbooks, tape recorders, calculators, typewriters, word-processors with spell-check, personal computers.

Auxiliary services: Alternative test arrangements, notetakers, priority registration, advocacy.

GENERAL COLLEGE INFORMATION

State-supported, 2-year, coed. Part of Utah System of Higher Education. Awards associate degrees. Founded 1937. *Setting:* 15-acre small-town campus. *Endowment:* $78.6 million. *Total enrollment:* 3,170. *Faculty:* 128 (78 full-time, 50 part-time); student–undergrad faculty ratio is 30:1.

Enrollment Profile: 3,170 students from 8 states and territories, 5 other countries. 49% women, 51% men, 52% part-time, 98% state residents, 5% transferred in, 1% international, 58% 25 or older, 9% Native American, 3% Hispanic, 1% black, 1% Asian or Pacific Islander. *Retention:* 35% of 1995 full-time freshmen returned. *Most popular recent major:* liberal arts/general studies.

First-Year Class: 1,373 total; 1,600 applied, 100% were accepted, 86% of whom enrolled.

Graduation Requirements: 93 credits; 1 math course; computer course.

Computers on Campus: 150 computers available on campus for general student use. A campus-wide network can be accessed from student residence rooms and from off-campus. Students can contact faculty members and/or advisers through e-mail. Computers for student use in computer labs, library provide access to the Internet/World Wide Web, on-campus e-mail addresses. Staffed computer lab on campus provides training in use of computers, software. *Academic computing expenditure 1995–96:* $438,214.

EXPENSES

Expenses for 1997–98: *Application fee:* $20. State resident tuition: $1001 full-time. Nonresident tuition: $4188 full-time. Part-time tuition per quarter ranges from $65.10 to $309.10 for state residents, $252 to $1292 for nonresidents. Part-time mandatory fees per quarter range from $10.35 to $103.50. Full-time mandatory fees: $311. College room and board: $2712 (minimum).

LD Services Contact: Mrs. Colleen Quigley, Director, Resource Center for Students with Disabilities, College of Eastern Utah, 451 East 400 North, Price, UT 84501-2699, 801-637-2120 Ext. 5326. Fax: 801-637-4102.

COLLEGE OF LAKE COUNTY

Grayslake, Illinois

LEARNING DISABILITIES SERVICES INFORMATION

Special Needs Office began offering services in 1984. Currently the program serves 125 undergraduates with LD. Students diagnosed with ADD/ADHD are eligible for the same services available to students with LD.

College of Lake County (continued)

Staff: 1 full-time, 3 part-time staff members, including coordinator. Services provided by tutors.

Special Fees: No special fees are charged for services to students with LD.

Applications and admissions: *Required:* personal interview, psychoeducational report completed within 3 years; *recommended:* high school transcript, grade point average, class rank, untimed or extended time ACT. Students may begin taking classes any term. *Application deadline:* continuous.

Special policies: The college has written policies regarding substitutions and waivers of degree requirements.

PROGRAM AND SERVICE COMPONENTS

Academic advising: Provided by unit staff members, academic advisers. Students with LD may take up to 15 credit hours each term; most take 9 to 12 credit hours; 12 credit hours required to maintain full-time status; 6 to 12 credit hours required to be eligible for financial aid.

Counseling services: Individual counseling, career counseling.

Basic skills remediation: Offered in class-size groups by regular teachers, tutors. Available in reading, math, written language, learning strategies.

Subject-area tutoring: Offered one-on-one by professional teachers, peer tutors. Available in all subjects.

Special courses: College survival skills, reading, learning strategies, time management, math. Some offered for credit.

Auxiliary aids: Taped textbooks, tape recorders, calculators, typewriters, word-processors with spell-check, talking computers, optical character readers.

Auxiliary services: Alternative test arrangements, notetakers, advocacy.

Campus support group: A special student organization is available to students with LD.

GENERAL COLLEGE INFORMATION

District-supported, 2-year, coed. Part of Illinois Community College System. Awards associate degrees. Founded 1967. *Setting:* 232-acre suburban campus with easy access to Chicago and Milwaukee. *Total enrollment:* 14,867. *Faculty:* 776 (180 full-time, 596 part-time); student–undergrad faculty ratio is 20:1.

Enrollment Profile: 14,867 students from 2 states and territories, 21 other countries. 58% women, 42% men, 80% part-time, 96% state residents, 9% transferred in, 1% international, 58% 25 or older, 1% Native American, 12% Hispanic, 7% black, 4% Asian or Pacific Islander. *Most popular recent majors:* liberal arts/general studies, data processing, business administration/commerce/management.

First-Year Class: 2,845 total; 2,987 applied, 100% were accepted, 95% of whom enrolled.

Graduation Requirements: 63 credit hours; math/science requirements vary according to program; computer course for architecture, business management, health information technology, library media technology, engineering technology, technical communications majors.

Computers on Campus: 800 computers available on campus for general student use. Computer purchase/lease plans available. A computer is recommended for all students. A campus-wide network can be accessed from off-campus. Students can contact faculty members and/or advisers through e-mail. Computers for student use in computer center, computer labs, learning resource center, classrooms, library, academic buildings provide access to the Internet/World Wide Web, on-campus e-mail addresses. Staffed computer lab on campus provides training in use of computers, software. *Academic computing expenditure 1995–96:* $293,679.

EXPENSES

Expenses for 1997–98: Area resident tuition: $1457 full-time, $47 per credit hour part-time. State resident tuition: $5906 full-time, $190.53 per credit hour part-time. Nonresident tuition: $7936 full-time, $255.99 per credit hour part-time. Part-time mandatory fees: $4 per credit hour. Full-time mandatory fees: $124.

LD Services Contact: Mr. Bill Freitag, Coordinator of Special Needs, College of Lake County, 19351 West Washington Street, Grayslake, IL 60030, 847-223-6601 Ext. 2474. Fax: 847-223-7690. Email: lac271@clc.cc.il.us.

COLLEGE OF SOUTHERN IDAHO

Twin Falls, Idaho

LEARNING DISABILITIES SERVICES INFORMATION

Learning Disabilities Services began offering services in 1995. Currently the program serves 19 undergraduates with LD. Students diagnosed with ADD/ADHD are eligible for the same services available to students with LD.

Staff: Includes director, coordinator. Services provided by tutors.

Special Fees: No special fees are charged for services to students with LD.

Applications and admissions: *Required:* high school transcript, grade point average, courses completed, psychoeducational report completed within 3 to 5 years. Students may begin taking classes in fall or spring. *Application deadline:* continuous.

PROGRAM AND SERVICE COMPONENTS

Special preparation or orientation: Optional orientation offered individually by arrangement.

Academic advising: Provided by unit staff members, academic advisers. Students with LD may take up to as many credits as an individual can handle each term; most take 12 to 18 credits; 12 credits required to maintain full-time status and be eligible for financial aid.

Subject-area tutoring: Offered one-on-one and in small groups by peer tutors. Available in most subjects.

Auxiliary services: Alternative test arrangements, notetakers; accommodations made on a case by case basis.

GENERAL COLLEGE INFORMATION

State and locally supported, 2-year, coed. Awards associate degrees. Founded 1964. *Setting:* 287-acre small-town campus. *Total enrollment:* 5,502. *Faculty:* 260 (120 full-time, 15% with terminal degrees, 140 part-time); student–undergrad faculty ratio is 18:1.

Enrollment Profile: 5,502 students from 16 states and territories, 24 other countries. 65% women, 35% men, 59% part-time, 95% state residents, 2% transferred in, 1% international, 57% 25 or older, 1% Native American, 5% Hispanic, 1% black, 1% Asian or Pacific Islander. *Retention:* 55% of 1995 full-time freshmen returned. *Most popular recent majors:* liberal arts/general studies, elementary education, nursing.

First-Year Class: 1,800 total. Of the students who applied, 100% were accepted.

Graduation Requirements: 64 credits; computer course for most majors.

Computers on Campus: 300 computers available on campus for general student use. A campus-wide network can be accessed from off-campus. Students can contact faculty members and/or advisers through e-mail. Computers for student use in computer labs, classrooms, library, dorms provide access to the Internet/World Wide Web, on- and off-campus e-mail addresses. Staffed computer lab on campus provides training in use of computers, software.

EXPENSES

Expenses for 1997–98: Area resident tuition: $1150 full-time, $57.50 per credit part-time. State resident tuition: $2150 full-time, $107.50 per credit part-time. Nonresident tuition: $3150 full-time, $157.50 per credit part-time. College room and board: $3380.

LD Services Contact: Ms. Marcia Yastrop, Learning Disabilities Coordinator, College of Southern Idaho, 315 Falls Avenue, Twin Falls, ID 83301, 208-733-9554 Ext. 2544. Fax: 208-736-3029. Email: myastrop@adc1.csi.cc.id.us.

COLLEGE OF THE CANYONS

Santa Clarita, California

LEARNING DISABILITIES SERVICES INFORMATION

Learning Assistance Program began offering services in 1979. Currently the program serves 110 undergraduates with LD. Students diagnosed with ADD/ADHD are eligible for the same services available to students with LD.

Staff: 1 full-time, 4 part-time staff members, including director, learning specialist, high-tech center specialist. Services provided by tutors, counselors, diagnostic specialists, learning skills assistant.

Special Fees: $6.50 for diagnostic testing.

Applications and admissions: *Required:* California Assessment System for Adults with Learning Disabilities. Students may begin taking classes in fall or spring. *Application deadline:* continuous.
Special policies: The college has written policies regarding grade forgiveness.

PROGRAM AND SERVICE COMPONENTS

Special preparation or orientation: Required orientation held before registration and individually by special arrangement.
Diagnostic testing: Intelligence, reading, math, spelling, written language, perceptual skills, learning strategies.
Academic advising: Provided by unit staff members, academic advisers. Students with LD may take up to as many units as an individual can handle each term; most take 12 units; 12 units required to maintain full-time status and be eligible for financial aid.
Counseling services: Individual counseling, career counseling, self-advocacy training.
Basic skills remediation: Offered one-on-one and in small groups by LD teachers; computer-aided instruction also offered. Available in reading, math, spelling, written language, learning strategies, study skills, time management, computer skills.
Subject-area tutoring: Offered one-on-one and in small groups by professional teachers, paraprofessional tutors. Available in most subjects.
Special courses: Learning strategies, word processing, study skills. None offered for credit; none enter into overall grade point average.
Auxiliary aids: Taped textbooks, tape recorders, calculators, typewriters, word-processors with spell-check, optical character readers.
Auxiliary services: Alternative test arrangements, notetakers, priority registration, advocacy.

GENERAL COLLEGE INFORMATION

State and locally supported, 2-year, coed. Part of California Community Colleges System. Awards associate degrees. Founded 1969. *Setting:* 158-acre suburban campus with easy access to Los Angeles. *Total enrollment:* 6,446. *Faculty:* 260 (70 full-time, 23% with terminal degrees, 190 part-time).
Enrollment Profile: 6,446 students from 15 states and territories, 14 other countries. 58% women, 42% men, 70% part-time, 98% state residents, 23% transferred in, 1% international, 43% 25 or older, 1% Native American, 10% Hispanic, 2% black, 3% Asian or Pacific Islander. *Most popular recent majors:* social science, business administration/commerce/management, science.
First-Year Class: 2,387 total. Of the students who applied, 100% were accepted, 95% of whom enrolled.
Graduation Requirements: 60 units; 1 math course.
Computers on Campus: 123 computers available on campus for general student use. Students can contact faculty members and/or advisers through e-mail. Computers for student use in computer center, classrooms, library provide access to the Internet/World Wide Web, on- and off-campus e-mail addresses.

EXPENSES

Estimated Expenses for 1997–98: State resident tuition: $0 full-time. Nonresident tuition: $3300 full-time, $110 per unit part-time. Part-time mandatory fees: $13 per unit. Full-time mandatory fees: $390.
LD Services Contact: Dr. Jane A. Feuerhelm, Learning Specialist, College of the Canyons, 26455 North Rockwell Canyon Road, Santa Clarita, CA 91355-1899, 805-259-7800 Ext. 3347. Fax: 805-259-8302.

COLLEGE OF THE DESERT

Palm Desert, California

LEARNING DISABILITIES SERVICES INFORMATION

Disabled Students Programs and Services began offering services in 1975. Currently the program serves 90 undergraduates with LD. Students diagnosed with ADD/ADHD are eligible for the same services available to students with LD.
Staff: 2 full-time, 8 part-time staff members, including director. Services provided by remediation specialists, tutors, counselors, diagnostic specialists, adapted technology specialist, speech therapist.
Special Fees: No special fees are charged for services to students with LD.
Applications and admissions: *Required:* California Assessment System for Adults with Learning Disabilities. Students may begin taking classes any term. *Application deadline:* continuous.
Special policies: The college has written policies regarding grade forgiveness.

PROGRAM AND SERVICE COMPONENTS

Special preparation or orientation: Required orientation held before registration and during registration.
Diagnostic testing: Intelligence, reading, math, spelling, handwriting, spoken language, written language, motor abilities, perceptual skills, social skills, speech, hearing, learning strategies.
Academic advising: Provided by unit staff members, academic advisers. Students with LD may take up to 18 units each term; most take 9 units; 12 units required to maintain full-time status; source of aid determines number of units required to be eligible for financial aid.
Counseling services: Individual counseling.
Basic skills remediation: Offered one-on-one and in small groups by LD teachers, regular teachers; computer-aided instruction also offered. Available in reading, math, spelling, written language, learning strategies, motor abilities, perceptual skills, study skills, time management, speech, computer skills.
Subject-area tutoring: Offered one-on-one by peer tutors. Available in all subjects.
Special courses: College survival skills, communication skills, learning strategies, word processing, personal psychology, study skills, information management. Some offered for credit; some enter into overall grade point average.
Auxiliary aids: Taped textbooks, tape recorders, calculators, typewriters, word-processors with spell-check, personal computers, talking computers, optical character readers.
Auxiliary services: Alternative test arrangements, notetakers, priority registration, advocacy.

GENERAL COLLEGE INFORMATION

State and locally supported, 2-year, coed. Part of California Community Colleges System. Awards associate degrees. Founded 1959. *Setting:* 160-acre small-town campus. *Total enrollment:* 9,710. *Faculty:* 320 (100 full-time, 220 part-time).
Enrollment Profile: 9,710 students from 23 states and territories. 58% women, 42% men, 80% part-time, 96% state residents, 11% transferred in, 60% 25 or older, 1% Native American, 37% Hispanic, 3% black, 2% Asian or Pacific Islander. *Retention:* 55% of 1995 full-time freshmen returned. *Areas of study chosen:* 4% education, 4% fine arts, 2% architecture, 2% communications and journalism, 2% performing arts, 2% premed, 1% agriculture, 1% engineering and applied sciences, 1% natural resource sciences, 1% prevet, 1% social sciences. *Most popular recent majors:* nursing, business administration/commerce/management, education.
First-Year Class: 1,553 total; 2,310 applied, 100% were accepted.
Graduation Requirements: 60 units; math proficiency; computer course for business, pre-engineering majors.
Computers on Campus: 43 computers available on campus for general student use. A campus-wide network can be accessed from off-campus. Computers for student use in library. Staffed computer lab on campus provides training in use of computers, software.

EXPENSES

Expenses for 1997–98: State resident tuition: $0 full-time. Nonresident tuition: $3660 full-time, $122 per unit part-time. Part-time mandatory fees per semester range from $23.25 to $155.75. Full-time mandatory fees: $418.
LD Services Contact: Mr. Michael O'Neill, Learning Disabilities Specialist/Assistant Professor of Special Education, College of the Desert, 43-500 Monterey Avenue, Palm Desert, CA 92260-9305, 760-773-2534. Fax: 760-776-0198. Email: michaelo@dccd.cc.ca.us.

COLLEGE OF THE MAINLAND

Texas City, Texas

LEARNING DISABILITIES SERVICES INFORMATION

Special Services began offering services in 1986. Currently the program serves 69 undergraduates with LD. Students diagnosed with ADD/ADHD are eligible for the same services available to students with LD.
Staff: Includes coordinators, consultant/diagnostic specialist. Services provided by remediation specialists, tutors, counselors.
Special Fees: No special fees are charged for services to students with LD.
Applications and admissions: *Required:* high school transcript, extended time SAT I or ACT; *recommended:* high school IEP (Individu-

College of the Mainland (continued)

alized Education Program), psychoeducational report. Students may begin taking classes in fall, spring, or summer. *Application deadline:* continuous.
Special policies: The college has written policies regarding grade forgiveness; substitutions and waivers of graduation and degree requirements.

PROGRAM AND SERVICE COMPONENTS

Special preparation or orientation: Optional orientation offered before registration.
Diagnostic testing: Intelligence, reading, math, spelling, handwriting, written language, motor abilities, perceptual skills, personality, psychoneurology, hearing.
Academic advising: Provided by unit staff members, academic advisers. Most students with LD take 6 to 9 hours each term; 12 hours required to maintain full-time status; 9 hours required to be eligible for financial aid.
Counseling services: Individual counseling, career counseling, self-advocacy training.
Basic skills remediation: Offered in class-size groups by LD teachers, regular teachers; computer-aided instruction also offered. Available in reading, math, spelling, handwriting, written language, speech.
Subject-area tutoring: Offered one-on-one by professional teachers, peer tutors. Available in all subjects.
Auxiliary aids: Taped textbooks, tape recorders, calculators, typewriters, word-processors with spell-check, voice computer.
Auxiliary services: Alternative test arrangements, notetakers, priority registration.
Campus support group: A special student organization is available to students with LD.

GENERAL COLLEGE INFORMATION

State and locally supported, 2-year, coed. Part of Texas Higher Education Coordinating Board. Awards associate degrees. Founded 1967. *Setting:* 120-acre small-town campus with easy access to Houston. *Total enrollment:* 3,564. *Faculty:* 180 (62 full-time, 118 part-time); student–undergrad faculty ratio is 25:1.
Enrollment Profile: 3,564 students from 2 states and territories, 6 other countries. 61% women, 39% men, 70% part-time, 98% state residents, 24% transferred in, 1% international, 60% 25 or older, 14% Hispanic, 16% black, 2% Asian or Pacific Islander. *Retention:* 38% of 1995 full-time freshmen returned. *Most popular recent majors:* nursing, computer science.
First-Year Class: 800 total; 1,000 applied, 100% were accepted, 80% of whom enrolled.
Graduation Requirements: 62 hours; 6 hours of math; 12 hours of lab science.
Computers on Campus: 275 computers available on campus for general student use. Computers for student use in computer center, computer labs, classrooms. Staffed computer lab on campus provides training in use of computers, software.

EXPENSES

Expenses for 1996–97: Area resident tuition: $434 full-time. State resident tuition: $922 full-time. Nonresident tuition: $1387 full-time. Part-time tuition per semester ranges from $84 to $154 for area residents, $178 to $327.25 for state residents, $280 to $492.25 for nonresidents. Part-time mandatory fees per semester range from $15 to $41.50. Full-time mandatory fees: $103.
LD Services Contact: Ms. Kelly Musick and Dr. Bill Spillak, Coordinators, Disabled Student Support Services, College of the Mainland, 1200 Amburn Road, Texas City, TX 77591, 409-938-1211 Ext. 496. Fax: 409-938-1306. Email: kmusick@campus.mainland.cc.tx.us.

COLLEGE OF THE SEQUOIAS

Visalia, California

LEARNING DISABILITIES SERVICES INFORMATION

Learning Disabilities Program currently serves 257 undergraduates with LD. Students diagnosed with ADD/ADHD are eligible for the same services available to students with LD.
Staff: 1 full-time, 6 part-time staff members, including director. Services provided by tutors, counselors, diagnostic specialists, instructional aides.
Special Fees: No special fees are charged for services to students with LD.
Applications and admissions: *Required:* personal interview, California Assessment System for Adults with Learning Disabilities. Students may begin taking classes in fall, spring, or summer. *Application deadline:* continuous.

PROGRAM AND SERVICE COMPONENTS

Diagnostic testing: Intelligence, reading, math, spelling, written language, perceptual skills.
Academic advising: Provided by unit staff members, academic advisers. Students with LD may take up to 18 semester units (more with approval) each term; most take 12 to 15 semester units; 12 semester units required to maintain full-time status; 6 to 12 semester units required to be eligible for financial aid.
Counseling services: Individual counseling, career counseling.
Basic skills remediation: Offered one-on-one and in small groups by teacher trainees, peer teachers. Available in reading, math, spelling, written language, learning strategies, perceptual skills, study skills, problem solving.
Subject-area tutoring: Offered one-on-one and in small groups by peer tutors, Fresno State education students. Available in all subjects.
Special courses: Reading, vocabulary development, composition, learning strategies, word processing, math, study skills. All offered for credit; none enter into overall grade point average.
Auxiliary aids: Taped textbooks, tape recorders, calculators, typewriters, word-processors with spell-check, optical character readers.
Auxiliary services: Alternative test arrangements, notetakers, priority registration, advocacy, readers.

GENERAL COLLEGE INFORMATION

State and locally supported, 2-year, coed. Part of California Community Colleges System. Awards associate degrees. Founded 1925. *Setting:* 215-acre suburban campus. *Endowment:* $1.2 million. *Educational spending 1995–96:* $1805 per undergrad. *Total enrollment:* 9,078. *Faculty:* 445 (145 full-time, 10% with terminal degrees, 300 part-time).
Enrollment Profile: 9,078 students from 23 states and territories, 10 other countries. 59% women, 41% men, 56% part-time, 87% state residents, 8% transferred in, 1% international, 43% 25 or older, 2% Native American, 34% Hispanic, 3% black, 4% Asian or Pacific Islander. *Areas of study chosen:* 58% vocational and home economics, 12% liberal arts/general studies, 10% agriculture, 4% business management and administrative services, 3% fine arts, 2% computer and information sciences, 2% engineering and applied sciences, 2% social sciences, 1% architecture, 1% biological and life sciences, 1% communications and journalism, 1% English language/literature/letters, 1% health professions and related sciences, 1% mathematics, 1% performing arts, 1% physical sciences. *Most popular recent majors:* liberal arts/general studies, business administration/commerce/management, social science.
First-Year Class: 3,125 total; 4,517 applied, 100% were accepted, 69% of whom enrolled.
Graduation Requirements: 60 units; 3 units of intermediate algebra; computer course for architecture, business, engineering majors.
Computers on Campus: 190 computers available on campus for general student use. A computer is recommended for some students. A campus-wide network can be accessed from off-campus. Students can contact faculty members and/or advisers through e-mail. Computers for student use in computer labs, classrooms, library, tutorial center provide access to the Internet/World Wide Web. Staffed computer lab on campus provides training in use of computers, software. *Academic computing expenditure 1995–96:* $323,612.

EXPENSES

Expenses for 1997–98: State resident tuition: $0 full-time. Nonresident tuition: $3810 full-time, $127 per unit part-time. Part-time mandatory fees per semester range from $25 to $155. Full-time mandatory fees: $414.
LD Services Contact: Mr. Don Mast, Associate Dean, College of the Sequoias, 915 South Mooney Boulevard, Visalia, CA 93277-2234, 209-730-3805. Fax: 209-737-4820.

COLORADO MOUNTAIN COLLEGE, ALPINE CAMPUS

Steamboat Springs, Colorado

LEARNING DISABILITIES SERVICES INFORMATION

Special Populations Services and Learning Lab began offering services in 1994. Currently the program serves 120 undergraduates with

LD. Students diagnosed with ADD/ADHD are eligible for the same services available to students with LD.
Staff: 1 part-time staff member (coordinator). Services provided by remediation specialists, tutors, counselors, diagnostic specialists.
Special Fees: $300 to $500 for diagnostic testing.
Applications and admissions: *Required:* high school transcript, psychoeducational report completed within 3 years. Students may begin taking classes in fall, spring, or summer. *Application deadline:* continuous.
Special policies: The college has written policies regarding grade forgiveness; substitutions and waivers of admissions, graduation, and degree requirements.

PROGRAM AND SERVICE COMPONENTS

Special preparation or orientation: Optional summer program offered prior to entering college. Optional orientation offered before registration and during registration.
Diagnostic testing: Reading, math, study skills.
Academic advising: Provided by unit staff members, academic advisers. Students with LD may take up to 18 credits each term; most take 12 credits; 12 credits required to maintain full-time status and be eligible for financial aid.
Counseling services: Individual counseling, career counseling, self-advocacy training.
Basic skills remediation: Offered in class-size groups by LD teachers, regular teachers. Available in reading, math, spoken language, written language, learning strategies, study skills, time management.
Subject-area tutoring: Offered one-on-one, in small groups, and in class-size groups by professional teachers, peer tutors. Available in most subjects.
Special courses: College survival skills, reading, vocabulary development, communication skills, composition, learning strategies, time management, math, study skills. Some offered for credit; some enter into overall grade point average.
Auxiliary aids: Taped textbooks, tape recorders, calculators, word-processors with spell-check.
Auxiliary services: Alternative test arrangements, notetakers.

GENERAL COLLEGE INFORMATION

District-supported, 2-year, coed. Part of Colorado Mountain College District System. Awards associate degrees. Founded 1965. *Setting:* 10-acre rural campus. *Total enrollment:* 1,262. *Faculty:* 132 (32 full-time, 25% with terminal degrees, 100 part-time).
Enrollment Profile: 1,262 students from 49 states and territories, 6 other countries. 50% women, 50% men, 64% part-time, 78% state residents, 12% live on campus, 25% transferred in, 2% international, 50% 25 or older, 1% Native American, 2% Hispanic, 1% black, 1% Asian or Pacific Islander. *Most popular recent major:* liberal arts/general studies.
First-Year Class: 198 total; 450 applied, 100% were accepted, 44% of whom enrolled.
Graduation Requirements: 62 credits; 3 credits of math; 4 credits of lab science; internship (some majors).
Computers on Campus: 60 computers available on campus for general student use. A campus-wide network can be accessed. Students can contact faculty members and/or advisers through e-mail. Computers for student use in computer center, computer labs, library provide access to the Internet/World Wide Web, on- and off-campus e-mail addresses.

EXPENSES

Expenses for 1997–98: Area resident tuition: $1020 full-time, $34 per credit part-time. State resident tuition: $1890 full-time, $63 per credit part-time. Nonresident tuition: $6000 full-time, $200 per credit part-time. Part-time mandatory fees per semester (9 to 11 credits): $50. Full-time mandatory fees: $130. College room and board: $4300.
LD Services Contact: Ms. Debra Farmer, Special Populations Coordinator, Colorado Mountain College, Alpine Campus, 1330 Bob Adams Drive, Steamboat Springs, CO 80487, 970-870-4450. Fax: 970-870-0485.

COLORADO NORTHWESTERN COMMUNITY COLLEGE

Rangely, Colorado

LEARNING DISABILITIES SERVICES INFORMATION

Supplemental Services began offering services in 1984. Currently the program serves 25 undergraduates with LD. Students diagnosed with ADD/ADHD are not eligible for the same services available to students with LD.

Staff: 2 full-time, 1 part-time staff members, including director, instructor. Services provided by remediation specialists, tutors, counselors.

Special Fees: No special fees are charged for services to students with LD.

Applications and admissions: Open admissions. Students may begin taking classes in fall only. *Application deadline:* continuous.

Special policies: The college has written policies regarding grade forgiveness; substitutions and waivers of admissions and graduation requirements.

PROGRAM AND SERVICE COMPONENTS

Special preparation or orientation: Optional summer program offered prior to entering college.

Diagnostic testing: Reading, spoken language, written language.

Academic advising: Provided by academic advisers. Students with LD may take up to 17 semester hours each term; most take 12 to 15 semester hours; 12 semester hours required to maintain full-time status and be eligible for financial aid.

Counseling services: Individual counseling, career counseling.

Basic skills remediation: Offered one-on-one and in class-size groups by regular teachers, Director. Available in reading, math, spelling, handwriting, written language, learning strategies, study skills, time management, phonics.

Subject-area tutoring: Offered one-on-one and in small groups by peer tutors, supplemental instruction leaders. Available in all subjects.

Special courses: College survival skills, reading, phonics. All offered for credit; all enter into overall grade point average.

Auxiliary aids: Taped textbooks, tape recorders, calculators, word-processors with spell-check, personal computers.

Auxiliary services: Alternative test arrangements, notetakers.

GENERAL COLLEGE INFORMATION

District-supported, 2-year, coed. Awards associate degrees. Founded 1962. *Setting:* 150-acre rural campus. *Research spending 1995–96:* $124,493. *Educational spending 1995–96:* $4024 per undergrad. *Total enrollment:* 563. *Faculty:* 201 (42 full-time, 5% with terminal degrees, 159 part-time).

Enrollment Profile: 563 students from 24 states and territories, 4 other countries. 55% women, 45% men, 25% part-time, 84% state residents, 8% transferred in, 1% international, 44% 25 or older, 2% Native American, 5% Hispanic, 2% black, 1% Asian or Pacific Islander. *Retention:* 49% of 1995 full-time freshmen returned. *Areas of study chosen:* 52% liberal arts/general studies, 17% engineering and applied sciences, 12% business management and administrative services, 8% health professions and related sciences, 5% agriculture, 3% computer and information sciences, 3% natural resource sciences. *Most popular recent majors:* liberal arts/general studies, dental services, law enforcement/police sciences.

First-Year Class: 155 total; 290 applied, 93% were accepted, 58% of whom enrolled. 3% from top 10% of their high school class, 16% from top quarter, 50% from top half. 3 valedictorians.

Graduation Requirements: 62 semester hours; computer course for all majors except dental hygiene.

Computers on Campus: 55 computers available on campus for general student use. Computers for student use in computer center, computer labs, learning resource center, library, dorms, off-campus apartments provide access to the Internet/World Wide Web, on- and off-campus e-mail addresses. Staffed computer lab on campus provides training in use of computers, software. *Academic computing expenditure 1995–96:* $221,608.

EXPENSES

Expenses for 1997–98: *Application fee:* $10. Area resident tuition: $0 full-time. State resident tuition: $1104 full-time, $46 per semester hour part-time. Nonresident tuition: $4200 full-time, $175 per semester hour part-time. Part-time mandatory fees: $11 per semester hour. Full-time mandatory fees: $470. College room and board: $3870. College room only: $1520.

LD Services Contact: Mr. Pete N. Kinnas, Director, Learning Assistance Center, Colorado Northwestern Community College, 500 Kennedy Drive, #5, Rangely, CO 81648, 970-675-3238. Fax: 970-675-3330. Email: pkinnas@cncc.cc.co.us.

COLUMBIA BASIN COLLEGE

Pasco, Washington

LEARNING DISABILITIES SERVICES INFORMATION

Educational Access Disability Resource Center began offering services in 1988. Currently the program serves 168 undergraduates with LD. Students diagnosed with ADD/ADHD are eligible for the same services available to students with LD.

Staff: 2 full-time, 2 part-time staff members, including coordinator. Services provided by counselor, instructional aide.

Special Fees: No special fees are charged for services to students with LD.

Applications and admissions: *Required:* high school transcript, IEP (Individualized Education Program), personal interview, psychoeducational report completed within 3 to 5 years. Students may begin taking classes any term. *Application deadline:* continuous.

PROGRAM AND SERVICE COMPONENTS

Special preparation or orientation: Optional orientation offered before registration.

Diagnostic testing: Reading, math, spelling, handwriting, perceptual skills, learning strategies.

Academic advising: Provided by unit staff members, academic advisers, coordinator and counselor liaison. Students with LD may take up to 16 quarter hours each term; most take 6 to 8 quarter hours; 12 quarter hours required to maintain full-time status; 6 quarter hours (part-time) required to be eligible for financial aid.

Counseling services: Individual counseling, career counseling.

Basic skills remediation: Offered one-on-one and in class-size groups by regular teachers. Available in reading, math, spelling, written language, study skills, time management.

Subject-area tutoring: Offered one-on-one by peer tutors, community volunteers. Available in most subjects.

Special courses: College survival skills, reading, vocabulary development, communication skills, time management, math, study skills, career planning, stress management. All offered for credit; most enter into overall grade point average.

Auxiliary aids: Taped textbooks, tape recorders, typewriters, word-processors with spell-check, optical character readers, word processors with voice and large print capability.

Auxiliary services: Alternative test arrangements, notetakers, priority registration, advocacy, proofreading.

Campus support group: A special student organization is available to students with LD.

GENERAL COLLEGE INFORMATION

State-supported, 2-year, coed. Part of Washington State Board for Community and Technical Colleges. Awards associate degrees. Founded 1955. *Setting:* 156-acre small-town campus. *Total enrollment:* 6,761. *Faculty:* 350 (100 full-time, 10% with terminal degrees, 250 part-time); student–undergrad faculty ratio is 18:1.

Enrollment Profile: 6,761 students from 9 states and territories, 24 other countries. 54% women, 46% men, 53% part-time, 98% state residents, 30% transferred in, 50% 25 or older, 1% Native American, 9% Hispanic, 1% black, 2% Asian or Pacific Islander. *Most popular recent majors:* liberal arts/general studies, nursing, computer science.

First-Year Class: Of the students who applied, 100% were accepted, 100% of whom enrolled.

Graduation Requirements: 92 quarter hours.

Computers on Campus: 450 computers available on campus for general student use. A campus-wide network can be accessed. Students can contact faculty members and/or advisers through e-mail. Computers for student use in computer center, computer labs, learning resource center, classrooms, library, academic buildings provide access to the Internet/World Wide Web, on-campus e-mail addresses. Staffed computer lab on campus.

EXPENSES

Expenses for 1996–97: State resident tuition: $1401 full-time, $46.70 per quarter hour part-time. Nonresident tuition: $5511 full-time, $183.70 per quarter hour part-time. Part-time mandatory fees: $7 per quarter. Full-time mandatory fees: $13.

LD Services Contact: Ms. Peggy Buchmiller, Coordinator, Education Access Disability Resource Center, Columbia Basin College, 2600 North 20th Avenue, Pasco, WA 99301-3397, 509-547-0511 Ext. 252. Fax: 509-546-0401. Email: pbuchmil@ctc.edu.

COLUMBIA-GREENE COMMUNITY COLLEGE

Hudson, New York

LEARNING DISABILITIES SERVICES INFORMATION

Learning Disabilities Support Program, Department of Alternative Learning began offering services in 1990. Currently the program serves 25 undergraduates with LD. Students diagnosed with ADD/ADHD are eligible for the same services available to students with LD.

Staff: 3 full-time, 2 part-time staff members, including coordinator. Services provided by remediation specialists, tutors, Vocational and Applied Technology Education Act (VATEA) counselor.

Special Fees: No special fees are charged for services to students with LD.

Applications and admissions: *Required:* high school transcript, grade point average, courses completed, IEP (Individualized Education Program), personal interview; *recommended:* high school class rank, extracurricular activities, autobiographical statement, psychoeducational report. Students may begin taking classes any term. *Application deadline:* continuous.

PROGRAM AND SERVICE COMPONENTS

Academic advising: Provided by academic advisers, coordinator. Students with LD may take up to 12 credits each term; most take 9 to 12 credits; 12 credits required to maintain full-time status and be eligible for financial aid.

Counseling services: Individual counseling, career counseling.

Basic skills remediation: Offered one-on-one, in small groups, and in class-size groups by regular teachers; computer-aided instruction also offered. Available in reading, math, spelling, handwriting, written language, learning strategies, study skills, time management.

Subject-area tutoring: Offered one-on-one and in small groups by professional teachers, peer tutors. Available in some subjects.

Special courses: College survival skills, reading, vocabulary development, communication skills, composition, learning strategies, word processing, time management, math, typing, study skills, career planning. None offered for credit.

Auxiliary aids: Taped textbooks, tape recorders, calculators, typewriters, word-processors with spell-check, personal computers.

Auxiliary services: Alternative test arrangements, notetakers, priority registration, advocacy.

GENERAL COLLEGE INFORMATION

State and locally supported, 2-year, coed. Part of State University of New York System. Awards associate degrees. Founded 1969. *Setting:* 143-acre rural campus. *Total enrollment:* 1,578. *Faculty:* 115 (48 full-time, 16% with terminal degrees, 67 part-time); student–undergrad faculty ratio is 15:1.

Enrollment Profile: 1,578 students from 4 states and territories, 15 other countries. 60% women, 40% men, 48% part-time, 92% state residents, 20% transferred in, 1% international, 56% 25 or older, 1% Native American, 8% Hispanic, 14% black, 1% Asian or Pacific Islander. *Retention:* 60% of 1995 full-time freshmen returned. *Areas of study chosen:* 28% interdisciplinary studies, 25% health professions and related sciences, 20% social sciences, 10% business management and administrative services, 10% computer and information sciences, 2% fine arts. *Most popular recent majors:* nursing, criminal justice, interdisciplinary studies.

First-Year Class: 511 total; 820 applied, 83% of whom enrolled.

Graduation Requirements: 62 credits; 1 course each in math and science; internship (some majors).

Computers on Campus: 90 computers available on campus for general student use. A campus-wide network can be accessed from off-campus. Students can contact faculty members and/or advisers through e-mail. Computers for student use in computer center, computer labs, learning resource center, library provide access to the Internet/World Wide Web, on- and off-campus e-mail addresses. Staffed computer lab on campus provides training in use of computers, software.

EXPENSES

Expenses for 1996–97: *Application fee:* $25. State resident tuition: $2064 full-time, $86 per credit part-time. Nonresident tuition: $4128 full-time, $172 per credit part-time. Part-time mandatory fees: $4 per credit. Full-time mandatory fees: $126.

LD Services Contact: Ms. Sherill Bolevice, Coordinator of Services to Students with Learning Disabilities, Columbia-Greene Community College, 4400 Route 23, Hudson, NY 12534, 518-828-4181 Ext. 3123. Fax: 518-828-8543.

COMMUNITY COLLEGE OF AURORA

Aurora, Colorado

LEARNING DISABILITIES SERVICES INFORMATION

Disability Services began offering services in 1983. Currently the program serves 150 undergraduates with LD. Students diagnosed with ADD/ADHD are eligible for the same services available to students with LD.

Staff: 1 full-time, 1 part-time staff members, including coordinator. Services provided by tutors.

Special Fees: No special fees are charged for services to students with LD.

Applications and admissions: *Required:* evaluations from high school counselors. Students may begin taking classes in fall, spring, or summer. *Application deadline:* continuous.

Special policies: The college has written policies regarding grade forgiveness.

PROGRAM AND SERVICE COMPONENTS

Academic advising: Provided by academic advisers. Most students with LD take 6 credit hours each term; 12 credit hours required to maintain full-time status; 6 credit hours required to be eligible for financial aid.

Counseling services: Career counseling.

Basic skills remediation: Offered one-on-one and in small groups by professional tutors, local retired teachers. Available in reading, math, spelling, written language, learning strategies, study skills.

Subject-area tutoring: Offered one-on-one and in small groups by peer tutors, professional tutors, local retired teachers. Available in all subjects.

Special courses: Learning strategies, word processing. All offered for credit; all enter into overall grade point average.

Auxiliary aids: Taped textbooks, tape recorders, typewriters, word-processors with spell-check, personal computers.

Auxiliary services: Alternative test arrangements, notetakers, advocacy.

GENERAL COLLEGE INFORMATION

State-supported, 2-year, coed. Awards associate degrees. Founded 1983. *Setting:* suburban campus with easy access to Denver. *Total enrollment:* 4,440. *Faculty:* 197 (18 full-time, 179 part-time); student–undergrad faculty ratio is 18:1.

Enrollment Profile: 4,440 students: 62% women, 38% men, 79% part-time, 95% state residents, 13% transferred in, 1% international, 60% 25 or older, 2% Native American, 8% Hispanic, 15% black, 5% Asian or Pacific Islander.

First-Year Class: 3,394 total.

Graduation Requirements: 60 semester hours; computer course for accounting, banking and financial services, insurance, flight attendant, management, marketing, metrology, criminal justice majors.

Computers on Campus: 160 computers available on campus for general student use. Computers for student use in computer center, computer labs, research center, learning resource center, classrooms, library, student center. Staffed computer lab on campus provides training in use of computers, software.

EXPENSES

Expenses for 1997–98: State resident tuition: $1629 full-time, $54.30 per semester hour part-time. Nonresident tuition: $7568 full-time, $252.25 per semester hour part-time. Part-time mandatory fees per semester range from $19.50 to $39.50. Full-time mandatory fees: $95.

LD Services Contact: Ms. Theresa Campbell Caron, Coordinator, Disability Services, Community College of Aurora, 16000 East Centre Tech Parkway, A-203, Aurora, CO 80011-9036, 303-360-4736. Fax: 303-360-4761.

COMMUNITY COLLEGE OF BEAVER COUNTY

Monaca, Pennsylvania

LEARNING DISABILITIES SERVICES INFORMATION

Vocational Education Supportive Services began offering services in 1990. Currently the program serves 45 undergraduates with LD. Students diagnosed with ADD/ADHD are eligible for the same services available to students with LD, as well as testing/tutoring/studying in soundproof booths.

Staff: 5 full-time, 1 part-time staff members, including director, coordinator. Services provided by remediation specialists, computer-assisted instruction specialist.

Special Fees: No special fees are charged for services to students with LD.

Applications and admissions: *Recommended:* personal interview, psychoeducational report completed within 4 years, college placement test. Students may begin taking classes any term. *Application deadline:* continuous.

PROGRAM AND SERVICE COMPONENTS

Special preparation or orientation: Optional orientation offered as students enter program.

Diagnostic testing: Reading, math, written language, learning strategies.

Academic advising: Provided by unit staff members, academic advisers. Students with LD may take up to 18 credits each term; most take 12 credits; 12 credits required to maintain full-time status and be eligible for financial aid.

Counseling services: Individual counseling.

Basic skills remediation: Offered one-on-one and in class-size groups by support specialists; computer-aided instruction also offered. Available in reading, math, written language, learning strategies, study skills, time management, social skills.

Subject-area tutoring: Offered one-on-one and in small groups by professional teachers, peer tutors, remediation specialists. Available in most subjects.

Auxiliary aids: Taped textbooks, tape recorders, calculators, typewriters, word-processors with spell-check, personal computers, talking computers, optical character readers, chroma CCD.

Auxiliary services: Alternative test arrangements, notetakers, advocacy, escorts, recorders.

Campus support group: A special student organization is available to students with LD.

GENERAL COLLEGE INFORMATION

State-supported, 2-year, coed. Awards associate degrees. Founded 1966. *Setting:* 75-acre small-town campus with easy access to Pittsburgh. *Total enrollment:* 2,352. *Faculty:* 149 (59 full-time, 90 part-time); student–undergrad faculty ratio is 20:1.

Enrollment Profile: 2,352 students from 21 states and territories, 4 other countries. 55% women, 45% men, 49% part-time, 94% state residents, 5% transferred in, 1% international, 56% 25 or older, 1% Native American, 1% Hispanic, 7% black, 0% Asian or Pacific Islander. *Retention:* 62% of 1995 full-time freshmen returned. *Most popular recent majors:* nursing, aviation technology, liberal arts/general studies.

First-Year Class: 870 total; 906 applied, 100% were accepted, 96% of whom enrolled. 10% from top 10% of their high school class, 20% from top quarter, 50% from top half.

Graduation Requirements: 60 credits; math/science requirements vary according to program; internship (some majors).

Computers on Campus: 79 computers available on campus for general student use. A campus-wide network can be accessed. Computers for student use in computer center, computer labs, learning resource center, library provide access to the Internet/World Wide Web, off-campus e-mail addresses. Staffed computer lab on campus provides training in use of computers, software.

EXPENSES

Expenses for 1997–98: *Application fee:* $25. Area resident tuition: $1980 full-time, $66 per credit part-time. State resident tuition: $4260 full-time, $142 per credit part-time. Nonresident tuition: $6540 full-time, $218 per credit part-time. Part-time mandatory fees: $50 per semester. Full-time mandatory fees: $100.

Community College of Beaver County (continued)

LD Services Contact: Ms. Lynda K. Kubik, Vocational Educational Special Populations Coordinator, Community College of Beaver County, One Campus Drive, Monaca, PA 15061, 412-775-8561 Ext. 272. Fax: 412-775-4055.

COMMUNITY COLLEGE OF PHILADELPHIA

Philadelphia, Pennsylvania

LEARNING DISABILITIES SERVICES INFORMATION

Center on Disability began offering services in 1984. Currently the program serves 180 undergraduates with LD. Students diagnosed with ADD/ADHD are eligible for the same services available to students with LD.

Staff: 5 full-time, 20 part-time staff members, including director. Services provided by remediation specialists, tutors, counselor, diagnostic specialist, reader, writer, computer trainer, disability aides, scribe.

Special Fees: No special fees are charged for services to students with LD.

Applications and admissions: *Required:* high school IEP (Individualized Education Program), psychoeducational report. Students may begin taking classes any term. *Application deadline:* continuous.

Special policies: The college has written policies regarding grade forgiveness; substitutions and waivers of graduation requirements.

PROGRAM AND SERVICE COMPONENTS

Special preparation or orientation: Optional orientation offered after registration, prior to the start of classes.

Diagnostic testing: Intelligence, reading, math, spelling, written language, perceptual skills.

Academic advising: Provided by unit staff members. Students with LD may take up to 16 credit hours each term; most take 9 credit hours; 12 credit hours required to maintain full-time status; source of aid determines number of credit hours required to be eligible for financial aid.

Counseling services: Individual counseling, small-group counseling, career counseling.

Basic skills remediation: Offered one-on-one and in small groups by LD teachers. Available in reading, math, spelling, learning strategies, study skills, time management.

Subject-area tutoring: Offered one-on-one and in small groups by professional teachers, peer tutors. Available in all subjects.

Special courses: College survival skills, reading, study skills, career planning. Some offered for credit; some enter into overall grade point average.

Auxiliary aids: Taped textbooks, tape recorders, calculators, typewriters, word-processors with spell-check, special study carrels.

Auxiliary services: Alternative test arrangements, notetakers, advocacy.

GENERAL COLLEGE INFORMATION

State and locally supported, 2-year, coed. Awards associate degrees. Founded 1964. *Setting:* 14-acre urban campus. *Total enrollment:* 18,713. *Faculty:* 1,182 (372 full-time, 810 part-time); student–undergrad faculty ratio is 22:1.

Enrollment Profile: 18,713 students: 66% women, 34% men, 71% part-time, 99% state residents, 3% transferred in, 53% 25 or older, 1% Native American, 5% Hispanic, 42% black, 7% Asian or Pacific Islander. *Most popular recent majors:* liberal arts/general studies, nursing, business administration/commerce/management.

First-Year Class: 4,125 total; 8,018 applied, 100% were accepted, 51% of whom enrolled.

Graduation Requirements: 62 credit hours; 1 math course; computer course for most majors.

Computers on Campus: 350 computers available on campus for general student use. Computers for student use in classrooms, library, learning lab. Staffed computer lab on campus provides training in use of computers.

EXPENSES

Expenses for 1997–98: Area resident tuition: $2139 full-time, $69 per credit hour part-time. State resident tuition: $4278 full-time, $138 per credit hour part-time. Nonresident tuition: $6417 full-time, $207 per credit hour part-time. Part-time mandatory fees: $5.50 per credit hour. Full-time mandatory fees: $171.

LD Services Contact: Ms. Francesca DiRosa, Director, Community College of Philadelphia, 1700 Spring Garden Street, Philadelphia, PA 19130-3991, 215-751-8050. Fax: 215-751-8806.

COMMUNITY COLLEGE OF RHODE ISLAND

Warwick, Rhode Island

LEARNING DISABILITIES SERVICES INFORMATION

Access to Opportunity began offering services in 1980. Currently the program serves 150 undergraduates with LD. Students diagnosed with ADD/ADHD are eligible for the same services available to students with LD.

Staff: 2 full-time, 2 part-time staff members, including director. Services provided by tutors, counselor, paraprofessional support staff.

Special Fees: No special fees are charged for services to students with LD.

Applications and admissions: *Required:* psychoeducational report completed within 3 years. Students may begin taking classes in fall or spring. *Application deadline:* continuous.

Special policies: The college has written policies regarding substitutions and waivers of admissions, graduation, and degree requirements.

PROGRAM AND SERVICE COMPONENTS

Special preparation or orientation: Required orientation held before registration.

Diagnostic testing: Reading, math, spelling, written language, study skills, learning strategies, career interests.

Academic advising: Provided by unit staff members. Students with LD may take up to 15 credits each term; most take 9 credits; 6 credits required to be eligible for financial aid.

Counseling services: Individual counseling, career counseling, self-advocacy training.

Basic skills remediation: Offered one-on-one, in small groups, and in class-size groups by regular teachers. Available in reading, math, written language, study skills.

Subject-area tutoring: Offered one-on-one by peer tutors, local college students. Available in most subjects.

Special courses: College survival skills. All offered for credit.

Auxiliary aids: Tape recorders, calculators, typewriters, word-processors with spell-check, personal computers, optical character readers, Franklin Speller, taped college materials, adaptive voice output computer system, assistive listening devices.

Auxiliary services: Alternative test arrangements, notetakers, priority registration, advocacy.

Campus support group: A special student organization is available to students with LD.

GENERAL COLLEGE INFORMATION

State-supported, 2-year, coed. Part of Community College of Rhode Island System. Awards associate degrees. Founded 1964. *Setting:* 205-acre suburban campus with easy access to Boston. *Educational spending 1995–96:* $3367 per undergrad. *Total enrollment:* 11,717. *Faculty:* 697 (293 full-time, 20% with terminal degrees, 404 part-time).

Enrollment Profile: 11,717 students from 3 states and territories, 11 other countries. 63% women, 37% men, 70% part-time, 95% state residents, 6% transferred in, 1% international, 55% 25 or older, 1% Native American, 7% Hispanic, 4% black, 2% Asian or Pacific Islander. *Most popular recent majors:* liberal arts/general studies, business administration/commerce/management, nursing.

First-Year Class: 3,712 total; 5,560 applied, 91% were accepted, 74% of whom enrolled.

Graduation Requirements: 60 credits; 1 math/science course; internship (some majors).

Computers on Campus: 260 computers available on campus for general student use. Computers for student use in computer labs, library, student center, departmental labs. Staffed computer lab on campus.

EXPENSES

Expenses for 1997–98: *Application fee:* $20. State resident tuition: $1776 full-time, $74 per credit part-time. Nonresident tuition: $5280 full-time, $220 per credit part-time. Part-time mandatory fees per semester range from $25 to $65. Nonresidents who are eligible for the New England Regional Student Program pay state resident tuition rates. Full-time mandatory fees: $180.

LD Services Contact: Tracy Karasinski, Counselor, Community College of Rhode Island, 400 East Avenue, Warwick, RI 02886-1807, 401-825-2305. Fax: 401-825-2282. Email: tkarasinski@ccri.cc.ri.us.

CORNING COMMUNITY COLLEGE

Corning, New York

LEARNING DISABILITIES SERVICES INFORMATION

Student Support Services Project (TRIO Program) began offering services in 1973. Currently the program serves 116 undergraduates with LD. Students diagnosed with ADD/ADHD are eligible for the same services available to students with LD, as well as assistance with organizational skills.
Staff: 5 full-time, 1 part-time staff members, including director. Services provided by remediation specialists, tutors, counselors, diagnostic specialist.
Special Fees: No special fees are charged for services to students with LD.
Applications and admissions: *Required:* high school transcript, grade point average, class rank, courses completed, IEP (Individualized Education Program), psychoeducational report completed as recently as determined necessary. Students may begin taking classes in fall, spring, or summer. *Application deadline:* continuous.
Special policies: The college has written policies regarding substitutions and waivers of admissions and degree requirements.

PROGRAM AND SERVICE COMPONENTS

Special preparation or orientation: Optional orientation offered before registration, during registration, after classes begin.
Diagnostic testing: Intelligence, reading, math, spelling, handwriting, spoken language, written language, perceptual skills, study skills, learning strategies.
Academic advising: Provided by unit staff members, academic advisers. Most students with LD take 9 to 12 credit hours each term; 12 credit hours required to maintain full-time status; 6 credit hours required to be eligible for financial aid.
Counseling services: Individual counseling, career counseling, self-advocacy training.
Basic skills remediation: Offered one-on-one and in class-size groups by LD teachers, regular teachers; computer-aided instruction also offered. Available in reading, math, spelling, written language, learning strategies, study skills, time management, social skills, computer skills.
Subject-area tutoring: Offered one-on-one and in small groups by professional teachers, peer tutors. Available in most subjects.
Special courses: College survival skills, reading, vocabulary development, communication skills, composition, learning strategies, word processing, time management, math, study skills, career planning. Some offered for credit; all enter into overall grade point average.
Auxiliary aids: Taped textbooks, tape recorders, calculators, word-processors with spell-check, personal computers, talking computers, optical character readers, reading machines, voice-activated computer software.
Auxiliary services: Alternative test arrangements, notetakers, advocacy.
Campus support group: A special student organization is available to students with LD.

GENERAL COLLEGE INFORMATION

State and locally supported, 2-year, coed. Part of State University of New York System. Awards associate degrees. Founded 1956. *Setting:* 275-acre rural campus. *Endowment:* $944,595. *Educational spending 1995–96:* $7120 per undergrad. *Total enrollment:* 3,220. *Faculty:* 188 (102 full-time, 95% with terminal degrees, 86 part-time); student–undergrad faculty ratio is 17:1.
Enrollment Profile: 3,220 students from 3 states and territories, 2 other countries. 56% women, 44% men, 35% part-time, 97% state residents, 6% transferred in, 38% 25 or older, 1% Native American, 1% Hispanic, 3% black, 1% Asian or Pacific Islander. *Retention:* 77% of 1995 full-time freshmen returned. *Areas of study chosen:* 23% vocational and home economics, 20% liberal arts/general studies, 17% business management and administrative services, 12% social sciences, 10% computer and information sciences, 8% health professions and related sciences, 6% engineering and applied sciences, 5% mathematics. *Most popular recent majors:* liberal arts/general studies, business administration/commerce/management, criminal justice.
First-Year Class: 983 total; 1,479 applied, 84% were accepted, 79% of whom enrolled. 3% from top 10% of their high school class, 14% from top quarter, 45% from top half.
Graduation Requirements: 62 credit hours; at least 1 course each in math and science; computer course for most majors; internship (some majors).
Computers on Campus: 350 computers available on campus for general student use. Computer purchase/lease plans available. A computer is recommended for some students. A campus-wide network can be accessed from off-campus. Students can contact faculty members and/or advisers through e-mail. Computers for student use in computer labs, learning resource center, classrooms, library, student center provide access to the Internet/World Wide Web. Staffed computer lab on campus provides training in use of computers, software.

EXPENSES

Expenses for 1996–97: *Application fee:* $25. State resident tuition: $2400 full-time, $100 per credit hour part-time. Nonresident tuition: $4800 full-time, $200 per credit hour part-time. Full-time mandatory fees: $166.
LD Services Contact: Ms. Judy Northrop, Counselor for Students with Learning Disabilities, Corning Community College, One Academic Drive, Corning, NY 14830, 607-962-9459. Fax: 607-962-9246.

CUYAHOGA COMMUNITY COLLEGE, EASTERN CAMPUS

Highland Hills, Ohio

LEARNING DISABILITIES SERVICES INFORMATION

Access Department began offering services in 1982. Currently the program serves 76 undergraduates with LD. Students diagnosed with ADD/ADHD are eligible for the same services available to students with LD.
Staff: 6 full-time, 12 part-time staff members, including director, coordinator, LD specialist, advisers, secretary/proctor. Services provided by tutors, counselors, diagnostic specialist.
Special Fees: No special fees are charged for services to students with LD.
Applications and admissions: *Required:* high school transcript, psychoeducational report completed within 3 years. Students may begin taking classes any term. *Application deadline:* continuous.
Special policies: The college has written policies regarding grade forgiveness; substitutions and waivers of graduation and degree requirements.

PROGRAM AND SERVICE COMPONENTS

Special preparation or orientation: Optional summer program offered prior to entering college. Orientation offered during registration for Fall quarter.
Academic advising: Provided by unit staff members. Students with LD may take up to 12 credit hours each term; most take 6 to 9 credit hours; 12 credit hours required to maintain full-time status; 6 credit hours (part-time), 12 credit hours (full-time) required to be eligible for financial aid.
Counseling services: Individual counseling, career counseling.
Basic skills remediation: Offered one-on-one, in small groups, and in class-size groups by regular teachers. Available in reading, math, written language, learning strategies, study skills, speech.
Subject-area tutoring: Offered one-on-one and in small groups by professional teachers, peer tutors, local retired teachers. Available in some subjects.
Auxiliary aids: Taped textbooks, tape recorders, calculators, typewriters, word-processors with spell-check, personal computers, computer adaptive technology and software.
Auxiliary services: Alternative test arrangements, notetakers, priority registration, advocacy, readers, writers.

GENERAL COLLEGE INFORMATION

State and locally supported, 2-year, coed. Part of Cuyahoga Community College District System. Awards associate degrees. Founded 1971. *Setting:* 25-acre suburban campus with easy access to Cleveland. *Total enrollment:* 4,959. *Faculty:* 201 (78 full-time, 23% with terminal degrees, 123 part-time); student–undergrad faculty ratio is 19:1.

Cuyahoga Community College, Eastern Campus (continued)

Enrollment Profile: 4,959 students: 68% women, 32% men, 73% part-time, 98% state residents, 1% international, 65% 25 or older, 0% Native American, 1% Hispanic, 45% black, 2% Asian or Pacific Islander. *Most popular recent major:* liberal arts/general studies.
First-Year Class: Of the students who applied, 100% were accepted.
Graduation Requirements: 93 credit hours; math/science requirements vary according to program; computer course for office administration, word processing, finance, business administration, accounting, agricultural technology, marketing, real estate, pharmacy majors; internship (some majors).
Computers on Campus: 200 computers available on campus for general student use. A campus-wide network can be accessed from off-campus. Computers for student use in computer labs, classrooms. Staffed computer lab on campus provides training in use of computers, software.

EXPENSES

Expenses for 1997–98: *Application fee:* $10. Area resident tuition: $1725 full-time, $36.70 per credit hour part-time. State resident tuition: $2338 full-time, $49.75 per credit hour part-time. Nonresident tuition: $4813 full-time, $102.40 per credit hour part-time. Part-time mandatory fees: $3.10 per credit hour. Full-time mandatory fees: $146.
LD Services Contact: Ms. Mary Syarto, Director of Access, Cuyahoga Community College, Eastern Campus, 4250 Richmond Road, Highland Hills, OH 44122-6104, 216-987-5106.

CUYAMACA COLLEGE

El Cajon, California

LEARNING DISABILITIES SERVICES INFORMATION

Disabled Students Programs and Services (DSP&S) began offering services in 1987. Currently the program serves 95 undergraduates with LD. Students diagnosed with ADD/ADHD are eligible for the same services available to students with LD.
Staff: 1 full-time, 6 part-time staff members, including coordinators. Services provided by tutors, counselors, diagnostic specialists.
Special Fees: No special fees are charged for services to students with LD.
Applications and admissions: *Recommended:* psychoeducational report completed within 3 years. Students may begin taking classes in fall, spring, or summer. *Application deadline:* continuous.
Special policies: The college has written policies regarding grade forgiveness; substitutions and waivers of degree requirements.

PROGRAM AND SERVICE COMPONENTS

Diagnostic testing: Intelligence, reading, math, spelling, spoken language, written language, perceptual skills, speech, hearing.
Academic advising: Provided by unit staff members. Students with LD may take up to as many units as an individual can handle each term; most take 9 units; 12 units required to maintain full-time status; 3 units required to be eligible for financial aid.
Counseling services: Individual counseling, career counseling.
Subject-area tutoring: Offered one-on-one and in small groups by peer tutors. Available in some subjects.
Auxiliary aids: Taped textbooks, tape recorders, calculators, word-processors with spell-check, personal computers, talking computers, optical character readers.
Auxiliary services: Alternative test arrangements, notetakers, priority registration, advocacy.

GENERAL COLLEGE INFORMATION

State-supported, 2-year, coed. Part of Grossmont-Cuyamaca Community College District System. Awards associate degrees. Founded 1978. *Setting:* 165-acre suburban campus with easy access to San Diego. *Total enrollment:* 4,469.
Enrollment Profile: 4,469 students: 49% women, 51% men, 86% part-time, 98% state residents, 32% transferred in, 1% international, 63% 25 or older, 2% Native American, 10% Hispanic, 2% black, 5% Asian or Pacific Islander.
First-Year Class: 1,825 total. Of the students who applied, 100% were accepted.
Graduation Requirements: 60 units; math/science requirements vary according to program.
Computers on Campus: 125 computers available on campus for general student use. Computers for student use in computer center. Staffed computer lab on campus.

EXPENSES

Expenses for 1997–98: State resident tuition: $0 full-time. Nonresident tuition: $3420 full-time, $114 per unit part-time. Part-time mandatory fees per semester range from $24 to $158. Full-time mandatory fees: $420.
LD Services Contact: Ms. O. Yvonette Murrell-Powell, DSP&S Coordinator/Counselor, Cuyamaca College, 900 Rancho San Diego Parkway, El Cajon, CA 92019, 619-670-1980. Fax: 619-660-4399. Email: yvonette_powell@gcccd.cc.ca.us.

CYPRESS COLLEGE

Cypress, California

LEARNING DISABILITIES SERVICES INFORMATION

Roosevelt Center began offering services in 1979. Currently the program serves 190 undergraduates with LD. Students diagnosed with ADD/ADHD are eligible for the same services available to students with LD, as well as referrals to community resources.
Staff: 5 full-time, 16 part-time staff members, including director. Services provided by remediation specialists, tutors, counselor, diagnostic specialist.
Special Fees: No special fees are charged for services to students with LD.
Applications and admissions: *Required:* California Community Colleges Learning Disabilities Eligibility Assessment. Students may begin taking classes any term. *Application deadline:* continuous.
Special policies: The college has written policies regarding grade forgiveness; substitutions and waivers of graduation requirements.

PROGRAM AND SERVICE COMPONENTS

Special preparation or orientation: Required orientation held before registration.
Diagnostic testing: Intelligence, reading, math, spelling, handwriting, spoken language, written language, motor abilities, perceptual skills.
Academic advising: Provided by unit staff members, academic advisers. Students with LD may take up to 19 units each term; most take 12 units; 12 units required to maintain full-time status; source of aid determines number of units required to be eligible for financial aid.
Counseling services: Individual counseling, career counseling.
Subject-area tutoring: Offered one-on-one and in small groups by peer tutors with LD training. Available in all subjects.
Special courses: College survival skills, study skills, career planning, adaptive computer courses. All offered for credit; all enter into overall grade point average.
Auxiliary aids: Taped textbooks, tape recorders, calculators, typewriters, word-processors with spell-check, personal computers, optical character readers.
Auxiliary services: Alternative test arrangements, notetakers, priority registration, advocacy.
Campus support group: A special student organization is available to students with LD.

GENERAL COLLEGE INFORMATION

State and locally supported, 2-year, coed. Part of California Community Colleges System. Awards associate degrees. Founded 1966. *Setting:* 108-acre suburban campus with easy access to Los Angeles. *Total enrollment:* 14,580. *Faculty:* 434 (209 full-time, 225 part-time); student–undergrad faculty ratio is 34:1.
Enrollment Profile: 14,580 students from 15 states and territories, 18 other countries. 58% women, 42% men, 66% part-time, 98% state residents, 13% transferred in, 1% international, 45% 25 or older, 1% Native American, 16% Hispanic, 4% black, 22% Asian or Pacific Islander.
First-Year Class: 9,362 total. Of the students who applied, 100% were accepted.
Graduation Requirements: 60 units; math/science requirements vary according to program; computer course.
Computers on Campus: 500 computers available on campus for general student use. Computers for student use in computer center, library, student center.

EXPENSES

Expenses for 1997–98: State resident tuition: $0 full-time. Nonresident tuition: $3540 full-time, $118 per unit part-time. Part-time mandatory fees: $13 per unit. Full-time mandatory fees: $390.

LD Services Contact: Ms. Cindy Owens, Learning Disabilities Specialist, Cypress College, 9200 Valley View, Cypress, CA 90630-5897, 714-826-2220 Ext. 215. Fax: 714-826-4042.

DABNEY S. LANCASTER COMMUNITY COLLEGE

Clifton Forge, Virginia

LEARNING DISABILITIES SERVICES INFORMATION

Achievement Center began offering services in 1985. Currently the program serves 20 undergraduates with LD. Students diagnosed with ADD/ADHD are eligible for the same services available to students with LD.

Staff: 3 full-time, 4 part-time staff members, including director. Services provided by tutors, counselors, peer tutors.

Special Fees: No special fees are charged for services to students with LD.

Applications and admissions: *Recommended:* high school transcript, courses completed, psychoeducational report completed within 3 years. Students may begin taking classes in fall, spring, or summer. *Application deadline:* continuous.

Special policies: The college has written policies regarding grade forgiveness.

PROGRAM AND SERVICE COMPONENTS

Academic advising: Provided by unit staff members, academic advisers. Most students with LD take 12 semester hours each term; 12 semester hours required to maintain full-time status; 6 semester hours required to be eligible for financial aid.

Counseling services: Individual counseling, small-group counseling, career counseling, self-advocacy training.

Subject-area tutoring: Offered one-on-one and in small groups by peer tutors, instructional assistants, paraprofessionals, tutors. Available in all subjects.

Auxiliary aids: Taped textbooks, tape recorders, word-processors with spell-check, personal computers.

Auxiliary services: Alternative test arrangements, notetakers, advocacy.

GENERAL COLLEGE INFORMATION

State-supported, 2-year, coed. Part of Virginia Community College System. Awards associate degrees. Founded 1964. *Setting:* 117-acre rural campus. *Total enrollment:* 1,722. *Faculty:* 160 (38 full-time, 122 part-time); student–undergrad faculty ratio is 14:1.

Enrollment Profile: 1,722 students from 5 states and territories, 1 other country. 60% women, 40% men, 65% part-time, 96% state residents, 9% transferred in, 1% international, 59% 25 or older, 1% Native American, 0% Hispanic, 6% black, 1% Asian or Pacific Islander. *Most popular recent majors:* liberal arts/general studies, business administration/commerce/management.

First-Year Class: 459 total. Of the students who applied, 100% were accepted, 85% of whom enrolled.

Graduation Requirements: 68 semester hours; math/science requirements vary according to program; computer course.

Computers on Campus: Computers for student use in computer center, library, Achievement Center.

EXPENSES

Expenses for 1997–98: State resident tuition: $1586 full-time, $46.65 per semester hour part-time. Nonresident tuition: $5304 full-time, $156 per semester hour part-time. Part-time mandatory fees: $1.75 per semester hour. Full-time mandatory fees: $59.50.

LD Services Contact: Ms. Elizabeth Davis, Project Director, Dabney S. Lancaster Community College, Box 1000, Clifton Forge, VA 24422, 540-862-4246. Fax: 540-862-2398. Email: oldavie@dl.cc.va.us.

DANVILLE AREA COMMUNITY COLLEGE

Danville, Illinois

LEARNING DISABILITIES SERVICES INFORMATION

Special Populations Program began offering services in 1986. Currently the program serves 18 undergraduates with LD. Students diagnosed with ADD/ADHD are eligible for the same services available to students with LD.

Staff: 2 full-time, 1 part-time staff members, including coordinators, office assistant. Services provided by remediation specialists, tutors.

Special Fees: No special fees are charged for services to students with LD.

Applications and admissions: *Required:* placement testing; *recommended:* high school transcript, IEP (Individualized Education Program), personal interview, psychoeducational report. Students may begin taking classes any term. *Application deadline:* continuous.

Special policies: The college has written policies regarding substitutions and waivers of admissions and degree requirements.

PROGRAM AND SERVICE COMPONENTS

Special preparation or orientation: Optional orientation offered during registration and individually by special arrangement.

Academic advising: Provided by unit staff members, academic advisers. Students with LD may take up to 16 credit hours each term; most take 8 to 12 credit hours; 12 credit hours required to maintain full-time status; 6 credit hours required to be eligible for financial aid.

Counseling services: Individual counseling, career counseling.

Basic skills remediation: Offered in class-size groups by regular teachers. Available in reading, math, spelling, spoken language, written language, learning strategies, study skills.

Subject-area tutoring: Offered one-on-one and in small groups by professional teachers, peer tutors. Available in most subjects.

Special courses: Study skills, career planning. None offered for credit.

Auxiliary aids: Taped textbooks, tape recorders, calculators, personal computers, voice-synthesized computer.

Auxiliary services: Alternative test arrangements, notetakers, advocacy.

GENERAL COLLEGE INFORMATION

State and locally supported, 2-year, coed. Part of Illinois Community College System. Awards associate degrees. Founded 1946. *Setting:* 50-acre small-town campus. *Endowment:* $978,329. *Total enrollment:* 2,662. *Faculty:* 134 (54 full-time, 6% with terminal degrees, 80 part-time); student–undergrad faculty ratio is 25:1.

Enrollment Profile: 2,662 students: 65% women, 35% men, 58% part-time, 93% state residents, 0% international, 52% 25 or older, 0% Native American, 1% Hispanic, 8% black, 1% Asian or Pacific Islander. *Retention:* 67% of 1995 full-time freshmen returned. *Most popular recent majors:* liberal arts/general studies, business administration/commerce/management.

First-Year Class: 429 total; 797 applied, 100% were accepted. 7% from top 10% of their high school class, 25% from top quarter, 60% from top half.

Graduation Requirements: 62 semester hours; math/science requirements vary according to program; computer course for accounting, marketing, mid-management, travel and tourism, criminal justice, law enforcement, early childhood education majors; internship (some majors).

Computers on Campus: 332 computers available on campus for general student use. A campus-wide network can be accessed from off-campus. Students can contact faculty members and/or advisers through e-mail. Computers for student use in computer labs, learning resource center, classrooms, library, math labs provide access to the Internet/World Wide Web, on- and off-campus e-mail addresses. Staffed computer lab on campus provides training in use of computers, software.

EXPENSES

Expenses for 1997–98: Area resident tuition: $1240 full-time, $40 per semester hour part-time. State resident tuition: $5124 full-time, $165.28 per semester hour part-time. Nonresident tuition: $6745 full-time, $217.57 per semester hour part-time.

LD Services Contact: Ms. Karen H. Davis, Coordinator, Special Populations Program, Danville Area Community College, 2000 East Main Street, Danville, IL 61832-5199, 217-443-8853. Fax: 217-443-8563.

DARTON COLLEGE

Albany, Georgia

LEARNING DISABILITIES SERVICES INFORMATION

Disabled Students Services began offering services in 1990. Currently the program serves 43 undergraduates with LD. Students diagnosed with ADD/ADHD are eligible for the same services available to students with LD, as well as separate studying and testing environment.

Staff: 2 part-time staff members, including coordinator, counselor. Services provided by remediation specialists, tutors, counselors, peer tutors (as needed), diagnostic specialist (through affiliated university).

Special Fees: No special fees are charged for services to students with LD.

Applications and admissions: *Required:* high school transcript, extended time SAT I; *recommended:* high school grade point average, class rank, courses completed, extracurricular activities, personal interview, letters of recommendation, psychoeducational report completed within 3 years. Students may begin taking classes any term. *Application deadline:* continuous.

Special policies: The college has written policies regarding substitutions and waivers of admissions, graduation, and degree requirements.

PROGRAM AND SERVICE COMPONENTS

Academic advising: Provided by unit staff members, academic advisers. Students with LD may take up to 15 quarter hours each term; most take 12 quarter hours; 12 quarter hours required to maintain full-time status and be eligible for financial aid.

Counseling services: Individual counseling, career counseling.

Basic skills remediation: Offered one-on-one and in class-size groups by regular teachers, lab tutors; computer-aided instruction also offered. Available in reading, math, written language, learning strategies, study skills, time management.

Subject-area tutoring: Offered one-on-one and in small groups by professional teachers, peer tutors. Available in all subjects.

Special courses: College survival skills, reading, composition, learning strategies, word processing, time management, math, study skills, career planning. Some offered for credit; some enter into overall grade point average.

Auxiliary aids: Taped textbooks, tape recorders, calculators, typewriters, word-processors with spell-check, personal computers.

Auxiliary services: Alternative test arrangements, notetakers, priority registration, advocacy.

GENERAL COLLEGE INFORMATION

State-supported, 2-year, coed. Part of University System of Georgia. Awards associate degrees. Founded 1965. *Setting:* 185-acre suburban campus. *Educational spending 1995–96:* $1861 per undergrad. *Total enrollment:* 2,265. *Faculty:* 150 (80 full-time, 31% with terminal degrees, 70 part-time); student–undergrad faculty ratio is 24:1.

Enrollment Profile: 2,265 students: 69% women, 31% men, 52% part-time, 95% state residents, 5% transferred in, 41% 25 or older, 1% Hispanic, 27% black, 1% Asian or Pacific Islander. *Retention:* 25% of 1995 full-time freshmen returned. *Areas of study chosen:* 30% health professions and related sciences, 8% social sciences, 7% business management and administrative services, 6% education, 5% communications and journalism, 5% fine arts, 3% engineering and applied sciences, 2% computer and information sciences, 2% physical sciences, 2% premed, 2% psychology, 1% biological and life sciences, 1% performing arts, 1% prevet. *Most popular recent majors:* nursing, business administration/commerce/management, early childhood education.

First-Year Class: 700 total; 1,350 applied, 99% were accepted, 52% of whom enrolled. 5% from top 10% of their high school class, 15% from top quarter, 40% from top half.

Graduation Requirements: 90 quarter hours; computer course for most majors.

Computers on Campus: 350 computers available on campus for general student use. Computer purchase/lease plans available. A campus-wide network can be accessed from off-campus. Students can contact faculty members and/or advisers through e-mail. Computers for student use in computer center, computer labs, library, classroom labs provide access to the Internet/World Wide Web, on- and off-campus e-mail addresses. Staffed computer lab on campus provides training in use of computers, software.

EXPENSES

Expenses for 1997–98: *Application fee:* $5. State resident tuition: $1281 full-time, $32 per quarter hour part-time. Nonresident tuition: $4455 full-time. Nonresident part-time tuition per quarter ranges from $605 to $1210. Part-time mandatory fees per quarter (6 to 11 quarter hours): $40.

LD Services Contact: Mr. Louis Emond, Coordinator, Disabled Student Services, Darton College, 2400 Gillionville Road, Albany, GA 31707, 912-430-6729. Fax: 912-430-3053. Email: lemond@cavalier.dartnet.peachnet.edu.

DAVIDSON COUNTY COMMUNITY COLLEGE

Lexington, North Carolina

LEARNING DISABILITIES SERVICES INFORMATION

Counseling Services currently serves undergraduate students with LD. Students diagnosed with ADD/ADHD are eligible for the same services available to students with LD.

Staff: 5 full-time staff members, including coordinator, admission counselor. Services provided by remediation specialists, tutors, counselors.

Special Fees: No special fees are charged for services to students with LD.

Applications and admissions: *Required:* high school transcript, IEP (Individualized Education Program), psychoeducational report completed within 3 years. Students may begin taking classes any term. *Application deadline:* continuous.

Special policies: The college has written policies regarding substitutions and waivers of graduation and degree requirements.

PROGRAM AND SERVICE COMPONENTS

Diagnostic testing: Reading, math, written language.

Academic advising: Provided by unit staff members, academic advisers. Students with LD required to take 12 semester hours to maintain full-time status and be eligible for financial aid.

Counseling services: Individual counseling, career counseling.

Basic skills remediation: Offered one-on-one, in small groups, and in class-size groups by regular teachers. Available in reading, math, written language, study skills.

Subject-area tutoring: Offered one-on-one by professional teachers, peer tutors. Available in most subjects.

Special courses: Reading, vocabulary development, communication skills, composition, math, study skills, career planning. Some offered for credit; some enter into overall grade point average.

Auxiliary aids: Taped textbooks, tape recorders, word-processors with spell-check, personal computers.

Auxiliary services: Alternative test arrangements, notetakers.

GENERAL COLLEGE INFORMATION

State and locally supported, 2-year, coed. Part of North Carolina Community College System. Awards associate degrees. Founded 1958. *Setting:* 83-acre rural campus. *Educational spending 1995–96:* $2914 per undergrad. *Total enrollment:* 2,193. *Faculty:* 346 (61 full-time, 16% with terminal degrees, 285 part-time); student–undergrad faculty ratio is 21:1.

Enrollment Profile: 2,193 students: 62% women, 38% men, 50% part-time, 99% state residents, 1% transferred in, 1% international, 33% 25 or older, 1% Native American, 1% Hispanic, 10% black, 1% Asian or Pacific Islander. *Most popular recent majors:* business administration/commerce/management, computer programming, liberal arts/general studies.

First-Year Class: 926 total; 1,363 applied, 100% were accepted, 68% of whom enrolled.

Graduation Requirements: Math/science requirements vary according to program.

Computers on Campus: 400 computers available on campus for general student use. Computer purchase/lease plans available. Computers for student use in computer center, computer labs, learning resource center, classrooms, library. Staffed computer lab on campus provides training in use of computers, software. *Academic computing expenditure 1995–96:* $291,512.

EXPENSES

Expenses for 1997–98: State resident tuition: $560 full-time, $20 per semester hour part-time. Nonresident tuition: $4564 full-time, $163 per semester hour part-time. Part-time mandatory fees: $5.40 per semester. Full-time mandatory fees: $19.

LD Services Contact: Dr. Ed Morse, Dean of Student Development Services, Davidson County Community College, PO Box 1287, Lexington, NC 27293, 910-249-8186. Fax: 910-249-2386.

DAWSON COMMUNITY COLLEGE

Glendive, Montana

LEARNING DISABILITIES SERVICES INFORMATION

Special Services for Disadvantaged Students began offering services in 1974. Currently the program serves 40 undergraduates with LD. Students diagnosed with ADD/ADHD are eligible for the same services available to students with LD.

Staff: 3 full-time, 4 part-time staff members, including director, coordinator. Services provided by remediation specialists, tutors, counselor, peer tutors.

Special Fees: No special fees are charged for services to students with LD.

Applications and admissions: *Required:* high school transcript, ACT or SAT, verification of disability; *recommended:* high school IEP (Individualized Education Program), autobiographical statement, letters of recommendation, psychoeducational report completed within 3 years. Students may begin taking classes in fall, spring, or summer. *Application deadline:* continuous.

Special policies: The college has written policies regarding grade forgiveness.

PROGRAM AND SERVICE COMPONENTS

Academic advising: Provided by unit staff members, academic advisers. Students with LD may take up to 18 semester hours each term; most take 9 to 15 semester hours; 12 semester hours required to maintain full-time status; 6 semester hours required to be eligible for financial aid.

Counseling services: Individual counseling, career counseling.

Basic skills remediation: Offered one-on-one and in small groups by LD teachers, regular teachers. Available in reading, math, written language, learning strategies, study skills, time management, computer skills.

Subject-area tutoring: Offered one-on-one and in small groups by professional teachers, peer tutors. Available in most subjects.

Special courses: College survival skills, reading, communication skills, composition, word processing, math, typing, study skills, career planning, health and nutrition, social relationships. Most offered for credit; most enter into overall grade point average.

Auxiliary aids: Taped textbooks, tape recorders, calculators, typewriters, word-processors with spell-check, personal computers.

Auxiliary services: Alternative test arrangements, notetakers, advocacy, typing services.

GENERAL COLLEGE INFORMATION

State and locally supported, 2-year, coed. Awards associate degrees. Founded 1940. *Setting:* 300-acre rural campus. *Endowment:* $259,561. *Educational spending 1995–96:* $3457 per undergrad. *Total enrollment:* 457. *Faculty:* 60 (25 full-time, 5% with terminal degrees, 35 part-time).

Enrollment Profile: 457 students from 2 states and territories. 56% women, 44% men, 31% part-time, 97% state residents, 18% live on campus, 4% transferred in, 0% international, 25% 25 or older, 3% Native American, 1% Hispanic, 0% black, 1% Asian or Pacific Islander. *Areas of study chosen:* 26% liberal arts/general studies, 8% business management and administrative services, 7% agriculture, 4% health professions and related sciences, 2% computer and information sciences. *Most popular recent majors:* liberal arts/general studies, business administration/commerce/management, human services.

First-Year Class: 129 total; 225 applied, 100% were accepted.

Graduation Requirements: 60 semester hours; computer course for agriculture, automotive, business, human services, office management majors, transfer associate degree programs; internship (some majors).

Computers on Campus: 70 computers available on campus for general student use. A campus-wide network can be accessed from off-campus. Students can contact faculty members and/or advisers through e-mail. Computers for student use in computer labs, learning resource center, library provide access to on-campus e-mail addresses. Staffed computer lab on campus provides training in use of computers, software. *Academic computing expenditure 1995–96:* $18,000.

EXPENSES

Expenses for 1996–97: *Application fee:* $30. Area resident tuition: $840 full-time, $30 per semester hour part-time. State resident tuition: $1442 full-time, $51.50 per semester hour part-time. Nonresident tuition: $3493 full-time, $124.75 per semester hour part-time. Part-time mandatory fees: $20 per semester hour. Nonresidents who are eligible for the Western Undergraduate Exchange pay state resident tuition rates. Full-time mandatory fees: $560. College room only: $1215.

LD Services Contact: Kent Dion, Director, Student Support Services, Dawson Community College, Box 421, Glendive, MT 59330, 406-365-5928. Fax: 406-365-8132. Email: kent_d@dawson.cc.mt.us.

DEAN COLLEGE

Franklin, Massachusetts

LEARNING DISABILITIES SERVICES INFORMATION

Personalized Learning Services (PLS) began offering services in 1989. Currently the program serves 150 undergraduates with LD. Students diagnosed with ADD/ADHD are eligible for the same services available to students with LD.

Staff: 2 full-time, 3 part-time staff members, including director, assistant director, coordinator, FACTS Advisor. Services provided by remediation specialist, tutors, learning specialists.

Special Fees: Special fees are charged for services to students with LD.

Applications and admissions: *Required:* high school transcript, courses completed, letters of recommendation, psychoeducational report completed within 2 years; *recommended:* high school class rank, untimed or extended time SAT I, personal interview, autobiographical statement. Students may begin taking classes in fall or spring. *Application deadline:* continuous.

Special policies: The college has written policies regarding substitutions and waivers of admissions, graduation, and degree requirements.

PROGRAM AND SERVICE COMPONENTS

Academic advising: Provided by academic advisers. Students with LD may take up to 18.5 credits each term; most take 12 to 15 credits; 12 credits required to maintain full-time status and be eligible for financial aid.

Subject-area tutoring: Offered one-on-one and in small groups by professional teachers, peer tutors. Available in all subjects.

Auxiliary aids: Taped textbooks, tape recorders, calculators, word-processors with spell-check, personal computers, screen enlargements.

Auxiliary services: Alternative test arrangements, notetakers, advocacy.

GENERAL COLLEGE INFORMATION

Independent, 2-year, coed. Awards associate degrees. Founded 1865. *Setting:* 100-acre small-town campus with easy access to Boston. *Endowment:* $9.8 million. *Total enrollment:* 1,950. *Faculty:* 111 (33 full-time, 10% with terminal degrees, 78 part-time); student–undergrad faculty ratio is 14:1.

Enrollment Profile: 1,950 students from 24 states and territories, 20 other countries. 45% women, 55% men, 53% part-time, 43% state residents, 80% live on campus, 5% transferred in, 10% international, 1% 25 or older, 0% Native American, 4% Hispanic, 10% black, 1% Asian or Pacific Islander. *Areas of study chosen:* 20% liberal arts/general studies, 17% social sciences, 14% performing arts, 13% health professions and related sciences, 12% business management and administrative services, 7% communications and journalism, 7% education, 3% computer and information sciences, 2% engineering and applied sciences, 1% biological and life sciences, 1% mathematics. *Most popular recent majors:* business administration/commerce/management, liberal arts/general studies, communication.

First-Year Class: 382 total; 1,466 applied, 86% were accepted, 30% of whom enrolled. 5% from top 10% of their high school class, 11% from top quarter, 30% from top half.

Graduation Requirements: 60 credits; completion of math proficiency test; computer course for business, criminal justice, math, pre-engineering, science, paralegal majors; internship (some majors).

Computers on Campus: 150 computers available on campus for general student use. A campus-wide network can be accessed from student residence rooms. Students can contact faculty members and/or advisers through e-mail. Computers for student use in computer center, library, writing center provide access to the Internet/World Wide Web, on-campus e-mail addresses. Staffed computer lab on campus (open 24 hours a day) provides training in use of computers, software. *Academic computing expenditure 1995–96:* $104,084.

Dean College (continued)

EXPENSES

Expenses for 1997–98: *Application fee:* $35. Comprehensive fee of $19,085 includes full-time tuition ($11,880 minimum), mandatory fees ($605 minimum), and college room and board ($6600). College room only: $4300. Full-time mandatory fees range from $605 to $805. Full-time tuition ranges up to $12,470 according to class level. Part-time tuition for continuing education program: $146 per credit. Part-time mandatory fees for continuing education program: $20 per semester. Tuition guaranteed not to increase for student's term of enrollment.
LD Services Contact: Ms. Francesca Purcell, FACTS Advisor, Dean College, 99 Main Street, Franklin, MA 02038-1994, 508-541-1558. Fax: 508-541-1549.

DEKALB COLLEGE

Decatur, Georgia

LEARNING DISABILITIES SERVICES INFORMATION

Center for Disability Services currently serves 300 undergraduates with LD. Students diagnosed with ADD/ADHD are eligible for the same services available to students with LD.
Staff: 9 full-time staff members, including director. Services provided by tutors, counselors, notetakers, readers.
Special Fees: No special fees are charged for services to students with LD.
Applications and admissions: *Required:* high school transcript, grade point average, courses completed, IEP (Individualized Education Program), untimed SAT I or ACT, psychoeducational report completed within 3 years, immunization records, psychological evaluation, high school college prep curriculum; *recommended:* extended time SAT I or ACT. Students may begin taking classes in fall, spring, or summer.
Special policies: The college has written policies regarding grade forgiveness; substitutions and waivers of admissions requirements.

PROGRAM AND SERVICE COMPONENTS

Special preparation or orientation: Optional orientation offered before registration.
Academic advising: Provided by unit staff members, academic advisers. Students with LD may take up to 18 semester hours each term; most take 12 to 15 semester hours; 12 semester hours required to maintain full-time status; 6 semester hours required to be eligible for financial aid.
Counseling services: Individual counseling, career counseling.
Basic skills remediation: Offered one-on-one and in small groups by tutors. Available in reading, math, written language.
Subject-area tutoring: Offered one-on-one and in small groups by professional teachers, peer tutors, subject specialists. Available in some subjects.
Auxiliary aids: Taped textbooks, tape recorders, calculators, word-processors with spell-check, personal computers, optical character readers, voice-activated computer, closed-captioned television.
Auxiliary services: Alternative test arrangements, notetakers, priority registration, advocacy.

GENERAL COLLEGE INFORMATION

State-supported, 2-year, coed. Part of University System of Georgia. Awards associate degrees. Founded 1964. *Setting:* 100-acre suburban campus with easy access to Atlanta. *Educational spending 1995–96:* $1261 per undergrad. *Total enrollment:* 15,690. *Faculty:* 1,050 (335 full-time, 23% with terminal degrees, 715 part-time); student–undergrad faculty ratio is 20:1.
Enrollment Profile: 15,690 students from 14 states and territories, 102 other countries. 61% women, 39% men, 65% part-time, 95% state residents, 6% transferred in, 4% international, 41% 25 or older, 1% Native American, 2% Hispanic, 30% black, 6% Asian or Pacific Islander. *Areas of study chosen:* 43% liberal arts/general studies, 18% health professions and related sciences, 15% business management and administrative services, 5% education, 3% computer and information sciences, 3% engineering and applied sciences, 3% psychology, 3% social sciences, 2% biological and life sciences, 1% agriculture, 1% communications and journalism, 1% English language/literature/letters, 1% fine arts, 1% foreign language and literature, 1% mathematics, 1% philosophy, 1% predentistry, 1% premed, 1% vocational and home economics. *Most popular recent majors:* business administration/commerce/management, nursing.
First-Year Class: 2,392 total; 2,932 applied, 100% were accepted, 82% of whom enrolled.
Graduation Requirements: 100 credit hours; computer course for business administration majors.
Computers on Campus: 50 computers available on campus for general student use. A campus-wide network can be accessed from off-campus. Students can contact faculty members and/or advisers through e-mail. Computers for student use in computer labs, classrooms, library provide access to the Internet/World Wide Web. Staffed computer lab on campus.

EXPENSES

Expenses for 1996–97: State resident tuition: $1225 full-time, $24.50 per credit hour part-time. Nonresident tuition: $4025 full-time, $80.50 per credit hour part-time. Part-time mandatory fees: $41 per quarter. Full-time mandatory fees: $123.
LD Services Contact: Dr. Louise B. Cebula, Counselor, Center for Disability Services, DeKalb College, 555 North Indian Creek Drive, Clarkston, GA 30021, 404-299-4120. Fax: 404-298-3830.

DEL MAR COLLEGE

Corpus Christi, Texas

LEARNING DISABILITIES SERVICES INFORMATION

Special Populations Office began offering services in 1984. Students diagnosed with ADD/ADHD are eligible for the same services available to students with LD.
Staff: 3 full-time staff members, including director, associate directors. Services provided by diagnostic specialist.
Special Fees: No special fees are charged for services to students with LD.
Applications and admissions: *Required:* high school transcript, psychoeducational report. Students may begin taking classes any term. *Application deadline:* continuous.

PROGRAM AND SERVICE COMPONENTS

Academic advising: Provided by academic advisers. Most students with LD take 9 semester hours each term; 9 semester hours required to maintain full-time status; 9 to 12 semester hours required to be eligible for financial aid.
Special courses: Reading.
Auxiliary aids: Typewriters, word-processors with spell-check, talking computers, optical character readers, electronic readers.
Auxiliary services: Alternative test arrangements, notetakers, priority registration, advocacy, scribes.

GENERAL COLLEGE INFORMATION

State and locally supported, 2-year, coed. Part of Texas Higher Education Coordinating Board. Awards associate degrees. Founded 1935. *Setting:* 159-acre urban campus. *Total enrollment:* 10,386. *Faculty:* 535.
Enrollment Profile: 10,386 students: 59% women, 41% men, 66% part-time, 98% state residents, 7% transferred in, 1% international, 68% 25 or older, 1% Native American, 52% Hispanic, 2% black, 1% Asian or Pacific Islander. *Areas of study chosen:* 20% health professions and related sciences, 9% business management and administrative services, 7% mathematics, 6% biological and life sciences, 5% vocational and home economics, 4% communications and journalism, 4% engineering and applied sciences, 4% English language/literature/letters, 4% social sciences, 3% computer and information sciences, 3% fine arts, 3% liberal arts/general studies.
First-Year Class: 1,984 total. Of the students who applied, 99% were accepted. 2% from top 10% of their high school class, 30% from top half.
Graduation Requirements: 61 semester hours; math/science requirements vary according to program; computer course (varies by major).
Computers on Campus: 450 computers available on campus for general student use. Computers for student use in computer center, computer labs, learning resource center, classrooms, library, student center, business building, English departmental lab.

EXPENSES

Expenses for 1997–98: Area resident tuition: $527 full-time. State resident tuition: $791 full-time. Nonresident tuition: $1550 full-time. Part-time tuition per credit ranges from $50 to $187 for area residents, $50 to $280.50 for state residents, $200 to $550 for nonresidents. Part-time mandatory fees per semester range from $30 to $130. Full-time mandatory fees: $350.

LD Services Contact: Dr. JoAnn Luckie, Director, Special Populations Office, Del Mar College, 101 Baldwin Boulevard, Corpus Christi, TX 78404, 512-886-1298. Fax: 512-886-1599. Email: jluckie@camino.delmar.edu.

DES MOINES AREA COMMUNITY COLLEGE

Ankeny, Iowa

LEARNING DISABILITIES SERVICES INFORMATION

Academic Achievement Department began offering services in 1986. Currently the program serves 130 undergraduates with LD. Students diagnosed with ADD/ADHD are eligible for the same services available to students with LD.

Staff: 7 full-time staff members, including director, tutoring coordinator, interpreter, placement specialist, counselor. Services provided by tutors, counselor.

Special Fees: No special fees are charged for services to students with LD.

Applications and admissions: *Required:* untimed ACT ASSET; *recommended:* high school transcript, courses completed, psychoeducational report completed within 3 years, transition plan. Students may begin taking classes in fall, spring, or summer. *Application deadline:* continuous.

PROGRAM AND SERVICE COMPONENTS

Diagnostic testing: Reading, math, spelling, written language, learning strategies.

Academic advising: Provided by unit staff members, academic advisers. Most students with LD take 9 to 12 semester hours each term; 12 semester hours required to maintain full-time status and be eligible for financial aid.

Counseling services: Individual counseling, career counseling, self-advocacy training.

Subject-area tutoring: Offered one-on-one and in small groups by peer tutors, former teachers, graduate students, paraprofessionals. Available in most subjects.

Special courses: College survival skills, reading, communication skills, composition, word processing, time management, math, typing, study skills, career planning. Some offered for credit; some enter into overall grade point average.

Auxiliary aids: Taped textbooks, tape recorders, calculators, typewriters, word-processors with spell-check, talking computers, optical character readers.

Auxiliary services: Alternative test arrangements, notetakers, priority registration, advocacy.

GENERAL COLLEGE INFORMATION

State and locally supported, 2-year, coed. Part of Iowa Area Community Colleges System. Awards associate degrees. Founded 1966. *Setting:* 362-acre small-town campus. *Educational spending 1995–96:* $2409 per undergrad. *Total enrollment:* 10,287. *Faculty:* 240 full-time; student–undergrad faculty ratio is 24:1.

Enrollment Profile: 10,287 students from 21 states and territories, 16 other countries. 61% women, 39% men, 58% part-time, 98% state residents, 5% transferred in, 2% international, 46% 25 or older, 1% Hispanic, 3% black, 2% Asian or Pacific Islander.

First-Year Class: 4,541 total. Of the students who applied, 100% were accepted. 8% from top 10% of their high school class, 35% from top quarter, 74% from top half.

Graduation Requirements: 64 semester hours; internship (some majors).

Computers on Campus: 700 computers available on campus for general student use. Computer purchase/lease plans available. Computers for student use in computer center, computer labs, classrooms, library. Staffed computer lab on campus provides training in use of computers, software.

EXPENSES

Expenses for 1997–98: State resident tuition: $1837 full-time, $57.40 per semester hour part-time. Nonresident tuition: $3469 full-time, $108.40 per semester hour part-time.

LD Services Contact: Ms. Carol Grimm, Counselor, Special Needs, Des Moines Area Community College, 2006 South Ankeny Boulevard, Ankeny, IA 50021-8995, 515-964-6268. Fax: 515-965-7080. Email: cagrimm@dmacc.cc.ia.us.

DIXIE COLLEGE

St. George, Utah

LEARNING DISABILITIES SERVICES INFORMATION

Academic Support Center began offering services in 1980. Currently the program serves 70 undergraduates with LD. Students diagnosed with ADD/ADHD are eligible for the same services available to students with LD.

Staff: 3 full-time, 1 part-time staff members, including coordinator. Services provided by remediation specialists, tutors.

Special Fees: No special fees are charged for services to students with LD.

Applications and admissions: *Required:* untimed ACT; *recommended:* high school transcript, extended time ACT, psychoeducational report completed within 4 years. Students may begin taking classes any term. *Application deadline:* continuous.

Special policies: The college has written policies regarding substitutions and waivers of admissions, graduation, and degree requirements.

PROGRAM AND SERVICE COMPONENTS

Special preparation or orientation: Optional orientation offered after classes begin and individually by special arrangement.

Academic advising: Provided by unit staff members, academic advisers. Students with LD may take up to as many credits as an individual can handle each term; most take 9 to 12 credits; 12 credits required to maintain full-time status and be eligible for financial aid.

Counseling services: Individual counseling, career counseling.

Basic skills remediation: Offered one-on-one, in small groups, and in class-size groups by regular teachers; computer-aided instruction also offered. Available in reading, math, spelling, written language, study skills.

Subject-area tutoring: Offered one-on-one and in small groups by peer tutors. Available in most subjects.

Special courses: College survival skills, reading, vocabulary development, communication skills, composition, math, study skills, career planning. Most offered for credit; most enter into overall grade point average.

Auxiliary aids: Taped textbooks, tape recorders, calculators, word-processors with spell-check, personal computers, optical character readers.

Auxiliary services: Alternative test arrangements, notetakers, priority registration, advocacy.

GENERAL COLLEGE INFORMATION

State-supported, 2-year, coed. Awards associate degrees. Founded 1911. *Setting:* 60-acre small-town campus. *Endowment:* $6.6 million. *Educational spending 1995–96:* $2119 per undergrad. *Total enrollment:* 3,132. *Faculty:* 198 (73 full-time, 85% with terminal degrees, 125 part-time); student–undergrad faculty ratio is 16:1.

Enrollment Profile: 3,132 students from 38 states and territories, 10 other countries. 52% women, 48% men, 25% part-time, 92% state residents, 7% live on campus, 4% transferred in, 1% international, 17% 25 or older, 2% Native American, 2% Hispanic, 1% black, 2% Asian or Pacific Islander. *Retention:* 43% of 1995 full-time freshmen returned. *Areas of study chosen:* 26% liberal arts/general studies, 18% vocational and home economics, 13% business management and administrative services, 9% education, 7% health professions and related sciences, 3% computer and information sciences, 3% foreign language and literature, 3% pre-med, 3% psychology, 2% biological and life sciences, 2% communications and journalism, 2% engineering and applied sciences, 2% fine arts, 2% performing arts, 2% social sciences, 1% agriculture, 1% English language/literature/letters, 1% predentistry. *Most popular recent majors:* liberal arts/general studies, education, business administration/commerce/management.

First-Year Class: 1,067 total; 2,006 applied, 100% were accepted, 53% of whom enrolled. 9% from top 10% of their high school class, 26% from top quarter, 50% from top half.

Graduation Requirements: 96 credits; 5 credits of math/science; computer course.

Computers on Campus: 450 computers available on campus for general student use. Computers for student use in computer labs, learning resource center, classrooms, library, student center, business departmental labs provide access to the Internet/World Wide Web. Staffed computer lab on campus provides training in use of computers, software.

Dixie College (continued)

EXPENSES

Expenses for 1997–98: *Application fee:* $25. State resident tuition: $1080 full-time, $30 per credit part-time. Nonresident tuition: $4721 full-time, $131.13 per credit part-time. Part-time mandatory fees per quarter (4 to 11 credits) range from $44.16 to $97.20. Full-time mandatory fees: $292. College room and board: $2757. College room only: $1095.

LD Services Contact: Mr. Matt Clark, Disabled Student Coordinator, Dixie College, 225 South 700 East, St. George, UT 84770-3876, 801-652-7516. Fax: 801-656-4006.

DOÑA ANA BRANCH COMMUNITY COLLEGE

Las Cruces, New Mexico

LEARNING DISABILITIES SERVICES INFORMATION

Disabled Student Services began offering services in 1990. Currently the program serves 21 undergraduates with LD. Students diagnosed with ADD/ADHD are eligible for the same services available to students with LD, as well as peer mentor program.

Staff: 2 full-time, 4 part-time staff members, including director, coordinator. Services provided by tutors, counselor, diagnostic specialist.

Special Fees: No special fees are charged for services to students with LD.

Applications and admissions: *Required:* high school transcript, ACT ASSET. Students may begin taking classes any term. *Application deadline:* continuous.

Special policies: The college has written policies regarding grade forgiveness; substitutions and waivers of admissions, graduation, and degree requirements.

PROGRAM AND SERVICE COMPONENTS

Diagnostic testing: Intelligence, reading, math, spelling, spoken language, written language, perceptual skills, speech, hearing, learning strategies.

Academic advising: Provided by academic advisers. Students with LD may take up to 12 credits each term; most take 9 to 12 credits; 12 credits (fewer with permission) required to maintain full-time status; 6 credits (part-time), 12 credits (full-time) required to be eligible for financial aid.

Counseling services: Individual counseling, career counseling, self-advocacy training.

Basic skills remediation: Offered one-on-one by LD teachers; computer-aided instruction also offered. Available in reading, math, spelling, written language, learning strategies, study skills, time management.

Subject-area tutoring: Offered one-on-one by peer tutors. Available in most subjects.

Auxiliary aids: Taped textbooks, tape recorders, typewriters, word-processors with spell-check, talking computers, Arkenstone Reader, Dragon Dictate.

Auxiliary services: Alternative test arrangements, notetakers, priority registration.

GENERAL COLLEGE INFORMATION

State and locally supported, 2-year, coed. Part of New Mexico State University System. Awards associate degrees. Founded 1973. *Setting:* 15-acre urban campus with easy access to Ciudad Juárez and El Paso. *Educational spending 1995–96:* $1444 per undergrad. *Total enrollment:* 3,949. *Faculty:* 65 full-time, 51% with terminal degrees, 157 part-time; student–undergrad faculty ratio is 20:1.

Enrollment Profile: 3,949 students from 15 states and territories, 3 other countries. 54% women, 46% men, 79% part-time, 84% state residents, 7% transferred in, 1% international, 39% 25 or older, 2% Native American, 48% Hispanic, 3% black, 1% Asian or Pacific Islander. *Retention:* 47% of 1995 full-time freshmen returned. *Areas of study chosen:* 12% business management and administrative services, 11% vocational and home economics, 4% computer and information sciences, 4% health professions and related sciences, 2% architecture, 2% natural resource sciences, 1% library and information studies. *Most popular recent majors:* secretarial studies/office management, water resources, computer technologies.

First-Year Class: 1,275 total. Of the students who applied, 100% were accepted, 80% of whom enrolled. 5% from top 10% of their high school class, 10% from top quarter, 70% from top half.

Graduation Requirements: 66 credits; intermediate algebra proficiency or 1 intermediate algebra course; computer course; internship (some majors).

Computers on Campus: 300 computers available on campus for general student use. A campus-wide network can be accessed from off-campus. Computers for student use in computer center, classrooms provide access to the Internet/World Wide Web, on- and off-campus e-mail addresses. Staffed computer lab on campus provides training in use of computers, software. *Academic computing expenditure 1995–96:* $300,000.

EXPENSES

Expenses for 1996–97: *Application fee.* $15. Area resident tuition: $768 full-time, $32 per credit part-time. State resident tuition: $864 full-time, $36 per credit part-time. Nonresident tuition: $1992 full-time, $83 per credit part-time. (Room and board are provided by New Mexico State University.). College room and board: $3229. College room only: $1669.

LD Services Contact: Ms. Trudy Meyer-Arrieta, Specialist, Services for Students with Disabilities, Doña Ana Branch Community College, Box 3DA NMSU, Las Cruces, NM 88003-8001, 505-527-7648. Fax: 505-527-7515. Email: tmeyerar@nmsu.edu.

DONNELLY COLLEGE

Kansas City, Kansas

LEARNING DISABILITIES SERVICES INFORMATION

Student Support Services began offering services in 1990. Currently the program serves 3 undergraduates with LD. Students diagnosed with ADD/ADHD are eligible for the same services available to students with LD.

Staff: 2 full-time, 1 part-time staff members, including director, coordinator. Services provided by remediation specialist, tutors, counselor.

Special Fees: No special fees are charged for services to students with LD.

Applications and admissions: *Required:* high school transcript; *recommended:* autobiographical statement, letters of recommendation, psychoeducational report completed in high school. Students may begin taking classes in fall, spring, or summer. *Application deadline:* 8/10 (fall term), 1/10 (spring term).

PROGRAM AND SERVICE COMPONENTS

Special preparation or orientation: Optional orientation offered individually by special arrangement.

Diagnostic testing: Intelligence, reading, math, perceptual skills, study skills, learning strategies.

Academic advising: Provided by unit staff members, academic advisers. Most students with LD take 6 credit hours each term; 12 credit hours required to maintain full-time status; source of aid determines number of credit hours required to be eligible for financial aid.

Counseling services: Individual counseling, career counseling.

Basic skills remediation: Offered one-on-one by regular teachers. Available in reading, math, spelling, written language, learning strategies, time management, speech.

Subject-area tutoring: Offered one-on-one by professional teachers, peer tutors. Available in some subjects.

Special courses: Reading, math. None offered for credit; none enter into overall grade point average.

Auxiliary aids: Taped textbooks, tape recorders, calculators, typewriters, word-processors with spell-check, personal computers.

Auxiliary services: Alternative test arrangements, notetakers.

GENERAL COLLEGE INFORMATION

Independent Roman Catholic, 2-year, coed. Awards associate degrees. Founded 1949. *Setting:* 4-acre urban campus. *Endowment:* $3 million. *Educational spending 1995–96:* $1945 per undergrad. *Total enrollment:* 409. *Faculty:* 48 (22 full-time, 25% with terminal degrees, 26 part-time); student–undergrad faculty ratio is 9:1.

Enrollment Profile: 409 students from 15 states and territories, 28 other countries. 65% women, 35% men, 28% part-time, 79% state residents, 11% transferred in, 7% international, 55% 25 or older, 2% Native American, 12% Hispanic, 46% black, 2% Asian or Pacific Islander. *Areas of study chosen:* 20% health professions and related sciences, 15% liberal arts/general studies, 10% education, 5% engineering and applied sciences, 2% communications and journalism, 2% prevet, 2% social sciences, 1% architecture.

First-Year Class: 55 total. Of the students who applied, 100% were accepted.
Graduation Requirements: 64 credit hours; 3 credit hours of math; 6 credit hours of science; computer course; internship (some majors).
Computers on Campus: 25 computers available on campus for general student use. Computers for student use in computer center, computer labs, library. Staffed computer lab on campus provides training in use of computers, software. *Academic computing expenditure 1995–96:* $65,000.

EXPENSES

Expenses for 1997–98: Tuition: $2800 full-time, $110 per credit hour part-time.
LD Services Contact: Ms. Lee Stephenson, Director, Student Support Services, Donnelly College, 608 North 18th Street, Kansas City, KS 66102-4298, 913-621-8764. Fax: 913-621-0354.

DUNDALK COMMUNITY COLLEGE

Baltimore, Maryland

LEARNING DISABILITIES SERVICES INFORMATION

Academic Support Services for Students with Disabilities began offering services in 1991. Currently the program serves 75 undergraduates with LD. Students diagnosed with ADD/ADHD are eligible for the same services available to students with LD, as well as distraction-free testing area.
Staff: 1 full-time, 1 part-time staff members, including coordinator. Services provided by assistant to coordinator.
Special Fees: No special fees are charged for services to students with LD.
Applications and admissions: *Recommended:* high school transcript. Students may begin taking classes any term. *Application deadline:* continuous.

PROGRAM AND SERVICE COMPONENTS

Academic advising: Provided by unit staff members, academic advisers. Most students with LD take 9 credits each term; 12 credits (fewer for insurance purposes) required to maintain full-time status; source of aid determines number of credits required to be eligible for financial aid.
Basic skills remediation: Offered one-on-one and in class-size groups by regular teachers, tutors, learning center faculty. Available in reading, math, written language, study skills.
Subject-area tutoring: Offered one-on-one by professional teachers, peer tutors. Available in all subjects.
Auxiliary aids: Taped textbooks, tape recorders, word-processors with spell-check.
Auxiliary services: Alternative test arrangements, notetakers, advocacy.
Campus support group: A special student organization is available to students with LD.

GENERAL COLLEGE INFORMATION

County-supported, 2-year, coed. Awards associate degrees. Founded 1970. *Setting:* 60-acre urban campus. *Total enrollment:* 2,946. *Faculty:* 157 (51 full-time, 22% with terminal degrees, 106 part-time); student–undergrad faculty ratio is 15:1.
Enrollment Profile: 2,946 students from 4 states and territories. 57% women, 43% men, 81% part-time, 76% state residents, 8% transferred in, 0% international, 68% 25 or older, 1% Native American, 2% Hispanic, 15% black, 2% Asian or Pacific Islander. *Areas of study chosen:* 25% interdisciplinary studies, 13% engineering and applied sciences, 10% business management and administrative services, 8% health professions and related sciences, 6% social sciences, 5% computer and information sciences, 4% education, 3% vocational and home economics, 2% agriculture, 2% performing arts, 1% communications and journalism. *Most popular recent majors:* liberal arts/general studies, paralegal studies, business administration/commerce/management.
First-Year Class: 753 total. Of the students who applied, 100% were accepted, 72% of whom enrolled.
Graduation Requirements: 60 credits; 2 math courses; 1 science course; computer course; internship (some majors).
Computers on Campus: 150 computers available on campus for general student use. Computers for student use in computer center, computer labs, learning resource center, business, math labs provide access to the Internet/World Wide Web. Staffed computer lab on campus provides training in use of computers, software.

EXPENSES

Expenses for 1997–98: *Application fee:* $10. Area resident tuition: $1800 full-time, $60 per credit part-time. State resident tuition: $3180 full-time, $106 per credit part-time. Nonresident tuition: $4980 full-time, $166 per credit part-time. Part-time mandatory fees: $6 per semester. Full-time mandatory fees: $82.
LD Services Contact: Ms. Laura Remchuk, Coordinator, Dundalk Community College, 7200 Sollers Point Road, Baltimore, MD 21222, 410-285-9781. Fax: 410-285-9903. Email: lremchuk@dundalk.cc.md.us.

EAST ARKANSAS COMMUNITY COLLEGE

Forrest City, Arkansas

LEARNING DISABILITIES SERVICES INFORMATION

Student Support Services began offering services in 1978. Currently the program serves 1 undergraduate with LD. Students diagnosed with ADD/ADHD are eligible for the same services available to students with LD.
Staff: 6 full-time staff members, including director. Services provided by tutors, lab instructors, transfer specialist.
Special Fees: No special fees are charged for services to students with LD.
Applications and admissions: *Required:* high school transcript, documentation of LD (for receipt of services); *recommended:* untimed or extended time SAT I or ACT. Students may begin taking classes in fall, spring, or summer. *Application deadline:* continuous.
Special policies: The college has written policies regarding grade forgiveness.

PROGRAM AND SERVICE COMPONENTS

Academic advising: Provided by academic advisers. Most students with LD take 12 to 15 hours each term; 12 hours required to maintain full-time status; 6 hours required to be eligible for financial aid.
Auxiliary aids: Taped textbooks, tape recorders, word-processors with spell-check.
Auxiliary services: Alternative test arrangements, notetakers.

GENERAL COLLEGE INFORMATION

State-supported, 2-year, coed. Awards associate degrees. Founded 1974. *Setting:* 40-acre small-town campus with easy access to Memphis. *Endowment:* $28,661. *Total enrollment:* 1,199. *Faculty:* 101 (42 full-time, 9% with terminal degrees, 59 part-time); student–undergrad faculty ratio is 13:1.
Enrollment Profile: 1,199 students from 4 states and territories. 72% women, 28% men, 44% part-time, 99% state residents, 20% transferred in, 0% international, 47% 25 or older, 0% Native American, 1% Hispanic, 38% black, 1% Asian or Pacific Islander. *Retention:* 47% of 1995 full-time freshmen returned. *Areas of study chosen:* 50% liberal arts/general studies, 25% health professions and related sciences, 15% computer and information sciences, 10% business management and administrative services. *Most popular recent majors:* liberal arts/general studies, practical nursing, criminal justice.
First-Year Class: 300 total; 480 applied, 100% were accepted, 63% of whom enrolled.
Graduation Requirements: 64 credits; college algebra for associate of arts degree, intermediate algebra for associate of applied science degree; computer course for associate of applied science degree programs.
Computers on Campus: 26 computers available on campus for general student use. Computers for student use in computer center. Staffed computer lab on campus provides training in use of computers, software. *Academic computing expenditure 1995–96:* $128,755.

EXPENSES

Expenses for 1997–98: Area resident tuition: $792 full-time, $33 per credit part-time. State resident tuition: $960 full-time, $40 per credit part-time. Nonresident tuition: $1164 full-time, $48.50 per credit part-time.
LD Services Contact: Mrs. Johnnie Hicks Culp, Director of Student Support Services, East Arkansas Community College, 1700 Newcastle Road, Forrest City, AR 72335, 870-633-4480 Ext. 233. Fax: 870-633-7222. Email: hicks@eacc.cc.ar.us.

EASTERN ARIZONA COLLEGE

Thatcher, Arizona

LEARNING DISABILITIES SERVICES INFORMATION

Student Support Services began offering services in 1983. Currently the program serves 4 undergraduates with LD. Students diagnosed with ADD/ADHD are eligible for the same services available to students with LD.

Staff: 2 full-time, 1 part-time staff members, including director, assistant director, coordinator. Services provided by tutors, counselor.

Special Fees: $20 to $40 for diagnostic testing.

Applications and admissions: Open admissions. Students may begin taking classes in fall, spring, or summer. *Application deadline:* continuous.

PROGRAM AND SERVICE COMPONENTS

Diagnostic testing: Reading, math, written language.

Academic advising: Provided by unit staff members, academic advisers. Students with LD may take up to 18 semester hours each term; most take 12 to 15 semester hours; 12 semester hours required to maintain full-time status; 6 semester hours (part-time), 12 semester hours (full-time) required to be eligible for financial aid.

Counseling services: Individual counseling, small-group counseling, career counseling, self-advocacy training.

Basic skills remediation: Offered in class-size groups by regular teachers. Available in reading, math, spoken language, written language, study skills, computer skills.

Subject-area tutoring: Offered one-on-one and in small groups by peer tutors. Available in most subjects.

Special courses: College survival skills, composition, math, typing, personal psychology, study skills, career planning. All offered for credit; most enter into overall grade point average.

Auxiliary services: Alternative test arrangements, notetakers, advocacy.

GENERAL COLLEGE INFORMATION

State and locally supported, 2-year, coed. Part of Arizona State Community College System. Awards associate degrees. Founded 1888. *Setting:* 40-acre rural campus. *Research spending 1995–96:* $64,225. *Total enrollment:* 2,686. *Faculty:* 232 (58 full-time, 100% with terminal degrees, 174 part-time).

Enrollment Profile: 2,686 students from 23 states and territories, 4 other countries. 59% women, 41% men, 39% part-time, 94% state residents, 10% transferred in, 1% international, 35% 25 or older, 8% Native American, 18% Hispanic, 3% black, 1% Asian or Pacific Islander. *Areas of study chosen:* 19% liberal arts/general studies, 18% business management and administrative services, 18% vocational and home economics, 16% education, 10% health professions and related sciences, 4% fine arts, 3% computer and information sciences, 3% premed, 2% engineering and applied sciences, 2% social sciences, 1% agriculture, 1% biological and life sciences, 1% communications and journalism, 1% performing arts, 1% prelaw, 1% psychology. *Most popular recent major:* liberal arts/general studies.

First-Year Class: 1,006 total. Of the students who applied, 100% were accepted.

Graduation Requirements: 64 semester hours; computer course for agricultural business, agricultural sciences, automotive technologies, bookkeeping, business education, office management majors.

Computers on Campus: 320 computers available on campus for general student use. Computer purchase/lease plans available. Computers for student use in computer center, computer labs, library, business classrooms provide access to the Internet/World Wide Web. Staffed computer lab on campus provides training in use of computers, software. *Academic computing expenditure 1995–96:* $537,428.

EXPENSES

Expenses for 1997–98: State resident tuition: $652 full-time. Nonresident tuition: $4380 full-time. Part-time tuition per semester ranges from $25 to $280 for state residents, $42 to $1839 for nonresidents. One-time mandatory fee: $40. College room and board: $2890 (minimum). College room only: $1090.

LD Services Contact: Ms. Sharon Allen, Project Director, Student Support Services, Eastern Arizona College, 3714 West Church Street, Thatcher, AZ 85552-0769, 520-428-8342. Fax: 520-428-8462. Email: sallen@eac.cc.az.us.

EASTERN NEW MEXICO UNIVERSITY–ROSWELL

Roswell, New Mexico

LEARNING DISABILITIES SERVICES INFORMATION

Special Services currently serves 24 undergraduates with LD. Students diagnosed with ADD/ADHD are eligible for the same services available to students with LD.

Staff: 6 full-time, 2 part-time staff members, including director. Services provided by remediation specialist, counselor, diagnostic specialist, vocational evaluator.

Special Fees: $60 per year for vocational courses.

Applications and admissions: *Required:* high school transcript, placement test (untimed is acceptable). Students may begin taking classes any term. *Application deadline:* continuous.

Special policies: The college has written policies regarding substitutions and waivers of degree requirements.

PROGRAM AND SERVICE COMPONENTS

Special preparation or orientation: Optional orientation offered during registration.

Diagnostic testing: Intelligence, reading, math, spelling.

Academic advising: Provided by unit staff members. Students with LD required to take 12 credit hours each term to maintain full-time status; 6 credit hours required to be eligible for financial aid.

Counseling services: Individual counseling, small-group counseling, career counseling.

Basic skills remediation: Offered one-on-one and in small groups by LD teachers, regular teachers. Available in reading, math, spelling.

Subject-area tutoring: Offered one-on-one and in small groups by professional teachers, peer tutors, lab technician. Available in most subjects.

Special courses: College survival skills.

Auxiliary aids: Taped textbooks, tape recorders, typewriters, word-processors with spell-check.

Auxiliary services: Alternative test arrangements, notetakers, priority registration, advocacy.

GENERAL COLLEGE INFORMATION

State-supported, 2-year, coed. Part of Eastern New Mexico University System. Awards associate degrees. Founded 1958. *Setting:* 241-acre small-town campus. *Educational spending 1995–96:* $1400 per undergrad. *Total enrollment:* 2,797. *Faculty:* 150 (50 full-time, 2% with terminal degrees, 100 part-time); student–undergrad faculty ratio is 22:1.

Enrollment Profile: 2,797 students from 11 states and territories, 2 other countries. 65% women, 35% men, 55% part-time, 98% state residents, 5% live on campus, 10% transferred in, 1% international, 75% 25 or older, 2% Native American, 38% Hispanic, 3% black, 1% Asian or Pacific Islander. *Retention:* 68% of 1995 full-time freshmen returned. *Most popular recent majors:* nursing, liberal arts/general studies, business administration/commerce/management.

First-Year Class: 725 applied, 99% were accepted, 80% of whom enrolled.

Graduation Requirements: 64 credit hours; internship (some majors).

Computers on Campus: 60 computers available on campus for general student use. A campus-wide network can be accessed. Students can contact faculty members and/or advisers through e-mail. Computers for student use in library provide access to the Internet/World Wide Web, on- and off-campus e-mail addresses. Staffed computer lab on campus provides training in use of computers, software.

EXPENSES

Expenses for 1996–97: Area resident tuition: $630 full-time, $26.25 per credit hour part-time. State resident tuition: $654 full-time, $27.25 per credit hour part-time. Nonresident tuition: $1890 full-time, $78.75 per credit hour part-time. Part-time mandatory fees: $2 per credit hour. Full-time mandatory fees: $48. College room only: $1086.

LD Services Contact: Ms. Linda Green, Director of Special Services, Eastern New Mexico University–Roswell, PO Box 6000, Roswell, NM 88202-6000, 505-624-7289. Fax: 505-624-7119.

EASTERN WYOMING COLLEGE

Torrington, Wyoming

LEARNING DISABILITIES SERVICES INFORMATION

Learning Skills Lab began offering services in 1994. Currently the program serves 5 undergraduates with LD. Students diagnosed with ADD/ADHD are eligible for the same services available to students with LD.

Staff: 7 part-time staff members, including director. Services provided by remediation specialists, tutors, counselors.

Special Fees: No special fees are charged for services to students with LD.

Applications and admissions: *Required:* high school transcript; *recommended:* personal interview. Students may begin taking classes in fall only. *Application deadline:* continuous.

Special policies: The college has written policies regarding grade forgiveness.

PROGRAM AND SERVICE COMPONENTS

Academic advising: Provided by unit staff members, academic advisers. Students with LD may take up to 16 credit hours each term; most take 12 to 14 credit hours; 12 credit hours required to maintain full-time status; 6 credit hours required to be eligible for financial aid.

Counseling services: Individual counseling, career counseling.

Basic skills remediation: Offered one-on-one, in small groups, and in class-size groups by regular teachers; computer-aided instruction also offered. Available in reading, math, spelling, learning strategies, study skills, time management.

Subject-area tutoring: Offered one-on-one by professional teachers, peer tutors. Available in all subjects.

Auxiliary aids: Taped textbooks, tape recorders, calculators, word-processors with spell-check, optical character readers.

Auxiliary services: Alternative test arrangements, advocacy.

GENERAL COLLEGE INFORMATION

State and locally supported, 2-year, coed. Part of Wyoming Community College Commission. Awards associate degrees. Founded 1948. *Setting:* 40-acre rural campus. *Endowment:* $607,654. *Total enrollment:* 1,651. *Faculty:* 136 (39 full-time, 11% with terminal degrees, 97 part-time); student–undergrad faculty ratio is 14:1.

Enrollment Profile: 1,651 students from 19 states and territories, 3 other countries. 66% women, 34% men, 71% part-time, 90% state residents, 8% live on campus, 10% transferred in, 1% international, 55% 25 or older, 1% Native American, 4% Hispanic, 1% black, 1% Asian or Pacific Islander. *Most popular recent majors:* education, veterinary technology, criminal justice.

First-Year Class: 155 total; 333 applied, 100% were accepted, 47% of whom enrolled. 10% from top 10% of their high school class, 15% from top quarter, 50% from top half.

Graduation Requirements: 64 credit hours; computer course for business, agriculture majors; internship (some majors).

Computers on Campus: 71 computers available on campus for general student use. Computer purchase/lease plans available. A campus-wide network can be accessed. Students can contact faculty members and/or advisers through e-mail. Computers for student use in computer center, computer labs, learning resource center, classrooms, student center provide access to the Internet/World Wide Web, off-campus e-mail addresses. Staffed computer lab on campus provides training in use of computers, software. *Academic computing expenditure 1995–96:* $51,923.

EXPENSES

Expenses for 1996–97: State resident tuition: $824 full-time, $36 per credit hour part-time. Nonresident tuition: $2472 full-time, $108 per credit hour part-time. Part-time mandatory fees: $12 per credit hour. Tuition for nonresidents who are eligible for the Western Undergraduate Exchange: $1236 full-time, $54 per credit hour part-time. Full-time mandatory fees: $384. College room and board: $2600.

LD Services Contact: Ms. Marilyn Cotant, Assistant Dean of Students, Eastern Wyoming College, 3200 West C Street, Torrington, WY 82240, 307-532-8200. Fax: 307-532-8222.

EASTFIELD COLLEGE

Mesquite, Texas

LEARNING DISABILITIES SERVICES INFORMATION

Services for Special Populations began offering services in 1972. Currently the program serves 136 undergraduates with LD. Students diagnosed with ADD/ADHD are eligible for the same services available to students with LD.

Staff: 10 full-time staff members, including director, assistant director. Services provided by tutors, counselors.

Special Fees: No special fees are charged for services to students with LD.

Applications and admissions: Open admissions. Students may begin taking classes in fall, spring, or summer. *Application deadline:* continuous.

PROGRAM AND SERVICE COMPONENTS

Academic advising: Provided by unit staff members, academic advisers. Most students with LD take 9 credit hours each term; 9 credit hours required to maintain full-time status.

Counseling services: Individual counseling, small-group counseling, career counseling.

Basic skills remediation: Offered one-on-one, in small groups, and in class-size groups by regular teachers, tutors. Available in reading, math, spelling, written language, learning strategies, study skills, social skills.

Subject-area tutoring: Offered one-on-one and in small groups by professional teachers, peer tutors. Available in all subjects.

Auxiliary aids: Tape recorders, typewriters, word-processors with spell-check, talking computers, optical character readers.

Auxiliary services: Alternative test arrangements, notetakers, advocacy.

GENERAL COLLEGE INFORMATION

State and locally supported, 2-year, coed. Part of Dallas County Community College District System. Awards associate degrees. Founded 1970. *Setting:* 244-acre suburban campus with easy access to Dallas–Fort Worth. *Total enrollment:* 8,056. *Faculty:* 105 (all full-time).

Enrollment Profile: 8,056 students: 57% women, 43% men, 71% part-time, 99% state residents, 25% transferred in, 1% international, 51% 25 or older, 1% Native American, 15% Hispanic, 16% black, 6% Asian or Pacific Islander. *Most popular recent majors:* liberal arts/general studies, computer programming, electrical and electronics technologies.

First-Year Class: 1,540 total; 1,540 applied, 100% were accepted, 100% of whom enrolled.

Graduation Requirements: 61 credit hours; math/science requirements vary according to program.

Computers on Campus: 50 computers available on campus for general student use. A campus-wide network can be accessed from off-campus. Students can contact faculty members and/or advisers through e-mail. Computers for student use in computer labs, library provide access to the Internet/World Wide Web, on- and off-campus e-mail addresses. Staffed computer lab on campus provides training in use of computers, software.

EXPENSES

Expenses for 1996–97: Area resident tuition: $520 full-time. State resident tuition: $900 full-time. Nonresident tuition: $2010 full-time. Part-time tuition per credit hour ranges from $54 to $196 for area residents, $110 to $386 for state residents, $201 to $737 for nonresidents. Part-time mandatory fees per semester range from $25 to $37. Full-time mandatory fees: $90.

LD Services Contact: Ms. Bobbi White, Access Services Grant Manager, Eastfield College, 3737 Motley Drive, Mesquite, TX 75150, 972-860-7032. Fax: 972-860-7622.

EAST LOS ANGELES COLLEGE

Monterey Park, California

LEARNING DISABILITIES SERVICES INFORMATION

Disabled Student Program and Services began offering services in 1985. Currently the program serves 143 undergraduates with LD.

Staff: 1 full-time staff member (director). Services provided by remediation specialist, tutors, counselors, diagnostic specialists.

Special Fees: No special fees are charged for services to students with LD.

East Los Angeles College (continued)

Applications and admissions: *Required:* high school transcript, California Assessment System for Adults with Learning Disabilities; *recommended:* psychoeducational report completed within 5 years. Students may begin taking classes in fall, spring, or summer. *Application deadline:* continuous.

Special policies: The college has written policies regarding substitutions and waivers of admissions, graduation, and degree requirements.

PROGRAM AND SERVICE COMPONENTS

Special preparation or orientation: Optional orientation offered before registration, during registration, after classes begin.

Diagnostic testing: Reading, math, spelling, spoken language, written language, motor abilities, perceptual skills, psychoneurology.

Academic advising: Provided by academic advisers. Students with LD may take up to 12 units each term; most take 9 units; 12 units required to maintain full-time status and be eligible for financial aid.

Counseling services: Individual counseling, small-group counseling, career counseling.

Basic skills remediation: Offered in class-size groups by LD teachers; computer-aided instruction also offered. Available in reading, math, spelling, handwriting, learning strategies, study skills.

Subject-area tutoring: Offered one-on-one and in small groups by peer tutors. Available in all subjects.

Special courses: College survival skills, reading, vocabulary development, communication skills, composition, learning strategies, word processing, math, typing, study skills, career planning. Most offered for credit; most enter into overall grade point average.

Auxiliary aids: Tape recorders, calculators, typewriters, word-processors with spell-check, personal computers, optical character readers.

Auxiliary services: Alternative test arrangements, notetakers, priority registration, advocacy.

GENERAL COLLEGE INFORMATION

State and locally supported, 2-year, coed. Part of Los Angeles Community College District System. Awards associate degrees. Founded 1945. *Setting:* 84-acre urban campus with easy access to Los Angeles. *Total enrollment:* 15,100. *Faculty:* 450 (250 full-time, 200 part-time).

Enrollment Profile: 15,100 students: 65% women, 35% men, 68% part-time, 95% state residents, 10% transferred in, 1% international, 60% 25 or older, 1% Native American, 67% Hispanic, 5% black, 15% Asian or Pacific Islander. *Most popular recent majors:* business administration/commerce/management, (pre)engineering sequence.

First-Year Class: 5,000 total; 19,632 applied, 100% were accepted, 80% of whom enrolled.

Graduation Requirements: 60 units; 1 course each in math and science.

Computers on Campus: Computers for student use in learning resource center.

EXPENSES

Expenses for 1996–97: State resident tuition: $0 full-time. Nonresident tuition: $3900 full-time, $130 per unit part-time. Part-time mandatory fees per semester range from $20.50 to $150.50. Full-time mandatory fees: $405.

LD Services Contact: Ms. Mary Seneker, Learning Disabilities Instructor, East Los Angeles College, 1301 Avenida Cesar Chavez, Monterey Park, CA 91754, 213-265-8744. Fax: 213-265-8714.

EDMONDS COMMUNITY COLLEGE

Lynnwood, Washington

LEARNING DISABILITIES SERVICES INFORMATION

Services for Students with Disabilities began offering services in 1983. Students diagnosed with ADD/ADHD are eligible for the same services available to students with LD.

Staff: 3 full-time, 2 part-time staff members, including coordinator. Services provided by tutors, counselors.

Special Fees: No special fees are charged for services to students with LD.

Applications and admissions: *Required:* documentation of disability; *recommended:* personal interview, psychoeducational report. Students may begin taking classes any term. *Application deadline:* continuous.

Special policies: The college has written policies regarding substitutions and waivers of admissions, graduation, and degree requirements.

PROGRAM AND SERVICE COMPONENTS

Special preparation or orientation: Optional orientation offered before registration.

Academic advising: Provided by unit staff members, academic advisers. Most students with LD take 10 to 12 credits each term; 10 credits required to maintain full-time status; 12 credits required to be eligible for financial aid.

Basic skills remediation: Offered one-on-one, in small groups, and in class-size groups by regular teachers, teacher trainees. Available in reading, math, spelling, written language, learning strategies, study skills, computer skills.

Subject-area tutoring: Offered one-on-one and in small groups by professional teachers, peer tutors. Available in most subjects.

Auxiliary aids: Taped textbooks, tape recorders, calculators, personal computers, talking computers, optical character readers.

Auxiliary services: Alternative test arrangements, priority registration.

GENERAL COLLEGE INFORMATION

State and locally supported, 2-year, coed. Part of Washington State Board for Community and Technical Colleges. Awards associate degrees. Founded 1967. *Setting:* 115-acre suburban campus with easy access to Seattle. *Total enrollment:* 10,089. *Faculty:* 440 (133 full-time, 307 part-time); student–undergrad faculty ratio is 24:1.

Enrollment Profile: 10,089 students: 63% women, 37% men, 64% part-time, 83% state residents, 36% transferred in, 10% international, 59% 25 or older, 2% Native American, 5% Hispanic, 2% black, 12% Asian or Pacific Islander.

First-Year Class: Of the students who applied, 100% were accepted.

Graduation Requirements: 90 credits; 1 college algebra course.

Computers on Campus: 220 computers available on campus for general student use. Computers for student use in computer center, computer labs, learning resource center, library. Staffed computer lab on campus provides training in use of computers, software.

EXPENSES

Expenses for 1996–97: *Application fee:* $15. State resident tuition: $1401 full-time, $46.70 per credit part-time. Nonresident tuition: $5511 full-time, $183.70 per credit part-time. College room and board: $3690.

LD Services Contact: Dee Olson, Instructional Technician, Edmonds Community College, 20000 68th Avenue West, Lynnwood, WA 98036, 206-640-1318. Fax: 206-771-3366. Email: dolson@edcc.ctc.edu.

EL CENTRO COLLEGE

Dallas, Texas

LEARNING DISABILITIES SERVICES INFORMATION

Special Services began offering services in 1980. Currently the program serves 85 undergraduates with LD. Students diagnosed with ADD/ADHD are eligible for the same services available to students with LD.

Staff: 1 full-time, 5 part-time staff members, including director, coordinators. Services provided by tutors, readers, scribes, test administrators.

Special Fees: No special fees are charged for services to students with LD.

Applications and admissions: *Recommended:* diagnostics from evaluation specialist. Students may begin taking classes any term. *Application deadline:* continuous.

Special policies: The college has written policies regarding grade forgiveness; substitutions and waivers of degree requirements.

PROGRAM AND SERVICE COMPONENTS

Academic advising: Provided by unit staff members, academic advisers. Students with LD may take up to 21 credit hours each term; most take 9 to 12 credit hours; 12 credit hours required to maintain full-time status; 6 credit hours required to be eligible for financial aid.

Counseling services: Individual counseling, career counseling.

Basic skills remediation: Offered in class-size groups by regular teachers; computer-aided instruction also offered. Available in reading, math, written language.

Subject-area tutoring: Offered one-on-one and in small groups by peer tutors. Available in most subjects.

Auxiliary aids: Taped textbooks, tape recorders, calculators, typewriters, word-processors with spell-check, personal computers, talking computers, optical character readers.

Auxiliary services: Alternative test arrangements, notetakers, priority registration.

GENERAL COLLEGE INFORMATION

County-supported, 2-year, coed. Part of Dallas County Community College District System. Awards associate degrees. Founded 1966. *Setting:* 2-acre urban campus. *Total enrollment:* 4,170. *Faculty:* 363 (117 full-time, 23% with terminal degrees, 246 part-time); student–undergrad faculty ratio is 16:1.
Enrollment Profile: 4,170 students from 38 states and territories, 36 other countries. 65% women, 35% men, 73% part-time, 98% state residents, 12% transferred in, 1% international, 56% 25 or older, 1% Native American, 19% Hispanic, 42% black, 2% Asian or Pacific Islander. *Retention:* 49% of 1995 full-time freshmen returned. *Areas of study chosen:* 26% health professions and related sciences, 17% interdisciplinary studies, 8% business management and administrative services, 8% fine arts, 3% education. *Most popular recent majors:* nursing, paralegal studies, food services management.
First-Year Class: 639 total; 1,510 applied, 100% were accepted, 52% of whom enrolled.
Graduation Requirements: 62 credit hours; 3 credit hours of math; computer course for business majors; internship (some majors).
Computers on Campus: 746 computers available on campus for general student use. Computers for student use in computer center, learning resource center, classrooms, library provide access to the Internet/World Wide Web. Staffed computer lab on campus provides training in use of computers, software.

EXPENSES

Expenses for 1997–98: Area resident tuition: $650 full-time. State resident tuition: $1030 full-time. Nonresident tuition: $2140 full-time. Part-time tuition per credit ranges from $79 to $245 for area residents, $135 to $435 for state residents, $226 to $786 for nonresidents.
LD Services Contact: Mr. Jim Handy, Director, El Centro College, Main and Lamar Street, Dallas, TX 75202-3604, 214-860-2073. Fax: 214-860-2335. Email: jlh5300@dcccd.edu.

ELGIN COMMUNITY COLLEGE

Elgin, Illinois

LEARNING DISABILITIES SERVICES INFORMATION

Learning Skills Center began offering services in 1989. Currently the program serves 80 undergraduates with LD. Students diagnosed with ADD/ADHD are eligible for the same services available to students with LD.
Staff: 1 full-time staff member (director). Services provided by tutors.
Special Fees: No special fees are charged for services to students with LD.
Applications and admissions: *Required:* high school transcript; *recommended:* high school IEP (Individualized Education Program), psychoeducational report completed within 3 years, testing reports. Students may begin taking classes any term. *Application deadline:* continuous.
Special policies: The college has written policies regarding grade forgiveness; substitutions and waivers of degree requirements.

PROGRAM AND SERVICE COMPONENTS

Diagnostic testing: Intelligence, reading, math, spelling, handwriting, spoken language, written language, perceptual skills, learning strategies, various other areas as appropriate.
Academic advising: Provided by academic advisers. Most students with LD take 9 to 12 credit hours each term; 12 credit hours required to maintain full-time status; 3 credit hours required to be eligible for financial aid.
Counseling services: Individual counseling, small-group counseling, career counseling.
Basic skills remediation: Offered one-on-one and in class-size groups by regular teachers. Available in reading, math, spelling, written language, learning strategies, study skills, time management.
Subject-area tutoring: Offered one-on-one by professional teachers. Available in all subjects.
Special courses: College survival skills, reading, vocabulary development, learning strategies, time management, study skills. Some offered for credit; some enter into overall grade point average.
Auxiliary aids: Taped textbooks, tape recorders, calculators, typewriters, word-processors with spell-check.
Auxiliary services: Alternative test arrangements, notetakers, advocacy.
Campus support group: A special student organization is available to students with LD.

GENERAL COLLEGE INFORMATION

State and locally supported, 2-year, coed. Part of Illinois Community College System. Awards associate degrees. Founded 1949. *Setting:* 119-acre suburban campus with easy access to Chicago. *Total enrollment:* 9,104. *Faculty:* 459 (109 full-time, 350 part-time); student–undergrad faculty ratio is 20:1.
Enrollment Profile: 9,104 students: 57% women, 43% men, 75% part-time, 99% state residents, 9% transferred in, 1% international, 50% 25 or older, 0% Native American, 19% Hispanic, 3% black, 4% Asian or Pacific Islander. *Retention:* 89% of 1995 full-time freshmen returned.
First-Year Class: 2,224 total. Of the students who applied, 100% were accepted. 15% from top quarter of their high school class, 42% from top half.
Graduation Requirements: 60 credit hours; internship (some majors).
Computers on Campus: 400 computers available on campus for general student use. A campus-wide network can be accessed. Computers for student use in computer center, computer labs, learning resource center, classrooms, library, student center provide access to the Internet/World Wide Web. Staffed computer lab on campus provides training in use of computers, software.

EXPENSES AND FINANCIAL AID

Expenses for 1997–98: *Application fee:* $15. Area resident tuition: $1275 full-time, $42.50 per credit hour part-time. State resident tuition: $5657 full-time, $188.55 per credit hour part-time. Nonresident tuition: $6657 full-time, $221.91 per credit hour part-time.
Financial aid specifically for students with LD: Scholarships: Doug Dvorak Scholarship, Lioness Club Scholarship.
LD Services Contact: Ms. Annabelle Rhoades, Director of Learning Skills Center, Elgin Community College, 1700 Spartan Drive, Elgin, IL 60123, 847-697-1000 Ext. 7220. Fax: 847-888-7995.

EL PASO COMMUNITY COLLEGE

El Paso, Texas

LEARNING DISABILITIES SERVICES INFORMATION

Center for Students with Disabilities began offering services in 1980. Currently the program serves 569 undergraduates with LD. Students diagnosed with ADD/ADHD are eligible for the same services available to students with LD.
Staff: 10 full-time, 34 part-time staff members, including director, coordinator. Services provided by remediation specialist, tutors, counselors.
Special Fees: No special fees are charged for services to students with LD.
Applications and admissions: *Required:* high school transcript, grade point average, courses completed, psychoeducational report completed within 3 years; *recommended:* extended time SAT I. Students may begin taking classes any term. *Application deadline:* continuous.
Special policies: The college has written policies regarding substitutions and waivers of admissions, graduation, and degree requirements.

PROGRAM AND SERVICE COMPONENTS

Special preparation or orientation: Required orientation held before registration and by individual arrangement.
Diagnostic testing: Intelligence, reading, math, spelling, written language, perceptual skills, study skills, personality, learning strategies.
Academic advising: Provided by unit staff members, academic advisers. Students with LD may take up to 12 credit hours each term; most take 9 to 12 credit hours; 12 credit hours required to maintain full-time status; 6 credit hours required to be eligible for financial aid.
Counseling services: Individual counseling, small-group counseling, career counseling.
Basic skills remediation: Offered one-on-one, in small groups, and in class-size groups by regular teachers. Available in reading, math, spelling, written language, learning strategies, study skills, time management, computer skills.
Subject-area tutoring: Offered one-on-one and in small groups by peer tutors. Available in most subjects.
Auxiliary aids: Taped textbooks, tape recorders, calculators, typewriters, word-processors with spell-check, personal computers, talking computers, optical character readers, assistive listening device, adaptive equipment.
Auxiliary services: Alternative test arrangements, notetakers, priority registration, advocacy, readers, scribes.

El Paso Community College (continued)

GENERAL COLLEGE INFORMATION

County-supported, 2-year, coed. Part of Texas Higher Education Coordinating Board. Awards associate degrees. Founded 1969. *Setting:* urban campus. *Endowment:* $19,419. *Educational spending 1995–96:* $1122 per undergrad. *Total enrollment:* 22,264. *Faculty:* 1,304 (332 full-time, 12% with terminal degrees, 972 part-time); student–undergrad faculty ratio is 17:1.

Enrollment Profile: 22,264 students from 33 states and territories, 43 other countries. 61% women, 39% men, 55% part-time, 95% state residents, 4% transferred in, 1% international, 48% 25 or older, 1% Native American, 80% Hispanic, 3% black, 1% Asian or Pacific Islander. *Areas of study chosen:* 18% health professions and related sciences, 17% English language/literature/letters, 15% business management and administrative services, 10% engineering and applied sciences, 8% interdisciplinary studies, 6% education, 5% computer and information sciences, 4% social sciences, 2% biological and life sciences, 2% communications and journalism, 2% psychology, 1% architecture, 1% fine arts, 1% foreign language and literature, 1% liberal arts/general studies, 1% natural resource sciences, 1% performing arts, 1% physical sciences. *Most popular recent majors:* liberal arts/general studies, business administration/commerce/management, nursing.

First-Year Class: 3,510 total; 5,000 applied, 100% were accepted.

Graduation Requirements: 60 credit hours; math/science requirements vary according to program; computer course.

Computers on Campus: 1,200 computers available on campus for general student use. A computer is recommended for all students. A campus-wide network can be accessed from off-campus. Students can contact faculty members and/or advisers through e-mail. Computers for student use in computer center, computer labs, learning resource center, classrooms, library provide access to the Internet/World Wide Web, on- and off-campus e-mail addresses. Staffed computer lab on campus provides training in use of computers, software. *Academic computing expenditure 1995–96:* $600,000.

EXPENSES

Expenses for 1996–97: *Application fee:* $10. State resident tuition: $950 full-time. Nonresident tuition: $3120 full-time. Part-time tuition per semester ranges from $97 to $367 for state residents, $262 to $1132 for nonresidents.

LD Services Contact: Ms. Anne L. Westbrook, Director, Center for Students with Disabilities, El Paso Community College, PO Box 20500, El Paso, TX 79998, 915-594-2426. Fax: 915-594-2244.

EVERETT COMMUNITY COLLEGE

Everett, Washington

LEARNING DISABILITIES SERVICES INFORMATION

Center for Disability Services (CDS) began offering services in 1979. Students diagnosed with ADD/ADHD are eligible for the same services available to students with LD.

Staff: 1 full-time, 1 part-time staff members, including coordinator.

Special Fees: No special fees are charged for services to students with LD.

Applications and admissions: *Required:* personal interview, psychoeducational report completed within 3 years. Students may begin taking classes any term. *Application deadline:* continuous.

PROGRAM AND SERVICE COMPONENTS

Special preparation or orientation: Optional orientation offered during registration and before the start of each quarter.

Academic advising: Provided by unit staff members, academic advisers. Most students with LD take 12 to 15 quarter credits each term; 12 quarter credits required to maintain full-time status and be eligible for financial aid.

Counseling services: Individual counseling, career counseling, self-advocacy training.

Basic skills remediation: Offered one-on-one, in small groups, and in class-size groups by regular teachers; computer-aided instruction also offered. Available in reading, math, spelling, written language, learning strategies, study skills.

Subject-area tutoring: Offered one-on-one by professional teachers, peer tutors. Available in all subjects.

Auxiliary aids: Taped textbooks, tape recorders, calculators, typewriters, word-processors with spell-check, personal computers, talking computers, optical character readers, adaptive computer lab.

Auxiliary services: Alternative test arrangements, notetakers, priority registration, advocacy.

GENERAL COLLEGE INFORMATION

State-supported, 2-year, coed. Part of Washington State Board for Community and Technical Colleges. Awards associate degrees. Founded 1941. *Setting:* 25-acre urban campus with easy access to Seattle. *Endowment:* $92,055. *Educational spending 1995–96:* $2200 per undergrad. *Total enrollment:* 7,303. *Faculty:* 288 (113 full-time, 10% with terminal degrees, 175 part-time).

Enrollment Profile: 7,303 students from 4 states and territories, 12 other countries. 60% women, 40% men, 50% part-time, 98% state residents, 3% transferred in, 1% international, 62% 25 or older, 3% Native American, 3% Hispanic, 1% black, 4% Asian or Pacific Islander. *Retention:* 52% of 1995 full-time freshmen returned. *Areas of study chosen:* 20% foreign language and literature, 15% business management and administrative services, 7% computer and information sciences, 3% communications and journalism, 3% engineering and applied sciences, 3% health professions and related sciences, 2% education, 1% architecture, 1% fine arts, 1% library and information studies, 1% natural resource sciences, 1% performing arts, 1% premed, 1% prevet, 1% social sciences. *Most popular recent majors:* liberal arts/general studies, business administration/commerce/management, engineering (general).

First-Year Class: 1,237 total; 1,730 applied, 100% were accepted, 72% of whom enrolled.

Graduation Requirements: 90 quarter credits; computer course for business technology majors.

Computers on Campus: 339 computers available on campus for general student use. A campus-wide network can be accessed from off-campus. Students can contact faculty members and/or advisers through e-mail. Computers for student use in computer center, computer labs, classrooms provide access to the Internet/World Wide Web, on- and off-campus e-mail addresses. Staffed computer lab on campus provides training in use of computers, software. *Academic computing expenditure 1995–96:* $512,826.

EXPENSES

Expenses for 1996–97: *Application fee:* $20. State resident tuition: $1430 full-time, $47.65 per credit part-time. Nonresident tuition: $5540 full-time, $184.65 per credit part-time.

LD Services Contact: Ms. Roxanna Hansen, Coordinator, Everett Community College, 801 Wetmore Avenue, Everett, WA 98201-1327, 425-388-9272. Fax: 425-388-9129. Email: hansen_roxanna/everet@ctc.edu.

EVERGREEN VALLEY COLLEGE

San Jose, California

LEARNING DISABILITIES SERVICES INFORMATION

Diagnostic Learning Program, Disabled Students Program began offering services in 1981. Currently the program serves 100 undergraduates with LD. Students diagnosed with ADD/ADHD are eligible for the same services available to students with LD.

Staff: 1 full-time, 2 part-time staff members, including instructors. Services provided by remediation specialists, tutors, counselors, diagnostic specialists, program aides.

Special Fees: No special fees are charged for services to students with LD.

Applications and admissions: *Required:* verification of disability (e.g., psychoeducational report, California Assessment System for Adults with Disabilities, Department of Vocational Rehabilitation Assessment). Students may begin taking classes any term. *Application deadline:* continuous.

Special policies: The college has written policies regarding grade forgiveness.

PROGRAM AND SERVICE COMPONENTS

Special preparation or orientation: Optional orientation offered before registration and individually with counselors.

Diagnostic testing: Intelligence, reading, math, spelling, written language, perceptual skills, personality, speech, hearing.

Academic advising: Provided by unit staff members. Students with LD may take up to as many units as an individual can handle each term;

most take 12 to 15 units (fewer with waiver); 12 units (fewer with waiver) required to maintain full-time status; 6 units (part-time), 12 units (full-time) required to be eligible for financial aid.
Counseling services: Individual counseling, career counseling.
Basic skills remediation: Offered in small groups by LD teachers, program aides; computer-aided instruction also offered. Available in reading, math, spelling, written language, learning strategies, perceptual skills, study skills, computer skills.
Subject-area tutoring: Offered one-on-one and in small groups by professional teachers, program aides. Available in some subjects.
Special courses: Vocabulary development, composition, word processing, math, typing, study skills. All offered for credit; none enter into overall grade point average.
Auxiliary aids: Taped textbooks, tape recorders, word-processors with spell-check, optical character readers.
Auxiliary services: Alternative test arrangements, notetakers, priority registration, advocacy.

GENERAL COLLEGE INFORMATION

State and locally supported, 2-year, coed. Part of California Community Colleges System. Awards associate degrees. Founded 1975. *Setting:* 175-acre urban campus. *Total enrollment:* 9,002. *Faculty:* 300 (103 full-time, 197 part-time).
Enrollment Profile: 9,002 students from 23 states and territories, 11 other countries. 54% women, 46% men, 80% part-time, 94% state residents, 2% transferred in, 1% international, 52% 25 or older, 1% Native American, 23% Hispanic, 5% black, 33% Asian or Pacific Islander. *Most popular recent majors:* liberal arts/general studies, business administration/commerce/management, drafting and design.
First-Year Class: 2,660 total; 3,409 applied, 100% were accepted, 78% of whom enrolled.
Graduation Requirements: 60 units; computer course.
Computers on Campus: 250 computers available on campus for general student use. Computer purchase/lease plans available. Computers for student use in computer center, learning resource center. Staffed computer lab on campus provides training in use of computers, software.

EXPENSES

Expenses for 1997–98: State resident tuition: $0 full-time. Nonresident tuition: $3780 full-time, $126 per unit part-time. Part-time mandatory fees per semester range from $28 to $158. Full-time mandatory fees: $420.
LD Services Contact: Ms. Bonnie Clark, Learning Disabilities Specialist, Evergreen Valley College, 3095 Yerba Buena Road, San Jose, CA 95135-1598, 408-270-6447. Fax: 408-239-0316.

FINGER LAKES COMMUNITY COLLEGE

Canandaigua, New York

LEARNING DISABILITIES SERVICES INFORMATION

Developmental Studies Department began offering services in 1985. Currently the program serves 126 undergraduates with LD. Students diagnosed with ADD/ADHD are eligible for the same services available to students with LD.
Staff: Includes coordinator, chairperson. Services provided by remediation specialists, counselor.
Special Fees: No special fees are charged for services to students with LD.
Applications and admissions: *Required:* high school transcript, IEP (Individualized Education Program), personal interview, psychoeducational report completed within 3 years; *recommended:* autobiographical statement, letters of recommendation. Students may begin taking classes in fall or spring. *Application deadline:* continuous.

PROGRAM AND SERVICE COMPONENTS

Diagnostic testing: Reading, math, written language.
Academic advising: Provided by unit staff members, academic advisers. Students with LD may take up to 15 credit hours each term; most take 12 credit hours; 12 credit hours required to maintain full-time status; 12 credit hours (full-time) required to be eligible for financial aid.
Counseling services: Individual counseling, small-group counseling, career counseling, self-advocacy training.
Basic skills remediation: Offered in class-size groups by regular teachers. Available in reading, math, written language, learning strategies, study skills, time management, social skills.
Subject-area tutoring: Offered one-on-one and in small groups by peer tutors, learning specialists. Available in all subjects.
Special courses: College survival skills, reading, composition, study skills. All offered for credit; all enter into overall grade point average.
Auxiliary aids: Taped textbooks, tape recorders, calculators, typewriters, word-processors with spell-check.
Auxiliary services: Alternative test arrangements, notetakers, readers.

GENERAL COLLEGE INFORMATION

State and locally supported, 2-year, coed. Part of State University of New York System. Awards associate degrees. Founded 1965. *Setting:* 300-acre small-town campus with easy access to Rochester. *Total enrollment:* 3,768. *Faculty:* 230 (94 full-time, 15% with terminal degrees, 136 part-time); student–undergrad faculty ratio is 18:1.
Enrollment Profile: 3,768 students: 57% women, 43% men, 45% part-time, 99% state residents, 5% transferred in, 1% international, 41% 25 or older, 1% Native American, 1% Hispanic, 2% black, 1% Asian or Pacific Islander. *Retention:* 59% of 1995 full-time freshmen returned. *Most popular recent majors:* business administration/commerce/management, criminal justice, conservation.
First-Year Class: 1,224 total; 2,192 applied, 98% were accepted, 57% of whom enrolled.
Graduation Requirements: 64 credit hours; computer course for business, engineering technology majors; internship (some majors).
Computers on Campus: 220 computers available on campus for general student use. A campus-wide network can be accessed. Students can contact faculty members and/or advisers through e-mail. Computers for student use in computer center, computer labs, learning resource center, classrooms, library, departmental labs provide access to the Internet/World Wide Web, on- and off-campus e-mail addresses. Staffed computer lab on campus provides training in use of computers, software.

EXPENSES

Expenses for 1996–97: *Application fee:* $30. State resident tuition: $2350 full-time, $87 per credit hour part-time. Nonresident tuition: $4700 full-time, $174 per credit hour part-time. Part-time mandatory fees: $3 per credit hour. Full-time mandatory fees: $130.
LD Services Contact: Ms. Amy Nichols, Coordinator of Services for Students with Learning Disabilities, Finger Lakes Community College, 4355 Lake Shore Drive, Canandaigua, NY 14424-8395, 716-394-3500 Ext. 390. Fax: 716-394-5005. Email: nicholal@snyflcc.fingerlakes.edu.

FIORELLO H. LAGUARDIA COMMUNITY COLLEGE OF THE CITY UNIVERSITY OF NEW YORK

Long Island City, New York

LEARNING DISABILITIES SERVICES INFORMATION

Office for Students with Disabilities (OSD) began offering services in 1976. Currently the program serves 175 undergraduates with LD. Students diagnosed with ADD/ADHD are eligible for the same services available to students with LD.
Staff: Includes director, coordinators, secretary. Services provided by remediation specialist, tutors, counselors, diagnostic specialist.
Special Fees: No special fees are charged for services to students with LD.
Applications and admissions: *Required:* high school transcript, IEP (Individualized Education Program), psychoeducational report completed within 3 years; *recommended:* personal interview. Students may begin taking classes in fall or spring. *Application deadline:* continuous.
Special policies: The college has written policies regarding grade forgiveness; substitutions and waivers of graduation requirements.

PROGRAM AND SERVICE COMPONENTS

Special preparation or orientation: Optional orientation offered on an individual basis.
Diagnostic testing: Intelligence, reading, math, spelling, written language, perceptual skills, learning strategies; ADD/ADHD screening also available.
Academic advising: Provided by unit staff members. Students with LD may take up to 12 credits each term; most take 12 credits; 12 credits required to maintain full-time status; 12 credits (6 with basic skills course load) required to be eligible for financial aid.

Fiorello H. LaGuardia Community College of the City University of New York (continued)

Counseling services: Individual counseling, career counseling, self-advocacy training, academic counseling.
Basic skills remediation: Offered one-on-one and in small groups by LD teachers, peer tutors. Available in reading, math, written language, learning strategies, study skills, time management, social skills, computer skills.
Subject-area tutoring: Offered one-on-one and in small groups by peer tutors. Available in most subjects.
Auxiliary aids: Tape recorders, calculators, typewriters, word-processors with spell-check, personal computers, talking computers, optical character readers, closed-captioned television.
Auxiliary services: Alternative test arrangements, notetakers, priority registration, advocacy.
Campus support group: A special student organization is available to students with LD.

GENERAL COLLEGE INFORMATION

State and locally supported, 2-year, coed. Part of City University of New York System. Awards associate degrees. Founded 1970. *Setting:* urban campus. *Total enrollment:* 10,341. *Faculty:* 604 (269 full-time, 46% with terminal degrees, 335 part-time).
Enrollment Profile: 10,341 students: 66% women, 34% men, 31% part-time, 7% transferred in, 44% 25 or older, 1% Native American, 38% Hispanic, 21% black, 12% Asian or Pacific Islander. *Retention:* 66% of 1995 full-time freshmen returned. *Areas of study chosen:* 29% business management and administrative services, 24% health professions and related sciences, 22% liberal arts/general studies, 17% computer and information sciences, 4% education. *Most popular recent majors:* accounting, business administration/commerce/management, tourism and travel.
First-Year Class: 2,248 total. Of the students who applied, 100% were accepted, 50% of whom enrolled.
Graduation Requirements: 64 units; internship (some majors).
Computers on Campus: 749 computers available on campus for general student use. Computer purchase/lease plans available. Computers for student use in computer center, computer labs, classrooms, library. *System-wide academic computing expenditure 1995–96:* $447,000.

EXPENSES

Expenses for 1996–97: Area resident tuition: $2500 full-time, $105 per unit part-time. State resident tuition: $3076 full-time, $130 per unit part-time. Nonresident tuition: $3076 full-time, $130 per unit part-time. Part-time mandatory fees: $20 per term. Full-time mandatory fees: $110.
LD Services Contact: Mr. Jhony Nelson, Coordinator for Services for Students with Disabilities, Fiorello H. LaGuardia Community College of the City University of New York, 31-10 Thomson Avenue, Room M119C, Long Island City, NY 11101-3071, 718-482-5260. Fax: 718-482-5599. Email: jhony@lagcc.cuny.edu.

FLATHEAD VALLEY COMMUNITY COLLEGE

Kalispell, Montana

LEARNING DISABILITIES SERVICES INFORMATION

Academic Reinforcement Center began offering services in 1988. Currently the program serves 35 undergraduates with LD. Students diagnosed with ADD/ADHD are eligible for the same services available to students with LD.
Staff: 6 full-time, 3 part-time staff members, including director. Services provided by remediation specialists, tutors, counselors, diagnostic specialists.
Special Fees: No special fees are charged for services to students with LD.
Applications and admissions: Open admissions. Students may begin taking classes in fall, spring, or summer. *Application deadline:* continuous.

PROGRAM AND SERVICE COMPONENTS

Diagnostic testing: Intelligence, reading, math, spelling, written language, personality.
Academic advising: Provided by unit staff members, academic advisers. Most students with LD take 12 semester hours each term; 12 semester hours required to maintain full-time status; source of aid determines number of semester hours required to be eligible for financial aid.
Counseling services: Individual counseling, small-group counseling, career counseling.
Basic skills remediation: Offered one-on-one, in small groups, and in class-size groups by regular teachers. Available in reading, math, spelling, written language, learning strategies, study skills.
Subject-area tutoring: Offered one-on-one, in small groups, and in class-size groups by professional teachers, peer tutors. Available in all subjects.
Special courses: College survival skills, reading, vocabulary development, composition, math, study skills, career planning. All offered for credit; most enter into overall grade point average.
Auxiliary aids: Taped textbooks, tape recorders, typewriters, word-processors with spell-check, talking computers, optical character readers, videocassette recorders, video cameras, Williams FM sound system.
Auxiliary services: Alternative test arrangements, notetakers, priority registration, advocacy.

GENERAL COLLEGE INFORMATION

State and locally supported, 2-year, coed. Awards associate degrees. Founded 1967. *Setting:* 40-acre small-town campus. *Educational spending 1995–96:* $2090 per undergrad. *Total enrollment:* 1,142. *Faculty:* 111 (36 full-time, 75 part-time).
Enrollment Profile: 1,142 students from 14 states and territories, 4 other countries. 63% women, 37% men, 52% part-time, 96% state residents, 9% transferred in, 1% international, 54% 25 or older, 2% Native American, 1% Hispanic, 1% black, 1% Asian or Pacific Islander.
First-Year Class: 250 total; 285 applied, 100% were accepted, 88% of whom enrolled.
Graduation Requirements: 64 semester hours; 1 college algebra course; computer course for associate of applied science degree programs; internship (some majors).
Computers on Campus: 90 computers available on campus for general student use. A campus-wide network can be accessed. Students can contact faculty members and/or advisers through e-mail. Computers for student use in library, instructional labs provide access to the Internet/World Wide Web, on-campus e-mail addresses. Staffed computer lab on campus. *Academic computing expenditure 1995–96:* $235,822.

EXPENSES

Expenses for 1996–97: Area resident tuition: $1505 full-time, $53.75 per semester hour part-time. State resident tuition: $2184 full-time, $78 per semester hour part-time. Nonresident tuition: $4599 full-time, $164.25 per semester hour part-time. Part-time mandatory fees: $15 per semester. Full-time mandatory fees: $30.
LD Services Contact: Mr. Brian R. Bechtold, Counselor, Flathead Valley Community College, 777 Grandview Drive, Kalispell, MT 59901, 406-756-3885. Fax: 406-756-3911. Email: bbechtol@fvcc.cc.mt.us.

FLOYD COLLEGE

Rome, Georgia

LEARNING DISABILITIES SERVICES INFORMATION

Office of Disabilities Support Services began offering services in 1993. Currently the program serves 5 undergraduates with LD. Students diagnosed with ADD/ADHD are eligible for the same services available to students with LD.
Staff: Includes coordinator, Disabilities Support Specialist.
Special Fees: $300 for diagnostic testing.
Applications and admissions: *Required:* high school transcript, untimed SAT I. Students may begin taking classes any term. *Application deadline:* continuous.
Special policies: The college has written policies regarding grade forgiveness.

PROGRAM AND SERVICE COMPONENTS

Diagnostic testing: The University System assigned center at Georgia State University.
Academic advising: Provided by academic advisers. Students with LD may take up to 17 quarter hours (without permission) each term; most take 12 to 17 quarter hours; 12 quarter hours required to maintain full-time status and be eligible for financial aid.
Counseling services: Individual counseling, career counseling.
Basic skills remediation: Offered in class-size groups by regular teachers; computer-aided instruction also offered. Available in reading, math, written language, study skills, time management.

Subject-area tutoring: Offered one-on-one by professional teachers. Available in most subjects.
Special courses: College survival skills, reading, composition, word processing, math, study skills. Most offered for credit; some enter into overall grade point average.
Auxiliary aids: Tape recorders, calculators, typewriters, word-processors with spell-check, personal computers, optical character readers.
Auxiliary services: Alternative test arrangements, notetakers.

GENERAL COLLEGE INFORMATION

State-supported, 2-year, coed. Part of University System of Georgia. Awards associate degrees. Founded 1970. *Setting:* 212-acre rural campus with easy access to Atlanta. *Educational spending 1995–96:* $1484 per undergrad. *Total enrollment:* 3,048. *Faculty:* 66 (51 full-time, 56% with terminal degrees, 15 part-time).
Enrollment Profile: 3,048 students from 2 states and territories, 4 other countries. 65% women, 35% men, 47% part-time, 98% state residents, 20% transferred in, 1% international, 1% Native American, 1% Hispanic, 8% black, 1% Asian or Pacific Islander. *Retention:* 38% of 1995 full-time freshmen returned. *Most popular recent majors:* nursing, business administration/commerce/management.
First-Year Class: 460 total; 617 applied, 100% were accepted, 55% of whom enrolled. 1 class president, 2 valedictorians.
Graduation Requirements: 102 quarter hours; 1 math course; computer course.
Computers on Campus: 175 computers available on campus for general student use. A campus-wide network can be accessed from off-campus. Students can contact faculty members and/or advisers through e-mail. Computers for student use in computer center, library provide access to the Internet/World Wide Web. Staffed computer lab on campus provides training in use of computers. *Academic computing expenditure 1995–96:* $99,006.

EXPENSES

Estimated Expenses for 1997–98: State resident tuition: $1146 full-time, $32 per quarter hour part-time. Nonresident tuition: $4320 full-time, $121 per quarter hour part-time. Part-time mandatory fees per quarter (6 to 11 quarter hours):$15. Full-time mandatory fees: $45.
LD Services Contact: Dr. Penelope Wills, Vice President for Student Development, Floyd College, PO Box 1864, Rome, GA 30162-1864, 706-295-6335. Fax: 706-295-6610.

FORT SCOTT COMMUNITY COLLEGE

Fort Scott, Kansas

LEARNING DISABILITIES SERVICES INFORMATION

Comprehensive Education and Employment Training Center (CE-ETC) began offering services in 1982. Currently the program serves 30 undergraduates with LD. Students diagnosed with ADD/ADHD are eligible for the same services available to students with LD.
Staff: Includes director, coordinators, testing coordinator, career counselor. Services provided by remediation specialists, tutors.
Special Fees: No special fees are charged for services to students with LD.
Applications and admissions: *Required:* ACT ASSET; *recommended:* high school grade point average, courses completed, extracurricular activities, personal interview, psychoeducational report completed within 1 year. Students may begin taking classes any term. *Application deadline:* continuous.
Special policies: The college has written policies regarding grade forgiveness.

PROGRAM AND SERVICE COMPONENTS

Diagnostic testing: Reading, math, written language, study skills, learning strategies.
Academic advising: Provided by unit staff members, academic advisers. Most students with LD take 12 semester hours each term; 12 semester hours required to maintain full-time status; source of aid determines number of semester hours required to be eligible for financial aid.
Counseling services: Individual counseling, career counseling.
Basic skills remediation: Offered one-on-one by LD teachers, regular teachers, remediation instructors, tutors. Available in reading, math, spelling, handwriting, written language, learning strategies, study skills, time management, social skills.
Subject-area tutoring: Offered one-on-one and in small groups by peer tutors, retired teachers, community volunteers. Available in all subjects.
Special courses: College survival skills, reading, vocabulary development, composition, learning strategies, word processing, math, study skills, career planning. All offered for credit; most enter into overall grade point average.
Auxiliary aids: Taped textbooks, tape recorders, calculators, typewriters, word-processors with spell-check, videocassettes.
Auxiliary services: Alternative test arrangements, notetakers.

GENERAL COLLEGE INFORMATION

State and locally supported, 2-year, coed. Awards associate degrees. Founded 1919. *Setting:* 147-acre small-town campus. *Total enrollment:* 1,651. *Faculty:* 59 (51 full-time, 8 part-time).
Enrollment Profile: 1,651 students from 24 states and territories, 7 other countries. 57% women, 43% men, 48% part-time, 86% state residents, 12% transferred in, 1% international, 40% 25 or older, 1% Native American, 1% Hispanic, 8% black, 1% Asian or Pacific Islander. *Retention:* 82% of 1995 full-time freshmen returned. *Most popular recent majors:* education, business administration/commerce/management, agricultural sciences.
First-Year Class: 1,104 total. Of the students who applied, 100% were accepted, 75% of whom enrolled. 30% from top 10% of their high school class, 70% from top half.
Graduation Requirements: 60 semester hours; 1 college algebra course; computer course; internship (some majors).
Computers on Campus: 95 computers available on campus for general student use. Computer purchase/lease plans available. Computers for student use in computer center, computer labs, learning resource center, classrooms, library provide access to the Internet/World Wide Web. Staffed computer lab on campus provides training in use of computers, software.

EXPENSES

Expenses for 1997–98: State resident tuition: $1200 full-time, $40 per semester hour part-time. Nonresident tuition: $2700 full-time, $90 per semester hour part-time. College room and board: $2700.
LD Services Contact: Dr. Linda James-Sours, Director, Fort Scott Community College, 2108 South Horton, Fort Scott, KS 66701, 316-223-2700 Ext. 80. Fax: 316-223-6530.

FOX VALLEY TECHNICAL COLLEGE

Appleton, Wisconsin

LEARNING DISABILITIES SERVICES INFORMATION

Student Services began offering services in 1978. Currently the program serves 133 undergraduates with LD. Students diagnosed with ADD/ADHD are eligible for the same services available to students with LD, as well as monitoring services, resource materials.
Staff: 2 full-time, 3 part-time staff members, including coordinator. Services provided by instructors.
Special Fees: No special fees are charged for services to students with LD.
Applications and admissions: *Required:* high school transcript, ACT ASSET; *recommended:* high school IEP (Individualized Education Program), personal interview, psychoeducational report. Students may begin taking classes any term. *Application deadline:* continuous.

PROGRAM AND SERVICE COMPONENTS

Diagnostic testing: Reading, math, spelling.
Academic advising: Provided by unit staff members. Most students with LD take 12 to 14 credits each term; 12 credits required to maintain full-time status; 6 credits (part-time), 12 credits (full-time) required to be eligible for financial aid.
Counseling services: Individual counseling, career counseling.
Basic skills remediation: Offered one-on-one by LD teachers, regular teachers. Available in reading, math, spelling, handwriting, written language, learning strategies, study skills, social skills.
Subject-area tutoring: Offered one-on-one by professional teachers, peer tutors. Available in all subjects.
Special courses: College survival skills, typing, career planning. Some offered for credit; some enter into overall grade point average.
Auxiliary aids: Taped textbooks, tape recorders, calculators, word-processors with spell-check, personal computers, talking computers, optical character readers, closed-captioned television.

Fox Valley Technical College (continued)

Auxiliary services: Alternative test arrangements, notetakers, advocacy.

GENERAL COLLEGE INFORMATION

State and locally supported, 2-year, coed. Part of Wisconsin Technical College System. Awards associate degrees. Founded 1967. *Setting:* 100-acre suburban campus. *Total enrollment:* 6,100. *Faculty:* 1,241 (244 full-time, 4% with terminal degrees, 997 part-time).

Enrollment Profile: 6,100 students from 4 states and territories, 20 other countries. 53% women, 47% men, 35% part-time, 94% state residents, 30% transferred in, 54% 25 or older, 2% Native American, 2% Hispanic, 2% black, 1% Asian or Pacific Islander. *Most popular recent majors:* marketing/retailing/merchandising, nursing, accounting.

First-Year Class: 2,150 total; 4,450 applied, 100% were accepted, 48% of whom enrolled.

Graduation Requirements: 74 credits; math/science requirements vary according to program.

Computers on Campus: 260 computers available on campus for general student use. Computer purchase/lease plans available. Computers for student use in computer center, computer labs, learning resource center, library, student center provide access to the Internet/World Wide Web. Staffed computer lab on campus.

EXPENSES

Expenses for 1997–98: *Application fee:* $25. State resident tuition: $2005 full-time, $54.20 per credit part-time. Nonresident tuition: $15,806 full-time, $427.20 per credit part-time. Part-time mandatory fees: $9.22 per credit. Full-time mandatory fees: $341.

LD Services Contact: Ms. Shary Schwabenlender, Special Needs Instructor-Coordinator, Fox Valley Technical College, 1825 North Bluemound Drive, Appleton, WI 54913-2277, 414-735-5679. Fax: 414-735-2582.

FREDERICK COMMUNITY COLLEGE

Frederick, Maryland

LEARNING DISABILITIES SERVICES INFORMATION

System for Student Success began offering services in 1987. Currently the program serves 85 undergraduates with LD. Students diagnosed with ADD/ADHD are eligible for the same services available to students with LD.

Staff: Includes director, coordinators, specialists. Services provided by tutors, diagnostic specialist, Director of Developmental Education.

Special Fees: No special fees are charged for services to students with LD.

Applications and admissions: *Required:* high school transcript, placement testing. Students may begin taking classes any term. *Application deadline:* continuous.

PROGRAM AND SERVICE COMPONENTS

Special preparation or orientation: Optional orientation offered before registration.

Diagnostic testing: Reading, math, spelling, handwriting, written language, perceptual skills.

Academic advising: Provided by unit staff members, academic advisers. Most students with LD take 3 to 12 credit hours each term; 12 credit hours required to maintain full-time status; 6 credit hours required to be eligible for financial aid.

Counseling services: Individual counseling, career counseling, self-advocacy training.

Basic skills remediation: Offered one-on-one and in small groups by regular teachers, learning specialist. Available in reading, math, spelling, written language, learning strategies, study skills, time management, computer skills.

Subject-area tutoring: Offered one-on-one by professional teachers, peer tutors, learning specialist. Available in all subjects.

Auxiliary aids: Tape recorders, calculators, word-processors with spell-check, personal computers, talking computers, optical character readers.

Auxiliary services: Alternative test arrangements, notetakers, readers.

GENERAL COLLEGE INFORMATION

State and locally supported, 2-year, coed. Awards associate degrees. Founded 1957. *Setting:* 125-acre small-town campus with easy access to Baltimore and Washington, DC. *Total enrollment:* 4,233. *Faculty:* 272 (72 full-time, 200 part-time); student–undergrad faculty ratio is 17:1.

Enrollment Profile: 4,233 students from 9 states and territories, 9 other countries. 62% women, 38% men, 69% part-time, 98% state residents, 15% transferred in, 1% international, 60% 25 or older, 1% Native American, 1% Hispanic, 6% black, 2% Asian or Pacific Islander. *Retention:* 66% of 1995 full-time freshmen returned. *Most popular recent majors:* liberal arts/general studies, business administration/commerce/management, nursing.

First-Year Class: 1,139 total. Of the students who applied, 100% were accepted.

Graduation Requirements: 60 credit hours; 1 course each in math and science; computer course for business majors.

Computers on Campus: Computers for student use in computer center, computer labs, learning resource center, classrooms, library, writing center provide access to the Internet/World Wide Web. Staffed computer lab on campus.

EXPENSES

Expenses for 1997–98: Area resident tuition: $2070 full-time, $69 per credit hour part-time. State resident tuition: $4140 full-time, $138 per credit hour part-time. Nonresident tuition: $6090 full-time, $203 per credit hour part-time. Part-time mandatory fees per semester range from $18.50 to $102. Full-time mandatory fees: $260.

LD Services Contact: Dr. Rosemary Wilkinson, Learning Specialist, Frederick Community College, 7932 Opossumtown Pike, Frederick, MD 21702, 301-846-2409. Fax: 301-846-2498. Email: rosemary_wilkinson@co.frederick.md.us.

FRESNO CITY COLLEGE

Fresno, California

LEARNING DISABILITIES SERVICES INFORMATION

Disabled Students Programs and Services, Learning Disabilities Program began offering services in 1975. Currently the program serves 250 undergraduates with LD. Students diagnosed with ADD/ADHD are eligible for the same services available to students with LD.

Staff: 10 full-time, 4 part-time staff members, including director. Services provided by tutors, counselors, diagnostic specialists, LD specialist.

Special Fees: No special fees are charged for services to students with LD.

Applications and admissions: *Required:* California Assessment System for Adults with Learning Disabilities; *recommended:* high school transcript, courses completed, IEP (Individualized Education Program). Students may begin taking classes in fall or spring. *Application deadline:* continuous.

Special policies: The college has written policies regarding grade forgiveness.

PROGRAM AND SERVICE COMPONENTS

Special preparation or orientation: Optional orientation offered before registration.

Diagnostic testing: Intelligence, reading, math, spelling, learning strategies.

Academic advising: Provided by unit staff members. Students with LD may take up to 15 units each term; most take 9 to 15 units; 12 units required to maintain full-time status; 6 units required to be eligible for financial aid.

Counseling services: Individual counseling, career counseling.

Basic skills remediation: Offered one-on-one and in small groups by LD teachers, teacher trainees. Available in reading, math, spelling, handwriting, written language, learning strategies, study skills.

Subject-area tutoring: Offered one-on-one and in small groups by professional teachers, peer tutors, graduate students. Available in most subjects.

Special courses: College survival skills, reading, vocabulary development, communication skills, composition, learning strategies, word processing, time management, math, typing, study skills, career planning, health and nutrition, social relationships. Some offered for credit.

Auxiliary aids: Taped textbooks, tape recorders, calculators, typewriters, word-processors with spell-check, optical character readers.

Auxiliary services: Alternative test arrangements, notetakers, advocacy.

Campus support group: A special student organization is available to students with LD.

GENERAL COLLEGE INFORMATION

District-supported, 2-year, coed. Part of California Community Colleges System. Awards associate degrees. Founded 1910. *Setting:* 103-acre urban campus. *Total enrollment:* 18,103. *Faculty:* 832 (271 full-time, 561 part-time); student–undergrad faculty ratio is 22:1.
Enrollment Profile: 18,103 students: 53% women, 47% men, 69% part-time, 97% state residents, 8% transferred in, 1% international, 46% 25 or older, 1% Native American, 30% Hispanic, 8% black, 13% Asian or Pacific Islander. *Retention:* 48% of 1995 full-time freshmen returned. *Most popular recent majors:* liberal arts/general studies, business administration/commerce/management.
First-Year Class: 4,067 total; 7,449 applied, 99% were accepted.
Graduation Requirements: 60 units; 1 algebra course; computer course for business administration majors.
Computers on Campus: 600 computers available on campus for general student use. Computers for student use in various locations. Staffed computer lab on campus provides training in use of computers, software.

EXPENSES

Expenses for 1997–98: State resident tuition: $0 full-time. Nonresident tuition: $3990 full-time, $130 per unit part-time. Part-time mandatory fees per semester range from $24 to $154. Full-time mandatory fees: $412.
LD Services Contact: Ms. Jeanette Covington, Learning Disabilities Specialist, Fresno City College, 1101 East University Avenue, Fresno, CA 93741-0002, 209-442-4600 Ext. 8157. Fax: 209-485-7304.

FRONT RANGE COMMUNITY COLLEGE

Westminster, Colorado

LEARNING DISABILITIES SERVICES INFORMATION

Special Services began offering services in 1987. Currently the program serves 150 undergraduates with LD. Students diagnosed with ADD/ADHD are eligible for the same services available to students with LD.
Staff: 1 full-time, 2 part-time staff members, including director, coordinator, counselor. Services provided by tutors, counselors, reading specialist, aides.
Special Fees: $150 for diagnostic testing.
Applications and admissions: *Required:* locally-administered basic skills assessment; *recommended:* psychoeducational report completed within 3 years, verification of disability (interview, testing, and/or records). Students may begin taking classes any term. *Application deadline:* continuous.

PROGRAM AND SERVICE COMPONENTS

Special preparation or orientation: Optional orientation offered individually by arrangement.
Diagnostic testing: Intelligence, reading, math, spelling, written language, motor abilities, perceptual skills, study skills.
Academic advising: Provided by unit staff members, academic advisers. Most students with LD take 6 to 9 credit hours each term; 12 credit hours required to maintain full-time status; 6 credit hours required to be eligible for financial aid.
Counseling services: Individual counseling, small-group counseling, career counseling, self-advocacy training.
Basic skills remediation: Offered one-on-one, in small groups, and in class-size groups by LD teachers, regular teachers, subject-area tutors; computer-aided instruction also offered. Available in reading, math, spelling, written language, learning strategies, perceptual skills, study skills, time management, social skills.
Subject-area tutoring: Offered one-on-one and in small groups by professional teachers, peer tutors, professional tutors. Available in all subjects.
Special courses: College survival skills, reading, vocabulary development, communication skills, composition, learning strategies, word processing, time management, math, typing, study skills, career planning, stress management, social relationships. Some offered for credit; some enter into overall grade point average.
Auxiliary aids: Taped textbooks, tape recorders, calculators, word-processors with spell-check, personal computers, talking computers, optical character readers, Arkenstone Reader.
Auxiliary services: Alternative test arrangements, notetakers, advocacy, readers.

GENERAL COLLEGE INFORMATION

State-supported, 2-year, coed. Awards associate degrees. Founded 1968. *Setting:* 90-acre suburban campus with easy access to Denver. *Endowment:* $54,500. *Total enrollment:* 11,027. *Faculty:* 765 (177 full-time, 11% with terminal degrees, 588 part-time); student–undergrad faculty ratio is 14:1.
Enrollment Profile: 11,027 students from 32 states and territories, 28 other countries. 59% women, 41% men, 71% part-time, 94% state residents, 15% transferred in, 3% international, 56% 25 or older, 1% Native American, 8% Hispanic, 1% black, 4% Asian or Pacific Islander. *Areas of study chosen:* 44% interdisciplinary studies, 19% vocational and home economics, 14% liberal arts/general studies, 9% biological and life sciences, 6% health professions and related sciences, 5% computer and information sciences, 3% business management and administrative services.
First-Year Class: 3,327 total; 6,050 applied, 100% were accepted, 55% of whom enrolled.
Graduation Requirements: 60 credit hours; 1 math course; computer course for most majors; internship (some majors).
Computers on Campus: 500 computers available on campus for general student use. A campus-wide network can be accessed from off-campus. Students can contact faculty members and/or advisers through e-mail. Computers for student use in computer labs, learning resource center, classrooms provide access to the Internet/World Wide Web. Staffed computer lab on campus provides training in use of computers. *Academic computing expenditure 1995–96:* $283,394.

EXPENSES

Expenses for 1996–97: State resident tuition: $1605 full-time, $53.50 per credit hour part-time. Nonresident tuition: $7313 full-time, $243.75 per credit hour part-time. Part-time mandatory fees per semester range from $46.45 to $120.95. Full-time mandatory fees: $302.
LD Services Contact: Ms. Karol Janice Bennett, Coordinator, Progressive Adult Learning, Front Range Community College, 3645 West 112th Avenue, Westminster, CO 80030-2105, 303-404-5243. Fax: 303-466-1623. Email: fr_karol@cccs.cccoes.edu.

FULLERTON COLLEGE

Fullerton, California

LEARNING DISABILITIES SERVICES INFORMATION

Learning Resource Services began offering services in 1981. Currently the program serves 500 to 540 undergraduates with LD. Students diagnosed with ADD/ADHD are eligible for the same services available to students with LD.
Staff: 5 full-time, 2 part-time staff members, including director. Services provided by tutors, counselor, diagnostic specialist.
Special Fees: No special fees are charged for services to students with LD.
Applications and admissions: *Required:* psychoeducational report completed within 3 years; *recommended:* California Assessment System for Adults with Learning Disabilities. Students may begin taking classes any term. *Application deadline:* continuous.
Special policies: The college has written policies regarding grade forgiveness; substitutions and waivers of admissions requirements.

PROGRAM AND SERVICE COMPONENTS

Special preparation or orientation: Optional orientation offered before registration and during registration.
Diagnostic testing: Intelligence, reading, math, spelling, written language, motor abilities, perceptual skills.
Academic advising: Provided by unit staff members, academic advisers. Students with LD may take up to 18 semester units each term; most take 8.5 semester units; 12 semester units required to maintain full-time status; 6 semester units required to be eligible for financial aid.
Counseling services: Individual counseling, career counseling, disability management.
Basic skills remediation: Offered one-on-one, in small groups, and in class-size groups by LD adaptive computer learning specialist. Available in reading, math, spelling, handwriting, spoken language, written language, learning strategies, motor abilities, perceptual skills, study skills, time management, social skills, speech.
Subject-area tutoring: Offered one-on-one and in small groups by peer tutors. Available in all subjects.
Special courses: Learning strategies, word processing. All offered for credit; none enter into overall grade point average.

Fullerton College (continued)

Auxiliary aids: Taped textbooks, tape recorders, calculators, typewriters, word-processors with spell-check, personal computers, talking computers, optical character readers, print enlargers, adaptive computers.
Auxiliary services: Alternative test arrangements, notetakers, priority registration, advocacy.
Campus support group: A special student organization is available to students with LD.

GENERAL COLLEGE INFORMATION

State and locally supported, 2-year, coed. Part of North Orange County Community College District System. Awards associate degrees. Founded 1913. *Setting:* 79-acre suburban campus with easy access to Los Angeles. *Total enrollment:* 18,339. *Faculty:* 678 (276 full-time, 402 part-time).
Enrollment Profile: 18,339 students: 52% women, 48% men, 49% part-time, 99% state residents, 10% transferred in, 1% international, 40% 25 or older, 2% Native American, 18% Hispanic, 2% black, 10% Asian or Pacific Islander. *Most popular recent majors:* liberal arts/general studies, business administration/commerce/management, law enforcement/police sciences.
First-Year Class: 3,459 applied, 100% were accepted, 100% of whom enrolled.
Graduation Requirements: 60 semester units; 3 semester units each of math and biological/physical science.
Computers on Campus: 600 computers available on campus for general student use. Computers for student use in computer labs, library, departmental labs. Staffed computer lab on campus provides training in use of computers, software.

EXPENSES

Expenses for 1997–98: State resident tuition: $0 full-time. Nonresident tuition: $3540 full-time, $118 per unit part-time. Part-time mandatory fees per semester range from $23 to $153. Full-time mandatory fees: $410.
LD Services Contact: Ms. Christine Terry, District Director, Disabled Student Programs and Services, Fullerton College, 321 East Chapman Avenue, Fullerton, CA 92832-2095, 714-992-7270. Fax: 714-871-9192. Email: terry@nocccd.cc.ca.us.

GALVESTON COLLEGE

Galveston, Texas

LEARNING DISABILITIES SERVICES INFORMATION

Special Populations began offering services in 1987. Currently the program serves 18 undergraduates with LD. Students diagnosed with ADD/ADHD are eligible for the same services available to students with LD, as well as appropriate referral services with local community agencies, organizations and/or institutions.
Staff: 1 full-time, 1 part-time staff members, including director. Services provided by remediation specialists, tutors, counselors, diagnostic specialists, community agencies and organizations.
Special Fees: No special fees are charged for services to students with LD.
Applications and admissions: *Required:* high school transcript, college's placement test; *recommended:* letters of recommendation, psychoeducational report completed within 1 year. Students may begin taking classes any term. *Application deadline:* continuous.
Special policies: The college has written policies regarding grade forgiveness.

PROGRAM AND SERVICE COMPONENTS

Special preparation or orientation: Required orientation held before registration and individually by special arrangement.
Diagnostic testing: Reading, math, written language.
Academic advising: Provided by unit staff members, academic advisers. Students with LD may take up to 12 credit hours each term; most take 6 credit hours; 9 credit hours required to maintain full-time status; 6 credit hours required to be eligible for financial aid.
Counseling services: Individual counseling, career counseling.
Basic skills remediation: Offered one-on-one by LD teachers, regular teachers, professional tutors; computer-aided instruction also offered. Available in reading, math, spelling, written language, learning strategies, perceptual skills, study skills, time management, speech.
Subject-area tutoring: Offered one-on-one and in small groups by professional teachers, peer tutors, community volunteers and service providers from community agencies. Available in all subjects.
Special courses: College survival skills, reading, vocabulary development, communication skills, composition, learning strategies, word processing, time management, math, typing, study skills, career planning. Most offered for credit; some enter into overall grade point average.
Auxiliary aids: Taped textbooks, tape recorders, calculators, typewriters, word-processors with spell-check, personal computers, optical character readers.
Auxiliary services: Alternative test arrangements, notetakers, priority registration.
Campus support group: A special student organization is available to students with LD.

GENERAL COLLEGE INFORMATION

State and locally supported, 2-year, coed. Part of Texas Higher Education Coordinating Board. Awards associate degrees. Founded 1967. *Setting:* 11-acre urban campus with easy access to Houston. *Educational spending 1995–96:* $1945 per undergrad. *Total enrollment:* 2,328. *Faculty:* 133 (49 full-time, 100% with terminal degrees, 84 part-time); student–undergrad faculty ratio is 19:1.
Enrollment Profile: 2,328 students from 29 states and territories, 21 other countries. 67% women, 33% men, 69% part-time, 96% state residents, 12% transferred in, 2% international, 51% 25 or older, 1% Native American, 20% Hispanic, 18% black, 3% Asian or Pacific Islander. *Most popular recent majors:* nursing, radiological technology, business administration/commerce/management.
First-Year Class: 418 total; 418 applied, 100% were accepted, 100% of whom enrolled.
Graduation Requirements: 60 credit hours; math/science requirements vary according to program; computer course for business, technology majors; internship (some majors).
Computers on Campus: 173 computers available on campus for general student use. Computers for student use in computer center, computer labs, learning resource center, classrooms, library. Staffed computer lab on campus provides training in use of computers, software. *Academic computing expenditure 1995–96:* $89,922.

EXPENSES

Expenses for 1996–97: State resident tuition: $244 full-time. Nonresident tuition: $600 full-time. Part-time tuition per semester ranges from $50 to $90 for state residents, $200 to $220 for nonresidents. Part-time mandatory fees per semester range from $35 to $190. Full-time mandatory fees: $500.
LD Services Contact: Dr. Gaynelle Hayes, Vice President and Dean of Student Development Services, Galveston College, 4015 Avenue Q, Galveston, TX 77550-7496, 409-763-6551 Ext. 205. Fax: 409-762-9367.

GARDEN CITY COMMUNITY COLLEGE

Garden City, Kansas

LEARNING DISABILITIES SERVICES INFORMATION

Comprehensive Learning Center (CLC) began offering services in 1990. Currently the program serves 4 undergraduates with LD. Students diagnosed with ADD/ADHD are eligible for the same services available to students with LD.
Staff: 3 full-time staff members, including director, coordinator, math instructor. Services provided by remediation specialists, tutors.
Special Fees: No special fees are charged for services to students with LD.
Applications and admissions: *Required:* psychoeducational report completed within 3 years. Students may begin taking classes any term. *Application deadline:* continuous.

PROGRAM AND SERVICE COMPONENTS

Academic advising: Provided by unit staff members, academic advisers. Most students with LD take 12 credit hours each term; 9 credit hours required to maintain full-time status and be eligible for financial aid.
Auxiliary aids: Taped textbooks, tape recorders, word-processors with spell-check, talking computers, optical character readers.
Auxiliary services: Alternative test arrangements.

GENERAL COLLEGE INFORMATION

District-supported, 2-year, coed. Part of Kansas State Board of Education. Awards associate degrees. Founded 1919. *Setting:* 12-acre rural campus. *Endowment:* $2 million. *Total enrollment:* 2,334. *Faculty:* 148 (67 full-time, 81 part-time); student–undergrad faculty ratio is 20:1.
Enrollment Profile: 2,334 students from 25 states and territories, 7 other countries. 58% women, 42% men, 65% part-time, 97% state residents, 12% live on campus, 4% transferred in, 1% international, 52% 25 or older, 1% Native American, 10% Hispanic, 3% black, 1% Asian or Pacific Islander. *Areas of study chosen:* 41% liberal arts/general studies, 12% business management and administrative services, 11% education, 7% health professions and related sciences, 7% vocational and home economics, 4% biological and life sciences, 4% premed, 3% agriculture, 2% performing arts, 1% architecture, 1% communications and journalism, 1% computer and information sciences, 1% engineering and applied sciences, 1% fine arts, 1% mathematics, 1% prevet, 1% psychology, 1% social sciences. *Most popular recent majors:* business administration/commerce/management, education, criminal justice.
First-Year Class: 485 total. Of the students who applied, 100% were accepted, 100% of whom enrolled. 17% from top 10% of their high school class, 19% from top quarter, 34% from top half. 7 class presidents, 5 valedictorians.
Graduation Requirements: 64 credit hours; 1 college algebra course; internship (some majors).
Computers on Campus: 150 computers available on campus for general student use. Computer purchase/lease plans available. A campus-wide network can be accessed. Computers for student use in computer center, computer labs, learning resource center, library, student center, dorms provide access to the Internet/World Wide Web, on-campus e-mail addresses. Staffed computer lab on campus provides training in use of computers, software. *Academic computing expenditure 1995–96:* $217,256.

EXPENSES

Expenses for 1996–97: State resident tuition: $896 full-time, $28 per credit hour part-time. Nonresident tuition: $2080 full-time, $65 per credit hour part-time. Part-time mandatory fees: $7 per credit hour. Full-time mandatory fees: $224. College room and board: $2770 (minimum).
LD Services Contact: Ms. Kitty Slover, Coordinator, Garden City Community College, 801 Campus Drive, Garden City, KS 67846, 316-276-9513. Fax: 316-276-9630.

GARLAND COUNTY COMMUNITY COLLEGE

Hot Springs, Arkansas

LEARNING DISABILITIES SERVICES INFORMATION

Student Support Services began offering services in 1979. Currently the program serves 18 undergraduates with LD. Students diagnosed with ADD/ADHD are eligible for the same services available to students with LD.
Staff: 1 full-time staff member (Counselor/Disability Specialist). Services provided by tutors, counselor.
Special Fees: No special fees are charged for services to students with LD.
Applications and admissions: *Required:* high school transcript, grade point average, courses completed, personal interview; *recommended:* psychoeducational report completed within 3 years, ACT ASSET (extended time acceptable). Students may begin taking classes any term. *Application deadline:* continuous.
Special policies: The college has written policies regarding grade forgiveness.

PROGRAM AND SERVICE COMPONENTS

Diagnostic testing: Reading, math.
Academic advising: Provided by unit staff members. Students with LD may take up to 12 credits each term; most take 9 to 12 credits; 9 credits required to maintain full-time status; 9 to 12 credits (full-time) required to be eligible for financial aid.
Counseling services: Individual counseling, career counseling.
Basic skills remediation: Offered in class-size groups by regular teachers. Available in reading, math, written language, learning strategies.
Subject-area tutoring: Offered one-on-one and in small groups by peer tutors. Available in some subjects.
Special courses: College survival skills, reading, vocabulary development, learning strategies, time management, math, study skills, career planning. Most offered for credit; most enter into overall grade point average.
Auxiliary aids: Taped textbooks, tape recorders, typewriters, word-processors with spell-check, voice synthesizer on computer, scanner.
Auxiliary services: Alternative test arrangements, notetakers, priority registration, advocacy.
Campus support group: A special student organization is available to students with LD.

GENERAL COLLEGE INFORMATION

State and locally supported, 2-year, coed. Awards associate degrees. Founded 1973. *Setting:* 50-acre suburban campus with easy access to Little Rock. *Total enrollment:* 1,866. *Faculty:* 106 (48 full-time, 14% with terminal degrees, 58 part-time); student–undergrad faculty ratio is 20:1.
Enrollment Profile: 1,866 students from 9 states and territories, 2 other countries. 66% women, 34% men, 58% part-time, 98% state residents, 24% transferred in, 1% international, 55% 25 or older, 2% Native American, 1% Hispanic, 6% black, 1% Asian or Pacific Islander. *Retention:* 47% of 1995 full-time freshmen returned. *Areas of study chosen:* 51% liberal arts/general studies, 29% health professions and related sciences, 10% business management and administrative services, 5% computer and information sciences, 3% performing arts, 2% engineering and applied sciences. *Most popular recent majors:* nursing, business administration/commerce/management, education.
First-Year Class: 591 total; 591 applied, 100% were accepted.
Graduation Requirements: 62 semester hours; math/science requirements vary according to program; computer course; internship (some majors).
Computers on Campus: 270 computers available on campus for general student use. A computer is recommended for some students. A campus-wide network can be accessed from off-campus. Students can contact faculty members and/or advisers through e-mail. Computers for student use in computer labs, learning resource center, classrooms, library provide access to the Internet/World Wide Web. Staffed computer lab on campus provides training in use of computers, software. *Academic computing expenditure 1995–96:* $183,378.

EXPENSES AND FINANCIAL AID

Expenses for 1997–98: Area resident tuition: $888 full-time, $37 per semester hour part-time. State resident tuition: $1104 full-time, $46 per semester hour part-time. Nonresident tuition: $2760 full-time, $115 per semester hour part-time. Part-time mandatory fees: $10 per semester. Full-time mandatory fees: $20.
Financial aid specifically for students with LD: Scholarship: GCCC Tuition Free Scholarship.
LD Services Contact: Ms. Annette Smelser, Counselor/Disability Specialist, Garland County Community College, 100 College Drive, Hot Springs, AR 71913, 501-760-4227.

GATEWAY TECHNICAL COLLEGE

Kenosha, Wisconsin

LEARNING DISABILITIES SERVICES INFORMATION

Learning Skills began offering services in 1972. Currently the program serves 236 undergraduates with LD. Students diagnosed with ADD/ADHD are eligible for the same services available to students with LD, as well as screening referrals to community specialists for diagnosis and therapy.
Staff: 11 full-time staff members. Services provided by remediation specialists, tutors, counselors, diagnostic specialist, adult basic education instructors, instructors for students with special needs.
Special Fees: No special fees are charged for services to students with LD.
Applications and admissions: *Required:* psychoeducational report completed within 3 years, intake via LD specialist who coordinates evaluation data; *recommended:* high school transcript. Students may begin taking classes in fall, spring, or summer. *Application deadline:* continuous.
Special policies: The college has written policies regarding grade forgiveness; substitutions and waivers of admissions requirements.

PROGRAM AND SERVICE COMPONENTS

Special preparation or orientation: Optional orientation offered individually by special arrangement.

Gateway Technical College (continued)

Diagnostic testing: Intelligence, reading, math, spelling, perceptual skills, speech, hearing, learning strategies, vision.
Academic advising: Provided by unit staff members, academic advisers. Most students with LD take 6 to 12 credits each term; 12 credits required to maintain full-time status; 6 credits required to be eligible for financial aid.
Counseling services: Individual counseling, small-group counseling, career counseling, self-advocacy training.
Basic skills remediation: Offered one-on-one, in small groups, and in class-size groups by LD teachers, regular teachers, peer tutors; computer-aided instruction also offered. Available in reading, math, spelling, written language, learning strategies, study skills, time management, social skills.
Subject-area tutoring: Offered one-on-one and in small groups by professional teachers, peer tutors, LD specialist. Available in all subjects.
Special courses: College survival skills, reading, vocabulary development, communication skills, composition, learning strategies, word processing, time management, math, typing, personal psychology, study skills, career planning. Most offered for credit; most enter into overall grade point average.
Auxiliary aids: Taped textbooks, tape recorders, calculators, typewriters, word-processors with spell-check, talking computers, optical character readers, colored overlays.
Auxiliary services: Alternative test arrangements, notetakers, advocacy.
Campus support group: A special student organization is available to students with LD.

GENERAL COLLEGE INFORMATION

State and locally supported, 2-year, coed. Part of Wisconsin Technical College System. Awards associate degrees. Founded 1911. *Setting:* 10-acre urban campus with easy access to Chicago and Minneapolis. *Research spending 1995–96:* $239,486. *Total enrollment:* 6,800. *Faculty:* 489 (232 full-time, 4% with terminal degrees, 257 part-time); student–undergrad faculty ratio is 18:1.
Enrollment Profile: 6,800 students from 8 states and territories, 2 other countries. 65% women, 35% men, 76% part-time, 97% state residents, 6% transferred in, 50% 25 or older, 1% Native American, 4% Hispanic, 10% black, 1% Asian or Pacific Islander. *Areas of study chosen:* 20% health professions and related sciences, 20% social sciences, 15% computer and information sciences, 5% business management and administrative services, 5% vocational and home economics, 3% architecture, 2% agriculture, 2% communications and journalism. *Most popular recent majors:* nursing, accounting, marketing/retailing/merchandising.
First-Year Class: 1,625 total; 2,575 applied, 75% were accepted, 70% of whom enrolled.
Graduation Requirements: 64 credits; computer course for all associate degree programs; internship (some majors).
Computers on Campus: 625 computers available on campus for general student use. Computer purchase/lease plans available. A computer is recommended for all students. A campus-wide network can be accessed from off-campus. Students can contact faculty members and/or advisers through e-mail. Computers for student use in computer center, computer labs, learning resource center, classrooms provide access to the Internet/World Wide Web, on-campus e-mail addresses. Staffed computer lab on campus provides training in use of computers, software. *Academic computing expenditure 1995–96:* $735,429.

EXPENSES

Expenses for 1997–98: *Application fee:* $25. State resident tuition: $1734 full-time, $54.20 per credit part-time. Nonresident tuition: $13,670 full-time, $427.20 per credit part-time. Part-time mandatory fees: $1.50 per credit. Full-time mandatory fees: $48.
LD Services Contact: Ms. Jo Bailey, Learning Skills Specialist, Gateway Technical College, 3520 30th Avenue, Kenosha, WI 53144, 414-656-6958. Fax: 414-656-6909. Email: baileyj@gateway.tec.wi.us.

GENESEE COMMUNITY COLLEGE

Batavia, New York

LEARNING DISABILITIES SERVICES INFORMATION

Center for Academic Progress (CAP) began offering services in 1986. Currently the program serves 100 undergraduates with LD. Students diagnosed with ADD/ADHD are eligible for the same services available to students with LD.
Staff: 6 full-time, 1 part-time staff members, including director. Services provided by remediation specialists, tutors, counselors.
Special Fees: No special fees are charged for services to students with LD.
Applications and admissions: *Required:* high school transcript, grade point average, class rank, courses completed, untimed ACT, personal interview, psychoeducational report completed within 3 years. Students may begin taking classes in fall or spring. *Application deadline:* continuous.

PROGRAM AND SERVICE COMPONENTS

Diagnostic testing: Intelligence, reading, math, spelling, written language, perceptual skills, personality.
Academic advising: Provided by unit staff members, academic advisers. Most students with LD take 12 credits each term; 12 credits required to maintain full-time status and be eligible for financial aid.
Counseling services: Individual counseling, small-group counseling, career counseling.
Basic skills remediation: Offered one-on-one, in small groups, and in class-size groups by regular teachers, professional tutors. Available in reading, math, spelling, written language, learning strategies, study skills, social skills, computer skills.
Subject-area tutoring: Offered one-on-one, in small groups, and in class-size groups by professional teachers, peer tutors. Available in most subjects.
Special courses: College survival skills, reading, composition, learning strategies, math, typing, personal psychology, study skills. Most offered for credit; most enter into overall grade point average.
Auxiliary aids: Taped textbooks, tape recorders, calculators, typewriters, word-processors with spell-check, personal computers, optical character readers.
Auxiliary services: Alternative test arrangements, notetakers, priority registration, advocacy.
Campus support group: A special student organization is available to students with LD.

GENERAL COLLEGE INFORMATION

State and locally supported, 2-year, coed. Part of State University of New York System. Awards associate degrees. Founded 1966. *Setting:* 256-acre small-town campus with easy access to Buffalo. *Total enrollment:* 4,059. *Faculty:* 219 (78 full-time, 10% with terminal degrees, 141 part-time); student–undergrad faculty ratio is 19:1.
Enrollment Profile: 4,059 students from 5 states and territories, 10 other countries. 62% women, 38% men, 50% part-time, 98% state residents, 8% transferred in, 1% international, 42% 25 or older, 1% Native American, 1% Hispanic, 2% black, 1% Asian or Pacific Islander. *Retention:* 60% of 1995 full-time freshmen returned. *Most popular recent majors:* liberal arts/general studies, business administration/commerce/management, criminal justice.
First-Year Class: 1,064 total; 2,095 applied, 100% were accepted, 51% of whom enrolled.
Graduation Requirements: 62 credit hours; 1 math course or completion of proficiency exam; computer course for business office technology, criminal justice, engineering, accounting, fashion buying and merchandising, paralegal, retail management majors; internship (some majors).
Computers on Campus: 325 computers available on campus for general student use. A campus-wide network can be accessed from off-campus. Students can contact faculty members and/or advisers through e-mail. Computers for student use in computer center, computer labs, learning resource center, classrooms, library provide access to the Internet/World Wide Web, on- and off-campus e-mail addresses. Staffed computer lab on campus provides training in use of computers, software. *Academic computing expenditure 1995–96:* $1 million.

EXPENSES

Expenses for 1997–98: State resident tuition: $2598 full-time, $97 per credit hour part-time. Nonresident tuition: $2848 full-time, $106 per credit hour part-time. Part-time mandatory fees: $8 per semester. (Housing is available through a cooperative agreement between the institution and an area landlord.). Full-time mandatory fees: $192.
LD Services Contact: Mr. Stuart Weinberg, Director, Center for Academic Progress, Genesee Community College, 1 College Road, Batavia, NY 14020-9704, 716-343-0055 Ext. 6353. Fax: 716-343-0433. Email: stuartw@sgccub.sunygenesee.cc.ny.us.

GEORGE C. WALLACE STATE COMMUNITY COLLEGE

Dothan, Alabama

LEARNING DISABILITIES SERVICES INFORMATION

Student Development/Counseling began offering services in 1984. Currently the program serves 18 undergraduates with LD. Students diagnosed with ADD/ADHD are eligible for the same services available to students with LD.
Staff: 1 full-time staff member (coordinator). Services provided by tutor, counselor.
Special Fees: No special fees are charged for services to students with LD.
Applications and admissions: *Required:* high school transcript, psychoeducational report completed within 3 years. Students may begin taking classes any term. *Application deadline:* continuous.

PROGRAM AND SERVICE COMPONENTS

Academic advising: Provided by unit staff members. Most students with LD take 12 to 15 quarter hours each term; 12 quarter hours required to maintain full-time status; 1 quarter hour required to be eligible for financial aid.
Counseling services: Individual counseling.
Auxiliary aids: Taped textbooks, tape recorders, calculators, typewriters, word-processors with spell-check, optical character readers, Book Wise.
Auxiliary services: Alternative test arrangements, notetakers, priority registration, advocacy.

GENERAL COLLEGE INFORMATION

State-supported, 2-year, coed. Awards associate degrees. Founded 1949. *Setting:* 200-acre rural campus. *Total enrollment:* 4,000. *Faculty:* 180.
Enrollment Profile: 4,000 students from 31 states and territories, 4 other countries. 58% women, 42% men, 52% part-time, 92% state residents, 12% transferred in, 43% 25 or older, 0% Native American, 1% Hispanic, 13% black, 1% Asian or Pacific Islander.
First-Year Class: Of the students who applied, 99% were accepted.
Graduation Requirements: 96 quarter hours; 1 math course; computer course; internship (some majors).
Computers on Campus: 75 computers available on campus for general student use. Computers for student use in computer center. Staffed computer lab on campus.

EXPENSES

Expenses for 1997–98: State resident tuition: $1200 full-time, $25 per quarter hour part-time. Nonresident tuition: $2400 full-time, $50 per quarter hour part-time. Part-time mandatory fees: $5.50 per quarter hour. Full-time mandatory fees: $264.
LD Services Contact: Ms. Jean Dagostin, Counselor, ADA/504 Coordinator, George C. Wallace State Community College, Route 6, PO Box 62, Dothan, AL 36303, 334-983-3521 Ext. 294. Fax: 334-983-6066.

GLEN OAKS COMMUNITY COLLEGE

Centreville, Michigan

LEARNING DISABILITIES SERVICES INFORMATION

Special Needs and Academic Opportunity Center began offering services in 1987. Currently the program serves 175 undergraduates with LD. Students diagnosed with ADD/ADHD are eligible for the same services available to students with LD.
Staff: Includes director, co-director, coordinator. Services provided by remediation specialist, tutor, counselor, diagnostic specialist.
Special Fees: No special fees are charged for services to students with LD.
Applications and admissions: *Required:* untimed ACT ASSET, LD evaluation and screening; *recommended:* high school transcript, courses completed, extracurricular activities, personal interview, psychoeducational report completed within 2 years. Students may begin taking classes any term. *Application deadline:* continuous.
Special policies: The college has written policies regarding grade forgiveness; substitutions and waivers of degree requirements.

PROGRAM AND SERVICE COMPONENTS

Special preparation or orientation: Orientation (required for some) held before registration.
Diagnostic testing: Intelligence, reading, spelling, written language, study skills, personality, social skills, learning strategies.
Academic advising: Provided by unit staff members, academic advisers. Students with LD may take up to 12 credit hours each term; most take 12 credit hours; 12 credit hours required to maintain full-time status; 6 to 12 credit hours (depending on assistance package) required to be eligible for financial aid.
Counseling services: Individual counseling, career counseling.
Basic skills remediation: Offered one-on-one and in class-size groups by LD teachers. Available in reading, math, spelling, spoken language, written language, learning strategies, perceptual skills, study skills, time management, speech.
Subject-area tutoring: Offered one-on-one and in class-size groups by professional teachers, peer tutors. Available in most subjects.
Special courses: College survival skills, reading, vocabulary development, communication skills, composition, learning strategies, math, typing, study skills, career planning, problem solving. Some offered for credit; some enter into overall grade point average.
Auxiliary aids: Taped textbooks, tape recorders, typewriters, word-processors with spell-check, personal computers, talking computers.
Auxiliary services: Alternative test arrangements, notetakers, priority registration, advocacy, readers.

GENERAL COLLEGE INFORMATION

State and locally supported, 2-year, coed. Part of Michigan Department of Education. Awards associate degrees. Founded 1965. *Setting:* 300-acre rural campus. *Total enrollment:* 1,447. *Faculty:* 96 (31 full-time, 7% with terminal degrees, 65 part-time); student–undergrad faculty ratio is 16:1.
Enrollment Profile: 1,447 students from 3 states and territories, 4 other countries. 57% women, 43% men, 63% part-time, 83% state residents, 9% transferred in, 1% international, 47% 25 or older, 1% Native American, 1% Hispanic, 2% black, 2% Asian or Pacific Islander. *Areas of study chosen:* 34% business management and administrative services, 30% liberal arts/general studies, 16% engineering and applied sciences, 10% health professions and related sciences, 5% physical sciences. *Most popular recent majors:* liberal arts/general studies, business administration/commerce/management, nursing.
First-Year Class: 214 total; 529 applied, 100% were accepted.
Graduation Requirements: 62 credit hours; math/science requirements vary according to program; computer course (varies by major).
Computers on Campus: 15 computers available on campus for general student use. Computers for student use in Academic Opportunity Center, media center provide access to software. Staffed computer lab on campus provides training in use of computers, software.

EXPENSES

Expenses for 1997–98: Area resident tuition: $1426 full-time, $46 per contact hour part-time. State resident tuition: $1674 full-time, $54 per contact hour part-time. Part-time mandatory fees: $7 per contact hour. Full-time mandatory fees: $217.
LD Services Contact: Mr. David Smith, Dean of Instruction, Glen Oaks Community College, 62249 Shimmel Road, Centreville, MI 49032-9719, 616-467-9945 Ext. 234. Fax: 616-467-4114.

GLOUCESTER COUNTY COLLEGE

Sewell, New Jersey

LEARNING DISABILITIES SERVICES INFORMATION

Office of Special Needs currently serves undergraduate students with LD. Students diagnosed with ADD/ADHD are eligible for the same services available to students with LD.
Staff: 2 full-time, 18 part-time staff members, including coordinator, technicians. Services provided by remediation specialist, tutor, counselor, notetakers.
Special Fees: No special fees are charged for services to students with LD.
Applications and admissions: *Required:* high school transcript, psychoeducational report completed most recently. *Application deadline:* continuous.
Special policies: The college has written policies regarding grade forgiveness.

Gloucester County College (continued)

PROGRAM AND SERVICE COMPONENTS

Academic advising: Provided by academic advisers. Students with LD may take up to 12 credit hours each term; most take 6 to 9 credit hours; 12 credit hours required to maintain full-time status; 9 credit hours required to be eligible for financial aid.
Counseling services: Individual counseling, career counseling.
Basic skills remediation: Offered in small groups and in class-size groups by regular teachers; computer-aided instruction also offered. Available in reading, math, written language, study skills.
Subject-area tutoring: Offered one-on-one by professional teachers, peer tutors. Available in most subjects.
Auxiliary aids: Taped textbooks, tape recorders, calculators, typewriters, word-processors with spell-check, optical character readers.
Auxiliary services: Alternative test arrangements, notetakers, advocacy.
Campus support group: A special student organization is available to students with LD.

GENERAL COLLEGE INFORMATION

County-supported, 2-year, coed. Part of New Jersey Commission on Higher Education. Awards associate degrees (the college has been approved to award the degree of associate of applied science in diagnostic medical sonography (ultrasound)). Founded 1967. *Setting:* 270-acre rural campus with easy access to Philadelphia. *Educational spending 1995–96:* $1522 per undergrad. *Total enrollment:* 4,811. *Faculty:* 215 (70 full-time, 20% with terminal degrees, 145 part-time); student–undergrad faculty ratio is 18:1.
Enrollment Profile: 4,811 students: 58% women, 42% men, 55% part-time, 99% state residents, 2% transferred in, 1% international, 48% 25 or older, 0% Native American, 1% Hispanic, 6% black, 2% Asian or Pacific Islander. *Areas of study chosen:* 29% liberal arts/general studies, 18% business management and administrative services, 12% education, 7% premed, 6% engineering and applied sciences, 6% health professions and related sciences, 5% computer and information sciences. *Most popular recent majors:* liberal arts/general studies, business administration/commerce/management, education.
First-Year Class: 1,566 total. Of the students who applied, 93% were accepted, 54% of whom enrolled.
Graduation Requirements: 63 credit hours; math/science requirements vary according to program; computer course for most majors.
Computers on Campus: 120 computers available on campus for general student use. Computers for student use in computer labs, library, student center.

EXPENSES

Expenses for 1997–98: *Application fee:* $10. Area resident tuition: $1736 full-time, $56 per credit hour part-time. State resident tuition: $1767 full-time, $57 per credit hour part-time. Nonresident tuition: $6944 full-time, $224 per credit hour part-time. Part-time mandatory fees: $9 per credit hour. Full-time mandatory fees: $279.
LD Services Contact: Ms. Sharon Lee, Technician, Gloucester County College, 1400 Tanyard Road, Sewell, NJ 08080, 609-468-5000 Ext. 361.

GREEN RIVER COMMUNITY COLLEGE

Auburn, Washington

LEARNING DISABILITIES SERVICES INFORMATION

Disabled Student Services began offering services in 1992. Currently the program serves 360 undergraduates with LD. Students diagnosed with ADD/ADHD are eligible for the same services available to students with LD, as well as special ADD handouts and materials.
Staff: Includes director, coordinator, assistant. Services provided by remediation specialists, tutors, counselor.
Special Fees: No special fees are charged for services to students with LD.
Applications and admissions: *Required:* psychoeducational report completed within 3 to 5 years. Students may begin taking classes any term. *Application deadline:* continuous.
Special policies: The college has written policies regarding substitutions and waivers of degree requirements.

PROGRAM AND SERVICE COMPONENTS

Special preparation or orientation: Required orientation held before registration and during registration.
Academic advising: Provided by unit staff members, academic advisers. Most students with LD take 10 to 12 quarter hours each term; 10 quarter hours required to maintain full-time status; 8 to 12 quarter hours required to be eligible for financial aid.
Counseling services: Individual counseling, career counseling.
Basic skills remediation: Offered one-on-one, in small groups, and in class-size groups by LD teachers, regular teachers. Available in reading, math, spelling, spoken language, written language, learning strategies, perceptual skills, study skills, time management, social skills.
Subject-area tutoring: Offered one-on-one and in small groups by professional teachers, peer tutors. Available in all subjects.
Special courses: College survival skills, reading, vocabulary development, communication skills, composition, learning strategies, time management, study skills, career planning. Most offered for credit.
Auxiliary aids: Taped textbooks, tape recorders, calculators, word-processors with spell-check, talking computers, optical character readers, enlarged screens.
Auxiliary services: Alternative test arrangements, notetakers, priority registration, scribes, readers.
Campus support group: A special student organization is available to students with LD.

GENERAL COLLEGE INFORMATION

State-supported, 2-year, coed. Part of Washington State Board for Community and Technical Colleges. Awards associate degrees. Founded 1965. *Setting:* 168-acre rural campus with easy access to Seattle. *Total enrollment:* 8,544. *Faculty:* 497 (115 full-time, 100% with terminal degrees, 382 part-time); student–undergrad faculty ratio is 25:1.
Enrollment Profile: 8,544 students from 21 states and territories, 30 other countries. 56% women, 44% men, 47% part-time, 91% state residents, 3% transferred in, 4% international, 52% 25 or older, 1% Native American, 3% Hispanic, 2% black, 5% Asian or Pacific Islander.
First-Year Class: 2,211 total; 3,896 applied, 100% were accepted, 57% of whom enrolled.
Graduation Requirements: 90 quarter hours; 15 quarter hours of math/science including at least 1 lab science course; computer course for most vocational majors.
Computers on Campus: 104 computers available on campus for general student use. Computer purchase/lease plans available. A campus-wide network can be accessed. Students can contact faculty members and/or advisers through e-mail. Computers for student use in library provide access to the Internet/World Wide Web. Staffed computer lab on campus (open 24 hours a day) provides training in use of computers, software.

EXPENSES

Expenses for 1996–97: State resident tuition: $1401 full-time, $46.70 per quarter hour part-time. Nonresident tuition: $5511 full-time, $183.70 per quarter hour part-time. Full-time mandatory fees: $15.
LD Services Contact: Ms. Karen Bruno, Coordinator, Disabled Student Services, Green River Community College, 12401 SE 320th Street, Auburn, WA 98092-3699, 206-833-9111 Ext. 412. Fax: 206-685-2026.

HAGERSTOWN JUNIOR COLLEGE

Hagerstown, Maryland

LEARNING DISABILITIES SERVICES INFORMATION

Office of Special Student Services began offering services in 1985. Currently the program serves 15 undergraduates with LD. Students diagnosed with ADD/ADHD are eligible for the same services available to students with LD.
Staff: 1 part-time staff member (coordinator). Services provided by tutors, counselors.
Special Fees: No special fees are charged for services to students with LD.
Applications and admissions: *Required:* high school transcript, IEP (Individualized Education Program), psychoeducational report. Students may begin taking classes any term. *Application deadline:* continuous.
Special policies: The college has written policies regarding grade forgiveness.

PROGRAM AND SERVICE COMPONENTS

Diagnostic testing: Reading, math, written language.
Academic advising: Provided by unit staff members, academic advisers. Students with LD may take up to as many credit hours as an individual

can handle each term; most take 9 credit hours; 12 credit hours required to maintain full-time status; source of aid determines number of credit hours required to be eligible for financial aid.
Counseling services: Individual counseling, career counseling, self-advocacy training.
Basic skills remediation: Offered one-on-one and in class-size groups by regular teachers. Available in reading, math, spelling, written language, learning strategies, study skills.
Subject-area tutoring: Offered one-on-one and in small groups by peer tutors, professional tutors. Available in all subjects.
Auxiliary aids: Taped textbooks, tape recorders, calculators, typewriters, word-processors with spell-check, personal computers, Dragon Dictate.
Auxiliary services: Alternative test arrangements, notetakers, advocacy.
Campus support group: A special student organization is available to students with LD.

GENERAL COLLEGE INFORMATION

County-supported, 2-year, coed. Awards associate degrees. Founded 1946. *Setting:* 187-acre suburban campus with easy access to Baltimore and Washington, DC. *Total enrollment:* 2,917. *Faculty:* 203 (55 full-time, 24% with terminal degrees, 148 part-time); student–undergrad faculty ratio is 18:1.
Enrollment Profile: 2,917 students from 8 states and territories. 62% women, 38% men, 63% part-time, 77% state residents, 10% transferred in, 0% international, 50% 25 or older, 1% Native American, 1% Hispanic, 6% black, 1% Asian or Pacific Islander. *Retention:* 64% of 1995 full-time freshmen returned. *Areas of study chosen:* 27% liberal arts/general studies, 15% business management and administrative services, 8% social sciences, 7% computer and information sciences, 7% education, 6% engineering and applied sciences, 5% health professions and related sciences, 2% biological and life sciences, 1% communications and journalism. *Most popular recent majors:* liberal arts/general studies, business administration/commerce/management, nursing.
First-Year Class: 807 total; 971 applied, 100% were accepted, 83% of whom enrolled.
Graduation Requirements: 64 credit hours; internship (some majors).
Computers on Campus: 200 computers available on campus for general student use. Computer purchase/lease plans available. A computer is recommended for some students. A campus-wide network can be accessed from off-campus. Students can contact faculty members and/or advisers through e-mail. Computers for student use in computer center, computer labs, learning resource center, classrooms, library, satellite labs provide access to the Internet/World Wide Web. Staffed computer lab on campus provides training in use of computers, software.

EXPENSES

Expenses for 1997–98: Area resident tuition: $2240 full-time, $70 per credit hour part-time. State resident tuition: $3200 full-time, $100 per credit hour part-time. Nonresident tuition: $4224 full-time, $132 per credit hour part-time. Part-time mandatory fees per semester range from $17 to $70. Full-time mandatory fees: $190.
LD Services Contact: Ms. Kathy Foltz, Coordinator, Special Student Services, Hagerstown Junior College, 11400 Robinwood Drive, Hagerstown, MD 21742-6590, 301-790-2800 Ext. 273. Fax: 301-791-9165.

HARFORD COMMUNITY COLLEGE

Bel Air, Maryland

LEARNING DISABILITIES SERVICES INFORMATION

Office of Learning Assistance began offering services in 1990. Currently the program serves 70 undergraduates with LD. Students diagnosed with ADD/ADHD are eligible for the same services available to students with LD.
Staff: 1 full-time, 3 part-time staff members, including coordinator, tutoring coordinator. Services provided by tutors, counselors.
Special Fees: No special fees are charged for services to students with LD.
Applications and admissions: Open admissions. Students may begin taking classes any term. *Application deadline:* continuous.

PROGRAM AND SERVICE COMPONENTS

Special preparation or orientation: Optional orientation offered after registration.
Academic advising: Provided by academic advisers. Students with LD may take up to 15 credit hours each term; most take 12 credit hours; 12 credit hours required to maintain full-time status.
Counseling services: Individual counseling, career counseling.
Basic skills remediation: Offered in small groups and in class-size groups by regular teachers. Available in reading, math, written language, study skills, time management.
Subject-area tutoring: Offered one-on-one by professional teachers, peer tutors. Available in all subjects.
Auxiliary aids: Taped textbooks, tape recorders, calculators, word-processors with spell-check, personal computers, Franklin Speller.
Auxiliary services: Alternative test arrangements, notetakers, signers, readers.

GENERAL COLLEGE INFORMATION

State and locally supported, 2-year, coed. Awards associate degrees. Founded 1957. *Setting:* 212-acre small-town campus with easy access to Baltimore. *Endowment:* $1.9 million. *Total enrollment:* 4,625. *Faculty:* 468 (85 full-time, 21% with terminal degrees, 383 part-time); student–undergrad faculty ratio is 19:1.
Enrollment Profile: 4,625 students from 4 states and territories, 9 other countries. 63% women, 37% men, 73% part-time, 98% state residents, 9% transferred in, 1% international, 52% 25 or older, 1% Native American, 2% Hispanic, 8% black, 2% Asian or Pacific Islander. *Retention:* 59% of 1995 full-time freshmen returned. *Areas of study chosen:* 24% business management and administrative services, 24% liberal arts/general studies, 10% communications and journalism, 8% health professions and related sciences, 8% interdisciplinary studies, 7% social sciences, 6% engineering and applied sciences, 4% education, 3% psychology, 2% architecture, 2% computer and information sciences, 1% physical sciences, 1% prelaw. *Most popular recent majors:* liberal arts/general studies, nursing, business administration/commerce/management.
First-Year Class: 986 total; 1,292 applied, 100% were accepted, 76% of whom enrolled. 5% from top 10% of their high school class, 50% from top half.
Graduation Requirements: 62 credits hours; 3 credit hours of math, 7 credit hours of science including at least 1 lab science course for associate of art and associate of science degree; 3 credit hours of math, 4 credits of science for associate of applied science degree; computer course for accounting, business administration, engineering majors.
Computers on Campus: 285 computers available on campus for general student use. A campus-wide network can be accessed. Students can contact faculty members and/or advisers through e-mail. Computers for student use in computer center, computer labs, learning resource center, classrooms, library provide access to the Internet/World Wide Web. Staffed computer lab on campus provides training in use of computers, software. *Academic computing expenditure 1995–96:* $139,303.

EXPENSES

Expenses for 1997–98: Area resident tuition: $1860 full-time, $60 per credit hour part-time. State resident tuition: $3100 full-time, $100 per credit hour part-time. Nonresident tuition: $5363 full-time, $173 per credit hour part-time. Part-time mandatory fees: $6 per credit hour. Full-time mandatory fees: $144.
LD Services Contact: Ms. Patricia Burton, Interim Coordinator of Learning Assistance, Harford Community College, 401 Thomas Run Road, Bel Air, MD 21015, 410-836-4414. Fax: 410-836-4198.

HARRISBURG AREA COMMUNITY COLLEGE

Harrisburg, Pennsylvania

LEARNING DISABILITIES SERVICES INFORMATION

Special Needs Services began offering services in 1973. Currently the program serves 197 undergraduates with LD. Students diagnosed with ADD/ADHD are eligible for the same services available to students with LD.
Staff: Includes coordinators, special services assistant. Services provided by remediation specialist, tutors, counselor, diagnostic specialists.
Special Fees: No special fees are charged for services to students with LD.
Applications and admissions: *Required:* high school transcript; *recommended:* personal interview, psychoeducational report, untimed placement testing. Students may begin taking classes any term. *Application deadline:* continuous.

Harrisburg Area Community College (continued)

Special policies: The college has written policies regarding substitutions and waivers of admissions, graduation, and degree requirements.

PROGRAM AND SERVICE COMPONENTS

Academic advising: Provided by academic advisers, counselors. Most students with LD take 6 to 12 credit hours each term; 12 credit hours required to maintain full-time status; 6 credit hours (federal), 12 credit hours (state) required to be eligible for financial aid.
Counseling services: Individual counseling, small-group counseling, career counseling.
Basic skills remediation: Offered in class-size groups by regular teachers. Available in reading, math, written language, learning strategies, study skills, time management.
Subject-area tutoring: Offered one-on-one by professional teachers, peer tutors. Available in most subjects.
Auxiliary aids: Taped textbooks, tape recorders, calculators, typewriters, word-processors with spell-check, personal computers.
Auxiliary services: Alternative test arrangements, notetakers, advocacy.

GENERAL COLLEGE INFORMATION

State and locally supported, 2-year, coed. Awards associate degrees. Founded 1964. *Setting:* 212-acre urban campus. *Total enrollment:* 10,719. *Faculty:* 612 (189 full-time, 15% with terminal degrees, 423 part-time); student–undergrad faculty ratio is 22:1.
Enrollment Profile: 10,719 students: 60% women, 40% men, 63% part-time, 99% state residents, 3% transferred in, 1% international, 48% 25 or older, 1% Native American, 3% Hispanic, 7% black, 4% Asian or Pacific Islander. *Retention:* 60% of 1995 full-time freshmen returned. *Areas of study chosen:* 22% business management and administrative services, 15% health professions and related sciences, 12% interdisciplinary studies, 8% computer and information sciences, 8% education, 5% social sciences, 4% communications and journalism, 4% vocational and home economics, 3% biological and life sciences, 3% engineering and applied sciences, 2% mathematics, 2% psychology, 1% fine arts, 1% natural resource sciences, 1% performing arts, 1% physical sciences. *Most popular recent majors:* business administration/commerce/management, nursing, criminal justice.
First-Year Class: 3,444 total; 4,246 applied, 99% were accepted, 82% of whom enrolled.
Graduation Requirements: 61 credit hours.
Computers on Campus: 260 computers available on campus for general student use. Computer purchase/lease plans available. Computers for student use in computer center, library provide access to the Internet/World Wide Web.

EXPENSES

Expenses for 1997–98: *Application fee:* $25. Area resident tuition: $1973 full-time, $65.75 per credit hour part-time. State resident tuition: $3855 full-time, $128.50 per credit hour part-time. Nonresident tuition: $5738 full-time, $191.25 per credit hour part-time.
LD Services Contact: Ms. Subrina Smith Taylor, Coordinator of Special Needs, Harrisburg Area Community College, One HACC Drive, Harrisburg, PA 17110, 717-780-2614. Fax: 717-231-7674. Email: sstaylor@hacc01b.hacc.edu.

HARTNELL COLLEGE

Salinas, California

LEARNING DISABILITIES SERVICES INFORMATION

Learning Disability Services, Disabled Student Services began offering services in 1983. Currently the program serves 190 to 275 undergraduates with LD. Students diagnosed with ADD/ADHD are eligible for the same services available to students with LD.
Staff: 2 full-time, 3 part-time staff members, including director, LD specialist. Services provided by remediation specialist, tutors, counselors.
Special Fees: $11.50 to $18 for diagnostic testing.
Applications and admissions: *Required:* personal interview, psychoeducational report completed within 3 years; *recommended:* high school transcript, IEP (Individualized Education Program), untimed SAT I or ACT. Students may begin taking classes in fall, spring, or summer. *Application deadline:* continuous.
Special policies: The college has written policies regarding substitutions and waivers of graduation and degree requirements.

PROGRAM AND SERVICE COMPONENTS

Special preparation or orientation: Optional orientation offered before registration and after classes begin.
Diagnostic testing: Intelligence, reading, math, spelling, written language, perceptual skills, learning strategies.
Academic advising: Provided by unit staff members, academic advisers. Most students with LD take 9 semester units each term; 12 semester units required to maintain full-time status.
Counseling services: Individual counseling, career counseling.
Basic skills remediation: Offered in small groups by LD teachers, teacher trainees, aide. Available in reading, math, spelling, written language, learning strategies, study skills.
Subject-area tutoring: Offered one-on-one and in small groups by professional teachers, peer tutors. Available in most subjects.
Special courses: College survival skills, reading, vocabulary development, learning strategies, word processing, time management, math, typing, personal psychology, study skills, career planning, stress management. All offered for credit; all enter into overall grade point average.
Auxiliary aids: Taped textbooks, tape recorders, word-processors with spell-check, personal computers.
Auxiliary services: Alternative test arrangements, notetakers, priority registration, advocacy.
Campus support group: A special student organization is available to students with LD.

GENERAL COLLEGE INFORMATION

District-supported, 2-year, coed. Part of California Community Colleges System. Awards associate degrees. Founded 1920. *Setting:* 50-acre small-town campus with easy access to San Jose. *Total enrollment:* 7,500. *Faculty:* 363 (95 full-time, 268 part-time).
Enrollment Profile: 7,500 students from 4 states and territories, 14 other countries. 54% women, 46% men, 70% part-time, 96% state residents, 5% transferred in, 1% international, 1% Native American, 39% Hispanic, 4% black, 5% Asian or Pacific Islander. *Areas of study chosen:* 20% liberal arts/general studies, 10% health professions and related sciences, 5% English language/literature/letters, 4% engineering and applied sciences, 4% fine arts, 3% foreign language and literature, 3% mathematics, 3% social sciences, 1% education, 1% library and information studies, 1% natural resource sciences, 1% performing arts. *Most popular recent majors:* liberal arts/general studies, business administration/commerce/management, nursing.
First-Year Class: 1,500 total. Of the students who applied, 97% were accepted, 75% of whom enrolled. 1% from top 10% of their high school class, 50% from top half.
Graduation Requirements: 60 semester units; math proficiency; 1 science course.
Computers on Campus: 100 computers available on campus for general student use. Computers for student use in computer labs, learning resource center, library provide access to the Internet/World Wide Web, on- and off-campus e-mail addresses. Staffed computer lab on campus.

EXPENSES

Expenses for 1997–98: State resident tuition: $0 full-time. Nonresident tuition: $3390 full-time, $113 per unit part-time. Part-time mandatory fees per semester range from $17 to $147. Full-time mandatory fees: $398.
LD Services Contact: Mrs. Theresa Carbajal, LD Specialist, Hartnell College, 156 Homestead Avenue, Salinas, CA 93901-1697, 408-755-6760 Ext. 5752.

HAWKEYE COMMUNITY COLLEGE

Waterloo, Iowa

LEARNING DISABILITIES SERVICES INFORMATION

Academic Support Area began offering services in 1980. Students diagnosed with ADD/ADHD are eligible for the same services available to students with LD.
Staff: 1 full-time, 4 part-time staff members, including coordinator. Services provided by remediation specialists, tutors, counselors, diagnostic specialists, instructors.
Special Fees: No special fees are charged for services to students with LD.

Applications and admissions: *Required:* high school transcript, untimed ACT ASSET (in lieu of high school transcripts). Students may begin taking classes in fall, spring, or summer. *Application deadline:* continuous.
Special policies: The college has written policies regarding grade forgiveness; substitutions and waivers of degree requirements.

PROGRAM AND SERVICE COMPONENTS

Special preparation or orientation: Optional summer program offered prior to entering college. Orientation offered during new student orientation.
Diagnostic testing: Reading, math, written language.
Academic advising: Provided by unit staff members, academic advisers. Students with LD may take up to 18 credits each term; most take 12 credits; 12 credits required to maintain full-time status; 6 credits required to be eligible for financial aid.
Counseling services: Individual counseling, career counseling.
Basic skills remediation: Offered one-on-one, in small groups, and in class-size groups by regular teachers. Available in reading, math, spelling, written language, learning strategies, study skills, time management.
Subject-area tutoring: Offered one-on-one by professional teachers, peer tutors. Available in all subjects.
Special courses: College survival skills, reading, vocabulary development, composition, learning strategies, word processing, time management, math, study skills, career planning. Most offered for credit; most enter into overall grade point average.
Auxiliary aids: Taped textbooks, tape recorders, typewriters, word-processors with spell-check, personal computers, optical character readers.
Auxiliary services: Alternative test arrangements, notetakers, advocacy.

GENERAL COLLEGE INFORMATION

State and locally supported, 2-year, coed. Part of Iowa Area Community Colleges System. Awards associate degrees. Founded 1967. *Setting:* 320-acre rural campus. *Total enrollment:* 3,538. *Faculty:* 207 (111 full-time, 87% with terminal degrees, 96 part-time); student–undergrad faculty ratio is 20:1.
Enrollment Profile: 3,538 students from 4 states and territories, 8 other countries. 56% women, 44% men, 29% part-time, 99% state residents, 12% transferred in, 1% international, 33% 25 or older, 1% Native American, 1% Hispanic, 6% black, 1% Asian or Pacific Islander. *Areas of study chosen:* 51% liberal arts/general studies, 15% engineering and applied sciences, 14% business management and administrative services, 9% health professions and related sciences, 4% agriculture, 4% fine arts, 2% architecture, 1% interdisciplinary studies. *Most popular recent majors:* liberal arts/general studies, criminal justice, practical nursing.
First-Year Class: 1,178 total; 2,196 applied, 97% were accepted, 55% of whom enrolled. 16% from top quarter of their high school class, 51% from top half.
Graduation Requirements: 64 credits; computer course for all associate of science and associate of applied science degree programs; internship (some majors).
Computers on Campus: 225 computers available on campus for general student use. A campus-wide network can be accessed. Computers for student use in computer labs, learning resource center, classrooms, library provide access to the Internet/World Wide Web, off-campus e-mail addresses. Staffed computer lab on campus.

EXPENSES AND FINANCIAL AID

Expenses for 1997–98: State resident tuition: $2048 full-time, $64 per credit part-time. Nonresident tuition: $4096 full-time, $128 per credit part-time. Part-time mandatory fees: $8.50 per credit. Full-time mandatory fees: $272.
Financial aid specifically for students with LD: Scholarship: Jimmie Robinson Scholarship.
LD Services Contact: Ms. Kathy Linda, Coordinator, Academic Support, Hawkeye Community College, PO Box 8015, Waterloo, IA 50704-8015, 319-236-1013. Fax: 319-296-1028.

HAYWOOD COMMUNITY COLLEGE

Clyde, North Carolina

LEARNING DISABILITIES SERVICES INFORMATION

Special Services began offering services in 1992. Currently the program serves 50 undergraduates with LD. Students diagnosed with ADD/ADHD are eligible for the same services available to students with LD.
Staff: 1 full-time staff member (coordinator). Services provided by tutors.
Special Fees: No special fees are charged for services to students with LD.
Applications and admissions: *Required:* high school transcript, psychoeducational report completed within 3 years; *recommended:* personal interview. Students may begin taking classes any term. *Application deadline:* continuous.
Special policies: The college has written policies regarding substitutions and waivers of admissions requirements.

PROGRAM AND SERVICE COMPONENTS

Special preparation or orientation: Optional orientation offered individually by arrangement.
Academic advising: Provided by unit staff members, academic advisers. Most students with LD take 14 semester hours each term; 14 semester hours required to maintain full-time status; 12 semester hours required to be eligible for financial aid.
Counseling services: Individual counseling, career counseling.
Subject-area tutoring: Offered one-on-one by professional teachers, peer tutors. Available in most subjects.
Auxiliary aids: Taped textbooks, tape recorders, calculators, typewriters, word-processors with spell-check, personal computers, optical character readers.
Auxiliary services: Alternative test arrangements, notetakers, priority registration.

GENERAL COLLEGE INFORMATION

State and locally supported, 2-year, coed. Part of North Carolina Community College System. Awards associate degrees. Founded 1964. *Setting:* 85-acre rural campus. *Educational spending 1995–96:* $3100 per undergrad. *Total enrollment:* 1,262. *Faculty:* 118 (57 full-time, 3% with terminal degrees, 61 part-time).
Enrollment Profile: 1,262 students from 20 states and territories. 54% women, 46% men, 43% part-time, 97% state residents, 8% transferred in, 0% international, 45% 25 or older, 1% Native American, 1% Hispanic, 1% black, 1% Asian or Pacific Islander. *Areas of study chosen:* 20% liberal arts/general studies, 14% natural resource sciences, 13% engineering and applied sciences, 8% health professions and related sciences, 7% business management and administrative services, 5% fine arts, 3% computer and information sciences, 2% social sciences. *Most popular recent majors:* liberal arts/general studies, business administration/commerce/management, fish and game management.
First-Year Class: 462 total; 703 applied, 80% were accepted, 82% of whom enrolled.
Graduation Requirements: 1 math course; computer course for all associate degree programs; internship (some majors).
Computers on Campus: 10 computers available on campus for general student use. Computers for student use in library provide access to word processing.

EXPENSES

Expenses for 1997–98: State resident tuition: $560 full-time, $20 per semester hour part-time. Nonresident tuition: $4564 full-time, $163 per semester hour part-time. Part-time mandatory fees per semester range from $4.75 to $8.75. Full-time mandatory fees: $18.
LD Services Contact: Dr. Nathan Hodges, President, Haywood Community College, 185 Freelander Drive, Clyde, NC 28721, 704-627-4544. Fax: 704-627-4513.

HIBBING COMMUNITY COLLEGE

Hibbing, Minnesota

LEARNING DISABILITIES SERVICES INFORMATION

Student Services began offering services in 1986. Currently the program serves 10 undergraduates with LD. Students diagnosed with ADD/ADHD are eligible for the same services available to students with LD.
Staff: 1 part-time staff member (director). Services provided by tutors, lab assistant.
Special Fees: No special fees are charged for services to students with LD.
Applications and admissions: *Required:* high school transcript; *recommended:* psychoeducational report completed within 3 years. Students may begin taking classes in fall, winter, or spring. *Application deadline:* continuous.

PROGRAM AND SERVICE COMPONENTS

Diagnostic testing: Reading, math, written language.

Hibbing Community College (continued)

Academic advising: Provided by unit staff members, academic advisers. Students with LD may take up to 18 credits each term; most take 12 to 13 credits; 12 credits required to maintain full-time status; 2 credits (part-time; otherwise 6 credits) required to be eligible for financial aid.
Counseling services: Individual counseling, career counseling, self-advocacy training.
Basic skills remediation: Offered one-on-one and in small groups by regular teachers. Available in reading, math, spelling, written language, learning strategies, study skills, time management.
Subject-area tutoring: Offered one-on-one by peer tutors. Available in most subjects.
Auxiliary aids: Taped textbooks, tape recorders, typewriters, word-processors with spell-check, personal computers, Soundproof software.
Auxiliary services: Alternative test arrangements, notetakers, priority registration, readers.

GENERAL COLLEGE INFORMATION

State-supported, 2-year, coed. Part of Minnesota State Colleges and Universities System. Awards associate degrees. Founded 1916. *Setting:* 100-acre small-town campus. *Total enrollment:* 1,042. *Faculty:* 65 (37 full-time, 28 part-time); student–undergrad faculty ratio is 22:1.
Enrollment Profile: 1,042 students from 5 states and territories, 1 other country. 58% women, 42% men, 51% part-time, 97% state residents, 5% transferred in, 1% international, 38% 25 or older, 4% Native American, 1% Hispanic, 1% black, 1% Asian or Pacific Islander. *Most popular recent majors:* liberal arts/general studies, (pre)engineering sequence, respiratory therapy.
First-Year Class: 401 total; 817 applied, 100% were accepted, 49% of whom enrolled. 7% from top 10% of their high school class, 54% from top half.
Graduation Requirements: 96 credits; 1 math course; 2 lab science courses.
Computers on Campus: 150 computers available on campus for general student use. Computers for student use in computer center, computer labs, learning resource center, classrooms, library provide access to the Internet/World Wide Web. Staffed computer lab on campus provides training in use of computers, software.

EXPENSES

Expenses for 1996–97: *Application fee:* $20. State resident tuition: $2105 full-time, $43.85 per credit part-time. Nonresident tuition: $4210 full-time, $87.70 per credit part-time. Part-time mandatory fees: $3.75 per credit. North Dakota, South Dakota and Wisconsin residents pay tuition at the rate they would pay if attending a comparable state-supported institution in their home state. Full-time mandatory fees: $180.
LD Services Contact: Ms. Barbara Anderson, Student Advisor, Hibbing Community College, 1515 East 25th Street, Hibbing, MN 55746, 218-262-6712. Fax: 218-262-6717.

HIGHLINE COMMUNITY COLLEGE

Des Moines, Washington

LEARNING DISABILITIES SERVICES INFORMATION

Access Services currently serves 30 to 35 undergraduates with LD. Students diagnosed with ADD/ADHD are eligible for the same services available to students with LD.
Staff: 2 full-time, 7 part-time staff members, including director, office staff, student assistants, psychologist.
Special Fees: No special fees are charged for services to students with LD.
Applications and admissions: *Required:* psychoeducational report completed within 3 years, IQ test, achievement test. Students may begin taking classes any term. *Application deadline:* continuous.
Special policies: The college has written policies regarding substitutions and waivers of graduation and degree requirements.

PROGRAM AND SERVICE COMPONENTS

Academic advising: Provided by academic advisers. Students with LD may take up to 18 credits (more with adviser's permission) each term; 12 credits required to maintain full-time status and be eligible for financial aid.
Auxiliary aids: Taped textbooks, tape recorders, calculators, word-processors with spell-check, talking computers.
Auxiliary services: Alternative test arrangements, notetakers, priority registration, special seating.

GENERAL COLLEGE INFORMATION

State-supported, 2-year, coed. Part of Washington State Board for Community and Technical Colleges. Awards associate degrees. Founded 1961. *Setting:* 81-acre suburban campus with easy access to Seattle. *Endowment:* $113,146. *Educational spending 1995–96:* $2320 per undergrad. *Total enrollment:* 7,185. *Faculty:* 223 (113 full-time, 95% with terminal degrees, 110 part-time); student–undergrad faculty ratio is 28:1.
Enrollment Profile: 7,185 students: 66% women, 34% men, 45% part-time, 93% state residents, 40% transferred in, 1% international, 50% 25 or older, 1% Native American, 3% Hispanic, 7% black, 14% Asian or Pacific Islander. *Most popular recent majors:* business administration/commerce/management, psychology, education.
First-Year Class: Of the students who applied, 100% were accepted.
Graduation Requirements: 90 quarter hours; college math; internship (some majors).
Computers on Campus: 300 computers available on campus for general student use. Computer purchase/lease plans available. A campus-wide network can be accessed. Students can contact faculty members and/or advisers through e-mail. Computers for student use in computer center, computer labs, learning resource center, classrooms, library provide access to the Internet/World Wide Web, on- and off-campus e-mail addresses. Staffed computer lab on campus provides training in use of computers, software. *Academic computing expenditure 1995–96:* $620,000.

EXPENSES

Expenses for 1996–97: State resident tuition: $1401 full-time, $46.70 per quarter hour part-time. Nonresident tuition: $5511 full-time, $183.70 per quarter hour part-time.
LD Services Contact: Mr. Jim Field, Director of Access Services, Highline Community College, PO Box 98000 M/S 6-10, Des Moines, WA 98198-9800, 206-878-3710 Ext. 3857. Fax: 206-870-3772. Email: jfield@hcc.ctc.edu.

HILL COLLEGE OF THE HILL JUNIOR COLLEGE DISTRICT

Hillsboro, Texas

LEARNING DISABILITIES SERVICES INFORMATION

Student Support Services began offering services in 1980. Currently the program serves 120 undergraduates with LD. Students diagnosed with ADD/ADHD are eligible for the same services available to students with LD, as well as self-help materials.
Staff: 2 part-time staff members, including director, coordinator. Services provided by remediation specialists, tutors, counselors.
Special Fees: No special fees are charged for services to students with LD.
Applications and admissions: *Required:* high school transcript, psychoeducational report, ACT ASSET, Texas Academic Skills Program (TASP); *recommended:* high school IEP (Individualized Education Program), untimed or extended time ACT, untimed SAT I. Students may begin taking classes in fall, spring, or summer. *Application deadline:* continuous.

PROGRAM AND SERVICE COMPONENTS

Special preparation or orientation: Orientation (required for some) held before registration and after classes begin.
Diagnostic testing: Reading, math, written language.
Academic advising: Provided by unit staff members, academic advisers. Students with LD may take up to 19 semester hours each term; most take 12 to 15 semester hours; 12 semester hours required to maintain full-time status and be eligible for financial aid.
Counseling services: Individual counseling, career counseling, support group.
Basic skills remediation: Offered one-on-one, in small groups, and in class-size groups by regular teachers; computer-aided instruction also offered. Available in reading, math, written language, study skills, time management.
Subject-area tutoring: Offered one-on-one, in small groups, and in class-size groups by professional teachers, peer tutors. Available in all subjects.

Special courses: College survival skills, reading, vocabulary development, learning strategies, word processing, Internet use, time management, math, typing, study skills, career planning, stress management. Some offered for credit; some enter into overall grade point average.
Auxiliary aids: Tape recorders, calculators, typewriters, word-processors with spell-check, personal computers.
Auxiliary services: Alternative test arrangements, notetakers, priority registration, advocacy.

GENERAL COLLEGE INFORMATION

District-supported, 2-year, coed. Part of Texas Higher Education Coordinating Board. Awards associate degrees. Founded 1923. *Setting:* 80-acre small-town campus with easy access to Dallas–Fort Worth. *Total enrollment:* 2,500. *Faculty:* 80 (60 full-time, 5% with terminal degrees, 20 part-time); student–undergrad faculty ratio is 25:1.
Enrollment Profile: 2,500 students from 16 states and territories, 3 other countries. 61% women, 39% men, 40% part-time, 95% state residents, 20% live on campus, 6% transferred in, 1% international, 40% 25 or older, 1% Native American, 6% Hispanic, 8% black, 1% Asian or Pacific Islander.
First-Year Class: 1,200 total. Of the students who applied, 100% were accepted, 100% of whom enrolled.
Graduation Requirements: 62 credit hours.
Computers on Campus: 150 computers available on campus for general student use. Computers for student use in computer center, computer labs, learning resource center, library provide access to the Internet/World Wide Web. Staffed computer lab on campus provides training in use of computers, software.

EXPENSES

Expenses for 1996–97: Area resident tuition: $768 full-time. State resident tuition: $1024 full-time. Nonresident tuition: $1424 full-time. Part-time tuition per quarter hour ranges from $96 to $264 for area residents, $128 to $352 for state residents, $328 to $552 for nonresidents. College room and board: $2560.
LD Services Contact: Mr. Louis N. Allen, Dean of Student Development, Hill College of the Hill Junior College District, PO Box 619, Hillsboro, TX 76645, 817-582-2555 Ext. 203. Fax: 817-582-7591.

HILLSBOROUGH COMMUNITY COLLEGE

Tampa, Florida

LEARNING DISABILITIES SERVICES INFORMATION

Services for Students with Disabilities began offering services in 1981. Currently the program serves 184 undergraduates with LD. Students diagnosed with ADD/ADHD are eligible for the same services available to students with LD.
Staff: 3 full-time staff members, including coordinators, LD specialist. Services provided by tutors, readers, interpreters.
Special Fees: No special fees are charged for services to students with LD.
Applications and admissions: *Required:* high school transcript, psychoeducational report. Students may begin taking classes in fall, spring, or summer. *Application deadline:* continuous.
Special policies: The college has written policies regarding grade forgiveness; substitutions and waivers of admissions, graduation, and degree requirements.

PROGRAM AND SERVICE COMPONENTS

Special preparation or orientation: Required orientation held individually once a student self-identifies.
Academic advising: Provided by unit staff members, academic advisers. Students with LD may take up to 15 credit hours each term; 12 credit hours required to maintain full-time status; 6 credit hours required to be eligible for financial aid.
Counseling services: Individual counseling, career counseling, self-advocacy training.
Basic skills remediation: Offered one-on-one by LD teachers, tutors. Available in reading, math, spelling, written language, learning strategies, study skills, social skills.
Subject-area tutoring: Offered one-on-one by professional teachers, peer tutors, LD specialists and tutors. Available in all subjects.
Special courses: Learning strategies. None offered for credit.
Auxiliary aids: Taped textbooks, tape recorders, calculators, typewriters, optical character readers, Franklin Speller, large print dictionaries.
Auxiliary services: Alternative test arrangements, notetakers, advocacy, readers.
Campus support group: A special student organization is available to students with LD.

GENERAL COLLEGE INFORMATION

State-supported, 2-year, coed. Awards associate degrees. Founded 1968. *Setting:* urban campus. *Endowment:* $1.1 million. *Educational spending 1995–96:* $2052 per undergrad. *Total enrollment:* 18,307. *Faculty:* 746 (253 full-time, 28% with terminal degrees, 493 part-time); student–undergrad faculty ratio is 26:1.
Enrollment Profile: 18,307 students: 58% women, 42% men, 71% part-time, 97% state residents, 7% transferred in, 2% international, 44% 25 or older, 1% Native American, 14% Hispanic, 12% black, 3% Asian or Pacific Islander. *Areas of study chosen:* 27% liberal arts/general studies, 13% business management and administrative services, 10% health professions and related sciences, 5% education, 4% computer and information sciences, 4% premed, 4% vocational and home economics, 3% engineering and applied sciences, 3% prelaw, 2% communications and journalism, 1% agriculture, 1% architecture, 1% biological and life sciences, 1% fine arts, 1% performing arts, 1% predentistry, 1% prevet. *Most popular recent majors:* liberal arts/general studies, nursing, optometric/ophthalmic technologies.
First-Year Class: 2,161 total; 2,673 applied, 100% were accepted, 81% of whom enrolled.
Graduation Requirements: 60 credit hours; computer course.
Computers on Campus: 600 computers available on campus for general student use. Computer purchase/lease plans available. Computers for student use in computer labs, learning resource center, classrooms, library provide access to the Internet/World Wide Web. Staffed computer lab on campus provides training in use of computers, software. *Academic computing expenditure 1995–96:* $548,205.

EXPENSES AND FINANCIAL AID

Expenses for 1996–97: *Application fee:* $20. State resident tuition: $1124 full-time, $37.47 per credit hour part-time. Nonresident tuition: $4187 full-time, $139.58 per credit hour part-time.
Financial aid specifically for students with LD: Scholarship: Students with Disabilities Incentive Scholarship.
LD Services Contact: Ms. Magali Pares, Coordinator of Services for Students with Disabilities, Hillsborough Community College, PO Box 31127, Tampa, FL 33631, 813-253-7031. Fax: 813-253-7506.

HOCKING COLLEGE

Nelsonville, Ohio

LEARNING DISABILITIES SERVICES INFORMATION

Center for Alternative Education began offering services in 1987. Currently the program serves 17 undergraduates with LD. Students diagnosed with ADD/ADHD are eligible for the same services available to students with LD.
Staff: 4 full-time, 1 part-time staff members, including director, coordinator, math specialist, communications specialist. Services provided by remediation specialists, tutors, counselors, diagnostic specialist.
Special Fees: No special fees are charged for services to students with LD.
Applications and admissions: Open admissions. Students may begin taking classes any term. *Application deadline:* continuous.

PROGRAM AND SERVICE COMPONENTS

Special preparation or orientation: Optional summer program offered prior to entering college.
Diagnostic testing: Reading, math, spelling, written language, study skills, personality, learning strategies.
Academic advising: Provided by unit staff members, academic advisers. Most students with LD take 12 to 15 credit hours each term; 12 credit hours required to maintain full-time status; source of aid determines number of credit hours required to be eligible for financial aid.
Counseling services: Individual counseling, career counseling.
Basic skills remediation: Offered in class-size groups by regular teachers. Available in reading, math, spelling, spoken language, written language, learning strategies, study skills, time management, social skills, speech.
Subject-area tutoring: Offered one-on-one and in small groups by professional teachers, peer tutors. Available in all subjects.

Hocking College (continued)

Special courses: College survival skills, reading, vocabulary development, communication skills, composition, learning strategies, math, study skills, career planning, stress management. All offered for credit; all enter into overall grade point average.
Auxiliary aids: Taped textbooks, tape recorders, calculators, typewriters, word-processors with spell-check, talking computers, optical character readers.
Auxiliary services: Alternative test arrangements, notetakers, advocacy.

GENERAL COLLEGE INFORMATION

State-supported, 2-year, coed. Part of Ohio Board of Regents. Awards associate degrees. Founded 1968. *Setting:* 1,600-acre rural campus with easy access to Columbus. *Endowment:* $2.1 million. *Total enrollment:* 5,071. *Faculty:* 253 (174 full-time, 98% with terminal degrees, 79 part-time); student–undergrad faculty ratio is 22:1.
Enrollment Profile: 5,071 students from 23 states and territories, 45 other countries. 44% women, 56% men, 31% part-time, 86% state residents, 9% transferred in, 1% international, 48% 25 or older, 0% Native American, 1% Hispanic, 1% black, 0% Asian or Pacific Islander. *Retention:* 50% of 1995 full-time freshmen returned. *Areas of study chosen:* 34% natural resource sciences, 23% health professions and related sciences, 15% engineering and applied sciences, 13% business management and administrative services, 2% computer and information sciences. *Most popular recent majors:* nursing, wildlife management, law enforcement/police sciences.
First-Year Class: 1,543 total; 2,247 applied, 91% were accepted, 75% of whom enrolled.
Graduation Requirements: 90 credit hours; 3 credit hours of math; computer course for most majors; internship (some majors).
Computers on Campus: 280 computers available on campus for general student use. A campus-wide network can be accessed from off-campus. Computers for student use in computer center, computer labs, learning resource center, classrooms, library, student center, dorms, career lab provide access to the Internet/World Wide Web. Staffed computer lab on campus provides training in use of computers, software. *Academic computing expenditure 1995–96:* $218,704.

EXPENSES

Expenses for 1997–98: *Application fee:* $15. State resident tuition: $2142 full-time, $60 per credit hour part-time. Nonresident tuition: $4284 full-time, $120 per credit hour part-time. Part-time mandatory fees: $5 per quarter. Full-time mandatory fees: $15. College room only: $1755 (minimum).
LD Services Contact: Ms. Kim Forbes Powell, Educational Coordinator for Students with Disabilities, Hocking College, 3301 Hocking Parkway, Nelsonville, OH 45764, 614-753-3591 Ext. 2230. Fax: 614-753-4097.

HUDSON COUNTY COMMUNITY COLLEGE

Jersey City, New Jersey

LEARNING DISABILITIES SERVICES INFORMATION

Center for Advisement and Counseling began offering services in 1992. Currently the program serves 55 undergraduates with LD. Students diagnosed with ADD/ADHD are eligible for the same services available to students with LD.
Staff: Includes director, counselors. Services provided by tutors, counselors.
Special Fees: No special fees are charged for services to students with LD.
Applications and admissions: *Recommended:* high school IEP (Individualized Education Program), personal interview, psychoeducational report completed within 4 years. Students may begin taking classes any term. *Application deadline:* continuous.

PROGRAM AND SERVICE COMPONENTS

Academic advising: Provided by academic advisers. Students with LD may take up to 15 credits each term; most take 9 to 12 credits; 12 credits required to maintain full-time status; 6 credits required to be eligible for financial aid.
Counseling services: Individual counseling, career counseling.
Subject-area tutoring: Offered in small groups by peer tutors. Available in most subjects.
Auxiliary aids: Tape recorders, calculators, word-processors with spell-check, personal computers.
Auxiliary services: Alternative test arrangements, advocacy.

GENERAL COLLEGE INFORMATION

State and locally supported, 2-year, coed. Part of New Jersey Commission on Higher Education. Awards associate degrees. Founded 1974. *Setting:* urban campus with easy access to New York City. *Endowment:* $10,445. *Total enrollment:* 4,249. *Faculty:* 237 (49 full-time, 21% with terminal degrees, 188 part-time); student–undergrad faculty ratio is 16:1.
Enrollment Profile: 4,249 students from 2 states and territories, 1 other country. 60% women, 40% men, 38% part-time, 99% state residents, 7% transferred in, 50% 25 or older, 1% Native American, 47% Hispanic, 18% black, 12% Asian or Pacific Islander. *Areas of study chosen:* 20% liberal arts/general studies, 10% health professions and related sciences, 8% business management and administrative services, 7% computer and information sciences, 5% education, 5% engineering and applied sciences, 5% vocational and home economics. *Most popular recent majors:* culinary arts, accounting, business administration/commerce/management.
First-Year Class: 1,596 total; 2,753 applied, 100% were accepted, 58% of whom enrolled.
Graduation Requirements: 66 credits; 1 college algebra course; computer course; internship (some majors).
Computers on Campus: 500 computers available on campus for general student use. Computers for student use in computer labs, learning resource center, data processing room. Staffed computer lab on campus provides training in use of computers, software.

EXPENSES

Expenses for 1997–98: *Application fee:* $10. Area resident tuition: $2063 full-time, $62.50 per credit part-time. State resident tuition: $4125 full-time, $125 per credit part-time. Nonresident tuition: $6188 full-time, $187.50 per credit part-time. Part-time mandatory fees per semester range from $40 to $290. Full-time mandatory fees: $855.
LD Services Contact: Janique Caffie, Director, Hudson County Community College, 25 Journal Square, Jersey City, NJ 07306, 732-714-5998. Fax: 732-714-7265.

HUDSON VALLEY COMMUNITY COLLEGE

Troy, New York

LEARNING DISABILITIES SERVICES INFORMATION

Disabled Student Services began offering services in 1987. Currently the program serves 170 undergraduates with LD. Students diagnosed with ADD/ADHD are eligible for the same services available to students with LD.
Staff: Includes coordinator, LD specialist, assistant coordinator. Services provided by tutors.
Special Fees: No special fees are charged for services to students with LD.
Applications and admissions: *Required:* high school transcript, IEP (Individualized Education Program), psychoeducational report completed within 3 years. Students may begin taking classes any term. *Application deadline:* continuous.

PROGRAM AND SERVICE COMPONENTS

Special preparation or orientation: Optional orientation offered before classes begin.
Academic advising: Provided by unit staff members, academic advisers. Students with LD may take up to 15 credits each term; most take 12 credits; 12 credits required to maintain full-time status; 6 credits required to be eligible for financial aid.
Counseling services: Individual counseling, career counseling.
Basic skills remediation: Offered in class-size groups by regular teachers. Available in reading, math, written language, learning strategies, time management.
Subject-area tutoring: Offered one-on-one and in small groups by peer tutors. Available in all subjects.
Special courses: Reading, composition, learning strategies, time management, math, study skills, career planning. None offered for credit; none enter into overall grade point average.

Auxiliary aids: Taped textbooks, tape recorders, calculators, word-processors with spell-check, optical character readers, taped encyclopedia, talking calculator.
Auxiliary services: Alternative test arrangements, notetakers, advocacy, readers.
Campus support group: A special student organization is available to students with LD.

GENERAL COLLEGE INFORMATION

State and locally supported, 2-year, coed. Part of State University of New York System. Awards associate degrees. Founded 1953. *Setting:* 135-acre suburban campus. *Total enrollment:* 9,644. *Faculty:* 511 (268 full-time, 13% with terminal degrees, 243 part-time); student–undergrad faculty ratio is 20:1.
Enrollment Profile: 9,644 students from 21 states and territories, 18 other countries. 48% women, 52% men, 17% part-time, 97% state residents, 5% transferred in, 1% international, 35% 25 or older, 1% Native American, 1% Hispanic, 5% black, 1% Asian or Pacific Islander. *Retention:* 50% of 1995 full-time freshmen returned. *Most popular recent majors:* liberal arts/general studies, criminal justice, accounting.
First-Year Class: 3,391 total; 5,500 applied, 85% were accepted, 65% of whom enrolled. 10% from top 10% of their high school class, 20% from top quarter, 50% from top half.
Graduation Requirements: 60 credits; 1 year of math; internship (some majors).
Computers on Campus: 500 computers available on campus for general student use. Computer purchase/lease plans available. A campus-wide network can be accessed from off-campus. Students can contact faculty members and/or advisers through e-mail. Computers for student use in computer center, computer labs, library, terminal clusters provide access to the Internet/World Wide Web, on- and off-campus e-mail addresses. Staffed computer lab on campus (open 24 hours a day) provides training in use of computers, software.

EXPENSES

Expenses for 1996–97: *Application fee:* $25. State resident tuition: $2150 full-time, $90 per credit part-time. Nonresident tuition: $5000 full-time, $180 per credit part-time. Part-time mandatory fees: $3 per credit. Full-time mandatory fees: $121.
LD Services Contact: Ms. Katherine P. Jetter, Learning Disabilities Specialist, Hudson Valley Community College, 80 Vandenburgh Avenue, Troy, NY 12180, 518-270-7552. Fax: 518-270-7509.

ILLINOIS CENTRAL COLLEGE

East Peoria, Illinois

LEARNING DISABILITIES SERVICES INFORMATION

Services for Students with Disabilities began offering services in 1981. Currently the program serves 156 undergraduates with LD. Students diagnosed with ADD/ADHD are eligible for the same services available to students with LD.
Staff: 1 part-time staff member (coordinator). Services provided by tutors, counselors.
Special Fees: No special fees are charged for services to students with LD.
Applications and admissions: *Required:* psychoeducational report; *recommended:* high school IEP (Individualized Education Program). Students may begin taking classes in fall, spring, or summer. *Application deadline:* continuous.

PROGRAM AND SERVICE COMPONENTS

Academic advising: Provided by unit staff members, academic advisers. Most students with LD take 6 to 12 semester hours each term; 12 semester hours required to maintain full-time status; 6 semester hours required to be eligible for financial aid.
Counseling services: Individual counseling, career counseling.
Basic skills remediation: Offered in class-size groups by regular teachers. Available in reading, math, spelling, written language, study skills.
Subject-area tutoring: Offered one-on-one by peer tutors, Math/Reading/Writing Lab staff. Available in all subjects.
Auxiliary aids: Taped textbooks, tape recorders, calculators, typewriters, word-processors with spell-check, optical character readers, Spellmasters.
Auxiliary services: Alternative test arrangements, notetakers, advocacy.

GENERAL COLLEGE INFORMATION

State and locally supported, 2-year, coed. Part of Illinois Community College System. Awards associate degrees. Founded 1967. *Setting:* 430-acre suburban campus. *Total enrollment:* 12,115. *Faculty:* 658 (172 full-time, 8% with terminal degrees, 486 part-time); student–undergrad faculty ratio is 20:1.
Enrollment Profile: 12,115 students: 59% women, 41% men, 69% part-time, 99% state residents, 5% transferred in, 1% international, 55% 25 or older, 1% Native American, 1% Hispanic, 6% black, 1% Asian or Pacific Islander. *Areas of study chosen:* 10% education, 5% fine arts, 3% agriculture, 3% architecture, 3% engineering and applied sciences, 3% library and information studies, 2% communications and journalism, 2% premed, 1% performing arts, 1% prevet, 1% social sciences. *Most popular recent majors:* liberal arts/general studies, science, business administration/commerce/management.
First-Year Class: 2,672 total. Of the students who applied, 100% were accepted, 80% of whom enrolled.
Graduation Requirements: 64 semester hours; math/science requirements vary according to program; internship (some majors).
Computers on Campus: 250 computers available on campus for general student use. A campus-wide network can be accessed from off-campus. Computers for student use in computer labs, departmental labs provide access to the Internet/World Wide Web, off-campus e-mail addresses. Staffed computer lab on campus provides training in use of computers, software. *Academic computing expenditure 1995–96:* $309,888.

EXPENSES AND FINANCIAL AID

Expenses for 1997–98: Area resident tuition: $1344 full-time, $42 per semester hour part-time. State resident tuition: $4832 full-time, $151 per semester hour part-time. Nonresident tuition: $6400 full-time, $200 per semester hour part-time.
Financial aid specifically for students with LD: work-study.
LD Services Contact: Ms. Nancy Davidson, Coordinator, Services for Students with Disabilities, Illinois Central College, 1 College Drive, East Peoria, IL 61635, 309-694-5749. Fax: 309-694-5450.

ILLINOIS EASTERN COMMUNITY COLLEGES, FRONTIER COMMUNITY COLLEGE

Fairfield, Illinois

LEARNING DISABILITIES SERVICES INFORMATION

Learning Skills Center currently serves undergraduate students with LD. Students diagnosed with ADD/ADHD are eligible for the same services available to students with LD.
Staff: Services provided by remediation specialist, tutors, counselor.
Special Fees: No special fees are charged for services to students with LD.
Applications and admissions: Open admissions. Students may begin taking classes any term. *Application deadline:* continuous.
Special policies: The college has written policies regarding grade forgiveness.

PROGRAM AND SERVICE COMPONENTS

Diagnostic testing: Intelligence, reading, math, spelling, spoken language, written language.
Academic advising: Provided by unit staff members. Students with LD may take up to 20 credit hours each term; most take 14 credit hours; 12 credit hours required to maintain full-time status; 6 credit hours (fall and spring), 3 credit hours (summer) required to be eligible for financial aid.
Counseling services: Individual counseling, career counseling.
Basic skills remediation: Offered one-on-one and in small groups by LD teachers, regular teachers. Available in reading, math, spelling, written language, learning strategies.
Subject-area tutoring: Offered one-on-one and in small groups by professional teachers, peer tutors. Available in most subjects.
Special courses: College survival skills, reading, communication skills, composition, math, study skills. All offered for credit; all enter into overall grade point average.
Auxiliary aids: Tape recorders.
Auxiliary services: Alternative test arrangements, notetakers.

Illinois Eastern Community Colleges, Frontier Community College (continued)

GENERAL COLLEGE INFORMATION

State and locally supported, 2-year, coed. Part of Illinois Eastern Community College System. Awards associate degrees. Founded 1976. *Setting:* 8-acre rural campus. *Total enrollment:* 2,302. *Faculty:* 128 (3 full-time, 125 part-time).
Enrollment Profile: 2,302 students: 67% women, 33% men, 90% part-time, 99% state residents, 0% transferred in, 0% international, 71% 25 or older, 0% Native American, 0% Hispanic, 0% black, 0% Asian or Pacific Islander. *Areas of study chosen:* 38% liberal arts/general studies, 34% health professions and related sciences, 10% vocational and home economics, 8% computer and information sciences, 7% business management and administrative services, 3% education.
First-Year Class: 1,569 total; 1,569 applied, 100% were accepted, 100% of whom enrolled.
Graduation Requirements: 64 credit hours.
Computers on Campus: 42 computers available on campus for general student use. Computers for student use in computer center.

EXPENSES

Expenses for 1997–98: *Application fee:* $10. Area resident tuition: $992 full-time, $31 per credit hour part-time. State resident tuition: $3939 full-time, $123.09 per credit hour part-time. Nonresident tuition: $4919 full-time, $153.72 per credit hour part-time. One-time mandatory fee: $10.
LD Services Contact: Ms. Rita Ladner, Program Director, College Support Services, Illinois Eastern Community Colleges, Frontier Community College, 233 East Chestnut Street, Olney, IL 62450, 618-393-2982 Ext. 5558. Fax: 618-392-4816.

ILLINOIS EASTERN COMMUNITY COLLEGES, LINCOLN TRAIL COLLEGE

Robinson, Illinois

LEARNING DISABILITIES SERVICES INFORMATION

Learning Skills Center currently serves undergraduate students with LD. Students diagnosed with ADD/ADHD are eligible for the same services available to students with LD.
Staff: Services provided by remediation specialist, tutors, counselor.
Special Fees: No special fees are charged for services to students with LD.
Applications and admissions: Open admissions. Students may begin taking classes any term. *Application deadline:* continuous.
Special policies: The college has written policies regarding grade forgiveness.

PROGRAM AND SERVICE COMPONENTS

Diagnostic testing: Intelligence, reading, math, spelling, spoken language, written language.
Academic advising: Provided by unit staff members. Most students with LD take 14 credit hours each term; 12 credit hours required to maintain full-time status; 6 credit hours (fall and spring), 3 credit hours (summer) required to be eligible for financial aid.
Counseling services: Individual counseling, career counseling.
Basic skills remediation: Offered one-on-one and in small groups by LD teachers, regular teachers. Available in reading, math, spelling, written language, learning strategies.
Subject-area tutoring: Offered one-on-one and in small groups by professional teachers, peer tutors. Available in most subjects.
Special courses: College survival skills, reading, communication skills, composition, math, study skills. All offered for credit; all enter into overall grade point average.
Auxiliary aids: Tape recorders.
Auxiliary services: Alternative test arrangements, notetakers.

GENERAL COLLEGE INFORMATION

State and locally supported, 2-year, coed. Part of Illinois Eastern Community College System. Awards associate degrees. Founded 1969. *Setting:* 120-acre rural campus. *Total enrollment:* 1,216. *Faculty:* 70 (23 full-time, 47 part-time).
Enrollment Profile: 1,216 students: 54% women, 46% men, 51% part-time, 87% state residents, 0% transferred in, 50% 25 or older, 0% Native American, 2% Hispanic, 8% black, 1% Asian or Pacific Islander. *Areas of study chosen:* 64% liberal arts/general studies, 21% vocational and home economics, 5% computer and information sciences, 4% architecture, 3% business management and administrative services, 2% education, 1% engineering and applied sciences.
First-Year Class: 855 total; 855 applied, 100% were accepted, 100% of whom enrolled.
Graduation Requirements: 64 credit hours; internship (some majors).
Computers on Campus: 96 computers available on campus for general student use. Computers for student use in learning resource center, classrooms, library.

EXPENSES

Expenses for 1997–98: *Application fee:* $10. Area resident tuition: $992 full-time, $31 per credit hour part-time. State resident tuition: $3939 full-time, $123.09 per credit hour part-time. Nonresident tuition: $4919 full-time, $153.72 per credit hour part-time. One-time mandatory fee: $10.
LD Services Contact: Ms. Rita Ladner, Program Director, College Support Services, Illinois Eastern Community Colleges, Lincoln Trail College, 233 East Chestnut Street, Olney, IL 62450, 618-393-2982 Ext. 5558. Fax: 618-392-4816.

ILLINOIS EASTERN COMMUNITY COLLEGES, OLNEY CENTRAL COLLEGE

Olney, Illinois

LEARNING DISABILITIES SERVICES INFORMATION

Learning Skills Center began offering services in 1986. Currently the program serves 10 undergraduates with LD. Students diagnosed with ADD/ADHD are eligible for the same services available to students with LD.
Staff: Services provided by remediation specialist, tutors, counselor.
Special Fees: No special fees are charged for services to students with LD.
Applications and admissions: *Required:* high school transcript; *recommended:* high school IEP (Individualized Education Program), personal interview. Students may begin taking classes any term. *Application deadline:* continuous.
Special policies: The college has written policies regarding grade forgiveness.

PROGRAM AND SERVICE COMPONENTS

Diagnostic testing: Intelligence, reading, math, spelling, spoken language, written language.
Academic advising: Provided by unit staff members, academic advisers. Most students with LD take 14 credit hours each term; 12 credit hours required to maintain full-time status; 6 credit hours (fall and spring), 3 credit hours (summer) required to be eligible for financial aid.
Counseling services: Individual counseling, career counseling.
Basic skills remediation: Offered one-on-one, in small groups, and in class-size groups by LD teachers, regular teachers; computer-aided instruction also offered. Available in reading, math, spelling, written language, learning strategies, study skills.
Subject-area tutoring: Offered one-on-one, in small groups, and in class-size groups by professional teachers, peer tutors. Available in all subjects.
Special courses: College survival skills, reading, communication skills, composition, math, study skills. All offered for credit; all enter into overall grade point average.
Auxiliary aids: Tape recorders, calculators, word-processors with spell-check, personal computers, talking computers.
Auxiliary services: Alternative test arrangements, notetakers.

GENERAL COLLEGE INFORMATION

State and locally supported, 2-year, coed. Part of Illinois Eastern Community College System. Awards associate degrees. Founded 1962. *Setting:* 128-acre rural campus. *Total enrollment:* 1,128. *Faculty:* 94 (41 full-time, 53 part-time).
Enrollment Profile: 1,128 students: 59% women, 41% men, 40% part-time, 99% state residents, 0% transferred in, 1% international, 38% 25 or older, 0% Native American, 0% Hispanic, 1% black, 1% Asian or Pacific Islander. *Areas of study chosen:* 60% liberal arts/general studies, 19% vocational and home economics, 13% health professions and related sciences, 5% prelaw, 3% computer and information sciences.

First-Year Class: 719 total; 719 applied, 100% were accepted, 100% of whom enrolled.
Graduation Requirements: 64 credit hours; internship (some majors).
Computers on Campus: 125 computers available on campus for general student use. Computers for student use in computer labs, learning resource center, classrooms, library.

EXPENSES

Expenses for 1997–98: *Application fee:* $10. Area resident tuition: $992 full-time, $31 per credit hour part-time. State resident tuition: $3939 full-time, $123.09 per credit hour part-time. Nonresident tuition: $4919 full-time, $153.72 per credit hour part-time. One-time mandatory fee: $10.
LD Services Contact: Ms. Rita Ladner, Program Director, College Support Services, Illinois Eastern Community Colleges, Olney Central College, 233 East Chestnut Street, Olney, IL 62450, 618-393-2982 Ext. 5558. Fax: 618-392-4816.

ILLINOIS EASTERN COMMUNITY COLLEGES, WABASH VALLEY COLLEGE

Mount Carmel, Illinois

LEARNING DISABILITIES SERVICES INFORMATION

Academic Assistance Service currently serves undergraduate students with LD. Students diagnosed with ADD/ADHD are eligible for the same services available to students with LD.
Staff: Includes director, coordinator. Services provided by remediation specialist, tutors, counselor.
Special Fees: No special fees are charged for services to students with LD.
Applications and admissions: *Required:* high school transcript, grade point average; *recommended:* high school courses completed, untimed ACT. Students may begin taking classes in fall, spring, or summer. *Application deadline:* continuous.
Special policies: The college has written policies regarding grade forgiveness.

PROGRAM AND SERVICE COMPONENTS

Diagnostic testing: Intelligence, reading, math, spelling, spoken language, written language.
Academic advising: Provided by unit staff members, academic advisers. Most students with LD take 14 credit hours each term; 12 credit hours required to maintain full-time status; 6 credit hours (fall and spring semesters), 3 credit hours (summer semester) required to be eligible for financial aid.
Counseling services: Individual counseling, career counseling.
Basic skills remediation: Offered one-on-one and in small groups by LD teachers, Academic Assistance staff; computer-aided instruction also offered. Available in reading, math, spelling, written language, learning strategies.
Subject-area tutoring: Offered one-on-one and in small groups by professional teachers, peer tutors, Academic Assistance staff. Available in most subjects.
Special courses: College survival skills, reading, communication skills, composition, math, study skills. All offered for credit; all enter into overall grade point average.
Auxiliary aids: Tape recorders, calculators, typewriters, word-processors with spell-check, personal computers.
Auxiliary services: Alternative test arrangements, notetakers.

GENERAL COLLEGE INFORMATION

State and locally supported, 2-year, coed. Part of Illinois Eastern Community College System. Awards associate degrees. Founded 1960. *Setting:* 40-acre rural campus. *Total enrollment:* 1,461. *Faculty:* 84 (40 full-time, 44 part-time).
Enrollment Profile: 1,461 students: 66% women, 34% men, 53% part-time, 97% state residents, 0% transferred in, 51% 25 or older, 0% Native American, 1% Hispanic, 1% black, 2% Asian or Pacific Islander. *Areas of study chosen:* 53% liberal arts/general studies, 33% vocational and home economics, 8% agriculture, 6% education, 3% communications and journalism, 3% computer and information sciences.
First-Year Class: 967 total; 967 applied, 100% were accepted, 100% of whom enrolled.
Graduation Requirements: 64 credit hours; internship (some majors).
Computers on Campus: 100 computers available on campus for general student use. Computers for student use in learning resource center, classrooms, library.

EXPENSES

Expenses for 1997–98: *Application fee:* $10. Area resident tuition: $992 full-time, $31 per credit hour part-time. State resident tuition: $3939 full-time, $123.09 per credit hour part-time. Nonresident tuition: $4919 full-time, $153.72 per credit hour part-time. One-time mandatory fee: $10.
LD Services Contact: Ms. Rita Ladner, Program Director, College Support Services, Illinois Eastern Community Colleges, Wabash Valley College, 233 East Chestnut Street, Olney, IL 62450, 618-393-2982 Ext. 5558. Fax: 618-392-4816.

ILLINOIS VALLEY COMMUNITY COLLEGE

Oglesby, Illinois

LEARNING DISABILITIES SERVICES INFORMATION

Special Needs Program began offering services in 1991. Currently the program serves 104 undergraduates with LD. Students diagnosed with ADD/ADHD are eligible for the same services available to students with LD.
Staff: 1 full-time, 1 part-time staff members, including director. Services provided by tutors, counselors.
Special Fees: No special fees are charged for services to students with LD.
Applications and admissions: *Required:* high school transcript, IEP (Individualized Education Program), personal interview, psychoeducational report. Students may begin taking classes any term. *Application deadline:* continuous.

PROGRAM AND SERVICE COMPONENTS

Special preparation or orientation: Optional summer program offered prior to entering college. Required orientation held before classes begin in the Fall.
Diagnostic testing: Reading, math, written language, perceptual skills, study skills, psychoneurology, learning strategies, learning processes.
Academic advising: Provided by academic advisers. Most students with LD take 12 semester hours each term; 12 semester hours required to maintain full-time status and be eligible for financial aid.
Counseling services: Individual counseling, career counseling.
Basic skills remediation: Offered one-on-one and in class-size groups by regular teachers. Available in reading, math, spelling, written language, learning strategies, study skills, time management.
Subject-area tutoring: Offered one-on-one and in small groups by peer tutors. Available in all subjects.
Special courses: College survival skills, reading, vocabulary development, composition, learning strategies, word processing, time management, math, typing, study skills, career planning. All offered for credit; some enter into overall grade point average.
Auxiliary aids: Taped textbooks, tape recorders, word-processors with spell-check, optical character readers, enlarging software programs, adaptive equipment.
Auxiliary services: Alternative test arrangements, notetakers, support group, scribes, scotopic screening.
Campus support group: A special student organization is available to students with LD.

GENERAL COLLEGE INFORMATION

District-supported, 2-year, coed. Part of Illinois Community College System. Awards associate degrees. Founded 1924. *Setting:* 410-acre rural campus with easy access to Chicago. *Total enrollment:* 4,281. *Faculty:* 189 (68 full-time, 121 part-time).
Enrollment Profile: 4,281 students: 61% women, 39% men, 64% part-time, 100% state residents, 11% transferred in, 0% international, 6% 25 or older, 0% Native American, 2% Hispanic, 2% black.
First-Year Class: 1,241 total. Of the students who applied, 100% were accepted, 73% of whom enrolled.
Graduation Requirements: 64 semester hours; computer course (varies by major); internship (some majors).
Computers on Campus: 420 computers available on campus for general student use. Computers for student use in library.

Illinois Valley Community College (continued)

EXPENSES

Expenses for 1997–98: Area resident tuition: $1248 full-time, $39 per semester hour part-time. State resident tuition: $4433 full-time, $138.54 per semester hour part-time. Nonresident tuition: $5598 full-time, $174.94 per semester hour part-time. Part-time mandatory fees per semester range from $5 to $25. Full-time mandatory fees: $67.

LD Services Contact: Ms. Marianne Dzik, Special Populations and Remediation Coordinator, Illinois Valley Community College, 815 Orlando Smith Road, Oglesby, IL 61348, 815-224-2720 Ext. 433. Fax: 815-224-3033. Email: dzik@rs6000.ivcc.edu.

IMPERIAL VALLEY COLLEGE

Imperial, California

LEARNING DISABILITIES SERVICES INFORMATION

Disabled Student Programs and Services began offering services in 1979. Currently the program serves 175 undergraduates with LD. Students diagnosed with ADD/ADHD are eligible for the same services available to students with LD.

Staff: 4 full-time, 7 part-time staff members, including director. Services provided by remediation specialist, tutors, counselors, diagnostic specialists, resource specialists, high-tech specialist, LD specialist.

Special Fees: No special fees are charged for services to students with LD.

Applications and admissions: *Required:* high school transcript, courses completed, personal interview, psychoeducational report completed within 3 years; *recommended:* high school grade point average, untimed or extended time SAT I or ACT. Students may begin taking classes in fall, spring, or summer. *Application deadline:* continuous.

Special policies: The college has written policies regarding grade forgiveness.

PROGRAM AND SERVICE COMPONENTS

Special preparation or orientation: Optional orientation offered before registration.

Diagnostic testing: Reading, math, written language, perceptual skills.

Academic advising: Provided by unit staff members. Students with LD may take up to 18 units each term; most take .5 to 18 units; 12 units required to maintain full-time status; 6 units required to be eligible for financial aid.

Counseling services: Individual counseling, career counseling.

Basic skills remediation: Offered one-on-one and in small groups by LD teachers, regular teachers. Available in reading, math, spelling.

Subject-area tutoring: Offered one-on-one and in small groups by peer tutors, resource persons. Available in all subjects.

Special courses: Reading, vocabulary development, composition, word processing, math, typing. All offered for credit; some enter into overall grade point average.

Auxiliary aids: Taped textbooks, tape recorders, typewriters, word-processors with spell-check, personal computers, optical character readers.

Auxiliary services: Alternative test arrangements, notetakers, priority registration, advocacy.

GENERAL COLLEGE INFORMATION

State and locally supported, 2-year, coed. Part of California Community Colleges System. Awards associate degrees. Founded 1922. *Setting:* 160-acre rural campus. *Endowment:* $680,000. *Total enrollment:* 5,841. *Faculty:* 310 (93 full-time, 7% with terminal degrees, 217 part-time); student–undergrad faculty ratio is 22:1.

Enrollment Profile: 5,841 students: 62% women, 38% men, 49% part-time, 98% state residents, 3% transferred in, 0% Native American, 83% Hispanic, 1% black, 2% Asian or Pacific Islander. *Areas of study chosen:* 25% liberal arts/general studies, 10% health professions and related sciences, 5% business management and administrative services, 4% vocational and home economics, 2% computer and information sciences, 2% fine arts. *Most popular recent majors:* liberal arts/general studies, social science, business administration/commerce/management.

First-Year Class: 1,372 total. Of the students who applied, 100% were accepted, 90% of whom enrolled.

Graduation Requirements: 60 units; 1 algebra course; 3 units of natural science; computer course for business majors; internship (some majors).

Computers on Campus: 200 computers available on campus for general student use. Computers for student use in computer center, learning resource center, business departmental lab, reading lab, writing lab. Staffed computer lab on campus provides training in use of computers, software.

EXPENSES AND FINANCIAL AID

Expenses for 1997–98: State resident tuition: $0 full-time. Nonresident tuition: $3540 full-time, $118 per unit part-time. Part-time mandatory fees: $13 per unit. Full-time mandatory fees: $390.

Financial aid specifically for students with LD: Scholarships; loans; work-study.

LD Services Contact: Ms. Norma Nava, Instructional Specialist, Imperial Valley College, PO Box 158, Imperial, CA 92251-0158, 760-355-6312. Fax: 760-355-6107.

INDIAN HILLS COMMUNITY COLLEGE

Ottumwa, Iowa

LEARNING DISABILITIES SERVICES INFORMATION

Success Center began offering services in 1978. Currently the program serves 150 undergraduates with LD. Students diagnosed with ADD/ADHD are eligible for the same services available to students with LD.

Staff: 5 full-time, 5 part-time staff members, including associate director. Services provided by remediation specialists, tutors, counselor.

Special Fees: No special fees are charged for services to students with LD.

Applications and admissions: *Required:* high school transcript, IEP (Individualized Education Program), psychoeducational report completed within 2 years. Students may begin taking classes in fall only. *Application deadline:* continuous.

PROGRAM AND SERVICE COMPONENTS

Special preparation or orientation: Optional summer program offered prior to entering college. Optional orientation offered before registration.

Academic advising: Provided by unit staff members. Students with LD may take up to 12 semester hours each term; most take 8 to 10 semester hours; 8 semester hours required to maintain full-time status; 4 semester hours required to be eligible for financial aid.

Counseling services: Individual counseling, small-group counseling, career counseling, self-advocacy training.

Basic skills remediation: Offered one-on-one, in small groups, and in class-size groups by LD teachers, regular teachers; computer-aided instruction also offered. Available in reading, math, spelling, spoken language, written language, study skills, time management, speech, computer skills.

Subject-area tutoring: Offered one-on-one, in small groups, and in class-size groups by professional teachers, peer tutors. Available in all subjects.

Auxiliary aids: Taped textbooks, tape recorders, calculators, typewriters, word-processors with spell-check, personal computers, talking computers.

Auxiliary services: Alternative test arrangements, notetakers, advocacy.

GENERAL COLLEGE INFORMATION

State and locally supported, 2-year, coed. Part of Iowa Area Community Colleges System. Awards associate degrees. Founded 1966. *Setting:* 400-acre small-town campus. *Total enrollment:* 3,424. *Faculty:* 143 (128 full-time, 4% with terminal degrees, 15 part-time).

Enrollment Profile: 3,424 students from 20 states and territories. 54% women, 46% men, 27% part-time, 90% state residents, 15% live on campus, 14% transferred in, 30% 25 or older, 1% Native American, 1% Hispanic, 1% black, 1% Asian or Pacific Islander. *Most popular recent majors:* liberal arts/general studies, practical nursing, electrical and electronics technologies.

First-Year Class: 1,444 total; 1,800 applied, 92% were accepted, 87% of whom enrolled. 20% from top 10% of their high school class.

Graduation Requirements: 61 credit hours; computer course for health science majors; internship (some majors).

Computers on Campus: 150 computers available on campus for general student use. A campus-wide network can be accessed. Computers for student use in computer center, computer labs, learning resource center, classrooms, library provide access to the Internet/World Wide Web. Staffed computer lab on campus provides training in use of computers, software.

EXPENSES

Expenses for 1997–98: State resident tuition: $1440 full-time, $48 per credit hour part-time. Nonresident tuition: $2160 full-time, $72 per credit hour part-time. Part-time mandatory fees: $7 per credit hour. Full-time mandatory fees: $210. College room and board: $1950.
LD Services Contact: Ms. Mary Stewart, Department Chairperson, Special Programs, Indian Hills Community College, 525 Grandview, Ottumwa, IA 52501-1398, 515-683-5218. Fax: 515-683-5263.

IOWA CENTRAL COMMUNITY COLLEGE

Fort Dodge, Iowa

LEARNING DISABILITIES SERVICES INFORMATION

Student Success Center began offering services in 1983. Currently the program serves 35 undergraduates with LD. Students diagnosed with ADD/ADHD are eligible for the same services available to students with LD.
Staff: 4 full-time, 11 part-time staff members, including coordinators. Services provided by tutors.
Special Fees: $70 for diagnostic testing.
Applications and admissions: *Required:* high school transcript, untimed ACT, ACT ASSET. Students may begin taking classes in fall or spring. *Application deadline:* continuous.

PROGRAM AND SERVICE COMPONENTS

Diagnostic testing: Motor abilities, perceptual skills, study skills, social skills, various other areas as appropriate.
Academic advising: Provided by unit staff members, academic advisers. Students with LD may take up to 17 semester hours each term; most take 12 to 14 semester hours; 12 semester hours required to maintain full-time status; 3 semester hours required to be eligible for financial aid.
Counseling services: Individual counseling, career counseling.
Basic skills remediation: Offered in class-size groups by regular teachers; computer-aided instruction also offered. Available in reading, math, written language, study skills, time management, computer skills.
Subject-area tutoring: Offered one-on-one by professional teachers, peer tutors, tutors with Bachelor's degrees in subject areas. Available in most subjects.
Auxiliary aids: Taped textbooks, tape recorders, calculators, typewriters, word-processors with spell-check.
Auxiliary services: Alternative test arrangements, notetakers, advocacy.

GENERAL COLLEGE INFORMATION

State and locally supported, 2-year, coed. Part of Iowa Department of Education Division of Community Colleges. Awards associate degrees. Founded 1966. *Setting:* 110-acre small-town campus. *Total enrollment:* 2,828. *Faculty:* 206 (79 full-time, 1% with terminal degrees, 127 part-time); student–undergrad faculty ratio is 16:1.
Enrollment Profile: 2,828 students from 22 states and territories, 14 other countries. 58% women, 42% men, 48% part-time, 97% state residents, 8% transferred in, 1% international, 32% 25 or older, 1% Native American, 1% Hispanic, 1% black, 1% Asian or Pacific Islander. *Most popular recent major:* business administration/commerce/management.
First-Year Class: 1,847 total; 2,400 applied, 90% of whom enrolled. 10% from top 10% of their high school class, 20% from top quarter, 40% from top half.
Graduation Requirements: 60 semester hours; 4 semester hours each of math and science; computer course for accounting, business majors; internship (some majors).
Computers on Campus: 510 computers available on campus for general student use. Computer purchase/lease plans available. A computer is required for some students. A campus-wide network can be accessed from off-campus. Students can contact faculty members and/or advisers through e-mail. Computers for student use in computer center, computer labs, learning resource center, library, student center, dorms, various locations provide access to the Internet/World Wide Web, on- and off-campus e-mail addresses. Staffed computer lab on campus.

EXPENSES

Expenses for 1997–98: State resident tuition: $1710 full-time, $57 per semester hour part-time. Nonresident tuition: $2565 full-time, $85.50 per semester hour part-time. Part-time mandatory fees: $8.25 per semester hour. Full-time mandatory fees: $248. College room and board: $3175.
LD Services Contact: Ms. Barbara McClannahan, Coordinator, Iowa Central Community College, 330 Avenue M, Fort Dodge, IA 50501-5798, 515-576-7201. Fax: 515-576-7206 Ext. 2374.

IOWA WESTERN COMMUNITY COLLEGE

Council Bluffs, Iowa

LEARNING DISABILITIES SERVICES INFORMATION

Special Services Department began offering services in 1978. Currently the program serves 30 undergraduates with LD. Students diagnosed with ADD/ADHD are eligible for the same services available to students with LD.
Staff: 5 full-time, 1 part-time staff members, including director, coordinator. Services provided by remediation specialists, tutors, counselors.
Special Fees: No special fees are charged for services to students with LD.
Applications and admissions: *Required:* high school transcript, institutional testing, Career Planning and Placement Test. Students may begin taking classes in fall, spring, or summer. *Application deadline:* continuous.
Special policies: The college has written policies regarding substitutions and waivers of admissions, graduation, and degree requirements.

PROGRAM AND SERVICE COMPONENTS

Special preparation or orientation: Optional orientation offered after registration and before classes begin.
Academic advising: Provided by unit staff members, academic advisers. Most students with LD take 12 credit hours each term; 12 credit hours required to maintain full-time status; 3 credit hours required to be eligible for financial aid.
Counseling services: Individual counseling, career counseling, self-advocacy training.
Basic skills remediation: Offered one-on-one, in small groups, and in class-size groups by regular teachers; computer-aided instruction also offered. Available in reading, math, spelling, handwriting, written language, learning strategies, study skills, time management.
Subject-area tutoring: Offered one-on-one and in small groups by professional teachers, peer tutors. Available in all subjects.
Special courses: Reading, vocabulary development, composition, time management, math, study skills, career planning. Some offered for credit; some enter into overall grade point average.
Auxiliary aids: Taped textbooks, tape recorders, calculators, typewriters, word-processors with spell-check.
Auxiliary services: Alternative test arrangements, notetakers, advocacy.

GENERAL COLLEGE INFORMATION

District-supported, 2-year, coed. Part of Iowa Department of Education Division of Community Colleges. Awards associate degrees. Founded 1966. *Setting:* 282-acre suburban campus with easy access to Omaha. *Total enrollment:* 3,887. *Faculty:* 218 (112 full-time, 98% with terminal degrees, 106 part-time); student–undergrad faculty ratio is 21:1.
Enrollment Profile: 3,887 students from 28 states and territories, 12 other countries. 57% women, 43% men, 51% part-time, 90% state residents, 5% transferred in, 1% international, 36% 25 or older, 1% Native American, 1% Hispanic, 1% black, 1% Asian or Pacific Islander. *Retention:* 55% of 1995 full-time freshmen returned. *Areas of study chosen:* 46% liberal arts/general studies, 16% business management and administrative services, 15% health professions and related sciences, 8% vocational and home economics, 7% computer and information sciences, 5% engineering and applied sciences, 3% agriculture. *Most popular recent majors:* business administration/commerce/management, nursing, criminal justice.
First-Year Class: 1,605 total; 1,837 applied, 96% were accepted, 91% of whom enrolled.
Graduation Requirements: 60 credit hours; math/science requirements vary according to program; computer course for all associate of science degree programs; internship (some majors).
Computers on Campus: 195 computers available on campus for general student use. Computers for student use in computer center, library, dorms. Staffed computer lab on campus provides training in use of computers, software. *Academic computing expenditure 1995–96:* $1.1 million.

EXPENSES

Expenses for 1997–98: *Application fee:* $15. State resident tuition: $1950 full-time, $65 per credit hour part-time. Nonresident tuition: $2925 full-time, $97.50 per credit hour part-time. Part-time mandatory fees: $7 per credit hour. Full-time mandatory fees: $210. College room and board: $3000. College room only: $1500.

Iowa Western Community College (continued)

LD Services Contact: Mr. Chris Holst, Special Population Advisor, Iowa Western Community College, 2700 College Road, Box 4-C, Council Bluffs, IA 51502, 712-325-3390. Fax: 712-325-3720.

IRVINE VALLEY COLLEGE

Irvine, California

LEARNING DISABILITIES SERVICES INFORMATION

Disabled Student Services and Programs began offering services in 1986. Currently the program serves 293 undergraduates with LD. Students diagnosed with ADD/ADHD are eligible for the same services available to students with LD, as well as quiet testing room.

Staff: 4 full-time, 4 part-time staff members, including coordinator. Services provided by counselor.

Special Fees: No special fees are charged for services to students with LD.

Applications and admissions: *Recommended:* high school IEP (Individualized Education Program), psychoeducational report completed within 3 years. Students may begin taking classes any term. *Application deadline:* continuous.

Special policies: The college has written policies regarding substitutions and waivers of admissions, graduation, and degree requirements.

PROGRAM AND SERVICE COMPONENTS

Diagnostic testing: Intelligence, reading, math, spelling, written language, perceptual skills.

Academic advising: Provided by academic advisers. Students with LD may take up to 19 units each term; most take 9 to 12 units; 12 units required to maintain full-time status and be eligible for financial aid.

Counseling services: Individual counseling, career counseling, self-advocacy training.

Basic skills remediation: Offered in class-size groups by LD teachers; computer-aided instruction also offered. Available in reading, math, spelling, written language, learning strategies, study skills, computer skills.

Special courses: College survival skills, reading, vocabulary development, composition, word processing, math, study skills. All offered for credit; all enter into overall grade point average.

Auxiliary aids: Taped textbooks, tape recorders, calculators, word-processors with spell-check, personal computers, talking computers, optical character readers.

Auxiliary services: Alternative test arrangements, notetakers, priority registration, advocacy, readers.

Campus support group: A special student organization is available to students with LD.

GENERAL COLLEGE INFORMATION

State and locally supported, 2-year, coed. Part of Saddleback Community College District. Awards associate degrees. Founded 1979. *Setting:* 20-acre suburban campus with easy access to Los Angeles. *Total enrollment:* 10,300. *Faculty:* 344 (94 full-time, 250 part-time).

Enrollment Profile: 10,300 students: 60% women, 40% men, 80% part-time, 90% state residents, 1% transferred in, 4% international, 55% 25 or older, 1% Native American, 5% Hispanic, 1% black, 2% Asian or Pacific Islander. *Most popular recent majors:* business administration/commerce/management, liberal arts/general studies.

First-Year Class: Of the students who applied, 100% were accepted, 95% of whom enrolled.

Graduation Requirements: 60 units; 1 math/analytical reasoning course.

Computers on Campus: 125 computers available on campus for general student use. Computer purchase/lease plans available. Computers for student use in computer center. Staffed computer lab on campus provides training in use of computers, software.

EXPENSES

Expenses for 1997–98: State resident tuition: $0 full-time. Nonresident tuition: $3930 full-time, $131 per unit part-time. Part-time mandatory fees per semester range from $24 to $154. Full-time mandatory fees: $412.

LD Services Contact: Ms. Julie Willard, Learning Disabilities Specialist, Irvine Valley College, 5500 Irvine Center Drive, Irvine, CA 92720, 714-451-5357. Fax: 714-451-5306.

ITASCA COMMUNITY COLLEGE

Grand Rapids, Minnesota

LEARNING DISABILITIES SERVICES INFORMATION

Office for Students with Disabilities began offering services in 1990. Currently the program serves 25 undergraduates with LD. Students diagnosed with ADD/ADHD are eligible for the same services available to students with LD.

Staff: 4 full-time, 2 part-time staff members, including director, tutoring coordinator. Services provided by remediation specialists, tutors, counselors.

Special Fees: No special fees are charged for services to students with LD.

Applications and admissions: *Required:* psychoeducational report completed within 3 years; *recommended:* high school counselor's report. Students may begin taking classes any term. *Application deadline:* continuous.

Special policies: The college has written policies regarding grade forgiveness; substitutions and waivers of graduation and degree requirements.

PROGRAM AND SERVICE COMPONENTS

Special preparation or orientation: Optional summer program offered prior to entering college. Optional orientation offered before registration.

Academic advising: Provided by unit staff members, academic advisers, counselors. Most students with LD take 6 to 12 credits each term; 12 credits required to maintain full-time status and be eligible for financial aid.

Counseling services: Career counseling, self-advocacy training.

Basic skills remediation: Offered one-on-one, in small groups, and in class-size groups by regular teachers. Available in reading, math, spelling, written language, learning strategies, study skills, time management.

Subject-area tutoring: Offered one-on-one and in small groups by peer tutors, paraprofessionals trained in LD. Available in all subjects.

Special courses: College survival skills, reading, vocabulary development, communication skills, composition, learning strategies, time management, math, study skills, career planning. All offered for credit; some enter into overall grade point average.

Auxiliary aids: Taped textbooks, tape recorders, calculators, typewriters, word-processors with spell-check, talking computers, voicetype.

Auxiliary services: Alternative test arrangements, notetakers, priority registration, advocacy, scribes.

GENERAL COLLEGE INFORMATION

State-supported, 2-year, coed. Part of Minnesota State Colleges and Universities System. Awards associate degrees. Founded 1922. *Setting:* 24-acre rural campus. *Total enrollment:* 1,308. *Faculty:* 68 (43 full-time, 30% with terminal degrees, 25 part-time).

Enrollment Profile: 1,308 students from 8 states and territories. 48% women, 52% men, 41% part-time, 97% state residents, 7% transferred in, 0% international, 35% 25 or older, 4% Native American, 1% Hispanic, 1% black, 1% Asian or Pacific Islander. *Retention:* 50% of 1995 full-time freshmen returned. *Most popular recent majors:* liberal arts/general studies, practical nursing.

First-Year Class: 390 total; 539 applied, 100% were accepted, 72% of whom enrolled.

Graduation Requirements: 96 credits; math/science requirements vary according to program; computer course for secretarial studies, accounting, forestry majors; internship (some majors).

Computers on Campus: 134 computers available on campus for general student use. A campus-wide network can be accessed. Students can contact faculty members and/or advisers through e-mail. Computers for student use in computer center, computer labs, learning resource center, classrooms, library, student center, dorms provide access to the Internet/World Wide Web, on- and off-campus e-mail addresses. Staffed computer lab on campus (open 24 hours a day) provides training in use of computers, software. *Academic computing expenditure 1995–96:* $153,855.

EXPENSES

Estimated Expenses for 1997–98: *Application fee:* $20. State resident tuition: $2218 full-time, $46.20 per credit part-time. Nonresident tuition: $4618 full-time, $96.20 per credit part-time. Part-time mandatory fees: $3.80 per credit. North Dakota, South Dakota and Wisconsin residents pay tuition at the rate they would pay if attending a comparable state-supported institution in their home state. Full-time mandatory fees: $182.

LD Services Contact: Ms. Beth Claussen, Director, Office for Students with Disabilities, Itasca Community College, 1851 Highway 169 East, Grand Rapids, MN 55744, 218-327-4166. Fax: 218-327-4350.

IVY TECH STATE COLLEGE–CENTRAL INDIANA

Indianapolis, Indiana

LEARNING DISABILITIES SERVICES INFORMATION

Special Needs Services began offering services in 1985. Currently the program serves 100 undergraduates with LD. Students diagnosed with ADD/ADHD are eligible for the same services available to students with LD.

Staff: 5 full-time staff members, including Manager. Services provided by remediation specialist, counselor, interpreters for the deaf.

Special Fees: No special fees are charged for services to students with LD.

Applications and admissions: *Required:* high school transcript, psychoeducational report completed within 3 years, Assessment and Placement Services for Community Colleges. Students may begin taking classes any term. *Application deadline:* continuous.

PROGRAM AND SERVICE COMPONENTS

Special preparation or orientation: Optional orientation offered before registration.

Diagnostic testing: Reading, math, spelling, handwriting, written language, learning strategies.

Academic advising: Provided by unit staff members. Students with LD may take up to 12 credits each term; most take 6 to 9 credits; 12 credits required to maintain full-time status; 6 credits (part-time), 12 credits (full-time) required to be eligible for financial aid.

Counseling services: Individual counseling, small-group counseling, career counseling.

Basic skills remediation: Offered in class-size groups by regular teachers. Available in reading, math, spelling, spoken language, written language, learning strategies.

Subject-area tutoring: Offered one-on-one and in small groups by professional teachers, peer tutors. Available in most subjects.

Auxiliary aids: Taped textbooks, tape recorders, calculators, typewriters, word-processors with spell-check, personal computers, optical character readers.

Auxiliary services: Alternative test arrangements.

GENERAL COLLEGE INFORMATION

State-supported, 2-year, coed. Part of Ivy Tech State College System. Awards associate degrees. Founded 1963. *Setting:* 10-acre urban campus. *System endowment:* $1.2 million. *Total enrollment:* 5,355. *Faculty:* 326 (117 full-time, 209 part-time); student–undergrad faculty ratio is 17:1.

Enrollment Profile: 5,355 students: 55% women, 45% men, 79% part-time, 100% state residents, 3% transferred in, 64% 25 or older, 1% Native American, 1% Hispanic, 19% black, 1% Asian or Pacific Islander. *Areas of study chosen:* 34% engineering and applied sciences, 26% liberal arts/general studies, 16% business management and administrative services, 12% computer and information sciences, 12% health professions and related sciences. *Most popular recent majors:* nursing, paralegal studies, respiratory therapy.

First-Year Class: 1,694 total. Of the students who applied, 100% were accepted, 62% of whom enrolled.

Graduation Requirements: 60 credits; computer course (varies by major); internship (some majors).

Computers on Campus: 120 computers available on campus for general student use. Computers for student use in computer center, computer labs, library. Staffed computer lab on campus.

EXPENSES

Expenses for 1997–98: State resident tuition: $1937 full-time, $64.55 per credit part-time. Nonresident tuition: $3561 full-time, $118.70 per credit part-time.

LD Services Contact: Ms. Sharon Dunn, Manager, Special Needs Services, Ivy Tech State College–Central Indiana, 1 West 26th Street, PO Box 1763, Indianapolis, IN 46206, 317-921-4908.

IVY TECH STATE COLLEGE–KOKOMO

Kokomo, Indiana

LEARNING DISABILITIES SERVICES INFORMATION

Disability Services began offering services in 1985. Currently the program serves 38 undergraduates with LD. Students diagnosed with ADD/ADHD are eligible for the same services available to students with LD.

Staff: 9 full-time, 1 part-time staff members, including coordinator, advocate. Services provided by tutors, counselors.

Special Fees: No special fees are charged for services to students with LD.

Applications and admissions: *Required:* high school transcript, IEP (Individualized Education Program), ACT ASSET; *recommended:* personal interview. Students may begin taking classes in fall, spring, or summer. *Application deadline:* continuous.

PROGRAM AND SERVICE COMPONENTS

Diagnostic testing: Intelligence, reading, math, spoken language, written language, motor abilities, perceptual skills, study skills.

Academic advising: Provided by academic advisers. Students with LD may take up to 15 credits each term; most take 8 credits; 12 credits required to maintain full-time status; 3 credits required to be eligible for financial aid.

Counseling services: Individual counseling, small-group counseling.

Basic skills remediation: Offered one-on-one, in small groups, and in class-size groups by regular teachers. Available in reading, math, spelling, spoken language, written language, learning strategies, study skills, time management.

Subject-area tutoring: Offered one-on-one, in small groups, and in class-size groups by professional teachers. Available in some subjects.

Special courses: Reading, vocabulary development, communication skills, composition, learning strategies, time management, math, typing, study skills, career planning. None offered for credit.

Auxiliary aids: Taped textbooks, tape recorders, calculators, typewriters, word-processors with spell-check, voice-activated computer (Dragon Dictate).

Auxiliary services: Alternative test arrangements, notetakers.

GENERAL COLLEGE INFORMATION

State-supported, 2-year, coed. Part of Ivy Tech State College System. Awards associate degrees. Founded 1968. *Setting:* 20-acre small-town campus with easy access to Indianapolis. *System endowment:* $1.2 million. *Total enrollment:* 1,659. *Faculty:* 141 (34 full-time, 107 part-time); student–undergrad faculty ratio is 11:1.

Enrollment Profile: 1,659 students: 61% women, 39% men, 76% part-time, 100% state residents, 1% transferred in, 66% 25 or older, 1% Native American, 2% Hispanic, 4% black, 1% Asian or Pacific Islander. *Areas of study chosen:* 30% engineering and applied sciences, 24% business management and administrative services, 19% computer and information sciences, 14% liberal arts/general studies, 13% health professions and related sciences. *Most popular recent majors:* secretarial studies/office management, computer information systems, medical assistant technologies.

First-Year Class: 623 total. Of the students who applied, 100% were accepted, 47% of whom enrolled.

Graduation Requirements: 60 credits; computer course (varies by major); internship (some majors).

Computers on Campus: 220 computers available on campus for general student use. Computers for student use in computer center, library. Staffed computer lab on campus.

EXPENSES

Expenses for 1997–98: State resident tuition: $1937 full-time, $64.55 per credit part-time. Nonresident tuition: $3561 full-time, $118.70 per credit part-time.

LD Services Contact: Mr. Russ Ragland, Disability Services Advocate, Ivy Tech State College–Kokomo, 1815 East Morgan Street, PO Box 1373, Kokomo, IN 46903-1373, 765-459-0561. Fax: 765-454-5111.

IVY TECH STATE COLLEGE–NORTHCENTRAL

South Bend, Indiana

LEARNING DISABILITIES SERVICES INFORMATION

General Education Office began offering services in 1985. Currently the program serves 50 undergraduates with LD. Students diagnosed with ADD/ADHD are eligible for the same services available to students with LD.

Staff: 1 part-time staff member (coordinator).

Special Fees: No special fees are charged for services to students with LD.

Applications and admissions: *Required:* high school transcript, psychoeducational report completed within 3 years. Students may begin taking classes any term. *Application deadline:* continuous.

PROGRAM AND SERVICE COMPONENTS

Academic advising: Provided by academic advisers. Most students with LD take 9 to 12 credits each term; 12 credits required to maintain full-time status.

Auxiliary aids: Taped textbooks, tape recorders, calculators, word-processors with spell-check, personal computers, talking computers.

Auxiliary services: Alternative test arrangements, notetakers, priority registration, advocacy.

GENERAL COLLEGE INFORMATION

State-supported, 2-year, coed. Part of Ivy Tech State College System. Awards associate degrees. Founded 1968. *Setting:* 4-acre suburban campus. *System endowment:* $1.2 million. *Total enrollment:* 2,552. *Faculty:* 226 (57 full-time, 169 part-time); student–undergrad faculty ratio is 12:1.

Enrollment Profile: 2,552 students from 4 states and territories. 59% women, 41% men, 78% part-time, 97% state residents, 5% transferred in, 70% 25 or older, 1% Native American, 2% Hispanic, 10% black, 1% Asian or Pacific Islander. *Areas of study chosen:* 33% engineering and applied sciences, 20% business management and administrative services, 17% liberal arts/general studies, 16% computer and information sciences, 14% health professions and related sciences. *Most popular recent majors:* nursing, accounting, secretarial studies/office management.

First-Year Class: 789 total. Of the students who applied, 100% were accepted, 49% of whom enrolled.

Graduation Requirements: 60 credits; computer course (varies by major); internship (some majors).

Computers on Campus: 80 computers available on campus for general student use. Computers for student use in computer center, library. Staffed computer lab on campus.

EXPENSES

Expenses for 1997–98: State resident tuition: $1937 full-time, $64.55 per credit part-time. Nonresident tuition: $3561 full-time, $118.70 per credit part-time.

LD Services Contact: Dr. Monica Smith, Coordinator of Services for Students with Disabilities, Ivy Tech State College–Northcentral, 1534 West Sample, South Bend, IN 46619-3837, 219-289-7001 Ext. 340.

IVY TECH STATE COLLEGE–NORTHEAST

Fort Wayne, Indiana

LEARNING DISABILITIES SERVICES INFORMATION

Disability Services Office began offering services in 1985. Currently the program serves 35 undergraduates with LD. Students diagnosed with ADD/ADHD are eligible for the same services available to students with LD.

Staff: 4 full-time, 3 part-time staff members, including director, assistant director, coordinator. Services provided by tutors, counselors.

Special Fees: No special fees are charged for services to students with LD.

Applications and admissions: *Required:* psychoeducational report completed within 3 years; *recommended:* ASSET skills assessment. Students may begin taking classes any term. *Application deadline:* continuous.

Special policies: The college has written policies regarding grade forgiveness; substitutions and waivers of admissions, graduation, and degree requirements.

PROGRAM AND SERVICE COMPONENTS

Academic advising: Provided by academic advisers. Most students with LD take 6 to 9 credits each term; 12 credits required to maintain full-time status; 6 credits required to be eligible for financial aid.

Counseling services: Individual counseling, career counseling.

Basic skills remediation: Offered in class-size groups by regular teachers. Available in reading, math, spelling, written language, learning strategies, study skills, time management, computer skills.

Subject-area tutoring: Offered one-on-one and in small groups by professional tutors. Available in some subjects.

Special courses: College survival skills, reading, vocabulary development, communication skills, composition, learning strategies, word processing, time management, math, study skills. Most offered for credit; none enter into overall grade point average.

Auxiliary aids: Tape recorders, calculators, typewriters, word-processors with spell-check, personal computers, talking computers, optical character readers, carbonless notepaper.

Auxiliary services: Alternative test arrangements, notetakers, priority registration, advocacy.

GENERAL COLLEGE INFORMATION

State-supported, 2-year, coed. Part of Ivy Tech State College System. Awards associate degrees. Founded 1969. *Setting:* 22-acre urban campus. *System endowment:* $1.2 million. *Total enrollment:* 3,305. *Faculty:* 280 (56 full-time, 224 part-time); student–undergrad faculty ratio is 12:1.

Enrollment Profile: 3,305 students from 5 states and territories. 58% women, 42% men, 76% part-time, 97% state residents, 3% transferred in, 63% 25 or older, 1% Native American, 1% Hispanic, 8% black, 1% Asian or Pacific Islander. *Areas of study chosen:* 32% engineering and applied sciences, 22% business management and administrative services, 22% health professions and related sciences, 16% liberal arts/general studies, 8% computer and information sciences. *Most popular recent majors:* medical assistant technologies, child care/child and family studies, accounting.

First-Year Class: 1,580 total. Of the students who applied, 100% were accepted, 64% of whom enrolled.

Graduation Requirements: 60 credits; computer course (varies by major); internship (some majors).

Computers on Campus: 158 computers available on campus for general student use. Computers for student use in computer center, computer labs, library. Staffed computer lab on campus.

EXPENSES

Expenses for 1997–98: State resident tuition: $1937 full-time, $64.55 per credit part-time. Nonresident tuition: $3561 full-time, $118.70 per credit part-time.

LD Services Contact: Mr. Rex Oechsle, Counselor, Ivy Tech State College–Northeast, 3800 North Anthony Boulevard, Fort Wayne, IN 46805, 219-482-9171. Fax: 219-480-4177.

IVY TECH STATE COLLEGE–SOUTHEAST

Madison, Indiana

LEARNING DISABILITIES SERVICES INFORMATION

Basic Skills and Learning Center began offering services in 1981. Currently the program serves 2 undergraduates with LD. Students diagnosed with ADD/ADHD are not eligible for the same services available to students with LD.

Staff: 6 full-time, 7 part-time staff members, including director, associate director. Services provided by remediation specialists, tutors, counselors, diagnostic specialists.

Special Fees: No special fees are charged for services to students with LD.

Applications and admissions: *Required:* ACT ASSET. Students may begin taking classes in fall, spring, or summer. *Application deadline:* continuous.

Special policies: The college has written policies regarding substitutions and waivers of graduation and degree requirements.

PROGRAM AND SERVICE COMPONENTS

Diagnostic testing: Reading, math, written language.

Academic advising: Provided by unit staff members, academic advisers. Students with LD may take up to 15 credits each term; most take 6 credits; 12 credits required to maintain full-time status; 6 credits required to be eligible for financial aid.
Counseling services: Individual counseling, small-group counseling, career counseling.
Basic skills remediation: Offered one-on-one, in small groups, and in class-size groups by LD teachers, regular teachers, teacher trainees. Available in reading, math, spelling, written language, learning strategies, study skills, time management, social skills.
Subject-area tutoring: Offered one-on-one, in small groups, and in class-size groups by professional teachers. Available in some subjects.
Special courses: College survival skills, reading, vocabulary development, composition, learning strategies, time management, math, typing, study skills, career planning. All offered for credit; none enter into overall grade point average.
Auxiliary aids: Taped textbooks, tape recorders, calculators, typewriters, word-processors with spell-check.
Auxiliary services: Alternative test arrangements.

GENERAL COLLEGE INFORMATION

State-supported, 2-year, coed. Part of Ivy Tech State College System. Awards associate degrees. Founded 1963. *Setting:* 5-acre small-town campus with easy access to Louisville. *System endowment:* $1.2 million. *Total enrollment:* 875. *Faculty:* 81 (30 full-time, 51 part-time); student–undergrad faculty ratio is 11:1.
Enrollment Profile: 875 students from 4 states and territories. 77% women, 23% men, 67% part-time, 93% state residents, 3% transferred in, 66% 25 or older, 0% Native American, 0% Hispanic, 1% black, 1% Asian or Pacific Islander. *Areas of study chosen:* 27% business management and administrative services, 22% health professions and related sciences, 20% liberal arts/general studies, 19% computer and information sciences, 12% engineering and applied sciences. *Most popular recent majors:* nursing, computer information systems, accounting.
First-Year Class: 282 total. Of the students who applied, 100% were accepted, 64% of whom enrolled. 5% from top 10% of their high school class, 25% from top quarter, 50% from top half.
Graduation Requirements: 60 credits; computer course (varies by major); internship (some majors).
Computers on Campus: Computers for student use in computer center. Staffed computer lab on campus.

EXPENSES

Expenses for 1997–98: State resident tuition: $1937 full-time, $64.55 per credit part-time. Nonresident tuition: $3561 full-time, $118.70 per credit part-time.
LD Services Contact: Ms. Margaret Seifert, Chair, General Education and Support Services, Ivy Tech State College–Southeast, Ivy Tech Drive, Madison, IN 47250, 812-265-2580. Fax: 812-265-4028.

IVY TECH STATE COLLEGE–SOUTHWEST

Evansville, Indiana

LEARNING DISABILITIES SERVICES INFORMATION

Special Needs Services/ACCESS began offering services in 1989. Currently the program serves 21 undergraduates with LD. Students diagnosed with ADD/ADHD are eligible for the same services available to students with LD.
Staff: 1 full-time, 1 part-time staff members, including director, associate director. Services provided by remediation specialist, tutors, counselors.
Special Fees: No special fees are charged for services to students with LD.
Applications and admissions: *Required:* high school transcript, personal interview, psychoeducational report completed within 3 years; *recommended:* high school IEP (Individualized Education Program). Students may begin taking classes in fall only. *Application deadline:* continuous.

PROGRAM AND SERVICE COMPONENTS

Academic advising: Provided by unit staff members, academic advisers. Most students with LD take 6 to 9 credit hours each term; 12 credit hours required to maintain full-time status; 3 credit hours required to be eligible for financial aid.
Basic skills remediation: Offered one-on-one, in small groups, and in class-size groups by LD teachers, regular teachers; computer-aided instruction also offered. Available in reading, math, spelling, written language, learning strategies, study skills, time management.
Special courses: College survival skills, reading, vocabulary development, communication skills, composition, learning strategies, word processing, time management, math, typing, study skills, career planning. Most offered for credit; some enter into overall grade point average.
Auxiliary aids: Taped textbooks, tape recorders, calculators, typewriters, word-processors with spell-check, personal computers, talking computers, optical character readers, speaking speller, carbonless notepaper, Arkenstone Open Book with DecTalk, Vocal Eyes.
Auxiliary services: Alternative test arrangements, notetakers, scribes.

GENERAL COLLEGE INFORMATION

State-supported, 2-year, coed. Part of Ivy Tech State College System. Awards associate degrees. Founded 1963. *Setting:* 15-acre suburban campus. *System endowment:* $1.2 million. *Total enrollment:* 2,765. *Faculty:* 235 (46 full-time, 189 part-time); student–undergrad faculty ratio is 12:1.
Enrollment Profile: 2,765 students from 4 states and territories. 58% women, 42% men, 75% part-time, 96% state residents, 10% transferred in, 63% 25 or older, 1% Native American, 0% Hispanic, 4% black, 0% Asian or Pacific Islander. *Areas of study chosen:* 38% engineering and applied sciences, 22% business management and administrative services, 15% health professions and related sciences, 15% liberal arts/general studies, 10% computer and information sciences. *Most popular recent majors:* nursing, secretarial studies/office management, medical assistant technologies.
First-Year Class: 710 total. Of the students who applied, 100% were accepted, 58% of whom enrolled.
Graduation Requirements: 60 credits; computer course (varies by major); internship (some majors).
Computers on Campus: 50 computers available on campus for general student use. Computers for student use in computer center, computer labs, learning resource center, library. Staffed computer lab on campus.

EXPENSES

Expenses for 1997–98: State resident tuition: $1937 full-time, $64.55 per credit part-time. Nonresident tuition: $3561 full-time, $118.70 per credit part-time.
LD Services Contact: Ms. Peg Ehlen, Special Needs Coordinator/General Education Instructor, Ivy Tech State College–Southwest, 3501 First Avenue, Evansville, IN 47710-3398, 812-429-1386. Fax: 812-429-1483.

IVY TECH STATE COLLEGE–WHITEWATER

Richmond, Indiana

LEARNING DISABILITIES SERVICES INFORMATION

Counseling Center began offering services in 1985. Currently the program serves 50 undergraduates with LD. Students diagnosed with ADD/ADHD are eligible for the same services available to students with LD.
Staff: 5 full-time, 4 part-time staff members, including assistant director, coordinator. Services provided by tutors, counselors.
Special Fees: No special fees are charged for services to students with LD.
Applications and admissions: Open admissions. Students may begin taking classes any term. *Application deadline:* 8/8 (fall term), 1/1 (spring term).

PROGRAM AND SERVICE COMPONENTS

Diagnostic testing: Reading, math, written language, study skills.
Academic advising: Provided by unit staff members, academic advisers. Students with LD may take up to as many credits as an individual can handle each term; 12 credits required to maintain full-time status.
Counseling services: Individual counseling, career counseling.
Basic skills remediation: Offered one-on-one and in small groups by regular teachers, teacher trainees. Available in reading, math, spelling, written language, study skills.
Subject-area tutoring: Offered one-on-one and in small groups by professional teachers, peer tutors. Available in most subjects.

Ivy Tech State College–Whitewater (continued)

Special courses: College survival skills, reading, communication skills, composition, math, typing, personal psychology, study skills. Some offered for credit.
Auxiliary aids: Taped textbooks, tape recorders, calculators, typewriters, word-processors with spell-check.
Auxiliary services: Alternative test arrangements, notetakers, advocacy.
Campus support group: A special student organization is available to students with LD.

GENERAL COLLEGE INFORMATION

State-supported, 2-year, coed. Part of Ivy Tech State College System. Awards associate degrees. Founded 1963. *Setting:* 23-acre small-town campus with easy access to Indianapolis. *System endowment:* $1.2 million. *Total enrollment:* 1,062. *Faculty:* 112 (21 full-time, 91 part-time); student–undergrad faculty ratio is 9:1.
Enrollment Profile: 1,062 students from 4 states and territories. 71% women, 29% men, 74% part-time, 97% state residents, 2% transferred in, 63% 25 or older, 1% Native American, 1% Hispanic, 4% black, 0% Asian or Pacific Islander. *Areas of study chosen:* 26% engineering and applied sciences, 23% business management and administrative services, 22% health professions and related sciences, 18% computer and information sciences, 11% liberal arts/general studies. *Most popular recent majors:* medical assistant technologies, nursing, computer information systems.
First-Year Class: 281 total. Of the students who applied, 100% were accepted, 51% of whom enrolled.
Graduation Requirements: 60 credits; computer course (varies by major); internship (some majors).
Computers on Campus: 80 computers available on campus for general student use. Computers for student use in computer center, classrooms. Staffed computer lab on campus.

EXPENSES

Expenses for 1997–98: State resident tuition: $1937 full-time, $64.55 per credit part-time. Nonresident tuition: $3561 full-time, $118.70 per credit part-time.
LD Services Contact: Ms. Gail D. Dimett, Counseling Center Secretary, Ivy Tech State College–Whitewater, Chester Boulevard, Richmond, IN 47374-1220, 765-966-2656 Ext. 305.

JACKSON COMMUNITY COLLEGE
Jackson, Michigan

LEARNING DISABILITIES SERVICES INFORMATION

Developmental Education currently serves 20 undergraduates with LD. Students diagnosed with ADD/ADHD are eligible for the same services available to students with LD.
Staff: 1 full-time staff member (coordinator). Services provided by tutors, notetakers, typists.
Special Fees: No special fees are charged for services to students with LD.
Applications and admissions: Students may begin taking classes in fall or winter. *Application deadline:* continuous.
Special policies: The college has written policies regarding grade forgiveness; substitutions and waivers of admissions, graduation, and degree requirements.

PROGRAM AND SERVICE COMPONENTS

Academic advising: Provided by counselors. Students with LD required to take 12 credit hours each term to maintain full-time status.
Counseling services: Individual counseling.
Auxiliary aids: Taped textbooks, tape recorders, calculators, typewriters, personal computers, talking computers.
Auxiliary services: Alternative test arrangements, notetakers, priority registration.

GENERAL COLLEGE INFORMATION

County-supported, 2-year, coed. Part of Michigan Department of Education. Awards associate degrees. Founded 1928. *Setting:* 580-acre suburban campus with easy access to Detroit. *Total enrollment:* 7,100. *Faculty:* 435 (110 full-time, 13% with terminal degrees, 325 part-time); student–undergrad faculty ratio is 18:1.
Enrollment Profile: 7,100 students from 4 states and territories. 62% women, 38% men, 73% part-time, 99% state residents, 8% transferred in, 0% international, 55% 25 or older, 1% Native American, 3% Hispanic, 5% black, 1% Asian or Pacific Islander.
First-Year Class: 1,100 total; 2,812 applied, 100% were accepted, 39% of whom enrolled.
Graduation Requirements: 63 credit hours; 3 credit hours of math; 4 credit hours of science; computer course.
Computers on Campus: 150 computers available on campus for general student use. Computer purchase/lease plans available. Computers for student use in computer center, computer labs, library, business, writing labs provide access to the Internet/World Wide Web. *Academic computing expenditure 1995–96:* $281,000.

EXPENSES

Expenses for 1997–98: Area resident tuition: $1535 full-time, $49.50 per credit hour part-time. State resident tuition: $2000 full-time, $64.50 per credit hour part-time. Nonresident tuition: $2248 full-time, $72.50 per credit hour part-time. Part-time mandatory fees per semester range from $10 to $30. Full-time mandatory fees: $78.
LD Services Contact: Ms. Sue Lewis, Special Needs Coordinator, Jackson Community College, 2111 Emmons Road, Jackson, MI 49201, 517-796-8553. Fax: 517-796-8631. Email: sue_lewis@jackson.cc.mi.us.

JAMES H. FAULKNER STATE COMMUNITY COLLEGE
Bay Minette, Alabama

LEARNING DISABILITIES SERVICES INFORMATION

Student Support Services began offering services in 1984. Students diagnosed with ADD/ADHD are not eligible for the same services available to students with LD.
Staff: 2 full-time, 1 part-time staff members, including director. Services provided by counselors.
Special Fees: No special fees are charged for services to students with LD.
Applications and admissions: *Required:* high school transcript; *recommended:* psychoeducational report completed within 5 years. Students may begin taking classes any term. *Application deadline:* continuous.
Special policies: The college has written policies regarding grade forgiveness.

PROGRAM AND SERVICE COMPONENTS

Diagnostic testing: Reading, math, written language.
Academic advising: Provided by academic advisers. Students with LD may take up to 21 quarter hours each term; most take 16 quarter hours; 12 quarter hours required to maintain full-time status and be eligible for financial aid.
Counseling services: Individual counseling, career counseling.
Basic skills remediation: Offered in class-size groups by regular teachers. Available in reading, math, spelling, spoken language, written language, study skills, time management.
Subject-area tutoring: Offered one-on-one by peer tutors. Available in most subjects.
Auxiliary aids: Word-processors with spell-check.
Auxiliary services: Alternative test arrangements, notetakers, readers.

GENERAL COLLEGE INFORMATION

State-supported, 2-year, coed. Awards associate degrees. Founded 1965. *Setting:* 105-acre small-town campus. *Educational spending 1995–96:* $1404 per undergrad. *Total enrollment:* 3,042. *Faculty:* 157 (52 full-time, 100% with terminal degrees, 105 part-time); student–undergrad faculty ratio is 22:1.
Enrollment Profile: 3,042 students from 12 states and territories, 4 other countries. 61% women, 39% men, 40% part-time, 98% state residents, 12% transferred in, 1% international, 39% 25 or older, 1% Native American, 1% Hispanic, 11% black, 1% Asian or Pacific Islander. *Retention:* 40% of 1995 full-time freshmen returned.
First-Year Class: 1,695 total; 2,000 applied, 90% were accepted, 94% of whom enrolled.
Graduation Requirements: 96 quarter hours; computer course; internship (some majors).
Computers on Campus: 175 computers available on campus for general student use. Computers for student use in computer center, com-

puter labs, learning resource center, library, business education departmental lab, counseling center. Staffed computer lab on campus provides training in use of computers, software. *Academic computing expenditure 1995–96:* $165,431.

EXPENSES

Estimated Expenses for 1997–98: State resident tuition: $1200 full-time, $25 per quarter hour part-time. Nonresident tuition: $2400 full-time, $50 per quarter hour part-time. College room and board: $2175.
LD Services Contact: Ms. Lena Dexter, Director of Federal Programs, James H. Faulkner State Community College, 1900 Highway 31 South, Bay Minette, AL 36507-2619, 334-580-2170. Fax: 334-580-2182.

JAMESTOWN COMMUNITY COLLEGE

Jamestown, New York

LEARNING DISABILITIES SERVICES INFORMATION

Disability Support Services Office began offering services in 1980. Currently the program serves 39 undergraduates with LD. Students diagnosed with ADD/ADHD are eligible for the same services available to students with LD.
Staff: 1 full-time, 1 part-time staff members, including director, coordinator. Services provided by remediation specialist, tutors, counselors.
Special Fees: No special fees are charged for services to students with LD.
Applications and admissions: *Required:* high school transcript, grade point average, class rank. Students may begin taking classes any term. *Application deadline:* 8/1.
Special policies: The college has written policies regarding substitutions and waivers of degree requirements.

PROGRAM AND SERVICE COMPONENTS

Special preparation or orientation: Optional orientation offered individually after application is submitted.
Diagnostic testing: Reading, math, written language, study skills, personality, learning strategies, vision.
Academic advising: Provided by unit staff members, academic advisers. Students with LD may take up to 19 semester hours each term; most take 9 to 12 semester hours; 12 semester hours required to maintain full-time status.
Subject-area tutoring: Offered one-on-one by professional teachers, peer tutors. Available in all subjects.
Auxiliary aids: Taped textbooks, tape recorders, calculators, typewriters, word-processors with spell-check, personal computers, optical character readers, reading pacers, Franklin spellers, Wordmasters.
Auxiliary services: Alternative test arrangements, notetakers, advocacy.
Campus support group: A special student organization is available to students with LD.

GENERAL COLLEGE INFORMATION

State and locally supported, 2-year, coed. Part of State University of New York System. Awards associate degrees. Founded 1950. *Setting:* 107-acre small-town campus. *Educational spending 1995–96:* $2938 per undergrad. *Total enrollment:* 3,343. *Faculty:* 263 (96 full-time, 16% with terminal degrees, 167 part-time); student–undergrad faculty ratio is 18:1.
Enrollment Profile: 3,343 students from 4 states and territories, 13 other countries. 60% women, 40% men, 45% part-time, 91% state residents, 6% transferred in, 1% international, 43% 25 or older, 1% Native American, 2% Hispanic, 2% black, 1% Asian or Pacific Islander. *Retention:* 58% of 1995 full-time freshmen returned. *Most popular recent majors:* business administration/commerce/management, criminal justice, nursing.
First-Year Class: 1,116 total; 1,138 applied, 99% were accepted, 98% of whom enrolled. 10% from top 10% of their high school class, 26% from top quarter, 52% from top half. 3 valedictorians.
Graduation Requirements: 60 semester hours; 1 math course; computer course for engineering majors; internship (some majors).
Computers on Campus: 200 computers available on campus for general student use. Computer purchase/lease plans available. A campus-wide network can be accessed from off-campus. Students can contact faculty members and/or advisers through e-mail. Computers for student use in computer center, computer labs, research center, learning resource center, classrooms, library, academic buildings provide access to the Internet/World Wide Web. Staffed computer lab on campus provides training in use of computers, software. *Academic computing expenditure 1995–96:* $292,000.

EXPENSES

Expenses for 1996–97: *Application fee:* $30. State resident tuition: $2600 full-time, $88 per semester hour part-time. Nonresident tuition: $5200 full-time, $154 per semester hour part-time. Part-time mandatory fees: $40.75 per semester. Full-time mandatory fees: $236.
LD Services Contact: Ms. Nancy Callahan, Coordinator, Services for Students with Disabilities, Jamestown Community College, 525 Falconer Street, Jamestown, NY 14701-1999, 716-665-5220 Ext. 459. Fax: 716-665-5518. Email: callahn@jccw22.cc.sunyjcc.edu.

JEFFERSON COLLEGE

Hillsboro, Missouri

LEARNING DISABILITIES SERVICES INFORMATION

Access-Ability Services began offering services in 1990. Currently the program serves 20 undergraduates with LD. Students diagnosed with ADD/ADHD are eligible for the same services available to students with LD.
Staff: 1 full-time staff member (coordinator). Services provided by tutors, counselors.
Special Fees: No special fees are charged for services to students with LD.
Applications and admissions: *Required:* high school transcript, psychoeducational report completed within the past several years; *recommended:* high school grade point average, class rank, courses completed, extracurricular activities, IEP (Individualized Education Program), untimed or extended time ACT, extended time SAT I, letters of recommendation. Students may begin taking classes any term. *Application deadline:* continuous.

PROGRAM AND SERVICE COMPONENTS

Special preparation or orientation: Required orientation held before registration, during registration, after classes begin.
Academic advising: Provided by unit staff members, academic advisers. Students with LD may take up to as many semester hours as an individual can handle each term; most take 6 to 12 semester hours; 12 semester hours required to maintain full-time status and be eligible for financial aid.
Counseling services: Individual counseling, career counseling, self-advocacy training.
Basic skills remediation: Offered one-on-one and in small groups by LD teachers, regular teachers; computer-aided instruction also offered. Available in reading, math, spelling, handwriting, spoken language, written language, learning strategies.
Subject-area tutoring: Offered one-on-one and in small groups by professional teachers, peer tutors. Available in all subjects.
Auxiliary aids: Taped textbooks, tape recorders, calculators, typewriters, word-processors with spell-check, personal computers, talking computers, optical character readers.
Auxiliary services: Alternative test arrangements, notetakers, advocacy.

GENERAL COLLEGE INFORMATION

State and locally supported, 2-year, coed. Part of Missouri Coordinating Board for Higher Education. Awards associate degrees. Founded 1963. *Setting:* 480-acre rural campus with easy access to St. Louis. *Educational spending 1995–96:* $1825 per undergrad. *Total enrollment:* 3,934. *Faculty:* 190 (90 full-time, 17% with terminal degrees, 100 part-time); student–undergrad faculty ratio is 19:1.
Enrollment Profile: 3,934 students from 2 states and territories, 3 other countries. 60% women, 40% men, 54% part-time, 98% state residents, 5% transferred in, 1% international, 50% 25 or older, 1% Native American, 1% Hispanic, 1% black, 1% Asian or Pacific Islander. *Retention:* 65% of 1995 full-time freshmen returned. *Areas of study chosen:* 26% liberal arts/general studies, 13% health professions and related sciences, 13% vocational and home economics, 10% business management and administrative services, 10% computer and information sciences, 7% social sciences, 5% biological and life sciences, 5% education, 3% performing arts, 2% engineering and applied sciences, 1% communications and journalism. *Most popular recent majors:* nursing, education, business administration/commerce/management.
First-Year Class: 1,713 total. Of the students who applied, 90% were accepted, 73% of whom enrolled. 11% from top 10% of their high school class, 35% from top quarter, 78% from top half.

Jefferson College (continued)

Graduation Requirements: 62 semester hours; 3 semester hours of college algebra for associate of arts degree; 6 semester hours of math/science for associate of applied science degree; computer course; internship (some majors).

Computers on Campus: 350 computers available on campus for general student use. A campus-wide network can be accessed. Students can contact faculty members and/or advisers through e-mail. Computers for student use in computer center, computer labs, library provide access to the Internet/World Wide Web. Staffed computer lab on campus provides training in use of software. *Academic computing expenditure 1995–96:* $297,633.

EXPENSES

Expenses for 1997–98: *Application fee:* $15. Area resident tuition: $1240 full-time, $40 per semester hour part-time. State resident tuition: $1612 full-time, $52 per semester hour part-time. Nonresident tuition: $1984 full-time, $64 per semester hour part-time. Part-time mandatory fees: $4 per semester hour. Full-time mandatory fees: $124.

LD Services Contact: Tracy Kopetzki, Assessment Counselor, Jefferson College, 1000 Viking Drive, Hillsboro, MO 63050, 314-942-3000 Ext. 169. Fax: 314-789-3954.

JEFFERSON COMMUNITY COLLEGE

Watertown, New York

LEARNING DISABILITIES SERVICES INFORMATION

Learning Skills Center began offering services in 1980. Currently the program serves 36 undergraduates with LD. Students diagnosed with ADD/ADHD are eligible for the same services available to students with LD, as well as time extensions and separate location for exams.

Staff: 3 full-time, 1 part-time staff members, including director. Services provided by remediation specialists, counselor.

Special Fees: No special fees are charged for services to students with LD.

Applications and admissions: *Required:* high school transcript, IEP (Individualized Education Program), psychoeducational report completed within 3 years. Students may begin taking classes any term. *Application deadline:* continuous.

PROGRAM AND SERVICE COMPONENTS

Diagnostic testing: Reading, math, written language.

Academic advising: Provided by academic advisers. Most students with LD take 9 to 12 credit hours each term; 12 credit hours required to maintain full-time status; 6 credit hours required to be eligible for financial aid.

Counseling services: Individual counseling, small-group counseling, career counseling.

Basic skills remediation: Offered one-on-one, in small groups, and in class-size groups by regular teachers; computer-aided instruction also offered. Available in reading, math, written language, study skills, time management.

Subject-area tutoring: Offered one-on-one and in small groups by professional teachers, peer tutors. Available in most subjects.

Special courses: College survival skills, reading, vocabulary development, composition, math, study skills. Some offered for credit; some enter into overall grade point average.

Auxiliary aids: Taped textbooks, tape recorders, calculators, typewriters, word-processors with spell-check, personal computers, talking computers, Visualtek machine.

Auxiliary services: Alternative test arrangements, notetakers, advocacy, readers.

Campus support group: A special student organization is available to students with LD.

GENERAL COLLEGE INFORMATION

State and locally supported, 2-year, coed. Part of State University of New York System. Awards associate degrees. Founded 1961. *Setting:* 90-acre small-town campus. *Total enrollment:* 3,500. *Faculty:* 193 (73 full-time, 11% with terminal degrees, 120 part-time); student–undergrad faculty ratio is 12:1.

Enrollment Profile: 3,500 students from 40 states and territories, 8 other countries. 56% women, 44% men, 36% part-time, 97% state residents, 13% transferred in, 1% international, 48% 25 or older, 1% Native American, 3% Hispanic, 8% black, 2% Asian or Pacific Islander. *Areas of study chosen:* 41% liberal arts/general studies, 26% business management and administrative services, 21% vocational and home economics, 5% health professions and related sciences, 4% computer and information sciences, 3% engineering and applied sciences. *Most popular recent major:* liberal arts/general studies.

First-Year Class: 1,140 total; 1,558 applied, 83% were accepted, 88% of whom enrolled.

Graduation Requirements: 62 credit hours; math/science requirements vary according to program; computer course for accounting, engineering, office technology majors; internship (some majors).

Computers on Campus: 125 computers available on campus for general student use. Computer purchase/lease plans available. A campus-wide network can be accessed. Students can contact faculty members and/or advisers through e-mail. Computers for student use in computer center, computer labs, learning resource center, classrooms, library provide access to the Internet/World Wide Web, on-campus e-mail addresses. Staffed computer lab on campus provides training in use of computers, software.

EXPENSES

Expenses for 1996–97: *Application fee:* $30. State resident tuition: $2136 full-time, $84 per credit hour part-time. Nonresident tuition: $4272 full-time, $168 per credit hour part-time. Part-time mandatory fees per semester range from $6 to $86. Full-time mandatory fees: $274.

LD Services Contact: Ms. Vickie Lewis, Learning Skills Specialist, Jefferson Community College, Outer Coffeen Street, Watertown, NY 13601, 315-786-2335.

JOHN A. LOGAN COLLEGE

Carterville, Illinois

LEARNING DISABILITIES SERVICES INFORMATION

Student Support Services began offering services in 1982. Currently the program serves 120 undergraduates with LD. Students diagnosed with ADD/ADHD are eligible for the same services available to students with LD, as well as support group.

Staff: 1 full-time staff member (director). Services provided by remediation specialists, tutors, counselor.

Special Fees: No special fees are charged for services to students with LD.

Applications and admissions: Open admissions. Students may begin taking classes any term. *Application deadline:* continuous.

Special policies: The college has written policies regarding grade forgiveness; substitutions and waivers of admissions, graduation, and degree requirements.

PROGRAM AND SERVICE COMPONENTS

Special preparation or orientation: Optional orientation offered during registration.

Diagnostic testing: Reading, math, handwriting, learning strategies.

Academic advising: Provided by unit staff members, academic advisers. Students with LD may take up to as many semester hours as an individual can handle each term; most take 12 semester hours; 12 semester hours required to maintain full-time status and be eligible for financial aid.

Counseling services: Individual counseling, small-group counseling, career counseling.

Subject-area tutoring: Offered one-on-one and in small groups by professional teachers, peer tutors. Available in most subjects.

Auxiliary aids: Taped textbooks, tape recorders, typewriters, word-processors with spell-check, assistive learning device.

Auxiliary services: Alternative test arrangements, notetakers.

Campus support group: A special student organization is available to students with LD.

GENERAL COLLEGE INFORMATION

State and locally supported, 2-year, coed. Part of Illinois Community College System. Awards associate degrees. Founded 1967. *Setting:* 160-acre rural campus. *Total enrollment:* 5,022. *Faculty:* 246 (93 full-time, 13% with terminal degrees, 153 part-time); student–undergrad faculty ratio is 25:1.

Enrollment Profile: 5,022 students: 56% women, 44% men, 42% part-time, 99% state residents, 20% transferred in, 0% international, 37% 25 or older, 0% Native American, 1% Hispanic, 7% black, 1% Asian or Pacific Islander. *Areas of study chosen:* 19% vocational and home economics, 9% business management and administrative services, 9% education, 6%

health professions and related sciences, 5% computer and information sciences, 4% liberal arts/general studies, 3% engineering and applied sciences, 3% psychology, 2% biological and life sciences, 1% communications and journalism, 1% English language/literature/letters, 1% fine arts, 1% mathematics, 1% physical sciences, 1% premed, 1% prevet, 1% social sciences.

First-Year Class: 1,238 total. 5% from top 10% of their high school class, 65% from top half.

Graduation Requirements: 62 semester hours; 5 semester hours of math; 12 semester hours of science; computer course for engineering majors.

Computers on Campus: 150 computers available on campus for general student use. Computers for student use in computer labs, library provide access to the Internet/World Wide Web. Staffed computer lab on campus provides training in use of computers, software.

EXPENSES

Estimated Expenses for 1997–98: Area resident tuition: $1023 full-time, $33 per semester hour part-time. State resident tuition: $3147 full-time, $101.52 per semester hour part-time. Nonresident tuition: $4231 full-time, $136.47 per semester hour part-time.

LD Services Contact: Ms. Jane Minton, Counselor, John A. Logan College, RR2 Box 145, Carterville, IL 62918, 618-549-7335 Ext. 289. Fax: 618-985-3899.

JOHN C. CALHOUN STATE COMMUNITY COLLEGE

Decatur, Alabama

LEARNING DISABILITIES SERVICES INFORMATION

Services for Special Student Populations currently serves 49 undergraduates with LD. Students diagnosed with ADD/ADHD are eligible for the same services available to students with LD.

Staff: 3 full-time staff members, including director. Services provided by counselor, secretary.

Special Fees: No special fees are charged for services to students with LD.

Applications and admissions: *Required:* high school transcript, high school diploma or GED. Students may begin taking classes any term. *Application deadline:* continuous.

Special policies: The college has written policies regarding grade forgiveness; substitutions and waivers of admissions, graduation, and degree requirements.

PROGRAM AND SERVICE COMPONENTS

Special preparation or orientation: Optional orientation offered on an individual basis.

Academic advising: Provided by unit staff members, academic advisers. Students with LD may take up to 20 quarter hours (more with permission of Dean of Instruction) each term; most take 10 quarter hours; 12 quarter hours required to maintain full-time status; 6 quarter hours (Pell Grant) required to be eligible for financial aid.

Counseling services: Individual counseling, career counseling, self-advocacy training.

Auxiliary aids: Taped textbooks, tape recorders, calculators, word-processors with spell-check, optical character readers, Dragon Dictate, electronic spellers, special notetaking paper.

Auxiliary services: Alternative test arrangements, notetakers, priority registration, liaison with faculty and others on an individual basis.

GENERAL COLLEGE INFORMATION

State-supported, 2-year, coed. Part of Alabama College System. Awards associate degrees. Founded 1965. *Setting:* 98-acre rural campus. *Research spending 1995–96:* $110,843. *Total enrollment:* 7,278. *Faculty:* 316 (118 full-time, 15% with terminal degrees, 198 part-time); student–undergrad faculty ratio is 20:1.

Enrollment Profile: 7,278 students: 53% women, 47% men, 74% part-time, 99% state residents, 23% transferred in, 1% international, 49% 25 or older, 2% Native American, 1% Hispanic, 20% black, 1% Asian or Pacific Islander. *Retention:* 39% of 1995 full-time freshmen returned. *Areas of study chosen:* 36% liberal arts/general studies, 14% interdisciplinary studies, 11% health professions and related sciences, 8% business management and administrative services, 6% computer and information sciences, 4% education, 2% fine arts, 2% mathematics, 1% agriculture, 1% biological and life sciences, 1% communications and journalism, 1% engineering and applied sciences, 1% English language/literature/letters, 1% performing arts, 1% prelaw, 1% premed, 1% prevet. *Most popular recent majors:* nursing, computer information systems, business administration/commerce/management.

First-Year Class: 1,370 total; 2,169 applied, 100% were accepted, 63% of whom enrolled.

Graduation Requirements: 96 quarter hours; computer course for agriculture, technology, science, education, health, medical, police science, real estate majors; internship (some majors).

Computers on Campus: 160 computers available on campus for general student use. Computers for student use in computer center, library, business, English buildings. *Academic computing expenditure 1995–96:* $374,002.

EXPENSES

Expenses for 1997–98: State resident tuition: $1200 full-time, $25 per quarter hour part-time. Nonresident tuition: $2400 full-time, $50 per quarter hour part-time. Part-time mandatory fees: $5 per quarter hour. Full-time mandatory fees: $237.

LD Services Contact: Ms. Virginia H. Smith, Counselor, John C. Calhoun State Community College, PO Box 2216, Decatur, AL 35609-2216, 205-306-2633. Fax: 205-350-2656. Email: vhs@calhoun.cc.al.us.

JOHN M. PATTERSON STATE TECHNICAL COLLEGE

Montgomery, Alabama

LEARNING DISABILITIES SERVICES INFORMATION

Project L.E.A.R.N.S. began offering services in 1990. Currently the program serves 91 undergraduates with LD. Students diagnosed with ADD/ADHD are eligible for the same services available to students with LD.

Staff: Includes director, coordinator. Services provided by remediation specialists, tutors, counselors.

Special Fees: No special fees are charged for services to students with LD.

Applications and admissions: *Required:* high school transcript, personal interview, ACT ASSET; *recommended:* psychoeducational report completed within 3 years. Students may begin taking classes any term. *Application deadline:* continuous.

Special policies: The college has written policies regarding grade forgiveness.

PROGRAM AND SERVICE COMPONENTS

Special preparation or orientation: Required orientation held before registration, during registration, after classes begin, during final year of high school (only for participants of the Program for Effective Transition (PET)).

Academic advising: Provided by academic advisers. Students with LD may take up to 16 semester hours each term; most take 15 semester hours; 12 semester hours required to maintain full-time status and be eligible for financial aid.

Counseling services: Individual counseling, career counseling.

Basic skills remediation: Offered one-on-one by regular teachers. Available in reading, math, written language.

Subject-area tutoring: Offered one-on-one and in small groups by professional teachers, peer tutors. Available in all subjects.

Special courses: College survival skills, reading, communication skills, math. None offered for credit.

Auxiliary aids: Taped textbooks, tape recorders.

Auxiliary services: Alternative test arrangements, notetakers, advocacy.

Campus support group: A special student organization is available to students with LD.

GENERAL COLLEGE INFORMATION

State-supported, 2-year, coed. Part of Alabama College System. Awards associate degrees. Founded 1962. *Setting:* 40-acre urban campus. *Total enrollment:* 1,144. *Faculty:* 63 (42 full-time, 21 part-time); student–undergrad faculty ratio is 20:1.

Enrollment Profile: 1,144 students from 3 states and territories, 1 other country. 42% women, 58% men, 48% part-time, 98% state residents, 27% transferred in, 1% international, 46% 25 or older, 1% Native American, 1% Hispanic, 51% black, 1% Asian or Pacific Islander. *Most popular recent majors:* cosmetology, computer information systems.

First-Year Class: 448 total; 1,041 applied, 43% of whom enrolled.

John M. Patterson State Technical College (continued)

Graduation Requirements: 114 credit hours; math/science requirements vary according to program; computer course for all associate degree programs.

Computers on Campus: 116 computers available on campus for general student use. Computers for student use in computer center, computer labs, classrooms, reading lab. Staffed computer lab on campus provides training in use of computers, software. *Academic computing expenditure 1995–96:* $299,173.

EXPENSES

Expenses for 1997–98: State resident tuition: $1425 full-time, $25 per credit hour part-time. Nonresident tuition: $2850 full-time, $50 per credit hour part-time. Part-time mandatory fees per quarter range from $3.50 to $37. Full-time mandatory fees: $159.

LD Services Contact: Ms. Sherryl Byrd, Coordinator for Student Services, John M. Patterson State Technical College, 3920 Troy Highway, Montgomery, AL 36116-2699, 334-288-1080.

JOHNSON TECHNICAL INSTITUTE

Scranton, Pennsylvania

LEARNING DISABILITIES SERVICES INFORMATION

Student Support Services currently serves 15 undergraduates with LD. Students diagnosed with ADD/ADHD are eligible for the same services available to students with LD.

Staff: 3 full-time staff members, including director, assistant director, coordinator. Services provided by remediation specialists, counselors, diagnostic specialist.

Special Fees: No special fees are charged for services to students with LD.

Applications and admissions: *Required:* high school transcript, grade point average, IEP (Individualized Education Program), personal interview, letters of recommendation, psychoeducational report completed within 4 years; *recommended:* high school class rank, extracurricular activities, untimed or extended time SAT I. Students may begin taking classes in summer only. *Application deadline:* continuous.

PROGRAM AND SERVICE COMPONENTS

Special preparation or orientation: Required summer program offered prior to entering college. Required orientation held before registration.

Academic advising: Provided by unit staff members. Students with LD may take up to 21 credit hours each term; most take 18 to 21 credit hours; 12 credit hours required to maintain full-time status and be eligible for financial aid.

Counseling services: Individual counseling, career counseling.

Basic skills remediation: Offered one-on-one and in small groups by regular teachers; computer-aided instruction also offered. Available in reading, math, spelling, spoken language, written language, learning strategies, study skills, time management, social skills, computer skills.

Subject-area tutoring: Offered one-on-one and in small groups by professional teachers, peer tutors. Available in all subjects.

Auxiliary aids: Tape recorders, calculators, typewriters, personal computers, Franklin Speller, Hooked on Phonics.

Auxiliary services: Alternative test arrangements, notetakers.

GENERAL COLLEGE INFORMATION

Independent, 2-year, primarily men. Awards associate degrees. Founded 1912. *Setting:* 65-acre urban campus. *Total enrollment:* 348. *Faculty:* 24 (21 full-time, 3 part-time); student–undergrad faculty ratio is 19:1.

Enrollment Profile: 348 students from 6 states and territories. 7% women, 93% men, 3% part-time, 92% state residents, 9% live on campus, 9% transferred in, 0% international, 11% 25 or older, 0% Native American, 1% Hispanic, 1% black, 1% Asian or Pacific Islander. *Retention:* 80% of 1995 full-time freshmen returned. *Most popular recent majors:* carpentry, biomedical technologies, electrical and electronics technologies.

First-Year Class: 191 total; 386 applied, 54% were accepted, 91% of whom enrolled. 6% from top 10% of their high school class, 12% from top quarter, 45% from top half.

Graduation Requirements: 76 credits; 1 algebra course; computer course; internship (some majors).

Computers on Campus: 70 computers available on campus for general student use. A computer is recommended for some students. Computers for student use in computer labs, learning resource center, library, student center, counseling center provide access to the Internet/World Wide Web. Staffed computer lab on campus provides training in use of computers, software.

EXPENSES

Expenses for 1997–98: *Application fee:* $25. Tuition: $6795 (minimum) full-time. Part-time mandatory fees: $115 per year. Full-time tuition ranges up to $7213 according to program. Part-time tuition per credit ranges from $100 to $210 according to program. Full-time mandatory fees: $115. College room only: $2800.

LD Services Contact: Ms. Carolyn L. Brozzetti, Admissions Director, Johnson Technical Institute, 3427 North Main Avenue, Scranton, PA 18508, 717-342-6404. Fax: 717-348-2181.

JOHN WOOD COMMUNITY COLLEGE

Quincy, Illinois

LEARNING DISABILITIES SERVICES INFORMATION

Support Services Center began offering services in 1988. Currently the program serves 50 undergraduates with LD. Students diagnosed with ADD/ADHD are eligible for the same services available to students with LD.

Staff: 11 full-time, 6 part-time staff members, including director, coordinators. Services provided by remediation specialists, tutors, counselors, diagnostic specialist, clerks.

Special Fees: No special fees are charged for services to students with LD.

Applications and admissions: *Required:* high school transcript, psychoeducational report completed within 3 years; *recommended:* high school grade point average, courses completed, IEP (Individualized Education Program), extended time ACT, personal interview, report from high school counselors. Students may begin taking classes any term. *Application deadline:* continuous.

Special policies: The college has written policies regarding substitutions and waivers of graduation and degree requirements.

PROGRAM AND SERVICE COMPONENTS

Special preparation or orientation: Optional orientation offered before registration and during registration.

Diagnostic testing: Reading, math, written language, study skills, personality, social skills, learning strategies, learning styles.

Academic advising: Provided by unit staff members, academic advisers. Most students with LD take 6 to 9 credit hours each term; 12 credit hours (fewer with special permission) required to maintain full-time status; 3 credit hours required to be eligible for financial aid.

Counseling services: Individual counseling, career counseling, self-advocacy training.

Basic skills remediation: Offered one-on-one and in small groups by regular teachers, peer tutors, learning specialists; computer-aided instruction also offered. Available in reading, math, spelling, spoken language, written language, learning strategies, perceptual skills, study skills, time management, social skills.

Subject-area tutoring: Offered one-on-one and in small groups by peer tutors, math and English specialists. Available in all subjects.

Auxiliary aids: Taped textbooks, tape recorders, calculators, typewriters, word-processors with spell-check, personal computers.

Auxiliary services: Alternative test arrangements, notetakers, priority registration, advocacy, readers, interpreters, TDD/(217)224-4309.

GENERAL COLLEGE INFORMATION

District-supported, 2-year, coed. Part of Illinois Community College System. Awards associate degrees. Founded 1974. *Setting:* small-town campus. *Total enrollment:* 2,300. *Faculty:* 156 (31 full-time, 125 part-time).

Enrollment Profile: 2,300 students from 3 states and territories. 65% women, 35% men, 62% part-time, 98% state residents, 3% transferred in, 1% international, 59% 25 or older, 1% Native American, 1% Hispanic, 2% black, 1% Asian or Pacific Islander.

First-Year Class: 950 total; 1,100 applied, 100% were accepted, 86% of whom enrolled. 5% from top 10% of their high school class, 8% from top quarter, 65% from top half.

Graduation Requirements: 64 credit hours; 1 math course; computer course.

Computers on Campus: 125 computers available on campus for general student use. Computer purchase/lease plans available. Staffed computer lab on campus provides training in use of computers, software.

EXPENSES AND FINANCIAL AID

Expenses for 1997–98: Area resident tuition: $1664 full-time, $52 per credit hour part-time. State resident tuition: $5037 full-time, $157.40 per credit hour part-time. Nonresident tuition: $7524 full-time, $235.11 per credit hour part-time.
Financial aid specifically for students with LD: Scholarship: Student Services Scholarship.
LD Services Contact: Ms. Rose-Marie Akers, Learning Specialist, John Wood Community College, 150 South 48th Street, Quincy, IL 62301-9147, 217-224-6500 Ext. 4352. Fax: 217-224-4208. Email: akers@jwcc.edu.

KANKAKEE COMMUNITY COLLEGE

Kankakee, Illinois

LEARNING DISABILITIES SERVICES INFORMATION

Special Populations Services currently serves 150 undergraduates with LD. Students diagnosed with ADD/ADHD are eligible for the same services available to students with LD.
Staff: 1 full-time, 6 part-time staff members, including director. Services provided by remediation specialists, tutors.
Special Fees: No special fees are charged for services to students with LD.
Applications and admissions: *Required:* high school transcript, IEP (Individualized Education Program), psychoeducational report completed within 2 years. Students may begin taking classes any term. *Application deadline:* continuous.
Special policies: The college has written policies regarding grade forgiveness.

PROGRAM AND SERVICE COMPONENTS

Special preparation or orientation: Optional orientation offered before registration.
Academic advising: Provided by academic advisers. Most students with LD take 6 credit hours each term; 12 credit hours required to maintain full-time status; 6 credit hours required to be eligible for financial aid.
Basic skills remediation: Offered in class-size groups by LD teachers, regular teachers. Available in reading, math, spelling, written language.
Subject-area tutoring: Offered one-on-one by professional tutors. Available in most subjects.
Auxiliary aids: Tape recorders, calculators, typewriters, word-processors with spell-check, adapted computers, Reading Edge, closed-captioned television, TTY (815) 935-9600.
Auxiliary services: Alternative test arrangements, notetakers, advocacy.

GENERAL COLLEGE INFORMATION

State and locally supported, 2-year, coed. Part of Illinois Community College Board. Awards associate degrees. Founded 1966. *Setting:* 178-acre small-town campus with easy access to Chicago. *Total enrollment:* 3,651. *Faculty:* 143 (52 full-time, 91 part-time); student–undergrad faculty ratio is 20:1.
Enrollment Profile: 3,651 students: 60% women, 40% men, 67% part-time, 97% state residents, 16% transferred in, 0% international, 0% Native American, 2% Hispanic, 11% black, 1% Asian or Pacific Islander. *Most popular recent majors:* nursing, liberal arts/general studies.
First-Year Class: Of the students who applied, 100% were accepted.
Graduation Requirements: 64 semester hours; computer course (varies by major).
Computers on Campus: 120 computers available on campus for general student use. Computers for student use in computer center, computer labs, learning resource center, library provide access to the Internet/World Wide Web, on- and off-campus e-mail addresses. Staffed computer lab on campus provides training in use of computers, software.

EXPENSES

Expenses for 1997–98: Area resident tuition: $1136 full-time, $35.50 per semester hour part-time. State resident tuition: $2398 full-time, $74.94 per semester hour part-time. Nonresident tuition: $6474 full-time, $202.31 per semester hour part-time. Part-time mandatory fees: $2.50 per semester hour. Full-time mandatory fees: $80.
LD Services Contact: Dr. Kevin Kennedy, Director of Special Populations and Institutional Programs, Kankakee Community College, Room L337, Kankakee, IL 60970, 815-933-0332.

KELLOGG COMMUNITY COLLEGE

Battle Creek, Michigan

LEARNING DISABILITIES SERVICES INFORMATION

Counseling Center began offering services in 1989. Currently the program serves 35 undergraduates with LD. Students diagnosed with ADD/ADHD are eligible for the same services available to students with LD.
Staff: 8 full-time staff members, including director. Services provided by remediation specialists, tutors, counselors.
Special Fees: No special fees are charged for services to students with LD.
Applications and admissions: *Required:* psychoeducational report completed within 3 years. Students may begin taking classes any term. *Application deadline:* continuous.

PROGRAM AND SERVICE COMPONENTS

Special preparation or orientation: Optional orientation offered before registration and during registration.
Diagnostic testing: Reading, math, spelling, handwriting, written language, study skills, learning strategies.
Academic advising: Provided by unit staff members. Students with LD may take up to as many credit hours as an individual can handle each term; most take 12 credit hours; 6 credit hours required to maintain full-time status and be eligible for financial aid.
Counseling services: Individual counseling, career counseling.
Basic skills remediation: Offered one-on-one and in small groups by paraprofessionals. Available in reading, math, spelling, handwriting, written language, learning strategies, study skills.
Subject-area tutoring: Offered one-on-one and in small groups by peer tutors. Available in most subjects.
Auxiliary aids: Taped textbooks, tape recorders, calculators, typewriters, word-processors with spell-check, optical character readers.
Auxiliary services: Alternative test arrangements, notetakers, advocacy.

GENERAL COLLEGE INFORMATION

State and locally supported, 2-year, coed. Part of Michigan Department of Education. Awards associate degrees. Founded 1956. *Setting:* 120-acre urban campus. *Endowment:* $1.2 million. *Research spending 1995–96:* $127,338. *Educational spending 1995–96:* $2831 per undergrad. *Total enrollment:* 7,920. *Faculty:* 325 (89 full-time, 100% with terminal degrees, 236 part-time); student–undergrad faculty ratio is 30:1.
Enrollment Profile: 7,920 students from 4 states and territories, 10 other countries. 57% women, 43% men, 76% part-time, 98% state residents, 5% transferred in, 1% international, 46% 25 or older, 1% Native American, 2% Hispanic, 9% black, 1% Asian or Pacific Islander. *Retention:* 62% of 1995 full-time freshmen returned. *Areas of study chosen:* 18% health professions and related sciences, 17% liberal arts/general studies, 15% engineering and applied sciences, 13% business management and administrative services, 9% social sciences, 6% education, 5% computer and information sciences, 2% communications and journalism, 1% premed. *Most popular recent majors:* business administration/commerce/management, nursing, law enforcement/police sciences.
First-Year Class: 755 total; 1,690 applied, 100% were accepted.
Graduation Requirements: 62 credit hours; computer course for accounting, business management, chemical technology, human services, legal assistant, communications technology, secretarial studies majors.
Computers on Campus: 550 computers available on campus for general student use. Computer purchase/lease plans available. Computers for student use in computer center, learning resource center, classrooms, library provide access to the Internet/World Wide Web. Staffed computer lab on campus provides training in use of computers, software. *Academic computing expenditure 1995–96:* $106,687.

EXPENSES

Expenses for 1997–98: Area resident tuition: $1364 full-time, $44 per credit hour part-time. State resident tuition: $2288 full-time, $73.80 per credit hour part-time. Nonresident tuition: $3594 full-time, $115.95 per credit hour part-time. Part-time mandatory fees: $4.50 per credit hour. Full-time mandatory fees: $140.
LD Services Contact: Mr. Ken Behmer, Dean for Student Development, Kellogg Community College, 450 North Avenue, Battle Creek, MI 49017-3306, 616-965-4124 Ext. 2603. Fax: 616-965-4133.

KENNEBEC VALLEY TECHNICAL COLLEGE

Fairfield, Maine

LEARNING DISABILITIES SERVICES INFORMATION

Student Services began offering services in 1988. Currently the program serves 15 undergraduates with LD. Students diagnosed with ADD/ADHD are eligible for the same services available to students with LD.

Staff: 4 full-time staff members, including director, coordinator. Services provided by remediation specialists, tutors, counselors, student counselor.

Special Fees: No special fees are charged for services to students with LD.

Applications and admissions: *Required:* high school transcript. Students may begin taking classes any term. *Application deadline:* continuous.

PROGRAM AND SERVICE COMPONENTS

Special preparation or orientation: Optional orientation offered before registration and after classes begin.

Academic advising: Provided by unit staff members, academic advisers. Students with LD may take up to 15 credit hours each term; most take 9 to 12 credit hours; 12 credit hours required to maintain full-time status; 1 to 3 credit hours required to be eligible for financial aid.

Counseling services: Individual counseling, small-group counseling, career counseling, self-advocacy training.

Basic skills remediation: Offered one-on-one, in small groups, and in class-size groups by regular teachers; computer-aided instruction also offered. Available in reading, math, spelling, written language, learning strategies, study skills, time management, social skills.

Subject-area tutoring: Offered one-on-one and in small groups by professional teachers, peer tutors, learning specialists (in professional writing, math, and science). Available in all subjects.

Special courses: College survival skills, learning strategies, time management, study skills, career planning, college writing, technical writing. None offered for credit.

Auxiliary aids: Taped textbooks, tape recorders, calculators, typewriters, word-processors with spell-check.

Auxiliary services: Alternative test arrangements, notetakers, advocacy.

GENERAL COLLEGE INFORMATION

State-supported, 2-year, coed. Part of Maine Technical College System. Awards associate degrees. Founded 1970. *Setting:* 58-acre small-town campus. *Total enrollment:* 701. *Faculty:* 34 full-time.

Enrollment Profile: 701 students from 3 states and territories, 2 other countries. 65% women, 35% men, 82% part-time, 95% state residents, 40% transferred in, 1% international, 40% 25 or older, 1% Native American, 0% Hispanic, 0% black, 1% Asian or Pacific Islander. *Most popular recent majors:* nursing, physical therapy, business administration/commerce/management.

First-Year Class: 761 applied, 49% were accepted, 90% of whom enrolled.

Graduation Requirements: 60 credit hours; math/science requirements vary according to program; computer course.

Computers on Campus: 57 computers available on campus for general student use. Computers for student use in computer labs, learning center.

EXPENSES

Expenses for 1997–98: *Application fee:* $15. State resident tuition: $1980 full-time, $66 per credit hour part-time. Nonresident tuition: $4290 full-time, $143 per credit hour part-time. Part-time mandatory fees: $9 per semester (minimum). Tuition for nonresidents who are eligible for the New England Regional Student Program: $2940 full-time, $98 per credit hour part-time. Full-time mandatory fees: $325.

LD Services Contact: Ms. Karen Normandin, Counselor for Students with Disabilities, Kennebec Valley Technical College, 92 Western Avenue, Fairfield, ME 04937, 207-453-5019. Fax: 207-453-5194.

KENT STATE UNIVERSITY, STARK CAMPUS

Canton, Ohio

LEARNING DISABILITIES SERVICES INFORMATION

Office of Student Disabilities Services began offering services in 1990. Currently the program serves 55 undergraduates with LD. Students diagnosed with ADD/ADHD are eligible for the same services available to students with LD.

Staff: Includes director, coordinator, specialist. Services provided by tutors.

Special Fees: No special fees are charged for services to students with LD.

Applications and admissions: *Required:* high school transcript, grade point average, courses completed, IEP (Individualized Education Program), extended time ACT, personal interview, psychoeducational report. Students may begin taking classes in fall, winter, or spring. *Application deadline:* continuous.

Special policies: The college has written policies regarding grade forgiveness.

PROGRAM AND SERVICE COMPONENTS

Academic advising: Provided by unit staff members, academic advisers. Students with LD may take up to 18 semester hours each term; 12 semester hours required to maintain full-time status; source of aid determines number of semester hours required to be eligible for financial aid.

Counseling services: Individual counseling, career counseling, self-advocacy training.

Basic skills remediation: Offered in class-size groups by regular teachers. Available in reading, math, written language, learning strategies, study skills.

Subject-area tutoring: Offered one-on-one and in small groups by professional teachers, peer tutors. Available in most subjects.

Auxiliary aids: Taped textbooks, word-processors with spell-check, personal computers.

Auxiliary services: Alternative test arrangements, notetakers, priority registration, advocacy, scribes.

GENERAL COLLEGE INFORMATION

State-supported, primarily 2-year, coed. Part of Kent State University System. Awards associate, bachelor's degrees (also offers some upper-level and graduate courses). Founded 1967. *Setting:* 200-acre suburban campus with easy access to Cleveland. *Total enrollment:* 2,607. *Faculty:*; student–undergrad faculty ratio is 26:1.

Enrollment Profile: 2,573 students from 2 states and territories. 60% women, 40% men, 46% part-time, 98% state residents, 10% transferred in, 0% international, 33% 25 or older, 1% Native American, 1% Hispanic, 7% black, 1% Asian or Pacific Islander. *Areas of study chosen:* 100% liberal arts/general studies.

First-Year Class: 904 total; 1,160 applied, 100% were accepted, 78% of whom enrolled. 6% from top 10% of their high school class, 22% from top quarter, 60% from top half.

Graduation Requirements: 65 semester hours for associate, 129 semester hours for bachelor's; 1 math/logic course; computer course for business administration majors; internship (some majors).

Computers on Campus: 76 computers available on campus for general student use. A computer is recommended for all student use. A campus-wide network can be accessed from off-campus. Students can contact faculty members and/or advisers through e-mail. Computers for student use in computer center, learning resource center, library, English lab, Writing Skills Center provide access to the Internet/World Wide Web, on- and off-campus e-mail addresses. Staffed computer lab on campus provides training in use of computers, software.

EXPENSES

Expenses for 1997–98: *Application fee:* $25. State resident tuition: $3056 full-time. Nonresident tuition: $7516 full-time. Part-time tuition (1 to 10 semester hours): $139 per semester hour for state residents, $341.75 per semester hour for nonresidents. Tuition guaranteed not to increase for student's term of enrollment.

LD Services Contact: Kelly Oster, Disability Specialist, Kent State University, Stark Campus, 6000 Frank Avenue, NW, Canton, OH 44720, 330-499-9600. Fax: 330-499-0301. Email: koster@stark.kent.edu.

KILGORE COLLEGE

Kilgore, Texas

LEARNING DISABILITIES SERVICES INFORMATION

Stepup To Education Prosperity-Special Learning Services (STEP-SLS) began offering services in 1991. Currently the program serves 120 undergraduates with LD. Students diagnosed with ADD/ADHD are eligible for the same services available to students with LD, as well as secluded testing environment.

Staff: 1 full-time staff member (counselor). Services provided by tutors, counselors.

Special Fees: No special fees are charged for services to students with LD.

Applications and admissions: *Required:* high school transcript, personal interview, psychoeducational report. Students may begin taking classes any term. *Application deadline:* continuous.

Special policies: The college has written policies regarding grade forgiveness.

PROGRAM AND SERVICE COMPONENTS

Special preparation or orientation: Optional summer program offered prior to entering college.

Academic advising: Provided by unit staff members, academic advisers. Students with LD may take up to 17 semester hours each term; most take 12 semester hours; 12 semester hours required to maintain full-time status; 3 semester hours required to be eligible for financial aid.

Counseling services: Individual counseling, career counseling.

Subject-area tutoring: Offered in small groups by peer tutors. Available in most subjects.

Auxiliary aids: Taped textbooks, tape recorders, optical character readers.

Auxiliary services: Alternative test arrangements, notetakers.

GENERAL COLLEGE INFORMATION

State and locally supported, 2-year, coed. Part of Texas Higher Education Coordinating Board. Awards associate degrees. Founded 1935. *Setting:* 35-acre small-town campus with easy access to Dallas. *Endowment:* $3.6 million. *Research spending 1995–96:* $46,652. *Educational spending 1995–96:* $2010 per undergrad. *Total enrollment:* 4,388. *Faculty:* 260 (163 full-time, 10% with terminal degrees, 97 part-time); student–undergrad faculty ratio is 19:1.

Enrollment Profile: 4,388 students from 16 states and territories, 12 other countries. 59% women, 41% men, 48% part-time, 96% state residents, 11% transferred in, 1% international, 36% 25 or older, 1% Native American, 3% Hispanic, 13% black, 1% Asian or Pacific Islander. *Retention:* 53% of 1995 full-time freshmen returned. *Areas of study chosen:* 18% liberal arts/general studies, 16% business management and administrative services, 15% health professions and related sciences, 14% engineering and applied sciences, 5% education, 4% computer and information sciences, 3% fine arts, 3% performing arts, 2% psychology, 2% social sciences, 1% agriculture, 1% architecture, 1% biological and life sciences, 1% communications and journalism, 1% English language/literature/letters, 1% interdisciplinary studies, 1% prelaw, 1% premed, 1% vocational and home economics. *Most popular recent majors:* nursing, liberal arts/general studies, business administration/commerce/management.

First-Year Class: 1,316 total; 1,316 applied, 100% were accepted, 100% of whom enrolled. 6% from top 10% of their high school class, 24% from top quarter, 59% from top half. 6 valedictorians.

Graduation Requirements: 64 credits; computer course (varies by major).

Computers on Campus: 250 computers available on campus for general student use. Computers for student use in computer labs, learning resource center, classrooms, library provide access to the Internet/World Wide Web, on- and off-campus e-mail addresses. Staffed computer lab on campus provides training in use of computers, software. *Academic computing expenditure 1995–96:* $113,816.

EXPENSES

Expenses for 1997–98: Area resident tuition: $832 full-time, $26 per semester hour part-time. State resident tuition: $1472 full-time, $46 per semester hour part-time. Nonresident tuition: $1984 full-time. Nonresident part-time tuition per semester ranges from $232 to $682. College room and board: $2600. College room only: $1100.

LD Services Contact: Ms. Deborah P. Kelley, Special Populations Counselor, Kilgore College, 1100 Broadway, Kilgore, TX 75662, 903-983-8682. Fax: 903-983-8660. Email: kelleyd@kcvm.kilgore.cc.tx.us.

KIRTLAND COMMUNITY COLLEGE

Roscommon, Michigan

LEARNING DISABILITIES SERVICES INFORMATION

Student Support Services began offering services in 1980. Currently the program serves 20 undergraduates with LD. Students diagnosed with ADD/ADHD are eligible for the same services available to students with LD.

Staff: Includes director, coordinator, secretary. Services provided by tutors, counselors, lead tutor.

Special Fees: No special fees are charged for services to students with LD.

Applications and admissions: *Required:* high school transcript, psychoeducational report completed within 3 years; *recommended:* high school IEP (Individualized Education Program), personal interview, ASSET placement test, registration with Recordings for the Blind (if disability is in reading). Students may begin taking classes any term. *Application deadline:* continuous.

Special policies: The college has written policies regarding grade forgiveness.

PROGRAM AND SERVICE COMPONENTS

Special preparation or orientation: Optional orientation offered on an individual basis.

Academic advising: Provided by unit staff members, academic advisers. Students with LD may take up to 18 credit hours (more with Dean's permission) each term; most take 6 to 9 credit hours (first semester), 9 to 12 credit hours (thereafter); 12 credit hours required to maintain full-time status; 3 credit hours required to be eligible for financial aid.

Counseling services: Individual counseling, career counseling, self-advocacy training.

Basic skills remediation: Offered in small groups and in class-size groups by regular teachers, tutors. Available in reading, math, spelling, written language, learning strategies, study skills, time management.

Subject-area tutoring: Offered one-on-one and in small groups by peer tutors, non-students with degrees. Available in most subjects.

Auxiliary aids: Taped textbooks, tape recorders, typewriters, word-processors with spell-check, personal computers, optical character readers.

Auxiliary services: Alternative test arrangements, notetakers, advocacy, scribes.

Campus support group: A special student organization is available to students with LD.

GENERAL COLLEGE INFORMATION

District-supported, 2-year, coed. Part of Michigan Department of Education. Awards associate degrees. Founded 1966. *Setting:* 180-acre rural campus. *Educational spending 1995–96:* $1925 per undergrad. *Total enrollment:* 1,352. *Faculty:* 95 (39 full-time, 56 part-time); student–undergrad faculty ratio is 19:1.

Enrollment Profile: 1,352 students: 66% women, 34% men, 65% part-time, 100% state residents, 20% transferred in, 45% 25 or older, 2% Native American, 1% Hispanic, 1% black, 1% Asian or Pacific Islander. *Areas of study chosen:* 25% liberal arts/general studies, 21% health professions and related sciences, 11% business management and administrative services, 9% engineering and applied sciences. *Most popular recent majors:* nursing, liberal arts/general studies, science.

First-Year Class: 296 total; 434 applied, 100% were accepted, 68% of whom enrolled.

Graduation Requirements: 60 credit hours; computer course for accounting, business management, real estate majors; internship (some majors).

Computers on Campus: 125 computers available on campus for general student use. Computers for student use in computer center, library.

EXPENSES

Expenses for 1997–98: Area resident tuition: $1460 full-time, $48.65 per credit hour part-time. State resident tuition: $2001 full-time, $66.70 per credit hour part-time. Nonresident tuition: $2550 full-time, $85 per credit hour part-time. Part-time mandatory fees: $4 per credit hour. Full-time mandatory fees: $120.

Kirtland Community College (continued)

LD Services Contact: Ms. Carole Chilton, Director of Special Populations, Kirtland Community College, 10775 North Saint Helen Road, Roscommon, MI 48653, 517-275-5121 Ext. 218. Fax: 517-275-8210.

KISHWAUKEE COLLEGE

Malta, Illinois

LEARNING DISABILITIES SERVICES INFORMATION

Special Needs Services began offering services in 1988. Currently the program serves 50 undergraduates with LD. Students diagnosed with ADD/ADHD are eligible for the same services available to students with LD.
Staff: 1 part-time staff member (coordinator). Services provided by tutors, counselors.
Special Fees: No special fees are charged for services to students with LD.
Applications and admissions: *Required:* high school transcript, IEP (Individualized Education Program); *recommended:* psychoeducational report. Students may begin taking classes any term. *Application deadline:* continuous.

PROGRAM AND SERVICE COMPONENTS

Academic advising: Provided by unit staff members. Most students with LD take 12 semester hours each term; 12 semester hours required to maintain full-time status; 6 semester hours required to be eligible for financial aid.
Counseling services: Individual counseling, career counseling, self-advocacy training.
Basic skills remediation: Offered in small groups by regular teachers. Available in reading, math, spelling, written language, learning strategies, study skills, time management.
Subject-area tutoring: Offered one-on-one and in small groups by professional teachers, peer tutors. Available in most subjects.
Auxiliary aids: Tape recorders, calculators, word-processors with spell-check, personal computers, talking computers.
Auxiliary services: Alternative test arrangements, notetakers, priority registration, advocacy.

GENERAL COLLEGE INFORMATION

State and locally supported, 2-year, coed. Part of Illinois Community College System. Awards associate degrees. Founded 1967. *Setting:* 120-acre rural campus with easy access to Chicago. *Total enrollment:* 4,500. *Faculty:* 198 (67 full-time, 10% with terminal degrees, 131 part-time); student–undergrad faculty ratio is 17:1.
Enrollment Profile: 4,500 students from 5 states and territories, 4 other countries. 58% women, 42% men, 52% part-time, 98% state residents, 22% transferred in, 1% international, 51% 25 or older, 1% Native American, 9% Hispanic, 7% black, 3% Asian or Pacific Islander. *Retention:* 67% of 1995 full-time freshmen returned. *Areas of study chosen:* 24% liberal arts/general studies, 11% health professions and related sciences, 5% education, 4% biological and life sciences, 3% business management and administrative services, 2% architecture, 2% communications and journalism, 2% engineering and applied sciences, 2% psychology, 1% agriculture, 1% computer and information sciences, 1% English language/literature/letters, 1% fine arts, 1% mathematics, 1% performing arts, 1% physical sciences, 1% prelaw, 1% premed, 1% prevet, 1% social sciences.
First-Year Class: 1,006 total. Of the students who applied, 100% were accepted.
Graduation Requirements: 64 semester hours; 3 semester hours of math; 7 semester hours of science; computer course for office management, agriculture, automotive technologies, drafting and design, electrical and electronics technology, horticulture, marketing, radiological technology majors; internship (some majors).
Computers on Campus: 200 computers available on campus for general student use. Computer purchase/lease plans available. Computers for student use in computer labs, learning resource center, library provide access to the Internet/World Wide Web. Staffed computer lab on campus provides training in use of computers, software.

EXPENSES

Expenses for 1997–98: Area resident tuition: $1280 full-time, $40 per semester hour part-time. State resident tuition: $5330 full-time, $166.55 per semester hour part-time. Nonresident tuition: $6574 full time, $205.43 per semester hour part-time. Part-time mandatory fees: $3.75 per semester hour. Full-time mandatory fees: $120.
LD Services Contact: Ms. Frances Loubere, Counselor/Coordinator of Special Needs Services, Kishwaukee College, 21193 Malta Road, Malta, IL 60150, 815-825-2086 Ext. 338. Fax: 815-825-2457. Email: floubere@kougars.kish.cc.il.us.

LABETTE COMMUNITY COLLEGE

Parsons, Kansas

LEARNING DISABILITIES SERVICES INFORMATION

LCC Learning Center began offering services in 1985. Currently the program serves 80 undergraduates with LD. Students diagnosed with ADD/ADHD are eligible for the same services available to students with LD.
Staff: 3 part-time staff members, including director. Services provided by remediation specialist, tutors.
Special Fees: No special fees are charged for services to students with LD.
Applications and admissions: *Required:* high school transcript; *recommended:* untimed ACT. Students may begin taking classes any term. *Application deadline:* continuous.
Special policies: The college has written policies regarding substitutions and waivers of admissions requirements.

PROGRAM AND SERVICE COMPONENTS

Diagnostic testing: Reading, math, spelling, spoken language, written language, study skills, learning strategies.
Academic advising: Provided by academic advisers. Students with LD may take up to 18 credit hours (more with special permission) each term; most take 3 to 12 credit hours; 12 credit hours required to maintain full-time status and be eligible for financial aid.
Counseling services: Individual counseling.
Basic skills remediation: Offered one-on-one by LD teachers, regular teachers. Available in reading, math, spelling, handwriting, written language, learning strategies, time management.
Subject-area tutoring: Offered one-on-one by professional teachers, peer tutors. Available in most subjects.
Special courses: Reading, vocabulary development, composition, learning strategies, time management, math, study skills, career planning. Some offered for credit; some enter into overall grade point average.
Auxiliary aids: Taped textbooks, tape recorders, calculators, typewriters, word-processors with spell-check, personal computers.
Auxiliary services: Alternative test arrangements, notetakers.

GENERAL COLLEGE INFORMATION

State and locally supported, 2-year, coed. Part of Kansas State Board of Education. Awards associate degrees. Founded 1923. *Setting:* 4-acre small-town campus. *Total enrollment:* 2,598. *Faculty:* 234 (36 full-time, 2% with terminal degrees, 198 part-time); student–undergrad faculty ratio is 16:1.
Enrollment Profile: 2,598 students from 7 states and territories, 4 other countries. 67% women, 33% men, 68% part-time, 96% state residents, 6% transferred in, 1% international, 40% 25 or older, 2% Native American, 1% Hispanic, 3% black, 1% Asian or Pacific Islander. *Areas of study chosen:* 4% education, 3% fine arts, 1% communications and journalism, 1% engineering and applied sciences, 1% performing arts, 1% social sciences.
First-Year Class: 1,286 total; 1,500 applied, 100% were accepted, 86% of whom enrolled. 13% from top 10% of their high school class, 49% from top half.
Graduation Requirements: 62 credit hours; 3 credit hours of college algebra; 5 credit hours of science; internship (some majors).
Computers on Campus: 66 computers available on campus for general student use. Computers for student use in computer center, classroom labs. Staffed computer lab on campus provides training in use of computers, software.

EXPENSES

Expenses for 1996–97: State resident tuition: $1147 full-time, $37 per credit hour part-time. Nonresident tuition: $2852 full-time, $92 per credit hour part-time. Full-time mandatory fees: $210. College room and board: $2200.

LD Services Contact: Ms. Viv Metcalf, Director of the Learning Center, Labette Community College, 200 South 14th, Parsons, KS 67357, 316-421-6700 Ext. 53. Fax: 316-421-0180.

LAKE CITY COMMUNITY COLLEGE

Lake City, Florida

LEARNING DISABILITIES SERVICES INFORMATION

Office of Disabled Student Services began offering services in 1988. Currently the program serves 30 undergraduates with LD. Students diagnosed with ADD/ADHD are eligible for the same services available to students with LD.
Staff: 1 full-time, 10 part-time staff members, including director, instructors, teacher's aides. Services provided by tutors, counselors, sign language interpreters, notetakers.
Special Fees: No special fees are charged for services to students with LD.
Applications and admissions: *Required:* high school transcript, psychoeducational report; *recommended:* untimed or extended time ACT, untimed SAT I. Students may begin taking classes any term. *Application deadline:* continuous.
Special policies: The college has written policies regarding grade forgiveness; substitutions and waivers of admissions, graduation, and degree requirements.

PROGRAM AND SERVICE COMPONENTS

Special preparation or orientation: Optional orientation offered individually by special arrangement.
Academic advising: Provided by unit staff members, academic advisers. Most students with LD take 6 to 12 semester hours each term; 12 semester hours required to maintain full-time status; 6 semester hours required to be eligible for financial aid.
Counseling services: Individual counseling, career counseling, self-advocacy training.
Basic skills remediation: Offered one-on-one and in small groups by regular teachers. Available in reading, math, spelling, written language, learning strategies, study skills, time management.
Subject-area tutoring: Offered one-on-one and in small groups by professional teachers, peer tutors. Available in all subjects.
Auxiliary aids: Tape recorders, calculators, typewriters, word-processors with spell-check.
Auxiliary services: Alternative test arrangements, notetakers, priority registration, advocacy.

GENERAL COLLEGE INFORMATION

State-supported, 2-year, coed. Part of Florida Community Colleges System. Awards associate degrees. Founded 1962. *Setting:* 132-acre small-town campus with easy access to Jacksonville. *Total enrollment:* 2,377. *Faculty:* 204 (55 full-time, 95% with terminal degrees, 149 part-time).
Enrollment Profile: 2,377 students from 18 states and territories, 8 other countries. 57% women, 43% men, 48% part-time, 95% state residents, 2% live on campus, 8% transferred in, 1% international, 52% 25 or older, 1% Native American, 2% Hispanic, 11% black, 1% Asian or Pacific Islander. *Retention:* 50% of 1995 full-time freshmen returned. *Areas of study chosen:* 55% vocational and home economics, 36% liberal arts/general studies, 9% health professions and related sciences, 5% business management and administrative services, 5% computer and information sciences. *Most popular recent majors:* liberal arts/general studies, nursing.
First-Year Class: 573 total; 1,391 applied, 100% were accepted, 41% of whom enrolled. 8% from top 10% of their high school class.
Graduation Requirements: 60 semester hours; 6 semester hours of math; 10 semester hours of science; computer course for emergency medical services, business, electronics engineering technology, forest management, golf course operations, landscaping technology majors; internship (some majors).
Computers on Campus: 150 computers available on campus for general student use. A campus-wide network can be accessed. Students can contact faculty members and/or advisers through e-mail. Computers for student use in computer center, learning resource center provide access to the Internet/World Wide Web. Staffed computer lab on campus provides training in use of computers, software.

EXPENSES

Expenses for 1997–98: *Application fee:* $15. State resident tuition: $1140 full-time, $38 per semester hour part-time. Nonresident tuition: $4425 full-time, $147.50 per semester hour part-time. College room and board: $3409.
LD Services Contact: Dr. Robert S. Sloat, Coordinator of Services for Disabled Students, Lake City Community College, Box 1030, Route 19, Lake City, FL 32025, 904-752-1822 Ext. 1393. Fax: 904-755-3144.

LAKELAND COMMUNITY COLLEGE

Kirtland, Ohio

LEARNING DISABILITIES SERVICES INFORMATION

Support Services for Students with Disabilities began offering services in 1980. Currently the program serves 152 undergraduates with LD. Students diagnosed with ADD/ADHD are eligible for the same services available to students with LD.
Staff: 1 full-time staff member (coordinator). Services provided by tutors, counselor.
Special Fees: No special fees are charged for services to students with LD.
Applications and admissions: *Required:* high school IEP (Individualized Education Program), personal interview, psychoeducational report completed within 3 years; *recommended:* high school transcript, grade point average, courses completed, extracurricular activities, untimed SAT I, letters of recommendation. Students may begin taking classes any term. *Application deadline:* continuous.
Special policies: The college has written policies regarding grade forgiveness; substitutions and waivers of admissions, graduation, and degree requirements.

PROGRAM AND SERVICE COMPONENTS

Special preparation or orientation: Optional summer program offered prior to entering college. Optional orientation offered before registration.
Academic advising: Provided by unit staff members, academic advisers. Most students with LD take 6 to 12 credit hours each term; 6 credit hours required to be eligible for financial aid.
Counseling services: Individual counseling, small-group counseling, career counseling, self-advocacy training.
Basic skills remediation: Offered one-on-one, in small groups, and in class-size groups by regular teachers; computer-aided instruction also offered. Available in reading, math, spelling, learning strategies, study skills, time management.
Subject-area tutoring: Offered one-on-one and in small groups by professional teachers. Available in all subjects.
Auxiliary aids: Taped textbooks, tape recorders, calculators, word-processors with spell-check, talking computers, optical character readers.
Auxiliary services: Alternative test arrangements, notetakers, priority registration, advocacy.
Campus support group: A special student organization is available to students with LD.

GENERAL COLLEGE INFORMATION

State and locally supported, 2-year, coed. Part of Ohio Board of Regents. Awards associate degrees. Founded 1967. *Setting:* 380-acre suburban campus with easy access to Cleveland. *Endowment:* $450,000. *Total enrollment:* 8,378. *Faculty:* 575 (126 full-time, 449 part-time); student–undergrad faculty ratio is 16:1.
Enrollment Profile: 8,378 students: 61% women, 39% men, 72% part-time, 99% state residents, 8% transferred in, 53% 25 or older, 1% Native American, 1% Hispanic, 3% black, 1% Asian or Pacific Islander. *Retention:* 74% of 1995 full-time freshmen returned. *Areas of study chosen:* 29% liberal arts/general studies, 27% business management and administrative services, 15% health professions and related sciences, 8% engineering and applied sciences, 1% vocational and home economics. *Most popular recent majors:* nursing, business administration/commerce/management, liberal arts/general studies.
First-Year Class: 2,146 total; 2,619 applied, 100% were accepted, 82% of whom enrolled.
Graduation Requirements: 96 credit hours; math/science requirements vary according to program; computer course for most majors.
Computers on Campus: 500 computers available on campus for general student use. A campus-wide network can be accessed from off-campus. Computers for student use in computer center, computer labs,

Lakeland Community College (continued)

learning resource center, classrooms, library provide access to the Internet/World Wide Web. Staffed computer lab on campus provides training in use of computers, software.

EXPENSES

Expenses for 1997–98: *Application fee:* $15. Area resident tuition: $1754 full-time, $36.55 per credit hour part-time. State resident tuition: $2208 full-time, $46 per credit hour part-time. Nonresident tuition: $4992 full-time, $104 per credit hour part-time. Part-time mandatory fees per quarter range from $15.15 to $66.65. Full-time mandatory fees: $262.

LD Services Contact: Mr. Alan B. Kirsh, Counselor for Students with Disabilities, Lakeland Community College, 7700 Clocktower Drive, Kirtland, OH 44094, 216-953-7245. Fax: 216-953-1692.

LAKESHORE TECHNICAL COLLEGE

Cleveland, Wisconsin

LEARNING DISABILITIES SERVICES INFORMATION

Instructional Support Services began offering services in 1987. Currently the program serves 40 undergraduates with LD. Students diagnosed with ADD/ADHD are eligible for the same services available to students with LD.

Staff: 2 full-time staff members, including director. Services provided by remediation specialists.

Special Fees: No special fees are charged for services to students with LD.

Applications and admissions: Open admissions. Students may begin taking classes in summer only. *Application deadline:* continuous.

Special policies: The college has written policies regarding grade forgiveness; substitutions and waivers of admissions and degree requirements.

PROGRAM AND SERVICE COMPONENTS

Special preparation or orientation: Optional orientation offered before registration.

Diagnostic testing: Intelligence, reading, math, spelling, handwriting, spoken language, written language, motor abilities, perceptual skills, study skills, personality, learning strategies.

Academic advising: Provided by academic advisers. Most students with LD take 6 to 10 credits each term; 12 credits required to maintain full-time status; 6 credits required to be eligible for financial aid.

Counseling services: Career counseling.

Basic skills remediation: Offered in small groups by reading specialist, math certified teachers. Available in reading, math, spelling, written language, learning strategies, study skills, time management, social skills.

Subject-area tutoring: Offered one-on-one and in small groups by professional teachers, peer tutors. Available in most subjects.

Special courses: College survival skills, reading, vocabulary development, learning strategies, word processing, time management, study skills.

Auxiliary aids: Taped textbooks, tape recorders, calculators, typewriters.

Auxiliary services: Alternative test arrangements, notetakers.

GENERAL COLLEGE INFORMATION

State and locally supported, 2-year, coed. Part of Wisconsin Technical College System. Awards associate degrees. Founded 1967. *Setting:* 160-acre rural campus with easy access to Milwaukee. *Total enrollment:* 2,409. *Faculty:* 300 (100 full-time, 200 part-time).

Enrollment Profile: 2,409 students from 12 states and territories. 60% women, 40% men, 70% part-time, 99% state residents, 7% transferred in, 0% international, 55% 25 or older, 0% Native American, 1% Hispanic, 0% black, 3% Asian or Pacific Islander. *Most popular recent majors:* marketing/retailing/merchandising, nursing, accounting.

First-Year Class: 1,069 total. Of the students who applied, 90% were accepted. 6% from top 10% of their high school class, 30% from top quarter, 65% from top half.

Graduation Requirements: 65 credits; math proficiency or 1 math course; internship (some majors).

Computers on Campus: 300 computers available on campus for general student use. Computers for student use in computer center, computer labs, learning resource center, classrooms, library, student center. Staffed computer lab on campus provides training in use of computers, software.

EXPENSES AND FINANCIAL AID

Expenses for 1997–98: *Application fee:* $25. State resident tuition: $1734 full-time, $54.20 per credit part-time. Nonresident tuition: $11,962 full-time, $373.80 per credit part-time.

Financial aid specifically for students with LD: work-study.

LD Services Contact: Mr. Tom Hilke, Dean of Special Services, Lakeshore Technical College, 1290 North Avenue, Cleveland, WI 53015-1414, 414-684-4409.

LAKE-SUMTER COMMUNITY COLLEGE

Leesburg, Florida

LEARNING DISABILITIES SERVICES INFORMATION

Office for Students with Disabilities (OSD) currently serves 35 undergraduates with LD. Students diagnosed with ADD/ADHD are eligible for the same services available to students with LD.

Staff: 1 full-time staff member (Specialist). Services provided by tutors, counselors.

Special Fees: No special fees are charged for services to students with LD.

Applications and admissions: *Required:* documentation of disability. Students may begin taking classes in fall, spring, or summer. *Application deadline:* continuous.

Special policies: The college has written policies regarding grade forgiveness; substitutions and waivers of admissions, graduation, and degree requirements.

PROGRAM AND SERVICE COMPONENTS

Academic advising: Provided by unit staff members, academic advisers. Most students with LD take 1 to 15 credit hours each term; 9 credit hours required to maintain full-time status and be eligible for financial aid.

Counseling services: Individual counseling, small-group counseling, career counseling.

Subject-area tutoring: Offered one-on-one by peer tutors. Available in most subjects.

Auxiliary aids: Taped textbooks, tape recorders, calculators, typewriters, word-processors with spell-check, optical character readers, Dragon Dictate, OSCAR.

Auxiliary services: Alternative test arrangements, notetakers, priority registration, advocacy.

GENERAL COLLEGE INFORMATION

State and locally supported, 2-year, coed. Part of Florida Community Colleges System. Awards associate degrees. Founded 1962. *Setting:* 110-acre rural campus with easy access to Orlando. *Total enrollment:* 2,700. *Faculty:* 117 (41 full-time, 76 part-time); student–undergrad faculty ratio is 20:1.

Enrollment Profile: 2,700 students from 4 states and territories, 2 other countries. 65% women, 35% men, 69% part-time, 98% state residents, 10% transferred in, 1% international, 52% 25 or older, 0% Native American, 1% Hispanic, 6% black, 0% Asian or Pacific Islander. *Most popular recent majors:* liberal arts/general studies, nursing, business administration/commerce/management.

First-Year Class: 699 total; 824 applied, 100% were accepted, 85% of whom enrolled.

Graduation Requirements: 60 semester hours; math/science requirements vary according to program; computer course for business-related majors.

Computers on Campus: 250 computers available on campus for general student use. A campus-wide network can be accessed from off-campus. Students can contact faculty members and/or advisers through e-mail. Computers for student use in computer center, media center.

EXPENSES

Expenses for 1997–98: *Application fee:* $15. State resident tuition: $1236 full-time, $41.20 per semester hour part-time. Nonresident tuition: $4686 full-time, $156.20 per semester hour part-time.

LD Services Contact: Mr. Ed Makovec, Specialist, Office for Students with Disabilities, Lake-Sumter Community College, 9501 Highway 441, Leesburg, FL 34788, 352-365-3559. Fax: 352-365-3501.

LAMAR COMMUNITY COLLEGE

Lamar, Colorado

LEARNING DISABILITIES SERVICES INFORMATION

Computer Access Center/Alternative Learning Center began offering services in 1988. Students diagnosed with ADD/ADHD are eligible for the same services available to students with LD.
Staff: 3 full-time staff members, including director. Services provided by tutors.
Special Fees: No special fees are charged for services to students with LD.
Applications and admissions: *Required:* high school transcript; *recommended:* high school IEP (Individualized Education Program), psychoeducational report. Students may begin taking classes in fall only. *Application deadline:* continuous.

PROGRAM AND SERVICE COMPONENTS

Special preparation or orientation: Optional orientation offered after classes begin.
Diagnostic testing: Reading, math, written language, study skills.
Academic advising: Provided by academic advisers. Students with LD may take up to 18 semester hours each term; most take 12 to 15 semester hours; 12 semester hours (for campus housing) required to maintain full-time status; 6 semester hours required to be eligible for financial aid.
Counseling services: Individual counseling, small-group counseling, career counseling, self-advocacy training.
Basic skills remediation: Offered one-on-one by regular teachers. Available in reading, math, written language, study skills, time management.
Subject-area tutoring: Offered one-on-one and in small groups by professional teachers, peer tutors. Available in all subjects.
Special courses: Reading, composition, time management, math, study skills. All offered for credit; all enter into overall grade point average.
Auxiliary aids: Taped textbooks, calculators, typewriters, word-processors with spell-check.
Auxiliary services: Alternative test arrangements, notetakers, advocacy.

GENERAL COLLEGE INFORMATION

State-supported, 2-year, coed. Part of Colorado Community College and Occupational Education System. Awards associate degrees. Founded 1937. *Setting:* 125-acre small-town campus. *Endowment:* $200,000. *Educational spending 1995–96:* $2122 per undergrad. *Total enrollment:* 701. *Faculty:* 63 (25 full-time, 12% with terminal degrees, 38 part-time); student–undergrad faculty ratio is 12:1.
Enrollment Profile: 701 students from 26 states and territories, 7 other countries. 58% women, 42% men, 44% part-time, 91% state residents, 8% transferred in, 2% international, 43% 25 or older, 2% Native American, 12% Hispanic, 3% black, 1% Asian or Pacific Islander. *Retention:* 50% of 1995 full-time freshmen returned. *Areas of study chosen:* 21% liberal arts/general studies, 12% agriculture, 12% biological and life sciences, 12% computer and information sciences, 6% vocational and home economics, 3% English language/literature/letters, 3% fine arts, 3% health professions and related sciences, 3% mathematics, 3% physical sciences, 3% psychology, 3% social sciences, 2% business management and administrative services, 2% education, 2% engineering and applied sciences, 2% predentistry, 2% prelaw, 2% premed, 2% prevet, 1% communications and journalism, 1% foreign language and literature, 1% natural resource sciences.
First-Year Class: 359 total; 427 applied, 100% were accepted, 84% of whom enrolled.
Graduation Requirements: 64 semester hours; 1 math course; computer course for most majors; internship (some majors).
Computers on Campus: 60 computers available on campus for general student use. Computer purchase/lease plans available. A campuswide network can be accessed. Computers for student use in computer center, computer labs, research center, learning resource center, classrooms, library, dorms. Staffed computer lab on campus provides training in use of computers, software. *Academic computing expenditure 1995–96:* $31,510.

EXPENSES

Expenses for 1997–98: State resident tuition: $1738 full-time, $54.30 per semester hour part-time. Nonresident tuition: $6061 full-time, $189.40 per semester hour part-time. Part-time mandatory fees per semester range from $16 to $86. Full-time mandatory fees: $294. College room and board: $4020. College room only: $1300.

LD Services Contact: Ms. Cynthia L. Baer, Director, Alternative Learning Center, Lamar Community College, 2401 South Main, Lamar, CO 81052-3999, 719-336-2248 Ext. 237. Fax: 719-336-2448. Email: cjbaer@iguana.ruralinternet.net.

LAMAR UNIVERSITY–PORT ARTHUR

Port Arthur, Texas

LEARNING DISABILITIES SERVICES INFORMATION

Learning Resource Center began offering services in 1984. Currently the program serves 30 undergraduates with LD. Students diagnosed with ADD/ADHD are eligible for the same services available to students with LD.
Staff: Includes coordinator. Services provided by tutors.
Special Fees: No special fees are charged for services to students with LD.
Applications and admissions: *Required:* high school transcript, instructor referral. Students may begin taking classes any term. *Application deadline:* continuous.
Special policies: The college has written policies regarding grade forgiveness.

PROGRAM AND SERVICE COMPONENTS

Diagnostic testing: Reading, math, written language.
Academic advising: Provided by academic advisers. Students with LD may take up to 15 credit hours each term; most take 6 credit hours; individual arrangement determines the number of credit hours required to maintain full-time status; 6 credit hours required to be eligible for financial aid.
Counseling services: Individual counseling, small-group counseling, career counseling.
Basic skills remediation: Offered one-on-one, in small groups, and in class-size groups by developmental education teachers. Available in reading, math, written language.
Subject-area tutoring: Offered one-on-one, in small groups, and in class-size groups by peer tutors. Available in some subjects.
Special courses: Composition, word processing, math, computer science. Most offered for credit; most enter into overall grade point average.
Auxiliary aids: Taped textbooks, tape recorders, calculators, word-processors with spell-check, talking computers.
Auxiliary services: Alternative test arrangements, notetakers.

GENERAL COLLEGE INFORMATION

State-supported, 2-year, coed. Part of The Texas State University System. Awards associate degrees. Founded 1909. *Setting:* 34-acre suburban campus. *Educational spending 1995–96:* $2030 per undergrad. *Total enrollment:* 2,476. *Faculty:* 141 (61 full-time, 10% with terminal degrees, 80 part-time); student–undergrad faculty ratio is 25:1.
Enrollment Profile: 2,476 students from 6 states and territories. 65% women, 35% men, 56% part-time, 97% state residents, 11% transferred in, 0% international, 45% 25 or older, 1% Native American, 7% Hispanic, 29% black, 4% Asian or Pacific Islander. *Areas of study chosen:* 55% vocational and home economics. *Most popular recent majors:* nursing, cosmetology, business administration/commerce/management.
First-Year Class: 520 total; 717 applied, 100% were accepted, 73% of whom enrolled.
Graduation Requirements: 62 credit hours; computer course for accounting, automotive technology, child care technology, electronics technology, hazardous material technology, legal assistant, management development, secretarial majors; internship (some majors).
Computers on Campus: 110 computers available on campus for general student use. A computer is required for some students. A campuswide network can be accessed from off-campus. Students can contact faculty members and/or advisers through e-mail. Computers for student use in computer center, computer labs, learning resource center, classrooms, library provide access to the Internet/World Wide Web, on- and off-campus e-mail addresses. Staffed computer lab on campus provides training in use of computers, software. *Academic computing expenditure 1995–96:* $679,000.

EXPENSES

Expenses for 1997–98: State resident tuition: $1054 full-time. Nonresident tuition: $7688 full-time, $248 per credit hour part-time. State resident part-time tuition per semester ranges from $120 to $374. Part-time mandatory fees per semester range from $56 to $319. Full-time mandatory fees: $764.

Lamar University Port Arthur (continued)

LD Services Contact: Dr. Gary Stretcher, Vice President of Academic Affairs, Lamar University–Port Arthur, PO Box 310, Port Arthur, TX 77641-0310, 409-984-6209. Fax: 409-984-6000.

LANE COMMUNITY COLLEGE

Eugene, Oregon

LEARNING DISABILITIES SERVICES INFORMATION

Disability Services Office began offering services in 1979. Currently the program serves 300 undergraduates with LD. Students diagnosed with ADD/ADHD are eligible for the same services available to students with LD.
Staff: 4 full-time, 1 part-time staff members, including coordinator, assistant coordinator, aide, sign language interpreters, administrative specialist. Services provided by remediation specialists.
Special Fees: No special fees are charged for services to students with LD.
Applications and admissions: *Required:* psychoeducational report completed within 3 years; *recommended:* high school IEP (Individualized Education Program), personal interview. Students may begin taking classes any term. *Application deadline:* continuous.
Special policies: The college has written policies regarding grade forgiveness.

PROGRAM AND SERVICE COMPONENTS

Academic advising: Provided by unit staff members, academic advisers. Most students with LD take 6 to 15 credit hours each term; 12 credit hours required to maintain full-time status; 6 credit hours required to be eligible for financial aid.
Counseling services: Individual counseling, career counseling.
Basic skills remediation: Offered in class-size groups by LD teachers, regular teachers. Available in reading, math, spelling, written language, learning strategies, study skills, time management, computer skills.
Subject-area tutoring: Offered one-on-one and in small groups by peer tutors. Available in all subjects.
Special courses: Reading, vocabulary development, composition, learning strategies, word processing, time management, math, typing, study skills. Some offered for credit.
Auxiliary aids: Taped textbooks, tape recorders, calculators, typewriters, word-processors with spell-check, talking computers, optical character readers, talking calculators.
Auxiliary services: Alternative test arrangements, notetakers, priority registration, advocacy.

GENERAL COLLEGE INFORMATION

State and locally supported, 2-year, coed. Awards associate degrees. Founded 1964. *Setting:* 240-acre suburban campus. *Endowment:* $2.9 million. *Total enrollment:* 9,441. *Faculty:* 537 (279 full-time, 91% with terminal degrees, 258 part-time).
Enrollment Profile: 9,441 students from 28 states and territories, 27 other countries. 54% women, 46% men, 60% part-time, 94% state residents, 18% transferred in, 3% international, 42% 25 or older, 3% Native American, 3% Hispanic, 1% black, 4% Asian or Pacific Islander. *Most popular recent majors:* nursing, business administration/commerce/management.
First-Year Class: 3,271 total; 4,904 applied, 100% were accepted, 67% of whom enrolled.
Graduation Requirements: 93 credit hours; math/science requirements vary according to program; computer course for most majors; internship (some majors).
Computers on Campus: 1,600 computers available on campus for general student use. Computer purchase/lease plans available. A campus-wide network can be accessed. Computers for student use in computer center, computer labs, classrooms, library. Staffed computer lab on campus provides training in use of computers, software. *Academic computing expenditure 1995–96:* $530,154.

EXPENSES

Expenses for 1997–98: State resident tuition: $1564 full-time, $34 per credit hour part-time. Nonresident tuition: $5336 full-time, $116 per credit hour part-time. Part-time mandatory fees: $25.25 per quarter. Full-time mandatory fees: $76.
LD Services Contact: Ms. Leigh Alice Petty, Coordinator of Disability Services, Lane Community College, 4000 East 30th Avenue, Eugene, OR 97405-0640, 541-747-4501 Ext. 2150. Fax: 541-744-4173. Email: pettyl@lanecc.edu.

LANSING COMMUNITY COLLEGE

Lansing, Michigan

LEARNING DISABILITIES SERVICES INFORMATION

Handicapped Support Services began offering services in 1982. Currently the program serves 84 undergraduates with LD. Students diagnosed with ADD/ADHD are eligible for the same services available to students with LD.
Staff: Includes director, facilitator for hearing impaired. Services provided by counselors, readers, scribes, interpreters, specialist for the visually impaired.
Special Fees: No special fees are charged for services to students with LD.
Applications and admissions: *Recommended:* psychoeducational report, medical or certified documentation. Students may begin taking classes any term. *Application deadline:* continuous.

PROGRAM AND SERVICE COMPONENTS

Academic advising: Provided by academic advisers. Most students with LD take 10 to 12 semester hours each term; 12 semester hours required to maintain full-time status; 6 semester hours required to be eligible for financial aid.
Counseling services: Individual counseling, career counseling.
Basic skills remediation: Offered one-on-one and in small groups by regular teachers. Available in reading, math, spelling, written language, learning strategies, study skills.
Subject-area tutoring: Offered one-on-one, in small groups, and in class-size groups by peer tutors, tutor technicians. Available in most subjects.
Special courses: Composition. All offered for credit; all enter into overall grade point average.
Auxiliary aids: Taped textbooks, word-processors with spell-check, optical character readers, Artic Vision.
Auxiliary services: Alternative test arrangements, notetakers, priority registration, readers, scribes, interpreters.

GENERAL COLLEGE INFORMATION

State and locally supported, 2-year, coed. Part of Michigan Department of Education. Awards associate degrees. Founded 1957. *Setting:* 120-acre urban campus. *Endowment:* $20,000. *Total enrollment:* 16,136. *Faculty:* 920 (170 full-time, 100% with terminal degrees, 750 part-time); student–undergrad faculty ratio is 13:1.
Enrollment Profile: 16,136 students: 57% women, 43% men, 74% part-time, 98% state residents, 2% transferred in, 1% international, 48% 25 or older, 1% Native American, 3% Hispanic, 7% black, 3% Asian or Pacific Islander. *Most popular recent major:* business administration/commerce/management.
First-Year Class: 3,924 total. Of the students who applied, 100% were accepted.
Graduation Requirements: 60 semester hours.
Computers on Campus: 288 computers available on campus for general student use. A campus-wide network can be accessed from off-campus. Students can contact faculty members and/or advisers through e-mail. Computers for student use in computer labs, classrooms provide access to the Internet/World Wide Web, on- and off-campus e-mail addresses. Staffed computer lab on campus provides training in use of computers, software. *Academic computing expenditure 1995–96:* $1.4 million.

EXPENSES

Expenses for 1996–97: *Application fee:* $10. Area resident tuition: $1290 full-time, $43 per semester hour part-time. State resident tuition: $2160 full-time, $72 per semester hour part-time. Nonresident tuition: $3030 full-time, $101 per semester hour part-time. Part-time mandatory fees per semester range from $21.50 to $27.50. Full-time mandatory fees: $55.
LD Services Contact: Ms. Pamela Davis, Counselor, Handicapped Support Services, Lansing Community College, PO Box 40010, Lansing, MI 48901-7210, 517-483-1207.

LARAMIE COUNTY COMMUNITY COLLEGE

Cheyenne, Wyoming

LEARNING DISABILITIES SERVICES INFORMATION

Learning Assistance Resource Center began offering services in 1986. Currently the program serves 130 undergraduates with LD. Students diagnosed with ADD/ADHD are not eligible for the same services available to students with LD.

Staff: 1 full-time, 5 part-time staff members, including coordinator, assistant coordinator. Services provided by remediation specialists, tutors.

Special Fees: No special fees are charged for services to students with LD.

Applications and admissions: *Recommended:* high school courses completed, IEP (Individualized Education Program), psychoeducational report completed within 3 years. Students may begin taking classes in fall, spring, or summer. *Application deadline:* continuous.

PROGRAM AND SERVICE COMPONENTS

Special preparation or orientation: Optional orientation offered before registration.

Diagnostic testing: Reading, math, spelling, spoken language, written language, study skills, speech, learning strategies.

Academic advising: Provided by unit staff members, academic advisers. Students with LD may take up to 15 credit hours each term; most take 6 to 9 credit hours; 12 credit hours required to maintain full-time status; 12 credit hours (for federal aid) required to be eligible for financial aid.

Counseling services: Individual counseling, small-group counseling, career counseling.

Basic skills remediation: Offered one-on-one, in small groups, and in class-size groups by regular teachers, teacher trainees, developmental studies instructors; computer-aided instruction also offered. Available in reading, math, spelling, spoken language, written language, study skills, time management, speech.

Subject-area tutoring: Offered one-on-one and in small groups by professional teachers, peer tutors. Available in most subjects.

Special courses: College survival skills, reading, vocabulary development, communication skills, composition, learning strategies, word processing, time management, math, typing, personal psychology, study skills, career planning, effective listening. Most offered for credit; most enter into overall grade point average.

Auxiliary aids: Taped textbooks, tape recorders, calculators, typewriters, word-processors with spell-check, personal computers, talking computers, optical character readers, print-to-voice computers.

Auxiliary services: Alternative test arrangements, notetakers, advocacy.

GENERAL COLLEGE INFORMATION

County-supported, 2-year, coed. Part of Wyoming Community College Commission. Awards associate degrees. Founded 1968. *Setting:* 270-acre small-town campus. *Total enrollment:* 4,282. *Faculty:* 255 (80 full-time, 20% with terminal degrees, 175 part-time); student–undergrad faculty ratio is 24:1.

Enrollment Profile: 4,282 students: 59% women, 41% men, 71% part-time, 90% state residents, 2% live on campus, 25% transferred in, 1% international, 60% 25 or older, 1% Native American, 5% Hispanic, 2% black, 1% Asian or Pacific Islander.

First-Year Class: 1,670 total; 1,974 applied, 100% were accepted, 85% of whom enrolled.

Graduation Requirements: 64 credit hours; 1 course each in college algebra and lab science; computer course for business-related majors; internship (some majors).

Computers on Campus: 600 computers available on campus for general student use. Computers for student use in computer center, computer labs, learning resource center, classrooms. Staffed computer lab on campus provides training in use of computers, software.

EXPENSES AND FINANCIAL AID

Expenses for 1997–98: *Application fee:* $10. State resident tuition: $894 full-time, $39 per credit hour part-time. Nonresident tuition: $2682 full-time, $117 per credit hour part-time. Part-time mandatory fees: $7.34 per credit hour. Tuition for nonresidents who are eligible for the Western Undergraduate Exchange: $1342 full-time, $59 per credit hour part-time. Full-time mandatory fees: $176. College room and board: $3360.

Financial aid specifically for students with LD: Scholarships: Laramie County Association for Children with Learning Disabilities (LCACLD), Venture Clubs of the Americas, Eddington Family Scholarship; work-study.

LD Services Contact: Ms. Patricia Pratz, Coordinator, System for Student Success, Laramie County Community College, 1400 East College Drive, Cheyenne, WY 82007-3299, 307-778-1262. Fax: 307-778-1344. Email: ppratz@mail.lcc.whecn.edu.

LEE COLLEGE

Baytown, Texas

LEARNING DISABILITIES SERVICES INFORMATION

Office of Disability Services began offering services in 1991. Currently the program serves 36 undergraduates with LD. Students diagnosed with ADD/ADHD are eligible for the same services available to students with LD.

Staff: 2 full-time, 5 part-time staff members. Services provided by interpreters.

Special Fees: No special fees are charged for services to students with LD.

Applications and admissions: Students may begin taking classes in spring or summer. *Application deadline:* continuous.

PROGRAM AND SERVICE COMPONENTS

Academic advising: Provided by unit staff members, academic advisers. Students with LD may take up to 18 credit hours each term; most take 9 credit hours; 12 credit hours required to maintain full-time status; source of aid determines number of credit hours required to be eligible for financial aid.

Counseling services: Career counseling, self-advocacy training.

Subject-area tutoring: Offered one-on-one by peer tutors. Available in most subjects.

Auxiliary aids: Taped textbooks, tape recorders.

Auxiliary services: Alternative test arrangements, notetakers, priority registration, advocacy.

GENERAL COLLEGE INFORMATION

District-supported, 2-year, coed. Part of Texas Higher Education Coordinating Board. Awards associate degrees. Founded 1934. *Setting:* 35-acre suburban campus with easy access to Houston. *Total enrollment:* 5,938. *Faculty:* 333 (156 full-time, 177 part-time); student–undergrad faculty ratio is 22:1.

Enrollment Profile: 5,938 students: 43% women, 57% men, 65% part-time, 99% state residents, 3% transferred in, 1% international, 52% 25 or older, 1% Native American, 16% Hispanic, 18% black, 1% Asian or Pacific Islander. *Most popular recent majors:* liberal arts/general studies, nursing, instrumentation technology.

First-Year Class: 1,110 total. Of the students who applied, 100% were accepted.

Graduation Requirements: 60 credit hours; math/science requirements vary according to program; computer course.

EXPENSES AND FINANCIAL AID

Expenses for 1997–98: Area resident tuition: $420 full-time. State resident tuition: $840 full-time. Nonresident tuition: $1200 full-time. Part-time tuition per course ranges from $84 to $154 for area residents, $98 to $308 for state residents, $200 to $440 for nonresidents. Part-time mandatory fees per semester range from $73 to $99. Full-time mandatory fees: $222.

Financial aid specifically for students with LD: Scholarships: Kevin Henderson Memorial Scholarship, Hou-Met Scholarship.

LD Services Contact: Ms. Rosemary Coffman, Counselor for Students with Disabilities, Lee College, PO Box 818, Baytown, TX 77522, 281-425-6384. Fax: 281-425-6382. Email: rcoffman@lee.edu.

LEHIGH CARBON COMMUNITY COLLEGE

Schnecksville, Pennsylvania

LEARNING DISABILITIES SERVICES INFORMATION

Services for Students with Disabilities began offering services in 1986. Currently the program serves 80 undergraduates with LD. Students diagnosed with ADD/ADHD are eligible for the same services available to students with LD.

Lehigh Carbon Community College (continued)

Staff: 2 full-time staff members, including director. Services provided by diagnostic specialist.

Special Fees: No special fees are charged for services to students with LD.

Applications and admissions: *Required:* high school transcript, courses completed, psychoeducational report completed within 3 years, achievement assessment. Students may begin taking classes in fall, spring, or summer. *Application deadline:* continuous.

Special policies: The college has written policies regarding grade forgiveness; substitutions and waivers of graduation and degree requirements.

PROGRAM AND SERVICE COMPONENTS

Special preparation or orientation: Orientation offered before registration.

Diagnostic testing: Reading, math, spelling, handwriting, spoken language, written language, perceptual skills, study skills, learning strategies.

Academic advising: Provided by unit staff members, academic advisers. Students with LD may take up to 18 credits each term; most take 9 to 12 credits; 12 credits required to maintain full-time status; source of aid determines number of credits required to be eligible for financial aid.

Counseling services: Individual counseling, career counseling.

Basic skills remediation: Offered in class-size groups by regular teachers. Available in reading, math, written language, study skills.

Subject-area tutoring: Offered one-on-one and in small groups by professional teachers, peer tutors, paraprofessionals. Available in most subjects.

Special courses: Technology. All offered for credit; all enter into overall grade point average.

Auxiliary aids: Taped textbooks, tape recorders, calculators, typewriters, word-processors with spell-check, talking computers, optical character readers.

Auxiliary services: Alternative test arrangements, notetakers.

Campus support group: A special student organization is available to students with LD.

GENERAL COLLEGE INFORMATION

State and locally supported, 2-year, coed. Awards associate degrees. Founded 1967. *Setting:* 100-acre rural campus. *Total enrollment:* 4,185. *Faculty:* 257 (73 full-time, 184 part-time); student–undergrad faculty ratio is 20:1.

Enrollment Profile: 4,185 students from 5 states and territories, 15 other countries. 60% women, 40% men, 55% part-time, 98% state residents, 16% transferred in, 2% international, 54% 25 or older, 0% Native American, 3% Hispanic, 1% black, 3% Asian or Pacific Islander. *Retention:* 70% of 1995 full-time freshmen returned. *Areas of study chosen:* 31% liberal arts/general studies, 14% vocational and home economics, 13% business management and administrative services, 8% computer and information sciences, 8% social sciences, 7% health professions and related sciences, 5% education, 2% biological and life sciences, 2% engineering and applied sciences, 1% mathematics. *Most popular recent majors:* liberal arts/general studies, accounting, business administration/commerce/management.

First-Year Class: 1,366 total; 1,991 applied, 90% were accepted, 76% of whom enrolled.

Graduation Requirements: 60 credits; computer course for business majors.

Computers on Campus: 175 computers available on campus for general student use. Computer purchase/lease plans available. Computers for student use in computer center, computer labs, learning resource center, library. Staffed computer lab on campus.

EXPENSES

Expenses for 1997–98: *Application fee:* $25. Area resident tuition: $2130 full-time, $71 per credit part-time. State resident tuition: $4290 full-time, $143 per credit part-time. Nonresident tuition: $6450 full-time, $215 per credit part-time.

LD Services Contact: Ms. Karen Goode-Ferguson, Director, Learning Assistance Grants, Lehigh Carbon Community College, 4525 Education Park Drive, Schnecksville, PA 18078-2598, 610-799-1542. Fax: 610-799-1159.

LIMA TECHNICAL COLLEGE

Lima, Ohio

LEARNING DISABILITIES SERVICES INFORMATION

Student Advising and Development Center currently serves undergraduate students with LD. Students diagnosed with ADD/ADHD are eligible for the same services available to students with LD.

Staff: 6 full-time staff members, including academic advisers. Services provided by academic advisers.

Special Fees: No special fees are charged for services to students with LD.

Applications and admissions: *Required:* high school transcript, IEP (if student requests accommodations); *recommended:* high school extracurricular activities, personal interview. Students may begin taking classes any term. *Application deadline:* continuous.

Special policies: The college has written policies regarding grade forgiveness; substitutions and waivers of admissions, graduation, and degree requirements.

PROGRAM AND SERVICE COMPONENTS

Academic advising: Provided by academic advisers. Students with LD may take up to 20 credit hours each term; most take 13 to 15 credit hours; 12 credit hours required to maintain full-time status and be eligible for financial aid.

Basic skills remediation: Offered in class-size groups by regular teachers. Available in reading, math, spelling.

Subject-area tutoring: Offered one-on-one by peer tutors. Available in all subjects.

Auxiliary aids: Taped textbooks, tape recorders, Phonic Ear, Arkenstone Reader, TTY machine, enlarged materials.

Auxiliary services: Alternative test arrangements, notetakers, readers, scribes.

Campus support group: A special student organization is available to students with LD.

GENERAL COLLEGE INFORMATION

State-supported, 2-year, coed. Awards associate degrees. Founded 1971. *Setting:* 565-acre rural campus. *Total enrollment:* 2,583. *Faculty:* 167 (100 full-time, 10% with terminal degrees, 67 part-time).

Enrollment Profile: 2,583 students: 68% women, 32% men, 48% part-time, 99% state residents, 9% transferred in, 1% international, 44% 25 or older, 0% Native American, 1% Hispanic, 6% black, 0% Asian or Pacific Islander. *Retention:* 75% of 1995 full-time freshmen returned. *Areas of study chosen:* 26% business management and administrative services, 23% liberal arts/general studies, 21% health professions and related sciences, 16% engineering and applied sciences, 14% social sciences.

First-Year Class: 744 total; 2,878 applied, 100% were accepted, 26% of whom enrolled. 5% from top 10% of their high school class, 20% from top quarter, 40% from top half.

Graduation Requirements: 106 credit hours; 1 math course; computer course; internship (some majors).

Computers on Campus: 150 computers available on campus for general student use. A computer is recommended for all students. A campus-wide network can be accessed from off-campus. Students can contact faculty members and/or advisers through e-mail. Computers for student use in computer center, computer labs, learning resource center, classrooms, library, business lab, Discover/Career Center provide access to the Internet/World Wide Web, on-campus e-mail addresses. Staffed computer lab on campus provides training in use of computers, software.

EXPENSES

Expenses for 1997–98: *Application fee:* $25. State resident tuition: $2308 full-time, $64.10 per credit hour part-time. Nonresident tuition: $4615 full-time, $128.20 per credit hour part-time. Part-time mandatory fees: $20 per quarter. Full-time mandatory fees: $60.

LD Services Contact: Ms. Tillie Schiffler Jr., Student Advising and Development Representative, Lima Technical College, 4240 Campus Drive, Lima, OH 45804, 419-995-8060. Fax: 419-995-8098. Email: schifflt@ltc.tec.oh.us.

LINCOLN LAND COMMUNITY COLLEGE

Springfield, Illinois

LEARNING DISABILITIES SERVICES INFORMATION

Special Needs Services began offering services in 1980. Currently the program serves 120 undergraduates with LD. Students diagnosed with ADD/ADHD are eligible for the same services available to students with LD.

Staff: 1 full-time staff member (coordinator). Services provided by remediation specialists, tutors, counselors, notetakers, tapers.

Special Fees: No special fees are charged for services to students with LD.

Applications and admissions: *Required:* psychoeducational report completed within 3 years, Compensatory Strategy Assessment administered by the school, ACT ASSET. Students may begin taking classes in fall, spring, or summer. *Application deadline:* continuous.

Special policies: The college has written policies regarding grade forgiveness; substitutions and waivers of admissions requirements.

PROGRAM AND SERVICE COMPONENTS

Special preparation or orientation: Orientation (required for some) held individually by special arrangement.

Academic advising: Provided by academic advisers. Students with LD may take up to as many credit hours as an individual can handle each term; most take 9 credit hours; 12 credit hours required to maintain full-time status; 6 credit hours required to be eligible for financial aid.

Counseling services: Individual counseling, career counseling.

Basic skills remediation: Offered one-on-one and in class-size groups by regular teachers, study skills specialists. Available in reading, math, written language, learning strategies.

Subject-area tutoring: Offered one-on-one by professional teachers, peer tutors. Available in all subjects.

Special courses: College survival skills, reading, vocabulary development, composition, learning strategies, time management, study skills, stress management. Some offered for credit; some enter into overall grade point average.

Auxiliary aids: Taped textbooks, tape recorders.

Auxiliary services: Alternative test arrangements, notetakers, priority registration, advocacy.

GENERAL COLLEGE INFORMATION

District-supported, 2-year, coed. Part of Illinois Community College System. Awards associate degrees. Founded 1967. *Setting:* 241-acre suburban campus with easy access to St. Louis. *Total enrollment:* 11,016. *Faculty:* 245 (115 full-time, 20% with terminal degrees, 130 part-time).

Enrollment Profile: 11,016 students from 6 states and territories, 4 other countries. 58% women, 42% men, 75% part-time, 96% state residents, 4% transferred in, 1% international, 50% 25 or older, 1% Native American, 1% Hispanic, 4% black, 1% Asian or Pacific Islander.

First-Year Class: Of the students who applied, 100% were accepted, 85% of whom enrolled.

Graduation Requirements: 60 credit hours; math/science requirements vary according to program; computer course for some majors; internship (some majors).

Computers on Campus: 130 computers available on campus for general student use. A computer is recommended for some students. Students can contact faculty members and/or advisers through e-mail. Computers for student use in computer center, computer labs, classrooms, library, off-campus locations provide access to the Internet/World Wide Web, on- and off-campus e-mail addresses. Staffed computer lab on campus provides training in use of computers, software. *Academic computing expenditure 1995–96:* $219,306.

EXPENSES

Expenses for 1997–98: Area resident tuition: $1193 full-time, $39.75 per credit hour part-time. State resident tuition: $3202 full-time, $106.72 per credit hour part-time. Nonresident tuition: $5142 full-time, $171.39 per credit hour part-time. Full-time mandatory fees: $5.

LD Services Contact: Ms. Linda Chriswell, Special Needs Professional, Lincoln Land Community College, Shepherd Road, Springfield, IL 62794-9256, 217-786-2828. Fax: 217-786-2828.

LINN-BENTON COMMUNITY COLLEGE

Albany, Oregon

LEARNING DISABILITIES SERVICES INFORMATION

Office of Disability Services began offering services in 1985. Currently the program serves 72 undergraduates with LD. Students diagnosed with ADD/ADHD are eligible for the same services available to students with LD.

Staff: 2 full-time, 10 part-time staff members, including coordinator. Services provided by remediation specialists, tutors, counselor, reader, interpreters, instructional assistants.

Special Fees: No special fees are charged for services to students with LD.

Applications and admissions: *Recommended:* psychoeducational report completed within 3 to 5 years, WAIS-R, Woodcock-Johnson Psychoeducational Battery, reading and writing tests. Students may begin taking classes any term. *Application deadline:* continuous.

Special policies: The college has written policies regarding grade forgiveness; substitutions and waivers of graduation requirements.

PROGRAM AND SERVICE COMPONENTS

Academic advising: Provided by unit staff members, academic advisers. Most students with LD take 9 to 12 credits each term; 12 credits required to maintain full-time status; 3 to 11 credits (part-time), 12 credits (full-time) required to be eligible for financial aid.

Counseling services: Individual counseling, career counseling.

Subject-area tutoring: Offered one-on-one and in small groups by professional teachers, peer tutors. Available in all subjects.

Auxiliary aids: Taped textbooks, tape recorders, calculators, word-processors with spell-check, talking computers, optical character readers, adaptive computer equipment.

Auxiliary services: Alternative test arrangements, notetakers, priority registration, advocacy, readers, scribes, tutors.

GENERAL COLLEGE INFORMATION

State and locally supported, 2-year, coed. Awards associate degrees. Founded 1966. *Setting:* 104-acre small-town campus. *Endowment:* $721,431. *Research spending 1995–96:* $66,701. *Total enrollment:* 5,455. *Faculty:* 475 (180 full-time, 295 part-time).

Enrollment Profile: 5,455 students: 54% women, 46% men, 61% part-time, 98% state residents, 1% international, 57% 25 or older, 2% Native American, 2% Hispanic, 1% black, 2% Asian or Pacific Islander.

First-Year Class: 1,871 total; 2,105 applied, 100% were accepted, 89% of whom enrolled.

Graduation Requirements: 90 quarter credit hours; 1 math course; computer course.

Computers on Campus: 500 computers available on campus for general student use. A campus-wide network can be accessed. Students can contact faculty members and/or advisers through e-mail. Computers for student use in computer labs, learning resource center, classrooms provide access to the Internet/World Wide Web, on-campus e-mail addresses. Staffed computer lab on campus provides training in use of computers, software. *Academic computing expenditure 1995–96:* $525,752.

EXPENSES

Expenses for 1997–98: *Application fee:* $20. State resident tuition: $1620 full-time, $36 per credit part-time. Nonresident tuition: $5535 full-time, $123 per credit part-time. Tuition for international students: $6210 full-time, $138 per credit part-time.

LD Services Contact: Ms. Paula Grigsby, Coordinator, Disability Services, Linn-Benton Community College, 6500 Southwest Pacific Boulevard, Albany, OR 97321, 541-917-4683. Fax: 541-917-4681. Email: grigsbp@gw.lbcc.cc.or.us.

LON MORRIS COLLEGE

Jacksonville, Texas

LEARNING DISABILITIES SERVICES INFORMATION

Department of Developmental Studies currently serves 17 undergraduates with LD. Students diagnosed with ADD/ADHD are eligible for the same services available to students with LD.

Staff: 1 full-time, 2 part-time staff members, including director. Services provided by developmental English and math instructors.

Lon Morris College (continued)

Special Fees: No special fees are charged for services to students with LD.

Applications and admissions: *Required:* high school transcript, grade point average, class rank, psychoeducational report; *recommended:* untimed or extended time ACT, extended time SAT I. Students may begin taking classes in fall, spring, or summer. *Application deadline:* continuous.

Special policies: The college has written policies regarding substitutions and waivers of graduation and degree requirements.

PROGRAM AND SERVICE COMPONENTS

Diagnostic testing: Intelligence, math, written language, learning strategies.

Academic advising: Provided by academic advisers. Students with LD may take up to 18 credits each term; most take 14 credits; 12 credits required to maintain full-time status; 6 credits required to be eligible for financial aid.

Basic skills remediation: Offered in class-size groups by regular teachers. Available in reading, math, written language.

Subject-area tutoring: Offered one-on-one by professional teachers, peer tutors. Available in some subjects.

Auxiliary aids: Tape recorders, calculators, word-processors with spell-check, personal computers.

Auxiliary services: Alternative test arrangements, notetakers.

GENERAL COLLEGE INFORMATION

Independent United Methodist, 2-year, coed. Awards associate degrees. Founded 1873. *Setting:* 76-acre small-town campus. *Total enrollment:* 350. *Faculty:* 30 (16 full-time, 14 part-time).

Enrollment Profile: 350 students from 11 states and territories, 9 other countries. 39% women, 61% men, 4% part-time, 85% state residents, 2% transferred in, 12% international, 4% 25 or older, 0% Native American, 2% Hispanic, 9% black, 0% Asian or Pacific Islander.

First-Year Class: 190 total; 240 applied, 94% were accepted, 84% of whom enrolled. 10% from top 10% of their high school class, 30% from top quarter, 70% from top half.

Graduation Requirements: 62 credits; math/science requirements vary according to program; computer course.

Computers on Campus: 20 computers available on campus for general student use. Computers for student use in computer center, library.

EXPENSES

Expenses for 1997–98: Tuition: $5900 full-time. Part-time tuition per semester ranges from $750 to $2250. Full-time mandatory fees: $690. College room only: $1990.

LD Services Contact: Dr. John Ross, Academic Dean, Lon Morris College, 800 College Avenue, Jacksonville, TX 75766, 903-589-4000. Fax: 903-586-8562.

LORAIN COUNTY COMMUNITY COLLEGE

Elyria, Ohio

LEARNING DISABILITIES SERVICES INFORMATION

Office for Special Needs Services began offering services in 1986. Currently the program serves 114 undergraduates with LD. Students diagnosed with ADD/ADHD are eligible for the same services available to students with LD, as well as distraction-free testing environment.

Staff: 1 full-time staff member (coordinator). Services provided by tutors.

Special Fees: No special fees are charged for services to students with LD.

Applications and admissions: *Recommended:* high school transcript, grade point average, class rank, courses completed, IEP (Individualized Education Program), personal interview, psychoeducational report completed within 3 years. Students may begin taking classes in fall, winter, or spring. *Application deadline:* continuous.

Special policies: The college has written policies regarding grade forgiveness.

PROGRAM AND SERVICE COMPONENTS

Academic advising: Provided by unit staff members, academic advisers. Students with LD may take up to as many credit hours as an individual can handle each term; most take 3 to 10 credit hours; 12 credit hours required to maintain full-time status; 6 credit hours (Pell Grant), 12 credit hours (Ohio Instructional Grant) required to be eligible for financial aid.

Counseling services: Individual counseling, career counseling, self advocacy training.

Subject-area tutoring: Offered one-on-one and in small groups by professional teachers, peer tutors. Available in all subjects.

Auxiliary aids: Taped textbooks, tape recorders, calculators, word-processors with spell-check.

Auxiliary services: Alternative test arrangements, notetakers, priority registration, advocacy, readers, TDD/(216)366-4135.

GENERAL COLLEGE INFORMATION

State and locally supported, 2-year, coed. Part of Ohio Board of Regents. Awards associate degrees. Founded 1963. *Setting:* 480-acre suburban campus with easy access to Cleveland. *Total enrollment:* 7,047. *Faculty:* 347 (112 full-time, 235 part-time); student–undergrad faculty ratio is 19:1.

Enrollment Profile: 7,047 students: 65% women, 35% men, 66% part-time, 99% state residents, 11% transferred in, 1% international, 54% 25 or older, 1% Native American, 5% Hispanic, 6% black, 1% Asian or Pacific Islander. *Retention:* 68% of 1995 full-time freshmen returned. *Most popular recent majors:* nursing, business administration/commerce/management, elementary education.

First-Year Class: 1,930 total; 2,100 applied, 100% were accepted, 92% of whom enrolled.

Graduation Requirements: 93 quarter credits; computer course for technology majors.

Computers on Campus: 300 computers available on campus for general student use. Computers for student use in library, academic buildings.

EXPENSES

Expenses for 1997–98: *Application fee:* $10. Area resident tuition: $2249 full-time, $48.90 per credit part-time. State resident tuition: $2732 full-time, $59.40 per credit part-time. Nonresident tuition: $5653 full-time, $122.90 per credit part-time. Part-time mandatory fees: $2 per credit. Full-time mandatory fees: $92.

LD Services Contact: Ms. Ruth Porter, Coordinator, Lorain County Community College, 1005 North Abbe Road, Elyria, OH 44035, 216-365-4191 Ext. 4058. Fax: 216-366-4127. Email: rporter@loraincc.edu.

LORD FAIRFAX COMMUNITY COLLEGE

Middletown, Virginia

LEARNING DISABILITIES SERVICES INFORMATION

Learning Assistance Center began offering services in 1986. Currently the program serves 200 undergraduates with LD. Students diagnosed with ADD/ADHD are eligible for the same services available to students with LD.

Staff: 1 full-time, 1 part-time staff members, including coordinator. Services provided by remediation specialist, tutors, counselors.

Special Fees: No special fees are charged for services to students with LD.

Applications and admissions: Open admissions. Students may begin taking classes any term. *Application deadline:* continuous.

Special policies: The college has written policies regarding grade forgiveness.

PROGRAM AND SERVICE COMPONENTS

Academic advising: Provided by unit staff members, academic advisers. Students with LD may take up to 15 semester credits each term; most take 12 semester credits; 12 semester credits required to maintain full-time status.

Counseling services: Individual counseling, small-group counseling, career counseling.

Basic skills remediation: Offered one-on-one, in small groups, and in class-size groups by regular teachers, learning specialist, tutors/assistants. Available in reading, math, written language, learning strategies, study skills, time management.

Subject-area tutoring: Offered one-on-one and in small groups by peer tutors. Available in all subjects.

Special courses: College survival skills, math, study skills, career planning. Some offered for credit; some enter into overall grade point average.

Auxiliary aids: Tape recorders, word-processors with spell-check, optical character readers.

Auxiliary services: Alternative test arrangements, notetakers, advocacy.

GENERAL COLLEGE INFORMATION

State-supported, 2-year, coed. Part of Virginia Community College System. Awards associate degrees. Founded 1969. *Setting:* 100-acre rural campus with easy access to Washington, DC. *Total enrollment:* 3,410. *Faculty:* 152 (42 full-time, 110 part-time); student–undergrad faculty ratio is 22:1.
Enrollment Profile: 3,410 students: 66% women, 34% men, 70% part-time, 94% state residents, 10% transferred in, 59% 25 or older, 1% Hispanic, 4% black. *Most popular recent majors:* business administration/commerce/management, education, liberal arts/general studies.
First-Year Class: 923 total; 950 applied, 100% were accepted, 97% of whom enrolled.
Graduation Requirements: 62 semester hours; math/science requirements vary according to program; computer course for business-related majors.
Computers on Campus: 200 computers available on campus for general student use. A campus-wide network can be accessed from off-campus. Students can contact faculty members and/or advisers through e-mail. Computers for student use in computer center, computer labs, learning resource center, classrooms, library provide access to the Internet/World Wide Web. Staffed computer lab on campus provides training in use of computers, software.

EXPENSES

Expenses for 1997–98: State resident tuition: $1430 full-time, $47.65 per semester hour part-time. Nonresident tuition: $4710 full-time, $157 per semester hour part-time. Part-time mandatory fees: $5 per semester. Full-time mandatory fees: $26.
LD Services Contact: Ms. Paula Dean, Coordinator, Learning Assistance Center, Lord Fairfax Community College, PO Box 47, Middletown, VA 22645-0047, 540-869-1120. Fax: 540-869-6424.

LOS ANGELES HARBOR COLLEGE

Wilmington, California

LEARNING DISABILITIES SERVICES INFORMATION

Disabled Student Programs and Services began offering services in 1979. Currently the program serves 200 undergraduates with LD. Students diagnosed with ADD/ADHD are eligible for the same services available to students with LD.
Staff: 3 full-time, 20 part-time staff members, including director, coordinator, LD specialist. Services provided by tutors, counselor.
Special Fees: No special fees are charged for services to students with LD.
Applications and admissions: *Required:* personal interview, autobiographical statement, psychoeducational report; *recommended:* high school transcript. Students may begin taking classes in fall, spring, or summer. *Application deadline:* continuous.

PROGRAM AND SERVICE COMPONENTS

Special preparation or orientation: Optional orientation offered before registration.
Diagnostic testing: Intelligence, reading, math, spelling, perceptual skills, study skills, learning strategies.
Academic advising: Provided by unit staff members, academic advisers. Students with LD may take up to as many units as an individual can handle each term; most take 6 to 12 units; 12 units required to maintain full-time status; 12 units (students can petition for fewer) required to be eligible for financial aid.
Counseling services: Individual counseling, small-group counseling, career counseling, self-advocacy training.
Basic skills remediation: Offered one-on-one and in small groups by LD teachers, regular teachers; computer-aided instruction also offered. Available in reading, math, spelling, written language, learning strategies, perceptual skills, time management.
Subject-area tutoring: Offered one-on-one and in small groups by peer tutors. Available in all subjects.
Special courses: College survival skills, reading, vocabulary development, learning strategies, word processing, time management, math, study skills, career planning. All offered for credit; all enter into overall grade point average.
Auxiliary aids: Taped textbooks, tape recorders, calculators, typewriters, word-processors with spell-check, personal computers.
Auxiliary services: Alternative test arrangements, notetakers, priority registration, advocacy.
Campus support group: A special student organization is available to students with LD.

GENERAL COLLEGE INFORMATION

State and locally supported, 2-year, coed. Part of Los Angeles Community College District System. Awards associate degrees. Founded 1949. *Setting:* 80-acre suburban campus. *Research spending 1995–96:* $26,000. *Total enrollment:* 7,603. *Faculty:* 259 (102 full-time, 157 part-time); student–undergrad faculty ratio is 25:1.
Enrollment Profile: 7,603 students from 14 states and territories, 16 other countries. 59% women, 41% men, 71% part-time, 98% state residents, 14% transferred in, 1% international, 49% 25 or older, 2% Native American, 36% Hispanic, 17% black, 18% Asian or Pacific Islander. *Most popular recent majors:* liberal arts/general studies, nursing, business administration/commerce/management.
First-Year Class: 2,272 total. Of the students who applied, 100% were accepted.
Graduation Requirements: 60 units; math/science requirements vary according to program; computer course for most majors.
Computers on Campus: 50 computers available on campus for general student use. A campus-wide network can be accessed. Students can contact faculty members and/or advisers through e-mail. Computers for student use in computer center, library, student center. Staffed computer lab on campus provides training in use of computers, software.

EXPENSES

Expenses for 1996–97: State resident tuition: $0 full-time. Nonresident tuition: $3570 full-time, $119 per unit part-time. Part-time mandatory fees per semester range from $20.50 to $150.50. Full-time mandatory fees: $405.
LD Services Contact: Ms. Deborah Tull, Coordinator, Los Angeles Harbor College, 1111 Figueroa Place, Wilmington, CA 90744-2397, 310-522-8281. Fax: 310-834-1882.

LOS ANGELES SOUTHWEST COLLEGE

Los Angeles, California

LEARNING DISABILITIES SERVICES INFORMATION

Disabled Student Programs and Services began offering services in 1988. Currently the program serves 28 undergraduates with LD. Students diagnosed with ADD/ADHD are eligible for the same services available to students with LD.
Staff: 3 full-time, 2 part-time staff members, including director. Services provided by tutors, counselor, diagnostic specialists.
Special Fees: No special fees are charged for services to students with LD.
Applications and admissions: *Required:* high school diploma or GED (student must be 18 years of age or receive special permission). Students may begin taking classes in fall, spring, or summer. *Application deadline:* 4/14.

PROGRAM AND SERVICE COMPONENTS

Diagnostic testing: Intelligence, reading, math, spelling, written language, perceptual skills, study skills, learning strategies.
Academic advising: Provided by unit staff members. Students with LD may take up to 17 units each term; most take 12 units; 12 units required to maintain full-time status; 3 units required to be eligible for financial aid.
Counseling services: Individual counseling, career counseling.
Basic skills remediation: Offered one-on-one, in small groups, and in class-size groups by LD teachers; computer-aided instruction also offered. Available in reading, math, spelling, written language, learning strategies, study skills, time management.
Subject-area tutoring: Offered one-on-one by peer tutors. Available in most subjects.
Special courses: Learning strategies, study skills. All offered for credit; none enter into overall grade point average.
Auxiliary aids: Taped textbooks, tape recorders, calculators, typewriters, personal computers.
Auxiliary services: Alternative test arrangements, notetakers, priority registration, advocacy.
Campus support group: A special student organization is available to students with LD.

Los Angeles Southwest College (continued)

GENERAL COLLEGE INFORMATION

State and locally supported, 2-year, coed. Part of Los Angeles Community College District System. Awards associate degrees. Founded 1967. *Setting:* 69-acre urban campus. *Research spending 1995–96:* $321,616. *Total enrollment:* 5,802. *Faculty:* 223 (75 full-time, 148 part-time); student–undergrad faculty ratio is 37:1.

Enrollment Profile: 5,802 students from 20 states and territories, 4 other countries. 72% women, 28% men, 77% part-time, 98% state residents, 16% transferred in, 63% 25 or older, 0% Native American, 24% Hispanic, 74% black, 1% Asian or Pacific Islander. *Retention:* 50% of 1995 full-time freshmen returned. *Areas of study chosen:* 41% liberal arts/general studies, 18% computer and information sciences, 9% health professions and related sciences, 4% communications and journalism, 2% engineering and applied sciences, 2% English language/literature/letters, 2% performing arts, 2% prelaw, 2% premed, 1% architecture, 1% area and ethnic studies, 1% biological and life sciences, 1% business management and administrative services, 1% education, 1% foreign language and literature, 1% interdisciplinary studies, 1% mathematics, 1% natural resource sciences, 1% psychology, 1% social sciences, 1% vocational and home economics.

First-Year Class: 485 total. Of the students accepted, 40% enrolled.

Graduation Requirements: 60 units; 1 course each in math and science; computer course for business administration, accounting, drafting, journalism, real estate majors.

Computers on Campus: 40 computers available on campus for general student use. A campus-wide network can be accessed from off-campus. Students can contact faculty members and/or advisers through e-mail. Computers for student use in computer center, library provide access to the Internet/World Wide Web. Staffed computer lab on campus provides training in use of computers, software. *Academic computing expenditure 1995–96:* $68,834.

EXPENSES

Expenses for 1996–97: State resident tuition: $0 full-time. Nonresident tuition: $4290 full-time, $143 per unit part-time. Part-time mandatory fees: $13 per unit. Full-time mandatory fees: $390.

LD Services Contact: Ms. Janice E. Lee, Counselor, Los Angeles Southwest College, 1600 West Imperial Highway, Los Angeles, CA 90047, 213-241-5480. Fax: 213-241-5278.

LOS ANGELES VALLEY COLLEGE

Van Nuys, California

LEARNING DISABILITIES SERVICES INFORMATION

Disabled Student Programs and Services Learning Center began offering services in 1982. Currently the program serves 180 undergraduates with LD. Students diagnosed with ADD/ADHD are eligible for the same services available to students with LD.

Staff: 2 full-time, 5 part-time staff members, including coordinator. Services provided by counselors, remediation/diagnostic specialist.

Special Fees: No special fees are charged for services to students with LD.

Applications and admissions: *Recommended:* high school transcript, IEP (Individualized Education Program), psychoeducational report completed within 5 years, California Assessment System for Adults with Learning Disabilities. Students may begin taking classes any term. *Application deadline:* continuous.

Special policies: The college has written policies regarding grade forgiveness.

PROGRAM AND SERVICE COMPONENTS

Special preparation or orientation: Optional orientation offered before registration, during registration, after classes begin.

Diagnostic testing: Intelligence, reading, math, spelling, written language, perceptual skills.

Academic advising: Provided by unit staff members, academic advisers. Students with LD may take up to 19 units each term; most take 12 units; 12 units required to maintain full-time status; 12 units (fewer for fee waiver only) required to be eligible for financial aid.

Counseling services: Individual counseling, career counseling, self-advocacy training, personal development.

Basic skills remediation: Offered in small groups and in class-size groups by LD teachers, regular teachers, teacher trainees; computer-aided instruction also offered. Available in reading, math, spelling, spoken language, written language, learning strategies, motor abilities, perceptual skills, study skills, time management, speech.

Subject-area tutoring: Offered in small groups by peer tutors. Available in some subjects.

Special courses: College survival skills, reading, vocabulary development, composition, learning strategies, math, study skills, career planning, spelling. All offered for credit; all enter into overall grade point average.

Auxiliary aids: Taped textbooks, tape recorders, calculators, word-processors with spell-check, optical character readers.

Auxiliary services: Alternative test arrangements, priority registration, advocacy, notetaking assistance.

Campus support group: A special student organization is available to students with LD.

GENERAL COLLEGE INFORMATION

State and locally supported, 2-year, coed. Part of Los Angeles Community College District System. Awards associate degrees. Founded 1949. *Setting:* 105-acre suburban campus. *Total enrollment:* 17,084. *Faculty:* 482.

Enrollment Profile: 17,084 students: 52% women, 48% men, 77% part-time, 99% state residents, 16% transferred in, 1% international, 50% 25 or older, 1% Native American, 22% Hispanic, 7% black, 12% Asian or Pacific Islander.

First-Year Class: 5,005 total; 10,000 applied, 100% were accepted, 50% of whom enrolled.

Graduation Requirements: 60 units; 1 math course; internship (some majors).

Computers on Campus: 40 computers available on campus for general student use. Computers for student use in computer center.

EXPENSES

Expenses for 1997–98: State resident tuition: $0 full-time. Nonresident tuition: $3900 full-time, $130 per unit part-time. Part-time mandatory fees per semester range from $21.50 to $151.50. Full-time mandatory fees: $407.

LD Services Contact: Dr. Cyndi Maddren, DSPS Program Assistant, Los Angeles Valley College, 5800 Fulton Avenue, Van Nuys, CA 91401-4062, 818-781-8542.

LUZERNE COUNTY COMMUNITY COLLEGE

Nanticoke, Pennsylvania

LEARNING DISABILITIES SERVICES INFORMATION

Institute for Developmental Educational Activities (IDEA) currently serves 49 undergraduates with LD. Students diagnosed with ADD/ADHD are eligible for the same services available to students with LD.

Staff: Includes co-directors, assistant director, coordinators, executive director. Services provided by tutors, counselors.

Special Fees: No special fees are charged for services to students with LD.

Applications and admissions: *Required:* high school transcript. Students may begin taking classes in fall, spring, or summer. *Application deadline:* continuous.

Special policies: The college has written policies regarding substitutions and waivers of graduation and degree requirements.

PROGRAM AND SERVICE COMPONENTS

Academic advising: Provided by academic advisers. Students with LD may take up to 18 semester hours (overload requires Dean's permission) each term; most take 9 semester hours; 12 semester hours required to maintain full-time status; 6 semester hours required to be eligible for financial aid.

Counseling services: Individual counseling, small-group counseling, career counseling.

Subject-area tutoring: Offered one-on-one and in small groups by professional teachers, peer tutors. Available in most subjects.

Auxiliary aids: Tape recorders, calculators, typewriters, word-processors with spell-check.

Auxiliary services: Alternative test arrangements, notetakers, priority registration.

Campus support group: A special student organization is available to students with LD.

GENERAL COLLEGE INFORMATION

County-supported, 2-year, coed. Awards associate degrees. Founded 1966. *Setting:* 122-acre suburban campus. *Total enrollment:* 6,137. *Faculty:* 399 (108 full-time, 7% with terminal degrees, 291 part-time).
Enrollment Profile: 6,137 students: 60% women, 40% men, 62% part-time, 99% state residents, 3% transferred in, 1% international, 51% 25 or older, 1% Native American, 1% Hispanic, 2% black, 1% Asian or Pacific Islander. *Areas of study chosen:* 32% liberal arts/general studies, 20% business management and administrative services, 7% health professions and related sciences, 6% computer and information sciences, 6% education, 4% engineering and applied sciences, 4% fine arts, 3% pre-med, 2% communications and journalism, 2% social sciences, 1% architecture, 1% English language/literature/letters, 1% mathematics.
First-Year Class: 1,966 total; 2,000 applied, 100% were accepted, 98% of whom enrolled.
Graduation Requirements: 60 semester hours; 3 semester hours of math; internship (some majors).
Computers on Campus: 650 computers available on campus for general student use. Computers for student use in computer center, computer labs, learning resource center, classrooms, library. Staffed computer lab on campus provides training in use of computers, software. *Academic computing expenditure 1995–96:* $264,897.

EXPENSES

Expenses for 1997–98: *Application fee:* $20. Area resident tuition: $1590 full-time, $53 per semester hour part-time. State resident tuition: $3180 full-time, $106 per semester hour part-time. Nonresident tuition: $4770 full-time, $159 per semester hour part-time. Part-time mandatory fees: $7 per semester hour. Full-time mandatory fees: $210.
LD Services Contact: Mr. Thomas P. Leary, Dean of Admissions/Student Affairs/Registrar, Luzerne County Community College, 1333 South Prospect Street, Nanticoke, PA 18634-3899, 717-740-0344. Fax: 717-740-0238. Email: admissions@luzerne.edu.

MADISON AREA TECHNICAL COLLEGE

Madison, Wisconsin

LEARNING DISABILITIES SERVICES INFORMATION

Alternative Learning Division began offering services in 1989. Currently the program serves 190 undergraduates with LD. Students diagnosed with ADD/ADHD are eligible for the same services available to students with LD.
Staff: 5 full-time staff members, including director, coordinators. Services provided by instructors.
Special Fees: No special fees are charged for services to students with LD.
Applications and admissions: *Required:* high school transcript; *recommended:* high school courses completed, psychoeducational report. Students may begin taking classes any term. *Application deadline:* 8/1 (fall term), 11/20 (spring term).
Special policies: The college has written policies regarding substitutions and waivers of admissions, graduation, and degree requirements.

PROGRAM AND SERVICE COMPONENTS

Special preparation or orientation: Optional summer program offered prior to entering college. Optional orientation offered during registration.
Diagnostic testing: Reading, math, written language.
Academic advising: Provided by academic advisers. Most students with LD take 10 to 12 credits each term; 12 credits required to maintain full-time status; 6 credits required to be eligible for financial aid.
Basic skills remediation: Offered one-on-one by LD teachers. Available in reading, math, spelling, handwriting, spoken language, written language, learning strategies, study skills, time management, social skills.
Subject-area tutoring: Offered one-on-one by peer tutors. Available in most subjects.
Special courses: College survival skills. None offered for credit; none enter into overall grade point average.
Auxiliary aids: Taped textbooks, personal computers, talking computers, optical character readers, Arkenstone Reader.
Auxiliary services: Alternative test arrangements, notetakers, advocacy, case management.
Campus support group: A special student organization is available to students with LD.

GENERAL COLLEGE INFORMATION

District-supported, 2-year, coed. Part of Wisconsin Technical College System. Awards associate degrees. Founded 1911. *Setting:* 150-acre urban campus. *Research spending 1995–96:* $195,238. *Total enrollment:* 19,050. *Faculty:* 1,881 (393 full-time, 1,488 part-time); student–undergrad faculty ratio is 8:1.
Enrollment Profile: 19,050 students from 9 states and territories. 57% women, 43% men, 65% part-time, 98% state residents, 10% transferred in, 0% international, 50% 25 or older, 1% Native American, 2% Hispanic, 3% black, 2% Asian or Pacific Islander. *Retention:* 54% of 1995 full-time freshmen returned. *Areas of study chosen:* 31% liberal arts/general studies, 26% business management and administrative services, 13% health professions and related sciences, 9% engineering and applied sciences, 5% computer and information sciences, 4% architecture, 4% fine arts, 3% social sciences, 3% vocational and home economics, 1% interdisciplinary studies. *Most popular recent majors:* accounting, nursing, marketing/retailing/merchandising.
First-Year Class: 1,757 total; 6,565 applied, 83% were accepted, 32% of whom enrolled. 1% from top 10% of their high school class, 31% from top half.
Graduation Requirements: 64 credits; internship (some majors).
Computers on Campus: 1,500 computers available on campus for general student use. Computers for student use in computer labs, learning resource center, library, student center provide access to the Internet/World Wide Web. Staffed computer lab on campus provides training in use of computers, software. *Academic computing expenditure 1995–96:* $1.4 million.

EXPENSES

Expenses for 1997–98: State resident tuition: $1734 (minimum) full-time. Nonresident tuition: $7862 (minimum) full-time. Part-time tuition per credit ranges from $54.20 to $71.55 for state residents, $245.70 to $427.20 for nonresidents. Part-time mandatory fees: $3.25 per credit. Full-time tuition ranges up to$2290 for state residents, $13,670 for nonresidents, according to program. Part-time tuition per credit ranges from $54.20 to $71.55 for state residents, $245.70 to $427.20 for nonresidents, according to program. Full-time mandatory fees: $104.
LD Services Contact: Ms. Diane McKenzie, LD Instructor, Madison Area Technical College, 3550 Anderson Street, Madison, WI 53704, 608-246-6277. Fax: 608-246-6880.

MANATEE COMMUNITY COLLEGE

Bradenton, Florida

LEARNING DISABILITIES SERVICES INFORMATION

Office of Disabled Student Services (ODSS) began offering services in 1980. Currently the program serves 93 undergraduates with LD. Students diagnosed with ADD/ADHD are eligible for the same services available to students with LD.
Staff: 2 full-time, 12 part-time staff members, including coordinator. Services provided by remediation specialist, tutors, scribes, notetakers, adaptive technicians.
Special Fees: No special fees are charged for services to students with LD.
Applications and admissions: *Required:* high school transcript, psychoeducational report completed within 3 years. Students may begin taking classes any term. *Application deadline:* continuous.
Special policies: The college has written policies regarding grade forgiveness; substitutions and waivers of admissions, graduation, and degree requirements.

PROGRAM AND SERVICE COMPONENTS

Special preparation or orientation: Optional orientation offered before registration.
Academic advising: Provided by unit staff members. Students with LD may take up to 15 credit hours each term; most take 12 credit hours; 12 credit hours required to maintain full-time status; 3 credit hours required to be eligible for financial aid.
Counseling services: Individual counseling, career counseling, self-advocacy training.
Basic skills remediation: Offered in small groups by teacher trainees; computer-aided instruction also offered. Available in reading, math, written language, learning strategies, study skills, time management, computer skills.
Subject-area tutoring: Offered in small groups by peer tutors. Available in most subjects.

Manatee Community College (continued)

Auxiliary aids: Taped textbooks, tape recorders, calculators, typewriters, word-processors with spell-check, personal computers, talking computers, optical character readers.

Auxiliary services: Alternative test arrangements, notetakers, priority registration, advocacy.

GENERAL COLLEGE INFORMATION

State-supported, 2-year, coed. Part of Florida Community Colleges System. Awards associate degrees. Founded 1957. *Setting:* 100-acre suburban campus with easy access to Tampa–St. Petersburg. *Total enrollment:* 7,308. *Faculty:* 260 (129 full-time, 17% with terminal degrees, 131 part-time); student–undergrad faculty ratio is 20:1.

Enrollment Profile: 7,308 students from 10 states and territories. 61% women, 39% men, 62% part-time, 96% state residents, 20% transferred in, 4% international, 41% 25 or older, 1% Native American, 3% Hispanic, 6% black, 1% Asian or Pacific Islander. *Areas of study chosen:* 80% library and information studies, 6% health professions and related sciences, 3% computer and information sciences, 2% business management and administrative services, 1% engineering and applied sciences. *Most popular recent majors:* liberal arts/general studies, nursing, legal studies.

First-Year Class: 1,003 total. Of the students who applied, 100% were accepted, 100% of whom enrolled.

Graduation Requirements: 60 credit hours; math/science requirements vary according to program; computer course.

Computers on Campus: 294 computers available on campus for general student use. A campus-wide network can be accessed. Computers for student use in computer labs, classrooms, technology building provide access to the Internet/World Wide Web. Staffed computer lab on campus provides training in use of computers, software.

EXPENSES

Expenses for 1997–98: *Application fee:* $15. State resident tuition: $1207 full-time, $40.22 per credit hour part-time. Nonresident tuition: $4437 full-time, $147.91 per credit hour part-time.

LD Services Contact: Mr. Gregory J. Fierro, Coordinator, Manatee Community College, PO Box 1849, Bradenton, FL 34206, 941-755-1511 Ext. 4295. Fax: 914-755-1511 Ext. 4288.

MANCHESTER COMMUNITY-TECHNICAL COLLEGE

Manchester, Connecticut

LEARNING DISABILITIES SERVICES INFORMATION

College Learning Center currently serves 1 undergraduate with LD. Students diagnosed with ADD/ADHD are eligible for the same services available to students with LD, as well as distraction-free testing environment.

Staff: 1 part-time staff member (coordinator).

Special Fees: No special fees are charged for services to students with LD.

Applications and admissions: *Required:* high school IEP (Individualized Education Program), psychoeducational report completed within 3 years; *recommended:* high school transcript, courses completed, personal interview. Students may begin taking classes in fall, spring, or summer. *Application deadline:* continuous.

PROGRAM AND SERVICE COMPONENTS

Academic advising: Provided by unit staff members. Most students with LD take 9 semester hours each term; 6 semester hours required to maintain full-time status and be eligible for financial aid.

Counseling services: Individual counseling, small-group counseling, self-advocacy training.

Special courses: Self-advocacy. None offered for credit.

Auxiliary aids: Word-processors with spell-check, optical character readers.

Auxiliary services: Alternative test arrangements, notetakers, priority registration, advocacy.

GENERAL COLLEGE INFORMATION

State-supported, 2-year, coed. Part of Connecticut Community–Technical College System. Awards associate degrees. Founded 1963. *Setting:* 160-acre small-town campus with easy access to Hartford. *Total enrollment:* 5,400. *Faculty:* 205 (100 full-time, 105 part-time).

Enrollment Profile: 5,400 students: 61% women, 39% men, 72% part-time, 98% state residents, 15% transferred in, 1% Hispanic, 4% black.

First-Year Class: Of the students who applied, 100% were accepted, 75% of whom enrolled.

Graduation Requirements: 60 credit hours; math/science requirements vary according to program; computer course for business-related majors.

Computers on Campus: Computers for student use in computer center, library, various buildings.

EXPENSES

Expenses for 1997–98: State resident tuition: $1608 full-time, $67 per credit hour part-time. Nonresident tuition: $5232 full-time, $218 per credit hour part-time. Part-time mandatory fees per semester range from $42 to $91. Full-time mandatory fees: $206.

LD Services Contact: Ms. Gail Hammond, Learning Disabilities Specialist, Manchester Community-Technical College, 60 Bidwell Street, Manchester, CT 06040, 860-647-6113.

MAPLE WOODS COMMUNITY COLLEGE

Kansas City, Missouri

LEARNING DISABILITIES SERVICES INFORMATION

Access Office began offering services in 1979. Currently the program serves 45 undergraduates with LD. Students diagnosed with ADD/ADHD are eligible for the same services available to students with LD.

Staff: 1 full-time, 1 part-time staff members, including director, coordinator. Services provided by tutors, special needs counselor, learning specialist.

Special Fees: No special fees are charged for services to students with LD.

Applications and admissions: *Required:* high school transcript, courses completed, psychoeducational report completed within 3 years, ASSET (with accommodations). Students may begin taking classes in fall, spring, or summer. *Application deadline:* continuous.

PROGRAM AND SERVICE COMPONENTS

Academic advising: Provided by academic advisers. Students with LD may take up to 12 credit hours each term; most take 6 to 12 credit hours; 12 credit hours required to maintain full-time status; 3 credit hours required to be eligible for financial aid.

Counseling services: Individual counseling, career counseling.

Basic skills remediation: Offered one-on-one and in class-size groups by regular teachers, learning specialist. Available in reading, math, spelling, written language, learning strategies, study skills, time management.

Subject-area tutoring: Offered one-on-one and in small groups by professional teachers, peer tutors. Available in most subjects.

Special courses: College survival skills, reading, time management, math, typing, study skills, career planning. Some offered for credit; all enter into overall grade point average.

Auxiliary aids: Tape recorders, word-processors with spell-check, personal computers, talking computers, Arkenstone Reader, electronic aids, scanners.

Auxiliary services: Alternative test arrangements, notetakers.

GENERAL COLLEGE INFORMATION

State and locally supported, 2-year, coed. Part of Metropolitan Community Colleges System. Awards associate degrees. Founded 1969. *Setting:* 205-acre suburban campus. *Total enrollment:* 4,558. *Faculty:* 189 (56 full-time, 98% with terminal degrees, 133 part-time); student–undergrad faculty ratio is 23:1.

Enrollment Profile: 4,558 students: 59% women, 41% men, 67% part-time, 99% state residents, 7% transferred in, 1% international, 41% 25 or older, 1% Native American, 2% Hispanic, 2% black, 2% Asian or Pacific Islander. *Retention:* 45% of 1995 full-time freshmen returned. *Areas of study chosen:* 62% liberal arts/general studies, 13% vocational and home economics, 12% business management and administrative services, 7% health professions and related sciences, 4% computer and information

sciences, 2% engineering and applied sciences. *Most popular recent majors:* liberal arts/general studies, secretarial studies/office management, veterinary technology.
First-Year Class: 813 total. Of the students who applied, 100% were accepted.
Graduation Requirements: 62 credit hours; 9 credit hours of math/science including at least 1 lab science course; computer course for business administration, most vocational majors; internship (some majors).
Computers on Campus: A campus-wide network can be accessed from off-campus. Students can contact faculty members and/or advisers through e-mail. Computers for student use in computer center, computer labs, learning resource center, classrooms, library, departmental labs provide access to the Internet/World Wide Web. Staffed computer lab on campus provides training in use of computers, software. *Academic computing expenditure 1995–96:* $361,876.

EXPENSES

Expenses for 1997–98: Area resident tuition: $1457 full-time, $47 per credit hour part-time. State resident tuition: $2449 full-time, $79 per credit hour part-time. Nonresident tuition: $3472 full-time, $112 per credit hour part-time.
LD Services Contact: Ms. Barbara Schaefer, Director, Access Office, Maple Woods Community College, 2601 Northeast Road, Kansas City, MO 64156-1299, 816-437-3192.

MARSHALLTOWN COMMUNITY COLLEGE

Marshalltown, Iowa

LEARNING DISABILITIES SERVICES INFORMATION

Student Success Center began offering services in 1982. Currently the program serves 22 undergraduates with LD. Students diagnosed with ADD/ADHD are eligible for the same services available to students with LD.
Staff: 1 full-time, 1 part-time staff members, including coordinator, Student Success Center assistant. Services provided by remediation specialists, tutors, counselors, diagnostic specialists.
Special Fees: No special fees are charged for services to students with LD.
Applications and admissions: *Required:* high school transcript, courses completed, IEP (Individualized Education Program), letters of recommendation, psychoeducational report completed within 1 year, psychological evaluation; *recommended:* untimed ACT, personal interview. Students may begin taking classes in fall, spring, or summer. *Application deadline:* continuous.
Special policies: The college has written policies regarding substitutions and waivers of admissions requirements.

PROGRAM AND SERVICE COMPONENTS

Special preparation or orientation: Summer program (required for some) held prior to entering college. Required orientation held before registration and after classes begin.
Diagnostic testing: Reading, math, spelling, spoken language, written language, motor abilities, perceptual skills, study skills, personality, social skills, learning strategies.
Academic advising: Provided by unit staff members, academic advisers. Students with LD may take up to 14 credits each term; most take 6 credits; 12 credits required to maintain full-time status; 6 credits required to be eligible for financial aid.
Counseling services: Individual counseling, small-group counseling, career counseling, self-advocacy training.
Basic skills remediation: Offered one-on-one and in small groups by regular teachers. Available in reading, math, spelling, learning strategies, motor abilities, perceptual skills, study skills, time management, social skills, speech, computer skills.
Subject-area tutoring: Offered one-on-one and in small groups by professional teachers, peer tutors. Available in most subjects.
Special courses: College survival skills, reading, vocabulary development, communication skills, learning strategies, word processing, time management, math, study skills, career planning. Some offered for credit; some enter into overall grade point average.
Auxiliary aids: Taped textbooks, tape recorders, calculators, typewriters, word-processors with spell-check, personal computers.
Auxiliary services: Alternative test arrangements, notetakers, priority registration, advocacy.

GENERAL COLLEGE INFORMATION

District-supported, 2-year, coed. Part of Iowa Valley Community College District System. Awards associate degrees. Founded 1927. *Setting:* 200-acre small-town campus. *Endowment:* $654,643. *Total enrollment:* 1,248. *Faculty:* 107 (39 full-time, 100% with terminal degrees, 68 part-time); student–undergrad faculty ratio is 15:1.
Enrollment Profile: 1,248 students from 3 states and territories, 6 other countries. 66% women, 34% men, 39% part-time, 99% state residents, 4% transferred in, 34% 25 or older, 2% Native American, 1% Hispanic, 1% black, 1% Asian or Pacific Islander. *Areas of study chosen:* 42% liberal arts/general studies, 20% business management and administrative services, 15% health professions and related sciences, 5% education, 4% computer and information sciences, 3% engineering and applied sciences, 2% social sciences, 1% agriculture, 1% biological and life sciences, 1% communications and journalism, 1% fine arts, 1% natural resource sciences, 1% prelaw, 1% prevet, 1% psychology, 1% vocational and home economics. *Most popular recent majors:* liberal arts/general studies, nursing, business administration/commerce/management.
First-Year Class: 177 total.
Graduation Requirements: 64 credits; math/science requirements vary according to program; internship (some majors).
Computers on Campus: 250 computers available on campus for general student use. Computers for student use in computer center, computer labs, learning resource center, library, student newspaper, Student senate offices. Staffed computer lab on campus provides training in use of computers, software. *Academic computing expenditure 1995–96:* $158,190.

EXPENSES

Expenses for 1997–98: *Application fee:* $25. State resident tuition: $1856 full-time, $58 per credit hour part-time. Nonresident tuition: $3712 full-time, $116 per credit hour part-time. Part-time mandatory fees: $96 per semester. Full-time mandatory fees range from $240 to $315.
LD Services Contact: Ms. Laura Browne, Coordinator, Marshalltown Community College, 3700 South Center Street, Marshalltown, IA 50158-4760, 515-752-7106 Ext. 246. Fax: 515-754-1442.

MARYMOUNT COLLEGE, PALOS VERDES, CALIFORNIA

Rancho Palos Verdes, California

LEARNING DISABILITIES SERVICES INFORMATION

Support Services for Students with Disabilities began offering services in 1989. Currently the program serves 60 undergraduates with LD. Students diagnosed with ADD/ADHD are eligible for the same services available to students with LD.
Staff: 1 full-time staff member (coordinator).
Applications and admissions: *Required:* high school transcript; *recommended:* autobiographical statement, letters of recommendation, psychoeducational report completed within 3 years. Students may begin taking classes any term. *Application deadline:* continuous.

PROGRAM AND SERVICE COMPONENTS

Special preparation or orientation: Optional orientation offered after classes begin.
Academic advising: Provided by unit staff members, academic advisers. Students with LD may take up to 16 units each term; most take 14 units; 12 units required to maintain full-time status and be eligible for financial aid.
Counseling services: Individual counseling, self-advocacy training.
Basic skills remediation: Offered one-on-one by LD teachers, regular teachers. Available in reading, math, spelling, learning strategies, study skills, time management.
Subject-area tutoring: Offered one-on-one by professional teachers, peer tutors. Available in most subjects.
Auxiliary aids: Taped textbooks.
Auxiliary services: Alternative test arrangements, notetakers, priority registration, advocacy.

GENERAL COLLEGE INFORMATION

Independent Roman Catholic, 2-year, coed. Awards associate degrees. Founded 1932. *Setting:* 26-acre suburban campus with easy access to Los Angeles. *Total enrollment:* 830. *Faculty:* 76 (44 full-time, 60% with terminal degrees, 32 part-time); student–undergrad faculty ratio is 14:1.

Marymount College, Palos Verdes, California (continued)

Enrollment Profile: 830 students from 24 states and territories, 27 other countries. 56% women, 44% men, 30% part-time, 70% state residents, 13% transferred in, 19% international, 20% 25 or older, 1% Native American, 15% Hispanic, 5% black, 9% Asian or Pacific Islander. *Retention:* 70% of 1995 full-time freshmen returned. *Areas of study chosen:* 100% liberal arts/general studies.

First-Year Class: 392 total; 803 applied, 90% were accepted, 54% of whom enrolled.

Graduation Requirements: 60 units.

Computers on Campus: 30 computers available on campus for general student use. Computer purchase/lease plans available. A campus-wide network can be accessed from student residence rooms and from off-campus. Students can contact faculty members and/or advisers through e-mail. Computers for student use in computer center, learning resource center, library provide access to the Internet/World Wide Web, on- and off-campus e-mail addresses. Staffed computer lab on campus provides training in use of computers, software. *Academic computing expenditure 1995–96:* $225,284.

EXPENSES

Expenses for 1997–98: *Application fee:* $25. Comprehensive fee of $20,190 includes full-time tuition ($13,400 minimum), mandatory fees ($140), and college room and board ($6650). Part-time tuition: $600 per unit. Part-time mandatory fees: $70 per year. Full-time tuition for international students: $14,150.

LD Services Contact: Ms. Ruth Proctor, Coordinator, Support Services for Students with Disabilities, Marymount College, Palos Verdes, California, 30800 Palos Verdes Drive East, Rancho Palos Verdes, CA 90275, 310-377-5501 Ext. 367. Fax: 310-377-6223.

MASSASOIT COMMUNITY COLLEGE

Brockton, Massachusetts

LEARNING DISABILITIES SERVICES INFORMATION

Academic Resource Center/LATCH Program began offering services in 1988. Currently the program serves 200 undergraduates with LD. Students diagnosed with ADD/ADHD are eligible for the same services available to students with LD.

Staff: 2 full-time, 5 part-time staff members, including co-directors. Services provided by remediation specialists, tutors, counselors.

Special Fees: No special fees are charged for services to students with LD.

Applications and admissions: *Required:* high school transcript; *recommended:* high school IEP (Individualized Education Program), personal interview, letters of recommendation, psychoeducational report completed within 1 year. Students may begin taking classes any term. *Application deadline:* continuous.

PROGRAM AND SERVICE COMPONENTS

Special preparation or orientation: Required orientation held after classes begin (for LATCH students only).

Academic advising: Provided by unit staff members, academic advisers. Students with LD may take up to 15 credits each term; most take 6 to 12 credits; 12 credits required to maintain full-time status; 6 credits required to be eligible for financial aid.

Counseling services: Individual counseling, small-group counseling, career counseling, self-advocacy training.

Basic skills remediation: Offered one-on-one, in small groups, and in class-size groups by regular teachers, LD tutors. Available in reading, math, spelling, written language, learning strategies, study skills.

Subject-area tutoring: Offered one-on-one and in small groups by professional teachers, peer tutors. Available in most subjects.

Special courses: College survival skills, reading, composition, learning strategies, math, study skills, career planning. Some offered for credit; some enter into overall grade point average.

Auxiliary aids: Taped textbooks, typewriters, word-processors with spell-check, optical character readers.

Auxiliary services: Alternative test arrangements, notetakers, advocacy.

Campus support group: A special student organization is available to students with LD.

GENERAL COLLEGE INFORMATION

State-supported, 2-year, coed. Awards associate degrees. Founded 1966. *Setting:* suburban campus with easy access to Boston. *Total enrollment:* 5,602. *Faculty:* 357 (153 full-time, 204 part-time); student–undergrad faculty ratio is 18:1.

Enrollment Profile: 5,602 students from 3 states and territories, 5 other countries. 56% women, 44% men, 50% part-time, 98% state residents, 12% transferred in, 1% international, 45% 25 or older, 1% Native American, 2% Hispanic, 6% black, 1% Asian or Pacific Islander. *Areas of study chosen:* 41% liberal arts/general studies, 22% business management and administrative services, 17% health professions and related sciences, 8% social sciences, 6% engineering and applied sciences, 4% computer and information sciences, 2% vocational and home economics, 1% architecture. *Most popular recent majors:* liberal arts/general studies, business administration/commerce/management.

First-Year Class: 1,002 total; 2,092 applied, 92% were accepted, 52% of whom enrolled. 5% from top 10% of their high school class, 15% from top quarter, 35% from top half.

Graduation Requirements: 60 credits; math/science requirements vary accorrding to program; computer course (varies by major); internship (some majors).

Computers on Campus: 350 computers available on campus for general student use. Computers for student use in computer center, computer labs, learning resource center, classrooms, library, student center. Staffed computer lab on campus provides training in use of computers, software.

EXPENSES

Expenses for 1997–98: State resident tuition: $1020 full-time, $34 per credit part-time. Nonresident tuition: $5880 full-time, $196 per credit part-time. Part-time mandatory fees: $43 per credit. Full-time mandatory fees: $1290.

LD Services Contact: Ms. Lorraine Simon, LATCH Counselor, Massasoit Community College, 1 Massasoit Boulevard, Brockton, MA 02402-3996, 508-588-9100 Ext. 1890. Fax: 508-427-1255.

MATER DEI COLLEGE

Ogdensburg, New York

LEARNING DISABILITIES SERVICES INFORMATION

Services for the Disabled began offering services in 1989. Currently the program serves 30 to 35 undergraduates with LD. Students diagnosed with ADD/ADHD are not eligible for the same services available to students with LD.

Staff: 1 full-time staff member (coordinator). Services provided by remediation specialists, tutors, counselors.

Special Fees: No special fees are charged for services to students with LD.

Applications and admissions: *Required:* high school transcript; *recommended:* untimed or extended time SAT I or ACT, personal interview. Students may begin taking classes in fall only. *Application deadline:* continuous.

PROGRAM AND SERVICE COMPONENTS

Special preparation or orientation: Required orientation held before registration and after classes begin.

Academic advising: Provided by unit staff members, academic advisers. Students with LD may take up to 12 credit hours each term; most take 12 credit hours; 12 credit hours required to maintain full-time status and be eligible for financial aid.

Counseling services: Individual counseling, career counseling.

Basic skills remediation: Offered one-on-one, in small groups, and in class-size groups by regular teachers. Available in reading, math, spelling, written language.

Subject-area tutoring: Offered one-on-one and in small groups by professional teachers, peer tutors. Available in most subjects.

Special courses: College survival skills, reading, composition, word processing, math, study skills. Some offered for credit; some enter into overall grade point average.

Auxiliary aids: Taped textbooks, tape recorders, calculators, typewriters, word-processors with spell-check, personal computers.

Auxiliary services: Alternative test arrangements, notetakers.

GENERAL COLLEGE INFORMATION

Independent Roman Catholic, 2-year, coed. Awards associate degrees. Founded 1960. *Setting:* 211-acre rural campus. *Endowment:* $1 million. *Educational spending 1995–96:* $2950 per undergrad. *Total enrollment:* 336. *Faculty:* 28 (17 full-time, 12% with terminal degrees, 11 part-time); student–undergrad faculty ratio is 14:1.
Enrollment Profile: 336 students from 4 states and territories, 2 other countries. 79% women, 21% men, 5% part-time, 99% state residents, 19% live on campus, 14% transferred in, 47% 25 or older, 13% Native American, 1% Hispanic, 1% black, 1% Asian or Pacific Islander. *Retention:* 48% of 1995 full-time freshmen returned. *Areas of study chosen:* 50% social sciences, 20% business management and administrative services, 15% education, 8% liberal arts/general studies, 7% health professions and related sciences. *Most popular recent majors:* business administration/commerce/management, social work, early childhood education.
First-Year Class: 91 total; 121 applied, 98% were accepted, 77% of whom enrolled.
Graduation Requirements: 61 credit hours; internship (some majors).
Computers on Campus: 45 computers available on campus for general student use. A campus-wide network can be accessed. Computers for student use in computer labs, learning resource center. Staffed computer lab on campus provides training in use of computers, software. *Academic computing expenditure 1995–96:* $44,700.

EXPENSES

Expenses for 1996–97: Comprehensive fee of $10,460 includes full-time tuition ($6360) and college room and board ($4100). Part-time tuition: $265 per credit hour. Tuition guaranteed not to increase for student's term of enrollment.
LD Services Contact: Mr. Anthony Puccia, Coordinator, Services for the Disabled, Mater Dei College, 5428 State Highway 37, Ogdensburg, NY 13669-9699, 315-393-5930.

MAYLAND COMMUNITY COLLEGE

Spruce Pine, North Carolina

LEARNING DISABILITIES SERVICES INFORMATION

S.O.A.R. Program began offering services in 1988. Students diagnosed with ADD/ADHD are eligible for the same services available to students with LD.
Staff: 4 full-time, 2 part-time staff members, including director, administrative secretary. Services provided by tutors, counselors, developmental instructors.
Special Fees: No special fees are charged for services to students with LD.
Applications and admissions: *Required:* high school transcript, grade point average, class rank, courses completed, personal interview, psychoeducational report completed within 3 years. Students may begin taking classes in fall, spring, or summer. *Application deadline:* continuous.

PROGRAM AND SERVICE COMPONENTS

Diagnostic testing: Intelligence, reading, math, spelling, handwriting, spoken language, written language, study skills, personality, learning strategies.
Academic advising: Provided by unit staff members, academic advisers. Most students with LD take 12 semester hours each term; 12 semester hours required to maintain full-time status; 6 semester hours required to be eligible for financial aid.
Counseling services: Individual counseling, career counseling.
Basic skills remediation: Offered one-on-one and in small groups by regular teachers. Available in reading, math, written language, learning strategies, study skills.
Subject-area tutoring: Offered one-on-one and in small groups by professional teachers, peer tutors. Available in most subjects.
Auxiliary aids: Taped textbooks, tape recorders, calculators, typewriters, personal computers, optical character readers, spell checkers.
Auxiliary services: Alternative test arrangements, notetakers, priority registration, advocacy.

GENERAL COLLEGE INFORMATION

State and locally supported, 2-year, coed. Part of North Carolina Community College System. Awards associate degrees. Founded 1971. *Setting:* 38-acre rural campus. *Total enrollment:* 814. *Faculty:* 35 (15 full-time, 20 part-time); student–undergrad faculty ratio is 23:1.
Enrollment Profile: 814 students from 3 states and territories. 60% women, 40% men, 50% part-time, 99% state residents, 15% transferred in, 0% international, 45% 25 or older, 1% Native American, 1% Hispanic, 3% black, 1% Asian or Pacific Islander. *Retention:* 60% of 1995 full-time freshmen returned. *Areas of study chosen:* 21% liberal arts/general studies, 17% business management and administrative services, 10% health professions and related sciences, 5% computer and information sciences, 4% engineering and applied sciences. *Most popular recent majors:* business administration/commerce/management, medical secretarial studies, nursing.
First-Year Class: 300 total; 417 applied, 96% were accepted, 75% of whom enrolled.
Computers on Campus: 80 computers available on campus for general student use. Computers for student use in computer labs, classrooms.

EXPENSES

Expenses for 1997–98: State resident tuition: $560 full-time, $20 per semester hour part-time. Nonresident tuition: $4564 full-time, $163 per semester hour part-time. Part-time mandatory fees: $38 per year. Full-time mandatory fees: $38.
LD Services Contact: Ms. Nancy H. Godwin, Director of S.O.A.R. Program, Mayland Community College, PO Box 547, Spruce Pine, NC 28777, 704-765-7351. Fax: 704-765-0728. Email: ngodwin@mayland.cc.nc.us.

MCDOWELL TECHNICAL COMMUNITY COLLEGE

Marion, North Carolina

LEARNING DISABILITIES SERVICES INFORMATION

Student Affairs began offering services in 1987. Currently the program serves 38 undergraduates with LD. Students diagnosed with ADD/ADHD are eligible for the same services available to students with LD, as well as small group and basic skills instruction.
Staff: 6 full-time, 12 part-time staff members, including director, assistant director. Services provided by remediation specialist, tutors, counselors, diagnostic specialist, psychologist.
Special Fees: No special fees are charged for services to students with LD.
Applications and admissions: *Required:* high school transcript, GED (in lieu of high school diploma), Computerized Placement Test (CPT); *recommended:* psychoeducational report completed within 3 years. Students may begin taking classes any term. *Application deadline:* continuous.
Special policies: The college has written policies regarding substitutions and waivers of admissions, graduation, and degree requirements.

PROGRAM AND SERVICE COMPONENTS

Special preparation or orientation: Optional summer program offered prior to entering college. Required orientation held before registration and after classes begin.
Diagnostic testing: Intelligence, reading, math, spelling, spoken language, written language, motor abilities, perceptual skills, study skills, social skills, learning strategies.
Academic advising: Provided by unit staff members, academic advisers.
Counseling services: Individual counseling, small-group counseling, career counseling.
Basic skills remediation: Offered one-on-one and in small groups by regular teachers, tutors; computer-aided instruction also offered. Available in reading, math, spelling, handwriting, spoken language, written language, learning strategies, study skills, time management, social skills, speech, computer skills.
Subject-area tutoring: Offered one-on-one and in small groups by professional teachers, peer tutors. Available in all subjects.
Special courses: College survival skills, reading, vocabulary development, communication skills, composition, learning strategies, word processing, Internet use, time management, math, typing, personal psychology, study skills, career planning, stress management. Most offered for credit; most enter into overall grade point average.
Auxiliary aids: Taped textbooks, tape recorders, calculators, typewriters, word-processors with spell-check, talking computers, optical character readers, Reading Edge.
Auxiliary services: Alternative test arrangements, notetakers, advocacy, readers.

McDowell Technical Community College (continued)

GENERAL COLLEGE INFORMATION

State-supported, 2-year, coed. Part of North Carolina Community College System. Awards associate degrees. Founded 1964. *Setting:* 31-acre rural campus. *Total enrollment:* 1,115. *Faculty:* 58 (40 full-time, 90% with terminal degrees, 18 part-time); student–undergrad faculty ratio is 17:1.
Enrollment Profile: 1,115 students: 63% women, 37% men, 54% part-time, 99% state residents, 9% transferred in, 0% international, 1% Native American, 1% Hispanic, 6% black, 1% Asian or Pacific Islander. *Retention:* 72% of 1995 full-time freshmen returned. *Areas of study chosen:* 8% health professions and related sciences, 5% computer and information sciences. *Most popular recent majors:* nursing, electrical and electronics technologies, accounting.
First-Year Class: 572 total; 720 applied, 87% were accepted, 91% of whom enrolled.
Graduation Requirements: 1 math course; computer course for most majors.
Computers on Campus: 70 computers available on campus for general student use. Computers for student use in computer center, computer labs, learning resource center, library, career center provide access to the Internet/World Wide Web. Staffed computer lab on campus provides training in use of computers, software.

EXPENSES

Expenses for 1997–98: State resident tuition: $560 full-time, $20 per semester hour part-time. Nonresident tuition: $4564 full-time, $163 per semester hour part-time. Part-time mandatory fees: $6.25 per semester. Full-time mandatory fees: $13.
LD Services Contact: Dr. James R. Robinson, Director of Counseling, McDowell Technical Community College, Route 1, Box 170, Marion, NC 28752, 704-652-6021. Fax: 704-652-1014.

MCHENRY COUNTY COLLEGE

Crystal Lake, Illinois

LEARNING DISABILITIES SERVICES INFORMATION

Special Needs Program began offering services in 1978. Currently the program serves 175 undergraduates with LD. Students diagnosed with ADD/ADHD are eligible for the same services available to students with LD.
Staff: 2 full-time, 13 part-time staff members, including director, coordinator. Services provided by tutors, counselor, diagnostic specialist.
Special Fees: No special fees are charged for services to students with LD.
Applications and admissions: *Required:* high school transcript, IEP (Individualized Education Program), personal interview, psychoeducational report completed within 3 years. Students may begin taking classes any term. *Application deadline:* continuous.

PROGRAM AND SERVICE COMPONENTS

Special preparation or orientation: Optional orientation offered during registration.
Diagnostic testing: Intelligence, reading, math, spelling, written language, perceptual skills.
Academic advising: Provided by unit staff members. Most students with LD take 9 to 14 semester hours each term; 12 semester hours required to maintain full-time status; 6 semester hours required to be eligible for financial aid.
Counseling services: Individual counseling, career counseling.
Subject-area tutoring: Offered one-on-one and in small groups by professional teachers, peer tutors. Available in all subjects.
Special courses: College survival skills, learning strategies, time management, study skills, career planning. Most offered for credit; none enter into overall grade point average.
Auxiliary aids: Taped textbooks, tape recorders, calculators, typewriters, word-processors with spell-check, personal computers, talking computers, optical character readers.
Auxiliary services: Alternative test arrangements, notetakers, advocacy.
Campus support group: A special student organization is available to students with LD.

GENERAL COLLEGE INFORMATION

State and locally supported, 2-year, coed. Part of Illinois Community College System. Awards associate degrees. Founded 1967. *Setting:* 109-acre suburban campus with easy access to Chicago. *Total enrollment:* 4,809. *Faculty:* 235 (73 full-time, 8% with terminal degrees, 162 part-time); student–undergrad faculty ratio is 18:1.
Enrollment Profile: 4,809 students: 61% women, 39% men, 73% part-time, 99% state residents, 6% transferred in, 0% international, 49% 25 or older, 0% Native American, 2% Hispanic, 0% black, 1% Asian or Pacific Islander. *Most popular recent majors:* liberal arts/general studies, science.
First-Year Class: 1,637 total; 2,360 applied, 100% were accepted, 69% of whom enrolled.
Graduation Requirements: 60 semester hours; 1 math course; 2 lab science courses; computer course.
Computers on Campus: 100 computers available on campus for general student use. Computers for student use in computer center, computer labs, learning resource center, classrooms, library provide access to the Internet/World Wide Web. Staffed computer lab on campus provides training in use of computers, software.

EXPENSES

Expenses for 1997–98: Area resident tuition: $1200 full-time, $40 per semester hour part-time. State resident tuition: $5433 full-time, $181.11 per semester hour part-time. Nonresident tuition: $6271 full-time, $209.03 per semester hour part-time. Part-time mandatory fees: $7 per semester. Full-time mandatory fees: $14.
LD Services Contact: Mr. Howard Foreman, Director of Special Needs, McHenry County College, 8900 US Highway 14, Crystal Lake, IL 60012-2761, 815-455-8710. Fax: 815-455-3999. Email: hforeman@pobox.mchenry.cc.il.us.

MCLENNAN COMMUNITY COLLEGE

Waco, Texas

LEARNING DISABILITIES SERVICES INFORMATION

Student Development began offering services in 1979. Currently the program serves 15 undergraduates with LD. Students diagnosed with ADD/ADHD are eligible for the same services available to students with LD.
Staff: 4 full-time staff members, including coordinator, counseling specialists. Services provided by tutors, counselors.
Special Fees: No special fees are charged for services to students with LD.
Applications and admissions: *Required:* high school transcript, personal interview, placement test; *recommended:* high school IEP (Individualized Education Program), psychoeducational report completed within 5 years. Students may begin taking classes any term. *Application deadline:* continuous.

PROGRAM AND SERVICE COMPONENTS

Academic advising: Provided by unit staff members, academic advisers. Students with LD may take up to 17 semester hours each term; most take 9 to 12 semester hours; 12 semester hours required to maintain full-time status; 6 semester hours (part-time), 12 semester hours (full-time) required to be eligible for financial aid.
Counseling services: Individual counseling, small-group counseling, career counseling.
Basic skills remediation: Offered one-on-one and in small groups by regular teachers, lab assistants, developmental education instructors. Available in reading, math, spelling, handwriting, written language, learning strategies, study skills, time management, social skills.
Subject-area tutoring: Offered one-on-one and in small groups by peer tutors, student workers. Available in all subjects.
Auxiliary aids: Taped textbooks, tape recorders, calculators, word-processors with spell-check, optical character readers, large screen computers.
Auxiliary services: Alternative test arrangements, notetakers, priority registration, readers.

GENERAL COLLEGE INFORMATION

County-supported, 2-year, coed. Part of Texas Higher Education Coordinating Board. Awards associate degrees. Founded 1965. *Setting:* 200-acre urban campus. *Total enrollment:* 5,561. *Faculty:* 284 (179 full-time, 10% with terminal degrees, 105 part-time); student–undergrad faculty ratio is 22:1.
Enrollment Profile: 5,561 students: 64% women, 36% men, 54% part-time, 98% state residents, 7% transferred in, 2% international, 55% 25 or older, 1% Native American, 10% Hispanic, 15% black, 1% Asian or Pacific Islander.

First-Year Class: 1,255 total; 2,528 applied, 100% were accepted, 50% of whom enrolled.
Graduation Requirements: 60 semester hours; computer course for most majors; internship (some majors).
Computers on Campus: 425 computers available on campus for general student use. Computers for student use in computer center, computer labs, research center, learning resource center, classrooms, library, accounting lab, learning center provide access to the Internet/World Wide Web. Staffed computer lab on campus provides training in use of computers, software.

EXPENSES

Expenses for 1997–98: Area resident tuition: $600 full-time. State resident tuition: $750 full-time. Nonresident tuition: $2400 full-time. Part-time tuition per semester ranges from $40 to $220 for area residents, $50 to $275 for state residents, $200 to $880 for nonresidents. Part-time mandatory fees per semester range from $46 to $221. Full-time mandatory fees: $620.
LD Services Contact: Ms. Vickie Hampton-Mitzel, Coordinator, Student Development, McLennan Community College, 1400 College Drive, Waco, TX 76708, 817-299-8428. Fax: 817-299-8681. Email: vhm@mcc.cc.tx.us.

MERCED COLLEGE

Merced, California

LEARNING DISABILITIES SERVICES INFORMATION

Disabled Student Services began offering services in 1988. Currently the program serves 120 undergraduates with LD. Students diagnosed with ADD/ADHD are eligible for the same services available to students with LD.
Staff: 1 full-time staff member (director). Services provided by tutors, counselors, diagnostic specialists, high-tech specialist, LD specialist.
Special Fees: No special fees are charged for services to students with LD.
Applications and admissions: *Recommended:* high school IEP (Individualized Education Program), psychoeducational report completed within 3 years. Students may begin taking classes in fall, spring, or summer. *Application deadline:* continuous.
Special policies: The college has written policies regarding grade forgiveness; substitutions and waivers of admissions, graduation, and degree requirements.

PROGRAM AND SERVICE COMPONENTS

Diagnostic testing: Intelligence, reading, math, spelling, written language, learning strategies.
Academic advising: Provided by unit staff members. Most students with LD take 9 to 12 units each term; 12 units required to maintain full-time status; 6 units (part-time), 12 units (full-time) required to be eligible for financial aid.

GENERAL COLLEGE INFORMATION

State and locally supported, 2-year, coed. Part of California Community Colleges System. Awards associate degrees. Founded 1962. *Setting:* 168-acre small-town campus. *Total enrollment:* 7,063. *Faculty:* 421 (145 full-time, 276 part-time); student–undergrad faculty ratio is 20:1.
Enrollment Profile: 7,063 students from 30 states and territories, 10 other countries. 60% women, 40% men, 55% part-time, 95% state residents, 8% transferred in, 1% international, 43% 25 or older, 2% Native American, 32% Hispanic, 6% black, 11% Asian or Pacific Islander. *Areas of study chosen:* 10% business management and administrative services, 10% health professions and related sciences, 8% social sciences, 7% liberal arts/general studies, 6% engineering and applied sciences, 6% vocational and home economics, 4% computer and information sciences, 2% agriculture, 2% English language/literature/letters, 2% fine arts, 2% performing arts, 1% biological and life sciences, 1% foreign language and literature, 1% mathematics, 1% natural resource sciences, 1% philosophy, 1% physical sciences, 1% prelaw, 1% psychology.
First-Year Class: 1,715 total; 2,950 applied, 100% were accepted.
Graduation Requirements: 60 units; algebra proficiency; computer course for business-related majors.
Computers on Campus: 400 computers available on campus for general student use. Computers for student use in computer center, learning resource center.

EXPENSES

Expenses for 1997–98: State resident tuition: $0 full-time. Nonresident tuition: $3540 full-time, $118 per unit part-time. Part-time mandatory fees per semester range from $24 to $154. Full-time mandatory fees: $412.
LD Services Contact: Mr. Richard Marashlian, Director of Student Services, Merced College, 3600 M Street, Merced, CA 95348-2898, 209-384-6155. Fax: 209-384-6084.

MERIDIAN COMMUNITY COLLEGE

Meridian, Mississippi

LEARNING DISABILITIES SERVICES INFORMATION

Special Populations Office began offering services in 1993. Currently the program serves 9 undergraduates with LD. Students diagnosed with ADD/ADHD are eligible for the same services available to students with LD.
Staff: 7 full-time staff members, including coordinator, Learning Lab Director. Services provided by tutors.
Special Fees: No special fees are charged for services to students with LD.
Applications and admissions: *Required:* high school transcript, grade point average, psychoeducational report completed within 3 years; *recommended:* untimed or extended time ACT. Students may begin taking classes in fall, spring, or summer. *Application deadline:* continuous.

PROGRAM AND SERVICE COMPONENTS

Academic advising: Provided by unit staff members, academic advisers. Students with LD may take up to 18 semester hours each term; most take 12 to 15 semester hours; 12 semester hours required to maintain full-time status and be eligible for financial aid.
Counseling services: Individual counseling, career counseling.
Basic skills remediation: Offered one-on-one by LD teachers, regular teachers; computer-aided instruction also offered. Available in reading, math, learning strategies, study skills, time management.
Auxiliary aids: Taped textbooks, optical character readers.
Auxiliary services: Alternative test arrangements, notetakers, priority registration, advocacy, time extensions for class assignments, extended office hours for meeting with instructors.

GENERAL COLLEGE INFORMATION

State and locally supported, 2-year, coed. Part of Mississippi State Board for Community and Junior Colleges. Awards associate degrees. Founded 1937. *Setting:* 62-acre small-town campus. *Educational spending 1995–96:* $2484 per undergrad. *Total enrollment:* 3,205. *Faculty:* 255 (190 full-time, 6% with terminal degrees, 65 part-time).
Enrollment Profile: 3,205 students from 8 states and territories, 14 other countries. 66% women, 34% men, 37% part-time, 93% state residents, 12% live on campus, 7% transferred in, 1% international, 39% 25 or older, 1% Native American, 1% Hispanic, 28% black, 1% Asian or Pacific Islander. *Retention:* 76% of 1995 full-time freshmen returned. *Areas of study chosen:* 42% vocational and home economics, 7% education, 6% business management and administrative services, 2% health professions and related sciences, 1% architecture, 1% biological and life sciences, 1% communications and journalism, 1% computer and information sciences, 1% engineering and applied sciences, 1% fine arts, 1% mathematics, 1% predentistry, 1% prelaw, 1% premed, 1% prevet, 1% psychology, 1% social sciences. *Most popular recent major:* nursing.
First-Year Class: 920 total; 1,451 applied, 80% were accepted, 79% of whom enrolled.
Graduation Requirements: 64 semester hours; 3 semester hours of math; 6 semester hours of science; computer course for marketing, medical records technology majors.
Computers on Campus: 123 computers available on campus for general student use. A computer is recommended for some students. Computers for student use in classrooms, library, career center. *Academic computing expenditure 1995–96:* $55,903.

EXPENSES

Expenses for 1996–97: State resident tuition: $960 full-time, $50 per semester hour part-time. Nonresident tuition: $2000 full-time, $100 per semester hour part-time. Part-time mandatory fees: $20 per semester. Full-time mandatory fees: $40. College room and board: $2200.
LD Services Contact: Ms. Kim L. Miller, Special Populations Coordinator, Meridian Community College, 910 Highway 19 North, Meridian, MS 39307, 601-484-8777. Fax: 601-484-8704.

MESABI RANGE COMMUNITY AND TECHNICAL COLLEGE

Virginia, Minnesota

LEARNING DISABILITIES SERVICES INFORMATION

Services to Students with Disabilities began offering services in 1985. Currently the program serves 90 to 100 undergraduates with LD. Students diagnosed with ADD/ADHD are eligible for the same services available to students with LD, as well as resources and information referrals.
Staff: 1 part-time staff member (director). Services provided by remediation specialists, tutors, counselors, diagnostic specialists.
Special Fees: No special fees are charged for services to students with LD.
Applications and admissions: *Required:* personal interview; *recommended:* high school IEP (Individualized Education Program), psychoeducational report completed within 3 years. Students may begin taking classes any term. *Application deadline:* continuous.
Special policies: The college has written policies regarding substitutions and waivers of admissions, graduation, and degree requirements.

PROGRAM AND SERVICE COMPONENTS

Special preparation or orientation: Optional summer program offered prior to entering college.
Academic advising: Provided by unit staff members, academic advisers. Students with LD may take up to 15 credits each term; most take 12 credits; 12 credits required to maintain full-time status and be eligible for financial aid.
Counseling services: Individual counseling, small-group counseling, career counseling, self-advocacy training.
Basic skills remediation: Offered one-on-one and in class-size groups by LD teachers, regular teachers. Available in reading, math, spelling, written language, learning strategies, study skills, time management.
Subject-area tutoring: Offered one-on-one and in small groups by professional teachers, peer tutors. Available in most subjects.
Special courses: College survival skills, reading, vocabulary development, composition, learning strategies, time management, math, study skills, career planning. All offered for credit; most enter into overall grade point average.
Auxiliary aids: Taped textbooks, tape recorders, calculators, word-processors with spell-check.
Auxiliary services: Alternative test arrangements, notetakers, priority registration, advocacy.

GENERAL COLLEGE INFORMATION

State-supported, 2-year, coed. Part of Minnesota State Colleges and Universities System. Awards associate degrees. Founded 1918. *Setting:* 30-acre small-town campus. *Total enrollment:* 998. *Faculty:* 71 (33 full-time, 9% with terminal degrees, 38 part-time).
Enrollment Profile: 998 students from 6 states and territories, 8 other countries. 60% women, 40% men, 42% part-time, 96% state residents, 10% live on campus, 5% transferred in, 1% international, 32% 25 or older, 4% Native American, 1% Hispanic, 2% black. *Areas of study chosen:* 59% liberal arts/general studies, 5% business management and administrative services, 5% education, 5% health professions and related sciences, 4% social sciences, 3% engineering and applied sciences, 3% psychology, 2% vocational and home economics, 1% architecture, 1% area and ethnic studies, 1% biological and life sciences, 1% communications and journalism, 1% computer and information sciences, 1% fine arts, 1% library and information studies, 1% mathematics, 1% natural resource sciences, 1% physical sciences, 1% predentistry, 1% prelaw, 1% premed, 1% prevet.
First-Year Class: 416 total; 341 applied, 100% were accepted, 82% of whom enrolled. 9% from top 10% of their high school class, 65% from top half.
Graduation Requirements: 96 credits; 1 math course; computer course; internship (some majors).
Computers on Campus: 80 computers available on campus for general student use. Computers for student use in computer center, computer labs, learning resource center, library provide access to the Internet/World Wide Web. Staffed computer lab on campus provides training in use of computers, software.

EXPENSES

Expenses for 1996–97: *Application fee:* $20. State resident tuition: $2286 full-time, $47.62 per credit part-time. Nonresident tuition: $4282 full-time, $89.20 per credit part-time. North Dakota, South Dakota and Wisconsin residents pay tuition at the rate they would pay if attending a comparable state-supported institution in their home state. College room only: $2115.
LD Services Contact: Ms. Jane Chilcote, Director of Disability Services, Mesabi Range Community and Technical College, 1001 Chestnut Street West, Virginia, MN 55792, 218-749-7791. Fax: 218-749-0318. Email: j.chilcote@me.cc.mn.us.

MIAMI-DADE COMMUNITY COLLEGE

Miami, Florida

LEARNING DISABILITIES SERVICES INFORMATION

Disabled Student Services began offering services in 1980. Currently the program serves 102 undergraduates with LD. Students diagnosed with ADD/ADHD are eligible for the same services available to students with LD.
Staff: 5 full-time, 24 part-time staff members, including director, lab manager, LD specialist, vocational education specialist. Services provided by remediation specialists, tutors, counselors, diagnostic specialists.
Special Fees: No special fees are charged for services to students with LD.
Applications and admissions: *Required:* high school diploma (for A.A./A.S.), certificate of completion (for vocational education courses); *recommended:* psychoeducational report completed within 3 years. Students may begin taking classes in fall, winter, or spring. *Application deadline:* continuous.
Special policies: The college has written policies regarding grade forgiveness; substitutions and waivers of admissions, graduation, and degree requirements.

PROGRAM AND SERVICE COMPONENTS

Special preparation or orientation: Required orientation held on an individual basis.
Diagnostic testing: Intelligence, reading, math, spelling, handwriting, spoken language, written language, learning strategies, cognitive skills.
Academic advising: Provided by unit staff members, academic advisers. Students with LD may take up to 12 credit hours each term; most take 6 to 12 credit hours; 12 credit hours (may be less for insurance purposes or transportation passes) required to maintain full-time status; 6 credit hours required to be eligible for financial aid.
Counseling services: Individual counseling, career counseling.
Basic skills remediation: Offered one-on-one and in small groups by LD specialist. Available in reading, math, spelling, handwriting, spoken language, written language, motor abilities, perceptual skills, study skills.
Subject-area tutoring: Offered one-on-one and in small groups by professional teachers, peer tutors, students with Bachelor's or Master's degrees. Available in most subjects.
Special courses: Reading, composition, math. All offered for credit; none enter into overall grade point average.
Auxiliary aids: Taped textbooks, tape recorders, calculators, optical character readers, voice synthesizers, braille writers, telecommunication devices for the deaf, screen enlargements, Franklin Speller, talking calculators.
Auxiliary services: Alternative test arrangements, notetakers, priority registration, advocacy, readers.
Campus support group: A special student organization is available to students with LD.

GENERAL COLLEGE INFORMATION

State and locally supported, 2-year, coed. Part of Florida Community Colleges System. Awards associate degrees. Founded 1960. *Setting:* urban campus. *Total enrollment:* 51,019. *Faculty:* 2,070 (886 full-time, 25% with terminal degrees, 1,184 part-time).
Enrollment Profile: 51,019 students from 31 states and territories, 97 other countries. 58% women, 42% men, 67% part-time, 92% state residents, 4% transferred in, 7% international, 43% 25 or older, 0% Native American, 59% Hispanic, 22% black, 2% Asian or Pacific Islander. *Retention:* 79% of 1995 full-time freshmen returned.
First-Year Class: 26,641 applied, 59% of whom enrolled. 9% from top 10% of their high school class, 23% from top quarter, 52% from top half.
Graduation Requirements: 60 credit hours; 6 credit hours of math/science.
Computers on Campus: 4,423 computers available on campus for general student use. Computer purchase/lease plans available. A campus-wide network can be accessed from off-campus. Students can contact

faculty members and/or advisers through e-mail. Computers for student use in computer labs, learning resource center, classrooms, library, student center provide access to the Internet/World Wide Web, on- and off-campus e-mail addresses. Staffed computer lab on campus provides training in use of computers, software.

EXPENSES

Expenses for 1997–98: *Application fee:* $15. State resident tuition: $1344 full-time, $44.80 per credit hour part-time. Nonresident tuition: $4724 full-time, $157.45 per credit hour part-time.
LD Services Contact: Ms. Nancy Stone-Sokoloff, Learning Disabilities Specialist, Miami-Dade Community College, 300 Northeast Second Avenue, Miami, FL 33132-2296, 305-237-3371. Fax: 305-237-3796.

MIAMI UNIVERSITY–MIDDLETOWN CAMPUS

Middletown, Ohio

LEARNING DISABILITIES SERVICES INFORMATION

Counseling/Learning Assistance Office began offering services in 1988. Students diagnosed with ADD/ADHD are eligible for the same services available to students with LD.
Staff: 2 full-time, 4 part-time staff members, including director, coordinator. Services provided by remediation specialists, tutors, counselor.
Special Fees: No special fees are charged for services to students with LD.
Applications and admissions: *Required:* high school transcript, grade point average, class rank, courses completed, extended time ACT, psychoeducational report completed within 3 years. Students may begin taking classes in fall, winter, or summer. *Application deadline:* continuous.
Special policies: The college has written policies regarding grade forgiveness; substitutions and waivers of admissions, graduation, and degree requirements.

PROGRAM AND SERVICE COMPONENTS

Academic advising: Provided by unit staff members, academic advisers. Students with LD may take up to 19 semester hours each term; most take 12 to 13 semester hours; 12 semester hours required to maintain full-time status.
Counseling services: Individual counseling, career counseling.
Basic skills remediation: Offered one-on-one and in small groups by regular teachers, peer tutors; computer-aided instruction also offered. Available in reading, math, written language, learning strategies, study skills.
Subject-area tutoring: Offered one-on-one and in small groups by peer tutors, writing/reading specialist, math specialist. Available in most subjects.
Special courses: College survival skills, reading, composition, math, study skills, career planning. Some offered for credit; all enter into overall grade point average.
Auxiliary aids: Taped textbooks, tape recorders, word-processors with spell-check.
Auxiliary services: Alternative test arrangements, notetakers.

GENERAL COLLEGE INFORMATION

State-supported, primarily 2-year, coed. Part of Miami University System. Awards associate, bachelor's degrees (also offers up to 2 years of most bachelor's degree programs offered at Miami University main campus). Founded 1966. *Setting:* 141-acre small-town campus with easy access to Cincinnati and Dayton. *Endowment:* $779,742. *Total enrollment:* 2,629. *Faculty:* 165 (65 full-time, 70% with terminal degrees, 100 part-time); student–undergrad faculty ratio is 19:1.
Enrollment Profile: 2,382 students: 63% women, 37% men, 59% part-time, 100% state residents, 4% transferred in, 0% international, 34% 25 or older, 1% Native American, 1% Hispanic, 2% black, 1% Asian or Pacific Islander. *Retention:* 65% of 1995 full-time freshmen returned. *Areas of study chosen:* 33% liberal arts/general studies, 18% business management and administrative services, 13% health professions and related sciences, 8% education, 5% social sciences, 4% computer and information sciences, 4% engineering and applied sciences, 3% biological and life sciences, 3% psychology, 2% communications and journalism, 1% agriculture, 1% English language/literature/letters, 1% fine arts, 1% foreign language and literature, 1% mathematics, 1% physical sciences. *Most popular recent majors:* elementary education, business machine technologies.
First-Year Class: 462 total; 653 applied, 100% were accepted, 71% of whom enrolled. 27% from top 10% of their high school class, 28% from top quarter, 40% from top half.
Graduation Requirements: 64 semester hours for associate, 128 semester hours for bachelor's; 1 math/science course.
Computers on Campus: 150 computers available on campus for general student use. A campus-wide network can be accessed from off-campus. Students can contact faculty members and/or advisers through e-mail. Computers for student use in computer center, computer labs, learning resource center, classrooms, library, academic buildings provide access to the Internet/World Wide Web, on- and off-campus e-mail addresses. Staffed computer lab on campus provides training in use of computers, software. *Academic computing expenditure 1995–96:* $270,000.

EXPENSES

Expenses for 1997–98: *Application fee:* $25. Part-time mandatory fees per semester range from $35 to $155. Full-time tuition ranges from $2792 to $3464 for state residents, $8892 to $9564 for nonresidents, according to course level. Part-time tuition per semester hour ranges from $116 to $144 for state residents, $370 to $398 for nonresidents, according to course level. Full-time mandatory fees: $326.
LD Services Contact: Ms. Linda Watkins, Coordinator of Counseling, Miami University–Middletown Campus, 4200 East University Boulevard, Middletown, OH 45042-3497, 513-727-3200. Fax: 513-727-3434. Email: lwatkins@miavx3.mid.muohio.edu.

MIDDLE GEORGIA COLLEGE

Cochran, Georgia

LEARNING DISABILITIES SERVICES INFORMATION

Office of Disability Services currently serves 40 undergraduates with LD. Students diagnosed with ADD/ADHD are eligible for the same services available to students with LD, as well as isolated testing room.
Staff: 1 full-time staff member (coordinator).
Special Fees: No special fees are charged for services to students with LD.
Applications and admissions: *Required:* high school transcript, extended time SAT I. Students may begin taking classes any term. *Application deadline:* continuous.
Special policies: The college has written policies regarding substitutions and waivers of graduation and degree requirements.

PROGRAM AND SERVICE COMPONENTS

Academic advising: Provided by academic advisers. Students with LD may take up to 20 quarter hours each term; most take 12 to 15 quarter hours; 12 quarter hours required to maintain full-time status and be eligible for financial aid.
Counseling services: Individual counseling, career counseling, self-advocacy training.
Auxiliary aids: Taped textbooks, tape recorders, personal computers, optical character readers.
Auxiliary services: Alternative test arrangements, notetakers.

GENERAL COLLEGE INFORMATION

State-supported, 2-year, coed. Part of University System of Georgia. Awards associate degrees. Founded 1884. *Setting:* 165-acre rural campus. *Endowment:* $843,966. *Total enrollment:* 2,061. *Faculty:* 120 (68 full-time, 40% with terminal degrees, 52 part-time); student–undergrad faculty ratio is 19:1.
Enrollment Profile: 2,061 students from 19 states and territories, 12 other countries. 56% women, 44% men, 47% part-time, 97% state residents, 4% transferred in, 1% international, 23% 25 or older, 1% Native American, 1% Hispanic, 27% black, 1% Asian or Pacific Islander. *Most popular recent majors:* nursing, business administration/commerce/management, engineering (general).
First-Year Class: 795 total; 1,604 applied, 93% were accepted, 54% of whom enrolled.
Graduation Requirements: 100 quarter hours; 1 college algebra course; computer course for engineering, business administration majors.
Computers on Campus: 288 computers available on campus for general student use. A campus-wide network can be accessed from student residence rooms and from off-campus. Students can contact faculty

Middle Georgia College (continued)

members and/or advisers through e-mail. Computers for student use in computer labs, learning resource center, classrooms, library provide access to the Internet/World Wide Web. Staffed computer lab on campus provides training in use of computers, software.

EXPENSES

Expenses for 1997–98: *Application fee:* $5. State resident tuition: $1206 full-time, $32 per quarter hour part-time. Nonresident tuition: $4380 full-time, $121 per quarter hour part-time. Part-time mandatory fees per quarter (6 to 11 quarter hours): $80. Full-time mandatory fees: $240. College room and board: $3000. College room only: $1365.

LD Services Contact: Ms. Tina K. Anderson, Coordinator of Counseling, Middle Georgia College, 1100 Second Street, SE, Cochran, GA 31014, 912-934-3023. Email: tanderso@warrior.mgc.peachnet.edu.

MIDLAND COLLEGE

Midland, Texas

LEARNING DISABILITIES SERVICES INFORMATION

Career Center began offering services in 1973. Currently the program serves 30 undergraduates with LD. Students diagnosed with ADD/ADHD are eligible for the same services available to students with LD.

Staff: Includes coordinator, support staff. Services provided by remediation specialists, tutors, counselors, readers, scribes, notetakers, mentor.

Special Fees: No special fees are charged for services to students with LD.

Applications and admissions: *Required:* high school transcript, personal interview, psychoeducational report, medical and school records; *recommended:* high school IEP (Individualized Education Program). Students may begin taking classes any term. *Application deadline:* continuous.

PROGRAM AND SERVICE COMPONENTS

Special preparation or orientation: Optional orientation offered before registration.

Academic advising: Provided by unit staff members, academic advisers. Most students with LD take 6 to 12 semester hours each term; 12 semester hours required to maintain full-time status; 6 semester hours required to be eligible for financial aid.

Counseling services: Individual counseling, career counseling, self-advocacy training.

Basic skills remediation: Offered one-on-one by Career Counselor.

Subject-area tutoring: Offered one-on-one and in small groups by professional teachers, peer tutors, Career Center staff. Available in all subjects.

Auxiliary aids: Taped textbooks, tape recorders, calculators, typewriters, word-processors with spell-check, personal computers, talking computers, optical character readers.

Auxiliary services: Alternative test arrangements, notetakers, priority registration, advocacy, mentors, role models, agency referrals.

GENERAL COLLEGE INFORMATION

State and locally supported, 2-year, coed. Part of Texas Higher Education Coordinating Board. Awards associate degrees. Founded 1969. *Setting:* 163-acre suburban campus. *Endowment:* $2.8 million. *Educational spending 1995–96:* $2769 per undergrad. *Total enrollment:* 4,000. *Faculty:* 194 (86 full-time, 67% with terminal degrees, 108 part-time); student–undergrad faculty ratio is 20:1.

Enrollment Profile: 4,000 students from 20 states and territories, 19 other countries. 57% women, 43% men, 68% part-time, 97% state residents, 23% transferred in, 1% international, 38% 25 or older, 0% Native American, 20% Hispanic, 5% black, 1% Asian or Pacific Islander. *Retention:* 65% of 1995 full-time freshmen returned. *Areas of study chosen:* 39% liberal arts/general studies, 16% health professions and related sciences, 13% business management and administrative services, 8% computer and information sciences, 7% vocational and home economics, 5% social sciences, 3% communications and journalism, 3% fine arts, 2% biological and life sciences, 1% architecture, 1% foreign language and literature, 1% mathematics. *Most popular recent majors:* nursing, business administration/commerce/management, paralegal studies.

First-Year Class: 1,449 total; 1,500 applied, 100% were accepted, 97% of whom enrolled. 10% from top 10% of their high school class, 20% from top quarter, 50% from top half.

Graduation Requirements: 62 semester hours; 3 semester hours of math/science; computer course for most majors; internship (some majors).

Computers on Campus: 40 computers available on campus for general student use. Computer purchase/lease plans available. A campus-wide network can be accessed from off-campus. Students can contact faculty members and/or advisers through e-mail. Computers for student use in computer labs, learning resource center, library provide access to the Internet/World Wide Web. Staffed computer lab on campus provides training in use of computers, software. *Academic computing expenditure 1995–96:* $125,975.

EXPENSES

Expenses for 1997–98: Area resident tuition: $900 full-time. State resident tuition: $960 full-time. Nonresident tuition: $1140 full-time. Part-time tuition per semester ranges from $104 to $334 for area residents, $112 to $356 for state residents, $236 to $422 for nonresidents.

LD Services Contact: Terry Clemmer, Career Counselor, Midland College, 3600 North Garfield, Midland, TX 79705, 915-685-4695. Fax: 915-685-4623. Email: tclemmer@midland.cc.tx.us.

MID MICHIGAN COMMUNITY COLLEGE

Harrison, Michigan

LEARNING DISABILITIES SERVICES INFORMATION

Student Educational Services began offering services in 1980. Currently the program serves 35 undergraduates with LD. Students diagnosed with ADD/ADHD are not eligible for the same services available to students with LD.

Special Fees: No special fees are charged for services to students with LD.

Applications and admissions: *Required:* high school transcript, grade point average; *recommended:* high school IEP (Individualized Education Program). Students may begin taking classes any term. *Application deadline:* continuous.

Special policies: The college has written policies regarding grade forgiveness; substitutions and waivers of graduation and degree requirements.

PROGRAM AND SERVICE COMPONENTS

Diagnostic testing: Reading, math, written language, learning strategies.

Academic advising: Provided by unit staff members, academic advisers. Most students with LD take 6 credit hours each term; 12 credit hours required to maintain full-time status; 6 credit hours required to be eligible for financial aid.

Counseling services: Individual counseling, career counseling.

Basic skills remediation: Offered one-on-one by regular teachers. Available in reading, math, spelling, written language, study skills.

Subject-area tutoring: Offered one-on-one by peer tutors, professional tutors, paraprofessional tutors. Available in all subjects.

Auxiliary aids: Taped textbooks, tape recorders, word-processors with spell-check, visual enlarger.

Auxiliary services: Alternative test arrangements, notetakers, advocacy.

GENERAL COLLEGE INFORMATION

State and locally supported, 2-year, coed. Part of Michigan Department of Education. Awards associate degrees. Founded 1965. *Setting:* 560-acre rural campus. *Educational spending 1995–96:* $903 per undergrad. *Total enrollment:* 3,304. *Faculty:* 227 (39 full-time, 188 part-time).

Enrollment Profile: 3,304 students: 64% women, 36% men, 60% part-time, 99% state residents, 5% transferred in, 1% international, 63% 25 or older, 1% Native American, 1% Hispanic, 1% black, 1% Asian or Pacific Islander. *Most popular recent majors:* nursing, business administration/commerce/management, art/fine arts.

First-Year Class: 460 total; 2,193 applied, 100% were accepted, 21% of whom enrolled.

Graduation Requirements: 62 credit hours; 1 course each in math and science; computer course.

Computers on Campus: 150 computers available on campus for general student use. Computers for student use in computer center, computer labs, learning resource center. Staffed computer lab on campus provides training in use of computers. *Academic computing expenditure 1995–96:* $186,158.

EXPENSES

Expenses for 1997–98: Area resident tuition: $1550 full-time, $50 per credit hour part-time. State resident tuition: $2294 full-time, $74 per

credit hour part-time. Nonresident tuition: $3007 full-time, $97 per credit hour part-time. Part-time mandatory fees: $15 per semester. Full-time mandatory fees: $60.
LD Services Contact: Ms. Susan M. Cobb, Coordinator/Counselor, Special Populations, Mid Michigan Community College, 1375 South Clare Avenue, Harrison, MI 48625-9447, 517-386-6636. Fax: 517-386-2411.

MINNEAPOLIS COMMUNITY AND TECHNICAL COLLEGE

Minneapolis, Minnesota

LEARNING DISABILITIES SERVICES INFORMATION

Office for Students with Disabilities began offering services in 1982. Currently the program serves 125 undergraduates with LD. Students diagnosed with ADD/ADHD are eligible for the same services available to students with LD, as well as earphones, assistance with organizational skills, private room.
Staff: 4 full-time staff members, including director, associate directors, coordinator. Services provided by peer tutors.
Special Fees: No special fees are charged for services to students with LD.
Applications and admissions: *Recommended:* high school transcript. Students may begin taking classes any term. *Application deadline:* continuous.
Special policies: The college has written policies regarding substitutions and waivers of admissions, graduation, and degree requirements.

PROGRAM AND SERVICE COMPONENTS

Special preparation or orientation: Optional summer program offered prior to entering college. Optional orientation offered before registration.
Academic advising: Provided by unit staff members. Most students with LD take 9 to 12 quarter credits each term; 12 quarter credits required to maintain full-time status; 1 to 6 quarter credits required to be eligible for financial aid.
Counseling services: Individual counseling.
Auxiliary aids: Taped textbooks, tape recorders, calculators, word-processors with spell-check, talking computers, optical character readers.
Auxiliary services: Alternative test arrangements, notetakers, priority registration, advocacy.
Campus support group: A special student organization is available to students with LD.

GENERAL COLLEGE INFORMATION

State-supported, 2-year, coed. Part of Minnesota State Colleges and Universities System. Awards associate degrees. *Setting:* 4-acre urban campus. *Total enrollment:* 5,777. *Faculty:* 435 (210 full-time, 81% with terminal degrees, 225 part-time).
Enrollment Profile: 5,777 students from 18 states and territories, 41 other countries. 59% women, 41% men, 52% part-time, 95% state residents, 48% transferred in, 3% international, 61% 25 or older, 2% Native American, 2% Hispanic, 21% black, 7% Asian or Pacific Islander. *Most popular recent majors:* liberal arts/general studies, nursing, human services.
First-Year Class: Of the students who applied, 95% were accepted, 90% of whom enrolled.
Graduation Requirements: 96 quarter credits; math/science requirements vary according to program; internship (some majors).
Computers on Campus: 150 computers available on campus for general student use. Computers for student use in computer center, computer labs, learning resource center. Staffed computer lab on campus provides training in use of software.

EXPENSES

Expenses for 1996–97: *Application fee:* $25. State resident tuition: $2105 full-time, $43.85 per credit part-time. Nonresident tuition: $4102 full-time, $85.45 per credit part-time. Part-time mandatory fees: $2.10 per credit. North Dakota, South Dakota and Wisconsin residents pay tuition at the rate they would pay if attending a comparable state-supported institution in their home state. Full-time mandatory fees: $101.
LD Services Contact: Ms. Carol Udstrand, Learning Disabilities Specialist, Minneapolis Community and Technical College, 1501 Hennepin Avenue, C262, Minneapolis, MN 55044, 612-341-7550. Fax: 612-370-9428.

MINNESOTA WEST COMMUNITY AND TECHNICAL COLLEGE–GRANITE FALLS CAMPUS

Granite Falls, Minnesota

LEARNING DISABILITIES SERVICES INFORMATION

Resource Room–Supplemental Services began offering services in 1976. Currently the program serves 6 undergraduates with LD. Students diagnosed with ADD/ADHD are eligible for the same services available to students with LD.
Staff: 1 full-time, 6 part-time staff members, including director. Services provided by tutors, counselor.
Special Fees: No special fees are charged for services to students with LD.
Applications and admissions: *Required:* high school transcript, IEP (Individualized Education Program), psychoeducational report; *recommended:* extended time ACT, personal interview. Students may begin taking classes in fall only. *Application deadline:* continuous.
Special policies: The college has written policies regarding substitutions and waivers of graduation requirements.

PROGRAM AND SERVICE COMPONENTS

Special preparation or orientation: Optional summer program offered prior to entering college.
Diagnostic testing: Reading, math, spelling, written language, motor abilities, perceptual skills, study skills, personality.
Academic advising: Provided by unit staff members, academic advisers. Most students with LD take 12 to 16 quarter credits each term; 12 quarter credits required to maintain full-time status; 12 quarter credits (for federal aid), 15 quarter credits (for state aid) required to be eligible for financial aid.
Counseling services: Individual counseling, career counseling.
Basic skills remediation: Offered in class-size groups by regular teachers. Available in math, written language, learning strategies, study skills, time management.
Subject-area tutoring: Offered one-on-one and in small groups by professional teachers. Available in most subjects.
Special courses: Composition, time management, study skills, stress management.
Auxiliary aids: Taped textbooks, tape recorders, calculators, typewriters, word-processors with spell-check, personal computers, talking computers, optical character readers.
Auxiliary services: Alternative test arrangements, notetakers, advocacy.

GENERAL COLLEGE INFORMATION

State-supported, 2-year, coed. Part of Minnesota State Colleges and Universities System. Awards associate degrees. Founded 1965. *Setting:* 15-acre small-town campus. *Total enrollment:* 450. *Faculty:* 38 (30 full-time, 8 part-time); student–undergrad faculty ratio is 17:1.
Enrollment Profile: 450 students: 43% women, 57% men, 10% part-time, 90% state residents, 10% transferred in, 1% international, 2% Native American, 1% Hispanic, 1% black. *Retention:* 85% of 1995 full-time freshmen returned. *Most popular recent majors:* mechanical engineering technology, robotics, machine and tool technologies.
First-Year Class: 200 total; 300 applied, 100% were accepted, 66% of whom enrolled.
Graduation Requirements: 96 quarter credits; computer course for most majors; internship (some majors).
Computers on Campus: 100 computers available on campus for general student use. A campus-wide network can be accessed. Students can contact faculty members and/or advisers through e-mail. Computers for student use in computer labs, classrooms, library provide access to the Internet/World Wide Web, off-campus e-mail addresses. Staffed computer lab on campus provides training in use of computers, software.

EXPENSES

Expenses for 1996–97: *Application fee:* $20. State resident tuition: $1997 full-time, $41.60 per credit part-time. Nonresident tuition: $3994 full-time, $83.20 per credit part-time. Part-time mandatory fees: $2.10 per credit. Full-time mandatory fees: $101.
LD Services Contact: Mr. John R. Joosten, Supplemental Services Supervisor, Minnesota West Community and Technical College–Granite Falls Campus, 1593 11th Avenue, Granite Falls, MN 56241, 320-564-4511. Fax: 320-564-4582. Email: jjoosten@tc-granitefalls.swg.tec.mn.us.

MINNESOTA WEST COMMUNITY AND TECHNICAL COLLEGE–WORTHINGTON CAMPUS

Worthington, Minnesota

LEARNING DISABILITIES SERVICES INFORMATION

Academic Achievement Center began offering services in 1987. Currently the program serves 15 undergraduates with LD. Students diagnosed with ADD/ADHD are eligible for the same services available to students with LD.

Staff: 2 part-time staff members, including coordinators. Services provided by remediation specialist, tutors, counselor.

Special Fees: No special fees are charged for services to students with LD.

Applications and admissions: *Required:* high school transcript, grade point average, class rank, courses completed, psychoeducational report; *recommended:* high school IEP (Individualized Education Program), untimed ACT, personal interview. Students may begin taking classes in fall, winter, or spring. *Application deadline:* continuous.

PROGRAM AND SERVICE COMPONENTS

Academic advising: Provided by academic advisers. Students with LD required to take 12 quarter credit hours each term to maintain full-time status.

Counseling services: Individual counseling, career counseling.

Basic skills remediation: Offered one-on-one and in small groups by regular teachers, Academic Achievement Center staff. Available in reading, math, spelling, written language.

Subject-area tutoring: Offered one-on-one by peer tutors. Available in most subjects.

Special courses: Reading, word processing, time management, study skills, career planning. Most offered for credit; none enter into overall grade point average.

Auxiliary aids: Taped textbooks, tape recorders, word-processors with spell-check, personal computers.

Auxiliary services: Alternative test arrangements, notetakers, priority registration, advocacy.

GENERAL COLLEGE INFORMATION

State-supported, 2-year, coed. Part of Minnesota State Colleges and Universities System. Awards associate degrees. Founded 1936. *Setting:* 70-acre small-town campus. *Total enrollment:* 903. *Faculty:* 60 (29 full-time, 10% with terminal degrees, 31 part-time); student–undergrad faculty ratio is 18:1.

Enrollment Profile: 903 students from 6 states and territories, 2 other countries. 64% women, 36% men, 49% part-time, 93% state residents, 5% transferred in, 1% international, 39% 25 or older, 0% Native American, 1% Hispanic, 2% black, 2% Asian or Pacific Islander. *Retention:* 50% of 1995 full-time freshmen returned. *Areas of study chosen:* 95% liberal arts/general studies, 1% agriculture. *Most popular recent majors:* liberal arts/general studies, business administration/commerce/management, nursing.

First-Year Class: 362 total. Of the students who applied, 98% were accepted, 81% of whom enrolled. 4% from top 10% of their high school class, 25% from top quarter, 60% from top half.

Graduation Requirements: 96 quarter credit hours; 1 math course; 2 science courses; computer course; internship (some majors).

Computers on Campus: 50 computers available on campus for general student use. A computer is recommended for all students. A campus-wide network can be accessed. Computers for student use in computer center, study skills center. Staffed computer lab on campus provides training in use of computers, software.

EXPENSES

Expenses for 1996–97: *Application fee:* $20. State resident tuition: $2208 full-time, $46 per credit hour part-time. Nonresident tuition: $4205 full-time, $87.60 per credit hour part-time. Part-time mandatory fees: $2.17 per credit hour. Full-time mandatory fees: $104.

LD Services Contact: Ms. Lu Ann Williamson, Developmental Learning Coordinator, Minnesota West Community and Technical College–Worthington Campus, 1450 College Way, Worthington, MN 56187, 507-372-2107. Fax: 507-372-5801.

MINOT STATE UNIVERSITY–BOTTINEAU

Bottineau, North Dakota

LEARNING DISABILITIES SERVICES INFORMATION

Student Opportunity Program began offering services in 1992. Currently the program serves 15 undergraduates with LD. Students diagnosed with ADD/ADHD are eligible for the same services available to students with LD.

Staff: Includes director, LD study skills teacher, math/science/computer instructor, English instructor, social science instructor. Services provided by remediation specialists, tutors.

Special Fees: No special fees are charged for services to students with LD.

Applications and admissions: *Required:* high school transcript, courses completed, untimed or extended time ACT; *recommended:* high school IEP (Individualized Education Program), personal interview, psychoeducational report completed within 3 years. Students may begin taking classes in fall or spring. *Application deadline:* continuous.

Special policies: The college has written policies regarding grade forgiveness.

PROGRAM AND SERVICE COMPONENTS

Diagnostic testing: Reading, math, written language, learning strategies.

Academic advising: Provided by unit staff members, academic advisers. Students with LD may take up to 19 credits each term; most take 15 credits; 12 credits required to maintain full-time status and be eligible for financial aid.

Counseling services: Individual counseling.

Basic skills remediation: Offered one-on-one and in small groups by LD teachers, regular teachers. Available in reading, math, spelling, written language, learning strategies, study skills, time management.

Subject-area tutoring: Offered one-on-one and in small groups by professional teachers, peer tutors. Available in all subjects.

Special courses: Reading, composition, word processing, math, study skills. Most offered for credit; most enter into overall grade point average.

Auxiliary aids: Taped textbooks, tape recorders, typewriters, word-processors with spell-check.

Auxiliary services: Alternative test arrangements, notetakers.

GENERAL COLLEGE INFORMATION

State-supported, 2-year, coed. Part of North Dakota University System. Awards associate degrees. Founded 1907. *Setting:* 35-acre rural campus. *Total enrollment:* 399. *Faculty:* 28 (22 full-time, 25% with terminal degrees, 6 part-time); student–undergrad faculty ratio is 15:1.

Enrollment Profile: 399 students from 31 states and territories, 2 other countries. 40% women, 60% men, 6% part-time, 67% state residents, 75% live on campus, 14% transferred in, 9% international, 16% 25 or older, 4% Native American, 0% Hispanic, 1% black, 0% Asian or Pacific Islander. *Areas of study chosen:* 38% natural resource sciences, 22% interdisciplinary studies, 6% education, 4% agriculture. *Most popular recent majors:* wildlife biology, liberal arts/general studies, business administration/commerce/management.

First-Year Class: 244 total; 293 applied, 100% were accepted, 83% of whom enrolled.

Graduation Requirements: 61 credits; computer course; internship (some majors).

Computers on Campus: 55 computers available on campus for general student use. Computers for student use in computer center, library provide access to the Internet/World Wide Web, on-campus e-mail addresses.

EXPENSES

Expenses for 1996–97: *Application fee:* $25. State resident tuition: $1805 full-time, $75.21 per credit part-time. Nonresident tuition: $4397 full-time, $183.21 per credit part-time. Tuition for Manitoba, Montana, Saskatchewan and South Dakota residents: $2193 full-time, $91.37 per credit part-time. Tuition for Minnesota residents: $2053 full-time, $85.54 per credit part-time. Tuition for nonresidents who are eligible for the Western Undergraduate Exchange: $2601 full-time, $107.54 per credit part-time. College room and board: $2444.

LD Services Contact: Ms. Faye Bernstein, Instructor, Student Learning Center, Minot State University–Bottineau, 105 Simrall Boulevard, Bottineau, ND 58318-1198, 701-228-5479. Fax: 701-228-2277. Email: bernstei@warp6.cs.misu.nodak.edu.

MIRACOSTA COLLEGE

Oceanside, California

LEARNING DISABILITIES SERVICES INFORMATION

Disabled Student Program and Services began offering services in 1983. Currently the program serves 125 undergraduates with LD. Students diagnosed with ADD/ADHD are eligible for the same services available to students with LD.

Staff: 1 full-time staff member. Services provided by LD specialist.

Special Fees: No special fees are charged for services to students with LD.

Applications and admissions: *Required:* California Assessment System for Adults with Learning Disabilities. Students may begin taking classes in fall, spring, or summer. *Application deadline:* continuous.

Special policies: The college has written policies regarding grade forgiveness.

PROGRAM AND SERVICE COMPONENTS

Diagnostic testing: Intelligence, reading, math, spelling, written language, perceptual skills.

Academic advising: Provided by unit staff members. Students with LD may take up to 18.5 units each term; most take 9 units; 12 units required to maintain full-time status; 6 units required to be eligible for financial aid.

Counseling services: Individual counseling.

Basic skills remediation: Offered one-on-one, in small groups, and in class-size groups by regular teachers, LD specialist. Available in reading, math, spelling, written language, learning strategies, study skills, time management, computer skills.

Subject-area tutoring: Offered one-on-one by peer tutors. Available in most subjects.

Special courses: Math, language arts. All offered for credit; all enter into overall grade point average.

Auxiliary aids: Taped textbooks, tape recorders, calculators, optical character readers, computers with spell check.

Auxiliary services: Alternative test arrangements, notetakers, priority registration, advocacy.

GENERAL COLLEGE INFORMATION

State-supported, 2-year, coed. Part of California Community Colleges System. Awards associate degrees. Founded 1934. *Setting:* 131-acre small-town campus with easy access to San Diego. *Research spending 1995–96:* $102,545. *Total enrollment:* 8,038. *Faculty:* 388 (93 full-time, 295 part-time); student–undergrad faculty ratio is 22:1.

Enrollment Profile: 8,038 students from 37 states and territories, 13 other countries. 59% women, 41% men, 72% part-time, 90% state residents, 20% transferred in, 1% international, 46% 25 or older, 3% Native American, 15% Hispanic, 5% black, 5% Asian or Pacific Islander. *Most popular recent majors:* business administration/commerce/management, liberal arts/general studies.

First-Year Class: 1,273 total; 7,187 applied, 100% were accepted, 18% of whom enrolled.

Graduation Requirements: 60 units; computer course for business majors; internship (some majors).

Computers on Campus: 275 computers available on campus for general student use. Computer purchase/lease plans available. Computers for student use in computer center, computer labs, learning resource center, classrooms, library, business, English departmental labs provide access to the Internet/World Wide Web. Staffed computer lab on campus provides training in use of computers, software.

EXPENSES

Expenses for 1997–98: State resident tuition: $0 full-time. Nonresident tuition: $3510 full-time, $117 per unit part-time. Part-time mandatory fees per semester range from $25 to $155. Full-time mandatory fees: $414.

LD Services Contact: Ms. Loretta Bohl, Coordinator/Enabler, MiraCosta College, One Barnard Drive, Oceanside, CA 92056-3899, 760-757-2121 Ext. 6658. Fax: 760-795-6609.

MISSISSIPPI DELTA COMMUNITY COLLEGE

Moorhead, Mississippi

LEARNING DISABILITIES SERVICES INFORMATION

Assistance for Success for Special Populations currently serves undergraduate students with LD. Students diagnosed with ADD/ADHD are eligible for the same services available to students with LD.

Staff: 3 full-time staff members, including coordinator. Services provided by remediation specialists.

Special Fees: No special fees are charged for services to students with LD.

Applications and admissions: *Required:* high school transcript, psychoeducational report completed within 3 years; *recommended:* high school IEP (Individualized Education Program), personal interview. Students may begin taking classes in fall, winter, or spring. *Application deadline:* 7/1 (fall term), 1/6 (spring term).

PROGRAM AND SERVICE COMPONENTS

Diagnostic testing: Reading, math, spelling, written language, motor abilities, perceptual skills, learning strategies, interest inventory.

Academic advising: Provided by unit staff members, academic advisers. Students with LD may take up to 21 semester hours each term; most take 12 semester hours; 12 semester hours required to maintain full-time status; 3 semester hours required to be eligible for financial aid.

Counseling services: Individual counseling, small-group counseling, career counseling, self-advocacy training.

Basic skills remediation: Offered in small groups by certified teachers; computer-aided instruction also offered. Available in reading, math, spelling, written language, learning strategies, study skills, communication skills, job skills.

Subject-area tutoring: Offered one-on-one. Available in all subjects.

Auxiliary services: Alternative test arrangements, notetakers, priority registration.

GENERAL COLLEGE INFORMATION

District-supported, 2-year, coed. Part of Mississippi State Board for Community and Junior Colleges. Awards associate degrees. Founded 1926. *Setting:* 425-acre small-town campus. *Total enrollment:* 2,497. *Faculty:* 130 (90 full-time, 3% with terminal degrees, 40 part-time).

Enrollment Profile: 2,497 students from 6 states and territories. 53% women, 47% men, 9% part-time, 99% state residents, 25% live on campus, 10% transferred in, 0% international, 7% 25 or older, 0% Native American, 1% Hispanic, 25% black, 1% Asian or Pacific Islander. *Retention:* 80% of 1995 full-time freshmen returned. *Areas of study chosen:* 28% business management and administrative services, 18% education, 13% biological and life sciences, 10% engineering and applied sciences, 10% health professions and related sciences, 3% agriculture, 3% liberal arts/general studies, 3% premed, 3% social sciences, 2% communications and journalism, 2% computer and information sciences, 2% prelaw, 1% mathematics, 1% predentistry, 1% prevet, 1% psychology.

First-Year Class: 1,054 total; 1,456 applied, 79% were accepted, 91% of whom enrolled. 4% from top 10% of their high school class, 20% from top quarter, 56% from top half.

Graduation Requirements: 64 semester hours; 1 college algebra course.

Computers on Campus: 80 computers available on campus for general student use. Computers for student use in computer center, library, vo-tech center.

EXPENSES

Expenses for 1997–98: State resident tuition: $920 full-time, $50 per semester hour part-time. Nonresident tuition: $2200 full-time, $50 per semester hour part-time. College room and board: $1450.

LD Services Contact: Ms. Wanda Thomas, Special Populations Coordinator, Mississippi Delta Community College, PO Box 668, Moorhead, MS 38761, 601-246-6550. Fax: 601-246-6517.

MOBERLY AREA COMMUNITY COLLEGE

Moberly, Missouri

LEARNING DISABILITIES SERVICES INFORMATION

Special Needs Counseling began offering services in 1989. Currently the program serves 250 undergraduates with LD. Students diagnosed with ADD/ADHD are eligible for the same services available to students with LD.

Staff: 1 full-time staff member (Associate Academic Dean). Services provided by tutors, counselors.

Special Fees: No special fees are charged for services to students with LD.

Applications and admissions: *Required:* high school transcript, courses completed, untimed SAT I or ACT, personal interview, psychoeducational report; *recommended:* high school grade point average, class rank, extracurricular activities, extended time SAT I or ACT, autobiographical statement, letters of recommendation, vocational rehabilitation report. Students may begin taking classes any term. *Application deadline:* continuous.

Special policies: The college has written policies regarding substitutions and waivers of graduation and degree requirements.

PROGRAM AND SERVICE COMPONENTS

Special preparation or orientation: Optional orientation offered after classes begin.

Academic advising: Provided by unit staff members. Students with LD may take up to 17 semester hours each term; most take 9 semester hours; 12 semester hours required to maintain full-time status and be eligible for financial aid.

Counseling services: Individual counseling, small-group counseling, career counseling.

Subject-area tutoring: Offered one-on-one by professional teachers, peer tutors. Available in most subjects.

Special courses: College survival skills, reading, communication skills, composition, learning strategies, time management, math, study skills, career planning. Most offered for credit; none enter into overall grade point average.

Auxiliary aids: Taped textbooks, tape recorders, word-processors with spell-check, personal computers, optical character readers, print enlarger.

Auxiliary services: Alternative test arrangements, notetakers, priority registration.

GENERAL COLLEGE INFORMATION

State and locally supported, 2-year, coed. Part of Missouri Coordinating Board for Higher Education. Awards associate degrees. Founded 1927. *Setting:* 23-acre small-town campus. *Total enrollment:* 2,014. *Faculty:* 95 (34 full-time, 20% with terminal degrees, 61 part-time); student–undergrad faculty ratio is 20:1.

Enrollment Profile: 2,014 students from 6 states and territories, 7 other countries. 63% women, 37% men, 44% part-time, 99% state residents, 1% live on campus, 20% transferred in, 1% international, 44% 25 or older, 1% Native American, 1% Hispanic, 6% black, 1% Asian or Pacific Islander. *Retention:* 40% of 1995 full-time freshmen returned. *Most popular recent majors:* liberal arts/general studies, nursing, business administration/commerce/management.

First-Year Class: 876 total. Of the students who applied, 100% were accepted, 70% of whom enrolled. 25% from top 10% of their high school class, 40% from top quarter, 75% from top half.

Graduation Requirements: 64 credit hours; 1 college algebra course; computer course.

Computers on Campus: 48 computers available on campus for general student use. Computers for student use in computer center, learning resource center, library provide access to the Internet/World Wide Web. *Academic computing expenditure 1995–96:* $111,419.

EXPENSES

Expenses for 1997–98: Area resident tuition: $1088 full-time, $34 per credit hour part-time. State resident tuition: $1920 full-time, $60 per credit hour part-time. Nonresident tuition: $3520 full-time, $110 per credit hour part-time. Part-time mandatory fees per semester (7 to 11 credit hours): $10. Full-time mandatory fees: $50. College room only: $1200.

LD Services Contact: Mr. Michael McGaugh, Special Needs Counselor, Moberly Area Community College, 101 College Avenue, Moberly, MO 65270, 816-263-4110 Ext. 278. Fax: 816-263-6448. Email: mikem@hp9000.macc.mo.us.

MOHAWK VALLEY COMMUNITY COLLEGE

Utica, New York

LEARNING DISABILITIES SERVICES INFORMATION

Office for Services to Students with Disabilities began offering services in 1985. Currently the program serves 100 undergraduates with LD. Students diagnosed with ADD/ADHD are eligible for the same services available to students with LD.

Staff: 1 full-time, 5 part-time staff members, including coordinator, student assistants. Services provided by LD specialist, office assistant, clerk.

Special Fees: No special fees are charged for services to students with LD.

Applications and admissions: *Required:* high school transcript, grade point average, courses completed, IEP (Individualized Education Program), psychoeducational report; *recommended:* untimed SAT I or ACT, personal interview, autobiographical statement, letters of recommendation. Students may begin taking classes in fall, spring, or summer. *Application deadline:* continuous.

PROGRAM AND SERVICE COMPONENTS

Academic advising: Provided by unit staff members, academic advisers. Students with LD may take up to 18 credits each term; most take 12 credits; 12 credits required to maintain full-time status; source of aid determines number of credits required to be eligible for financial aid.

Counseling services: Individual counseling, career counseling, self-advocacy training.

Basic skills remediation: Offered one-on-one, in small groups, and in class-size groups by regular teachers. Available in reading, math, spelling, written language, learning strategies, study skills.

Subject-area tutoring: Offered one-on-one, in small groups, and in class-size groups by professional teachers, peer tutors. Available in most subjects.

Special courses: College survival skills, reading, vocabulary development, composition, math. Some offered for credit.

Auxiliary aids: Taped textbooks, tape recorders, calculators, typewriters, word-processors with spell-check, optical character readers, enlargers, videotape recorders, Phonic Ears.

Auxiliary services: Alternative test arrangements, notetakers, priority registration, advocacy.

GENERAL COLLEGE INFORMATION

State and locally supported, 2-year, coed. Part of State University of New York System. Awards associate degrees. Founded 1946. *Setting:* 80-acre suburban campus. *Total enrollment:* 4,423. *Faculty:* 274 (137 full-time, 13% with terminal degrees, 137 part-time); student–undergrad faculty ratio is 18:1.

Enrollment Profile: 4,423 students from 5 states and territories, 8 other countries. 52% women, 48% men, 29% part-time, 98% state residents, 6% live on campus, 6% transferred in, 1% international, 37% 25 or older, 1% Native American, 2% Hispanic, 6% black, 1% Asian or Pacific Islander. *Areas of study chosen:* 25% liberal arts/general studies, 16% health professions and related sciences, 14% business management and administrative services, 14% fine arts, 14% vocational and home economics, 7% engineering and applied sciences, 4% social sciences, 3% computer and information sciences, 1% biological and life sciences, 1% mathematics, 1% physical sciences. *Most popular recent majors:* nursing, liberal arts/general studies, art/fine arts.

First-Year Class: 1,559 total; 2,767 applied, 94% were accepted, 60% of whom enrolled.

Graduation Requirements: 62 credits; math/science requirements vary according to program; computer course for most majors; internship (some majors).

Computers on Campus: 200 computers available on campus for general student use. A campus-wide network can be accessed from off-campus. Students can contact faculty members and/or advisers through e-mail. Computers for student use in computer center, computer labs, learning resource center, classrooms, library provide access to the Internet/World Wide Web, on- and off-campus e-mail addresses. Staffed computer lab on campus provides training in use of computers, software.

EXPENSES

Expenses for 1996–97: *Application fee:* $30. State resident tuition: $2500 full-time, $85 per credit part-time. Nonresident tuition: $5000

full-time, $170 per credit part-time. Part-time mandatory fees: $1 per credit. Full-time mandatory fees: $116. College room and board: $3900 (minimum). College room only: $2250.
LD Services Contact: Ms. Lynn Igoe, Coordinator, Office for Services to Students with Disabilities, Mohawk Valley Community College, Academic Building 137, 1101 Sherman Drive, Utica, NY 13501, 315-792-5413. Fax: 315-792-5527. Email: ligoe@mvcc.edu.

MONTANA STATE UNIVERSITY COLLEGE OF TECHNOLOGY–GREAT FALLS

Great Falls, Montana

LEARNING DISABILITIES SERVICES INFORMATION

Student Services began offering services in 1988. Currently the program serves 45 undergraduates with LD. Students diagnosed with ADD/ADHD are eligible for the same services available to students with LD.
Staff: 3 full-time staff members, including director, Student Services counselor, retention specialist. Services provided by tutors, counselors, retention specialist.
Special Fees: No special fees are charged for services to students with LD.
Applications and admissions: *Required:* high school transcript, psychoeducational report; *recommended:* personal interview, ACT ASSET, verification of disability/testing. Students may begin taking classes any term. *Application deadline:* continuous.

PROGRAM AND SERVICE COMPONENTS

Academic advising: Provided by unit staff members, academic advisers. Most students with LD take 9 credits each term; 12 credits required to maintain full-time status; 6 credits required to be eligible for financial aid.
Counseling services: Individual counseling, career counseling, self-advocacy training, peer mentoring.
Basic skills remediation: Offered one-on-one, in small groups, and in class-size groups by regular teachers, tutors, interpreters, readers; computer-aided instruction also offered. Available in reading, math, spelling, handwriting, spoken language, written language, learning strategies, study skills, time management, social skills, computer skills.
Subject-area tutoring: Offered one-on-one, in small groups, and in class-size groups by professional teachers, peer tutors, interpreters (American sign language), professional tutors, readers. Available in most subjects.
Special courses: College survival skills, reading, vocabulary development, communication skills, composition, learning strategies, word processing, Internet use, time management, math, typing, personal psychology, study skills, career planning, stress management, health and nutrition, social relationships. All offered for credit; all enter into overall grade point average.
Auxiliary aids: Taped textbooks, tape recorders, calculators, typewriters, word-processors with spell-check, personal computers, talking computers, optical character readers, Arkenstone Reader.
Auxiliary services: Alternative test arrangements, notetakers, priority registration, advocacy, readers, interpreters.

GENERAL COLLEGE INFORMATION

State-supported, 2-year, coed. Part of Montana University System. Awards associate degrees. Founded 1969. *Setting:* 35-acre urban campus. *Total enrollment:* 1,020. *Faculty:* 65 full-time, 1% with terminal degrees; student–undergrad faculty ratio is 15:1.
Enrollment Profile: 1,020 students: 66% women, 34% men, 33% part-time, 95% state residents, 20% transferred in, 1% international, 60% 25 or older, 10% Native American, 2% Hispanic, 3% black, 1% Asian or Pacific Islander. *Areas of study chosen:* 60% business management and administrative services, 36% health professions and related sciences, 4% vocational and home economics. *Most popular recent major:* business administration/commerce/management.
First-Year Class: 530 total; 600 applied, 100% were accepted, 88% of whom enrolled.
Graduation Requirements: 60 credits; computer course for business, allied health majors; internship (some majors).
Computers on Campus: 150 computers available on campus for general student use. Computer purchase/lease plans available. A campuswide network can be accessed from off-campus. Students can contact faculty members and/or advisers through e-mail. Computers for student use in computer labs, classrooms, library provide access to the Internet/World Wide Web. Staffed computer lab on campus provides training in use of computers, software.

EXPENSES

Expenses for 1997–98: *Application fee:* $30. State resident tuition: $1872 full-time. Nonresident tuition: $4654 full-time. Part-time tuition per semester ranges from $99.35 to $742.86 for state residents, $198.70 to $1837 for nonresidents.
LD Services Contact: Ms. Diana Wyatt, Counselor, Montana State University College of Technology–Great Falls, 2100 16th Avenue South, Great Falls, MT 59405, 406-791-4311. Fax: 406-771-4317. Email: zgf1009@maia.oscs.montana.edu.

MONTCALM COMMUNITY COLLEGE

Sidney, Michigan

LEARNING DISABILITIES SERVICES INFORMATION

Special Populations Program began offering services in 1984. Currently the program serves 200 undergraduates with LD. Students diagnosed with ADD/ADHD are eligible for the same services available to students with LD.
Staff: 1 full-time, 31 part-time staff members, including director. Services provided by tutors, student aides.
Special Fees: No special fees are charged for services to students with LD.
Applications and admissions: *Required:* high school transcript, grade point average, courses completed; *recommended:* high school counselor's special education report, Michigan Rehabilitative Services referral. Students may begin taking classes in fall only. *Application deadline:* continuous.
Special policies: The college has written policies regarding substitutions and waivers of admissions, graduation, and degree requirements.

PROGRAM AND SERVICE COMPONENTS

Special preparation or orientation: Optional summer program offered prior to entering college. Optional orientation offered before registration.
Diagnostic testing: Reading, math, spelling, written language, study skills.
Academic advising: Provided by academic advisers. Students with LD may take up to 18 credit hours (more with Dean's permission) each term; most take 6 credit hours; 12 credit hours required to maintain full-time status; 1 credit hour required to be eligible for financial aid.
Counseling services: Individual counseling, career counseling.
Basic skills remediation: Offered one-on-one, in small groups, and in class-size groups by Developmental Lab teachers. Available in reading, math, spelling, written language, learning strategies, study skills.
Subject-area tutoring: Offered one-on-one and in small groups by professional teachers, peer tutors. Available in most subjects.
Auxiliary aids: Taped textbooks, tape recorders, typewriters, word-processors with spell-check.
Auxiliary services: Alternative test arrangements, notetakers, advocacy.

GENERAL COLLEGE INFORMATION

State and locally supported, 2-year, coed. Part of Michigan Department of Education. Awards associate degrees. Founded 1965. *Setting:* 248-acre rural campus. *Endowment:* $47,401. *Educational spending 1995–96:* $1643 per undergrad. *Total enrollment:* 1,945. *Faculty:* 153 (25 full-time, 5% with terminal degrees, 128 part-time).
Enrollment Profile: 1,945 students: 56% women, 44% men, 74% part-time, 100% state residents, 6% transferred in, 56% 25 or older, 1% Native American, 2% Hispanic, 14% black, 1% Asian or Pacific Islander. *Retention:* 40% of 1995 full-time freshmen returned. *Areas of study chosen:* 33% liberal arts/general studies, 22% business management and administrative services, 15% health professions and related sciences, 13% vocational and home economics, 11% engineering and applied sciences, 6% computer and information sciences. *Most popular recent majors:* liberal arts/general studies, nursing, business administration/commerce/management.
First-Year Class: 759 applied, 100% were accepted, 85% of whom enrolled. 4% from top 10% of their high school class, 11% from top quarter, 34% from top half.
Graduation Requirements: 60 credit hours; computer course for industrial technology, electronics, drafting, business administration, paralegal studies, accounting majors.

Montcalm Community College (continued)

Computers on Campus: 400 computers available on campus for general student use. Computers for student use in computer center, computer labs, learning resource center, classrooms, library provide access to the Internet/World Wide Web, on- and off-campus e-mail addresses. Staffed computer lab on campus provides training in use of computers, software. *Academic computing expenditure 1995–96:* $188,402.

EXPENSES

Expenses for 1997–98: Area resident tuition: $1464 full-time, $48.80 per credit hour part-time. State resident tuition: $2246 full-time, $74.85 per credit hour part-time. Nonresident tuition: $2865 full-time, $95.50 per credit hour part-time. Part-time mandatory fees: $5.50 per credit hour. Full-time mandatory fees: $165.

LD Services Contact: Ms. Charlotte Fokens, Special Populations Counselor, Montcalm Community College, 2800 College Drive, Sidney, MI 48885-0300, 517-328-2111 Ext. 356. Fax: 517-328-2950.

MORAINE PARK TECHNICAL COLLEGE

Fond du Lac, Wisconsin

LEARNING DISABILITIES SERVICES INFORMATION

Student Services/Support Services currently serves 300 undergraduates with LD. Students diagnosed with ADD/ADHD are eligible for the same services available to students with LD.

Staff: 9 full-time staff members, including learning specialists, Special Services Associate. Services provided by remediation specialist, diagnostic specialists, interpreter, support services specialists.

Special Fees: No special fees are charged for services to students with LD.

Applications and admissions: *Recommended:* high school IEP (Individualized Education Program), psychoeducational report, Student Learner Transition Profile, M-Team report, educational evaluation. Students may begin taking classes in fall, spring, or summer. *Application deadline:* continuous.

Special policies: The college has written policies regarding grade forgiveness.

PROGRAM AND SERVICE COMPONENTS

Special preparation or orientation: Summer program (required for some) held prior to entering college. Required orientation held before registration.

Academic advising: Provided by unit staff members, academic advisers, learning specialist. Most students with LD take 9 to 12 credits each term; 12 credits required to maintain full-time status; 6 credits required to be eligible for financial aid.

Counseling services: Individual counseling, career counseling.

Basic skills remediation: Offered one-on-one and in small groups by Goal Oriented Learning lab (GOAL). Available in reading, math, spelling, handwriting, spoken language, written language, learning strategies.

Subject-area tutoring: Offered one-on-one and in small groups by peer tutors. Available in most subjects.

Special courses: College survival skills, study skills. None offered for credit; none enter into overall grade point average.

Auxiliary aids: Taped textbooks, tape recorders, calculators, typewriters, word-processors with spell-check, spelling aces.

Auxiliary services: Alternative test arrangements, notetakers, advocacy, TDD/(414)929-2109.

GENERAL COLLEGE INFORMATION

State and locally supported, 2-year, coed. Part of Wisconsin Technical College System. Awards associate degrees. Founded 1967. *Setting:* 40-acre small-town campus with easy access to Milwaukee. *Endowment:* $15,500. *Research spending 1995–96:* $74,561. *Total enrollment:* 5,811. *Faculty:* 351 (151 full-time, 200 part-time); student–undergrad faculty ratio is 19:1.

Enrollment Profile: 5,811 students: 55% women, 45% men, 80% part-time, 99% state residents, 1% transferred in, 0% international, 66% 25 or older, 1% Native American, 1% Hispanic, 2% black, 1% Asian or Pacific Islander. *Areas of study chosen:* 38% business management and administrative services, 20% vocational and home economics, 19% health professions and related sciences, 12% engineering and applied sciences, 3% agriculture, 3% computer and information sciences, 1% architecture.

First-Year Class: 845 total; 1,200 applied, 100% were accepted, 70% of whom enrolled.

Graduation Requirements: 68 credits; computer course for most majors; internship (some majors).

Computers on Campus: A campus-wide network can be accessed. Computers for student use in computer center, computer labs. Staffed computer lab on campus provides training in use of computers, software. *Academic computing expenditure 1995–96:* $782,167.

EXPENSES

Expenses for 1997–98: *Application fee:* $25. State resident tuition: $1843 full-time, $54.20 per credit part-time. Nonresident tuition: $14,525 full-time, $427.20 per credit part-time.

LD Services Contact: Mr. Craig Finley, Re-entry/Special Services Associate, Moraine Park Technical College, 235 North National Avenue, PO Box 1940, Fond du Lac, WI 54936-1940, 414-924-3192.

MORAINE VALLEY COMMUNITY COLLEGE

Palos Hills, Illinois

LEARNING DISABILITIES SERVICES INFORMATION

Learning Development Support System/Center for Disability Services began offering services in 1983. Currently the program serves 120 undergraduates with LD. Students diagnosed with ADD/ADHD are eligible for the same services available to students with LD.

Staff: 2 full-time, 7 part-time staff members, including director, coordinator. Services provided by tutors, counselor, diagnostic specialist.

Special Fees: $100 for diagnostic testing.

Applications and admissions: *Required:* high school transcript, personal interview, psychoeducational report completed within 3 years, high school diploma or GED; *recommended:* high school IEP (Individualized Education Program). Students may begin taking classes any term. *Application deadline:* continuous.

Special policies: The college has written policies regarding grade forgiveness.

PROGRAM AND SERVICE COMPONENTS

Special preparation or orientation: Optional orientation offered before registration.

Diagnostic testing: Intelligence, reading, math, spelling, written language, perceptual skills, study skills, social skills.

Academic advising: Provided by unit staff members. Students with LD may take up to 16 semester hours each term; most take 10 to 12 semester hours; 12 semester hours required to maintain full-time status; 6 semester hours (part-time), 12 semester hours (full-time) required to be eligible for financial aid.

Counseling services: Individual counseling, small-group counseling, career counseling.

Basic skills remediation: Offered in class-size groups by regular teachers. Available in reading, math, written language, learning strategies, study skills, time management.

Subject-area tutoring: Offered one-on-one and in small groups by professional teachers, peer tutors. Available in most subjects.

Special courses: College survival skills, personal psychology, career planning. Most offered for credit; most enter into overall grade point average.

Auxiliary aids: Taped textbooks, tape recorders, typewriters, word-processors with spell-check, optical character readers.

Auxiliary services: Alternative test arrangements, notetakers, priority registration.

Campus support group: A special student organization is available to students with LD.

GENERAL COLLEGE INFORMATION

State and locally supported, 2-year, coed. Part of Illinois Community College System. Awards associate degrees. Founded 1967. *Setting:* 292-acre suburban campus with easy access to Chicago. *Endowment:* $9.6 million. *Educational spending 1995–96:* $1319 per undergrad. *Total enrollment:* 13,234. *Faculty:* 570 (163 full-time, 12% with terminal degrees, 407 part-time); student–undergrad faculty ratio is 23:1.

Enrollment Profile: 13,234 students from 5 states and territories, 28 other countries. 58% women, 42% men, 65% part-time, 96% state residents, 11% transferred in, 4% international, 41% 25 or older, 1% Native American, 5% Hispanic, 4% black, 1% Asian or Pacific Islander. *Retention:* 71% of 1995 full-time freshmen returned. *Areas of study chosen:* 39% liberal arts/general studies, 13% business management and admin-

istrative services, 7% engineering and applied sciences, 7% health professions and related sciences, 5% interdisciplinary studies, 3% vocational and home economics, 1% education. *Most popular recent majors:* liberal arts/general studies, science, nursing.
First-Year Class: 3,871 total; 4,973 applied, 100% were accepted, 78% of whom enrolled. 7% from top 10% of their high school class, 26% from top quarter, 58% from top half.
Graduation Requirements: 62 semester hours; 3 semester hours of math; 8 semester hours of science; computer course for medical records services, drafting and design, quality control technology, most business majors; internship (some majors).
Computers on Campus: 464 computers available on campus for general student use. A campus-wide network can be accessed. Computers for student use in computer center, computer labs, learning resource center, classrooms, library. Staffed computer lab on campus provides training in use of computers, software. *Academic computing expenditure 1995–96:* $1.7 million.

EXPENSES AND FINANCIAL AID

Estimated Expenses for 1997–98: Area resident tuition: $1302 full-time, $42 per semester hour part-time. State resident tuition: $4991 full-time, $161 per semester hour part-time. Nonresident tuition: $5611 full-time, $181 per semester hour part-time. Part-time mandatory fees: $5 per semester hour. Full-time mandatory fees: $155.
Financial aid specifically for students with LD: Scholarship: Moraine Valley Disability Services Scholarship.
LD Services Contact: Ms. Mary Schafer, Director, Disability Services, Moraine Valley Community College, 10900 South 88th Avenue, Palos Hills, IL 60465, 708-974-5711. Fax: 708-974-1184. Email: schafer@moraine.cc.il.us.

MORGAN COMMUNITY COLLEGE

Fort Morgan, Colorado

LEARNING DISABILITIES SERVICES INFORMATION

Learning Center began offering services in 1988. Currently the program serves 9 undergraduates with LD. Students diagnosed with ADD/ADHD are eligible for the same services available to students with LD.
Staff: 1 full-time staff member (instructor). Services provided by tutors, instructor, manager of Computer Access Center.
Special Fees: No special fees are charged for services to students with LD.
Applications and admissions: *Recommended:* high school transcript, courses completed, psychoeducational report. *Application deadline:* continuous.

PROGRAM AND SERVICE COMPONENTS

Diagnostic testing: Reading, math, written language, perceptual skills.
Academic advising: Provided by unit staff members, academic advisers. Students with LD may take up to 12 credit hours each term; most take 9 credit hours; 12 credit hours required to maintain full-time status and be eligible for financial aid.
Counseling services: Individual counseling, career counseling.
Basic skills remediation: Offered one-on-one, in small groups, and in class-size groups by regular teachers; computer-aided instruction also offered. Available in reading, math, written language, learning strategies, study skills, time management, computer skills.
Subject-area tutoring: Offered one-on-one by professional teachers, peer tutors. Available in some subjects.
Special courses: Career planning, customized basic skills. All offered for credit; none enter into overall grade point average.
Auxiliary aids: Taped textbooks, tape recorders, calculators, word-processors with spell-check, personal computers, talking computers, adaptive software, instructive classes (Computer Access Center).
Auxiliary services: Alternative test arrangements, notetakers.

GENERAL COLLEGE INFORMATION

State-supported, 2-year, coed. Part of Colorado Community College and Occupational Education System. Awards associate degrees. Founded 1967. *Setting:* 20-acre rural campus with easy access to Denver. *Total enrollment:* 1,200. *Faculty:* 142 (29 full-time, 113 part-time); student–undergrad faculty ratio is 9:1.
Enrollment Profile: 1,200 students: 66% women, 34% men, 69% part-time, 99% state residents, 7% transferred in, 0% international, 52% 25 or older, 9% Hispanic, 1% black.
First-Year Class: 422 total; 450 applied, 100% were accepted, 94% of whom enrolled.
Graduation Requirements: 62 credit hours; math/science requirements vary according to program; computer course.
Computers on Campus: 60 computers available on campus for general student use. Computers for student use in computer center, library. Staffed computer lab on campus provides training in use of computers, software.

EXPENSES

Expenses for 1997–98: State resident tuition: $1683 full-time, $54.30 per credit hour part-time. Nonresident tuition: $7820 full-time, $252.25 per credit hour part-time. Part-time mandatory fees: $3.50 per credit hour. Full-time mandatory fees: $109.
LD Services Contact: Ms. Evelyn Kral, Instructor, Developmental Education, Morgan Community College, 17800 Road 20, Fort Morgan, CO 80701, 970-867-3081. Fax: 970-867-6608.

MOTLOW STATE COMMUNITY COLLEGE

Tullahoma, Tennessee

LEARNING DISABILITIES SERVICES INFORMATION

Student Affairs began offering services in 1990. Currently the program serves 15 undergraduates with LD. Students diagnosed with ADD/ADHD are eligible for the same services available to students with LD.
Staff: 1 full-time, 1 part-time staff members, including coordinator. Services provided by tutors, counselors.
Special Fees: No special fees are charged for services to students with LD.
Applications and admissions: *Required:* high school transcript, grade point average, class rank, courses completed, IEP (Individualized Education Program), untimed or extended time SAT I, psychoeducational report completed within 3 years, ACT ASSET (may be substituted for ACT or SAT I); *recommended:* untimed or extended time ACT, letters of recommendation. Students may begin taking classes any term. *Application deadline:* continuous.

PROGRAM AND SERVICE COMPONENTS

Academic advising: Provided by unit staff members, academic advisers. Students with LD may take up to 15 credits each term; most take 12 credits; 12 credits required to maintain full-time status; 6 credits (federal assistance), 15 credits (state assistance; fewer with special permission) required to be eligible for financial aid.
Counseling services: Individual counseling, career counseling.
Basic skills remediation: Offered in class-size groups by regular teachers. Available in reading, math, study skills, English.
Subject-area tutoring: Offered one-on-one by peer tutors. Available in all subjects.
Auxiliary aids: Taped textbooks, tape recorders, calculators, word-processors with spell-check, personal computers, enlarger reading machines.
Auxiliary services: Alternative test arrangements, notetakers, priority registration.

GENERAL COLLEGE INFORMATION

State-supported, 2-year, coed. Part of State University and Community College System of Tennessee. Awards associate degrees. Founded 1969. *Setting:* 187-acre small-town campus with easy access to Nashville. *Total enrollment:* 3,160. *Faculty:* 210 (79 full-time, 10% with terminal degrees, 131 part-time).
Enrollment Profile: 3,160 students: 67% women, 33% men, 48% part-time, 99% state residents, 5% transferred in, 1% international, 43% 25 or older, 1% Native American, 1% Hispanic, 6% black, 1% Asian or Pacific Islander. *Most popular recent majors:* liberal arts/general studies, nursing.
First-Year Class: 750 total; 2,000 applied, 100% were accepted. 12% from top 10% of their high school class, 33% from top quarter, 42% from top half.
Graduation Requirements: 66 credits; 2 science courses; computer course.
Computers on Campus: 245 computers available on campus for general student use. A campus-wide network can be accessed from off-campus. Students can contact faculty members and/or advisers through e-mail. Computers for student use in computer center, computer labs, library, math lab. Staffed computer lab on campus (open 24 hours a day).

Motlow State Community College (continued)

EXPENSES

Expenses for 1997–98: *Application fee:* $5. State resident tuition: $1086 full-time, $48 per semester hour part-time. Nonresident tuition: $4342 full-time, $190 per semester hour part-time. Part-time mandatory fees per semester range from $7 to $22. Full-time mandatory fees: $52.

LD Services Contact: Ms. Ann Simmons, Dean of Student Development, Motlow State Community College, PO Box 88100, Tullahoma, TN 37388-8100, 615-393-1762. Fax: 615-393-1681. Email: asimmons@mscc.cc.tn.us.

MOUNTAIN VIEW COLLEGE

Dallas, Texas

LEARNING DISABILITIES SERVICES INFORMATION

Special Services began offering services in 1970. Currently the program serves 81 undergraduates with LD. Students diagnosed with ADD/ADHD are eligible for the same services available to students with LD.

Staff: 1 full-time, 3 part-time staff members, including rehabilitation specialist, sign language interpreter. Services provided by tutors, counselor.

Special Fees: No special fees are charged for services to students with LD.

Applications and admissions: *Required:* high school transcript, autobiographical statement, psychoeducational report completed within 2 years, Texas Academic Skills Program test (TASP); *recommended:* high school grade point average. Students may begin taking classes any term. *Application deadline:* continuous.

Special policies: The college has written policies regarding grade forgiveness; substitutions and waivers of admissions, graduation, and degree requirements.

PROGRAM AND SERVICE COMPONENTS

Academic advising: Provided by unit staff members. Students with LD may take up to 18 credit hours each term; most take 12 credit hours; 12 credit hours required to maintain full-time status and be eligible for financial aid.

Counseling services: Individual counseling, small-group counseling, career counseling, self-advocacy training.

Basic skills remediation: Offered one-on-one and in small groups by regular teachers, teacher trainees. Available in reading, math.

Subject-area tutoring: Offered one-on-one and in small groups by professional teachers, peer tutors. Available in all subjects.

Auxiliary aids: Taped textbooks, tape recorders, calculators, typewriters, word-processors with spell-check, personal computers, optical character readers.

Auxiliary services: Alternative test arrangements, notetakers, priority registration.

GENERAL COLLEGE INFORMATION

County-supported, 2-year, coed. Part of Dallas County Community College District System. Awards associate degrees. Founded 1970. *Setting:* 200-acre urban campus. *Total enrollment:* 5,569. *Faculty:* 264 (79 full-time, 185 part-time); student–undergrad faculty ratio is 25:1.

Enrollment Profile: 5,569 students: 56% women, 44% men, 69% part-time, 98% state residents, 24% transferred in, 1% international, 40% 25 or older, 1% Native American, 27% Hispanic, 25% black, 5% Asian or Pacific Islander. *Most popular recent majors:* liberal arts/general studies, aviation technology, accounting.

First-Year Class: 1,259 total; 1,560 applied, 100% were accepted, 81% of whom enrolled.

Graduation Requirements: 61 credit hours; 1 math course.

Computers on Campus: 188 computers available on campus for general student use. Computers for student use in computer center, computer labs, learning resource center, classrooms, library, student center. Staffed computer lab on campus provides training in use of computers, software.

EXPENSES

Expenses for 1997–98: Area resident tuition: $650 full-time. State resident tuition: $1030 full-time. Nonresident tuition: $2140 full-time. Part-time tuition per semester ranges from $79 to $245 for area residents, $135 to $435 for state residents, $226 to $786 for nonresidents.

LD Services Contact: Ms. Donna Richards, Dean, Mountain View College, 4849 West Illinois Avenue, Dallas, TX 75211-6599, 214-860-8691. Fax: 214-333-8570.

MT. HOOD COMMUNITY COLLEGE

Gresham, Oregon

LEARNING DISABILITIES SERVICES INFORMATION

Disability Services began offering services in 1987. Currently the program serves 180 undergraduates with LD. Students diagnosed with ADD/ADHD are eligible for the same services available to students with LD.

Staff: 3 full-time, 3 part-time staff members, including coordinator, access technology specialist, assistant. Services provided by tutors, auxiliary aides.

Special Fees: No special fees are charged for services to students with LD.

Applications and admissions: *Required:* psychoeducational report; *recommended:* high school transcript, grade point average, class rank, courses completed, college placement test. Students may begin taking classes any term. *Application deadline:* continuous.

Special policies: The college has written policies regarding grade forgiveness; substitutions and waivers of degree requirements.

PROGRAM AND SERVICE COMPONENTS

Special preparation or orientation: Orientation (required for some) held during registration.

Academic advising: Provided by unit staff members, academic advisers. Students with LD may take up to 19 credits each term; most take 9 to 12 credits; 12 credits required to maintain full-time status; 6 credits required to be eligible for financial aid.

Counseling services: Individual counseling, small-group counseling, career counseling, self-advocacy training.

Basic skills remediation: Offered one-on-one, in small groups, and in class-size groups by regular teachers, professional tutors. Available in reading, math, spelling, handwriting, spoken language, written language, learning strategies, study skills, time management, social skills.

Subject-area tutoring: Offered one-on-one and in small groups by professional teachers, peer tutors. Available in most subjects.

Special courses: College survival skills, reading, vocabulary development, learning strategies, time management, study skills, career planning. All offered for credit; some enter into overall grade point average.

Auxiliary aids: Taped textbooks, tape recorders, typewriters, word-processors with spell-check, talking computers, optical character readers, adaptive software, enlargers.

Auxiliary services: Alternative test arrangements, notetakers, priority registration, advocacy, scribes.

GENERAL COLLEGE INFORMATION

State and locally supported, 2-year, coed. Awards associate degrees. Founded 1966. *Setting:* 212-acre suburban campus with easy access to Portland. *Research spending 1995–96:* $75,611. *Total enrollment:* 7,171. *Faculty:* 547 (167 full-time, 95% with terminal degrees, 380 part-time).

Enrollment Profile: 7,171 students from 16 states and territories, 6 other countries. 60% women, 40% men, 70% part-time, 80% state residents, 10% transferred in, 1% international, 56% 25 or older, 1% Native American, 2% Hispanic, 2% black, 3% Asian or Pacific Islander. *Retention:* 70% of 1995 full-time freshmen returned. *Most popular recent majors:* liberal arts/general studies, nursing, physical therapy.

First-Year Class: 2,198 total. Of the students who applied, 100% were accepted.

Graduation Requirements: 90 credits; math/science requirements vary according to program; computer course for all transfer associate of applied arts degree programs; internship (some majors).

Computers on Campus: 100 computers available on campus for general student use. Computers for student use in computer center, computer labs, classrooms, library, art, writing labs provide access to the Internet/World Wide Web. Staffed computer lab on campus provides training in use of computers, software. *Academic computing expenditure 1995–96:* $200,000.

EXPENSES

Expenses for 1997–98: State resident tuition: $1530 full-time, $34 per credit part-time. Nonresident tuition: $5265 full-time, $117 per credit part-time. Part-time mandatory fees: $2 per credit. Tuition for international students: $5985 full-time, $133 per credit part-time. Full-time mandatory fees: $90.

LD Services Contact: Mr. David Blessman, Coordinator, Disability Services, Mt. Hood Community College, 26000 Southeast Stark, Gresham, OR 97030-3300, 503-667-7650. Fax: 503-667-7388. Email: blessmad@mhcc.or.us.

MOUNT WACHUSETT COMMUNITY COLLEGE

Gardner, Massachusetts

LEARNING DISABILITIES SERVICES INFORMATION

Services for Students with Learning Disabilities began offering services in 1982. Currently the program serves 175 undergraduates with LD. Students diagnosed with ADD/ADHD are eligible for the same services available to students with LD.

Staff: 2 full-time, 2 part-time staff members. Services provided by remediation specialists, tutors, counselors.

Special Fees: No special fees are charged for services to students with LD.

Applications and admissions: *Recommended:* high school transcript, IEP (Individualized Education Program), psychoeducational report. Students may begin taking classes in fall, spring, or summer. *Application deadline:* continuous.

Special policies: The college has written policies regarding substitutions and waivers of admissions, graduation, and degree requirements.

PROGRAM AND SERVICE COMPONENTS

Special preparation or orientation: Optional orientation offered before classes begin.

Academic advising: Provided by unit staff members, academic advisers. Students with LD may take up to 17 credits each term; most take 12 credits; 12 credits required to maintain full-time status; 3 credits required to be eligible for financial aid.

Counseling services: Individual counseling, career counseling, self-advocacy training.

Basic skills remediation: Offered in class-size groups by regular teachers. Available in reading, math, written language, study skills.

Auxiliary aids: Taped textbooks, tape recorders, calculators, typewriters, word-processors with spell-check.

Auxiliary services: Alternative test arrangements, notetakers, advocacy.

Campus support group: A special student organization is available to students with LD.

GENERAL COLLEGE INFORMATION

State-supported, 2-year, coed. Part of Massachusetts Public Higher Education System. Awards associate degrees. Founded 1963. *Setting:* 270-acre small-town campus with easy access to Boston. *Total enrollment:* 2,814. *Faculty:* 112 (72 full-time, 30% with terminal degrees, 40 part-time); student–undergrad faculty ratio is 20:1.

Enrollment Profile: 2,814 students: 63% women, 37% men, 59% part-time, 98% state residents, 35% transferred in, 1% international, 82% 25 or older, 1% Native American, 5% Hispanic, 2% black, 2% Asian or Pacific Islander. *Most popular recent majors:* business administration/commerce/management, criminal justice.

First-Year Class: 576 total; 996 applied, 61% were accepted, 95% of whom enrolled.

Graduation Requirements: 61 credits; computer course for business administration majors.

Computers on Campus: 125 computers available on campus for general student use. A campus-wide network can be accessed. Students can contact faculty members and/or advisers through e-mail. Computers for student use in computer center provide access to the Internet/World Wide Web, on-campus e-mail addresses.

EXPENSES AND FINANCIAL AID

Expenses for 1997–98: *Application fee:* $10. State resident tuition: $1020 full-time, $34 per credit part-time. Nonresident tuition: $6120 full-time, $204 per credit part-time. Part-time mandatory fees: $63 per credit. Tuition for nonresidents who are eligible for the New England Regional Student Program: $1530 full-time, $51 per credit part-time. Full-time mandatory fees: $1890.

Financial aid specifically for students with LD: Scholarship: George Wallace Scholarship.

LD Services Contact: Ms. Jo Ann Brooks, Learning Disability Specialist, Mount Wachusett Community College, 444 Green Street, Gardner, MA 01440-1337, 508-632-6600 Ext. 325.

MUSKEGON COMMUNITY COLLEGE

Muskegon, Michigan

LEARNING DISABILITIES SERVICES INFORMATION

Special Service Programs Office began offering services in 1993. Currently the program serves 25 undergraduates with LD. Students diagnosed with ADD/ADHD are eligible for the same services available to students with LD.

Staff: 1 full-time, 1 part-time staff members, including director.

Special Fees: No special fees are charged for services to students with LD.

Applications and admissions: *Required:* high school transcript, IEP (Individualized Education Program), psychoeducational report completed in high school. Students may begin taking classes any term. *Application deadline:* continuous.

Special policies: The college has written policies regarding substitutions and waivers of graduation and degree requirements.

PROGRAM AND SERVICE COMPONENTS

Academic advising: Provided by unit staff members, academic advisers. Most students with LD take 9 to 12 credit hours each term; 12 credit hours required to maintain full-time status; no minimum number of credit hours required to be eligible for financial aid.

Counseling services: Individual counseling, career counseling.

Basic skills remediation: Offered one-on-one by regular teachers. Available in reading, math, written language, learning strategies, study skills.

Subject-area tutoring: Offered one-on-one by professional teachers, peer tutors. Available in all subjects.

Auxiliary aids: Taped textbooks, word-processors with spell-check, closed-captioned television.

Auxiliary services: Alternative test arrangements, notetakers, readers (for exams).

GENERAL COLLEGE INFORMATION

State and locally supported, 2-year, coed. Part of Michigan Department of Education. Awards associate degrees. Founded 1926. *Setting:* 112-acre urban campus with easy access to Grand Rapids. *Total enrollment:* 5,169. *Faculty:* 150 (100 full-time, 50 part-time); student–undergrad faculty ratio is 33:1.

Enrollment Profile: 5,169 students from 3 states and territories, 5 other countries. 52% women, 48% men, 57% part-time, 95% state residents, 8% transferred in, 2% international, 52% 25 or older, 2% Native American, 2% Hispanic, 10% black. *Most popular recent majors:* nursing, business administration/commerce/management, liberal arts/general studies.

First-Year Class: 1,788 total. Of the students who applied, 100% were accepted.

Graduation Requirements: 62 credit hours.

Computers on Campus: 30 computers available on campus for general student use. Computers for student use in computer center.

EXPENSES

Expenses for 1997–98: Area resident tuition: $1457 full-time, $47 per credit hour part-time. State resident tuition: $2093 full-time, $67.50 per credit hour part-time. Nonresident tuition: $2573 full-time, $83 per credit hour part-time. Part-time mandatory fees: $15 per semester. Full-time mandatory fees: $30.

LD Services Contact: Ms. Eunice Merwin, Special Service Programs Director/Counselor, Muskegon Community College, 221 South Quarterline Road, Muskegon, MI 49442-1493, 616-777-0309. Fax: 616-777-0255.

MUSKINGUM AREA TECHNICAL COLLEGE

Zanesville, Ohio

LEARNING DISABILITIES SERVICES INFORMATION

Student Services Center began offering services in 1989. Currently the program serves 30 undergraduates with LD. Students diagnosed with ADD/ADHD are eligible for the same services available to students with LD.

Staff: 1 full-time, 4 part-time staff members. Services provided by tutors, counselors.

Muskingum Area Technical College (continued)

Special Fees: No special fees are charged for services to students with LD.
Applications and admissions: *Required:* high school transcript, grade point average, IEP (Individualized Education Program), personal interview. Students may begin taking classes any term. *Application deadline:* continuous.
Special policies: The college has written policies regarding grade forgiveness; substitutions and waivers of admissions, graduation, and degree requirements.

PROGRAM AND SERVICE COMPONENTS

Academic advising: Provided by academic advisers. Students with LD may take up to 15 credits each term; most take 12 credits; 12 credits required to maintain full-time status; 6 credits required to be eligible for financial aid.
Counseling services: Individual counseling, career counseling.
Basic skills remediation: Offered in class-size groups by regular teachers; computer-aided instruction also offered. Available in reading, math, written language, learning strategies, study skills, time management, social skills, computer skills.
Subject-area tutoring: Offered one-on-one, in small groups, and in class-size groups by professional teachers, peer tutors. Available in all subjects.
Special courses: College survival skills, reading, vocabulary development, communication skills, composition, word processing, Internet use, time management, math, study skills, career planning. Most offered for credit; most enter into overall grade point average.
Auxiliary aids: Taped textbooks, tape recorders, calculators, typewriters, word-processors with spell-check, personal computers, talking computers, optical character readers.
Auxiliary services: Alternative test arrangements, notetakers, advocacy.

GENERAL COLLEGE INFORMATION

State and locally supported, 2-year, coed. Awards associate degrees. Founded 1969. *Setting:* 170-acre small-town campus with easy access to Columbus. *Total enrollment:* 2,135. *Faculty:* 104 (40 full-time, 64 part-time).
Enrollment Profile: 2,135 students: 63% women, 37% men, 65% part-time, 99% state residents, 5% transferred in, 45% 25 or older, 1% Native American, 1% Hispanic, 3% black, 1% Asian or Pacific Islander. *Most popular recent majors:* criminal justice, accounting, business administration/commerce/management.
First-Year Class: 895 applied, 100% were accepted.
Graduation Requirements: 110 credits; math/science requirements vary according to program; computer course.
Computers on Campus: 110 computers available on campus for general student use. Computers for student use in computer labs, business lab. Staffed computer lab on campus.

EXPENSES

Expenses for 1997–98: *Application fee:* $25. State resident tuition: $2750 full-time, $50 per credit hour part-time. Nonresident tuition: $3555 full-time, $80 per credit hour part-time. Part-time mandatory fees: $5 per credit hour. Full-time mandatory fees: $160.
LD Services Contact: Mr. David C. Wells, Director of Advising, Muskingum Area Technical College, 1555 Newark Road, Zanesville, OH 43701, 614-454-2501 Ext. 121. Fax: 614-454-0035. Email: dwells@matc.tec.oh.us.

NASHVILLE STATE TECHNICAL INSTITUTE

Nashville, Tennessee

LEARNING DISABILITIES SERVICES INFORMATION

Office of Affirmative Action began offering services in 1992. Currently the program serves 100 undergraduates with LD. Students diagnosed with ADD/ADHD are eligible for the same services available to students with LD.
Staff: 3 full-time, 8 part-time staff members, including co-directors, coordinator. Services provided by tutors, counselors, LD specialist.
Special Fees: No special fees are charged for services to students with LD.
Applications and admissions: *Required:* high school transcript, grade point average, courses completed, psychoeducational report completed within 3 years; *recommended:* high school IEP (Individualized Education Program), extended time ACT, personal interview. Students may begin taking classes any term. *Application deadline:* continuous.

PROGRAM AND SERVICE COMPONENTS

Academic advising: Provided by unit staff members, academic advisers. Most students with LD take 12 semester hours each term; 12 semester hours required to maintain full-time status; 12 semester hours (Federal Pell), 15 semester hours (State Vocational Rehabilitation) required to be eligible for financial aid.
Counseling services: Individual counseling, career counseling, self-advocacy training, community referrals.
Subject-area tutoring: Offered one-on-one and in small groups by peer tutors, staff tutors. Available in all subjects.
Auxiliary aids: Tape recorders, typewriters, word-processors with spell-check, personal computers, optical character readers.
Auxiliary services: Alternative test arrangements, notetakers, priority registration, advocacy.

GENERAL COLLEGE INFORMATION

State-supported, 2-year, coed. Part of State University and Community College System of Tennessee. Awards associate degrees. Founded 1970. *Setting:* 60-acre urban campus. *Total enrollment:* 7,013. *Faculty:* 294 (94 full-time, 200 part-time); student–undergrad faculty ratio is 19:1.
Enrollment Profile: 7,013 students: 46% women, 54% men, 48% part-time, 99% state residents, 9% transferred in, 1% international, 71% 25 or older, 0% Native American, 1% Hispanic, 17% black, 2% Asian or Pacific Islander. *Areas of study chosen:* 7% engineering and applied sciences, 5% communications and journalism, 2% architecture.
First-Year Class: 3,112 total. Of the students who applied, 100% were accepted, 90% of whom enrolled.
Graduation Requirements: 65 credits; 1 course each in math and science; computer course.
Computers on Campus: 518 computers available on campus for general student use. A computer is recommended for some students. A campus-wide network can be accessed from off-campus. Students can contact faculty members and/or advisers through e-mail. Computers for student use in classrooms provide access to the Internet/World Wide Web, on- and off-campus e-mail addresses.

EXPENSES

Expenses for 1997–98: *Application fee:* $5. State resident tuition: $1086 full-time, $48 per semester hour part-time. Nonresident tuition: $4342 full-time, $190 per semester hour part-time. Part-time mandatory fees per semester range from $3.50 to $29. Full-time mandatory fees: $58.
LD Services Contact: Ms. Diane Wood, LD Coordinator, Academic Skills Department, Nashville State Technical Institute, 120 White Bridge Road, Nashville, TN 37209-4515, 615-353-3720.

NASSAU COMMUNITY COLLEGE

Garden City, New York

LEARNING DISABILITIES SERVICES INFORMATION

Disabled Student Services began offering services in 1978. Currently the program serves 221 undergraduates with LD. Students diagnosed with ADD/ADHD are eligible for the same services available to students with LD.
Staff: 5 full-time, 4 part-time staff members, including coordinator, administrative assistant. Services provided by tutors, counselors, job developer, LD specialists.
Special Fees: No special fees are charged for services to students with LD.
Applications and admissions: *Required:* high school transcript, psychoeducational report, high school diploma or GED. Students may begin taking classes any term. *Application deadline:* continuous.
Special policies: The college has written policies regarding substitutions and waivers of degree requirements.

PROGRAM AND SERVICE COMPONENTS

Special preparation or orientation: Optional orientation offered before classes begin.
Academic advising: Provided by unit staff members. Students with LD may take up to 17 credits each term; most take 9 to 12 credits; 12 credits (or the equivalent of required non-credit remedial courses) required to maintain full-time status and be eligible for financial aid.
Counseling services: Individual counseling, career counseling, self-advocacy training.

Basic skills remediation: Offered one-on-one and in small groups by LD teachers, regular teachers. Available in reading, math, spelling, written language, learning strategies, study skills, time management, social skills, computer skills.
Subject-area tutoring: Offered one-on-one and in small groups by professional teachers, peer tutors. Available in some subjects.
Auxiliary aids: Taped textbooks, tape recorders, calculators, typewriters, word-processors with spell-check, personal computers, talking computers, optical character readers, voice synthesizer.
Auxiliary services: Alternative test arrangements, notetakers, priority registration, advocacy.

GENERAL COLLEGE INFORMATION

State and locally supported, 2-year, coed. Part of State University of New York System. Awards associate degrees. Founded 1959. *Setting:* 225-acre suburban campus with easy access to New York City. *Total enrollment:* 20,620. *Faculty:* 1,523 (512 full-time, 30% with terminal degrees, 1,011 part-time).
Enrollment Profile: 20,620 students: 53% women, 47% men, 43% part-time, 99% state residents, 9% transferred in, 32% 25 or older, 1% Native American, 8% Hispanic, 11% black, 3% Asian or Pacific Islander. *Retention:* 70% of 1995 full-time freshmen returned. *Areas of study chosen:* 49% liberal arts/general studies, 17% business management and administrative services, 6% health professions and related sciences, 2% communications and journalism, 2% computer and information sciences, 2% engineering and applied sciences, 2% fine arts, 1% performing arts. *Most popular recent majors:* liberal arts/general studies, business administration/commerce/management.
First-Year Class: 4,928 total; 7,960 applied, 84% were accepted, 73% of whom enrolled. 1% from top 10% of their high school class, 9% from top quarter, 32% from top half.
Graduation Requirements: 64 credits; 3 credits of math; 4 credits of lab science; computer course for business, accounting, marketing majors; internship (some majors).
Computers on Campus: 1,000 computers available on campus for general student use. A campus-wide network can be accessed from off-campus. Students can contact faculty members and/or advisers through e-mail. Computers for student use in computer center, computer labs, learning resource center, classrooms, library provide access to the Internet/World Wide Web, on-campus e-mail addresses. Staffed computer lab on campus provides training in use of computers, software.

EXPENSES

Expenses for 1996–97: *Application fee:* $20. State resident tuition: $2120 full-time, $86 per credit part-time. Nonresident tuition: $4240 full-time, $172 per credit part-time. Part-time mandatory fees: $4 per credit. Full-time mandatory fees: $100.
LD Services Contact: Prof. Janis Schimsky, Coordinator, Center for Students with Disabilities, Nassau Community College, 1 Education Drive, Garden City, NY 11530-6793, 516-572-7138.

NAUGATUCK VALLEY COMMUNITY–TECHNICAL COLLEGE

Waterbury, Connecticut

LEARNING DISABILITIES SERVICES INFORMATION

Office for Students with Learning Disabilities began offering services in 1987. Currently the program serves 85 undergraduates with LD. Students diagnosed with ADD/ADHD are eligible for the same services available to students with LD.
Staff: 1 full-time, 1 part-time staff members, including coordinator. Services provided by tutors, counselors.
Special Fees: No special fees are charged for services to students with LD.
Applications and admissions: *Required:* high school transcript, psychoeducational report completed most recently, evaluations from high school counselors; *recommended:* high school IEP (Individualized Education Program). Students may begin taking classes any term. *Application deadline:* continuous.
Special policies: The college has written policies regarding grade forgiveness.

PROGRAM AND SERVICE COMPONENTS

Special preparation or orientation: Optional orientation offered before registration, during registration, after classes begin.
Academic advising: Provided by unit staff members, academic advisers. Students with LD may take up to 15 credits each term; most take 6 to 9 credits; 12 credits required to maintain full-time status.
Counseling services: Individual counseling, small-group counseling, career counseling.
Basic skills remediation: Offered one-on-one and in class-size groups by regular teachers, teacher trainees. Available in reading, math, spelling, spoken language, written language, learning strategies, study skills, time management.
Subject-area tutoring: Offered one-on-one by professional teachers, peer tutors. Available in most subjects.
Auxiliary aids: Taped textbooks, tape recorders, calculators, word-processors with spell-check, personal computers, videocassettes on academic skills.
Auxiliary services: Alternative test arrangements, notetakers, priority registration, advocacy.

GENERAL COLLEGE INFORMATION

State-supported, 2-year, coed. Part of Connecticut Community–Technical College System. Awards associate degrees. Founded 1992. *Setting:* 110-acre urban campus. *Total enrollment:* 5,239. *Faculty:* 299 (110 full-time, 97% with terminal degrees, 189 part-time); student–undergrad faculty ratio is 25:1.
Enrollment Profile: 5,239 students from 4 states and territories, 31 other countries. 55% women, 45% men, 70% part-time, 98% state residents, 25% transferred in, 1% international, 54% 25 or older, 1% Native American, 7% Hispanic, 6% black, 2% Asian or Pacific Islander. *Retention:* 65% of 1995 full-time freshmen returned. *Areas of study chosen:* 38% liberal arts/general studies, 16% business management and administrative services, 13% engineering and applied sciences, 12% social sciences, 6% computer and information sciences, 6% education, 5% health professions and related sciences, 4% vocational and home economics. *Most popular recent majors:* liberal arts/general studies, early childhood education, business administration/commerce/management.
First-Year Class: 1,175 total; 1,847 applied, 100% were accepted, 64% of whom enrolled.
Graduation Requirements: 60 credits; math/science requirements vary according to program; computer course for business, engineering technology, hospitality management, automotive technician, legal assistant, nursing, radiologic technology majors; internship (some majors).
Computers on Campus: 450 computers available on campus for general student use. A campus-wide network can be accessed. Students can contact faculty members and/or advisers through e-mail. Computers for student use in computer labs, learning resource center, classrooms provide access to the Internet/World Wide Web, on- and off-campus e-mail addresses. Staffed computer lab on campus. *Academic computing expenditure 1995–96:* $51,531.

EXPENSES

Expenses for 1997–98: *Application fee:* $20. State resident tuition: $1608 full-time, $67 per credit part-time. Nonresident tuition: $5232 full-time, $218 per credit part-time. Part-time mandatory fees per semester range from $42 to $91. Tuition for nonresidents who are eligible for the New England Regional Student Program: $2412 full-time, $100.50 per credit part-time. Full-time mandatory fees: $206.
LD Services Contact: Ms. Louise L. Myers, Coordinator and Instructor of Learning Disabilities Program, Naugatuck Valley Community–Technical College, 750 Chase Parkway, Waterbury, CT 06708, 203-575-8161. Email: mt_markos_ay@apollo.commnet.edu.

NEOSHO COUNTY COMMUNITY COLLEGE

Chanute, Kansas

LEARNING DISABILITIES SERVICES INFORMATION

Center for Academic and Vocational Excellence (CAVE) began offering services in 1993. Currently the program serves 3 to 4 undergraduates with LD. Students diagnosed with ADD/ADHD are eligible for the same services available to students with LD.
Staff: 2 full-time, 1 part-time staff members, including assistant director. Services provided by tutor.
Special Fees: No special fees are charged for services to students with LD.

Neosho County Community College (continued)

Applications and admissions: *Required:* high school transcript, IEP (Individualized Education Program). Students may begin taking classes any term. *Application deadline:* continuous.

Special policies: The college has written policies regarding grade forgiveness; substitutions and waivers of admissions, graduation, and degree requirements.

PROGRAM AND SERVICE COMPONENTS

Academic advising: Provided by academic advisers. Students with LD may take up to 18 semester hours each term; most take 12 to 15 semester hours; 12 semester hours required to maintain full-time status; 12 semester hours (full-time), 6 semester hours (part-time) required to be eligible for financial aid.

Counseling services: Individual counseling.

Subject-area tutoring: Offered one-on-one and in small groups by professional teachers, peer tutors. Available in all subjects.

Auxiliary services: Alternative test arrangements.

GENERAL COLLEGE INFORMATION

State and locally supported, 2-year, coed. Part of Kansas State Board of Education. Awards associate degrees. Founded 1936. *Setting:* 50-acre small-town campus. *Endowment:* $370,000. *Educational spending 1995–96:* $1400 per undergrad. *Total enrollment:* 1,185. *Faculty:* 96 (10% of full-time faculty have terminal degrees).

Enrollment Profile: 1,185 students from 15 states and territories, 3 other countries. 65% women, 35% men, 60% part-time, 98% state residents, 5% live on campus, 10% transferred in, 58% 25 or older, 1% Native American, 3% Hispanic, 5% black, 1% Asian or Pacific Islander. *Areas of study chosen:* 25% business management and administrative services, 25% education, 15% health professions and related sciences, 5% architecture, 2% engineering and applied sciences, 2% premed, 2% social sciences. *Most popular recent majors:* accounting, business machine technologies, nursing.

First-Year Class: 350 total; 479 applied, 100% were accepted, 73% of whom enrolled. 8% from top 10% of their high school class, 20% from top quarter, 60% from top half.

Graduation Requirements: 62 semester hours; computer course.

Computers on Campus: 100 computers available on campus for general student use. Computers for student use in computer center, library, dorms, English lab. Staffed computer lab on campus provides training in use of computers, software. *Academic computing expenditure 1995–96:* $74,731.

EXPENSES

Expenses for 1996–97: State resident tuition: $1147 full-time, $37 per semester hour part-time. Nonresident tuition: $2759 full-time, $89 per semester hour part-time. College room and board: $2600.

LD Services Contact: Ms. Judith Luther, Director of Basic Skills, Neosho County Community College, 1000 South Allen, Chanute, KS 66720, 316-431-2820 Ext. 279.

NEW ENGLAND INSTITUTE OF TECHNOLOGY

Warwick, Rhode Island

LEARNING DISABILITIES SERVICES INFORMATION

Academic Skills Center began offering services in 1988. Currently the program serves 50 undergraduates with LD. Students diagnosed with ADD/ADHD are eligible for the same services available to students with LD.

Staff: 1 full-time, 8 part-time staff members, including director, coordinators. Services provided by remediation specialists, tutors, counselor, skills specialist.

Special Fees: No special fees are charged for services to students with LD.

Applications and admissions: *Required:* NEIT Placement Tests in math, reading and writing (untimed), documentation of disability. Students may begin taking classes any term. *Application deadline:* continuous.

PROGRAM AND SERVICE COMPONENTS

Academic advising: Provided by unit staff members, academic advisers. Students with LD may take up to 12 credits each term; most take 10 to 12 credits; 10 credits required to maintain full-time status; source of aid determines number of credits required to be eligible for financial aid.

Counseling services: Individual counseling.

Basic skills remediation: Offered one-on-one and in small groups by LD teachers, regular teachers. Available in reading, math, spelling, spoken language, written language, learning strategies, study skills, time management.

Subject-area tutoring: Offered one-on-one and in small groups by professional teachers. Available in all subjects.

Special courses: College survival skills, reading, vocabulary development, composition, learning strategies, word processing, time management, math, personal psychology, study skills. Some offered for credit; some enter into overall grade point average.

Auxiliary aids: Taped textbooks, tape recorders, calculators, typewriters, word-processors with spell-check.

Auxiliary services: Alternative test arrangements, notetakers, priority registration, advocacy.

GENERAL COLLEGE INFORMATION

Independent, primarily 2-year, coed. Awards associate, bachelor's degrees. Founded 1940. *Setting:* 10-acre suburban campus with easy access to Boston. *Total enrollment:* 2,200. *Faculty:* 168 (71 full-time, 97 part-time).

Enrollment Profile: 2,200 students from 8 states and territories, 6 other countries. 22% women, 78% men, 60% state residents, 1% transferred in, 2% international, 36% 25 or older, 0% Native American, 2% Hispanic, 3% black, 1% Asian or Pacific Islander. *Most popular recent majors:* electrical and electronics technologies, automotive technologies.

First-Year Class: 700 total.

Graduation Requirements: 90 credits for associate, 180 credits for bachelor's; math/science requirements vary according to program; computer course for business-related, medical assistant majors; internship (some majors).

Computers on Campus: 175 computers available on campus for general student use. Computers for student use in computer center, computer labs, learning resource center, classrooms provide access to the Internet/World Wide Web. Staffed computer lab on campus provides training in use of computers, software.

EXPENSES

Expenses for 1997–98: *Application fee:* $25. Tuition: $18,300 per degree program. Full-time mandatory fees: $300. Tuition guaranteed not to increase for student's term of enrollment.

LD Services Contact: Ms. Doreen Lasiewski, Director of Instructional Development, New England Institute of Technology, 2500 Post Road, Warwick, RI 02886-2244, 401-739-5000 Ext. 3428. Fax: 401-738-5122. Email: dlasiewski@ids.net.

NEW HAMPSHIRE COMMUNITY TECHNICAL COLLEGE, MANCHESTER/STRATHAM

Manchester, New Hampshire

LEARNING DISABILITIES SERVICES INFORMATION

Student Services Office/Academic Support Center began offering services in 1992. Currently the program serves 75 undergraduates with LD. Students diagnosed with ADD/ADHD are eligible for the same services available to students with LD.

Staff: 1 part-time staff member (director).

Special Fees: No special fees are charged for services to students with LD.

Applications and admissions: *Required:* high school transcript, grade point average, courses completed, IEP (Individualized Education Program), letters of recommendation, psychoeducational report completed within 3 years; *recommended:* untimed or extended time ACT. Students may begin taking classes in fall or spring. *Application deadline:* continuous.

Special policies: The college has written policies regarding substitutions and waivers of degree requirements.

PROGRAM AND SERVICE COMPONENTS

Special preparation or orientation: Optional summer program offered prior to entering college. Required orientation held during registration.

Diagnostic testing: Reading, math, written language.

Academic advising: Provided by academic advisers. Students with LD may take up to 15 credit hours (unless special requirements are set) each term; most take 12 credit hours; 12 credit hours required to maintain full-time status; 6 credit hours required to be eligible for financial aid.
Counseling services: Individual counseling, small-group counseling, career counseling, support group.
Basic skills remediation: Offered in class-size groups by regular teachers; computer-aided instruction also offered. Available in reading, math, spelling, study skills.
Subject-area tutoring: Offered one-on-one and in small groups by peer tutors. Available in most subjects.
Auxiliary aids: Taped textbooks, tape recorders, calculators, word-processors with spell-check, personal computers, talking computers, optical character readers, pocket spell checkers.
Auxiliary services: Alternative test arrangements, notetakers, advocacy.

GENERAL COLLEGE INFORMATION

State-supported, 2-year, coed. Part of New Hampshire Post-Secondary Technical Education System. Awards associate degrees. Founded 1945. *Setting:* 60-acre urban campus with easy access to Boston. *Total enrollment:* 942. *Faculty:* 200 (50 full-time, 10% with terminal degrees, 150 part-time).
Enrollment Profile: 942 students from 5 states and territories. 55% women, 45% men, 40% part-time, 85% state residents, 20% transferred in, 0% Native American, 2% Hispanic, 1% black, 1% Asian or Pacific Islander. *Retention:* 60% of 1995 full-time freshmen returned. *Areas of study chosen:* 8% communications and journalism.
First-Year Class: 451 total; 876 applied, 62% were accepted, 83% of whom enrolled.
Graduation Requirements: 64 credit hours; computer course (varies by major); internship (some majors).
Computers on Campus: 75 computers available on campus for general student use. A campus-wide network can be accessed. Students can contact faculty members and/or advisers through e-mail. Computers for student use in computer center, computer labs, learning resource center, library provide access to the Internet/World Wide Web, on- and off-campus e-mail addresses. Staffed computer lab on campus provides training in use of computers, software.

EXPENSES AND FINANCIAL AID

Expenses for 1997–98: *Application fee:* $10. State resident tuition: $3080 full-time, $110 per credit hour part-time. Nonresident tuition: $7084 full-time, $253 per credit hour part-time. Part-time mandatory fees: $3 per credit hour. Tuition for nonresidents who are eligible for the New England Regional Student Program: $4620 full-time, $165 per credit hour part-time. Full-time mandatory fees: $84.
Financial aid specifically for students with LD: loan: flexible loan fund for students with disabilities.
LD Services Contact: Ms. Cathryn Weir, Coordinator of Support Services for Students with Disabilities, New Hampshire Community Technical College, Manchester/Stratham, 1066 Front Street, Manchester, NH 03102, 603-668-6706. Fax: 603-668-5354.

NEW HAMPSHIRE TECHNICAL INSTITUTE

Concord, New Hampshire

LEARNING DISABILITIES SERVICES INFORMATION

Learning and Career Center began offering services in 1990. Currently the program serves 188 undergraduates with LD. Students diagnosed with ADD/ADHD are eligible for the same services available to students with LD.
Staff: 4 full-time, 1 part-time staff members, including director, co-directors, receptionist. Services provided by tutors.
Special Fees: No special fees are charged for services to students with LD.
Applications and admissions: *Required:* high school transcript, courses completed, letters of recommendation; *recommended:* high school grade point average, class rank, extracurricular activities, untimed or extended time SAT I or ACT, personal interview, psychoeducational report completed within 3 years. Students may begin taking classes any term. *Application deadline:* continuous.

PROGRAM AND SERVICE COMPONENTS

Special preparation or orientation: Optional summer program offered prior to entering college. Optional orientation offered before classes begin and after general orientation for all students.
Academic advising: Provided by unit staff members, academic advisers. Students with LD may take up to 19 credit hours each term; most take 6 to 9 credit hours; 6 credit hours required to maintain full-time status and be eligible for financial aid.
Counseling services: Individual counseling, small-group counseling, career counseling, self-advocacy training.
Basic skills remediation: Offered one-on-one by Coordinator, special tutors; computer-aided instruction also offered. Available in reading, math, spelling, written language, learning strategies, study skills, time management, social skills.
Subject-area tutoring: Offered one-on-one and in small groups by professional teachers, peer tutors. Available in all subjects.
Auxiliary aids: Taped textbooks, tape recorders, calculators, word-processors with spell-check, optical character readers.
Auxiliary services: Alternative test arrangements, notetakers, priority registration, advocacy.
Campus support group: A special student organization is available to students with LD.

GENERAL COLLEGE INFORMATION

State-supported, 2-year, coed. Part of New Hampshire Post-Secondary Technical Education System. Awards associate degrees. Founded 1964. *Setting:* 225-acre small-town campus with easy access to Boston. *Educational spending 1995–96:* $6000 per undergrad. *Total enrollment:* 1,453. *Faculty:* 145 (110 full-time, 35 part-time); student–undergrad faculty ratio is 10:1.
Enrollment Profile: 1,453 students from 6 states and territories. 54% women, 46% men, 30% part-time, 90% state residents, 43% transferred in, 70% 25 or older, 0% black. *Areas of study chosen:* 30% health professions and related sciences, 20% business management and administrative services, 20% engineering and applied sciences, 10% computer and information sciences, 10% psychology, 10% social sciences. *Most popular recent majors:* nursing, engineering technology, business administration/commerce/management.
First-Year Class: 550 total. Of the students who applied, 60% were accepted, 45% of whom enrolled. 22% from top quarter of their high school class, 41% from top half.
Graduation Requirements: 64 credit hours; computer course for business, criminal justice, radiology, engineering technology majors.
Computers on Campus: 110 computers available on campus for general student use. Computers for student use in computer center, computer labs, library, dorms. *Academic computing expenditure 1995–96:* $606,000.

EXPENSES AND FINANCIAL AID

Estimated Expenses for 1997–98: *Application fee:* $10. State resident tuition: $2756 full-time, $106 per credit hour part-time. Nonresident tuition: $6344 full-time, $244 per credit hour part-time. Part-time mandatory fees: $10 per credit hour. Tuition for nonresidents who are eligible for the New England Regional Student Program: $4134 full-time, $159 per credit hour part-time. Full-time mandatory fees: $260. College room and board: $4135.
Financial aid specifically for students with LD: loan: flexible student loan fund.
LD Services Contact: Mr. Frank Meyer, Director of Admissions, New Hampshire Technical Institute, 11 Institute Drive, Concord, NH 03301-7412, 603-225-1865. Fax: 603-225-1895.

NEW MEXICO JUNIOR COLLEGE

Hobbs, New Mexico

LEARNING DISABILITIES SERVICES INFORMATION

Special Needs Students Services began offering services in 1983. Currently the program serves 30 undergraduates with LD. Students diagnosed with ADD/ADHD are eligible for the same services available to students with LD.
Staff: Includes director, coordinator. Services provided by remediation specialists, tutors, diagnostic specialists, instructors.
Special Fees: No special fees are charged for services to students with LD.

New Mexico Junior College (continued)

Applications and admissions: *Required:* high school transcript, IEP (Individualized Education Program), untimed or extended time SAT I or ACT, COMPASS or ASSET (only as substitute for SAT I or ACT); *recommended:* psychoeducational report. Students may begin taking classes any term. *Application deadline:* continuous.

Special policies: The college has written policies regarding grade forgiveness.

PROGRAM AND SERVICE COMPONENTS

Special preparation or orientation: Required orientation held during registration and after classes begin, individually by special arrangement.

Diagnostic testing: Intelligence, reading, math, spelling, written language, motor abilities, perceptual skills, learning strategies.

Academic advising: Provided by unit staff members, academic advisers. Students with LD may take up to 18 semester hours each term; most take 12 semester hours; 12 semester hours required to maintain full-time status; 6 semester hours required to be eligible for financial aid.

Counseling services: Individual counseling, small-group counseling, career counseling.

Basic skills remediation: Offered one-on-one, in small groups, and in class-size groups by regular teachers; computer-aided instruction also offered. Available in reading, math, spelling, spoken language, written language, learning strategies, study skills, time management, computer skills.

Subject-area tutoring: Offered one-on-one and in small groups by peer tutors. Available in all subjects.

Auxiliary aids: Taped textbooks, tape recorders, calculators, typewriters, word-processors with spell-check, personal computers, talking computers.

Auxiliary services: Alternative test arrangements, notetakers, advocacy, readers.

GENERAL COLLEGE INFORMATION

State and locally supported, 2-year, coed. Part of New Mexico Commission on Higher Education. Awards associate degrees. Founded 1965. *Setting:* 185-acre small-town campus. *Research spending 1995–96:* $21,370. *Total enrollment:* 2,882. *Faculty:* 129 (68 full-time, 17% with terminal degrees, 61 part-time); student–undergrad faculty ratio is 20:1.

Enrollment Profile: 2,882 students from 16 states and territories, 6 other countries. 66% women, 34% men, 58% part-time, 82% state residents, 4% transferred in, 1% international, 50% 25 or older, 1% Native American, 26% Hispanic, 3% black, 1% Asian or Pacific Islander. *Retention:* 70% of 1995 full-time freshmen returned. *Areas of study chosen:* 23% liberal arts/general studies, 18% health professions and related sciences, 14% business management and administrative services, 12% education, 5% computer and information sciences, 3% engineering and applied sciences, 2% architecture, 1% agriculture, 1% biological and life sciences, 1% fine arts, 1% mathematics. *Most popular recent majors:* liberal arts/general studies, nursing, business administration/commerce/management.

First-Year Class: 783 total; 965 applied, 100% were accepted, 81% of whom enrolled. 9% from top 10% of their high school class, 24% from top quarter, 72% from top half. 5 valedictorians.

Graduation Requirements: 64 semester hours; intermediate algebra proficiency; internship (some majors).

Computers on Campus: 275 computers available on campus for general student use. Computer purchase/lease plans available. A campus-wide network can be accessed from off-campus. Students can contact faculty members and/or advisers through e-mail. Computers for student use in computer labs, learning resource center, classrooms, library, student center, dorms, testing center provide access to on- and off-campus e-mail addresses. Staffed computer lab on campus provides training in use of computers, software.

EXPENSES

Expenses for 1997–98: Area resident tuition: $312 full-time, $13 per semester hour part-time. State resident tuition: $720 full-time, $30 per semester hour part-time. Nonresident tuition: $840 full-time, $35 per semester hour part-time. Part-time mandatory fees per semester range from $2 to $10. Full-time mandatory fees: $40. College room and board: $3000.

LD Services Contact: Ms. Connie Brumley, Special Needs Coordinator, New Mexico Junior College, 5317 Lovington Highway, Hobbs, NM 88240-9123, 505-392-5411.

NIAGARA COUNTY COMMUNITY COLLEGE

Sanborn, New York

LEARNING DISABILITIES SERVICES INFORMATION

Disabled Student Services began offering services in 1975. Currently the program serves 123 undergraduates with LD. Students diagnosed with ADD/ADHD are eligible for the same services available to students with LD.

Staff: 1 full-time staff member (coordinator).

Special Fees: No special fees are charged for services to students with LD.

Applications and admissions: *Required:* high school transcript, IEP (Individualized Education Program), psychoeducational report completed within 3 years, college placement tests. Students may begin taking classes any term. *Application deadline:* continuous.

PROGRAM AND SERVICE COMPONENTS

Special preparation or orientation: Optional orientation offered in August before registration.

Academic advising: Provided by unit staff members, academic advisers. Students with LD may take up to 18 credit hours each term; most take 12 credit hours; 12 credit hours required to maintain full-time status; source of aid determines number of credit hours required to be eligible for financial aid.

Counseling services: Individual counseling, career counseling, self-advocacy training.

Basic skills remediation: Offered one-on-one and in class-size groups by regular teachers, peer teachers. Available in reading, math, spelling, spoken language, written language, learning strategies, study skills.

Auxiliary aids: Taped textbooks, tape recorders, calculators, typewriters, word-processors with spell-check, voice-synthesized computers, Voyager print enlargement system.

Auxiliary services: Alternative test arrangements, notetakers, advocacy, readers.

GENERAL COLLEGE INFORMATION

State and locally supported, 2-year, coed. Part of State University of New York System. Awards associate degrees. Founded 1962. *Setting:* 287-acre rural campus with easy access to Buffalo. *Endowment:* $1 million. *Educational spending 1995–96:* $2810 per undergrad. *Total enrollment:* 5,118. *Faculty:* 449 (214 full-time, 9% with terminal degrees, 235 part-time); student–undergrad faculty ratio is 18:1.

Enrollment Profile: 5,118 students from 2 states and territories, 14 other countries. 58% women, 42% men, 38% part-time, 98% state residents, 6% transferred in, 1% international, 39% 25 or older, 2% Native American, 1% Hispanic, 5% black, 1% Asian or Pacific Islander. *Retention:* 57% of 1995 full-time freshmen returned. *Areas of study chosen:* 38% liberal arts/general studies, 16% health professions and related sciences, 13% business management and administrative services, 13% social sciences, 8% engineering and applied sciences, 4% computer and information sciences, 3% communications and journalism, 2% fine arts, 1% biological and life sciences, 1% performing arts, 1% vocational and home economics. *Most popular recent majors:* liberal arts/general studies, social science, nursing.

First-Year Class: 1,246 total; 2,317 applied, 91% were accepted, 59% of whom enrolled. 2% from top 10% of their high school class, 11% from top quarter, 36% from top half.

Graduation Requirements: 62 credit hours; computer course for most majors; internship (some majors).

Computers on Campus: 220 computers available on campus for general student use. Computers for student use in computer center, computer labs, learning resource center, classrooms, library, learning labs provide access to the Internet/World Wide Web. Staffed computer lab on campus provides training in use of computers, software. *Academic computing expenditure 1995–96:* $611,971.

EXPENSES

Expenses for 1996–97: State resident tuition: $2350 full-time, $85 per credit hour part-time. Nonresident tuition: $3525 full-time, $127.50 per credit hour part-time. Part-time mandatory fees per semester range from $3.50 to $28.50. Full-time mandatory fees: $104.

LD Services Contact: Ms. Karen A. Drilling, Counselor/Coordinator, Disabled Student Services, Niagara County Community College, 3111 Saunders Settlement Road, Sanborn, NY 14132-9460, 716-731-3271 Ext. 530. Fax: 716-731-4053.

NICOLET AREA TECHNICAL COLLEGE

Rhinelander, Wisconsin

LEARNING DISABILITIES SERVICES INFORMATION

Special Needs Support Program (SNSP) began offering services in 1989. Currently the program serves 74 undergraduates with LD. Students diagnosed with ADD/ADHD are eligible for the same services available to students with LD.

Staff: 1 full-time, 2 part-time staff members, including director. Services provided by counselors, accommodation trainers, lab technician.

Special Fees: No special fees are charged for services to students with LD.

Applications and admissions: *Required:* high school transcript, courses completed; *recommended:* high school extracurricular activities, IEP (Individualized Education Program), extended time SAT I, personal interview, autobiographical statement, letters of recommendation, psychoeducational report completed within 2 years. Students may begin taking classes any term. *Application deadline:* continuous.

PROGRAM AND SERVICE COMPONENTS

Special preparation or orientation: Optional summer program offered prior to entering college. Optional orientation offered individually by special arrangement.

Diagnostic testing: Intelligence, reading, math, spelling, handwriting, written language, study skills, social skills, learning strategies.

Academic advising: Provided by unit staff members, academic advisers. Students with LD may take up to as many credit hours as an individual can handle each term; most take 9 to 12 credit hours; 12 credit hours required to maintain full-time status; 6 credit hours (part-time), 12 credit hours (full-time) required to be eligible for financial aid.

Counseling services: Individual counseling, small-group counseling, career counseling, self-advocacy training.

Basic skills remediation: Offered one-on-one, in small groups, and in class-size groups by LD teachers, regular teachers; computer-aided instruction also offered. Available in reading, math, spelling, handwriting, written language, learning strategies, study skills, time management, social skills, computer skills.

Subject-area tutoring: Offered one-on-one and in small groups by professional teachers, peer tutors. Available in most subjects.

Special courses: College survival skills, reading, vocabulary development, communication skills, composition, learning strategies, word processing, Internet use, time management, math, typing, personal psychology, study skills, career planning, Accommodation Skill Identification and Training. Most offered for credit; some enter into overall grade point average.

Auxiliary aids: Taped textbooks, tape recorders, calculators, typewriters, word-processors with spell-check, personal computers, talking computers, optical character readers, interactive video, scanners, talking computer interface, adaptive equipment and course materials.

Auxiliary services: Alternative test arrangements, notetakers, priority registration, advocacy, readers, scribes, TDD/(717)365-4426.

GENERAL COLLEGE INFORMATION

State and locally supported, 2-year, coed. Part of Wisconsin Technical College System. Awards associate degrees. Founded 1968. *Setting:* 280-acre rural campus. *Total enrollment:* 1,433. *Faculty:* 84 (65 full-time, 19 part-time).

Enrollment Profile: 1,433 students from 3 states and territories. 68% women, 32% men, 64% part-time, 99% state residents, 10% transferred in, 0% international, 64% 25 or older, 4% Native American, 1% Hispanic, 1% black, 0% Asian or Pacific Islander. *Areas of study chosen:* 30% liberal arts/general studies, 15% business management and administrative services, 9% health professions and related sciences, 4% computer and information sciences. *Most popular recent majors:* liberal arts/general studies, accounting, law enforcement/police sciences.

First-Year Class: 560 total; 830 applied, 90% were accepted, 75% of whom enrolled.

Graduation Requirements: 64 credit hours; math/science requirements vary according to program; computer course.

Computers on Campus: 50 computers available on campus for general student use. Computers for student use in computer center, classrooms, library. Staffed computer lab on campus provides training in use of computers.

EXPENSES AND FINANCIAL AID

Expenses for 1997–98: *Application fee:* $25. State resident tuition: $2290 full-time, $71.55 per credit hour part-time. Nonresident tuition: $7862 full-time, $245.70 per credit hour part-time. Part-time mandatory fees: $1.60 per credit hour. Full-time mandatory fees: $48.

Financial aid specifically for students with LD: Scholarships: NATC Foundation Scholarships, WTCS Special Needs Grants; work-study.

LD Services Contact: Mr. Todd Allgood, Special Needs, Evaluation, Testing and Job Placement Director, Nicolet Area Technical College, Box 518, Rhinelander, WI 54501-0518, 715-365-4448. Fax: 715-365-4542.

NORMANDALE COMMUNITY COLLEGE

Bloomington, Minnesota

LEARNING DISABILITIES SERVICES INFORMATION

Designing Educational Experiences for Disabled Students (DEEDS) began offering services in 1980. Currently the program serves 160 undergraduates with LD. Students diagnosed with ADD/ADHD are eligible for the same services available to students with LD, as well as priority registration for medication effectiveness (if needed).

Staff: 1 full-time, 4 part-time staff members, including coordinators. Services provided by remediation specialists.

Special Fees: No special fees are charged for services to students with LD.

Applications and admissions: Open admissions. Students may begin taking classes any term. *Application deadline:* continuous.

PROGRAM AND SERVICE COMPONENTS

Special preparation or orientation: Optional orientation offered before registration.

Academic advising: Provided by unit staff members, academic advisers. Most students with LD take 12 quarter credits each term; 12 quarter credits required to maintain full-time status; 1 quarter credit required to be eligible for financial aid.

Counseling services: Individual counseling.

Basic skills remediation: Offered in class-size groups by LD teachers, regular teachers. Available in reading, math, written language, learning strategies, study skills, time management.

Special courses: College survival skills, reading, vocabulary development, composition, learning strategies, word processing, time management, math, study skills. All offered for credit; all enter into overall grade point average.

Auxiliary aids: Taped textbooks, tape recorders, typewriters, word-processors with spell-check, personal computers, optical character readers.

Auxiliary services: Alternative test arrangements, notetakers, priority registration, advocacy, proofreaders.

GENERAL COLLEGE INFORMATION

State-supported, 2-year, coed. Part of Minnesota State Colleges and Universities System. Awards associate degrees. Founded 1968. *Setting:* 90-acre suburban campus with easy access to Minneapolis–St. Paul. *Total enrollment:* 7,365. *Faculty:* 230 (170 full-time, 12% with terminal degrees, 60 part-time); student–undergrad faculty ratio is 30:1.

Enrollment Profile: 7,365 students from 17 states and territories, 12 other countries. 61% women, 39% men, 56% part-time, 98% state residents, 6% transferred in, 1% international, 42% 25 or older, 1% Native American, 1% Hispanic, 3% black, 4% Asian or Pacific Islander. *Areas of study chosen:* 38% liberal arts/general studies, 7% business management and administrative services, 4% health professions and related sciences, 3% education, 3% engineering and applied sciences, 1% architecture, 1% communications and journalism, 1% computer and information sciences, 1% natural resource sciences, 1% premed.

First-Year Class: 2,363 total; 3,534 applied, 100% were accepted, 67% of whom enrolled. 4% from top 10% of their high school class, 23% from top quarter, 70% from top half.

Graduation Requirements: 90 quarter credits; computer course for accounting, business administration and management, hospitality services, mechanical engineering technology, office management majors; internship (some majors).

Computers on Campus: 421 computers available on campus for general student use. Computer purchase/lease plans available. A campuswide network can be accessed from off-campus. Students can contact faculty members and/or advisers through e-mail. Computers for student use in computer center, computer labs, learning resource center, class-

Normandale Community College (continued)

rooms, library provide access to the Internet/World Wide Web. Staffed computer lab on campus provides training in use of computers, software. *Academic computing expenditure 1995–96:* $400,000.

EXPENSES

Expenses for 1996–97: *Application fee:* $20. State resident tuition: $2160 full-time, $48 per quarter hour part-time. Nonresident tuition: $4140 full-time, $92 per quarter hour part-time. North Dakota, South Dakota and Wisconsin residents pay tuition at the rate they would pay if attending a comparable state-supported institution in their home state.
LD Services Contact: Ms. Mary Jibben, Student Needs Coordinator, Normandale Community College, 9700 France Avenue South, Bloomington, MN 55431, 612-832-6422. Fax: 612-832-6391.

NORTHAMPTON COUNTY AREA COMMUNITY COLLEGE

Bethlehem, Pennsylvania

LEARNING DISABILITIES SERVICES INFORMATION

Services for Students with Disabilities began offering services in 1982. Currently the program serves 125 undergraduates with LD. Students diagnosed with ADD/ADHD are eligible for the same services available to students with LD.
Staff: 1 full-time, 2 part-time staff members, including coordinator. Services provided by tutor, counselors.
Special Fees: No special fees are charged for services to students with LD.
Applications and admissions: *Required:* high school transcript, personal interview, psychoeducational report completed within 3 years. Students may begin taking classes in fall, spring, or summer. *Application deadline:* continuous.

PROGRAM AND SERVICE COMPONENTS

Special preparation or orientation: Optional orientation offered during registration.
Academic advising: Provided by unit staff members, academic advisers. Students with LD may take up to 15 credit hours each term; most take 9 to 12 credit hours; 12 credit hours required to maintain full-time status; 6 credit hours required to be eligible for financial aid.
Counseling services: Individual counseling, small-group counseling, career counseling, self-advocacy training.
Basic skills remediation: Offered one-on-one, in small groups, and in class-size groups by LD teachers, regular teachers. Available in reading, math, written language, learning strategies, study skills, time management, social skills.
Subject-area tutoring: Offered one-on-one and in small groups by peer tutors, paraprofessionals. Available in most subjects.
Auxiliary aids: Taped textbooks, tape recorders, calculators, typewriters, word-processors with spell-check, personal computers, optical character readers.
Auxiliary services: Alternative test arrangements, notetakers, priority registration, advocacy.

GENERAL COLLEGE INFORMATION

State and locally supported, 2-year, coed. Awards associate degrees. Founded 1967. *Setting:* 165-acre suburban campus with easy access to Philadelphia. *Endowment:* $5.9 million. *Educational spending 1995–96:* $2359 per undergrad. *Total enrollment:* 5,542. *Faculty:* 464 (71 full-time, 393 part-time); student–undergrad faculty ratio is 17:1.
Enrollment Profile: 5,542 students from 10 states and territories, 16 other countries. 61% women, 39% men, 62% part-time, 96% state residents, 4% live on campus, 20% transferred in, 1% international, 47% 25 or older, 0% Native American, 5% Hispanic, 3% black, 3% Asian or Pacific Islander. *Retention:* 57% of 1995 full-time freshmen returned. *Areas of study chosen:* 36% liberal arts/general studies, 21% business management and administrative services, 10% health professions and related sciences, 8% education, 5% social sciences, 4% communications and journalism, 4% computer and information sciences, 4% engineering and applied sciences, 2% architecture, 2% biological and life sciences, 2% vocational and home economics, 1% library and information studies, 1% physical sciences. *Most popular recent majors:* liberal arts/general studies, business administration/commerce/management, education.
First-Year Class: 1,247 total; 1,862 applied, 98% were accepted, 69% of whom enrolled.
Graduation Requirements: 60 credit hours; computer course for most majors; internship (some majors).
Computers on Campus: 441 computers available on campus for general student use. A campus-wide network can be accessed. Computers for student use in computer labs, learning resource center, classrooms, library, off-campus centers provide access to the Internet/World Wide Web. Staffed computer lab on campus provides training in use of computers, software. *Academic computing expenditure 1995–96:* $205,186.

EXPENSES AND FINANCIAL AID

Expenses for 1997–98: *Application fee:* $25. Area resident tuition: $1860 full-time, $62 per credit hour part-time. State resident tuition: $4230 full-time, $141 per credit hour part-time. Nonresident tuition: $6600 full-time, $220 per credit hour part-time. Tuition for residents of Monroe county: $3330 full-time, $111 per credit hour part-time. College room and board: $4410. College room only: $2550.
Financial aid specifically for students with LD: Scholarship: Bethlehem Kiwanis Club Scholarship.
LD Services Contact: Ms. Laraine A. Demshock, Coordinator of Disability Services, Northampton County Area Community College, 3835 Green Pond Road, Bethlehem, PA 18017, 610-861-5342. Fax: 610-861-8577.

NORTH CENTRAL MICHIGAN COLLEGE

Petoskey, Michigan

LEARNING DISABILITIES SERVICES INFORMATION

Special Populations Office began offering services in 1991. Currently the program serves 16 undergraduates with LD. Students diagnosed with ADD/ADHD are eligible for the same services available to students with LD.
Staff: 1 full-time, 1 part-time staff members.
Special Fees: No special fees are charged for services to students with LD.
Applications and admissions: *Required:* high school transcript, psychoeducational report completed within 3 years, ACT COMPASS (with accommodations); *recommended:* high school IEP (Individualized Education Program). Students may begin taking classes any term. *Application deadline:* continuous.
Special policies: The college has written policies regarding substitutions and waivers of admissions requirements.

PROGRAM AND SERVICE COMPONENTS

Special preparation or orientation: Optional orientation offered individually by appointment.
Academic advising: Provided by unit staff members, academic advisers. Students with LD may take up to 18 credit hours each term; most take 6 to 12 credit hours; 12 credit hours required to maintain full-time status; 6 credit hours required to be eligible for financial aid.
Counseling services: Individual counseling, career counseling.
Subject-area tutoring: Offered one-on-one by peer tutors, professionals in the particular subject area. Available in all subjects.
Special courses: Learning strategies. All offered for credit; all enter into overall grade point average.
Auxiliary aids: Taped textbooks, tape recorders, calculators, word-processors with spell-check, personal computers, talking computers, optical character readers, closed-captioned television.
Auxiliary services: Alternative test arrangements, notetakers, advocacy.

GENERAL COLLEGE INFORMATION

County-supported, 2-year, coed. Part of Michigan Department of Education. Awards associate degrees. Founded 1958. *Setting:* 270-acre small-town campus. *Educational spending 1995–96:* $884 per undergrad. *Total enrollment:* 2,032. *Faculty:* 146 (28 full-time, 3% with terminal degrees, 118 part-time).
Enrollment Profile: 2,032 students from 4 states and territories, 2 other countries. 68% women, 32% men, 71% part-time, 98% state residents, 3% live on campus, 8% transferred in, 1% international, 55% 25 or older, 3% Native American, 1% Hispanic, 1% black, 1% Asian or Pacific Islander. *Retention:* 71% of 1995 full-time freshmen returned. *Most popular recent majors:* business administration/commerce/management, liberal arts/general studies, nursing.
First-Year Class: 472 total; 998 applied, 100% were accepted, 75% of whom enrolled. 10% from top 10% of their high school class, 80% from top half.

Graduation Requirements: 60 credit hours; 8 credit hours of math/science; computer course for business majors.
Computers on Campus: 133 computers available on campus for general student use. Computers for student use in computer center, computer labs, learning resource center, library provide access to the Internet/World Wide Web. Staffed computer lab on campus provides training in use of computers, software. *Academic computing expenditure 1995–96:* $12,000.

EXPENSES

Expenses for 1997–98: Area resident tuition: $1380 full-time, $46 per credit hour part-time. State resident tuition: $1920 full-time, $64 per credit hour part-time. Nonresident tuition: $2430 full-time, $81 per credit hour part-time. Part-time mandatory fees per semester range from $13.50 to $53.50. Full-time mandatory fees: $135. College room and board: $4482. College room only: $1440.
LD Services Contact: Mr. Daniel M. Linnenberg, Special Populations Coordinator, North Central Michigan College, 1515 Howard Street, Petoskey, MI 49770, 616-348-6687. Fax: 616-348-6628.

NORTH CENTRAL MISSOURI COLLEGE

Trenton, Missouri

LEARNING DISABILITIES SERVICES INFORMATION

Academic Reinforcement Center and the Counseling Center began offering services in 1986. Students diagnosed with ADD/ADHD are eligible for the same services available to students with LD.
Staff: 1 full-time, 2 part-time staff members, including director. Services provided by remediation specialists, tutors, counselors.
Special Fees: No special fees are charged for services to students with LD.
Applications and admissions: *Required:* high school transcript, GED (in lieu of high school diploma). Students may begin taking classes any term. *Application deadline:* continuous.
Special policies: The college has written policies regarding grade forgiveness; substitutions and waivers of admissions, graduation, and degree requirements.

PROGRAM AND SERVICE COMPONENTS

Academic advising: Provided by unit staff members, academic advisers. Most students with LD take 12 semester hours each term; 12 semester hours required to maintain full-time status; 3 semester hours required to be eligible for financial aid.
Auxiliary aids: Taped textbooks, tape recorders, calculators, word-processors with spell-check.
Auxiliary services: Alternative test arrangements, notetakers, advocacy.

GENERAL COLLEGE INFORMATION

District-supported, 2-year, coed. Part of Missouri Coordinating Board for Higher Education. Awards associate degrees. Founded 1925. *Setting:* 1-acre small-town campus. *Total enrollment:* 704. *Faculty:* 77 (28 full-time, 20% with terminal degrees, 49 part-time); student–undergrad faculty ratio is 16:1.
Enrollment Profile: 704 students from 6 states and territories, 1 other country. 70% women, 30% men, 40% part-time, 99% state residents, 11% live on campus, 6% transferred in, 33% 25 or older, 0% Native American, 0% Hispanic, 0% black, 0% Asian or Pacific Islander. *Retention:* 55% of 1995 full-time freshmen returned. *Areas of study chosen:* 51% liberal arts/general studies, 6% agriculture, 4% business management and administrative services. *Most popular recent majors:* liberal arts/general studies, nursing, accounting.
First-Year Class: 249 total. Of the students who applied, 100% were accepted, 90% of whom enrolled. 3% from top 10% of their high school class, 18% from top quarter, 47% from top half.
Graduation Requirements: 60 credit hours; computer course for accounting, office occupations, agriculture, business majors; internship (some majors).
Computers on Campus: 101 computers available on campus for general student use. A campus-wide network can be accessed. Students can contact faculty members and/or advisers through e-mail. Computers for student use in computer labs, library, student center, Academic Reinforcement Center, career center. Staffed computer lab on campus provides training in use of computers, software. *Academic computing expenditure 1995–96:* $66,878.

EXPENSES

Expenses for 1997–98: Area resident tuition: $1140 full-time, $38 per credit hour part-time. State resident tuition: $1770 full-time, $59 per credit hour part-time. Nonresident tuition: $2490 full-time, $83 per credit hour part-time. Part-time mandatory fees: $9.50 per credit hour. Full-time mandatory fees: $285. College room and board: $2900.
LD Services Contact: Ms. Ginny Wikoff, Counselor, North Central Missouri College, 1301 Main Street, Trenton, MO 64683-1824, 816-359-3948 Ext. 405. Fax: 816-359-2211. Email: ginny@ncmc.cc.mo.us.

NORTHCENTRAL TECHNICAL COLLEGE

Wausau, Wisconsin

LEARNING DISABILITIES SERVICES INFORMATION

GOAL Program began offering services in 1976. Currently the program serves 50 undergraduates with LD. Students diagnosed with ADD/ADHD are eligible for the same services available to students with LD.
Staff: 3 full-time, 15 part-time staff members, including director. Services provided by tutors, counselor, remediation instructors.
Special Fees: No special fees are charged for services to students with LD.
Applications and admissions: *Required:* high school transcript, IEP (Individualized Education Program); *recommended:* untimed ACT. Students may begin taking classes in fall, spring, or summer. *Application deadline:* continuous.

PROGRAM AND SERVICE COMPONENTS

Special preparation or orientation: Orientation optional.
Academic advising: Provided by unit staff members, academic advisers. Most students with LD take 9 to 12 credits each term; 12 credits required to maintain full-time status and be eligible for financial aid.
Counseling services: Individual counseling, career counseling.
Subject-area tutoring: Offered one-on-one and in small groups by professional teachers, peer tutors, technical assistants. Available in all subjects.
Special courses: Reading, vocabulary development, communication skills, composition, math, study skills, career planning. Some offered for credit.
Auxiliary aids: Taped textbooks, tape recorders, calculators, typewriters, word-processors with spell-check, personal computers, talking computers, optical character readers, talking dictionary.
Auxiliary services: Alternative test arrangements, notetakers, advocacy.

GENERAL COLLEGE INFORMATION

District-supported, 2-year, coed. Part of Wisconsin Technical College System. Awards associate degrees. Founded 1912. *Setting:* 96-acre small-town campus. *Total enrollment:* 3,500. *Faculty:* 218 (153 full-time, 17% with terminal degrees, 65 part-time).
Enrollment Profile: 3,500 students from 3 states and territories, 2 other countries. 58% women, 42% men, 69% part-time, 98% state residents, 5% transferred in, 1% international, 65% 25 or older, 1% Native American, 1% Hispanic, 1% black, 2% Asian or Pacific Islander. *Most popular recent majors:* nursing, computer information systems, architectural technologies.
First-Year Class: 2,010 applied, 89% of whom enrolled.
Graduation Requirements: 64 credits; computer course for business majors; internship (some majors).
Computers on Campus: 90 computers available on campus for general student use. Computers for student use in computer center, computer labs, library provide access to the Internet/World Wide Web. Staffed computer lab on campus provides training in use of computers, software.

EXPENSES

Expenses for 1996–97: *Application fee:* $25. State resident tuition: $1638 full-time, $51.20 per credit part-time. Nonresident tuition: $12,640 full-time, $395 per credit part-time. Part-time mandatory fees: $2.65 per credit. Full-time mandatory fees: $85.
LD Services Contact: Mr. Joe Mielczarek, Instructional/Vocational Counselor, Center for Students with Disabilities (DHH/VIP Programs), Northcentral Technical College, 1000 West Campus Drive, Wausau, WI 54401, 715-675-3331 Ext. 4087. Fax: 715-675-9776. Email: mielczar?ntc@mail.northcentral.tec.wi.us.

NORTH DAKOTA STATE COLLEGE OF SCIENCE

Wahpeton, North Dakota

LEARNING DISABILITIES SERVICES INFORMATION

Study Services for Students with Disabilities began offering services in 1982. Currently the program serves 90 undergraduates with LD. Students diagnosed with ADD/ADHD are eligible for the same services available to students with LD.

Staff: 5 full-time, 5 part-time staff members, including co-directors, coordinator, career guidance coordinators, secretary. Services provided by remediation specialists, tutors, counselors, diagnostic specialists, readers.

Special Fees: No special fees are charged for services to students with LD.

Applications and admissions: *Required:* high school transcript, courses completed, IEP (Individualized Education Program), untimed or extended time ACT, psychoeducational report completed most recently; *recommended:* high school extracurricular activities, personal interview. Students may begin taking classes any term. *Application deadline:* continuous.

PROGRAM AND SERVICE COMPONENTS

Special preparation or orientation: Optional summer program offered prior to entering college.

Diagnostic testing: Reading, math, spelling, written language, motor abilities, perceptual skills, personality, learning strategies.

Academic advising: Provided by unit staff members, academic advisers. Students with LD may take up to 18 credits each term; most take 12 to 18 credits; 12 credits required to maintain full-time status and be eligible for financial aid.

Counseling services: Individual counseling, career counseling.

Basic skills remediation: Offered one-on-one, in small groups, and in class-size groups by Academic Services Center staff. Available in reading, math, spelling, written language, learning strategies, perceptual skills, study skills, time management, computer skills.

Subject-area tutoring: Offered one-on-one and in small groups by professional teachers, peer tutors. Available in all subjects.

Special courses: Reading, vocabulary development, composition, learning strategies, word processing, time management, math, typing, study skills. Most offered for credit; none enter into overall grade point average.

Auxiliary aids: Taped textbooks, tape recorders, calculators, typewriters, word-processors with spell-check, personal computers.

Auxiliary services: Alternative test arrangements, notetakers.

GENERAL COLLEGE INFORMATION

State-supported, 2-year, coed. Awards associate degrees. Founded 1903. *Setting:* 125-acre rural campus. *Endowment:* $4000. *Educational spending 1995–96:* $3275 per undergrad. *Total enrollment:* 2,581. *Faculty:* 159 (144 full-time, 2% with terminal degrees, 15 part-time); student–undergrad faculty ratio is 17:1.

Enrollment Profile: 2,581 students from 25 states and territories, 9 other countries. 40% women, 60% men, 9% part-time, 69% state residents, 58% live on campus, 32% transferred in, 1% international, 15% 25 or older, 2% Native American, 0% Hispanic, 1% black, 0% Asian or Pacific Islander. *Areas of study chosen:* 44% engineering and applied sciences, 25% liberal arts/general studies, 14% health professions and related sciences, 9% business management and administrative services, 4% agriculture, 4% computer and information sciences. *Most popular recent majors:* liberal arts/general studies, architectural technologies, practical nursing.

First-Year Class: 932 total; 1,155 applied, 94% were accepted, 86% of whom enrolled.

Graduation Requirements: 64 credits; computer course for most majors; internship (some majors).

Computers on Campus: 450 computers available on campus for general student use. Computer purchase/lease plans available. A computer is recommended for some students. A campus-wide network can be accessed from student residence rooms and from off-campus. Students can contact faculty members and/or advisers through e-mail. Computers for student use in computer center, learning resource center, classrooms, library, student center provide access to the Internet/World Wide Web, on- and off-campus e-mail addresses. Staffed computer lab on campus provides training in use of computers, software. *Academic computing expenditure 1995–96:* $418,539.

EXPENSES

Expenses for 1997–98: *Application fee:* $25. State resident tuition: $1552 full-time, $64.67 per credit part-time. Nonresident tuition: $4144 full-time, $172.67 per credit part-time. Part-time mandatory fees: $9.03 per credit. Manitoba, Minnesota, Montana, Saskatchewan and South Dakota resident tuition: $1940 full-time, $80.84 per credit part-time. Full-time mandatory fees: $217. College room and board: $2180. College room only: $914.

LD Services Contact: Ms. Doris Bruesch, Coordinator, Academic Services Center, North Dakota State College of Science, Academic Services Center, Wahpeton, ND 58076, 701-671-2623. Email: bruesch@plains.nodak.edu.

NORTHEAST ALABAMA COMMUNITY COLLEGE

Rainsville, Alabama

LEARNING DISABILITIES SERVICES INFORMATION

Office of the Dean of Instruction began offering services in 1980. Currently the program serves 15 undergraduates with LD. Students diagnosed with ADD/ADHD are eligible for the same services available to students with LD, as well as isolated testing (if needed).

Staff: 1 full-time staff member (coordinator). Services provided by tutors.

Special Fees: No special fees are charged for services to students with LD.

Applications and admissions: Students may begin taking classes any term. *Application deadline:* continuous.

Special policies: The college has written policies regarding grade forgiveness; substitutions and waivers of admissions requirements.

PROGRAM AND SERVICE COMPONENTS

Special preparation or orientation: Optional orientation offered individually by special arrangement.

Academic advising: Provided by academic advisers. Students with LD may take up to 21 quarter hours each term; most take 10 to 15 quarter hours; 12 quarter hours required to maintain full-time status; 12 quarter hours (Pell Grant), 15 quarter hours (academic) required to be eligible for financial aid.

Counseling services: Individual counseling, career counseling.

Basic skills remediation: Offered one-on-one by tutors. Available in reading, math, written language, perceptual skills, time management, social skills, speech.

Subject-area tutoring: Offered one-on-one by professional teachers, peer tutors. Available in all subjects.

Auxiliary aids: Taped textbooks, tape recorders, word-processors with spell-check, personal computers, speech synthesizer, text telephones, other aids as necessary.

Auxiliary services: Alternative test arrangements, notetakers, advocacy.

Campus support group: A special student organization is available to students with LD.

GENERAL COLLEGE INFORMATION

State-supported, 2-year, coed. Part of Alabama College System. Awards associate degrees. Founded 1963. *Setting:* 100-acre rural campus. *Total enrollment:* 1,838. *Faculty:* 51 (36 full-time, 10% with terminal degrees, 15 part-time).

Enrollment Profile: 1,838 students: 62% women, 38% men, 37% part-time, 99% state residents, 15% transferred in, 1% international, 40% 25 or older, 2% Native American, 1% Hispanic, 1% black, 1% Asian or Pacific Islander. *Retention:* 60% of 1995 full-time freshmen returned. *Areas of study chosen:* 30% health professions and related sciences, 20% computer and information sciences, 15% business management and administrative services, 15% education, 5% biological and life sciences, 5% engineering and applied sciences, 5% mathematics, 4% vocational and home economics, 1% psychology. *Most popular recent majors:* nursing, liberal arts/general studies, computer science.

First-Year Class: 506 total; 650 applied, 100% were accepted, 78% of whom enrolled.

Graduation Requirements: 96 quarter hours; 20 quarter hours of math/science for associate of arts degree; 15 quarter hours of math/science for associate of science degree; computer course for most majors.

Computers on Campus: 50 computers available on campus for general student use. Computers for student use in computer center, computer labs, library. Staffed computer lab on campus provides training in use of computers, software.

EXPENSES

Estimated Expenses for 1997–98: State resident tuition: $1197 full-time, $25 per quarter hour part-time. Nonresident tuition: $2157 full-time, $45 per quarter hour part-time.

LD Services Contact: Ms. Elaine S. Hayden, Assistant to the Dean of Instruction/ADA Compliance Representative/Student Contact, Northeast Alabama Community College, PO Box 159, Rainsville, AL 35986, 205-638-4418 Ext. 330. Fax: 205-228-6558.

NORTHEAST COMMUNITY COLLEGE

Norfolk, Nebraska

LEARNING DISABILITIES SERVICES INFORMATION

Special Services began offering services in 1986. Currently the program serves 40 undergraduates with LD. Students diagnosed with ADD/ADHD are eligible for the same services available to students with LD.

Staff: 1 full-time, 2 part-time staff members, including director, coordinator. Services provided by remediation specialists, tutors, counselors, diagnostic specialists, readers.

Special Fees: No special fees are charged for services to students with LD.

Applications and admissions: *Required:* high school transcript, ASSET; *recommended:* high school IEP (Individualized Education Program), personal interview. Students may begin taking classes any term. *Application deadline:* continuous.

PROGRAM AND SERVICE COMPONENTS

Special preparation or orientation: Optional summer program offered prior to entering college. Optional orientation offered before registration.

Diagnostic testing: Intelligence, reading, math, spelling, spoken language, written language, perceptual skills, learning strategies.

Academic advising: Provided by unit staff members, academic advisers. Most students with LD take 12 to 13 semester hours each term; 12 semester hours required to maintain full-time status; 6 to 12 semester hours required to be eligible for financial aid.

Counseling services: Individual counseling, career counseling, self-advocacy training.

Basic skills remediation: Offered one-on-one and in small groups by LD teachers, regular teachers; computer-aided instruction also offered. Available in reading, math, spelling, handwriting, written language, learning strategies, study skills, time management, computer skills.

Subject-area tutoring: Offered one-on-one, in small groups, and in class-size groups by professional teachers, peer tutors. Available in most subjects.

Special courses: College survival skills, reading, vocabulary development, communication skills, composition, learning strategies, word processing, time management, math, study skills, career planning, stress management, health and nutrition, social relationships. Most offered for credit; most enter into overall grade point average.

Auxiliary aids: Taped textbooks, tape recorders, word-processors with spell-check, personal computers.

Auxiliary services: Alternative test arrangements, notetakers, priority registration, advocacy.

GENERAL COLLEGE INFORMATION

State and locally supported, 2-year, coed. Part of Nebraska Coordinating Commission for Postsecondary Education. Awards associate degrees. Founded 1973. *Setting:* 205-acre small-town campus. *Total enrollment:* 4,285. *Faculty:* 194 (93 full-time, 94% with terminal degrees, 101 part-time); student–undergrad faculty ratio is 25:1.

Enrollment Profile: 4,285 students from 13 states and territories, 5 other countries. 47% women, 53% men, 59% part-time, 98% state residents, 15% live on campus, 15% transferred in, 1% international, 27% 25 or older, 2% Native American, 2% Hispanic, 3% black, 1% Asian or Pacific Islander.

First-Year Class: 589 total; 1,080 applied, 100% were accepted, 55% of whom enrolled.

Graduation Requirements: 60 semester hours; math/science requirements vary according to program; computer course for agriculture, technical, office technology majors; internship (some majors).

Computers on Campus: 150 computers available on campus for general student use. A computer is recommended for some students. A campus-wide network can be accessed. Computers for student use in computer center, computer labs, classrooms, library, dorms provide access to the Internet/World Wide Web. Staffed computer lab on campus provides training in use of computers, software.

EXPENSES

Expenses for 1997–98: State resident tuition: $1140 full-time, $38 per semester hour part-time. Nonresident tuition: $1425 full-time, $47.50 per semester hour part-time. Part-time mandatory fees: $4 per semester hour. Full-time mandatory fees: $120. College room and board: $2054 (minimum). College room only: $1520 (minimum).

LD Services Contact: Ms. Louise Torkelson, Coordinator of Special Services, Northeast Community College, 801 East Benjamin Avenue, Norfolk, NE 68702-0469, 402-644-0682. Fax: 402-644-0650.

NORTHEASTERN JUNIOR COLLEGE

Sterling, Colorado

LEARNING DISABILITIES SERVICES INFORMATION

Study Skills Services began offering services in 1984. Currently the program serves 35 undergraduates with LD. Students diagnosed with ADD/ADHD are eligible for the same services available to students with LD.

Staff: 8 full-time staff members, including coordinator. Services provided by tutors, counselor.

Special Fees: No special fees are charged for services to students with LD.

Applications and admissions: *Required:* high school transcript, psychoeducational report completed within 3 years, ACT ASSET; *recommended:* untimed or extended time ACT. Students may begin taking classes any term. *Application deadline:* continuous.

PROGRAM AND SERVICE COMPONENTS

Diagnostic testing: Reading, math, spelling, spoken language, written language, perceptual skills, study skills, learning strategies.

Academic advising: Provided by unit staff members, academic advisers. Students with LD may take up to 16 credit hours each term; most take 12 to 16 credit hours; 12 credit hours required to maintain full-time status; 6 credit hours (partial assistance), 12 credit hours (full assistance) required to be eligible for financial aid.

Counseling services: Individual counseling, small-group counseling, career counseling.

Basic skills remediation: Offered one-on-one, in small groups, and in class-size groups by regular teachers. Available in reading, math, spelling, written language, learning strategies, study skills, time management.

Subject-area tutoring: Offered one-on-one, in small groups, and in class-size groups by professional teachers, peer tutors. Available in most subjects.

Auxiliary aids: Taped textbooks, tape recorders, calculators, typewriters, word-processors with spell-check, personal computers, talking computers.

Auxiliary services: Alternative test arrangements, notetakers, advocacy, readers.

GENERAL COLLEGE INFORMATION

State-supported, 2-year, coed. Part of Colorado Community College and Occupational Education System. Awards associate degrees. Founded 1941. *Setting:* 65-acre small-town campus. *Endowment:* $483,000. *Total enrollment:* 3,408. *Faculty:* 79 (65 full-time, 14 part-time).

Enrollment Profile: 3,408 students from 13 states and territories, 4 other countries. 54% women, 46% men, 25% part-time, 96% state residents, 3% transferred in, 2% international, 16% 25 or older, 1% Native American, 3% Hispanic, 2% black. *Areas of study chosen:* 30% liberal arts/general studies, 15% agriculture, 15% business management and administrative services, 10% health professions and related sciences, 5% biological and life sciences, 5% computer and information sciences, 5% engineering and applied sciences, 3% education, 3% psychology, 2% premed, 2% prevet, 2% social sciences, 1% communications and journalism, 1% mathematics, 1% performing arts. *Most popular recent majors:* business administration/commerce/management, psychology, agricultural business.

First-Year Class: 470 total; 820 applied, 99% were accepted, 65% of whom enrolled. 6% from top 10% of their high school class, 47% from top half.

Graduation Requirements: 62 credit hours; internship (some majors).

Computers on Campus: 50 computers available on campus for general student use. A campus-wide network can be accessed. Computers

Northeastern Junior College (continued)

for student use in computer labs, library provide access to the Internet/World Wide Web. Staffed computer lab on campus provides training in use of computers, software. *Academic computing expenditure 1995–96:* $50,000.

EXPENSES

Estimated Expenses for 1997–98: *Application fee:* $15. Area resident tuition: $0 full-time, $50 per credit hour part-time. State resident tuition: $1344 full-time, $56 per credit hour part-time. Nonresident tuition: $4464 full-time, $186 per credit hour part-time. Full-time mandatory fees: $218. College room and board: $3600 (minimum).

LD Services Contact: Ms. Nancy Mann, Coordinator, Study Skills Services, Northeastern Junior College, 100 College Drive, Sterling, CO 80751, 970-522-6600 Ext. 679. Fax: 970-522-4945.

NORTHEAST IOWA COMMUNITY COLLEGE, CALMAR CAMPUS

Calmar, Iowa

LEARNING DISABILITIES SERVICES INFORMATION

Learning Center began offering services in 1990. Currently the program serves 120 undergraduates with LD. Students diagnosed with ADD/ADHD are eligible for the same services available to students with LD.

Staff: 6 full-time, 1 part-time staff members, including coordinators. Services provided by remediation specialists, tutors.

Special Fees: No special fees are charged for services to students with LD.

Applications and admissions: *Required:* high school transcript, psychoeducational report; *recommended:* extended time ASSET. Students may begin taking classes any term. *Application deadline:* continuous.

Special policies: The college has written policies regarding grade forgiveness; substitutions and waivers of graduation and degree requirements.

PROGRAM AND SERVICE COMPONENTS

Academic advising: Provided by unit staff members, academic advisers. Most students with LD take 9 to 12 credits each term; 12 credits required to maintain full-time status; 6 credits (loans) required to be eligible for financial aid.

Auxiliary aids: Taped textbooks, tape recorders, calculators, typewriters, word-processors with spell-check.

Auxiliary services: Alternative test arrangements, notetakers, test readers and scribes.

GENERAL COLLEGE INFORMATION

State and locally supported, 2-year, coed. Part of Iowa Area Community Colleges System. Awards associate degrees. Founded 1966. *Setting:* 210-acre small-town campus. *Total enrollment:* 900. *Faculty:* 137 (93 full-time, 44 part-time).

Enrollment Profile: 900 students: 62% women, 38% men, 23% part-time, 99% state residents, 12% transferred in, 38% 25 or older, 2% Native American, 2% Hispanic, 0% black, 2% Asian or Pacific Islander.

First-Year Class: 500 total. Of the students who applied, 100% were accepted. 7% from top 10% of their high school class, 25% from top half.

Graduation Requirements: 64 credits; computer course; internship (some majors).

Computers on Campus: 120 computers available on campus for general student use. Computers for student use in computer center, library.

EXPENSES

Expenses for 1997–98: State resident tuition: $2016 full-time, $63 per credit part-time. Nonresident tuition: $2822 full-time, $88.20 per credit part-time. Part-time mandatory fees: $9.75 per credit. Full-time mandatory fees: $312.

LD Services Contact: Ms. Myra Benzer, Coordinator of Developmental Education, Northeast Iowa Community College, Calmar Campus, 10250 Sundown Road, Peosta, IA 52068, 319-556-5110. Fax: 319-556-5058.

NORTHEAST IOWA COMMUNITY COLLEGE, PEOSTA CAMPUS

Peosta, Iowa

LEARNING DISABILITIES SERVICES INFORMATION

Developmental Education/Learning Center currently serves 90 undergraduates with LD. Students diagnosed with ADD/ADHD are eligible for the same services available to students with LD.

Staff: 6 full-time, 1 part-time staff members, including director, instructors. Services provided by remediation specialists, tutors, counselors.

Special Fees: No special fees are charged for services to students with LD.

Applications and admissions: *Required:* high school transcript, grade point average, class rank, courses completed, IEP (Individualized Education Program), personal interview, psychoeducational report, ACT ASSET. Students may begin taking classes any term. *Application deadline:* continuous.

Special policies: The college has written policies regarding substitutions and waivers of admissions and graduation requirements.

PROGRAM AND SERVICE COMPONENTS

Academic advising: Provided by academic advisers. Most students with LD take 12 credits each term; 12 credits required to maintain full-time status.

Counseling services: Individual counseling, career counseling.

Basic skills remediation: Offered one-on-one by regular teachers; computer-aided instruction also offered. Available in reading, math, spelling, written language, learning strategies, study skills, time management.

Subject-area tutoring: Offered one-on-one, in small groups, and in class-size groups by peer tutors. Available in most subjects.

Special courses: Reading, composition, learning strategies, time management, study skills, career planning. Some offered for credit.

Auxiliary aids: Taped textbooks, tape recorders, word-processors with spell-check.

Auxiliary services: Alternative test arrangements, notetakers, advocacy.

GENERAL COLLEGE INFORMATION

State and locally supported, 2-year, coed. Part of Iowa Area Community Colleges System. Awards associate degrees. Founded 1970. *Setting:* 95-acre small-town campus. *Total enrollment:* 1,700. *Faculty:* 66 (48 full-time, 18 part-time).

Enrollment Profile: 1,700 students from 5 states and territories, 5 other countries. 69% women, 31% men, 35% part-time, 96% state residents, 20% transferred in, 27% 25 or older, 1% Native American, 1% Hispanic, 1% black, 1% Asian or Pacific Islander. *Most popular recent majors:* nursing, human services, business administration/commerce/management.

First-Year Class: 800 total. Of the students who applied, 100% were accepted.

Graduation Requirements: 64 credit hours; 9 credit hours of math/science; computer course.

Computers on Campus: 80 computers available on campus for general student use. Computers for student use in computer center, library.

EXPENSES

Expenses for 1997–98: State resident tuition: $2016 full-time, $63 per credit hour part-time. Nonresident tuition: $2822 full-time, $88.20 per credit hour part-time. Part-time mandatory fees: $9.75 per credit hour. Full-time mandatory fees: $312.

LD Services Contact: Ms. Myra Benzer, Coordinator, Developmental Education, Northeast Iowa Community College, Peosta Campus, 10250 Sundown Road, Peosta, IA 52068-9776, 319-556-5110 Ext. 280. Fax: 319-556-5058.

NORTHERN OKLAHOMA COLLEGE

Tonkawa, Oklahoma

LEARNING DISABILITIES SERVICES INFORMATION

Counseling Center began offering services in 1990. Currently the program serves 40 undergraduates with LD. Students diagnosed with ADD/ADHD are eligible for the same services available to students with LD, as well as readers, study sessions.

Staff: 4 part-time staff members, including director. Services provided by tutors, counselors, diagnostic specialists.
Special Fees: No special fees are charged for services to students with LD.
Applications and admissions: *Required:* high school transcript, grade point average, class rank, courses completed, untimed or extended time ACT, psychoeducational report; *recommended:* high school IEP (Individualized Education Program). Students may begin taking classes in summer only. *Application deadline:* continuous.
Special policies: The college has written policies regarding grade forgiveness; substitutions and waivers of admissions and graduation requirements.

PROGRAM AND SERVICE COMPONENTS

Special preparation or orientation: Orientation optional.
Diagnostic testing: Reading, math, written language, psychoneurology.
Academic advising: Provided by unit staff members. Students with LD may take up to 15 credit hours each term; most take 12 to 15 credit hours; 9 credit hours required to maintain full-time status; 6 credit hours required to be eligible for financial aid.
Counseling services: Individual counseling, career counseling.
Basic skills remediation: Offered in small groups by regular teachers. Available in reading, math, written language.
Subject-area tutoring: Offered one-on-one by peer tutors, educational therapist. Available in all subjects.
Special courses: College survival skills, time management, study skills. None offered for credit.
Auxiliary aids: Taped textbooks, tape recorders.
Auxiliary services: Alternative test arrangements, notetakers, advocacy.

GENERAL COLLEGE INFORMATION

State-supported, 2-year, coed. Part of Oklahoma State Regents for Higher Education. Awards associate degrees. Founded 1901. *Setting:* 10-acre rural campus. *Total enrollment:* 2,350. *Faculty:* 80 (45 full-time, 35 part-time); student–undergrad faculty ratio is 25:1.
Enrollment Profile: 2,350 students: 60% women, 40% men, 44% part-time, 99% state residents, 20% live on campus, 13% transferred in, 1% international, 40% 25 or older, 8% Native American, 1% Hispanic, 2% black. *Retention:* 75% of 1995 full-time freshmen returned. *Most popular recent majors:* business administration/commerce/management, nursing, liberal arts/general studies.
First-Year Class: 541 total. Of the students who applied, 100% were accepted, 90% of whom enrolled.
Graduation Requirements: 60 credit hours; 1 algebra course; computer course for business majors.
Computers on Campus: 150 computers available on campus for general student use. Computers for student use in computer center, computer labs, learning resource center, classrooms, library, dorms, student rooms, departmental labs provide access to the Internet/World Wide Web. Staffed computer lab on campus.

EXPENSES

Expenses for 1997–98: *Application fee:* $15. State resident tuition: $840 full-time, $28 per credit hour part-time. Nonresident tuition: $2640 full-time, $88 per credit hour part-time. Part-time mandatory fees per semester range from $10.50 to $97.50. Full-time mandatory fees: $263. College room and board: $1880 (minimum).
LD Services Contact: Ms. LaDonna McCune, Counselor, Northern Oklahoma College, 1220 East Grand, Tonkawa, OK 74653-0310, 405-628-6654. Fax: 405-628-6209.

NORTH HARRIS COLLEGE

Houston, Texas

LEARNING DISABILITIES SERVICES INFORMATION

Office of Disability Services (ODS) began offering services in 1986. Currently the program serves 315 undergraduates with LD. Students diagnosed with ADD/ADHD are eligible for the same services available to students with LD, as well as personal amplification systems.
Staff: 3 full-time, 1 part-time staff members, including coordinator, counselor, diagnostician. Services provided by remediation specialists, counselors, diagnostic specialists.
Special Fees: No special fees are charged for services to students with LD.
Applications and admissions: *Required:* extended time SAT I, personal interview, college placement exam; *recommended:* high school transcript, grade point average, courses completed, IEP (Individualized Education Program). Students may begin taking classes any term. *Application deadline:* continuous.
Special policies: The college has written policies regarding grade forgiveness.

PROGRAM AND SERVICE COMPONENTS

Special preparation or orientation: Optional summer program offered prior to entering college.
Diagnostic testing: Intelligence, reading, math, spelling, written language, study skills, learning strategies.
Academic advising: Provided by unit staff members. Students with LD may take up to 18 semester hours each term; most take 12 to 13 semester hours; 12 semester hours required to maintain full-time status; 6 semester hours required to be eligible for financial aid.
Counseling services: Individual counseling, career counseling, self-advocacy training.
Special courses: College survival skills, learning strategies, time management, study skills. All offered for credit; none enter into overall grade point average.
Auxiliary aids: Taped textbooks, tape recorders, calculators, word-processors with spell-check, personal computers, talking computers, optical character readers, voice-activated computer.
Auxiliary services: Alternative test arrangements, notetakers, priority registration, advocacy.
Campus support group: A special student organization is available to students with LD.

GENERAL COLLEGE INFORMATION

State and locally supported, 2-year, coed. Part of North Harris Montgomery Community College District. Awards associate degrees. Founded 1972. *Setting:* 185-acre suburban campus. *Total enrollment:* 9,398. *Faculty:* 196 (56 full-time, 140 part-time).
Enrollment Profile: 9,398 students from 41 states and territories, 25 other countries. 59% women, 41% men, 69% part-time, 98% state residents, 11% transferred in, 1% international, 44% 25 or older, 1% Native American, 18% Hispanic, 13% black, 9% Asian or Pacific Islander.
First-Year Class: 1,292 total; 1,292 applied, 100% were accepted, 100% of whom enrolled.
Graduation Requirements: 62 credits; computer course for most majors; internship (some majors).
Computers on Campus: 39 computers available on campus for general student use. A computer is recommended for all students. A campus-wide network can be accessed. Students can contact faculty members and/or advisers through e-mail. Computers for student use in library provide access to the Internet/World Wide Web, on- and off-campus e-mail addresses. Staffed computer lab on campus provides training in use of computers, software.

EXPENSES

Estimated Expenses for 1997–98: Area resident tuition: $682 full-time. State resident tuition: $1767 full-time, $57 per credit part-time. Nonresident tuition: $2077 full-time. Part-time tuition per semester ranges from $25 to $242 for area residents, $200 to $737 for nonresidents. Part-time mandatory fees per semester range from $16 to $56. Full-time mandatory fees: $148.
LD Services Contact: Ms. Sandi Patton, Coordinator, Office of Disability Services, North Harris College, 2700 W.W. Thorne, Houston, TX 77073, 281-443-5482. Fax: 281-443-5402.

NORTH IOWA AREA COMMUNITY COLLEGE

Mason City, Iowa

LEARNING DISABILITIES SERVICES INFORMATION

Student Support Services began offering services in 1973. Currently the program serves 15 undergraduates with LD. Students diagnosed with ADD/ADHD are eligible for the same services available to students with LD.
Staff: 4 full-time, 5 part-time staff members, including coordinator. Services provided by tutors, counselor, faculty members.
Special Fees: No special fees are charged for services to students with LD.
Applications and admissions: *Required:* high school transcript; *recommended:* high school grade point average, class rank, courses com-

North Iowa Area Community College (continued)

pleted, psychoeducational report. Students may begin taking classes in fall, spring, or summer. *Application deadline:* continuous.
Special policies: The college has written policies regarding grade forgiveness.

PROGRAM AND SERVICE COMPONENTS

Special preparation or orientation: Optional orientation offered before registration.
Diagnostic testing: Reading, math, written language, personality.
Academic advising: Provided by academic advisers. Most students with LD take 12 to 14 semester hours each term; 12 semester hours required to maintain full-time status; 6 semester hours required to be eligible for financial aid.
Counseling services: Individual counseling, career counseling, self-advocacy training.
Basic skills remediation: Offered in small groups and in class-size groups by regular teachers. Available in reading, math, spelling, written language, learning strategies, study skills, time management.
Subject-area tutoring: Offered one-on-one by professional teachers, peer tutors. Available in most subjects.
Special courses: College survival skills, reading, composition, math, study skills, career planning. Most offered for credit; most enter into overall grade point average.
Auxiliary aids: Taped textbooks, tape recorders, word-processors with spell-check, personal computers.
Auxiliary services: Alternative test arrangements, notetakers, priority registration, advocacy.

GENERAL COLLEGE INFORMATION

State and locally supported, 2-year, coed. Part of Iowa Area Community Colleges System. Awards associate degrees. Founded 1918. *Setting:* 320-acre rural campus. *Total enrollment:* 2,728. *Faculty:* 107 (87 full-time, 20 part-time).
Enrollment Profile: 2,728 students from 18 states and territories, 9 other countries. 56% women, 44% men, 36% part-time, 97% state residents, 5% transferred in, 1% international, 30% 25 or older, 1% Native American, 1% Hispanic, 1% black, 1% Asian or Pacific Islander. *Retention:* 78% of 1995 full-time freshmen returned. *Most popular recent majors:* liberal arts/general studies, nursing, business administration/commerce/management.
First-Year Class: 1,892 total. 5% from top 10% of their high school class, 14% from top quarter, 31% from top half. 2 National Merit Scholars.
Graduation Requirements: 60 semester hours; 1 course each in math and science.
Computers on Campus: 350 computers available on campus for general student use. A campus-wide network can be accessed from off-campus. Students can contact faculty members and/or advisers through e-mail. Computers for student use in computer center, library, departmental labs provide access to the Internet/World Wide Web, on- and off-campus e-mail addresses. Staffed computer lab on campus provides training in use of computers, software.

EXPENSES

Expenses for 1997–98: State resident tuition: $1727 full-time, $57.55 per semester hour part-time. Nonresident tuition: $2591 full-time, $86.35 per semester hour part-time. Part-time mandatory fees per semester range from $14.90 to $92.90. Full-time mandatory fees: $248. College room and board: $3032.
LD Services Contact: Ms. Jonnie Webster, Special Needs Coordinator, North Iowa Area Community College, 500 College Drive, Mason City, IA 50401-7299, 515-422-4365. Fax: 515-423-1711.

NORTH LAKE COLLEGE

Irving, Texas

LEARNING DISABILITIES SERVICES INFORMATION

Special Services Program began offering services in 1979. Currently the program serves 65 undergraduates with LD. Students diagnosed with ADD/ADHD are eligible for the same services available to students with LD, as well as quiet rooms.
Staff: 2 full-time, 20 part-time staff members, including coordinator, rehabilitation specialist, department assistant. Services provided by tutors, readers, LD specialist, disabled student specialist, interpreters.
Special Fees: No special fees are charged for services to students with LD.
Applications and admissions: *Required:* psychoeducational report completed within 3 to 5 years. Students may begin taking classes any term. *Application deadline:* continuous.
Special policies: The college has written policies regarding grade forgiveness.

PROGRAM AND SERVICE COMPONENTS

Academic advising: Provided by unit staff members. Students with LD may take up to 15 credit hours each term; most take 6 to 12 credit hours; 12 credit hours required to maintain full-time status; 6 credit hours required to be eligible for financial aid.
Counseling services: Individual counseling, career counseling, self-advocacy training.
Subject-area tutoring: Offered one-on-one by professional teachers, peer tutors. Available in all subjects.
Special courses: Reading. All offered for credit; all enter into overall grade point average.
Auxiliary aids: Taped textbooks, tape recorders, calculators, typewriters, word-processors with spell-check, personal computers, optical character readers.
Auxiliary services: Alternative test arrangements, notetakers, priority registration, advocacy.

GENERAL COLLEGE INFORMATION

County-supported, 2-year, coed. Part of Dallas County Community College District System. Awards associate degrees. Founded 1977. *Setting:* 250-acre suburban campus with easy access to Dallas. *Total enrollment:* 6,233. *Faculty:* 342 (92 full-time, 250 part-time).
Enrollment Profile: 6,233 students: 52% women, 48% men, 75% part-time, 98% state residents, 12% transferred in, 1% international, 51% 25 or older, 1% Native American, 13% Hispanic, 10% black, 8% Asian or Pacific Islander. *Most popular recent majors:* liberal arts/general studies, electrical and electronics technologies, business administration/commerce/management.
First-Year Class: Of the students who applied, 99% were accepted. 2% from top 10% of their high school class, 85% from top half.
Graduation Requirements: 62 semester hours; 1 math course.
Computers on Campus: 65 computers available on campus for general student use. A campus-wide network can be accessed. Computers for student use in computer center provide access to the Internet/World Wide Web. Staffed computer lab on campus.

EXPENSES

Expenses for 1997–98: Area resident tuition: $650 full-time. State resident tuition: $1030 full-time. Nonresident tuition: $2140 full-time. Part-time tuition per semester ranges from $79 to $245 for area residents, $136 to $435 for state residents, $226 to $786 for nonresidents.
LD Services Contact: Ms. Mary G. Ciminelli, Coordinator/Counselor, Special Services Program, North Lake College, 5001 North MacArthur, Irving, TX 75038-3899, 972-273-3165. Fax: 972-273-3014. Email: mgc7341@dcccd.edu.

NORTHLAND COMMUNITY AND TECHNICAL COLLEGE

Thief River Falls, Minnesota

LEARNING DISABILITIES SERVICES INFORMATION

Services to Students with Disabilities, Student Services Office began offering services in 1978. Currently the program serves 56 undergraduates with LD. Students diagnosed with ADD/ADHD are eligible for the same services available to students with LD.
Staff: 2 full-time, 2 part-time staff members, including director. Services provided by tutors, instructors.
Special Fees: No special fees are charged for services to students with LD.
Applications and admissions: *Required:* high school transcript, courses completed, IEP or other documentation of disability; *recommended:* high school class rank, extracurricular activities, psychoeducational report completed within 3 years. Students may begin taking classes any term. *Application deadline:* continuous.
Special policies: The college has written policies regarding substitutions and waivers of graduation requirements.

PROGRAM AND SERVICE COMPONENTS

Academic advising: Provided by unit staff members, academic advisers. Students with LD may take up to 18 credits (over 18 requires written approval) each term; most take 12 credits; 12 credits required to maintain full-time status; 12 credits (Federal), 15 credits (State grants) required to be eligible for financial aid.
Counseling services: Individual counseling, career counseling, self-advocacy training.
Basic skills remediation: Offered one-on-one and in class-size groups by regular teachers, Learning Center instructors. Available in reading, math, spelling, spoken language, written language, learning strategies, study skills, time management, computer skills.
Subject-area tutoring: Offered one-on-one and in small groups by professional teachers, peer tutors. Available in most subjects.
Auxiliary aids: Taped textbooks, tape recorders, calculators, word-processors with spell-check, personal computers, optical character readers, voice-activated computers.
Auxiliary services: Alternative test arrangements, notetakers, priority registration, advocacy, scribes, writers.

GENERAL COLLEGE INFORMATION

State-supported, 2-year, coed. Part of Minnesota State Colleges and Universities System. Awards associate degrees. Founded 1965. *Setting:* rural campus. *Total enrollment:* 1,214. *Faculty:* 82 (68 full-time, 10% with terminal degrees, 14 part-time); student–undergrad faculty ratio is 22:1.
Enrollment Profile: 1,214 students from 13 states and territories, 2 other countries. 51% women, 49% men, 31% part-time, 92% state residents, 25% transferred in, 1% international, 23% 25 or older, 3% Native American, 1% Hispanic, 1% black, 1% Asian or Pacific Islander. *Retention:* 65% of 1995 full-time freshmen returned. *Areas of study chosen:* 73% vocational and home economics, 27% liberal arts/general studies. *Most popular recent majors:* law enforcement/police sciences, nursing, aviation technology.
First-Year Class: 626 total; 693 applied, 100% were accepted, 90% of whom enrolled.
Graduation Requirements: 96 credits; computer course for education, business administration, electrical and electronics technology majors.
Computers on Campus: 154 computers available on campus for general student use. Computer purchase/lease plans available. A computer is recommended for all students. A campus-wide network can be accessed. Students can contact faculty members and/or advisers through e-mail. Computers for student use in computer center, computer labs, learning resource center, classrooms, library provide access to the Internet/World Wide Web, on-campus e-mail addresses. Staffed computer lab on campus.

EXPENSES

Expenses for 1996–97: *Application fee:* $20. State resident tuition: $2105 full-time, $43.85 per credit part-time. Nonresident tuition: $4102 full-time, $85.45 per credit part-time. Part-time mandatory fees: $5.42 per credit. North Dakota, South Dakota and Wisconsin residents pay tuition at the rate they would pay if attending a comparable state-supported institution in their home state. Full-time mandatory fees: $260.
LD Services Contact: Ms. Carol Torgerson, Learning Center Director, Northland Community and Technical College, Highway 1 East, Thief River Falls, MN 56701, 218-681-0835.

NORTHLAND PIONEER COLLEGE

Holbrook, Arizona

LEARNING DISABILITIES SERVICES INFORMATION

Office for Special Needs currently serves 21 undergraduates with LD.
Staff: 1 full-time staff member (coordinator). Services provided by tutors, readers, proctors, notetakers.
Special Fees: No special fees are charged for services to students with LD.
Applications and admissions: *Recommended:* high school IEP (Individualized Education Program), psychoeducational report completed within 5 years. Students may begin taking classes any term. *Application deadline:* continuous.
Special policies: The college has written policies regarding substitutions and waivers of graduation and degree requirements.

PROGRAM AND SERVICE COMPONENTS

Academic advising: Provided by unit staff members, academic advisers. Most students with LD take 6 to 12 semester hours each term; 12 semester hours required to maintain full-time status.
Counseling services: Individual counseling, career counseling.
Basic skills remediation: Offered one-on-one and in small groups by regular teachers; computer-aided instruction also offered. Available in reading, math, spelling, handwriting, study skills, time management, speech, computer skills.
Subject-area tutoring: Offered one-on-one by peer tutors. Available in most subjects.
Auxiliary aids: Taped textbooks, word-processors with spell-check, personal computers.
Auxiliary services: Alternative test arrangements, notetakers, priority registration.

GENERAL COLLEGE INFORMATION

State and locally supported, 2-year, coed. Awards associate degrees. Founded 1974. *Setting:* 40-acre rural campus. *Total enrollment:* 4,779. *Faculty:* 400 (50 full-time, 15% with terminal degrees, 350 part-time); student–undergrad faculty ratio is 16:1.
Enrollment Profile: 4,779 students from 15 states and territories. 67% women, 33% men, 85% part-time, 99% state residents, 5% transferred in, 0% international, 77% 25 or older, 26% Native American, 8% Hispanic, 1% black, 1% Asian or Pacific Islander. *Most popular recent majors:* early childhood education, business administration/commerce/management, liberal arts/general studies.
First-Year Class: 1,800 total. Of the students who applied, 100% were accepted.
Graduation Requirements: 64 semester hours; math/science requirements vary according to program; computer course for office administration support, business majors.
Computers on Campus: 200 computers available on campus for general student use. Computers for student use in computer labs, classrooms, library. Staffed computer lab on campus provides training in use of computers, software. *Academic computing expenditure 1995–96:* $110,000.

EXPENSES

Expenses for 1996–97: State resident tuition: $660 full-time, $22 per semester hour part-time. Nonresident tuition: $2760 full-time. Nonresident part-time tuition per semester hour ranges from $42 to $92. College room only: $1400.
LD Services Contact: Dr. Joseph Reynolds, Coordinator for Special Needs, Northland Pioneer College, PO Box 610, Holbrook, AZ 86025, 520-524-6111 Ext. 508. Fax: 520-524-2124.

NORTH SHORE COMMUNITY COLLEGE

Danvers, Massachusetts

LEARNING DISABILITIES SERVICES INFORMATION

Student Support Center began offering services in 1975. Currently the program serves 100 undergraduates with LD. Students diagnosed with ADD/ADHD are eligible for the same services available to students with LD.
Staff: 15 full-time, 12 part-time staff members, including director, coordinator, educational specialists. Services provided by remediation specialists, tutors, counselors, diagnostic specialists, notetakers, scribes.
Special Fees: No special fees are charged for services to students with LD.
Applications and admissions: *Required:* high school transcript, personal interview; *recommended:* psychoeducational report completed within 3 years. Students may begin taking classes in fall, spring, or summer. *Application deadline:* continuous.
Special policies: The college has written policies regarding grade forgiveness; substitutions and waivers of graduation and degree requirements.

PROGRAM AND SERVICE COMPONENTS

Special preparation or orientation: Optional orientation offered individually by special arrangement.
Diagnostic testing: Reading, math, spelling, handwriting, written language, perceptual skills, learning strategies.
Academic advising: Provided by unit staff members, academic advisers. Students with LD may take up to 12 credits each term; most take 6 to 12 credits; 12 credits required to maintain full-time status; 6 credits required to be eligible for financial aid.

North Shore Community College (continued)

Counseling services: Individual counseling, small-group counseling, career counseling, computerized self-paced programs.
Basic skills remediation: Offered in small groups and in class-size groups by LD teachers, regular teachers; computer-aided instruction also offered. Available in reading, math, spelling, written language, learning strategies, study skills, time management.
Subject-area tutoring: Offered in small groups and in class-size groups by professional teachers, peer tutors. Available in most subjects.
Special courses: College survival skills, reading, vocabulary development, communication skills, composition, learning strategies, word processing, time management, math, typing, study skills, career planning, stress management, freshman seminar. Most offered for credit; some enter into overall grade point average.
Auxiliary aids: Taped textbooks, tape recorders, calculators, typewriters, word-processors with spell-check, personal computers, optical character readers, electronic devices for vision and/or hearing impaired, videos for tutorial support, reading machines, adaptive computer equipment and instruction.
Auxiliary services: Alternative test arrangements, notetakers, priority registration, readers.

GENERAL COLLEGE INFORMATION

State-supported, 2-year, coed. Awards associate degrees. Founded 1965. *Setting:* suburban campus with easy access to Boston. *Total enrollment:* 4,238. *Faculty:* 339 (104 full-time, 235 part-time).
Enrollment Profile: 4,238 students: 63% women, 37% men, 65% part-time, 98% state residents, 6% transferred in, 57% 25 or older, 1% Native American, 11% Hispanic, 5% black, 2% Asian or Pacific Islander. *Retention:* 75% of 1995 full-time freshmen returned. *Most popular recent majors:* liberal arts/general studies, business administration/commerce/management, nursing.
First-Year Class: 1,261 total; 1,935 applied, 89% were accepted, 73% of whom enrolled.
Graduation Requirements: 60 credits; math proficiency; computer course (varies by major); internship (some majors).
Computers on Campus: 300 computers available on campus for general student use. A campus-wide network can be accessed. Computers for student use in computer labs, learning resource center, classrooms, computer classrooms, student support center provide access to the Internet/World Wide Web. Staffed computer lab on campus provides training in use of computers, software.

EXPENSES

Expenses for 1997–98: State resident tuition: $1020 full-time, $34 per credit part-time. Nonresident tuition: $6120 full-time, $204 per credit part-time. Part-time mandatory fees: $46 per credit. Full-time mandatory fees: $1380.
LD Services Contact: Ms. Jean Keith, Director, Student Support Center, North Shore Community College, 1 Ferncroft Road, Danvers, MA 01923, 508-762-4000 Ext. 2132. Fax: 617-477-2144.

NORTHWESTERN COLLEGE

Lima, Ohio

LEARNING DISABILITIES SERVICES INFORMATION

Learning Lab began offering services in 1993. Currently the program serves 42 undergraduates with LD. Students diagnosed with ADD/ADHD are eligible for the same services available to students with LD.
Staff: 1 full-time, 1 part-time staff members, including coordinator. Services provided by remediation specialists, tutors, counselor.
Special Fees: No special fees are charged for services to students with LD.
Applications and admissions: *Required:* high school transcript, grade point average, IEP (Individualized Education Program), psychoeducational report completed within 3 years; *recommended:* high school class rank, courses completed. Students may begin taking classes any term. *Application deadline:* continuous.
Special policies: The college has written policies regarding grade forgiveness; substitutions and waivers of graduation requirements.

PROGRAM AND SERVICE COMPONENTS

Special preparation or orientation: Optional orientation offered before registration, during registration, after classes begin.
Academic advising: Provided by unit staff members. Most students with LD take 15 quarter hours each term; 12 quarter hours required to maintain full-time status; 6 to 12 quarter hours (for business division loans and grants), 3 to 6 credit hours (for tech division loans and grants) required to be eligible for financial aid.
Counseling services: Individual counseling, career counseling, self-advocacy training.
Basic skills remediation: Offered one-on-one by LD teachers, regular teachers. Available in reading, math, spelling, learning strategies, study skills, time management.
Subject-area tutoring: Offered one-on-one by professional teachers, peer tutors. Available in all subjects.
Auxiliary services: Alternative test arrangements, notetakers, advocacy.

GENERAL COLLEGE INFORMATION

Independent, 2-year, coed. Awards associate degrees. Founded 1920. *Setting:* 35-acre small-town campus with easy access to Dayton and Toledo. *Total enrollment:* 1,800. *Faculty:* 67 (48 full-time, 19 part-time); student–undergrad faculty ratio is 25:1.
Enrollment Profile: 1,800 students from 10 states and territories. 29% women, 71% men, 12% part-time, 90% state residents, 1% transferred in, 0% international, 15% 25 or older, 0% Native American, 1% Hispanic, 4% black, 0% Asian or Pacific Islander. *Retention:* 80% of 1995 full-time freshmen returned. *Areas of study chosen:* 61% vocational and home economics, 32% business management and administrative services, 5% health professions and related sciences, 1% agriculture, 1% computer and information sciences. *Most popular recent majors:* automotive technologies, secretarial studies/office management.
First-Year Class: 1,200 total. Of the students who applied, 98% were accepted, 58% of whom enrolled. 5% from top 10% of their high school class, 20% from top quarter, 75% from top half.
Graduation Requirements: 108 credits; 1 math course; computer course.
Computers on Campus: 65 computers available on campus for general student use. A computer is recommended for some students. A campus-wide network can be accessed from off-campus. Students can contact faculty members and/or advisers through e-mail. Computers for student use in computer center, computer labs, auto school classroom provide access to the Internet/World Wide Web, on- and off-campus e-mail addresses. Staffed computer lab on campus provides training in use of computers, software. *Academic computing expenditure 1995–96:* $75,000.

EXPENSES

Expenses for 1996–97: *Application fee:* $50. Full-time tuition ranges from $10,584 to $14,308 according to program. Part-time tuition: $98 per credit. College room only: $2400. Tuition guaranteed not to increase for student's term of enrollment.
LD Services Contact: Ms. Karen Meyer, Learning Lab Coordinator, Northwestern College, 1441 North Cable Road, Lima, OH 45805-1498, 419-998-3157. Fax: 419-998-3080. Email: meyer_k@nc.edu.

NORTHWEST IOWA COMMUNITY COLLEGE

Sheldon, Iowa

LEARNING DISABILITIES SERVICES INFORMATION

Learning Center began offering services in 1980. Students diagnosed with ADD/ADHD are eligible for the same services available to students with LD.
Staff: 3 part-time staff members. Services provided by tutors.
Special Fees: No special fees are charged for services to students with LD.
Applications and admissions: *Required:* high school transcript, courses completed, ASSET; *recommended:* high school grade point average, class rank, extracurricular activities. Students may begin taking classes any term. *Application deadline:* continuous.

PROGRAM AND SERVICE COMPONENTS

Special preparation or orientation: Optional summer program offered prior to entering college.
Diagnostic testing: Reading, math, motor abilities, perceptual skills, personality.
Academic advising: Provided by academic advisers. Most students with LD take 15 credit hours each term; 12 credit hours required to maintain full-time status and be eligible for financial aid.

Counseling services: Individual counseling.
Basic skills remediation: Offered one-on-one and in small groups by Learning Center instructors. Available in reading, math, spelling, spoken language, written language, learning strategies, study skills, time management, social skills, speech, vocational training.
Subject-area tutoring: Offered one-on-one and in small groups by professional teachers. Available in all subjects.
Special courses: College survival skills, reading, learning strategies, time management, math, typing, study skills, career planning. Some offered for credit; none enter into overall grade point average.
Auxiliary aids: Taped textbooks, tape recorders, calculators, typewriters, word-processors with spell-check, personal computers.
Auxiliary services: Alternative test arrangements.

GENERAL COLLEGE INFORMATION

State-supported, 2-year, coed. Part of Iowa Department of Education Division of Community Colleges. Awards associate degrees. Founded 1966. *Setting:* 263-acre small-town campus. *Educational spending 1995–96:* $3277 per undergrad. *Total enrollment:* 742. *Faculty:* 60 (35 full-time, 6% with terminal degrees, 25 part-time); student–undergrad faculty ratio is 12:1.
Enrollment Profile: 742 students from 9 states and territories. 49% women, 51% men, 37% part-time, 96% state residents, 6% live on campus, 11% transferred in, 0% international, 17% 25 or older, 1% black, 0% Asian or Pacific Islander. *Retention:* 41% of 1995 full-time freshmen returned.
First-Year Class: 366 total; 761 applied, 94% were accepted, 51% of whom enrolled.
Graduation Requirements: 60 credit hours; math/science requirements vary according to program; internship (some majors).
Computers on Campus: 89 computers available on campus for general student use. A campus-wide network can be accessed. Computers for student use in computer center, computer labs, learning resource center, classrooms, library provide access to the Internet/World Wide Web. Staffed computer lab on campus. *Academic computing expenditure 1995–96:* $127,080.

EXPENSES

Expenses for 1997–98: *Application fee:* $10. State resident tuition: $1650 full-time, $55 per credit hour part-time. Nonresident tuition: $2475 full-time, $82.50 per credit hour part-time. Part-time mandatory fees per credit hour range from $7 to $13. Full-time mandatory fees range from $210 to $390. College room only: $1800.
LD Services Contact: Ms. Marlys Schwebach, Instructor, Learning Center, Northwest Iowa Community College, 603 West Park Street, Sheldon, IA 51201, 712-324-5061. Fax: 712-324-4136.

NORTHWEST STATE COMMUNITY COLLEGE

Archbold, Ohio

LEARNING DISABILITIES SERVICES INFORMATION

Learning Support Center began offering services in 1995. Currently the program serves 10 to 15 undergraduates with LD. Students diagnosed with ADD/ADHD are eligible for the same services available to students with LD.
Staff: 1 full-time staff member (coordinator). Services provided by remediation specialist, tutors, counselors.
Special Fees: No special fees are charged for services to students with LD.
Applications and admissions: *Required:* high school transcript, IEP (Individualized Education Program), personal interview, psychoeducational report. Students may begin taking classes in fall, spring, or summer. *Application deadline:* continuous.

PROGRAM AND SERVICE COMPONENTS

Academic advising: Provided by academic advisers. Students with LD may take up to 15 semester hours each term; most take 12 semester hours; 12 semester hours required to maintain full-time status and be eligible for financial aid.
Counseling services: Individual counseling, career counseling.
Basic skills remediation: Offered in small groups by regular teachers. Available in reading, math, written language, study skills, time management.
Subject-area tutoring: Offered one-on-one and in small groups by peer tutors. Available in all subjects.
Auxiliary aids: Taped textbooks, tape recorders, typewriters, word-processors with spell-check, talking computers.
Auxiliary services: Alternative test arrangements, notetakers, advocacy.

GENERAL COLLEGE INFORMATION

State-supported, 2-year, coed. Part of Ohio Board of Regents. Awards associate degrees. Founded 1968. *Setting:* 84-acre rural campus with easy access to Toledo. *Educational spending 1995–96:* $1398 per undergrad. *Total enrollment:* 2,119. *Faculty:* 136 (41 full-time, 12% with terminal degrees, 95 part-time); student–undergrad faculty ratio is 14:1.
Enrollment Profile: 2,119 students from 3 states and territories. 63% women, 37% men, 67% part-time, 98% state residents, 26% transferred in, 0% international, 50% 25 or older, 1% Native American, 5% Hispanic, 1% black, 1% Asian or Pacific Islander. *Retention:* 59% of 1995 full-time freshmen returned. *Areas of study chosen:* 26% business management and administrative services, 20% health professions and related sciences, 11% engineering and applied sciences, 6% social sciences, 4% computer and information sciences, 4% liberal arts/general studies. *Most popular recent majors:* accounting, nursing, business administration/commerce/management.
First-Year Class: 741 total; 1,135 applied, 100% were accepted, 65% of whom enrolled. 5% from top 10% of their high school class, 25% from top quarter, 55% from top half.
Graduation Requirements: 62 semester hours; 1 college algebra course; computer course; internship (some majors).
Computers on Campus: 214 computers available on campus for general student use. A campus-wide network can be accessed. Students can contact faculty members and/or advisers through e-mail. Computers for student use in computer center, computer labs, learning resource center, classrooms, library provide access to the Internet/World Wide Web, on- and off-campus e-mail addresses. Staffed computer lab on campus provides training in use of computers, software. *Academic computing expenditure 1995–96:* $318,920.

EXPENSES

Expenses for 1997–98: *Application fee:* $10. State resident tuition: $3030 full-time, $97.75 per semester hour part-time. Nonresident tuition: $5720 full-time, $184.50 per semester hour part-time.
LD Services Contact: Mr. Dennis Gable, Dean of Student Services, Northwest State Community College, 22-600 State Route 34, Archbold, OH 43502-9542, 419-267-5511. Fax: 419-267-3688. Email: dennisga@nscc.cc.oh.us.

NORTHWEST TECHNICAL COLLEGE

Bemidji, Minnesota

LEARNING DISABILITIES SERVICES INFORMATION

Learning Center began offering services in 1976. Currently the program serves 15 undergraduates with LD. Students diagnosed with ADD/ADHD are eligible for the same services available to students with LD.
Staff: Includes disability coordinators. Services provided by remediation specialists, tutors, counselors.
Special Fees: No special fees are charged for services to students with LD.
Applications and admissions: *Required:* high school transcript, grade point average, IEP (Individualized Education Program), personal interview; *recommended:* documentation of disability. Students may begin taking classes any term. *Application deadline:* continuous.

PROGRAM AND SERVICE COMPONENTS

Academic advising: Provided by unit staff members, academic advisers. Most students with LD take 15 credits each term; 15 credits required to maintain full-time status and be eligible for financial aid.
Counseling services: Individual counseling, small-group counseling, career counseling, self-advocacy training.
Auxiliary aids: Taped textbooks, tape recorders, calculators, typewriters, word-processors with spell-check, personal computers.
Auxiliary services: Alternative test arrangements, notetakers, priority registration, advocacy.

GENERAL COLLEGE INFORMATION

State-supported, 2-year. Part of Minnesota State Colleges and Universities System. Awards associate degrees (branch locations: Detroit Lakes, East Grand Forks, Moorhead, Wadena). Founded 1993. *Total enrollment:* 5,000. *Faculty:* 400 (300 full-time, 100 part-time).

Northwest Technical College (continued)

First-Year Class: 3,500 total; 6,000 applied, 100% were accepted, 58% of whom enrolled.
Graduation Requirements: 96 credits.
Computers on Campus: Computer purchase/lease plans available. A computer is required for some students. A campus-wide network can be accessed from off-campus. Students can contact faculty members and/or advisers through e-mail. Computers for student use in computer center, computer labs, learning resource center, classrooms provide access to the Internet/World Wide Web, on-campus e-mail addresses. Staffed computer lab on campus provides training in use of computers, software.

EXPENSES

Expenses for 1996–97: State resident tuition: $1997 full-time, $41.60 per credit part-time. Nonresident tuition: $3792 full-time, $79 per credit part-time. Part-time mandatory fees: $2 per quarter. Full-time mandatory fees: $6.
LD Services Contact: Ms. Jeanne Johnson, Disabilities Coordinator, Northwest Technical College, 906 Grant Avenue, SE, Bemidji, MN 56601, 218-755-4270. Fax: 218-755-4289.

OAKTON COMMUNITY COLLEGE

Des Plaines, Illinois

LEARNING DISABILITIES SERVICES INFORMATION

ASSIST Services began offering services in 1980. Currently the program serves 350 undergraduates with LD. Students diagnosed with ADD/ADHD are eligible for the same services available to students with LD.
Staff: 2 full-time, 9 part-time staff members, including director, associate director, coordinator. Services provided by remediation specialists, tutors, counselors, diagnostic specialist.
Special Fees: $150 for diagnostic testing.
Applications and admissions: *Required:* high school IEP (Individualized Education Program), psychoeducational report completed within 3 years, intake interview. Students may begin taking classes any term. *Application deadline:* continuous.

PROGRAM AND SERVICE COMPONENTS

Special preparation or orientation: Optional orientation offered during registration.
Diagnostic testing: Reading, math, written language, perceptual skills, study skills, learning strategies.
Academic advising: Provided by unit staff members, academic advisers. Most students with LD take 9 semester hours each term; 12 semester hours required to maintain full-time status.
Counseling services: Individual counseling, career counseling.
Basic skills remediation: Offered one-on-one by LD teachers. Available in reading, math, spelling, handwriting, spoken language, written language, learning strategies, study skills, time management.
Subject-area tutoring: Offered one-on-one and in small groups by professional teachers. Available in most subjects.
Auxiliary aids: Taped textbooks, tape recorders, calculators, typewriters, word-processors with spell-check, talking computers, optical character readers.
Auxiliary services: Alternative test arrangements, advocacy.

GENERAL COLLEGE INFORMATION

District-supported, 2-year, coed. Part of Illinois Community College System. Awards associate degrees. Founded 1969. *Setting:* 160-acre suburban campus. *Research spending 1995–96:* $311,702. *Total enrollment:* 10,404. *Faculty:* 625 (151 full-time, 474 part-time); student–undergrad faculty ratio is 25:1.
Enrollment Profile: 10,404 students: 56% women, 44% men, 74% part-time, 86% state residents, 12% transferred in, 0% international, 46% 25 or older, 0% Native American, 4% Hispanic, 4% black, 10% Asian or Pacific Islander. *Areas of study chosen:* 51% liberal arts/general studies, 8% business management and administrative services, 7% health professions and related sciences, 5% computer and information sciences, 3% biological and life sciences, 3% engineering and applied sciences, 1% architecture.
First-Year Class: 2,034 total. Of the students who applied, 99% were accepted, 99% of whom enrolled. 1% from top 10% of their high school class, 10% from top quarter, 45% from top half.
Graduation Requirements: 60 semester hours; internship (some majors).
Computers on Campus: 750 computers available on campus for general student use. Computers for student use in computer center, computer labs provide access to the Internet/World Wide Web. Staffed computer lab on campus provides training in use of computers, software. *Academic computing expenditure 1995–96:* $128,320.

EXPENSES

Expenses for 1997–98: *Application fee:* $25. Area resident tuition: $1110 full-time, $37 per semester hour part-time. State resident tuition: $4140 full-time, $138 per semester hour part-time. Nonresident tuition: $5190 full-time, $173 per semester hour part-time. Part-time mandatory fees per semester range from $16.75 to $34.25. Tuition and fees for district residents over 60 years of age: $17.50 per semester hour. Full-time mandatory fees: $83.
LD Services Contact: Ms. Linda McCann, Special Needs Coordinator, Oakton Community College, 1600 East Golf Road, Des Plaines, IL 60016, 847-635-1759. Fax: 847-635-1987.

OHIO STATE UNIVERSITY AGRICULTURAL TECHNICAL INSTITUTE

Wooster, Ohio

LEARNING DISABILITIES SERVICES INFORMATION

Learning Assistance Center, Program for Students with Learning Disabilities currently serves 86 undergraduates with LD. Students diagnosed with ADD/ADHD are eligible for the same services available to students with LD, as well as support group.
Staff: 3 part-time staff members, including coordinator. Services provided by diagnostic specialist, tutor coordinator.
Special Fees: $125 for diagnostic testing.
Applications and admissions: *Required:* high school transcript, psychoeducational report completed within 3 years; *recommended:* extended time SAT I or ACT. Students may begin taking classes any term. *Application deadline:* 8/15 (fall term), 3/1 (spring term).
Special policies: The college has written policies regarding grade forgiveness; substitutions and waivers of admissions, graduation, and degree requirements.

PROGRAM AND SERVICE COMPONENTS

Special preparation or orientation: Optional orientation offered before registration and after classes begin.
Diagnostic testing: Intelligence, reading, math, spelling, handwriting, spoken language, written language, perceptual skills, study skills, learning strategies.
Academic advising: Provided by unit staff members, academic advisers. Most students with LD take 12 to 15 quarter hours each term; 12 quarter hours required to maintain full-time status; 12 quarter hours (can be prorated) required to be eligible for financial aid.
Counseling services: Individual counseling, small-group counseling, career counseling.
Basic skills remediation: Offered one-on-one, in small groups, and in class-size groups by LD teachers, regular teachers. Available in reading, math, spelling, learning strategies, perceptual skills, study skills, time management, social skills.
Subject-area tutoring: Offered one-on-one and in small groups by professional teachers, peer tutors, LD specialist. Available in most subjects.
Special courses: College survival skills, reading, communication skills, composition, learning strategies, time management, math, study skills. Some offered for credit; some enter into overall grade point average.
Auxiliary aids: Taped textbooks, tape recorders, calculators, typewriters, word-processors with spell-check, personal computers, talking computers, optical character readers.
Auxiliary services: Alternative test arrangements, notetakers, priority registration, advocacy, scribes, readers.

GENERAL COLLEGE INFORMATION

State-supported, 2-year, coed. Part of Ohio State University. Awards associate degrees. Founded 1971. *Setting:* 136-acre small-town campus with easy access to Cleveland and Columbus. *Total enrollment:* 827. *Faculty:* 55 (35 full-time, 20 part-time); student–undergrad faculty ratio is 15:1.
Enrollment Profile: 827 students from 10 states and territories, 2 other countries. 26% women, 74% men, 14% part-time, 97% state residents, 22% live on campus, 12% transferred in, 1% international, 20% 25 or

older, 1% Native American, 1% Hispanic, 3% black, 1% Asian or Pacific Islander. *Retention:* 64% of 1995 full-time freshmen returned. *Areas of study chosen:* 100% agriculture.
First-Year Class: 264 total; 422 applied, 92% were accepted, 68% of whom enrolled. 2% from top 10% of their high school class, 15% from top quarter, 55% from top half.
Graduation Requirements: 100 quarter hours; math/science requirements vary according to program; computer course for most majors.
Computers on Campus: 85 computers available on campus for general student use. Computers for student use in computer center, learning resource center, library, dorms.

EXPENSES

Expenses for 1997–98: *Application fee:* $30. State resident tuition: $3570 full-time. Nonresident tuition: $10,653 full-time. Part-time tuition per quarter ranges from $98 to $1092 for state residents, $195 to $3256 for nonresidents. College room only: $2700.
LD Services Contact: Ms. Tanya Kunze, Learning Disabilities Specialist, Ohio State University Agricultural Technical Institute, 1328 Dover Road, Wooster, OH 44691, 330-264-3911. Fax: 330-262-7634.

OKALOOSA-WALTON COMMUNITY COLLEGE

Niceville, Florida

LEARNING DISABILITIES SERVICES INFORMATION

Department of Student Services currently serves 61 undergraduates with LD. Students diagnosed with ADD/ADHD are eligible for the same services available to students with LD, as well as distraction-free testing environment.
Staff: 1 full-time staff member (coordinator). Services provided by tutors, counselor, notetakers, scribes.
Special Fees: No special fees are charged for services to students with LD.
Applications and admissions: Open admissions. Students may begin taking classes any term. *Application deadline:* continuous.
Special policies: The college has written policies regarding grade forgiveness; substitutions and waivers of admissions, graduation, and degree requirements.

PROGRAM AND SERVICE COMPONENTS

Academic advising: Provided by academic advisers. Students with LD may take up to as many semester hours as an individual can handle each term; most take 9 to 12 semester hours; 12 semester hours required to maintain full-time status; 3 semester hours required to be eligible for financial aid.
Counseling services: Individual counseling, career counseling.
Basic skills remediation: Offered in class-size groups by regular teachers. Available in reading, math, written language.
Subject-area tutoring: Offered one-on-one by peer tutors, faculty volunteers. Available in most subjects.
Special courses: College survival skills, reading, vocabulary development, study skills. Some offered for credit; some enter into overall grade point average.
Auxiliary aids: Tape recorders.
Auxiliary services: Alternative test arrangements, notetakers.

GENERAL COLLEGE INFORMATION

State and locally supported, 2-year, coed. Part of Florida Community Colleges System. Awards associate degrees. Founded 1963. *Setting:* 264-acre small-town campus. *Total enrollment:* 5,820. *Faculty:* 274 (74 full-time, 20% with terminal degrees, 200 part-time); student–undergrad faculty ratio is 21:1.
Enrollment Profile: 5,820 students: 55% women, 45% men, 95% part-time, 99% state residents, 6% transferred in, 55% 25 or older, 1% Native American, 2% Hispanic, 8% black, 3% Asian or Pacific Islander. *Retention:* 36% of 1995 full-time freshmen returned. *Most popular recent majors:* liberal arts/general studies, drafting and design, electronics engineering technology.
First-Year Class: 1,569 applied, 100% were accepted, 100% of whom enrolled. 6% from top 10% of their high school class, 16% from top quarter, 31% from top half.
Graduation Requirements: 60 semester hours; math/science requirements vary according to program.
Computers on Campus: 200 computers available on campus for general student use. Computer purchase/lease plans available. Computers for student use in computer labs, learning resource center, classrooms, library, teaching labs. *Academic computing expenditure 1995–96:* $497,147.

EXPENSES AND FINANCIAL AID

Expenses for 1997–98: *Application fee:* $15. State resident tuition: $1080 full-time, $36 per semester hour part-time. Nonresident tuition: $4122 full-time, $137.40 per semester hour part-time.
Financial aid specifically for students with LD: Scholarship: Destin Kiwanis Scholarship.
LD Services Contact: Ms. Jody Swenson, Counselor/Coordinator of Services to Students with Special Needs, Okaloosa-Walton Community College, 100 College Boulevard, Niceville, FL 32578-1295, 904-729-5236. Fax: 904-729-5323.

OKLAHOMA STATE UNIVERSITY, OKLAHOMA CITY

Oklahoma City, Oklahoma

LEARNING DISABILITIES SERVICES INFORMATION

Wellness Center began offering services in 1990. Currently the program serves 32 undergraduates with LD. Students diagnosed with ADD/ADHD are eligible for the same services available to students with LD.
Staff: 3 full-time, 7 part-time staff members, including director, Vice Provost. Services provided by tutors, counselors, Student Support Services staff.
Special Fees: No special fees are charged for services to students with LD.
Applications and admissions: *Required:* high school transcript, documentation of disability. Students may begin taking classes in fall, spring, or summer. *Application deadline:* continuous.
Special policies: The college has written policies regarding grade forgiveness; substitutions and waivers of admissions, graduation, and degree requirements.

PROGRAM AND SERVICE COMPONENTS

Academic advising: Provided by unit staff members, academic advisers. Students with LD may take up to 12 credit hours each term; most take 9 credit hours; 9 credit hours required to maintain full-time status and be eligible for financial aid.
Counseling services: Individual counseling, small-group counseling, career counseling, self-advocacy training.
Basic skills remediation: Offered in class-size groups by regular teachers; computer-aided instruction also offered. Available in reading, math, spelling, handwriting, written language, learning strategies, perceptual skills, study skills, time management, social skills, computer skills.
Subject-area tutoring: Offered one-on-one by professional teachers, peer tutors. Available in most subjects.
Auxiliary aids: Taped textbooks, tape recorders, calculators, typewriters, word-processors with spell-check, personal computers, optical character readers.
Auxiliary services: Alternative test arrangements, notetakers, advocacy, signers.

GENERAL COLLEGE INFORMATION

State-supported, 2-year, coed. Part of Oklahoma State University. Awards associate degrees. Founded 1961. *Setting:* 80-acre urban campus. *Educational spending 1995–96:* $1044 per undergrad. *Total enrollment:* 4,000. *Faculty:* 205 (61 full-time, 1% with terminal degrees, 144 part-time); student–undergrad faculty ratio is 18:1.
Enrollment Profile: 4,000 students from 18 states and territories, 15 other countries. 53% women, 47% men, 70% part-time, 90% state residents, 24% transferred in, 1% international, 76% 25 or older, 5% Native American, 2% Hispanic, 8% black, 4% Asian or Pacific Islander. *Most popular recent major:* nursing.
First-Year Class: 836 total. 10% from top 10% of their high school class, 15% from top half.
Graduation Requirements: 60 semester hours; math/science requirements vary according to program; computer course for architectural technology, environment systems technology, technical communications majors.
Computers on Campus: 55 computers available on campus for general student use. Computers for student use in computer center, library

Oklahoma State University, Oklahoma City (continued)

provide access to the Internet/World Wide Web. Staffed computer lab on campus. *Academic computing expenditure 1995–96:* $312,315.

EXPENSES

Expenses for 1996–97: State resident tuition: $1539 full-time, $51.30 per semester hour part-time. Nonresident tuition: $3714 full-time, $123.80 per semester hour part-time. Part-time mandatory fees: $17.50 per semester. Full-time mandatory fees: $35.

LD Services Contact: Ms. Karen Smith, Coordinator of Student Activities/Family Resource Center, Oklahoma State University, Oklahoma City, 900 North Portland, Oklahoma City, OK 73107-6120, 405-945-3378. Fax: 405-945-9131.

OLYMPIC COLLEGE

Bremerton, Washington

LEARNING DISABILITIES SERVICES INFORMATION

Disability Support Services began offering services in 1980. Currently the program serves 111 undergraduates with LD. Students diagnosed with ADD/ADHD are eligible for the same services available to students with LD.

Staff: 2 full-time, 2 part-time staff members, including coordinator, Program Manager, tutorial coordinator, instructional technician. Services provided by remediation specialists, tutors, counselors.

Special Fees: No special fees are charged for services to students with LD.

Applications and admissions: Students may begin taking classes any term. *Application deadline:* continuous.

Special policies: The college has written policies regarding grade forgiveness; substitutions and waivers of graduation and degree requirements.

PROGRAM AND SERVICE COMPONENTS

Special preparation or orientation: Orientation offered upon individual arrangement.

Academic advising: Provided by unit staff members, academic advisers. Most students with LD take 8 to 10 quarter credits each term; 12 quarter credits required to maintain full-time status; 6 to 8 quarter credits (half-time), 12 quarter credits (full-time) required to be eligible for financial aid.

Counseling services: Individual counseling, small-group counseling, career counseling, self-advocacy training.

Subject-area tutoring: Offered one-on-one and in small groups by professional teachers, peer tutors, retired teachers. Available in most subjects.

Auxiliary aids: Taped textbooks, tape recorders, calculators, word-processors with spell-check, talking computers, optical character readers.

Auxiliary services: Alternative test arrangements, notetakers, priority registration, advocacy.

GENERAL COLLEGE INFORMATION

State-supported, 2-year, coed. Part of Washington State Board for Community and Technical Colleges. Awards associate degrees. Founded 1946. *Setting:* 27-acre suburban campus with easy access to Seattle. *Total enrollment:* 12,038. *Faculty:* 339 (99 full-time, 84% with terminal degrees, 240 part-time).

Enrollment Profile: 12,038 students: 58% women, 42% men, 52% part-time, 99% state residents, 10% transferred in, 1% international, 70% 25 or older, 2% Native American, 3% Hispanic, 4% black, 10% Asian or Pacific Islander. *Retention:* 60% of 1995 full-time freshmen returned. *Areas of study chosen:* 15% business management and administrative services, 6% computer and information sciences, 4% health professions and related sciences. *Most popular recent majors:* liberal arts/general studies, business economics, nursing.

First-Year Class: 2,400 total. Of the students who applied, 100% were accepted.

Graduation Requirements: 90 credits; 1 college algebra course; 4 natural science courses; computer course (varies by major).

Computers on Campus: 260 computers available on campus for general student use. Computer purchase/lease plans available. A campus-wide network can be accessed from off-campus. Students can contact faculty members and/or advisers through e-mail. Computers for student use in computer center, computer labs, learning resource center provide access to the Internet/World Wide Web. Staffed computer lab on campus provides training in use of computers, software. *Academic computing expenditure 1995–96:* $590,753.

EXPENSES

Expenses for 1997–98: State resident tuition: $1458 full-time, $48.60 per credit part-time. Nonresident tuition: $5733 full-time, $191.10 per credit part-time. Part-time mandatory fees: $15 per quarter. Full-time mandatory fees: $45.

LD Services Contact: Ms. Anna Hoey-Dorsey, Program Manager, Olympic College, 16th and Chester, Bremerton, WA 98337-1699, 360-478-4607. Fax: 360-792-6058.

OUR LADY OF THE LAKE COLLEGE

Baton Rouge, Louisiana

LEARNING DISABILITIES SERVICES INFORMATION

Counseling Services began offering services in 1994. Currently the program serves 25 undergraduates with LD. Students diagnosed with ADD/ADHD are eligible for the same services available to students with LD.

Staff: 1 full-time staff member (director). Services provided by tutors, counselor, diagnostic specialist.

Special Fees: No special fees are charged for services to students with LD.

Applications and admissions: *Required:* high school transcript, courses completed, personal interview, psychoeducational report completed within 5 years; *recommended:* high school grade point average, IEP (Individualized Education Program), untimed or extended time ACT, letters of recommendation. Students may begin taking classes in fall, spring, or summer. *Application deadline:* 8/25 (fall term), 1/9 (spring term).

Special policies: The college has written policies regarding grade forgiveness; substitutions and waivers of admissions requirements.

PROGRAM AND SERVICE COMPONENTS

Special preparation or orientation: Required orientation held before registration.

Diagnostic testing: Intelligence, reading, math, spelling, handwriting, written language, motor abilities, perceptual skills, study skills, personality, social skills, psychoneurology, learning strategies.

Academic advising: Provided by unit staff members, academic advisers. Students with LD may take up to 15 credit hours each term; most take 7 credit hours; 9 credit hours (12 for General Studies program) required to maintain full-time status; 6 credit hours required to be eligible for financial aid.

Counseling services: Individual counseling, small-group counseling, career counseling, self-advocacy training.

Basic skills remediation: Offered in small groups by regular teachers; computer-aided instruction also offered. Available in reading, math, spelling, written language, learning strategies, study skills, time management, social skills, computer skills.

Subject-area tutoring: Offered one-on-one by professional teachers, peer tutors. Available in all subjects.

Special courses: College survival skills, reading, communication skills, composition, learning strategies, word processing, Internet use, time management, math, study skills, career planning, stress management, health and nutrition, social relationships. Some offered for credit; some enter into overall grade point average.

Auxiliary aids: Tape recorders, typewriters, word-processors with spell-check, personal computers.

Auxiliary services: Alternative test arrangements, notetakers, advocacy, priority seating.

GENERAL COLLEGE INFORMATION

Independent Roman Catholic, 2-year, coed. Awards associate degrees. Founded 1990. *Setting:* 5-acre suburban campus with easy access to New Orleans. *Total enrollment:* 869. *Faculty:* 50 (34 full-time, 18% with terminal degrees, 16 part-time); student–undergrad faculty ratio is 25:1.

Enrollment Profile: 869 students from 3 states and territories. 84% women, 16% men, 66% part-time, 99% state residents, 0% international, 61% 25 or older, 1% Native American, 1% Hispanic, 12% black, 1% Asian or Pacific Islander. *Areas of study chosen:* 100% health professions and related sciences. *Most popular recent majors:* nursing, operating room technology, radiological technology.

First-Year Class: 218 total. Of the students who applied, 100% were accepted, 80% of whom enrolled.
Graduation Requirements: 69 credit hours; 1 college algebra course.
Computers on Campus: 25 computers available on campus for general student use. A campus-wide network can be accessed. Students can contact faculty members and/or advisers through e-mail. Computers for student use in learning resource center provide access to the Internet/World Wide Web. Staffed computer lab on campus provides training in use of computers, software. *Academic computing expenditure 1995–96:* $100,000.

EXPENSES

Expenses for 1997–98: *Application fee:* $25. Tuition: $5440 full-time, $160 per credit hour part-time. Part-time mandatory fees: $60 per semester. Full-time mandatory fees: $120.
LD Services Contact: Dr. Mark D. Viator, Director, Counseling Services, Our Lady of the Lake College, 5345 Brittany Drive, Baton Rouge, LA 70808, 504-768-1700. Fax: 504-768-1726. Email: mviator@ololcollege.cc.la.us.

OWENS COMMUNITY COLLEGE

Toledo, Ohio

LEARNING DISABILITIES SERVICES INFORMATION

Disability Resource Center began offering services in 1985. Currently the program serves 105 undergraduates with LD. Students diagnosed with ADD/ADHD are eligible for the same services available to students with LD, as well as distraction-free testing environment.
Staff: 2 full-time, 1 part-time staff members, including coordinator.
Special Fees: No special fees are charged for services to students with LD.
Applications and admissions: *Required:* high school transcript; *recommended:* high school IEP (Individualized Education Program), psychoeducational report. Students may begin taking classes in fall, spring, or summer. *Application deadline:* continuous.

PROGRAM AND SERVICE COMPONENTS

Special preparation or orientation: Optional orientation offered before registration and during registration.
Diagnostic testing: Intelligence, reading, math, spelling, written language, perceptual skills, study skills, personality, social skills, learning strategies.
Academic advising: Provided by academic advisers. Most students with LD take 12 semester hours each term; 12 semester hours required to maintain full-time status; source of aid determines number of semester hours required to be eligible for financial aid.
Counseling services: Individual counseling, small-group counseling, career counseling.
Basic skills remediation: Offered in small groups and in class-size groups by regular teachers. Available in reading, math, spelling, written language, learning strategies, study skills, time management.
Subject-area tutoring: Offered one-on-one and in small groups by professional teachers, peer tutors. Available in most subjects.
Special courses: College survival skills, reading, vocabulary development, learning strategies, time management, math, typing, personal psychology, study skills, career planning. All offered for credit; most enter into overall grade point average.
Auxiliary aids: Taped textbooks, typewriters, personal computers.
Auxiliary services: Alternative test arrangements, notetakers, advocacy.

GENERAL COLLEGE INFORMATION

State-supported, 2-year, coed. Part of Owens Community College System. Awards associate degrees. Founded 1966. *Setting:* 100-acre suburban campus. *Total enrollment:* 10,432. *Faculty:* 622 (120 full-time, 15% with terminal degrees, 502 part-time).
Enrollment Profile: 10,432 students from 2 states and territories, 2 other countries. 49% women, 51% men, 69% part-time, 98% state residents, 9% transferred in, 1% international, 54% 25 or older, 1% Native American, 4% Hispanic, 9% black, 1% Asian or Pacific Islander. *Areas of study chosen:* 33% business management and administrative services, 26% health professions and related sciences, 23% engineering and applied sciences, 17% liberal arts/general studies, 1% agriculture. *Most popular recent majors:* nursing, business administration/commerce/management.
First-Year Class: 3,166 total; 4,717 applied, 100% were accepted, 67% of whom enrolled. 5% from top 10% of their high school class, 10% from top quarter, 50% from top half.
Graduation Requirements: 65 semester hours; computer course; internship (some majors).
Computers on Campus: 200 computers available on campus for general student use. A campus-wide network can be accessed. Students can contact faculty members and/or advisers through e-mail. Computers for student use in computer center, computer labs, learning resource center, classrooms, library. Staffed computer lab on campus provides training in use of computers, software.

EXPENSES

Expenses for 1997–98: State resident tuition: $1896 full-time, $79 per semester hour part-time. Nonresident tuition: $3552 full-time, $148 per semester hour part-time. Part-time mandatory fees: $10 per semester. Full-time mandatory fees: $20.
LD Services Contact: Ms. Debra Sanchez, Coordinator of Disability Resource Services, Owens Community College, PO Box 10000, Toledo, OH 43699-1947, 419-661-7504.

OXNARD COLLEGE

Oxnard, California

LEARNING DISABILITIES SERVICES INFORMATION

Disabled Students Programs and Services began offering services in 1978. Currently the program serves 210 undergraduates with LD. Students diagnosed with ADD/ADHD are eligible for the same services available to students with LD.
Staff: 5 full-time, 6 part-time staff members, including coordinator, LD specialist, job developer/instructor, ACT specialist, adaptive physical education instructor. Services provided by counselor, diagnostic specialist, support services specialist, LD technician, test proctor, ASL interpreter.
Special Fees: $6.50 for diagnostic testing.
Applications and admissions: *Recommended:* high school transcript, personal interview, psychoeducational report, California Assessment System for Adults with Learning Disabilities. Students may begin taking classes in fall, spring, or summer. *Application deadline:* continuous.
Special policies: The college has written policies regarding substitutions and waivers of graduation requirements.

PROGRAM AND SERVICE COMPONENTS

Special preparation or orientation: Required orientation held during registration.
Diagnostic testing: Intelligence, reading, math, spelling, handwriting, written language, perceptual skills, study skills, social skills.
Academic advising: Provided by unit staff members. Students with LD may take up to 18 units each term; most take 9 to 14 units; 12 units required to maintain full-time status; 6 to 12 units required to be eligible for financial aid.
Counseling services: Individual counseling, career counseling.
Basic skills remediation: Offered in small groups and in class-size groups by LD teachers, regular teachers, teacher trainees; computer-aided instruction also offered. Available in reading, math, spelling, written language, learning strategies, study skills, time management, social skills.
Subject-area tutoring: Offered one-on-one and in small groups by professional teachers, peer tutors. Available in most subjects.
Special courses: Reading, vocabulary development, communication skills, composition, learning strategies, word processing, math, typing, personal psychology, career planning. All offered for credit; most enter into overall grade point average.
Auxiliary aids: Taped textbooks, tape recorders, calculators, typewriters, word-processors with spell-check, personal computers, electronic dictionary, Phonic Ears, Arkenstone Reader.
Auxiliary services: Alternative test arrangements, notetakers, priority registration, advocacy.

GENERAL COLLEGE INFORMATION

County-supported, 2-year, coed. Part of Ventura County Community College District System. Awards associate degrees. Founded 1975. *Setting:* 119-acre urban campus. *Total enrollment:* 5,073. *Faculty:* 288 (79 full-time, 209 part-time).
Enrollment Profile: 5,073 students from 10 states and territories, 11 other countries. 53% women, 47% men, 79% part-time, 98% state residents, 18% transferred in, 1% international, 62% 25 or older, 1% Native American, 37% Hispanic, 5% black, 12% Asian or Pacific Islander.
First-Year Class: Of the students who applied, 100% were accepted, 65% of whom enrolled.

Oxnard College (continued)

Graduation Requirements: 60 units; math/science requirements vary according to program; computer course for most majors.
Computers on Campus: 116 computers available on campus for general student use. Computers for student use in computer center, classrooms.

EXPENSES AND FINANCIAL AID

Expenses for 1997–98: *Application fee:* $10. State resident tuition: $0 full-time. Nonresident tuition: $3420 full-time, $114 per unit part-time. Part-time mandatory fees per semester range from $23 to $153. Full-time mandatory fees: $410.
Financial aid specifically for students with LD: Scholarship: Special Education Scholarship.
LD Services Contact: Ms. Carole A. Frick, Learning Disabilities Specialist, Oxnard College, 4000 South Rose Avenue, Oxnard, CA 93033-6699, 805-986-5830. Fax: 805-986-5806.

PALOMAR COLLEGE

San Marcos, California

LEARNING DISABILITIES SERVICES INFORMATION

Disabled Student Programs and Services (DSP&S) began offering services in 1976. Currently the program serves 150 to 200 undergraduates with LD. Students diagnosed with ADD/ADHD are eligible for the same services available to students with LD.
Staff: 4 full-time, 4 part-time staff members, including director, LD specialist. Services provided by counselors, LD instructor, adaptive computer specialist.
Special Fees: No special fees are charged for services to students with LD.
Applications and admissions: *Recommended:* psychoeducational report completed within 3 years. Students may begin taking classes in fall, spring, or summer. *Application deadline:* continuous.
Special policies: The college has written policies regarding grade forgiveness; substitutions and waivers of graduation and degree requirements.

PROGRAM AND SERVICE COMPONENTS

Diagnostic testing: Intelligence, reading, math, written language, learning strategies.
Academic advising: Provided by unit staff members. Students with LD may take up to as many units as an individual can handle each term; most take 9 to 12 units; 12 units (fewer with waiver) required to maintain full-time status; 12 units (full-time) required to be eligible for financial aid.
Counseling services: Individual counseling, small-group counseling, career counseling, self-advocacy training.
Basic skills remediation: Offered in class-size groups by LD teachers. Available in math, spoken language, written language, learning strategies.
Subject-area tutoring: Offered one-on-one, in small groups, and in class-size groups by campus tutoring center staff. Available in most subjects.
Special courses: College survival skills, composition, learning strategies, word processing, time management, math, study skills, career planning. All offered for credit; none enter into overall grade point average.
Auxiliary aids: Taped textbooks, tape recorders, calculators, word-processors with spell-check, personal computers, talking computers, optical character readers, carbonless notepaper.
Auxiliary services: Alternative test arrangements, notetakers, priority registration.

GENERAL COLLEGE INFORMATION

State and locally supported, 2-year, coed. Part of California Community Colleges System. Awards associate degrees. Founded 1946. *Setting:* 156-acre suburban campus with easy access to San Diego. *Total enrollment:* 24,013. *Faculty:* 1,097 (307 full-time, 790 part-time); student–undergrad faculty ratio is 25:1.
Enrollment Profile: 24,013 students: 54% women, 46% men, 62% part-time, 89% state residents, 10% transferred in, 6% international, 3% 25 or older, 1% Native American, 19% Hispanic, 3% black, 4% Asian or Pacific Islander. *Retention:* 46% of 1995 full-time freshmen returned. *Most popular recent majors:* liberal arts/general studies, accounting.
First-Year Class: 5,622 total; 10,000 applied, 100% were accepted, 47% of whom enrolled.
Graduation Requirements: 60 units; internship (some majors).
Computers on Campus: 922 computers available on campus for general student use. Computer purchase/lease plans available. Computers for student use in computer center, computer labs, library provide access to the Internet/World Wide Web. Staffed computer lab on campus provides training in use of computers, software.

EXPENSES

Expenses for 1997–98: State resident tuition: $0 full-time. Nonresident tuition: $3540 full-time, $118 per unit part-time. Part-time mandatory fees per semester range from $24 to $154. Full-time mandatory fees: $412.
LD Services Contact: Ms. Suzann M. Norton, Associate Professor/LD Specialist, Palomar College, 1140 West Mission Avenue, San Marcos, CA 92069-1487, 619-744-1150 Ext. 2707. Fax: 619-761-3509.

PARIS JUNIOR COLLEGE

Paris, Texas

LEARNING DISABILITIES SERVICES INFORMATION

Student Development Center/Special Services began offering services in 1992. Currently the program serves 20 undergraduates with LD. Students diagnosed with ADD/ADHD are eligible for the same services available to students with LD.
Staff: 1 part-time staff member (director). Services provided by remediation specialists, tutors, counselors.
Special Fees: No special fees are charged for services to students with LD.
Applications and admissions: *Required:* high school transcript, IEP (Individualized Education Program), personal interview, psychoeducational report. Students may begin taking classes in fall, spring, or summer. *Application deadline:* continuous.

PROGRAM AND SERVICE COMPONENTS

Academic advising: Provided by unit staff members, academic advisers. Most students with LD take 12 semester hours each term; 12 semester hours required to maintain full-time status and be eligible for financial aid.
Counseling services: Individual counseling, career counseling.
Subject-area tutoring: Offered one-on-one and in small groups by peer tutors. Available in most subjects.
Auxiliary aids: Taped textbooks, tape recorders, calculators, typewriters, word-processors with spell-check.
Auxiliary services: Alternative test arrangements, notetakers, priority registration.

GENERAL COLLEGE INFORMATION

State and locally supported, 2-year, coed. Part of Texas Higher Education Coordinating Board. Awards associate degrees. Founded 1924. *Setting:* 54-acre rural campus. *Total enrollment:* 2,450. *Faculty:* 117 (89 full-time, 28 part-time); student–undergrad faculty ratio is 20:1.
Enrollment Profile: 2,450 students from 16 states and territories, 9 other countries. 60% women, 40% men, 50% part-time, 95% state residents, 1% transferred in, 1% international, 41% 25 or older, 1% Native American, 1% Hispanic, 12% black, 1% Asian or Pacific Islander. *Most popular recent majors:* nursing, jewelry and metalsmithing, liberal arts/general studies.
First-Year Class: 1,680 total. Of the students who applied, 100% were accepted.
Graduation Requirements: 64 semester hours; 6 semester hours of lab science.
Computers on Campus: 82 computers available on campus for general student use. Computers for student use in computer center, library. Staffed computer lab on campus provides training in use of computers, software.

EXPENSES

Expenses for 1996–97: Area resident tuition: $672 full-time. State resident tuition: $1056 full-time. Nonresident tuition: $1920 full-time. Part-time tuition per semester ranges from $52 to $231 for area residents, $80 to $363 for state residents, $252 to $660 for nonresidents. Part-time mandatory fees per semester range from $44 to $84. Oklahoma residents pay state resident tuition rates. Full-time mandatory fees: $238. College room and board: $2678 (minimum).

LD Services Contact: Ms. Barbara O. Thomas, Director of Student Development, Paris Junior College, 2400 Clarksville Street, Paris, TX 75460, 903-782-0434. Fax: 903-782-0370.

PASADENA CITY COLLEGE

Pasadena, California

LEARNING DISABILITIES SERVICES INFORMATION

Disabled Student Programs and Services, Learning Disabilities began offering services in 1976. Currently the program serves 450 undergraduates with LD. Students diagnosed with ADD/ADHD are eligible for the same services available to students with LD, as well as referrals to doctors, CHADD groups, psychological services for counseling.
Staff: 3 full-time, 22 part-time staff members, including Teacher Specialist. Services provided by tutors, counselor, interns, program adviser.
Special Fees: No special fees are charged for services to students with LD.
Applications and admissions: *Required:* high school transcript, courses completed, psychoeducational report completed within 3 years; *recommended:* high school grade point average. Students may begin taking classes any term. *Application deadline:* continuous.

PROGRAM AND SERVICE COMPONENTS

Special preparation or orientation: Optional orientation offered before registration and individually by special arrangement after eligibility is verified.
Diagnostic testing: Intelligence, reading, math, spelling, handwriting, spoken language, written language, perceptual skills, study skills, speech, hearing, learning strategies.
Academic advising: Provided by unit staff members, academic advisers. Most students with LD take 6 to 9 units each term; 12 units required to maintain full-time status; 6 units required to be eligible for financial aid.
Counseling services: Individual counseling, small-group counseling, career counseling, self-advocacy training.
Basic skills remediation: Offered one-on-one and in class-size groups by regular teachers, teacher trainees, instructional aides; computer-aided instruction also offered. Available in reading, math, spelling, spoken language, written language, learning strategies, study skills, time management, speech, computer skills.
Subject-area tutoring: Offered in small groups by peer tutors. Available in most subjects.
Special courses: College survival skills, communication skills, learning strategies, word processing, personal psychology, study skills, career planning, computer-assisted instruction. All offered for credit; none enter into overall grade point average.
Auxiliary aids: Taped textbooks, tape recorders, calculators, word-processors with spell-check, talking computers, optical character readers.
Auxiliary services: Alternative test arrangements, priority registration (in some cases).

GENERAL COLLEGE INFORMATION

State and locally supported, 2-year, coed. Part of California Community Colleges System. Awards associate degrees. Founded 1924. *Setting:* 55-acre urban campus with easy access to Los Angeles. *Total enrollment:* 21,673. *Faculty:* 824 (308 full-time, 100% with terminal degrees, 516 part-time); student–undergrad faculty ratio is 27:1.
Enrollment Profile: 21,673 students from 15 states and territories, 50 other countries. 56% women, 44% men, 70% part-time, 95% state residents, 14% transferred in, 3% international, 39% 25 or older, 1% Native American, 33% Hispanic, 8% black, 36% Asian or Pacific Islander. *Most popular recent major:* business administration/commerce/management.
First-Year Class: 4,332 total; 17,600 applied, 98% were accepted, 25% of whom enrolled.
Graduation Requirements: 60 units; internship (some majors).
Computers on Campus: 274 computers available on campus for general student use. Computers for student use in computer center, computer labs, learning resource center, classrooms. Staffed computer lab on campus provides training in use of computers, software.

EXPENSES

Expenses for 1997–98: State resident tuition: $0 full-time. Nonresident tuition: $3510 full-time, $117 per unit part-time. Part-time mandatory fees per semester range from $24 to $154. Full-time mandatory fees: $412.
LD Services Contact: Dr. Emy Lu Weller, Teacher Specialist, Pasadena City College, 1570 East Colorado Boulevard, Pasadena, CA 91106-2003, 818-585-7127. Email: elweller@paccd.cc.ca.us.

PATRICK HENRY COMMUNITY COLLEGE

Martinsville, Virginia

LEARNING DISABILITIES SERVICES INFORMATION

Student Support Services began offering services in 1988. Currently the program serves 35 to 40 undergraduates with LD. Students diagnosed with ADD/ADHD are eligible for the same services available to students with LD.
Staff: 5 full-time, 1 part-time staff members, including director. Services provided by tutors, counselors.
Special Fees: No special fees are charged for services to students with LD.
Applications and admissions: *Recommended:* psychoeducational report completed within 3 years, Comparative Guidance and Placement Program. Students may begin taking classes any term. *Application deadline:* continuous.
Special policies: The college has written policies regarding grade forgiveness.

PROGRAM AND SERVICE COMPONENTS

Diagnostic testing: Reading, spelling, study skills, learning strategies.
Academic advising: Provided by unit staff members, academic advisers. Students with LD may take up to 15 semester hours each term; most take 12 semester hours; 12 semester hours for financial aid (fewer for academic and other purposes) required to maintain full-time status; 12 semester hours required to be eligible for financial aid.
Counseling services: Individual counseling, small-group counseling, career counseling, self-advocacy training.
Basic skills remediation: Offered one-on-one, in small groups, and in class-size groups by LD teachers, regular teachers; computer-aided instruction also offered. Available in reading, math, spelling, written language, learning strategies, study skills, time management, social skills.
Subject-area tutoring: Offered one-on-one and in small groups by professional teachers, peer tutors. Available in most subjects.
Auxiliary aids: Taped textbooks, tape recorders, calculators, typewriters, word-processors with spell-check, personal computers, electronic dictionary.
Auxiliary services: Alternative test arrangements, notetakers, priority registration, advocacy.
Campus support group: A special student organization is available to students with LD.

GENERAL COLLEGE INFORMATION

State-supported, 2-year, coed. Part of Virginia Community College System. Awards associate degrees. Founded 1962. *Setting:* 137-acre rural campus. *Total enrollment:* 2,700. *Faculty:* 113 (38 full-time, 75 part-time).
Enrollment Profile: 2,700 students from 3 states and territories. 60% women, 40% men, 69% part-time, 98% state residents, 7% transferred in, 0% international, 52% 25 or older, 1% Native American, 1% Hispanic, 19% black, 3% Asian or Pacific Islander. *Most popular recent majors:* liberal arts/general studies, business administration/commerce/management, nursing.
First-Year Class: 550 total. Of the students who applied, 100% were accepted, 63% of whom enrolled.
Graduation Requirements: 62 semester hours; 3 semester hours of math; computer course.
Computers on Campus: 100 computers available on campus for general student use. A computer is recommended for some students. A campus-wide network can be accessed. Students can contact faculty members and/or advisers through e-mail. Computers for student use in computer center, library provide access to the Internet/World Wide Web. Staffed computer lab on campus provides training in use of computers, software.

EXPENSES

Expenses for 1997–98: State resident tuition: $1477 full-time, $47.65 per semester hour part-time. Nonresident tuition: $4867 full-time, $157 per semester hour part-time. Part-time mandatory fees: $5 per semester. Full-time mandatory fees: $10.
LD Services Contact: Ms. Angela P. Oliver, Learning Disabilities Specialist, Patrick Henry Community College, PO Box 5311, Martinsville, VA 24115-5311, 540-656-0223. Fax: 540-656-0327.

PAUL SMITH'S COLLEGE OF ARTS AND SCIENCES

Paul Smiths, New York

LEARNING DISABILITIES SERVICES INFORMATION

Center for Accommodative Services began offering services in 1986. Currently the program serves 80 undergraduates with LD. Students diagnosed with ADD/ADHD are eligible for the same services available to students with LD, as well as assistance with medications (in connection with Health Services), information/classes on organizational skills.
Staff: 2 full-time staff members. Services provided by diagnostic specialist, learning specialist.
Special Fees: No special fees are charged for services to students with LD.
Applications and admissions: *Required:* high school transcript, courses completed, extended time SAT I or ACT; *recommended:* high school grade point average, class rank, extracurricular activities, personal interview, letters of recommendation. Students may begin taking classes in fall or spring. *Application deadline:* continuous.
Special policies: The college has written policies regarding substitutions and waivers of admissions, graduation, and degree requirements.

PROGRAM AND SERVICE COMPONENTS

Special preparation or orientation: Optional orientation offered during registration.
Diagnostic testing: Reading, math, spelling, handwriting, spoken language, written language, perceptual skills, study skills, personality, social skills, learning strategies.
Academic advising: Provided by unit staff members, academic advisers. Students with LD may take up to the number of credit hours prescribed by a student's course of study each term; most take 12 to 15 credit hours; 12 credit hours required to maintain full-time status and be eligible for financial aid.
Counseling services: Individual counseling, small-group counseling, career counseling, self-advocacy training.
Subject-area tutoring: Offered one-on-one and in small groups by professional teachers, peer tutors. Available in all subjects.
Special courses: College survival skills, communication skills, learning strategies, word processing, Internet use, time management, study skills, career planning, stress management, social relationships. None offered for credit; none enter into overall grade point average.
Auxiliary aids: Taped textbooks, tape recorders, calculators, word-processors with spell-check, optical character readers.
Auxiliary services: Alternative test arrangements, notetakers, priority registration, advocacy, readers.

GENERAL COLLEGE INFORMATION

Independent, 2-year, coed. Awards associate degrees. Founded 1937. *Setting:* 13,400-acre rural campus. *Endowment:* $7.2 million. *Total enrollment:* 700. *Faculty:* 59 (57 full-time, 10% with terminal degrees, 2 part-time); student–undergrad faculty ratio is 12:1.
Enrollment Profile: 700 students from 31 states and territories, 4 other countries. 30% women, 70% men, 3% part-time, 70% state residents, 6% transferred in, 4% international, 1% 25 or older, 2% Native American, 2% Hispanic, 2% black, 1% Asian or Pacific Islander. *Retention:* 60% of 1995 full-time freshmen returned. *Most popular recent majors:* ecology, hotel and restaurant management, forestry.
First-Year Class: 379 total; 1,270 applied, 83% were accepted, 36% of whom enrolled. 5% from top quarter of their high school class, 35% from top half.
Graduation Requirements: 60 credit hours; 2 semesters each of math and science; computer course for surveying, travel and tourism, hotel and restaurant management majors; internship (some majors).
Computers on Campus: 65 computers available on campus for general student use. Computers for student use in learning resource center. Staffed computer lab on campus.

EXPENSES

Expenses for 1996–97: *Application fee:* $25. Comprehensive fee of $16,130 includes full-time tuition ($11,000 minimum) and college room and board ($4780 minimum). College room only: $2300 (minimum). Part-time tuition: $260 per credit hour. Part-time mandatory fees: $255 per semester. Full-time mandatory fees range from $350 to $1150 according to program. Tuition guaranteed not to increase for student's term of enrollment.

LD Services Contact: Ms. Carol McKillip, Learning Specialist/Diagnostician, Paul Smith's College of Arts and Sciences, Paul Smiths, NY 12970, 518-327-6425. Fax: 518-327-6369. Email: mckillc@paulsmiths.edu.

PEIRCE COLLEGE

Philadelphia, Pennsylvania

LEARNING DISABILITIES SERVICES INFORMATION

Perkins Center began offering services in 1984. Currently the program serves 15 undergraduates with LD. Students diagnosed with ADD/ADHD are eligible for the same services available to students with LD.
Staff: 5 full-time, 10 part-time staff members, including director, coordinator. Services provided by remediation specialists, tutors, counselors.
Special Fees: No special fees are charged for services to students with LD.
Applications and admissions: *Required:* high school transcript; *recommended:* untimed ACT ASSET. Students may begin taking classes any term. *Application deadline:* continuous.

PROGRAM AND SERVICE COMPONENTS

Academic advising: Provided by unit staff members, academic advisers. Students with LD may take up to 15 credits each term; most take 12 credits; 12 credits required to maintain full-time status; 6 credits (part-time), 12 credits (full-time) required to be eligible for financial aid.
Counseling services: Individual counseling, small-group counseling, career counseling, time management and study skills workshops.
Basic skills remediation: Offered one-on-one, in small groups, and in class-size groups by regular teachers, teacher trainees, learning specialists; computer-aided instruction also offered. Available in reading, math, spelling, handwriting, spoken language, written language, learning strategies, study skills, time management, social skills, computer skills.
Subject-area tutoring: Offered one-on-one, in small groups, and in class-size groups by professional teachers, peer tutors, learning specialists, professional tutors. Available in all subjects.
Special courses: College survival skills, reading, vocabulary development, communication skills, composition, learning strategies, word processing, Internet use, time management, math, typing, personal psychology, study skills, career planning. Some offered for credit; some enter into overall grade point average.
Auxiliary aids: Tape recorders, calculators, typewriters, word-processors with spell-check, personal computers, CSR computer tutorial program.
Auxiliary services: Alternative test arrangements, notetakers, advocacy, IEP for remedial classes.

GENERAL COLLEGE INFORMATION

Independent, 2-year, coed. Awards associate degrees. Founded 1865. *Setting:* 2-acre urban campus. *Total enrollment:* 1,200. *Faculty:* 123 (25 full-time, 16% with terminal degrees, 98 part-time); student–undergrad faculty ratio is 19:1.
Enrollment Profile: 1,200 students from 9 states and territories, 13 other countries. 76% women, 24% men, 32% part-time, 81% state residents, 3% live on campus, 5% transferred in, 3% international, 35% 25 or older, 1% Native American, 3% Hispanic, 65% black, 2% Asian or Pacific Islander. *Retention:* 81% of 1995 full-time freshmen returned. *Areas of study chosen:* 49% business management and administrative services, 19% computer and information sciences. *Most popular recent majors:* business administration/commerce/management, paralegal studies, computer information systems.
First-Year Class: 510 total; 780 applied, 78% were accepted, 84% of whom enrolled.
Graduation Requirements: 60 credits; 1 math course; computer course; internship (some majors).
Computers on Campus: 225 computers available on campus for general student use. A campus-wide network can be accessed from off-campus. Students can contact faculty members and/or advisers through e-mail. Computers for student use in computer center, computer labs, learning resource center, classrooms, library provide access to the Internet/World Wide Web, on-campus e-mail addresses. Staffed computer lab on campus provides training in use of computers, software.

EXPENSES

Expenses for 1996–97: *Application fee:* $20. Tuition: $6920 full-time. Part-time mandatory fees per semester range from $39 to $102. Part-time

tuition: $246 per credit for day classes, $193 per credit for evening classes. Full-time mandatory fees: $192. College room only: $3675.
LD Services Contact: Pascale Marko-Dzambela, Special Populations Coordinator/ESL Facilitator, Peirce College, 1420 Pine Street, Philadelphia, PA 19102-4603, 215-545-6400 Ext. 326. Fax: 215-546-5996.

PENNSYLVANIA COLLEGE OF TECHNOLOGY

Williamsport, Pennsylvania

LEARNING DISABILITIES SERVICES INFORMATION

Academic Support Services began offering services in 1977. Currently the program serves 315 undergraduates with LD. Students diagnosed with ADD/ADHD are eligible for the same services available to students with LD.
Staff: 2 full-time, 2 part-time staff members, including coordinator. Services provided by counselors, LD specialist, accommodations clerk.
Special Fees: No special fees are charged for services to students with LD.
Applications and admissions: *Required:* high school transcript, psychoeducational report completed within 4 years; *recommended:* high school IEP (Individualized Education Program), untimed SAT I. Students may begin taking classes any term. *Application deadline:* continuous.

PROGRAM AND SERVICE COMPONENTS

Special preparation or orientation: Optional orientation offered before registration.
Academic advising: Provided by unit staff members, academic advisers. Students with LD may take up to 18 credits each term; most take 12 to 15 credits; 12 credits required to maintain full-time status; 6 to 9 credits required to be eligible for financial aid.
Counseling services: Individual counseling, career counseling, self-advocacy training.
Special courses: Learning strategies. All offered for credit; all enter into overall grade point average.
Auxiliary aids: Tape recorders, calculators, optical character readers.
Auxiliary services: Alternative test arrangements, notetakers, advocacy.

GENERAL COLLEGE INFORMATION

State-related, primarily 2-year, coed. Part of Pennsylvania State University. Awards associate, bachelor's degrees. Founded 1965. *Setting:* 899-acre small-town campus. *Total enrollment:* 4,744. *Faculty:* 350 (222 full-time, 77% with terminal degrees, 128 part-time); student–undergrad faculty ratio is 17:1.
Enrollment Profile: 4,744 students from 13 states and territories, 6 other countries. 41% women, 59% men, 22% part-time, 96% state residents, 6% transferred in, 1% international, 33% 25 or older, 1% Native American, 1% Hispanic, 3% black, 1% Asian or Pacific Islander. *Retention:* 65% of 1995 full-time freshmen returned. *Areas of study chosen:* 16% health professions and related sciences, 13% engineering and applied sciences, 7% business management and administrative services, 5% natural resource sciences, 3% computer and information sciences, 3% liberal arts/general studies, 2% architecture, 1% biological and life sciences, 1% communications and journalism, 1% education, 1% military science. *Most popular recent majors:* heating/refrigeration/air conditioning, automotive technologies, nursing.
First-Year Class: 2,078 total; 2,079 applied, 90% were accepted, 52% of whom enrolled. 5% from top 10% of their high school class, 18% from top quarter, 40% from top half.
Graduation Requirements: 60 credits for associate, 120 credits for bachelor's; math/science requirements vary according to program; computer course (varies by major); internship (some majors).
Computers on Campus: 1,000 computers available on campus for general student use. Computer purchase/lease plans available. Computers for student use in computer center, computer labs, classrooms, library provide access to the Internet/World Wide Web. Staffed computer lab on campus provides training in use of computers, software.

EXPENSES

Expenses for 1996–97: *Application fee:* $35. State resident tuition: $6200 full-time, $208.80 per credit part-time. Nonresident tuition: $7400 full-time, $247.90 per credit part-time. Part-time mandatory fees: $10.20 per credit. Full-time mandatory fees: $306. College room and board: $1400.
LD Services Contact: Ms. Mary Lou Morollo, Coordinator of Services for Students with Learning Disabilities, Pennsylvania College of Technology, One College Avenue, Williamsport, PA 17701-5778, 717-326-3761 Ext. 7429. Fax: 717-321-5539.

PENNSYLVANIA STATE UNIVERSITY MONT ALTO CAMPUS OF THE COMMONWEALTH COLLEGE

Mont Alto, Pennsylvania

LEARNING DISABILITIES SERVICES INFORMATION

Learning Center began offering services in 1988. Currently the program serves 35 undergraduates with LD. Students diagnosed with ADD/ADHD are eligible for the same services available to students with LD.
Staff: 1 full-time, 2 part-time staff members, including director. Services provided by remediation specialists.
Special Fees: No special fees are charged for services to students with LD.
Applications and admissions: *Required:* high school transcript, grade point average, class rank, courses completed, untimed SAT I, psychoeducational report completed within 3 years; *recommended:* high school extracurricular activities, extended time SAT I, autobiographical statement, letters of recommendation. Students may begin taking classes in fall, spring, or summer. *Application deadline:* continuous.

PROGRAM AND SERVICE COMPONENTS

Special preparation or orientation: Optional orientation offered after classes begin.
Academic advising: Provided by unit staff members, academic advisers. Most students with LD take 12 to 15 credits each term; 12 credits required to maintain full-time status; 26 credits per year required to be eligible for financial aid.
Counseling services: Individual counseling, small-group counseling, career counseling.
Basic skills remediation: Offered one-on-one, in small groups, and in class-size groups by professional and peer tutors. Available in reading, math, spelling, written language, learning strategies, study skills, time management.
Subject-area tutoring: Offered one-on-one, in small groups, and in class-size groups by professional teachers, peer tutors. Available in some subjects.
Special courses: College survival skills, reading, vocabulary development, communication skills, composition, learning strategies, word processing, Internet use, time management, math, typing, study skills, career planning, stress management. Some offered for credit; some enter into overall grade point average.
Auxiliary aids: Taped textbooks, word-processors with spell-check.
Auxiliary services: Alternative test arrangements, notetakers, priority registration, advocacy.
Campus support group: A special student organization is available to students with LD.

GENERAL COLLEGE INFORMATION

State-related, 2-year, coed. Part of Pennsylvania State University. Awards associate degrees (also offers up to 2 years of most bachelor's degree programs offered at University Park campus; of students entering the associate degree program, 25% complete the degree and an additional 35% change to a bachelor's degree program). Founded 1929. *Setting:* 62-acre small-town campus. *Research spending 1995–96:* $18,732. *Total enrollment:* 1,205. *Faculty:* 71 (50 full-time, 81% with terminal degrees, 21 part-time); student–undergrad faculty ratio is 19:1.
Enrollment Profile: 1,134 students from 17 states and territories. 52% women, 48% men, 24% part-time, 88% state residents, 39% live on campus, 4% transferred in, 0% international, 16% 25 or older, 0% Native American, 1% Hispanic, 3% black, 2% Asian or Pacific Islander. *Retention:* 76% of 1995 full-time freshmen returned. *Areas of study chosen:* 20% liberal arts/general studies, 19% engineering and applied sciences, 15% business management and administrative services, 13% interdisciplinary studies, 8% education, 8% health professions and related sciences, 4% agriculture, 4% communications and journalism, 2% social sciences, 2% vocational and home economics, 1% computer and information sciences, 1% natural resource sciences, 1% performing arts, 1% physical sciences, 1% psychology.

Pennsylvania State University Mont Alto Campus of the Commonwealth College (continued)

First-Year Class: 371 total; 797 applied, 87% were accepted, 54% of whom enrolled. 8% from top 10% of their high school class, 56% from top quarter, 82% from top half.
Graduation Requirements: 60 credits; computer course for engineering, technology, business, science majors; internship (some majors).
Computers on Campus: 58 computers available on campus for general student use. Computers for student use in computer labs.

EXPENSES

Expenses for 1996–97: *Application fee:* $35. State resident tuition: $5262 full-time, $211 per credit part-time. Nonresident tuition: $8178 full-time, $341 per credit part-time. Part-time mandatory fees per semester range from $33 to $95. Full-time mandatory fees: $190. College room and board: $4170.
LD Services Contact: Mr. Bill Hughes, Division of Undergraduate Studies Coordinator, Pennsylvania State University Mont Alto Campus of the Commonwealth College, Campus Drive, Mont Alto, PA 17237-9703, 717-749-6054. Fax: 717-749-6069.

PENNSYLVANIA STATE UNIVERSITY WILKES-BARRE CAMPUS OF THE COMMONWEALTH COLLEGE

Lehman, Pennsylvania

LEARNING DISABILITIES SERVICES INFORMATION

Learning Support Center began offering services in 1979. Currently the program serves 3 undergraduates with LD. Students diagnosed with ADD/ADHD are eligible for the same services available to students with LD.
Staff: 1 full-time, 2 part-time staff members, including director, assistant director. Services provided by remediation specialists, tutors, counselor, diagnostic specialist.
Special Fees: No special fees are charged for services to students with LD.
Applications and admissions: *Required:* high school transcript, grade point average, courses completed, untimed or extended time SAT I or ACT; *recommended:* high school class rank, extracurricular activities, IEP (Individualized Education Program), personal interview, autobiographical statement, letters of recommendation, psychoeducational report. Students may begin taking classes in fall only. *Application deadline:* continuous.
Special policies: The college has written policies regarding substitutions and waivers of admissions, graduation, and degree requirements.

PROGRAM AND SERVICE COMPONENTS

Diagnostic testing: Intelligence, reading, spelling, written language, learning strategies.
Academic advising: Provided by academic advisers. Most students with LD take 13 credits each term; 13 credits required to maintain full-time status and be eligible for financial aid.
Counseling services: Individual counseling, small-group counseling, career counseling.
Subject-area tutoring: Offered one-on-one, in small groups, and in class-size groups by professional teachers, peer tutors. Available in all subjects.
Auxiliary aids: Taped textbooks, tape recorders, calculators, word-processors with spell-check.
Auxiliary services: Alternative test arrangements, notetakers; other services as determined necessary through needs assessment.

GENERAL COLLEGE INFORMATION

State-related, 2-year, coed. Part of Pennsylvania State University. Awards associate degrees (also offers up to 2 years of most bachelor's degree programs offered at University Park campus; of students entering the associate degree program, 25% complete the degree and an additional 35% change to a bachelor's degree program). Founded 1916. *Setting:* 58-acre rural campus. *Research spending 1995–96:* $51,192. *Total enrollment:* 807. *Faculty:* 80 (35 full-time, 78% with terminal degrees, 45 part-time).
Enrollment Profile: 780 students from 7 states and territories. 34% women, 66% men, 18% part-time, 95% state residents, 4% transferred in, 0% international, 10% 25 or older, 0% Native American, 1% Hispanic, 7% black, 1% Asian or Pacific Islander. *Retention:* 76% of 1995 full-time freshmen returned. *Areas of study chosen:* 20% liberal arts/general studies, 19% engineering and applied sciences, 15% business management and administrative services, 13% interdisciplinary studies, 8% education, 8% health professions and related sciences, 4% agriculture, 4% communications and journalism, 2% social sciences, 2% vocational and home economics, 1% computer and information sciences, 1% natural resource sciences, 1% performing arts, 1% physical sciences, 1% psychology.
First-Year Class: 245 total; 553 applied, 90% were accepted, 49% of whom enrolled. 8% from top 10% of their high school class, 56% from top quarter, 82% from top half.
Graduation Requirements: 60 credits; computer course for engineering, technology, business, science majors; internship (some majors).
Computers on Campus: 150 computers available on campus for general student use. Computers for student use in computer labs.

EXPENSES

Expenses for 1996–97: *Application fee:* $35. State resident tuition: $5262 full-time, $211 per credit part-time. Nonresident tuition: $8178 full-time, $341 per credit part-time. Part-time mandatory fees per semester range from $33 to $95. Full-time mandatory fees: $190.
LD Services Contact: Ms. Patricia G. Cole, Director, Learning Support Services, Pennsylvania State University Wilkes-Barre Campus of the Commonwealth College, PO Box PSU, Lehman, PA 18627, 717-675-9217. Fax: 717-675-8308.

PENSACOLA JUNIOR COLLEGE

Pensacola, Florida

LEARNING DISABILITIES SERVICES INFORMATION

Disabled Student Services began offering services in 1978. Currently the program serves 154 undergraduates with LD. Students diagnosed with ADD/ADHD are eligible for the same services available to students with LD.
Staff: 3 full-time, 6 part-time staff members, including director, coordinator, interpreter. Services provided by tutors, counselors.
Special Fees: No special fees are charged for services to students with LD.
Applications and admissions: *Recommended:* high school transcript, IEP (Individualized Education Program), extended time ACT, psychoeducational report completed within 5 years. Students may begin taking classes any term. *Application deadline:* continuous.
Special policies: The college has written policies regarding substitutions and waivers of admissions, graduation, and degree requirements.

PROGRAM AND SERVICE COMPONENTS

Special preparation or orientation: Optional summer program offered prior to entering college. Optional orientation offered before registration and during registration.
Diagnostic testing: Reading, math, spelling, written language, perceptual skills, study skills, achievement, cognition.
Academic advising: Provided by unit staff members, academic advisers. Students with LD may take up to 15 semester hours each term; most take 12 semester hours; 12 semester hours required to maintain full-time status and be eligible for financial aid.
Counseling services: Individual counseling, small-group counseling, career counseling.
Basic skills remediation: Offered one-on-one, in small groups, and in class-size groups by regular teachers, peer teachers. Available in reading, math, spelling, written language, study skills, time management, social skills.
Subject-area tutoring: Offered one-on-one and in small groups by professional teachers, peer tutors. Available in most subjects.
Auxiliary aids: Taped textbooks, tape recorders, calculators, typewriters, word-processors with spell-check, personal computers, talking computers, optical character readers.
Auxiliary services: Alternative test arrangements, notetakers, priority registration, advocacy, readers, interpreters.
Campus support group: A special student organization is available to students with LD.

GENERAL COLLEGE INFORMATION

State-supported, 2-year, coed. Awards associate degrees. Founded 1948. *Setting:* 160-acre suburban campus. *Endowment:* $852,309. *Total enrollment:* 12,000. *Faculty:* 819 (207 full-time, 26% with terminal degrees, 612 part-time).

Enrollment Profile: 12,000 students from 37 states and territories. 60% women, 40% men, 71% part-time, 98% state residents, 10% transferred in, 50% 25 or older, 1% Native American, 1% Hispanic, 13% black, 3% Asian or Pacific Islander.
First-Year Class: Of the students who applied, 100% were accepted.
Graduation Requirements: 60 semester hours; 6 semester hours of math; 10 semester hours of science.
Computers on Campus: 175 computers available on campus for general student use. A campus-wide network can be accessed. Students can contact faculty members and/or advisers through e-mail. Computers for student use in computer labs, library, business education departmental lab provide access to the Internet/World Wide Web, on-campus e-mail addresses. Staffed computer lab on campus provides training in use of computers, software. *Academic computing expenditure 1995–96:* $600,000.

EXPENSES

Expenses for 1997–98: *Application fee:* $20. State resident tuition: $1304 full-time, $43.45 per semester hour part-time. Nonresident tuition: $4691 full-time, $156.35 per semester hour part-time.
LD Services Contact: Ms. Linda Sheppard, Coordinator, Disabled Student Services, Pensacola Junior College, 1000 College Boulevard, Pensacola, FL 32504-8998, 904-484-2094 Ext. 1637. Fax: 904-484-1637.

PIEDMONT VIRGINIA COMMUNITY COLLEGE

Charlottesville, Virginia

LEARNING DISABILITIES SERVICES INFORMATION

Office of the Counselor for Special Needs Students began offering services in 1987. Currently the program serves 152 undergraduates with LD. Students diagnosed with ADD/ADHD are eligible for the same services available to students with LD, as well as quiet testing rooms, counseling in various areas.
Staff: 1 full-time staff member (counselor). Services provided by remediation specialists, tutors, counselor, developmental teachers.
Special Fees: No special fees are charged for services to students with LD.
Applications and admissions: *Required:* personal interview, psychoeducational report completed within 5 years; *recommended:* high school transcript. Students may begin taking classes in summer only. *Application deadline:* continuous.

PROGRAM AND SERVICE COMPONENTS

Academic advising: Provided by unit staff members. Students with LD may take up to 18 semester hours each term; most take 10 to 12 semester hours; 12 semester hours required to maintain full-time status; no minimum number of semester hours required to be eligible for financial aid.
Counseling services: Individual counseling, small-group counseling, career counseling, self-advocacy training.
Basic skills remediation: Offered in class-size groups by regular teachers. Available in reading, math, written language.
Subject-area tutoring: Offered one-on-one and in small groups by professional teachers, peer tutors. Available in all subjects.
Auxiliary aids: Taped textbooks, tape recorders, calculators, typewriters, word-processors with spell-check, voice computer, voice calculators, 4-track tape recorders (Recordings for the Blind).
Auxiliary services: Alternative test arrangements, notetakers, priority registration, advocacy, a copy of class notes.
Campus support group: A special student organization is available to students with LD.

GENERAL COLLEGE INFORMATION

State-supported, 2-year, coed. Part of Virginia Community College System. Awards associate degrees. Founded 1972. *Setting:* 100-acre suburban campus with easy access to Richmond. *Total enrollment:* 4,436. *Faculty:* 262 (71 full-time, 191 part-time).
Enrollment Profile: 4,436 students from 11 states and territories, 18 other countries. 61% women, 39% men, 81% part-time, 96% state residents, 2% transferred in, 60% 25 or older, 1% Hispanic, 11% black, 1% Asian or Pacific Islander. *Most popular recent majors:* nursing, business administration/commerce/management, liberal arts/general studies.
First-Year Class: 845 total. Of the students who applied, 100% were accepted, 98% of whom enrolled. 80% from top half of their high school class.
Graduation Requirements: 67 semester hours; 1 math course; computer course.
Computers on Campus: 110 computers available on campus for general student use. Computers for student use in computer center.

EXPENSES

Expenses for 1996–97: State resident tuition: $1620 full-time, $47.65 per semester hour part-time. Nonresident tuition: $5338 full-time, $157 per semester hour part-time. Part-time mandatory fees per semester range from $3 to $6. Full-time mandatory fees: $12.
LD Services Contact: Ms. Marlene Herakovich, Counselor, Piedmont Virginia Community College, 501 College Drive, Charlottesville, VA 22902-8714, 804-961-5281. Fax: 804-971-8232. Email: mvh2d@jade.pvcc.cc.va.us.

PIMA COMMUNITY COLLEGE

Tucson, Arizona

LEARNING DISABILITIES SERVICES INFORMATION

Disabled Student Resources began offering services in 1980. Students diagnosed with ADD/ADHD are eligible for the same services available to students with LD.
Staff: 6 full-time staff members, including services coordinator, support staff. Services provided by tutors, diagnostic specialists, LD specialists.
Special Fees: No special fees are charged for services to students with LD.
Applications and admissions: Open admissions. Students may begin taking classes in fall, spring, or summer. *Application deadline:* continuous.
Special policies: The college has written policies regarding grade forgiveness; substitutions and waivers of graduation and degree requirements.

PROGRAM AND SERVICE COMPONENTS

Special preparation or orientation: Optional orientation offered before registration and individually by special arrangement.
Academic advising: Provided by unit staff members, academic advisers. Students with LD may take up to 12 credit hours each term; most take 9 to 12 credit hours; 9 credit hours required to maintain full-time status; 3 credit hours required to be eligible for financial aid.
Counseling services: Individual counseling, career counseling.
Basic skills remediation: Offered one-on-one and in small groups by tutors. Available in reading, math, spelling, written language, learning strategies, study skills, social skills, word processing.
Special courses: College survival skills, reading, vocabulary development, composition, learning strategies, math, study skills, career planning, spelling. All offered for credit; all enter into overall grade point average.
Auxiliary aids: Taped textbooks, tape recorders, calculators, typewriters, word-processors with spell-check, talking computers, optical character readers.
Auxiliary services: Alternative test arrangements, notetakers, priority registration, advocacy, readers, interpreters, mobility assistance.

GENERAL COLLEGE INFORMATION

State-supported, 2-year, coed. Part of Arizona State Community College System. Awards associate degrees. Founded 1966. *Setting:* 350-acre urban campus. *Endowment:* $460,000. *Educational spending 1995–96:* $1902 per undergrad. *Total enrollment:* 27,960. *Faculty:* 1,567 (319 full-time, 85% with terminal degrees, 1,248 part-time); student–undergrad faculty ratio is 20:1.
Enrollment Profile: 27,960 students from 48 states and territories, 80 other countries. 55% women, 45% men, 74% part-time, 94% state residents, 11% transferred in, 2% international, 50% 25 or older, 3% Native American, 26% Hispanic, 4% black, 4% Asian or Pacific Islander. *Most popular recent majors:* liberal arts/general studies, business administration/commerce/management, education.
First-Year Class: 4,924 total; 4,924 applied, 100% were accepted, 100% of whom enrolled. 6% from top 10% of their high school class, 36% from top quarter, 70% from top half.
Graduation Requirements: 60 credit hours; math/science requirements vary according to program.
Computers on Campus: 1,500 computers available on campus for general student use. Computer purchase/lease plans available. Comput-

Pima Community College (continued)

ers for student use in computer labs, classrooms. Staffed computer lab on campus provides training in use of computers, software. *Academic computing expenditure 1995–96:* $88,285.

EXPENSES AND FINANCIAL AID

Expenses for 1996–97: State resident tuition: $930 full-time, $31 per credit hour part-time. Nonresident tuition: $4500 full-time. Part-time mandatory fees: $5 per semester. Nonresident part-time tuition: $51 per credit hour for 1 to 6 credit hours, $150 per credit hour for 7 or more credit hours. Full-time mandatory fees: $10.
Financial aid specifically for students with LD: Scholarships.
LD Services Contact: Dean of Student Development, Pima Community College, 4907 East Broadway, Tucson, AZ 85709, 520-884-6939.

PITTSBURGH TECHNICAL INSTITUTE

Pittsburgh, Pennsylvania

LEARNING DISABILITIES SERVICES INFORMATION

Student Development Office currently serves 12 undergraduates with LD. Students diagnosed with ADD/ADHD are not eligible for the same services available to students with LD.
Staff: 3 full-time staff members, including director. Services provided by remediation specialist, tutors, diagnostic specialist.
Special Fees: No special fees are charged for services to students with LD.
Applications and admissions: *Required:* high school transcript, grade point average, class rank, courses completed, personal interview; *recommended:* high school IEP (Individualized Education Program), extended time SAT I, letters of recommendation, psychoeducational report. Students may begin taking classes in fall, winter, or summer. *Application deadline:* continuous.

PROGRAM AND SERVICE COMPONENTS

Special preparation or orientation: Required summer program offered prior to entering college. Required orientation held before registration.
Diagnostic testing: Reading, math, spelling, handwriting, spoken language, written language, study skills, social skills, learning strategies.
Academic advising: Provided by unit staff members. Students with LD may take up to 12 credit hours each term; most take 12 credit hours; 12 credit hours required to maintain full-time status and be eligible for financial aid.
Counseling services: Individual counseling, career counseling.
Basic skills remediation: Offered by LD teachers, regular teachers; computer-aided instruction also offered. Available in reading, math, spelling, written language, learning strategies, study skills, time management, social skills, computer skills.
Subject-area tutoring: Offered one-on-one and in small groups by professional teachers, peer tutors. Available in all subjects.
Special courses: Communication skills, study skills. None offered for credit.
Auxiliary aids: Calculators, typewriters, word-processors with spell-check, personal computers, opticon reader.
Auxiliary services: Alternative test arrangements.

GENERAL COLLEGE INFORMATION

Proprietary, 2-year, coed. Awards associate degrees (also offers courses at 1 branch campus with significant enrollment reflected in profile). Founded 1946. *Setting:* urban campus. *Total enrollment:* 833. *Faculty:* 45 (42 full-time, 100% with terminal degrees, 3 part-time).
Enrollment Profile: 833 students from 5 states and territories. 20% women, 80% men, 0% part-time, 88% state residents, 7% transferred in, 8% 25 or older, 1% Hispanic, 7% black, 1% Asian or Pacific Islander. *Retention:* 93% of 1995 full-time freshmen returned. *Areas of study chosen:* 90% vocational and home economics, 5% business management and administrative services, 5% computer and information sciences. *Most popular recent majors:* drafting and design, graphic arts, business administration/commerce/management.
First-Year Class: 574 total; 839 applied, 96% were accepted, 71% of whom enrolled. 7% from top 10% of their high school class, 17% from top quarter, 40% from top half.
Graduation Requirements: 98 credit hours; computer course; internship.
Computers on Campus: 160 computers available on campus for general student use. Computer purchase/lease plans available. A campus-wide network can be accessed. Computers for student use in computer center, computer labs, learning resource center, library provide access to the Internet/World Wide Web. Staffed computer lab on campus provides training in use of computers, software.

EXPENSES AND FINANCIAL AID

Expenses for 1997–98: *Application fee:* $40. Tuition per degree program ranges from $23,120 to $26,160. Tuition guaranteed not to increase for student's term of enrollment.
Financial aid specifically for students with LD: loans; work-study.
LD Services Contact: Mr. Robert Havey Jr., Director of Student Development, Pittsburgh Technical Institute, 635 Smithfield Street, Pittsburgh, PA 15222, 412-471-1011 Ext. 246. Fax: 412-471-9014.

PORTLAND COMMUNITY COLLEGE

Portland, Oregon

LEARNING DISABILITIES SERVICES INFORMATION

Office for Students with Disabilities began offering services in 1981. Currently the program serves 210 undergraduates with LD. Students diagnosed with ADD/ADHD are eligible for the same services available to students with LD.
Staff: 3 full-time, 5 part-time staff members, including director, LD specialists. Services provided by tutors, counselors, diagnostic specialists.
Special Fees: No special fees are charged for services to students with LD.
Applications and admissions: *Required:* documentation of LD. Students may begin taking classes any term. *Application deadline:* continuous.
Special policies: The college has written policies regarding substitutions and waivers of graduation and degree requirements.

PROGRAM AND SERVICE COMPONENTS

Special preparation or orientation: Optional orientation offered during registration.
Diagnostic testing: Intelligence, reading, math, spelling, handwriting, spoken language, written language, motor abilities, perceptual skills, study skills, learning strategies.
Academic advising: Provided by unit staff members, academic advisers. Students with LD may take up to 18 credit hours each term; most take 9 to 12 credit hours; 12 credit hours required to maintain full-time status; 6 credit hours required to be eligible for financial aid.
Counseling services: Individual counseling, career counseling, support group (available according to student interest).
Subject-area tutoring: Offered one-on-one by peer tutors. Available in some subjects.
Special courses: Study skills. All offered for credit; all enter into overall grade point average.
Auxiliary aids: Taped textbooks, tape recorders, calculators, typewriters, word-processors with spell-check, personal computers, talking computers, optical character readers.
Auxiliary services: Alternative test arrangements, notetakers, priority registration, advocacy.

GENERAL COLLEGE INFORMATION

State and locally supported, 2-year, coed. Awards associate degrees. Founded 1961. *Setting:* 400-acre urban campus. *Total enrollment:* 27,594. *Faculty:* 1,215 (390 full-time, 825 part-time).
Enrollment Profile: 27,594 students from 20 states and territories, 56 other countries. 56% women, 44% men, 68% part-time, 98% state residents, 1% international, 67% 25 or older, 1% Native American, 5% Hispanic, 4% black, 8% Asian or Pacific Islander. *Most popular recent majors:* science, nursing, radiological technology.
First-Year Class: Of the students who applied, 100% were accepted, 90% of whom enrolled.
Graduation Requirements: 90 credit hours; internship (some majors).
Computers on Campus: 240 computers available on campus for general student use. A campus-wide network can be accessed from off-campus. Students can contact faculty members and/or advisers through e-mail. Computers for student use in computer center, computer labs, learning resource center, library provide access to the Internet/World Wide Web. Staffed computer lab on campus provides training in use of computers, software.

EXPENSES

Estimated Expenses for 1997–98: State resident tuition: $1620 full-time, $36 per credit hour part-time. Nonresident tuition: $5850 full-time, $130 per credit hour part-time.
LD Services Contact: Ms. Carolee Schmeer, Learning Disabilities Specialist, Portland Community College, PO Box 19000, Portland, OR 97280-0990, 503-977-4340. Fax: 503-977-4882.

POTOMAC STATE COLLEGE OF WEST VIRGINIA UNIVERSITY

Keyser, West Virginia

LEARNING DISABILITIES SERVICES INFORMATION

Student Support Services (SSS) began offering services in 1987. Currently the program serves 15 undergraduates with LD. Students diagnosed with ADD/ADHD are eligible for the same services available to students with LD.
Staff: 4 full-time, 4 part-time staff members, including director. Services provided by tutors, counselor, peer tutors.
Special Fees: No special fees are charged for services to students with LD.
Applications and admissions: *Required:* high school transcript, grade point average, courses completed, untimed SAT I or ACT, personal interview, psychoeducational report, completed Student Support Services (SSS) application; *recommended:* high school class rank, IEP (Individualized Education Program), extended time SAT I or ACT. Students may begin taking classes in fall, spring, or summer. *Application deadline:* continuous.
Special policies: The college has written policies regarding grade forgiveness; substitutions and waivers of admissions, graduation, and degree requirements.

PROGRAM AND SERVICE COMPONENTS

Special preparation or orientation: Required orientation held after classes begin and individually in meetings scheduled during first week of classes.
Diagnostic testing: Intelligence, reading, math, written language, motor abilities, perceptual skills, study skills, personality, social skills, learning strategies.
Academic advising: Provided by unit staff members, academic advisers. Most students with LD take 12 to 15 credit hours each term; 12 credit hours required to maintain full-time status; 11 credit hours required to be eligible for financial aid.
Counseling services: Individual counseling, small-group counseling, career counseling.
Basic skills remediation: Offered one-on-one, in small groups, and in class-size groups by regular teachers, professional tutors and peer tutors. Available in reading, math, spelling, written language, learning strategies, study skills, time management.
Subject-area tutoring: Offered one-on-one and in small groups by peer tutors, professional tutors. Available in most subjects.
Auxiliary aids: Taped textbooks, tape recorders, calculators, typewriters, word-processors with spell-check, magnifying sheets.
Auxiliary services: Alternative test arrangements, priority registration, advocacy, oral exams.
Campus support group: A special student organization is available to students with LD.

GENERAL COLLEGE INFORMATION

State-supported, 2-year, coed. Part of University System of West Virginia. Awards associate degrees. Founded 1901. *Setting:* 391-acre small-town campus. *Endowment:* $1 million. *Total enrollment:* 1,108. *Faculty:* 83 (39 full-time, 50% with terminal degrees, 44 part-time); student–undergrad faculty ratio is 19:1.
Enrollment Profile: 1,108 students from 25 states and territories. 49% women, 51% men, 32% part-time, 83% state residents, 35% live on campus, 5% transferred in, 16% 25 or older, 1% Native American, 1% Hispanic, 6% black. *Retention:* 40% of 1995 full-time freshmen returned. *Areas of study chosen:* 40% liberal arts/general studies, 15% business management and administrative services, 13% biological and life sciences, 10% agriculture, 7% health professions and related sciences, 3% education, 2% natural resource sciences, 1% communications and journalism, 1% computer and information sciences, 1% engineering and applied sciences, 1% performing arts, 1% premed, 1% prevet, 1% psychology. *Most popular recent majors:* business administration/commerce/management, (pre)engineering sequence, agricultural sciences.
First-Year Class: 552 total; 1,311 applied, 98% were accepted, 27% of whom enrolled. 13% from top 10% of their high school class, 24% from top quarter, 70% from top half.
Graduation Requirements: 64 credit hours; math/science requirements vary according to program; computer course for agriculture majors.
Computers on Campus: 113 computers available on campus for general student use. Computers for student use in computer center, computer labs, learning resource center, classrooms, library, dorms provide access to the Internet/World Wide Web. Staffed computer lab on campus provides training in use of computers.

EXPENSES

Expenses for 1997–98: State resident tuition: $1926 full-time. Nonresident tuition: $6252 full-time. Part-time tuition per semester ranges from $77.50 to $903.50 for state residents, $257.75 to $2886 for nonresidents. College room and board: $3954.
LD Services Contact: Mr. William M. Letrent, Director, Student Support Services, Potomac State College of West Virginia University, Fort Avenue, Keyser, WV 26726, 304-788-6856. Fax: 304-788-6848. Email: pscsupport@miworld.net.

PRAIRIE STATE COLLEGE

Chicago Heights, Illinois

LEARNING DISABILITIES SERVICES INFORMATION

Disabled Student Services began offering services in 1984. Currently the program serves 55 undergraduates with LD. Students diagnosed with ADD/ADHD are eligible for the same services available to students with LD.
Staff: 2 full-time, 2 part-time staff members, including director. Services provided by tutors, counselor.
Special Fees: No special fees are charged for services to students with LD.
Applications and admissions: *Required:* high school transcript, extended time SAT I, personal interview, ACT ASSET. Students may begin taking classes any term. *Application deadline:* continuous.

PROGRAM AND SERVICE COMPONENTS

Special preparation or orientation: Required summer program offered prior to entering college. Optional orientation offered during the summer.
Academic advising: Provided by unit staff members. Students with LD may take up to 12 credit hours each term; most take 6 to 9 credit hours; 12 credit hours required to maintain full-time status; 6 credit hours required to be eligible for financial aid.
Counseling services: Individual counseling.
Subject-area tutoring: Offered one-on-one and in small groups by professional teachers, peer tutors. Available in all subjects.
Special courses: College survival skills, reading, composition, math, career planning. All enter into overall grade point average.
Auxiliary aids: Taped textbooks, tape recorders, calculators, typewriters, word-processors with spell-check, personal computers, talking computers, optical character readers.
Auxiliary services: Alternative test arrangements, notetakers.

GENERAL COLLEGE INFORMATION

State and locally supported, 2-year, coed. Part of Illinois Community College System. Awards associate degrees. Founded 1958. *Setting:* 68-acre suburban campus with easy access to Chicago. *Total enrollment:* 5,000. *Faculty:* 289 (89 full-time, 200 part-time).
Enrollment Profile: 5,000 students from 2 states and territories. 60% women, 40% men, 76% part-time, 92% state residents, 1% transferred in, 0% international, 53% 25 or older, 5% Hispanic, 25% black, 1% Asian or Pacific Islander. *Most popular recent majors:* liberal arts/general studies, nursing.
First-Year Class: 1,000 total. Of the students who applied, 100% were accepted, 74% of whom enrolled.
Graduation Requirements: 62 credit hours; 1 math course.
Computers on Campus: Computers for student use in learning resource center, student labs provide access to the Internet/World Wide Web. Staffed computer lab on campus.

EXPENSES

Expenses for 1997–98: *Application fee:* $10. Area resident tuition: $1736 full-time, $56 per credit hour part-time. State resident tuition: $5208 full-time, $168 per credit hour part-time. Nonresident tuition: $5487 full-time, $177 per credit hour part-time.
LD Services Contact: Ms. Sheila Lewis, Coordinator, Disabled Student Services, Prairie State College, 202 South Halsted Street, Chicago Heights, IL 60411-1275, 708-709-3689.

PUEBLO COMMUNITY COLLEGE

Pueblo, Colorado

LEARNING DISABILITIES SERVICES INFORMATION

Learning Center currently serves 30 to 35 undergraduates with LD. Students diagnosed with ADD/ADHD are eligible for the same services available to students with LD.
Staff: 1 full-time, 2 part-time staff members, including director. Services provided by tutors, counselors, interpreter for the deaf.
Special Fees: No special fees are charged for services to students with LD.
Applications and admissions: *Required:* high school transcript, personal interview, documentation of disability; *recommended:* untimed ACT. Students may begin taking classes any term. *Application deadline:* continuous.
Special policies: The college has written policies regarding grade forgiveness.

PROGRAM AND SERVICE COMPONENTS

Academic advising: Provided by unit staff members, academic advisers. Students with LD may take up to 20 semester hours (more with approval from Vice President of Instruction) each term; most take 6 to 12 semester hours; 12 semester hours required to maintain full-time status; 6 semester hours (part-time), 12 semester hours (full-time) required to be eligible for financial aid.
Counseling services: Individual counseling, career counseling.
Basic skills remediation: Offered one-on-one and in small groups by regular teachers. Available in reading, math, study skills.
Subject-area tutoring: Offered one-on-one, in small groups, and in class-size groups by professional teachers, peer tutors. Available in most subjects.
Auxiliary aids: Taped textbooks, tape recorders, calculators, typewriters, word-processors with spell-check, personal computers, Arkenstone Reader.
Auxiliary services: Alternative test arrangements, notetakers, advocacy.

GENERAL COLLEGE INFORMATION

State-supported, 2-year, coed. Part of Colorado Community College and Occupational Education System. Awards associate degrees. Founded 1933. *Setting:* 35-acre urban campus. *Endowment:* $1.6 million. *Total enrollment:* 4,127. *Faculty:* 310 (101 full-time, 100% with terminal degrees, 209 part-time); student–undergrad faculty ratio is 16:1.
Enrollment Profile: 4,127 students: 65% women, 35% men, 58% part-time, 99% state residents, 5% transferred in, 1% international, 55% 25 or older, 2% Native American, 31% Hispanic, 2% black, 1% Asian or Pacific Islander. *Areas of study chosen:* 10% business management and administrative services, 8% health professions and related sciences, 7% social sciences, 4% computer and information sciences, 1% agriculture, 1% vocational and home economics. *Most popular recent majors:* nursing, criminal justice.
First-Year Class: 1,472 total; 2,388 applied, 100% were accepted, 62% of whom enrolled.
Graduation Requirements: 60 credits; math/science requirements vary according to program; computer course for students without computer competency; internship (some majors).
Computers on Campus: 365 computers available on campus for general student use. A campus-wide network can be accessed. Students can contact faculty members and/or advisers through e-mail. Computers for student use in computer labs, learning resource center, classrooms, library, learning center provide access to the Internet/World Wide Web. Staffed computer lab on campus provides training in use of computers, software. *Academic computing expenditure 1995–96:* $413,170.

EXPENSES

Expenses for 1997–98: State resident tuition: $1605 full-time, $53.50 per credit hour part-time. Nonresident tuition: $7313 full-time, $243.75 per credit hour part-time. Part-time mandatory fees: $18.05 per semester. Full-time mandatory fees: $186.
LD Services Contact: Mr. Bill Conner, Vocational Services Counselor, Pueblo Community College, 900 West Orman Avenue, Pueblo, CO 81004-1499, 719-549-3382.

RAINY RIVER COMMUNITY COLLEGE

International Falls, Minnesota

LEARNING DISABILITIES SERVICES INFORMATION

Disability Services began offering services in 1988. Currently the program serves 14 undergraduates with LD. Students diagnosed with ADD/ADHD are eligible for the same services available to students with LD, as well as special class schedules.
Staff: 1 full-time, 4 part-time staff members, including director. Services provided by remediation specialists, tutors, counselors.
Special Fees: No special fees are charged for services to students with LD.
Applications and admissions: *Required:* high school transcript, immunization record, GED (in lieu of high school diploma); *recommended:* psychoeducational report completed within 3 years, skill level placement assessment. Students may begin taking classes any term. *Application deadline:* continuous.
Special policies: The college has written policies regarding grade forgiveness.

PROGRAM AND SERVICE COMPONENTS

Diagnostic testing: Intelligence, reading, math, spelling, spoken language, written language, perceptual skills, personality.
Academic advising: Provided by academic advisers. Students with LD may take up to 18 credits each term; most take 12 to 15 credits; 12 credits required to maintain full-time status and be eligible for financial aid.
Counseling services: Individual counseling, career counseling.
Basic skills remediation: Offered one-on-one, in small groups, and in class-size groups by regular teachers, professional tutor; computer-aided instruction also offered. Available in reading, math, spelling, written language, learning strategies, study skills, time management.
Subject-area tutoring: Offered one-on-one and in small groups by professional teachers, peer tutors. Available in all subjects.
Special courses: College survival skills, reading, vocabulary development, composition, learning strategies, word processing, Internet use, time management, math, typing, study skills, career planning, stress management. Most offered for credit; most enter into overall grade point average.
Auxiliary aids: Taped textbooks, tape recorders, calculators, word-processors with spell-check, talking computers, optical character readers, Soundproof software.
Auxiliary services: Alternative test arrangements, notetakers, priority registration, advocacy, scribes.

GENERAL COLLEGE INFORMATION

State-supported, 2-year, coed. Part of Minnesota State Colleges and Universities System. Awards associate degrees. Founded 1967. *Setting:* 80-acre small-town campus. *Total enrollment:* 669. *Faculty:* 37 (25 full-time, 12 part-time).
Enrollment Profile: 669 students from 7 states and territories, 1 other country. 69% women, 31% men, 62% part-time, 80% state residents, 10% live on campus, 10% transferred in, 8% international, 54% 25 or older, 5% Native American, 1% Hispanic, 3% black, 1% Asian or Pacific Islander. *Retention:* 49% of 1995 full-time freshmen returned.
First-Year Class: 202 total; 243 applied, 100% were accepted, 96% of whom enrolled.
Graduation Requirements: 96 credits; 5 credits of math; 12 credits of science; computer course.
Computers on Campus: 70 computers available on campus for general student use. Computer purchase/lease plans available. A computer is recommended for some students. A campus-wide network can be accessed from off-campus. Students can contact faculty members and/or advisers through e-mail. Computers for student use in computer center, computer labs, learning resource center, classrooms, library provide

access to the Internet/World Wide Web, on- and off-campus e-mail addresses. Staffed computer lab on campus provides training in use of computers, software.

EXPENSES

Expenses for 1996–97: *Application fee:* $20. State resident tuition: $2143 full-time, $44.65 per credit part-time. Nonresident tuition: $4286 full-time, $89.30 per credit part-time. Part-time mandatory fees: $2.85 per credit. Manitoba, North Dakota, South Dakota, and Wisconsin residents pay tuition at the rate they would pay if attending a comparable state-supported institution in their home state. Full-time mandatory fees: $137. College room and board: $3150. College room only: $1935.
LD Services Contact: Ms. Carol Grim, Disability Services Coordinator, Rainy River Community College, 1501 Highway 71, International Falls, MN 56649, 218-285-2238. Fax: 218-285-2239. Email: twood@rr.cc.mn.us.

RANDOLPH COMMUNITY COLLEGE

Asheboro, North Carolina

LEARNING DISABILITIES SERVICES INFORMATION

Special Services/College Preparatory Studies began offering services in 1981. Currently the program serves 43 undergraduates with LD. Students diagnosed with ADD/ADHD are eligible for the same services available to students with LD, as well as preferential scheduling/seating.
Staff: 4 full-time staff members, including director. Services provided by remediation specialists.
Special Fees: No special fees are charged for services to students with LD.
Applications and admissions: *Required:* high school transcript, personal interview. Students may begin taking classes any term. *Application deadline:* continuous.

PROGRAM AND SERVICE COMPONENTS

Diagnostic testing: Intelligence, reading, math, spelling, written language, study skills.
Academic advising: Provided by unit staff members, academic advisers. Students with LD may take up to 18 semester hours each term; most take 12 semester hours; 12 semester hours required to maintain full-time status; 6 semester hours required to be eligible for financial aid.
Counseling services: Individual counseling, career counseling.
Basic skills remediation: Offered one-on-one and in class-size groups by regular teachers. Available in reading, math, spelling, handwriting, written language, learning strategies, study skills.
Subject-area tutoring: Offered one-on-one by professional teachers, peer tutors. Available in most subjects.
Special courses: Reading, vocabulary development, composition, math, study skills. All offered for credit; none enter into overall grade point average.
Auxiliary aids: Tape recorders, typewriters, personal computers.
Auxiliary services: Alternative test arrangements, advocacy.

GENERAL COLLEGE INFORMATION

State-supported, 2-year, coed. Part of North Carolina Community College System. Awards associate degrees. Founded 1962. *Setting:* 27-acre small-town campus. *Total enrollment:* 1,427. *Faculty:* 73 (43 full-time, 30 part-time); student–undergrad faculty ratio is 22:1.
Enrollment Profile: 1,427 students from 12 states and territories, 1 other country. 60% women, 40% men, 51% part-time, 99% state residents, 10% transferred in, 48% 25 or older, 1% Native American, 1% Hispanic, 5% black, 0% Asian or Pacific Islander. *Retention:* 40% of 1995 full-time freshmen returned. *Areas of study chosen:* 20% liberal arts/general studies, 19% business management and administrative services, 11% health professions and related sciences, 9% computer and information sciences. *Most popular recent majors:* photography, interior design, business administration/commerce/management.
First-Year Class: 189 total.
Graduation Requirements: Computer course for photography, accounting, commercial graphics, business administration, criminal justice majors; internship (some majors).
Computers on Campus: 125 computers available on campus for general student use. Computer purchase/lease plans available. Computers for student use in computer center, learning resource center, library provide access to the Internet/World Wide Web, Novell network. Staffed computer lab on campus provides training in use of computers, software.

EXPENSES

Expenses for 1997–98: State resident tuition: $560 full-time, $20 per semester hour part-time. Nonresident tuition: $4564 full-time, $163 per semester hour part-time. Full-time mandatory fees: $22.
LD Services Contact: Dr. Rebekah Megerian, Director of Special Services, Randolph Community College, PO Box 1009, Asheboro, NC 27204-1009, 910-629-1471 Ext. 230. Fax: 910-629-4695.

RARITAN VALLEY COMMUNITY COLLEGE

Somerville, New Jersey

LEARNING DISABILITIES SERVICES INFORMATION

Learning Disability Support Services began offering services in 1990. Currently the program serves 160 undergraduates with LD. Students diagnosed with ADD/ADHD are eligible for the same services available to students with LD.
Staff: 1 full-time staff member (coordinator). Services provided by tutors.
Special Fees: No special fees are charged for services to students with LD.
Applications and admissions: *Required:* psychoeducational report completed within 3 years. Students may begin taking classes any term. *Application deadline:* continuous.

PROGRAM AND SERVICE COMPONENTS

Special preparation or orientation: Optional orientation offered during general orientation.
Academic advising: Provided by unit staff members, academic advisers. Students with LD may take up to as many credits as an individual can handle each term; most take 9 to 12 credits; 12 credits required to maintain full-time status; source of aid determines number of credits required to be eligible for financial aid.
Counseling services: Individual counseling, career counseling, self-advocacy training.
Basic skills remediation: Offered in class-size groups by regular teachers. Available in reading, math, written language, learning strategies, study skills, time management.
Subject-area tutoring: Offered one-on-one by professional teachers, peer tutors. Available in most subjects.
Special courses: College survival skills. None offered for credit.
Auxiliary aids: Taped textbooks, tape recorders, calculators, word-processors with spell-check.
Auxiliary services: Alternative test arrangements, priority registration.

GENERAL COLLEGE INFORMATION

County-supported, 2-year, coed. Awards associate degrees. Founded 1965. *Setting:* 225-acre small-town campus with easy access to New York City and Philadelphia. *Research spending 1995–96:* $90,979. *Total enrollment:* 5,470. *Faculty:* 289 (87 full-time, 30% with terminal degrees, 202 part-time); student–undergrad faculty ratio is 18:1.
Enrollment Profile: 5,470 students from 2 states and territories, 14 other countries. 59% women, 41% men, 58% part-time, 98% state residents, 8% transferred in, 1% international, 49% 25 or older, 1% Native American, 3% Hispanic, 4% black, 4% Asian or Pacific Islander. *Areas of study chosen:* 25% liberal arts/general studies, 21% business management and administrative services, 7% interdisciplinary studies, 4% health professions and related sciences, 4% performing arts, 3% computer and information sciences, 3% social sciences, 2% biological and life sciences, 2% education, 2% engineering and applied sciences, 2% fine arts, 1% communications and journalism. *Most popular recent majors:* business administration/commerce/management, liberal arts/general studies, nursing.
First-Year Class: 1,610 total; 2,087 applied, 92% were accepted, 84% of whom enrolled.
Graduation Requirements: 60 credits; algebra proficiency; internship (some majors).
Computers on Campus: 120 computers available on campus for general student use. Computers for student use in computer center, computer labs, classrooms, library provide access to the Internet/World Wide Web. Staffed computer lab on campus provides training in use of computers, software. *Academic computing expenditure 1995–96:* $647,013.

Raritan Valley Community College (continued)

EXPENSES

Expenses for 1997–98: *Application fee:* $25. Area resident tuition: $1800 full-time, $60 per credit part-time. State resident tuition: $3600 full-time, $120 per credit part-time. Nonresident tuition: $7200 full-time, $240 per credit part-time. Part-time mandatory fees per semester range from $24 to $114. Full-time mandatory fees: $300.

LD Services Contact: Ms. Linda Baum, Learning Disability Specialist, Raritan Valley Community College, Box 3300, Somerville, NJ 08876-1265, 973-526-1200 Ext. 8418.

READING AREA COMMUNITY COLLEGE

Reading, Pennsylvania

LEARNING DISABILITIES SERVICES INFORMATION

Center for Counseling and Academic Development began offering services in 1983. Currently the program serves 40 undergraduates with LD. Students diagnosed with ADD/ADHD are eligible for the same services available to students with LD.

Staff: 2 full-time, 2 part-time staff members, including coordinators, managers. Services provided by remediation specialist, tutors, counselors.

Special Fees: No special fees are charged for services to students with LD.

Applications and admissions: *Required:* psychoeducational report completed within 3 years, special education transcripts. Students may begin taking classes any term. *Application deadline:* continuous.

PROGRAM AND SERVICE COMPONENTS

Special preparation or orientation: Optional orientation offered before registration.

Academic advising: Provided by unit staff members, academic advisers. Students with LD may take up to 9 credits each term; most take 6 credits; 6 credits required to maintain full-time status and be eligible for financial aid.

Counseling services: Individual counseling, small-group counseling, career counseling.

Basic skills remediation: Offered one-on-one, in small groups, and in class-size groups by regular teachers, professional tutors; computer-aided instruction also offered. Available in reading, math, spelling, written language, learning strategies, study skills, time management, social skills.

Subject-area tutoring: Offered one-on-one and in small groups by professional teachers, peer tutors, professional tutors. Available in all subjects.

Special courses: College survival skills, reading, composition, time management, math, personal psychology, study skills, career planning, stress management. All offered for credit; all enter into overall grade point average.

Auxiliary aids: Taped textbooks, tape recorders, calculators, typewriters, word-processors with spell-check, personal computers.

Auxiliary services: Alternative test arrangements, notetakers, advocacy, video taping.

GENERAL COLLEGE INFORMATION

County-supported, 2-year, coed. Awards associate degrees. Founded 1971. *Setting:* urban campus with easy access to Philadelphia. *Endowment:* $745,770. *Total enrollment:* 2,756. *Faculty:* 249 (59 full-time, 190 part-time).

Enrollment Profile: 2,756 students: 68% women, 32% men, 68% part-time, 99% state residents, 35% transferred in, 1% international, 56% 25 or older, 1% Native American, 9% Hispanic, 9% black, 1% Asian or Pacific Islander. *Retention:* 69% of 1995 full-time freshmen returned.

First-Year Class: 857 total; 1,144 applied, 100% were accepted, 75% of whom enrolled.

Graduation Requirements: 60 credits; 1 course each in math and science; computer course for business majors; internship (some majors).

Computers on Campus: 80 computers available on campus for general student use. Computers for student use in computer center, computer labs, learning resource center, classrooms, library. Staffed computer lab on campus provides training in use of computers, software. *Academic computing expenditure 1995–96:* $125,000.

EXPENSES

Expenses for 1996–97: *Application fee:* $20. Area resident tuition: $1740 full-time, $58 per credit part-time. State resident tuition: $3480 full-time, $116 per credit part-time. Nonresident tuition: $5220 full-time, $174 per credit part-time. Mandatory fees: $300 full-time, $10 per credit part-time for area residents; $360 full-time, $12 per credit part-time for state and nonresidents.

LD Services Contact: Ms. Tomma Lee Furst, Tutorial Coordinator, Reading Area Community College, PO Box 1706, Reading, PA 19603-1706, 610-372-4721 Ext. 250.

RIDGEWATER COLLEGE

Willmar, Minnesota

LEARNING DISABILITIES SERVICES INFORMATION

Resource Center began offering services in 1975. Currently the program serves 150 undergraduates with LD. Students diagnosed with ADD/ADHD are eligible for the same services available to students with LD.

Staff: 8 full-time, 5 part-time staff members, including President, Department Chair. Services provided by remediation specialists, tutors.

Special Fees: No special fees are charged for services to students with LD.

Applications and admissions: *Required:* high school transcript, IEP (Individualized Education Program). Students may begin taking classes any term. *Application deadline:* continuous.

PROGRAM AND SERVICE COMPONENTS

Special preparation or orientation: Optional summer program offered prior to entering college. Required orientation held before registration.

Diagnostic testing: Reading, math, spelling, spoken language, written language, study skills, learning strategies.

Academic advising: Provided by unit staff members, academic advisers. Students with LD may take up to as many credits as an individual can handle each term; most take 16 credits; 12 credits required to maintain full-time status and be eligible for financial aid.

Counseling services: Individual counseling, career counseling.

Basic skills remediation: Offered one-on-one and in small groups by LD teachers, regular teachers. Available in reading, math, spelling, spoken language, written language, learning strategies, study skills, time management, social skills.

Subject-area tutoring: Offered one-on-one and in small groups by professional teachers, peer tutors. Available in most subjects.

Special courses: College survival skills, reading, vocabulary development, communication skills, composition, learning strategies, math, study skills. All offered for credit; none enter into overall grade point average.

Auxiliary aids: Taped textbooks, tape recorders, calculators, typewriters, word-processors with spell-check, personal computers, optical character readers.

Auxiliary services: Alternative test arrangements, notetakers.

GENERAL COLLEGE INFORMATION

State-supported, 2-year, coed. Part of Minnesota State Colleges and Universities System. Awards associate degrees. Founded 1961. *Setting:* 83-acre small-town campus. *Total enrollment:* 3,840. *Faculty:* 236 (127 full-time, 1% with terminal degrees, 109 part-time); student–undergrad faculty ratio is 20:1.

Enrollment Profile: 3,840 students from 18 states and territories, 6 other countries. 45% women, 55% men, 41% part-time, 98% state residents, 24% transferred in, 1% international, 27% 25 or older, 1% Native American, 3% Hispanic, 1% black, 1% Asian or Pacific Islander. *Retention:* 61% of 1995 full-time freshmen returned. *Areas of study chosen:* 22% liberal arts/general studies, 19% business management and administrative services, 11% health professions and related sciences, 8% education, 3% agriculture, 2% computer and information sciences, 2% engineering and applied sciences, 2% psychology, 2% social sciences, 1% communications and journalism, 1% fine arts, 1% natural resource sciences, 1% prelaw, 1% prevet.

First-Year Class: 1,786 total; 1,796 applied, 100% were accepted, 99% of whom enrolled. 6% from top 10% of their high school class, 20% from top quarter, 51% from top half. 1 class president, 3 valedictorians.

Graduation Requirements: 96 quarter hours; 1 math course; 2 lab science courses; computer course for business administration, accounting, agricultural-business, drafting, radiological technology, vetinary technology majors; internship (some majors).

Computers on Campus: 200 computers available on campus for general student use. A computer is recommended for some students. A campus-wide network can be accessed. Students can contact faculty members and/or advisers through e-mail. Computers for student use in computer center, computer labs, learning resource center, library, counseling center provide access to the Internet/World Wide Web, on-campus e-mail addresses. Staffed computer lab on campus provides training in use of computers, software. *Academic computing expenditure 1995–96:* $150,000.

EXPENSES

Expenses for 1996–97: *Application fee:* $20. State resident tuition: $1997 full-time, $41.60 per quarter hour part-time. Nonresident tuition: $3994 full-time, $83.20 per quarter hour part-time. Part-time mandatory fees: $3.17 per quarter hour. North Dakota, South Dakota and Wisconsin residents pay tuition at the rate they would pay if attending a comparable state-supported institution in their home state. Fees vary according to program. Full-time mandatory fees: $244 (minimum).

LD Services Contact: Ms. Mary Casey Allen, Department Chair, Ridgewater College, 2101 15th Avenue NW, PO Box 1097, Willmar, MN 56201-1097, 320-231-2959. Fax: 320-231-7695. Email: mallen@hut.tec.mn.us.

RIVERLAND COMMUNITY COLLEGE

Austin, Minnesota

LEARNING DISABILITIES SERVICES INFORMATION

Student Success Center began offering services in 1991. Students diagnosed with ADD/ADHD are eligible for the same services available to students with LD.

Staff: 1 full-time staff member (director). Services provided by tutors, readers, scribes.

Special Fees: No special fees are charged for services to students with LD.

Applications and admissions: Open admissions. Students may begin taking classes any term. *Application deadline:* continuous.

PROGRAM AND SERVICE COMPONENTS

Academic advising: Provided by unit staff members, academic advisers. Most students with LD take 9 to 12 quarter hours each term; 12 quarter hours required to maintain full-time status; 6 quarter hours required to be eligible for financial aid.

Counseling services: Individual counseling, career counseling, self-advocacy training.

Basic skills remediation: Offered in class-size groups by regular teachers; computer-aided instruction also offered. Available in reading, math, written language, learning strategies, study skills, time management.

Subject-area tutoring: Offered one-on-one and in small groups by peer tutors. Available in all subjects.

Auxiliary aids: Taped textbooks, tape recorders, calculators, word-processors with spell-check, personal computers, optical character readers, Franklin Speller.

Auxiliary services: Alternative test arrangements, notetakers, priority registration, advocacy.

GENERAL COLLEGE INFORMATION

State-supported, 2-year, coed. Part of Minnesota State Colleges and Universities System. Awards associate degrees. Founded 1940. *Setting:* 187-acre small-town campus with easy access to Minneapolis–St. Paul. *Total enrollment:* 2,571. *Faculty:* 161 (103 full-time, 58 part-time).

Enrollment Profile: 2,571 students: 54% women, 46% men, 48% part-time, 98% state residents, 45% 25 or older.

First-Year Class: 1,296 applied, 100% were accepted.

Graduation Requirements: 96 quarter hours; 12 quarter hours of math/science; computer course; internship (some majors).

Computers on Campus: 175 computers available on campus for general student use. A campus-wide network can be accessed from student residence rooms. Computers for student use in computer center, library. Staffed computer lab on campus provides training in use of computers.

EXPENSES

Expenses for 1996–97: *Application fee:* $20. State resident tuition: $1997 full-time, $41.60 per quarter hour part-time. Nonresident tuition: $3994 full-time, $83.20 per quarter hour part-time. Part-time mandatory fees: $3.42 per quarter hour. North Dakota, South Dakota and Wisconsin residents pay tuition at the rate they would pay if attending a comparable state-supported institution in their home state. Full-time mandatory fees: $164.

LD Services Contact: Ms. Mindi Askelson, Director, Riverland Community College, 1600 8th Avenue, NW, Austin, MN 55912, 507-433-0569. Fax: 507-433-0515. Email: maskelso@river.cc.mn.us.

RIVERSIDE COMMUNITY COLLEGE

Riverside, California

LEARNING DISABILITIES SERVICES INFORMATION

Learning Disabilities Program began offering services in 1980. Currently the program serves 300 undergraduates with LD. Students diagnosed with ADD/ADHD are eligible for the same services available to students with LD.

Staff: 3 full-time, 1 part-time staff members. Services provided by remediation specialists, counselor, instructional assistant.

Special Fees: No special fees are charged for services to students with LD.

Applications and admissions: *Recommended:* psychoeducational report completed within 3 years. Students may begin taking classes any term. *Application deadline:* continuous.

Special policies: The college has written policies regarding grade forgiveness.

PROGRAM AND SERVICE COMPONENTS

Special preparation or orientation: Optional orientation offered before registration.

Diagnostic testing: Intelligence, reading, math, spelling.

Academic advising: Provided by academic advisers. Most students with LD take 9 to 12 units each term; 12 units required to maintain full-time status and be eligible for financial aid.

Counseling services: Individual counseling, career counseling.

Basic skills remediation: Offered in class-size groups by LD teachers, regular teachers. Available in reading, math, spelling, written language, learning strategies, study skills.

Special courses: Reading, learning strategies. Most offered for credit; all enter into overall grade point average.

Auxiliary aids: Taped textbooks, tape recorders, calculators, word-processors with spell-check, personal computers, talking computers, optical character readers.

Auxiliary services: Alternative test arrangements, notetakers, priority registration.

GENERAL COLLEGE INFORMATION

State and locally supported, 2-year, coed. Part of California Community Colleges System. Awards associate degrees. Founded 1916. *Setting:* 109-acre suburban campus with easy access to Los Angeles. *Total enrollment:* 20,845. *Faculty:* 550 (250 full-time, 300 part-time).

Enrollment Profile: 20,845 students from 40 states and territories, 31 other countries. 60% women, 40% men, 74% part-time, 97% state residents, 15% transferred in, 2% international, 54% 25 or older, 2% Native American, 24% Hispanic, 11% black, 6% Asian or Pacific Islander. *Retention:* 62% of 1995 full-time freshmen returned. *Areas of study chosen:* 13% health professions and related sciences, 12% business management and administrative services, 5% education, 4% psychology, 3% engineering and applied sciences, 3% liberal arts/general studies, 2% biological and life sciences, 2% English language/literature/letters, 2% fine arts, 2% prelaw, 2% premed, 1% agriculture, 1% communications and journalism, 1% computer and information sciences, 1% foreign language and literature, 1% library and information studies, 1% mathematics, 1% philosophy, 1% physical sciences, 1% predentistry, 1% prevet, 1% social sciences, 1% vocational and home economics.

First-Year Class: 5,350 total. Of the students who applied, 100% were accepted.

Graduation Requirements: 60 units; math proficiency; 3 units of natural science; computer course (varies by major).

Computers on Campus: 200 computers available on campus for general student use. Computers for student use in computer center, library, writing lab. Staffed computer lab on campus.

EXPENSES

Expenses for 1997–98: State resident tuition: $0 full-time. Nonresident tuition: $3540 full-time, $118 per unit part-time. Part-time mandatory fees per semester range from $33 to $163. Full-time mandatory fees: $430.

LD Services Contact: Ms. Maureen E. Fry, Learning Disabilities Instructor/ Counselor, Riverside Community College, 4800 Magnolia Avenue, Riverside, CA 92506-1299, 909-222-8641. Fax: 909-222-8790. Email: mfry@rccd.cc.ca.us.

ROCHESTER COMMUNITY AND TECHNICAL COLLEGE

Rochester, Minnesota

LEARNING DISABILITIES SERVICES INFORMATION

Academic Support Center began offering services in 1977. Currently the program serves 63 undergraduates with LD. Students diagnosed with ADD/ADHD are eligible for the same services available to students with LD.

Staff: 2 full-time staff members, including coordinator. Services provided by tutor, advisers.

Special Fees: No special fees are charged for services to students with LD.

Applications and admissions: Students may begin taking classes any term. *Application deadline:* continuous.

PROGRAM AND SERVICE COMPONENTS

Special preparation or orientation: Optional orientation offered before registration.

Academic advising: Provided by unit staff members, academic advisers. Students with LD may take up to 15 quarter hours each term; most take 12 quarter hours; 12 quarter hours required to maintain full-time status; 6 quarter hours (part-time), 12 quarter hours (full-time) required to be eligible for financial aid.

Counseling services: Individual counseling, small-group counseling.

Basic skills remediation: Offered one-on-one, in small groups, and in class-size groups by LD teachers, regular teachers. Available in reading, math, spelling, written language, learning strategies, study skills, time management.

Subject-area tutoring: Offered one-on-one and in small groups by professional teachers, peer tutors. Available in all subjects.

Special courses: College survival skills, reading, vocabulary development, composition, word processing, math, typing, study skills, career planning. All offered for credit; some enter into overall grade point average.

Auxiliary aids: Tape recorders, calculators, typewriters, word-processors with spell-check.

Auxiliary services: Alternative test arrangements, notetakers, priority registration, advocacy.

GENERAL COLLEGE INFORMATION

State-supported, 2-year, coed. Part of Minnesota State Colleges and Universities System. Awards associate degrees. Founded 1915. *Setting:* 160-acre small-town campus. *Endowment:* $437,000. *Total enrollment:* 4,350. *Faculty:* 225 (92 full-time, 133 part-time); student–undergrad faculty ratio is 18:1.

Enrollment Profile: 4,350 students from 18 states and territories, 36 other countries. 63% women, 37% men, 44% part-time, 93% state residents, 1% international, 38% 25 or older, 1% Native American, 1% Hispanic, 2% black, 4% Asian or Pacific Islander. *Areas of study chosen:* 46% liberal arts/general studies, 20% vocational and home economics, 9% health professions and related sciences, 3% computer and information sciences, 3% education, 1% communications and journalism, 1% engineering and applied sciences. *Most popular recent majors:* liberal arts/general studies, nursing, secretarial studies/office management.

First-Year Class: Of the students who applied, 99% were accepted.

Graduation Requirements: 96 quarter hours; computer course for business management majors; internship (some majors).

Computers on Campus: 170 computers available on campus for general student use. A campus-wide network can be accessed. Students can contact faculty members and/or advisers through e-mail. Computers for student use in computer center, computer labs, learning resource center, writing center. Staffed computer lab on campus.

EXPENSES

Expenses for 1996–97: *Application fee:* $20. State resident tuition: $1997 full-time, $41.60 per quarter hour part-time. Nonresident tuition: $3994 full-time, $83.20 per quarter hour part-time. Part-time mandatory fees: $4.35 per quarter hour. North Dakota, South Dakota and Wisconsin residents pay tuition at the rate they would pay if attending a comparable state-supported institution in their home state. Full-time mandatory fees: $209.

LD Services Contact: Ms. Janell Holter, Director, Disability Support Services, Rochester Community and Technical College, Highway 14 East, Rochester, MN 55904-4999, 507-280-2968. Fax: 507-285-7496.

ROCKLAND COMMUNITY COLLEGE

Suffern, New York

LEARNING DISABILITIES SERVICES INFORMATION

Office of Disability Services began offering services in 1985. Currently the program serves 350 undergraduates with LD. Students diagnosed with ADD/ADHD are eligible for the same services available to students with LD.

Staff: 1 full-time, 4 part-time staff members, including director, LD specialist, assistant to LD specialist. Services provided by tutors, tutor/counselor.

Special Fees: No special fees are charged for services to students with LD.

Applications and admissions: *Required:* high school IEP (Individualized Education Program); *recommended:* psychoeducational report. Students may begin taking classes any term. *Application deadline:* continuous.

PROGRAM AND SERVICE COMPONENTS

Special preparation or orientation: Optional summer program offered prior to entering college. Optional orientation offered before registration.

Academic advising: Provided by unit staff members. Students with LD may take up to 12 credits each term; most take 12 credits; 12 credits required to maintain full-time status; 6 credits (part-time), 12 credits (full-time) required to be eligible for financial aid.

Counseling services: Individual counseling, career counseling.

Basic skills remediation: Offered in class-size groups by regular teachers. Available in reading, math, written language, learning strategies, study skills, social skills.

Subject-area tutoring: Offered one-on-one by professional teachers, peer tutors. Available in most subjects.

Special courses: College survival skills, study skills. All offered for credit; all enter into overall grade point average.

Auxiliary aids: Taped textbooks, tape recorders, calculators, typewriters, word-processors with spell-check, Franklin Speller.

Auxiliary services: Alternative test arrangements, notetakers, priority registration, advocacy.

GENERAL COLLEGE INFORMATION

State and locally supported, 2-year, coed. Part of State University of New York System. Awards associate degrees. Founded 1959. *Setting:* 150-acre suburban campus with easy access to New York City. *Research spending 1995–96:* $952,214. *Total enrollment:* 6,446. *Faculty:* 586 (167 full-time, 21% with terminal degrees, 419 part-time).

Enrollment Profile: 6,446 students from 6 states and territories, 22 other countries. 57% women, 43% men, 50% part-time, 96% state residents, 5% transferred in, 2% international, 39% 25 or older, 8% Hispanic, 17% black, 6% Asian or Pacific Islander. *Retention:* 58% of 1995 full-time freshmen returned. *Areas of study chosen:* 66% liberal arts/general studies, 19% health professions and related sciences, 12% business management and administrative services, 2% communications and journalism, 1% computer and information sciences.

First-Year Class: 1,526 total; 2,186 applied, 100% were accepted, 70% of whom enrolled. 10% from top 10% of their high school class, 21% from top quarter, 69% from top half.

Graduation Requirements: 60 credits; computer course for business majors.

Computers on Campus: 177 computers available on campus for general student use. Computer purchase/lease plans available. A campus-wide network can be accessed. Students can contact faculty members and/or advisers through e-mail. Computers for student use in computer center, computer labs, library provide access to the Internet/World Wide Web, on-campus e-mail addresses. Staffed computer lab on campus provides training in use of computers, software.

EXPENSES

Expenses for 1997–98: State resident tuition: $2325 full-time, $97 per credit part-time. Nonresident tuition: $5812 full-time, $243 per credit part-time. Part-time mandatory fees: $2.50 per credit. Full-time mandatory fees: $75.

LD Services Contact: Ms. Marge Zemek, Learning Disabilities Specialist, Rockland Community College, 145 College Road, Suffern, NY 10901-3699, 914-574-4316.

ROGUE COMMUNITY COLLEGE

Grants Pass, Oregon

LEARNING DISABILITIES SERVICES INFORMATION

Vocational Special Services began offering services in 1984. Currently the program serves 46 undergraduates with LD. Students diagnosed with ADD/ADHD are eligible for the same services available to students with LD.

Staff: 2 full-time, 12 part-time staff members, including coordinator, adviser, assistant to coordinator. Services provided by remediation specialists, tutors, diagnostic specialist, readers, scribes.

Special Fees: No special fees are charged for services to students with LD.

Applications and admissions: *Required:* personal interview, psychoeducational report completed within 3 years (or as an adult), college placement test; *recommended:* high school IEP (Individualized Education Program), autobiographical statement, instructor evaluations, college transition forms. Students may begin taking classes any term. *Application deadline:* continuous.

PROGRAM AND SERVICE COMPONENTS

Diagnostic testing: Intelligence, reading, math, spelling, handwriting, written language, perceptual skills, study skills, learning strategies.

Academic advising: Provided by unit staff members, academic advisers. Most students with LD take 6 to 12 credits each term; 12 credits for financial aid (fewer for scholarship eligibility) required to maintain full-time status.

Counseling services: Individual counseling, career counseling.

Basic skills remediation: Offered one-on-one, in small groups, and in class-size groups by regular teachers, developmental studies instructors, tutors, peer teachers; computer-aided instruction also offered. Available in reading, math, spelling, handwriting, written language, learning strategies, study skills, time management, social skills, computer skills.

Subject-area tutoring: Offered one-on-one, in small groups, and in class-size groups by professional teachers, peer tutors, subject area experts. Available in most subjects.

Special courses: College survival skills, reading, vocabulary development, communication skills, composition, word processing, math, typing, study skills, career planning. All offered for credit; some enter into overall grade point average.

Auxiliary aids: Taped textbooks, tape recorders, calculators, typewriters, word-processors with spell-check, personal computers, talking computers, optical character readers, electronic spell checkers, personal listening system.

Auxiliary services: Alternative test arrangements, notetakers, priority registration, advocacy.

GENERAL COLLEGE INFORMATION

State and locally supported, 2-year, coed. Awards associate degrees. Founded 1970. *Setting:* 90-acre rural campus. *Total enrollment:* 2,425. *Faculty:* 459 (76 full-time, 1% with terminal degrees, 383 part-time).

Enrollment Profile: 2,425 students from 3 states and territories. 63% women, 37% men, 57% part-time, 99% state residents, 0% international, 56% 25 or older, 2% Native American, 7% Hispanic, 1% black, 2% Asian or Pacific Islander. *Retention:* 43% of 1995 full-time freshmen returned. *Areas of study chosen:* 14% liberal arts/general studies, 13% health professions and related sciences, 12% business management and administrative services, 10% engineering and applied sciences, 5% computer and information sciences, 5% social sciences, 4% psychology, 3% education, 2% fine arts, 1% agriculture, 1% biological and life sciences, 1% English language/literature/letters, 1% premed, 1% vocational and home economics. *Most popular recent majors:* liberal arts/general studies, business administration/commerce/management, nursing.

First-Year Class: 382 total. Of the students who applied, 100% were accepted, 100% of whom enrolled.

Graduation Requirements: 90 credits; 6 credits of math, 8 credits of science; computer course for business administration, office technology majors.

Computers on Campus: 96 computers available on campus for general student use. A campus-wide network can be accessed. Students can contact faculty members and/or advisers through e-mail. Computers for student use in computer center, computer labs, learning resource center, student center provide access to the Internet/World Wide Web. Staffed computer lab on campus.

EXPENSES

Expenses for 1997–98: State resident tuition: $1620 full-time, $36 per credit part-time. Nonresident tuition: $4905 full-time, $109 per credit part-time.

LD Services Contact: Ms. Bonnie Reeq, Coordinator, Vocational Special Services, Rogue Community College, 3345 Redwood Highway, Grants Pass, OR 97527-9298, 503-471-3500 Ext. 234. Fax: 503-471-3588. Email: breeq@rogue.cc.or.us.

SADDLEBACK COLLEGE

Mission Viejo, California

LEARNING DISABILITIES SERVICES INFORMATION

Special Services began offering services in 1967. Currently the program serves 350 undergraduates with LD. Students diagnosed with ADD/ADHD are eligible for the same services available to students with LD.

Staff: 5 full-time, 8 part-time staff members, including director. Services provided by remediation specialists, tutors, counselors, diagnostic specialists.

Special Fees: No special fees are charged for services to students with LD.

Applications and admissions: *Required:* student must be at least 18 years of age; *recommended:* high school transcript, courses completed, IEP (Individualized Education Program), personal interview. Students may begin taking classes any term. *Application deadline:* continuous.

Special policies: The college has written policies regarding grade forgiveness; substitutions and waivers of graduation and degree requirements.

PROGRAM AND SERVICE COMPONENTS

Special preparation or orientation: Optional summer program offered prior to entering college. Optional orientation offered before registration.

Diagnostic testing: Intelligence, reading, math, spelling, spoken language, written language, motor abilities, perceptual skills.

Academic advising: Provided by unit staff members. Students with LD may take up to 18 units each term; most take 6 units; 12 units required to maintain full-time status; 12 units (less with justification by specialist) required to be eligible for financial aid.

Counseling services: Individual counseling, career counseling, self-advocacy training.

Basic skills remediation: Offered in small groups by LD teachers; computer-aided instruction also offered. Available in math, spelling, written language, learning strategies, study skills, time management, social skills, computer skills.

Subject-area tutoring: Offered in small groups by peer tutors. Available in some subjects.

Special courses: College survival skills, composition, learning strategies, word processing, Internet use, time management, math, study skills, career planning. Most offered for credit; most enter into overall grade point average.

Auxiliary aids: Taped textbooks, tape recorders, calculators, word-processors with spell-check, talking computers, optical character readers.

Auxiliary services: Alternative test arrangements, notetakers, priority registration.

Campus support group: A special student organization is available to students with LD.

GENERAL COLLEGE INFORMATION

State and locally supported, 2-year, coed. Part of Saddleback Community College District. Awards associate degrees. Founded 1967. *Setting:* 100-acre suburban campus with easy access to Los Angeles and San Diego. *Total enrollment:* 16,917. *Faculty:* 606 (196 full-time, 40% with terminal degrees, 410 part-time).

Enrollment Profile: 16,917 students from 37 states and territories, 23 other countries. 62% women, 38% men, 60% part-time, 95% state residents, 10% transferred in, 1% international, 52% 25 or older, 1% Native American, 14% Hispanic, 1% black, 13% Asian or Pacific Islander. *Retention:* 65% of 1995 full-time freshmen returned. *Most popular recent majors:* liberal arts/general studies, nursing.

First-Year Class: 6,200 total; 11,070 applied, 100% were accepted, 56% of whom enrolled.

Graduation Requirements: 64 units; completion of math proficiency exam or 1 algebra course; computer course for accounting, science, business majors.

Computers on Campus: 200 computers available on campus for general student use. Computer purchase/lease plans available. A computer

Saddleback College (continued)

is recommended for some students. A campus-wide network can be accessed. Students can contact faculty members and/or advisers through e-mail. Computers for student use in computer center, computer labs, learning resource center, library provide access to the Internet/World Wide Web, on- and off-campus e-mail addresses. Staffed computer lab on campus provides training in use of computers, software.

EXPENSES

Expenses for 1997–98: State resident tuition: $0 full-time. Nonresident tuition: $4160 full-time, $130 per unit part-time. Part-time mandatory fees per semester range from $23 to $153. Full-time mandatory fees: $436.

LD Services Contact: Mr. Randy Anderson, Director, Special Services, Saddleback College, 28000 Marguerite Parkway, Mission Viejo, CA 92692, 714-582-4885. Fax: 714-347-1526. Email: anderson_r@sccd.cc.ca.us.

SAINT CHARLES COUNTY COMMUNITY COLLEGE

St. Peters, Missouri

LEARNING DISABILITIES SERVICES INFORMATION

Disabled Student Services currently serves 74 undergraduates with LD. Students diagnosed with ADD/ADHD are eligible for the same services available to students with LD.

Staff: 1 full-time, 1 part-time staff members, including coordinator, proctor/assistant.

Special Fees: No special fees are charged for services to students with LD.

Applications and admissions: *Required:* psychoeducational report completed within 5 years; *recommended:* high school IEP (Individualized Education Program). Students may begin taking classes any term. *Application deadline:* continuous.

Special policies: The college has written policies regarding substitutions and waivers of graduation and degree requirements.

PROGRAM AND SERVICE COMPONENTS

Special preparation or orientation: Optional orientation offered before registration.

Academic advising: Provided by unit staff members. Most students with LD take 9 to 12 credits each term; 12 credits required to maintain full-time status; 6 credits required to be eligible for financial aid.

Counseling services: Individual counseling, self-advocacy training.

Auxiliary aids: Taped textbooks, tape recorders, word-processors with spell-check, talking computers, optical character readers.

Auxiliary services: Alternative test arrangements, notetakers, advocacy.

GENERAL COLLEGE INFORMATION

State-supported, 2-year, coed. Part of Missouri Coordinating Board for Higher Education. Awards associate degrees. Founded 1986. *Setting:* 135-acre small-town campus with easy access to St. Louis. *Total enrollment:* 4,564. *Faculty:* 231 (63 full-time, 16% with terminal degrees, 168 part-time); student–undergrad faculty ratio is 18:1.

Enrollment Profile: 4,564 students from 21 states and territories, 3 other countries. 64% women, 36% men, 72% part-time, 98% state residents, 6% transferred in, 1% international, 40% 25 or older, 1% Native American, 1% Hispanic, 2% black, 1% Asian or Pacific Islander. *Retention:* 45% of 1995 full-time freshmen returned. *Areas of study chosen:* 55% liberal arts/general studies, 14% business management and administrative services, 11% health professions and related sciences, 5% social sciences, 4% education, 4% engineering and applied sciences, 3% computer and information sciences, 2% fine arts, 1% biological and life sciences, 1% communications and journalism, 1% English language/literature/letters, 1% psychology, 1% vocational and home economics. *Most popular recent majors:* liberal arts/general studies, nursing, practical nursing.

First-Year Class: 1,110 total; 1,135 applied, 100% were accepted, 98% of whom enrolled. 3% from top 10% of their high school class, 21% from top quarter, 49% from top half.

Graduation Requirements: 64 semester hours; computer course for all majors except nursing.

Computers on Campus: 279 computers available on campus for general student use. A campus-wide network can be accessed from off-campus. Students can contact faculty members and/or advisers through e-mail. Computers for student use in computer center, computer labs, learning resource center, classrooms, library, student center provide access to the Internet/World Wide Web, on- and off-campus e-mail addresses. Staffed computer lab on campus provides training in use of computers, software. *Academic computing expenditure 1995–96:* $170,490.

EXPENSES

Expenses for 1997–98: Area resident tuition: $1290 full-time, $43 per semester hour part-time. State resident tuition: $1890 full-time, $63 per semester hour part-time. Nonresident tuition: $2910 full-time, $97 per semester hour part-time. Part-time mandatory fees: $5 per semester hour. Full-time mandatory fees: $150.

LD Services Contact: Ms. Pam Bova, Coordinator, Disabled Student Services, Saint Charles County Community College, 4601 Mid Rivers Mall Drive, St. Peters, MO 63376, 314-922-8247. Fax: 314-922-8251. Email: pbova@chuck.stchas.edu.

ST. CLAIR COUNTY COMMUNITY COLLEGE

Port Huron, Michigan

LEARNING DISABILITIES SERVICES INFORMATION

Student Learning Center began offering services in 1978. Currently the program serves 40 undergraduates with LD. Students diagnosed with ADD/ADHD are eligible for the same services available to students with LD.

Staff: 4 full-time, 1 part-time staff members, including coordinator. Services provided by tutors, counselors, notetakers, readers, instructional assessment specialist, tutoring assistant.

Special Fees: No special fees are charged for services to students with LD.

Applications and admissions: *Required:* certification of learning disability; *recommended:* high school transcript, grade point average, courses completed, personal interview, psychoeducational report completed within 3 years, referral by Vocational Rehabilitation Services. Students may begin taking classes any term. *Application deadline:* continuous.

PROGRAM AND SERVICE COMPONENTS

Special preparation or orientation: Optional orientation offered individually by special arrangement.

Academic advising: Provided by unit staff members, academic advisers. Students with LD may take up to 18 credits each term; most take 6 to 12 credits; 12 credits required to maintain full-time status; 1 credit required to be eligible for financial aid.

Counseling services: Individual counseling, career counseling.

Basic skills remediation: Offered one-on-one and in class-size groups by regular teachers, tutors. Available in reading, math, spelling, written language, learning strategies, study skills, word processing, biology.

Subject-area tutoring: Offered one-on-one and in small groups by professional teachers, peer tutors, professional tutors. Available in all subjects.

Auxiliary aids: Tape recorders, typewriters, word-processors with spell-check, personal computers, optical character readers.

Auxiliary services: Alternative test arrangements, notetakers, readers.

GENERAL COLLEGE INFORMATION

County-supported, 2-year, coed. Part of Michigan Department of Education. Awards associate degrees. Founded 1923. *Setting:* 22-acre small-town campus with easy access to Detroit. *Endowment:* $1.4 million. *Research spending 1995–96:* $2000. *Total enrollment:* 4,132. *Faculty:* 270 (80 full-time, 100% with terminal degrees, 190 part-time); student–undergrad faculty ratio is 19:1.

Enrollment Profile: 4,132 students: 63% women, 37% men, 68% part-time, 99% state residents, 6% transferred in, 1% international, 45% 25 or older, 1% Native American, 1% Hispanic, 2% black, 1% Asian or Pacific Islander. *Most popular recent majors:* nursing, liberal arts/general studies, business administration/commerce/management.

First-Year Class: 838 total; 1,094 applied, 100% were accepted, 77% of whom enrolled.

Graduation Requirements: 62 credits; math/science requirements vary according to program; internship (some majors).

Computers on Campus: 350 computers available on campus for general student use. Computer purchase/lease plans available. A campus-wide network can be accessed. Computers for student use in computer center, computer labs, classrooms, library provide access to the Internet/World Wide Web. Staffed computer lab on campus. *Academic computing expenditure 1995–96:* $464,779.

EXPENSES

Expenses for 1997–98: *Application fee:* $10. Area resident tuition: $1767 full-time, $57 per credit part-time. State resident tuition: $2620 full-time, $84.50 per credit part-time. Nonresident tuition: $3534 full-time, $114 per credit part-time. Part-time mandatory fees per semester range from $22.50 to $47.50. Full-time mandatory fees: $118.

LD Services Contact: Ms. Nancy Pecorilli, Counselor, St. Clair County Community College, 323 Erie Street, PO Box 5015, Port Huron, MI 48061-5015, 810-989-5557. Fax: 810-984-4730.

ST. CLOUD TECHNICAL COLLEGE

St. Cloud, Minnesota

LEARNING DISABILITIES SERVICES INFORMATION

Learning Support Center began offering services in 1974. Currently the program serves 40 undergraduates with LD. Students diagnosed with ADD/ADHD are eligible for the same services available to students with LD.

Staff: 5 full-time staff members. Services provided by remediation specialists, tutors, counselor.

Special Fees: No special fees are charged for services to students with LD.

Applications and admissions: *Required:* high school transcript, grade point average, class rank, courses completed, IEP (Individualized Education Program), psychoeducational report completed within 3 years; *recommended:* personal interview. Students may begin taking classes any term. *Application deadline:* continuous.

Special policies: The college has written policies regarding grade forgiveness.

PROGRAM AND SERVICE COMPONENTS

Diagnostic testing: Reading, math, spelling, learning strategies.

Academic advising: Provided by unit staff members, academic advisers. Students with LD may take up to 16 credits each term; most take 12 credits; 12 credits required to maintain full-time status and be eligible for financial aid.

Counseling services: Individual counseling, career counseling.

Basic skills remediation: Offered one-on-one, in small groups, and in class-size groups by LD teachers, regular teachers. Available in reading, math, spelling, written language, study skills, time management.

Subject-area tutoring: Offered one-on-one and in small groups by professional teachers, peer tutors. Available in all subjects.

Auxiliary aids: Taped textbooks, tape recorders, calculators, typewriters, word-processors with spell-check, personal computers, optical character readers.

Auxiliary services: Alternative test arrangements, notetakers, priority registration, advocacy.

GENERAL COLLEGE INFORMATION

State-supported, 2-year, coed. Part of Minnesota State Colleges and Universities System. Awards associate degrees. Founded 1948. *Setting:* urban campus with easy access to Minneapolis–St. Paul. *Total enrollment:* 2,558. *Faculty:* 121 (78 full-time, 43 part-time); student–undergrad faculty ratio is 20:1.

Enrollment Profile: 2,558 students from 5 states and territories. 49% women, 51% men, 41% part-time, 98% state residents, 19% transferred in, 0% international, 47% 25 or older, 1% Native American, 1% Hispanic, 1% black, 1% Asian or Pacific Islander. *Retention:* 80% of 1995 full-time freshmen returned. *Areas of study chosen:* 44% vocational and home economics, 22% business management and administrative services, 12% health professions and related sciences, 8% engineering and applied sciences, 5% computer and information sciences, 4% architecture, 3% communications and journalism, 2% natural resource sciences. *Most popular recent majors:* practical nursing, marketing/retailing/merchandising, business administration/commerce/management.

First-Year Class: 1,249 total; 1,843 applied, 99% were accepted, 75% of whom enrolled.

Graduation Requirements: 96 credits; 1 developmental math course; computer course for most majors; internship (some majors).

Computers on Campus: 350 computers available on campus for general student use. A computer is recommended for some students. A campus-wide network can be accessed. Students can contact faculty members and/or advisers through e-mail. Computers for student use in computer center, computer labs, learning resource center, library, student labs provide access to the Internet/World Wide Web. Staffed computer lab on campus provides training in use of computers, software.

EXPENSES

Expenses for 1997–98: *Application fee:* $20. State resident tuition: $1997 full-time, $41.60 per credit part-time. Nonresident tuition: $3994 full-time, $83.20 per credit part-time. Part-time mandatory fees: $3.35 per credit. Tuition for North Dakota residents: $2208 full-time, $46 per credit part-time. Full-time mandatory fees: $161.

LD Services Contact: Mr. Robert Thienes, Supplemental Support Service Counselor, St. Cloud Technical College, 1540 Northway Drive, St. Cloud, MN 56303, 320-654-5959. Fax: 320-654-5981. Email: blt@cloud.tec.mn.us.

ST. GREGORY'S COLLEGE

Shawnee, Oklahoma

LEARNING DISABILITIES SERVICES INFORMATION

Partners in Learning began offering services in 1997. Currently the program serves 12 undergraduates with LD. Students diagnosed with ADD/ADHD are eligible for the same services available to students with LD.

Staff: 1 full-time staff member (director). Services provided by remediation specialist, tutors, counselors, diagnostic specialist.

Special Fees: $5000 per year.

Applications and admissions: *Required:* high school transcript, grade point average, courses completed, personal interview, psychoeducational report completed in 12th grade or within 1 year of application; *recommended:* high school extracurricular activities, IEP (Individualized Education Program), extended time SAT I or ACT, autobiographical statement, letters of recommendation, Weschler International Scale score. Students may begin taking classes in fall only. *Application deadline:* continuous.

PROGRAM AND SERVICE COMPONENTS

Special preparation or orientation: Required orientation held before registration and after classes begin.

Academic advising: Provided by unit staff members, academic advisers. Students with LD may take up to 18 credit hours each term; most take 12 to 15 credit hours; 12 credit hours required to maintain full-time status; 6 credit hours required to be eligible for financial aid.

Counseling services: Individual counseling, small-group counseling, career counseling, self-advocacy training.

Basic skills remediation: Offered one-on-one, in small groups, and in class-size groups by regular teachers, teacher trainees, reading specialists; computer-aided instruction also offered. Available in reading, math, spelling, spoken language, written language, learning strategies, study skills, time management, social skills, computer skills.

Subject-area tutoring: Offered one-on-one and in small groups by professional teachers, peer tutors. Available in all subjects.

Special courses: College survival skills, reading, vocabulary development, communication skills, composition, learning strategies, word processing, Internet use, time management, math, typing, study skills, career planning. Some offered for credit; some enter into overall grade point average.

Auxiliary aids: Taped textbooks, tape recorders, calculators, word-processors with spell-check, personal computers, talking computers, optical character readers.

Auxiliary services: Alternative test arrangements, notetakers, priority registration, advocacy.

GENERAL COLLEGE INFORMATION

Independent Roman Catholic, 2-year, coed. Awards associate degrees. Founded 1875. *Setting:* 640-acre small-town campus with easy access to Oklahoma City. *Endowment:* $3.2 million. *Total enrollment:* 490. *Faculty:* 30 (12 full-time, 30% with terminal degrees, 18 part-time); student–undergrad faculty ratio is 16:1.

Enrollment Profile: 490 students from 12 states and territories, 6 other countries. 52% women, 48% men, 26% part-time, 76% state residents, 16% transferred in, 11% international, 16% 25 or older, 11% Native American, 6% Hispanic, 4% black, 2% Asian or Pacific Islander. *Retention:* 41% of 1995 full-time freshmen returned. *Areas of study chosen:* 35% liberal arts/general studies, 21% social sciences, 13% business management and administrative services, 9% education, 3% engineering and applied sciences, 2% communications and journalism, 2% English

St. Gregory's College (continued)

language/literature/letters, 2% fine arts, 2% physical sciences, 1% theology/religion. *Most popular recent majors:* business administration/commerce/management, natural sciences, engineering sciences.
First-Year Class: 263 total; 368 applied, 99% were accepted, 72% of whom enrolled. 20% from top 10% of their high school class, 38% from top quarter, 78% from top half.
Graduation Requirements: 64 credit hours; 3 credit hours of math; 8 credit hours of natural science; computer course for business majors.
Computers on Campus: 35 computers available on campus for general student use. Computer purchase/lease plans available. Computers for student use in computer labs, learning resource center, dorms provide access to the Internet/World Wide Web. Staffed computer lab on campus provides training in use of computers, software. *Academic computing expenditure 1995–96:* $41,302.

EXPENSES

Expenses for 1996–97: *Application fee:* $25. Comprehensive fee of $9624 includes full-time tuition ($5310), mandatory fees ($550), and college room and board ($3764). Part-time tuition: $160 per credit hour. Part-time mandatory fees: $30 per credit hour.
LD Services Contact: Ms. Gay Faulk, Director, Partners in Learning, St. Gregory's College, 1900 West MacArthur Drive, Shawnee, OK 74801, 405-878-5100. Fax: 405-878-5198. Email: 75033.1040@compuserve.com.

ST. JOHNS RIVER COMMUNITY COLLEGE

Palatka, Florida

LEARNING DISABILITIES SERVICES INFORMATION

Auxiliary Aids for Handicapped Student Services began offering services in 1983. Currently the program serves 30 undergraduates with LD. Students diagnosed with ADD/ADHD are eligible for the same services available to students with LD.
Staff: 4 part-time staff members, including coordinator. Services provided by tutors, counselors.
Special Fees: No special fees are charged for services to students with LD.
Applications and admissions: *Required:* high school transcript, extended time SAT I, high school diploma or GED; *recommended:* high school grade point average, courses completed, extended time ACT. Students may begin taking classes any term. *Application deadline:* continuous.
Special policies: The college has written policies regarding grade forgiveness; substitutions and waivers of graduation requirements.

PROGRAM AND SERVICE COMPONENTS

Academic advising: Provided by unit staff members, academic advisers. Students with LD may take up to 13 credit hours each trimester for first term (subsequent course loads determined by GPA) each term; most take 12 credit hours; 12 credit hours required to maintain full-time status; 6 credit hours required to be eligible for financial aid.
Counseling services: Individual counseling, career counseling.
Basic skills remediation: Offered in class-size groups by regular teachers, peer teachers. Available in reading, math, spelling, written language, study skills.
Subject-area tutoring: Offered one-on-one by peer tutors. Available in all subjects.
Auxiliary aids: Taped textbooks, tape recorders, calculators, typewriters, word-processors with spell-check, personal computers, optical character readers.
Auxiliary services: Alternative test arrangements, notetakers, priority registration.

GENERAL COLLEGE INFORMATION

State-supported, 2-year, coed. Awards associate degrees. Founded 1958. *Setting:* 105-acre small-town campus with easy access to Jacksonville. *Total enrollment:* 3,500. *Faculty:* 157 (61 full-time, 13% with terminal degrees, 96 part-time); student–undergrad faculty ratio is 22:1.
Enrollment Profile: 3,500 students: 61% women, 39% men, 60% part-time, 99% state residents, 13% transferred in, 41% 25 or older, 1% Native American, 2% Hispanic, 11% black, 2% Asian or Pacific Islander.
First-Year Class: Of the students who applied, 99% were accepted.
Graduation Requirements: 60 credit hours; 1 math course; computer course for technology, business majors.
Computers on Campus: 203 computers available on campus for general student use. Computers for student use in computer center, computer labs, classrooms, library. Staffed computer lab on campus provides training in use of computers, software.

EXPENSES

Expenses for 1997–98: *Application fee:* $20. State resident tuition: $1167 full-time, $38.90 per credit hour part-time. Nonresident tuition: $4378 full-time, $145.95 per credit hour part-time.
LD Services Contact: Dr. Shirley Kennedy, Counselor, Auxiliary Aids for Handicapped Student Services, St. Johns River Community College, 2990 College Drive, St. Augustine, FL 32095-1197, 904-808-7417. Fax: 904-808-7420.

ST. LOUIS COMMUNITY COLLEGE AT FLORISSANT VALLEY

St. Louis, Missouri

LEARNING DISABILITIES SERVICES INFORMATION

ACCESS Office began offering services in 1980. Currently the program serves 100 undergraduates with LD. Students diagnosed with ADD/ADHD are eligible for the same services available to students with LD.
Staff: 2 full-time, 2 part-time staff members, including coordinator, Manager. Services provided by counselor, ACCESS office specialist.
Special Fees: No special fees are charged for services to students with LD.
Applications and admissions: *Required:* high school transcript. Students may begin taking classes any term. *Application deadline:* continuous.
Special policies: The college has written policies regarding grade forgiveness.

PROGRAM AND SERVICE COMPONENTS

Special preparation or orientation: Optional orientation offered during registration.
Academic advising: Provided by unit staff members. Students with LD may take up to 18 credit hours each term; most take 9 to 12 credit hours; 12 credit hours required to maintain full-time status; 3 credit hours required to be eligible for financial aid.
Counseling services: Individual counseling, small-group counseling, career counseling, self-advocacy training.
Basic skills remediation: Offered one-on-one, in small groups, and in class-size groups by regular teachers. Available in reading, math, spelling, written language, learning strategies, study skills, time management, social skills, computer skills.
Auxiliary aids: Taped textbooks, tape recorders, calculators, word-processors with spell-check, personal computers, talking computers, optical character readers.
Auxiliary services: Alternative test arrangements, notetakers, advocacy.

GENERAL COLLEGE INFORMATION

District-supported, 2-year, coed. Part of St. Louis Community College System. Awards associate degrees. Founded 1963. *Setting:* 108-acre suburban campus. *Total enrollment:* 7,664. *Faculty:* 380 (133 full-time, 247 part-time); student–undergrad faculty ratio is 19:1.
Enrollment Profile: 7,664 students: 63% women, 37% men, 69% part-time, 97% state residents, 6% transferred in, 1% international, 51% 25 or older, 1% Native American, 1% Hispanic, 32% black, 1% Asian or Pacific Islander. *Retention:* 38% of 1995 full-time freshmen returned. *Areas of study chosen:* 39% interdisciplinary studies, 12% business management and administrative services, 8% communications and journalism, 7% engineering and applied sciences, 4% computer and information sciences, 4% fine arts, 2% education, 2% health professions and related sciences, 1% biological and life sciences, 1% mathematics.
First-Year Class: 1,434 total; 2,321 applied, 99% were accepted, 62% of whom enrolled.
Graduation Requirements: 64 credit hours.
Computers on Campus: 470 computers available on campus for general student use. A campus-wide network can be accessed. Computers for student use in computer center, computer labs, learning resource center, engineering, technical learning center provide access to the Internet/World Wide Web. Staffed computer lab on campus provides training in use of computers, software.

EXPENSES

Expenses for 1997–98: Area resident tuition: $1344 full-time, $42 per credit hour part-time. State resident tuition: $1696 full-time, $53 per credit hour part-time. Nonresident tuition: $2144 full-time, $67 per credit hour part-time.

LD Services Contact: Ms. Suelaine Matthews, Manager, ACCESS Office, St. Louis Community College at Florissant Valley, 3400 Pershall Road, St. Louis, MO 63135, 314-595-4551. Fax: 314-595-4544. Email: smatthew@fv.stlcc.cc.mo.us.

ST. LOUIS COMMUNITY COLLEGE AT FOREST PARK

St. Louis, Missouri

LEARNING DISABILITIES SERVICES INFORMATION

ACCESS OFFICE - disAbility Support Services began offering services in 1982. Currently the program serves 50 undergraduates with LD. Students diagnosed with ADD/ADHD are eligible for the same services available to students with LD.

Staff: 2 full-time staff members, including director, specialist. Services provided by counselor.

Special Fees: No special fees are charged for services to students with LD.

Applications and admissions: *Required:* high school transcript, psychoeducational report completed since age 16 or older, GED (in lieu of high school diploma), placement tests in English, reading, and math; *recommended:* high school IEP (Individualized Education Program). Students may begin taking classes any term. *Application deadline:* continuous.

Special policies: The college has written policies regarding grade forgiveness; substitutions and waivers of admissions, graduation, and degree requirements.

PROGRAM AND SERVICE COMPONENTS

Academic advising: Provided by unit staff members, academic advisers. Students with LD may take up to 15 credit hours each term; most take 9 to 14 credit hours; 12 credit hours required to maintain full-time status.

Counseling services: Individual counseling, career counseling.

Basic skills remediation: Offered one-on-one, in small groups, and in class-size groups by regular teachers. Available in reading, math, spelling, written language, study skills.

Subject-area tutoring: Offered one-on-one and in small groups by peer tutors. Available in some subjects.

Auxiliary aids: Taped textbooks, tape recorders, calculators, typewriters, word-processors with spell-check, talking computers, optical character readers, spell checkers.

Auxiliary services: Alternative test arrangements, notetakers, priority registration, readers.

Campus support group: A special student organization is available to students with LD.

GENERAL COLLEGE INFORMATION

District-supported, 2-year, coed. Part of St. Louis Community College System. Awards associate degrees. Founded 1962. *Setting:* 34-acre suburban campus. *Total enrollment:* 8,197. *Faculty:* 366 (131 full-time, 235 part-time).

Enrollment Profile: 8,197 students from 13 states and territories, 29 other countries. 61% women, 39% men, 76% part-time, 95% state residents, 13% transferred in, 1% international, 62% 25 or older, 0% Native American, 0% Hispanic, 32% black, 5% Asian or Pacific Islander. *Areas of study chosen:* 27% business management and administrative services, 24% physical sciences, 20% engineering and applied sciences, 10% liberal arts/general studies, 8% computer and information sciences, 5% biological and life sciences, 5% mathematics, 1% fine arts.

First-Year Class: 1,722 applied, 100% were accepted.

Graduation Requirements: 64 credit hours; math/science requirements vary according to program; computer course for business-related majors.

Computers on Campus: 302 computers available on campus for general student use. Computers for student use in computer center, library. Staffed computer lab on campus.

EXPENSES

Expenses for 1997–98: Area resident tuition: $1344 full-time, $42 per credit hour part-time. State resident tuition: $1696 full-time, $53 per credit hour part-time. Nonresident tuition: $2144 full-time, $67 per credit hour part-time.

LD Services Contact: Ms. Monica L. Hébert, Manager, ACCESS OFFICE, St. Louis Community College at Forest Park, G-215, 5600 Oakland Avenue, St. Louis, MO 63110, 314-644-9039. Fax: 314-951-9439.

ST. LOUIS COMMUNITY COLLEGE AT MERAMEC

Kirkwood, Missouri

LEARNING DISABILITIES SERVICES INFORMATION

Access Office began offering services in 1978. Currently the program serves 380 undergraduates with LD. Students diagnosed with ADD/ADHD are eligible for the same services available to students with LD.

Staff: 7 full-time staff members, including coordinator, counselors/advisers, secretaries. Services provided by remediation specialists, tutors, counselors, diagnostic specialists.

Special Fees: No special fees are charged for services to students with LD.

Applications and admissions: *Required:* high school transcript, adult assessment; *recommended:* untimed or extended time ACT, psychoeducational report completed within 3 years. Students may begin taking classes any term. *Application deadline:* continuous.

Special policies: The college has written policies regarding grade forgiveness; substitutions and waivers of admissions, graduation, and degree requirements.

PROGRAM AND SERVICE COMPONENTS

Special preparation or orientation: Required orientation held during registration and individually by special arrangement before classes begin.

Diagnostic testing: Reading, math, written language, personality.

Academic advising: Provided by unit staff members, academic advisers. Most students with LD take 10 to 12 credit hours each term; 12 credit hours (fewer with supporting documentation) required to maintain full-time status; 3 credit hours required to be eligible for financial aid.

Counseling services: Individual counseling, small-group counseling, career counseling, self-advocacy training.

Basic skills remediation: Offered in class-size groups by regular teachers. Available in reading, math, written language, learning strategies, study skills, time management.

Subject-area tutoring: Offered one-on-one, in small groups, and in class-size groups by professional teachers, peer tutors, educational assistants, supplemental instructors. Available in some subjects.

Auxiliary aids: Taped textbooks, tape recorders, calculators, typewriters, word-processors with spell-check, personal computers, optical character readers, FM systems, Dragon Dictate, Soundproof Gold.

Auxiliary services: Alternative test arrangements, notetakers, advocacy, interpreters, stenographers, readers, writers.

GENERAL COLLEGE INFORMATION

District-supported, 2-year, coed. Part of St. Louis Community College System. Awards associate degrees. Founded 1963. *Setting:* 80-acre suburban campus with easy access to St. Louis. *Educational spending 1995–96:* $1304 per undergrad. *Total enrollment:* 13,570. *Faculty:* 570 (185 full-time, 14% with terminal degrees, 385 part-time).

Enrollment Profile: 13,570 students from 10 states and territories, 18 other countries. 58% women, 42% men, 64% part-time, 98% state residents, 7% transferred in, 1% international, 42% 25 or older, 1% Native American, 1% Hispanic, 3% black, 2% Asian or Pacific Islander. *Retention:* 50% of 1995 full-time freshmen returned. *Areas of study chosen:* 60% liberal arts/general studies, 14% business management and administrative services, 4% communications and journalism, 3% computer and information sciences, 3% education, 3% health professions and related sciences, 2% architecture, 2% engineering and applied sciences, 2% fine arts, 2% social sciences, 1% physical sciences, 1% vocational and home economics.

First-Year Class: 2,595 total. Of the students who applied, 100% were accepted.

Graduation Requirements: 64 credit hours.

Computers on Campus: 420 computers available on campus for general student use. Computers for student use in computer center, computer labs, classrooms, library, student center, departmental labs provide

St. Louis Community College at Meramec (continued)

access to the Internet/World Wide Web. Staffed computer lab on campus provides training in use of computers, software. *Academic computing expenditure 1995–96:* $186,380.

EXPENSES

Expenses for 1996–97: Area resident tuition: $1344 full-time, $42 per credit hour part-time. State resident tuition: $1696 full-time, $53 per credit hour part-time. Nonresident tuition: $2144 full-time, $67 per credit hour part-time. Part-time mandatory fees: $2 per credit hour. Full-time mandatory fees: $64.

LD Services Contact: Ms. Debbie Koenig, Secretary, St. Louis Community College at Meramec, 11333 Big Bend Boulevard, Kirkwood, MO 63122-5720, 314-984-7673. Fax: 314-984-7117.

ST. PAUL TECHNICAL COLLEGE

St. Paul, Minnesota

LEARNING DISABILITIES SERVICES INFORMATION

Services for Students with Disabilities began offering services in 1988. Currently the program serves 110 undergraduates with LD. Students diagnosed with ADD/ADHD are eligible for the same services available to students with LD, as well as quiet testing room, weekly check-ins with Disability Coordinator.

Staff: 1 full-time staff member (coordinator). Services provided by tutors, counselors.

Special Fees: No special fees are charged for services to students with LD.

Applications and admissions: *Required:* ACT ASSET; *recommended:* high school transcript, psychoeducational report completed within 3 years. Students may begin taking classes any term. *Application deadline:* continuous.

Special policies: The college has written policies regarding substitutions and waivers of admissions, graduation, and degree requirements.

PROGRAM AND SERVICE COMPONENTS

Special preparation or orientation: Optional orientation offered before registration, during registration, after classes begin, individually by special arrangement.

Diagnostic testing: Reading, math, study skills, hearing, occupational interests.

Academic advising: Provided by unit staff members, academic advisers. Students with LD may take up to 15 credits each term; most take 6 to 12 credits; 12 credits required to maintain full-time status; source of aid determines number of credits required to be eligible for financial aid.

Counseling services: Career counseling, self-advocacy training.

Basic skills remediation: Offered in small groups and in class-size groups by LD teachers, regular teachers, interactive computer technology lab. Available in reading, math, spelling, handwriting, spoken language, written language, learning strategies, study skills, time management, social skills, speech, occupational chemistry, physics, developmental medical terminology, anatomy.

Subject-area tutoring: Offered one-on-one and in small groups by peer tutors. Available in all subjects.

Special courses: College survival skills, reading, vocabulary development, communication skills, composition, learning strategies, word processing, time management, math, typing, study skills, career planning. Most offered for credit.

Auxiliary aids: Taped textbooks, tape recorders, calculators, typewriters, word-processors with spell-check, personal computers, talking computers, optical character readers.

Auxiliary services: Alternative test arrangements, notetakers, priority registration, advocacy, readers, editing assistance, modified scheduling.

GENERAL COLLEGE INFORMATION

State-related, 2-year, coed. Part of Minnesota State Colleges and Universities System. Awards associate degrees. Founded 1922. *Setting:* urban campus. *Total enrollment:* 3,400. *Faculty:* 565 (115 full-time, 450 part-time).

Enrollment Profile: 3,400 students: 51% women, 49% men, 27% part-time, 93% state residents, 21% transferred in, 0% international, 50% 25 or older, 1% Native American, 4% Hispanic, 11% black, 12% Asian or Pacific Islander. *Retention:* 40% of 1995 full-time freshmen returned.

First-Year Class: Of the students who applied, 100% were accepted.

Graduation Requirements: 110 credits; 4 credits of math/science; computer course for most majors; internship (some majors).

Computers on Campus: 520 computers available on campus for general student use. Computers for student use in computer center, computer labs, learning resource center, classrooms, library provide access to the Internet/World Wide Web. Staffed computer lab on campus provides training in use of computers, software.

EXPENSES

Expenses for 1996–97: *Application fee:* $20. State resident tuition: $2288 full-time, $41.60 per credit part-time. Nonresident tuition: $4576 full-time, $83.20 per credit part-time. Part-time mandatory fees: $1.80 per credit. Wisconsin residents pay state resident tuition rates. Tuition for North Dakota residents: $2638 full-time, $47.85 per credit part-time. Full-time mandatory fees: $100.

LD Services Contact: Ms. Carolyn Sorenson, Disability Coordinator, St. Paul Technical College, 235 Marshall Avenue, St. Paul, MN 55102-1800, 612-228-4300. Fax: 612-221-1416.

ST. PETERSBURG JUNIOR COLLEGE

St. Petersburg, Florida

LEARNING DISABILITIES SERVICES INFORMATION

Office of Services for Students with Disabilities began offering services in 1989. Currently the program serves 340 undergraduates with LD. Students diagnosed with ADD/ADHD are eligible for the same services available to students with LD.

Staff: 3 full-time, 5 part-time staff members, including coordinators. Services provided by tutors, counselors, diagnostic specialists, learning specialists, job specialists.

Special Fees: No special fees are charged for services to students with LD.

Applications and admissions: Open admissions. Students may begin taking classes any term. *Application deadline:* continuous.

Special policies: The college has written policies regarding grade forgiveness; substitutions and waivers of admissions, graduation, and degree requirements.

PROGRAM AND SERVICE COMPONENTS

Special preparation or orientation: Optional orientation offered before registration and during summer prior to enrollment.

Diagnostic testing: Reading, math, spelling, spoken language, written language, motor abilities, perceptual skills, learning strategies.

Academic advising: Provided by unit staff members, academic advisers. Most students with LD take 9 to 12 semester hours each term; 12 semester hours required to maintain full-time status; 6 semester hours (part-time), 12 semester hours (full-time) required to be eligible for financial aid.

Counseling services: Individual counseling, small-group counseling.

Basic skills remediation: Offered one-on-one, in small groups, and in class-size groups by regular teachers, LD trained tutors. Available in reading, math, learning strategies, study skills, time management.

Subject-area tutoring: Offered one-on-one and in small groups by professional teachers, peer tutors. Available in most subjects.

Auxiliary aids: Taped textbooks, tape recorders, calculators, typewriters, word-processors with spell-check, personal computers, optical character readers, spell checkers (speaking, non-speaking, medical), speaking computer peripherals and software, video and computer testing, video subject tutoring, Reading Edge, FM receivers (personal).

Auxiliary services: Alternative test arrangements, notetakers, priority registration, readers, scribes.

GENERAL COLLEGE INFORMATION

State and locally supported, 2-year, coed. Awards associate degrees. Founded 1927. *Setting:* suburban campus. *Endowment:* $2.4 million. *Total enrollment:* 17,535. *Faculty:* 899 (299 full-time, 22% with terminal degrees, 600 part-time).

Enrollment Profile: 17,535 students from 45 states and territories, 30 other countries. 62% women, 38% men, 76% part-time, 86% state residents, 18% transferred in, 1% international, 49% 25 or older, 2% Native American, 3% Hispanic, 7% black, 4% Asian or Pacific Islander.

First-Year Class: 2,422 total. Of the students who applied, 100% were accepted, 100% of whom enrolled. 2% from top 10% of their high school class, 30% from top quarter, 68% from top half.

Graduation Requirements: 60 semester hours; math/science requirements vary according to program; computer course.

Computers on Campus: A campus-wide network can be accessed from off-campus. Students can contact faculty members and/or advisers through e-mail. Computers for student use in computer labs, classrooms, library provide access to the Internet/World Wide Web, on- and off-campus e-mail addresses. Staffed computer lab on campus provides training in use of computers, software. *Academic computing expenditure 1995–96:* $555,258.

EXPENSES

Expenses for 1997–98: *Application fee:* $22. State resident tuition: $1245 full-time, $41.50 per semester hour part-time. Nonresident tuition: $4581 full-time, $152.71 per semester hour part-time.
LD Services Contact: Ms. Melanie Johnson, Learning Specialist, St. Petersburg Junior College, PO Box 13489, St. Petersburg, FL 33733, 813-791-2710.

ST. PHILIP'S COLLEGE

San Antonio, Texas

LEARNING DISABILITIES SERVICES INFORMATION

Learning Disabilities Program began offering services in 1987. Currently the program serves 416 undergraduates with LD. Students diagnosed with ADD/ADHD are eligible for the same services available to students with LD.
Staff: 2 full-time, 14 part-time staff members, including director, coordinator. Services provided by remediation specialists, tutors, counselor, diagnostic specialists, computer lab technicians.
Special Fees: No special fees are charged for services to students with LD.
Applications and admissions: *Required:* psychoeducational report completed within 3 years. Students may begin taking classes any term. *Application deadline:* continuous.
Special policies: The college has written policies regarding substitutions and waivers of admissions and graduation requirements.

PROGRAM AND SERVICE COMPONENTS

Special preparation or orientation: Optional orientation offered during summer transition program or 16-week fall program after classes begin.
Diagnostic testing: Intelligence, reading, math, spelling, handwriting, written language, perceptual skills, study skills, personality, psychoneurology, learning strategies.
Academic advising: Provided by unit staff members, academic advisers. Students with LD may take up to 18 credits each term; most take 9 to 12 credits; 12 credits (fewer with special permission) required to maintain full-time status; 9 credits required to be eligible for financial aid.
Counseling services: Individual counseling, small-group counseling, career counseling, self-advocacy training.
Basic skills remediation: Offered one-on-one, in small groups, and in class-size groups by LD teachers, regular teachers, LD specialist, education skills specialist; computer-aided instruction also offered. Available in reading, math, spelling, written language, learning strategies, perceptual skills, study skills, time management, computer skills.
Subject-area tutoring: Offered one-on-one and in small groups by professional teachers, peer tutors, professional tutors. Available in most subjects.
Special courses: College survival skills, reading, communication skills, learning strategies, word processing, time management, math, study skills, concentration on test anxiety reduction. Most offered for credit; most enter into overall grade point average.
Auxiliary aids: Taped textbooks, tape recorders, calculators, typewriters, word-processors with spell-check, talking computers, optical character readers.
Auxiliary services: Alternative test arrangements, advocacy, test readers and scribes.
Campus support group: A special student organization is available to students with LD.

GENERAL COLLEGE INFORMATION

District-supported, 2-year, coed. Part of Alamo Community College District System. Awards associate degrees. Founded 1898. *Setting:* 16-acre urban campus. *Total enrollment:* 7,867. *Faculty:* 462 (200 full-time, 262 part-time); student–undergrad faculty ratio is 17:1.
Enrollment Profile: 7,867 students from 50 states and territories, 5 other countries. 54% women, 46% men, 67% part-time, 86% state residents, 13% transferred in, 55% 25 or older, 1% Native American, 46% Hispanic, 21% black, 2% Asian or Pacific Islander. *Areas of study chosen:* 20% health professions and related sciences, 6% business management and administrative services, 4% education, 2% computer and information sciences, 1% biological and life sciences, 1% fine arts, 1% psychology, 1% social sciences. *Most popular recent majors:* nursing, business administration/commerce/management.
First-Year Class: 1,534 total; 1,534 applied, 100% were accepted, 100% of whom enrolled.
Graduation Requirements: 60 credits; computer course for business administration majors.
Computers on Campus: 255 computers available on campus for general student use. Computer purchase/lease plans available. A campus-wide network can be accessed from off-campus. Students can contact faculty members and/or advisers through e-mail. Computers for student use in computer labs, learning resource center, library, student center provide access to the Internet/World Wide Web, on- and off-campus e-mail addresses. Staffed computer lab on campus provides training in use of computers, software.

EXPENSES

Expenses for 1997–98: Area resident tuition: $720 full-time. State resident tuition: $1380 full-time. Nonresident tuition: $2760 full-time. Part-time tuition per semester hour ranges from $120 to $264 for area residents, $230 to $506 for state residents, $460 to $1012 for nonresidents. Part-time mandatory fees per semester range from $74 to $79. Full-time mandatory fees: $158.
LD Services Contact: Ms. Rhonda H. Rapp, Learning Disabilities Specialist, St. Philip's College, 1801 Martin Luther King Drive, San Antonio, TX 78203-2098, 210-531-3474. Fax: 210-531-3513. Email: rrapp@accdvm.accd.edu.

SALISH KOOTENAI COLLEGE

Pablo, Montana

LEARNING DISABILITIES SERVICES INFORMATION

ACCESS currently serves undergraduate students with LD. Students diagnosed with ADD/ADHD are eligible for the same services available to students with LD.
Staff: Includes director, coordinator. Services provided by remediation specialists, tutors, counselors, diagnostic specialists.
Special Fees: No special fees are charged for services to students with LD.
Applications and admissions: *Required:* high school transcript. Students may begin taking classes any term. *Application deadline:* continuous.
Special policies: The college has written policies regarding grade forgiveness; substitutions and waivers of admissions and graduation requirements.

PROGRAM AND SERVICE COMPONENTS

Academic advising: Provided by unit staff members, academic advisers. Students with LD may take up to as many credits as an individual can handle each term; most take 12 to 18 credits; 12 credits required to maintain full-time status.
Counseling services: Individual counseling, small-group counseling, career counseling, self-advocacy training.
Auxiliary aids: Taped textbooks, tape recorders, calculators, typewriters, word-processors with spell-check, personal computers.
Auxiliary services: Alternative test arrangements, notetakers, priority registration, advocacy.

GENERAL COLLEGE INFORMATION

Independent, primarily 2-year, coed. Awards associate, bachelor's degrees. Founded 1977. *Setting:* 4-acre rural campus. *Total enrollment:* 750. *Faculty:* 55 (20 full-time, 35 part-time); student–undergrad faculty ratio is 18:1.
Enrollment Profile: 750 students from 3 states and territories. 56% women, 44% men, 50% part-time, 90% state residents, 30% transferred in, 0% international, 48% 25 or older, 65% Native American, 0% Hispanic, 0% black, 0% Asian or Pacific Islander. *Most popular recent majors:* nursing, human services, secretarial studies/office management.
First-Year Class: 150 total; 300 applied, 100% were accepted, 50% of whom enrolled. 50% from top half of their high school class.
Graduation Requirements: 92 credits for associate, 180 credits for bachelor's; 1 college algebra course; computer course.

Salish Kootenai College (continued)

Computers on Campus: 20 computers available on campus for general student use. Computers for student use in computer labs.

EXPENSES

Expenses for 1996–97: State resident tuition: $2432 full-time, $106 per credit part-time. Nonresident tuition: $6600 full-time, $205 per credit part-time. Part-time mandatory fees per quarter range from $63.25 to $195.75. Tuition for reservation residents: $1890 full-time, $91.25 per credit part-time. Full-time mandatory fees: $471.

LD Services Contact: Ms. Mary Herak, Counselor, Salish Kootenai College, PO Box 117, Pablo, MT 59855-0117, 406-675-4800 Ext. 205. Fax: 406-675-4801. Email: herak@skc.edu.

SAN BERNARDINO VALLEY COLLEGE

San Bernardino, California

LEARNING DISABILITIES SERVICES INFORMATION

Disabled Students Programs and Services currently serves 550 undergraduates with LD. Students diagnosed with ADD/ADHD are eligible for the same services available to students with LD.

Staff: 6 full-time, 4 part-time staff members, including coordinator. Services provided by remediation specialists, tutors, counselors, diagnostic specialists.

Special Fees: No special fees are charged for services to students with LD.

Applications and admissions: *Recommended:* psychoeducational report completed within 3 years. Students may begin taking classes in fall, spring, or summer. *Application deadline:* continuous.

PROGRAM AND SERVICE COMPONENTS

Special preparation or orientation: Required orientation held before registration.

Diagnostic testing: Intelligence, reading, math, spelling, handwriting, written language, learning strategies.

Academic advising: Provided by unit staff members. Students with LD may take up to 18 semester units each term; most take 6 to 12 semester units; 12 semester units required to maintain full-time status and be eligible for financial aid.

Counseling services: Individual counseling, self-advocacy training, academic and personal counseling.

Basic skills remediation: Offered one-on-one and in small groups by LD teachers, teacher trainees. Available in reading, math, spelling, written language.

Subject-area tutoring: Offered one-on-one and in small groups by peer tutors. Available in most subjects.

Special courses: Reading, math. None offered for credit.

Auxiliary aids: Taped textbooks, tape recorders, calculators, typewriters, word-processors with spell-check, personal computers, talking computers, optical character readers.

Auxiliary services: Alternative test arrangements, notetakers, priority registration, advocacy.

GENERAL COLLEGE INFORMATION

State and locally supported, 2-year, coed. Part of San Bernardino Community College District System. Awards associate degrees. Founded 1926. *Setting:* 82-acre campus with easy access to Los Angeles. *Total enrollment:* 10,156. *Faculty:* 375 (175 full-time, 200 part-time).

Enrollment Profile: 10,156 students from 2 states and territories. 52% women, 48% men, 70% part-time, 90% state residents, 22% transferred in, 55% 25 or older, 5% Native American, 20% Hispanic, 14% black, 7% Asian or Pacific Islander.

First-Year Class: 1,591 total. Of the students who applied, 100% were accepted.

Graduation Requirements: 60 semester units; 1 math course or completion of proficiency exam; 6 semester units of science.

Computers on Campus: 180 computers available on campus for general student use. Computers for student use in computer center, learning resource center, library. Staffed computer lab on campus provides training in use of computers.

EXPENSES

Expenses for 1997–98: State resident tuition: $0 full-time. Nonresident tuition: $3540 full-time, $118 per unit part-time. Part-time mandatory fees per semester range from $21 to $163. Full-time mandatory fees: $434.

LD Services Contact: Ms. Rebeccah Warren Marlatt, Department Head, San Bernardino Valley College, 701 South Mt. Vernon Avenue, San Bernardino, CA 92410, 909-888-6511 Ext. 1642.

SANDHILLS COMMUNITY COLLEGE

Pinehurst, North Carolina

LEARNING DISABILITIES SERVICES INFORMATION

Handicapped Services began offering services in 1981. Currently the program serves 10 to 15 undergraduates with LD. Students diagnosed with ADD/ADHD are eligible for the same services available to students with LD.

Staff: Includes coordinator. Services provided by remediation specialists, tutors.

Special Fees: No special fees are charged for services to students with LD.

Applications and admissions: *Required:* high school transcript, psychoeducational report completed within 5 years. Students may begin taking classes in fall only. *Application deadline:* continuous.

PROGRAM AND SERVICE COMPONENTS

Academic advising: Provided by academic advisers. Students with LD may take up to 18 semester hours each term; most take 12 to 14 semester hours; 12 semester hours required to maintain full-time status.

Counseling services: Individual counseling.

Subject-area tutoring: Offered one-on-one by peer tutors. Available in most subjects.

Auxiliary aids: Taped textbooks, tape recorders, calculators, typewriters, word-processors with spell-check.

Auxiliary services: Alternative test arrangements, notetakers, advocacy.

GENERAL COLLEGE INFORMATION

State and locally supported, 2-year, coed. Part of North Carolina Community College System. Awards associate degrees. Founded 1963. *Setting:* 230-acre small-town campus. *Endowment:* $1.2 million. *Educational spending 1995–96:* $3316 per undergrad. *Total enrollment:* 2,489. *Faculty:* 148 (102 full-time, 98% with terminal degrees, 46 part-time); student–undergrad faculty ratio is 17:1.

Enrollment Profile: 2,489 students: 62% women, 38% men, 42% part-time, 98% state residents, 21% transferred in, 1% international, 40% 25 or older, 3% Native American, 1% Hispanic, 20% black, 1% Asian or Pacific Islander. *Retention:* 47% of 1995 full-time freshmen returned. *Areas of study chosen:* 23% health professions and related sciences, 15% business management and administrative services, 12% liberal arts/general studies, 7% social sciences, 6% computer and information sciences, 6% vocational and home economics, 5% engineering and applied sciences, 4% agriculture, 4% biological and life sciences, 3% education, 2% architecture, 2% fine arts, 1% communications and journalism, 1% English language/literature/letters, 1% mathematics, 1% natural resource sciences, 1% performing arts, 1% physical sciences, 1% predentistry, 1% prelaw, 1% premed, 1% prevet, 1% psychology. *Most popular recent majors:* liberal arts/general studies, nursing, business administration/commerce/management.

First-Year Class: 545 total; 1,040 applied, 100% were accepted, 52% of whom enrolled.

Graduation Requirements: Computer course for most majors; internship (some majors).

Computers on Campus: 300 computers available on campus for general student use. A campus-wide network can be accessed from off-campus. Students can contact faculty members and/or advisers through e-mail. Computers for student use in computer center, computer labs, learning resource center, classrooms, library, writing center provide access to the Internet/World Wide Web, on- and off-campus e-mail addresses. Staffed computer lab on campus provides training in use of computers, software. *Academic computing expenditure 1995–96:* $129,115.

EXPENSES

Expenses for 1997–98: State resident tuition: $560 full-time, $20 per semester hour part-time. Nonresident tuition: $4564 full-time, $163 per semester hour part-time. Part-time mandatory fees: $14 per semester. Full-time mandatory fees: $28.

LD Services Contact: Ms. Peggie R. Chavis, Testing/Disabilities Coordinator, Sandhills Community College, 2200 Airport Road, Pinehurst, NC 28374-8299, 910-695-3733.

SAN DIEGO CITY COLLEGE

San Diego, California

LEARNING DISABILITIES SERVICES INFORMATION

Learning Development Program: Disabled Student Services began offering services in 1977. Currently the program serves 241 undergraduates with LD. Students diagnosed with ADD/ADHD are eligible for the same services available to students with LD.

Staff: 1 full-time, 16 part-time staff members, including coordinator. Services provided by remediation specialist, tutors, counselor, diagnostic specialists, educational technician.

Special Fees: No special fees are charged for services to students with LD.

Applications and admissions: Open admissions. Students may begin taking classes in fall or spring. *Application deadline:* continuous.

Special policies: The college has written policies regarding substitutions and waivers of graduation and degree requirements.

PROGRAM AND SERVICE COMPONENTS

Special preparation or orientation: Required orientation held during registration.

Diagnostic testing: Intelligence, reading, math, spelling, spoken language, written language, perceptual skills, speech, hearing, receptive vocabulary.

Academic advising: Provided by unit staff members. Students with LD may take up to 16 credits each term; most take 9 to 12 credits; 12 credits required to maintain full-time status and be eligible for financial aid.

Counseling services: Individual counseling, small-group counseling, career counseling.

Basic skills remediation: Offered one-on-one and in small groups by LD teachers; computer-aided instruction also offered. Available in reading, math, spelling, written language, learning strategies, perceptual skills, study skills, time management, speech.

Subject-area tutoring: Offered one-on-one and in small groups by professional teachers, peer tutors. Available in most subjects.

Special courses: College survival skills, reading, vocabulary development, word processing, math, typing, study skills, career planning, spelling, sentence writing strategy. All offered for credit; all enter into overall grade point average.

Auxiliary aids: Taped textbooks, tape recorders, word-processors with spell-check, talking computers, optical character readers.

Auxiliary services: Alternative test arrangements, notetakers, priority registration, advocacy.

Campus support group: A special student organization is available to students with LD.

GENERAL COLLEGE INFORMATION

State and locally supported, 2-year, coed. Part of San Diego Community College District System. Awards associate degrees. Founded 1914. *Setting:* 56-acre urban campus. *Total enrollment:* 12,652. *Faculty:* 250 (180 full-time, 70 part-time).

Enrollment Profile: 12,652 students: 52% women, 48% men, 75% part-time, 97% state residents, 14% transferred in, 1% international, 63% 25 or older, 1% Native American, 23% Hispanic, 22% black, 13% Asian or Pacific Islander.

First-Year Class: 1,289 total; 1,289 applied, 100% were accepted, 49% of whom enrolled.

Graduation Requirements: 60 semester units; math/science requirements vary according to program; computer course for business; internship (some majors).

Computers on Campus: 396 computers available on campus for general student use. Computer purchase/lease plans available. A campuswide network can be accessed. Computers for student use in computer center, computer labs, learning resource center, library, graphics room provide access to the Internet/World Wide Web. Staffed computer lab on campus provides training in use of computers, software. *Academic computing expenditure 1995–96:* $200,101.

EXPENSES

Expenses for 1997–98: State resident tuition: $0 full-time. Nonresident tuition: $3300 full-time, $110 per unit part-time. Part-time mandatory fees: $13 per unit. Full-time mandatory fees: $390.

LD Services Contact: Mr. Vince Ceccacci, Counselor, San Diego City College, 1313 12th Avenue, San Diego, CA 92101-4787, 619-230-2513.

SAN DIEGO MESA COLLEGE

San Diego, California

LEARNING DISABILITIES SERVICES INFORMATION

Learning Disabilities Program began offering services in 1976. Currently the program serves 225 undergraduates with LD. Students diagnosed with ADD/ADHD are eligible for the same services available to students with LD.

Staff: 4 full-time, 4 part-time staff members, including department chair, supervisors. Services provided by remediation specialists, tutors, counselor/diagnostic specialist, computer education technician.

Special Fees: A fee is charged for diagnostic testing.

Applications and admissions: *Required:* California Assessment System for Adults with Learning Disabilities; *recommended:* high school transcript, IEP (Individualized Education Program), psychoeducational report completed within 3 years. Students may begin taking classes in fall, spring, or summer. *Application deadline:* continuous.

Special policies: The college has written policies regarding grade forgiveness.

PROGRAM AND SERVICE COMPONENTS

Special preparation or orientation: Required orientation held before registration, during registration, after classes begin, during the summer.

Diagnostic testing: Intelligence, reading, math, spelling, perceptual skills.

Academic advising: Provided by unit staff members, academic advisers. Students with LD may take up to 20 semester units each term; most take 6 to 12 semester units; 12 semester units required to maintain full-time status and be eligible for financial aid.

Counseling services: Individual counseling, career counseling.

Basic skills remediation: Offered one-on-one, in small groups, and in class-size groups by LD teachers, trained tutors; computer-aided instruction also offered. Available in reading, math, spelling, learning strategies, study skills.

Subject-area tutoring: Offered one-on-one and in small groups by professional teachers, peer tutors, trained tutors. Available in most subjects.

Special courses: College survival skills, learning strategies, word processing, Internet use, study skills, spelling. All offered for credit; some enter into overall grade point average.

Auxiliary aids: Taped textbooks, tape recorders, word-processors with spell-check, talking computers, optical character readers, carbonless notepaper.

Auxiliary services: Alternative test arrangements, notetakers, priority registration, advocacy.

Campus support group: A special student organization is available to students with LD.

GENERAL COLLEGE INFORMATION

District-supported, 2-year, coed. Part of San Diego Community College District System. Awards associate degrees. Founded 1964. *Setting:* 104-acre suburban campus. *Total enrollment:* 22,677. *Faculty:* 676 (228 full-time, 448 part-time).

Enrollment Profile: 22,677 students: 53% women, 47% men, 71% part-time, 97% state residents, 16% transferred in, 1% international, 51% 25 or older, 2% Native American, 12% Hispanic, 7% black, 19% Asian or Pacific Islander. *Areas of study chosen:* 7% business management and administrative services, 5% liberal arts/general studies, 5% vocational and home economics, 4% biological and life sciences, 4% health professions and related sciences, 3% computer and information sciences, 3% psychology, 2% engineering and applied sciences, 1% architecture, 1% English language/literature/letters, 1% library and information studies, 1% social sciences.

First-Year Class: Of the students who applied, 100% were accepted.

Graduation Requirements: 60 semester hours; math/science requirements vary according to program; 2 courses in a foreign language.

Computers on Campus: 350 computers available on campus for general student use. Computers for student use in computer center, computer labs, learning resource center, library. Staffed computer lab on campus provides training in use of computers, software.

EXPENSES

Expenses for 1997–98: State resident tuition: $0 full-time. Nonresident tuition: $3540 full-time, $118 per unit part-time. Part-time mandatory fees per semester range from $24 to $154. Full-time mandatory fees: $412.

San Diego Mesa College (continued)

LD Services Contact: Mrs. Glenyth A. Turner, Learning Disabilities Assessment Specialist/Counselor, San Diego Mesa College, 7250 Mesa College Drive, San Diego, CA 92111-4998, 619-627-2780. Fax: 619-627-2460. Email: gturner@sdccd.cc.ca.us.

SAN DIEGO MIRAMAR COLLEGE

San Diego, California

LEARNING DISABILITIES SERVICES INFORMATION

Disabled Students Program and Services (DSPS) began offering services in 1990. Currently the program serves 120 undergraduates with LD. Students diagnosed with ADD/ADHD are eligible for the same services available to students with LD.

Staff: 1 full-time, 4 part-time staff members, including coordinator. Services provided by tutors, counselor, diagnostic specialist.

Special Fees: $6.50 for diagnostic testing

Applications and admissions: *Required:* psychoeducational report completed within 3 years, California Community College Eligibility Model; *recommended:* personal interview. Students may begin taking classes any term. *Application deadline:* continuous.

PROGRAM AND SERVICE COMPONENTS

Diagnostic testing: Intelligence, reading, math, spelling, written language, perceptual skills, study skills, personality, social skills, learning strategies, word recognition, academic attributes.

Academic advising: Provided by academic advisers. Students with LD may take up to 12 credits each term; most take 3 to 9 credits; 12 credits required to maintain full-time status; 12 credits (fewer with special permission) required to be eligible for financial aid.

Counseling services: Individual counseling.

Basic skills remediation: Offered one-on-one and in small groups by LD teachers; computer-aided instruction also offered. Available in reading, math, spelling, written language, learning strategies, study skills, time management, social skills, computer skills.

Subject-area tutoring: Offered one-on-one by peer tutors, professional tutors. Available in most subjects.

Special courses: College survival skills, word processing, Internet use, typing, study skills, individualized courses in math, reading, spelling, writing and test taking strategies. All offered for credit; all enter into overall grade point average.

Auxiliary aids: Taped textbooks, tape recorders, word-processors with spell-check, talking computers, optical character readers.

Auxiliary services: Alternative test arrangements, notetakers, priority registration, advocacy.

GENERAL COLLEGE INFORMATION

State and locally supported, 2-year, coed. Part of San Diego Community College District System. Awards associate degrees. Founded 1969. *Setting:* 120-acre suburban campus. *Faculty:* 243 (64 full-time, 20% with terminal degrees, 179 part-time).

Enrollment Profile: 41% women, 59% men, 89% part-time, 98% state residents, 14% transferred in, 1% international, 62% 25 or older, 1% Native American, 11% Hispanic, 6% black, 23% Asian or Pacific Islander. *Most popular recent majors:* liberal arts/general studies, fire science, law enforcement/police sciences.

First-Year Class: Of the students who applied, 100% were accepted, 99% of whom enrolled.

Graduation Requirements: 60 credits; math proficiency; computer course for fire technology majors.

Computers on Campus: 230 computers available on campus for general student use. Computers for student use in computer center, computer labs, learning resource center, classrooms, library. Staffed computer lab on campus provides training in use of computers, software.

EXPENSES

Expenses for 1997–98: State resident tuition: $0 full-time. Nonresident tuition: $3540 full-time, $118 per unit part-time. Part-time mandatory fees per semester range from $15.50 to $145.50. Full-time mandatory fees: $395.

LD Services Contact: Mrs. Kathleen Doorly, DSPS Coordinator, San Diego Miramar College, 10440 Black Mountain Road, San Diego, CA 92126-2999, 619-536-7212. Fax: 619-536-4302. Email: kdoorly@sdccd.cc.ca.us.

SAN JACINTO COLLEGE–CENTRAL CAMPUS

Pasadena, Texas

LEARNING DISABILITIES SERVICES INFORMATION

Special Populations began offering services in 1991. Currently the program serves 34 undergraduates with LD. Students diagnosed with ADD/ADHD are eligible for the same services available to students with LD.

Staff: 2 full-time staff members, including director, coordinator. Services provided by remediation specialists, tutors, counselors.

Special Fees: No special fees are charged for services to students with LD.

Applications and admissions: *Required:* high school transcript, basic skills testing; *recommended:* personal interview, psychoeducational report completed within 3 years. Students may begin taking classes any term. *Application deadline:* continuous.

PROGRAM AND SERVICE COMPONENTS

Academic advising: Provided by academic advisers. Students with LD may take up to 18 credit hours each term; most take 9 to 12 credit hours; 12 credit hours required to maintain full-time status; 3 to 6 credit hours required to be eligible for financial aid.

Counseling services: Individual counseling, career counseling.

Basic skills remediation: Offered one-on-one and in small groups by regular teachers, lab assistants; computer-aided instruction also offered. Available in reading, math, spelling, written language, learning strategies, study skills, time management.

Subject-area tutoring: Offered one-on-one and in small groups by professional teachers, peer tutors, lab assistants. Available in most subjects.

Auxiliary aids: Taped textbooks, tape recorders, calculators, typewriters, word-processors with spell-check, personal computers.

Auxiliary services: Alternative test arrangements, notetakers, advocacy.

GENERAL COLLEGE INFORMATION

State and locally supported, 2-year, coed. Part of San Jacinto College District. Awards associate degrees. Founded 1961. *Setting:* 141-acre suburban campus with easy access to Houston. *Faculty:* 539 (282 full-time, 257 part-time).

Enrollment Profile: 67% part-time, 67% state residents, 17% transferred in, 48% 25 or older, 0% Native American, 13% Hispanic, 4% black, 3% Asian or Pacific Islander. *Areas of study chosen:* 30% vocational and home economics, 11% education, 9% business management and administrative services, 9% health professions and related sciences, 8% interdisciplinary studies, 7% social sciences, 4% psychology, 3% computer and information sciences, 3% engineering and applied sciences, 3% English language/literature/letters, 2% biological and life sciences, 2% communications and journalism, 2% fine arts, 2% premed, 1% architecture, 1% foreign language and literature, 1% mathematics, 1% predentistry, 1% prelaw. *Most popular recent majors:* nursing, business administration/commerce/management, computer science.

First-Year Class: 6,500 applied, 99% were accepted, 100% of whom enrolled.

Graduation Requirements: 62 credit hours; 1 math course; computer course; internship (some majors).

Computers on Campus: 58 computers available on campus for general student use. Computers for student use in computer center, computer labs, learning resource center.

EXPENSES

Expenses for 1996–97: Area resident tuition: $584 full-time. State resident tuition: $944 full-time. Nonresident tuition: $1814 full-time. Part-time tuition per semester ranges from $116 to $238 for area residents, $152 to $382 for state residents, $281 to $730 for nonresidents.

LD Services Contact: Mrs. Judy Ellison, Special Populations Coordinator, San Jacinto College–Central Campus, 8060 Spencer Highway, Pasadena, TX 77505, 281-476-1501 Ext. 1638. Fax: 281-478-2790.

SAN JACINTO COLLEGE–NORTH CAMPUS

Houston, Texas

LEARNING DISABILITIES SERVICES INFORMATION

Special Populations currently serves 27 undergraduates with LD. Students diagnosed with ADD/ADHD are eligible for the same services available to students with LD.
Staff: 1 part-time staff member (coordinator). Services provided by remediation specialists.
Special Fees: No special fees are charged for services to students with LD.
Applications and admissions: *Required:* high school transcript, basic skills testing; *recommended:* personal interview, psychoeducational report completed within 3 years. Students may begin taking classes any term. *Application deadline:* continuous.

PROGRAM AND SERVICE COMPONENTS

Diagnostic testing: Personality, temperament.
Academic advising: Provided by academic advisers. Students with LD may take up to 18 credit hours each term; most take 6 to 12 credit hours; 12 credit hours required to maintain full-time status; 3 to 6 credit hours required to be eligible for financial aid.
Counseling services: Individual counseling, career counseling.
Basic skills remediation: Offered in class-size groups by regular teachers, lab assistants; computer-aided instruction also offered. Available in reading, math, written language.
Subject-area tutoring: Offered one-on-one and in small groups by professional teachers, peer tutors. Available in some subjects.
Auxiliary aids: Taped textbooks, tape recorders, calculators, typewriters, word-processors with spell-check, personal computers.
Auxiliary services: Alternative test arrangements, notetakers, advocacy.

GENERAL COLLEGE INFORMATION

State and locally supported, 2-year, coed. Part of San Jacinto College District. Awards associate degrees. Founded 1974. *Setting:* 105-acre suburban campus. *Total enrollment:* 4,080. *Faculty:* 213 (88 full-time, 15% with terminal degrees, 125 part-time).
Enrollment Profile: 4,080 students from 14 states and territories, 46 other countries. 57% women, 43% men, 65% part-time, 98% state residents, 13% transferred in, 1% international, 41% 25 or older, 1% Native American, 24% Hispanic, 21% black, 2% Asian or Pacific Islander. *Most popular recent majors:* social science, secretarial studies/office management, computer information systems.
First-Year Class: 954 total. Of the students who applied, 100% were accepted, 100% of whom enrolled.
Graduation Requirements: 62 credits; 1 college algebra course; computer course (varies by major); internship (some majors).
Computers on Campus: 400 computers available on campus for general student use. Computers for student use in computer labs, classrooms, library. Staffed computer lab on campus provides training in use of computers, software.

EXPENSES

Expenses for 1996–97: Area resident tuition: $434 full-time. State resident tuition: $806 full-time. Nonresident tuition: $1705 full-time. Part-time tuition per semester ranges from $75 to $154 for area residents, $87 to $286 for state residents, $240 to $605 for nonresidents. Part-time mandatory fees per semester range from $35 to $66. Full-time mandatory fees: $168.
LD Services Contact: Ms. Jennifer Rheinhardt, Coordinator of Special Populations, San Jacinto College–North Campus, 5800 Uvalde Street, Houston, TX 77049-4599, 281-458-4050 Ext. 7250.

SAN JUAN COLLEGE

Farmington, New Mexico

LEARNING DISABILITIES SERVICES INFORMATION

Students with Disabilities on Campus (SDOC), Student Success Center began offering services in 1988. Students diagnosed with ADD/ADHD are eligible for the same services available to students with LD.
Staff: 8 full-time, 9 part-time staff members, including director, coordinators. Services provided by remediation specialists, tutors, counselor, support staff.
Special Fees: No special fees are charged for services to students with LD.
Applications and admissions: *Required:* high school IEP (Individualized Education Program), California Placement Test; *recommended:* high school transcript, courses completed, extended time SAT I or ACT, psychoeducational report completed within 3 years. Students may begin taking classes any term. *Application deadline:* continuous.

PROGRAM AND SERVICE COMPONENTS

Special preparation or orientation: Optional orientation offered throughout the year.
Diagnostic testing: Intelligence, reading, math, spelling, handwriting, spoken language, written language, motor abilities, perceptual skills, study skills, social skills, psychoneurology, learning strategies.
Academic advising: Provided by unit staff members, academic advisers. Most students with LD take 9 to 12 credit hours each term; 12 credit hours required to maintain full-time status and be eligible for financial aid.
Counseling services: Individual counseling, career counseling, self-advocacy training.
Basic skills remediation: Offered one-on-one and in small groups by regular teachers; computer-aided instruction also offered. Available in reading, math, spelling, written language, learning strategies, study skills, time management, social skills, computer skills.
Auxiliary aids: Taped textbooks, tape recorders, calculators, typewriters, word-processors with spell-check, personal computers, talking computers, optical character readers.
Auxiliary services: Alternative test arrangements, notetakers, priority registration, advocacy.

GENERAL COLLEGE INFORMATION

County-supported, 2-year, coed. Part of New Mexico Commission on Higher Education. Awards associate degrees. Founded 1958. *Setting:* 698-acre small-town campus. *Total enrollment:* 4,231. *Faculty:* 252 (72 full-time, 25% with terminal degrees, 180 part-time); student–undergrad faculty ratio is 18:1.
Enrollment Profile: 4,231 students: 62% women, 38% men, 64% part-time, 96% state residents, 4% transferred in, 0% international, 61% 25 or older, 26% Native American, 11% Hispanic, 0% black, 0% Asian or Pacific Islander. *Areas of study chosen:* 26% business management and administrative services, 15% health professions and related sciences, 15% liberal arts/general studies, 12% computer and information sciences, 5% education, 4% social sciences, 2% biological and life sciences, 2% communications and journalism, 2% engineering and applied sciences, 2% English language/literature/letters, 1% fine arts, 1% performing arts, 1% premed.
First-Year Class: 838 total; 1,197 applied, 100% were accepted, 70% of whom enrolled.
Graduation Requirements: 64 credits; internship (some majors).
Computers on Campus: 144 computers available on campus for general student use. Computer purchase/lease plans available. A computer is recommended for all students. A campus-wide network can be accessed from off-campus. Students can contact faculty members and/or advisers through e-mail. Computers for student use in computer center, computer labs, learning resource center, library, writing lab provide access to the Internet/World Wide Web. Staffed computer lab on campus provides training in use of computers, software.

EXPENSES

Expenses for 1996–97: *Application fee:* $10. State resident tuition: $360 full-time, $15 per credit part-time. Nonresident tuition: $600 full-time, $25 per credit part-time.
LD Services Contact: Ms. LuAnn Wood, Adult Education Specialist, San Juan College, 4601 College Boulevard, Farmington, NM 87402, 505-599-0340. Fax: 505-599-0385.

SANTA BARBARA CITY COLLEGE

Santa Barbara, California

LEARNING DISABILITIES SERVICES INFORMATION

Disabled Student Programs and Services (DSPS) began offering services in 1981. Currently the program serves 500 undergraduates with LD. Students diagnosed with ADD/ADHD are eligible for the same services available to students with LD.

Santa Barbara City College (continued)

Staff: 4 full-time, 17 part-time staff members, including coordinator. Services provided by tutors, counselor, disability specialists, support staff.
Special Fees: No special fees are charged for services to students with LD.
Applications and admissions: *Required:* psychoeducational report completed within 3 years. Students may begin taking classes any term. *Application deadline:* continuous.
Special policies: The college has written policies regarding substitutions and waivers of admissions, graduation, and degree requirements.

PROGRAM AND SERVICE COMPONENTS

Special preparation or orientation: Optional orientation offered before registration.
Diagnostic testing: Intelligence, reading, math, spelling.
Academic advising: Provided by unit staff members, academic advisers. Students with LD may take up to 18 units (more with counselor's approval) each term; most take 12 to 15 units; 12 units required to maintain full-time status and be eligible for financial aid.
Counseling services: Individual counseling, small-group counseling, career counseling, self-advocacy training.
Special courses: Learning strategies, word processing, assistive technology, self-advocacy. All offered for credit; none enter into overall grade point average.
Auxiliary aids: Taped textbooks, word-processors with spell-check, personal computers, talking computers, optical character readers, shared notes.
Auxiliary services: Alternative test arrangements, notetakers, priority registration, advocacy.

GENERAL COLLEGE INFORMATION

District-supported, 2-year, coed. Part of California Community Colleges System. Awards associate degrees. Founded 1908. *Setting:* 65-acre small-town campus. *Total enrollment:* 11,288. *Faculty:* 562 (205 full-time, 18% with terminal degrees, 357 part-time).
Enrollment Profile: 11,288 students from 20 states and territories, 60 other countries. 50% women, 50% men, 58% part-time, 94% state residents, 13% transferred in, 4% international, 34% 25 or older, 1% Native American, 25% Hispanic, 2% black, 7% Asian or Pacific Islander. *Retention:* 63% of 1995 full-time freshmen returned. *Most popular recent majors:* liberal arts/general studies, criminal justice, business administration/commerce/management.
First-Year Class: 2,260 total. Of the students who applied, 100% were accepted.
Graduation Requirements: 60 units; 1 course each in intermediate algebra and lab science; internship (some majors).
Computers on Campus: 225 computers available on campus for general student use. Computer purchase/lease plans available. A campus-wide network can be accessed from off-campus. Students can contact faculty members and/or advisers through e-mail. Computers for student use in computer center, computer labs, learning resource center provide access to the Internet/World Wide Web, on- and off-campus e-mail addresses. Staffed computer lab on campus provides training in use of computers, software.

EXPENSES

Expenses for 1997–98: State resident tuition: $0 full-time. Nonresident tuition: $3540 full-time, $118 per unit part-time. Part-time mandatory fees per semester range from $36.50 to $166.50. Full-time mandatory fees: $437.
LD Services Contact: Ms. Mary Lawson, Learning Disabilities Specialist, Santa Barbara City College, 721 Cliff Drive, Santa Barbara, CA 93109, 805-965-0581 Ext. 2374. Fax: 805-963-7222. Email: lawson@gate1.sbcc.cc.ca.us.

SANTA FE COMMUNITY COLLEGE

Gainesville, Florida

LEARNING DISABILITIES SERVICES INFORMATION

Disabilities Resource Center began offering services in 1993. Currently the program serves 271 undergraduates with LD. Students diagnosed with ADD/ADHD are eligible for the same services available to students with LD.
Staff: 3 full-time staff members, including coordinator. Services provided by tutors, counselors.
Special Fees: No special fees are charged for services to students with LD.
Applications and admissions: *Required:* high school transcript, psychoeducational report completed within 3 years. Students may begin taking classes any term. *Application deadline:* continuous.
Special policies: The college has written policies regarding grade forgiveness; substitutions and waivers of admissions, graduation, and degree requirements.

PROGRAM AND SERVICE COMPONENTS

Academic advising: Provided by unit staff members, academic advisers. Students with LD may take up to 12 credits each term; most take 12 credits; 12 credits required to maintain full-time status; 12 credits (full-time) required to be eligible for financial aid.
Counseling services: Individual counseling, career counseling.
Subject-area tutoring: Offered one-on-one and in small groups by peer tutors. Available in most subjects.
Auxiliary aids: Taped textbooks, tape recorders, calculators, typewriters, word-processors with spell-check, talking computers, optical character readers.
Auxiliary services: Alternative test arrangements, notetakers, priority registration, advocacy, readers.

GENERAL COLLEGE INFORMATION

State and locally supported, 2-year, coed. Part of Florida Community Colleges System. Awards associate degrees (offers bachelor's degrees in conjunction with Saint Leo College). Founded 1966. *Setting:* 175-acre suburban campus with easy access to Jacksonville. *Total enrollment:* 12,058. *Faculty:* 611 (232 full-time, 379 part-time); student–undergrad faculty ratio is 18:1.
Enrollment Profile: 12,058 students from 47 states and territories, 60 other countries. 54% women, 46% men, 50% part-time, 94% state residents, 11% transferred in, 2% international, 35% 25 or older, 1% Native American, 7% Hispanic, 10% black, 3% Asian or Pacific Islander. *Areas of study chosen:* 33% liberal arts/general studies, 16% business management and administrative services, 10% health professions and related sciences, 6% education, 5% engineering and applied sciences, 4% psychology, 3% communications and journalism, 3% fine arts, 3% premed, 3% social sciences, 2% agriculture, 2% architecture, 2% biological and life sciences, 2% English language/literature/letters, 1% mathematics, 1% natural resource sciences, 1% performing arts, 1% physical sciences, 1% predentistry, 1% prevet. *Most popular recent majors:* nursing, radiological technology, dental services.
First-Year Class: 1,803 total.
Graduation Requirements: 60 semester hours; 6 semester hours of math; 7 semester hours of science; computer course (varies by major).
Computers on Campus: Computers for student use in computer center provide access to the Internet/World Wide Web. Staffed computer lab on campus provides training in use of computers, software.

EXPENSES

Expenses for 1997–98: *Application fee:* $30. State resident tuition: $1245 full-time, $41.50 per semester hour part-time. Nonresident tuition: $4634 full-time, $154.45 per semester hour part-time.
LD Services Contact: Ms. Martha Zimmerman, Administrative Assistant, Santa Fe Community College, 3000 Northwest 83rd Street, Building S, Room 110, Gainesville, FL 32606-6200, 352-395-5948. Fax: 352-395-4100. Email: martha.zimmerman@santafe.cc.fl.us.

SANTA FE COMMUNITY COLLEGE

Santa Fe, New Mexico

LEARNING DISABILITIES SERVICES INFORMATION

Office of Special Services began offering services in 1984. Currently the program serves 75 to 100 undergraduates with LD. Students diagnosed with ADD/ADHD are eligible for the same services available to students with LD.
Staff: 1 full-time, 1 part-time staff members, including coordinators. Services provided by remediation specialists.
Special Fees: No special fees are charged for services to students with LD.
Applications and admissions: *Required:* documentation of disability. Students may begin taking classes any term. *Application deadline:* continuous.

PROGRAM AND SERVICE COMPONENTS

Diagnostic testing: The form of a psychoeducational diagnostic battery.
Academic advising: Provided by unit staff members. Students with LD may take up to 12 credit hours each term; most take 6 to 12 credit hours; 12 credit hours required to maintain full-time status; 6 credit hours required to be eligible for financial aid.
Counseling services: Individual counseling, career counseling, self-advocacy training.
Basic skills remediation: Offered in class-size groups by regular teachers. Available in reading, math, written language, learning strategies.
Subject-area tutoring: Offered one-on-one and in small groups by LD specialists. Available in most subjects.
Auxiliary aids: Taped textbooks, tape recorders, word-processors with spell-check, talking computers.
Auxiliary services: Alternative test arrangements, priority registration, advocacy.
Campus support group: A special student organization is available to students with LD.

GENERAL COLLEGE INFORMATION

State and locally supported, 2-year, coed. Part of New Mexico Commission on Higher Education. Awards associate degrees. Founded 1983. *Setting:* 366-acre suburban campus. *Faculty:* 275 (46 full-time, 229 part-time); student–undergrad faculty ratio is 12:1.
Enrollment Profile: 49% part-time, 78% state residents, 12% transferred in, 78% 25 or older, 3% Native American, 40% Hispanic, 1% black, 1% Asian or Pacific Islander. *Areas of study chosen:* 6% liberal arts/general studies, 5% business management and administrative services, 3% health professions and related sciences, 2% computer and information sciences, 1% biological and life sciences, 1% communications and journalism, 1% education, 1% engineering and applied sciences, 1% social sciences, 1% vocational and home economics.
First-Year Class: Of the students who applied, 100% were accepted.
Graduation Requirements: 64 credits; 3 credits of math; 8 credits of lab science; computer course; internship (some majors).
Computers on Campus: 225 computers available on campus for general student use. A campus-wide network can be accessed. Students can contact faculty members and/or advisers through e-mail. Computers for student use in computer center, Academic Center for Enrichment provide access to the Internet/World Wide Web, on- and off-campus e-mail addresses. Staffed computer lab on campus provides training in use of computers, software.

EXPENSES

Expenses for 1996–97: Area resident tuition: $408 full-time, $17 per credit part-time. State resident tuition: $552 full-time, $23 per credit part-time. Nonresident tuition: $1080 full-time, $45 per credit part-time. Full-time mandatory fees: $31.
LD Services Contact: Ms. Jill Douglass, Special Services Director, Santa Fe Community College, 6401 Richards Avenue, Santa Fe, NM 87505, 505-438-1331. Fax: 505-438-1338.

SANTA ROSA JUNIOR COLLEGE

Santa Rosa, California

LEARNING DISABILITIES SERVICES INFORMATION

Disability Resources Department began offering services in 1975. Currently the program serves 300 undergraduates with LD. Students diagnosed with ADD/ADHD are eligible for the same services available to students with LD.
Staff: 3 full-time, 26 part-time staff members, including coordinator. Services provided by tutors, diagnostic specialists.
Special Fees: $20 for diagnostic testing.
Applications and admissions: *Required:* psychoeducational report completed within 3 years. Students may begin taking classes in fall, spring, or summer. *Application deadline:* 8/15.
Special policies: The college has written policies regarding grade forgiveness; substitutions and waivers of degree requirements.

PROGRAM AND SERVICE COMPONENTS

Diagnostic testing: Intelligence, reading, math, spelling, written language, perceptual skills, speech, hearing, vision.
Academic advising: Provided by unit staff members. Students with LD may take up to 16 units each term; most take 12 units; 12 units required to maintain full-time status; 9 units for part-time, 12 units for full-time required to be eligible for financial aid.
Counseling services: Individual counseling, career counseling.
Basic skills remediation: Offered one-on-one, in small groups, and in class-size groups by LD teachers, trained instructional aides, part-time teachers. Available in reading, math, spelling, handwriting, spoken language, written language, learning strategies, motor abilities, perceptual skills, study skills, time management, social skills, speech.
Subject-area tutoring: Offered one-on-one and in small groups by instructional aides. Available in most subjects.
Special courses: College survival skills, reading, vocabulary development, communication skills, composition, learning strategies, word processing, time management, math, typing, study skills, career planning. All offered for credit; all enter into overall grade point average.
Auxiliary aids: Taped textbooks, tape recorders, typewriters, word-processors with spell-check.
Auxiliary services: Alternative test arrangements, notetakers, priority registration, advocacy.

GENERAL COLLEGE INFORMATION

State and locally supported, 2-year, coed. Part of California Community Colleges System. Awards associate degrees. Founded 1918. *Setting:* 93-acre urban campus with easy access to San Francisco. *Endowment:* $12 million. *Educational spending 1995–96:* $2004 per undergrad. *Total enrollment:* 27,885. *Faculty:* 1,062 (277 full-time, 11% with terminal degrees, 785 part-time).
Enrollment Profile: 27,885 students from 39 states and territories, 43 other countries. 59% women, 41% men, 62% part-time, 98% state residents, 9% transferred in, 1% international, 59% 25 or older, 1% Native American, 11% Hispanic, 2% black, 3% Asian or Pacific Islander. *Most popular recent majors:* liberal arts/general studies, science.
First-Year Class: 3,937 total; 3,937 applied, 100% were accepted, 100% of whom enrolled.
Graduation Requirements: 60 units.
Computers on Campus: 1,062 computers available on campus for general student use. A campus-wide network can be accessed from off-campus. Students can contact faculty members and/or advisers through e-mail. Computers for student use in computer center, computer labs, learning resource center, classrooms, library, tutorial center, various locations provide access to the Internet/World Wide Web. Staffed computer lab on campus provides training in use of computers, software.

EXPENSES

Expenses for 1997–98: State resident tuition: $0 full-time. Nonresident tuition: $3570 full-time, $119 per unit part-time. Part-time mandatory fees per semester range from $23 to $153. Tuition for international students: $3930 full-time, $131 per unit part-time. Full-time mandatory fees: $410. College room only: $1850.
LD Services Contact: Ms. Catherine Reisman, Learning Disability Specialist, Santa Rosa Junior College, 1501 Mendocino Avenue, Santa Rosa, CA 95401-4395, 707-527-4279. Fax: 707-524-1768. Email: catherine_reisman@garfield.santarosa.edu.

SAUK VALLEY COMMUNITY COLLEGE

Dixon, Illinois

LEARNING DISABILITIES SERVICES INFORMATION

The Learning Disabilities special services program currently serves 45 undergraduates with LD. Students diagnosed with ADD/ADHD are eligible for the same services available to students with LD.
Staff: 1 part-time staff member (LD specialist).
Special Fees: No special fees are charged for services to students with LD.
Applications and admissions: *Required:* personal interview; *recommended:* IEP or psychoeducational report. Students may begin taking classes any term. *Application deadline:* continuous.

PROGRAM AND SERVICE COMPONENTS

Special preparation or orientation: Optional orientation offered individually once a student self-identifies.
Academic advising: Provided by unit staff members, academic advisers.
Counseling services: Individual counseling.
Auxiliary aids: Taped textbooks, tape recorders, calculators, typewriters, word-processors with spell-check, personal computers.
Auxiliary services: Alternative test arrangements, notetakers, priority registration.

Sauk Valley Community College (continued)

GENERAL COLLEGE INFORMATION

District-supported, 2-year, coed. Part of Illinois Community College System. Awards associate degrees. Founded 1965. *Setting:* 165-acre rural campus. *Total enrollment:* 2,635. *Faculty:* 152 (62 full-time, 90 part-time).
Enrollment Profile: 2,635 students: 59% women, 41% men, 60% part-time, 99% state residents, 2% transferred in, 50% 25 or older, 1% Native American, 5% Hispanic, 1% black, 1% Asian or Pacific Islander.
First-Year Class: 560 total; 1,250 applied, 100% were accepted, 45% of whom enrolled. 5% from top 10% of their high school class, 21% from top quarter, 53% from top half.
Graduation Requirements: 64 semester hours.
Computers on Campus: 100 computers available on campus for general student use. Computers for student use in computer center provide access to the Internet/World Wide Web. Staffed computer lab on campus provides training in use of computers, software. *Academic computing expenditure 1995–96:* $175,000.

EXPENSES

Expenses for 1997–98: Area resident tuition: $1408 full-time, $44 per semester hour part-time. State resident tuition: $4133 full-time, $129.17 per semester hour part-time. Nonresident tuition: $5364 full-time, $167.64 per semester hour part-time.
LD Services Contact: Ms. Ann Edmonds, LD Specialist, Sauk Valley Community College, 173 Illinois Route 2, Dixon, IL 61021, 815-288-5511 Ext. 246. Fax: 815-288-5958. Email: edmonda@svcc.edu.

SCHENECTADY COUNTY COMMUNITY COLLEGE

Schenectady, New York

LEARNING DISABILITIES SERVICES INFORMATION

Disabled Student Services began offering services in 1980. Currently the program serves 59 undergraduates with LD. Students diagnosed with ADD/ADHD are eligible for the same services available to students with LD.
Staff: 1 full-time, 1 part-time staff members, including coordinator.
Special Fees: No special fees are charged for services to students with LD.
Applications and admissions: *Required:* documentation of disability. Students may begin taking classes in fall, spring, or summer. *Application deadline:* continuous.

PROGRAM AND SERVICE COMPONENTS

Special preparation or orientation: Optional orientation offered during registration.
Academic advising: Provided by unit staff members, academic advisers. Most students with LD take 6 to 12 credit hours each term; 12 credit hours required to maintain full-time status and be eligible for financial aid.
Counseling services: Individual counseling, career counseling, self-advocacy training.
Basic skills remediation: Offered in class-size groups by regular teachers. Available in reading, math, written language, learning strategies, study skills, time management.
Subject-area tutoring: Offered one-on-one and in small groups by peer tutors. Available in all subjects.
Auxiliary aids: Taped textbooks, tape recorders, calculators, typewriters, word-processors with spell-check.
Auxiliary services: Alternative test arrangements, notetakers, advocacy, scribes.

GENERAL COLLEGE INFORMATION

State and locally supported, 2-year, coed. Part of State University of New York System. Awards associate degrees. Founded 1968. *Setting:* 50-acre urban campus. *Endowment:* $230,490. *Total enrollment:* 3,510. *Faculty:* 211 (58 full-time, 25% with terminal degrees, 153 part-time); student–undergrad faculty ratio is 17:1.
Enrollment Profile: 3,510 students from 6 states and territories. 58% women, 42% men, 51% part-time, 99% state residents, 10% transferred in, 0% international, 52% 25 or older, 1% Native American, 2% Hispanic, 7% black, 2% Asian or Pacific Islander. *Retention:* 70% of 1995 full-time freshmen returned. *Most popular recent majors:* hotel and restaurant management, humanities, business administration/commerce/management.
First-Year Class: 973 total; 1,927 applied, 83% were accepted, 61% of whom enrolled.
Graduation Requirements: 60 credit hours.
Computers on Campus: A campus-wide network can be accessed. Students can contact faculty members and/or advisers through e-mail. Computers for student use in computer center, learning resource center, library provide access to the Internet/World Wide Web, on- and off-campus e-mail addresses. Staffed computer lab on campus provides training in use of computers, software. *Academic computing expenditure 1995–96:* $95,800.

EXPENSES

Expenses for 1996–97: *Application fee:* $25. State resident tuition: $2240 full-time, $94 per credit hour part-time. Nonresident tuition: $4480 full-time, $188 per credit hour part-time. Full-time mandatory fees: $105.
LD Services Contact: Mr. Tom Dotson, Coordinator, Disabled Student Services, Schenectady County Community College, 78 Washington Avenue, Schenectady, NY 12305-2294, 518-381-1345.

SCHOOLCRAFT COLLEGE

Livonia, Michigan

LEARNING DISABILITIES SERVICES INFORMATION

Learning Assistance Center began offering services in 1980. Currently the program serves 200 undergraduates with LD. Students diagnosed with ADD/ADHD are eligible for the same services available to students with LD, as well as support group.
Staff: 4 full-time, 5 part-time staff members, including director. Services provided by remediation specialists, tutors, counselors, learning specialists.
Special Fees: No special fees are charged for services to students with LD.
Applications and admissions: *Required:* high school transcript, professional documentation of LD (for receipt of services). Students may begin taking classes any term. *Application deadline:* continuous.
Special policies: The college has written policies regarding grade forgiveness.

PROGRAM AND SERVICE COMPONENTS

Special preparation or orientation: Optional summer program offered prior to entering college. Optional orientation offered before registration.
Academic advising: Provided by academic advisers. Students with LD may take up to 12 credit hours each term; most take 6 to 8 credit hours; 12 credit hours required to maintain full-time status; source of aid determines number of credit hours required to be eligible for financial aid.
Counseling services: Individual counseling, small-group counseling, career counseling, self-advocacy training.
Basic skills remediation: Offered one-on-one, in small groups, and in class-size groups by LD teachers, regular teachers, developmental education teachers; computer-aided instruction also offered. Available in reading, math, spelling, written language, learning strategies, study skills, time management, computer skills.
Subject-area tutoring: Offered one-on-one and in small groups by professional teachers, peer tutors. Available in all subjects.
Special courses: College survival skills, reading, vocabulary development, communication skills, composition, learning strategies, time management, math, typing, study skills, career planning. Most offered for credit; most enter into overall grade point average.
Auxiliary aids: Taped textbooks, tape recorders, calculators, word-processors with spell-check, optical character readers.
Auxiliary services: Alternative test arrangements, notetakers, advocacy, readers.
Campus support group: A special student organization is available to students with LD.

GENERAL COLLEGE INFORMATION

District-supported, 2-year, coed. Part of Michigan Department of Education. Awards associate degrees. Founded 1961. *Setting:* 183-acre suburban campus with easy access to Detroit. *Endowment:* $1.7 million. *Research spending 1995–96:* $222,890. *Total enrollment:* 9,307. *Faculty:* 421 (125 full-time, 96% with terminal degrees, 296 part-time); student–undergrad faculty ratio is 22:1.

Enrollment Profile: 9,307 students: 58% women, 42% men, 75% part-time, 99% state residents, 38% transferred in, 1% international, 45% 25 or older, 1% Native American, 1% Hispanic, 3% black, 1% Asian or Pacific Islander. *Areas of study chosen:* 12% engineering and applied sciences, 4% education, 2% fine arts, 1% architecture, 1% communications and journalism, 1% library and information studies, 1% natural resource sciences, 1% performing arts, 1% premed, 1% prevet, 1% social sciences. *Most popular recent majors:* science, liberal arts/general studies, business administration/commerce/management.
First-Year Class: 1,406 total; 2,474 applied, 100% were accepted, 57% of whom enrolled. 5% from top 10% of their high school class, 20% from top quarter, 70% from top half.
Graduation Requirements: 60 credit hours; math proficiency; computer course; internship (some majors).
Computers on Campus: 700 computers available on campus for general student use. Computers for student use in computer center, computer labs, learning resource center, classrooms, library, applied science building. Staffed computer lab on campus provides training in use of computers, software. *Academic computing expenditure 1995–96:* $319,668.

EXPENSES

Expenses for 1997–98: *Application fee:* $10. Area resident tuition: $1530 full-time, $51 per credit hour part-time. State resident tuition: $2250 full-time, $75 per credit hour part-time. Nonresident tuition: $3360 full-time, $112 per credit hour part-time. Part-time mandatory fees per semester range from $27 to $47. Full-time mandatory fees: $110.
LD Services Contact: Ms. Pat Hurick, Counselor, Schoolcraft College, 18600 Haggerty Road, Livonia, MI 48152, 313-462-4436. Fax: 313-462-4542. Email: phurick@schoolcraft.cc.mi.us.

SEATTLE CENTRAL COMMUNITY COLLEGE

Seattle, Washington

LEARNING DISABILITIES SERVICES INFORMATION

Differently-abled Student Services (DSS) began offering services in 1980. Currently the program serves 80 undergraduates with LD. Students diagnosed with ADD/ADHD are eligible for the same services available to students with LD.
Staff: 1 full-time, 1 part-time staff members, including coordinators. Services provided by counselors.
Special Fees: No special fees are charged for services to students with LD.
Applications and admissions: *Required:* high school transcript, ACT ASSET. Students may begin taking classes any term. *Application deadline:* 8/1 (fall term), 3/1 (spring term).

PROGRAM AND SERVICE COMPONENTS

Special preparation or orientation: Optional orientation offered before registration, during registration, after classes begin.
Academic advising: Provided by academic advisers. Students with LD may take up to 18 credits each term; most take 12 credits; 12 credits required to maintain full-time status and be eligible for financial aid.
Counseling services: Individual counseling, small-group counseling.
Subject-area tutoring: Offered one-on-one by professional teachers, peer tutors. Available in most subjects.
Auxiliary aids: Taped textbooks, tape recorders, calculators, typewriters, word-processors with spell-check, personal computers.
Auxiliary services: Alternative test arrangements, notetakers, priority registration, advocacy.
Campus support group: A special student organization is available to students with LD.

GENERAL COLLEGE INFORMATION

State-supported, 2-year, coed. Part of Seattle Community College District System. Awards associate degrees. Founded 1966. *Setting:* 15-acre urban campus. *Total enrollment:* 10,333. *Faculty:* 388 (139 full-time, 249 part-time); student–undergrad faculty ratio is 25:1.
Enrollment Profile: 10,333 students: 59% women, 41% men, 51% part-time, 93% state residents, 8% transferred in, 1% international, 63% 25 or older, 1% Native American, 6% Hispanic, 13% black, 20% Asian or Pacific Islander.
First-Year Class: 2,541 total. Of the students who applied, 100% were accepted, 50% of whom enrolled.
Graduation Requirements: 90 credits; 1 college algebra course.
Computers on Campus: 366 computers available on campus for general student use. Computers for student use in computer center, computer labs, classrooms, library. Staffed computer lab on campus provides training in use of computers, software.

EXPENSES

Expenses for 1997–98: State resident tuition: $1452 full-time, $48.40 per credit part-time. Nonresident tuition: $5727 full-time, $190.90 per credit part-time. Part-time tuition (1 to 9 credits): $48.40 per credit for state residents, $190.90 per credit for nonresidents. Part-time mandatory fees per quarter (5 to 9 credits): $15. Full-time mandatory fees: $75.
LD Services Contact: Mr. Al Souma, DSS Coordinator, Seattle Central Community College, 1701 Broadway, Seattle, WA 98122, 206-587-4169.

SEMINOLE COMMUNITY COLLEGE

Sanford, Florida

LEARNING DISABILITIES SERVICES INFORMATION

Disability Support Services (DSS) began offering services in 1988. Currently the program serves 156 undergraduates with LD. Students diagnosed with ADD/ADHD are eligible for the same services available to students with LD.
Staff: 1 full-time, 2 part-time staff members, including coordinator. Services provided by remediation specialist, tutor.
Special Fees: No special fees are charged for services to students with LD.
Applications and admissions: *Required:* high school transcript, psychoeducational report completed within 3 years, placement test. Students may begin taking classes any term. *Application deadline:* continuous.
Special policies: The college has written policies regarding grade forgiveness; substitutions and waivers of graduation and degree requirements.

PROGRAM AND SERVICE COMPONENTS

Academic advising: Provided by unit staff members, academic advisers. Most students with LD take 12 credit hours each term; 12 credit hours required to maintain full-time status and be eligible for financial aid.
Counseling services: Individual counseling.
Subject-area tutoring: Offered one-on-one by peer tutors. Available in most subjects.
Auxiliary aids: Taped textbooks, tape recorders, calculators, word-processors with spell-check, personal computers, talking computers, optical character readers.
Auxiliary services: Alternative test arrangements, notetakers.

GENERAL COLLEGE INFORMATION

State and locally supported, 2-year, coed. Awards associate degrees. Founded 1966. *Setting:* 200-acre small-town campus with easy access to Orlando. *Total enrollment:* 6,924. *Faculty:* 502 (130 full-time, 17% with terminal degrees, 372 part-time).
Enrollment Profile: 6,924 students from 25 states and territories, 12 other countries. 56% women, 44% men, 64% part-time, 95% state residents, 5% transferred in, 1% international, 43% 25 or older, 1% Native American, 9% Hispanic, 9% black, 4% Asian or Pacific Islander. *Most popular recent majors:* liberal arts/general studies, nursing, paralegal studies.
First-Year Class: 1,192 total. Of the students who applied, 98% were accepted.
Graduation Requirements: 64 credit hours; 6 credit hours of math; 9 credit hours of science; 2 years of a foreign language in high school or 6 credit hours in college; internship (some majors).
Computers on Campus: A campus-wide network can be accessed from off-campus. Students can contact faculty members and/or advisers through e-mail. Computers for student use in computer center, computer labs, learning resource center provide access to the Internet/World Wide Web, on- and off-campus e-mail addresses. Staffed computer lab on campus provides training in use of computers, software.

EXPENSES

Expenses for 1997–98: *Application fee:* $25. State resident tuition: $1328 full-time, $41.50 per credit hour part-time. Nonresident tuition: $4943 full-time, $154.46 per credit hour part-time.

Seminole Community College (continued)

LD Services Contact: Ms. Dottie Paishon, Coordinator, Disability Support Services, Seminole Community College, 100 Weldon Boulevard, Sanford, FL 32773, 407-328-2109. Fax: 407-328-2139. Email: dpaishon@ipo.seminole.cc.fl.us.

SEMINOLE STATE COLLEGE

Seminole, Oklahoma

LEARNING DISABILITIES SERVICES INFORMATION

Student Services began offering services in 1990. Currently the program serves 11 undergraduates with LD. Students diagnosed with ADD/ADHD are eligible for the same services available to students with LD.
Staff: 1 part-time staff member (Counselor). Services provided by counselors.
Special Fees: No special fees are charged for services to students with LD.
Applications and admissions: *Required:* high school transcript, courses completed, personal interview, psychoeducational report completed within 3 years; *recommended:* high school grade point average, class rank, IEP (Individualized Education Program). Students may begin taking classes in fall, spring, or summer. *Application deadline:* continuous.

PROGRAM AND SERVICE COMPONENTS

Academic advising: Provided by unit staff members. Students with LD may take up to as many credit hours as an individual can handle each term; most take 6 to 12 credit hours; 12 credit hours required to maintain full-time status; 3 credit hours required to be eligible for financial aid.
Auxiliary aids: Tape recorders, optical character readers, spell checkers.
Auxiliary services: Alternative test arrangements, notetakers, priority registration, advocacy.

GENERAL COLLEGE INFORMATION

State-supported, 2-year, coed. Part of Oklahoma State Regents for Higher Education. Awards associate degrees. Founded 1931. *Setting:* 40-acre small-town campus with easy access to Oklahoma City. *Educational spending 1995–96:* $1398 per undergrad. *Total enrollment:* 1,600. *Faculty:* 85 (46 full-time, 20% with terminal degrees, 39 part-time); student–undergrad faculty ratio is 20:1.
Enrollment Profile: 1,600 students from 11 states and territories, 4 other countries. 64% women, 36% men, 38% part-time, 94% state residents, 8% live on campus, 5% transferred in, 1% international, 42% 25 or older, 15% Native American, 1% Hispanic, 5% black, 1% Asian or Pacific Islander. *Retention:* 60% of 1995 full-time freshmen returned. *Areas of study chosen:* 40% liberal arts/general studies, 12% health professions and related sciences, 10% business management and administrative services, 8% education, 4% psychology, 2% computer and information sciences, 2% social sciences, 1% biological and life sciences, 1% communications and journalism, 1% English language/literature/letters, 1% fine arts, 1% mathematics, 1% physical sciences. *Most popular recent majors:* elementary education, behavioral sciences, business administration/commerce/management.
First-Year Class: 781 total; 850 applied, 100% were accepted, 92% of whom enrolled.
Graduation Requirements: 60 credit hours.
Computers on Campus: 100 computers available on campus for general student use. A computer is recommended for some students. A campus-wide network can be accessed from off-campus. Students can contact faculty members and/or advisers through e-mail. Computers for student use in computer labs, library provide access to the Internet/World Wide Web, on- and off-campus e-mail addresses. Staffed computer lab on campus provides training in use of computers, software. *Academic computing expenditure 1995–96:* $109,500.

EXPENSES

Expenses for 1996–97: *Application fee:* $15. State resident tuition: $840 full-time, $28 per credit hour part-time. Nonresident tuition: $2640 full-time, $88 per credit hour part-time. Part-time mandatory fees: $8.50 per credit hour. Full-time mandatory fees: $255. College room and board: $1830.
LD Services Contact: Tracy Wood Jacomo, Counselor, Seminole State College, PO Box 351, Seminole, OK 74868, 405-382-9950. Fax: 405-382-3122.

SHASTA COLLEGE

Redding, California

LEARNING DISABILITIES SERVICES INFORMATION

Health and Learning Services began offering services in 1977.
Staff: Includes director. Services provided by tutors, counselor, paraprofessional.
Special Fees: No special fees are charged for services to students with LD.
Applications and admissions: *Required:* California Assessment System for Adults with Learning Disabilities. Students may begin taking classes any term. *Application deadline:* continuous.

PROGRAM AND SERVICE COMPONENTS

Special preparation or orientation: Optional orientation offered before registration.
Diagnostic testing: Various areas as appropriate (by outside referral).
Academic advising: Provided by academic advisers. Students with LD may take up to 18 semester units each term; most take 12 semester units; 12 semester units required to maintain full-time status.
Counseling services: Individual counseling, career counseling.
Subject-area tutoring: Offered one-on-one by peer tutors. Available in all subjects.
Special courses: Reading. All offered for credit; all enter into overall grade point average.
Auxiliary aids: Taped textbooks, tape recorders, calculators, word-processors with spell-check, personal computers.
Auxiliary services: Alternative test arrangements, notetakers, priority registration, advocacy.

GENERAL COLLEGE INFORMATION

State and locally supported, 2-year, coed. Part of California Community Colleges System. Awards associate degrees. Founded 1948. *Setting:* 336-acre campus. *Endowment:* $1.2 million. *Total enrollment:* 10,650. *Faculty:* 397 (132 full-time, 15% with terminal degrees, 265 part-time); student–undergrad faculty ratio is 26:1.
Enrollment Profile: 10,650 students from 6 states and territories, 5 other countries. 60% women, 40% men, 77% part-time, 99% state residents, 19% transferred in, 60% 25 or older, 4% Native American, 5% Hispanic, 1% black, 2% Asian or Pacific Islander. *Retention:* 55% of 1995 full-time freshmen returned.
First-Year Class: 2,130 total. Of the students who applied, 100% were accepted, 90% of whom enrolled.
Graduation Requirements: 60 semester units; internship (some majors).
Computers on Campus: 200 computers available on campus for general student use. Computers for student use in computer center, computer labs, learning resource center, classrooms provide access to the Internet/World Wide Web. Staffed computer lab on campus provides training in use of computers, software.

EXPENSES

Expenses for 1997–98: State resident tuition: $0 full-time. Nonresident tuition: $3330 full-time, $111 per unit part-time. Part-time mandatory fees per semester range from $26 to $156. Full-time mandatory fees: $416. College room and board: $3176. College room only: $1976.
LD Services Contact: Ms. Carla Tracy, Learning Disabilities Services Instructor, Shasta College, PO Box 6006, Redding, CA 96049-6006, 916-225-4937.

SHAWNEE COMMUNITY COLLEGE

Ullin, Illinois

LEARNING DISABILITIES SERVICES INFORMATION

Office of Special Needs began offering services in 1984. Students diagnosed with ADD/ADHD are eligible for the same services available to students with LD.
Staff: 1 full-time staff member (coordinator). Services provided by tutors, counselors.
Special Fees: No special fees are charged for services to students with LD.
Applications and admissions: *Required:* high school transcript, ACT ASSET. Students may begin taking classes any term. *Application deadline:* continuous.

PROGRAM AND SERVICE COMPONENTS

Diagnostic testing: Reading, math, spelling, written language.
Academic advising: Provided by unit staff members, academic advisers. Most students with LD take 12 semester hours each term; 12 semester hours required to maintain full-time status; 6 semester hours required to be eligible for financial aid.
Counseling services: Individual counseling, career counseling.
Basic skills remediation: Offered one-on-one and in class-size groups by regular teachers. Available in reading, math, spelling, written language.
Subject-area tutoring: Offered one-on-one by professional teachers, peer tutors. Available in most subjects.
Special courses: Reading, composition, math. Some offered for credit.
Auxiliary aids: Taped textbooks, tape recorders.
Auxiliary services: Alternative test arrangements, notetakers.

GENERAL COLLEGE INFORMATION

State and locally supported, 2-year, coed. Part of Illinois Community College System. Awards associate degrees. Founded 1967. *Setting:* 163-acre rural campus. *Total enrollment:* 2,109. *Faculty:* 166 (42 full-time, 10% with terminal degrees, 124 part-time).
Enrollment Profile: 2,109 students from 3 states and territories. 66% women, 34% men, 62% part-time, 89% state residents, 1% transferred in, 1% international, 54% 25 or older, 0% Native American, 1% Hispanic, 14% black, 1% Asian or Pacific Islander. *Most popular recent majors:* liberal arts/general studies, science.
First-Year Class: 1,464 total. Of the students who applied, 100% were accepted. 5% from top 10% of their high school class, 20% from top quarter, 60% from top half.
Graduation Requirements: 64 semester hours; 8 semester hours of math/science; computer course for accounting, business administration majors.
Computers on Campus: 40 computers available on campus for general student use. A computer is recommended for some students. A campus-wide network can be accessed from off-campus. Students can contact faculty members and/or advisers through e-mail. Computers for student use in computer center, library provide access to the Internet/World Wide Web, on- and off-campus e-mail addresses.

EXPENSES

Expenses for 1997–98: Area resident tuition: $1080 full-time, $33.75 per semester hour part-time. State resident tuition: $2818 full-time, $88.06 per semester hour part-time. Nonresident tuition: $6759 full-time, $211.23 per semester hour part-time. Part-time mandatory fees: $1.25 per semester hour. Tuition for residents of participating counties: $1816 full-time, $56.75 per semester hour part-time. Full-time mandatory fees: $40.
LD Services Contact: Ms. Annie Hubbard, Special Needs Coordinator, Shawnee Community College, Route 1, Box 53, Ullin, IL 62992-9725, 618-634-2242. Fax: 618-634-9028.

SHELBY STATE COMMUNITY COLLEGE

Memphis, Tennessee

LEARNING DISABILITIES SERVICES INFORMATION

Disabled Student Services began offering services in 1992. Currently the program serves 120 undergraduates with LD. Students diagnosed with ADD/ADHD are eligible for the same services available to students with LD.
Staff: 3 full-time, 5 part-time staff members, including director, coordinator, secretary. Services provided by tutors, counselors, notetakers, interpreters, readers.
Special Fees: No special fees are charged for services to students with LD.
Applications and admissions: *Required:* high school transcript; *recommended:* high school IEP (Individualized Education Program), untimed or extended time ACT, psychoeducational report. Students may begin taking classes in fall, spring, or summer. *Application deadline:* continuous.
Special policies: The college has written policies regarding grade forgiveness.

PROGRAM AND SERVICE COMPONENTS

Special preparation or orientation: Required orientation held before registration.
Academic advising: Provided by unit staff members, academic advisers. Students with LD may take up to 18 semester hours (more with approval) each term; 6 semester hours required to be eligible for financial aid.
Counseling services: Individual counseling, small-group counseling, career counseling, self-advocacy training.
Basic skills remediation: Offered in class-size groups by regular teachers; computer-aided instruction also offered. Available in reading, math, written language, learning strategies, study skills, time management.
Subject-area tutoring: Offered one-on-one and in small groups by tutors. Available in some subjects.
Auxiliary aids: Taped textbooks, tape recorders, calculators, typewriters, word-processors with spell-check, personal computers, optical character readers, Dragon Dictate.
Auxiliary services: Alternative test arrangements, notetakers, advocacy.

GENERAL COLLEGE INFORMATION

State-supported, 2-year, coed. Part of State University and Community College System of Tennessee. Awards associate degrees. Founded 1970. *Setting:* 22-acre urban campus. *Endowment:* $31,452. *Educational spending 1995–96:* $1600 per undergrad. *Total enrollment:* 5,862. *Faculty:* 342 (134 full-time, 19% with terminal degrees, 208 part-time); student–undergrad faculty ratio is 21:1.
Enrollment Profile: 5,862 students from 15 states and territories. 70% women, 30% men, 53% part-time, 98% state residents, 7% transferred in, 0% international, 46% 25 or older, 0% Native American, 1% Hispanic, 66% black, 1% Asian or Pacific Islander. *Areas of study chosen:* 55% liberal arts/general studies, 38% health professions and related sciences, 5% business management and administrative services, 2% social sciences. *Most popular recent majors:* emergency medical technology, nursing, liberal arts/general studies.
First-Year Class: 912 total.
Graduation Requirements: 64 semester hours; science requirement varies according to program; 1 college algebra course; computer course.
Computers on Campus: 220 computers available on campus for general student use. A campus-wide network can be accessed from off-campus. Students can contact faculty members and/or advisers through e-mail. Computers for student use in computer labs, classrooms provide access to the Internet/World Wide Web. Staffed computer lab on campus provides training in use of computers, software. *Academic computing expenditure 1995–96:* $24,872.

EXPENSES

Expenses for 1997–98: *Application fee:* $5. State resident tuition: $1086 full-time, $48 per semester hour part-time. Nonresident tuition: $4342 full-time, $190 per semester hour part-time. Part-time mandatory fees per semester range from $16 to $26. Full-time mandatory fees: $66.
LD Services Contact: Mrs. Geraldine Young, Director, Shelby State Community College, 737 Union Avenue, Memphis, TN 38174, 901-544-5084. Fax: 901-544-5643.

SINCLAIR COMMUNITY COLLEGE

Dayton, Ohio

LEARNING DISABILITIES SERVICES INFORMATION

Learning Disabilities Program, Office of Disability Services began offering services in 1985. Currently the program serves 250 undergraduates with LD. Students diagnosed with ADD/ADHD are eligible for the same services available to students with LD.
Staff: 3 full-time, 17 part-time staff members. Services provided by tutors, LD specialist.
Special Fees: No special fees are charged for services to students with LD.
Applications and admissions: *Required:* personal interview, psychoeducational report completed within 3 years, most recent IEP. Students may begin taking classes any term. *Application deadline:* continuous.
Special policies: The college has written policies regarding grade forgiveness; substitutions and waivers of degree requirements.

PROGRAM AND SERVICE COMPONENTS

Academic advising: Provided by academic advisers. Students with LD may take up to 20 quarter hours (more with special permission) each term; most take 6 to 9 quarter hours; 12 quarter hours required to maintain full-time status.
Counseling services: Individual counseling, small-group counseling, career counseling.
Basic skills remediation: Offered in class-size groups by developmental faculty. Available in reading, math, spelling, study skills, science.
Subject-area tutoring: Offered one-on-one, in small groups, and in class-size groups by peer tutors. Available in all subjects.

Sinclair Community College (continued)

Special courses: College survival skills, reading, vocabulary development, composition, math, study skills, career planning. All offered for credit; none enter into overall grade point average.
Auxiliary aids: Taped textbooks, tape recorders, calculators, typewriters, word-processors with spell-check, personal computers, optical character readers, Visualtek machine.
Auxiliary services: Alternative test arrangements, notetakers, advocacy.
Campus support group: A special student organization is available to students with LD.

GENERAL COLLEGE INFORMATION

State and locally supported, 2-year, coed. Part of Ohio Board of Regents. Awards associate degrees. Founded 1887. *Setting:* 50-acre urban campus. *Total enrollment:* 19,360. *Faculty:* 880 (300 full-time, 580 part-time); student–undergrad faculty ratio is 22:1.
Enrollment Profile: 19,360 students from 10 states and territories. 62% women, 38% men, 71% part-time, 99% state residents, 7% transferred in, 0% international, 62% 25 or older, 1% Native American, 1% Hispanic, 16% black, 2% Asian or Pacific Islander. *Areas of study chosen:* 20% health professions and related sciences, 17% liberal arts/general studies, 11% engineering and applied sciences, 8% business management and administrative services, 3% communications and journalism, 3% computer and information sciences, 1% architecture, 1% fine arts, 1% performing arts. *Most popular recent majors:* nursing, liberal arts/general studies, business administration/commerce/management.
First-Year Class: 4,464 total; 6,552 applied, 100% were accepted, 68% of whom enrolled.
Graduation Requirements: 94 quarter hours; math requirement varies according to program; computer course for students without computer competency; internship (some majors).
Computers on Campus: 700 computers available on campus for general student use. A campus-wide network can be accessed from off-campus. Computers for student use in computer labs, learning resource center, classrooms, library provide access to the Internet/World Wide Web. Staffed computer lab on campus provides training in use of computers, software. *Academic computing expenditure 1995–96:* $921,837.

EXPENSES

Expenses for 1997–98: *Application fee:* $10. Area resident tuition: $1457 full-time, $31 per quarter hour part-time. State resident tuition: $2303 full-time, $49 per quarter hour part-time. Nonresident tuition: $3760 full-time, $80 per quarter hour part-time.
LD Services Contact: Mrs. Lisa Badia Rhine, Program Manager, Disability Services, Sinclair Community College, 444 West Third Street, Dayton, OH 45402-1460, 937-449-5113. Fax: 937-449-5370. Email: lrhine@sinclair.edu.

SKAGIT VALLEY COLLEGE

Mount Vernon, Washington

LEARNING DISABILITIES SERVICES INFORMATION

Disabled Student Services (DSS) began offering services in 1985. Currently the program serves 60 undergraduates with LD. Students diagnosed with ADD/ADHD are eligible for the same services available to students with LD.
Staff: 1 full-time, 1 part-time staff members, including director, coordinator. Services provided by counselors.
Special Fees: No special fees are charged for services to students with LD.
Applications and admissions: *Required:* personal interview, psychoeducational report completed within 3 years. Students may begin taking classes any term. *Application deadline:* continuous.
Special policies: The college has written policies regarding substitutions and waivers of graduation and degree requirements.

PROGRAM AND SERVICE COMPONENTS

Academic advising: Provided by unit staff members. Students with LD may take up to 18 credits each term; most take 8 to 12 credits; 12 credits required to maintain full-time status and be eligible for financial aid.
Counseling services: Individual counseling, career counseling.
Basic skills remediation: Offered in small groups and in class-size groups by regular teachers. Available in reading, math, spelling, written language, learning strategies, study skills, time management.
Subject-area tutoring: Offered one-on-one by peer tutors. Available in most subjects.
Special courses: College survival skills, reading, time management, math, study skills, career planning. All offered for credit; all enter into overall grade point average.
Auxiliary aids: Taped textbooks, tape recorders, word-processors with spell-check, talking computers, optical character readers.
Auxiliary services: Alternative test arrangements, notetakers, priority registration.
Campus support group: A special student organization is available to students with LD.

GENERAL COLLEGE INFORMATION

State-supported, 2-year, coed. Part of Washington State Board for Community and Technical Colleges. Awards associate degrees. Founded 1926. *Setting:* 85-acre small-town campus with easy access to Seattle and Vancouver. *Total enrollment:* 6,538. *Faculty:* 344 (105 full-time, 2% with terminal degrees, 239 part-time); student–undergrad faculty ratio is 18:1.
Enrollment Profile: 6,538 students from 20 states and territories, 10 other countries. 60% women, 40% men, 54% part-time, 94% state residents, 4% transferred in, 1% international, 68% 25 or older, 2% Native American, 3% Hispanic, 1% black, 3% Asian or Pacific Islander. *Retention:* 56% of 1995 full-time freshmen returned. *Areas of study chosen:* 64% liberal arts/general studies.
First-Year Class: 1,150 total; 2,150 applied, 100% were accepted, 53% of whom enrolled.
Graduation Requirements: 90 credits; 1 intermediate college algebra course; 15 credits of science; computer course for most majors.
Computers on Campus: 90 computers available on campus for general student use. A campus-wide network can be accessed. Students can contact faculty members and/or advisers through e-mail. Computers for student use in computer center provide access to the Internet/World Wide Web, on- and off-campus e-mail addresses. Staffed computer lab on campus provides training in use of computers, software.

EXPENSES

Expenses for 1996–97: State resident tuition: $1401 full-time, $46.70 per credit part-time. Nonresident tuition: $5511 full-time, $183.70 per credit part-time.
LD Services Contact: Mr. Eric Anderson, Guidance Counselor/Disabled Student Services Coordinator, Skagit Valley College, 2405 College Way, Mt. Vernon, WA 98273, 360-416-7818. Fax: 360-416-7698.

SOUTH CENTRAL TECHNICAL COLLEGE

North Mankato, Minnesota

LEARNING DISABILITIES SERVICES INFORMATION

Supplemental Services began offering services in 1976. Currently the program serves 45 undergraduates with LD. Students diagnosed with ADD/ADHD are eligible for the same services available to students with LD.
Staff: 4 full-time, 2 part-time staff members, including coordinator. Services provided by remediation specialists, tutors.
Special Fees: No special fees are charged for services to students with LD.
Applications and admissions: *Required:* high school transcript, grade point average, courses completed, IEP (Individualized Education Program), personal interview. Students may begin taking classes in fall, winter, or spring. *Application deadline:* continuous.

PROGRAM AND SERVICE COMPONENTS

Special preparation or orientation: Required orientation held before registration.
Diagnostic testing: Reading, math, written language.
Academic advising: Provided by academic advisers. Students with LD may take up to 16 credits each term; most take 12 credits; 12 credits required to maintain full-time status and be eligible for financial aid.
Counseling services: Individual counseling.
Basic skills remediation: Offered in small groups by regular teachers; computer-aided instruction also offered. Available in reading, math, written language, study skills, time management, computer skills.
Subject-area tutoring: Offered in small groups by professional teachers, peer tutors. Available in all subjects.
Auxiliary aids: Taped textbooks, tape recorders, calculators, word-processors with spell-check, talking computers, optical character readers.

Auxiliary services: Alternative test arrangements, notetakers.

GENERAL COLLEGE INFORMATION

State-supported, 2-year. Part of Minnesota State Colleges and Universities System. Awards associate degrees (branch location: Fairibault). Founded 1946. *Total enrollment:* 3,590.
Enrollment Profile: 3,590 students.
First-Year Class: 410 total.
Graduation Requirements: 110 credits.
Computers on Campus: 300 computers available on campus for general student use. A campus-wide network can be accessed. Students can contact faculty members and/or advisers through e-mail. Computers for student use in computer center, computer labs, learning resource center, classrooms, library, student center provide access to the Internet/World Wide Web, on- and off-campus e-mail addresses. Staffed computer lab on campus provides training in use of computers, software.

EXPENSES

Expenses for 1996–97: State resident tuition: $2200 full-time, $40 per credit part-time. Nonresident tuition: $4400 full-time, $80 per credit part-time. Part-time mandatory fees: $2.80 per credit. Full-time mandatory fees: $154.
LD Services Contact: Mr. Lowell Raschke, Supplemental Services Supervisor, South Central Technical College, 1920 Lee Boulevard, North Mankato, MN 56003, 507-389-7350. Fax: 507-388-9951. Email: lowellr@tc-mankato.scm.tec.mn.us.

SOUTHEAST COMMUNITY COLLEGE, BEATRICE CAMPUS

Beatrice, Nebraska

LEARNING DISABILITIES SERVICES INFORMATION

Rural Career Development Center began offering services in 1987. Currently the program serves 6 undergraduates with LD. Students diagnosed with ADD/ADHD are not eligible for the same services available to students with LD.
Staff: 2 full-time staff members, including coordinator, vocational teacher. Services provided by tutors, counselors, diagnostic specialists.
Special Fees: $90 for diagnostic testing.
Applications and admissions: *Required:* Woodcock-Johnson Revised; *recommended:* high school transcript, grade point average, class rank, courses completed, extracurricular activities, extended time SAT I or ACT, psychoeducational report completed within 3 years. Students may begin taking classes any term. *Application deadline:* continuous.
Special policies: The college has written policies regarding grade forgiveness.

PROGRAM AND SERVICE COMPONENTS

Special preparation or orientation: Required orientation held individually by special arrangement.
Diagnostic testing: Intelligence, reading, math, spelling, spoken language, written language, personality, learning strategies.
Academic advising: Provided by academic advisers. Students with LD may take up to 16 credit hours each term; most take 12 credit hours; 12 credit hours required to maintain full-time status and be eligible for financial aid.
Counseling services: Individual counseling, career counseling.
Basic skills remediation: Offered one-on-one and in small groups by regular teachers. Available in reading, math, written language, learning strategies.
Subject-area tutoring: Offered one-on-one by peer tutors. Available in most subjects.
Special courses: Reading, communication skills, learning strategies, math, study skills, career planning. None offered for credit.
Auxiliary aids: Taped textbooks, tape recorders, word-processors with spell-check.
Auxiliary services: Alternative test arrangements, advocacy.

GENERAL COLLEGE INFORMATION

District-supported, 2-year, coed. Part of Southeast Community College System. Awards associate degrees. Founded 1976. *Setting:* 640-acre small-town campus. *Total enrollment:* 920. *Faculty:* 65 (40 full-time, 5% with terminal degrees, 25 part-time); student–undergrad faculty ratio is 20:1.
Enrollment Profile: 920 students from 9 states and territories, 7 other countries. 60% women, 40% men, 36% part-time, 93% state residents, 22% live on campus, 4% transferred in, 1% international, 40% 25 or older, 1% Hispanic, 1% black, 1% Asian or Pacific Islander. *Retention:* 90% of 1995 full-time freshmen returned.
First-Year Class: 300 total; 600 applied, 100% were accepted, 50% of whom enrolled.
Graduation Requirements: 60 credit hours; 3 credit hours of math; 1 lab science course; computer course; internship (some majors).
Computers on Campus: 75 computers available on campus for general student use. Computers for student use in computer center, computer labs, classrooms, library, dorms. Staffed computer lab on campus provides training in use of computers.

EXPENSES

Expenses for 1997–98: State resident tuition: $1193 full-time, $39.75 per credit hour part-time. Nonresident tuition: $1418 full-time, $47.25 per credit hour part-time. Part-time mandatory fees: $3.50 per credit hour. Colorado, Iowa, Kansas, Missouri, South Dakota and Wyoming residents pay state resident tuition rates. Full-time mandatory fees: $84. College room only: $588.
LD Services Contact: Mr. Jim Rakers, Counselor, Southeast Community College, Beatrice Campus, Route 2, Box 35A, Beatrice, NE 68310-9683, 402-228-3468. Fax: 402-288-3468.

SOUTHEAST COMMUNITY COLLEGE, MILFORD CAMPUS

Milford, Nebraska

LEARNING DISABILITIES SERVICES INFORMATION

Student Services, Maximum Achievement Project began offering services in 1988. Students diagnosed with ADD/ADHD are eligible for the same services available to students with LD.
Staff: 1 full-time staff member (coordinator). Services provided by tutors, counselors.
Special Fees: No special fees are charged for services to students with LD.
Applications and admissions: *Required:* high school transcript, courses completed, psychoeducational report completed within 3 to 4 years; *recommended:* personal interview. Students may begin taking classes any term. *Application deadline:* continuous.
Special policies: The college has written policies regarding grade forgiveness.

PROGRAM AND SERVICE COMPONENTS

Diagnostic testing: Intelligence, reading, math, spoken language, written language, perceptual skills.
Academic advising: Students with LD may take up to the number of quarter credits prescribed by a student's course of study each term; 12 quarter credits required to maintain full-time status and be eligible for financial aid.
Counseling services: Individual counseling, small-group counseling, career counseling.
Basic skills remediation: Offered one-on-one and in small groups by regular teachers. Available in reading, math, written language, learning strategies, study skills, time management.
Subject-area tutoring: Offered one-on-one and in small groups by professional teachers, peer tutors. Available in some subjects.
Special courses: College survival skills, reading, vocabulary development, communication skills, learning strategies, word processing, time management, math, study skills. All offered for credit; some enter into overall grade point average.
Auxiliary aids: Taped textbooks, tape recorders, calculators, word-processors with spell-check, personal computers.
Auxiliary services: Alternative test arrangements, notetakers, priority registration.
Campus support group: A special student organization is available to students with LD.

GENERAL COLLEGE INFORMATION

District-supported, 2-year, coed. Part of Southeast Community College System. Awards associate degrees. Founded 1941. *Setting:* 50-acre small-town campus with easy access to Omaha. *Total enrollment:* 955. *Faculty:* 89 (86 full-time, 3 part-time).

Southeast Community College, Milford Campus (continued)

Enrollment Profile: 955 students: 3% women, 97% men, 3% part-time, 95% state residents, 33% live on campus, 5% transferred in, 1% international, 20% 25 or older, 0% Native American, 0% Hispanic, 0% black, 0% Asian or Pacific Islander. *Most popular recent majors:* architectural technologies, automotive technologies, construction technologies.
First-Year Class: 157 total. Of the students who applied, 100% were accepted.
Graduation Requirements: 108 credits.
Computers on Campus: 72 computers available on campus for general student use. Computer purchase/lease plans available. Computers for student use in computer center, library. Staffed computer lab on campus provides training in use of computers, software.

EXPENSES

Expenses for 1997–98: State resident tuition: $1431 full-time, $26.50 per credit part-time. Nonresident tuition: $1701 full-time, $31.50 per credit part-time. Part-time mandatory fees: $12 per quarter. Colorado, Iowa, Kansas, Missouri, South Dakota and Wyoming residents pay state resident tuition rates. Full-time mandatory fees: $36. College room and board: $2145.
LD Services Contact: Ms. Joan Sterns, Coordinator, Student Assessment and Learning Disabilities, Southeast Community College, Milford Campus, 600 State Street, Milford, NE 68405-9397, 402-761-2131 Ext. 8202. Fax: 402-761-2324.

SOUTHEASTERN COMMUNITY COLLEGE, NORTH CAMPUS

West Burlington, Iowa

LEARNING DISABILITIES SERVICES INFORMATION

Learning Center began offering services in 1984. Currently the program serves 50 undergraduates with LD. Students diagnosed with ADD/ADHD are eligible for the same services available to students with LD.
Staff: 3 full-time, 1 part-time staff members, including coordinator. Services provided by tutors, instructors.
Special Fees: No special fees are charged for services to students with LD.
Applications and admissions: *Required:* high school transcript, psychoeducational report completed within 12 months, referral from high school special education instructor (may be substituted for psychoeducational report); *recommended:* high school courses completed. Students may begin taking classes in fall, spring, or summer. *Application deadline:* continuous.
Special policies: The college has written policies regarding grade forgiveness.

PROGRAM AND SERVICE COMPONENTS

Diagnostic testing: Intelligence, reading, math, spoken language, written language, motor abilities, study skills, personality, social skills, learning strategies.
Academic advising: Provided by unit staff members, academic advisers. Students with LD may take up to 18 credit hours each term; most take 12 credit hours; 12 credit hours required to maintain full-time status; 3 credit hours (part-time), 12 credit hours (full-time) required to be eligible for financial aid.
Counseling services: Individual counseling, career counseling.
Basic skills remediation: Offered one-on-one and in small groups by regular teachers. Available in reading, math, spelling, written language, learning strategies, study skills, time management, social skills.
Subject-area tutoring: Offered one-on-one and in small groups by peer tutors. Available in some subjects.
Auxiliary aids: Taped textbooks, tape recorders, calculators, word-processors with spell-check.
Auxiliary services: Alternative test arrangements, notetakers, advocacy.

GENERAL COLLEGE INFORMATION

State and locally supported, 2-year, coed. Part of Iowa Department of Education Division of Community Colleges. Awards associate degrees. Founded 1968. *Setting:* 160-acre small-town campus. *Total enrollment:* 1,881. *Faculty:* 94 (12 full-time, 82 part-time); student–undergrad faculty ratio is 19:1.
Enrollment Profile: 1,881 students from 8 states and territories. 61% women, 39% men, 34% part-time, 92% state residents, 3% live on campus, 18% transferred in, 0% international, 34% 25 or older, 0% Native American, 1% Hispanic, 2% black, 1% Asian or Pacific Islander. *Retention:* 50% of 1995 full-time freshmen returned.
First-Year Class: 760 total; 1,382 applied, 100% were accepted, 55% of whom enrolled.
Graduation Requirements: 62 credit hours; computer course for medical assistant technologies majors; internship (some majors).
Computers on Campus: 100 computers available on campus for general student use. Computers for student use in computer center, library. Staffed computer lab on campus provides training in use of computers, software.

EXPENSES

Expenses for 1997–98: State resident tuition: $1566 full-time, $50.50 per credit hour part-time. Nonresident tuition: $2348 full-time, $75.75 per credit hour part-time. Mandatory fees: $233 full-time, $7.50 per credit hour part-time for state residents; $279 full-time, $9 per credit hour part-time for nonresidents. College room and board: $1990 (minimum). College room only: $1500.
LD Services Contact: Ms. Danna Fienburg, Enrollment Representative, Southeastern Community College, North Campus, Drawer F, 1015 South Gear Avenue, West Burlington, IA 52655-0605, 319-752-2731. Fax: 319-752-4957.

SOUTHEASTERN ILLINOIS COLLEGE

Harrisburg, Illinois

LEARNING DISABILITIES SERVICES INFORMATION

Office of Student Affairs/Office of Instruction/Academic Affairs began offering services in 1981. Currently the program serves 5 undergraduates with LD. Students diagnosed with ADD/ADHD are eligible for the same services available to students with LD.
Staff: 2 part-time staff members, including director, coordinator. Services provided by tutors, counselors, professional tutor.
Special Fees: No special fees are charged for services to students with LD.
Applications and admissions: *Required:* high school transcript, psychoeducational report, ACT ASSET (for placement). Students may begin taking classes any term. *Application deadline:* 9/10.

PROGRAM AND SERVICE COMPONENTS

Academic advising: Provided by unit staff members, academic advisers. Most students with LD take 12 to 15 semester hours each term; 12 semester hours required to maintain full-time status and be eligible for financial aid.
Counseling services: Individual counseling, small-group counseling, career counseling.
Basic skills remediation: Offered one-on-one, in small groups, and in class-size groups by regular teachers. Available in reading, math, spelling, written language, learning strategies, study skills, time management, social skills.
Subject-area tutoring: Offered one-on-one and in small groups by peer tutors, professional tutors. Available in most subjects.
Auxiliary aids: Taped textbooks, tape recorders, calculators, typewriters, word-processors with spell-check, personal computers.
Auxiliary services: Alternative test arrangements, notetakers, advocacy.

GENERAL COLLEGE INFORMATION

State-supported, 2-year, coed. Part of Illinois Community College System. Awards associate degrees. Founded 1960. *Setting:* 140-acre rural campus. *Total enrollment:* 2,964. *Faculty:* 184 (47 full-time, 14% with terminal degrees, 137 part-time); student–undergrad faculty ratio is 20:1.
Enrollment Profile: 2,964 students from 5 states and territories, 2 other countries. 48% women, 52% men, 69% part-time, 95% state residents, 5% transferred in, 2% international, 40% 25 or older, 1% Native American, 1% Hispanic, 13% black, 1% Asian or Pacific Islander. *Most popular recent majors:* nursing, business administration/commerce/management.
First-Year Class: 1,119 total. Of the students who applied, 100% were accepted.
Graduation Requirements: 62 semester hours; math/science requirements vary according to program; internship (some majors).
Computers on Campus: 78 computers available on campus for general student use. Computers for student use in classrooms, library, learning electronics labs. Staffed computer lab on campus provides training in use of computers, software.

EXPENSES

Expenses for 1997–98: Area resident tuition: $1023 full-time, $33 per semester hour part-time. State resident tuition: $4262 full-time, $137.48 per semester hour part-time. Nonresident tuition: $5538 full-time, $178.66 per semester hour part-time.

LD Services Contact: Dr. Catherine Packard, Director of Developmental Education, Southeastern Illinois College, 3575 College Road, Harrisburg, IL 62946, 618-252-6376 Ext. 433. Fax: 618-252-2713. Email: cpackard@sic.cc.il.us.

SOUTHERN MAINE TECHNICAL COLLEGE

South Portland, Maine

LEARNING DISABILITIES SERVICES INFORMATION

Learning Assistance Center began offering services in 1978. Currently the program serves 58 undergraduates with LD. Students diagnosed with ADD/ADHD are eligible for the same services available to students with LD.

Staff: Includes coordinator. Services provided by tutors, LD certified instructor.

Special Fees: No special fees are charged for services to students with LD.

Applications and admissions: *Required:* high school transcript, courses completed; *recommended:* untimed or extended time SAT I, personal interview, letters of recommendation, psychoeducational report completed within 3 years. Students may begin taking classes in fall or spring. *Application deadline:* continuous.

PROGRAM AND SERVICE COMPONENTS

Diagnostic testing: Reading, math, spelling, written language, study skills, learning strategies.

Academic advising: Provided by unit staff members, academic advisers. Students with LD may take up to 15 credits each term; most take 9 to 12 credits; 12 credits required to maintain full-time status and be eligible for financial aid.

Counseling services: Individual counseling, career counseling.

Basic skills remediation: Offered one-on-one, in small groups, and in class-size groups by LD teachers, regular teachers; computer-aided instruction also offered. Available in reading, math, spelling, written language, learning strategies, study skills, time management.

Subject-area tutoring: Offered one-on-one and in small groups by professional teachers, peer tutors. Available in most subjects.

Special courses: College survival skills, reading, composition, word processing, math, typing, personal psychology, study skills, career planning. All offered for credit; most enter into overall grade point average.

Auxiliary aids: Taped textbooks, tape recorders, calculators, typewriters, word-processors with spell-check, personal computers.

Auxiliary services: Alternative test arrangements, notetakers, advocacy.

GENERAL COLLEGE INFORMATION

State-supported, 2-year, coed. Part of Maine Technical College System. Awards associate degrees. Founded 1946. *Setting:* 65-acre suburban campus. *Total enrollment:* 2,412. *Faculty:* 148 (98 full-time, 5% with terminal degrees, 50 part-time); student–undergrad faculty ratio is 12:1.

Enrollment Profile: 2,412 students from 12 states and territories. 38% women, 62% men, 52% part-time, 91% state residents, 10% live on campus, 44% transferred in, 1% international, 40% 25 or older, 1% Native American, 1% Hispanic, 1% black, 1% Asian or Pacific Islander. *Retention:* 71% of 1995 full-time freshmen returned. *Most popular recent majors:* law enforcement/police sciences, culinary arts, computer technologies.

First-Year Class: 839 total; 1,960 applied, 59% were accepted, 72% of whom enrolled. 5% from top 10% of their high school class, 30% from top quarter, 65% from top half.

Graduation Requirements: 60 credit hours; math proficiency; computer course for allied health, hotel management, machine tool technology, drafting, medical assisting, culinary arts, marine biology, graphics, design majors; internship (some majors).

Computers on Campus: 45 computers available on campus for general student use. Computers for student use in computer center, computer labs, student center, study center provide access to the Internet/World Wide Web. Staffed computer lab on campus provides training in use of computers, software.

EXPENSES

Expenses for 1996–97: *Application fee:* $20. State resident tuition: $1920 full-time, $64 per credit hour part-time. Nonresident tuition: $4230 full-time, $141 per credit hour part-time. Part-time mandatory fees: $4 per credit hour. Tuition for nonresidents who are eligible for the New England Regional Student Program: $2400 full-time, $80 per credit hour part-time. Full-time mandatory fees: $230. College room and board: $3640 (minimum).

LD Services Contact: Mr. Bob Weimont, Director of Admissions, Southern Maine Technical College, Fort Road, South Portland, ME 04106, 207-767-9520.

SOUTHERN WEST VIRGINIA COMMUNITY AND TECHNICAL COLLEGE

Mount Gay, West Virginia

LEARNING DISABILITIES SERVICES INFORMATION

Disabled Student Services began offering services in 1991. Currently the program serves 9 undergraduates with LD. Students diagnosed with ADD/ADHD are eligible for the same services available to students with LD.

Staff: 1 full-time staff member (director). Services provided by counselor.

Special Fees: No special fees are charged for services to students with LD.

Applications and admissions: *Required:* high school transcript, untimed ACT; *recommended:* high school grade point average, class rank, courses completed, extracurricular activities, extended time ACT, autobiographical statement, letters of recommendation. Students may begin taking classes in fall, spring, or summer. *Application deadline:* continuous.

Special policies: The college has written policies regarding grade forgiveness.

PROGRAM AND SERVICE COMPONENTS

Special preparation or orientation: Orientation (required for some) held during registration.

Diagnostic testing: Intelligence, reading, math, spelling, written language, personality, vocational interests, career values.

Academic advising: Provided by unit staff members, academic advisers. Students with LD may take up to 18 credit hours each term; most take 12 credit hours; 12 credit hours required to maintain full-time status and be eligible for financial aid.

Counseling services: Individual counseling, career counseling.

Basic skills remediation: Offered in small groups by regular teachers. Available in reading, math, spelling, written language, study skills.

Subject-area tutoring: Offered one-on-one by peer tutors. Available in most subjects.

Auxiliary aids: Taped textbooks, tape recorders, typewriters, personal computers, optical character readers, spell check on computers.

Auxiliary services: Alternative test arrangements, notetakers, advocacy.

GENERAL COLLEGE INFORMATION

State-supported, 2-year, coed. Part of State College System of West Virginia. Awards associate degrees. Founded 1971. *Setting:* 23-acre rural campus. *Total enrollment:* 3,014. *Faculty:* 184 (52 full-time, 6% with terminal degrees, 132 part-time).

Enrollment Profile: 3,014 students from 2 states and territories. 68% women, 32% men, 41% part-time, 91% state residents, 48% transferred in, 80% 25 or older, 1% Native American, 1% Hispanic, 2% black, 1% Asian or Pacific Islander. *Areas of study chosen:* 66% interdisciplinary studies, 3% social sciences, 1% communications and journalism, 1% engineering and applied sciences. *Most popular recent majors:* liberal arts/general studies, business administration/commerce/management, nursing.

First-Year Class: 897 total; 960 applied, 100% were accepted, 93% of whom enrolled. 1% from top 10% of their high school class, 36% from top half.

Graduation Requirements: 63 semester hours; math/science requirements vary according to program; computer course.

Computers on Campus: 92 computers available on campus for general student use. A campus-wide network can be accessed from off-campus. Students can contact faculty members and/or advisers through e-mail. Computers for student use in computer labs, library provide access to the Internet/World Wide Web, on- and off-campus e-mail addresses. Staffed computer lab on campus.

Southern West Virginia Community and Technical College (continued)

EXPENSES

Expenses for 1997–98: *Application fee:* $10. State resident tuition: $1170 full-time. Nonresident tuition: $4454 full-time. Part-time tuition per semester (1 to 10 semester hours): $49 to $489 for state residents, $186 to $1857 for nonresidents, according to course load.

LD Services Contact: Ms. Sherry Dempsey, Program Manager, Disabled Student Services, Southern West Virginia Community and Technical College, Box 2900, Mount Gay, WV 25637, 304-792-7098 Ext. 225. Fax: 304-792-7024. Email: sherryd@swvcc.wvnet.edu.

SOUTH MOUNTAIN COMMUNITY COLLEGE

Phoenix, Arizona

LEARNING DISABILITIES SERVICES INFORMATION

Learning Assistance Center began offering services in 1982. Students diagnosed with ADD/ADHD are eligible for the same services available to students with LD.

Staff: 2 full-time, 3 part-time staff members, including director, testing personnel. Services provided by tutors.

Special Fees: No special fees are charged for services to students with LD.

Applications and admissions: Neurological reports, IEP, or vocational rehabilitation documentation may serve as documentation of disability. Students may begin taking classes in fall, spring, or summer. *Application deadline:* continuous.

PROGRAM AND SERVICE COMPONENTS

Academic advising: Provided by academic advisers. Students with LD may take up to 15 credit hours each term; 12 credit hours required to maintain full-time status; 6 credit hours required to be eligible for financial aid.

Counseling services: Individual counseling, small-group counseling, career counseling, workshops.

Basic skills remediation: Offered one-on-one, in small groups, and in class-size groups by regular teachers, video instruction; computer-aided instruction also offered. Available in reading, math, spelling, spoken language, written language, learning strategies, study skills, time management, computer skills, computer instruction, basic skills (GED program).

Subject-area tutoring: Offered one-on-one and in small groups by peer tutors, professional tutors. Available in some subjects.

Special courses: College survival skills, reading, vocabulary development, communication skills, composition, learning strategies, time management, math, typing, personal psychology, study skills, career planning, computer skills. All offered for credit; all enter into overall grade point average.

Auxiliary aids: Taped textbooks, tape recorders, calculators, typewriters, word-processors with spell-check, personal computers, talking computers, optical character readers.

Auxiliary services: Alternative test arrangements, notetakers, advocacy.

GENERAL COLLEGE INFORMATION

State and locally supported, 2-year, coed. Part of Maricopa County Community College District System. Awards associate degrees. Founded 1979. *Setting:* 108-acre suburban campus. *Total enrollment:* 2,423. *Faculty:* 184 (42 full-time, 32% with terminal degrees, 142 part-time); student–undergrad faculty ratio is 20:1.

Enrollment Profile: 2,423 students: 58% women, 42% men, 72% part-time, 96% state residents, 23% transferred in, 4% international, 40% 25 or older, 4% Native American, 43% Hispanic, 16% black, 3% Asian or Pacific Islander. *Retention:* 25% of 1995 full-time freshmen returned. *Most popular recent major:* liberal arts/general studies.

First-Year Class: 2,317 total. Of the students who applied, 100% were accepted, 85% of whom enrolled.

Graduation Requirements: 62 credit hours; 1 math course; computer course.

Computers on Campus: 150 computers available on campus for general student use. Computers for student use in computer center, computer labs, library, business building classrooms provide access to the Internet/World Wide Web, electronic forum career guidance. Staffed computer lab on campus (open 24 hours a day) provides training in use of computers, software.

EXPENSES

Expenses for 1996–97: Area resident tuition: $744 full-time, $24 per credit hour part-time. State resident tuition: $4464 full-time. Nonresident tuition: $4619 full-time. Part-time tuition per credit hour ranges from $24 to $144 for state residents, $49 to $149 for nonresidents. Part-time mandatory fees per semester range from $15 to $115. Residents of participating Arizona counties pay area resident tuition rates. Full-time mandatory fees: $320.

LD Services Contact: Ms. Henrietta Harris, Associate Dean of Student Services, South Mountain Community College, 7050 South Twenty-Fourth Street, Phoenix, AZ 85040, 602-243-8064. Fax: 602-243-8329.

SOUTH SEATTLE COMMUNITY COLLEGE

Seattle, Washington

LEARNING DISABILITIES SERVICES INFORMATION

Special Student Services began offering services in 1983. Currently the program serves 40 undergraduates with LD. Students diagnosed with ADD/ADHD are eligible for the same services available to students with LD.

Staff: 2 full-time, 30 part-time staff members, including director. Services provided by remediation specialists, tutors, counselors.

Special Fees: No special fees are charged for services to students with LD.

Applications and admissions: Open admissions. Students may begin taking classes any term. *Application deadline:* continuous.

PROGRAM AND SERVICE COMPONENTS

Academic advising: Provided by unit staff members, academic advisers. Students with LD may take up to 18 quarter credits each term; most take 10 to 12 quarter credits; 12 quarter credits required to maintain full-time status.

Counseling services: Individual counseling, career counseling.

Basic skills remediation: Offered one-on-one, in small groups, and in class-size groups by regular teachers, peer teachers. Available in reading, math, spelling, written language, learning strategies, study skills.

Subject-area tutoring: Offered one-on-one and in small groups by peer tutors. Available in most subjects.

Auxiliary aids: Taped textbooks, tape recorders, calculators, typewriters, word-processors with spell-check, personal computers, talking computers, optical character readers, ScreenPower/OSCAR.

Auxiliary services: Alternative test arrangements, notetakers, priority registration, advocacy.

GENERAL COLLEGE INFORMATION

State-supported, 2-year, coed. Part of Seattle Community College District System. Awards associate degrees. Founded 1970. *Setting:* 65-acre urban campus. *Total enrollment:* 2,837. *Faculty:* 194 (76 full-time, 118 part-time).

Enrollment Profile: 2,837 students from 4 states and territories, 24 other countries. 48% women, 52% men, 54% part-time, 91% state residents, 4% transferred in, 7% international, 54% 25 or older, 2% Native American, 3% Hispanic, 10% black, 22% Asian or Pacific Islander.

First-Year Class: 914 total. Of the students who applied, 100% were accepted.

Graduation Requirements: 90 credits; math/science requirements vary according to program; computer course.

Computers on Campus: 300 computers available on campus for general student use. A campus-wide network can be accessed. Students can contact faculty members and/or advisers through e-mail. Computers for student use in computer center, library provide access to the Internet/World Wide Web, on- and off-campus e-mail addresses. Staffed computer lab on campus provides training in use of computers, software.

EXPENSES

Expenses for 1996–97: State resident tuition: $1379 full-time, $45.95 per credit part-time. Nonresident tuition: $5489 full-time, $182.95 per credit part-time. Full-time mandatory fees: $30.

LD Services Contact: Ms. Roxanne Tillman, Director, Disabled Student Services, South Seattle Community College, 6000 16th Avenue, SW, Seattle, WA 98106-1499, 206-763-5137. Fax: 206-763-5155. Email: rtillman@seaccd.sccd.ctc.edu.

SOUTH TEXAS COMMUNITY COLLEGE

McAllen, Texas

LEARNING DISABILITIES SERVICES INFORMATION

Student Support Services began offering services in 1993. Students diagnosed with ADD/ADHD are not eligible for the same services available to students with LD.

Staff: 1 full-time, 1 part-time staff members, including coordinator. Services provided by tutors, counselor.

Special Fees: No special fees are charged for services to students with LD.

Applications and admissions: *Required:* high school transcript, grade point average, class rank, courses completed; *recommended:* untimed or extended time SAT I or ACT. Students may begin taking classes any term. *Application deadline:* 7/1 (fall term), 12/2 (spring term).

PROGRAM AND SERVICE COMPONENTS

Special preparation or orientation: Required orientation held individually during registration.

Academic advising: Provided by unit staff members. Students with LD may take up to as many hours as an individual can handle each term; most take 6 to 12 hours; 12 hours required to maintain full-time status; 6 hours required to be eligible for financial aid.

Counseling services: Individual counseling, career counseling.

Subject-area tutoring: Offered one-on-one and in small groups by peer tutors. Available in most subjects.

Auxiliary aids: Taped textbooks, tape recorders, calculators, typewriters, personal computers, optical character readers.

Auxiliary services: Alternative test arrangements, notetakers, priority registration, advocacy.

GENERAL COLLEGE INFORMATION

District-supported, 2-year, coed. Awards associate degrees. Founded 1993. *Setting:* 20-acre suburban campus. *Endowment:* $17,971. *Total enrollment:* 6,050. *Faculty:* 108 (10% of full-time faculty have terminal degrees).

Enrollment Profile: 6,050 students: 58% women, 42% men, 60% part-time, 99% state residents, 44% transferred in, 1% international, 35% 25 or older, 91% Hispanic, 1% black, 1% Asian or Pacific Islander. *Retention:* 45% of 1995 full-time freshmen returned. *Areas of study chosen:* 29% interdisciplinary studies, 17% mathematics, 11% education, 7% liberal arts/general studies, 5% health professions and related sciences, 3% biological and life sciences, 2% business management and administrative services, 1% computer and information sciences, 1% engineering and applied sciences. *Most popular recent majors:* nursing, automotive technologies.

First-Year Class: 1,194 total; 2,612 applied, 100% were accepted, 46% of whom enrolled.

Graduation Requirements: 60 semester hours; computer course for teacher preparation, interdisciplinary studies, child care and development, heating, ventilation and air conditioning majors.

Computers on Campus: 240 computers available on campus for general student use. A computer is recommended for some students. A campus-wide network can be accessed from off-campus. Students can contact faculty members and/or advisers through e-mail. Computers for student use in computer center, computer labs, learning resource center, classrooms, library provide access to the Internet/World Wide Web. Staffed computer lab on campus provides training in use of computers, software. *Academic computing expenditure 1995–96:* $538,601.

EXPENSES

Expenses for 1996–97: Area resident tuition: $1202 full-time. State resident tuition: $1462 full-time. Nonresident tuition: $6660 full-time, $222 per semester part-time. Part-time tuition per semester ranges from $118 to $457 for area residents, $168 to $559 for state residents.

LD Services Contact: Mr. Wayne Williams, Academic Counselor, South Texas Community College, Box 9701, McAllen, TX 78501, 210-618-8367. Fax: 210-668-6477. Email: waynew@stcc.cc.tx.us.

SOUTHWESTERN COMMUNITY COLLEGE

Creston, Iowa

LEARNING DISABILITIES SERVICES INFORMATION

Comprehensive Learning Center began offering services in 1972. Currently the program serves 45 undergraduates with LD. Students diagnosed with ADD/ADHD are not eligible for the same services available to students with LD.

Staff: 2 full-time, 1 part-time staff members. Services provided by remediation specialists, counselors.

Special Fees: $25 to $50 for diagnostic testing.

Applications and admissions: *Required:* high school transcript, grade point average, class rank, courses completed, personal interview, psychoeducational report completed within 3 years, ACT ASSET; *recommended:* high school IEP (Individualized Education Program). Students may begin taking classes in fall, spring, or summer. *Application deadline:* continuous.

Special policies: The college has written policies regarding substitutions and waivers of admissions requirements.

PROGRAM AND SERVICE COMPONENTS

Diagnostic testing: Reading, math, spelling, perceptual skills, study skills.

Academic advising: Provided by academic advisers. Students with LD may take up to 16 credit hours each term; most take 15 credit hours; 12 credit hours required to maintain full-time status; 6 credit hours required to be eligible for financial aid.

Counseling services: Individual counseling, career counseling.

Basic skills remediation: Offered one-on-one by regular teachers. Available in reading, math, spelling, written language, learning strategies, study skills.

Subject-area tutoring: Offered one-on-one by peer tutors. Available in some subjects.

Special courses: College survival skills, reading, vocabulary development, communication skills, math, typing, study skills, career planning. Most offered for credit; most enter into overall grade point average.

Auxiliary aids: Taped textbooks, tape recorders, calculators, word-processors with spell-check.

Auxiliary services: Alternative test arrangements, notetakers.

GENERAL COLLEGE INFORMATION

State-supported, 2-year, coed. Part of Iowa Department of Education Division of Community Colleges. Awards associate degrees. Founded 1966. *Setting:* 420-acre rural campus. *Educational spending 1995–96:* $3424 per undergrad. *Total enrollment:* 1,228. *Faculty:* 69 (43 full-time, 100% with terminal degrees, 26 part-time).

Enrollment Profile: 1,228 students: 60% women, 40% men, 38% part-time, 94% state residents, 6% live on campus, 6% transferred in, 1% international, 39% 25 or older, 0% Native American, 1% Hispanic, 1% black, 0% Asian or Pacific Islander. *Retention:* 53% of 1995 full-time freshmen returned. *Areas of study chosen:* 62% liberal arts/general studies, 38% vocational and home economics. *Most popular recent major:* business administration/commerce/management.

First-Year Class: 426 total; 690 applied, 91% were accepted, 68% of whom enrolled. 1% from top 10% of their high school class, 13% from top quarter, 42% from top half.

Graduation Requirements: 62 credit hours; computer course for business administration, accounting, secretarial studies majors; internship (some majors).

Computers on Campus: 115 computers available on campus for general student use. A campus-wide network can be accessed from off-campus. Computers for student use in computer center, computer labs, learning resource center, library. Staffed computer lab on campus.

EXPENSES

Expenses for 1997–98: State resident tuition: $1674 full-time, $54 per credit hour part-time. Nonresident tuition: $2511 full-time, $81 per credit hour part-time. Part-time mandatory fees: $12 per credit hour. Full-time mandatory fees: $372. College room and board: $2760.

LD Services Contact: Mr. Gary O'Daniels, Special Needs Coordinator, Southwestern Community College, 1501 Townline Road, Creston, IA 50801, 515-782-7081. Fax: 515-782-3312.

SOUTHWESTERN COMMUNITY COLLEGE

Sylva, North Carolina

LEARNING DISABILITIES SERVICES INFORMATION

Student Support Services began offering services in 1989. Currently the program serves 12 undergraduates with LD. Students diagnosed with ADD/ADHD are eligible for the same services available to students with LD, as well as customized modifications and diagnostics.
Staff: 4 full-time, 3 part-time staff members, including director. Services provided by remediation specialists, tutors, counselors, diagnostic specialists, part-time teachers.
Special Fees: No special fees are charged for services to students with LD.
Applications and admissions: *Required:* high school transcript, psychoeducational report completed within 3 years; *recommended:* high school IEP (Individualized Education Program), documentation from high school counselors, Vocational Rehabilitation, or another Student Support Services project. Students may begin taking classes any term. *Application deadline:* continuous.
Special policies: The college has written policies regarding grade forgiveness; substitutions and waivers of admissions, graduation, and degree requirements.

PROGRAM AND SERVICE COMPONENTS

Diagnostic testing: Intelligence, reading, math, written language.
Academic advising: Provided by unit staff members. Most students with LD take 12 to 15 quarter hours each term; 12 quarter hours required to maintain full-time status and be eligible for financial aid.
Counseling services: Individual counseling, career counseling.
Basic skills remediation: Offered one-on-one, in small groups, and in class-size groups by regular teachers, Student Success Center instructors. Available in reading, math, spelling, written language, learning strategies, study skills, time management, computer skills.
Subject-area tutoring: Offered one-on-one and in small groups by peer tutors. Available in most subjects.
Auxiliary aids: Taped textbooks, tape recorders, word-processors with spell-check, optical character readers.
Auxiliary services: Alternative test arrangements, notetakers.

GENERAL COLLEGE INFORMATION

State-supported, 2-year, coed. Part of North Carolina Community College System. Awards associate degrees. Founded 1964. *Setting:* 55-acre small-town campus. *Total enrollment:* 1,735. *Faculty:* 45 full-time, 156 part-time; student–undergrad faculty ratio is 10:1.
Enrollment Profile: 1,735 students: 66% women, 34% men, 46% part-time, 95% state residents, 7% transferred in, 0% international, 46% 25 or older, 11% Native American, 0% Hispanic, 2% black, 0% Asian or Pacific Islander.
First-Year Class: 867 total. Of the students who applied, 75% were accepted.
Graduation Requirements: 1 math course; computer course.
Computers on Campus: 120 computers available on campus for general student use. A computer is recommended for all students. A campus-wide network can be accessed from off-campus. Computers for student use in computer center, computer labs, learning resource center, classrooms provide access to the Internet/World Wide Web, on-campus e-mail addresses. Staffed computer lab on campus.

EXPENSES

Expenses for 1997–98: State resident tuition: $560 full-time, $20 per semester hour part-time. Nonresident tuition: $4564 full-time, $163 per semester hour part-time. Part-time mandatory fees per semester range from $2 to $7. Full-time mandatory fees: $16.
LD Services Contact: Mr. Steve Conlin, Director, Student Support Services, Southwestern Community College, 275 Webster Road, Sylva, NC 28779-9578, 704-586-4091 Ext. 226. Fax: 704-586-3129.

SOUTHWEST WISCONSIN TECHNICAL COLLEGE

Fennimore, Wisconsin

LEARNING DISABILITIES SERVICES INFORMATION

Vocational Educational Support Program (VESP) began offering services in 1980. Currently the program serves 21 undergraduates with LD. Students diagnosed with ADD/ADHD are eligible for the same services available to students with LD.
Staff: 2 full-time staff members, including coordinators. Services provided by remediation specialists, tutors, counselors, transition specialist.
Special Fees: No special fees are charged for services to students with LD.
Applications and admissions: *Required:* high school transcript, grade point average, class rank, courses completed, psychoeducational report, multidisciplinary team reports; *recommended:* high school IEP (Individualized Education Program), vocational evaluations for Division of Vocational Rehabilitation students. Students may begin taking classes any term. *Application deadline:* 8/9 (fall term), 1/9 (spring term).
Special policies: The college has written policies regarding substitutions and waivers of graduation and degree requirements.

PROGRAM AND SERVICE COMPONENTS

Special preparation or orientation: Optional summer program offered prior to entering college.
Diagnostic testing: Reading, math, spelling, written language, learning strategies.
Academic advising: Provided by unit staff members. Students with LD may take up to 20 credits each term; most take 12 to 18 credits; 12 credits required to maintain full-time status; 1 credit required to be eligible for financial aid.
Counseling services: Individual counseling, career counseling.
Basic skills remediation: Offered one-on-one and in small groups by regular teachers. Available in reading, math, spelling, spoken language, written language.
Subject-area tutoring: Offered one-on-one and in small groups by professional teachers, peer tutors. Available in all subjects.
Auxiliary aids: Taped textbooks, tape recorders, calculators, typewriters, word-processors with spell-check, personal computers, optical character readers, laptop computers.
Auxiliary services: Alternative test arrangements, notetakers, advocacy.

GENERAL COLLEGE INFORMATION

State and locally supported, 2-year, coed. Part of Wisconsin Technical College System. Awards associate degrees. Founded 1967. *Setting:* 53-acre rural campus. *Endowment:* $214,997. *Research spending 1995–96:* $99,422. *Total enrollment:* 3,870. *Faculty:* 101 (80 full-time, 100% with terminal degrees, 21 part-time).
Enrollment Profile: 3,870 students from 4 states and territories, 1 other country. 58% women, 42% men, 79% part-time, 98% state residents, 10% transferred in, 54% 25 or older, 1% Native American, 1% Hispanic, 1% black, 1% Asian or Pacific Islander. *Retention:* 75% of 1995 full-time freshmen returned. *Areas of study chosen:* 29% engineering and applied sciences, 27% business management and administrative services, 26% health professions and related sciences, 11% vocational and home economics, 7% agriculture. *Most popular recent majors:* nursing, human services, accounting.
First-Year Class: 979 applied, 88% were accepted, 73% of whom enrolled.
Graduation Requirements: 64 credits; computer course for most majors; internship (some majors).
Computers on Campus: 250 computers available on campus for general student use. Computers for student use in computer center, computer labs, classrooms, library. Staffed computer lab on campus provides training in use of computers, software. *Academic computing expenditure 1995–96:* $163,224.

EXPENSES

Expenses for 1996–97: *Application fee:* $25. State resident tuition: $1638 full-time, $51.20 per credit part-time. Nonresident tuition: $12,640 full-time, $395 per credit part-time. Part-time mandatory fees: $4.65 per credit. Full-time mandatory fees: $149.
LD Services Contact: Mr. Alan Propst, Special Services Coordinator, Southwest Wisconsin Technical College, Kramer Administration Building, 1800 Bronson Boulevard, Fennimore, WI 53809, 608-822-3262 Ext. 115. Fax: 608-822-6019. Email: apropst@southwest.tec.wi.us.

SPARTANBURG TECHNICAL COLLEGE

Spartanburg, South Carolina

LEARNING DISABILITIES SERVICES INFORMATION

Student Disability Services Center currently serves 50 to 75 undergraduates with LD. Students diagnosed with ADD/ADHD are eligible for the same services available to students with LD.

Staff: 1 full-time, 3 part-time staff members, including director. Services provided by remediation specialist, tutors, counselor.
Special Fees: No special fees are charged for services to students with LD.
Applications and admissions: *Required:* high school transcript, personal interview, documentation of disability. Students may begin taking classes any term. *Application deadline:* continuous.

PROGRAM AND SERVICE COMPONENTS

Special preparation or orientation: Optional orientation offered individually by arrangement.
Academic advising: Provided by unit staff members, academic advisers. Most students with LD take 6 to 12 semester hours each term; 12 semester hours (can vary with individual needs) required to maintain full-time status and be eligible for financial aid.
Counseling services: Individual counseling, career counseling, self-advocacy training.
Basic skills remediation: Offered one-on-one and in class-size groups by regular teachers; computer-aided instruction also offered. Available in reading, math, written language, learning strategies, study skills, time management.
Auxiliary aids: Taped textbooks, tape recorders, word-processors with spell-check, personal computers, large print DOS, voice synthesizer.
Auxiliary services: Alternative test arrangements, notetakers, advocacy.

GENERAL COLLEGE INFORMATION

State-supported, 2-year, coed. Part of South Carolina State Board for Technical and Comprehensive Education. Awards associate degrees. Founded 1961. *Setting:* 104-acre urban campus. *Total enrollment:* 2,562. *Faculty:* 98 full-time, 100% with terminal degrees; student–undergrad faculty ratio is 25:1.
Enrollment Profile: 2,562 students from 4 states and territories. 53% women, 47% men, 50% part-time, 99% state residents, 1% transferred in, 41% 25 or older, 1% Native American, 1% Hispanic, 20% black, 1% Asian or Pacific Islander.
First-Year Class: 1,392 total; 2,026 applied, 84% were accepted, 82% of whom enrolled.
Graduation Requirements: 60 semester hours; 1 math/science course; computer course.
Computers on Campus: 225 computers available on campus for general student use. A campus-wide network can be accessed from off-campus. Computers for student use in computer labs, learning resource center, classrooms, library provide access to the Internet/World Wide Web. Staffed computer lab on campus provides training in use of computers, software.

EXPENSES

Expenses for 1997–98: *Application fee:* $10. Area resident tuition: $1100 full-time, $46 per semester hour part-time. State resident tuition: $1370 full-time, $58 per semester hour part-time. Nonresident tuition: $3050 full-time, $128 per semester hour part-time.
LD Services Contact: Ms. Sharon Bellwood, Director of Student Disability Services, Spartanburg Technical College, PO Box 4386, Spartanburg, SC 29305, 864-591-3811. Fax: 864-591-3609. Email: bellwoods@spt.tec.sc.us.

SPOKANE FALLS COMMUNITY COLLEGE

Spokane, Washington

LEARNING DISABILITIES SERVICES INFORMATION

Disability Support Services began offering services in 1978. Currently the program serves 30 to 40 undergraduates with LD. Students diagnosed with ADD/ADHD are eligible for the same services available to students with LD, as well as FM systems.
Staff: 3 full-time, 20 part-time staff members, including director, coordinator, program assistant. Services provided by counselors, peer tutors, teachers, specialists (reading, writing, and study skills).
Special Fees: $10 for diagnostic testing.
Applications and admissions: *Required:* high school transcript, psychoeducational report, one of the following: ACT, SAT I, or ACT ASSET. Students may begin taking classes any term. *Application deadline:* continuous.

PROGRAM AND SERVICE COMPONENTS

Diagnostic testing: Reading, math, written language, study skills.
Academic advising: Provided by unit staff members, academic advisers. Most students with LD take 12 to 15 credits each term; 12 credits required to maintain full-time status; 6 to 12 credits required to be eligible for financial aid.
Counseling services: Individual counseling, career counseling.
Basic skills remediation: Offered one-on-one, in small groups, and in class-size groups by regular teachers, instructional aides. Available in reading, math, spelling, written language, learning strategies, study skills, time management.
Subject-area tutoring: Offered one-on-one and in small groups by peer tutors. Available in most subjects.
Auxiliary aids: Taped textbooks, tape recorders, calculators, typewriters, word-processors with spell-check, talking computers, optical character readers, Franklin Speller, Inspiration software, Franklin Language Master (with speech).
Auxiliary services: Alternative test arrangements, notetakers, priority registration.

GENERAL COLLEGE INFORMATION

State-supported, 2-year, coed. Part of State Board for Washington Community and Technical Colleges. Awards associate degrees. Founded 1967. *Setting:* 125-acre urban campus. *Endowment:* $33,407. *Total enrollment:* 5,700. *Faculty:* 565 (163 full-time, 402 part-time).
Enrollment Profile: 5,700 students from 6 states and territories, 14 other countries. 59% women, 41% men, 31% part-time, 96% state residents, 36% transferred in, 1% international, 35% 25 or older, 3% Native American, 3% Hispanic, 2% black, 3% Asian or Pacific Islander. *Areas of study chosen:* 77% liberal arts/general studies, 9% business management and administrative services, 4% health professions and related sciences, 4% performing arts, 4% vocational and home economics, 1% computer and information sciences, 1% library and information studies. *Most popular recent majors:* liberal arts/general studies, early childhood education, graphic arts.
First-Year Class: 1,850 total. Of the students who applied, 100% were accepted.
Graduation Requirements: 90 credits; computer course for accounting, business, office administration majors; internship (some majors).
Computers on Campus: 360 computers available on campus for general student use. Computer purchase/lease plans available. A campus-wide network can be accessed. Computers for student use in computer labs, learning resource center, classrooms, library provide access to the Internet/World Wide Web. Staffed computer lab on campus provides training in use of computers, software. *Academic computing expenditure 1995–96:* $379,818.

EXPENSES

Expenses for 1996–97: *Application fee:* $10. State resident tuition: $1401 full-time. Nonresident tuition: $5511 full-time. State resident part-time tuition: $93.40 per credit for 1 to 2 credits, $46.70 per credit for 3 or more credits. Nonresident part-time tuition: $367.40 per credit for 1 to 2 credits, $183.70 per credit for 3 or more credits.
LD Services Contact: Mr. Ben Webinger, Counselor, Disability Support Services, Spokane Falls Community College, 3410 West Fort George Wright Drive, MS 3010, Spokane, WA 99224-5288, 509-533-3543. Fax: 509-533-3225. Email: benw@sfcc.spokane.cc.wa.us.

SPOON RIVER COLLEGE

Canton, Illinois

LEARNING DISABILITIES SERVICES INFORMATION

Special Needs Assistance Program (SNAP) began offering services in 1987. Currently the program serves 55 undergraduates with LD. Students diagnosed with ADD/ADHD are eligible for the same services available to students with LD, as well as interactive computer programs.
Staff: 1 full-time, 1 part-time staff members, including coordinator. Services provided by tutor, counselor.
Special Fees: No special fees are charged for services to students with LD.
Applications and admissions: *Required:* high school transcript, psychoeducational report completed within 3 years. Students may begin taking classes any term. *Application deadline:* continuous.

PROGRAM AND SERVICE COMPONENTS

Diagnostic testing: Reading, math.

Spoon River College (continued)

Academic advising: Provided by academic advisers. Students with LD may take up to 12 semester hours each term; most take 9 to 12 semester hours; 12 semester hours required to maintain full-time status; 6 semester hours required to be eligible for financial aid.
Counseling services: Individual counseling, career counseling.
Basic skills remediation: Offered in small groups by regular teachers. Available in reading, math, spelling, study skills.
Subject-area tutoring: Offered one-on-one and in small groups by peer tutors. Available in most subjects.
Special courses: Career planning. None offered for credit.
Auxiliary aids: Taped textbooks, tape recorders, calculators, typewriters, computer software, Language Masters, adaptive computer equipment.
Auxiliary services: Alternative test arrangements, notetakers.

GENERAL COLLEGE INFORMATION

State-supported, 2-year, coed. Part of Illinois Community College System. Awards associate degrees. Founded 1959. *Setting:* 160-acre rural campus. *Total enrollment:* 1,922. *Faculty:* 189 (39 full-time, 8% with terminal degrees, 150 part-time); student–undergrad faculty ratio is 18:1.
Enrollment Profile: 1,922 students from 2 states and territories, 5 other countries. 62% women, 38% men, 45% part-time, 97% state residents, 10% transferred in, 1% international, 42% 25 or older, 0% Native American, 1% Hispanic, 4% black, 1% Asian or Pacific Islander. *Most popular recent majors:* business administration/commerce/management, communication, electrical and electronics technologies.
First-Year Class: 1,093 total. Of the students who applied, 100% were accepted, 90% of whom enrolled.
Graduation Requirements: 64 semester hours; computer course.
Computers on Campus: 34 computers available on campus for general student use. Computers for student use in computer labs, library. Staffed computer lab on campus provides training in use of computers, software.

EXPENSES

Expenses for 1997–98: Area resident tuition: $1376 full-time, $43 per semester hour part-time. State resident tuition: $3682 full-time, $115.05 per semester hour part-time. Nonresident tuition: $6614 full-time, $206.69 per semester hour part-time. Part-time mandatory fees: $5 per semester hour. Full-time mandatory fees: $160.
LD Services Contact: Ms. Gail L. Ham, Student Development Specialist–Special Needs, Spoon River College, 23235 North County 22, Canton, IL 61520-9801, 309-647-4645. Fax: 309-647-6498. Email: gham@macomb.com.

SPRINGFIELD TECHNICAL COMMUNITY COLLEGE

Springfield, Massachusetts

LEARNING DISABILITIES SERVICES INFORMATION

Disabilities Services Office began offering services in 1980. Currently the program serves 100 undergraduates with LD. Students diagnosed with ADD/ADHD are eligible for the same services available to students with LD.
Staff: 8 full-time, 3 part-time staff members, including coordinator. Services provided by tutor, counselors, career services and technology specialist.
Special Fees: No special fees are charged for services to students with LD.
Applications and admissions: *Required:* high school transcript. Students may begin taking classes any term. *Application deadline:* continuous.

PROGRAM AND SERVICE COMPONENTS

Diagnostic testing: Reading, math, study skills, personality, learning strategies, career aptitude/interests.
Academic advising: Provided by academic advisers, LD counselor. Students with LD may take up to 15 credits each term; most take 6 to 9 credits; 6 credits (for insurance purposes) required to maintain full-time status; 3 credits required to be eligible for financial aid.
Counseling services: Individual counseling, small-group counseling, career counseling, self-advocacy training, academic support group.
Auxiliary aids: Taped textbooks, tape recorders, calculators, word-processors with spell-check, personal computers, talking computers, math audio tutorial, DecTalk, Oscar Reading Machines, adaptive software.
Auxiliary services: Alternative test arrangements, notetakers, advocacy

GENERAL COLLEGE INFORMATION

State-supported, 2-year, coed. Awards associate degrees. Founded 1967. *Setting:* 34-acre urban campus. *Total enrollment:* 6,211. *Faculty:* 308 (173 full-time, 16% with terminal degrees, 135 part-time); student–undergrad faculty ratio is 16:1.
Enrollment Profile: 6,211 students from 6 states and territories, 21 other countries. 57% women, 43% men, 61% part-time, 98% state residents, 6% transferred in, 1% international, 57% 25 or older, 1% Native American, 8% Hispanic, 8% black, 2% Asian or Pacific Islander. *Retention:* 54% of 1995 full-time freshmen returned. *Areas of study chosen:* 34% interdisciplinary studies, 19% health professions and related sciences, 15% business management and administrative services, 10% vocational and home economics, 8% computer and information sciences, 7% engineering and applied sciences, 2% performing arts, 1% agriculture, 1% architecture, 1% communications and journalism, 1% education.
First-Year Class: 1,078 total; 1,893 applied, 93% were accepted, 61% of whom enrolled. 10% from top 10% of their high school class, 50% from top half.
Graduation Requirements: 60 credits; math/science requirements vary according to program; computer course for business administration majors.
Computers on Campus: 415 computers available on campus for general student use. Computer purchase/lease plans available. A campus-wide network can be accessed from off-campus. Students can contact faculty members and/or advisers through e-mail. Computers for student use in computer labs, learning resource center, classrooms, library provide access to the Internet/World Wide Web, on- and off-campus e-mail addresses. Staffed computer lab on campus provides training in use of computers, software. *Academic computing expenditure 1995–96:* $350,000.

EXPENSES

Expenses for 1996–97: *Application fee:* $10. State resident tuition: $1080 full-time, $36 per credit part-time. Nonresident tuition: $5880 full-time, $196 per credit part-time. Part-time mandatory fees per semester range from $75 to $575. Tuition for nonresidents who are eligible for the New England Regional Student Program: $1620 full-time, $54 per credit part-time. Full-time mandatory fees: $1550.
LD Services Contact: Ms. Deena Shriver, Counselor for Students with Learning Disabilities, Springfield Technical Community College, Armory Square, Springfield, MA 01105-1296, 413-781-7822. Fax: 413-781-5805.

STATE TECHNICAL INSTITUTE AT MEMPHIS

Memphis, Tennessee

LEARNING DISABILITIES SERVICES INFORMATION

Developmental Studies Department began offering services in 1974. Currently the program serves 150 to 250 undergraduates with LD. Students diagnosed with ADD/ADHD are eligible for the same services available to students with LD.
Staff: 28 full-time, 80 part-time staff members, including director, associate directors, coordinator. Services provided by counselors, faculty members.
Special Fees: No special fees are charged for services to students with LD.
Applications and admissions: *Required:* high school transcript, extended time ACT, personal interview, psychoeducational report completed within 3 years, Tennessee Academic Assessment and Placement Program Test (AAPP). Students may begin taking classes any term. *Application deadline:* continuous.

PROGRAM AND SERVICE COMPONENTS

Diagnostic testing: Reading, math, spelling, written language, learning strategies.
Academic advising: Provided by academic advisers. Students with LD may take up to 20 semester hours each term; most take 12 semester hours; 12 semester hours required to maintain full-time status; 8 semester hours for part-time, 12 semester hours for full-time required to be eligible for financial aid.
Counseling services: Individual counseling, career counseling.

Basic skills remediation: Offered in class-size groups by regular teachers. Available in reading, math, spelling, written language, learning strategies, time management.
Subject-area tutoring: Offered one-on-one by professional teachers, professional tutors. Available in most subjects.
Special courses: Reading, composition, math, study skills. All offered for credit; all enter into overall grade point average.
Auxiliary aids: Personal computers.
Auxiliary services: Alternative test arrangements, notetakers, interpreters.
Campus support group: A special student organization is available to students with LD.

GENERAL COLLEGE INFORMATION

State-supported, 2-year, coed. Part of State University and Community College System of Tennessee. Awards associate degrees. Founded 1967. *Setting:* 100-acre urban campus. *Educational spending 1995–96:* $1534 per undergrad. *Total enrollment:* 10,195. *Faculty:* 620 (161 full-time, 14% with terminal degrees, 459 part-time); student–undergrad faculty ratio is 18:1.
Enrollment Profile: 10,195 students from 3 states and territories, 15 other countries. 54% women, 46% men, 74% part-time, 95% state residents, 16% transferred in, 1% international, 65% 25 or older, 1% Native American, 1% Hispanic, 31% black, 3% Asian or Pacific Islander. *Retention:* 48% of 1995 full-time freshmen returned. *Areas of study chosen:* 21% business management and administrative services, 14% computer and information sciences, 14% engineering and applied sciences. *Most popular recent majors:* electronics engineering technology, accounting, secretarial studies/office management.
First-Year Class: 984 total; 2,528 applied, 100% were accepted, 39% of whom enrolled.
Graduation Requirements: 64 credits; 2 math courses; computer course; internship (some majors).
Computers on Campus: 800 computers available on campus for general student use. Computer purchase/lease plans available. A campus-wide network can be accessed from off-campus. Computers for student use in computer center, computer labs, learning resource center, classrooms provide access to the Internet/World Wide Web. Staffed computer lab on campus provides training in use of computers, software. *Academic computing expenditure 1995–96:* $850,038.

EXPENSES

Expenses for 1997–98: *Application fee:* $5. State resident tuition: $1086 full-time, $48 per semester hour part-time. Nonresident tuition: $4342 full-time, $190 per semester hour part-time. Part-time mandatory fees per semester range from $12 to $25. Full-time mandatory fees: $50.
LD Services Contact: Mr. Paul Dudenhefer, Chairman, Developmental Studies, State Technical Institute at Memphis, 5983 Macon Cove, Memphis, TN 38134-7693, 901-383-4123. Fax: 901-383-2503.

STATE UNIVERSITY OF NEW YORK AT FARMINGDALE

Farmingdale, New York

LEARNING DISABILITIES SERVICES INFORMATION

Support Services for Students with Disabilities began offering services in 1971. Currently the program serves 150 undergraduates with LD. Students diagnosed with ADD/ADHD are eligible for the same services available to students with LD.
Staff: Includes director, LD specialists, psychologists, counselor. Services provided by tutors, counselors.
Special Fees: No special fees are charged for services to students with LD.
Applications and admissions: *Required:* high school transcript, grade point average, courses completed; *recommended:* personal interview, letters of recommendation. Students may begin taking classes any term. *Application deadline:* continuous.

PROGRAM AND SERVICE COMPONENTS

Special preparation or orientation: Optional orientation offered during registration.
Academic advising: Provided by unit staff members. Students with LD may take up to as many credits as an individual can handle each term; most take 12 credits; 12 credits required to maintain full-time status and be eligible for financial aid.
Counseling services: Individual counseling, small-group counseling, career counseling.
Basic skills remediation: Offered one-on-one and in small groups by LD teachers. Available in reading, math, spelling, learning strategies, study skills, social skills.
Subject-area tutoring: Offered one-on-one and in small groups by professional teachers, peer tutors, LD specialist. Available in some subjects.
Auxiliary aids: Taped textbooks, word-processors with spell-check, personal computers.
Auxiliary services: Alternative test arrangements, notetakers, advocacy, time extensions for assignments, test readers, scribes.

GENERAL COLLEGE INFORMATION

State-supported, primarily 2-year, coed. Part of State University of New York System. Awards associate, bachelor's degrees (some bachelor's degree programs are upper level). Founded 1912. *Setting:* 380-acre small-town campus with easy access to New York City. *Endowment:* $293,905. *Research spending 1995–96:* $1.2 million. *Educational spending 1995–96:* $3580 per undergrad. *Total enrollment:* 5,697. *Faculty:* 285 (152 full-time, 37% with terminal degrees, 133 part-time); student–undergrad faculty ratio is 20:1.
Enrollment Profile: 5,697 students from 4 states and territories. 43% women, 57% men, 44% part-time, 99% state residents, 9% live on campus, 13% transferred in, 37% 25 or older, 1% Native American, 9% Hispanic, 12% black, 4% Asian or Pacific Islander. *Retention:* 62% of 1995 full-time freshmen returned. *Areas of study chosen:* 30% business management and administrative services, 26% liberal arts/general studies, 22% engineering and applied sciences, 13% health professions and related sciences, 5% computer and information sciences. *Most popular recent majors:* liberal arts/general studies, business administration/commerce/management.
First-Year Class: 1,459 total; 3,555 applied, 52% were accepted, 78% of whom enrolled. 10% from top 10% of their high school class, 20% from top quarter, 70% from top half.
Graduation Requirements: 60 credits for associate, 128 credits for bachelor's; 6 credits of math/science for associate degree; 12 credits of math/science for bachelor's degree; computer course for business administration, engineering technology, horticulture, nutrition majors.
Computers on Campus: 285 computers available on campus for general student use. A campus-wide network can be accessed from off-campus. Students can contact faculty members and/or advisers through e-mail. Computers for student use in computer labs, learning resource center, classrooms, library, dorms, writing center provide access to the Internet/World Wide Web, on- and off-campus e-mail addresses. Staffed computer lab on campus provides training in use of computers, software. *Academic computing expenditure 1995–96:* $260,000.

EXPENSES

Expenses for 1996–97: *Application fee:* $30. State resident tuition: $3200 (minimum) full-time. Nonresident tuition: $8300 full-time, $346 per credit part-time. State resident part-time tuition per credit ranges from $128 to $137. Part-time mandatory fees: $11.10 per credit. Full-time tuition ranges up to $3400 for state residents according to program. Full-time mandatory fees: $465. College room and board: $5414. College room only: $2790.
LD Services Contact: Ms. Malka Edelman, Director, Support Services for Students with Disabilities, State University of New York at Farmingdale, Memorial Hall, Farmingdale, NY 11735, 516-420-2411 Ext. 2296. Fax: 516-420-2163. Email: edelmamp@snyfarva.cc.farmingdale.edu.

STATE UNIVERSITY OF NEW YORK COLLEGE OF AGRICULTURE AND TECHNOLOGY AT COBLESKILL

Cobleskill, New York

LEARNING DISABILITIES SERVICES INFORMATION

Academic Support Center began offering services in 1985. Currently the program serves 125 undergraduates with LD. Students diagnosed with ADD/ADHD are eligible for the same services available to students with LD.
Staff: 2 full-time, 2 part-time staff members, including director, coordinator. Services provided by remediation specialists, tutor, counselor.
Special Fees: No special fees are charged for services to students with LD.

State University of New York College of Agriculture and Technology at Cobleskill (continued)

Applications and admissions: *Required:* high school transcript. Students may begin taking classes in fall or spring. *Application deadline:* continuous.

PROGRAM AND SERVICE COMPONENTS

Academic advising: Provided by unit staff members, academic advisers. Students with LD may take up to 18 credit hours each term; most take 12 credit hours; 12 credit hours required to maintain full-time status and be eligible for financial aid.

Counseling services: Individual counseling, career counseling.

Basic skills remediation: Offered one-on-one and in class-size groups by regular teachers. Available in reading, math, written language, study skills, time management.

Subject-area tutoring: Offered one-on-one by professional teachers, peer tutors. Available in most subjects.

Auxiliary aids: Taped textbooks, tape recorders, calculators, word-processors with spell-check, personal computers, talking computers, optical character readers, Franklin Speller, Alpha Smart Pro Keyboards.

Auxiliary services: Alternative test arrangements, notetakers, priority registration, advocacy, readers, scribes.

GENERAL COLLEGE INFORMATION

State-supported, primarily 2-year, coed. Part of State University of New York System. Awards associate, bachelor's degrees. Founded 1916. *Setting:* 750-acre rural campus. *Endowment:* $750,000. *Research spending 1995–96:* $1 million. *Total enrollment:* 2,213. *Faculty:* 145 (125 full-time, 10% with terminal degrees, 20 part-time); student–undergrad faculty ratio is 20:1.

Enrollment Profile: 2,213 students from 13 states and territories, 1 other country. 45% women, 55% men, 7% part-time, 95% state residents, 7% transferred in, 1% international, 10% 25 or older, 1% Native American, 3% Hispanic, 5% black, 1% Asian or Pacific Islander. *Retention:* 62% of 1995 full-time freshmen returned. *Areas of study chosen:* 40% agriculture, 15% liberal arts/general studies, 12% education, 10% business management and administrative services, 8% foreign language and literature, 7% social sciences, 5% biological and life sciences, 3% computer and information sciences, 3% health professions and related sciences, 2% mathematics. *Most popular recent majors:* business administration/commerce/management, early childhood education.

First-Year Class: 813 total; 3,500 applied, 63% were accepted, 37% of whom enrolled. 4% from top 10% of their high school class, 30% from top quarter, 45% from top half.

Graduation Requirements: 66 credit hours for associate, 126 credit hours for bachelor's; algebra proficiency.

Computers on Campus: 100 computers available on campus for general student use. Computer purchase/lease plans available. A campus-wide network can be accessed from student residence rooms and from off-campus. Students can contact faculty members and/or advisers through e-mail. Computers for student use in computer center, computer labs, learning resource center, classrooms, library, dorms, student rooms provide access to the Internet/World Wide Web, on- and off-campus e-mail addresses. Staffed computer lab on campus provides training in use of computers, software. *Academic computing expenditure 1995–96:* $837,800.

EXPENSES

Expenses for 1996–97: *Application fee:* $30. State resident tuition: $3200 (minimum) full-time. Nonresident tuition: $5000 full-time, $208 per credit hour part-time. State resident part-time tuition per credit hour ranges from $99 to $137. Part-time mandatory fees: $21.12 per credit hour. Full-time tuition ranges up to $3400 for state residents according to program. Full-time mandatory fees: $535. College room and board: $5600.

LD Services Contact: Ms. Anne E. Campbell, Coordinator of Students with Learning Disabilities, State University of New York College of Agriculture and Technology at Cobleskill, Frisbie 009, Cobleskill, NY 12122, 518-234-5624. Fax: 518-234-5333. Email: campbea@cobleskill.edu.

STATE UNIVERSITY OF NEW YORK COLLEGE OF TECHNOLOGY AT ALFRED

Alfred, New York

LEARNING DISABILITIES SERVICES INFORMATION

Services for Students with Disabilities (SSD) began offering services in 1980. Currently the program serves 235 undergraduates with LD. Students diagnosed with ADD/ADHD are eligible for the same services available to students with LD.

Staff: 2 full-time staff members, including coordinator. Services provided by tutors, counselors.

Special Fees: No special fees are charged for services to students with LD.

Applications and admissions: *Required:* high school transcript; *recommended:* high school IEP (Individualized Education Program), personal interview, psychoeducational report completed within 3 years. Students may begin taking classes in fall or spring. *Application deadline:* continuous.

Special policies: The college has written policies regarding grade forgiveness.

PROGRAM AND SERVICE COMPONENTS

Academic advising: Provided by unit staff members, academic advisers. Students with LD may take up to 18 credit hours each term; most take 12 to 15 credit hours; 12 credit hours required to maintain full-time status; source of aid determines number of credit hours required to be eligible for financial aid.

Counseling services: Individual counseling, career counseling, assertiveness training.

Basic skills remediation: Offered one-on-one and in small groups by regular teachers, academic counselors; computer-aided instruction also offered. Available in reading, math, written language, learning strategies, study skills, time management, computer skills.

Subject-area tutoring: Offered one-on-one and in small groups by peer tutors, professional tutors. Available in most subjects.

Special courses: College survival skills, reading, composition, study skills, career planning. Most offered for credit; some enter into overall grade point average.

Auxiliary aids: Taped textbooks, tape recorders, calculators, typewriters, word-processors with spell-check, personal computers, optical character readers, talking calculators, VISTEK, Franklin Speller, closed-captioned television.

Auxiliary services: Alternative test arrangements, notetakers, priority registration, advocacy, readers, scribes, transcribers.

GENERAL COLLEGE INFORMATION

State-supported, primarily 2-year, coed. Part of State University of New York System. Awards associate, bachelor's degrees. Founded 1908. *Setting:* 175-acre rural campus. *Endowment:* $20 million. *Research spending 1995–96:* $210,865. *Total enrollment:* 3,100. *Faculty:* 176; student–undergrad faculty ratio is 19:1.

Enrollment Profile: 3,100 students from 6 states and territories, 2 other countries. 37% women, 63% men, 6% part-time, 98% state residents, 63% live on campus, 5% transferred in, 1% international, 17% 25 or older, 1% Native American, 1% Hispanic, 6% black, 1% Asian or Pacific Islander. *Retention:* 93% of 1995 full-time freshmen returned. *Areas of study chosen:* 23% vocational and home economics, 19% engineering and applied sciences, 11% social sciences, 9% business management and administrative services, 9% liberal arts/general studies, 7% health professions and related sciences, 6% biological and life sciences, 6% computer and information sciences, 5% agriculture. *Most popular recent majors:* nursing, liberal arts/general studies, human services.

First-Year Class: 1,354 total; 3,385 applied, 77% were accepted, 52% of whom enrolled. 5% from top 10% of their high school class, 21% from top quarter, 50% from top half.

Graduation Requirements: 60 credit hours for associate, 120 credit hours for bachelor's; computer course (varies by major); internship (some majors).

Computers on Campus: 1,400 computers available on campus for general student use. Computer purchase/lease plans available. A campus-wide network can be accessed from student residence rooms and from off-campus. Students can contact faculty members and/or advisers through e-mail. Computers for student use in computer center, computer labs, learning resource center, classrooms, library, dorms, student rooms, academic buildings provide access to the Internet/World Wide Web, on-

and off-campus e-mail addresses. Staffed computer lab on campus provides training in use of computers, software. *Academic computing expenditure 1995–96:* $460,100.

EXPENSES

Expenses for 1996–97: *Application fee:* $30. State resident tuition: $3200 (minimum) full-time. Nonresident tuition: $5000 full-time. Full-time tuition ranges up to $3400 for state residents according to program. Full-time mandatory fees: $457. College room and board: $4856.
LD Services Contact: Dr. Cora Dzubak, Coordinator, SSD, State University of New York College of Technology at Alfred, Alfred, NY 14802, 607-587-4122. Fax: 607-587-3210.

STATE UNIVERSITY OF NEW YORK COLLEGE OF TECHNOLOGY AT CANTON

Canton, New York

LEARNING DISABILITIES SERVICES INFORMATION

Accommodative Services began offering services in 1983. Currently the program serves 105 to 115 undergraduates with LD. Students diagnosed with ADD/ADHD are eligible for the same services available to students with LD, as well as medical supervision (through Health Services).
Staff: 2 full-time, 1 part-time staff members, including coordinator. Services provided by remediation specialists, tutors, counselors, diagnostic specialists.
Special Fees: No special fees are charged for services to students with LD.
Applications and admissions: *Required:* high school transcript, courses completed, IEP (Individualized Education Program), psychoeducational report completed within 3 years; *recommended:* high school grade point average, extracurricular activities, untimed or extended time ACT, autobiographical statement, letters of recommendation. Students may begin taking classes in fall or spring. *Application deadline:* continuous.
Special policies: The college has written policies regarding substitutions and waivers of admissions, graduation, and degree requirements.

PROGRAM AND SERVICE COMPONENTS

Diagnostic testing: Reading, math, written language, study skills, learning strategies.
Academic advising: Provided by unit staff members, academic advisers. Students with LD may take up to 18 credit hours each term; most take 14 credit hours; 12 credit hours required to maintain full-time status and be eligible for financial aid.
Counseling services: Individual counseling, small-group counseling, career counseling, self-advocacy training.
Basic skills remediation: Offered one-on-one and in class-size groups by regular teachers, academic counselor. Available in reading, math, spelling, handwriting, written language, learning strategies, study skills, time management.
Subject-area tutoring: Offered one-on-one and in small groups by professional teachers, peer tutors. Available in most subjects.
Special courses: College survival skills, reading, composition, math, study skills. Some offered for credit; some enter into overall grade point average.
Auxiliary aids: Taped textbooks, tape recorders, calculators, typewriters, word-processors with spell-check, optical character readers.
Auxiliary services: Alternative test arrangements, notetakers, priority registration, advocacy.

GENERAL COLLEGE INFORMATION

State-supported, 2-year, coed. Part of State University of New York System. Awards associate degrees. Founded 1906. *Setting:* 555-acre small-town campus. *Research spending 1995–96:* $42,119. *Educational spending 1995–96:* $2995 per undergrad. *Total enrollment:* 2,004. *Faculty:* 107 (92 full-time, 11% with terminal degrees, 15 part-time); student–undergrad faculty ratio is 18:1.
Enrollment Profile: 2,004 students from 11 states and territories, 3 other countries. 45% women, 55% men, 16% part-time, 99% state residents, 55% live on campus, 7% transferred in, 26% 25 or older, 1% Native American, 2% Hispanic, 5% black, 1% Asian or Pacific Islander. *Retention:* 45% of 1995 full-time freshmen returned. *Areas of study chosen:* 24% business management and administrative services, 21% liberal arts/general studies, 20% interdisciplinary studies, 19% engineering and applied sciences, 8% health professions and related sciences, 2% computer and information sciences, 2% social sciences. *Most popular recent majors:* interdisciplinary studies, business administration/commerce/management, nursing.
First-Year Class: 1,189 total; 2,571 applied, 90% were accepted, 51% of whom enrolled. 3% from top 10% of their high school class, 12% from top quarter, 40% from top half.
Graduation Requirements: 61 credit hours; math/science requirements vary according to program; computer course; internship (some majors).
Computers on Campus: 215 computers available on campus for general student use. Computer purchase/lease plans available. A campus-wide network can be accessed from student residence rooms. Computers for student use in computer center, library, dorms, academic buildings provide access to the Internet/World Wide Web, on- and off-campus e-mail addresses. Staffed computer lab on campus provides training in use of computers, software. *Academic computing expenditure 1995–96:* $166,064.

EXPENSES

Estimated Expenses for 1997–98: *Application fee:* $30. State resident tuition: $3200 full-time, $128 per credit hour part-time. Nonresident tuition: $5000 full-time, $210 per credit hour part-time. Part-time mandatory fees: $11.85 per credit hour. Full-time mandatory fees: $300. College room and board: $5024. College room only: $2818.
LD Services Contact: Ms. Debora L. Camp, Coordinator of Accommodative Services, State University of New York College of Technology at Canton, FOB 214, Canton, NY 13617, 315-386-7121. Fax: 315-386-7930.

SUFFOLK COUNTY COMMUNITY COLLEGE–AMMERMAN CAMPUS

Selden, New York

LEARNING DISABILITIES SERVICES INFORMATION

Office of Special Services began offering services in 1980. Currently the program serves 230 undergraduates with LD. Students diagnosed with ADD/ADHD are eligible for the same services available to students with LD.
Staff: 5 full-time staff members, including director. Services provided by remediation specialists, tutors, counselors, professors, textbook recorder.
Special Fees: No special fees are charged for services to students with LD.
Applications and admissions: *Required:* high school transcript, IEP (Individualized Education Program), extended time SAT I, psychoeducational report completed within 1 year. Students may begin taking classes any term. *Application deadline:* continuous.
Special policies: The college has written policies regarding grade forgiveness.

PROGRAM AND SERVICE COMPONENTS

Special preparation or orientation: Optional orientation offered before registration.
Diagnostic testing: Reading, math, written language.
Academic advising: Provided by unit staff members. Students with LD may take up to 14 credits each term; most take 12 credits; 12 credits required to maintain full-time status; 6 credits (for state aid) required to be eligible for financial aid.
Counseling services: Individual counseling, career counseling.
Basic skills remediation: Offered in small groups by regular teachers. Available in reading, math, spelling, written language.
Subject-area tutoring: Offered one-on-one by professional teachers, peer tutors. Available in most subjects.
Special courses: College survival skills, reading, vocabulary development, communication skills, composition, learning strategies, math. All offered for credit.
Auxiliary aids: Taped textbooks, tape recorders, calculators, word-processors with spell-check, optical character readers.
Auxiliary services: Alternative test arrangements, notetakers, priority registration, advocacy.

GENERAL COLLEGE INFORMATION

State and locally supported, 2-year, coed. Part of State University of New York System. Awards associate degrees. Founded 1962. *Setting:* 200-acre small-town campus with easy access to New York City. *Total enrollment:* 13,154. *Faculty:* 782 (287 full-time, 495 part-time).

Suffolk County Community College–Ammerman Campus (continued)

Enrollment Profile: 13,154 students: 61% women, 39% men, 53% part-time, 5% transferred in, 1% international, 37% 25 or older, 1% Native American, 4% Hispanic, 4% black, 2% Asian or Pacific Islander. *Retention:* 76% of 1995 full-time freshmen returned.
First-Year Class: 3,645 total. Of the students who applied, 95% were accepted.
Graduation Requirements: 68 credits; math/science requirements vary according to program; computer course for business administration majors; internship (some majors).
Computers on Campus: 200 computers available on campus for general student use. A computer is recommended for some students. A campus-wide network can be accessed. Computers for student use in computer center, computer labs, learning resource center, library provide access to on- and off-campus e-mail addresses. Staffed computer lab on campus provides training in use of computers, software. *Academic computing expenditure 1995–96:* $499,443.

EXPENSES

Expenses for 1996–97: *Application fee:* $25. State resident tuition: $2180 full-time, $94 per credit part-time. Nonresident tuition: $4360 full-time, $188 per credit part-time. Part-time mandatory fees: $4.50 per credit. Full-time mandatory fees: $106.
LD Services Contact: Dr. Elmira Johnson, Director of Special Services, Suffolk County Community College–Ammerman Campus, 533 College Road, Selden, NY 11784-2851, 516-451-4045. Fax: 516-451-4953.

SUFFOLK COUNTY COMMUNITY COLLEGE–EASTERN CAMPUS

Riverhead, New York

LEARNING DISABILITIES SERVICES INFORMATION

Special Services Office of the Student Affairs Department began offering services in 1988. Currently the program serves 90 undergraduates with LD. Students diagnosed with ADD/ADHD are eligible for the same services available to students with LD.
Staff: 2 part-time staff members. Services provided by counselor, diagnostic specialists.
Special Fees: No special fees are charged for services to students with LD.
Applications and admissions: *Required:* high school transcript, extracurricular activities, psychoeducational report completed most recently; *recommended:* high school IEP (Individualized Education Program). Students may begin taking classes in fall, spring, or summer. *Application deadline:* 8/15 (fall term), 1/15 (spring term).
Special policies: The college has written policies regarding grade forgiveness; substitutions and waivers of admissions, graduation, and degree requirements.

PROGRAM AND SERVICE COMPONENTS

Academic advising: Provided by unit staff members. Students with LD may take up to 14 credits (first semester, 19 credits thereafter) each term; most take 14 credits; 12 credits required to maintain full-time status; 3 credits required to be eligible for financial aid.
Counseling services: Individual counseling, career counseling, academic counseling.
Basic skills remediation: Offered one-on-one and in small groups by regular teachers, LD specialist. Available in reading, math, study skills, time management, various other areas as appropriate.
Subject-area tutoring: Offered one-on-one and in small groups by professional teachers, peer tutors. Available in most subjects.
Auxiliary aids: Taped textbooks, tape recorders, word-processors with spell-check, personal computers, Franklin Speller.
Auxiliary services: Alternative test arrangements, notetakers, priority registration, advocacy.
Campus support group: A special student organization is available to students with LD.

GENERAL COLLEGE INFORMATION

State and locally supported, 2-year, coed. Part of State University of New York System. Awards associate degrees. Founded 1977. *Setting:* 192-acre small-town campus. *Faculty:* 216 (42 full-time, 174 part-time).
Enrollment Profile: 68% women, 32% men, 68% part-time, 100% state residents, 40% transferred in, 0% international, 51% 25 or older, 1% Native American, 3% Hispanic, 3% black, 1% Asian or Pacific Islander. *Most popular recent majors:* liberal arts/general studies, business administration/commerce/management, accounting.
First-Year Class: 2% from top 10% of their high school class, 19% from top quarter, 43% from top half.
Graduation Requirements: 66 credits; math/science requirements vary according to program; computer course for most majors; internship (some majors).
Computers on Campus: 45 computers available on campus for general student use. A computer is recommended for some students. A campus-wide network can be accessed. Computers for student use in computer center, learning resource center, library. *Academic computing expenditure 1995–96:* $87,130.

EXPENSES

Expenses for 1996–97: *Application fee:* $25. State resident tuition: $2180 full-time, $94 per credit part-time. Nonresident tuition: $4360 full-time, $188 per credit part-time. Part-time mandatory fees: $4.50 per credit. Full-time mandatory fees: $126.
LD Services Contact: Ms. Michele Artez or Ms. Mary Respoli, Disabilities Advisors, Suffolk County Community College–Eastern Campus, Speonk-Riverhead Road, Riverhead, NY 11901, 516-548-2527. Fax: 516-369-2641.

SULLIVAN COUNTY COMMUNITY COLLEGE

Loch Sheldrake, New York

LEARNING DISABILITIES SERVICES INFORMATION

Center for Learning Assistance currently serves undergraduate students with LD. Students diagnosed with ADD/ADHD are eligible for the same services available to students with LD.
Staff: 2 full-time, 15 part-time staff members, including coordinator. Services provided by remediation specialists, tutors.
Special Fees: No special fees are charged for services to students with LD.
Applications and admissions: *Required:* high school transcript, IEP (Individualized Education Program); *recommended:* personal interview, psychoeducational report completed in high school. Students may begin taking classes any term. *Application deadline:* continuous.
Special policies: The college has written policies regarding grade forgiveness; substitutions and waivers of admissions, graduation, and degree requirements.

PROGRAM AND SERVICE COMPONENTS

Special preparation or orientation: Optional orientation offered after classes begin and individually with Coordinator after student self-identifies by letter.
Academic advising: Provided by academic advisers. Most students with LD take 12 to 15 credits each term; 12 credits required to maintain full-time status and be eligible for financial aid.
Counseling services: Individual counseling.
Subject-area tutoring: Offered one-on-one and in small groups by peer tutors, professional tutors. Available in all subjects.
Auxiliary aids: Taped textbooks, calculators, optical character readers.
Auxiliary services: Alternative test arrangements, notetakers, priority registration, advocacy.

GENERAL COLLEGE INFORMATION

State and locally supported, 2-year, coed. Part of State University of New York System. Awards associate degrees. Founded 1962. *Setting:* 405-acre rural campus. *Endowment:* $759,333. *Educational spending 1995–96:* $2942 per undergrad. *Total enrollment:* 1,781. *Faculty:* 106 (56 full-time, 23% with terminal degrees, 50 part-time); student–undergrad faculty ratio is 18:1.
Enrollment Profile: 1,781 students from 4 states and territories, 7 other countries. 56% women, 44% men, 33% part-time, 95% state residents, 9% transferred in, 3% international, 43% 25 or older, 0% Native American, 11% Hispanic, 23% black, 2% Asian or Pacific Islander. *Most popular recent majors:* liberal arts/general studies, hospitality services, commercial art.
First-Year Class: 517 total; 2,100 applied, 98% were accepted, 25% of whom enrolled. 28% from top half of their high school class.
Graduation Requirements: 63 credits; 8 credits of science; internship (some majors).

Computers on Campus: 80 computers available on campus for general student use. A campus-wide network can be accessed. Students can contact faculty members and/or advisers through e-mail. Computers for student use in computer center, library, science labs provide access to the Internet/World Wide Web, on- and off-campus e-mail addresses. Staffed computer lab on campus provides training in use of computers, software. *Academic computing expenditure 1995–96:* $249,151.

EXPENSES

Expenses for 1996–97: *Application fee:* $30. State resident tuition: $2300 full-time, $80 per credit part-time. Nonresident tuition: $4400 full-time, $180 per credit part-time. Part-time mandatory fees: $5.25 per credit. Full-time mandatory fees: $156.

LD Services Contact: Ms. Sari Rosenheck, Technical Assistant, Sullivan County Community College, 1000 Leroy Road, Loch Sheldrake, NY 12759, 914-434-5750 Ext. 229. Fax: 914-434-4806.

TALLAHASSEE COMMUNITY COLLEGE

Tallahassee, Florida

LEARNING DISABILITIES SERVICES INFORMATION

Disabled Student Services began offering services in 1981. Currently the program serves 320 undergraduates with LD. Students diagnosed with ADD/ADHD are eligible for the same services available to students with LD, as well as multi-sensorally taught math at specific levels.

Staff: 3 full-time, 2 part-time staff members, including director, coordinator. Services provided by tutors, counselors.

Special Fees: No special fees are charged for services to students with LD.

Applications and admissions: Open admissions (psychoeducational report highly recommended). Students may begin taking classes any term. *Application deadline:* 7/18 (fall term), 12/21 (spring term).

Special policies: The college has written policies regarding grade forgiveness; substitutions and waivers of admissions, graduation, and degree requirements.

PROGRAM AND SERVICE COMPONENTS

Special preparation or orientation: Optional orientation offered before registration and during registration.

Academic advising: Provided by unit staff members. Students with LD may take up to 12 semester hours each term; most take 3 to 12 semester hours; 12 semester hours required to maintain full-time status and be eligible for financial aid.

Counseling services: Individual counseling, career counseling.

Basic skills remediation: Offered one-on-one by teacher trainees, peer teachers. Available in reading, math, written language.

Subject-area tutoring: Offered one-on-one by professional teachers, peer tutors. Available in all subjects.

Special courses: Math. Some offered for credit.

Auxiliary aids: Taped textbooks, tape recorders, calculators, word-processors with spell-check, personal computers.

Auxiliary services: Alternative test arrangements, notetakers, advocacy.

Campus support group: A special student organization is available to students with LD.

GENERAL COLLEGE INFORMATION

State and locally supported, 2-year, coed. Part of Florida Community Colleges System. Awards associate degrees. Founded 1966. *Setting:* 183-acre suburban campus. *Total enrollment:* 9,737. *Faculty:* 372 (132 full-time, 37% with terminal degrees, 240 part-time); student–undergrad faculty ratio is 26:1.

Enrollment Profile: 9,737 students from 40 states and territories, 39 other countries. 55% women, 45% men, 56% part-time, 96% state residents, 38% transferred in, 1% international, 27% 25 or older, 1% Native American, 4% Hispanic, 25% black, 2% Asian or Pacific Islander. *Retention:* 79% of 1995 full-time freshmen returned. *Areas of study chosen:* 92% liberal arts/general studies, 6% health professions and related sciences, 1% business management and administrative services.

First-Year Class: 1,701 total; 2,566 applied, 100% were accepted, 66% of whom enrolled.

Graduation Requirements: 60 semester hours; 6 semester hours each of math and science.

Computers on Campus: 170 computers available on campus for general student use. Computer purchase/lease plans available. A campus-wide network can be accessed from off-campus. Students can contact faculty members and/or advisers through e-mail. Computers for student use in computer labs, classrooms, library, counseling, skills labs provide access to the Internet/World Wide Web, on- and off-campus e-mail addresses. Staffed computer lab on campus provides training in use of computers, software. *Academic computing expenditure 1995–96:* $1.5 million.

EXPENSES

Expenses for 1997–98: State resident tuition: $1185 full-time, $39.50 per semester hour part-time. Nonresident tuition: $4530 full-time, $151 per semester hour part-time. Part-time mandatory fees: $10 per semester. Full-time mandatory fees: $20.

LD Services Contact: Mr. Mark Linehan, Counselor, Tallahassee Community College, 444 Appleyard Drive, Tallahassee, FL 32304-2895, 904-413-0004. Fax: 904-921-4386. Email: linehanm@mail.tallahassee.cc.fl.us.

TERRA STATE COMMUNITY COLLEGE

Fremont, Ohio

LEARNING DISABILITIES SERVICES INFORMATION

Office of Disabled Student Services began offering services in 1991. Currently the program serves 33 undergraduates with LD. Students diagnosed with ADD/ADHD are not eligible for the same services available to students with LD.

Staff: 1 full-time staff member (coordinator). Services provided by remediation specialists, tutors, counselors, readers, scribes, proctors.

Special Fees: No special fees are charged for services to students with LD.

Applications and admissions: *Required:* high school transcript, IEP (Individualized Education Program), personal interview, psychoeducational report completed within 3 years; *recommended:* high school grade point average, class rank, courses completed, extracurricular activities. Students may begin taking classes any term. *Application deadline:* continuous.

Special policies: The college has written policies regarding grade forgiveness.

PROGRAM AND SERVICE COMPONENTS

Special preparation or orientation: Optional orientation offered before registration.

Academic advising: Provided by unit staff members. Most students with LD take 12 quarter hours each term; 12 quarter hours required to maintain full-time status; 6 to 12 quarter hours required to be eligible for financial aid.

Counseling services: Individual counseling, career counseling.

Basic skills remediation: Offered one-on-one and in small groups by developmental classroom director; computer-aided instruction also offered. Available in reading, math, written language, study skills, time management, social skills.

Subject-area tutoring: Offered one-on-one and in small groups by professional teachers, peer tutors. Available in most subjects.

Special courses: College survival skills, reading, time management, math, study skills, career planning. None offered for credit; none enter into overall grade point average.

Auxiliary aids: Taped textbooks, tape recorders, calculators, word-processors with spell-check, personal computers.

Auxiliary services: Alternative test arrangements, notetakers, priority registration, advocacy.

Campus support group: A special student organization is available to students with LD.

GENERAL COLLEGE INFORMATION

State-supported, 2-year, coed. Part of Ohio Board of Regents. Awards associate degrees. Founded 1968. *Setting:* 100-acre small-town campus with easy access to Toledo. *Total enrollment:* 2,512. *Faculty:* 159 (49 full-time, 76% with terminal degrees, 110 part-time); student–undergrad faculty ratio is 18:1.

Enrollment Profile: 2,512 students from 5 states and territories. 45% women, 55% men, 63% part-time, 99% state residents, 1% transferred in, 0% international, 50% 25 or older, 1% Native American, 4% Hispanic, 2% black, 1% Asian or Pacific Islander. *Most popular recent majors:* engineering (general), business administration/commerce/management, law enforcement/police sciences.

First-Year Class: 859 total; 1,041 applied, 100% were accepted, 83% of whom enrolled.

Graduation Requirements: 90 credit hours; 1 math course; computer course.

Terra State Community College (continued)

Computers on Campus: 300 computers available on campus for general student use. A computer is recommended for all students. Students can contact faculty members and/or advisers through e-mail. Computers for student use in computer center, computer labs, classrooms, library. Staffed computer lab on campus provides training in use of computers, software.

EXPENSES

Expenses for 1997–98: State resident tuition: $2103 full-time, $49 per credit hour part-time. Nonresident tuition: $5412 full-time, $126 per credit hour part-time. Part-time mandatory fees per quarter range from $13 to $43. Full-time mandatory fees: $165.
LD Services Contact: Mr. Richard Newman, Coordinator, Disabled Student Services, Terra State Community College, 2830 Napoleon Road, Fremont, OH 43420, 419-334-8400 Ext. 208. Fax: 419-334-9035.

TEXAS STATE TECHNICAL COLLEGE–HARLINGEN

Harlingen, Texas

LEARNING DISABILITIES SERVICES INFORMATION

Special Support Services currently serves 150 undergraduates with LD. Students diagnosed with ADD/ADHD are eligible for the same services available to students with LD.
Staff: 4 full-time staff members, including director, student assistant, clerk. Services provided by remediation specialists, tutors, counselors.
Special Fees: No special fees are charged for services to students with LD.
Applications and admissions: *Required:* high school transcript, documentation of disability. Students may begin taking classes any term. *Application deadline:* continuous.
Special policies: The college has written policies regarding grade forgiveness; substitutions and waivers of admissions requirements.

PROGRAM AND SERVICE COMPONENTS

Diagnostic testing: Reading, math, written language, motor abilities.
Academic advising: Provided by unit staff members, academic advisers. Students with LD may take up to 15 credit hours each term; most take 9 credit hours; 12 credit hours required to maintain full-time status; 6 credit hours required to be eligible for financial aid.
Counseling services: Individual counseling.
Basic skills remediation: Offered in class-size groups by regular teachers. Available in reading, math, written language.
Subject-area tutoring: Offered one-on-one by peer tutors. Available in all subjects.
Special courses: Reading, math, computer lab. None offered for credit; none enter into overall grade point average.
Auxiliary aids: Taped textbooks, tape recorders, word-processors with spell-check, talking computers, optical character readers, closed-captioned television, talking calculators.
Auxiliary services: Alternative test arrangements, notetakers, priority registration, advocacy.

GENERAL COLLEGE INFORMATION

State-supported, 2-year, coed. Part of Texas State Technical College System. Awards associate degrees. Founded 1967. *Setting:* 118-acre small-town campus. *Research spending 1995–96:* $20,795. *Total enrollment:* 3,082. *Faculty:* 151 (134 full-time, 4% with terminal degrees, 17 part-time); student–undergrad faculty ratio is 20:1.
Enrollment Profile: 3,082 students: 47% women, 53% men, 44% part-time, 99% state residents, 13% live on campus, 20% transferred in, 1% international, 30% 25 or older, 0% Native American, 87% Hispanic, 1% black, 1% Asian or Pacific Islander. *Retention:* 16% of 1995 full-time freshmen returned. *Areas of study chosen:* 21% computer and information sciences, 15% health professions and related sciences, 11% engineering and applied sciences, 8% vocational and home economics, 1% agriculture, 1% natural resource sciences. *Most popular recent majors:* chemical engineering technology, computer technologies, information science.
First-Year Class: 993 total. Of the students who applied, 100% were accepted, 75% of whom enrolled. 6% from top 10% of their high school class, 13% from top quarter, 24% from top half. 1 valedictorian.
Graduation Requirements: 90 credit hours; math/science requirements vary according to program; computer course.
Computers on Campus: 40 computers available on campus for general student use. A campus-wide network can be accessed. Computers for student use in learning resource center, library provide access to the Internet/World Wide Web. Staffed computer lab on campus provides training in use of computers, software. *Academic computing expenditure 1995–96:* $1.2 million.

EXPENSES

Expenses for 1996–97: State resident tuition: $810 full-time. Nonresident tuition: $3600 full-time, $80 per credit hour part-time. State resident part-time tuition per quarter ranges from $90 to $198. Part-time mandatory fees per quarter range from $13.75 to $151.25. Full-time mandatory fees: $453. College room and board: $3060. College room only: $1275.
LD Services Contact: Ms. Kathleen Garcia, Disabilities Coordinator, Texas State Technical College–Harlingen, 2424 Boxwood, Harlingen, TX 78550, 956-425-0777. Fax: 956-412-4423.

TEXAS STATE TECHNICAL COLLEGE–WACO/MARSHALL CAMPUS

Waco, Texas

LEARNING DISABILITIES SERVICES INFORMATION

Deaf and Disabled Student Services (DSS) currently serves 90 undergraduates with LD. Students diagnosed with ADD/ADHD are eligible for the same services available to students with LD.
Staff: 13 full-time, 2 part-time staff members, including director, coordinator. Services provided by remediation specialists, tutors, notetakers, interpreters, interpreters for the deaf.
Special Fees: No special fees are charged for services to students with LD.
Applications and admissions: *Required:* high school transcript, IEP (Individualized Education Program), psychoeducational report, computerized placement test; *recommended:* high school class rank, extracurricular activities. Students may begin taking classes any term. *Application deadline:* continuous.
Special policies: The college has written policies regarding grade forgiveness; substitutions and waivers of graduation and degree requirements.

PROGRAM AND SERVICE COMPONENTS

Academic advising: Provided by unit staff members, academic advisers. Students with LD may take up to 20 quarter hours each term; most take 12 to 15 quarter hours; 12 quarter hours required to maintain full-time status; 12 quarter hours (Federal), 9 quarter hours (State Vocational Rehabilitation) required to be eligible for financial aid.
Counseling services: Individual counseling, career counseling.
Subject-area tutoring: Offered one-on-one, in small groups, and in class-size groups by professional teachers, peer tutors, computerized tutorial programs. Available in most subjects.
Auxiliary aids: Tape recorders, calculators, word-processors with spell-check, personal computers, optical character readers.
Auxiliary services: Alternative test arrangements, notetakers, advocacy, tutors.

GENERAL COLLEGE INFORMATION

State-supported, 2-year, coed. Part of Texas State Technical College System. Awards associate degrees. Founded 1965. *Setting:* 200-acre suburban campus. *Total enrollment:* 3,448. *Faculty:* 331 (242 full-time, 89 part-time); student–undergrad faculty ratio is 15:1.
Enrollment Profile: 3,448 students from 37 states and territories, 8 other countries. 22% women, 78% men, 18% part-time, 97% state residents, 38% transferred in, 1% international, 40% 25 or older, 1% Native American, 10% Hispanic, 12% black, 1% Asian or Pacific Islander. *Retention:* 49% of 1995 full-time freshmen returned. *Most popular recent majors:* computer technologies, laser technologies, automotive technologies.
First-Year Class: 1,310 total; 1,857 applied, 100% were accepted, 71% of whom enrolled.
Graduation Requirements: 100 quarter hours; 1 college algebra course; computer course for most majors.
Computers on Campus: 700 computers available on campus for general student use. A campus-wide network can be accessed from student residence rooms. Students can contact faculty members and/or advisers through e-mail. Computers for student use in computer center, computer labs, learning resource center, classrooms, library, student center provide access to the Internet/World Wide Web, on- and off-campus

e-mail addresses, various software packages. Staffed computer lab on campus provides training in use of computers, software.

EXPENSES

Expenses for 1996–97: State resident tuition: $900 full-time. Nonresident tuition: $4000 full-time, $80 per quarter hour part-time. State resident part-time tuition per quarter ranges from $90 to $198. Part-time mandatory fees per quarter range from $13.75 to $151.25. Full-time mandatory fees: $490. College room only: $2300 (minimum).

LD Services Contact: Mr. Andrew Sanchez, Supervisor, Texas State Technical College–Waco/Marshall Campus, 3801 Campus Drive, Waco, TX 76705, 254-867-3600. Fax: 254-867-3601. Email: asanchez@tstc.edu.

THOMAS NELSON COMMUNITY COLLEGE

Hampton, Virginia

LEARNING DISABILITIES SERVICES INFORMATION

Services for Students with Disabilities began offering services in 1978. Currently the program serves 78 undergraduates with LD. Students diagnosed with ADD/ADHD are eligible for the same services available to students with LD.

Staff: 1 full-time, 12 part-time staff members, including director, Associate Coordinator. Services provided by remediation specialists, tutors, counselors.

Special Fees: No special fees are charged for services to students with LD.

Applications and admissions: *Required:* high school transcript, psychoeducational report completed within 3 years. Students may begin taking classes in fall, spring, or summer. *Application deadline:* continuous.

Special policies: The college has written policies regarding grade forgiveness; substitutions and waivers of degree requirements.

PROGRAM AND SERVICE COMPONENTS

Special preparation or orientation: Optional summer program offered prior to entering college. Optional orientation offered after classes begin.

Academic advising: Provided by academic advisers. Students with LD may take up to 18 semester hours (without special permission) each term; most take 9 to 12 semester hours; 12 semester hours required to maintain full-time status; 3 semester hours required to be eligible for financial aid.

Counseling services: Individual counseling, small-group counseling, career counseling, self-advocacy training.

Basic skills remediation: Offered in class-size groups by regular teachers, peer tutors. Available in reading, math, spelling, written language, learning strategies, study skills, time management.

Subject-area tutoring: Offered one-on-one by peer tutors. Available in most subjects.

Auxiliary aids: Taped textbooks, tape recorders, calculators, word-processors with spell-check, personal computers, talking computers, optical character readers.

Auxiliary services: Alternative test arrangements, notetakers, priority registration, advocacy.

Campus support group: A special student organization is available to students with LD.

GENERAL COLLEGE INFORMATION

State-supported, 2-year, coed. Part of Virginia Community College System. Awards associate degrees. Founded 1968. *Setting:* 85-acre suburban campus with easy access to Virginia Beach. *Total enrollment:* 7,192. *Faculty:* 320 (100 full-time, 21% with terminal degrees, 220 part-time); student–undergrad faculty ratio is 24:1.

Enrollment Profile: 7,192 students from 46 states and territories. 58% women, 42% men, 73% part-time, 92% state residents, 25% transferred in, 0% international, 62% 25 or older, 1% Native American, 2% Hispanic, 28% black, 3% Asian or Pacific Islander. *Retention:* 72% of 1995 full-time freshmen returned.

First-Year Class: 1,274 total; 2,000 applied, 99% were accepted.

Graduation Requirements: 65 semester hours; 1 math course; internship (some majors).

Computers on Campus: 80 computers available on campus for general student use. A campus-wide network can be accessed. Students can contact faculty members and/or advisers through e-mail. Computers for student use in computer labs, library, academic buildings provide access to the Internet/World Wide Web. Staffed computer lab on campus provides training in use of computers, software.

EXPENSES AND FINANCIAL AID

Expenses for 1997–98: State resident tuition: $1525 full-time, $47.65 per semester hour part-time. Nonresident tuition: $5024 full-time, $157 per semester hour part-time. Part-time mandatory fees: $10.50 per semester. Full-time mandatory fees: $21.

Financial aid specifically for students with LD: Scholarship: Project Start Scholarship.

LD Services Contact: Mr. Thomas C. Kellen, Associate Coordinator, Services for Students with Disabilities, Thomas Nelson Community College, PO Box 9407, Hampton, VA 23670-0407, 757-825-2827. Fax: 757-825-3697.

TOMBALL COLLEGE

Tomball, Texas

LEARNING DISABILITIES SERVICES INFORMATION

Student Life Office began offering services in 1988. Currently the program serves 200 undergraduates with LD. Students diagnosed with ADD/ADHD are eligible for the same services available to students with LD.

Staff: 3 full-time staff members. Services provided by remediation specialists, tutors, counselors, diagnostic specialists.

Special Fees: No special fees are charged for services to students with LD.

Applications and admissions: *Required:* high school courses completed, personal interview, psychoeducational report completed within 3 years; *recommended:* high school transcript. Students may begin taking classes any term. *Application deadline:* continuous.

Special policies: The college has written policies regarding grade forgiveness; substitutions and waivers of admissions requirements.

PROGRAM AND SERVICE COMPONENTS

Diagnostic testing: Intelligence, reading, math, spelling, written language, perceptual skills, learning strategies.

Academic advising: Provided by unit staff members, academic advisers. Students with LD may take up to 12 credit hours each term; most take 6 to 12 credit hours; 12 credit hours required to maintain full-time status; 1 credit hour required to be eligible for financial aid.

Counseling services: Individual counseling, career counseling.

Basic skills remediation: Offered in small groups and in class-size groups by regular teachers; computer-aided instruction also offered. Available in reading, math, written language, learning strategies, study skills, social skills.

Subject-area tutoring: Offered one-on-one by professional teachers, peer tutors. Available in most subjects.

Auxiliary aids: Taped textbooks, tape recorders, calculators, word-processors with spell-check, talking computers, optical character readers, Comtek (personal amplifier).

Auxiliary services: Alternative test arrangements, notetakers.

Campus support group: A special student organization is available to students with LD.

GENERAL COLLEGE INFORMATION

State and locally supported, 2-year, coed. Part of North Harris Montgomery Community College District. Awards associate degrees. Founded 1988. *Setting:* 210-acre suburban campus with easy access to Houston. *Educational spending 1995–96:* $1073 per undergrad. *Total enrollment:* 3,805. *Faculty:* 230 (60 full-time, 36% with terminal degrees, 170 part-time); student–undergrad faculty ratio is 24:1.

Enrollment Profile: 3,805 students: 61% women, 39% men, 56% part-time, 99% state residents, 15% transferred in, 1% international, 32% 25 or older, 1% Native American, 7% Hispanic, 2% black, 2% Asian or Pacific Islander. *Retention:* 45% of 1995 full-time freshmen returned. *Areas of study chosen:* 13% fine arts, 11% education, 5% premed.

First-Year Class: 1,025 total. Of the students who applied, 100% were accepted, 100% of whom enrolled.

Graduation Requirements: 62 credit hours; computer course for accounting, criminal justice, geology majors; internship (some majors).

Computers on Campus: 92 computers available on campus for general student use. A computer is required for some students. A campus-wide network can be accessed from off-campus. Students can contact faculty members and/or advisers through e-mail. Computers for student

Tomball College (continued)

use in computer center, computer labs, learning resource center, library provide access to the Internet/World Wide Web, campus network. Staffed computer lab on campus provides training in use of computers, software. *Academic computing expenditure 1995–96:* $135,699.

EXPENSES AND FINANCIAL AID

Expenses for 1996–97: Area resident tuition: $682 full-time. State resident tuition: $1767 full-time. Nonresident tuition: $2077 full-time. Part-time tuition per semester ranges from $60 to $242 for area residents, $95 to $627 for state residents, $200 to $737 for nonresidents. Part-time mandatory fees per semester range from $16 to $56. Full-time mandatory fees: $148.
Financial aid specifically for students with LD: Scholarship: Houmet Scholarship.
LD Services Contact: Ms. Shaheen Ansari, Educational Diagnostician, Tomball College, 30555 Tomball Parkway, Tomball, TX 77375-4036, 281-351-3380. Fax: 281-351-3384.

TREASURE VALLEY COMMUNITY COLLEGE

Ontario, Oregon

LEARNING DISABILITIES SERVICES INFORMATION

Services for Students with Disabilities (SSD), Developmental Education Program began offering services in 1995. Currently the program serves 30 undergraduates with LD. Students diagnosed with ADD/ADHD are eligible for the same services available to students with LD.
Staff: 10 part-time staff members, including director, coordinator, instructors. Services provided by remediation specialists, tutors, counselors.
Special Fees: No special fees are charged for services to students with LD.
Applications and admissions: *Required:* high school transcript, psychoeducational report completed within 3 years; *recommended:* personal interview. Students may begin taking classes any term. *Application deadline:* continuous.

PROGRAM AND SERVICE COMPONENTS

Special preparation or orientation: Optional summer program offered prior to entering college.
Diagnostic testing: Reading, math, personality, learning strategies.
Academic advising: Provided by unit staff members, academic advisers. Students with LD may take up to 20 credits each term; most take 12 to 14 credits; 12 credits required to maintain full-time status and be eligible for financial aid.
Counseling services: Individual counseling, career counseling.
Basic skills remediation: Offered one-on-one, in small groups, and in class-size groups by regular teachers, tutor, aides; computer-aided instruction also offered. Available in reading, math, spelling, written language, learning strategies, study skills, time management, computer skills.
Subject-area tutoring: Offered one-on-one and in small groups by peer tutors, teacher/lab assistants. Available in all subjects.
Special courses: College survival skills, reading, communication skills, composition, math, career planning, Learning Skills Lab. Most offered for credit.
Auxiliary aids: Taped textbooks, tape recorders, calculators, word-processors with spell-check, talking computers, Brain Train software, Inspiration software.
Auxiliary services: Alternative test arrangements, notetakers, advocacy.

GENERAL COLLEGE INFORMATION

State and locally supported, 2-year, coed. Awards associate degrees. Founded 1962. *Setting:* 95-acre small-town campus. *Total enrollment:* 3,625. *Faculty:* 110 (42 full-time, 68 part-time); student–undergrad faculty ratio is 20:1.
Enrollment Profile: 3,625 students from 8 states and territories, 3 other countries. 60% women, 40% men, 75% part-time, 92% state residents, 6% live on campus, 2% transferred in, 1% international, 45% 25 or older, 1% Native American, 5% Hispanic, 1% black, 1% Asian or Pacific Islander. *Retention:* 60% of 1995 full-time freshmen returned. *Most popular recent majors:* liberal arts/general studies, education, business administration/commerce/management.
First-Year Class: 502 total; 800 applied, 100% were accepted, 63% of whom enrolled.
Graduation Requirements: 90 credits; 1 college algebra course; computer course for business majors.
Computers on Campus: 70 computers available on campus for general student use. A campus-wide network can be accessed. Students can contact faculty members and/or advisers through e-mail. Computers for student use in computer center, computer labs, library provide access to the Internet/World Wide Web, on- and off-campus e-mail addresses. Staffed computer lab on campus.

EXPENSES

Estimated Expenses for 1997–98: State resident tuition: $1620 full-time, $36 per credit part-time. Nonresident tuition: $2385 full-time, $53 per credit part-time. Part-time mandatory fees: $10 per quarter. Full-time mandatory fees: $60. College room and board: $3261.
LD Services Contact: Ms. Joy Bloch, Counselor, Services for Students with Disabilities, Treasure Valley Community College, 650 College Boulevard, Ontario, OR 97914, 541-889-6493 Ext. 234. Fax: 541-881-2721. Email: joy_bloch@mailman.tvcc.cc.or.us.

TRIDENT TECHNICAL COLLEGE

Charleston, South Carolina

LEARNING DISABILITIES SERVICES INFORMATION

Counseling and Career Development/Services for Students with Disabilities began offering services in 1982. Currently the program serves 250 undergraduates with LD. Students diagnosed with ADD/ADHD are eligible for the same services available to students with LD.
Staff: 3 full-time staff members, including director. Services provided by counselors.
Special Fees: No special fees are charged for services to students with LD.
Applications and admissions: *Required:* high school transcript, College Placement Test (if SAT I not taken), documentation of disability; *recommended:* untimed or extended time SAT I. Students may begin taking classes in fall, spring, or summer. *Application deadline:* continuous.

PROGRAM AND SERVICE COMPONENTS

Special preparation or orientation: Optional orientation offered during registration.
Diagnostic testing: Study skills.
Academic advising: Provided by unit staff members, academic advisers. Students with LD may take up to 18 credit hours (more with departmental approval) each term; most take 6 to 12 credit hours; 12 credit hours required to maintain full-time status; 6 credit hours required to be eligible for financial aid.
Counseling services: Individual counseling, career counseling.
Basic skills remediation: Offered in class-size groups by regular teachers. Available in reading, math, written language, study skills, time management.
Subject-area tutoring: Offered one-on-one and in small groups by professional teachers, peer tutors. Available in some subjects.
Special courses: College survival skills, learning strategies, time management, study skills, career planning. Some offered for credit; some enter into overall grade point average.
Auxiliary aids: Taped textbooks, tape recorders, calculators, typewriters, word-processors with spell-check, personal computers.
Auxiliary services: Alternative test arrangements, notetakers, priority registration.
Campus support group: A special student organization is available to students with LD.

GENERAL COLLEGE INFORMATION

State and locally supported, 2-year, coed. Part of South Carolina Technical and Comprehensive Education System. Awards associate degrees. Founded 1964. *Setting:* urban campus. *Total enrollment:* 9,079. *Faculty:* 523 (236 full-time, 287 part-time).
Enrollment Profile: 9,079 students: 57% women, 43% men, 65% part-time, 96% state residents, 1% international, 1% Native American, 1% Hispanic, 21% black, 2% Asian or Pacific Islander. *Areas of study chosen:* 12% health professions and related sciences, 10% business management and administrative services, 10% engineering and applied sciences, 5% computer and information sciences, 2% vocational and home economics.
First-Year Class: 1,638 total.
Graduation Requirements: 60 credit hours; computer course.
Computers on Campus: 500 computers available on campus for general student use. Computer purchase/lease plans available. Computers

for student use in computer center, computer labs, learning resource center, classrooms, library. Staffed computer lab on campus provides training in use of computers, software. *Academic computing expenditure 1995–96:* $592,424.

EXPENSES

Expenses for 1997–98: *Application fee:* $20. Area resident tuition: $1024 full-time, $44 per credit hour part-time. State resident tuition: $1224 full-time, $52 per credit hour part-time. Nonresident tuition: $3162 full-time, $133 per credit hour part-time. Part-time mandatory fees: $20 per semester. Full-time mandatory fees: $40.

LD Services Contact: Ms. Pamela Middleton, Counselor for Students with Disabilities, Trident Technical College, PO Box 118067, Charleston, SC 29423-8067, 803-574-6303. Fax: 803-574-6645. Email: zpmiddletonp@trident.tec.sc.us.

TRINIDAD STATE JUNIOR COLLEGE

Trinidad, Colorado

LEARNING DISABILITIES SERVICES INFORMATION

Special Populations Department, Learning Center began offering services in 1992. Currently the program serves 20 undergraduates with LD. Students diagnosed with ADD/ADHD are eligible for the same services available to students with LD.

Staff: 2 full-time, 1 part-time staff members, including coordinators. Services provided by tutors, counselors, diagnostic specialists.

Special Fees: No special fees are charged for services to students with LD.

Applications and admissions: *Required:* high school transcript, courses completed, personal interview, autobiographical statement, psychoeducational report completed within 3 years; *recommended:* high school grade point average, class rank, extracurricular activities, IEP (Individualized Education Program), untimed or extended time SAT I or ACT, letters of recommendation. Students may begin taking classes any term. *Application deadline:* continuous.

Special policies: The college has written policies regarding substitutions and waivers of admissions, graduation, and degree requirements.

PROGRAM AND SERVICE COMPONENTS

Special preparation or orientation: Optional orientation offered during first week of classes in Fall.

Diagnostic testing: Intelligence, reading, math, spelling, handwriting, written language, study skills, social skills, learning strategies, psychoeducation.

Academic advising: Provided by unit staff members, academic advisers. Most students with LD take 12 semester hours each term; 12 semester hours required to maintain full-time status and be eligible for financial aid.

Counseling services: Individual counseling.

Basic skills remediation: Offered in class-size groups by regular teachers. Available in reading, math, spelling, learning strategies, study skills, time management, computer skills.

Subject-area tutoring: Offered one-on-one by peer tutors. Available in most subjects.

Special courses: Vocabulary development, word processing, Internet use, typing. All offered for credit; none enter into overall grade point average.

Auxiliary aids: Taped textbooks, tape recorders, typewriters, word-processors with spell-check, personal computers, talking computers, screen enlargers.

Auxiliary services: Alternative test arrangements, notetakers, advocacy.

GENERAL COLLEGE INFORMATION

State-supported, 2-year, coed. Part of Colorado Community College and Occupational Education System. Awards associate degrees. Founded 1925. *Setting:* 17-acre small-town campus. *Educational spending 1995–96:* $1542 per undergrad. *Total enrollment:* 2,281. *Faculty:* 140 (79 full-time, 61 part-time); student–undergrad faculty ratio is 17:1.

Enrollment Profile: 2,281 students from 33 states and territories, 11 other countries. 46% women, 54% men, 28% part-time, 80% state residents, 23% transferred in, 1% international, 26% 25 or older, 1% Native American, 42% Hispanic, 2% black, 1% Asian or Pacific Islander.

First-Year Class: 380 total. Of the students who applied, 100% were accepted.

Graduation Requirements: 64 semester hours; math/science requirements vary according to program; computer course for most majors.

Computers on Campus: 125 computers available on campus for general student use. A campus-wide network can be accessed from off-campus. Students can contact faculty members and/or advisers through e-mail. Computers for student use in computer center, computer labs, learning resource center, classrooms, library provide access to the Internet/World Wide Web, on-campus e-mail addresses. Staffed computer lab on campus provides training in use of computers, software. *Academic computing expenditure 1995–96:* $263,888.

EXPENSES

Expenses for 1997–98: *Application fee:* $10. State resident tuition: $1738 full-time, $54.30 per semester hour part-time. Nonresident tuition: $6061 full-time, $189.40 per semester hour part-time. Part-time mandatory fees per semester range from $10 to $20. Full-time mandatory fees: $193. College room and board: $3172.

LD Services Contact: Special Populations Coordinator, Trinidad State Junior College, 600 Prospect Street, Trinidad, CO 81082, 719-846-5589. Fax: 719-846-5667.

TROCAIRE COLLEGE

Buffalo, New York

LEARNING DISABILITIES SERVICES INFORMATION

Academic Learning Center/Office for the Handicapped Person (ALC/OH) began offering services in 1988. Currently the program serves 7 undergraduates with LD. Students diagnosed with ADD/ADHD are eligible for the same services available to students with LD.

Staff: 2 full-time, 4 part-time staff members, including director, co-directors, nursing resource person. Services provided by remediation specialists, tutors, diagnostic specialists.

Special Fees: No special fees are charged for services to students with LD.

Applications and admissions: *Required:* high school transcript, class rank, untimed or extended time SAT I, personal interview, autobiographical statement. Students may begin taking classes in fall, spring, or summer. *Application deadline:* continuous.

Special policies: The college has written policies regarding substitutions and waivers of admissions, graduation, and degree requirements.

PROGRAM AND SERVICE COMPONENTS

Diagnostic testing: Reading, math, written language, perceptual skills, learning strategies.

Academic advising: Provided by academic advisers, coordinator. Students with LD may take up to 12 credit hours each term; 12 credit hours required to maintain full-time status and be eligible for financial aid.

Counseling services: Individual counseling, career counseling.

Basic skills remediation: Offered one-on-one and in small groups by LD teachers, regular teachers. Available in reading, math, spelling, handwriting, written language, learning strategies, perceptual skills, study skills, time management.

Subject-area tutoring: Offered one-on-one and in small groups by professional teachers, peer tutors. Available in all subjects.

Special courses: College survival skills, reading, vocabulary development, learning strategies, time management, math, study skills, career planning. Some offered for credit; some enter into overall grade point average.

Auxiliary aids: Tape recorders, calculators, typewriters, word-processors with spell-check, personal computers.

Auxiliary services: Alternative test arrangements, notetakers, advocacy.

GENERAL COLLEGE INFORMATION

Independent, 2-year, coed. Awards associate degrees. Founded 1958. *Setting:* 1-acre urban campus. *Endowment:* $2.7 million. *Educational spending 1995–96:* $2885 per undergrad. *Total enrollment:* 960. *Faculty:* 113 (43 full-time, 5% with terminal degrees, 70 part-time); student–undergrad faculty ratio is 12:1.

Enrollment Profile: 960 students: 87% women, 13% men, 45% part-time, 99% state residents, 11% transferred in, 1% international, 63% 25 or older, 1% Native American, 1% Hispanic, 9% black, 1% Asian or Pacific Islander. *Retention:* 86% of 1995 full-time freshmen returned. *Areas of study chosen:* 59% health professions and related sciences, 27% liberal arts/general studies, 10% business management and administrative services, 4% education. *Most popular recent majors:* nursing, radiological technology, operating room technology.

Trocaire College (continued)

First-Year Class: 272 total; 624 applied, 55% were accepted, 79% of whom enrolled. 6% from top 10% of their high school class, 18% from top quarter, 47% from top half.
Graduation Requirements: 60 credit hours; computer course for medical assistant, radiologic technology, hotel management, health information technology, business administration majors; internship (some majors).
Computers on Campus: 55 computers available on campus for general student use. A campus-wide network can be accessed. Computers for student use in computer center, computer labs, learning resource center. Staffed computer lab on campus provides training in use of computers, software. *Academic computing expenditure 1995–96:* $30,000.

EXPENSES

Expenses for 1997–98: *Application fee:* $15. Tuition: $6150 full-time, $180 per credit hour part-time. Part-time mandatory fees: $10 per credit hour. Full-time mandatory fees: $220 (minimum).
LD Services Contact: Sr. M. Norine Truax, Coordinator of ALC/OH, Trocaire College, 110 Red Jacket, Buffalo, NY 14220, 716-826-1200. Fax: 716-826-4704.

TRUETT-MCCONNELL COLLEGE

Cleveland, Georgia

LEARNING DISABILITIES SERVICES INFORMATION

Office of Special Support Services began offering services in 1996. Currently the program serves 35 undergraduates with LD. Students diagnosed with ADD/ADHD are eligible for the same services available to students with LD.
Staff: 1 full-time staff member (director).
Special Fees: No special fees are charged for services to students with LD.
Applications and admissions: *Required:* documentation of disability. Students may begin taking classes any term. *Application deadline:* 9/1 (fall term), 3/1 (spring term).

PROGRAM AND SERVICE COMPONENTS

Academic advising: Provided by academic advisers. Students with LD required to take 12 quarter hours each term to maintain full-time status.
Auxiliary aids: Taped textbooks, tape recorders, calculators, word-processors with spell-check.
Auxiliary services: Alternative test arrangements, notetakers, priority registration.

GENERAL COLLEGE INFORMATION

Independent Baptist, 2-year, coed. Awards associate degrees. Founded 1946. *Setting:* 310-acre rural campus with easy access to Atlanta. *Endowment:* $5.9 million. *Total enrollment:* 2,090. *Faculty:* 162 (37 full-time, 17% with terminal degrees, 125 part-time); student–undergrad faculty ratio is 17:1.
Enrollment Profile: 2,090 students from 2 states and territories, 7 other countries. 51% women, 49% men, 23% part-time, 99% state residents, 13% live on campus, 5% transferred in, 1% international, 21% 25 or older, 0% Native American, 1% Hispanic, 8% black, 0% Asian or Pacific Islander. *Retention:* 34% of 1995 full-time freshmen returned.
First-Year Class: 388 total.
Graduation Requirements: 90 quarter hours; 1 math course; computer course for business majors.
Computers on Campus: 60 computers available on campus for general student use. A campus-wide network can be accessed. Students can contact faculty members and/or advisers through e-mail. Computers for student use in computer labs, learning resource center, library provide access to the Internet/World Wide Web, on- and off-campus e-mail addresses. Staffed computer lab on campus provides training in use of computers, software.

EXPENSES

Expenses for 1997–98: *Application fee:* $20. Comprehensive fee of $8475 includes full-time tuition ($5550) and college room and board ($2925). College room only: $1425. Part-time tuition: $110 per quarter hour.
LD Services Contact: Ms. Kathy Yohn, Director, Special Support Services, Truett-McConnell College, 100 Alumni Drive, Cleveland, GA 30528, 706-865-2134 Ext. 172. Fax: 706-865-5135. Email: kathy@truett.cc.ga.us.

TULSA COMMUNITY COLLEGE

Tulsa, Oklahoma

LEARNING DISABILITIES SERVICES INFORMATION

disABLED Student Resource Center currently serves 350 undergraduates with LD. Students diagnosed with ADD/ADHD are eligible for the same services available to students with LD.
Staff: 4 full-time, 4 part-time staff members, including Counselor. Services provided by counselor, readers, computer specialist, clerks, disABLED Student Resource Center specialists.
Special Fees: No special fees are charged for services to students with LD.
Applications and admissions: *Required:* high school transcript, SAT I or ACT (for placement purposes); *recommended:* high school IEP (Individualized Education Program), psychoeducational report completed within 3 years. Students may begin taking classes any term. *Application deadline:* continuous.

PROGRAM AND SERVICE COMPONENTS

Special preparation or orientation: Optional orientation offered before registration and after classes begin, individually by special arrangement.
Academic advising: Provided by unit staff members, academic advisers. Students with LD may take up to 15 credit hours each term; most take 6 to 9 credit hours; 12 credit hours required to maintain full-time status; 6 credit hours required to be eligible for financial aid.
Counseling services: Individual counseling, career counseling.
Basic skills remediation: Offered in class-size groups by regular teachers. Available in reading, math, spelling, spoken language, written language, learning strategies, study skills, time management, social skills, computer skills.
Subject-area tutoring: Offered one-on-one by peer tutors. Available in most subjects.
Special courses: College survival skills, reading, vocabulary development, composition, learning strategies, word processing, Internet use, time management, math, typing, study skills, career planning, stress management, social relationships. Some offered for credit; some enter into overall grade point average.
Auxiliary aids: Taped textbooks, tape recorders, calculators, typewriters, word-processors with spell-check, personal computers, talking computers, optical character readers.
Auxiliary services: Alternative test arrangements, notetakers, advocacy.
Campus support group: A special student organization is available to students with LD.

GENERAL COLLEGE INFORMATION

State-supported, 2-year, coed. Part of Oklahoma State Regents for Higher Education. Awards associate degrees. Founded 1968. *Setting:* 160-acre urban campus. *Total enrollment:* 20,000. *Faculty:* 1,200 (250 full-time, 90% with terminal degrees, 950 part-time); student–undergrad faculty ratio is 25:1.
Enrollment Profile: 20,000 students: 60% women, 40% men, 80% part-time, 99% state residents, 25% transferred in, 50% 25 or older, 7% Native American, 3% Hispanic, 15% black, 2% Asian or Pacific Islander. *Retention:* 25% of 1995 full-time freshmen returned. *Most popular recent majors:* business administration/commerce/management, computer information systems, nursing.
First-Year Class: 4,000 total; 4,000 applied, 100% were accepted, 100% of whom enrolled.
Graduation Requirements: 60 credit hours; computer course for most majors; internship (some majors).
Computers on Campus: 1,000 computers available on campus for general student use. A computer is recommended for all students. A campus-wide network can be accessed from off-campus. Students can contact faculty members and/or advisers through e-mail. Computers for student use in computer center, computer labs, learning resource center, library provide access to the Internet/World Wide Web. Staffed computer lab on campus provides training in use of computers, software.

EXPENSES

Expenses for 1996–97: *Application fee:* $15. State resident tuition: $855 full-time, $28.50 per credit hour part-time. Nonresident tuition: $2693 full-time, $89.75 per credit hour part-time. Part-time mandatory fees: $9.50 per credit hour. Full-time mandatory fees: $285.

LD Services Contact: Mrs. Yolanda R. Williams, Counselor, disABLED Student Resource Center, Tulsa Community College, Room 331B, 909 South Boston Avenue, Tulsa, OK 74119, 918-595-7115. Fax: 918-595-7298. Email: ywillia@vm.tulsa.cc.ok.us.

UMPQUA COMMUNITY COLLEGE

Roseburg, Oregon

LEARNING DISABILITIES SERVICES INFORMATION

Disability Services began offering services in 1984. Currently the program serves 31 undergraduates with LD. Students diagnosed with ADD/ADHD are eligible for the same services available to students with LD.
Staff: 1 full-time, 1 part-time staff members, including coordinator, instructor. Services provided by tutors, diagnostic specialist.
Special Fees: No special fees are charged for services to students with LD.
Applications and admissions: *Recommended:* personal interview, psychoeducational report completed within 3 years. Students may begin taking classes any term. *Application deadline:* continuous.
Special policies: The college has written policies regarding grade forgiveness.

PROGRAM AND SERVICE COMPONENTS

Diagnostic testing: Intelligence, reading, math, spelling, spoken language, written language, personality, learning styles.
Academic advising: Provided by unit staff members, academic advisers. Students with LD may take up to 16 credits each term; most take 9 to 12 credits; 12 credits required to maintain full-time status; 6 credits (part-time), 12 credits (full-time) required to be eligible for financial aid.
Counseling services: Individual counseling, career counseling, self-advocacy training.
Basic skills remediation: Offered one-on-one, in small groups, and in class-size groups by regular teachers. Available in reading, math, spelling, handwriting, written language, learning strategies, study skills, time management, computer skills, critical thinking, test taking.
Subject-area tutoring: Offered one-on-one and in small groups by peer tutors. Available in most subjects.
Special courses: College survival skills, reading, vocabulary development, composition, learning strategies, word processing, Internet use, time management, math, typing, personal psychology, study skills, career planning, stress management, health and nutrition, college orientation. Most offered for credit; some enter into overall grade point average.
Auxiliary aids: Taped textbooks, tape recorders, calculators, typewriters, word-processors with spell-check, personal computers, talking computers.
Auxiliary services: Alternative test arrangements, notetakers, advocacy, readers.
Campus support group: A special student organization is available to students with LD.

GENERAL COLLEGE INFORMATION

State and locally supported, 2-year, coed. Awards associate degrees. Founded 1964. *Setting:* 100-acre rural campus. *Endowment:* $1.3 million. *Educational spending 1995–96:* $2395 per undergrad. *Total enrollment:* 2,100. *Faculty:* 148 (73 full-time, 25% with terminal degrees, 75 part-time).
Enrollment Profile: 2,100 students from 7 states and territories, 5 other countries. 53% women, 47% men, 45% part-time, 98% state residents, 10% transferred in, 1% international, 60% 25 or older, 1% Native American, 1% Hispanic, 1% black, 1% Asian or Pacific Islander. *Areas of study chosen:* 58% library and information studies, 20% vocational and home economics, 5% business management and administrative services, 5% education, 5% health professions and related sciences, 5% psychology, 2% engineering and applied sciences. *Most popular recent majors:* liberal arts/general studies, nursing, business administration/commerce/management.
First-Year Class: 1,350 total; 1,700 applied, 100% were accepted, 79% of whom enrolled.
Graduation Requirements: 93 credits; math/science requirements vary according to program; computer course for office technology, business, automotive, digital systems majors.
Computers on Campus: 200 computers available on campus for general student use. Computer purchase/lease plans available. A campus-wide network can be accessed. Computers for student use in computer center, library provide access to the Internet/World Wide Web, off-campus e-mail addresses. Staffed computer lab on campus. *Academic computing expenditure 1995–96:* $130,000.

EXPENSES

Expenses for 1997–98: State resident tuition: $1610 full-time, $35 per credit part-time. Nonresident tuition: $4738 full-time, $103 per credit part-time.
LD Services Contact: Ms. Barbara Stoner, Evaluation Specialist/Disability Services Coordinator, Umpqua Community College, PO Box 967, Roseburg, OR 97470, 541-440-4600 Ext. 741. Fax: 541-440-4665. Email: stonerb@umpqua.cc.or.us.

THE UNIVERSITY OF AKRON–WAYNE COLLEGE

Orrville, Ohio

LEARNING DISABILITIES SERVICES INFORMATION

Learning Center began offering services in 1985. Currently the program serves 15 undergraduates with LD. Students diagnosed with ADD/ADHD are eligible for the same services available to students with LD.
Staff: 2 full-time staff members, including director, administrative assistant. Services provided by tutors.
Special Fees: No special fees are charged for services to students with LD.
Applications and admissions: *Required:* psychoeducational report completed within 3 years. Students may begin taking classes any term. *Application deadline:* continuous.
Special policies: The college has written policies regarding grade forgiveness.

PROGRAM AND SERVICE COMPONENTS

Diagnostic testing: Intelligence, reading, math, spelling, study skills, personality, speech, hearing, learning strategies.
Academic advising: Provided by academic advisers. Most students with LD take 6 to 10 credit hours each term; 12 credit hours (fewer with special permission) required to maintain full-time status and be eligible for financial aid.
Counseling services: Individual counseling, career counseling.
Basic skills remediation: Offered in class-size groups by regular teachers. Available in reading, math, written language, learning strategies, time management.
Subject-area tutoring: Offered one-on-one by professional teachers, peer tutors. Available in all subjects.
Special courses: College survival skills, reading, composition, learning strategies, time management, math, study skills, career planning. None offered for credit; none enter into overall grade point average.
Auxiliary aids: Taped textbooks, tape recorders, calculators, typewriters, word-processors with spell-check, personal computers, talking computers, optical character readers.
Auxiliary services: Alternative test arrangements, notetakers.

GENERAL COLLEGE INFORMATION

State-supported, 2-year, coed. Part of University of Akron. Awards associate degrees. Founded 1972. *Setting:* 163-acre rural campus. *Total enrollment:* 1,458. *Faculty:* 109 (24 full-time, 85 part-time).
Enrollment Profile: 1,458 students: 70% women, 30% men, 64% part-time, 100% state residents, 9% transferred in, 41% 25 or older, 1% Native American, 0% Hispanic, 2% black. *Most popular recent majors:* business administration/commerce/management, science, social work.
First-Year Class: 238 total; 334 applied, 77% of whom enrolled. 1 National Merit Scholar.
Graduation Requirements: 64 credits; math/science requirements vary according to program; computer course (varies by major).
Computers on Campus: 223 computers available on campus for general student use. A campus-wide network can be accessed from off-campus. Students can contact faculty members and/or advisers through e-mail. Computers for student use in computer center, computer labs, learning resource center, classrooms, library provide access to the Internet/World Wide Web, on-campus e-mail addresses. Staffed computer lab on campus.

The University of Akron–Wayne College (continued)

EXPENSES

Expenses for 1997–98: *Application fee:* $25. State resident tuition: $4275 full-time, $133.60 per credit part-time. Nonresident tuition: $9478 full-time, $296.20 per credit part-time. Part-time mandatory fees: $4 per credit. Full-time mandatory fees: $128.

LD Services Contact: Ms. Julia Beyeler, Director of Learning Support Services, The University of Akron–Wayne College, 1901 Smucker Road, Orrville, OH 44667-9192, 330-684-8963. Fax: 330-684-8989. Email: juliabeyeler@uakron.edu.

UNIVERSITY OF HAWAII–HAWAII COMMUNITY COLLEGE

Hilo, Hawaii

LEARNING DISABILITIES SERVICES INFORMATION

Ha'awi Kokua Program began offering services in 1992. Students diagnosed with ADD/ADHD are eligible for the same services available to students with LD.

Staff: 1 full-time staff member (director). Services provided by student workers.

Special Fees: No special fees are charged for services to students with LD.

Applications and admissions: *Required:* special education certification or doctor's letter or psychological test results; *recommended:* high school IEP (Individualized Education Program). Students may begin taking classes in fall or spring. *Application deadline:* continuous.

PROGRAM AND SERVICE COMPONENTS

Academic advising: Provided by unit staff members, academic advisers. Students with LD may take up to 15 credits each term; most take 12 credits; 1 credit required to be eligible for financial aid.

Auxiliary aids: Taped textbooks, tape recorders, calculators, typewriters, word-processors with spell-check, optical character readers.

GENERAL COLLEGE INFORMATION

State-supported, 2-year, coed. Part of University of Hawaii System. Awards associate degrees. Founded 1954. *Setting:* small-town campus. *Total enrollment:* 2,500. *Faculty:* 149 (71 full-time, 78 part-time).

Enrollment Profile: 2,500 students from 12 states and territories, 32 other countries. 58% women, 42% men, 50% part-time, 95% state residents, 19% transferred in, 1% international, 40% 25 or older, 6% Native American, 2% Hispanic, 1% black, 59% Asian or Pacific Islander. *Areas of study chosen:* 41% liberal arts/general studies, 22% vocational and home economics, 14% business management and administrative services, 12% health professions and related sciences, 5% education, 3% computer and information sciences, 2% agriculture. *Most popular recent major:* liberal arts/general studies.

First-Year Class: 530 total; 1,154 applied, 94% were accepted, 49% of whom enrolled.

Graduation Requirements: 60 credit hours; 1 math/science course.

Computers on Campus: 100 computers available on campus for general student use. Computer purchase/lease plans available. A campus-wide network can be accessed from off-campus. Students can contact faculty members and/or advisers through e-mail. Computers for student use in computer labs, learning resource center, classrooms provide access to the Internet/World Wide Web, on- and off-campus e-mail addresses. Staffed computer lab on campus provides training in use of computers, software.

EXPENSES

Expenses for 1997–98: State resident tuition: $936 full-time, $39 per credit hour part-time. Nonresident tuition: $5712 full-time, $238 per credit hour part-time. Part-time mandatory fees per semester range from $7 to $25. Full-time mandatory fees: $50. College room and board: $3826. College room only: $1748.

LD Services Contact: Ms. Karen Kane, Counselor/Coordinator of the Ha'awi Kokua Program, University of Hawaii–Hawaii Community College, 200 West Kawili Street, Hilo, HI 96720, 808-974-7741. Fax: 808-974-7692.

UNIVERSITY OF KENTUCKY, HAZARD COMMUNITY COLLEGE

Hazard, Kentucky

LEARNING DISABILITIES SERVICES INFORMATION

Student Support Services/Learning Lab currently serves 30 undergraduates with LD. Students diagnosed with ADD/ADHD are eligible for the same services available to students with LD.

Staff: 15 full-time, 4 part-time staff members, including director. Services provided by remediation specialists, tutors, counselor.

Special Fees: No special fees are charged for services to students with LD.

Applications and admissions: *Required:* high school transcript, grade point average, courses completed; *recommended:* high school class rank, extracurricular activities, extended time SAT I. Students may begin taking classes in fall, spring, or summer. *Application deadline:* continuous.

PROGRAM AND SERVICE COMPONENTS

Diagnostic testing: Reading, math, study skills, personality, learning strategies.

Academic advising: Provided by academic advisers. Students with LD may take up to 12 credit hours each term; most take 10 to 12 credit hours; 12 credit hours required to maintain full-time status; 6 credit hours (part-time) required to be eligible for financial aid.

Counseling services: Career counseling.

Basic skills remediation: Offered in small groups by regular teachers. Available in reading, math, written language, learning strategies, study skills, time management.

Subject-area tutoring: Offered one-on-one, in small groups, and in class-size groups by professional teachers, peer tutors. Available in most subjects.

Auxiliary aids: Taped textbooks, tape recorders, word-processors with spell-check, talking computers.

Auxiliary services: Alternative test arrangements, notetakers, priority registration, advocacy.

Campus support group: A special student organization is available to students with LD.

GENERAL COLLEGE INFORMATION

State-supported, 2-year, coed. Part of University of Kentucky Community College System. Awards associate degrees. Founded 1968. *Setting:* 34-acre rural campus. *Total enrollment:* 2,358. *Faculty:* 156 (88 full-time, 68 part-time); student–undergrad faculty ratio is 17:1.

Enrollment Profile: 2,358 students from 3 states and territories. 70% women, 30% men, 41% part-time, 99% state residents, 32% transferred in, 0% international, 35% 25 or older, 1% Native American, 0% Hispanic, 1% black, 0% Asian or Pacific Islander. *Most popular recent majors:* nursing, radiological technology, business administration/commerce/management.

First-Year Class: 695 total; 1,125 applied, 100% were accepted, 62% of whom enrolled. 15% from top 10% of their high school class, 50% from top half.

Graduation Requirements: 60 credit hours; 1 course each in math and science; computer course.

Computers on Campus: 28 computers available on campus for general student use. Computers for student use in computer labs, learning resource center, library.

EXPENSES

Expenses for 1997–98: State resident tuition: $1020 full-time, $43 per credit hour part-time. Nonresident tuition: $3060 full-time, $126 per credit hour part-time. Part-time mandatory fees per semester range from $4 to $40. Full-time mandatory fees: $80.

LD Services Contact: Ms. Cynthia Plummer, ADA Contact, University of Kentucky, Hazard Community College, 1 College Drive, Hazard, KY 41701, 606-436-5721 Ext. 555. Fax: 606-439-1600.

UNIVERSITY OF KENTUCKY, LEXINGTON COMMUNITY COLLEGE

Lexington, Kentucky

LEARNING DISABILITIES SERVICES INFORMATION

Disability Support Services began offering services in 1984. Currently the program serves 105 undergraduates with LD. Students diagnosed with ADD/ADHD are eligible for the same services available to students with LD.

Staff: 2 full-time, 10 part-time staff members, including coordinator, instructional specialist. Services provided by tutors, counselors.

Special Fees: No special fees are charged for services to students with LD.

Applications and admissions: *Required:* psychoeducational report completed within 3 years. Students may begin taking classes in fall, spring, or summer. *Application deadline:* 8/1 (fall term), 12/1 (spring term).

PROGRAM AND SERVICE COMPONENTS

Academic advising: Provided by unit staff members. Students with LD may take up to 12 credit hours each term; most take 12 credit hours; 12 credit hours required to maintain full-time status and be eligible for financial aid.

Counseling services: Individual counseling, small-group counseling, career counseling, self-advocacy training.

Basic skills remediation: Offered in class-size groups by regular teachers. Available in reading, math, written language, learning strategies.

Subject-area tutoring: Offered one-on-one and in small groups by professional teachers, peer tutors. Available in all subjects.

Special courses: College survival skills, reading, math, study skills, career planning. None offered for credit.

Auxiliary aids: Taped textbooks, tape recorders, calculators, typewriters, word-processors with spell-check.

Auxiliary services: Alternative test arrangements, notetakers, advocacy.

Campus support group: A special student organization is available to students with LD.

GENERAL COLLEGE INFORMATION

State-supported, 2-year, coed. Part of University of Kentucky Community College System. Awards associate degrees. Founded 1965. *Setting:* 10-acre urban campus. *Educational spending 1995–96:* $1246 per undergrad. *Total enrollment:* 5,505. *Faculty:* 302 (132 full-time, 170 part-time); student–undergrad faculty ratio is 19:1.

Enrollment Profile: 5,505 students from 30 states and territories, 23 other countries. 58% women, 42% men, 42% part-time, 99% state residents, 39% transferred in, 39% 25 or older, 1% Native American, 1% Hispanic, 7% black, 1% Asian or Pacific Islander. *Retention:* 50% of 1995 full-time freshmen returned. *Most popular recent majors:* nursing, liberal arts/general studies.

First-Year Class: 2,472 total. Of the students who applied, 100% were accepted.

Graduation Requirements: 60 credit hours; math/science requirements vary according to program; computer course; internship (some majors).

Computers on Campus: 80 computers available on campus for general student use. A computer is recommended for some students. A campus-wide network can be accessed. Students can contact faculty members and/or advisers through e-mail. Computers for student use in computer center, library provide access to the Internet/World Wide Web, on-campus e-mail addresses. Staffed computer lab on campus provides training in use of computers, software. *Academic computing expenditure 1995–96:* $449,296.

EXPENSES

Expenses for 1997–98: State resident tuition: $1956 full-time, $74 per credit hour part-time. Nonresident tuition: $5196 full-time, $209 per credit hour part-time. Part-time mandatory fees per semester range from $4 to $40. Full-time mandatory fees: $80.

LD Services Contact: Ms. Veronica Miller, Coordinator, Disability Support Services, University of Kentucky, Lexington Community College, 103F Oswald Building, Cooper Drive, Lexington, KY 40506-0235, 606-257-6068. Fax: 606-257-4339.

UNIVERSITY OF KENTUCKY, SOMERSET COMMUNITY COLLEGE

Somerset, Kentucky

LEARNING DISABILITIES SERVICES INFORMATION

Disabilities Services began offering services in 1992. Currently the program serves 42 undergraduates with LD. Students diagnosed with ADD/ADHD are eligible for the same services available to students with LD.

Staff: 1 full-time, 2 part-time staff members, including coordinator. Services provided by remediation specialists, tutors, counselors.

Special Fees: No special fees are charged for services to students with LD.

Applications and admissions: *Required:* high school transcript, courses completed, IEP (Individualized Education Program); *recommended:* untimed or extended time ACT, ACT ASSET (in lieu of ACT for students over 21 years of age). Students may begin taking classes any term.

PROGRAM AND SERVICE COMPONENTS

Academic advising: Provided by unit staff members, academic advisers. Students with LD may take up to 18 credit hours each term; most take 12 credit hours; 12 credit hours required to maintain full-time status; 6 credit hours required to be eligible for financial aid.

Counseling services: Individual counseling, career counseling.

Basic skills remediation: Offered one-on-one and in small groups by Coordinator, instructional specialist. Available in reading, math, spelling, handwriting, spoken language, written language, learning strategies, study skills, time management, speech, computer skills.

Subject-area tutoring: Offered one-on-one, in small groups, and in class-size groups by professional teachers, peer tutors, instructional specialists, professional tutors. Available in most subjects.

Auxiliary aids: Taped textbooks, tape recorders, calculators, typewriters, word-processors with spell-check, personal computers, talking computers.

GENERAL COLLEGE INFORMATION

State-supported, 2-year, coed. Part of University of Kentucky Community College System. Awards associate degrees. Founded 1965. *Setting:* 70-acre small-town campus. *Total enrollment:* 2,498. *Faculty:* 153 (55 full-time, 98 part-time); student–undergrad faculty ratio is 17:1.

Enrollment Profile: 2,498 students from 3 states and territories, 2 other countries. 70% women, 30% men, 45% part-time, 99% state residents, 5% transferred in, 45% 25 or older, 1% Native American, 0% Hispanic, 1% black, 0% Asian or Pacific Islander. *Most popular recent majors:* business administration/commerce/management, nursing.

First-Year Class: 1,600 total; 2,100 applied, 100% were accepted.

Graduation Requirements: 60 credit hours; 1 college algebra course, 2 science courses for associate of arts degree; 1 course each in college algebra and trigonometry, 4 science courses for associate of science degree; computer course.

Computers on Campus: 175 computers available on campus for general student use. Computers for student use in computer labs, learning resource center, library provide access to the Internet/World Wide Web.

EXPENSES

Expenses for 1997–98: State resident tuition: $1020 full-time, $43 per credit hour part-time. Nonresident tuition: $3060 full-time, $126 per credit hour part-time. Part-time mandatory fees per semester range from $4 to $40. Full-time mandatory fees: $80.

LD Services Contact: Ms. Louanne Lane, Special Needs Coordinator, University of Kentucky, Somerset Community College, 808 Monticello Road, Somerset, KY 42501, 606-679-8501. Fax: 606-679-5139.

UNIVERSITY OF NEW MEXICO–VALENCIA CAMPUS

Los Lunas, New Mexico

LEARNING DISABILITIES SERVICES INFORMATION

Student Enrichment Center/Special Services Program currently serves 74 undergraduates with LD. Students diagnosed with ADD/ADHD are eligible for the same services available to students with LD.

University of New Mexico–Valencia Campus (continued)

Staff: 3 full-time, 20 part-time staff members, including Program Manager. Services provided by remediation specialists, tutors, diagnostic specialists, academic counselors.
Special Fees: No special fees are charged for services to students with LD.
Applications and admissions: *Required:* psychoeducational report completed within 3 years; *recommended:* high school IEP (Individualized Education Program). Students may begin taking classes in fall, spring, or summer. *Application deadline:* 8/26 (fall term), 1/1 (spring term).

PROGRAM AND SERVICE COMPONENTS

Diagnostic testing: Intelligence, reading, math, spelling, spoken language, written language, perceptual skills, learning strategies.
Academic advising: Provided by unit staff members, academic advisers. Most students with LD take 6 to 12 credit hours each term; 6 credit hours required to be eligible for financial aid.
Counseling services: Career counseling.
Basic skills remediation: Offered one-on-one and in small groups by regular teachers, professional tutors. Available in reading, math, spelling, written language, learning strategies, study skills, time management.
Subject-area tutoring: Offered one-on-one, in small groups, and in class-size groups by professional teachers, peer tutors, professional tutors. Available in most subjects.
Auxiliary aids: Taped textbooks, tape recorders, calculators, typewriters, word-processors with spell-check, personal computers, talking computers, optical character readers.
Auxiliary services: Alternative test arrangements, notetakers, advocacy, transcribers/readers, TDD/(505)865-9598.

GENERAL COLLEGE INFORMATION

State-supported, 2-year, coed. Part of New Mexico Commission on Higher Education. Awards associate degrees. Founded 1981. *Setting:* small-town campus with easy access to Albuquerque. *Total enrollment:* 1,550. *Faculty:* 93 (19 full-time, 80% with terminal degrees, 74 part-time).
Enrollment Profile: 1,550 students from 4 states and territories, 2 other countries. 68% women, 32% men, 59% part-time, 97% state residents, 5% transferred in, 76% 25 or older, 4% Native American, 49% Hispanic, 1% black, 0% Asian or Pacific Islander. *Most popular recent majors:* liberal arts/general studies, education, secretarial studies/office management.
First-Year Class: 300 total. Of the students who applied, 100% were accepted, 95% of whom enrolled.
Graduation Requirements: 60 credit hours.
Computers on Campus: 65 computers available on campus for general student use. A campus-wide network can be accessed from off-campus. Students can contact faculty members and/or advisers through e-mail. Computers for student use in computer labs, tutorial center. Staffed computer lab on campus provides training in use of computers, software.

EXPENSES

Expenses for 1996–97: *Application fee:* $15. State resident tuition: $720 full-time, $30 per credit hour part-time. Nonresident tuition: $1776 full-time, $74 per credit hour part-time.
LD Services Contact: Ms. Stella Creek, Assistant, Student Enrichment Center, University of New Mexico–Valencia Campus, 280 La Entrada, Los Lunas, NM 87031, 505-925-8931. Fax: 505-925-8933.

UNIVERSITY OF NORTH DAKOTA–LAKE REGION

Devils Lake, North Dakota

LEARNING DISABILITIES SERVICES INFORMATION

Learning Center currently serves 26 undergraduates with LD. Students diagnosed with ADD/ADHD are eligible for the same services available to students with LD.
Staff: 1 part-time staff member (director). Services provided by remediation specialists, tutors, counselors.
Special Fees: No special fees are charged for services to students with LD.
Applications and admissions: *Required:* high school transcript, grade point average, untimed ACT; *recommended:* high school class rank, courses completed, extracurricular activities, IEP (Individualized Education Program), extended time SAT I, personal interview, autobiographical statement, letters of recommendation, psychoeducational report. Students may begin taking classes in fall only. *Application deadline:* continuous.
Special policies: The college has written policies regarding grade forgiveness; substitutions and waivers of degree requirements.

PROGRAM AND SERVICE COMPONENTS

Special preparation or orientation: Optional orientation offered before registration and during registration.
Academic advising: Provided by unit staff members, academic advisers. Students with LD may take up to 16 semester hours each term; most take 12 to 14 semester hours; 12 semester hours required to maintain full-time status; 3 semester hours required to be eligible for financial aid.
Counseling services: Individual counseling, career counseling, self-advocacy training.
Basic skills remediation: Offered in class-size groups by regular teachers. Available in reading, math, spoken language, written language, learning strategies, study skills, time management, social skills.
Subject-area tutoring: Offered one-on-one, in small groups, and in class-size groups by professional teachers, peer tutors. Available in all subjects.
Special courses: College survival skills, reading, communication skills, composition, learning strategies, time management, math, study skills, career planning. Some offered for credit; some enter into overall grade point average.
Auxiliary aids: Taped textbooks, tape recorders, word-processors with spell-check, talking computers, optical character readers.
Auxiliary services: Alternative test arrangements, notetakers, advocacy.

GENERAL COLLEGE INFORMATION

State-supported, 2-year, coed. Part of North Dakota University System. Awards associate degrees. Founded 1941. *Setting:* 15-acre small-town campus. *Educational spending 1995–96:* $2670 per undergrad. *Total enrollment:* 704. *Faculty:* 54 (26 full-time, 8% with terminal degrees, 28 part-time).
Enrollment Profile: 704 students from 6 states and territories. 58% women, 42% men, 49% part-time, 98% state residents, 12% transferred in, 0% international, 40% 25 or older, 6% Native American, 0% Hispanic, 0% black, 0% Asian or Pacific Islander. *Areas of study chosen:* 49% liberal arts/general studies, 15% business management and administrative services, 11% agriculture, 4% computer and information sciences, 4% health professions and related sciences, 1% vocational and home economics. *Most popular recent majors:* liberal arts/general studies, agricultural business, marketing/retailing/merchandising.
First-Year Class: 270 total; 322 applied.
Graduation Requirements: 60 semester hours; internship (some majors).
Computers on Campus: 127 computers available on campus for general student use. A campus-wide network can be accessed. Students can contact faculty members and/or advisers through e-mail. Computers for student use in computer labs, classrooms, dorms provide access to the Internet/World Wide Web. Staffed computer lab on campus (open 24 hours a day) provides training in use of computers, software. *Academic computing expenditure 1995–96:* $218,512.

EXPENSES

Expenses for 1996–97: *Application fee:* $25. State resident tuition: $1552 full-time, $64.67 per semester hour part-time. Nonresident tuition: $4144 full-time, $172.67 per semester hour part-time. Part-time mandatory fees: $10.21 per semester hour. Full-time mandatory fees: $326. College room and board: $2440.
LD Services Contact: Ms. Theresa Leiphon, Director of Learning Resources, University of North Dakota–Lake Region, 1801 College Drive North, Devils Lake, ND 58301, 701-662-1537. Fax: 701-662-1570.

UNIVERSITY OF WISCONSIN CENTER–BARABOO/SAUK COUNTY

Baraboo, Wisconsin

LEARNING DISABILITIES SERVICES INFORMATION

Student Services currently serves 3 undergraduates with LD. Students diagnosed with ADD/ADHD are eligible for the same services available to students with LD.
Staff: 2 part-time staff members, including coordinators.

Special Fees: No special fees are charged for services to students with LD.
Applications and admissions: *Required:* high school transcript, class rank, IEP (Individualized Education Program), untimed or extended time ACT, extended time SAT I. Students may begin taking classes in fall, spring, or summer. *Application deadline:* continuous.
Special policies: The college has written policies regarding substitutions and waivers of admissions, graduation, and degree requirements.

PROGRAM AND SERVICE COMPONENTS

Academic advising: Provided by academic advisers. Most students with LD take 6 to 12 credits each term; 12 credits required to maintain full-time status; 6 credits required to be eligible for financial aid.
Auxiliary aids: Taped textbooks, tape recorders.
Auxiliary services: Alternative test arrangements, notetakers.

GENERAL COLLEGE INFORMATION

State-supported, 2-year, coed. Part of University of Wisconsin System. Awards associate degrees. Founded 1968. *Setting:* 68-acre small-town campus. *Total enrollment:* 415. *Faculty:* 31 (20 full-time, 75% with terminal degrees, 11 part-time); student–undergrad faculty ratio is 15:1.
Enrollment Profile: 415 students: 60% women, 40% men, 47% part-time, 99% state residents, 10% transferred in, 1% international, 30% 25 or older, 1% Native American, 1% Hispanic, 1% black, 1% Asian or Pacific Islander. *Retention:* 41% of 1995 full-time freshmen returned.
First-Year Class: 173 total; 250 applied, 96% were accepted, 72% of whom enrolled. 8% from top 10% of their high school class, 23% from top quarter, 60% from top half. 1 valedictorian.
Graduation Requirements: 60 credits.
Computers on Campus: 20 computers available on campus for general student use. A campus-wide network can be accessed from off-campus. Students can contact faculty members and/or advisers through e-mail. Computers for student use in computer labs, library, student center provide access to the Internet/World Wide Web, on- and off-campus e-mail addresses. Staffed computer lab on campus provides training in use of software.

EXPENSES

Expenses for 1996–97: *Application fee:* $28. State resident tuition: $1949 full-time. Nonresident tuition: $6558 full-time. Part-time tuition per semester ranges from $82.25 to $895.25 for state residents, $274.25 to $3007 for nonresidents. Minnesota residents pay tuition at the rate they would pay if attending a comparable state-supported institution in Minnesota. Full-time mandatory fees: $2.
LD Services Contact: Mr. Tom Martin, Director, Student Services, University of Wisconsin Center–Baraboo/Sauk County, 1006 Connie Road, Baraboo, WI 53913-1015, 608-356-8724. Fax: 608-356-4074. Email: boouinfo@uwc.edu.

UNIVERSITY OF WISCONSIN CENTER–FOX VALLEY

Menasha, Wisconsin

LEARNING DISABILITIES SERVICES INFORMATION

Student Services Office began offering services in 1988. Currently the program serves 20 undergraduates with LD. Students diagnosed with ADD/ADHD are eligible for the same services available to students with LD.
Staff: 6 full-time, 2 part-time staff members, including director, coordinator. Services provided by tutors, counselors.
Special Fees: No special fees are charged for services to students with LD.
Applications and admissions: *Required:* high school transcript, grade point average, class rank, courses completed, untimed or extended time ACT. Students may begin taking classes in fall, spring, or summer. *Application deadline:* continuous.
Special policies: The college has written policies regarding substitutions and waivers of admissions and degree requirements.

PROGRAM AND SERVICE COMPONENTS

Academic advising: Provided by academic advisers. Students with LD may take up to 18 credits each term; most take 12 credits; 12 credits required to maintain full-time status; 6 credits required to be eligible for financial aid.
Counseling services: Individual counseling, small-group counseling, career counseling.
Subject-area tutoring: Offered one-on-one and in small groups by peer tutors. Available in most subjects.
Special courses: College survival skills. All offered for credit; none enter into overall grade point average.
Auxiliary aids: Taped textbooks, tape recorders, typewriters, word-processors with spell-check, optical character readers.
Auxiliary services: Alternative test arrangements, notetakers, priority registration, advocacy.
Campus support group: A special student organization is available to students with LD.

GENERAL COLLEGE INFORMATION

State-supported, 2-year, coed. Part of University of Wisconsin System. Awards associate degrees. Founded 1933. *Setting:* 33-acre urban campus. *Total enrollment:* 1,250. *Faculty:* 58 (36 full-time, 75% with terminal degrees, 22 part-time); student–undergrad faculty ratio is 25:1.
Enrollment Profile: 1,250 students from 2 states and territories. 52% women, 48% men, 55% part-time, 99% state residents, 4% transferred in, 0% international, 40% 25 or older, 1% Native American, 2% Hispanic, 1% black, 2% Asian or Pacific Islander. *Retention:* 60% of 1995 full-time freshmen returned.
First-Year Class: 396 total; 640 applied, 86% were accepted, 72% of whom enrolled. 3% from top 10% of their high school class, 13% from top quarter, 45% from top half. 2 valedictorians.
Graduation Requirements: 60 credit hours; 3 credit hours of math/science.
Computers on Campus: 50 computers available on campus for general student use. A campus-wide network can be accessed from off-campus. Students can contact faculty members and/or advisers through e-mail. Computers for student use in computer labs, learning resource center provide access to the Internet/World Wide Web, on- and off-campus e-mail addresses. Staffed computer lab on campus provides training in use of computers, software.

EXPENSES

Estimated Expenses for 1997–98: State resident tuition: $2079 full-time, $87.68 per credit hour part-time. Nonresident tuition: $6918 full-time, $288 per credit hour part-time. Minnesota residents pay tuition at the rate they would pay if attending a comparable state-supported institution in Minnesota. Full-time mandatory fees: $2.
LD Services Contact: Ms. Carla Rabe, Student Services Coordinator, University of Wisconsin Center–Fox Valley, 1478 Midway Road, Menasha, WI 54952-8002, 414-832-2620. Fax: 414-832-2674. Email: crabe@uwc.edu.

UNIVERSITY OF WISCONSIN CENTER–MARATHON COUNTY

Wausau, Wisconsin

LEARNING DISABILITIES SERVICES INFORMATION

Tutoring Services currently serves undergraduate students with LD. Students diagnosed with ADD/ADHD are eligible for the same services available to students with LD.
Staff: 1 full-time, 3 part-time staff members, including director. Services provided by remediation specialists, tutor.
Special Fees: A fee is charged for diagnostic testing.
Applications and admissions: *Required:* high school transcript, grade point average, class rank, courses completed. Students may begin taking classes in fall only. *Application deadline:* 3/1 (fall term), 11/1 (spring term).

PROGRAM AND SERVICE COMPONENTS

Diagnostic testing: Intelligence, reading, math, spelling, handwriting, spoken language, written language, motor abilities, perceptual skills, study skills, personality, social skills, psychoneurology, speech, hearing, learning strategies.
Academic advising: Provided by academic advisers. Students with LD may take up to 12 credits each term; most take 12 credits; 12 credits required to maintain full-time status.
Subject-area tutoring: Offered one-on-one by peer tutors. Available in some subjects.

University of Wisconsin Center Marathon County (continued)

GENERAL COLLEGE INFORMATION

State-supported, 2-year, coed. Part of University of Wisconsin System. Awards associate degrees. Founded 1933. *Setting:* 7-acre small-town campus. *Total enrollment:* 815. *Faculty:* 71 (49 full-time, 85% with terminal degrees, 22 part-time); student–undergrad faculty ratio is 16:1.
Enrollment Profile: 815 students from 3 states and territories, 13 other countries. 55% women, 45% men, 30% part-time, 97% state residents, 6% transferred in, 1% international, 26% 25 or older, 1% Native American, 1% Hispanic, 1% black, 1% Asian or Pacific Islander. *Areas of study chosen:* 13% business management and administrative services, 13% education, 13% liberal arts/general studies, 10% health professions and related sciences, 6% engineering and applied sciences, 5% fine arts, 5% natural resource sciences, 5% psychology, 5% social sciences, 3% biological and life sciences, 3% communications and journalism, 3% prelaw, 2% computer and information sciences, 2% English language/literature/letters, 2% premed, 1% agriculture, 1% architecture, 1% foreign language and literature, 1% mathematics, 1% performing arts, 1% philosophy, 1% physical sciences, 1% predentistry, 1% prevet, 1% vocational and home economics.
First-Year Class: 274 total. Of the students who applied, 95% were accepted. 10% from top 10% of their high school class, 28% from top quarter, 63% from top half. 2 National Merit Scholars, 9 valedictorians.
Graduation Requirements: 60 credits; math proficiency; 12 credits in natural and mathematical science.
Computers on Campus: 50 computers available on campus for general student use. Computer purchase/lease plans available. A campus-wide network can be accessed. Students can contact faculty members and/or advisers through e-mail. Computers for student use in computer center, classrooms, library provide access to the Internet/World Wide Web, on- and off-campus e-mail addresses. Staffed computer lab on campus provides training in use of computers, software. *Academic computing expenditure 1995–96:* $47,938.

EXPENSES

Expenses for 1996–97: *Application fee:* $28. State resident tuition: $1953 full-time. Nonresident tuition: $6562 full-time. Part-time tuition per semester ranges from $88.85 to $903.95 for state residents, $280.85 to $3016 for nonresidents. College room and board: $2580.
LD Services Contact: Ms. Joanne Judes, Director of Tutoring Services, University of Wisconsin Center–Marathon County, 518 South 7th Avenue, Wausau, WI 54401, 715-261-6255. Fax: 715-261-6333. Email: jjudes@uwc.edu.

UNIVERSITY OF WISCONSIN CENTER–MARINETTE COUNTY

Marinette, Wisconsin

LEARNING DISABILITIES SERVICES INFORMATION

Student Services currently serves undergraduate students with LD. Students diagnosed with ADD/ADHD are eligible for the same services available to students with LD.
Staff: 1 part-time staff member (coordinator).
Special Fees: No special fees are charged for services to students with LD.
Applications and admissions: *Required:* high school transcript, courses completed; *recommended:* high school IEP (Individualized Education Program), untimed or extended time SAT I or ACT, personal interview, autobiographical statement, letters of recommendation, psychoeducational report. Students may begin taking classes in fall or spring. *Application deadline:* continuous.

PROGRAM AND SERVICE COMPONENTS

Academic advising: Provided by unit staff members. Most students with LD take 12 credits each term; 12 credits required to maintain full-time status; 6 credits required to be eligible for financial aid.
Counseling services: Individual counseling.
Basic skills remediation: Offered one-on-one by regular teachers; computer-aided instruction also offered. Available in reading, math.
Subject-area tutoring: Offered one-on-one by peer tutors. Available in some subjects.
Special courses: Study skills. Most offered for credit; most enter into overall grade point average.
Auxiliary aids: Taped textbooks, word-processors with spell-check.
Auxiliary services: Alternative test arrangements, notetakers.

GENERAL COLLEGE INFORMATION

State-supported, 2-year, coed. Part of University of Wisconsin System. Awards associate degrees. Founded 1965. *Setting:* 36-acre small-town campus. *Endowment:* $200,000. *Total enrollment:* 354. *Faculty:* 14 full-time, 57% with terminal degrees, 7 part-time; student–undergrad faculty ratio is 20:1.
Enrollment Profile: 354 students from 2 states and territories, 6 other countries. 53% women, 1% men, 35% part-time, 61% state residents, 4% transferred in, 3% international, 33% 25 or older, 1% Native American, 1% Hispanic, 1% black, 1% Asian or Pacific Islander. *Areas of study chosen:* 100% liberal arts/general studies.
First-Year Class: 111 total; 234 applied, 100% were accepted, 47% of whom enrolled. 9% from top 10% of their high school class, 25% from top quarter, 58% from top half. 1 valedictorian.
Graduation Requirements: 60 credits; 12 credits of math/natural science.
Computers on Campus: 48 computers available on campus for general student use. A campus-wide network can be accessed. Students can contact faculty members and/or advisers through e-mail. Computers for student use in computer labs, library. Staffed computer lab on campus provides training in use of computers, software.

EXPENSES

Expenses for 1996–97: *Application fee:* $28. State resident tuition: $1904 full-time, $79.45 per credit part-time. Nonresident tuition: $6514 full-time, $271.45 per credit part-time. Full-time mandatory fees: $2.
LD Services Contact: Student Services Coordinator, University of Wisconsin Center–Marinette County, 750 West Bay Shore Street, Marinette, WI 54143-4299, 715-735-4301. Fax: 715-735-4307.

UNIVERSITY OF WISCONSIN CENTER–MARSHFIELD/WOOD COUNTY

Marshfield, Wisconsin

LEARNING DISABILITIES SERVICES INFORMATION

Student Services currently serves 14 undergraduates with LD. Students diagnosed with ADD/ADHD are eligible for the same services available to students with LD.
Staff: 4 full-time staff members, including director, associate director.
Special Fees: No special fees are charged for services to students with LD.
Applications and admissions: *Required:* high school transcript, class rank, courses completed, untimed ACT; *recommended:* high school grade point average, personal interview, psychoeducational report completed within 2 to 3 years. Students may begin taking classes in fall, spring, or summer. *Application deadline:* continuous.

PROGRAM AND SERVICE COMPONENTS

Special preparation or orientation: Optional orientation offered before registration.
Academic advising: Provided by unit staff members, academic advisers. Students with LD may take up to 18 credits each term; most take 6 to 15 credits; 12 credits required to maintain full-time status; 6 credits required to be eligible for financial aid.
Counseling services: Individual counseling.
Basic skills remediation: Offered one-on-one, in small groups, and in class-size groups by regular teachers. Available in math, written language.
Subject-area tutoring: Offered one-on-one, in small groups, and in class-size groups by professional teachers, peer tutors. Available in most subjects.
Special courses: Composition, math. None offered for credit.
Auxiliary aids: Taped textbooks, tape recorders, calculators, typewriters, word-processors with spell-check, personal computers.
Auxiliary services: Alternative test arrangements, notetakers, priority registration, advocacy.

GENERAL COLLEGE INFORMATION

State-supported, 2-year, coed. Part of University of Wisconsin System. Awards associate degrees. Founded 1964. *Setting:* 71-acre small-town campus. *Endowment:* $500,000. *Total enrollment:* 536. *Faculty:* 38 (18 full-time, 33% with terminal degrees, 20 part-time); student–undergrad faculty ratio is 14:1.

Enrollment Profile: 536 students from 9 states and territories, 2 other countries. 66% women, 34% men, 35% part-time, 99% state residents, 5% transferred in, 25% 25 or older, 1% Native American, 1% Hispanic, 1% black, 1% Asian or Pacific Islander. *Retention:* 82% of 1995 full-time freshmen returned.
First-Year Class: 198 total; 209 applied, 99% were accepted, 96% of whom enrolled. 11% from top 10% of their high school class, 31% from top quarter, 68% from top half. 2 valedictorians.
Graduation Requirements: 60 credits; 12 credits of math/science.
Computers on Campus: 20 computers available on campus for general student use. A computer is recommended for all students. A campus-wide network can be accessed. Students can contact faculty members and/or advisers through e-mail. Computers for student use in computer center, library provide access to the Internet/World Wide Web, on- and off-campus e-mail addresses. Staffed computer lab on campus provides training in use of computers, software. *Academic computing expenditure 1995–96:* $94,027.

EXPENSES

Expenses for 1996–97: *Application fee:* $28. State resident tuition: $1937 full-time, $80.85 per credit part-time. Nonresident tuition: $6546 full-time, $272.85 per credit part-time. Minnesota residents pay tuition at the rate they would pay if attending a comparable state-supported institution in Minnesota. Full-time mandatory fees: $2.
LD Services Contact: Dr. Susan Adams, Associate Director, Student Services, University of Wisconsin Center–Marshfield/Wood County, 2000 West 5th Street, Marshfield, WI 54449-0150, 715-389-6529.

UNIVERSITY OF WISCONSIN CENTER–ROCK COUNTY

Janesville, Wisconsin

LEARNING DISABILITIES SERVICES INFORMATION

Academic Skills Center began offering services in 1979. Currently the program serves 15 undergraduates with LD. Students diagnosed with ADD/ADHD are eligible for the same services available to students with LD.
Staff: 1 full-time, 8 part-time staff members, including director, associate director. Services provided by remediation specialists, tutors, counselor.
Special Fees: No special fees are charged for services to students with LD.
Applications and admissions: *Required:* high school transcript, grade point average, class rank, courses completed, untimed or extended time ACT, untimed SAT I, verification of disability and any information regarding necessary accommodations; *recommended:* extended time SAT I. Students may begin taking classes any term. *Application deadline:* continuous.

PROGRAM AND SERVICE COMPONENTS

Academic advising: Provided by unit staff members, academic advisers. Students with LD may take up to 16 credits each term; 12 credits required to maintain full-time status; 6 credits required to be eligible for financial aid.
Counseling services: Individual counseling, career counseling.
Basic skills remediation: Offered one-on-one, in small groups, and in class-size groups by LD teachers. Available in reading, math, spelling, written language, study skills.
Subject-area tutoring: Offered one-on-one and in small groups by professional teachers, peer tutors. Available in most subjects.
Special courses: College survival skills, composition, math, study skills. Most offered for credit; none enter into overall grade point average.
Auxiliary aids: Typewriters, word-processors with spell-check.
Auxiliary services: Advocacy.

GENERAL COLLEGE INFORMATION

State-supported, 2-year, coed. Part of University of Wisconsin System. Awards associate degrees. Founded 1966. *Setting:* 50-acre suburban campus with easy access to Milwaukee. *Total enrollment:* 700. *Faculty:* 38 (28 full-time, 68% with terminal degrees, 10 part-time); student–undergrad faculty ratio is 20:1.
Enrollment Profile: 700 students: 61% women, 39% men, 54% part-time, 99% state residents, 7% transferred in, 34% 25 or older, 1% Native American, 1% Hispanic, 5% black, 1% Asian or Pacific Islander.
First-Year Class: 172 total; 314 applied, 84% were accepted, 65% of whom enrolled. 4% from top 10% of their high school class, 18% from top quarter, 52% from top half.
Graduation Requirements: 60 credits; 2 science courses, including at least 1 lab science course; 2 math courses.
Computers on Campus: 40 computers available on campus for general student use. A campus-wide network can be accessed. Students can contact faculty members and/or advisers through e-mail. Computers for student use in computer center, computer labs, library provide access to the Internet/World Wide Web, on- and off-campus e-mail addresses. Staffed computer lab on campus provides training in use of computers, software.

EXPENSES

Expenses for 1996–97: *Application fee:* $28. State resident tuition: $1929 full-time, $80.55 per credit part-time. Nonresident tuition: $6538 full-time, $272.55 per credit part-time. Minnesota residents pay tuition at the rate they would pay if attending a comparable state-supported institution in Minnesota. Full-time mandatory fees: $2.
LD Services Contact: Dr. Mary Schlais, Associate Director, Academic Skills Center, University of Wisconsin Center–Rock County, 2909 Kellogg Avenue, Janesville, WI 53546, 608-758-6513.

UNIVERSITY OF WISCONSIN CENTER–SHEBOYGAN COUNTY

Sheboygan, Wisconsin

LEARNING DISABILITIES SERVICES INFORMATION

Student Services currently serves 10 undergraduates with LD. Students diagnosed with ADD/ADHD are eligible for the same services available to students with LD.
Staff: 2 full-time, 2 part-time staff members, including director, coordinator. Services provided by remediation specialists, tutors, counselors, diagnostic specialists.
Special Fees: No special fees are charged for services to students with LD.
Applications and admissions: *Required:* high school transcript, grade point average, class rank, psychoeducational report completed within 3 years; *recommended:* high school courses completed, extracurricular activities, IEP (Individualized Education Program), untimed or extended time ACT, letters of recommendation. Students may begin taking classes in fall, spring, or summer. *Application deadline:* continuous.
Special policies: The college has written policies regarding substitutions and waivers of admissions and degree requirements.

PROGRAM AND SERVICE COMPONENTS

Academic advising: Provided by unit staff members, academic advisers. Students with LD may take up to 16 credit hours each term; most take 12 credit hours; 12 credit hours required to maintain full-time status; 6 credit hours required to be eligible for financial aid.
Counseling services: Individual counseling, career counseling.
Basic skills remediation: Offered in class-size groups by regular teachers. Available in reading, math, spelling, written language, learning strategies, study skills, time management.
Subject-area tutoring: Offered one-on-one and in small groups by professional teachers, peer tutors. Available in all subjects.
Auxiliary aids: Taped textbooks, tape recorders, calculators, word-processors with spell-check, personal computers.
Auxiliary services: Alternative test arrangements, notetakers, priority registration, advocacy.

GENERAL COLLEGE INFORMATION

State-supported, 2-year, coed. Part of University of Wisconsin System. Awards associate degrees. Founded 1933. *Setting:* 75-acre small-town campus with easy access to Milwaukee. *Total enrollment:* 507. *Faculty:* 28 (23 full-time, 52% with terminal degrees, 5 part-time); student–undergrad faculty ratio is 18:1.
Enrollment Profile: 507 students: 53% women, 47% men, 46% part-time, 99% state residents, 5% transferred in, 0% international, 31% 25 or older, 1% Native American, 2% Hispanic, 1% black, 1% Asian or Pacific Islander. *Retention:* 69% of 1995 full-time freshmen returned. *Areas of study chosen:* 25% liberal arts/general studies, 10% education, 9% business management and administrative services, 3% psychology, 2% communications and journalism, 2% computer and information sciences, 2% engineering and applied sciences, 2% health professions and related

University of Wisconsin Center–Sheboygan County (continued)

sciences, 1% agriculture, 1% architecture, 1% biological and life sciences, 1% English language/literature/letters, 1% fine arts, 1% library and information studies, 1% predentistry, 1% premed.
First-Year Class: 163 total; 206 applied, 100% were accepted, 79% of whom enrolled. 1% from top 10% of their high school class, 22% from top quarter, 53% from top half.
Graduation Requirements: 60 credit hours; math/science requirements vary according to program.
Computers on Campus: 40 computers available on campus for general student use. A computer is recommended for some students. A campus-wide network can be accessed. Students can contact faculty members and/or advisers through e-mail. Computers for student use in computer labs, library, physics lab provide access to the Internet/World Wide Web, on- and off-campus e-mail addresses. Staffed computer lab on campus provides training in use of computers.

EXPENSES

Expenses for 1996–97: *Application fee:* $28. State resident tuition: $1941 full-time, $81.90 per credit hour part-time. Nonresident tuition: $6550 full-time, $273.90 per credit hour part-time. Minnesota residents pay tuition at the rate they would pay if attending a comparable state-supported institution in Minnesota. Full-time mandatory fees: $2.
LD Services Contact: Dr. Mary Ann Searle, Director of Student Services, University of Wisconsin Center–Sheboygan County, 1 University Drive, Sheboygan, WI 53081-4789, 414-459-6633. Fax: 414-459-6602. Email: msearle@uwc.edu.

UTICA SCHOOL OF COMMERCE

Utica, New York

LEARNING DISABILITIES SERVICES INFORMATION

Learning Center began offering services in 1994. Currently the program serves 6 undergraduates with LD. Students diagnosed with ADD/ADHD are eligible for the same services available to students with LD.
Staff: 2 part-time staff members, including director. Services provided by tutors.
Special Fees: No special fees are charged for services to students with LD.
Applications and admissions: *Required:* high school transcript, grade point average, class rank, courses completed, extended time SAT I or untimed ACT, psychoeducational report completed within 3 years; *recommended:* high school extracurricular activities, extended time ACT, personal interview, letters of recommendation. Students may begin taking classes any term. *Application deadline:* continuous.

PROGRAM AND SERVICE COMPONENTS

Academic advising: Provided by academic advisers. Students with LD may take up to 18 quarter credits each term; most take 12 to 15 quarter credits; 12 quarter credits required to maintain full-time status and be eligible for financial aid.
Basic skills remediation: Offered one-on-one and in small groups by regular teachers, teacher trainees; computer-aided instruction also offered. Available in reading, math, spoken language, written language, learning strategies, study skills, time management, social skills, speech.
Subject-area tutoring: Offered one-on-one, in small groups, and in class-size groups by professional teachers, peer tutors, professional tutors trained in the particular subject area. Available in all subjects.
Special courses: College survival skills, reading, vocabulary development, communication skills, composition, learning strategies, word processing, time management, math, typing, study skills, career planning. Some offered for credit; some enter into overall grade point average.
Auxiliary aids: Tape recorders, calculators, typewriters, word-processors with spell-check, personal computers, large print reader.
Auxiliary services: Alternative test arrangements, notetakers, advocacy.

GENERAL COLLEGE INFORMATION

Proprietary, 2-year, primarily women. Awards associate degrees. Founded 1896. *Setting:* 2-acre urban campus. *Total enrollment:* 573. *Faculty:* 70 (2% of full-time faculty have terminal degrees); student–undergrad faculty ratio is 13:1.
Enrollment Profile: 573 students from 3 states and territories. 83% women, 17% men, 19% part-time, 99% state residents, 21% transferred in, 0% international, 29% 25 or older, 2% Hispanic, 2% black. *Retention:* 66% of 1995 full-time freshmen returned. *Areas of study chosen:* 100% business management and administrative services. *Most popular recent majors:* business administration/commerce/management, data processing, accounting.
First-Year Class: 193 total; 325 applied. 15% from top 10% of their high school class, 50% from top half.
Graduation Requirements: 90 quarter credits; 1 semester of math; computer course.
Computers on Campus: 156 computers available on campus for general student use. Computers for student use in learning resource center, classrooms, library. Staffed computer lab on campus provides training in use of computers, software.

EXPENSES

Expenses for 1996–97: *Application fee:* $20. Tuition: $5550 full-time, $125 per credit hour part-time.
LD Services Contact: Mrs. Wendy Cary, Director of Special Programs/Placement, Utica School of Commerce, 201 Bleecker Street, Utica, NY 13501, 315-697-8200. Fax: 315-697-2805.

VANCE-GRANVILLE COMMUNITY COLLEGE

Henderson, North Carolina

LEARNING DISABILITIES SERVICES INFORMATION

Student Services Office currently serves 25 undergraduates with LD. Students diagnosed with ADD/ADHD are eligible for the same services available to students with LD.
Staff: 30 full-time staff members, including director, assistant director. Services provided by remediation specialists, tutors, counselors, diagnostic specialist.
Special Fees: No special fees are charged for services to students with LD.
Applications and admissions: *Required:* high school transcript, courses completed, untimed ACT, psychoeducational report completed within 2 years; *recommended:* personal interview. Students may begin taking classes in fall, spring, or summer. *Application deadline:* continuous.
Special policies: The college has written policies regarding grade forgiveness; substitutions and waivers of admissions, graduation, and degree requirements.

PROGRAM AND SERVICE COMPONENTS

Special preparation or orientation: Optional summer program offered prior to entering college.
Academic advising: Provided by unit staff members. Students with LD may take up to 15 semester credit hours each term; most take 12 semester credit hours; 12 semester credit hours required to maintain full-time status and be eligible for financial aid.
Counseling services: Individual counseling, small-group counseling, career counseling.
Basic skills remediation: Offered in class-size groups by regular teachers. Available in reading, math, spoken language, written language.
Subject-area tutoring: Offered one-on-one by peer tutors. Available in most subjects.
Auxiliary aids: Taped textbooks, tape recorders, calculators, typewriters, word-processors with spell-check, talking computers.
Auxiliary services: Alternative test arrangements, notetakers, priority registration.

GENERAL COLLEGE INFORMATION

State-supported, 2-year, coed. Part of North Carolina Community College System. Awards associate degrees. Founded 1969. *Setting:* 83-acre rural campus with easy access to Raleigh. *Endowment:* $2.2 million. *Educational spending 1995–96:* $2003 per undergrad. *Total enrollment:* 4,234. *Faculty:* 262 (86 full-time, 5% with terminal degrees, 176 part-time); student–undergrad faculty ratio is 16:1.
Enrollment Profile: 4,234 students from 7 states and territories. 66% women, 34% men, 52% part-time, 99% state residents, 4% transferred in, 0% international, 56% 25 or older, 1% Native American, 1% Hispanic, 44% black, 0% Asian or Pacific Islander. *Retention:* 71% of 1995 full-time freshmen returned. *Areas of study chosen:* 25% business management and administrative services, 21% liberal arts/general studies, 21% vocational and home economics, 15% computer and information sciences, 10% health professions and related sciences, 5% education, 3% engineering and applied sciences. *Most popular recent majors:* business administration/commerce/management, liberal arts/general studies.

First-Year Class: 792 total; 1,215 applied, 95% were accepted, 69% of whom enrolled. 4% from top 10% of their high school class, 20% from top quarter, 45% from top half.
Graduation Requirements: 1 math course; computer course (varies by major); internship (some majors).
Computers on Campus: 184 computers available on campus for general student use. A campus-wide network can be accessed from off-campus. Students can contact faculty members and/or advisers through e-mail. Computers for student use in computer center, computer labs, learning resource center, library provide access to the Internet/World Wide Web, on- and off-campus e-mail addresses. Staffed computer lab on campus provides training in use of computers, software. *Academic computing expenditure 1995–96:* $218,396.

EXPENSES

Expenses for 1997–98: State resident tuition: $560 full-time, $20 per semester hour part-time. Nonresident tuition: $4564 full-time, $163 per semester hour part-time. Part-time mandatory fees: $10 per semester. Full-time mandatory fees: $28.
LD Services Contact: Ms. Lynn Blackburn, Dean of Student Services, Vance-Granville Community College, PO Box 917, Henderson, NC 27536, 919-492-2061. Fax: 919-430-0460.

VERMILION COMMUNITY COLLEGE

Ely, Minnesota

LEARNING DISABILITIES SERVICES INFORMATION

Student Support Services/Office of Disability Services began offering services in 1986. Currently the program serves 64 undergraduates with LD. Students diagnosed with ADD/ADHD are eligible for the same services available to students with LD.
Staff: 1 full-time staff member (coordinator). Services provided by tutors, counselor.
Special Fees: No special fees are charged for services to students with LD.
Applications and admissions: *Required:* high school transcript, grade point average, class rank, courses completed; *recommended:* high school extracurricular activities, untimed SAT I or ACT, personal interview, autobiographical statement, letters of recommendation, psychoeducational report completed within 4 years. Students may begin taking classes any term. *Application deadline:* continuous.

PROGRAM AND SERVICE COMPONENTS

Academic advising: Provided by academic advisers. Students with LD may take up to 18 quarter hours each term; most take 16 quarter hours; 12 quarter hours required to maintain full-time status and be eligible for financial aid.
Counseling services: Individual counseling, career counseling.
Basic skills remediation: Offered in class-size groups by regular teachers. Available in reading, math, study skills.
Subject-area tutoring: Offered one-on-one by peer tutors. Available in all subjects.
Special courses: Reading, composition, math, study skills, career planning, physical and biological sciences. All offered for credit; all enter into overall grade point average.
Auxiliary aids: Taped textbooks, tape recorders, calculators, typewriters, word-processors with spell-check, spell checkers, phonetic dictionaries.
Auxiliary services: Alternative test arrangements, notetakers, priority registration, advocacy.

GENERAL COLLEGE INFORMATION

State-supported, 2-year, coed. Part of Minnesota State Colleges and Universities System. Awards associate degrees. Founded 1922. *Setting:* 5-acre rural campus. *Total enrollment:* 735. *Faculty:* 102 (32 full-time, 70 part-time); student–undergrad faculty ratio is 15:1.
Enrollment Profile: 735 students from 12 states and territories, 4 other countries. 35% women, 65% men, 13% part-time, 89% state residents, 50% live on campus, 1% international, 18% 25 or older, 1% Native American, 0% Hispanic, 8% black. *Retention:* 73% of 1995 full-time freshmen returned. *Areas of study chosen:* 50% natural resource sciences, 10% biological and life sciences, 10% education, 10% liberal arts/general studies, 5% computer and information sciences, 5% engineering and applied sciences, 5% health professions and related sciences, 5% psychology. *Most popular recent majors:* law enforcement/police sciences, natural resource management, water resources.
First-Year Class: 390 total. Of the students who applied, 96% were accepted, 61% of whom enrolled.
Graduation Requirements: 96 quarter hours; math/science requirements vary according to program; computer course; internship (some majors).
Computers on Campus: 30 computers available on campus for general student use. A campus-wide network can be accessed from off-campus. Students can contact faculty members and/or advisers through e-mail. Computers for student use in computer labs, library, clerical lab provide access to the Internet/World Wide Web, on- and off-campus e-mail addresses. Staffed computer lab on campus provides training in use of computers, software.

EXPENSES

Expenses for 1996–97: *Application fee:* $20. State resident tuition: $2286 full-time, $47.62 per quarter hour part-time. Nonresident tuition: $4283 full-time, $89.22 per quarter hour part-time. College room and board: $3420 (minimum). College room only: $2040.
LD Services Contact: Ms. Lisa C. Bestul, Student Support Services Director/Disabilities Coordinator, Vermilion Community College, 1900 East Camp Street, Ely, MN 55731, 218-365-7214. Fax: 218-365-7207. Email: l.bestul@vr.cc.mn.us.

VERMONT TECHNICAL COLLEGE

Randolph Center, Vermont

LEARNING DISABILITIES SERVICES INFORMATION

Services for Students with Disabilities began offering services in 1988. Students diagnosed with ADD/ADHD are eligible for the same services available to students with LD.
Staff: 1 full-time, 25 part-time staff members, including director. Services provided by remediation specialists, tutors, counselors, diagnostic specialists.
Special Fees: No special fees are charged for services to students with LD.
Applications and admissions: *Required:* high school transcript, grade point average, courses completed, psychoeducational report completed within 3 years; *recommended:* high school class rank, extracurricular activities, IEP (Individualized Education Program), extended time SAT I or ACT, personal interview, autobiographical statement, letters of recommendation. Students may begin taking classes in fall, spring, or summer. *Application deadline:* continuous.

PROGRAM AND SERVICE COMPONENTS

Special preparation or orientation: Optional orientation offered before registration.
Diagnostic testing: Intelligence, reading, math, spelling, handwriting, spoken language, written language, motor abilities, perceptual skills, personality, psychoneurology, hearing.
Academic advising: Provided by unit staff members, academic advisers. Students with LD may take up to 19 credit hours each term; most take 15 credit hours; 12 credit hours required to maintain full-time status and be eligible for financial aid.
Counseling services: Individual counseling, small-group counseling, career counseling.
Basic skills remediation: Offered one-on-one, in small groups, and in class-size groups by regular teachers, tutors, paraprofessional tutors, math/science specialist; computer-aided instruction also offered. Available in reading, math, spoken language, written language, learning strategies, study skills, time management, computer skills, self-advocacy skills.
Subject-area tutoring: Offered one-on-one and in small groups by peer tutors, paraprofessional tutors. Available in most subjects.
Special courses: Reading, vocabulary development, composition, learning strategies, word processing, math. Most offered for credit; some enter into overall grade point average.
Auxiliary aids: Tape recorders, personal computers, Arkenstone Reader, computers and miscellaneous resources of Rehabilitation Engineering Technology Department.
Auxiliary services: Alternative test arrangements, priority registration, advocacy.

GENERAL COLLEGE INFORMATION

State-supported, primarily 2-year, coed. Part of Vermont State Colleges System. Awards associate, bachelor's degrees. Founded 1866. *Setting:* 544-acre rural campus. *Endowment:* $1.8 million. *Educational spending*

1995–96: $4615 per undergrad. *Total enrollment:* 848. *Faculty:* 86 (66 full-time, 32% with terminal degrees, 20 part-time); student–undergrad faculty ratio is 12:1.
Enrollment Profile: 848 students from 13 states and territories, 3 other countries. 34% women, 66% men, 9% part-time, 99% state residents, 60% live on campus, 15% transferred in, 1% international, 19% 25 or older, 0% Native American, 0% Hispanic, 1% black, 1% Asian or Pacific Islander. *Retention:* 75% of 1995 full-time freshmen returned. *Areas of study chosen:* 58% engineering and applied sciences, 12% agriculture, 12% health professions and related sciences, 9% business management and administrative services, 7% computer and information sciences, 2% biological and life sciences.
First-Year Class: 342 total; 662 applied, 89% were accepted, 58% of whom enrolled. 15% from top 10% of their high school class, 45% from top quarter, 80% from top half. 3 class presidents.
Graduation Requirements: 67 credit hours for associate, 132 credit hours for bachelor's; computer course; internship (some majors).
Computers on Campus: 175 computers available on campus for general student use. A campus-wide network can be accessed from student residence rooms and from off-campus. Students can contact faculty members and/or advisers through e-mail. Computers for student use in computer center, computer labs, learning resource center, classrooms, library, student center, dorms provide access to the Internet/World Wide Web, on- and off-campus e-mail addresses. Staffed computer lab on campus (open 24 hours a day) provides training in use of computers, software. *Academic computing expenditure 1995–96:* $200,226.

EXPENSES

Expenses for 1997–98: *Application fee:* $30. State resident tuition: $4584 full-time, $191 per credit hour part-time. Nonresident tuition: $9168 full-time, $382 per credit hour part-time. Part-time mandatory fees per semester range from $21.50 to $293.37. Tuition for nonresidents who are eligible for the New England Regional Student Program: $6912 full-time, $288 per credit hour part-time. Full-time mandatory fees: $640. College room and board: $4960 (minimum). College room only: $2928 (minimum).
LD Services Contact: Ms. Barbara Bendix, Director of Services for Students with Disabilities, Vermont Technical College, PO Box 500, Randolph Center, VT 05061, 802-728-1278. Fax: 802-728-1390. Email: bbendix@vtc.vsc.edu.

VILLA MARIA COLLEGE OF BUFFALO

Buffalo, New York

LEARNING DISABILITIES SERVICES INFORMATION

Learning Support Center began offering services in 1985. Currently the program serves 20 undergraduates with LD. Students diagnosed with ADD/ADHD are eligible for the same services available to students with LD.
Staff: 4 full-time, 7 part-time staff members, including director, tutors. Services provided by tutors.
Special Fees: No special fees are charged for services to students with LD.
Applications and admissions: *Required:* high school transcript, grade point average, class rank, courses completed, IEP (Individualized Education Program), extended time SAT I, personal interview, psychoeducational report completed within 2 years. Students may begin taking classes in fall, spring, or summer. *Application deadline:* continuous.
Special policies: The college has written policies regarding grade forgiveness; substitutions and waivers of admissions and degree requirements.

PROGRAM AND SERVICE COMPONENTS

Special preparation or orientation: Optional summer program offered prior to entering college.
Diagnostic testing: Reading, math, spelling, written language, study skills, learning strategies.
Academic advising: Provided by academic advisers. Students with LD may take up to 17 credits each term; most take 12 credits; 12 credits required to maintain full-time status; 6 credits required to be eligible for financial aid.
Counseling services: Individual counseling, small-group counseling, career counseling, self-advocacy training.
Basic skills remediation: Offered in class-size groups by regular teachers. Available in reading, math, spelling, spoken language, written language, learning strategies, study skills, time management, social skills.
Subject area tutoring: Offered one-on-one and in small groups by peer tutors, professional tutors. Available in most subjects.
Special courses: Reading, vocabulary development, communication skills, composition, time management, math, study skills, career planning. Some offered for credit; some enter into overall grade point average.
Auxiliary aids: Taped textbooks, tape recorders, calculators, word-processors with spell-check.
Auxiliary services: Alternative test arrangements, notetakers, advocacy.
Campus support group: A special student organization is available to students with LD.

GENERAL COLLEGE INFORMATION

Independent Roman Catholic, 2-year, coed. Awards associate degrees. Founded 1960. *Setting:* 9-acre suburban campus. *Endowment:* $581,063. *Research spending 1995–96:* $36,440. *Educational spending 1995–96:* $2742 per undergrad. *Total enrollment:* 334. *Faculty:* 51 (15 full-time, 15% with terminal degrees, 36 part-time).
Enrollment Profile: 334 students: 81% women, 19% men, 27% part-time, 99% state residents, 14% transferred in, 44% 25 or older, 2% Native American, 2% Hispanic, 17% black, 0% Asian or Pacific Islander. *Retention:* 58% of 1995 full-time freshmen returned. *Areas of study chosen:* 22% education, 19% business management and administrative services, 18% architecture, 11% liberal arts/general studies, 11% performing arts, 8% communications and journalism, 5% computer and information sciences, 4% health professions and related sciences, 2% fine arts. *Most popular recent majors:* early childhood education, interior design, liberal arts/general studies.
First-Year Class: 158 total; 278 applied, 78% were accepted, 73% of whom enrolled. 6% from top 10% of their high school class, 14% from top quarter, 38% from top half.
Graduation Requirements: 61 credits; math/science requirements vary according to program; computer course for graphic design, interior design, photography, business majors; internship (some majors).
Computers on Campus: 76 computers available on campus for general student use. Computer purchase/lease plans available. A campus-wide network can be accessed from off-campus. Students can contact faculty members and/or advisers through e-mail. Computers for student use in computer labs, learning resource center, classrooms, library, career center provide access to the Internet/World Wide Web, on-campus e-mail addresses. Staffed computer lab on campus provides training in use of computers, software. *Academic computing expenditure 1995–96:* $74,375.

EXPENSES

Expenses for 1997–98: *Application fee:* $25. Tuition: $7200 full-time, $240 per credit part-time. Part-time mandatory fees per semester range from $25.90 to $34.90. Full-time mandatory fees: $230.
LD Services Contact: Ms. Arlene Sullivan, Director, Learning Support Center, Villa Maria College of Buffalo, 240 Pine Ridge Road, Buffalo, NY 14225-3999, 716-896-0700 Ext. 417. Fax: 716-896-0705.

VIRGINIA HIGHLANDS COMMUNITY COLLEGE

Abingdon, Virginia

LEARNING DISABILITIES SERVICES INFORMATION

Project EXCEL began offering services in 1989. Currently the program serves 20 undergraduates with LD. Students diagnosed with ADD/ADHD are eligible for the same services available to students with LD.
Staff: 4 full-time staff members, including director, program assistant. Services provided by tutors, counselors.
Special Fees: No special fees are charged for services to students with LD.
Applications and admissions: *Required:* high school transcript; *recommended:* psychoeducational report completed within 3 years. Students may begin taking classes in summer only. *Application deadline:* continuous.

PROGRAM AND SERVICE COMPONENTS

Academic advising: Provided by unit staff members, academic advisers. Students with LD may take up to 12 semester hours each term; most take 12 semester hours; 12 semester hours required to maintain full-time status and be eligible for financial aid.
Counseling services: Individual counseling, small-group counseling, career counseling.

Basic skills remediation: Offered in class-size groups by regular teachers. Available in reading, math, handwriting, written language, learning strategies, study skills, time management.
Subject-area tutoring: Offered one-on-one by peer tutors. Available in most subjects.
Special courses: Learning strategies. All offered for credit; all enter into overall grade point average.
Auxiliary aids: Taped textbooks, tape recorders, calculators, typewriters, word-processors with spell-check, personal computers, spell checkers.
Auxiliary services: Alternative test arrangements, notetakers.

GENERAL COLLEGE INFORMATION

State-supported, 2-year, coed. Part of Virginia Community College System. Awards associate degrees. Founded 1967. *Setting:* 100-acre small-town campus. *Total enrollment:* 1,834. *Faculty:* 131 (47 full-time, 84 part-time); student–undergrad faculty ratio is 17:1.
Enrollment Profile: 1,834 students from 7 states and territories. 59% women, 41% men, 53% part-time, 96% state residents, 9% transferred in, 0% international, 52% 25 or older, 1% Native American, 1% Hispanic, 3% black, 0% Asian or Pacific Islander. *Most popular recent majors:* business administration/commerce/management, education, liberal arts/general studies.
First-Year Class: 446 total; 700 applied, 100% were accepted, 64% of whom enrolled. 15% from top 10% of their high school class, 35% from top quarter, 65% from top half.
Graduation Requirements: 65 semester hours; math/science requirements vary according to program; computer course for most majors.
Computers on Campus: 240 computers available on campus for general student use. A campus-wide network can be accessed from off-campus. Students can contact faculty members and/or advisers through e-mail. Computers for student use in computer center, computer labs, library, learning, CAD, math labs provide access to the Internet/World Wide Web, on- and off-campus e-mail addresses. Staffed computer lab on campus.

EXPENSES

Expenses for 1997–98: State resident tuition: $1493 full-time, $46.65 per semester hour part-time. Nonresident tuition: $4992 full-time, $156 per semester hour part-time. Part-time mandatory fees: $1 per semester hour. Full-time mandatory fees: $32.
LD Services Contact: Ms. Charlotte L. Faris, Director, Project EXCEL, Virginia Highlands Community College, PO Box 828, Abingdon, VA 24210, 540-628-6094. Fax: 540-628-7576.

VIRGINIA WESTERN COMMUNITY COLLEGE

Roanoke, Virginia

LEARNING DISABILITIES SERVICES INFORMATION

Student Support Services currently serves undergraduate students with LD. Students diagnosed with ADD/ADHD are eligible for the same services available to students with LD.
Staff: 4 full-time, 1 part-time staff members, including director. Services provided by tutors, counselors, LD specialists.
Special Fees: No special fees are charged for services to students with LD.
Applications and admissions: *Required:* psychoeducational report completed within 3 years; *recommended:* high school transcript, grade point average, personal interview. Students may begin taking classes any term. *Application deadline:* continuous.
Special policies: The college has written policies regarding grade forgiveness; substitutions and waivers of graduation and degree requirements.

PROGRAM AND SERVICE COMPONENTS

Diagnostic testing: Intelligence, reading, math, written language, study skills, learning strategies.
Academic advising: Provided by unit staff members. Students with LD may take up to 18 semester hours each term; most take 6 to 9 semester hours.
Counseling services: Individual counseling, career counseling, self-advocacy training.
Basic skills remediation: Offered one-on-one and in class-size groups by regular teachers, remediation specialists. Available in reading, math, spelling, written language, learning strategies, study skills, time management, social skills.
Subject-area tutoring: Offered one-on-one by peer tutors. Available in most subjects.
Special courses: College survival skills, learning strategies, study skills, career planning. All offered for credit; all enter into overall grade point average.
Auxiliary aids: Taped textbooks, tape recorders, calculators, typewriters, word-processors with spell-check, personal computers, talking computers, optical character readers, grammar checkers.
Auxiliary services: Alternative test arrangements, notetakers, priority registration, advocacy, readers.
Campus support group: A special student organization is available to students with LD.

GENERAL COLLEGE INFORMATION

State-supported, 2-year, coed. Part of Virginia Community College System. Awards associate degrees. Founded 1966. *Setting:* 70-acre urban campus. *Total enrollment:* 7,201. *Faculty:* 290 (90 full-time, 200 part-time).
Enrollment Profile: 7,201 students from 52 states and territories, 10 other countries. 58% women, 42% men, 76% part-time, 98% state residents, 20% transferred in, 55% 25 or older, 1% Native American, 1% Hispanic, 8% black, 1% Asian or Pacific Islander. *Most popular recent majors:* liberal arts/general studies, business administration/commerce/management, science.
First-Year Class: 1,654 total. Of the students who applied, 100% were accepted, 66% of whom enrolled. 7% from top 10% of their high school class, 15% from top quarter, 50% from top half.
Graduation Requirements: 60 semester hours; computer course.
Computers on Campus: 200 computers available on campus for general student use. A campus-wide network can be accessed from off-campus. Students can contact faculty members and/or advisers through e-mail. Computers for student use in computer center, library, engineering building provide access to the Internet/World Wide Web, on- and off-campus e-mail addresses. Staffed computer lab on campus (open 24 hours a day) provides training in use of computers, software.

EXPENSES

Expenses for 1997–98: State resident tuition: $1430 full-time, $47.65 per semester hour part-time. Nonresident tuition: $4710 full-time, $157 per semester hour part-time. Part-time mandatory fees: $2 per semester. Full-time mandatory fees: $4.
LD Services Contact: Mr. Michael C. Henderson, Director, Student Support Services, Virginia Western Community College, PO Box 14007, Roanoke, VA 24038, 540-857-7286. Fax: 540-857-7302.

VISTA COMMUNITY COLLEGE

Berkeley, California

LEARNING DISABILITIES SERVICES INFORMATION

Disabled Students Program and Services began offering services in 1993. Currently the program serves 40 undergraduates with LD. Students diagnosed with ADD/ADHD are eligible for the same services available to students with LD.
Staff: 1 full-time, 2 part-time staff members, including coordinator, LD specialists. Services provided by tutors, counselors.
Special Fees: $6.50 for testing class (one-time charge).
Applications and admissions: *Required:* General Assessment Test (for math and English); *recommended:* psychoeducational report completed within 3 years. Students may begin taking classes any term. *Application deadline:* continuous.

PROGRAM AND SERVICE COMPONENTS

Diagnostic testing: Intelligence, reading, math, spelling, handwriting, spoken language, written language, perceptual skills, personality, learning strategies.
Academic advising: Provided by academic advisers. Students with LD may take up to 18 semester units each term; most take 9 to 12 semester units; LD specialist determines the number of semester units required to maintain full-time status; 12 semester units required to be eligible for financial aid.
Counseling services: Individual counseling, career counseling.
Subject-area tutoring: Offered one-on-one and in small groups by LD specialists. Available in some subjects.
Auxiliary aids: Taped textbooks, tape recorders, calculators, typewriters, word-processors with spell-check, spell checkers (hand-held).

Vista Community College (continued)

Auxiliary services: Alternative test arrangements, notetakers, priority registration.

GENERAL COLLEGE INFORMATION

State and locally supported, 2-year, coed. Part of Peralta Community College District System. Awards associate degrees. Founded 1974. *Setting:* urban campus with easy access to San Francisco. *Research spending 1995–96:* $23,897. *Educational spending 1995–96:* $485 per undergrad. *Total enrollment:* 3,318. *Faculty:* 125 (18 full-time, 107 part-time).

Enrollment Profile: 3,318 students: 66% women, 34% men, 81% part-time, 99% state residents, 17% transferred in, 0% international, 63% 25 or older, 1% Native American, 12% Hispanic, 35% black, 9% Asian or Pacific Islander. *Retention:* 48% of 1995 full-time freshmen returned. *Areas of study chosen:* 15% interdisciplinary studies, 8% business management and administrative services, 8% education, 7% computer and information sciences, 4% fine arts, 4% liberal arts/general studies, 4% social sciences, 2% biological and life sciences, 2% engineering and applied sciences, 2% health professions and related sciences, 2% psychology, 1% architecture, 1% communications and journalism, 1% foreign language and literature.

First-Year Class: 722 total. Of the students who applied, 100% were accepted.

Graduation Requirements: 60 semester hours; 3 semester hours of math; computer course.

Computers on Campus: 10 computers available on campus for general student use. Computers for student use in computer labs.

EXPENSES

Expenses for 1997–98: State resident tuition: $0 full-time. Nonresident tuition: $3660 full-time, $122 per semester hour part-time. Part-time mandatory fees: $13 per semester hour. Full-time mandatory fees: $394.

LD Services Contact: Ms. Ponnie Rasmussen, Disabled Students Program and Services Coordinator/Counselor, Vista Community College, 2020 Milvia Street, Berkeley, CA 94704, 510-841-8431 Ext. 221. Fax: 510-841-7333.

WARREN COUNTY COMMUNITY COLLEGE

Washington, New Jersey

LEARNING DISABILITIES SERVICES INFORMATION

Office of Student Development began offering services in 1993. Currently the program serves 90 undergraduates with LD. Students diagnosed with ADD/ADHD are eligible for the same services available to students with LD.

Staff: 1 full-time staff member (director).

Special Fees: No special fees are charged for services to students with LD.

Applications and admissions: *Required:* psychoeducational report completed within 3 years; *recommended:* high school transcript, courses completed, IEP (Individualized Education Program), personal interview. Students may begin taking classes any term. *Application deadline:* continuous.

Special policies: The college has written policies regarding grade forgiveness; substitutions and waivers of degree requirements.

PROGRAM AND SERVICE COMPONENTS

Academic advising: Provided by unit staff members, academic advisers. Most students with LD take 3 to 12 credits each term; 3 credits required to be eligible for financial aid.

Counseling services: Individual counseling, small-group counseling, career counseling.

Auxiliary aids: Word-processors with spell-check, personal computers.

Auxiliary services: Alternative test arrangements, notetakers, priority registration.

GENERAL COLLEGE INFORMATION

State and locally supported, 2-year, coed. Part of New Jersey Commission on Higher Education. Awards associate degrees. Founded 1981. *Setting:* 77-acre rural campus. *Total enrollment:* 1,619. *Faculty:* 61 (17 full-time, 14% with terminal degrees, 44 part-time).

Enrollment Profile: 1,619 students from 4 states and territories, 64% women, 36% men, 77% part-time, 97% state residents, 16% transferred in, 0% international, 57% 25 or older, 0% Native American, 2% Hispanic, 3% black, 0% Asian or Pacific Islander. *Most popular recent majors:* liberal arts/general studies, business administration/commerce/management, paralegal studies.

First-Year Class: 607 total. Of the students who applied, 100% were accepted.

Graduation Requirements: 64 credits; 3 credits of math/science.

Computers on Campus: 85 computers available on campus for general student use. A campus-wide network can be accessed from off-campus. Students can contact faculty members and/or advisers through e-mail. Computers for student use in computer center, computer labs, learning resource center, classrooms, library, science labs provide access to the Internet/World Wide Web, on- and off-campus e-mail addresses. Staffed computer lab on campus provides training in use of computers.

EXPENSES

Expenses for 1997–98: *Application fee:* $15. Area resident tuition: $2144 full-time, $67 per credit part-time. State resident tuition: $4288 full-time, $134 per credit part-time. Nonresident tuition: $6432 full-time, $201 per credit part-time. Part-time mandatory fees: $9.50 per credit. Full-time mandatory fees: $304.

LD Services Contact: Ms. Peggy Heim, Director of Admissions and Counseling, Warren County Community College, 475 Route 57 West, Washington, NJ 07882, 973-835-9222. Fax: 973-689-5824. Email: pheim@mail.warren.cc.nj.us.

WASHINGTON STATE COMMUNITY COLLEGE

Marietta, Ohio

LEARNING DISABILITIES SERVICES INFORMATION

Student Support Services/Opportunity Scholars began offering services in 1988. Currently the program serves 63 undergraduates with LD. Students diagnosed with ADD/ADHD are eligible for the same services available to students with LD.

Staff: 2 full-time, 2 part-time staff members, including director, coordinator. Services provided by diagnostic specialists.

Special Fees: No special fees are charged for services to students with LD.

Applications and admissions: *Required:* personal interview; *recommended:* high school transcript, IEP (Individualized Education Program), psychoeducational report completed within 3 years. Students may begin taking classes any term. *Application deadline:* continuous.

Special policies: The college has written policies regarding substitutions and waivers of admissions, graduation, and degree requirements.

PROGRAM AND SERVICE COMPONENTS

Academic advising: Provided by unit staff members, academic advisers. Most students with LD take 12 credit hours each term; 12 credit hours required to maintain full-time status; 6 credit hours required to be eligible for financial aid.

Counseling services: Individual counseling, small-group counseling, career counseling.

Auxiliary aids: Taped textbooks, tape recorders, calculators, word-processors with spell-check, optical character readers.

Auxiliary services: Alternative test arrangements, notetakers.

GENERAL COLLEGE INFORMATION

State-supported, 2-year, coed. Part of Ohio Board of Regents. Awards associate degrees. Founded 1971. *Setting:* small-town campus. *Total enrollment:* 2,019. *Faculty:* 132 (61 full-time, 71 part-time).

Enrollment Profile: 2,019 students from 5 states and territories. 60% women, 40% men, 46% part-time, 90% state residents, 5% transferred in, 0% international, 51% 25 or older, 1% Native American, 1% Hispanic, 2% black, 1% Asian or Pacific Islander. *Retention:* 67% of 1995 full-time freshmen returned. *Areas of study chosen:* 16% business management and administrative services, 12% engineering and applied sciences, 10% health professions and related sciences, 4% computer and information sciences, 4% education, 4% liberal arts/general studies, 3% social sciences, 2% biological and life sciences, 2% communications and journalism, 1% mathematics, 1% physical sciences. *Most popular recent majors:* automotive technologies, nursing, secretarial studies/office management.

First-Year Class: 659 total; 915 applied, 100% were accepted, 72% of whom enrolled.
Graduation Requirements: 90 credit hours; computer course.
Computers on Campus: 175 computers available on campus for general student use. Computers for student use in computer center, computer labs, learning resource center, classrooms, library provide access to the Internet/World Wide Web. Staffed computer lab on campus.

EXPENSES

Expenses for 1997–98: State resident tuition: $2520 full-time, $56 per credit part-time. Nonresident tuition: $5040 full-time, $112 per credit part-time. Part-time mandatory fees: $15 per quarter. Full-time mandatory fees: $45.
LD Services Contact: Ms. Deborah Thomas, Learning Specialist, Washington State Community College, 710 Colegate Drive, Marietta, OH 45750, 614-374-8716. Fax: 614-376-9435. Email: dthomas@wscc.edu.

WASHTENAW COMMUNITY COLLEGE

Ann Arbor, Michigan

LEARNING DISABILITIES SERVICES INFORMATION

Learning Support Services began offering services in 1986. Currently the program serves 50 undergraduates with LD. Students diagnosed with ADD/ADHD are eligible for the same services available to students with LD.
Staff: 2 full-time, 4 part-time staff members, including director, assistant director. Services provided by tutors, counselor, diagnostic specialist.
Special Fees: No special fees are charged for services to students with LD.
Applications and admissions: *Required:* high school transcript, IEP (Individualized Education Program), personal interview, psychoeducational report completed within 3 years. Students may begin taking classes in fall or winter. *Application deadline:* continuous.

PROGRAM AND SERVICE COMPONENTS

Diagnostic testing: Intelligence, reading, math, written language, motor abilities, perceptual skills, psychoneurology, learning strategies.
Academic advising: Provided by unit staff members. Students with LD may take up to 12 credit hours each term; 6 credit hours required to be eligible for financial aid.
Counseling services: Individual counseling, career counseling.
Subject-area tutoring: Offered one-on-one by professional teachers, peer tutors. Available in most subjects.
Special courses: College survival skills, reading, vocabulary development, communication skills, composition, learning strategies, time management, math, study skills, career planning, social relationships. Some offered for credit; all enter into overall grade point average.
Auxiliary aids: Taped textbooks, tape recorders, typewriters, talking computers.
Auxiliary services: Alternative test arrangements, notetakers, priority registration, advocacy.

GENERAL COLLEGE INFORMATION

State and locally supported, 2-year, coed. Awards associate degrees. Founded 1965. *Setting:* 235-acre suburban campus with easy access to Detroit. *Endowment:* $2 million. *Research spending 1995–96:* $96,000. *Educational spending 1995–96:* $1490 per undergrad. *Total enrollment:* 10,560. *Faculty:* 759 (179 full-time, 12% with terminal degrees, 580 part-time); student–undergrad faculty ratio is 17:1.
Enrollment Profile: 10,560 students from 10 states and territories, 41 other countries. 56% women, 44% men, 81% part-time, 94% state residents, 32% transferred in, 2% international, 38% 25 or older, 1% Native American, 2% Hispanic, 14% black, 4% Asian or Pacific Islander. *Retention:* 82% of 1995 full-time freshmen returned. *Areas of study chosen:* 29% liberal arts/general studies, 25% business management and administrative services, 18% health professions and related sciences, 16% engineering and applied sciences, 6% biological and life sciences, 6% mathematics.
First-Year Class: 3,280 total; 3,310 applied, 100% were accepted, 99% of whom enrolled. 2% from top 10% of their high school class, 10% from top quarter, 24% from top half. 3 valedictorians.
Graduation Requirements: 60 credit hours; 1 course each in math and science; computer course; internship (some majors).
Computers on Campus: 211 computers available on campus for general student use. A campus-wide network can be accessed. Students can contact faculty members and/or advisers through e-mail. Computers for student use in computer center, computer labs, learning resource center, classrooms, library provide access to the Internet/World Wide Web. Staffed computer lab on campus provides training in use of computers, software. *Academic computing expenditure 1995–96:* $1.5 million.

EXPENSES

Expenses for 1996–97: *Application fee:* $15. Area resident tuition: $1560 full-time, $52 per credit hour part-time. State resident tuition: $2250 full-time, $75 per credit hour part-time. Nonresident tuition: $2850 full-time, $95 per credit hour part-time. Part-time mandatory fees: $23 per semester. Full-time mandatory fees: $46.
LD Services Contact: Ms. Marjorie Olivier-Cash, Coordinator, Learning Support Services, Washtenaw Community College, 4800 E Huron River Dr, PO Box D-1, Ann Arbor, MI 48106, 313-973-3342. Fax: 313-677-5414.

WAYCROSS COLLEGE

Waycross, Georgia

LEARNING DISABILITIES SERVICES INFORMATION

Student Life Office began offering services in 1994. Currently the program serves 4 undergraduates with LD. Students diagnosed with ADD/ADHD are eligible for the same services available to students with LD.
Staff: 3 full-time staff members, including director, coordinator.
Special Fees: No special fees are charged for services to students with LD.
Applications and admissions: *Required:* high school transcript, grade point average, untimed SAT I. Students may begin taking classes any term. *Application deadline:* continuous.
Special policies: The college has written policies regarding grade forgiveness; substitutions and waivers of admissions, graduation, and degree requirements.

PROGRAM AND SERVICE COMPONENTS

Academic advising: Provided by unit staff members. Most students with LD take 10 to 12 quarter hours each term; 12 quarter hours required to maintain full-time status; source of aid determines number of quarter hours required to be eligible for financial aid.
Counseling services: Individual counseling.
Special courses: College survival skills, learning strategies, time management, study skills, career planning, stress management, social relationships. None offered for credit; none enter into overall grade point average.
Auxiliary aids: Taped textbooks, tape recorders, word-processors with spell-check, personal computers, talking computers.
Auxiliary services: Alternative test arrangements, notetakers, advocacy.

GENERAL COLLEGE INFORMATION

State-supported, 2-year, coed. Part of University System of Georgia. Awards associate degrees. Founded 1976. *Setting:* 150-acre small-town campus. *Endowment:* $85,583. *Total enrollment:* 885. *Faculty:* 51 (21 full-time, 30 part-time).
Enrollment Profile: 885 students: 71% women, 29% men, 35% part-time, 99% state residents, 10% transferred in, 1% international, 43% 25 or older, 1% Hispanic, 13% black, 1% Asian or Pacific Islander. *Areas of study chosen:* 33% health professions and related sciences, 12% education, 11% social sciences, 8% biological and life sciences, 7% business management and administrative services, 4% engineering and applied sciences, 3% computer and information sciences, 3% mathematics, 2% liberal arts/general studies. *Most popular recent majors:* education, business administration/commerce/management, psychology.
First-Year Class: 166 total. 15% from top 10% of their high school class, 25% from top quarter, 75% from top half.
Graduation Requirements: 93 quarter hours; math/science requirements vary according to program; computer course for business administration, forestry majors.
Computers on Campus: 56 computers available on campus for general student use. Computers for student use in computer center, writing lab. Staffed computer lab on campus provides training in use of computers, software. *Academic computing expenditure 1995–96:* $24,931.

EXPENSES

Expenses for 1996–97: State resident tuition: $1080 full-time, $30 per quarter hour part-time. Nonresident tuition: $3984 full-time, $111 per quarter hour part-time. Part-time mandatory fees per quarter (6 to 11 quarter hours): $17.50. Full-time mandatory fees: $53.

Waycross College (continued)

LD Services Contact: Ms. Lynda Page, Director of Student Life, Waycross College, 2001 South Georgia Parkway, Waycross, GA 31503, 912-285-6012. Fax: 912-287-4909. Email: lap385@fox.way.peachnet.edu.

WENATCHEE VALLEY COLLEGE

Wenatchee, Washington

LEARNING DISABILITIES SERVICES INFORMATION

Disability and Support Services began offering services in 1985. Currently the program serves 35 undergraduates with LD. Services are also available to graduate students. Students diagnosed with ADD/ADHD are eligible for the same services available to students with LD.
Staff: 1 full-time staff member (coordinator).
Special Fees: No special fees are charged for services to students with LD.
Applications and admissions: *Required:* high school transcript, courses completed, personal interview, psychoeducational report completed within 3 years. Students may begin taking classes any quarter after registration. *Application deadline:* continuous.
Special policies: The college has written policies regarding substitutions and waivers of degree requirements.

PROGRAM AND SERVICE COMPONENTS

Academic advising: Provided by unit staff members, academic advisers. Students with LD may take up to 19 credits (with special permission of Dean of Student Services or Dean of Instruction) each term; most take 10 to 15 credits; 12 credits required to maintain full-time status and be eligible for financial aid.
Counseling services: Individual counseling, career counseling.
Basic skills remediation: Offered in small groups and in class-size groups by regular teachers. Available in reading, math, spelling, spoken language, written language, learning strategies, study skills, time management.
Subject-area tutoring: Offered one-on-one and in small groups by professional teachers, peer tutors. Available in some subjects.
Auxiliary aids: Taped textbooks, tape recorders, calculators, word-processors with spell-check, talking computers, optical character readers.
Auxiliary services: Alternative test arrangements, notetakers, priority registration, advocacy.

GENERAL COLLEGE INFORMATION

State and locally supported, 2-year, coed. Part of Washington State Board for Community and Technical Colleges. Awards associate degrees. Founded 1939. *Setting:* 56-acre rural campus. *Endowment:* $358,000. *Total enrollment:* 3,368. *Faculty:* 203 (67 full-time, 136 part-time).
Enrollment Profile: 3,368 students: 58% women, 42% men, 49% part-time, 96% state residents, 3% transferred in, 1% international, 54% 25 or older, 5% Native American, 5% Hispanic, 1% black, 1% Asian or Pacific Islander. *Areas of study chosen:* 22% business management and administrative services, 17% health professions and related sciences, 9% education, 6% agriculture, 6% biological and life sciences, 6% computer and information sciences, 6% engineering and applied sciences, 6% English language/literature/letters, 6% social sciences. *Most popular recent majors:* liberal arts/general studies, nursing, business administration/commerce/management.
First-Year Class: 329 total; 843 applied, 100% were accepted, 39% of whom enrolled.
Graduation Requirements: 93 credits; math/science requirements vary according to program; computer course for health science majors; internship (some majors).
Computers on Campus: 54 computers available on campus for general student use. Computers for student use in computer center, computer labs, classrooms, library provide access to the Internet/World Wide Web. Staffed computer lab on campus provides training in use of computers, software. *Academic computing expenditure 1995–96:* $100,000.

EXPENSES

Expenses for 1997–98: State resident tuition: $1455 full-time, $48.50 per credit part-time. Nonresident tuition: $5730 full-time, $191 per credit part-time. Part-time mandatory fees: $2 per quarter. Full-time mandatory fees: $6. College room and board: $3315.

LD Services Contact: Ms. Marilee Clark, Special Populations Coordinator/Disability and Support Services, Wenatchee Valley College, 1300 Fifth Street, Wenatchee, WA 98801, 509-662-1651. Fax: 509-664-2538. Email: clark_marilee/wenval.ctc.edu.

WESTCHESTER COMMUNITY COLLEGE

Valhalla, New York

LEARNING DISABILITIES SERVICES INFORMATION

Services for Students with Disabilities began offering services in 1986. Currently the program serves 400 undergraduates with LD. Students diagnosed with ADD/ADHD are eligible for the same services available to students with LD.
Staff: 2 full-time, 2 part-time staff members, including LD specialist, counselor/coordinator. Services provided by remediation specialists, tutors, counselors.
Special Fees: No special fees are charged for services to students with LD.
Applications and admissions: *Required:* high school transcript, psychoeducational report completed within 3 years. Students may begin taking classes in fall, winter, or spring. *Application deadline:* continuous.
Special policies: The college has written policies regarding grade forgiveness.

PROGRAM AND SERVICE COMPONENTS

Special preparation or orientation: Required orientation held before registration, during registration, after classes begin, after placement testing.
Academic advising: Provided by unit staff members, academic advisers. Students with LD may take up to 19 credits each term; most take 6 to 12 credits; 12 credits required to maintain full-time status; 6 credits (part-time), 12 credits (full-time) required to be eligible for financial aid.
Counseling services: Individual counseling, career counseling, self-advocacy training.
Basic skills remediation: Offered one-on-one, in small groups, and in class-size groups by regular teachers, tutors; computer-aided instruction also offered. Available in reading, math, written language, learning strategies, study skills, time management, social skills.
Auxiliary aids: Tape recorders, calculators, typewriters, word-processors with spell-check, personal computers, talking computers, optical character readers.
Auxiliary services: Alternative test arrangements, priority registration, advocacy.

GENERAL COLLEGE INFORMATION

State and locally supported, 2-year, coed. Part of State University of New York System. Awards associate degrees. Founded 1946. *Setting:* 218-acre suburban campus with easy access to New York City. *Total enrollment:* 11,127. *Faculty:* 788 (159 full-time, 23% with terminal degrees, 629 part-time).
Enrollment Profile: 11,127 students from 7 states and territories, 105 other countries. 57% women, 43% men, 59% part-time, 98% state residents, 9% transferred in, 1% international, 46% 25 or older, 1% Native American, 11% Hispanic, 15% black, 5% Asian or Pacific Islander. *Retention:* 38% of 1995 full-time freshmen returned. *Areas of study chosen:* 15% business management and administrative services, 6% liberal arts/general studies, 5% engineering and applied sciences, 4% computer and information sciences, 4% health professions and related sciences, 3% performing arts, 3% vocational and home economics, 2% communications and journalism, 2% library and information studies, 1% fine arts, 1% interdisciplinary studies, 1% natural resource sciences, 1% social sciences.
First-Year Class: 2,723 total; 6,242 applied, 100% were accepted, 44% of whom enrolled.
Graduation Requirements: 64 credits; computer course for accounting, business administration, international business, engineering science, marketing majors; internship (some majors).
Computers on Campus: 650 computers available on campus for general student use. A campus-wide network can be accessed from off-campus. Students can contact faculty members and/or advisers through e-mail. Computers for student use in computer center, computer labs, learning resource center, classrooms, library provide access to the Internet/World Wide Web. Staffed computer lab on campus provides training in use of computers, software. *Academic computing expenditure 1995–96:* $2.3 million.

EXPENSES

Expenses for 1996–97: *Application fee:* $25. State resident tuition: $2350 full-time, $98 per credit part-time. Nonresident tuition: $5874 full-time, $245 per credit part-time. Part-time mandatory fees: $45.50 per semester. Full-time mandatory fees: $233.

LD Services Contact: Prof. Suzanne Putnam, Learning Disability Specialist, Westchester Community College, 75 Grasslands Road, Valhalla, NY 10595-1698, 914-785-6626.

WESTERN IOWA TECH COMMUNITY COLLEGE

Sioux City, Iowa

LEARNING DISABILITIES SERVICES INFORMATION

Career Learning Center began offering services in 1972. Students diagnosed with ADD/ADHD are eligible for the same services available to students with LD.

Staff: 7 full-time, 3 part-time staff members, including coordinator. Services provided by remediation specialists, tutors.

Special Fees: No special fees are charged for services to students with LD.

Applications and admissions: *Required:* high school transcript; *recommended:* high school IEP (Individualized Education Program), assessment materials from JTPA, vocational rehabilitation, school records, computerized placement test. Students may begin taking classes any term. *Application deadline:* continuous.

PROGRAM AND SERVICE COMPONENTS

Academic advising: Provided by academic advisers. Most students with LD take 11 to 13 semester credit hours each term; 8 semester credit hours required to maintain full-time status; 4 semester credit hours (part-time) required to be eligible for financial aid.

Counseling services: Individual counseling, career counseling.

Basic skills remediation: Offered one-on-one, in small groups, and in class-size groups by regular teachers, developmental educators. Available in reading, math, spelling, spoken language, written language, learning strategies, study skills, time management, medical terminology.

Subject-area tutoring: Offered one-on-one and in small groups by professional teachers, peer tutors, computerized instructional labs. Available in all subjects.

Auxiliary aids: Taped textbooks, tape recorders, calculators, typewriters, word-processors with spell-check, personal computers, optical character readers, Franklin Speller, talking calculators, Phonic Ear, screen reading system (Soundproof), screen text enlarger software (Magic).

Auxiliary services: Alternative test arrangements, notetakers, advocacy.

GENERAL COLLEGE INFORMATION

State-supported, 2-year, coed. Part of Iowa Department of Education Division of Community Colleges. Awards associate degrees. Founded 1966. *Setting:* 145-acre urban campus. *Total enrollment:* 3,200. *Faculty:* 157; student–undergrad faculty ratio is 15:1.

Enrollment Profile: 3,200 students: 42% women, 58% men, 2% part-time, 88% state residents, 12% transferred in, 28% 25 or older, 1% Native American, 2% Hispanic, 1% black, 3% Asian or Pacific Islander. *Most popular recent majors:* nursing, law enforcement/police sciences, architectural technologies.

First-Year Class: 1,800 total. Of the students who applied, 97% were accepted.

Graduation Requirements: 64 semester credit hours; computer course.

Computers on Campus: 50 computers available on campus for general student use. A campus-wide network can be accessed. Students can contact faculty members and/or advisers through e-mail. Computers for student use in learning resource center, classrooms provide access to the Internet/World Wide Web, on- and off-campus e-mail addresses. Staffed computer lab on campus.

EXPENSES

Expenses for 1997–98: *Application fee:* $10. State resident tuition: $1888 full-time, $59 per semester hour part-time. Nonresident tuition: $3776 full-time, $118 per semester hour part-time. Part-time mandatory fees: $8 per semester hour. Full-time mandatory fees: $256.

LD Services Contact: Ms. Brenda Porter, Coordinator, Student Success Center, Western Iowa Tech Community College, PO Box 5199, Sioux City, IA 51102-5199, 712-274-6400 Ext. 1247. Fax: 712-274-6412. Email: porterb@witcc.cc.ia.us.

WESTERN NEVADA COMMUNITY COLLEGE

Carson City, Nevada

LEARNING DISABILITIES SERVICES INFORMATION

Disabled Student Services Program began offering services in 1995. Students diagnosed with ADD/ADHD are eligible for the same services available to students with LD.

Staff: Includes director, coordinator. Services provided by counselors.

Special Fees: No special fees are charged for services to students with LD.

Applications and admissions: *Required:* personal interview, psychoeducational report completed within 3 years. Students may begin taking classes any term.

PROGRAM AND SERVICE COMPONENTS

Academic advising: Provided by unit staff members, academic advisers. Most students with LD take 6 to 9 credits each term; 12 credits required to maintain full-time status; 6 credits required to be eligible for financial aid.

Counseling services: Individual counseling, small-group counseling, career counseling.

Basic skills remediation: Offered one-on-one, in small groups, and in class-size groups by regular teachers, teacher trainees; computer-aided instruction also offered. Available in reading, math, spelling, written language, learning strategies, study skills, time management, social skills.

Subject-area tutoring: Offered one-on-one and in small groups by professional teachers, peer tutors. Available in most subjects.

Special courses: College survival skills, reading, vocabulary development, communication skills, composition, learning strategies, word processing, time management, math, typing, study skills. All offered for credit; most enter into overall grade point average.

Auxiliary aids: Tape recorders.

Auxiliary services: Alternative test arrangements, notetakers, advocacy.

GENERAL COLLEGE INFORMATION

State-supported, 2-year, coed. Part of University and Community College System of Nevada. Awards associate degrees. Founded 1971. *Setting:* 200-acre small-town campus. *Total enrollment:* 5,143. *Faculty:* 358 (93 full-time, 265 part-time); student–undergrad faculty ratio is 16:1.

Enrollment Profile: 5,143 students from 21 states and territories, 4 other countries. 62% women, 38% men, 91% part-time, 97% state residents, 13% transferred in, 1% international, 60% 25 or older, 3% Native American, 9% Hispanic, 1% black, 2% Asian or Pacific Islander.

First-Year Class: 1,437 total; 1,437 applied, 100% were accepted.

Graduation Requirements: 60 credits; computer course for most majors.

Computers on Campus: 125 computers available on campus for general student use. Computers for student use in computer labs, library, student center.

EXPENSES

Expenses for 1997–98: *Application fee:* $5. State resident tuition: $1095 full-time, $36.50 per credit part-time. Nonresident tuition: $4294 full-time. Nonresident part-time tuition per semester ranges from $52 to $1952.

LD Services Contact: Ms. Barbara Leger, Accommodations Specialist, Western Nevada Community College, 2201 West College Parkway, Carson City, NV 89703-7316, 702-887-3059. Fax: 702-885-0642.

WESTERN WISCONSIN TECHNICAL COLLEGE

La Crosse, Wisconsin

LEARNING DISABILITIES SERVICES INFORMATION

Disability Services began offering services in 1972. Currently the program serves 100 undergraduates with LD. Students diagnosed with ADD/ADHD are eligible for the same services available to students with LD, as well as preferential seating, distraction-free testing environment.

Staff: 2 full-time staff members, including coordinator. Services provided by remediation specialist, Disability Services assistant.

Special Fees: No special fees are charged for services to students with LD.

Western Wisconsin Technical College (continued)

Applications and admissions: *Required:* high school transcript, ACT ASSET; *recommended:* high school IEP (Individualized Education Program), psychoeducational report completed within 3 years. Students may begin taking classes any term. *Application deadline:* continuous.

Special policies: The college has written policies regarding substitutions and waivers of admissions, graduation, and degree requirements.

PROGRAM AND SERVICE COMPONENTS

Special preparation or orientation: Optional orientation offered individually by special arrangement.

Diagnostic testing: Reading, math, spelling, spoken language, written language, perceptual skills, study skills, learning strategies.

Academic advising: Provided by unit staff members, academic advisers. Most students with LD take 6 to 15 credit hours each term; 12 credit hours required to maintain full-time status; 6 to 12 credit hours (depending on assistance package) required to be eligible for financial aid.

Counseling services: Individual counseling, career counseling.

Basic skills remediation: Offered one-on-one, in small groups, and in class-size groups by LD teachers, regular teachers. Available in reading, math, spelling, written language, learning strategies, study skills, time management.

Subject-area tutoring: Offered one-on-one and in small groups by professional teachers, peer tutors. Available in all subjects.

Special courses: College survival skills, reading, vocabulary development, communication skills, composition, learning strategies, study skills, career planning. Some offered for credit; some enter into overall grade point average.

Auxiliary aids: Taped textbooks, tape recorders, calculators, typewriters, word-processors with spell-check, personal computers, optical character readers.

Auxiliary services: Alternative test arrangements, notetakers, advocacy.

GENERAL COLLEGE INFORMATION

District-supported, 2-year, coed. Part of Wisconsin Technical College System. Awards associate degrees. Founded 1911. *Setting:* 10-acre urban campus. *Research spending 1995–96:* $367,172. *Total enrollment:* 4,438. *Faculty:* 184 (all full-time, 6% with terminal degrees); student–undergrad faculty ratio is 24:1.

Enrollment Profile: 4,438 students: 55% women, 45% men, 60% part-time, 93% state residents, 1% live on campus, 8% transferred in, 0% international, 52% 25 or older, 1% Native American, 1% Hispanic, 1% black, 1% Asian or Pacific Islander. *Retention:* 56% of 1995 full-time freshmen returned. *Areas of study chosen:* 39% health professions and related sciences, 25% business management and administrative services, 14% engineering and applied sciences, 8% agriculture, 5% computer and information sciences, 3% vocational and home economics, 1% architecture, 1% communications and journalism. *Most popular recent majors:* nursing, accounting, law enforcement/police sciences.

First-Year Class: 1,148 total; 3,190 applied, 42% were accepted, 85% of whom enrolled.

Graduation Requirements: 68 credit hours; computer course for most majors except vocational majors; internship (some majors).

Computers on Campus: 800 computers available on campus for general student use. A campus-wide network can be accessed from student residence rooms and from off-campus. Students can contact faculty members and/or advisers through e-mail. Computers for student use in computer center, computer labs, learning resource center, classrooms, student services department. Staffed computer lab on campus provides training in use of computers, software.

EXPENSES

Expenses for 1997–98: *Application fee:* $25. State resident tuition: $1843 full-time, $54.20 per credit hour part-time. Nonresident tuition: $14,525 full-time, $427.20 per credit hour part-time. College room only: $1250.

LD Services Contact: Ms. Kristina Puent, Instructional Support Specialist, Western Wisconsin Technical College, 304 North Sixth Street, La Crosse, WI 54602-0908, 608-785-9875.

WESTERN WYOMING COMMUNITY COLLEGE

Rock Springs, Wyoming

LEARNING DISABILITIES SERVICES INFORMATION

Learning Opportunities Program, Student Development Center began offering services in 1992. Currently the program serves 27 undergraduates with LD. Students diagnosed with ADD/ADHD are eligible for the same services available to students with LD.

Staff: 4 part-time staff members, including co-directors, coordinator. Services provided by remediation specialist, counselor.

Special Fees: No special fees are charged for services to students with LD.

Applications and admissions: *Required:* personal interview, psychoeducational report completed within 3 years; *recommended:* high school transcript, grade point average, courses completed, IEP (Individualized Education Program). Students may begin taking classes any term. *Application deadline:* continuous.

Special policies: The college has written policies regarding grade forgiveness; substitutions and waivers of graduation and degree requirements.

PROGRAM AND SERVICE COMPONENTS

Academic advising: Provided by unit staff members, academic advisers. Most students with LD take 12 credit hours each term; 12 credit hours required to maintain full-time status and be eligible for financial aid.

Counseling services: Individual counseling, small-group counseling, career counseling.

Basic skills remediation: Offered one-on-one and in class-size groups by LD teachers, regular teachers, reading specialist; computer-aided instruction also offered. Available in reading, math, spelling, written language, learning strategies, study skills, time management, computer skills, computer-based assistive technology training.

Subject-area tutoring: Offered one-on-one and in small groups by peer tutors. Available in all subjects.

Auxiliary aids: Taped textbooks, tape recorders, optical character readers, Dragon Dictate.

Auxiliary services: Alternative test arrangements, notetakers.

GENERAL COLLEGE INFORMATION

State and locally supported, 2-year, coed. Awards associate degrees. Founded 1959. *Setting:* 10-acre small-town campus. *Total enrollment:* 3,094. *Faculty:* 232 (72 full-time, 25% with terminal degrees, 160 part-time); student–undergrad faculty ratio is 18:1.

Enrollment Profile: 3,094 students from 15 states and territories, 11 other countries. 63% women, 37% men, 63% part-time, 96% state residents, 2% transferred in, 64% 25 or older, 1% Native American, 5% Hispanic, 1% black, 1% Asian or Pacific Islander. *Retention:* 80% of 1995 full-time freshmen returned. *Areas of study chosen:* 18% education, 17% business management and administrative services, 12% computer and information sciences, 11% liberal arts/general studies, 7% psychology, 6% biological and life sciences, 6% health professions and related sciences, 4% communications and journalism, 4% fine arts, 4% social sciences, 2% engineering and applied sciences. *Most popular recent majors:* education, psychology, business administration/commerce/management.

First-Year Class: 1,950 total; 3,000 applied, 100% were accepted, 65% of whom enrolled. 100% from top half of their high school class.

Graduation Requirements: 64 credit hours; 1 course each in math and lab science; computer course; internship (some majors).

Computers on Campus: 120 computers available on campus for general student use. A campus-wide network can be accessed. Students can contact faculty members and/or advisers through e-mail. Computers for student use in computer labs, learning resource center, classrooms, library, writing lab provide access to the Internet/World Wide Web. Staffed computer lab on campus provides training in use of computers, software.

EXPENSES

Expenses for 1997–98: State resident tuition: $1098 full-time, $46 per credit hour part-time. Nonresident tuition: $2886 full-time, $124 per credit hour part-time. Tuition for nonresidents who are eligible for the Western Undergraduate Exchange: $1546 full-time, $66 per credit hour part-time. College room and board: $2610. College room only: $1180.

LD Services Contact: Randy Bodenhamer, Director, Student Development Center, Western Wyoming Community College, PO Box 428, B-601, Rock Springs, WY 82902, 307-382-1645. Fax: 307-382-7665. Email: bodenha@wwcc.cc.wy.us.

WILKES COMMUNITY COLLEGE

Wilkesboro, North Carolina

LEARNING DISABILITIES SERVICES INFORMATION

Student Support Services began offering services in 1987. Currently the program serves 17 undergraduates with LD. Students diagnosed with ADD/ADHD are eligible for the same services available to students with LD.

Staff: 4 full-time staff members, including director. Services provided by tutors, counselors.

Special Fees: No special fees are charged for services to students with LD.

Applications and admissions: *Recommended:* psychoeducational report. Students may begin taking classes any term. *Application deadline:* continuous.

PROGRAM AND SERVICE COMPONENTS

Diagnostic testing: Intelligence, reading, math, spelling, handwriting, written language, study skills.

Academic advising: Provided by unit staff members, academic advisers. Most students with LD take 12 to 15 semester hours each term; 12 semester hours required to maintain full-time status and be eligible for financial aid.

Counseling services: Individual counseling, small-group counseling, career counseling.

Basic skills remediation: Offered in small groups by regular teachers. Available in reading, math, written language, study skills.

Subject-area tutoring: Offered one-on-one by professional teachers, peer tutors. Available in most subjects.

Auxiliary aids: Taped textbooks, tape recorders, calculators, word-processors with spell-check, 4-track tape player.

Auxiliary services: Alternative test arrangements, notetakers, advocacy.

GENERAL COLLEGE INFORMATION

State-supported, 2-year, coed. Part of North Carolina Community College System. Awards associate degrees. Founded 1965. *Setting:* 140-acre small-town campus. *Endowment:* $801,634. *Educational spending 1995–96:* $3183 per undergrad. *Total enrollment:* 2,240. *Faculty:* 171 (52 full-time, 6% with terminal degrees, 119 part-time); student–undergrad faculty ratio is 15:1.

Enrollment Profile: 2,240 students from 5 states and territories, 1 other country. 67% women, 33% men, 49% part-time, 99% state residents, 2% transferred in, 48% 25 or older, 1% Native American, 1% Hispanic, 5% black, 1% Asian or Pacific Islander. *Retention:* 56% of 1995 full-time freshmen returned. *Areas of study chosen:* 32% liberal arts/general studies, 22% business management and administrative services, 17% health professions and related sciences, 15% computer and information sciences, 5% engineering and applied sciences, 4% education, 1% architecture, 1% communications and journalism, 1% fine arts, 1% performing arts, 1% vocational and home economics. *Most popular recent majors:* liberal arts/general studies, business administration/commerce/management.

First-Year Class: 1,223 applied, 100% were accepted, 66% of whom enrolled.

Graduation Requirements: 1 math course; computer course; internship (some majors).

Computers on Campus: 235 computers available on campus for general student use. Computers for student use in computer center, computer labs, learning resource center, classrooms, library provide access to the Internet/World Wide Web. Staffed computer lab on campus provides training in use of computers, software.

EXPENSES

Expenses for 1997–98: State resident tuition: $560 full-time, $20 per credit hour part-time. Nonresident tuition: $4564 full-time, $163 per credit hour part-time. Part-time mandatory fees: $28 per year. Full-time mandatory fees: $28.

LD Services Contact: Dr. Barbara Holt, Director of Student Support Services, Wilkes Community College, PO Box 120, Wilkesboro, NC 28697, 910-838-6244. Fax: 910-838-6277.

WILSON TECHNICAL COMMUNITY COLLEGE

Wilson, North Carolina

LEARNING DISABILITIES SERVICES INFORMATION

Student Support Services began offering services in 1970. Currently the program serves 17 undergraduates with LD. Students diagnosed with ADD/ADHD are eligible for the same services available to students with LD.

Staff: 3 full-time, 1 part-time staff members, including director. Services provided by tutors, counselors.

Special Fees: No special fees are charged for services to students with LD.

Applications and admissions: *Required:* high school transcript, psychoeducational report completed within 5 years; *recommended:* personal interview. Students may begin taking classes any term. *Application deadline:* continuous.

Special policies: The college has written policies regarding grade forgiveness.

PROGRAM AND SERVICE COMPONENTS

Special preparation or orientation: Optional orientation offered before registration.

Academic advising: Provided by unit staff members, academic advisers. Students with LD may take up to 18 credit hours each term; most take 6 to 14 credit hours; 12 credit hours required to maintain full-time status; 6 credit hours required to be eligible for financial aid.

Counseling services: Individual counseling, small-group counseling, career counseling.

Basic skills remediation: Offered one-on-one, in small groups, and in class-size groups by regular teachers. Available in reading, math, spelling, written language, study skills, time management, computer skills.

Subject-area tutoring: Offered one-on-one, in small groups, and in class-size groups by peer tutors. Available in most subjects.

Special courses: College survival skills, reading, vocabulary development, communication skills, composition, Internet use, time management, math, typing, personal psychology, study skills, career planning, stress management. Some offered for credit; some enter into overall grade point average.

Auxiliary aids: Taped textbooks, typewriters, word-processors with spell-check, personal computers.

Auxiliary services: Alternative test arrangements, notetakers.

GENERAL COLLEGE INFORMATION

State-supported, 2-year, coed. Part of North Carolina Community College System. Awards associate degrees. Founded 1958. *Setting:* 35-acre small-town campus. *Endowment:* $537,786. *Total enrollment:* 1,379. *Faculty:* 92 (47 full-time, 45 part-time); student–undergrad faculty ratio is 18:1.

Enrollment Profile: 1,379 students from 11 states and territories, 1 other country. 61% women, 39% men, 54% part-time, 98% state residents, 17% transferred in, 51% 25 or older, 0% Native American, 1% Hispanic, 33% black, 0% Asian or Pacific Islander. *Retention:* 40% of 1995 full-time freshmen returned. *Areas of study chosen:* 29% vocational and home economics, 26% business management and administrative services, 16% liberal arts/general studies, 10% computer and information sciences, 9% health professions and related sciences, 6% engineering and applied sciences, 4% education. *Most popular recent majors:* nursing, business administration/commerce/management, accounting.

First-Year Class: 487 total; 883 applied, 87% were accepted, 63% of whom enrolled.

Graduation Requirements: Math/science requirements vary according to program; computer course for most majors.

Computers on Campus: 200 computers available on campus for general student use. Computers for student use in computer center, computer labs, classrooms, library. Staffed computer lab on campus provides training in use of computers, software.

EXPENSES

Expenses for 1997–98: State resident tuition: $560 full-time, $20 per credit hour part-time. Nonresident tuition: $4564 full-time, $163 per credit hour part-time. Full-time mandatory fees: $21.

LD Services Contact: Ms. Rhonda Treadaway, Counselor for Students with Disabilities, Wilson Technical Community College, PO Box 4305, Wilson, NC 27893-3310, 919-291-1195. Fax: 919-243-7148.

WISCONSIN INDIANHEAD TECHNICAL COLLEGE, SUPERIOR CAMPUS

Superior, Wisconsin

LEARNING DISABILITIES SERVICES INFORMATION

Student Success Center began offering services in 1982. Currently the program serves 25 undergraduates with LD. Students diagnosed with ADD/ADHD are eligible for the same services available to students with LD.
Staff: 4 full-time, 1 part-time staff members, including director. Services provided by remediation specialist, tutors, counselor, instructors.
Special Fees: No special fees are charged for services to students with LD.
Applications and admissions: *Required:* psychoeducational report completed within 3 years; *recommended:* high school transcript, IEP (Individualized Education Program). Students may begin taking classes any term. *Application deadline:* continuous.
Special policies: The college has written policies regarding substitutions and waivers of admissions and graduation requirements.

PROGRAM AND SERVICE COMPONENTS

Academic advising: Provided by unit staff members, academic advisers. Students with LD may take up to 17 credits each term; most take 8 to 12 credits; 12 credits required to maintain full-time status; 6 to 12 credits required to be eligible for financial aid.
Counseling services: Individual counseling, career counseling.
Basic skills remediation: Offered one-on-one by regular teachers; computer-aided instruction also offered. Available in reading, math, spelling, learning strategies, study skills, time management.
Subject-area tutoring: Offered one-on-one by peer tutors. Available in all subjects.
Auxiliary aids: Taped textbooks, tape recorders, calculators, word-processors with spell-check, talking computers, optical character readers.
Auxiliary services: Alternative test arrangements, notetakers, advocacy.

GENERAL COLLEGE INFORMATION

District-supported, 2-year, coed. Part of Wisconsin Technical College System. Awards associate degrees. Founded 1912. *Setting:* 6-acre small-town campus. *Total enrollment:* 800. *Faculty:* 76 (41 full-time, 4% with terminal degrees, 35 part-time).
Enrollment Profile: 800 students from 3 states and territories. 57% women, 43% men, 34% part-time, 88% state residents, 3% transferred in, 0% international, 55% 25 or older, 3% Native American, 0% Hispanic, 0% Asian or Pacific Islander.
First-Year Class: Of the students who applied, 80% were accepted.
Graduation Requirements: 68 credits; computer course.
Computers on Campus: 100 computers available on campus for general student use. Computers for student use in classrooms, library. Staffed computer lab on campus.

EXPENSES

Expenses for 1997–98: *Application fee:* $10. State resident tuition: $1843 full-time, $54.20 per credit part-time. Nonresident tuition: $14,525 full-time, $427.20 per credit part-time. Part-time mandatory fees: $2.45 per credit. (College housing is available through University of Wisconsin-Superior.). Full-time mandatory fees: $83.
LD Services Contact: Ms. Wendy Ecklund, Study Skills Instructor, Wisconsin Indianhead Technical College, Superior Campus, 600 North 21st Street, Superior, WI 54880, 715-394-6677 Ext. 6363. Fax: 715-394-3771.

WOR-WIC COMMUNITY COLLEGE

Salisbury, Maryland

LEARNING DISABILITIES SERVICES INFORMATION

Services to Students with Disabilities began offering services in 1985. Currently the program serves 52 undergraduates with LD. Students diagnosed with ADD/ADHD are eligible for the same services available to students with LD.
Staff: 1 full-time staff member (director). Services provided by tutors, diagnostic specialists.
Special Fees: No special fees are charged for services to students with LD.
Applications and admissions: *Required:* high school transcript, psychoeducational report completed within 3 years. Students may begin taking classes any term. *Application deadline:* continuous.
Special policies: The college has written policies regarding substitutions and waivers of graduation and degree requirements.

PROGRAM AND SERVICE COMPONENTS

Diagnostic testing: Reading, math, written language.
Academic advising: Provided by unit staff members, academic advisers. Students with LD may take up to 16 credit hours each term; most take 6 to 9 credit hours; 12 credit hours required to maintain full-time status.
Counseling services: Individual counseling, career counseling, self-advocacy training.
Basic skills remediation: Offered one-on-one and in class-size groups by regular teachers, tutors/counselors. Available in reading, math, spelling, handwriting, spoken language, written language, learning strategies, study skills, time management.
Subject-area tutoring: Offered one-on-one and in small groups by professional teachers, peer tutors. Available in all subjects.
Auxiliary aids: Taped textbooks, tape recorders, calculators, word-processors with spell-check, personal computers, optical character readers.
Auxiliary services: Alternative test arrangements, notetakers, priority registration.

GENERAL COLLEGE INFORMATION

State and locally supported, 2-year, coed. Part of Maryland State Community Colleges System. Awards associate degrees. Founded 1976. *Setting:* small-town campus. *Total enrollment:* 1,989. *Faculty:* 103 (37 full-time, 66 part-time).
Enrollment Profile: 1,989 students from 3 states and territories. 76% women, 24% men, 82% part-time, 99% state residents, 21% transferred in, 50% 25 or older, 1% Native American, 1% Hispanic, 20% black, 1% Asian or Pacific Islander. *Most popular recent majors:* liberal arts/general studies, accounting, business administration/commerce/management.
First-Year Class: 669 total. Of the students who applied, 100% were accepted. 5% from top 10% of their high school class, 15% from top quarter, 50% from top half.
Graduation Requirements: 60 credit hours.
Computers on Campus: 50 computers available on campus for general student use. A campus-wide network can be accessed. Computers for student use in computer center, secretarial studies lab provide access to the Internet/World Wide Web.

EXPENSES

Expenses for 1997–98: Area resident tuition: $1560 full-time, $52 per credit hour part-time. State resident tuition: $3870 full-time, $129 per credit hour part-time. Nonresident tuition: $4440 full-time, $148 per credit hour part-time. Part-time mandatory fees: $12 per semester. Full-time mandatory fees: $24.
LD Services Contact: Ms. Suzanne Alexander, Director of Counseling, Wor-Wic Community College, 32000 Campus Drive, Salisbury, MD 21804, 410-334-2899. Fax: 410-543-6568.

WRIGHT STATE UNIVERSITY, LAKE CAMPUS

Celina, Ohio

LEARNING DISABILITIES SERVICES INFORMATION

Learning Resource Center began offering services in 1986. Currently the program serves 12 undergraduates with LD. Students diagnosed with ADD/ADHD are eligible for the same services available to students with LD.
Staff: 1 full-time, 22 part-time staff members, including director. Services provided by remediation specialists, tutors.
Special Fees: No special fees are charged for services to students with LD.
Applications and admissions: *Required:* high school transcript, untimed ACT, psychoeducational report completed within 3 years; *recommended:* personal interview. Students may begin taking classes any term. *Application deadline:* continuous.
Special policies: The college has written policies regarding grade forgiveness.

PROGRAM AND SERVICE COMPONENTS

Academic advising: Provided by unit staff members, academic advisers. Most students with LD take 6 to 12 credit hours each term; 12 credit hours required to maintain full-time status; 6 credit hours (part-time), 12 credit hours (full-time) required to be eligible for financial aid.
Counseling services: Self-advocacy training.
Basic skills remediation: Offered one-on-one, in small groups, and in class-size groups by regular teachers; computer-aided instruction also offered. Available in reading, math, spelling, written language, study skills, time management.
Subject-area tutoring: Offered one-on-one, in small groups, and in class-size groups by professional teachers, peer tutors. Available in most subjects.
Special courses: College survival skills, reading, vocabulary development, composition, time management, math, study skills. All offered for credit; some enter into overall grade point average.
Auxiliary aids: Taped textbooks, tape recorders, personal computers.
Auxiliary services: Alternative test arrangements, notetakers, advocacy.

GENERAL COLLEGE INFORMATION

State-supported, 2-year, coed. Part of Ohio Board of Regents. Awards associate degrees. Founded 1969. *Setting:* 173-acre rural campus. *Total enrollment:* 654. *Faculty:* 48 (18 full-time, 30 part-time).
Enrollment Profile: 654 students from 3 states and territories, 1 other country. 60% women, 40% men, 52% part-time, 99% state residents, 6% transferred in, 52% 25 or older, 1% Native American, 0% Hispanic, 0% black, 1% Asian or Pacific Islander. *Areas of study chosen:* 27% business management and administrative services, 19% education, 13% engineering and applied sciences, 5% social sciences, 3% biological and life sciences, 3% health professions and related sciences, 2% communications and journalism, 2% psychology, 1% computer and information sciences, 1% English language/literature/letters, 1% fine arts, 1% foreign language and literature, 1% mathematics, 1% physical sciences. *Most popular recent majors:* business administration/commerce/management, secretarial studies/office management, accounting.
First-Year Class: 186 total; 262 applied, 99% were accepted, 72% of whom enrolled.
Graduation Requirements: 94 credit hours.
Computers on Campus: 115 computers available on campus for general student use. A campus-wide network can be accessed from off-campus. Students can contact faculty members and/or advisers through e-mail. Computers for student use in computer center, computer labs, learning resource center, library, secreterial lab provide access to the Internet/World Wide Web, on- and off-campus e-mail addresses. Staffed computer lab on campus provides training in use of computers, software.

EXPENSES

Expenses for 1997–98: *Application fee:* $30. State resident tuition: $3270 full-time, $102 per credit hour part-time. Nonresident tuition: $7629 full-time, $217 per credit hour part-time. Part-time tuition per credit hour (1 to 10 credit hours): $102 for state residents, $217 for nonresidents.
LD Services Contact: Dr. John Wolfe, Director, Learning Resource Center, Wright State University, Lake Campus, 7600 State Route 703, Celina, OH 45822-2921, 419-586-0326. Fax: 419-586-0358. Email: jwolfe@lake.wright.edu.

YAVAPAI COLLEGE

Prescott, Arizona

LEARNING DISABILITIES SERVICES INFORMATION

Student Support Services, TRIO began offering services in 1986. Currently the program serves 50 to 75 undergraduates with LD. Students diagnosed with ADD/ADHD are eligible for the same services available to students with LD.
Staff: 5 full-time, 1 part-time staff members, including director, coordinator. Services provided by remediation specialist, tutors, counselor, LD specialist.
Special Fees: No special fees are charged for services to students with LD.
Applications and admissions: *Required:* high school transcript, psychoeducational report, documentation of learning disability; *recommended:* high school IEP (Individualized Education Program). Students may begin taking classes any term. *Application deadline:* continuous.
Special policies: The college has written policies regarding substitutions and waivers of graduation and degree requirements.

PROGRAM AND SERVICE COMPONENTS

Special preparation or orientation: Optional orientation offered before registration, during registration, after classes begin, individually by appointment.
Diagnostic testing: Reading, math, spelling, handwriting, spoken language, written language, study skills, learning strategies.
Academic advising: Provided by LD counselor/specialist. Students with LD may take up to as many credits as an individual can handle each term; most take 12 to 15 credits; 12 credits required to maintain full-time status and be eligible for financial aid.
Counseling services: Individual counseling, career counseling, self-advocacy training.
Basic skills remediation: Offered one-on-one, in small groups, and in class-size groups by LD teachers, regular teachers, reading specialist. Available in reading, math, spelling, handwriting, spoken language, written language, learning strategies, study skills, time management, social skills, computer skills.
Subject-area tutoring: Offered one-on-one and in small groups by professional teachers, peer tutors, professional LD expert. Available in all subjects.
Auxiliary aids: Taped textbooks, tape recorders, calculators, typewriters, word-processors with spell-check, personal computers, talking computers, optical character readers, computer voice simulator for text, text enlarger.
Auxiliary services: Alternative test arrangements, notetakers, advocacy, taped lectures.

GENERAL COLLEGE INFORMATION

State and locally supported, 2-year, coed. Part of Arizona State Community College System. Awards associate degrees. Founded 1966. *Setting:* 100-acre small-town campus. *Endowment:* $1.2 million. *Total enrollment:* 6,121. *Faculty:* 487 (87 full-time, 24% with terminal degrees, 400 part-time); student–undergrad faculty ratio is 15:1.
Enrollment Profile: 6,121 students: 63% women, 37% men, 80% part-time, 94% state residents, 7% live on campus, 5% transferred in, 1% international, 67% 25 or older, 8% Native American, 4% Hispanic, 1% black, 1% Asian or Pacific Islander. *Retention:* 70% of 1995 full-time freshmen returned. *Most popular recent majors:* nursing, liberal arts/general studies, business administration/commerce/management.
First-Year Class: 1,748 total. Of the students who applied, 100% were accepted.
Graduation Requirements: 64 credits; math/science requirements vary according to program.
Computers on Campus: 150 computers available on campus for general student use. Computers for student use in computer labs, classrooms, library, learning center provide access to the Internet/World Wide Web. Staffed computer lab on campus provides training in use of computers.

EXPENSES

Expenses for 1997–98: State resident tuition: $1002 full-time. Nonresident tuition: $6002 full-time. Part-time tuition per semester ranges from $50 to $326 for state residents, $60 to $2614 for nonresidents. College room and board: $3030 (minimum).
LD Services Contact: Ms. Patricia Quinn-Kane, Learning Specialist, Yavapai College, 1100 East Sheldon Street, Prescott, AZ 86301-3297, 520-776-2091. Fax: 520-776-2083. Email: lc_patricia@sizzle.yavapai.cc.az.us.

▶ INDEX ◀

The names of colleges with **comprehensive programs** for students with LD are printed in bold-face type; those with special services for students with LD are in regular type.

A

B

C

D

E

O

P

Q

R

S

ABOUT THE AUTHORS

Charles T. Mangrum II, Ed.D.

Dr. Mangrum is Professor of Special Education and Reading at the University of Miami, Coral Gables, Florida. He attended high school in Chicago and then graduated from Northern Michigan University with a degree in education. He taught in elementary and secondary schools before entering graduate school. Dr. Mangrum earned an Ed.D. from Indiana University in 1968. He has been on the faculty at the University of Miami since 1968, where he trains teachers who teach students with reading and learning disabilities.

Stephen S. Strichart, Ph.D.

Dr. Strichart is Professor of Special Education and Learning Disabilities at Florida International University, Miami, Florida. He grew up in New York City, where he attended school from kindergarten through graduate school. He taught children with various types of disabilities before entering graduate school. Dr. Strichart earned a Ph.D. from Yeshiva University in 1972. He has been on the faculty at Florida International University since 1975, where he trains teachers to work with students with learning disabilities.

Dr. Mangrum and Dr. Strichart have evaluated and counseled several thousand students with learning disabilities. Over the past two decades, much of their work has focused on the needs of college-bound students with learning disabilities. They coauthored *College and the Learning Disabled Student*, which was first published in 1984. This book was used by personnel at colleges and universities throughout the nation to establish programs and services for students with learning disabilities. The first edition of *Peterson's Guide to Colleges with Programs for Students with Learning Disabilities* appeared in 1986 to meet the needs of students, parents, and advocates for a source of accurate and complete information about college opportunities for students with learning disabilities. The fifth edition of this guide, retitled *Peterson's Colleges with Programs for Students with Learning Disabilities or Attention Deficit Disorders* to reflect the inclusion of information about services for students with ADD, continues their efforts to provide the most accurate, complete, and useful guide on the subject.